FOUNDATIONS OF CRIMINAL JUSTICE

A TREATISE

ON

THE CRIMINAL LAW

VOL. I

FOUNDATIONS OF CRIMINAL JUSTICE

FOUNDATIONS OF CRIMINAL JUSTICE

TREATISE
ON
THE CRIMINAL LAW

BY

EMLIN McCLAIN

with a new preface by

Alton R. Waldon, Jr.

VOL. I

AMS PRESS
NEW YORK, 1974

Library of Congress Cataloging in Publication Data

McClain, Emlin, 1851-1915.
A treatise on the criminal law as now administered in the United States.

(Foundations of criminal justice)
1. Criminal law—United States. 2. Criminal procedure—United States. I. Title. II. Series.
KF9219.M3 1974 345'.73'05 74-156026
ISBN 0-404-01927-X

International Standard Book Number:
Complete Set: 0-404-01927-X
Volume I: 0-404-09166-0

Foundations of Criminal Justice Series
General Editors: Richard H. Ward and Austin Fowler,
John Jay College of Criminal Justice

Published in the United States by AMS Press, Inc.
56 E. 13th Street, New York, N.Y. 10003

Manufactured in the United States of America

An Invaluable History

A Preface to the New Edition of

TREATISE ON THE CRIMINAL LAW AS NOW ADMINISTERED IN THE UNITED STATES

Emlin McClain was born on November 26, 1851, in Salem, Ohio. He attended the State University of Iowa and from there received his Ph.B. in 1871; A.B., 1872; LL.B., 1873. He distinguished himself as an undergraduate student and, for his academic achievement, was elected to Phi Beta Kappa.

The brilliant, analytical mind of Emlin McClain destined him to occupy the ultimate pinnacle for the advocate, the judicial bench. His elevation to the role of jurist occurred in 1901, when he became a judge of the Supreme Court of Iowa. In 1906 he became the Chief Justice and remained in that position until 1912.

Emlin McClain's preparation to assume the role of the jurist was both diversified and notable. Immediately upon his graduation from law school he was awarded a professorship in the Law Department at the State University of Iowa. He occupied that position until 1881. In 1887 he relinquished his private practice to become Vice Chancellor of his Alma Mater and he was elevated to the position of Chancellor in 1890. His writings and publications were prolific. However, not all of his publications had a lasting effect on the legal and judicial community. Those which did render such an impact were: *McClain's Annotated Statutes of Iowa,* published in 1880; his reports, in conjunction with commissioners from other states, on uniform laws in 1894; his annotations to the new code of Iowa, which were published in 1894; and lastly, his major work, these volumes.

Emlin McClain toiled for seven long years in the preparation of this treatise. He had taught criminal law for eight years prior to devoting his energies toward this publication. It is not an expansion of the outlines developed and employed by him for his lectures but rather the culmination of a life's work intertwined with the status of the criminal law as it was in 1897.

Many states were functioning under a non-statutory or recently codified criminal law and McClain intended for this work not to be a mere collaboration of more or less conflicting decisions, leaving the lawyer or student or judge using it at sea in a mass of confusing cases. Instead, he attempted to permit an analysis of the cases in the light of the fundamental principles of the criminal and the civil law where applicable and their historical development. He wished to bring about a reconciliation of apparently conflicting cases whenever possible, to the end that the true rule would be arrived at; and, in those cases of conflicting rules which could not be reconciled, he made an honest attempt to determine which should prevail.

Pervading the two volumes is the keen awareness of what is required to isolate the culpable act in question, the procedure to be followed to defend or prosecute such act, and—because of precedents—the logical resolution of the legal question involved. The experience obtained from his many years as a professor, practicioner and researcher evidences itself throughout this work.

The treatise obviously must have influenced the legal practitioners of the late nineteenth and early twentieth century era. It was written by an outstanding member of the bar and was an attempt to place at the fingertips of lawyers a comprehensive statement of where the criminal law had been, was, and would be in future years.

This work, for the contemporary lawyer, is a guide to the development of the criminal law in the United States. It is replete with historical "legal nostalgia," as is evidenced with its statements on the actions *qui tam* and the merger doctrine. The latter was rule of law which, in many states, provided for conviction of an included misdemeanor under a felony charge. There was an allowance in many jurisdictions to resist unlawful arrest violently. If such resistance resulted in a homicide, it was automatically reduced to manslaughter because "unlawful arrest is deemed such provocation as to cause heat of blood in an ordinary person." There was also the unique Texas statute of the late 1890s which viewed insulting words to a femal relative as sufficient provocation to reduce homicide of the perpetrator/speaker to manslaughter.

This treatise is a history of the criminal law of the United States circa 1897. For a member of the bar to understand well the progress, change and origin of today's criminal law he must be fully consonant with its past.

To encounter and peruse *Treatise on the Criminal Law as now Administered in the United States,* is to know the past and thereby facilitate the understanding of the present and future of criminal law.

Alton R. Waldon, Jr.
New York City Housing Authority
New York, N.Y.

A TREATISE

ON

THE CRIMINAL LAW

A TREATISE

ON

THE CRIMINAL LAW

AS NOW ADMINISTERED IN THE
UNITED STATES

BY

EMLIN McCLAIN, A. M., LL. D.

CHANCELLOR OF THE LAW DEPARTMENT OF THE STATE UNIVERSITY OF IOWA

IN TWO VOLUMES

VOLUME I

CHICAGO
CALLAGHAN AND COMPANY
1897

PREFACE.

It is proper that the author of a law book should state its general nature and scope and the principles in accordance with which it is constructed so that the reader may make intelligent use of it and understand how far it is to be relied upon. The object, then, of this treatise is to present under a convenient and methodical arrangement the principles of the criminal law as they have been established by adjudication, so far as they are now recognized and applied in the states of this Union. The primary and controlling purpose has been to state the law for lawyers; and while in so doing it has been deemed of the utmost importance to clearly and succinctly present the general rules relating to the subject as announced by text-writers and judges, yet the fact has also been recognized that it is in the application of these general rules, and not in the broad statement of them, that the difficulties arise which lawyers must contend with and courts must settle.

The principles of the criminal law are comparatively simple and quite definitely established, but it would be misleading to assume that this branch of the law has ceased to develop, and that the full statement of it as made in one decade will serve every purpose for succeeding decades; for new applications of established doctrines are constantly being made, which in themselves become a part of the established law and must be understood and made use of in solving new cases as they arise. Even in states where the criminal law has been codified this development is constantly going on, and the interpretation and application of the statutory rules and definitions give as much occasion for the development of the law as does the explanation of common-law principles in states where codification is not attempted. Indeed, legislative modifications of the common law of crimes have become so general that even in states where there is no formal codification there is a large body of statutory law on the subject, covering not only new offenses, but also, to a great extent, the ordinary common-law crimes, and it is therefore wholly futile to attempt to distinguish between the common law and the statutory law of the subject; but it is important to give prominence to the common-law principles as compared with such statutory provisions as are not uniform and relate to minor matters.

The attempt to state the criminal law as found in the decisions, having in mind the general principles of the subject but stating them with reference to their applications, has led to the citation of a very large number of cases, the endeavor of the author having been to make use of every criminal case of any general value decided in the courts of last resort in the United States and those accessible in the standard English reports, including the cases from both these sources so far as accessible in the official reports up to within eight months of the date of publication, and including also some important cases not accessible in the official reports when the book goes to press. In handling this great body of cases, the aim has been to so differentiate them into groups by the statements of the text, and further explanations made in the notes, that there shall not be a large number of them cited indiscriminately to any one general proposition. But where many cases embody the application of the same principle, the author has not hesitated to cite all of them, realizing that for the lawyer or the judge it is frequently of great importance that he be able, by searching through the cases in which the proposition is applied, to find minor differences which may not be amplified in a text-book without undue prolixity, and yet which may be very important in the solution of the particular question under consideration. It is seldom that two cases are exactly alike, and their differences may in subsequent cases be made the basis of an important distinction which could not have been anticipated and its consequences pointed out at the time the cases themselves were decided. But in handling this mass of decisions embodying the criminal law, the greatest care has been exercised to avoid mere digesting, and to state in a methodical manner and according to proper classification the principles of the subject, and not merely the points adjudicated.

In the development of our common law the functions of the text-writer necessarily change from time to time under changing circumstances. When authorities are few he may be to some extent a prophet and an originator; but as the ground is more fully covered in detail by judicial decisions, he necessarily limits himself more strictly to an orderly arrangement and concise statement of that which has been determined; and finally when the number of adjudications on the subject which he is considering has become so great as to cover practically all the important questions which are likely to arise, his function is to put all in order and preserve a proper perspective which shall make general and well-established principles stand out boldly among the bewildering details of complicated cases, without obliterating distinctions which may be of the greatest importance when they are pertinent, but would mislead if magnified into prominent dividing lines. It is futile to speak of one of these functions as greater than another. The business of the text-writer is to make the law as available as possible to the lawyer, and he may well allow the direction and extent of the exercise of his individual talents to depend upon the nature and circumstances of the particular question under discussion.

The law in almost any subject may be so stated by generalization that there can be no conflict in the decisions cited, or it may, on the other hand, be so technically and minutely stated that as to almost any proposition conflicts among the decisions shall appear. It should be so stated, however, as to avoid differences in the authorities which are apparent rather than real; but where, as is frequently the case in making an application to particular circumstances of general rules, contradictory conclusions have been reached, the discrepancy should be noted, so that, as between different views, that one may be chosen which is consonant with reason and the weight of authority. It may be a question, however, how far an author should attempt by his own reasoning and judgment to settle the questions as to which the courts entertain conflicting views. Frequently such questions are not to be settled by mere reasoning, but rather on grounds of practical expediency; and usually the cases themselves furnish better guidance to the solution of the difficulty than the reasoning of a text-writer set out within the limits of the space which he may properly devote to any one such question.

While it is not the plan of this treatise to cover criminal procedure in general nor the rules of criminal evidence, yet in connection with each crime there are rules as to the form of the indictment and the evidence admissible on questions peculiar to that particular crime which can be better stated as a part of the substantive law of that crime than in connection with a discussion of the general law of procedure, for these peculiarities usually depend on the nature of the crime. Such rules as to procedure and evidence as relate to the particular crime are therefore here stated in the discussion of that crime. In other words, the object borne in mind has been to give the lawyer with reference to any particular branch of the criminal law that information which he is likely to want in the consideration and trial of a case arising under that branch. In this view it is clear that the forms of indictment for each crime are properly given in connection with the discussion of that crime. The forms which have been selected are almost without exception based upon those which have been found sufficient in particular cases and therefore have judicial sanction. It has not been thought desirable to present a multitude of forms, but to give only such as indicate the ordinary language used in stating the ingredients of each offense.

Civil cases have been sparingly cited, it being thought that in the statement of the criminal law the authorities should be limited to cases in which the principles of the criminal law are applied. Nevertheless so far as has been necessary civil cases have been made use of as illustrating principles not otherwise covered or explaining necessary distinctions. In citing cases the official reference is uniformly given, from which it will be possible to find them in any series not official in which they may be included. While duplicate references may in some cases be a matter of convenience, yet to give them in every instance would involve more space than the corresponding advantage would warrant.

It may be proper for the author to say, by way of explanation as to his fitness for dealing with this subject, that not only has the present treatise been in preparation for more than seven years, but that for eight years prior to commencing the work he had been engaged in teaching criminal law, having prepared during that time for the use of his classes an Outline of Criminal Law and Procedure in about two hundred and fifty pages, stating the general principles of the subject, which is still in use as the class book in criminal law in the school with which he is connected. The present treatise, however, is in no sense an expansion or outgrowth of that Outline, but is the result of an attempt to gather together and state in connected form the principles of the criminal law established by adjudication as they have been worked out in detail in the courts, for it is thus that the law grows and will continue to grow, all efforts at generalization, condensation and codification to the contrary notwithstanding.

E. McC.

LAW DEPARTMENT, STATE UNIVERSITY OF IOWA,
IOWA CITY, February, 1897.

ANALYSIS OF CONTENTS.

VOLUME I.

PART I.

NATURE AND SOURCES.

CHAPTER 1.

ORIGIN OF CRIMINAL LAW; DEFINITION AND NATURE OF CRIME.

§ 1. Theory of criminal punishment.
2. History of criminal law.
3. Place of criminal law in jurisprudence.
4. Definition.
5. What deemed criminal proceeding.
6. Breach of city ordinance.
7. Penal statutes; actions *qui tam.*
8. Penalty, exclusive or concurrent.
9. Contempts.
10. Crime distinct from tort and from breach of contract.
11. Civil remedy not merged or suspended.

CHAPTER 2.

HOW CRIMES PRESCRIBED; WHAT DEEMED CRIMINAL; CLASSIFICATION OF CRIMES.

§ 12. Written and unwritten law.
13. Common-law offenses not recognized.
14. In the federal courts.
15. Common-law definitions and general principles.
16. What deemed criminal.
17. Classes of offenses.
18. Felony and misdemeanor.
19. Other classifications; high crimes and misdemeanors.
§ 20. Infamous crimes.
21. Misdemeanors.
22. Merger.

CHAPTER 3.

OFFENSES PRESCRIBED UNDER GENERAL POLICE POWER AND MUNICIPAL ORDINANCES.

§ 23. Criminal law a part of the police power.
24. Various grounds of regulation.
25. Evil course of life.
26. Common scold.
27. Common barrator.
28. Habitual criminals.
29. Regulation of business; sale of liquors, opium, dangerous articles.
30. Protection of public health.
31. Health of employees.
32. Unwholesome provisions.
33. Adulterated food and drinks.
34. Imitation butter, cheese and lard; oleomargarine.
35. Inspection laws.
36. Regulations of professions; physicians, pharmacists, dentists.
37. Practice of law.
38. Licenses in other callings.
39. Regulation of business in particular localities.
40. Public callings.
41. Insurance.
42. Bankers; factors; mercantile agencies.
43. Corporate business.

§ 44. Occupation tax; peddlers, itinerant merchants.
45. Protection of public interests.
46. Protection of game and fish.
47. Protection of brands.
48. False weights and measures; frauds.
49. Regulation of warehousemen.
50. Regulation of sales.
51. Enticing away servants.
52. Rescue of distrained property.
53. Usury.
54. Civil rights.
55. Regulation of employment.
56. Sale of diseased animals.
57. Regulation of marriage.
58. Abandonment of wife or child; care of children.
59. Protection of minors.
60. Indecency and profanity.
61. Vagrants.
62. Municipal regulations.
63. Ordinances and statutes on same subject.
64. Impose punishments.
65. Reasonableness of ordinances.
66. Suppression of nuisances.
67. Quarantine.
68. Sale of liquors.
69. Power to regulate does not include power to prohibit.
70. Regulation of streets and public places.
71. Regulation of markets and market places.
72. Regulations as to fire.
73. Regulation of employments.

CHAPTER 4.

CONSTITUTIONAL LIMITATIONS.

§ 74. Applicable to criminal statutes.
75. Interference with obligation of contracts and other vested rights.
§ 76. Interference with interstate commerce.
77. Uniformity of operation; equality of protection.
78. *Ex post facto* laws.
79. Bills of attainder.
80. Cruel and unusual punishments.

CHAPTER 5.

PENAL STATUTES; CONSTRUCTION; REPEAL.

§ 81. Construction.
82. Reason of the statute.
83. Strict construction.
84. Not so as to defeat intent.
85. Letter and spirit.
86. Legislative intent.
87. Statutes *in pari materia.*
88. Civil code.
89. General and special provisions.
90. General clause; particular enumeration.
91. Implied repeal.
92. Implied repeals not favored.
93. What amounts to a repeal.
94. As between general and special provisions.
95. Effect of statute upon preexisting common law.
96. Effect of repeals as to offenses already committed.
97. Effect on pending prosecutions.
98. Repeal after conviction.
99. Repeal after judgment pending an appeal.
100. Effect of partial repeal or partial invalidity.
101. Saving clause.
102. Repeal of repealing statute.
103. Statutes construed prospectively.
104. Effect of invalidity of statute.
105. Construction of terms.
106. Grammar and punctuation.
107. Singular for plural.
108. "And," "or."
109. "May."
110. Definition of terms.

PART II.

CRIMINAL INTENT AND CAPACITY.

CHAPTER 6.

THE CRIMINAL INTENT.

§ 111. Tort and crime distinct as to intent.
112. Intent, essential element in crime.
113. Acting under claim of right.
114. Legal advice.
115. Acting under legal or other authority.
116. Compulsion.
117. Acting as detective.
118. Decoying to crime.
119. Other illustrations.
120. Motive and intent distinguished.
121. Malice.
122. Specific criminal intent.
123. Intent presumed.
124. Allegation and proof of intent.
125. Statements as to intent.
126. Variance of the act from the intent.
127. Intent alone.
128. Intent in statutory offenses.

CHAPTER 7.

CRIMINAL NEGLIGENCE.

§ 129. As supplying intent.
130. Causing injury.

CHAPTER 8.

IGNORANCE OR MISTAKE.

§ 131. When a defense.
132. Ignorance or mistake of law.
133. Ignorance or mistake of fact.
134. Duty to know the facts.
135. Mixed mistake of law and fact.

CHAPTER 9.

NECESSITY AND COMPULSION.

§ 136. How far excuse.
137. Avoiding injury to one's self.
§ 138. Defense of person or property.
139. Extent of right to defend the person.
140. Defense of family and others.
141. Resisting unlawful arrest.
142. Defense of property.
143. Power of custodian of building.
144. Protection of dwelling.

CHAPTER 10.

COVERTURE.

§ 145. Presumption of coercion.
146. Exception in case of murder.
147. Presumption not conclusive.
148. Wife's separate business.

CHAPTER 11.

INFANCY.

§ 149. When complete defense.
150. Presumption of innocence.
151. Over fourteen years.
152. Evidence of capacity; question for the jury.
153. Proof of age.

CHAPTER 12.

INSANITY AND INTOXICATION.

§ 154. Lack of mind; imbecility.
155. Deaf and dumb.
156. Complete insanity; right and wrong theory.
157. Uncontrollable impulses; moral insanity.
158. Partial insanity; insane delusions.
159. Insanity caused by intoxication.
160. Intoxication alone no defense.
161. Intoxication as bearing upon the specific intent.
162. In cases of homicide.
163. Voluntary intoxication.

§ 164. Defense of insanity; how raised.
165. Question for the jury.
166. Preliminary investigation.
167. Evidence of insanity.
168. Acts and declarations of accused.
169. Mental condition before and after the crime.
170. Hereditary.
171. Other evidence.
172. Opinions of experts.
173. Opinions of those not experts.
174. Presumption.
175. Burden of proof.
§ 176. Amount of evidence; various rules.
177. Beyond a reasonable doubt.
178. By preponderance of evidence.
179. Reasonable doubt sufficient.

CHAPTER 13.

CORPORATIONS.

§ 180. Liability to indictment.
181. Whether deemed "person."
182. Liable for non-feasance.
183. Also for misfeasance.
184. Criminal intent.
185. Allegation and proof of corporate existence.

PART III.

CONNECTION WITH THE ACT.

CHAPTER 14.

AGENCY.

§ 186. As affecting criminal liability.
187. Principal's liability.
188. Whether authority presumed.
189. Illegal sales of liquor by servant.
190. Liability of agent or servant.
191. Liability of partners.
192. Management of property.

CHAPTER 15.

COMBINATIONS; PRINCIPAL AND ACCESSORY.

I. In General.

§ 193. Acts, as well as intent, essential.
194. Participation necessary.
195. Persons acting together.
196. Whether or not act contemplated in the original design.
197. Acts outside of original design.
§ 198. Abandonment of original design.
199. Accomplices; aiders and abettors.
200. What is sufficient procurement or participation.
201. Detectives.
202. Consent to crime; *particeps criminis.*
203. Acts or declarations of accomplices or confederates.

II. Principal and Accessory.

204. Distinction.
205. Principals in first and second degree.
206. Constructive presence.
207. Accessory before the fact.
208. Accessory in manslaughter.
209. Accessory after the fact.
210. Crimes in which accessories not recognized.

III. Procedure as to Accessories.

211. Jurisdiction and venue.
212. Indictment; joinder.
213. Charging principals.
214. Charging accessories.

§ 215. Accessory not tried before principal.
216. Guilt of principal must be shown.
§ 217. Statutory provisions.
218. Statutes making accessory guilty of substantive offense.

PART IV.

UNCOMPLETED ACT; WHEN CRIMINAL.

§ 219. How far intent must have been carried.

CHAPTER 16.

ATTEMPTS.

§ 220. Solicitations.
221. Attempts deemed criminal.
222. Intent involved.
223. What acts sufficient.
224. Preparation distinguished from attempt.
225. Illustrations.
226. Impossibility.
227. Attempts to poison.
228. Indictment.
228*a*. Forms.
229. Included offense.

CHAPTER 17.

ASSAULTS.

§ 230. How classified.

I. SIMPLE ASSAULT AND ASSAULT AND BATTERY.

231. What constitutes; attempt to commit battery.
232. Cases of attempt; menace not enough.
233. Putting in fear.
234. Present ability.
235. What acts sufficient; battery.
236. Administering injurious drug.
237. Wilful or negligent exposure, or improper treatment of another.
238. Indecent assault.
239. Intent.
240. Unlawfulness.
§ 241. Justification.
242. Lawful chastisement.
243. Correction of wife.
244. Control of premises.
245. Protection of property.
246. Self-defense.
247. Effect of civil action.
248. Mitigation or aggravation.
249. Effect of consent.
250. Principal and accessory.
251. Jurisdiction.
252. Indictment.
252*a*. Form.
253. Included offense.

II. AGGRAVATED ASSAULTS.

254. How classified.
255. What constitutes aggravation.
256. Shooting, cutting, stabbing, wounding, inflicting great bodily harm, etc.
257. Assaults with dangerous or deadly weapons.
258. Loaded weapons.
259. Intent.
260. Indictment.
261. Forms.
262. Included offense.

III. ASSAULTS WITH FELONIOUS INTENT.

263. Whether felonious or not.
264. What included.
265. The intent involved.
266. Ability to commit the injury threatened.
267. Justification, excuse, or mitigation.
268. Indictment; charging assault.

§ 269. Charging the intent.
270. Forms.
271. Included offenses.
272. Joinder.

IV. ASSAULT WITH INTENT TO KILL OR MURDER.

273. The assault.
274. The intent.
275. Allegation and proof of intent.
276. Connection of intent and act.
§ 277. Justification or excuse.
278. With intent to commit manslaughter.
279. Assault with intent to kill.

V. ASSAULT TO DO GREAT BODILY INJURY.

280. What constitutes; how shown.

VI. ASSAULT WITH INTENT TO ROB.

281. What constitutes.

PART V.

OFFENSES AGAINST THE PERSON.

CHAPTER 18.

HOMICIDE.

§ 282. Scope of the chapter.
282*a*. Table of homicide.

I. CAUSATION.

283. Means of killing.
284. Threats, fear.
285. Accident.
286. Negligence; failure to provide for dependent persons.
287. Physicians and chemists.
288. Railroad companies.
289. Wrongful act.
290. Suicide.
291. By act of another; combination; conspiracy.
292. Proximate or remote cause; death from wound.
293. Time of death.

II. WHO DEEMED PERSON.

294. Human being; child unborn.
295. Person in the king's peace.

III. HOMICIDES NOT CRIMINAL; JUSTIFIABLE OR EXCUSABLE; SELF-DEFENSE.

296. How distinguished.
297. In executing sentence of death.
§ 297*a*. In acting under military command.
298. In arresting or detaining criminals.
299. Resisting commission of felony.
300. Accidental killing.
301. Self-defense.
302. Danger to life or of injury to the person.
303. Imminent danger.
304. Apparent danger.
305. Belief of danger.
306. Reasonableness of belief.
307. Threats and character of deceased.
308. Necessity.
309. Party in the wrong.
310. Duty to withdraw.
311. Duty to retreat.
312. Where felony threatened, or invasion of home.
313. Protection of others.
314. Right to pursue.
315. Instruction as to self-defense.
316. Burden of proof.

IV. MURDER.

317. Felonious.
318. Division into murder and manslaughter.
319. Malice aforethought.

§ 320. Meaning of term.
321. Malice in general.
322. Express or implied.
323. Intent to kill the person killed or another.
324. Dueling; fighting by consent.
325. General recklessness; acts dangerous to life.
326. In the attempt to commit a felony.
327. Attempt to procure abortion.
328. In resisting lawful arrest.
329. "Aforethought;" deliberation; premeditation.
330. Evidence of malice.
331. Intoxication or insanity as affecting the question of malice.
332. Whether malice presumed; use of deadly weapon.
333. Presumption of malice from killing.
334. Instructions as to malice.

MANSLAUGHTER.

335. How distinguished.
336. Intentional killing; when manslaughter.
337. Provocation.
338. What sufficient.
339. Quarrel; mutual combat; tumult.
340. Resisting unlawful arrest.
341. Wife in adultery; insults to females, etc.
342. Homicide irrespective of provocation.
343. Cooling time.
344. Sufficiency of provocation as affected by intoxication or insanity of defendant, character of deceased, etc.
345. Question of law or fact.
346. Burden of proof; sufficiency of evidence.
347. Unintentional killing in doing wrongful act; attempted abortion.
348. Unlawful violence in doing lawful act.
§ 349. Death from negligence.
350. What deemed negligence.
351. Examples.

VI. STATUTORY DEGREES OF MURDER AND MANSLAUGHTER.

352. To determine extent of punishment.
353. Degrees of murder.
354. First degree; by poison or lying in wait.
355. In perpetrating certain felonies.
356. Wilful, deliberate, and premeditated killing.
357. Wilfulness; intentional killing.
358. Deliberate and premeditated.
359. Evidence of deliberation and premeditation.
360. Intoxication or insanity as showing want of deliberation or premeditation.
361. Indictment for first degree.
362. Finding as to degree.
363. Fixing the punishment.
364. Fixing the degree of punishment on plea of guilty.
365. Murder in second degree.
366. Question of law and fact.
367. Conviction of second degree under indictment of first degree.
368. Degrees of manslaughter.

VII. JURISDICTION AND VENUE.

369. Jurisdiction.
370. Venue.

VIII. THE INDICTMENT.

371. Murder and manslaughter distinguished.
372. Elements.
373. Name of the party charged; "sound mind."
373*a*. The person killed.
374. Human being; in the king's peace.
375. Killing two or more persons.
376. Time and place of wrongful act.
377. The means of killing.

§ 378. Method; assault, weapon, strangulation, poison, etc.
379. Negligence.
380. Description of wound.
381. Death.
382. Allegations of intent; feloniously, wilfully, with malice aforethought.
383. Intent to kill.
384. Opening and conclusion.
385. In general; allegations of fact; clerical errors.
386. Under statutes.
387. Form of indictment in general.
388. Particular forms.

IX. PROCEDURE AND PUNISHMENT.

389. Included offenses.
390. Effect of conviction of lower degree or included offense.
391. Instructions as to lower degree or included offense.
392. Verdict.
393. Punishment.
394. Sentence.

X. THE EVIDENCE.

395. Venue.
396. *Corpus delicti.*
397. When corroboration necessary.
398. Identity of body.
399. *Alibi* of alleged deceased.
400. Cause of death.
401. Proof of suicide.
402. Death from natural causes.
403. Identity of accused.
404. Guilt of third persons.
405. Real evidence.
406. Photographs.
407. Experiments.
408. Circumstantial evidence.
409. Weight and sufficiency of circumstantial evidence.
410. Best evidence; eye-witnesses.
411. *Res gestæ.*
412. Declarations as part of *res gestæ.*
413. Antecedent acts and declarations.
§ 414. Narrative of past transaction.
415. Declarations as to physical condition.
416. Motive.
417. Relations of parties.
418. Evidence of intent.
419. Threats and hostile acts of accused.
420. Confessions and admissions by defendant.
421. Acts and behavior of defendant subsequent to the homicide.
422. Defendant's character.
423. Threats, character, and occupation of deceased.
424. Declarations of deceased.
425. Dying declarations.
426. Sense of impending death.
427. As to what matters admissible.
428. Competency of evidence; opinions.
429. Form of statement.
430. Admissibility for the court.
431. Credibility and weight.

CHAPTER 19.

MAYHEM AND MAIMING.

§ 432. Mayhem; maiming.
433. Whether felony.
434. What constitutes maiming.
435. Intent.
436. Indictment.
436*a*. Forms.
437. Included offense.

CHAPTER 20.

RAPE AND CARNAL ABUSE OF FEMALE CHILDREN.

§ 438. Rape defined.
439. The force involved.
440. Resistance.
441. Without consent.
442. Age of the female as bearing upon the question of consent.
443. Carnal abuse of females under the age of consent.

§ 444. What deemed the age of consent.
445. Woman insensible.
446. Consent obtained by fraud.
447. Woman imbecile or insane.
448. Consent through fear.
449. Who may commit: husband; boy; woman; joint principals.
450. The act; penetration; emission.
451. The intent.
452. Indictment.
453. Forms.
454. Included offenses.
455. Evidence; outcry or complaint.
456. Evidence of complaints only corroborative.
457. Other discrediting evidence.
458. Corroboration of prosecutrix.
459. Physical condition.
460. Previous unchastity; relations between parties, etc.
461. Other crimes; burden of proof, etc.

CHAPTER 21.

ASSAULT WITH INTENT TO COMMIT RAPE; OR ATTEMPT TO COMMIT RAPE.

§ 462. What acts necessary; included assault.
463. Intent.
464. Consent.
465. Effect of incapacity to commit rape.
466. Indictment.
467. Forms.

CHAPTER 22.

ROBBERY.

§ 468. Definition.
469. The violence.
470. Putting in fear.
471. The taking and carrying away.
472. The value.
473. The property of another.
474. From the person.
475. Against the owner's will.
476. Participation.
477. Injury to different persons.
478. Degrees of the offense; aggravation.
479. The intent.
480. Indictment.
481. Description of property; value.
482. Statutory provisions.
483. Form of indictment.
484. Included offense.

CHAPTER 23.

KIDNAPPING; FALSE IMPRISONMENT.

§ 485. Nature of offenses.
486. False imprisonment.
487. Unlawfulness.
488. Method of detention.
489. Kidnapping.
490. Against the will.
491. Intent.
492. Indictment; form.

PART VI.

OFFENSES AGAINST THE HABITATION.

CHAPTER 24.

BURGLARY AND STATUTORY BREAKINGS AND ENTERINGS.

§ 493. Definition.
494. The habitation.
495. House of another.
§ 496. Buildings connected with or appurtenant to the dwelling; common roof.
497. Within the curtilage.
498. Buildings adjacent.
499. Buildings not connected with a dwelling; statutory provisions.

§ 500. The breaking.
501. Constructive breaking.
502. Breaking out.
503. The entry.
504. Night-time; day-time under statutes.
505. The intent.
506. Evidence of intent.
507. Intent disproved.
508. Indictment; description of property.
509. Description of offense intended; goods stolen or intended to be stolen.
509*a*. Venue.
510. "Burglariously," "feloniously," etc.
511. Joinder of offenses; included offenses.
512. Aggravation; degrees.
513. Forms of indictment.
514. Evidence; recent possession of stolen property.
515. Other evidence.
516. Possession of burglars' tools.

CHAPTER 25.

ARSON AND OTHER BURNINGS.

§ 517. Definition.
518. What constitutes "the house."
519. Other buildings within the curtilage; adjacent buildings; barns.
520. Buildings not part of the dwelling; grain, hay, etc.
521. The house of another.
522. Intent to defraud insurance companies and others.
523. The burning.
524. Person in the building.
525. Other matters of aggravation; degrees; night-time.
526. The intent.
527. Indictment; venue.
528. Description of property.
529. Description of ownership.
530. Allegation of intent.
531. Forms of indictment.
532. Included offenses.
533. Evidence.

PART VII.

OFFENSES AGAINST PROPERTY.

CHAPTER 26.

LARCENY.

I. Definition.

§ 534. Technical.
535. In brief.

II. What Property Subject to Larceny.

536. Not realty.
537. Where the severance and carrying away are not continuous.
538. Animals *feræ naturæ* or without value.
539. Dogs and cats.
540. Domestic animals or fowl, and their product.
§ 541. Animals, alive or dead.
542. Other instances of property.
543. Things of value; written instruments; choses in action.

III. Ownership of the Property.

544. Property without owner; abandoned.
545. Property temporarily out of owner's control; lost or left in another's custody.
546. What sufficient ownership; special owner, bailee or custodian; part owner.
547. One's own property; intent to charge another.

IV. The Act; Taking and Carrying Away.

§ 548. What sufficient asportation.
549. Trespass necessary.
550. What constitutes trespass.
551. Continuous trespass; distinct articles; different owners.
552. Taking goods from one county to another.
553. Taking goods from one state or country to another.
554. Misappropriation by bailee.
555. Carriers or other bailees breaking bulk.
556. Larceny by servant or mere custodian.
557. Consent of owner; collusion.
558. Consent of servant or custodian or wife.
559. Further as to consent; force, duress, fraud.
560. Property obtained by trick or fraud.
561. Mutual mistake and subsequent wrongful appropriations.
562. Obtaining possession only, but with intent to appropriate.
563. Obtaining property by false pretenses.

V. Intent.

564. An essential element.
565. Under claim of right.
566. Intent to appropriate; temporary use.
567. Pecuniary advantage without permanent appropriation.
568. For the thief's benefit; *lucri causa.*
569. Intent contemporaneous with act.
570. Intent relating back.
571. Lost property.
572. Intent; how charged and proved or disproved.
573. Connection with the offense; principal and accessory; receiver.

VI. Compound Larcenies.

§ 574. Elements of aggravation.
575. From the person.
576. From the dwelling-house.
577. From the house.
578. From a building, store-house, warehouse, vessel, etc.
579. In night-time or day-time.
580. Common thief.

VII. Value as Determining Punishment; Grand and Petit.

581. Felony.
582. Some value essential.
583. What essential for grand larceny.
584. Aggregate value.
585. Value, how estimated.
586. Allegation and proof of value.
587. Finding as to value.
588. What sufficient finding.
589. Cases where value immaterial; horse-stealing, etc.

VIII. Procedure.

590. Jurisdiction and venue.
591. Indictment.
592. Description of the property.
593. Sufficiency of description in particular cases.
594. Description of animals.
595. Written instruments, bills and notes.
596. Bank-notes, treasury notes, etc.
597. Money, coin.
598. Money not goods and chattels.
599. Evidence of identity and value.
600. "Personal property," "goods and chattels."
601. Ownership.
602. Joint ownership; several owners.
603. What sufficient ownership.
604. Ownership in corporation.
605. Effect of mistake in name.
606. Defective indictment cured by verdict.

§ 607. Allegation of "stealing, taking, and carrying away."
608. Felonious intent.
609. As an included offense; joinder.
610. Forms of indictment.
611. Restitution of property.

IX. EVIDENCE.

612. *Corpus delicti.*
613. Identification of property.
614. Identification of defendant; declarations; circumstantial evidence.
615. Other crimes.
616. Recent possession of stolen goods.
617. Effect of such evidence; presumption; burden of proof.
618. Sufficiency of explanation.
619. When possession deemed sufficiently recent.
620. Possession exclusive.

CHAPTER 27.

EMBEZZLEMENT.

I. NATURE OF THE OFFENSE.

§ 621. What constitutes.
622. Definition.
623. How distinguished from larceny.
624. Whether statute exclusive.
625. Whether embezzlement is a form of larceny.

II. BY SERVANT, CLERK, AGENT, ETC.

626. Who deemed servant or clerk.
627. Who deemed agent.
628. For hire.
629. Trustees, attorneys, collectors, etc.
630. Custodian.
631. Partnerships and associations.
632. Officers or agents of corporations.
633. Persons under the age of sixteen years.
634. Property received by virtue of employment.
§ 635. Illegally received.
636. What property subject to embezzlement; value.
637. What acts sufficient.
638. Conversion of property.
639. Conversion of money; demand and refusal.
640. Failure to account or pay over.
641. Intent necessary.
642. Other acts.
643. Without employer's consent.

III. BY CARRIER OR OTHER BAILEE.

644. Carrier liable.

IV. BY PUBLIC OFFICERS.

645. Special statutory provisions.
646. Who deemed public officer.
647. *De facto* officer.
648. Public funds.
649. What constitutes conversion.

V. PROCEDURE.

650. Venue.
651. Time.
652. Description of money or property.
653. Ownership of property.
654. The relation under which the property is received.
655. Description of the act.
656. Joinder of counts; duplicity.
656*a*. Forms of indictment.

CHAPTER 28.

FALSE PRETENSES; CHEATS AND FRAUDS.

I. NATURE OF THE OFFENSES.

§ 657. General scope of this chapter.
658. General divisions.
659. Distinguished from larceny.
660. Cheat defined.
661. Cheating by false tokens.
662. Swindling by gambling devices, etc.
663. False packing.
663*a*. Frauds on hotel-keepers.
664. False personation.
665. False pretenses; general nature of the offense.

II. SUFFICIENCY OF THE FALSE PRETENSE.

§ 666. False pretense; what constitutes.
667. Relevancy of the pretense, continued.
668. Misrepresentation of fact.
669. Distinguished from opinion.
670. Statements as to value, or indebtedness.
671. Incumbrance on property.
672. Fraudulent second sale.
673. Misrepresentation of authority.
674. Checks, drafts, orders, or accounts.
675. Using false money, notes, or checks.
676. Contract; warranty.
677. False representations in sale of horse.
678. False promises; statement of fact as distinguished from promise.
679. False statements of financial ability.

III. CONNECTION BETWEEN THE FALSE PRETENSE AND THE WRONG DONE.

680. Fraud accomplished.
681. By means of the false pretense.
682. Illegality of mutual purpose.
683. Made to or by agent or third person.
684. Pretense relied upon.
685. Falsity of pretense; fraud perpetrated.
686. Controlling cause.
687. Want of prudence of person defrauded.

IV. INTENT AND KNOWLEDGE.

688. Purpose to defraud.
689. Intent.
690. Knowledge of falsity.
691. Evidence of intent; other transactions.

V. THE FRAUD PERPETRATED.

§ 692. What constitutes property.
693. Notes, checks and other instruments.
694. Obtaining signature.
695. Obtaining charity.

VI. INDICTMENT AND EVIDENCE.

696. Venue.
697. Parties indictable; combination.
698. The indictment; statutory form.
699. Statement of the false pretenses.
700. Setting out the words or instrument.
701. Several pretenses.
702. Falsity of the pretenses.
703. Intent.
704. Person defrauded.
705. Corporation deemed person.
706. How fraud effected; means.
707. Name of party defrauded; ownership of property.
708. Description of the property.
709. Value.
710. Variance.
711. Forms of indictment.
712. Restitution.

CHAPTER 29.

RECEIVING STOLEN GOODS.

§ 713. Nature of the offense.
714. What acts sufficient.
715. What goods.
716. Guilty knowledge.
717. Intent.
718. Indictment; description of the property.
719. Description of the larceny.
720. Jurisdiction and venue.
721. Allegation of intent and knowledge.
722. Joinder.
723. Finding of value.
724. Evidence.
725. Recent possession.
726. Guilty knowledge.
727. Forms of indictment.

CHAPTER 30.

OBTAINING PROPERTY BY THREATS; BLACKMAIL.

§ 728. What constitutes.
729. Sending threatening letters.
730. Threats for the purpose of extortion.
731. American statutes.
732. The threat.
733. Must be communicated.
§ 734. The thing threatened; violence.
735. Injury to business.
736. Injury to character.
737. Threat to prosecute.
738. The advantage obtained.
739. Venue.
740. The indictment.
741. Forms of indictment.
742. Evidence; other acts.

VOLUME II.

PART VII.

OFFENSES AGAINST PROPERTY (CONTINUED).

CHAPTER 31.

FORGERY AND COUNTERFEITING.

§ 743. General nature.

I. FORGERY.

744. Defined.
745. Written instruments.
746. Part false.
747. Classes of instruments.
748. Effect of statutes; felony or misdemeanor.
749. What instruments.
750. Public records or process; wills.
751. Bonds and deeds.
752. Notes, bills, checks and other instruments.
753. Undertakings, warrants, or orders for the payment of money or the delivery of goods.
754. Receipts.
755. Books of account.
756. Validity or legal effect of the writing.
757. Apparent legal efficacy.
758. Invalid instrument.
759. Invalid for lack of authority.
§ 760. Delivery not essential.
761. False signature; similarity not essential.
762. Unauthorized signature.
763. By procurement.
764. Fictitious name.
765. Alteration.
766. Intent to defraud.
767. Intent inferred.
768. Execution of the intent.
769. Fraudulent tendency of the act.
770. Person to be defrauded.
771. Name of person intended to be defrauded.
772. Existence of corporation.
773. Perpetration of fraud.

II. COUNTERFEITING.

774. What deemed counterfeit; similitude.
775. Foreign coin or notes.
776. Intent.

III. POSSESSION OF COUNTERFEITING TOOLS.

777. What criminal.
778. Of intent.
779. How charged.

IV. UTTERING, PASSING, OR HAVING IN POSSESSION.

§ 780. Offenses defined.
781. What constitutes an uttering.
782. Passing counterfeit money.
783. What constitutes a passing.
784. Having in possession.
785. What constitutes possession.
786. Possession with intent.
787. Representation of genuineness.
788. The intent.
789. Guilty knowledge.

V. PROCEDURE.

790. Jurisdiction of state and United States.
791. Venue.
792. Indictment.
793. Description of instrument.
794. Setting out the instrument.
795. Foreign language; translation.
796. Purport.
797. Immaterial matters.
798. Variance.
799. Name forged; *idem sonans*.
800. Statutory provisions as to indictment.
801. Allegations as to the act.
802. Allegation of intent; feloniously.
803. Different offenses; duplicity.
804. Form of indictment.

VI. EVIDENCE.

805. Production of instrument.
806. Comparison of handwriting.
807. Capacity of defendant and other matters.
808. Evidence of other crimes.
809. Inferences from the act or possession.
810. In cases of conspiracy.

CHAPTER 32.

MALICIOUS MISCHIEF; WILFUL TRESPASS.

§ 811. Nature of these crimes.
812. Malicious mischief by early statutes; Black Act.
§ 813. Distinguished from larceny.
814. Injuries to personal property.
815. Injuries to animals.
816. Altering brand, etc.
817. Injuries to machinery.
818. Injuries to vessels.
819. Injury to public property.
820. Forcible trespass.
821. Injury to buildings.
822. Hunting or fishing without permission.
823. Injuries to real property.
824. Trespass after warning, or when forbidden.
825. Offenses against possession.
826. The intent; malice.
827. Under claim of right.
828. Under claim of authority.
829. Malice against owner.
830. Indictment; ownership of property.
831. Other description.
832. The act, how charged.
833. As to intent.
834. Value of property.
835. Joinder.

CHAPTER 33.

FORCIBLE ENTRY AND DETAINER.

§ 836. Common-law offenses.
837. What constitutes forcible entry.
838. Forcible detainer.
839. Possession involved.
840. Description of premises.
841. Restitution.

CHAPTER 34.

FRAUDULENT CONVEYANCES; CONCEALMENT OF PROPERTY.

§ 842. General characteristics.
843. Concealing or disposing of property to defraud creditors.
844. Fraudulent conveyances.

§ 845. Fraud perpetrated.
846. Removal or disposal of property covered by chattel mortgage.
847. Consent of mortgagee.
§ 848. Selling or removing property subject to lien.
849. The intent.
850. Venue.
851. Indictment.

PART VIII.

OFFENSES AGAINST PUBLIC JUSTICE.

CHAPTER 35.

PERJURY.

I. WHAT CONSTITUTES.
§ 852. Definition.
853. Elements of the offense.

II. THE OATH.
854. Essential.
855. Before authorized officer.
856. Acting officer.
857. State officer acting under federal statute.

III. IN A COURT HAVING JURISDICTION.
858. Jurisdiction essential.

IV. WHERE AN OATH IS AUTHORIZED.
859. Collateral proceedings in court.
860. Proceedings not in court.

V. MATERIALITY.
861. Essential.
862. Collateral facts.
863. Illustrations.
864. As to credibility of witness.
865. Effect immaterial.
866. Materiality is for the court.

VI. FALSITY.
867. Essential.
868. Statement of fact.

VII. INTENT.
869. What essential.
870. Advice of counsel.

VIII. THE INDICTMENT.
871. Jurisdiction.
872. Requisites.
§ 873. The proceeding.
874. Description of the oath.
875. Authority of officer.
876. Jurisdiction of the court.
877. The matter falsely sworn.
878. Materiality.
879. Availability and effect.
880. The averment as to falsity.
881. Intent; knowledge.
882. Time and place.
883. Separate counts; several assignments.
884. Joinder of defendants.
885. Forms of indictment.

IX. THE EVIDENCE.
886. As to the proceedings or issue.
887. Administration of the oath.
888. The testimony or statement.
889. Materiality.
890. Wilful falsity.
891. Sufficiency of testimony; contradictory statements of accused.
892. One witness not sufficient.

X. SUBORNATION; ATTEMPT TO PROCURE.
893. What constitutes.
894. Attempt to procure or incite.
895. Form of indictment.

CHAPTER 36.

BRIBERY.

§ 896. What constitutes.
897. Who subject to bribery.
898. Bribing witness.
899. Bribing jurors; embracery.

§ 900. Venue.
901. Indictment.
902. Forms of indictment.
903. Evidence.

CHAPTER 37.

OFFICIAL MISCONDUCT; EXTORTION.

§ 904. Usurpation.
905. Abuse of authority.
906. Misconduct.
907. Refusal to act.
908. Disregard of duty.
909. Neglect of duty.
910. Permitting a prisoner to escape.
911. Public contracts.
912. Who deemed officer.
913. Intent.
914. xtortion.
915. Indictment for misconduct or neglect.
916. Stating the office.
917. Alleging the intent.
918. Describing the act or omission.
919. Removal; penalty.

CHAPTER 38.

OBSTRUCTING JUSTICE.

I. In General.

§ 920. What constitutes.

II. Resisting an Officer.

§ 921. When criminal.
922. What officers; authority.
923. What constitutes resistance.
924. Intent; justifiable resistance.
925. Indictment.
926. Allegation of act.
927. Charging the intent.
928. Duplicity.
929. Evidence.

III. Breaking Jail; Escape; Rescue.

930. What criminal.
931. Legality of arrest or confinement.
932. Pound-breach.
933. Intent.
934. Indictment.
935. Practice.
936. Evidence.

IV. Tampering with a Witness.

937. Nature of the offense.

CHAPTER 39.

MISPRISION OF FELONY; COMPOUNDING OFFENSES.

§ 938. What constitutes misprision.
939. Compounding offenses.
940. Further as to the crime of compounding.

PART IX.

OFFENSES AGAINST THE ELECTIVE FRANCHISE.

CHAPTER 40.

VIOLATION OF ELECTION LAWS.

§ 941. Under statutes.
942. What deemed an election.
943. Illegal voting.
944. Disqualified voters.
§ 945. Crimes by election officers.
946. Interference with elections.
947. Improperly influencing voters.
948. Federal election laws.
949. Intent.
950. Indictment.
951. Evidence.

PART X.

OFFENSES AGAINST PUBLIC PEACE AND SECURITY.

CHAPTER 41.

CONSPIRACY; UNLAWFUL COMBINATION.

I. WHAT CONSTITUTES THE OFFENSE.

§ 952. General nature.
953. Definitions.
954. Purpose or means as criminal or unlawful.
955. Common-law conspiracy.
956. Conspiracies to commit a crime.
957. To charge with crime.
958. To slander.
959. To seduce female or entice to prostitution.
960. To defraud private persons.
961. To deprive of a right.
962. To injure the public.
963. In restraint of trade.
964. To defraud the government.
965. To overthrow the government.
966. Overt act.
967. Impossibility.
968. The combination.
969. Joining in the execution.
970. Liability of one for acts of all.
971. Intent.

II. PROCEDURE.

972. Jurisdiction and venue.
973. Limitation.
974. The indictment; allegation of wrongful purpose.
975. Setting out the unlawful means.
976. Bills of particulars.
977. Charging overt act.
978. Duplicity.
979. Merger.
980. Joinder of offenses.
981. Joinder of defendants.
982. The person to be injured.
983. Description of property.
984. Statutory language.
§ 985. Variance.
986. Form of indictment.
987. Punishment.

III. EVIDENCE.

988. Declarations and acts of co-conspirators.
989. Proof of the existence of the conspiracy.
990. Necessity of corroboration.

CHAPTER 42.

RIOT; UNLAWFUL ASSEMBLY.

I. IN GENERAL.

§ 991. Nature of offenses.

II. RIOT AND ROUT.

992. Definition.
993. Unlawfulness of act or manner.
994. Numbers of persons.
995. Participation.
996. Conviction of one alone.
997. Reading the riot act.
998. Indictment.
999. Forms of indictment.
1000. Description of property.
1001. Included crime.
1002. Punishment.

III. UNLAWFUL ASSEMBLY.

1003. Defined.
1004. Intent sufficient.
1005. Statutory definition.

CHAPTER 43.

AFFRAYS AND BREACHES OF THE PEACE.

I. AFFRAY.

§ 1006. Defined.
1007. Fighting by consent; mere words not enough.
1008. In a public place.
1009. Indictment.
1010. Conviction of joint offense.
1011. Included offense.

II. BREACH OF THE PEACE AND DISORDERLY CONDUCT.

1012. What constitutes.
1013. Prize-fighting.
1014. Injuries to property.
1015. Shooting in streets or highways.
1016. Noise and disturbance.
1017. Threatening and insulting language.
1018. Disorderly persons; vagrants; drunkards.
1019. Public place.
1020. Disturbance of family or neighborhood.
1021. Method of charging offense.

III. DISTURBANCE OF MEETINGS.

1022. What constitutes.
1023. What deemed public meeting.
1024. Congregation assembled for worship.
1025. Disturbance of school.
1026. What deemed a disturbance.
1027. The intent.
1028. The indictment.

CHAPTER 44.

CARRYING CONCEALED WEAPONS.

§ 1029. At common law.
1030. Constitutionality of statutes.
1031. What made criminal.
1032. The intent.
1033. What weapons.
1034. Exceptions; apprehension of attack.
1035. On one's own premises.
1036. Travelers.
§ 1037. Officers.
1038. Indictment.
1039. Evidence.

CHAPTER 45.

LIBEL AND SLANDER.

§ 1040. Nature of the offenses.
1041. Definition.
1042. Common law or statutory.
1043. As against private individuals.
1044. As against a family or class or corporation.
1045. As against wife.
1046. As against the dead.
1047. As against public officers.
1048. As against government.
1049. Blasphemous or obscene publications.
1050. Freedom of the press.
1051. The truth as a defense.
1052. Privileged publications.
1053. Intent; malice.
1054. Mitigation.
1055. Publication.
1056. Liability for acts of servants or agents.
1057. Slander.
1058. Venue.
1059. Indictment.
1060. Colloquium and innuendo.
1061. Setting out the language.
1062. In foreign language.
1063. Whole publication.
1064. Indecent matter not set out.
1065. Alleging publication.
1066. Description of the person.
1067. Allegation of intent.
1068. Duplicity.
1069. Forms of indictment.
1070. Functions of court and jury.

PART XI.

OFFENSES AGAINST CONJUGAL AND PARENTAL RIGHTS.

CHAPTER 46.

BIGAMY.

§ 1071. Definition.
1072. What constitutes.
§ 1073. The second marriage.
1074. Validity of prior marriage.
1075. Prior marriage terminated by divorce.

§ 1076. Intent; belief as to death of former consort.
1077. Jurisdiction and venue.
1078. Limitation.
1079. Indictment.
1080. Negativing proviso.
1081. Allegation of intent.
1082. Evidence; proof of former marriage.
1083. Admissions of defendant.
1084. Evidence that former spouse is still living.
1085. Testimony of husband or wife.

CHAPTER 47.

ADULTERY.

§ 1086. What constitutes.
1087. Living in adultery; habitual intercourse.
1088. Validity of marriage.
1089. Presumption of continuance.
1090. Termination by divorce.
1091. Intent; knowledge.
1092. Mutual criminal intent.
§ 1093. Complaint of husband or wife.
1094. Indictment.
1095. Joinder; included offenses.
1096. Evidence as to the marriage.
1097. Proof of act.
1098. Proof of other acts.
1099. Competency of husband or wife as a witness.

CHAPTER 48.

ABDUCTION OF FEMALES.

§ 1100. In case of girls.
1101. From the custody of parent or guardian.
1102. Consent.
1103. What constitutes a taking.
1104. Purpose of the abduction.
1105. Knowledge as to age.
1106. Chastity of the female.
1106*a*. Abduction or enticement of woman; pimping or procuring.
1107. The indictment.
1108. Evidence.

PART XII.

OFFENSES AGAINST CHASTITY, DECENCY AND MORALITY.

CHAPTER 49.

SEDUCTION.

§ 1109. Classification of sexual crimes.
1110. Table of sexual crimes.
1111. What constitutes seduction.
1112. Seductive arts; promise of marriage.
1113. Prosecutrix unmarried and chaste.
1114. Indictment.
1115. Included offenses.
1116. Marriage a bar.
1117. Evidence in general.
1118. Evidence of chastity.
1119. Sufficiency of evidence; corroboration.

CHAPTER 50.

INCEST.

§ 1120. What constitutes.
1121. Mutuality.
1122. The act.
1123. Indictment.
1124. Evidence.

CHAPTER 51.

FORNICATION AND BASTARDY.

§ 1125. Fornication; when punishable.
1126. Bastardy.
1127. Jurisdiction and venue.
1128. Complaint.
1129. Evidence.

CHAPTER 52.

ILLICIT COHABITATION.

§ 1130. How far criminal.
1131. Intent; joint offenses.
1132. Other incidents of indictment and evidence.

CHAPTER 53.

PROSTITUTION AND LEWDNESS.

§ 1133. Prostitution and nightwalking.
1134. Frequenting houses of ill-fame.
1135. Lewdness.
1136. Indecent exposure.

CHAPTER 54.

KEEPING DISORDERLY HOUSES.

§ 1137. What deemed criminal.
1138. Keeping houses of ill-fame.
1139. What deemed a house.
1140. What constitutes a keeping.
1141. Procuring or encouraging.
1142. Permitting the use or leasing for the purpose.
1143. Indictment.
1144. Forms of indictment.
1145. Evidence.

CHAPTER 55.

PROCURING ABORTION; CONCEALING BIRTH OF BASTARD.

§ 1146. Procuring abortion.
1147. Where death results.
1148. Attempting; advising.
1149. Consent; necessity.
1150. The indictment.
§ 1151. Evidence.
1152. Concealing birth of a bastard.

CHAPTER 56.

SODOMY.

§ 1153. What constitutes.
1154. Indictment.
1155. Evidence.

CHAPTER 57.

OBSCENITY AND INDECENCY.

§ 1156. Obscene language.
1157. Indecent exhibitions and prints.
1158. Indictment and evidence.

CHAPTER 58.

BLASPHEMY AND PROFANITY.

§ 1159. What constitutes.
1160. Indictment.

CHAPTER 59.

CRUELTY TO ANIMALS.

§ 1161. What punishable.
1162. What deemed animal.
1163. Intent.
1164. Indictment.

CHAPTER 60.

VIOLATION OF RIGHT OF SEPULTURE.

§ 1165. Failure to bury; preventing inquest.
1166. Disposal of dead bodies.
1167. Violation of graves.
1168. Desecration of cemeteries.

PART XIII.

OFFENSES AGAINST PUBLIC HEALTH AND GENERAL WELFARE.

CHAPTER 61.

PUBLIC NUISANCE.

§ 1169. What constitutes.
1170. Further as to what constitutes a nuisance.
1171. Whether public benefit a defense.
1172. Acts under public authority.
1173. Illegal continuance of use.
1174. Liability of owner or servant.
1175. Effect of contribution to the nuisance.
1176. Intent and knowledge.
1177. Venue.
1178. Indictment; charging public nature.
1179. Charging the act.
1180. Joinder of different acts; continuance.
1181. Description of locality.
1182. Abatement.
1183. Forms of indictment.

CHAPTER 62.

OFFENSES AS TO HIGHWAYS.

I. OBSTRUCTION OR NON-REPAIR OF HIGHWAYS.

§ 1184. Deemed a nuisance.
1185. Failure to open or repair.
1186. Obstruction; what constitutes.
1187. Obstruction by railroads.
1188. Continuance of obstruction.
1189. The intent.
1190. What deemed highway.
1191. Private ways.
1192. Streets, alleys and public places.
1193. Indictment.
1194. Title in defendant.

II. OBSTRUCTION OF NAVIGABLE RIVERS.

§ 1195. When criminal.

III. INTERFERENCE WITH THE OPERATION OF RAILROADS.

1196. What criminal.

IV. LAW OF THE ROAD.

1197. Turning to the right; bicycles.
1198. Racing on the highway.

CHAPTER 63.

VIOLATION OF LIQUOR LAWS.

I. GENERAL STATUTORY REGULATIONS; CONSTITUTIONALITY AND CONSTRUCTION OF STATUTES; CONCURRENT FEDERAL, STATE AND CITY REGULATIONS.

§ 1199. General character of statutory regulations.
1200. Constitutionality of liquor legislation.
1201. Federal constitution; fourteenth amendment.
1202. Regulation of commerce.
1203. Restriction of transportation into the state.
1204. Sale in original package.
1205. Effect of Wilson law.
1206. Under state constitutions.
1207. Due process of law; taking private property for public use.
1208. Jury trial.
1209. License; impairing obligation of contract.
1210. Local or special laws; local option.
1211. Uniformity of taxation.
1212. Conditions for granting license.
1213. Constitutional prohibition.

§ 1214. Sale by public agent.
1215. Constitutionality of provisions as to evidence.
1216. Construction of statutes.
1217. Concurrent effect of federal, state and city provisions.

II. WHAT DEEMED INTOXICATING LIQUOR.

1218. Law or fact; judicial notice.
1219. Mixed or compounded liquor.
1220. Particular classes of liquors.
1221. Other descriptions; "spirituous," "fermented," etc.
1222. Evidence as to character of liquor; knowledge by defendant.

III. SYSTEMS OF REGULATION; LICENSE; LOCAL OPTION.

1223. The license system.
1224. License not retroactive.
1225. Direct and collateral attack; appeal.
1226. Forfeiture or revocation.
1227. Not assignable; who protected by; agent or partner.
1228. Authority to issue, discretionary.
1229. Selling without license; allegation and proof of license.
1230. Carrying on the business without a license.
1231. Place of sale.
1232. Local option.

IV. ILLEGAL SELLING OR KEEPING FOR SALE.

1233. What deemed a sale.
1234. Consideration; barter or exchange.
1235. Giving; furnishing; disposing of.
1236. When sale complete; place of sale.
§ 1237. Liability for sales by servant.
1238. Sales by partner or wife.
1239. Liability of agent.
1240. Furnishing to members of club.
1241. Purchaser not punishable.
1242. Transporting.
1243. Unlawfully keeping for sale.
1244. The business of selling; being common seller.
1245. Retailing; wholesaling.
1246. Selling by small measure.
1247. To be drunk on the premises.
1248. Nuisance; keeping place for illegal sale.
1249. Charging and proving the nuisance.
1250. Regulations as to receipts, hour of closing, screens, etc.
1251. Intent.

V. SPECIAL EXCEPTIONS IN CASES OF PHYSICIANS, DRUGGISTS, PRODUCERS, ETC.

1252. Exceptions by statute; need not be negatived.
1253. Sales by physicians and druggists.
1254. Sales by producers or manufacturers.

VI. SPECIAL PROHIBITIONS.

1255. Provisions in general.
1256. Sales to prohibited persons.
1257. Intent or knowledge in such cases.
1258. Sale to minor or intoxicated person for another.
1259. Furnishing to minor or intoxicated person.
1260. Who deemed minor; allegation and proof of age.
1261. Consent of parent or guardian.
1262. Sales to habitual drunkard or intoxicated person.
1263. Sales to Indians.

§ 1264. Selling on Sundays or holidays.
1265. Selling on election day.
1266. Selling near churches, educational institutions, etc.

VII. The Procedure; Seizure; Indictment; Evidence.

1267. Seizure; property in liquors.
1268. Second offense.
1269. Venue.
1270. Indictment.
1271. Further as to description of the particular act.
1272. Time and place.
1273. Description of kind, quantity, price, etc.
1274. Name of purchaser.
1275. Joinder of offenses.
1276. Variance; election.
1277. Double punishment; included offenses; previous jeopardy.
1278. Negativing exceptions.
1279. Evidence.
1280. License as evidence.
1281. Burden of proof as to lawfulness of sales.

CHAPTER 64.

GAMING AND BETTING.

I. Gaming in General.

§ 1282. Introductory.
1283. Gaming in general.
1284. Statutory provisions.
1285. What deemed games.
1286. What deemed a wager.
1287. When offense complete.
1288. Aiding or procuring.
1289. Indictment in general.
1290. Names of parties.
1291. Charging the game played.
1292. The wager.
1293. Time and place.
1294. Joinder of defendants.
1295. Charging different offenses; duplicity.
1296. Evidence.

II. Betting.

§ 1297. In general; on horse-races.
1298. Betting on elections.
1299. Indictment; evidence.

III. Common Gambler.

1300. Who is.

IV. Gaming in Public Places.

1301. In general.
1302. The place.
1303. Further as to public place.
1304. Indictment and evidence.

V. Pool Selling.

1305. Statutory provisions.

VI. Keeping a Gaming House.

1306. What criminal.
1307. Place and time.
1308. The keeper.
1309. The indictment and evidence.

VII. Keeping and Exhibiting Gaming Devices and Tables.

1310. What constitutes.
1311. Procedure; indictment.
1312. Penalty; destruction of implements.

VIII. Allowing Games to be Played on the Premises.

1313. When criminal.

IX. Gaming by Minors.

1314. Permitting to game or to resort.

CHAPTER 65.

LOTTERIES.

§ 1315. Definition.
1316. Statutes.
1317. Constitutionality.
1318. Indictment.

CHAPTER 66.

VIOLATION OF SUNDAY LAWS.

§ 1319. Nature of regulations; constitutionality.
1320. What deemed Sunday.

§ 1321. Works of charity or necessity excepted.
1322. Sunday traveling.
1323. Operation of railroads or telegraph lines.
§ 1324. Carrying on business.
1325. Sunday amusements.
1326. Indictment.

PART XIV.

OFFENSES UNDER FEDERAL REGULATIONS.

CHAPTER 67.

POSTAL CRIMES.

§ 1327. In general.
1328. Obstruction of mails.
1329. Robbery of the mails.
1330. Larceny or embezzlement by postal servants.
1331. Use of mails to defraud.
1332. Sending obscene matter through the mails.
1333. Defamatory or threatening matter.
1334. Lottery advertisements.
1335. Decoy letters.

CHAPTER 68.

REGULATIONS AS TO COMMERCE.

§ 1336. Discrimination.
1337. Unlawful combinations.
1338. Carriage of live-stock.
1338*a*. Trading with the Indians.

CHAPTER 69.

OFFENSES AGAINST BANKING ACT.

§ 1339. False entries.
1340. Embezzlement; misapplication of funds.

CHAPTER 70.

OFFENSES AGAINST NEUTRALITY, IMMIGRATION AND NATURALIZATION LAWS.

§ 1341. Violations of neutrality.
1342. Violence to foreign minister.
§ 1343. Immigration laws; contract labor.
1344. Exclusion of Chinese.
1345. To whom applicable.
1346. Naturalization.

CHAPTER 71.

VIOLATION OF NAVIGATION LAWS.

§ 1347. What criminal.

CHAPTER 72.

VIOLATION OF PENSION LAWS.

§ 1348. What criminal.

CHAPTER 73.

VIOLATION OF REVENUE LAWS; MAKING FALSE CLAIMS.

§ 1349. Forfeiture of goods.
1350. Licenses and stamps.
1351. Customs duties.
1352. Presenting false claims.

CHAPTER 74.

VIOLATION OF LAND LAWS.

§ 1353. What punishable.

PART XV.

OFFENSES AGAINST SOVEREIGNTY.

CHAPTER 75.

TREASON.

§ 1354. History of the crime.
1355. Constitutional definitions.
1356. Statutory definitions.
§ 1357. Levying war; rendering aid and comfort.
1358. Overt act.

CHAPTER 76.

PIRACY.

§ 1359. Nature of the offense.

CRIMINAL LAW.

PART I.

NATURE AND SOURCES.

CHAPTER 1.

ORIGIN OF CRIMINAL LAW — DEFINITION AND NATURE OF CRIME.

§ 1. **Theory of criminal punishment.**— The infliction by the governing power, in any community, of punishment for acts deemed so far detrimental to the public welfare as to make such repressive measures necessary, seems to be a useful and inherent function of government. But the theory under which such power is exercised is by no means so simple as the universal acceptance, without question, of the practical fact would lead us to suppose. Indeed there are many conflicting and inconsistent theories propounded, for the most part by moralists and philosophers, on which the right and duty of the state to punish crime is upheld.[1] This whole theoretical discussion, however, seems to be of no consequence whatever in determining what the criminal law is. It does not throw any light on the solution of the questions which come before the courts for determination. It is of interest, nevertheless, to notice that the so-called absolute theory, making it the duty of the government to punish crime because it is wrong,— the wrongness, of course, depending on the notions of right prevailing with those who make and administer the law,— gave way to preventive or general welfare theories with the introduction of notions of natural law and a social compact, as illustrated in Blackstone[2] and Beccaria;[3] and that when in turn

[1] These theories are collected and discussed in Whart. Cr. L., ch. 1, where the authorities on the subject are referred to.

[2] 4 Com., ch. 1.

[3] See his Essay on Crimes and Punishments, especially ch. 7.

the social compact and natural law theories of government were abandoned, they had already revolutionized the existing ideas as to criminal punishment, and had brought about conceptions which were quite in harmony with the theory of government developed by reason of the peculiar origin of our state and federal governments, and thus paved the way for what may perhaps be called the American theory of criminal law, that punishment is to be inflicted for the protection of the people against the repetition of similar wrongs on the part of the criminal himself or others.[1] The American system, which follows the English, as contrasted with the continental, in treating all men as equals before the law and presuming innocence until the contrary appears, has pushed even farther than the English doctrine the notion of justice in criminal punishment, recognizing that even the criminal shall not be unjustly, unfairly and unequally dealt with; and the adjustment of the punishment to the nature of the act and the moral capability of the actor is made a prominent consideration.[2] Any contrast to be drawn between the American and the English systems relates, however, rather to the English system as it prevailed in the time of Blackstone, just prior to American Independence, than to its present state, for the same moral movement toward humanity and justice, which is so noticeable in the development of the criminal law in America, has had the effect in England of revolutionizing the whole system as it existed in Blackstone's time, and there is perhaps no appreciable difference between the theories recognized in the English criminal law of to-day and those which are assumed in America.

§ 2. **History of criminal law.**— Of more importance than the discussion of theories of criminal responsibility would be the accurate statement of the exact facts with reference to the development of the different features of our criminal law. But such a statement would involve investigations quite outside of the proper scope of a general treatise. It will be sufficiently accurate for present purposes to say that among the Anglo-

[1] The whole subject as looked at from the American point of view is fully discussed in 2 Wilson's Works (Andrews' ed.), part 3, ch. 1, p. 337. See, also, Livingston's report on the Penal Code for Louisiana.

[2] 2 Wilson's Works (Andrews' ed.), 344–6. This view is the basis for the constitutional provisions against cruel and unusual punishments, and other like clauses in the federal and state constitutions.

Saxons was found a somewhat elaborate system of police supervision and a complicated scheme of compensation to be paid by wrong-doers, both to the ruler and to the injured party. That prominence was given to the making of some sort of reparation to the injured party rather than to punishment for the general public benefit is apparent, not only from the provisions for payment of such compensation adjusted to the rank of the injured party and the wrong done him, called the weregild,[1] but also from the prevalence of the system of appeals of felony, which amounted practically to the infliction of punishment by the government on the wrong-doer, not on behalf of the government itself, but on behalf of the injured party or his relatives, and which was deemed so far a private right that the prerogative of mercy could not be exercised by the government, on account of the private interest involved.[2] There was also, however, a well-recognized right to punish corporally, usually by death or some form of mutilation, the wrong-doer who did not pay the penalty imposed for his wrongful act, or whose act was so atrocious as to be deemed beyond pecuniary satisfaction. Corporal punishment was also allowed in some cases of second offense, where the first offense subjected the wrong-doer only to a pecuniary penalty. It seems to have been considered that the payment of the penalty was an absolution from the private vengeance which would otherwise be permissibly inflicted by the injured party or his friends, it being to the interest of the public that private feuds be suppressed and the peace maintained. And where corporal punishment was still permitted, it was perhaps looked upon as a lawful exercise of vengeance on the part of those injured, being regulated, however, by the public authorities, or inflicted by them in behalf of those injured. It is, indeed, claimed by some that the whole criminal law is based on this early notion of vengeance,[3] and that therefore the punishment inflicted is not intended merely as preventive, but also as a satisfaction of the natural instinct of revenge which arises on the part of the individuals of a community as against one who has done an atrocious wrong. It appears, however, that even among the Germanic tribes, be-

[1] 4 Bl. Com. 413.

[2] 2 Wilson's Works (Andrews' ed.), 340, 341.

[3] Holmes' Com. L. 2, 37, 41.

fore the Anglo-Saxons transferred themselves to Great Britain, there was a well-recognized right on the part of the people in their public capacity to inflict capital punishment for public wrongs; a right which is supposed to have been in the nature of self-defense, a power to exclude from the community those who could not be allowed to continue in the community without injury to others. This power was exercised in the Anglo-Saxon system of government by the great Council of State as a matter of public administration, and an outgrowth thereof was the process of outlawry, which was a prominent feature of civil as well as of criminal procedure. The outlaw was simply regarded as a public enemy, having no longer any right whatever in the public state.[1] The system of criminal law which we have derived from the Anglo-Saxons, and which has been molded in England and America during the centuries of its development by changing theories of criminal responsibility and individual rights, is drawn therefore, perhaps, from at least two distinct sources, the one involving redress to the individual, the other protection to the state. It is worthy of note, also, that the present marked distinction between a tort and a crime, the one being an injury to the individual, for which the wrong-doer must make compensation, and the other an injury to the public growing out of the same wrong, for which criminal punishment should be inflicted, was not known to the Anglo-Saxon law.[2] The relations between crime and tort will be hereafter discussed.[3]

§ 3. **Place of criminal law in jurisprudence.**— When the notion of crime has become so well defined that an offense of that character is looked upon as a wrong to the public, distinct from the wrong to any private person who may be injuriously affected, then it is evident that the criminal law is a part of the public law, that is, the law affecting the relation of the state or governing power to the subject, and not a part of the private law which affects the relations of subjects to each other;[4] for although many acts are punishable because they are

[1] See Hammond's Notes to 4 Bl. Com., ch. 1.

[2] See in general, 2 Pollock & Maitland's Hist. Eng. L. 446; 1 Steph. Hist. Cr. L. 51.

[3] *Infra*, § 10.

[4] Holland, Jurisp., chs. 9 and 10, criticising Austin, Jurisp., lec. 44.

infringements of private right, yet the punishment is for the protection of the whole public and not for the satisfaction of the injured party. The natural division of the law relating to crime is into criminal law proper, that is, the substantive law of crime, which determines what is punishable, and criminal procedure, the adjective law of crime, which prescribes the method by which it is determined whether a crime has been committed, and in accordance with which punishment is inflicted. The plan of discussion which has been adopted for this work, however, combines with the criminal law proper so much of criminal procedure as relates peculiarly to each particular crime.

§ 4. **Definition.**— A crime is an act or omission punishable as an offense against the state.[1] It is thus distinguished from

[1] An old definition is found in Staundforde's Plees Del Coron (1583), where it is said that "pleas of the crown are the pleas which relate to (*conteignont*) offenses done against the crown and dignity of the king." And the author then proceeds to describe crimes, such as treason, homicide, rape, larceny, burglary, etc. This illustrates the view of a crime as a direct injury to the sovereign, for the punishment of which a proceeding in his name, as the party wronged, was allowed. The notion that the king is the representative only of the public and that the proceeding is for the benefit of the public seems to be modern. Other definitions are as follows: —

"A crime or misdemeanor is an act committed or omitted in violation of a public law, either forbidding or commanding it: " 4 Bl. Com. 5. Quoted in U. S. v. Eaton, 144 U. S. 677, 688; Ex parte Hollwedell, 74 Mo. 395, 401; S. v. Bishop, 7 Conn. 181, 185; Ex parte Hickey, 4 Sm. & M. 751, 783; In re Bergin, 31 Wis. 383, 386. And see cases cited *infra*, § 17, as to whether crime includes misdemeanor, which quote the whole definition.

"A crime is any wrong which the government deems injurious to the public at large, and punishes through a judicial proceeding in its own name: " 1 Bish. Cr. L., § 32.

"A crime may be defined as an act or omission, in respect of which legal punishment may be inflicted on the person who is in default, either by acting or omitting to act: " 1 Steph. Hist. Cr. L. 1. But this author proceeds to say that his definition is too wide for practical purposes, and that if applied in its full latitude it would embrace all law whatever, for one specific peculiarity, by which all law is distinguished, is that it is coercive, and all coercion at some stage involves the possibility of punishment: Ibid. 2.

In Colorado the penal code defines a crime or misdemeanor to be the violation of a public law, in the commission of which there shall be a union or joint operation of act and intention, or criminal negligence: Kent v. P., 8 Colo. 563. And as to union of act and intent, see Buckner v. C., 14 Bush, 601; Roberts v. P., 19 Mich. 401, and *infra*, § 112.

The term "crime" includes the more trivial offenses known as misa civil injury, which is considered only as a wrong against an individual. As will hereafter appear, some acts or omissions may be both crimes and civil injuries;[1] but the distinction is that, in case of a crime, the state is deemed the injured party and punishes the wrong-doer in the interests of the general public and in its own name, while in the case of a civil injury, although the state furnishes means for redress, the proceeding is directly in the name and under the control of the party injured. The state in the sense here intended is simply the governing power acting in behalf of the people; in England it means the sovereign and parliament; in the United States it means the federal or state government, according as the offense is one against the United States or one of the states.[2]

§ 5. **What deemed criminal proceeding.**— As the definition of a crime involves the fact that cognizance is taken of it in a criminal proceeding, it becomes important to know what is deemed a criminal proceeding. If the object of the proceeding is to recover a penalty, in the nature of damages to the injured party, and not as a punishment only in behalf of the state, the proceeding is not criminal.[3] All acts for which the remedy is

demeanors, as well as the more atrocious ones called felonies. Although Blackstone's definition, as above given, would seem to indicate that misdemeanors are not crimes, he proceeds immediately afterward to explain his meaning to the contrary. And in general to the effect that the term crime includes misdemeanor, see In re Bergin, 31 Wis. 383, 386; In re Clark, 9 Wend. 212, 222; In re Voorhees, 32 N. J. 141; Van Meter v. P., 60 Ill. 168, 170; Lehigh County v. Schock, 113 Pa. St. 373; and see *infra*, § 17. The term "criminal offense" as used in a state constitution is held to cover misdemeanors: Slaughter v. P., 2 Doug. (Mich.) 334, note. A conviction before a police judge of the offense of intoxication is a conviction of a crime: P. v. French, 102 N. Y. 583.

1 *Infra*, § 10.

2 The fact that a proceeding is in behalf of the public is indicated in England by its being brought in the name of the King (or Queen) against the offender, the title of the prosecution being Rex (or Reg.) v. ——. And in accordance with the same view the indictment concludes, "against the peace of the King (or Queen)." In the United States the form of expression varies in the different states. In some the title is "The State of —— v. ——," in others "The Commonwealth of —— v. ——," in still others, "The People of the State of —— v. ——;" and correspondingly the indictment concludes, "against the peace and dignity of the state of ——," or "the commonwealth of ——," or "the people of the state of ——."

3 So held where statute provided for recovery by indictment against a railway company of a penalty for the benefit of the widow and child or heirs, in case of the death of any person through its negligence: S. v. Grand Trunk R. Co., 58 Me. 176.

by indictment are not necessarily criminal.[1] The fact that a statute provides for the recovery of a penalty by civil action for the use of the county,[2] or for the forfeiture of some right or license as a penalty,[3] does not render the proceeding criminal.[4] On the other hand, the fact that a fine imposed is to be for the benefit of any party, municipality, or person, injured by the offense, does not make it necessary that the proceeding be in the name of the person or corporation to be benefited, but it may be in the usual form of a criminal case.[5] However, even where a penalty is to be recovered by an action for debt, the proceeding may be in some respects governed by the rules of criminal actions, so that the declaration must be equally certain in charging the facts necessary to bring defendant within the statute, as though it were a criminal accusation.[6] The form of the action does not determine whether an act forbidden by statute is a crime, but the object of the statute will control. If it is designed to prevent a public injury or wrong, the act forbidden is criminal; but if merely to redress a private wrong it is civil, whatever the form of the action.[7] Nor does

[1] Where a statute provided for the removal of the register of deeds on presentment by the grand jury, or on information, it was held that the proceeding was not criminal: S. v. Leach, 60 Me. 58. So where a statute provided that money drawn in a lottery should be forfeited and might be recovered for the use of the commonwealth by indictment, it was held that the proceeding was not necessarily criminal: C. v. Howes, 15 Pick. 231. Under a statute providing that fines imposed for violation of a statute duty, when no other mode of collection is expressly stated, may be recovered by indictment, it was held that indictment would lie to enforce against a railway company a forfeiture for obstructing a highway by its engines and cars: S. v. Grand Trunk Ry., 59 Me. 189. So a proceeding by indictment to recover damages against a city for death caused by leaving the streets in a dangerous condition was held not to be an action for a penalty or forfeiture: S. v. Bangor, 30 Me. 341; and see case cited in last preceding note. The fact that remedy is by complaint does not conclusively show that the action is criminal, but the fact that the proceedings provided for are such as are usual in criminal cases is strong evidence of an intention that the proceeding be criminal: S. v. Stearns, 31 N. H. 106.

[2] S. v. Ford, 70 Mo. 469.

[3] S. v. Burnett, 77 Mo. 570.

[4] *Quasi*-criminal actions to enforce a fine for the breach of some police regulation, in which imprisonment is not a part of the punishment, but only a means for enforcing payment of the penalty, are not criminal in such sense that defendant necessarily has a right to a trial by jury: Inwood v. S., 42 Ohio St. 186.

[5] C. v. Newell, 5 Gray, 76.

[6] S. v. Androscoggin R. Co., 76 Me. 411.

[7] S. v. Shoemaker, 20 N. J. 153; S. v. Stearns, 31 N. H. 106. Thus,

the fact that the tribunal in which the action is prosecuted has no power to enforce payment by imprisonment affect the nature of the prohibited act.[1] Where the statute provides that, upon conviction of an act specified, the person guilty thereof shall be fined, etc., the proceeding to enforce the penalty is criminal;[2] and in general an offense against the public good which may be penal is punishable as a crime.[3] The fact that an act or omission renders a party liable to a pecuniary forfeiture, which when collected goes into the public treasury, does not necessarily render the act a crime;[4] but a prosecution by indictment in which a fine is to be imposed is a criminal prosecution.[5]

§ 6. **Breach of city ordinance.**— Where a city is given authority to enact ordinances and punish violations thereof by imprisonment, or by fine enforcible by imprisonment, a prose-

forcible entry may be punished by indictment as a breach of the peace, while restitution may be enforced by a civil suit. Cruiser v. S., 18 N. J. 206.

[1] Hinman v. Taylor, 2 Conn. 357; S. v. Keenan, 57 Conn. 286; S. v. Stearns, 31 N. H. 106.

[2] P. v. Goshen, etc. Turnpike Road, 11 Wend. 597.

[3] S. v. Bishop, 7 Conn. 181. Thus, a failure to construct fish-ways in a dam and thereby obstructing the passage of fish, contrary to the statute, is criminal: C. v. Essex Co., 13 Gray, 239. Statutes prohibiting the sale of liquors without a license are criminal, and prosecutions thereunder will be governed by rules applicable to criminal procedure: S. v. Volmer, 6 Kan. 379; Haug v. Gillett, 14 Kan. 140, 142. A prosecution under a statute requiring a certificate for the practice of medicine is a criminal prosecution: Ex parte Wong You Ting, 106 Cal. 296. Violation by an officer of a statutory regulation as to payment of warrants is a criminal offense: Ex parte Howe, 26 Ore. 181.

[4] The fact that the judgment for the violation of a liquor law is made a lien upon the property used for that purpose does not make the proceeding to enforce such judgment a criminal prosecution: Polk County v. Hierb, 37 Ia. 361. So a penalty imposed for violation of a police regulation is not necessarily a criminal punishment: S. v. Grove, 77 Wis. 448. A penalty imposed for the offense of disturbing the public ditches, to be recovered by the overseer for the benefit of the ditch, and to be enforced by compulsory labor on the public works, is not punishment for a crime: T. v. Baca, 2 N. Mex. 183; T. v. Tafoya, 2 N. Mex. 191. On the other hand, a statute providing that penalty and damages for trespass may be recovered by civil action or on indictment and for imprisonment for non-payment of the judgment in such civil suit is not unconstitutional as providing imprisonment for debt: Blewett v. Smith, 74 Mo. 404. A statute providing for recovery of double damages by an injured party is penal, as imposing a penalty or forfeiture: Union Pac. R. Co. v. Proctor, 12 Colo. 194.

[5] In re Clark, 9 Wend. 212, 221.

cution under such an ordinance, although in the name of the city, is generally held to be a criminal proceeding.[1] This is particularly true where the act prohibited by the ordinance is one which is against the public at large, rather than the municipality as such, and falls within the legal notion of a crime; and in such a case the constitutional provisions as to jury trial in criminal cases are applicable.[2] But violations of municipal police regulations, as, for example, those concerning markets, streets, water-works, city officers, etc., which do not come within the general criminal legislation of the state, are not to be deemed crimes in the constitutional sense, and may be prosecuted in a summary manner.[3] Proceedings for violations of a city ordinance may be in the name of the city when so provided by statute[4] without a violation of constitutional provisions requiring that all prosecutions shall be conducted in the name and by the authority of the state.[5]

§ 7. **Penal statutes; actions qui tam.**— Statutes sometimes provide for forfeiture enforcible by the state, or by a private

[1] S. v. West, 42 Minn. 147; P. v. Hanrahan, 75 Mich. 611, 620; Davenport v. Bird, 34 Ia. 524; Jaquith v. Royce, 42 Ia. 406; S. v. Vail, 57 Ia. 103; Columbus City v. Cutcomp, 61 Ia. 672. But in Indiana it is held that an action by a city to recover a penalty for the violation of an ordinance is a civil action, even though process is by warrant, and the fine may be enforced by imprisonment: Goshen v. Croxton, 34 Ind. 239; Quigley v. Aurora, 50 Ind. 28; Greensburgh v. Corwin, 58 Ind. 518. In Louisiana and Missouri it is held that the term "crime" as used in the constitution means a breach of the general law of the state, and does not refer to the violation of a city ordinance: S. v. Heuchert, 42 La. An. 270; Kansas v. Clark, 68 Mo. 588. In Georgia it is said that the words "criminal case" in the constitution do not apply to the violation of police regulations of cities and towns: Williams v. Augusta, 4 Ga. 509. So in Ohio it is held that the violation of a city ordinance is not a felony or a misdemeanor: S. v. Rouch, 47 Ohio St. 478. A city cannot punish criminally the violation of an ordinance unless such power is expressly conferred: S. v. Bright, 38 La. An. 1.

[2] Taylor v. Reynolds, 92 Cal. 573, quoting from 1 Dill. Mun. Corp., § 433; Ex parte Wong You Ting, 106 Cal. 296.

[3] Callan v. Wilson, 127 U. S. 540, quoting from 1 Dill. Mun. Corp., § 433. See, also, Ibid., § 411. Violations of municipal ordinances are usually prosecuted summarily, and the right of trial by jury is not guarantied: S. v. Fourcade, 45 La. An. 717; Board of Police, etc. of Opelousas v. Giron, 46 La. An. 1364.

[4] S. v. King, 37 Ia. 462.

[5] Davenport v. Bird, 34 Ia. 524; Bautsch v. S., 27 Tex. Ap. 342. But in Missouri this result is reached on the theory that a proceeding to recover a pecuniary penalty for violation of a city ordinance is not a criminal prosecution: Ex parte Hollwedell, 74 Mo. 395.

informer on his own behalf, or by a private informer who is allowed to prosecute an action for the penalty, a portion of which is to go to him individually. Actions of the last class are called *qui tam* actions on account of the use of these words at the beginning of the information by which the proceeding is instituted.[1] These penal actions, however, whether in the name of the state or of an individual informer, are civil and not criminal.[2] They may be perhaps criminal in their nature;[3] but, as already indicated,[4] the fact that a pecuniary forfeiture, when collected, goes into the public treasury, does not make the act for which it is imposed criminal.

§ 8. **Penalty, exclusive or concurrent.**— A statute giving a civil remedy for an act already criminal does not take away the right to proceed by indictment unless expressly so provided.[5] The fact that the statute provides a civil punishment for an offense does not prevent its also being punishable criminally. The punishment may be cumulative.[6] The intention of the legislature is to be considered. If the act prohibited has been previously an indictable offense, it will be presumed that the civil penalty therefor is cumulative;[7] but when the act creates a new offense and makes that unlawful which was lawful before, and prescribes a particular penalty and mode of procedure, that penalty alone can be enforced.[8] A civil action to recover damages for an injury cannot, of course, be joined with a criminal prosecution for the same act as an offense.[9]

1 3 Bl. Com. 159; Bacon, Abr., s. v. Actions *qui tam;* 1 Steph. Hist. Cr. L. 4; 1 Jacob L. Dic. 30, s. v. Actions popular; 3 id. 434, s. v. Information.

2 Wilson v. Rastall, 4 Term R. 753; Atcheson v. Everitt, Cowp. 382; U. S. v. Simms, 1 Cranch, 252; U. S. v. Gadsby, 1 Cranch, C. C. 55; Stevens v. Dimond, 6 N. H. 330.

3 State ex rel. v. Kansas City R. Co., 32 Fed. R. 722; State v. Androscoggin R. Co., 76 Me. 411.

4 *Supra*, § 5.

5 Susquehannah, etc. Turnpike Co. v. P., 15 Wend. 267; P. v. Safford, 5 Denio, 112; S. v. Miskimmons, 2 Ind. 440; S. v. Virt, 3 Ind. 447.

6 P. v. Stevens, 13 Wend. 341. A licensed retailer of intoxicants may be proceeded against on his bond for injury resulting from his business, and also prosecuted for maintaining a public nuisance: S. v. Mullikin, 8 Blackf. 260.

7 Behan v. P., 17 N. Y. 516. So a statute providing punishment for an offense is not superseded by giving to a city the power to fix a punishment for the same act: P. v. Mallette, 79 Mich. 600.

8 P. v. Hislop, 77 N. Y. 331; C. v. Evan, 13 Serg. & R. 426; McElhiney v. C., 22 Pa. St. 365; Hellings v. C., 5 Rawle, 63. The existence of a civil remedy does not necessarily exclude a remedy by prosecution: Pittsburgh, etc. R. Co. v. C., 101 Pa. St. 192.

9 Manville v. Felter, 19 Kan. 253.

§ 9. **Contempts.**—Courts have power to punish as contempts any interference with their proceedings or resistance of their authority. This is a power inherent in courts of superior jurisdiction and essential to their existence.[1] It is not simply an incident of the exercise of judicial functions, but is the highest exercise of judicial power.[2] Contempts are sometimes spoken of as criminal when they involve interference with the action of the court, and civil, when they are an injury to a private party by reason of the violation of some order or proceeding of the court to protect his rights.[3] Criminal contempts may be punishable by fine and imprisonment, even though imprisonment for debt is prohibited.[4] In such cases there is no constitutional right to jury trial,[5] or to be confronted by the witnesses against him,[6] but the defendant may be relieved from punishment by executive pardon, as in case of conviction for crime.[7] The procedure is governed by the analogies of a criminal prosecution,[8] and it is said that the imposition of a fine in such cases is a judgment in a criminal case.[9] Civil contempts are not analogous to crimes, but the remedy afforded is civil in its nature.[10] It is evident that, even in cases of criminal contempt, the contempt as such is not deemed a crime; for instance, no indictment is required.[11] The same act may constitute both a contempt and a crime, and may be dealt with as either without regard to proceedings of the

[1] U. S. v. Hudson, 7 Cranch, 32; Fishback v. S., 131 Ind. 304.

[2] In re Mason, 43 Fed. R. 510.

[3] S. v. Knight, 3 S. Dak. 509. If contempt of a federal court is to be classed at all as a crime, it is a misdemeanor and not a felony: In re Acker, 66 Fed. R. 290.

[4] P. v. Cowles, 4 Keyes (N. Y.), 38, 46; P. v. Bennett, 4 Paige, Ch. 282; P. v. Spalding, 10 Paige, Ch. 284.

[5] Bates' Case, 55 N. H. 325; Ex parte Grace, 12 Ia. 208.

[6] S. v. Mitchell, 3 S. Dak. 223.

[7] Ex parte Hickey, 4 Sm. & M. 751.

[8] Bates' Case, 55 N. H. 325; S. v. Matthews, 37 N. H. 450; In re Sims, 54 Kan. 1; In re Manning, 44 Fed. R. 275; U. S. v. Jose, 63 Fed. R. 951.

[9] New Orleans v. Steamship Co., 20 Wall. 387, 392; Fischer v. Hayes, 6 Fed. R. 63.

[10] Hawley v. Bennett, 4 Paige, Ch. 162; S. v. Becht, 23 Minn. 411; Beck v. S., 72 Ind. 250; Leopold v. P., 140 Ill. 552; First Cong. Church v. City of Muscatine, 2 Ia. 69; Jordan v. Circuit Court, 69 Ia. 177; U. S. v. Lancaster, 44 Fed. R. 885. Jury trial cannot be refused where the proceeding is substantially to determine a private right: Ex parte Grace, 12 Ia. 208.

[11] Arnold v. C., 80 Ky. 300; Ex parte Wall, 107 U. S. 265.

other character.[1] At common law, many acts now considered only as contempts were punishable criminally.[2]

§ 10. Crime distinct from tort and from breach of contract.— As has already been suggested,[3] crimes differ from torts in that the wrong in one case is deemed to be to the public, and in the other case to the individual injured.[4] The same act may constitute both a crime and a tort. A tort may, or may not, constitute a crime; and likewise, a crime may, or may not, be a tort. It is to be noticed that crimes and torts are similar in this: each is the breach of a general duty imposed upon all. Breaches of contract, that is, violations of obligations arising merely by assent of the parties, are not torts;[5] neither are they criminal. While there may be a crime involved in the violation of duties growing out of a relation assumed by contract, it is the breach of general duty and not the breach of the contract obligation which is deemed criminal.[6]

[1] Foster v. C., 8 Watts & S. 77; Brooker v. C., 12 Serg. & R. 175; In re Brule, 71 Fed. R. 943; Burke v. T., 2 Okl. 499: Rex v. Lord Ossulston, 2 Strange, 1107.

[2] Rex v. Lord Ossulston, 2 Strange, 1107; Foster v. C., 8 W. & S. 77; Brooker v. C., 12 Serg. & R. 175.

[3] *Supra*, § 4.

[4] Austin's Jurisp., lectures 17 and 27; 1 Bish. Cr. L., ch. 16. It may be that, in general terms, every crime includes a private injury (see 4 Bl. Com. 5; 2 Wilson's Works, Andrews' ed., 339); but there are crimes, such as treason, bribing election officers, or sending obscene literature through the mails, in which the element of private injury can be considered present only by the merest fiction: Hammond's note to 4 Bl. Com. 5.

[5] While some torts are said to be based upon breach of contract, the fact seems to be that in such cases it is not the breach of the contract which constitutes a tort, but the violation of a duty which may arise from a special contract relation and which is imposed upon all who occupy that relation; so that the wrong is not merely a breach of contract, but also a breach of general duty. Thus, a carrier who has received goods for transportation may be sued in tort for not delivering them safely; but such an action is founded on his general duty as carrier, not on the violation of the special contract under which the goods may have been accepted: Tattan v. Great Western R. Co., 2 El. & El. 844; Smith v. Seward, 3 Pa. St. 342.

[6] That mere breach of contract not involving any fraud or breach of trust is not criminal, see Rex v. Wheatly, 2 Burr. 1125; S. C., 1 Bennett & Heard, Lead. Cr. Cas. 1 and note. In South Carolina there is a statute making the violation of a contract between land-owner and laborer an indictable offense, but it has been held unconstitutional, not as imposing involuntary servitude, but as making a discrimination in the punishment imposed as between the two parties: S. v. Williams, 32 S. C. 123. In Alabama there is a statute by which one convicted of an offense may contract with the party who becomes his surety for

§ 11. **Civil remedy not merged or suspended.**— In England there is a rule of the common law to the effect that no civil action against one who has committed a felony can be maintained for damages caused thereby, until a criminal proceeding for the wrong to the public has been prosecuted.[1] This rule was in some early cases recognized as prevailing here,[2] but the decided weight of authority in the United States is to the effect that this doctrine of the common law is not in force with us, and that a civil suit for damages may be maintained against the wrong-doer regardless of whether a criminal prosecution for the act has been commenced or brought to a conclusion.

the fine and costs to render personal services in liquidation thereof, and making it criminal to fail to carry out such contract: Wade v. S., 94 Ala. 109. And such statute is held valid even as to an infant: Wynn v. S., 82 Ala. 55. But there can be no such punishment imposed for failure to repay money advanced, as this would amount to imprisonment for debt: Smith v. S., 82 Ala. 40.

1 Gimson v. Woodfull, 2 C. & P. 41; Crosby v. Leng, 12 East, 409; Lutterell v. Reynell, 1 Mod. 282; Markham v. Cob, Latch, 144; Cooper v. Witham, Lev. 247; Higgins v. Butcher, Yelv. 89; Dawkes v. Coveneigh, Style, 346; Wellock v. Constantine, 2 H. & C. 146; Chowne v. Baylis, 31 Beav. 351. But this doctrine has been held not applicable to an action against a person other than the wrong-doer; for instance, the purchaser of stolen goods: White v. Spettigue, 13 M. & W. 603; Peer v. Humphrey, 2 A. & E. 495; Stone v. Marsh, 6 B. & C. 551. The doctrine only applies so far as is required by public policy: Wickham v. Gatrill, 2 Sm. & G. 353; Dudley, etc. Banking Co. v. Spittle, 1 Johns. & H. 14. The recent English cases throw discredit upon if they do not overthrow the entire doctrine: Wells v. Abrahams, L. R. 7 Q. B. 554 (1872); Midland Ins. Co. v. Smith, 6 Q. B. D. 561 (1881).

2 Grafton Bank v. Flanders, 4 N. H. 239; Story v. Hammond, 4 Ohio, 376; Foster v. Tucker, 3 Me. 458; Boody v. Keating, 4 Me. 164; Crowell v. Merrick, 19 Me. 392; McGrew v. Cato, Minor, 8; Bell v. Troy, 35 Ala. 184; Adams v. Barrett, 5 Ga. 404. In some states this supposed rule has been abolished by statute: Belknap v. Milliken, 23 Me. 381; Van Duzer v. Howe, 21 N. Y. 531; Chiles v. Drake, 2 Met. (Ky.) 146.

3 Boston, etc. R. Co. v. Dana, 1 Gray, 83; Boardman v. Gore, 15 Mass. 331; Pettingill v. Rideout, 6 N. H. 454; Hollis v. Davis, 56 N. H. 74, 85; Quimby v. Blackey, 63 N. H. 77; Allison v. Farmers' Bank, 6 Rand. 204, 223; Cross v. Guthery, 2 Root, 90; Patton v. Freeman, 1 Coxe, 113, note; White v. Fort, 3 Hawks, 251; S. C., 1 Bennett & Heard, Lead. Cr. Cas. 34 and note; Hepburn's Case, 3 Bland, 114; Robinson v. Culp, 3 Brev. 302; Nash v. Primm, 1 Mo. 178; Mann v. Trabue, 1 Mo. 709; Ballew v. Alexander, 6 Humph. 433; Mitchell v. Mims, 8 Tex. 7; Smith v. Weaver, 2 Hayw. 108; Lofton v. Vogles, 17 Ind. 105; Short v. Baker, 22 Ind. 148; Hutchinson v. Bank, 41 Pa. St. 42; Foster v. C., 8 Watts & S. 77; Piscataqua v. Turnley, 1 Miles, 312; Blassingame v. Glaves, 6 B. Mon. 38; Ocean Ins. Co. v. Fields, 2 Story, 59. That an act is so far injurious to the whole people as to be

Various reasons are assigned for not recognizing in the United States the rule of the common law in this respect, the principal of which are that, as there are prosecuting officers with us specially charged with instituting and carrying on criminal proceedings for the state without the intervention of a private prosecutor, it is not necessary to hold out the same inducement to the injured party to be active in the prosecution of the offense as it was in England, where there were no prosecuting officers, and a criminal proceeding must be carried on at private expense; and that as felonies are not with us generally punishable capitally and by forfeiture of goods, the civil proceeding has a value which it did not have in England, where conviction of the felon resulted in his execution and the confiscation of his goods.[1] The common-law rule postponing a civil suit to a criminal prosecution was never applied in cases of misdemeanor,[2] but in such cases courts have sometimes suspended the criminal prosecution until the determination of a civil action for the same act.[3] The injured party, however, cannot be required to elect between a criminal prosecution and a civil action.[4] The fact that criminal punishment may be inflicted will not prevent the giving of vindictive or exemplary damages in a civil suit for the same injury.[5] But if by law the prosecutor is entitled to and has received a portion of the penalty imposed in a criminal prosecution, it has been held that plaintiff may be limited in his civil suit for the same injury to nominal damages.[6]

criminal is no defense in a civil action for private injury resulting therefrom: Story v. Hammond, 4 Ohio, 376.

[1] Boston, etc. R. Co. v. Dana, 1 Gray, 83.

[2] Foster v. C., 8 Watts & S. 77; Fissington v. Hutchinson, 15 L. T. 390.

[3] P. v. Genesee General Sessions, 13 Johns. 85; C. v. Bliss, 1 Mass. 32. In a subsequent Massachusetts case, however, the court refused to continue a criminal proceeding to await the result of the civil action, it not appearing that the injured party was needed as a witness for the government: C. v. Elliott, 2 Mass. 372.

[4] Jones v. Clay, 1 Bos. & P. 191.

[5] Wilson v. Middleton, 2 Cal. 54; Cook v. Ellis, 6 Hill, 466; Klopfer v. Bromme, 26 Wis. 372; Brown v. Swineford, 44 Wis. 282; Wolff v. Cohen, 8 Rich. 144; Roberts v. Mason, 10 Ohio St. 277; Boetcher v. Staples, 27 Minn. 308; Chiles v. Drake, 2 Met. (Ky.) 146; Hendrickson v. Kingsbury, 21 Ia. 379; Guengerich v. Smith, 36 Ia. 587; Wheatley v. Thorn, 23 Miss. 62; Corwin v. Walton, 18 Mo. 71; Cole v. Tucker, 6 Tex. 266. *Contra*, Fay v. Parker, 53 N. H. 342; Murphy v. Hobbs, 7 Colo. 541; Taber v. Hutson, 5 Ind. 322; Humphries v. Johnson, 20 Ind. 190.

[6] Jacks v. Bell, 3 C. & P. 316.

CHAPTER 2.

HOW CRIMES PRESCRIBED — WHAT DEEMED CRIMINAL — CLASSIFICATION OF CRIMES.

§ 12. **Written and unwritten law.**— What acts and omissions are punishable as offenses against the state must be determined by law. In this as in other respects the law may be unwritten as well as written. From a historical point of view there is no doubt but that acts injurious to the public were punishable as crimes by the courts without having been prohibited by any statute, the criminal law, like other portions of the law, being in its origin unwritten or customary. It is also true that there have been statutory modifications of the unwritten law as to crimes, so that many of them were specifically defined by statute and punishment therefor prescribed and the procedure regulated from very early times. And thus the unwritten criminal law has been continually modified and supplanted by written law. The criminal law of England as thus composed of both written and unwritten portions, including statutes of England passed prior to the English settlements in this country, became common law in the states of the Union and remained in force after their independence, so far as it was adapted to the conditions of the people and in harmony with the genius of their institutions and not changed by the constitution or statutes of the particular state.[1] English statutes

[1] C. v. Chapman, 13 Met. 68; S. v. Rollins, 8 N. H. 550; S. v. Moore, 26 N. H. 448; Green v. S., 3 Colo. 68. As to how far the common law is in force in the states of the Union, see Boyer v. Sweet, 4 Ill. 120; Wagner v. Bissell, 3 Ia. 396; Kerwhacker v. Cleveland, etc. R. Co., 3 Ohio St. 172; Van Ness v. Pacard, 2 Peters, 137, 144. In the states composed of territory acquired from Spain, France and Mexico, which was already settled at the time of acquisition, the civil law and not the common law was the prevailing system; but by special action in these states the common law has been adopted as a body, except in Louisiana, where it is made the basis of the criminal law only, while the civil law as it had prevailed under the French rule still remains as the prevailing system in other cases: S. v. Mullen, 14 La. An. 570; Grinder v. S., 2 Tex. 338. The adoption in Louisiana in 1805 of the common law of England as

passed after the English colonization of this country and prior to the independence of the states are a part of the common law so far as they were applicable to and recognized in the colonies.[1] The adoption of a written constitution or of statutes with reference to crimes does not abrogate the common law[2] so far as the doctrines of the common law are not covered by constitutional or statutory enactments;[3] nor does the fact that the statutes provide for the punishment of certain classes of cases recognized as crimes by the common law preclude punishment under the common law of cases not falling within the statutes.[4] Thus, an indictment may be sufficient to charge an offense at common law, although not sufficient to show a crime under a statute passed in regard to similar cases.[5] But where an act not previously criminal is made punishable by a statute providing a special method of enforcing the penalty, that method is exclusive;[6] and if the statute fully provides for the punishment of a certain class of crimes, the common law as to such crimes is abrogated.[7] If the common-law punishment for a

the basis of criminal jurisprudence did not operate to adopt subsequent English statutes: S. v. Davis, 22 La. An. 77. In the portions of the territory acquired in the Louisiana purchase, not settled at the time of such purchase, the common law has been introduced, both in civil and criminal matters: See Prell v. McDonald, 7 Kan. 426, 450.

[1] Opinion of Baldwin, J., in Bains v. Schooner James and Catharine, Bald. 544; S. v. Mairs, 1 N. J. 335; Morris' Lessee v. Vanderen, 1 Dall. 64, 67; Resp. v. Mesca, 1 Dall. 73; Opinion of Judges, 3 Binn. 595; Calvert's Lessee v. Eden, 2 Har. & McH. 335; Moore's Lessee v. Pearce, 2 Har. & McH. 241.

[2] S. v. Danforth, 3 Conn. 112.

[3] C. v. Mohn, 52 Pa. St. 243; Rolland v. C., 85 Pa. St. 66; Wilson v. C., 96 Pa. St. 56; S. v. Wilson, 3 Mo. 125; T. v. Ye Wan, 2 Mon. T. 478; T. v. Flowers, 2 Mon. T. 531.

[4] C. v. Farrell, 5 Allen, 130. If the legislature enacts statutes affirmatory of the common law, adding new regulations and supplying additional remedies, this does not repeal the common law unless the intention of the legislature is plain to supersede it on the whole general subject: C. v. Rumford Chemical Works, 16 Gray, 231; C. v. Flannelly, 15 Gray, 195. When two different acts constitute a common-law offense, a statute specially providing a penalty for one does not supersede the common-law punishment; S. v. Mullikin, 8 Blackf. 260. Thus, a statute granting to the city the right to prohibit gaming and card-playing does not abrogate the common-law crime of keeping a gaming-house: S. v. Crummey, 17 Minn. 72.

[5] S. v. Appling, 25 Mo. 315; S. v. Rose, 32 Mo. 560.

[6] Thus, if the method provided is a civil action, indictment will not lie: S. v. Huffschmidt, 47 Mo. 73. But if the act is merely prohibited, indictment will lie: Journey v. S., 1 Mo. 428.

[7] McNamee v. P., 31 Mich. 473; Smith v. S., 14 Mo. 147; S. v. Wacker,

criminal act is uncertain or obsolete, in the absence of any statute on the subject, fine and imprisonment may be imposed at the discretion of the court.[1] So where an act is made criminal by statute, but no procedure or punishment is provided, the omission will be supplied from the common law.[2]

§ 13. Common-law offenses not recognized.— In some states the common law has been expressly repealed as to crimes, so that nothing is punishable unless made so by statute.[3] In other states where criminal codes have been adopted, which are apparently intended to cover the whole ground, it is held that the common law is repealed without any special statutory provision to that effect, and that there are no crimes except as specified by statute.[4] The supreme court of Iowa suggests

71 Wis. 672. As to repeal of common law by statute, see *infra*, § 95.

[1] James v. C., 12 Serg. & R. 220; C. v. Mohn, 52 Pa. St. 243; Wilson v. C., 96 Pa. St. 56. If an act has been punishable at common law, or by previous statute, it will continue under the criminal code to be punishable as a misdemeanor: Foote v. P., 56 N. Y. 321.

[2] Jim v. S., 3 Mo. 108; Sanders v. S., 85 Ind. 318; S. v. Parker, 91 N. C. 650; S. v. Fletcher, 5 N. H. 257; Beery v. U. S., 2 Colo. 186; Mackey v. P., 2 Colo. 13. But to the contrary it has been said that if the offense is created by statute, but no punishment is provided, none can be imposed: S. v. Ashley, Dudley, 188. So a constitutional prohibition is not self-executing: In re Breene, 14 Colo. 401.

[3] Thus, in Indiana, the statute provides that crimes shall be defined and punishments therefor fixed by statute, and not otherwise; and it was held that a statute must define the offense with some degree of minuteness: Hackney v. S., 8 Ind. 494; Jennings v. S., 16 Ind. 335; Marvin v. S., 19 Ind. 181; and that an information or indictment must enumerate and charge all the substantial elements entering into the statutory description of the offense: Cranor v. S., 39 Ind. 64; Howard v. S., 67 Ind. 401. But it was afterwards said that this statutory provision, abrogating the common law, was not binding on subsequent legislatures, and if, by later statute, punishment was provided for acts enumerated but not defined, such statute would be valid and repeal the prior general statute as to common-law offenses to that extent: Wall v. S., 23 Ind. 150 (overruling the cases first cited in this note); S. v. Oskins, 28 Ind. 364; Hood v. S., 56 Ind. 263; Ardery v. S., 56 Ind. 328; Peachee v. S., 63 Ind. 399; Hartford v. S., 96 Ind. 461. But these cases do not, when properly construed, hold that there can be common-law crimes, but only that if punishment is provided for what was a common-law offense, without a full definition of it, the common-law definition will be resorted to: Ledgerwood v. S., 134 Ind. 81; and see Stephens v. S., 107 Ind. 185; Jones v. S., 59 Ind. 229.

[4] Smith v. S., 12 Ohio St. 466; Sovereign v. S., 4 Ohio St. 489; Allen v. S., 10 Ohio St. 287, 301; Key v. Vattier, 1 Ohio, 132, 144; Estes v. Carter, 10 Ia. 400; S. v. Gaunt, 13 Oreg. 115; S. v. Young, 55 Kan. 349. In Missouri it is held that no punishment

that as the constitution gives criminal jurisdiction to the district court as prescribed by law, and the legislature has provided a general criminal code, it must be understood that the jurisdiction of the court is limited to the crimes and modes of procedure specified in such code.[1] But in Minnesota, where there is also a general criminal code, it is held that the common law as to crimes is still in force except so far as abrogated by statute, either expressly or by implication.[2]

§ 14. **In the federal courts.**— The federal government being one of specified powers, its courts have only limited authority, and cannot exercise jurisdiction to punish crimes except so far as such jurisdiction is expressly conferred by the constitution or by statutes in accordance therewith; and therefore no common-law crimes are recognized.[3] Although general admiralty jurisdiction is conferred by the federal constitution upon the government of the United States, and such jurisdiction includes the criminal as well as the civil branch of admiralty, yet no general criminal jurisdiction in admiralty cases has thus far been conferred upon the federal courts. Under the admiralty power,

can be imposed except as authorized by statute: Ex parte Meyers, 44 Mo. 279. So in Michigan, although unenumerated crimes are recognized, the punishment must be provided by statute: In re Lamphere, 61 Mich. 105. The criminal code of Ohio is not amendatory of, nor in addition to, the common law, but an entirely new and independent system: Lasure v. S., 19 Ohio St. 43. In California the penal code is to be considered without reference to the common law, in determining the sufficiency of informations or indictments: P. v. Mahlman, 82 Cal. 585; P. v. Goggins, 80 Cal. 229; P. v. Tomlinson, 66 Cal. 344. And to same effect, see S. v. Gaster, 45 La. An. 636.

1 Estes v. Carter, 10 Ia. 400.

2 S. v. Pulle, 12 Minn. 164 (overruling Benson v. S., 5 Minn. 19).

3 U. S. v. Hudson, 7 Cranch, 32; U. S. v. Coolidge, 1 Wheat. 415; U. S. v. Bevans, 3 Wheat. 336; U. S. v. Wiltberger, 5 Wheat. 76; U. S. v. Hall, 98 U. S. 343, 345; U. S. v. Britton, 108 U. S. 199; U. S. v. Eaton, 144 U. S. 677; U. S. v. Walsh, 5 Dill. 58; U. S. v. Barney, 5 Blatch. 294; U. S. v. Taylor, 1 Hughes, 514; U. S. v. De Groat, 30 Fed. R. 764; In re Greene, 52 Fed. R. 104. Early cases in the circuit court were conflicting on this point: Case of Henfield, Whart. St. Tr. 49; Case of Williams, Whart. St. Tr. 652; U. S. v. Ravara, 2 Dall. 297; U. S. v. Worrall, 2 Dall. 384; U. S. v. Burr, 2 Robertson, 481. The Hudson and Coolidge cases above cited were decided without argument, and in the second one the court was not agreed, but the result reached has since been generally acquiesced in, although no subsequent case involving the exact question has been before the supreme court. That the United States has no common law, see Manchester v. Massachusetts, 139 U. S. 240; Gatton v. Chicago, R. I. & P. R. Co. (Ia.), 63 N. W. R. 589.

congress has defined crimes which are punishable in the federal courts; but no criminal jurisdiction is conferred, even in admiralty cases, aside from that given by these statutes. Therefore, whatever might be the authority of congress to confer general admiralty jurisdiction in criminal cases, thus far the admiralty crimes, as well as the common-law crimes, cognizable by the federal courts, are only those defined by statute.[1]

§ 15. Common-law definitions and general principles.— Without regard to whether the common law is in any particular state superseded as the source of criminal jurisdiction, it remains the basis of criminal jurisprudence in the courts of the states of the Union,[2] and of the United States also, and the terms and provisions found in statutes are to be construed in reference thereto;[3] therefore, if the statute provides a punishment for a crime which is not fully defined by the statute, the common law will be resorted to for a definition, even though the common law as to crimes is not in force.[4]

§ 16. What deemed criminal.— Those acts and omissions are criminal which are made so by law; that is, by the common law or by statute. While the criminal law remained largely unwritten, it was for the courts to determine what acts were so far detrimental to the public as to be punished as crimes, the distinction being borne in mind that, to constitute a criminal offense, the act must be such as to injuriously affect the public, and not merely a breach of contract or a private injury.[5] It thus appears that where the common law as to crimes

[1] U. S. v. Bevans, 3 Wheat. 336; U. S. v. Wiltberger, 5 Wheat. 76; U. S. v. Rodgers, 150 U. S. 249; C. v. Peters, 12 Met. 387.

[2] As to Louisiana, see *supra*, note to § 12.

[3] Smith v. S., 12 Ohio St. 466; Estes v. Carter, 10 Ia. 400; Nicholls v. S., 68 Wis. 416; S. v. Bertheol, 6 Blackf. 474; S. v. Boll, 59 Mo. 321.

[4] Ledgerwood v. S., 134 Ind. 81; Hedderich v. S., 101 Ind. 564; S. v. Berdetta, 73 Ind. 185; P. v. Miller, 82 Cal. 107; S. v. Twogood, 7 Ia. 252; Houston v. C., 87 Va. 257; S. v. Gaster, 45 La. An. 636; U. S. v. De Groat, 30 Fed. R. 764; U. S. v. King, 34 Fed. R. 302; U. S. v. Boyd, 45 Fed. R. 851; In re Greene, 52 Fed. R. 104. The fact that an ordinance provides a punishment for playing or carrying on the game of "policy," without defining it, does not render it invalid: S. v. Carpenter, 60 Conn. 97.

[5] Rex v. Wheatly, 2 Burr. 1125; S. C., 1 Bennett & Heard, Lead. Cr. Cas. 1, and note; Rex v. Storr, 3 Burr. 1698; Rex v. Atkyns, 3 Burr. 1706; S. v. Burroughs, 7 N. J. 426. All crimes that injuriously affect public society are indictable at common law. The test is not whether precedents can be found in the books, but whether they affect the public pol-

is still in force, the courts have the power to punish acts injurious to the public other than those prescribed by statute; yet very few instances will be found among the modern cases in which the courts have taken it upon themselves to declare acts criminal which do not come within the description of well-recognized common-law offenses. It would not be improper to generalize as to what classes of acts are at common law deemed so far injurious to the public as to be punishable, yet such a discussion would be unprofitable, for it would involve a discussion of the essential features of the different common-law crimes, which can best be considered under the discussion of the crimes themselves. But some groups of offenses, mainly statutory, which may be distinguished as made such by virtue of the general police powers of the state, are discussed in the next chapter.

§ **17. Classes of offenses.**— At common law all offenses were said to be treasons, felonies, or misdemeanors;[1] but as to treasons, it will appear hereafter that what was formerly in England known as petit treason is now felony,[2] and even high treason was said to be a felony and something more.[3] In the United States, treason is, perhaps, not anywhere regarded as a class of crime distinct from felony. Some classification of offenses, based on their relative criminality, seems in the nature of things important, and whatever may be the origin of the division into felonies and misdemeanors, the fact that particular distinctions in the proceedings and the punishment are still made to depend on whether the offense in question is of the one grade or the other, makes the grouping of offenses into felonies and misdemeanors of present consequence, although the basis of the grouping may be to some extent uncertain, and lacking in uniformity in the different states. Although Blackstone, after his definition of "crime,"[4] recognizes a use of the term "misdemeanor" to indicate something less than a crime,

icy or economy: C. v. Randolph, 146 Pa. St. 83. Thus, bribery of an elector is punishable at common law: S. v. Jackson, 73 Me. 91; C. v. McHale, 97 Pa. St. 397. But there must be something more than a private injury, e. g., false pretense without false token. "We are not to indict one man for making a fool of another:" Reg. v. Jones, 1 Salk. 379.

[1] 1 Bish. Cr. L., ch. 43.

[2] *Infra*, ch. 75

[3] 1 Hale, P. C. 497; 1 Hawk. P. C., ch. 25, § 2; 4 Bl. Com. 94; 3 Inst. 15; 2 Wilson's Works (Andrews' ed.), 348.

[4] *Supra*, § 4, note.

yet the whole passage shows that for legal purposes misdemeanors are included in the general word "crimes," and to that effect his language is quoted in many cases.[1]

§ 18. **Felony and misdemeanor.**— Assuming that, for present practical purposes, all crimes are either felonies or misdemeanors,[2] and that felonies include the offenses deemed more serious in their nature, and therefore attended with a more severe punishment, it becomes important to explain the basis on which such division is made. By the early common law in England, felonies were those crimes punishable capitally, or by forfeiture of land, or goods, or both,[3] but the term was not one of settled meaning, and by some authorities the test was the liability to forfeiture rather than the liability to capital punishment.[4] As used in the American colonies, the popular distinction seems to have been, however, between offenses punishable with death and those not so punishable.[5] In statutes creating or defining offenses, the language usually expressly indicates whether the offense is to be deemed a felony or misdemeanor, and for practical purposes it may be said that those crimes which, by the common law, were punishable capitally, or which are expressly made felonies by statute, are now to be considered of that class, while all other criminal offenses are to be deemed misdemeanors,[6] and no offense is to be deemed a felony unless it comes within this description.[7] But if the of-

[1] 4 Bl. Com. 5; Sevier v. Justices, Peck (Tenn.), 334, 357; Smith v. Smith, 34 Tenn. 472, 477; S. v. Collins, 1 McCord, 355, 357; S. v. Peterson, 41 Vt. 504, 511; S. v. Savannah, 1 T. U. P. Charl. 235; Lehigh County v. Schrock, 113 Pa. St. 373, 378; Illies v. Knight, 3 Tex. 312, 314; Morton v. Skinner, 48 Ind. 123; Van Meter v. P., 60 Ill. 168; In re Clark, 9 Wend. 212, 222; and see *supra*, § 4, note.

[2] P. v. French, 102 N. Y. 583; S. v. Rouch, 47 Ohio St. 478.

[3] Lynch v. C., 89 Pa. St. 189; 1 Bish. Cr. L., § 615.

[4] 4 Bl. Com. 94; 2 Steph. Hist. Cr. L. 192; 1 Hawk. P. C., ch. 25; Adams v. Barrett, 5 Ga. 404. For the history of the early use of the term, see 2 Pollock & Maitland, Hist. Eng. L. 460. In Wilson's Works (Andrews' ed.), vol. 2, p. 348, the view of Blackstone that the term "felony" is feudal in origin is vigorously combated, and an earlier origin of the word is insisted on.

[5] Lynch v. C., 88 Pa. St. 189; 2 Swift's System, 384; C. v. Newell, 7 Mass. 245; C. v. Barlow, 4 Mass. 439. Originally, petty larceny was a felony, althogh never punishable capitally, but later it was considered a misdemeanor: 1 Steph. Hist. Cr. L. 192; C. v. Keith, 8 Met. 531.

[6] S. v. Murphy, 17 R. I. 698.

[7] S. v. Hord, 8 S. C. 84; Bruguier v. U. S., 1 Dak. T. 5. The fact that by statute an assault of a particular character is designated as a felonious assault does not make the offense

fense has been a felony, the mere reduction of the punishment will not of itself change it to a misdemeanor.[1] In most of the states the statutes expressly provide a definition for the term "felony," and make it to mean any offense punishable with death or confinement in the penitentiary;[2] and under this definition it is almost universally held that it is the liability to such punishment, rather than the fact that such punishment is actually imposed, which makes the offense a felony; so that if, under any circumstances, the court might for an offense impose a sentence of death or imprisonment in the penitentiary, such offense is a felony, although the court has the discretion to impose and does impose another penalty.[3] This statutory description of felony is applicable in all cases and for all purposes where a distinction between felony and misdemeanor is necessary to be made.[4] But it has been said in some cases that the statutory definition serves only to explain the term as used in the statutes and does not change the grade of common-law offenses.[5]

§ 19. Other classifications; high crimes and misdemeanors.— In Connecticut the higher grade of crimes is defined as consisting of high crimes and misdemeanors, corresponding substantially to felony at common law, although the term "fel-

a felony: C. v. Barlow, 4 Mass. 439. Statutes regulating crimes against the United States may reduce what was a felony to a misdemeanor, unless the penalty is fixed by the constitution: U. S. v. Cross, 1 MacArthur, 149.

1 S. v. Dewer, 65 N. C. 572.

2 Nichols v. S., 35 Wis. 308; Wilson v. S., 1 Wis. 184; Buford v. C., 14 B. Mon. 24; Tharp v. C., 3 Met. (Ky.) 411; P. v. War, 20 Cal. 117; In re Pratt, 19 Colo. 138; Rafferty v. S., 91 Tenn. 655.

3 S. v. Smith, 32 Me. 369; S. v. Goddard, 69 Me. 181; C. v. Pemberton, 118 Mass. 36; P. v. Hughes, 137 N. Y. 29; S. v. Magoon, 61 Vt. 45; Johnston v. S., 7 Mo. 183; S. v. Green, 66 Mo. 631; S. v. Reeves, 97 Mo. 668; S. v. Melton, 117 Mo. 618; Benton v. C., 89 Va. 570; In re Stevens, 52 Kan. 56; Miller v. S., 58 Ga. 200; S. v. Waller, 43 Ark. 381. Some offenses may be punishable either as felonies or as misdemeanors, and it is said the punishment inflicted may determine the grade: P. v. Cornell, 16 Cal. 187; but see P. v. War, 20 Cal. 117. In New Jersey the statute ignores the distinction between felony and misdemeanor, and all statutory offenses are either misdemeanors or high misdemeanors, the latter being practically the same as felonies: Jackson v. S., 49 N. J. 252.

4 P. v. Lyon, 99 N. Y. 210; Shay v. P., 22 N. Y. 317; P. v. Park, 41 N. Y. 21.

5 Drennan v. P., 10 Mich. 169; S. v. Hurt, 7 Mo. 321; Nichols v. S., 35 Wis. 308; Wilson v. S., 1 Wis. 184; Lynch v. C., 89 Pa. St. 189.

ony" is not used.[1] The term "high crimes and misdemeanors" is used in the federal constitution[2] in specifying the grounds for impeachment of president, vice-president, or other civil officer of the United States, but as used in this connection it does not necessarily imply a criminal offense, much less a felony.[3]

§ 20. **Infamous crimes.**—The constitution of the United States[4] requires that prosecutions in the federal court for capital or otherwise infamous crimes shall be only on indictment, and under this provision it has been held that any crime punishable by imprisonment in a state prison or penitentiary, with or without hard labor, is an infamous crime.[5] The construction of the term in the state courts, as used in the state constitutions or statutes, has left the meaning to depend on whether the crime itself was infamous, rather than on the degree of the punishment.[6] An infamous crime in this sense includes not

[1] S. v. Lockwood, Kirby, 106; S. v. Danforth, 3 Conn. 112; Southworth v. S., 5 Conn. 325; S. v. Howard, 6 Conn. 475; S. v. Knapp, 6 Conn. 415; S. v. Smith, 7 Conn. 428.

[2] Art. 2, sec. 4.

[3] Cooley's Prin. Const. L. 165.

[4] Amendments, art. 5.

[5] Ex parte Wilson, 114 U. S. 417; Mackin v. U. S., 117 U. S. 348; Ex parte Bain, 121 U. S. 1; Parkinson v. U. S., 121 U. S. 281; U. S. v. De Walt, 128 U. S. 393; In re Mills, 135 U. S. 263; In re Claasen, 140 U. S. 200; Bannon v. U. S., 156 U. S. 464. Prior to the leading case it had been held that what was an infamous crime would depend on the nature of the crime, and not the extent of the punishment, and it was thought that the term was to be construed according to the same principle which determines at common law whether a witness previously convicted of crime is incompetent to testify: U. S. v. Block, 4 Sawyer, 211; and see U. S. v. Reilley, 20 Fed. R. 46; T. v. Farnsworth, 5 Mont. 303. For further illustrations of the application of the rule on this subject, see U. S. v. Johannesen, 35 Fed. R. 411; U. S. v. Smith, 40 Fed. R. 755. Inasmuch as it is provided by Revised Statutes, section 5541, that a sentence for imprisonment for a longer term than one year may be ordered to be executed in any state jail or penitentiary, a crime under the laws of the United States punishable by sentence for a longer period of imprisonment than one year will be an infamous crime: U. S. v. Cobb, 43 Fed. R. 570. And it is immaterial whether the punishment actually imposed is imprisonment in a state jail or penitentiary, provided it is within the power of the court to award such punishment: In re Claasen, 140 U. S. 200; Ex parte McClusky, 40 Fed. R. 71. The fact that the crime is infamous gives a right of appeal to the supreme court from a conviction in the circuit court of the United States: In re Claasen, 140 U. S. 200; but not from a conviction in the supreme court of the District of Columbia: In re Heath, 144 U. S. 92; nor from the supreme court of a territory: Farnsworth v. Montana, 129 U. S. 104.

[6] S. v. Cram, 84 Me. 271; S. v. Nolan, 15 R. I. 529.

only treason and felony, but also every species of the *crimen falsi*, such as perjury, conspiracy, and barratry.[1]

§ 21. **Misdemeanor.**— From the discussion in the preceding paragraph it will appear that every criminal offense not a felony is a misdemeanor, but it is sometimes specially provided by statute that when a public duty is imposed, or the doing of any act is prohibited by statute, the omission or the prohibited act, as the case may be, shall constitute a misdemeanor, and if no other punishment is provided, then such omission or wrongful act shall be punished as directed in that connection.[2] In general, violations of statutory duties imposed for the protection of the people are punishable at common law, even though no penalty is fixed by the statute itself.[3]

§ 22. **Merger.**— The same act cannot be punishable both as a felony and as a misdemeanor. It was said at common law that the misdemeanor was merged in the felony.[4] But the question whether on an indictment for a misdemeanor the defendant may be convicted, though the evidence shows the commission of a felony involving the misdemeanor charged, or whether on an indictment for felony defendant may be convicted of a misdemeanor thus involved, is one of procedure rather than of law. It is sufficient to suggest here that at common law the misdemeanor and the felony, though the misdemeanor is included in the felony, are deemed distinct crimes, and proof of one will not warrant conviction of the other; but that in many states of this Union, either by statute or by judicial legislation, a conviction of an included misdemeanor may be had under a charge of felony. This question will be found discussed under the head of the separate crimes where a misdemeanor is deemed included in a felony.[5]

[1] Barker v. P., 20 Johns. 457; C. v. Rogers, 7 Met. 500.

[2] P. v. Long Island R. Co., 134 N. Y. 506; P. v. Meakim, 133 N. Y. 214; S. v. Conlee, 25 Ia. 237; and see Foote v. P., 56 N. Y. 321. If the statute provides that acts or omissions shall be deemed misdemeanors within the meaning of the statute, when specially declared by law to be such, it is the statute law of the state and not the common law that is meant: S. v. Grove, 77 Wis. 448.

[3] C. v. Silsbee, 9 Mass. 417; S. v. Startup, 39 N. J. 423; Reg. v. Walker, L. R. 10 Q. B. 355.

[4] Rex v. Harmwood, 1 East P. C. 411; Reg. v. Button, 11 Q. B. 929; C. v. Roby, 12 Pick. 496; C. v. Parr, 5 Watts & S. 345; Johnson v. S., 29 N. J. 453; S. v. Durham, 72 N. C. 447.

[5] See as to homicide, *infra*, § 389; as to assaults, *infra*, § 253; as to robbery, *infra*, § 484.

CHAPTER 3.

OFFENSES PRESCRIBED UNDER GENERAL POLICE POWER, AND MUNICIPAL ORDINANCES.

§ 23. **Criminal law a part of the police power.**—Undoubtedly the authority to determine what crimes are punishable and to provide for their punishment is a part of the general police power of a sovereign and independent state, and, not being conferred by the constitution of the United States upon the federal government, remains with the separate states of this Union. But, aside from the crimes recognized at common law and resting on the general principles of protection to life, the person, and property, new offenses are constantly being created by statute to prevent the commission of acts deemed by the legislature to be inimical to the public welfare, some of which are so analogous to common-law crimes that no other reason for their punishment need be suggested than the better protection of the public against classes of acts which have before been recognized as criminal, while others rest on doctrines of expediency not of such general recognition, and yet deemed sufficient by the legislature to warrant the infliction of a criminal punishment upon the violator. Some such distinction as this seems to be indicated by the terms *malum in se* and *malum prohibitum;*[1] that is, a crime which is such by reason of its inherent nature, and a crime existing by reason of statutory prohibition only. The distinction is perhaps of no practical utility, and some crimes which are only *mala prohibita* have become so generally recognized by statute in different jurisdictions that they may be spoken of as covered by the criminal law

[1] 1 Bl. Com. 54, 57; 2 id. 420; 4 id. 29, 42. Offenses against the statutes prohibiting gaming and lotteries are *mala prohibita*, not *mala in se:* Stone v. Mississippi, 101 U.S. 814, 821. Carrying concealed weapons, though not evil in itself, may be prohibited as tending to breach of the peace or other public injury: S. v. Shelby, 90 Mo. 302; and further as to this offense, see *infra*, ch. 44. *Mali prohibiti* are taken judicial notice of as criminal when committed in a country where the common law prevails: Morrissey v. P., 11 Mich. 327.

in the same general sense as the crimes which are universally recognized as *mala in se.* But it is nevertheless true that in each state of the Union, as well as in England, are many statutes providing for the criminal punishment of particular acts or omissions which are made punishable only by reason of peculiar circumstances, or in order to effect some statutory purpose which would not be regarded as common to all jurisdictions.

§ 24. **Various grounds of regulation.**— The grounds on which these various police regulations are based are not always easy to determine. Some of the offenses thus defined are analogous to offenses well recognized, and hereafter separately discussed, but it is difficult in many instances to determine just what particular object the legislature had in mind in making the act penal — whether to prevent it as a nuisance, or as a breach of the peace, or as a species of fraud, or as detrimental to public health, or whether the prevention is merely a means of raising revenue. The police power is so varied in its application that it is impossible to anticipate and classify the grounds on which it may, by the legislature, be deemed expedient and proper to regulate human action, and therefore in this chapter are grouped a variety of instances of the exercise of such power without any pretense that they cover the whole field, and without any definite reason, more than that of convenience, for separating them from the well-recognized groups of crimes to be hereafter discussed.

§ 25. **Evil course of life.**— Under the general police power it is proper to provide for the punishment of those who pursue a course of life prejudicial to the public welfare, such as common thieves, gamblers, night-walkers, etc., without regard to their guilt of any one particular criminal offense.[1] But the

[1] Morgan v. Nolte, 37 Ohio St. 23; C. v. Hopkins, 2 Dana, 418; S. v. Noyes, 30 N. H. 279; World v. S., 50 Md. 49. The offense of being a common night-walker consists in the habit of being out late at night for some wicked purpose: Watson v. Carr, 1 Lewin, 6; Roscoe, Cr. Ev. 262. The term includes eaves-droppers, mischief-makers, persons of ill-fame and their associates: 1 Burns, Justice, 765. But a general statute making it a misdemeanor to commit any act injurious to the public health or public morals, or tending to the perversion of public justice or the due administration of the laws, is void for indefiniteness: Ex parte Jackson, 45 Ark. 158. The offense of being a common night-walker, like that of being a common scold, etc., may be charged in general terms: S. v. Dowers, 46 N. H. 543.

state cannot punish conduct which does not itself constitute an injury to the public, nor show intention or preparation to commit an offense, such as associating with persons reputed to be thieves and prostitutes.[1]

§ 26. **Common scold.**— On analogous principles the common law recognizes the crime of being a common scold.[2] This offense, while recognized, as shown by the cases just cited, in those states where the common law of crimes prevails, is in fact, however, only one example of the crime of nuisance, and analogous offenses may be found considered under that general head.[3] It is also analogous to the offenses punishable as breaches of the peace.[4] A similar offense is that of being a common railer and brawler as defined by statute, which may be committed by the use of immoderate and vituperative language, even in one's own house, and in sudden altercation, if such use is so frequent and notorious as to amount to a disturbance of the public peace.[5]

§ 27. **Common barrator.**—An offense known to the common law, but which has found only the slightest recognition in the United States, is that of common barratry, which consists in frequently exciting and stirring up of suits and quarrels, either at law or otherwise.[6]

§ 28. **Habitual criminals.**—It is not unusual to provide by statute a heavier punishment in case of larceny, receiving stolen goods, forgery and like crimes, for a second or subsequent offense of the same character than for the first offense, the reason for such additional punishment being that the first punishment has been ineffectual or that the criminal has evinced a depravity which merits a greater punishment and needs to be restrained by severer penalties.[7] Such additional

[1] St. Louis v. Fitz, 53 Mo. 582.

[2] 4 Bl. Com. 168; 1 Hawk. P. C., ch. 75, § 14; 1 Bishop, Crim. Law, § 1102; Baker v. S., 53 N. J. 45; C. v. Mohn, 53 Pa. St. 243; James v. C., 12 Serg. & R. 220; U. S. v. Royall, 3 Cranch, C. C. 620; Reg. v. Foxby, 6 Mod. 11.

[3] *Infra*, ch. 61.

[4] *Infra*, ch. 43.

[5] C. v. Foley, 99 Mass. 497; Stratton v. C., 10 Met. 217.

[6] 4 Bl. Com. 134; Case of Barretry, 8 Co. 36b; C. v. Davis, 11 Pick. 432; C. v. McCulloch, 15 Mass. 227.

[7] S. v. Moore, 121 Mo. 514; S. C., Moore v. Missouri, 159 U. S. 673; P. v. Stanley, 47 Cal. 113; Kelly v. P., 115 Ill. 583; Blackburn v. S., 50 Ohio St. 428; Ingalls v. S., 48 Wis. 647; Maguire v. S., 47 Md. 485; Johnson v. P., 55 N. H. 512; Wood v. P., 53 N. Y. 511; P. v. Butler, 3 Cow. 347; Palmer v. P., 5 Hill, 427; Sturtevant v. C., 158 Mass. 598; C. v. Graves, 155 Mass. 163; C. v. Harrington, 130

punishment is not deemed a second punishment for a former offense, but a punishment for a subsequent aggravated offense.[1] It is the last offense which is punished, and therefore such a statute will not be *ex post facto*, although the first offense relied on as an aggravation was committed before the statute authorizing the increased punishment for the subsequent offense.[2] An indictment under which it is sought to impose a higher penalty by reason of a previous conviction must allege the fact of such conviction.[3] There may be a conviction for the first offense if the aggravation is not sufficiently alleged or proved.[4] Sometimes the third conviction at the same term of court, for the same crime, is made punishable in a higher degree.[5]

§ 29. Regulation of business; sale of liquors, opium, dangerous articles.— No branch of the police power is now better established than that which regulates kinds of business which may be injurious to the public, even though no wrong is necessarily involved therein.[6] The best illustration of the

Mass. 35; Garvey v. C., 8 Gray, 382; Plumbly v. C., 2 Met. 413; Ross' Case, 2 Pick. 165; Rand v. C., 9 Grat. 738; Reg. v. Clark, 6 Cox, 210. The former conviction must be for a similar offense, but it is not necessary that the punishment be identical with that of the offense which is charged as a second offense: C. v. Marchand, 155 Mass. 8; Kelly v. P., 115 Ill. 583.

[1] Moore v. Missouri, 159 U. S. 673; S. C., S. v. Moore, 121 Mo. 514; C. v. Marchand, 155 Mass. 8; Sturtevant v. C., 158 Mass. 598; Kelly v. P., 115 Ill. 583. The same act relied upon to constitute a third offense under the statute may again be relied upon to aggravate a subsequent offense. Relying upon it once does not effect a merger: C. v. Hughes, 133 Mass. 496.

[2] Blackburn v. S., 50 Ohio St. 428; Ex parte Gutierrez, 45 Cal. 429; C. v. Graves, 155 Mass. 163; Ross' Case, 2 Pick. 165; Rand v. C., 9 Grat. 738; and see *infra*, § 78. The New York statute was construed to require that the second offense must have been committed after conviction for the first offense: P. v. Butler, 3 Cow. 347.

[3] P. v. Powers, 6 N. Y. 50; Stevens v. P., 1 Hill, 261; C. v. Harrington, 130 Mass. 35; Garvey v. C., 8 Gray, 382. And the prior conviction must have preceded the commission of the second offense: S. v. Volmer, 6 Kan. 379.

[4] Palmer v. P., 5 Hill, 427; P. v. O'Brien, 64 Cal. 53; Good v. S., 61 Ind. 69; Myers v. S., 92 Ind. 390. If the increased punishment makes the offense a felony, the crime must be charged as feloniously committed even though the first offense would be a misdemeanor: S. v. Weldon, 70 Mo. 572.

[5] S. v. Nelson, 29 Me. 329: Stevens v. C., 6 Met. 241. In Virginia a statute was upheld which imposed an additional penalty if the accused was found to have been convicted in the United States for a similar offense: Reed v. C., 9 Gratt. 738.

[6] C. v. Vrooman, 164 Pa. St. 306.

exercise of power in this direction is the regulation of the sale of intoxicating liquors, by way either of entire prohibition, or the imposition of restrictions as to time, place and manner of carrying on the business. There is no uniformity in the reasons given for such regulations. In some states all sales, except for a few authorized purposes, are forbidden, evidently on the theory that the use of intoxicating liquors is injurious to the health and morals; in others, restriction is thrown about the business on the theory that the use of intoxicating liquors may be injurious and that improper use ought to be prevented; while in still other cases, the regulation amounts to little more than the enforcement of the payment of a tax to the state or municipal corporation for the privilege of conducting the business.[1] It is believed that in no state is the drinking of liquor made criminal,[2] though there are frequently statutes for the punishment of drunkenness.[3] The whole subject of the statutory regulation of the sale of intoxicating liquors is discussed elsewhere.[4] The validity of these statutes as against every possible constitutional objection is fully established.[5] While

[1] A statute requiring a license for the sale of intoxicating liquors should not be treated as a mere revenue law: Campbell v. S., 46 Ala. 116: Lillensteine v. S., 46 Ala. 498. The South Carolina Dispensary Act is not a police regulation: In re Langford, 57 Fed. R. 570; Ex parte Jervey, 61 Fed. R. 957; and it is unconstitutional as interfering with interstate commerce, inasmuch as it not only attempts to regulate the sale, but also the bringing into the state, of intoxicating liquors: Ex parte Edgerton, 59 Fed. R. 115; but it is sustained by the last decision of the state court: S. v. City Council, 42 S. C. 222 (overruling S. v. Jacobs, 41 S. C. 220). There is no vested right in a citizen to carry on the business of selling intoxicating liquors, and a deprivation of the privilege does not interfere with any rights under the Fourteenth Amendment of the Federal Constitution: S. v. Brennan, 2 S. Dak. 384.

[2] As bearing upon the question whether a prohibition of the use would be constitutional, it may be noted that a statute punishing as a misdemeanor the smoking of opium has been sustained: Ah Lim v. T., 1 Wash. 156. And see *infra*, § 1241.

[3] C. v. Morrissey, 157 Mass. 471. And see *infra*, § 1018.

[4] *Infra*, ch. 63.

[5] Bartemeyer v. Iowa, 18 Wall. 129; Beer Co. v. Massachusetts, 97 U. S. 25; Foster v. Kansas, 112 U. S. 201; Mugler v. Kansas, 123 U. S. 623. Earlier cases in the state courts held that a prohibition of sale could not be made applicable to liquor already on hand: Wynehamer v. P., 13 N. Y. 378; and that the legislature could not appropriate to itself any such business or declare it a nuisance, it being one generally recognized throughout the civilized world as a useful industry: Herman v. S., 8 Ind. 545; Beebe v. S., 6 Ind. 501. The requiring of a license to

the United States may collect a revenue from the business of selling liquor, the power of regulation for the public good is in the state, and the payment of a license tax to the federal government does not exempt the business from state control.[1] On similar grounds the sale of opium may be regulated.[2] It is not improper to prohibit the sale, or keeping for sale, of dangerous articles, such as naphtha, except in accordance with regulations fixed by statute.[3]

§ 30. **Protection of public health.**— As a general principle of law, aside from any statutory regulation, the doing of acts detrimental to the general public health is punishable as a nuisance;[4] but aside from the prevention of nuisances, there is a general power to legislate with reference to the protection of the public health; for instance, it may be made criminal to contaminate the water supply,[5] or to prevent the use, or danger of use, of contaminated water in preparing food for sale.[6] Owners of tenement houses may be required to put in a water supply on the order of the board of health.[7] The methods of using machinery in manufacturing may be regulated so as to protect the health of employees.[8] But regulations made by a board of health under authority given to it must be reasonable.[9] Regulations discussed in the following paragraphs are supported to a considerable extent on the ground of being a proper exercise of the power to preserve the public health.

§ 31. **Health of employees.**— A statute requiring street railway companies to protect their employees against the inclemency of the weather has been held constitutional.[10]

§ 32. **Unwholesome provisions.**— The sale of unwholesome food is a misdemeanor at common law,[11] and it is not necessary

sell liquor is not an unwarrantable interference with individual rights when not unreasonable: Thomasson v. S., 15 Ind. 449. That this legislation must not interfere with interstate commerce, see *infra*, § 76. And see Heisembrittle v. Charleston, 2 McMull. 233.

[1] McGuire v. C., 3 Wall. 387; License Tax Cases, 5 Wall. 462; C. v. Holbrook, 10 Allen, 200.

[2] Ex parte Yung Jon, 28 Fed. R. 308; S. v. Ah Chew, 16 Nev. 50; S. v. Ching Gang, 16 Nev. 62.

[3] C. v. Wentworth, 118 Mass. 441; Anderson v. Savannah, 69 Ga. 472.

[4] *Infra*, ch. 61.

[5] S. v. Wheeler, 44 N. J. 88; P. v. Borda, 105 Cal. 636; S. v. Frieberg, 49 Ohio St. 585.

[6] S. v. Schlemmer, 42 La. An. 1166.

[7] Health Dep't v. Rector, 145 N. Y. 32.

[8] P. v. Smith, — Mich. — 66 N. W. R. 382.

[9] S. v. Speyer, 67 Vt. 502.

[10] S. v. Smith, 58 Minn. 35.

[11] Goodrich v. P., 19 N. Y. 574.

that it shall have actually caused sickness, to come within the prohibition;[1] but the provisions must be in such a state that they would by their noxious, unwholesome and adulterous quality have affected the consumer.[2] Under statutes relating to the same subject, it is held that the sale must be for food, and that, if for some other purpose, the offense is not committed.[3] But it is said that it is not necessary to allege the particular use for which the article was intended, either by the seller or the purchaser.[4] In general, it is sufficient to charge the selling of the unwholesome food as good wholesome food, without alleging that it was to be eaten, or that it was eaten, or the particulars in which it was unwholesome.[5] And if the statute describes the offense as selling with knowledge of the unwholesomeness, such knowledge must be alleged with reference to the condition of the food, and not merely with reference to the sale itself.[6] The question as to whether there can be a conviction in such cases, without proof of knowledge and intent on the part of the accused, is discussed fully under the subject of intent.[7]

§ **33. Adulterated food and drinks.**— The prohibition of the sale of adulterated articles of food and drink is sustained, not only on the ground of danger to the public health, but also by way of preventing fraud; and therefore the fact that the adulterated article is of equal utility with the genuine one, or is of an inferior quality, without being injurious, will be immaterial.[8] Such prohibition is usual as to the sale of milk, and it is immaterial in what the adulteration consists.[9] Within such a statute a sale is made when milk is sold by the glass at a restaurant,[10] or as part of a meal.[11] As a means of securing evidence

[1] Goodrich v. P., 19 N. Y. 574.
[2] S. v. Norton, 2 Ired. 40.
[3] Schmidt v. S., 78 Ind. 41.
[4] C. v. Raymond, 97 Mass. 567.
[5] Goodrich v. P., 19 N. Y. 574.
[6] C. v. Boynton, 12 Cush. 499.
[7] *Infra*, § 128.
[8] C. v. Judd, 2 Mass. 329; C. v. Evans, 132 Mass. 11; S. v. Campbell, 64 N. H. 402.
[9] S. v. Smyth, 14 R. I. 100; C. v. Wetherbee, 153 Mass. 159. Under such a statute the sale of cream to which boracic acid had been added was held criminal: C. v. Gordon, 159 Mass. 8. The power to make such regulations may be conferred upon a city: Littlefield v. S., 42 Neb. 223.
[10] C. v. Vieth, 155 Mass. 442.
[11] C. v. Warren, 160 Mass. 533; C. v. Worcester, 126 Mass. 256; and to the same effect as to oleomargarine, see C. v. Miller, 131 Pa. St. 118. Delivery under a contract covering a considerable period constitutes a sale: C. v. Holt, 146 Mass. 38.

for the violation of such a statute, it is usual to provide for the taking and examination by a health officer of samples of the article,[1] and this provision is not unconstitutional as depriving the accused of evidence in his defense, inasmuch as the public analysis is not conclusive.[2] But this right to take samples can only be exercised by virtue of some positive provision,[3] and the analysis must be conducted in accordance with the provisions of the statute; otherwise the general rules of evidence apply in such cases.[4] As a means of preventing fraud in the sale of adulterated articles which, though not unwholesome, are deemed inferior to the genuine article, it is sometimes provided that the sale can only be made where the article bears a stamp or label showing its genuine character, and such a requirement is not unconstitutional as applied to a patented article.[5] To the same end the sale of vinegar containing any coloring matter may be prohibited entirely.[6]

§ **34. Imitation butter, cheese and lard; oleomargarine.** The exercise of the power mentioned in the preceding section of preventing fraud, even where the article sold is not injurious, is found in statutes which prohibit entirely the sale of products made in the semblance of butter or cheese, but not from milk; that is, manufactured by the use of animal fat. Substitutes for butter have been quite extensively manufactured, designated as oleomargarine, margarine, or butterine, and it is against the sale of these substances that most of the statutes are directed. It has now been distinctly settled that the manufacture or sale of such substances may be absolutely prohibited on account of the danger of fraud involved therein, although the substance may not in itself be harmful.[7] Lard compounds and substitutes are subject to similar regulation.[8] There was an inclination in some of the courts to hold that the absolute

[1] C. v. Carter, 132 Mass. 12; C. v. Coleman, 157 Mass. 460.

[2] S. v. Groves, 15 R. I. 208; C. v. Spear, 143 Mass. 172.

[3] C. v. Smith, 141 Mass. 135; S. v. Stone, 46 La. An. 147.

[4] C. v. Lockhardt, 144 Mass. 132.

[5] Palmer v. S., 39 Ohio St. 236; In re Brosnahan, 18 Fed. R. 62. As to the labeling of oleomargarine, see the next section.

[6] P. v. Girard, 145 N. Y. 105.

[7] Powell v. C., 114 Pa. St. 265; S. C., Powell v. Pennsylvania, 127 U. S. 678; C. v. Shirley, 152 Pa. St. 170; McAllister v. S., 72 Md. 390; Pierce v. S., 63 Md. 592; C. v. Huntley, 156 Mass. 236; Plumley v. C., 155 U. S. 461; S. v. Addington, 77 Mo. 110; P. v. Arensberg, 105 N. Y. 123; S. v. Newton, 50 N. J. 534.

[8] S. v. Aslesen, 50 Minn. 5.

prohibition was not constitutional as long as the article was not injurious, and was not so sold as to perpetrate a fraud.[1] Most of the statutes recognize the justness of this distinction and authorize the sale under such restrictions as shall prevent fraud; for instance, without coloration,[2] or only with the display of placards in the place where sold, and by the labeling of the article itself.[3] The offense of exposing for sale such article is not committed where the article is kept in a closed receptacle not subject to public inspection.[4] Furnishing oleomargarine as a part of a meal constitutes a sale, within the terms of the statute.[5] The question as to whether knowledge or intent is essential to constitute the offense will be fully discussed under the heading of intent.[6] As these statutes with reference to the prohibition or regulation of the sale of oleomargarine would probably not be applicable to the sale of such article brought into the state as a subject of interstate commerce,[7] congress has passed a statute intended to accomplish the same object in regard to the article thus imported;[8] but the federal statute does not render invalid the prohibition or regulation of such traffic by state legislation so far as it affects the article not subject to interstate commerce.[9]

§ 35. **Inspection laws.**— There is a provision of the federal constitution[10] which prohibits the levying of a tax by a state upon exports or imports from or to the state, except in

[1] P. v. Marx, 99 N. Y. 377.

[2] C. v. Kelly, 163 Mass. 169.

[3] C. v. Crane, 162 Mass. 506; C. v. Russell, 162 Mass. 520; C. v. McDonnell, 157 Mass. 407; C. v. Mills, 157 Mass. 405; C. v. Stewart, 159 Mass. 113; C. v. Crane, 158 Mass. 218; C. v. Bean, 148 Mass. 172; C. v. Schollenberger, 156 Pa. St. 201; P. v. Arensberg, 103 N. Y. 388; Pierce v. S., 63 Md. 592; S. v. Marshall, 64 N. H. 579.

[4] C. v. Byrnes, 158 Mass. 172. But it may be exposed for sale although still wrapped up: Wheat v. Brown, 1 Q. B. D. (1892), 418. Oleomargarine and butterine are "provisions" within the terms of a statute with reference to carrying provisions from place to place and exposing them for sale without a license: C. v. Lutton, 157 Mass. 392.

[5] C. v. Miller, 131 Pa. St. 118. And see C. v. Warren, 160 Mass. 533, with reference to a similar provision as to adulterated milk.

[6] See *infra*, § 128.

[7] In re McAllister, 51 Fed. R. 282; In re Worthen, 58 Fed. R. 467. But it has been held that such regulations are valid even as to the sale of such article brought from another state: C. v. Schollenberger, 156 Pa. St. 201; C. v. Paul, 148 Pa. St. 559.

[8] U. S. v. Eaton, 144 U. S. 677; U. S. v. Ford, 50 Fed. R. 467.

[9] Plumley v. Massachusetts, 155 U. S. 461; C. v. Crane, 158 Mass. 218; S. v. Newton, 50 N. J. 534.

[10] Art. I, sec. 10.

the enforcement of its inspection laws; and from this it is inferred that the state may, as has been done in various instances, require an inspection of articles held for sale in the state, either for export or for sale after being imported.[1] Such inspection is usually required, however, for the purpose of preserving the character of the state's productions and to prevent the reputation thereof from being injured by exports of an inferior quality, or of packages intended to deceive as to the weight or quantity.[2] But they are also supported as a means of preventing the import of articles in such form that they may be used for the purpose of fraud or imposition;[3] for instance, the inspection of illuminating oil is thus provided for in some states.[4] Such inspection may properly be required to prevent the property of the people of the state from being unlawfully taken out of the state for the purpose of depriving them of such property, and on this ground a statute may require an inspection of hides for export in order that a register of the brands thereof may be preserved and the export of unbranded hides prevented.[5] But inspection laws will be unconstitutional that are so unreasonable in their provisions as to practically prevent the sale in the state of goods brought from another state.[6]

§ 36. Regulation of professions; physicians, pharmacists, dentists.— In the exercise of the inherent power to prescribe such rules as will protect the health and safety of the people, the state may determine the qualifications necessary to entitle persons to practice medicine;[7] but it is not a violation

[1] Gibbons v. Ogden, 9 Wheat. 1, 203.

[2] Gibbons v. Ogden, 9 Wheat. 1, 203; Turner v. Maryland, 107 U. S. 38, 51, 53; P. v. Compagnie Generale Transatlantique, 107 U. S. 59; C. v. King, 1 Whart. 448. Examples of state inspection laws are collected in a note to 9 Wheat. 119.

[3] Brown v. Maryland, 12 Wheat. 419; Clintsman v. Northrop, 8 Cow. 45.

[4] Patterson v. Kentucky, 97 U. S. 501; Downing v. S., 66 Ga. 160; Ex parte Robinson, 29 Tex. Ap. 186.

[5] Neilson v. Garza, 2 Woods, 287.

[6] Minnesota v. Barber, 136 U. S. 313; Brimmer v. Rebman, 138 U. S. 78; Voight v. Wright, 141 U. S. 62; Bowman v. Chicago & N. W. R. Co., 125 U. S. 465, 488.

[7] Dent v. West Virginia, 129 U. S. 114; S. C., S. v. Dent, 25 W. Va. 1; Driscoll v. C., 93 Ky. 393; S. v. Gregory, 83 Mo. 123; S. v. Medical Society, 32 Minn. 324; Harding v. P., 10 Colo. 387; Eastman v. S., 109 Ind. 278; Williams v. P., 121 Ill. 84; P. v. Moorman, 86 Mich. 433; Nicholson v. S., 100 Ala. 132; S. v. Carey, 4 Wash. 424; Gee Woo v. S., 36 Neb. 241. Such a regulation is not an *ex post facto* law as to physicians already in practice: Fox v. T., 2 Wash.

of the usual statutory provisions on this subject to advise or give medicine to a sick person merely as a neighbor or friend, where no compensation is received or expected; it is the holding one's self out as a physician which is prohibited.[1] But some statutes make it immaterial whether or not any compensation is received or expected.[2] It is usual to provide for a board which shall issue licenses on proof of proper qualifications, and revoke them on proof of lack of such qualifications, or for misconduct.[3] To sustain a prosecution under the statutes on this subject, all the facts necessary to show an act of the defendant to have been such as the statute forbids must be alleged.[4] But it is not necessary to specify any particular person whom the defendant treated.[5] Under the provisions in many states requiring report to be made of deaths and the cause thereof, a physician may be punished for failing to make such report.[6] The wicked, ignorant, unskilful, rash and improper treatment of a patient by one acting as a physician, whether licensed or not, was a misdemeanor at common law.[7] The practice of pharmacy, or conducting the business of a drug-store, is regulated by statute on the same principle as the practice of medicine.[8] Itinerant vendors of drugs and patent

T. 297; nor, if it exempts from its regulations those who have been five years in practice, is it invalid for lack of uniformity: S. v. Hathaway, 115 Mo. 36.

[1] Nelson v. S., 97 Ala. 79. Where the statute defines what shall constitute the crime of practicing medicine without a license, anything which is not covered by the statute will not be punishable: S. v. Carey, 4 Wash. 424. In such a statute "physician" and "person practicing medicine" are synonymous: Harrison v. S., 102 Ala. 170. But the regulations usually extend to those who profess to heal, by whatever means, and not merely to those who profess to practice medicine as the term is generally used: S. v. Buswell, 40 Neb. 158. As to what is an "emergency" within such a statute, see P. v. Lee Wah, 71 Cal. 80.

[2] Whitlock v. C., 89 Va. 337. But even without such express provision it is not necessary to prove the actual receipt of compensation: S. v. Hale, 15 Mo. 606.

[3] S. v. Mosher, 78 Ia. 321; Ex parte McNulty, 77 Cal. 164; S. v. Schultz, 11 Mont. 429.

[4] S. v. Hathaway, 106 Mo. 236; S. C., 115 Mo. 36; Brooks v. S., 88 Ala. 122; Stough v. State, 88 Ala. 234. For instance, the fact that defendant had no license must be expressly alleged: S. v. Fussell, 45 Ark. 65; Dee v. S., 68 Miss. 601.

[5] S. v. Van Doran, 109 N. C. 864; S. v. Little, 76 Mo. 52.

[6] P. v. Brady, 90 Mich. 459.

[7] Rice v. S., 8 Mo. 561. As to when a physician will be liable for murder or manslaughter in causing the death of a patient, see *infra*, § 287.

[8] S. v. Forcier, 65 N. H. 42; S. v. Heinemann, 80 Wis. 253; S. v. Jones, 18 Oreg. 256.

medicines are also brought within the provisions of some of the statutes.[1] On like principles as those above indicated, the practice of dentistry may be regulated.[2]

§ 37. **Practice of law.**— The right to practice as an attorney at law is within the control of the legislature and the courts, on other grounds than those applied to the professions of medicine and pharmacy. An attorney is a part of the court for the administration of its functions. Thus, public officers may be prohibited from practicing as attorneys.[3] But the business of an attorney is such that it may be regulated apart from this power to control his conduct as an officer of the court, and therefore a statute prohibiting attorneys from "shaving" notes has been upheld.[4]

§ 38. **Licenses in other callings.**— In the exercise of the general police power to protect the public health, it is competent for the legislature to require a license upon examination to carry on the business of plumbing.[5] Also for the purpose of protecting the traveling public, and perhaps railroad employees as well, from unnecessary danger, it may be required that locomotive engineers shall have a license procured from a board created for that purpose, upon proper examination.[6] So, in general, licenses may be required for certain trades[7] or for places of common entertainment, such as taverns, restaurants, etc.[8] But such a license does not constitute a contract or confer any vested right which the legislature may not impair or take away even before the expiration of the license.[9] It is no protection against subsequent police regulation.[10] In granting such licenses there must not be discrimination against citizens of other states.[11]

1 P. v. Blue Mountain Joe, 129 Ill. 370; S. v. Van Doran, 109 N. C. 864; S. v. Ragland, 31 W. Va. 453; Love v. S., 31 Tex. Ap. 469.

2 S. v. Creditor, 44 Kan. 565; Gosnell v. S., 52 Ark. 228; S. v. Vandersluis, 42 Minn. 129.

3 McCracken v. S., 27 Ind. 491.

4 P. v. Walbridge, 3 Wend. 120.

5 Singer v. S., 72 Md. 464; Davidson v. S., 77 Md. 388; P. v. Warden, 144 N. Y. 529.

6 Smith v. Alabama, 124 U. S. 465; McDonald v. S., 81 Ala. 279. An examination for color-blindness may be required: Nashville, C. & St. L. R. v. Alabama, 128 U. S. 96.

7 Stokes v. N. Y. Corp., 14 Wend. 87; S. v. Cummings, 36 Mo. 263.

8 S. v. Freeman, 38 N. H. 426; St. Louis v. Siegrist, 46 Mo. 593.

9 S. v. Holmes, 38 N. H. 225; Gutzweller v. P., 14 Ill. 142; Hirn v. S., 1 Ohio St. 15. *Contra*, Hannibal v. Guyott, 18 Mo. 515.

10 Gray v. Connecticut, 159 U. S. 74.

11 S. v. Lancaster, 63 N. H. 267; S. v. Wiggin, 64 N. H. 508.

§ 39. Regulation of business in particular localities.— A business may be such as is proper and necessary in itself, and yet improper by reason of danger to other property, or annoyance to persons within the thickly settled portions of a city, so as to justify its regulation or even prohibition. It has been so held as to public laundries, wash-houses, etc.;[1] as to the business of rendering fat from dead animals,[2] and as to slaughter-houses.[3] On the same principle, sales of liquor within certain limits may be subjected to special regulations not imposed on the business as elsewhere conducted.[4] So any business may be regulated and prohibited, even on the premises of the owner, within a specified distance of a camp meeting so far as such regulation is necessary to protect the meeting from disturbance.[5] The use of shades upon the public street may be regulated, although the title to the street is in the abutting owner subject to the easement.[6] A business, such as operating public vehicles upon the streets of a city, may be prohibited, except on payment of a license tax.[7] The beating of drums within the compact portions of a city may be prohibited.[8] So express permission of an officer may be required for operating a bicycle on a certain turnpike.[9]

§ 40. Public callings.— Some kinds of business are recognized as public in their nature in such sense as to be subject to regulation on that ground alone. Thus, it is held that elevator charges may be regulated by state statute,[10] and the charges of grist mills;[11] and the same principle applies to the business of carriers,[12] ferrymen,[13] wharfingers, warehousemen, etc.[14] Police

[1] Barbier v. Connolly, 113 U. S. 27; Soon Hing v. Crowley, 113 U. S. 703.

[2] S. v. Fisher, 52 Mo. 174.

[3] Slaughter-House Cases, 16 Wall. 36; Taylor v. S., 35 Wis. 298.

[4] S. v. Shroeder, 51 Ia. 197; Heck v. S., 44 Ohio St. 536; S. v. Chambers, 93 N. C. 600; and see S. v. Partlow, 91 N. C. 550.

[5] C. v. Bearse, 132 Mass. 542; C. v. Porter, 1 Gray, 476; Meyers v. Baker, 120 Ill. 567; S. v. Cate, 58 N. H. 240.

[6] S. v. Merrill, 37 Me. 329.

[7] Marmet v. S., 45 Ohio St. 63.

[8] S. v. White, 64 N. H. 48.

[9] S. v. Yopp, 97 N. C. 477.

[10] Munn v. Illinois, 94 U. S. 113; Budd v. New York, 143 U. S. 517; Brass v. Stoeser, 153 U. S. 391.

[11] S. v. Edwards, 86 Me. 102. And see Head v. Manufacturing Co., 113 U. S. 9; Burlington v. Beasley, 94 U. S. 310.

[12] Ruggles v. Illinois, 108 U. S. 526; Chicago, B. & Q. R. Co. v. Iowa, 94 U. S. 155; Chicago, M. & St. P. R. Co. v. Minnesota, 134 U. S. 418. Thus the sale of passenger tickets may be regulated: S. v. Corbett, 57 Minn. 345.

[13] It may be made a public offense for a ferryman to detain a traveler at his ferry: S. v. Sewell, 45 Ark. 387.

[14] The whole subject is fully dis-

regulations in regard to the operation of railroads are common, and are upheld without question.[1] Thus, railroads may be required to make stops at county seats.[2] A statute forbidding the running of freight trains on Sunday is not unconstitutional as an interference with interstate commerce.[3] But a regulation of stops which impedes interstate commerce and the transportation of the mails is unconstitutional.[4]

§ **41. Insurance.**— The business of soliciting insurance or acting as an insurance agent may be regulated.[5] The company itself may be required to have a license for the privilege of carrying on the business,[6] and foreign insurance companies are specially subject to regulation, as they may be excluded from doing business in the state except on such terms as the state may prescribe.[7] Discriminations in insurance rates, not based upon differences in risk or expectation of life, may be prohibited.[8]

§ **42. Bankers; factors; mercantile agencies.**— It is often made criminal for bankers to receive deposits when insolvent,[9] or to issue notes to circulate as money.[10] But it is not

cussed in Munn v. Illinois, 94 U. S. 113. See Blair v. Cuming County, 111 U. S. 363; Stone v. Trust Co., 116 U. S. 307.

1 Fuller v. Chicago & N. W. R. Co., 31 Ia. 187; S. C., Railroad Co. v. Fuller, 17 Wall. 560; S. v. Railroad, 59 N. H. 85; P. v. Detroit, Grand Haven & Milwaukee R. Co., 79 Mich. 471; Davis v. S., 6 Tex. Ap. 166. As to separate accommodations for colored persons, see *infra*, § 54. Railroads may be subjected to criminal liability for death caused by negligence: Boston, C. & M. R. Co. v. S., 32 N. H. 215. And see *infra*, § 288.

2 S. v. Gladson, 57 Minn. 385.

3 Hennington v. Georgia, 163 U. S. 299.

4 Illinois Central R. Co. v. Illinois, 163 U. S. 142.

5 S. v. Farmer, 49 Wis. 459; C. v. Vrooman, 164 Pa. St. 306; List v. C., 118 Pa. St. 322; C. v. Wetherbee, 105 Mass. 149; S. v. Hosmer, 81 Me. 506; S. v. Johnson, 43 Minn. 350; S. v. Williams, 46 La. An. 922; Fort v. S., 92 Ga. 8; S. v. Hover, 58 Vt. 496; Brown v. S., 26 Tex. Ap. 540; Smith v. S., 18 Tex. Ap. 69.

6 Lee Mut. Fire Ins. Co. v. S., 60 Miss. 395; S. v. Case, 53 Mo. 246.

7 C. v. Biddle, 139 Pa. St. 605; Moses v. S., 65 Miss. 56. It may be made a misdemeanor to procure insurance to be taken by a resident in a company not authorized to do business in the state: Hooper v. California, 155 U. S. 648.

8 S. v. Schwarzschild, 83 Me. 261; C. v. Morningstar, 144 Pa. St. 103.

9 S. v. Cadwell, 79 Ia. 432; S. v. Fields (Ia.), 62 N. W. R. 653; Baker v. S., 54 Wis. 368; Koetting v. S., 88 Wis. 502; S. v. Myers, 54 Kan. 206; Collins v. S., 33 Fla. 429; S. v. Kelsey, 89 Mo. 623; C. v. Junkin, 170 Pa. St. 194, 31 L. R. A. 124 and note; S. v. Buck, 108 Mo. 622. But such regulations do not apply to a trust company: S. v. Reid, 125 Mo. 43. A state statute punishing usury as a misdemeanor is applicable to a national bank: S. v. First Nat. Bank, 2 S. Dak. 568.

10 S. v. Watson, 4 Ind. 595; Steedman v. S., 11 Ohio St. 82; S. v. James, 63 Mo. 570.

proper to prohibit usual banking operations except as carried on by a corporation.[1] Those who receive the property of others on trust, as factors, or manufacturers of butter and cheese who receive milk with the agreement to return the product made therefrom, may be required to make monthly reports and give a bond.[2] Mercantile or commercial agencies are not instruments of commerce in such sense that state regulation thereof is invalid as interfering with interstate commerce.[3]

§ **43. Corporate business.**— Fraudulent issue of corporate stock may be punished criminally.[4] And so may the making of false entries on the books with intent to defraud.[5] Under penalty, corporations may be required to make annual statements,[6] and foreign corporations may be required to secure a permit before transacting business in the state.[7] A proper regulation of corporate business is applicable to corporations already created as well as those afterwards chartered.[8]

§ **44. Occupation tax; peddlers, itinerant merchants.**— Some kinds of business are frequently subjected to a tax, mainly for the purpose of raising revenue, though other objects may also be involved. Thus, the regulation of the sale of intoxicating liquors may be by means of a license, though the object is the regulation of the business as well as the raising of revenue.[9] So a tax on the business of packing oysters has been upheld.[10] Peddlers, or hawkers as they were sometimes called, are usually required to pay some form of tax, which is said to be not merely a revenue provision, though at present that is probably its principal purpose, but also a means of keeping under control a class of persons who, in past times, were looked upon with distrust as possible perpetrators of fraud;[11] and the exposing for sale as well as the sale of goods

[1] S. v. Scougal, 3 S. Dak. 55.

[2] Hawthorn v. P., 109 Ill. 302.

[3] S. v. Morgan, 2 S. Dak. 32.

[4] West v. P., 137 Ill. 189.

[5] P. v. Leonard, 103 Cal. 200.

[6] S. v. Hanna, 84 Ind. 183.

[7] List v. C., 118 Pa. St. 322; Paul v. Virginia, 8 Wall. 168.

[8] S. v. Mathews, 44 Mo. 523.

[9] S. v. Green, 27 Neb. 64. So a license tax may be required to be paid for the privilege of selling immoral publications: Thompson v. S., 17 Tex. Ap. 253.

[10] S. v. Applegarth, 81 Md. 293.

[11] Emert v. Missouri, 156 U. S. 296; S. C., S. v. Emert, 103 Mo. 241; S. v. Parsons, 124 Mo. 436; C. v. Ober, 12 Cush. 493; C. v. Brinton, 132 Pa. St. 69; C. v. Harmel, 166 Pa. St. 89; Cherokee v. Fox, 34 Kan. 16; Morrill v. S., 38 Wis. 428; Shiff v. S., 84 Ala. 454; S. v. Gorham, 115 N. C. 721. Peddlers may be required to pay a

by such itinerants without a license may be punished.[1] But one who goes about with samples taking orders to be subsequently filled is not a peddler.[2] Itinerant vendors or merchants, not coming strictly within the definition of a peddler, may also be subjected to a license tax.[3] So brokers may be required to pay a license tax.[4] So may itinerant musicians.[5] As to the constitutionality of these statutes, it has been held that, if the license is imposed only on those who are non-residents of the state, or only on those who sell goods manufactured outside of the state, they are unconstitutional; in the one case, because interfering with the privileges and immunities of citizens of another state;[6] and in the other because interfering with interstate commerce.[7] Even if there is no discrimination a statute is unconstitutional which imposes a tax on the privilege of selling within the state the products or manufactures of another state; for even this is an interference with interstate commerce.[8] But so far as such statutes apply

municipal as well as a state license: C. v. Ellis, 158 Mass. 555.

[1] Morrill v. S., 38 Wis. 428.

[2] Ballou v. S., 87 Ala. 144; S. v. Fetterer, 65 Conn. 287; C. v. Eichenburg, 140 Pa. St. 158; S. v. Lee, 113 N. C. 681; S. v. Gibbs, 115 N. C. 700. And it is immaterial that he makes occasional sales and deliveries, that not being the general method of conducting his business: C. v. Ober, 12 Cush. 493; C. v. Farnum, 114 Mass. 267; but see S. v. Snoddy, 128 Mo. 523.

[3] C. v. Crowell, 156 Mass. 215; Weaver v. S., 89 Ga. 639. One who travels merely as agent for a manufacturer in the sale and delivery of small articles may still be a peddler: C. v. Gardner, 133 Pa. St. 284. Dealing in railroad tickets may be required to be by a duly authorized agent: S. v. Ray, 109 N. C. 736. Those who sell goods at auction may be required to pay a license tax for the privilege: C. v. Harnden, 19 Pick. 482; Crandall v. S., 28 Ohio St. 479. Such a license is not transferable: Stone v. S., 12 Mo. 400. Dealers in pistols may be required to pay a privilege tax: Graham v. S., 71 Miss. 208.

[4] Henderson v. S., 50 Ind. 234.

[5] C. v. Plaisted, 148 Mass. 375.

[6] U. S. Const., art. IV, sec. 2; Ward v. Maryland, 12 Wall. 418; Guy v. Baltimore, 100 U. S. 434; Marshalltown v. Blum, 58 Ia. 184; Pacific Junction v. Dyer, 64 Ia. 38; S. v. Lancaster, 63 N. H. 267.

[7] Welton v. Missouri, 91 U. S. 275; Walling v. Michigan, 116 U. S. 446; Webber v. Virginia, 103 U. S. 344; S. v. Furbush, 72 Me. 493; S. v. North, 27 Mo. 464. Views to the contrary are found in S. v. Welton, 55 Mo. 288; Morrill v. S., 38 Wis. 428; Fry v. S., 63 Ind. 552. The state cannot require the filing of a bond by sellers of fruit trees grown out of the state: In re Schechter, 63 Fed. R. 695.

[8] Asher v. Texas, 128 U. S. 129; Brennan v. Titusville, 153 U. S. 289; Robbins v. Shelby County Taxing Dist., 120 U. S. 489; In re Houston, 47 Fed. R. 539; In re Nichols, 48 Fed. R. 164; In re Rozelle, 57 Fed. R. 155; In re Flinn, 57 Fed. R. 496; S. v. Agee,

to peddlers, without regard to whether or not they are residents of the state, or are selling goods produced or manufactured in the state, they are constitutional.[1] But a heavier burden cannot be imposed on account of the sale of patented articles.[2] A license in the nature of a monopoly cannot be justified as to a business merely because it is transient.[3]

§ 45. **Protection of public interests.**— The use of private property in such way as to be an injury to the public may be prohibited, as where such use would injure public property. Thus, the removal of sand from a beach, where such act would injure a harbor and prejudice public shipping, may be prevented as a public nuisance.[4] The removal of landmarks which determine boundaries may be prohibited.[5] So it may be made criminal to inclose public land.[6] It may be made criminal to deface or obliterate a public notice.[7] The return of an untrue list of property for taxation may be punished.[8] Failure to work out a road tax may be made criminal.[9] It may be made criminal in a county officer to buy warrants at a discount.[10]

§ 46. **Protection of game and fish.**— The preservation of game and fish is within the proper domain of the state's police

83 Ala. 110; Hurford v. S., 91 Tenn. 669. To the contrary: Ex parte Asher, 23 Tex. Ap. 662; T. v. Farnsworth, 5 Mont. 303. The producer or manufacturer of goods or his agent may sell them without the payment of a privilege tax: Folkes v. S., 63 Miss. 81; S. v. Bracco, 103 N. C. 349. But, *contra*, see Beall v. S., 4 Blackf. 107. So an agent for a foreign transportation company cannot be required to pay a license tax: McCall v. California, 136 U. S. 104. Nor can a foreign railway company be required to pay a tax for the privilege of maintaining an office for the transaction of its business: Norfolk & W. R. Co. v. Pennsylvania, 136 U. S. 114. Nor can an express company engaged in interstate commerce be required to pay a license tax: Crutcher v. Kentucky, 141 U. S. 47. Nor can a license be imposed on a telegraph company doing both state and interstate business: Leloup v. Mobile, 127 U. S. 240. But a license fee on a local business of telegraph companies is valid: Postal Tel. Cable Co. v. Charleston, 153 U. S. 692.

[1] Emert v. Missouri, 156 U. S. 296; S. C., S. v. Emert, 103 Mo. 241; Ficklin v. Taxing Dist., 145 U. S. 1; S. v. Richards, 32 W. Va. 348.

[2] In re Sheffield, 64 Fed. Rep. 833.

[3] S. v. Conlon, 65 Conn. 478.

[4] C. v. Tewksbury, 11 Met. 55.

[5] S. v. Bryant, 111 N. C. 693; S. v. Beckman, 58 N. H. 399; Stratton v. S., 45 Ind. 468. And see *infra*, § 819.

[6] U. S. v. Buford, 8 Utah, 173.

[7] T. v. Lannon, 9 Mont. 1; T. v. Mackey, 8 Mont. 168; *infra*, § 819.

[8] Lose v. S., 72 Ind. 285; Burns v. S., 5 Ind. Ap. 385; S. v. Welch, 28 Mo. 600.

[9] S. v. Gillikin, 114 N. C. 832; S. v. Wainright, 60 Ark. 280.

[10] Marks v. S., 71 Miss. 206.

power.[1] Wild game running at large and fish in the public waters are deemed the property of the state in a peculiar sense, and it is usual to regulate by somewhat elaborate provisions the taking of such game or fish, and the having possession, transportation and sale of the same. Thus, as to the right of hunting and fishing, a statute may discriminate between residents and non-residents without interfering with any of the privileges and immunities of citizens of another state.[2] And the having in possession or selling game or fish contrary to the requirements of the statute may be punished, even though it is not taken contrary to the law of the state, or is brought in from other states;[3] so it may be made illegal to transport game without regard to whether it was killed in violation of the game laws; and this is not unconstitutional as affecting interstate commerce;[4] so the having in possession may be criminal without regard to the killing.[5] An exception to the game law may be made in behalf of the owner of the land, but such exception is not a transferable right, and he cannot give to another permission to

[1] Lawton v. Steele, 152 U. S. 133. The power of the legislature in this respect is derived from the common law: Parker v. P., 111 Ill. 581.

[2] McCready v. Virginia, 94 U. S. 391; Manchester v. Massachusetts, 139 U. S. 240; S. v. Medbury, 3 R. I. 138; Crandall v. S., 10 Conn. 339; Slaughter v. C., 13 Gratt. 767; P. v. Coleman, 4 Cal. 46; Allen v. Wyckoff, 48 N. J. 90; S. v. Tower, 84 Me. 444; P. v. Lowndes, 130 N. Y. 455; S. v. Conner, 107 N. C. 931. *Contra,* In re Ah Chong, 6 Sawyer, 451.

[3] Roth v. S., 51 Ohio St. 209; Ex parte Maier, 103 Cal. 476; In re Asbill, 104 Cal. 205; Magner v. P., 97 Ill. 320; S. v. Craig, 80 Me. 85; S. v. Beal, 75 Me. 289; S. v. Rodman, 58 Minn. 393. Thus, it may be unlawful during the close season to sell fish artificially propagated, even though the right of private ownership in such fish is fully recognized: C. v. Gilbert, 160 Mass. 157. But such statutes will be construed in the light of the intent and object of the law: C. v. Hall, 128 Mass. 410. And under such construction it may be found that the prohibition relates only to game killed in the state: C. v. Wilkinson, 139 Pa. St. 298; S. v. Barnes, 24 Oreg. 366; Guyer v. Reg., 23 Q. B. D. 100.

[4] Geer v. Connecticut, 161 U. S. 519; S. C., S. v. Geer, 61 Conn. 144; Organ v. State, 56 Ark. 267. As to prohibition of shipping, see, also, American Express Co. v. P., 133 Ill. 649; S. v. Northern Pacific Express Co., 58 Minn. 403; S. v. Swett, 87 Me. 99. Selling may be made illegal, even though the game is brought from another state: S. v. Randolph, 1 Mo. Ap. 15. But in some cases statutes as to transportation have been thought unconstitutional: S. v. Saunders, 19 Kan. 127; T. v. Evans, 2 Idaho, 634.

[5] S. v. Rodman, 58 Me. 393; Phelps v. Racey, 60 N. Y. 10. As to the validity of the game laws in general, see, also, Organ v. S., 56 Ark. 267; Gentile v. S., 29 Ind. 409; S. v. Farrell, 23 Mo. Ap. 176.

do that which he is himself, by the law, permitted to do.[1] Sometimes it is provided that hunting on private premises may be rendered criminal by notice posted forbidding it.[2] The regulation of the method in which fish may be captured is within the police power, even as applicable to waters within private boundaries.[3] No individual right attaches to fish in public waters, and the legislature has exclusive control over the manner of capture;[4] especially as to migratory fish is it proper that the taking of them should be under the control of the state, regardless of the locality in which they may happen to be found.[5] Indeed, at common law an obstruction to the passage of migratory fish, by which they were prevented from going into the public waters, was a nuisance.[6] A statute may, however, exempt from its regulations the taking of fish in private ponds,[7] or fish artificially propagated.[8] So, while the method of taking oysters by dredging, etc., may be regulated,[9] such regulations may be restricted in their application to natural oyster-beds, as distinct from private beds.[10] The exclusive fishing rights in a public pond may be granted on such conditions as the state may specify.[11] For the purpose of making the restrictions as to the method of fishing effectual, it may be made a misdemeanor for any one to have in his possession such a net or seine as is forbidden to be used, and the confiscation thereof will not be unconstitutional.[12]

[1] Hart v. S., 29 Ohio St. 666.

[2] S. v. Shannon, 36 Ohio St. 423.

[3] Gentile v. S., 29 Ind. 409; S. v. Blount, 85 Mo. 543; P. v. Bridges, 142 Ill. 30; P. v. Miller, 88 Mich. 383; S. v. Houghten, 65 Vt. 328; S. v. Roberts, 59 N. H. 256, 484; C. v. Look, 108 Mass. 452.

[4] S. v. Lewis, 134 Ind. 250; C. v. Cavey, 97 Mass. 541; S. v. Dunning, 83 Me. 178; S. v. Smith, 61 Vt. 346; P. v. Brooks, 101 Mich. 98.

[5] P. v. Collison, 85 Mich. 105; Parker v. P., 111 Ill. 581; S. v. Roberts, 59 N. H. 256, and 484. Where the catching of certain fish only is forbidden, the accidental taking of such fish while in good faith fishing for those which may lawfully be caught will not be criminal: C. v. Look, 108 Mass. 452.

[6] S. v. Franklin, etc. Co. 49 N. H. 240

[7] Reynolds v. C., 93 Pa. St. 458; S. v. Welch, 66 N. H. 178.

[8] C. v. Gilbert, 160 Mass. 157.

[9] S. v. Conner, 107 N. C. 931; Smith v. Maryland, 18 How. 71.

[10] P. v. Hazen, 121 N. Y. 313; S. v. Willis, 104 N. C. 764.

[11] C. v. Wetherhead, 110 Mass. 175.

[12] Lawton v. Steele, 152 U. S. 133; S. v. Lewis, 134 Ind. 250. So the forfeiture of a vessel for illegal fishing may be provided for; but to authorize such forfeiture where there is no fault on the part of the owner, there must be a proceeding against the vessel: Boggs v. C., 76 Va. 989.

§ 47. **Protection of brands.**— By way of protecting property it is common to provide for the punishment of falsely branding or changing brands, where branding is a means of identifying property for the purpose of proving the ownership. Thus, it is criminal to falsely brand, or alter the brand, of horses, cattle, or sheep, with the purpose of thereby destroying the evidence of another's ownership of them.[1] So it is criminal to destroy the brand on logs, provision being made by statute for recording such brands as evidence of ownership.[2] So it may be provided that stamps on bottles may be registered, and the possession by second-hand dealers of such bottles without the written consent of the owner of the stamp may be made *prima facie* evidence of unlawful use or traffic.[3] Brands are also authorized in some cases as a means of determining the quality or value of an article sold, or offered for sale, and the false branding for the purpose of deception would be criminal.[4]

§ 48. **False weights and measures; frauds.**— The states regulate to some extent the weights and measures which are authorized to be used in business transactions, and make it criminal to use false weights and measures.[5] So the states usually provide a weight for various articles which shall constitute a bushel, for purposes of sale, and make it criminal to sell except at the weight and measure prescribed by law.[6] The weighing of coal at coal mines as the basis on which to pay the miners has been made a subject of legislation.[7] So the weight of loaves of bread offered for sale may be regulated.[8] Fraud, constituting cheating by false pretenses, is hereafter considered in a separate chapter, but it may be suggested here

[1] Murrah v. S., 51 Miss. 652; P. v. Swasey, 6 Utah, 93; S. v. Haws, 41 Tex. 161; Alford v. S., 31 Tex. Ap. 299. So it is made criminal for a butcher to slaughter an unbranded animal: Hunt v. S., 33 Tex. Ap. 93.

[2] C. v. Puckett, 92 Ky. 206.

[3] P. v. Cannon, 139 N. Y. 32.

[4] S. v. Burge, 7 Ia. 255.

[5] S. v. Kellner, 22 Neb. 668. And see Reg. v. Justices, 24 Q. B. D. 181.

[6] Blanchard v. S., 3 Ind. Ap. 395. In this case it is said that if the purchaser had knowledge of the fact that the sale was at a less number of pounds per bushel than that required by statute, and was not deceived, there could be no conviction.

[7] Smith v. S., 90 Tenn. 575; S. v. Jenkins, 90 Tenn. 580. As to whether statutes requiring such weighing, for the protection of employees, notwithstanding contracts of parties to the contrary, are constitutional, see *infra*, § 55.

[8] P. v. Wagner, 86 Mich. 594.

that in some states fraud on hotel-keepers is made a special subject of statutory punishment.[1]

§ 49. **Regulation of warehousemen.**— For the protection of those who purchase property by means of the transfer of warehouse receipts, it is sometimes made criminal for the warehouseman to sell or remove goods for which a receipt has been given by him without the written assent of the holder thereof.[2]

§ 50. **Regulation of sales.**— To prevent the fraud which may be perpetrated in the selling or buying of the property belonging to another, it is provided in Texas that it shall be criminal to buy cattle without taking a bill of sale.[3] In other states, the sale of cotton or other farm produce after sunset or at night is criminal.[4] For a similar reason it is provided that seed cotton shall not be sold in less than the usual quantity for baling, and without reducing the sale to writing and delivering the receipt to the nearest justice of the peace to be docketed, and such a statute is held constitutional.[5] Notes given for patent rights may be required to show the consideration.[6]

§ 51. **Enticing away servants.**— In some of the southern states it is made criminal to induce a servant to leave the services of his employer, with whom he has a written contract, before the expiration of the time contracted for.[7] So it may be made criminal to entice a minor from the employ of a person to whom the parent has hired him.[8]

§ 52. **Rescue of distrained property.**— When cattle running at large are lawfully taken up, which fact must appear, the act of rescuing them from distraint may be criminal.[9]

§ 53. **Usury.**— The usury laws generally affect the validity of the contract or attach a penalty by way of forfeiture

[1] Such a statute is not unconstitutional as providing for imprisonment for debt: See *infra*, § 663*a*.

[2] S. v. Kirby, 115 Mo. 440; S. v. Miller, 140 Ind. 168; S. v. Koshland, 25 Or. 178; S. v. Stevenson, 52 Ia. 701; Sykes v. P., 127 Ill. 117; Bucher v. C., 103 Pa. St. 528.

[3] Long v. S., 6 Tex. Ap. 643; Huston v. S., 13 Tex. Ap. 595.

[4] S. v. Padgett, 18 S. C. 317; Reese v. S., 73 Ala. 18; Gilliam v. S., 71 Ala. 10; Mangan v. S. 76 Ala. 60; Davis v. S. 68 Ala. 58.

[5] S. v. Moore, 104 N. C. 714.

[6] S. v. Peck, 25 Ohio St. 26.

[7] Tarpley v. S., 79 Ala. 271; Tartt v. S., 86 Ala. 26; Prestwood v. S., 87 Ala. 147; Ward v. S., 70 Miss. 245; S. v. Harwood, 104 N. C. 724; S. v. Anderson, 104 N. C. 771; S. v. Hoover, 107 N. C. 795. And see, as to indentured servants, S. v. Owens, 1 Houst. Cr. C. 72; S. v. Hooper, 1 Houst. Cr. C. 17.

[8] Winslow v. S., 92 Ala. 78.

[9] S. v. Barrett, 42 N. H. 466; *infra*, § 932.

of interest, but a criminal punishment is also sometimes imposed.[1]

§ 54. **Civil rights.**—In the protection of all persons in equality of rights, it is common to prohibit the owners or managers of places of amusement or entertainment from excluding any person on account of race or color.[2] But even since the abolition of slavery it has been held constitutional to impose a severer penalty for adultery or fornication between persons of different races than between persons of the same race.[3] The statutes of the United States, which attempted to prevent discrimination against the colored race in their enjoyment of equal civil rights, was held unconstitutional as beyond the power of congress, such rights being within the protection of the states.[4] A state regulation requiring carriers within the state to furnish separate accommodations for white and colored passengers is not invalid as a regulation of interstate commerce;[5] otherwise if it applies to the carrying of passengers beyond the state limits.[6]

§ 55. **Regulation of employment.**—It is undoubtedly competent for the legislature to specially protect the interests of employees who, by reason of their lack of maturity, are not in a situation to make a valid contract.[7] But special restrictions

[1] C. v. Frost, 5 Mass. 53; Groves v. S., 6 Blackf. 489; Merriman v. S., 6 Blackf. 449; Crawford v. S., 2 Ind. 112; Wilkerson v. S., 2 Ind. 546; S. v. Williams, 4 Ind. 234; Marble v. S., 13 Ind. 362; Malone v. S., 14 Ind. 219; Swinney v. S., 14 Ind. 315; Block v. S., 14 Ind. 425; Sumner v. P., 29 N. Y. 337; Kenyon v. S., 31 Tex. Ap. 13. Such statutes are not unconstitutional as applied to national banks: S. v. First Nat. Bank, 2 S. Dak. 568.

[2] P. v. King, 110 N. Y. 418; C. v. Colton, 8 Gray, 488; C. v. Sylvester, 13 Allen, 247; Messenger v. S., 25 Neb. 674; S. v. Hall, 72 Ia. 525; U. S. v. Taylor, 3 Fed. R. 563. Discriminative statutes based on race distinctions were recognized before the abolition of slavery: S. v. Manuel, 4 Dev. & B. 20; S. v. Cooper, 5 Blackf. 258; Baptiste v. S., 5 Blackf. 283; Hatwood v. S., 18 Ind. 492; Pendleton v. S., 6 Ark. 509; Hickland v. S., 8 Ark. 365; S. v. Claiborne, 1 Meigs, 331.

[3] Green v. S., 58 Ala. 190; Pace v. S., 69 Ala. 231; S. C., Pace v. Alabama, 106 U. S. 583.

[4] Civil Rights Cases, 109 U. S. 3. But the right of a citizen of the United States in the custody of a marshal under lawful commitment, to be secure against lawless violence, is a right under the constitution and laws of the United States: Logan v. U. S., 144 U. S. 263. The right of suffrage is not guarantied by the Fifteenth Amendment to the Federal Constitution, but only the right to freedom from discrimination therein on account of race: U. S. v. Amsden, 6 Fed. R. 819.

[5] Louisville, etc. R. Co. v. Mississippi, 133 U. S. 587.

[6] Hall v. De Cuir, 95 U. S. 485.

[7] C. v. Hamilton Mfg. Co., 120 Mass. 383.

as to female labor are not constitutional.[1] Recently, statutes have been passed in many of the states intended to protect employees in general against their own contracts, which have been contested on the ground that such legislation interferes with that freedom of contract and right to the management of one's own services and property which the constitutions protect in general terms, if not in express provisions. In many instances these regulations have been held unconstitutional, but in some cases they have been sustained. The illustrations which are here given will furnish as definite a guide as is now practicable as to the scope of this legislative power. A restriction of the number of hours of labor which may be contracted for, or performed by an employee, per day or per week, is unconstitutional;[2] so is a contract requiring weekly payment of employees;[3] so is a statute prohibiting the payment of employees in orders or evidences of indebtedness, and not in lawful money;[4] so is a statute requiring the weighing of coal at mines;[5] so is a statute prohibiting an arrangement by which damages for bad work shall not be deducted from the pay of the employee;[6] so is a statute requiring payment for services to be made at the completion of the work;[7] so is

[1] In re Maguire, 57 Cal. 604; Ritchie v. P., 155 Ill. 98. But sale of liquor in dance-houses where there are female waitresses may be prohibited: Ex parte Hayes, 98 Cal. 555. And as to uniform operation of laws, see *infra*, § 77.

[2] Low v. Rees Ptg. Co., 41 Neb. 127; In re Eight Hour Law, — Colo. —, 39 Pac. R. 328; Ritchie v. P., 155 Ill. 98; Ex parte Kuback, 85 Cal. 274. As to the eight-hour law applicable to United States officers, contractors, etc., see U. S. v. Ollinger, 55 Fed. R. 959. It is applicable to seamen on a government vessel: U. S. v. Jefferson, 60 Fed. R. 736.

[3] Braceville Coal Co. v. P., 147 Ill. 66. The contrary decision in S. v. Brown, etc. Mfg. Co., 18 R. I. 16, is based to some extent on the fact that the statute in that case was applicable to corporations only, as to which see subsequent note to this section.

[4] S. v. Loomis, 115 Mo. 307; S. v. Peel Splint Coal Co., 36 W. Va. 802; S. v. Goodwill, 33 W. Va. 179. A similar provision that mining and manufacturing companies should not sell merchandise or supplies to their employees at a greater profit than to others not employed, was held unconstitutional: S. v. Fire Creek Coal & Coke Co., 33 W. Va. 188. The so-called "truck-store" statutes are unconstitutional: Frorer v. P., 141 Ill. 171.

[5] Millett v. P., 117 Ill. 294; Ramsey v. P., 142 Ill. 380; In re House Bill, — Colo. —, 39 Pac. R. 431. Such a statute is not constitutional, even though for the avowed purpose of securing statistics: Millett v. P., 117 Ill. 294.

[6] C. v. Perry, 155 Mass. 117.

[7] Leep v. St. Louis, etc. R. Co., 58 Ark. 407.

a statute requiring employers to give to employees a written statement of the reasons for their discharge;[1] so is a statute prohibiting employers from requiring laborers not to belong to labor organizations.[2] It has been suggested that such statutes may be valid as to corporations whose charters are subject to legislative regulation, even though unconstitutional as to natural persons.[3] Prohibition of labor and business on Sunday, works of necessity and charity excepted, is constitutional;[4] but a prohibition of a particular employment being exercised on that day, such as barbering, which is not specially objectionable, is unconstitutional, on the ground that it unjustly discriminates between classes.[5]

§ 56. **Sale of diseased animals.**— The right of the state to protect the owners of animals from the risk of contagion communicated by the animals of other owners known to be diseased, even to the extent of causing the destruction of the diseased animals, is not questioned.[6] Such legislation is not unconstitutional, either as an invasion of the privileges and immunities of citizens of another state, or as an interference with interstate commerce.[7]

§ 57. **Regulation of marriage.**— The state may properly require a record to be preserved of the solemnization of marriages, and punish those charged with the duty of having that fact recorded for failure to do so;[8] and it is competent to prohibit intermarriage between whites and blacks, there being in such a regulation no interference with the equality of rights guarantied by the Fourteenth Amendment of the Federal Constitution.[9]

[1] Wallace v. Georgia, etc. R. Co., 94 Ga. 732.

[2] S. v. Julow, 129 Mo. 163.

[3] Leep v. St. Louis, etc. R. Co., 58 Ark. 407. And see S. v. Brown, etc. Mfg. Co., 18 R. I. 16, where a statute applicable to corporations was upheld. The argument of the court, however, is in behalf of the constitutionality of such legislation, even as applied to natural persons.

[4] See SUNDAY LAWS, *infra*, ch. 66.

[5] Eden v. P., 161 Ill. 296; Ex parte Jentzsch (Cal.), 44 Pac. R. 803; S. v. Granneman (Mo.), 33 S. W. R. 784. *Contra*, P. v. Havnor, 149 N. Y. 195.

[6] Thus, a statute making it criminal to bring into the state, or to suffer to run at large, or to sell diseased sheep or to contract for the sale of such sheep, will be valid: Caldwell v. Bridal, 48 Ia. 15; and as to such statutes see S. v. Sterritt, 19 Oreg. 352.

[7] Kimmish v. Ball, 129 U. S. 217.

[8] S. v. Madden, 81 Mo. 421; S. v. Walker, 36 Kan. 297.

[9] S. v. Gibson, 36 Ind. 389; S. v. Jackson, 80 Mo. 175.

§ 58. Abandonment of wife or child; neglect of children. Under homicide it will appear that, for one charged with the support of a child to fail to furnish such support, so that the child dies, is manslaughter.[1] But even if death does not result, the failure to support a child is usually made criminal by statute.[2] Such offense may be committed by the head of a charitable institution which assumes the care and custody of poor children, if he knowingly allows a child in such institution to be without proper food, clothing and medical attendance.[3] The elements of the offense are that the child is of tender age or unable to take care of itself; that defendant is under obligations to support it, or at least that it is in his care or keeping, and that the defendant did not do what he could in furnishing the necessary support to the child so that it suffered injury.[4] If defendant voluntarily assumes the care and support he is not excusable on account of not having the means, unless, when such incapacity has arisen, he does what he can to resign such care and applies to the public authorities for relief.[5] In some states the offense is described as the abandonment by parents of their children.[6] In some states, as also in England, the offense of exposing children is made punishable by statute.[7] There are also statutory provisions requiring one who receives a child of tender age with the agreement to care for it, taking compensation therefor, to notify a state board of charity.[8] Some statutes with reference to abandonment or failure to support, make it criminal for a husband to abandon his wife, or wife and children.[9] In charging such offense the words of the statute may be followed, without setting out the facts con-

[1] *Infra*, § 286.

[2] Cowley v. P., 83 N. Y. 464; C. v. Burlington, 136 Mass. 435; C. v. Ellis, 160 Mass. 165.

[3] Cowley v. P., 83 N. Y. 464.

[4] C. v. Stoddard, 9 Allen, 280; Reg. v. Hogan, 2 Den. 277.

[5] Cowley v. P., 83 N. Y. 464.

[6] Bull v. S., 80 Ga. 704; Bennefield v. S., 80 Ga. 107. By early English statute such person was punishable as disorderly: Duffy v. P., 6 Hill, 75. A parent who thus abandons a child in one state is not punishable therefor in another, though the child is afterwards in destitute circumstances in the latter: Jemmerson v. S., 80 Ga. 111.

[7] S. v. Smith, 46 Ia. 670; Reg. v. Cooper, 1 Den. 459; Reg. v. White, L. R. 1 C. C. 311; Reg. v. Falkigham, L. R. 1 C. C. 222; Reg. v. Renshaw, 2 Cox, 385.

[8] C. v. Johnson, 162 Mass. 596.

[9] C. v. Baldwin, 149 Pa. St. 305; S. v. Witham, 70 Wis. 473; Carney v. S., 84 Ala. 7. Under such a statute the husband may be punished for failing to provide for the child alone without regard to the wife: S. v. Kerby, 110 N. C. 558.

stituting the abandonment,[1] and the wife is competent to make the complaint, the crime being one against her.[2] Misconduct on the part of the wife is a defense to such a charge so far as she is concerned.[3] The inability to support which will usually constitute a defense under the statute does not mean simply the lack of such accumulated property as would enable the husband to furnish such support, but mental and physical inability to earn support for the wife.[4] If the husband has earnings which he spends otherwise, though for a lawful purpose, he may be punished for the omission of duty.[5]

§ 59. **Protection of minors.**— The care of the state with reference to minors is sometimes exercised by providing that they shall not be allowed to remain in billiard halls or saloons,[6] or to play games in such places, at least without the consent of their parents.[7] And it is immaterial whether the minor bet on the game so that it should constitute the offense of gambling.[8] In an indictment charging this offense it is necessary to allege that the minor played as prohibited by statute, and the name of the person with whom he played.[9] The fact that the person charged with the offense in good faith believed the minor to be of age has been held to constitute a defense.[10] Statutes regulating the numbers of hours per day for which they may be employed in manufacturing, etc., have been upheld.[11]

[1] S. v. Davis, 70 Mo. 467.

[2] S. v. Newberry, 43 Mo. 429.

[3] S. v. Schweitzer, 57 Conn. 532; C. v. Ham, 156 Mass. 485. But misconduct before marriage, of which the husband had knowledge, is no excuse: S. v. Ransell, 41 Conn. 433. Nor is misconduct after abandonment any defense: Hall v. S., 100 Ala. 86.

[4] S. v. Witham, 70 Wis. 473; C. v. Baldwin, 149 Pa. St. 305. To sustain a charge against a minor husband it is necessary to prove his emancipation and that he owns property: P. v. Todd, 61 Mich. 234.

[5] S. v. Ransell, 41 Conn. 433.

[6] S. v. Probasco, 62 Ia. 400.

[7] Kiley v. S., 120 Ind. 65; Conyers v. S., 50 Ga. 103. See *infra*, § 1314.

[8] Green v. C., 5 Bush, 327; S. v. Ward, 57 Ind. 537; Bond v. S., 52 Ind. 457; Ready v. S., 62 Ind. 1.

[9] Donniger v. S., 52 Ind. 326; Alexander v. S., 48 Ind. 394; Zook v. S., 47 Ind. 463. And it must be alleged that the act was unlawful, or the facts must be stated showing that it was so; for instance, to show that it was a public table as provided by statute: S. v. Dupies, 91 Ind. 233.

[10] Stern v. S., 53 Ga. 229. But it has been otherwise held as to the offense of selling liquor to minors: See *infra*, § 128.

[11] C. v. Hamilton Mfg. Co., 120 Mass. 383. So in New York it is made criminal for the parent to consent to the employment or exhibition of a female child, under fourteen years of age, as a dancer, in violation of police regulations with reference

§ 60. **Indecency and profanity.**— The offense of making obscene publications, blaspheming, etc., will be elsewhere discussed, but it may be suggested here that it is competent for the legislature to suppress newspaper publications which are devoted largely to scandals, lecheries, assignations, etc.,[1] and that the use of profane and indecent language may be made punishable as a nuisance.[2]

§ 61. **Vagrants.**—In some states vagrancy is made a crime in itself, and punishment therefor is provided where the case is brought within the particular description of the offense in the statute.[3] The usual method of dealing with vagrants, however, is to require them to give security for good behavior, or to commit them to compulsory labor. A statute which provides for binding them out to labor is not unconstitutional, as imposing slavery or involuntary servitude.[4]

§ 62. **Municipal regulations.**— A municipal corporation may be given authority to make police regulations in the discharge of the powers conferred upon it by law and to punish the violation of such regulations, and such a grant of authority is not an unconstitutional delegation of legislative power.[5] But the authority of the municipality in this respect is closely restricted to the express powers given in the charter, or contained in the general laws defining the rights, duties and powers of such corporations, or such powers as are necessarily implied therefrom or involved therein.[6] In passing ordinances a municipality must comply with the provisions of the general statutes,[7] and exercise them within the limits imposed by the

thereto; and such a statute is not unconstitutional: P. v. Ewer, 141 N. Y. 129.

[1] In re Banks (Kan.), 42 Pac. R. 694.

[2] S. v. Warren, 113 N. C. 683.

[3] Ex parte McCarthy, 72 Cal. 384; Price v. S., 67 Ga. 723; Allen v. S., 51 Ga. 264; Walters v. S., 52 Ga. 574; Taylor v. S., 59 Ala. 19; Boulo v. S., 49 Ala. 22; Taylor v. S., 100 Ala. 68; S. v. Custer, 65 N. C. 339; Brown v. S., 2 Lea, 158; In re Smith, 54 Kan. 702; Walton v. S., 12 Tex. Ap. 117.

[4] In re Thompson, 117 Mo. 83.

[5] S. v. Tryon, 39 Conn. 183; S. v. Carpenter, 60 Conn. 97; S. v. Noyes, 30 N. H. 279; S. v. King, 37 Ia. 462; Des Moines v. Hillis, 55 Ia. 643; St. Louis v. McCoy, 18 Mo. 238; St. Louis v. Boffinger, 19 Mo. 13; S. v. Garibaldi, 44 La. An. 809.

[6] S. v. Hunter, 106 N. C. 796; S. v. Horne, 115 N. C. 739; S. v. Zeigler, 32 N. J. 262; Keokuk v. Scroggs, 39 Ia. 447; C. v. Wilkins, 121 Mass. 356; S. v. Miller, 41 La. An. 53; S. v. Garibaldi, 44 La. An. 809.

[7] C. v. Young, 135 Mass. 526.

constitution on legislative action,[1] and an ordinance in excess of the power vested in the city is void.[2] The authority to make ordinances involves also the power to repeal them;[3] and also to delegate to an officer a discretion which the council might exercise, for instance, as to granting licenses for the sale of liquors,[4] or permitting the repair of wooden buildings within the fire limits,[5] or authorizing the beating of drums on the streets which is prohibited without such authority.[6] The municipal authority to maintain peace and good order is not a constitutional privilege, but may be taken away by legislative action and vested in a general board having control of all such municipalities.[7]

§ 63. **Ordinances and statutes on same subject.**— As a general rule the municipality is not given authority to pass ordinances as to subjects which are fully covered by the general laws of the state,[8] but an ordinance to regulate matters which are within the general power of the city is not invalid because such matters are also regulated in a different way by statute, if there is no necessary repugnance between the ordinance and the statute.[9] Thus, a city may be authorized to regulate as a nuisance things which would not be nuisances under the state statute, although statutory punishment for nuisances is provided for;[10] and may, for instance, regulate and prohibit the sale of liquors, although its action goes beyond the regulations

[1] S. v. Hunter, 106 N. C. 796. For instance, a city cannot prescribe a penalty for failing to perform a duty, when there is no ordinance commanding such duty: City of Kansas v. Corrigan, 86 Mo. 67. It cannot make that unlawful which is within the scope of proper personal liberty, for instance, visiting for a lawful purpose a place where opium is sold: In re Ah Jow, 29 Fed. R. 181.

[2] S. v. Hammond, 40 Minn. 43; Fayette v. Shafroth, 25 Mo. 445.

[3] City of Kansas v. White, 69 Mo. 26.

[4] Swarth v. P., 109 Ill. 621.

[5] Ex parte Fiske, 72 Cal. 125.

[6] In re Flaherty, 105 Cal. 558.

[7] C. v. Plaisted, 148 Mass. 375.

[8] C. v. Turner, 1 Cush. 493; S. v. Lindsay, 34 Ark. 372; S. v. McCoy, 115 N. C. 1059.

[9] C. v. Goodnow, 117 Mass. 114; S. v. Plunkett, 18 N. J. 5; S. v. Zeigler, 46 N. J. 307; S. v. King, 37 Ia. 462; St. Louis v. Cafferata, 24 Mo. 94; S. v. Binder, 38 Mo. 450; Ex parte Hayes, 98 Cal. 555; Ex parte Boswell, 86 Cal. 232; S. v. Priester, 43 Minn. 373; Paton v. P., 1 Colo. 77.

[10] S. v. Wilson, 106 N. C. 718; P. v. Detroit Lead Works, 82 Mich. 471; S. v. Flint, 63 Conn. 248. Although there is a statute regulating the sale of poisons, a city may by ordinance make special regulations as to selling opium: Ex parte Hong Shen, 98 Cal. 681.

made by general statute.[1] An ordinance providing punishment for what is also punishable under state statute is therefore not necessarily void;[2] and even if an ordinance and a statute are in conflict, the repeal of the statute may leave the ordinance in force.[3] If both the ordinance and the statute can be given effect, each will be valid.[4] The city cannot, however, interfere with a right or privilege derived by license from the state under a statute.[5] In general it is said that the power to enforce police regulations by the city does not extend to creating crimes and fixing punishment therefor.[6]

§ **64. Impose punishments.**— The power given to a city to suppress and prohibit a class of acts implies a power to inflict punishment therefor.[7] If the city is authorized to enforce its ordinances by fine only, it cannot provide a criminal punishment thereunder by way of imprisonment;[8] but it may be given authority to impose imprisonment as a punishment,[9] even as a means of enforcing a regulation requiring citizens to work upon the streets.[10]

§ **65. Reasonableness of ordinances.**—An ordinance which the city passes in the exercise of the powers given it must be reasonable, and the courts have authority to inquire into that question to a greater extent than they have with reference to state statutes.[11]

[1] S. v. Clark, 28 N. H. 176; Hannibal v. Guyott, 18 Mo. 515; Independence v. Noland, 21 Mo. 394; St. Louis v. Caffarata, 24 Mo. 94; In re Thomas, 53 Kan. 659; Deitz v. Central City, 1 Colo. 323; Rogers v. P., 9 Colo. 450; Heinssen v. S., 14 Colo. 228; Ex parte Taylor, 87 Cal. 91. But if the matter is one requiring general regulation throughout the state, a general statute on the subject will prevail over a city ordinance. In re Sic, 73 Cal. 142.

[2] Bloomfield v. Trimble, 54 Ia. 399.

[3] S. v. Zeigler, 46 N. J. 307.

[4] S. v. Welch, 36 Conn. 215; S. v. Brady, 41 Conn. 588.

[5] Hannibal v. Guyott, 18 Mo. 515; S. v. Ferguson, 33 N. H. 424; Ex parte Keeney, 84 Cal. 304. But a city ordinance will not be rendered invalid by a statute in conflict therewith until it goes into effect, although the statute is already passed when the ordinance is enacted: Swarth v. P., 109 Ill. 621.

[6] Slaughter v. P., 2 Doug. (Mich.) 334; S. v. Bright, 38 La. An. 1.

[7] Rogers v. P., 9 Colo. 450. But no punishment can be provided for except as authorized by law: S. v. Lochte, 45 La. An. 1405.

[8] S. v. Earnhardt, 107 N. C. 789; S. v. Mannessier, 32 La. An. 1308.

[9] S. v. Mack, 41 La. An. 1079; P. v. Hanrahan, 75 Mich. 611.

[10] S. v. Smith, 103 N. C. 403; Tipton v. Norman, 72 Mo. 380.

[11] P. v. Armstrong, 73 Mich. 288; S. v. Dering, 84 Wis. 585; Ex parte Hodges, 87 Cal. 162; Ex parte Robinson, 30 Tex. Ap. 493; Ex parte Bell,

§ 66. Suppression of nuisances.— The power granted to municipalities usually involves the authority to determine what are nuisances in a city and to suppress them, even though the matters referred to may not be nuisances under the general state law;[1] and they may make municipal regulations for the suppression of nuisances which are also within state control.[2] But the city cannot, under the power to suppress nuisances, make that a nuisance which is not such in fact.[3] The general power given to cities is broad enough to authorize the prohibition of the sale of lottery tickets,[4] or the sale of adulterated milk,[5] or the operation of a carpet-beating machine near a residence.[6] Minors may be prohibited from entering bar-rooms.[7]

32 Tex. Ap. 308; Ex parte Neill, 32 Tex. Ap. 275; S. v. Dubarry, 44 La. An. 1117; S. v. Garibaldi, 44 La. An. 809.

1 So held as to an ordinance imposing a fine for abusive or indecent language, swearing, loud talking and other disorderly conduct: S. v. Earnhardt, 107 N. C. 789. So held also as to smoking in street cars: S. v. Heidenhain, 42 La. An. 483; and as to delivering addresses in public grounds without permission: C. v. Davis, 140 Mass. 485; C. v. Abrahams, 156 Mass. 57; and as to street parades; but such an ordinance was held invalid which made unreasonable discriminations and conferred arbitrary power upon the mayor: S. v. Dering, 84 Wis. 585; and as to placing placards on sidewalks or carrying them displayed: C. v. McCafferty, 145 Mass. 384; P. v. Armstrong, 73 Mich. 288; and as to keeping swine in populous parts of the city: C. v. Patch, 97 Mass. 221; S. v. Holcomb, 68 Ia. 107; or allowing such animals to be at large: S. v. Tweedy, 115 N. C. 704; and as to driving cattle through the streets: C. v. Curtis, 9 Allen, 266; and as to removing garbage in closed carts: P. v. Gordon, 81 Mich. 306; and as to restaurants and eating-houses: S. v. Clark, 28 N. H. 176; and as to garbage or filth on land adjoining private way: C. v. Cutter, 156 Mass. 52. While a license may be required for dogs (C. v. Palmer, 134 Mass. 537; S. v. Topeka, 36 Kan. 76), yet where deemed property, policemen cannot be authorized to shoot them because unmuzzled. Such killing is destruction of property without due process of law; Lynn v. S., 33 Tex. Ap. 153.

2 So held as to houses of ill fame: P. v. Hanrahan, 75 Mich. 611; S. v. Mack, 41 La. An. 1079; S. v. Webber, 107 N. C. 962. So as to slaughter-houses: Cronin v. P., 82 N. Y. 318; and bowling alleys: S. v. Hay, 29 Me. 457; S. v. Noyes, 30 N. H. 279; and billiard and gaming rooms: S. v. Pamperin, 42 Minn. 320; S. v. Carpenter, 60 Conn. 97.

3 Ex parte Robinson, 30 Tex. Ap. 493; Ex parte Bell, 32 Tex. Ap. 308; Ex parte Neill, 32 Tex. Ap. 275; P. v. Armstrong, 73 Mich. 288; Poyer v. Desplaines, 22 Ill. Ap. 30. But the city may punish persons whose modes of life and practices are inimical to the public: Morgan v. Nolte, 37 Ohio St. 23.

4 S. v. Dobard, 45 La. An. 1412.

5 S. v. Stone, 46 La. An. 147.

6 Ex parte Lacey, 108 Cal. 326.

7 S. v. Austin, 114 N. C. 855.

§ 67. **Quarantine.**— The enforcement of a reasonable quarantine is within the police power usually delegated to cities.[1]

§ 68. **Sale of liquors.**— Under the same general police power the city may regulate the sale of liquors, and in this direction it may, in promoting the general welfare or morals of the people, go beyond the state legislation on the same subject.[2]

§ 69. **Power to regulate does not include power to prohibit.**— Under a statute authorizing a city to regulate, or to regulate, license and tax the sale of intoxicating liquors, the city has no authority to prohibit the sale of liquors.[3] Similarly it has been held that the power to suppress and restrain disorderly houses does not authorize an ordinance making the keeping of such houses a misdemeanor, imposing punishment therefor.[4] The power to regulate implies the power to impose a license[5] and exact a fee for such license sufficient to meet the expense of enforcing it,[6] but it does not authorize the levying of a tax for revenue.[7] However, a license, if exacted for a privilege or franchise, may lawfully be collected as revenue.[8] On the other hand, the power to prohibit does not include the power to regulate by license,[9] nor does the power to suppress imply the power to punish as a crime an act connected with the business to be suppressed.[10]

§ 70. **Regulation of streets and public places.**— The city may make regulations as to the use of omnibuses and stagecoaches upon its streets, with the view of promoting the safety and convenience of travelers;[11] and it may regulate the speed

[1] St. Louis v. McCoy, 18 Mo. 238; St. Louis v. Boffinger, 19 Mo. 13.

[2] Deitz v. Central City, 1 Colo. 323; S. v. Clark, 28 N. H. 176.

[3] Miller v. Jones, 80 Ala. 89; Ex parte Reynolds, 87 Ala. 138; Ex parte Mayor of Anniston, 90 Ala. 516; S. v. Pamperin, 42 Minn. 320.

[4] Chariton v. Barber, 54 Ia. 360.

[5] Huntington v. Cheesbro, 57 Ind. 74; S. v. Stone, 46 La. An. 147.

[6] C. v. Plaisted, 148 Mass. 375; Ash v. P., 11 Mich. 347.

[7] C. v. Stodder, 2 Cush. 562; Burlington v. Bumgardner, 42 Ia. 673.

[8] Chilvers v. P., 11 Mich. 43.

[9] S. v. Fay, 44 N. J. 474.

[10] Mt. Pleasant v. Breeze, 11 Ia. 399; New Hampton v. Conroy, 56 Ia. 498; Chariton v. Barber, 54 Ia. 360; Nevada v. Hutchins, 59 Ia. 506; Slaughter v. P., 2 Doug. (Mich.) 334. But held that under the power to prevent disturbances, etc., the city might provide a punishment for keeping a place where persons are permitted to engage in loud and profane language to the disturbance of others: Centerville v. Miller, 57 Ia. 56, 225. So under the general authority to provide for preserving order, the city may punish intoxication: Bloomfield v. Trimble, 54 Ia. 399.

[11] C. v. Stodder, 2 Cush. 562. But

of vehicles driven through the streets,[1] and prohibit the stopping of vehicles for more than a certain time,[2] or fix the place at which hackney coaches may stand to solicit hire,[3] and regulate the rate to be charged by hackney coaches and other public conveyances.[4] It may regulate the use by railways of the city streets,[5] and the speed of railway cars on the streets.[6] In the exercise of the police power with reference to the streets, a city may require a license for the use of bicycles.[7] The power to establish wharves and fix the rate of wharfage includes the power to punish for using other places for landing.[8]

§ 71. Regulation of markets and market-places.— The power usually given to cities with reference to markets, as well as the power to regulate the use of streets, involves the authority to regulate the time at which market carts may stand in a market which is also a public thoroughfare,[9] and to determine at what places, or within what limits in the streets, vehicles and carts containing produce for sale shall be allowed to stand.[10] So the exposing of merchandise, provisions, vegetables, etc., in front of stores, and the use of the sidewalk therefor, may be regulated;[11] and the offering of meats for sale at places other than those designated by ordinance may be punished.[12]

the power to regulate, license and tax vehicles used within the city does not authorize the imposing of a license on wagons hauling goods into and out of the city: St. Charles v. Nolle, 51 Mo. 122; Wells v. Weston, 22 Mo. 384. But the power of the state to impose such tax is not thus restricted: Langhorne v. Robinson, 20 Grat. 661.

[1] C. v. Worcester, 3 Pick. 462; C. v. Roy, 140 Mass. 432. The city may be authorized to regulate the use of public parks: C. v. Davis, 162 Mass. 510.

[2] C. v. Fenton, 139 Mass. 195. But a licensed push-cart peddler is not subject to punishment for allowing his cart to stand in the street: S. v. Rayantis, 55 Minn. 126.

[3] C. v. Matthews, 122 Mass. 60.

[4] C. v. Duane, 98 Mass. 1.

[5] S. v. Cozzens, 42 La. An. 1069.

[6] Whitson v. Franklin, 34 Ind. 392. Under the power given to police juries in Louisiana, it is held that the regulation of the speed of railway trains is not included: S. v. Miller, 41 La. An. 53. But in the same state it is said that much discretion is left to municipal corporations, and that they may make smoking in street cars a punishable nuisance: S. v. Heidenhain, 42 La. An. 483.

[7] St. Louis v. Green, 70 Mo. 562.

[8] Dubuque v. Stout, 32 Ia. 80.

[9] C. v. Brooks, 109 Mass. 355.

[10] P. v. Keir, 78 Mich. 98.

[11] S. v. Summerfield, 107 N. C. 895.

[12] Davenport v. Kelley, 7 Ia. 102; St. Louis v. Jackson, 25 Mo. 37. Sales within the designated limits in violation of the ordinance, even by producers or dealers from outside the limits, are subject to the city

The use of public markets may be restricted to those living beyond a distance named from the city.[1] The right to establish and regulate markets and prescribe at what places within the city limits marketable things may be sold covers the right to provide for the election of a cotton weigher and his compensation, and require that all persons selling cotton within the city limits shall have their cotton weighed by such officer.[2] The setting up of a private market within a stipulated distance from the public market may be prohibited.[3] But the requirement that no private market shall be set up without the permission of the council is not valid, as it does not constitute a regulation or prescribe the conditions on which such privilege shall be granted.[4] So it is not proper to make the right to conduct a private market dependent upon the consent of neighboring property owners, all the police and sanitary regulations of the city being complied with.[5]

§ 72. **Regulations as to fire.**— Under the usual powers given to cities, fire limits may be established and the erection of wooden buildings within them prohibited.[6] But this is not one of the incidental or implied powers which may be exercised in the absence of express legislative authority.[7] The alteration and repairing of an old building for the purpose of converting it into a dwelling-house is not the offense of erecting a wooden dwelling-house within said limits;[8] but the construction of a material addition to a building is within a statute prohibiting the building or erection of a wooden house.[9] In general, the police powers extend to the regulation of buildings dangerous to life, or in case of fire.[10] Under the police power, also, it may be made a crime to give a false alarm of

regulations: S. v. Wernwag, 116 N. C. 1061; S. v. Sarradat, 46 La. An. 700.

[1] C. v. Rice, 9 Met. 253.

[2] S. v. Tyson, 111 N. C. 687.

[3] S. v. Natal, 41 La. An. 887.

[4] S. v. Dubarry, 44 La. An. 1117.

[5] S. v. Garibaldi, 44 La. An. 809.

[6] Booth v. S., 4 Conn. 65; Tuttle v. S., 4 Conn. 68. Discretion as to allowing repairs on wooden buildings within fire limits may be left to an officer: Ex parte Fiske, 72 Cal. 125. If such regulations are intended as a discrimination against a class, as the Chinese, they are invalid: Yick Wo v. Hopkins, 118 U. S. 356.

[7] S. v. Schuchardt, 42 La. An. 49.

[8] Booth v. S., 4 Conn. 65.

[9] Douglas v. C., 2 Rawle, 262.

[10] St. Paul v. Hennessy, 38 Minn. 94. Rebuilding of a partly-burned wooden building may be within the prohibition: S. v. Johnson, 114 N. C. 846.

fire by the fire-alarm telegraph.[1] Smoking in the streets may be made criminal.[2]

§ 73. **Regulation of employments.**— The powers conferred upon cities are usually broad enough to authorize regulations as to the number of hours during which a person may be employed in a particular business;[3] to require physicians to report cases of infectious diseases;[4] to require attorneys to procure licenses for conducting their business,[5] and to require licenses of undertakers.[6] But a license and bond cannot be required for the conducting of a legitimate business.[7]

[1] Koppersmith v. S., 51 Ala. 6.
[2] C. v. Thompson, 12 Met. 231.
[3] C. v. Hamilton Mfg. Co., 120 Mass. 383.
[4] S. v. Wordin, 56 Conn. 216.
[5] St. Louis v. Sternberg, 69 Mo. 289.
[6] C. v. Goodrich, 13 Allen, 546.
[7] S. v. Von Sachs, 45 La. An. 1416.

CHAPTER 4.

CONSTITUTIONAL LIMITATIONS.

§ 74. Applicable to criminal statutes.— The power of congress, or of a state legislature, to make acts criminal is subject to the general constitutional limitations upon legislative power, applicable in civil as well as criminal matters,[1] and also to certain special constitutional limitations having direct reference to the legislative power to define and punish crimes, and the procedure with reference thereto. The constitutionality of various statutes relating to particular crimes is discussed in connection with those crimes specifically, and it is only necessary in this chapter to notice some of the constitutional provisions which are likely to be involved in different classes of cases. But it may be said generally that the unreasonableness of a statute will not render it invalid, and that it can be unconstitutional (in the case of state legislation) only where it is in violation of some constitutional restriction.[2]

§ 75. Interference with obligation of contracts and other vested rights.— The legislative power cannot make acts criminal in such a way as to impair the obligations of a contract,[3] but a privilege or franchise granted to individuals or corporations to carry on a particular business does not put such business beyond the police control of the state, which may, at any time, by general law regulate or prohibit the carrying on of

[1] For instance, a statute making it criminal for judges and state school officers to electioneer is unconstitutional as interfering with civil equality and freedom of speech and the press: Louthan v. C., 79 Va. 196. But a statute forbidding the levying and collection of political assessments on government officers and employees is not unconstitutional: Ex parte Curtis, 106 U. S 371.

[2] Giozza v. Tiernan, 148 U. S. 657; Hedderich v. S., 101 Ind. 564; S. v. Clottu, 33 Ind. 409; Wynehamer v. P., 13 N. Y. 378, 390.

[3] It was so held with reference to charters or licenses for the conduct of lotteries: S. v. Hawthorn, 9 Mo. 385; S. v. Morrow, 26 Mo. 131; S. v. Miller, 50 Mo. 129; Kellum v. S., 66 Ind. 588. But it has since been held that the police power extends even to the regulation of lotteries under charters or licenses already granted: See cases in a subsequent note under this section.

the business which has been authorized by such grant. It is so held with reference to the business of manufacturing or selling intoxicating liquors under a charter or privilege granted by the state, such business being unquestionably subject to police regulation.[1] So a state may annul the charter of a corporation authorized to carry on a lottery, and make it criminal to transact the business authorized by such charter.[2] So the granting of letters patent by the United States, under which property has been acquired, does not prevent the regulation of such property by the states in the exercise of their police power.[3] Unnecessary interference with business or the use of property, will be unconstitutional as depriving of liberty and property without due process of law.[4]

§ 76. Interference with interstate commerce.— In a previous section the limitation of the power to regulate and tax occupations, such as that of itinerant vendors and agents, resulting from the investment of the United States government with the power to regulate foreign commerce and commerce among the states, has been already discussed.[5] It is proper here, however, to suggest the additional proposition that a state cannot, in the exercise of its police power, interfere with the bringing into the state,[6] or with the sale within the state,

[1] C. v. Intoxicating Liquors, 115 Mass. 153; Beer Co. v. Massachusetts, 97 U. S. 25. A license is not a contract though granted upon consideration paid by the licensee; he takes it on the implied understanding that it may be revoked: C. v. Kinsley, 133 Mass. 578; S. v. Fairfield, 37 Me. 517; Columbus City v. Cutcomp, 61 Ia. 672. But a statute will not be construed as revoking existing licenses, where such construction is not necessary: Hirn v. S., 1 Ohio St. 15; S. v. Andrews, 28 Mo. 14.

[2] Stone v. Mississippi, 101 U. S. 814; Boyd v. Alabama, 94 U. S. 645; S. v. Woodward, 89 Ind. 110; S. v. Morris, 77 N. C. 512; Moore v. S., 48 Miss. 147; Freleigh v. S., 8 Mo. 606.

[3] Patterson v. Kentucky, 97 U. S. 501.

[4] See the discussion under various sections of the preceding chapter on Police Power, especially § 55.

[5] *Supra*, § 44.

[6] So held as to intoxicating liquors: Bowman v. Chicago & N. W. R. Co., 125 U. S. 465; and as to garden seeds: In re Sanders, 52 Fed. R. 802; and as to baking powder: In re Ware, 53 Fed. R. 783. The act of congress referred to in the next note, which subjects intoxicating liquors brought into the state to the regulations of the state law as to the sale does not apply to the bringing into the state, and therefore the South Carolina Dispensary Act, which vests the traffic in intoxicating liquors exclusively in the state, is unconstitutional so far as it attempts to prohibit the bringing of such liquor into the state: Ex parte Edgerton, 59 Fed. R. 115. See *infra*, §§ 1205, 1214.

by the importer in the original package, of goods thus brought in, as such interference is a restriction of the freedom of interstate commerce.[1] But the exercise of the police power of the state to exclude from the state articles which are not a legitimate subject of commerce, but are generally recognized as injurious to the public, such as cattle infected with a contagious disease, is not interfered with by the rule as to freedom of interstate commerce, and such property may be excluded.[2] Nor does the power of congress to regulate commerce preclude the existence in the state of a power to make local regulations, as to matters which could not be the subject of general regulation, such as the operation of bridges, which interfere with commerce, over a particular navigable stream.[3]

§ 77. Uniformity of operation; equality of protection.— Most state constitutions require in some form that legislation shall be of uniform operation, and therefore a statute punishing acts which are in effect injurious to the public must be applicable to all acts of the same character; but a statute may

[1] Brown v. Maryland, 12 Wheat. 419; Waring v. Mayor, 8 Wall. 110; Leisy v. Hardin, 135 U. S. 100; Lyng v. Michigan, 135 U. S. 161; S. v. Shapleigh, 27 Mo. 344; P. v. Maring, 3 Keyes, 374; C. v. Paul, 148 Pa. St. 559; In re Worthen, 58 Fed. R. 467; In re McAllister, 51 Fed. R. 282; Ex parte Loeb, 72 Fed. R. 657. *Contra*, Pierce v. S., 13 N. H. 536. Sale of cigarettes in original packages by the agent of the importer cannot be regulated by state statute: In re Minor, 69 Fed. R. 233. So far as state statutes regulating the sale of intoxicating liquors were interfered with by the announcement of this doctrine by the supreme court of the United States in the case of Leisy v. Hardin, *supra*, the obstacle to the enforcement of the statute is removed by an act of congress subjecting intoxicating liquors taken into a state to the regulations imposed by the state law: Wilkerson v. Rahrer, 140 U. S. 545. By this act the original package, when it reaches its destination, is subject to the state law: In re Langford, 57 Fed. R. 570. As to what constitutes an original package, see the chapter on intoxicating liquors, *infra*, § 1204. The South Carolina Dispensary Act, vesting the exclusive right to sell intoxicating liquors in the state, is not a police regulation, and is therefore invalid as an interference with interstate commerce: In re Langford, 57 Fed. R. 570; Ex parte Jervey, 66 Fed. R. 957; Ex parte Edgerton, 59 Fed. R. 115. The last decision in the state court, however, upholds the law: S. v. City Council, 42 S. C. 222 (overruling S. v. Jacobs, 41 S. C. 220).

[2] Kimmish v. Ball, 129 U. S. 217. Transportation of game may be prohibited: See *supra*, § 46.

[3] Escanaba Co. v. Chicago, 107 U. S. 678; and see Barnaby v. S., 21 Ind. 450. But a city ordinance requiring a license fee for tugs used in interstate commerce is unconstitutional; Harman v. Chicago, 147 U. S. 396.

be passed to meet special local requirements and be limited in its operation without being objectionable.[1] Thus, police regulations as to selling intoxicating liquors, gambling, etc., may be applicable only within certain localities.[2] The requirement of uniformity of operation has been held sufficient to render invalid a statute making it a misdemeanor on the part of an officer of a railroad company that stock is killed in the operation of the road, and providing that the fact of killing shall be *prima facie* evidence of negligence.[3] But in another state, a statute somewhat similar in its purpose has been held constitutional.[4] A statute providing a heavier punishment for adultery between a white person and a negro, than that provided for a similar offense between those of the same race, is not unconstitutional, as it provides merely a penalty for an offense which can only exist when the parties are of different races.[5] So a statute requiring licenses to be procured by physicians, but exempting from its operation physicians who had been already in practice for a specified period, was held not unconstitutional as class legislation.[6] It is not constitutional to discriminate against any particular class of persons in the matter of employment. Thus, an act prohibiting a special calling, such as that of barbering, which is not particularly objectionable, being exercised on Sunday, is unconstitutional.[7] So is an act restricting the hours of labor of women, when no such regulation is applicable in case of men;[8] but an ordinance prohibiting the sale of liquors

[1] Marmet v. S., 45 Ohio St. 63. It is not necessary that the regulation affect the whole community if it is applicable to all of a class: Hawthorn v. P., 109 Ill. 302. Local option liquor laws are constitutional: S. v. Noyes, 30 N. H. 279.

[2] See *supra*, § 39. Thus, a statute prohibiting gambling or the sale of intoxicating liquors within a certain distance of a particular lake has been held unconstitutional: S. v. Winch, 45 Ohio St. 663. An act curing a defect in prosecutions, not applying generally to all such cases, nor to all localities, is unconstitutional: S. v. Flemming, 66 Me. 142. A constitutional provision requiring that laws shall be of uniform operation is not retroactive so as to affect laws passed prior to its adoption: S. v. Thompson, 2 Kan. 432.

[3] S. v. Divine, 98 N. C. 778.

[4] Bannon v. S., 49 Ark. 167.

[5] Pace v. Alabama, 106 U. S. 583; S. C., 69 Ala. 231. As to protection of civil rights, see *supra*, § 54.

[6] S. v. Hathaway, 115 Mo. 36.

[7] Eden v. P., 161 Ill. 296, 43 N. E. R. 1108; S. v. Granneman, — Mo. —, 33 S. W. R. 784; Ex parte Jentzsch, — Cal. —, 44 Pac. R. 803. *Contra*, P. v. Havnor, 149 N. Y. 195, 43 N. E. R. 541.

[8] Ritchie v. P., 155 Ill. 98; Ex parte Kuback, 85 Cal. 274; In re Maguire, 57 Cal. 604.

in dance-houses, or other places where females attend as waitresses, or in places where women and minors are employed, is not such a discrimination on account of sex as to be invalid.[1] So sales of liquors to Indians may be prohibited.[2] An ordinance which gives to a mayor of a city the absolute power to decide what particular parades may, and what may not, march on the city streets, is invalid as authorizing unreasonable discriminations and depriving citizens of the equal protection of the laws.[3] While it is unconstitutional to discriminate against residents of other states so as to deprive them of the privileges and immunities enjoyed by citizens of the same state,[4] yet some privileges may be allowed to citizens of a state which are refused to non-residents; such as the right to hunt and fish within the state limits.[5] The privileges and immunities of citizens of the United States which are protected by the Fourteenth Amendment to the Federal Constitution are those granted or secured by that constitution, or arising out of the nature and essential character of the federal government.[6] Special legislation does not deprive any person of the equal protection of the laws guarantied by that amendment if all persons coming within the class affected thereby are treated alike.[7]

§ 78. Ex post facto laws.—Both federal and state constitutions contain provisions that no *ex post facto* laws shall be passed.[8] An *ex post facto* law, as the term is thus used, is a law which makes an act criminal which was not criminal when done, or which, with reference to a crime already committed,

[1] Ex parte Hayes, 98 Cal. 555; S. ex rel. v. Reynolds, 14 Mont. 383.

[2] P. v. Bray, 105 Cal. 344.

[3] S. v. Dering, 84 Wis. 585. But the mayor of a city may be given authority to determine whether a liquor license shall be granted: Swarth v. P., 109 Ill. 621. And discretion to allow repairs on wooden buildings within fire limits may be given to an officer: Ex parte Fiske, 72 Cal. 125.

[4] S. v. Wiggin, 64 N. H. 508; S. v. Lancaster, 63 N. H. 267; Ward v. Maryland, 12 Wall. 418; Guy v. Baltimore, 100 U. S. 434; Marshalltown v. Blum, 58 Ia. 184; Pacific Junction v. Dyer, 64 Ia. 38.

[5] See *supra*, § 46.

[6] Duncan v. Missouri, 152 U. S. 377; Giozza v. Tiernan, 148 U. S. 67; Mugler v. Kansas, 123 U. S. 623; Miller v. Texas, 153 U. S. 535; Kimmish v. Ball, 129 U. S. 217; McElvaine v. Brush, 142 U. S. 155; Davis v. Texas, 139 U. S. 651.

[7] Duncan v. Missouri, 152 U. S. 377; Hayes v. Missouri, 120 U. S. 68; Fielden v. Illinois, 143 U. S. 452.

[8] U. S. Const., art. I, secs. 9 and 10.

increases the punishment, or makes it harder for the accused to defend himself against the charge.[1] With reference to making acts criminal which were not criminal when done, it simply means that an act imposing a criminal punishment shall not have retroactive effect.[2] If a statute imposes a severer penalty for an offense than was imposed by the law in force when the act was committed, it cannot be applicable to acts committed before its passage.[3] If the manner of punishment is changed the act is *ex post facto*, whether the new punishment may be generally considered lighter or not, as, for instance, where the punishment is changed from the death penalty to imprisonment for life.[4] But if a statute manifestly mitigates the punishment

[1] Calder v. Bull, 3 Dall. 386; Watson v. Mercer, 8 Pet. 88; Fletcher v. Peck, 6 Cranch, 87, 138; Locke v. New Orleans, 4 Wall. 172; Carpenter v. Pennsylvania, 17 How. 456; Burgess v. Salmon, 97 U. S. 381; Kring v. Missouri, 107 U. S. 221; Hopt v. Utah, 110 U. S. 574; In re Sawyer, 124 U. S. 200; Strong v. S., 1 Blackf. 193, 196; Ex parte Bethurum, 66 Mo. 545; S. v. Squires, 26 Ia. 340; Byrne v. Stewart, 3 Desau. 466; Perry v. C., 3 Grat. 632; Municipality v. Wheeler, 10 La. An. 745; Article in 5 Cr. L. Mag. 325. Thus, a statute inflicting solitary confinement on one sentenced to death, until the execution of the sentence, or which makes the time of the execution of the death penalty indefinite as to the particular date, by reposing a discretion in the warden, is void as to an offense already committed: In re Medley, 134 U. S. 160. But a mere regulation as to the time and manner of inflicting the death penalty, as, for instance, that it shall be before sunrise, etc., is not objectionable on that ground: Holden v. Minnesota, 137 U. S. 483. A statute providing that one who is declared a bankrupt shall be punished for obtaining goods by false pretenses within three months preceding such bankruptcy is unconstitutional, as *ex post facto:* U. S. v. Fox, 95 U. S. 670. A statute providing for cumulative imprisonment or reducing the convict's credit for good conduct is not applicable to crimes already committed: Hannahan v. S., 7 Tex. Ap. 664; Ex parte Hunt, 28 Tex. Ap. 361. A statute giving double damages to a party injured is not applicable to an injury already suffered: Union Pac. R. Co. v. Proctor, 12 Colo. 194.

[2] S. v. Ryan, 13 Minn. 370; S. v. Gut, 13 Minn. 341.

[3] S. v. Ingersoll, 17 Wis. 631. Even though a severer penalty is only possible and not necessary: C. v. McDonough, 13 Allen, 581.

[4] Shepherd v. P., 25 N. Y. 406; P. v. Dane, 81 Mich. 36. Unless the punishment is separable, and one of its parts is abrogated or lessened: Ratzky v. P., 29 N. Y. 124; Hartung v. P., 28 N. Y. 400; S. C., 26 N. Y. 167; S. C., 22 N. Y. 95. It is said in one case, however, that a change of form of punishment is not invalid as being *ex post facto*, unless the punishment is manifestly increased or intensified in severity: Strong v. S., 1 Blackf. 193. If the lighter punishment involves the forfeiture of some special privilege, the statute imposing it is not applicable to offenses already committed: S. v. Arlin, 39 N. H. 179.

it is not invalid,[1] especially if the offender is allowed to choose the original punishment if desired.[2] A law is *ex post facto* which is made to apply to an act already committed, whether it was criminal or innocent when it was done.[3] Thus, the status of an individual being fixed by law with reference to an offense already committed, by reason of the period of the statute of limitations on the prosecution for such offenses having already expired, the offender cannot be, by subsequent statute, subject to punishment for such offense.[4] So an offender who has been pardoned by general amnesty or otherwise cannot by subsequent statute be subjected to punishment for the crime.[5] Therefore the statute of congress passed after the close of the rebellion, requiring public officers, attorneys, ministers and others, before being allowed to discharge the duties of the office, or engage in the callings specified, to take an oath that they had not engaged in hostilities against the United States, was held unconstitutional as imposing a penalty for the act of engaging in rebellion, which did not exist at the time of such act.[6] However, a statute imposing a severer penalty for a second offense than that imposed upon conviction for the first offense of like character, is not unconstitutional as applied to a second offense committed after the statute takes effect, although the commission of the former offense, on account of which the heavier penalty is imposed, preceded the taking effect of the act.[7] So a constitutional provision denying the right of suffrage to those who have been convicted of crime is not unconstitutional as to one whose conviction antedated the constitutional provision.[8] A statute for the punishment of con-

[1] S. v. Kent, 65 N. C. 311; Clarke v. S., 23 Miss. 261; P. v. Hayes, 140 N. Y. 484; Turner v. S., 40 Ala. 21.

[2] McInturf v. S., 20 Tex. Ap. 335; Cockrum v. S., 24 Tex. 394; Wall v. S., 18 Tex. 682; Veal v. S., 8 Tex. Ap. 474; Perez v. S., 8 Tex. Ap. 610; S. v. McClure, 25 Mo. 338. The defendant is entitled to the benefit of a statute mitigating the punishment passed after the crime is committed: C. v. Gardner, 11 Gray, 438.

[3] Moore v. S., 43 N. J. 203.

[4] Moore v. S., 43 N. J. 203; S. v. Sneed, 25 Tex. (Supp.) 66.

[5] Ex parte Garland, 4 Wall. 333; S. v. Keith, 63 N. C. 140.

[6] Cummings v. Missouri, 4 Wall. 277; Ex parte Garland, 4 Wall. 333. So held also as to a statute requiring a similar oath from a party asking a new trial: Pierce v. Carskadon, 16 Wall. 234.

[7] Ross' Case, 2 Pick. 165; Riley's Case, 2 Pick. 172; C. v. Graves, 155 Mass. 163; S. v. Woods, 68 Me. 409; P. v. Raymond, 96 N. Y. 38; Rand v. C., 9 Gratt. 738; and see *supra*, § 28.

[8] Washington v. S., 75 Ala. 582.

tinuing acts is not *ex post facto*, since each continuance after the statute takes effect is criminal in itself.[1] In general a statute which affects the procedure only,[2] as by fixing the place for the trial of the offense,[3] or providing that cases shall be heard on appeal by a divided supreme court,[4] are not invalid as applied to crimes already committed. A statute will be operative as to subsequent offenses, although *ex post facto* as to acts already committed to which it may be sought to apply it.[5] In general a penal statute is not to be construed as retrospective if such construction can be avoided.[6]

§ 79. **Bills of attainder.**— There are in the federal constitution, and most of the state constitutions, provisions prohibiting the passage of any bills of attainder. By this term is meant a legislative act inflicting punishment without a judicial trial. Within the meaning of the constitution the term includes bills of pains and penalties.[7] The act which disqualified

[1] S. v. Railroad Co., 86 Ind. 114. Thus, under statute making it criminal for a husband to abandon his wife and neglect to provide for her support, a punishment may be inflicted, although the abandonment took place prior to the passage of the act; the failure to provide for support, after the taking effect of the act, being sufficient to constitute a crime: S. v. Witham, 70 Wis. 473. A statute validating a municipal ordinance adopted before it was authorized by the municipal charter is not void as an *ex post facto* law, for the reason that it would authorize punishment only after the passage of the statute: Morris v. S., 62 Tex. 728.

[2] Jones v. C., 86 Va. 661; Wilson v. C., 86 Va. 666; Sage v. S., 127 Ind. 15; Lovett v. S., 33 Fla. 389; S. v. Ah Jim, 9 Mont. 167; Potter v. S., 42 Ark. 29; Perry v. S., 87 Ala. 30; Gibson v. Mississippi, 162 U. S. 565.

[3] Cook v. U. S., 138 U. S. 157; Gut v. Minnesota, 9 Wall. 35. But *contra*, see S. v. Sweat, 16 S. C. 624.

[4] Duncan v. Missouri, 152 U. S. 377; S. v. Jackson, 105 Mo. 196. Or a statute which creates a new court, or extends the jurisdiction or powers of an existing court: C. v. Phillips, 11 Pick. 27; S. v. Sullivan, 14 Rich. 281. Otherwise as to a statute giving exclusive jurisdiction to a court in a case where it has had only concurrent jurisdiction: S. v. Littlefield, 93 N. C. 614. But a statute increasing the costs which may be taxed on conviction is *ex post facto* as to a crime already committed: Caldwell v. S., 55 Ala. 133.

[5] Jaehne v. New York, 128 U. S. 189; P. v. O'Neil, 109 N. Y. 251. As to the effect of a repealing statute upon crimes already committed, see *infra*, § 96.

[6] C. v. Boston, etc. R. Co., 11 Cush. 512; C. v. Homer, 153 Mass. 343; Hirn v. S., 1 Ohio St. 15; S. v. Andrews, 28 Mo. 14; S. v. Littlefield, 93 N. C. 614; In re Jaehne, 35 Fed. R. 357.

[7] Cummings v. Missouri, 4 Wall. 277, 325. And see, also, dissenting opinion in Ex parte Garland, 4 Wall. 333, 386.

public officers, attorneys, ministers, etc., from holding office or pursuing their calling without taking oath that they had not been engaged in hostilities against the government during the rebellion was held unconstitutional, not only on the ground indicated in the previous section, as being *ex post facto*, but also as depriving persons who had engaged in the rebellion of their rights, without any of the ordinary forms and safeguards provided for the security of the citizen in the administration of justice before established tribunals.[1] A legislative act which undertakes to inflict punishment, or expel from the United States a citizen thereof, for any cause or no cause, or because of race or color, is a bill of attainder within the prohibition of the constitution, and therefore void.[2] But the statute passed by congress[3] requiring all alien resident Chinese to register, on penalty of expulsion from the United States, was held constitutional as a regulation by congress of the right of aliens to reside in the United States.[4]

§ 80. **Cruel and unusual punishments.**— The provisions in federal and state constitutions against the imposition of cruel and unusual punishments do not prevent the infliction of whipping as a criminal punishment.[5] A statute providing for the infliction of the death penalty by electricity does not impose a cruel and unusual punishment,[6] nor is a sentence to death by being shot void on that ground, if it is valid otherwise;[7] nor is a statute objectionable on this ground which provides for solitary confinement prior to the execution of the death penalty.[8] It has been held, however, that the cutting off of the hair as part of a punishment may be cruel as to persons entertaining peculiar religious and social views as to the effect of such infliction.[9] The fact that a punishment is severe by reason of a long term of imprisonment being possible for a slight

1 Cummings v. Missouri, 4 Wall. 277, 325.

2 In re Yung Sing Hee, 36 Fed. R. 437.

3 Act of May 5, 1892, ch. 60; 27 Stat. at Large, 25.

4 Fong Yue Ting v. U. S., 149 U. S. 698.

5 Foote v. S., 59 Md. 264; C. v. Wyatt, 6 Rand. 694; Garcia v. T., 1 N. M. 415.

6 P. v. Kemmler, 119 N. Y. 580; In re Kemmler, 136 U. S. 436.

7 Wilkerson v. Utah, 99 U. S. 130.

8 McElvaine v. Brush, 142 U. S. 155.

9 Ho Ah Kow v. Nunan, 5 Sawyer, 552.

offense will not make the statute imposing such punishment unconstitutional.[1] The provision of the amendment to the federal constitution prohibiting the infliction of cruel and unusual punishments applies only to the federal courts.[2]

[1] Pervear v. Massachusetts, 5 Wall. 475; O'Neil v. Vermont, 144 U. S. 323; S. C., S. v. O'Neil, 58 Vt. 140; S. v. Williams, 77 Mo. 310. An ordinance imposing labor on the public streets in case of default of paying a fine is not invalid: Ex parte Bedell, 20 Mo. Ap. 125. A heavy punishment imposed on the second conviction for the same offense is not objectionable: Sturtevant v. C., 158 Mass. 598.

[2] Pervear v. Massachusetts, 5 Wall. 475.

CHAPTER 5.

PENAL STATUTES; CONSTRUCTION; REPEAL.

§ 81. **Construction.**— It is not proposed to here discuss the principles of construction and interpretation of statutes, so far as they are applicable to both civil and criminal cases; but there are some rules peculiar to penal statutes which need to be discussed, and there are also applications of the general rules specially pertinent in criminal cases, and illustrated thereby, that may properly be given here.

§ 82. **Reason of the statute.**—The old law, the mischief and the remedy are to be taken into account in construing the provisions of a statute,[1] and it is to be so construed as to suppress the mischief, advance the remedy and suppress all evasions for a continuance of the mischief.[2] The reason of the act, in view of the evil to be remedied, will prevail over the literal terms used.[3] Thus, the reason of the statute will be taken into account to limit its general terms.[4] The construction which best comports with the reason and the general purview of the statute

[1] S. v. Smith, 13 Kan. 274.

[2] S. v. Clarke, 33 N. H. 329; Magdalene College Cases, 11 Co. 66.

[3] Smith v. S., 28 Ind. 321; S. v. Robinson, 33 Me. 564; Rice v. S., 3 Kan. 141. And this will be true even though the construction, which is in accordance with reason, may be less favorable to the prisoner than the literal terms of the statute: S. v. Thomas, 29 Ind. 109.

[4] Alcott v. S., 8 Blackf. 6; S. v. Benton, 18 N. H. 47; S. v. Clark, 29 N. J. 96. The statute will not be construed so as to multiply offenses, nor enlarge by mere implication a class of offenses: C. v. Wyman, 8 Met. 247. Where the complete act is not punishable the statute will not be held to apply to attempts to effect such act, unless plainly expressed: C. v. Homer, 5 Met. 555. An intention to abrogate the general law as respects a particular locality should be very apparent to justify a construction of a special act so as to lead to that result: S. v. Nolan, 37 Minn. 16. Where a statute, out of abundant caution, enumerates a great variety of possible places within which crimes committed are punishable, it should not be regarded as an assertion that there are such places within jurisdiction: P. v. Tyler, 17 Mich. 161. For the purpose of avoiding giving an absurd meaning to parts of a statute, the whole will be construed together and the meaning of particular words departed from: Arbuckle v. S., 32 Ind. 34.

will be adopted when the terms are ambiguous,[1] and the letter of the statute will not be strictly followed when it would render the law unreasonable or iniquitous in its construction,[2] or unconstitutional.[3] Indeed, the reason and plain intention of the statute will be followed even to the extent of correcting a mistaken reference to another statute,[4] or omitting the word "not" where the sense requires it.[5] The whole statute should be so construed as that it may have effect, and not be found vain and illusive[6] or absurd.[7] But the language used is the first guide, and if that be plain and unambiguous and leads in its application to no absurd or improbable results, there is no room for construction.[8]

§ 83. **Strict construction.**— If a penal statute is susceptible of two constructions the court will give to it that which is the more favorable to the defendant;[9] in other words, penal statutes are to be taken strictly and literally and cannot be extended by construction.[10] Otherwise stated, the rule is that

[1] Foster v. P., 1 Colo. 293.

[2] The judiciary should not, except where the intent is too palpable to admit of doubt, adjudge an unnatural and unjust consequence as in contemplation of the law: Bradley v. P., 8 Colo. 599. But the fact that the punishment provided by the legislature for a statutory offense is apparently incommensurably excessive will not take the case out of the statute which evidently covers it: Griffin v. S., 34 Ohio St. 299. That a statute will be construed as not retrospective, if such a result can possibly be reached, see *supra*, § 78.

[3] Pierce v. S., 13 N. H. 536.

[4] P. v. Hill, 3 Utah, 334; Chambers v. S., 25 Tex. 307; Hearn v. S., 25 Tex. 336. And see Thurston v. S., 3 Coldw. 115, in which "following causes" was made to read "following clauses."

[5] Chapman v. S., 16 Tex. Ap. 76.

[6] Bailey v. C., 11 Bush, 688.

[7] P. v. Tanner, 128 N. Y. 416.

[8] S. v. Long, 48 Ohio St. 509.

[9] Kent v. S., 8 Blackf. 163; Brooks v. P., 14 Colo. 413. "Tenderness ought always to prevail, so far at least as to take care that a man may not suffer otherwise than by due course of law or for any hardship done him, or severity exercised upon him, where the construction may admit of a reasonable doubt or difficulty." (Lord Mansfield, J., in Rex v. Royce, 4 Burr. 2073, 2082; but this was a case of the construction of a special verdict.) Resp. v. Newell, 3 Yeates, 407, 411. The statute will not be extended beyond its terms to include an act not within the language used. This is what is meant by construing penal statutes in favor of the defendant: C. v. Macomber, 3 Mass. 254; C. v. Boston & A. R. Co., 121 Mass. 36; Fagan v. S., 47 N. J. 175.

[10] Rawson v. S., 19 Conn. 292; S. v. Crowley, 60 Me. 103; Hall v. S., 20 Ohio, 7; Warner v. C., 1 Pa. St. 154; Ferrett v. Atwill, 1 Blatch. 151; Steel v. S., 26 Ind. 82; Horner v. S., 1 Oreg. 268; Remmington v. S., 1 Oreg. 281; S. v. Solomons, 3 Hill (S. C.), 96; Bettis v. Taylor, 8 Port. 564; Williams v. S., 91 Ala. 14; Lair

criminal statutes are inelastic and cannot be extended to cover cases not within the letter, though they may be within the reason and policy of the law.[1] There can be no constructive violations of a penal statute.[2] It is said, however, in some cases that this strictness of construction was adopted at the common law in favor of life,[3] or the liberty of the citizen,[4] and has never been observed in the construction of statutes enacted for the punishment of mere misdemeanors.[5] So statutes for the prevention of fraud and suppression of public wrong, or to effect a public good by prohibiting the doing of an act without certain prerequisite conditions being complied with, although a penalty is imposed for violating them, are often remedial, rather than penal, and are to be construed liberally so as to effect the remedy contemplated by their passage;[6] and in general, strict construction is not required in a statute relating to procedure.[7]

v. Killmer, 25 N. J. 522; Simms v. Bean, 10 La. An. 346; Andrews v. U. S., 2 Story, 202; The Enterprise, 1 Paine, 32; U. S. v. Starr, 1 Hempst. 469; U. S. v. Ramsay, id. 481; U. S. v. Beaty, id. 487; U. S. v. Ragsdale, id. 497; U. S. v. Mitchell, 36 Fed. R. 492; U. S. v. Huggett, 40 Fed. R. 636; U. S. v. Garretson, 42 Fed. R. 22. A statute which awards a penalty not known to the common law and is in a high degree penal will be limited to such cases as are clearly within its terms: C. v. Phillips, 11 Pick. 27; C. v. Martin, 130 Mass. 465. Where a statute does not indicate whether a term of imprisonment provided for shall be in a county jail or in the penitentiary, it will be construed to be in the county jail: Brooks v. P., 14 Colo. 413. Under a statute providing for punishments by imprisonment for breaking out of a place of confinement, the term to commence at the expiration of the term for which the prisoner was confined, it was held that it could not be extended to a case of imprisonment to enforce a fine: S. v. Chapman, 33 Kan. 134. An ordinance punishing the erection of a frame or wooden building will not be extended to cover the erection of a building partly of wood and partly of brick: Stewart v. C., 10 Watts, 306.

1 S. v. Lovell, 23 Ia. 304; Cearfoss v. S., 42 Md. 403; S. v. Bruner, 135 Ind. 419; Johnson v. S., 63 Miss. 228; S. v. Peters, 37 La. An. 730; U. S. v. Lacher, 134 U. S. 624; Todd v. U. S., 158 U. S. 278. Before a man can be punished his case must be plainly and unmistakably within the statute: U. S. v. Brewer, 139 U. S. 278. Doubtful words are not to be extended beyond their natural meaning: Baldwin v. Franks, 120 U. S. 678.

2 Todd v. U. S., 158 U. S. 278.

3 Gibson v. S., 38 Ga. 571.

4 Pierce's Case, 16 Me. 255; Elam v. Rawson, 21 Ga. 139; Ramsey v. Foy, 10 Ind. 493.

5 Randolph v. S., 9 Tex. 521.

6 Taylor v. U. S., 3 How. 197; Harding v. P., 10 Colo. 387.

7 S. v. Chadbourne, 74 Me. 506.

§ 84. **Not so as to defeat intent.**—The rule of strict construction is not to be so applied as to defeat the obvious intention of the legislature, which will govern so far as the terms of the statute will reasonably allow.[1] The rule is not to be so applied as to exclude the application of common sense to the language used, nor the giving of words their ordinary acceptance or their obvious meaning, so as to defeat the legislative intent.[2] In some states the rule of strict construction is abolished, either by statute or by decision of the courts.[3]

§ 85. **Letter and spirit.**—As just stated, the act must be within the strict terms of the statute as well as within its spirit and intention.[4] It is not enough that the act comes within the reason and mischief of the statute, if it is not strictly within the enumeration and terms thereof, although it is of equal atrocity or of kindred character with acts enumerated.[5] The words creating an offense will not be construed beyond their plain letter.[6] On the other hand, a penal statute is not

[1] Douglas v. C., 2 Rawle, 262; S. v. Crowley, 39 N. J. 264; C. v. Loring, 8 Pick. 369; Brown v. C., 8 Mass. 59; C. v. Martin, 17 Mass. 359; Woodworth v. S., 26 Ohio St. 196; Butler v. Ricker, 6 Me. 268; Fairbanks v. Antrim, 2 N. H. 105; Crosby v. Hawthorne, 25 Ala. 221; Crawford v. S., Minor, 143; Doe v. Avaline, 8 Ind. 6; Parkinson v. S., 14 Md. 184; Broadwell v. Conger, 2 N. J. 210; Jones v. Estis, 2 Johns. 375; Sprague v. Birdsal, 2 Cow. 419; Daggett v. S., 4 Conn. 60; State v. McCrystol, 43 La. An. 907; U. S. v. Wiltberger, 5 Wheat. 76. The strictness required is not such as would exclude an act plainly intended to be included, but where the meaning is ambiguous the doubt should be in favor of the accused: S. v. Wilson, 47 N. H. 101. The kindred rule must not be disregarded that the intention of the law-maker, to be gathered from the words employed, governs in the construction of all statutes: In re Coy, 31 Fed. R. 794. Unless the terms are ambiguous the full effect of the statute should be given: S. v. Barter, 58 N. H. 604.

[2] Rawson v. S., 19 Conn. 292; S. v. Lovell, 23 Ia. 304; Walton v. S., 62 Ala. 197; Huffman v. S., 29 Ala. 40; U. S. v. Wilson, Baldw. 78; U. S. v. Ellis, 51 Fed. R. 808; U. S. v. Athens Armory, 2 Abb. C. C. 129. The rule of strict construction is not violated by giving the words in some cases their full meaning, or the more extended of two meanings; for instance, a wider popular, instead of a narrower technical one: S. v. Thatcher, 35 N. J. 445.

[3] P. v. Fowler, 88 Cal. 136; P. v. Soto, 49 Cal. 67; C. v. Davis, 12 Bush, 240.

[4] Daggett v. S., 4 Conn. 60; Davis v. S., 19 Ohio St. 270. Thus, a statute referring to logs taken from the river was held not applicable to logs on the bank: S. v. Adams, 16 Me. 67.

[5] S. v. Brewer, 8 Mo. 373; P. v. Reiley, 50 Mich. 384.

[6] Warner v. C., 1 Pa. St. 154; Brabham v. S., 18 Ohio St. 485; Ex parte McNulty, 77 Cal. 164. Thus, a statute

to be extended to any act not within the spirit and intention thereof, although it may be within its strict terms.[1] General terms will be limited by the obvious meaning and spirit,[2] so that even when the language is unambiguous and fairly covers the case, the literal meaning will be limited by the intent and spirit of the law.[3]

§ 86. **Legislative intent.**— It has already been stated that the legislative intent is to govern. This is the first of all rules of construction, and is applicable in criminal as well as in civil cases.[4] To reach this meaning the court may consider the statements of those who had charge of the passage of the act in the legislature.[5] Thus, the statements of members of the legislature in debate may be adverted to as part of the history of the times,[6] and contemporaneous and uniform construction given to the statute by those charged with its execution is entitled to weight;[7] but the court cannot take into view the motives of the legislators further than they are expressed in the statute,[8] and evidence to establish bribery and corruption in securing its passage is not admissible.[9]

§ 87. **Statutes in pari materia.**— When the statute is ambiguous and susceptible of more than one construction, the

prohibiting sales of liquor within two miles of the premises of a military academy was held not to include sales within such premises: P. v. Gadway, 61 Mich. 285. So also a statute requiring licenses on the part of certain classes of liquor-sellers will not be extended beyond the classes plainly referred to: Jaeger v. S., 63 Mo. 403. The legislative intent is to be found, if possible, in the enactment itself, and statutes are not to be extended by construction to cases not fairly and clearly embraced within their terms. Of course, a statute is not to be frittered away by forced construction, by metaphysical niceties, or by mere verbal or sharp criticism; nevertheless, the doctrine is fundamental that there can be no constructive offenses; that before a man can be punished his case must be plainly and unmistakably within the statute, and if there be any fair doubt whether the statute embraces it, that doubt is to be resolved in favor of the accused: U. S. v. Clayton, 2 Dill. 219.

1 S. v. McMahon, 53 Conn. 407.

2 S. v. Craig, 80 Me. 85.

3 S. v. Wacker, 71 Wis. 672. This will, of course, be especially true where the words are susceptible of two meanings: S. v. Howard, 72 Me. 459.

4 Ex parte Evers, 29 Tex. Ap. 539; Murray v. S., 21 Tex. Ap. 620; Cain v. S., 20 Tex. 355.

5 Ex parte Farley, 40 Fed. R. 66.

6 U. S. v. Wilson, 58 Fed. R. 768.

7 Brown v. U. S., 113 U. S. 568; U. S. v. Johnston, 124 U. S. 236; U. S. v. Hill, 120 U. S. 169; U. S. v. Philbrick, 120 U. S. 52.

8 S. v. King, 12 La. An. 593.

9 S. v. Fagan, 22 La. An. 545.

court may, for the purpose of arriving at the legislative intent, as in civil cases, consider together the provisions of the statute in question and other statutes relating to the same subject-matter.[1]

§ 88. **Civil code.**—The provisions of the civil code will not be construed as applicable to criminal cases unless it plainly appears that such was the legislative intent.[2] Whether provisions as to practice and evidence, general in their terms, will be applicable in criminal as well as civil cases, will be determined by the context, the relative positions of the chapters, and surrounding circumstances.[3] In general, the civil code will be resorted to for the purpose of supplying an omission in the criminal code only in a case totally unprovided for in the latter.[4]

§ 89. **General and special provisions.**—In thus construing together the general provisions of one statute on the subject, and the special provisions of another as to the same subject, the particular intent will override a general intent incompatible therewith.[5] This doctrine is to be applied, not only where

[1] S. v. Robinson, 33 Me. 564; C. v. Wyman, 8 Met. 247; Smith v. P., 47 N. Y. 303; S. v. Stimson, 24 N. J. 478; Farrell v. S., 54 N. J. 421; Rice v. S., 3 Kan. 141; S. v. Smith, 13 Kan. 274; U. S. v. Benson, 31 Fed. R. 896. The meaning of terms used in one statute not there defined may be determined by reference to other statutes on the same subject, and for this an amendment to the statute may be considered, being applied only to cases arising after its passage: S. v. Hughes, 16 R. I. 403. After amendment an act is generally to be interpreted as though the amended section had originally read as it does after the amendment is made. But if a part of the statute cannot be accommodated by construction to the new reading, then it is to be regarded as retaining its original sense: Kiser v. S., 89 Ga. 421. So an amendment to a section of a statute which would render the section referred to by the amendment senseless and nugatory, while in connection with another section it would be sensible and consistent with previous law, will be construed as a part of the latter section and not the former: Bledsoe v. S., 10 Mo. 388.

[2] Williams v. P., 33 N. Y. 688.

[3] S. v. Moulton, 48 N. H. 485.

[4] Hackney v. S., 8 Ind. 494.

[5] Resp. v. Richards, 1 Yeates, 480; O'Connell v. S., 6 Minn. 279. Thus, a provision in a state charter permitting a city to regulate houses of ill-fame will control a general law prohibiting such houses: S. v. Clarke, 54 Mo. 17. And a statute as to the entering of any building, with or without breaking, will not apply to dwelling-houses, the breaking and entering of which is otherwise made punishable: Rolland v. C., 82 Pa. St. 306. So a statute directing the mode of prosecution and manner of punishment of an offense is not controlled by general statute so as

a later special statute conflicts with a prior general one,[1] but also where a later general statute conflicts with an earlier special one, and in such cases there is not an implied repeal.[2]

§ **90. General clause; particular enumeration.**— A general clause at the end of a special enumeration of particulars will be limited to things analogous to those in such special enumeration.[3] But where the terms used are unequivocal, and the legislative intent evidently does not require a limited meaning to be applied, the general terms used will be given their full effect.[4] On the other hand, where a general term is made to include a certain class in some provisions of the statute, it will be considered to include that class in the other provisions thereof.[5] But in general, a specific enumeration will exclude cases not enumerated.[6] If one seeks to bring himself within a special exemption, he must show himself to be clearly within the terms and conditions of such exemption.[7]

§ **91. Implied repeal.**— It is a principle of universal application in the construction of statutes, that, if two legislative provisions are found to be inconsistent, the court in construing them will give effect to the later expression of the legislative will. Therefore, if two statutes make inconsistent provisions for the punishment of the same act, the later repeals the earlier;[8] but

to impose a different penalty: S. v. Henley, 30 Mo. 509; S. v. Green, 87 Mo. 583; S. v. Wingo, 89 Ind. 204. But a statute for the punishment of lighter forms of an offense will be exclusive of the provisions of a general statute covering the same acts, as well as others defined as a general offense: Bork v. P., 91 N. Y. 5; Johnson v. P., 123 Ill. 624. The provisions of a statute as to murder will prevail, in reference to that crime, over those found in a chapter relating to petit treason: S. v. Bilansky, 3 Minn. 246.

1 S. v. Hope, 15 Ind. 474; C. v. Railing, 113 Pa. St. 37.

2 Mobile, etc. R. Co. v. S., 29 Ala. 573; S. v. Falkenham, 73 Md. 463; McCracken v. S., 71 Md. 150; T. v. McPherson, 6 Dak. 27. But a statute which is broader and more exact in its terms will repeal a prior statute more limited in its application: S. v. Giles, 125 Ind. 124.

3 S. v. Bryant, 90 Mo. 534; S. v. Grisham, 90 Mo. 163; S. v. Black, 75 Wis. 490; Jensen v. S., 60 Wis. 582; Shirk v. P., 121 Ill. 61.

4 S. v. Stimson, 24 N. J. 9; S. v. Cleveland, 80 Mo. 108; S. v. Hays, 78 Mo. 600; Rau v. P., 63 N. Y. 277; O'Keefe v. S., 24 Ohio St. 175; S. v. Holman, 3 McCord, 306.

5 S. v. Kelsey, 89 Mo. 623.

6 S. v. Grant, 76 Mo. 236. But this maxim, *inclusio unius exclusio alterius est*, is too general to govern in the construction of criminal statutes: S. v. Connor, 7 La. An. 379.

7 S. v. Intoxicating Liquors, 68 Me. 187.

8 C. v. Kimball, 21 Pick. 373; C. v. Davis, 11 Gray, 48; Huber v. S., 25

if a subsequent statute simply reduces the penalty, or allows discretion to the court to assess a lower degree of punishment, the former statute is not thereby repealed;[1] in order, however, that the later statute shall repeal the former, the two must be repugnant or inconsistent. Even a general repealing clause as to all previous inconsistent statutes must be construed as repealing only those which are plainly repugnant.[2]

§ 92. **Implied repeals not favored.**—Repeals by implication are not favored by the law; and when two statutes on the same subject can both stand and be effective, no repeal will be implied.[3] In the absence of an express repealing clause, a subsequent statute repeals a former one only so far as the two are inconsistent;[4] and if it is possible to construe the later statute as cumulative, such construction will be given to it, although its provisions differ from those found in the earlier statute.[5] In determining whether there is a repeal by implication, the intention of the legislature is the prime object of inquiry.[6]

§ 93. **What amounts to a repeal.**— A statute which assumes to cover the whole subject-matter embraced in a former statute, re-enacting it with changes, will operate as a repeal of the former, even though there is no expressed repeal.[7] But a stat-

Ind. 175; Hayes v. S., 55 Ind. 99; Wall v. S., 23 Ind. 150; S. v. Craig, 23 Ind. 185; U. S. v. Irwin, 5 McLean, 178.

[1] C. v. Gardner, 11 Gray, 438; C. v. Evans, 16 Pick. 448; C. v. Wyman, 12 Cush. 237; Allen v. S., 5 Wis. 329. But the imposition of a further penalty does not operate to repeal a former act as to the same crime, the provisions not being necessarily repugnant: S. v. Shoemaker, 20 N. J. 153. Where the punishment which may be inflicted by a justice is reduced, such provision will operate as a reduction of the punishment for offenses exclusively punishable by a justice: Gordon v. P., 44 Mich. 485.

[2] S. v. Anderson, 40 N. J. 224.

[3] Shepherd v. P., 25 N. Y. 406; Hartung v. P., 28 N. Y. 400; Homer v. C., 106 Pa. St. 221; C. v. Cromley, 1 Ashmead, 179; P. v. Hanrahan, 75 Mich. 611; P. v. Gustin, 57 Mich. 407; Gordon v. P., 44 Mich. 485; C. v. Duff, 87 Ky. 586; Sosat v. S., 2 Ind. Ap. 586.

[4] S. v. Tibbetts, 36 Me. 553; C. v. McGuirk, 78 Pa. St. 298.

[5] Myers v. S., 92 Ind. 390; Coghill v. S., 37 Ind. 111; P. v. Smith, 69 N. Y. 175; P. v. Krank, 110 N. Y. 488; Sifred v. C., 104 Pa. St. 179; Prohibitory Amendment Cases, 24 Kan. 700; S. v. Green, 87 Mo. 583; Cate v. S., 3 Sneed, 120; P. v. Gustin, 57 Mich. 407; P. v. Bussell, 59 Mich. 104; S. v. Van Vliet, — Ia. —, 61 N. W. R. 241.

[6] P. v. Hanrahan, 75 Mich. 611.

[7] C. v. Kelliher, 12 Allen, 480; Hirschburg v. P., 6 Colo. 145; Cullen v. S., 42 Conn. 55; S. v. Roller, 77 Mo. 120; S. v. Christman, 67 Ind. 328; Douglass v. S., 72 Ind. 385; Wagoner v. S., 90 Ind. 504; P. v. Bussell, 59 Mich. 104; C. v. Cromley, 1 Ashmead, 179; Stirman v. S., 21 Tex. 734.

ute or amendment which enlarges the class of cases made punishable by a former statute, but leaves the punishment the same, does not operate as a repeal;[1] so a revision of the statutes or of the ordinances of a city is not to be deemed a repeal, but so far as not changed they remain in full force as if no revision had been made;[2] and in general a mere modification of a statute, or amendment of it, by additions, will not be construed as the repeal of the portions not affected, even though the change is made by way of repeal and re-enactment.[3] A subsequent statute in aid of an existing statute will not operate to repeal it.[4]

§ 94. **As between general and special provisions.**— It is an application of a rule already stated[5] that a special statute will not be deemed to be repealed by implication by a subsequent general statute on the subject. The special provision will be deemed still in force unless it is plainly evident that the general statute was intended to supersede the special one, or the two are plainly irreconcilable.[6]

§ 95. **Effect of statute upon pre-existing common law.**— A statute revising an entire subject-matter repeals the common law as to that matter;[7] but a statute only repeals the common law as to a particular crime when it covers the whole ground. If both the statute and common law can consistently take effect together, they are to be construed as concurrent, and the statute is cumulative.[8]

So held where an act declared that a former act "is hereby amended so as to read as follows:" S. v. Ingersoll, 17 Wis. 631.

[1] P. v. Safford, 5 Denio, 112; C. v. Herrick, 6 Cush. 465; S. v. Herzog, 25 Minn. 490. That in such cases an offense committed prior to the repeal and re-enactment may still be prosecuted, see *infra*, § 96.

[2] U. S. v. Le Bris, 121 U. S. 278; U. S. v. Lacher, 134 U. S. 624; St. Louis v. Foster, 52 Mo. 513.

[3] Gordon v. P., 44 Mich. 485; S. v. Gumber, 37 Wis. 298; C. v. Phillips, 11 Pick. 27; S. v. Van Vliet, — Ia. —, 61 N. W. R. 241.

[4] S. v. Taylor, 2 McCord, 483; S. v. Cole, 2 McCord, 1.

[5] *Supra*, § 89.

[6] Seifried v. C., 101 Pa. St. 200; P. v. Jaehne, 103 N. Y. 182; P. v. Quigg, 59 N. Y. 83; Sykes v. P., 127 Ill. 117; Ochs v. P., 124 Ill. 399; Kollenberger v. P., 9 Colo. 233; C. v. Ballou, 124 Mass. 26; Keiser v. S., 78 Ind. 430; Ex parte Van Hagan, 25 Ohio St. 426; P. v. Hanrahan, 75 Mich. 611; P. v. Furman, 85 Mich. 110.

[7] C. v. Cooley, 10 Pick. 37.

[8] S. v. Wilson, 43 N. H. 415; S. v. Burnham, 9 N. H. 34; C. v. Ayer, 3 Cush. 150; Jennings v. C., 17 Pick. 80; C. v. King, 13 Met. 115; S. v. Norton, 23 N. J. 33; Kelly v. C., 11 Serg. & R. 345; Wood v. C., 12 Serg. & R. 213; Beard v. S., 74 Md. 130; Lewis v. S., 3 Head, 127.

§ 96. Effect of repeals as to offenses already committed. No conviction can take place for an offense after the statute creating it has been repealed.[1] Therefore, if the prior law is superseded by a statute inconsistent therewith, offenses already committed under the prior law cannot be punished unless there is a saving clause, for the prior law is no longer in force and the subsequent statute is not applicable to the offense already committed, because as to such offense it is *ex post facto*. There can be no legal conviction for an offense unless the act complained of be contrary to law at the time it is committed, nor can there be a judgment unless the law be in force at the time the indictment is found and judgment rendered thereunder.[2] And the repeal of the repealing act will not restore the original law in such way that offenses committed under it will be punishable, for the reason that the last repealing act will itself be *ex post facto*;[3] but a mere amendment, or repeal and reenactment, substantially without change, will not defeat a prosecution under the previous statute.[4] It is not necessary to

[1] Taylor v. S., 7 Blackf. 93; S. v. Loyd, 2 Ind. 659; Howard v. S., 5 Ind. 183; Lunning v. S., 9 Ind. 309; Calkins v. S., 14 Ohio St. 222; S. v. Fletcher, 1 R. I. 193; S. v. Ingersoll, 17 Wis. 631; S. v. Meader, 62 Vt. 458; S. v. Cross, 4 Jones, 421; S. v. O'Connor, 13 La. An. 486; S. v. Henderson, 13 La. An. 489; Wall v. S., 18 Tex. 682; Greer v. S., 22 Tex. 588; Hubbard v. S., 2 Tex. Ap. 506; Montgomery v. S., 2 Tex. Ap. 618; Tuton v. S., 4 Tex. Ap. 472; Wheeler v. S., 64 Miss. 462; C. v. Leftwich, 5 Rand. 657; Scutt v. C., 2 Va. Cas. 54; Attoo v. C., 2 Va. Cas. 382; S. v. Cole, 2 McCord, 1; Griffin v. S., 39 Ala. 541; S. v. Allaire, 14 Ala. 435; S. v. Tombeckbee Bank, 1 Stew. 347; C. v. Welch, 2 Dana, 330; Genkinger v. C., 32 Pa. St. 99; S. v. Oliver, 12 Wash. 547; U. S. v. Passmore, 4 Dall. 372.

[2] C. v. Marshall, 11 Pick. 350; C. v. Kimball, 21 Pick. 373; Heald v. S., 36 Me. 62; C. v. McDonough, 13 Allen, 581; S. v. Ingersoll, 17 Wis. 631; S. v. Stone, 43 Wis. 481; S. v. McDonald, 20 Minn. 136; S. v. Daley, 29 Conn. 272; C. v. Duane, 1 Binn. 601; The Irresistible, 7 Wheat. 551; S. v. King, 12 La. An. 593; S. v. Bank, 12 Rich. 609; Keller v. S., 12 Md. 322; Smith v. S., 45 Md. 49; Whitehurst v. S., 43 Ind. 473. This is true also as to repealing ordinances: Kansas City v. Clark, 68 Mo. 588.

[3] Hartung v. P., 26 N. Y. 167; S. C., 28 N. Y. 400; S. C., 22 N. Y. 95; S. v. Van Stralen, 45 Wis. 437.

[4] S. v. Miller, 58 Ind. 399; Sage v. S., 127 Ind. 15; Cheezem v. S., 2 Ind. 149; Beard v. S., 74 Md. 130; S. v. Wish, 15 Neb. 448; C. v. Sullivan, 150 Mass. 315; S. v. Sutton, 100 N. C. 474; S. v. Massey, 103 N. C. 356; S. v. Baldwin, 45 Conn. 134; S. v. Gumber, 37 Wis. 298; S. v. Kibling, 63 Vt. 636; P. v. Sloan, 2 Utah, 326; S. v. King, 12 La. An. 593. If a statute specially repeals one portion only of a prior act, the other portions will be deemed to be continued in force: S. v. Morrow, 26 Mo. 131.

negative in the indictment the possible commission of the crime before the statute under which it is prosecuted went into effect.[1]

§ 97. **Effect on pending prosecutions.**— A prosecution begun under one statute cannot be continued under a subsequent statute which supersedes or repeals it, unless there is a saving clause.[2]

§ 98. **Repeal after conviction.**— The time of conviction fixes the liability of the defendant to punishment, and a subsequent change of the statute will not affect the case.[3] But even after a verdict, a repeal before rendition of judgment will defeat the prosecution.[4]

§ 99. **Repeal after judgment pending an appeal.**—It is said that the repeal of the statute after judgment in the inferior court, and pending appeal, discharges the defendant on the presumption of legislative pardon.[5] If a judgment is reviewed by *certiorari* instead of by appeal, and is affirmed, the repeal of the statute between the rendition of judgment and affirmance will not render the sentence invalid.[6]

§ 100. **Effect of partial repeal or partial invalidity.**— Where a later statute only repeals a former one so far as the provisions of the two are inconsistent, prosecutions under the former statute are not affected so far as such statute is not repealed.[7] The portion of the statute not repealed continues in force.[8] If the provisions of the repealing act are in any way inoperative, the former statute or the common law will continue in force.[9]

§ 101. **Saving clause.**— To obviate the result which a repealing statute may have by way of preventing prosecutions

[1] S. v. Halford, 104 N. C. 874; S. v. Fleming, 107 N. C. 905; Wilder v. S., 3 Mo. 291.

[2] Hartung v. P., 22 N. Y. 95; Abbott v. C., 8 Watts, 517; Hale v. S., 15 Conn. 242; Mullinix v. S., 43 Ind. 511; S. v. Trimble, 2 Ind. 655; S. v. Lackey, 2 Ind. 285; Sprigs v. S., 2 Ind. 75; Laughlin v. C., 13 Bush, 261; Keller v. S., 12 Md. 322; S. v. King, 12 La. An. 593; Hubbard v. S., 2 Tex. Ap. 506; Montgomery v. S., 2 Tex. Ap. 618.

[3] C. v. McDonough, 13 Allen, 581; Aaron v. S., 40 Ala. 307.

[4] C. v. Pattee, 12 Cush. 501; S. v. Williams, 97 N. C. 455.

[5] S. v. Brewer, 22 La. An. 273.

[6] P. v. Hobson, 48 Mich. 27.

[7] S. v. Grady, 34 Conn. 118; Packer v. P., 8 Colo. 361.

[8] S. v. Andrews, 28 Mo. 14; C. v. Dow, 10 Met. 382; P. v. Whiting, 64 Cal. 67.

[9] S. v. Newton, 59 Ind. 173; S. v. Hallock, 14 Nev. 202; Jim v. S., 3 Mo. 108.

for offenses committed under the prior statute, it is usual to insert a saving clause providing that the statute is to operate only prospectively and not to affect any prosecutions pending, or the punishment of any offenses already committed;[1] and a general saving clause, by which it is declared that the repeal of a previous statute, whether express or implied, shall in all cases be prospective only, unless the contrary intent is expressly declared, and shall not affect crimes already committed, or prosecutions pending under the act repealed, is effectual for the same purpose.[2] A special saving clause in the statute will, however, prevent the application of the general saving clause.[3] A general saving provision applicable to actions, not in terms, however, embracing criminal prosecutions, will not be construed as applicable to such prosecutions for offenses committed before the repeal of the statute;[4] nor will a saving clause as to prosecutions apply to preliminary proceedings pending before a committing magistrate;[5] nor will such a clause preserve the common law as previously existing, and a common-law punishment cannot be inflicted after the passage of a statute in abrogation thereof.[6] But a saving clause providing that crimes committed before the passage of the repealing statute may still be prosecuted does not imply that the procedure shall be in accordance with the previous statute, and such procedure may be required to be in accordance with the new statute.[7]

[1] C. v. Marshall, 11 Pick. 350; C. v. Grover, 16 Gray, 602; Ratzky v. P., 29 N. Y. 124; McKee v. P., 32 N. Y. 239; Sanders v. C., 117 Pa. St. 293; P. v. Gill, 7 Cal. 356; Packer v. P., 8 Colo. 361; U. S. v. Kohnstamm, 5 Blatchf. 222.

[2] C. v. Desmond, 123 Mass. 407; C. v. Grover, 16 Gray, 602; P. v. McNulty, 93 Cal. 427; P. v. Quinn, 18 Cal. 122; Bergin v. S., 31 Ohio St. 111; Richardson v. S., 3 Coldw. 122; S. v. Shaffer, 21 Ia. 486; Sanders v. S., 77 Ind. 227; McCalmen v. S., 77 Ind. 250; S. v. Mathews, 14 Mo. 133; S. v. Ross, 49 Mo. 416; S. v. Proctor, 90 Mo. 334; S. v. Crawford, 11 Kan. 32; S. v. Boyle, 10 Kan. 113; S. v. Showers, 34 Kan. 269; Acree v. C., 13 Bush, 353; Volmer v. S., 34 Ark. 487; McCuen v. S., 19 Ark. 630; Jordan v. S., 38 Ga. 585; Gibson v. S., 35 Ga. 224; Tempe v. S., 40 Ala. 350; U. S. v. Barr, 4 Sawyer, 254; U. S. v. Reisinger, 128 U. S. 398.

[3] S. v. Showers, 34 Kan. 269; S. v. Schmidt, 34 Kan. 399.

[4] Calkins v. S., 14 Ohio St. 222.

[5] S. v. Arlin, 39 N. H. 179.

[6] S. v. Boogher, 71 Mo. 631.

[7] Powers v. S., 87 Ind. 144; S. v. Phillips, 24 Mo. 475. A statute increasing the punishment will leave the old law in effect as to offenses already committed: Miles v. S., 40 Ala. 39; Moore v. S., 40 Ala. 49; Stephen v. S., 40 Ala. 67; Wade v. S., 40 Ala. 74.

§ 102. Repeal of repealing statute.— The repeal of a statute which repealed a prior statute will reinstate the statute repealed thereby, and will revive any liability which existed at the time of the former repeal.[1] The repeal of an amendatory act leaves the act which it amends in full force and effect, as if the amendatory act had never been passed.[2] In some states there are statutory provisions preventing the revival of a former statute by the repeal of the repealing statute.[3] The repeal of a statute which supersedes the common law with reference to an offense is in some cases said to revive the common law as to such offenses.[4] But in other cases it is said that the repeal of a statute in derogation of the common law does not revive the common law.[5]

§ 103. Statutes construed prospectively.— While a statute will be construed with reference to the state of facts existing at the time of its passage,[6] yet a statute punishing acts under

[1] C. v. Getchell, 16 Pick. 452; C. v. Mott, 21 Pick. 492; C. v. Churchill, 2 Met. 118; P. v. Wintermute, 1 Dak. 60; S. v. Chadbourne, 74 Me. 506; Campbell v. S., 35 Ohio St. 70; U. S. v. Philbrick, 120 U. S. 52. A legislative declaration that a statute already passed shall not repeal a prior statute does not operate as a revivor or re-enactment of such prior statute: S. v. Conkling, 19 Cal. 501. So the correction of a statute already repealed does not revive it: U. S. v. Auffmordt, 122 U. S. 197. A statute creating an offense and fixing the penalty by reference to another statute so incorporates the statute thus referred to that the implied repeal of the later statute by another statute on the subject does not revive the statute thus incorporated: C. v. Kendall, 144 Mass. 357. The repeal of a statute defining a term does not prevent such statute being still used to show the meaning of the term as employed elsewhere: U. S. v. Le Bris, 121 U. S. 278. So the adoption in a local statute of the provisions of a general statute does not imply the adoption of changes afterwards made in the general law: In re Heath, 144 U. S. 92.

[2] S. v. Thornton, 63 N. H. 114; Hannibal v. Guyott, 18 Mo. 515. After a statute is repealed as applicable to certain cases, it is not revived as to such cases by a subsequent amendment of it: P. v. Tyler, 36 Cal. 522. Where an act was amended in a particular section and thereafter that section of the original act was repealed, held, that the repeal applied to the section as amended: Greer v. S., 22 Tex. 588.

[3] S. v. Huffschmidt, 47 Mo. 73. Even under such a provision, however, the repeal of an ordinance which has superseded the general law does not prevent the revival of the general law upon such repeal: Heinssen v. S., 14 Colo. 228.

[4] S. v. Rollins, 8 N. H. 550; S. v. Franklin Falls Co., 49 N. H. 240.

[5] S. v. Loney, 82 Mo. 82; S. v. Slaughter, 70 Mo. 484.

[6] An act forbidding the sale of intoxicants on a legal holiday will not render illegal a sale made on a holiday created by subsequent enactment: Ruge v. S., 62 Ind. 388.

circumstances depending upon legislative action for their existence will be construed as applicable to subsequent as well as preceding legislative action, so that a penalty provided for acts committed on election day is applicable to election days provided for by subsequent statutes;[1] and a statute providing a punishment for embezzlement by public officers will be applicable to an officer whose office is afterwards created, as well as where the office exists at the time of the passage of the statute.[2] A statute prescribing requirements for a valid indictment will not affect pending indictments.[3]

§ **104. Effect of invalidity of statute.**— Even though a statute be declared invalid and unconstitutional, yet such part of it as expressly repeals prior inconsistent statutes will be effectual to prevent a punishment under the former statute of offenses committed after the repeal.[4] If a statute which is indivisible is unconstitutional with reference to some acts covered by it, the whole must fall, since the court cannot say that it would have been passed if it had been deemed applicable only to the acts to which it is constitutionally applicable.[5] But plainly, the fact that the statute is unconstitutional as to offenses already committed will not make it invalid as to subsequent offenses;[6] nor will the fact that it is not applicable to articles of interstate commerce make it unconstitutional as to property within the state.[7] The invalidity of one part will not render the other part invalid, unless the two parts are so mutually connected with and dependent on each other as to warrant a belief that the legislature intended them as a whole, and that if all could not be carried into effect they would not have passed the residue.[8] Thus, if it is claimed that a proviso is invalid, the party

Where the sale of liquor within three miles of a factory is prohibited, the prohibition will not be applicable to a factory not then existing: Hall v. S., 20 Ohio, 8.

[1] S. v. Kidd, 74 Ind. 554.

[2] S. v. Hays, 78 Mo. 600; S. v. Cleveland, 80 Mo. 108.

[3] S. v. Smith, 38 Conn. 397.

[4] Ingersoll v. S., 11 Ind. 464; Meshmeier v. S., 11 Ind. 482.

[5] Wynehamer v. P., 13 N. Y. 378.

[6] *Supra*, § 78.

[7] In re Rahrer, 140 U. S. 545. So if a statute is invalid with reference to acts punishable only in the federal courts, it remains valid as to other acts: S. v. Tuller, 34 Conn. 280. A state bankruptcy statute suspended by the passage of a federal bankrupt law revives without re-enactment on the repeal of the federal law: Butler v. Goreley, 146 U. S. 303.

[8] S. v. Wheeler, 25 Conn. 290; S. v. Newton, 59 Ind. 173.

making such claim must show that his case is one affected by the proviso.[1]

§ 105. **Construction of terms.**— A statute is to be construed in the ordinary popular meaning of its terms, thus giving it the effect which the legislature obviously intended.[2] Terms of art, trade, or science will be construed in accordance with the interpretation of those learned in the particular art, trade, or science.[3] If a word used in a statute has attained a meaning at common law, the same meaning will be applied to it in the statute.[4] Where a term or phrase has been used with a certain meaning in one statute, it will be given the same meaning in a later statute, unless there is something to show that a different meaning was intended.[5] In determining what acts are included, the description of the same offense in other sections of the same statute, or statutes on the same subject, will be considered.[6]

§ 106. **Grammar and punctuation.**— Neither the ungrammatical and inaccurate structure of the statute, nor the fact that a sentence is wrongly pointed, will be allowed to interfere with giving it a construction in accordance with its plain intent and meaning.[7] Typographical errors and clerical mistakes will be disregarded, and the meaning which the legislature intended will be applied.[8]

§ 107. **Singular for plural.**— A plural word may be construed as singular or to include the singular when common sense and the plain intention of the legislature require it.[9]

[1] McGuire v. S., 42 Ohio St. 530.

[2] Hedderich v. S., 101 Ind. 564.

[3] S. v. Farrand, 8 N. J. 333.

[4] S. v. Farrand, 8 N. J. 333; Turner v. S., 1 Ohio St. 422; Mayo v. Wilson, 1 N. H. 53; Bradley v. P., 8 Colo. 599. But if an offense is defined in the statute such definition controls: Benson v. S., 5 Minn. 19. As to common-law crimes in states having a criminal code, see *supra*, § 13.

[5] S. v. Stimson, 24 N. J. 9; Norris v. S., 25 Ohio St. 217; Bradley v. P., 8 Colo. 599.

[6] Hallett v. S., 29 Ohio St. 168; S. v. Kelsey, 89 Mo. 623.

[7] S. v. Murphy, 27 N. J. 112. The court will read the statute with such stops as are manifestly required for the purpose of arriving at the true meaning: U. S. v. Lacher, 134 U. S. 624.

[8] S. v. Beasley, 5 Mo. 91; S. v. Acuff, 6 Mo. 54.

[9] S. v. Main, 31 Conn. 572. Thus, a statute providing punishment for stealing obligations or bonds includes the stealing of one such instrument: C. v. Messinger, 1 Binn. 273; Resp. v. Cleaver, 4 Yeates, 69.

§ **108. "And," "or."**—In construing a statute the word "and" may be substituted for "or," even as against the defendant, when the context and the analogy of the other statutes on the same subject require it;[1] but if a statute directs fine *or* imprisonment, the court is not authorized to inflict both,[2] nor *vice versa*.[3]

§ **109. "May."**—The word "may" is construed as imperative when the circumstances show that such was the intention.[4] Thus, "may be punished" will be mandatory when the offense is not otherwise provided for; but if provided for by other statutes, and an aggravating circumstance is referred to, the provision will be deemed discretionary.[5]

§ **110. Definition of terms.**—It would not be practicable to give here a list of the words and phrases which have received construction in criminal cases. Some of them are construed in civil cases as well, and others will be considered in connection with particular crimes. But some which are of special significance in the criminal law, and of application in considering different offenses, may properly be mentioned. A municipal or *quasi*-corporation is not included in the term "body corporate" or "public company," but must be expressly included.[6] The word "person," when used to designate the party defrauded, or whose property is injured, may include the United States,[7] or a state;[8] and the words "person or persons" may, in the same way, extend to corporations.[9] The term "state" may mean one of the United States.[10] "Punishable" must be construed to mean that which may be punished.[11] "Wilfully" may mean corruptly and unlawfully, or simply intentionally, according to the context, and if the statute requires knowledge as well as wilfulness, the word "wilfully" means only intentionally,[12] but it may mean more than voluntarily and knowingly;[13] in other connections it may mean that the act is done without reasonable ground to believe it to be

[1] S. v. Brandt, 41 Ia. 593; Rolland v. C., 82 Pa. St. 306.

[2] S. v. Walters, 97 N. C. 489.

[3] U. S. v. Vickery, 1 Har. & J. 427.

[4] C. v. Gable, 7 Serg. & R. 423.

[5] Williams v. P., 24 N. Y. 405.

[6] C. v. Beamish, 81 Pa. St. 389; S. v. Bancroft, 22 Kan. 170.

[7] S. v. Herold, 9 Kan. 194.

[8] Martin v. S., 24 Tex. 62.

[9] U. S. v. Amedy, 11 Wheat. 392.

[10] U. S. v. Pirates, 5 Wheat. 184.

[11] S. v. Neuner, 49 Conn. 232.

[12] C. v. Bradford, 9 Met. 268.

[13] Rose v. S., 19 Tex. Ap. 470.

lawful.[1] "Maliciously" usually implies an unlawful, wilful act without excuse, and does not require specific malice against the injured party.[2] The term "indictment," as well as "complaint," may be construed as applicable to all forms of accusation.[3] "Conviction," as a ground of disqualification or impeachment of a witness, implies a judgment,[4] but the general meaning of the term is a plea or verdict of guilty.[5]

[1] Owens v. S., 19 Tex. Ap. 242; Loyd v. S., 19 Tex. Ap. 321.

[2] C. v. Goodwin, 122 Mass. 19; C. v. Hicks, 7 Allen, 573. See, also, *infra*, § 121; P. v. Petheram, 64 Mich. 252.

[3] C. v. Gillon, 2 Allen, 502; C. v. Haynes, 107 Mass. 194.

[4] C. v. Gorham, 99 Mass. 420.

[5] C. v. Lockwood, 109 Mass. 323.

PART II.

CRIMINAL INTENT AND CAPACITY.

CHAPTER 6.

THE CRIMINAL INTENT.

§ 111. Tort and crime distinct as to intent.— There is a marked distinction between the civil and the criminal law in regard to the importance of the intent with which an act is done. In an action for tort, or for breach of contract, the intent with which the wrong was done is usually immaterial. It is reasonable that the one doing the wrongful act shall reimburse the one suffering injury therefrom, even though the act was not the result of a wrongful intent, provided it was unlawful.[1] But the basis on which criminal punishment is inflicted is wholly different from that upon which civil liability is founded, the object of the criminal law being preventive rather than compensative, and the intent with which the act is done will be of great importance in determining whether it shall be criminally punished.

§ 112. Intent, essential element in crime.— In determining whether criminal punishment shall be inflicted, the intent with which the act is done is material; and it is true as a gen-

[1] 1 Hale, P. C., ch. II. It is thus in a case of tort committed by an insane person: Morain v. Devlin, 132 Mass. 87; Dickinson v. Barber, 9 Mass. 225. So it was held that a soldier who, in a sham fight, injured a comrade by the discharge of his gun, was liable in damages in a civil action, although he was guilty of no intentional wrong: Weaver v. Ward, Hobart, 134. So one may be civilly liable for the acts of his agent, although there is no criminal liability: Rex v. Fell, 1 Salk. 272; S. v. Berkshire, 2 Ind. 207; Campbell v. Phelps, 17 Mass. 244. And in general as to criminal liability for acts of agents, see *infra*, § 187. In cases of slander and libel, lack of wrongful intent is no defense in a civil action for damages: Barr v. Moore, 87 Pa. St. 385; Wilson v. Noonan, 35 Wis. 321, 353; Rodgers v. Kline, 56 Miss. 808; Shepheard v. Whitaker, L. R. 10 C. P. 502.

eral proposition that such punishment should not be imposed where criminal intent, or, as it is sometimes called, *mens rea*, is absent.[1] Thus, in a prosecution for unlawfully engraving a portion of a bank note, it was held that evidence that such engraving was not made with the intention of reproducing the note for unlawful purposes, but only for the purpose of furnishing a specimen of skill in that kind of work, was admissible as a defense.[2] So it has been held that in cases of misfeasance in office, it is necessary that the unlawful act shall have been done knowingly or with an improper motive.[3]

§ 113. Acting under claim of right.— The fact that defendant in doing a wrongful act believed that he had a right to do so, such belief being founded on a mistake as to title to property, or the like, will constitute a defense.[4]

§ 114. Legal advice.— It will hereafter appear[5] that ignorance of the law is no defense. Therefore, one who does a criminal act will not be excused by the fact that he had legal advice that the act would not be criminal.[6] Thus, the official

[1] McCourt v. P., 64 N. Y. 583; Wagstaff v. Schippel, 27 Kan. 450; 1 Bish. Cr. L., ch. XVIII; 2 Steph. Hist. Cr. L., ch. XVIII; 3 Coke's Inst. 6. As pointed out in 2 Pollock & Maitland's Hist. Eng. L. 474, the maxim "*actus non facit reum nisi mens sit rea*," as found in Coke and also in the laws of Henry I, is borrowed from St. Augustine, and does not at all represent the early English conception under which crimes were punished.

[2] Rex v. Harris, 7 C. & P. 428. But as will be seen further on, the act may be by statute made criminal, regardless of the intent, and in such case the doing of the act without any purpose to commit an offense will not be excused; and it was so held as to the statutory crime of making and circulating due-bills to be used as money: Norvell v. S., 50 Ala. 174.

[3] S. v. Kite, 81 Mo. 97; S. v. Gardner, 5 Nev. 377. But where a public officer is indicted for failure to perform a duty required by law, there is a presumption, in the absence of evidence to the contrary, that such failure was wilful: S. v. Heaton, 77 N. C. 505. But here again it is to be noticed that the intent may be rendered immaterial by the statute: See *infra*, § 128.

[4] S. v. Crosset, 81 N. C. 579; S. v. Deal, 64 N. C. 270; Newton Mfg. Co. v. White, 63 Ga. 697; U. S. v. Railroad Cars, 1 Abbott, C. C. 196; Reg. v. Twose, 14 Cox, 327. But in case of trespass, mere belief of a right to enter, after being forbidden, is not a sufficient excuse: S. v. Bryson, 81 N. C. 595. And as to claim of right in larceny, see *infra*, § 565.

[5] *Infra*, § 132.

[6] Barnett v. S., 89 Ala. 165; S. v. Goodenow, 65 Me. 30; S. v. Marsh, 36 N. H. 196; Weston v. C., 111 Pa. St. 251; S. v. Sheeley, 15 Ia. 404; S. v. Downs, 116 N. C. 1064. But if the criminality depends on knowledge of the fact that the act is illegal, defendant may show that he took

opinion of a public officer, such as the attorney-general, as to the proper construction of a particular statute, even with reference to the duties of public officers thereunder, will not constitute a protection to one acting in reliance thereon.[1]

§ 115. **Acting under legal or other authority.**— No one has authority to set aside the law. Therefore, it is no defense to one who has done a criminal act that he was directed to do so by an officer who had no power to permit or command the act done.[2] So the command of a principal will not be a defense in the prosecution of an agent for doing an unlawful act.[3]

§ 116. **Compulsion.**— The fact that an act is done under compulsion may, under some circumstances, constitute a defense, as will be hereafter shown.[4]

§ 117. **Acting as detective.**— Another illustration of the doctrine that the intent determines criminality is found in the rule that a detective who joins with persons in the commission of a crime for the purpose of securing their arrest and conviction is not punishable, although he so far co-operates as to be guilty if his intention had been the same as theirs.[5] Thus, a detective who has co-operated with a criminal in committing an offense is not to be deemed an accomplice whose evidence must be corroborated.[6]

advice of counsel for the purpose of proving *bona fides:* C. v. Bradford, 9 Met. 268. One who claims good faith by reason of acting on advice of counsel must show that he followed such advice: P. v. Long, 50 Mich. 249.

[1] Dodd v. S., 18 Ind. 56.

[2] Nichols v. S., 89 Ind. 298; C. v. Blodgett, 12 Met. 56; P. v. McLeod, 1 Hill, 377; Cox v. S., 3 Blackf. 193. And see *infra,* § 297*a*. License to carry on a business which is only lawful to persons having such license will not authorize the business to be done in an unlawful manner: Garrett v. S., 49 N. J. 94. But the authority of the United States to do an act within the scope of federal regulation will be a defense in a prosecution for violation of state law in doing such act: C. v. Knox, 6 Mass. 76. When a statute makes knowledge essential to the crime, it may be a defense to show that it was done under authority of the officers having control of such matter: Hess v. S., 45 N. J. 445.

[3] *Infra,* §§ 136, 190.

[4] *Infra,* § 136. As to coverture being a defense in the prosecution of the wife for a wrongful act done in the presence of her husband, see *infra,* § 145.

[5] Price v. P., 109 Ill. 109; S. v. McKean, 36 Ia. 343; Campbell v. C., 84 Pa. St. 187; C. v. Hollister, 157 Pa. St. 13.

[6] Campbell v. C., 84 Pa. St. 187; P. v. Farrell, 30 Cal. 316; P. v. Barric, 49 Cal. 342; P. v. Bolanger, 71 Cal. 17; Wright v. S., 7 Tex. Ap. 574;

§ **118. Decoying to crime.**—A question analogous to that discussed in the preceding section, and yet depending for its solution on somewhat different principles, is as to whether one who has been decoyed into the commission of a criminal act for the purpose of securing his detection and punishment is relieved from criminal liability by that fact. It is sometimes suggested that it is very improper and unworthy conduct on the part of prosecuting officers to induce men to be criminals for the purpose of securing their conviction, and such conduct has been criticised.[1] But it is a well-settled principle that the wrongful acts of the officers of the state in connection with a prosecution will not be imputed to the state so as to excuse the defendant from criminal liability for what he actually does. Thus, although the officers for the prosecution secure the bringing of the defendant within the jurisdiction of the court without right, and unlawfully, nevertheless the jurisdiction of the court to try the offense is not thereby defeated.[2] Therefore it is immaterial that an officer had knowledge of the threatened offense and allowed it to be committed with the intention of arresting the criminal.[3] The only question in the case of decoys is as to whether defendant has committed a criminal act; of course, if he has joined with one who pretends to be a confederate, but in reality is acting as a detective, and therefore has no criminal intent, he will not be criminally liable for acts done by the detective, although present to aid and assist; for while such presence and aid would make him a confederate in the case of a real crime, it cannot render him guilty where no real crime is committed. Thus, it is held that if in burglary an officer or a servant, under the instructions of the owner, admits the intended burglar to the house, pretending to be in collusion with

Reg. v. Bernard, 1 F. & F. 240. So held where the detective was a purchaser of intoxicating liquors sold contrary to law: C. v. Downing, 4 Gray, 29; C. v. Graves, 97 Mass. 114. Also where he engaged in gambling for the express purpose of detecting that crime: C. v. Baker, 155 Mass. 287. Also where he was a purchaser of a lottery ticket: P. v. Noelke, 94 N. Y. 137. As to whether the subject of the offense in abortion, or the purchaser of intoxicating liquors sold criminally, is to be deemed an accomplice, see *infra*, § 199.

[1] Saunders v. P., 38 Mich. 218; P. v. McCord, 76 Mich. 200, 8 Am. Cr. R. 117, and note; Love v. P., 160 Ill. 501; U. S. v. Whittier, 5 Dill. 35.

[2] Ker v. Illinois, 119 U. S. 436; Mahon v. Justice, 127 U. S. 700; Cook v. Hart, 146 U. S. 183; S. v. Ross, 21 Ia. 467. See also *infra*, § 405 n.

[3] P. v. Greening, 102 Cal. 384.

him, there is no burglary committed.[1] And so in larceny, if the property is delivered to the intending thief by the owner, the element of want of consent would be absent and the offense would not be committed.[2] Thus, if one consents to be robbed so that a reward may be secured, there can be no conviction for such robbery.[3] But the fact that the owner of property puts it where he expects it will be stolen, marking it so that the thief may be detected, does not so far constitute consent as to prevent the conviction of the one who wrongfully takes the property.[4] The rule may be said to be that the fact that the owner, or servant or detective acting for him, puts himself or his property in the way of one who, it is supposed, will commit a crime with reference thereto, does not prevent the conviction of the person who commits such crime, provided he actually does the criminal act, and the opportunity or inducement held out to him will constitute no defense.[5] In general, then, it is no defense that accused was decoyed into committing the particular offense charged. Accordingly it is held criminal for one to sell libelous publications, although the purchase was made for the purpose of exposure and prosecution.[6] So in regard to offenses consisting in the improper use of the mails, or larceny of letters, it is held to be no excuse that the crime was committed in response to inquiries or suggestions, or in consequence of the sending of fictitious or decoy letters for the purpose of detection.[7]

§ 119. Other illustrations.— The doctrine that the criminal intent is essential is better illustrated, however, by rules

1 Reg. v. Johnson, Car. & M. 218; Allen v. S., 40 Ala. 334; Speiden v. S., 3 Tex. Ap. 156; Johnson v. S., 3 Tex. Ap. 590. And see *infra*, § 501.

2 Kemp v. S., 11 Humph. 320; Williams v. S., 55 Ga. 391; Connor v. P., 18 Colo. 373, 25 L. R. A. 341, and note.

3 Rex v. McDaniel, Foster, 121.

4 Reg. v. Williams, 1 C. & K. 95; Rex v. Egginton, 2 Bos. & P. 508; Reg. v. Bannen, 1 C. & K. 295; S. v. Covington, 2 Bailey, 569.

5 P. v. Hanselman, 76 Cal. 460, Thompson v. S., 18 Ind. 386; S. v. Jansen, 22 Kan. 498; S. v. Stickney, 53 Kan. 308; Dodge v. Brittain, Meigs, 84; Harrington v. S., 36 Ala. 236; S. v. Anone, 2 Nott & M. 27; *infra*, § 557.

6 Rex v. Burdett, 4 B. & Ald. 95; Rex v. Wegener, 2 Stark. 245; C. v. Blanding, 3 Pick. 304; S. v. Avery, 7 Conn. 266; Swindle v. S., 2 Yerg. 581.

7 Grimm v. U. S., 156 U. S. 604; Goode v. U. S., 159 U. S. 663; Andrews v. U. S., 162 U. S. 420; Montgomery v. U. S., 162 U. S. 410. And further as to improper use of the mails, see *infra*, ch. 67.

hereafter to be discussed as to the liability of infants, insane persons, persons acting under compulsion or mistake of fact, etc., each of which cases furnishes an illustration of the doctrine that the intent is an essential element of criminality.

§ 120. **Motive and intent distinguished.**— The fact that the criminal act is done with an innocent or laudable motive will not, however, furnish an excuse. The distinction between intent and motive seems to be, that intent relates to the doing of the act, while motive relates to the object sought to be accomplished thereby. The question involved in determining criminality of intent depends upon the intent accompanying the act and not upon the motive actuating such act. In this sense good motives do not constitute a defense.[1]

§ 121. **Malice.**— By the term "malice," as commonly used in criminal law, is meant in general simply the intention of doing a criminal act without justification or excuse, and it is for most purposes synonymous with criminal intent. It does not imply bad feeling toward, or desire to injure, any particular person.[2] The term as used in the definition of murder will be

[1] In re Bininger, 7 Blatchf. 262, 277; C. v. Waterman, 122 Mass. 43; Guiteau Case, 10 Fed. R. 161, 175. Thus, the circulation of an obscene book is not excused by the fact that its intent is to expose improper practices. Reg. v. Hicklin, L. R. 3 Q. B. 360. Nor is polygamy excused by religious belief as to its being obligatory: Reynolds v. U. S., 98 U. S. 145. So violations of Sunday laws are punishable without regard to the conscientious convictions of the person charged: C. v. Has, 122 Mass. 40; Specht v. C., 8 Pa. St. 312. Motive is that which excites and stimulates to action; intent is the purpose or fixed direction of the mind to the accomplishment of some particular act. "The intent to do the act exists for all criminal purposes when it is wilfully done, although the act itself was merely intended as a means of obtaining some ulterior object:" Broom's Com. 870, quoting from Eng. Cr. L. Com., 4 Rep., p. 15. "When any act is defined by law to be illegal and criminal, every one is punishable who does the prohibited act without some legal justification or excuse furnished by the action and the circumstances, and without regard to his real motive and intention. To hold that a man should be absolved from penal responsibility, merely because his motives were benevolent, would be to set private opinion above the law:" Broom's Com. 866, quoting from Eng. Cr. L. Com., 6 Rep., p. 52. There can be nothing more dangerous than to allow the obligation to obey the law to depend upon the opinion entertained by individuals of its propriety, that opinion being so liable to be influenced by interest, prejudice, or passion: Per Lord Campbell in Ferguson v. Earl of Kinnoull, 9 Cl. & Fin. 251.

[2] C. v. Goodwin, 122 Mass. 19; C. v. Hicks, 7 Allen, 573; C. v. York, 9 Met. 93; C. v. Temple, 14 Gray, 69;

more fully discussed in that connection.[1] It is also sometimes used in the statutory definitions of offenses, such as malicious trespass, and the like, in which cases it means more than the mere intentional doing of an act which is wrongful.[2] Where wilfulness is the essence of the crime, evidence tending to show that the crime was not wilful is admissible.[3]

§ 122. **Specific criminal intent.**— In some cases an act is made punishable, or more severely punishable, by reason of the specific intent with which it is done; that is, by reason of an intent to do something more than is involved in the act itself. For instance, some acts which would otherwise be innocent are criminal if done with wrongful intent, and such intent must therefore be alleged and proved.[4] Thus, the offense of administering a drug to a pregnant woman with intent to procure an abortion may be committed, although the drug administered is not harmful.[5] On the other hand, some acts which are in themselves criminal, such as assault, may be criminal in a higher degree by reason of the ultimate intent with which the assault is made, although such intent is not accomplished; as, for instance, assault with intent to commit murder, or rape, or great bodily injury, or any felony.[6] Burglary is a pertinent example of a case where the gist of the offense is the intent with which the act is committed; the act of breaking and entering alone, without intent to commit any other wrong, would be an offense of a low grade, if criminal at all, but if committed with intent to effect a felony (or in some states any public offense) it is a crime severely punished.[7] There may be

S. v. Malloy, 34 N. J. 410; S. v. Hambleton, 22 Mo. 452; S. v. Schoenwald, 31 Mo. 147; Davison v. P., 90 Ill. 221; In re Murphy, 109 Ill. 31; Spies v. P., 122 Ill. 1.

[1] See *infra*, §§ 319–321.

[2] C. v. Williams, 110 Mass. 401.

[3] Potter v. U. S., 155 U. S. 438.

[4] S. v. Weller, 20 N. J. 521; S. v. Norton, 76 Mo. 180. By statute in some states it is sufficient to allege generally the intent to defraud without naming the person intended to be defrauded: S. v. Scott, 48 Mo. 422. But even in such case, if the intent to defraud a specified person is alleged, it must be proved: C. v. Harley, 7 Met. 506. If the act itself is by statute made criminal, intent to defraud is not material: S. v. Czizek, 38 Minn. 192. In larceny the specific intent to convert is essential: S. v. Gresser, 19 Mo. 247. And as to larceny, see *infra*, § 564.

[5] C. v. Morrison, 16 Gray, 224.

[6] *Infra*, § 264. See, also, the discussion under the head of attempts: *Infra*, § 222. Intent is essential in a prosecution for simple assault: S. v. Sears, 86 Mo. 169.

[7] *Infra*, § 505.

a double intent, so that the same act would constitute two different crimes.[1]

§ 123. Intent presumed.— Although intent is thus found to be an essential element in crime, without which the criminal act is in general not punishable, yet it is not required of the prosecution that it shall accomplish the impossible by proving the actual intent which existed in the mind of the accused when the act was done. It is according to the ordinary course of human affairs that men intend the acts which they voluntarily do, and, upon proof of doing a criminal act, the criminal intent is in general presumed.[2] It has sometimes been stated to be the rule that a criminal intent will be conclusively presumed from the doing of a criminal act, as in the case of publication of a libel,[3] or improper use of funds by the cashier of a bank,[4] or homicide.[5] But the statement of the rule now generally accepted is that the intent is a question for the jury, they being justified, however, in inferring the existence of criminal intent from the doing of a criminal act where no justification or excuse appears.[6] Where a specific intent, as

[1] P. v. Carmichael, 5 Mich. 10. But *contra*, see S. v. Chinault, 55 Kan. 326.

[2] C. v. Mash, 7 Met. 472; Olive v. C., 5 Bush, 376; S. v. Heaton, 77 N. C. 505; S. v. King, 86 N. C. 603; S. v. Voight, 90 N. C. 741; S. v. Smith, 93 N. C. 516; S. v. Patterson, 116 Mo. 505; Lane v. S., 16 Tex. Ap. 172; Hill v. S., 63 Ga. 578; S. v. Milholland, 89 Ia. 5; Rosin v. U. S., 161 U. S. 29; U. S. v. McFarland, 1 Cranch, C. C. 140; U. S. v. Baldridge, 11 Fed. Rep. 552; Ambrose Light, 25 Fed. R. 408, 422; Rex v. Moore, 3 B. & Ad. 184, 188.

[3] Rex v. Woodfall, 5 Burr. 2661.

[4] U. S. v. Taintor, 11 Blatchf. 374.

[5] C. v. Webster, 5 Cush. 295.

[6] P. v. D'Argencour, 95 N. Y. 624; P. v. Conroy, 97 N. Y. 62; P. v. Herrick, 13 Wend. 87; C. v. Randall, 4 Gray, 36; C. v. Reynolds, 120 Mass. 190; S. v. Knight, 43 Me. 11; S. v. Malloy, 34 N. J. 410; S. v. Patterson, 45 Vt. 308; S. v. Evans, 65 Mo. 574; S. v. Hays, 23 Mo. 287; Hopkins v. C., 50 Pa. St. 9; S. v. Lautenschlager, 22 Minn. 514; Ridenour v. S., 38 Ohio St. 272; Reg. v. Farnborough, 2 Q. B. D. (1895) 484; Clark v. Reg., 14 Q. B. D. 92. The court should not instruct as to intent unless there is some evidence furnishing a basis for such instruction: P. v. Bennett, 49 N. Y. 137. Criminal intent may be implied from the fact that defendant was engaged in some other unlawful act at the time the act charged was committed, but any such unlawful act thus relied on must be unlawful in itself, and not a mere breach of police regulations: C. v. Adams, 114 Mass. 323. It will not be implied from a subsequent unlawful act; for instance, to commit a crime while trespassing does not necessarily make the trespass criminal from the beginning: S. v. Moore, 12 N. H. 42. In homicide cases the rule that the act of killing gives rise to the presumption of malice, which must be rebutted by evidence, applies only where there is the en-

above explained, is necessary to constitute the crime, such intent is not to be inferred from acts alone, which, without such specific intent, would not constitute the crime charged.[1] Nevertheless, specific intent also, as well as the general intent, may be inferred from defendant's acts.[2] In cases of assault with intent to kill, a specific intent may be inferred from the nature of the weapon used or the injury inflicted;[3] but in such cases, unless the specific intent is proved, the offense is not made out.[4]

§ **124. Allegation and proof of intent.**— The general criminal intent presumed from the doing of the wrongful act is at common law sufficiently alleged by charging the act as having been done maliciously, or wilfully, or feloniously, according to the approved forms of indictment for each particular crime. No general rule on the subject can be stated, but it will be found that as to almost every crime there is some form of allegation directly or indirectly imputing intentional wrong to defendant. In statutory crimes the intent will be alleged, or not, in accordance with the language of the statute;[5] if that describes the act as criminal when knowingly, or intentionally, or maliciously, or wilfully done, the indictment must contain such an allegation.[6] But even where the statute does not specifically use these terms, the nature of the act may be such as to make a particular allegation of the intent necessary to show a crime.[7] Where knowledge is essential it must be

tire absence of qualifying or explanatory evidence: P. v. Potter, 5 Mich. 1. As to the presumption in cases of homicide, see *infra*, §§ 332, 333.

1 Simpson v. S., 59 Ala. 1; Patterson v. S., 85 Ga. 131; Roberts v. P., 19 Mich. 401; Maher v. P., 10 Mich. 212.

2 Weaver v. P., 132 Ill. 536; Van Houten v. S., 46 N. J. 16. So in cases of burglary, the fact that the breaking and entering is with intent to commit a felony may be inferred from defendant's acts: S. v. Teeter, 69 Ia. 717; S. v. McBryde, 97 N. C. 393. A specific intent to defraud may be inferred from the acts done: Hutchinson v. C., 82 Pa. St. 472; S. v. Kimball, 50 Me. 409; S. v. Scott, 48 Mo. 422; C. v. Tuckerman, 10 Gray, 173. It is a question for the jury: C. v. Harnden, 19 Pick. 482.

3 Doolittle v. S., 93 Ind. 272; Dunaway v. P., 110 Ill. 333; Crosby v. P., 137 Ill. 325; S. v. Doyle, 107 Mo. 36; Shinn v. S., 68 Ind. 423. But the intent to kill is not conclusively presumed from such an assault: S. v. Stewart, 29 Mo. 419. But see *infra*, § 275.

4 S. v. King, 86 N. C. 603. And see cases in third preceding note.

5 S. v. Aleck, 41 La. An. 83; Halsted v. S., 41 N. J. 552; S. v. Cutter, 36 N. J. 125; Harding v. P., 10 Colo. 387.

6 S. v. Ross, 25 Mo. 426.

7 C. v. Shaw, 7 Met. 52; S. v. Startup,

proved, the burden being upon the prosecution,[1] and it will not be imputed merely from carelessness in failing to make inquiry.[2] But ignorance of the probable results of the act will not be an excuse if the act itself is wrongful and injurious.[3] Where specific intent is required it must be directly alleged, and proven as alleged;[4] but it seems that it is not necessary that such specific intent be alleged with the same particularity as would be required in charging the commission of the crime.[5]

§ 125. **Statements as to intent.**— The intent of the defendant in doing the act charged is to be proved, when essential, by evidence of his acts rather than by his declarations.[6] But where the question is one of specific intent, the defendant may be allowed (in states where defendant is a competent witness in criminal cases) to testify as to what his intent was.[7] By means of the acts of defendant the intent can in most cases be proved with as much certainty as if it were a thing to be tangibly perceived, and therefore no person should be punished for an act as to which the intent forms a material part of the

39 N. J. 423. Thus, in an indictment for selling diseased or unwholesome meat, knowledge of the condition of the article sold must be alleged, and it is not sufficient to charge defendant with knowingly selling such meat: C. v. Boynton, 12 Cush. 499. But if the proof shows the meat to have been of that character, defendant, to escape the penalty of the law, must prove that the sale was not unlawful: Seibright v. S., 2 W. Va. 591.

1 Hess v. S., 45 N. J. 445.

2 P. v. Brown, 74 Cal. 306.

3 C. v. Stratton, 114 Mass. 303; Reg. v. Button, 8 C. & P. 660.

4 C. v. Hersey, 2 Allen, 173; C. v. Shaw, 7 Met. 52; S. v. Learned, 47 Me. 426; S. v. Bloedow, 45 Wis. 279; Slattery v. P., 76 Ill. 217. But the allegation may be in general terms: Evans v. U. S., 153 U. S. 584.

5 S. v. Newberry, 26 Ia. 467; S. v. Mecum, — Ia. —, 64 N. W. R. 286. As to this matter, however, there is some conflict in the decisions. See as to burglary, *infra*, § 509; and as to assaults and attempts, *infra*, §§ 228, 269.

6 Henderson v. P., 124 Ill. 607. Any evidence as to intent which would make the act lawful is admissible: Filkins v. P., 69 N. Y. 101. Evidence as to absence of intent need not be limited to the time covered by the charge: C. v. Hill, 145 Mass. 305.

7 P. v. Baker, 96 N. Y. 340; Delano v. Goodwin, 48 N. H. 203; Bolen v. S., 26 Ohio St. 371; Wohlford v. P., 148 Ill. 296; article in 22 Cent. L. J. 271; note in 21 Am. St. R. 314. In Alabama it is held, contrary to the weight of authority elsewhere, that the defendant cannot testify as to his uncommunicated intention: Brown v. S., 79 Ala. 51; Lewis v. S., 96 Ala. 6; S. ex rel. v. Tally, 102 Ala. 25. But proof of declarations made before the act, tending to show the intention or belief under which the act was done, is admissible: Jones v. S., 103 Ala. 1.

offense until the intent has been demonstrated beyond a reasonable doubt.[1]

§ 126. **Variance of the act from the intent.**— From the rule above stated with reference to inferring the intent from the act, it follows that where a specific intent is required it may be inferred from the doing of an unlawful act implying such intent, even though the actual intent was different. Thus, if the charge is of shooting with intent to kill A., the crime will be made out by proof of unlawfully shooting and injuring A., and it will be immaterial that defendant actually intended to kill B., and hit A. by mistake.[2] If after the doing of an act a new intent is formed, it cannot be considered in determining the criminality of the act.[3]

§ 127. **Intent alone.**— Notwithstanding the importance which is given to the criminal intent, it is a well-settled doctrine of criminal law that intent alone, not accompanied with a criminal act, is not punishable. This will be fully discussed under the subject of attempts.[4]

§ 128. **Intent in statutory offenses.**— Where an act in itself not criminal is prohibited by statute on grounds of public policy, and the statute does not make the criminality of the act depend upon its being wilfully, or maliciously, or knowingly done, it has frequently been held that the criminal intent is immaterial.[5] A statute may throw on the defendant the burden of keeping within its requirements, and may make the doing of the prohibited act criminal without regard to the intent.[6] In such cases it is not necessary to allege or prove

[1] Mullins v. S., 37 Tex. 337.

[2] Walker v. S., 8 Ind. 290; Callahan v. S., 21 Ohio St. 306; Hollywood v. P., 3 Keyes, 55; S. v. Montgomery, 91 Mo. 52; Reg. v. Latimer, 17 Q. B. D. 359. *Contra,* McCormack v. S., 102 Ala. 156. But if the act as intended would have been justifiable or excusable, then the accidental injury to another thereby will also be justifiable or excusable, provided, of course, there is no negligence: Pinder v. S., 27 Fla. 370; Plummer v. S., 4 Tex. Ap. 310; Aaron v. S., 31 Ga. 167.

[3] S. v. Craft, 72 Mo. 456.

[4] *Infra,* § 222.

[5] P. v. Walbridge, 6 Cow. 512; Walls v. S., 7 Blackf. 572; S. v. James, 63 Mo. 570. Ignorance of the duties of an engineer will be no excuse for statutory misconduct in discharging such duties: U. S. v. Taylor, 5 McLean, 242.

[6] S. v. Farr, 34 W. Va. 84; S. v. Hughes, 16 R. I. 403; Strahan v. S., 68 Miss. 347; U. S. v. Adams, 2 Dak. 305; U. S. v. Leathers, 6 Sawyer, 17; U. S. v. Malone, 20 Blatch. C. C. 137; U. S. v. Thomasson, 4 Biss. 99; Reg. v. Bishop, 5 Q. B. D. 259. In a prosecution for twice voting at the same election

intent or knowledge.[1] Where the statute makes it criminal to conduct without a license a business which is subject to police regulations, the person carrying on such business may be required to act at his peril with reference to the validity of such a license.[2] So a principal will be liable for the acts of his agent in conducting such a business in violation of statutory

intent is not material: S. v. Welch, 21 Minn. 22. Nor is intent material in a prosecution for selling liquor to minors or habitual drunkards or slaves in violation of statute: Barnes v. S., 19 Conn. 398; S. v. Heck, 23 Minn. 549; S. v. Presnell, 12 Ired. 103. And proof of a mistake as to the age or character of the person to whom sale is made will not be admissible: Barnes v. S., 19 Conn. 398; C. v. Green, 163 Mass. 103; McCutcheons v. P., 69 Ill. 601; Jamison v. Burton, 43 Ia. 282; Dudley v. Sautbine, 49 Ia. 650; Redmond v. S., 36 Ark. 58; S. v. Scoggins, 107 N. C. 959. So knowledge of age is immaterial in a prosecution for admitting minors to billiard saloons: C. v. Emmons, 98 Mass. 6. So a prosecution for obstruction of the highway is not dependent on knowledge of the existence of the highway: S. v. Wells, 70 Mo. 635; McKibbin v. S., 40 Ark. 480. So religious worship accompanied with exercises forbidden by statute may be punished, the intent being immaterial: S. v. White, 64 N. H. 48. In a prosecution for the statutory offense of maiming, the intent with which the injury is inflicted is immaterial: S. v. Moore, 65 Mo. 606. And the intent to maim may be inferred from the infliction of the injury: S. v. Hair, 37 Minn. 351. As to mistake of fact as a defense in bigamy, see *infra*, § 133.

1 Sykes v. P., 127 Ill. 117; S. v. Walters, 64 Ind. 226; S. v. Hartfiel, 24 Wis. 60. So held as to the selling of adulterated food or liquors contrary to statute: S. v. Stanton, 37 Conn. 421; C. v. Nichols, 10 Allen, 199; C. v. Smith, 103 Mass. 444; C. v. Evans, 132 Mass. 11; C. v. Warren, 160 Mass. 533; P. v. Kibler, 106 N. Y. 321; P. v. West, 106 N. Y. 293; S. v. Smith, 10 R. I. 258; Barton v. S., 99 Ind. 89; Betts v. Armstead, 20 Q. B. D. 771; Pain v. Boughtwood, 24 Q. B. D. 353; or adulterated milk: C. v. Farren, 9 Allen, 489; and having in possession adulterated tobacco: Reg. v. Woodrow, 15 Mees. & W. 404. So held also as to sale of oleomargarine in violation of statutory regulations: C. v. Weiss, 139 Pa. St. 247. But if the offense is selling oleomargarine as an article of food, it must appear that the article sold was intended for use as food: C. v. Schollenberger, 156 Pa. St. 201. So held as to sale of beer, it being incumbent upon the seller to know whether the article sold was beer or not: S. v. Tomasi, 67 Vt. 312. So held, also, as to the violation of a statute prohibiting the sale of the flesh of a calf, under a prescribed age, for veal: C. v. Raymond, 97 Mass. 567; and as to the keeping of naphtha for sale in violation of statute: C. v. Wentworth, 118 Mass. 441; and as to the offense of selling obscene and indecent pictures: P. v. Muller, 96 N. Y. 408; and as to the offense of secreting the body of a newly-born infant: S. v. White, 76 Mo. 96. As to violation of game or fish laws, see *supra*, § 46.

2 S. v. Putnam, 38 Me. 296; S. v. Keen, 34 Me. 500. And an employee who relies on his employer's license will be punishable for acting outside of the scope of such license: C. v. Holstine, 132 Pa. St. 357.

regulations, though the act is done without the principal's knowledge or direction.[1] This doctrine, that one who violates a penal statute is absolutely liable regardless of knowledge of the facts which render his act a violation thereof, applies only to the regulation of kinds of business which may, or may not, be prosecuted at the option of the party, and which he does prosecute at his peril. But it does not apply to a business which is in its nature lawful, such as that of carrier, which there is a public duty to perform.[2] And therefore it is held that there could be no punishment of a carrier for bringing into the state cattle infected with Texas fever where there was no negligence shown.[3] Indeed, on the whole question as to whether absence of intent may be shown as a defense in a prosecution for violating statutory regulations, the authorities are irreconcilably in conflict; and in contradiction to cases previously cited in this section, it has been held that mistake or want of knowledge as to the facts which bring the case within the statutory prohibition may be shown as a defense.[4] Thus, mistake or want of knowledge as to the age or character of the person to whom liquors are sold in violation of statute may, according to some authorities, be shown.[5] So in a prosecution for removing and concealing dead bodies, it has been held that one who purchases such bodies to supply a medical institute was not punishable for violation of the statute, unless he knew them to have been illegally procured.[6] Other illustrations of the same principle

[1] C. v. Gray, 150 Mass. 327; P. v. Roby, 52 Mich. 577; S. v. O'Connor, 58 Minn. 193.

[2] Where the statute makes it criminal to have in possession short lobsters, such possession on the part of a carrier, without knowledge of or reason to know the character of the consignment, will not be criminal: S. v. Swett, 87 Me. 99.

[3] Furley v. Chicago, M. & St. P. R. Co., 90 Ia. 146.

[4] So in a prosecution for selling diseased meat, knowledge has been held essential: Schmidt v. S., 78 Ind. 41; Teague v. S., 25 Tex. Ap. 577. Where an officer liberated a prisoner under what he believed to be a valid discharge, he was held not guilty of "voluntarily permitting a convict to escape:" Meehan v. S., 46 N. J. 355.

[5] Miller v. S., 5 Ohio St. 275; Crabtree v. S., 30 Ohio St. 382; Falks v. P., 39 Mich. 200; Ball v. S., 50 Ind. 595; Robinius v. S., 63 Ind. 235; Hunter v. S., 101 Ind. 241; Waldstien v. S., 29 Tex. Ap. 82. And held that in a prosecution for the sale of bitters, in fact intoxicating, defendant might show that he acted under the belief that there was no alcohol contained therein: Farrell v. S., 32 Ohio St. 456. So in a prosecution for allowing a minor to play billiards it has been held that evidence of an honest mistake as to age could not be disregarded: Stern v. S., 53 Ga. 229.

[6] Schneider v. S., 40 Ohio St. 336.

may be found.[1] The apparent conflict in the cases on this subject is to be explained upon the principle that the question whether or not intent is material must be determined by the construction of the particular statute in question, and if the construction excluding the element of intent would lead to an absurdity, the defense of want of intent must be admitted. On the other hand, if the prohibition is in respect to some duty of a public nature, plain and simple of performance, want of intent or knowledge may, by the terms of the statute, be deemed excluded.[2] But it may be observed in this connection that the cases which hold that an absolute statutory prohibition admits of no exception based on want of criminality in the intent, unless such exception is expressly recognized in the statute, go too far. Criminal statutes seldom make any exception on the ground of infancy, insanity, coverture, or mistake, and yet there is no doubt that these common-law exceptions are recognized with reference to statutory offenses as fully as they are in regard to those which are *mala in se*.[3] The rule of construction which would allow the ordinary exceptions to be made to the criminal liability under a statutory provision will be especially applicable where the statute is merely an expression of the common law;[4] and it has been suggested that the omission in a statutory definition of any requirement of criminal intent has only the effect of throwing the burden of introducing evidence of the absence of such intent upon the defendant.[5]

[1] In a prosecution for secreting a slave, *scienter* is essential: Birney v. S., 8 Ohio, 230. In a prosecution for letting a carriage for use on Sunday in violation of statute, a good-faith belief that it was desired for a proper purpose was held a defense: Myers v. S., 1 Conn. 502. In a prosecution for sale of bread in the manufacture of which alum had been used, it was held necessary to show knowledge: Core v. James, L. R. 7 Q. B. 135. Under a statute declaring the branding of the cattle of another larceny, felonious intent was held to be essential: Bradley v. P., 8 Colo. 599. Intent is essential to a conspiracy to do an act not criminal *per se:* P. v. Powell, 63 N. Y. 88.

[2] Halsted v. S., 41 N. J. 552; Startup v. S., 39 N. J. 423; S. v. Cutter, 36 N. J. 125; S. v. Stimson, 24 N. J. 478; P. v. Stevens, 109 N. Y. 159; P. v. Powell, 63 N. Y. 88. Even where the word "knowingly" is used in a statute punishing neglect of official duty, such knowledge will be construed as relating to the facts and not the law: P. v. Burns, 75 Cal. 627.

[3] S. v. Brown, 38 Kan. 390; Bradley v. P., 8 Colo. 599. See, also, these various headings for examples, and especially as to mistake of fact, see *infra*, § 133.

[4] S. v. Cutter, 36 N. J. 125.

[5] Bradley v. P., 8 Colo. 599.

CHAPTER 7.

CRIMINAL NEGLIGENCE.

§ 129. **As supplying intent.**— The general rule requiring criminal intent to render an act punishable does not prevent criminal liability for wrongs resulting from carelessness or negligence. This is perhaps simply an extension of the principle that the natural consequence of that which one does is presumed to have been intended. It would evidently not be open to one charged with the commission of a crime to claim that through inadvertence or lack of forethought he did not realize the consequence of an act which, in its nature, might be injurious to others. The best illustrations of this doctrine are to be found in cases of homicide, where death caused by negligence is classed as manslaughter;[1] but it will appear in that connection that the carelessness or negligence which is criminally punishable is the omission of some duty, and in general omissions are criminal only where they relate to a duty imposed. There is an obligation to so regulate one's actions and conduct in the control of property, or the exercise of rights, as not to injure others; but aside from this there is no obligation to see that others shall not be injured.

§ 130. **Causing injury.**— Cases where carelessness or negligence are held to be criminal will be found to be those in which there is the breach of some legal duty likely to be injurious; and in such cases the intent is presumed from the negligence or carelessness in the omission of such duty.[2] Thus, a person carelessly handling a dangerous instrument is guilty of manslaughter if death inadvertently results.[3] But even in such a case, if the consequence was not such as to have been anticipated there will be no criminal liability.[4] A person pretend-

[1] *Infra*, § 349.

[2] Belk v. P., 125 Ill. 584; Seacord v. P., 22 Ill. Ap. 279; Reg. v. Benge, 4 F. & F. 504. Simply to permit does not necessarily imply the element of carelessness: C. v. Curtis, 9 Allen, 266.

[3] S. v. Hardie, 47 Ia. 647.

[4] Robertson v. S., 2 Lea, 239. Recklessly shooting into a crowd and

ing to act as a physician and causing the death of his patient by gross want of skill or knowledge in his profession is guilty of manslaughter.[1] One knowingly or carelessly employing in competent servants to perform an act resulting in injury, by reason of such incompetency, may be criminally liable therefor.[2] Mere failure to furnish support is not criminal, unless a legal duty is violated;[3] but by voluntarily taking upon one's self the care of a helpless person, the obligation to provide for such person may arise, and it may be a crime not to furnish support;[4] but in order that there shall be any criminal liability, the person injured must have been helpless and dependent on the person charged with failure to support, either by reason of tender years or other incapacity,[5] and there must have been actual injury resulting from the negligence.[6] Of course where there is a direct wrong, such as that of exposure,[7] or supplying unwholesome or unfit food,[8] the wrong is one of commission and not merely of omission.

wounding some one is criminal, though there is no intent to inflict the particular injury which results: S. v. Myers, 19 Ia. 517; S. v. Vance, 17 Ia. 138. And see a full discussion on this question under the head of Homicide: *Infra*, § 350.

[1] C. v. Pierce, 138 Mass. 165; Rex v. Spiller, 5 Car. & P. 333. And see *infra*, § 351.

[2] Rex v. Dixon, 3 Maule & S. 11; Rex v. Medley, 6 C. & P. 292; Rex v. Smith, 2 C. & P. 449.

[3] Rex v. Smith, 2 C. & P. 449; Rex v. Ridley, 2 Camp. 650; Rex v. Friend, Russ. & Ry. 20; Rex v. Meridith, Russ. & Ry. 46; Rex v. Warren, Russ. & Ry. 47, n.

[4] Reg. v. Smith, 14 Cox, 398; Reg. v. Porter, L. & C. 394; Reg. v. Rundle, Dears. 482.

[5] Anon., 5 Cox, 279; Reg. v. Pelham, 8 Q. B. 959.

[6] Reg. v. Phillpot, Dears. 179.

[7] Rex v. Ridley, 2 Camp. 650.

[8] Rex v. Treeve, 2 East, P. C. 821.

CHAPTER 8.

IGNORANCE OR MISTAKE.

§ 131. **When a defense.**— One of the methods of showing absence of criminal intent, such as to constitute a defense for a criminal act, is by proof of want of knowledge, or mistake as to the nature of the act done. But it will be apparent from what has been said in the preceding chapter as to the nature of criminal intent, and the presumption arising from the doing of a criminal act, that such a defense is limited in its scope.[1]

§ 132. **Ignorance or mistake of law.**— The general proposition that every one is conclusively presumed to know the law, and that ignorance or mistake of law will not constitute a defense or excuse for an unlawful act, is recognized in civil as well as criminal jurisprudence, and needs no consideration here except by way of illustration as to its application in criminal cases.[2] It is immaterial, therefore, that the rule of law which it is sought to apply to the defendant in a criminal prosecution was not generally known even to the legal profession.[3] A belief that the act is lawful will constitute no defense.[4] A criminal act knowingly and intentionally done, so far as the fact is concerned, is not excused by any misinformation or mistake of judgment as to the law applicable thereto.[5] Therefore, advice

[1] 1 Bish. Cr. L., ch. 19; 2 Steph. Hist. Cr. L. 114.

[2] Winehart v. S., 6 Ind. 30; Derixson v. S., 65 Ind. 385; S. v. Marsh, 36 N. H. 196. The law is administered upon the principle that every one must be taken conclusively to know without proof that he does not know it: Per Tindall, Ch. J., in McNaghten's Case, 10 Cl. & Fin. 200. An indictment need not allege knowledge on the part of defendant that the act charged was criminal: S. v. Ryan, 81 Me. 107.

[3] C. v. Everson, 140 Mass. 292.

[4] So held where one whose wife had deserted him for more than three years was informed and believed that the marriage had thereby become void, and married again: Medrano v. S., 32 Tex. Ap. 214. And for an analogous case see S. v. Goodenow, 65 Me. 30.

[5] Gardner v. P., 62 N. Y. 299; P. v. Brooks, 1 Denio, 457; C. v. Bagley, 7 Pick. 279; S. v. Cutter, 36 N. J. 125; S. v. Vasel, 47 Mo. 416; S. v. Mainey, 65 Ind. 404.

of counsel will be immaterial.[1] This conclusive presumption as to knowledge of the law is applicable even to a foreigner who has not yet had opportunity to become familiar with it;[2] and it is applicable in case of a statute so recently enacted that the person affected thereby has not had opportunity to be advised concerning it.[3] Indeed, the obligation to know the law applies generally to statutory offenses, as well as those existing by the common law, and ignorance of the statute will be no defense.[4] But a quarantine order of a health officer is not a law, in this sense, and knowledge thereof will be essential to render its violation criminal.[5]

§ 133. **Ignorance or mistake of fact.**— One who, by reason of a mistake as to the facts, does an act which would be innocent if the facts were as he supposes them to be, is not punishable, although under the facts as they really exist the act is criminal, it being understood that this ignorance or mistake is not due to negligence or bad faith.[6] Thus, where a railroad agent, having the right to eject from the station hackmen who had previously been guilty of violating rules of the company in this respect, who ejected such a hackman actually possessing a passenger ticket, which he did not disclose, it was held that the agent was not liable for an assault.[7] So, one who killed an officer without knowledge of his official character, and in the belief that he was a member of a pursuing mob, was held excusable.[8] On the same principle, one who kills another as the result of an insane delusion is not accountable, if the facts, had they been as the insane person supposed them to be, would have justified the killing.[9] So, where a woman, with good reason to believe her husband dead, married again, she was held not guilty of bigamy, although the first husband was still living.[10] The general proposition that a mistake of

[1] C. v. Bradford, 9 Met. 268; S. v. Goodenow, 65 Me. 30. And see *supra*, § 114.

[2] In re Barronet, 1 El. & B. 1; Rex v. Esop, 7 C. & P. 456.

[3] The Ann, 1 Gall. 61.

[4] S. v. Wilforth, 74 Mo. 528; S. v. Welch, 73 Mo. 284. In a prosecution of an Indian under a statute which made certain crimes committed by Indians even in tribal relations cognizable by the federal courts, held, that it was no defense that notice of the statute had not been given: U. S. v. Whaley, 37 Fed. R. 145.

[5] S. v. Butts, 3 S. Dak. 577.

[6] Pettit v. S., 28 Tex. Ap. 240.

[7] C. v. Power, 7 Met. 596.

[8] Yates v. P., 32 N. Y. 509. And see Isham v. S., 38 Ala. 213.

[9] C. v. Rogers, 7 Met. 500.

[10] Reg. v. Tolson, 23 Q. B. D. 168.

fact will excuse for a criminal act is sometimes embodied in general statutory provisions as to criminal liability;[1] but this is a mere declaration of the common law and does not materially assist in the solution of the question.

§ 134. **Duty to know the facts.**— Notwithstanding the general proposition of the last paragraph that a mistake of fact will constitute a defense, there are many cases in which ignorance or mistake is held no defense for the doing of an act prohibited by statute, on the theory that a statute may throw upon a person, acting with reference to a matter regulated by it, the obligation to know whether or not the facts are such as to make his action proper. This question has already been discussed under the subject of intent.[2] In further illustration of the same principle, cases may be cited in which violations of statutes as to abducting girls under a specified age,[3] or having carnal knowledge of girls under the age of consent,[4] have been held criminal, although the offender acted under a mistaken belief as to the age, and would not have been guilty if the fact as to age had been as he supposed it to be. So in cases of adultery it has been held no excuse that the offender was mistaken in believing the other party not to be married.[5]

§ 135. **Mixed mistake of law and fact.**— The knowledge of law which is conclusively presumed, and the absence of which will constitute no excuse, is knowledge of the existence of the law. If a judicial discretion is reposed in an officer in the discharge of his duties, he will not be criminally liable if he exercises this discretion in good faith in acting upon the facts as they appear to him.[6] But if the prohibition in respect to duties of public officers is plain and simple, the intent or knowl-

And see Squire v. S., 46 Ind. 459. But bigamy is a statutory offense, and the principle that as to acts regulated by statute a party may be required to proceed at his peril has been applied: C. v. Mash, 8 Met. 472. So the fact of acting in such a case in reliance on an invalid decree of divorce is immaterial: S. v. Armington, 25 Minn. 29. And see as to bigamy, *infra*, § 1076. The question as to whether a statute is to be construed as requiring persons to act at their peril with reference thereto has already been considered in the chapter relating to intent: *Supra*, § 128; and is also referred to in the next section. See, also, *infra*, § 163.

[1] P. v. Bushton, 80 Cal. 160; Neely v. S., 8 Tex. Ap. 64.

[2] *Supra*, § 128.

[3] Reg. v. Prince, L. R. 2 C. C. 154. And see *infra*, § 1105.

[4] S. v. Newton, 44 Ia. 45.

[5] C. v. Elwell, 2 Met. 190.

[6] Byrne v. S., 12 Wis. 519.

edge is immaterial.[1] There are cases where a mistake as to the right to do an act, though in one sense a question of law, is dependent on the title to property, which may be regarded as a question of fact, and in such cases the mistake, though one of both law and fact, is treated as a mistake of fact which will excuse. Thus, a trespass committed under a mistake as to the ownership of property will not be criminal.[2] On the other hand, it has been held that one who votes under a mistaken belief of a right to vote, as a matter of law, is not excused for illegal voting.[3]

[1] Halsted v. S., 41 N. J. 552; Startup v. S., 39 N. J. 423. And see *supra*, § 128.

[2] S. v. Crosset, 81 N. C. 579; S. v. Bryson, 81 N. C. 595. But if the party might have ascertained by reasonable inquiry that he did not have the right which he claims, he will not be excused: Clark v. S., 50 Ark. 570. Where a game-keeper took possession of wires and game caught therein, and the person setting the wires compelled the keeper to surrender the game by threats of violence, it was held that, as defendant believed he was entitled to the game, his act did not constitute robbery: Rex v. Hall, 3 C. & P. 409. So where the finder of a note believed himself entitled thereto and appropriated it to his own use, held, that such belief might be taken into account by the jury: Reg. v. Reed, Car. & M. 306; but contrary to this case, see S. v. Welch, 73 Mo. 284, cited in the third preceding paragraph.

[3] U. S. v. Anthony, 11 Blatch. 200. See note to this case in 2 Green's Cr. L. R. 215. If one is disqualified from voting by reason of conviction of a felony, he is presumed to be aware of such disqualification and can properly be punishable for illegal voting: Thompson v. S., 26 Tex. Ap. 94.

CHAPTER 9.

NECESSITY AND COMPULSION.

§ **136. How far excuse.**— An act which is involuntary, and due to overmastering constraint imposed by another, is not criminal in the one who commits it, because the criminal intent is lacking.[1] But the doctrine of necessity and compulsion does not have regard merely to cases where the action is wholly involuntary, as to which, of course, there could be no doubt whatever, but also to cases where the act is done under fear of injury of some kind threatened to the person doing it.[2] In such cases there is an intent to do the act, but it is sought to excuse from criminal liability therefor on the ground that it was not the result of a free will. The defense seems to be analogous to that of duress in case of contracts;[3] but this doctrine of duress, relating as it does to the question of assent to a contract, and not to the intent with which the act is done, has evidently no application in criminal law. Neither is it any excuse that the accused was directed or commanded by a superior to do the wrongful act, as no one has authority to authorize a violation of law;[4] nor is the necessity, which is sometimes urged, of preserving one's own life by the taking of provisions

[1] **Hpynotism.**— The claim that the act was done under hypnotic influence exercised by another would, if recognized as a defense, furnish an example of a case of compulsion; but while such a claim has been, in a few instances, made in trial courts (see Hypnotism in the Criminal Courts, 13 Med. Leg. Jour. 351, Mar. 1896), it has not as yet received any recognition in courts of last resort. Evidence of the effects of hypnotism was held properly rejected where it did not appear that the act was due to any such influence: P. v. Worthington, 105 Cal. 166.

[2] 1 Hale, P. C. 434; Broom's Leg. Max. 17, 18; 1 East, P. C. 225; 1 Russ. Cr. L. 660; 1 Bish. Cr. L., § 346; 1 Whart. Cr. L., § 94.

[3] 1 Bl. Com. 130, 131.

[4] U. S. v. Carr, 1 Woods, 480; Sarah v. S., 18 Ark. 114. And see as to principal and agent, or master and servant, the discussion *infra*, § 190. The only exception to the doctrine that compulsion of authority will not excuse a criminal act is that found in the case of married women; as to which, see *infra*, § 145.

belonging to another to keep from starving, such a necessity as the law regards as an excuse for larceny.[1] But where a parent was indicted for not providing for the burial of his deceased child, it was held to be an excuse that he had no means to do so.[2] A case of emergency has been held to be a sufficient excuse for violation of a general liquor law as to sales in quantities less than a quart.[3]

§ **137. Avoiding injury to one's self.**— The real question is whether the purpose of avoiding threatened injury to one's self or to another will serve as an excuse for doing an act which would otherwise be criminal; and it may be further simplified by distinguishing between cases where the act, which would otherwise be criminal, is directed against one who brings about a threatened danger, or against one who has no connection with producing such threatened danger. Examples of the latter class of cases do not often occur, and on principle they may be easily disposed of. There is in the reason of the thing no ground for excusing one who inflicts a wrong upon another in order to avoid a similar and substantially equivalent wrong threatened to himself.[4] It may be that one should be excused for doing a slight injury to another to avoid a great injury to himself, as, for instance, loss of life.[5] And this would be especially true where the offense committed consists rather in the intent than in the enormity of the act itself. Thus, it is suggested that one who to save his life should join in treasonable acts, escaping, however, from those who coerce him into such acts as soon as he can do so with safety, will not be guilty of

[1] 4 Bl. Com. 31; 1 Hale, P. C. 54, 565; 1 Hawk. P. C., ch. 33, § 20.

[2] Reg. v. Vann, 2 Den. 325.

[3] S. v. Wray, 72 N. C. 253. But where the statute specifically forbade sales to minors, it was held that a physician's prescription would not furnish a justification for a violation of the law: S. v. McBrayer, 98 N. C. 619.

[4] 1 Hale, P. C. 434; 4 Bl. Com. 30; Reg. v. Tyler, 8 C. & P. 616; Arp v. S., 97 Ala. 5. The law will not warrant one in exposing the life or property of another to peril in order to seek safety by escape from a danger against which he would be justified in defending himself: P. v. Macard, 73 Mich. 152.

[5] So where one was compelled by a mob to go with them to break a threshing machine, he was held excusable for his act in breaking the machine, it appearing that he escaped at the first opportunity: Rex v. Crutchley, 5 C. & P. 133. It has been said that, to justify an unlawful act on the ground of fear of injury, the threatened injury must involve life or grievous bodily harm. The Georgia statute so provides: Burns v. S., 89 Ga. 527.

the crime of treason.[1] But in such cases mere threat of injury to one's property will not serve as an excuse.[2] It has been suggested that the rule of necessity found in the law of nature justifies one person in taking the life of another for his own preservation, where the two stand on an equal footing.[3] But in the recent English case of "The Mignonette," in which sailors were prosecuted for having in extremity killed one of their number with a view to preserving their own lives, it was held that the necessity constituted no excuse for taking the life of one innocent of any wrong, and their conviction of murder was unanimously sustained.[4] In another case it was said that the commission of rape would not be excused on the ground that it was by reason of threats against the life of the person committing the act.[5] In a prosecution for perjury committed on the trial of a criminal case it was held to be no defense that the false testimony was given by reason of threats against the life of the witness, made out of court and some time before the trial.[6]

§ 138. **Defense of person or property.**— While the law attempts to furnish redress to one whose rights of person or property have been interfered with, it does not deny to him the right to prevent such injury by his own act.[7] Thus, where the owner of a mill-pond destroyed the boat which another had repeatedly, and without right, placed in such pond, it was held that he was not guilty of malicious mischief.[8] Moreover it is always an excuse for violence toward another that such violence was employed to prevent a wrongful act on the latter, which would have immediately resulted in injury to the

[1] 1 East, P. C. 294; 1 Hawk. P. C., ch. 17, § 24.

[2] Resp. v. McCarty, 2 Dall. 86; U. S. v. Greiner, 4 Phila. 396; Rex v. McGrowther, 1 East, P. C. 71.

[3] 4 Bl. Com. 186. This principle was approved in a prosecution of sailors for having thrown passengers overboard with a view to their own preservation; but the judge instructed the jury that the parties were not on an equal footing, and that the sailors owed the passengers the duty of protection and were not therefore excused: U. S. v. Holmes, 1 Wall. Jr. 1.

[4] Reg. v. Dudley, 14 Q. B. D. 273.

[5] This was a case where a husband, by threats of instant death, attempted to compel a negro to ravish his wife, the court considering that the threatened danger would have been no excuse had the crime been consummated: S. v. Dowell, 106 N. C. 722.

[6] Bain v. S., 67 Miss. 557; Burns v. S., 89 Ga. 527.

[7] 3 Bl. Com. 3.

[8] P. v. Kane, 131 N. Y. 111.

person or property of the former; but this right of self-protection is subject to the important limitation that the violence used in defense is reasonably calculated to prevent the threatened injury and is not disproportionate to it. In other words, there must be an immediate necessity for the employment of some force, and the force employed must not go beyond that reasonably necessary for the purpose. These very general propositions are illustrated by, rather than fully stated in, judicial decisions, but they explain the points actually decided.[1]

§ 139. Extent of right to defend the person.— Where circumstances are such as, under the principle just stated, give rise to the right of self-defense, the next question is as to the extent of the right — that is, as to how far the person assailed or put in danger is justified in offering resistance to the assailant,— and this evidently will depend on the nature of the injury threatened as it appears to the person assailed. It is not every assault, or assault and battery, that will be a defense to the party assailed in maiming or wounding his assailant, but such resistance will only be justifiable when called out by the nature of the assault.[2] Thus, the assailed is not justified in resisting a mere assault and battery, or other non-felonious assault, with a deadly weapon, and thus killing his assailant.[3] A party cannot claim justification in such cases, or indeed where the assault is felonious, on the ground of necessity, unless every other remedy has been exhausted.[4] In the case of

[1] The defense based on the ground of necessity is usually self-defense relied on in cases of homicide, and the whole question affecting such cases will be discussed under the head of justifiable or excusable homicide: See *infra*, §§ 299–316.

[2] Hayden v. S., 4 Blackf. 546; C. v. Ford, 5 Gray, 475; S. v. Thompson, 9 Ia. 188; U. S. v. Wiltberger, 3 Wash. C. C. 515; C. v. Selfridge, Whart. Hom. 417; P. v. Gatewood, 20 Cal. 147. The question whether the degree of force used was greater than necessary must be submitted to the jury: Gallagher v. S., 3 Minn. 270; C. v. Bush, 112 Mass. 280; C. v. Mann, 116 Mass. 58.

[3] Stewart v. S., 1 Ohio St. 66; C. v. Drum, 58 Pa. St. 9; Brooks v. C., 61 Pa. St. 352; C. v. McKie, 1 Gray, 61; Shorter v. P., 2 N. Y. 193; S. v. Neeley, 20 Ia. 108; Isaacs v. S., 25 Tex. 174; Stockton v. S., 25 Tex. 772.

[4] Fahnestock v. S., 23 Ind. 231; Shorter v. P., 2 N. Y. 193; P. v. Gonzales, 71 Cal. 569; Sawyer v. P., 91 N. Y. 667. A prisoner claiming that his food was unwholesome and insufficient was held not justified in killing the warden of the prison on that account, at least unless every other remedy had been exhausted: S. v. Wilson, 38 Conn. 126.

a mere affray, no matter by whom commenced, if no deadly weapon is employed, and there is no material advantage of one party over another in the affray, there is no right to use a deadly weapon in defense.[1] Thus, also, one who is disturbed in his dwelling by a riotous assemblage not gathered for the avowed purpose of committing a felony, is not justified in using force, such as is likely to imperil life, in securing the dispersion of the rioters.[2] It is only where an assault is of such nature as to indicate that the person assailed is in danger of suffering death or great bodily harm, that he is warranted in making defense by means which involve taking the life of the assailant.[3] That is, one in protecting his own person against an assault is not justified in imperiling the life of the assailant unless his own life is imperiled, or he is put in danger of great bodily harm.[4] But it is not required that the person assailed should nicely gauge the quantum of force necessary to avoid the danger. It is sufficient that danger to life or great bodily harm appears imminent.[5]

§ **140. Defense of family and others.**— The same right which exists on behalf of a person assailed to protect himself, exists also for the protection of those dependent upon him, such, for instance, as members of his family, the justification being the same as though the danger were threatened to the person himself.[6] Where the act is in defense of another, the

[1] Shorter v. P., 2 N. Y. 193; S. v. Newland, 27 Kan. 764. Nor in such case is a person not engaged in the affray justified in taking life to stop it: Conner v. S., 4 Yerg. 136; Johnston's Case, 5 Grat. 660; P. v. Cole, 4 Park. Cr. R. 35.

[2] Patten v. P., 18 Mich. 314.

[3] Clifford v. S., 58 Wis. 477; Jackson v. S., 94 Ala. 85.

[4] Nailor's Case, Foster, 278; S. v. Wells, 1 N. J. 424; Shorter v. P., 2 N. Y. 193; P. v. Gonzales, 71 Cal. 569; S. v. Sloan, 47 Mo. 604; West v. S., 59 Ind. 113; Hays v. S., 77 Ind. 450; Batten v. S., 80 Ind. 394; Duncan v. S., 84 Ind. 204. The burden of proving that the assault was of this nature is on defendant: Sawyer v. P., 91 N. Y. 667; U. S. v. Crow Dog, 3 Dak. 106.

[5] S. v. Palmer, 88 Mo. 568. The party assaulted may strike in anticipation, provided he does not use unreasonable force in repelling the threatened assault; Myers v. S., 62 Ala. 599. The jury are sole judges as to the time when the danger becomes such that defendant is justified in striking: Gallagher v. S., 3 Minn. 270; S. v. Stockton, 61 Mo. 382. But the jury should be instructed as to what are sufficient grounds for self-defense: S. v. Hickam, 95 Mo. 322.

[6] West v. S., 59 Ind. 113; S. v. Hickam, 95 Mo. 322; S. v. Melton, 102 Mo. 683. One is not justified in forc-

danger must be imminent.[1] Thus, where a riotous assemblage causes noise and disturbance likely to produce serious bodily injury to an inmate of the house, of which fact the rioters are advised as far as is possible, another inmate of the house is justified in using the same force to compel them to leave as though great bodily harm were threatened to his own person.[2] But if the person in whose behalf the resistance is made would not himself be justified in making such resistance, another having knowledge of such facts has no right to make it in his behalf.[3]

§ **141. Resisting unlawful arrest.**— Necessity in the case of homicide cannot be predicated on the ground of restraint of personal freedom,[4] but one held in unlawful restraint may use any force necessary, short of taking life, to effect escape.[5] So such force may be used as is necessary in resisting arrest by an officer having no writ or other authority.[6] But if such arrest is lawful, even though made by a private citizen under circumstances where such arrest is proper, resistance is not justified.[7] Where the officer attempts to make an arrest without warrant and without making known the circumstances under which he claims the right to act, the prisoner will not be guilty of assault in threatening him.[8] But if the person sought to be arrested must, under the circumstances, know the character and purpose of the officer, it will be unlawful to resist, even though notice of the purpose has not been formally given to him.[9] An attempted unlawful arrest will not be a defense in the prosecution for killing the officer if there is no reasonable ground of apprehension of great bodily harm, or other felony, in connection with such arrest.[10]

ing entrance into the house of another to obtain possession of his child, the owner of the house not being the party guilty of the wrongful detention: C. v. Beals, 133 Mass. 396; C. v. Brown, 121 Mass. 69.

[1] P. v. Cook, 39 Mich. 236.

[2] Patten v. P., 18 Mich. 314.

[3] Bush v. P., 10 Colo. 566; S. v. Linney, 52 Mo. 40; P. v. Curtis, 52 Mich. 616; S. v. Melton, 102 Mo. 683; Sharp v. S., 19 Ohio, 379; S. v. Herdina, 25 Minn. 161. As to homicide in defense of others, see *infra*, § 313.

[4] Clifford v. S., 58 Wis. 477.

[5] Goodman v. S., 4 Tex. Ap. 349.

[6] Redman v. S., 28 Ind. 205.

[7] S. v. Mowry, 37 Kan. 369.

[8] Drennan v. P., 10 Mich. 169; Franklin v. S., 27 Tex. Ap. 136.

[9] S. v. Mowry, 37 Kan. 369.

[10] S. v. Cantieny, 34 Minn. 1. As to homicide in resisting arrest, see *infra*, §§ 328–340.

§ 142. Defense of property.— One who is in lawful possession of property is justified in opposing force to force in the protection thereof, and will not be guilty of assault and battery in so doing when he uses no more force than is necessary.[1] So one is justified in using force in attempting to remove another from his premises after requesting him to leave;[2] or in retaking his property from another who is in the act of carrying it off,[3] so long as he uses no more force than is necessary to obtain possession of it.[4] But as against one who is attempting to take property under a mistaken claim of right, the owner is not justifiable in using such force as would be proper in opposition to a felonious taking, and perhaps should not use violence to the person at all.[5] The owner of goods is not justified in resisting a levy or attachment under legal process, even though the process be against the goods of another, if the officer acts in good faith; the owner must rely upon the legal remedy.[6] But as against a levy under a judgment which is not valid,[7] or upon exempt property,[8] resistance is justified. While the right to possession may thus be involved in determining the right to defend property, the law will not permit the parties in such cases to go into the question of title.[9] It is not, however, every trespass or invasion of a right in prop-

[1] Filkins v. P., 69 N. Y. 101; P. v. Kane, 142 N. Y. 366; C. v. Clark, 2 Met. 23; P. v. Foss, 80 Mich. 559. Further as to defense of property, see *infra*, § 245 and § 299.

[2] S. v. Elliot, 11 N. H. 540; C. v. Donahue, 148 Mass. 529; C. v. Lynn, 123 Mass. 218.

[3] S. v. Woodward, 50 N. H. 527; McCoy v. S., 8 Ark. 451; S. v. Clements, 32 Me. 279. Violence cannot be used to compel a traveler to pay toll; the penalty in such case must be recovered as provided by law: S. v. Dearborn, 15 Me. 402. As to resisting a felony or threatened danger to life in the protection of property, see *infra*, § 299.

[4] S. v. Elliot, 11 N. H. 540. As to protection of property against trespassing animals, see Aldrich v. Wright, 53 N. H. 398.

[5] S. v. Fifield, 18 N. H. 34; S. v. Richardson, 38 N. H. 208; S. v. Downer, 8 Vt. 424; S. v. Buchanan, 17 Vt. 573; S. v. Miller, 12 Vt. 437. *Contra*, C. v. Kennard, 8 Pick. 132. It is criminal to resist with force the censor appointed to make inventory of an estate, though he enter without permission and refuse to leave when requested: S. v. Hyde, 29 Conn. 564.

[6] P. v. Dann, 53 Mich. 490.

[7] P. v. Clements, 68 Mich. 655.

[8] S. v. Zellers, 7 N. J. 220; P. v. Stone, 82 Cal. 36; S. v. Yeaton, 53 Me. 125; P. v. Honshell, 10 Cal. 83. But one in possession as a servant and not as the tenant of the owner has no right to resist the owner by force for the purpose of retaining possession: Kerrains v. P., 60 N. Y. 221.

[9] S. v. Yeaton, 53 Me. 125.

erty that will justify violence in resistance;[1] especially is it true that the protection of property will not justify an assault with intent to kill. One will not be held guiltless for having in this manner resisted a threatened trespass.[2] Death caused by a spring gun or poison in preventing a trespass to property will be criminal.[3] Resistance of a trespass to property is not on the same footing even with resistance to coercion of the person in protection of property only other than the dwelling-house; the owner is not justified in using violence such as to endanger life, as, for instance, by employing a deadly weapon.[4] But where the owner in resisting an invasion of his property simply opposes force to force, without using undue violence, and the aggressor prosecutes his attack until it threatens loss of life or great bodily harm to the person assailed, the latter may then protect himself even to the extent of taking life.[5] So in attempting to eject a trespasser, the owner, if resisted, may proceed to the extent of taking life, if necessary to protect his life or person.[6]

§ 143. **Power of custodian of building.**— Those who have custody of buildings and grounds which the public have a license to enter may use force in ejecting any one making im-

[1] S. v. Gilman, 69 Me. 163; Harrison v. S., 24 Ala. 67; Rex v. Scully, 1 C. & P. 319.

[2] Simpson v. S., 59 Ala. 1; Johnson v. Patterson, 14 Conn. 1. But death thus caused in preventing a felony will be justifiable: S. v. Moore, 31 Conn. 479; Gray v. Coombs, 7 J. J. Marsh. 478. And see McClelland v. Kay, 14 B. Mon. 103.

[3] Roberts v. S., 14 Mo. 138; S. v. Barr, 11 Wash. 481, 29 L. R. A. 154 and note.

[4] C. v. Drew, 4 Mass. 391; S. v. Taylor, 20 Kan. 643; S. v. Hoyt, 13 Minn. 132; S. v. Zellers, 7 N. J. 220; Kunkle v. S., 32 Ind. 220; S. v. Forsythe, 89 Mo. 667. If the trespass is in pursuance of a purpose to drive the owner from his premises, such resistance would be justifiable: P. v. Clark, 84 Cal. 573. And see *infra*, § 144.

[5] P. v. Dann, 53 Mich. 490; S. v. Thompson, 71 Ia. 503; P. v. Payne, 8 Cal. 341; P. v. Batchelder, 27 Cal. 69; Ross v. S., 10 Tex. Ap. 455; S. v. Dugan, 1 Houst. Cr. C. 563; Rex v. Scully, 1 C. & P. 319. But under the Texas penal code it is lawful to repel an aggression on property to the extent of taking life, all other means having been exhausted, and this is independent of the right to resist a person attacked: Lilly v. S., 20 Tex. Ap. 1. If the attack is such as to produce reasonable apprehension of death or serious bodily harm, the owner may take life in resistance without resorting to other means; otherwise taking life will be justifiable only when no other means of preventing the wrong are available: Ledbetter v. S., 26 Tex. Ap. 22.

[6] Ayers v. S., 60 Miss. 709.

proper use of the premises, the force, however, being only such as is necessary to effect the purpose.[1]

§ 144. Protection of dwelling.— Where one is assaulted in his home, or invasion thereof is threatened, he may use all necessary means to repel the assailant, even to the extent of taking life.[2] But if the assailant is already lawfully in the dwelling and the assault is purely personal in its nature, the locality will not in itself justify a resistance endangering life.[3] In cases of defense of the dwelling, as well as in other cases, the rule applies that the person making resistance must do so in a careful and proper manner, and employ means dangerous to life only in the *bona fide* belief, upon reasonable grounds, that such extreme measure is necessary to repel the assailant or prevent forcible entry.[4] The right to resist a felony involving the security of the dwelling is considered elsewhere;[5] so is the question as to the duty to retreat from the dwelling,[6] and the protection of the dwelling by persons merely lodging therein.[7]

[1] C. v. Dougherty, 107 Mass. 243; C. v. Power, 7 Met. 596. Thus, the servant of a railroad company may eject from the cars a passenger riding without compliance with the requirements of the company: S. v. Overton, 24 N. J. 435. The whole subject is further considered in the chapter on assaults: See *infra*, § 244.

[2] S. v. Peacock, 40 Ohio St. 333; Pond v. P., 8 Mich. 150; S. v. Scheele, 57 Conn. 307; S. v. Patterson, 45 Vt. 308; S. v. Medlin, 1 Wins. 99. By provisions of the penal code in California and Georgia, homicide in resisting an attack on a habitation is justifiable only where the attempt to enter the habitation of another is made in a riotous or tumultous manner with intention to do personal violence: P. v. Walsh, 43 Cal. 447; Hudgins v. S., 2 Ga. 173. A separate building used in conjunction with a dwelling as the living place for servants, and situated a short distance from, it may be deemed a part of the dwelling: Pond v. P., 8 Mich. 150; but this right of defense does not extend to lands, etc., not part of the curtilage: Lee v. S., 92 Ala. 15.

[3] S. v. Martin, 30 Wis. 216; S. v. Umfried, 76 Mo. 404; Turner v. S., 16 Tex. Ap. 378. The general license arising from usage of persons to go uninvited to entertainments at houses of neighbors will not deprive a householder of the right to maintain the privacy and inviolability of his home: Davis v. S., 92 Ala. 20.

[4] S. v. Peacock, 40 Ohio St. 333; S. v. Scheele, 57 Conn. 307.

[5] *Infra*, § 312.

[6] *Infra*, § 312.

[7] *Infra*, § 312, n.

CHAPTER 10.

COVERTURE.

§ **145. Presumption of coercion.**— As has already been seen, the rule that necessity excuses does not extend to cases of mere authority. But the relation of husband and wife is considered at common law to be such that a criminal act committed by the wife in the presence of her husband is presumed to be done, not of her own free will, but under coercion, and is therefore excusable. For such an act the wife is not, therefore, punishable criminally.[1] And this rule is still recognized in states having codes which change entirely the common-law *status* of married women,[2] unless it is expressly otherwise provided.[3] This presumption does not arise from the coverture alone, but only when the act is done in the presence of the

[1] S. v. Jonathan, 3 N. H. 65; C. v. Eagan, 103 Mass. 71; C. v. Trimmer, 1 Mass. 476; C. v. Neal, 10 Mass. 152; S. v. Williams, 65 N. C. 398; Rex v. Knight, 1 C. & P. 116; Rex v. Price, 8 C. & P. 19; Reg. v. Matthews, 1 Den. 596; Anon., 2 East, P. C. 559. It is said in one case that this presumption is against the husband, as well as in favor of the wife; but the case is one of sale of liquor in the husband's presence: S. v. Boyle, 13 R. I. 537. The presumption would arise in such case on the theory of agency: See *infra*, §§ 148, 1238. Further than this there should be no presumption against the husband. The wife is not guilty in receiving stolen goods from the husband: Reg. v. Brooks, Dears. 184; and see *infra*, § 714; nor in giving him aid and comfort after the commission of a felony: Reg. v. Good, 1 C. & K. 185; and see *infra*, § 209. The instruments or fruits of crime found in the husband's house are presumed to be in his possession and not in that of his wife: Reg. v. Booker, 2 Cox, 272; Reg. v. Laugher, 2 C. & K. 225. Whether received by the wife in the husband's absence is for the jury: Reg. v. Wardroper, Bell, 249; Rex v. Archer, 1 Moody, 143.

[2] P. v. Miller, 82 Cal. 107; C. v. Gannon, 97 Mass. 547; S. v. Kelly, 74 Ia. 589; S. v. Fitzgerald, 49 Ia. 260. But it is held otherwise in Kansas, the court deciding, without any special statutory provision, that the statutes giving women equal property and other rights exclude the operation of the common-law rule. (But this was a murder case, and the court also refers to the fact that the common-law exemption with reference to coverture did not apply in treason and murder): S. v. Hendricks, 32 Kan. 559. In Georgia the statute provides that the wife is not excused by mere presence of the husband, but only by his violent threats, commands, or coercion: Bell v. S., 92 Ga. 49.

[3] Freel v. S., 21 Ark. 212; Edwards v. S., 27 Ark. 493.

husband.[1] But if the act is in his presence, the liability is not that of agent, even though she acts under his command, but she is exonerated entirely, if at all.[2] If the act is not in the presence of the husband, even though under his command, she is held accountable.[3] Immediate presence of the husband is not, however, necessary if he is near enough so that the wife might be under his control.[4] To entitle the wife to this exemption the marriage must be established, the mere fact of cohabitation or reputation not being sufficient unless the jury finds therefrom that the marriage existed.[5] The wife is indictable alone, or jointly with her husband, and it is only as a defense that coverture is available.[6]

§ 146. **Exception in case of murder.**— The presumed coercion has never been recognized, however, as a defense to the wife in crimes involving a high degree of criminality, such as that of murder.[7]

§ 147. **Presumption not conclusive.**— This presumption in behalf of the wife is *prima facie* only. If the circumstances indicate that she took an active and willing part in the offense, independently of any control exercised by her husband, she may be held criminally accountable.[8] But even where there is evi-

[1] C. v. Butler, 1 Allen, 4; C. v. Murphy, 2 Gray, 510; Rex v. Morris, Russ. & Ry. 220; Reg. v. John, 13 Cox, 100.

[2] C. v. Burk, 11 Gray, 437.

[3] C. v. Feeney, 13 Allen, 560; C. v. Coughlin, 14 Gray, 389; S. v. Haines, 35 N. H. 207; S. v. Potter, 42 Vt. 495.

[4] C. v. Flaherty, 140 Mass. 454; C. v. Munsey, 112 Mass. 287; Connolly's Case, 2 Lewin, 229. But mere proximity of the husband, not actually present, is not sufficient: S. v. Shea, 13 R. I. 535.

[5] Davis v. S., 15 Ohio, 72. But mere irregularity or invalidity of the marriage under which the woman is living with the man as her husband would perhaps not deprive her of the presumption: Reg. v. Good, 1 C. & K. 185. If the two are indicted as husband and wife, perhaps no evidence of the marriage is necessary: Rex v. Knight, 1 C. & P. 116. But where the woman is not so named, the fact may sufficiently appear circumstantially and without any such claim on her part: Reg. v. McGinnes, 11 Cox, 391; Reg. v. Woodward, 8 C. & P. 561.

[6] 1 Ben. & H. Lead. Cr. Cas. 82.

[7] Bibb v. S., 94 Ala. 31; S. v. Hendricks, 32 Kan. 559; Reg. v. Manning, 2 C. & K. 886. Treason as well as murder is usually said to be within the exception: 1 Hale, P. C. 45; 1 Bl. Com. 444. Robbery also is included: 1 Hawk. P. C., ch. 1, § 11. *Contra*, Reg. v. Torpey, 12 Cox, 45. For cases of robbery where the wife was found to have acted without coercion, see P. v. Wright, 38 Mich. 744; Miller v. S., 25 Wis. 384. The presumption in favor of the wife arises in misdemeanors as well as felonies: Reg. v. Torpey, 12 Cox, 45.

[8] S. v. Dyer, 59 Me. 303; Miller v. S., 25 Wis. 384; Tabler v. S., 34 Ohio St. 127; Seiler v. P., 77 N. Y. 411; Gold-

dence to rebut the presumption, the wife is still entitled to have it considered in her favor, and the jury should be instructed on the question.[1] It is not necessary in the indictment of a married woman to negative the existence of coercion; it is a matter of defense.[2]

§ **148. Wife's separate business.**— Some kinds of business, however, are of such nature that, when carried on by the wife, the presumption of the husband's control does not arise, and, if criminal, there is no presumption of coercion. Such, for instance, is the keeping of a house of ill-fame.[3] If the property which is criminally used is the separate property of the wife, the husband is only responsible for the acts of the wife in the control thereof when they are done with his knowledge and consent.[4] In the keeping of houses of ill-fame, places for illegal sale of liquors, and other nuisances, the wife is jointly liable with the husband, and therefore the conviction of the husband thereof is not a bar to the subsequent prosecution of the wife.[5] But when husband and wife live together he is presumed to be the head of the family, and regardless of ownership he is presumed to be liable for an unlawful use of the house, such as permitting gaming, and to render her liable it must appear that she was active in giving such permission and not merely passive in failing to prevent such use.[6]

stein v. P., 82 N. Y. 231; Nolan v. Traber, 49 Md. 460; S. v. Parkerson, 1 Strobh. 169; Reg. v. Cohen, 11 Cox, 99; Reg. v. Torpey, 12 Cox, 45; Reg. v. Dicks, 1 Russ. Cr. 19; Rex v. Hughes, 2 Lewin, 229. For instance, where it appears that the husband was bedridden and unable, therefore, to exercise any coercion: C. v. Gormley, 133 Mass. 580; or, where she is shown to have suggested the crime and to have participated individually in the results: P. v. Ryland, 97 N. Y. 126. The presumption may be overcome by evidence that, although in the same room, the husband exercised no control over her: U. S. v. Terry, 42 Fed. R. 317. If the coercion exists, the fact of the activity of the wife will not render her liable: S. v. Houston, 29 S. C. 108.

1 C. v. Eagan, 103 Mass. 71.

2 S. v. Nelson, 29 Me. 329.

3 C. v. Cheney, 114 Mass. 281. But the husband is liable also, although the premises on which the offense is committed and on which both reside belong to the wife, unless he uses all available means to prevent the illegal business: C. v. Wood, 97 Mass. 225; C. v. Pratt, 126 Mass. 462. The married woman's property act does not alter the husband's liability in regard to the control of his own household: C. v. Barry, 115 Mass. 146; C. v. Kennedy, 119 Mass. 211; C. v. Gannon, 97 Mass. 547.

4 C. v. Hill, 145 Mass. 305.

5 C. v. Tryon, 99 Mass. 442; C. v. Heffron, 102 Mass. 148.

6 Bell v. S., 92 Ga. 49.

CHAPTER 11.

INFANCY.

§ **149. When complete defense.**— The doctrine finds universal recognition in the text-books, although few direct adjudications in its support can be cited, that an infant under seven years of age is by law conclusively presumed incapable of entertaining a criminal intent, and is therefore not criminally punishable.[1]

§ **150. Presumption of innocence.**— Between the ages of seven and fourteen an infant is presumed incapable of criminal intent, but this presumption is not conclusive and may be overthrown by proof of mental capacity sufficient to enable him to understand the nature of the act and its consequences.[2] The presumption grows less strong, however, with advance of years from seven to fourteen.[3] The question as to incapacity of a boy under fourteen years of age to commit rape or similar crimes is discussed elsewhere.[4]

[1] 4 Bl. Com. 22; 1 Bish. Cr. L., §§ 367–373; 1 Whart. Cr. L., § 67; 1 Russ. Cr. 1; 1 Hawk. P. C. 2; 1 Hale, P. C. 27; 2 Steph. Cr. L. 97; Broom's Leg. Max. 311; P. v. Townsend, 3 Hill, 479; Godfrey v. S., 31 Ala. 323; Rex v. Inhabitants, 1 Stra. 631; Marsh v. Loader, 14 C. B. (N. S.) 535. By a statute in Illinois there can be no criminal liability under ten years: Angelo v. P., 96 Ill. 209. For a Texas statute on the subject see notes to next section.

[2] S. v. Guild, 10 N. J. 163; Law v. C., 75 Va. 885; S. v. Fowler, 52 Ia. 103; S. v. Learnard, 41 Vt. 585; Hill v. S., 63 Ga. 578; S. v. Doherty, 2 Overt. 80; S. v. Goin, 9 Humph. 175; Godfrey v. S., 31 Ala. 323; Martin v. S., 90 Ala. 602; C. v. Smith, 119 Mass. 305; Willet v. C., 13 Bush, 230; S. v. Pugh, 7 Jones, 61; S. v. Nickleson, 45 La. An. 1172; Rex v. Owen, 4 C. & P. 236; York's Case, Foster, 70; Reg. v. Vamplew, 3 F. & F. 520; Reg. v. Booker, 2 Cox, 272. By statute in Texas the ages fixed between which there is a rebuttable presumption of innocence are nine and thirteen: Carr v. S., 24 Tex. Ap. 562; Parker v. S., 20 Tex. Ap. 451; Wusnig v. S., 33 Tex. 651; Keith v. S., 33 Tex. Ap. 341. The presumption of incapacity does not, therefore, apply to a criminal act done on the day preceding the thirteenth birthday: Lenhart v. S., 33 Tex. Ap. 504.

[3] S. v. Aaron, 4 N. J. 231; S. v. Guild, 10 N. J. 163; Law v. C., 75 Va. 885.

[4] *Infra*, § 449.

§ 151. Over fourteen years.— The presumption of lack of criminal capacity ends at the age of fourteen years, and an infant over that age is subject to the same rules and presumptions as to criminal capacity which apply to adults.[1] The evidence of the age of such an infant when accused of crime, and that he acted under the control and direction of another, will not be admissible.[2] His own testimony that he did not know the act to be wrong, in the absence of evidence of mental infirmity, will not tend to remove the presumption of accountability.[3]

§ 152. Evidence of capacity, question for the jury.— The question as to the capacity of an infant between seven and fourteen years of age is for the jury, and they may consider all the facts and circumstances of the case bearing upon that question;[4] but direct evidence of mental capacity is not required.[5] The confession of the infant, properly corroborated, may in itself be sufficient to establish this capacity;[6] so may statements made by him;[7] but to warrant a conviction there must be something in the evidence tending to show mental capacity sufficient to rebut the presumption arising from immaturity of age,[8] and such evidence tending to show knowledge and discretion should be strong and clear beyond all doubt and contradiction;[9] especially is this true in a capital case.[10]

§ 153. Proof of age.— Where the defense is that the accused was under the age of presumed capacity the burden of proof as to age is upon him,[11] but direct evidence is not necessary; the jury may take into account the appearance of defendant, in determining the question.[12] The opinion of a non-expert is not admissible.[13]

[1] P. v. Kendall, 25 Wend. 399; S. v. Handy, 4 Harr. 566; Irby v. S., 32 Ga. 496.

[2] P. v. Richmond, 29 Cal. 414.

[3] S. v. Kluseman, 53 Minn. 541.

[4] S. v. Milholland, 89 Ia. 5; Willis v. S., 89 Va. 188; McCormack v. S., 102 Ala. 156.

[5] C. v. Mead, 10 Allen, 398; Law v. C., 75 Va. 885; Carr v. S., 24 Tex. Ap. 562; S. v. Toney, 15 S. C. 409.

[6] S. v. Guild, 10 N. J. 163.

[7] Willis v. S., 89 Ga. 188.

[8] S. v. Tice, 90 Mo. 112.

[9] Angelo v. S., 96 Ill. 209; S. v. Adams, 76 Mo. 355; Godfrey v. S., 31 Ala. 323; 1 Hale, P. C. 27.

[10] S. v. Aaron, 4 N. J. 231.

[11] S. v. Arnold, 13 Ired. 184. In Texas this is so by statute: Ellis v. S., 30 Tex. Ap. 601; Ake v. S., 6 Tex. Ap. 398.

[12] S. v. Arnold, 13 Ired. 184; Martin v. S., 90 Ala. 602.

[13] Martin v. S., 90 Ala. 602.

CHAPTER 12.

INSANITY AND INTOXICATION.

§ 154. **Lack of mind, imbecility.**— From a preceding discussion of intent it is evident that entire absence of a rational mind would render criminality impossible.[1] Thus, idiocy, a congenital absence of mind, would of course be a complete defense to any prosecution for an act criminal in its nature.[2] Imbecility, a weakness of mind due to arrest of mental development in infancy, is also a defense; for the mental capacity of the imbecile being not greater than that of a child would not justify his being held accountable any further than a child would be.[3] Insanity, which is a more or less complete disorder of mind resulting from disease or defect in the brain, is or is not a defense, depending upon the degree to which the mental capacity of the subject is thereby affected, as will be seen in this chapter.[4]

§ 155. **Deaf and dumb.**— Whatever may have been the early theories on the subject,[5] it is now a fully-recognized fact that persons without the senses of speech and of hearing may be possessed of perfectly sound minds, and may be indicted and tried for a criminal offense just as other persons, the only difficulty being as to the procedure.[6]

[1] 1 Hawk. P. C., ch. 1; 1 Hale, P. C. ch. 4; 4 Bl. Com. 24; 1 Russ. Cr. 6; 1 Bish. Cr., § 374; 1 Whart. Cr. L., § 32; Bac. Abr., s. v. Idiots, E.

[2] Beverley's Case, 4 Co. 123; 1 Hale, P. C. 29.

[3] S. v. Richards, 39 Conn. 591; Pettigrew v. S., 12 Tex. Ap. 225.

[4] For definitions of Insanity in Medical Jurisprudence, see Hammond's Treatise on Insanity, 265; Ray's Medical Jurisp. of Ins., § 54; Elwell's Malprac. 338. Judges and law writers have not indulged to any considerable extent in mere definitions. They discuss what has been held by the courts to be such insanity as to excuse for crime.

[5] In an early case in this country it was said that the burden of proof was on the prosecution to show that the person was of sound mind when he committed the crime: S. v. Draper, 1 Houst. Cr. C. 291.

[6] C. v. Hill, 14 Mass. 207, where it is said that the indictment may be interpreted to the defendant by signs, and, a plea of not guilty being entered, he may be put on trial. But where, in a prosecution against a deaf

§ 156. Complete insanity; right-and-wrong theory.— An early well-settled rule as to the degree of insanity which would relieve from criminal responsibility was, that if the lack of mental capacity was such that the accused, by reason of defective reasoning powers, did not know that he was doing wrong, he was not accountable.[1] This inability to distinguish right from wrong is still very frequently announced as the test in determining whether the insanity is such as to constitute an excuse for crime, the usual form of statement being that it is sufficient if the accused did not know right from wrong, or did not know the nature and consequences of the act done as being wrong.[2] Other authorities, however, add to this test another, as to whether accused had sufficient mental power to regulate his action in accordance with his knowledge of what was right; that is, whether he had control over his acts.[3] Other cases still further modify the rigors of the rule as to capacity to distinguish right from wrong, so as to excuse the accused if he had not sufficient mental capacity to understand the nature of

and dumb person, it appeared that defendant was not capable of understanding, and did not understand, the nature of the proceeding, it was held that he could not be convicted, but must be detained the same as a person of unsound mind would be under similar circumstances: Reg. v. Berry, 1 Q. B. D. 447. There may be a preliminary investigation of the capacity of the deaf and dumb person to understand the nature of a trial and its incidents, as in case of insanity: S. v. Harris, 8 Jones, 136.

[1] This proposition was laid down with others by fourteen judges of England in response to certain questions propounded to them by the House of Lords: McNaghten's Case, 10 Cl. & F. 200.

[2] Flanagan v. P., 52 N. Y. 467; P. v. Mills, 98 N. Y. 176; Loeffner v. S., 10 Ohio St. 598; S. v. Kotovsky, 74 Mo. 247; S. v. Mowry, 37 Kan. 369; S. v. Nixon, 32 Kan. 205; S. v. Gut, 13 Minn. 341; Dove v. S., 3 Heisk. 348; Casat v. S., 40 Ark. 511; S. v. Murray, 11 Ore. 413; S. v. Windsor, 5 Harr. 512; S. v. Haywood, Phill. 376; Grissom v. S., 62 Miss. 167; Brinkley v. S., 58 Ga. 296; Clark v. S., 8 Tex. Ap. 350; U. S. v. Shults, 6 McLean, 121; U. S. v. Young, 25 Fed. R. 710; Rex v. Offord, 5 C. & P. 168; Reg. v. Oxford, 9 C. & P. 525; Reg. v. Higginson, 1 C. & K. 129; Reg. v. Davies, 1 F. & F. 69.

[3] S. v. Shippey, 10 Minn. 223; Dunn v. P., 109 Ill. 635; Williams v. S., 50 Ark. 511. For instance, it is said that the question to be submitted to the jury is whether the defendant was a free agent in forming the purpose to do the criminal act, or was at the time capable of judging whether that act was right or wrong: Blackburn v. S., 23 Ohio St. 146; Farrer v. S., 2 Ohio St. 54. But to the contrary it is said that if accused had the ability to know whether the act was wrong, the law

his act and its effect upon the subject thereof, and power to control the impulses of his mind.[1] But mere mental weakness or lack of sufficient will power to control the impulses is not an excuse,[2] and the lack of ability to distinguish right from wrong must be from a lack of mental capacity, not merely from a perverted moral nature, which prevents the criminal from appreciating the heinousness of the crime.[3]

§ 157. Uncontrollable impulses; moral insanity.— As indicated in the preceding paragraph, there are some cases which lend countenance to the idea that an irresistible impulse to the commission of the crime will be an excuse; but in many cases, and indeed by a great weight of authority, irresistible impulse, or uncontrollable passion, is held not to be a defense. Where the criminal has sufficient mental capacity to distinguish between right and wrong,[4] mere passion or frenzy produced by anger, jealousy, or other passions, will not excuse.[5] There may indeed be insane impulses which are so far uncontrollable that there is no criminal liability therefor, but they must be shown to be the result of a diseased mind, and not merely of passion or impulse;[6] though it is said in one case that uncontrollable impulses, due to provocation and disappointment, exaggerated by a disordered mind, might be taken into account to relieve the degree of homicide.[7] But what is called moral or emotional insanity is distinctly repudiated as

presumes the power to choose, and it is not for the court or jury to speculate as to the non-existence of such power: P. v. Taylor, 138 N. Y. 398.

[1] Bennett v. S., 57 Wis. 69; Bradley v. S., 31 Ind. 492; Stevens v. S., 31 Ind. 485; P. v. Cummins, 47 Mich. 334.

[2] S. v. Miller, 111 Mo. 542; Fitzpatrick v. C., 81 Ky. 357; P. v. Leary, 105 Cal. 486; Wilcox v. S., 94 Tenn. 106; S. v. Leehman, 2 S. Dak. 171.

[3] Loyd v. S., 45 Ga. 57; Flanigan v. P., 52 N. Y. 467; S. v. Swift, 57 Conn. 496; Reg. v. Burton, 3 F. & F. 772.

[4] Walker v. P., 88 N. Y. 81; P. v. Carpenter, 102 N. Y. 238; P. v. Hoin, 62 Cal. 120; S. v. Turlington, 102 Mo. 642; S. v. Pagels, 92 Mo. 300; S. v. Miller, 111 Mo. 542; Smith v. S., 55 Ark. 259; Bolling v. S., 54 Ark. 588; S. v. Harrison, 36 W. Va. 729; S. v. Alexander, 30 S. C. 74; Cunningham v. S., 56 Miss. 269; U. S. v. Guiteau, 1 Mackey, 498; S. C., 10 Fed. R. 161, and note; Reg. v. Barton, 3 Cox, 275; Reg. v. Haynes. 1 F. & F. 666.

[5] Guetig v. S., 66 Ind. 94; P. v. Mortimer, 48 Mich. 37; P. v. Finley, 38 Mich. 482; Welch v. Ware, 32 Mich. 77; S. v. Spencer, 21 N. J. 196; P. v. Foy, 138 N. Y. 664.

[6] S. v. Jones, 50 N. H. 369; C. v. Rogers, 7 Met. 500; P. v. Durfee, 62 Mich. 487; C. v. Mosler, 4 Pa. St. 264; S. v. Brandon, 8 Jones, 463.

[7] Anderson v. S., 43 Conn. 514.

an excuse in perhaps all the cases in which such defense has been directly considered.[1]

§ 158. Partial insanity; insane delusions.— Partial insanity, not so great in degree as to interfere with knowledge of the nature of the act and ability to control action on the part of the accused, will not constitute a defense.[2] The unsoundness of mind relied on as a defense must be of such degree as to obliterate the sense of right as to the particular act and create an uncontrollable impulse to do the wrong by overriding the reason and judgment.[3] Accordingly there may be monomania upon a particular subject which will not constitute a defense for a criminal act.[4] Monomania in the form of an insane delusion as to particular facts will excuse if the accused acted in a manner which would have been lawful had the facts been as he believed them to be.[5] But the act must be connected with the particular delusion under which the accused was laboring,[6] and if, notwithstanding the delusion, the accused could distinguish between right and wrong and knew the act he was doing to be wrong, the delusion will be no defense.[7]

[1] P. v. Kerrigan, 73 Cal. 222; S. v. Mowry, 37 Kan. 369; Walker v. S., 91 Ala. 76; Smith v. C., 1 Duv. 224; S. v. Potts, 100 N. C. 457; Scott v. C., 4 Met. (Ky.) 227; Smith v. S., 55 Ark. 259; Parsons v. S., 81 Ala. 577.

[2] Taylor v. C., 109 Pa. St. 262; S. v. Huting, 21 Mo. 464; Dejarnette v. C., 75 Va. 867. Whether there must be ability to control the impulses arising from the diseased condition of the mind in order to render the person whose mind is unbalanced criminally responsible for his acts will, of course, depend on whether irresistible insane impulses are an excuse, as considered in the preceding paragraph. The cases just cited in this note seem to recognize insane impulses as constituting a defense; but to the contrary, see S. v. Harrison, 36 W. Va. 729.

[3] Lilly v. P., 148 Ill. 467; U. S. v. Faulkner, 35 Fed. R. 730. It will not do to say that insanity without regard to the degree thereof will excuse: P. v. Best, 39 Cal. 690. A higher degree of insanity must be proved to absolve from the guilt of a criminal act than to discharge from a contract: Webb v. S., 5 Tex. Ap. 596.

[4] Reg. v. Layton, 4 Cox, 149; Reg. v. Townley, 3 F. & F. 839. Thus, on a trial for homicide, evidence of erotomania is not pertinent: S. v. Simms, 71 Mo. 538.

[5] McNaghten's Case, 10 Cl. & Fin. 200; S. v. Spencer, 21 N. J. 196; S. v. Lawrence, 57 Me. 574; Baldwin v. S., 12 Mo. 223; S. v. Simms, 68 Mo. 305; Boswell v. S., 63 Ala. 307; Cunningham v. S., 56 Miss. 269; Bolling v. S., 54 Ark. 588; P. v. Taylor, 138 N. Y. 398.

[6] Roberts v. S., 3 Ga. 310; S. v. Gut, 13 Minn. 341; Bovard v. S., 30 Miss. 600; S. v. Huting, 21 Mo. 464.

[7] Bolling v. S., 54 Ark. 588; Smith v. S., 55 Ark. 259; S. v. Maier, 36 W. Va. 757; Wilcox v. S., 94 Tenn. 106; Stephens' Dig. Cr. L., art. 27.

But the view of insane delusions which considers them simply as mistakes of fact, and holds persons subject to them accountable for acts not connected with such delusions, or for acts which would be criminal even if the facts were as they appeared to be, is from a medical point of view unsound. It is perfectly well known that a mind which is unsound on one subject is an unbalanced mind, and not a sound mind even as to other subjects, and though no defect in the mental operations outside of the particular delusion may be apparent.[1] Whether, however, from the legal point of view it is wise to allow partial insanity to be taken account of as a defense where it cannot be directly shown to have dethroned the reason as to the very act in question, may be doubtful. But partial insanity is entitled to consideration in determining whether the act in question was the result of a sane mind, and so the fact that the accused is subject to delusions may properly be considered even though the delusion if true would not have rendered the act lawful.[2] Even though the insanity be not such as to constitute a defense, it may, in homicide, be considered as affecting the degree of the crime.[3]

§ 159. Insanity caused by intoxication.— As will appear in a subsequent paragraph, the fact that a criminal act is done while in a condition of intoxication constitutes no defense, but continuous or repeated intoxication may cause such a condition of mind more or less permanent as may amount to insanity, and constitute a defense on that ground. Thus, delirium tremens or *mania-a-potu* may be shown as a defense for criminal acts done during the continuance of such disease.[4] And even though this specific form of disease does not exist, it may nevertheless appear that mental unsoundness, such as will destroy the capacity of distinguishing between right and wrong, has been superinduced by excessive drunkenness, and extends beyond the immediate condition of intoxication, and this will constitute the defense of insanity.[5] But the insanity which is the immedi-

[1] Maudsley, Mental Disease, p. 197; note in 5 Am. Cr. R. 317.

[2] C. v. Rogers, 7 Met. 500.

[3] P. v. Walter, 1 Ida. (N. S.) 386.

[4] Maconnehey v. S., 5 Ohio St. 77; S. v. Dillahunt, 3 Harr. 551; S. v. Hurley, 1 Houst. Cr. C. 28; Reg. v. Davis, 14 Cox, 563.

[5] P. v. Blake, 65 Cal. 275; Beasley v. S., 50 Ala. 149; Beck v. S., 76 Ga. 452; S. v. Robinson, 20 W. Va. 713; S. v. McGonigal, 5 Harr. 510; Mercer v. S., 17 Ga. 146; Tyra v. C., 2 Met. (Ky.) 1; Schaller v. S., 14 Mo. 502; Kenny v. P., 31 N. Y. 330; Carter v. S., 12 Tex. 500; Evers v. S., 30 Tex. Ap. 318;

ate result of voluntary intoxication is no defense.[1] It must appear that the accused was under the delirium at the time the act was perpetrated; and there is not the same presumption of continuance, on evidence of previous fits of delirium or long-continued habit of excessive drinking, there would be in previous evidence of insanity.[2] There may be a tendency to insanity which intoxication will develop into an insane condition, and if the person affected thereby should bring on the insane condition by becoming intoxicated, not having reason from experience or information to anticipate such result, he would not be liable for acts due to such insanity.[3] But the mere fact that accused was, by reason of infirmity, more liable to be overcome by liquor than another will not excuse him for acts done while in an insane condition produced by voluntary intoxication.[4] Drunkenness is only a defense where it has produced actual idiocy or insanity, not merely where it has caused bad habits of mind or any other want of moral discrimination and mental control.[5] The question whether there is a disease of the mind due to intoxication, and whether the crime was a product thereof, is a question of fact for the jury;[6] and the burden is upon the accused to show that the intoxication relied on had actually caused insanity which was the occasion of the commission of the crime.[7]

§ 160. Intoxication alone no defense.— There is an unanimous concurrence of the authorities in the proposition that the fact of voluntary intoxication or drunkenness at the time

U. S. v. Forbes, Crabbe, 558; U. S. v. Drew, 5 Mason, 28; U. S. v. McGlue, 1 Curt. 1; U. S. v. Clarke, 2 Cranch, C. C. 158; Hill v. S., 42 Neb. 503. This rule applies, even under the Texas statute which relates only to temporary intoxication: Ex parte Evers, 29 Tex. Ap. 539; Kelley v. S., 31 Tex. Ap. 216.

1 P. v. Lewis, 36 Cal. 531; Bennett v. S., Mart. & Y. 133; Cornwell v. S., Mart. & Y. 147; Upstone v. P., 109 Ill. 169. Dipsomania is no defense: S. v. Potts, 100 N. C. 457.

2 Real v. P., 42 N. Y. 270; S. v. Sewell, 3 Jones, 245; Spence v. S., 15 Lea, 539. But in those cases where intoxication may be proved as bearing on the question of intent (see *infra*, § 161), it may be shown that a short time previous to the commission of the offense the accused was intoxicated, for the purpose of indicating the continuance of that condition up to the commission of the crime: Pierce v. S., 53 Ga. 365.

3 Roberts v. P., 19 Mich. 401; Terrill v. S., 74 Wis. 278.

4 Choice v. S., 31 Ga. 424.

5 Fisher v. S., 64 Ind. 435.

6 S. v. Pike, 49 N. H. 399.

7 P. v. Bell, 49 Cal. 485. Further, as to burden of proof, however, see *infra*, § 175.

of the commission of a criminal act constitutes no defense therefor.[1] Indeed, it has sometimes been said that intoxication is rather an aggravation than an excuse for crime;[2] but it is probably unnecessary to speak of it as an aggravation, and it is not practically so considered; it simply has no bearing on the offense committed.[3] Proof of intoxication is admissible, however, in a proper case, to show that the defendant was physically incapable of the act with which he is charged.[4]

§ 161. Intoxication as bearing upon the specific intent.— As has already been explained,[5] some crimes consist not merely in the committing of a criminal act and the criminal intent inferred therefrom, but in whole or in part in the specific intent with which the act is done; and in such cases it is a well-established doctrine that intoxication may be shown for the purpose of negativing the existence of such specific intent by showing that the accused was at the time of committing the

[1] Dunn v. P., 109 Ill. 635; Cluck v. S., 40 Ind. 263; Smurr v. S., 88 Ind. 504; Sanders v. S., 94 Ind. 147; Colee v. S., 75 Ind. 511; S. v. Welch, 21 Minn. 22; C. v. Curry, 150 Mass. 509; Cornwell v. S., 1 Mart. & Y. 147; S. v. Harlow, 21 Mo. 446; S. v. Dearing, 65 Mo. 530; S. v. Eddings, 71 Mo. 545; S. v. Ramsey, 82 Mo. 133; Tidwell v. S., 70 Ala. 33; Fonville v. S., 91 Ala. 39; Estes v. S., 55 Ga. 31; S. v. Paulk, 18 S. C. 514; S. v. John, 8 Ired. 330; Wilkerson v. C., 88 Ky. 29; P. v. Jones, 63 Cal. 168; S. v. Thompson, 12 Nev. 140; T. v. Franklin, 2 N. Mex. 307; Scott v. S., 12 Tex. Ap. 31; Ex parte Evers, 29 Tex. Ap. 539; Pearson's Case, 2 Lewin, 144. An instruction that drunkenness is no excuse is correct notwithstanding the rule to be hereafter stated that it may be shown as affecting the question of specific intent: Cross v. S., 55 Wis. 261. Intoxication is no excuse for manslaughter, though committed in a cruel and unusual manner and while blinded by uncontrollable passion: Boyle v. S., 61 Wis. 440. Notwithstanding the general principle that intent is an essential element in crime, intoxication is not to be considered for the purpose of showing absence of such intent: S. v. Harlow, 21 Mo. 446; S. v. Hundley, 46 Mo. 414; O'Herrin v. S., 14 Ind. 420; State v. Avery, 44 N. H. 392; Nichols v. S., 8 Ohio St. 435. Nor to repel the inference of manslaughter: S. v. Dearing, 65 Mo. 530; Flanigan v. P., 86 N. Y. 554; Friery v. P., 2 Keyes (N. Y.), 424. It does not rebut the intent presumed from the act: Upstone v. P., 109 Ill. 169. It has been said, however, that evidence of intoxication may be admissible on the question of malice: Kelly v. S., 11 Miss. 518; P. v. Rogers, 18 N. Y. 9. And as to its bearing on the question of specific intent, see the next section.

[2] 1 Inst. 247; 4 Bl. Com. 25; S. v. Smith, 49 Conn. 376; C. v. Hart, 2 Brews. 546; S. v. Hundley, 46 Mo. 414; Beck v. S., 76 Ga. 452; Ex parte Evers, 29 Tex. Ap. 539.

[3] Haile v. S., 11 Humph. 154.

[4] Ingalls v. S., 48 Wis. 647; Jenkins v. S., 93 Ga. 1.

[5] *Supra*, § 122.

act charged incapable of entertaining the intent which is relied on as constituting or increasing the criminality of such act.[1] Thus, if the charge is assault with intent to murder, the fact of intoxication may be shown as tending to disprove the specific intent to murder, although it would not excuse the assault.[2] So in case of robbery the intoxication of accused may be considered in determining the intent.[3] In a prosecution for larceny intoxication may be considered on the question whether accused had the intent to steal.[4] Where knowledge is essential to constitute a crime, the fact of intoxication may be shown for the purpose of negativing such knowledge; it is so held as to the passing of counterfeit money.[5] So in perjury it has been said that the fact of intoxication at the time of the transaction about which a witness afterwards testifies may be considered for the purpose of showing whether he knew or remembered what took place;[6] so intoxication may be taken into account as affecting the presumption arising from declarations of accused as to his intent.[7] But there may be wrongful intent even where there is intoxication; and so where one was charged with shooting at a railroad train with intent to injure, it was held that his intent was properly submitted to the jury, although the evidence showed that he was very drunk at the time;[8] and so where the charge was of assault with intent to

[1] Roberts v. P., 19 Mich. 401; C. v. Hagenlock, 140 Mass. 125; O'Grady v. S., 36 Neb. 320; P. v. Harris, 29 Cal. 678; P. v. Young, 102 Cal. 411; White v. S., 103 Ala. 72; Golliher v. C., 2 Duv. 163; S. v. White, 14 Kan. 538; Chrisman v. S., 54 Ark. 283; Wenz v. S., 1 Tex. Ap. 36; Ferrell v. S., 43 Tex. 503; U. S. v. Meagher, 37 Fed. R. 875; Reg. v. Cruse, 8 C. & P. 541; Reg. v. Gamlen, 1 F. & F. 90. This is so, even though drunkenness is no excuse: Crosby v. P., 137 Ill. 325; Reagan v. S., 28 Tex. Ap. 227.

[2] S. v. Fiske, 63 Conn. 388; S. v. Garvey, 11 Minn. 154; S. v. Bullock, 13 Ala. 413; Mooney v. S., 33 Ala. 419; S. v. Mullen, 14 La. An. 570; Lancaster v. S., 2 Lea, 575, 3 Am. Cr. R. 160 and note. *Contra*, Jeffries v. S., 9 Tex. Ap. 598. Intoxication is not material where the assault is with a deadly weapon; but it may be if the assault is by intemperate use of a weapon not deadly: Rex v. Meakin, 7 C. & P. 297. In a prosecution for assault to do great bodily harm, intoxication may be shown: S. v. Grear, 28 Minn. 426.

[3] Keeton v. C., 92 Ky. 522.

[4] P. v. Walker, 38 Mich. 156; S. v. Schingen, 20 Wis. 74; Chatham v. S., 92 Ala. 47; King v. S., 90 Ala. 612; Chrisman v. S., 54 Ark. 283; Wood v. S., 34 Ark. 341.

[5] Pigman v. S., 14 Ohio, 555; U. S. v. Roudenbush, 1 Baldw. 514.

[6] Lyle v. S., 31 Tex. Ap. 103.

[7] Nichols v. S., 8 Ohio St. 435.

[8] S. v. Barbee, 92 N. C. 820.

commit rape, it was held immaterial that defendant had voluntarily drank to intoxication and made the assault while in that condition.[1] On a charge of attempting to commit suicide, intoxication, while not a defense, may be shown as bearing on whether accused did really intend to take his own life.[2]

§ **162. In cases of homicide.**—According to the weight of authority, intoxication may be shown in homicide cases as bearing on the question whether the killing was with malice aforethought so as to constitute murder, or without malice aforethought and therefore manslaughter. Thus, if the question is whether the killing was under provocation, proof of intoxication may be admissible as tending, together with evidence of provocation, to show that the act was done in heat of passion and not in cold blood.[3] Indeed, some cases go so far as to admit intoxication generally in prosecutions for murder, as bearing on the question whether the offense is murder or manslaughter.[4] But there is a decided dissent from this doctrine in many cases in which it is held that voluntary intoxication, being no excuse for crime, will not excuse the malice which is implied from intentionally taking life;[5] and that one who is sober enough to intend to take the life of another and actually

[1] S. v. Carter, 98 Mo. 176.

[2] Reg. v. Moore, 3 C. & K. 319; Reg. v. Doody, 6 Cox, 463.

[3] Kenny v. P., 31 N. Y. 330; P. v. Rogers, 18 N. Y. 9; Pennsylvania v. McFall, Addison, 255; S. v. Johnson, 40 Conn. 136; S. C., 41 Conn. 584; Wilkerson v. C., 88 Ky. 29; Morrison v. S., 84 Ala. 405; Davis v. S., 25 Ohio St. 369; Cartwright v. S., 8 Lea, 376; U. S. v. King, 34 Fed. R. 302; Rex v. Thomas, 7 C. & P. 817. So the fact that the deceased was intoxicated is admissible as bearing on the question as to whether his language constituted a sufficient provocation for an assault by the accused: Harris v. S., 34 Ark. 469. So where declarations and previous acts of accused are relied on to show malice aforethought, intoxication may be proved to negative such malice: Bolzer v. P., 129 Ill. 112; Jones v. S., 29 Ga. 594; Curry v. C., 2 Bush, 67; S. v. McCants, 1 Spears, 384; Pirtle v. S., 9 Humph. 663; Rex v. Thomas, 7 C. & P. 817. But the whole doctrine that intoxication may be considered in determining the provocation is repudiated in C. v. Hawkins, 3 Gray, 463; Keenan v. C., 44 Pa. St. 55. Unjustifiable belief as to the necessity of taking life in self-defense, due to intoxication, will be no excuse: Springfield v. S., 96 Ala. 81.

[4] King v. S., 90 Ala. 612; Smith v. C., 1 Duv. 224; Buckhannon v. C., 86 Ky. 110; Wilkerson v. C., 88 Ky. 29; Burkhard v. S., 18 Tex. Ap. 599; Reg. v. Doherty, 16 Cox, 306.

[5] Upstone v. P., 109 Ill. 169; S. v. Morgan, 40 S. C. 345; Warner v. S., 56 N. J. 686; S. v. Johnson, 41 Conn. 584.

does so is sober enough to form the specific intent to murder.[1] And in several cases it has been said generally that intoxication is not material in determining whether the offense is murder in the second degree or manslaughter.[2] As bearing on the question whether the homicide is murder in the first degree or in the second degree, the authorities almost unanimously agree that intoxication is admissible for the purpose of disproving wilfulness, deliberation and premeditation essential to constitute the first degree of the crime.[3] But even though there is intoxication, there may be deliberation and premeditation, and if the evidence shows those elements of murder in the first degree to have been present, the intoxication will not reduce the degree.[4] And certainly one who while sober deliberately resolves to kill another, and makes himself drunk for that purpose, will be guilty of murder in the first degree.[5] Great caution is to be observed in admitting evidence of intoxication, even to reduce the offense below the first degree, because intoxication may have thus been resorted to as the very

[1] Estes v. S., 55 Ga. 31; Marshall v. S., 59 Ga. 154; P. v. Leonardi, 143 N. Y. 360; S. v. Gut, 13 Minn. 341; Shannahan v. C., 8 Bush, 463; S. v. Willis, 43 La. An. 407.

[2] S. v. Smith, 49 Conn. 376; P. v. Langton, 67 Cal. 427; P. v. Moan, 65 Cal. 532; S. v. Tatro, 50 Vt. 483.

[3] Hopt v. P., 104 U. S. 631; Jones v. C., 75 Pa. St. 403; Meyers v. C., 83 Pa. St. 131; Kelly v. C., 1 Grant, 484; C. v. Hart, 2 Brews. 546; P. v. Balencia, 21 Cal. 544; P. v. King, 27 Cal. 507; P. v. Williams, 43 Cal. 344; S. v. Johnson, 41 Conn. 584; Willis v. C., 32 Grat. 929; Smith v. S., 4 Neb. 277; Schlencker v. S., 9 Neb. 241; S. v. Mowry, 37 Kan. 369; Kriel v. C., 5 Bush, 362; Walker v. S., 91 Ala. 76; S. v. Shores, 31 W. Va. 491; Swan v. S., 4 Humph. 136; Huile v. S., 11 Humph. 154; Wilcox v. S., 94 Tenn. 106; Colbath v. S., 2 Tex. Ap. 391. But mere evidence of intemperate habits is not admissible where it does not tend to show actual drunkenness to such extent that a deliberate design was impossible: Warren v. C., 37 Pa. St. 45. By a statute in Texas intoxication is not to be considered to mitigate the degree of crime, and therefore it will not reduce murder from the first to the second degree: Ex parte Evers, 29 Tex. Ap. 539; Clore v. S., 26 Tex. Ap. 624 (but this view is disapproved in Lyle v. State, 31 Tex. Ap. 103, which is not, however, a case of homicide).

[4] P. v. Rogers, 18 N. Y. 9; Flanigan v. P., 86 N. Y. 554; P. v. Mills, 98 N. Y. 176; Nevling v. C., 98 Pa. St. 322; S. v. Cross, 27 Mo. 332; S. v. McDaniel, 115 N. C. 807. Indeed in a late case it is said that voluntary intoxication should not be taken into account in determining whether defendant acted wilfully, deliberately and premeditatedly: State v. O'Reilly, 126 Mo. 597. But this is contrary to the weight of authority as indicated above.

[5] S. v. Robinson, 20 W. Va. 713.

means of providing a mitigation for the offense.[1] Of course, neither as reducing homicide from murder to manslaughter, nor as mitigating the offense from the first to the second degree of murder, does evidence of intoxication constitute an excuse for a homicide.[2] Where evidence of intoxication is admissible, the burden of proof is determined by the same principles as those which govern in cases of insanity.[3]

§ 163. **Voluntary intoxication.**— In cases in which it is said that intoxication is not a defense the courts frequently speak of it as voluntary intoxication. It is thus sometimes assumed, rather than stated, that the rule would be different in cases of involuntary intoxication.[4] While drunkenness occasioned by fraud, artifice, or contrivance of another for the purpose of having a crime perpetrated might furnish an excuse, yet if one gives liquor to another in a social way, with no view or purpose at the time of inducing him to commit a crime, and afterwards, while he is so drunk that he does not know what he is doing, procures a crime to be committed by him, the intoxicated person is legally responsible for his own acts.[5]

§ 164. **Defense of insanity; how raised.**— The fact of insanity should not be considered by the grand jury as a reason for not finding an indictment; they should bring in a bill and let the question be determined on the trial.[6] The question is one of defense, to be tried as a part of the case, and if, on being raised, the prosecution is dismissed and the jury discharged, the accused cannot be again put on trial.[7] It is sometimes expressly provided by statute that defendant shall interpose insanity by a special plea, if at all;[8] and under such a statute it is not proper, where the special plea is interposed, to authorize the jury to return a simple verdict of guilty or not guilty, because a verdict of not guilty on the ground of insanity involves,

[1] S. v. Welch, 36 W. Va. 690; P. v. Ferris, 55 Cal. 588. Little effect can be given to intoxication where the homicide is with a deadly weapon procured for the occasion: Golden v. S., 25 Ga. 527.

[2] Cleveland v. S., 86 Ala. 1; Williams v. S., 81 Ala. 1.

[3] See *infra*, §§ 175, 178.

[4] Upstone v. P., 109 Ill. 169; 1 Hale, P. C. 32. A statute making it a public offense to be drunk is not applicable to intoxicating liquors drank in ignorance of their effect: S. v. Brown, 38 Kan. 390; 8 Am. Cr. R. 165.

[5] McCook v. S., 91 Ga. 740.

[6] Reg. v. Hodges, 8 C. & P. 195.

[7] Gruber v. S., 3 W. Va. 699.

[8] Perry v. S., 87 Ala. 30; Anderson v. S., 42 Ga. 9.

under such statutes, a committal to an insane asylum.[1] But the general plea of not guilty may be interposed in addition to the special plea of insanity;[2] and under such statute, unless the special plea is interposed, evidence of defendant's mental condition at the time of the commission of the crime should be rejected.[3] In most states there are no provisions for raising a special issue as to insanity, and evidence thereof as a defense may be introduced on the general issue of not guilty.[4] It is therefore erroneous to speak of the issue of insanity in a criminal case, or of the defendant pleading insanity. This point is, however, discussed under a succeeding section of this chapter relating to the burden of proof. To raise the question there must be some evidence, and the court is not bound to instruct as to insanity where no evidence definitely pointing to insanity is before the jury.[5]

§ **165. Question for the jury.**— The question whether the defendant was insane at the time of the commission of the offense, and the crime was induced thereby, is to be left to the jury as one of fact.[6] In a late case it is said that the inquiries to be submitted to the jury in a criminal trial in which insanity is relied on as a defense are: First. Was the defendant, at the time of the commission of the alleged crime, as matter of fact, afflicted with a disease of the mind so as to be either idiotic or otherwise insane? Second. If such be the case, did he know right from wrong as applied to the particular act in question? If he did not have such knowledge, he is not legally responsible. Third. If he did have such knowledge, he

[1] Maxwell v. S., 89 Ala. 150.

[2] Long v. S., 38 Ga. 491; Perry v. S., 87 Ala. 30.

[3] Ward v. S., 96 Ala. 100. *Contra,* P. v. Olwell, 28 Cal. 456.

[4] Where, on arraignment, defendant admitted the killing, but claimed that he was insane and therefore pleaded not guilty, it was held that this amounted simply to a general plea of not guilty: S. v. Potts, 100 N. C. 457.

[5] S. v. Ward, 74 Mo. 253. Evidence that defendant has been subject to epilepsy, which is conducive to insanity, will not, alone, require instructions as to insanity as a defense: S. v. Worrell, 25 Mo. 205; Guetig v. S., 63 Ind. 278. Instructions on the forms of insanity are not necessary where there is no evidence as to any particular form: S. v. Lawrence, 57 Me. 574. Where general instructions as to insanity are given, it is not necessary to instruct as to insanity produced by any special drug or liquor: S. v. Mahn, 25 Kan. 182.

[6] S. v. Jones, 50 N. H. 369; S. v. Pike, 49 N. H. 399; S. v. Smith, 53 Mo. 267.

may, nevertheless, not be legally responsible if the two following conditions concurred: (1) If, by reason of the duress of such mental disease, he had so far lost the power to choose between the right and wrong and to avoid doing the act in question as that his free agency was at the time destroyed; (2) and whether at the time the alleged crime was so connected with such mental disease in the relation of cause and effect as to have been the product of it solely.[1]

§ 166. **Preliminary investigation.**— Entirely apart from the question whether the defendant was insane at the time of the commission of the crime is that of the present existence of insanity, which may be raised at any stage of the proceeding from the arrest to the final completion of the imprisonment under the sentence; for if he is insane he ought not, according to modern humanitarian views, to be subjected to a trial or imprisoned by way of punishment, but should be kept in custody only as an insane person. Statutes usually make some provision for an investigation of this kind in the case of a prisoner under arrest before trial, and also in regard to prisoners in the penitentiary, but this matter is of no consequence here. The question, however, whether defendant is insane when arraigned and put on trial is a much more important one; for as he has a constitutional right to be present, and as presence in felonies is essential to the jurisdiction of the court, it is evident that the law contemplates that he shall be in a condition to make his defense. If, by reason of insanity, he is not in such condition, he should not be put on trial, and this question is the subject of a preliminary investigation,[2] which should be awarded by the court on the suggestion of the prisoner or his attorney, or upon the affidavit of even a disinterested person,[3] or upon the court's own motion.[4] But the court is not required to order such an examination unless reasonable ground to doubt the sanity of the prisoner is made to appear. In the determination of the question the court may examine and inspect the prisoner, consider his actions and demeanor, read affidavits, and inquire of physicians and others touching his condition.[5]

[1] Parsons v. S., 81 Ala. 577.

[2] Freeman v. P., 4 Denio, 9.

[3] Guagando v. S., 41 Tex. 626; Reg. v. Dwerryhouse, 2 Cox, 446.

[4] S. v. Reed, 41 La. An. 581.

[5] S. v. Harrison, 36 W. Va. 729.

The question is to be tried by a jury specially summoned for that purpose,[1] the evidence of insanity being first introduced in behalf of the defendant.[2] The jury are to act, however, on the demeanor of the accused before them, as well as on the evidence presented.[3] The question may be raised at any stage of the proceeding down to the time of sentence,[4] but, if raised pending trial, it seems that the issue may be submitted to the trial jury in connection with the issue arising on the plea of not guilty.[5] It is sometimes provided by statute that if the jury impaneled to try the preliminary question should disagree, the question shall be submitted to the jury impaneled to try the issue in the case.[6] If the suggestion is made after conviction, judgment should be suspended until the fact can be tried;[7] but after conviction the court may refuse to allow the inquiry to be made if, on its inspection, it is satisfied that the claim is false; if there is any doubt, however, a venire should be awarded returnable instanter to ascertain the facts.[8] Where the fact of present insanity did not appear until on the hearing of the appeal, the supreme court recommended commutation by the government of capital sentence to imprisonment for life, after which the prisoner could be transferred to the hospital for the insane in accordance with statutory regulations.[9] Jurors who have passed on the question of the prisoner's sanity at the time of the trial are not competent to serve on the trial of the offense which may involve the same issue.[10] The finding on the preliminary investigation that the prisoner is not insane will of course not preclude his proving on the trial that he was insane at the time of the commission of the crime.[11] A

1 P. v. Farrell, 31 Cal. 576. And the investigation may be repeated as often as the occasion may require: Ibid.

2 Reg. v. Turton, 6 Cox, 385. But it seems that if the inquiry is at the suggestion of the prosecution, it should first call its witnesses to prove the prisoner's sanity: Reg. v. Davis, 3 C. & K. 328.

3 Reg. v. Goode, 7 A. & E. 536.

4 In re Chandler, 45 La. An. 696.

5 S. v. Reed, 41 La. An. 581; Reg. v. Southey, 4 F. & F. 864.

6 French v. S., 85 Wis. 400.

7 S. v. Vann, 84 N. C. 722. Even after judgment the execution should be stayed on such suggestion: Ibid.

8 Bonds v. S., Mart. & Y. 143. Under the Texas statute, providing for an inquiry as to insanity after conviction, the judgment of the trial court upon said inquiry is conclusive and no appeal lies: Darnell v. S., 24 Tex. Ap. 6.

9 Green v. S., 88 Tenn. 634.

10 French v. S., 85 Wis. 400.

11 Inskeep v. S., 35 Ohio St. 482.

preliminary investigation similar to that as to the prisoner's sanity may be had, where it is claimed that he is by reason of being deaf and dumb incapable of understanding the nature of the trial and its incidents, and his rights under it.[1]

§ 167. **Evidence of insanity.**— From the preceding discussion as to what is sufficient insanity to constitute an excuse for crime, it is plain that the evidence must go beyond proof of a mere state of mental excitement or passion;[2] nor will mere absence of motive,[3] or absurd and eccentric behavior, coupled with excessive intemperance,[4] or a tendency to commit suicide,[5] or the unnatural atrocity of the crime,[6] or the fact of a homicide unexplained,[7] be sufficient; but the lack of motive, the attempt at suicide, and preceding fits of madness, or other physical conditions tending to loss of mental control, may be shown in connection with other facts as indicating insanity.[8] An attempt to commit suicide does not, however, of itself show such mental impairment as to render the person irresponsible.[9]

§ 168. **Acts and declarations of accused.**— Acts, declarations, conversations and exclamations by the accused, shortly before, at the time of, or after the commission of the offense, may be shown.[10] And to rebut such evidence the prosecution may introduce evidence of other acts and declarations within the same period.[11] For instance, in rebuttal, the prosecution may prove intoxication as tending to account for strange words and actions attributed to insanity.[12] And so where the accused

[1] S. v. Harris, 8 Jones, 136; Reg. v. Berry, 1 Q. B. D. 447.

[2] P. v. Hurley, 8 Cal. 390; Williams v. S., 50 Ark. 511; S. v. Ward, 74 Mo. 253; Montag v. P., 141 Ill. 75; S. v. Graviotte, 22 La. An. 587; Fisher v. S., 30 Tex. Ap. 502.

[3] Reg. v. Dixon, 11 Cox, 341.

[4] Spence v. S., 15 Lea, 539; Reg. v. Leigh, 4 F. & F. 915.

[5] P. v. Messersmith, 61 Cal. 246.

[6] S. v. Coleman, 20 S. C. 441.

[7] Williams v. S., 50 Ark. 511.

[8] P. v. Messersmith, 61 Cal. 246; Reg. v. Vyse, 3 F. & F. 247; Reg. v. Law, 2 F. & F. 836; Reg. v. Richards, 1 F. & F. 87.

[9] P. v. Taylor, 138 N. Y. 398.

[10] Bolling v. State, 54 Ark. 588. Subsequent acts and conduct are often competent but not admissible as of course: S. v. Leehman, 2 S. Dak. 171. Mere narration or statement by accused should be excluded, but testimony of deportment, complaints, etc., such as usually and naturally accompany and furnish proof of an existing malady, ought to be freely admitted: S. v. Hays, 22 La. An. 39.

[11] U. S. v. Holmes, 1 Cliff. 98.

[12] P. v. Miles, 143 N. Y. 383.

relies on strange actions as accounted for only by insanity, the prosecution may show in rebuttal particular acts, and conduct contemporaneous with the conduct referred to, tending to show that they were consistent with his sanity.[1] While the statement of the accused as to his sanity may be admissible, his declarations that he was not insane will not preclude such defense,[2] and insane statements made by him should be disregarded so far as it is sought to bind him thereby.[3]

§ **169. Mental condition before and after the crime.**— As a general proposition, evidence of mental condition before and after the commission of the offense is admissible, for it would be practically impossible to limit the evidence to such condition at the exact time.[4] Evidence of mental condition of the accused before the commission of the crime is admissible on the theory that, at least where the insanity is of a permanent type or continuing nature, or possesses all the characteristics of a confirmed disorder, such a condition proved to have once existed is presumed to have continued until the time of the commission of the criminal act.[5] In some cases this presumption is limited to a state of insanity shown to have existed shortly before the crime was committed.[6] But even when previous insanity has been established, it may still be a question whether it did in fact continue until the time of the commission of the act, and of this the jury should be satisfied in order to warrant an acquittal.[7] Moreover, the presumption of continuance is applicable only to habitual insanity, and not to a spasmodic or temporary mania.[8] Thus, where delirium tremens is relied on, the accused must show that he was under a delirium

[1] U. S. v. Guiteau, 1 Mackey, 498 (10 Fed. R. 161).

[2] Reg. v. Pearce, 9 C. & P. 667.

[3] P. v. Wreden, 59 Cal. 392.

[4] P. v. March, 6 Cal. 543; Gardner v. S., 96 Ala. 12; Montgomery v. C., 88 Ky. 509.

[5] Armstrong v. S., 30 Fla. 170; P. v. Francis, 38 Cal. 183; Vance v. C., 2 Va. Cas. 132. Previous conviction of insanity raises no presumption of continuance, but is simply evidence for the jury: Hunt v. S., 33 Tex. Ap. 252.

[6] P. v. Smith, 57 Cal. 130. But evidence of insanity existing several months before the criminal act has been admitted: S. v. Harrigan, 9 Houst. 369.

[7] S. v. Vann, 82 N. C. 631. As to whether a defendant must make out insanity to the satisfaction of the jury, see *infra*, § 178.

[8] P. v. Francis, 38 Cal. 183; P. v. Lane, 101 Cal. 513; S. v. Spencer, 21 N. J. 196.

at the time the act was perpetrated, and there is no presumption of continuance on proof of an insane fit from which he had recovered.[1] In Texas, the presumption of continuance of insanity is entirely discarded.[2] The same presumption as to continuance of mental condition operates to render admissible evidence of insanity subsequent to the commission of the offense;[3] thus, the testimony of a physician as to the mental condition of accused a day or two after the commission of the crime is competent.[4] But this rule is even more strictly guarded than that with reference to proof of insanity before the commission of the offense, and the evidence of subsequent insanity must be so connected with the criminal act as to warrant an inference that the insanity existed when the act was committed.[5] In some cases the mental condition at the time of trial has been admitted for the purpose of indicating that the accused was insane at the time of committing the criminal act.[6] In other cases, such evidence has been refused on the theory that it is too remote.[7]

§ **170. Hereditary.**— Where there is evidence of want of motive or other evidence furnishing a basis for inquiry as to the sanity of the accused at the time of committing the criminal act, evidence of hereditary insanity may be introduced by proving the insanity of a parent[8] or a brother or sister,[9] or perhaps of more distant blood relations. But it must appear that the kind of insanity proposed to be proven is not a temporary malady, but notorious and of the same species as that

[1] Real v. P., 42 N. Y. 270; S. v. Sewell, 3 Jones, 245. But it is said that where intoxication is relied on, it is competent to prove that accused was, a short time previous to the commission of the offense, in an intoxicated condition, provided the testimony makes it probable that the intoxication still existed when the act was done: Pierce v. S., 53 Ga. 365.

[2] Leache v. S., 22 Tex. Ap. 279; Smith v. S., 22 Tex. Ap. 316.

[3] Moore v. C., 92 Ky. 630; Bolling v. S., 54 Ark. 588.

[4] Murphy v. C., 92 Ky. 485.

[5] C. v. Pomeroy, 117 Mass. 143. Where a prisoner committed homicide in the evening, evidence as to what he said the next morning was held not admissible to show derangement at the time the crime was committed: S. v. Scott, 1 Hawks, 24.

[6] McAllister v. S., 17 Ala. 434; Freeman v. P., 4 Denio, 9.

[7] Jones v. S., 13 Ala. 153; P. v. Ward, 105 Cal. 335; Shultz v. S., 13 Tex. 401.

[8] P. v. Smith, 31 Cal. 466; Murphy v. C., 92 Ky. 485; Lovegrove v. S., 31 Tex. Ap. 491.

[9] Hagan v. S., 5 Baxter, 615; S. v. Hoyt, 47 Conn. 518.

with which other members of the family have been afflicted.[1] Where evidence of the insanity of a sister was relied on, it was held proper for the state to inquire into the cause of such insanity in order to show that it was not hereditary.[2] Mere proof of insanity in a parent will not be sufficient to constitute a defense, if the other evidence negatives the presence of insanity in the accused.[3]

§ 171. **Other evidence.**— As insanity is a subject of investigation in various classes of civil cases as well as in criminal prosecutions, it is not proper here to go into the entire subject, but further illustrations of what has been decided in criminal cases may perhaps be proper. For instance, insanity is not to be proved by reputation,[4] nor by hearsay testimony.[5]

§ 172. **Opinions of experts.**— Experts may, of course, in answer to hypothetical questions, give their opinions as to the sanity of the accused as indicated by the evidence bearing upon his sanity.[6] Thus it was held that defendant's family physician might testify as to his being weak-minded.[7] Likewise, defendant's physician may be called to testify in behalf of the state on that question, the rule making such relations privileged not being applicable in criminal cases.[8] But the expert should not give his opinion as to whether the accused is responsible or capable of judging between right and wrong, but as to the state of mind, whether sane or insane. The responsibility of the accused is for the jury.[9] The testimony of the expert is for the purpose of enlightening the jury and not of controlling their judgment. They are not bound to accept his conclusions as their own.[10] The defendant may read ex-

[1] S. v. Christmas, 6 Jones, 471.

[2] S. v. Hoyt, 47 Conn. 518.

[3] Lovegrove v. S., 31 Tex. Ap. 491.

[4] S. v. Hoyt, 47 Conn. 518; Brinkley v. S., 58 Ga. 296; Ellis v. S., 33 Tex. Ap. 86.

[5] P. v. Pico, 62 Cal. 50.

[6] Reg. v. Frances, 4 Cox, 57. In some cases it has even been held admissible to have an expert, who has been present in court and heard the evidence, testify as to whether the evidence stated by the witness, supposing it to be true, showed a state of mind incapable of distinguishing between right and wrong: S. v. Hayden, 51 Vt. 296; McNaghten's Case, 10 Cl. & Fin. 200. And see Rex v. Wright, Russ. & Ry. 456.

[7] P. v. Worthington, 105 Cal. 166.

[8] P. v. Lane, 101 Cal. 513.

[9] Reg. v. Richards, 1 F. & F. 87; Reg. v. Layton, 4 Cox, 149. *Contra*, U. S. v. Guiteau, 1 Mackey, 498 (10 Fed. R. 161).

[10] Williams v. State, 50 Ark. 511.

tracts from books of high medical authority,[1] but scientific works are not legal authorities, except so far as the facts expressed are supported by judicial decisions.[2]

§ 173. **Opinions of those not experts.**— As a general rule persons who are not experts are not competent to give an opinion as to the sanity of the accused.[3] But it is now well established that witnesses who are not experts may give an opinion as to the sanity of accused in connection with a statement of the particular conduct and expressions which form the basis of such opinion; such conduct and expressions being testified to as of the witness' knowledge.[4]

§ 174. **Presumption.**— As bearing on the question of proving insanity it is important to state that every person is presumed to be sane and possessed of a sufficient degree of reason to be responsible for his crimes until the contrary appears.[5] This rule relieves the prosecution from any obligation to introduce in the first instance proof of the sanity of the accused.

§ 175. **Burden of proof.**— It is usually assumed as following from the proposition that sanity is presumed until evidence is introduced to the contrary, that therefore the burden of proof is on the defendant to show his insanity, and not on the prosecution to show sanity. The correctness of this assumption will depend entirely on the sense in which the term "burden of proof" is used. If it refers to the issue in the case, then it is erroneous; for in a criminal case there is, as a rule, but one

[1] Bales v. State, 63 Ala. 30.

[2] State v. West, 1 Houst. Cr. C. 371.

[3] Choice v. S., 31 Ga. 424; Gehrke v. S., 13 Tex. 568; Ellis v. S., 33 Tex. Ap. 86; S. v. Coleman, 27 La. An. 691; S. v. Crisp, 126 Mo. 605.

[4] S. v. Maier, 36 W. Va. 757; Shults v. S., 37 Neb. 481; Brown v. C., 14 Bush, 398; Jamison v. P., 145 Ill. 357; S. v. Hayden, 51 Vt. 296; P. v. Borgetto, 99 Mich. 336; Armstrong v. S., 30 Fla. 170; S. v. Williamson, 106 Mo. 162; Parsons v. S., 81 Ala. 577; Ford v. S., 71 Ala. 385; Norris v. S., 16 Ala. 776; S. v. Potts, 100 N. C. 457; Bolling v. S., 54 Ark. 588; S. v. Leehman, 2 S. Dak. 171; Holcomb v. S., 41 Tex. 125. A contrary opinion expressed in S. v. Pike, 49 N. H. 399, and S. v. Archer, 54 N. H. 465, is overruled in Hardy v. Merrill, 56 N. H. 227.

[5] C. v. Heath, 11 Gray, 303; Walter v. P., 32 N. Y. 147; Loeffner v. S., 10 Ohio St. 598; Fisher v. P., 23 Ill. 283; Montag v. P., 141 Ill. 75; McKensie v. S., 42 Ga. 334; Graham v. C., 16 B. Mon. 587; S. v. McCoy, 34 Mo. 531; Newcomb v. S., 37 Miss. 383; S. v. Starling, 6 Jones, 366; S. v. Coleman, 27 La. An. 691; Fisher v. S., 30 Tex. Ap. 502; U. S. v. McGlue, 1 Curt. 1; U. S. v. Lawrence, 4 Cranch, C. C. 514; McNaghten's Case, 10 Cl. & Fin. 200.

issue, and that is as to whether defendant is guilty, and (except under statutes which require insanity to be specially pleaded)[1] evidence of insanity is introduced under this general issue and does not constitute an issue in itself, but bears simply on the question of guilt. The whole proposition is obscured by speaking of defendant's plea of insanity or defense of insanity as though it were new matter pleaded by way of confession and avoidance. It is plain that there is no issue, in a strict sense, as to the defendant's insanity, any more than there is an issue of *alibi*, evidence of insanity being admissible on that element of crime involved in the general issue which relates to defendant's accountability, just as evidence of defendant's presence at a place other than that where he must have been in order to be guilty under the evidence for the prosecution is admissible as bearing on another element of the crime involved in the general plea of not guilty, that is, the connection of the defendant with the criminal act. If, therefore, the term "burden of proof" is used with reference to the issue in the case, it is erroneous to speak of the burden being upon the defendant, for the weight of authority is that in a criminal case the burden of proof is on the prosecution throughout to establish every material element of the offense.[2] But if the term "burden of proof" is used simply to indicate which party must first introduce evidence upon the particular question of fact, then, inasmuch as the presumption of sanity exists until there is evidence to the contrary, it may properly be said that the burden of proving insanity rests upon the defendant, and this is what the cases usually decide.[3]

§ 176. **Amount of evidence; various rules.**— Closely connected with the rule as to burden of proof is the question as to how much proof will be sufficient to entitle the defendant

[1] *Supra*, § 164; P. v. Dillon, 8 Utah, 92.

[2] Brotherton v. P., 75 N. Y. 159; O'Connell v. P., 87 N. Y. 377; C. v. Heath, 11 Gray, 303; Central Bridge Co. v. Butler, 2 Gray, 130; C. v. Pomeroy, 117 Mass. 143; S. v. Flye, 26 Me. 312; S. v. Bartlett, 43 N. H. 224; Davis v. U. S., 160 U. S. 469. And see as to the term "burden of proof," articles by Dr. Thayer in 4 Harv. L. Rev. 45, by Dr. Abbott in 6 Harv. L. Rev. 125, and by the author in 17 Amer. L. Rev. 892.

[3] Moore v. C., 92 Ky. 630; Ball v. C., 81 Ky. 662; McKensie v. S., 42 Ga. 334; S. v. Potts, 100 N. C. 457; Leache v. S., 22 Tex. Ap. 279; Mendiola v. S., 18 Tex. Ap. 462; Williams v. S., 50 Ark. 511; P. v. Walter, 1 Idaho (N. S.), 286; U. S. v. Ridgeway, 31 Fed. R. 144; Reg. v. Layton, 4 Cox, 149.

to an acquittal. Three distinctly different rules have been laid down on this question, which will be stated in separate paragraphs.

§ 177. **Beyond a reasonable doubt.**— In a few cases, evidently decided by courts actuated by the early hostility that prevailed in regard to the excuse of insanity at a time when the nature of the disease was but little understood, it has been held that, to be entitled to an acquittal on that ground, the accused must establish his insanity beyond a reasonable doubt;[1] but this rule has been expressly repudiated in some cases,[2] and is entirely inconsistent with the cases which support either of the other rules.

§ 178. **By preponderance of evidence.**— The statement of the second rule is not uniform in the cases which support it. It is sometimes said that the defendant, having the burden of proof, must clearly establish his insanity,[3] or that he must establish it to the satisfaction of the jury.[4] These statements are probably simply different forms of expression for the rule that insanity must be made out by a preponderance of evidence.[5] The great weight of authority is in favor of the proposition that the defendant, relying upon insanity as an excuse for his criminal act, must establish such insanity by a preponderance of evidence;[6] that is, by such weight of evi-

[1] S. v. Pratt, 1 Houst. Cr. C. 249; S. v. Danby, 1 Houst. Cr. C. 166; S. v. Spencer, 21 N. J. 196; S. v. Brinyea, 5 Ala. 241; S. v. De Rance, 34 La. An. 186; S. v. Hansen, 25 Oreg. 271. In this last case, which is recent, the point is not directly raised, but an instruction to that effect is held good as against a different objection, and there is no intimation that it does not correctly state the rule.

[2] Hodge v. S., 26 Fla. 11; P. v. Coffman, 24 Cal. 230; P. v. Wilson, 49 Cal. 13; S. v. Paulk, 18 S. C. 514.

[3] P. v. McDonnell, 47 Cal. 134; Smith v. S., 19 Tex. Ap. 95; McNaghten's Case, 10 Cl. & Fin. 200.

[4] Boswell v. C., 20 Grat. 860; Baccigalupo v. C., 33 Grat. 807; Parsons v. S., 81 Ala. 577; S. v. Potts, 100 N. C. 457; S. v. Coleman, 20 S. C. 441; Graham v. C., 16 B. Mon. 587; S. v. Coleman, 27 La. An. 691; P. v. Hamilton, 62 Cal. 377; Ortwein v. C., 76 Pa. St. 414, 424; Meyers v. C., 83 Pa. St. 131, 141; Loeffner v. S., 10 Ohio St. 598; S. v. Klinger, 43 Mo. 127; Johnson v. S., 10 Tex. Ap. 571; Reg. v. Layton, 4 Cox, 149.

[5] In one case, however, it is said that while it would be erroneous to charge that the burden is on defendant to prove insanity by preponderance of evidence, yet a charge that insanity must be established to the satisfaction of the jury was proper: S. v. Payne, 86 N. C. 609.

[6] S. v. Lawrence, 57 Me. 574; S. v. Hoyt, 46 Conn. 330; Ortwein v. C., 76 Pa. St. 414; Lynch v. C., 77 Pa. St. 205; C. v. Bezek, 168 Pa. St. 603; S. v.

dence as would entitle him to succeed on an issue in a civil case as to which he has the burden of proof.[1] In harmony with this rule it has been held that where the accused attempts to show irresponsibility by reason of intoxication, he must do so by a preponderance of evidence.[2]

§ 179. **Reasonable doubt sufficient.**— The reasoning on which the cases cited in the preceding section are decided is based, as has been indicated, on assumptions with reference to the connection between the presumption of sanity and the burden of proof of insanity which are more specious than sound. The fact that a state of sanity is presumed until evidence of insanity is introduced does not at all necessitate the conclusion that the presumption exists until overcome by a preponderance of evidence. It is more in accordance with the correct use of terms to say that the presumption simply supplies the place of direct evidence until evidence is introduced, and that then the burden of proof is on the prosecution to establish defendant's guilt, as well with reference to his capacity to entertain a criminal intent as to the fact of his having committed a criminal act. And as the prosecution can sustain the burden which rests upon it only by evidence which establishes the guilt of defendant beyond a reasonable doubt, if, on the entire evidence relating to the insanity of the accused, there is left a reasonable doubt as to whether he was sufficiently sane to be criminally accountable for his act, he should be acquitted. This course of reasoning has been followed in a number of well-considered cases,[3] and has received the strong indorsement of the supreme

Gut, 13 Minn. 341; Bonfanti v. S., 2 Minn. 123; P. v. Coffman, 24 Cal. 230; P. v. Myers, 20 Cal. 518; P. v. McDonnell, 47 Cal. 134; P. v. Bell, 49 Cal. 485; P. v. Wilson, 49 Cal. 13; P. v. Messersmith, 61 Cal. 246; P. v. Travers, 88 Cal. 233; P. v. Bemmerly, 98 Cal. 299; P. v. Ward, 105 Cal. 335; S. v. Hansen, 25 Oreg. 391; Bond v. S., 23 Ohio St. 349; P. v. Walter, 1 Idaho (N. S.), 386; State v. Felter, 32 Ia. 49; P. v. Redemeier, 71 Mo. 173; Dove v. S., 3 Heisk. 348; S. v. Lewis, 20 Nev. 333; Boswell v. S., 63 Ala. 307; Parsons v. S., 81 Ala. 490; Maxwell v. S., 89 Ala. 150; S. v. Paulk, 18 S. C. 514; S. v. Alexander, 30 S. C. 74; Casat v. S., 40 Ark. 511; Coates v. S., 50 Ark. 330; Williams v. S., 50 Ark. 511; Bolling v. S., 54 Ark. 588; Fisher v. S., 30 Tex. Ap. 502; Lovegrove v. S., 31 Tex. Ap. 491; Webb v. S., 9 Tex. Ap. 490.

1 P. v. Messersmith, 61 Cal. 246.

2 S. v. Grear, 29 Minn. 221; S. v. Hill, 46 La. An. 27.

3 P. v. Garbutt, 17 Mich. 9; Brotherton v. P., 75 N. Y. 159; O'Connell v. P., 87 N. Y. 377; Walker v. P., 88 N. Y. 81; P. v. McCann, 16 N. Y. 58; C. v. Heath, 11 Gray, 303; C. v. McKie, 1 Gray, 61; C. v. Pomeroy, 117

court of the United States in a recent decision.[1] In some of the cases just cited, the courts, without holding that the burden of proof is on the prosecution, or even while maintaining directly that the burden is on the defendant as to proof of insanity, nevertheless say that if on the whole evidence, including the evidence relating to insanity, there is a reasonable doubt of defendant's guilt, he should be acquitted. This is, of course, practically the same thing as saying that to warrant conviction, where there is evidence of insanity, the prosecution must establish the sanity beyond a reasonable doubt. Some cases which are noticeable for putting the question in this rather inconsistent form are cited in the note;[2] but as a rule the courts holding defendant to have the burden of proof as to insanity consistently adhere to the doctrine as stated in the preceding section, and require the evidence to establish insanity to preponderate, and authorize the jury to disregard defendant's insanity unless it is thus established; and the proposition that a reasonable doubt of sanity will entitle to acquittal is in many of those cases expressly repudiated.[3]

Mass. 143; S. v. Bartlett, 43 N. H. 224; Cunningham v. S., 56 Miss. 269; Polk v. S., 19 Ind. 170; Guetig v. S., 66 Ind. 94; Plake v. S., 121 Ind. 433; Chase v. P., 40 Ill. 352; Montag v. P., 141 Ill. 75; S. v. Crawford, 11 Kan. 32; S. v. Nixon, 32 Kan. 205; Ballard v. S., 19 Neb. 609; Dove v. S., 3 Heisk. 348; Hodge v. S., 26 Fla. 11; Armstrong v. S., 27 Fla. 366; Armstrong v. S., 30 Fla. 170; U. S. v. Faulkner, 35 Fed. R. 730; Guiteau's Case, 10 Fed. R. 161.

1 Davis v. U. S., 160 U. S. 469. The author of this work does not claim to be a prophet as to future decisions of courts, but some years ago he ventured to predict that courts not already committed by precedent in their respective states on this question would, in the future, recognize the soundness of the position stated in this paragraph; and the prediction seems to be in a measure, at least, justified by the view which the supreme court of the United States has now taken. See the author's article on Burden of Proof in Criminal Prosecutions, 17 Amer. L. Rev. 892.

2 Westmoreland v. S., 45 Ga. 225; King v. S., 91 Tenn. 617; Stuart v. S., 1 Baxter, 178; S. v. Paulk, 18 S. C. 514.

3 Maxwell v. S., 89 Ala. 150; Boswell v. S., 63 Ala. 307; Ford v. S., 71 Ala. 385; Parsons v. S., 81 Ala. 577; Gunter v. S., 83 Ala. 96; Baccigalupo v. C., 33 Grat. 807; Boswell v. C., 20 Grat. 860; P. v. Myers, 20 Cal. 518; Kriel v. C.. 5 Bush, 362; S. v. Strauder, 11 W. Va. 745, 823; S. v. Stark, 1 Strob. 479; S. v. Hurley, 1 Houst. Cr. C. 28; Reg. v. Stokes, 3 C. & K. 185.

CHAPTER 13.

CORPORATIONS.

§ 180. Liability to indictment.— There was formerly some question as to whether a corporation, being a purely artificial person, was within the reach of the criminal law, it being suggested that the liability, if any, must be that of the members and not of the corporation as such;[1] but it seems now to be well settled that a corporation is at common law subject to indictment.[2] The difficulty has been in determining the method of securing jurisdiction of the defendant, inasmuch as a corporal arrest is not practicable; but in England before the passage of any statute on the subject, it was suggested that the corporation might be brought into court by a distress infinite.[3] Any difficulty as to procedure has been removed, both in England and the various states of this Union, by statutory provisions.[4] The officers or agents of the corporation being criminally liable are of course also punishable under the general principles of liability of agents and officers, discussed elsewhere.[5]

§ 181. Whether deemed "person." — Another difficulty which sometimes arises as to the criminal liability of a corporation is based on the language of the statutes defining crimes, and declaring that any "person" guilty of the prohibited acts shall be punished. And it has been said that in such case the

[1] Anon., 12 Mod. 559; S. v. Great Works, etc. Co., 20 Me. 41; C. v. Swift Run Gap Turnpike Co., 2 Va. Cas. 361; Fertilizer Co. v. S., 24 Ohio St. 611.

[2] Reg. v. Birmingham, etc. R. Co., 9 C. & P. 469; C. v. Lehigh Valley R. Co., 165 Pa. St. 162; Boston, etc. R. Co. v. S., 32 N. H. 215; S. v. Baltimore, etc. R. Co., 15 W. Va. 362; S. v. Security Bank, 2 S. Dak. 538. A national bank may thus be indicted for usury under a state statute: S. v. First Nat. Bank, 2 S. Dak. 568.

[3] Reg. v. Birmingham, etc. R. Co., 9 C. & P. 469; or, as more fully explained in a recent case where the subject is discussed, by a *venire facias* and a *distringas:* C. v. Lehigh Valley R. Co., 165 Pa. St. 162.

[4] S. v. West. N. C. R. Co., 89 N. C. 584.

[5] *Infra*, § 190. And see Kane v. P., 8 Wend. 203; S. v. Morris & E. R. Co., 23 N. J. 360; Cowley v. P., 83 N. Y. 464. But if a penalty is imposed by statute upon the president,

word "person" does not embrace a corporation;[1] but this rule of construction has not been elsewhere followed and is unsound.[2]

§ 182. **Liable for non-feasance.**— Where a duty is specially imposed by law, which is such that it covers acts which a corporation may do, it is now well settled that a corporation may be criminally liable for its breach.[3] Thus, corporations have been criminally punished for failing to maintain a bridge in a safe condition,[4] or for not reconstructing a highway or bridge as required by the corporate charter.[5]

§ 183. **Also for misfeasance.**— It was maintained in some of the early cases that a corporation was indictable only for breach of duty, that is, for non-feasance, and not for wrongful acts or misfeasance;[6] but this supposed distinction between non-feasance and misfeasance has been entirely discarded,[7] and this applies to municipal as well as private corporations.[8] Thus, a corporation is indictable for nuisance,[9] or for keeping a dis-

directors and company, the president and directors are not individually indictable: C. v. Demuth, 12 Serg. & R. 389.

1 Fertilizer Co. v. S., 24 Ohio St. 611. And even where a general statute declares that the word "person" shall be construed to include corporations, it has been said that such provision is applicable only in civil cases: S. v. Pres. of O. & M. R. Co., 23 Ind. 362. Where the statute required persons or companies engaged in the business of money brokers and exchange dealers to take out a license, it was held that such provision was not applicable to corporations but only to moral agents capable of taking an oath: S. v. Field, 49 Mo. 270.

2 S. v. Baltimore, etc. R. Co., 15 W. Va. 362; C. v. Boston, etc. R. Co., 11 Cush. 512. A state or other municipal corporation is a "person" capable of being defrauded or injured: Stewart v. S., 4 Blackf. 171.

3 S. v. Cox, 88 Ind. 254.

4 C. v. Central Bridge Corp., 12 Cush. 242; Reg. v. Birmingham, etc. R. Co., 9 C. & P. 469.

5 C. v. Penn. R. Co., 117 Pa. St. 637; S. v. Inhabitants of Madison, 63 Me. 546. But if a duty is imposed upon a board of a municipal corporation, the inhabitants collectively are relieved from their common-law liability: S. v. Inhabitants of Hudson County, 30 N. J. 137.

6 S. v. Great Works, etc. Co., 20 Me. 41.

7 C. v. Proprietor, etc., 2 Gray, 339; Reg. v. Great N. of E. Ry., 9 Q. B. 315; Pittsburg, etc. R. Co. v. C., 101 Pa. St. 192; S. v. Vermont Central R. Co., 27 Vt. 103; S. v. Morris & E. R. Co., 23 N. J. 360.

8 C. v. Bredin, 165 Pa. St. 224; Dillon, Mun. Corp., § 932.

9 P. v. Albany, 11 Wend. 539; C. v. Proprietors, etc., 2 Gray, 339; C. v. Gloucester, 110 Mass. 491; Delaware, etc. Canal Co. v. C., 60 Pa. St. 367; C. v. Bredin, 165 Pa. St. 224; S. v. Portland, 74 Me. 268; S. v. Louisville, N. A. & C. R. Co., 86 Ind. 114; P. v. Detroit, etc. Works, 82 Mich. 471.

orderly house,[1] or for obstructing a public highway[2] or a navigable river.[3] So, a corporation may be criminally punished for libel,[4] or for violating the Sunday laws,[5] or the statute as to the sale of intoxicating liquors.[6] So, a corporation may be punished for contempt.[7]

§ 184. **Criminal intent.**— The numerous cases in which corporations have been held criminally liable show that such liability arises either from not doing that which it is made the duty of the corporation to do, or from doing that which it is authorized to do, but doing it in such manner as to constitute a violation of law. As a corporation can only act through its directors, officers, and agents, whose authority is limited to acts within the scope of the charter, and as a charter could not authorize directly the doing of an unlawful act, it is evident that there is a large class of crimes, including perhaps all the common-law felonies, that cannot be committed by a corporation because criminality is dependent upon the intent with which the criminal act is done. If murder, larceny, or assault and battery are committed by the officers or agents of a corporation, even though in the prosecution of the corporate business, such acts are the individual acts of the officers or agents and not the acts of the corporation, it being impossible that such acts could have been authorized, being necessarily *ultra vires*.[8] Thus, to render a corporation criminally liable, it must appear that the act was one authorized by the company and not the mere unauthorized act of the officer or agent.[9] If a statute imposes a penalty for knowingly and wilfully doing an act which the statute declares wrongful, as, for instance, wilfully

[1] S. v. Passaic County Agl. Soc'y, 54 N. J. 260.

[2] Northern Cent. R. Co. v. C., 90 Pa. St. 300; Susquehanna, etc. Turnpike Co. v. P., 15 Wend. 267; C. v. Vermont, etc. R. Co., 4 Gray, 22; C. v. Boston, etc. R. Co., 97 Mass. 555; S. v. Morris & E. R. Co., 23 N. J. 360; S. v. Western, etc. R. Co., 96 N. C. 602; Reg. v. Great N. of E. Ry., 9 Q. B. 315.

[3] S. v. Freeport, 43 Me. 198.

[4] S. v. Atchison, etc. R. Co., 3 Lea, 729.

[5] S. v. Baltimore, etc. R. Co., 15 W. Va. 362.

[6] Stewart v. Waterloo Turn Verein, 71 Ia. 226.

[7] U. S. ex rel. v. Memphis, etc. R. Co., 6 Fed. R. 237.

[8] Cumberland, etc. Canal Corp. v. Portland, 56 Me. 77; C. v. Proprietors, etc. Co., 2 Gray, 339, 345.

[9] S. v. Baltimore, etc. R. Co., 15 W. Va. 362. So an indictment must show the duty on the part of the corporation which is violated: S. v. Patton, 4 Ired. 16.

converting the property of another or knowingly employing children under a certain age in manufacturing establishments, it is not to be deemed directed against corporations, but against their officers or agents, who alone can knowingly and wilfully do the prohibited act.[1] But by statute in some states railroad corporations are made liable to fines for the benefit of the representatives of any person whose death is caused by the carelessness or negligence of their servants, and in such cases the proceeding is against the corporation.[2]

§ 185. Allegation and proof of corporate existence.— An indictment must, of course, aver the legal existence of the corporation;[3] but the want of corporate existence, if properly averred, must be raised by special plea. A plea of not guilty is an admission of the existence of the corporation.[4]

[1] Benson v. Manufacturing. Co., 9 Met. 562; Cumberland, etc. Canal Corp. v. Portland, 56 Me. 79; Androscoggin Water-power Co. v. Bethel Steam Mill Co., 64 Me. 441; C. v. Swift Run Gap Turnpike Co., 2 Va. Cas. 361.

[2] S. v. Maine Central R. Co., 81 Me. 84; C. v. Boston, etc. R. Co., 134 Mass. 211.

[3] S. v. Vermont Central R. Co., 28 Vt. 583.

[4] S. v. Western, etc. R. Co., 96 N. C. 602.

PART III.

CONNECTION WITH THE ACT.

CHAPTER 14.

AGENCY.

§ 186. **As affecting criminal liability.**—The general doctrine as to the liability of those who combine in the commission of crime is discussed elsewhere.[1] This chapter is limited to the consideration of the liability of principal and agent respectively for criminal acts done by the agent as such.

§ 187. **Principal's liability.**—The general maxim "*Qui facit per alium facit per se*" is applicable in criminal law to make one accountable for acts done for him by an agent under his instruction or by his consent.[2] And in regard to the liability of the principal it is wholly immaterial whether the act is procured to be done through a guilty or an innocent agent.[3] If the act is done through an innocent agent, the one who procures it to be done is guilty as principal, as though he had done the act himself.[4] But if the agent or servant through whom the act is done is guilty, the principal or master is deemed an accessory before the fact only, unless present.[5] But in misdemeanors there are no accessories, and one who procures the commission of such an offense through an agent is guilty thereof as though he had himself done the act.[6] In such cases the offense may be alleged as committed by the principal or

[1] *Infra*, § 195.

[2] Carey v. S., 83 Ind. 597; S. v. Wagster, 75 Mo. 107; S. v. Lichliter, 95 Mo. 402; S. v. Scoggins, 107 N. C. 959; Reg. v. Clifford, 2 C. & K. 202. The act of an innocent agent, for instance an irresponsible child, is not necessarily to be referred to a responsible person who is present rather than to one who is absent but has procured the doing of the act: S. v. Learnard, 41 Vt. 585.

[3] S. v. Basserman, 54 Conn. 88.

[4] C. v. Hill, 11 Mass. 136; Reg. v. Michael, 9 C. & P. 356; Rex v. Giles, 1 Moody, 166; Reg. v. Bannen, 1 C. & K. 295; Reg. v. Butcher, Bell, 6; Reg. v. Clifford, 2 C. & K. 202; Reg. v. Bleasdale, 2 C. & K. 765; Reg. v. Dowey, 11 Cox, 115.

[5] P. v. Lyon, 99 N. Y. 210. And see *infra*, § 207.

[6] C. v. Stevens, 10 Mass. 181; S. v. Fox, 16 N. J. 152; S. v. Morris, etc.

master and established by proof of the committing of the act through an agent or servant.[1] Thus, by means of an agent one may commit crime in another state or county than that in which he is at the time of its commission.[2]

§ 188. **Whether authority presumed.**— As a general proposition the principal or master is not criminally liable for acts of his agent or servant even though done in the general course of the employment, unless authorized or consented to by him, for authority to do a criminal act will not be presumed.[3] There are cases where the essence of the crime seems to be the unlawful carrying on of a business, in which the principal is held liable for the acts of his agent though done without his knowledge and consent. It is so held in regard to the sale of a libelous publication.[4] And in other cases the master has been held liable for his servant's improper acts in the conduct of the business, on the same principle;[5] for instance, where the business is so conducted as to create a nuisance.[6] In such cases direct proof of authority is not necessary, but it may be inferred by

R. Co., 23 N. J. 360; S. v. Brown, 31 Me. 520. And see *infra*, § 210.

[1] C. v. Hill, 11 Mass. 136; S. v. Hinckley, 38 Me. 21; C. v. Park, 1 Gray, 553; C. v. Gray, 150 Mass. 327. So held even where the statute made the sale of intoxicating liquors by any person or servant or agent punishable: S. v. Stewart, 31 Me. 515. And see *infra*, § 213.

[2] C. v. Gillespie, 7 Serg. & R. 469; C. v. Eggleston, 128 Mass. 408; Rex v. Brisac, 4 East, 164. And see *infra*, § 211.

[3] C. v. Stevens, 153 Mass. 421; Hipp v. S., 5 Blackf. 149; Sloan v. S., 8 Ind. 312; S. v. James, 63 Mo. 570; S. v. Smith, 10 R. I. 258; Rex v. Huggins, 2 Ld. Raym. 1574; Reg. v. Bennett, Bell, 1; Reg. v. Hutchinson, 9 Cox, 555. So held where, without knowledge of the proprietor, an employee in a drug store made an illegal sale, not being a registered pharmacist: S. v. Robinson, 55 Minn. 169. Even knowledge of the act will not render the principal liable if it was done without his consent: C. v. Putnam, 4 Gray, 16.

[4] C. v. Morgan, 107 Mass. 199: S. v. Mason, 26 Oreg. 273, 26 L. R. A. 779, and note; Rex v. Almon, 5 Burr. 2686; S. C., 1 Ben. & H. Lead. Cr. Cas. 145, and note; Rex v. Gutch, Moody & M. 433; Reg. v. Holbrook, 3 Q. B. D. 60, 4 id. 42.

[5] C. v. Gray, 150 Mass. 327; C. v. King, 1 Whart. 448; Hipes v. S., 73 Ind. 39; S. v. Dawson, 2 Bay, 360; Redgate v. Haynes, 1 Q. B. D. 89. So in cases of sale of adulterated milk: C. v. Vieth, 155 Mass. 442. If the servant in making bread use an improper amount of alum, so as to render the product unwholesome within statutory prohibition, the master is liable: Rex v. Dixon, 3 M. & S. 11. A penalty for smuggling may be enforced against the master although the act is done without his authority by the servant in prosecuting the master's business; Attorney-General v. Siddon, 1 Cromp. & J. 220.

[6] Reg. v. Stephens, L. R. 1 Q. B. 702.

the jury from the acts of the parties.[1] But the presumption is *prima facie* only, and may be rebutted by showing that the act of the agent or servant was contrary to his employer's directions.[2]

§ 189. Illegal sales of liquor by servant.— There has been difficulty in applying the principles of the preceding section in case of violation by a servant of the statutory regulations in regard to the sale of liquors. In general, if the business is being lawfully conducted, but the particular sale is contrary to the master's instruction and without his knowledge, the master will not be liable, although such sale was in violation of statutory regulations.[3] And it has been said in some of the cases that the burden of showing that the illegal sales were made by the servant with the authority or consent of the master is upon the prosecution.[4] In other cases it is said that there is a *prima facie* liability of the master for illegal sales by the servant.[5] But, even then, evidence that the act was forbidden by the master should be admitted.[6] The Massachusetts courts have held that proof of the illegal sales by the servant does not furnish even *prima facie* evidence of the sale by the master, but that it is simply a matter for the jury to consider in determining whether the sale was with the master's knowledge and consent.[7] Some cases, however, hold the master absolutely liable for an improper sale made by the servant in the conduct of the business, it being deemed the duty of the master to see that the business is lawfully conducted.[8] Of course, if the sale is made by the servant in the master's presence, the master is liable.[9]

[1] S. v. Foster, 23 N. H. 348.

[2] C. v. Nichols, 10 Met. 259; C. v. Park, 1 Gray, 553; P. v. Parks, 49 Mich. 333; Barnes v. S., 19 Conn. 398.

[3] C. v. Stevens, 153 Mass. 421; S. v. McGrath, 73 Mo. 181; S. v. Mahoney, 23 Minn. 181, 2 Am. Cr. R. 408; Lauer v. S., 24 Ind. 131; Stevenson v. S., 65 Ind. 409: S. v. Hays, 67 Ia. 27; Newman v. Jones, 17 Q. B. D. 132. So held as to illegal sales on Sunday: S. v. Burke, 15 R. I. 324. And as to allowing a minor in a room where liquors are sold: P. v. Hughes, 86 Mich. 180. And as to sales after hours: C. v. Wachendorf, 141 Mass. 270.

[4] C. v. Hayes, 145 Mass. 289; Parker v. S., 4 Ohio St. 563.

[5] S. v. Wentworth, 65 Me. 234; S. v. Reiley, 75 Mo. 521; S. v. O'Connor, 58 Minn. 193.

[6] S. v. Baker, 71 Mo. 475; Anderson v. S., 22 Ohio St. 305; Barnes v. S., 19 Conn. 398.

[7] C. v. Briant, 142 Mass. 463; C. v. Stevenson, 142 Mass. 466; C. v. Hayes, 145 Mass. 289.

[8] Carroll v. S., 63 Md. 551; S. v.

[9] Schmidt v. S., 14 Mo. 137; Hofner v. S., 94 Ind. 84; S. v. Scoggins, 107 N. C. 959.

§ 190. Liability of agent or servant.— One who, though acting as the agent or servant of another, professes to act for himself, will be held criminally accountable for his acts without regard to his agency.[1] But even if the agent or servant purports to act only for his principal or master, yet if he knowingly commits an offense, even by the direction of his superior, he is liable.[2] Indeed, in prosecutions for selling liquor without a license, it is said that the servant may be convicted if the master has not a license, without regard to whether the servant had knowledge of that fact or not.[3] And even where the statute makes clerks, servants, and agents equally liable with their principals, the agent need not be indicted as such but simply as principal.[4] So, an insurance agent may be criminally liable for soliciting insurance for a company not authorized as required by statute.[5] So, a deputy sheriff may be liable to indictment for neglect in the discharge of the duties of his office.[6] In general, the agent cannot be held to a higher degree of guilt than the principal who procured the act to be done would have incurred if the principal himself had committed the act.[7] Where the principal may lawfully do an act he may usually do it through an agent, and the agent will not be held criminally responsible for such act, though it would be criminal in him if he were doing it in his own right.[8] Where the manner of conducting a business is the offense, and the agent or servant con-

Denoon, 31 W. Va. 122; S. v. Kittelle, 110 N. C. 560; Martin v. S., 30 Neb. 507; Mullins v. Collins, L. R. 9 Q. B. 292. As to whether knowledge is necessary to warrant a conviction for illegal sales, see *supra*, § 128.

[1] C. v. Frost, 5 Mass. 53.

[2] C. v. Drew, 3 Cush. 279; C. v. Sinclair, 138 Mass. 493; C. v. Fisher, 138 Mass. 504; C. v. Burke, 114 Mass. 261; C. v. Dowling, 114 Mass. 259; S. v. Hoxsie, 15 R. I. 1; S. v. Marchant, 15 R. I. 539; S. v. Walker, 16 Me. 241; S. v. Sullivan, 83 Me. 417; S. v. McGuire, 64 N. H. 529; Delaware Div. Canal Co. v. C., 60 Pa. St. 367; Hays v. S., 13 Mo. 246; Elsberry v. S., 52 Ala. 8; P. v. Ackerman, 80 Mich. 588.

[3] S. v. Chastain, 19 Oreg. 176; C. v. Nickerson, 5 Allen, 518. But it is not correct to say as an absolute rule that one acting under authority from another must know that the other has the right to give it. So held in regard to violation by a servant of the owner as to handling stock of more than one brand: Wills v. S., 40 Tex. 69.

[4] P. v. Price, 74 Mich. 37.

[5] P. v. Howard, 50 Mich. 239.

[6] S. v. Berkshire, 2 Ind. 207.

[7] S. v. Haynes, 66 Me. 307.

[8] So held in regard to the taking of oysters by non-residents acting as servants for a resident, the law not allowing non-residents to take oysters: S. v. Conner, 107 N. C. 931.

trols or aids and assists in the regulation of the business, he may be liable as well as the principal.[1] But if the offense consists in maintaining a nuisance or otherwise using premises in an unlawful manner, one unlawful act of the kind done on the premises by a servant will not render him guilty, the offense of maintaining being that of the principal.[2]

§ 191. **Liability of partners.**— There can be no partnership in crime; but if the members of a partnership are connected in one joint criminal act, as keeping a gaming-house, making a joint assault, or the like, they may be indicted jointly or severally,[3] but they cannot both be convicted upon proof that one alone committed the offense, even though the partnership is shown.[4] If one partner, as agent for the firm and by agreement with the other members, does an act the fruits of which are shared by all, the other members become criminally liable therefor.[5] Indeed, where the business is one subject to regulation, and one partner conducts it unlawfully, all the partners may be rendered liable.[6] As the partners are joint owners of partnership property, there cannot be embezzlement thereof committed by one partner.[7]

§ 192. **Management of property.**— Cases somewhat analogous to those of agency, arising out of the management of the property of one by another, are to be determined on analogous principles. The lessor is not criminally liable for the acts of the lessee in managing the leased property, unless the statute especially so provides.[8] Nor is the lessee responsible for the acts of a contractor carrying on business on the premises without the lessee's control.[9] Where the general title to real property is in a trustee, the *cestui que trust* is not answerable for a nuisance, unless he is in some way directly connected therewith.[10]

1 C. v. Mann, 4 Gray, 213; C. v. Drew, 3 Cush. 279; C. v. Brady, 147 Mass. 583; Stout v. S., 93 Ind. 150.

2 C. v. Churchill, 136 Mass. 148; C. v. Galligan, 144 Mass. 171; C. v. Murphy, 145 Mass. 250; S. v. Gravelin, 16 R. I. 407.

3 S. v. Gay, 10 Mo. 440; S. v. Brown, 49 Vt. 437.

4 Stevens v. S. 14 Ohio, 386. The advancing of money by partners in a faro table is not indictable as the offense of betting under a statute: O'Blennis v. S., 12 Mo. 311. Further as to joinder of partners as defendants, see Barada v. S., 13 Mo. 94; S. v. Presbury, 13 Mo. 342.

5 S. v. Neal, 27 N. H. 131.

6 S. v. Wiggin, 20 N. H. 449.

7 S. v. Kusnick, 45 Ohio St. 535.

8 S. v. Coe, 72 Me. 456.

9 S. v. Emerson, 72 Me. 455.

10 P. v. Townsend, 3 Hill, 479.

CHAPTER 15.

COMBINATIONS; PRINCIPAL AND ACCESSORY.

I. IN GENERAL.
II. PRINCIPAL AND ACCESSORY.
III. PROCEDURE IN CASE OF ACCESSORIES.

I. IN GENERAL.

§ 193. **Act, as well as intent, essential.**— Although, as pointed out in a previous chapter,[1] the criminal intent is an essential element in crime, yet it is the criminal act which furnishes the foundation for criminal liability. Intent alone does not subject to criminal punishment. But one who procures an act to be done, or assists in doing it, may be properly punished therefor; and it is the purpose of this chapter to discuss the various ways in which one may become criminally liable by being connected more or less directly with the commission of an offense. Several distinct propositions are involved: First, the joint liability of all who participate in any way in doing the criminal act; second, the liability of those encouraging the crime, although not actually participating in the act; and third, the liability of those who assist the criminal in his attempts to evade the law after the crime has been committed. But some technical distinctions have, for historical reasons, found a place in this branch of the law which must be recognized and explained, although they interfere with the orderly presentation and logical treatment of the subject.

§ 194. **Participation necessary.**— Some degree of participation in the criminal act must be shown in order to establish any criminal liability. Proof that one has stood by at the commission of a crime, without taking any steps to prevent it, does not alone indicate such participation or combination in the wrong done as to show criminal liability,[2] although he ap-

[1] *Supra*, § 136.

[2] Connaughty v. S., 1 Wis. 159; Hilmes v. Stroebel, 59 Wis. 74; Brown v. Perkins, 1 Allen, 89; P. v.

proves of the act.[1] Even the fact of previous knowledge that a felony was intended will not render one who has concealed such knowledge, and is present at the commission of the offense, a party thereto.[2] But it may be inferred that one who is present and assents in the doing of an act from which he derives a benefit has procured it to be done;[3] and mere presence is a fact to go to the jury in connection with the other facts in the case as tending to show participation.[4] On the other hand, the fact that some benefit may have accrued to the accused from the doing of the wrongful act will not establish his liability, if he was absent at the time of the commission of the act. Thus, a sale of liquor in the prosecution of the business of the husband, made by the wife in his absence, will not establish the husband's criminal liability.[5] But the circumstances may show that in such case the wife was acting as the husband's agent and under his authority so as to render him liable.[6] The general doctrine as to liability of the principal for criminal acts of his agent has been already considered.[7] As presence with knowledge is not enough to show criminal liability, so previous knowledge without presence or encouragement will not be sufficient.[8] But here again evidence of privity in the plot to commit a crime may go to the jury as tending to show criminal participation.[9] As will be seen in subsequent sections, participation in the crime may be shown by evidence of entering into a combination to do the wrongful act, even though the

Woodward, 45 Cal. 293; P. v. Ah Ping, 27 Cal. 489; S. v. Farr, 33 Ia. 553; S. v. Cox, 65 Mo. 29; Butler v. C., 2 Duv. 435; Kemp v. C., 80 Va. 443; S. v. Hildreth, 9 Ired. 440; Wicks v. S., 44 Ala. 398; U. S. v. Jones, 3 Wash. C. C. 220; Burrell v. S., 18 Tex. 713; Jackson v. S., 20 Tex. Ap. 190; Floyd v. S., 29 id. 245; Sharp v. S., 29 id. 211; Rountree v. S., 10 id. 110; Foster, 350.

[1] Cabbell v. S., 46 Ala. 195; True v. C., 90 Ky. 651; Cooper v. Johnson, 81 Mo. 483.

[2] Noftsinger v. S., 7 Tex. Ap. 301; Rucker v. S., 7 Tex. Ap. 549; Smith v. S., 23 Tex. Ap. 357. So one who is present without approving, and subsequently assists in concealing the fact of the commission of the crime, is not a principal: White v. P., 81 Ill. 333.

[3] C. v. Stevens, 10 Mass. 181.

[4] Brown v. Perkins, 1 Allen, 89; Burrell v. S., 18 Tex. 713; Foster, 350.

[5] Pennybaker v. S., 2 Blackf. 484.

[6] C. v. Lafayette, 148 Mass. 130. And for a similar case as to violation of the revenue laws, see Attorney-General v. Riddle, 2 Cr. & J. 493.

[7] *Supra*, § 187.

[8] Melton v. S., 43 Ark. 367; Reg. v. Talfourd, 6 Cox, 333.

[9] Reg. v. Bernard, 1 F. & F. 240.

accused took no actual part, but without some evidence of such combination the accused can be held liable only for acts done or procured by him;[1] so if the evidence tends to show that one or the other of two persons committed the offense without any agreement or concert of action, but does not fasten the crime on either one beyond a reasonable doubt, neither can properly be convicted.[2]

§ 195. **Persons acting together.**— Two or more persons may combine to commit one criminal act, and each may be punished therefor as though the act were his alone.[3] Thus, all who participate in a criminal enterprise are equally guilty of the crime committed by one of their number in which the others, being present, either participate or are ready to assist.[4] And where there is a common enterprise, the presence of the accused at the actual commission of the offense which is contemplated is immaterial. All who take part in the enterprise are equally guilty, though the part which they take involves their absence from the place of actual commission of the offense with which they are charged;[5] and one who executes a distinct part of

[1] S. v. Westfall, 49 Ia. 328; Rex v. Isaacs, 1 Russ., C. & M. 63; Reg. v. Luck, 3 F. & F. 483. Evidence of motive and opportunity to commit the crime will not be sufficient in the absence of evidence connecting the accused personally with the act: Johnson v. C., 29 Grat. 796.

[2] P. v. Woody, 45 Cal. 289; Washington v. S., 16 Tex. Ap. 376; Reg. v. Turner, 4 F. & F. 339. But somewhat *contra*, see T. v. Yarberry, 2 N. Mex. 391. If two persons, without concert, inflict wounds consecutively, the last of which is fatal, the one inflicting the first wound is not guilty of murder: Jordan v. S., 79 Ala. 9.

[3] Dumas v. S., 62 Ga. 58; S. v. Brown, 49 Vt. 437; P. v. Weber, 66 Cal. 391; Jordan v. S., 82 Ala. 1; Mayhew v. Wardly, 14 C. B. (N. S.) 550.

[4] S. v. Gooch, 105 Mo. 392; S. v. Nelson, 98 Mo. 414; S. v. Murray, 126 Mo. 526; P. v. Cotta, 49 Cal. 166; P. v. Geiger, 49 Cal. 643; S. v. Rawles, 65 N. C. 334; S. v. Lucy, 41 Minn. 60; Holtz v. S., 76 Wis. 99; Smith v. P., 1 Colo. 121; T. v. Olsen, 6 Utah, 284; S. v. O'Neal, 1 Houst. Cr. C. 58; Dunman v. S., 1 Tex. Ap. 593; Sharp v. S., 6 Tex. Ap. 650; Reed v. S., 11 Tex. Ap. 587; Kirby v. S., 23 Tex. Ap. 13; Reg. v. Bird, 2 C. & K. 817; Reg. v. Bowen, Car. & M. 149; Reg. v. Sheppard, 9 C. & P. 121; Reg. v. Thompson, 11 Cox, 362; Reg. v. Whithorne, 3 C. & P. 394; Reg. v. Nezzell, 3 C. & K. 150.

[5] Mitchell v. C., 33 Grat. 845; C. v. Ahearn, 160 Mass. 300; Blaine v. S., 24 Tex. Ap. 626; Rex v. Skerritt, 2 C. & P. 427; Reg. v. Hornby, 1 C. & K. 305; Rex v. County, 2 Russ., C. & M. 230, 329; Reg. v. Greenwood, 2 Den. 453; Reg. v. Hurse, 2 M. & R. 360; Rex v. Standley, Russ. & Ry. 305; Reg. v. Kelly, 2 Cox, 171. Thus, in poaching, those who do not enter the premises are equally guilty with those who do, if they were engaged in the common enterprise: Rex v.

the criminal act, as the execution of part of a forged instrument, is chargeable with the entire crime, even though he does not know who does the other part.[1] This subject is further discussed in a subsequent section in regard to constructive presence of those charged as principals.[2] The rule does not depend in any way on the technical distinction between principal and accessory, but is a proposition founded on its own sound reason and the general principles involving the joint liability of all whose acts have a direct connection with the commission of the offense.[3] It is evident, however, that the liability in these cases depends on the combination or conspiracy to do the criminal act, and that, unless such connection with it can be shown, one of the parties is not responsible for acts done by the others.[4] Thus, though one person engages in a fight in which another commits murder, the one participating but not inflicting the fatal injury is not criminally responsible for the murder, if there is no prior conspiracy between the parties, or any incitement or encouragement of the overt act on his part.[5]

§ 196. Whether or not act contemplated in the original design.— It results from the principle stated in the preceding section that every one connected with carrying out a common design to commit a criminal act is concluded and bound by the act of any member of the combination perpetrated in the prosecution of the common design.[6] But it is not necessary that the crime committed shall have been originally intended. Each is accountable for all the acts of the others done in carrying out the common purpose, whether such acts were originally contemplated or not, if they were the natural and proximate result of carrying out such purpose;[7] and the question whether

Dowsell, 6 C. & P. 398; Rex v. Passey, 7 C. & P. 282; Reg. v. Whittaker, 2 C. & K. 636; Reg. v. Eaton, 2 Den. 274.

1 Rex v. Dade, 1 Moody, 307; Rex v. Kirkwood, 1 Moody, 304; Rex v. Bingley, Russ. & Ry. 446; S. v. Stutson, Kirby, 52; Sasser v. S., 13 Ohio, 453; S. v. Mix, 15 Mo. 153.

2 *Infra*, § 206.

3 As to the causal connection in cases of joint crime, see article by Dr. Wharton, 20 Cent. L. J. 3.

4 Wright v. S., 43 Tex. 170; S. v. Brewer, 109 Mo. 648; Reg. v. Cruse, 8 C. & P. 541; Reg. v. Lee, 4 F. & F. 63.

5 Woolweaver v. S., 50 Ohio St. 277; Goins v. S., 46 Ohio St. 457; P. v. Elder, 100 Mich. 515; S. v. White, 10 Wash. 611; S. v. Howard, 112 N. C. 859; S. v. Carson, 36 S. C. 524.

6 P. v. Olsen, 80 Cal. 122.

7 Pierson v. S., 99 Ala. 148; Turner v. S., 97 Ala. 57; Jolly v. S., 94 Ala. 19; Tanner v. S., 92 Ala. 1; Williams v. S., 81 Ala. 1; Martin v. S., 89 Ala.

the result is the natural and probable effect of the wrongful act intended is for the jury.[1] Thus, if several persons agree to commit and enter upon the commission of a crime involving danger to human life, such as robbery,[2] or assault and battery,[3] or resisting an officer,[4] or resisting arrest,[5] all are criminally accountable for death caused in the common enterprise. Thus, also, if the unlawful enterprise is likely to meet violent resistance, all will be liable for a felonious assault committed by one of their number in consequence of such resistance;[6] and if the common design in general involves acts of violence, all who participate in the common plan are equally answerable for acts of others done in pursuance thereof, although the result was not specially intended by them all.[7] If a conspiracy contemplates the destruction of human life and that result follows, all who are connected with the conspiracy, or any of the steps taken in carrying it out, will be responsible for the result, even though the object may not be effected in exactly the manner contemplated.[8] Even where the result is wholly unexpected, as, for instance, if there is a plot to murder one person by means of an explosive machine, and another person is accidentally killed by the explosion, all participating in the original conspiracy are accountable for the result.[9] The mere fact that by mistake injury falls on one not intended to be injured

115; Gibson v. S., 89 Ala. 121; Smith v. S., 88 Ala. 23; C. v. Glover, 111 Mass. 395; C. v. Campbell, 7 Allen, 541; S. v. Beebe, 17 Minn. 241; S. v. David, 4 Jones, 353; S. v. Johnson, 7 Oreg. 210; Green v. S., 51 Ark. 189; U. S. v. Boyd, 45 Fed. R. 851; Reg. v. Swindall, 2 C. & K. 230; 1 Hale, P. C. 441.

1 Spies v. P., 122 Ill. 1; Bowers v. S., 24 Tex. Ap. 542.

2 Boyd v. U. S., 142 U. S. 450; S. v. Barrett, 40 Minn. 77; Stephens v. S., 42 Ohio St. 150; Reg. v. Jackson, 7 Cox, 357. Even though the accused did not himself intend to take life and prohibited others from doing so: P. v. Vasquez, 49 Cal. 560.

3 Williams v. S., 81 Ala. 1; Peden v. S., 61 Miss. 267; Brennan v. P., 15 Ill. 511; S. v. Simmons, 6 Jones, 21; S. v. Maloy, 44 Ia. 104; S. v. Herdina, 25 Minn. 161.

4 S. v. Zeibart, 40 Ia. 169.

5 Moody v. S., 6 Coldw. 299; Huling v. S., 17 Ohio St. 583; Reg. v. McNaughten, 14 Cox, 576.

6 Hamilton v. P., 113 Ill. 34.

7 Williams v. S., 47 Ind. 568; Weston v. C., 111 Pa. St. 251; U. S. v. Ross, 1 Gall. 624; Reg. v. Harrington, 5 Cox, 231.

8 Spies v. P., 122 Ill. 1.

9 Reg. v. Bernard, 1 F. & F. 240. But the result may be so far disconnected from the act that those engaged in the original wrong will not be accountable. Thus, where accused engaged in a riot, and the death of an innocent person was caused by the firing of a pistol by the police engaged in the suppres-

by the wrong-doers will not excuse them from liability for the act done.[1] And even though the participation consists only in distributing inflammatory circulars, or publishing newspaper articles of that character, inciting others to a course of action the result of which would be homicide, such person is guilty of a homicide committed in consequence thereof.[2] In the cases cited in this section there has been either such a previous agreement or such combination in the acts done as to indicate on the part of the accused the intention that violence shall be used involving danger to life. And if there is such intention it is immaterial how trivial the wrong originally intended.[3] And probably if a felony is contemplated, a criminal homicide resulting in connection with the commission thereof is chargeable to all who conspire to commit the felony.[4] But if the unlawful act intended was a mere trespass or misdemeanor, the parties will not all be responsible for an unintended homicide committed by one of them in connection with the carrying out of the wrong intended.[5] In cases of prize-fighting it has been said that all who are present as spectators are indictable for an assault committed in the fight,[6] or even for death resulting to one of the combatants.[7] But the court of Queen's Bench was afterwards divided as to whether mere spectators were liable for an assault thus committed in a prize-fight, the majority holding that they could not be deemed to be aiding and abetting in the assault.[8] Certainly a mere stake-holder, having nothing to do with the fight, and having no reason to suppose that the life of a combatant would be imperiled, would not be liable for manslaughter on account of death having unexpectedly resulted from injuries received by such combat-

sion of the riot, it was held that the accused was not liable for the homicide: Butler v. P., 125 Ill. 641.

1 Wynn v. S., 63 Miss. 260; S. v. Greenwade, 72 Mo. 298.

2 Spies v. P., 122 Ill. 1. So the editor of a newspaper may be guilty of the statutory crime of encouraging or endeavoring to persuade persons to commit murder by reason of inflammatory articles published by him, although they are not addressed to any one in particular: Reg. v. Most, 7 Q. B. D. 244.

3 Ritzman v. P., 110 Ill. 362; Ruloff v. P., 45 N. Y. 213; Washington v. S., 36 Ga. 222.

4 Miller v. S., 25 Wis. 384; S. v. Beebe, 17 Minn. 241; S. v. Shelledy, 8 Ia. 477; Reg. v. Howell, 9 C. & P. 437.

5 Reg. v. Skeet, 4 F. & F. 931.

6 Rex v. Perkins, 4 C. & P. 537.

7 Rex v. Murphy, 6 C. & P. 103.

8 Reg. v. Coney, 8 Q. B. D. 534.

ant.[1] As indicated in a preceding section, there must be some evidence or combination or conspiracy to render one of the parties liable for acts of the others.[2] But the evidence of combination need not be direct and positive. Such combination may be shown from the circumstances connected with the transaction.[3] If, however, the injury is done by a person who is not co-operating with the accused, the accused will not be liable, although he was present at the time and engaged in the unlawful act.[4]

§ **197. Acts outside of original design.**— Those who participate in the original unlawful combination or conspiracy are not, however, liable for the acts of one of their number, who, independently and not in pursuance of the original plan, commits a crime.[5] Thus, all are not liable for unlawful acts done by one of the number after the purpose of the combination has been completed, or when he departs from the common plan to do a wrongful act of his own intention.[6] So, those who engage in a conspiracy to beat another will not be guilty of murder in a homicide committed by one of their number without the knowledge of the others and not in pursuance of the common plan, as, for instance, by the use of a deadly weapon when the use of a deadly weapon was not intended by the others.[7] So, if the combination is to commit burglary, one of the conspirators is not guilty of murder committed by another not contemplated in the plan nor committed in his presence.[8]

[1] Reg. v. Taylor, L. R. 2 C. C. 147.

[2] *Supra*, § 194. And see P. v. Leith, 52 Cal. 251; Rex v. Mastin, 6 C. & P. 396. Where a particular intent is essential to the crime, the one who assists must have knowledge of such intent to render him liable therefor: Wagner v. S., 43 Neb. 1.

[3] Miller v. Dayton, 57 Ia. 423; S. v. Lucas, 57 Ia. 501; S. v. Squaires, 2 Nev. 226; S. v. Mix, 15 Mo. 153; Tanner v. S., 92 Ala. 1; Pierson v. S., 99 Ala. 148; Taylor v. S., 9 Tex. Ap. 100; Blain v. S., 33 Tex. Ap. 236.

[4] Tharpe v. S., 13 Lea, 138; Brabston v. S., 68 Miss. 208 (disapproving Beets v. S., Meigs, 106); Rex v. Murphy, 6 C. & P. 103.

[5] P. v. Olsen, 80 Cal. 122; Watts v. S., 5 W. Va. 532; C. v. Drew, 4 Mass. 391; C. v. Nickerson, 5 Allen, 518; S. v. Lucas, 55 Ia. 321; P. v. Hooghkerk, 96 N. Y. 149; Rex v. Collison, 4 C. & P. 565.

[6] P. v. Knapp, 26 Mich. 112; Reg. v. Nickless, 8 C. & P. 757; Rex v. Hawkins, 3 C. & P. 392; Rex v. White, Russ. & Ry. 99.

[7] S. v. Hickam, 95 Mo. 322; Nye v. P., 35 Mich. 16; Brown v. S., 28 Ga. 199; Blain v. S., 30 Tex. Ap. 702; Turner v. S., 20 Tex. Ap. 56; Mercersmith v. S., 8 Tex. Ap. 211; Reg. v. Caton, 12 Cox, 624.

[8] Lamb v. P., 96 Ill. 73.

So, if the combination is to commit personal injury, one of the conspirators will not be liable for property wrongfully taken by another from the person of the party injured.[1]

§ 198. **Abandonment of original design.**— One of the parties to a combination to do an unlawful act may abandon the common purpose so as to relieve himself from liability for the acts subsequently done in pursuance thereof.[2] But such abandonment must be evidenced by some act or word calculated to apprise the other confederates of such intention.[3]

§ 199. **Accomplices; aiders and abettors.**— These terms are used in a loose way to indicate those who are not the principal actors in or instigators of the commission of the crime, but who, to some extent, assist in its commission, or encourage it beforehand.[4] The term "accomplice" is sometimes used as equivalent to accessory before the fact, hereafter to be considered.[5] An aider and abettor may be one who so far participates as to be present for the purpose of assisting if necessary, and in such case he will be liable as principal, as will hereafter appear.[6] The relation of aider and abettor does not refer especially, however, to the distinction hereafter made between principal and accessory.[7] Either an accomplice or an aider and abettor will in general be principal or accessory, depending upon whether he is present or absent when the crime is committed.[8] As already indicated, something more than mere presence, even accompanied with approval of the act done, is necessary to make one an aider and abettor. There must be some participation, either in the plan or its execution.[9] As is

[1] Duffy v. P., 26 N. Y. 588; Reg. v. Barnett, 2 C. & K. 594.

[2] S. v. Allen, 47 Conn. 121; Harris v. S., 15 Tex. Ap. 629.

[3] S. v. Allen, 47 Conn. 121; S. v. Gray, 55 Kan. 135; Phillips v. S., 26 Tex. Ap. 228; Rex v. Edmeads, 3 C. & P. 390.

[4] Thus, an indictment for maliciously shooting, and aiding and abetting therein, is defective: C. v. Patrick, 80 Ky. 605. So under a statute providing for the punishment of the principal only, an accomplice is not punishable: Stamper v. C., 7 Bush, 612.

[5] Smith v. S., 13 Tex. Ap. 507; Cook v. S., 14 Tex. Ap. 96; Allison v. S., 14 Tex. Ap. 122; O'Neal v. S., 14 Tex. Ap. 582; Ogle v. S., 16 Tex. Ap. 361

[6] Jordan v. S., 81 Ala. 20; Raiford v. S., 59 Ala. 106; S. ex rel. v. Tally, 102 Ala. 25; McCarty v. S., 26 Miss. 299; U. S. v. Henry, 4 Wash. C. C. 428; Green v. S., 13 Mo. 382. As to the whole subject of principal and accessory, see the subsequent sections of this chapter.

[7] U. S. v. Gooding, 12 Wheat. 460.

[8] Johnson v. S., 2 Ind. 652; Cross v. P., 47 Ill. 152.

[9] *Supra*, § 194.

suggested in a subsequent section,[1] consent to the crime on the part of the person injured sometimes prevents any criminal liability for the act. At any rate, the person upon whom the wrong is done cannot be deemed an accomplice. Thus, the woman upon whom an abortion is procured, or attempted, is not an accomplice in the crime.[2] So a person to whom liquor is illegally sold is not guilty of any offense.[3] These conclusions are not easily fitted into a general rule, but perhaps it may be safely said that where a penal statute is intended for the protection of a particular class of persons, one of that class does not become an accomplice by submitting to the injury, while another person, not of that class, by encouraging the wrong, may be guilty as an accomplice. Thus, where it was made criminal for slaves to sell liquor, a white person purchasing from a slave was held an accomplice in the crime.[4]

§ **200. What is sufficient procurement or participation.**— One who procures the crime to be committed is, of course, criminally liable therefor, though his liability may be termed that of an accessory rather than of a principal, as will hereafter be shown.[5] But direct procurement, in the sense of originating the design, is not essential. One who encourages the carrying out of the criminal plan is equally guilty with the one who plans and procures its execution;[6] and where one advises the

[1] *Infra*, § 202.

[2] C. v. Wood, 11 Gray, 85; C. v. Boynton, 116 Mass. 343; C. v. Drake, 124 Mass. 21; Dunn v. P., 29 N. Y. 523; S. v. Owens, 22 Minn. 238; S. v. Pearce, 56 Minn. 226. And see Ash v. S., 81 Ala. 76; S. v. Quinlan, 40 Minn. 55; Rex v. Jellyman, 8 C. & P. 604. As to corroboration of accomplice as witness, see *infra*, § 203.

[3] S. v. Cullins, 53 Kan. 100; Harney v. S., 8 Lea, 113. Therefore the purchaser may be compelled to testify as to such purchases: C. v. Willard, 22 Pick. 476; S. v. Rand, 51 N. H. 361; Wakeman v. Chambers, 69 Ia. 169.

[4] S. v. Bonner, 2 Head, 135 (distinguished in Harney v. S., 8 Lea, 113, cited above).

[5] U. S. v. Sykes, 58 Fed. R. 1000; P. v. Ryland, 97 N. Y. 126; S. v. Rucker, 93 Mo. 88; P. v. Ward, 85 Cal. 585; Rex v. Sawyer, 1 Russ., C. & M. 670; Rex v. Soares, 2 East, P. C. 974; Reg. v. Gaylor, Dears. & B. 288. Thus, the lessor of a house to be used for purposes of prostitution is guilty of keeping a disorderly house: P. v. Erwin, 4 Denio, 129; Troutman v. S., 49 N. J. 33. One who procures another to be inveigled out of the state is equally guilty with those who do the act: Hadden v. P., 25 N. Y. 373.

[6] Keithler v. S., 10 Sm. & M. 192; Reg. v. Manning, 2 C. & K. 887; Reg. v. Clayton, 1 C. & K. 128; Reg. v. Hollis, 28 L. T. 455. But to render one guilty by reason of acts or words of encouragement they must have been done or used with the intention of encouraging or abetting: Hicks v. U. S., 150 U. S. 442.

commission of a crime, the presumption is that the advising had the effect intended by the adviser, if the crime is committed accordingly, unless the contrary is shown.[1] Indeed, it is not essential that there should have been any direct communication between the adviser and principal criminal. It is enough if, through an intermediate agent, the commission of the crime is procured.[2] Nor is it essential that the aid or encouragement given was a necessary factor in the result, without which it would not have followed. It is enough if it facilitates the result, which might have been otherwise attained.[3] There may be criminal liability for inciting generally to the commission of the particular crime or crimes of that character, though no particular person is thus incited.[4] One who beforehand does some act intended to assist in the subsequent commission of a crime is liable therefor, though he was not present when the crime was committed,[5] and though no particular method of execution was agreed upon.[6] One who, after the commission of a crime, takes advantage thereof, or assists in disposing of the proceeds, may be an accessory after the fact, as will hereafter appear.[7] If a statute defining the offense is silent in regard to criminality for aiding or assisting therein, there may be liability on the part of the one who thus aids and assists, though he does not participate in the act itself.[8] Although manslaughter consists of a homicide not purposely or maliciously caused, yet

[1] C. v. Bowen, 13 Mass. 356; Thompson v. C., 1 Met. (Ky.) 13.

[2] Rex v. Cooper, 5 C. & P. 535.

[3] S. ex rel. v. Tally, 102 Ala. 25.

[4] Reg. v. Most, 7 Q. B. D. 244; Spies v. P., 122 Ill. 1.

[5] Reg. v. Tuckwell, Car. & M. 215. As, for instance, where one furnishes tools to a confederate with which to commit burglary, even though the tools are not actually used, provided the burglary is committed: S. v. Tazwell, 30 La. An., pt. II, 884. But where tools were conveyed into a jail to assist prisoners to escape, it was held that one who made use of such tools was not an accomplice in the crime of conveying the tools into the jail: Peeler v. S., 3 Tex. Ap. 533; Ash v. S., 81 Ala. 76.

[6] Griffith v. S., 90 Ala. 583; Ex parte Willoughby, 14 Nev. 451.

[7] Norton v. P., 8 Cow. 137; Minor v. S., 58 Ga. 551; House v. S., 16 Tex. Ap. 25; Rex v. King, Russ. & Ry. 332; Reg. v. Manning, Dears. 21. But the fact that the participation was only in disposing of the property does not prove that the accused was only an accessory after the fact. He may beforehand have procured or encouraged the commission of the crime, and in that way may be accessory before the fact, or even principal if, though not present, he did some act in the general plan of committing the crime: Conner v. S., 25 Ga. 515.

[8] U. S. v. Mills, 7 Pet. 138; U. S. v. Sykes, 58 Fed. R. 1000; C. v. Carter,

there may be an aider and abettor therein;[1] but not if the aider and abettor in the act which results, but was not intended to result, in a homicide, did not participate in any way in the use of a deadly weapon, and therefore had no knowledge of any intended wrong which would result in killing.[2] To incite to the commission of a crime may be in itself a crime, distinct from the crime committed.[3] Thus it is a misdemeanor to incite to the commission of a misdemeanor.[4]

§ **201. Detectives.**— One whose participation in the crime only as a detective, for the purpose of discovering and bringing to punishment the criminal, is not an accomplice, nor an aider and abettor, as he has not the criminal intent.[5] This subject has, however, been already discussed in the chapter relating to intent.[6]

§ **202. Consent to crime; particeps criminis.**— In discussing the subject of intent it has already appeared that, where the offense is against property, consent of the owner will prevent the injury thereto being criminal.[7] It will hereafter appear, in discussing homicide, mayhem, assault and other crimes that consent to serious physical injury cannot be given so as to deprive it of its criminal character. Where fraud is perpetrated, the fact that the person injured is a party to the fraud will deprive the transaction of its criminal character;[8] but where a fictitious check was given in payment of an illegal and immoral debt, it was held that the wrong on the part of the person defrauded would not prevent the punishment of the fraud.[9] This question must be discussed with reference to each crime as to which it may arise, and any general discussion would be superficial and inadequate.[10]

94 Ky. 527 (overruling Stamper v. C., 7 Bush, 612); Baker v. S., 12 Ohio St. 214; Rex v. Potts, Russ. & Ry. 353. *Contra*, S. v. Hendry, 10 La. An. 207.

[1] Hagan v. S., 10 Ohio St. 459. And see *infra*, § 208.

[2] Adams v. S., 65 Ind. 565.

[3] Reg. v. Brawn, 1 C. & K. 144; Reg. v. Quail, 4 F. & F. 1076.

[4] C. v. Hurley, 99 Mass. 433; Baker v. S., 12 Ohio St. 214. And as to incitement or solicitation as an attempt, see *infra*, § 220.

[5] C. v. Hollister, 157 Pa. St. 13; Harrington v. S., 36 Ala. 236; Williams v. S., 55 Ga. 391; S. v. Brownlee, 84 Ia. 473; Reg. v. Bannen, 1 C. & K. 295; Reg. v. Johnson, Car. & M. 218.

[6] *Supra*, § 117.

[7] *Supra*, § 118.

[8] McCord v. P., 46 N. Y. 470.

[9] Dunn v. P., 4 Colo. 126.

[10] A general discussion may be found in 1 Whart. Cr. L., §§ 141–150; 1 Bish. Cr. L., §§ 258–263.

§ 203. **Acts or declarations of accomplices or confederates.**— Under the principle that all who participate in the commission of an offense, either by way of procurement or encouragement, or by doing acts in carrying out the criminal purpose, are accountable therefor,[1] it is held that the acts or declarations of one of the parties combining to commit the offense may be shown as against the others so far as such acts or declarations were done or made in the prosecution of the common plan.[2] But this is a matter of evidence rather than of substantive law. On the other hand, it is a general rule of evidence that the testimony of an accomplice will not warrant conviction without corroboration.[3]

II. PRINCIPAL AND ACCESSORY.

§ 204. **Distinction.**— There is a technical distinction between different methods of participation in crime which depends on historical rather than on logical reasons, and therefore is difficult to explain as conformable to any rational analysis of the subject. The early idea of classification was to designate those as principals in a felony who committed the overt act, while those who were present aiding and abetting were deemed accessories at the fact, and those who, not being present, had advised or encouraged the perpetration of the crime, were deemed accessories before the fact.[4] There was also the relation to the crime of accessory after the fact, which will be explained hereafter. But the accessory at the fact was deemed equally guilty with the principal, and came to be called a principal in the second degree;[5] so that the relations to be here

[1] *Supra*, § 195.

[2] S. v. Soper, 16 Me. 293; S. v. Myers, 19 Ia. 517; S. v. Phillips, 117 Mo. 389; Smith v. S., 46 Ga. 298; P. v. Stanley, 47 Cal. 113; P. v. Lane, 101 Cal. 513; S. v. Thaden, 43 Minn. 253; Baker v. S., 7 Tex. Ap. 612; Heard v. S., 9 Tex. Ap. 1; Post v. S., 10 Tex. Ap. 598.

[3] An accessory after the fact is not an accomplice in such sense as to require corroboration: Lowery v. S., 72 Ga. 649; Allen v. S., 74 Ga. 769; S v. Umble, 115 Mo. 452; P. v. Chadwick, 7 Utah, 134. *Contra*, Chumley v. S., 28 Tex. Ap. 87; Polk v. S., 36 Ark. 117. Where the witness' relation to the crime constitutes a substantive offense and not merely the relation of accessory after the fact, corroboration is not required: Harris v. S., 7 Lea, 124. The woman upon whom an abortion is procured or attempted is not an accomplice in such sense as to require corroboration: *Supra*, § 199.

[4] Usselton v. P., 149 Ill. 612.

[5] Accessories at the fact in murder

discussed are those of principal in the first and second degree, accessory before the fact, and accessory after the fact. But it must be carefully noticed in the first place that these terms do not necessarily indicate differing degrees of criminality. The principal in the first degree and in the second degree are guilty of the same crime and subject to the same punishment;[1] and this is also true as to accessory before the fact and principal.[2] The distinction is based entirely upon technical reasons, and not upon any inherent difference in moral accountability.[3] In the second place, this distinction is not based on the difference between simply procuring another to commit a felony and actually doing the criminal act; for one who not only procures but assists in the preliminary preparations does not thereby become principal, while one who only advises or encourages will be a principal in the second degree if present. The distinction between principal and accessory before the fact is this: The principal is the one who actually does the criminal act or participates in the doing of it, whether actually or only constructively present, or who is actually present at the doing of it, aiding and abetting; while the accessory is one who has such connection with the crime, by reason of preparation, procurement, advice, or encouragement, as to be deemed criminally liable therefor, but does not participate in the final commission of the crime and is not present thereat.[4]

§ **205. Principals in first and second degree.**— No further description of the principal in the first degree, being the person who directly commits the criminal act, is necessary, but it is important to consider some questions with reference to who is principal in the second degree. To constitute this form of connection with the offense, the accused must have been present when the offense was committed,[5] although, as will be seen

are principals: S. v. Arden, 1 Bay, 487.

[1] Brown v. S., 28 Ga. 199.

[2] Nuthill v. S., 11 Humph. 247; Freel v. S., 21 Ark. 212.

[3] Usselton v. P., 149 Ill. 612.

[4] Warden v. S., 24 Ohio St. 143; S. v. Larkin, 49 N. H. 39; S. v. Clarke, 33 N. H. 329; P. v. Trim, 39 Cal. 75; P. v. Gassaway, 28 Cal. 404; Wicks v. S., 44 Ala. 398; Able v. C., 5 Bush, 698; Albritton v. S., 32 Fla. 358; Hately v. S., 15 Ga. 346; S. v. Maxent, 10 La. An. 743; Bean v. S., 17 Tex. Ap. 60; Reg. v. Jeffries, 3 Cox, 85; Rex v. Stewart, Russ. & Ry. 363; Rex v. Davis, Russ. & Ry. 113; Rex v. Kelly, Russ. & Ry. 421; Rex v. Badcock, Russ. & Ry. 249; Rex v. Soares, 2 East, P. C. 974.

[5] U. S. v. Holland, 3 Cranch, C. C. 254; U. S. v. Wilson, Bald. 78, 103;

in the next paragraph, this presence may be constructive. Mere presence, however, is not enough without some form of participation.[1] But those who, being present, aid and abet, or are present for that purpose, although they actually do no wrongful act whatever, are principals in the second degree.[2] It seems not to be very well settled just what amount of participation will make the person who is present principal in the first degree, rather than in the second degree, and the point is not of importance, inasmuch as there is no distinction whatever, either in the guilt or in the method of procedure, between the two.[3] As will be seen in a subsequent section, an indictment of a principal in the second degree as principal simply is sufficient, and will authorize his conviction.[4] But certainly one who is present and actually renders assistance in the commission of the crime is principal in the first degree.[5]

§ 206. **Constructive presence.**— It has already been stated in this chapter[6] that one who participates in the crime, by way of preparation, is guilty thereof even though not present at its commission. But if he does not participate in the final criminal act, he is deemed accessory rather than principal. If, however, he takes some part in the criminal act itself, then, though he is not personally present, he is said to be constructively present and a principal in the first degree; and it is not necessary that the part he thus takes be an active one, if in the carrying out of the final criminal act he is participating in the common plan by doing something, or being ready to do something, in furtherance thereof, at a place other than that where the act is consummated.[7] It is not necessary that accused shall

Rex v. Manners, 7 C. & P. 801; Reg. v. Hurse, 2 M. & Rob. 360; Reg. v. Jones, 9 C. & P. 761.

[1] Clem v. S., 33 Ind. 418; Wade v. S., 71 Ind. 535. And see *supra*, § 194.

[2] C. v. Stevens, 10 Mass. 181; C. v. Chapman, 11 Cush. 422; C. v. Roberts, 108 Mass. 296; Blackburn v. S., 23 Ohio St. 146; State v. Gorham, 55 N. H. 152; S. v. McGregor, 41 N. H. 407; S. v. Valwell, 66 Vt. 558; Washington v. S., 68 Ga. 570; C. v. Carter, 94 Ky. 527; S. v. Putnam, 18 S. C. 175; Alterberry v. S., 56 Ark. 515; Thomas v. S., 43 Ark. 149; S. v. Ellis, 12 La. An. 390; Rex v. Royce, 4 Burr. 2073; Reg. v. Cuddy, 1 C. & K. 210; Reg. v. Young, 8 C. & P. 644; Reg. v. McPhane, Car. & M. 212; Rex v. Dyson, Russ. & Ry. 523; Rex v. Potts, Russ. & Ry. 353.

[3] S. v. Davis, 29 Mo. 391.

[4] *Infra*, § 213.

[5] S. v. Hollenscheit, 61 Mo. 302.

[6] *Supra*, §§ 195, 200.

[7] Tate v. S., 6 Blackf. 110; Stipp v. S., 11 Ind. 62; Green v. S., 13 Mo. 382; C. v. Harley, 7 Met. 462; Trim

have been in sight or hearing of those who committed the crime, in order to render him a principal, if he participated in the common design.[1] For instance, one who keeps surveillance over the owner of the property, and endeavors to keep him away from the place of the crime, is constructively present;[2] or one who in robbery stays outside of the building on guard;[3] or one who is near by for the purpose of assisting in carrying away the property stolen.[4] Where the agent of a railroad company stayed away from his post of duty in order to facilitate the stealing of property from the company, he was held to be a principal.[5]

§ **207. Accessory before the fact.**—The preceding discussion as to what is such instigation or procurement as to render one punishable for an act which he does not directly commit,[6] and as to the distinction between principal and accessory,[7] has substantially covered the ground as to who are to be deemed accessories before the fact. But some questions still remain for elucidation. It will be apparent from the preceding discussion that guilt as an accessory presupposes the existence of a guilty principal, and this furnishes the reason for the rule to be hereafter stated, that one charged as accessory cannot be convicted until the conviction of the principal.[8] If one procures the doing of a criminal act through an innocent agent, though he may not be present at the time the act is done, he

v. C., 18 Grat. 983; S. v. Hamilton, 13 Nev. 386; S. ex rel. v. Tally, 102 Ala. 25; S. v. Douglass, 34 La. An. 523; Berry v. S., 4 Tex. Ap. 492; Phillips v. S., 26 Tex. Ap. 228; Truitt v. S., 8 Tex. Ap. 148; Welsh v. S., 3 Tex. Ap. 413; U. S. v. Boyd, 45 Fed. R. 851; Reg. v. Kelly, 2 C. & K. 379; Rex v. Jordan, 7 C. & P. 432; Rex v. Gogerly, Russ. & Ry. 343; Reg. v. Moland, 2 Moody, 276; Reg. v. Murphy, 6 Cox, 340; Rex v. Passey, 7 C. & P. 282.

[1] McCarney v. P., 83 N. Y. 408; Williams v. P., 54 Ill. 422; Spies v. P., 122 Ill. 1.

[2] Breese v. S., 12 Ohio St. 146.

[3] Stephens v. S., 42 Ohio St. 150.

[4] C. v. Lucas, 2 Allen, 170; Selvidge v. S., 30 Tex. 60; Rex v. Owen, 1 Moody, 96. In Texas it has even been held that one who participated in the original plan, and afterwards assisted in another state or county in disposing of the property, was principal: Sutton v. S., 16 Tex. Ap. 490; Scales v. S., 7 Tex. Ap. 361; McKeen v. S., 7 Tex. Ap. 631. But subsequent assistance without any participation in the intent to commit the crime itself will not render one a principal: Walker v. S., 29 Tex. Ap. 621.

[5] S. v. Poynier, 36 La. An. 572.

[6] *Supra*, § 200.

[7] *Supra*, § 204.

[8] *Infra*, §§ 215, 216.

is principal and not accessory;[1] while if a felony is committed through a guilty agent, the one who causes it to be committed is accessory only, and must be indicted as such.[2] Moreover, if the principal in a transaction is not criminally liable under the laws of the jurisdiction where the act is done, another person cannot be guilty of crime in aiding and abetting the doing of such act, unless he has himself done an act rendering him criminally liable as principal.[3] In general, one cannot be indicted for counseling another to commit a felony, unless the felony is actually committed.[4] So in cases of suicide, the one who incites another to the commission of a suicide is not guilty in the suicide committed in pursuance of such instigation, for there is no guilty principal, and there cannot, therefore, be an accessory.[5]

§ 208. **Accessory in manslaughter.**—Although manslaughter is a form of homicide in which the killing is usually not intended, yet it is held in some cases that there may be such connection, on the part of an accessory before the fact, with the wrongful act which is intended and which causes death in its perpetration, that the accessory, as well as the principal, will be guilty.[6] There is venerable authority, however, for the proposition that there can be no accessories in manslaughter;[7] and while it has been attempted to limit these statements to manslaughter of the character generally known as involuntary, and to argue that there may be an accessory before the fact to some forms of homicide committed without malice aforethought — for instance, where death results, unintended, from a criminal act not amounting to a felony, which act defendant procured or encouraged the commission of, not being present,[8]—

[1] S. v. Wyckoff, 31 N. J. 65. Thus, a person in one jurisdiction may, by means of an innocent agent, be principal in the commission of a crime in another jurisdiction, and may be there punished if his presence can be secured: P. v. Adams, 3 Denio, 190; C. v. Hill, 11 Mass. 136. Further as to liability for crime committed in another jurisdiction, see *infra*, § 211.

[2] P. v. Lyon, 99 N. Y. 210.

[3] U. S. v. Libby, 1 Woodb. & M. 221.

[4] Reg. v. Gregory, L. R. 1 C. C. 77.

[5] Reg. v. Leddington, 9 C. & P. 79; Rex v. Russell, 1 Moody, 356; Reg. v. Fretwell, 9 Cox, 152.

[6] Hagan v. S., 10 Ohio St. 459; P. v. Newberry, 20 Cal. 439; Brown v. S., 28 Ga. 199; Freel v. S., 21 Ark. 212; S. v. Coleman, 5 Port. 32; S. v. Robinson, 12 Wash. 349.

[7] Bibithe's Case, 4 Coke, 43, b; 1 Hale, P. C. 437.

[8] Reg. v. Gaylor, Dears. & B. 288; S. v. Hermann, 117 Mo. 629 (over-

yet it is doubtful if there is any case directly holding that there can be a conviction of manslaughter under such circumstances. Of course one who is present, aiding and abetting, though without participation in the act, may be guilty of the manslaughter,[1] and that seems to be practically all that is decided in the cases cited to the first note under this section. Perhaps under statutes making accessories guilty as principals the result might be different.[2] If the person charged as accessory did not aid and abet in any act tending to imperil life, it would seem that he should not be held guilty of the homicide.[3]

§ **209. Accessory after the fact.**— One who is not connected with the crime until after its commission cannot in general be punished as principal.[4] But the common law recognizes guilt on the part of one who, after the commission of the felony, assists the felon to escape punishment, and the person occupying this relation to the crime is called an accessory after the fact to that crime; but the wife of the felon is said not to be guilty in rendering such assistance to her husband.[5] The theory of liability of accessory after the fact is undoubtedly that he is guilty of the crime committed by the felon, and punishable therefor.[6] But the principal cannot at the same time be deemed an accessory after the fact; if he is present at the commission of the crime he would at least be principal in the second degree and not an accessory.[7] To render one an accessory after the fact it must appear a felony had been com-

ruling S. v. Phillips, 117 Mo. 389, where there is a *dictum* the other way. But the statement in the Hermann case is also *dictum*, for the accused was present, and was therefore principal and not accessory). A question somewhat analogous arises as to assaults with intent to commit manslaughter (*infra*, § 278), but the absence of the accessory makes a manifest distinction.

[1] Stipp v. S., 11 Ind. 62; Goff v. Prime, 26 Ind. 196; Rex v. Murphy, 6 C. & P. 103.

[2] S. v. Hermann, 117 Mo. 629.

[3] Adams v. S., 65 Ind. 565; Reg. v. Caton, 12 Cox, 624.

[4] P. v. Sligh, 48 Mich. 54; Rex v. McMakin, Russ. & Ry. 333, n.; Rex v. Dyer, 2 East, P. C. 767.

[5] 1 Hawk. P. C., ch. 1, § 10. By Texas statute relatives in the direct line of consanguinity or affinity cannot be accessories: Gray v. S., 24 Tex. Ap. 611.

[6] Long v. S., 1 Swan, 287; S. v. Payne, 1 Swan, 383; S. v. Reed, 85 Mo. 194; Reg. v. Richards, 2 Q. B. D. 311; Rex v. Greenacre, 8 C. & P. 35; Reg. v. Munday, 2 F. & F. 170; Rex v. Morris, 2 East, P. C. 748.

[7] P. v. Chadwick, 7 Utah, 134; Reg. v. Perkins, 2 Den. 459.

pleted, that the accused had knowledge of the guilt of the felon, and that he received, relieved, comforted, or assisted him.[1] Thus, if it appears that no felony was actually committed,[2] or that it was not completed at the time the assistance was rendered, the accused is not punishable as accessory after the fact to such felony.[3] The mere concealment of the crime, or failure to take any steps to apprehend the felon, will not constitute one an accessory after the fact.[4] There must be a harboring of the criminal, or aid and assistance furnished to him with a view to assist him in escaping from justice.[5] But the rendering of assistance of that kind, either by accused or by another through his procurement, will be sufficient to constitute guilt.[6] Such assistance must be rendered, however, with knowledge of the commission of the crime.[7] As to whether at common law the receiving and aiding in concealing or disposing of property procured by larceny or robbery would render the one thus assisting an accessory after the fact to the felony seems not to have been well settled under the common-law authorities, but there are some cases which indicate that this was deemed a sufficient connection with the crime to establish the common-law liability;[8] there are, however, cases to the contrary.[9] But receiving stolen goods is generally punishable as a substantive offense.[10] There cannot, of course, be an accessory after the fact unless there is a guilty principal.[11] The

[1] Wren v. C., 26 Grat. 952; Tully v. C., 11 Bush, 154.

[2] Poston v. S., 12 Tex. Ap. 408.

[3] Harrel v. S., 39 Miss. 702. In this case accused was charged as accessory after the fact to murder, but it appearing that the supposed deceased had not yet died from the injuries received at the time the assistance was rendered to the assailant, it was held that accused was not guilty as accessory after the fact to the murder, though he might have been guilty in occupying that relation to the crime of assault with intent to kill.

[4] S. v. Hann, 40 N. J. 228; Carroll v. S., 45 Ark. 539; Green v. S., 51 Ark. 189.

[5] Reg. v. Chapple, 9 C. & P. 355.

[6] Blakely v. S., 24 Tex. Ap. 616; Rex v. Jarvis, 2 M. & Rob. 40; Rex v. Lee, 6 C. & P. 536; Reg. v. Smith, L. R. 1 C. C. 266.

[7] S. v. Davis, 14 R. I. 281; Robbins v. S., 33 Tex. Ap. 573; Rex v. Greenacre, 8 C. & P. 35; Reg. v. Butterfield, 1 Cox, 39.

[8] Reg. v. Butterfield, 1 Cox, 39. At least this was made so by English statute (3 W. & M., ch. 9, §§ 4 and 5; Ann, ch. 31, § 5): 1 Hawk. P. C. 232.

[9] P. v. Shepardson, 48 Cal. 189; S. v. Calvin, 22 N. J. 207; Rex v. Morris, 2 East, P. C. 748.

[10] *Infra*, § 218. And in general as to receiving stolen goods, see *infra*, § 713.

[11] Edwards v. S., 80 Ga. 127.

general rules hereafter stated as to the necessity of a conviction of the principal before the trial or conviction of the accessory, are applicable to accessories after the fact as well as to accessories before the fact. The indefiniteness of the law as to accessory after the fact is largely due to the interference of legislation, which has made substantive crimes out of the receiving of stolen goods, the assisting of felons to escape, etc., which may at common law have been deemed sufficient to justify a conviction for the felony of one related thereto as accessory after the fact. Moreover, English statutes took away benefit of clergy in many cases from principals and accessories before the fact, and left accessories after the fact entitled to this privilege, which amounted substantially to an exemption from punishment; and finally the whole theory on which an accessory after the fact was deemed guilty of the felony committed is repugnant to enlightened views of criminal liability and has fallen into disuse; and it may be stated as the present law, both in England and the United States, that one who harbors or assists the felon, or aids him in disposing of the fruits of the crime, is punishable only as his case comes within the description of some substantive offense created by statute.[1]

§ 210. Crimes in which accessories not recognized.—The distinction between principal and accessory is peculiar to felonies. In misdemeanors, those who, if the offense had been a felony, would be deemed accessories before the fact, are considered simply as principals, presence or absence at the time of the commission of the offense being immaterial.[2] And it seems that this is also true in petit larceny, though at common law it was a felony.[3] It is important to notice that the doctrine that there are no accessories before the fact in misdemeanors

[1] 1 Bish. Cr. L., § 692 et seq.

[2] C. v. Harrington, 3 Pick. 26; C. v. Ray, 3 Gray, 441; C. v. Brockway, 150 Mass. 322; C. v. Ahearn, 160 Mass. 300; S. v. Murdoch, 71 Me. 454; P. v. Erwin, 4 Denio, 129; Stratton v. S., 45 Ind. 468; S. v. Gurnee, 14 Kan. 111; Wagner v. S., 43 Neb. 1; Williams v. S., 20 Miss. 58; S. v. Westfield, 1 Bailey, 132; Whitaker v. English, 1 Bay, 15; Curlin v. S., 4 Yerg. 143; Atkins v. S., 95 Tenn. 474; U. S. v. Gooding, 12 Wheat. 460; U. S. v. Sykes, 58 Fed. R. 1000; U. S. v. Snyder, 14 Fed. R. 554; U. S. v. Williams, 1 Cranch, C. C. 174; Reg. v. Waudby, 2 Q. B. D. (1895) 482; Reg. v. Greenwood, 2 Den. 453; Reg. v. Clayton, 1 C. & K. 128; Reg. v. Whittaker, 1 Den. 310.

[3] Ward v. P., 6 Hill, 144; S. v. Fox, 94 N. C. 928; U. S. v. Holland, 3 Cranch, C. C. 254; 12 Coke R. 81; 2 Inst. 183.

does not mean that there is no criminal liability for procuring or instigating the commission of the offense, but that on the other hand there is such liability wherever the procurement or instigation has a causal connection with the commission of the crime under the principles heretofore discussed;[1] the only difference, so far as it appears, between a felony and misdemeanor in this respect, being that the technical distinction recognized in felonies between the presence and the absence of the accused at the commission of the act is not noticed in cases of misdemeanor.[2] It is also said that there can be no accessories after the fact in a misdemeanor;[3] but this does not mean that accessories after the fact to a misdemeanor are deemed principals, but on the contrary they are not guilty of any offense,[4] unless, of course, of some substantive crime described by statute. The text-books also say that no accessories are recognized in treason,[5] thus coupling the highest and the lowest grades of offenses, and this statement is repeated in some of the cases,[6] but there do not seem to be direct adjudications illustrative of the doctrine.

III. Procedure as to Accessories.

§ 211. Jurisdiction and venue.— The general proposition that one who commits a crime is amenable therefor in the jurisdiction where it is committed disposes of most of the cases in which the question of jurisdiction has arisen. Thus, if a person in one state or country, by means of an innocent agent, causes a crime to be committed in another state or country, he thereby violates the law of the jurisdiction where the act is done by

[1] *Supra*, § 200.

[2] It is said in C. v. Ahearn, 160 Mass. 300, that there may be exceptions to this rule, and reference is made to 1 Bish. Cr. L., § 657, and 1 Whart. Cr. L., § 225. But no adjudications have been found which justify the statement of any distinction. It is doubtless true, however, as suggested in the authorities cited, that the instigation or procurement deemed sufficient to constitute guilt must be more closely related to the commission of the act in case of petty misdemeanors than where the crime is one of greater magnitude.

[3] C. v. Macomber, 3 Mass. 254; C. v. Barlow, 4 Mass. 439.

[4] 12 Coke R. 81; Ward v. P., 6 Hill, 144.

[5] 1 Hale, P. C. 133; 1 Hawk. P. C., ch. 17, § 39; Foster, 213; 4 Bl. Com. 35; 1 Bish. Cr. L., § 681; 12 Coke R. 81; 2 Inst. 183; 3 id. 138.

[6] Whitaker v. English, 1 Bay, 15; Chanet v. Parker, 1 Mill, Const. 333; C. v. Ahearn, 160 Mass. 300.

the innocent agent, and may be tried and punished there if the court can acquire jurisdiction of his person, just as he would be amenable to punishment if the crime had been accomplished by putting in motion some material force not involving the intervention of any independent human agency.[1] In cases of misdemeanor all the participants in the crime being deemed principal whether present or absent,[2] those who take part in the common enterprise resulting in the commission of a misdemeanor are guilty thereof in the jurisdiction where the misdemeanor is committed.[3] In cases of conspiracy, conspirators who are absent from the state are guilty of the conspiracy with those who carry it out in the jurisdiction where it is executed;[4] and, in general, all who may be charged as principals in the offense are punishable for the crime in the jurisdiction where it is committed.[5] But where the relation to the crime is that of accessory and not of principal, some courts hold that the jurisdiction is in the state or county where the acts were done, constituting the accused an accessory, and not where the crime was committed with which he is charged as being accessory.[6] It is insisted, however, that this doctrine is founded on an improper conception or application of the common-law rule as to venue in cases of accessories, to be explained in the latter part of this section, and should not be followed in determining the question of jurisdiction; but that all who are guilty of the crime, whether in the relation of principal or accessory, are amenable to punishment where the crime is committed.[7] As the English cases usually referred to in this connection are nearly all cases in which the question is between different counties in England, they bear on the question of venue rather than that of jurisdic-

[1] P. v. Adams, 3 Denio, 190; P. v. Rathbun, 21 Wend. 509; Noyes v. S., 41 N. J. 418; S. v. Chapin, 17 Ark. 561; C. v. Pettes, 114 Mass. 307; C. v. Hill, 11 Mass. 136; Rex v. Brisac, 4 East, 164; Reg. v. Garret, Dears. 232; Foster, 349; 1 Chitty, Cr. L. 191.

[2] *Supra*, § 210.

[3] C. v. Eggleston, 128 Mass. 408; C. v. Gillespie, 7 Serg. & R. 469; Barkhamsted v. Parsons, 3 Conn. 1; Duckett v. S., 93 Ga. 415.

[4] C. v. Gillespie, 7 Serg. & R. 469; Noyes v. S., 41 N. J. 418.

[5] S. v. Hamilton, 13 Nev. 386; Sutton v. S., 16 Tex. Ap. 490; Scales v. S., 7 Tex. Ap. 361; Berry v. S., 4 Tex. Ap. 492; Bybee v. S., 4 Tex. Ap. 505; Carlisle v. S., 31 Tex. Ap. 537; Rex v. Andrews, 2 M. & Rob. 37.

[6] Noyes v. S., 41 N. J. 418; S. v. Chapin, 17 Ark. 561; S. v. Moore, 26 N. H. 448.

[7] S. v. Grady, 34 Conn. 118; 1 Bish. Cr. L., § 111.

tion between independent sovereignties, and throw but little light on the ques...on; and the position taken in the note last above seems to be reasonable and essential to the administration of justice, for clearly there can be no adequate prosecution of the accessory in the foreign jurisdiction in which his accessorial acts are done. If the crime is in the same jurisdiction as that in which the accused became accessory, though in another county, the situation is quite different. The question is then one of venue only, which may be settled by statute. It is true that in England it was thought at one time that if the accused became accessory to a crime in a different county from that in which the crime was committed, he could be indicted in neither.[1] But there seems to have been a difference of opinion on this question;[2] at any rate the difficulty was settled by statute,[3] which provided that the crime of the accessory might be inquired into in the county where his acts as accessory were done; and there are statutes in the various states making the accessory punishable in accordance with the English statute, in the county where he acts, or in accordance with a more liberal and effectual policy, either in the county where the accessorial act is done, or in the county where the crime itself is committed.[4]

§ 212. **Indictment; joinder.**— The general rules of procedure in criminal cases authorize joinder in one indictment of all who are criminally liable for the crime charged. As applicable to principals there is no question as to the correctness of such practice, the rule being the general one of procedure.[5] So an accessory before the fact may be charged in the same count with the principal, the facts making him an accessory being alleged in addition to the facts showing the commission of the crime by the principal;[6] and where the accessory is

[1] 1 Hale, P. C. 623.

[2] 1 East, P. C. 362.

[3] 2 & 3 Edward 6, ch. 24; 1 Hale, P. C. 623.

[4] P. v. Hodges, 27 Cal. 340; Tully v. C., 13 Bush, 142; S. v. Moore, 26 N. H. 448; Baron v. P., 1 Parker, Cr. R. 246; P. v. Mather, 4 Wend. 229; Carlisle v. S., 31 Tex. Ap. 537; S. v. Hamilton, 13 Nev. 386.

[5] 1 Bish. Cr. Pr., § 463; Reg. v. Caspar, 9 C. & P. 289. And this is true under a statute declaring that aiders and abettors may be charged as principals: S. v. King, 9 Mont. 445; or where the statute makes the aiding, abetting or procuring, and the commission of the crime, distinct offenses: Hartshorn v. S., 29 Ohio St. 635.

[6] C. v. Glover, 111 Mass. 395; Pettes v. C., 126 Mass. 242; S. v. Atkinson, 40 S. C. 363; Loyd v. S., 45 Ga. 57; Rex v. Morris, 2 Leach, 1096.

charged in the same count with the principal, it is not necessary to repeat in the portion thereof referring to the accessory the allegations already made in the same count as to the commission of the offense by the principal, if such allegations are properly referred to.[1] Principal and accessory may, however, be charged in separate counts,[2] and if there is any doubt as to whether a particular defendant was principal or accessory, the indictment should charge both forms of guilt in separate counts.[3] So in different counts the same defendant may be charged with being an accessory before the fact and an accessory after the fact.[4] The count charging one or more of the defendants as accessories may be rejected as surplusage, if the evidence shows all to have been principals.[5] It seems that the prosecution cannot be compelled to elect between counts charging as principal and as accessory.[6] The right of separate trials where principal and accessory are jointly indicted is usually regulated by statute and left within the discretion of the court.[7] If the principal and accessory are jointly indicted, they may be tried together.[8]

§ 213. **Charging principals.**— The accused may be charged as principal, although he procured a crime to be committed by another, if he was so related to the crime as to be deemed in law the principal in its commission. Thus, a charge as principal is supported by proof of the doing of the act by an agent.[9] And so in misdemeanors, all the participants being principals may be charged as such whether present or not.[10] It is imma-

1 C. v. Cohen, 120 Mass. 198; C. v. Adams, 127 Mass. 15; S. v. Ruby, 68 Me. 543; Everett v. S., 33 Fla. 661. But where the accessory is charged in a separate count it should be complete in itself: T. v. Conley, 2 Wyo. 324.

2 Miller v. S., 25 Wis. 384; C. v. Chiovaro, 129 Mass. 489.

3 C. v. Knapp, 10 Pick. 477; S. v. Testerman, 68 Mo. 408; P. v. Valencia, 43 Cal. 552.

4 Rex v. Blackson, 8 C. & P. 43.

5 P. v. Ah Hop, 1 Idaho (N. S.), 698.

6 S. v. Sawtelle, 66 N. H. 488; Rex v. Blackson, 8 C. & P. 43. But after the evidence for the prosecution is in, an election may perhaps be required: Simms v. S., 10 Tex. Ap. 131. This question, however, is one of procedure and need not be further discussed here.

7 Loyd v. S., 45 Ga. 57; S. v. Yancy, 1 Treadw. Const. 241; S. v. Washington, 33 La. An. 1473; Reg. v. Fisher, 3 Cox, 68.

8 Sampson v. C., 5 Watts & S. 385; S. v. York, 37 N. H. 175.

9 Parker v. S., 4 Ohio St. 563; Collins v. S., 88 Ga. 347.

10 C. v. Harrington, 3 Pick. 26; C. v. Wallace, 108 Mass. 12; Stratton v. S., 45 Ind. 468. And in such cases it is immaterial that the charge is of aid-

terial as to one who is properly charged as principal that he is said to have acted with another.[1] No distinction in the form of the charge is necessary between principals in the first and in the second degree. Those charged as principals in the crime, without designation of the degree, and therefore as principals in the first degree, may be convicted on proof of being present, aiding and abetting.[2] So, if the indictment charges one of the defendants with aiding and abetting, he may be convicted on proof of his being the actual perpetrator.[3] Even where the indictment charges the aiding and abetting on the part of the accused, it is not necessary to state the particulars of the aid or assistance rendered by him.[4]

§ 214. **Charging accessories.**—Under the common-law distinction between principal and accessory, one indicted as principal cannot be convicted as an accessory.[5] So, on the other hand, one who is charged as accessory cannot be convicted if the evidence shows him to have been principal.[6] The indictment must be specific as to whether the charge is as principal or as accessory;[7] and in charging one as accessory it must allege the facts showing the commission of the crime.[8] So under a charge as principal one cannot be convicted as accessory after the fact.[9] If the indictment in charging the accessory erroneously

ing and abetting: S. v. Nowell, 60 N. H. 199.

[1] Watson v. S., 28 Tex. Ap. 34; S. v. Davis, 29 Mo. 391.

[2] C. v. Chapman, 11 Cush. 422; S. v. Ross, 29 Mo. 32; S. v. Dalton, 27 Mo. 13; S. v. Blan, 69 Mo. 317; Warden v. S., 24 Ohio St. 143; Doan v. S., 26 Ind. 495; Williams v. S., 47 Ind. 568; Hill v. S., 42 Neb. 503; S. v. Kirk, 10 Oreg. 505; Young v. C., 8 Bush, 366; Collins v. S., 88 Ga. 347; U. S. v. Douglass, 2 Blatch. 207. But it seems to have been held, contrary to the weight of authority, that where the accused is charged as an actor or absolute perpetrator he cannot be convicted on evidence of aiding and abetting: Washington v. S., 36 Ga. 222; Shaw v. S., 40 Ga. 120; S. v. White, 7 La. An. 531; S. v. Blackman, 35 La. An. 483; Davis v. S., 3 Tex. Ap. 91.

[3] Benge v. C., 92 Ky. 1; S. v. Littell, 45 La. An. 655.

[4] Coffin v. U. S., 156 U. S. 432; S. v. Buzzell, 59 N. H. 65; S. v. Wyckoff, 31 N. J. 65; Wade v. S., 71 Ind. 535.

[5] Philipps v. S., 26 Tex. Ap. 228; Rix v. S., 33 Tex. Ap. 353; Smith v. S., 37 Ark. 274; Hughes v. S., 12 Ala. 458.

[6] Rex v. Gordon, 1 East, P. C. 352.

[7] P. v. Schwartz, 32 Cal. 160.

[8] P. v. Crenshaw, 46 Cal. 65. In murder, if the indictment charges the principal offense as with malice aforethought, etc., it is sufficient as to the accessory to charge that he advised and encouraged the principal to commit the crime "in manner and form as aforesaid:" Jones v. S., 58 Ark. 390.

[9] P. v. Keefer, 65 Cal. 232; McCoy v. S., 52 Ga. 287; Jordan v. S., 56 Ga.

names the principal offender, the mistake will be fatal;[1] but it may in different counts name different persons as principal, or may allege the principals to be unknown.[2] But it seems that if the charge is that the principal is unknown, it cannot be supported should it appear that the name of the principal offender was known to the grand jury.[3] By statute it is sometimes made sufficient to charge the accessory simply as principal,[4] and it is not necessary in such cases to allege the particular facts showing the connection of the accused with the offense.[5]

§ 215. **Accessory not tried before principal.**— At common law the accessory can be tried either with the principal or after the conviction of the principal, but not before the principal.[6] Therefore, if for any reason such as the escape of the principal, or his death before conviction, or on account of his being insane, the conviction of the principal is not secured, the accessory cannot be tried.[7] And this rule is applicable also to accessories after the fact.[8] But it is not applied as between principals in the first and second degree,[9] nor in misdemeanors where all are principals.[10] It is not necessary, however, that the principal be tried before the indictment of the accessory, nor that the fact of previous trial of the principal be alleged in the indictment. All that is necessary is that the accessory be not put on trial before the trial and conviction of the principal.[11] If the accessory is charged with an offense committed

92; S. v. Allen, 37 La. An. 685; Reg. v. Fallon, L. & C. 217.

[1] S. v. Houston, 19 Mo. 211.

[2] Spies v. P., 122 Ill. 1.

[3] Rex v. Walker, 3 Camp. 264. But see Rex v. Bush, Russ. & Ry. 372.

[4] Baxter v. P., 8 Ill. 368; S. v. Zeibart, 40 Ia. 169; Bonsell v. U. S., 1 Greene (Ia.), 111; P. v. Ah Fat, 48 Cal. 61; P. v. Davidson, 5 Cal. 133; Doan v. S., 26 Ind. 495.

[5] Campbell v. C., 84 Pa. St. 187; P. v. Bigler, 5 Cal. 23; S. v. Duncan, 7 Wash. 336; S. v. Golden, 11 Wash. 422; S. v. White, 10 Wash. 611; S. v. Cassady, 12 Kan. 550. And further as to statutory provisions, see *infra*, § 217.

[6] Ex parte Hays, 25 Fla. 279; S. v. Pybass, 4 Humph. 441; S. v. Groff, 1 Murph. 270; U. S. v. Crane, 4 McLean, 317. But conviction of the principal without judgment is sufficient to warrant the trial of the accessory: C. v. Williamson, 2 Va. Cas. 211.

[7] C. v. Phillips, 16 Mass. 423; Harty v. S., 3 Blackf. 386; S. v. McDaniel, 41 Tex. 229; U. S. v. Crane, 4 McLean, 317; Reg. v. Tyler, 8 C. & P. 616.

[8] C. v. Andrews, 3 Mass. 126.

[9] Boyd v. S., 17 Ga. 194.

[10] U. S. v. Gooding, 12 Wheat. 460; C. v. Brockway, 150 Mass. 322.

[11] Holmes v. C., 25 Pa. St. 221; Harty v. S., 3 Blackf. 386; S. v. Crank, 2 Bailey, 66; S. v. Sims, 2 Bailey, 29.

by several principals, he may be tried as accessory to those who have been convicted, but if he is tried as accessory to any who are not yet convicted it is error.[1] The objection that the principal has not been put on trial and convicted may be made before or after the impaneling of the jury.[2] It may be waived by the accessory,[3] but the mere fact of going to trial without raising the objection does not constitute a waiver.[4] Even in case of waiver the accessory will not be sentenced until conviction of the principal.[5] It seems, however, that the accessory is not necessarily to be discharged on a showing of the mere fact that the principal has not been convicted. He may either be held to await the conviction of the principal, or may be discharged in the discretion of the court.[6] But of course on the acquittal of the principal the accessory is entitled to his discharge.[7] These requirements in regard to the previous trial or conviction of the principal are relaxed by statute in many states;[8] but even under such a statute, without more, the accessory should not be sentenced if the principal is acquitted before sentence is passed.[9] Where a crime, which is accessorial in its nature, is by statute made a substantive offense, the rule requiring the previous trial and conviction of the principal no longer applies.[10]

§ 216. **Guilt of principal must be shown.**—The reason for the doctrine stated in the preceding section seems to be that if there is no principal guilty of the offense the accessory cannot be convicted therefor;[11] so that even though the technical rule requiring the previous trial and conviction of the principal before the trial of the accessory is removed by statute, nevertheless proof of the guilt of the principal is still essen-

1 Stoops v. C., 7 Serg. & R. 491.

2 Starin v. P., 45 N. Y. 333.

3 1 Hale, P. C. 623; C. v. Andrews, 3 Mass. 126.

4 Ex parte Hayes, 25 Fla. 214; Stoops v. C., 7 Serg. & R. 491.

5 C. v. Andrews, 3 Mass. 126.

6 C. v. Sheriff, 16 Serg. & R. 304; S. v. Pybass, 4 Humph. 441.

7 U. S. v. Crane, 4 McLean, 317.

8 P. v. Bearss, 10 Cal. 68. And see as to statutory regulations in regard to trial of accessories, *infra*, § 217.

9 McCarty v. S., 44 Ind. 214.

10 Ex parte Bowen, 25 Fla. 214; S. v. Ricker, 29 Me. 84; Reg. v. Pulham, 9 C. & P. 280; Reg. v. Hughes, Bell, 242; Holloway v. Reg., 17 Q. B. 317; Reg. v. Hansell, 3 Cox, 597.

11 Bowen v. S., 25 Fla. 645; T. v. Dwenger, 2 N. Mex. 73; Simmons v. S., 4 Ga. 465; Ogden v. S., 12 Wis. 532; Whitehead v. S., 4 Humph. 278.

tial.[1] But this rule has no application as between principals in the first and second degree, and one may be convicted as principal in the second degree without the guilt of the principal in the first degree being shown, or of a higher degree of the offense than that of which the principal in the first degree has been convicted.[2] Proof that the principal has been tried and convicted is made by introducing the record of such conviction, and this is also *prima facie* evidence of his guilt,[3] and it is immaterial whether the judgment is erroneous or not;[4] and parol evidence is not sufficient;[5] nor is the conviction of the principal admissible in evidence until judgment on such conviction has been rendered.[6] But notwithstanding the conviction of the principal the accessory may controvert the fact of his guilt by parol evidence;[7] so, on the other hand, the state may introduce on its part other evidence of the principal's guilt than the record of his conviction.[8]

§ 217. **Statutory provisions.**— In both England and the United States statutes have been passed to obviate the difficulty arising out of the technical rules as to prosecution and conviction of accessories. Some of these statutes are narrow in their application, and simply remove the obstacle due to the requirement that the accessory can only be put on trial in connection with, or after the conviction of, the principal, and leave

[1] Hatchett v. C., 75 Va. 925; Tully v. C., 11 Bush, 154.

[2] P. v. Bearss, 10 Cal. 68; Goins v. S., 46 Ohio St. 457; Weston v. C., 111 Pa. St. 251; S. v. Lee, 91 Ia. 499; S. v. Whitt, 113 N. C. 716; Rex v. Taggart, 1 C. & P. 201; Shaw's Case, 1 East, P. C. 351. If, however, the guilt of the principal in the second degree necessarily depends on evidence of the guilt of some one else as principal in the first degree, of course the principal in the second degree should not be convicted without such evidence: Jones v. S., 64 Ga. 697.

[3] S. v. Chittem, 2 Dev. 49; Anderson v. S., 63 Ga. 675; S. v. Sims, 2 Bailey, 29; S. v. Crank, 2 Bailey, 66; West v. S., 27 Tex. Ap. 472. On a trial of principal in the second degree, the record of the conviction of the principal in the first degree is *prima facie* evidence of that fact: Studstill v. S., 7 Ga. 2.

[4] Rex v. Baldwin, 3 Camp. 265; S. v. Duncan, 6 Ired. 236.

[5] Rex v. Turner, 1 Moody, 347. But if the accessory is charged with being present aiding and abetting (and therefore as principal), parol evidence of the conviction of the one who actually committed the crime is admissible: S. v. Crank, 2 Bailey, 66. In Texas the guilt of the principal may be shown by any evidence which would be competent as against him: Armstrong v. S., 33 Tex. Ap. 417.

[6] S. v. Duncan, 6 Ired. 98.

[7] C. v. Knapp, 10 Pick. 477; Rex v. Smith, 1 Leach, 288.

[8] Levy v. P., 80 N. Y. 327.

it still necessary that the accessory shall be indicted and tried as such and not as principal.[1] Such a provision does not authorize the conviction of the accessory after the acquittal of the principal.[2] But the statutory provision which has generally been adopted is one declaring that the accessory may be tried and convicted as principal, and this obviates the distinction, not only as to trial, but as to method of indictment; so that where these provisions are found, one who at common law would be only an accessory in felony may be directly charged as principal with its commission, just as has been done at common law in cases of misdemeanor, and it is not necessary to describe his connection with the offense as being that of accessory;[3] and it is not necessary that the statute specially authorize the indictment of the accessory as principal if it declares that the accessory shall be deemed guilty as principal.[4] It is not improper, even where the statute broadly declares that all who encourage, advise, aid, etc., shall be guilty as principals, to charge such persons directly as principals.[5] There may be crimes, however, which can only be committed by persons of a certain class, and it seems that a person not of such a class cannot be charged as principal in such a crime.[6] Where

[1] S. v. Ricker, 29 Me. 84; S. v. York. 37 N. H. 175. And see *supra*, § 215. Such a statute does not change the rules of evidence, but the actual commission of the principal offense must be shown as before: S. v. Rand, 33 N. H. 216.

[2] McCarty v. S., 44 Ind. 214.

[3] S. v. Hamlin, 47 Conn. 95; P. v. Valencia, 43 Cal. 552; P. v. Outeveras, 48 Cal. 19; P. v. Shepardson, 48 Cal. 189; Spies v. P., 122 Ill. 1; Usselton v. P., 149 Ill. 612; Dempsey v. P., 47 Ill. 323; Baxter v. P., 8 Ill. 368; S. v. Kent, 4 N. Dak. 577; Hanoff v. S., 37 Ohio St. 178; S. v. Brown, 21 Kan. 38; S. v. Bogue, 52 Kan. 79; S. v. Beebe, 17 Minn. 241; Campbell v. C., 84 Pa. St. 187; Brandt v. C., 94 Pa. St. 290; S. v. Frederick, 85 Mo. 145; S. v. Payton, 90 Mo. 220; S. v. Stacy, 103 Mo. 11; Doan v. S., 26 Ind. 495; Harty v. S., 3 Blackf. 386; S. v. Chapman, 6 Nev. 320; Griffith v. S., 90 Ala. 583; Raiford v. S., 59 Ala. 106; S. v. Littell, 45 La. An. 655; Reg. v. Manning, 2 C. & K. 887. Under such a statute all persons concerned in the commission of a felony, including aiders and abettors, may be indicted and convicted as principals: S. v. Brown, 25 Ia. 561; S. v. Thornton, 26 Ia. 79; S. v. Stanley, 48 Ia. 221; S. v. Hessian, 58 Ia. 68; S. v. Pugsley, 75 Ia. 742. And two or more may be jointly indicted for a criminal act which is of such nature that it can be actually committed by but one person: S. v. Comstock, 46 Ia. 265. As to charging accessory as principal, under statute, see, also, *supra*, § 214.

[4] P. v. Bliven, 112 N. Y. 79.

[5] P. v. Rozelle, 78 Cal. 84, explaining P. v. Schwartz, 32 Cal. 160.

[6] Shannon v. P., 5 Mich. 71; al-

the statute makes the accessory guilty as principal, he may be punished without regard to the punishment of the principal, and therefore may be punished for a higher degree of crime than that of which the one who commits the crime is actually convicted,[1] and of course may be convicted whether the principal is convicted or not.[2] Under such a statute the accessory should be charged as principal with the commission of the crime and not as accessory to the commission of the crime.[3] Such a statute applies to statutory felonies as well as to felonies at common law.[4]

§ 218. Statutes making accessory guilty of substantive offense.— There is still another form of statutory provision found in some states, which, instead of making the accessory guilty as principal, makes him guilty of a substantive offense in procuring the commission of the crime;[5] and under such statute the accessory may be charged either with this substantive offense or as a common-law accessory.[6] A statute providing for the punishment of the accessory in the same manner as the principal thus makes his offense a substantive crime.[7] If the statute provides for two offenses, one the committing of the act, the other the procuring of the act to be done, a person guilty of the latter cannot be charged as principal, but only as authorized by the statute;[8] and knowledge on the part of the accused must be affirmatively alleged[9] and the commission of the principal crime must be proven.[10] But, on the other hand, the acquittal of a person charged with the principal crime will be competent evidence that it was not committed.[11] Even under such a statute, however, one who is present aiding and abet-

though several may be charged as principals in an offense which can be committed by but one person: S. v. Comstock, 46 Ia. 265.

[1] S. v. Patterson, 52 Kan. 335; S. v. Gray, 55 Kan. 135.

[2] S. v. Bogue, 52 Kan. 79; Pettes v. C., 126 Mass. 242; Brown v. S., 18 Ohio St. 497.

[3] Usselton v. P., 149 Ill. 612; Fixmer v. P., 153 Ill. 123. But a common-law indictment as accessory may be sufficient: S. v. Gleim, 17 Mont. 17; P. v. Rozelle, 78 Cal. 84.

[4] Nichols v. S., 35 Wis. 308.

[5] S. v. Ricker, 29 Me. 84. But a statute which simply names aiders and abettors in describing the crime does not make the aiding and abetting a separate offense: U. S. v. Douglass, 2 Blatch. 207.

[6] Brandt v. C., 94 Pa. St. 290; S. v. Hamlin, 47 Conn. 95; P. v. Valencia, 43 Cal. 552.

[7] Noland v. S., 19 Ohio, 131.

[8] Meister v. P., 31 Mich. 99.

[9] S. v. Seran, 28 N. J. 519.

[10] Ogden v. S., 12 Wis. 532.

[11] P. v. Buckland, 13 Wend. 592.

ting may be charged as principal as at common law.[1] If the procuring, etc., is made a substantive offense, the name of the principal may be charged as unknown, and it will not be necessary to prove who committed the act as principal.[2] Even where the aiding and abetting is made a substantive offense, it may still be charged in the same indictment and in the same count with the principal offense.[3]

1 Warden v. S., 24 Ohio St. 143.
2 C. v. Glover, 111 Mass. 395.
3 S. v. Ruby, 68 Me. 543; Hartshorn v. S., 29 Ohio St. 635.

PART IV.

UNCOMPLETED ACT; WHEN CRIMINAL.

§ 219. How far intent must have been carried.—It has already been suggested that intent alone is not punishable.[1] But the question may arise under a variety of circumstances as to how far the intent may be carried out before criminality attaches, or, on the other hand, what is a sufficient act in pursuance of the intent to become a crime. Frequently when a crime intended has not been committed, there has been enough done to merit punishment, and it is the discussion of this ground which is contemplated in the following two chapters, the first of which relates to attempts and the second to assaults, which are in their essence a kind of attempt, though they involve usually something more than a mere attempt. Frequently assault involves an act in itself wrongful apart from any further specific intent, the simplest case being that of a battery, which, though it is a completed crime, is for practical convenience considered in connection with assaults. Moreover, if the battery is attended with aggravating circumstances, it may constitute a higher offense, such as that of malicious wounding, stabbing, etc.; and further still, the assault, or the assault and battery, may be coupled with an intent to commit a still higher injury, such as murder, robbery, or the like, and become closely akin to felony, or even by statute be made a felony, and these assaults can be conveniently discussed under the general heading of assaults with felonious intent. Assaults with intent to commit rape, while they might properly be included in assaults with a felonious intent, are more conveniently discussed in connection with the crime of rape, and are postponed until that chapter.

[1] *Supra*, § 127.

CHAPTER 16.

ATTEMPTS.

§ **220. Solicitations.**— The form of intent which perhaps involves the least degree of criminality is that of a solicitation of another to do an act which, if done, would constitute a crime, and such solicitation is generally held to be punishable as a misdemeanor, although the offense solicited is never committed.[1] There is probably no real difference in criminality between a solicitation and an attempt; the solicitation is in itself such an overt act as is necessary to constitute an attempt within the general principle of attempts to be hereafter stated.[2] There are cases, however, holding a mere solicitation not to be punishable as an attempt.[3] If the offense is one requiring the con-

[1] P. v. Bush, 4 Hill, 133; S. v. Murphy, 27 N. J. 112; S. v. Avery, 7 Conn. 266; C. v. Flag, 135 Mass. 545. Thus, a solicitation to commit arson with promise of money therefor and an offer of means to accomplish the purpose is criminal, notwithstanding the offer is repudiated: S. v. Bowers, 35 S. C. 262. So held also as to solicitations to commit murder, accompanied by an offer of money as an inducement: C. v. Randolph, 146 Pa. St. 83. Earlier Pennsylvania cases held that to constitute an attempt there must be some act which would constitute an indictable offense: Randolph v. C., 6 Serg. & R. 398; Smith v. C., 54 Pa. St. 209; Stabler v. C., 95 Pa. St. 318. But in this respect these cases are practically overruled by the one just cited.

[2] S. v. Avery, 7 Conn. 266; S. v. Ames, 64 Me. 386; C. v. Randolph, 146 Pa. St. 83.

[3] S. v. Baller, 26 W. Va. 90; and see Pennsylvania cases referred to in the first note to this section. Thus, where the accused wrote and posted a letter to another requesting him to commit murder, which letter never reached the person to whom it was addressed, it was held that there could be no conviction for the solicitation as an attempt: Reg. v. Fox, 19 W. R. 109. Where a statute made it punishable to set fire to buildings of a certain class, or to set fire to material with intent to cause the burning of such buildings, or by any other means to attempt to cause such burning, it was held that the attempt thus specified did not include an attempt to induce another person to fire the buildings, and that some physical act of causation was essential: McDade v. P., 29 Mich. 50. Under a statute punishing the attempt to procure a slave to commit a crime or misdemeanor, held, that the crime or misdemeanor intended was an offense which, if committed, would constitute such crime or misdemeanor in a white person: Grady v. S., 11 Ga. 253.

current action of two or more persons, it is doubtful whether a solicitation of one person by another to commit the offense is in itself criminal. Thus, the weight of authority is to the effect that a solicitation to commit adultery is not in itself a crime,[1] and it is so held as to a solicitation to commit incest,[2] and also as to a solicitation for criminal connection with a female under the age of consent.[3] So it is held that one who purchases liquor illegally sold is not guilty of a crime.[4]

§ 221. **Attempts deemed criminal.**— At common law an attempt to commit a felony is a misdemeanor;[5] but where the common law is superseded by a complete criminal code, an attempt to commit a felony is punishable only when made so by statute.[6] Moreover, at common law an attempt to commit a misdemeanor — that is, an actual attempt and not merely an intent — is also a misdemeanor.[7] Possession of burglar's tools with intent to use them is in the nature of an attempt to commit burglary, and may be made criminal by statute, although the intent is to use them outside of the state.[8]

§ 222. **Intent involved.**— To constitute an attempt there must be the intent to commit a crime and some act done toward its consummation.[9] The intent alone will not be criminal,

[1] Smith v. C., 54 Pa. St. 209; S. v. Butler, 8 Wash. 194, 9 Am. Cr. R. 661, and note; S. v. Goodrich, 84 Wis. 359. *Contra*, S. v. Avery, 7 Conn. 266.

[2] Cox v. P., 82 Ill. 191. But it is said that solicitation to commit sodomy is criminal: Rex v. Hickman, 1 Moody, 34; Reg. v. Ransford, 13 Cox, 9.

[3] S. v. Harney, 101 Mo. 470.

[4] *Supra*, § 199.

[5] C. v. Barlow, 4 Mass. 439; Hackett v. C., 15 Pa. St. 95; Nicholson v. S., 9 Baxt. 258; S. v. Jordan, 75 N. C. 27; C. v. Blackburn, 1 Duv. 4. Thus, an assault to commit murder was at common law a misdemeanor: Green v. P., 3 Colo. 68; S. v. Clayton, 100 Mo. 516. An attempt to commit suicide is not indictable where attempts are by statute punishable in the same manner as completed offenses, suicide not being punishable in any manner: C. v. Dennis, 105 Mass. 162 (distinguishing C. v. Bowen, 13 Mass. 356). Mayhem being a felony by statute, the attempt to maim is punishable: S. v. Brown, 60 Mo. 141.

[6] Smith v. S., 12 Ohio St. 466. And see Hill v. S., 53 Ga. 125.

[7] Reg. v. Martin, 9 C. & P. 215; Rex v. Meredith, 8 C. & P. 589; Reg. v. Chapman, 2 C. & K. 846. And it is immaterial whether the offense is statutory or by the common law: Rex v. Roderick, 7 C. & P. 795; Rex v. Butler, 6 C. & P. 368. Attempt to commit a statutory misdemeanor is not indictable unless made so by statute: Whitesides v. S., 11 Lea, 474.

[8] Davis v. S., 87 Ala. 10.

[9] Hicks v. C., 86 Va. 223; Glover v. C., 86 Va. 382; Davis v. S., 87 Ala. 10; 1 Bish. Cr. L., § 728. Thus, an assault to commit murder is something more than the intent to murder

but when an act is done toward carrying it out the law judges not only of the act but of the intent also; even if the act alone would be innocent, the intent may make it criminal. The term "attempt" signifies both an act and the intent with which it is done.[1]

§ **223. What acts sufficient.**— Under the doctrine of intent it has already been stated that a mere intent to commit a crime, no overt act toward its commission being done, is not criminal;[2] but there may be such overt act short of actual commission of the crime as to constitute a criminal attempt to commit.[3] Thus, if the means adopted for committing larceny are such that had the parties to be affected by defendant's acts done what he supposed they would do he would have succeeded in his purpose, the attempt is complete.[4] So the act of placing an explosive bomb in such way that a person driving along the highway would explode it and probably be killed is an attempt to murder.[5] Where defendant had prepared an explosive for the purpose of putting it upon the track of a railroad, and had started so to place it a short distance from his house, he was held guilty of an attempt to place an obstruction upon such track.[6] Where material was prepared for the purpose of setting fire to a building, and defendant went off to procure a match, leaving another person who was to do the act at the place, it was held that the acts were sufficient to constitute an

with ability to carry out such intent; there must be an attempt: P. v. Devine, 59 Cal. 630. Attempt involves intent: Felker v. S., 54 Ark. 489. Where a woman to escape violence from her husband jumped from a window and was injured, held, that he was not guilty of attempt to murder unless he intended to cause her to jump from the window: Reg. v. Donovan, 4 Cox, 400.

[1] Cunningham v. S., 49 Miss. 685.

[2] *Supra*, § 127.

[3] Watts v. S., 30 Tex. Ap. 533; S. v. Montgomery, 109 Mo. 645; P. v. Stites, 75 Cal. 570; P. v. McDonnell, 80 Cal. 285; Sipple v. S., 46 N. J. 197. There is no such crime as attempt to commit an assault with intent to commit murder: Wilson v. S., 53 Ga. 205; White v. S., 22 Tex. 608; or with intent to commit rape: Brown v. S., 7 Tex. Ap. 569. Under a statute prescribing a penalty for an attempt at insurrection there cannot be a conviction for an attempt to incite an insurrection: Gibson v. S., 38 Ga. 571.

[4] Sipple v. S., 46 N. J. 197. To take the impression of a warehouse key for the purpose of having a false key made is an attempt to commit larceny, whether the defendant intended to use the false key himself or procure another to do so: Griffin v. S., 26 Ga. 493.

[5] Jambor v. S., 75 Wis. 664.

[6] P. v. Stites, 75 Cal. 570.

attempt.[1] So where a lighted candle was placed among hay with intent that a building should burn by means of fire communicated from the candle to the hay, it was held that the statutory offense of setting fire to material with intent to burn, etc., was complete.[2] On the principle of an attempt it may be made criminal to visit a house for the purpose of gambling.[3] Where it appeared that accused, having threatened violence, took from his pocket a loaded revolver and pointed it at the person threatened, with words indicating an intention to discharge it, but he was seized and disarmed before doing so, it was held that the crime of attempting to discharge loaded arms at another was established.[4] An attempt to commit burglary may be established on proof of breaking with intent to rob without actual entry;[5] or an attempt to feloniously break and enter a shop with intent to commit a felony, by proof of making a hole in the roof with intent to enter and steal.[6] An attempt to obtain money or property under false pretenses may be punished, although the party to be defrauded is not deceived,[7] or the money or property is not actually obtained.[8] When an act has been done in pursuance of the intent, the attempt is complete although the intention is abandoned before the consummation of the crime, or, by reason of consent to the act on the part of the other party, no crime is actually committed.[9]

§ 224. **Preparation distinguished from attempt.**— Mere preliminary preparation is not, however, such an overt act as to constitute an attempt. There must be some act done directed toward the particular party and toward the particular offense, the result of which would be the completed offense if not hindered by extraneous causes.[10] There must be some overt

1 S. v. Hayes, 78 Mo. 307.

2 S. v. Johnson, 19 Ia. 230.

3 Ex parte Lane, 76 Cal. 587.

4 Reg. v. Duckworth, 2 Q. B. D. (1892), 83 (overruling Reg. v. St. George, 9 C. & P. 483, and distinguishing Reg. v. Lewis, 9 C. & P. 523).

5 Reg. v. Spanner, 12 Cox, 155.

6 Reg. v. Bain, L. & C. 129.

7 Reg. v. Hensler, 11 Cox, 570.

8 Reg. v. Holloway, 1 Den. 370; Reg. v. Eagleton, Dears. 515; Reg. v. Ball, Car. & M. 249; Reg. v. Cheeseman, L. & C. 140.

9 So in case of attempt to rape: Glover v. C., 86 Va. 382; Lewis v. S., 35 Ala. 380. And further as to the same point, see cases of assault with intent to rape, *infra*, § 463.

10 Sipple v. S., 46 N. J. 197; S. v. Montgomery, 63 Mo. 296; Reg. v. Collins, L. & C. 471. An indictable attempt to commit a crime is such an intentional preliminary guilty act as will apparently result in a de-

act alleged which is as a matter of law illegal.[1] To make an act indictable as an attempt, "it must be a *cause* as distinguished from a *condition*" of the contemplated offense.[2] Until an unlawful act is committed there is *locus pœnitentiæ*, time for repentance, and such repentance and abandonment of the unlawful intent may prevent such intent from becoming a criminal attempt.[3] Where the design is changed, the subsequent intent is not to be so connected with the preceding act as to constitute an attempt to commit a new crime.[4] An assault is a form of attempt.[5] Thus in every assault there must be the intent to injure, coupled with an act which must at least be the beginning of an attempt to injure, and not merely an act of preparation for such contemplated injury.[6] In a recent case the court endeavors to cover the whole ground by saying that "an act must reach far enough towards the accomplishment of the desired result to amount to the commencement of the consummation, and must not be merely preparatory." In other words, while it need not be the last proximate act to the consummation of the offense attempted to be perpetrated, it must approach sufficiently near to it to stand either as the first or some subsequent step in the direct movement towards the commission of the offense after the preparations are made.[7] As said in another case, "it need not be the last proximate act to the consummation of the crime in contemplation, but is sufficient if it be an act apparently adapted to produce the result intended. It must be something more than mere preparation."[8] Mere preparation to commit a violent injury upon the person

liberate crime: S. v. Brown, 95 N. C. 685.

[1] Randolph v. C., 6 Serg. & R. 398. One who stands by when an attempt is made to commit a crime, but gives no assistance therein, is not guilty of the attempt: P. v. Woodward, 45 Cal. 293.

[2] 1 Whart. Cr. L. 181; Patrick v. P., 132 Ill. 529; Hicks v. C., 86 Va. 223.

[3] Shannon v C., 14 Pa. St. 226; P. v. Lilley, 43 Mich. 521; Pinkard v. S., 30 Ga. 757; S. v. McDaniel, Winst. 249. But where the wrongful intent is coupled with an overt act, the criminal attempt is completed, although the crime intended does not result: S. v. Hayes, 78 Mo. 307. And see cases cited in subsequent notes to this section.

[4] S. v. Craft, 72 Mo. 456.

[5] 2 Bish. Cr. L., § 52. And see *infra*, § 231.

[6] Johnson v. S., 43 Tex. 576.

[7] Hicks v. C., 86 Va. 223. And see Uhl v. C., 6 Grat. 706.

[8] Glover v. C., 86 Va. 382.

of another, unaccompanied by a physical offer to commit such injury, will not justify a conviction for an assault.[1]

§ 225. **Illustrations.**— The general statements of the preceding section may be rendered more intelligible by further illustration. Thus, it has been said (by way of illustration only) that the purchase or loading of a gun with intent to commit murder does not constitute an indictable offense, being only in the nature of a preliminary preparation;[2] and so the act of picking up a stone with the intention of throwing it to injure another is not an assault.[3] Where one person sent to another a box containing gunpowder and appliances to cause its explosion when the box should be opened, it was held that this was not an attempt to discharge loaded arms at such other person, within an English statute.[4] Delivering poison to another to be administered to a third person, the one to whom it is delivered not agreeing or combining to carry out such intent, does not constitute an attempt to administer poison.[5] An attempt to contract an incestuous marriage is not proven by evidence of an elopement and sending for a magistrate to perform the ceremony, such acts being preparatory only;[6] nor is a solicitation to commit fornication or adultery a criminal attempt.[7] The act of procuring tools and implements, and delivering them to another to be given to one who is confined in jail to be used in making his escape, is not an attempt to commit the offense of rescue, even though an intermediate party actually attempts to convey them into the jail; it is preparation only.[8] The attempt to introduce spirituous liquors into Alaska in violation of United States statutes is not committed by ordering liquor of a dealer with the intention of taking it to Alaska.[9] The crime of attempting to burn a building does not include the act of attempting to induce another to fire the building, and of providing such other person with material for

[1] Brown v. S., 95 Ga. 481.

[2] Hicks v. C., 86 Va. 223; P. v. Murray, 14 Cal. 159; Johnson v. S., 27 Neb. 687.

[3] Brown v. S., 95 Ga. 481.

[4] Rex v. Mountford, 7 C. & P. 242.

[5] Stabler v. C., 95 Pa. St. 318; Hicks v. C., 86 Va. 223; Reg. v. Williams, 1 C. & K. 589. But that such a solicitation may constitute an attempt, see *infra*, § 227.

[6] P. v. Murray, 14 Cal. 159.

[7] Smith v. C., 54 Pa. St. 209. And see *supra*, § 220.

[8] Patrick v. P., 132 Ill. 529.

[9] U. S. v. Stephens, 12 Fed. R. 52.

the purpose.[1] One who tries to ascertain whether another's pocket contains anything to be stolen, but does not insert his hand into the pocket for the purpose of stealing, is not guilty of an attempt to commit larceny.[2]

§ **226. Impossibility.**— To constitute a criminal attempt the act attempted must be a possibility. For instance, when the charge is an attempt to suborn perjury, there must be a cause or proceeding pending in which the perjury might be committed.[3] So, it has been suggested that if a man should undertake to ravish, under circumstances making the crime of ravishment absolutely impossible, such attempt would not be criminal;[4] and it has been held that a boy under fourteen, not being capable of committing rape, cannot be guilty of an assault with intent to commit rape.[5] It has been said also that it is not an assault to point a pistol at another which is not loaded;[6] but these cases are overruled or distinguished in recent English cases.[7] As will be seen, however, under the head of Assault, that offense has a dual character, being to some extent an attempt, but, on the other hand, consisting also in the act of putting in fear even where the threatened injury could not be committed,[8] so that assault cases are not conclusive as to the present doctrine. But it will be found that if there is an attempt with present ability to commit the injury, this constitutes an assault;[9] also, that in an assault with intent to kill, it is not necessary that the weapon used should have been such as to effect the result intended.[10] And in general, where there is the intent to commit a crime and an act is done tending to effect the commission thereof, the attempt is punishable, although by reason of extraneous circumstances the actual

[1] McDade v. P., 29 Mich. 50.

[2] Reg. v. Taylor, 25 L. T. 75.

[3] S. v. Joaquin, 69 Me. 218.

[4] 1 Bish. Cr. L., § 742.

[5] Rex v. Eldershaw, 3 C. & P. 396; Reg. v. Philips, 8 C. & P. 736. On this question the authorities are not in harmony. See, to the contrary, C. v. Green, 2 Pick. 380. This question is further discussed under the head of Assault with Intent to Commit Rape, *infra*, § 467.

[6] Reg. v. James, 1 C. & K. 530; Reg. v. St. George, 9 C. & P. 483; Reg. v. Lewis, 9 C. & P. 523; Reg. v. Gamble, 10 Cox, 545.

[7] Reg. v. Brown, 10 Q. B. D. 381; Reg. v. Duckworth, 2 Q. B. D. (1892), 83.

[8] *Infra*, § 231.

[9] S. v. Malcolm, 8 Ia. 413; P. v. Lilley, 43 Mich. 521.

[10] C. v. Creed, 8 Gray, 387; Kunkle v. S., 32 Ind. 220; S. v. Rigg, 10 Nev. 284.

commission of the crime is impossible.[1] Thus, where there is an attempt to commit larceny by picking a pocket, and in the prosecution of the attempt the hand is thrust into the pocket of the other person, the attempt is complete, although it turns out that there is nothing in the pocket to be stolen.[2] So, in an assault with intent to rob, it is not necessary that the person upon whom the crime was attempted shall have had the money which the assailant intended to steal.[3] So, one who opens a money drawer with the purpose of stealing money therefrom is guilty of an attempt, although there is no money in the drawer.[4] So, the crime of burglary is committed by breaking and entering with intent to steal money from a safe, although the safe is not at the time used as a place for keeping money and contains none.[5] Under an indictment for using an instrument to procure a miscarriage it is immaterial whether the woman is pregnant.[6]

§ 227. **Attempts to poison.**— Some peculiar questions arise in regard to the attempt to kill by the use of poison. To constitute an administering of poison, the substance must be taken into the stomach.[7] One who puts poison into coffee, intending that another shall drink it, is guilty of causing poison to be taken if the coffee is drank.[8] So, intentionally placing poison where it is likely to be found and taken is an attempt to administer it;[9] so, if poison is sent to A. with intent that he shall take it, and it comes into the possession of B., who does take it, the crime of administering poison to B. is committed.[10] But it has been said that giving poison to a guilty agent with the direction to cause it to be administered is not in itself an attempt to administer.[11] The thing administered must be of a

[1] P. v. Moran, 123 N. Y. 254, 10 L. R. A. 109, and note; S. v. Beal, 37 Ohio St. 108; C. v. Jacobs, 9 Allen, 274; P. v. Lee Kong, 95 Cal. 666; Kunkle v. S., 32 Ind. 220. See, also, *infra*, § 234.

[2] C. v. McDonald, 5 Cush. 365; S. v. Wilson, 30 Conn. 500; P. v. Jones, 46 Mich. 441; Rogers v. C., 5 Serg. & R. 463; P. v. Moran, 123 N. Y. 254. The case of Reg. v. Collins, L. & C. 471 (and by inference that of Reg. v. McPherson, Dears. & B. 197, which is analogous to it), is overruled by *dict.* in Reg. v. Brown, 24 Q. B. D. 357.

[3] Hamilton v. S., 36 Ind. 280.

[4] Clark v. S., 86 Tenn. 511.

[5] S. v. Beal, 37 Ohio St. 108.

[6] Reg. v. Goodchild, 2 C. & K. 293 (s. n. Reg. v. Goodhall, 1 Den. 187); Reg. v. Goodall, 2 Cox, 41. And see P. v. Gardner, 144 N. Y. 119.

[7] Rex v. Cadman, 1 Moody, 114.

[8] Rex v. Harley, 4 C. & P. 369.

[9] Reg. v. Dale, 6 Cox, 14.

[10] Rex v. Lewis, 6 C. & P. 161.

[11] Reg. v. Williams, 1 C. & K. 589.

deleterious nature;[1] and an indictment for attempting to poison must allege that the substance was a deadly poison.[2] An attempt to poison where no injury is done is not an assault.[3] There may be a crime committed in administering a harmful drug, where the intent is not to kill but to facilitate the commission of some unlawful act, such as robbery or seduction, and in such cases it is not necessary that the substance should be calculated to cause any direct physical injury. Any intention to suspend the natural functions of the body, though the result would not be painful or permanently harmful, is sufficient to constitute a crime.[4]

§ 228. Indictment.— It is evident from the discussion as to what constitutes an attempt that an indictment therefor must charge both the intent and the overt act;[5] but it is not necessary to allege the act attempted with the same particularity as would be required in charging the attempted act as a completed crime.[6] Thus, it is not necessary to use all the qualifying words required in alleging the crime involved in the completed act.[7] In charging the attempt to commit larceny it is not necessary to specifically describe the article which defendant intended to steal;[8] but an indictment charging an attempt to poison must specifically allege that the substance employed was a deadly poison.[9] The particular means used

Certainly not if the person solicited does not promise to administer it and does not do so: Hicks v. C., 86 Va. 223. And see *supra*, § 225.

[1] Rex v. Powels, 4 C. & P. 571; Reg. v. Cluderoy, 2 C. & K. 907.

[2] Anthony v. S., 29 Ala. 27.

[3] Garnet v. S., 1 Tex. Ap. 605; Collins v. S., 3 Heisk. 14. But, for a further discussion of this point, see Assault, *infra*, § 236, n.

[4] P. v. Carmichael, 5 Mich. 10; P. v. Adwards, 5 Mich. 22.

[5] S. v. Wilson, 30 Conn. 500; C. v. Clark, 6 Grat. 675.

[6] Coffin v. U. S., 156 U. S. 432; C. v. Doherty, 10 Cush. 52. To similar effect, see cases with reference to assault with intent, *infra*, § 269, and burglary, *infra*, § 509.

[7] C. v. McLaughlin, 105 Mass. 460.

[8] S. v. Hughes, 76 Mo. 323; Buntin v. S., 68 Ind. 38; Dickinson v. S., 70 Ind. 247; Hayes v. S., 15 Lea, 64; Reg. v. Johnson, L. & C. 489. But where the indictment described the goods which defendant was indicted for breaking and entering a dwelling-house with intent to steal, held, that a conviction could not be sustained, it appearing that the goods described were not in the house at the time: Reg. v. McPherson, Dears. & B. 197.

[9] Anthony v. S., 29 Ala. 27. To merely describe the drug as a poisonous drug is not sufficient: Shackleford v. S., 79 Ala. 26. But an indictment charging defendant with an attempt to poison A., and that in such attempt he delivered knowingly and unlawfully to A. a pill

towards committing the attempted crime need not be alleged,[1] but the acts constituting the alleged attempt should be set forth;[2] and an indictment merely stating that defendant "did attempt to take, steal and carry away" certain chattels, etc., without setting out the acts done or the mode and manner of the attempt, was held insufficient to charge the attempt to commit larceny.[3] The allegation of the attempt implies the intent to do the act attempted.[4] In fact, the allegation of attempt implies both the intent and an actual offer to consummate the intent, and therefore such an allegation has been held in itself sufficient.[5] It is not necessary to allege a present ability to accomplish the act intended, or the possibility of the commission of the crime.[6]

§ **228a. Forms.**— A few forms will sufficiently illustrate the method of charging attempts:

ATTEMPT TO STEAL FROM DWELLING-HOUSE.

That E. J., in ——, on the —— day of ——, A. D. ——, the goods and chattels of T. R., in the dwelling-house of T. R., situate in the county of ——, did attempt feloniously to steal, take and carry away.[7]

containing a large quantity of deadly poison, and solicited A. to swallow it, with intent to murder A., was held sufficient to charge an attempt to murder by poison: Bittle v. S., 78 Md. 526.

[1] P. v. Bush, 4 Hill, 133.

[2] S. v. Brown, 95 N. C. 685; S. v. Frazier, 53 Kan. 87.

[3] S. v. Brannan, 3 Nev. 238.

[4] Felker v. S., 54 Ark. 489.

[5] The indictment in question charged that defendant "did attempt to feloniously take and carry away," etc., and was held to charge an attempt to commit larceny, the court refusing to follow the views of Dr. Wharton (1 Whart. Cr. L., §§ 190–2): Jackson v. S., 91 Ala. 55. But where the indictment merely charged defendant with attempting, fraudulently, etc., to obtain from A. a large sum of money, with intent to cheat and defraud him, it was held insufficient: Reg. v. Marsh, 3 Cox, 571. Where the statute makes it an offense to provoke, or attempt to provoke, a person to commit an assault and battery, it is not erroneous to allege that defendant did provoke and attempt to provoke: Marshall v. S., 123 Ind. 128.

[6] C. v. Creed, 8 Gray, 387; C. v. McDonald, 5 Cush. 365; Marshall v. S., 123 Ind. 128. And as to similar question, see cases under the chapter on assaults, *infra*, §§ 234, 252.

[7] This is practically the form approved in Reg. v. Johnson, L. & C. 489. Substantially the same form of indictment is upheld in S. v. Hughes, 76 Mo. 323.

ATTEMPT TO ROB.

That A. H., in said county, on the —— day of ——, A. D. ——, in a rude, insolent and angry manner, did unlawfully touch one J. M., with intent forcibly and feloniously by violence and putting in fear to take from his person the goods and chattels of him, the said J. M.[1]

ATTEMPT TO STEAL FROM THE PERSON.

That G. W., in said county, on the —— day of ——, A. D. ——, wilfully and maliciously did make an assault on one X. Y., and then and there did thrust his hand into the pocket of the said X. Y., with intent in so doing the money, goods and chattels of the said X. Y., if any such should then be found in his personal possession, feloniously to take, steal and carry away from his person.[2]

§ 229. **Included offense.**— Attempts are generally deemed to be included in an indictment charging the complete offense.[3]

[1] This is held sufficient in Buntin v. S., 68 Ind. 38. An indictment more elaborately setting out the assault and battery is found in Dickinson v. S., 70 Ind. 247.

[2] This form is held sufficient in S. v. Wilson, 30 Conn. 500; but another count charging that defendant did feloniously attempt to steal, take and carry away from the person of X. Y. the money and personal property of the said X. Y., then and there in his possession, was held insufficient as not alleging the overt act.

[3] S. v. Archer, 54 N. H. 465; S. v. Frank, 103 Mo. 120; Reg. v. Bain, L. & C. 129; Reg. v. Hapgood, L. R. 1 C. C. 221. And there may be a conviction for an attempt without formal acquittal of the commission of the offense charged: Miller v. S., 58 Ga. 200. But of course if the offense itself is proven it is error to convict of an attempt only: Reg. v. Nicholls, 2 Cox, 182.

CHAPTER 17.

ASSAULTS.

I. Simple Assault and Assault and Battery.
II. Aggravated Assaults.
III. Assaults with Felonious Intent.
IV. Assault with Intent to Kill or Murder.
V. Assault to do Great Bodily Injury.
VI. Assault with Intent to Rob.

§ 230. **How classified.**— The general subject of assault is closely connected with that of attempt, which is discussed in the preceding chapter, but it covers also cases not included in the doctrine of attempt, such as putting in fear where there is no intent to injure. Although an assault may be committed without any actual injury, yet it is not practicable to separate the discussion of the assault alone from that of an assault in which some injury is inflicted constituting a battery, and therefore assault and battery is necessarily included in this chapter. Moreover, aggravated assaults and assaults with intent to commit a felony, such as murder, robbery, rape, etc., are recognized as distinct forms of assault, and are by statute usually made felonies, although at common law an attempt to commit a felony was, as has already appeared, only a misdemeanor.[1] Assaults with intent to commit rape are, however, discussed in connection with the crime of rape.[2]

I. Simple Assault and Assault and Battery.

§ 231. **What constitutes; attempt to commit battery.**— Some authorities treat an assault as a form of attempt, and the definitions given are based on the idea that the offense consists in an attempt to commit a battery or other physical injury.[3]

[1] *Supra*, § 221.

[2] *Infra*, ch. 21.

[3] "An assault is an attempt or offer with force and violence to do a corporal hurt to another:" 1 Hawk. P. C., ch. 62, § 1; 1 East, P. C. 406; 1 Russ. Cr. 750. It is an "attempt or offer to beat another without touching him:" 3 Bl. Com. 120; 4 id. 216. "An assault is an apparent attempt

Other authorities, however, recognize the offense as consisting of putting another in fear of violence.[1] It is believed that each of these classes of cases constitutes an assault, and that the two must be considered as distinct branches of the crime and discussed separately. The recognition of this distinction will explain somewhat the confusion among the cases.

§ 232. Cases of attempt; menace not enough.—Where the offense consists of an attempt to do injury there must be, as in other cases of attempt, something more than a mere intention. Some step must be taken toward carrying out the intent.[2] Thus, mere preparation is not enough,[3] nor mere threats unaccompanied with any offer of violence,[4] nor the presentation of a dangerous weapon without manifestation of intention to use it,[5] or accompanied with language indicating the intention not to use it.[6] But pointing a loaded weapon with words indicating the intention to discharge it is enough without an attempt made to actually discharge it, the further prosecution of the attempt being prevented by interference.[7] Mere words will not constitute an assault,[8] but words may be important as giv-

by violence to do corporal hurt to another:" 1 Whart. Cr. L., § 603. And as cases where the notion of attempt is recognized, see Tarver v. S., 43 Ala. 354; S. v. Davis, 1 Ired. 125: U. S. v. Hand, 2 Wash. C. C. 435. Under a statute providing for the punishment of an assault with intent to commit a crime, it was held that an attempt to commit larceny was included and not assaults on the person only: Hayes v. S., 15 Lea, 64.

1 "An assault is an unlawful physical force partly or fully put in motion creating a reasonable apprehension of immediate physical injury to a human being:" 2 Bish. Cr. L., § 23. And see S. v. Gorham, 55 N. H. 152. In Rapalje's Law Dic. under the word "assault," both definitions are recognized.

2 Carter v. S., 87 Ala. 113. And as to attempts in general, see *supra*, § 223.

3 Johnson v. S., 43 Tex. 576.

4 Smith v. S., 39 Miss. 521; S. v. Mooney, Phil. 434. The use of insulting language and the act of picking up a stone without offer to throw it, held not an assault: S. v. Milsaps, 82 N. C. 549. Violence must be offered, menaced. or designed. An indignity involving dishonor offered to a consenting female is not an assault: P. v. Bransby, 32 N. Y. 525; Keefe v. S., 19 Ark. 190. And see *infra*, § 464.

5 Flournoy v. S., 25 Tex. Ap. 244; S. v. Blackwell, 9 Ala. 79; Cutler v. S., 59 Ind. 300.

6 S. v. Crow, 1 Ired. 375; Richels v. S., 1 Sneed, 606; Warren v. S., 33 Tex. 517; C. v. Eyre, 1 Serg. & R. 347. And see Tuberville v. Savage, 1 Mod. 3.

7 U. S. v. Kierman, 3 Cranch, C. C. 435; S. v. Reavis, 113 N. C. 677; Reg. v. Duckworth, 2 Q. B. D. (1892), 83.

8 Smith v. S., 39 Miss. 521; P. v. Bransby, 32 N. Y. 525; Warren v. S., 33 Tex. 517.

ing color to acts, and may make that an assault which would not otherwise be one.[1] The line of criminality is to be drawn between menace only and violence begun to be executed.[2] There must be an act in pursuance of a wrongful intent, and such act must involve, as is frequently said, the present ability on the part of the assailant to commit the threatened injury.[3] Thus, to constitute an assault with a weapon it is necessary that the weapon should be presented at the party assaulted within the distance at which it may do execution.[4] But if there is intent to injure and the means resorted to is believed to be adapted to the end, it seems to be immaterial whether such means could have produced the injury intended.[5] The question whether there is ability on the part of the assailant to inflict the threatened injury, as, for instance, in case of a gun loaded with powder only, whether the assailant is near enough to the assailed so that the discharge of the weapon thus loaded would inflict an injury, is for the jury;[6] but it is not necessary that assailant, attempting to strike the assailed with a club or otherwise, be actually within reach of him. It is enough if he be so near as to cause imminent danger if not stopped that the

[1] S. v. Rawles, 65 N. C. 334; S. v. Shipman, 81 N. C. 513; S. v. Martin, 85 N. C. 508; S. v. Horne, 92 N. C. 805; Crow v. S., 41 Tex. 468.

[2] S. v. Myerfield, Phil. 108; S. v. Davis, 1 Ired. 125; Smith v. S., 39 Miss. 521.

[3] U. S. v. Hand, 2 Wash. C. C. 435; C. v. Hagenlock, 140 Mass. 125; Higginbotham v. S., 23 Tex. 574; S. v. Epperson, 27 Mo. 255; S. v. Myerfield, Phil. 108; S. v. Church, 63 N. C. 15; Vaughan v. S., 3 Sm. & M. 553.

[4] Tarver v. S., 43 Ala. 354; Chapman v. S., 78 Ala. 463; P. v. Dodel, 77 Cal. 293; S. v. Godfrey, 17 Oreg. 300; Vaughan v. S., 3 Sm. & M. 553. And, further, as to intent in felonious assaults, see *infra*, § 259. And the gun must be loaded: Henry v. S., 18 Ohio, 32; S. v. Godfrey, 17 Oreg. 300; S. v. Sears, 86 Mo. 169; S. v. Swails, 8 Ind. 524; Pratt v. S., 49 Ark. 179; McKay v. S., 44 Tex. 43; Robinson v. S., 31 Tex. 170 (but this last case is overruled in Bradberry v. S., 22 Tex. Ap. 273). And see further as to necessity of ability to commit: Jarnigan v. S., 6 Tex. Ap. 465; Boles v. S., 18 Tex. Ap. 422. Where "present ability" is a part of the statutory definition, it must be charged and proved: S. v. Hubbs, 58 Ind. 415; Howard v. S., 67 Ind. 401; Klein v. S., 9 Ind. Ap. 365. Otherwise such allegation is not necessary: P. v. Forney, 81 Cal. 118. Nor is it necessary, in order to warrant a conviction for assault under an indictment for assault with intent to do great bodily harm: Kennedy v. P., 122 Ill. 649.

[5] S. v. Glover, 27 S. C. 602. See, also, cases in attempt, *supra*, § 226; and assault with intent, *infra*, § 266.

[6] Clark v. S., 84 Ga. 577; P. v. Lilley, 43 Mich. 521.

injury will be immediately inflicted;[1] and the assault is completed if the attempt has thus been made, although it has been interrupted or abandoned before an injury has actually been committed,[2] the actual infliction of personal injury not being necessary to an assault.[3] If the threatened injury, coupled with present ability to inflict it, is conditioned on the party assailed refusing to do something which the assailant has no right to require him to do, it will constitute an assault even though the conditions are complied with and therefore no violence is used.[4]

§ **233. Putting in fear.**— As already indicated, the doctrine stated in the preceding section, in accordance with which actual threatened injury is essential to constitute an assault, is not universally recognized, and indeed the general proposition supported by the weight of authority is that, if assailant makes threats to injure, being in apparent position to carry them out, and does acts with the apparent intention of carrying them out, thus putting the assailed in fear, an assault is committed even though by reason of facts not known to the person assailed it would be impossible for assailant to commit the injury threatened.[5] Thus, to point a gun or pistol at a person who

[1] S. v. Davis, 1 Ired. 125; P. v. Lilley, 43 Mich. 521; P. v. Yslas, 27 Cal. 630; S. v. Vannoy, 65 N. C. 532; S. v. Malcolm, 8 Ia. 413; Stephens v. Myers, 4 C. & P. 349.

[2] Bishop v. S., 86 Ga. 329; S. v. Malcolm, 8 Ia. 413; S. v. McAfee, 107 N. C. 812; Cato v. S., 4 Tex. Ap. 87. So, where defendant was detected standing in a state of indecent exposure within a few feet of a female under the age of consent, he having induced her to accompany him to a place of retirement, it was held that an assault was proven: Hays v. P., 1 Hill, 351.

[3] S. v. Myers, 19 Ia. 517.

[4] U. S. v. Richardson, 5 Cranch, C. C. 348; U. S. v. Myers, 1 Cranch, C. C. 310; S. v. Morgan, 3 Ired. 186; S. v. Horne, 92 N. C. 805; S. v. Martin, 85 N. C. 508; S. v. Rawles, 65 N. C. 334; S. v. Hampton, 63 N. C. 13; S. v. Church, 63 N. C. 15; Bloomer v. S., 3 Sneed, 66. But under statutory provisions, held that to point an unloaded pistol at another within shooting distance accompanied with an order to kneel, which was obeyed through fear, was not a criminal assault: McKay v. S., 44 Tex. 43.

[5] C. v. White, 110 Mass. 407; S. v. Gorham, 55 N. H. 152; S. v. Cherry, 11 Ired. 475; S. v. Benedict, 11 Vt. 236; Atteberry v. S., 33 Tex. Ap. 88; Reg. v. St. George, 9 C. & P. 483. Thus, to ride a horse so near another as to endanger his person and create a belief in his mind that it is the intention of the rider to ride over him, constitutes an assault: S. v. Sims, 3 Strobh. 137; or to threaten injury to another with a knife held in the hand, causing the other to go away by fear: S. v. Shipman, 81 N. C. 513. There seems to be no difference in

does not know but that it is loaded, and has no reason to believe that it is not, is an assault.[1] It is therefore unnecessary, in such cases, that the indictment allege that the weapon was loaded, or otherwise show present ability to inflict an injury;[2] but on this point authorities to the contrary are cited in the preceding section.[3]

§ 234. **Present ability.**— It is evident from the discussion in the two preceding sections that the question of ability to commit a threatened injury is of importance for different reasons under different circumstances. In general there must be something more than mere menace or threat, and unless there is ability, at least apparent, to carry it out, there is no assault whatever. If there is apparent ability so as to cause fear on the part of the person assailed, then under the doctrine of the preceding section an assault is committed. If there is actual ability and intention to carry out the threat, then there is an assault under the doctrine of the second preceding section, in accordance with the general theory of assaults; and under the doctrine of attempts there might evidently be an assault where the assailant should threaten and intend to do an injury believing himself to be in a position to do it, and attempting to carry out his purpose, although by reason of some fact not within his knowledge the act should be really impossible.[4]

§ 235. **What acts sufficient; battery.**— As has already been said, an attempt to commit an injury to the person of another, either real or apparent, is an assault, and in so far as an assault is thus looked upon as an attempt, the thing attempted, unless

this respect between civil and criminal cases; Beach v. Hancock, 27 N. H. 223.

[1] S. v. Shepard, 10 Ia. 126; Crumbley v. S., 61 Ga. 582; S. v. Triplett, 52 Kan. 678; S. v. Smith, 2 Humph. 457; Crow v. S., 41 Tex. 468; Kief v. S., 10 Tex. Ap. 286.

[2] S. v. Shepard, 10 Ia. 126; S. v. Rigg, 10 Nev. 284.

[3] Some English cases which are cited in support of this contrary view are without bearing, for the reason that they involve construction of statutes punishing the offense of attempting to discharge a loaded weapon at another: Reg. v. Baker, 1 C. & K. 254; Reg. v. James, 1 C. & K. 530. The case of Reg. v. St. George, heretofore cited, is of the same character, but Parke, B., says that the putting in fear would constitute an assault. In other cases defendant was held not to have committed an assault where the weapon was unloaded, because of variance from the allegations of the indictment: Blake v. Barnard, 9 C. & P. 626; Reg. v. Oxford, 9 C. & P. 525.

[4] *Supra*, § 226.

it constitutes some other crime, such as murder, robbery, rape, etc., is a battery, and the two things, the assault and the battery, must usually be considered together. In this sense it is properly said that a battery is a completed assault, just as on the other hand an assault is an attempt to commit a battery, and a battery, therefore, necessarily includes an assault.[1] Leaving out of view for the present, therefore, aggravated assaults and assaults with intent to commit specific felonies, to be considered hereafter, it is important now to determine what kind of an injury it is which attempted is an assault, and completed is a battery. Such injury must be to the person, rather than to property, reputation, etc., and yet the offense of battery is committed not only by striking the person, but by striking or pulling the clothing, or a cane, or otherwise infringing the personal immunity from harm. That such act must, however, be not merely accidental or in sport, or with an innocent purpose, will hereafter appear in considering the intent as an element of an assault.[2] Thus, it has been held that merely taking hold of the coat, or laying the hand gently on the person of another, if done in an angry, insolent, or hostile manner, amounts to an assault and battery;[3] but to strike the horse which another is driving is not sufficient.[4] So spitting or throwing water upon another or jostling him, or even touching him in a rude, insolent, or angry manner,[5] or driving against or riding over him,

[1] S. v. Twogood, 7 Ia. 252. But of course an assault does not necessarily include a battery: Furnish v. C., 14 Bush, 180. It seems that there is no such offense by federal statute as an assault alone, in territory exclusively under federal jurisdiction: U. S. v. Barnaby, 51 Fed. R. 20.

[2] *Infra*, § 239.

[3] U. S. v. Ortega, 4 Wash. C. C. 531; U. S. v. Hand, 2 Wash. C. C. 435; Johnson v. S., 17 Tex. 515; Resp. v. De Longchamps, 1 Dall. 111; S. v. Davis, 1 Hill (S. C.), 46. Pushing one with the open hand, accompanied with the use of threatening language, is an assault and battery: S. v. Baker, 65 N. C. 332. So is the act of cutting off a pauper's hair against his will: Forde v. Skinner, 4 C. & P. 239.

[4] Kirland v. S., 43 Ind. 146.

[5] Bonner v. S., 97 Ala. 47. So held in Indiana under a statute following the common-law definition, and requiring that the manner be rude, insolent, or angry: McCulley v. S., 62 Ind. 428; S. v. Wright, 52 Ind. 307. And the indictment must charge the manner accordingly: Howard v. S., 67 Ind. 401. But it is sufficient if the allegation is of an injury in one of those three ways: S. v. Philley, 67 Ind. 304. Even without touching, if there is an intent to injure, the act may constitute an assault: Jackson v. S., 91 Ga. 322.

if wilfully done, will be a battery.[1] But as will be seen hereafter, where actual injury is inflicted, the question of whether the act is criminal will depend on the intent with which it is done.[2] Unlawful arrest or imprisonment includes a battery.[3]

§ 236. **Administering injurious drug.**— One who administers to another deleterious substances without his consent, and thereby causes an injury, is guilty of assault and battery.[4] It is not necessary to allege knowledge of the poisonous or injurious nature of the thing administered, if the allegation is that the act was wilful and malicious or wanton.[5]

§ 237. **Wilful or negligent exposure, or improper treatment of another.**— Exposing and abandoning a helpless infant will constitute an assault.[6] One who attempts to act as a phy-

[1] 1 Hawk. P. C., ch. 62, § 2; 1 Russ. Cr. 751; Reg. v. Cotesworth, 6 Mod. 172. But merely touching the hand of another in snatching an article therefrom with intent to steal it, if done without intent to hurt and without violence, does not constitute an assault with force and violence with intent to steal: C. v. Ordway, 12 Cush. 270.

[2] *Infra*, § 239.

[3] Long v. Rogers, 17 Ala. 540; Bissell v. Gold, 1 Wend. 210; S. v. Parker, 75 N. C. 249; U. S. v. Benner, Baldw. 234; 1 Russ. Cr. 753.

[4] C. v. Stratton, 114 Mass. 303; Carr v. S., 135 Ind. 1; Reg. v. Button, 8 C. & P. 660. Administering poison is an assault: Hall v. S., 132 Ind. 317. But in England administering deleterious substances in food or drink has been held not indictable as an assault: Reg. v. Hanson, 2 C. & K. 912; Reg. v. Dilworth, 2 M. & Rob. 531; but is made criminal by statute: Reg. v. Wilkins, L. & C. 89; Reg. v. Hennah, 13 Cox, 547. Attempting to poison does not involve an assault: Collins v. S., 3 Heisk. 14; Garnet v. S., 1 Tex. Ap. 605. In determining whether a substance is noxious within a statute punishing the administration of noxious substances, the question is whether the intent in administering it was to injure. If it is of such nature that it might properly superinduce the injury intended, the act will be criminal, although in other circumstances and other quantities it might not be injurious: Dougherty v. P., 1 Colo. 514. By the California code the word "poison" refers to an inherent destructive quality and not to a mechanical action on the system, but it is otherwise as to the words "other noxious substances or liquors:" P. v. Van Deleer, 53 Cal. 147.

[5] C. v. Hobbs, 140 Mass. 443; C. v. Stratton, 114 Mass. 303. So, under an indictment for mixing poison with food with intent to kill, it is not necessary to allege that the substance was known by the defendant to be poisonous: C. v. Galavan, 9 Allen, 271; C. v. Bearse, 108 Mass. 487. The statutory description of "poisonous substances" is sufficient: P. v. Keeley, 81 Cal. 210.

[6] C. v. Stoddard, 9 Allen, 280; Reg. v. March, 1 C. & K. 496. But somewhat contrary as to abandoning an infant, see Reg. v. Renshaw, 2 Cox, 385; and as to keeping an idiot brother without supplies or necessaries: Rex v. Smith, 2 C. & P. 449. A master is not bound to provide medical advice for a servant, but he is for an apprentice: Reg. v. Smith,

sician, and as such prescribes injurious treatment, even with good intentions, but with gross negligence and ignorance as to the probable effect, is guilty of an assault.[1]

§ 238. **Indecent assault.**— It is an assault for an adult male to touch or handle a female without her consent in an indecent manner or with undue familiarity,[2] as by putting his arm about her neck and kissing her.[3] So unnecessarily stripping a female patient naked for the purpose of medical examination is an assault.[4] Where one justified in administering punishment upon a female does so in an indecent manner it may be an assault.[5] While, as will hereafter appear, an assault with an attempt to commit rape is not committed where the attempt to have connection with her is by her consent, yet the connection may in itself be so brutal as to constitute an assault, even where consent to the act appears.[6] So where there is consent, there may be assault and battery in communicating to the female a venereal disease, the existence of the disease in the male not being known to the female.[7] But this is doubted and the contrary is held as between husband and wife.[8] Attempt to commit an unnatural crime with a boy is an assault upon him even though he submit, if he is too young to understand the nature of the act.[9]

§ 239. **Intent.**— Intent to injure is essential to constitute an assault;[10] and a stroke given by inadvertence or for self-protection is not an assault.[11] Therefore, evidence of other assaults

8 C. & P. 153. An indictment for assault to kill an adopted daughter by failing and refusing to nourish her is insufficient without charging that defendant had the means and was pecuniarily able to provide for her: S. v. Merkley, 74 Ia. 695. *Contra*, Reg. v. Ryland, L. R. 1 C. C. 99. And see further under homicide, *infra*, § 286.

[1] C v. Pierce, 138 Mass. 165.

[2] Rex v. Nichol, Russ. & Ry. 130; Ridout v. S., 6 Tex. Ap. 249; Veal v. S., 8 Tex. Ap. 474; Donaldson v. S., 10 Tex. Ap. 307; Reg. v. McGavaran, 6 Cox, 64.

[3] Goodrum v. S., 60 Ga. 509; Reg. v. Dungey, 4 F. & F. 99.

[4] Rex v. Rosinski, 1 Moody, 19.

[5] Reg. v. Miles, 6 Jur. 243.

[6] Richie v. S., 58 Ind. 355.

[7] Reg. v. Sinclair, 13 Cox, 28; Reg. v. Bennett, 4 F. & F. 1105.

[8] Reg. v. Clarence, 22 Q. B. D. 23.

[9] Reg. v. Lock, L. R. 2 C. C. 10. But where the boy was fourteen years of age, *held*, no assault: Reg. v. Wollaston, 12 Cox, 180. Further as to consent, see *infra*, § 249.

[10] Richels v. S., 1 Sneed, 606; S. v. Sears, 86 Mo. 169; White v. S., 29 Tex. Ap. 530; Rutherford v. S., 13 Tex. Ap. 92.

[11] C. v. Ruggles, 6 Allen, 588.

and threats by the same person immediately preceding that complained of is admissible to show with what intent the assault in question was made.[1] But an assault may be committed without intending to injure a particular person, as by recklessly shooting into a crowd,[2] or by accidentally injuring another person than the one for whom the injury is intended.[3] So mere recklessness without intent to injure any one, but resulting in injury, may constitute an assault.[4] However, the intent to injure the person assaulted must be alleged; the legal presumption of an intent to injure from the fact of injury does not dispense with the necessity of such an allegation.[5] Mistake as to facts will not excuse if the intent was to do an unlawful act.[6]

§ **240. Unlawfulness.**— If the act is unlawful, the intent with which it is done is immaterial; as where one negligently aims and discharges a fire-arm toward another, supposing it not to be loaded;[7] or negligently throws a stone at another in sport, causing an injury.[8] Unlawful intent will be inferred from an illegal act.[9] One who is engaged in an affray or riot is responsible for committing an assault thereby.[10] But the mere fact that one is driving at greater speed than permitted by ordinance in a city will not make the act of unintentionally running over another in the highway an assault.[11]

§ **241. Justification.**— Under some circumstances it is lawful to use violence towards or commit an injury upon another,

[1] Ross v. S., 62 Ala. 224. But evidence, disconnected, of previous threats of personal violence, is inadmissible: S. v. Skidmore, 87 N. C. 509.

[2] S. v. Myers, 19 Ia. 517; Scott v. S., 49 Ark. 156. And see the famous squib case: Scott v. Shepherd, 2 W. Bl. 892. An indiscriminate assault upon several is an assault upon each: S. v. Merritt, Phil. 134; S. v. Nash, 86 N. C. 650. As to the intent, in case of assault to kill or murder, see *infra*, § 274.

[3] Hollywood v. P., 3 Keyes (N. Y.), 55; James v. Campbell, 5 C. & P. 372. Thus, one firing a pistol through the door of a house commits an assault upon the inmates, although his intent is to injure not them but some one else supposed to be therein: Cowley v. S., 10 Lea, 282.

[4] Smith v. C., 100 Pa. St. 324.

[5] Grayson v. S., 37 Tex. 228.

[6] For instance, an indecent assault upon a woman, mistaking her for another who is a prostitute, will be criminal: Carter v. S., 87 Ala. 113. So one who fired into a crowd in the mistaken belief that they had committed an injury to his child was held guilty of an assault: S. v. Nash, 88 N. C. 618.

[7] C. v. McLaughlin, 5 Allen, 507.

[8] Hill v. S., 63 Ga. 578.

[9] S. v. Allen, 30 Tex. 59; S. v. Boynton, 75 Ia. 753; Smith v. C., 100 Pa. St. 324.

[10] S. v. Dineen, 10 Minn. 407.

[11] C. v. Adams, 114 Mass. 323.

and therefore it is not every attempt to use such violence or do such injury that will constitute an assault; the act must be without legal excuse.[1] But the provocation of offensive or threatening language will not justify an assault.[2] In some states, however, by statute, insulting or opprobrious language may be shown in mitigation or even in justification.[3] Resistance to unlawful arrest will be justified;[4] and so will the act of an officer in attempting to make a lawful arrest,[5] or in preserving the peace,[6] unless the violence used in the resistance to such unlawful arrest, or in attempting to make a lawful arrest or preserve the peace, was uncalled for and excessive.[7]

§ **242. Lawful chastisement.**— There are various relations in life which make some degree of violence or restraint under proper circumstances lawful. Thus, moderate restraint or correction may be employed by the parent,[8] or by one *in loco parentis*.[9] But if such correction or restraint is unreasonable it constitutes an assault.[10] In the relation between teacher and pupil the teacher stands *in loco parentis*, and may enforce obedience to reasonable demands by corporal punishment administered with proper motives and within reasonable limits.[11] But

[1] S. v. Wyatt, 76 Ia. 328; S. v. Bateswell, 105 Mo. 609; Rex v. Osmer, 5 East, 304; Rex v. Cheere, 4 B. & C. 902; Reg. v. Meredith, 8 C. & P. 589.

[2] S. v. Herrington, 21 Ark. 195, S. v. Gamble, 119 Mo. 427; S. v. Wood, 1 Bay, 351; Coleman v. S., 28 Ga. 78; Boon v. S., 31 Tex. 557; Nash v. S., 2 Tex. Ap. 362. Evidence of provocation may be introduced by the state to explain and show a motive of resentment for defendant's act: S. v. Griffis, 3 Ired. 504. But see S. v. Jowers, 11 Ired. 555.

[3] Spigner v. S., 103 Ala. 30; Riddle v. S., 49 Ala. 389; Brown v. S., 74 Ala. 42; Wood v. S., 64 Miss. 761; Hodgkins v. S., 89 Ga. 761. But even under such statutes opprobrious language will not excuse an assault with intent to kill: Jones v. S., 33 Tex. Ap. 492.

[4] S. v. Bateswell, 105 Mo. 609; S. v. Denkins, 24 La. An. 29.

[5] S. v. Pugh, 101 N. C. 737; S. v. McNinch, 90 N. C. 695.

[6] Patterson v. S., 91 Ala. 58. But a police officer cannot justify assault and battery as a means of repressing disorder: Stone v. S., 56 Ark. 345.

[7] C. v. Cooley, 6 Gray, 350; Delafoile v. S., 54 N. J. 381; S. v. Pugh, 101 N. C. 737; S. v. Hedrick, 95 N. C. 624; Rasberry v. S., 1 Tex. Ap. 664.

[8] Davis v. S., 6 Tex. Ap. 133.

[9] Snowden v. S., 12 Tex. Ap. 105.

[10] Hinkle v. S., 127 Ind. 490; S. v. Bitman, 13 Ia. 485. For instance, if the weapon used is improper: Neal v. S., 54 Ga. 281. But if no permanent injury is inflicted there must be legal malice or wicked motive, the parent being intrusted by law with discretion: Dean v. S., 89 Ala. 46; S. v. Jones, 95 N. C. 588.

[11] Danenhoffer v. S., 69 Ind. 295; Dowlen v. S., 14 Tex. Ap. 61; Hutton

if the punishment is excessive he is guilty of assault and battery.[1] In determining whether the punishment is excessive, the nature of the instrument used in connection with the offense is to be considered by the jury.[2] If in the judgment of the jury the punishment inflicted is immoderate or excessive, they may infer malice from the act.[3] And as a general rule the reasonable limit is exceeded when the punishment causes lasting injury.[4] In other relations where authority is conferred upon one person over another, moderate chastisement may be lawful, as by the keeper of an almshouse upon an inmate so far as is necessary to preserve order and proper discipline.[5] But those who hire from the state the service of convicts have not any such authority over them as will justify flogging.[6]

§ 243. **Correction of wife.**— It seems generally to be supposed that by the earlier common law the husband might lawfully inflict physical chastisement on his wife in exercising over her a reasonable control, and that unless some permanent injury should be inflicted, or there should be an excess of violence, or such a degree of cruelty as to show that the act was for the gratification of his own bad passions rather than for proper restraint, the husband was not guilty of an assault.[7] But this authority on the part of the husband has been expressly repudiated in all the recent cases on the subject, even in the two states from which earlier cases are cited in the last preceding note.[8] The consent of the wife to sexual connec-

v. S., 23 Tex. Ap. 386; Bolding v. S., 23 Tex. Ap. 172.

1 Gardner v. S., 4 Ind. 632.

2 C. v. Randall, 4 Gray, 36.

3 Boyd v. S., 88 Ala. 169; S. v. Stafford, 113 N. C. 635; Whitley v. S., 33 Tex. Ap. 172. Immoderate whipping of an apprentice, even for committing larceny, will not be excused as without malice: S. v. Dickerson, 98 N. C. 708.

4 S. v. Pendergrass, 2 Dev. & B. 365.

5 S. v. Neff, 58 Ind. 516; S. v. Hull, 34 Conn. 132.

6 Cornell v. S., 6 Lea, 624; Prewitt v. S., 51 Ala. 33; Werner v. S., 44 Ark. 122.

7 S. v. Black, 1 Winst. 266; S. v. Rhodes, Phill. 453; S. v. Mabrey, 64 N. C. 592; Bradley v. S., 1 Walk. (Miss.). 156; 1 Bl. Com. 444 (but see Hammond's note to this passage, p. 752).

8 Harris v. S., 71 Miss. 462; S. v. Oliver, 70 N. C. 60 (but a still later North Carolina case, in a dictum, restates the earlier rule: S. v. Edens, 95 N. C. 693); C. v. McAfee, 108 Mass. 458; P. v. Winters, 2 Park. Cr. 10; Fulgham v. S., 46 Ala. 143; S. v. Buckley, 2 Harr. 552; Reg. v. Jackson, 1 Q. B. D. (1891), 671.

tion with the husband having been given by the act of marrying, he is not guilty of an assault in having such connection.[1]

§ 244. **Control of premises.**— One lawfully in charge and control of premises used by the public may properly eject therefrom persons unlawfully coming upon such premises, or guilty of improper conduct thereon, without being liable for assault, as, for instance, the proprietor of a public house.[2] But a station-master will be guilty of assault in ejecting a passenger without good cause;[3] so will a conductor in ejecting a person from a train while in motion.[4]

§ 245. **Protection of property.**— Assault and battery may be justified in defense of real or personal property,[5] as where the owner or person in charge of premises without unnecessary force removes an intruder,[6] or attempts to prevent another from wrongfully entering upon his premises.[7] But in ejecting a trespasser there must first be a request to depart before violence is resorted to, and then only such violence should be used as is necessary under the circumstances.[8] So the unlawful act of an officer in attempting to seize property will justify violence in preventing him from taking the property,[9] but not in attempting to retake property from the officer, though wrongfully taken by him.[10] Assault and battery is not justified in attempting to take possession of a house which is in the peaceable possession of another,[11] or in attempting to retake from another, who is in possession, property claimed to have been stolen from the assailant.[12] One tenant in common cannot lawfully

[1] This is said by a majority of the court in a prosecution of the husband for assault in having connection with his wife by consent, but communicating to her venereal disease which he had, unknown to her: Reg. v. Clarence, 22 Q. B. D. 23.

[2] S. v. Steele, 106 N. C. 766.

[3] P. v. McKay, 46 Mich. 439.

[4] S. v. Kinney, 34 Minn. 311.

[5] Souther v. S., 18 Tex. Ap. 352.

[6] U. S. v. Bartle, 1 Cranch, C. C. 236; S. v. Marsteller, 84 N. C. 726; P. v. Adams, 52 Mich. 105; P. v. Foss, 80 Mich. 559; Clarke v. S., 89 Ga. 768; S. v. Weeks, 1 Dev. 135.

[7] S. v. Stoke, 80 Ia. 68. Even though the owner of premises is unlawfully obstructing a right of way, he has a right to protect his premises, and his act in doing so will not justify an assault on him by the person entitled to the right of way: S. v. White, 18 R. I. 473.

[8] C. v. Goodwin, 3 Cush. 154; S. v. Lazarus, 1 Treadw. (S. C.) 34; S. v. Burke, 82 N. C. 551; S. v. Taylor, 82 N. C. 554; S. v. Yancey, 74 N. C. 244; Parrish v. S., 32 Tex. Ap. 583.

[9] S. v. Briggs, 3 Ired. 357.

[10] S. v. Black, 109 N. C. 856; Cokely v. S., 4 Ia. 477.

[11] S. v. McKinley, 82 Ia. 445.

[12] Hendrix v. S., 50 Ala. 148. But

use violence in resisting the entry of another tenant upon the common premises, though with the declared purpose of committing an unlawful act.[1] In all cases the violence threatened must be reasonably proportioned to the wrongful act which is resisted. Thus, it is an assault to point a pistol at another who, without right, has stopped the assailant from driving along the highway,[2] or to repel a trespass on premises by an attempt to murder.[3]

§ 246. **Self-defense.**— One who is struck at may strike back to prevent a repetition,[4] not, however, to avenge himself, but only in self-defense.[5] And in self-protection no more violence should be used than is necessary under the circumstances.[6] In general, self-defense is a justification;[7] but where defendant relies upon reasonable apprehension of danger, he must show that his belief was founded on reasonable grounds,[8] the jury being judge of the apparent necessity.[9] One who has brought on a difficulty cannot justify striking in self-defense.[10] But he will not by reason of his own wrong in provoking the difficulty be entirely cut off from defending himself from ensuing violence,[11] unless he might by retreating have avoided the danger.[12] A son may use violence when necessary to defend or protect his father, but he may not interpose in a fight in which his father is engaged with another on equal terms.[13] The whole subject

assault is said to be justifiable in attempting to recover money fraudulently taken and in possession of the person wrongfully taking it: Anderson v. S., 6 Baxter, 608.

1 C. v. Lakeman, 4 Cush. 597.

2 Hairston v. S., 54 Miss. 689.

3 S. v. Donyes, 14 Mont. 70; S. v. Montgomery, 65 Ia. 483.

4 Anon., 2 Lewin, 48; U. S. v. Beyer, 31 Fed. R. 35.

5 Reg. v. Driscoll, Car. & M. 214. Although by statute opprobrious words are made a justification, a prior blow is not a defense: Riddle v. S., 49 Ala. 389.

6 Stevens v. S., 1 Tex. Ap. 591; Cotton v. S., 4 Tex. 260; Mooney v. S., 33 Ala. 419; S. v. Quin, 3 Brev. 515; Floyd v. S., 36 Ga. 91; Gallagher v. S., 3 Minn. 270; Reid v. S., 71 Ga. 865.

7 Sharp v. S., 19 Ohio, 379; S. v. Gibson, 10 Ired. 214; McAfee v. S., 31 Ga. 411; S. v. Davis, 7 Jones, 52; Edwards v. S., 5 Tex. Ap. 593. It is not proper to speak of assault in self-defense; an act done in lawful self-defense cannot be an assault: P. v. Lynch, 101 Cal. 229.

8 S. v. Bryson, 1 Wins. (No. 2), 86; May v. S., 6 Tex. Ap. 191.

9 S. v. McGreer, 13 S. C. 464.

10 S. v. Bryson, 1 Wins. (No. 2), 86.

11 Daniel v. S., 10 Lea, 261; Smith v. S., 8 Lea, 402; Yoes v. S., 9 Ark. 42.

12 S. v. McKinley, 82 Ia. 445.

13 S. v. Johnson, 75 N. C. 174; Waddell v. S., 1 Tex. Ap. 720.

of self-defense is considered under homicide,[1] and to some extent under assaults with intent to commit a felony.[2]

§ 247. Effect of civil action.— Acknowledgment of satisfaction by the injured party will not authorize a discharge of defendant after conviction.[3] The prosecution of a civil action to recover damages for an assault will not bar a criminal prosecution for the same assault.[4] Nor will judgment in favor of one party against another for damages for assault bar a prosecution of the former for an assault in the same difficulty, since each may have been guilty of an assault.[5] Where the assault is committed in view of the court and is punished as a contempt, that fact will not bar prosecution for the crime.[6]

§ 248. Mitigation or aggravation.— Extenuating circumstances not amounting to a complete defense of justification should not be proven under a plea of not guilty, but are to be submitted to the court on sentence day.[7] For instance, evidence that defendant had been informed before the assault that the injured party had agreed with defendant's wife to help her get a divorce and then marry her is not admissible.[8] But on the other hand it has been held that by way of mitigation for assault and battery on the wife the husband may show that at the time of the assault he was immediately provoked to its commission by her bad behavior,[9] and that in explanation of what would otherwise appear to have been a wanton and incomprehensible assault upon his wife, defendant might show that her prior undue intimacy with another man had been communicated to him.[10] It seems also that circumstances of aggravation may be proven.[11] But the general subject of aggravated assaults will be treated of in the next chapter.[12]

§ 249. Effect of consent.— An assault implies an attempt to use force on the one side, and repulsion, or at least want of assent, on the other, and it must be, therefore, committed against

[1] *Infra*, §§ 301-316.

[2] *Infra*, § 267.

[3] P. v. Bishop, 5 Wend. 111.

[4] C. v. Elliott, 2 Mass. 372; P. v. Judges, etc., 13 Johns. 85; S. v. Frost, 1 Brev. 385 (overruling S. v. Blyth, 1 Bay, 166); Buckner v. Beck, Dudley (S. C.), 168.

[5] P. v. Keuhn, 93 Mich. 619.

[6] S. v. Yancy, Law Rep. (N. C.) 519.

[7] S. v. Smith, 2 Bay, 62.

[8] S. v. Jackson, 17 Mo. 544.

[9] Robbins v. S., 20 Ala. 36.

[10] Greta v. S., 10 Tex. Ap. 36.

[11] Murdock v. S., 65 Ala. 520; S. v. Dearborn, 54 Me. 442.

[12] See *infra*, § 254 et seq.

the will of the party assaulted.[1] Thus, where parties engage in a fight at fisticuffs there is no assault, although the act may constitute an affray, which is a distinct offense.[2] But even a boxing-match or fist-fight engaged in by consent may constitute or tend to a breach of the peace, and the parties thus be guilty of an assault.[3] Especially is a prize-fight illegal, and all persons aiding and abetting therein are guilty of assault, the consent of the persons actually engaged not affording any answer to the criminal charge.[4] The consent of the patient to improper and injurious medical treatment, in reliance on the advice of a physician, will not be a defense to the physician when charged with such improper and dangerous treatment as constitutes an assault.[5] So consent to carnal connection, under the pretense of medical treatment, will not prevent the act being an assault.[6] On the principle that there is no assault where there is consent, an indignity offered to a female, where she is the consenting party to an act involving her own dishonor, is not an assault.[7] The general effect of proof of consent in prosecutions for rape will be discussed in connection with that subject.[8] Where the female is under the age of consent, so that the act of connection is criminal (sometimes called rape), even if she does consent, the authorities are not agreed whether the attempt to have such connection with her consent is an assault.[9] So in case of indecent acts committed by a man

[1] Duncan v. C., 6 Dana, 295; Smith v. S., 12 Ohio St. 466.

[2] Champer v. S., 14 Ohio St. 437; Duncan v. C., 6 Dana, 295.

[3] C. v. Collberg, 119 Mass. 350; S. v. Burnham, 56 Vt. 445; Reg. v. Lewis, 1 C. & K. 419. And even in civil actions for assault it has been held that consent to fight will not prevent recovery for assault and battery: Bell v. Hansley, 3 Jones, 131; Stout v. Wren, 1 Hawks, 420; Logan v. Austin, 1 Stew. 476; Adams v. Waggoner, 33 Ind. 531.

[4] Reg. v. Coney, 8 Q. B. D. 534. Further, as to prize-fights, see *infra*, § 1013.

[5] C. v. Pierce, 138 Mass. 165.

[6] Reg. v. Case, 1 Den. 580.

[7] P. v. Bransby, 32 N. Y. 525.

[8] See *infra*, § 464.

[9] As holding that such an attempt even with consent is an assault, see Cliver v. S., 45 N. J. 46; Hays v. P., 1 Hill, 351; P. v. McDonald, 9 Mich. 150; Murphy v. S., 120 Ind. 115. Mere submission of a child of tender years does not show consent: Reg. v. Day, 9 C. & P. 722; Reg. v. Lock, L. R. 2 C. C. 10. On the other hand, as holding that in such a case the act that would be rape, if completed, does not involve an assault if by consent of the female, see S. v. Pickett, 11 Nev. 255; Smith v. S., 12 Ohio St. 466; Rhodes v. S., 1 Coldw. 350; Reg. v. Martin, 9 C. & P. 215; Reg. v. Banks, 8 C. & P. 574; Reg. v. Meredith, 8 C.

with a boy too young to understand the nature of such acts (eight years of age, for instance), the man was held guilty of an assault.[1] But where such act was committed with a boy above fourteen years of age by his consent, it was held that there was no assault.[2] Consent obtained by fraud, as where by personating a woman's husband another man has connection with her, will not prevent the act being an assault.[3] Where the act goes beyond the consent there may be an assault; for instance, where, though there is consent to sexual connection, it is brutal and excessive.[4] So it has been thought there may be an assault where, in sexual connection consented to, the male is, without the knowledge of the female, affected with venereal disease, which is thus communicated to the female.[5] But these cases have been doubted, and by a divided court it has been held that it is not an assault for a husband to communicate venereal disease to the wife.[6]

§ 250. **Principal and accessory.**— As assaults, or assaults and batteries, are misdemeanors and not felonies, there is no distinction between principal and accessory, and one who incites others to the commission of such an offense may be convicted under a charge for the offense itself;[7] and those who are present aiding and abetting are equally guilty with those who do the act.[8]

§ 251. **Jurisdiction.**— Where the lower grade of offenses are cognizable only in an inferior court, the offense of assault or assault and battery is usually of such inferior grade that it may be prosecuted only in such court, even though some form of aggravation is alleged, provided such additional allegation does not raise the offense to a higher grade.[9] But it may be,

& P. 589; Reg. v. Read, 2 Car. & K. 957. As to assault with intent to rape, see, in general, *infra*, § 464 *et seq.*

[1] Reg. v. Lock, L. R. 2 C. C. 10.

[2] Reg. v. Wollaston, 12 Cox, 180.

[3] Reg. v. Saunders, 8 C. & P. 265; Reg. v. Williams, 8 C. & P. 286. As to whether the act would be rape. see *infra*, § 446.

[4] Richie v. S., 58 Ind. 355.

[5] Reg. v. Bennett, 4 F. & F. 1105; Reg. v. Sinclair, 13 Cox, 28.

[6] Reg. v. Clarence, 22 Q. B. D. 23.

[7] C. v. Hurley, 99 Mass. 433; S. v. Lymburn, 1 Brev. 397; S. v. McClintock, 8 Ia. 203; Thompson v. S., 25 Ala. 41; U. S. v. Ricketts, 1 Cranch, C. C. 164.

[8] S. v. Morris, 3 Hawks, 388; S. v. Merritt, Phil. 134; Hansford v. S., 54 Ga. 55.

[9] C. v. Cunningham, 13 Mass. 245; C. v. O'Donnell, 150 Mass. 502; T. v. Valdez, 1 New Mex. 548. But a court of general criminal jurisdic-

under peculiar provisions as to jurisdiction, that the question of whether the offense is of a higher grade can only be determined on the evidence and not by the pleadings, and in such case the higher court would have jurisdiction.[1] Where assault and battery is by statute a criminal offense, and the provision is such that all criminal offenses are tried upon presentment or indictment only, then such proceeding would be necessary in case of this crime.[2] A question of territorial jurisdiction arises when a person in one state shoots across the line at a person in another, and it has been held that there is in such case a crime committed in the state where the person is who is assailed.[3] Similar questions are considered in the chapter on homicide.[4]

§ 252. **Indictment.**— The indictment may be as at common law,[5] but where special terms are used in the statute the indictment must correspond therewith.[6] Matter of aggravation not necessary to charge the crime may be alleged without vitiating the indictment.[7] It is not necessary to set out the particular acts of violence done,[8] nor to allege the nature of the weapon used, or the manner of its use.[9] Even if the means is stated, other means may be proven without constituting a variance.[10] As in other cases, time should be alleged (although not material),[11] unless by statutory provision such allegation is not necessary.[12] Facts showing the present ability to commit

tion can entertain the prosecution unless it directly appears that it is exclusively in the jurisdiction of some other court: S. v. Earnest, 98 N. C. 740.

[1] S. v. Jones, 73 Me. 280.

[2] Rector v. S., 6 Ark. 187; Durr v. Howard, 6 Ark. 461.

[3] Simpson v. S., 92 Ga. 41.

[4] *Infra*, § 369.

[5] Evans v. S., 25 Tex. 304.

[6] S. v. Trulock, 46 Ind. 289; Rollins v. S., 62 Ind. 46; Howard v. S., 67 Ind. 401; Slusser v. S., 71 Ind. 280. "Touch, strike and wound" are equivalent to the statutory words "touch in a rude, insolent or angry manner, unlawfully:" S. v. Miller, 27 Ind. 15; but "violently beat, bruise, wound and ill-treat" are sufficient without "in an angry and wilful manner," where the latter words are not used in the statute: S. v. Boynton, 75 Ia. 753. Similar words were held sufficient in Reg. v. Crespin, 11 Q. B. 913.

[7] Murdock v. S., 65 Ala. 520; S. v. Dearborn, 54 Me. 442; S. v. Inskeep, 49 Ohio St. 228.

[8] Bloomer v. S., 3 Sneed, 66; Roberson v. S., 15 Tex. Ap. 317.

[9] P. v. Casey, 72 N. Y. 393; S. v. Clayton, 100 Mo. 516. As to alleging the manner or means in aggravated assaults or assaults with intent, see *infra*, §§ 260, 268.

[10] Ryan v. S., 52 Ind. 167; P. v. Casey, 72 N. Y. 393.

[11] S. v. Eubanks, 41 Tex. 291.

[12] Myers v. S., 121 Ind. 15. The fact

the offense on the part of the defendant at the time of the assault need not be alleged; the words of the statute are sufficient.[1] The unlawful character of the assault need not be alleged nor need the intent to injure be stated.[2] It is not necessary to allege that the person beaten was in the peace of the state, nor are the words "with force and arms" necessary.[3] Nor is it necessary to say that the party wronged was "late of said county," or that he was damaged.[4] The act may be charged as felonious where the statute defining the offense brings it within the definition of a felony.[5] Where the offense is statutory the conclusion of the indictment should be, "against the form of the statute," as in other indictments for statutory offenses.[6] The name of the person injured, if known, must be alleged;[7] if not known, that fact must be stated.[8] The name of the person upon whom the assault is charged to have been committed is material, and proof of an assault upon such person or another will not support a conviction;[9] but identity of the name of the person assaulted with the name used in the indictment is sufficient, although there are two persons of the same name.[10] An assault may be charged as made upon two persons without the allegation being objectionable as charging two offenses.[11] So two persons may commit an assault and battery each on the other, but each will be guilty of a separate offense.[12]

of correspondence between the date of an assault as charged in an indictment and the date of an assault for which prosecution was previously dismissed will indicate, in the absence of evidence to the contrary, that they were the same assault: Reg. v. Westley, 11 Cox, 139.

[1] Shinn v. S., 68 Ind. 423. Further as to whether present ability must be alleged, see *supra*, § 233, and *infra*, § 266.

[2] S. v. Hays, 41 Tex. 526; S. v. Hartman, 41 Tex. 562; S. v. Lutterloh, 22 Tex. 210.

[3] S. v. Elliott, 7 Blackf. 280.

[4] S. v. Wimple, 8 Blackf. 214.

[5] S. v. Goddard, 69 Me. 181.

[6] S. v. McKettrick, 14 S. C. 346. But see Noles v. S., 24 Ala. 672.

[7] S. v. Bitman, 13 Ia. 485.

[8] Rutherford v. S., 13 Tex. Ap. 92; S. v. Snow, 41 Tex. 596; S. v. Elmore, 44 Tex. 102.

[9] Brown v. S., 16 Tex. Ap. 197.

[10] Rex v. Peace, 3 B. & Ald. 579; Rex v. Clendon, 2 Ld. Ray. 1572, cited in argument in Rex v. Benfield, 2 Burr. 980; Anon., Lofft. 272.

[11] Kenney v. S., 5 R. I. 385; S. v. Nash, 86 N. C. 650; S. v. Merritt, Phill. 134; Fowler v. S., 3 Heisk. 154. But old English cases seem *contra:* Rex v. Clendon, 2 Ld. Ray. 1572, cited in argument in Rex v. Benfield, 2 Burr. 980; Anon., Lofft. 272.

[12] S. v. Lonon, 19 Ark. 577.

§ 252a. Forms.— The recognized forms of complaint for assault and battery are exceedingly simple. They do not contain, as a rule, the method or means, either of the assault or the injury. The following will be sufficient illustrations:

ASSAULT AND BATTERY.

That A. B., on ——, in the county of ——, in and upon one C. D. did make an assault, and him, the said C. D., then and there did beat, bruise, wound and ill-treat, and other wrongs to the said C. D. then and there did.[1]

ASSAULT WITHOUT BATTERY.

That A. B., on ——, in the county of ——, in and upon one C. D., with a certain instrument called a rake, did make an assault, and other wrongs to the said C. D. then and there did and committed.

§ 253. Included offense.— An assault is necessarily included in a battery,[2] and under an indictment for assault and battery the defendant may be convicted of an assault only.[3] But under an indictment for simple assault there cannot be a conviction of a battery.[4] The offense of maiming and disfiguring necessarily includes an assault and battery;[5] so does false imprisonment;[6] but an indictment for an affray will not sustain a conviction for assault and battery unless it contains substantive allegations such as to admit proof of the other offense.[7] In discussing aggravated assaults and assaults with intent, it will appear that they include necessarily an assault and sometimes an assault and battery.[8]

II. AGGRAVATED ASSAULTS.

§ 254. How classified.— The circumstances under which an assault is committed or the intent with which it is committed may show a higher degree of criminality than would be indi-

[1] This is substantially the form recognized in the common-law form books and adopted by the modern writers. It omits some of the phraseology of the older books, but nothing that is material. It is usual to thus charge battery, as well as assault, even though an assault only has been committed. The form would doubtless be sufficient for an assault if the allegations as to beating, etc., were omitted.

[2] S. v. Twogood, 7 Ia. 252.

[3] Lewis v. S., 33 Ga. 131.

[4] Furnish v. C., 14 Bush, 180.

[5] Benham v. S., 1 Ia. 542.

[6] Francisco v. S., 24 N. J. 30.

[7] Childs v. S., 15 Ark. 204.

[8] See *infra*, §§ 262 and 271; also as to assault with intent to commit rape, see § 462.

cated by the acts alone, and assaults which are thus made especially criminal may therefore be divided into aggravated assaults, or those in which the circumstances or manner of the assault are made a ground of aggravation, and assaults with felonious intent, or those in which the intent of the assailant renders the crime of a higher degree. It will be difficult to fully distinguish these two kinds, for the reason that they are for the most part provided for by statute, and the statutes sometimes combine in the description of the offense both circumstances or means, and the intent; but in the main these divisions will be found practicable and useful. The cases included under this subheading are those in which the increased criminality of the assault is made to depend on the circumstances under which or the means by which it is committed.

§ 255. **What constitutes aggravation.**— At common law all assaults were misdemeanors only, punishable by fine and imprisonment, but the circumstances of aggravation could be taken into account by the court in affixing punishment. Statutes have made some aggravated assaults felonious.[1] Under statutes providing generally for cases of aggravated assault, an aggravation in the manner or character of an assault or battery, as, for instance, by reason of its wantonness, its violence, or the injury inflicted, may be considered sufficient to render it of an aggravated nature;[2] but it was held that striking and beating with a pistol in a manner calculated to inflict serious bodily pain and injury did not *per se* constitute an aggravated assault.[3] The offense of "endangering the life" of another may be committed by shooting at him, though he is not hit.[4] Unnecessary beating of a prisoner by an officer for refusing to go with him upon being arrested may constitute an aggravated assault.[5] By statute, in one state at least, an assault and battery committed upon a decrepit person is made specially punishable.[6] Assaults upon females are sometimes specially mentioned by statute.[7] By the Texas statute an assault by an adult

[1] Cornelison v. C., 84 Ky. 583; T. v. Conrad, 1 Dak. T. 363.

[2] Norton v. S., 14 Tex. 387.

[3] Miles v. S., 23 Tex. Ap. 410.

[4] S. v. Agee, 68 Mo. 264.

[5] Skidmore v. S., 2 Tex. Ap. 20.

[6] Hall v. S., 16 Tex. Ap. 6.

[7] Ridout v. S., 6 Tex. Ap. 249; Atkins v. S., 11 Tex. Ap. 8; Munday v. Maiden, 33 L. T. 377; Wilkinson v. Dutton, 3 B. & S. 821. But the Texas statute describes the offense

upon a child,[1] or an assault in the house of a private family, is an aggravated assault.[2] An assault is sometimes declared aggravated if committed in resisting an officer in the discharge of his duty.[3] In England cutting or stabbing with intent to resist lawful apprehension has been made specially punishable by statutory provision.[4] An assault committed in a court of justice is in Texas made an aggravated assault.[5] In North Carolina there is provision as to a secret and malicious assault with a deadly weapon.[6]

§ 256. **Shooting, cutting, stabbing, wounding, inflicting great bodily harm, etc.**—The nature of the injury inflicted, or the intent to inflict serious injury, is by some statutes made an element of increased criminality, as, for instance, an assault by wilful shooting, in which case the indictment need not allege that the shooting was done with a dangerous weapon,[7]

as by an adult male upon a female and the indictment should so allege: Blackburn v. S., 39 Tex. 153; Lawson v. S., 13 Tex. Ap. 83; Andrews v. S., 13 Tex. Ap. 343; Kemp v. S., 25 Tex. Ap. 589. To constitute an aggravated assault upon a female it must be shown that defendant attempted to use force with intent to injure the person: Floyd v. S., 29 Tex. Ap. 349. A woman may be joint principal, in connection with an adult male, in such assault: Kemp v. S., 25 Tex. Ap. 589. An injury resulting in a sense of shame from violence to the person is by Texas statute an aggravated assault: Young v. S., 31 Tex. Ap. 24.

1 Under such statute an adult is a person twenty-one years of age: George v. S., 11 Tex. Ap. 95; Schenault v. S., 10 Tex. Ap. 410. The term "child," not being specially defined, must be taken in its ordinary sense as indicating a boy under fourteen, or a girl under twelve, and not as synonymous with minor: McGregor v. S., 4 Tex. Ap. 599; Bell v. S., 18 Tex. Ap. 53. In such cases it is not the instrument used, nor the manner of its use, that constitutes the aggravation: Stanfield v. S., 43 Tex. 167.

2 S. v. Cass, 41 Tex. 552; Pederson v. S., 21 Tex. Ap. 485. But shooting *in* a dwelling-house does not constitute the statutory offense of shooting *into* a dwelling: S. v. Kye, 46 La. An. 424.

3 Johnson v. S., 26 Tex. 117; S. v. Coffey, 41 Tex. 46; Johnson v. S., 5 Tex. Ap. 43; U. S. v. McEwan, 44 Fed. R. 594. In England beating a deer-keeper in the discharge of his duty is specially punished: Rex v. Amey, Russ. & Ry. 500. But "beating" must be more than a simple battery: Reg. v. Hale, 2 C. & K. 326.

4 Reg. v. Price, 8 C. & P. 282; Reg. v. Walker, Dears. 358; Rex v. Williams, 1 Moody, 387; Rex v. Howarth, 1 Moody, 207; Rex v. Gardener, 1 Moody, 390; Rex v. Fraser, 1 Moody, 419; Rex v. Ricketts, 3 Camp. 68; Rex v. Dyson, 1 Stark. 246.

5 S. v. Hunter, 44 Tex. 94; S. v. Murrah, 25 Tex. 759.

6 S. v. Jennings, 104 N. C. 774; S. v. Gunter, 116 N. C. 1068; S. v. Patton, 115 N. C. 753; S. v. Shade, 115 N. C. 757.

7 S. v. Cognovitch, 34 La. An. 529.

although the statute was evidently intended to cover shooting with such weapon.[1] In charging such offense it is not necessary to describe the weapon nor the method of its use.[2] Malicious stabbing does not necessarily involve such malice as would be necessary to make death resulting therefrom murder in the first degree.[3] The offense of cutting or stabbing with a knife, sword, or other deadly weapon, includes the offense of cutting another with an ax.[4] To constitute stabbing, the knife need not penetrate further than to draw blood,[5] and the allegation that defendant did "cut, penetrate and wound," sufficiently shows a stabbing.[6] Striking upon the head with the claw part of a hammer may constitute a cutting;[7] but an indictment for cutting and maiming with intent to murder and disable is not supported by evidence of a cutting with intent to produce a temporary disability.[8] A wounding may consist in an injury which breaks the skin and draws blood, although the instrument used is not one calculated to inflict a wound.[9] The

But the indictment must charge wilful shooting, not merely a wilful assault by shooting: S. v. Langston, 45 La. An. 1182.

[1] S. v. Mosely, 42 La. An. 975.

[2] S. v. Ladd, 2 Swan, 225. An assault need not be alleged, the statutory terms being sufficient: S. v. Phelan, 65 Mo. 547. The fact that the weapon was loaded with powder and paper only will not prevent the offense being that of malicious shooting if the circumstances indicated an intent to kill or do other grievous bodily harm: Rex v. Kitchen, Russ. & Ry. 95. Method of firing off the gun is immaterial: Rex v. Coates, 6 C. & P. 394. In West Virginia the statute provides for the punishment of malicious shooting and unlawful shooting, in either case with intent to maim, disfigure, disable or kill: S. v. Harr, 38 W. Va. 58.

[3] Wright v. S., 9 Yerg. 342; Tyra v. C., 2 Met. (Ky.) 1. If the offense by statute is stabbing with intent to maim, etc., the intent must be found: Marshall v. C., 5 Grat. 663. But a general allegation of the intent is enough: Woodson's Case, 9 Leigh, 669.

[4] Wilson v. C., 3 Bush, 105. Thrusting with a dangerous weapon includes thrusting with an iron bolt, whether the point be sharp or not: S. v. Lowry, 33 La. An. 1224.

[5] Ward v. S., 56 Ga. 408.

[6] Starks v. S., 7 Baxt. 64.

[7] Rex v. Atkinson, Russ. & Ry. 104.

[8] Rex v. Boyce, 1 Moody, 29.

[9] S. v. Leonard, 22 Mo. 449; Rex v. Payne, 4 C. & P. 558; Rex v. Withers, 4 C. & P. 446; Reg. v. Briggs, 1 Moody, 318; Reg. v. Smith, 8 C. & P. 173; Rex v. Beckett, 1 M. & Rob. 526; but a separation of the cuticle or upper skin only is not sufficient: Reg. v. McLoughlin, 8 C. & P. 635. Breaking collar-bone and bruising is not a wounding: Rex v. Wood, 4 C. & P. 381. Injury from a kick which causes a flow of blood will be a wounding if the flow of blood is due to rupture of the skin: Reg. v. Waltham, 3 Cox, 442; Reg v. Jones,

wound must be direct, and therefore an injury occasioned by falling in consequence of a blow is not a wounding;[1] but where a wound was occasioned by a violent blow with a weapon, upon prosecutor's hat, although the weapon did not come in contact with the head, the offense was held to be a wounding.[2] An injury from oil of vitriol thrown in the face is not a wounding,[3] nor is biting off the end of the nose or the joint of a finger a wounding, the intent of the statute appearing to be to punish wounding by some instrument and not merely by the hands or teeth.[4] Throwing another down with violence, or scratching his face, is not a striking and wounding.[5] Inflicting serious bodily injury, or great bodily harm, etc., is sometimes by statute made an aggravated assault; but to constitute such injury or harm something more than mere pain and anguish must be shown.[6] Breaking a rib in an attempt to beat, but without intent to do serious injury, was held not a serious bodily injury;[7] but it is not necessary that the injury should be premeditated or dangerous.[8] Under a statute providing a punishment for an assault by means likely to produce great bodily injury, one may be indicted for throwing another out of a third-story window.[9]

§ 257. Assaults with dangerous or deadly weapons.— It is often made an element of aggravation that the assault is com-

3 Cox, 441. A wounding less than mayhem has a definite meaning when used in a statute as descriptive of an offense: S. v. Hagan, 45 La. An. 839.

[1] Reg. v. Spooner, 6 Cox, 392.

[2] Rex v. Sheard, 7 C. & P. 846.

[3] Rex v. Murrow, 1 Moody, 456; Henshawel's Case, 2 Lewin, 135. Throwing vitriol with intent to injure is a statutory offense, and includes an assault: P. v. Stanton, 106 Cal. 139.

[4] Rex v. Harris, 7 C. & P. 446; Jennings' Case, 2 Lewin, 130.

[5] C. v. Gallagher, 6 Met. 565.

[6] S. v. Nash, 109 N. C. 824.

[7] Halsell v. S., 29 Tex. Ap. 22.

[8] Reg. v. Ashman, 1 F. & F. 88; Rex v. Cox, Russ. & Ry. 362. A mother exposing her infant child so as to imperil its life, but not causing a lesion of any organ, was held not guilty of causing bodily injury: Reg. v. Gray, Dears. & B. 903. An indictment for inflicting actual bodily harm is sustained by proof of communicating an infectious disease to a female by sexual connection, without knowledge on her part of the diseased condition of the male: Reg. v. Sinclair, 13 Cox, 28; Reg. v. Bennett, 4 F. & F. 1105. One who, by producing a panic in a theater, caused the people to rush against an iron bar placed by him across the door, thus producing serious injury, was held guilty of inflicting grievous bodily harm: Reg. v. Martin, 8 Q. B. D. 54.

[9] P. v. Emmons, 61 Cal. 487.

mitted with, or by one who is armed with, a dangerous or a deadly weapon.[1] Where the statute uses the term "dangerous weapon," without describing any particular kind of weapon as dangerous, the character of the weapon is a fact for the jury,[2] a dangerous weapon being one likely to produce death or great bodily harm.[3] It is not necessary to allege the assault specifically as "with a dangerous weapon" where the indictment states facts showing that a dangerous weapon was used,[4] nor that, if a pistol, loaded, was used, that it was used to shoot.[5] The question as to what is a dangerous weapon may depend upon the nature of the assault.[6] The offense of assault and battery with a cowhide, etc., having at the time in possession a pistol or other deadly weapon,[7] is sufficiently shown by proof

[1] There is no punishment provided for an assault with a dangerous weapon, committed within the exclusive jurisdiction of the United States on land: U. S. v. Williams, 2 Fed. R. 61; but such an assault committed on the high seas, on board an American vessel, is criminal: U. S. v. Lewis, 36 Fed. R. 449.

[2] S. v. Brown, 41 La. An. 345; Nelson v. P., 23 N. Y. 293; P. v. Irving, 95 N. Y. 541; U. S. v. Small, 2 Curtis, 241.

[3] S. v. Dineen, 10 Minn. 407; S. v. Godfrey, 17 Oreg. 300. The "danger" involved, that the weapon may be dangerous, is danger to life: U. S. v. Small, 2 Curtis, 241; or of great bodily harm: S. v. Godfrey, 17 Oreg. 300.

[4] S. v. Mosley, 42 La. An. 975. By the Texas statute an assault with a stick, which is a dangerous but not a deadly weapon, is not an aggravated assault, unless with premeditated design or with the infliction of great bodily injury: Pinson v. S., 23 Tex. 579. Thus an aggravated assault can be committed with the fists: Keley v. S., 12 Tex. Ap. 245. But unless the nature of the weapon is stated there can be no conviction of an assault with a dangerous weapon: Garcia v. S., 19 Tex. Ap. 389.

[5] C. v. Fenno, 125 Mass. 387.

[6] A pocket-knife is not, in terms, a dangerous weapon, but it may be such if used to inflict a dangerous wound: S. v. Hertzog, 41 La. An. 775; S. v. Scott, 38 La. An. 387; further as to knife, see Weaver v. S., 24 Tex. 387. A belaying-pin may be a dangerous weapon: U. S. v. Small, 2 Curtis, 241. An unloaded gun may be a dangerous weapon within striking distance; otherwise not: S. v. Godfrey, 17 Oreg. 300. The allegation of stabbing with a knife, in a charge for inflicting a wound with a dangerous weapon, is sufficiently supported by evidence of cutting with a knife, the term "stabbing," in such connection, not having a technical meaning: Ruby v. S., 7 Mo. 206. Threatening to strike with a pound-weight or a large stone may constitute an aggravated assault by use of a dangerous weapon: Brown v. S., 58 Ga. 212; S. v. Dineen, 10 Minn. 407. A large piece of timber may be a dangerous weapon: S. v. Alfred, 44 La. An. 582; so an iron auger: Jennings v. S., 9 Mo. 852. As bearing on this question, see cases in notes to this section as to what is a deadly weapon.

[7] As provided by statute: Clarke v. T., 1 Wash. T. 68; Lawson v. S., 62

of possession of the weapon, although such possession was not ostensible nor known to the party assaulted.[1] The charge of assault while armed with a dangerous weapon is supported by proof of arming with the weapon prior to the assault, whether at the place of the assault or elsewhere.[2] In defining assault with a deadly weapon, statutes sometimes enumerate certain weapons, concluding the enumeration with a general specification of "other deadly weapons," and in such case the enumerated weapons are not exclusive, but others not included in the enumeration must, to bring the crime within the statute, be alleged to be deadly.[3] But if the weapon is of a kind included in the statutory enumeration it is not necessary to allege it to be a dangerous or deadly weapon;[4] and if the weapon is of this character, then it is not necessary to allege the assault to have been committed in a manner calculated to produce death.[5] Where no particular weapons are enumerated by statute as deadly, it is sometimes held that the court may judge from the nature of the weapon as described whether it is deadly in the manner used.[6] It is sufficient to allege the assault to have been with a deadly weapon.[7] An ax may be described in the indictment in terms as a deadly weapon without any allegation as to size, weight, etc.;[8] and it is so held, also, as to a club;[9] so held, also, as to the handle of a hoe.[10] Such allegation is sufficient even though the weapon or instrument is not one which is usually considered to be deadly;[11] but an allegation of an assault "with a deadly weapon, to wit, a certain stick," is,

Miss. 556; Higginbotham v. S., 50 Ala. 133.

1 Lawson v. S., 62 Miss. 556.

2 S. v. Dineen, 10 Minn. 407.

3 S. v. Sebastian, 81 Mo. 514.

4 S. v. Hoffman, 78 Mo. 256; S. v. Greenhalgh, 24 Mo. 373.

5 S. v. Painter, 67 Mo. 84.

6 P. v. Guidice, 73 Cal. 226; S. v. Swann, 65 N. C. 330. Therefore, in such case, an instruction as to simple assault may be necessary: S. v. Schloss, 93 Mo. 88. Guns, swords, pistols, knives and the like are deadly, as matter of law, when used within striking distance; others are deadly or not, according to their capacity to cause death or great bodily harm in the manner used, and of this the jury must judge: S. v. Godfrey, 17 Oreg. 300; Stevens v. S., 27 Tex. Ap. 461.

7 P. v. Congleton, 44 Cal. 92. But in another case it is said that the character of the weapon must be averred: S. v. Russell, 91 N. C. 624.

8 S. v. Schields, 110 N. C. 497. An ax is a deadly weapon: Wilson v. C., 3 Bush, 105. So is a sledge-hammer: Philpot v. C., 86 Ky. 595.

9 S. v. Phillips, 104 N. C. 786.

10 S. v. Thompson, 30 Mo. 470; Hamilton v. P., 113 Ill. 34.

11 P. v. Casey, 72 N. Y. 393; S. v. Harper, 69 Mo. 425.

on the contrary, held not sufficient to show an assault with a deadly weapon;[1] and even in the case of an ax, or a fence-post, or brass knuckles (enumerated by statute among the deadly weapons which are forbidden to be carried), it is held that there must be proof that the weapon or instrument is of a deadly character.[2] The question whether or not a weapon is deadly is for the jury.[3] If the assault is shown to have been with a knife, there must be evidence that it was a deadly weapon to sustain a conviction.[4] The question whether the weapon is deadly or not will often depend on the manner of its use, and the jury must determine whether, in the manner in which it appears to have been used, it was deadly or not.[5] To sustain a charge of assault with a deadly weapon it must appear that there was present ability on the part of accused to commit the threatened injury with the weapon used;[6] but some cases hold that where an assault is charged to have been made with a weapon in its nature deadly, as a gun, it is not necessary to allege the present ability;[7] and that the fact that such weapon was not loaded is matter of defense;[8] and that such weapon, though unloaded, is still deadly.[9] Any weapon is a deadly weapon which is likely to produce death; but a weapon capable of producing death is not necessarily a deadly

[1] S. v. Porter, 101 N. C. 713.

[2] Melton v. S., 30 Tex. Ap. 273; Wilson v. S., 15 Tex. Ap. 150; Wilks v. S., 3 Tex. Ap. 34.

[3] P. v. Irving, 95 N. Y. 541; Nelson v. P., 23 N. Y. 293.

[4] Hilliard v. S., 17 Tex. Ap. 210. Proof as to size of blade and manner of use *held* sufficient in Briggs v. S., 6 Tex. Ap. 144.

[5] P. v. Leyba, 74 Cal. 407; Hunt v. S., 6 Tex. Ap. 663; Blige v. S., 20 Fla. 742; so held as to a chair: Kouns v. S., 3 Tex. Ap. 13; so held as to a pistol used to strike with but not to shoot: S. v. Franklin, 36 Tex. 155; Pierce v. S., 21 Tex. Ap. 540; Jenkins v. S., 30 Tex. Ap. 379; Key v. S., 12 Tex. Ap. 506; Stephenson v. S., 33 Tex. Ap. 162; so held as to a fork with prongs ten inches long: Reynolds v. S., 4 Tex. Ap. 327; so held as to a stone: C. v. Duncan, 91 Ky. 592. But proof of intent to kill is not necessary: S. v. Hertzog, 41 La. An. 775.

[6] If with a gun, accused must have been within shooting distance: S. v. Godfrey, 17 Oreg. 300; or if a weapon used for striking, within striking distance: P. v. Dodel, 77 Cal. 293.

[7] Forrest v. S., 3 Tex. Ap. 232. If with a loaded pistol, it is not necessary to allege a shooting rather than a striking: S. v. Fenno, 125 Mass. 387. The offense of pointing a fire-arm at another may be committed although there is a wall between the parties: Lange v. S., 95 Ind. 114.

[8] Allen v. P., 82 Ill. 610; Burton v. S., 3 Tex. Ap. 408; Cross v. S., 55 Wis. 261; S. v. Herron, 12 Mont. 230.

[9] Johnson v. S., 26 Ga. 611; Allen v. S., 28 Ga. 395; Flournoy v. S., 16 Tex. 31.

weapon.[1] If a weapon is not one deadly *per se*, the jury should be instructed as to the meaning of the phrase.[2] The indictment may charge an assault with two weapons, and the state is not required to elect between them.[3] As in other cases of assault, there must be either an attempt to injure or something done which causes apprehension of such intent.[4]

§ 258. **Loaded weapons.**— Under English statutory provisions against attempting to discharge loaded fire-arms, a weapon was held not to be loaded which, for want of priming, could not go off.[5] The weapon must have been so loaded as to be capable of doing the mischief intended.[6] If the allegation is of maliciously shooting with a loaded gun, that is sufficient without alleging how it is loaded.[7]

§ 259. **Intent.**— Where the increased criminality of the assault depends on the fact that it was made in such manner that life was thereby endangered, the intent is immaterial;[8] and, in general, where the crime consists in an assault with a dangerous or a deadly weapon, the intent is sufficiently shown by proof of words indicating the purpose of committing injury with such weapon, although the accused was not yet in the immediate act of using the weapon.[9] Intent to kill is not necessarily an ingredient in a charge of malicious stabbing,[10] and under such a charge the accused may be convicted even though the circumstances show that death resulting from such an assault would be manslaughter and not murder, malicious intent

[1] Pittman v. S., 25 Fla. 648. Perhaps there is a distinction in this respect between a deadly weapon and a dangerous weapon, the latter being defined as one by the use of which death or great bodily harm may be inflicted: S. v. Godfrey, 17 Oreg. 300. And see other case under note, *supra*, in this section.

[2] Howard v. S., 18 Tex. Ap. 348.

[3] Johnson v. S., 35 Ala. 363.

[4] Young v. S., 7 Tex. Ap. 75; S. v. Painter, 67 Mo. 84.

[5] Reg. v. James, 1 C. & K. 530. So if the touch-hole was plugged: Rex v. Harris, 5 C. & P. 159.

[6] Rex v. Carr, Russ. & Ry. 377; Rex v. Whitley, 1 Lewin, 123. But the crime is committed if the weapon is presented with intent to shoot, although the assailant is disarmed before the weapon is discharged: Reg. v. Duckworth, 2 Q. B. D. (1892), 83.

[7] Reg. v. Cox, 3 Cox, 58.

[8] S. v. Hays, 67 Mo. 692.

[9] S. v. Epperson, 27 Mo. 255; Johnson v. S., 7 Tex. Ap. 210.

[10] Tyra v. C., 2 Metc. (Ky.) 1. And see *supra*, § 256. Nor is intent to kill essential in the offense of inflicting a wound with a dangerous weapon: S. v. Hertzog, 41 La. An. 775.

being general malice and not malice aforethought.[1] In such case malice against the individual is not essential, general malice being sufficient.[2] So where the charge is of assaulting, being armed with a dangerous weapon, no intent to inflict death or great bodily harm need be proved. No other intent need be shown than that involved in being armed with such weapon and making an assault.[3] But if the statute makes the offense to consist in assault with a deadly weapon with intent to inflict bodily injury, etc., the intent must be alleged.[4] The attempt to commit a violent injury on another by the explosion of gunpowder constitutes an assault with a deadly weapon though the accused was not present when the explosion occurred.[5] In a charge of aggravated assault, where the aggravation consists in the manner of the assault or the danger of injury therefrom, defendant may testify as to his purpose.[6] If the act of defendant was, under the circumstances, justifiable, as, for instance, in using a gun in self-defense, the act will not be an aggravated assault.[7]

§ 260. **Indictment.**— Something more than a mere statement that the offense was an aggravated assault is necessary in the indictment; as, for instance, that a deadly weapon was used.[8] The indictment should state the facts constituting the aggravation.[9] Nor is it sufficient to charge that accused made an aggravated assault with a pistol; the facts must be set forth.[10] But it is sufficient if the indictment proceed to charge

[1] Nichols v. S., 8 Ohio St. 435; Taylor v. S., 6 Lea, 234. Gross negligence in the discharge of a pistol in violation of a city ordinance may indicate the criminal intent: C. v. Hawkins, 157 Mass. 551.

[2] Rex v. Hunt, 1 Moody, 93. So if the injury is accidental in the attempt to unlawfully and maliciously wound another, there may be a conviction on the charge of unlawfully and maliciously wounding the person injured: Reg. v. Latimer, 17 Q. B. D. 359.

[3] S. v. Godfrey, 17 Oreg. 300. And see P. v. Savercool, 81 Cal. 650; S. v. Moore, 65 Mo. 606.

[4] S. v. Eschbach, 13 Mont. 399.

[5] P. v. Pape, 66 Cal. 366.

[6] Berry v. S., 30 Tex. Ap. 423.

[7] Fondren v. S., 16 Tex. Ap. 48.

[8] Flynn v. S., 8 Tex. Ap. 368. To charge that defendant was armed with a deadly weapon and did assault is not enough to show an assault with a deadly weapon: P. v. Vierra, 52 Cal. 451.

[9] S. v. Beadon, 17 S. C. 55; Griffin v. S., 12 Tex. Ap. 423; Marshall v. S., 13 Tex. Ap. 492.

[10] Key v. S., 12 Tex. Ap. 506. The indictment must be more specific than the common-law indictment for assault and battery: S. v. McKettrick, 14 S. C. 346. But where the method of procedure providing for

that accused presented the pistol to the person assaulted and did then and there shoot at him.[1] The charge must in general be proved as alleged,[2] but it will not constitute a fatal variance if the charge is of an assault with a knife while the evidence is of an assault with some other weapon, inflicting the same kind of a wound.[3] Where the charge was of an assault in a school-house, and the evidence disclosed an assault upon a minister in a congregation assembled for religious worship in a brush arbor near such school-house, it was held that there was not a fatal variance, either act being criminal under the same statutory provision;[4] but under an information charging aggravated assault committed with a certain deadly weapon, to wit, a shovel, proof of an assault committed with an ax was held to constitute a fatal variance.[5] Under the Texas statute defining various forms of aggravated assault, the distinguishing circumstances constituting the aggravation so as to indicate under which subdivision a conviction is sought must be alleged; it is not sufficient to simply charge that accused did make an aggravated assault on, etc., with intent to injure him.[6] An indictment for an assault with a deadly weapon need not specify the weapon;[7]

aggravated assaults involves a certificate by the magistrate, under which the offense is thereupon cognizable by a higher court, it is not necessary to make any distinction in the charging of the offense, the fact of the certificate having been given being alleged in the higher court: S. v. Hilton, 32 N. H. 285; S. v. Bean, 36 N. H. 122; S. v. Stevens, 36 N. H. 59. In such case the objection that the indictment does not recite such previous certificate must be taken before plea: S. v. Thompson, 20 N. H. 250.

[1] S. v. Lutterloh, 22 Tex. 210.

[2] Anderson v. S., 16 Tex. Ap. 132; Pinson v. S., 23 Tex. 579.

[3] S. v. Dame, 11 N. H. 271; Hull v. S., 79 Ala. 32.

[4] Blackwell v. S., 30 Tex. Ap. 416.

[5] Ferguson v. S., 4 Tex. Ap. 156; and see Walker v. S., 73 Ala. 17.

[6] Browning v. S., 2 Tex. Ap. 47. But under such statute it is not necessary to describe the assault as aggravated: Meier v. S., 10 Tex. Ap. 39. It is sufficient to state the facts showing the offense to be an aggravated assault: Rasberry v. S., 1 Tex. Ap. 664. Under such statute aggravated assault is synonymous with aggravated assault and battery, and the terms may be used interchangeably: Smith v. S., 9 Tex. Ap. 315; and a verdict of guilty of aggravated assault and battery is good although no battery is charged or proven: Bittick v. S., 40 Tex. 117. Further as to the construction of the Texas statute, see Bronson v. S., 2 Tex. Ap. 46; Bowden v. S., 2 Tex. Ap. 56; Coney v. S., 2 Tex. Ap. 62; Haynes v. S., 2 Tex. Ap. 84; Nelson v. S., 2 Tex. Ap. 227; Chamberlain v. S., 2 Tex. Ap. 451; Pugh v. S., 2 Tex. Ap. 539.

[7] S. v. Tidwell, 43 Ark. 71; P. v. Congleton, 44 Cal. 92; P. v. Savercool, 81 Cal. 650.

and where the offense consists by statute of an assault with a deadly weapon, or by any means or force likely to produce great bodily injury, the allegation of an assault with a deadly weapon need not allege that it was made with intent to produce such injury.[1] It is not bad to charge an assault as committed with several different kinds of dangerous weapons.[2] Where the statutory words are "unlawfully and maliciously," an allegation of the assault as committed feloniously, wilfully and maliciously is bad as not following the terms of the statute.[3] The use of the word "assault" sufficiently charges illegality in the act.[4] Under the Texas statute making an assault committed in a court of justice an aggravated assault, the allegation that the assault was committed in a court of justice is sufficient,[5] and it is not necessary even to specify the court or to state that it was legally in session.[6] An indictment for assaulting a peace officer need not aver his official character.[7]

§ 261. **Forms.**— Assaults of this character are dependent entirely for their definition upon statute, and therefore no general forms can be given which will be of much value. The following illustrations may, however, be suggestive:

ASSAULT WITH DANGEROUS WEAPON.

That A. B., on ——, in the county of ——, upon one C. D. did wilfully and feloniously make an assault with a certain dangerous weapon called a hatchet, and him, the said C. D., did then and there beat, bruise, wound and ill-treat, to the great injury of him, the said C. D.

[1] P. v. Turner, 65 Cal. 540. So where the statute describes the offense as shooting at another or assaulting with a deadly weapon in resisting execution of process, it is sufficient to charge the shooting at the officer without alleging an assault or the use of a dangerous weapon: S. v. Estis, 70 Mo. 427.

[2] S. v. McDonald, 67 Mo. 13.

[3] Rex v. Ryan, 7 C. & P. 854. So a charge of maliciously assaulting and shooting is not sufficient for the offense of maliciously shooting: Allen v. S., 4 Baxt. 21. But where the charge was that accused did "inflict" grievous bodily harm instead of using the statutory word "cause," *held*, that the indictment was sufficient: Reg. v. Bray, 15 Cox, 197.

[4] U. S. v. Lunt, 1 Sprague, 311. It is not necessary to allege the assault as committed feloniously: U. S. v. Gallagher, 2 Paine, 447.

[5] S. v. Hunter, 44 Tex. 94.

[6] S. v. Murrah, 25 Tex. 759.

[7] S. v. Belk, 76 N. C. 10. But to the contrary it was held that such an indictment should set forth the authority of the officer and the capacity in which he was acting at the time: Rountree v. U. S., 1 Pinney, 59.

ASSAULT AND STABBING.

That A. B., on ——, in the county of ——, upon one C. D. did wilfully and feloniously make an assault with a dangerous weapon called a knife, held open in the hand of him, the said A. B., and did, with said knife held open as aforesaid, then and there wilfully and feloniously cut and stab him, the said C. D.

§ 262. **Included offense.**— As the various forms of aggravated assaults are simply assaults with some additional element of criminality, there may be a conviction of the assault alone where the additional element is not established;[1] therefore it is error to refuse to instruct the jury as to conviction of an assault under the charge of an aggravated assault.[2] But if the evidence shows that if the assault was committed at all it was committed in such way as to constitute an aggravated assault, no charge as to simple assault is required.[3] An aggravated assault does not necessarily include an assault and battery;[4] but if the aggravation as charged consists in the injury done to the person of the assailed, then upon failure to prove that kind of injury, if the evidence shows some injury there may be a conviction of assault and battery.[5]

III. ASSAULTS WITH FELONIOUS INTENT.

§ 263. Whether felonious or not.— At common law assaults with intent to commit a felony are misdemeanors,[6] but assaults

[1] Kennedy v. P., 122 Ill. 649; Bryant v. S., 41 Ark. 359; Harrison v. S., 10 Tex. Ap. 93; T. v. Conrad, 1 Dak. 363; Reg. v. Taylor, L. R. 1 C. C. 194; Reg. v. Yeadon, L. & C. 81; Reg. v. Oliver, Bell, 287. Thus, under the Texas statute, a higher and lower degree of assault may be charged in the same indictment if both are charged as the result of one act: S. v. Bradley, 34 Tex. 95. Similar questions arise under indictments for felonious assaults: See *infra*, § 271.

[2] Harrison v. S., 10 Tex. Ap. 93; Jackson v. S., 25 Tex. (Sup.) 229.

[3] S. v. Guidice, 73 Cal. 226; Ward v. S., 56 Ga. 408.

[4] For instance, where the assault is with a deadly weapon: Young v. P., 6 Ill. Ap. 434; Moore v. P., 26 Ill. Ap. 137.

[5] P. v. Casey, 72 N. Y. 393; Higginbotham v. S., 50 Ala. 133; Whilden v. S., 25 Ga. 396; Clarke v. T., 1 Wash. T. 68. Under an indictment for stabbing there may be conviction for assault and battery: Rives v. S., 74 Ga. 375.

[6] Green v. P., 3 Colo. 68; Rice v. C., 3 Bush, 14; S. v. Swann, 65 N. C. 330; even an assault with intent to commit murder: P. v. Pettit, 3 Johns. 511; C. v. Barlow, 4 Mass. 439; Bacon's Case, 1 Lev. 146; 1 East, P. C. 411. Assault with intent to kill is by some statutes a misdemeanor only: Kennedy v. S., 15 Fla.

with intent to commit felonies are frequently by statute made felonies.[1]

§ 264. **What included.**— In many states the statutes make an assault with intent to commit any felony punishable to a greater degree than a simple assault. They also usually specify some particular assaults of this kind, as assaults to murder or to kill, assaults to commit rape, assaults to rob, etc., providing a special punishment for each. The assault with intent to commit rape will be discussed in connection with that offense, and the assault with intent to murder or to kill, with intent to do great bodily harm, and with intent to rob, will be treated in subsequent sections of this chapter.[2]

§ 265. **The intent involved.**— The various assaults with felonious intent are examples of the different attempts in which the intent gives color to the act rendering it punishable on account of the evil involved in the intent.[3] It is therefore not sufficient to prove merely a general felonious intent, but a particular intent must be alleged and proven,[4] and proof of the intent is just as indispensable as proof of the act.[5] There must be something more than the malice implied from the act itself,[6]

635; S. v. Hord, 8 S. C. 84. Sometimes by statute aggravated assaults are misdemeanors, while assaults with intent to kill, etc., are felonies: Ex parte Brown, 40 Fed. R. 81.

[1] Hughes v. S., 12 Ala. 458. See, in case of sodomy, Davis v. S., 3 Har. & J. 154; in case of maiming, S. v. Brown, 60 Mo. 141; in case of larceny, Corneille v. S., 16 Ind. 232. Where a statute provides a punishment for an assault with intent to commit murder, larceny, or other felony, assault with intent to commit petit larceny is included, although it is only a misdemeanor: Kelly v. P., 132 Ill. 363.

[2] *Infra*, §§ 273, 280, 281.

[3] Cunningham v. S., 49 Miss. 685. And see attempts, *supra*, § 222. Without either intent to injure or injury, there can be no conviction: S. v. Moran, 46 Kan. 318. In crimes requiring force in their commission, there is no material difference between assault with intent and assault with attempt to commit a crime: Johnson v. S., 14 Ga. 55. And see Prince v. S., 35 Ala. 367. But it is said that there is no such an offense as an assault with an attempt to murder, the attempt not being equivalent to the intent: S. v. Marshall, 14 Ala. 411; nor as an attempt to commit an assault with intent to murder: White v. S., 22 Tex. 608. Under a statute making it an offense to assault with intent to commit a crime, it was held that an attempt to commit larceny was included, and not assaults on the person merely: Hayes v. S., 15 Lea, 64.

[4] Ogletree v. S., 28 Ala. 693; Watson v. S., 2 Wash. 504; Marshall v. C., 5 Grat. 663; Davis v. S., 15 Tex. Ap. 475; S. v. Seymour, 1 Houst. Cr. C. 508.

[5] Botsch v. S., 43 Neb. 501.

[6] Pennsylvania v. McBirnie, Add. 28.

and the intent is not necessarily to be inferred from the act done, but must be made out from the circumstances.[1] However, the intent may be inferred from the acts done, on the principle that each person is presumed to intend the natural and probable consequences of his acts unless a different intent appears.[2] The specified intent may be negatived in the same way as in other cases where specific intent is essential.[3] Evidence of threats or quarrels as showing the intent is admissible.[4] Two or more may be liable in case of combination for the same assault with intent,[5] or one may be liable as aiding and abetting another,[6] but there must be some participation or abetting.[7] Where parties combine in the assault, evidence of acts afterwards committed by one of them will not be admissible to show the intent of the other, unless the act committed was in pursuance of the common plan.[8] It is a sufficient finding of the intent that the jury find defendant guilty of the act

[1] S. v. Glovery, 10 Nev. 24.

[2] P. v. Landman, 103 Cal. 577; S. v. Gillett, 56 Ia. 459; Krchnavy v. S., 43 Neb. 337; Ex parte Brown, 40 Fed. R. 81. The presumption, however, is one of fact, merely, to be drawn by the jury, if they see fit to do so; it is not a presumption of law: Murphey v. S., 43 Neb. 34. It is error to authorize the intent to kill to be inferred from the use of a deadly weapon without regard to the circumstances under which the assault is made: Friederich v. P., 147 Ill. 310. While a person is presumed to intend the consequences ordinarily resulting from the act, expert evidence is not admissible to show what result might have been apprehended by a skilled physician from the acts done: S. v. Redfield, 73 Ia. 643. The result of a kick should not be considered as evidence of the intent with which the kick was given, without other evidence that the result was contemplated, but the result as showing the force used may be taken as evidence of the intent: P. v. Miller, 91 Mich. 639. Further as to presumption of intent in assaults with intent to murder, see *infra*, §§ 275, 276.

[3] S. v. Fiske, 63 Conn. 388; P. v. Gordon, 103 Cal. 568. And as to specific intent in general, see *supra*, § 122.

[4] Sharp v. P., 29 Ill. 464; but not threats against some other than the person assailed: Ogletree v. S., 28 Ala. 693; S. v. Ackles, 8 Wash. 462; S. v. Pennington, 124 Mo. 388. Evidence showing ill-will toward assailed is admissible as bearing on the state of mind of the accused: Moore v. S., 31 Tex. Ap. 234.

[5] Garrett v. S., 89 Ga. 446; King v. S., 21 Ga. 220.

[6] S. v. Pile, 5 Ala. 72; Mills v. S., 13 Tex. Ap. 487.

[7] White v. P., 139 Ill. 143; Cabbell v. S., 46 Ala. 195.

[8] Watts v. S., 5 W. Va. 532; Reg. v. Sullivan, Car. & M. 209. And, in general, as to joint liability in cases of combination, see *supra*, § 195. The question of common intent is for the jury: Hudgins v. S., 61 Ga. 182.

alleged as charged in the indictment, where the indictment itself sufficiently charges intent.[1]

§ 266. **Ability to commit the injury threatened.**— The same difficulty arises here as was discussed in connection with assaults, in regard to whether ability to commit the injury threatened is essential in order to constitute the offense of assault with intent to commit a crime.[2] An assault merely by putting in fear is not enough, without ability to do some injury; for it is evident that, if there is mere putting in fear without intent to injure, the crime cannot be assault with intent, though it might be assault.[3] The weight of authority seems to be here, as with reference to simple assault, that it is not necessary to allege the present ability to complete the injury intended.[4] For instance, to substantiate the charge of assault with intent to commit robbery, it is not necessary that there should have been anything in the possession of the assailed which could be stolen.[5] While it is doubtless true that some adaptability, real or apparent, of the means employed to the end charged to have been intended must appear,[6] yet in a charge of assault with intent to kill by means of a pistol it need not be stated in the in-

[1] Jones v. C., 31 Grat. 830.

[2] *Supra*, § 234.

[3] McCollough v. S., 24 Tex. Ap. 128.

[4] C. v. Creed, 8 Gray, 387; S. v. Rigg, 10 Nev. 284; S. v. O'Flaherty, 7 Nev. 153; Kunkle v. S., 32 Ind. 220. Where the statute as to assaults requires the present ability to be alleged, it must be alleged also in assault with intent: S. v. Swails, 8 Ind. 524; Adell v. S., 34 Ind. 543; Howard v. S., 67 Ind. 401. But in Illinois it is said that in charging assault with a deadly weapon it is not necessary to allege a present ability, as that is implied in the term "assault" itself: Kennedy v. P., 122 Ill. 649. And where the assault is properly charged, it is not necessary to state the means with which the crime was intended to be made to show the present ability to commit such crime: Freel v. S., 125 Ind. 166.

[5] Hamilton v. S., 36 Ind. 280.

[6] Kunkle v. S., 32 Ind. 220. But even then it is sufficient that the adaptability be apparent, although there is some inadequacy not known to the assailant which would prevent his carrying out his purpose: Ibid. Where the gun used was only loaded with powder and wadding, and was fired at such a distance as not to be dangerous, *held*, that the act did not constitute the offense of shooting at one with intent to kill: Henry v. S., 18 Ohio, 32. But it is said that the charge of assault in itself implies the ability to do the act threatened, and therefore it is not necessary to charge that the person assailed was within the distance to which the gun would carry: Shaw v. S., 18 Ala. 547. Present ability held to be sufficiently shown in particular cases: S. v. Sheerin, 12 Mont. 539; Hatton v. S., 31 Tex. Ap. 586.

dictment that defendant was within pistol range of the person assailed,[1] nor that the pistol was loaded.[2] Where the defendant was charged with shooting at another, it was held that he could not be convicted on proof of firing a gun into a room of the latter's house where he supposed the latter to be.[3] But where defendant fired at a place where another was supposed to be, with intention of killing him, and the person at whom the shot was fired was some little distance away from the exact place, it was held that the offense of assault with intent to kill was complete.[4] Where the evidence to support a charge of assault and battery with intent to kill showed that defendant believed that a certain drug was a deadly poison, and administered such drug to another with intent to kill him, it was held wholly immaterial to inquire whether the drug was in fact poisonous or what quantity would endanger life.[5]

§ 267. **Justification, excuse, or mitigation.**— Facts which, if the threatened act had been completed, would have justified, excused, or mitigated the offense, are admissible as affecting the intent, where the charge is of an assault with intent to commit such an offense. Thus, the intoxication of the accused at the time of the assault is material to show that he was incapable of the intent charged.[6] So facts showing that the assault was justifiable in self-defense will negative the crime.[7] But the cir-

[1] Mayfield v. S., 44 Tex. 59. It is sufficient in alleging the gun with which the assault was made to be loaded to state that it was loaded with gunpowder, as that might render it dangerous: S. v. Sears, 86 Mo. 169. But under an indictment charging intent to murder with a pistol loaded with gunpowder and leaden bullets, it is said that the state must show that the pistol was so loaded as to produce death, although it may establish this fact by circumstantial evidence: Porter v. S., 57 Miss. 300.

[2] Bradberry v. S., 22 Tex. Ap. 273.

[3] Rex v. Lovell, 2 M. & Rob. 236.

[4] P. v. Lee Kong, 95 Cal. 666.

[5] S. v. Glover, 27 S. C. 602.

[6] Mooney v. S., 33 Ala. 419; S. v. Garvey, 11 Minn. 154.

[7] Vandermark v. P., 47 Ill. 122; Christian v. S., 96 Ala. 89; Hobbs v. S., 16 Tex. Ap. 517; Black v. S., 8 Tex. Ap. 329. As in cases of self-defense, reasonable belief of danger is sufficient: Rapp v. C., 14 B. Mon. 614; Howell v. S., 5 Ga. 48; Rodriguez v. S., 8 Tex. Ap. 129; Spearman v. S., 23 Tex. Ap. 224; S. v. Dennison, 108 Mo. 541. For the purpose of showing such belief, previous threats of the assailed are admissible: Gray v. S., 63 Ala. 66; Black v. S., 8 Tex. Ap. 329. But proof that defendant had previously made complaint before a peace officer, charging assailed with having threatened his life, and asking to have him bound over to keep the peace, is not admissible: S. v. Doty, 5 Oreg. 491; nor evidence of a fight between prosecutor and defendant two years before the alleged

cumstances must be such as to make the case a proper one for self-defense.[1] If the offense charged is an assault with intent to commit murder, provocation may be shown as indicating that the assault was in heat of passion, and, therefore, that there was no intent to murder.[2] If the circumstances under which a husband shoots at a person found in criminal intercourse with his wife would reduce the crime, if death had resulted, to manslaughter, the attempt to kill will not be assault with intent to commit murder.[3] But that which would not be an adequate provocation in homicide to reduce to manslaughter will not be a defense in assault with intent to commit murder.[4] Some statutes require that, to constitute assault with intent to commit murder, it shall appear that there was no considerable provocation or just excuse.[5]

§ **268. Indictment; charging assault.**— The assault is to be alleged as at common law,[6] and that which would be an assault

crime: Hatcher v. S., 18 Ga. 460. But there must be apprehension of bodily danger or some other felonious violence: Reg. v. Hewlett, 1 F. & F. 91. Assault with intent to kill cannot be justified in defense of property: S. v. Morgan, 3 Ired. 186; or to eject a trespasser: S. v. Smith, 12 Mont. 378. The fact that the person assailed has a weapon in his possession will not be a justification if the situation is such that he is unable to use it: Connaghan v. P., 88 Ill. 460. The defendant, claiming that he acted in self-defense, must prove it by a preponderance of evidence: S. v. Jones, 20 W. Va. 764.

1 As that, if the assailant commenced the difficulty, he withdrew therefrom as far as possible before attempting to kill: Crane v. S., 41 Tex. 494; Wilson v. S., 4 Tex. Ap. 637; Sullivan v. S., 31 Tex. Ap. 486; Crowder v. S., 8 Lea, 669; Aldrige v. S., 59 Miss. 250.

2 Williams v. S., 25 Tex. Ap. 216. And where the charge was of assault with intent to kill, *held*, that provocation might reduce the offense to assault and battery: Smith v. S., 86 Ala. 28. So if the assault is in resistance of unlawful arrest, it will not be assault with intent to commit murder: C. v. McLaughlin, 12 Cush. 615; Davis v. S., 79 Ga. 767.

3 Biggs v. S., 29 Ga. 723. As to a case of shooting at another under belief that he is having illicit intercourse with defendant's daughter, see Lewis v. S., 18 Tex. Ap. 116. That mere belief of previous illicit intercourse with defendant's wife will not be a defense, see Reed v. S., 62 Miss. 405; Stewart v. S., 66 Ga. 90.

4 Allen v. S., 52 Ala. 391. Mere words or opprobrious epithets are not enough: Steffy v. P., 130 Ill. 98; Brown v. S., 58 Ga. 212; nor a previous injury or insult: S. v. Lawry, 4 Nev. 161; nor a charivari: Minaghan v. S., 77 Wis. 643 (but on the other hand, see S. v. Adams, 78 Ia. 292); nor resisting lawful arrest: Johnson v. S., 30 Ga. 426; Phillips v. S., 66 Ga. 755.

5 Baker v. P., 49 Ill. 308; P. v. Fairbanks, 7 Utah, 3. But it is not necessary to negative the exception in the indictment: Jenkins v. S., 92 Ga. 470.

6 Beasley v. S., 18 Ala. 535. An al-

if uncombined with a felonious intent will be such when it is thus combined.[1] The acts constituting an assault should be specified as in any other case;[2] but the allegation of an assault with a deadly weapon, naming it, with intent to kill, is sufficient under a statute making such act a felony, without stating the mode of making the assault.[3] Indeed, it is generally held that it is not necessary to charge the manner, means, or instrument with which the assault is made.[4] But if the offense is assault with a deadly weapon, the weapon should be stated and it should be alleged that an assault was made therewith.[5] There is some apparent conflict between the cases on the ques-

legation of attempt to kill sufficiently shows an assault: S. v. Feamster, 12 Wash. 461.

[1] S. v. Malcolm, 8 Ia. 413.

[2] Beasley v. S., 18 Ala. 535; Trexler v. S., 19 Ala. 21. An assault is not a postulate; it must be defined to the jury and the law applied to the facts: Campbell v. S., 9 Tex. Ap. 147. But failure to state in the indictment the acts constituting an assault cannot be taken advantage of after verdict: S. v. Doty, 5 Oreg. 491.

[3] S. v. Chandler, 24 Mo. 371. But if the charge is of assault with a pistol loaded with powder and a leaden bullet, it was formerly held that it must appear that the pistol was loaded with a bullet: Rex v. Hughes, 5 C. & P. 126. And see Reg. v. Oxford, 9 C. & P. 525. Under a statutory description of the offense, it has been held sufficient to charge a crime in the language of the statute without stating the means with which the assault was committed: Murphey v. S., 43 Neb. 34.

[4] S. v. Smith, 80 Mo. 516; S. v. Keele, 105 Mo. 38; S. v. Chandler, 24 Mo. 371; Connors v. S., 45 N. J. 211; Hamilton v. P., 113 Ill. 34; Williams v. S., 47 Ind. 568; Baker v. S., 134 Ind. 657; Ash v. S., 56 Ga. 583; Fulford v. S., 50 Ga. 591; S. v. Gainus, 86 N. C. 632; Harrison v. S., 2 Coldw. 232; Lacefield v. S., 34 Ark. 275; S. v. Jackson, 37 La. An. 768; S. v. Smith, 41 La. An. 791; S. v. Croft, 15 Tex. 575; Martin v. S., 40 Tex. 19; Bittick v. S., 40 Tex. 117; Mayfield v. S., 44 Tex. 59; Nash v. S., 2 Tex. Ap. 362; Hines v. S., 3 Tex. Ap. 483; Montgomery v. S., 4 Tex. Ap. 140; Payne v. S., 5 Tex. Ap. 35; Price v. S., 22 Tex. Ap. 110; Hernandez v. S., 32 Tex. Ap. 271; Reg. v. Briggs, 1 Moody, 318. Variance as to the instrument used will not be fatal: Douglass v. S., 26 Tex. Ap. 109. Several different methods of making assault may be alleged: C. v. Creed, 8 Gray, 387. An indictment charging two with a joint assault with intent to murder, the one with a gun, the other with a knife, is not objectionable for duplicity: Shaw v. S., 18 Ala. 547. And to the same effect, see Hamilton v. P., 113 Ill. 34. If the assault and the stroke are charged as unlawful and felonious, that is enough: S. v. Bailey, 21 Mo. 484. The offense may be charged and described in the words of the statute: S. v. Chumley, 67 Mo. 41; S. v. Collyer, 17 Nev. 275; S. v. Sheerin, 12 Mont. 539; S. v. Brady, 39 La. An. 687; S. v. Aleck, 41 La. An. 83; S. v. Daley, 41 Vt. 564; Rice v. P., 15 Mich. 9. See, also, as to assault to kill or murder, *infra*, § 274.

[5] S. v. Jordan, 19 Mo. 212; S. v. Johnston, 11 Tex. 22.

tion as to whether the means must be alleged, but this seems to grow out of confusing the requirements as to allegation of the assault with those as to allegation of the intent. As will be seen in the next section, it is not necessary to allege the means by which the felony intended was to be carried out, but there is certainly no reason why the assault should not be charged with as much definiteness at least as is required in an indictment for assault alone.[1] When a statute defines what shall constitute an assault, it is necessary to charge the assault in such statutory terms in case of an assault with felonious intent.[2] The fact that the indictment also charges a battery,[3] or an aggravated assault,[4] will not render it objectionable; nor will it be a ground of objection that the indictment alleges a stabbing in addition to the assault.[5] If the statute defines the offense as assault and battery with intent to kill, etc., the indictment must allege a battery as well as an assault.[6] A constructive assault, as by besetting the house of another, will not constitute the crime, but there must be an actual assault on the person, coupled with a felonious intent.[7] The act must be charged as felonious if by statute the offense is made a felony.[8] But if the proper allegation as to felonious intent is made, that is sufficient.[9] If the statute uses the term "wilful" in describing

[1] U. S. v. Barnaby, 51 Fed. R. 20; Gordon v. S., 23 Tex. Ap. 219. An indictment charging the crime of stabbing, in the perpetration of robbery, with intent to murder, should allege the robbery and stabbing with the same particularity as if those offenses alone were charged: S. v. Brown, 21 La. An. 347.

[2] Adell v. S., 34 Ind. 543. But the statutory language will be sufficient without a specific description of the assault: Williams v. S., 47 Ind. 568; P. v. Pettit, 3 Johns. 511. Where the statute defines shooting with intent to kill as a crime, the words of the statute may be followed without charging an assault: S. v. Phelan, 65 Mo. 547. If the offense consists of inflicting a wound less than mayhem, these words must be used: S. v. Jackson, 43 La. An. 183.

[3] Cokely v. S., 4 Ia. 477.

[4] Young v. S., 44 Tex. 98; Johnson v. S., 1 Tex. Ap. 130; S. v. Parker, 42 La. An. 972.

[5] Cole v. S., 10 Ark. 318.

[6] U. S. v. Turley, 4 Cranch, C. C. 334. And the allegation of the intent may be made following the allegation of a battery without making it also in connection with the assault: S. v. Schloss, 93 Mo. 361.

[7] Evans v. S., 1 Humph. 394; S. v. Freels, 3 Humph. 228.

[8] S. v. Clayton, 100 Mo. 516.

[9] Wood v. S., 64 Miss. 761. It was held the other way, however, in a case of assault with intent to commit a rape: Williams v. S., 8 Humph. 584.

the offense, an allegation that it was felonious is sufficient, as the term "felonious" includes "wilful."[1]

§ 269. Charging the intent.— The specific intent must be averred, as the intent is the gist of the offense,[2] and the felony intended must be specifically alleged.[3] But such felony need not be described with the particularity required in an indictment for the crime itself.[4] For instance, if the assault charged is with intent to steal or rob, the particular goods need not be described.[5] But the intent as to the person to be injured must be correctly described; and if the intent is to murder A. and B. is actually assaulted, an indictment for assault with intent to murder B. cannot be sustained.[6] It has been held necessary to allege the intent to have been felonious as well as the assault.[7] It is not necessary, however, to repeat the allegation of time and place in connection with the felonious intent, having alleged them as to assault.[8] A charge of assault and attempt to murder is a sufficient allegation of assault with intent to murder;[9] and so a verdict of assault to kill is sufficient for assault with intent to kill.[10]

[1] S. v. McDaniel, 45 La. An. 686.

[2] Conolly v. P., 4 Ill. 474; S. v. Child, 42 Kan. 611. If the offense is defined as assault with intent to kill, etc., which would, if death should result, constitute murder or manslaughter, the latter qualification need not be stated: S. v. Van Zant, 71 Mo. 541; Jennings v. S., 9 Mo. 852. Where the intent alleged was to murder, it was held that a conviction for the act with intent to prevent wilful apprehension was not warranted: Rex v. Duffin, Russ. & Ry. 365. If in separate prosecutions the same assault is charged with different intents, conviction or acquittal in one will bar the other: S. v. Chinault, 55 Kan. 326.

[3] Davis v. S., 35 Fla. 614.

[4] S. v. Montgomery, 7 Baxt. 162; S. v. Newberry, 26 Ia. 467; S. v. Lynch, 20 Oreg. 389; Ridenour v. S., 38 Ohio St. 272.

[5] Rogers v. C., 5 Serg. & R. 463; S. v. Blake, 39 Me. 322; Grogan v. S., 63 Miss. 147; Hayes v. S., 15 Lea, 64; Reg. v. Huxley, Car. & M. 596. And in regard to attempts on the same point, see *supra*, § 228.

[6] McCormack v. S., 102 Ala. 156. And see *infra*, § 276.

[7] S. v. Yates, 21 W. Va. 761; S. v. Howell, Ga. Dec., pt. I, 158; Milan v. S., 24 Ark. 346; S. v. Davis, 121 Mo. 404; S. v. Hang Tong, 115 Mo. 389. *Contra*, S. v. Davis, 29 Mo. 391. But if the intent is described as felonious, that sufficiently qualifies the act: S. v. Sonnier, 38 La. An. 962.

[8] Buntin v. S., 68 Ind. 38; S. v. Murphy, 35 La. An. 622.

[9] Felker v. S., 54 Ark. 489. But there is no such crime as an attempt to make an assault: Wilson v. S., 53 Ga. 205; White v. S., 22 Tex. 608.

[10] S. v. Dooley, 121 Mo. 591.

§ **270. Forms.**— These offenses are usually fully described by statute, and the statutory language is on general principles sufficient,[1] but a few examples may profitably be given.

ASSAULT WITH FELONIOUS INTENT.

That A. B., on ——, in the county of ——, in and upon one C. D. did make an assault, and him, the said C. D., did then and there beat and ill-treat with intent [*here state the felony intended*].[2]

ASSAULT WITH INTENT TO ROB.

That A. B., on ——, at ——, in and upon R. B. feloniously did make an assault with intent the money, goods and chattels of the said R. B. from the person and against the will of him, the said R. B., then and there feloniously and violently to rob, steal, take and carry away.[3]

ASSAULT WITH INTENT TO KILL OR MURDER.

That A. B., on ——, at ——, with a certain loaded pistol, the same being a deadly weapon, which said pistol the said A. B. then and there held in his hand, did then and there unlawfully and feloniously make an assault upon one S. P., then and there being, with intent then and there with the pistol aforesaid, unlawfully, feloniously, and with malice aforethought to kill and murder the said S. P.[4]

ANOTHER FORM UNDER STATUTE.

That M. H., on the —— in the ——, unlawfully and feloniously and with malice aforethought did assault W. W. with intent to commit murder in the first degree upon him, the said W. W.[5]

ASSAULT WITH DANGEROUS WEAPON WITH INTENT TO COMMIT MURDER.

That A. B., on ——, at ——, in and upon one J. H. with a certain dangerous weapon, to wit, with a pistol then and there loaded with powder and a leaden ball, with which dangerous

1 See *supra*, § 260.

2 1 Archbold's Cr. Pr. & Pl. (8th ed.) 929.

3 Reg. v. Huxley, Car. & M. 596. See a similar form for attempt to rob and steal, *supra*, § 228*a*.

4 This substantially follows the indictment held sufficient in Hamilton v. P., 113 Ill. 34.

5 Harrison v. S., 2 Coldw. 232. In Indiana it was held sufficient to allege assault and battery in the language of the statute, and then to allege that such assault and battery was "with the intent then and there thereby unlawfully, feloniously, purposely and with premeditated malice to kill him, the said," etc.: Williams v. S., 47 Ind. 568.

weapon the said A. B. was then and there armed, feloniously, wilfully, and with his malice aforethought did make an assault with intent the said J. H. then and there, with the pistol aforesaid, feloniously and wilfully and with his malice aforethought to kill and murder.[1]

§ 271. **Included offenses.**— There are frequently statutory provisions by which, on charges of assault with intent to commit the various felonies, there may be conviction of the included offenses.[2] But even where there is no such special provision, there is usually a general provision authorizing conviction of lower degrees or included crimes which would authorize the same result, and the cases may properly be considered without regard to any special statutory provision authorizing the conviction of the lower offense. Thus, there may be conviction of an aggravated assault under an indictment charging assault with intent to murder,— the former offense being of the same general character as, and of a lower grade than, that charged.[3] So under an indictment for assault with intent to commit murder, defendant may be convicted of felonious assault.[4] Under indictment for assault and stabbing with a dangerous weapon with intent to murder, there may be a conviction of assault with a dangerous weapon.[5] A charge of assault and battery with intent to commit murder includes assault and battery with intent to commit murder in the second degree, or involuntary manslaughter, or simple assault and battery.[6] Assault with intent to kill is included in a charge of assault with intent to kill with malice aforethought.[7] An assault with intent to commit mur-

[1] This was held sufficient as against the objection that it did not set forth an assault. But a majority of the court also held that it sufficiently alleged an assault with a pistol by shooting, and not merely by striking as with a club: C. v. Fenno, 125 Mass. 387. A fuller form containing the averments of shooting, wounding, etc., may be found in C. v. Creed, 8 Gray, 387.

[2] S. v. Gummell, 22 Minn. 51; S. v. Melton, 102 Mo. 683; S. v. Baldridge, 105 Mo. 319; Nelson v. P., 23 N. Y. 293; Foley v. S., 9 Ind. 363; P. v. Odell, 1 Dak. T. 199; T. v. Conrad, 1 Dak. T. 363.

[3] S. v. Robinson, 31 S. C. 453; Pittman v. S., 25 Fla. 648; Corley v. S., 95 Ga. 465; Blackwell v. S., 33 Tex. Ap. 278; Moore v. S., 33 Tex. Ap. 306. So under a charge of felonious assault there may be conviction of aggravated assault, although no circumstances of aggravation are alleged: Bolding v. S., 23 Tex. Ap. 172; Davis v. S., 20 Tex. Ap. 302.

[4] S. v. Baldridge, 105 Mo. 319. But the jury must be limited to some specified felonious assault: S. v. Schleagel, 50 Kan. 325.

[5] S. v. De Laney, 28 La. An. 431.

[6] Behymer v. S., 95 Ind. 140.

[7] S. v. Berning, 91 Mo. 82.

der in the second degree is included in a charge of intent to commit murder in the first degree;[1] therefore, if the indictment is not sufficient to charge assault with intent to commit murder in the first degree, because it fails to charge deliberation and premeditation, there may be a trial and conviction under it as an indictment for assault with intent to commit murder in the second degree.[2] And assault with intent to commit murder necessarily includes assault with intent to commit manslaughter.[3] It is therefore error, under an indictment for assault with intent to commit murder, to instruct the jury that if they find defendant guilty they must convict him of the offense charged, for they might convict him of a lower offense.[4] If, under an indictment charging assault with intent to kill and murder, the jury find defendant guilty of assault with intent to kill, this will be considered as negativing intent to murder.[5] And if the assault with intent to kill is not a crime in itself in the state, then defendant can be convicted only of assault or assault and battery.[6] An assault with a deadly weapon with intent to murder covers assault with a deadly weapon with intent to do bodily harm.[7] It has been held that a charge of assault with intent to kill includes an assault with a deadly weapon,[8] and also an assault with a deadly weapon with intent to inflict bodily injury.[9] But assault with malice aforethought and assault with a deadly weapon with intent to kill, etc., are distinct offenses, and the latter is not included in the former.[10] So maliciously shooting at another with intent to kill is a different crime than assault to murder, even when committed by shooting.[11] An indictment for assault with intent to murder by

[1] Wall v. S., 23 Ind. 150.

[2] S. v. Saylor, 6 Lea, 586.

[3] S. v. Butman, 42 N. H. 490; S. v. White, 45 Ia. 325; Spivey v. S., 30 Tex. Ap. 343. Further, as to assault with intent to commit manslaughter, see *infra*, § 278.

[4] P. v. Fine, 53 Cal. 263.

[5] Nancy v. S., 6 Ala. 483.

[6] S. v. Burns, 8 Ala. 313.

[7] P. v. Congleton, 44 Cal. 92; Beckwith v. P., 26 Ill. 500; S. v. Johnson, 3 N. Dak. 150. Where the verdict was of assault with intent to commit great bodily injury, there being no such crime by statute, *held*, that it imported only a simple assault: Ex parte Ah Cha, 40 Cal. 426. But assault with intent to commit murder does not include assault with intent to do great bodily harm: Hungate v. P., 7 Ill. Ap. 101.

[8] P. v. Bentley, 75 Cal. 470; P. v. Gordon, 103 Cal. 568; P. v. Gordon, 99 Cal. 227.

[9] S. v. Collyer, 17 Nev. 275.

[10] S. v. Burk, 89 Mo. 635.

[11] Wilson v. S., 18 Ohio, 143.

stabbing includes the minor offense of stabbing.[1] But an indictment for shooting with intent to murder will not justify a verdict of inflicting with a dangerous weapon a wound less than mayhem.[2] An assault is necessarily included in any of the offenses described as assault with felonious intent, etc.;[3] thus, there may be conviction of simple assault under a charge of assault with intent to murder;[4] or assault to do great bodily injury;[5] or assault with intent to commit mayhem;[6] or assault with intent to rob.[7] Where the statute does not provide for any such offense as assault with intent to kill, a charge of that kind will nevertheless be a sufficient charge of an assault.[8] But a conviction for a less offense can only be had when such offense is necessarily proved in making proof of the greater offense charged; therefore, a charge of assault with intent to kill will not authorize a conviction of wounding,[9] or of malicious shooting.[10] In view of the general principle that accused can only be convicted of an offense charged, there can be no conviction, as for an included offense, of an offense some element or condition of which is not covered by the higher crime charged.[11] Thus, under an indictment charging assault with intent to murder, there cannot be conviction of assault and battery, as the charge does not necessarily include a battery[12] (unless, of course, the indictment states facts showing a bat-

[1] Isom v. S., 83 Ga., 378.

[2] S. v. Murdoch, 35 La. An. 729. But it does include shooting with intent to kill or wound: Robinson v. C., 16 B. Mon. 609.

[3] Winburn v. S., 28 Fla. 339.

[4] S. v. Triplett, 52 Kan. 678; S. v. Reynolds, 126 Mo. 516; P. v. Defoor, 100 Cal. 150; S. v. Coy, 2 Aikens, 181; Bedell v. S., 50 Miss. 492; S. v. Jarvis, 21 Ia. 44; S. v. Shepard, 10 Ia. 126; Horn v. S., 98 Ala. 23. If the indictment is insufficient to support a conviction for assault with intent to murder, there may still be a conviction under it for simple assault: S. v. Archer, 34 Tex. 646.

[5] Orton v. S., 4 Greene (Ia.), 140; S. v. Schele, 52 Ia. 608; S. v. King, 111 Mo. 576; Reg. v. Phillips, 3 Cox, 225. And see Reg. v. St. George, 9 C. & P. 483.

[6] McBride v. S., 7 Ark. 374.

[7] Dickerson v. C., 2 Bush, 1.

[8] Wilson v. S., 25 Tex. 169.

[9] S. v. Melton, 102 Mo. 683.

[10] McCroskey v. S., 2 Coldw. 178.

[11] S. v. Ackles, 8 Wash. 462; S. v. Largent, 9 Wash. 691.

[12] Sweeden v. S., 19 Ark. 205; T. v. Dooley, 4 Mont. 295. So the offense of aggravated assault with a dangerous weapon with intent to do bodily harm does not include assault and battery: S. v. Marcks, 3 N. Dak. 532. But under charge of assault with intent to kill, a verdict of aggravated assault and battery was held to support a conviction for aggravated assault alone: S. v. Robinson, 31 S. C. 453.

tery).[1] If the crime described by statute and charged in the indictment expressly involves assault and battery, such as felonious assault and battery;[2] or assault and battery with intent to kill;[3] or assault and battery with intent to commit a felony,[4] there may properly be a conviction for assault and battery, the intent not being proven.[5] There are some cases, however, which seem to justify conviction for assault and battery under a charge of assault with intent not involving a battery, as, for instance, under a charge of assault with a deadly weapon with intent to kill;[6] or assault to kill;[7] or assault with intent to inflict great bodily injury;[8] or assault with intent to commit murder.[9] Of course, under an assault with intent to commit a crime defendant cannot be found guilty of the crime itself.[10] Where the evidence indicates that, if the defendant is guilty at all, he is guilty of the crime charged, there is no necessity of instructing the jury with reference to the included crime.[11] But if in a prosecution for assault with intent to murder there is evidence of aggravated assault, which, if death had resulted, would have been manslaughter, an instruction as to manslaughter is called for.[12] If the crime charged is one of which the court has jurisdiction, there may properly be a conviction of an included offense, which, if charged alone, would not have been within the jurisdiction of the court, but only within the jurisdiction of an inferior court.[13] Under the same

[1] Clark v. S., 12 Ga. 350; S. v. Graham, 51 Ia. 72. But even if the indictment does show a battery, a verdict for assault will be sustained: Bard v. S., 55 Ga. 319. The charge of maliciously, etc., shooting a pistol to, at, and against another includes an assault and battery: Hays v. S., 77 Ind. 450.

[2] Mears v. C., 2 Grant, 385.

[3] S. v. Stedman, 7 Port. 495.

[4] Foley v. S., 9 Ind. 363.

[5] Greer v. S., 50 Ind. 267; McGuire v. S., 50 Ind. 284; S. v. Murphy, 21 Ind. 441.

[6] S. v. Schreiber, 41 Kan. 307.

[7] Kruget v. S., 1 Neb. 365.

[8] S. v. Welsh, 73 Ia. 106.

[9] Ferrell v. S., 2 Lea, 25; S. v. Bowling, 10 Humph. 52; Gardenheir v. S., 6 Tex. 348; Reynolds v. S., 11 Tex. 120; Johnson v. S., 17 Tex. 515.

[10] Manigault v. S., 53 Ga. 113.

[11] Spivey v. S., 30 Tex. Ap. 343; S. v. Johnson, 129 Mo. 26; S. v. Maguire, 113 Mo. 670; S. v. Woods, 124 Mo. 412; S. v. Moran, 46 Kan. 318. And see *supra*, § 262.

[12] Spivey v. S., 30 Tex. Ap. 343. If there is such instruction and the jury convicts of assault to murder, there will be no error even if there is no such crime as assault to commit manslaughter: Long v. P., 102 Ill. 331.

[13] Gillespie v. S., 9 Ind. 380; S. v. Johnson, 81 Mo. 60; S. v. De Laney, 28 La. An. 431; S. v. Berritt, 17 N. H. 268; Pittman v. S., 25 Fla. 648. In

principle there may be a conviction for a lower offense under a charge for the higher brought within the proper period of limitation for the higher, although the time for prosecuting the included offense has expired.[1]

§ 272. **Joinder.**— On the same principle which allows conviction for an included crime, different crimes when one is necessarily included within the other may be charged in the same indictment without subjecting it to the objection of duplicity.[2] Or the two crimes may be charged in the same count in the conjunctive.[3] If there are two counts, a general verdict of guilty will be considered as a conviction of the higher offense.[4] So if there is but one count charging an offense which necessarily includes less offenses, a general verdict of guilty will support a conviction for the offense charged.[5]

IV. ASSAULT WITH INTENT TO KILL OR MURDER.

§ 273. **The assault.**— The previous discussion has covered many questions which arise in connection with the crime of assault with intent to murder.[6] As in other cases of assault with intent, there must be something more than the intent alone; there must be an assault, that is, an attempt.[7] The assault may be by the administration of poison.[8]

Indiana, before the passage of the statute allowing conviction for lower offenses, it was held otherwise: Nelson v. S., 2 Ind. 249. See, also, S. v. Smalls, 17 S. C. 62. But if the court does not have jurisdiction of the major offense it cannot have jurisdiction to try accused for an included offense: Ex parte Brown, 40 Fed. R. 81.

[1] S. v. Bowling, 10 Humph. 52; Clarke v. S., 12 Ga. 350.

[2] People v. Beam, 66 Cal. 394; S. v. Cryer, 20 Ark. 64. It is otherwise if the offenses are such that under the charge of one there could not be a conviction for the other: S. v. Johns, 32 La. An. 812.

[3] S. v. Reed, 40 Vt. 603.

[4] Manly v. S., 7 Md. 135; S. v. Glover, 27 S. C. 602; S. v. Scott, 15 S. C. 434. But where one count charged assault and battery with intent to kill, and the other charged aggravated assault and battery, and the jury found a verdict for assault and battery, *held*, that this must be considered as for assault and battery only and not for the aggravated crime charged: S. v. Smalls, 17 S. C. 62.

[5] Curry v. S., 5 Neb. 412.

[6] See *supra*, § 264. Forms are given in § 270.

[7] P. v. Devine, 59 Cal. 630; Cooley v. S., 88 Tenn. 250. But it is said that an attempt to murder is not equivalent to an assault with intent to murder: S. v. Marshall, 14 Ala. 411. It is not necessary, however, to use the word "assault" if the acts charged constitute an assault: S. v. Munco, 12 La. An. 625. It is not essential that there be any actual injury: S. v. O'Flaherty, 7 Nev. 153; S. v. Roderigas, 7 Nev. 328.

[8] Johnson v. S., 92 Ga. 36. Further as to assaults by poisoning, see *supra*, § 236.

§ 274. The intent.— The specific intent must be alleged,[1] and the weight of authority is that there must be specific intent to kill,[2] and it must appear that the killing, had death resulted, would have been murder;[3] that is, the intent must be such as to involve malice aforethought in the killing, had death resulted,[4] and the indictment must charge the intent in that form.[5] But by statutory provision it is sometimes rendered unnecessary to charge more than simple intent to murder.[6] If the killing, had death resulted, would have been only manslaughter, the assault may be an assault with intent to kill,[7] or an assault with intent to commit manslaughter.[8] But the fact that the killing, had death ensued, would have been murder is

[1] S. v. Bloedow, 45 Wis. 279; Bartlett v. S., 21 Tex. Ap. 500.

[2] Walls v. S., 90 Ala. 618 (overruling Smith v. S., 88 Ala. 23); McCormack v. S., 102 Ala. 156; Moore v. S., 18 Ala. 532; Jeff v. S., 39 Miss. 593; Williams v. S., 30 Tex. Ap. 429; White v. S., 13 Tex. Ap. 259; Courtney v. S., 13 Tex. Ap. 502; Moore v. S., 26 Tex. Ap. 322; Reg. v. Cruse, 8 C. & P. 541. But it is not necessary that the intent should have been formed at the beginning of the difficulty: Henderson v. S., 12 Tex. 525. An attempt to commit suicide is not an attempt to commit murder: Reg. v. Burgess, L. & C. 258; nor is an assault to commit great bodily harm the same thing as an assault with intent to commit murder, even though, if death had resulted, the crime would have been murder: Harrell v. S., 13 Tex. Ap. 374; Gillespie v. S., 13 Tex. Ap. 415; White v. S., 13 Tex. Ap. 259.

[3] P. v. Landman, 103 Cal. 577; McCoy v. S., 8 Ark. 451; King v. S., 21 Ga. 220; S. v. Boyden, 13 Ired. 505; Seborn v. S., 51 Ga. 164; Jackson v. S., 51 Ga. 402; Smith v. S., 52 Ga. 88; Thomas v. S., 91 Ga. 204; Revels v. S., 33 Fla. 308; Hopkinson v. P., 18 Ill. 264; Hooper v. S., 29 Tex. Ap. 614.

[4] S. v. Miller, 27 Ind. 15; Vaughan v. S., 128 Ind. 14; S. v. Fiske, 63 Conn. 388; S. v. Keasling, 74 Ia. 528; S. v. Newberry, 26 Ia. 467; P. v. McFadden, 65 Cal. 445; nor need the assault be charged as felonious: Wood v. S., 64 Miss. 761. A charge of assault to kill with malice aforethought is a sufficient charge of assault to murder, the legal effect being the same: Smith v. S., 31 Tex. Ap. 33.

[5] S. v. Fee, 19 Wis. 562; Hungate v. P., 7 Ill. Ap. 101; S. v. Howell, Ga. Dec., part I, 158.

[6] Cross v. S., 55 Wis. 261; Kilkelly v. S., 43 Wis. 604; Rice v. P., 15 Mich. 9; Robinson v. C., 16 B. Mon. 609. Particular indictments were considered in this respect in the following cases: Hanrahan v. P., 91 Ill. 142; S. v. Doyle, 107 Mo. 36; S. v. Maguire, 113 Mo. 670; Anthony v. S., 13 Sm. & M. 263; Burns v. C., 3 Met. (Ky.) 13; S. v. Munco, 12 La. An. 625; S. v. Green, 36 La. An. 99; S. v. Frances, 36 La. An. 336.

[7] Ex parte Brown, 40 Fed. R. 81. But the charge of assault with intent to kill and murder will support a conviction of assault with intent to murder.

[8] Maher v. P., 10 Mich. 212; S. v. Neal, 37 Me. 468; Rapp v. C., 14 B. Mon. 614; Williams v. S., 43 Tex. 382; Elliott v. S., 46 Ga. 159; Read v. C., 22 Grat. 924. And further as to assault with intent to commit manslaughter, see *infra*, § 278.

not conclusive as to the intent to murder, for an act resulting in death is sometimes murder where there is no intent to kill, and therefore no intent to murder;[1] as, for instance, where death results in pursuance of an attempt to do great bodily injury, the death would be murder though the assault would not be an assault with intent to commit murder.[2] As the malice aforethought is an essential element of the crime it must be explained to the jury.[3] It is not necessary, however, to specify whether the intent is to commit murder in the first or in the second degree, there being in general no such degrees in the crime of assault with intent to commit murder;[4] and it is not necessary to show that if death had resulted it would have been murder in the first degree;[5] but by some statutes there may be assault with intent to commit murder in the first degree, and in such case the intent is to be described by the terms proper in an indictment charging murder in that degree.[6]

§ 275. **Allegation and proof of intent.**— It is not necessary to charge specifically the acts showing that the intent was to murder;[7] nor need the intent be shown by direct and positive testimony, as it may be inferred from the circumstances.[8]

[1] P. v. Mize, 80 Cal. 41; S. v. Evans, 39 La. An. 912; Gallery v. S., 92 Ga. 463; Carter v. S., 28 Tex. Ap. 355.

[2] Harrell v. S., 13 Tex. Ap. 374; Pruitt v. S., 20 Tex. Ap. 129.

[3] Garza v. S., 11 Tex. Ap. 345; Williams v. S., 3 Tex. Ap. 316; Hodges v. S., 3 Tex. Ap. 470; Ewing v. S., 4 Tex. Ap. 417; Daniels v. S., 4 Tex. Ap. 429; Johnson v. S., 4 Tex. Ap. 598; Caruthers v. S., 13 Tex. Ap. 339. But there need be no explanation of the distinction between express and implied malice, that not being material under the statute: Wilson v. S., 4 Tex. Ap. 637.

[4] S. v. Jarvis, 21 Ia. 44; Meredith v. S., 60 Ala. 441; P. v. Scott, 6 Mich. 287; Sharp v. S., 19 Ohio, 379; Curry v. S., 4 Neb. 545; S. v. Williams, 23 N. H. 321. Allegations of deliberation and premeditation are not essential: S. v. Keasling, 74 Ia. 528; S. v. Newberry, 26 Ia. 467.

[5] Ogletree v. S., 28 Ala. 693; Stapp v. S., 3 Tex. Ap. 138. *Contra*, Bonfanti v. S., 2 Minn. 123.

[6] S. v. Jenkins, 120 Ind. 268; Cooley v. S., 88 Tenn. 250; Logan v. S., 2 Lea, 222.

[7] Williams v. S., 47 Ind. 568. *Contra*, Williams v. S., 42 Miss. 328; T. v. Sevailles, 1 N. M. 119. See *supra*, § 269.

[8] Conn v. P., 116 Ill. 458; Weaver v. P., 132 Ill. 536; Jackson v. S., 94 Ala. 85; Trevinio v. S., 27 Tex. Ap. 372; Cole v. S., 10 Ark. 318; S. v. Woodward, 84 Ia. 172. For instance, where it appeared that the accused armed himself and provoked the quarrel: Steffy v. P., 130 Ill. 98; or used the weapon in a manner or under circumstances indicating an intent to kill without justification or excuse: King v. S., 4 Tex. Ap. 54; Ferguson v. S., 6 Tex. Ap. 504. Some Alabama cases hold that an instruc-

And in this sense it is said the person is presumed to intend the consequences of his acts,[1] and that from the unlawful use of a deadly weapon[2] there will be a presumption of intent to murder, unless such presumption is overcome by other testimony in the case.[3] Indeed, it has been said that in such a case the burden is on defendant to show that there was no malice.[4] But such a statement of the law as to burden of proof is not warranted by the weight of authority, as will appear in a discussion of the same question under the subject of homicide;[5] and much less is it justifiable to speak of a legal presumption of intent from the use of a deadly weapon where the assault with intent only is charged; for while the rule has sometimes been stated that the law implies malice where death results from the use of a deadly weapon, this does not warrant the presumption of malice from a portion of the facts, that is, from the use of a deadly weapon without death resulting.[6] The question of intent is for the jury, even if the facts from which it is sought to draw the presumption are admitted.[7] And it is erroneous to direct the jury to infer the intent from any facts not including the whole evidence.[8] Previous difficulties between the parties

tion to the jury requiring evidence of positive intention or specific intent to murder may be refused as misleading: Moore v. S., 18 Ala. 532; Jackson v. S., 94 Ala. 85.

[1] S. v. Gilman, 69 Me. 163; Garza v. S., 11 Tex. Ap. 345. And see a further discussion of this subject under the head of intent, *supra*, § 123, and homicide. *infra*, § 332.

[2] A pistol used for striking may be a deadly weapon for this purpose: Prior v. S., 41 Ga. 155. But on the contrary it is said, to render a gun a deadly weapon, it is necessary to show that it was loaded with powder and ball, and a mere threat to shoot is not sufficient to give rise to the presumption of intent to kill: Fastbinder v. S., 42 Ohio St. 341. The question as to whether the instrument used is a deadly weapon is one of fact for the jury: S. v. Nueslein, 25 Mo. 111. The fact, however, that the weapon used in the assault is one not likely to cause death does not necessarily show that there was not an intent to murder: Tatum v. S., 59 Ga. 638; Monday v. S., 32 Ga. 672. Further, as to deadly weapon, see the discussion under homicide, *infra*, § 330, and aggravated assault, *supra*, § 257.

[3] Jeff v. S., 39 Miss. 593; Wood v. S., 27 Tex. Ap. 393; Watts v. S., 30 Tex. Ap. 533.

[4] Hogan v. S., 61 Ga. 43; Collier v. S., 39 Ga. 31.

[5] *Infra*, § 332.

[6] Gallery v. S., 92 Ga. 463.

[7] Patterson v. S., 85 Ga. 131; Chrisman v. S., 54 Ark. 283; Agitone v. S., 41 Tex. 501; Anderson v. S., 1 Tex. Ap. 730; Walker v. S., 7 Tex. Ap. 627; Seitz v. S., 23 Ala. 42; Morgan v. S., 33 Ala. 413; S. v. Stewart, 29 Mo. 419.

[8] Simpson v. S., 59 Ala. 1.

may be shown as bearing on the question of intent;[1] so may evidence of previous threats,[2] and of violent language during the assault[3] or immediately afterward.[4] The fact that defendant, before the assault, armed himself with a secreted weapon is evidence of a murderous intent.[5] Where the defense is temporary insanity from intoxication, evidence of previous assaults and threats is admissible to show malice and the condition of defendant's mind.[6]

§ 276. **Connection of intent and act.**— In alleging an assault with intent to kill or murder, the accused must be charged with the assault of a certain person with intent to kill that person, and a mere general intent to kill evidenced by recklessness and depravity will not support the charge.[7] There are cases, however, the other way.[8] At any rate it is not essential that there be malice toward the particular person upon whom the assault is made.[9] There seems to be no reason, however, why, if an act is done with intent to murder A., but injury or danger sufficient to constitute an assault results therefrom to B., the wrong-doer may not properly be prosecuted for an assault with intent to murder B., just as he might have been prosecuted for killing B. with malice aforethought if B. had died from the injury.[10] But there are cases holding to the contrary.[11] There may certainly be assault with intent to murder, even though

[1] S. v. Schleagel, 50 Kan. 325; Sullivan v. S., 31 Tex. Ap. 486. But the circumstances of the previous difficulty are not admissible: Tarver v. S., 43 Ala. 354.

[2] Lawrence v. S., 84 Ala. 424; Smith v. S., 92 Ala. 30; Bingham v. S., 6 Tex. Ap. 169. So where the assault was upon the agent of a railroad company, *held*, that previous threats against the company were admissible: Newton v. S., 92 Ala. 33.

[3] McMahon v. S., 16 Tex. Ap. 357; Wims v. S., 90 Ala. 623; Brown v. S., 55 Ga. 169.

[4] Henderson v. S., 70 Ala. 29; Meeks v. S., 51 Ga. 429.

[5] Price v. S., 36 Miss. 531.

[6] Hall v. S., 31 Tex. Ap. 565.

[7] Jones v. S., 11 Sm. & M. 315; Morgan v. S., 13 Sm. & M. 242; Scott v. S., 49 Ark. 156; Reg. v. Lallement, 6 Cox, 204.

[8] Perry v. P., 14 Ill. 496; Vandermark v. P., 47 Ill. 122; Dunaway v. P., 110 Ill. 333; Conn v. P., 116 Ill. 458; Weaver v. P., 132 Ill. 536.

[9] P. v. Raher, 92 Mich. 165; Johnson v. S., 92 Ga. 36; Harrell v. S., 75 Ga. 842; Reg. v. Fretwell, L. & C. 443.

[10] S. v. Gilman, 69 Me. 163, 3 Am. Cr. R. 15 and note; S. v. Montgomery, 91 Mo. 52; McGehee v. S., 62 Miss. 772; S. v. Meadows, 18 W. Va. 658; Hollywood v. P., 3 Keyes, 55; Reg. v. Smith, Dears. 559; Rex v. Jarvis, 2 M. & Rob. 40. One count may charge intent to murder A. and another intent to murder B.: Rex v. Holt, 7 C. & P. 518. And see § 323.

[11] Lacefield v. S., 34 Ark. 275; C. v. Morgan, 11 Bush, 601; McCormack

the intent be to kill a person not knowing who he is.[1] So there may be assault with intent to murder two persons,[2] and in such case there may be a conviction on proof of intent to murder one of the persons named.[3]

§ 277. **Justification or excuse.**— If it appears that the assault, though with intent to kill, was under such circumstances as to make it justifiable or excusable, it will not be an assault with intent to murder.[4]

§ 278. **With intent to commit manslaughter.**— As there may be intentional killing which is only manslaughter, it is evident that there may, in principle, be an assault with intent to commit manslaughter, and such a charge is not impossible or repugnant.[5] Such an offense would be committed where there was an assault with intent to kill, but in such heat of blood arising from provocation that if death had resulted manslaughter only would have been committed.[6] The offense is identical with that of assault with intent to commit murder except that the element of malice aforethought is lacking,[7] and therefore, under an indictment for assault with intent to commit murder, a conviction may be supported for assault with intent to commit manslaughter as an included offense.[8] In charging the offense it is not necessary to allege malice.[9] If the statute does not specifically provide for the punishment of assault with intent to commit manslaughter, the act is still punishable under general statutory provisions as an assault with intent to commit a felony.[10]

v. S., 102 Ala. 156: Reg. v. Hewlett, 1 F. & F. 91. An indictment charging that defendant caused A. to take poison with intent to murder him is not supported by proof that the poison, though taken by A., was intended for B.: Reg. v. Ryan, 2 M. & Rob. 213.

1 Washington v. S., 53 Ala. 29.

2 C. v. McLaughlin, 12 Cush. 615.

3 Tuberville v. S., 40 Ala. 715.

4 Long v. S., 46 Ind. 582; Field v. S., 50 Ind. 15; Pickens v. S., 13 Tex. Ap. 353.

5 S. v. Calligan, 17 N. H. 253; S. v. Butman, 42 N. H. 490; S. v. Nichols, 8 Conn. 496; Jarrell v. S., 58 Ind. 293; S. v. White, 45 Ia. 325; S. v. Connor, 59 Ia. 357; S. v. Postal, 83 Ia. 460; S. v. McGuire, 87 Ia. 142; Smith v. S., 83 Ala. 26. *Contra*, Moore v. P., 146 Ill. 600; Morman v. S., 24 Miss. 54; Bedell v. S., 50 Miss. 492. In Tennessee there is no such offense as assault with intent to commit involuntary manslaughter: Stevens v. S., 91 Tenn. 726.

6 S. v. Clair, 84 Me. 248; S. v. Lang, 65 N. H. 284; Spearman v. S., 23 Tex. Ap. 224.

7 S. v. Leary, 88 N. C. 615.

8 *Supra*, § 271.

9 Pierce v. S., 75 Ind. 199.

10 S. v. Williams, 6 Baxt. 655; S. v. White, 45 Ia. 325; S. v. Keasling, 74 Ia. 528.

§ 279. Assault with intent to kill.— At common law assault or assault and battery with intent to kill is a misdemeanor,[1] and by statutes in many states providing for the punishment of such offense it is still a misdemeanor.[2] But in other states no such offense being specified by statute, it is in effect only an assault.[3] In construing the provisions of statutes on the subject, difficulty has arisen as to whether by intent to kill was meant intent to kill with malice aforethought — that is, such as that if death should result it would be murder — or whether it includes an intent to kill formed in heat of blood under provocation such that a resulting death would be manslaughter only. In New York the statute has been held to be so framed as to indicate that the offense contemplated was an assault with intent to kill under circumstances which would make the crime at least murder in the second degree.[4] In Ohio it is held that "intent to kill" was an unauthorized change in the statute made by the code commissioners in substituting that expression for "intent to murder."[5] And it seems to be held in some other states that intent to kill means intent to murder, and means more than intent to commit manslaughter.[6] But with more reason it has been said in other cases that, as intentional killing may be manslaughter, it is not necessary that assault with intent to kill be an assault with malice aforethought.[7] Under such construction, if there is assault with intent to commit murder under the statute, assault with intent to kill would be assault with intent to commit manslaughter.[8] The intent to kill may be inferred from the

[1] S. v. Danforth, 3 Conn. 112.

[2] S. v. Hord, 8 S. C. 84; Kennedy v. S., 15 Fla. 635; Rice v. C., 3 Bush, 14; S. v. Swann, 65 N. C. 330.

[3] Wilson v. P., 24 Mich. 410; Long v. S., 34 Tex. 566; Sheffield v. S., 1 Tex. Ap. 640; Lockwood v. S., 1 Tex. Ap. 749.

[4] Pontius v. P., 82 N. Y. 339; Slatterly v. P., 58 N. Y. 354.

[5] S. v. Stout, 49 Ohio St. 270.

[6] Bradley v. S., 10 Sm. & M. 618; Milan v. S., 24 Ark. 346. A verdict of assault with intent to kill will not sustain a conviction for assault with intent to commit murder where there is no such offense as assault with intent to kill: Sheffield v. S., 1 Tex. Ap. 640.

[7] S. v. Waters, 39 Me. 54; S. v. Nichols, 8 Conn. 496; Scott v. C., 6 S. & R. 224; U. S. v. Lloyd, 4 Cranch, C. C. 468; U. S. v. Tharp, 5 Cranch, C. C. 390. And see preceding section.

[8] S. v. Waters, 39 Me. 54. But see S. v. Scannell, 39 Me. 68, which seems not intelligible in view of the preceding case.

nature of the act done.[1] But the fact that death might reasonably be anticipated from the injury inflicted will not necessarily show intent to kill.[2] And the indictment should charge the assault as made with a deadly weapon.[3] In order to show that the killing intended was not lawful, the indictment should allege that the intent was unlawful and felonious.[4] The fact that the indictment alleges intent to murder as well as to kill will not vitiate it as an indictment for assault with intent to kill.[5] And although the evidence shows the assault to have been with intent to kill with malice aforethought, a conviction under the indictment will not be improper.[6] An indictment charging assault with a deadly weapon with intent to kill is not improper under a statute providing for the punishment of an assault with intent to kill.[7]

V. ASSAULT TO DO GREAT BODILY INJURY.

§ 280. **What constitutes; how shown.**— An assault with intent to do great bodily injury or harm is a misdemeanor only, unless the statute provides otherwise.[8] But it is sometimes made a felony [9] by reason of the seriousness of the specific intent,[10] especially where it involves the use of a deadly weapon.[11] The offense is not the same as assault with intent to maim.[12] It is not necessary that the intent to injure be of such character that death resulting would be murder.[13] An indictment

[1] Lane v. S., 85 Ala. 11; Nixon v. P., 3 Ill. 267.

[2] P. v. Comstock, 49 Mich. 330; P. v. Odell, 1 Dak. 189.

[3] Kruget v. S., 1 Neb. 365.

[4] Curtis v. P., 2 Ill. 285. But the omission of the words "unlawfully and feloniously" will not vitiate the indictment if other apt words to express the same meaning are used: Perry v. P., 14 Ill. 496; S. v. Daley, 41 Vt. 564.

[5] S. v. Lynch, 20 Oreg. 389; P. v. Odell, 1 Dak. 189; S. v. Johnson, 9 Nev. 175.

[6] S. v. Parmelee, 9 Conn. 259. The fact that the crime is named assault with intent to murder while the charge is of administering poison with intent to kill will not be fatal to a conviction of the latter offense: P. v. Cuddihi, 54 Cal. 53.

[7] S. v. Rigg, 10 Nev. 284. Further, as to sufficiency of indictments in Nevada, see S. v. O'Connor, 11 Nev. 416.

[8] P. v. Murat, 45 Cal. 281; Ex parte Max, 44 Cal. 579.

[9] P. v. Troy, 96 Mich. 530.

[10] Smith v. S., 34 Neb. 689.

[11] Ex parte Ah Cha, 40 Cal. 426.

[12] S. v. Meadows, 18 W. Va. 658.

[13] Harrell v. S., 13 Tex. Ap. 374; Reg. v. Griffiths, 8 C. & P. 248.

for the offense is sufficient which accuses defendant of an assault and battery, alleging the wilful and malicious striking and beating of another with intent of doing him great bodily injury.[1] And it is immaterial that the battery is alleged.[2] A great bodily injury is injury to the person of a more grave and serious character than ordinary battery. The question whether the injury in a particular case is of such character is for the jury.[3] The intent may be inferred from the ordinary consequences of the act done.[4] But the specific intent must appear.[5] It is not necessary, however, that it be the principal intent, if involved in that which is intended.[6] If the intent is to do a lawful act in defense of property or person a crime is not committed.[7] But it may be committed in acting in self-defense without having retreated as far as necessary to authorize such violence.[8] The result of the injury is not to be considered as evidence of the intent with which it is inflicted, unless the jury find that such result was contemplated, but may be taken into account in determining the force actually employed, and therefore the intent to be inferred therefrom.[9] It is not necessary that accused should have contemplated the very thing which resulted from the assault, if serious and permanent bodily injury of any kind was intended.[10] Specific intent to injure the person injured is not essential if the acts of accused indicate a reckless disregard of the safety of others.[11]

VI. Assault with Intent to Rob.

§ 281. What constitutes.— As in other cases of assault with intent, the intent is the gist of the offense, and must be alleged.[12] But the allegation need not specifically state the acts indicat-

[1] S. v. Carpenter, 23 Ia. 506. The means need not be stated nor the precise injury intended: Murphey v. S., 43 Neb. 34.

[2] Cokely v. S., 4 Ia. 477.

[3] S. v. Gillett, 56 Ia. 459. And see Rex v. Shadbolt, 5 C. & P. 504.

[4] S. v. Gillett, 56 Ia. 459; S. v. Redfield, 73 Ia. 643.

[5] S. v. Vosburgh, 82 Wis. 168; Tarpley v. P., 42 Ill. 340.

[6] Rex v. Gillow, 1 Moody, 85.

[7] Filkins v. P., 69 N. Y. 101.

[8] Reg. v. Odgers, 2 M. & Rob. 479.

[9] P. v. Miller, 91 Mich. 639. This was a case of kicking, as to which, see, also, Rex v. Shadbolt, 5 C. & P. 504.

[10] P. v. Miller, 91 Mich. 639.

[11] P. v. Raher, 92 Mich. 165.

[12] Conolly v. P., 4 Ill. 474. Conviction cannot be sustained upon evidence of nothing beyond mere assault: Garrity v. P., 70 Ill. 83.

ing such intent.[1] The indictment may allege both violence and putting in fear.[2] It is not necessary to specify what accused intended to take;[3] and if the intent alleged is to rob one of his watch and money, it is enough to prove an intent to rob him of either.[4] It is not necessary that the property belong to the one assaulted, mere possession being sufficient.[5]

[1] Dickerson v. C., 2 Bush, 1; Taylor v. C., 3 Bush, 508; Hollohan v. S., 32 Md. 399; Morris v. S., 13 Tex. Ap. 65. But in another case it is said that the acts must be stated with the particularity necessary in an indictment for the offense of robbery: S. v. Brown, 21 La. An. 347.

[2] S. v. Montgomery, 109 Mo. 645.

[3] Conolly v. P., 4 Ill. 474; Crumes v. S., 28 Tex. Ap. 516.

[4] Phillips v. S., 36 Ark. 282.

[5] Durand v. P., 47 Mich. 332.

PART V.

OFFENSES AGAINST THE PERSON.

CHAPTER 18.

HOMICIDE.

I. Causation.
II. Who Deemed Person.
III. Homicides Not Criminal; Justifiable and Excusable; Self-defense.
IV. Murder.
V. Manslaughter.
VI. Statutory Degrees.
VII. Jurisdiction and Venue.
VIII. The Indictment.
IX. Procedure and Punishment.
X. The Evidence.

§ 282. **Scope of the chapter.**— It will be necessary to consider in this chapter what is a killing, including various questions as to causation and as to proximate and remote cause, and also who is such human being as to be subject of homicide. Homicide is not, however, the name of a crime or group of crimes; it is the name of an act, and the act may or may not be criminal, depending upon the motives actuating it and the circumstances under which it is done. It will be necessary, therefore, to further consider what homicides are justifiable or excusable — that is, not criminal; and as to those which are criminal, to divide them into grades and degrees.[1] Finally, the method of charging, proving and punishing these offenses will be discussed.

[1] **Table of homicide.**— The analysis of the subject placed in tabular form, and shown on the following page, will perhaps be of assistance as presenting the usual classification. It will be understood that only the principal divisions can be shown in a table, and that for explanations and application of the principles resort must be had to the text.

§ 282a. Table of homicide.—

HOMICIDE (*i. e.*, causing the death of a human being by an injury resulting in death within a year and a day).	Non-felonious.	Justifiable (in discharge of legal duty).	By an officer executing sentence of death, or by an officer or a private person in making lawful arrest.	
			By any person in preventing a felony.	
		Excusable (without fault).	By accident or misadventure.	
			In an affray, to save life after withdrawal.	
	Felonious.	Manslaughter (without malice aforethought).	By negligence	In failure to provide support where there is a legal duty to do so.
				In careless use of dangerous instrumentalities.
			In self-defense, chastisement, or arrest, where unnecessary violence is used, without intent to kill.	
			In committing a misdemeanor.	
			By intentional killing in heat of blood, *i. e.*, under provocation.	
			By intentional killing in resisting unlawful arrest.	
		Murder (with malice aforethought, express or implied).	In committing a felony.	In first degree (by statute usually including murder by poison, or by lying in wait, or in commission of certain felonies, or with wilful, deliberate and premeditated intent to kill).
			In attempting to cause great bodily harm, or in a riot.	
			In resisting legal arrest.	
			By intentional unlawful killing.	In second degree (all other murders).

I. CAUSATION.

§ 283. **Means of killing.**— The ordinary methods of causing death, such as wounding, poisoning, strangling, etc., need no special illustration.[1] But there are some questions of difficulty as to what are such acts as that when death follows the doer of the act can be said to have caused the death. It is thought that formerly it was deemed to be criminal homicide if, with intent to cause death, one should falsely swear to the commission of a crime by another and thus secure his conviction and execution,[2] but this is not now the recognized law.[3]

§ 284. **Threats, fear.**— Where one is induced by fear of violence, caused by threats or otherwise, to do an act likely to cause his death and which does cause it, the person thus bringing about the fatal result is responsible therefor.[4] But it seems that death from fear alone cannot be considered as criminally chargeable to the one causing the fear.[5]

§ 285. **Accident.**— If the death is accidental and not the probable or necessary result of the act done, it does not constitute homicide in the person doing the act.[6] In general, there is no criminal liability for the accidental result of an act done

[1] 4 Bl. Com. 196; 1 Hawk. P. C., ch. 31, §§ 4-8.

[2] 1 Russ. Cr. 494; 4 Bl. Com. 196.

[3] Rex v. Macdaniel, 1 East, P. C. 333.

[4] Rex v. Evans, 1 Russ., C. & M. 676; Reg. v. Pitts, Car. & M. 284. But where the wife was able to contend with her husband, who was a cripple, it was held that the jury should have been allowed to inquire whether it was reasonable fear of the husband's violence which caused the wife to leave the house and resulted in death from freezing: Hendrickson v. C., 85 Ky. 281.

[5] 1 Hale, P. C. 429. Death occasioned by grief or terror cannot, in law, be deemed murder: C. v. Webster, 5 Cush. 295. But where, as the result of an unlawful assault upon the mother, an infant held in her arms was so frightened that it had convulsions, from the effects of which it died, *held*, that the person making the assault was guilty of manslaughter if the jury should think that the assault was the direct cause of death: Reg. v. Towers, 12 Cox, 530.

[6] U. S. v. Meagher, 37 Fed. R. 875. So held where one wrongfully knocked another off a horse, the latter being killed by the horse jumping upon him and kicking him: P. v. Rockwell, 39 Mich. 503. But *contra*, where the assault was such as to give apprehension that the life of the person assailed was in danger, and in spurring his horse to escape he was thrown and killed: Rex v. Hickman, 5 C. & P. 151. An accident is something that occurs notwithstanding the exercise of the care required by law to prevent its occurrence: U. S. v. Boyd, 45 Fed. R. 851.

in sport.[1] The liability for accidental death will be further considered under excusable homicide and also under the head of manslaughter.[2]

§ 286. Negligence; failure to provide for dependent persons.— While mere negligence not the proximate cause of the death does not amount to homicide,[3] yet homicide may consist in an injury or series of injuries caused by neglect, restraint, exposure, and depriving of sufficient food and nourishment.[4] Thus, failure to provide medical attendance for a sick child, as required by statute,[5] or proper food and clothing,[6] or failing to care for a new-born infant[7] or other dependent person,[8] may constitute criminal homicide. But to render one thus criminally liable for death caused by neglect, it must appear that he was chargeable with the care of the person neglected and had the means of supplying his needs, and that the person neglected was entirely dependent on the one sought to be charged and could not himself have avoided the result.[9] A husband is not

[1] Reg. v. Bruce, 2 Cox, 262.

[2] See *infra*, §§ 300 and 347.

[3] As where a captain refused to take steps to rescue a sailor who had fallen overboard, his death being caused by the fall: U. S. v. Knowles, 4 Sawyer, 517. Where the person having charge of a steam-engine stopped it and went away, and another party set it in motion whereby a person was killed, it was held that the first party was not guilty of manslaughter: Hilton's Case, 2 Lewin, 214. Where A. and B. were engaged in an altercation and A. pushed away B.'s boat, and B., catching at another boat to prevent his boat drifting, fell into the water and was drowned, *held*, that A. was not guilty of manslaughter: Rex v. Waters, 6 C. & P. 328.

[4] C. v. Macloon, 101 Mass. 1.

[5] Reg. v. Downes, 1 Q. B. D. 8. But it must appear that the death was caused or accelerated by the neglect to provide medical aid: Reg. v. Morby, 8 Q. B. D. 571. Aside from statute it is not criminal to thus fail to call medical attendance, if it is in pursuance of a religious conviction: Reg. v. Wagstaffe, 10 Cox, 530.

[6] Reg. v. Bubb, 4 Cox, 455; Rex v. Friend, Russ. & Ry. 20; Rex v. Squire, 1 Russ., C. & M. 80, 678; Reg. v. Conde, 10 Cox, 547.

[7] Reg. v. Middleship, 5 Cox, 275; Reg. v. Handley, 13 Cox, 79. It is not necessary in such case to allege that defendant was in duty bound to provide for such child, or that it was unable to help itself: S. v. Behm, 72 Ia. 533. But the mere failure of a woman who knows she is to be confined to take the necessary precautions to preserve the life of the child, after its birth, will not render her criminally responsible for its death: Reg. v. Knights, 2 F. & F. 46.

[8] S. v. Smith, 65 Me. 257; Reg. v. Instan, 1 Q. B. D. (1893), 450. So, where a servant is helpless in body and mind, and under the dominion of the master, death from the master's neglect will render the latter guilty of manslaughter: Reg. v. Smith, L. & C. 607.

[9] 2 Bish. Cr. L., §§ 659–662; Rex v.

criminally liable on account of the death of his wife, whom he has driven from the house by cruelty and threats, unless it appear that the death of the wife by exposure was the natural and probable consequence of her leaving the house at the time and under the circumstances.[1] Where there is criminal neglect causing death, the offense will be manslaughter.[2]

§ 287. **Physicians and chemists.**— Other acts, not in themselves wrongful, but calculated to injure another if not done with proper skill and care, may render the person doing them criminally responsible for death resulting; thus, one who as physician undertakes to treat another is bound to have competent skill and to use care and attention, and if death results from want of skill or care the physician is criminally responsible.[3] While it may not be criminal in one who has not proper medical training to administer in good faith a remedy the dangerous character of which is not known to him and which causes death,[4] yet one who rashly administers remedies the effect of which he does not know, and which cause death, is criminally

Smith, 2 C. & P. 449; Reg. v. Edwards, 8 C. & P. 611; Reg. v. Waters, 2 C. & K. 864; Reg. v. Nicholls, 13 Cox, 75. If the person charged has not the means to supply the necessities of the dependent person there is no criminal liability: S. v. Merkley, 74 Ia. 695; Rex v. Saunders, 7 C. & P. 277; Reg. v. Rugg, 12 Cox, 16. It seems that where the person charged has not the means of supplying necessities, he will not be held criminally liable by reason of having failed to apply for relief to proper authorities: Reg. v. Chandler, Dears. 453; Reg. v. Rugg, 12 Cox, 16. *Contra*, Reg. v. Mabbett, 5 Cox, 339. Where a daughter went to her mother's house to be confined, and died because a midwife was not called, *held*, that the mother was under no duty and was not guilty of manslaughter: Reg. v. Shepherd, 9 Cox, 123.

[1] Hendrickson v. C., 85 Ky. 281. So, where the wife, after being assaulted and beaten by her husband, and after he had gone to bed, voluntarily left the house and unnecessarily exposed herself, *held*, that he was not responsible for her death: S. v. Preslar, 3 Jones, 421. Where husband and wife are living apart by mutual consent, the husband is not responsible for her death by reason of the lack of shelter, unless he is made acquainted with the fact that she is without shelter and refuses to provide her with it: Reg. v. Plummer, 1 C. & K. 600.

[2] *Infra*, § 349.

[3] Rex v. Long, 4 C. & P. 423; Rex v. Spiller, 5 C. & P. 333; Reg. v. Spilling, 2 M. & Rob. 107. But it is otherwise if death arises from mere error of judgment: Reg. v. Macleod, 12 Cox, 534. Consent to the operation will not be an excuse: S. v. Gile, 8 Wash. 12.

[4] C. v. Thompson, 6 Mass. 134; Rice v. S., 8 Mo. 561; 1 Hale, P. C. 429.

responsible.[1] One who *bona fide* and honestly exercises his best skill to cure a patient and performs an operation causing death is not criminally responsible.[2] It seems that, in determining the criminal responsibility of one who gives medical treatment, the fact that he is not regularly licensed to practice will not, in itself, show such negligence as to render him criminally responsible.[3] Mistake of a physician or chemist, causing death, will not necessarily show criminal liability in the absence of any evidence of negligence.[4]

§ 288. **Railroad companies.**— In Massachusetts, Maine and New Hampshire are found statutes authorizing indictment of a railroad company where the negligence of the corporation or its agents has caused death.[5] But the proceeding is to enforce a penalty in behalf of certain named persons, such as widow, heirs, etc.[6] Though criminal in form, the proceeding is in effect civil, and subject to the rules applicable in actions for damages as to amount of evidence, burden of proof, contributory negligence, etc.[7] It is provided to supply a defect

[1] C. v. Pierce, 138 Mass. 165; S. v. Hardister, 38 Ark. 605; Rex v. Long, 4 C. & P. 398; Rex v. Simpson, 1 Lewin, 172; Reg. v. Crook, 1 F. & F. 521; Reg. v. Crick, 1 F. & F. 519; Reg. v. Markuss, 4 F. & F. 356; Reg. v. Chamberlain, 10 Cox, 486; Rex v. Webb, 1 M. & Rob. 405.

[2] S. v. Schulz, 55 Ia. 628; S. v. Hardister, 38 Ark. 605; Rex v. Van Butchell, 3 C. & P. 629; Rex v. Williamson, 3 C. & P. 635. Where death resulted from the operation of sounding, with a usual instrument, to determine pregnancy, *held*, that the physician was not criminally responsible in the absence of negligence: S. v. Reynolds, 42 Kan. 320.

[3] C. v. Thompson, 6 Mass. 134; Rex v. Long, 4 C. & P. 398; Rex v. Van Butchell, 3 C. & P. 629.

[4] Reg. v. Noakes, 4 F. & F. 920; Reg. v. Bull, 2 F. & F. 201; Reg. v. Spencer, 10 Cox, 525. As to sufficiency of indictment against a druggist for negligence in administering a drug causing death, see S. v. Smith, 66 Mo. 92.

[5] C. v. Boston & Worcester R. Co., 11 Cush. 512; C. v. Fitchburg R. Co., 126 Mass. 472; C. v. Coburn, 132 Mass. 555; S. v. Maine Central R. Co., 60 Me. 490; S. v. Gilmore, 24 N. H. 461; S. v. Railroad, 52 N. H. 528.

[6] C. v. Eastern R. Co., 5 Gray, 473; C. v. Boston & Albany R. Co., 121 Mass. 36; S. v. Gilmore, 24 N. H. 461; S. v. Railroad, 58 N. H. 510; S. v. Grand Trunk R. Co., 60 Me. 145.

[7] C. v. Fitchburg R. Co., 10 Allen, 189; C. v. Boston & Maine R. Co., 129 Mass. 500; C. v. Boston & Lowell R. Co., 134 Mass. 211; S. v. European & N. A. R. Co., 67 Me. 479; S. v. Maine Central R. Co., 76 Me. 357; S. v. Maine Central R. Co., 77 Me. 538; S. v. Maine Central R. Co., 77 Me. 244; S. v. Boston & Maine R. Co., 80 Me. 430; S. v. Railroad, 52 N. H. 528; S. v. Railroad, 58 N. H. 198.

in the common law,[1] but it is not unconstitutional as class legislation.[2]

§ 289. **Wrongful act.**— In considering the distinction between murder and manslaughter it will appear that death resulting from doing a wrongful act will be criminal, the degree of crime depending to some extent on the degree of wrong in the act done.[3] In considering what homicides are accidental so as to be excusable, and what are so far the result of wrong as to constitute manslaughter, other cases of death from wrongful acts will also be considered.[4] It is sufficient here to say, in general, that a wrongful act causing death will render the one doing it criminally responsible, even though death was not intended, if the wrong is one in any way calculated to produce such result.[5] Whether an attempt to procure an abortion is such wrongful act that the death of the woman thereby caused is criminal will be considered under the head of manslaughter.[6]

§ 290. **Suicide.**— While one who commits suicide does take the life of a human being, yet the impossibility of inflicting any punishment has prevented any adjudication as to whether such an act is to be deemed criminal; but it certainly does not come within the definition of excusable or justifiable homicide as hereafter discussed. If the killing is the accidental result of a lawful act, it evidently does not come within the definition of suicide at all. If it is the unintended result of an un-

[1] S. v. Grand Trunk Ry., 58 Me. 176; S. v. Maine Central R. Co., 60 Me. 490.

[2] Boston, C. & M. R. Co. v. S., 32 N. H. 215.

[3] See *infra*, § 289.

[4] See *infra*, § 300.

[5] Where one induced another to drink an excessive quantity of liquor from which death resulted, *held*, that he was criminally responsible for the homicide: Reg. v. Packard, Car. & M. 236. But where it was claimed that defendant had caused the death of another by setting a fire, it was held necessary to prove that the fire could not have originated from any other cause than defendant's act: Reg. v. Gardner, 1 F. & F. 669. Where it appeared that defendant, charged with murder, had wilfully set fire to a stack of straw, not near to any dwelling-house, and a person was thereby burned to death, *held* that, to warrant conviction, it must appear that deceased was there when the fire was set: Reg. v. Horsey, 3 F. & F. 287. Accidental homicide in illegally carrying away furniture to avoid distress for rent may be murder: Rex v. Hubson, 1 East, P. C. 258. In Kentucky special provision is made as to death caused by shooting, stabbing, striking, etc., and such offense is not included under an indictment for murder: Trimble v. C., 78 Ky. 176; Peoples v. C., 87 Ky. 487.

[6] *Infra*, § 347.

lawful act, as, for instance, the taking of poison to procure a miscarriage, it is deemed unlawful.[1] Although intentional self-destruction cannot, in the nature of the case, be punished, there are various questions collaterally involving its lawfulness from which a legal inference that it to be deemed unlawful may conclusively be drawn. For instance, if two mutually attempt to commit suicide and one survives, he is guilty of murder of the one who dies, by reason of the doctrine of unlawful combinations.[2] If in attempting to commit suicide the accidental death of another is caused, such death will be chargeable as a crime to the one making the attempt[3] (which would not be so if death were the accidental result of a lawful act); and the attempt itself is a misdemeanor at common law in the person making it,[4] but it is not attempt to murder.[5] One who advises and counsels another to commit suicide is an accessory before the fact to murder.[6] Both from the reasoning which makes an accessory before the fact to the suicide guilty of murder, and from the forfeiture imposed until recently by the English law as a penalty, it is evident that the wrong involved in the act is felonious in its nature.[7]

§ 291. By act of another; combination; conspiracy.— Under the general doctrine of combination the criminal responsibility of one person for acts done by another has been already considered.[8] But in determining what is sufficient causation in such cases to render one liable for death due to the acts of another, some further illustration may be given. Of course, if by the command of one person another is killed, the one commanding commits homicide.[9] Where two combine to commit a felony or make an assault, and in carrying out the common purpose another is killed, the one who enters into the combination but does not personally commit the wrongful act

[1] Rex v. Russell, 1 Moody, 356.

[2] Reg. v. Alison, 8 C. & P. 418; Rex v. Dyson, Russ. & Ry. 523.

[3] S. v. Levelle, 34 S. C. 120.

[4] Reg. v. Doody, 6 Cox, 463; Reg. v. Burgess, L. & C. 258.

[5] Reg. v. Burgess, L. & C. 258.

[6] C. v. Bowen, 13 Mass. 356; C. v. Mink, 123 Mass. 422; Blackburn v. S., 23 Ohio St. 146; 1 Hale, P. C. 412, 413. And see S. v. Avery, 113 Mo. 475.

[7] 3 Stephen's Hist. Cr. L. 104; 4 Bl. Com. 189. And in general, as to suicides, 1 Hawk. P. C., ch. 27; 2 Bish. Cr. L., § 1187; Reg. v. Leddington, 9 C. & P. 79; C. v. Dennis, 105 Mass. 162.

[8] See *supra*, §§ 195, 196.

[9] Washington v. S., 68 Ga. 570; Rex v. Sawyer, 1 Russ., C. & M. 670.

is equally responsible for the homicide with the one who directly causes it;[1] and the conviction of the one who personally does the act will not prevent the punishment of the other also.[2] So, if one advise a killing, and the person advised perpetrates it, the presumption is that the advice had the effect intended unless the contrary be shown, and the act will be homicide in the person giving the advice.[3] But the mere sanction, or presence at the commission of a homicide, will not alone render the person thus present guilty.[4] Where death results from acts of persons unlawfully assembled to obstruct the officers of the law, all who are thus assembled are responsible for a homicide committed in consequence of such assembling.[5] So, if several persons conspire to seize a vessel with force, and death ensues to another party opposing the design, it is criminal in all who conspired to do the wrongful act.[6] So, if one by force, persuasion, or threats induces another to take poison, he is criminally responsible for the death resulting, whether he furnished the poison or not, and without regard to whether the deceased knew the nature of what he was taking.[7] As has already been shown, a master is not criminally responsible for the wrongful acts done by his servant.[8] So where, in artillery practice, a ball by accident hits a by-stander, the officer in charge, and in obedience to whose general orders the ball is fired, is not criminally responsible.[9]

§ 292. Proximate or remote cause; death from wound.— One who strikes a blow or inflicts a wound from which death ensues has committed a homicide, although if properly treated the injury would not have been fatal. The unskilfulness of the surgeon (the improper treatment not being intentional,

[1] S. v. Barrett, 40 Minn. 77; S. v. Davis, 87 N. C. 514; Mitchell v. C., 33 Grat. 845; Williams v. S., 81 Ala. 1; S. v. Simmons, 6 Jones, 21; Beets v. S., Meigs, 106; Taylor v. S., 9 Tex. Ap. 100; U. S. v. Ross, 1 Gall. 624; Brennan v. P., 15 Ill. 511.

[2] Dumas v. S., 62 Ga. 58.

[3] Thompson v. C., 1 Met. (Ky.) 13.

[4] Butler v. C., 2 Duv. 435; Connaughty v. S., 1 Wis. 159; Jordan v. S., 81 Ala. 20; Rountree v. S., 10 Tex. Ap. 110. And see *supra*, § 194.

[5] Reg. v. McNaughten, 14 Cox, 576. If a man begin a riot by which an officer is killed he is criminally liable for the homicide: Reg. v. Wallis, 1 Salk. 334.

[6] U. S. v. Ross, 1 Gall. 624.

[7] Blackburn v. S., 23 Ohio St. 146.

[8] See *supra*, § 187.

[9] Reg. v. Hutchinson, 9 Cox, 555.

but the result of ignorance or carelessness),[1] or the negligence of the injured party,[2] or of others,[3] will not relieve the person inflicting the original injury from the consequences of his act, which will be charged to such original injury and not to this intervening cause.[4] So if the wound is the mediate cause it is no defense to the person inflicting the wound that the immediate cause was disease resulting therefrom.[5] But the person causing the original injury is not responsible for death resulting alone from improper treatment or disease subsequently contracted, and not from the injury itself.[6] It must plainly

[1] S. v. Bantley, 44 Conn. 537; P. v. Cook, 39 Mich. 236; S. v. Landgraf, 95 Mo. 97; Clark v. C., 90 Va. 360; S. v. Scott, 12 La. An. 274; S. v. Barnes, 34 La. An. 395.

[2] Bowles v. S., 58 Ala. 335; Williams v. S., 2 Tex. Ap. 271; for instance, his refusal to submit to a surgical operation: Reg. v. Holland, 2 M. & Rob. 351.

[3] Failure of a third person to interpose in preventing a fatal consequence from defendant's act will not relieve defendant: Belk v. P., 125 Ill. 584, 8 Am. Cr. R. 507 and note.

[4] C. v. McPike, 3 Cush. 181; C. v. Hackett, 2 Allen, 136; C. v. Costley, 118 Mass. 1. A wound given in malice, not in its nature fatal, but through mismanagement or neglect resulting in death, will render the person inflicting it guilty of the homicide, unless it appears that the neglect or mismanagement and not the wound was the sole cause of death (overruling McBeth v. S., 50 Miss. 81): Crum v. S., 64 Miss. 1.

[5] Denman v. S., 15 Neb. 138; Burnett v. S., 14 Lea, 439: S. v. Corbett, 1 Jones, 264; S. v. Hambright, 111 N. C. 707; C. v. Green, 1 Ashm. 289; Kee v. S., 28 Ark. 155; Powell v. S., 13 Tex. Ap. 244; 1 Hale, P. C. 428. So, where the injury inflicted renders an operation advisable and the injured person dies by reason of the administration of chloroform in connection with such operation: Reg. v. Davis, 15 Cox, 174. If the wound indirectly causes the death, through a chain of natural causes and effects, unchanged by human action, the death is chargeable to the one inflicting it: Kelley v. S., 53 Ind. 311. It is not necessary that it be the sole cause if it contributed, mediately or immediately, to the death: S. v. Matthews, 38 La. An. 795; S. v. Smith, 10 Nev. 106.

[6] Coffman v. C., 10 Bush, 495; Bush v. C., 78 Ky. 268; Smith v. S., 50 Ark. 545. And the jury should be instructed, if requested, that they cannot convict for such homicide unless satisfied that the death resulted from the wound and not from the malpractice of the surgeon: Brown v. S., 38 Tex. 482; Parsons v. S., 21 Ala. 300. Where an injured party lived for nine months, and the evidence left it in doubt whether death was caused by the injury or by other causes, *held*, that a conviction was erroneous: Treadwell v. S., 16 Tex. Ap. 560. If death is due to disease subsequently contracted, the person inflicting the wound will not be chargeable therewith, although the progress of the disease is quickened by the enfeebled condition due to the wound: Livingston v. C., 14 Grat. 592. Of course, if it is doubtful whether death resulted from the injury in question or some other in-

appear, however, that the death was caused, not by the wound, but only by misconduct, malpractice, or ill-treatment on the part of other persons than the accused.[1] If, however, after a fatal blow is inflicted, death is caused by the independent act of another person without concert with or procurement of the first, the person inflicting the first wound cannot be held responsible for the death;[2] but the one inflicting the subsequent injury, thereby hastening death, will be held responsible for it.[3] To hasten the death of one who would soon have otherwise died from incurable disease will constitute homicide.[4] The fact that the person killed was in feeble condition, so that his

jury, there can be no conviction: McNamee v. S., 34 Neb. 288.

[1] S. v. Morphy, 33 Ia. 270; S. v. Scott, 12 La. An. 274. By reason of the language of the Texas statute defining homicide, it is held in that state that the rule of the common law whereby the neglect or improper treatment must produce the death in order to relieve the person inflicting the original injury is changed, and that gross neglect and improper treatment which allow, suffer, or permit the death to result will relieve the person doing the injury as well as where they directly produce the destruction of life: Morgan v. S., 16 Tex. Ap. 593. Where the defendant was charged with having caused death of deceased by beatings, and it was sought to show that the death was in consequence of a severe burn, *held*, that evidence as to whether the burn was received after death, and also as to statements by deceased that he had received a burn, were admissible: S. v. Harris, 63 N. C. 1. Evidence of the health of the deceased immediately before the infliction of the wound is admissible as showing whether death was caused thereby: Phillips v. S., 68 Ala. 468. The jury is the exclusive judge of the cause of death when there is conflicting evidence as to whether it resulted from a wound or from natural disease or from another injury: P. v. Dunne, 80 Cal. 34.

[2] S. v. Wood, 53 Vt. 560; S. v. Scates, 5 Jones, 420; Jordan v. S., 79 Ala. 9. *Contra*, Tidwell v. S., 70 Ala. 33.

[3] P. v. Ah Fat, 48 Cal. 61; Fisher v. S., 10 Lea, 151. A subsequent injury not affecting the result will not constitute homicide: S. v. Grinden, 91 Ia. 505. If a fatal wound is given in self-defense, but a second wound is inflicted by the same person without justification, there is criminal homicide if the second wound contributes to or hastened death: Rogers v. S., 60 Ark. 76.

[4] C. v. Fox, 7 Gray. 585; P. v. Moan, 65 Cal. 532; S. v. Morea, 2 Ala. 275; S. v. Smith, 73 Ia. 32; Williams v. S., 2 Tex. Ap. 271; Reg. v. Murton, 3 F. & F. 492. It is for the jury to determine whether the injury inflicted, and not the disease, caused the death, but ignorance on the part of the defendant of the deceased's physical condition will constitute no excuse: S. v. O'Brien, 81 Ia. 88. Although where there is doubt as to which of two persons, not acting in concert, caused the death, neither can be convicted (see *supra*, § 194), yet a doubt as to which of two acts by the same person in the same transaction caused the death will not relieve: P. v. Ah Luck, 62 Cal. 503. If two persons at the same time inflict

death was caused by a blow which would not have caused the death of a healthy person, will be no defense.[1]

§ 293. **Time of death.**— It is evident the longer the injured person lives after the injury the more doubtful it becomes whether the death is the result of such injury or of independent causes, and it is convenient to have a definite period after which death shall not be deemed due to the particular injury under investigation. This definite period is fixed by the common law at a year and a day.[2] The origin of this rule and the reason for fixing this particular period are not made clear. The cases above referred to assume the existence of the rule, without adjudicating or explaining it, but it is definitely laid down in all the books that refer to the question at all. In computing the period "the whole of the day on which the hurt was done shall be reckoned the first," and if death does not occur until after the end of the corresponding day of the next year the act is not deemed a homicide in the person inflicting the injury.[3]

II. Who Deemed Person.

§ 294. **Human being; child unborn.**— A child in its mother's womb is not a human being in such sense that to cause the death thereof before birth is a homicide.[4] In order that the child shall be so far born as to be considered a human being, the causing the death of which is homicide, it must have an independent circulation.[5] It is not enough that the child may have breathed in the progress of birth, if the whole body was

mortal wounds and death results, an instruction with regard to a doubt as to which caused the death need not be given: T. v. Yarberry, 2 N. Mex. 391.

[1] S. v. Castello, 62 Ia. 404. But such fact may bear on the question of malice: C. v. Fox, 7 Gray, 585.

[2] 1 Hale, P. C. 427; 2 Bish. Cr. L., § 640. The indictment must show the death to have been within a year and a day after the injury: S. v. Orrell, 1 Dev. 139; S. v. Huff, 11 Nev. 17; P. v. Kelly, 6 Cal. 210; P. v. Wallace, 9 Cal. 30; Lester v. S., 9 Mo. 658; S. v. Mayfield, 66 Mo. 125.

[3] 1 Hawk. P. C., ch. 31, § 9; 3 Inst. 53.

[4] 2 Bish. Cr. L., § 632; 1 Hawk. P. C., ch. 31, § 16; 3 Inst. 50; 1 Hale, P. C. 433; Abrams v. Foshee, 3 Ia. 274. For some purposes a child in the womb has a legal existence, but not in criminal law except by statute, as in New York, where it is manslaughter to cause the death of the fœtus after it is quick: Evans v. P., 49 N. Y. 86; and see Williams v. S., 34 Fla. 217.

[5] Reg. v. Wright, 9 C. & P. 754; S. v. Winthrop, 43 Ia. 519; Sheppard v. S., 17 Tex. Ap. 74. It is not necessary that it shall have breathed if fully born alive: Rex v. Brain, 6 C. & P. 349.

not brought alive into the world.[1] But the fact that the child is still attached to its mother by the umbilical cord will not prevent its being considered a human being if it has been wholly produced from the body of its mother and has an independent circulation.[2] If the child be actually born alive, although prematurely, its death, caused by reason of the fact that it is prematurely brought into the world, will constitute homicide in the person thus causing its premature birth.[3] One who before the birth of the child counsels the mother to kill it when born is criminally responsible for its death if his advice is acted upon.[4]

§ 295. **Person in the king's peace.**— The old definitions of criminal homicide refer to the killing of a person in the king's peace,[5] but this phrase seems to be used in later times only to exclude cases of killing an alien enemy in war. In general, every person is entitled to protection against unlawful violence, and, whether he be a felon or an alien or a person outlawed, to cause his death except in a lawful manner, or in a way such as to render the homicide justifiable or excusable, will be criminal.[6]

III. HOMICIDES NOT CRIMINAL; JUSTIFIABLE AND EXCUSABLE; SELF-DEFENSE.

§ 296. **How distinguished.**— The previous discussion has related to what shall be deemed a homicide; but in determining whether or not a homicide constitutes a crime, that is, what homicides are not punishable as distinguished from those which

[1] Rex v. Poulton, 5 C. & P. 329; Rex v. Enoch, 5 C. & P. 539; Rex v. Sellis, 7 C. & P. 850. There must be a complete expulsion, alive, from the body of the mother: Wallace v. S., 10 Tex. Ap. 255.

[2] Reg. v. Trilloe, Car. & M. 650; Reg. v. Handley, 13 Cox, 79. In a case as to descent of property, *held*, that a child was born alive which made an effort to breathe after expulsion, although still attached by the umbilical cord: Goff v. Anderson, 91 Ky. 303.

[3] Reg. v. West, 2 C. & K. 784; Rex v. Senior, 1 Lewin, 183.

[4] 1 Hale, P. C. 433; 4 Bl. Com. 198; 7 Co. Rep. 9; Dwyer, 186; 1 Hawk. P. C., ch. 31, § 17; 3 Inst. 51.

[5] 3 Inst. 50; Pennsylvania v. Robertson, Addison, 246.

[6] 1 Hale, P. C. 433; 1 Hawk. P. C., ch. 28, § 8; Id., ch. 31, § 15; 4 Bl. Com. 197, 198; 1 Bish. Cr. L., § 134; C. v. Holland, 1 Duv. 182; S. v. Cook, Phil. 535. Thus, it is criminal unlawfully to kill a horse-thief: Rye v. S., 8 Tex. Ap. 153, or a person of color: Campbell v. P., 16 Ill. 17, or an Indian: S. v. Gut, 13 Minn. 341; Jim v. T., 1 Wash. 76.

are punishable, or what are lawful and what are unlawful, further classification is necessary. At one time a distinction was maintained between justifiable homicides, that is, those committed under lawful authority, for instance, in the course of justice or in war, and excusable homicides, such as those resulting from accident or in self-defense. The excusable class were like the justifiable in not being punishable in a criminal proceeding; but, while the justifiable were deemed wholly without blame, the excusable were attended with some penalty, such as the forfeiture to the crown of the thing causing the death and of the goods of the homicide.[1] But by the present law, forfeitures of this kind are in no way recognized, and all practical distinctions between justifiable and excusable homicide have ceased to exist. The cases of homicide which are not punishable will be considered, therefore, without regard to whether they would have been deemed justifiable or excusable, it being impossible to now determine in all cases within which class each particular kind of non-criminal homicide would fall. The two being synonymous, it is not error, in charging the jury, to use one term for the other.[2]

§ 297. **In executing sentence of death.**— A duly authorized officer who, in pursuance of a writ issued by a court having jurisdiction, executes sentence of death upon a prisoner, is justifiable in the act, and no criminality attaches thereto.[3]

§ 297a. **In acting under military command.**— The act of a soldier in causing death in lawful military operations is, of course, justifiable.[4] But the mere command of a military superior will not render an act of homicide justifiable unless the order is lawful.[5]

§ 298. **In arresting or detaining criminals.**— The general questions as to what is a lawful arrest, and whether arrest may be made by an officer without warrant or by a private person, pertain to the law of arrest, and cannot be discussed here. But an officer or private person acting under circumstances authorizing an arrest may use all the force necessary in overcoming

[1] 1 Bl. Com. 300; 4 Bl. Com. 186–188; 1 Bish. Cr. L., § 968; Foster, 265; Reg. v. Polwart, 1 Q. B. 818.

[2] S. v. Row, 81 Ia. 138; Bone v. S., 86 Ga. 108.

[3] 4 Bl. Com. 178; 1 Hale, P. C. 496–502; 1 Hawk. P. C., ch. 28, §§ 4–10; Foster, 267; 1 Russ. Cr. 665.

[4] U. S. v. Clark, 31 Fed. R. 710.

[5] U. S. v. Carr, 1 Woods, 480; U. S. v. Gut, 13 Minn. 341. And see *supra*, § 115.

resistance and defending himself against violence from the person sought to be arrested,[1] and if in doing so he takes life, it is justifiable, being in pursuance of public justice.[2] In attempting to make an arrest, however, where the person to be arrested, instead of resisting, seeks to make his escape, there is a difference, depending on the gravity of the offense for which the arrest is being made, as to whether the officer may do an act calculated to take life. If the offense for which the arrest is being made is a felony, the person (whether an officer or not, provided he is lawfully arresting) may take life if necessary in order to effect the arrest.[3] But if the offense for which the arrest is being made is a misdemeanor, there is no right to take life, and the person seeking to make the arrest will be guilty of a crime in doing so.[4] As to resisting the escape of a prisoner under arrest or in confinement, it seems that the officer may resist so far as necessary, and if the attempt is so violent as to make it necessary to take life in preventing such escape, the officer will be justified in doing so, whether the prisoner is under arrest for felony or misdemeanor, or even (at common

[1] Carter v. S., 30 Tex. Ap. 551; S. v. Turlington, 102 Mo. 642.

[2] 1 Hawk. P. C., ch. 28, §§ 11-14; 1 Russ. Cr. 665-667; 4 Bl. Com. 179; 2 Bish. Cr. L., §§ 647-655; Head v. Martin, 85 Ky. 480; Adams v. S., 72 Ga. 85; Clements v. S., 50 Ala. 117; S. v. Dierberger, 96 Mo. 666; S. v. Fuller, 96 Mo. 165; S. v. Anderson, 1 Hill (S. C.), 327; S. v. Roane, 2 Dev. 58; U. S. v. Jailer, 2 Abb. (U. S.) 265. An officer who neglects to use proper means to detain a prisoner is not justified in the use of a deadly weapon to prevent escape: Reneau v. S., 2 Lea, 720. If by a private person, belief that the crime has been committed is not enough; there must have been an actual crime: S. v. Rutherford, 1 Hawks, 457. As to lawfulness of arrest without warrant, see, also, Nelson v. S., 33 Neb. 528; Lacy v. S., 7 Tex. Ap. 403; Carter v. S., 30 Tex. Ap. 551. But this subject properly pertains to the law of arrest.

[3] 1 Hale, P. C., 481, 489; 1 Hawk. P. C., ch. 28, §§ 11, 12; Foster, 271; 3 Inst. 221; 1 East, P. C. 298; 1 Russ. Cr. 666; Carr v. S., 43 Ark. 99. It is for the jury to say, under all the circumstances, whether it was necessary to kill in order to effect the arrest, and on that question the officer is entitled to the benefit of a reasonable doubt: Jackson v. S., 66 Miss. 89.

[4] See authorities in last note; also, 2 Hale, P. C. 117; 1 East, P. C. 302; Dilger v. C., 88 Ky. 550; Handley v. S., 96 Ala. 48. Even if he cannot otherwise be taken: Rex v. Smith, 1 Russ., C. & M. 749. Larceny of a horse, though felony by statute, does not justify killing the thief, though necessary in order to recapture the horse: Storey v. S., 71 Ala. 329. It is held in Texas that an officer may not kill to prevent escape of prisoner under arrest even if for grand larceny: Caldwell v. S., 41 Tex. 86.

law) merely under civil process.[1] It is probable, however, that even as to preventing escape the officer is justified in taking life only to prevent escape for felony, or where, the offense being a misdemeanor, in resisting force with force his own life is put in peril, and not where he takes life merely to prevent escape of one charged with a misdemeanor.[2] But the officer will be justified in taking life only where he has reasonable ground to believe and does believe that it is necessary in making the arrest or preventing escape or defending himself, and the jury must judge of this on the facts.[3] Where there is no right to take life in making the arrest or preventing escape, it will be murder or manslaughter to kill, depending upon circumstances;[4] or if the officer does not use violence calculated to imperil the life of the person whom he is seeking to arrest, but is using only proper force for the purpose, and death results by accident, it will be excusable.[5] Homicide in unlawful arrest, that is, an arrest without authority, is murder.[6] There is no right to resist arrest, to the extent of taking life, as will hereafter appear.[7] But if the person to be arrested has no knowledge that the person arresting is an officer, or as a private person is seeking to make an arrest, he may resist as in other cases of threatened wrong.[8] But if the officer or arresting person is acting properly, it will be murder to cause death in resistance.[9]

§ 299. **Resisting commission of felony.**— On the same principle which makes it justifiable in an officer to take life in the discharge of his duties, it is justifiable homicide to take the life of another, when necessary to prevent the commission, by

[1] Foster, 321; 1 Hawk. P. C., ch. 28, § 13; 1 Russ. Cr. 667; S. v. Turlington, 102 Mo. 642; Jackson v. S., 76 Ga. 473. But this right does not extend to an officer attempting to re-arrest an escaped convict. He has only such authority as belongs to an ordinary peace officer in making an arrest: Wright v. S., 44 Tex. 645. As to cases of civil arrest, see 1 Hawk. P. C., ch. 28, §§ 17–20; 1 East, P. C. 306; Mackalley's Case, 9 Coke, 65; Calfield's Case, 1 Rol. 189.

[2] Reneau v. S., 2 Lea, 720.

[3] Jackson v. S., 76 Ga. 473; S. v. Bland, 97 N. C. 438; S. v. Rollins, 113 N. C. 722. But if the facts are undisputed the question is for the court: P. v. Kilvington, 104 Cal. 86.

[4] *Infra*, § 347.

[5] Plummer v. S., 4 Tex. Ap. 310.

[6] Rex v. Longden, Russ. & Ry. 228; Rex v. Dixon, Russ. & Ry. 53; 1 East, P. C. 312, 313.

[7] *Infra*, §§ 328, 340.

[8] Starr v. U. S., 153 U. S. 614; Plummer v. S., 135 Ind. 308.

[9] S. v. Turlington, 102 Mo. 642. And see *infra*, § 328.

him, of a felony.[1] And this is true as to acts which are felonious only by statute as well as those recognized as felonious at common law.[2] But it is not justifiable to take life to prevent a mere misdemeanor,[3] nor in the mere protection of property.[4] The extent of the right to protect property by force has already been discussed under the doctrine of necessity.[5] The killing must take place while the person killed was in the act of committing the offense and before its actual completion.[6]

[1] 1 Hale, P. C. 484–9; 1 Hawk. P. C., ch. 28, §§ 21–27; 4 Bl. Com. 180; 1 Bish. Cr. L., §§853, 867; Cooper's Case, Cro. Car. 544; P. v. Payne, 8 Cal. 341; P. v. Flanagan, 60 Cal. 2; P. v. De Los Angeles, 61 Cal. 188; Hicks v. S., 51 Ind. 407; Aldrich v. Wright, 53 N. H. 398; McPherson v. S., 22 Ga. 478; 1 Houst. Cr. C. 116. If one is killed while resisting a felony it will be murder: Dill v. S., 25 Ala. 15.

[2] S. v. Moore, 31 Conn. 479; Pond v. P., 8 Mich. 150. Assault with intent to do great bodily harm not being a felony by statute, *held* erroneous to instruct with reference to resisting such assault as though it were a felony: S. v. Stockton, 61 Mo. 382. But the killing must be necessary in preventing the felony: Weaver v. S., 19 Tex. Ap. 547.

[3] As, for instance, larceny, which by the Tennessee code is not a felony: Marks v. Borum, 57 Tenn. 87; or an assault with intent to do great bodily harm, such offense not being a felony; although if the assault were such as to cause fear of great bodily harm, the assailed might be excused for taking life in self-defense: S. v. Stockton, 61 Mo. 382. And see further as to fear of bodily harm, *infra*, § 302. In Carmouche v. Bouis, 6 La. An. 96, it is said that homicide is not justifiable to prevent a felony threatened without force. In Texas, adultery being only a misdemeanor, *held*, the husband apprehending another in the commission of adultery with his wife is not justified in taking life, and the person assailed will be guilty only of manslaughter in taking the life of the husband to save his own: Reed v. S., 9 Tex. Ap. 317; Reed v. S., 11 Tex. Ap. 509. But under the penal code of Texas, making homicide justifiable when committed by the husband on one taken in the act of adultery with his wife, *held*, that under the facts of the case deceased was taken in adultery in such sense as that homicide was justifiable: Price v. S., 18 Tex. Ap. 474. With reference to a similar statutory provision in Georgia, see Biggs v. S., 29 Ga. 723; Cloud v. S., 81 Ga. 444. But a husband is justifiable in slaying another under the apprehension of a design to commit a felony on his wife: Staten v. S., 30 Miss. 619. There is no justification for a husband who kills on account of a past adultery or attempt to debauch the wife: Farmer v. S., 91 Ga. 720; Jackson v. S., 91 Ga. 271.

[4] S. v. Morgan, 3 Ired. 186; Weston v. C., 111 Pa. St. 251.

[5] *Supra*, § 142. See, also, *infra*, § 313.

[6] Under a statute in Texas, however, such killing is justifiable in case of burglary or theft by night, if at the place where such crime is committed, and it is held that if a thief by night be shot while within reach of gunshot from the place of committing the theft, although he has abandoned the goods, the homicide is justifiable: Whitten v. S., 29 Tex. Ap. 504. But if the killing is

§ 300. Accidental killing.— It has already been said that a homicide by accident is not criminal, but was, at common law, deemed not justifiable but excusable only, some penalty by way of forfeiture being involved.[1] The doctrine that accidental homicide in attempting to do a wrongful act will be murder or manslaughter, depending on the question whether the act attempted was a felony or a misdemeanor, will be hereafter discussed.[2] If, in resisting an assault, death results by accident, the homicide will be excusable although the assault was not such as to make the taking of life justifiable.[3] So, accidental killing of a third person in making proper self-defense will be excused in the same way as though the person killed were the aggressor.[4]

§ 301. Self-defense.— Aside from the doctrine that it is justifiable homicide to take life, if necessary, in preventing a felony,[5] is the general proposition that one is excused in taking the life of a person who threatens his own life.[6] This is the general doctrine of self-defense, which must be discussed, however, with reference, first, to the kind of danger which will excuse taking the life of the assailant; and second, the necessity, or the imminence of the danger, which will make such violent resistance proper.

with malice and not to prevent a theft or in consequence of a theft, it is not justifiable: Laws v. S., 26 Tex. Ap. 643. Evidence indicating the purpose of the deceased to have been to commit a felony is admissible: C. v. Pipes, 158 Pa. St. 25.

[1] *Supra*, §§ 285, 296. The burden to prove accident, with use of proper care, is said to be on the accused: Reg. v. Cavendish, 8 Ir. R. C. L. 178; S. v. Bond, 2 Nev. 265. The evidence must be more than simply enough to lead to conjecture that the homicide is accidental: S. v. Haywood, Phill. 376.

[2] *Infra*, §§ 326, 347.

[3] Hicks v. S., 51 Ind. 407. But reasonable care must have been exercised: S. v. Morgan, 40 S. C. 345.

[4] Aaron v. S., 31 Ga. 167; Butler v. S., 92 Ga. 601; Hart v. C., 85 Ky. 77; Plummer v. S., 4 Tex. Ap. 310; Pinder v. S., 27 Fla. 370; Reg. v. Knock, 14 Cox, 1. But one who fires at random into a crowd and kills a bystander cannot claim to be excused on the ground of self-defense: S. v. Smith, 114 Mo. 406.

[5] *Supra*, § 299.

[6] Bohannon v. C., 8 Bush, 481; Wall v. S., 51 Ind. 453; Jim v. S., 15 Ga. 535; Underwood v. S., 25 Tex. Supp. 389. If two assailants are acting in concert the acts of one may justify the killing of the other: Jones v. S., 20 Tex. Ap. 665. A statute making it a crime to fight in a public place with a deadly weapon does not impair the right of self-defense: Hunter v. S., 62 Miss. 540.

§ **302. Danger to life or of injury to the person.**— Not only will one be excused for taking the life of one who puts his life in peril, but one will be equally excused in taking the life of an assailant who threatens to inflict upon him great bodily injury.[1] Danger of a battery alone will not be sufficient.[2] If unlawful violence is resorted to in the attempt to make an arrest for a misdemeanor where it is not lawful to imperil life, the person whose arrest is attempted will be justified in taking life.[3]

§ **303. Imminent danger.**— To warrant taking life in self-defense the danger must be imminent.[4] Mere words or gestures however insulting, not indicating immediate danger to the person assailed, will not be sufficient;[5] neither will threats

[1] C. v. Carey, 2 Brews. 404; Holmes v. S., 23 Ala. 17; Meredith v. C., 18 B. Mon. 49; Minton v. C., 79 Ky. 461; Shorter v. P., 2 N. Y. 193; Pond v. P., 8 Mich. 150; Young v. S., 11 Humph. 200; Hunt v. S., 72 Miss. 413; Kingen v. S., 45 Ind. 518; Fields v. S., 134 Ind. 46; Cheek v. S., 4 Tex. Ap. 444; Fuller v. S., 30 Tex. Ap. 559. The terms, "great bodily harm," "danger of loss of life or limb," "enormous bodily harm," "great personal injury," "enormous bodily injury," "enormous injury," "dreadful injury," may be used in describing the danger which will excuse taking life in self-defense: S. v. Murdy, 81 Ia. 603; Green v. S., 28 Miss. 687. But it is error to require danger of "enormous bodily harm:" McDonald v. S., 89 Tenn. 161.

[2] Eiland v. S., 52 Ala. 322; Scales v. S., 96 Ala. 69; S. v. Thompson, 9 Ia. 188; S. v. Jones, 89 Ia. 182; C. v. Drum, 58 Pa. St. 9; Reg. v. Hewlett, 1 F. & F. 91; and see note to next section. But when a fight is actually going on, sticks and clubs, though perhaps not in themselves dangerous weapons, may become weapons of a very deadly character, and their use may give rise to the extreme right of self-defense: Allen v. U. S., 157 U. S. 675. If in making proper self-defense death results by accident the homicide is excusable: *Supra*, § 300.

[3] Tiner v. S., 44 Tex. 128. As to arrest, see *supra*, § 298.

[4] Nailor's Case, Foster, 278; C. v. Selfridge, 1 Whart. Hom. 417; Dolan v. S., 81 Ala. 11. By "imminent" is meant immediate, such as must be instantly met, and cannot be guarded against by calling upon others or seeking the protection of the law: U. S. v. Outerbridge, 5 Sawyer, 620. But it need not be impending at the very moment. A party may anticipate attack if the danger exists, the jury being judges as to the necessity: Cotton v. S., 31 Miss. 504; Fortenberry v. S., 55 Miss. 403; Goodall v. S., 1 Oreg. 333; Philips v. C., 2 Duv. 328. Previous threats cannot be made an excuse when unaccompanied with present hostile demonstrations: Turner v. C., 89 Ky. 78; U. S. v. Leighton, 3 Dak. 29.

[5] U. S. v. Wiltberger, 3 Wash. C. C. 515; U. S. v. Carr, 1 Woods, 480; S. v. Martin, 30 Wis. 216; Price v. P., 131 Ill. 223; P. v. Lombard, 17 Cal. 316; P. v. Tamkin, 62 Cal. 468; P. v. Taing, 53 Cal. 602; P. v. Campbell, 59 Cal. 243; Lander v. S., 12 Tex. 462; Taylor v. S., 48 Ala. 180; S. v. McCollum, 119 Mo. 469; S. v. Harris, 59 Mo. 550; S. v. Evans, 65 Mo. 574; Evans v. S., 44 Miss. 762; Rippy v.

which do not indicate a present purpose to carry them out;[1] nor the violent and lawless character of one from whom danger is apprehended.[2] The fact of antecedent threats or difficulties, even though such as to induce the fear on the part of the person threatened that the other may seek to kill on opportunity, will not justify killing the other without a manifestation of present purpose to carry out such threats or continue the difficulty.[3] There must be such a demonstration of an immediate intention to execute the threat, or such overt act, as it is usually called, as to induce a reasonable belief that the party threatened will lose his life or suffer serious bodily injury unless he immediately defends himself against the attack;[4] for it is only danger imminent at the time of the homicide (or believed to be imminent, as will hereafter be explained) which will justify or excuse the killing.[5] The overt act must be one

S., 2 Head, 217; Bohannon v. C., 8 Bush, 481; S. v. Harrigan, 9 Houst. 369. The wounded pride or sense of shame which may result from declining to fight will not justify killing in self-defense: Springfield v. S., 96 Ala. 81.

[1] Hughey v. S., 47 Ala. 97; Byrd v. C., 89 Va. 536; Harris v. S., 47 Miss. 318; Edwards v. S., 47 Miss. 581; Irwin v. S., 43 Tex. 236; Williams v. S., 2 Tex. Ap. 271; Mize v. S., 36 Ark. 653: Roberts v. S., 65 Ga. 430; U. S. v. Outerbridge, 5 Sawyer, 620.

[2] S. v. Field, 14 Me. 244; Franklin v. S., 29 Ala. 14; P. v. Lamb, 2 Keyes, 360.

[3] Crabtree v. S., 1 Lea, 267; Parsons v. C., 78 Ky. 102; Payne v. S., 60 Ala. 80; Myers v. S., 62 Ala, 599; Tidwell v. S., 70 Ala. 33; S. v. Hall, 9 Nev. 58; S. v. Ferguson, 9 Nev. 106; S. v. Stewart, 9 Nev. 120; S. v. Mullen, 14 La. An. 570; S. v. Bradley, 6 La. An. 555; Carter v. S., 8 Tex. Ap. 372; Penland v. S., 19 Tex. Ap. 365.

[4] P. v. Scoggins, 37 Cal. 676; Barnards v. S., 88 Tenn. 183; Mitchell v. S., 41 Ga. 527; Williams v. S., 3 Heisk. 376; Turpin v. S., 55 Md. 462; Myers v. S., 33 Tex. 525; Peck v. S., 5 Tex. Ap. 611; Johnson v. S., 27 Tex. 758; Thomas v. S., 11 Tex. Ap. 315; McDade v. S., 27 Tex. Ap. 641; S. v. Cosgrove, 42 La. An. 753; S. v. Jackson, 33 La. An. 1087; S. v. Jackson, 44 La. An. 160; S. v. Williams, 46 La. An. 709. Evidence of threats is not admissible where there is no evidence of any overt act: Rutledge v. S., 88 Ala. 85; Smith v. S., 25 Fla. 517; Moriarty v. S., 62 Miss. 654; Allen v. S., 17 Tex. Ap. 637; West v. S., 18 Tex. Ap. 640; S. v. Demareste, 41 La. An. 617; S. v. Labuzan, 37 La. An. 489; S. v. Janvier, 37 La. An. 645; S. v. Jackson, 37 La. An. 896; S. v. Birdwell, 36 La. An. 859. So as to evidence of bad character: S. v. Mitchell, 41 La. An. 1073; S. v. Vance, 32 La. An. 1177; Wesley v. S., 37 Miss. 327.

[5] S. v. Thompson, 9 Ia. 188; S. v. Neeley, 20 Ia. 108; S. v. Field, 14 Me. 244; Holt v. S., 9 Tex. Ap. 571; Kennedy v. C., 14 Bush, 340; Farris v. C., 14 Bush, 362; Payne v. C., 1 Met. (Ky.) 370; Draper v. S., 4 Bax. 246; Rippy v. S., 2 Head, 217; Williams v. S., 3 Heisk. 376; P. v. Morine, 61 Cal. 367; P. v. Herbert, 61 Cal. 544; P. v. Cochran, 61 Cal. 548; P. v. Williams, 32 Cal. 280; P. v. Gonzales, 71 Cal.

indicating an intent to take life or cause great bodily harm; a mere intent to assault will not be enough.[1] As to what constitutes such an overt act as will justify homicide in self-defense must depend on circumstances,[2] and is a question for the jury, for which no general rule can be laid down, each case depending upon its own circumstances.[3] One who is about to be assailed with a deadly weapon is not required to wait until his assailant gets upon equal terms with himself before proceeding to make self-defense,[4] and it is erroneous to limit self-defense to a case of extreme necessity and as a last resort.[5]

§ **304. Apparent danger.**— It is evident that notwithstanding the language of cases which hold that the danger must be real and imminent, what is meant is, real and imminent to the mind of the person assailed; and that apparent danger is enough to excuse his acting in self-defense, that is, a danger which to his mind is real and imminent, that he is about to suffer death or great bodily injury unless he resists the assault.[6] The necessity need not be actual, provided the circumstances are such as to impress the mind of the person assailed with the reasonable belief that such necessity is impending.[7] If the acts of the as-

569; Scott v. S., 56 Miss. 287; S. v. Newcomb, 1 Houst. Cr. C. 66; S. v. Hollis, 1 Houst. Cr. C. 24; S. v. Vines, 1 Houst. Cr. C. 424; Jackson v. S., 94 Ala. 85; Dupree v. S., 33 Ala. 380; Harrison v. S., 24 Ala. 67; Hull v. S., 79 Ala. 32; S. v. O'Connor, 31 Mo. 389; S. v. Horne, 9 Kan. 119; S. v. Swift, 14 La. An. 827; Johnson v. S., 58 Ark. 57; Reg. v. Bull, 9 C. & P. 22; P. v. Cole, 4 Park. Cr. Rep. 35.

1 Wortham v. S., 70 Ga. 336; Bailey v. S., 70 Ga. 617; S. v. Brittain, 89 N. C. 481; S. v. Shreves, 81 Ia. 615; S. v. Thompson, 9 Ia. 188; Eiland v. S., 52 Ala. 322. An attempt to carry out a conspiracy to take life without more will not be enough: Henderson v. S., 77 Ala. 77.

2 Oder v. C., 80 Ky. 32. That one assailed with threats and offensive language puts his hand into his pocket does not authorize the inference that he is about to draw a weapon: Mitchell v. S., 41 Ga. 527; nor will the possession by one assaulted of a weapon warrant such inference, at least where the circumstances are such that he could not use it: Connaghan v. P., 88 Ill. 460.

3 Jackson v. S., 6 Baxt. 452; Allison v. U. S., 160 U. S. 203.

4 See *supra*, § 302, n. Where one killed a pursuer who was aiming a deadly weapon at him, *held*, that the crime was not murder: Underwood v. S., 25 Tex. Supp. 389.

5 King v. S., 13 Tex. Ap. 277.

6 Evans v. S., 44 Miss. 762; Rapp v. C., 14 B. Mon. 614.

7 Shorter v. P., 2 N. Y. 193; Pond v. P., 8 Mich. 150; Patten v. P., 18 Mich. 314; Murray v. C., 79 Pa. St. 311; P. v. Lamb, 2 Keyes (N. Y.), 360; Wall v. S., 51 Ind. 453; West v. S., 59 Ind. 113; Hays v. S., 77 Ind. 450; Duncan v. S., 84 Ind. 204; Cockrill v. C., 95 Ky. 22; S. v. Neeley, 20 Ia. 108; S. v. Sorenson, 32 Minn. 118; S. v. Howard, 14 Kan. 173; S. v. Sloan,

sailant, in view of previous threats or the character of the deceased, of which the person assailed is aware, indicate an imminent danger, the assailed is justified in acting with reference thereto,[1] and it will be immaterial that, as a matter of fact, deceased was not in a position to inflict the injury which seemed imminent.[2] If there is any evidence, however slight, of reasonable grounds of apprehension of danger, an instruction as to the law of self-defense should be given.[3]

§ **305. Belief of danger.**— Therefore, a well-grounded belief of danger will excuse.[4] It will be immaterial as affecting the criminality of the act of the person assailed that he supposed the assailant to be armed with a deadly weapon, whereas, in fact, although the person assailed had reasonable grounds to believe his assailant was thus armed (there being also an overt

47 Mo. 604; Oliver v. S., 16 Ala. 587; Dill v. S., 25 Ala. 15; Keener v. S., 18 Ga. 194; Boatwright v. S., 89 Ga. 140; Ingram v. S., 62 Miss. 142; P. v. Flahave, 58 Cal. 249; Jordan v. S., 11 Tex. Ap. 435; Smith v. S., 15 Tex. Ap. 338; Nalley v. S., 30 Tex. Ap. 456; Wilson v. S., 18 Tex. Ap. 576; Honnicutt v. S., 20 Tex. Ap. 632; S. v. Chandler, 5 La. An. 489; S. v. Peterson, 41 La. An. 85. One is justified in resisting an apparent attempt to take his life, although it afterward appears that the person resisted was in fact an officer seeking to make an arrest: Logue v. C., 38 Pa. St. 265; Plummer v. S., 135 Ind. 308; Starr v. U. S., 153 U. S. 614.

[1] Sims v. S., 9 Tex. Ap. 586; S. v. Mullen, 14 La. An. 570. Further as to effect of threats and character of deceased, see *infra*, § 307. The real intention of the deceased will be immaterial, as accused must be judged by his apparent intention: P. v. Fitchpatrick, 106 Cal. 286.

[2] P. v. Scoggins, 37 Cal. 676. The surrounding circumstances are the test: Williams v. C., 80 Ky. 313; Lightfoot v. C., 80 Ky. 516. And the accused is to be judged by the facts as they reasonably appear to him, and not as they actually are: S. v. Reed, 53 Kan. 767; Barr v. S., 45 Neb. 458; Rodriguez v. S., 8 Tex. Ap. 129.

[3] Batten v. S., 80 Ind. 394; S. v. Alley, 68 Mo. 124; Johnson v. S., 72 Ga. 679. But there is no necessity for an instruction as to apparent danger when the real nature of the assault is plain: S. v. Umfried, 76 Mo. 404. And it will be error to instruct as to necessity without qualification as to apparent danger: Enright v. P., 155 Ill. 32; Stanley v. C., 86 Ky. 440; Cockrell v. C., 95 Ky. 22; Barnards v. S., 88 Tenn. 183.

[4] S. v. Rutherford, 1 Hawks, 457; S. v. Roane, 2 Dev. 58; Rogers v. S., 62 Ala. 170; Hathaway v. S., 32 Fla. 56; Marnoch v. S., 7 Tex. Ap. 269; Pinder v. S., 27 Fla. 370; S. v. St. Geme, 31 La. An. 302. Further illustrations will be found in cases cited under the preceding section, the doctrine as to belief being practically the same as that with reference to apparent danger. It is not belief on the part of the jury that the danger existed, but belief on the part of defendant as to its existence which is material: Cockrill v. C., 95 Ky. 22.

act), the assailant was in fact not armed.[1] As bearing on the reasonableness of the belief on the part of the person assailed, the relative physical strength of the parties, the condition of health of the person assailed, and other like matters, may be taken into account.[2] If there is no belief of danger, actual danger will be immaterial. The question is whether defendant did believe, on reasonable grounds, and not whether there were grounds on which he might reasonably believe.[3]

§ 306. **Reasonableness of belief.**— The question is, however, not merely as to the existence of the belief, but also as to whether, under the circumstances as they appeared to defendant, there was reasonable ground of belief of danger.[4] The doctrine as to

[1] S. v. Potter, 13 Kan. 414; De Arman v. S., 71 Ala. 351; Everett v. S., 30 Tex. Ap. 682; Bode v. S., 6 Tex. Ap. 424; P. v. Anderson, 44 Cal. 65; Bang v. S., 60 Miss. 571. And for other illustrations of danger apparent, but not real, see Brown v. C., 86 Va. 466; S. v. Evans, 33 W. Va. 417; S. v. Cain, 20 W. Va. 679; Murray v. C., 79 Pa. St. 311; Roach v. P., 77 Ill. 25; Holloway v. C., 11 Bush, 344; Fain v. C., 78 Ky. 183.

[2] Hinch v. S., 25 Ga. 699; S. v. Sterrett, 80 Ia. 609; S. v. Harrod, 102 Mo. 590; Stoneham v. C., 86 Va. 523; Pease v. S., 13 Tex. Ap. 18. By a provision of the penal code in Texas, the use of a deadly weapon by the assaulting party justifies the belief that the assailant intended to kill: Ward v. S., 30 Tex. Ap. 687; Kendall v. S., 8 Tex. Ap. 569. For other illustrations of appearances supporting a belief of danger, see Williams v. S., 30 Tex. Ap. 429; Fuller v. S., 30 Tex. Ap. 559; S. v. Rhodes, 1 Houst. Cr. C. 476; Reg. v. Weston, 14 Cox, 346.

[3] Trogdon v. S., 133 Ind. 1; Lovett v. S., 30 Fla. 142.

[4] C. v. Selfridge, Whart. Hom. 417; Campbell v. P., 16 Ill. 17; Kinney v. P., 108 Ill. 519; Panton v. P., 114 Ill. 505; S. v. Parker, 106 Mo. 217; Morgan v. S., 3 Sneed, 475; McDermott v. S., 89 Ind. 187; S. v. Abbott, 8 W. Va. 741; Holley v. S., 75 Ala. 14; Poe v. S., 87 Ala. 65; Askew v. S., 94 Ala. 4; Parker v. S., 55 Miss. 414; Kendrick v. S., 55 Miss. 436; Wilson v. S., 30 Fla. 234; Tillery v. S., 24 Tex. Ap. 251. The reasonableness of the grounds of belief is to be judged by the jury from the standard of ordinary men and not from that of defendant: S. v. Shoultz, 25 Mo. 128; S. v. Thompson, 9 Ia. 188. The grounds must be such as reasonable men would act on: S. v. Horne, 9 Kan. 119; S. v. Bohan, 19 Kan. 28. Nevertheless, the question is as to reasonable belief on the part of defendant, and not on the part of an ideal reasonable man. The jury should be directed with reference to the actual persons and circumstances: Batten v. S., 80 Ind. 394. It has been held in some cases that the question was as to the actual belief on the part of defendant, and not as to whether such belief was one which a reasonable man would have entertained: Grainger v. S., 5 Yerg. 459. The Grainger case has been followed with modifications in other cases in the same state: Rippy v. S., 2 Head, 217; Copeland v. S., 7 Humph. 479; Williams v. S., 3 Heisk. 376; Jackson v. S., 6 Baxt. 452. But it has been repeatedly criticised in

reasonable belief does not dispense with the necessity of an overt act and imminent danger. Fear alone will not be sufficient.[1] The person assailed in acting upon appearance and taking the life of his fellow-man does so at his peril, and will not be excused unless the circumstances are such as would induce a reasonable man to believe it necessary to save his own life or save himself from great personal injury.[2] But the reasonableness of the apprehension is to be judged from the standpoint of the defendant at the time and not from that of the jury.[3] By this is not meant, however, that the jury should ask themselves the question what they would have done under the circumstances surrounding the accused at the time, but that as sworn officers of the law they should look carefully at all the circumstances surrounding the accused as they appeared to him, and ask themselves, 1st. Did the accused believe himself in imminent danger? and 2d. Were there circumstances such as would justify such a belief in the mind of a person of ordinary firmness and reason?[4]

§ **307. Threats and character of deceased.**— It has already been said that threats alone, not accompanied with such overt

other states: See S. v. Shippey, 10 Minn. 223; Gladden v. S., 12 Fla. 562; S. v. Thompson, 9 Ia. 188. That case went too far. It is not enough that the party believed himself in danger, unless the facts and circumstances were such that the jury can say that he had reasonable grounds for his belief: Shorter v. P., 2 N. Y. 193. That mere fear, which is not a fear such as would be entertained by a reasonable person, is not sufficient, is held in P. v. Stonecifer, 6 Cal. 405; P. v. Hurley, 8 Cal. 390; P. v. Williams, 32 Cal. 280; Creek v. S., 24 Ind. 151; Teal v. S., 22 Ga. 75. The circumstances must be such as would excite the fears of a person of ordinary firmness and reason: Thompson v. S., 55 Ga. 47; Teal v. S., 22 Ga. 75; S. v. Littlejohn, 33 S. C. 599; Palmore v. S., 29 Ark. 248; Wall v. S., 51 Ind. 453; S. v. Stockton, 61 Mo. 382. Evidence that defendant was nervous and peculiarly sensitive is inadmissible: S. v. Shoultz, 25 Mo. 128. Defendant may testify as to his belief: Wallace v. U. S., 162 U. S. 466.

[1] Dyson v. S., 26 Miss. 362; Stoneman v. C., 25 Grat. 887; Hinton v. S., 24 Tex. 454; S. v. Jackson, 44 La. An. 160. But one need not be in terror to justify killing: Arto v. S., 19 Tex. Ap. 126.

[2] Pinder v. S., 27 Fla. 370; Smith v. S., 25 Fla. 517; Smith v. S., 59 Ark. 132; Branch v. S., 15 Tex. Ap. 96.

[3] Bell v. S., 20 Tex. Ap. 445; S. v. Cain, 20 W. Va. 679. It is not proper to require that defendant should have exercised mature deliberation in determining whether the circumstances were such as to require him to act in self-defense: Fields v. S., 134 Ind. 46.

[4] S. v. Wyse, 33 S. C. 582; S. v. Jackson, 32 S. C. 27. And see S. v. Jones, 29 S. C. 201; S. v. Harris, 1 Jones, 190; S. v. Evans, 33 W. Va. 417. What circumstances constitute

act as to indicate an intention to put them into execution, will not warrant the person threatened in taking life in self-defense. But threats accompanying an overt act will, of course, tend to show the character of the act,[1] and antecedent threats made by deceased and known to the defendant will be admissible in connection with proof of an overt act to show that he had reasonable ground to fear that he was in peril of loss of life or great bodily injury, and was therefore excused in taking life in self-defense.[2] Threats by deceased which have not come to the knowledge of defendant prior to the killing cannot be proven for this purpose, as they would not bear upon the question of the reasonable belief of defendant at the commission of the homicide.[3] There are cases, however, which hold that uncommunicated threats made by deceased against the defendant are admissible as tending to show the intention and *animus* of deceased.[4] The violent, vicious or lawless character of deceased

apparent danger is primarily a mixed question of law and fact, but when all the facts are ascertained it is a question of law alone: Long v. S., 52 Miss. 23.

[1] *Supra*, §§ 303, 304.

[2] Wallace v. U. S., 162 U. S. 466; P. v. Arnold, 15 Cal. 476; P. v. Scoggins, 37 Cal. 676; S. v. Nett, 50 Wis. 524; S. v. Sloan, 47 Mo. 604; Wood v. S., 92 Ind. 269; Monroe v. S., 5 Ga. 85; Carico v. C., 7 Bush, 124; Rapp v. C., 14 B. Mon. 614; Rutledge v. S., 88 Ala. 85; Dupree v. S., 33 Ala. 380; Powell v. S., 52 Ala. 1; Hawthorne v. S., 61 Miss. 749; King v. S., 65 Miss. 576; S. v. Abbott, 8 W. Va. 741; S. v. Dodson, 4 Oreg. 64; Pridgen v. S., 31 Tex. 420; Logan v. S., 17 Tex. Ap. 50. In connection with proof of threats, evidence of previous affrays and attacks is admissible, its weight being for the jury: Russell v. S., 11 Tex. Ap. 288. There must be proof of an assault or hostile demonstrations by deceased to warrant the introduction of proof of communicated threats: Bond v. S., 21 Fla. 738; S. v. Spell, 38 La. An. 20. A general threat having no reference to defendant is not sufficient: S. v. Guy, 69 Mo. 430. But threats may be made by innuendo: S. v. Tarter, 26 Oreg. 38. Threats are not admissible which would not lead the accused to fear: P. v. Deitz, 86 Mich. 419. Derogatory statements by deceased in regard to accused not amounting to threats are not admissible: S. v. Sullivan, 43 S. C. 205.

[3] Powell v. S., 19 Ala. 577; P. v. Henderson, 28 Cal. 465; Keener v. S., 18 Ga. 194; Lingo v. S., 29 Ga. 470; S. v. Dumphey, 4 Minn. 438; Atkins v. S., 16 Ark. 568; Cocker v. S., 20 Ark. 53; Harris v. S., 34 Ark. 469; S. v. McCoy, 29 La. An. 593; S. v. Ryan, 30 La. An., pt. II, 1176; S. v. Fisher, 33 La. An. 1344; S. v. Bowser, 42 La. An. 936.

[4] Cornelius v. C., 15 B. Mon. 539; Roberts v. S., 68 Ala. 156; Green v. S., 69 Ala. 6; S. v. Turpin, 77 N. C. 473; Fitzhugh v. S., 13 Lea, 258; Keener v. S., 18 Ga. 194; S. v. Abbott, 8 W. Va. 741; S. v. Evans, 33 W. Va. 417; West v. S., 2 Tex. Ap. 460; King v. S., 9 Tex. Ap. 515; S. v. Donohoe, 78 Ia. 486; S. v. Williams, 40 La. An. 168; S. v. Harrod, 102 Mo. 590.

as known to defendant before the homicide may be proven for the same purpose as antecedent threats, that is, to show the apparent danger to the person assailed.[1] But there must be also proof of some overt act.[2] Moreover, where the homicide has been committed in an encounter, and defendant claims to have been acting in self-defense, but it does not appear which was the aggressor, the character of deceased as a violent man may be shown as indicating that it was he who brought on the conflict and that defendant acted in necessary self-defense.[3] And previous threats, not communicated, are admissible under the same circumstances for the same purpose.[4] But antecedent threats or the bad character of deceased, not known to the defendant, are not thus admissible according to most authorities, unless the circumstances of the homicide are such as to leave

[1] Marts v. S., 26 Ohio St. 162; Brownell v. P., 38 Mich. 732; S. v. Tackett, 1 Hawks, 210; Monroe v. S., 5 Ga. 85; Quesenberry v. S., 3 Stew. & P. 308; Pritchett v. P., 22 Ala. 39; King v. S., 90 Ala. 612; Dukes v. S., 11 Ind. 557; S. v. Collins, 32 Ia. 36; S. v. Graham, 61 Ia. 608; S. v. Keene, 50 Mo. 357; S. v. Hicks, 27 Mo. 588; S. v. Elkins, 63 Mo. 159; S. v. Brown, 63 Mo. 439; S. v. Bryant, 55 Mo. 75; S. v. Smith, 12 Rich. 430; Hudson v. S., 6 Tex. Ap. 565; Grissom v. S., 8 Tex. Ap. 386; Warren v. S., 31 Tex. Ap. 573. But proof that deceased was reckless is not admissible: S. v. Middleham, 62 Ia. 150. Proof that deceased was a man of great physical strength and bad character is admissible: S. v. Nett, 50 Wis. 524; S. v. Collins, 32 Ia. 36; Wellar v. P., 30 Mich. 16; Smith v. U. S., 161 U. S. 85. General character for violence will be presumed to have been known to defendant: S. v. Turner, 29 S. C. 34.

[2] Karr v. S., 100 Ala. 4; Lang v. S., 84 Ala. 1; S. v. Carter, 45 La. An. 1326; S. v. Harris, 45 La. An. 842. As to necessity of overt act, see *supra*, § 303.

[3] S. v. Turpin, 77 N. C. 473; S. v. Tackett, 1 Hawks, 210; S. v. Spendlove, 44 Kan. 1; S. v. Bryant, 55 Mo. 75; S. v. Keene, 50 Mo. 357; P. v. Murray, 10 Cal. 309; S. v. Morey, 25 Oreg. 241; S. v. Keefe, 54 Kan. 197; Basye v. S., 45 Neb. 261.

[4] Stokes v. P., 53 N. Y. 164; Campbell v. P., 16 Ill. 17; Wiggins v. P., 93 U. S. 465; P. v. Arnold, 15 Cal. 476; P. v. Scoggins, 37 Cal. 676; P. v. Travis, 56 Cal. 251; P. v. Alivtre, 55 Cal. 263; Davidson v. P., 4 Colo. 145; S. v. Brown, 22 Kan. 222; Vaughn v. S., 88 Ga. 731; Pittman v. S., 92 Ga. 480; Miller v. C., 89 Ky. 653; Hart v. C., 85 Ky. 77; Holler v. S., 37 Ind. 57; Keener v. S., 18 Ga. 194; Burns v. S., 49 Ala. 370; Johnson v. S., 54 Miss. 430; Johnson v. S., 66 Miss. 189; S. v. Elliott, 45 Ia. 486; S. v. Helm, — Ia. —, 61 N. W. R. 246; S. v. Harris, 59 Mo. 550; Little v. S., 6 Baxt. 491; Binfield v. S., 15 Neb. 484; Dickson v. S., 39 Ohio St. 73; Myers v. S., 62 Ala. 599; S. v. Tarter, 26 Oreg. 38; Wilson v. S., 30 Fla. 234; P. v. Palmer, 96 Mich. 580; S. v. Faile, 43 S. C. 52; Brown v. S., 55 Ark. 593; Reg. v. Weston, 14 Cox, 346. Abandonment by deceased of his hostile purpose may be shown: Trumbull v. S., 25 Tex. Ap. 631. Uncommunicated threats do not bear on manslaughter: Levy v. S., 28 Tex. Ap. 203.

it in doubt which party was the aggressor.[1] In some cases, however, a more liberal rule in regard to allowing evidence of the bad character of deceased is recognized, it being thought that it is not for the court to say whether the case is a doubtful one as to who is the aggressor.[2] Other cases do not make the admissibility of evidence of bad character of deceased, not known to defendant, depend entirely upon its being doubtful as to who made the attack, but allow such evidence generally where it is sought to excuse the homicide on the ground of self-defense.[3] But aside from the question of self-defense, evidence of the dangerous, quarrelsome and vicious character of the deceased is not admissible.[4] Where the bad character of the deceased becomes material it is to be proved by reputa-

[1] Vaughan v. S., 88 Ga. 731; Doyal v. S., 70 Ga. 134; Monroe v. S., 5 Ga. 85; Harrison v. C., 79 Va. 374; Eiland v. S., 52 Ala. 322; Bowles v. S., 58 Ala. 335; Pritchett v. S., 22 Ala. 39; Franklin v. S., 29 Ala. 14; Fields v. S., 47 Ala. 603; S. v. Barfield, 8 Ired. 344; S. v. Rollins, 113 N. C. 722; S. v. Pearce, 15 Nev. 188; P. v. Stock, 1 Ida. 218; C. v. Straesser, 153 Pa. St. 451; P. v. Murray, 10 Cal. 309; P. v. Lombard, 17 Cal. 316; P. v. Edwards, 41 Cal. 640; Wesley v. S., 37 Miss. 327; Newcomb v. S., 37 Miss. 383; Creswell v. S., 14 Tex. Ap. 1; S. v. Elliott, 45 Ia. 486; S. v. Alexander, 66 Mo. 148; Steele v. S., 33 Fla. 348; S. v. Depass, 45 La. An. 1151. Where it appears that the accused was armed and was the aggressor, evidence of violent character of deceased, who was unarmed, is immaterial: Skaggs v. S., 31 Tex. Ap. 563. Thus, where it appears beyond question that the defendant was the attacking party, evidence of the bad character of deceased is not admissible: S. v. Watson, 36 La. An. 148; S. v. Ford, 37 La. An. 443; S. v. Paterno, 43 La. An. 514; S. v. Burns, 30 La. An., part I, 679; S. v. Cooper, 32 La. An. 1084; S. v. Claude, 35 La. An. 71; S. v. Hays, 23 Mo. 287; Gonzales v. S., 31 Tex. 495.

[2] P. v. Stewart, 28 Cal. 395; Pridgen v. S., 31 Tex. 420. And generally as recognizing the admissibility of evidence of bad character beyond the limits fixed by the rules stated in the text with reference to who is the aggressor, see S. v. Ricks, 32 La. An. 1098; S. v. McNeeley, 34 La. An. 1022; Palmore v. S., 29 Ark. 248; Payne v. C., 1 Met. (Ky.) 370; Riley v. C., 94 Ky. 266; Branch v. S., 15 Tex. Ap. 96.

[3] Williams v. S., 74 Ala. 18; S. v. Donohoe, 78 Ia. 486; S. v. McNally, 87 Mo. 644; S. v. Hayden, 83 Mo. 198; S. v. Matthews, 78 N. C. 523; Williams v. S., 14 Tex. Ap. 102; Moore v. S., 15 Tex. Ap. 1. Such evidence is also admissible on the degree of defendant's guilt: Smith v. S., 88 Ala. 73.

[4] S. v. Thawley, 4 Harr. 562; S. v. Field, 14 Me. 244; C. v. Ferrigan, 44 Pa. St. 386; Abbott v. P., 86 N. Y. 460; P. v. Garbutt, 17 Mich. 9; S. v. Hogue, 6 Jones, 381; Drake v. S., 75 Ga. 413; S. v. Kennade, 121 Mo. 405; S. v. Riddle, 20 Kan. 711; S. v. Tilly, 3 Ired. 424; Chase v. S., 46 Miss. 683; S. v. Jackson, 12 La. An. 679; McKeone v. P., 6 Colo. 346; Jones v. P., 6 Colo. 452; May v. P., 8 Colo. 210; Bond v. S., 21 Fla. 738. And see, in general, *infra*, § 423.

tion, actual character not being material on the question of reasonable belief.[1] Opinions of witnesses are not admissible on the question.[2] So bad character cannot be shown by proof of particular acts of violence or bad conduct.[3] Whether or not a proper foundation has been laid for the introduction of evidence of the threats or character of deceased is a matter to be decided by the trial court;[4] but the weight of the evidence is for the jury.[5]

§ 308. **Necessity.**— The excuse for homicide in all these cases of self-defense rests on the doctrine of necessity as showing absence of criminal intent. If the person assailed may safely avoid the danger without resorting to the use of a deadly weapon, he must do so.[6] If, notwithstanding the danger, or apparent danger, it appears that the killing was with wrongful motives and not in self-defense, it will be criminal.[7] Where

[1] P. v. Anderson, 39 Cal. 703.

[2] Harrison v. C., 79 Va. 374. For instance, it is not proper to ask a witness whether deceased was a man likely to use weapons in a difficulty: Bingham v. S., 6 Tex. Ap. 169. And see Hudson v. S., 6 Tex. Ap. 565; Lewallen v. S., 6 Tex. Ap. 475.

[3] Pound v. S., 43 Ga. 88; Campbell v. S., 38 Ark. 498; Steele v. S., 83 Ala. 20; Thomas v. P., 67 N. Y. 218; S. v. Abarr, 39 Ia. 185. *Contra*, P. v. Harris, 95 Mich. 87. Thus, evidence that the general character of deceased for honesty was bad is not admissible: Plasters v. S., 1 Tex. Ap. 673. A record of conviction of deceased for manslaughter may be introduced: Brunet v. S., 12 Tex. Ap. 521. But it is not competent to show that he was an escaped convict: Dupree v. S., 33 Ala. 380; Franklin v. S., 29 Ala. 14. Where the physical strength of deceased is admissible it is not to be proved by evidence of specific acts: Wellar v. P., 30 Mich. 16; C. v. Mead, 12 Gray, 167.

[4] King v. S., 90 Ala. 612; S. v. Christian, 44 La. An. 950; S. v. Spell, 38 La. An. 20; S. v. Stewart, 45 La. An. 1164; S. v. Green, 46 La. An. 1522.

[5] Garner v. S., 28 Fla. 113; Wilson v. S., 30 Fla. 234.

[6] S. v. Johnson, 76 Mo. 121; S. v. Brooks, 99 Mo. 137. The repellant force must be protective and not aggressive: Lewis v. S., 51 Ala. 1. One who resisted an assault by another who was drunk and unarmed, by stabbing him, was held guilty of murder in the second degree: Fitzgerald v. S., 15 Lea, 99.

[7] S. v. Scheele, 57 Conn. 307 (distinguishing C. v. Carey, 12 Cush. 246); De Arman v. S., 77 Ala. 10; Mitchell v. S., 22 Ga. 211; Stiles v. S., 57 Ga. 183; P. v. Miller, 49 Mich. 23; S. v. Jones, 89 Ia. 182; Kinney v. P., 108 Ill. 519; S. v. Hudson, 59 Mo. 135; S. v. Brown, 63 Mo. 439; S. v. Paxton, 126 Mo. 500; Barnett v. S., 100 Ind. 171; S. v. Scott, 41 Minn. 365; S. v. Wells, 1 N. J. 424; Turner v. C., 89 Ky. 78; Varnell v. S., 26 Tex. Ap. 56; C. v. Drum, 58 Pa. St. 9; S. v. Martin, 2 Ired. 101. But where there is reasonable cause for believing that there is imminent danger, and defendant acts in such belief, it is immaterial whether the circumstances actually caused the belief of danger. (This was said in construc-

defendant claims to have acted upon reasonable ground of apprehension, he will not be excused if it appears that he did not really apprehend danger, although he had ground to do so, but acted from other motives.[1] So, after the danger is past, killing will not be excused in self-defense.[2] Where the homicide is the result of a preconceived intention on the part of the defendant and is not brought on by the deceased, even though there is apparent necessity by reason of the first assault being made by the other party, the homicide will not be excusable.[3]

§ **309. Party in the wrong.**— One may, by his conduct, put himself so far in the wrong that he is not afterwards excusable for acting in self-defense, even though he is put in peril. If by his wilful, wrongful act, he brings about the necessity for killing to save his own life, he will not be excused.[4] Therefore, one who commences an assault which is resisted with violence is not excused in going to the extent of taking life in avoiding a danger to his own life, which arises by reason of the violence of the party whom he has assaulted.[5] It has even been said

tion of a statute): Clifford v. S., 58 Wis. 477.

[1] S. v. Matthews, 78 N. C. 523. It must appear that the act was done as a result of the belief: P. v. Gonzales, 71 Cal. 569.

[2] Evans v. S., 33 Ga. 4; Guice v. S., 60 Miss. 714; S. v. Chavis, 80 N. C. 353; Lewis v. S., 51 Ala. 1; S. v. Mitchell, 41 La. An. 1073; S. v. Rutherford, 1 Hawks, 457; S. v. Roane, 2 Dev. 58; P. v. Pierson, 2 Ida. 71.

[3] P. v. Miller, 49 Mich. 23; Kinney v. P., 108 Ill. 519; S. v. Hudson, 59 Mo. 135; S. v. Brown, 63 Mo. 439; Murphy v. S., 37 Ala. 142; Coker v. S., 20 Ark. 53; Helm v. S., 67 Miss. 562; S. v. Hensley, 94 N. C. 1021. The right of self-defense is a shield and not a sword to be used for the purpose of excusing an injury to the party provoked: Barnett v. S., 100 Ind. 171. If defendant, armed with a deadly weapon, sought out the deceased, and, by insulting language, intentionally provoked an assault from the deceased, he is not justified in taking life in resistance to such assault: S. v. Scott, 41 Minn. 365. One who provides a weapon to be used in overcoming opposition cannot be excused on the ground of self-defense: Thomas v. S., 61 Miss. 60. But see the next section and notes.

[4] Eiland v. S., 52 Ala. 322; S. v. Hill, 4 Dev. & B. 491; Meuly v. S., 26 Tex. Ap. 274; Reg. v. Mawgridge, J. Kel. 119; Rex v. Oneby, 2 Stra. 766. Thus, an officer attempting to make an unlawful arrest cannot defend himself against one who resists such arrest with violence; S. v. Campbell, 107 N. C. 948; Zaner v. S., 90 Ala. 651; Carter v. S., 30 Tex. Ap. 551; Roberson v. S., 53 Ark. 516. So one who attempts to resist or escape from arrest cannot defend himself against violence on the part of the officer seeking to affect such arrest: Floyd v. S., 82 Ala. 16.

[5] S. v. Rogers, 18 Kan. 78; S. v. Neeley, 20 Ia. 108; Clifford v. S., 58 Wis. 477; Story v. S., 99 Ind. 413; S.

that one who provokes a difficulty with abusive language, or seeks a quarrel, will not be excused in defending himself against violence which he has thus incited,[1] though in such case, if his original intention was not to kill or inflict great bodily injury, the necessity which afterwards arises for taking life may reduce the homicide to manslaughter.[2] But the mere provocation of insulting language will not, according to many cases, deprive the person who thus brings on the combat of the right of ultimately resorting to violence, even to the extent of taking life, to defend himself if that is his only available resort.[3] The mere preparation for the perpetration of a wrongful act unaccompanied by a demonstration toward its commission will

v. Starr, 38 Mo. 270; S. v. McDonald, 67 Mo. 13; S. v. Johnson, 76 Mo. 121; S. v. Davidson, 95 Mo. 155; S. v. Gilmore, 95 Mo. 554; Lewis v. S., 88 Ala. 11; Leonard v. S., 66 Ala. 461; Page v. S., 69 Ala. 229; Johnson v. S., 69 Ala. 253; Tesney v. S., 77 Ala. 33; Waller v. S., 89 Ala. 79; Gibson v. S., 91 Ala. 64; Davis v. S., 92 Ala. 20; P. v. Stonecifer, 6 Cal. 405; P. v. Lamb, 17 Cal. 323; P. v. Westlake, 62 Cal. 303; P. v. Douglass, 87 Cal. 281; Lingo v. S., 29 Ga. 470; Roach v. S., 34 Ga. 78; Mitchell v. S., 22 Ga. 211; Stewart v. S., 1 Ohio St. 66; S. v. Edwards, 112 N. C. 901; Vaiden v. C., 12 Grat. 717; Harrison v. C., 79 Va. 374; Gilleland v. S., 44 Tex. 356; Thumm v. S., 24 Tex. Ap. 667; Brazzil v. S., 28 Tex. Ap. 584; Roberts v. S., 30 Tex. Ap. 291; Polk v. S., 30 Tex. Ap. 657.

1 S. v. Talmage, 107 Mo. 543; Adams v. P., 47 Ill. 376; Jackson v. S., 81 Ala. 33; Baker v. S., 81 Ala. 38; Henry v. S., 79 Ala. 43; S. v. Trammell, 40 S. C. 331. It is said that the law admits of no qualification of the requirement that defendant must have been free from all fault tending to provoke or bring on the difficulty: McQueen v. S., 103 Ala. 12. But one who returns a verbal insult does not thereby deprive himself of the privilege of afterward making self-defense when violently assaulted: Howell v. S., 79 Ala. 283.

2 This is called, in some cases, the imperfect right of self-defense: S. v. Partlow, 90 Mo. 608; S. v. Gilmore, 95 Mo. 554; S. v. Bryant, 102 Mo. 24; S. v. Parker, 96 Mo. 382; S. v. Parker, 106 Mo. 217; S. v. Evans, 128 Mo. 406; S. v. Lewis, 118 Mo. 79; Johnson v. S., 26 Tex. Ap. 631; Meuly v. S., 26 Tex. Ap. 274; Gonzales v. S., 28 Tex. Ap. 130. It is even said that in such cases there is a perfect right of self-defense: S. v. Culler, 82 Mo. 623; S. v. Anderson, 89 Mo. 312, 331; but this view is disclaimed in the same state: S. v. Parker, 106 Mo. 217.

3 P. v. Curtis, 52 Mich. 616; Brown v. S., 58 Ga. 212; Boatwright v. S., 89 Ga. 140; Bush v. P., 10 Colo. 566; S. v. Anderson, 86 Mo. 309. And an instruction that if defendant provoked the difficulty he cannot be excused for homicide in self-defense is erroneous: Brinkley v. S., 89 Ala. 34; S. v. Harrison, 5 Jones, 115; P. v. Bush, 65 Cal. 129; Logan v. S., 17 Tex. Ap. 50. Publication of a libel is not such a wrong as to preclude resort to self-defense as against a violent assault by the person libeled: C. v. Selfridge, Whart. Hom. 417.

not preclude self-defense;[1] nor will mere malice or ill-will toward assailant deprive the assailed of that right;[2] nor the mere fact of arming in anticipation of an encounter.[3] So the fact that defendant armed himself and prepared for the encounter which he anticipated might result from the attempt on his part to do that which he had a right to do, will not preclude a rightful self-defense on his part if attacked.[4] But, of course, if he prepares for an attack with the intention of taking advantage thereof in order to wreak his vengeance on his adversary, there will be no question of self-defense.[5] And a homicide, even upon sudden combat, is not excusable if undue advantage is taken of the adversary.[6] One who is engaged in perpetrating a felony will not be excused for taking life to preserve his own life, as the danger is one growing out of his own wrong;[7] and the same reasoning applies to one who kills in resisting lawful arrest.[8] So, where defendant had gone to the house of deceased for the purpose of committing adultery with deceased's wife, it was held that he could not excuse himself for homicide in defending against an assault made by the husband;[9] but where, having desisted from the attempt, he was seeking to escape, it was held that in defending himself against a murderous assault from the husband he might be excusable in killing.[10] Although

[1] Cartwright v. S., 14 Tex. Ap. 486; Meuly v. S., 26 Tex. Ap. 274.

[2] P. v. Macard, 73 Mich. 15.

[3] P. v. Stone, 82 Cal. 36; S. v. Rider, 90 Mo. 54; Fussell v. S. 94 Ga. 78

[4] P. v. Gonzales, 71 Cal. 569; S. v. Evans, 124 Mo. 397; Milrainey v. S., 33 Tex. Ap. 577; Gilcrease v. S., 33 Tex. Ap. 619; Gourko v. U. S., 153 U. S. 183; Allen v. U. S., 157 U. S. 675. A person anticipating an attack is not obliged to remain at home to avoid the difficulty, but may arm himself and pursue his legitimate avocations and defend himself when it becomes necessary: P. v. Macard, 73 Mich. 15. The accused will not be deemed to have been in fault by reason of having, after a quarrel, returned to secure a settlement of his rights from the other party: Johnson v. S., 26 Tex. Ap. 631. Nor will a threat by defendant to compel deceased to do an act be imputed to him as a wrong so as to deprive him of the right of self-defense: S. v. Thompson, 83 Mo. 257. A party may have a perfect right of self-defense, though not free from blame, if the wrong being done was not intended to produce the occasion, nor an act which was under the circumstances reasonably calculated to produce the occasion for the killing or to provoke the difficulty: Franklin v. S., 30 Tex. Ap. 628.

[5] Allen v. S., 66 Miss. 385; S. v. Herrell, 97 Mo. 105; Allen v. S., 24 Tex. Ap. 216.

[6] P. v. Perdue, 49 Cal. 425; S. v. Christain, 66 Mo. 138.

[7] Dill v. S., 25 Ala. 15.

[8] Floyd v. S., 82 Ala. 16.

[9] Franklin v. S., 30 Tex. Ap. 628.

[10] McSpatten v. S., 30 Tex. Ap. 616. So where defendant laid a trap to

one who is in the wrong cannot properly make self-defense, his wrong will not be imputed to relatives or friends who assist him after he is in imminent danger, they not being aware of anything which deprives him of his right to make defense.[1]

§ **310. Duty to withdraw.**— As appears from the preceding section, one who voluntarily enters into a combat or is the original aggressor cannot excuse a subsequent homicide committed in consequence thereof on the ground of self-defense, it being his duty to withdraw;[2] but there must be allowed room for repentance and abandonment of the evil and unlawful purpose, and if the defendant, though originally in the wrong, does thus abandon his purpose, he may afterwards exercise the right of self-defense.[3] The withdrawal, however, must be in good faith; if the original assailant merely ceases to advance for the purpose of watching his opponent's movements and without attempting to avoid the encounter, he will not be excused for what he afterwards does on the ground of self-defense;[4] and

catch defendant in the act of adultery with the wife, it was held that as against an assault made by the husband, the defendant was excusable for defending himself: Wilkerson v. S., 91 Ga. 729. So where accused had been guilty of fornication with defendant's daughter, it was held that, as against an assault afterwards made upon him by reason thereof, he might exercise the right of self-defense: Varnell v. S., 26 Tex. Ap. 56. And in general one who has merely attempted a felony, or is being pursued on suspicion thereof, may defend himself against a murderous assault: Felker v. S., 54 Ark. 489; Luera v. S., 12 Tex. Ap. 257. Further as to making defense on the part of one originally in the wrong, but who has withdrawn therefrom, see the next section.

[1] Bush v. P., 10 Colo. 566. As to the right to protect others, see *infra*, § 313.

[2] Presser v. S., 77 Ind. 274; S. v. Cain, 20 W. Va. 679; Deal v. S., 140 Ind. 354; S. v. Spears, 46 La. An. 1524. As to burden of proof in regard to withdrawal see *infra*, § 316. It is suggested that in these cases the difference between excusable homicide and manslaughter is that in the one case the slayer could not escape if he would, and in the other he would not escape if he could: U. S. v. King, 34 Fed. R. 302.

[3] Stoffer v. S., 15 Ohio St. 47; Parker v. S., 88 Ala. 4; P. v. Robertson, 67 Cal. 646; P. v. Simons, 60 Cal. 72; P. v. Wong Ah Teak, 63 Cal. 544; P. v. Button, 106 Cal. 628; S. v. Cable, 117 Mo. 380; S. v. Talmage, 107 Mo. 543; S. v. Partlow, 90 Mo. 608; Hittner v. S., 19 Ind. 48; Wall v. S., 51 Ind. 453; Terrell v. C., 13 Bush, 246; S. v. Smith, 10 Nev. 106; S. v. Hill, 4 Dev. & B. 491; S. v. Ingold, 4 Jones, 216; Aikin v. S., 58 Ark. 544; Johnson v. S., 58 Ark. 57; Brazzil v. S., 28 Tex. Ap. 584; Roberts v. S., 30 Tex. Ap. 291; Johnson v. S., 26 Tex. Ap. 631; S. v. Thompson, 45 La. An. 969; 4 Bl. Com. 184.

[4] S. v. Rogers, 18 Kan. 78; Parker v. S., 88 Ala. 4.

the fact of change of purpose must be known to the other party.[1] Perhaps this duty to withdraw does not exist where the danger has become such that a reasonably prudent man would consider that withdrawal would imperil his life.[2] But a distinction must be introduced between the duty to withdraw here referred to and the duty to retreat discussed in the next section, for in the cases now under consideration the party who seeks to avail himself of the right of self-defense has been originally in the wrong, and it is doubtful whether he ought to be excused for killing in self-defense before a definite withdrawal, no matter how dangerous such withdrawal might be.[3]

§ 311. **Duty to retreat.**— The right of self-defense being a part of the doctrine of necessity, it follows that, in order to justify the taking of life, the one who is assailed must employ all the means within his power and consistent with his safety to avoid the danger and avert the necessity.[4] Therefore, it is well settled that one who is assailed must retreat if he can do so without danger, and thus avoid the necessity of taking life in self-defense.[5] However, a distinction as to the duty to retreat is made between cases where the assault indicates a purpose to commit a felony, and those where the assault is not felonious, and it is sometimes said that in the cases of the former class there is no necessity to retreat.[6] One who is not in fault, and is in a place where he has a right to be, may, without re-

[1] S. v. Edwards, 112 N. C. 901.

[2] S. v. Jones, 89 Ia. 182; Brown v. C., 86 Va. 466.

[3] S. v. Jacobs, 28 S. C. 29.

[4] McPherson v. S., 29 Ark. 225; Levells v. S., 32 Ark. 585; Kendall v. S., 8 Tex. Ap. 569.

[5] C. v. Drum, 58 Pa. St. 9; Shorter v. P., 2 N. Y. 193; Holmes v. S., 100 Ala. 80; Ingram v. S., 67 Ala. 67; Sullivan v. S., 102 Ala. 135; Poe v. S., 87 Ala. 65; Goodwin v. S., 102 Ala. 87; Squire v. S., 87 Ala. 114; Finch v. S., 81 Ala. 41; P. v. Giancoli, 74 Cal. 642; S. v. Johnson, 76 Mo. 121; S. v. Kennedy, 91 N. C. 572; S. v. Crane, 95 N. C. 619; S. v. Jones, 89 Ia. 182 (overruling Tweedy v. S., 5 Ia. 433); Brown v. C., 86 Va. 466; Clark v. C., 90 Va. 360; S. v. Trammell, 40 S. C. 331. And it is said that defendant is not excused from retreating by the fact that he will not be placed in a better position or in less peril, but that he must retreat unless his danger would thereby be increased: Carter v. S., 82 Ala. 13; Roden v. S., 97 Ala. 54; McDaniel v. S., 97 Ala. 14. It is stating the duty to retreat too strongly, however, to say that it must appear that the assailed had no other possible or probable means of escape: Babcock v. P., 13 Colo. 515.

[6] S. v. Dickson, 75 N. C. 275; Erwin v. S., 29 Ohio St. 186; Meuly v. S., 26 Tex. Ap. 274. This is the rule by statute in Texas: Parker v. S., 22 Tex. Ap. 105; Williams v. S., 22 Tex. Ap. 497.

treating, resist an attack which reasonably appears to imperil his life or threaten him grievous bodily harm, and take the life of the aggressor if necessary;[1] nor is the rule as to duty to retreat applicable to one who is in pursuance of a legal duty, such as an officer or one acting under his command;[2] or a person charged with the custody of property;[3] nor is the rule applicable where retreat without danger is impractical,[4] or, what is the same thing, if it is impracticable to the reasonable apprehension of the party assailed.[5]

§ 312. Where felony threatened or invasion of home.— It has already been suggested in the preceding section that one who is proceeding in the discharge of a duty, or going about his own lawful business, is not bound to desist therefrom and retreat for fear of bringing on a difficulty with some one who threatens to unlawfully interfere with him. This rule is especially applicable where a felony is threatened; and, without retreating, one who is opposing the commission of a felony may resist the attempt by whatever force may be necessary, even to the extent of taking life.[6] On the same principle, one who is assailed in his home is not bound to retreat therefrom, but may resist the invasion thereof for the purpose of committing a felony or doing personal violence to the inmates, and may justifiably take life, if necessary, without retreating from the threatened danger.[7] This exemption does not extend, how-

[1] Beard v. U. S., 158 U. S. 550; Baker v. C., 93 Ky. 302; Estep v. C., 86 Ky. 39; Eversole v. C., 95 Ky. 623; Sparks v. C., 89 Ky. 644; Harris v. S., 96 Ala. 24. But such an instruction is not applicable to a case where the assault is committed in a public place, which, though belonging to the defendant, is one where the deceased also had a right to be: Hall v. C., 94 Ky. 322.

[2] Cockrill v. C., 95 Ky. 22.

[3] High v. S., 26 Tex. Ap. 545.

[4] Philips v. C., 2 Duv. 328; Holloway v. C., 11 Bush, 344; Riley v. C., 94 Ky. 266; Jones v. S., 90 Ala. 628; Haynes v. S., 17 Ga. 465; Brown v. C., 86 Va. 466; Gallagher v. S., 3 Minn. 270; S. v. Thompson, 45 La. An. 969. Under the language of the penal code of Texas, retreat from danger is not required: Foster v. S., 11 Tex. Ap. 105; Bell v. S., 17 Tex. Ap. 538; Parker v. S., 18 Tex. Ap. 72; Williams v. S., 30 Tex. Ap. 429; Nalley v. S., 30 Tex. Ap. 456; May v. S., 23 Tex. Ap. 146.

[5] Baltrip v. S., 30 Tex. Ap. 545; Stoneham v. C., 86 Va. 523; Poe v. S., 87 Ala. 65; Erwin v. S., 29 Ohio St. 186; S. v. Thompson, 9 Ia. 188; Runyan v. S., 57 Ind. 80.

[6] Stoneham v. C., 86 Va. 523; Pond v. P., 8 Mich. 150. That one will be justified in killing to prevent a felony, see *supra*, § 299.

[7] Pond v. P., 8 Mich. 150; P. v. Lilly, 38 Mich. 270; Miller v. S., 74 Ind. 1;

ever, to premises not included within the curtilage;[1] and it does not afford protection to one who has emerged from his dwelling to voluntarily enter upon a combat.[2]

§ 313. **Protection of others.**— It has already been suggested that the doctrine of necessity justifies the protection of others against a threatened felony, as well as the protection of one's self.[3] Those circumstances which will justify or excuse a homicide where the assault is upon one's self will also justify or excuse taking life in defense of a wife, husband, parent, child, master, or servant.[4] In this case the necessity for taking life must be established to the same extent as though justification were claimed for taking life in one's own defense.[5] Indeed, the broad principle has been laid down in some cases that homicide is justified in the protection of the life of another to the same extent that it would be in protecting one's own life.[6] But the case must be one where killing on the part of the person assailed would be justified in self-defense.[7]

§ 314. **Right to pursue.**— It is sometimes said that where there is a right to make self-defense without retreat, the person assailed may even pursue his adversary, instead of retreating, until danger from the assault is passed.[8]

S. v. Harman, 78 N. C. 515; Brown v. S., 55 Ark. 593. But the resistance should be by means not imperiling life, if practicable: King v. S., 55 Ark. 604. The protection of the home does not justify the shooting of an invited guest in the home without notice to leave: S. v. McIntosh, 40 S. C. 349. A lodger may resist invasion of the premises to the same extent as the owner: Cooper's Cas. Cro. Car. 544.

[1] Lee v. S., 92 Ala. 15. Whether it applies to a place of business or other premises not constituting a dwelling-house, see *supra*, § 311.

[2] Watkins v. S., 89 Ala. 82. As to protection of property, see *supra*, § 142.

[3] *Supra*, § 140.

[4] Hathaway v. S., 32 Fla. 56; Staten v. S., 30 Miss. 619; Estep v. C., 86 Ky. 39; Campbell v. C., 88 Ky. 402; Alberty v. U. S., 162 U. S. 499; Reg. v. Rose, 15 Cox, 540. But where the justification claimed is that the person assailed was the wife of the slayer, the fact of the marital relation must be established: P. v. Pierson, 2 Ida. 71; Parker v. S., 31 Tex. 132.

[5] S. v. Wilson, 10 Wash. 402; P. v. Pierson, 2 Ida. 71.

[6] In re Neagle, 135 U. S. 1; Dyson v. S., 14 Tex. Ap. 454; Glover v. S., 33 Tex. Ap. 224.

[7] S. v. Greer, 22 W. Va. 800; Whatley v. S., 91 Ala. 108; Bostic v. S., 94 Ala. 45; Risby v. S., 17 Tex. Ap. 517. It seems, however, that if a person defending another has no knowledge of facts precluding the right of self-defense, he will be excusable for acting in accordance with appearances: Bush v. P., 10 Colo. 566.

[8] Philips v. C., 2 Duv. 328; Holloway v. C., 11 Bush, 344; Luby v. C., 12 Bush, 1; Pond v. P., 8 Mich. 150;

§ 315. Instruction as to self-defense.— Where there is evidence in support of the claim that defendant acted in self-defense, the law regarding it should be explained to the jury.[1]

§ 316. Burden of proof.— It is said in many cases that the burden is on the defendant to show by preponderance of evidence that he acted in proper self-defense, that is, that the circumstances as they appeared to him were such as to justify him in taking the life of his assailant, under the principles already set out.[2] Accordingly it has been held that defendant had the burden of showing that he could not safely retreat without apparently increasing his peril.[3] But in reason it is not proper to throw the burden of proof as to any element in the crime

Luckinbell v. S., 52 Ark. 45; West v. S., 2 Tex. Ap. 460; S. v. Thompson, 45 La. An. 969. But in a later Kentucky case the doctrine of Philips v. C., *supra*, is somewhat discredited, and it is said that certainly no case justifies one who may think his life in danger in lying in wait to slay his adversary without warning: Turner v. C., 89 Ky. 78. Certainly if the assailant has desisted from the assault and is in retreat, and danger from him is over, the assailant will not be justified in pursuing him and taking his life: P. v. Pierson, 2 Ida. 71.

[1] Hinch v. S., 25 Ga. 699; S. v. Donahoe, 78 Ia. 486; Fields v. S., 134 Ind. 46; Bradley v. S., 31 Ind. 492; Souey v. S., 13 Lea, 472; Munday v. C., 81 Ky. 233; P. v. Ye Park, 62 Cal. 204; Bennett v. S., 12 Tex. Ap. 15; Short v. S., 15 Tex. Ap. 370; Jackson v. S., 15 Tex. Ap. 84; Cartwright v. S., 16 Tex. Ap. 473; Tillery v. S., 24 Tex. Ap. 251. The distinction between the right of perfect and imperfect self-defense (see *supra*, § 309, n.) should be explained where there is any doubt as to the character of the intent: Meuly v. S., 26 Tex. Ap. 274. Where the evidence showed that the accused was not in serious peril and had no reasonable cause to believe there was a necessity for taking life, *held*, that it was not erroneous to ignore such defense: Taylor v. S., 48 Ala. 180.

[2] C. v. Drum, 58 Pa. St. 9; Silvus v. S., 22 Ohio St. 90; Weaver v. S., 24 Ohio St. 584; Crews v. P., 120 Ill. 317; P. v. Stonecifer, 6 Cal. 405; P. v. Flahave, 58 Cal. 249; P. v. Hong Ah Duck, 61 Cal. 387; Stit v. S., 91 Ala. 10; Cleveland v. S., 86 Ala. 1; Smith v. S., 86 Ala. 28; S. v. Brown, 34 S. C. 41; P. v. Schryver, 42 N. Y. 1; S. v. Bertrand, 3 Oreg. 61; S. v. Jones, 20 W. Va. 764; S. v. West, 1 Houst. Cr. C. 371. Or as it is perhaps better stated in another case, the *onus* to show the facts which authorize the taking of life to preserve life is upon the defendant who relies on them in justification of the killing: Lewis v. S., 88 Ala. 11. But it is not proper to require self-defense to be made out beyond a reasonable doubt: U. S. v. Crow Dog, 3 Dak. 106; S. v. Ariel, 38 S. C. 221; S. v. Summers, 36 S. C. 479. Where it is claimed that the homicide, though committed by defendant, was accidental and therefore excusable, the burden, it is said, is on defendant to prove due care: S. v. Bonds, 2 Nev. 265; Reg. v. Cavendish, 8 Ir. R. C. L. 178; Foster, 255. *Contra*, Richardson v. S., 32 Tex. Ap. 524.

[3] Gibson v. S., 89 Ala. 121; T. v. Edmonson, 4 Mont. 141; T. v. Tunnell, 4 Mont. 148.

upon the defendant, and it has accordingly been held, in accordance with what is a more reasonable doctrine, that defendant has no such burden even as to self-defense; but that if the evidence in regard to self-defense raises a reasonable doubt of the defendant's guilt, he should be acquitted.[1] Even where the burden of proof is on defendant to show that he acted in self-defense, he is not required to go further and prove that he was not at fault in bringing on the difficulty, and if this is relied on to overcome the evidence of acting in self-defense, it must be established by the prosecution.[2] Certainly where the evidence for the prosecution leaves a doubt as to the character of the homicide, whether justifiable or not, the person is entitled to the doubt.[3] The question whether the evidence is sufficient to establish self-defense is for the jury.[4]

IV. MURDER.

§ **317. Felonious.**— All homicides, not justifiable or excusable, are criminal and felonious. This is so at common law and also under statutes in the several states. There are probably not in any state any cases of homicide punishable at all which are not punishable as felonies.

§ **318. Division into murder and manslaughter.**—The common-law division of the law of criminal homicides into two classes constituting distinct crimes of murder and manslaughter is universally recognized in the states of the Union, and, in-

[1] C. v. McKie, 1 Gray, 61; Stokes v. P., 53 N. Y. 164; P. v. Downs, 123 N. Y. 558; P. v. Pallister, 138 N. Y. 601; S. v. Porter, 34 Ia. 131; S. v. Fowler, 52 Ia. 103; S. v. Donahoe, 78 Ia. 486; S. v. Patterson, 45 Vt. 308; S. v. Wingo, 66 Mo. 181; S. v. Alexander, 66 Mo. 148; McKenna v. S., 61 Miss. 589; S. v. Ellick, 1 Winst., ii., 56; Goodall v. S., 1 Oreg. 333; S. v. Conahan, 10 Wash. 268; S. v. McCluer, 5 Nev. 132; March v. Walker, 48 Tex. 372; Richardson v. S., 9 Tex. Ap. 612; Babb v. S., 8 Tex. Ap. 173; Ainsworth v. S., 8 Tex. Ap. 532. An instruction that the burden is on defendant, but that the state must make out its whole case beyond a reasonable doubt, is not objectionable as requiring defendant to prove his innocence: S. v. McIntosh, 40 S. C. 349.

[2] McCormack v. S., 102 Ala. 156; McDaniel v. S., 76 Ala. 1; Brown v. S., 83 Ala. 33; Harris v. S., 96 Ala. 24; Keith v. S., 97 Ala. 32; Holmes v. S., 100 Ala. 80.

[3] This is the result of statutory provision in California: P. v. Arnold, 15 Cal. 476; P. v. West, 49 Cal. 610.

[4] P. v. Young, 64 Cal. 212; Lister v. S., 3 Tex. Ap. 17. The court may direct the jury that there is no evidence tending to excuse the homicide if such is the fact: T. v. Gay, 2 Dak. 125.

deed, probably in all English-speaking countries, and involves one of the most perplexing distinctions to be met in the law. This distinction is expressed by the term "malice aforethought," the presence of which renders an unlawful homicide murder, and the absence of which makes it manslaughter.

§ **319. Malice aforethought.**— The history of the introduction of this term into the law as indicating the distinction between murder and manslaughter is exceedingly interesting, but not important, as it throws little light on the distinction itself, which is the work of modern refinements. Originally there was no difference in the punishment, all criminal homicides being felonies and punishable with death and forfeiture of land and goods. But at an early day some special provision was made in regard to secret killings, by which, in such cases, an amercement was to be paid by the township or hundred, unless it should be made to appear at the inquest that the person killed was an Englishman, and this was called presentment of Englishery. These provisions are said to have been introduced by King Canute to protect his Danish subjects against the English, and to have been revived under similar circumstances by William the Conqueror to protect his French followers.[1] This secret killing was denominated *murdrum*, and thus furnished the name for one division of criminal homicide, although it did not furnish the definition for it. The use of the term "malice aforethought" first appears, so far as is now known, in Fitz Herbert,[2] as a part of the finding of the jury in determining that a homicide was not intentional (that is, was by accident or in chance medley) and therefore subject for a pardon.[3] Even in this connection the term had no relation to its present meaning, but it seems to have connected itself subsequently with the term "malice prepensed," used in 23 Henry VIII., chapter 1, and in other similar statutes, as designating the kinds of homicide which should not be entitled to benefit of clergy. And this distinction at a time when benefit of clergy was becoming so general that a crime as to which it was allowed, although a felony, ceased practically to be punishable by death, created a real distinction, leaving homicides which were denied benefit of clergy punishable according to the full rigor of the

[1] 1 Hale, P. C. 447; 4 Bl. Com. 194.

[2] Corone, 284 (3 Edw. III.).

[3] Hammond's note to 4 Bl. Com. 195; 3 Stephen's Hist. Cr. L. 38.

common law, and homicide to which it still attached punishable only slightly, as by branding of the thumb, fine, etc.[1]

§ 320. **Meaning of term.**— All definitions of murder make use of the term "malice aforethought" in distinguishing it from manslaughter,[2] but the words themselves give no real indication of the distinction intended to be made. Foster,[3] followed by Blackstone,[4] speaks of the words as indicating "that the fact hath been attended with such circumstances as are the ordinary symptoms of a wicked, depraved and malignant spirit," and some such language is occasionally found in statutes defining murder,[5] while it is constantly used in the definition of murder by the courts.[6]

§ 321. **Malice, in general.**—The term "malice" is sometimes discussed in connection with homicide as though it indicated something different from malice in other crimes, that is, a wrongful act intentionally done. But in fact nothing more seems to be intended by malice in this case than in any other.[7]

1 2 Bish. Cr. L. 623–625; 3 Stephen's Hist. Cr. L., ch. 26; S. v. Pike, 49 N. H. 399.

2 The following definition is from Coke: "Murder is when a man of sound memory and of the age of discretion unlawfully killeth, within any county of the realm, any reasonable creature *in rerum natura*, under the king's peace, with malice forethought, either expressed by the party or implied by law, so as the party wounded, or hurt, etc., die of the wound or hurt, etc., within a year and a day after the same:" 3 Inst. 47. Blackstone somewhat modernizes this, as follows: "Murder is . . . when a person of sound memory and discretion unlawfully killeth any reasonable creature in being and under the king's peace with malice aforethought, either express or implied:" 4 Com. 195. This definition is constantly quoted. See Darry v. P., 10 N. Y. 120, 149; S. v. Conley, 39 Me. 78, 87; P. v. Garbutt, 17 Mich. 9, 21; Fouts v. S., 8 Ohio St. 98, 109; McDougal v. S., 88 Ind. 24, 26; Schaffer v. S., 22 Neb. 557, 560; S. v. Crawford, 11 Kan. 32, 42; Garvey's Case, 7 Colo. 384, 387; U. S. v. Meagher, 37 Fed. R. 875.

3 Foster, 256, 257.

4 4 Bl. Com. 198.

5 For instance in Alabama, see Washington v. S., 60 Ala. 10.

6 C. v. Webster, 5 Cush. 295; S. v. Smith, 2 Strob. 77; McAdams v. S., 25 Ark. 405; S. v. Douglass, 28 W. Va. 297; P. v. McDonald, 2 Ida. 14; Vela v. S., 33 Tex. Ap. 322.

7 S. v. Schoenwald, 31 Mo. 147; Darry v. P., 10 N. Y. 120; Dozier v. S., 26 Ga. 156; Carson v. S., 80 Ga. 170; Lovett v. S., 30 Fla. 142. Malice in general has already been discussed in connection with the general subject of criminal intent: *Supra*, § 121. "Aforethought" implies only that the act is of purpose or design, in contradiction to an act resulting from accident or mischance: C. v. Webster, 5 Cush. 295. And see *infra*, § 329. As in other crimes, malice is inferred from an act causing death, which is not justifiable or

Malice in this connection does not mean personal hatred or revenge.[1]

§ **322. Express or implied.**— It is often said in older definitions of malice aforethought, which are also copied into statutes, that malice aforethought, distinguishing murder from manslaughter, may be either express or implied.[2] By express malice is meant an intent to take life or cause great bodily harm;[3] while implied malice indicates, according to Foster's definition,[4] "that the fact hath been attended with such circumstances as carry in them the plain indications of a heart regardless of social duty and fatally bent upon mischief." This definition of implied malice is, however, too general to be of any value, although it is still frequently used.[5] The real distinction between express and implied malice seems to be that in the former there are circumstances indicating an intent to kill or do great bodily harm; while in the latter, though there may be no apparent intent to kill, there is some other wicked intention sufficiently aggravated to make the offense murder. Such implied malice may consist in a general recklessness imperiling the lives of others;[6] or in the intent to commit a felony, no matter what it may be, and even though its tendency in itself is not to cause death; or in an intent to resist lawful arrest. The classes of acts constituting malice aforethought, express or implied, will be considered hereafter.[7]

excusable, or accompanied with such circumstances as to reduce it to manslaughter: U. S. v. Boyd, 45 Fed. R. 851; P. v. McDonald, 2 Ida. 14; S. v. Douglass, 28 W. Va. 297. And see *infra*, § 332.

[1] Reg. v. Tyler, 8 C. & P. 616; Reg. v. Mawgridge, J. Kel. 119; Rex v. Oneby, 2 Stra. 766; C. v. York, 9 Met. 93; S. v. Pike, 49 N. H. 399; Revel v. S., 26 Ga. 275; Brennan v. P., 15 Ill. 511; S. v. Decklotts, 19 Ia. 447; Warren v. S., 4 Cold. 130; McAdams v. S., 25 Ark. 405; U. S. v. Meagher, 37 Fed. R. 875; U. S. v. Ross, 1 Gall. 624.

[2] 4 Bl. Com. 199; 1 Hale, P. C. 451; 1 East, P. C. 222, § 9.

[3] Exp. Wray, 30 Miss. 673. If the intent be to do bodily harm, it must be serious bodily harm: Wellar v. P., 30 Mich. 16.

[4] Foster, 257.

[5] McDonel v. S., 90 Ind. 320; Harris v. S., 8 Tex. Ap. 90; Ellis v. S., 30 Tex. Ap. 601; Mayes v. P., 106 Ill. 306; Nye v. P., 35 Mich. 16; Carr v. S., 23 Neb. 749; Vollmer v. S., 24 Neb. 838.

[6] S. v. Smith, 2 Strob. 77. And see *infra*, § 325.

[7] In Texas express malice makes murder in the first degree, and for that reason the meaning of the term has been there fully discussed: McCoy v. S., 25 Tex. 33; Ake v. S., 30 Tex. 466; Moore v. S., 31 Tex. 572; Gaitan v. S., 11 Tex. Ap. 544; Bohannon v. S., 14 Tex. Ap. 271; Lewis v.

§ 323. Intent to kill the person killed or another.— Illustrations of cases where the intent is to kill the person killed are unnecessary. All such homicides, if criminal at all, will be murder unless there is such provocation as to reduce the case to manslaughter, as will be discussed hereafter.[1] But in determining the criminality of the act of killing it will be immaterial whether the intent was to kill the person killed, or whether the death of such person was the accidental or otherwise unintended result of the intent to kill some one else; the criminality of the act will be deemed the same.[2] In such cases a conviction for the homicide may be based on the ordinary allegation of striking, etc., with malice aforethought, it being immaterial that the malice was not towards the person injured. But where the offense is for shooting at another with intent to kill, it must be shown, as has already appeared, that there was a specific intent to kill the person named, and proof of injury to such person caused with the intent to kill some one else will not constitute the offense.[3] Of course, the criminal intent may be executed by another and still the person originating or participating in it may be guilty of murder in the act resulting.[4]

§ 324. Dueling; fighting by consent.— Killing in a duel is murder in the principals, seconds, and all others aiding or encouraging.[5] Indeed, if by any mutual agreement parties enter into a fight in a manner calculated to endanger life, death

S., 15 Tex. Ap. 647; Sherar v. S., 30 Tex. Ap. 349. The court must instruct as to the distinction: See *infra*, § 334.

[1] *Infra*, § 336.

[2] S. v. Gilman, 69 Me. 163; C. v. Breyessee, 160 Pa. St. 451; Wareham v. S., 25 Ohio St. 601; S. v. Renfrow, 111 Mo. 589; S. v. Raymond, 11 Nev. 98; Durham v. S., 70 Ga. 264; Wills v. S., 74 Ala. 21; S. v. Dugan, 1 Houst. Cr. C. 563; S. v. Fulkerson, Phill. 233; S. v. Smith, 2 Strob. 77; Clark v. S., 19 Tex. Ap. 495; Gore's Case, 9 Coke, 81. Where the offense indicates an intent to kill some one else, and that is relied on as showing the malice aforethought, it must appear that such person was, or might be supposed to be, at or near the spot at or about the time of the fatal blow: Reg. v. Cleary, 2 F. & F. 850.

[3] Morgan v. S., 13 Sm. & M. 242; Barcus v. S., 49 Miss. 17; Rex v. Holt, 7 C. & P. 518. And see *supra*, § 275.

[4] S. v. Green, 7 La. An. 518. But the participation must be in the malicious intent: Savage v. S., 18 Fla. 909; Frank v. S., 27 Ala. 37. And in general, on the question of combinations, see *supra*, §§ 195, 276.

[5] Reg. v. Young, 8 C. & P. 644; Reg. v. Cuddy, 1 C. & K. 210. All are joint principals if present: C. v. Boott, Thatch. Cr. 390; Moody v. C., 4 Met. (Ky.) 1; S. v. Dupont, 2 McCord, 334.

resulting therefrom will be murder.[1] Consent to fight on the part of the one killed will not prevent the homicide being murder.[2] There are statutes in many of the states in regard to dueling, and it seems that some of these relieve the death thus caused from its common-law consequences as murder and impose a special penalty;[3] they also provide a punishment for dueling even though no death results therefrom.[4] So punishment is provided for consenting to be a second in a duel,[5] and for sending or carrying a challenge to fight a duel.[6] It is also sometimes made criminal to leave the state in order to elude statutory provisions for the suppression of dueling.[7] Aside from statute, an indictment charging the fighting of a duel with pistols states no offense.[8] Under a statute punishing dueling it is sufficient to use the statutory language, naming the parties, and designating the place where the engagement was made and the fight was had without particulars.[9] In charging the offense of aiding and abetting in fighting a duel, it must be clearly alleged that the duel was fought.[10] In charging consent to a challenge under statute it is not necessary to set out the words of the challenge nor even the substance thereof.[11] There are sometimes constitutional provisions disqualifying from holding office on account of having been engaged in a duel, but there must be some legal proceedings in

[1] S. v. Christian, 66 Mo. 138. If the means used involve personal injury not of dangerous character, death resulting will be manslaughter: See *infra*, § 339.

[2] Rex v. Rice, 3 East, 581.

[3] P. v. Bartlett, 14 Cal. 651.

[4] S. v. Herriott, 1 McMull. 126; S. v. Taylor, 1 Treadw. Const. 107.

[5] Harris v. S., 58 Ga. 332.

[6] S. v. Gibbons, 4 N. J. 40; S. v. Perkins, 6 Blackf. 20; Ivey v. S., 12 Ala. 276; Smith v. S., 1 Stew. 506; S. v. Dupont, 2 McCord, 334; S. v. Strickland, 2 Nott & McC. 181; Cunningham v. S., 2 Spears, 246; S. v. Taylor, 3 Brev. 243; S. v. Farrier, 1 Hawks, 487; Moody v. C., 4 Met. (Ky.) 1; Heffren v. C., 4 Met. (Ky.) 5; C. v. Hart, 6 J. J. Marsh. 119; S. v. S. S., 1 Tyler (Vt.), 180. Under an indictment for unlawfully carrying a challenge to fight a duel, *scienter* must be proved: U. S. v. Shackelford, 3 Cranch, C. C. 178. To constitute a challenge a letter must be something more than an invitation or incitement to a challenge: Aulger v. P., 34 Ill. 486.

[7] S. v. Warren, 14 Tex. 406.

[8] C. v. Lambert, 9 Leigh, 603.

[9] C. v. Barrett, 108 Mass. 302.

[10] C. v. Dudley, 6 Leigh, 613.

[11] Brown v. C., 2 Va. Cas. 516; S. v. Farrier, 1 Hawks, 487. Although a challenge is set out by copy it may be helped with an averment that it was intended and understood as a challenge to fight with deadly weapons, although the fact does not appear from the language itself: C. v. Pope, 3 Dana, 418.

which the question can be determined before the right to hold office for violence of the provision is forfeited.[1]

§ 325. **General recklessness; acts dangerous to life.**— Where an act in itself unlawful is intentionally done for the purpose of killing or inflicting serious bodily injury and death ensues, it is murder at common law, although the intention is not directed toward any particular person.[2] So it is where death results from discharging a fire-arm in the direction of another with reckless indifference to consequences, if the act is likely to result in the death of the person toward whom the shot is fired,[3] or where it is caused by discharging a fire-arm into a crowd of persons with intent to kill some one, or with criminal recklessness;[4] so, where life is taken by setting a spring-gun to defend property other than the dwelling-house against trespass,[5] or otherwise attempting by unlawful violence to prevent a mere trespass or personal injury not threatening life or likely to cause great bodily harm.[6] So it is murder to cause the death of another by threats and show of violence, thereby recklessly and wilfully inducing him to do an act imminently dangerous to life.[7] In general, to cause death by wilfully doing an act calculated to endanger life or cause great bodily harm will be murder, although there is no specific intent to kill.[8] But if the intention, though unlawful, was not

[1] C. v. Jones, 10 Bush, 725. But under a Virginia statute there may be removal from office by *quo warranto* without conviction in a criminal prosecution: Royall v. Thomas, 28 Grat. 130.

[2] Mayes v. P., 106 Ill. 306. And see Howard v. S., 25 Tex. Ap. 686.

[3] Conn v. P., 116 Ill. 458. It is not necessary in order that this be murder that it be in the commission of some unlawful act: Pool v. S., 87 Ga. 526.

[4] Dunaway v. P., 110 Ill. 333; S. v. Edwards, 71 Mo. 312; Aiken v. S., 10 Tex. Ap. 610; Golliher v. C., 2 Duv. 163; Washington v. S., 60 Ala. 10.

[5] Simpson v. S., 59 Ala. 1; S. v. Barr, 11 Wash. 481. Further as to injury from spring-gun, see *supra*, § 142.

[6] Harrison v. S., 24 Ala. 67; S. v. Shippey, 10 Minn. 223; S. v. Smith, 3 Dev. & B. 117; S. v. McDonald, 4 Jones, 19; S. v. Brandon, 8 Jones, 463; Lyon v. S., 22 Ga. 399; S. v. Ferguson, 2 Hill, 619.

[7] Adams v. P., 109 Ill. 444.

[8] Boyle v. S., 57 Wis. 472. As by running over a child: Lee v. S., 1 Coldw. 62. Or by omitting to provide for a child where such omission is likely to cause death: Lewis v. S., 72 Ga. 164. Or by using means dangerous to life in attempting to procure an abortion: Peoples v. C., 87 Ky. 487; S. v. Moore, 25 Ia. 128. (Further as to homicide in attempting to procure an abortion, see *infra*, § 327.) Or by ordering a seaman who is in a state of debility so that he cannot safely go aloft to do so, compelling

to cause death or great bodily injury, and death accidentally or unexpectedly resulted, the offense is not murder but manslaughter. The negligence or unlawfulness may be sufficient to make the act criminal, although not sufficient to show malice aforethought.[1]

§ 326. **In the attempt to commit a felony.**— Design to kill is not necessary to constitute malice aforethought,[2] except as may be specially provided by statute.[3] The state of mind involved in the attempt to commit a felony constitutes malice aforethought (implied); so that death resulting, although entirely unintended, will be murder.[4] Thus, if persons conspire to commit a felony, death resulting will be murder in all, although it happened beside the original design.[5] But if homicide is committed as a preliminary to the perpetration of the felony, it is a homicide of express malice.[6] So it is if the felony is one such as mayhem, which in itself involves great bodily harm.[7] In each of these cases the offense will not be of the lower degree of murder provided for by statute, where the death results from the attempt to commit a felony, but of the degree involved in the intentional killing or causing great bodily injury.[8] But to constitute murder by killing in the execution of a felony it is necessary that the death and the felonious action from which the necessary implied malice is derived have

him with brutal malignity to obey so that death results: U. S. v. Freeman, 4 Mason, 505. Or by beating another in a cruel and inhuman manner: Duebbe v. S., 1 Tex. Ap. 159; especially a child: Powell v. S., 67 Miss. 119; or a person in feeble health with knowledge of his condition: C. v. Fox, 7 Gray, 585; S. v. O'Brien, 81 Ia. 88. Intent to kill is not essential in such cases: Adams v. P., 109 Ill. 444; S. v. Walker, 37 La. An. 560; Warren v. S., 4 Coldw. 130; Scott v. S., 37 Ala. 117; Howard v. S., 34 Ark. 433; Boyle v. S., 57 Wis. 472.

[1] Pool v. S., 87 Ga. 526; C. v. Thompson, 6 Mass. 134; Errington's Case, 2 Lewin, 217; Ann v. S., 11 Humph. 158. And further as to cases of unlawful intent, not felonious, and negligence, see manslaughter, *infra*, §§ 347, 349.

[2] S. v. Alexander, 30 S. C. 74; Brassfield v. S., 55 Ark. 556; Sweeney v. S., 35 Ark. 585; P. v. Wilson, 145 N. Y. 628.

[3] Fouts v. S., 8 Ohio St. 98; Robbins v. S., 8 Ohio St. 131; Jones v. S., 51 Ohio St. 331; S. v. Young, 55 Kan. 349.

[4] Keefe v. P., 40 N. Y. 348; Terrill v. S., 74 Wis. 278; T. v. McAndrews, 3 Mont. 158.

[5] S. v. Shelledy, 8 Ia. 477; P. v. Olsen, 80 Cal. 122; Smith v. P., 1 Colo. 121.

[6] S. v. Worrell, 25 Mo. 205.

[7] Foster v. P., 50 N. Y. 598.

[8] As to homicide caused in the attempt to perpetrate any of the principal felonies, it is usually made murder in the first degree: See *infra*.

at least some intimate relation and close connection, so that the danger to life is naturally consequent upon the felony committed.[1] The felony attempted must be other than that involved in the act of violence itself,[2] and must be alleged.[3]

§ 327. **Attempt to procure abortion.**— An illustration of the difference as to whether the intent is felonious or not in determining whether a consequent death unintended is murder or manslaughter is found in the cases of attempting to procure an abortion. At common law such attempt is not felonious, and therefore death resulting is manslaughter, not murder.[4]

§ 328. **In resisting lawful arrest.**— Death resulting from resistance to lawful arrest will be murder,[5] and it is immaterial whether the person arrested is guilty of the crime charged or not.[6] To make the crime murder it is not necessary that the warrant be strictly legal if it be within the jurisdiction of the magistrate issuing it.[7] Nor is it necessary that the appointment of the officer be shown by record evidence; it is sufficient that it appear that he was acting as officer, which fact was generally known.[8] It will equally be murder to kill a private

[1] Pliemling v. S., 46 Wis. 516; Reg. v. Serne, 16 Cox, 311.

[2] S. v. Downs, 91 Mo. 19; S. v. Sloan, 47 Mo. 604.

[3] Titus v. S., 49 N. J. 36.

[4] Reg. v. Fretwell, 9 Cox, 152; Smith v. S., 33 Me. 48; Evans v. P., 49 N. Y. 86; S. v. Barker, 28 Ohio St. 583. But by statute death thus caused is sometimes made murder: S. v. McNab, 20 N. H. 160. If the means used are such as are calculated to endanger life, malice aforethought will be implied from the act unlawfully and unjustifiably committed: S. v. Moore, 25 Ia. 128; Peoples v. C., 87 Ky. 487. But to make the death criminal it must appear that the act was unnecessary: Willey v. S., 46 Ind. 363; S. v. Fitzporter, 93 Mo. 390. If causing death by an attempted abortion is made a distinct offense, punishable in a different manner from that of murder or manslaughter, it must be charged under the special statute: C. v. Railing, 113 Pa. St. 37.

[5] Dilger v. C., 88 Ky. 550; S. v. Green, 66 Mo. 631; Simmerman v. S., 16 Neb. 615; Minniard v. C., 87 Ky. 213; Washington v. S., 1 Tex. Ap. 647; Reg. v. Porter, 12 Cox, 444. So, if in making such resistance a third person is accidentally killed it is murder: Angell v. S., 36 Tex. 542. So, it is murder to kill an officer in attempting to escape: Wilson v. S., 11 Lea, 310. So, it is murder to kill an officer seeking to recapture an escaped convict: Wallace v. S., 20 Tex. Ap. 360. It is immaterial who fires the first shot, if the person seeking to make the arrest is acting within the scope of his duties: Tolbert v. S., 71 Miss. 179.

[6] Roten v. S., 31 Fla. 514.

[7] Boyd v. S., 17 Ga. 194. Informality in the warrant should be taken advantage of by proper proceeding and not by a murderous assault with the purpose of effecting escape: Reg. v. Allen, 17 L. T. 222.

[8] Martin v. S., 89 Ala. 115; Weather-

person making arrest where the circumstances authorize an arrest by such person.[1] Also, it is murder to kill an officer acting without warrant under circumstances where a warrant is not required.[2] As will hereafter be seen,[3] death caused in resisting unlawful arrest, although not justifiable, is manslaughter and not murder. Therefore, if the person being arrested does not know, and has no reason to know, that the arrest is lawful, death caused by him in resistance will be only manslaughter.[4] But if the person arrested have reason to believe that the person attempting to make the arrest is an officer, it will be murder if he takes life in resistance although the officer does not in terms state his official character.[5] The reason for making homicide, in resisting unlawful arrest, manslaughter, is that the unlawful arrest is deemed a provocation.[6] Therefore, if the killing is with malice, irrespective of the provocation of illegal arrest, it is murder and not manslaughter.[7] In charging the murder of an officer while making an arrest it is not necessary to allege that he was an officer, nor the fact of the arrest and its legality, but the charge may be made as of the murder of a private citizen.[8] Whether the arrest is lawful or not is not a question wholly for the jury, but is a mixed question of law and fact.[9]

ford v. S., 31 Tex. Ap. 530; Rex v. Gordon, 1 East, P. C. 352. That the deceased was an officer *de facto* is sufficient: S. v. Zeibart, 40 Ia. 169; S. v. McMahan, 103 N. C. 379.

[1] Snelling v. S., 87 Ga. 50; S. v. Mowry, 37 Kan. 369.

[2] Ballard v. S., 43 Ohio St. 340; Rex v. Curran, 3 C. & P. 397; Rex v. Hems, 7 C. & P. 312; Reg. v. Hagan, 8 C. & P. 167; Rex v. Ford, Russ. & Ry. 329; Rex v. Ball, 1 Moody, 330.

[3] *Infra*, § 340.

[4] Croom v. S., 85 Ga. 718; Mockabee v. C., 78 Ky. 380; Fleetwood v. C., 80 Ky. 1; Rex v. Gordon, 1 East, P. C. 315.

[5] P. v. Pool, 27 Cal. 572; Rex v. Woolmer, 1 Moody, 334. One who attempts to escape has no right to express information that the person seeking to arrest him is an officer: Thomas v. S., 91 Ga. 204; S. v. Mowry, 37 Kan. 369.

[6] *Infra*, § 340.

[7] Rafferty v. P., 72 Ill. 37; P. v. Brown, 59 Cal. 345; Muscoe v. C., 86 Va. 443; C. v. Drew, 4 Mass. 391; Roberts v. S., 14 Mo. 138; S. v. Johnson, 76 Mo. 121; S. v. Oliver, 2 Houst. 58; Miller v. S., 32 Tex. Ap. 319. So where defendant had for some time been in custody without knowledge of any informality in the warrant, *held*, that homicide in the attempted escape was murder, notwithstanding such defect: Graham v. S., 29 Tex. Ap. 31; Reg. v. Allen, 17 L. T. 222.

[8] S. v. Roberts, 15 Mo. 28.

[9] Pritchett v. S., 92 Ga. 65; Muscoe v. C., 86 Va. 443.

§ 329. **"Aforethought;" deliberation; premeditation.**— The term "aforethought," as applied to the malice necessary to constitute murder, does not imply anything further than an intentional act as distinguished from an act done on sudden provocation in heat of passion.[1] It is not necessary that the intent shall have been entertained for any length of time.[2] But the malice must exist at the time of the killing; a predetermination to kill will not be sufficient where the killing is not the result of such predetermination, but of some other intent not in itself constituting malice.[3] What is such deliberation and premeditation as to constitute murder in the first degree will be considered hereafter.[4]

§ 330. **Evidence of malice.**— Malice may be proven by circumstances, and this even applies to express malice, which involves the intent to kill or do great bodily harm.[5] From circumstances indicating a manifest disregard of human life and a wicked, depraved and malignant spirit, malice may be inferred.[6] Previous threats are evidence of malice.[7] Previous ill-treatment of a child or an inferior will tend to show malice in a subsequent act of ill-treatment causing death of such person.[8] So declarations after the act may tend to show express malice.[9] But proof of threats and previous preparation should

[1] C. v. York, 9 Met. 93.

[2] P. v. Clark, 7 N. Y. 385; S. v. McDonnell, 32 Vt. 491; S. v. Decklotts, 19 Ia. 447; Peri v. P., 65 Ill. 17; Spies v. P., 122 Ill. 1; U. S. v. Cornell, 2 Mason, 60; Jones v. S., 29 Ga. 594; McQueen v. S., 103 Ala. 12; Green v. S., 13 Mo. 382; C. v. Drum, 58 Pa. St. 9; Lewis v. S., 15 Tex. Ap. 647; McKenzie v. S., 26 Ark. 334; McAdams v. S., 25 Ark. 405. When it is said that the homicide must be deliberate, it is only meant that it must be intentional and malicious: Nichols v. C., 11 Bush, 575. It is sufficient that the malicious intent was formed at the moment of striking the fatal blow: McDaniel v. C., 77 Va. 281; Brown v. C., 90 Va. 671; Cook v. S., 77 Ga. 96.

[3] Domingus v. S., 94 Ala. 9; Clements v. S., 50 Ala. 117; McMillan v. S., 35 Ga. 54; S. v. Anderson, 2 Overt. 6; Bristow v. C., 15 Grat. 634; Brooks v. S., 90 Ind. 428.

[4] *Infra*, § 358.

[5] Gomez v. S., 15 Tex. Ap. 327; Sharpe v. S., 17 Tex. Ap. 486; Farrer v. S., 42 Tex. 265; Resp. v. Langcake, 1 Yeates, 415. It may appear otherwise than by verbal declarations, as, by lying in wait, antecedent menaces, the character of the act done, etc.: Singleton v. S., 1 Tex. Ap. 501.

[6] Adams v. P., 109 Ill. 444; S. v. O'Hara, 92 Mo. 59; S. v. Smith, 2 Strob. 77.

[7] Moon v. S., 68 Ga. 687; Nichols v. C., 11 Bush, 575; Anderson v. S., 15 Tex. Ap. 447; T. v. Egan, 3 Dak. 119.

[8] Burnett v. S., 14 Lea, 439; Williams v. S., 64 Md. 384; S. v. Harris, 63 N. C. 1.

[9] Lewis v. S., 29 Tex. Ap. 201.

be such as to show that they were made in contemplation of a homicide without justification or excuse. If they indicate intention and preparation to resist an expected attack, they will not be proof of malice.[1] Where deliberate malice is once ascertained, its continuance down to the perpetration of a homicide must be presumed unless there is evidence to repel it and show an abandonment of the wicked purpose.[2] But if a subsequent reconciliation, followed by fresh provocation, is proved, the law will refer the motive of the slayer to the recent provocation unless special circumstances forbid such presumption.[3] It is for the jury to say whether the killing was the result of previous malice or of a subsequent provocation or necessity.[4] So where there has been an antecedent provocation it may still appear from the circumstances that the killing was the result of malice aforethought and not of provocation.[5]

§ 331. Intoxication or insanity as affecting the question of malice.— The deliberate intent to kill not being necessary in murder (unless in the first degree), evidence of intoxication is not admissible for the purpose of reducing the offense from murder to manslaughter.[6] But while intoxication is not to be considered as showing want of malice, it may be shown in cases where defendant relies upon provocation as reducing the crime to manslaughter, as indicating that the homicide was the result of the provocation, and not in cold blood.[7]

§ 332. Whether malice presumed; use of deadly weapon. When the homicide is committed in such a manner and by such means that death or greatly bodily injury is the probable result, such facts will indicate malice aforethought.[8] The defend-

[1] Bolzer v. P., 129 Ill. 112. Proof of anticipation of an attack is therefore admissible on the part of defendant: Long v. S., 52 Miss. 23.

[2] S. v. Johnson, 1 Ired. 354; S. v. Tully, 4 Ired. 424.

[3] S. v. Barnwell, 80 N. C. 466; Cannon v. S., 57 Miss. 147.

[4] S. v. Tachanatah, 64 N. C. 614; Read v. C., 22 Grat. 924; McCoy v. S., 25 Tex. 33.

[5] S. v. Dillon, 74 Ia. 653; Johnson v. S., 30 Tex. 748. And, in general, as to provocation, see *infra*, § 342.

[6] S. v. Smith, 49 Conn. 376; P. v. Langton, 67 Cal. 427, 7 Am. Cr. R. 439 and note; Boyle v. S., 61 Wis. 440. But it is said that intoxication may be shown on the question whether a dangerous weapon was used with intent to do great bodily harm: Reg. v. Doherty, 16 Cox, 306.

[7] S. v. McCants, 1 Spears, 384; S. v. Johnson, 40 Conn. 136; S. v. Johnson, 41 Conn. 584; Wilkerson v. C., 88 Ky. 29; Bolzer v. P., 129 Ill. 112. See the whole question discussed, *supra*, § 162.

[8] C. v. Webster, 5 Cush. 295; Boatwright v. S., 89 Ga. 140. Malice is

ant will be presumed to have intended the natural consequences of his act.[1] The use of a dangerous or deadly weapon, in the absence of circumstances indicating provocation or excuse, indicates intent to kill, and therefore is evidence of malice aforethought.[2] What is meant by the cases just cited evidently is, that the use of a deadly weapon indicates an intention to take life or do great bodily injury. In many other cases it is said, in a general way, but evidently in the same sense, that the unlawful use of a deadly weapon is evidence of malice,[3] or gives

presumed where it does not appear that there was any apprehension of great bodily harm, or such provocation as to cause heat of blood: Peri v. P., 65 Ill. 17; Boatwright v. S., 89 Ga. 140. The fact that the injured party exposed himself will not tend to show that the wound was not, in itself, dangerous: S. v. Stokely, 16 Minn. 282.

[1] Doherty v. S., 84 Wis. 152; U. S. v. Boyd, 45 Fed. R. 851. Thus, the age, condition and strength of the person assailed may be considered as well as the nature of the weapon used and the blow inflicted: C. v. Fox, 7 Gray, 585; Murphy v. P., 9 Colo. 435. Even if the fact be that the deceased was in a feeble condition, so that a blow of less force would cause his death than would be required to take the life of a healthy man, this will not constitute a defense: S. v. Castello, 62 Ia. 404. Shooting at a person is dangerous, and where death ensues and the circumstances afford evidence of malice, the homicide is murder: S. v. Sisson, 3 Brev. 58. So where the death of a child resulted from giving it sufficient laudanum to kill it, the offense was held to be murder: S. v. Leak, Phill. 450. So in other cases where the circumstances indicate an intention to kill without excuse or provocation: Beltram v. S., 9 Tex. Ap. 280; S. v. Ah Lee, 8 Oreg. 214. Otherwise if an excuse for the killing appears: Petty v. S., 6 Baxt. 610. It is erroneous, however, where the act does not indicate an intent to kill, to instruct the jury that a person is liable for all possible consequences of his acts: P. v. Munn, 65 Cal. 211. If the killing is not the result of an act calculated to take life or cause great bodily harm, it will not indicate malice unless such intent otherwise appears: Wellar v. P., 30 Mich. 16; S. v. Shirley, 64 N. C. 610.

[2] Beauchamp v. S., 6 Blackf. 299; U. S. v. McGlue, 1 Curtis, 1; Oliver v. S., 17 Ala. 587; Hornsby v. S., 94 Ala. 55; Sullivan v. S., 102 Ala. 135; P. v. Wolf, 95 Mich. 625; Clifford v. S., 58 Wis. 477; Green v. S., 28 Miss. 687; State v. Gillick, 7 Ia. 287; S. v. Zeibart, 40 Ia. 169; S. v. Jones, 64 Ia. 349; S. v. Sullivan, 51 Ia. 142; S. v. Hockett, 70 Ia. 442; S. v. Hogue, 6 Jones, 381; Brown v. C., 90 Va. 671; S. v. Willis, 63 N. C. 26; Bivens v. S., 11 Ark. 455; McAdams v. S., 25 Ark. 405; U. S. v. Crow Dog, 3 Dak. 106; S. v. Des Champs, 42 La. An. 567. Under like circumstances, if death does not ensue the jury may infer that the assault was with intent to murder: S. v. Gilman, 69 Me. 163; Walker v. S., 8 Ind. 290; Chrisman v. S., 54 Ark. 283. And see *supra*, § 275.

[3] S. v. Ward, 5 Harr. 496; Walter v. P., 32 N. Y. 147; S. v. Hargett, 65 N. C. 669; Kriel v. C., 5 Bush, 362.

rise to a presumption of malice.[1] It has been said that this presumption from the use of a deadly weapon can only be overcome by evidence offered by defendant to show sufficient provocation.[2] But by the great weight of authority there is no such presumption in law, and the whole question of whether there is malice aforethought is for the jury, the evidence of the use of a deadly weapon being for their consideration as indicating malice in the absence of evidence of provocation or excuse.[3] It is not the intention to use a deadly weapon, but the intention to kill, of which such use is evidence, that indicates murder.[4] By statute the use of a deadly weapon is sometimes made evidence of malice.[5] When the question is as to whether the weapon was deadly or whether it was used in a deadly man-

[1] C. v. Drum, 58 Pa. St. 9; S. v. Talmage, 107 Mo. 543; S. v. Evans, 65 Mo. 574; S. v. Hays, 23 Mo. 287; S. v. Levelle, 34 S. C. 120; Moon v. S., 68 Ga. 687. An instruction that malice is implied from the unlawful and intentional use of a deadly weapon is not erroneous where there is no evidence that the homicide was accidental or under provocation: S. v. Rainsbarger, 71 Ia. 746. But malice is not proved by such evidence; the fact merely raises a presumption of malice subject to be rebutted: S. v. Townsend, 66 Ia. 741. It has also been said that where the evidence shows a deliberate killing, without provocation or excuse, murder in the first degree may be presumed: P. v. Wolf, 95 Mich. 625; S. v. Martin, 124 Mo. 514; S. v. Mahn, 25 Kan. 182.

[2] Kilpatrick v. C., 31 Pa. St. 198.

[3] Farris v. C., 14 Bush, 362; Hornsby v. S., 94 Ala. 55; Tesney v. S., 77 Ala. 33; Cross v. S., 68 Ala. 476; Eiland v. S., 52 Ala. 322; S. v. McKinzie, 102 Mo. 620; Hawthorne v. S., 58 Miss. 778; S. v. McDonell, 32 Vt. 491; Madden v. S., 1 Kan. 340; C. v. Hawkins, 3 Gray, 463. It is erroneous to instruct the jury that the presumption of malice arises from the fact of using a deadly weapon: Erwin v. S., 29 Ohio St. 186; Smith v. C., 1 Duv. 224; S. v. Newton, 4 Nev. 410. While the use of a deadly weapon, not in self-defense, is evidence of malice, it does not follow that every homicide thus committed is murder: Dunnellan v. C., 7 Bush, 676; Hill v. S., 41 Ga. 484. For it may appear that there was such provocation as to reduce the murder to manslaughter: Murphy v. S., 31 Ind. 511; Miller v. S., 37 Ind. 432; P. v. Curtis, 52 Mich. 616; S. v. Hoyt, 13 Minn. 132. Indeed, an intent to kill is not necessarily presumed from the use of a deadly weapon: Anderson v. S., 3 Heisk. 86; Floyd v. S., 3 Heisk. 342; Miller v. S., 37 Ind. 432; Hurd v. P., 25 Mich. 405.

[4] Palmore v. S., 29 Ark. 248; P. v. Crowey, 56 Cal. 33.

[5] As in Texas, where a homicide committed with a bowie-knife or dagger is made murder: Isaacs v. S., 25 Tex. 174. And such statute is constitutional: Cockrum v. S., 24 Tex. 394. But the fact that the weapon with which the homicide was committed was carried in violation of the law in regard to carrying concealed weapons will not in itself imply malice aforethought: Alfred v. S., 33 Ga. 303.

ner, it is for the jury.[1] But where the weapon is one necessarily dangerous and it is used in a deadly manner, the court may, as matter of law, declare its nature.[2] Thus, an ax may be a deadly weapon.[3] It cannot be said as matter of law that a pocket-knife is not a deadly weapon.[4] An instrument may or may not be a deadly weapon, depending upon the manner in which it is used;[5] so held as to a stick of wood.[6] A deadly weapon is not one a blow from which would ordinarily produce death, but one from which, as used, death would probably result;[7] an instrument designed for offensive and defensive purposes, by means of destruction of life or infliction of bodily injury.[8] Where death was caused by the use by a school-boy of a twenty-two calibre pistol, held, that it was not error to instruct the jury on the theory that such instrument was a deadly weapon.[9] The question as to what is a deadly weapon is also considered under the head of aggravated assaults.[10]

§ 333. **Presumption of malice from killing.**—In some cases it has been said that malice is presumed from evidence of intentional killing, the burden to overcome this presumption being on defendant.[11] In other cases it is said that this presumption arises in the absence of any evidence indicating that the

[1] S. v. Levigne, 17 Nev. 435; S. v. Olds, 18 Oreg. 440.

[2] S. v. Levigne, 17 Nev. 435; S. v. Craton, 6 Ired. 164. See *supra*, 265.

[3] S. v. Ostrander, 18 Ia. 435; Mask v. S., 36 Miss. 77.

[4] Sylvester v. S., 71 Ala. 17. If so used as to cause death it is deadly: Webb v. S., 100 Ala. 47. The use of a pocket-knife may be considered as indicating malice aforethought: Gatlin v. S., 5 Tex. Ap. 531.

[5] If not in nature deadly, the use of the weapon cannot be held to indicate an intent to kill unless by reason of the manner of its use: Nichols v. S., 24 Tex. Ap. 137.

[6] S. v. Brown, 67 Ia. 289; Kelly v. S., 68 Miss. 343. So as to a large bottle thrown at another: Weeks v. S., 79 Ga. 36. A pin is a deadly weapon when pushed down an infant's throat in a manner likely to cause death: S. v. Norwood, 115 N. C. 789.

[7] Sylvester v. S., 72 Ala. 201.

[8] C. v. Branham, 8 Bush, 387.

[9] S. v. Sterrett, 80 Ia. 609.

[10] See *supra*, § 257.

[11] C. v. York, 9 Met. 93; C. v. Webster, 5 Cush. 295; Dejarnette v. C., 75 Va. 867; S. v. Norwood, 115 N. C. 789; S. v. Payne, 10 Wash. 545; S. v. Knight, 43 Me. 11. And this is the English rule: Rex v. Oneby, 2 Stra. 766; Rex v. Greenacre, 8 C. & P. 35; Reg. v. Kirkham, 8 C. & P. 115; 4 Bl. Com. 201. Homicide is presumed by law to be murder in the second degree until circumstances of justification, excuse, or mitigation are shown: S. v. Miller, 9 Houst. 564; Myers v. C., 90 Va. 705; Davis v. S., 25 Ohio St. 369; Clements v. S., 50 Ala. 117.

killing was justifiable, excusable, or under provocation,[1] and it devolves upon the defendant to repel the presumption.[2] But this rule is properly qualified, so as to give defendant the benefit of any justification, excuse, or mitigation appearing from the evidence for the prosecution as well as from the evidence introduced on his behalf.[3] Where, however, all the circumstances of the transaction are disclosed in evidence, there is no presumption, but the question is for the jury upon the evidence.[4] It is also said that where there is proof of killing, the burden is upon defendant to show justification, excuse, or mitigation;[5] and, in accordance with the same theory, it is held that the mitigation must be proven by a preponderance of evidence, and that it is not enough if the evidence merely raises a reasonable doubt of guilt.[6] But in other cases this whole doctrine of presumption, with the resulting rule as to burden of proof and amount of evidence to show mitigation, is repudiated, and the more reasonable and logical rule is announced that the

[1] O'Mara v. C., 75 Pa. St. 424; C. v. Drew, 4 Mass. 391; Murphy v. P., 37 Ill. 447; Upstone v. P., 109 Ill. 169; S. v. Lautenschlager, 22 Minn. 514; S. v. Brown, 41 Minn. 319; Clarke v. S., 35 Ga. 75; Wilson v. S., 69 Ga. 224; Mitchell v. S., 5 Yerg. 340; S. v. Johnson, 3 Jones, 266; Green v. S., 28 Miss. 687; Hague v. S., 34 Miss. 616; S. v. Town, Wright, 75; Davis v. S., 25 Ohio St. 369; Clements v. S., 50 Ala. 117; Brown v. S., 4 Tex. Ap. 275; Schlencker v. S., 9 Neb. 300.

[2] P. v. March, 6 Cal. 543; Williams v. S., 6 Neb. 334; Milton v. S., 6 Neb. 136.

[3] P. v. Elliott, 80 Cal. 296; Hawthorne v. S., 58 Miss. 778; Gladden v. S., 13 Fla. 623; Jordan v. S., 79 Ala. 9; Dixon v. S., 13 Fla. 636; Alexander v. S., 17 Tex. Ap. 614; Robinson v. S., 16 Tex. Ap. 347; Turner v. S., 16 Tex. Ap. 378; U. S. v. Armstrong, 2 Curt. 446; Conner v. S., 4 Yerg. 136; S. v. Dugan, 1 Houst. Cr. C. 563.

[4] C. v. Hawkins, 3 Gray, 463; P. v. Potter, 5 Mich. 1; S. v. Alexander, 30 S. C. 74; S. v. Ariel, 38 S. C. 221; S. v. Coleman, 6 S. C. 185; Hampton v. S., 45 Ala. 82; Dukes v. S., 14 Fla. 499; Vollmer v. S., 24 Neb. 838; S. v. Wright, 46 La. An. 1403. By statute in Florida the rule formerly recognized as to presumption from the fact of killing is changed and proof of malice must be made by the state: Adams v. S., 28 Fla. 511. The charge that malice is implied unless justification or mitigation appears from the evidence is erroneous, as infringing upon the doctrine of reasonable doubt: Morgan v. S., 16 Tex. Ap. 593; Bryant v. S., 7 Baxt. 67; Smith v. P., 142 Ill. 117.

[5] Vann v. S., 83 Ga. 44; Hill v. C., 2 Grat. 594; S. v. Brittain, 89 N. C. 481; S. v. Whitson, 111 N. C. 695; S. v. Hobbs, 37 W. Va. 812; S. v. Evans, 124 Mo. 397; T. v. McAndrews, 3 Mont. 158; S. v. Bonds, 2 Nev. 265; S. v. Briscoe, 30 La. An., pt. I, 433; Rex v. Greenacre, 8 C. & P. 35; 4 Bl. Com. 201.

[6] C. v. York, 9 Met. 93; S. v. Cox, 110 N. C. 503; S. v. Smith, 77 N. C. 488; S. v. Haywood, Phill. 376; S. v. Byers, 100 N. C. 512.

burden of proof is throughout upon the prosecution; and if upon the evidence a reasonable doubt arises as to whether the homicide was upon malice aforethought, the defendant is entitled to the doubt.[1]

§ 334. Instructions as to malice.— Malice aforethought being an essential, therefore, in murder, it has been held in Texas that it must be explained to the jury by the instructions, and that a failure to instruct in that respect will constitute error even though no instruction on the subject were asked.[2] But in other jurisdictions there seems to be no such specific rule, and the sufficiency of the instructions in this respect will depend upon the nature of the case.[3] In Texas it is also required that the distinction between express and implied malice be explained.[4]

V. MANSLAUGHTER.

§ 335. How distinguished.— From the explanation already given of what constitutes non-criminal homicide, either justifiable or excusable, on the one hand, and murder, that is, killing with malice aforethought, on the other, the general scope of the crime of manslaughter, which includes all criminal homicides not amounting to murder, is quite definitely indicated. Cases of manslaughter, however, fall into classes having different characteristics. They may be, 1st, cases in which it appears that the intent was to take life or do great bodily harm, and which would therefore be murder but for some mitigating circumstance; 2d, cases where death unintentionally

[1] Stokes v. P., 53 N. Y. 164; P. v. Fish, 125 N. Y. 136; S. v. Patterson, 45 Vt. 308; S. v. Hopkins, 15 S. C. 153; S. v. Jones, 29 S. C. 201; P. v. Powell, 87 Cal. 348; P. v. Ah Gee Yung, 86 Cal. 144; P. v. Bushton, 80 Cal. 160 (overruling P. v. Knapp, 71 Cal. 1); Kent v. P., 8 Colo. 563; Perry v. S., 44 Tex. 473; Murray v. S., 1 Tex. Ap. 417; S. v. Trivas, 32 La. An. 1086; S. v. Swayze, 32 La. An., pt. II, 1323. If the facts are not in controversy the question is for the court, otherwise for the jury: S. v. Hildreth, 9 Ired. 429; T. v. Gay, 2 Dak. 125.

[2] Holmes v. S., 11 Tex. Ap. 223; Babb v. S., 12 Tex. Ap. 491; Hayes v. S., 14 Tex. Ap. 330. And this is not cured by an instruction as to the distinction between express and implied malice: Ainsworth v. S., 29 Tex. Ap. 599; Callahan v. S., 30 Tex. Ap. 275; Moody v. S., 30 Tex. Ap. 422.

[3] Kennedy v. P., 40 Ill. 488; Peri v. P., 65 Ill. 17; S. v. Forney, 24 La. An. 191; Holley v. S., 75 Ala. 14.

[4] Jones v. S., 5 Tex. Ap. 397; Pickett v. S., 12 Tex. Ap. 86.

results from doing an unlawful act not constituting a felony, the unlawfulness of the act separating them from cases of accidental homicide, and the nature of the act as less heinous than that of a felony, making them less than murder; and 3d, cases of negligence where, although there was no intent to kill, there was the doing or omission of an act, which doing or omission, though not in itself wrongful, was attended with circumstances endangering life. Blackstone designates the first of these classes as voluntary and the last two as involuntary manslaughter.[1] All these classes are characterized on the one hand by the presence of some wrong, and on the other by absence of malice aforethought, so that a short definition of manslaughter would be criminal homicide without malice aforethought.[2] This definition is sometimes embodied in statutes, in which case it is necessary to resort to the common law to determine what killings are and what are not within the definition.[3] Manslaughter is not a degree of murder, but a distinct crime, included, however, in the crime of murder.[4]

§ **336. Intentional killing, when manslaughter.**— Intent to kill or do great bodily harm does not necessarily make homicide resulting murder. If it appears that by reason of passion, caused by what is deemed an adequate provocation (to be hereafter explained), the homicide is without malice aforethought, it is manslaughter only.[5] In such case "the law pays that regard to human frailty as not to put a hasty and a deliberate act upon the same footing with regard to guilt."[6] Intentional homicide may be murder in either degree (as will be hereafter explained), or it may be manslaughter; and the

[1] 4 Bl. Com. 191. As to voluntary and involuntary, see, also, *infra*, § 368.

[2] Rex v. Taylor, 2 Lewin, 215.

[3] Hornsby v. S., 94 Ala. 55; S. v. Shelledy, 8 Ia. 477; S. v. Moore, 25 Ia. 128; S. v. Abarr, 39 Ia. 185; S. v. Hockett, 70 Ia. 442.

[4] S. v. White, 45 Ia. 325. As to assault to commit manslaughter, see *supra*, § 278.

[5] P. v. Freel, 48 Cal. 436; P. v. Doyell, 48 Cal. 85; P. v. Kernaghan, 72 Cal. 609; C. v. Drum, 58 Pa. St. 9; Brown v. C., 86 Va. 466; Hoss v. S., 18 Ind. 349; Dennison v. S., 13 Ind. 510; Murphy v. S., 31 Ind. 511; Exp. Moore, 30 Ind. 197; S. v. Cooper, 71 Mo. 436; Erwin v. S., 29 Ohio St. 186; Burden v. P., 26 Mich. 162; S. v. Decklotts, 19 Ia. 447; S. v. Spangler, 40 Ia. 365; Quarles v. S., 1 Sneed, 407; Perry v. S., 43 Ala. 21; Hinton v. S., 24 Tex. Ap. 454; S. v. Anderson, 1 Houst. Cr. C. 38.

[6] 4 Bl. Com. 191; P. v. Freel, 48 Cal. 436; Preston v. S., 25 Miss. 383. In such case the law imputes the homicide to inherent frailty, instead of malice or formed design: Smith v. S., 83 Ala. 26.

difference in such case between murder in the second degree and manslaughter is not in the intention with which the injury is inflicted, but in the fact that in manslaughter the act is done under heat of blood upon provocation.[1] If done under such circumstances, although not justifiable or excusable, the homicide is deemed to be without malice and therefore manslaughter.[2]

§ **337. Provocation.**—In general, provocation consists in circumstances of such nature as are calculated to produce and do produce such excitement and passion as might obscure the reason of an ordinary man, and render him liable to do the act which causes the homicide.[3] Some cases seem to make it simply a question whether the circumstances would, in a reasonable person, create heat of blood or passion;[4] but as to some particular classes of cases the law has determined what is and what is not a sufficient provocation.

§ **338. What sufficient.**— Mere words or gestures, no matter how insulting, opprobrious, or abusive, are not sufficient to reduce an intentional killing to manslaughter.[5] Mere trespass

[1] S. v. Spangler, 40 Ia. 365; S. v. Decklotts, 19 Ia. 447; S. v. Ellis, 74 Mo. 207; S. v. Hoyt, 13 Minn. 132.

[2] Nye v. P.,35 Mich. 16. The provocation reduces the homicide to manslaughter, but does not render it justifiable or excusable: S. v. Vance, 17 Ia. 138.

[3] Maher v. P., 10 Mich. 212; S. v. Hoyt, 13 Minn. 132; Seals v. S., 3 Baxt. 459; S. v. Rhodes, 1 Houst. Cr. C. 476. The passion contemplated is some emotion of the mind, such as anger, rage, sudden resentment, or terror rendering it incapable of cool reflection: Boyett v. S., 2 Tex. Ap. 93. Provocation does not excuse or justify, it only mitigates: S. v. Murphy, 61 Me. 56. But a charge to such effect may be misleading as excluding self-defense: Smith v. S., 68 Ala. 424.

[4] Maher v. P., 10 Mich. 212; Seals v. S., 3 Baxt. 495; S. v. Zellers, 7 N. J. 220; Murray v. S., 85 Ga. 378. Thus, abuse of and assault upon a married daughter by her husband may constitute sufficient provocation to mitigate the killing of the husband by the father: Campbell v. C., 88 Ky. 402. One who, on seeing his friend shot down, kills the slayer in sudden passion caused thereby, is guilty of manslaughter only: Moore v. S., 26 Tex. Ap. 322. But the killing of a friend will not be sufficient provocation if not done in defendant's presence: S. v. Gut, 13 Minn. 341. The fact that the deceased was drunk when he uttered insulting words may be considered in determining whether such words would palliate an assault upon him by the other party: Harris v. S., 34 Ark. 469.

[5] Steffy v. P., 130 Ill. 98; S. v. Levelle, 34 S. C. 120; S. v. McNeill, 92 N. C. 812; S. v. Carter, 76 N. C. 20; Jackson v. S., 77 Ala. 18; Exp. Brown, 65 Ala. 446; Smith v. S., 103 Ala. 4; Johnson v. S., 102 Ala. 1; P. v. Turley, 50 Cal. 469; P. v.

to property will not be sufficient.[1] The provocation should be sudden and sufficiently great, that is, calculated to exasperate, both in its character and in respect to the person against whom it is directed.[2] In general, a blow or other personal violence is sufficient.[3] But circumstances may affect the question by indicating whether or not the blow was such as would arouse uncontrollable passion in an ordinary person.[4] The sufficiency

Murback, 64 Cal. 369; P. v. Biggins, 65 Cal. 564; P. v. Butler, 8 Cal. 435; Malone v. S., 49 Ga. 210; Bird v. S., 55 Ga. 317; Ross v. S., 59 Ga. 248; Hawkins v. S., 25 Ga. 207; Fry v. S., 81 Ga. 645; S. v. Hockett, 70 Ia. 442; S. v. Berkley, 109 Mo. 665; S. v. Martin, 124 Mo. 514; S. v. Buchanan, 1 Houst. Cr. C. 79; S. v. Draper, 1 Houst. Cr. C. 531; Rapp v. C., 14 B. Mon. 614; Wall v. S., 18 Tex. 682; S. v. Fuentes, 5 La. An. 427; S. v. Leonard, 6 La. An. 420. There must be personal violence or injury and not mere words or gestures: Beauchamp v. S., 6 Blackf. 299; Reg. v. Welsh, 11 Cox, 336; Rex v. Oneby, 2 Stra. 766. By statute in Georgia threats are not sufficient: Jackson v. S., 45 Ga. 198; Freeman v. S., 70 Ga. 736. Disgraceful conduct on the part of a wife, though long continued, will not constitute such provocation as to reduce the act of the husband in killing her to manslaughter: Murphy v. P., 9 Colo. 435.

[1] S. v. Zellers, 7 N. J. 220; S. v. Buchanan, 1 Houst. Cr. C. 79; S. v. Woodward, 1 Houst. Cr. C. 455. But where a person armed with a club enters upon the premises of another in a threatening manner and provokes the quarrel, in the excitement of which the other with a stick fells the aggressor, inflicting a wound from which he dies, it is at most manslaughter: Silgar v. P., 107 Ill. 563. Where deceased having violently assailed defendant and followed him up into his own house in a threatening manner, the act of defendant in taking his life after he had ordered him to stop before entering the house will not constitute more than manslaughter: Hurd v. P., 25 Mich. 405. Attempt to unlawfully seize property under a mortgage without warrant may constitute provocation although the owner does not resort to all other available means of preventing the seizure before taking life: Ledbetter v. S., 26 Tex. Ap. 22.

[2] Flanagan v. S., 46 Ala. 703.

[3] S. v. Branstetter, 65 Mo. 149; Exp. Warrick, 73 Ala. 57; Nichols v. C., 11 Bush, 575. The blow need not be one endangering life: S. v. Sizemore, 7 Jones, 206. Opprobrious and insulting epithets accompanying the offer of personal violence may make it sufficient: S. v. Umfried, 76 Mo. 404. It is error to charge that in all cases there must be some actual assault: Mack v. S., 63 Ga. 693; Reg. v. Smith, 4 F. & F. 1066. One who is not assaulted, but voluntarily interposes in a fight between others, and purposely using a dangerous weapon causes death, is guilty of murder: Johnston's Case, 5 Grat. 660.

[4] Stewart v. S., 78 Ala. 436; Nichols v. C., 11 Bush, 575. Personal restraint or a slight blow, proper under the circumstances, will not constitute provocation: Thompson v. S., 55 Ga. 47; Holmes v. S., 88 Ala. 26; Rex v. Willoughby, 1 East, P. C. 288. So it is not every slight provocation

of the provocation does not depend alone on whether it actually caused passion and heat of blood in the defendant, but also on whether it was calculated to cause such state of mind in a reasonable person,[1] that is, there must be an adequate cause.[2] The terms "reasonable" or "lawful" or "adequate" or "sufficient" or "legal" may be used in describing the provocation which will be sufficient.[3] The nature of the weapon or method of injury must be considered in determining the adequacy of the provocation. It will require great provocation to mitigate a homicide committed with a deadly weapon.[4]

§ 339. **Quarrel; mutual combat; tumult.** — It would seem from the authorities cited in the notes to the preceding section that a mere quarrel with words will not constitute a provocation extenuating an intentional killing, although such circumstances might extenuate an assault and battery not in its nature calculated to cause death, but which by accident results fatally, so that the homicide would be only manslaughter. In general, however, a quarrel leading to a fight with deadly weapons, in the course of which death is caused in passion, will reduce the homicide to manslaughter.[5] But even if the combat

which will mitigate killing with a deadly weapon to manslaughter: Rex v. Lynch, 5 C. & P. 324. But if the provocation is sufficient it is immaterial how violent and disproportionate was the defendant's act. Degree of force does not constitute an element in determining whether the crime is manslaughter or not: Beaty v. S., 30 Tex. Ap. 677.

[1] Davis v. P., 114 Ill. 86; Maher v. P., 10 Mich. 212; Reese v. S., 90 Ala. 624; Preston v. S., 25 Miss. 383; S. v. Shippey, 10 Minn. 223; Reg. v. Welsh, 11 Cox, 336. It is not the fact that the blow is given in passion, but rather that there is provocation for such passion, that reduces it to manslaughter: S. v. Ellis, 74 Mo. 207; Reg. v. Noon, 6 Cox, 137; Smith v. S., 49 Ga. 482. In Texas the statute describes an assault and battery, severe pain, or bloodshed as an adequate cause constituting a provocation: Tickle v. S., 6 Tex. Ap. 623; Reed v. S., 9 Tex. Ap. 317. But other adequate causes aside from those described may be considered: Rutherford v. S., 15 Tex. Ap. 236; Williams v. S., 15 Tex. Ap. 617; Wadlington v. S., 19 Tex. Ap. 266; Bonner v. S., 29 Tex. Ap. 223.

[2] McKinney v. S., 8 Tex. Ap. 626; P. v. Bruggy, 93 Cal. 476.

[3] S. v. Ellis, 74 Mo. 207; S. v. Smith, 10 Rich. 341.

[4] S. v. Shippey, 10 Minn. 223; S. v. Hoyt, 13 Minn. 132.

[5] S. v. McDonnell, 32 Vt. 491; Golden v. S., 25 Ga. 527; S. v. Roberts, 1 Hawks, 349; S. v. Floyd, 6 Jones, 392; Atkins v. S., 16 Ark. 568; U. S. v. Mingo, 2 Curtis, 1; S. v. Costen, 1 Houst. Cr. Cas. 340; S. v. O'Neal, 1 Houst. Cr. Cas. 58. But the homicide may be such as to show an intention of killing regardless of provocation and constitute murder: P. v. Sanchez, 24 Cal. 17; S. v. Gooch, 94 N. C. 987; McAllister v. T., 1 Wash.

is not with deadly weapons, and one takes the life of the other in sudden heat,[1] even with the use of a deadly weapon, it is still only manslaughter.[2] No matter how disproportionate the violence is to the provocation (provided the provocation is such as is calculated to cause heat of blood and does cause it), the homicide will be manslaughter only.[3] One who brings on or voluntarily enters into an affray or combat cannot, as has already been said,[4] justify the taking of life in self-defense in the continuance thereof, although his life may be put in peril; but if he does thus kill he is guilty of manslaughter and not murder.[5] So one is not excused in killing after a murderous assault on him is discontinued,[6] but his act, if in heat of blood, will be manslaughter only.[7] The assembling of persons for the purpose of charivari, accompanied with tumult and confusion, has been held sufficient provocation to those annoyed and insulted by it to reduce a homicide, caused by firing into the crowd, from murder to manslaughter.[8] But it has also

360; Rex v. Shaw, 6 C. & P. 372. And further as to killing which is not the result of provocation, although following the provocation, see *infra*, § 342.

[1] S. v. Miller, 112 N. C. 878; Williams v. S., 25 Tex. Ap. 216.

[2] Silgar v. P., 107 Ill. 563; Perkins v. S., 78 Wis. 551; Smith v. S., 73 Ga. 31; Battle v. S., 92 Ga. 465; Patterson v. S., 66 Ind. 185; S. v. Murphy, 61 Me. 56; S. v. Henderson, 24 Oreg. 100; Tate v. S., 46 Ga. 148; S. v. Massage, 65 N. C. 480; Allen v. S., 5 Yerg. 453; S. v. Levigne, 17 Nev. 435; Bonnard v. S., 25 Tex. Ap. 173; Carter v. S., 30 Tex. Ap. 551; S. v. Davis, 1 Houst. Cr. Cas. 13; Rex v. Snow, 1 East, P. C. 244; Rex v. Taylor, 5 Burr. 2793; Rex v. Anderson, 1 Russ., C. & M. 731; Rex v. Ayes, Russ. & Ry. 166; Rex v. Rankin, Russ. & Ry. 43; Rex v. Kessal, 1 C. & P. 437. For a construction of the Georgia code provision as to mutual combat, see Hinch v. S., 25 Ga. 699.

[3] Judge v. S., 58 Ala. 406; Kelly v. S., 68 Miss. 343; S. v. Blunt, 91 Mo. 503; McGuffie v. S., 17 Ga. 497; S. v. Curry, 1 Jones, 280; S. v. Ramsey, 5 Jones, 195; Cotton v. S., 31 Miss. 504; Holly v. S., 10 Humph. 141; Franklin v. S., 30 Tex. Ap. 628; Rex v. Thomas, 7 C. & P. 817. If the occasion is sudden, the blood heated and the killing during actual combat, it is manslaughter: S. v. Havercamp, 54 Ia. 350. But an actual struggle is not conclusive. Other facts may show malice or its absence: S. v. White, 30 La. An., pt. I, 364; Cochran v. S., 28 Tex. Ap. 422; Bracken v. S., 29 Tex. Ap. 362.

[4] See *supra*, § 309.

[5] S. v. Davidson, 95 Mo. 155; S. v. Partlow, 90 Mo. 608; Kinney v. P., 108 Ill. 518; Childers v. S., 33 Tex. Ap. 509; Wallace v. U. S., 162 U. S. 466. But if the act is unnecessary and intentional, even after retreating, it is murder: S. v. Scott, 4 Ired. 409.

[6] *Supra*, § 308.

[7] S. v. Gaskins, 93 N. C. 547.

[8] S. v. Adams, 78 Ia. 292. Evidence that chiravaris were customary in

been said that the fact that a homicide occurs in a melee does not necessarily reduce it below murder.[1] One who, not a party to a combat, interferes therein, cannot claim heat of blood as mitigating his act of homicide to manslaughter.[2] If a murderous blow is dealt under such circumstances that the death of the person against whom it is directed would be manslaughter only, the death of a by-stander caused thereby will be of no higher degree.[3] Cases where the killing of a master by a slave were held to be reduced by provocation arising from the master's acts to manslaughter are cited in the note.[4]

§ 340. **Resisting unlawful arrest.**— A homicide committed in resisting unlawful arrest is manslaughter and not murder.[5] The reason of this seems to be that an unlawful arrest is deemed such a provocation as is likely to cause heat of blood in an ordinary person, and therefore the homicide is manslaughter only.[6] Some cases seem to announce the doctrine that, if the attempted arrest would be illegal, the homicide committed in resisting it will be manslaughter only, although the resistance was with a deadly weapon prepared beforehand for the purpose,[7] and although resistance is made with unnecessary violence.[8] Other cases make an exception where the killing is with express

the neighborhood is inadmissible to increase the provocation: Minaghan v. S., 77 Wis. 643.

[1] Smith v. S., 88 Ala. 73; Patten v. P., 18 Mich. 314.

[2] Johnston's Case, 5 Grat. 660. And see note to § 342. But where defendant, on seeing his friend shot down, had, in sudden passion resulting therefrom, killed the slayer, *held*, that he was guilty of manslaughter only: Moore v. S., 26 Tex. Ap. 322.

[3] Rex v. Brown, 1 East, P. C. 231, 245, 274.

[4] S. v. Will, 1 Dev. & B. 121; S. v. Brodnax, Phill. 41; S. v. Caesar, 9 Ired. 391; Maria v. S., 28 Tex. 698.

[5] C. v. Drew, 4 Mass. 391; Rafferty v. P., 72 Ill. 37; Ballard v. S., 43 Ohio St. 340; Roberts v. S., 14 Mo. 138; Harrison v. S., 24 Ala. 67; Poteete v. S., 9 Baxter, 261; S. v. List, 1 Houst. Cr. Cas. 133; Ross v. S., 10 Tex. Ap. 455; Reg. v. Phelps, Car. & M. 180; Rex v. Addis, 6 C. & P. 388; Rex v. Davis, 7 C. & P. 785; Rex v. Withers, 1 East, P. C. 295, 360; Rex v. Curvan, 1 Moody, 132. Unless attended with cruelty and barbarity: S. v. Craton, 6 Ired. 164. Homicide in attempting to escape from an officer holding in custody under an unlawful arrest is only manslaughter: Goodman v. S., 4 Tex. Ap. 349. So, homicide by accident in unlawfully attempting to arrest another will be manslaughter: See *infra*, § 347.

[6] Foster, 312; 1 Bish. Cr. L., sec. 868 (2).

[7] C. v. Carey, 12 Cush. 246; Rex v. Thompson, 1 Moody, 80. *Contra*, Rex v. Patience, 7 C. & P. 775.

[8] Brown v. U. S., 159 U. S. 100; Ross v. S., 10 Tex. Ap. 455.

malice,[1] and other cases go even further in making exceptions to the rule and refuse to consider as sufficient mitigation an illegal arrest which is unaccompanied by any imminent danger.[2] If the party threatened with arrest has reason to believe and does believe the arrest to be legal, homicide committed in resistance will be murder, as the circumstances negative passion.[3] Therefore mere error in the process will not reduce the killing to manslaughter.[4]

§ 341. Wife in adultery; insults to females, etc.— Where the husband discovers another with his wife in the act of committing adultery, the killing of either of them, as the result of the sudden passion thus aroused, will be manslaughter, the circumstances being deemed to constitute a sufficient provocation.[5] But it is only when the husband has detected the parties in the very act that the provocation will be deemed sufficient.[6] If a homicide is the result of previous knowledge of adulterous relations,[7] and after some time has elapsed,[8] or upon suspicion

[1] Rafferty v. P., 69 Ill. 111; S. v. Holcomb, 86 Mo. 371.

[2] Noles v. S., 26 Ala. 31; Galvin v. S., 6 Coldw. 283. But if the threatened illegal arrest is with violence and a show of deadly weapons, homicide in resistance will be manslaughter only: P. v. Burt, 51 Mich. 199.

[3] Ex parte Sherwood, 29 Tex. Ap. 334. But in a proceeding in a case in the same court it was said that the lawfulness of the arrest, not the information of the accused respecting its legality, was the criterion in connection with the character of the means used to effect the arrest upon the one hand and those used to resist it upon the other: Alford v. S., 8 Tex. Ap. 545.

[4] Mackaley's Case, Cro. Jac. 279. But if the warrant is issued in blank and afterwards filled in by the officer, the arrest under it will be so far illegal that homicide in resistance will be manslaughter only: Rafferty v. P., 69 Ill. 111; Rex v. Hood, 1 Moody, 281.

[5] Shufflin v. P., 62 N. Y. 229; Galvin v. S., 6 Coldw. 283; Pearson's Case, 2 Lewin, 216; Manning's Case, T. Raym. 212; s. c. (s. n., Maddy's Case), Ventr. 158.

[6] S. v. France, 76 Mo. 681; Hooks v. S., 99 Ala. 166; Reg. v. Kelly, 2 C. & K. 814. In a prosecution of a husband for killing his wife, evidence of infidelity on the part of the wife, unknown to the husband, is not admissible: P. v. Osmond, 138 N. Y. 80. One who is employed by the husband to watch the wife and detect her in adultery is guilty of murder in killing her paramour, although he detects the parties in the act: P. v. Horton, 4 Mich. 67. While perhaps a father, seeing a person committing an unnatural offense with his son, will be guilty of manslaughter only if he kills instantly, he would be guilty of murder if, hearing of such conduct, he goes in search of the person and kills him: Reg. v. Fisher, 8 C. & P. 182.

[7] S. v. Pratt, 1 Houst. Cr. Cas. 249; Alfred v. S., 37 Miss. 296.

[8] Sanchez v. P., 22 N. Y. 147; S. v.

producing a frenzy,[1] or after preparation and lying in wait,[2] the offense will be murder. The fact that deceased has been criminally intimate with defendant's wife's sister is not sufficient provocation to reduce the homicide to manslaughter.[3] In another case it is said that obscene language used in the presence of defendant's family in connection with other vexatious conduct could be taken into account in determining whether the circumstances were calculated to produce and did produce such excitement and passion as would obscure the reason of an ordinary man.[4] So the resentment felt by the father on seeing his daughter violently assailed by her husband was held sufficient provocation to reduce the killing of the latter by the father to manslaughter.[5] In Texas, by statute, insulting words to a female relative may constitute such provocation as to reduce a homicide in consequence thereof to manslaughter.[6]

Samuel, 3 Jones, 74; S. v. Neville, 6 Jones, 423; S. v. John, 8 Ired. 330; S. v. Herrell, 97 Mo. 105; McNeill v. S., 102 Ala. 121; Sawyer v. S., 35 Ind. 80; Pickens v. S., 31 Tex. Ap. 554. By statute in Texas the provocation will be sufficient if the killing is upon first learning of the fact: Paulin v. S., 21 Tex. Ap. 436.

[1] Sanchez v. P., 22 N. Y. 147; S. v. Avery, 64 N. C. 608.

[2] Breedlove v. S., 26 Tex. Ap. 445. See, also, as to killing to prevent the commission of adultery, *supra*, § 299.

[3] S. v. Hockett, 70 Ia. 442. And see as to killing a man who appeared to have committed adultery with defendant's sister, but where the homicide seemed to have been deliberately planned: Lynch v. C., 77 Pa. St. 205. Improper conduct on the part of a wife living apart from her husband will not constitute such provocation as to reduce his act in killing her to manslaughter: S. v. Bulling, 105 Mo. 204.

[4] Seals v. S., 3 Baxt. 459.

[5] Reg. v. Harrington, 10 Cox, 370.

[6] The statute covers insulting words used concerning a female relative who is absent, as well as such words used in the presence of such relative: Hudson v. S., 6 Tex. Ap. 565; Niland v. S., 19 Tex. Ap. 166. To be excusable, the homicide must be immediately upon the happening of the conduct or utterance of the language, or on the first meeting after being informed of the insult: Evers v. S., 31 Tex. Ap. 318; Orman v. S., 22 Tex. Ap. 604; Norman v. S., 26 Tex. Ap. 221; Howard v. S., 23 Tex. Ap. 265; Melton v. S., 24 Tex. Ap. 47; Pitts v. S., 29 Tex. Ap. 374. And it must appear that the fact of the insult had become known to defendant: Gibson v. S., 23 Tex. Ap. 414; or that defendant believed the insult to have been given, even though it had not been given in fact: Jones v. S., 33 Tex. Ap. 492. It must also appear that the killing was the result of the provocation: Hill v. S., 5 Tex. Ap. 2; Eanes v. S., 10 Tex. Ap. 421; Ex parte Jones, 31 Tex. Ap. 422; Richardson v. S., 28 Tex. Ap. 216. It is immaterial what length of time had elapsed between the reception of the information and the meeting: Jones v. S., 33 Tex. Ap. 492. The statute provides that any female under the permanent or temporary

§ 342. Homicide irrespective of provocation.— The theory of these various kinds of provocation is that heat of blood has been produced by circumstances which would produce such condition in the mind of a reasonable person and that the homicide is the result thereof.[1] But unless the provocation does cause heat of blood, which exists at the time of the commission of the homicide,[2] then the offense is not mitigated to manslaughter. If it appears that the moving cause of a homicide was revenge and not an insult,[3] that is, that the homicide was the result of express malice, notwithstanding the provocation,[4] the offense will be murder. If a former threat or grudge is the cause of the homicide, it will be immaterial what provocation immediately preceded the killing.[5] So, if one goes into the combat with a preconceived purpose of taking life, as shown by his having provided himself with a deadly weapon, and thus with an undue advantage,[6] or prepares to kill in anticipation of

protection of the slayer at the time of the killing shall be included within the meaning of the term "relation," and held that the difference between the case of an actual relation and that of the statutory relation of protection is that in the latter case the killing must occur while the female is still under the protection of the slayer: Ex parte Jones, 31 Tex. Ap. 422. During the lifetime of a man's wife her daughter is his female relation: Clanton v. S., 20 Tex. Ap. 615. To call one a "son of a bitch" is not within the statute as to insulting words towards a female relative: Simmons v. S., 23 Tex. Ap. 653; Levy v. S., 28 Tex. Ap. 203; Shields v. S., 89 Ga. 549. One woman killing another for insulting words about herself does not make a case within the statute: Moore v. S., 33 Tex. Ap. 351. Insult to a male relative, however infirm or closely related, is not within the statute: Ex parte Jones, 31 Tex. Ap. 422.

[1] S. v. Talmadge, 107 Mo. 543. Thus, one who as a volunteer engages in an affray between others and commits homicide is guilty of murder. As to him there is no provocation: Conner v. S., 4 Yerg. 136; Johnston's Case, 5 Grat. 660; P. v. Cole, 4 Parker Cr. R. 35; Holland v. S., 12 Fla. 117.

[2] S. v. Ellis, 74 Mo. 207; Roman v. S., 41 Wis. 312.

[3] Escareno v. S., 16 Tex. Ap. 85.

[4] S. v. Pankey, 104 N. C. 840; S. v. Lane, 4 Ired. 113; S. v. Nelson, 101 Mo. 464; S. v. Gee, 85 Mo. 647; McNeill v. S., 102 Ala. 121; Miles v. S., 18 Tex. Ap. 156; Reg. v. Kirkham, 8 C. & P. 115; Rex v. Mason, 1 East, P. C. 239; Reg. v. Selten, 11 Cox, 674.

[5] Riggs v. S., 30 Miss. 635; Pickens v. S., 61 Miss. 52; S. v. Johnson, 1 Ired. 354; C. v. Mosler, 4 Pa. St. 264; S. v. Downham, 1 Houst. Cr. Cas. 45; Boyett v. S., 2 Tex. Ap. 93.

[6] S. v. Dunn, 80 Mo. 681; S. v. Christian, 66 Mo. 138; Scales v. S., 96 Ala. 69; Kennedy v. S., 85 Ala. 326; S. v. Ferguson, 2 Hill (S. C.), 619; S. v. Kearley, 26 Kan. 77; Rex v. Whiteley, 1 Lewin, 173; Rex v. Kessal, 1 C. & P. 437. But the mere fact of the possession of a deadly weapon will not be sufficient to show such purpose: Reg. v. Smith, 8 C. & P. 160; Atkins v. S., 16 Ark. 568. Arm-

unlawful arrest,[1] or where the circumstances otherwise show a premeditated design to take life,[2] or where the act is cowardly and unmanly,[3] the homicide will be murder. If there is reflection or deliberation, the law does not measure the length of time, but pronounces the offense murder.[4] If the slayer acts coolly and vengefully, or with violence out of all proportion to the provocation, the offense will be murder, although the killing immediately follows the provocation.[5] If one party to a conflict retreats and the other follows him up and kills him, it is murder.[6] But the law will not presume a homicide to be the result of previous malice where an adequate provocation appears.[7] The question whether the homicide is in pursuance of previous malice or of passion produced by the provocation is for the jury.[8]

§ **343. Cooling time.**— The preceding discussion has shown that homicide under provocation is reduced to manslaughter on account of the heat of passion thereby engendered, which, out of charity to the weakness of human nature, is assumed to deprive the killing of that malignant character which would otherwise be supposed to exist and to constitute malice aforethought. And it has also appeared that the provocation must be such as would have influenced a reasonable person, and that the killing must be the result of passion. Therefore, if such time has elapsed after the provocation as that a reasonable person would have regained self-control, then the act must be deemed malicious and not the result of the provocation, and, therefore, murder. In other words, if there has been sufficient time for

ing for a proper self-defense will not prevent a subsequent intentional killing on provocation being reduced to manslaughter though not in self-defense: Gourko v. U. S., 153 U. S. 183; Allen v. U. S., 157 U. S. 675.

[1] Rafferty v. P., 72 Ill. 37; Miller v. S., 32 Tex. 319.

[2] Lynch v. C., 77 Pa. St. 205; Ex parte Nettles, 58 Ala. 268. So if there is a mutual intention to kill: Bonnard v. S., 25 Tex. Ap. 173.

[3] C. v. Mosler, 4 Pa. St. 264; S. v. Kloss, 117 Mo. 591.

[4] Ex parte Brown, 65 Ala. 446.

[5] S. v. Boon, 82 N. C. 637; S. v. Snell, 78 Mo. 240; S. v. Scott, 36 W. Va. 704.

[6] S. v. Howell, 9 Ired. 485; Green v. S., 45 Ark. 281. So where the assailed, after the assailant was disabled by a blow, gave another fatal blow unnecessarily, the homicide was held to be murder: P. v. Beckwith, 103 N. Y. 360.

[7] S. v. Barfield, 7 Ired. 299; S. v. Horn, 116 N. C. 1037; Copeland v. S., 7 Humph. 479; Murray v. S., 1 Tex. Ap. 417.

[8] Bolzer v. P., 129 Ill. 112; Meuly v. S., 26 Tex. Ap. 274.

the passion to cool, the provocation will not mitigate a subsequent killing to manslaughter.[1] The question is not whether the blow was actually struck in a continuance of the passion, but whether there had been a reasonable time for the passion to cool in the case of an ordinary person, or whether the defendant did actually commit the homicide in cold blood.[2] This must depend on the circumstances of the case, and is a question for the jury.[3] There are cases which seem to make the question as to whether there has been sufficient time to cool one for the court and not the jury;[4] but these cases, as well as others holding that the question of the sufficiency of the provocation is for the court, seem to be capable of a different interpretation.[5] In the note are given cases in which the question of the sufficiency of time under particular circumstances is discussed.[6] Whether the time for cooling has been sufficient will not be affected by the fact that defendant was intoxicated.[7]

§ 344. Sufficiency of provocation as affected by intoxication or insanity of defendant, character of deceased, etc.— It has already been said that the provocation must be such as would cause heat of blood in an ordinary person; therefore, the fact that defendant was intoxicated will be immaterial on the question of the sufficiency of the provocation.[8] But where the question is not whether there was adequate provocation,

[1] S. v. Kotovsky, 74 Mo. 247; Achey v. S., 64 Ind. 56; McNeill v. S., 102 Ala. 121; Fitzpatrick v. S., 37 Ark. 238; Rex v. Hayward, 6 C. & P. 157; Rex v. Oneby, 2 Stra. 766. But if the homicide is in a continuing general affray, it will be recognized that the opportunity for cooling does not occur and that the provocation continues: P. v. Curtis, 52 Mich. 616.

[2] P. v. Sullivan, 7 N. Y. 396; S. v. Grayor, 89 Mo. 600; S. v. McCants, 1 Spears, 384; S. v. Holmes, 12 Wash. 169.

[3] Maher v. P., 10 Mich. 212; Ferguson v. S., 49 Ind. 33; Kilpatrick v. C., 31 Pa. St. 198; S. v. Yarborough, 39 Kan. 581; T. v. Bannigan, 1 Dak. 432.

[4] Rex v. Oneby, 2 Strange, 766; Reg. v. Fisher, 8 C. & P. 182; S. v. Moore, 69 N. C. 267.

[5] See *infra*, § 345.

[6] Hurd v. P., 25 Mich. 405; McWhirt's Case, 3 Grat. 594; Cates v. S., 50 Ala. 166; Ex parte Moore, 30 Ind. 197; S. v. Moore, 69 N. C. 267; T. v. Bannigan, 1 Dak. 451. The court may instruct that an interval of three days is sufficient, but if the time is short the question should be left to the jury: Rockmore v. S., 93 Ga. 123.

[7] C. v. Hawkins, 3 Gray, 463. Further, as to whether the intoxicated condition of defendant can be considered in determining the sufficiency of the provocation, see the next section.

[8] C. v. Hawkins, 3 Gray, 463; Gaitan v. S., 11 Tex. Ap. 544.

but whether the defendant acted under the provocation or in cold blood, evidence of his intoxication is admissible as tending to show that he acted in passion.[1] Violent character of deceased, not known to defendant, is not admissible under the question of provocation.[2]

§ 345. **Question of law or fact.**— It is sometimes said that the question as to the sufficiency of the provocation is for the court;[3] but it will be found on examining these cases that what is meant in most of them is, either that the sufficiency of the provocation to affect an ordinary person and not the idiosyncrasy of defendant in this respect is the legal test,[4] or that where there is no legal evidence of provocation the court may disregard that issue.[5] The reasonable view seems to be that, under proper instructions as to what will constitute sufficient provocation, the question of its existence and whether defendant acted under it is for the jury.[6]

§ 346. **Burden of proof; sufficiency of evidence.**— While it is sometimes said that the burden of proving extenuation, such as will reduce a homicide to manslaughter, is upon defendant,[7] yet it appears that what is meant by such statement is simply that, where no extenuating circumstances are indicated in the evidence offered by the defendant or in the evidence offered by the prosecution, the jury should not merely on conjecture, without evidence, find the defendant guilty of manslaughter instead of murder.[8] It is not necessary that the extenuating facts should be affirmatively proved by de-

[1] S. v. McCants, 1 Spears, 384. And see *supra*, § 162.

[2] C. v. Hilliard, 2 Gray, 294. But where homicide was committed in a melee, *held*, that the violent and bloodthirsty character of deceased might be taken into account in determining the degree of defendant's guilt: Smith v. S., 88 Ala. 73.

[3] Lynch v. C., 77 Pa. St. 205; S. v. Craton, 6 Ired. 164; Rex v. Oneby, 2 Strange, 766; Reg. v. Fisher, 8 C. & P. 182; S. v. Moore, 69 N. C. 267; S. v. Sizemore, 7 Jones, 206; S. v. Jones, 20 Mo. 58; S. v. Dunn, 18 Mo. 519; S. v. Nueslein, 25 Mo. 111; S. v. Ellis, 74 Mo. 207.

[4] Small v. C., 91 Pa. St. 304; Lynch v. C., 77 Pa. St. 205; Beauchamp v. S., 6 Blackf. 299.

[5] Hill v. S., 11 Tex. Ap. 456; Lum v. S., 11 Tex. Ap. 483; S. v. Nueslein, 25 Mo. 111; S. v. Moore, 69 N. C. 267; P. v. Estrado, 49 Cal. 171.

[6] Crawford v. P., 12 Colo. 290; Parrish v. S., 18 Neb. 405; Vollmer v. S., 24 Neb. 838; Mackey v. S., 13 Tex. Ap. 360; Meuly v. S., 26 Tex. Ap. 274; Dennison v. S., 13 Ind., 510; Reg. v. Eagle, 2 F. & F. 827.

[7] P. v. Gibson, 17 Cal. 283.

[8] U. S. v. Armstrong, 2 Curtis, 446.

fendant; it is sufficient if they appear from the evidence introduced by the state.[1] And therefore it is error to instruct that the burden of proof is upon the defendant to establish the mitigation and that he must do it by a preponderance of evidence.[2] If the jury are not convinced of the malice they should convict only of manslaughter.[3]

§ 347. Unintentional killing in doing wrongful act; attempted abortion.— The cases of manslaughter already discussed are those where the killing is intentional, but under such provocation as to indicate absence of malice and reduce the offense to manslaughter. But there are also cases of unintentional homicide amounting to manslaughter, just as there are of unintentional homicide amounting to murder, the difference being as to the magnitude of the wrong which was intended and from which the death has resulted. Thus, if a wrongful blow is given, resulting in death, the act will not be less than manslaughter, even though the blow was one in its nature not likely to cause death, or otherwise shown to have been inflicted with intent to cause death.[4] Death resulting from an act wrongful *per se*, such as an attempt to procure an abortion, where not necessary to save the life of the woman, will be manslaughter at least.[5] So, if a man, in order to have unlawful sexual connection with a woman, uses artificial means, from

[1] Reid v. S., 50 Ga. 556.

[2] P. v. West, 49 Cal. 610; S. v. McCluer, 5 Nev. 132. But if there is no evidence in mitigation, such instruction will do the defendant no harm: P. v. Ah Kong, 49 Cal. 6. The question as to presumptions and burden of proof has already been considered in connection with justification and excuse: See *supra*, § 316.

[3] Short v. S., 7 Yerg. 510.

[4] C. v. Woodward, 102 Mass. 155; P. v. Rector, 19 Wend. 569; Wellar v. P., 30 Mich. 16; Sutcliffe v. S., 18 Ohio, 469; Rex v. Brown, 1 East, P. C. 231, 245, 274; Rex v. Conner, 7 C. & P. 438; Rex v. Fray, 1 East, P. C. 236. If a woman abandons her young infant in a place where it is likely to be found and taken care of, the resulting death of the infant will be manslaughter. But if the child is left in a remote place where it is not likely to be found, and death ensues, it will be murder: Reg. v. Walters, Car. & M. 164.

[5] Peoples v. C., 87 Ky. 487; Reg. v. Gaylor, Dears. & B. 288. In some states wilful killing of an unborn quick child is manslaughter: See *supra*, § 294. By statute in Wisconsin, actual necessity, or the advice of two physicians that such necessity exists, must be shown to excuse the act: Hatchard v. S., 79 Wis. 357. A mere examination with a usual instrument, to determine pregnancy, will not render a physician liable for death resulting therefrom: S. v. Reynolds, 42 Kan. 320.

which death results, it is manslaughter.[1] So, if one person causes the death of another by an act which is in violation of law, it will be manslaughter, although not shown to be wilful or intentional.[2] An officer, killing in making an unlawful arrest, or having unwarrantably made an arrest in preventing escape, will be guilty at least of manslaughter.[3] Where a party placed an obstruction upon a railroad track, intending to give information thereof, and thus secure a position as a reward, and an accident resulting in death was caused by a train, not expected by the wrong-doer, running into the obstruction, the wrong-doer was held guilty of manslaughter.[4] Where a trespasser was ejected from premises with unwarrantable violence, though not in a manner likely to cause death, but death resulted, it was held to be manslaughter.[5] Where an unlawful attempt was made to take a gun from deceased, and he was accidentally killed, it was held to be manslaughter.[6] So held, also, where death of a gamekeeper was caused by a poacher who unlawfully resisted the taking of his gun.[7] Where an encounter was commenced by defendant by snatching the hat of deceased in a rude or angry manner, it was held that death subsequently resulting in the encounter from the act of defendant, although by misadventure and not likely to ensue, rendered defendant guilty of manslaughter.[8] So, if in a game one player does an unlawful act causing the death of another, he is guilty of manslaughter.[9] The distinction between these cases and those of accident or misadventure, which are excusable homicide, is the element of wrong or unlawfulness in the act done.[10] But it is not every unlawful act from which death results that will constitute manslaughter. It is only where the unlawful

[1] S. v. Center, 35 Vt. 378.

[2] Cases under navigation laws: U. S. v. Farnham, 2 Blatch. 528; U. S. v. Keller, 19 Fed. R. 633; U. S. v. Holtzhauer, 40 Fed. R. 76. So death resulting from pointing a gun at another in sport is manslaughter where the statute makes it a misdemeanor to point a gun at another: Henderson v. S., 98 Ala. 35. So where one unlawfully discharges his pistol in the street: Sparks v. C., 3 Bush, 111; P. v. Fuller, 2 Park. Cr. R. 16; but this might be murder: See *supra*, § 326.

[3] S. v. Craton, 6 Ired. 164; C. v. Drew, 4 Mass. 391; O'Connor v. S., 64 Ga. 125; Alford v. S., 8 Tex. Ap. 545; as to this see, also, *supra*, § 298.

[4] S. v. Brown, 1 Houst. Cr. C. 539.

[5] Wild's Case, 2 Lewin, 214.

[6] Reg. v. Archer, 1 F. & F. 361.

[7] Reg. v. Skeet, 4 F. & F. 931.

[8] Jenkins v. S., 82 Ala. 25.

[9] Reg. v. Bradshaw, 14 Cox, 83.

[10] Johnson v. S., 94 Ala. 35.

act is intentionally done, under such conditions as will be dangerous to another. Therefore, held, that where defendant unlawfully sought to drive through a toll-gate without paying toll, and the death of the toll-keeper resulted from his attempting to stop defendant's horses, the act would not be manslaughter unless it should appear that defendant had reason to know that an attempt on the part of the toll-keeper to stop the horses would be dangerous.[1] So, where the mere civil wrong of throwing a box, belonging to another, wantonly into the sea caused the death of a bather, held, that unless there was negligence in doing the act the homicide was not manslaughter.[2]

§ **348. Unlawful violence in doing lawful act.**— In cases where some force or violence is lawful, but not to the extent of endangering life or threatening great bodily injury, death resulting from the force or violence used may be of any one of the three grades of homicide. If no more force or violence is used than is proper and death results by accident it will be excusable as by misadventure.[3] If such violence is used as would naturally cause death or great bodily harm, intent to kill will be presumed and the offense will be murder.[4] But if, although undue violence is used, the circumstances do not indicate an intent to cause death or great bodily harm, death resulting will be manslaughter; that is, it will be homicide resulting from an unlawful act not indicating an intent to cause death or commit a felony. Thus, death resulting from unnecessary violence of an officer making an arrest,[5] or from unreasonable chastisement of a child by the father,[6] or by a schoolmaster,[7] is manslaughter. If a child of such tender years as to not be capable of appreciating correction is subjected to physical punishment and death results, it is manslaughter.[8] The officers of a vessel unreasonably punishing a seaman, and thus causing his death, will be guilty of manslaughter.[9] So it is in case of an apprentice,[10] or a boy employed as a servant.[11] There being no right

[1] Estell v. S., 51 N. J. 182.

[2] Reg. v. Franklin, 15 Cox, 163.

[3] *Supra*, § 300.

[4] *Supra*, §§ 323, 325.

[5] Doherty v. S., 84 Wis. 152; Carter v. S., 30 Tex. Ap. 551.

[6] Anon., 1 East, P. C. 261; Rex v. Cheeseman, 7 C. & P. 455; or by another person: Hill v. S., 11 Tex. Ap. 456.

[7] Reg. v. Hopley, 2 F. & F. 202.

[8] Reg. v. Griffin, 11 Cox, 402.

[9] Reg. v. Leggett, 8 C. & P. 191.

[10] Rex v. Friend, Russ. & Ry. 20; Reg. v. Crumpton, Car. & M. 597.

[11] Rex v. Wiggs, 1 Leach, 379.

in Massachusetts in the husband to use violence in the correction of the wife, death resulting from such violent correction will be at least manslaughter.[1] Excessive violence in self-defense or in defense of another, which causes death, will be manslaughter.[2]

§ 349. **Death from negligence.**— Where one by his negligence has caused or contributed to the death of another he is guilty of manslaughter.[3] It is not necessary that there be any intent or will concurring in the negligence or omission of duty which causes death.[4] If the act were intentional and with a purpose of causing death the homicide would be murder.[5] Of course, under the general doctrine of combinations, if the negligence of others as well as that of defendant has contributed to the result, he will nevertheless be responsible.[6] It is immaterial that there was negligence on the part of deceased himself contributing to the result, the doctrine of contributory negligence having no place in the law of crimes.[7] But the death must have been the direct result wholly or in part of defendant's negligence. If the negligence of deceased or others intervened so as to constitute the proximate, efficient cause of the death, it will not be criminal homicide in defendant.[8] In one case it was said that one is not to be held criminally responsible for the death of another on account of negligence where he would not have been civilly liable in an action at the suit of the party injured if the injury sustained had not caused death.[9] The question of how closely the death

[1] C. v. McAfee, 108 Mass. 458.

[2] Brooks v. C., 61 Pa. St. 352; S. v. Fitzsimmons, 63 Ia. 656; S. v. Elliott, 98 Mo. 150; Rex v. Bourne, 5 C. & P. 120.

[3] Robins v. S., 9 Tex. Ap. 666; U. S. v. Meagher, 37 Fed. R. 875; Reg. v. Swindall, 2 C. & K. 230; Reg. v. Hughes, Dears. & B. 248.

[4] S. v. O'Brien, 32 N. J. 169. And see *supra*, §§ 129, 130.

[5] S. v. Smith, 65 Me. 257; Reg. v. Marriott, 8 C. & P. 425; Reg. v. Conde, 10 Cox, 547; Rex v. Self, 1 East, P. C. 226. To charge that defendant wilfully, and with culpable negligence, killed deceased, is inconsistent: S. v. Lockwood, 119 Mo. 463.

[6] Reg. v. Haines, 2 C. & K. 368; S. v. Shelledy, 8 Ia. 477, 507.

[7] Reg. v. Kew, 12 Cox, 355; Reg. v. Longbottom, 3 Cox, 439; Reg. v. Jones, 11 Cox, 544. For instance, the fact that deceased might have avoided the result of defendant's negligence if he had not been intoxicated, will be no defense: Rex v. Walker, 1 C. & P. 320; or that deceased was deaf and dumb: Reg. v. Swindall, 2 Cox, 141.

[8] Reg. v. Jones, 11 Cox, 544; Reg. v. Ledger, 2 F. & F. 857.

[9] Reg. v. Birchall, 4 F. & F. 1087.

must be related to the act to constitute homicide has already been discussed.[1] It is not sufficient in charging manslaughter by negligence to simply allege that by the negligence and misconduct of defendant the death of deceased was caused; the facts must be set out.[2] But in charging death from neglect it is sufficient to charge that defendant wilfully and feloniously neglected and refused to provide necessary food, clothing, shelter, etc., without charging that it was knowingly.[3]

§ **350. What deemed negligence.**— Negligence which will render unintentional homicide criminal is such carelessness or recklessness as is incompatible with a proper regard for human life.[4] An act of omission as well as of commission may be so criminal as to render death resulting therefrom manslaughter.[5] But the omission must be one likely to cause death. Failure to perform the official duty of repairing a highway, from which death results, will not be homicide.[6] The omission must be of a public duty.[7]

§ **351. Examples.**— A great variety of cases of negligent homicide may be enumerated. It has been held manslaughter to strike another with a stick and leave him exposed, helpless, to the elements;[8] or to cause the death of a child by giving it spirituous liquors in a quantity unfit for its tender age;[9] or to confine an aged person without provision for necessaries.[10] Neglect of an officer in charge of seamen is made criminal by act of congress, and death resulting therefrom will be manslaughter.[11] Persons on board a ship are necessarily subject to something like despotic government, and the law should regulate the conduct of those who exercise dominion over them.[12] Cases where the failure to provide necessaries for a child or

[1] *Supra*, § 292.

[2] U. S. v. Holtzhauer, 40 Fed. R. 76.

[3] S. v. Smith, 65 Me. 257.

[4] S. v. Emery, 78 Mo. 77; Darry v. P., 10 N. Y. 120; Reg. v. Finney, 12 Cox, 625. But a mere omission through forgetfulness of something which a reasonably prudent person might omit will not be sufficient: S. v. O'Brien, 32 N. J. 169. If there is no omission of duty and no neglect, there is no responsibility: Thomas v. P., 2 Colo. Ap. 513.

[5] Reg. v. Lowe, 3 C. & K. 123.

[6] Reg. v. Pocock, 17 Q. B. 34.

[7] Reg. v. Smith, 11 Cox, 210.

[8] Reg. v. Martin, 11 Cox, 136.

[9] Rex v. Martin, 3 C. & P. 211.

[10] Reg. v. Marriott, 8 C. & P. 425.

[11] U. S. v. Farnham, 2 Blatch. 528; U. S. v. Warner, 4 McLean, 463; U. S. v. Taylor, 5 McLean, 242; U. S. v. Keller, 19 Fed. R. 633.

[12] Reg. v. Leggett, 8 C. & P. 191.

other dependent person is held to amount to homicide if death results have been already cited.[1] These cases, unless the facts indicate an intention to cause death, will be cases of manslaughter. Reckless negligence and foolhardy presumption on the part of a physician in pursuing a course of treatment dangerous in its nature and uncalled for, will render death resulting therefrom manslaughter.[2] Homicide, resulting from negligence in the discharge of a perfectly lawful business, may be manslaughter;[3] it is so in case of negligent driving.[4] A similar rule applies to navigation of a vessel where another boat is run down and death results.[5] Negligence in the management of machinery likely to be dangerous if not carefully managed, and causing death, will be manslaughter.[6] One who so negligently makes or repairs a cannon that it bursts and causes

[1] *Supra*, § 286.

[2] C. v. Pierce, 138 Mass. 165. Further as to negligence of physicians, druggists, etc., see *supra*, § 287.

[3] Chrystal v. C., 9 Bush, 669. For instance, in the construction of a building: Deford v. S., 30 Md. 179.

[4] Rex v. Walker, 1 C. & P. 320; Rex v. Grout, 6 C. & P. 629; Rex v. Timmins, 7 C. & P. 499; Reg. v. Dalloway, 2 Cox, 273. But not if the accident happens through some chance which could not have been foreseen or avoided: Reg. v. Murray, 5 Cox, 509. Where two persons engage in racing their horses at a furious rate on the highway, and one of them runs over a man and kills him, each of the two persons is guilty of manslaughter: Reg. v. Swindall, 2 C. & K. 230. But in another case it was held that only the one doing the injury was guilty: Rex v. Mastin, 6 C. & P. 396.

[5] Reg. v. Taylor, 9 C. & P. 672; Rex v. Green, 7 C. & P. 156; Rex v. Allen, 7 C. & P. 153.

[6] For instance, where a person incompetent for the management of machinery to hoist colliers was temporarily left in charge, and death of some of the men resulted, it was held manslaughter in the engineer: Reg. v. Lowe, 3 C. & K. 123. Where by the neglect of defendant in placing a stage over the mouth of a shaft the death of a miner was caused, *held*, that defendant was properly convicted of manslaughter: Reg. v. Hughes, Dears. & B. 248. So where the person whose duty it was to cause a mine to be ventilated, neglected such duty and an explosion occurred causing death, *held*, that he was properly convicted of manslaughter if a person using reasonable diligence would have attended to the ventilation: Reg. v. Haines, 2 C. & K. 368. The engineer of a railway train may be guilty of manslaughter in the negligent management of his engine so as to cause a collision resulting in death: Reg. v. Birchall, 4 F. & F. 1087. But it must be clearly shown that the negligence was that of the defendant: Reg. v. Gregory, 2 F. & F. 153; Reg. v. Gray, 4 F. & F. 1098; Reg. v. Trainer, 4 F. & F. 105. It is not necessary that defendant should have known what would be the result of his act, if he did the act intentionally and it was dangerous in its character: White v. S., 84 Ala. 421.

death is guilty of manslaughter.[1] Where, in a frolic, a lad took the stick out of the front part of a cart, in consequence of which it was upset and the carman who was in it was killed, it was held that the lad was guilty of manslaughter.[2] Where one by the careless use of a pistol in sport kills another by accident, it is manslaughter.[3] It is negligence in such case to fail to ascertain whether the weapon is loaded.[4] The wanton and reckless discharge of fire-arms causing death will be manslaughter, although there is no intent to kill or do bodily injury.[5] One turning loose a vicious animal where there are passers-by likely to be injured will be guilty of manslaughter if the animal causes death.[6]

VI. STATUTORY DEGREES OF MURDER AND MANSLAUGHTER.

§ 352. To determine extent of punishment.— In much the same way as criminal homicide, which was originally punishable in but one way, was divided into the crimes of murder and manslaughter with regard to the degree of wrong involved, so in the further attempt to distinguish between grades of guilt in these two crimes they have been by statutes, in the various states of the Union, divided to a greater or less extent into degrees punishable in different measure.[7]

§ 353. Degrees of murder.— The first step in this direction was the division of murder into the first and the second degrees, and some such division has become universal in the states although it is made in somewhat varying terms. The laws of

[1] Rex v. Carr, 8 C. & P. 163, n.

[2] Rex v. Sullivan, 7 C. & P. 641.

[3] S. v. Vines, 93 N. C. 493; P. v. Slack, 90 Mich. 448; S. v. Benham, 23 Ia. 154; Nelson v. S., 6 Baxt. 418; Reg. v. Weston, 14 Cox, 346; Reg. v. Salmon, 6 Q. B. D. 79.

[4] S. v. Hardie, 47 Ia. 647; Johnson v. S., 94 Ala. 35; Reg. v. Campbell, 11 Cox, 323; Reg. v. Jones, 12 Cox, 628. But in one case it was held that, unless the circumstances were such as to constitute an assault, the mere playful and negligent handling of a pistol believed to be empty, with no intent to harm, would not make death resulting therefrom manslaughter: Robertson v. S., 2 Lea, 239.

[5] P. v. Stubenvoll, 62 Mich. 329; S. v. Grote, 109 Mo. 345; Sparks v. C., 3 Bush, 111; P. v. Fuller, 2 Parker, Cr. R. 16.

[6] Reg. v. Dant, 10 Cox, 102.

[7] In Illinois the statute does not make degrees, but it allows a discrimination in punishment based on similar considerations: Fletcher v. P., 117 Ill. 184. And evidence of facts in mitigation is admissible, although such facts would not reduce the offense to manslaughter: Nowacryk v. P., 139 Ill. 336.

the United States do not, however, make any such distinction.[1] The various statutes involve at least three distinct characteristics, some one of which must be present to constitute murder in the first degree, to wit: Murder by certain forms of killing, such as poison, or lying in wait; in the commission of any one of certain named felonies; or by any other wilful, deliberate and premeditated killing. But this language does not imply that to make murder by poison, or lying in wait, or in the commission of a specified felony, the first degree, it must be wilful, deliberate and premeditated. These forms furnish in themselves the element of extreme criminality required for the first degree.[2] It is evident that, where the designation of the first degree is as broad as above, it will include some cases of express malice and some cases of implied malice;[3] thus, it will include cases where there is no intent to kill, but only an intent to unlawfully injure by poison, or to commit one of the specified felonies, as well as cases where there is an intent to kill. On the other hand, the first degree will not include all cases of intent to kill, for from it are excluded cases where the killing, though intentional, is not accompanied with delibera-

[1] U. S. v. Outerbridge, 5 Sawyer, 620.

[2] C. v. Jones, 1 Leigh, 598; P. v. Bealoba, 17 Cal. 389; C. v. Desmarteau, 16 Gray, 1; S. v. Harris, 12 Nev. 414; S. v. Wagner, 78 Mo. 644; Washington v. S., 25 Tex. Ap. 387. *Contra*, holding that the poisoning referred to is wilful and deliberate poisoning, see C. v. Keeper of Prison, 2 Ashm. 227; Robbins v. S., 8 Ohio St. 131. See, further, as to poisoning, the discussion in the following section.

[3] In some states "express malice," and not deliberation and premeditation, is the test of first degree: S. v. Verrill, 54 Me. 408; S. v. Jones, 1 Houst. Cr. Cas. 21; Ake v. S., 30 Tex. 466; Jones v. S., 29 Tex. Ap. 338. Therefore, a killing without justification, mitigation or excuse, with a formed design to kill, and a cool and sedate mind, is murder in the first degree: Summers v. S., 5 Tex. Ap. 365; Cox v. S., 5 Tex. Ap. 493; Stanley v. S., 14 Tex. Ap. 315; Campbell v. S., 15 Tex. Ap. 506. An indictment alleging facts indicating express malice is sufficient for the first degree: Banks v. S., 24 Tex. Ap. 559. If the act is the result of a rash and sudden design, springing from impulse, passion or excitement, it is not with express malice, and therefore not in the first degree: Jones v. S., 29 Tex. Ap. 338; Burnham v. S., 43 Tex. 322. But design to kill is not essential to constitute express malice; a design to do serious bodily harm by an unlawful act may be enough: Primus v. S., 2 Tex. Ap. 369. Evidence of express malice is admissible where accused can be convicted only of the second degree: McLaughlin v. S., 10 Tex. Ap. 340.

tion and premeditation. It will be necessary to discuss these various classes separately, but it should be first said that the statutes do not, in general, change the definition of murder; and the distinction between murder and manslaughter remains as at common law, except that in a very few instances what was at common law a form of murder is by statute made a grade or degree of manslaughter. Therefore, the second degree of murder must still have the characteristics of murder at common law.[1] Malice aforethought is essential in both degrees.[2] To constitute murder in the first degree so far as it is made to depend upon deliberation and premeditation, there must be proof of something more than the malice, express or implied, which constitutes murder.[3] It seems that murder in the second degree is to be looked upon as mitigated murder, in much the same way as manslaughter is mitigated criminal homicide.[4] But this question will need further discussion in considerating how murder in the first degree is to be charged in the indictment.[5] Some statutes provide for a third degree of murder.[6]

§ 354. **First degree; by poison or lying in wait.**— The statutes on the subject uniformly make a murder, perpetrated by means of poisoning or lying in wait, of the first degree, and they sometimes couple with these forms of killing others of similar atrocity.[7] The use of poison in causing death indicates deliberation and premeditation, and thus makes the homicide of the same degree of atrocity as though wilful, deliberate and premeditated within the other portion of the statute.[8] In an early case in Pennsylvania, construing the first statute on this

[1] P. v. Haun, 44 Cal. 96; Gehrke v. S., 13 Tex. 568. And see *infra*, § 365.

[2] P. v. Potter, 5 Mich. 1; Fouts v. S., 4 Greene (Ia.), 500; S. v. Johnson, 8 Ia. 525; Babcock v. P., 13 Colo. 515; S. v. Curtis, 70 Mo. 594; Craft v. S., 3 Kan. 450.

[3] Smith v. S., 68 Ala. 424; S. v. Foster, 61 Mo. 549; S. v. Lane, 64 Mo. 319; S. v. Evans, 65 Mo. 574; Finn v. S., 5 Ind. 400; Palmore v. S., 29 Ark. 248; S. v. Garrand, 5 Oreg. 216; P. v. Guance, 57 Cal. 154; P. v. Long, 39 Cal. 694; Beers v. S., 24 Neb. 614; Milton v. S., 6 Neb. 136; Schlencker v. S., 9 Neb. 300; Anderson v. S., 26 Neb. 387; Sullivan v. C., 93 Pa. St. 284; S. v. Raymond, 11 Nev. 98; Guffee v. S., 8 Tex. Ap. 187.

[4] See, by way of illustration, C. v. Gardiner, 11 Gray, 438; Boyd v. S., 7 Coldw. 69.

[5] *Infra*, § 361.

[6] Marshall v. S., 32 Fla. 462.

[7] See P. v. White, 24 Wend. 520.

[8] Zell v. C., 94 Pa. St. 258; S. v. Wells, 61 Ia. 629; S. v. Baldwin, 36 Kan. 1.

subject, it was said that homicide committed by administering a drug or using an instrument upon a woman to commit an abortion was not murder in the first degree, even though the drug was a poison, the poisoning contemplated by statute being wilful and deliberate poisoning.[1] To the contrary, it has been decided in Missouri that homicide by poison administered, not with intent to kill, but in order to accomplish some unlawful act, being murder at common law, will be murder in the first degree under the statute, because it is murder which is committed by means of poison.[2] The question will be in construing such a statute whether it includes only intentional killing by poison in the first degree or whether it includes all murder by poison in that degree. In Ohio, where the statute makes murder in the first degree to consist of any act of "purposely and of deliberate and premeditated malice, . . . or by administering poison, killing another," it is held that intent to kill the specific person must be shown.[3] In Texas the form of the statute is such that a common-law murder committed by poison or lying in wait is of the first degree, although these forms are not expressly enumerated.[4] The expression, "lying in wait," means lying in ambush or concealment.[5] And it may be shown that the killing was of this form under an indictment for murder in the first degree, although alleged to be by wilful, deliberate and premeditated killing, instead of by lying in wait, for the evidence of this form of killing would show wilfulness, deliberation and premeditation.[6] Under a construction of the Missouri statute similar to that given in case of a death by poisoning, it is held that if the murder is committed by lying in wait it is of the first degree, without reference to whether the intent was to kill the party killed or another, either of such cases being murder at common law.[7] And in a Tennessee case it is said that, under such circumstances, evidence as to the extent of the injury which the party assailing intended to inflict is irrelevant, as the use of a deadly weapon would show

[1] C. v. Keeper of Prison, 2 Ashm. 227.

[2] S. v. Wagner, 78 Mo. 644.

[3] Robbins v. S., 8 Ohio St. 131.

[4] Tooney v. S., 5 Tex. Ap. 163. But they are not so *per se:* Osborne v. S., 23 Tex. Ap. 431.

[5] S. v. Cross, 68 Ia. 180.

[6] S. v. Green, 66 Mo. 631; S. v. Kilgore, 70 Mo. 546; Riley v. S., 9 Humph. 646.

[7] S. v. Payton, 90 Mo. 220.

malice aforethought, such as to make the case murder.[1] So, in Virginia, it is said that murder by lying in wait or by poison will be of the first degree, whether the killing was intended or not.[2] The term "concealed" is not synonymous with "lying in wait;" a person may, while concealed, kill another without committing the crime of murder. It is only where he conceals himself for the purpose of killing another unawares that he is lying in wait.[3]

§ 355. **In perpetrating certain felonies.**— The statutes defining murder in the first degree, perhaps without exception, include cases where the homicide results during the perpetration or attempt to perpetrate certain felonies named, those usually included being arson, rape, robbery, mayhem and burglary. As has been shown, a homicide resulting from the commission or attempt to commit a felony is with malice aforethought and is therefore murder.[4] And the effect of the statutory provision as to the first degree is to make criminal in that degree the murder resulting from committing or attempting to commit the particular felonies specified. No intent to kill and no deliberation and premeditation are necessary, the implied malice involved in the felonious intent being sufficient.[5] The intent to commit one of the named felonies, in itself constitutes deliberation and premeditation, and therefore, under an indictment for the first degree charging the offense as wilful, deliberate and premeditated, evidence is admissible that the homicide was committed in the perpetration of robbery, one of such felonies.[6] Or where a common-law form of indictment is sufficient for the first degree, proof of the first degree by the commission of a named felony may be made under such an indictment.[7] The

[1] Riley v. S., 9 Humph. 646.

[2] C. v. Jones, 1 Leigh, 598.

[3] P. v. Miles, 55 Cal. 207.

[4] See *supra*, § 326.

[5] Moynihan v. S., 70 Ind. 126; Stephens v. S., 42 Ohio St. 150; S. v. Pike, 49 N. H. 399; Cox v. P., 80 N. Y. 500; C. v. Pemberton, 118 Mass. 36: P. v. Bealoba, 17 Cal. 389; Pharr v. S., 7 Tex. Ap. 472; Singleton v. S., 1 Tex. Ap. 501; Gonzales v. S., 19 Tex. Ap. 394; Washington v. S., 25 Tex. Ap. 387; Smith v. S., 31 Tex. Ap. 14.

[6] S. v. Johnson, 72 Ia. 393; S. v. Meyers, 99 Mo. 107. Wilfulness and premeditation are shown by proving that the homicide was committed as the initiatory act in the perpetration of the crime of robbery: S. v. Worrell, 25 Mo. 205; Duran v. S., 14 Tex. Ap. 195; Meradez v. S., 29 Tex. Ap. 608.

[7] C. v. Flanagan, 7 W. & S. 415; Cox v. P., 80 N. Y. 500; Titus v. S., 49 N. J. 36. And see, as to indictment for first degree, *infra*, § 361.

indictment may, however, allege fully the commission of the felony, and the murder may then be charged as having been committed while in the perpetration of such felony.[1] The killing is committed in the perpetration or attempt to perpetrate one of the named felonies if it occurs at any time while the perpetrator is engaged in any acts immediately connected with such felony, even though the felony may have been already completed.[2] In New York a killing perpetrated in the commission of any felony is murder in the first degree, regardless of any intent to kill, and regardless of whether the violence causing death is part of the other felony or separate and distinct.[3] In Wisconsin the court, construing a similar statute, holds that the felony must be separate and in addition to the mere act of causing death, and is not supplied or evidenced by intent presumed from the act itself, so that, although any homicide unexplained would be a felony, the intent to commit a felony would not be presumed therefrom so as to make the homicide murder of the first degree; as the court say, this would be presuming the felony from the act and then qualifying the act by the felony.[4] The doctrine of the New York court was also recognized under a similar statute in Missouri,[5] but has been modified by later cases in the same state; and it is now held that under the language of the statute which makes murder, committed in the perpetration of a felony, of the first degree, it is not enough that death results from the murderous assault, but there must be some collateral felony attempted distinct from the acts of personal violence causing the homicide.[6]

[1] Dolan v. P., 64 N. Y. 485.

[2] Dolan v. P., 64 N. Y. 485. Thus, where defendant, having committed a robbery, and while carrying off the plunder, was pursued by an officer whom he shot at, and in so doing killed a by-stander, *held*, that the murder was of the first degree: S. v. Brown, 7 Oreg. 186.

[3] Buel v. P., 78 N. Y. 492. Thus, an attempt to escape from lawful custody on a charge of felony, being punishable by confinement in the penitentiary, is in itself such felony that homicide committed in the attempt is murder in the first degree: P. v. Johnson, 110 N. Y. 134. So, murder committed in the perpetration of a felonious assault will be in the first degree: P. v. Giblin, 115 N. Y. 196.

[4] S. v. Hammond, 35 Wis. 315.

[5] S. v. Nueslein, 25 Mo. 111.

[6] S. v. Shock, 68 Mo. 552. To the point that it is the murder, and not merely the killing committed in the perpetration of a felony, that constitutes murder in the first degree, see, also, S. v. Earnest, 70 Mo. 520; S. v. Hopper, 71 Mo. 425. But these cases

There must be, however, something more than the mere intent to commit a felony; there must also be an overt act,[1] and the killing must have been in the attempt to commit the felony, and not after the attempt has been abandoned and as the result of an independent intent.[2]

§ 356. **Wilful, deliberate and premeditated killing.**— The statutes almost uniformly make of the first degree, murder which is committed by means of wilful, deliberate and premeditated killing or with wilful, deliberate and premeditated malice aforethought. The general meaning of these terms, as grouped together, is that suggested by the words themselves.[3] In using the term "other killing," as qualified by wilful, deliberate and premeditated, and after specifying "by poison or lying in wait," the statute does not restrict such killing to killing by like means, but includes wilful, deliberate and premeditated killing by any means.[4] In Massachusetts, where the statute defines murder of the first degree as "deliberate and premeditated," or "committed with extreme cruelty and atrocity," or committed in the "commission of certain felonies," proof of either of these attending elements is sufficient; and "deliberation and premeditation" are held not applicable to the other two forms.[5] The method of taking life in case of a homicide by poison is by statute equivalent to deliberate and premeditated homicide; but in cases not specified by statute, the deliberation and premeditation must be found by the jury to make the case of the first degree.[6] However a separate discussion of these terms is necessary.

have again been modified to the extent of deciding that, if the homicide would have been murder at common law, then it would be of the first degree under the statute, even though the subject of the felony and the murder is the same person: S. v. Hopkirk, 84 Mo. 278. The distinction thus made in Missouri between killing and murder in the perpetration of a felony is not recognized in the courts of Pennsylvania: Kelly v. C., 1 Grant, 484.

[1] Kelly v. C., 1 Grant, 484.

[2] Hoffman v. S., 88 Wis. 166.

[3] Dale v. S., 10 Yerg. 550.

[4] C. v. Jones, 1 Leigh, 598; P. v. Bealoba, 17 Cal. 389; S. v. Fairlamb, 121 Mo. 137; S. v. Harris, 12 Nev. 414.

[5] C. v. Desmarteau, 16 Gray, 1. And see *supra*, § 353.

[6] P. v. Sanchez, 24 Cal. 17. So in Texas, where the statute does not specify killing by poison or lying in wait as first degree: Osborne v. S., 23 Tex. Ap. 431; Tooney v. S., 5 Tex. Ap. 163.

§ 357. **Wilfulness; intentional killing.**— Intent to kill is essential to constitute murder in the first degree under the statutory provision as to wilful, deliberate and premeditated killing. Implied or constructive malice is not sufficient to make the homicide of that degree.[1] Therefore it has been said that if with premeditated intent to slay one person death is caused to another, this will not be murder in the first degree.[2] But with more reason it has been held in other cases that defendant may be guilty of murder in the first degree in a wilful, deliberate and premeditated killing although his intent was not directed toward any particular individual, but involved only the killing of some one generally.[3] In instructing the jury as to the killing being intentional, it is erroneous to say that if defendant "intentionally shot" the deceased, "killing him," it is murder in the first degree; the instruction should be that if he shot intending to kill, and did kill, that degree of murder would be shown.[4] As to the expression "wilful," used in the statute, it means nothing more than an intentional killing,[5] and may be omitted from the instruction entirely if other equivalent words, such as "maliciously, deliberately and premeditatedly," are used.[6] Wilfulness alone does not make the murder of the first degree.[7]

§ 358. **"Deliberate and premeditated."**— The word "deliberately" is not equivalent to "intentionally" or "wilfully," but means more.[8] It has been said that the word "premedi-

[1] C. v. Green, 1 Ashm. 289; P. v. Bealoba, [illegible] Cal. 389; S. v. Gillick, 7 Ia. 287, [illegible]; P. v. Clark, 7 N. Y. 385; P. v. White, 24 Wend. 520; Donnelly v. S., 26 N. J. 463, 509; S. v. Herrell, 97 Mo. 105; Anthony v. S., Meigs, 265; Keenan v. C., 44 Pa. St. 55; P. v. Foren, 25 Cal. 361; Clark v. S., 8 Humph. 671; Dains v. S., 2 Humph. 438.

[2] Bratton v. S., 10 Humph. 103; McConnell v. S., 13 Tex. Ap. 390; Taylor v. S., 3 Tex. Ap. 387. But where defendant on hearing of a fight ran into the crowd with a stick, striking several persons, among others a by-stander, who died from the effects of the blow, *held*, that he was guilty of murder in the first degree: Wright v. C., 75 Va. 914.

[3] Hopkins v. C., 50 Pa. St. 9; Spies v. P., 122 Ill. 1; Wright v. C., 75 Va. 914. Thus, two persons may be guilty of the same murder in the first degree: Phelps v. S., 15 Tex. Ap. 45; Ruloff v. P., 45 N. Y. 213.

[4] Savage v. S., 18 Fla. 909. But in Pennsylvania it is enough if the act was deliberate: Keenan v. C., 44 Pa. St. 55.

[5] S. v. Townsend, 66 Ia. 741.

[6] Fisher v. S., 10 Lea, 151.

[7] S. v. Keasling, 74 Ia. 528.

[8] S. v. Sharp, 71 Mo. 218. Where defendant by slight insult or assault has brought on the retaliation of de-

tated" does not indicate anything different from the malice aforethought of the common law when applied to the express intent to take life, and a premeditated design to effect death simply means express malice.[1] Therefore, deliberation is the only element added to distinguish the two degrees as applied to an intended killing.[2] On the contrary, it is said in another case that premeditation implies more than deliberation, and means to meditate and deliberate before concluding to do the act, and that this distinctive peculiarity is what characterizes the first degree.[3] So far as deliberation implies that the act must have been thought of beforehand, it distinguishes murder in the first degree from manslaughter.[4] "Premeditated" means "thought of beforehand," and an instruction which defines it as indicating that the act was "thought of," without adding the word "beforehand," is erroneous.[5] But it does not mean "thought over," which would be equivalent to deliberation.[6] It is doubtful, however, whether any precise distinction in meaning between the terms "deliberate" and "premeditated" can be made. They have been said in some cases to be synonymous,[7] or to mean about the same thing.[8] The insertion of the word "or" instead of "and" between "deliberate" and "premeditated" has been held immaterial.[9] The words "deliberate and premeditated" are intended to restrict the first degree to cases where deliberation is shown to have taken place before the commission of the act,[10] and require that the killing shall have been done with reflection and conceived of beforehand.[11]

ceased and then has immediately killed him with a dangerous weapon, this indicates murder in the first degree, since if the intention to kill had been a sudden impulse the first attack would not have been a slight one, which indicates a certain amount of control: S. v. Wieners, 66 Mo. 13.

[1] P. v. Clark, 7 N. Y. 385; S. v. Taylor, 126 Mo. 531.

[2] Darry v. P., 10 N. Y. 120; S. v. Curtis, 70 Mo. 594. Deliberation includes premeditation: S. v. Dale, 108 Mo. 205.

[3] S. v. Johnson, 8 Ia. 525. And see Wiggins v. S., 23 Fla. 180.

[4] S. v. Robinson, 73 Mo. 306; S. v. Lewis, 74 Mo. 222; Craft v. S., 3 Kan. 450.

[5] S. v. Harris, 76 Mo. 361.

[6] S. v. Ellis, 74 Mo. 207. "Premeditated design" includes malice aforethought: S. v. Duvall, 26 Wis. 415.

[7] S. v. Lopez, 15 Nev. 407.

[8] Cleveland v. S., 86 Ala. 1; Bower v. S., 5 Mo. 364; S. v. Wieners, 66 Mo. 13; S. v. Kotovsky, 74 Mo. 247.

[9] P. v. Pool, 27 Cal. 572.

[10] Beers v. S., 24 Neb. 614; Milton v. S., 6 Neb. 136.

[11] Zimmerman v. S., 14 Neb. 568; Boulden v. S., 102 Ala. 78; S. v.

The intent must have preceded the killing long enough to admit of premeditation and deliberation, although they need not have existed for any particular length of time.[1] There must be a deliberately formed design.[2] Some time, however short, should have intervened between the formation of the design and its execution, in which the intention was deliberated upon.[3] But the length of time is not material;[4] no particular length of time is necessary.[5] The law fixes no measure of time for deliberation and premeditation.[6] It is not necessary that there be any appreciable space of time.[7] Premeditation may exist, although not for an extended time;[8] "some moments,"[9] "a moment,"[10] will be sufficient. No matter for how short a time deliberation and premeditation are entertained, if they exist the murder will be of the first degree.[11] It is not necessary that the deliberate, premeditated intention should be formed and matured prior to the occasion at which the act is done; if executed the moment it is formed the offense is in the first degree.[12] The jury must determine in the particular case whether there was reflection in the act and a choice and deliberation as the result of mental action.[13]

Reed, 117 Mo. 604. If the intent to kill formed beforehand is conditional, it will nevertheless make the offense of the first degree: S. v. Kearley, 26 Kan. 77.

1 S. v. Sopher, 70 Ia. 494; S. v. Hockett, 70 Ia. 442.

2 Swan v. S., 4 Humph. 136; S. v. Green, 1 Houst. Cr. C. 217.

3 Fahnestock v. S., 23 Ind. 231; Lovett v. S., 30 Fla. 142.

4 S. v. Smith, 49 Conn. 376; Shoemaker v. S., 12 Ohio, 43; Donnelly v. S., 26 N. J. 463; S. v. McCormac, 116 N. C. 1033.

5 Wright v. C., 33 Grat. 880; P. v. Bealoba, 17 Cal. 389; S. v. Dunn, 18 Mo. 419; P. v. Sanchez, 24 Cal. 17; S. v. Ah Mook, 12 Nev. 369; S. v. Brown, 41 Minn. 319; S. v. Dennison, 44 La. An. 135; Whiteford v. C., 6 Rand. 721; Wright v. C., 75 Va. 914; S. v. Carr, 53 Vt. 37; S. v. Johnson, 8 Ia. 525.

6 S. v. Rhodes, 1 Houst. Cr. C. 476; Carter v. S., 22 Fla. 553.

7 P. v. Cotta, 49 Cal. 166; Binns v. S., 66 Ind. 428; Miller v. S., 54 Ala. 155; Halbert v. S., 3 Tex. Ap. 656; Green v. S., 51 Ark. 189.

8 Ernest v. S., 20 Fla. 383.

9 S. v. Peffers, 80 Ia. 580.

10 Keenan v. C., 44 Pa. St. 55; Anthony v. S., Meigs, 265; S. v. Jennings, 18 Mo. 435; Lang v. S., 84 Ala. 1; Donnelly v. S., 26 N. J. 463; Shoemaker v. S., 12 Ohio, 43; Green v. S., 98 Ala. 14.

11 Donnelly v. S., 26 N. J. 601; P. v. Moore, 8 Cal. 90; S. v. Jones, 64 Mo. 391; Jones v. S., 90 Ala. 628; S. v. Fairlamb, 121 Mo. 137.

12 Herrin v. S., 33 Tex. 638; Wright v. C., 33 Grat. 880.

13 P. v. Hawkins, 109 N. Y. 408; P. v. Gibson, 17 Cal. 283; S. v. Brown, 41 Minn. 319; Lovett v. S., 30 Fla. 142; Westcott v. S., 31 Fla. 458; S. v. Morey, 25 Oreg. 241.

§ 359. Evidence of deliberation and premeditation.— It has been said in some cases that an intentional killing, the intent to kill being shown by the use of a deadly weapon, will, in the absence of any evidence of justification, excuse, or mitigation, be murder in the first degree.[1] Such a presumption is denied, however, in other cases, and it is said that killing with a deadly weapon is not enough alone to show deliberation and premeditation.[2] But even where such a presumption is recognized it is not conclusive, but may be overcome by evidence showing an absence of deliberation.[3] However, according to the great weight of authority such presumption does not arise from proof of intentional killing alone, and from such evidence, without more, the jury would not be justified in convicting of the first degree.[4] The question whether the killing was deliberate and premeditated is for the jury, and it is erroneous to charge that certain facts will show deliberation and premeditation;[5] or that there are no circumstances in the case to reduce the offense below that of murder in the first degree.[6] Circumstances indicating premeditation and deliberation are to be construed by the jury only as evidence and not as conclusive in law.[7] Even where the statute provides that murder perpetrated by means of poison or by any other kind of wilful, deliberate and premeditated killing, etc., shall be murder in the first degree, the jury may still find a verdict for the second degree under a charge of murder by poison, the statute especially prescribing that the degree shall be determined by the jury.[8] What is meant by saying that the question is for the

[1] C. v. Green, 1 Ashm. 289; Kilpatrick v. C., 31 Pa. St. 198; Warren v. C., 37 Pa. St. 45; McCue v. C., 78 Pa. St. 185; Lanahan v. C., 84 Pa. St. 80; Abernethy v. C., 101 Pa. St. 322; S. v. Gillick, 7 Ia. 287, 311; S. v. Welch, 36 W. Va. 690; Irvin v. S., 19 Fla. 872; P. v. Bealoba, 17 Cal. 389.

[2] Dains v. S., 2 Humph. 438.

[3] Kelly v. C., 1 Grant, 484.

[4] Stokes v. P., 53 N. Y. 164; Dukes v. S., 14 Fla. 499; Hall v. S., 40 Ala. 698; S. v. Foster, 61 Mo. 549; S. v. Carver, 22 Oreg. 602; S. v. Olds, 19 Oreg. 397; Witt v. S., 6 Coldw. 5; Fouts v. S., 4 Greene (Ia.), 500; S. v. McCormick, 27 Ia. 402; Schlencker v. S., 9 Neb. 300; P. v. Gibson, 17 Cal. 283; P. v. Belencia, 21 Cal. 544; P. v. Williams, 73 Cal. 531; S. v. Hicks, 27 Mo. 588; Watson v. C., 85 Va. 867; S. v. Hobbs, 37 W. Va. 812; S. v. Fuller, 114 N. C. 885; Hamby v. S., 36 Tex. 523; Baltrip v. S., 30 Tex. Ap. 545.

[5] P. v. Williams, 73 Cal. 531.

[6] P. v. Ah Lee, 60 Cal. 85.

[7] Hill v. P., 1 Colo. 436.

[8] S. v. Dowd, 19 Conn. 388.

jury is that, where there is evidence tending to show deliberation and premeditation, the verdict will not be disturbed.[1] But if there is not sufficient evidence of these elements, the trial court may so direct the jury, or its sufficiency may be considered on appeal.[2] While it is necessary, therefore, that the premeditation and deliberation shall be found by the jury, such finding is not necessarily based upon express or positive evidence thereof, but may be predicated upon all the circumstances connected with the killing.[3] Although, as already indicated, the mere act of killing will not be sufficient evidence of deliberation and premeditation,[4] yet, if the circumstances show that the defendant had time to consider the act and select the manner or weapon to be used, he may be convicted of the first degree.[5] Direct proof of previous animosity or other motive is not necessary in addition to proof of killing where there are no attendant circumstances to show justification or mitigation.[6] If all the circumstances surrounding the act are consistent with premeditated, deliberate intent, the jury may find the first degree.[7] There is, however, no presumption of the first degree, and the introduction of evidence of previous intent to kill, tending to show premeditation and deliberation, does not throw the burden upon defendant to prove that such intention had been abandoned.[8] Premeditation and deliberation may be shown by proof of the nature of the murderous assault;[9] or by proof of previous hostility and threats;[10] of declarations just preceding the killing indicating the intent,[11] together with procuring and employing a deadly weapon in a fatal manner,[12]

[1] T. v. Johnson, 9 Mont. 21.

[2] S. v. Olds, 19 Oreg. 397.

[3] S. v. Dunn, 18 Mo. 419; S. v. Shoultz, 25 Mo. 128; S. v. Starr, 38 Mo. 270; S. v. Joeckel, 44 Mo. 234; S. v. Holme, 54 Mo. 153; S. v. Underwood, 57 Mo. 40; S. v. Foster, 61 Mo. 549; S. v. Mitchell, 64 Mo. 191; S. v. Kilgore, 70 Mo. 546; S. v. Walker, 98 Mo. 95; P. v. Bowman, 81 Cal. 566; Hicks v. S., 25 Fla. 535; Yates v. S., 26 Fla. 484; S. v. Brown, 41 Minn. 319; T. v. Romine, 2 N. Mex. 114.

[4] S. v. Cushing, 29 Mo. 215. And see *supra*, § 358.

[5] S. v. Holme, 54 Mo. 153; S. v. Wisdom, 84 Mo. 177; P. v. Beckwith, 103 N. Y. 360; S. v. Brown, 41 Minn. 319; S. v. Hansen, 25 Oreg. 391.

[6] McKee v. P., 36 N. Y. 113; Sindram v. P., 88 N. Y. 196.

[7] P. v. Conroy, 97 N. Y. 62.

[8] Murray v. C., 79 Pa. St. 311.

[9] C. v. Murray, 2 Ashm. 41.

[10] P. v. Bezy, 73 Cal. 186; Kehoe v. C., 85 Pa. St. 127.

[11] Smith v. S., 7 Tex. Ap. 414.

[12] T. v. Johnson, 9 Mont. 21; P. v. Goslaw, 73 Cal. 323.

or arranging a plan for the homicide.[1] But evidence of previous brutal and cruel treatment will not suffice.[2]

§ 360. Intoxication or insanity as showing want of deliberation or premeditation.— While, as has been said elsewhere,[3] intoxication is no excuse for crime, yet, where the question is between murder in the first degree and second degree, it may be proven as tending to show that there was not deliberation and premeditation in the act.[4] But one who deliberately resolves to kill another and makes himself drunk for that purpose is guilty of murder in the first degree.[5] Mere drunkenness will not negative the specific intent to kill evidenced by actual shooting and killing, no motive for the act being shown.[6] Insanity may be taken into account as well as intoxication for the purpose of affecting the degree.[7]

§ 361. Indictment for first degree.— The general requisites of an indictment for murder will be hereafter considered, but in direct connection with a discussion of the difference between the degrees of murder it will be well to notice whether any change by reason of such division of the crime into degrees is made necessary in the usual form of indictment for murder. In the state where the statutory division into degrees was first adopted it was held that the degrees as defined were not new offenses created by statute, and therefore to be charged in the language of the statute, but were simply classes of the previous crime of murder made with reference to the penalty to be inflicted, and therefore no change in the common-law indictment for murder was required, punishment for the first degree being properly inflicted under the usual indictment.[8]

[1] Garlitz v. S., 71 Md. 293.

[2] Shelton v. S., 34 Tex. 662.

[3] *Supra*, § 160.

[4] Willis v. C., 32 Grat. 929; Kelly v. C., 1 Grant, 484; Jones v. C., 75 Pa. St. 403; P. v. Williams, 43 Cal. 344; S. v. Johnson, 40 Conn. 136; S. v. Johnson, 41 Conn. 584; Tidwell v. S., 70 Ala. 33. *Contra*, S. v. O'Reilly, 126 Mo. 597. And see *supra*, § 162.

[5] S. v. Robinson, 20 W. Va. 713.

[6] Estes v. S., 55 Ga. 31; Nevling v. C., 98 Pa. St. 322.

[7] Anderson v. S., 43 Conn. 514; P. v. Walter, 1 Idaho (N. S.), 386. This whole subject is considered in the chapter on insanity and intoxication, *supra*, § 162.

[8] White v. C., 6 Binn. 179; C. v. Flanagan, 7 W. & S. 415. And see Greer v. S., 3 Baxt. 321. The statute creating degrees does not create new offenses: Garvey's Case, 7 Colo. 384. Where the statute simply describes conditions of the crime, but does not make them separate degrees, the common-law indictment is sufficient: P. v. Enoch, 13 Wend. 159.

And this view has been approved in other states.[1] This result is also supported in the same states on the ground that the statute specially directs that the jury shall find the degree in their verdict, or on a plea of guilty such finding shall be made by the court (or in some states by a jury specially impaneled) on the evidence received for that purpose, which provisions would have been unnecessary if it was intended that the degree should be specially charged, as in that case a verdict or plea of guilty would have determined the degree.[2] In some states it is specially provided by statute that no change in the form of indictment shall be made necessary by the division into degrees.[3] And such statutory provision has been held not to be in conflict with the usual constitutional provision requiring the defendant to be informed of the offense of which he is charged.[4] Other cases reach the same result on the theory that the ordinary indictment for murder alleging the killing as done feloniously, wilfully and of malice aforethought sufficiently charges the first degree.[5] According to the great weight of authority, a finding of guilt in the first degree may be made under an indictment in the common-law form for murder.[6] In accordance with this general doctrine

[1] C. v. Gardner, 11 Gray, 438; C. v. Desmarteau, 16 Gray, 1; P. v. Haun, 44 Cal. 96; S. v. Pike, 49 N. H. 399.

[2] White v. C., 6 Binn. 179; C. v. Flanagan, 7 W. & S. 415; P. v. Doe, 1 Mich. 451; Redus v. P., 10 Colo. 208.

[3] C. v. Gardner, 11 Gray, 438; Redus v. P., 10 Colo. 208; Garvey's Case, 7 Colo. 384. In Minnesota a form of indictment provided by statute and not specifying the degree was held sufficient for the first degree: S. v. Dumphey, 4 Minn. 438. So, in California it has been held that the statutory definition of murder, which corresponds to the common-law definition, covers both degrees and that it is sufficient to follow it (as in the common-law form) without charging the characteristics of the first degree: P. v. De La Cour Soto, 63 Cal. 165; P. v. Hyndman, 99 Cal. 1.

[4] C. v. Gardner, 11 Gray, 438; Graves v. S., 45 N. J. 347. The decision in a state court that the common-law indictment will support conviction for the first degree raises no question under the federal constitution: In re Robertson, 156 U. S. 183; Bergemann v. Backer, 157 U. S. 655; Kohl v. Lehlback, 160 U. S. 293.

[5] S. v. Verrill, 54 Me. 408; S. v. Hing, 16 Nev. 307; P. v. Ah Choy, 1 Idaho (N. S.), 317. In accordance with the Maine case it is held in the same state that under a common-law indictment a verdict of guilty implies guilty in the first degree: S. v. Cleveland, 58 Me. 564. But the cases cited in the opinion do not support that conclusion.

[6] In addition to the cases already cited in this section the following support this proposition: Mitchell v. S., 5 Yerg. 340; S. C., 8 Yerg. 513; Hines v. S., 8 Humph. 597; Taylor v.

as to deliberation and premeditation, it has also been held that proof of the killing in the perpetration of a felony, such as by the statute will make the offense murder of the first degree, may be proved and found by the jury under the common-law indictment.[1] Opposed, however, to the authorities already cited in this section are some cases indicating and approving a general practice in their respective states of specially charging the first degree in the indictment when a conviction for that degree is sought by alleging the killing to have been wilful, deliberate and premeditated, or by poison or lying in wait, or in the commission of some specified felony.[2] It should be said of these cases, however, before citing them, that in not one of them (except perhaps the first case from Iowa) is the exact question passed on; yet they doubtless indicate an opinion on the part of the courts rendering them which would lead to the reversal of a conviction in the first degree on an indictment containing no allegation indicating the crime to have been of that degree. In Ohio it is held that as in that state there are no common-law offenses, but all crimes are statutory, and the statute is explicit in describing murder in the first degree, the allegations must follow the statute as in the case of other statutory offenses.[3] In Missouri it is held that the form of indictment charging the killing as wilful, deliberate and premeditated is in use, and that a particular indictment under consideration

S., 11 Lea, 708; Williams v. S., 3 Heisk. 37; Hogan v. S., 30 Wis. 428; Green v. C., 12 Allen, 155; Fitzgerald v. P., 37 N. Y. 413; Kennedy v. P., 39 N. Y. 245; Dolan v. P., 64 N. Y. 485; P. v. Conroy, 97 N. Y. 63; P. v. Giblin, 115 N. Y. 196; S. v. Jones, 50 N. H. 369; Gehrke v. S., 13 Tex. 568; Wall v. S., 18 Tex. 682; Roach v. S., 8 Tex. Ap. 478; C. v. Miller, 1 Va. Cas. 310; Livingston v. C., 14 Grat. 592; McGee v. S., 8 Mo. 495; S. v. Dunkley, 3 Ired. 116; Davis v. S., 39 Md. 355; McAdams v. S., 25 Ark. 405; S. v. Lessing, 16 Minn. 75; Hill v. P., 1 Colo. T. 436; Noles v. S., 24 Ala. 672; S. v. Millain, 3 Nev. 409; Leschi v. T., 1 Wash. T. 13; T. v. Bannigan, 1 Dak. 432; Davis v. Utah, 151 U. S. 262. And see 1 Whart. Cr. L., § 393.

[1] C. v. Flanagan, 7 W. & S. 415; Cox v. P., 80 N. Y. 500; P. v. Giblin, 115 N. Y. 196; Titus v. S., 49 N. J. 36; S. v. Meyers, 99 Mo. 107; Roach v. S., 8 Tex. Ap. 478.

[2] Bishop gives his unqualified approval to this doctrine: See 2 Bish. Cr. L., § 726; 2 Bish. Cr. P., § 561 *et seq.*

[3] Fouts v. S., 8 Ohio St. 98; Kain v. S., 8 Ohio St. 306; Hagan v. S., 10 Ohio St. 459. Intent to kill must be alleged: Robbins v. S., 8 Ohio St. 131. But purposely and with deliberate and premeditated malice giving a mortal wound is sufficient allegation of such intent: Loeffner v. S., 10 Ohio St. 598.

was not sufficient in that respect.[1] In Iowa, without citing any of the cases on the point, but after dissenting from some of the arguments made in support of the general rule, the court held an indictment which did not use the words "deliberately and premeditatedly" insufficient to sustain a conviction of the first degree.[2] In the later Iowa cases indictments have been held insufficient to support a conviction in the first degree which alleged a wilful, deliberate and premeditated assault and the infliction of an injury from which death resulted, but did not allege that the killing was wilful, deliberate and premeditated.[3] The same conclusion has been reached in Kansas, following the Iowa cases.[4] In Indiana the doctrine of the Ohio court is adopted and it is said that the indictment must allege a purpose to kill.[5] In Idaho the circumstances constituting the

[1] This was not, however, the principal point in the case: S. v. Jones, 20 Mo. 58. In a previous case the court had passed on the sufficiency of the evidence to show wilfulness, deliberation and premeditation, and, one of the judges dissenting, had assumed by way of argument that the indictment must contain such allegations: Bower v. S., 5 Mo. 364.

[2] Fouts v. S., 4 Greene (Ia.), 500. This case is said by the same court to be against the weight of authority, but is not directly overruled, the precise question not arising: S. v. Johnson, 8 Ia. 525.

[3] S. v. McCormick, 27 Ia. 402; S. v. Watkins, 27 Ia. 415; S. v. Knouse, 29 Ia. 118; S. v. Thompson, 31 Ia. 393; S. v. Baldwin, 79 Ia. 714; S. v. Andrews, 84 Ia. 88. And see Kain v. S., 8 Ohio St. 306. But indictments have been held sufficient which thus allege the assault and that defendant did thereby wilfully, deliberately and premeditatedly inflict a mortal wound with specific intent to kill, without saying that the intent to kill was deliberate and premeditated: S. v. Shelton, 64 Ia. 333; S. v. Townsend, 66 Ia. 741; S. v. Stanley, 33 Ia. 526. And see Loeffner v. S., 10 Ohio St. 598. It is also held prejudicial error to put a party on trial for murder in the first degree under an indictment not sufficiently charging that degree, although he is only convicted of the second degree: S. v. Boyle, 28 Ia. 522; S. v. Knouse, 29 Ia. 118. Sentence for second degree cannot be imposed where conviction for first degree is reversed on account of insufficiency of indictment to charge that degree: S. v. Watkins, 27 Ia. 415. But see S. v. McCormick, 27 Ia. 402.

[4] S. v. Brown, 21 Kan. 38. The necessity of charging wilfulness, deliberation and premeditation in order to warrant a conviction in the first degree was recognized in Smith v. S., 1 Kan. 365; but in that case it was held that the conclusion to the indictment in which the grand jury charged wilful, deliberate and premeditated killing made the indictment sufficient. This, however, is contrary to the Ohio and Iowa cases: Kain v. S., 8 Ohio St. 306; Hagan v. S., 10 Ohio St. 459; S. v. McCormick, 27 Ia. 402; S. v. Andrews, 84 Ia. 88.

[5] Snyder v. S., 59 Ind. 105.

first degree must be charged.[1] In Connecticut the statute requires that the indictment shall allege the degree of the crime charged, and the courts of that state, while recognizing the weight of authority in favor of the general doctrine that the statute simply divides the crime into degrees and therefore a common-law indictment is sufficient, requires the indictment to show that the first degree is charged, but holds this need not be done by formal averment, but may be by any appropriate words indicating that the grand jury intend to charge the first degree — a statement of that fact in the conclusion of the indictment being sufficient.[2] The foregoing review of the cases leads to the conclusion that the peculiar Ohio doctrine, that there are no common-law crimes and that the statutory description of murder in the first degree is the description of a new crime, has been the source of the rule that the first degree must be specifically charged. In determining the form to be used in this respect the pleader must be guided by the precedents in his own state.[3]

§ 362. **Finding as to degree.**— The provisions of the statutes differ as to how the degree is to be determined and the punishment affixed. In states where it is not necessary to specifically charge the first degree, a general verdict of guilty under a common-law indictment for murder will not establish the first degree of the crime.[4] There are a few cases, however,

[1] P. v. O'Callaghan, 2 Idaho, 143.

[2] S. v. Dowd, 19 Conn. 388; S. v. Hamlin, 47 Conn. 95; Smith v. S., 50 Conn. 193.

[3] For forms, see *infra*, § 388; also, Whart. Prec., Forms 139–141; 2 Bish. Cr. P., § 561 *et seq.;* Bish. Direc. & Forms, § 517.

[4] Johnson v. C., 24 Pa. St. 386; Hogan v. S., 30 Wis. 428; Kirby v. S., 7 Yerg. 258; McPherson v. S., 9 Yerg. 279; S. v. Montgomery, 98 Mo. 399; Cobia v. S., 16 Ala. 781; Johnson v. S., 17 Ala. 618; Hall v. S., 40 Ala. 698; Story v. S., 71 Ala. 329; Dover v. S., 75 Ala. 40; Levison v. S., 54 Ala. 520; P. v. Marquis, 15 Cal. 38; P. v. Campbell, 40 Cal. 129; Tully v. P., 6 Mich. 273; Williams v. S., 60 Md. 402; Ford v. S., 12 Md. 514; S. v. Dowd, 19 Conn. 388; Thompson v. S., 26 Ark. 323; S. v. Rover, 10 Nev. 388; Slaughter v. S., 24 Tex. 410; Krebs v. S., 3 Tex. Ap. 348; Dubose v. S., 13 Tex. Ap. 418. Even where the jury fixes the punishment at that which is provided for the second degree, this will not dispense with the finding of the degree: Johnson v. S., 30 Tex. Ap. 419; Slaughter v. S., 24 Tex. 410. It is held in S. v. Cleveland, 58 Me. 564, that "guilty as charged" is a sufficient finding of the first degree even under a common-law indictment, but this doctrine is not supported by the authorities cited in the opinion and is contrary to the view of the court as expressed in S. v. Verrill, 54 Me. 408.

in which it is held that a verdict of guilty under such an indictment will support a sentence for the first degree without any finding by the jury.[1] Even in states where the first degree must be specified in the indictment it is held that a verdict of guilty as charged is not a sufficient finding of the degree where the statute requires the degree to be found by the jury, one reason assigned being that such an indictment also charges the lower degree.[2] If the statute requires that the jury find the degree, a verdict which does not find the degree is a nullity and will support no conviction whatever.[3] It has been held, however, that where the indictment alleges murder committed by poison or by lying in wait, or in the perpetration of robbery, burglary, or some other of the felonies specified in the description of the first degree, a verdict of guilty as charged will be a sufficient finding of the degree.[4] It has also been held that if the verdict in the first degree is not supported by the evidence, the court may sentence as on a verdict for the second degree.[5] In general, where the statute directs the jury to find the degree, the court can give no instructions with reference thereto.[6] The provisions as to the finding of the degree by the jury have no application to a case where the jury might find a lower included crime, such as manslaughter; and if a verdict of guilty is rendered under an indictment charging murder, it is sufficient to sustain a sentence for murder although the jury might, under the indictment, have rendered a verdict for manslaughter or some other lower offense.[7] It seems also that if the indictment charges only the second degree, a verdict of guilty simply is sufficient.[8]

[1] S. v. Gilchrist, 113 N. C. 673; White v. S., 16 Tex. 206; Curtis v. S., 26 Ark. 439; Leschi v. T., 1 Wash. T. 23; T. v. Romine, 2 N. Mex. 114; T. v. Yarberry, 2 N. Mex. 391.

[2] Dick v. S., 3 Ohio St. 89; Parks v. S., 3 Ohio St., 101; McGee v. S., 8 Mo. 495; S. v. Upton, 20 Mo. 397; Colbath v. S., 2 Tex. Ap. 391. *Contra*, Bilansky v. S., 3 Minn. 427.

[3] Allen v. S., 85 Wis. 22; In re Eckart, 85 Wis. 681; Hall v. S., 31 Fla. 176; Nelson v. S., 32 Fla. 244; S. v. Montgomery, 98 Mo. 399; S. v. Jackson, 99 Mo. 60.

[4] C. v. Earl, 1 Whart. 525; White v. C., 6 Binn. 179; S. v. Weese, 53 Ia. 92 (overruling to some extent S. v. Moran, 7 Ia. 236, which was in harmony with the cases cited in the second preceding note). *Contra*, Kendall v. S., 65 Ala. 492; S. v. Dowd, 19 Conn. 388.

[5] Simpson v. S., 56 Ark. 8.

[6] Lane v. C., 59 Pa. St. 371.

[7] St. Clair v. U. S., 154 U. S. 134.

[8] Porter v. S., 57 Ark. 267.

§ 363. Fixing the punishment.— By some statutes a discretion is left to the jury in determining the punishment. If the provision is such as to authorize a mitigation merely by the jury, then if they do not in their verdict fix the penalty, it is the duty of the court to impose the higher penalty provided by statute;[1] but some statutes leave the penalty within certain limits entirely to the jury, and in such a case a verdict not fixing the penalty will be invalid.[2] And the court should not in any way interfere by instructions with the discretion of the jury.[3] A statutory provision that the jury shall fix the penalty is not unconstitutional.[4] If the statute leaves the punishment to the jury only in case of conviction of the first degree, then if the verdict is in the second degree the punishment is to be imposed by the court.[5] Where the fixing of the punishment is for the jury, evidence in mitigation is admissible, though it would not be legally sufficient to reduce the homicide to manslaughter.[6]

§ 364. Fixing the degree of punishment on plea of guilty. Statutes sometimes contain the provision that, in case of a plea of guilty, witnesses are to be examined by the court and the degree of the crime thus fixed, and the record should therefore show that these steps were taken;[7] and such a method of procedure is not unconstitutional.[8] In Texas the degree must be fixed by jury, even where defendant pleads guilty.[9] Where the degree is to be fixed by the court on such a plea, it is not error, after hearing the witnesses and determining the degree, but before entry of judgment, to overrule an application of defendant to withdraw the plea.[10]

[1] P. v. Welch, 49 Cal. 174; Green v. S., 55 Miss. 454; Fleming v. S., 60 Miss. 434.

[2] Doran v. S., 7 Tex. Ap. 385; Marshall v. S., 33 Tex. 664; Buster v. S., 42 Tex. 315; Walston v. S., 54 Ga. 242.

[3] Hill v. S., 72 Ga. 131; Spain v. S., 59 Miss. 19; S. v. Johnson, 30 La. An. (pt. II), 921; S. v. Foster, 36 La. An. 857; P. v. Leary, 105 Cal. 486 (apparently overruling P. v. Bawden, 90 Cal. 195, and earlier cases).

[4] S. v. Hockett, 70 Ia. 442.

[5] S. v. Howard, 118 Mo. 127; White v. S., 30 Ala. 518.

[6] Nowacryk v. P., 139 Ill. 336; Fletcher v. P., 117 Ill. 184.

[7] McCauley v. U. S., Morris, 486. But in another case it was held that the presumption that the court acted properly would be sufficient: In re Brown, 32 Cal. 48.

[8] Hallinger v. Davis, 146 U. S. 314.

[9] Sanders v. S., 18 Tex. Ap. 372.

[10] P. v. Lennox, 67 Cal. 113.

§ 365. Murder in second degree.— Where murder is divided into two degrees and the facts do not show any of the classes of cases which by statute are made to constitute the first degree, but do show what would at common law be murder,[1] the crime is murder in the second degree, unless excluded by some peculiarity in the statutory definition of that degree. In general, all common-law murders which are not by statute of the first degree are of the second degree.[2] The prosecution may elect to try for the second degree only,[3] and the fact that defendant is put on trial for the second degree while the evidence shows the first degree will not render a conviction of the second degree improper.[4] The presumption, on proof of homicide without circumstances of mitigation or excuse, will be as already stated,[5] that there was malice aforethought, and therefore that the crime is murder; but such presumption will be of murder in the second and not in the first degree.[6] Neither deliberation nor premeditation is essential to murder in the second degree;[7] nor is specific intention to kill.[8] Murder in the perpetration of a felony, not being one of the felonies named in the statutory provision with reference to murder in the first degree, will be murder in the second degree.[9] So, murder by carelessly throwing a stone into a crowd without any intention of killing any particular person, but thereby causing death, is of the second degree.[10] Murder committed

[1] Keefe v. P., 40 N. Y. 348.

[2] S. v. Conley, 39 Me. 78; Weighorst v. S., 7 Md. 442; P. v. Doyell, 48 Cal. 85; Fields v. S., 52 Ala. 348; Gray v. S., 4 Baxter, 331.

[3] S. v. Moxley, 115 Mo. 644; S. v. Baldwin, 79 Ia. 714.

[4] Fuller v. S., 30 Tex. Ap. 559.

[5] See *supra*, §§ 332, 333.

[6] Schlencker v. S., 9 Neb. 300; Preuit v. P., 5 Neb. 378; Milton v. S., 6 Neb. 136; S. v. Testerman, 68 Mo. 408; S. v. Underwood, 57 Mo. 40; S. v. Holme, 54 Mo. 153; Pennsylvania v. Lewis, Addison, 279; Harris v. S., 8 Tex. Ap. 90; Douglass v. S., 8 Tex. Ap. 520; Hubby v. S., 8 Tex. Ap. 597.

[7] S. v. Keasling, 74 Ia. 528.

[8] S. v. Decklotts, 19 Ia. 447; S. v. Morphy, 33 Ia. 270; S. v. Mewherter, 46 Ia. 88; S. v. O'Hara, 92 Mo. 59; except in Ohio and Kansas: See *supra*, § 326.

[9] S. v. Leeper, 70 Ia. 748; S. v. Boice, 1 Houst. Cr. C. 355.

[10] Golding v. S., 26 Fla. 530. So, in Wisconsin, under a statute defining murder in the second degree as homicide when perpetrated by an act imminently dangerous to others and evincing a depraved mind regardless of human life, although without any premeditated design to effect the death of any particular individual, *held*, that this degree includes cases where the actual intent to take life is absent, the act being of such nature as to be inherently

without deliberation and premeditation, but upon such intent to kill as arises involuntarily on some sudden provocation or hasty impulse, not sufficient, however, to reduce homicide to manslaughter, is of the second degree.[1] Where the killing is the result of a sudden impulse due to an insult, even though by words alone, the murder will be of the second degree, there not being sufficient provocation to reduce the homicide to manslaughter.[2] So, disrespectful words spoken of defendant's wife may be sufficient to indicate that the killing was not deliberate and premeditated.[3] But provocation by insulting words will only reduce the crime to the second degree when the act is the immediate result of rashness and impetuous temper without consciousness of any purpose except to do bodily harm, and not when it is the result of hate and revenge with sufficient consciousness to select a deadly weapon with the purpose of taking life.[4] So, other evidence may show that the killing, though in a sudden combat or upon a sudden occasion, was wilful and deliberate.[5] If there has been time for the passion to subside,[6] or the passion is without reasonable cause,[7] it will not reduce the killing to the second degree. Other cases where death in a quarrel was held to be murder in the second degree will be found in the note.[8] On the other hand, where, after a

an assault dangerous to human life, whether to the person against whom it is directed or to persons in general: Hogan v. S., 36 Wis. 226. And as to a similar statute in Minnesota, see S. v. Stokely, 16 Minn. 282.

[1] S. v. Wieners, 66 Mo. 13; S. v. Lane, 64 Mo. 319; S. v. Packwood, 26 Mo. 340; P. v. Barberi, — N. Y. — (43 N. E. R. 635); Bohanan v. S., 15 Neb. 209; Hornsby v. S., 94 Ala. 55; Anderson v. S., 31 Tex. 440; Ake v. S., 31 Tex. 416. Absence of previous grudge may be shown to indicate that the murder was only of the second degree: Kelly v. C., 1 Grant, 484. But even if there appears an old grudge, the killing may be the result of a sudden impulse without premeditation, and, therefore, of the second degree: McQueen v. S., 1 Lea, 285; S. v. Till, 1 Houst. Cr. Cas. 233.

[2] Watson v. S., 82 Ala. 10; S. v. Hill, 69 Mo. 451; S. v. Lewis, 74 Mo. 222; S. v. Kotovsky, 74 Mo. 247; S. v. McGinnis, 76 Mo. 326.

[3] S. v. Collins, 81 Mo. 652; S. C., 86 Mo. 245.

[4] Green v. C., 83 Pa. St. 75.

[5] S. v. Burgess, 78 Mo. 234; S. v. Wisdom, 84 Mo. 177; S. v. McDaniel, 94 Mo. 301. A conspiracy implies premeditation, and is therefore inconsistent with the second degree: S. v. Swain, 68 Mo. 605.

[6] P. v. Kerrigan, 147 N. Y. 210; Ex parte Jones, 31 Tex. Ap. 422.

[7] Smith v. S., 103 Ala. 4.

[8] Harris v. S., 36 Ark. 127; McDaniel v. C., 77 Va. 281; Wilson v. S., 6 Tex. Ap. 427; Evans v. S., 6 Tex. Ap. 513; Cunningham v. S., 17 Tex. Ap. 89; Hull v. S., 6 Lea, 249; Allsup v. S., 5 Lea, 362.

fight is over, one of the parties turns deliberately and kills the other, the murder is of the first degree.[1] Killing in resisting rightful ejectment from premises will not be murder in the second degree, though done in the scuffle arising from the attempt to eject.[2] Where an officer in seeking to arrest for a misdemeanor (and therefore having no right to take life) fired at the person attempting to escape and accidentally killed a by-stander, he was held guilty of murder in the second degree.[3] While infidelity of the wife may cause such frenzy that the killing of the wife by the husband will be only murder in the second degree, yet where there has been time to cool and for deliberation in view of the circumstances, the killing will be of the first degree.[4] Although the second degree of murder is without deliberation and specific intent to kill, yet there may be an accessory before the fact to murder in the second degree.[5]

§ 366. Question of law and fact.— Whether the provocation is sufficient to show that the murder was of the second degree and not deliberate is a question for the court, and whether the state of mind involving want of deliberation in an intentional killing was in fact produced by such provocation is a question for the jury.[6]

§ 367. Conviction of second degree under indictment of first degree.— Defendant being put on trial under an indictment properly charging the first degree, in those states where the indictment must show the degree, may be convicted of the second degree on failure of the evidence to show the premeditated malice or the attempt to commit a felony necessary to establish the first degree.[7] Therefore it is proper to instruct as to the second degree.[8] But no instruction as to the second degree is necessary where, under the evidence, the defendant is guilty of the first degree or not guilty of any crime; for in-

[1] S. v. Gardner, 1 Houst. Cr. Cas. 146; S. v. Rhodes, 1 Houst. Cr. Cas. 476.

[2] Keenan v. C., 44 Pa. St. 55.

[3] S. v. O'Neil, 1 Houst. Cr. Cas. 468.

[4] S. v. Bulling, 105 Mo. 204; S. v. Anderson, 98 Mo. 461; Garlitz v. S., 71 Md. 293.

[5] Jones v. S., 13 Tex. 168.

[6] S. v. Ellis, 74 Mo. 207.

[7] Keefe v. P., 40 N. Y. 348.

[8] S. v. Baker, 13 Mont. 160. This subject is discussed hereafter in connection with instructions as to other crimes necessarily included in murder: See *infra*, § 391.

stance, where defendant relies for justification or excuse on insanity or accident.[1]

§ 368. Degrees of manslaughter. — In some states manslaughter remains as at common law, but in others it has been divided more or less elaborately into degrees. Such division is sometimes made into voluntary and involuntary manslaughter, the voluntary corresponding to that kind of manslaughter already described as consisting in intentional killing under such provocation as to negative malice and therefore prevent the offense being murder;[2] the involuntary including all the other common-law classes of manslaughter, that is, those in which the offense does not indicate an intention to cause death.[3] In Texas manslaughter is limited to voluntary homicide, other

[1] Boren v. S., 32 Tex. Ap. 637; S. v. Reed, 117 Mo. 604; S. v. Fairlamb, 121 Mo. 137.

[2] Voluntary manslaughter is on sudden heat, without malice, but with intent to kill: Creek v. S., 24 Ind. 151; Bruner v. S., 58 Ind. 159; Norton v. S., 98 Ind. 347; Luck v. S., 96 Ind. 16. But it is not necessary that actual intent to kill appear, nor that instruments or means usually fatal shall have been employed from which such intent may be implied. The intent may be implied from the infliction of violence, which would not be likely to prove fatal in case of an ordinary person, upon one in such physical condition that the use of such violence would be probably followed by death or great danger to life. It is the element of a probably fatal result from the injury that distinguishes voluntary from involuntary manslaughter: Murphy v. P., 9 Colo. 435. The death need not be by a deadly weapon in order to make the manslaughter voluntary; it is enough that it is with violence dangerous to life: Thompson v. S., 24 Ga. 297; Ray v. S., 15 Ga. 223; Brown v. S., 28 Ga. 199. Under the Georgia statute, including death resulting from an attempt to commit a serious personal injury in voluntary manslaughter, *held*, that this expression meant an attempt to commit an injury greater than a provocation by mere words and less than a felony: Buchanan v. S., 24 Ga. 282. In a similar case of killing with a deadly weapon, *held*, that the circumstances supported a conviction for voluntary manslaughter: Irby v. S., 32 Ga. 496.

[3] Homicide committed in the perpetration of an act which is in itself unlawful, or not done with sufficient caution, but without intention to kill or do serious bodily harm, is involuntary manslaughter: C. v. Gable, 7 Serg. & R. 423. It is not included in a charge of murder or involuntary manslaughter, but must be specially charged in a separate count: Walters v. C., 44 Pa. St. 135. Drawing a deadly weapon upon another, being an unlawful act, is sufficient to make death resulting, although unintended, involuntary manslaughter: Surber v. S., 99 Ind. 71. Homicide resulting from doing a wrongful act is involuntary manslaughter: S. v. Johnson, 102 Ind. 247. Negligently running over and killing a child will support a conviction of involuntary manslaughter: Lee v. S., 1 Coldw. 62. Negligence in performing a surgical

forms of the common-law offense being otherwise named.[1] In some states manslaughter is divided into degrees according to the wrongfulness of the act. The cases with reference to the construction of these statutory provisions as to degrees are sufficiently stated in the note.[2]

operation from which death results may be involuntary manslaughter: S. v. Gile, 8 Wash. 12. Where a statute creates two grades of the offense of involuntary manslaughter, a verdict of guilt of involuntary manslaughter without specifying the grade will not support a judgment: Thomas v. S., 38 Ga. 117.

[1] Therefore a common-law indictment for manslaughter is not sufficient: Jennings v. S., 7 Tex. Ap. 350.

[2] In Alabama an act amounting to manslaughter voluntarily committed is of the first degree without regard to provocation: Oliver v. S., 17 Ala. 587; McManus v. S., 36 Ala. 285; Collier v. S., 69 Ala. 247. But in a later case it is said that to constitute the first degree there must be either a positive intention to kill or an act of violence from which, in the usual course of events, death or great bodily harm may result: Harrington v. S., 83 Ala. 9; Williams v. S., 83 Ala. 16. In Wisconsin manslaughter in the first degree is what would at common law be murder with malice aforethought implied from the use of a dangerous weapon, without intent to take life or do great bodily harm: Rowan v. S., 30 Wis. 129; Boyle v. S., 57 Wis. 472; while manslaughter in the fourth degree is the involuntary killing of another by any weapon or any means neither cruel or unusual in heat of passion: Schlecht v. S., 75 Wis. 486. Under the same statute defining a degree of manslaughter as consisting of killing which is not in a cruel and unusual manner, and there is evidence of killing by means of cutting and stabbing with a knife, the question of whether the manner was cruel and unusual is for the jury: Keenan v. S., 8 Wis. 132. So held also under a similar statute in Missouri: S. v. Gassert, 65 Mo. 352. By the Missouri statute manslaughter in the fourth degree includes negligent killing: S. v. Morrison, 104 Mo. 638. Under the same statute death from negligence while engaged in the perpetration of any other felony refers to death resulting from some other wrong than the act of violence itself: S. v. Sloan, 47 Mo. 604; S. v. Downs, 91 Mo. 19. The distinction between the third and fourth degree of manslaughter in that state turns on the question of whether the killing in heat of passion was by a dangerous weapon or by means cruel or unusual: S. v. Wilson, 98 Mo. 440. But there may be manslaughter of the fourth degree even where there is intent to kill, if the act is without malice and in the heat of passion: S. v. McKinzie, 102 Mo. 620. Common-law voluntary manslaughter does not fall within the statutory degree of manslaughter defined as being without design: S. v. Edwards, 70 Mo. 480. The statutory crime defined as the unlawful killing of another on a sudden quarrel without malice does not necessarily imply intent to kill: Montgomery v. S., 11 Ohio, 424. And in such offense there may be an aider and abettor: Hagan v. S., 10 Ohio St. 459. But there can be no aider and abettor in involuntary manslaughter where there is no conspiracy to use a dangerous weapon, even though there is a conspiracy to do an unlawful act.

VII. JURISDICTION AND VENUE.

§ **369. Jurisdiction.**— The general subject of jurisdiction belongs to procedure rather than the substantive criminal law, but in homicide a peculiar question arises which requires attention here. In general, criminality is determined by the nature of the act done and the intent with which it is done; but a criminal homicide is not committed until the death of the injured person, although the connection of the accused with the crime is already completed. It is true that the act itself accompanied with the criminal intent may be some form of assault, but until death occurs it is not criminal homicide. Therefore, where the act of the accused is committed in one jurisdiction, while the death of the injured party takes place in another, some difficulty has been supposed to arise in determining in which jurisdiction the offense is to be punished. The origin of the difficulty is to be found in some peculiar rules of common-law procedure relating to the venue, which are considered in the next section; but the jurisdictional question is less easily disposed of, for while the venue as between different counties in the same jurisdiction may be regulated by statute, no statutory regulation can cure the trouble growing out of a defect in jurisdiction. It is not competent for one sovereignty to punish as a crime against it an act which is done outside of its territorial limits.[1] Therefore the question is, whether the homicide is a crime in the jurisdiction where the wound is inflicted, or the jurisdiction where the death occurs; and notwithstanding some doubts which have been expressed on the subject, it is now definitely settled that the criminality of the one who inflicts the wound, or other injury which subsequently causes death, is fixed by the completion of his act, provided death subsequently follows within a year and a day, and he may be punished within the jurisdiction where the act is thus completed without regard to where the death occurs.[2] In some cases this result is held to be

[1] S. v. Carter, 27 N. J. 499; Tyler v. P., 8 Mich. 320; S. v. Hall, 114 N. C. 909; Reg. v. Keyn, L. R. 2 Exch. 63.

[2] U. S. v. Guiteau, 1 Mackey, 498, 47 Am. R. 247; S. v. Hall, 114 N. C. 909; S. v. Gessert, 21 Minn. 369. This view is enforced by cases cited in the next section as to venue: See especially S. v. Bowen, 16 Kan. 475; Green v. S., 66 Ala. 40; Riley v. S., 9 Humph. 646. It is also supported by decisions to the effect that in deter-

reached only by virtue of statutory provisions,[1] and it is said that without legislation the homicide cannot be punished in the jurisdiction where the wound is inflicted if the death occurs in another jurisdiction.[2] Statutes have, however, been upheld which make the offense punishable in the jurisdiction where the death occurs, on the theory that the crime is a continuous one and may be punished where it is completed.[3] The reasoning of these cases would seem to be inconsistent with that of the cases just cited, in which it is held that the offense is complete when the mortal wound is inflicted, provided only that death subsequently occurs. On the other hand there are cases apparently not supported by sound reasoning which hold that if a wound is inflicted on the high seas, and death subsequently occurs on land, the crime of murder on the high seas is not committed.[4] Where a person standing on one side of the boundary line between two jurisdictions, as, for instance, two states of the Union, fires across the line at a person within the other jurisdiction, and thus commits a criminal homicide, the crime is committed in the jurisdiction where the injury is inflicted, and not in that where the offender is when he fires the shot.[5] And even if no actual injury whatever is inflicted, the crime of assault with intent to commit murder is committed within the jurisdiction where the person is who is assaulted,[6] although it is difficult to see why an assault is not also committed within the jurisdiction of the assailant, as a wrongful act in the nature of assault and the criminal intent there concur.

§ 370. **Venue.**— At common law there was at one time a doubt whether, if the wound was inflicted in one county and death occurred in another, an indictment could be found in

mining when the crime was committed, for instance whether prior or subsequent to the passing of a certain statute, the date of inflicting the wound and not that of the death is to be considered the date of the crime: P. v. Gill, 6 Cal. 637; Dibney v. S., 45 Neb. 856.

[1] Hunter v. S., 40 N. J. 495, 546.

[2] C. v. Linton, 2 Va. Cas. 205.

[3] C. v. Macloon, 101 Mass. 1; S. v. Caldwell, 115 N. C. 794; Reg. v. Azzopardi, 1 C. & K. 203; Reg. v. Lewis, 7 Cox, 277. And see Hunter v. S., 40 N. J. 495, 548.

[4] U. S. v. McGill, 1 Wash. C. C. 463; U. S. v. Armstrong, 2 Curt. 446.

[5] S. v. Hall, 114 N. C. 909, 28 L. R. A. 59 and note. But there can be no extradition in such a case, as the criminal does not flee from the state where the crime was committed: Ibid. And see Jones v. Leonard, 50 Ia. 106; Hartman v. Aveline, 63 Ind. 344.

[6] Simpson v. S., 92 Ga. 41.

either county.[1] But this doubt was resolved in England by a statute providing that the prosecution might take place in either county, and similar provisions will be found in the statutes of the various states;[2] and it is not essential to allege the circumstances, but the whole transaction may be charged as taking place in the county where the prosecution is brought.[3] Sometimes the statute makes the offense punishable only in the county where the blow was struck.[4]

VIII. THE INDICTMENT.

§ 371. **Murder and manslaughter distinguished.**— The discussion under the third principal heading of this chapter as to the division of criminal homicide into murder and manslaughter has indicated in what respect the two crimes differ, and from that discussion it appears that the crimes are alike as to the fact and unlawfulness of the killing, and differ only in the nature of the intent, express or implied, with which the unlawful act is done. It is apparent, therefore, that it is only in this respect that indictments for these two kinds of criminal homicide will differ, and that in the main their allegations may be, as they practically are, the same. Indictments for these two offenses may therefore be discussed indiscriminately, except with reference to the intent, where the distinction will be pointed out.

§ 372. **Elements.**— An analysis of the common-law form of indictment for criminal homicide[5] will disclose that such indictment may be divided into the following principal elements (omitting the introduction, which is the same in this as in other indictments for felony): (1) The name of the party charged; (2) the name or description of the person killed; (3) the act done; (4) with reference to the means employed; (5) the injury inflicted; (6) the result of such injury; (7) the time and place and fact of the death; and (8) the conclusion.

[1] 1 Hale, P. C. 426; 1 East, P. C. 361; 1 Hawk. P. C., ch. 31, § 13.

[2] Nash v. S., 2 Greene (Ia.), 286; C. v. Parker, 2 Pick. 550; Dula v. S., 8 Yerg. 510; S. v. Blunt, 110 Mo. 322; Green v. S., 66 Ala. 40; S. v. Bowen, 16 Kan. 475; Riley v. S., 9 Humph. 646.

[3] S. v. Jones, 38 La. An. 792.

[4] Stout v. S., 76 Md. 317; 9 Am. Cr. R. 398, and note.

[5] See *infra*, § 388.

§ 373. Name of the party charged; "sound mind."— No different principles apply to indictments for criminal homicide from those applicable in other indictments as to naming the defendant or accused, and therefore no general discussion of the question is here material. It is not necessary to describe defendant as "of sound mind and memory" or to otherwise indicate his sanity.[1]

§ 373a. The person killed.— In general, indictments for homicide do not differ from other indictments as to the necessity and method of naming or describing the injured party, but some peculiar rules in that respect arise from the fact that it is the death of the injured party that is complained of. The indictment must in some way name or describe the person killed. Even though the name of the person assaulted is given, if the indictment is blank as to the name of the person killed it is insufficient.[2] The name by which the deceased was generally or commonly known is sufficient.[3] Where the name of deceased is to the grand jury unknown, that fact may be alleged,[4] coupled with some other description, such as a "female child,"[5] or "infant child,"[6] a "woman,"[7] a certain "Wyandott Indian."[8] But the allegation that the name is to the grand jury unknown must be proven. If it appears that the name was known to the grand jury, the misdescription will be fatal.[9]

[1] Jerry v. S., 1 Blackf. 395; Fahnestock v. S., 23 Ind. 231; Dumas v. S., 63 Ga. 600; Bean v. S., 17 Tex. Ap. 60.

[2] S. v. Pemberton, 30 Mo. 376; Dias v. S., 7 Blackf. 20. *Contra* where the only omission of the name was in the conclusion, the body of the indictment being in proper form: Evans v. P., 12 Mich. 27.

[3] P. v. Freeland, 6 Cal. 96. And it is immaterial that he has another name: Jones v. S., 65 Ga. 147; Hunter v. S., 8 Tex. Ap. 75.

[4] Reese v. S., 90 Ala. 624; Edmonds v. S., 34 Ark. 720; Rex v. Clark, Russ. & Ry. 358. If the Christian name is unknown that fact may be stated, the surname being given: Bryan v. S., 36 Ala. 270. So, if the surname is unknown the Christian name may be given: Reg. v. Stroud, 1 C. & K. 187; Edmonds v. S., 34 Ark. 720.

[5] S. v. Richmond, 42 La. An. 299.

[6] Tempe v. S., 40 Ala. 350. It is not necessary to aver the sex of the child: S. v. Morrissey, 70 Me. 401.

[7] Reg. v. Campbell, 1 C. & K. 82. Or a "white woman:" Rothschild v. S., 7 Tex. Ap. 519.

[8] Reed v. S., 16 Ark. 499. Where the indictment undertakes to describe deceased by his race, the description must be proved: Reed v. S., 16 Ark. 499.

[9] Reese v. S., 90 Ala. 624. Where the Christian name is known it should be stated. It would be erroneous to allege that the name is to the grand jurors unknown: Reg. v.

The indictment must give the name or account for the omission.[1] But an allegation in an indictment for the killing of an infant child that it was not named is sufficient.[2] In the case of illegitimate children the surname of the mother may be used if the child has been known by that name,[3] otherwise it should not be described by that name.[4] Although the name should be proved as alleged,[5] yet, where there is no controversy as to the identity, it need not be fully proven, no variance appearing.[6] Error in the middle name is not material.[7] The general doctrine in all crimes where description of a person is necessary, that it is sufficient if the name used in the indictment has, or may be given, the same sound as that proven (or, as it is generally expressed, is *idem sonans* with the name proven), is illustrated by a few cases cited in the note.[8]

§ 374. **Human being; in the king's peace.**— It is not necessary to allege in terms that the person killed was a human being; the name imports such fact.[9] Nor is necessary to al-

Stroud, 1 C. & K. 187; Rothschild v. S., 7 Tex. Ap. 519; Reg. v. Campbell, 1 C. & K. 82.

[1] Reg. v. Hicks, 2 M. & Rob. 302.

[2] Reg. v. Waters, 2 C. & K. 864. "Not baptized" would not be sufficient: Ibid.; Reg. v. Bliss, 8 C. & P. 773. In case of a bastard child the absence of a name is sufficiently accounted for by describing it as "lately before born of the body of," etc.: Reg. v. Hogg, 2 M. & Rob. 380. In such case, the bastard not having acquired a name, it would be error to describe it as of a name unknown; Reg. v. Willis, 1 C. & K. 722.

[3] Reg. v. Evans, 8 C. & P. 765.

[4] Rex v. Clark, Russ. & Ry. 358; Rex v. Waters, 1 Moody, 457. But where there is some evidence that the child has been known by a name, its name may be said to be to the grand jurors unknown: Rex v. Smith, 6 C. & P. 151; Rex v. Poulton, 5 C. & P. 329.

[5] S. v. Angel, 7 Ired. 27; Davis v. P., 19 Ill. 74. But proof of identity is not necessarily restricted to proof of name: Shepherd v. P., 72 Ill. 480. If deceased is described by his Christian and surname, proof of the surname only is not sufficient: Penrod v. P., 89 Ill. 150.

[6] Rutherford v. S., 11 Lea, 31. Discrepancy between the name in the indictment and the description in the order to the attorney-general to prosecute *ex officio* is immaterial: Boyd v. S., 14 Lea, 161.

[7] P. v. Lockwood, 6 Cal. 205.

[8] "Churchill" and "Churchwell:" Reddick v. S., 25 Fla. 112, 433. "Preyer" and "Prior:" Page v. S., 61 Ala. 16. "Boredet" and "Burdet:" Aaron v. S., 37 Ala. 106. "Giddings," "Gidings" and "Gidines:" State v. Lincoln, 17 Wis. 579. "Herron" and "Herring:" Herron v. S., 93 Ga. 554.

[9] S. v. Stanley, 33 Ia. 526, 531; Palmer v. P., 138 Ill. 356; Merrick v. S., 63 Ind. 327; P. v. McNulty, 93 Cal. 427; S. v. Day, 4 Wash. 104; Bohannon v. S., 14 Tex. Ap. 271; Ogden v. S., 15 Tex. Ap. 454.

lege that the person killed was a reasonable creature in being,[1] or was in the king's peace or "in the peace of the state."[2]

§ 375. **Killing two or more persons.**— The killing of two or more persons may be charged in the same count when it is the result of one act.[3] And under such indictment defendant may be convicted on proof of a murder of one of the parties named.[4] But in order that two acts of felonious killing may constitute a single offense, something more should appear than that they were committed on the same occasion or in the progress of the same affray.[5]

§ 376. **Time and place of wrongful act.**— The general principle as to all crimes, that the time and place of the wrongful act, while necessarily alleged in an indictment as a part of the description, need not be proved as alleged, applies also to cases of criminal homicide, and it is only necessary here to give cases in which that principle has been thus applied.[6] As to most crimes there is a period of limitation for the prosecution, and the indictment must bring the act within the period of such limitation; but there is usually in such statutes an exception with reference to murder, the prosecution for which is thus generally left without limitation, and therefore as the allegation in the indictment need not have reference to any prescription of time, any time prior to the finding thereof will be sufficient,

[1] Perryman v. S., 36 Tex. 321; Bohannon v. S., 14 Tex. Ap. 271; Bean v. S., 17 Tex. Ap. 60; Wade v. S., 23 Tex. Ap. 308.

[2] C. v. Murphy, 11 Cush. 472; Dumas v. S., 63 Ga. 600. Under an indictment stating that the person murdered was in the king's peace, *held*, sufficient to show that he was a British subject (the charge being of murder of a British subject abroad): Rex v. Sawyer, 2 C. & K. 101.

[3] Womack v. S., 7 Coldw. 508; Griffith v. S., 90 Ala. 583; Clem v. S., 42 Ind. 420; Rucker v. S., 7 Tex. Ap. 549; Chivarrio v. S., 15 Tex. Ap. 330. *Contra*, P. v. Alibez, 49 Cal. 452.

[4] Haunstine v. S., 31 Neb. 112.

[5] Womack v. S., 7 Coldw. 508. But even where it appears that two persons were killed by separate blows, defendant cannot take advantage of the objection in arrest of judgment, though he might have required the state to elect upon which homicide it would proceed: Forrest v. S., 13 Lea, 103.

[6] Livingston v. C., 14 Grat. 592; S. v. Polite, 33 La. An. 1016; S. v. Kane, 33 La. An. 1269; Ball v. U. S., 140 U. S. 118. The offense may be proved to have been committed at any time before the finding of the indictment, whether before or after the time charged: O'Connell v. S., 18 Tex. 343. So under a statute: P. v. Kelly, 6 Cal. 210. The indictment may charge the violence as on different days where it consists of several acts of ill-treatment: C. v. Stafford, 12 Cush. 619.

no matter how remote.[1] The place is material in showing the jurisdiction of the court, but beyond that it is immaterial and need not be proven as alleged.[2] The particular place in the county where the crime was committed was formerly alleged in the common-law indictment, but is now not material.[3] The venue is where the blow is struck and not where the death takes place.[4] Under the federal statute with reference to murder committed on an American vessel, it is sufficient to allege that the vessel was owned by an American citizen.[5] Where the venue was alleged as, "In the district court of the United States of America for the first judicial district of Idaho Territory," it was held that the venue was properly alleged, the words "United States of America" being mere surplusage.[6] The venue being properly alleged and the time once stated, the words "then and there" sufficiently refer to such time and place.[7]

§ 377. **The means of killing.**— At common law the manner and means of killing must be set out,[8] and if by a weapon the

[1] S. v. Williams, 30 La. An., part II, 843. Although there is no limitation as to murder, lapse of time may be a strong consideration with the jury in weighing the testimony: P. v. Hancock, 7 Utah, 170. The crime is deemed committed when the fatal wound is inflicted, although death does not immediately result, and accused is to be tried under the law then in force: P. v. Gill, 6 Cal. 637; Debney v. S., 45 Neb. 856.

[2] S. v. Reed, 12 Md. 263. In North Carolina, unless the jurisdiction is put in issue by plea in abatement, the allegation that the killing was within the jurisdiction of the court will be presumed to be true: S. v. Outerbridge, 82 N. C. 617. So in Maryland, a wrong allegation of venue must be taken advantage of by demurrer: S. v. Reed, 12 Md. 263. In Arkansas, by statute, the indictment not alleging the venue is construed as charging it within the jurisdiction of the court: Brassfield v. S., 55 Ark. 556. Where the offense is murder committed on the high seas, the place is sufficiently charged by alleging that it was committed on board an American vessel on the high seas within the jurisdiction of the court and the admiralty and maritime jurisdiction of the United States and not within the jurisdiction of any particular state: St. Clair v. U. S., 154 U. S. 134.

[3] P. v. Robinson, 17 Cal. 363; Studstill v. S., 7 Ga. 2.

[4] S. v. Gessert, 21 Minn. 369. And see *supra*, § 370.

[5] U. S. v. Demarchi, 5 Blatch. 84.

[6] Pickett v. U. S., 1 Idaho (N. S.), 523.

[7] Woodsides v. S., 2 How. 655; S. v. Stewart, 26 S. C. 125; S. v. Taylor, 21 Mo. 477; S. v. Lamon, 3 Hawks, 175; S. v. Cherry, 3 Murph. 7. The omission of the word "there" in the phrase "then and there" is immaterial with reference to the assault where the averment of the place is otherwise sufficiently made: Jackson v. P., 18 Ill. 269.

[8] Rex v. Sharwin, 1 East, P. C. 341,

name of the weapon.[1] But it is sufficient to describe the weapon as a loaded pistol,[2] or a "certain wooden stick," without giving its length or thickness.[3] It is not necessary to describe the weapon as dangerous or deadly.[4] A variance as to the means between the allegations in the indictment and the evidence is fatal.[5] But, aside from any statutory modifications, much greater liberality with reference to the allegation of the means has been sanctioned in this country.[6] Allegations in different counts of various means, although inconsistent, will support a general verdict on evidence proving death to have resulted from some one of the means thus alleged.[7] And the prosecution cannot be compelled to elect as between such

421; White v. C., 9 Bush, 178; S. v. Owen, 1 Murph. 452; Guedel v. P., 43 Ill. 226; Haney v. S., 34 Ark. 263; P. v. Wallace, 9 Cal. 30; S. v. Williams, 36 Tex. 352; Drye v. S., 14 Tex. Ap. 185. But it is not necessary to allege the causes merely natural conducing to the death of the party, the act being properly alleged: Rex v. Webb, 1 M. & Rob. 405. To charge murder as committed with a shotgun, without setting forth the manner of its use, is not enough: Edwards v. S., 27 Ark. 493.

1 Hornsby v. S., 94 Ala. 55.

2 P. v. Choiser, 10 Cal. 310. It is not necessary to allege that it was loaded with powder and ball: Peterson v. S., 47 Ga. 524.

3 S. v. Smith, Phill. 340.

4 S. v. McDaniel, 94 Mo. 301; T. v. Tenorio, 1 N. Mex. 279. The nature of the instrument used or blow inflicted is not material except to determine the malice: C. v. Fox, 7 Gray, 585.

5 Thus, an allegation of the striking and beating with a piece of brick was held not supported by proof of the prisoner having knocked down the deceased with his fist, and that the death was caused by the deceased striking his head in falling on a piece of brick in consequence of the blow: Rex v. Kelly, 1 Moody, 113. So an indictment alleging a blow from a hammer, held not supported by proof of death from being pushed against the lock of a door: Rex v. Martin, 5 C. & P. 128; or the allegation of a mortal wound received by falling on the ground, by proof that the prisoner knocked deceased down by a blow upon the head: Rex v. Thompson, 1 Moody, 139. But an indictment charging death to have been caused by a mortal wound on the head inflicted with a swingle was held sufficiently supported by evidence of a blow upon the head with a piece of wood resulting in a contused wound and death from effusion of blood: Reg. v. Warman, 2 C. & K. 195. And the allegation of death caused by a plaster applied by defendant, held sufficiently proved by showing death from the application of three plasters, two applied by the defendant and the third made from materials furnished by him: Rex v. Spiller, 5 C. & P. 333.

6 P. v. Hyndman, 99 Cal. 1; S. v. Fox, 25 N. J. 566.

7 Jackson v. S., 39 Ohio St. 37; S. v. Blan, 69 Mo. 317; S. v. Baker, 63 N. C. 276; Smith v. C., 21 Grat. 809; Lazier v. C., 10 Grat. 708; Jones v. S., 65 Ga. 621; Hunter v. S., 40 N. J. 495; C. v. Macloon, 101 Mass. 1; Reg. v. O'Brian, 2 C. & K. 115.

counts.[1] So in the same count different instruments may be named, and proof of death by any one of them is sufficient.[2] The allegations as to means or instrument need not be strictly proven; it is sufficient if the mode of applying the violence is the same in kind as that alleged.[3] It is not necessary to charge in which hand the weapon was held.[4] So several may be charged with inflicting the wound, or even with holding in their hands the same weapon, and proof of the infliction of the wound by one and aiding and abetting by the others will be sufficient.[5] But if the indictment attempts to allege the acts of each defendant, and those alleged as to one are insufficient, the indictment as to him should be quashed.[6] Aside from statutory provisions, it is still insisted in some cases that it is not competent to prove the killing to have been done with a weapon or in a manner totally different from that named in the indictment.[7] Without regard to statutory modifications, it is sufficient to describe the crime as committed by some weapon or means to the grand jurors unknown, where the circumstances of the case are such as will not admit of greater certainty.[8] In

[1] Joy v. S., 14 Ind. 139; Dill v. S., 1 Tex. Ap. 278; Pierce v. U. S., 160 U. S. 355. This is so where different means are alleged in one count: Gonzales v. S., 5 Tex. Ap. 534.

[2] Beavers v. S., 58 Ind. 530; Pierce v. U. S., 160 U. S. 355. Inconsistency in this respect is immaterial: S. v. Taylor, 126 Mo. 531.

[3] State v. Jenkins, 14 Rich. 215; S. v. Smith, 32 Me. 369; Donnelly v. S., 26 N. J. 463; C. v. McAfee, 108 Mass. 458; State v. Gould, 90 N. C. 658. Proof of shooting with a pistol will support an allegation of shooting with a gun, the weapons being of the same character: Turner v. S., 97 Ala. 57. Proof of killing with a different weapon than that described will not constitute a fatal variance: Douglass v. S., 26 Tex. Ap. 109. So proof of killing with a pistol was held admissible under the charge of killing with a hatchet: P. v. Colt, 3 Hill, 432. So, where the allegation was of killing by cutting off the head of deceased with a knife, *held*, that proof of death by some sort of cutting about the neck was sufficient, no matter what weapon was used: Rodgers v. S., 50 Ala. 102.

[4] C. v. Robertson, 162 Mass. 90; C. v. Costley, 118 Mass. 1.

[5] C. v. Chapman, 11 Cush. 422; C. v. Roberts, 108 Mass. 296; Ritzman v. P., 110 Ill. 362; S. v. Payton, 90 Mo. 220; Evans v. S., 58 Ark. 47.

[6] Williams v. S., 42 Tex. 392.

[7] Witt v. S., 6 Coldw. 5. Thus, a charge of shooting with a gun is not supported by proof of beating upon the head with a gun: Guedel v. P., 43 Ill. 226.

[8] Rex v. Grounsell, 7 C. & P. 788; C. v. Webster, 5 Cush. 295; C. v. Holmes, 157 Mass. 233; S. v. Williams, 7 Jones, 446; Edmonds v. S., 34 Ark. 720; S. v. Parker, 65 N. C. 453; S. v. Burke, 54 N. H. 92. And under such allegation it is not necessary to offer any evidence of the particular means or instrument by which

most of the states statutes have been passed making it unnecessary to allege the means or manner.[1] By such statutes it is sometimes made sufficient simply to charge that accused did feloniously, etc., kill and murder the deceased;[2] but where the form given in the statute retains a description of the means used, an allegation of killing by a particular instrument "or other weapon" is insufficient,[3] and in such case a charge that defendant did "kill and murder" the deceased is insufficient.[4] Such statutes are not unconstitutional.[5] These statutes usually obviate any difficulty arising from the technical description of the means employed or the character of the weapon used.[6]

§ 378. **Method — Assault, weapon, strangulation, poison, etc.**—It is usual to charge an assault as well as the giving of the mortal wound.[7] As to the method of using the weapon, it is

the death was effected: C. v. Martin, 125 Mass. 394. Such form of allegation is proper notwithstanding the constitutional provision that the crime must be fully and plainly described: S. v. Burke, 54 N. H. 92.

1 Wolf v. S., 19 Ohio St. 248; Williams v. S., 35 Ohio St. 175; Cathcart v. C., 37 Pa. St. 108; Campbell v. C., 84 Pa. St. 187; Goersen v. C., 99 Pa. St. 388; S. v. Verrill, 54 Me. 408; S. v. Morrissey, 70 Me. 401; P. v. Hong Ah Duck, 61 Cal. 387; P. v. Davis, 73 Cal. 355; P. v. King, 27 Cal. 507; P. v. Cronin, 34 Cal. 191; Newcomb v. S., 37 Miss. 383; S. v. Moore, 104 N. C. 743; Dwyer v. S., 12 Tex. Ap. 535; Peterson v. S., 12 Tex. Ap. 650; S. v. Shay, 30 La. An. (Part I), 114; S. v. Bartley, 34 La. An. 147. Under a statute providing for prosecutions by information, a general charge of murder, without alleging the means, is not objectionable; the prisoner being entitled to a preliminary examination, the returns of which are filed with the information: P. v. Bemis, 51 Mich. 422.

2 S. v. Shay, 30 La. An. (Part I), 114; Williams v. S., 35 Ohio St. 175; Nichols v. S., 46 Miss. 284; S. v. Moore, 104 N. C. 743; Goersen v. C., 99 Pa. St. 388; S. v. Florenza, 28 La. An. 945; Scott v. S., 31 Tex. Ap. 405. Or, did assault and kill the deceased: S. v. Verrill, 54 Me. 408; Alexander v. S., 3 Heisk. 475. "Did wilfully, etc., kill and murder," etc., by administering poison, held sufficient under statute: Jane v. C., 3 Met. (Ky.) 18. But held that an indictment simply charging that defendant did unlawfully kill the deceased was not sufficient, although the statute provided that the manner or means of killing need not be set out, the indictment being, however, for manslaughter, and it being necessary to indicate whether it was voluntary or involuntary: S. v. Lay, 93 Ind. 341.

3 Hornsby v. S., 94 Ala. 55.

4 S. v. Blan, 69 Mo. 317; Littell v. S., 133 Ind. 577.

5 Wolf v. S., 19 Ohio St. 248; Campbell v. C., 84 Pa. St. 187; S. v. Moore, 104 N. C. 743; C. v. Robertson, 162 Mass. 90.

6 S. v. Morrissey, 70 Me. 401; P. v. Ybarra, 17 Cal. 166; P. v. Stevenson, 9 Cal. 273; S. v. Anderson, 4 Nev. 265; S. v. McLane, 15 Nev. 345; S. v. Noblett, 2 Jones, 418.

7 Lester v. S., 9 Mo. 658; Haney v. S., 34 Ark. 263.

sufficient to say that the gun or pistol, loaded with gunpowder and a leaden bullet, the defendant did shoot off and discharge;[1] and a variance arising from proof of a death caused by shot, under an allegation as to discharging a bullet, will not be fatal.[2] The indictment need not allege that the weapon was held in defendant's hand.[3] Where there is an averment of stabbing with a dirk, the allegation of "giving one mortal wound" sufficiently shows that it was inflicted by the stab.[4] An allegation of killing "by strangulation in this, to wit, that he choked her to death," is sufficiently descriptive of the means.[5] In an indictment for murder by poisoning it is sufficient to allege the administering of a deadly poison and mortal sickness occasioned thereby.[6] It is not necessary to allege the amount of poison administered, it being clearly charged that the death was occasioned by such poisoning.[7] An allegation of actual poisoning includes by implication an allegation that the substance employed was poison; but under an indictment for attempt to poison, the substance employed must be specially alleged to have been a deadly poison.[8] It is not necessary to allege knowl-

[1] Reg. v. Stokes, 2 C. & K. 536; S. v. Freeman, 1 Spears, 57.

[2] Goodwyn v. S., 4 Sm. & M. 520.

[3] C. v. Costley, 118 Mass. 1; T. v. Young, 5 Mont. 242.

[4] Gibson v. C., 2 Va. Cas. 111. So the connection between the act of defendant and the injury to deceased may be made to appear by the expression "by reason whereof:" Mayes v. P., 106 Ill. 306. And see Reg. v. Ellis, 2 C. & K. 470. But where the allegation was that defendant discharged a gun at deceased, and by thus striking, etc., with no averment that he did strike, etc., the connection was held not to be sufficiently made out: S. v. Green, 111 Mo. 585. "Did kill, etc., by shooting with a gun," is not a sufficiently direct charge of killing: Pierce v. S., 21 Tex. Ap. 669.

[5] Redd v. S., 69 Ala. 255. Where the suffocation results from suffering of the throat due to wounds occasioned by forcing things into it, the statement may be that the things were forced into the throat and deceased choked thereby: Rex v. Tye, Russ. & Ry. 345. A charge of suffocation by placing the hand on the mouth is made out if the jury is satisfied that any violence was used in causing the suffocation: Rex v. Waters, 7 C. & P. 250. Under a charge of suffocation by placing both hands upon the neck, etc., defendant may be convicted if the suffocation was caused in any manner either by defendant or any other person in her presence and by her procurement: Rex v. Culkin, 5 C. & P. 121.

[6] Reg. v. Sandys, Car. & M. 345. Purpose to kill is thus sufficiently shown: Snyder v. S., 59 Ind. 105.

[7] Epps v. S., 102 Ind. 539.

[8] Anthony v. S., 29 Ala. 27.

edge on the part of the defendant of the nature of the poisonous substance administered.[1]

§ 379. **Negligence.**— Where the indictment alleges the nature and extent of the defendant's negligence, the allegation must be proved as alleged.[2] Where neglect to signal an obstruction on a railway track was the negligence charged, it was held not necessary to allege what particular act was omitted in reference to such signaling;[3] nor, in general, is it necessary that the indictment should charge that the injury was caused by an act of omission.[4] The indictment may allege the act which is wrongful, because negligent, as an assault, even though the wrongful act was with the consent of the deceased.[5] The indictment must show the circumstances giving rise to a duty on the part of the defendant, the neglect of which has caused death;[6] but an allegation of wilful and felonious neglect to perform the duties devolved upon him by law in the premises imports an allegation of knowledge, and further statement of the intent is unnecessary.[7] The connection between the negligence and the death must appear.[8]

§ 380. **Description of wound.**— It seems to have been usual in the common-law indictment to describe the wound where death is alleged to have been caused by the infliction of a wound, and in one case in this country such description was said to be necessary.[9] It was also said in an early case that the way of administering the fatal blow must be proven as

[1] Westmoreland v. U. S., 155 U. S. 545; S. v. Slagle, 83 N. C. 630; Jane v. C., 3 Met. (Ky.) 18. The point was discussed but not decided in C. v. Earle, 1 Whart. 525. Administration of poison may be shown to have been by hypodermic injection or otherwise as well as by its having been taken into the stomach: Westmoreland v. U. S., 150 U. S. 545; and a charge of administering one kind of poison may be supported by proof of administering another: Ibid.

[2] C. v. Hartwell, 128 Mass. 415.

[3] Reg. v. Pargeter, 3 Cox, 191.

[4] Reg. v. Smith, 11 Cox, 210.

[5] So held in case of a physician: Reg. v. Ellis, 2 C. & K. 470.

[6] Reg. v. Barrett, 2 C. & K. 343.

[7] So held in an indictment of a husband for causing the death of his wife by neglecting to provide proper shelter and clothing: S. v. Smith, 65 Me. 257.

[8] Therefore, held, that an allegation of negligence in compounding a prescription and of death resulting from taking the prescription was not sufficient, it not appearing that the powders compounded were delivered to be administered to deceased: S. v. Smith, 66 Mo. 92.

[9] S. v. Owen, 1 Murphy, 452. But a contrary conclusion seems to have been reached in a later case in the same state: S. v. Moses, 2 Dev. 452.

alleged.[1] It was usual to state also that defendant gave deceased a mortal wound.[2] But the wound need not be particularly described otherwise than as a mortal wound.[3] While it is usual in the common-law indictment to allege the part of the body on which the wound was inflicted,[4] such allegation is deemed so far immaterial that a variance is not fatal.[5] And, therefore, under statutes usually found in the various states by which it is declared that indictments shall not be deemed defective on account of such immaterial matters, it is not now necessary to allege the part of the body on which the wound was inflicted.[6] And a repugnancy in the description of the wound will be immaterial.[7] By statute the description of the wound is sometimes expressly made unnecessary.[8] It is immaterial that the wound particularly described appears from the evidence not to have been the wound causing death.[9] It is also usual, in the common-law indictment alleging death from a wound, to describe the length and depth of the wound, but that is also immaterial.[10]

§ **381. Death.**— It is necessary to allege in some form that the death of the person named in the indictment resulted from

[1] S. v. Townsend, 1 Houst. Cr. Cas. 337.

[2] Rex v. Lad, 1 Leach, 96. But held that this was not necessary to warrant a verdict for manslaughter: Brown v. S., 18 Fla. 472. The description of the wound as mortal, held unnecessary where the fact otherwise appeared: P. v. Judd, 10 Cal. 313. The indictment may charge more than one mortal wound (under statute): S. v. Patterson, 73 Mo. 695.

[3] C. v. Chapman, 11 Cush. 422; C. v. Robertson, 162 Mass. 90.

[4] And it was accordingly said that a repugnancy in the averments as to the parts of the body upon which the wounds were inflicted was fatal: Dias v. S., 7 Blackf. 20.

[5] Sanchez v. P., 22 N. Y. 147; C. v. Coy, 157 Mass. 200; Cordell v. S., 22 Ind. 1; S. v. Waller, 88 Mo. 402; Bryan v. S., 19 Fla. 864; Nelson v. S., 1 Tex. Ap. 41.

[6] Sanchez v. S., 22 N. Y. 147; S. v. Edmundson, 64 Mo. 398; Cordell v. S., 22 Ind. 1; Whelchell v. S., 23 Ind. 89; Jones v. S., 35 Ind. 122; P. v. Judd, 10 Cal. 313; S. v. Day, 4 Wash. 104; Walker v. S., 34 Fla. 167.

[7] S. v. Ramsey, 82 Mo. 133 (overruling S. v. Jones, 20 Mo. 58); S. v. Anderson, 98 Mo. 461.

[8] Wilkerson v. S., 2 Tex. Ap. 255.

[9] Real v. P., 42 N. Y. 270; S. v. Hoyt, 13 Minn. 132.

[10] S. v. Conley, 39 Me. 78; Stone v. P., 2 Scam. 326; S. v. Jones, 20 Mo. 58; S. v. Snell, 78 Mo. 240; Dukes v. S., 11 Ind. 557; West v. S., 48 Ind. 483; Powers v. S., 80 Ind. 77; Nash v. S., 2 Greene (Ia.), 286; Hodge v. S., 26 Fla. 11; Smith v. S., 43 Tex. 643; S. v. Robertson, 30 La. An. (Part I), 340; Rex v. Mosley, 1 Moody, 98; Rex v. Tomlinson, 6 C. & P. 370. Description of the wound as "mortal" is sufficient: S. v. Snell, 78 Mo. 240; S. v. Conley, 39 Me. 78.

the acts alleged.[1] Thus, if there is an allegation of an assault and the inflicting of a stroke or blow, the indictment should state the inflicting of a "mortal wound" of which deceased died.[2] While the general statement that defendant did "kill and murder" the deceased is a sufficient allegation that death resulted from the assault and that it was defendant's act,[3] yet the mere allegation in the conclusion of the indictment that defendant did "kill and murder" deceased is not sufficient to charge the death.[4] It is usual, after stating the assault and the wound, to say: "from which said mortal wound the said —— —— did then and there instantly die," or from the date named until a later date did "suffer and languish, and languishing did live," and on the last date "languishing did die." But under the latter form of averment, which is intended to cover cases where the death did not occur at the time and place of the injury, it is sufficient to say that deceased on a subsequent day "did languish and die."[5] These forms of averment state the time and place of the death, and such statement is essential.[6] And the word "immediately" is not equivalent to "instantly" as indicating the time,[7] nor is "instantly" sufficient without "then and there."[8] But where "then and there" has been used in connection with the allegation of the giving of the wound, the statement that deceased "did instantly die" from such wound is sufficient.[9] The allegation that deceased of said mortal wound "did languish and then and there did die" is sufficient as to time.[10] The allegation that deceased was killed on a day named sufficiently indicates, under a statute allow-

[1] S. v. Wimberly, 3 McCord, 190; Lutz v. C., 29 Pa. St. 441; Edmondson v. S., 41 Tex. 496.

[2] S. v. Morgan, 85 N. C. 581.

[3] Wood v. S., 92 Ind. 269; P. v. Sanford, 43 Cal. 29; S. v. Day, 4 Wash. 104; Cook v. S., 72 Miss. 517. Other equivalent words may be sufficient: S. v. O'Niel, 23 Ia. 272; Walker v. S., 14 Tex. Ap. 609; Caldwell v. S., 28 Tex. Ap. 566. But an allegation that defendant did murder A., etc., is not sufficient to show that defendant killed A.: Strickland v. S., 19 Tex. Ap. 518. But "killed" without "murdered" is sufficient for manslaughter: Evans v. P., 12 Mich. 27.

[4] S. v. Blan, 69 Mo. 317. The allegation that defendant did kill and murder, or the like, without stating the means, is in some states, by statute, sufficient: See *supra*, § 377.

[5] S. v. Conley, 39 Me. 78; U. S. v. Ball, 163 U. S. 662.

[6] Lester v. S., 9 Mo. 658; S. v. Mayfield, 66 Mo. 125; S. v. Testerman, 68 Mo. 408; S. v. Sundheimer, 93 Mo. 311; Edmondson v. S., 41 Tex. 496.

[7] S. v. Testerman, 68 Mo. 408.

[8] S. v. Lakey, 65 Mo. 217.

[9] Hardin v. S., 4 Tex. Ap. 355.

[10] S. v. Haney, 67 N. C. 467; C. v. Robertson, 162 Mass. 90.

ing that form of allegation, that the death took place on that day.[1] But the object of alleging the time being merely to show that the death occurred within a year and a day,[2] evidence of death within that time, although subsequent to the date alleged in the indictment, will not be a material variance, although the indictment charges that deceased then and there instantly died.[3] In a common-law indictment the place of the death should be stated.[4] But as has already been seen, it is no longer regarded material that the place of death was in the same county as that where the wound was inflicted.[5] So that the repugnancy between two counts in this respect which allege the place of death in different counties is not material.[6] It is not, at common law, necessary to prove the place of death further than to bring the case within the jurisdiction of the court, and by code provisions it is in some states rendered unnecessary to allege the place of death at all.[7]

§ 382. Allegations of intent; feloniously, wilfully, with malice aforethought.— It is usual, in the common-law indictment, to allege the assault and the infliction of the wound to have been felonious and wilful, and in case of murder, with malice aforethought, and similar terms are used in the conclusion. The

[1] Thomas v. S., 71 Ga. 44. A clerical error in the allegation of the date of death where the indictment is plain, notwithstanding such error, will not be a ground for arresting judgment: C. v. Ailstock, 3 Grat. 650.

[2] As already explained, *supra*, § 293. And see S. v. Haney, 67 N. C. 467. If it appears that the indictment, which alleges the death, was found within a year and a day after the date of the injury as charged, the death within a year and a day is sufficiently charged: Brassfield v. S., 55 Ark. 556.

[3] S. v. Baker, 1 Jones, 267; S. v. Hobbs, 33 La. An. 226; Cudd v. S., 28 Tex. Ap. 124. Where, in pursuance of statute, it was charged that on a day named defendant did assault, etc., and did kill and murder the deceased, *held*, that evidence that death occurred on a subsequent day constituted a variance, as the murder was not completed by the assault but only by the death: Chapman v. P., 39 Mich. 357.

[4] S. v. Coleman, 17 S. C. 473; S. v. Blakeney, 33 S. C. 111; Riggs v. S., 26 Miss. 51; S. v. Cummings, 5 La. An. 330. But this is sufficiently alleged where the place of the assault and the wounding is stated, and subsequently, without any other place having been mentioned, it is alleged in the conclusion that the accused did then and there, etc., kill and murder deceased, although it appears from the indictment that the death did not immediately follow the wound: S. v. Blakeney, 33 S. C. 111.

[5] *Supra*, § 370.

[6] Hunter v. S., 40 N. J. 495.

[7] Roche v. S., 34 Ga. 78; S. v. Bowen, 16 Kan. 475.

omission of "feloniously" is fatal,[1] unless it is rendered immaterial by statute.[2] "Unlawfully" is not necessary.[3] "Wilfully" is not essential,[4] unless required by the statutory definition.[5] Wilfulness, deliberation and premeditation are usually required by statute to constitute murder in the first degree, but need not be charged in the indictment in those states where the common-law form of indictment is held sufficient for murder in either degree; otherwise they must be alleged to support a conviction in the first degree.[6] "Malice aforethought" is essential in an indictment for murder.[7] But this expression may, perhaps, be supplied by words of equivalent import;[8] such, for instance, as "premeditated malice."[9] It is not necessary to describe the malice aforethought as "express" or "implied."[10] The averment as to malice aforethought, etc., must be made

[1] S. v. Thomas, 29 La. An. 601; Kaelin v. C., 84 Ky. 354; S. v. Fairlamb, 121 Mo. 137; Edwards v. S., 25 Ark. 444; Witt v. S., 6 Coldw. 5; S. v. Wimberly, 3 McCord, 190.

[2] Williams v. S., 3 Heisk. 376; Riddle v. S., 3 Heisk. 401.

[3] Beavers v. S., 58 Ind. 530; Bean v. S., 17 Tex. Ap. 60; S. v. Arnold, 107 N. C. 861; for the allegation of malice aforethought necessarily shows the unlawfulness: Hunter v. S., 30 Tex. Ap. 314; Jackson v. S., 25 Tex. Ap. 314. But the unlawfulness must in some form appear: Henry v. S., 33 Ala. 389; Dukes v. S., 11 Ind. 557. Under the statute of Tennessee "unlawfully" is unnecessary: Williams v. S., 3 Heisk. 376; Riddle v. S., 3 Heisk. 401. So it is immaterial in Texas, although the statute uses the term, the other allegations being such as to show the act to be unlawful: Thompson v. S., 36 Tex. 326.

[4] S. v. Arnold, 107 N. C. 861; S. v. Thompson, 12 Nev. 140; S. v. Crozier, 12 Nev. 300.

[5] S. v. Thomas, 29 La. An. 601; S. v. Williams, 37 La. An. 776; S. v. Scott, 38 La. An. 387.

[6] *Supra,* § 361. And see Poole v. S., 2 Baxt. 288; Brannigan v. P., 3 Utah, 488; Bird v. S., 18 Fla. 493.

[7] Witt v. S., 6 Coldw. 5; Jesse v. S., 28 Miss. 100; Wall v. S., 51 Ind. 453; S. v. Newberry, 26 Ia. 467; S. v. Green, 42 La. An. 644; McElroy v. S., 14 Tex. Ap. 235; Rex v. Nicholson, 1 East, P. C. 346. But the use of that phrase in the conclusion is sufficient if there is nothing inconsistent with it in the body of the indictment: Chase v. S., 50 Wis. 510. But "maliciously" in the conclusion is not sufficient, even where malice aforethought is used in describing the assault and wound: C. v. Gibson, 2 Va. Cas. 70. After "malice aforethought" is once charged, "malice aforesaid" is sufficient: Maile v. C., 9 Leigh, 661.

[8] P. v. Schmidt, 63 Cal. 28; P. v. Vance, 21 Cal. 400; S. v. Neeley, 20 Ia. 108; S. v. Thurman, 66 Ia. 693. But "without just cause or provocation, but with an abandoned and malignant heart," is not sufficient as a substitute for malice aforethought: P. v. Urias, 12 Cal. 325.

[9] Edwards v. S., 25 Ark. 444.

[10] Henrie v. S., 41 Tex. 573; P. v. Bonilla, 38 Cal. 699; T. v. Bannigan, 1 Dak. 432.

with reference to the homicidal act and not merely with reference to the assault.[1] But this may be done by proper connecting words, without necessarily repeating such averment with reference to the act after once making them with reference to the assault.[2] Where the homicide is committed in the commission of a felony, the common-law form of indictment, alleging the injury as felonious and with malice aforethought, is sufficient.[3] As malice aforethought is not essential in manslaughter, it is sufficient in charging that offense to allege that the act was maliciously done.[4]

§ 383. **Intent to kill.**— Where the definition of murder is statutory as to both the first and second degrees, and the statute makes the intent or purpose to kill a part of the definition, such intent or purpose must be charged, and it is not enough to use the common-law form.[5] It is not sufficient that the intent to kill is alleged in the conclusion if it does not appear from the charging part of the indictment.[6] But it is sufficient to say that defendant committed the assault "with intent to kill and murder deceased."[7] So, it has been decided in states where it is held necessary to allege wilfulness, deliberation and premeditation in an indictment for the first degree,[8] that such wilfulness, deliberation and premeditation must be alleged with reference to the killing as well as with reference to the assault.[9] But if it is charged that the mortal wound was inflicted with specific intent to kill, and that it was wilfully, deliberately and premeditatedly inflicted, that is sufficient without an allegation that the killing was wilful, deliberate and premeditated.[10] And

[1] S. v. Herrell, 97 Mo. 105; Simmons v. S., 32 Fla. 387; S. v. Jones, 45 La. An. 1454.

[2] St. Clair v. U. S., 154 U. S. 134; P. v. Davis, 73 Cal. 355; S. v. Owen, 1 Murph. 452; P. v. Davis, 8 Utah, 412.

[3] P. v. Willett, 102 N. Y. 251; S. v. Worrell, 25 Mo. 205; Hill v. S., 42 Neb. 503; Mitchell v. S., 1 Tex. Ap. 194; Reyes v. S., 10 Tex. Ap. 1; Sharpe v. S., 17 Tex. Ap. 486.

[4] Reed v. S., 8 Ind. 200.

[5] Fouts v. S., 8 Ohio St. 98; Kain v. S., 8 Ohio St. 306; Shaffer v. S., 22 Neb. 557; S. v. McCormick, 27 Ia. 402.

[6] Hagan v. S., 10 Ohio St. 459; S. v. McCormick, 27 Ia. 402; S. v. Watkins, 27 Ia. 415; Leonard v. T., 2 Wash. T. 381; Blanton v. S., 1 Wash. 265.

[7] Rufer v. S., 25 Ohio St. 464.

[8] *Supra*, § 361.

[9] S. v. McCormick, 27 Ia. 402; S. v. Watkins, 27 Ia. 415; Shaffer v. S., 22 Neb. 557; Loeffner v. S., 10 Ohio St. 598; S. v. Brown, 21 Kan. 38; Leonard v. T., 2 Wash. T. 381; Blanton v. S., 1 Wash. 265.

[10] S. v. Stanley, 33 Ia. 526; S. v. Shelton, 64 Ia. 333; S. v. Townsend, 66 Ia. 741; S. v. Perigo, 70 Ia. 657.

the unlawful administration of poison sufficiently shows the intent to kill.[1] The intent to kill need not necessarily be alleged in the words of the statute.[2] Where the purpose to kill is alleged to be wilful, deliberate and premeditated and with malice aforethought, such allegations need not be made with reference to the assault.[3]

§ 384. Opening and conclusion.—Although it is usual to name the offense in the beginning of the indictment, as, for instance: "The grand jury, etc., accuse —— —— of the crime of murder committed as follows," yet a failure to thus name it will be immaterial if it is properly charged in the body of the indictment.[4] And even a mistake, as by charging manslaughter when the body of the indictment shows the offense to be murder, will not prevent the defendant being put on trial for the offense shown by the allegations.[5] It is said that the concluding portion of the indictment for murder should state that defendant murdered deceased, not merely that he made a murderous assault;[6] but in general the conclusion is not an essential part of the indictment, and if the body of the indictment shows murder it will be immaterial that the conclusion charges defendant with manslaughter only.[7] And malice aforethought need not be alleged in the conclusion.[8] The conclusion may, when not consistent with the indictment, be disregarded as surplusage.[9]

§ 385. In general; allegations of fact; clerical errors.—The indictment should state the facts constituting the offense,[10] but it need not state the evidence. For instance, where the person killed is an officer it is not necessary to allege that fact;[11]

And see S. v. Hunter, 42 La. An. 814. The allegation of the wilful, etc., infliction of a mortal wound implies intent to kill: Loeffner v. S., 10 Ohio St. 598.

[1] C. v. Hersey, 2 Allen, 173; S. v. Wells, 61 Ia. 629.

[2] Loeffner v. S., 10 Ohio St. 598.

[3] S. v. France, 76 Mo. 681; Plake v. S., 121 Ind. 433; S. v. Bradford, 33 La. An. 921. Even under the common-law form, if the allegation is of the infliction of the injury with premeditated design to effect the death of a particular individual, this allegation, although not essential, will limit the proof: P. v. White, 24 Wend. 520.

[4] Dias v. S., 7 Blackf. 20.

[5] Camp v. S., 25 Ga. 689.

[6] Anderson v. S., 5 Ark. 444.

[7] S. v. Hessenkamp, 17 Ia. 25. *Contra*, S. v. Meyers, 99 Mo. 107.

[8] S. v. Davis, 41 Ia. 311.

[9] Hawley v. C., 75 Va. 847.

[10] P. v. Wallace, 9 Cal. 30.

[11] Boyd v. S., 17 Ga. 194; S. v. Green, 66 Mo. 631.

nor that the homicide occurred in the prosecution of a riot to which the prisoner was a party, although such fact must be proven in order to show his concurrence in the act.[1] Clerical errors cannot be taken advantage of after verdict.[2] Grammatical and rhetorical errors which do not render the indictment so obscure as not to sufficiently advise defendant of the crime of which he is charged do not vitiate it.[3]

§ **386. Under statutes.**— Indictments in the form presented in the statute are in general held sufficient.[4]

§ **387. Form of indictment in general.**— There are very great difficulties attending any effort to give a form of indictment for criminal homicide, even in the simplest cases, which will be sufficient in all the states. These difficulties grow out of the fact that the forms early used at common law were extremely technical and verbose, being literal translations of the Latin, in which indictments were originally framed, and preserving to some extent the peculiar arrangement of the Latin sentences; and that the forms thus derived by translation have been materially modified by usage, and have been further modified by express statutes both in England and in the states of the Union. By usage, sanctioned in some cases by the decisions of the courts, in others not expressly authorized, some portions of the earlier forms are omitted entirely; other portions, while still retained and held necessary as matters of form, are deemed immaterial in such sense that a variance between the allegation and the proof with reference thereto will not prevent a conviction; and in some states, by statutes, it is provided that these immaterial matters need not be alleged. Statutory modifications are so various in the different states that no uniform result thereof can be stated. In the preceding sections the different elements of the indictment have been considered in the light of

[1] S. v. Jenkins, 14 Rich. 215.

[2] S. v. Rinehart, 75 N. C. 58; Shay v. P., 4 Park. Cr. R. 353; S. v. Harrington, 9 Nev. 91. So, under a statute requiring the service of a copy of an indictment, *held*, that a clerical error in substituting "same" for "name" in the introductory clause was not a ground of objection that a copy had not been served: Johnson v. S., 4 Tex. Ap. 268.

[3] S. v. Turlington, 102 Mo. 642.

[4] Aikin v. S., 35 Ala. 399; P. v. Murray, 10 Cal. 309; P. v. De La Cour Soto, 63 Cal. 165; P. v. Murphy, 39 Cal. 52; P. v. Campbell, 59 Cal. 243; Dillon v. S., 9 Ind. 408; O'Kelly v. T., 1 Oreg. 51; Cathcart v. C., 37 Pa. St. 108.

the decisions. It only remains here to give some forms illustrative of the indictments in common use, and as nearly as may be in accordance with the practice in all the states.

§ 388. **Particular forms.**— It is unnecessary to take the space requisite for setting out in full the earlier form of an indictment in England at common law, as there is no usage in any state making such a form necessary or desirable; but the first form given is a full common-law indictment such as would now be sufficient anywhere, except as in some states additional averments may be required to charge the first degree of murder. The previous discussion,[1] however, has indicated that some of the terms used in this indictment are unnecessary, and this will be illustrated by shorter forms following.

MURDER WITH A WEAPON.

That W. C., on ——, in the county of ——, with force and arms in and upon one J. W., feloniously, wilfully, and of his malice aforethought, did make an assault, and that he, the said W. C., then and there, with a certain ax, which he, the said W. C., in his hands then and there had and held, him, the said J. W., in and upon the head of him, the said J. W., on the left side of the head of him, the said J. W., in front of the ear and near to the left ear of his, the said J. W.'s, said head, then and there feloniously, wilfully, and of his malice aforethought did strike, giving unto him, the said J. W., then and there with the ax aforesaid, by the stroke aforesaid, in the manner aforesaid, in and upon the head of him, the said J. W., on the left side of his said head, in front of and near the left ear of his, the said J. W.'s, said head, one mortal wound of the length of four inches, of the breadth of one inch, and of the depth of one-half inch, of which said mortal wound the said J. W. then and there instantly died; and so the jurors aforesaid, upon their oath aforesaid, do say and present that the said W. C., him, the said J. W., in manner and form aforesaid, then and there feloniously, wilfully, and of his malice aforethought, did kill and murder, against the peace of said commonwealth, and contrary to the form of the statute in such case made and provided.[2]

[1] *Supra*, § 372 *et seq.*

[2] This follows the language of the second count in C. v. Coy, 157 Mass. 200, with the omission of the particular locality at which the crime was committed. It is well settled that it is sufficient to lay the venue in the county without naming any particular locality: *Supra*, § 376.

SECOND COUNT; BY MEANS UNKNOWN.

And the jurors aforesaid, upon their oath aforesaid, do further present that the said W. C. on ——, in the county of —— aforesaid, in and upon the said J. W., feloniously, wilfully, and of his malice aforethought, did make an assault, and him, the said J. W., in some way and manner, and by some means, instruments and weapons to the jurors aforesaid unknown, did then and there feloniously, wilfully, and of his malice aforethought, deprive of life, so that he, the said J. W., then and there died; and so the jurors aforesaid, etc.[1]

SHORTER FORM.

That D. R., in the county of ——, on ——, in and upon one M. R., feloniously, wilfully, and of his malice aforethought, an assault did make, and with a certain weapon, to wit, a knife, which the said D. R. then and there held, her, the said M. R., feloniously, wilfully, and of his malice aforethought, did strike, cut, stab and thrust in and upon the head of her, the said M. R., giving to her, the said M. R., by the striking, cutting, stabbing and thrusting in and upon the head of her, the said M. R., one mortal wound, of which mortal wound the said M. R. then and there died.[2]

MURDER IN FIRST DEGREE IN CALIFORNIA.

T. K. is accused by the grand jury of the county of —— aforesaid, by this indictment, of the crime of murder of the first degree, committed as follows: The said T. K. on ——, at the county of ——, in and upon one J. D., feloniously, wilfully,

[1] This is another count in the same indictment referred to in the preceding note. The evidence being that the death was caused by cutting the throat with an ax, and not by a blow with an ax upon the temple, it was contended, on behalf of defendant, that a conviction could not be sustained; but it was held that the injury shown was nearly enough of the same character as that charged to warrant a conviction under the first count alleging a stroke with an ax, and also that a conviction might be sustained under this count alleging the means to have been unknown, and that the presumption in favor of this allegation would warrant the jury in believing that it was true, even though it appeared that there was some evidence before the grand jury showing that the means by which death was caused was known to them.

[2] This is the form of the indictment in C. v. Robertson, 162 Mass. 90, found also in 10 Harv. L. Rev. 105, and held sufficient as against the objections that it did not allege how defendant held the knife, nor fully describe the wound or the portion of the head upon which the wound was inflicted, nor state whether or not the death was instantaneous.

and of his malice aforethought, did make an assault, and did then and there feloniously, wilfully, and of his malice aforethought, cut, stab and wound him, the said J. D., and did then and there give him, the said J. D., one mortal wound, of which said mortal wound the said J. D. afterwards, on the ——, did die. So the grand jurors aforesaid, etc.[1]

MURDER IN FIRST DEGREE IN IOWA.

That said G. S., on the ——, in the county aforesaid, in and upon the body of one W. P., then and there being, wilfully, feloniously, deliberately, premeditatedly, by lying in wait and of his malice aforethought, did commit an assault with a deadly weapon, being a pistol then and there held in the hands of the said G. S., and loaded and charged with powder and bullet; and then and there the said G. S. did, by lying in wait with the specific intent to kill and murder the said W. P., wilfully, feloniously, deliberately, premeditatedly, and of his malice aforethought, shoot off and discharge the contents of said deadly weapon, being the powder and bullet aforesaid, at, against, into and through the head and body of the said W. P., thereby wilfully, feloniously, deliberately, premeditatedly, and of his malice aforethought, inflicting upon the head and body of the said W. P. a mortal wound, of which mortal wound the said W. P. then and there did die.[2]

MURDER BY POISON.

That the said A. B., on the ——, in the county aforesaid, did unlawfully, fraudulently and feloniously, and with his malice aforethought and with certain drugs and poisons, to wit, strychnine, and certain poisons to the grand jurors unknown, then and there given and administered by the said A. B. to one

[1] This is taken from P. v. King, 27 Cal. 507, and illustrates the usual form held sufficient under statutes where it is not necessary to allege particularly the matter showing the offense to be in the first degree. It will be understood from the previous discussion (*supra*, § 361) that under either of the preceding forms there might be a conviction in the first degree in Massachusetts, or other states in which it is held not necessary to specify the degree in any form.

[2] See S. v. Stanley, 33 Ia. 526, and substantially the same form in S. v. Shelton, 64 Ia. 333, and S. v. Dooley, 89 Ia. 584, except that the phrase "by lying in wait" is not there used. That phrase may be omitted and still leave the indictment for the first degree. If the words "deliberately" and "premeditatedly" were omitted it would be an indictment for the second degree. The phrase "with specific intent to kill" is deemed important in charging the first degree also in Ohio (see Fouts v. S., 8 Ohio St. 98, 109; *supra*, § 361, n.) though not in general use elsewhere.

C. D., make an assault upon the said C. D. with the unlawful and felonious intent of the said A. B. then and there to take the life of him, the said C. D., and he, the said A. B., did then and there, by administering said poison as aforesaid, unlawfully, knowingly and feloniously poison him, the said C. D., from the effects of which said poison, he, the said C. D., did languish, and languishing did then and there die, on the said ——, and within a year and a day from said date.[1]

MURDER BY POISON; ANOTHER FORM.

That C. M., contriving and intending to kill and murder G. M., on ——, at ——, upon the said G. M. feloniously, etc., did make an assault, and that the said C. M. a large quantity, to wit, half an ounce weight, of a certain deadly poison called laudanum, feloniously, etc., did give and administer unto the said G. M. with intent that he should take and swallow the same down into his body (the said C. M. then and there well knowing the said laudanum to be a deadly poison), and the said G. M. the said laudanum so given and administered unto him by the said C. M. as aforesaid did take and swallow down into his body, by reason and by means of which said taking and swallowing down the said laudanum into his body as aforesaid, the said G. M. became and was mortally sick and distempered in his body, of which said mortal sickness and distemper the said G. M. from, etc., till, etc., did languish, etc., and died.[2]

MANSLAUGHTER.

That J. T., on ——, at ——, in and upon one J. L. feloniously and wilfully did make an assault, and that he, the said J. T., with a certain stone, which he, the said J. T., in his right hand then and there had and held, in and upon the left side of the head of him, the said J. L., then and there feloniously and wilfully did cast and throw, and that the said J. T., with the stone aforesaid, so as aforesaid cast and thrown, the aforesaid J. L. in and upon the left side of the head of him, the said J. L., then and there feloniously and wilfully did strike, penetrate and wound, giving to the said J. L., by the casting and throwing of the stone aforesaid in and upon the left side of the head of him, the said J. L., one mortal wound of the length of one inch and of the

[1] This follows the indictment in Westmoreland v. U. S., 155 U. S. 545, which was in the circuit court of the United States for a crime committed in the Indian country, and contains allegations as to defendant not being an Indian which have not been retained in the form. The indictment was held good as against the objection that it did not allege knowledge by defendant that the substance administered was a deadly poison, and also that it did not allege that the poison was taken into the stomach of the deceased.

[2] See Reg. v. Michael, 9 C. & P. 356.

breadth of half an inch, of which said mortal wound he, the said J. L., from the said —— day of —— in the year aforesaid to the —— day of ——, at —— aforesaid, in the county aforesaid, did languish, and languishing did live, on which —— day of ——, at —— aforesaid, the said J. L. of the mortal wound aforesaid died; and so the said jurors, etc.[1]

MANSLAUGHTER BY NEGLECTING TO PROVIDE.

That H. S., on the ——, at ——, being then and there the husband of one L. S., his wife, and being then and there under the legal duty to provide for his said wife necessary clothing, shelter, and protection from the frost, cold and inclemency of the weather, and then and there having the means to provide the same, and she, the said L. S., being then and there weak, feeble, destitute and infirm, and unable to go abroad, did then and there feloniously and wilfully neglect and refuse to provide necessary clothing, shelter and protection from the frost, cold and inclemency of the weather for his said wife, whereby her health was greatly injured; and he, the said H. S., afterward, to wit, on the next succeeding day, and on every day between the said —— and ——, then next ensuing, did there feloniously and wilfully continue to neglect and refuse to provide her, the said L. S., with necessary clothing, shelter, and protection from the frost, cold and inclemency of the weather, the said H. S. being there on all days and times her husband as aforesaid, and having the means to provide the same as aforesaid, and under the legal duty to provide the same as aforesaid, and she, the said L. S., having no means to provide the same as aforesaid, and being weak, feeble, destitute, infirm, and unable to go abroad as aforesaid. By reason whereof the said L. S. there on all the days and times before mentioned, until the —— day of —— in the year aforesaid, sickened and languished with a mortal sickness and feebleness of body so as aforesaid created and produced by the said H. S. until the —— day of —— now last past, on which said last mentioned day at ——, she, the said L. S., there of said mortal sickness and feebleness of body died. And so the jurors aforesaid, upon their oath aforesaid, do say that the said H. S. her the said

[1] This is abbreviated from the form given in Turns v. C., 6 Met. 224, by the omission of some matter plainly superfluous. But much of that retained is also superfluous, as will be seen by comparing it with the indictment for murder which was held sufficient in C. v. Robinson, as given above. It is usual in such cases to charge murder and convict for manslaughter if the circumstances indicating malice aforethought do not appear. Indeed, all the preceding forms of charging murder would become indictments for manslaughter if the allegations with reference to malice aforethought were omitted.

L. S. in manner and by the means aforesaid feloniously did kill and slay, against the peace of said state and contrary to the form of the statute in such case made and provided.[1]

IX. PROCEDURE AND PUNISHMENT.

§ 389. Included offenses.— Under the general rule that the jury may convict for any offense sufficiently charged in the indictment, an indictment for murder includes a charge of all forms of criminal homicide.[2] Thus, a verdict for manslaughter may properly be returned under an indictment for murder.[3] So in states where a special form of indictment for the first degree is held necessary, the defendant may under such indictment be found guilty of the second degree.[4] Involuntary manslaughter is included under a charge for murder or voluntary manslaughter.[5] But to sustain a conviction for a lower degree or an included offense, it is necessary that the allegations of the indictment show such lower offense to be necessarily included in the one charged. Thus, if the statutory form of the indictment for murder does not include a charge of an assault, a con-

[1] This is copied *verbatim* from S. v. Smith, 65 Me. 257, and illustrates a case where the facts necessarily indicate manslaughter and not murder, and where the indictment should be drawn accordingly.

[2] Davis v. S., 39 Md. 355; S. v. Grant, 7 Oreg. 414; Buckner v. C., 14 Bush, 601. And a plea of not guilty puts in issue the guilt of a lower degree or included offense, as well as that of the crime charged: Reynolds v. S., 34 Fla. 175.

[3] S. v. Gordon, 3 Ia. 410; P. v. McDonnell, 92 N. Y. 657; Evans v. S., 33 Ga. 4; Reynolds v. S., 1 Ga. 222; Roy v. S., 2 Kan. 405; McPherson v. S., 29 Ark. 225; King v. S., 5 How. (Miss.) 730; Watson v. S., 5 Mo. 497; Plummer v. S., 6 Mo. 231; Brooks v. S., 3 Humph. 24; Conner v. C., 13 Bush, 714; U. S. v. Meagher, 37 Fed. R. 875. Therefore rejection of evidence tending to reduce the offense to manslaughter, or error in instructions as to murder, will not be ground for reversal where defendant is convicted of manslaughter only: P. v. Wyman, 15 Cal. 70; Smith v. S., 59 Ark. 132. Under an indictment for murder the jury may return a verdict for manslaughter by criminal negligence: Burton v. S., 92 Ga. 449. But this will depend upon the circumstances of the case: Lucas v. S., 71 Miss. 471; Reg. v. French, 14 Cox, 328. Under the charge of being accessory to murder there may be a conviction for manslaughter: S. v. Robinson, 12 Wash. 349.

[4] S. v. Ostrander, 30 Mo. 13; P. v. Dolan, 9 Cal. 576; S. v. Grant, 7 Oreg. 414. By permission of the court, defendant indicted for the first degree may be tried for the second degree: S. v. Talmage, 107 Mo. 543.

[5] Isham v. S., 38 Ala. 213; Price v. C., 33 Grat. 819; Powers v. S., 87 Ind. 144. But this is so only by statute: Hilands v. C., 114 Pa. St. 372.

viction of an assault with intent to commit murder cannot be sustained;[1] but under the usual indictment for murder by means of an assault there may be a conviction for assault with intent to murder,[2] or for assault and battery,[3] but not for an assault not involved in the transaction charged in the indictment.[4] Under an indictment for child-murder, conviction for concealing the birth of the child cannot be supported.[5] Under an indictment for murder defendant cannot be convicted of the statutory offense of killing by wilfully striking, etc., as defined by the statute of Kentucky.[6] There can be no conviction of manslaughter or assault under an indictment for murder if the statutory period for the prosecution for manslaughter or assault has expired.[7]

§ 390. Effect of conviction of lower degree or included offense.— Where a defendant is put on trial for murder and convicted of manslaughter, such conviction amounts to an acquittal of murder, whether so specified by the jury or not, and even if the conviction for manslaughter is afterwards set aside on application by defendant for a new trial or on appeal he cannot again be tried for murder.[8] It has been held also that a conviction of murder in the second degree is an acquittal of murder in the first degree, and defendant cannot, where the verdict is set aside and a new trial granted, be subsequently convicted of the first degree.[9] But it is insisted, on the other hand, that the

[1] Scott v. S., 60 Miss. 268.

[2] P. v. McDonnell, 92 N. Y. 657; Peterson v. S., 12 Tex. Ap. 650. *Contra*, S. v. Guillory, 42 La. An. 581.

[3] S. v. Scott, 24 Vt. 127. *Contra*, Burns v. P., 1 Park. Cr. R. 182.

[4] Reg. v. Phelps, Car. & M. 180.

[5] Reg. v. Hicks, 2 M. & Rob. 302.

[6] Conner v. C., 13 Bush, 714; Buckner v. C., 14 Bush, 601; Trimble v. C., 78 Ky. 176. But where the charge is of murder by striking, beating, etc., there may be conviction for an aggravated assault: Bean v. S., 25 Tex. Ap. 346.

[7] P. v. Miller, 12 Cal. 291; White v. S., 4 Tex. Ap. 488; Fulcher v. S., 33 Tex. Ap. 22; S. v. Cobbs, 7 La. An. 107; S. v. Foster, 7 La. An. 525. It is not error in a prosecution for murder to instruct the jury that a prosecution for manslaughter is already barred, that being the fact: Riggs v. S., 30 Miss. 635.

[8] S. v. Tweedy, 11 Ia. 350; P. v. Gilmore, 4 Cal. 376; S. v. Ross, 29 Mo. 32; Brennan v. P., 15 Ill. 511; Barnett v. P., 54 Ill. 325; Slaughter v. S., 6 Humph. 410; S. v. Flannigan, 6 Md. 167; Jordan v. S., 22 Ga. 545; Hurt v. S., 25 Miss. 378; S. v. Dunn, 41 La. An. 610.

[9] Sylvester v. S., 72 Ala. 201; Johnson v. S., 29 Ark. 31; S. v. Belden, 33 Wis. 120; S. v. Helm, — Ia. —, 61 N. W. Rep. 246; S. v. Ball, 27 Mo. 324; Golding v. S., 31 Fla. 262; Jones v. S., 13 Tex. 168. The court

division of murder into two degrees does not make two offenses, and therefore the same rule should not apply as where the conviction is of a lower offense, as manslaughter.[1] The whole proposition that the verdict for the lower degree or for the included offense amounts to an acquittal of the higher degree or higher offense, and that therefore to put defendant on trial again for the higher degree or higher offense would be putting him twice in jeopardy, is forcibly controverted in some cases on the ground that when defendant procures the setting aside of the verdict or the reversal of a judgment based thereon he waives all advantage from such verdict or judgment, which must be regarded as an entirety, and is thereby placed in the same position as he was before trial.[2] But the weight of authority seems to be in support of the proposition that a new trial secured by defendant operates only to set aside the verdict so far as it constitutes a conviction, and does not affect it so far as it constitutes, even by implication, an acquittal of the higher degree or higher offense.[3] By statute in some states this matter has been regulated so that where a new trial is granted defendant is put on trial on the original indictment.[4] But the objection to putting defendant a second time on trial for the higher degree or offense is one based upon the constitutional provision against putting a defendant twice in jeopardy and therefore is not to be disposed of by a mere statutory provision. If the conviction for the lower degree or offense amounts to an acquittal of the higher degree or offense, then nothing else than a constitutional amendment which shall limit

may allude to the former conviction of the second degree as explaining why it becomes immaterial to consider whether the evidence indicates the first degree: Pharr v. S., 10 Tex. Ap. 485.

[1] P. v. Keefer, 65 Cal. 232; Bohanan v. S., 18 Neb. 57; S. v. Bradley, 67 Vt. 465. Verdict of guilty with mitigating circumstances, as authorized by statute, will not prevent a verdict, on a new trial, of guilty without mitigating circumstances: Greer v. S., 3 Baxt. 321.

[2] Bohanan v. S., 18 Neb. 57; S. v. Behimer, 20 Ohio St. 572; S. v. McCord, 8 Kan. 232; Veatch v. S., 60 Ind. 291; C. v. Arnold, 83 Ky. 1; S. v. Kring, 11 Mo. Ap. 92. Indeed, it has been held that this is the result where the offense is charged in several counts upon one of which defendant is acquitted while he is convicted upon others: Lesslie v. S., 18 Ohio St. 390.

[3] S. v. Martin, 30 Wis. 216; S. v. Belden, 33 Wis. 120; Jones v. S., 13 Tex. 168.

[4] C. v. Arnold, 83 Ky. 1.

in this respect the general provision as to former jeopardy can cure the difficulty.[1] But if, on the other hand, the asking for a new trial by defendant is a waiver of the entire effect of the conviction and not merely a waiver of previous jeopardy as to the portion of the crime for which he has been convicted, then of course the constitutional provision as to former jeopardy does not affect the question, for it is well settled that the constitutional provision in defendant's behalf may be waived and a new trial granted at his request.[2] Where it is held that defendant can only be put on trial the second time for the degree or offense of which he has been convicted, such trial may be had on the original indictment, without a new arraignment,[3] the jury being instructed that they are not to convict him of a higher offense than that for which he was previously convicted;[4] or he may be tried on a new or amended indictment.[5] It will be error to try the case as though defendant were on trial for the higher degree or higher offense, even though he is convicted only of that degree or offense of which he was previously convicted,[6] and an instruction discussing the higher degree or higher offense as though defendant were on trial therefor will constitute error.[7] The trial is no longer one for the higher degree or higher offense,[8] but defendant may on the second trial be convicted of the offense for which he was previously convicted, or any included offense, and the fact that the evidence shows a higher offense or higher degree will not constitute a variance.[9]

§ 391. Instructions as to lower degree or included offense. As the jury may convict of a lower grade of homicide than that charged in the indictment, or of an offense necessarily included in that charged, it is error to so instruct the jury as to exclude or influence the exercise by them of this power.[10]

[1] Kring v. Missouri, 107 U. S. 221. Such constitutional amendments have been adopted in Missouri and Colorado, and perhaps other states.

[2] Stewart v. S., 15 Ohio St. 155; S. v. Clark, 69 Ia. 196; S. v. Blaisdell, 59 N. H. 328; S. v. Hart, 33 Kan. 218; Veatch v. S., 60 Ind. 291; Gannon v. P., 127 Ill. 507; P. v. Olwell, 28 Cal. 456; 1 Bish. Cr. L., § 1003.

[3] Reynolds v. S., 34 Fla. 175.

[4] S. v. Dunn, 41 La. An. 610.

[5] Gannon v. P., 127 Ill. 507.

[6] S. v. Boyle, 28 Ia. 522; S. v. Knouse, 29 Ia. 118.

[7] S. v. Tweedy, 11 Ia. 350.

[8] Baker v. S., 4 Tex. Ap. 223; Cheek v. S., 4 Tex. Ap. 444.

[9] Fuller v. S., 30 Tex. Ap. 559.

[10] That is, it is improper to say to

The court should explain to the jury all the grades of homicide, it being the province of the jury, and not that of the court, to say of what grade, if any, defendant is guilty.[1] Thus, on a trial for murder the jury should be instructed as to what constitutes manslaughter.[2] More definitely, however, the rule seems to be that the court must instruct the jury fully and explicitly on the legal effect of all the circumstances developed on the trial tending to determine the degree of the prisoner's guilt.[3] Even where the defense on which the prisoner relies is equally a defense as to all degrees of criminality in the act, the court should instruct as to the lower degrees and offenses if there is anything in the evidence indicating that the guilt is of a lower grade of crime.[4] But it is not necessary to instruct as to the

the jury that an atrocious and dastardly murder has been committed: Hopt v. Utah, 110 U. S. 574; or to say that they must find defendant guilty of murder or voluntary manslaughter or not guilty, thereby precluding inquiry as to any other grade of offense: Holder v. S., 5 Ga. 441.

[1] Jones v. S., 29 Ga. 594; Craft v. S., 3 Kan. 450; P. v. Dunn, 1 Idaho T. 75; Brannigan v. P., 3 Utah, 488. And the jury may convict of manslaughter, though the evidence shows the crime to have been murder: Fagg v. S., 50 Ark. 506. In some states the judge must instruct as to lower degrees and included crimes and leave the matter entirely to the jury: S. v. Greer, 11 Wash. 244; S. v. Brown, 40 La. An. 725; S. v. Clark, 46 La. An. 704. Similarly the judge should instruct as to what circumstances will justify or excuse homicide: Pinder v. S., 27 Fla. 370. But failure to instruct as to lower offenses will not be ground of reversal if no such instructions are asked: Lovett v. S., 30 Fla. 142.

[2] S. v. Clemons, 51 Ia. 274; Rutherford v. C., 13 Bush, 608; Payne v. C., 1 Met. (Ky.) 370; Maria v. S., 28 Tex. 698; S. v. Brown, 41 La. An. 410. It is error to so charge as to lead the jury to infer that, if they find defendant not guilty of the first degree of murder, they must find him guilty in the second: Greta v. S., 9 Tex. Ap. 429. In Texas by statute the court is required to present to the jury the law applicable to the case: Holmes v. S., 11 Tex. Ap. 223; Carter v. S., 30 Tex. Ap. 551; Sanders v. S., 41 Tex. 306.

[3] Nelson v. S., 2 Swan, 237; Crawford v. S., 12 Ga. 142; Washington v. S., 36 Ga. 222; S. v. Kirkland, 14 Rich. 230; S. v. Meyer, 58 Vt. 457; S. v. Hartzell, 58 Ia. 520; S. v. Talmage, 107 Mo. 543; Elliston v. S., 10 Tex. Ap. 361; Whitaker v. S., 12 Tex. Ap. 436; Green v. S., 12 Tex. Ap. 445; Reynolds v. S., 14 Tex. Ap. 427; Moore v. S., 15 Tex. Ap. 1; Rutherford v. S., 16 Tex. Ap. 649; Lindsay v. S., 36 Tex. 337; Ellison v. S., 12 Tex. Ap. 557; McLaughlin v. S., 10 Tex. Ap. 340; Williams v. S., 7 Tex. Ap. 396. On a joint trial the judge should, if it appears that either prisoner is guilty of a less offense than that charged, so instruct the jury without regard to its effect upon the other prisoner: S. v. Pratt, 88 N. C. 639.

[4] So where the defense is an *alibi:* S. v. Ah Lee, 7 Oreg. 237; or insanity: S. v. Patton, 12 La. An. 288.

lower degrees or offense where there is nothing in the evidence tending to show defendant to be guilty of such lower degree or offense and not guilty of a higher degree or offense charged.[1] Indeed, it has been held that where there is no evidence of a lower degree or included crime the court may tell the jury that they must convict of the crime charged or acquit.[2] It is not error to instruct the jury as to murder, or murder in the first degree, when defendant can be convicted only of manslaughter or murder in the second degree, provided the jury are instructed also as to what crime or degree of crime defendant may be convicted of.[3] But erroneous instructions as to a higher degree or offense than that of which defendant is convicted will not be error without prejudice, but ground for reversal.[4]

[1] P. v. Byrnes, 30 Cal. 206; P. v. Quincy, 8 Cal. 89; P. v. Welch, 49 Cal. 174; S. v. Anderson, 98 Mo. 461; S. v. Phillips, 117 Mo. 389; S. v. Duncan, 116 Mo. 288; S. v. Nelson, 118 Mo. 124; S. v. Schoenwald, 31 Mo. 147; O'Brien v. C., 89 Ky. 354; S. v. Smith, 56 Minn. 78; Jackson v. S., 88 Ga. 784; Dozier v. S., 26 Ga. 156; Choice v. S., 31 Ga. 424; Hicks v. S., 25 Fla. 535; King v. S., 71 Ala. 1; Pierson v. S., 99 Ala. 148; O'Connell v. S., 18 Tex. 343; Holden v. S., 1 Tex. Ap. 225; Washington v. S., 1 Tex. Ap. 647; Berry v. S., 8 Tex. Ap. 515; Homberg v. S., 12 Tex. Ap. 1; Evans v. S., 13 Tex. Ap. 225; Neyland v. S., 13 Tex. Ap. 536; Anderson v. S., 15 Tex. Ap. 447; Smith v. S., 15 Tex. Ap. 139; Gilly v. S., 15 Tex. Ap. 287; Hughes v. S., 29 Tex. Ap. 565; Trumble v. S., 25 Tex. Ap. 631; Angus v. S., 29 Tex. Ap. 52; Spivey v. S., 30 Tex. Ap. 343; White v. S., 30 Tex. Ap. 652. Indeed, where there is no evidence to reduce the crime to manslaughter, an instruction as to manslaughter will require a reversal if the conviction is of manslaughter: S. v. Punshon, 124 Mo. 448; Virgil v. S., 63 Miss. 317. But instances are comparatively rare in which a charge as to the second degree, on a prosecution for the first degree, may safely be dispensed with: Blocker v. S., 27 Tex. Ap. 16; Nalley v. S., 28 Tex. Ap. 387; Benevides v. S., 14 Tex. Ap. 378. Instructions to the jury which, after properly defining the first and second degrees of manslaughter and justifiable homicide, direct the jury as to the form of the verdict for murder in the first degree and for murder in the second degree, and not guilty, do not constitute error in failing to instruct as to the form of verdict for manslaughter: S. v. St. Clair, 16 Nev. 207.

[2] Sparf v. U. S., 156 U. S. 51; S. v. McKinney, 111 N. C. 683. But if there is any evidence relevant to the issue of manslaughter, that issue should be submitted to the jury: Stevenson v. U. S., 162 U. S. 313.

[3] Goaler v. S., 5 Baxt. 678. Otherwise, if an instruction as to a higher degree of murder is given than that of which the defendant may properly be convicted: Tweedy v. S., 11 Ia. 350. An instruction as to murder is not necessary where defendant is on trial for manslaughter: S. v. Hartzell, 58 Ia. 520.

[4] Mitchell v. S., 60 Ala. 26. *Contra,*

§ **392. Verdict.**— The statutes which divide murder into two degrees usually provide that the jury shall by their verdict determine the degree; and under these statutes it is held that a verdict of guilty which does not thus specify the degree of murder is invalid, even where the indictment shows with what degree of murder the defendant is charged.[1] But a verdict of guilty under an indictment for murder is sufficient to show that the conviction is for that crime and not for the included offense of manslaughter.[2] Aside from this question, there is little to be said with reference to verdicts in cases of homicide that is not equally applicable in other cases. If the indictment is in several counts referring to one transaction, a general verdict is sufficient.[3] Several defendants jointly indicted and tried may be convicted of different offenses included within the indictment.[4] The verdict must respond to the indictment, and where it is coupled with a statement that the jury believe the act to have been committed without premeditation the judge may refuse to receive it and direct the jury to say guilty or not guilty.[5] So a finding of mitigating circumstances may be disregarded.[6] The court may direct the jury that a recommendation of mercy will be of no avail.[7] Where the verdict was of manslaughter in the second degree, no such degree of manslaughter being specified by the statute, a conviction for manslaughter was sustained, the words relating to the degree being rejected as surplusage.[8] Cases of verdicts in prosecutions for homicide which have been called in question because of misspelling or similar irregularity are cited in the note.[9] It is

P. v. Swift, 66 Cal. 348. It will not be construed as prejudicial that the court instructs that certain circumstances will not amount to more than manslaughter, defendant being convicted of manslaughter: S. v. Hutchinson, 7 Nev. 53; nor to fail to accurately define manslaughter in a prosecution for murder, where the theory of the defense is that the homicide committed was manslaughter and defendant is convicted of that offense: P. v. Harper, 83 Mich. 273.

[1] See *supra*, § 362.

[2] P. v. March, 6 Cal. 543; O'Connor v. S., 9 Fla. 215; S. v. Upton, 1 Dev. 513.

[3] Scott v. S., 37 Ala. 117; S. v. Baker, 63 N. C. 276; Kilgore v. S., 74 Ala. 1; Jackson v. S., 74 Ala. 26.

[4] Mask v. S., 32 Miss. 405; S. v. Arden, 1 Bay, 487.

[5] Reg. v. Maloney, 9 Cox, 6.

[6] Eason v. S., 6 Baxt. 431.

[7] Shaw v. S., 60 Ga. 246.

[8] Traube v. S., 56 Miss. 153.

[9] Guilty in "fist" degree held insufficient: Wooldridge v. S., 13 Tex. Ap. 443; but held that the misspell-

sufficient, where there is but one defendant, that the indictment finds "defendant" guilty; and therefore it is not error to amend such a verdict afterwards by the insertion of the name of the defendant.[1]

§ 393. **Punishment.**—The provision in statutes dividing murder into two degrees and leaving it to the jury to affix the punishment in case of conviction in the first degree has already been considered.[2] The punishment at common law for manslaughter is burning in the hand,[3] but such punishment may be respited that the party may avail himself of the right of soliciting a pardon.[4]

§ 394. **Sentence.**—Time and place of execution form no part of the sentence of death,[5] and a mistake in that respect may be corrected.[6] If the conviction does not specify the day, the appellate court on affirming the judgment may appoint a day.[7]

X. THE EVIDENCE.

§ 395. **Venue.**—The general rule that the venue must be proven in this as in other criminal cases need not be specially discussed. A few illustrations, however, of its application to this crime may properly be given. The proof of the venue must not be left to inference, and it was therefore held that evidence that the homicide was committed about seventy-five yards from a certain house, and that the house was in the county where the indictment was found, was not sufficient to show the venue.[8] But in another case,[9] it is said that the venue need not be proved affirmatively, and it is enough if the witness states generally that the transaction occurred in the county of the indictment.[10] Whether the venue is proved is a question

ing of "mrder" for "murder" was not a fatal defect: Walker v. S., 13 Tex. Ap. 618. Where the statute did not require a verdict in writing, *held*, that a verdict written "gulty without capitel parnish," but properly read by the clerk, was sufficient: S. v. Ross, 32 La. An. 854.

[1] Martin v. S., 25 Ga. 494; S. v. Yancey, 3 Brev. 142.

[2] *Supra*, § 363.

[3] S. v. Henderson, 2 Dev. & B. 543.

[4] Allen v. S., Mart. & Y. 294.

[5] Rex v. Doyle, 1 Leach, 67.

[6] Rex v. Wyatt, Russ. & Ry. 230.

[7] Russell v. S., 33 Ala. 366.

[8] Franklin v. S., 5 Baxt. 613.

[9] S. v. Dent, 6 S. C. 383.

[10] Laydon v. S., 52 Ind. 459. So where the proof was that the crime was committed in the house of the witness in the county of the indictment, the proof was held sufficient: Mitchum v. S., 11 Ga. 615.

for the jury,[1] but if not established, the verdict should be set aside as against the evidence.[2] The venue may be established by circumstantial evidence;[3] and if the evidence raises a violent presumption that the offense was committed in the county, or that fact may be reasonably inferred from the evidence, it is sufficient. The doctrine of reasonable doubt does not apply, it is said, to proof of the venue.[4] Where a body with marks of injuries sufficient to cause death was found in a river in the heart of the county in a condition showing that it must have been placed there by human agency and had not drifted there by the current, it was held that the evidence warranted a finding that the homicide was committed in that county.[5] So where the evidence showed that defendant, in company with deceased, on the evening of the alleged murder, left one county going toward another county in which the body of the deceased was found, it was held that the venue of the killing was sufficiently shown to have been in the latter.[6]

§ **396. Corpus delicti.**— There is nothing peculiar to crimes of homicide in the rule that the fact of the commission of the crime must be proven, but in homicide cases the rule requiring proof of the *corpus delicti* has been especially insisted upon. The earlier statement of the rule in these cases seems to have involved the necessity of direct and positive proof of the death of the alleged deceased.[7] But this strict statement of the rule has been much questioned and later authorities have modified it, so that while proof of the *corpus delicti* is still insisted upon as an essential part of the case, no particular emphasis is laid upon its being established by direct and positive evidence;[8] and circumstantial evidence is by the decided preponderance

[1] S. v. Miller, 9 Houst. 564.

[2] Jones v. S., 58 Ark. 390.

[3] S. v. West, 69 Mo. 401.

[4] Andrews v. S., 21 Fla. 598.

[5] C. v. Costley, 118 Mass. 1.

[6] Beavers v. S., 58 Ind. 530.

[7] 2 Hale, P. C. 290; 4 Bl. Com. 358; 1 Stark. Ev. 575; 2 id. 710; Ruloff v. P., 18 N. Y. 179; P. v. Bennett, 49 N. Y. 137. A statement of the strict rule, not in a homicide case, but showing the view of the judge as applicable to such cases, may be found in Evans v. Evans, 1 Hag. Con. 35, 79. The *corpus delicti* should be first shown, so far as the testimony can be separately given, and especially so far as can be shown from a *post-mortem* examination: P. v. Hall, 48 Mich. 482; Joe v. S., 6 Fla. 591.

[8] 3 Greenl. Ev., § 131; Best, Ev. (Chamberlain's ed.), § 441; 1 Bish. Cr. Proc., § 1056; S. v. Williams, 7 Jones, 446. And see Reg. v. Burton, Dears. 282; C. v. Bell, 164 Pa. St. 517.

of authority sufficient to establish the *corpus delicti* if it is strong and unequivocal.[1] There are some cases where the body of the deceased cannot possibly be produced or identified, as where it is destroyed by fire or thrown overboard at sea, and circumstantial evidence alone can be relied on.[2] In cases of criminal homicide the *corpus delicti* has two components: death as the result, and the criminal agency of another as the means;[3] and it has been said that as to the death the evidence must be direct and positive.[4] But the authorities cited in the previous note as to proving the *corpus delicti* by circumstantial evidence do not make any such distinction between the death and the criminal agency, and it is doubtful if it is of any value. There are numerous illustrations, however, of the insufficiency of the evidence to prove the *corpus delicti*.[5] It must be established beyond a reasonable doubt.[6]

§ **397. When corroboration necessary.**— It is a general rule of criminal evidence which has found application in cases of

[1] U. S. v. Williams, 1 Cliff. 5; P. v. Alviso, 55 Cal. 230; Zoldoske v. S., 82 Wis. 580; S. v. Keeler, 28 Ia. 551; S. v. Dickson, 78 Mo. 438; Johnson v. C., 81 Ky. 325, 4 Am. Cr. R. 140 and note; Campbell v. P., — Ill. —, 42 N. E. R. 123; Peters v. S., 67 Ga. 29; Rex v. Hindmarsh, 2 Leach, 569.

[2] S. v. Williams, 7 Jones, 446; S. v. Smith, 9 Wash. 341; St. Clair v. U. S., 154 U. S. 134; U. S. v. Williams, 1 Cliff. 5; Cavaness v. S., 43 Ark. 331. In Texas the body or a portion of it must be found and sufficiently identified to establish the fact of death: Puryear v. S., 28 Tex. Ap. 73.

[3] It has been said that the *corpus delicti* involves defendant's agency in producing the death: S. v. Dickson, 78 Mo. 438; Harris v. S., 28 Tex. Ap. 308; Whart. Cr. Ev., § 325. But this is erroneous; it involves only the existence of the criminal fact: P. v. Palmer, 109 N. Y. 110: 3 Greenl. Ev., § 30; 1 Bish. Cr. Pr., § 1060; Bouv. L. Dic.

[4] P. v. Bennett, 49 N. Y. 137; Pitts v. S., 43 Miss. 472; Jackson v. S., 29 Tex. Ap. 458. The identity of defendant as the murderer may be established by a lower degree of evidence: P. v. Palmer, 109 N. Y. 110.

[5] P. v. Ah Fung, 16 Cal. 137; Lucas v. S., 19 Tex. Ap. 79; Lovelady v. S., 14 Tex. Ap. 545; S. C., 17 Tex. Ap. 286; High v. S., 26 Tex. Ap. 545; Reg. v. Hopkins, 8 C. & P. 591. Where there was evidence of the finding of the skeleton of a human being corresponding in sex and size to the body of the alleged deceased, it was held that there was sufficient to justify the admission of circumstantial evidence to identify the skeleton as that of the murdered party: McCulloch v. S., 48 Ind. 109. Mere suspicious circumstances are not enough to establish the *corpus delicti:* Conde v. S., — Tex. Ap. —, 34 S. W. R. 286.

[6] S. v. Taylor, 1 Houst. Cr. C. 436; Walker v. S., 14 Tex. Ap. 609; S. v. Flanagan, 26 W. Va. 116; Griffith v. S., 90 Ala. 583; Dreessen v. S., 38 Neb. 375.

criminal homicide that the extra-judicial confession of the defendant, without corroboration,[1] or the uncorroborated evidence of an accomplice, is insufficient to prove the *corpus delicti*.[2]

§ 398. **Identity of body.**— In proving the *corpus delicti* it is essential that the proof correspond with the indictment as to the identity of the person charged to have been killed.[3] But it is not necessary to have an express identification of the body where the circumstances are sufficient to establish such identity.[4] The jury may, in determining the identity, consider the entire evidence and the attendant circumstances.[5] It is not essential that the body of the deceased be found.[6] And where identification is attempted in case of a body which has been partially destroyed, slight clues have been held sufficient in connection with other evidence.[7] The proof of the identification in such cases may be the same as that which is admissible to identify the person on trial with the one charged with the crime.[8]

§ 399. **Alibi of alleged deceased.**— It has been said that where defendant attempts to prove that the person charged to have been killed was alive after the evidence for the prosecution shows him to have been dead, and thus seeks to show that

[1] Smith v. C., 21 Grat. 809; S. v. German, 54 Mo. 526; P. v. Lane, 49 Mich. 340; S. v. Miller, 9 Houst. 564; Jackson v. S., 29 Tex. Ap. 458; Harris v. S., 30 Tex. Ap. 549. And held that a confession sworn to by the defendant in a preliminary examination was a judicial confession and not within the rule: Jackson v. S., 29 Tex. Ap. 458. If the *corpus delicti* is otherwise established, a conviction of defendant may be had on his confession alone: Mose v. S., 36 Ala. 211.

[2] Elizando v. S., 31 Tex. Ap. 237. Evidence of the *corpus delicti* and defendant's confession will sufficiently corroborate the evidence of an accomplice: Schaefer v. S., 93 Ga. 177.

[3] Smith v. C., 21 Grat. 809; Lightfoot v. S., 20 Tex. Ap. 77; Walker v. S., 14 Tex. Ap. 609.

[4] S. v. Patterson, 73 Mo. 695; Reg. v. Cheverton, 2 F. & F. 833.

[5] Spear v. S., 16 Tex. Ap. 98. A witness testifying as to identity need not be absolutely certain with reference thereto in order that his evidence be admissible: P. v. Young, 102 Cal. 411.

[6] Stocking v. S., 7 Ind. 326. Otherwise in Texas by statute: Walker v. S., 14 Tex. Ap. 609.

[7] C. v. Webster, 5 Cush. 295; Wilson v. S., 43 Tex. 472; Jackson v. S., 29 Tex. Ap. 458; S. v. Williams, 7 Jones, 446. A witness who is not an expert may testify that the bones found are those of a human being: Jackson v. S., 29 Tex. Ap. 458.

[8] Taylor v. S., 35 Tex. 97. Identification may be made by a photograph: Udderzook v. C., 76 Pa. St. 340.

the crime with which the accused is charged was not committed, the burden of proving that fact is upon the defendant.[1] But these cases are based on the theory that an *alibi* as to accused must be made out by him by preponderance of evidence, which is not in accordance with the weight of authority, and therefore this proposition is probably not correct.[2] On the other hand, it is not necessary that the state shall show that deceased was alive immediately preceding the time of the alleged homicide. Having shown him to be alive shortly before, the presumption of life remains.[3]

§ **400. Cause of death.**— For the purpose of establishing the death as due to the act of the accused it is necessary to establish the cause of death.[4] But if the circumstances proved indicate the death as the result of injuries inflicted by the accused without any other cause appearing, it is sufficient.[5] Thus, evidence as to a gunshot wound is admissible as bearing on the cause of death, although the indictment does not describe the wound.[6] If the accused has been convicted of assault and battery and the evidence shows that death afterwards resulted therefrom, the record of the former conviction is admissible.[7] While expert evidence is admissible as to the cause of death, as indicated by blood stains, etc.,[8] yet the testimony of those not experts as to the cause of death may also be received.[9]

§ **401. Proof of suicide.**— In behalf of the accused it may be shown that the death was the result of suicide and not of the acts of the accused,[10] and for this purpose evidence of sui-

[1] S. v. Vincent, 24 Ia. 570; Fahnestock v. S., 23 Ind. 231. Where there is evidence that the supposed deceased was seen alive after the homicide, it is not admissible for the state to show that about that time a person resembling deceased was seen in the neighborhood: C. v. Webster, 5 Cush. 295.

[2] 17 Am. L. Rev. 904, 906.

[3] C. v. Harman, 4 Pa. St. 269.

[4] Cole v. S., 59 Ark. 50.

[5] U. S. v. Wiltberger, 3 Wash. C. C. 515; P. v. Lewis, 36 Cal. 531.

[6] Dukes v. S., 11 Ind. 557.

[7] C. v. McPike, 3 Cush. 181.

[8] S. v. Morgan, 95 N. C. 641; Batten v. S., 80 Ind. 394; S. v. Miller, 9 Houst. 564; C. v. Piper, 120 Mass. 185; S. v. Sullivan, 43 S. C. 205; Rash v. S., 61 Ala. 89; Cannon v. P., 141 Ill. 270; Von Pollnitz v. S., 92 Ga. 16. An expert may be asked whether in his opinion a certain wound did or did not cause death, or whether such wound would or would not be fatal: Davidson v. S., 135 Ind. 254.

[9] Everett v. S., 62 Ga. 65; P. v. Bell, 49 Cal. 485; P. v. Gibson, 106 Cal. 458; C. v. Sturtivant, 117 Mass. 122; C. v. Dunan, 128 Mass. 422; S. v. Bradley, 67 Vt. 465; Smith v. S., 43 Tex. 643.

[10] S. v. Billings, 81 Ia. 99.

cidal disposition is competent where the circumstances do not negative the possibility of suicide.[1] The presumption against the commission of suicide will not prevail against the presumption of innocence so as to require proof of the suicide by preponderance of evidence.[2] But the state may rebut the evidence as to suicide by proof that the condition in life and personal surroundings of the deceased tended to show the absence of any motive likely to impel to suicide.[3]

§ 402. **Death from natural causes.**— It is of course open to defendant to show that the evidence for prosecution is not inconsistent with the theory of death from natural causes.[4]

§ 403. **Identity of accused.**— There is nothing so peculiar in homicide cases in regard to the proof of the identity of the accused with the person committing the injury as to render a special citation of cases important. There must be some participation shown, which cannot be inferred from the mere fact that accused received an injury at the time the deceased appears to have suffered violence causing his death.[5] Previous threats by accused are admissible as tending to identify him as the one who caused the death of the deceased.[6] Circumstantial evidence connecting the accused with the crime may

[1] Boyd v. S., 14 Lea, 161; C. v. Trefethen, 157 Mass. 180. Evidence of threats to commit suicide six years before has been held admissible: Blackburn v. S., 23 Ohio St. 146. *Contra*, see Siebert v. P., 143 Ill. 571. Where insanity is relied on as tending to show suicide, declarations of deceased, offered to prove sanity, should be received with great caution: Jumpertz v. P., 21 Ill. 375.

[2] Persons v. S., 90 Tenn. 291. Where there is a general instruction as to reasonable doubt it is not necessary to instruct specially as to reasonable doubt due to evidence that the death was suicidal: S. v. Bradley, 64 Vt. 466.

[3] S. v. Lentz, 45 Minn. 177. So evidence of the death of another person in a similar way, and as a part of the same scheme to get money, is admissible to rebut the theory of suicide or accident: Goersen v. C., 99 Pa. St. 388.

[4] Dreessen v. S., 38 Neb. 375. Evidence of a life of license and debauchery being admitted to prove a probable cause of death, drunkenness on a particular occasion not connected with the death cannot be shown: C. v. Ryan, 134 Mass. 223. So proof of declarations of deceased as to being subject to fits is not admissible: S. v. Dart, 29 Conn. 153. Where the crime charged is manslaughter from attempted abortion, proof that deceased previously attempted to procure an abortion on herself is not admissible: S. v. Glass, 5 Oreg. 73.

[5] S. v. Harrison, 5 Jones, 115. But accused may show that immediately after the combat he had a fresh bruise: Scott v. S., 56 Miss. 287.

[6] Nichols v. C., 11 Bush, 575.

be sufficient.[1] Various circumstances tending to establish this connection will be discussed under other headings.

§ 404. **Guilt of third persons.**— It is open to the accused to prove that the crime was committed by someone else, for the purpose of relieving himself from responsibility, and such proof is admissible even though the person to whom the crime is thus charged has already been acquitted thereof.[2] But it is not competent to prove confessions or admissions by a third person showing such person to have committed the crime charged to defendant.[3] Such evidence is mere hearsay.[4] So it is incompetent to show that another had malice toward the deceased and a motive and opportunity to take his life, and made threats of taking it.[5] But, on the contrary, any evidence tending proximately to show the commission of the crime by another than the defendant is admissible whether it be direct and positive or circumstantial only, and therefore threats, motive and opportunity pointing to another person as the guilty party may be shown.[6]

§ 405. **Real evidence.**— Clothing worn by the deceased showing evidence of the violence causing the death may be shown to the jury as indicating the location and direction of the wound, its fatal character, etc.;[7] or blood stains on the cloth-

[1] C. v. Johnson, 162 Pa. St. 63. An impression as to identity of a person whom witness saw near the place of the homicide as the defendant is not admissible: Woodward v. S., 4 Baxt. 322. The witness may be cross-examined as to the extent of his acquaintance with defendant: Olive v. S., 11 Neb. 1.

[2] P. v. Mitchell, 100 Cal. 328.

[3] Greenfield v. P., 85 N. Y. 75; Davis v. C., 95 Ky. 19; Holt v. S., 9 Tex. Ap. 571; Rhea v. S., 10 Yerg. 257.

[4] S. v. Terrell, 12 Rich. 321; S. v. Fletcher, 24 Oreg. 295; West v. S., 76 Ala. 98; 1 Bish. Cr. Pr., § 1248; Whart. Cr. Ev., § 225.

[5] S. v. Lambert, 93 N. C. 618; S. v. Davis, 77 N. C. 483; S. v. Bishop, 73 N. C. 44; Stephens v. P., 19 N. Y. 549; C. v. Abbott, 130 Mass. 472; S. v. Beaudet, 53 Conn. 536; Woolfolk v. S., 81 Ga. 551; S. C., 85 Ga. 69; Banks v. S., 72 Ala. 522; Alston v. S., 63 Ala. 178; Crookham v. S., 5 W. Va. 510; S. v. Laque, 41 La. An. 1070; S. v. Myers, 12 Wash. 77. At least such evidence is not admissible without showing the name and circumstances: S. v. Johnson, 31 La. An. 368.

[6] Dubose v. S., 10 Tex. Ap. 230; Ex parte Gilstrap, 14 Tex. Ap. 240; Leonard v. T., 2 Wash. 381; Morgan v. C., 14 Bush, 106; Sawyers v. S., 15 Lea, 694; S. v. Brown, 21 Kan. 38; S. v. Hawley, 63 Conn. 47; S. v. Johnson, 30 La. An., Part II, 921. The Texas cases here cited overrule general statements to the contrary found in Boothe v. S., 4 Tex. Ap. 202; Walker v. S., 6 Tex. Ap. 576.

[7] Story v. S., 99 Ind. 413; S. v. Winter, 72 Ia. 627; Hart v. S., 15

ing of accused worn on the day of, or soon after, the homicide may be put in evidence.[1] And so shoes corresponding to the tracks of the supposed murderer and fitting the accused or shown to belong to him may be introduced.[2] A question has been raised in this connection as to whether it is not compelling the defendant to be a witness against himself, in violation of the constitution, to thus put in evidence his personal belongings; but it is well settled that while the accused cannot be compelled to exhibit those portions of his body usually covered for the purpose of securing his identification, yet his personal effects may be taken from him and used upon his trial for what they may be worth.[3] If the accused makes no objection it is not improper to have his foot measured or make other tests to determine his identity by such means.[4] The weapon used by defendant may be shown to the jury.[5] So it was held that a stick used by defendant shortly after the homicide and showing blood stains might be introduced.[6]

§ **406. Photographs.**— Photographic views taken near the time of the homicide showing the condition of the premises on discovery of the crime, and satisfactorily verified, are admissible.[7] So a photograph of the wound is admissible.[8] A photograph of the alleged deceased may be introduced for the purpose of enabling the witnesses by comparison to say whether the dead body is that of such person.[9]

Tex. Ap. 202; King v. S., 13 Tex. Ap. 277; Levy v. S., 28 Tex. Ap. 203. So the bedclothes found in deceased's room stained with blood are admissible: Painter v. P., 147 Ill. 444.

[1] S. v. Stair, 87 Mo. 268.

[2] S. v. Nordstrom, 7 Wash. 506. The witness should only describe or identify; he should not give his opinion as to correspondence; that is for the jury: Hodge v. S., 97 Ala. 37.

[3] S. v. Nordstrom, 7 Wash. 506; Drake v. S., 75 Ga. 413. Though the evidence is improperly obtained, it will not, on that account, be inadmissible: Siebert v. P., 143 Ill. 571; S. v. Graham, 74 N. C. 646; S. v. Griswold, — Conn. —, 34 Atl. Rep. 1046; Shields v. S., 104 Ala. 35, 9 Am. Cr. R. 149 and note; P. v. Gardner, 144 N. Y. 119, 28 L. R. A. 699 and note. And see *supra*, § 118.

[4] S. v. Nordstrom, 7 Wash. 506.

[5] Siberry v. S., 133 Ind. 677.

[6] Thomas v. S., 67 Ga. 460. And a non-expert witness may testify as to whether stains are blood stains or not: S. v. Welch, 36 W. Va. 690; Greenfield v. P., 85 N. Y. 75.

[7] C. v. Robertson, 162 Mass. 90. In the photograph may be included persons grouped as those present were shown to have been at the commission of the crime: S. v. O'Reilly, 126 Mo. 597; P. v. Jackson, 111 N. Y. 362.

[8] Franklin v. S., 69 Ga. 36.

[9] Udderzook v. C., 76 Pa. St. 340; Wilson v. U. S., 162 U. S. 613. Also to show his physical characteristics, if important: P. v. Webster, 139 N. Y. 73.

§ 407. **Experiments.**— Evidence of experiments of non-professional witnesses with guns and targets for the purpose of showing that the shooting charged as homicide was done at short range is not admissible.[1] And so the court may reject experiments by means of a dynamometer for the purpose of measuring the force of the blow with a stick with substantially the same form and weight as that with which it is claimed the murder was committed. The difficulty in such cases is to show that the experiments were made under conditions the same as those existing in the case on trial.[2] Similarly it was held that the sheriff could not be allowed to discharge the revolver alleged to have been used by the prisoner to see if it would go off at half cock as was claimed.[3] But the opinion of an expert given as the result of experiments as to the distance of the deceased from the gun with which the fatal wound was inflicted, based on the character of the wound, is admissible.[4]

§ 408. **Circumstantial evidence.**— It is not proper here to go into the whole field of circumstantial evidence and the rules covering it, but some pertinent illustrations of such evidence in homicide cases may be properly given. Within this description comes evidence of correspondence between the shoes of defendant and the tracks of the person supposed to be guilty of the homicide.[5] So it has been held admissible to show that a hound, trained to follow the tracks of a human being, was shortly after the homicide put on what appeared to be the track of the guilty

[1] S. v. Justus, 11 Oreg. 178.

[2] C. v. Piper, 120 Mass. 185. See also, S. v. Fletcher, 24 Oreg. 295. But in a prosecution for manslaughter, where it was claimed that death resulted from the application of a lotion to the skin, evidence of the effect of the lotion when applied to other patients was permitted: Rex v. Long, 4 C. & P. 398.

[3] Polin v. S., 14 Neb. 540. Experiments before the jury as to the possibility of death having been suicide should be permitted with great caution: Jumpertz v. S., 21 Ill. 375. The court is not required to allow pistols which are in the custody of the court as connected with the crime to be used by an expert for the purpose of making experiments: S. v. Smith, 49 Conn. 376.

[4] S. v. Jones, 41 Kan. 309; Boyd v. S., 14 Lea, 161; Sullivan v. C., 93 Pa. St. 284. It will not be error for the court to allow the weapon with which the crime was committed to be experimented with to determine such fact: U. S. v. Ball, 163 U. S. 662.

[5] Ruloff v. P., 45 N. Y. 213; Russell v. C., 78 Va. 400; Bouldin v. S., 8 Tex. Ap. 332; or correspondence between a horse's tracks near the place of the homicide and those of defendant's horse: Campbell v. S., 23 Ala. 44.

person and followed such track to the house where defendant was shown to have been after the killing.[1] Recent possession of property taken at the time of and in connection with the homicide may be shown.[2] In order to make out a chain of circumstances, the prosecution may be allowed to give in evidence even minute and remote circumstances tending to connect the defendant with the crime.[3] Thus, evidence in relation to the examination of guns in the neighborhood of the homicide to ascertain whether any of them carried a ball of the size of the one found in the body of deceased was held admissible.[4] Circumstances indicating a motive for the crime may be proved.[5]

§ 409. Weight and sufficiency of circumstantial evidence. Even though the evidence be wholly circumstantial it may be sufficient to convict;[6] but it must be of such character as to preclude every hypothesis inconsistent with the guilt of the accused.[7] It is not enough that the mystery of the crime cannot be solved from the evidence except upon the supposition of the defendant's guilt; the facts proved must be susceptible of explanation upon no reasonable hypothesis consistent with his innocence.[8] The hypothesis, however, which will require the jury to acquit the defendant in such cases should be a rea-

[1] Hodge v. S., 98 Ala. 10. And see 54 Alb. L. Jour. 113.

[2] Williams v. C., 29 Pa. St. 102; Mimms v. S., 16 Ohio St. 221; Poe v. S., 10 Lea, 673; Reg. v. Franz, 2 F. & F. 580.

[3] Mendum v. C., 6 Rand. 704. And see Anderson v. S., 79 Ala. 5; S. v. Atkinson, 40 S. C. 363; S. v. Craemer, 12 Wash. 217.

[4] Dean v. C., 32 Grat. 912. For the purpose of corroborating the confession of the defendant and a dying declaration of deceased, it was held admissible to show the finding of a buck-shot of the described size in a tree within range of the gun said to have been used: Mose v. S., 36 Ala. 211.

[5] Russell v. C., 78 Va. 400; Hogan v. S., 13 Tex. Ap. 319. The subject of motive and relation between the parties is discussed *infra*, §§ 416, 417.

[6] Dean v. C., 32 Grat. 912; P. v. Hampton, 144 N. Y. 639; S. v. Pagano, 7 Wash. 549; Jim v. S., 5 Humph. 145; S. v. Atkinson, 40 S. C. 363; Shultz v. S., 13 Tex. 401; Williams v. S., 3 Tex. Ap. 123. As to circumstantial evidence of the *corpus delicti*, see *supra*, § 396.

[7] P. v. Strong, 30 Cal. 151; Coleman v. S., 26 Fla. 61; Dreessen v. S., 38 Neb. 375; Johnson v. S., 18 Tex. Ap. 385; Crow v. S., 33 Tex. Ap. 264; Pogue v. S., 12 Tex. Ap. 283; Hodges Case, 2 Lewin, 227.

[8] Schusler v. S., 29 Ind. 394; Horne v. S., 1 Kan. 42. Where simultaneous shots were fired by two persons not acting in combination, it was held that if there was any doubt as to the one fired by defendant having caused the death he should be acquitted: P. v. Woody, 45 Cal. 289.

sonable hypothesis arising out of the testimony and inconsistent with his guilt.[1] Though the failure of defendant to explain circumstances apparently connecting him with the crime, when it is in his power to do so, may be considered against him, yet such failure is not conclusive of his guilt,[2] and has no weight unless satisfactory proof of guilt is offered.[3] Where a chain of facts is relied on to establish the main fact in issue, each fact in the chain must be proved by competent evidence of the same weight as if that fact were the main fact in issue.[4] The court should instruct as to the law of circumstantial evidence where it is relied on for a conviction.[5]

§ **410. Best evidence; eye-witnesses.**— The general doctrine that the best evidence should be produced of which the case will admit has been so applied as to require the production of the evidence of eye-witnesses, if attainable, and render circumstantial evidence inadmissible in such cases.[6] A rule is also rec-

[1] Kendrick v. S., 55 Miss. 436.

[2] Gordon v. P., 33 N. Y. 501.

[3] C. v. Hardiman, 9 Gray, 136; Findley v. S., 5 Blackf. 576.

[4] C. v. Webster, 5 Cush. 295; P. v. Phipps, 39 Cal. 333; P. v. Anthony, 56 Cal. 397; Clare v. P., 9 Colo. 122; Dossett v. U. S., 3 Okl. 591; Harrison v. S., 6 Tex. Ap. 42; Crow v. S., 33 Tex. Ap. 264. But it is not error to refuse to charge that if one link in the chain of circumstantial evidence is wanting the state fails to make out a case, for such an instruction would be misleading: Grant v. S., 97 Ala. 35.

[5] Riley v. S., 20 Tex. Ap. 100; Hunt v. S., 7 Tex. Ap. 212; Wallace v. S., 7 Tex. Ap. 570; Struckman v. S., 7 Tex. Ap. 581; Myers v. S., 7 Tex. Ap. 640. But it was held error to charge that circumstantial evidence is legal evidence, and is often as conclusive as that which is termed direct and positive evidence, on the ground that such instruction was an intimation as to the opinion of the court on the weight of evidence of defendant's guilt: Harrison v. S., 9 Tex. Ap. 407. On the other hand, a charge that circumstantial evidence is as good as any other kind of evidence was held not to be error: West v. S., 76 Ala. 98. The defendant is not entitled to a charge that the jury should not convict upon circumstantial evidence unless it is as fully satisfactory to their minds as would be the positive swearing of one credible witness that he saw the act: Rea v. S., 8 Lea, 356; S. v. Carson, 115 N. C. 743. After counsel for defendant had read over cases where conviction of innocent persons had been secured on circumstantial evidence, it was held proper for the court to caution the jury against attaching too much importance to such cases: P. v. Ah Fook, 64 Cal. 380. It is only where the inculpatory evidence is wholly circumstantial that an instruction as to its weight is required: Smith v. S., 28 Tex. Ap. 309; Self v. S., 28 Tex. Ap. 398; Jones v. S., 31 Tex. Ap. 177.

[6] Thompson v. S., 30 Tex. Ap. 325; Hunnicutt v. S., 20 Tex. Ap. 632.

ognized in England, and in some of the states, requiring the prosecution to call all the witnesses who were present at the transaction, whether they are supposed to be favorable to the prosecution or the defense, the theory being that in a criminal case the prosecution should have no other object than to get at the truth.[1] Of course, if the witness shows an unfair bias, the prosecution will be allowed great latitude in his examination,[2] but should examine him to some extent as to the facts, so as to give the defense an opportunity for cross-examination.[3] This doctrine has not received general support, however, in the United States, it being thought that the opportunity which defendant has of securing witnesses, and in many states of testifying in his own behalf, is sufficient to protect him against any improper suppression of evidence on the part of the prosecution;[4] and in states where some recognition to the rules is given it is interpreted to mean only that the prosecution must show the whole transaction, and not suppress a part of it and ask a conviction on a partial showing of the facts.[5]

§ **411. Res gestæ.**— It is not necessary in this connection to discuss the general doctrine as to admissibility of evidence of the *res gestæ* in all its phases, but some pertinent illustrations may properly be given showing its application in homicide cases. The general principle is that evidence of the entire

[1] Maher v. P., 10 Mich. 212, 225; Hurd v. P., 25 Mich. 405, 415; Thomas v. P., 39 Mich. 309; P. v. Swetland, 77 Mich. 53; P. v. Deitz, 86 Mich. 419; P. v. Germaine, 101 Mich. 485; P. v. Kindra, 102 Mich. 147; S. v. Magoon, 50 Vt. 333; Donaldson v. C., 95 Pa. St. 21; Reg. v. Holden, 8 C. & P. 606; Reg. v. Chapman, 8 C. & P. 558; Reg. v. Orchard, Ibid., note; Reg. v. Stroner, 1 C. & K. 650; Reg. v. Bull, 9 C. & P. 22; Whart. Cr. Ev., § 448; Roscoe, Cr. Ev., § 139.

[2] Wellar v. P., 30 Mich. 16; S. v. Magoon, 50 Vt. 333; Reg. v. Chapman, 8 C. & P. 558; Reg. v. Stroner, 1 C. & K. 650.

[3] Reg. v. Bull, 9 C. & P. 22.

[4] C. v. Haskell, 140 Mass. 128; C. v. Schmous, 162 Pa. St. 326; S. v. Eaton, 75 Mo. 586; S. v. Johnson, 76 Mo. 121; S. v. Cain, 20 W. Va. 679; S. v. Martin, 2 Ired. 101; S. v. Smallwood, 75 N. C. 106; Hale v. S., 72 Miss. 140; Clark v. C., 90 Va. 360. At any rate, where there is evidence of eye-witnesses as to the whole transaction, it is not obligatory on the state to call all the witnesses to the transaction: S. v. Middleham, 62 Ia. 150; S. v. McGahey, 3 N. Dak. 293.

[5] Bonker v. P., 37 Mich. 4; T. v. Hanna, 5 Mont. 248.

transaction is admissible,[1] and of the surroundings.[2] In proving the whole transaction it is competent to give evidence of what happened after or before the homicide if it is connected therewith.[3] Where there has been a continuous quarrel or difficulty between the parties preceding the homicide, the evidence may cover the entire difficulty.[4] While of course evidence of any other transaction in which defendant was involved, even though near the time of the transaction in question, is not admissible,[5] yet if the two acts are connected as a part of one transaction, both may be shown although one of them involves a crime distinct from that for which the defendant is on trial.[6]

§ 412. **Declarations as part of res gestæ.**— Declarations of the parties to the transaction involving the homicide are admissible as a part of the transaction itself.[7] And in this way

[1] P. v. Potter, 5 Mich. 1; Rees v. S., 7 Ga. 373; S. v. Donelon, 45 La. An. 744. Thus, where the homicide committed was connected with a controversy about a mining claim, evidence by defendant of his ownership of the claim was held admissible: P. v. Costello, 15 Cal. 350. But where the defendant was charged with killing a highway commissioner in a controversy as to the existence of a road over defendant's land, it was held that evidence that the place where the offense was committed was not a public road was not admissible: Davison v. P., 90 Ill. 221. Proof as to the articles found in defendant's possession immediately after the commission of the crime is admissible as part of the *res gestæ:* P. v. Smith, 106 Cal. 73.

[2] For instance, the existence of blood stains at or near the place where violence has been inflicted: Wilson v. U. S., 162 U. S. 613.

[3] P. v. Marble, 38 Mich. 117; O'Mara v. C., 75 Pa. St. 424; Howser v. C., 51 Pa. St. 332; S. v. Kennade, 121 Mo. 405. Proof of statements made by one party to the controversy in the presence of the other, and denied by the latter, may be shown for the purpose of proving the circumstances, though the statements are not evidence of the truth of what was said: Haile v. S., 1 Swan, 248.

[4] Stit v. S., 91 Ala. 10; P. v. Stonecifer, 6 Cal. 405; Poindexter v. C., 33 Grat. 766; McGinnis v. S., 31 Ga. 236. Thus, where defendant was on trial for the murder of an officer while in pursuit of defendant for a crime, proof of the commission of the crime and defendant's connection with it was held admissible: P. v. Pool, 27 Cal. 572.

[5] P. v. Lane, 100 Cal. 379.

[6] S. v. Lapage, 57 N. H. 245; Brown v. C., 76 Pa. St. 319; C. v. Sturtivant, 117 Mass. 122; P. v. Johnson, 139 N. Y. 358; P. v. Pallister, 138 N. Y. 601; S. v. Sanders, 76 Mo. 35; S. v. Mathews, 98 Mo. 125; S. v. Dooley, 89 Ia. 584; Johnson v. S., 88 Ga. 203; Heath v. C., 1 Rob. (Va.) 735; Killins v. S., 28 Fla. 313; Smith v. S., 88 Ala. 73; Glory v. S., 13 Ark. 236; Fernandez v. S., 4 Tex. Ap. 419; Wilkerson v. S., 31 Tex. Ap. 86; S. v. Deschamps, 42 La. An. 567.

[7] P. v. Roach, 17 Cal. 297; S. v. Henderson, 24 Oreg. 100; Warren v. S.,

the declarations of accused accompanying his act become admissible in his own behalf as showing the motive with which the act was done.[1] In the same way declarations and exclamations made by bystanders have been held admissible as a part of the transaction.[2] But some cases hold the other way on the ground that such evidence is mere hearsay.[3] Even threats made at the time the act is done, which they are supposed to characterize and harmonize with it as one transaction, may be shown as part of the *res gestæ*. This is especially true as to threats of deceased where the accused seeks to show that he acted in self-defense.[4] Of course acts or declarations by accused not a part of the transaction are not admissible in his behalf, as they would be open to the objection of being self-serving acts;[5] but they may be shown against him as in the nature of confessions or admissions.[6]

§ 413. **Antecedent acts and declarations.**— It has already appeared that if they form part of the transaction involving the homicide, antecedent acts and declarations are admissible.[7]

9 Tex. Ap. 619; Bejarano v. S., 6 Tex. Ap. 265; Cox v. S., 8 Tex. Ap. 254.

[1] S. v. Walker, 77 Me. 488; S. v. Abbott, 8 W. Va. 741. But no weight is to be given to a declaration of accused in his own behalf unless the jury are satisfied that it was forced from him as the utterance of truth by the particular event itself, and at a time so closely connected with the transaction that there was no opportunity to determine as to what it might be wise to say: U. S. v. King, 34 Fed. R. 302.

[2] Flanegan v. S., 64 Ga. 52; McRae v. S., 71 Ga. 96; S. v. Duncan, 116 Mo. 288; S. v. Kaiser, 124 Mo. 651. So acts of a third person connected with the subject-matter may be shown: Alexander v. U. S., 138 U. S. 353. Statements of persons who examined the body immediately after the killing and at the place of the homicide may be shown: S. v. Robinson, 12 Wash. 491. Where it was sought to show the exclamations of a child, it was held that if the child had not such capacity as that its evidence would be admissible, its exclamations were not competent: Adams v. S., 34 Fla. 185.

[3] Bradshaw v. C., 10 Bush, 576; S. v. Riley, 42 La. An. 995.

[4] Wilson v. P., 94 Ill. 299; S. v. Gregor, 21 La. An. 473; even though such threats may not have been communicated to defendant: Pitman v. S., 22 Ark. 354; Reynolds v. S., 1 Ga. 222. So the character and habits of the deceased may be shown as a part of the circumstances: Wise v. S., 2 Kan. 419. Further, as to threats and character of deceased and threats of accused, see *infra*, §§ 419, 422, 423.

[5] S. v. Smith, 114 Mo. 406; S. v. Talbert, 41 S. C. 526; U. S. v. King, 34 Fed. R. 302.

[6] *Infra*, § 420.

[7] *Supra*, § 411. And see Reg. v. Edwards, 12 Cox, 230; Howard v. S., 8 Tex. Ap. 53.

But if separated from the homicide and constituting independent transactions, they are not admissible. There must be some connection between the two.[1] But where previous acts are so connected with the homicide as that evidence of them is admissible, declarations explanatory of such acts, made at the time of and in connection with the acts themselves, are also admissible.[2]

§ **414. Narrative of past transaction.**— As a general proposition a narrative of a past transaction, even by one of the parties to it, is not admissible as *res gestæ*.[3] And it is immaterial as to the length of time after the transaction, if such time has elapsed as to make the statements, having regard to their form and substance, mere narration.[4] And therefore in several cases it has been held that statements of deceased made a few minutes after the injury were not admissible.[5] And the same rule is applicable to declarations of the accused.[6] But the cases just cited apply the rule of exclusion of subsequent statements with a strictness not supported by the weight of authority. It is evident that statements made after the infliction of the injury may be so closely connected with it as to be a part of the transaction, and therefore admissible under the general principle of *res gestæ*.[7] Thus, declarations of the deceased made immediately after the injury as to how it was

[1] S. v. Woodward, 1 Houst. Cr. Cas. 455; Fonville v. S., 91 Ala. 39; Henry v. S., 79 Ala. 43; S. v. Anderson, 4 Nev. 265; Newcomb v. S., 37 Miss. 383; P. v. Smith, 26 Cal. 665; Montag v. P., 141 Ill. 75; Kahlenbeck v. S., 119 Ind. 118; S. v. Swain, 68 Mo. 605; S. v. Baker, 30 La. An., Part II, 1134.

[2] Hunter v. S., 40 N. J. 495; P. v. Shea, 8 Cal. 538; Garber v. S., 4 Coldw. 161; S. v. Howard, 32 Vt. 380; Price v. S., 72 Ga. 441; Jones v. S., 103 Ala. 1; Harris v. S., 96 Ala. 24; T. v. Couk, 2 Dak. 188; Carr v. S., 43 Ark. 99; S. v. Dula, Phill. 211; Reg. v. Buckley, 13 Cox, 293; Reg. v. Wainwright, 13 Cox, 171; Reg. v. Pook, 13 Cox, 172, n.

[3] Parker v. S., 136 Ind. 284; Doles v. S., 97 Ind. 555; P. v. O'Brien, 92 Mich. 17; Hall v. S., 132 Ind. 317; Scaggs v. S., 8 Sm. & M. 722; Denton v. S., 1 Swan, 278; P. v. Dewey, 2 Idaho, 79; Pharr v. S., 9 Tex. Ap. 129; Cockerell v. S., 32 Tex. Ap. 585; S. v. Johnson, 35 La. An. 968; S. v. Harris, 45 La. An. 842; S. v. Frazier, 1 Houst. Cr. Cas. 176; Steele v. S., 61 Ala. 213; Evans v. S., 58 Ark. 47.

[4] Parker v. S., 136 Ind. 284; Jones v. S., 71 Ind. 66.

[5] P. v. Wong Ark, 96 Cal. 125; S. v. Carlton, 48 Vt. 636; S. v. Davidson, 30 Vt. 377; Reg. v. Bedingfield, 14 Cox, 341.

[6] Hall v. S., 40 Ala. 698; Gardner v. P., 4 Ill. 83; S. v. Jackson, 17 Mo. 544.

[7] S. v. Harris, 45 La. An. 842.

received have been held admissible.[1] So, declarations of the accused under the same circumstances are admissible either for or against him.[2] Especially are such declarations admissible in behalf of the defendant where they are made concurrently with his acts and explanatory thereof.[3] The principle is that if the declarations are a part of the facts of the case inseparable from the crime, if they are voluntary and spontaneous, and made at a time so near to it as reasonably to preclude the idea of design, then they are to be deemed admissible.[4]

§ **415. Declarations as to physical condition.**— Another extension of the doctrine with reference to declarations is found in the principle that where the physical condition of the person is in question the usual expressions of feeling with reference to such injury are admissible. And such expressions may therefore be proven although made after the infliction of the injury.[5]

§ **416. Motive.**— Where the question is whether defendant was guilty of the homicide charged it is proper to prove any facts tending to show motive or want of motive for the killing of deceased by defendant; and such evidence is admissible in behalf of defendant as well as of the state.[6] But, though proof of the motive is important, especially where circumstantial evidence is relied on, it is not necessary to estab-

[1] C. v. Hackett, 2 Allen, 136; C. v. McPike, 3 Cush. 181; S. v. Martin, 124 Mo. 514; Burns v. S., 61 Ga. 192; Stevenson v. S., 69 Ga. 68; Von Pollnitz v. S., 92 Ga. 16; S. v. Talbert, 41 S. C. 526; Lambright v. S., 34 Fla. 564; Craig v. S., 30 Tex. Ap. 619; Stagner v. S., 9 Tex. Ap. 440; White v. S., 30 Tex. Ap. 652; Fulcher v. S., 28 Tex. Ap. 465; Reg. v. Lunny, 6 Cox, 477; Rex v. Foster, 6 C. & P. 325.

[2] Mitchum v. S., 11 Ga. 615; Thomas v. S., 27 Ga. 287; S. v. Crawford, 115 Mo. 620; Little v. C., 25 Grat. 921; Harrison v. S., 20 Tex. Ap. 387; Foster v. S., 8 Tex. Ap. 248.

[3] Washington v. S., 19 Tex. Ap. 521; Means v. S., 10 Tex. Ap. 16. But they should be limited to statements of fact, and not include statements of opinion: Monroe v. S., 5 Ga. 85.

[4] Craig v. S., 30 Tex. Ap. 619; S. v. Euzebe, 42 La. An. 727.

[5] Livingston v. C., 14 Grat. 592; Denton v. S., 1 Swan, 278; Field v. S., 57 Miss. 474; Johnson v. S., 30 Tex. Ap. 419; Tooney v. S., 8 Tex. Ap. 452; Edmonds v. S., 34 Ark. 720. On a somewhat analogous principle it was held admissible to show declarations of deceased before the injury as to what his name was and as to the fact that he received letters in that name: Rex v. Timmins, 7 C. & P. 499.

[6] Story v. S., 68 Miss. 609; Noles v. S., 26 Ala. 31; Flanagan v. S., 46 Ala. 703; Hunter v. S., 43 Ga. 483. If there is evidence of a conspiracy, proof of motive on the part of another conspirator is admissible as against defendant: Rufer v. S., 25 Ohio St. 464.

lish a motive in order to warrant a conviction, provided the offense be otherwise made out.[1] There are many illustrations as to what may be shown for the purpose of establishing a motive. Proof that deceased had money;[2] especially if it appears that the fact was known to the accused;[3] or that the accused supposed that deceased had money;[4] or that accused had proposed to another to rob one who was supposed to have money;[5] or that accused attempted to realize insurance money on the life of deceased;[6] or that a robbery had been committed by defendant, and that the homicide was committed in the attempt to conceal stolen goods taken in such robbery,[7] is admissible. So it is competent for the same purpose to show that after the homicide the prisoner had much more money in his possession than previously.[8] Likewise it is competent to prove that accused was a rejected and deceased an accepted suitor for the hand of the same woman;[9] or that accused and deceased both visited or sustained illicit relations with the same woman;[10] or that illicit relations existed between defendant and the wife of deceased;[11] or that after the homicide the wife of deceased had illicit relations with defendant;[12] or in case of uxoricide that the accused had illicit relations with another;[13]

[1] Hornsby v. S., 94 Ala. 55; S. v. Morgan, 35 W. Va. 260; Powell v. S., 67 Miss. 119; Green v. S., 38 Ark. 304; C. v. Hudson, 97 Mass. 565; C. v. Vaughan, 9 Cush. 594; S. v. Miller, 9 Houst. 564; Vaughan v. C., 85 Va. 671; Pointer v. U. S., 151 U. S. 396; Johnson v. U. S., 157 U. S. 320. The question as to whether a motive is shown is for the jury: P. v. Johnson, 139 N. Y. 358.

[2] Kennedy v. P., 39 N. Y. 245; Early v. S., 9 Tex. Ap. 476; S. v. Crowley, 33 La. An. 782.

[3] Ettinger v. C., 98 Pa. St. 338; Howser v. C., 51 Pa. St. 332; Marable v. S., 89 Ga. 425. Thus, the fact that defendant had declared his intention to take W.'s money and that defendant knew that deceased had charge of such money as employee is admissible: Mimms v. S., 16 Ohio St. 221.

[4] S. v. Howard, 82 N. C. 623; P. v. Wolf, 95 Mich. 625.

[5] Stafford v. S., 55 Ga. 592.

[6] S. v. West, 1 Houst. Cr. Cas. 371.

[7] McConkey v. C., 101 Pa. St. 416.

[8] S. v. Wintzingerode, 9 Oreg. 153; Clough v. S., 7 Neb. 320.

[9] Hunter v. S., 43 Ga. 483.

[10] McCue v. C., 78 Pa. St. 185; C. v. Ferrigan, 44 Pa. St. 386; S. v. Larkin, 11 Nev. 314.

[11] Pate v. S., 94 Ala. 14; S. v. Reed, 53 Kan. 767; Siebert v. P., 143 Ill. 571.

[12] Traverse v. S., 61 Wis. 144; Miller v. S., 68 Miss. 221; or that the defendant immediately married the widow of deceased: Pierson v. P., 79 N. Y. 424.

[13] St. Louis v. S., 8 Neb. 405; Wilkerson v. S., 31 Tex. Ap. 86; O'Brien v. C., 89 Ky. 354.

and in such cases proof of dissatisfaction of the accused with the deceased as husband or wife is admissible.[1] On the other hand, evidence that deceased had made improper advances to the wife of defendant may be shown.[2] In case of a killing of husband by wife, unchastity on the part of the wife may be proven.[3] Proof of seduction of deceased by accused is admissible.[4] The pendency of a divorce suit by the wife against the husband may be shown as indicating a motive for the killing of the wife by the husband.[5] The fact that deceased was or might be an important witness against accused in the divorce suit may also be shown;[6] or that deceased was an obstacle to the marriage of accused to another;[7] or that deceased had entered into a combination with a third person to induce defendant's wife to elope, that fact having come to the knowledge of defendant.[8] The fact that deceased had been instrumental in instituting or threatening a criminal prosecution against defendant is admissible as indicating motive, the fact being known to defendant.[9] Likewise it may be shown that deceased was or was likely to be a witness in such prosecution.[10] In general, as will be more fully pointed out in the following section, any facts showing a ground for ill-will on the part of

[1] Duncan v. S., 88 Ala. 31; Wharton v. S., 73 Ala. 366; S. v. Green, 35 Conn. 203; Marler v. S., 67 Ala. 55.

[2] Utzman v. S., 32 Tex. Ap. 426. But improper intimacy between deceased and the wife of the accused not known to the accused before the killing cannot be shown: Polin v. S., 14 Neb. 540.

[3] Weyrich v. P., 89 Ill. 90.

[4] S. v. Kline, 54 Ia. 183.

[5] Binns v. S., 66 Ind. 428; Pinckford v. S., 13 Tex. Ap. 468. But the record of the suit is not admissible, as its pendency may be shown by parol evidence: Binns v. S., 57 Ind. 46. The allegations of the petition for divorce cannot be shown: Pinckford v. S., 13 Tex. Ap. 468; nor the final disposition made of the suit after the homicide: C. v. Madan, 102 Mass. 1.

[6] C. v. Madan, 102 Mass. 1; Marler v. S., 68 Ala. 580.

[7] Marler v. S., 67 Ala. 55; S. v. Lentz, 45 Minn. 177.

[8] Cheek v. S., 35 Ind. 492.

[9] S. v. Moelchen, 53 Ia. 310; Martin v. C., 93 Ky. 189; Franklin v. C., 92 Ky. 612; Turner v. S., 70 Ga. 765; Gillum v. S., 62 Miss. 547; Walker v. S., 63 Ga. 150; Dunn v. S., 2 Ark. 229; S. v. Patza, 3 La. An. 512; Powell v. S., 13 Tex. Ap. 244; Coward v. S., 6 id. 59; Hudson v. S., 28 id. 323.

[10] Murphy v. P., 63 N. Y. 590; Hodge v. S., 97 Ala. 37; Williams v. S., 69 Ga. 11; S. v. Morris, 84 N. C. 756; S. v. Brantley, 84 N. C. 766; Rex v. Clewes, 4 C. & P. 221. The fact that deceased was on the bail bond of one who was charged with an assault with intent to murder defendant was held admissible: P. v. Chin Hane, 108 Cal. 597.

accused against deceased may be proven.[1] The fact that defendant was a member of a secret association (known as the Molly Maguires), one object of which was to commit murder, was held admissible where the homicide appeared to be connected with the carrying out of the objects of the association.[2] In many of the illustrations above given, the evidence tended to prove another crime, but it was held that it should not be excluded on that ground.[3]

§ **417. Relations of parties.**— The previous relations of the defendant and the deceased may be shown as of more or less importance in explaining conduct and motives;[4] and this rule includes social and business relations, where the homicide appears to have been in any way connected with such relations.[5] Thus, proof of a family feud is admissible.[6] Indeed, any state of ill-feeling may become material.[7] In cases of uxoricide the previous relations of the husband and wife and a course of ill-treatment by one towards the other may be shown.[8] And such evidence has been held admissible though relating to quarrels and ill-treatment antedating by two or three years the homicide.[9] But it would seem that where the evidence

[1] S. v. Lawlor, 28 Minn. 216; Thompson v. S., 55 Ga. 47; Fraser v. S., 55 Ga. 325; Kelose v. S., 47 Ala. 573.

[2] McManus v. C., 91 Pa. St. 57; Carroll v. C., 84 Pa. St. 107; Campbell v. C., 84 Pa. St. 187; Hester v. C., 85 Pa. St. 139.

[3] S. v. Reed, 53 Kan. 767; P. v. Lane, 101 Cal. 513; S. v. Williamson, 106 Mo. 162.

[4] Wellar v. P., 30 Mich. 16.

[5] Clough v. S., 7 Neb. 320; Everett v. S., 30 Tex. Ap. 682.

[6] P. v. Walters, 98 Cal. 138. Evidence of a quarrel with a member of the family of the deceased is admissible: Gravely v. S., 45 Neb. 878.

[7] P. v. Dennis, 39 Cal. 625; P. v. Kern, 61 Cal. 244; McMillen v. S., 13 Mo. 30; S. v. Moelchen, 53 Ia. 310; S. v. Stackhouse, 24 Kan. 445; Myers v. S., 62 Ala. 599; Commander v. S., 60 Ala. 1; Evans v. S., 62 Ala. 6; Haynes v. S., 17 Ga. 465; Coxwell v. S., 66 Ga. 309; Spivey v. S., 58 Miss. 858; Marnoch v. S., 7 Tex. Ap. 269; Reg. v. Hagan, 12 Cox, 357. Where deceased had been absent from the neighborhood of the accused for eight to ten months, the state of feeling between deceased and accused immediately preceding such absence was held incompetent: Dillin v. P., 8 Mich. 357.

[8] Painter v. P., 147 Ill. 444; S. v. Cole, 63 Ia. 695; Boyle v. S., 61 Wis. 440; S. v. Rash, 12 Ired. 382; S. v. Bradley, 67 Vt. 465; Malce v. S., 33 Tex. Ap. 14; Thiede v. Utah, 159 U. S. 510.

[9] Sayres v. C., 88 Pa. St. 291; Koerner v. S., 98 Ind. 7; C. v. Holmes, 157 Mass. 233. Where the prosecution has given proof of the conduct and expressions of the wife to show unpleasant relations of this kind, the defense may rebut such evidence by letters of the wife to a third person: S. v. Leabo, 84 Mo. 168. Declarations by defendant before the homi-

relates to remote difficulties there should be something to connect them with the homicide.[1] Evidence that the homicide grew out of a charge by deceased against accused of undue familiarity with the wife of the former was held inadmissible, as the jealousy of deceased could furnish no explanation of the circumstances under which his life was taken.[2]

§ 418. **Evidence of intent.**— Testimony going to show motive is material also as bearing on the question of malice, for there can be no malice without motive.[3] Facts showing intent are always admissible,[4] such as pre-existing enmity between accused and deceased,[5] threats against the accused,[6] or preparation for the homicide.[7] Any evidence tending to explain such preparation on a theory contradicting the malice, such as fear of danger, etc., is admissible for defendant.[8] As bearing on the intention with which an act is done, evidence of similar acts is admissible, even though showing a distinct crime.[9] Thus, in poisoning cases, if it is claimed that the poisoning was acci-

cide relating to troubles between him and his wife, the deceased, are inadmissible unless forming a part of the *res gestæ:* Billingslea v. S., 68 Ala. 486.

[1] C. v. Abbott, 130 Mass. 472.

[2] Costley v. S., 48 Md. 175. But evidence tending to show, in such a case, that no improper relations existed was held admissible: Wadlington v. S., 19 Tex. Ap. 266.

[3] Fraser v. S., 55 Ga. 325; Ryan v. S., 100 Ala. 105. Where defendant had made hostile demonstrations toward A., mistaking him for B., *held,* that this might be shown in a prosecution of defendant for the murder of B.: Angus v. S., 29 Tex. Ap. 52.

[4] Austin v. S., 14 Ark. 556.

[5] Marler v. S., 67 Ala. 55; Holmes v. S., 100 Ala. 80; S. v. D'Angelo, 9 La. An. 46; Stone v. S., 4 Humph. 26; S. v. Johnson, 2 Jones, 247; Starke v. S., 81 Ga. 593. Acts and statements of defendant preceding the homicide indicating a grudge against deceased may be shown: Ortiz v. S., 30 Fla. 256; S. v. Green, 1 Houst. Cr. Cas. 217.

[6] S. v. Birdwell, 36 La. An. 859. So threats showing an intention to kill somebody are evidences of malice, although not directed against deceased: Hopkins v. C., 50 Pa. St. 9. So an expression of a wish to kill the deceased will indicate malice: Clampitt v. S., 9 Tex. Ap. 27.

[7] Bolling v. S., 54 Ark. 588. Testimony of a third person that he told defendant to take a brick and look for deceased held admissible, it appearing that defendant acted on the advice: Fisher v. S., 77 Ind. 42.

[8] S. v. Claire, 41 La. An. 191.

[9] C. v. Ferrigan, 44 Pa. St. 386; Goerson v. C., 99 Pa. St. 388; Pierson v. P., 79 N. Y. 424; P. v. Shea, 147 N. Y. 78; S. v. Dooley, 89 Ia. 584. But evidence of distinct crimes not connected with that in question is not admissible: Shaffner v. C., 72 Pa. St. 60; S. v. Martin, 74 Mo. 547; Hall v. U. S., 150 U. S. 76; Boyd v. U. S., 142 U. S. 450; Billings v. S., 52 Ark. 303.

dental, evidence of similar poisonings may be introduced.[1] But it is error to admit evidence of another transaction for the purpose of showing intent, when it is not made to appear that defendant had any connection with such transaction.[2] Circumstances attending the homicide may show the malice with which the act was done.[3] So the violence of the efforts made to escape may tend to show the animus of defendant.[4] On behalf of defendant the circumstances may be shown as they appeared to him for the purpose of excusing his acts.[5] So the fact of a recent communication made to defendant likely to cause and actually causing great excitement on his part may be shown, but the truth of the communication made will be immaterial.[6]

§ 419. **Threats and hostile acts of accused.**— Prior acts, declarations and threats of accused, even though not a part of the *res gestæ*, are admissible against him when they legitimately tend to establish motive or intention to commit the crime.[7] And it is immaterial whether these threats had been known to deceased; the doctrine in regard to threats of deceased being admissible when communicated to defendant has no application to defendant's threats.[8] Even though the threats be general in their terms and not expressly directed against deceased, yet if they can be shown to have included or to have had reference to deceased they are admissible.[9] Indeed it has been held that

[1] Zoldoske v. S., 82 Wis. 580; Reg. v. Garner, 4 F. & F. 346; Reg. v. Heeson, 14 Cox, 14; Reg. v. Cotton, 12 Cox, 400; Reg. v. Geering, 18 L. J. M. C. 215; Reg. v. Roden, 12 Cox, 630.

[2] P. v. Hancock, 7 Utah, 170; Reg. v. Winslow, 8 Cox, 397; Reg. v. Whitehead, 3 C. & K. 202.

[3] P. v. Walters, 98 Cal. 138; C. v. Salyards, 158 Pa. St. 501; Shackleford v. S., 79 Ala. 26. But the use of superior weapons on the part of the accused is not in itself evidence of malice: P. v. Barry, 31 Cal. 357.

[4] Revel v. S., 26 Ga. 275; C. v. Salyards, 158 Pa. St. 501.

[5] Yates v. P., 32 N. Y. 509; Williams v. P., 54 Ill. 422. And, in general as to intent, see *supra*, §§ 112, 121.

[6] P. v. Hurtado, 63 Cal. 288.

[7] S. v. Edwards, 34 La. An. 1012; S. v. Brown, 63 Mo. 439; S. v. Nugent, 71 Mo. 136. A prior assault may be shown only where it tends to show enmity or is in pursuance of threats: Hale v. S., 72 Miss. 140. In general as to such threats, see S. v. Harrod, 102 Mo. 590; Burgess v. S., 93 Ga. 304; Jones v. S., 76 Ala. 8; Beavers v. S., 103 Ala. 36; White v. S., 32 Tex. Ap. 625. A witness may give an opinion as to whether defendant on a particular occasion manifested anger toward deceased: S. v. Shelton, 64 Ia. 333.

[8] S. v. Black, 42 La. An. 861; S. v. Elkins, 63 Mo. 159; S. v. Guy, 69 Mo. 430.

[9] Parker v. S., 136 Ind. 284; Hardy v. S., 31 Tex. Ap. 289; Everett v. S., 62 Ga. 65; Dixon v. S., 13 Fla. 636;

general threats to kill somebody, made shortly before the homicide, may be shown as indicating the state of mind of the accused at the time.[1] But if such threats are not so connected with the homicide as to serve this purpose they are not admissible.[2] Even evidence of conditional threats may be admissible.[3] With reference to the time elapsing between the threat and the homicide as affecting the admissibility of the evidence, it may be stated as a general proposition that the lapse of time goes to the weight rather than to the admissibility of the evidence.[4] And such threats made months or even years before the commission of the crime have therefore been admitted.[5] But in the cases just cited there was nothing to indicate that the state of feeling evidenced by the threat was not still in existence. If there has been a good-faith reconciliation after the making of the threats they doubtless would become entirely inadmissible.[6] Where there is a conspiracy to commit the crime, acts and threats of those thus conspiring may be shown against any of them.[7] It is not necessary to put in evidence the whole conversation in connection with which the threat is made.[8] It is unnecessary to say that a particular threat alone will not warrant conviction of one accused of the homicide though no other perpetrator is disclosed.[9]

§ **420. Confessions and admissions by defendant.**—The general rules as to the admissibility of evidence of confessions or admissions against the party making them need not be here stated, but it is proper to give some illustrations of the application of these rules in prosecutions for homicide. Declara-

S. v. Hymer, 15 Nev. 49; S. v. Hoyt, 47 Conn. 518; Anderson v. S., 79 Ala. 5; Jordan v. S., 79 Ala. 9; Harrison v. S., 79 Ala. 29.

[1] Benedict v. S., 14 Wis. 423; Muscoe v. C., 87 Va. 460; Hopkins v. C., 50 Pa. St. 9.

[2] Abernethy v. C., 101 Pa. St. 322; S. v. Grant, 79 Mo. 113.

[3] S. v. Adams, 76 Mo. 355.

[4] Griffin v. S., 90 Ala. 596; Pate v. S., 94 Ala. 14.

[5] Redd v. S., 68 Ala. 492; Griffin v. S., 90 Ala. 596; Pulliam v. S., 88 Ala. 1; S. v. Bradley, 64 Vt. 466; Hodge v. S., 26 Fla. 11; S. v. Campbell, 35 S. C. 28; U. S. v. Neverson, 1 Mackey, 152. In one case threats made thirty years before the homicide were held admissible: Goodwin v. S., 96 Ind. 550.

[6] P. v. Hyndman, 99 Cal. 1.

[7] Kehoe v. C., 85 Pa. St. 127; Gardner v. P., 4 Ill. 83.

[8] Stit v. S., 91 Ala. 10; S. v. Oliver, 43 La. An. 1003. But it is error to exclude part of the threat if it throws light by way of explanation on the balance: P. v. Curtis, 52 Mich. 616.

[9] Jones v. S., 57 Miss. 684.

tions of the accused which are not a part of the *res gestæ* are of course in no case admissible for him.[1] As against him such declarations are admissible on the presumption that a person will not make an untrue statement against his own interests, but even in that view they are to be received with great caution because of the danger of mistake and also because influences of hope or fear often induce the making of an untrue confession. Subject, however, to these qualifications, confessions are among the most effectual proofs.[2] The question whether the declarations sought to be shown as admissions relate to the crime charged or to another matter is for the jury.[3] Where a confession is admissible it is not competent for defendant to rebut it by proving other declarations showing that it was false.[4] As a form of confession or admission the prosecution may prove statements made by the accused before a coroner's inquest;[5] or on preliminary examination;[6] or on a previous trial.[7] But on this question there are a few cases holding to the contrary.[8] In order that a declaration or statement made by the defendant may be proven it must of course have some connection with the homicide in question, and it was accordingly held that a statement that "if she had killed one woman she would kill another" was not admissible.[9] But the matters that may be proven as constituting declarations or admissions having some bearing on the case will depend on the questions in issue under the evidence; thus, where the capacity for speed of a horse which accused appeared to have been riding became material on account of the distance he had to ride within a given time under the evidence, his statements as to

[1] S. v. Brandon, 8 Jones, 463.

[2] P. v. Borgetto, 99 Mich. 336. As to the sufficiency of such evidence in particular cases, see Paul v. S., 65 Ga. 152; Rex v. Morrison, 8 C. & P. 22.

[3] U. S. v. Beebe, 2 Dak. 292.

[4] Honeycutt v. S., 8 Baxt. 371; P. v. Ah Choy, 1 Idaho (N. S.), 317. Apparently to the contrary, Shrivers v. S., 7 Tex. Ap. 450.

[5] S. v. Gilman, 51 Me. 206; Snyder v. S., 59 Ind. 105; S. v. Wisdom, 119 Mo. 539.

[6] S. v. Miller, 35 Kan. 328.

[7] Dumas v. S., 63 Ga. 600.

[8] S. v. Dufour, 31 La. An. 804; S. v. Johnson, 10 La. An. 456; S. v. Parker, 7 La. An. 84; S. v. Young, 1 Wins. 126.

[9] Ledbetter v. S., 61 Miss. 22. A statement in regard to meat from a hog which was the occasion of the homicide appearing to be clotted with blood was held to be irrelevant when standing alone: S. v. Mikle, 81 N. C. 552.

such capacity were held admissible.[1] And statements by accused as to how he could kill a man were allowed to be shown as a part of his conduct, indicating the workings of his mind, although not in any way connected with the homicide in question.[2] A writing identified as that of defendant, containing a suggestion as to the best method of disposing of a dead body, was held admissible;[3] and also a letter written long after the homicide containing a threat connected in its motive with the homicide in question.[4] Admissions by accused of previous knowledge or possession of articles found near the place of the homicide may be shown.[5] Admissions as to previous wrongful acts having some connection with the homicide in question may be shown.[6] Declarations indicating apprehension by the prisoner on account of the condition of deceased were held admissible.[7] So an offer by accused to tell all he knew about the homicide on certain conditions, which conditions were not accepted, was held admissible.[8] Declarations of a third person in the presence of accused may be shown in connection with his reply thereto or acquiescence therein when they tend to implicate him;[9] but this principle does not apply to declarations calling for no response or disclaimer.[10] Where concert of action between accused and another with reference to the homicide appears, the declarations of the other may be shown as against defendant;[11] but complicity must be shown.[12]

§ 421. **Acts and behavior of defendant subsequent to the homicide.**— Where the evidence is circumstantial, unnatural be-

[1] Fraser v. S., 55 Ga. 325.

[2] Moore v. S., 2 Ohio St. 500; C. v. Crossmire, 156 Pa. St. 304. So evidence that defendant, who belonged to a Masonic lodge, had said that any one injuring a member of the lodge would pass away, was held admissible, there being some evidence inculpating other members of the lodge also: Jones v. S., 4 Tex. Ap. 436.

[3] State v. Stair, 87 Mo. 268.

[4] Stephens v. P., 19 N. Y. 549.

[5] Murphy v. P., 63 N. Y. 590; Aikin v. S., 35 Ala. 399.

[6] Shaw v. S., 60 Ga. 246; Washington v. S., 8 Tex. Ap. 377.

[7] Tooney v. S., 8 Tex. Ap. 452.

[8] Perkins v. S., 60 Ala. 7.

[9] Liles v. S., 30 Ala. 24; Franklin v. S., 69 Ga. 36.

[10] Loggins v. S., 8 Tex. Ap. 434; S. v. Murray, 126 Mo. 611.

[11] Malone v. S., 8 Ga. 408; Ake v. S., 31 Tex. 416; Williams v. S., 81 Ala. 1; Huling v. S., 17 Ohio St. 583; S. v. Ellis, 101 N. C. 765; S. v. Payne, 10 Wash. 545; St. Clair v. U. S., 154 U. S. 134.

[12] S. v. Carroll, 31 La. An. 860; Preston v. S., 4 Tex. Ap. 186.

havior of defendant shortly after the homicide may be shown;[1] for instance, the fact that, when accused of the murder of his wife, he showed no concern or emotion.[2] The conduct of the accused in the presence of the dead body is admissible, but his declarations made at the time cannot be shown in his own behalf.[3] The fact of concealment of the death of a child is evidence of guilt.[4] Conduct of the accused when the crime is mentioned in his presence,[5] or his failure to reply when charged with the offense, may be shown.[6] Proof of flight after the crime was committed is competent as against the defendant;[7] so is proof of an attempt to escape after arrest.[8] So any evidence of concealment of the homicide or misrepresentations as to the disappearance of deceased are admissible;[9] or as to the property of the deceased taken in connection with the homicide.[10] But evidence of flight or concealment is not conclusive.[11] The prisoner may rebut the presumption from flight by showing other reasons therefor;[12] but he cannot introduce such

[1] S. v. Brabham, 108 N. C. 793; Noftsinger v. S., 7 Tex. Ap. 301; Miller v. S., 18 Tex. Ap. 232.

[2] Greenfield v. P., 85 N. Y. 75.

[3] U. S. v. Neverson, 1 Mackay, 152.

[4] S. v. Love, 1 Bay, 167.

[5] S. v. Nash, 7 Ia. 347.

[6] S. v. Reed, 62 Me. 129; S. v. Bowman, 80 N. C. 432; Kendrick v. S., 55 Miss. 436; Ford v. S., 34 Ark. 649.

[7] S. v. Anderson, 10 Oreg. 448; Batten v. S., 80 Ind. 394; Revel v. S., 26 Ga. 275; P. v. Fredericks, 106 Cal. 554; C. v. Bezek, 168 Pa. St. 603. And where there was ambiguity as to the occasion of the defendant leaving the neighborhood after the homicide, it was held admissible to prove in behalf of the prosecution that he had a contract to work there, which he did not carry out: Welsh v. S., 97 Ala. 1. The fact of flight is a circumstance to be considered by the jury as tending to increase the probability of defendant being the guilty person. It does not give rise to a legal presumption of guilt: Hickory v. U. S., 160 U. S. 408; Alberty v. U. S., 162 U. S. 499.

[8] Hittner v. S., 19 Ind. 48; S. v. Dufour, 31 La. An. 804. But proof of forfeiture of appeal bond and eluding arrest was held properly rejected: Morgan v. C., 14 Bush, 106. Threats by defendant to kill a person sent to identify him in jail, held admissible: P. v. Chin Hane, 108 Cal. 597.

[9] S. v. Dickson, 78 Mo. 438.

[10] Betts v. S., 66 Ga. 508. Possession of the fruits of the crime soon after its commission constitutes *prima facie* evidence of guilt: Wilson v. U. S., 162 U. S. 613. But if the concealed property is found in a house which is in the joint occupancy of defendant and another, such fact should be referred to by the court as affecting the weight of the evidence: Hall v. S., 65 Ga. 36. As to evidence of recent possession in case of larceny, see *infra*, § —.

[11] Waybright v. S., 56 Ind. 122; Hickory v. U. S., 160 U. S. 408.

[12] S. v. Barham, 82 Mo. 67.

explanatory evidence unless the flight is proved as tending to show guilt.[1] A subsequent attempt to carry out the same criminal purpose as that involved in the homicide may be shown as against the defendant;[2] but not a subsequent crime having no connection with the homicide.[3]

§ 422. **Defendant's character.**— As the admissibility of proof respectively of defendant's bad character and good character are in no way peculiar to homicide, it need not be even illustrated here. It is suggested, however, that on a trial for murder, proof of defendant's good character is entitled to less weight than in trials for offenses of a lower grade.[4]

§ 423. **Threats, character and occupation of deceased.**— The admissibility of antecedent threats of deceased against accused and his character for violence as bearing on the question of self-defense has already been fully considered.[5] Threats are also admissible as showing the relations of the parties and a motive for the homicide;[6] and as a part of the *res gestæ* if frequent and continuous down to the time of the killing.[7] Evidence of the character of the deceased as a quiet and peaceable man is not admissible as original evidence in behalf of the prosecution.[8] The general character of deceased as a violent and quarrelsome man cannot be shown in behalf of defendant,[9] except as bearing on the question of self-defense, as already explained.[10] Where such evidence is admitted in behalf of defendant, the state may in rebuttal prove that deceased was of a

[1] S. v. Hays, 23 Mo. 287.

[2] McManus v. S., 36 Ala. 285.

[3] S. v. Hoyt, 13 Minn. 132.

[4] C. v. Webster, 5 Cush. 295.

[5] *Supra*, § 307.

[6] Painter v. P., 147 Ill. 444. But not if the threats have not been communicated to the accused: S. v. Helm, — Ia. —, 61 N. W. R. 246; Combs v. S., 75 Ind. 215. Even if communicated they may be so indefinite as not to be admissible: S. v. Guy, 69 Mo. 430.

[7] S. v. Sloan, 47 Mo. 604.

[8] P. v. Bezy, 67 Cal. 223; S. v. Potter, 13 Kan. 414; Ben v. S., 37 Ala. 103; S. v. Eddon, 8 Wash. 292; S. v. McCarthy, 43 La. An. 541. In a Texas case it appears to be held that the general character of deceased may be shown as against defendant: Russell v. S., 11 Tex. Ap. 288. But in a later case it is said that while such evidence is not admissible except in rebuttal of evidence to the contrary introduced in behalf of defendant, yet, if a conviction is otherwise supported by competent evidence, it will not be reversed on that account: Graves v. S., 14 Tex. Ap. 113.

[9] S. v. Thawley, 4 Harr. 562; S. v. Hogue, 6 Jones, 381; Chase v. S., 46 Miss. 683; S. v. Tilly, 3 Ired. 424; S. v. Jackson, 12 La. An. 679.

[10] *Supra*, § 307.

peaceful character.[1] Even in such cases the evidence should go to the general character as to violence or quarrelsomeness, and not to such character under the circumstances of intoxication.[2] The question in such cases is as to the general character in that respect.[3] In behalf of the prosecution the occupation of the deceased may be shown, but the illegal or immoral nature of the business carried on by him is not a matter which can be inquired into on behalf of defendant as showing an excuse for the homicide.[4]

§ **424. Declarations of deceased.**— As a general rule, declarations of the deceased in regard to the transaction are not admissible in behalf of the prosecution.[5] Nor are such declarations admissible in behalf of defendant.[6] An affidavit or deposition by the injured party, who afterwards dies, being an *ex parte* statement, cannot be shown.[7] Of course, declarations of the deceased made before the homicide are not admissible as against the defendant.[8]

§ **425. Dying declarations.**— To the general proposition stated in the preceding paragraph, that the declarations of the deceased are not admissible, there is the important exception that such declarations relating to the transaction, and made in contemplation of approaching death, may be proven in a prosecution for criminal homicide.[9] This is said to be a doctrine of necessity, and to be based on the theory that the solemnity of the circumstances surrounding the declaration are such as to give to it the sanction which would result from the administration of an oath.[10] But even though this be admitted, there is

[1] Davis v. P., 114 Ill. 86.

[2] Fahnestock v. S., 23 Ind. 231.

[3] Jackson v. S., 77 Ala. 18.

[4] P. v. Butler, 8 Cal. 435; S. v. Kennade, 121 Mo. 405.

[5] Binns v. S., 57 Ind. 46; S. v. Curtis, 70 Mo. 594; S. v. Brandon, 8 Jones, 463; Johnson v. S., 63 Miss. 313; S. v. Wyse, 32 S. C. 45.

[6] C. v. Dunan, 128 Mass. 422; C. v. Densmore, 12 Allen, 535; Kane v. C., 109 Pa. St. 541; Fahnestock v. S., 23 Ind. 231; S. v. Patrick, 3 Jones, 443; S. v. Punshon, 124 Mo. 448.

[7] Collier v. S., 13 Ark. 676; Reg. v. Clarke, 2 F. & F. 2.

[8] P. v. Carkhuff, 24 Cal. 640; P. v. Carlton, 57 Cal. 83; Kirby v. S., 9 Yerg. 383; Cheek v. S., 35 Ind. 492; P. v. Gress, 107 Cal. 461.

[9] 1 East, P. C. 353; 1 Bish. Cr. Proc., § 1207; 1 Greenl. Ev., § 156; Best, Ev., § 505; S. v. Faile, 43 S. C. 52; Mattox v. U. S., 146 U. S. 140.

[10] Mattox v. U. S., 156 U. S. 237; P. v. Glenn, 10 Cal. 32; Donnelly v. S., 26 N. J. 463; C. v. Murray, 2 Ashmead, 41; S. v. Pearce, 56 Minn. 226; Walston v. C., 16 B. Mon. 15; 1 East, P. C. 353. But the inadmissibility does not depend upon whether there is in fact other evidence: S. v. Wilson,

yet lacking the opportunity for cross-examination for the purpose of developing the truth which would have been open to the party against whom the declaration is introduced, had it been given by a living witness.[1] Notwithstanding these difficulties, such declarations are uniformly held to be admissible.[2] As to the objection which has been made in such cases, that when the declarations are introduced against the defendant he is deprived of his constitutional right to be confronted with the witnesses against him, it is uniformly held that the deceased is not a witness, within the scope of this provision, and that the defendant, being confronted with the witness who testifies to the declaration, the requirement of the constitutional provision is complied with.[3] But such evidence is limited to the declarations of one deceased whose death is the subject of the charge; that is, to cases of criminal homicide.[4] Thus, in a civil action to recover damages for injuries causing death, dying declarations of the injured party are not admissible.[5] Nor are such declarations admissible in any prosecution except for criminal homicide, although homicide may have been involved in, or resulted from, other crime.[6] In a prosecution for administering

24 Kan. 189. Belief in the doctrine of the efficiency of repentance at any time before death is immaterial; North v. P., 139 Ill. 81.

[1] The objections to such evidence are set out in detail in Shell v. S., 88 Ala. 14.

[2] Ward v. S., 8 Blackf. 101; Thompson v. S., 24 Ga. 297; S. v. Freeman, 1 Spears, 57; S. v. Quick, 15 Rich. 342; S. v. Brunneto, 13 La. An. 45; U. S. v. McGurk, 1 Cranch, C. C. 71; U. S. v. Veitch, 1 Cranch, C. C. 115; U. S. v. Taylor, 4 Cranch, C. C. 338.

[3] Mattox v. U. S., 156 U. S. 237; S. v. Dickinson, 41 Wis. 299; Miller v. S., 25 Wis. 384; Robbins v. S., 8 Ohio St. 131; C. v. Carey, 12 Cush. 246; Walston v. C., 16 B. Mon. 15; S. v. Nash, 7 Ia. 347; Campbell v. S., 11 Ga. 353; Woodsides v. S., 2 How. (Miss.) 655; P. v. Glenn, 10 Cal. 32; Brown v. C., 73 Pa. St. 321; Burrell v. S., 18 Tex. 713; S. v. Price, 6 La. An. 691. This rule of evidence was in force when the state constitutions were adopted: S. v. Dickinson, 41 Wis. 299.

[4] Rex v. Mead, 2 B. & C. 605; Wilson v. Boerem, 15 Johns. 286; Duling v. Johnson, 32 Ind. 155; S. v. Bohan, 15 Kan. 407; Resp. v. Langcake, 1 Yeates, 415. They must be by the party whose death is the subject of the charge: S. v. Jefferson, 77 Mo. 136.

[5] Daily v. N. Y. etc. R. Co., 32 Conn. 356, Marshall v. Chi. etc. R. Co., 48 Ill. 475; Brownell v. Pacific R. Co., 47 Mo. 239. Therefore held, in an action by the father for the seduction of his minor daughter, that the dying declarations of the daughter as to who was the father of her child were inadmissible: Wooten v. Wilkins, 39 Ga. 223.

[6] Rex v. Mead, 2 B. & C. 605; Reg. v. Newton, 1 F. & F. 641; Rex v. Lloyd, 4 C. & P. 233.

medicine or using instruments for the purpose of procuring an abortion, where death has resulted, the dying declarations of the victim are not admissible,[1] even though under the statute the fact of the death may be material in determining the degree of the crime.[2] Dying declarations of another whose death resulted from the same cause as that for which the defendant is being prosecuted are not admissible.[3] Dying declarations of one who confesses the homicide for which defendant is on trial are not admissible in behalf of defendant.[4] In general, dying declarations, when admissible at all, are admissible in behalf of defendant as well as of the prosecution.[5]

§ **426. Sense of impending death.**— It is essential to the admissibility of a dying declaration that it was made under a sense of impending death.[6] This preliminary fact must be established by the party offering to prove the declaration.[7]

[1] Rex v. Hutchinson, 2 B. & C. 608, n.; Reg. v. Hind, Bell, 253.

[2] S. v. Harper, 35 Ohio St. 78; P. v. Davis, 56 N. Y. 95; Railing v. C., 110 Pa. St. 109. But in another case it is said that the death of the victim being necessarily involved in the investigation, her dying declarations should be admitted: Montgomery v. S., 80 Ind. 338.

[3] Brown v. C., 73 Pa. St. 321; S. v. Westfall, 49 Ia. 328; Fitzhugh v. S., 2 Oreg. 227; S. v. Bohan, 15 Kan. 407; Krebs v. S., 3 Tex. Ap. 348; Radford v. S., 33 Tex. Ap. 520. *Contra*, S. v. Terrell, 12 Rich. 321; S. v. Wilson, 23 La. An. 558; Rex v. Baker, 2 M. & Rob. 53.

[4] Davis v. C., 95 Ky. 19; Mora v. P., 19 Colo. 255.

[5] P. v. Knapp, 26 Mich. 112; Brock v. C., 92 Ky. 183; Brown v. S., 74 Ala. 478; Mattox v. U. S., 146 U. S. 140; Rex v. Scaife, 2 Lewin, 150. *Contra*, Moeck v. P., 100 Ill. 242; Adams v. P., 47 Ill. 376.

[6] Kelly v. U. S., 27 Fed. R. 616; C. v. Roberts, 108 Mass. 296; Sullivan v. C., 93 Pa. St. 284; Starkey v. P., 17 Ill. 17; P. v. Knapp, 26 Mich. 112; S. v. Johnson, 118 Mo. 491; S. v. Bradley, 34 S. C. 136; Pulliam v. S., 88 Ala. 1; S. v. Garrand, 5 Oreg. 216; P. v. Lee, 17 Cal. 76; P. v. Ybarra, 17 Cal. 166; P. v. Sanchez, 24 Cal. 17; Brown v. S., 32 Miss. 433; Lewis v. S., 9 Sm. & M. 115; Bell v. S., 72 Miss. 507; Montgomery v. S., 11 Ohio, 424; Brakefield v. S., 1 Sneed, 214; Nelson v. S., 7 Humph. 541; Smith v. S., 9 Humph. 9; Logan v. S., 9 Humph. 24; S. v. Center, 35 Vt. 378; Bull v. C., 14 Grat. 613; Hill v. C., 2 Grat. 594; Vass v. C., 3 Leigh, 786; Vaughan v. C., 86 Ky. 431; Benavides v. S., 31 Tex. 580; Irby v. S., 25 Tex. Ap. 203; U. S. v. Woods, 4 Cranch, C. C. 484; U. S. v. Veitch, 1 Cranch, C. C. 115; Reg. v. Whitworth, 1 F. & F. 382; Reg. v. Howell, 1 C. & K. 689. While the old expression of the rule was that the declaration must be made *in extremis* or *in articulo mortis*, all that is contemplated is that there be the belief of impending death and that death afterward results: S. v. Tilghman, 11 Ired. 513.

[7] Kelly v. U. S., 27 Fed. R. 616; S. v. Swift, 57 Conn. 496. If there is any reasonable doubt as to belief of impending death and absence of hope, the declaration should not be

Evidence is admissible showing the condition of the deceased at the time the declarations were made.[1] For while the declarations of deceased as to the fact of the apprehension of death are admissible,[2] yet the consciousness of the near approach of death may be shown by other circumstances, and it is not necessary that the deceased shall have expressly declared his belief in that fact.[3] It is proper to prove that the deceased was told that he could not recover, even though no reply was made to such information, if his conduct indicated his realization of the fact,[4] and this consciousness may be shown by all the circumstances.[5] But the judge is not to receive the declarations merely on his own notion as to the nature and probable effect of the wound as described, without evidence that deceased believed himself about to die, unless the wound appears to have been such as would necessarily cause death in a short time and would lead the deceased as a reasonable per-

received: S. v. Medlicott, 9 Kan. 257. But the court on appeal will not interfere with the action of the lower court in admitting the declaration if there is reasonable evidence to support it: Robbins v. S., 8 Ohio St. 131. And see Donnelly v. S., 26 N. J. 463. As to the preliminary showing, see, also, *infra*, § 430.

[1] Sullivan v. C., 93 Pa. St. 284; Price v. S., 72 Ga. 441. The vindictive spirit of deceased at the time the declaration was made, and his use of profane language at that time, may be shown, and the declaration may be excluded on that ground: Tracy v. P., 97 Ill. 101. But it is not necessary to show that deceased stated explicitly that he was at peace with God and the world: S. v. Black, 42 La. An. 861.

[2] C. v. Thompson, 159 Mass. 56; S. v. Cronin, 64 Conn. 293; Hammil v. S., 90 Ala. 577; Westbrook v. P., 126 Ill. 81.

[3] C. v. Murray, 2 Ashmead, 41; C. v. Williams, 2 Ashmead, 69; Kilpatrick v. C., 31 Pa. St. 198; Donnelly v. S., 26 N. J. 463; Nelson v. S., 7 Humph. 541; P. v. Lee Save Bo, 72 Cal. 623; S. v. Gillick, 7 Ia. 287; S. v. Nash, 7 Ia. 347; S. v. Wilson, 24 Kan. 189; Dumas v. S., 62 Ga. 58; Fitzgerald v. S., 11 Neb. 577; McLean v. S., 16 Ala. 672; Justice v. S., 99 Ala. 180; S. v. Russell, 13 Mont. 164; S. v. Scott, 12 La. An. 274; Morgan v. S., 31 Ind. 198; Rex v. Woodcock, 1 East, P. C. 356; Rex v. Dingler, 1 East, P. C. 356; Rex v. John, 1 East, P. C. 357; Rex v. Spilsbury, 7 C. & P. 187; Rex v. Bonner, 6 C. & P. 386; Reg. v. Hunt, 2 Cox, 239. Statements of deceased that he did not expect to recover are not conclusive that the declarations are under a sense of *impending* death: Morgan v. S., 31 Ind. 198; Digby v. P., 113 Ill. 123.

[4] Reg. v. Perkins, 9 C. & P. 395; P. v. Simpson, 48 Mich. 474. On the other hand, it may appear that the person believed he was about to die, although his physician and others held out to him a hope of recovery: S. v. Caldwell, 115 N. C. 794.

[5] C. v. Murray, 2 Ashmead, 41; Donnelly v. S., 26 N. J. 463; P. v. Lee Save Bo, 72 Cal. 623; P. v. Farmer, 77 Cal. 1; Westbrook v. P., 126 Ill. 81.

son to so believe.[1] It is not necessary that deceased shall have been told that he is about to die if his actions indicate his consciousness of that fact and he so states in his declaration.[2] But where there has been no medical advice nor apparent cause to believe that death is approaching, nor evidence that the deceased does so believe, the declaration is not admissible.[3] Many cases illustrating what has been held sufficient proof of the consciousness of the near approach of death are given in the note without further particularization, which would be impracticable and of little value.[4] On the other hand, if it appears that the deceased had at the time the statement was made any hope of recovery the declaration is not admissible.[5] Other cases in which the showing as to the sense of impending death was held not sufficient are given in the note.[6] It is not sufficient that the deceased was actually dying, but it must appear that he was conscious of that fact;[7] and such consciousness must appear to have existed at the time of the statement.[8] It is not enough that deceased should have thought that he would

[1] Reg. v. Cleary, 2 F. & F. 850.

[2] Hammil v. S., 90 Ala. 577.

[3] S. v. Johnson, 118 Mo. 491.

[4] Kehoe v. C., 85 Pa. St. 127; Small v. C., 91 Pa. St. 304; Brotherton v. P., 75 N. Y. 159; C. v. Haney, 127 Mass. 455; S. v. Wilson, 24 Kan. 189; Westbrook v. P., 126 Ill. 81; Simons v. P., 150 Ill. 66; S. v. Johnson, 76 Mo. 121; S. v. Wensell, 98 Mo. 137; S. v. Umble, 115 Mo. 452; P. v. Hawes, 98 Cal. 648; C. v. Matthews, 89 Ky. 287; S. v. Fletcher, 24 Oreg. 295; Scales v. S., 96 Ala. 69; McQueen v. S., 94 Ala. 50; Hussey v. S., 87 Ala. 121; Anderson v. S., 79 Ala. 5; Gibson v. C., 2 Va. Cas. 111; S. v. Jones, 38 La. An. 792; Reg. v. Peel, 2 F. & F. 21; Ashton's Case, 2 Lewin, 147; Reg. v. Goddard, 15 Cox, 7.

[5] C. v. Roberts, 108 Mass. 296; Peak v. S., 50 N. J. 179; S. v. Simon, 50 Mo. 370; Jackson v. C., 19 Grat. 656; Adwell v. C., 17 B. Mon. 310; Whitaker v. S., 79 Ga. 87; Reg. v. Jenkins, L. R. 1 C. C. 187; Rex v. Crockett, 4 C. & P. 544; Rex v. Hayward, 6 C. & P. 157; Rex v. Welbourn, 1 East, P. C. 358; Reg. v. Megson, 9 C. & P. 418; Rex v. Fagent, 7 C. & P. 238; Errington's Case, 2 Lewin, 148; Rex v. Christie, Car. C. L. 232. A mere suggestion of recovery will not prevent the introduction of the declaration if from other evidence it appears deceased had no hope: Allison v. C., 99 Pa. St. 17.

[6] Digby v. P., 113 Ill. 123; Tracy v. P., 97 Ill. 101; S. v. Nash, 7 Ia. 347; Blackburn v. S., 98 Ala. 63; Justice v. S., 99 Ala. 180; Lewis v. S., 9 Sm. & M. 115; Irby v. S., 25 Tex. Ap. 203; Stewart v. S., 2 Lea, 598; Reg. v. Qualter, 6 Cox, 357; Reg. v. Nicolas, 6 Cox, 120; Reg. v. Osman, 15 Cox, 1; Reg. v. Mackay, 11 Cox, 148; Reg. v. Taylor, 3 Cox, 84.

[7] Reg. v. Mooney, 5 Cox, 318.

[8] Reg. v. Qualter, 6 Cox, 357. But where the opinion of deceased that he was about to die was expressed at the end of the conversation instead of at the beginning, it was held to sufficiently appear that the

ultimately never recover, but it must appear that he was conscious that death was actually imminent.[1] If, however, consciousness of impending death, without hope of recovery, existed at the time the declaration was made, it is immaterial that deceased afterwards entertained a hope of recovery.[2] It is the impression of impending death and not the succession of death in point of fact which renders the testimony admissible;[3] and the declaration will be admissible although deceased lived for some days thereafter. Indeed the time of death is immaterial; and there are cases where the declaration was admitted although the deceased lived two or three weeks after the declaration was made.[4]

§ 427. As to what matters admissible.— Nothing can be evidence in a dying declaration which would not be so if the party was being examined as a witness.[5] In general such dec-

whole statement was made with that consciousness: S. v. Peace, 1 Jones, 251.

[1] Rex v. Van Butchell, 3 C. & P. 629; Reg. v. Forrester, 4 F. & F. 857; Morgan v. S., 31 Ind. 193; Digby v. P., 113 Ill. 123. Even if the sense of impending dissolution is not sufficiently shown to have existed when the declaration was originally made, yet if such declaration was subsequently referred to and affirmed as true at the time when such consciousness existed, it is sufficient: Young v. C., 6 Bush, 312; P. v. Crews, 102 Cal. 174; S. v. Evans, 124 Mo. 397; Johnson v. S., 102 Ala. 1; Carver v. U. S., 160 U. S. 553; Reg. v. Steele, 12 Cox, 168.

[2] S. v. Tilghman, 11 Ired. 513; S. v. Turlington, 102 Mo. 642; S. v. Kilgore, 70 Mo. 546; S. v. Reed, 53 Kan. 767; Swisher v. C., 26 Grat. 963; Hall v. C., 89 Va. 171; Reg. v. Reany, Dears. & B. 151; Reg. v. Hubbard, 14 Cox, 565. The mere fact that deceased had at the time the declaration was made a hope of present ease or relief is not such a hope as will render the declaration inadmissible: Johnson v. S., 17 Ala. 618; Donnelly v. S., 26 N. J. 463; Rex v. Tinckler, 1 East, P. C. 354; Reg. v. Howell, 1 Den. 1. The repetition of a dying declaration, made after hope of recovery has revived, is not admissible: Carver v. U. S., 160 U. S. 553. Sending for a physician may indicate a hope of recovery: Justice v. S., 99 Ala. 180; but not necessarily: S. v. Evans, 124 Mo. 397; McQueen v. S., 103 Ala. 12.

[3] Pulliam v. S., 88 Ala. 1; P. v. Simpson, 48 Mich. 474; S. v. Kilgore, 70 Mo. 546.

[4] S. v. Nocton, 121 Mo. 537; S. v. Wilson, 121 Mo. 434; C. v. Cooper, 5 Allen, 495; C. v. Haney, 127 Mass. 455; Jones v. S., 71 Ind. 66; Hall v. C., 89 Va. 171; Swisher v. C., 26 Grat. 963; S. v. Banister, 35 S. C. 290; Oliver v. S., 17 Ala. 587; Boulden v. S., 102 Ala. 78; Justice v. S., 99 Ala. 180; Bryant v. S., 80 Ga. 272; McDaniel v. S., 8 Sm. & M. 401: Peoples v. C., 87 Ky. 487; S. v. Dániel, 31 La. An. 91; Reg. v. Bernadotte, 11 Cox, 316; Rex v. Mosley, 1 Moody, 98; Rex v. Tinckler, 1 East, P. C. 354.

[5] Montgomery v. S., 80 Ind. 338; P. v. Lanagan, 81 Cal. 142; Rex v. Sellers, Car. C. L. 233. And as to

larations are admissible only so far as they relate to the killing and the facts and circumstances attending it and constituting a part of the *res gestæ*, and the connection of the accused with the offense.[1] So far as such declarations relate to former and distinct transactions, even though other evidence of such transactions might be admissible, the declarations cannot be received.[2] In such cases they do not come within the principle of necessity which justifies the admission of dying declarations.[3]

§ 428. **Competency of evidence; opinions.**— In general the declaration is admissible as to any matter which deceased, if alive, would have been competent to testify to.[4] So far as the declaration is a mere narrative or statement and not a declaration as to the facts, it is not admissible.[5] Declarations which cover the opinion or belief only of the deceased are not admissible, for the deceased if a living witness would not be allowed to give such testimony.[6] But declarations such as that accused had no reason for shooting deceased, or that the wound was given without provocation, or that it was given by accident, are not excluded as mere matter of opinion, but are admissible as statements of fact.[7]

opinions not being admissible, see next paragraph.

[1] S. v. Draper, 65 Mo. 335; P. v. Knapp, 26 Mich. 112; Pulliam v. S., 88 Ala. 1; Moore v. S., 12 Ala. 764; Johnson v. S., 102 Ala. 1; North v. P., 139 Ill. 81; S. v. Arnold, 13 Ired. 184; Wilkerson v. S., 91 Ga. 729; S. v. Shelton, 2 Jones, 360; Hudson v. S., 3 Coldw. 355; S. v. Donnelly, 26 N. J. 601 (in dissenting opinion, at 623). They must refer distinctly to the subject of the homicide and cannot be connected with it by inference or supposition: P. v. Olmstead, 30 Mich. 431.

[2] S. v. Draper, 65 Mo. 335; Leiber v. C., 9 Bush, 11; Ben v. S., 37 Ala. 103; Johnson v. S., 17 Ala. 618; Montgomery v. S., 80 Ind. 338; Jones v. S., 71 Ind. 66; West v. S., 7 Tex. Ap. 150. But in one case it has been held that the declaration might be considered in evidence as showing previous conduct of the prisoner: S. v. Terrell, 12 Rich. 321. A part of a declaration which is proper should not be excluded because another part relates to antecedent threats: Jones v. S., 71 Ind. 66.

[3] Nelson v. S., 7 Humph. 541.

[4] P. v. Green, 1 Denio, 614; S. v. Foot You, 24 Oreg. 61; S. v. Elkins, 101 Mo. 344.

[5] P. v. Olmstead, 30 Mich. 431; Jones v. S., 71 Ind. 66; S. v. Elkins, 101 Mo. 344.

[6] Binns v. S., 46 Ind. 311; Montgomery v. S., 80 Ind. 338; P. v. Lanagan, 81 Cal. 142; S. v. Parker, 96 Mo. 382; S. v. Chambers, 87 Mo. 406; S. v. Vansant, 80 Mo. 67; S. v. Rider, 90 Mo. 54; McPherson v. S., 22 Ga. 478; Whitley v. S., 38 Ga. 50; S. v. Black, 42 La. An. 861; U. S. v. Veitch, 1 Cranch, C. C. 115.

[7] Boyle v. S., 97 Ind. 322; S. C., 105 Ind. 469; P. v. Farmer, 77 Cal. 1; C. v. Matthews, 89 Ky. 287; Sullivan v. S., 102 Ala. 135; Wroe v. S., 20 Ohio

§ 429. Form of statement.— It is immaterial in what form the statement is made so that it is the declaration of the deceased. Thus, where he is able to understand what is said to him but is unable to speak, his answers to questions put to him, communicated by signs, may be proven.[1] If it appears that while the questions are being asked or the statements read to him he is unconscious or in a stupor, the statement cannot be received.[2] It is no objection that the statement is made in response to questions,[3] and not a continuous narrative.[4] It is not necessary that the exact words of deceased be proved.[5] Where the dying declaration was at the time reduced to writing and read over to the deceased and signed or assented to by him, the writing must be produced or its absence accounted for before parol evidence of the declaration is admissible;[6] but not if the writing is a memorandum only, made by a bystander, not signed by deceased or read over and assented to.[7] The writing will not preclude parol evidence of unwritten declarations on other occasions.[8] A copy of the written declarations is not admissible;[9] and of course a memorandum not signed

St. 460; Roberts v. S., 5 Tex. Ap. 141. Thus, the statement of deceased that he had been butchered by the doctors was held admissible in a trial for manslaughter of the surgeon who performed an operation resulting in death: S. v. Gile, 8 Wash. 12. So a statement that deceased did not recognize the accused until he "commenced his pranks" was held admissible: Brotherton v. P., 75 N. Y. 159.

[1] C. v. Casey, 11 Cush. 417; Jones v. S., 71 Ind. 66.

[2] McHugh v. S., 31 Ala. 318.

[3] C. v. Haney, 127 Mass. 455; Boyle v. S., 97 Ind. 322; P. v. Brady, 72 Cal. 490; White v. S., 30 Tex. Ap. 652; even though the questions are leading: Reg. v. Smith, L. & C. 607, and by the state's attorney, without any representation on the part of the accused: North v. P., 139 Ill. 81; S. v. Foot You, 24 Oreg. 61.

[4] S. v. Nettlebush, 20 Ia. 257; Rex v. Fagent, 7 C. & P. 238.

[5] P. v. Bemmerley, 87 Cal. 117; Montgomery v. S., 11 Ohio, 424; Ward v. S., 8 Blackf. 101.

[6] Rex v. Trowter, 1 East, P. C. 356; Rex v. Gay, 7 C. & P. 230; S. v. Sullivan, 51 Ia. 142; S. v. Kindle, 47 Ohio St. 358; Turner v. S., 89 Tenn. 547; Boulden v. S., 102 Ala. 78; Drake v. S., 25 Tex. Ap. 293.

[7] Allison v. C., 99 Pa. St. 17; S. v. Patterson, 45 Vt. 308; S. v. Sullivan, 51 Ia. 142. If the memorandum is made to refresh the recollection of the witness, it is not primary evidence even though signed and sworn to by deceased: S. v. Whitson, 111 N. C. 695.

[8] S. v. Tweedy, 11 Ia. 350; S. v. Walton, — Ia. —, 61 N. W. R. 179; P. v. Simpson, 48 Mich. 474; Krebs v. S., 8 Tex. Ap. 1; P. v. Glenn, 10 Cal. 32; Collier v. S., 20 Ark. 36.

[9] Beets v. S., 1 Meigs, 106; Rex v. Gay, 7 C. & P. 230.

cannot be introduced except as a part of the testimony of the witness who made it.[1] The fact that the declaration is sworn to by the deceased is not material.[2]

§ 430. Admissibility for the court.— The question of the admissibility of the dying declaration is in the first instance for the court, which must determine whether the declaration was made under the sense of impending death.[3] But if a *prima facie* case for the introduction of the declaration is established, it should be allowed to go to the jury, who will determine ultimately whether the circumstances under which it is shown to have been made were such as to justify its consideration.[4] The preliminary showing should precede the introduction of the declaration as evidence for the jury,[5] and may include the declaration itself and the conversation in which it was made, and facts not relating to the killing but bearing on the question as to the consciousness of impending death on the part of declarant.[6] Even after the declaration has been admitted without objection, the facts touching this question may be shown.[7] It is in the discretion of the court whether the preliminary evi-

[1] S. v. Wilson, 24 Kan. 189; Beets v. S., Meigs, 106. When proved by the person making it to be in the words of deceased, the writing is admissible though not signed by deceased: Pa. v. Stoops, Addison, 381.

[2] S. v. Frazier, 1 Houst. Cr. Cas. 176; S. v. Talbert, 41 S. C. 526; Turner v. S., 89 Tenn. 547; Reg. v. Bernadotte, 11 Cox, 316. The sworn statement is not admissible as a deposition. It is simply evidence of the declaration: C. v. Haney, 127 Mass. 455.

[3] Smith v. S., 9 Humph. 9; Donnelly v. S., 26 N. J. 463; S. v. Burns, 33 Mo. 483; McLean v. S., 8 Mo. 153; S. v. Cantieny, 34 Minn. 1; Roten v. S., 31 Fla. 514; S. v. Reed, 53 Kan. 767; C. v. Sullivan, 13 Phila. 410; Rex v. John, 1 East, P. C. 357; Rex v. Welbourn, 1 East, P. C. 358; Rex v. Hucks, 1 Stark. 521. And see *supra*, § 426. And if allowed to go to the jury when the grounds for admission are not shown, the introduction will constitute error: S. v. Johnson, 118 Mo. 491. The court determines the admissibility of the evidence produced by the state, without hearing evidence from the other side: S. v. Frazier, 1 Houst. Cr. C. 176. The admission of such evidence is to some extent discretionary with the court hearing the witnesses: S. v. Ah Lee, 7 Oreg. 237.

[4] C. v. Murray, 2 Ashmead, 41; Jones v. S., 71 Ind. 66; Varnedoe v. S., 75 Ga. 181; S. v. Banister, 35 S. C. 290. The question of admissibility is one of law blended with fact, and the court may receive the evidence in the first instance for the purpose of determining the question: S. v. Seiley, 41 La. An. 141; Donnelly v. S., 26 N. J. 463.

[5] Montgomery v. S., 11 Ohio, 424.

[6] P. v. Smith, 104 N. Y. 491.

[7] S. v. Swift, 57 Conn. 496.

dence as to the admissibility of the declaration shall be given in the presence of the jury.[1]

§ **431. Credibility and weight.**—As has been stated in the preceding section, the ultimate question as to whether the circumstances were such as to render the declaration admissible is for the jury, and even if the evidence leaves the question doubtful the evidence is to go to the jury for what it is worth.[2] Facts bearing upon the credibility of the declarations as constituting the testimony of the deceased may be considered by the jury, such as that, where the declaration relates to the identity of defendant, he was in the habit of mistaking persons;[3] and the whole statement is to be admitted and other conversations on the same subject under the same circumstances.[4] But this rule does not require that the evidence shall show everything that concerned the *res gestæ*, but only that the declarant's statements of any given fact should be a full expression of all that he intended to say as conveying his meaning as to such fact.[5] On the question whether other statements made by the deceased not under such circumstances as to entitle them to admission as dying declarations may be proven to contradict the statements in the dying declaration, authorities are divided. Technically such other statements are not admissible as impeaching evidence, because the foundation cannot be laid by calling the attention of the deceased thereto and giving him an opportunity to explain them.[6] But by the decided weight of authority such declarations are admissible, the lack of oppor-

[1] Doles v. S., 97 Ind. 555; S. v. Johnson, 41 La. An. 1076.

[2] P. v. Knapp, 26 Mich. 112. But see *supra*, § 426. So if the declarations bear in any degree on the homicide they are admissible, though vague and indefinite, their effect being for the jury: C. v. Murray, 2 Ashmead, 41.

[3] C. v. Cooper, 5 Allen, 495.

[4] Nelms v. S., 13 Sm. & M. 500; S. v. Martin, 30 Wis. 216; Mattox v. U. S., 146 U. S. 140.

[5] S. v. Patterson, 45 Vt. 308; P. v. Brady, 72 Cal. 490; Boyle v. S., 97 Ind. 322.

[6] Wroe v. S., 20 Ohio St. 460; Maine v. P., 9 Hun, 113; S. v. Burt, 41 La. An. 787. This is on the same principle on which, where the evidence of a deceased witness given on a former trial is allowed to be proven, declarations inconsistent therewith are excluded: Craft v. C., 81 Ky. 250; Ayers v. Watson, 132 U. S. 394; Mattox v. U. S., 156 U. S. 237; Griffith v. S., 37 Ark. 324; Hubbard v. Briggs, 31 N. Y. 518, 536; Unis v. Charlton's Adm'r, 12 Grat. 484; Kimball v. Davis, 19 Wend. 437. And see 9 Harvard Law Rev. 432, 472.

tunity for cross-examination of the deceased as to his declaration being deemed an offset to the lack of opportunity to the deceased to explain his inconsistent statements.[1] Of course, contradictory statements made in the declaration itself or in different declarations which are admissible as dying declarations may be considered as affecting their credibility.[2] In other respects the credibility of the deceased may be tested as that of any other witness, as by showing that he was intoxicated at the time of making them;[3] or that he was of such immature years as not to be competent to give testimony;[4] or that he was a disbeliever in a future state of rewards and punishments.[5] So, bad character of the deceased, such as would affect his credibility as a living witness, may be shown, and in such case the declaration may be corroborated by proof that deceased made other declarations to the same purport.[6] It is said that the dying declarations are to be received with the same degree of credit as the testimony of the deceased would have been, had he been examined on oath.[7] But in other cases it is held that it is error to instruct the jury that such declarations are entitled to the same credit and force as the testimony of a witness regularly testifying on oath.[8] Such an instruction inter-

[1] S. v. Lodge, 9 Houst. 542, 33 Atl. R. 312; P. v. Lawrence, 21 Cal. 368; Shell v. S., 88 Ala. 14; Battle v. S., 74 Ga. 101; Morelock v. S., 90 Tenn. 528; Felder v. S., 23 Tex. Ap. 477; Carver v. U. S. — U. S. —, 17 S. C. R. 228; Wharton, Cr. Ev., § 298; 1 Bish. Cr. Proc., § 1209.

[2] McPherson v. S., 9 Yerg. 279. Lack of exact correspondence between a previous affidavit and the dying declaration will not be material unless they are contradictory: Leigh v. P., 113 Ill. 372.

[3] S. v. Nolan, — Ia. —, 61 N. W. R. 181.

[4] Rex v. Pike, 3 C. & P. 598; Reg. v. Perkins, 9 C. & P. 395.

[5] Goodall v. S., 1 Oreg. 333; Donnelly v. S., 26 N. J. 463. But of course such disbelief would not under usual rules of evidence render the declaration inadmissible, but would affect its credibility only: S. v. Ah Lee, 8 Oreg. 214. Attainder might be shown under the early common-law doctrine as to the effect thereof, for the purpose of excluding the declarations: Rex v. Drummond, 1 East, P. C. 353, n.

[6] S. v. Thomason, 1 Jones, 274.

[7] P. v. Knapp, 1 Edm. Sel. Cas. 177; Kennedy v. S., 85 Ala. 326; Ashton's Case, 2 Lewin, 147. Or, as said in another case, the declaration is to have the same weight as the testimony of a witness who cannot be cross-examined: S. v. Eddon, 8 Wash. 292. And see Jones v. S., 70 Miss. 401.

[8] Lambeth v. S., 23 Miss. 322; S. v. Vansant, 80 Mo. 67, overruling Green v. S., 13 Mo. 382; S. v. Mathes, 90 Mo. 571.

feres with the province of the jury to determine the weight of the evidence.[1] It is better to say that the jury may consider the character of the dying declarations and the circumstances under which they are made in determining the weight to which they are entitled.[2]

[1] S. v. McCanon, 51 Mo. 160; S. v. Pearce, 56 Minn. 226.

[2] Jordan v. S., 81 Ala. 20; Jones v. S., 70 Miss. 401; S. v. Pearce, 56 Minn. 226. In general, as to admissibility and weight of dying declarations, see Hill v. S., 41 Ga. 484.

CHAPTER 19.

MAYHEM AND MAIMING.

§ 432. **Mayhem; maiming.**— The offense of mayhem as known at common law, aside from any statutory modification, is defined as the violently depriving another of the use of such of his members as may render him less able in fighting either to defend himself or to annoy his adversary.[1] But by various statutes in England, one of which (22 and 23 Car. II., ch. 1) is known as the Coventry Act, the scope of the offense was extended to include various acts, such as cutting out or disabling the tongue, putting out the eye, slitting the nose or lip, or otherwise maiming or disfiguring, thus covering various injuries which were included in common-law mayhem.[2] Notwithstanding this statute became a part of the common law in the states of the Union, some statutory provision has been almost uniformly made for the punishment of such acts, and these statutes now provide the definition of the offense.[3] "Maim," as used in the statute, is not a synonym of mayhem, but is an equivalent for mutilate,[4] and involves an injury of a permanent nature.[5] But any such offense made punishable by statute may be denominated mayhem in an indictment.[6]

§ 433. **Whether felony.**— Mayhem at early common law was a felony involving the punishment of loss of member for member, but it was not punishable by death except in case of

[1] 4 Bl. Com. 205. Hawkins and East use the term "maim" as synonymous with "mayhem," and define it as a bodily hurt whereby one is rendered less able, etc.: 1 Hawk. P. C., ch. 44, § 1; 1 East, P. C. 393. And see 1 Whart. Cr. L., § 581; 2 Bish. Cr. L., § 1001; Terrell v. S., 86 Tenn. 523, 8 Am. Cr. R. 532, and note.

[2] 4 Bl. Com. 207; 1 Hawk. P. C., ch. 44, § 4; 1 East, P. C. 394.

[3] Foster v. P., 50 N. Y. 598; S. v. Briley, 8 Port. 472; S. v. Green, 7 Ired. 39; P. v. Golden, 62 Cal. 542; S. v. Vowels, 4 Oreg. 324. To the same effect is an act of congress: U. S. v. Scroggins, Hempst. 478.

[4] C. v. Newell, 7 Mass. 245.

[5] Bish. Stat. Cr., § 316.

[6] S. v. Vowels, 4 Oreg. 324.

castration, and therefore was not, with that exception, properly a felony.[1]

§ 434. **What constitutes maiming.**— At common law knocking out a front tooth,[2] or putting out an eye,[3] is mayhem. The statutory provisions in regard to disabling contemplate a permanent injury.[4] Thus, an injury inflicted with intent to break the skull is not done with intent to maim, but with intent to kill, and the injury is not maiming under the statute.[5] But an injury depriving a person of the use of a limb, or rendering him permanently lame or defective in bodily vigor, is a maim.[6] If there is a loss of a member such as to deprive the person of it at the time of the injury, the offense is complete, though the member is at once restored to its proper place and grows there.[7] Whether biting off a small portion of the ear is maiming or disfiguring within the statute depends upon whether the loss is such as to attract attention;[8] but such injury has been held to be covered by a statute defining the offense of mayhem so as to include the disabling or disfiguring of a member of the body.[9] A statute with reference to wounding or disfiguring the private parts of another relates to the private parts of a female as well as to those of a male.[10] The act must be within the statutory description;[11] but the means or instrument is immaterial unless specified in such description.[12] Various statutory offenses of wounding with a dangerous weapon, and stabbing, cutting, etc., are discussed under the head of aggravated assaults.[13]

§ 435. **Intent.**— As to mayhem proper, the intent, aside from the unlawful intent essential in all crime, is not material,

[1] 1 Hawk. P. C., ch. 44, § 3; 1 Whart. Cr. L. 583; 2 Bish. Cr. Pr. 852; 3 Bl. Com. 121; C. v. Lester, 2 Va. Cas. 198; Terrell v. S., 86 Tenn. 523; C. v. Newell, 7 Mass. 245.

[2] High v. S., 26 Tex. Ap. 545.

[3] Chick v. S., 7 Humph. 161.

[4] S. v. Briley, 8 Port. 472. The term is used in the same sense in regard to injuries to animals: Baker v. S., 4 Ark. 56; Bish. St. Cr., § 316; Roscoe, Cr. Ev. 389.

[5] Foster v. P., 50 N. Y. 598. But see 1 East, P. C. 393.

[6] Baker v. S., 4 Ark. 56.

[7] Slattery v. S., 41 Tex. 619.

[8] S. v. Abram, 10 Ala. 928; S. v. Harrison, 30 La. An., pt. II, 1329; U. S. v. Askins, 4 Cranch, C. C. 98.

[9] P. v. Golden, 62 Cal. 542. And see S. v. Green, 7 Ired. 39.

[10] Kitchens v. S., 80 Ga. 810.

[11] Foster v. P., 50 N. Y. 598.

[12] Baker v. S., 4 Ark. 56; C. v. Hawkins, 11 Bush, 603.

[13] *Supra*, §§ 256, 257. As to wounding, see, also, S. v. Brown, 41 La. An. 345; S. v. Hertzog, 41 La. An. 775.

the proof of the commission of the act being sufficient to give rise to the presumption of wrongful intent.[1] Evidence of malice aforethought or a preconceived intention is not necessary.[2] In general, specific intent to maim is not essential.[3] Under statutes similar to the Coventry Act, premeditated design is essential, but the act of lying in wait which evinces such intention need not be charged;[4] and it is not necessary, in order to show premeditated design, that malice aforethought or lying in wait, referred to by the statute, should be on purpose to maim or disfigure, specific intent not being necessary under that clause, although it is held necessary under the clause "shall voluntarily, maliciously and on purpose put out an eye," etc.[5] Whether there was such premeditated design is a question for the jury.[6] But an act done in a sudden affray or assault without some evidence of preparation or previous intent does not come within the statutory provision.[7] If the result does not show that an injury of the kind was intended, a conviction cannot be sustained.[8] Where, however, the statute provides a punishment for unlawfully or maliciously disabling or disfiguring, an intent to do a wrongful act, either established by proof or presumption, is sufficient.[9] Where specific intent to disfigure is made an essential element, such intent may be inferred or presumed if the act is done deliberately and the disfigurement is reasonably to be apprehended as the natural and probable consequence.[10] The statutes do not make the occasion material, and self-defense will not be an excuse.[11] Consent to the offense is immaterial.[12] The intent to disfigure may be inferred from an

[1] Foster v. P., 1 Colo. 293; S. v. Simmons, 3 Ala. 497.

[2] S. v. Gerkin, 1 Ired. 121; S. v. Crawford, 2 Dev. 425; Terrell v. S., 86 Tenn. 523; U. S. v. Gunther, 5 Dak. 234.

[3] S. v. Clark, 69 Ia. 196; 1 East, P. C. 400. It is not necessary that the blow be struck for the purpose of inflicting the particular injury: Werley v. S., 11 Humph. 171.

[4] Tully v. P., 67 N. Y. 15.

[5] Resp. v. Langcake, 1 Yeates, 415; Rex v. Tickner, 1 East, P. C. 398.

[6] Tully v. P., 67 N. Y. 15.

[7] Godfrey v. P., 63 N. Y. 207.

[8] S. v. Cody, 18 Oreg. 506.

[9] P. v. Wright, 93 Cal. 564.

[10] S. v. Jones, 70 Ia. 505; S. v. Clark, 69 Ia. 196. So the use of an instrument which ordinarily would result in maiming and does so result shows the required intent: Davis v. S., 22 Tex. Ap. 45; S. v. Ma Foo, 110 Mo. 7.

[11] Molette v. S., 49 Ala. 18; Foster v. P., 1 Colo. 293.

[12] Rex v. Wright, 1 East, P. C. 396; Foster v. P., 1 Colo. 293.

act which does in fact disfigure unless that presumption is repelled.[1]

§ **436. Indictment.**— It seems that the indictment must allege that the injured party was maimed, disabled, or disfigured, as the case may be.[2] But under statute it is sufficient, generally, to use the language of the statute, without specifically charging the effect.[3] Where several intents are mentioned disjunctively in the statute they may be properly alleged conjunctively in the indictment, and proof of either will support a conviction.[4] "Maim" is a word of art and should be used when made the essential part of the statutory description.[5] "Maliciously" is usually an essential part of the statutory description and must be used in the indictment,[6] "feloniously" not being sufficient.[7]

§ **436a. Forms.**— As the various offenses of mayhem and maiming are now entirely regulated by statute, the form of the indictment must be based on the language of the particular statute under which it is drawn; nevertheless the following forms may be suggestive:

PUTTING OUT AN EYE.

That A. B., at ——, on ——, unlawfully and feloniously and with malice aforethought in and upon one W. M. an assault did make, and then and there unlawfully and feloniously and with malice aforethought, with the thumb and fingers of the right hand of the said A. B., the left eye of the said W. M. did put out and destroy, with malicious intent the said W. M. to maim and disfigure; whereby the said W. M. was then and there, by the said putting out and destroying of his said eye as aforesaid, maimed and disfigured.[8]

[1] S. v. Gerkin, 1 Ired. 121; S. v. Crawford, 2 Dev. 425; S. v. Evans, 1 Hayw. 281.

[2] C. v. Lester, 2 Va. Cas. 198; Chick v. S., 7 Humph. 161.

[3] U. S. v. Gunther, 5 Dak. 234. It is not necessary, where biting off an ear is charged, to specify which ear: S. v. Green, 7 Ired. 39.

[4] Angel v. C., 2 Va. Cas. 231.

[5] Chick v. S., 7 Humph. 161.

[6] S. v. Cook, 42 La. An. 85; S. v. Mason, 42 La. An. 714.

[7] C. v. Lester, 2 Va. Cas. 198; S. v. Watson, 41 La. An. 598.

[8] This follows to some extent the indictment in Chick v. S., 7 Humph. 161, with the addition of such averments as are thought necessary to fully obviate the objections sustained to that indictment. It is difficult to see any advantage in the averment that the person assaulted was maimed, when it is distinctly alleged that his eye was put out with intent to maim him. Possibly

DISABLING THE THUMB.

That A. B., at ——, on ——, in and upon one W. M. wilfully and feloniously and with premeditated design did make an assault, and that the said A. B. with his teeth the thumb of the said W. M. then and there wilfully and feloniously and from premeditated design did cut, bite, slit and destroy on purpose with intent the said W. M. then and there to maim and disfigure.[1]

§ 437. **Included offense.**— On an indictment for maiming defendant may be convicted of an aggravated assault and battery, the two offenses being of the same generic class, and the latter included in the former.[2] So, one charged with mayhem may be found guilty of beating only,[3] or of a misdemeanor.[4] So a sentence on a verdict for fighting by mutual agreement under an indictment for maiming may be sustained.[5] Under an indictment in two counts, one for aiding and abetting in mayhem, the other for assault and battery, a conviction on the second count, with an acquittal on the first count, cannot be sustained.[6]

if the intent to maim had been alleged in the indictment which was before the court, it would have been thought sufficient without the direct allegation that the party was maimed.

[1] This follows substantially the indictment in Tully v. P., 67 N. Y. 15.

[2] Guest v. S., 19 Ark. 405. Assault is an essential ingredient of mayhem: S. v. Taylor, 35 La. An. 834.

[3] S. v. Absence, 4 Port. 397.

[4] Foster v. P., 1 Colo. 293. Under a charge of felonious wounding there may be conviction for the misdemeanor of unlawfully wounding: Reg. v. Waudby, 2 Q. B. D. (1895), 482.

[5] Strawn v. S., 14 Ark. 541.

[6] S. v. Bridges, 1 Murph. 134.

CHAPTER 20.

RAPE AND CARNAL ABUSE OF FEMALE CHILDREN.

§ **438. Rape defined.**— There is a general concurrence among later authors in the definition of this offense as "the unlawful carnal knowledge of a woman by force and against her will."[1] The only material question which has arisen as to the correctness of this definition is as to the expression "against her will," it being contended that want of consent on the part of the woman is sufficient to constitute the offense.[2] It is suggested in one case that there is no real difference in meaning between the two forms of expression.[3] But it will be evident by subsequent discussion of the cases which relate to the different elements of the offense that the authorities are not entirely harmonious on this question, and that some support the proposition that actual opposition overcome is essential, while others are to the effect that lack of consent is enough.

§ **439. The force involved.**— The act must be by force, either actual or constructive,[4] and by force is meant, according to some definitions, not merely the force necessary to accomplish the act of connection, but force overcoming resistance on the part of the female. According to this theory, connection with a girl under the age of consent is not rape if there is no opposition on her part, although by reason of her want of maturity she is not deemed capable of consent.[5] But in other

[1] 1 East, P. C., 434; 1 Hawk. P. C., ch. 41, § 1; 4 Bl. Com. 210; 1 Russ. Cr. 675. So by statute: Garrison v. P., 6 Neb. 274; Sutton v. P., 145 Ill. 279, and probably in other states.

[2] 2 Bish. Cr. L., § 1115; Reg. v. Camplin, 1 C. & K. 746; Reg. v. Fletcher, Bell, 63; Mooney v. S., 29 Tex. Ap. 257. Against consent is synonymous with against the will: S. v. Gaul, 50 Conn. 578. So by statute in some states: Leoni v. S., 44 Ala. 110.

[3] C. v. Burke, 105 Mass. 376. And see S. v. Gaul, 50 Conn. 578; Harvey v. S., 53 Ark. 425.

[4] McNair v. S., 53 Ala. 453. But it is not necessary that the force be such as to cause apprehension of death: Waller v. S., 40 Ala. 325.

[5] Vasser v. S., 55 Ala. 264; Williams v. S., 1 Tex. Ap. 90; Walton v. S., 29 Tex. Ap. 163; Bonner v. S., 65 Miss. 293. Further as to whether this is rape, see *infra*, § 443.

cases it is suggested that force is simply a test of consent, and that if want of consent is otherwise shown force is immaterial.[1] And as supporting the theory that force is simply a test of consent may be cited cases in which it is said that the force necessary depends upon the relative mental and physical strength of the parties and the circumstances surrounding them,[2] acts of violence being unnecessary where there is no consent, if the intent is to use force if required in accomplishing the purpose.[3] The question whether connection procured by fraud or during insensibility or by fear is sufficient will be discussed in subsequent sections.

§ **440. Resistance.**— The theory which requires actual force also requires that there shall have been resistance on the part of the female to her utmost ability.[4] The cases cited in the last note are evidently authority for the proposition that actual force overcoming the will is essential; but the weight of authority seems to be in support of the proposition that the resistance is merely evidence bearing on the question of want of consent.[5] Thus, as will appear in a subsequent paragraph, no resistance need be shown if it appears that the consent was procured through threats and fear.[6] As excusing the want of resistance, the strength and capacity of the female mentally as well as physically may be shown, including her lack of development and lack of knowledge of the nature of the act.[7] In the case of a child, although above the age of consent, mere submission does not necessarily show such consent as to prevent the act being rape;[8] and the fact that the child is young and unde-

[1] Mooney v. S., 29 Tex. Ap. 257; S. v. Cunningham, 100 Mo. 382. Thus, it is said that force is implied if it appears that the connection was had against the consent of the woman: S. v. Riggs, 1 Houst. Cr. C. 120.

[2] Jenkins v. S., 1 Tex. Ap. 346.

[3] S. v. Smith, 80 Mo. 516. So where the female was imbecile, *held*, that there was no necessity for showing that opposition was actually made: S. v. Tarr, 28 Ia. 397.

[4] P. v. Dohring, 59 N. Y. 374; P. v. Morrison, 1 Park. Cr. R. 625; Brown v. P., 36 Mich. 203; Strang v. P., 24 Mich. 1; S. v. Burgdorf, 53 Mo. 65; P. v. Brown, 47 Cal. 447; Oleson v. S., 11 Neb. 276; Mathews v. S., 19 Neb. 330; Rhea v. S., 30 Tex. Ap. 483. Opposition by mere words is not enough: Huber v. S., 126 Ind. 185.

[5] C. v. McDonald, 110 Mass. 405; S. v. Shields, 45 Conn. 256.

[6] *Infra*, § 448.

[7] P. v. Lynch, 29 Mich. 274; Hollis v. S., 27 Fla. 387; S. v. Tarr, 28 Ia. 397; P. v. Connor, 126 N. Y. 278; Hawkins v. S., 136 Ind. 630.

[8] Reg. v. Day, 9 C. & P. 722; S. v. Cross, 12 Ia. 66. In such case the same resistance as required in case of an older female need not be

veloped, and lacks intelligence as to the nature of the act, may be shown as tending to prove want of consent, though resistance does not appear to have been made.[1] But even in such cases there must not be consent. If there is capacity to consent, and consent is given, the offense is not committed.[2] Even, however, if the view be taken that evidence of want of consent alone is sufficient, yet it must appear that there was resistance, unless some excuse for want of resistance is shown.[3] And if such resistance was given over before the accomplishment of the unlawful purpose, without excuse, there will be such consent as to prevent the act being rape.[4] The force involved in an attempt to commit rape is such as to justify the repelling of the attempt by the use of a deadly weapon in case of reasonable belief of actual danger of the accomplishment of the crime.[5] There seems to have been at one time some recognition of the idea that the fact of conception indicated consent and therefore negatived rape, but this doctrine has long been repudiated.[6]

§ 441. Without consent.— Consent of the female (except when the will is overcome by fear, as hereafter to be explained) will prevent the act from constituting rape,[7] and this is true no matter how reluctantly or tardily consent is given or how much force has been previously employed.[8] But subsequent condonation will not constitute a defense, though it may be shown as tending to prove that there was in fact consent.[9]

shown: Hammond v. S., 39 Neb. 252; Thompson v. S., 44 Neb. 366.

[1] S. v. Cross, 12 Ia. 66; S. v. McCaffrey, 63 Ia. 479; Joiner v. S., 62 Ga. 560; Bailey v. C., 82 Va. 107; Anschicks v. S., 6 Tex. Ap. 524; Coates v. S., 50 Ark. 330, 7 Am. Cr. R. 585 and note; S. v. Niles, 47 Vt. 82, 1 Am. Cr. R. 646 and note.

[2] Pounds v. S., 95 Ga. 475; Thompson v. S., 33 Tex. Ap. 472; T. v. Potter, 1 Ariz. 421.

[3] Austine v. P., 110 Ill. 248.

[4] Reg. v. Hallett, 9 C. & P. 748; Reg. v. Rudland, 4 F. & F. 495. So if resistance is made in consequence of a banter, and not in good faith, it will not be sufficient: S. v. Chapman, 88 Ia. 254.

[5] P. v. De Los Angeles, 61 Cal. 188. And see *supra*, § 299.

[6] 1 Hawk. P. C., ch. 41, § 2; 1 East, P. C. 445; U. S. v. Dickinson, Hemp. 1.

[7] Hull v. S., 22 Wis. 580; Whittaker v. S., 50 Wis. 518; P. v. Bransby, 32 N. Y. 525.

[8] Conners v. S., 47 Wis. 523; Reynolds v. S., 27 Neb. 90; T. v. Potter, 1 Ariz. 421; Sutton v. P., 145 Ill. 279. The prosecuting witness may be asked whether the act was with or without consent: Coates v. S., 2 Tex. Ap. 16.

[9] C. v. Slattery, 147 Mass. 423. Consent subsequent to the act is no defense: S. v. Bagan, 41 Minn. 285; Wright v. S., 4 Humph. 194.

§ 442. Age of the female as bearing upon the question of consent.— Under the discussion of the subject of resistance in a previous paragraph,[1] it has been shown that less resistance is to be required in a child of tender years and ignorant of the nature of the act; and as will be shown in the next section, there are statutes both in England and in the various states making the act of having connection with a female under the age of consent (such age being fixed by statute) a crime without regard to the consent of the female. But some courts seem to have so connected these two phases of the doctrine of consent on the part of females of tender years as to reach the result that such a child is incapable of giving consent, and therefore such connection is rape, want of consent being presumed.[2] Such presumption of incapacity of consent may be rebutted by evidence that the child understood the nature of the act.[3] But these cases are unsatisfactory. The early English statute (18 Eliz., ch. 7, § 4), which is common law in this country, made carnal knowledge of a woman child under the age of ten years a felony, but did not describe the felony as rape; and as will be seen in the next section there is authority to the effect that the offense is distinguished from rape, but similar, the fact of consent being immaterial. According to this view, even though the female be under the age of consent, the crime of rape cannot be established without proof of want of consent;[4] but the immaturity of the female may be shown for the purpose of showing that the act was really without consent, although there was not such resistance as would be necessary in a person of more mature years.[5] Notwithstanding a definition of Lord Hale's, which speaks of rape as being upon a woman over the age of consent;[6] the crime of rape can be committed upon a child under the age of consent,[7] but want of con-

[1] *Supra*, § 440.

[2] Coates v. S., 50 Ark. 330; Williams v. S., 47 Miss. 609; Moore v. S., 17 Ohio St. 521; S. v. Miller, 42 La. An. 1186.

[3] O'Meara v. S., 17 Ohio St. 516.

[4] Vasser v. S., 55 Ala. 264; Bonner v. S., 65 Miss. 293; Greer v. S., 50 Ind. 267; S. v. Worden, 46 Conn. 349; S. v. Wheat, 63 Vt. 673.

[5] *Supra*, § 440.

[6] 1 Hale, P. C. 628. This definition includes, it is true, carnal knowledge of a girl under age of consent as rape, but as will be seen in the next section this is perhaps erroneous: See Reg. v. Shott, 3 C. & K. 206.

[7] C. v. Sugland, 4 Gray, 7; Reg. v. Ratcliffe, 10 Q. B. D. 74; Reg v. Dicken, 14 Cox, 8; Reg. v. Neale, 1 C. & K. 591.

sent should be alleged and proven as in other cases.[1] And where the indictment properly charges the act as by force and against the will, etc., an allegation that the female was under the age of consent will be immaterial and may be rejected as surplusage, leaving the indictment a proper one for rape.[2] On the other hand, it is unnecessary in an indictment for rape by force, etc., to allege that the female was over the age of consent.[3]

§ 443. Carnal abuse of females under the age of consent. The history of the early English statutes relating to rape seems to indicate that the offense as at first defined involved force and want of consent, and that a subsequent statute, referred to in the preceding section, was passed making connection with females under ten years a crime without regard to consent, and these are properly stated as distinct crimes.[4] Apparently, however, without any authority found in the statutes, Lord Hale[5] combines the two into one offense. And most of the statutes in this country follow this form of definition, thus making the crime of rape to consist of either the forcible act without consent, or of carnal knowledge of a female child under the age specified regardless of her consent.[6] Under this consolidation of the two offenses it seems that there may be a conviction under an indictment charging the act to be forcible and against the consent of the female, on proof that she was under the age of consent.[7] If the indictment charges the female to have

[1] S. v. Worden, 46 Conn. 349; Charles v. S., 11 Ark. 389. It is therefore not necessary to allege the age: Hall v. S., 40 Neb. 320.

[2] C. v. Sugland, 4 Gray, 7; C. v. Scannel, 11 Cush. 547; S. v. Casford, 76 Ia. 330; Nicholas v. S., 23 Tex. Ap. 317; Coates v. S., 50 Ark. 330; Dawson v. S., 29 Ark. 116; S. v. Houx, 109 Mo. 654.

[3] S. v. Gaul, 50 Conn. 578; O'Meara v. S., 17 Ohio St. 516; S. v. Farmer, 4 Ired. 224; S. v. Storkey, 63 N. C. 7. And see *infra*, § 452.

[4] 2 Bish. Cr. L., §§ 1108–1112.

[5] 1 Hale, P. C. 628, citing 3 Coke, Inst., ch. 11, p. 60. And see Givens v. C., 29 Grat. 830.

[6] S. v. Dalton, 106 Mo. 463; S. v. Lacey, 111 Mo. 513; McMath v. S., 55 Ga. 303; C. v. Roosnell, 143 Mass. 32; S. v. Newton, 44 Ia. 45; S. v. Wright, 25 Neb. 38; Davis v. S., 31 Neb. 240; S. v. White, 44 Kan. 514; S. v. Woods, 49 Kan. 237; Lawrence v. C., 30 Grat. 845; McKinny v. S., 29 Fla. 565; Mayo v. S., 7 Tex. Ap. 342; Rodgers v. S., 30 Tex. Ap. 510. The two may be charged in counts of the same indictment: Wright v. S., 4 Humph. 194.

[7] Lawrence v. C., 30 Grat. 845; Davis v. S., 42 Tex. 226; S. v. Jackson, 46 La. An. 547. And see cases cited in preceding section.

been under the age of consent it is not necessary to allege the act to have been forcible and against the will, the allegation of age being sufficient in this respect.[1] But in accordance with what seems better reason, it is said in other cases that if the indictment charges that the act was forcible and against the will of the female it must be so proven, and conviction cannot be had upon evidence that the female was under the age of consent, without proof of actual want of consent, even though such evidence would have sustained a conviction had the indictment been framed with reference thereto.[2] The difficulty is as to whether carnal knowledge of a female child under the age of consent shall be called rape, it being held, on the one hand, that if the indictment shows an assault with intent to have such carnal knowledge, it charges an assault to commit rape,[3] and on the other that such an allegation does not show intent to commit a common-law rape and therefore does not indicate an attempt to commit rape.[4] From the foregoing discussion it is evident that unless the statute indicates without equivocation that the two forms of the crime are consolidated into one, it is better to treat them as distinct offenses and draw the indictment accordingly. It is plain that under a statute punishing carnal knowledge of a female child under the age of consent the indictment need not describe the offense as rape.[5] Under a statute providing for the punishment of carnal knowledge of such child or abuse in the attempt to have such knowledge, the indictment may state that defendant did carnally know, or abuse in the attempt to know,[6] or it may charge the carnal knowledge only.[7] In such statute the

[1] S. v. Black, 63 Me. 210; Holton v. S., 28 Fla. 303; C. v. Sullivan, 6 Gray, 477; P. v. Mills, 17 Cal. 276; S. v. Miller, 111 Mo. 542; Farrell v. S., 54 N. J. 416.

[2] S. v. Johnson, 100 N. C. 494; Warner v. S., 54 Ark. 660; Evans v. S., 52 N. J. 261; Vasser v. S., 55 Ala. 264; Bonner v. S., 65 Miss. 293; Greer v. S., 50 Ind. 267.

[3] Cliver v. S., 45 N. J. 46; Hays v. P., 1 Hill, 351; P. v. McDonald, 9 Mich. 150; Proper v. S., 85 Wis. 615; McKinny v. S., 29 Fla. 565; S. v. Meinhart, 73 Mo. 562; P. v. Gordon, 70 Cal. 467; P. v. Verdegreen, 106 Cal. 211.

[4] Smith v. S., 12 Ohio St. 466; Rhodes v. S., 1 Coldw. 350; Brown v. S., 6 Baxt. 422; S. v. Pickett, 11 Nev. 255.

[5] S. v. Smith, Phill. 302.

[6] McGuff v. S., 88 Ala. 147. A charge of assault with intent to know does not sufficiently show abuse: Toullet v. S., 100 Ala. 72.

[7] Reg. v. Holland, 10 Cox, 478.

term "abuse" has reference to the sexual organs only and does not relate to other ill usage.[1] Under an indictment charging in one count carnal knowledge and abuse, and in another the taking of improper and indecent liberties, evidence of the former will not support a conviction for the latter.[2] It is no defense to the charge of having connection with a girl under the age of consent that accused did not know she was under age.[3] It is for the prosecution to prove the age to be below that of consent.[4]

§ 444. **What deemed the age of consent.**— There seems to have been a discrepancy in the English law at one time with reference to the age of consent, in that twelve years was deemed the age of puberty and the age at which a female could consent to a valid marriage, while the statute punishing carnal knowledge and abuse of female children related to females under the age of ten years.[5] So there are English authorities to the effect that connection with a girl under twelve and over ten with her consent will be a misdemeanor, that is, not the felony of rape, and that such consent will prevent there being an assault with intent to commit rape under such circumstances.[6] But in this country age of consent means simply the age fixed by statutes defining the offense of carnal knowledge and abuse of girls, and making such act rape without regard to the girl's consent. It varies in different states from the age of ten, named in the first English statute on the subject, to that of eighteen, fixed by some of the recent statutes.[7] In these various statutes the terms "woman" and "child" indicate respectively a female above the age of puberty and one under that age.[8] But where the age of consent was fixed at fourteen, it was held that the term "female child" indicated a female under

[1] Dawkins v. S., 58 Ala. 376.

[2] P. v. Partridge, 86 Mich. 243.

[3] See *infra*, § 451.

[4] S. v. Houx, 109 Mo. 654.

[5] 1 Hale, P. C. 630. And see S. v. Pierson, 44 Ark. 265.

[6] Reg. v. Martin, 9 C. & P. 213; Reg. v. Johnson, L. & C. 632; Reg. v. Beale, L. R. 1 C. C. 10; 1 Hale, P. C. 631; 4 Bl. Com. 212; 1 Russ. Cr. 693.

[7] S. v. Newton, 44 Ia. 45; S. v. Wright, 25 Neb. 38; S. v. Woods, 49 Kan. 237. The objections to statutes raising the age of consent to an age beyond the period of puberty are discussed in S. v. White, 44 Kan. 514. And similar objections to a statute making connection with consent punishable more severely than the offense of rape itself are pointed out in S. v. Wentler, 76 Wis. 89.

[8] Greer v. S., 50 Ind. 267; Blackburn v. S., 22 Ohio St. 102.

that age.[1] Under a statute providing a punishment for the ravishing by a negro of a white "woman," it was held that a girl under twelve years of age was included in the term "woman."[2] But under a somewhat similar statute it was held that an assault with intent to commit rape on a white woman did not cover an assault with intent to have carnal knowledge of a girl under ten years of age.[3] The age may be found by the jury from the testimony of prosecutrix and her appearance.[4]

§ 445. **Woman insensible.**— Where the connection is had by reason of the fact that the woman is insensible, as, for instance, through sleep, the act is rape, for the woman does not consent, being incapable of resistance.[5] It was so held, also, where the woman had been rendered insensible by liquor administered to her by defendant, although the jury found that the liquor was administered for the purpose of exciting her, and not with the intention of rendering her insensible.[6] These cases evidently support the proposition that want of consent is enough, and that it is not necessary that the act be against the will of the woman.[7] Taking advantage of insensibility for the purpose of having connection is not, however, having carnal intercourse by means of fraud within the Texas statute, which was passed for the purpose of protecting married women against attempts to have connection by personation of the husband.[8]

§ 446. **Consent obtained by fraud.**— If the consent of the woman to sexual intercourse is given, the act will not, aside from statutory provisions, constitute rape, though it is procured by reason of the belief on the part of the woman, fraudulently induced, that the person having connection with her is her husband.[9] It is not rape to have carnal intercourse with a weak-

[1] P. v. Miller, 96 Mich. 119.

[2] C. v. Watts, 4 Leigh, 672.

[3] Sydney v. S., 3 Humph. 478.

[4] C. v. Phillips, 162 Mass. 504.

[5] Reg. v. Mayers, 12 Cox, 311; Reg. v. Young, 38 L. T. 540; Harvey v. S., 53 Ark. 425.

[6] Reg. v. Champlin, 1 C. & K. 746.

[7] See C. v. Burke, 105 Mass. 376.

[8] King v. S., 22 Tex. Ap. 650; Mooney v. S., 29 Tex. Ap. 257.

[9] Lewis v. S., 30 Ala. 54; Wyat v. S., 2 Swan, 394; Reg. v. Barrow, L. R. 1 C. C. 156; Rex v. Jackson, Russ. & Ry. 47; Reg. v. Clarke, Dears. 397; Reg. v. Sweenie, 8 Cox, 223. But such connection constitutes an assault: Reg. v. Williams, 8 C. & P.

minded woman by fraudulent pretense of a fictitious marriage.[1] But if the fraud consists in inducing the woman to submit to a pretended surgical operation or form of medical treatment so that there is no consent whatever to sexual intercourse, then the act constitutes rape.[2] Such connection amounts to an assault, there being no consent to the thing done.[3]

§ **447. Woman imbecile or insane.**— There may be such idiocy or insanity on the part of the female as to negative any consent by her, and therefore make the connection had with her by reason of her condition rape.[4] But if, even though the woman be imbecile, she consent to the act, the crime is not rape,[5] and force must be shown,[6] although less resistance would be required in such cases than in case of a woman of sound mind.[7] By statute in some states it is made criminal, however, to have carnal knowledge of a woman who is imbecile; and such provision is intended to cover cases of the kind where the act is accomplished without force and without consent.[8]

§ **448. Consent through fear.**— Threats of great bodily injury sufficient to overpower the mind of the female and thus compel consent are equivalent to the force required to constitute the crime of rape.[9] The rule is otherwise stated, but to the same effect, in cases which say that evidence that the connection was had by reason of violence negatives consent on the part of the female and excuses want of resistance.[10] But the threatened violence must be such as to make resistance seem hopeless and utterly useless,[11] although in case of a child of

286; Reg. v. Saunders, 8 C. & P. 265. And by statute in Texas it is rape: King v. S., 22 Tex. Ap. 650; Mooney v. S., 29 Tex. Ap. 257; Ledbetter v. S., 33 Tex. Ap. 400.

[1] Bloodworth v. S., 6 Baxt. 614; S. v. Murphy, 6 Ala. 765.

[2] Pomeroy v. S., 94 Ind. 96; S. v. Nash, 109 N. C. 824; Reg. v. Flattery, 2 Q. B. D. 410; Reg. v. Stanton, 1 C. & K. 415.

[3] Reg. v. Case, 1 Den. 580.

[4] S. v. Shields, 45 Conn. 256; Huston v. P., 121 Ill. 497; Felton v. S., 139 Ind. 531; P. v. Lenon, 79 Cal. 625; S. v. Ruth, 21 Kan. 583; Rice v. S., 35 Fla. 236; Reg. v. Woodhurst, 12 Cox, 443; Reg. v. Jones, 4 L. T. 154.

[5] S. v. Shields, 45 Conn. 256; Oleson v. S., 11 Neb. 276.

[6] P. v. Lenon, 79 Cal. 625; Sharp v. S., 15 Tex. Ap. 171.

[7] Waller v. S., 40 Ala. 325.

[8] Ledley v. S., 4 Ind. 580.

[9] Jones v. S., 10 Tex. Ap. 552.

[10] Williams v. S., 1 Tex. Ap. 90; S. v. Vorey, 41 Minn. 134. But evidence of threats may be admissible for other purposes: Bass v. S., 16 Tex. Ap. 62.

[11] Sharp v. S., 15 Tex. Ap. 171; Cooper v. S., 22 Tex. Ap. 419.

tender years the overcoming of the will by a long course of ill-treatment may be sufficient.[1] It is not necessary that the force used or injury threatened be such as to create a reasonable apprehension of death in order to excuse want of resistance.[2] The question whether resistance is overcome by duress is for the jury;[3] and the court should explicitly instruct with reference to the matter.[4] Where the statute defines rape in different forms, by force and also by putting in fear, evidence that the connection is had through fear will not be admissible under an indictment charging the offense to have been committed by force.[5] If, however, the indictment charges the offense in both forms, the state is not compelled to elect which form it will rely on.[6]

§ 449. **Who may commit — Husband; boy; woman; joint principals.**— The crime may be committed by any male of the age of fourteen or over, not the husband of the female.[7] Under the age of fourteen, by the common law of England, a boy is conclusively presumed incapable of the act necessary to constitute rape,[8] or having carnal knowledge of a female child under the age of consent.[9] In some of the United States, however, the doctrine has been established that capacity in a boy under fourteen may be proven, and if the fact is shown he may be convicted of the crime.[10] But the presumption of incapacity

[1] Reg. v. Barratt, L. R. 2 C. C. 81; Reg. v. Fletcher, Bell, 63; S. v. Tarr, 28 Ia. 397; S. v. Atherton, 50 Ia. 189.

[2] Crosswell v. P., 13 Mich. 427; Reg. v. Fletcher, L. R. 1 C. C. 39.

[3] Baldwin v. S., 15 Tex. Ap. 275.

[4] S. v. Cunningham, 100 Mo. 382.

[5] S. v. Enright, 90 Ia. 520. Connection procured by duress or threats may constitute statutory defilement, though the resistance is not such as to show rape: S. v. Fernald, 88 Ia. 553; S. v. Montgomery, 79 Ia. 737; Pollard v. S., 2 Ia. 567; Beyer v. P., 86 N. Y. 369; S. v. Rogers, 108 Mo. 202.

[6] Don Moran v. P., 25 Mich. 356; Pleasant v. S., 13 Ark. 360.

[7] The husband cannot be guilty of a rape committed by himself upon his lawful wife: 1 Hale, P. C. 629. But it is unnecessary to charge that the defendant is not the husband: See *infra*, § 452.

[8] 1 Hale, P. C. 630; S. v. Sam, 1 Wins. i, 300; Williams v. S., 20 Fla. 777; Reg. v. Waite, 2 Q. B. (1892), 600. If under age no evidence is admissible showing capacity: Reg. v. Jordan, 9 C. & P. 118; Reg. v. Philips, 8 C. & P. 736.

[9] Reg. v. Jordan, 9 C. & P. 118; Reg. v. Brimilow, 9 C. & P. 366; Reg. v. Williams, 1 Q. B. D. (1893), 320; Reg. v. Waite, 2 Q. B. D. (1892), 600.

[10] Hiltabiddle v. S., 35 Ohio St. 52; Williams v. S., 14 Ohio St. 222; O'Meara v. S., 17 Ohio St., 516; Moore v. S., 17 Ohio St. 521; P. v. Randolph, 2 Park. Cr. 174; Heilman v. C., 84 Ky. 457; Wagoner v. S., 5 Lea, 352; Gordon v. S., 93 Ga. 531; McKinny v. S., 29 Fla. 565. In Louisiana it is

of a boy under fourteen will prevail until overcome by evidence.[1] The question of liability of a boy, incapable of committing the offense, for an assault with intent to commit rape, will be discussed under that head.[2] The fact that the person charged with the offense is under the age of capacity is one to be shown by evidence and need not be negatived in the indictment.[3] Two or more persons may be guilty of the crime as principals, those who are present, aiding and abetting, being principals in the second degree;[4] the distinction between principals in the first and second degree being now, however, wholly immaterial.[5] Thus, a boy, or a woman, or a husband, though incapable of committing the crime, may be guilty thereof as principal by being present, aiding and assisting in its commission.[6]

§ 450. The act; penetration; emission.—Penetration of the body of the female by the virile organ of the male is essential to constitute the crime.[7] But the slightest penetration is sufficient.[8] It is not necessary that the hymen be ruptured.[9] So in case of abuse of a female child, perfect penetration is

doubted whether the common-law presumption has any force in view of the conditions being different from those prevailing in England, where the rule originated: S. v. Jones, 39 La. An. 935.

1 Heilman v. C., 84 Ky. 457. It is said that even proof of actual penetration by a boy under fourteen will not be sufficient without other evidence of capacity to complete the act: Hiltabiddle v. S., 35 Ohio St. 52.

2 *Infra*, § 465.

3 *Infra*, § 452.

4 Reg. v. Cray, 7 C. & P. 164; Rex v. Folkes, 1 Moody, 354; Reg. v. Crisham, Car. & M. 187; Dennis v. S., 5 Ark. 230; Montague v. S., 17 Fla. 662; S. v. Duffy, 124 Mo. 1.

5 See *supra*, § 217.

6 S. v. Jones, 83 N. C. 605; Kessler v. C., 12 Bush, 18; C. v. Fogerty, 8 Gray, 489; P. v. Chapman, 62 Mich. 280; S. v. Dowell, 106 N. C. 722; Audley's Case, 3 How. St. Tr. 401; 1 Hawk. P. C., ch. 41, § 6; 1 East, P. C. 446; 2 Bish. Cr. L., § 1135.

7 Hardtke v. S., 67 Wis. 552; S. v. Grubb, 55 Kan. 678. And must be proven beyond a reasonable doubt: Davis v. S., 43 Tex. 189. But it may be proved by circumstantial evidence where the victim has been reduced to insensibility: Word v. S., 12 Tex. Ap. 174. "Carnal knowledge" implies the act necessary to constitute the crime: McMath v. S., 55 Ga. 303; Burk v. S., 8 Tex. Ap. 336; Lujano v. S., 32 Tex. Ap. 414.

8 P. v. Crowley, 102 N. Y. 234; S. v. Hargrave, 65 N. C. 466; Brown v. S., 76 Ga. 623; S. v. Le Blanc, 1 Treadw. Const. 354; Reg. v. Allen, 9 C. & P. 31. The male organ must pass within the labia of the pudendum: Reg. v. Lines, 1 C. & K. 393. There must be *res in re:* 3 Inst. 60; 2 Bish. Cr. L., § 1132; 1 Hale, P. C. 428; P. v. Courier, 79 Mich. 366.

9 Brauer v. S., 25 Wis. 413; Reg. v. Russen, 1 East, P. C. 438; Reg. v. McRue, 8 C. & P. 641; Reg. v. Hughes, 9 C. & P. 752; Reg. v. Jordan, 9 C. & P. 118.

not necessary.[1] But mere proof of an attempt or of indecent liberties is not sufficient.[2] It is not necessary, however, that the act of copulation should have been completed.[3] No particular form of words on the part of the prosecuting witness is necessary in testifying to the fact of penetration. Her statement that the defendant had full connection or sexual intercourse with her is sufficient if the jury therefrom believe that the penetration was effected. There is a doubt as to whether, by the common law, proof of emission of semen was necessary to establish the offense. It is said in several English cases that, prior to the statute on the subject, the fact of emission must be alleged and proven.[4] But Lord Hale speaks of this doctrine as erroneous.[5] There is an English statute (9 Geo. 4, ch. 31) which renders proof of emission unnecessary,[6] and there are similar statutes in the various states, so that with us, in general, emission is immaterial.[7] But there are cases in the United States holding that, in the absence of statutes on the subject, emission must be proven.[8] While it thus appears that perhaps at common law, and generally by statute, the fact of emission is deemed immaterial, yet the capacity to emit is essential, so that mere penetration by a boy so young as to be incapable of emission, or by an adult who is impotent, is perhaps not rape.[9]

[1] P. v. Courier, 79 Mich. 366; Reg. v. Lines, 1 C. & K. 393.

[2] Wesley v. S., 65 Ga. 731; S. v. Dalton, 106 Mo. 463.

[3] Rodgers v. S., 30 Tex. Ap. 510; Reg. v. Allen, 9 C. & P. 31.

[4] Rex v. Hill, 1 East, P. C. 439; Rex v. Cave, 1 East, P. C. 438; Rex v. Burrows, Russ. & Ry. 519; Rex v. Cozins, 6 C. & P. 351.

[5] 1 Hale, P. C. 628.

[6] Rex v. Jennings, 4 C. & P. 249; Rex v. Reekspear, 1 Moody, 342; Johnson v. S., 27 Tex. Ap. 163. This statute is applicable also to carnal knowledge of a girl: Reg. v. Marsden, 2 Q. B. D. (1891), 149.

[7] Waller v. S., 40 Ala. 325; S. v. Burton, 1 Houst. Cr. C. 363; C. v. Thomas, 1 Va. Cases, 307. It is said that emission is presumed from the fact of penetration: Pennsylvania v. Sullivan, Addison, 143; Comstock v. S., 14 Neb. 205.

[8] S. v. Gray, 8 Jones, 170; Williams v. S., 14 Ohio, 222; Blackburn v. S., 22 Ohio St. 102; Brown v. S., 76 Ga. 623. Thus, where there was a statute rendering proof of emission in sodomy unnecessary, which statute was subsequently repealed, *held*, that after the repeal proof of emission was essential to establish the offense: P. v. Hodgkin, 94 Mich. 27.

[9] Hiltabiddle v. S., 35 Ohio St. 52; Nugent v. S., 18 Ala. 521. Though as to the case of impotency, Lord Hale is of the contrary opinion: 1 Hale, P. C. 628.

§ **451. The intent.**— The only intention necessary to constitute the offense is that of having connection by force and without consent. As will be seen hereafter in discussing assaults with intent to commit rape, this intent is material, and if the purpose was only to secure connection by consent, no such assault would be committed.[1] If the purpose of the defendant was not to effect the connection by force sufficient to overcome resistance on the part of the female, there would not be an intent to commit rape.[2] But in a prosecution for having carnal knowledge of a girl under the age of consent it is not essential that there be any intent to use force or overcome the will.[3] It is not, however, the intent with which the act is entered upon, but the force actually used, that determines whether rape has been committed.[4] As tending to show intent, prior assaults or declarations may be proven;[5] but evidence of prior indecent liberties and lewd acts should not be received.[6] As bearing on the question of intent, it has been held admissible for the defendant to prove conduct on the part of the female from which a belief on his part that she had consented might reasonably result, although, as a matter of fact, no consent was given.[7] Where the offense is in having connection with a child under the age of consent, belief on the part of the defendant that she was over the age of consent, and that therefore consent on her part would prevent the act from being criminal, cannot be shown. Connection with a child under the age of consent being criminal, one who has connection with a female, which would in any event be unlawful, must know, at his peril, whether her age is such as to make the act a rape.[8]

[1] *Infra*, § 463.

[2] Taylor v. S., 50 Ga. 79; Walton v. S., 29 Tex. Ap. 163; Reagan v. S., 28 Tex. Ap. 227; Reg. v. Stanton, 1 C. & K. 415; Reg. v. Wright, 4 F. & F. 967. Intent to surprise is not enough: McNair v. S., 53 Ala. 453, 2 Am. Cr. R. 583 and note.

[3] P. v. Courier, 79 Mich. 366.

[4] Dawson v. S., 29 Ark. 116.

[5] S. v. Patrick, 107 Mo. 147; Massey v. S., 31 Tex. Ap. 371.

[6] C. v. Merrill, 14 Gray, 415; Thompson v. S., 43 Tex. 583; Rex v. Lloyd, 7 C. & P. 318. Testimony of medical experts as to the effect of indecent liberties upon the mind of the female is inadmissible: P. v. Royal, 53 Cal. 62.

[7] Allen v. S., 87 Ala. 107.

[8] Lawrence v. C., 30 Grat. 845; S. v. Newton, 44 Ia. 45; S. v. Houx, 109 Mo. 654; S. v. Baskett, 111 Mo. 271; Holton v. S., 28 Fla. 303; Reg. v. Prince, L. R. 2 C. C. 154.

§ 452. **Indictment.**— The common-law form of indictment charges that the defendant "did feloniously ravish and carnally know," and it is not necessary to allege the force or want of consent, the term "ravish" implying both.[1] It seems to be not unusual, however, to use words indicating the force and want of consent, and for that purpose the term "violently" is equivalent to "forcibly."[2] The word "ravish," however, is the essential word in the common-law indictment,[3] and the allegation of carnal knowledge is a mere repetition.[4] As a substitute for "ravish" the word "rape" is insufficient.[5] Whatever the statutory expression may be, the allegation of the facts constituting the offense will be sufficient,[6] and it is held that words charging carnal knowledge "by force and against the will" are equivalent to the statutory term "ravish."[7] As in other cases of felony, the act should be charged as feloniously done;[8] but it seems that an allegation of a felonious assault and of an act forcibly and against the will is sufficient, without alleging the act as felonious.[9] The particular manner of the accomplishment of the act need not be alleged.[10] It is not necessary, even where the statute describes the methods of committing the offense, as by fraud, or artifice, or force and violence, to state in which of these methods the act was accomplished.[11] But in one case it is said that, under a statute specifying different methods of committing the offense, the acts constituting the alleged offense should be so stated as to advise the accused of the different ways in which he was charged to have committed the crime.[12] It is not necessary, though usual, to charge

[1] Harman v. C., 12 Serg. & R. 69; C. v. Fogerty, 8 Gray, 489; Williams v. S., 1 Tex. Ap. 90. But in a North Carolina case it is said that the allegation "forcibly and against the will" is necessary: S. v. Jim, 1 Dev. 142.

[2] Gutierrez v. S., 44 Tex. 587; Walling v. S., 7 Tex. Ap. 625; S. v. Williams, 32 La. An. 335; S. v. Johnson, 67 N. C. 55. To the contrary, see S. v. Blake, 39 Me. 322.

[3] Christian v. C., 23 Grat. 954.

[4] Gibson v. S., 17 Tex. Ap. 574.

[5] Davis v. S., 42 Tex. Ap. 226.

[6] P. v. McDonald, 9 Mich. 150; S. v. Mueller, 85 Wis. 203.

[7] S. v. Little, 67 Mo. 624.

[8] Hays v. S., 57 Miss. 783.

[9] S. v. Casford, 76 Ia. 330.

[10] McMath v. S., 55 Ga. 303.

[11] P. v. Snyder, 75 Cal. 323. If two methods are charged the state cannot be required to elect: Thompson v. S., 33 Tex. Ap. 472. An indictment charging both rape and carnal knowledge of a girl under age is not so defective as to deprive the court of jurisdiction: In re Lane, 135 U. S. 443.

[12] S. v. Vorey, 41 Minn. 134.

an assault.[1] Even if an assault is alleged there must be also allegation of the act in such manner as to indicate a ravishment, an allegation that the defendant did, by means of an assault, obtain carnal knowledge, etc., not being sufficient.[2] It is not necessary to allege specifically the sex of the person on whom the crime is alleged to have been committed, if the fact appears from the general language of the indictment.[3] Neither is it necessary to allege that the female was of the human species.[4] The term "female" is equivalent to the term "woman" used in a statute.[5] Even when the statute makes the offense of having carnal knowledge of a female child under ten years of age distinct from that of rape, it is not necessary, in an indictment for rape, to allege the age of the female to be over the age of consent.[6] Even under the theory that the two offenses are distinct, the crime of rape may be committed on a child under the age of consent.[7] It is not necessary to allege in the indictment that the woman is not the wife of the defendant;[8] nor that the accused is a male;[9] nor that he is over fourteen years of age.[10]

[1] Reg. v. Allen, 9 C. & P. 521.

[2] Elschlep v. S., 11 Tex. Ap. 301.

[3] S. v. Fielding, 32 Me. 585; Taylor v. C., 20 Grat. 825; S. v. Hussey, 7 Ia. 409; S. v. Warner, 74 Mo. 83; Warner v. S., 54 Ark. 660; S. v. Farmer, 4 Ired. 224; S. v. Terry, 4 Dev. & B. 152; Hill v. S., 3 Heisk. 317.

[4] S. v. Ward, 35 Minn. 182; S. v. Tom, 2 Jones, 414; Anderson v. S., 34 Ark. 257; O'Rourke v. S., 8 Tex. Ap. 70.

[5] Myers v. S., 84 Ala. 11; Gibson v. S., 17 Tex. Ap. 574.

[6] S. v. Fielding, 32 Me. 585; C. v. Sugland, 4 Gray, 7; Hill v. S., 3 Heisk. 317; Mobley v. S., 46 Miss. 501.

[7] See *supra*, § 442.

[8] C. v. Scannel, 11 Cush. 547; C. v. Fogerty, 8 Gray, 489; S. v. Williams, 9 Mont. 179. Even where the statute defines the offense as having connection, etc., with a woman not the wife of the accused, the fact that the woman, in a particular case, was not the wife of the accused may appear from the name, etc., without being specifically alleged: S. v. White, 44 Kan. 514. Where the crime is defined by statute in connection with that of incest as having carnal connection with any other woman than a sister or daughter forcibly, etc., it is necessary to allege that the woman was not the daughter or sister, in order to specify the form of the offense charged: Howard v. S., 11 Ohio St. 328.

[9] S. v. Tom, 2 Jones, 414; Brown v. S., 72 Miss. 997; Warner v. S., 54 Ark. 660; Cornelius v. S., 13 Tex. Ap. 349.

[10] S. v. Ward, 35 Minn. 182; P. v. Ah Yek, 29 Cal. 575; Davis v. S., 42 Tex. 226; Word v. S., 12 Tex. Ap. 174; Cornelius v. S., 13 Tex. Ap. 349. Want of physical capacity is a matter of defense: P. v. Wessel, 98 Ca' 352.

§ **453. Forms.**— There is a well-settled common-law form which is simple and direct, and applicable to all cases except those where the female is under the age of consent. Such variations from it as are likely to be found are pointed out in the note:

FOR RAPE.

That A. B., in the county aforesaid, on the ——, in and upon one C. D. feloniously and violently did make an assault, and her, the said C. D., then and there violently and against her will feloniously did ravish and carnally know.[1]

FOR CARNAL KNOWLEDGE OF FEMALE CHILD.

That A. B., in the county aforesaid, on ——, did then and there in a rude, insolent and angry manner unlawfully and feloniously touch one S. M., a woman child then and there under twelve years of age, to wit, of the age of nine years, and did then and there unlawfully and feloniously have carnal knowledge of her, the said S. M.[2]

§ **454. Included offenses.**— An indictment for the offense necessarily includes an assault with intent to commit the offense.[3] So there may be a conviction, under an indictment for

[1] This form from Archbold is substantially copied into all the form books. Sometimes the age of the female is given so as to show that she was above the age of consent: See C. v. Fogerty, 8 Gray, 489; P. v. Jackson, 3 Park. Cr. 391; but this averment is unnecessary, as already shown. A slightly different form of averment is illustrated by the indictment for assault with intent to commit rape, given *infra*, § 467.

[2] See Batterson v. S., 63 Ind. 531. The indictment in that case averred as to the age of the child simply that she was under twelve years of age, that being the age of consent fixed by statute. But it is usual in such cases to aver also the actual age under a *videlicet*, and such an averment has been introduced in the form here given, though it is probably unnecessary anywhere. It has been held that the allegation that the girl was of the age of eleven years was sufficient to charge that she was under the age of fourteen, the statutory age of consent: P. v. Gardner, 98 Cal. 127. As the offense is statutory the language must be adapted in each state to that found in the statute.

[3] P. v. Courier, 79 Mich. 366; P. v. Abbott, 97 Mich. 484; Prindeville v. P., 42 Ill. 217; S. v. Mueller, 85 Wis. 203; Pratt v. S., 51 Ark. 167; Polson v. S., 137 Ind. 519; S. v. Cross, 12 Ia. 66; S. v. Atherton, 50 Ia. 189; S. v. Vinsant, 49 Ia. 241; S. v. Peters, 56 Ia. 263; S. v. Kendall, 73 Ia. 255; S. v. Frazier, 53 Kan. 87; S. v. May, 42 La. An. 82. It is error to instruct the jury with reference to the completed crime where the evidence shows only an assault to commit it, even though the jury convict of the assault only: S. v. Kyne, 86 Ia. 616.

the offense, of an attempt to commit it.[1] The defendant is entitled to an instruction with reference to an assault with intent to commit when put on trial for the completed offense;[2] and even if the evidence shows the completion of the act, a conviction for the assault with intent will not be erroneous.[3] As the assault with intent to commit the crime is included in a charge of the crime itself, a count charging the assault may be united with one charging the offense.[4] So the offense of simple assault is necessarily included in the charge of rape.[5] If the assault is charged in such form as to show a battery, there may be a conviction of an assault and battery as an included offense.[6] Where rape and the offense of having carnal knowledge of a female child under the age of consent are regarded

[1] Glover v. C., 86 Va. 382; S. v. Frazier, 53 Kan. 87. But an attempt to commit does not necessarily amount to an assault with intent to commit: P. v. Gardner, 98 Cal. 127. And see P. v. Lee Kong, 95 Cal. 666; S. v. Godfrey, 17 Oreg. 300.

[2] Bethel v. C., 80 Ky. 526; Massey v. S., 31 Tex. Ap. 371; P. v. Abbott, 97 Mich. 484. But where the crime is established it is not error to refuse to instruct as to an assault with intent: P. v. Chavez, 103 Cal. 407.

[3] S. v. Archer, 54 N. H. 465; S. v. Smith, 43 Vt. 324; P. v. Miller, 96 Mich. 119; Pratt v. S., 51 Ark. 167. *Contra*, S. v. Mitchell, 54 Kan. 516; S. v. Frazier, 54 Kan. 719. It was held otherwise under statute: Kelsey v. S., 62 Ga. 558. Also in England before statutory provisions on the subject: Rex v. Harmwood, 1 East, P. C. 411; Reg. v. Nicholls, 2 Cox, 182; but now such a conviction is sustained: Reg. v. Ryland, 11 Cox, 101. For the discussion of a similar question, involving an assault by a slave upon a white woman, see Wash v. S., 14 Sm. & M. 120. Under charge of assault with intent, there may be a conviction, though the evidence shows the completed crime: P. v. Creadon, 162 Mass. 466.

[4] Harman v. C., 12 Serg. & R. 69; P. v. Tyler, 35 Cal. 553; S. v. Sutton, 4 Gill, 494.

[5] P. v. McDonald, 9 Mich. 150; Campbell v. P., 34 Mich. 351; P. v. Courier, 79 Mich. 366; S. v. Vinsant, 49 Ia. 241; S. v. Peters, 56 Ia. 263; S. v. Bagan, 41 Minn. 285; Reg. v. Guthrie, L. R. 1 C. C. 241; Reg. v. Hapgood, L. R. 1 C. C. 221; Reg. v. Folkes, 2 M. & Rob. 460; Rex v. Dawson, 3 Stark. 62; Reg. v. Catherall, 13 Cox, 109; Reg. v. Dungey, 4 F. & F. 99.

[6] Hanna v. P., 19 Mich. 316; Richardson v. S., 54 Ala. 158; Mills v. S., 52 Ind. 187; S. v. McDevitt, 69 Ia. 549; S. v. Kyne, 86 Ia. 616. Where the evidence shows a battery, instructions as to assault and battery are sufficient without any instruction as to simple assault: S. v. Sigg, 86 Ia. 746. Even if it appears that the intercourse was consented to, there may still be a conviction for the assault and battery if the act was done in such a brutal and violent manner as to involve personal injury, the consent to the intercourse not necessarily involving consent to such injury: Richie v. S., 58 Ind. 355.

as distinct crimes, an indictment for the latter will not sustain a conviction for the former.[1] Under an indictment for rape, defendant may be convicted of fornication.[2] Whether rape may also amount to adultery or incest will be considered in discussing those crimes.[3]

§ **455. Evidence; outcry or complaint.**— Evidence of complaint made by the female with reference to the act is admissible in two ways. In the first place her outcries and declarations immediately connected with the act may be shown as part of the *res gestæ*,[4] and for the same purpose marks of violence on the person may be shown.[5] In the second place, as it is essential that the female should have resisted so far as possible,[6] it is important to show, in corroboration of her evidence, that she made outcry at the time, and complaint afterwards.[7] Therefore, where it appears there was no outcry and that no complaint was made immediately or as soon as reasonable opportunity offered, there should not be a conviction,[8] the absence of outcry or complaint being admissible as discrediting and overcoming the otherwise uncorroborated testimony of the prosecutrix.[9] Failure to make outcry or complaint may be ex-

[1] S. v. Erickson, 45 Wis. 86; S. v. Cherry, 1 Swan, 160.

[2] C. v. Parker, 146 Pa. St. 343. But it must appear that the parties were not married to each other, that being an essential fact in a charge of fornication: C. v. Murphy, 2 Allen, 163. There are cases holding that the crime of fornication is not included in a charge of rape: S. v. Shear, 51 Wis. 460; Speer v. S., 60 Ga. 381.

[3] See *infra*, §§ 1092 and 1121.

[4] McMath v. S., 55 Ga. 303; P. v. Flynn, 96 Mich. 276; Castillo v. S. 31 Tex. Ap. 145; S. v. Shettleworth, 18 Minn. 208; Rex v. Clarke, 2 Stark. 241.

[5] S. v. Shettleworth, 18 Minn. 208.

[6] *Supra*, § 440.

[7] S. v. Brown, 54 Kan. 71; Hannon v. S., 70 Wis. 448.

[8] S. v. Patrick, 107 Mo. 147; P. v. O'Sullivan, 104 N. Y. 481; Monroe v. S., 71 Miss. 196; Richards v. S., 36 Neb. 17; S. v. Cone, 1 Jones, 18; Gazley v. S., 17 Tex. Ap. 267; Lawson v. S., 17 Tex. Ap. 292; Thompson v. S., 33 Tex. Ap. 472.

[9] Pefferling v. S., 40 Tex. 486; Topolanck v. S., 40 Tex. 160; Rhea v. S., 30 Tex. Ap. 483; Whitney v. S., 35 Ind. 503; Eyler v. S., 71 Ind. 49; S. v. Tomlinson, 11 Ia. 401; Barney v. P., 22 Ill. 160; S. v. Wilkins, 66 Vt. 1; Smith v. S., 77 Ga. 705. Evidence that the prosecutrix cried continuously while going home after the alleged assault is admissible, as indication of distress is material and competent: S. v. Bedard, 65 Vt. 278. So it may be shown that the female alleged to have been injured requested another to go before a magistrate and report the offense: Smith v. S., 47 Ala. 540. Failure to make outcry will not prevent conviction for assault to commit rape

cused, however, where it is shown that the female refrained from doing so on account of fear,[1] or by reason of youth and inexperience.[2] The inference arising against the truth of the charge from long silence on the part of the female is not a presumption of law but a matter of fact for the consideration of the jury.[3] While delay in making complaint may tend to discredit the evidence of the prosecutrix, the mere lapse of time is not a test of admissibility in evidence of such complaint, but is only matter for the consideration of the jury in determining the weight to be given to it.[4] Evidence of subsequent complaint by the prosecutrix being admissible, therefore, not as original evidence or as a part of the *res gestæ*, but to overcome a suspicion which would otherwise attach to evidence tending to show her want of consent and to corroborate her testimony, the fact that such complaint was made is alone admissible and not its particulars or details.[5] But evidence of the complaint

if it appears that actual resistance was made which was effectual: S. v. Brown, 54 Kan. 71.

[1] For instance, in the case of rape committed by the father on his daughter of fourteen years of age: S. v. Wilcox, 111 Mo. 569. But such relation between the parties was held not to excuse want of outcry in S. v. Cone, 1 Jones, 18, and Lawson v. S., 17 Tex. Ap. 292.

[2] Sutton v. P., 145 Ill. 279; S. v. Marshall, Phil. 49; S. v. Cross, 12 Ia. 66.

[3] S. v. Peter, 8 Jones, 19; S. v. Cross, 12 Ia. 66; S. v. Tarr, 28 Ia. 397; S. v. Hagerman, 47 Ia. 151; Crockett v. S., 49 Ga. 185.

[4] S. v. Niles, 47 Vt. 82; S. v. Mulkern, 85 Me. 106; S. v. Witten, 100 Mo. 525; Hill v. S., 5 Lea, 725. The delay may be explained by showing excuse therefor: S. v. Shettleworth, 18 Minn. 208.

[5] Lacy v. S., 45 Ala. 80; Barnett v. S., 83 Ala. 40; Lee v. S., 74 Wis. 45; McMurrin v. Rigby, 80 Ia. 322; S. v. Clark, 69 Ia. 294; S. v. Richards, 33 Ia. 420; P. v. Mayes, 66 Cal. 597; P. v. Stewart, 97 Cal. 238; P. v. Graham, 21 Cal. 261; Oleson v. S., 11 Neb. 276; Ellis v. S., 25 Fla. 702; Pefferling v. S., 40 Tex. 486; Holst v. S., 23 Tex. Ap. 1; McGee v. S., 21 Tex. Ap. 670; S. v. Robertson, 38 La. An. 618; S. v. Langford, 45 La. An. 1177; Reg. v. Megson, 9 C. & P. 420; Reg. v. Mercer, 6 Jur. 243. Thus, the statement of the prosecutrix as to who committed the offense cannot be shown: Bean v. P., 124 Ill. 576; Stephens v. S., 11 Ga. 225; S. v. Hill, 2 Hill, 607; S. v. Shettleworth, 18 Minn. 208. *Contra*, S. v. Cook, — Ia. —, 61 N. W. R. 185. She may be asked whether, in making complaint, she named a person as having committed the offense without being allowed to give the name: Reg. v. Osborne, Car. & M. 622. It is not competent to show that the prosecutrix, when making complaint, said that certain scratches on her neck were made by the accused in attempting to ravish her: Scott v. S., 48 Ala. 420. Evidence of complaints is receivable as confirmatory evidence only: S. v. Peter, 14 La. An. 521.

may extend to showing what the person made complaint of.[1] This rule which forbids the prosecution from showing, either by the prosecutrix or others, the details of her complaint made after the commission of the offense, though thus supported by the overwhelming weight of authority, has not been universally recognized. In a few cases it has been said that the same reasons which permit the introduction of evidence that the complaint was made, require that the complaint in detail should also be shown.[2]

§ 456. **Evidence of complaints only corroborative.**— The doctrine that evidence of subsequent complaint is admissible is based on the theory of a corroboration of the testimony of prosecutrix, and all the cases are of that kind,[3] and therefore it has no applicability where the prosecutrix does not testify as a witness;[4] for instance, where she is dead,[5] or is incompetent because so young that her testimony is not admissible,[6] or because imbecile.[7] Her complaints are not to be shown as independent evidence,[8] but the authorities generally agree that, after prosecutrix has testified as to having made complaint, the particulars of her complaint may, on cross-examination, be in-

[1] S. v. Mitchell, 68 Ia. 116. It is proper to show the statement of prosecutrix as to who did the act and that it was without her consent: S. v. Cook, — Ia. —, 61 N. W. R. 185; S. v. Carroll, 67 Vt. 477.

[2] S. v. Kinney, 44 Conn. 153; McCombs v. S., 8 Ohio St. 643; Phillips v. S., 9 Humph. 245; Benstine v. S., 2 Lea, 169. And see Barnett v. S., 83 Ala. 40, and S. v. Freeman, 100 N. C. 429. See, also, language of Baron Parke in Reg. v. Walker, 2 M. & Rob. 212.

[3] See, especially, Johnson v. S., 17 Ohio, 593; Laughlin v. S., 18 Ohio, 99; Phillips v. S., 9 Humph. 246.

[4] Reg. v. Guttridges, 9 C. & P. 471.

[5] Reg. v. Megson, 9 C. & P. 420.

[6] Weldon v. S., 32 Ind. 81; Hornbeck v. S., 35 Ohio St. 277. It was at one time thought that in such cases the statement of the child not under oath might be taken where she was too young to be examined under oath: 1 Hale. P. C. 634; Rex v. Brasier, 1 East, P. C. 443. But it was afterwards held that if the child was too immature to be sworn, her statements not under oath were likewise inadmissible: 1 East, P. C. 444; 4 Bl. Com. 214; 1 Chit. Cr. L. 590; Reg. v. Guttridges, 9 C. & P. 471; Reg. v. Nicholas, 2 C. & K. 246. An English statute now provides that a statement not under oath may be received in such cases: Reg. v. Wealand, 20 Q. B. D. 827; Reg. v. Paul, 25 Q. B. D. 202. A five-year-old child held not too young to testify on oath as to such a crime: S. v. Juneau, 88 Wis. 180.

[7] P. v. McGee, 1 Denio, 19; S. v. Meyers, — Neb. —, 64 N. W. R. 697; Hornbeck v. S., 35 Ohio St. 277.

[8] Hornbeck v. S., 35 Ohio St. 277; Oleson v. S., 11 Neb. 276; P. v. Gage, 62 Mich. 274; P. v. Hicks, 98 Mich. 86.

quired into,[1] and that thereupon, if the cross-examination has developed only a portion of such complaint, the balance may be brought out on re-direct;[2] and further, that if an attempt is made to impeach the credibility of her testimony, she may show the details of her complaint by way of corroboration.[3]

§ 457. **Other discrediting evidence.**— On the same theory on which evidence of outcry or complaint is important, it is held that the continuance of friendly relations between the prosecutrix and the defendant after the time of the alleged crime will tend to disprove the offense.[4] Statements of the prosecutrix inconsistent with the fact of the commission of the crime are, of course, admissible.[5]

§ 458. **Corroboration of prosecutrix.**— The charge of rape is one which, as Lord Hale observes, is "an accusation easily to be made, hard to be proved, and harder to be defended by the party accused, though never so innocent,"[6] and the court may properly warn the jury of the danger in convicting a defendant on the uncorroborated testimony of the prosecutrix.[7] As has already been pointed out,[8] an important corroboration is the making of outcry at the time, if it would be of any avail, and speedy complaint afterward.[9] However, corroboration of the testimony of the prosecutrix by other evidence is not, in the absence of statute, absolutely essential,[10] and a conviction may be had even on the uncorroborated evidence of an infant, under the years of discretion, where it appears that she is competent to testify, or upon the uncorroborated evidence of the prosecutrix, although she is shown to be unchaste.[11] But

[1] Barnett v. S., 83 Ala. 40; Reg. v. Walker, 2 M. & Rob. 212; Reg. v. Wood, 14 Cox, 46; Reg. v. Eyre, 2 F. & F. 579.

[2] Barnett v. S., 83 Ala. 40.

[3] Barnett v. S., 83 Ala. 40; Scott v. S., 48 Ala. 420; Griffin v. S., 76 Ala. 29; S. v. Freeman, 100 N. C. 429; S. v. Clark, 69 Ia. 294.

[4] S. v. Patrick, 107 Mo. 147; Barney v. P., 22 Ill. 160; Sutton v. P., 145 Ill. 279.

[5] Allen v. S., 87 Ala. 107; Austine v. P., 110 Ill. 248; Sherwin v. P., 69 Ill. 55; Kennedy v. P., 44 Ill. 283; S. v. Cassidy, 85 Ia. 145.

[6] 1 Hale, P. C. 635.

[7] P. v. Benson, 6 Cal. 221; S. v. Hagerman, 47 Ia. 151.

[8] *Supra*, § 455.

[9] S. v. Cook, — Ia. —, 61 N. W. R. 185. And see 1 Hale, P. C. 633; 1 East, P. C. 445; Topolanck v. S., 40 Tex. 160.

[10] Garrison v. P. 6 Neb. 274; P. v. Stewart, 90 Cal. 212; P. v. Mesa, 93 Cal. 580; Gonzales v. S., 32 Tex. Ap. 611.

[11] McGuff v. S., 88 Ala. 147; Boddie v. S., 52 Ala. 395; P. v. Mayes, 66 Cal. 597; Anonymous, 1 Russ., C. & M. 932.

the court may find the uncorroborated evidence of the prosecutrix not entitled to sufficient weight, under the circumstances, to support a conviction.[1] Where the defendant is entitled to be a witness, and clearly and explicitly denies the commission of the offense, there must be evidence corroborating the testimony of the prosecutrix to authorize a conviction.[2] But to constitute such corroboration of the prosecutrix, it is not necessary that she be supported by other witnesses as to the particular act constituting the offense. If she is corroborated as to material facts and circumstances which tend to support her testimony, and from which, together with her testimony as to the principal facts, the inference of guilt may be drawn, this is sufficient.[3] In some states there are statutes requiring the corroboration of the prosecutrix to warrant a conviction.[4]

§ 459. **Physical condition.**— As tending to show the commission of the offense, the state and appearance of the person claimed to have been injured, marks of violence on her person, the condition of her dress, etc., shortly after the alleged injury, may be proven as original evidence.[5] Evidence as to stains on the clothing of the prosecutrix is also admissible;[6] and so is evidence of physical examination showing bruises and other

[1] P. v. Ardaga, 51 Cal. 371; Leoni v. S., 44 Ala. 110.

[2] Mathews v S., 19 Neb. 330; Oleson v. S., 11 Neb. 276; Fisk v. S., 9 Neb. 62.

[3] Fager v. S., 22 Neb. 332; Hammond v. S., 39 Neb. 252.

[4] In Iowa the statute requires that the testimony of the prosecutrix be corroborated by other evidence tending to connect the defendant with the commission of the crime, and it is held that the fact of the commission of the crime may be established by the testimony of the prosecutrix alone, and the admission by the defendant of having had sexual connection with the prosecutrix at the time complained of may furnish sufficient corroboration of his connection with the offense: S. v. McLaughlin, 44 Ia. 82; S. v. Cassidy, 85 Ia. 145; so may his conduct: S. v. Watson, 81 Ia. 380. But evidence that prosecutrix was bruised and made complaint would not, under such statute, be sufficient corroboration: S. v. Stowell, 60 Ia. 535. The sufficiency of the corroboration is for the jury: S. v. Moore, 81 Ia. 578. As to sufficiency of corroboration in particular cases, see S. v. Comstock, 46 Ia. 265; S. v. Mitchell, 68 Ia. 116. Under this statute corroboration is not required in case of assault with intent to commit rape: S. v. Hatfield, 75 Ia. 592; Rogers v. Winch, 76 Ia. 546; S. v. Grossheim, 79 Ia. 75; S. v. Cook, — Ia. —, 61 N. W. R. 185; or in case of forcible defilement: S. v. Montgomery, 79 Ia. 737.

[5] Pefferling v. S., 40 Tex. 486; Hornbeck v. S., 35 Ohio St. 277; Polson v. S., 137 Ind. 519; S. v. Sanford, 124 Mo. 484; Rex v. Clarke, 2 Stark. 241.

[6] S. v. Montgomery, 79 Ia. 737.

injuries received, the weight of such evidence depending upon the length of time that has elapsed after the alleged injury before the making of the examination; but the length of time is a matter going to the credibility of the evidence, and not to its competency.[1] There is, however, no authority on the part of the court to require an examination of the person of the prosecutrix by medical experts,[2] and the defendant is not entitled to an instruction that a failure of the prosecution to call expert testimony to the fact of the existence of such injuries as would result from penetration should operate in favor of the defendant.[3]

§ 460. Previous unchastity; relations between parties, etc. While the want of chastity of the female is no defense, for the crime of rape may be committed upon a prostitute or upon the mistress of the assailant,[4] yet the bad character of the prosecutrix as to chastity is material as tending to show that the evidence of want of consent is not sufficient.[5] The bad character of the prosecutrix in this respect is to be shown by proof of general reputation only, and not by proof of particular instances of unchastity.[6] The prosecutrix cannot be cross-

[1] S. v. Teipner, 36 Minn. 535; C. v. Allen, 135 Pa. St. 483; S. v. McLaughlin, 44 Ia. 82; S. v. Watson, 81 Ia. 380.

[2] McGuff v. S., 88 Ala. 147.

[3] Comstock v. S., 14 Neb. 205.

[4] 1 Hawk. P. C., ch. 41, § 2; 1 Hale, P. C. 629; Pratt v. S., 19 Ohio St. 277; Pleasant v. S., 13 Ark. 360; S. C., 15 Ark. 624; Wright v. S., 4 Humph. 194; P. v. Hartman, 103 Cal. 242; Wilson v. S., 17 Tex. Ap. 525; McQuirk v. S., 84 Ala. 435; Rex v. Barker, 3 C. & P. 589.

[5] McQuirk v. S., 84 Ala. 435; O'Blenis v. S., 47 N. J. 279; S. v. Daniel, 87 N. C. 507; S. v. Murray, 63 N. C. 31; S. v. Jefferson, 6 Ired. 305; Sherwin v. P., 69 Ill. 55; P. v. Benson, 6 Cal. 221; Rice v. S., 35 Fla. 236; Shields v. S., 32 Tex. Ap. 498; Rex v. Barker, 3 C. & P. 589; Reg. v. Clay, 5 Cox, 146. In rebuttal of evidence of bad reputation for chastity the prosecution may show the good character of prosecutrix in that respect: P. v. Tyler, 36 Cal. 522. And it is said that evidence of good character is competent by way of confirming her credibility. (But this is probably not correct as a general proposition): Turney v. S., 8 Sm. & M. 104. Where there is no question as to force and want of consent, previous unchastity cannot be shown: Steinke v. S., 33 Tex. Ap. 65.

[6] S. v. White, 35 Mo. 500; S. v. Knapp, 45 N. H. 148; S. v. Forshner, 43 N. H. 89; McCombs v. S., 8 Ohio St. 643; McDermott v. S., 13 Ohio St. 332; McQuirk v. S., 84 Ala. 435; Camp v. S., 3 Ga. 417; Boddie v. S., 52 Ala. 395; S. v. Jefferson, 6 Ired. 305; S. v. Brown, 55 Kan. 766; Mitchell v. Work, 13 R. I. 645; P. v. McLean, 71 Mich. 309; Strang v. P., 24 Mich. 1; C. v. Harris, 131 Mass. 336; P. v. Jackson, 3 Park. Cr. R. 391; Pleasant v. S., 15 Ark. 624; Rice v. S., 35 Fla. 236; Wilson v. S., 17 Tex.

examined as to specific unchaste conduct with others than the defendant.[1] While the great weight of authority is in support of the proposition that evidence of specific acts of unchastity on the part of the prosecutrix with others than the defendant is not admissible, there are a few cases in which the introduction of such evidence is upheld on the ground that such acts show the probability of consent in the case in question.[2] The general prohibition in regard to showing specific acts of unchastity does not apply to previous illicit intercourse with the accused.[3] Such prior intercourse is admissible to give rise to a presumption of consent to the act in question.[4] As evidence of unchastity on the part of prosecutrix goes to the question of consent, it is immaterial in a prosecution for having carnal

Ap. 525; Dorsey v. S., 1 Tex. Ap. 33; Rogers v. S., 1 Tex. Ap. 187; Reg. v. Hodgson, Russ. & Ry. 211; Rex v. Clarke, 2 Stark. 241. A particular act of lewdness by prosecutrix, not known to defendant at the time of his assault upon her, is not admissible: S. v. Henry, 5 Jones, 65. Testimony to show previous promiscuous sexual intercourse on the part of prosecutrix is admissible: Woods v. P., 55 N. Y. 515; Brown v. S., 72 Miss. 997. Where the prosecutrix claims that the connection with her was while she was unconscious and proves subsequent want of the physical evidences of virginity, the effect of such testimony may be overcome by proof of specific acts of unchastity: Sherwin v. P., 69 Ill. 55. So where the prosecutrix is shown after the alleged injury to be bruised and infected with venereal disease, proof of sexual intercourse with other specific persons about the time of the commission of the alleged offense is admissible: Nugent v. S., 18 Ala. 521. Evidence as to the reputation of the prosecutrix for unchastity should be limited to such reputation before the alleged commission of the crime: S. v. Ward, 73 Ia. 532.

[1] Shartzer v. S., 63 Md. 149; S. v. Turner, 1 Houst. Cr. C. 76. *Contra*, S. v. Johnson, 28 Vt. 512; S. v. Reed, 39 Vt. 417; Titus v. S., 7 Baxt. 132; Brown v. S., 72 Miss. 997. It is said that if prosecutrix is asked on cross-examination whether she had previously had connection with a particular person, her answer is final and cannot be contradicted: Reg. v. Holmes, L. R. 1 C. C. 334; P. v. McLean, 71 Mich. 309. But if she denies that she had connection with other men, presumably those men may be called to contradict her: Reg. v. Robins, 2 M. & Rob. 512. If the question as to particular acts becomes proper on cross-examination the prosecutrix is not privileged from answering: Titus, v. S. 7 Baxt. 132; Brown v. S., 72 Miss. 997; Bedgood v. S., 115 Ind. 275; P. v. Abbot, 19 Wend. 192.

[2] Benstine v. S., 2 Lea, 169; P. v. Abbot, 19 Wend. 192; S. v. Freeman, 100 N. C. 429.

[3] Pleasant v. S., 15 Ark. 624; Bedgood v. S., 115 Ind. 275; Wilson v. S., 17 Tex. Ap. 525; McQuirk v. S., 84 Ala. 435; Reg. v. Hodgson, Russ. & Ry. 211.

[4] P. v. Goulette, 82 Mich. 36; Hall v. P., 47 Mich. 636; Barnes v. S., 88 Ala. 204; S. v. Cook, 65 Ia. 560; Rex v. Martin, 6 C. & P. 562; Reg. v. Riley, 18 Q. B. D. 481.

knowledge of a girl under the age of consent, for in such a case want of consent to the act is not essential.[1]

§ 461. **Other crimes; burden of proof, etc.**— Proof of other distinct and disconnected crimes of the same character by defendant is not admissible.[2] But in sexual crimes a greater latitude is allowed in proving other like occurrences than is deemed proper in other cases, and proof of previous assaults or attempts as against the prosecutrix, made by the defendant, may be shown as indicating his intention and disposition toward her.[3] It is said in one case that where several acts of unlawful intercourse are testified to by the prosecutrix, the state must elect to rely upon a particular act, and the court must thereupon exclude from the consideration of the jury all testimony with reference to other acts not tending to directly prove the commission of the particular act relied upon for conviction.[4] But in other cases it is said that the prosecution may show repeated acts, and that they were committed against the will of the prosecutrix, in explanation of her conduct at the time of the specific act relied on.[5] Evidence of other ill-usage, not sexual in character, is not admissible.[6] Statements made by the accused prior to the alleged offense

[1] P. v. Abbott, 97 Mich. 484; P. v. Glover, 71 Mich. 303; S. v. Duffey, 128 Mo. 549; P. v. Johnson, 106 Cal. 289. But the prosecution may show previous relations between prosecutrix and accused as indicating his opportunity and the like: P. v. Abbott, 97 Mich. 484. And see cases cited under the following section.

[2] S. v. Walters, 45 Ia. 389; Porath v. S., 90 Wis. 527; Janzen v. P., — Ill. —, 42 N. E. R. 862; Parkinson v. P., 135 Ill. 401.

[3] Proper v. S., 85 Wis. 615; Palin v. S., 38 Neb. 862; Williams v. S., 8 Humph. 584; P. v. O'Sullivan, 104 N. Y. 481; S. v. Walters, 45 Ia. 389; S. v. Knapp, 45 N. H. 148; Sharp v. S., 15 Tex. Ap. 171. A similar principle is recognized in cases of adultery: P. v. Jenness, 5 Mich. 305; C. v. Merriam, 14 Pick. 518; C. v. Nichols, 114 Mass. 285; S. v. Stice, 88 Ia. 27. Evidence in a prosecution for carnal knowledge of a girl under the age of consent that defendant took her to a house of prostitution kept by himself is admissible, although it proves his guilt of the crime of keeping such a house: Cross v. S., 138 Ind. 254.

[4] S. v. Bonsor, 49 Kan. 758; P. v. Jenness, 5 Mich. 305. But evidence that the act relied upon was at another time and place than that testified to by the prosecution will not constitute a defense: P. v. Ten Elshof, 92 Mich. 167. If the prosecution is for connection by consent with a girl under the age of consent, evidence of connection after she attained the age of consent is inadmissible: P. v. Etter, 81 Mich. 570.

[5] S. v. Parish, 104 N. C. 679; Reg. v. Rearden. 4 F. & F. 76.

[6] P. v. Tyler, 36 Cal. 522.

with reference to his carnal passion for prosecutrix and the belief that she would not yield to his desires is admissible,[1] and also evidence that defendant had at previous times made improper proposals to the prosecutrix.[2] The prosecution should establish the offense beyond a reasonable doubt,[3] and has the burden throughout.[4]

[1] Barnes v. S., 88 Ala. 204.

[2] P. v. Manahan, 32 Cal. 68.

[3] Austine v. P., 51 Ill. 236.

[4] P. v. McWhorter, 93 Mich. 641.

CHAPTER 21.

ASSAULT WITH INTENT TO COMMIT RAPE; OR ATTEMPT TO COMMIT RAPE.

§ 462. **What acts necessary; included assault.**— This offense is one of the forms of assault with felonious intent which have been elsewhere discussed in connection with the general subject of assault;[1] but the nature of the intent required connects it so closely with the crime of rape that it seems better to consider it here. As to the assault itself, little need be added to the general doctrines of assault discussed in the chapter on that subject. To constitute an assault with intent to commit rape there must be an assault for that purpose upon the person intended to be ravished.[2] If there is no intent to use the force necessary to constitute rape there may be a conviction for an assault involved in the purpose of having sexual connection, or for an aggravated assault, depending on the circumstances.[3] Thus, a simple or an aggravated assault is an included offense under the charge of an assault with intent to commit rape.[4] Such a charge does not necessarily include assault and battery,[5] but by charging violence used a battery may also be included.[6] To what extent assault and battery and assault with intent to commit rape are included in a charge of rape itself has already been considered.[7] There is in some states provision for punishing attempts to commit crime, in-

[1] *Supra*, §§ 263–272.

[2] Garrison v. P., 6 Neb. 274. A mere attempt may not constitute an assault: Preisker v. P., 47 Ill. 382.

[3] S. v. Priestley, 74 Mo. 24; Skinner v. S., 28 Neb. 814; Outlaw v. S., 35 Tex. 481; Thompson v. S., 43 Tex. 583; Irving v. S., 9 Tex. Ap. 66; Sanford v. S., 12 Tex. Ap. 196; Shields v. S., 32 Tex. Ap. 498; Porter v. S., 33 Tex. Ap. 385; Reg. v. Case, 1 Den. 580; Reg. v. Guthrie, L. R. 1 C. C. 241; Rex v. Nichol, Russ. & Ry. 130; Reg. v. Folkes, 2 M. & R. 460; Reg. v. Stanton, 1 C. & K. 415; Reg. v. Williams, 8 C. & P. 286. And see Alexander v. Blodgett, 44 Vt. 476.

[4] Curry v. S., 4 Tex. Ap. 574; Hemanus v. S., 7 Tex. Ap. 372.

[5] S. v. McDevitt, 69 Ia. 549.

[6] S. v. Fontenette, 38 La. An. 61; S. v. Keen, 10 Wash. 93; Barnard v. C., 94 Ky. 285.

[7] See *supra*, § 454.

cluding attempts to commit rape, and not necessarily involving an assault.[1]

§ **463. Intent.**— The intent is an essential element of an assault with intent to commit rape and must in some way appear.[2] To warrant a conviction the jury must be satisfied, not only that the prisoner intended to gratify his passion on the person of the prosecutrix, but that he intended to do so at all events and notwithstanding any resistance on her part.[3] And the intention must be to penetrate, otherwise the assault would not be with intent to commit rape.[4] But according to the authorities hereafter to be discussed, which hold that an attempt to have carnal knowledge of a girl under the age of consent is an assault with intent to commit rape, even though she is a consenting party, intent in such cases to overcome resistance is not essential.[5] Even in such case there must be an attempt to have connection; mere solicitation will not constitute the crime.[6] If the purpose of the accused appears to have been to procure consent, if possible, to the act, but upon resistance or outcry being made he abandon his purpose, the crime is not assault with intent to commit rape.[7] But if it appears that

P. v. Gardner, 98 Cal. 127; S. v. Berzaman, 10 Wash. 277. And see Rex v. Butler, 6 C. & P. 368; Reg. v. Martin, 9 C. & P. 213; Reg. v. Johnson, L. & C. 632.

2 Barr v. P., 113 Ill. 471; Peterson v. S., 14 Tex. Ap. 162; Hunter v. S., 29 Fla. 486. Therefore the court should instruct the jury as to the constituents of the crime of rape: Fulcher v. S., 41 Tex. 233. A husband who by threats and violence attempts to compel another person to commit rape on the former's wife is guilty of assault with intent to commit rape: S. v. Dowell, 106 N. C. 722.

3 Rex v. Lloyd, 7 C. & P. 318; Reg. v. Wright, 4 F. & F. 967; Joice v. S., 53 Ga. 50; S. v. Cross, 12 Ia. 66; S. v. Hagerman, 47 Ia. 151; S. v. Canada, 68 Ia. 397; White v. S., 136 Ind. 308; Moore v. S., 79 Wis. 546; Hunter v. S., 29 Fla. 486; Bradley v. S., 32 Ark. 704; Walton v. S., 29 Tex. Ap. 163; Brown v. S., 27 Tex. Ap. 330; Langan v. S., 27 Tex. Ap. 498; Passmore v. S., 29 Tex. Ap. 241. The intent must appear beyond a reasonable doubt: Krum v. S., 19 Neb. 728; House v. S., 9 Tex. Ap. 567. Defendant's testimony as to his intent is admissible: Lewellen v. S., 33 Tex. Ap. 412. The court should instruct as to the force which must have been intended: Shields v. S., 32 Tex. Ap. 498.

4 McGee v. S., 21 Tex. Ap. 670; Robertson v. S., 30 Tex. Ap. 498. But it may be an assault: P. v. Courier, 79 Mich. 366.

5 P. v. Goulette, 82 Mich. 36. And see cases *infra*, § 464.

6 S. v. Harney, 101 Mo. 470; Toullet v. S., 100 Ala. 72.

7 P. v. Fleming, 94 Cal. 308; S. v. Owsley, 102 Mo. 678; S. v. Priestley, 74 Mo. 24; House v. S., 9 Tex. Ap. 53.

the intent was to have connection by force, regardless of consent, the crime is complete, and the fact that the assailant subsequently abandoned his purpose will not purge him of the offense.[1] There may be an assault with intent to commit rape although, by reason of the subsequent consent of the female to the completion of the act, the crime of rape is not committed.[2] If the purpose is to have connection by personation of the husband,[3] or while the woman is insensible,[4] or by fraud,[5] an assault with intent to commit rape is not committed. It is even said that where the attempt to secure connection is by threats there is no assault although there may be an attempt to commit rape.[6] The question as to whether the assault was with intent to have connection by force will be determined by the circumstances under which the assault is made.[7] Mere evidence of violence alone will not be sufficient,[8] or the mere entry of the room of the female,[9] or mere pursuit of the female where the words accompanying the act do not indicate an intention to have sexual connection.[10] But it is not necessary that the intent be shown by words accompanying the

[1] C. v. Roosnell, 143 Mass. 32; Glover v. C., 86 Va. 382; Lewis v. S., 35 Ala. 380; P. v. Stewart, 97 Cal. 238; S. v. Elick, 7 Jones, 58; Carter v. S., 35 Ga. 263. The fact of relinquishment of purpose to have connection upon outcry and resistance being made is to be considered in determining the question of intent: Taylor v. S., 50 Ga. 79. The force employed may be only constructive. It is not necessary that there be intention to inflict personal injury: Norris v. S., 87 Ala. 85. But if the act, though some force is used, is with the woman's consent, there is no assault with intent to commit rape: P. v. Bransby, 32 N. Y. 525. And further as to consent to the act as negativing an assault, see *infra*, § 464.

[2] S. v. Cross, 12 Ia. 66; S. v. Atherton, 50 Ia. 189; S. v. Pilkington, — Ia. —, 60 N. W. R. 502; S. v. Bagan, 41 Minn. 285; S. v. Hartigan, 32 Vt. 607; Reg. v. Hallett, 9 C. & P. 748.

[3] Reg. v. Williams, 8 C. & P. 286; S. v. Brooks, 76 N. C. 1.

[4] C. v. Fields, 4 Leigh, 648; Saddler v. S., 12 Tex. Ap. 194.

[5] Reg. v. Stanton, 1 C. & K. 415; Milton v. S., 23 Tex. Ap. 204.

[6] Burney v. S., 21 Tex. Ap. 565. In such case there is an attempt, but not an assault: Taylor v. S., 22 Tex. Ap. 529. A conspiracy to abduct does not constitute an assault with intent to ravish: Jacques v. P., 66 Ill. 84.

[7] Hunter v. S., 29 Fla. 486; Skinner v. S., 28 Neb. 814. Evidence of intoxication is admissible to negative the intent: S. v. Donovan, 61 Ia. 369, so is evidence that accused acted in jest: S. v. Warner, 25 Ia. 200.

[8] Jones v. S., 18 Tex. Ap. 485; Green v. S., 67 Miss. 356.

[9] Carroll v. S., 24 Tex. Ap. 366.

[10] S. v. Massey, 86 N. C. 658 (overruling S. v. Neely, 74 N. C. 425); S. v. Donovan, 61 Ia. 369. So pursuing

assault.[1] Acts may sufficiently indicate the intent to use violence though no violence on the person is actually used.[2] And of course violence to the person of the female, otherwise unexplained, will be strong evidence of the intent to have connection by force.[3] Other cases in which the evidence is held insufficient to show the intent are stated in the note.[4] As bearing on the intent, former intimacy and friendly relations between the defendant and the prosecutrix are material.[5] But criminal intimacy of the defendant with others is not material.[6] Nor can previous assaults of the same character on others be shown, but previous assaults on the prosecutrix are admissible.[7]

§ **464. Consent.**— The general rule applicable in other assaults is applicable here, that there can be no assault where the party complaining was assenting to what was proposed.[8] In England this doctrine has been applied also to cases of attempt to have carnal knowledge of a female child under the age of consent, it being considered that although, by statute, such connection is criminal without regard to the consent of the child, yet that the consent negatives the element of assault.[9] Therefore in England, where the age of consent being

a woman after solicitation, apparently with a view merely to repeat such solicitations, will not necessarily show the intent to commit rape: Thomas v. S., 16 Tex. Ap. 535.

1 Fitzpatrick v. P., 98 Ill. 269.

2 S. v. Shroyer, 104 Mo. 441; S. v. Chaims, 25 Oreg. 221; Dibrell v. S., 3 Tex. Ap. 456.

3 Ware v. S., 67 Ga. 349; S. v. Mitchell, 89 N. C. 521; S. v. Boon, 13 Ired. 244.

4 Johnson v. S., 27 Neb. 687; Skinner v. S., 28 Neb. 814; S. v. McIntire, 66 Ia. 339.

5 Hall v. P., 47 Mich. 636. But of course prior liberties with the prosecutrix, taken by the defendant, will not necessarily show that he did not have, on the occasion in question, the intent to commit rape: Rex v. Lloyd, 7 C. & P. 318.

6 Sutton v. Johnson, 62 Ill. 209. Nor are declarations of the defendant concerning misconduct with other females admissible: P. v. Bowen, 49 Cal. 654.

7 S. v. Walters, 45 Ia. 389. On the whole subject of evidence in such cases, see *supra*, §§ 456–461, where cases of assault are given.

8 P. v. Bransby, 32 N. Y. 525. But consent to the act done, under pretense of medical treatment, will not be a defense in a charge of an assault with intent to commit rape by fraud, unless it appears that the female consented with the knowledge that the defendant was not acting in good faith as a physician: S. v. Nash, 109 N. C. 824.

9 Reg. v. Martin, 9 C. & P. 213; Reg. v. Johnson, L. & C. 632; Reg. v. Read, 2 C. & K. 957; Reg. v. Cockburn, 3 Cox, 543; Reg. v. Roadley, 14 Cox, 463.

fixed at ten years, but the age of puberty being recognized as twelve years in the case of a female, the connection with a female child between the ages of ten and twelve by consent was neither rape nor carnal abuse of a female child but a misdemeanor only, the attempt to commit such misdemeanor was not punishable as an assault.[1] This doctrine is recognized in some of the states of the Union, and consent, even of a child, will prevent the attempt to have carnal connection with her from being an assault although the completed act would be criminal.[2] In those states where the offense of having carnal knowledge of a female child under the age of consent is regarded as a different crime from that of rape, the attempt to have such connection is not an assault with intent to commit rape.[3] But where (as is the rule in most states) the connection with a female child under the age of consent is considered as rape, it is almost universally held that an attempt to have such connection is an assault with intent to commit rape, the consent of the child being wholly immaterial.[4] In such a case, according to other authorities, the doctrine that a child under the age of consent cannot give a valid assent to an act of intercourse is applicable also to the assault.[5] And under this

[1] Reg. v. Martin, 9 C. & P. 213; Reg. v. Johnson, L. & C. 632; Reg. v. Beale, L. R. 1 C. C. 10.

[2] S. v. Pickett, 11 Nev. 255; Whitcher v. S., 2 Wash. 286.

[3] Rhodes v. S., 1 Coldw. 350; Brown v. S., 6 Baxt. 422; Hardwick v. S., 6 Lea, 103; Smith v. S., 12 Ohio St. 466.

[4] P. v. McDonald, 9 Mich. 150; Crosswell v. P., 13 Mich. 427; P. v. Courier, 79 Mich. 366; P. v. Ten Elshof, 92 Mich. 167; Fizell v. S., 25 Wis. 364; S. v. Meinhart, 73 Mo. 562; S. v. Wray, 109 Mo. 594; S. v. Wheat, 63 Vt. 673; Davis v. S., 31 Neb. 247; Murphy v. S., 120 Ind. 115; S. v. Newton, 44 Ia. 45; T. v. Keyes, 5 Dak. 244; S. v. Johnston, 76 N. C. 209; S. v. Dancy, 83 N. C. 608; S. v. Staton, 88 N. C. 654; Glover v. C., 86 Va. 382; McKinny v. S., 29 Fla. 565. The indictment in such cases will be sufficient although it does not designate the attempted crime as rape, if the facts with reference to the intent to have carnal knowledge, etc., of the female child which are alleged would constitute rape if the act had been completed: S. v. Meinhart, 73 Mo. 562.

[5] Hays v. P., 1 Hill, 351; C. v. Roosnell, 143 Mass. 32; Farrell v. S., 54 N. J. 416; Fizell v. S., 25 Wis. 364; S. v. Grossheim, 79 Ia. 75. And see *supra*, § 443. But where the two offenses of rape and carnal knowledge of a female child are distinct, an indictment for assault with intent to commit rape charging force and not alleging the female to be under the age of consent, will not support a conviction if it appears that she did consent, although it is also shown that she was under age: Moore v. S., 20 Tex. Ap. 275; Craig v. S., 18 Tex. Ap. 321.

doctrine ignorance on the part of the defendant that the female was under the age of consent is immaterial.[1]

§ 465. Effect of incapacity to commit rape.— Under the doctrine that a boy under the age of fourteen is incapable of the offense of rape, it has been questioned whether such a person can be guilty of the crime of assault with intent to commit rape. There is some authority that he may,[2] but the weight of authority seems to be to the contrary.[3] But he may be convicted of an indecent assault.[4]

§ 466. Indictment.— The indictment need not strictly follow the words of the statute.[5] But it must show the essential facts and that the act was with intention of accomplishing the purpose by force and against the will of the female.[6] Some cases hold that it is not sufficient to allege the intent in general terms, as, for instance, "with intent to commit rape," but that the technical language necessary to charge the crime of rape must be used.[7] But in other cases it is held that the general words "with intent to commit rape" or "with intent to ravish" are sufficient.[8] In charging an attempt, something more than the general allegation of an attempt to commit the crime should be set out; the physical acts done toward the commission of the crime should be specified.[9] In an allegation of an

[1] S. v. Newton, 44 Ia. 45. And see further, as to want of knowledge in such cases, *supra*, § 451.

[2] C. v. Green, 2 Pick. 380. So it is said that impotency is no defense to a charge of assault with intent to commit rape: T. v. Keyes, 5 Dak. 244.

[3] S. v. Sam, 1 Wins. i, 300; McKinny v. S., 29 Fla. 565; Rex v. Eldershaw, 3 C. & P. 396; Reg. v. Philips, 8 C. & P. 736; Rex v. Groombridge, 7 C. & P. 582. And see *supra*, § 449.

[4] Reg. v. Williams, 1 Q. B. D. (1893), 320.

[5] P. v. Girr, 53 Cal. 629; T. v. Keyes, 5 Dak. 244. Thus, "with intent to rape" is sufficient: P. v. Girr, 53 Cal. 629. "Intention to ravish" may be used in place of "intent to ravish:" S. v. Tom, 2 Jones, 414.

[6] S. v. Powell, 106 N. C. 635; Mears v. C., 2 Grant, 385; Stout v. C., 11 Serg. & R. 177; Hewitt v. S., 15 Tex. Ap. 80; P. v. O'Neil, 48 Cal. 257. Such an indictment may be sufficient to support a conviction for simple assault or for assault and battery: Stout v. C., 11 Serg. & R. 177; P. v. O'Neil, 48 Cal. 257; S. v. Goldston, 103 N. C. 323.

[7] S. v. Blake, 39 Me. 322; S. v. Moore, 82 N. C. 659; S. v. Hooper, 82 N. C. 663; S. v. Benthall, 82 N. C. 664; Sullivant v. S., 8 Ark. 400.

[8] P. v. Mesa, 93 Cal. 580; S. v. Hanlon, 62 Vt. 334; Witherby v. S., 39 Ala. 702; Green v. S., 23 Miss. 509; S. v. Langford, 45 La. An. 1177. Analogous cases as to other assaults with intent to commit specific felonies are discussed in connection with felonious assaults: *Supra*, § 269.

[9] S. v. Frazier, 53 Kan. 87. If the

assault with intent to have carnal knowledge of a female under the age of consent, the age is material in those states where that offense is a different one from the offense of rape.[1] Where the assault is a felony the word "feloniously" should be used.[2] As in an indictment for rape,[3] it is not essential to allege that the accused is a male;[4] nor that the person assaulted is a female where that fact appears from the general tenor of the language used;[5] nor that she was not the wife of defendant.[6]

§ 467. **Forms.**— The examples of indictments for assaults with felonious intent[7] will furnish a guide for charging this form of felonious assault. But the following specific forms may be noticed:

THE ORDINARY FORM.

That said A. B., in the county aforesaid, on ——, in and upon the body of S. A. feloniously an assault did make, and her, the said S. A., did then and there beat, bruise, strike and wound, with intent then and there her, the said S. A., feloniously and violently to ravish and carnally know by force and against her will.[8]

ASSAULT ON FEMALE CHILD.

That said A. B., in the county aforesaid, on ——, in and upon one M. B., a female child under the age of ten years, to wit, of the age of seven years, did unlawfully and feloniously make an assault, and her, the said M. B., did then and there beat, wound and ill-treat, with intent her, the said M. B., unlawfully, feloniously and carnally to know and abuse.[9]

crime is that of abusing a female child, something more than an "assault with intent to carnally know" must be charged: Toullet v. S., 100 Ala. 72.

1 Mosely v. S., 9 Tex. Ap. 137; Hall v. S., 40 Neb. 320.

2 S. v. Scott, 72 N. C. 461; Williams v. S., 8 Humph. 584.

3 *Supra*, § 452.

4 Greenlee v. S., 4 Tex. Ap. 345.

5 Battle v. S., 4 Tex. Ap. 595; Joice v. S., 53 Ga. 50.

6 P. v. Estrada, 53 Cal. 600.

7 See *supra*, § 270.

8 See C. v. Thompson, 116 Mass. 346. It would of course be entirely proper that the latter part should conform exactly to the general indictment for rape given above: *Supra*, § 453. But the exact form used in the case cited is retained as illustrating another form of allegation which is in use in charging rape. Substantially the same form of charging the assault is found in O'Meara v. S., 17 Ohio St. 516, except that an averment is there found with reference to the female not being the daughter or sister of defendant, which is made necessary by peculiar statutory provisions in that state. In the form here given, beating is alleged so that there might be a conviction for assault and battery as an included crime if a felonious intent should not appear.

9 See P. v. McDonald, 9 Mich. 150.

CHAPTER 22.

ROBBERY.

§ 468. **Definition.**—The offense is best described perhaps as the felonious taking of the money or goods of another from his person by violence or putting him in fear.[1] The elements in the offense are either violence or putting in fear, and larceny committed thereby from the person of the owner.[2] It has been suggested that the crime might be described as larceny by an assault, as either actual violence or putting in fear of violence constitutes an assault; and either form of assault may be shown. The conjunctive allegation of both violence and putting in fear will not render the count repugnant.[3] But where it was attempted to put this form of definition into the statute, it was held that there were three separate modes — by assault, by violence, and by putting in fear — in which the offense might be committed.[4] It is not necessary that there be both violence and putting in fear; either is sufficient, if alleged and proven.[5] Robbery is distinguished from forcible trespass by the difference in the intent with which the act is done;[6] and from larceny from the person by the violence or

[1] This definition is practically, although not exactly, that found in 2 East, P. C. 707; 4 Bl. Com. 242. Bishop's definition (2 Bish. Cr. L. 1156) is "larceny committed by violence from the person of one put in fear," which seems not to be accurate, in that it implies both violence and fear; whereas it is not necessary that each of these elements be present, as will be seen in the subsequent discussion.

[2] Houston v. C., 87 Va. 257; Acker v. C., 94 Pa. St. 284; Stevens v. S., 19 Neb. 647; C. v. Brooks, 1 Duv. 150; S. v. Davidson, 38 Mo. 374; McDaniel v. S., 8 Sm. & M. 401; Seymour v. S., 15 Ind. 288; U. S. v. Jones, 3 Wash. C. C. 209.

[3] S. v. Gorham, 55 N. H. 152.

[4] Bond v. S., 20 Tex. Ap. 421; Leonard v. S., 20 Tex. Ap. 442. But these modes do not constitute distinct felonies: S. v. Montgomery, 109 Mo. 645.

[5] C. v. Humphries, 7 Mass. 242; S. v. Stinson, 124 Mo. 447; S. v. Broderick, 59 Mo. 318; Young v. S., 50 Ark. 501; Clary v. S., 33 Ark. 561; S. v. Burke, 73 N. C. 83; Chappell v. S., 52 Ala. 359.

[6] S. v. Sowls, Phil. 151.

putting in fear.[1] While robbery is usually defined by statute, the definition remains practically the same as at common law.[2]

§ 469. The violence.— Where violence is relied upon as constituting the offense there must be violence to the person, something more than the mere force involved in the taking of the property without resistance.[3] But the degree of violence is immaterial if the violence used is the means by which the property is obtained.[4] Thus, if the taking of a watch is by means of sufficient violence to break the guard,[5] or in any other way any form of attachment of the property to the person or any resistance is overcome, the offense is complete.[6] But the mere snatching of property from the hand of another before any resistance is made is not sufficient.[7] If resistance, however slight, is overcome, the violence is sufficient.[8] The violence must precede or accompany the taking; if it is used only in attempting to escape after the taking,[9] or in resisting the attempt of the owner to recover his property,[10] it will not constitute the offense. But if unlawful physical force is put in motion by the assailant before the owner is fully deprived of the control and possession of his property, it is sufficient.[11] As has been indicated in the preceding section, if violence is used it is not necessary to show that such violence resulted in putting the owner of the property in fear.[12]

[1] Burke v. S., 74 Ga. 372.

[2] Houston v. C., 87 Va. 257; Turner v. S., 1 Ohio St. 422; Crews v. S., 3 Coldw. 350; P. v. Shuler, 28 Cal. 490.

[3] Brennon v. S., 25 Ind. 403; S. v. Miller, 83 Ia. 291.

[4] Seymour v. S., 15 Ind. 288. Where an officer handcuffed a prisoner to convey him to jail and by means of this violence extorted money, he was held guilty of robbery: Rex v. Gascoigne, 2 East, P. C. 709.

[5] S. v. McCune, 5 R. I. 60; S. v. Broderick, 59 Mo. 318; Rex v. Mason, Russ. & Ry. 419.

[6] Rex v. Lapier, 2 East, P. C. 557, 708; Rex v. Moore, 1 Leach, 335; U. S. v. Simms, 4 Cranch, C. C. 618. Where a handbag carried on the arm was taken with such force as to bruise the arm, the violence was held sufficient: Klein v. P., 113 Ill. 596.

[7] Rex v. Baker, 2 East, P. C. 702; Rex v. Gnosil, 1 C. & P. 304; Reg. v. Hughes, 2 C. & K. 214; Rex v. Macaulay, 1 Leach, 287; S. v. John, 5 Jones, 163; Fanning v. S., 66 Ga. 167. *Contra*, S. v. Carr, 43 Ia. 418.

[8] Evans v. S., 80 Ala. 4.

[9] Hanson v. S., 43 Ohio St. 376. It is sufficient if the violence is contemporaneous with the taking: S. v. Miller, 53 Kan. 324.

[10] Shinn v. S., 64 Ind. 13; Thomas v. S., 91 Ala. 34.

[11] S. v. Gorham, 55 N. H. 152.

[12] S. v. Broderick, 59 Mo. 318.

§ **470. Putting in fear.**— The putting in fear which will be sufficient to constitute the crime where violence is not used must be fear of personal harm. Threats of a criminal prosecution [1] or of a legal imprisonment [2] will not be sufficient; but the English cases furnish an exception in holding that to obtain money or property from another by threatening to charge him with an unnatural offense is robbery.[3] There are perhaps no adjudications in this country directly supporting this exception to the general rule, although it is recognized in two or three cases in the definition of the crime.[4] But it is clearly anomalous and out of harmony with the general theory as to what constitutes robbery.[5] It seems that threats to cause the destruction of one's dwelling by a mob may be a sufficient putting in fear to constitute robbery.[6] It is not necessary that the object of the actual or threatened violence from which fear results be to procure money; it is enough that money be parted with to the assailant as the result of such fear;[7] but the parting with the money or property must be in consequence of the fear; if fear results afterwards in regard to the detention of the property by the assailant it is not enough;[8] nor is it enough that there shall have been fear, provided suf-

[1] Britt v. S., 7 Humph. 45; Long v. S., 12 Ga. 293.

[2] Williams v. S., 12 Tex. Ap. 240; Kimble v. S., 12 Tex. Ap. 420; Rex v. Wood, 2 East, P. C. 732. But where violence is threatened under the pretense of being an officer, and money is paid in consequence thereof, the crime is complete: Bussey v. S., 71 Ga. 100; McCormick v. S., 26 Tex. Ap. 678. So, if violence is used in taking a person before a magistrate to accuse him of an offense, it may constitute an assault with intent to rob, if the object was to extort money: Reg. v. Stringer, 1 C. & K. 188.

[3] Rex v. Jones, 1 Leach, 139; Rex v. Donnally, 2 East, P. C. 713, 783; Rex v. Hickman, 2 East, P. C. 728; Rex v. Gardner, 1 C. & P. 479; Rex v. Edwards, 5 C. & P. 518; Rex v. Cannon, Russ. & Ry. 146; Rex v. Egerton, Russ. & Ry. 375; Reg v. Fuller, Russ. & Ry. 408; Rex v. Elmstead, 2 Russ., C. & M. 128; Rex v. Stringer, 2 Moody, 261; Rex v. Jackson, 1 East, P. C., Ad. XXI.

[4] Long v. S., 12 Ga. 293; Houston v. C., 87 Va. 257; Britt v. S., 7 Humph. 45; P. v. McDaniels, 1 Park. Cr. R. 198.

[5] 2 Bishop, Cr. L., § 1172.

[6] Rex v. Astley, 2 East, P. C. 729; Rex v. Brown, 2 East, P. C. 731; Rex v. Simons, 2 East, P. C. 731. So where money was given to one of a mob during the London riots upon knocking at the prosecutor's door in a threatening manner, it was held robbery: Rex v. Taplin, 2 East, P. C. 712.

[7] Rex v. Blackham, 2 East, P. C. 711; McCormick v. S., 26 Tex. Ap. 678.

[8] Thomas v. S., 91 Ala. 34.

ficient time has elapsed before the taking so that there has been opportunity to deliberate and procure assistance.[1] It is said that the taking must be under such circumstances as would be likely to create an apprehension of danger in the mind of a man of ordinary experience;[2] but on the other hand it has been decided that the means used need not be such as would put in fear one used to the ways of the world and that it is sufficient if actual fear is proved.[3] If there is no actual fear (and no violence) the offense is not robbery, even though there is reasonable ground for fear.[4] The prosecuting witness may testify as to whether or not he was put in fear.[5]

§ **471. The taking and carrying away.**— Robbery is simply an aggravated form of larceny, that is, larceny with an added element of taking from the person by violence or putting in fear, and so far as the taking and carrying away in relation to the act of larceny are concerned, little need be said, as the doctrines discussed under the head of larceny are applicable.[6] Therefore, if the property is dropped by the person assaulted, but is not carried away by the assailant, the offense of robbery is not committed.[7] But the fact that the property is returned to the owner after being taken does not prevent the offense being complete.[8] If the property is taken by one with whom the defendant is acting in concert, the defendant who has been guilty of the violence and putting in fear may be convicted of the robbery.[9]

[1] Rex v. Jackson, 1 East, P. C., Ad. XXI. But if the taking is while the fear or apprehension of danger still continues it may be robbery: Long v. S., 12 Ga. 293.

[2] Long v. S., 12 Ga. 293.

[3] S. v. Carr, 43 Ia. 418.

[4] Rex v. Reane, 2 East, P. C. 734.

[5] Long v. S., 12 Ga. 293; Dill v. S., 6 Tex. Ap. 113.

[6] C. v. Clifford, 8 Cush. 215; Terry v. S., 13 Ind. 70; Brennon v. S., 25 Ind. 403; 2 Bishop, Cr. L. 1158-1162. Thus, the offense of receiving stolen goods as defined by statute covers goods taken by robbery as well as larceny: Levi v. S., 14 Neb. 1; Shriedley v. S., 23 Ohio St. 130. And the charge of robbery necessarily includes that of larceny: See *infra*, § 484.

[7] Rex v. Farrel, 2 East, P. C. 557; Hale, P. C. 533. But it is said that the averment of carrying away is not necessary where the allegation shows a taking: Terry v. S., 13 Ind. 70. To remove an earring from the curls of a lady's hair, where it has accidentally lodged, is a sufficient carrying away: Rex v. Lapier, 2 East, P. C. 557, 708.

[8] Rex v. Peat, 2 East, P. C. 557.

[9] Ashworth v. S., 31 Tex. Ap. 419.

§ 472. **The value.**— As in larceny, the value of the property is immaterial, so that it have some value.[1] There is no occasion, as there is in larceny, for alleging the value, as the punishment is not made to depend on the value of the property taken.[2]

§ 473. **The property of another.**— As in larceny, it must appear that the property taken was that of another than the accused.[3] And even where the statute does not expressly require that the property be that of another, but defines the taking required as of any property which may be the subject of larceny, it must be alleged that the property was that of another, as such a statute is merely affirmative of the common law;[4] but a special property in the one from whom it is taken is sufficient.[5] And the property taken may be properly charged as the property of the person from whom it was taken.[6] Indeed, it seems that the charge of taking property from another sufficiently implies in him the ownership necessary to constitute robbery.[7] There is even some authority for the proposition that it is immaterial whether the property taken is that of the person from whom it is taken or of another person, if it is the property of another than the accused.[8] But the indictment must give the name of the person from whom the property

[1] Rex v. Bingley, 5 C. & P. 602.

[2] S. v. Howerton, 58 Mo. 581; S. v. Perley, 86 Me. 427; Williams v. S., 10 Tex. Ap. 8; S. v. Brown, 113 N. C. 645; P. v. Chuey Ying Git, 100 Cal. 437. See *infra*, § 481.

[3] Smedly v. S., 30 Tex. 214; Barnes v. S., 9 Tex. Ap. 128. The owner of property is not guilty of robbery in taking it from one in possession: P. v. Vice, 21 Cal. 344.

[4] C. v. Clifford, 8 Cush. 215. Under such a statute, the taking of property which is made the subject of larceny by statute will be robbery, although such property was not the subject of larceny at common law: S. v. Gorham, 55 N. H. 152.

[5] S. v. Ah Loi, 5 Nev. 99; P. v. Clark, 106 Cal. 32. Possession and apparent ownership in the person described as owner are sufficient: S. v. Hobgood, 46 La. An. 855. Possession is *prima facie* evidence of ownership, and may be proved to show ownership: Bradley v. S., 103 Ala. 29.

[6] Brooks v. P., 49 N. Y. 436.

[7] P. v. Hicks, 66 Cal. 103; P. v. Shuler, 28 Cal. 490.

[8] P. v. Anderson, 80 Cal. 205; Clemons v. S., 92 Tenn. 282. And it is said that if the ownership is wrongfully described, such description may be rejected as surplusage under statutory provision curing a variance which does not prejudice the rights of defendant: P. v. Anderson, 80 Cal. 205.

is taken.[1] Ownership may be laid in the real owner or in the person who is in custody as the servant of the real owner.[2]

§ 474. **From the person.**— Robbery involves not merely the taking of the property of another, but the taking of it from his person.[3] But it is not necessary that the property be in any way attached to the owner's person, and it is sufficient if the taking is from his immediate personal presence.[4] Some cases give a liberal construction to the expression "from the presence of the owner," and hold it sufficient that the taking is effected by violent restraint of the owner, although the property is not actually within his sight or manual custody at the time it is taken.[5]

§ 475. **Against the owner's will.**— The taking must of course be against the will of the owner in order to constitute robbery;[6] and such a statement is sometimes embodied in the statute describing the offense, but certainly there is no different requirement in this respect than in case of larceny. It is said that such an averment is not necessary where the taking is charged to have been effected by force.[7]

§ 476. **Participation.**— If two or more associate together to commit the offense and take different parts in the transaction, each will be guilty; and if the offense is consummated through

[1] Smedly v. S., 30 Tex. 214. And it must allege that the party robbed was the party assailed and put in fear: Trimble v. S., 16 Tex. Ap. 115. A mistake in the name of the person robbed is not material under statutes curing immaterial variance unless the accused has been prejudiced: S. v. Carr, 43 Ia. 418.

[2] S. v. Nelson, 11 Nev. 334. But if the property in the possession of the servant has been received by him for the owner but not delivered to the owner's possession, it should not be charged as the property of the owner, under the rule applicable in cases of larceny: Reg. v. Rudick, 8 C. & P. 237.

[3] Kit v. S., 11 Humph. 167; P. v. Beck, 21 Cal. 385; Rex v. Fallows, 5 C. & P. 508; Reg. v. Wilkins, 10 Cox, 363.

[4] Crews v. S., 3 Coldw. 350; Turner v. S., 1 Ohio St. 422; Hill v. S., 42 Neb. 503; P. v. Ah Sing, 95 Cal. 654; S. v. Davidson, 38 Mo. 374; S. v. McDowell, 1 Hawks, 449. And this is true though the language of the statute is "taking from the person:" Turner v. S., 1 Ohio St. 422; In re Ezeta, 62 Fed. R. 672. Where the robber was traveling with the owner of the property, who had intrusted such property to his custody, and took it by violence, it was held that the taking was sufficiently from the owner's presence: James v. S., 53 Ala. 380.

[5] S. v. Calhoun, 72 Ia. 432; Clements v. S., 84 Ga. 660, 8 Am. Cr. R. 692, and note.

[6] Kit v. S., 11 Humph. 167.

[7] P. v. Riley, 75 Cal. 98.

the act of one alone, the others will be deemed constructively present and equally punishable.[1] And if all act together, each in his own way, all will be equally guilty, although they do not actually meet and agree to commit the robbery.[2] But if they all participate in the assault, while one only, without agreement with the others, takes the property, he alone is guilty of the robbery.[3] One who stands by, without interfering, there being no evidence of complicity, cannot be held guilty of the crime committed in his presence;[4] nor will the receipt of the goods taken render the party receiving guilty of the robbery.[5] But one who is present, aiding and abetting, may be guilty of the offense, though he does not participate in the proceeds.[6] As in case of larceny, recent possession of the property is evidence of guilt.[7]

§ **477. Injury to different persons.**— It has been said that taking at the same time the several property of different persons who are put in fear by the same act may be charged as one crime of robbery.[8] But other cases hold, and apparently

[1] S. v. Heyward, 2 Nott & M. 312.

[2] Miller v. P., 39 Ill. 457. Where all who act together are charged as principals, it is not necessary to allege a conspiracy: Bell v. S., 1 Tex. Ap. 598. Defendant may be charged in different counts with being principal, and also with acting with others in the commission of the offense, and the prosecution should not be required to elect: S. v. Cook, 20 La. An. 145. It seems, however, that if one only is indicted and it is sought to hold him for the acts of all, it should be averred that he committed the offense together with others: Raffety's Case, 2 Lewin, 271. But under a statute which specially describes it as one method of committing the offense that it is done by several persons acting together, the defendant may be convicted for having acted as one of several, although the indictment charges a robbery by one: Farris v. S., 26 Tex. Ap. 105.

[3] Rex v. Hawkins, 3 C. & P. 392. But if the whole transaction is carried out by all, it is immaterial that those participating did not beforehand have the intention to rob: Ferguson v. S., 32 Ga. 658.

[4] Golden v. S., 18 Tex. Ap. 637.

[5] P. v. Shepardson, 48 Cal. 189.

[6] S. v. Brown, 104 Mo. 365. Evidence that defendant was seen in company with other persons near the scene of the crime may be admissible to prove his connection with the offense: Odle v. S., 13 Tex. Ap. 612; but not to prove the *corpus delicti:* S. v. Davidson, 30 Vt. 377.

[7] S. v. Wyatt, 124 Mo. 537; *infra*, § 616.

[8] Reg. v. Giddins, Car. & M. 634. And see S. v. Christmas, 101 N. C. 749; Clark v. S., 28 Tex. Ap. 189. If two offenses are charged in different indictments, one as to each of the persons assailed, evidence of the taking of property from B., which is found on the pris-

with better reason, that where the assault is upon several different persons there will be distinct offenses of robbery committed as to each of them, although the transaction is continuous.[1]

§ 478. **Degrees of the offense; aggravation.**— Some statutes divide the offense into degrees, depending on whether the crime is committed by violence or by putting in fear, or whether the fear is of immediate injury or injury to be inflicted in the future.[2] By other statutes the crime is more severely punished where the assailant is armed with a dangerous weapon;[3] or in or near the public highway;[4] or by killing or wounding.[5]

§ 479. **The intent.**— It is essential to allege and prove not merely the violence or putting in fear and the taking of the property from the person of defendant, but also that such taking was with intent to commit larceny.[6] Thus, if the property is taken under a *bona fide* claim of right, though it be done by violence or putting in fear, the act will not be robbery.[7] Nor will it constitute robbery that by violence or putting in fear one is compelled to pay over money which is due.[8] So if the taking is under supposed military command there will be no robbery.[9] The fact that the assailant compels the party from whom the property is taken to receive pay therefor to an

oner, may be shown under the indictment charging robbery from A.; but evidence of violence offered to B. will not be admissible: Rex v. Rooney, 7 C. & P. 517.

[1] In re Allison, 13 Colo. 525; Keeton v. C., 92 Ky. 522.

[2] Lampkin v. S., 87 Ga. 516; Long v. S., 12 Ga. 293; S. v. Stoffel, 48 Kan. 364.

[3] U. S. v. Wood, 3 Wash. C. C. 440; U. S. v. Wilson, Bald. 78; S. v. Calhoun, 72 Ia. 432; Rex v. Pelfryman, 2 East, P. C. 783.

[4] S. v. Burke, 73 N. C. 83; S. v. Anthony, 7 Ired. 234; S. v. Cowan, 7 Ired. 239; S. v. Johnson, Phill. 140.

[5] C. v. Gallagher, 6 Metc. 565; C. v. Martin, 17 Mass. 359.

[6] Matthews v. S., 4 Ohio St. 539; Boose v. S., 10 Ohio St. 575; C. v. White, 133 Pa. St. 182; S. v. O'Connor, 105 Mo. 121; Chappell v. S., 52 Ala. 359; Ward v. C., 14 Bush, 233; Reg. v. Edwards, 1 Cox, 32. If the person committing the act is so much under the influence of liquor as not to know what he is doing, he will not be deemed to have taken the property with felonious intent: Keeton v. C., 92 Ky. 522. Other acts of robbery, in pursuance of the same general plan, may be shown to prove the intent: S. v. Lee, 91 Ia. 499.

[7] Reg. v. Boden, 1 C. & K. 395; Rex v. Hall, 3 C. & P. 409; Brown v. S., 28 Ark. 126.

[8] S. v. Hollyway, 41 Ia. 200; S. v. Brown, 104 Mo. 365; Reg. v. Hemmings, 4 F. & F. 50.

[9] S. v. Sowls, Phill. 151; C. v. Holland, 1 Duv. 182.

amount less than its value will not, however, prevent the act being robbery by converting it into a sale.[1]

§ 480. **Indictment.**— The indictment must allege the offense as committed either by violence or putting in fear;[2] but if violence is charged it is not necessary to charge also putting in fear.[3] The use of the word "forcibly" does not sufficiently charge violence or putting in fear;[4] but the charge that the property was taken "feloniously and violently" sufficiently alleges the putting in fear.[5] It is not necessary to specially charge an assault if the putting in fear is otherwise alleged.[6] The fear alleged must be of injury to the person.[7] The taking of the property may be alleged as in larceny,[8] and though it is usual it is not necessary to employ the term "rob;"[9] but the taking must be alleged as from the person.[10] It is not essential to charge the taking as "against the will" if the larceny is otherwise sufficiently charged.[11] The word "steal" implies intent to steal,[12] but it is not necessary where the indictment alleges feloniously taking and carrying away.[13] The putting in fear need not be alleged as felonious where the assault is so charged.[14]

§ 481. **Description of property; value.**— No greater particularity is necessary in describing the property than in case of larceny;[15] but as in that case, ownership must be alleged.[16] It is not necessary to allege the value of the property.[17] As to

[1] Rex v. Simons, 2 East, P. C. 712; Rex v. Spencer, 2 East, P. C. 712.

[2] Collins v. P., 39 Ill. 233.

[3] Houston v. C., 87 Va. 257.

[4] Landringham v. S., 49 Ind. 186.

[5] S. v. Cowan, 7 Ired. 239. It is not necessary, however, that the indictment charge specifically that the act was done "violently:" Rex v. Smith, 2 East, P. C. 783.

[6] S. v. Brewer, 53 Ia. 735.

[7] S. v. Smith, 119 Mo. 439.

[8] S. v. Kegan, 62 Ia. 106; Houston v. C., 87 Va. 257; Reg. v. Huxley, Car. & M. 596.

[9] S. v. Ready, 44 Kan. 697, 700; S. v. Robinson, 29 La. An. 364; S. v. Kegan, 62 Ia. 106.

[10] S. v. Leighton, 56 Ia. 595.

[11] Terry v. S., 13 Ind. 70; S. v. Patterson, 42 La. An. 934.

[12] Turner v. S., 1 Ohio St. 422.

[13] S. v. Brown, 113 N. C. 645.

[14] S. v. Brown, 104 Mo. 365.

[15] Arnold v. S., 52 Ind. 281. Where the property is unnecessarily described, such description need not be proven: Burke v. P., 148 Ill. 70; but the indictment ought to allege the name of the person robbed: Parker v. S., 9 Tex. Ap. 351. The allegation that a more particular description is unknown will cure insufficiency: T. v. Bell, 5 Mont. 562.

[16] Boles v. S., 58 Ark. 35.

[17] S. v. Howerton, 58 Mo. 581; Williams v. S., 10 Tex. Ap. 8. And see *supra*, § 472. The same rules in

the method of describing and alleging the value of bank notes, the same rules apply as in larceny, the cases cited in the note serving as illustrations.[1]

§ 482. **Statutory provisions.**— While the requirements of the common law as to the indictment are to some extent modified by statute,[2] yet the indictment must still state the essentials of the crime as defined by the statute.[3] But even where there is a statutory form the common-law form will be sufficient;[4] and it will not render the indictment bad for duplicity that it charges larceny, although the formal charge of larceny is not necessary.[5]

§ 483. **Form of indictment.**— It is usual to charge the offense both by violence and by putting in fear, in substantially the following form:

That A. B., on ——, in said county, in and upon C. D. feloniously did make an assault, and then and there one gold watch of the goods and chattels of him, the said C. D., from the person and against the will of the said C. D., then and there feloniously, forcibly and by violence, and by putting him, the said C. D., in fear, did take, steal and carry away.[6]

§ 484. **Included offenses.**— As the indictment for robbery must allege everything necessary to constitute larceny, there may be a conviction for larceny under an indictment for robbery.[7] So there may be conviction for larceny from the per-

proving value are said to be applicable in robbery as in larceny: C. v. Cahill, 12 Allen, 540.

[1] McEntee v. S., 24 Wis. 43; S. v. Helvin, 65 Ia. 289; Terry v. S., 13 Ind. 70; McCarty v. S., 127 Ind. 223; Taylor v. S., 130 Ind. 66; Wesley v. S., 61 Ala. 282; Winston v. S., 9 Tex. Ap. 143; Menear v. S., 30 Tex. Ap. 475; Coffelt v. S. 27 Tex. Ap. 608.

[2] S. v. Swafford, 3 Lea, 162.

[3] S. v. Cook, 20 La. An. 145.

[4] Burns v. S., 12 Tex. Ap. 269.

[5] McTigue v. S., 4 Baxt. 313.

[6] S. v. Gorham, 55 N. H. 152; Terry v. S., 13 Ind. 70; S. v. Kegan, 62 Ia. 106; 2 Archbold, Cr. Pr. & Pl. 417; 2 Chitty, Cr. L. 807. The following form of allegation is also used: "In and upon one C. D. feloniously did make an assault, and him, the said C. D., in bodily fear did feloniously put, and one (describe the article) of the moneys, goods and chattels of the said C. D. from the person and against the will of the said C. D. then and there feloniously and violently did steal, take and carry away:" Houston v. C., 87 Va. 257; 1 Wharton, Prec. 375. Where this form was used, but "seize" was substituted for "steal," it was held that the intent was not sufficiently alleged, there being no presumption of criminal intent from the acts charged, such as would have arisen had the term "steal" been used: Matthews v. S., 4 Ohio St. 539. But *contra*, see S. v. Brown, 113 N. C. 645.

[7] P. v. Nelson, 56 Cal. 77; Stevens v. S., 19 Neb. 647; Tucker v. S., 3

son.[1] It seems that if the indictment, in setting out the violence or putting in fear, does so in such form as to constitute a valid charge of assault, there may be a conviction for assault under an indictment for robbery.[2]

Heisk. 484; Haley v. S., 49 Ark. 147; Morris v. S., 97 Ala. 82.

[1] Brown v. S., 33 Neb. 354; S. v. Graff, 66 Ia. 482.

[2] Hardy v. C., 17 Grat. 592; Reg. v. Mitchell, 3 C. & K. 181; Reg. v. Greenwood, 2 C. & K. 339; Reg. v. Birch, 2 C. & K. 193; Reg. v. Barnett, 2 C. & K. 594; Reg. v. Reid, 2 Den. 88. As to assault with intent to rob, see Reg. v. Reid, 2 Den. 88; Rex v. Edwards, 6 C. & P. 521. The assault must be on the person intended to be robbed: Rex v. Thomas, 1 East, P. C. 417; but must be coupled with demand of money or property to constitute robbery: Rex v. Parfait, 1 East, P. C. 416. An assault with intent to steal, and the misdemeanor of attempting to steal, may be charged in different counts of the same indictment: Reg. v. Ferguson, Dears. 427.

CHAPTER 23.

KIDNAPPING; FALSE IMPRISONMENT.

§ 485. **Nature of offenses.**—The offenses of kidnapping and false imprisonment are violations of the right of liberty, and also involve, presumptively at least, the crime of assault.[1] An offense somewhat analogous is that of abduction of a child, which is an offense against the parent rather than the child.[2] The abduction of females for illicit purposes is considered elsewhere.[3]

§ 486. **False imprisonment.**— To unlawfully detain another, thus interfering with his liberty, is not only a ground of action for damages, but is also a common-law crime.[4] Every confinement of the person is an imprisonment, whether it be in a prison, in a private house, or even by forcible detention in the public streets.[5] Thus, if persons without authority take and detain one under pretended charge of a crime and not in pursuance of lawful arrest, it is false imprisonment.[6] Where the purpose is to arrest without warrant, even though that would be justifiable, yet if the person arrested is detained an unreasonable time before taking him to a magistrate, as is required in such cases, there is false imprisonment.[7] So it is false imprisonment

[1] Click v. S., 3 Tex. 282; Smith v. S., 7 Humph. 43; 1 East, P. C. 428.

[2] Burns v. C., 129 Pa. St. 138; though if the act is against the will of the parent, it is deemed to be without the child's consent: C. v. Nickerson, 5 Allen, 518. And see *infra*, § 490. Some statutes, however, specifically provide for child-stealing: C. v. Myers, 146 Pa. St. 24; P. v. Congdon, 77 Mich. 351; S. v. Angel, 42 Kan. 216. To constitute the latter offense there must be intent to unlawfully detain or conceal: Mays v. S., 43 Ohio St. 567; P. v. Congdon, 77 Mich. 351. Under such statutes one parent may be guilty in taking the child from another to whom possession has been awarded: C. v. Nickerson, 5 Allen, 518; otherwise the taking by one parent from another is not criminal: Burns v. C., 129 Pa. St. 138.

[3] *Infra*, §§ 1100, 1106*a*.

[4] 4 Bl. Com. 218; 2 Bish. Cr. L., § 747. And see *infra*, § 906.

[5] Floyd v. S., 12 Ark. 43; 1 East, P. C. 428. Restraint of liberty, if not justifiable, is false imprisonment: C. v. Nickerson, 5 Allen, 518.

[6] Jones v. C., 1 Rob. (Va.) 748.

[7] Lavina v. S., 63 Ga. 513.

for persons acting under the military authority of one state to go into another state and forcibly seize and confine any person there or carry him out of the state.[1]

§ 487. **Unlawfulness.**— In cases of arrest the question whether the detention resulting therefrom constitutes false imprisonment depends on the lawfulness of the arrest; if the persons making it act without authority they will be guilty of false imprisonment.[2] And in general the burden is on the defendant to show that he acted under lawful authority;[3] but the indictment must allege the want of lawful authority.[4] If an officer acts under lawful warrant in making the arrest, he is usually protected;[5] and the mere fact that he delays to take bail when he should do so will not render him criminally liable.[6] But if he conspires with others to procure the process to be wrongfully issued, and does not act in good faith thereunder, he commits a crime although the process may be regular on its face.[7] So if after making the arrest the officer makes an improper disposition of the prisoner, or otherwise fails to properly execute and return the process, he is criminally liable.[8] A magistrate who exercises his authority entirely without jurisdiction, and thereby causes persons to be unlawfully imprisoned, is punishable criminally.[9] An arrest under military authority, if within the scope of the military power, will not be criminal.[10]

[1] C. v. Blodgett, 12 Met. 56.

[2] Kirbie v. S., 5 Tex. Ap. 60. And see cases cited to previous section. But in mitigation the defendant may show that he made the arrest having reason to believe that it was justifiable: Staples v. S., 14 Tex. Ap. 136. Where the arrest was on an indorsed warrant, but the person was taken before the magistrate issuing the warrant in another county instead of before the magistrate indorsing the warrant as required by law, *held*, that the officer was punishable: Francisco v. S., 24 N. J. 30.

[3] Floyd v. S., 12 Ark. 43; Mitchell v. S., 12 Ark. 50; P. v. McGrew, 77 Cal. 570.

[4] Barber v. S., 13 Fla. 675; Waterman v. S., 13 Fla. 683; S. v. Kimmerling, 124 Ind. 382. But it is sufficient to charge that defendant was unlawfully and feloniously imprisoned, as that implies that it was without legal authority: U. S. v. Lapoint, 1 Morris (Ia.), 146.

[5] Ex parte Sternes, 82 Cal. 245.

[6] Cargill v. S., 8 Tex. Ap. 41.

[7] Slomer v. P., 25 Ill. 70; P. v. Fick, 89 Cal. 144.

[8] P. v. Fick, 89 Cal. 144.

[9] Vanderpool v. S., 34 Ark. 174; Campbell v. S., 48 Ga. 353. But where a judge without jurisdiction caused a person to be brought before him on *habeas corpus*, he was held not punishable, for, the proceedings being void, the detention was proper under the original process: S. v. Guest, 6 Ala. 778.

[10] Oglesby v. S., 39 Tex. 53; Reg. v. Lesley, Bell, 220.

A parent may properly exercise restraint over his minor child, but if this power is wantonly and inhumanly exercised it may amount to false imprisonment.[1]

§ 488. **Method of detention.**— To constitute false imprisonment it is not necessary that there be any actual arrest or assault. It is sufficient that the person be detained by threats or violence, and prevented from going where he wishes by reasonable apprehension of personal danger.[2] Nor is it necessary that the person be detained in one particular place. It is enough to constitute false imprisonment if he is prevented by force or threats of violence from going in any direction he sees proper, this being a sufficient interference with his liberty to constitute a crime.[3]

§ 489. **Kidnapping.**— The common-law offense of kidnapping seems to consist in the "forcible abduction or stealing away of a man, woman or child from their own country and sending them into another."[4] It is an aggravated species of false imprisonment.[5] But by statutes in England and in the various states, the offense has been extended to cover any transportation of a person against his will from one place to another.[6] It is not necessary that there be any actual violence.[7] It is enough if the object is attained by exciting the fears, by threats, fraud, etc., amounting substantially to a coercion of the

[1] Fletcher v. P., 52 Ill. 395.

[2] Smith v. S., 7 Humph. 43; Pike v. Hanson, 9 N. H. 491; Herring v. S., 3 Tex. Ap. 108. And the threats may be by acts or gestures as well as by words: Maner v. S., 8 Tex. Ap. 361; Reg. v. Jones, 11 Cox, 393. But to fraudulently induce one to go with persons who pretended they were seeking another person in order to make an arrest, the scheme being merely a practical joke, was held not criminal: S. v. Lunsford, 81 N. C. 528.

[3] Smith v. S., 7 Humph. 43; Harkins v. S., 6 Tex. Ap. 452; Woods v. S., 3 Tex. Ap. 204.

[4] 4 Bl. Com. 219. Where the statute punishes the transporting of any person to parts beyond the sea, the carrying must be to some foreign country: Campbell v. Rankins, 11 Me. 103; C. v. Nickerson, 5 Allen, 518.

[5] 1 East, P. C. 429; 2 Bish. Cr. L., § 750; Click v. S., 3 Tex. 282; Ross v. S., 15 Fla. 55; P. v. Fick, 89 Cal. 228.

[6] S. v. Rollins, 8 N. H. 550; S. v. Backarow, 38 La. An. 316; P. v. Chu Quong, 15 Cal. 332; Ex parte Keil, 85 Cal. 309; Smith v. S., 63 Wis. 453. During the existence of slavery in the southern states there were statutes punishing the carrying of slaves out of the state: Thomas v. C., 2 Leigh, 741; or the stealing for purposes of sale of free negroes: Davenport v. C., 1 Leigh, 588; S. v. Whaley, 2 Har. (Del.) 538; S. v. Griffin, 3 Harr. (Del.) 539; S. v. Weaver, Busb. 9; S. v. Watkins, 4 Humph. 256.

[7] S. v. Rollins, 8 N. H. 550.

will.[1] So where a woman was induced to go out of the country by fraudulent representations of employment abroad, the intent being to take her to a house of ill-fame, it was held that the crime was committed.[2] So where a sailor, being first made drunk, was induced while in that condition to go on board a vessel, the intent being to take him out of the country without his consent, it was held that the act was criminal.[3] But there must be some act of taking or detaining; a mere solicitation or inducement will not be sufficient.[4]

§ 490. **Against the will.**— It is implied that the detention and transportation shall be against the will, or at least without the consent, of the person taken, but consent on the part of a child of such immature years as not to be competent to give a valid consent will be immaterial;[5] and where the child is in the custody of a parent or guardian, the taking without the consent of such parent or guardian, even though the child may be of considerable maturity and consent to the act, will be criminal.[6] But where there is consent on the part of the person to be abducted, who is of sufficient maturity to give a valid consent, the offense is not usually regarded as kidnapping,[7] although the act might be a violation of some statutory provision against abduction.

§ 491. **Intent.**—Under most of the statutes the intent must be to cause the person to be unlawfully transported, or in some states concealed.[8] If an act is in pursuance of lawful authority, such as taking an insane person to an asylum to which he

[1] Moody v. P., 20 Ill. 315.

[2] P. v. De Leon, 109 N. Y. 226. That threats are enough without force, see In re Kelly, 46 Fed. R. 653. The crime is committed where the inveiglement takes place, not in the county in which the transportation is completed: Ib.

[3] Hadden v. P., 25 N. Y. 373. As to enticing persons out of the state for enlistment, see C. v. Jacobs, 9 Allen, 274; C. v. McGovern, 10 Allen, 193.

[4] P. v. Parshall, 6 Park. Cr. R. 129. This was a charge under a statute punishing the taking, etc., of a woman against her will, with intent to have carnal knowledge of her. Under a similar statute it was held that the fact that the woman was unconscious or insane would be immaterial: Malone v. C., 91 Ky. 307; Higgins v. C., 94 Ky. 54.

[5] S. v. Rollins, 8 N. H. 550; S. v. Farrar, 41 N. H. 53; C. v. Nickerson, 5 Allen, 518; U. S. v. Aucarola, 17 Blatchf. 423.

[6] Gravett v. S., 74 Ga. 191. In such a case harsh treatment of the child by the parent cannot be shown as an excuse: Ibid.

[7] Eberling v. S., 136 Ind. 117; Cochran v. S., 91 Ga. 763.

[8] Smith v. S., 63 Wis. 453; Mayo v. S., 43 Ohio St. 567.

has been committed, there is no crime whether he is really insane or not.[1] An unlawful intent must be alleged.[2]

§ 492. Indictment; form.— As both of the offenses discussed in this chapter are practically regulated by statute, the form of the indictment will be determined by the statutory provisions.[3] The following forms are under statutes of particular states and therefore are suggestive only:

FALSE IMPRISONMENT.

That A. B., in the county aforesaid, on ——, did then and there unlawfully and wilfully arrest and detain one W. M. against his consent, and without any express warrant or authority of law, the said detention being then and there effected by the said A. B. by threats of violence, and the threats being then and there of such a character as was calculated to operate upon and to inspire the said W. M. with a just fear of serious injury to his person, and then and there to restrain the said W. M. from removing from one place to another as he might then and there see proper.[4]

KIDNAPPING.

That A. B., in the county aforesaid, on ——, did unlawfully make an assault on one C. D., and him, the said C. D., did then and there beat, bruise and ill-treat, and without lawful authority did then and there unlawfully, forcibly and feloniously, and without any authority or lawful excuse, restrain and imprison against his will, with intent that the said C. D. should be unlawfully and against his will carried and conveyed and sent out of this state into another state, to wit, into the state of ——, against the will of the said C. D.; and that the said A. B. did then and there without lawful authority forcibly and feloniously kidnap, carry and send the said C. D. out of this state into another state, to wit, the said state of ——, against the will of the said C. D.[5]

1 P. v. Camp, 139 N. Y. 87.

2 S. v. Sutton, 116 Ind. 527.

3 S. v. Sutton, 116 Ind. 527, 8 Am. Cr. R. 452, and note; S. v. McRoberts, 4 Blackf. 178; Boies v. S., 125 Ind. 255.

4 Herring v. S., 3 Tex. Ap. 108.

5 This form covers assault and battery, false imprisonment, imprisonment with intention to transport out of the state, and finally kidnaping. It is believed, however, that it is not open to the charge of duplicity, inasmuch as the various subjects are all involved in the final act charged, and that there might be conviction of any one of the included offenses in a prosecution for the principal offense.

ARREST WITH INTENT TO KIDNAP.

That A. B., in the county aforesaid, on the —— day of ——, did then and there feloniously, forcibly and fraudulently arrest J. R. with the felonious and fraudulent intention of carrying him, the said J. R., forcibly and against his will from his place of residence, the said forcible and fraudulent arrest not being then and there made in pursuance of any law of this state or of the United States.[1]

[1] S. v. Sutton, 116 Ind. 527.

PART VI.

OFFENSES AGAINST THE HABITATION.

CHAPTER 24.

BURGLARY AND STATUTORY BREAKINGS AND ENTERINGS.

§ **493. Definition.**— Burglary is the breaking and entering of the dwelling-house of another by night with intent to commit a felony therein.[1] All the authors use substantially the same terms with slight variations in arrangement.[2]

§ **494. The habitation.**— Burglary is, like arson, an offense especially against the habitation, that is, against the security of the home. By the early law of England various forms of breaking and entering seem to have been popularly known as burglary, but the offense was, by the decisions of the court, narrowed to that above defined.[3] It is proper, therefore, to first describe the offense with reference to the place where it may be committed, that is, as to what is such a building as to come within the definition. The technical term of the common-law description is "mansion-house."[4] The technical term in arson is "house;"[5] but whatever distinction there may formerly have been between the two terms (and it is doubtful if there was any) they are now apparently synonymous. At any rate the term "dwelling" or "dwelling-house" is sufficient in burglary.[6] To constitute a dwelling-house the building must be used for the purpose of a dwelling;[7] and if it has never been slept in

[1] See S. v. McCall, 4 Ala. 643; Stephen, Dig. Cr. L., art. 316; 2 Bish. Cr. L., § 90.

[2] 1 Hawk. P. C., ch. 38; 2 East, P. C. 484; 1 Hale, P. C. 549; 4 Bl. Com. 224; 3 Inst. 63. And see Clarke v. C., 25 Grat. 908; S. v. Wilson, 1 N. J. 439.

[3] 1 Hale, P. C. 547; 4 Bl. Com. 223.

[4] C. v. Pennock, 3 S. & R. 199; 1 Hawk. P. C., ch. 38, § 10. And see the definitions already referred to as given by Hale, East and Blackstone.

[5] See *infra*, § 518.

[6] 2 Bish. Cr. Proc., § 135.

[7] Fuller v. S., 48 Ala. 273.

by the person whose dwelling-house it is charged to be, or by his family or servants, it is not a dwelling-house with respect to this crime.[1] It is the fact that the house is a place for sleeping at night which fixes its character as a dwelling.[2] It is not essential to the crime that some one should be in the house at the time.[3] A house uninhabited because undergoing repairs is not the dwelling-house of the owner, though part of his property is still deposited therein;[4] but the fact that the owner temporarily locks up his house and leaves it, even for some months, with intention of returning, does not render it any less a dwelling-house.[5] The house may be a dwelling-house although occupied only by the servants of the owner.[6] But a building only occasionally and temporarily used as a lodging place is not a dwelling-house.[7] It is unnecessary, however, that the building be solely or principally used as a dwelling; even though its principal use is for other purposes, if it is also occupied to sleep in, it is a dwelling-house in such sense that burglary may be committed therein. It was so held with reference to a baker's shop in a portion of which a workman and his family resided;[8] and as to a workshop rented with a sleeping-room attached and occupied by the renter;[9] also as to a public building in which persons sleep;[10] also as to the corner of a warehouse used as an office and to sleep in;[11] and as to a building used as a store-house in some rooms of which the

[1] The fact that it has been used for meals and purposes of business is not enough: Rex v. Martin, Russ. & Ry. 108; or that goods have been moved into it with the intention of using it for a dwelling, it not yet having been slept in: Rex v. Harris, 2 East, P. C. 498; Rex v. Thompson, 2 East, P. C. 498. But these cases are doubted on the authority of an earlier statement in 1 Hawk. P. C., ch. 38, § 11; and it is said that a house, to which the owner has moved his furniture with the purpose of occupying it on his return from the country, is his dwelling: C. v. Brown, 3 Rawle, 207. The same person may have two dwellings: U. S. v. Johnson, 2 Cranch, C. C. 21.

[2] U. S. v. Johnson, 2 Cranch, C. C. 21.

[3] S. v. Reid, 20 Ia. 413.

[4] Rex v. Lyons, 2 East, P. C. 497.

[5] S. v. Meerchouse, 34 Mo. 344; Harrison v. S., 74 Ga. 801.

[6] Rex v. Gibbons, Russ. & Ry. 442; Rex v. Westwood, Russ. & Ry. 495; Buchanan v. S., 24 Tex. Ap. 195.

[7] S. v. Jenkins, 5 Jones, 430; Scott v. S., 62 Miss. 781.

[8] Rex v. Stock, Russ. & Ry. 185.

[9] Rex v. Carrell, 2 East, P. C. 506. And see Rex v. Bailey, 1 Moody, 23.

[10] Rex v. Smith, 1 M. & Rob. 256. Thus, a county jail in which the keeper and his family reside is a dwelling-house: S. v. Abbott, 16 N. H. 507; so is a sheriff's office similarly used: Bigham v. S., 31 Tex. Ap. 244.

[11] Anderson v. S., 17 Tex. Ap. 305.

owner or his clerks sleep.[1] But a building used as a store-house in which a person sleeps merely as watchman to protect the premises or goods therein is not a dwelling-house.[2] It is said, however, that if the store-house is used regularly as a sleeping apartment, although for the sole purpose of protecting the premises, it is a dwelling-house.[3] There are statutory provisions in some states with reference to breaking and entering which render it immaterial whether the building is inhabited.[4]

§ 495. **House of another.**— The house must be the dwelling of another than the defendant, for one cannot be guilty of burglary in breaking and entering his own building. Therefore, it is necessary to allege the ownership of the house.[5] The sufficiency of the description as to ownership will be discussed hereafter in the section relating to the indictment.[6] But the owner, within the meaning of the law with reference to burglary, is the person occupying the premises as a dwelling, the offense being one against the possession rather than against the mere ownership; and it is proper, therefore, in alleging the ownership, to lay it in the person who, as against the burglar, is in rightful occupancy.[7] Therefore, the allegation that the house broken and entered was "the dwelling-house of A. B." is a sufficient allegation that it was at the time occupied by A. B. as his dwelling-house.[8] So in case of a tenant occupying premises, the ownership should be laid in the tenant and not in the landlord.[9] And it seems that a tenant of only a portion of a house may be deemed the owner for this purpose of that portion.[10] But where the owner of the premises leases rooms only to lodgers, the whole premises are deemed the dwelling

[1] Ex parte Vincent, 26 Ala. 145; U. S. v. Johnson, 2 Cranch, C. C. 21; S. v. Leedy, 95 Mo. 76; Ashton v. S., 68 Ga. 25; S. v. Frank, 41 La. An. 596.

[2] S. v. Potts, 75 N. C. 129; Rex v. Smith, 2 East, P. C. 497; Rex v. Brown, 2 East, P. C. 501; Rex v. Davis, 2 East, P. C. 499; Rex v. Flannagan, Russ. & Ry. 187.

[3] S. v. Outlaw, 72 N. C. 598; S. v. Williams, 90 N. C. 724.

[4] C. v. Reynolds, 122 Mass. 454; P. v. Stickman, 34 Cal. 242; S. v. Dan, 18 Nev. 345. And see as to store-houses and other buildings, *infra*, § 499.

[5] C. v. Perris, 108 Mass. 1; Wilson v. S., 34 Ohio St. 199.

[6] See *infra*, § 508.

[7] Smith v. P., 115 Ill. 17; S. v. Rivers, 68 Ia. 611; Kennedy v. S., 81 Ind. 379; McCrillis v. S., 69 Ind. 159; Houston v. S., 38 Ga. 165; Ducher v. S., 18 Ohio, 308; Leslie v. S., 35 Fla. 171; Lenhart v. S., 33 Tex. Ap. 504.

[8] Bell v. S., 20 Wis. 599.

[9] Rex v. Collett, Russ. & Ry. 498.

[10] Smith v. P., 115 Ill. 17.

of the owner who resides in a portion of the premises.[1] The room of a guest in a hotel is not a dwelling-house.[2] Where the building is rented to different tenants, the landlord not occupying any portion of it, the tenants are to be regarded, with respect to burglary, as owners of their respective portions, although they use a common outer door;[3] and more so where the outer doors are separate.[4] Where the premises are occupied by the husband and wife they are to be described as the dwelling-house of the husband, even though the wife has the legal title.[5] And the husband may be deemed to be in constructive possession of the premises occupied by his wife and family although he is absent.[6] Indeed, it is the doctrine of the English cases that the dwelling-house in which the wife lives separate from her husband is to be described as his dwelling.[7]

§ 496. Buildings connected with or appurtenant to the dwelling; common roof.— The fact that portions of a building under a common roof are used for business or other purposes not incident to the occupation of the building as a dwelling will not prevent the whole building being deemed the dwelling, including the part used for other purposes.[8] Thus, a breaking and entering of a cellar may be burglary, although the cellar is not used in connection with the dwelling and

[1] S. v. Pressly, 90 N. C. 730.

[2] Rex v. Prosser, 2 East, P. C. 502. And this is true whether the proprietor of the hotel lives therein or not: Rodgers v. P., 86 N. Y. 360. The sample room in a hotel cannot be considered a dwelling: Thomas v. S., 97 Ala. 3. So apartments in a college, not occupied by the students, are to be laid in the indictment as owned by the college: Rex v. Maynard, 2 East, P. C. 501. In Georgia a room in an inn is deemed the dwelling of the guest who occupies it: Jones v. S., 75 Ga. 825.

[3] Mason v. P., 26 N. Y. 200; Rex v. Trapshaw, 2 East, P. C. 506. And it is the same where the owner of the whole building, not used principally as a dwelling, occupies rooms therein separate from rooms occupied by other tenants: S. v. Rand, 33 N. H. 216. Under statutory provisions in California, the occupant of a room or apartment is to be deemed the owner thereof with respect to burglary: P. v. St. Clair, 38 Cal. 137.

[4] Rex v. Rogers, 2 East, P. C. 506; Rex v. Bailey, 1 Moody, 23; Rex v. Turner, 2 East, P. C. 492; Rex v. Jones, 2 East, P. C. 504.

[5] S. v. Short, 54 Ia. 392; Yarborough v. S., 86 Ga. 396; Morgan v. S., 63 Ga. 307; Young v. S., 100 Ala. 126; Jackson v. S., 102 Ala. 167. *Contra*, S. v. Trapp, 17 S. C. 467.

[6] C. v. Dailey, 110 Mass. 503.

[7] Rex v. Smyth, 5 C. & P. 201; Rex v. French, Russ. & Ry. 491; Rex v. Wilford, Russ. & Ry. 517.

[8] P. v. Dupree, 98 Mich. 26; Rex v. Lithgo, Russ. & Ry. 357; Reg. v. Wenmouth, 8 Cox, 348. But see Rex v. Jenkins, Russ. & Ry. 244.

has no internal communication with the other parts of the building.[1] Provision for such cases is sometimes made by statute.[2] Although where the parts of the building having such diverse use are under a common roof, internal communication is, perhaps, not essential in order that the whole building shall be deemed the dwelling,[3] yet the fact of internal communication is often referred to as important in showing that all the parts of the building are included in the dwelling, though they are subjected to use for other purposes.[4] And where there is no internal communication, and the portion of the premises used for other purposes than a dwelling is not, properly speaking, a part of the dwelling, the breaking and entering of the business part will not be a breaking and entering of the dwelling.[5]

§ 497. **Within the curtilage.**— The common-law notion of a mansion involved a common inclosure protected originally by a surrounding wall for purposes of defense, or, later, by some sort of fence for the purpose of excluding strangers and securing privacy. This common inclosure is designated as the curtilage, and all the buildings within it are considered as parts of the mansion-house or dwelling.[6] Thus, a barn, used for purposes incident to the use of the dwelling and in the common inclosure, is a part of the dwelling in such sense that to break and enter the barn with felonious intent may be burglary.[7] The same principle covers a goose-house,[8] a smoke-house,[9] a

[1] Mitchell v. C., 88 Ky. 349.

[2] Moore v. P., 47 Mich. 639; Mitchell v. C., 88 Ky. 349; S. v. Hutchinson, 111 Mo. 257.

[3] Rex v. Gibson, 2 East, P. C. 508; Rex v. Chalking, Russ. & Ry. 334; Rex v. Burrows, 1 Moody, 274.

[4] P. v. Griffin, 77 Mich. 585; Rex v. Sefton, Russ. & Ry. 202; Rex v. Stock, Russ. & Ry. 185.

[5] Rex v. Eggington, 2 East, P. C. 494, 666. And as illustrating the same principle, see Rex v. Paine, 7 C. & P. 135; Reg. v. Higgs, 2 C. & K. 322.

[6] C. v. Barney, 10 Cush. 478; S. v. Hecox, 83 Mo. 531, 5 Am. Cr. R. 98, and note.

[7] Pitcher v. P., 16 Mich. 142. And the statute defining the offense as the breaking and entering of a dwelling, etc., covers the offense of breaking and entering the barn: Ibid. A building used for the purposes of a barn comes within a statutory definition of burglary which embraces the barn: Ratekin v. S., 26 Ohio St. 420; Barnett v. S., 38 Ohio St. 7. A charge of breaking and entering the stable implies that the stable was a building: Orrell v. P., 94 Ill. 456.

[8] Rex v. Clayburn, Russ. & Ry. 360.

[9] Fletcher v. S., 10 Lea, 338; S. v. White, 4 Jones, 349. But the smoke-house must be appurtenant to the

summer-house,[1] a store-house used also as a sleeping-room,[2] and other outhouses; that is, houses appurtenant to the mansion-house but not a parcel of it.[3] A building which has an entrance inside the curtilage, and also one outside, is deemed within the curtilage in such sense that a breaking and entering, even of that part outside, may be burglary.[4] A breaking and entry through the door of the wall or the fence itself surrounding the curtilage, but not forming the entrance into any building, does not constitute burglary.[5] A division of the inclosure by a fence or wall so as to separate it into yards for purposes appropriate to the dwelling will not prevent a portion of the general inclosure from being a part of the curtilage.[6] Nor will the fact that the inclosure is appurtenant to different dwellings and common to them prevent a barn or other building therein, which is to some extent used as appurtenant to one of the dwellings, from being deemed a part thereof.[7]

§ 498. **Buildings adjacent.**— The entire change from the conditions of life under which the conception of a mansion-house was formed has made necessary new notions of the house and common inclosure requisite to render the adjacent buildings parts of the dwelling, and it is believed that at the present time the question is twofold, depending, first, upon the nature of the building, and second, upon the proximity to the dwelling. If the building is not used for purposes incident to the use of the principal building as a dwelling, it is not subject to burglary, though it may be near the dwelling, under common ownership, and even in a common inclosure.[8] Thus, it is held that there cannot be burglary of a tobacco barn,[9] or a mill-house,[10] or a building used for the sale of goods.[11] If the build-

dwelling-house: Palmer v. S., 7 Coldw. 82.

1 Rex v. Norris, Russ. & Ry. 69.

2 S. v. Mordecai, 68 N. C. 207.

3 S. v. Bailey, 10 Conn. 144; Bryant v. S., 60 Ga. 358; Rex v. Hancock, Russ. & Ry. 170.

4 Fisher v. S., 43 Ala. 17; Washington v. S., 82 Ala. 31.

5 Rex v. Bennett, Russ. & Ry. 289; Rex v. Davis, Russ. & Ry. 322.

6 Reg. v. Gilbert, 1 C. & K. 84; P. v. Aplin, 86 Mich. 393. And see P. v. Taylor, 2 Mich. 250.

7 P. v. Aplin, 86 Mich. 393; Rex v. Hancock, Russ. & Ry. 170; Rex v. Walters, 1 Moody, 13.

8 See Mitchell v. C., 88 Ky. 349.

9 White v. C., 87 Ky. 454.

10 S. v. Sampson, 12 S. C. 567.

11 Armour v. S., 3 Humph. 379; S. v. Langford, 1 Dev. 253; P. v. Parker, 4 Johns. 424; S. v. Ginns, 1 Nott & M. 583.

ing is thus appurtenant to the house, the fact of a common inclosure is immaterial.[1] But remoteness from the dwelling-house may deprive the building of the character of an appurtenance to the dwelling where not within a common inclosure.[2] Thus, buildings separated from the dwelling by a public road are said to be necessarily excluded from the category of buildings appurtenant to the dwelling-place for the reason that they could not be deemed even constructively within the curtilage.[3] In Missouri a division of the offense into degrees separates the breaking and entering of the dwelling proper from the breaking and entering of the building appurtenant.[4]

§ 499. Buildings not connected with a dwelling; statutory provisions.— At common law the breaking and entering in the night-time, with felonious intent, of a building not occupied as a dwelling or appurtenant thereto, was not the crime of burglary, although it was made punishable by various statutory provisions.[5] Under the broader definition of burglary suggested by Lord Hale, and already referred to,[6] a walled town or church might be subject to burglary.[7] But there is probably no modern authority making the breaking and entry of a church burglary, aside from statutory provisions. Statutes having specific reference to the breaking and entry of churches are to be found, however, in England and some of the states.[8] Statutes have been generally passed in the various states providing for the punishment, as crimes, of acts of break-

[1] S. v. Wilson, 1 Hayw. 242; S. v. Twitty, 1 Hayw. 102; Wait v. S., 99 Ala. 164; S. v. Shaw, 31 Me. 523; Rex v. Brown, 2 East, P. C. 493.

[2] S. v. Sampson, 12 S. C. 567; S. v. Jake, 1 Wins., ii, 80.

[3] Curkendall v. P., 36 Mich. 309; S. v. Stewart, 6 Conn. 47; Rex v. Westwood, Russ. & Ry. 495.

[4] S. v. Hecox, 83 Mo. 531.

[5] Hollister v. C., 60 Pa. St. 103; Koster v. P., 8 Mich. 431; S. v. Dozier, 73 N. C. 117; Conners v. S., 45 N. J. 340.

[6] See *supra*, § 494.

[7] 4 Bl. Com. 224; 1 Hawk. P. C., ch. 38, § 10; 2 East, P. C. 491. And Lord Coke supports this doctrine as to the church by the suggestion that it is the mansion-house of God: 3 Inst. 64.

[8] Under the English statute a dissenting meeting-house was not a church within its terms: Rex v. Richardson, 6 C. & P. 335; Rex v. Nixon, 7 C. & P. 442. The vestry is held to be a part of the church: Reg. v. Evans, Car. & M. 298; so is the tower: Rex v. Wheeler, 3 C. & P. 585. Where the statute refers to breaking and entering a church and stealing therefrom of some chattel, taking a fixture is not sufficient: Reg. v. Baker, 3 Cox, 581. A box containing money is not deemed a fixture: Reg. v. Wortly, 1 Den. 162. It is not neces-

ing and entering in the night-time buildings not used for dwelling purposes nor appurtenant thereto. A provision for the punishment of such breaking and entering of an outhouse, whether appurtenant to the mansion-house or not, in which goods, etc., are deposited, includes a barn in which animals and produce are kept, irrespective of its distance from the dwelling-house.[1] And where the statute defines the building as one not adjacent to or occupied with a dwelling-house, such description is intended to cover cases where the building is not appurtenant to the dwelling, and the negative words need not be used in the indictment.[2] A statute covering the breaking and entering of a building in which goods, wares and merchandise are deposited, includes an apartment so used, even the cabin of a vessel.[3] The indictment should describe the building as used for such purposes.[4] Under such a statute, a "store or building" includes an unfinished building where tools are temporarily stored.[5] A "store" is a place where merchandise is kept for sale.[6] The term "shop" is not synonymous with "store,"[7] but, under the English statute, is a place for the sale of goods, and not a work-shop.[8] The term "store-house" may include a room occupied as a news depot.[9] The term "warehouse" may include a cellar, used merely for the deposit of goods,[10] or a railroad depot.[11] A railroad depot may also be in-

sary that the chattels be such as are used in divine service: Rex v. Rourke, Russ. & Ry. 386.

[1] S. v. Brooks, 4 Conn. 446.

[2] Devoe v. C., 3 Met. 316; Larned v. C., 12 Met. 240; S. v. Kane, 63 Wis. 260. But in Michigan, the fact that the building is not adjoining, etc., seems to be deemed material to the offense under the statute: Koster v. P., 8 Mich. 431; the question being for the jury: P. v. Shaughnessy, 89 Mich. 130.

[3] S. v. Carrier, 5 Day, 131.

[4] Crawford v. S., 44 Ala. 382; Thomas v. S., 97 Ala. 3; Bearden v. S., 95 Ga. 459. But such description is not necessary under the Iowa statute: S. v. Emmons, 72 Ia. 265. As to how the offense is to be charged so as to distinguish it from burglary, see S. v. Franks, 64 Ia. 39. As to the description of the goods in such cases, see *infra*, § 509.

[5] Clark v. S., 69 Wis. 203. But the indictment must allege that the building was of the character described by statute: S. v. Savage, 32 Me. 583.

[6] C. v. Whalen, 131 Mass. 419.

[7] S. v. Canney, 19 N. H. 135.

[8] Reg. v. Sanders, 9 C. & P. 79. A butcher shop does not necessarily imply that animals are slaughtered or dressed there: Green v. S., 56 Ark. 386. Under later English statutes, a work-shop is covered by the term "shop:" Reg. v. Carter, 1 C. & K. 173.

[9] Bauer v. S., 25 Ohio St. 70.

[10] Reg. v. Hill, 2 M. & Rob. 458.

[11] S. v. Bishop, 51 Vt. 287.

cluded in the term "other building."[1] Indeed, the term "other building" is broadly construed to cover an office,[2] a court-house,[3] a buggy-house,[4] or a granary;[5] but where those words in the statute followed "shop, store," etc., it was held that they must be limited to buildings of the same general character, and would not cover a "chicken-house."[6] A description of the building, in the disjunctive, as a dwelling-house or a shop, store-house, warehouse or other building, will be proper under a statute including all of them.[7] The term "factory," used in a statute, will cover a place used for the purpose of depositing ashes and converting them into potash.[8] As to the construction of other terms covering houses and places of business, see cases in note.[9] A statute as to a "building" does not cover the breaking into a corn crib;[10] nor does the term "building or other inclosure" thus used include a cemetery vault.[11] Though the statute does not describe the breaking and entering of store buildings as burglary, it is not objectionable that the offense is so named in the indictment if otherwise correctly described.[12]

§ 500. **The breaking.**— Some breaking of the building is essential to the crime of burglary,[13] though by statute, in some states, the offense is made to consist of the entry in the night-time with felonious intent without regard to the breaking.[14] The breaking must be such as will afford the burglar an opportunity to enter for the purpose of committing the intended felony.[15] Thus, it is sufficient to break a pane of glass for the purpose of opening a window in order to enter, although the window is not in fact opened.[16] So it is burglary to break further a partially broken pane and thus open the window, the

[1] S. v. Edwards, 109 Mo. 315. Breaking and entering a railway car with intent, etc., is sometimes covered by statute: Lyons v. P., 68 Ill. 271.

[2] P. v. Young, 65 Cal. 225; S. v. Sufferin, 6 Wash. 107.

[3] S. v. Rogers, 54 Kan. 683.

[4] S. v. Garrison, 52 Kan. 180.

[5] S. v. Hecox, 83 Mo. 531.

[6] S. v. Schuchmann, — Mo. —, 33 S. W. R. 35 (overruling S. v. Hecox, *supra*).

[7] Ward v. S., 50 Ala. 120.

[8] Blackford v. S., 11 Ohio St. 327.

[9] Reg. v. Potter, 2 Den. 235; Womack v. S., 6 Lea, 146; Bethune v. S., 48 Ga. 505; McElreath v. S., 55 Ga. 562.

[10] Wood v. S., 18 Fla. 967.

[11] P. v. Richards, 108 N. Y. 137.

[12] S. v. Gillett, — Ia. —, 61 N. W. R. 169.

[13] S. v. Boon, 13 Ired. 244; P. v. McCord, 76 Mich. 200.

[14] Martin v. S., 1 Tex. Ap. 525; S. v. Watkins, 11 Nev. 30.

[15] Rex v. Hughes, 2 East, P. C. 491.

[16] Rex v. Perkes, 1 C. & P. 300.

offense consisting in opening the window, however, and not in the breaking further the pane already broken,[1] or in pushing in a pane of glass which had been previously cut.[2] But it was held not enough to break open a shutter of the window for the purpose of reaching the sash and glass, the latter not being broken.[3] If the breaking is such as to enable the prisoner to take the property stolen through the breach with his hands, that is sufficient.[4] So it has been held that one who, intending to steal shelled corn, bored a hole through the floor of the crib from the outside and drew the corn into a sack below, was guilty of sufficient breaking to constitute burglary;[5] but that one who neither effected nor enlarged the opening through which corn was taken from a crib was not guilty of burglary.[6] A breaking may be effected by fire if that is the means employed for obtaining entrance with a felonious purpose.[7] The term "breaking" does not imply the use of any degree of force and violence in order to injure or destroy any part of the building, but simply the force that is necessary to remove the impediments to entering.[8] The violation of any mode of security adopted by the occupant is a breaking.[9] Thus, opening a door fastened in the usual way, by lifting the latch,[10] or by unhooking a chain by which the door is fastened,[11] or by pushing open a door which is closed and held in place by reason of fitting closely within the casing,[12] even though the door is not locked or bolted,[13] is sufficient. The same principle is applicable to a transom,[14] and to a window opening upon hinges.[15] Opening a closed window by raising the sash from the bottom or pulling it down from the top, although the sash is only held in place by gravity or by a pulley weight, is a breaking.[16] So-

1 Rex v. Robinson, 1 Moody, 327.

2 Reg. v. Bird, 9 C. & P. 44.

3 S. v. McCall, 4 Ala. 643.

4 Fisher v. S., 43 Ala. 17.

5 Walker v. S., 63 Ala. 49.

6 Miller v. S., 77 Ala. 41.

7 White v. S., 49 Ala. 344.

8 S. v. O'Brien, 81 Ia. 93.

9 S. v. Cash, 38 Kan. 50.

10 Bass v. S., 1 Lea, 444; S. v. O'Brien, 81 Ia. 93; S. v. Jansen, 22 Kan. 498; S. v. Groning, 33 Kan. 18.

11 S. v. Hecox, 83 Mo. 531.

12 Kent v. S., 84 Ga. 438.

13 Finch v. C., 14 Grat. 643; S. v. Reid, 20 Ia. 413; Lyons v. P., 68 Ill. 271; Hild v. S., 67 Ala. 39; S. v. Boon, 13 Ired. 244; S. v. Fleming, 107 N. C. 905; Grimes v. S., 77 Ga. 762.

14 Timmons v. S., 34 Ohio St. 426; even though the transom be not shut down close into the frame, if some force is necessary to open it: Dennis v. P., 27 Mich. 151.

15 Rex v. Hall, Russ. & Ry. 355.

16 S. v. Carpenter, 1 Houst. Cr. C.

the breaking or cutting out of a screen or light net-work in a window, preventing entrance, is sufficient though the sash is open.[1] But if the window is partially open, and all that is necessary to effect entrance is to push it further open, that act is not a breaking,[2] the reason assigned for this distinction being that in the latter case there has not been an effort to protect the building from entry, and, as is sometimes said, the leaving open of the window or door is an invitation to enter.[3] The question is whether the closing is such as is intended to exclude, and if it is merely for convenience, with intent that all who desire to come in may do so, it is not a breaking whatever the purpose of entry may be;[4] it was so held as to the removal of a plank which was loose and could be pulled back at pleasure.[5] On this principle it has been held that lifting the flap of a cellar door, held in place by its own weight, is not a breaking.[6] But these cases must be regarded as doubtful. There is authority the other way.[7] While there must be force in a legal sense, actual force and violence are not necessary if the entry is unlawful.[8] Of course, the entry through a window or other opening which is not in any way closed to prevent ingress is not burglary.[9] But entry through an opening left for other purposes than entry, and which is not customarily closed for the purpose of excluding entrance to the building, as, for in-

367; Frank v. S., 39 Miss. 705; S. v. Moore, 117 Mo. 395; Rex v. Haines, Russ. & Ry. 451; Rex v. Hyams, 7 C. & P. 441. Where defendant in the day-time slightly raised a sash so that the lock would not catch, and then at night entered by putting up the sash, he was held guilty of breaking at night: P. v. Dupree, 98 Mich. 26.

1 C. v. Stephenson, 8 Pick. 354; Sims v. S., 136 Ind. 358.

2 C. v. Strupney, 105 Mass. 588; Rex v. Smith, 1 Moody, 178.

3 C. v. Stephenson, 8 Pick. 354; S. v. Wilson, 1 N. J. 439; S. v. Boon, 13 Ired. 244; Stone v. S., 63 Ala. 115; Rex v. Lewis, 2 C. & P. 628.

4 S. v. Newbegin, 25 Me. 500.

5 C. v. Trimmer, 1 Mass. 476.

6 Rex v. Russell, 1 Moody, 377; Rex v. Lawrence, 4 C. & P. 231; Rex v. Brown, 2 East, P. C. 487. And see Rex v. Callan, Russ. & Ry. 157, where the judges were equally divided in opinion.

7 P. v. Nolan, 22 Mich. 229.

8 Pritchett v. S., 92 Ga. 33. Thus, to open a door with the owner's key is a breaking though it is left within the reach of every comer: Colbert v. S., 91 Ga. 705. By Oregon statute unlawful entry is sufficient, and such evidence will support the indictment though it charge an entry by forcible breaking: S. v. Huntley, 25 Oreg. 349.

9 Green v. S., 68 Ala. 539; Pines v. S., 50 Ala. 153; Williams v. S., 52 Ga. 580; Melton v. S., 24 Tex. Ap. 287; Rex v. Lewis, 2 C. & P. 628.

stance, an open chimney, is a breaking.[1] And the breaking and entry is complete although the person does not get further down than into the chimney.[2] The same principle applies to other openings not intended for entry.[3] Even though entry is effected into the building through a door or window left open, so that it is not preceded by a breaking, yet, if with the purpose of carrying out the felonious intent, there is a breaking into a room through an inner door which is closed, this will constitute a sufficient breaking.[4] Thus, one who is lawfully in the house may be convicted of burglary in breaking into another part of it where he has not the right to enter.[5] But this doctrine as to the breaking of an inner door is not applicable to the opening of the door of a cupboard, closet or chest.[6] Evidence that access to the building could only have been had by some form of breaking is sufficient although the particular manner is not made to appear.[7]

§ 501. **Constructive breaking.**— The forms of breaking already described involve force, but procuring entrance by fraud is considered as a constructive breaking and sufficient to constitute the crime. Thus, if accused has obtained entrance under the guise of friendship, or by fraud, as where the door was opened in response to what was supposed to be a friendly summons by ringing the bell or otherwise, the breaking is sufficient.[8] Where the prisoner, with intent to rob the agent

1 S. v. Willis, 7 Jones, 190; Walker v. S., 52 Ala. 376.

2 Donohoo v. S., 36 Ala. 281; Olds v. S., 97 Ala. 81; Rex v. Brice, Russ. & Ry. 450.

3 Painter v. S., 26 Tex. Ap. 454; Stone v. S., 63 Ala. 115; Marshall v. S., 94 Ga. 589.

4 U. S. v. Bowen, 4 Cranch, C. C. 604; Carter v. S., 68 Ala. 96; S. v. Scripture, 42 N. H. 485; P. v. Young, 65 Cal. 225; Rex v. Johnson, 2 East, P. C. 488. And it is said that the same rule is applicable whether the design is to commit the felony in the room to which access is thus gained or not: Rolland v. C., 85 Pa. St. 66.

5 A guest in a hotel: S. v. Clark, 42 Vt. 629. And see S. v. Moore, 12 N. H. 42. So held as to an employee left in charge of a house, but entering a room which he had no right to enter: Hild v. S., 67 Ala. 39; Van Walker v. S., 33 Tex. Ap. 359. In Texas by statute a burglary by an inhabitant of the house can be committed only by an actual breaking: Peters v. S., 33 Tex. Ap. 170.

6 S. v. Wilson, 1 N. J. 439; 2 East, P. C. 489. And see Peters v. S., 33 Tex. Ap. 170.

7 S. v. Kenney, 101 Mo. 160; S. v. Warford, 106 Mo. 55.

8 Johnston v. C., 85 Pa. St. 54; Rolland v. C., 82 Pa. St. 306; S. v. Carter, 1 Houst. Cr. C. 402; S. v. Mordecai, 68 N. C. 207. But a mere entry through stealth is not a fraudulent

on an express car, had himself packed and shipped as an express package and thus obtained entry to the car, it was held that there was a constructive breaking.[1] An entry obtained by threats is by constructive breaking.[2] There may be a constructive breaking by conspiracy with a servant,[3] and the offense will be burglary in both the servant and the prisoner who thus procures admission.[4] But there cannot be such constructive breaking where the entry is allowed by one who has the right to enter, as, for instance, a joint occupant.[5] Though the entry by a person having a right to enter is for a wrongful purpose, the fraud does not render the entry criminal as a constructive breaking.[6] Neither can one who thus has the right to enter be himself guilty of constructive breaking in entering without breaking, though he have a felonious intent.[7] Though the entry by a person having a right to enter is with a wrongful purpose, the fraud does not render the entry criminal as a constructive breaking.[8] So if, with the purpose of entrapping an intending burglar, the owner, or his servant under his direction, or the servant by direction of an officer, admits the intending burglar, there is not a constructive breaking.[9] But the fact that the owner has knowledge of the intended burglary and takes no steps to prevent it, intending to capture the burglar, does not prevent the breaking from being burglary.[10] If a person pretends to conspire to commit burglary, and, acting under the direction of another, breaks and enters, and the other does not himself commit any act of

entry: Hamilton v. S., 11 Tex. Ap. 116. Where the owner was enticed from his house by fraud and left the door open behind him, and sometime subsequently an entry was made by accomplices, the door not having been closed by the family in the meantime, *held,* that there was not a breaking: S. v. Henry, 9 Ired. 463.

[1] Nicholls v. S., 68 Wis. 416.

[2] Rex v. Swallow, 2 Russ., C. & M. 9.

[3] S. v. Rowe, 98 N. C. 629.

[4] Clarke v. C., 25 Grat. 908; Neiderluck v. S., 23 Tex. Ap. 38.

[5] Clarke v. C., 25 Grat. 908.

[6] Lowder v. S., 63 Ala. 143.

[7] Neiderluck v. S., 23 Tex. Ap. 38.

[8] S. v. Moore, 12 N. H. 42.

[9] Allen v. S., 40 Ala. 334; Love v. P., 160 Ill. 501; P. v. McCord, 76 Mich. 200, 8 Am. Cr. R. 117, and note; Speiden v. S., 3 Tex. Ap. 156; Reg. v. Johnson, Car. & M. 218; Rex v. Dannelly, Russ. & Ry. 310. Under a Texas statute with reference to actual breaking, excluding entry by collusion with a domestic servant, *held,* that a farm hand, sleeping and eating outside the house, was not included: Waterhouse v. S., 21 Tex. Ap. 663.

[10] Thompson v. S., 18 Ind. 386; S. v. Sneff, 22 Neb. 481; S. v. Jansen, 22 Kan. 498; S. v. Stickney, 53 Kan. 308. And see *supra,* §§ 117, 118.

breaking and entering, the latter is not guilty of burglary though he would have been guilty had the supposed accomplice been a real one.[1] So if one accomplice secures entry without breaking and admits the other, there is no burglary,[2] unless the entry of the first is procured by fraud.[3]

§ 502. **Breaking out.**— Where there has been an entry with intent to commit a felony, but no such breaking as is necessary in burglary, and the person committing the offense breaks out of the house in attempting to escape after the intended felony has been either completed or desisted from, the offense is not burglary, aside from any statutory provision.[4] In England, since the statute on the subject (12 Anne, ch. 7), the breaking out will make the offense burglary.[5] The term "forcibly" used in the definition of the offense by statute has been held to imply no more than at common law, and an entrance by fraud has been held to come within such statute.[6] But where the statute specifies different forms of burglary, it has been held that if the offense is charged to have been committed by force it cannot be shown to have been committed by threats or fraud.[7]

§ 503. **The entry.**— An entry must be alleged and proven.[8] Getting into the chimney is a sufficient entry.[9] An entry of any portion of the body into the house, whether for the purpose of effecting the breaking or the entry, or of committing the felony intended, will constitute an entry.[10] Thus, the fact that the finger goes inside of the window in breaking it is an entry.[11] So introducing the hand between the glass of an outer

[1] S. v. Hayes, 105 Mo. 76; P. v. Collins, 53 Cal. 185.

[2] Ray v. S., 66 Ala. 281.

[3] C. v. Lowry, 158 Mass. 18.

[4] Wine v. S., 25 Ohio St. 69; White v. S., 51 Ga. 285; Adkinson v. S., 5 Baxt. 569; Brown v. S., 55 Ala. 123.

[5] Rex v. Lawrence, 4 C. & P. 231; Reg. v. Wheeldon, 8 C. & P. 747; Rex v. Compton, 7 C. & P. 139. This statute is probably common law in this country even if not declaratory of the common law previously existing: S. v. Ward, 43 Conn. 489. If the case is to be brought within a statute with reference to breaking out, the breaking must be alleged in that form: S. v. McPherson, 70 N. C. 239; and the entry must be in the night-time as well as the breaking out: Conner v. S., 14 Mo. 561.

[6] Ducher v. S., 18 Ohio, 308.

[7] Buntain v. S., 15 Tex. Ap. 485, Lott v. S., 17 Tex. Ap. 598; Ross v. S., 16 Tex. Ap. 554.

[8] Reg. v. Meal, 3 Cox, 70; Reg. v. Davis, 6 Cox, 367.

[9] Donohoo v. S., 36 Ala. 281; Olds v. S., 97 Ala. 81; Rex v. Brice, Russ. & Ry. 450.

[10] S. v. McCall, 4 Ala. 643.

[11] Rex v. Davis, Russ. & Ry. 499.

window and an inner shutter,[1] or pushing up a trap door with the hand,[2] will be an entry; and also, it would seem, that putting in an instrument for the purpose of effecting the felony intended, as, for instance, a hook with which to remove articles from the house for the purpose of stealing them, would be an entry.[3] But if no part of the prisoner's body is inside the premises, the introduction of an instrument for the purpose of effecting an entry does not constitute an entry, although the instrument be partially inside the house.[4] By virtue of statutory provisions in Texas, shooting into a house with intent to commit a felony is a sufficient entry, and in such case breaking and entering need not be alleged.[5] By the Texas statute, also, there is a requirement that the entry be without the consent of the owner or any one authorized to give consent; but it is held that the indictment need not negative the fact of such consent.[6] Sometimes, by statute, the entry alone without breaking, the intent being to commit larceny, is made burglary, and in such case an entry in the usual way into a store building open to customers, the entry being, however, with the unlawful intent, constitutes the offense.[7]

§ 504. **Night-time; day-time under statutes.**— At the common law, and under statutes drawn in conformity therewith, it is necessary to allege and prove the offense to have been committed in the night-time.[8] Such fact must be proven by positive testimony, and if it is doubtful there should be an acquittal.[9] But in a prosecution for breaking and entering a store building or shop in the night-time, evidence that it was entered

[1] Rex v. Bailey, Russ. & Ry. 341.

[2] Nash v. S., 20 Tex. Ap. 384.

[3] Rex v. Gibbons, 2 East, P. C. 490; Foster, 107; 1 Hale, P. C. 553; 1 Hawk. P. C., ch. 38, § 7; 4 Bl. Com. 227; 2 Bish. Cr. L., § 92; S. v. McCall, 4 Ala. 643.

[4] Reg. v. O'Brien, 4 Cox, 398; Rex v. Rust, 1 Moody, 183; Rex v. Roberts, 2 East, P. C. 487.

[5] Garner v. S., 31 Tex. Ap. 22.

[6] S. v. Williams, 41 Tex. 98; Sullivan v. S., 13 Tex. Ap. 462; Reed v. S., 14 Tex. Ap. 662; Smith v. S., 22 Tex. Ap. 350; Taylor v. S., 23 Tex. Ap. 639 (overruling earlier cases). The consent, if it exists, is a matter of defense: Willis v. S., 33 Tex. Ap. 168.

[7] P. v. Barry, 94 Cal. 481. And see S. v. Huntley, 25 Oreg. 349.

[8] S. v. Mather, N. Chip. 32; C. v. Marks, 4 Leigh, 658; Davis v. S., 3 Coldw. 77; S. v. White, 4 Jones, 349. The heinousness of the crime consists largely in its being committed at night: S. v. Frahm, 73 Ia. 355.

[9] Waters v. S., 53 Ga. 567. But circumstantial evidence may be sufficient, and the jury may consider the probability of the entry taking place in the daylight: S. v. Bancroft, 10 N. H. 105. This element must be es-

and the goods taken between the time of closing after dark and the time of opening at sunrise has been held sufficient.[1] At common law it was a question whether the hour of the night need be alleged.[2] Statutory definitions of burglary say "in the night-time," and an allegation in that form is universally held sufficient.[3] An allegation of the particular hour, if such as to show the commission of the offense in the night-time, will be sufficient;[4] but the hour need not be proven as alleged.[5] Both the breaking and the entry must be in the night-time, but they need not be on the same night.[6] If the breaking and entry are in the night-time the offense is burglary, although the intended felony is not completed in the night-time.[7] The fact that the accused, after breaking and entering and carrying away goods in the night-time, returned after an interval and took away other goods in the day-time, does not show two distinct offenses, but the whole transaction is one burglary.[8] While time is essential to the extent that the acts must be in the night-time, yet the precise date need not be proven as alleged any more than in other cases.[9] Some statutes extend the offense of burglary so as to cover a breaking and entering in the day-time; others make breaking and entering in the day-time a distinct offense. Under the former class of statutory provisions, the fact that the offense is committed in the night-time is usually made material in aggravation; under the latter it is punishable to a greater degree than the

tablished: Ashford v. S., 36 Neb. 38. But the accused is not entitled to any presumption that he entered by day and secreted himself: U. S. v. Lantry, 30 Fed. R. 232.

1 Howser v. S., 58 Ga. 78; Brown v. S., 59 Ga. 456; Smith v. S., 62 Ga. 663; P. v. Dupree, 98 Mich. 26.

2 The hour was held necessary in Rex v. Waddington, 2 East, P. C. 513. And see 1 Russ. Cr. 826. But other authorities hold generally an allegation of the night-time sufficient: 1 Hale, P. C. 549; Mackally's Case, 9 Coke, 65. Where the act was alleged as burglariously done, that was held a sufficient allegation that it was done in the night-time: Reg. v. Thompson, 2 Cox, 445. But to the contrary see Lewis v. S., 16 Conn. 32.

3 Lewis v. S., 16 Conn. 32; P. v. Burgess, 35 Cal. 115; S. v. Robinson, 35 N. J. 71; S. v. Ruby, 61 Ia. 86; C. v. Williams, 2 Cush. 582.

4 S. v. Seymour, 36 Me. 225. Thus, to allege that the act was committed on a certain day "about the hour of twelve o'clock in the night of that day" is sufficient: Shelton v. C., 89 Va. 450.

5 P. v. Burgess, 35 Cal. 115.

6 Rex v. Smith, Russ. & Ry. 417.

7 C. v. Glover, 111 Mass. 395.

8 P. v. Gibson, 58 Mich. 368.

9 S. v. Branham, 13 S. C. 389.

offense of breaking and entering in the day-time. If the statutory provision is such that breaking and entry in the daytime is burglary, it is not necessary to allege the breaking and entry as committed in the day-time, and an indictment will support a conviction for breaking and entering in the day-time where it does not make an allegation as to the time.[1] If it is an aggravation of the offense that it is committed in the nighttime, it should be alleged as committed at night.[2] If the statute makes the breaking and entering in the day-time a distinct offense from burglary, then it seems that the offense must be alleged and proven with the same definiteness as to time as is required in burglary.[3] Some statutes make breaking and entering by day-time, and entering by day or night without breaking, offenses distinct from burglary.[4] The night-time, within the meaning of the previous discussion, is the time when, by reason of the absence of daylight (not taking into account moonlight), a person's features are not reasonably discernible.[5] When the statute uses the term "night-time" it means that which was night-time at common law.[6]

§ 505. **The intent.**— The intent to commit a felony (that is, an offense distinct from the breaking and entering, and for the

[1] Butler v. P., 4 Denio, 68; C. v. Reynolds, 122 Mass. 454; C. v. Carson, 166 Pa. St. 179; S. v. Hutchinson, 111 Mo. 257; S. v. Miller, 3 Wash. 131; Bravo v. S., 20 Tex. Ap. 188. The breaking and entering in the day-time may be regarded as a lower degree of the offense of burglary: S. v. Jordan, 87 Ia. 86.

[2] Hall v. P., 43 Mich. 417; S. v. Anselm, 43 La. An. 195. *Contra*, holding it sufficient that the evidence shows the offense to have been committed in the night: Buchanan v. S., 24 Tex. Ap. 195. If the offense committed in the day-time is made burglary in the second degree, the indictment may charge burglary generally and the degree may be determined on the proof: P. v. Jefferson, 52 Cal. 452; P. v. Barnhart, 59 Cal. 381.

[3] P. v. Taggart, 43 Cal. 81; S. v. Mack, 20 Oreg. 234; Davis v. S., 3 Coldw. 77; Bromley v. P., 150 Ill. 297; Jones v. S., 63 Ga. 141; Guynes v. S., 25 Tex. Ap. 584; Coates v. S., 31 Tex. Ap. 257. In such case under a charge for burglary defendant must be found guilty or not guilty of the offense of breaking and entering in the night-time: Williams v. S., 46 Ga. 212; Wood v. S., 46 Ga. 322.

[4] Rolland v. C., 85 Pa. St. 66; Williams v. S., 46 Ga. 212.

[5] S. v. Morris, 47 Conn. 179; S. v. Bancroft, 10 N. H. 105; P. v. Griffin, 19 Cal. 578; Thomas v. S., 5 How. (Miss.) 20; 2 East, P. C. 509; 1 Hale, P. C. 550. In some states the nighttime is more accurately defined by statute: Laws v. S., 26 Tex. Ap. 643.

[6] S. v. Robinson, 35 N. J. 71; C. v. Williams, 2 Cush. 582; Kleiforth v. S., 88 Wis. 163.

purpose of committing which in the house the breaking and entry was made[1]) must be alleged and proven;[2] such intent must accompany the act but need not precede it.[3] Intent to commit a misdemeanor will not be sufficient.[4] At common law petit larceny was a felony, so that breaking and entry with intent to steal, whether the value of the goods was such as to make the intended offense grand larceny or not, was burglary.[5] A compound larceny, such as stealing in a house, may be a felony, without regard to the value of the goods stolen.[6] Sometimes by statute the definition expressly covers all forms of larceny.[7] But intent to commit another felony than larceny will equally make the breaking and entry burglary; as, for instance, murder,[8] aiding a felon to escape,[9] arson,[10] rape,[11] or adultery where that offense is a felony, or the statute makes intent to commit any public offense sufficient.[12] Under the felonious intent sufficient to constitute the offense is included intent to commit statutory felonies as well as those which are such by the common law.[13] The indictment must allege what specific felony was intended, and the proof must

[1] Harris v. S., 20 Tex. Ap. 652; Benton v. C., 89 Va. 570; Winslow v. S., 26 Neb. 308. "With intent then and there" sufficiently shows the intent to commit the proposed crime in the house: Burke v. S., 5 Tex. Ap. 74; Reg. v. Andrews, Car. & M. 121.

[2] S. v. Carter, 1 Houst. Cr. C. 402; Price v. P., 109 Ill. 109; S. v. Green, 15 Mont. 424; Reeves v. S., 7 Tex. Ap. 276; Walton v. S., 29 Tex. Ap. 163; S. v. Meche, 42 La. An. 273. But there may be a statutory offense of house-breaking in which intent need not be alleged: Pardue v. S., 4 Baxt. 10.

[3] Jackson v. S., 102 Ala. 167.

[4] C. v. Newell, 7 Mass. 245; Wood v. S., 18 Fla. 967.

[5] Stevenson v. S., 5 Baxt. 681. Where petit larceny is not a felony the evidence must show the value of the goods to be such as to constitute grand larceny: Clifton v. S., 26 Fla. 523; unless, as in Iowa, the statute extends the crime to cover such an intent, as by the substitution of "any public offense" for "a felony:" S. v. Jones, 10 Ia. 206.

[6] S. v. Scott, 109 Mo. 226.

[7] P. v. Smith, 86 Cal. 238; P. v. Urquidas, 96 Cal. 239; P. v. Stapleton, 2 Idaho, 49; Simms v. S., 2 Tex. Ap. 110. And the intent may be alleged to be to commit "grand and petit larceny:" P. v. Hall, 94 Cal. 595.

[8] S. v. Manluff, 1 Houst. Cr. C. 208; S. v. Willis, 43 La. An. 407.

[9] S. v. Abbott, 16 N. H. 507.

[10] S. v. Ely, 35 La. An. 895.

[11] S. v. Powell, 94 N. C. 965; Harvey v. S., 53 Ark. 425; Walton v. S., 29 Tex. Ap. 163; Colman v. S., 26 Tex. Ap. 252; Mitchell v. S., 32 Tex. Ap. 479; 1 Hawk. P. C., ch. 38, § 14.

[12] S. v. Cooper, 16 Vt. 551; S. v. Corliss, 85 Ia. 18.

[13] 1 Hawk. P. C., ch. 38, § 19; Griffin v. S., 34 Ohio St. 299.

correspond;[1] but the indictment may charge two or more different felonious intents, and proof of one or more of them will support a conviction.[2] The intent charged must be proved beyond a reasonable doubt as any other ingredient of the crime;[3] and the court should instruct the jury as to the elements of the crime intended as well as with reference to burglary.[4] But it is not necessary to prove the commission of the offense which it is alleged the defendant intended to commit.[5]

§ 506. **Evidence of intent.**— The specific intent to commit a felony is to be proved as in other cases of specific intent.[6] Thus, previous preparation or antecedent circumstances may be shown,[7] or conversation at the time.[8] It may be inferred from acts done after the breaking and entering and apparently in pursuance of the original plan. Thus, if the acts indicate an intent to violate a female, a conviction may be had of breaking and entering with intent to commit rape;[9] or where injuries are inflicted on a person within, not making resistance, an assault to kill may be presumed.[10] Where no other motive for the breaking and entering appears, the intent to steal may be in-

[1] Mason v. P., 26 N. Y. 200; P. v. Mulkey, 65 Cal. 501; S. v. Eaton, 3 Harr. 554; Ashford v. S., 36 Neb. 38; S. v. Carroll, 13 Mont. 246; S. v. Lockhart, 24 Ga. 420; S. v. Williamson, 3 Heisk. 483; Portwood v. S., 29 Tex. 47; Wilburn v. S., 41 Tex. 237; Black v. S., 18 Tex. Ap. 124; S. v. Meche, 42 La. An. 273; Rex v. Vandercomb, 2 East, P. C. 514, 517. But proof of intent to commit robbery will support a charge of intent to commit larceny: P. v. Crowley, 100 Cal. 478; S. v. Halford, 104 N. C. 874; S. v. Cody, 1 Wins., i, 197. *Contra*, Miller v. S., 28 Tex. Ap. 445.

[2] S. v. Fox, 80 Ia. 312; Rex v. Thompson, 2 East, P. C. 515. And it is also said that where the indictment alleges breaking and entry with intent to steal the goods of the person named, and the evidence shows the stealing and carrying away of the goods of another person, there is not a misjoinder of offenses: S. v. Brady, 14 Vt. 353.

[3] S. v. Carpenter, 1 Houst. Cr. C. 367.

[4] Castenada v. S., 11 Tex. Ap. 390; Walton v. S., 29 Tex. Ap. 163; S. v. Yohe, 87 Ia. 33.

[5] Olive v. C., 5 Bush, 376; S. v. McDaniel, 1 Wins., i, 249; Bush v. S., 65 Ga. 658. But there may be a statutory offense of stealing from the dwelling-house requiring proof of actual larceny: Reg. v. Wenmouth, 8 Cox, 348.

[6] As to specific intent in general, see *supra*, § 122.

[7] S. v. Cowell, 12 Nev. 337; S. v. McDaniel, 1 Wins., i, 249.

[8] S. v. Powell, 94 N. C. 965.

[9] Harvey v. S., 53 Ark. 425; Burke v. S., 5 Tex. Ap. 74. Evidence of such intent in a particular case held insufficient: Hamilton v. S., 11 Tex. Ap. 116.

[10] S. v. Manluff, 1 Houst. Cr. C. 208.

ferred.[1] If the entry is made noisily, the intent may be presumed to be to rob rather than to steal.[2] Impossibility of carrying out the intent is immaterial.[3] Thus, the intent being to steal money from a safe, it is held to be immaterial whether there is any money in the safe or not, the crime existing in the intent.[4] While the issue with reference to the intent is as to the intent entertained at the time of breaking and entering and not as to the actual commission of the crime after breaking and entering,[5] yet the actual commission of the crime in the building after breaking and entering it is the best evidence of the intent which accompanied the breaking and entering.[6] It is so held with reference to larceny.[7] And therefore, by common-law precedents, it is proper to allege the breaking and entry and the commission of larceny, on the theory that the allegation of the commission of the act is a sufficient allegation of the intent to commit it.[8] But if the evidence does not show the commission of the offense, then the prosecution, under an indictment charging its commission but not alleging an intent to commit it, will fail, it not being admissible, under that form of indictment, to introduce other evidence of the intention to commit.[9] It seems that when the indictment charges the actual commission of larceny in connection with breaking and

[1] Steadman v. S., 81 Ga. 736; S. v. Teeter, 69 Ia. 717; S. v. Fox, 80 Ia. 312; Franco v. S., 42 Tex. 276; Alexander v. S., 31 Tex. Ap. 359; P. v. Soto, 53 Cal. 415; P. v. Winters, 93 Cal. 277. By statute the breaking and entry alone may be made presumptive evidence of an intent to commit a felony or misdemeanor, it not being required to state the particular offense intended: Linbeck v. S., 1 Wash. 336.

[2] Lowe v. S., 14 Lea, 204.

[3] Burke v. S., 5 Tex. Ap. 74 (where the intent alleged was to commit rape on a certain woman, and it appeared that she was not in the house).

[4] S. v. Beal, 37 Ohio St. 108; Harvick v. S., 49 Ark. 514. But *contra*, see Lee v. S., 56 Ga. 477; Reg. v. McPherson, Dears. & B. C. C. 197. And as to the effect of impossibility of committing the crime intended, see the discussion under assault, *supra*, §§ 234, 266.

[5] P. v. Jenkins, 16 Cal. 431; S. v. Ayer, 23 N. H. 301.

[6] S. v. Ayer, 23 N. H. 301.

[7] Stokes v. S., 84 Ga. 258; Allen v. S., 12 Lea, 424; S. v. Golden, 49 Ia. 48; S. v. Woods, 31 La. An. 267.

[8] Jones v. S., 11 N. H., 269; S. v. Ayer, 23 N. H. 301; S. v. Henley, 30 Mo. 509; C. v. Brown, 3 Rawle, 207; Murray v. S., 48 Ala. 675; Rex v. Dobbs, 2 East, P. C. 513; Rex v. Furnival, Russ. & Ry. 445. *Contra*, Hammons v. S., 29 Tex. Ap. 445. This applies to the statutory offense of entering a building with felonious intent: Devoe v. C., 3 Met. 316.

[9] Rex v. Vandercomb, 2 East, P. C. 514; Reg. v. McPherson, Dears. & B. 197; Jones v. S., 11 N. H. 269.

entering for the purpose of showing burglary, the larceny need not be alleged with the same technicality as in an indictment for that substantive offense.[1] An indictment which thus charges breaking and entering and also the commission of larceny does not charge two offenses, as the allegation with reference to the commission of larceny is simply a form of charging the intent.[2]

§ 507. **Intent disproved.**— The specific intent may be disproved as in other cases; for instance, evidence of intoxication may be considered for that purpose,[3] or evidence of accident or mistake,[4] or that the breaking and entry was with some other intent than that charged.[5] If the intended taking of the goods as charged would not constitute larceny if the goods were taken, the breaking and entry with that intent will not be burglary.[6]

§ 508. **Indictment; description of property.**— Some description of the building broken and entered is essential, and that description should, in general, show that it was the kind of a building required to constitute the crime[7] and the name of the owner.[8] The name of the owner must be proved as

[1] Larned v. C., 12 Met. 240; Barber v. S., 78 Ala. 19. But where neither the intent to steal nor the ownership of the property stolen was alleged, *held*, that the indictment was insufficient: P. v. Stewart, 44 Mich. 484. And further as to the form of charging the offense intended, see *infra*, § 509.

[2] See *infra*, § 511.

[3] S. v. Bell, 29 Ia. 316.

[4] P. v. Griffin, 77 Mich. 585.

[5] Robinson v. S., 53 Md. 151.

[6] Rex v. Knight, 2 East, P. C. 510; Wilson v. S., 18 Tex. Ap. 270.

[7] That is, a mansion-house or dwelling-house. See *supra*, § 494. The character of the building should be alleged according to its real occupancy or use, and not in accordance with the name which it may have acquired: Thalls v. S., 21 Ohio St. 233.

[8] P. v. Parker, 91 Cal. 91; S. v. Reece, 27 W. Va. 375; Graves v. S., 63 Ala. 134; S. v. Hupp, 31 W. Va. 355; S. v. Morrissey, 22 Ia. 158; Webster v. C., 80 Va. 598; Butler v. C., 81 Va. 159; Rex v. White, 2 East, P. C. 513, 780. An indictment charging the breaking and entering of a building not alleged to be the property of any one is insufficient: Pells v. S., 20 Fla. 774. Where the indictment described the house as the "property of the estate of John Tate," *held*, that it was fatally defective because not containing an averment of ownership: Beall v. S., 53 Ala. 460 (overruling Anderson v. S., 48 Ala. 665; Murray v. S., 48 Ala. 675). "The dwelling-house of" or "dwelling-house belonging to" is a sufficient allegation: S. v. Fox, 80 Ia. 312; S. v. Miller, 3 Wash. 131; or a "certain building of," where the crime is the breaking and entering of a building: S. v. Tyrrell, 98 Mo. 354.

alleged; if not known it should be so stated.[1] Liberal provisions in some states as to what shall be sufficient in an indictment are held to make the allegation of ownership immaterial, so that a variance of the proof from the allegations in that respect will not be fatal.[2] Thus, if the property is described as that of one person, while the proof shows such person to be one of two or more joint tenants, the variance has, under such statutes, been held immaterial.[3] But aside from statutes such a variance is fatal.[4] These statutory provisions do not obviate the necessity of all description, and if there is none other sufficient to identify the building, that of ownership is essential.[5] The situation of the building is not a material allegation, except so far as necessary to show jurisdiction.[6] In alleging the ownership, the name of the person occupying the premises should be used, the offense being, as already explained, an offense against the possession;[7] and this is true although the possession is wrongful.[8] In case of joint occupancy, the ownership may properly be laid in the occupants

[1] Jackson v. S., 55 Wis. 589.

[2] P. v. Bitancourt, 74 Cal. 188; P. v. McGilver, 67 Cal. 55; P. v. Edwards, 59 Cal. 359; S. v. Wright, 19 Oreg. 258; S. v. Emmons, 72 Ia. 265; S. v. Clifton, 30 La. An., part II, 951.

[3] White v. S., 72 Ala. 195; Johnson v. C., 87 Ky. 189; P. v. Bitancourt, 74 Cal. 188; P. v. Edwards, 59 Cal. 359.

[4] Rex v. Jenkins, Russ. & Ry. 244.

[5] P. v. Parker, 91 Cal. 91.

[6] Spencer v. S., 13 Ohio, 401; Reg. v. Brookes, Car. & M. 544.

[7] Winslow v. S., 26 Neb. 308; S. v. Golden, 49 Ia. 48; S. v. Teeter, 69 Ia. 717; S. v. Betsall, 11 W. Va. 703. And see *supra*, § 495. Thus, if a servant lives in the house of his master at a yearly rent, the house should be described as the servant's: Rex v. Jarvis, 1 Moody, 7. But where the servant occupies merely by virtue of his service, without separate rental, the house may be described either as his or his master's: Rex v. Rees, 7 C. & P. 568; Rex v. Jobling, Russ. & Ry. 525; Rex v. Camfield, 1 Moody, 42. If a part of the house is used as the master's store-room, a breaking and entry of that part should be charged as in the dwelling-house of the master: Reg. v. Courtenay, 5 Cox, 218; Rex v. Wilson, Russ. & Ry. 115. But to the contrary see Rex v. Witt, 1 Moody, 248. A burglary committed in the house belonging to a trading company occupied by an agent for the purpose of carrying on the business may be charged as in the house of the agent: Rex v. Margetts, 2 Leach, 930. But a burglary in the apartments of an officer of a company in the building of the company should be charged as in the mansion-house of such company: Rex v. Hawkins, 2 East, P. C. 501. If the occupant is a mere care-taker the house should be alleged as that of the owner: Rex v. Rawlins, 7 C. & P. 150.

[8] Houston v. S., 38 Ga. 165.

jointly.[1] Where the occupancy is in husband and wife, or in the wife living separate from her husband, the allegation of ownership should be in the husband.[2] In case of a building occupied by a corporation, the ownership should be alleged as in the corporation.[3] Thus, the ownership of depots, cars, etc., of a railroad company should be alleged as in the company.[4] If the building belongs to a public corporation it may be so described.[5]

§ 509. Description of offense intended; goods stolen or intended to be stolen.— As to the description of the offense intended, there is much the same discrepancy among the cases as under the head of assault with felonious intent.[6] While it is not sufficient (unless by virtue of some statute) to allege generally the intent to commit a felony,[7] the weight of authority is to the effect that the crime intended need not be alleged with the particularity that would be necessary in an indictment charging the intended offense as a substantive crime; at least, this is true under statutory definitions of burglary, where it is generally sufficient to charge the offense in the terms of the statute.[8] Thus, in charging burglary with intent to com-

[1] Webb v. S., 52 Ala. 422; Rex v. Athea, 1 Moody, 329. But where a barn was in the occupancy of a tenant who allowed another a temporary and revocable right to keep goods therein, *held*, that the ownership laid in the tenant alone was proper: State v. Betsall, 11 W. Va. 703.

[2] See *supra*, § 495.

[3] Aldridge v. S., 88 Ala. 113. But if the allegation shows the ownership of a company without alleging such company to be a corporation, it is insufficient: Emmonds v. S., 87 Ala. 12.

[4] C. v. Moriarty, 135 Mass. 540; S. v. Parker, 16 Nev. 79; Johnson v. S., 73 Ala. 483; Hamilton v. S., 26 Tex. Ap. 206. If the building is in the joint occupancy of two railroad companies it may be so described: S. v. Scripture, 42 N. H. 485. Ownership of a railroad car may be described as in the person occupying it: Pyland v. S., 33 Tex. Ap. 382.

[5] C. v. Williams, 2 Cush. 582. And if the building is used as a dwelling-house, for instance, as a work-house or infirmary, it may be charged as the dwelling-house of the county or parish or guardians of the poor, as the case may be: Davis v. S., 38 Ohio St. 505; Reg. v. Frowen, 4 Cox, 266. If the building is a church, the ownership may be alleged in the trustees: Wilson v. S., 34 Ohio St. 199.

[6] See *supra*, § 269.

[7] Wilburn v. S., 41 Tex. 237. If the crime intended is properly described it is not necessary to describe it as a felony: P. v. Young, 65 Cal. 225.

[8] C. v. Doherty, 10 Cush. 52; Larned v. C., 12 Met. 240; P. v. Burns, 63 Cal. 614; P. v. Murray, 67 Cal. 103; Houser v. S., 58 Ga. 78; Coleman v. S., 2 Tex. Ap. 512. But proper allegation of

mit larceny, it is said not to be necessary to aver what specific goods or chattels were intended to be stolen, or the name of the owner,[1] and that, if the indictment charges intent to commit "the crime of larceny," it is sufficient under a statute describing burglary as the breaking and entering with intent to commit a felony or other infamous crime;[2] also that it is not necessary to say that the taking was with the felonious intent of depriving the owner permanently of his property;[3] so that variance as to ownership of property intended to be stolen is immaterial.[4] But it is held in other cases that the statutory description of the crime intended to be committed must be used;[5] and that, if the larceny intended must, under the statute, be grand larceny in order that the breaking and entering shall be burglary, the value of the goods must be alleged in order to show that the intended larceny was of that description.[6] Where breaking and entering with intent to commit larceny is burglary, irrespective of whether the intended larceny is grand or petit, an allegation of the value of the goods intended to be stolen or actually stolen, as the case may be, is immaterial.[7] But the value is essential where burglary consists of breaking and entering with intent to commit a felony,

the crime intended must be made: P. v. St. Clair, 56 Cal. 406.

[1] Jones v. S., 18 Fla. 889; Spencer v. S., 13 Ohio, 401; Josslyn v. C., 6 Met. 236; S. v. Jennings, 79 Ia. 513; S. v. Tyrrell, 98 Mo. 354; Hunter v. S., 29 Ind. 80; Reinhold v. S., 130 Ind. 467; Neiderluck v. S., 23 Tex. Ap. 38; Washington v. S., 17 Tex. Ap. 197; Martin v. S., 1 Tex. Ap. 525; Reg. v. Clarke, 1 C. & K. 421; Reg. v. Lawes, 1 C. & K. 62. But if the owner's name is given, it must be proven as alleged: C. v. Moore, 130 Mass. 45; S. v. Lee, 1 Houst. Cr. C. 335; Rex v. Jenks, 2 East, P. C. 514. But *contra*, holding that a variance as to the given name of the owner of the goods was immaterial: S. v. Hutchinson, 111 Mo. 257.

[2] S. v. Tytus, 98 N. C. 705; S. v. Mecum, — Ia. —, 64 N. W. R. 286.

[3] Mitchell v. C., 88 Ky. 349.

[4] S. v. Wincroft, 76 N. C. 38; S. v. Matthews, 76 N. C. 41; Harris v. S., 61 Miss. 304.

[5] Reed v. S., 14 Tex. Ap. 662; Webster v. S., 9 Tex. Ap. 75; Taylor v. S., 23 Tex. Ap. 639; O'Brien v. S., 27 Tex. Ap. 448; S. v. Williams, 41 Tex. 98. But if the statutory description of the intended offense is used, either in charging the intent or the act done, that is enough: Williams v. S., 24 Tex. Ap. 69; Bigham v. S., 31 Tex. Ap. 244.

[6] T. v. Duncan, 5 Mont. 478.

[7] Collins v. S., 20 Tex. Ap. 197; Henderson v. S., 70 Ala. 29; Kelly v. S., 72 Ala. 244; Duncan v. C., 85 Ky. 614; S. v. Kane, 63 Wis. 260; Hall v. S., 48 Wis. 688; S. v. Beckworth, 68 Mo. 82; Hunter v. S., 29 Ind. 80; Short v. S., 63 Ind. 376; Reinhold v. S., 130 Ind. 467; P. v. Ah Ye, 31 Cal. 451. And see *supra*, § 505.

and petit larceny is not a felony.[1] Where the statutory offense consists in breaking and entering a house in which any "goods or merchandise or other valuable thing is kept," etc., it is necessary to specify "the valuable thing" and its value.[2] But where "the thing of value" was described as "meal and flour," it was held that such description implied value and the money value need not be stated.[3] So, if the allegation is of stealing "goods and chattels" or "goods and merchandise," under the statutory description it is not necessary to allege value.[4]

§ 509a. **Venue.**— It is sometimes provided by statute that the offense may be prosecuted not only in the county where committed, but also in any county to which goods stolen in connection with the burglary are taken by the accused,[5] and in such cases the indictment must allege the facts; and it is not proper to charge the breaking and entering as in the county to which the goods are thus taken.[6]

§ 510. **"Burglariously;" "feloniously," etc.**— The indictment must, at common law, charge the act as being burglarious and felonious,[7] and these terms are commonly used in indictments under a statute.[8] But the word "burglariously"

[1] P. v. Murray, 8 Cal. 519.

[2] Neal v. S., 53 Ala. 465; Norris v. S., 50 Ala. 126; Robinson v. S., 52 Ala. 587; Pickett v. S., 60 Ala. 77; Webb v. S., 52 Ala. 422; Davis v. S., 54 Ala. 88; Danner v. S., 54 Ala. 127; Rouland v. S., 55 Ala. 210. If the indictment unnecessarily alleges that there were goods in the house, that fact must be proven: Gilmore v. S., 99 Ala. 154.

[3] Hurt v. S., 55 Ala. 214; Matthews v. S., 55 Ala. 65; Wicks v. S., 44 Ala. 398.

[4] Henderson v. S., 70 Ala. 29; Spencer v. S., 13 Ohio, 401. Where the ownership of the property intended to be, or actually, stolen is alleged, it may be in the name of the bailee thereof rather than in the name of the real owner: Stokes v. S., 84 Ga. 258; Wimbish v. S, 89 Ga. 294; S. v. Hill, 1 Houst. Cr. C. 421; Reg. v. Bird, 9 C. & P. 44. Thus, where the charge was of breaking into a church and stealing a box of money therefrom, *held*, that the property was rightfully laid in the vicar and others in their individual names; Reg. v. Wortley, 1 Den. 162. And where the goods stolen were forfeited to the crown, *held*, that they might properly be described as the property of the queen: Reg. v. Whitehead, 9 C. & P. 429.

[5] P. v. Jockinsky, 106 Cal. 638.

[6] P. v. Scott, 74 Cal. 94; Haskins v. P., 16 N. Y. 344. In ordinary cases the venue must be proved as in other crimes: Harlan v. S., 134 Ind. 339.

[7] S. v. McDonald, 9 W. Va. 456; S. v. Meadows, 22 W. Va. 766; S. v. Curtis, 30 La. An., part II, 814.

[8] P. v. Long, 43 Cal. 444; Shotwell v. S., 43 Ark. 345. Where the statute provides a punishment for "wilfully and maliciously" entering, an

is not essential where the statute does not use that term in the description of the offense.[1] Whether the offense must be charged as felonious will depend on the rule in any particular state as to the necessity of using that term in describing offenses which are felonies. The fact that the offense is described by statute specially defining the hours, the punishment, etc., does not make it necessary to conclude the indictment "against the form of the statute."[2]

§ 511. **Joinder of offenses; included offenses.**—It has already been shown that it is proper to allege the intent by alleging the actual commission of the substantive crime following the breaking and entry,[3] and this is a common form of indictment.[4] The indictment is not open, therefore, to the objection of duplicity if it alleges in the same count the breaking and entry and the commission of larceny.[5] Even if the intent to steal is alleged, the allegation also of theft following the breaking and entry will not be objectionable.[6] But the question arises in such cases as to whether, under an indictment for burglary alleging the commission of larceny as indicating the intent, there can be a conviction for both burglary and larceny or for larceny alone. As two offenses cannot properly be charged in the same count, it is evident that there cannot be a conviction under one count for both burglary and larceny,[7] and a general verdict of guilty under such indictment will constitute a conviction for burglary, though it

indictment charging the act as felonious instead of malicious will be good: C. v. Carson, 166 Pa. St. 179.

[1] Tully v. C., 4 Met. 357; S. v. Short, 54 Ia. 392; Reed v. S., 14 Tex. Ap. 662; S. v. Jordan, 39 La. An. 340.

[2] Reg. v. Polly, 1 C. & K. 77.

[3] *Supra*, § 506.

[4] *Infra*, § 513.

[5] S. v. Squires, 11 N. H. 37; C. v. Eaton, 15 Pick. 273; S. v. Colter, 6 R. I. 195; Breese v. S., 12 Ohio St. 146; Murray v. S., 48 Ala. 675; Snow v. S., 54 Ala. 138; Walker v. S., 97 Ala. 85; S. v. Ah Sam, 7 Nev. 127; S. v. Crawford, 38 S. C. 330; Wilcox v. S., 31 Tex. 586; Shepherd v. S., 42 Tex. 501. This rule is applicable also to statutory burglary of shops or other buildings, even though the commission of larceny in such a building is made a distinct crime: S. v. Ayer, 23 N. H. 301.

[6] S. v. Squires, 11 N. H. 37; Murray v. S., 48 Ala. 675; S. v. Colter, 6 R. I. 195; C. v. Carson, 166 Pa. St. 179; Shepherd v. S., 42 Tex. 501.

[7] S. v. McClung, 35 W. Va. 280. The two offenses being charged in the same count will be deemed one transaction and the larceny will be merged in the burglary: Crowley v. C., 11 Met. 575; Kite v. C., 11 Met. 581; Josslyn v. C., 6 Met. 236.

is not so specified in the verdict itself.[1] If the indictment is, for any reason, defective, so that a conviction for burglary could not be sustained under it, it will support a conviction for larceny, provided that offense is sufficiently charged.[2] And, according to some authorities, if the jury do not, under the indictment, find the defendant guilty of burglary, but do find the larceny to have been committed, they may convict of the latter offense.[3] But it seems that in such a case the verdict should be special for the larceny and that a general verdict will not be sustained for larceny, the indictment being defective as to burglary.[4] This doctrine may be well enough under the common-law rules of procedure, which do not forbid that defendant shall be put on trial under one indictment for different felonies, though, even in such case, it would seem that the prosecution might be required to elect whether it should proceed for burglary or for larceny;[5] but under statutory provisions requiring that an indictment shall charge but one offense, it seems that an indictment charging in one count burglary and larceny would either be open to objection for duplicity,[6] or would be considered only as an indictment for burglary, the allegation as to larceny being deemed merely a charge of the intent, in which event a conviction for larceny would not be proper; and this latter conclusion is not only reasonable, but has some support in authority.[7] But in other

[1] Yarborough v. S., 86 Ga. 396; Roberts v. S., 55 Miss. 421; S. v. McClung, 35 W. Va. 280; Hobbs v. S., 44 Tex. 353; S. v. Crenshaw, 45 La. An. 496.

[2] S. v. Hupp, 31 W. Va. 355; S. v. Richardson, 45 La. An. 692. The charge for larceny must be well laid to warrant a conviction for such offense: S. v. McClung, 35 W. Va. 280; P. v. Stewart, 44 Mich. 484.

[3] C. v. Lowery, 149 Mass. 67; C. v. Hope, 22 Pick. 1; S. v. Ayer, 23 N. H. 301; Clarke v. C., 25 Grat. 908; Hall's Case, 3 Grat. 593; S. v. Barker, 64 Mo. 282; S. v. Grisham, 1 Hayw. 12; S. v. Cocker, 3 Harr. 554; Rex v. Withal, 2 East, P. C. 515. The conviction in such a case will be for grand or petit larceny, depending upon the allegations and the proof as to the value of the property stolen: S. v. Brown, 73 Mo. 631; S. v. Owens, 79 Mo. 619; S. v. Hecox, 83 Mo. 531; S. v. Kennedy, 88 Mo. 341. The prosecution may dismiss as to burglary and secure a conviction as to larceny: C. v. Jennings, 105 Mass. 586; Dunham v. S., 9 Tex. Ap. 330; S. v. Christian, 30 La. An., part I, 367. In England the matter is somewhat affected by statute: Rex v. Compton, 3 C. & P. 418; Rex v. Butterworth, Russ. & Ry. 520.

[4] Hollister v. C., 60 Pa. St. 103; Rex v. Hungerford, 2 East, P. C. 518.

[5] Gilbert v. S., 65 Ga. 449.

[6] S. v. Smith, 2 N. Dak. 515; S. v. McFarland, 49 Ia. 99.

[7] S. v. Shaffer, 59 Ia. 290.

cases it is said that the fact that there may be a conviction for larceny if the burglary is not proven does not render the indictment double, and it is to be considered as an indictment for burglary only.[1] The statutes which thus prohibit charging two offenses in the same indictment contain exceptions of compound offenses where the same act constitutes different crimes, or where the crime charged necessarily includes other crimes or lower degrees of the same crime; but larceny is not included in the crime of burglary committed by breaking and entering with intent to commit larceny, for the larceny itself is necessarily distinct from the breaking and entering and is not a part of the same transaction.[2] Therefore a conviction or acquittal for burglary with intent to commit larceny will not bar a subsequent prosecution for larceny.[3] The burglary and the larceny are distinct offenses and may be prosecuted separately,[4] and a prosecution for larceny will not bar a subsequent prosecution for burglary.[5] In jurisdictions where two distinct felonies may be charged in different counts of the same indictment, burglary and larceny may be joined in separate counts,[6] and it is said a conviction may be had for each,[7] though in most states where such joinder is allowed the conviction can be for but one of the offenses.[8] By statute it is sometimes authorized to prosecute for the burglary and the larceny jointly and to punish for each,[9] but in

[1] C. v. Hope, 22 Pick. 1; S. v. Ayer, 23 N. H. 301.

[2] S. v. Ridley, 48 Ia. 370; S. v. Rhodes, 48 Ia. 702; Fisher v. S., 46 Ala. 717; S. v. Ford, 30 La. An., part I. 311; P. v. Curtis, 76 Cal. 57; S. v. Thompson, R. M. Charl. (Ga.) 80; S. v. Malony, id. 84. *Contra*, Choen v. S., 85 Ind. 209.

[3] P. v. Parrow, 80 Mich. 567; S. v. Warner, 14 Ind. 572; S. v. Martin, 76 Mo. 337. *Contra*, Rex v. Comer, 1 Leach, 36; Shepherd v. S., 42 Tex. 501.

[4] S. v. Hackett, 47 Minn. 425; S. v. Turney, 77 Ia. 269. One who receives stolen goods is not an accomplice in the burglary committed for the purpose of stealing them: S. v. Hayden, 45 Ia. 11.

[5] Smith v. S., 22 Tex. Ap. 350; Copenhaven v. S., 15 Ga. 264. A conviction of burglary does not bar a prosecution for conspiracy to commit the burglary: Whitford v. S., 24 Tex. Ap. 489.

[6] Choen v. S., 85 Ind. 209; Bell v. S., 48 Ala. 684; Lyons v. P., 68 Ill. 271. But petit larceny, if a misdemeanor, cannot be joined with burglary: Adams v. S., 55 Ala. 143.

[7] Ex parte Peters, 2 McCrary, 403.

[8] Bell v. S., 48 Ala. 684; Lyons v. P., 68 Ill. 271.

[9] S. v. Barker, 64 Mo. 282; S. v. Henley, 30 Mo. 509; S. v. Kelsoe, 76 Mo. 505; S. v. Hutchinson, 111 Mo. 257; Rust v. S., 31 Tex. Ap. 75; Loakman v. S., 32 Tex. Ap. 563.

such case the larceny must be charged with the same certainty and exactness as in a separate indictment for the offense.[1] Although, as has just been said, larceny is not properly an included crime in the charge of burglary, yet if the offense is the statutory one of breaking and entering a building and stealing therefrom, a conviction for larceny may be had.[2] The statutory offense of breaking and entering a storehouse, etc., is not included in a charge of burglary,[3] but burglary does include entering a house in the night-time with felonious intent, the only element lacking being the breaking.[4] So the statutory offense of forcibly breaking into a dwelling armed with a dangerous weapon with intent to kill includes the offense of forcibly entering without being armed.[5] The charge of burglary does not include an assault, although the crime intended is one involving an assault.[6]

§ 512. **Aggravation; degrees.**— There have been English statutes for the punishment of burglary committed with violence, for instance, "burglary and striking," and in such case the indictment must allege both the burglary and the striking, and if the proof shows the person struck to have been another than the one named in the indictment, there can be a conviction for burglary only.[7] So if the statutory offense of burglary committed by one armed with a dangerous weapon is charged, and the latter element is not proved, there may be conviction of burglary alone.[8] There are similar statutes in some of the states, and under them it is held that where violence toward some person was made the aggravating element of the crime, subjecting the defendant to higher punishment, such violence must be alleged in the indictment.[9] So if the aggravation, as provided by statute, consists in the fact that there is some one in the dwelling at the time of the breaking and entry, that

[1] S. v. Dooley, 64 Mo. 146.

[2] S. v. Savage, 32 Me. 583.

[3] Hollister v. C., 60 Pa. St. 103.

[4] S. v. Moore, 12 N. H. 42; S. v. Maxwell, 42 Ia. 208.

[5] S. v. Morris, 27 La. An. 480.

[6] Reg. v. Watkins, Car. & M. 264. And see S. v. Fitzsimon, 18 R. I. 236.

[7] Reg. v. Parfitt, 8 C. & P. 288.

[8] S. v. Miller, 45 La. An. 1170.

[9] Hobbs v. S., 44 Tex. 353. Where assault with intent to murder was charged as the aggravation, *held*, that the state might dismiss that part of the charge notwithstanding a plea of former acquittal with reference thereto, and proceed for simple burglary: S. v. Struble, 71 Ia. 11.

fact must be alleged or the conviction can be for burglary only.[1] Where the aggravation is attempting to do personal violence in connection with the commission of the offense, proof of pointing a dangerous weapon at a person in the house is sufficient to establish the crime.[2] In California burglary is, by statute, divided into degrees, breaking and entering in the daytime with felonious intent being the second degree, and it is held that the indictment should charge burglary only and leave the degree to be determined on the trial.[3] But in Kansas it is held proper to charge expressly the first degree, and under such an indictment the jury must find the degree or their verdict will not support a judgment.[4] There may, of course, be a conviction of the lower degree under an indictment for the higher.[5]

§ **513. Forms of indictment.**— The language of the common-law indictment is definite and easily made use of in any ordinary case, but statutory modifications of the crime have necessitated the introduction of other forms which will be sufficiently illustrated by those here given.

WITH INTENT TO STEAL.

That A. B., in the county aforesaid, on ——, about the hour of eleven in the night of the same day, the dwelling-house of C. D. there situate, feloniously and burglariously did break and enter, with intent the goods and chattels of the said C. D. in said dwelling-house then and there being, then and there feloniously and burglariously to steal, take and carry away, and the said A. B., then in the said dwelling-house, thirty-nine fleeces of wool of the goods and chattels of said C. D., then and there being found, feloniously and burglariously did steal, take and carry away.[6]

1 S. v. Fleming, 107 N. C. 905.

2 Seling v. S., 18 Neb. 548.

3 P. v. Jefferson, 52 Cal. 452; P. v. Barnhart, 59 Cal. 381.

4 S. v. Treadwell, 54 Kan. 513. But it is said that such a judgment, while erroneous, would not be a nullity: In re Black, 52 Kan. 64.

5 Moore v. Missouri, 159 U. S. 673.

6 This follows substantially the form in Archbold's Criminal Practice and Pleading, and is also based to some extent on the form found in Pitcher v. P., 16 Mich. 142. In that case, and in Fletcher v. S., 10 Lea, 338, the indictment states only that the breaking and entering were "in the night-time" of said day, whereas in the absence of statutory provisions it is usual, if not necessary, to allege the hour of night: See Shelton v. C., 89 Va. 450; S. v. Seymour, 36 Me. 225; *supra*, § 504. The cases first cited also illustrate the proposition that under the charge of breaking and entering the dwelling or man-

WITH INTENT TO COMMIT RAPE.

That A. B., in the county aforesaid, on ——, did unlawfully, feloniously and burglariously, about the hour of eleven o'clock at night of said day, break and enter the dwelling-house of J. R., there situate, with intent then and there unlawfully, feloniously and burglariously, one F. R. violently to ravish and carnally know by force and against her will.

FOR BREAKING AND ENTERING IN DAY-TIME.

That A. B., on ——, in the county aforesaid, a certain building there situate, to wit, the dwelling-house of one I. S., did break and enter, with intent to commit the crime of larceny therein.[2]

FOR BREAKING AND ENTERING BUILDING.

That A. B., on ——, in the county aforesaid, the store building of H. K., there situate, in the night-time of the same day, then and there unlawfully, feloniously and burglariously did break and enter, with intent then and there the personal goods,

sion-house there may be a conviction where the proof shows the breaking and entering of a barn, smoke-house or other such building connected with the dwelling-house and situated within the curtilage. A subsequent form is for the statutory offense of breaking and entering a building not itself connected with and adjacent to the dwelling-house.

[1] This follows to some extent indictments found in Burke v. S., 5 Tex. Ap. 74, and Hamilton v. S., 11 Tex. Ap. 116. The latter part, charging the intent, is analogous to the form given for assault with intent to commit rape, *supra*, § 467. The forms found in the cases here cited charge the intent to have been "to ravish and carnally know by force and by assaulting the said," etc., but certainly the phrase "by assaulting" is unnecessary: See 1 Whart. Prec. 377. The phrase "with force and arms" as applied to the breaking, used in the forms given in the cases here referred to, are plainly superfluous, as they are everywhere: See Bish. Direc. & Forms, § 43.

[2] This form, found in C. v. Reynolds, 122 Mass. 454, was held sufficient for the statutory offense of breaking and entering in the day-time, on the theory that the crime thus defined was only a lower degree of the crime of burglary, defined in a preceding section of the same statute as breaking and entering in the night-time; and that therefore the time became immaterial so long as it was not intended to charge the offense as committed in the night-time. The same reasoning is recognized in Butler v. P., 4 Denio, 68. But it is not safe, perhaps, to omit the averment that the act was done in the day-time, in a state where there is no express authority for it. The form given also omits the allegation that the act was feloniously and burglariously committed, which was necessary at common law, and charges the intent in a general way instead of specifically, which is not a safe practice, unless authorized by statute or decisions in the particular state.

chattels and property of said H. K., then and there in the said store building being found, then and there feloniously and burglariously to steal, take and carry away.[1]

FOR BREAKING AND ENTERING BUILDING IN WHICH GOODS, ETC., ARE KEPT.

That A. B., in the county aforesaid, on ——, in the night-time of said day, unlawfully, feloniously and burglariously did break and enter the store of one J. S. there situate, in which store goods, merchandise and valuable things were then and there kept for use, sale and deposit, with intent then and there the personal goods, chattels, money and property of the said J. S. in said store then and there being, then and there unlawfully, feloniously and burglariously to steal, take and carry away; and two caddies of tobacco of the value of twelve dollars of the personal goods, chattels and property of the said J. S. in the said store then and there being found, then and there unlawfully, feloniously and burglariously did steal, take and carry away.[2]

FOR BREAKING AND ENTERING A RAILROAD CAR.

That A. B., on the ——, at the county of ——, in the night-time of the same day, a freight railroad car of the Illinois Central Railroad Company, incorporated as such railroad company under the laws of the state of Illinois by virtue of an act of the General Assembly thereof, feloniously, wilfully, maliciously and forcibly did then and there break and enter with intent the goods and chattels of the said Illinois Central Railroad Company in the said freight railroad car then and there being, feloniously to steal, take and carry away.[3]

[1] In S. v. Kane, 63 Wis. 260, this was held to be sufficient under a statute defining the offense of breaking and entering in the night-time an office, shop, etc., not adjoining or occupied in connection with a dwelling-house, etc., the context of the statute showing that the breaking and entering of a building not thus situated was regarded as a lower offense than the breaking and entering of a building adjoining or occupied in connection with a dwelling, and therefore it was unnecessary to charge that the building was not adjoining, etc. A similar indictment was sustained under the same reasoning in Larned v. C., 12 Met. 240; but a contrary conclusion under a similar statute was reached in Koster v. P., 8 Mich. 431, and it would doubtless be wise to use the language of the full statutory provision, unless the question has been expressly settled otherwise.

[2] In S. v. Ridley, 48 Ia. 370, it was held that this indictment would not sustain a conviction of larceny from the store, the allegation of such larceny being only material as further indicating the intent with which the breaking and entering were effected. The same form of indictment was held sufficient for breaking and entering in S. v. Hayden, 45 Ia. 11.

[3] Lyons v. P., 68 Ill. 271.

§ 514. Evidence; recent possession of stolen property.— If the breaking and entering are charged as with the intent to commit larceny, the possession by defendant, soon after the crime, of goods shown to have been stolen from the premises broken and entered tends to show that defendant is the one who committed the burglary, unless such possession is in some way explained. Such recent possession is evidence of guilt of larceny, as will be explained in connection with that offense;[1] and as proof of the commission of larceny by the person breaking and entering is evidence of his intent in breaking and entering, the finding of the goods in his possession is evidence of the commission by him of the burglary.[2] The authorities do not agree, however, as to the weight to be given to such evidence. The rule sustained by a preponderance of authority is that it is *prima facie* or presumptive evidence of the guilt of burglary,[3] and will warrant conviction.[4] Indeed, it has been said that proof of recent possession of the stolen goods casts on the defendant, prosecuted for burglary, the burden of explaining such possession;[5] but this is an incorrect expression of the rule, as the burden of proof does not shift, and it is not correct to impose on the defendant the necessity of giving a particular explanation.[6] There are many cases which authorize the evidence of recent possession of stolen goods to be considered in determining the prisoner's guilt without sanctioning the proposition that such proof is in itself presumptive evi-

[1] *Infra*, § 615.

[2] C. v. Millard, 1 Mass. 6; S. v. Rivers, 68 Ia. 611; S. v. Frahm, 73 Ia. 355; S. v. Babb, 76 Mo. 501; Frank v. S., 39 Miss. 705; Smith v. P., 115 Ill. 17; P. v. Wood, 99 Mich. 620; P. v. Jockinsky, 106 Cal. 638; Hays v. S., 30 Tex. Ap. 472. Such evidence is admissible although the indictment does not charge that any goods were stolen: Stokes v. S., 84 Ga. 258.

[3] Reg. v. Exall, 4 F. & F. 922; Magee v. P.. 139 Ill. 138; Harris v. S., 61 Miss. 304; Lundy v. S., 71 Ga. 360; S. v. Warford, 106 Mo. 55. Some cases say it is presumptive evidence of guilt if unexplained: Davis v. S., 76 Ga. 16; S. v. Owens, 79 Mo. 619; S. v. Golden, 49 Ia. 48.

[4] Morgan v. S., 25 Tex. Ap. 513; S. v. Owsley, 111 Mo. 450; P. v. Smith, 79 Cal. 554; Brown v. S., 61 Ga. 311; Mangham v. S., 87 Ga. 549; but other Georgia cases do not go to the same extent: Falvey v. S., 85 Ga. 157; Bryan v. S., 62 Ga. 179; Houser v. S., 58 Ga. 78.

[5] Cooper v. S., 87 Ala. 135; S. v. Edwards, 109 Mo. 315; S. v. Scott, 109 Mo. 226; Knickerbocker v. P., 43 N. Y. 177.

[6] S. v. Jennings, 79 Ia. 513; Falvey v. S., 85 Ga. 157; Griffin v. S., 86 Ga. 257.

dence of guilt as to the burglary.[1] The rule is perhaps best stated by saying that the presumption arising from proof of such recent possession is not conclusive, but is to be dealt with by the jury only as the basis for a mere inference of fact,[2] and that the recent possession without other evidence of guilt of the burglary is not of itself sufficient to warrant conviction.[3] There must be other evidence of the fact that burglary has been committed,[4] though the recent possession may be sufficient to connect defendant with the crime,[5] or to corroborate the testimony of an accomplice.[6] A false or contradictory or improbable account by defendant of how he obtained the goods will tend to corroborate the inference drawn from mere recent possession.[7] Evidence explaining the possession consistently with defendant's innocence is to be received;[8] and some cases say that, if reasonable, such explanation throws on the state the burden of proving its falsity.[9] The question as to how soon after the burglary the goods are found in defendant's possession is important as affecting the weight of the evidence rather than its admissibility,[10] and also as affecting the amount of evidence necessary to identify the goods as those stolen at the time of the burglary.[11] The possession must be shown to have been in the defendant in order to make the finding of the goods evidence against him. If it is jointly in him and another, not charged with the burglary, it will not be admissible,[12] or at least that fact will prevent the evidence being conclusive.[13] But, of course, joint possession of two persons

[1] Gravely v. C., 86 Va. 396; Taliaferro v. C., 77 Va. 411; Walker v. C., 28 Grat. 969; Hall's Case, 3 Grat. 593; Ryan v. S., 83 Wis. 486; P. v. Carroll, 54 Mich. 334; P. v. Beaver, 49 Cal. 57; S. v. Reid, 20 Ia. 413; S. v. Jennings, 79 Ia. 513; Prince v. S., 44 Tex. 480.

[2] C. v. McGorty, 114 Mass. 299.

[3] S. v. Shaffer, 59 Ia. 290; S. v. Tilton, 63 Ia. 117; P. v. Bielfus, 59 Mich. 576; Methard v. S., 19 Ohio St. 363; P. v. Hart, 10 Utah, 204.

[4] Fuller v. S., 48 Ala. 273.

[5] Neubrandt v. S., 53 Wis. 89.

[6] Pritchett v. S., 92 Ga. 33; Boswell v. S., 92 Ga. 581.

[7] Smith v. S., 62 Ga. 663; Wynn v. S., 81 Ga. 744; Magee v. P., 139 Ill. 138; Gravely v. C., 86 Va. 396.

[8] Henderson v. S., 70 Ala. 29; Shuler v. S., 23 Tex. Ap. 182; Morgan v. S., 25 Tex. Ap. 513.

[9] Leslie v. S., 35 Fla. 171; Tarver v. S., 95 Ga. 222.

[10] Smith v. P., 115 Ill. 17.

[11] Gravely v. C., 86 Va. 396.

[12] S. v. Warford, 106 Mo. 55; S. v. Owsley, 111 Mo. 450; Reg. v. Coots, 2 Cox, 188.

[13] Shropshire v. S., 69 Ga. 273.

jointly implicated may be shown.[1] It is not essential, however, that the fruits of the crime be traced to the defendant in order to warrant his conviction of the burglary, if he is sufficiently connected with it by other evidence.[2] The various phases of the rule relating to recent possession are more fully discussed under the head of larceny.[3]

§ 515. **Other evidence.**—Proof of the commission of other crimes of burglary is admissible when the crimes are connected together or the result of a general plan.[4] Evidence is also admissible to show the previous presence of the defendant in and about the house, inquiries as to weapons kept in the house, knowledge that there was money in the house, etc.[5] The articles stolen, having been found in defendant's possession, are themselves admissible in evidence.[6]

§ 516. **Possession of burglar's tools.**— The possession of burglar's tools soon after the commission of the crime may be proven as tending to connect the defendant with it.[7] The having of burglar's tools in possession is by statute made a substantive offense without proof of intention to use them in any particular burglary;[8] and it is not essential that the intent with which they are kept is to commit burglary in the state, the place where they are intended to be used not being material.[9] Indeed the intent to commit a felony with the instruments is not an essential element of the crime of having them in possession.[10] Keys are instruments of house breaking if the

[1] P. v. Arthur, 93 Cal. 536; Ryan v. S., 83 Wis. 486; Murphy v. S., 86 Wis. 626; S. v. Harrison, 66 Vt. 523; Frazier v. S., 135 Ind. 38; Jackson v. S., 28 Tex. Ap. 370.

[2] Garrity v. P., 107 Ill. 162.

[3] *Infra*, §§ 616–620.

[4] Mason v. S., 42 Ala. 532; S. v. Robinson, 35 S. C. 340; S. v. Valwell, 66 Vt. 558; Kelley v. S., 31 Tex. Ap. 211; Dawson v. S., 32 Tex. Ap. 535; Reg. v. Cobden, 3 F. & F. 833; Reg. v. Rearden, 4 F. & F. 76. But evidence of a distinct and disconnected crime is not admissible: S. v. Johnson, 38 La. An. 686.

[5] S. v. Ward, 103 N. C. 419; S. v. Bill, 6 Jones, 34; P. v. Flynn, 73 Cal. 511. Where the crime charged was breaking and entering a railway car with intent to steal, the bill of goods shipped in the car was held admissible to show that some of the goods shipped were gone: S. v. Russell, 90 Ia. 493.

[6] Walker v. S., 97 Ala. 85.

[7] S. v. Franks, 64 Ia. 39; P. v. Hope, 62 Cal. 291; P. v. Winters, 29 Cal. 658.

[8] C. v. Tivnon, 8 Gray, 375; P. v. Edwards, 93 Mich. 636. Otherwise under English statutes: Reg. v. Jarrald, L. & C. 301.

[9] Davis v. S., 87 Ala. 10.

[10] Reg. v. Bailey, Dears. 244.

jury find that they are had in possession for that purpose instead of a lawful purpose.[1] Several may be jointly guilty for having such tools in possession, although they are actually in the custody of but one of them;[2] and proof of the fact that a confederate was a burglar and "safe-blower" was held competent in showing the intention with which defendant had such tools in his possession.[3]

[1] Reg. v. Oldham, 2 Den. 472.

[2] Reg. v. Thompson, 11 Cox, 362; C. v. Tivnon, 8 Gray, 375.

[3] P. v. Howard, 73 Mich. 10.

CHAPTER 25.

ARSON AND OTHER BURNINGS.

§ 517. **Definition.**— The common-law crime of arson consists in the malicious burning of the house of another.[1]

§ 518. **What constitutes "the house."**— Although the term "house" is used in arson,[2] while "dwelling-house" is the term in burglary, yet, as already stated under the discussion of burglary,[3] the meaning of the two terms is practically if not exactly the same.[4] A building, in order to constitute a house within the meaning of the definition of arson, must have been not only finished and ready for occupancy,[5] but actually occupied.[6] It must be a building such as is usually occupied as a dwelling.[7] If, though it has been occupied, such occupancy has terminated and it is vacant, the burning will not be arson.[8] But temporary absence of the occupants will not deprive it of the character of a dwelling-house.[9] A penitentiary or jail in which officers and others are lodged is a dwelling-house.[10] The

[1] The definitions in the different books are the same in effect with slight variations in the terms used: 3 Inst. 66; 1 Hale, P. C. 566; 1 Hawk. P. C., ch. 39; 2 East, P. C. 1015; 4 Bl. Com. 220; 2 Bish. Cr. L., § 8. Coke, followed by Hale and Hawkins, adds "by night or by day," but this unnecessary phrase, probably used by contrast to "in the night-time" in burglary, is omitted by East, Blackstone and Bishop.

[2] C. v. Barney, 10 Cush. 478; and see the definitions cited in the preceding note.

[3] *Supra*, § 494.

[4] The term "house" used in an indictment imports a dwelling-house and is sufficient: C. v. Posey, 4 Call, 109; but in the forms for indictment, "dwelling-house" is commonly used as in burglary: See *infra*, § 531.

[5] Reg. v. Edgell, 11 Cox, 132. A structure not entirely completed may nevertheless be a building; whether it is or not is a question for the jury. There are in some states statutes as to the burning of buildings in the process of erection: McGary v. P., 45 N. Y. 153; S. v. Wolfenberger, 20 Ind. 242.

[6] C. v. Barney, 10 Cush. 478; Elsmore v. St. Briavels, 8 B. & C. 461.

[7] S. v. Warren, 33 Me. 30; P. v. Handley, 93 Mich. 46; Reg. v. England, 1 C. & K. 533.

[8] S. v. Clark, 7 Jones, 167; Hooker v. C., 13 Grat. 763.

[9] S. v. Warren, 33 Me. 30: Johnson v. S., 48 Ga. 116.

[10] S. v. Johnson, 93 Mo. 73; P. v. Van Blarcum, 2 Johns. 105; Stevens v. C., 4 Leigh, 683; Rex v. Donnevan, 2 W. Bl. 682; but not a jail which

description of the building in an indictment as a dwelling-house is sufficient without further allegation that it is used as a place of abode.[1] Parts of the building not connected by internal communication, nor used by the occupants of the dwelling, are not to be deemed parts of such dwelling;[2] and such separate and unconnected portion, if used for other purposes, is not a dwelling at all for the purpose of arson, but the setting fire to it would constitute one of the statutory crimes hereafter to be described.[3] If there are several lodgers in the building it may be described as the dwelling of any one of them,[4] and, in general, the ownership should be laid in the occupant, as in cases of burglary, without regard to the legal title.[5] If the owner lets part of the building to lodgers it should be described as the house of the owner although the portion set fire to is occupied by a lodger.[6]

§ 519. Other buildings within the curtilage; adjacent buildings; barns.— The same rule applies here as in burglary, that buildings within the curtilage occupied in connection with the house as a dwelling are deemed a part of the dwelling in such sense that setting fire thereto is arson.[7] There are sometimes statutory provisions as to the burning of outbuildings adjoining a dwelling-house;[8] and under a statute with reference to outhouses not adjoining a dwelling nor under the same roof, but in which some person usually lodges at night, it is not necessary to show that a barn claimed to be under such description is

is occupied by none but prisoners: Reg. v. Connor, 2 Cox, 65.

[1] McClaine v. T., 1 Wash. 345. The word "house" imports the same thing: C. v. Barney, 10 Cush. 478.

[2] S. v. Sandy, 3 Ired. 570. And an internal communication will not make the portion occupied as a store a part of the dwelling if it is used by a different tenant and has a separate outside entrance: P. v. Nolan, 22 Mich. 229.

[3] P. v. Fairchild, 48 Mich. 31; S. v. Biles, 6 Wash. 186.

[4] Levy v. P., 80 N. Y. 327; Shepherd v. P., 19 N. Y. 537. If a portion of the house is let to tenants, and in such portion fire is set, the indictment may describe the dwelling as that of the tenant: S. v. Toole, 29 Conn. 342.

[5] S. v. Toole, 29 Conn. 342. As to burglary see *supra*, § 508.

[6] Rex v. Ball, 1 Moody, 30.

[7] S. v. Shaw, 31 Me. 523; C. v. Barney, 10 Cush. 480. But a barn separated from the house by a highway is not within the curtilage: S. v. Stewart, 6 Conn. 47; Curkendall v. P., 36 Mich. 309.

[8] But "adjoining" in such a statute was held to mean "contiguous to," and not merely "near to:" S. v. Downs, 59 N. H. 320.

within the curtilage.[1] At common law it is said that the burning of a barn with hay and grain in it is arson;[2] and, of course, a barn within the curtilage and used in connection with the dwelling would be deemed a part thereof, as already suggested;[3] but there are in many states provisions as to setting fire to barns, stables, etc., and the question whether the barn is within the curtilage, under such a statute, would be immaterial.[4] The burning of a barn so situated that its destruction would endanger the dwelling-house is the burning of any building "a parcel of, belonging to, or adjoining the dwelling-house," within statutory description.[5]

§ 520. Buildings not part of the dwelling; grain, hay, etc. Aside from the common-law felony of arson consisting in the burning of the dwelling-house or a building appurtenant thereto, there are in all the states provisions for the punishment of the burning of other buildings or chattels. There is scarcely any harmony among these statutes, and all that can be done is to mention some of the principal classes of buildings and property with reference to which such provisions may be found. Where the statute describes arson as the burning of a building with intent to destroy it, the offense may be so alleged although the statute elsewhere defines "building" as including a house, structure, vessel, etc.[6] Where the statute defined the crime as the wilful burning of any house, and then defined "house" as any building or structure inclosed with walls and covered, it was held that a crib which had been torn down ceased to be a building or structure.[7] An unfinished house substantially completed as to walls and roof, though not plastered or ready for occu-

[1] Page v. C., 26 Grat. 943. If the building is described, in accordance with the statutory definition, as a building not parcel of a dwelling, it need not appear that there is any dwelling-house owned by the person owning the building: S. v. Price, 11 N. J. 203.

[2] Sampson v. C., 5 Watts & S. 385; S. v. Porter, 90 N. C. 719.

[3] Statutes sometimes especially refer to the burning of a barn within the curtilage: P. v. Taylor, 2 Mich. 250; Nabors v. S., 82 Ala. 8. And see Gibson v. S., 54 Md. 447.

[4] S. v. Taylor, 45 Me. 322. As to what constitutes a barn, under such statute, in North Carolina, see S. v. Jim, 8 Jones, 459; S. v. Laughlin, 8 Jones, 455; S. v. Cherry, 63 N. C. 439.

[5] Hill v. C., 98 Pa. St. 192.

[6] P. v. Giacamella, 71 Cal. 48; P. v. Russell, 81 Cal. 616. In such a statute "house" may include other buildings than a dwelling-house: Pike v. S., 8 Lea, 577.

[7] Mulligan v. S., 25 Tex. Ap. 199.

pancy, may be a building.[1] The question whether a building in the process of construction is sufficiently advanced to be termed a building is for the jury.[2] Statutory provisions as to buildings, houses, etc., are broad enough to cover a church or school-house.[3] Statutes frequently cover by special designation the burning of "outhouses," and it is held that this term is not synonymous with "house,"[4] but is a technical term referring to a building appurtenant in some way to a dwelling-house.[5] Other cases with reference to what particular buildings are, or are not, within the description of an outhouse are given in the note.[6] Setting fire to barns, stables, sheds, etc., is also specially provided for by statute. The cases are sufficiently collected in the note.[7] Statutes also refer to the burning of warehouses, store-houses, etc.[8] Where the offense would be greater if the building were adjacent to a dwelling-house or within the curtilage, it is not necessary, in order to convict of the lower offense of burning a building, structure, etc., to allege that it was not adjoining a dwelling-house, etc.[9] There are statutes

[1] Reg. v. Manning, L. R. 1 C. C. 338.

[2] C. v. Squire, 1 Met. 258.

[3] Watt v. S., 61 Ga. 66; Wallace v. Young, 5 T. B. Mon. 155; S. v. O'Brien, 2 Root, 516; Jones v. Hungerford, 4 Gill & J. 402; S. v. Bedell, 65 Vt. 541; McDonald v. C., 86 Ky. 10.

[4] Whiteside v. S., 4 Coldw. 175; Hester v. S., 17 Ga. 130.

[5] S. v. Roper, 88 N. C. 656; S. v. Stewart, 6 Conn. 47.

[6] Rex v. Nash, 2 East, P. C. 1021; Rex v. Haughton, 5 C. & P. 555; Rex v. Parrott, 6 C. & P. 402; Rex v. Winter, Russ. & Ry. 295; Rex v. Stallion, 1 Moody, 398; Rex v. Ellison, 1 Moody, 336; Reg. v. Jones, 1 C. & K. 303; Elsmore v. St. Briavels, 8 B. & C. 461; Reg. v. Munson, 2 Cox, 186; S. v. O'Brien, 2 Root, 516.

[7] As to what is a barn, see Elsmore v. St. Briavels, 8 B. & C. 461; S. v. Thornton, 56 Vt. 35; a stable, see Dugle v. S., 100 Ind. 259; Reg. v. Munson, 2 Cox, 186; Reg. v. Haughton, 5 C. & P. 555. As to sheds, see Reg. v. Munson, 2 Cox, 186; Reg. v. Amos, 2 Den. 55. The charge of burning a stable is not supported by proof of burning a shed not used for the purposes of a stable: Reg. v. Colley, 2 M. & Rob. 475. But under an indictment for burning a certain building "called a barn," evidence that the building burned was only a shed was held not to constitute a variance: S. v. Smith, 28 Ia. 565. As to the burning of a corn-crib, see Brown v. S., 52 Ala. 345; S. v. Millican, 15 La. An. 557. A description of the building as a "barn or stable," or a "barn, house or building," is defective: Horton v. S., 60 Ala. 72.

[8] As to a warehouse, see Allen v. S., 10 Ohio St. 287; store-house, S. v. Sandy, 3 Ired. 570; cotton-house, Washington v. S., 68 Ala. 85; mill, S. v. Upchurch, 9 Ired. 454; S. v. Livermore, 44 N. H. 386; shop, S. v. Morgan, 98 N. C. 641; S. v. O'Connell, 26 Ind. 266.

[9] S. v. Emerson, 53 N. H. 619; Staeger v. C., 103 Pa. St. 469; C. v.

with reference to the burning of railroad bridges.[1] Although, as will hereafter appear, the burning of personal property is not arson, such burning is made criminal by various statutes. Thus, it is made a crime to burn stacks of hay, grain, straw, etc.[2] So it is made criminal to set fire to another's grain, grass, etc.,[3] or to another's woods.[4]

§ 521. **The house of another.**— In arson, as in burglary, the offense consists in putting in danger another's home, and therefore the house must be the dwelling of another than the accused. It is not common-law arson for one to burn his own house;[5] nor for a wife to burn her husband's house, she being an occupant as well as he.[6] The element of wrong in arson is the injury of another with reference to his dwelling, and therefore one who burns the dwelling-house of another by the owner's procurement is not guilty.[7] The person in possession is deemed the owner, and therefore a tenant is not guilty of arson in burning the house occupied by him, injury to the person occupying rather than to the holder of the title being the criterion.[8] But the landlord in such case may be guilty of the crime, for he thereby does burn the dwelling of

Hamilton, 15 Gray, 480; S. v. Ambler, 56 Vt. 672; S. v. Gregory, 33 La. An. 737. Even though the building is actually a part of the dwelling so that the common-law crime of arson is committed, yet there may be a conviction therefor under a charge of burning a building or out-house: C. v. Smith, 151 Mass. 491; Rex v. North, 2 East, P. C. 1021. But if the building is described as a dwelling there cannot be a conviction for the burning of a building other than a dwelling; the description must be proved as laid: C. v. Hayden, 150 Mass. 332.

[1] Duncan v. S., 29 Fla. 439.

[2] S. v. Pope, 9 S. C. 273; Black v. S., 2 Md. 376; Erskine v. C., 8 Grat. 624; Rex v. Judd, 2 East, P. C. 1018; Rex v. Swatkins, 4 C. & P. 548; Rex v. Reader, 4 C. & P. 245; Rex v. Aris, 6 C. & P. 348; Rex v. Tottenham, 7 C. & P. 237; Reg. v. Satchwell, L. R. 2 C. C. 21; Reg. v. Spencer, Dears. & B. 131; Rex v. Woodward, 1 Moody, 323; Reg. v. Baldock, 2 Cox, 55; Reg. v. Munson, 2 Cox, 186; Reg. v. McKeever, 5 Ir. R. C. L. 86.

[3] S. v. Lewis, 10 Rich. 20; S. v. Avery, 109 N. C. 798.

[4] Hall v. Cranford, 5 Jones, 3; Earhart v. C., 9 Leigh, 671; Reg. v. Price, 9 C. & P. 729.

[5] Roberts v. S., 7 Coldw. 359; Heard v. S., 81 Ala. 55; P. v. De Winton, — Cal. —, 45 Pac. R. 708. But in Louisiana the statute renders it immaterial that the house is the property of the accused: S. v. Elder, 21 La. An. 157; S. v. Rohfrischt, 12 La. An. 382.

[6] Snyder v. P., 26 Mich. 106; Rex v. March, 1 Moody, 182.

[7] S. v. Haynes, 66 Me. 307; C. v. Makely, 131 Mass. 421; Heard v. S., 81 Ala. 55.

[8] S. v. Fish, 27 N. J. 323. One in possession, even by wrong, is not guilty of arson in burning the house: Sullivan v. S., 5 Stew. & P. 175.

another, that is, the tenant.[1] One who is in possession as a mere servant of the owner, and not a tenant, is guilty of arson in burning the house, for the house is that of another.[2] The ownership should be alleged as in the person in possession.[3] These distinctions are, to a considerable extent, modified or abolished by statutory provisions. Thus, it is made criminal for a tenant in occupancy of premises to burn them, the injury being deemed to be to the rights of the landlord.[4] If it is made an offense to burn a building in which there is a living person at the time,[5] this would include the burning of one's own house, another person being at the time therein.[6] At common law it is a misdemeanor, although not arson, to burn a building, even one's own, whereby the dwelling of another is endangered,[7] and statutes sometimes make this arson.[8] Of course, it would be arson, and not merely a statutory offense, if, as a natural consequence of the setting fire to one's own building or property, the dwelling of another near by should be burned.[9]

§ 522. Intent to defraud insurance companies and others. A further illustration of cases where the burning of one's own building, not being arson at common law, is made a crime by statute because resulting in injury to others, is the case of burning one's own building with intent to defraud the insurer of such building. Such a statutory provision is found in England and most of the states. And thereunder it must be alleged that the building was insured and that the act was with intent to injure the insurers,[10] and the fact of insurance must

[1] S. v. Fish, 27 N. J. 323; Erskine v. C., 8 Grat. 624; Rex v. Harris, 2 East, P. C. 1023.

[2] Rex v. Gowen, 2 East, P. C. 1027.

[3] See *infra*, § 529.

[4] P. v. Fisher, 51 Cal. 319; P. v. Simpson, 50 Cal. 304; Allen v. S., 10 Ohio St. 287; S. v. Fish, 27 N. J. 323.

[5] *Infra*, § 524.

[6] Shepherd v. P., 19 N. Y. 537; Levy v. P., 80 N. Y. 327; S. v. Hayes, 78 Mo. 307; Tuller v. S., 8 Tex. Ap. 501; Reg. v. McGrath, 14 Cox, 598.

[7] Rex v. Probert, 2 East, P. C. 1030; Rex v. Isaac, 2 East, P. C. 1031; Rex v. Scofield, 2 East, P. C. 1028; S. v. Fish, 27 N. J. 323; Heard v. S., 81 Ala. 55.

[8] Gage v. Shelton, 3 Rich. 242; Grimes v. S., 63 Ala. 166.

[9] S. v. Laughlin, 8 Jones, 354; Early v. C., 86 Va. 921; Rex v. Cooper, 5 C. & P. 535. Whether the defendant intended to burn another building than that in which the combustibles were placed is a question of fact: C. v. Harney, 10 Met. 422. But it is said in another case that the fire must be set to the dwelling itself in order to constitute common-law arson: P. v. Fairchild, 48 Mich. 31.

[10] Staaden v. P., 82 Ill. 432.

have been known to the defendant,[1] but it is immaterial that the policy is invalid.[2] It is immaterial also that the policy is made payable to the mortgagee of the premises.[3] The offense in this class of cases consists in the destruction or burning of the building rather than in merely setting fire to it, but a partial destruction is sufficient to constitute a burning.[4] This offense is a kind of fraud, and evidence tending to show or to negative an intent to defraud is admissible.[5] But the intent to defraud need not be shown by the allegation of particular circumstances, unless required by statute.[6] As in other cases where the crime consists in an intent to defraud, the name of the person or corporation intended to be defrauded should be alleged, and in case the fraud is against a corporation or partnership, with the corporate or partnership capacity.[7] But proof of the *de facto* existence of the corporation is sufficient.[8] This offense is distinct from the offense of arson, and a conviction therefor cannot be had under an indictment for arson.[9]

§ **523. The burning.**— If any part of the house be consumed by fire there is such burning as to constitute the offense.[10] If the wood of the house is charred so as to destroy its fiber, the crime is completed though there is no blaze and the burning does not proceed further.[11] It is not necessary that some part of the house be destroyed or consumed; burning is sufficient.[12] But there must be something more than a mere scorching or blackening.[13] The allegation should be that defendant did "burn" the building, not merely set fire to it.[14] The question whether the house is actually burnt within the foregoing de-

[1] Martin v. S., 28 Ala. 71.

[2] McDonald v. P., 47 Ill. 533.

[3] S. v. Byrne, 45 Conn. 273.

[4] S. v. Babcock, 51 Vt. 570.

[5] Reg. v. Grant, 4 F. & F. 322; Reg. v. Gray, 4 F. & F. 1102; Rogers v. S., 26 Tex. Ap. 404.

[6] Reg. v. Heseltine, 12 Cox, 404.

[7] P. v. Schwartz, 32 Cal. 160.

[8] P. v. Hughes, 29 Cal. 257; P. v. Schwartz, 32 Cal. 160; S. v. Tucker, 84 Mo. 23; S. v. Byrne, 45 Conn. 273; U. S. v. Amedy, 11 Wheat. 392.

[9] C. v. Makely, 131 Mass. 421; Roberts v. S., 7 Coldw. 359.

[10] C. v. Van Schaack, 16 Mass. 105; S. v. Sandy, 3 Ired. 570; S. v. Mitchell, 5 Ired. 350; P. v. Butler, 16 Johns. 203.

[11] P. v. Haggerty, 46 Cal. 354; S. v. Taylor, 45 Me. 322; Reg. v. Parker, 9 C. & P. 45; Rex v. Stallion, 1 Moody, 398.

[12] C. v. Tucker, 110 Mass. 403.

[13] Woolsey v. S., 30 Tex. Ap. 346; Reg. v. Russell, Car. & M. 541.

[14] Howell v. C., 5 Grat. 664; Cochrane v. S., 6 Md. 400; Mary v. S., 24 Ark. 44; Polsten v. S., 14 Mo. 463.

scription is for the jury, even when a portion of the wood showing the extent of the injury is introduced in evidence.[1] Some of the statutory offenses of burning involve such destruction as to cause injury and are not completed merely by setting the building on fire.[2] The burning must be of the building or some part of it;[3] if the fire is set to and burns only chattel property in the house, and no portion of the house itself, the offense of arson is not committed.[4] Setting fire to matter with intent to cause a burning of the house is made a statutory crime in the nature of an attempt,[5] and under indictment therefor the burning may be alleged, not as a distinct crime, but as a statement showing the intent with which the fire was set.[6]

§ 524. **Person in the building.**— There are statutory provisions in some states with reference to setting fire to a building in which there is at the time a human being, or which is used as a lodging place. Under such statute the presence of a person in the building or its use as a lodging place is the important fact,[7] and the ownership of the building is immaterial.[8] In such case it is not necessary to allege the name of the person nor that the accused knew of his presence in the building at the time.[9] But if the statute specifies that such person must be lawfully in the building to constitute the crime, then that fact must be specifically stated, and the mere identity of the name with that of the owner of the building as alleged will not be sufficient.[10] The person must be actually in the building when the fire is set.[11] The gist of this offense is the danger involved to the person in the building and not the injury to the building itself, and, therefore, if the presence of some person

[1] C. v. Betton, 5 Cush. 427.

[2] Hester v. S., 17 Ga. 130; S. v. De Bruhl, 10 Rich. 23; Rex v. Salmon, Russ. & Ry. 26.

[3] P. v. Simpson, 50 Cal. 304.

[4] Graham v. S., 40 Ala. 659; Rex v. Taylor, 2 East, P. C. 1020; Reg. v. Child, L. R. 1 C. C. 307; Reg. v. Batstone, 10 Cox, 20; Reg. v. Harris, 15 Cox, 75; Reg. v. Nattrass, 15 Cox, 73; Reg. v. Lyons, Bell, 38.

[5] S. v. Dennin, 32 Vt. 158; S. v. Johnson, 19 Ia. 230; S. v. Clay, 12 La. An. 431; Reg. v. Taylor, 1 F. & F. 511.

[6] S. v. Hull, 83 Ia. 112.

[7] Childress v. S., 86 Ala. 77; S. v. Jones, 106 Mo. 302.

[8] S. v. Hayes, 78 Mo. 307. This crime can be committed by burning one's own house: See *supra*, § 521.

[9] S. v. Aguila, 14 Mo. 130.

[10] Lacy v. S., 15 Wis. 13.

[11] C. v. Buzzell, 16 Pick. 153; Reg. v. Fletcher, 2 C. & K. 215. But it is immaterial whether he had an opportunity to escape: Woodford v. P., 62 N. Y. 117.

is not proven, it is said there can be no conviction for a burning with intent to injure or defraud,[1] though of course there may be for arson. The offense provided for by such statutes is usually made the first degree of arson where the crime is divided into degrees;[2] but the burning of a dwelling-house is also usually included in the first degree, in which case it is not necessary to allege and prove that there was a person in the house.[3] There is an English statute with reference to the damaging of any building by dynamite or other explosive substance whereby the lives of persons are endangered.[4]

§ 525. **Other matters of aggravation; degrees; night-time.**— By statute the offense is sometimes divided into degrees, some elements of aggravation being taken into account in determining the higher degrees.[5] Setting fire to a building in which there is any human being is sometimes made a higher degree of the offense,[6] and it is also sometimes made the first degree of the offense that the house is set fire to in the night-time;[7] but the common-law offense is committed either in the day or night, and, therefore, if the allegation is not sufficient to sustain a conviction for the aggravated offense of setting fire in the night-time, there may be a conviction for setting fire in the day-time.[8] But to warrant a conviction of the aggravated offense the facts constituting such offense should be alleged.[9]

§ 526. **The intent.**—While the definitions usually speak of the act as malicious and wilful,[10] yet arson is not a crime involving any specific intent in addition to the act done. The intent to burn is the only intent required and that is necessarily

[1] Reg. v. Paice, 1 C. & K. 73.

[2] Woodford v. P., 62 N. Y. 117.

[3] Paine v. S., 89 Ala. 26.

[4] Reg. v. McGrath, 14 Cox, 598; Reg. v. Brown, 3 F. & F. 821. Under a statute punishing the throwing of any explosive against a building, the explosive must be in a condition to explode when it is thrown, although an actual explosion is not necessary: Reg. v. Sheppard, 11 Cox, 302.

[5] As to form of indictment for the third degree, see Leonard v. S., 96 Ala. 108.

[6] See preceding section.

[7] S. v. Nolan, 48 Kan. 723.

[8] Curran's Case, 7 Grat. 619; Brown v. S., 52 Ala. 345; Cheatham v. S., 59 Ala. 40; Dick v. S., 53 Miss. 384; Brightwell v. S., 41 Ga. 482.

[9] Dick v. S., 53 Miss. 384; Davis v. S., 52 Ala. 357. But this will depend upon the statute, and under some statutes the aggravation is a mere matter of proof and not of allegation: Brightwell v. S., 41 Ga. 482.

[10] Jesse v. S., 28 Miss. 100; Young v. C., 12 Bush, 243.

implied in the act,[1] unless some excuse, such as accident, appears.[2] An intentional wrongful burning makes the act wilful and malicious, and no special malice or ill-will toward the owner is necessary.[3] Nor is it necessary that there be an intent that the building be destroyed, the wilful and malicious burning being sufficient.[4] There must be an intent, however, to burn the house which is burned in order to support an indictment therefor, and if fire is set to another building and a dwelling-house is thereby burned, to convict the accused of the burning of the latter it must appear that such was the intent with which the fire was set.[5] But the intent to burn the building which is burned may be inferred from the fact that such result is a natural consequence of the burning of the building to which the fire is set.[6] So if an act is done with the purpose of causing a fire which will be criminal, and a fire naturally results therefrom, the crime is committed.[7] If there is a combination to do an unlawful act, and in the prosecution of the design and as a result and necessary consequence a house is burned, all are guilty of arson.[8] Under some statutes, acts of burning which would not constitute arson are, as has already been seen,[9] criminal if done with intent to defraud, and in such case the intent to defraud becomes material and must be alleged and proven.[10] But such an allegation is supported by evidence that the natural consequence of the burning of the building would be injury to the owner.[11] But an ordinary indictment

[1] S. v. Watson, 63 Me. 128; S. v. Hill, 55 Me. 365. The co-operation of a detective will not prevent the act being criminal: P. v. Greening, 102 Cal. 384. And see *supra*, §§ 117, 118.

[2] Reg. v. Faulkner, 13 Cox, 550; S. v. Carroll, 85 Ia. 1.

[3] S. v. McCarter, 98 N. C. 637; Reg. v. Davies, 1 F. & F. 69; Rex v. Salmon, R. & R. 26.

[4] P. v. Fanshawe, 137 N. Y. 68. Thus, if the intention in setting fire to a building was to obtain a reward for giving the earliest information of the fire at the engine station, the crime would be complete: Reg. v. Regan, 4 Cox, 335.

[5] Woodford v. P., 62 N. Y. 117; S. v. Watson, 63 Me. 128; S. v. Hill, 55 Me. 365; Combs v. C., 93 Ky. 313.

[6] Woodford v. P., 62 N. Y. 117.

[7] Overstreet v. S., 46 Ala. 30, which was a case where matches were put in cotton in a gin-house with the intention and expectation that they would be ignited in the necessary and probable handling of the cotton, and they were so ignited and the gin-house was burned.

[8] Lusk v. S., 64 Miss. 845.

[9] *Supra*, § 522.

[10] Rex v. Smith, 4 C. & P. 569; Reg. v. Newboult, L. R. 1 C. C. 344; Reg. v. Connor, 2 Cox, 65.

[11] Rex v. Farrington, Russ. & Ry.

for arson need not aver an intent thereby to injure and defraud.[1] It has been suggested that the setting fire by an inmate of a jail or poor-house with the intent to burn a hole therein for the purpose of effecting escape would not be arson;[2] but in reason and on authority this doctrine is not supported, and it is immaterial what is the ultimate intent in the burning if it is unlawful.[3]

§ 527. **Indictment; venue.**— It is not necessary to describe the house or building with reference to any particular city, town or village.[4] It is only essential that the offense be so described in this respect as to show it to have been committed within the jurisdiction of the court.[5] A mistake as to the name of the place is immaterial, the crime being transitory and not local.[6]

§ 528. **Description of property.**— The allegation that the house was "used as a dwelling-house" is sufficient to charge that it was a dwelling-house;[7] so to describe the building as a "dwelling-house used as a shop" is a sufficient allegation to bring it within the statute as to the burning of a shop.[8] The value is immaterial unless the punishment is in some way made to depend upon value.[9]

§ 529. **Description of ownership.**— The indictment must show that the house was that of another (except where circumstances are alleged showing the offense to be a crime when committed with reference to one's own house), and the indictment must state the name of the owner and the proof must correspond.[10] The name of the owner is a necessary part of the

207; Rex v. Newell, 1 Moody, 458. Where the building set on fire was a common jail kept in repair by rates levied upon the inhabitants of the liberty in and for which the jail was kept, *held*, that an indictment for setting fire to the jail should allege it to be with intent to injure the inhabitants of the liberty: Reg. v. Connor, 2 Cox, 65.

[1] S. v. Thompson, 97 N. C. 496.

[2] P. v. Cotteral, 18 Johns. 115; Jenkins v. S., 53 Ga. 33.

[3] Lockett v. S., 63 Ala. 5; Smith v. S., 23 Tex. Ap. 357 (overruling Delany v. S., 41 Tex. 601); Willis v. S., 32 Tex. Ap. 534.

[4] Smith v. S., 64 Ga. 605.

[5] C. v. Lamb, 1 Gray, 493; C. v. Barney, 10 Cush. 478; P. v. Wooley, 44 Cal. 494; Duncan v. S., 29 Fla. 439.

[6] Rex v. Woodward, 1 Moody, 323.

[7] McLane v. S., 4 Ga. 335.

[8] S. v. Morgan, 98 N. C. 641.

[9] Ritchey v. S., 7 Blackf. 168.

[10] C. v. Mahar, 16 Pick. 120; Martha v. S., 26 Ala. 72; S. v. Keena, 63 Conn. 329; Rex v. Rickman, 2 East, P. C. 1034.

description, and cannot be rejected as surplusage,[1] and the allegation as to ownership must be direct and certain.[2] Therefore, an allegation of the burning of a building containing the property of a person named, without allegation as to the ownership of the building, is insufficient;[3] and the allegation of the ownership of the property in the building and its value is immaterial.[4] Under statutes with reference to the burning of public buildings, the ownership is sometimes not required to be stated.[5] The form of alleging ownership is not essential, and the house named may be described as "belonging to" "the property of," "owned by," or "in possession of," or simply "of," a person named.[6] As already indicated, the house is to be described as that of the person in possession of it, rather than as that of the owner of the title,[7] and if the indictment state the name of the occupant that is sufficient.[8] So ownership may be laid in the widow of the deceased owner who occupies the premises, although dower has not yet been assigned;[9] and while general ownership is to be laid in the husband rather than in the wife,[10] yet, where a wife occupied and cultivated the premises in the husband's absence and had a corn-pen built, it was held that an indictment for the burning of the corn-pen properly laid ownership in the wife.[11] In a charge of burning a jail, possession may be laid in the jailer.[12] Where the name of the occupant is stated it is redundant, although not fatal, to allege also the name of the general owner.[13] But it is said that an allegation showing property in one person, and that the house is the dwelling of another, is fatally defective for uncertainty.[14] The question being as to the occupant and not as to the title, evidence of title is immaterial.[15] The doctrine with reference to

[1] McGary v. P., 45 N. Y. 153.

[2] P. v. Myers, 20 Cal. 76.

[3] Smoke v. S., 87 Ala. 143.

[4] C. v. Brailey, 134 Mass. 527.

[5] Mott v. S., 29 Ark. 147; S. v. Roe, 12 Vt. 93. Otherwise it should be described as the property of the public corporation to which it belongs: Lockett v. S., 63 Ala. 5; Sands v. S., 80 Ala. 201.

[6] Woodford v. P., 62 N. Y. 117.

[7] *Supra*, § 521.

[8] Young v. C., 12 Bush, 243; P. v. Wooley, 44 Cal. 494; P. v. Handley, 100 Cal. 370.

[9] S. v. Gailor, 71 N. C. 88.

[10] *Supra*, § 495.

[11] May v. S., 85 Ala. 14.

[12] Reg. v. Connor, 2 Cox, 65.

[13] Rogers v. S., 26 Tex. Ap. 404; P. v. Shainwold, 51 Cal. 468; P. v. Handley, 100 Cal. 370; S. v. McCarter, 98 N. C. 637.

[14] P. v. Myers, 20 Cal. 76.

[15] P. v. Scott, 32 Cal. 200; S. v. Burrows, 1 Houst. Cr. C. 74.

occupancy being sufficient is applicable to statutory offenses of burning as well as to arson.[1] Where the premises are in the occupation of a tenant, the house should be alleged as that of the tenant and not of the landlord.[2] So where the premises are in possession of a servant, but as tenant during the continuance of the relation of servant, the ownership may be laid in such servant.[3] Proof of possession unquestioned will be sufficient evidence of property, although the title is in another.[4] Where one of two tenants in common is in possession, the house may be properly described as his;[5] and where it is described as occupied by two persons as tenants, proof that one is a tenant and the other a subtenant under him does not create a material variance.[6] If the ownership is laid in a private corporation, proof of *de facto* existence is sufficient.[7]

§ **530. Allegation of intent.**— The indictment should allege the act as malicious in accordance with the definition,[8] but as the malice which is required is simply the intent to do the wrongful act, it is held sufficient to allege that the act was wilfully done.[9] The allegation that the act was unlawful will be sufficient without stating it to have been wilful, it being charged as malicious and felonious.[10] But an allegation that it was felonious, voluntary and malicious was held insufficient where it was not charged that it was unlawful.[11]

§ **531. Forms of indictment.**— The form of indictment for arson is simple, and the variations rendered necessary by statutory provisions are usually plainly indicated by the language.

FOR COMMON-LAW ARSON.

That A. B., in the county aforesaid, on ——, the dwelling-house of one C. D., there situate, did unlawfully, wilfully, maliciously and feloniously set fire to and burn.[12]

[1] S. v. Kroscher, 24 Wis. 64.

[2] S. v. Tennery, 9 Ia. 436; S. v. Bradley, 1 Houst. Cr. C. 164; P. v. Gates, 15 Wend. 159; C. v. Buckley, 148 Mass. 27. But held that under an allegation of possession by a certain person, evidence of possession by his tenant will not constitute a variance: Harvey v. S., 67 Ga. 639.

[3] Davis v. S., 52 Ala. 357.

[4] S. v. Thompson, 97 N. C. 496.

[5] Adams v. S., 62 Ala. 177.

[6] Woolsey v. S., 30 Tex. Ap. 346.

[7] Duncan v. S., 29 Fla. 439.

[8] Maxwell v. S., 68 Miss. 339.

[9] Thomas v. S., 41 Tex. 27; S. v. Nickleson, 45 La. An. 1172. *Contra*, Kellenbeck v. S., 10 Md. 431.

[10] S. v. Thorne, 81 N. C. 555.

[11] Rex v. Reader, 4 C. & P. 245.

[12] No exact precedent for the order of arrangement of the terms in this

FOR BURNING DWELLING-HOUSE IN NIGHT-TIME, HUMAN BEING THEREIN.

That A. B., in the county aforesaid, on ——, about the hour of ten in the night-time of said day, unlawfully, maliciously and feloniously did set fire to and burn the dwelling-house of T. H. then and there situate, in which said dwelling-house there was then and there a human being.[1]

FOR BURNING BUILDING TO DEFRAUD INSURER.

That A. B., in the county aforesaid, on ——, did set fire to and burn the dwelling-house of him, the said A. B., there situate, with intent thereby to defraud a certain insurance company called the ——, said dwelling-house then and there being insured against loss or damage by fire by the said company for the sum of one thousand dollars.[2]

§ 532. **Included offenses.**— The burning of a building not a dwelling is not included in the charge of burning a dwelling-house; the term "dwelling-house," being matter of description, must be proved as laid.[3] Neither is the crime of burning insured property with intent to defraud included in a charge of common-law arson.[4]

§ 533. **Evidence.**— Prior difficulties between the defendant and the owner may be shown for the purpose of supplying a motive.[5] So the presence in the building of property of a person not the owner, against whom the defendant had malice,

indictment can be cited, but it certainly contains the essentials of all the various forms.

[1] See S. v. Aguila, 14 Mo. 130; Woodford v. P., 62 N. Y. 117. In Wisconsin the statute requires that the human being shall have been lawfully in the house, and that fact must be alleged to constitute the first degree: Lacy v. S., 15 Wis. 13. In the Wisconsin case the name of the person who was in the house is stated in the indictment, and Bishop regards such a statement as essential: Bish. Direc. & Forms, § 188 and note. But in S. v. Aguila, *supra*, it is expressly held not to be necessary, and it is not found in the indictment given in Woodford v. P., *supra*, though the question is not there passed upon.

[2] This is substantially the form authorized in Archbold's Criminal Practice and Pleading, with the addition, however, of the allegation that the property was insured in said company, which is necessary under some statutory provisions.

[3] C. v. Hayden, 150 Mass. 332; P. v. Handley, 93 Mich. 46.

[4] Dedieu v. P., 22 N. Y. 178.

[5] Hudson v. S., 61 Ala. 333; Oliver v. S., 33 Tex. Ap. 541. In case of burning a jail the indictments against defendant and others under which they were held in confinement in such jail may be shown: Lockett v. S., 63 Ala. 5.

may be shown;[1] or that defendant had charged that his wife was living in improper relations with the owner of the property;[2] or that defendant charged with burning with intent to defraud an insurance company had other insurance on the property.[3] Prior attempts of defendant to burn the same building may be shown as indicating his intent;[4] and, indeed, it is said that previous attempts to burn the premises may be shown without evidence that such attempts were made by the defendant,[5] and that the presence of the defendant at the time of such previous attempts, and his demeanor, may be shown;[6] and also the presence and demeanor of defendant at other similar fires.[7] But it is not competent to show similar fires on other premises.[8] A general conspiracy to burn houses entered into between defendant and another, and a subsequent agreement to burn the particular house, may be proven.[9] Previous presence of the defendant in a suspicious way about the premises may be shown,[10] and in behalf of the defendant it may perhaps be shown that another person had threatened to burn the house and was in the vicinity at the time it was burned;[11] but threats alone, made by a third person, are not admissible.[12] Where it appears that the crime was committed in the absence of the occupant, evidence that goods were found in defendant's possession which were in the building just before the fire is admissible;[13] and as tending to show motive, the fact of the commission of larceny may be proven.[14] Before circumstantial evidence is admissible to connect the prisoner with the burning, it must appear that the building was feloniously and not accidentally burned.[15] Evidence of experiments in order to show the way in which the building was set on fire is admissible.[16]

1 McAdory v. S., 62 Ala. 154.

2 S. v. Rhodes, 111 N. C. 647.

3 S. v. Cohn, 9 Nev. 179.

4 P. v. Shainwold, 51 Cal. 468; S. v. Ward, 61 Vt. 153.

5 Reg. v. Bailey, 2 Cox, 311. And see Brock v. S., 26 Ala. 104; S. v. Rohfrischt, 12 La. An. 382.

6 Reg. v. Dossett, 2 C. & K. 306; but *contra*, see Reg. v. Harris, 4 F. & F. 342.

7 Reg. v. Taylor, 5 Cox, 136.

8 Reg. v. Regan, 4 Cox, 335.

9 Hall v. S., 3 Lea, 552.

10 S. v. Crawford, 99 Mo. 74.

11 Hensley v. S., 9 Humph. 243.

12 Carlton v. P., 150 Ill. 181.

13 S. v Vatter, 71 Ia. 557. For a full discussion of the question as to admissibility and weight of evidence as to recent possession of stolen goods, see *supra*, § 514, and *infra*, § 616.

14 Jones v. S., 63 Ga. 395.

15 Phillips v. S., 29 Ga. 105.

16 Reg. v. Heseltine, 12 Cox, 404.

PART VII.

OFFENSES AGAINST PROPERTY.

CHAPTER 26.

LARCENY.

I. DEFINITION.
II. WHAT PROPERTY SUBJECT OF LARCENY.
III. OWNERSHIP OF THE PROPERTY.
IV. THE ACT: TAKING AND CARRYING AWAY.
V. THE INTENT.
VI. COMPOUND LARCENIES.
VII. VALUE AS DETERMINING PUNISHMENT; GRAND AND PETIT.
VIII. PROCEDURE.
IX. EVIDENCE.

I. DEFINITION.

§ **534. Technical.**— This offense is the most technical in its distinctions of all the common-law felonies.[1] The reason for this is perhaps to be found in the fact that, inasmuch as the higher grade of the offense was, until since Blackstone's time, punishable capitally,[2] the courts were inclined to find technical reasons to avoid the infliction of that penalty for mere wrong done with reference to property. By reason of the depreciation of money, and the consequent appreciation of the money value of property, which took place within about two centuries and a half after the passage of the statute of Westminster I. (A. D. 1275), chapter 15 of which made grand larceny to consist of the stealing of property "above the value of twelve pence," cases of larceny became capital which would not have been such at the time the statute was passed, and therefore Lord Coke suggests that the valuation of property in determining whether the offense was grand larceny ought to be "reasonable."[3]

[1] For the origin of some of its intricacies, see 3 Stephen, Hist. Cr. L. 121.

[2] 4 Bl. Com. 236; but with benefit of clergy for the first offense: 4 Bl. Com. 238.

[3] 2 Inst. 189; 2 East, P. C. 736; 4 Bl. Com. 237; Spelman, Gloss., s. v. Laricinium; 1 Bish. Cr. L., § 679; 1 Green, Cr. L. R. 339, note. According to Coke, money had by his time decreased to about one-third of its

§ **535. In brief.**— It has been found by writers on the subject to be impossible to give any short description of the offense which shall be accurate and at the same time embody the various technical distinctions which have been recognized in administering the law with reference to this crime. Inasmuch, therefore, as no definition however elaborate can satisfactorily present its peculiarities, it seems better to adhere to some simple and well-recognized form of statement which shall not be inaccurate in itself, leaving the explanation and elaboration of the definition to be presented in the discussion of the different doctrines of the offense as they have been worked out by the courts. For that purpose there is probably no definition which is better than that of Blackstone, "the felonious taking and carrying away of the personal goods of another."[1]

II. WHAT PROPERTY SUBJECT OF LARCENY.

§ **536. Not realty.**— The definition indicates that the crime can be committed only with reference to personal property, and therefore not as to anything which is a part of the realty. But as the taking and carrying away would necessarily terminate the character of the property as realty, even if it were such before, the important point in this distinction is, that if the severance from the realty of anything which is a part thereof, or annexed thereto, so as to go with the realty by descent or in case of conveyance, is made by the wrong-doer himself, so

value at the time the statute of Westminster I. was passed. As to the depreciation of English money, see Encyc. Brit. s. v. Money, 6.

[1] 4 Bl. Com. 229. For other analogous short definitions substantially the same in purport as that of Blackstone, see 3 Inst. 107; 1 Hawk. P. C., ch. 33, § 1; 1 Hale, P. C. 503; 2 East, P. C. 553. These definitions are quoted in the following cases among others: S. v. Chambers, 22 W. Va. 779; Holly v. S., 54 Ala. 238; Edmonds v. S., 70 Ala. 8; Johnson v. P., 113 Ill. 99; Mead v. S., 25 Neb. 444; Thompson v. P., 4 Neb. 524; Dignowitty v. S., 17 Tex. 521. For more elaborate definitions, see Stephen, Dig. Cr. Law, art. 295; 2 Bish. Cr. L., § 758; Grose, J., in Rex v. Hammond, 2 Leach, 1083, 1089; and other definitions collected in 2 Russ. Cr. 2; 3 Stephen, Hist. Cr. L. 129–141; 2 Bish. Cr. L. § 758, note. Under the Texas statute, "theft" and "stealing" are synonymous, and include all unlawful acquisitions of personal property punishable by law: Carr v. S., 9 Tex. Ap. 463; Martin v. S., 9 Tex. Ap. 293; Quitzow v. S., 1 Tex. Ap. 65; Marshall v. S., 4 Tex. Ap. 549. But the mere fraudulent taking is not enough; the statute enumerates other elements of the offense: Johnston v. S., 25 Tex. Ap. 731.

that the taking and carrying away is a continuous act, the offense is not larceny, because the taking and carrying away is not of the personal property of another, that which was severed not having been in his possession as a chattel but only as a portion of the realty. Thus, if ore which has not been mined or otherwise severed so as to convert it into a chattel of the owner is severed and carried away by a wrong-doer, the offense is not larceny.[1] On the same reasoning, water or ice is not subject of larceny while remaining a part of the realty; but if the ice is cut and stored in an ice-house,[2] or the water is pumped into supply pipes,[3] it is subject of larceny like other personal property. Seaweed lying ungathered on the shore is a part of the realty and not subject of larceny.[4] So, it is not larceny to wrongfully detach from a building and carry away a portion of it, such as metal pipes or troughs or other things attached to and part thereof.[5] But the courts have expressed their disapproval of doctrines so technical, even while compelled to follow them;[6] and in cases where the annexation is constructive only, have held the taking and carrying away to be larceny. It has been so held as to window sashes not permanently annexed to the building,[7] chandeliers,[8] doors taken from their hinges,[9] rails in a fence,[10] belts belonging to a mill,[11]

[1] S. v. Burt, 64 N. C. 619; S. v. Berryman, 8 Nev. 262. Where the indictment charged that the defendant did "unlawfully and feloniously take, steal and carry away fifty-two pounds of gold-bearing quartz of the property, etc., of the value, etc.," *held*, that it did not appear but that the ore had been first severed by the wrong-doer in the act of carrying it away and that the indictment was bad: P. v. Williams, 35 Cal. 671. But where the indictment was for stealing a quantity of specimens of gold and silver ore, etc., *held*, that the description was sufficient to indicate that the ores were personal property: P. v. Freeman, 1 Idaho (N. S.), 322.

[2] Ward v. P., 6 Hill, 144; S. v. Pottmeyer, 33 Ind. 402.

[3] Ferens v. O'Brien, 11 Q. B. D. 21.

[4] Reg. v. Clinton, 4 Ir. R. C. L. 6. But where waste coal was carried upon land by a stream, *held*, that although it was realty as thus deposited along the shore, one who gathered it into a boat and appropriated it was guilty of larceny: C. v. Steimling, 156 Pa. St. 400, 27 Atl. R. 297.

[5] S. v. Hall, 5 Harr. 492; Smith v. C., 14 Bush, 31; S. v. Davis, 22 La. An. 77; Langston v. S., 96 Ala. 44; Lee v. Risdon, 3 Taunt. 188.

[6] P. v. Williams, 35 Cal. 671. And see Holly v. S., 54 Ala. 238, and other cases cited in the notes immediately following.

[7] Rex v. Hedges, 1 Leach, 201.

[8] Smith v. C., 14 Bush, 31.

[9] Ex parte Wilke, 34 Tex. 155.

[10] Harberger v. S., 4 Tex. Ap. 26.

[11] Jackson v. S., 11 Ohio St. 104.

valves in a portable pump,[1] and the key of a door.[2] So, trees and shrubs, or fruit thereon, or grass or crops growing upon or still remaining attached to the soil, are realty, and one who severs and carries away such portion of the realty is not guilty of larceny.[3] The wrongful severing and carrying away of metal attached in some way to the land, as pipes, etc.,[4] or products of the soil,[5] are made misdemeanors by statute in England and some of the states. The stealing of grain, fruit, etc., remaining ungathered in some states is made larceny.[6] In other states the taking of the products of the soil is punishable as malicious trespass, which will be elsewhere considered.[7]

§ 537. **Where the severance and carrying away are not continuous.**— If, after the wrongful severance, in cases such as are described in the preceding section, the wrong-doer abandons the property, even for a short space of time, and subsequently carries it away, the offense is larceny because the abandonment has placed the property in the possession of the owner of the realty as a chattel and the subsequent taking is the tak-

[1] Langston v. S., 96 Ala. 44.

[2] Hoskins v. Tarrence, 5 Blackf. 417.

[3] 3 Inst. 109; 4 Bl. Com. 232; Gregg v. S., 55 Ala. 116; Pinckard v. S., 62 Ala. 167; S. v. Foy, 82 N. C. 679; C. v. Steimling, 156 Pa. 400, 27 Atl. R. 297; Bartlett v. Brown, 6 R. I. 37; S. v. Prince, 42 La. An. 817.

[4] Reg. v. Jones, Dears. & B. 655; Reg. v. Rice, Bell, 87; Reg. v. Gooch, 8 C. & P. 293; Rex v. Davis, 2 East, P. C. 593; Rex v. Blick, 4 C. & P. 377; Rex v. Richards, Russ. & Ry. 28; Rex v. Finch, 1 Moody, 418.

[5] Rex v. Hodges, Moody & M. 341; Rex v. Brumby, 3 C. & K. 315.

[6] S. v. Liles, 78 N. C. 496; S. v. Thompson, 93 N. C. 537; S. v. Washington, 26 S. C. 604; S. v. Nelson, 28 S. C. 16; S. v. Fife, 2 Bailey, 337; Wiswell v. S., 21 Ohio St. 658; S. v. Sheppard, 33 La. An. 1216. Under such a statute, peas are included in the general term "other grain:" S. v. Williams, 2 Strobh. 474; but it will not cover a case of entering upon the land and carrying away money, such act not being within its general purpose: S. v. Vosburg, 111 N. C. 718. In Alabama the offense is described as the carrying away of any outstanding crop: Schamberger v. S., 68 Ala. 543; Harris v. S., 60 Ala. 50. But under an indictment for that offense there cannot be a conviction for larceny: Pinckard v. S., 62 Ala. 167; Gregg v. S., 55 Ala. 116; and to the same effect, see S. v. Washington, 26 S. C. 604. Such a statute, if it covers generally the stealing of property from a field, may cover also cases of petit larceny where the taking from the field is of a crop already severed: S. v. Shuler, 19 S. C. 140; S. v. Nelson, 28 S. C. 16. As to the construction of a statute with reference to larceny of corn, etc., or other product "cultivated for food or market, growing, standing or remaining ungathered," see S. v. Bragg, 86 N. C. 687; S. v. Ballard, 97 N. C. 443.

[7] *Infra*, § 823.

ing of personal property from the possession of the owner within the definition of larceny.[1] The question is whether the severance and carrying away are parts of one continuous transaction.[2] If there is no abandonment, but the thing severed is only temporarily placed on the ground with the continuous intention of taking it away,[3] or even is concealed with the purpose of returning for it,[4] the subsequent carrying away is deemed a part of the same transaction and does not constitute larceny; but the cases just cited indicate a reluctance on the part of the courts to countenance so technical a rule, and in a recent case of a similar character, where waste coal washed upon land by a stream was gathered in small quantities and subsequently taken away, the court refused to follow it and held the act to be larceny.[5] So where a trespasser caused turpentine to flow from trees on the land of another and subsequently collected it and carried it away, it was said that the act might be larceny, although as the indictment was for the stealing of "two barrels" of turpentine, it was held that the acts proved did not constitute the offense charged.[6]

§ 538. **Animals feræ naturæ or without value.**—Larceny can only be committed of that which is a subject of ownership. Wild animals running at large belong to no one, and therefore to take them from the premises of another, either by capture or by killing and taking away the carcasses, is not larceny.[7] Where such animals are reduced to control by being killed or

[1] Holly v. S., 54 Ala. 238; S. v. Parker, 34 Ark. 158; S. v. Berryman, 8 Nev. 262; S. v. Prince, 42 La. An. 817; Lee v. Risdon, 7 Taunt. 188; Emmerson v. Annison, 1 Mod. 89; Reg. v. Foley, 17 Cox, 142. Where dead rabbits were concealed by one intending to wrongfully take them away, but the agent of the owner discovered and marked them, for the purpose of detecting the thief, *held*, that the act was not such reduction to possession of the owner as to make the subsequent taking away a larceny: Reg. v. Petch, 14 Cox, 17.

[2] S. v. Hall, 5 Harr. 492; Bradford v. S., 6 Lea, 634; Bell v. S., 4 Baxt. 426.

[3] Bradford v. S., 6 Lea, 634; Bell v. S., 4 Baxt. 426; S. v. Bragg, 86 N. C. 687.

[4] Reg. v. Townley, L. R. 1 C. C. 315. And see Reg. v. Petch, 14 Cox, 17.

[5] C. v. Steimling, 156 Pa. 400, 27 Atl. R. 297. For a somewhat similar case see S. v. Berryman, 3 Nev. 262.

[6] S. v. Moore, 11 Ired. 70. And see S. v. King, 98 N. C. 648.

[7] 4 Bl. Com. 235; 1 Hale, P. C. 511; Staundford, P. C., ch. 16; Pollock & Maitland, Hist. Eng. L. 497; 2 Bish. Cr. L., § 771; Aldrich v. Wright, 53 N. H. 398; Reg. v. Townley, L. R. 1 C. C. 315.

captured and kept in confinement or tamed,[1] another question arises, that is, whether they are of value. If the flesh is suitable for food or the skin or fur is valuable,[2] then they are subject of larceny when they have been thus reduced to control. Thus, doves are subject of larceny if kept and fed under the control of an owner in a pigeon-house or cote;[3] and so are pigeons though they have liberty of ingress and egress from the cote if they are so far tamed that they return to roost in boxes provided for them.[4] So partridges or pheasants reared and kept in confinement, or so far tamed as to remain on the owner's premises, are subject of larceny.[5] So fish are subject of larceny if confined in a tank, but the facts showing their reduction to possession must appear.[6] So oysters are subject of larceny, and it is a sufficient reduction to possession that they have been planted in a bed.[7] Bees are *feræ naturæ*, but they become property by being reclaimed and hived and are then subject of larceny, for while they are not fit for food themselves, their honey is.[8] Animals which, though reclaimed by

[1] S. v. House, 65 N. C. 315. And the facts showing such reduction to control must be averred: Harvey v. C., 23 Grat. 941; Rex v. Rough, 2 East, P. C. 607; Rex v. Hundson, 2 East, P. C. 611; Reg. v. Cheafor, 2 Den. 361. A turkey may be subject of larceny though not tamed: S. v. Turner, 66 N. C. 618. As to what is such reduction of a wild animal to control by chasing and attempting to capture it as that it becomes property, see Pierson v. Post, 3 Caines, 175; Buster v. Newkirk, 20 Johns. 75; Taber v. Jenny, 1 Sprague, 315.

[2] An otter: S. v. House, 65 N. C. 315.

[3] C. v. Chace, 9 Pick. 15.

[4] Rex v. Brooks, 4 C. & P. 131. But these illustrations are of taking from the cote. Where tame doves were taken while at large as "free tenants of the air," *held*, that there was no larceny: C. v. Chace, 9 Pick. 15.

[5] Reg. v. Head, 1 F. & F. 350; Reg. v. Garnham, 2 F. & F. 347; Reg. v. Cory, 10 Cox, 23; Reg. v. Shickle, L. R. 1 C. C. 158. But where a wild partridge was wounded, and in this condition was taken by another, *held*, that there could be no conviction for larceny: Reg. v. Roe, 11 Cox, 554.

[6] S. v. Krider, 78 N. C. 481; S. v. Donovan, 1 Houst. Cr. C. 43; Reg. v. Steer, 6 Mod. 183; Wickes v. Clutterbuck, 2 Bing. 483; Rex v. Sadler, 2 Chitty, 519; Rex v. Caradice, Russ. & Ry. 205; Rex v. Mallinson, 2 Burr. 679.

[7] Fleet v. Hegeman, 14 Wend. 42; S. v. Tayler, 27 N. J. 117. The taking of oysters from a private bed is sometimes made an offense distinct from that of larceny: S. v. Taylor, 13 R. I. 541.

[8] Harvey v. C., 23 Grat. 941; S. v. Murphy, 8 Blackf. 498. As to property in bees, see, also, Rexroth v. Coon, 15 R. I. 35; Gillet v. Mason, 7 Johns. 16; Wallis v. Mease, 3 Binn. 546.

being tamed, confined, or killed, do not possess the elements of value as above suggested, but are mere objects of fancy, are not subject of larceny. Among these are enumerated ferrets, squirrels, parrots, singing birds, martens and coons.[1] Apparently contrary to this general statement it has been held that a tame mocking-bird is subject of larceny.[2] Hawks, tamed and trained for use in hunting, have been regarded in England of such nature that the taking of them is larceny.[3] The hides and fur of wild animals are subject of larceny, having been reduced to possession.[4]

§ **539. Dogs and cats.**— The animals referred to in the preceding section are by nature wild, but in the particular instance reduced to control. Some animals which are by nature tame are still not regarded as subject of larceny. The principal examples of this class of animals are the dog and the cat.[5] Though dogs are regarded in civil suits as having value,[6] yet at common law, recognized in practically all the cases where it is not modified by statute, the stealing of them is not criminal.[7] Where the definition of larceny has by statute been enlarged to cover personal property in general, it has been held that a dog, being property of value for other purposes, is subject of larceny;[8] but to the contrary it is held that, by the use of the term "personal property" in defining larceny, it is not intended to include dogs,

[1] 1 Hawk. P. C., ch. 33, § 23; 2 Bish. Cr. L., § 773. And see as to ferrets: Rex v. Searing, Russ. & Ry. 350; and coons: Warren v. S., 1 Greene (Ia.), 106. In Norton v. Ladd, 5 N. H. 203, a sable caught in a trap was said not to be subject of larceny, though it is difficult to see why in such case the value of the fur would not bring it within the description of an animal of value.

[2] Haywood v. S., 41 Ark. 479.

[3] 3 Inst. 109; 1 Hale, P. C. 512; 1 Hawk. P. C., ch. 33, § 23.

[4] Pennsylvania v. Becomb, Addis. 386; Norton v. Ladd, 5 N. H. 203; Reg. v. Gallears, 1 Den. 501.

[5] 3 Inst. 109; 1 Hale, P. C. 512; 1 Hawk. P. C., ch. 33, § 23; 2 East, P. C. 614; 2 Bish. Cr. L., § 773.

[6] Findley v. Bear, 8 S. & R. 571; Smith v. Forehand, 100 Mass. 136; Railway Co. v. Hauks, 78 Tex. 300.

[7] Reg. v. Robinson, Bell, 34; S. v. Holder, 81 N. C. 527; Ward v. S., 48 Ala. 161; S. v. Doe, 79 Ind. 9; S. v. Limus, 26 Ohio St. 400; S. v. Harriman, 75 Me. 562; S. v. Marshall, 13 Tex. 58.

[8] Mullaly v. P., 86 N. Y. 365; P. v. Campbell, 4 Park. Cr. R. 386; P. v. Maloney, 1 Park. Cr. R. 593; Harrington v. Miles, 11 Kan. 480; S. v. Brown, 9 Baxt. 53; Hurley v. S., 30 Tex. Ap. 333. And it is said that a statutory enlargement of the definition of larceny so as to include "anything of value" is sufficient to render a dog subject of larceny: S. v. Yates (Ohio Com. Pl.), 10 Cr. L. Mag. 439.

which at common law were not such property as could be stolen.[1] In some cases it is suggested that, by subjecting dogs to taxation, the legislature so far recognizes them as property that they are made the subject of larceny under the description of a thing of value;[2] but it has been well pointed out that taxes on dogs are not imposed on the theory that they are property, but as a police regulation, and therefore that such taxation does not in itself render them subject of larceny.[3] Dogs are so far domestic animals as to be within statutes punishing malicious mischief in injuring or destroying animals of that kind.[4] By statute in England the taking of dogs was made punishable, but not as larceny.[5] This distinction as to dogs is generally reprobated, but in the absence of some statutory modification upon which an intention to change the common-law rule can be predicated, it is still upheld, as the cases above referred to clearly show.

§ 540. **Domestic animals or fowl, and their products.**— The discussion in the second preceding section has no reference to animals or fowl generally recognized as domestic and the subject of property. These are goods and chattels within the strict terms of the definition of larceny.[6] So it is larceny to take wool from live sheep or milk from a cow.[7] Under an indictment for larceny of eggs it was held that it should have been stated of what species the eggs were, so as to show them to be the subject of larceny.[8]

§ 541. **Animals, alive or dead.**— An indictment for stealing an animal, naming it, will be construed as charging the stealing of a living animal. If the intent is to charge the stealing of the carcass of a dead animal, proper descriptive words must

[1] Ward v. S., 48 Ala. 161.

[2] C. v. Hazelwood, 84 Ky. 681; Mullaly v. P., 86 N. Y. 365. Such statutes sometimes expressly make dogs subject of larceny: C. v. Depuy, 148 Pa. St. 201. Such a statute declaring the taking of a dog, registered under the act, to be larceny, but not expressly making dogs property, was held invalid for uncertainty, because not furnishing any basis for determining whether the offense would be grand or petit larceny: Johnston v. S., 100 Ala. 32.

[3] S. v. Doe, 79 Ind. 9; S. v. Limas, 26 Ohio St. 400.

[4] S. v. Sumner, 2 Ind. 377; S. v. Latham, 13 Ired. 33; S. v. McDuffie, 34 N. H. 523; Hurley v. S., 30 Tex. Ap. 333. *Contra*, S. v. Harriman, 75 Me. 562; S. v. Marshall, 13 Tex. 55.

[5] 1 Hawk. P. C., ch. 33, § 23.

[6] 1 Hale, P. C. 511; C. v. Beaman, 8 Gray, 497; S. v. Turner, 66 N. C. 618; Reg. v. Edwards, 13 Cox, 384.

[7] Rex v. Martin, 2 East, P. C. 618.

[8] Reg. v. Cox, 1 C. & K. 494.

be used.[1] In England there are statutory provisions for the punishment of the killing of an animal with intent to steal its carcass, but this is not larceny.[2]

§ 542. **Other instances of property.**— There is such property in illuminating gas that it is subject of larceny.[3] The dead body of a human being is not subject of larceny,[4] but the clothing or shroud of such body[5] or the coffin[6] may be stolen. By a statute, stealing letters or other matter from the mail is punishable.[7] The fact that a person in possession of property has no ownership therein because it is stolen property,[8] or that he holds it for some unlawful purpose,[9] such as liquors, to be unlawfully sold,[10] or chips for gambling,[11] will not prevent such thing being subject of larceny.

§ 543. **Things of value; written instruments; choses in action.**— Smallness of value of the property will not prevent the wrongful taking of it from being larceny. It is not necessary that it be of the value of some known coin,[12] and a mere piece of paper is of such value that larceny may be committed thereof.[13] Thus, a paper containing a list of names of sub-

[1] C. v. Beaman, 8 Gray, 497; Kollenberger v. P., 9 Colo. 233; Rex v. Edwards, Russ. & Ry. 497; Rex v. Halloway, 1 C. & P. 127. The case of Rex v. Puckering, 1 Moody, 242, seems to be contrary to this, but is probably not authority on the point.

[2] Reg. v. Sutton, 8 C. & P. 291; Rex v. Clay, Russ. & Ry. 387; Rex v. Williams, 1 Moody, 107. And see Beavers v. S., 14 Tex. Ap. 541, holding that the unlawfully killing alone does not constitute larceny.

[3] C. v. Shaw, 4 Allen, 308; S. v. Wellman, 34 Minn. 221; Reg. v. White, 3 C. & K. 363; Reg. v. Firth, L. R. 1 C. C. 172.

[4] 2 East, P. C. 652.

[5] Hayne's Case, 12 Coke, 113; 1 Hale, P. C. 515; 1 Hawk. P. C., ch. 33, § 29; Wonson v. Sayward, 13 Pick. 402.

[6] S. v. Doepke, 68 Mo. 208.

[7] Farnum v. U. S., 1 Colo. 309; Beery v. U. S., 2 Colo. 186; Reg. v. Wynn, 2 C. & K. 859. Further as to robbing the mails, see *infra*, § 1329.

[8] 1 Hale, P. C. 507. Larceny is an offense against the possession: See *infra*, § 546.

[9] C. v. Smith, 129 Mass. 104, distinguishing Reg. v. Hunt, 8 C. & P. 642, where it was held that an illegal combination, being incapable of owning property, a taking from it was not larceny.

[10] S. v. May, 20 Ia. 305; C. v. Coffee, 9 Gray, 139; C. v. Rourke, 10 Cush. 397.

[11] Bales v. S., 3 W. Va. 685.

[12] Reg. v. Morris, 9 C. & P. 349. Further as to value, see *infra*, §§ 581, 589.

[13] For instance, a piece of paper on which a void check is written, the property being described in the count on which the conviction is had as a piece of paper and not as a check: Reg. v. Perry, 1 C. & K. 725. It was so held as to country bankers'

scribers to a fund was held to be a chattel subject of larceny.[1] But if the value of the paper exists not in itself, but in the relation which it bears to some other thing which cannot be stolen, it is by common law not subject of larceny, being only the evidence or representative of a right.[2] On this theory and also because they were considered to pertain to the realty, title deeds and other instruments representing ownership of or an interest in the land were not subject of larceny.[3] But this rule has been changed in England by statute.[4] Written instruments evidencing a right of action, usually called choses in action, are not subject of larceny for the same reason. The taking of the paper does not constitute a taking of the right represented by it, and looked at as a mere instrument of evidence the paper is not a thing of value, not being essential to the existence of the right which it represents.[5] This principle of the common law is well settled and universally applied, where not changed by statute; but there are statutes so extending the definition of larceny by general terms as to include the ordinary forms of commercial paper,[6] or covering notes, bills and checks, etc., by special description in such definition.[7] Under such statutes the description of the property stolen as one promissory note, or one due-bill, is sufficient.[8] And it is not necessary to allege with reference to a promissory note that it was "for the payment of money."[9] A due-bill is an "obligation" within such statutes.[10] Checks are the subject of larceny within the usual statutory description.[11] A

notes which had been paid: Rex v. Vyse, 1 Moody, 218. And see Rex v. Mead, 4 C. & P. 535; Rex v. Clark, Russ. & Ry. 181; Reg. v. Godfrey, Dears. & B. 426.

[1] S. v. James, 58 N. H. 67.

[2] 1 Hawk. P. C., ch. 33, § 22; 2 East, P. C. 597; 4 Bl. Com. 234; 2 Bish. Cr. L., § 768–770.

[3] 3 Inst. 109; 4 Bl. Com. 234; 1 Hale, P. C. 510, n.; Rex v. Westbeer, 2 Stra. 1133; S. C., 1 Leach, 12.

[4] Rex v. John, 7 C. & P. 324; Rex v. Walker, 1 Moody, 155.

[5] Reg. v. Morrison, Bell, 158; Reg. v. Watts, Dears. 326; Reg. v. Powell, 2 Den. 403; U. S. v. Davis, 5 Mason, 356; Culp v. S., 1 Port. 33; C. v. Eichelberger, 119 Pa. St. 254.

[6] Garfield v. S., 74 Ind. 60; Turner v. S., 1 Ohio St. 422.

[7] Rex v. Chard, Russ. & Ry. 488; C. v. Brettun, 100 Mass. 206; Payne v. P., 6 Johns. 103; P. v. Wiley, 3 Hill (N. Y.), 194; Moore v. C., 8 Pa. St. 260; S. v. Campbell, 103 N. C. 344.

[8] C. v. Henry, 2 Brewst. 556; C. v. Byerly, 2 Brewst. 566.

[9] C. v. Brettun, 100 Mass. 206.

[10] S. v. Campbell, 103 N. C. 344.

[11] C. v. Yerkes, 29 Leg. Int. 60; S. C., 119 Pa. St. 266; Reg. v. Heath, 2 Moody, 33; Reg. v. Godfrey, Dears. & B. 426.

postoffice order is within such a statute,[1] but not a county order.[2] The statutes expressly include valuable securities or securities for the payment of money;[3] and are broad enough to cover a mortgage of real estate.[4] Books of account are by statute made the subject of larceny, and such description is not confined to books of original entry, but includes any books in which the owner keeps statements of his accounts with others.[5] The statutes also cover receipts and releases[6] and vouchers.[7] Public records would not be the subject of larceny under the common-law rule, but are made so by statute.[8] Bank-bills are usually specified in the statutes.[9] Bank-bills although not specified are covered by the general description of promissory notes.[10] Where the definition of larceny is extended to cover personal property, treasury notes of the United States are included without special designation,[11] and such treasury notes are also bank-notes under that description.[12] At common law, money, according to the original meaning of the term, that is, coin, has always been subject of larceny.[13] But the term "money" as used in the statutory definitions of larceny includes bank-

1 Reg. v. Gilchrist, Car. & M. 224.

2 Warner v. C., 1 Pa. St. 154.

3 Reg. v. Smith, Dears. 561; Reg. v. Williams, 6 Cox, 49; Reg. v. Lowrie, L. R. 1 C. C. 61.

4 C. v. Concannon, 5 Allen, 502.

5 C. v. Williams, 9 Met. 273.

6 C. v. Williams, 9 Met. 273.

7 S. v. Hickman, 8 N. J. 299.

8 Reg. v. Bailey, L. R. 1 C. C. 347; Wilson v. S., 5 Ark. 513.

9 C. v. Stebbins, 8 Gray, 492; Cummings v. C., 2 Va. Cas. 128; Pomeroy v. C., 2 Va. Cas. 342; S. v. Carr, 43 Ia. 418; Greeson v. S., 6 Miss. 33; Damewood v. S., 2 Miss. 262; U. S. v. Moulton, 5 Mason, 537; Ex parte Prince, 27 Fla. 196.

10 S. v. Wilson, Treadw. Const. 495; S. v. Tillery, 1 Nott & M. 9; S. v. Casados, 1 Nott & M. 91; S. v. Wilson, 2 Brev. 196. But aside from statutory provisions, paper money is not subject of larceny: C. v. McDowell, 1 Browne (Pa.), 359; C. v. Boyer, 1 Binn. 201; S. v. Dill, 75 N. C. 57. Further as to larceny of bank-bills, see *infra*, §§ 595, 598.

11 Collins v. P., 39 Ill. 233.

12 Ex parte Prince, 27 Fla. 196; Sally v. S., 39 Ala. 691; Sansbury v. S., 4 Tex. Ap. 99.

13 Rex v. Fry, Russ. & Ry. 482; P. v. Williams, 24 Mich. 156; Hall v. S., 3 Ohio St. 575. The form of indictment given in Archbold describes it as "certain money of C. D.:" 2 Archbold, Cr. Pr. & Pl. 354. But it is said that the indictment should describe the pieces: Rex v. Fry, Russ. & Ry. 482; S. v. Longbottom, 11 Humph. 39. It seems that coin is not to be described as "goods and chattels:" Reg. v. Radley, 1 Den. 453. But it is said in another case that money is in general covered by the words "goods and chattels:" Hall v. S., 3 Ohio St. 575. Under an English statute with reference to the taking of goods, wares and merchandise from a shop, it was held that those terms did not include

notes and other forms of paper money as well as coin.[1] The question as to how money is to be described in the indictment will be considered in a subsequent section.[2] Under these statutes extending the definition of larceny to include commercial paper, bank-notes and other instruments in writing, the question arises whether an instrument of such character which is of no value can be the subject of larceny, and it has sometimes been said that if the instrument is invalid the crime cannot be committed with reference thereto;[3] for instance, where the instrument is still in the hands of the maker and has not yet been executed and delivered.[4] But the reasonable doctrine seems to be that if the instrument becomes of value when it passes from the maker's possession, that is, if when taken from him it shows an apparent liability, the taking will be larceny.[5] Thus bank-notes, before issue and not yet put in circulation, are subject of larceny.[6] But blank railroad tickets or passes, not valid until countersigned, are not subject of larceny.[7] An instrument which has been paid or redeemed, if it would be good in the hands of an innocent holder or valuable for reissue, is subject of larceny.[8] There must be some evidence, however, of the genuineness of the instrument to warrant a conviction.[9] It seems that the doctrine in regard to written

money: Rex v. Leigh, 1 Leach, 52; Rex v. Grimes, 2 East, P. C. 647. Under the English statute as to receiving stolen goods, although the terms used are "goods and chattels," the receiving of stolen money is not included: Guy's Case and Morris's Case, 2 East, P. C. 748. And to the same effect, see S. v. Calvin, 22 N. J. 207. *Contra*, Hall v. S., 3 Ohio St. 575.

[1] S. v. Moore, 66 Mo. 372; Ex parte Prince, 27 Fla. 196; S. v. Carr, 43 Ia. 418; U. S. v. Moulton, 5 Mason 537. *Contra*, Pryor v. C., 2 Dana, 298.

[2] *Infra*, §§ 596, 597.

[3] Wilson v. S., 1 Porter, 118.

[4] P. v. Loomis, 4 Denio, 380; Rex v. Hart, 6 C. & P. 106; Rex v. Walsh, Russ. & Ry. 215; Rex v. Phipoe, 2 East, P. C. 599. And this was decided also as to reissuable notes which had been taken up and not yet reissued: Rex v. Clark, Russ. & Ry. 181. A man cannot be convicted of larceny of a deed made and executed by himself: P. v. Mackinley, 9 Cal. 250.

[5] S. v. Thatcher, 35 N. J. 445; C. v. Rand, 7 Met. 475; Reg. v. Heath, 2 Moody, 33; Rex v. Metcalf, 1 Moody, 433; Rex v. Aslett, Russ. & Ry. 67. And see with reference to fraudulently securing a signature to an instrument: P. v. Genung, 11 Wend. 18.

[6] P. v. Wiley, 3 Hill (N. Y.), 194; Reg. v. West, Dears. & B. 109.

[7] S. v. Musgang, 51 Minn. 556; S. v. Hill, 1 Houst. Cr. C. 421.

[8] C. v. Rand, 4 Met. 475. *Contra* as to a due-bill which has been paid: S. v. Campbell, 103 N. C. 344.

[9] S. v. Tillery, 1 Nott & M. 8; Cummings v. C., 2 Va. Cas. 128; Collins v.

instruments evidencing a chose in action is not applicable to an instrument which directly represents property and not merely a right of action, and it is accordingly held that a pawnbroker's ticket is the subject of larceny inasmuch as it stands for the goods themselves.[1] And under analogous reasoning it is said that a railroad ticket is the subject of larceny although such a ticket does not of course stand for any specific property.[2] But railway tickets are included by express designation or general terms in the statutory definitions of larceny in most of the states.[3] A ticket or pass stolen from the company before issuance is not yet such a complete instrument as to be the subject of larceny.[4]

III. OWNERSHIP OF THE PROPERTY.

§ 544. Property without owner; abandoned.— It has already been said that some things are incapable of ownership, and cannot, therefore, be subject of larceny.[5] So, abandoned property, having no owner, cannot be stolen.[6] But the fact that the owner makes his property public, to be taken by others without compensation as they wish in a manner contemplated, will not constitute an abandonment so that a taking in some other way may not be larceny.[7]

§ 545. Property temporarily out of owner's control; lost or left in another's custody.— It will appear from the next section that possession may be constructive in the owner, so

P., 39 Ill. 233; Hildreth v. P., 32 Ill. 36; S. v. Dobson, 3 Harr. 563; Simpson v. S., 10 Tex. Ap. 681. But the production of the note itself is sufficient proof of genuineness: U. S. v. Byers, 4 Cranch, C. C. 171.

[1] Reg. v. Morrison, Bell, 158.

[2] Reg. v. Boulton, 1 Den. 508; Reg. v. Beecham, 6 Cox, 181; Millner v. S., 15 Lea, 179.

[3] McDaniels v. P., 118 Ill. 301; S. v. Musgang, 51 Minn. 556.

[4] S. v. Musgang, 51 Minn. 556; S. v. Hill, 1 Houst. Cr. C. 421. This is in accordance with the doctrine stated in the earlier part of this paragraph.

[5] See *supra*, §§ 538, 539.

[6] U. S. v. Smiley, 6 Sawyer, 640; Johnson v. S., 36 Tex. 375; Ritcher v. S., 38 Tex. 643; Debbs v. S., 43 Tex. 650. But where carcasses of animals were buried by the owner, without intent to make use of them, *held*, that they were, nevertheless, not abandoned, and that the taking of them might be larceny: Reg. v. Edwards, 13 Cox, 384. By statute in Arkansas it is not larceny to take unbranded stock over a year of age found running at large: Thompson v. S., 60 Ark. 59.

[7] A box of matches set out on a store counter for the use of purchasers of cigars is subject of larceny: Mitchum v. S., 45 Ala. 29.

that a taking thereof may be larceny from him, although he is not in immediate possession. An analogous rule is to be applied to property which, though not abandoned, has been temporarily and unintentionally given to or left by the owner on the premises or in the custody of another. Such property is deemed still in the possession of the owner, and a wrongful taking of it by the person on whose premises or in whose custody it is left,[1] or by a third person,[2] will be larceny from the owner. Cases of lost property, converted by the finder, are somewhat analogous, but are discussed under a subsequent section relating to intent,[3] where it will appear that the finder who takes with the intent of appropriating is guilty of larceny. It has been attempted to explain the doctrine as to lost goods on the theory of constructive possession in the owner and trespass by the finder, as in the case of property temporarily and unintentionally left on another's premises, and to limit the doctrine of larceny by the finder to such cases;[4] but such a theory is not sustained.[5] The difference is this: If the property is temporarily left by the owner on another's premises, a third person taking it commits trespass and is guilty of larceny, but if the property is really lost, the finder does not commit trespass unless he has at the time the intention to wrongfully convert.[6] If there is originally a trespass, the subsequent conversion, according to some cases, relates back and renders the whole transaction larceny.[7]

§ 546. What sufficient ownership; special owner, bailee or custodian; part owner.—As will appear in a subsequent section under the head of indictment,[8] the name of the owner

[1] P. v. McGarren, 17 Wend. 460; Reg. v. West, Dears. 402; property accidentally left in a coach and appropriated by the driver: Rex v. Wynne, 2 East, P. C. 664, 697; money left in a bureau and appropriated by the person into whose possession the bureau comes: Cartwright v. Green, 2 Leach, C. C. 952; Merry v. Green, 7 M. & W. 623; property taken from a trunk purchased from the owner's clerk in ignorance of its contents: Robinson v. S., 11 Tex. Ap. 403; property left in a railway coach and appropriated by a servant of the company: Reg. v. Pierce, 6 Cox, 117.

[2] Pyland v. S., 4 Sneed, 357; S. v. McCann, 19 Mo. 249; Brooks v. S., 35 Ohio St. 46.

[3] *Infra*, § 571.

[4] Porter v. S., Mart. & Yerg. 226; Lawrence v. S., 1 Humph. 228.

[5] Tanner v. C., 14 Grat. 635.

[6] Griggs v. S., 58 Ala. 425; Rountree v. S., 58 Ala. 381.

[7] See *infra*, § 550.

[8] *Infra*, § 601.

of the property must be alleged and proven as alleged. It cannot be charged as the property of a person who has never had either actual or constructive possession of it.[1] But possession need not be actual, it may be constructive only.[2] Thus, cattle at large may be deemed in the possession of the owner.[3] The ownership which must be proven to support the indictment charging that the property was that of the person named therein is not absolute or full ownership; for example, ownership may be laid in one who is the part owner only, in possession of the property.[4] A receiver has such ownership of property in his possession that in an indictment for stealing the same it may be charged as his property.[5] One who has taken up an estray may be deemed the owner.[6] Even a thief or person wrongfully in possession may be deemed the owner in such sense that the taking from him may be properly charged and proven as larceny of his property.[7] Where there is general ownership in one person and possession in another, as special owner, bailee or custodian, it is optional to charge the ownership as in the real owner or in the person in possession.[8] Thus,

[1] Brooks v. S., 5 Baxt. 607; King v. S., 44 Ind. 285; Hite v. S., 9 Yerg. 197; Rex v. Adams, Russ. & Ry. 225.

[2] Rex v. Remnant, Russ. & Ry. 136; C. v. Lawless, 103 Mass. 425.

[3] Owen v. S., 6 Humph. 330; Burger v. S., 83 Ala. 36; Pritchett v. S., 2 Sneed, 285; S. v. Martin, 28 Mo. 530; S. v. Casteel, 53 Mo. 124; Moore v. S., 8 Tex. Ap. 496; McGrew v. S., 31 Tex. Ap. 336; Bennett v. S., 32 Tex. Ap. 216; Trimble v. S., 33 Tex. Ap. 397; S. v. Everage, 33 La. An. 120; S. v. Kane, 33 La. An. 1269. It is larceny to take up and appropriate a trespassing animal: C. v. Mason, 105 Mass. 163. As to larceny of estrays or other lost property, see *infra*, § 571.

[4] Reg. v. Webster, L. & C. 77; Rex v. Bramley, Russ. & Ry. 478; Reg. v. Watts, 2 Den. 14. At least this is so by statute in some states: C. v. Arrance, 5 Allen, 517; Fairy v. S., 18 Tex. Ap. 314; Samora v. S., 4 Tex. Ap. 508.

[5] S. v. Rivers, 60 Ia. 381. Though the receiver is appointed by a federal court the crime is punishable in a state court: S. v. Coss, 12 Wash. 673.

[6] Quinn v. P., 123 Ill. 333; Jinks v. S., 5 Tex. Ap. 68; Smith v. S., 7 Tex. Ap. 382; Lowe v. S., 11 Tex. Ap. 253; Swink v. S., 32 Tex. Ap. 530.

[7] Ward v. S., 6 Hill (N. Y.), 144; C. v. Rourke, 10 Cush. 397.

[8] S. v. Gorham, 55 N. H. 152; C. v Sullivan, 104 Mass. 552; C. v. O'Hara, 10 Gray, 469; C. v. Morse, 14 Mass 217; Norton v. P., 8 Cowen. 137; Phelps v. P., 72 N. Y. 334; S. v. Mullen, 30 Ia. 203; Quinn v. P., 123 Ill. 333; S. v. Moore, 101 Mo. 316; Kennedy v. S., 31 Fla. 428; Fowler v. S., 100 Ala. 96; Langford v. S., 8 Tex. 115; Cox v. S., 43 Tex. 101; Rex v. Todd, 1 Leach, 357, n.; Rex v. Wymer, 4 C. & P. 391; Reg. v. Vincent, 3 C. & K. 246.

the property may be charged to be that of the real owner although in the possession of another,[1] unless by virtue of statutory provisions it is specially required that possession be properly alleged; as, for instance, where it is made essential that the taking be without the consent of the person in possession.[2] Even at common law ownership only is alleged, and it is not necessary to say that the owner was in possession or that the taking was from his possession.[3] It is entirely proper, however, and in accordance with the general practice, to describe the property as that of the person who is in possession thereof, evidence of the possession being sufficient to sustain the allegation. So it is as to one who is in possession as bailee.[4] And evidence of possession is sufficient proof of ownership under such an indictment.[5] So chattels in the possession of an agent may be

[1] C. v. Lawless, 103 Mass. 425; U. S. v. Burroughs, 3 McLean, 405; Reg. v. Kendall, 12 Cox, 598.

[2] Gadson v. S., 36 Tex. 350; Otero v. S., 30 Tex. Ap. 450; Littleton v. S., 20 Tex. Ap. 168; Spruill v. S., 10 Tex. Ap. 695; White v. S., 33 Tex. Ap. 94.

[3] S. v. Leavitt, 66 Me. 440; Angel v. C., 2 Va. Cas. 228; Thompson v. C., 2 Va. Cas. 135. In Texas, by virtue of a statutory provision, the possession must be alleged, and if the property is not in the possession of the general owner, the ownership and the possession should both be alleged: Garner v. S., 36 Tex. 693; Johnson v. S., 4 Tex. Ap. 594; West v. S., 6 Tex. Ap. 485; Watts v. S., 6 Tex. Ap. 263; Calloway v. S., 7 Tex. Ap. 585; Hannahan v. S., 7 Tex. Ap. 664; Case v. S., 12 Tex. Ap. 228; Bailey v. S., 20 Tex. Ap. 68; Briggs v. S., 20 Tex. Ap. 106; Hall v. S., 22 Tex. Ap. 632; Alexander v. S., 24 Tex. Ap. 126; Tinney v. S., 24 Tex. Ap. 112; Connor v. S., 24 Tex. Ap. 245. But ownership and possession may be charged as in the person who is actually in possession, although another is the general owner: Gaines v. S., 4 Tex. Ap. 330; Crockett v. S., 5 Tex. Ap. 526; Duren v. S., 15 Tex. Ap. 624. As to the necessity, under the Texas statute, of alleging want of consent by the person actually in possession, see *infra*, § 557.

[4] S. v. Ayer, 23 N. H. 301; S. v. Gorham, 55 N. H. 152; S. v. Allen, 103 N. C. 433; S. v. McRae, 111 N. C. 665; P. v. Buelna, 81 Cal. 135; S. v. Fitzpatrick, 9 Houst. 385; Blackburn v. S., 44 Tex. 457; Moseley v. S., 42 Tex. 78; Yates v. S., 10 Yerg. 548; Reg. v. Rowe, Bell, 93; Reg. v. Wortley, 2 C. & K. 283; Rex v. Wymer, 4 C. & P. 391; 2 East, P. C. 653; so in case of a lodger in furnished lodgings: Rex v. Belstead, R. & R. 411; Rex v. Brunswick, 1 Moody, 26. So in case of larceny from a carrier the property may be charged as that of the carrier: S. v. Casavant, 64 Vt. 405; Bruley v. Rose, 57 Ia. 657; but it may be alleged in the consignee: Walker v. S., 9 Tex. Ap. 38. And see cases cited in the section following with reference to larceny by the owner from his bailee in possession with intent to charge such bailee.

[5] S. v. Somerville, 21 Me. 14; Adams v. S., 45 N. J. 448; S. v. Hardison, 75 N. C. 203; Morningstar v. S., 52 Ala. 405; U. S. v. Duffy, 1 Cranch, C. C.

charged as his property.[1] But if the chattels are in the custody of a servant they should be charged as the property of the master.[2] A general allegation as to ownership of the property will be supported by proof of a conditional ownership.[3] In case of guardianship or other possession of the property of a minor or other person under disability, the ownership may be properly charged in the guardian or custodian in possession.[4] Clothing furnished to a minor by his father may be laid as that of the minor, and this is usual;[5] but it may be laid as that of the father,[6] unless furnished under some contract obligation, as where the son is an apprentice of the father, and the clothing is furnished according to the terms of the apprenticeship.[7] Property belonging to an estate may be charged as that of an heir in possession.[8] The property of the wife in the husband's possession or control or management may be charged as his property.[9] The husband has a qualified ownership of the property of the wife which is in the house or used in the family such as to support a charge of the stealing of it as his property.[10] And

164; S. v. Stanley, 48 Ia. 221; P. v. Nelson, 56 Cal. 77; P. v. Davis, 97 Cal. 194. And see other cases *infra*, § 603.

[1] Arcia v. S., 28 Tex. Ap. 198; Reg. v. Jennings, Dears. & B. 447; Reg. v. Burgess, L. & C. 299. This is true in embezzlement when it appears that defendant was in the employ of the agent and received the property by such employment: Campbell v. S., 35 Ohio St. 70.

[2] C. v. Morse, 14 Mass. 217; Norton v. P., 8 Cowen, 137; P. v. Bennett, 37 N. Y. 117; Murphy v. P., 104 Ill. 528; S. v. Jenkins, 78 N. C. 478; S. v. Edwards, 86 N. C. 666; Heygood v. S., 59 Ala. 49; S. v. Myers, 82 Mo. 558; Clark v. S., 23 Tex. Ap. 612; Rex v. Wilkins, 2 East, P. C. 673; Rex v. Pearce, 2 East, P. C. 603; Reg. v. Kay, Dears. & B. 231; Reg. v. Green, Dears. & B. 113; Rex v. Hutchinson, Russ. & Ry. 412.

[3] S. v. Pettis, 63 Me. 124; Robinson v. S., 1 Ga. 563.

[4] Thomasson v. S., 22 Ga. 499; Jones v. Jones, 71 Cal. 89; S. v. Koch, 4 Harr. 570.

[5] Rex v. Haynes, 12 Coke, 113; 2 East, P. C. 654; 2 Archb. Cr. Pr. & Pl. 357, n.; 2 Bish. Cr. Pr., § 721; S. v. Koch, 4 Harr. 570; S. v. Williams, 2 Strob. 229.

[6] Reg. v. Hughes, Car. & M. 593.

[7] Rex v. Forsgate, 1 Leach, 463.

[8] Dreyer v. S., 11 Tex. Ap. 503. See, also, 2 East, P. C. 655; Reg. v. Tippin, Car. & M. 545; Reg. v. King, 4 F. & F. 493; Rex v. Scott, Russ. & Ry. 13; Rex v. Gaby, Russ. & Ry. 178. In England, where there was no will proved and before administration, the property might be laid in the ordinary: Rex v. Smith, 7 C. & P. 147; Reg. v. Johnson, Dears. & B. 340.

[9] Davis v. S., 17 Ala. 415; Lavender v. S., 60 Ala. 60; U. S. v. Murphy, 4 Cranch, C. C. 681; Alexander v. S., 9 Tex. Ap. 48; S. v. Jackson, 1 Houst. Cr. C. 561.

[10] Petre v. S., 35 N. J. 64; P. v. Swalm, 80 Cal. 46. It is so in Texas

this is so even as to separate property of the wife in her possession, the husband being deemed to have presumptively the possession and a qualified ownership thereof.[1] An officer has sufficient possession of property levied upon by him so that larceny from him may be charged as of his property.[2] In case of an unincorporated association, property may be laid in trustees.[3]

§ 547. **One's own property; intent to charge another.**— The definition of larceny indicates that the property taken must be that of another, and it is evident that one cannot be guilty of larceny in taking his own property.[4] Yet that statement is subject to many explanations, most of them to be hereafter considered in determining what is a taking and carrying away. One principle may, however, be properly stated here, though it is of application, also, under other headings; that is, that one who takes property which is his own, but under such circumstances that he thereby throws liability for the loss of such property upon another, does, in effect, take the property of another so as to constitute larceny.[5] But this proposition is

by statute: Merriweather v. S., 33 Tex. 789; Wilson v. S., 3 Tex. Ap. 206. Husband and wife may be deemed in joint possession of property in the custody of the wife: Kennedy v. S., 31 Fla. 428.

[1] C. v. Williams, 7 Gray, 337; C. v. Cullins, 1 Mass. 116; Ellis v. S., 76 Ala. 90; Rex v. Roberts, 7 C. & P. 485. But it has been held otherwise where the statute gives the wife separate property: Rollins v. S., 98 Ala. 79; Johnson v. S., 100 Ala. 55; Pratt v. S., 35 Ohio St. 514. A female minor may be deemed the owner of clothing belonging to and used by her: Phillips v. S., 85 Tenn. 551.

[2] Hill v. S., 1 Head, 454; S. v. Harris, 38 Ia. 242. But it may also be charged as the property of the owner: Rex v. Eastall, 2 Russ., C. & M. 291, 382.

[3] Reg. v. Cain, Car. & M. 309; Reg. v. Webster, L. & C. 77; Reg. v. Loose, Bell, 259; Rex v. Sherrington, 1 Leach, 513; Reg. v. Atkinson, Car. & M. 525; Rex v. Boulton, 5 C. & P. 537.

[4] Thus, one who, having made an assignment of his goods for the benefit of creditors, but before delivering possession, removed them with intent to deprive his creditors of them, was held not guilty of larceny: Reg. v. Pratt, Dears. 360. For a somewhat similar case, where the purpose was only to prevent the seizure of the property by creditors, see C. v. Greene, 111 Mass. 392. Where there is a contract of sale, but title has not passed, the property is still that of the seller, so that he cannot commit larceny thereof: Love v. State, 78 Ga. 66. An indictment will not lie against a tenant for larceny of crops belonging jointly to him and the landlord: S. v. McCoy, 89 N. C. 466. And see *infra*, § 550.

[5] Palmer v. P., 10 Wend. 165; Adams v. S., 45 N. J. 448; P. v. Stone,

involved in another of more general application, to be discussed in the next section, that a bailee of property is to be considered the owner thereof with reference to larceny. In accordance with that principle, the general owner may be guilty of the offense in wrongfully taking the property from the possession of such bailee.[1] So the owner of property which has been levied upon and is in the possession of the officer under such levy is guilty of larceny in wrongfully taking the property from such officer.[2] But if the owner only retakes a portion of such property, leaving enough to satisfy the claim, his purpose being to prevent the seizure of the remainder for other debts, he does not commit larceny.[3] Another proposition which is applicable here, but runs into one that must be discussed under taking and carrying away, is that as to property in one's own possession he cannot commit larceny;[4] therefore where one gets another to write a receipt or obligation on stamped paper which the former furnishes, he does not commit larceny by misappropriating or misusing it, though he had the wrongful purpose from the beginning, because the paper is his and he cannot steal his own property.[5]

IV. The Act; Taking and Carrying Away.

§ 548. **What sufficient asportation.**— That the taking must be wrongful, that is, with fraudulent intent, will hereafter appear in discussing intent.[6] It is necessary now to consider what acts will constitute such taking and carrying away as is contemplated by the definition of larceny.[7] A temporary taking

16 Cal. 369; P. v. Thompson, 34 Cal. 671; S. v. Fitzpatrick, 9 Houst. 385; 2 East, P. C. 654. As to taking with intention of returning and claiming reward, see *infra*, § 567.

[1] P. v. Long, 50 Mich. 249; Kirksey v. Fike, 29 Ala. 206; S. v. Stephens, 32 Tex. 155; Connell v. S., 2 Tex. Ap. 422; Rex v. Wilkinson, Russ. & Ry. 470. *Contra*, C. v. Tobin, 2 Brews. 570.

[2] C. v. Greene, 111 Mass. 392; Palmer v. P., 10 Wend. 165.

[3] C. v. Greene, 111 Mass. 392.

[4] This is the distinction between larceny and embezzlement: See *infra*, § 554.

[5] Rex v. Hart, 6 C. & P. 106; Reg. v. Smith, 2 Den. 449· Reg. v. Frampton, 2 C. & K. 47.

[6] See *infra*, § 564.

[7] The words used in the indictment to indicate the act are "steal, take and carry away." See, as to indictment, *infra*, § 607. The omission of "away" is fatal: C. v. Adams, 7 Gray, 43; Rountree v. S., 58 Ala. 381. Under some statutes "steal" is enough: Barnes v. S., 40 Neb. 545. It is not essential that there be a

of wrongful possession and having the property under control, even for a short space of time, is sufficient, although the property is abandoned before being effectually appropriated by the wrong-doer.[1] Thus, if a pickpocket thrusts his hand into the pocket of another and seizes his pocket-book, partially removing it, and then is compelled to desist, he has committed larceny.[2] There may be sufficient removal to constitute larceny, even though the property which the thief is attempting to take from the person of another remains to some extent attached, as by a chain or otherwise.[3] There must be at least a temporary possession in the thief; and where the property is dropped by the owner as a result of fear or violence, but is not taken up by the intending thief, there is no larceny.[4] Any removal during which the thief has, though only for an instant, entire and absolute possession of the property is sufficient.[5]

taking from the person: S. v. Pratt, 20 Ia. 267; and if the taker knows that he has no authority to take he is guilty of larceny: S. v. Rivers, 60 Ia. 381.

[1] S. v. Gray, 106 N. C. 734. To take animals of another with intent to fraudulently mark them with one's own brand and claim ownership thereof is sufficient to constitute larceny: Scott v. Harbor, 18 Cal. 705. The wrongful taking of an animal may be larceny, though it is not disposed of: Davis v. S., 10 Lea, 707. But mere possession with intent to steal, but without any wrongful act, is not larceny: S. v. Newman, 9 Nev. 48.

[2] S. v. Chambers, 22 W. Va. 779. So where the prisoner lifted a bag from the boot of a coach and then abandoned it, he was held guilty of larceny: Rex v. Walsh, 1 Moody, 14. So where money in a drawer was taken into the hand of the thief but was dropped back, *held*, that larceny had been committed: Eckels v. S., 20 Ohio St. 508. So one who had taken a horse and was leading it away, but before he had removed it from the owner's premises was compelled to desist, was held guilty of larceny: S. v. Gazell, 30 Mo. 92. So the removal of money from the money drawer to the floor was held a sufficient taking and carrying away: S. v. Higgins, 88 Mo. 354.

[3] Harrison v. P., 50 N. Y. 518; Reg. v. Simpson, Dears. 421. But the offense of larceny from the person would not be committed in such case: Harrison v. P., 50 N. Y. 518; Rex v. Thompson, 1 Moody, 78. Where there was an attempt to carry away goods fastened to the counter and the string attaching them was not broken, *held*, that the offense of larceny was not committed: Anon., 2 East, P. C. 556; and where a coat at a store door was removed from the dummy, but still remained fastened by a chain, it was held there was no larceny: P. v. Meyers, 75 Cal. 383.

[4] Rex v. Farrell, 1 Leach, 322, n.; Thompson v. S., 94 Ala. 535. The act may be an attempt, but if abandoned before a removal of the property in pursuance of the act will not be larceny: C. v. Luckis, 99 Mass. 431.

[5] S. v. Jackson, 65 N. C. 305; Gar-

Thus, it has been held, where a package was removed from one end of a wagon to another with intent to wrongfully take it away, the act was larceny;[1] or an animal from one portion of the owner's premises to another;[2] or goods from one part of a vessel to another;[3] or wheat from one bin into another;[4] or wheat from the bin to sacks;[5] or money from a drawer, though afterward returned;[6] or a letter by a mail carrier from his pouch to his pocket.[7] But there must be, though for an instant only, complete possession. To set up a bale upon end in a wagon and open it, yet without removing any portion of the contents, was held not larceny.[8] So the mere upsetting of a barrel of turpentine, although with felonious intent, was held not sufficient asportation to constitute larceny.[9] Merely to kill a domestic animal, without in any way removing the carcass, is not larceny, but malicious mischief.[10] But there may be such taking possession of the carcass after the killing as to make the act larceny, although no part of it is actually carried away and appropriated.[11] Larceny of an animal may be committed by taking or enticing it away with intent to appropriate it.[12]

riss v. S., 35 Ga. 247; Gettinger v. S., 13 Neb. 308.

[1] Rex v. Cozlett, 2 East, P. C. 556.

[2] Delk v. S., 64 Miss. 77.

[3] Nutzel v. S., 60 Ga. 264.

[4] S. v. Craige, 89 N. C. 475.

[5] S. v. Hecox, 83 Mo. 531.

[6] S. v. Green, 81 N. C. 560.

[7] Reg. v. Poynton, L. & C. 247.

[8] Rex v. Cherry, 2 East, P. C. 556.

[9] S. v. Jones, 65 N. C. 395. But where the indictment was for stealing five pints of porter, and it appeared that the defendant had, by boring a hole in the barrel, allowed that quantity of the liquor to run into a can on the ground, *held*, that the asportation was sufficient: Reg. v. Wallis, 3 Cox, 67.

[10] P. v. Murphy, 47 Cal. 103; S. v. Butler, 65 N. C. 309; S. v. Alexander, 74 N. C. 232; S. v. Seagler, 1 Rich. 30; Williams v. S., 63 Miss. 58; Molton v. S., — Ala. —, 16 So. R. 795; Minter v. S., 26 Tex. Ap. 217; Beavers v. S., 14 Tex. Ap. 541. In such case there may be enough to show an intent to steal: Williams v. S., 63 Miss. 58.

[11] Croom v. S., 71 Ala. 14; Kemp v. S., 89 Ala. 52; Coombes v. S., 17 Tex. Ap. 258. So held where the defendant partially skinned the carcass: Lundy v. S., 60 Ga. 143; McPhail v. S., 9 Tex. Ap. 164. An indictment for stealing an animal is sustained by proof of killing the animal and taking the skin, although the carcass is not removed: Rex v. Rawlins, 2 East, P. C. 617.

[12] P. v. Smith, 15 Cal. 408; S. v. Wisdom, 8 Port. 511; S. v. Hawkins, 8 Port. 461; S. v. Whyte, 2 Nott & McC. 174. This form of taking may be proven under the usual form of allegations: P. v. Strong, 46 Cal. 302. But where the animal was enticed for a short distance and then abandoned without being taken from the owner's premises, *held*, that the crime was not committed: Edmonds v. S., 70 Ala. 8.

There may be larceny of gas by wrongfully drawing it off from the mains or pipes,[1] and there may be larceny of water in the same way.[2] The taking and carrying away may be committed by setting in motion an agency, innocent or otherwise, by which the property is asported from the possession of the owner to that of the thief or his accomplice. Thus, the change of a check of another's baggage, by which possession of it is secured, is larceny.[3] The criminal act may be done by an innocent agent. Thus, where a thief at an inn stable pointed out an animal as his, directing the hostler to lead him out, which was done, it was held that there was sufficient taking to constitute larceny.[4] And it was so held where an auctioneer, employed to sell impounded animals, sold one of them as his own, and it was taken away by the purchaser.[5] But if the intending thief merely points out an animal not in his possession, representing it to be his, and selling it to be taken away, the act is not larceny, as he has not taken possession of the animal.[6] The Texas statute makes asportation unnecessary, a fraudulent taking being sufficient;[7] thus, to open a drawer in which there is money, and take a part thereof with intent to take all, is larceny as to all.[8]

§ 549. **Trespass necessary.**— It is one of the early and thoroughly established doctrines of the law of larceny that the act must be such as to constitute a trespass, otherwise there is not such wrongful taking as to be larceny.[9] Many more cases might be cited to the same proposition, but if they be examined the uselessness of further citations, and, indeed, the uselessness of the proposition itself, becomes at once apparent. As

[1] C. v. Shaw, 4 Allen, 308; Reg. v. White, 3 C. & K. 363; Reg. v. Firth, L. R. 1 C. C. 172.

[2] Ferens v. O'Brien, 11 Q. B. D. 21.

[3] C. v. Barry, 125 Mass. 390.

[4] Rex v. Pitman, 2 C. & P. 423.

[5] S. v. Hunt, 45 Ia. 673. In general where one wrongfully sells property of another as his own, and it is taken away by the purchaser, the act is larceny: Dale v. S., 32 Tex. Ap. 78.

[6] Hardeman v. S., 12 Tex. Ap. 207; Madison v. S., 16 Tex. Ap. 435; P. v. Gillis, 6 Utah, 84.

[7] Prim v. S., 32 Tex. 158; Musquez v. S., 41 Tex. 226; Hall v. S., 41 Tex. 287; Purtell v. S., 43 Tex. 483; Martindale v. S., 19 Tex. Ap. 333; Lott v. S., 20 Tex. Ap. 230; Doss v. S., 21 Tex. Ap. 505; Dukes v. S., 22 Tex. Ap. 192.

[8] Harris v. S., 29 Tex. Ap. 101.

[9] S. v. Braden, 2 Tenn. 68; S. v. Hite, 9 Yerg. 197; Robinson v. S., 1 Coldw. 120; Morehead v. S., 9 Humph. 635; Thorne v. Turck, 94 N. Y. 90; Pennsylvania v. Campbell, Addis. 232; Rex v. Raven, J. Kel. 24; Rex v. Hart, 6 C. & P. 106; Reg. v. Smith, 2 Den. 449; Rex v. Webb, 1 Moody, 431.

these cases show, the general proposition is one incapable of definite application and of no value as furnishing in itself a solution of any particular case. The more definite rules which are generally derived from it, and a discussion of which is of importance, are: First, that one who is in rightful possession of the property of another does not commit larceny by a misappropriation thereof, no matter how fraudulent and wrongful such act may be in itself; second, that there is, however, a distinction in this respect between possession and mere custody, and that a servant who has mere custody may commit larceny of the property of the master which he has within his control; third, that as there can be no trespass against one who consents to the act done, it is not larceny to obtain property from an owner by his consent, even though he is induced by false pretenses to part with the property. There are many other ramifications of the general doctrine in regard to trespass as an essential element of larceny, but these three main divisions are the controlling ones.

§ 550. **What constitutes trespass.**— The trespass necessary to constitute larceny may be committed by various acts of wrongful taking and appropriating as already described.[1] If the original taking is wrongful, it constitutes a trespass even though it is not with fraudulent intent, and subsequent appropriation and disposal with fraudulent intent will relate back, as it were, and make the whole transaction felonious.[2] And it is said that a subsequent misuse and appropriation of property obtained by false representations as to the purpose for which it is to be used will constitute larceny.[3] But there must be something more than a mere technical conversion without disposal.[4] In case of joint owners, each being equally entitled to possession, there can be no trespass by the one against the other, and a wrongful appropriation and disposal by one of such joint owners will not constitute larceny.[5] But if the right of possession is in one of the joint owners to the exclusion of the other, then a wrongful taking of possession by the other would constitute larceny.[6] Tenants or croppers who cultivate land on shares are joint owners with the landlord who is

[1] See *supra*, §§ 545–548.

[2] C. v. White, 11 Cush. 483.

[3] S. v. Coombs, 55 Me. 477.

[4] Berg v. S., 2 Tex. Ap. 148.

[5] Pennsylvania v. Campbell, Addis. 232; Alfele v. Wright, 17 Ohio St. 238.

[6] Pennsylvania v. Campbell, Addis. 232; Bell v. S., 7 Tex. Ap. 25.

entitled to a share of the crop, and a wrongful appropriation and disposal of a portion of the crop by the tenant will not constitute larceny,[1] the crop being the joint property of the tenant and landlord.[2] But after delivery of the landlord's share to him, or abandonment of the crop to the landlord, a subsequent taking by the tenant may be larceny.[3] The cases of a wrongful appropriation or disposal of property of which the wrong-doer has custody or possession will be considered in the sections following, and it will appear that the instances in which the person thus having control of the property can be deemed to commit trespass with reference thereto, so as to be guilty of larceny, are: (1) When he is the servant or other custodian without a right to possession; (2) when his possession has been obtained by fraud with the intent to deprive the owner of his property; and (3) where there is such wrongful act with reference to the property in possession as to constitute a trespass against the owner notwithstanding such possession, *e. g.*, breaking of bulk by carrier. In other cases of possession acquired by the consent of the owner, a subsequent wrongful act with reference to the property will not be larceny.[4]

§ 551. Continuous trespass; distinct articles; different owners.— Although several articles are involved which are taken away successively but in one transaction and as the result of one intent, the whole will constitute but one larceny.[5] So the wrongful taking of gas from time to time as needed, by means of an unauthorized and secret connecting pipe, is but one larceny.[6] So there is but one trespass involved in taking at the same time several articles belonging to the same owner and therefore but one larceny.[7] And even if portions of the property belong to different owners, if the whole is taken in

[1] S. v. Copeland, 86 N. C. 691; S. v. McCoy, 89 N. C. 466; Bell v. S., 7 Tex. Ap. 25.

[2] S. v. Frame, 4 Harr. 569; McNealy v. S., 17 Fla. 198.

[3] S. v. Webb, 87 N. C. 558; Bonham v. S., 65 Ala. 456.

[4] Johnson v. P., 113 Ill. 99. And see *infra*, § 554.

[5] S. v. Martin, 82 N. C. 672; S. v. Weaver, 104 N. C. 758; S. v. Larson, 85 Ia. 659.

[6] Reg. v. Firth, L. R. 1 C. C. 172.

[7] Kelly v. S., 7 Baxt. 323; Fisher v. C., 1 Bush, 211; S. v. Williams, 10 Humph. 101; S. v. Daniels, 32 Mo. 558; S. v. Wagner, 118 Mo. 626; S. v. Johnson, 3 Hill (S. C.), 1; S. v. McCormack, 8 Oreg. 236; S. v. Faulkner, 32 La. An. 725; Quitzow v. S., 1 Tex. Ap. 47; T. v. Heywood, 2 Wash. T. 180; Reg. v. Brettel, Car. & M. 609.

one act there is but a single larceny.[1] But if acts of taking are not the same, although at about the same time, they will not constitute a single larceny.[2] In an English case it is held that an interval of two minutes could not make two takings distinct larcenies, but an interval of half an hour would.[3] The question of prosecution in one jurisdiction for larceny of property stolen in and brought from another jurisdiction will be discussed in the next section. By various statutory provisions which will be referred to in the succeeding discussion, such as those relating to larceny by bailees, those making embezzlement larceny, and those making larceny out of obtaining property by false pretenses, the doctrine as to the necessity of trespass in order to constitute larceny has been, in some directions, broken down.[4]

§ 552. **Taking goods from one county to another.**—Where goods have been stolen in one county and by the thief carried into another, the continuing exercise of control over the goods is considered a continuing trespass, and larceny is therefore committed in the county into which the goods are brought as well as in the county where the original wrongful taking was committed.[5] The same reason has been applied where the act of larceny was committed prior to the passing of a certain statute with reference to the punishment of larceny and the unlawful possession was continued until after the taking effect of such act, and it was held that the prisoner might be punished under the new act on the theory of a continuing trespass.[6]

[1] S. v. Hennessey, 23 Ohio St. 339; S. v. Warren, 77 Md. 121; Alexander v. C., 90 Va. 809; Hoiles v. U. S., 3 MacArthur, 370; Hudson v. S., 9 Tex. Ap. 151; S. v. Larson, 85 Ia. 659. That the prosecution may in such cases elect to prosecute for a single larceny of the entire goods or for distinct larcenies of the property of the several owners, see S. v. Lambert, 9 Nev. 321; Lorton v. S., 7 Mo. 55; S. v. Morphin, 37 Mo. 373; Reg. v. Bleasdale, 2 C. & K. 765. *Contra*, U. S. v. Beerman, 5 Cranch, C. C. 412.

[2] Nichols v. C., 78 Ky. 180; S. v. English, 14 Mont. 399; Reg. v. Lonsdale, 4 F. & F. 56. If larceny of several articles is charged in the indictment on one day, and there is proof that a part was stolen on that day, it is not proper to prove that another part was stolen on a subsequent day: Fisher v. S., 33 Tex. 792.

[3] Rex v. Birdseye, 4 C. & P. 386.

[4] S. v. Brown, 25 Ia. 561.

[5] Stinson v. P., 43 Ill. 397; Myers v. P., 26 Ill. 173; S. v. McCoy, 42 La. An. 228; S. v. Smith, 66 Mo. 61; S. v. Grant, 76 Mo. 236.

[6] S. v. Somerville, 21 Me. 14. On the same principle of continuance of possession it is held that a horse borrowed in one state and unlawfully sold in another might be con-

This rule as between counties originated with and has uniformly been followed by the English court,[1] and has been accepted without question in the United States.[2] In some states the rule is made statutory.[3] The indictment may properly charge the larceny in the county to which the goods are brought and in which the prosecution is commenced as though the wrongful taking had been there committed;[4] but it will not render the indictment bad that it states the facts, that is, the wrongful taking in another county and the bringing into the county where the prosecution is commenced.[5] The party who commits larceny in one county and sends the goods to a confederate in another county is guilty of larceny in the second county, because his constructive possession still continues and his accountability is the same as though he himself had gone with the goods into the second county.[6] But there must be pos-

sidered as in the hands of the defendant in the statė where sold as bailee, and the act therefore a larceny by bailee: Brooks v. S., 26 Tex. Ap. 184.

[1] Rex v. Thompson, 2 Russ., C. & M. 328; Rex v. Parkin, 1 Moody, 45; Reg. v. Newland, 2 Cox, 283; 4 Bl. Com. 305; 2 Russ. Cr. 116; 1 Hawk. P. C., ch. 33, § 9; 2 East, P. C. 771.

[2] C. v. Rand, 7 Met. 475; C. v. Simpson, 9 Met. 138; C. v. Dewitt, 10 Mass. 154; Haskins v. P., 16 N. Y. 344; S. v. Douglas, 17 Me. 193; S. v. Bryant, 9 Rich. 113; C. v. Cousins, 2 Leigh, 708; Myers v. P., 26 Ill. 173; S. v. McCoy, 42 La. An. 228.

[3] Aaron v. S., 39 Ala. 684; Kidd v. S., 83 Ala. 58; S. v. Seay, 3 Stew. 123; S. v. Hunter, 50 Kan. 302; S. v. Lillard, 59 Ia. 479; S. v. Williams, 35 Mo. 229; S. v. Smith, 66 Mo. 61; S. v. Brown, 8 Nev. 208; Shubert v. S., 20 Tex. Ap. 320; Clark v. S., 23 Tex. Ap. 612; Givens v. S., 32 Tex. Ap. 457. Such a statutory provision is not unconstitutional as depriving the accused of the right of trial by jury of the county where the offense is committed where such right is guarantied: S. v. Price, 55 Kan. 606.

[4] Haskins v. P., 16 N. Y. 344; Morissey v. P., 11 Mich. 327; P. v. Mellon, 40 Cal. 648; Johnson v. S., 47 Miss. 671. But if property stolen in another county at different times is held by defendant, he cannot be prosecuted for larceny of the whole of it under one indictment in the latter county, but the prosecution must elect between the two transactions: Rex v. Smith, Russ. & M. 295.

[5] Hurt v. S., 26 Ind. 106; Jones v. S., 53 Ind. 235; Connell v. S., 2 Tex. Ap. 422. Of course, if the indictment shows the wrongful taking to have been in another county, and does not allege facts sufficient to show larceny in the county where the prosecution is commenced, it cannot be maintained: Johnson v. S., 47 Miss. 671. On the whole subject, see, as to venue, *infra*, § 590.

[6] C. v. Dewitt, 10 Mass. 154; Ferrill v. C., 1 Duv. 153; Lucas v. S., 62 Ala. 26; Reg. v. Rogers, L. R. 1 C. C. 136; Reg. v. Cryer, Dears. & B. 324. But the court of the county where the goods are taken cannot inquire into the guilt of the receiver in another county: P. v. Stakem, 40 Cal. 599.

session by the thief in some form. If he is taken by an officer with the property into another county, there will be no jurisdiction of the offense in the county to which he is thus taken;[1] nor will there be, if he disposes of the property in the county where it is taken, and accompanies the purchaser into another county.[2] The value of the property in a case where a thief is prosecuted in the county to which the property is taken is that which it has in that county, or, if only a portion of the property originally stolen is brought to that county, then the value of that portion is alone to be considered.[3] If the nature of the property has been changed before being brought into the county of the prosecution, it must be described in the form in which it was brought into the county.[4]

§ 553. **Taking goods from one state or country to another.** The doctrine of the preceding section with reference to stolen goods taken from one county to another was not recognized in English courts as applicable to goods stolen out of the kingdom and afterwards brought into England.[5] The reason for this failure to follow in such a case the theory that each subsequent asportation was a new larceny is not apparent. The courts of the different states do not agree as to whether they shall adhere to the doctrine of the English courts on this question, or shall recognize as conclusive the reasoning which is universally adopted with reference to goods stolen in one county and taken into another. In some cases it is decided that where goods are stolen in one state and carried into another, no larceny is committed in the latter.[6] In other cases it is held that the thief may be prosecuted for larceny in the state to which the stolen

[1] Rex v. Simmonds, 1 Moody, 408. Where defendant was seen with the stolen property in another county taking it toward the county of his residence, but it was not found in his possession in the county of his residence, *held*, that an indictment for larceny in the latter county could not be sustained: Moore v. S., 55 Miss. 432.

[2] Lucas v. S., 62 Ala. 26.

[3] Roth v. S., 10 Tex. Ap. 27; Clark v. S., 23 Tex. Ap. 612.

[4] C. v. Beaman, 8 Gray, 497, a case where an animal was killed in one county and its carcass was brought into the other. See, also, Rex v. Halloway, 1 C. & P. 127.

[5] 1 Hawk. P. C., ch. 33, § 9; 3 Inst. 113; 13 Co. 53; 2 East, P. C. 772; 2 Russ. Cr. 119; Rex v. Prowes, 1 Moody, 349; Reg. v. Madge, 9 C. & P. 29; Reg. v. Debruiel, 11 Cox, 207.

[6] P. v. Schenck, 2 Johns. 479; P. v. Gardner, 2 Johns. 477; Simmons v. C., 5 Bin. 617; S. v. Le Blanch, 31 N. J. 82; Stanley v. S., 24 Ohio St. 166; Beal v. S., 15 Ind. 378; Lee v. S., 64 Ga. 203; P. v. Loughridge, 1 Neb. 11; S. v. Newman, 9 Nev. 48; S.

goods are taken.[1] The Massachusetts court hold that the states of the Union are not foreign to each other, and that bringing goods into one of them from another is not similar to bringing goods into England from without the kingdom, but rather like bringing them from one county of England into another,[2] and that the bringing of stolen goods into the state from a foreign country is not larceny;[3] and the Ohio court has refused to apply to goods brought from a foreign country the rule applied by it in an earlier case to goods brought from another state.[4] But most courts place the bringing into the state from a foreign country on the same basis as the bringing from another state.[5] In many of the states statutes are passed regulating this subject and providing for the punishment for larceny of one who brings stolen goods into the state, and such statutes are constitutional.[6] The offense is deemed committed in the county where the thief is in possession of the stolen goods, and his trial in such county is not for an offense committed elsewhere.[7] Where the larceny is a compound one, it can be pun-

v. Reonnals, 14 La. An. 278; Simpson v. S., 4 Humph. 456; S. v. Brown, 1 Hayw. 100.

[1] C. v. Cullins, 1 Mass. 116; C. v. Andrews, 2 Mass. 14; C. v. Holder, 9 Gray, 7; S. v. Ellis, 3 Conn. 185; S. v. Cummings, 33 Conn. 260; S. v. Underwood, 49 Maine, 181; Watson v. S., 36 Miss. 593; Cummings v. S., 1 Harr. & J. 340; Hamilton v. S., 11 Ohio, 435; S. v. Bennett, 14 Ia. 479; Worthington v. S., 58 Md. 403; S. v. Hill, 19 S. C. 435; S. v. Johnson, 2 Oreg. 115; Tippins v. S., 14 Ga. 492; U. S. v. Tolson, 1 Cranch, C. C. 269; U. S. v. Haukey, 2 Cranch, C. C. 65.

[2] C. v. Holder, 9 Gray, 7; C. v. Rand, 7 Met. 475.

[3] C. v. Uprichard, 3 Gray, 434.

[4] Stanley v. S., 24 Ohio St. 166.

[5] P. v. Burke, 11 Wend. 129; S. v. Bartlett, 11 Vt. 650; S. v. Morrill, — Vt. —, 33 Atl. R. 1070; S. v. Underwood, 49 Maine, 181.

[6] P. v. Williams, 24 Mich. 156; Morrissey v. P., 11 Mich. 327; Tyler v. P., 8 Mich. 320; P. v. Staples, 91 Cal. 23; Alsey v. S., 39 Ala. 664; S. v. Matthews, 87 Tenn. 689; Henry v. S., 7 Coldw. 331; S. v. Butler, 67 Mo. 59; Hemmaker v. S., 12 Mo. 453; S. v. Johnson, 38 Ark. 568; Norris v. S., 33 Miss. 373; S. v. Kief, 12 Mont. 92; McFarland v. S., 4 Kan. 68.

[7] S. v. Johnson, 38 Ark. 568; Worthington v. S., 58 Md. 403. Evidence of the larceny out of the state is admissible to show the possession within the state to be felonious: McFarland v. S., 4 Kan. 68; Watson v. S., 36 Miss. 593. But it is not necessary to show the offense to have been a felony by the laws of the state where the goods were first taken, the laws of that state being immaterial: Hemmaker v. S., 12 Mo. 453; S. v. Kief, 12 Mont. 92. The nature of the act in the other state is material in determining whether continuance in possession is in pursuance of a crime: Alsey v. S., 39 Ala. 664. In Texas the statute makes the criminality depend upon the law of the state where the goods were taken,

ished as such only where the original taking is committed. The aggravation will not be deemed to constitute a part of the facts in the county or state to which the stolen property is taken.[1]

§ 554. **Misappropriation by bailee.**— The fundamental proposition that there can be no larceny by one who has already a rightful possession before conceiving a fraudulent intent serves as a line of distinction between larceny and embezzlement. It is not necessary to cite many authorities as to this distinction. Those which could be cited would be in the main illustrations turning on details to be elsewhere considered rather than authorities for the proposition itself. A few are given in the note by way of illustration.[2] While in both England and the United States there are statutes for the punishment of embezzlement, and most cases of wrongful appropriation of property of which one has rightful custody are covered by such statutes, yet there are also statutes in England and in some of the states making a misappropriation of property by a bailee larceny, thus obviating the technical difficulty as to trespass in such cases.[3] Such statutes relate to the misappropriation by a bailee of property to be returned in specie;[4] and this distinguishes larceny by a bailee from embezzlement under such statutes. But where fungible property is delivered for storage, the failure to return it may be larceny by bailee although it was not intended that the identical property be returned but only property of the same kind.[5] Such statutory provision is not intended

which therefore becomes an issuable fact: Cummins v. S., 12 Tex. Ap. 121; Carmisales v. S., 11 Tex. Ap. 474; Clark v. S., 27 Tex. Ap. 405; Edwards v. S., 29 Tex. Ap. 452.

1 Smith v. S., 55 Ala. 59; Gage v. S., 22 Tex. Ap. 123; Nichols v. S., 28 Tex. Ap. 105; 1 Hale, P. C. 507, 536.

2 Rex v. Smith, 1 Moody, 473; Reg. v. Thristle, 2 C. & K. 842; Reg. v. Hey, 2 C. & K. 983; Reg. v. Glass, 2 C. & K. 395; Reg. v. Marsh, 3 F. & F. 523; Reg. v. Saward, 5 Cox, 295; Wright v. Lindsay, 20 Ala. 428; S. v. White, 2 Tyler, 352; S. v. Fann, 65 N. C. 317; S. v. England, 8 Jones, 399; S. v. Hayes, 111 N. C. 727; Johnson v. P., 113 Ill. 99; Jones v. S., 59 Ind. 229; Hill v. S., 57 Wis. 377; Moore v. U. S., 160 U. S. 268. Money of which the prisoner obtained possession without intent to wrongfully appropriate is not subject of larceny: S. v. McDougal, 20 Wis. 482; Shinn v. C., 32 Grat. 899.

3 Truslow v. S., 95 Tenn. 189; S. v. Turner, 10 Wash. 94; Torres v. S., 33 Tex. Ap. 125; Neel v. S., 33 Tex. Ap. 408; S. v. Lucas, 24 Oreg. 168. Such a statute is constitutional: S. v. Hopkins, 56 Vt. 250.

4 Krause v. C., 93 Pa. St. 418; Dotson v. S., 51 Ark. 119; Reg. v. Hassall, 8 Cox, 491; Reg. v. Ashwell, 16 Q. B. D. 190.

5 Hutchinson v. C., 82 Pa. St. 472. The Pennsylvania statute was intended to apply to carriers, so as to

to apply to cases which would be larceny at common law.[1] The intent to steal is essential as in other larcenies.[2] A bailment within such statute may arise by mere license without special contract,[3] and thus may exist as to property received for another as well as with reference to property received directly from the person for whom it is to be kept.[4] And so where money is to be delivered to be used in a certain way and it is misappropriated, the offense is committed although the specific money was not to be returned.[5] The same principle applies to goods given to another for sale and which are by him misappropriated.[6] So there may be such misuse of bills of exchange or other securities given to be used for a particular purpose as to constitute larceny by bailee.[7] But property which is in possession otherwise than as a bailment is not the subject of this offense even though there is a perversion of it from its intended and proper use.[8] Furthermore, if the property was received with an original wrongful intent to convert, the crime is not larceny by bailee but simple larceny, the fraudulent intent negativing the rightful possession.[9] Mere failure by bailee to return property will not constitute the offense. There must be something showing a conversion.[10] And where

obviate the difficulties referred to in the next section in regard to breaking bulk; but it is not limited in its application to carrier cases: C. v. Chathams, 50 Pa. St. 181.

1 Johnson v. P., 113 Ill. 99; Reg. v. McDonald, 15 Q. B. D. 323. *Contra*, S. v. Shirer, 20 S. C. 392; S. v. Taberner, 14 R. I. 272. If constructive possession is in the owner and the wrong-doer has custody only, the wrongful taking is larceny and not embezzlement: Holebrook v. S., — Ala. —, 18 So. R. 109. A conviction for larceny as bailee cannot be had under an indictment for larceny in the usual form: Taylor v. S., 25 Tex. Ap. 96; Huntsman v. S., 12 Tex. Ap. 619; Williams v. S., 30 Tex. Ap. 153.

2 Phelps v. P., 55 Ill. 334.

3 Reg. v. Robson, L. & C. 93; Reg. v. Reeves, 5 Jur. (N. S.) 716.

4 Reg. v. Bunkall, 9 Cox, 419; Reg. v. De Banks, 13 Q. B. D. 29; Dotson v. S., 51 Ark. 119; P. v. Sherman, 133 N. Y. 349; Rucker v. S., 95 Ga. 465.

5 Reg. v. Wells, 1 F. & F. 109; Reg. v. Aden, 12 Cox, 512; Reg. v. Dartnell, 20 L. T. 1020; Crofton v. S., 79 Ga. 584; S. v. Dale, 8 Oreg. 229.

6 Reg. v. Henderson, 11 Cox, 593; Reg. v. Richmond, 29 L. T. 408; Reg. v. Hey, 2 C. & K. 983.

7 Reg. v. Casser, 13 Cox, 187; Reg. v. Oxenham, 13 Cox, 349; Reg. v. Tonkinson, 14 Cox, 603.

8 Rex v. Palmer, 2 East, P. C. 586; Reg. v. Mattheson, 5 Cox, 276; Reg. v. Hoare, 1 F. & F. 647; Reg. v. Marsh, 3 F. & F. 523; Zschocke v. P., 62 Ill. 127.

9 Reg. v. Waller, 10 Cox, 360; Rex v. Banks, Russ. & Ry. 441. And see *infra*, § 562.

10 Rex v. Banks, Russ. & Ry. 441; Reg. v. Jackson, 9 Cox, 505. But the

the duty is to account only on demand, there must be a demand and failure to account in order to show the commission of the crime.[1] Especially is this so where the case is not one of specific property, but, as is contemplated under some statutes, one of obligation to account for funds which the bailee has a right to mingle with his own.[2] Although an infant cannot make a valid contract of bailment, yet, if over fourteen years of age, he may be guilty of the offense of larceny as bailee, the validity of the contract of bailment being immaterial.[3] There has been a question in England whether a married woman could be a bailee so as to commit this offense,[4] but clearly no such question would arise under the law as to married women as it now exists in most of the states. The offense is to be deemed a statutory one and described as other statutory offenses.[5] The indictment must allege the facts showing a relation of trust, either express or implied, and a conversion of the property with intent to steal.[6]

§ 555. **Carriers or other bailees breaking bulk.** — The doctrine of the preceding paragraph, that a bailee does not commit trespass in misappropriation of the property in his possession, and therefore is not guilty of larceny, has an exception of as great antiquity apparently as the rule itself, based also on the technical doctrines of the common law as to trespass, to the effect that if the bailee, instead of appropriating the property as a whole, does an unauthorized act with reference thereto, such as breaking open the package and removing a portion of the contents, he has thereby committed trespass against the owner and may be guilty of larceny. This doctrine seems to have been first applied to carriers, and the peculiarly technical nature of it is recognized in a discussion thereof, during the reign of Charles II, by Chief Justice Kelynge, who criticises a case in the time of Elizabeth in which the

mere misappropriation may be made the crime without fraudulent intent: S. v. Hopkins, 56 Vt. 250.

1 Soule v. S., 71 Ga. 267; S. v. Chew Muck You, 20 Oreg. 215.

2 Snell v. S., 50 Ga. 219; Hoyt v. S., 50 Ga. 313.

3 Reg. v. McDonald, 15 Q. B. D. 323.

4 Reg. v. Robson, L. & C. 93; Reg. v. Denmour, 8 Cox, 440; Reg. v. Warren, 10 Cox, 359.

5 Johnson v. P., 113 Ill. 99; Kibs v. P., 81 Ill. 599; Reg. v. Haigh, 7 Cox, 403.

6 Wilbur v. T., 3 Wyo. 268; S. v. Kaspar, 5 Wash. 174; Sanders v. S., 86 Ga. 717.

proposition seems to have been laid down.[1] But this doctrine has received modern recognition and is the rule of the common law, except as it may have been modified by statute, and if there has been a breaking of bulk the carrier is held guilty,[2] while, if there is no breaking of bulk, the offense of larceny is not committed.[3] Where the cargo is in bulk and not in packages, the taking of a portion thereof by the carrier is larceny.[4] The doctrine of this section, though usually laid down with reference to carriers, is applicable to other bailees, for instance, a miller misappropriating a part of a quantity of grain delivered to him for grinding.[5] So, where a warehouseman, to whom sacks of wheat were intrusted for keeping, took the wheat out of one bag, it was held larceny.[6] So, where a letter or parcel is given to another to be mailed or delivered for transportation, a breaking open of the letter or package and appropriation of the contents will be larceny.[7] So, when a person employed to sell cloths, which were delivered to him in a bundle, broke open the bundle with the fraudulent purpose of pawning a part of them and subsequently misappropriated the remainder, it was held that he was guilty of larceny.[8] A fraudulent conversion after the privity of contract has terminated will be larceny.[9]

§ **556. Larceny by servant or mere custodian.**— There is a well-recognized distinction between possession such as that of a bailee and mere custody as that of a servant, and the doctrine by which a bailee is held not guilty of larceny in misappropriating goods in his possession does not apply to the act of a servant in wrongfully converting or disposing of his master's property of which he has the mere custody. In such case there is a trespass, for the possession is in the master and not in the servant, and the servant may be guilty of larceny in

[1] J. Kel. 81, 82.

[2] C. v. Brown, 4 Mass. 580; S. v. Fairclough, 29 Conn. 47; Nichols v. P., 17 N. Y. 114; P. v. Poggi, 19 Cal. 600; S. v. Thurston, 2 McMull. 382; Rex v. Pratley, 5 C. & P. 533; Rex v. Howell, 7 C. & P. 325.

[3] Rex v. Fletcher, 4 C. & P. 545; Reg. v. Cornish, Dears. 425; Rex v. Madox, Russ. & Ry. 92.

[4] Nichols v. P., 17 N. Y. 114.

[5] C. v. James, 1 Pick. 375.

[6] Rex v. Brazier, Russ. & Ry. 337.

[7] Rex v. Jones, 7 C. & P. 151; Reg. v. Jenkins, 9 C. & P. 38.

[8] Reg. v. Poyser, 2 Den. 233.

[9] Rex v. Charlewood, 2 East, P. C. 689.

the wrongful disposal of his master's property even though he has it at the time under his entire control.[1] And it is sufficient that the servant forms the intent to misappropriate and attempts to carry it out although he does not actually part with the property.[2] It is sometimes difficult to distinguish a servant from a bailee to whom property is given into possession for a specific purpose. One who is employed to drive cattle generally or to a particular place, and misappropriates them, is guilty of larceny.[3] But if he is given general authority to dispose of the property, he is something more than a mere servant, and does not commit larceny in making a wrongful disposition.[4] A person who is engaged about the business of his employer, such as a clerk or salesman, is a servant within the doctrine of this section, and does not have possession of his employer's property, but only the custody of it, and therefore is guilty of larceny in fraudulently misappropriating it.[5] So one who is employed in general labor, having control of his employer's property for that purpose, is guilty of larceny in wrongfully taking such property.[6] It is not necessary that the employment be continuous; it may be for a special purpose, and the misappropriation of property received in pursuance of such purpose, larceny.[7] So, where a clerk authorized to pay out money to workmen misappropriates the money given to him

[1] C. v. Brown, 4 Mass. 580; C. v. Collins, 12 Allen, 181; C. v. Berry, 99 Mass. 428; Phelps v. P., 72 N. Y. 334; S. v. McCartey, 17 Minn. 76; S. v. Schlingen, 20 Wis. 74; Smith v. S., 28 Ind. 321; Powell v. S., 34 Ark. 693; Brown v. P., 20 Colo. 161; Crocheron v. S., 86 Ala. 64; Case v. S., 26 Ala. 17; Rex v. Bass, 2 East, P. C. 566; Rex v. Somerton, 7 B. & C. 463; Reg. v. White, 9 C. & P. 344; Reg. v. Privett, 2 C. & K. 114; 1 Hale, P. C. 506; T. Kel. 35.

[2] S. v. Schlingen, 20 Wis. 74. But the mere formation of the purpose is not enough: Reg. v. Roberts, 3 Cox, 74.

[3] Rex v. McNamee, 1 Moody, 368; Reg. v. Jackson, 2 Moody, 32.

[4] Reg. v. Goodbody, 8 C. & P. 665; Reg. v. Leppard, 4 F. & F. 51; Reg. v. Jones, Car. & M. 611; Reg. v. Evans, Car. & M. 632.

[5] Jenkins v. S., 62 Wis. 49; Marcus v. S., 26 Ind. 101; Walker v. C., 8 Leigh, 743; U. S. v. Clew, 4 Wash. 700; Rex v. Hammon, 4 Taunt. 304; Reg. v. Harvey, 9 C. & P. 353; Rex v. Chipchase, 2 East, P. C. 567; Reg. v. Wright, Dears. & B. 431; Reg. v. Flanagan, 10 Cox, 561.

[6] C. v. Brown, 4 Mass. 580; P. v. Belden, 37 Cal. 51; Reg. v. Winbow, 5 Cox, 346.

[7] Reg. v. Goode, Car. & M. 582; Reg. v. Beaman, Car. & M. 595; Reg. v. Smith, 1 C. & K. 423; Reg. v. Hawkins, 4 Cox, 224. The driver of a coach hired for the day is not the servant of the person hiring: Rex v. Haydon, 7 C. & P. 445.

for that purpose, he is guilty of larceny.[1] In order that the servant shall be guilty of larceny of his master's property, the property must have been, up to the time of the wrongful taking by the servant, in the possession of the master; so that, as to goods given to the servant by another to be delivered to his master, it is said that the servant cannot commit larceny, the possession of the master not having yet attached.[2] But where coals had been received by the servant into his master's cart, it was held that they were so far in the master's possession that the servant was guilty of larceny in misappropriating them;[3] and where money was given to the servant by the agent of the master for delivery to the master, it was held that the previous possession of the agent was that of the master in such sense that the misappropriation by the servant was larceny.[4] If, however, the property is received from the master for delivery to another, it continues in the master's possession till such delivery is made, and therefore the servant misappropriating it is guilty of larceny.[5] There may be other custodians who stand in the same relation to the property as that of a servant, and who, therefore, may be guilty of larceny in misappropriating the property, although they are not technically servants.[6] Thus, where an instrument is handed to one for indorsement, he does not have possession, but mere custody thereof, and may be guilty of trespass in appropriating it, and if the act is with

[1] Reg. v. Cooke, L. R. 1 C. C. 295; Reg. v. Low, 10 Cox, 168. But where the wages of several employees were drawn by one and misappropriated, it was held that he was not guilty of larceny from the employer: Reg. v. Barnes, L. R. 1 C. C. 45.

[2] C. v. Ryan, 155 Mass. 523. So held as to cash received for a check or change for a bill: C. v. King, 9 Cush. 284; Rex v. Sullens, 1 Moody, 129; or money received for goods sold: Reg. v. Betts, Bell, 90; Reg. v. Brockett, 4 Cox, 274. And see *infra*, § 562.

[3] Reg. v. Reed, Dears. 257. And see Reg. v. Hayward, 1 C. & K. 518; Rex v. Harding, Russ. & Ry. 125; 2 East, P. C. 568.

[4] P. v. McDonald, 43 N. Y. 61. So where money was paid in the usual course of business to the agent of a partnership who misappropriated it, *held*, that he was not guilty of the statutory offense of larceny by breach of trust as to the party paying, as his relation to the money was solely that of clerk of the partnership: McNish v. S., 88 Ga. 499.

[5] Rex v. Metcalf, 1 Moody, 433; Reg. v. Heath, 2 Moody, 33; Reg. v. Hawkins, 1 Den. 584.

[6] C. v. O'Malley, 97 Mass. 584; S. v. Jarvis, 63 N. C. 556; S. v. Self, 1 Bay, 242; Gill v. Bright, 6 T. B. Mon. 130; Robinson v. S., 1 Coldw. 120.

fraudulent intent he will be guilty of larceny.[1] A brakeman or railway conductor will be guilty of larceny in the wrongful taking of property in the possession of the company. He is not a carrier.[2] The assistant foreman of a warehouse, having no authority to dispose of the property stored therein, but only to deliver it upon orders, has been held guilty of larceny rather than embezzlement in attempting to sell it.[3] One who is intrusted with the custody of money for a special purpose may commit larceny thereof although he is entitled to a portion of the money by way of compensation, such portion not having been selected.[4] Under statutes with reference to conversion by a servant in connection with embezzlement, it is held that such a conversion cannot be prosecuted as larceny, but only as a statutory offense, although in the absence of statute it might be larceny.[5]

§ 557. Consent of owner; collusion.— The essential element of trespass is absent where the taking is with the owner's consent.[6] In view of this doctrine the question has sometimes been raised whether, where the owner for the purpose of capturing the thief takes no steps to prevent the intended larceny of which he has knowledge, he does not thereby so far consent as that the act when committed is not larceny; but this view is not sustained, and the crime is committed although the owner takes no steps to prevent it.[7] Thus, if marked money is placed where it may be taken by one who is planning to commit larceny, there will not be such consent as to prevent punishment for the felony.[8] It is so where the marked money

[1] P. v. Call, 1 Denio, 120.

[2] Manson v. S., 24 Ohio St. 590; Brown v. P., 20 Colo. 161.

[3] P. v. Perini, 94 Cal. 573.

[4] C. v. Lannan, 153 Mass. 287. And see Reg. v. Wright, Dears. & B. 431.

[5] S. v. Wingo, 89 Ind. 204.

[6] 2 East, P. C. 665; 2 Bish. Cr. L., § 811; Moye v. S., 65 Ga. 754; Dodd v. Hamilton, 2 Tayl. 31; Marshall v. S., 31 Tex. 471.

[7] Varner v. S., 72 Ga. 745; P. v. Hanselman, 76 Cal. 460; Connor v. S., 24 Tex. Ap. 245; Rex v. Egginton, 2 East, P. C. 494, 666. But the crime of receiving stolen goods is not committed where the goods are by procurement of the owner delivered to the receiver: See *infra*, § 717. In general as to decoying to crime, see *supra*, § 118.

[8] Reg. v. Williams, 1 C. & K. 195. Where rabbits had been killed and concealed, with the purpose of afterwards taking them away, it was held that the discovery of the bodies by the owner, and marking them for subsequent identification, was not such taking into possession that a subsequent taking, in continuance of the original purpose, would be larceny: Reg. v. Petch, 14 Cox, 17.

is put in a letter which is stolen, the letter being sent for the purpose of detecting larceny from the mails.[1] And it will not prevent the punishment of the criminal that one who acts in the interest of the owner has pretended to join with the criminal in committing the crime, not, however, having been instrumental in suggesting it.[2] It is not necessary in general to negative the consent of the owner in the indictment,[3] but under the particular definition of larceny in the Texas statute it is required that such consent be directly negatived;[4] and if the ownership is alleged to be in two, or ownership in one and possession in another, the want of consent of both must be alleged and shown.[5] Where the question of want of consent of the owner becomes material, it is not necessary to prove such want of consent by the evidence of the owner himself. It may be shown by others having knowledge of the facts.[6] But it is said that the rule as to the introduction of the best evidence makes it necessary to introduce the evidence of the owner on that question unless some reason for not doing so appears.[7] Where the evidence of the owner is not obtainable, his want of consent may be shown by circumstantial evidence.[8]

[1] Reg. v. Rathbone, Carr. & M. 220; Reg. v. Young, 2 C. & K. 466; though it is said in some cases that such a letter is not a post letter within the English statute as to stealing letters from the mails: Reg. v. Shepherd, Dears. 606; Reg. v. Rathbone, *supra;* Reg. v. Gardner. 1 C. & K. 628. But the last case seems to be overruled in Reg. v. Young, *supra.* As to larceny from the mails, see *infra*, § 1330.

[2] McAdams v. S., 8 Lea, 456; Pigg v. S., 43 Tex. 108.

[3] Wedge v. S., 7 Lea, 687; P. v. Davis, 97 Cal. 194.

[4] Garcia v. S., 26 Tex. 209; Johnson v. S., 39 Tex. 393; Bland v. S., 18 Tex. Ap. 12; Jackson v. S., 7 Tex. Ap. 363; Otero v. S., 30 Tex. Ap. 450; McMahon v. S., 1 Tex. Ap. 102; Bowling v. S., 13 Tex. Ap. 338.

[5] Taylor v. S., 18 Tex. Ap. 449; Williams v. S., 19 Tex. Ap. 276; Willey v. S., 22 Tex. Ap. 408; Spruill v. S., 10 Tex. Ap. 695; Rains v. S., 7 Tex. Ap. 588; Jones v. S., 28 Tex. Ap. 42; Swink v. S., 32 Tex. Ap. 530. Where there is mere temporary custody in the person from whom the property is taken, his consent need not be negatived: Burns v. S., 35 Tex. 724; Bailey v. S., 18 Tex. Ap. 426. In case of custody of property of an infant by his guardian, it is sufficient to negative the consent of such guardian: Frazier v. S., 18 Tex. Ap. 434. Where the property is in possession of bailee, want of consent of such bailee is sufficient: Skipworth v. S., 8 Tex. Ap. 135. It being permitted by statute to allege ownership in one of two joint owners, it is not necessary to prove want of consent of the other: Coates v. S., 31 Tex. Ap. 257. As to consent, see, also, *supra*, § 546.

[6] P. v. Jack, 76 Mich. 218.

[7] S. v. Osborne, 28 Ia. 9; Bubster v. S., 33 Neb. 663; Perry v. S., 44 Neb. 414; S. v. Moon, 41 Wis. 684.

[8] Clayton v. S., 15 Tex. Ap. 348;

§ 558. Consent of servant, or custodian, or wife.—The fact that the servant, in whose possession the property is, consents to its taking will not prevent the act being larceny, he having no authority to consent and the wrong-doer being aware of that fact.[1] So where the property was obtained from a bailee on the false representation that the owner consented, the act was held larceny.[2] But the doctrine as to the necessity of trespass, already stated, prevents the taking of the property of the husband or wife by the other from being larceny, as they have such joint possession that the wrongful act of the one is not a trespass as against the other.[3] And so where the wife elopes, carrying with her the property of the husband, there is no larceny committed by one who subsequently obtains the property from her.[4] And one who assists the wife in taking the property from her husband is not guilty of larceny, for the consent of the wife prevents the act from being a trespass.[5] But this doctrine is subject to a well-settled exception, that if the person who assists the wife does so in pursuance of a mutual intention that they shall commit adultery, the consent of the wife is no excuse, for the adulterer must have known that such taking was without the husband's consent.[6] And this doctrine, that

Love v. S., 15 Tex. Ap. 563; Schultz v. S., 20 Tex. Ap. 308.

[1] S. v. McCartey, 17 Minn. 76; P. v. Griswold, 64 Mich. 722; S. v. Edwards, 36 Mo, 394; Reg. v. Tuckwell, Car. & M. 215; Rex v. Hench, Russ. & Ry. 163; Reg. v. Sheppard, 9 C. & P. 121; Reg. v. White, 9 C. & P. 344; Reg. v. Robins, Dears. 418; Rex v. Longstreeth, 1 Moody, 137; Reg. v. Simpson, 2 Cox, 235; Reg. v. Webb, 5 Cox, 154; Reg. v. Little, 10 Cox, 559. These cases run into the doctrine of obtaining possession by false pretenses with the purpose of stealing, which will be discussed hereafter: See *infra*, § 563.

[2] Reg. v. Steer, 2 C. & K. 988.

[3] Thomas v. Thomas, 51 Ill. 162; Watkins v. S., 60 Miss. 323; Reg. v. Kenny, 2 Q. B. D. 307; Rex v. Willis, 1 Moody, 375. *Contra*, Beasley v. S., 138 Ind. 552. The crime of larceny from a building cannot be committed by the wife of goods in a building belonging to the husband; but the court seems to have thought that the wife in such case could be convicted for the simple larceny: C. v. Hartnett, 3 Gray, 450.

[4] Reg. v. Kenny, 2 Q. B. D. 207; Reg. v. Fitch, Dears. & B. 87; Reg. v. Rosenberg, 1 C. & K. 233; Reg. v. Prince, 11 Cox, 145; Reg. v. Taylor, 12 Cox, 627.

[5] S. v. Banks, 48 Ind. 197; Lamphier v. S., 70 Ind. 317; Rex v. Harrison, 2 East, P. C. 559; Reg. v. Avery, Bell, 150; Rex v. Tolfree, 1 Moody, 243.

[6] P. v. Swalm, 80 Cal. 46; P. v. Schuyler, 6 Cowen, 572; Reg. v. Tollett, Car. & M. 112; Reg. v. Berry, Bell, 95; Reg. v. Featherstone, Dears. 369; Reg. v. Thompson, 1 Den. 549; Reg. v. Mutters, L. & C. 511; Reg. v.

any knowledge on the part of the person assisting the wife that the consent of the wife is not the consent of the husband, is applicable to other cases where the person thus assisting has knowledge that the wife is going away without the husband's consent, even though he is not intending to commit adultery with her.[1] The fact that property thus taken by the wife and given to another without the husband's consent is her own wearing apparel will not, under the statutes as to separate property of the wife, give rise to any presumption that such apparel does not belong to the husband.[2]

§ 559. **Further as to consent; force, duress, fraud.**—Where the consent of the owner to the taking is procured only by force or duress it does not, of course, prevent the act being a crime.[3] So a fraudulent taking is equivalent to a wrongful taking and may constitute larceny.[4] But this line of reasoning leads to great difficulties, and some of the most intricate distinctions in larceny are involved in cases where the property is procured by fraud. These cases may perhaps be conveniently divided into three classes: First, where the property is obtained by some trick or device; second, where the purpose of the owner is only to surrender possession, in which case the party obtaining possession will be guilty of larceny if he obtained such possession with the fraudulent purpose of appropriating the property and depriving the owner thereof, but not if he originally took possession for an innocent purpose, and subsequently appropriated the property wrongfully to his own use; and third, where the owner intends to part with the title to the property, such intention, however, being brought about by fraud. These three classes of cases run into each other in so many ways that it seems almost impossible to draw clear dividing lines. The method conducing to clearness will be to discuss the three, bearing in mind under each heading the controlling principle and seeking in the cases for its application.

§ 560. **Property obtained by trick or fraud.**— The general proposition is a plain one, that where the owner does not in-

Harrison, 12 Cox, 19; Reg. v. Flatman, 14 Cox, 396.

[1] P. v. Cole, 43 N. Y. 508; P. v. Schuyler, 6 Cowen, 572.

[2] P. v. Swalm, 80 Cal. 46.

[3] Reg. v. McGrath, L. R. 1 C. C. 205; Reg. v. Lovell, 8 Q. B. D. 185; Reg. v. Hazell, 11 Cox, 597; S. v. Bryant, 74 N. C. 124.

[4] P. v. Shaw, 57 Mich. 403; C. v. Wilde, 5 Gray, 83; Shipply v. P., 86 N. Y. 375.

tend to part with his property, but only with temporary possession, and it is obtained from him by trick or fraud with the intention of depriving him of it, the offense is larceny.[1] Thus, if one obtains money by a pretended game of chance so artfully devised that the person from whom the money is obtained has no chance of winning, the act constitutes larceny.[2] An early case in England held such an act not to be larceny, on the theory that the owner voluntarily parted with his money, not expecting to get it back if he should lose;[3] but the modern cases cited in the last preceding note take a more reasonable view of the transaction and consider that the fraud is a wrongful taking, and that larceny is committed. Where the trick consists in inducing another to make a wager, the owner intending to part with his money if he loses the wager, but the purpose of the wrong-doer being that, irrespective of the result of the wager, the owner shall not have back his money, the offense is larceny.[4] Other frauds and tricks by which the owner voluntarily parts with his money under an entire misapprehension brought about by fraud of the opposite party will make the taking larceny;[5] so, where one procured goods to be sent to him C. O. D., and then got the goods from the carrier by a worthless check, that being a part of his original plan, it was held that larceny was committed;[6] and it was so held where one bought coal, but by covering it with slack got it at the

[1] C. v. Lannan, 153 Mass. 287; C. v. Barry, 124 Mass. 325; Frazier v. S., 85 Ala. 17; Wilson v. S., 1 Port. 118; S. v. Lindenthall, 5 Rich. 237; Rex v. Munday, 2 East, P. C. 594. But the application of this doctrine raises the questions, whether the owner intended to part with his property, and whether, if he intended only to part with possession, there was a fraudulent purpose in the wrong-doer from the beginning, which questions are for subsequent discussion.

[2] Miller v. C., 78 Ky. 15; Defrese v. S., 3 Heisk. 53; Hall v. S., 6 Baxt. 522; U. S. v. Murphy, McA. & M. 375; for instance, by a pretended illustration of lottery drawing, the money used being kept instead of being returned: P. v. Johnson, 91 Cal. 265.

[3] Rex v. Nicholson, 2 East, P. C. 669; Reg. v. Wilson, 8 C. & P. 111.

[4] Stinson v. P., 43 Ill. 397; Reg. v. Buckmaster, 20 Q. B. D. 182.

[5] Thus, where a cigarette was procured from a slot machine by putting in a worthless brass disk instead of a penny, *held*, that the act was larceny: Reg. v. Hands, 16 Cox, 188; 8 Am. Cr. R. 469. Where money was obtained under pretense that an act had been done which defendant had agreed to do, and for which the money was to have been paid, but the act had in fact not been done, *held*, that there was larceny: P. v. Berlin, 9 Utah, 383.

[6] Shipply v. P., 86 N. Y. 375.

price of slack instead of at the price of lump coal;[1] also where defendant, having intentionally killed and concealed a hog belonging to his neighbor, represented that the hog had died and was only valuable for soap grease and obtained it as such.[2] Where, by the assistance of a confederate, defendant procured a loan from a traveling companion on pretended security, but with the intention of appropriating the money, the act was held larceny.[3] Where it appeared that the prisoner had obtained a horse from the bailee of another by fraudulently representing that it was with the owner's consent, well knowing that the owner was not willing that the horse should be delivered to him, the act was held larceny.[4] There are other cases falling under the same doctrine involving a transaction in which the owner is induced to part with his property by a pretended exchange which is so fraudulently carried out that the owner does not get in exchange the thing which was intended.[5] In such cases, although the owner intends to part with his property and never get it back, yet the fraudulent plan of the wrongdoer prevents the consent being voluntary, and the property is therefore wrongfully taken.[6] Cases similar to this and governed by the same principle are those where there is ostensible purchase with pretended intent to pay at once, but the property, having been got into custody by the pretense, is taken without payment in pursuance of an original wrongful purpose.[7]

[1] Rex v. Bramley, L. & C. 21.

[2] Frazier v. S., 85 Ala. 17.

[3] P. v. Rae, 66 Cal. 423. So where money is obtained on deposit as security in case of a pretended employment, and is then retained wrongfully, the act is larceny: P. v. Tomlinson, 102 Cal. 19; P. v. Fehrenback, 102 Cal. 394. So where money is thus appropriated after being obtained as security for a contract: Devore v. T., 2 Okl. 562.

[4] Reg. v. Steer, 2 C. & K. 988.

[5] C. v. Eichelberger, 119 Pa. St. 254; Grunson v. S., 89 Ind. 533; Huber v. S., 57 Ind. 341; Taylor v. S., 32 Tex. Ap. 110; Rex v. Oliver, 2 Russ., C. & M. 122; Reg. v. Russett, 2 Q. B. D. (1892) 312, 9 Am. Cr. R. 511 and note.

[6] Reg. v. Rodway, 9 C. & P. 784. This was a case of obtaining a receipt with the expectation on the part of the person giving it that he should receive the money called for, which, however, was not paid. A similar case was that where, by means of fraudulent checks, an order for property was secured, and the property was thus obtained without payment being actually made: Reg. v. North, 8 Cox, 43. It is larceny to get money as compensation under the false pretense of being able to secure the return of stolen property: Cantwell v. P., 138 Ill. 602.

[7] Vaughn v. C., 10 Grat. 758; Blunt v. C., 4 Leigh, 689; Hildebrand v. P., 56 N. Y. 394; S. v. Shoaf, 68 N. C.

In such cases as these the question whether there was a *bona fide* intent to pay is material; if there was, a subsequent failure to pay will not constitute larceny.[1] Thus, if a pretended buyer gets possession of the goods for the purpose of inspection and makes off with the property without payment, that being his original intent, larceny is committed.[2] Another class of cases rests on the same principle, namely, where the owner gives money to the wrong-doer with the expectation of having change in return, and the wrong-doer takes the money and appropriates it with the intention, from the first, of not returning the expected change.[3] The difficulty in these cases is in determining whether there was a wrongful purpose at the beginning or only a subsequent wrongful conversion of the money intrusted, and there is early English authority holding that under such circumstances there is no larceny;[4] but even by the older cases, if the original intention was to deprive the owner of his property, the crime was committed,[5] and under the later cases there is no doubt that, although the reasoning may not be entirely in accord with the technical doctrines, a conviction will be supported.[6] Somewhat analogous to these cases are those where, by artfully "ringing the changes," as it is called, the wrong-doer confuses the person who attempts to make change, and procures more money in exchange than he is entitled to.[7]

375; U. S. v. Rodgers, 1 Mackey, 419; Rex v. Sharpless, 2 East, P. C. 675; Rex v. Pratt, 1 Moody, 250; Rex v. Gilbert, 1 Moody, 185; Reg. v. Morgan, Dears. 395; Reg. v. Box, 9 C. & P. 126; Reg. v. Slowly, 12 Cox, 269; Rex v. Campbell, 1 Moody, 179; Reg. v. Cohen, 2 Den. 249.

[1] Reg. v. Richardson, 1 F. & F. 488; Rex v. Harvey, 2 East, P. C. 669; P. v. Raschke, 73 Cal. 378.

[2] S. v. Hall, 76 Ia. 85, 8 Am. Cr. 463 and note. So where one gets possession of a note under pretense of intent to pay and then destroys it, he is guilty of larceny: State v. Fenn, 41 Conn. 590, 1 Am. Cr. 378 and note. One who gets permission to sample cotton, but with intent to appropriate the samples, is guilty of larceny. S. v. McRae, 111 N. C. 665.

[3] Murphy v. P., 120 Ill. 234; Farrell v. P., 16 Ill. 506; Levy v. S., 79 Ala. 259; Walters v. S., 17 Tex. Ap. 226. Where a child was allowed to pay a gold piece for a small purchase and given change for a dollar, the receiver was held guilty of swindling, not larceny: Jones v. S., — Ga. —, 25 S. E. R. 319.

[4] Reg. v. Thomas, 9 C. & P. 741. And see Reg. v. Bird, 12 Cox, 257.

[5] Rex v. Aickles, 2 East, P. C. 675; Rex v. Williams, 6 C. & P. 390. And see Reg. v. Twist, 29 L. T. 546.

[6] Justices v. P., 90 N. Y. 12; C. v. Barry, 124 Mass. 325; Hildebrand v. P., 56 N. Y. 394.

[7] Reg. v. Johnson, 2 Den. 310; Reg v. McKale, L. R. 1 C. C. 125. And see Fleming v. S., 136 Ind. 149.

§ 561. Mutual mistake and subsequent wrongful appropriations.—Notwithstanding the well-recognized rule already discussed,[1] that a subsequent wrongful appropriation of property rightfully obtained is not larceny because there is no trespass, that is, no taking from the owner, it is now well settled that if by mutual mistake a bill or coin of a larger denomination than that intended is given and received, and the person receiving it, on discovering the mistake, does not return the money or the excess, he is guilty of larceny; the theory being that, in such case, the owner does not really part with his money, and that a trespass is committed when the person receiving it uses it as his own.[2] Unquestionably, also, one who knowingly receives an overpayment made by mistake is guilty of larceny of the excess, for there is no intention on the part of the person making payment to transfer such excess, and the acceptance and conversion are wrongful.[3] But where the overpayment was not known at the time and the excess was, on its discovery by the person receiving, retained, it was held that larceny had not been committed.[4]

§ 562. Obtaining possession only, but with intent to appropriate.— Notwithstanding the doctrine that, where the wrong-doer already has lawful possession, there is no larceny in a subsequent wrongful appropriation,[5] the principle that fraud vitiates any transaction into which it enters would furnish a theoretical reason for the rule that, where the wrong-doer thus obtains possession for the purpose and with the intent of appropriating the property, the act will be larceny; and this doctrine is fully recognized by the cases, the older ones emphasizing the fact that the taking of possession in the first in-

[1] See *supra*, § 550.

[2] S. v. Ducker, 8 Oreg. 394; Bailey v. S., 58 Ala. 414; S. v. Williamson, 1 Houst. Cr. C. 155; Reg. v. Ashwell, 16 Q. B. D. 190. The English court does not, however, abandon the doctrine that the receipt and the wrongful appropriation must be contemporaneous: Reg. v. Flowers, 16 Q. B. D. 643. Where a money order was delivered to the wrong person by mistake, and he, knowing the mistake, had it cashed, *held*, that he was not guilty of larceny of the order: Reg. v. Davis, Dears. 640.

[3] Reg. v. Middleton, L. R. 2 C. C. 38. In this case the judges were divided in their views. This does not constitute larceny by bailee under Texas statute: Fulcher v. S., 32 Tex. Ap. 621.

[4] Reg. v. Flowers, 16 Q. B. D. 643. And see Reg. v. Hehir, 29 Ir. L. T. 323; Article 8 Harv. L. Rev. 317.

[5] *Supra*, § 550.

stance by the wrong-doer must have been *animo furandi*, that is, with intent to steal.[1] A typical illustration of this doctrine is found in cases where property is ostensibly borrowed or hired, but with the purpose on the part of the borrower of appropriating instead of returning it.[2] In such cases, the fact that the owner consents to the delivery of possession to the wrong-doer does not prevent the act being larceny, not only because the consent is procured by fraud, but because it is not the parting with title, but only the delivery of possession; and the cases are thus distinguished from those to be discussed in the next section, where the owner by fraudulent pretenses or otherwise is induced to part with his property. In the cases now being considered the title remains in the owner, and the subsequent conversion and the original intent to deprive the owner of his property supply the necessary elements of larceny.[3] Obtaining possession of property by falsely personating another, or false representation of authority to purchase or take for another, is larceny.[4] It is evidently necessary, to bring a case within this doctrine, that there should have been the original wrongful intent to deprive the owner of his property, for otherwise there is only a conversion after rightful possession, which does not constitute the crime of larceny.[5] If there is an original wrongful but not felonious intent, as to make use of

[1] Rex v. Horner, 1 Leach, 270; Rex v. Pear, 2 East, P. C. 685, 697; Rex v. Tunnard, 2 East, P. C. 687; Rex v. Semple, 2 East, P. C. 691; Reg. v. Box, 9 C. & P. 126; Rex v. Stock, 1 Moody, 87; Reg. v. Cole, 3 Cox, 340; Reg. v. Janson, 4 Cox, 82; Reg. v. Waller, 10 Cox, 360.

[2] S. v. Humphrey, 32 Vt. 569; Loomis v. P., 67 N. Y. 322; P. v. Jersey, 18 Cal. 337; Starkie v. C., 7 Leigh, 752; Richards v. C., 13 Grat. 803; Quinn v. P., 123 Ill. 333; Felter v. S., 9 Yerg. 397; Coldwell v. S., 59 Tenn. 429; S. v. Woodruff, 47 Kan. 151; Dignowitty v. S., 17 Tex. 521; White v. S., 11 Tex. 769; Rex v. Semple, 2 East, P. C. 691; Rex v. Pear, 2 East, P. C. 685, 697; Reg. v. Bunce, 1 F. & F. 523; Reg. v. Gillings, 1 F. & F. 36. One who obtained property from the minor son of the owner, intending to convert it to his own use, was held guilty of larceny: P. v. Camp, 56 Mich. 548.

[3] C. v. Barry, 124 Mass. 325; Loomis v. P., 67 N. Y. 322; Smith v. P., 53 N. Y. 111; S. v. Watson, 41 N. H. 533; P. v. Raischke, 83 Cal. 501; S. v. Williams, 35 Mo. 229; S. v. Gorman, 2 Nott & McC. 90.

[4] C. v. Collins, 12 Allen, 181; C. v. Whitman, 121 Mass. 361; Harris v. S., 81 Ga. 758; Madden v. S., 1 Tex. Ap. 204. So by statute: S. v. Brown, 25 Ia. 561; S. v. Smith, 9 Wash. 248.

[5] P. v. Cruger, 102 N. Y. 510; S. v. Shermer, 55 Mo. 83; Johnson v. P., 113 Ill. 99; Reg. v. Matthews, 28 L. T. 645. And see further cases collected on this subject in relation to intent, *infra*, § 569. That wrongful appro-

the property for an unauthorized purpose, a subsequent appropriation will be larceny, for there was not consent to the intended use.[1] But there must be a subsequent appropriation; the mere technical conversion involved in the misuse is not enough.[2] The mere fact of the subsequent conversion is not, in itself, sufficient evidence of the wrongful intent.[3] It is not necessary, however, to bring a case within the doctrine here discussed, to show that the owner was to have back the identical property. The person to whom it is delivered may have possession only and not title, although he is intrusted with the property with the purpose on the part of the owner that he shall dispose of it; and if there is the intent to deprive the owner of his property when it is taken under such an arrangement, the offense is larceny.[4] Cases analogous to this have already been discussed under the section relating to larceny by trick.[5] It is necessary to bear in mind here also the distinction between possession and custody; for, as already has been said in relation to larceny by servants and other custodians, if such mere custodian wrongfully converts the property he is guilty of larceny, because he has not even possession, and is therefore guilty of trespass in such misappropriation.[6] If the original wrongful intent exist at the time possession is taken, there may be sufficient subsequent conversion in pursuance of such intent, although the property is not actually disposed of, the wrong-doer intending to appropriate it and treat it as his own.[7] But there must be something constituting a conversion.[8] In some states the statute defining larceny is so drawn as to expressly cover the class of cases considered in this section.[9]

priation after lawful possession is not larceny has already been stated: *Supra*, § 549.

[1] S. v. Coombs, 55 Me. 477. So a trespass not felonious in taking property may become larceny by a subsequent wrongful appropriation and disposal: C. v. White, 11 Cush. 483.

[2] Berg v. S., 2 Tex. Ap. 148.

[3] P. v. Carabin, 14 Cal. 438; Pitts v. S., 3 Tex. Ap. 210. And see other cases under the head of intent, *infra*, § 571.

[4] S. v. Watson, 41 N. H. 533; C. v. Yerkes, 29 Leg. Int. 60, reported in 119 Pa. St. 266; Mitchell v. S., 92 Tenn. 668; Reg. v. Brown, Dears. 616; Reg. v. Thompson, 9 Cox, 244.

[5] *Supra*, § 560.

[6] Reg. v. Jones, Car. & M. 611; Reg. v. Evans, Car. & M. 632, and cases *supra*, § 556.

[7] S. v. Humphrey, 32 Vt. 569; Reg. v. Janson, 4 Cox, 82.

[8] Blunt v. C., 4 Leigh, 689; S. v. Hayes, 111 N. C. 727; Berg v. S., 2 Tex. Ap. 148.

[9] P. v. Laurence, 137 N. Y. 517; Coldwell v. S., 59 Tenn. 429.

§ 563. Obtaining property by false pretenses.— Where the owner of property delivers it to another intending to part with title, there can be no trespass on the part of the person thus obtaining the title to the property, and therefore no larceny, although the owner was induced to part with his property by fraud or false pretenses. Such a case is plainly distinguishable from one where the owner intends to deliver the custody or possession only to another, retaining the title.[1] Therefore the well-known offense of obtaining property by false pretenses is a distinct one from larceny.[2] Thus, if the owner parts with his property not intending to have it back, but intending that it shall become the property of the wrong-doer, the fact that he was deceived as to the object or purpose for which the wrong-doer obtained the property will not make the offense larceny;[3] nor will it where the owner is deceived as to what he is receiving for the property.[4] It has even been held that where one fraudulently obtains property intended for another,[5] or delivers property, expecting it to be paid for on delivery, and it is fraudulently taken without payment,[6] there is no larceny; but more recent cases do not carry the doctrine to this extent.[7] If the property is obtained by duress, then no title passes, and

[1] Zink v. P., 77 N. Y. 114; Loomis v. P., 67 N. Y. 322; Farrell v. P., 16 Ill. 506; Murphy v. P., 104 Ill. 528; Kellogg v. S., 26 Ohio St. 15; Elliott v. C., 12 Bush, 176; Hill v. S., 57 Wis. 377; C. v. Eichelberger, 119 Pa. St. 254; Pease v. S., 94 Ga. 615; Reg. v. Prince, L. R. 1 C. C. 150.

[2] S. v. Porter, 25 W. Va. 685; Haley v. S., 49 Ark. 147; Williams v. S., 49 Ind. 367; Ross v. P., 5 Hill (N. Y.), 294; Pitts v. S., 5 Tex. Ap. 122; Taylor v. S., 32 Tex. Ap. 110; Reg. v. Wilson, 8 C. & M. 111; Reg. v. Thompson, L. & C. 233; Reg. v. Green, Dears. 323; Reg. v. Essex, Dears. & B. 371; Reg. v. Barnes, 2 Den. 59; Reg. v. Hunt, 8 Cox, 495. In some of these cases the facts are such as would now be deemed to constitute a trick or artifice rendering the wrong-doer guilty of larceny under the principle stated *supra*, § 560, which see. Where a servant induces his master to give him money for a particular expenditure, but intends to and does appropriate the money to his own use, he is not guilty of larceny, the offense being false pretenses: Reg. v. Barnes, 2 Den. 59; Reg. v. Green, Dears. 323; Reg. v. Essex, Dears. & B. 371; Reg. v. Hunt, 8 Cox, 495; Reg. v. Thompson, L. & C. 233.

[3] Collins v. S., 15 Lea, 68.

[4] Reg. v. Adams, 1 Den. 38; Rex v. Jackson, 1 Moody, 119.

[5] Rex v. Adams, Russ. & Ry. 225.

[6] Rex v. Parks, 2 East, P. C. 671.

[7] Reg. v. Russett, 2 Q. B. D. (1892), 312; Harris v. S., 81 Ga. 758; S. v. Hall, 76 Ia. 85. See *supra*, §§ 560, 562.

the offense is larceny.[1] This very technical rule as to larceny, the application of which has been found extremely difficult in practice, is, in some states, abrogated by statute, making it larceny to obtain property by false pretenses, and abolishing the distinction between the two offenses.[2] But even under such a statute, where it appeared that the property was delivered by the agent of the owner under a false representation by the wrong-doer that he had bought the property, it was held that the offense was swindling and not theft.[3] Where the statute makes the obtaining of property by false pretenses larceny, the false pretenses cannot be proven under a common-law indictment for larceny, but the false pretenses must be averred.[4]

V. INTENT.

§ 564. **An essential element.**— The mere unlawful taking and carrying away of the property of another is not larceny unless it is done with a criminal intent or *animo furandi*.[5] Even though the taking away is without the owner's consent and with the intention of converting the property, the act will not be larceny unless it is done with intent to steal.[6] In speaking of this intent various terms are used, such as felonious, fraudulent, etc., but no particular significance attaches to these terms. The question is whether the intent is a criminal one. There may be, therefore, such a wrongful taking as to consti-

[1] Perkins v. S., 65 Ind. 317. And see *supra*, § 559.

[2] Fay v. C., 28 Grat. 912; Davison v. S., 12 Tex. Ap. 214; Atterberry v. S., 19 Tex. Ap. 401; S. v. Vickery, 19 Tex. 326; Hornbeck v. S., 10 Tex. Ap. 408. And proof of obtaining property under false pretenses may be introduced under an indictment for larceny: Anable v. C., 24 Grat. 563; Leftwich v. C., 20 Grat. 716.

[3] Frank v. S., 30 Tex. Ap. 381.

[4] P. v. Dumar, 106 N. Y. 502.

[5] Williams v. S., 44 Ala. 396; Phelps v. P., 55 Ill. 334; Smith v. Shultz, 2 Ill. 490; Moore v. Watts, Beech. Bre. 42; S. v. Campbell, 108 Mo. 611; S. v. Fritchler, 54 Mo. 424; Hart v. S., 57 Ind. 102; Thompson v. P., 4 Neb. 524; Waidley v. S., 34 Neb. 250; Barnes v. S., 40 Neb. 545; S. v. Ledford, 67 N. C. 60; S. v. Butler, 21 S. C. 353; Mullin v. S., 37 Tex. 337; Riojas v. S., 8 Tex. Ap. 49; Landin v. S., 10 Tex. Ap. 63; Taylor v. S., 12 Tex. Ap. 489; Knutson v. S., 14 Tex. Ap. 570; Fletcher v. S., 16 Tex. Ap. 635; Winn v. S., 17 Tex. Ap. 284; White v. S., 23 Tex. Ap. 643; Holsey v. S., 24 Tex. Ap. 35. The question whether the act is done *animo furandi* is for the jury: Reg. v. Farnborough, 2 Q. B. D. (1893), 484.

[6] Witt v. S., 9 Mo. 663; P. v. Raschke, 73 Cal. 378.

tute trespass without the crime of larceny having been committed.[1] If the taking is under a *bona fide* claim of right there is no larceny.[2] Thus, if the purpose of the taking is only to test a right,[3] or to protect one's own property,[4] the act will not be larceny.

§ 565. Under claim of right.— If the taking is under a *bona fide* belief on the part of the person taking that he has a right to the property, the act will not constitute larceny, although the belief is unfounded. Even if the facts would not, if true, justify the taking, nevertheless if they give rise to a belief on the part of defendant that he has a legal right to the property they will disprove the crime of larceny.[5] Any claim of right to the property may be shown as a defense if made in good faith.[6] Mistake as to the ownership of the property may be shown in defendant's behalf.[7] Thus, it will disprove criminal intent of defendant that the property was taken in pursuance

[1] Adams v. S., 45 N. J. 448; Bray v. S., 41 Tex. 203; Gooch v. S., 60 Ark. 5.

[2] Miller v. P., 4 Colo. 182. And see the next section.

[3] Kinnersley v. Orpe, 2 Doug. 517.

[4] Taylor v. Newman, 4 B. & S. 89; McPhail v. S., 9 Tex. Ap. 164.

[5] P. v. Eastman, 77 Cal. 171; P. v. Hillhouse, 80 Mich. 580; P. v. Shultz, — Mich. —, 38 N. W. R. 868; S. v. Deal, 64 N. C. 270; Barnes v. S., 103 Ala. 44; Durrett v. S., 62 Ala. 434; Morningstar v. S., 55 Ala. 148; Morningstar v. S., 59 Ala. 30; Kay v. S., 40 Tex. 29; Smith v. S., 42 Tex. 444; Heath v. S., 7 Tex. Ap. 464. Payment will excuse taking by mortgagor from mortgagee: P. v. Stone, 16 Cal. 369.

[6] S. v. Caddle, 35 W. Va. 73; P. v. Devine, 95 Cal. 227; Baker v. S., 17 Fla. 406; Long v. S., 11 Fla. 295; Mead v. S., 25 Neb. 444; S. v. Homes, 17 Mo. 379; Randle v. S., 49 Ala. 14; Spivey v. S., 26 Ala. 90; S. v. Larson, 85 Ia. 659; Fields v. S., 6 Coldw. 524; Johnson v. S., 41 Tex. 608; Varas v. S., 41 Tex. 527; Camplin v. S., 1 Tex. Ap. 108; Miles v. S., 1 Tex. Ap. 510; Vincent v. S., 9 Tex. Ap. 303; Henry v. S., 9 Tex. Ap. 358; Sigler v. S., 9 Tex. Ap. 427; Evans v. S., 15 Tex. Ap. 31; Harris v. S., 17 Tex. Ap. 177; Small v. S., 18 Tex. Ap. 336; Boyd v. S., 18 Tex. Ap. 339; Howard v. S., 25 Tex. Ap. 602. Thus, declarations of defendant, made while claiming to be in search of a lost animal, were held admissible in his behalf in a prosecution for taking an animal which he claimed to have taken under the belief that it was his own: S. v. Daley, 53 Vt. 442. Where one takes under leave of a pretended agent of the owner, the question is whether he believed such person to be the agent: Heskew v. S., 18 Tex. Ap. 275.

[7] Long v. S., 11 Fla. 295; Parks v. S., 29 Tex. Ap. 597; Reg. v. Halford, 11 Cox, 88. If one is charged with wrongfully taking his own property from the possession of another who has a right to possession, ignorance of such right, or the belief that it is terminated, will constitute a defense: S. v. De Witt, 32 Mo. 571; Taylor v. S., 7 Tex. Ap. 659.

of a supposed purchase.[1] So if the prisoner believes the property to have been delivered to him as his own,[2] or that the property was lost and abandoned,[3] there will be no larceny. One who disposes of the property of another under the well-founded though erroneous belief that he is authorized so to do is not guilty of larceny.[4] But the belief of ownership of right which will constitute a defense must be an honest belief and not a mere impression or pretense.[5] It is said in one case that the defendant might testify that he held a claim against the owner of the property taken and took the property with the belief that he could set off his claim against the action of the owner for the value of the property.[6] But with better reason it is said that the supposition of the thief that the article stolen belonged to one indebted to him, and the intention to appropriate it to the payment of his debt, would not, even if true, disprove larceny.[7]

§ **566. Intent to appropriate; temporary use.**— The essential intent on the part of the wrong-doer must be to appropriate the property to his own use. Though he interferes unlawfully with the property, yet if his purpose is not to appropriate it he is not guilty of larceny.[8] Thus, where accused took and carried away muskets to which he had no right, in order to prevent others from using them against himself and his friends, it was held that he was not guilty of larceny.[9] There must be an intention to deprive the owner permanently of his property, and taking for a mere temporary use will not constitute larceny.[10] Thus, it has been held that one who, for the purpose

Bond v. S., 23 Tex. Ap. 180; Ray v. S., 13 Tex. Ap. 51; Dreyer v. S., 11 Tex. Ap. 631.

[2] S. v. Shores, 31 W. Va. 491.

[3] S. v. Swayze, 11 Oreg. 357.

[4] S. v. Barrackmore, 47 Ia. 684; Chambers v. S., 62 Miss. 108.

[5] Morrisette v. S., 77 Ala. 71; S. v. Bond, 8 Ia. 540; S. v. Thompson, 95 N. C. 596; Peck v. S., 9 Tex. Ap. 70; Reg. v. Wade, 11 Cox, 549. And the claim must be of a present, not a prospective, right: S. v. Jones, 2 Dev. & B. 544.

[6] S. v. Williams, 95 Mo. 247.

[7] C. v. Stebbins, 8 Gray, 492; Gettinger v. S., 13 Neb. 308. As to whether a mistake of law would excuse, see the general discussion under that head, *supra*, § 132.

[8] To take from an officer warrants under which he has seized property, with the purpose of thus depriving him of his authority, does not constitute larceny: Reg. v. Bailey, L. R. 1 C. C. 347.

[9] U. S. v. Durkee, 1 McAll. 196.

[10] Rex v. Phillips, 2 East, P. C. 662; Reg. v. Guernsey, 1 F. & F. 394; Reg. v. Holloway, 2 C. & K. 942; Rex v.

of escaping with stolen property, takes a horse not intending to keep it but only to use it temporarily, is not guilty of larceny of the horse.[1] So it has been held as to other similar temporary appropriations.[2] But some recent cases give to this doctrine a more reasonable interpretation, and hold that if the person taking the property does not intend that it shall be returned to the owner, but to abandon it after his temporary use is ended, thus, so far as he is concerned, intending to deprive the owner permanently of his property, the act will be larceny, even though the owner subsequently recovers possession.[3] And it may be stated as a general proposition that an intent to deprive the owner permanently of his property is sufficient to constitute the necessary criminal intent in larceny.[4]

§ 567. Pecuniary advantage without permanent appropriation.— Although intent to appropriate is essential, yet such appropriation may be made even though there is a purpose to return the property to the owner, if the purpose is to make use of the temporary possession and subsequent return with a view to obtaining a pecuniary advantage. Thus, one who takes another's property intending to return it when a reward shall be offered is guilty of larceny;[5] so is one who

Dickinson, Russ. & Ry. 420. Wrongfully pawning property of another, intending to redeem and return it, may not be larceny: Reg. v. Phetheon, 9 C. & P. 552. But there must be the ability as well as the intent to redeem: Reg. v. Medland, 5 Cox, 292; Reg. v. Trebilcock, Dears. & B. 453. And if in consequence of the wrongful act the property is lost to the owner, the act is larceny: Truslow v. S., 95 Tenn. 189.

[1] Schultz v. S., 30 Tex. Ap. 94; Rex v. Crump, 1 C. & P. 658; S. v. York, 5 Harr. 493. And see Mahoney v. S., 33 Tex. Ap. 388.

[2] Dove v. S., 37 Ark. 261; In re Mutchler, 55 Kan. 164; P. v. Brown, 105 Cal. 66; S. v. Ryan, 12 Nev. 401; Umphrey v. S., 63 Ind. 223; Lucas v. S., 33 Tex. Ap. 290; Bryant v. S., 25 Tex. Ap. 75, 8 S. W. R. 937; Reg. v. Gardner, L. & C. 243.

[3] S. v. Davis, 38 N. J. 176, 1 Am. Cr. R. 398; S. v. South, 28 N. J. 28; P. v. Flynn, 7 Utah, 378. In Alabama one taking for temporary use without the consent of the owner or person having control may be convicted of larceny on complaint of the owner. Consent must be negatived in the indictment: Blackman v. S., 98 Ala. 77. But it is not necessary to allege that the prosecution is on the owner's complaint. That the prosecution is not by him is matter of defense: Bellinger v. S., 92 Ala. 86; Blackman v. S., 98 Ala. 77.

[4] Williams v. S., 52 Ala. 411.

[5] Berry v. S., 31 Ohio St. 219; C. v. Mason, 105 Mass. 163; Baker v. S., 58 Ark. 513; P. v. Wiley, 3 Hill (N. Y.), 194. But where defendant took up a stray horse having heard who was the owner, with intent to return him to such owner, *held*, that he was not guilty of larceny: Micheaux v. S., 30 Tex. Ap. 660.

takes property with the purpose of selling it back to the owner.[1] So, the taking of property with the intent to assert a lien for work pretended to be done upon it, or to receive pay for such work, is larceny.[2] But there must be a taking from the possession of the owner in such case; and if the act is that of a servant in removing the property of the owner from one place to another without taking possession of it, larceny is not committed, although there is an intent to fraudulently receive pay for work not really done.[3] It has already been said that one may be guilty of larceny in taking his own property from another with intent to charge such other therewith.[4]

§ 568. **For the thief's benefit; lucri causa.**— Some expressions have been used in text-books and opinions indicating that, to constitute larceny, the taking must be with a view to the benefit of the wrong-doer, or, as it is sometimes expressed, the taking must be *lucri causa*.[5] There may be some reason for this doctrine in the attempt to distinguish between larceny and malicious trespass, and for the purpose of making such distinction it may be proper to say that an intent merely to deprive the owner of his property is not sufficient in larceny; but where the intention of the wrong-doer is to deprive the owner of his property by taking it from him, and such intention is carried out by an act which constitutes a taking and carrying away, it certainly ought to be immaterial whether the motive of the wrong-doer is benefit to himself or only injury to the owner, and the great weight of authority supports such a proposition. For instance, where the prisoner, for the purpose of preventing a horse from being used in evidence against an accomplice, took it from the prosecutor's stable and killed it by backing it into a coal pit, it was held that the offense was larceny;[6] and this

[1] Reg. v. Hall, 2 C. & K. 947; Reg. v. Manning, Dears. 21.

[2] Fort v. S., 82 Ala. 50; Reg. v. Richards, 1 C. & K. 532.

[3] Reg. v. Poole, Dears. & B. 345; Rex v. Webb, 1 Moody, 431.

[4] *Supra*, § 547.

[5] 4 Bl. Com. 232; Reg. v. Godfrey, 8 C. & P. 563; S. v. Hawkins, 8 Port. 461; U. S. v. Durkee, 1 McAll. 196; Pence v. S., 110 Ind. 95.

[6] Rex v. Cabbage, Russ. & Ry. 292. (Some of the judges, however, dissented, on the ground that there was no intention on the part of the prisoner to benefit himself.) And see Reg. v. Jones, 2 C. & K. 236. Where a postal servant, to conceal a mistake in sorting letters, threw two letters containing money into a water-closet, *held*, that he was guilty of larceny from the mails: Reg. v. Wynn, 2 C. & K. 859. But see Reg. v. Godfrey, 8 C. & P. 563.

doctrine has been generally followed in the United States.[1] But it still is true that there must be an intent to take the property and not merely to injure it.[2]

§ 569. **Intent contemporaneous with act.**— It is a general principle already discussed under the head of criminal intent, that the criminal intent must concur with the criminal act, and that a subsequent criminal intent will not render criminal an act which was not criminal when done. This principle finds various applications in the law of larceny. Thus, it has already been seen that if one having obtained possession of property for a lawful purpose subsequently conceives the intent to wrongfully appropriate it and does so, his act is not larceny;[3] while if, though he makes pretense of a lawful purpose in obtaining possession, he really intends at that time to wrongfully appropriate the property, larceny is committed.[4] The distinction hinges on whether at the time the possession was taken there was an intent to steal.[5] But if the criminal intent is conceived at any time before the taking and carrying away is completed, it is sufficient.[6] Moreover, while the intent must have existed when the act was done, it may be shown by subsequent acts and conduct.[7] Whether the felonious intent was contemporaneous with the procuring of possession or subsequently conceived is for the jury.[8]

[1] P. v. Jaurez, 28 Cal. 380; Warden v. S., 60 Miss. 638; Hamilton v. S., 35 Miss. 214; Delk v. S., 64 Miss. 77; S. v. Caddle, 35 W. Va. 73; Keely v. S., 14 Ind. 36; Dignowitty v. S., 17 Tex. 521; Stegall v. S., 32 Tex. Ap. 100.

[2] S. v. Hawkins, 8 Port. 461; McDaniel v. S., 8 Smed. & M. 401; S. v. Ware, 10 Ala. 814.

[3] *Supra*, § 549.

[4] *Supra*, § 562.

[5] P. v. Cruger, 102 N. Y. 510; Wilson v. P., 39 N. Y. 459; P. v. Morino, 85 Cal. 515; P. v. Abbott, 53 Cal. 284; Hill v. S., 57 Wis. 377; Lyon v. S., 61 Ala. 224; Weaver v. S., 77 Ala. 26; Beatty v. S., 61 Miss. 18; P. v. Taugher, 102 Mich. 598; S. v. Shermer, 55 Mo. 83; S. v. Stone, 68 Mo. 101; S. v. Larson, 85 Ia. 659; Ennis v. S., 3 Greene (Ia.), 67; Smith v. Shultz, 2 Ill. 490; Fulton v. S., 13 Ark. 168; Quitzow v. S., 1 Tex. Ap. 65; Pitts v. S., 3 Tex. Ap. 210; Dow v. S., 12 Tex. Ap. 343; Wolf v. S., 14 Tex. Ap. 210; Morrison v. S., 17 Tex. Ap. 34; Hernandez v. S., 20 Tex. Ap. 151; Wilson v. S., 20 Tex. Ap. 662; Roberts v. S., 21 Tex. Ap. 460; Porter v. S., 23 Tex. Ap. 295; Guest v. S., 24 Tex. Ap. 235; Stokely v. S., 24 Tex. Ap. 509; Boyd v. S., 24 Tex. Ap. 570; Cunningham v. S., 27 Tex. Ap. 479; Rumbo v. S., 28 Tex. Ap. 30; Nichols v. S., 28 Tex. Ap. 105; Rex v. Leigh, 2 East, P. C. 694; Rex v. Charlewood, 2 East, P. C. 689; Reg. v. Matthews, 28 L. T. 645; Rex v. Mucklow, 1 Moody, 160.

[6] S. v. Anderson, 25 Minn. 66.

[7] S. v. Wood, 46 Ia. 116; C. v. Rubin, — Mass. —, 43 N. E. R. 200.

[8] Hill v. S., 57 Wis. 377.

§ 570. Intent relating back.— There is authority for the proposition that when the original taking is wrongful, though without criminal intent, and subsequently, by reason of the possession thus obtained, the wrong-doer is able to and does convert the property to his own use, his subsequent wrongful intent will be coupled with his original act so as to make the original taking larceny.[1] But the cases cited in support of this proposition can be better explained by the suggestion that the original taking was not wrongful and was not a trespass, there being some mistake or doubt as to the actual possession of the property, and that the wrongful taking was after all contemporaneous with the formation of the wrongful intent.[2] The cases are thus rendered analogous with those where the wrongdoer is a mere custodian, and subsequently is guilty of larceny in the wrongful appropriation of the property which up to such appropriation was deemed in the possession of the owner.[3] In the same manner are to be explained the cases which hold that one who, in taking property which he intends to steal, also takes, without his knowledge, other property incident to or contained in that which he intends to take, is guilty also of larceny of the property thus unconsciously taken, by appropriating it when he finds it in his possession.[4]

§ 571. Lost property.— The proposition of a preceding section to the effect that the attempt to steal must be contemporaneous with the taking is illustrated by the rule as to the taking of lost property. The finder of such property, who takes possession thereof, becomes a bailee, and as such his possession is rightful. If, having thus a rightful possession, he subsequently converts the property to his own use in derogation of the owner's right, even though, upon learning who the owner is, he decides to conceal the property and prevent the restoration of it, he is not guilty of larceny, because there is no wrongful tak-

[1] C. v. White, 11 Cush. 483; S. v. Coombs, 55 Me. 477. And see C. v. Rubin, — Mass. —, 43 N. E. R. 200. Thus, where one driving his own animals inadvertently drove away the animal of another, but when he discovered the fact appropriated the other animal to his own use, he was held guilty of larceny: Reg. v. Riley, Dears. 149. Taking and carrying away, followed by felonious appropriation, is enough: S. v. Davenport, 38 S. C. 348.

[2] P. v. Call, 1 Denio, 120.

[3] *Supra*, § 556.

[4] C. v. Lawless, 103 Mass. 425; Stevens v. S., 19 Neb. 647.

ing;[1] and the proposition as generally stated is that, to make the finder guilty of larceny, he must have conceived a fraudulent purpose of converting the property to his own use at the time he took possession of it.[2] In determining whether there was a contemporaneous intention to fraudulently appropriate in disregard of the rights of the owner, the fact that the finder knew or had reasonable means of knowing the owner is important.[3] There is no obligation on the part of the finder to take steps to ascertain the owner and to restore the property to him, and a failure to do so will not constitute larceny.[4] The question whether or not the finder believes or has ground to believe, when he takes possession of the property, that the owner can be found, is important in determining whether there is at that time a criminal intent. For, even if he then intends to appropriate the property, yet if he has no reasonable means of knowing the owner he is not guilty of larceny.[5] But it is immaterial that the finder does not know the name of the owner if he knows the person or has reason to know that the owner will appear or be ascertained.[6] The intent of the finder is to be determined as a fact by the jury from all the circumstances and defendant's conduct.[7] But after allowing to the

[1] P. v. Anderson, 14 Johns. 294; Tyler v. P., Beech. Bre. 293; Lane v. P., 10 Ill. 305; Griggs v. S., 58 Ala. 425; Allen v. S., 91 Ala. 19; Bailey v. S., 52 Ind. 462; Starck v. S., 63 Ind. 285; S. v. Conway, 18 Mo. 321; S. v. England, 8 Jones, 399.

[2] Ransom v. S., 22 Conn. 153; Weaver v. S., 77 Ala. 26; Smith v. S., 103 Ala. 40; Beckham v. S., 100 Ala. 15; Lamb v. S., 40 Neb. 312; Martinez v. S., 16 Tex. Ap. 122; Reg. v. Christopher, Bell, 27; Reg. v. Yorke, 2 C. & K. 841; Reg. v. Preston, 2 Den. 353.

[3] Allen v. S., 91 Ala. 19; Lane v. P., 10 Ill. 305; S. v. Cummings, 33 Conn. 260; S. v. Taylor, 25 Ia. 273; Reg. v. Mole, 1 C. & K. 417; Reg. v. Dixon, Dears. 580.

[4] S. v. Dean, 49 Ia. 73; Hunt v. C., 13 Grat. 757; Perrin v. C., 87 Va. 554; Reg. v. Dixon, Dears. 580; Reg. v. Knight, 12 Cox, 102. By the law of Vermont the finder is bound to advertise the property, and if he conceals or converts it he commits larceny: S. v. Jenkins, 2 Tyler, 377. By the statute of Missouri it is made larceny to convert the found property within a year after posting notice of it, and an indictment for conversion before posting will not be sustained: S. v. Casteel, 53 Mo. 124.

[5] Reg. v. Glyde, L. R. 1 C. C. 139; Reg. v. Thurborn, 1 Den. 387; Reg. v. Deaves, 11 Cox, 227.

[6] Brooks v. S., 35 Ohio St. 46; S. v. Martin, 28 Mo. 530; S. v. Casteel, 53 Mo. 124; S. v. McCann, 19 Mo. 249; S. v. White, 126 Mo. 591; Reg. v. West, Dears. 402.

[7] Ransom v. S., 22 Conn. 153. If the found property is marked with the owner's name, and the finder knows that some one has lost such

proposition, which requires that the wrongful intent shall be contemporaneous with the taking, its full force, it still remains true, as shown by many cases, that the finder of lost property in converting it to his own use, having knowledge or reasonable means of knowledge as to who is the owner, and with the intention to deprive the owner thereof, is guilty of larceny.[1] Where a father received from his children property found by them, knowing it to be lost, he was held to have assumed the same relations to the owner as the finder.[2] The question of knowledge or means of knowledge as to the owner is one of fact, but there is no legal conclusion created by the fact as to the guilt or innocence of the finder. The question of intent is for the jury.[3] The intent may be proved by acts after the finding, so far as they are relevant for that purpose.[4] The difference between finding lost property and taking property not lost, but only temporarily and inadvertently left by the owner, has been already considered;[5] with a view to this distinction, the place of finding is material as indicating whether the goods were lost or only left by mistake.[6] Statutes providing for the taking up of estrays sometimes provide that after a certain length of time and on certain conditions the title shall vest in the party taking up; in such case larceny by such party may be charged by alleging the conversion by him before the title had vested in him according to law.[7]

§ 572. **Intent; how charged and proved or disproved.**— In the absence of some statutory requirement (such as is found in Texas),[8] it is not necessary to allege specifically the intent, but the statement that the defendant feloniously did steal, take

property, he is sufficiently put on notice of the ownership so as to make the appropriation larceny: Stepp v. S., 31 Tex. Ap. 349.

[1] S. v. Roper, 3 Dev. 473; S. v. Ferguson, 2 McMull. 502; Baker v. S., 29 Ohio St. 184; Brooks v. S., 35 Ohio St. 46; S. v. Weston, 9 Conn. 527; S. v Levy, 23 Minn. 104; S. v. Boyd, 36 Minn. 538; P. v. Buelna, 81 Cal. 135; C. v. Titus, 116 Mass. 42, 1 Am. Cr. R. 416 and note; Reg. v. Peters, 1 C. & K. 245; Reg. v. Reed, Car. & M. 306; S. v. Pratt, 20 Ia. 267; S. v. Bolander, 71 Ia. 706; S. v. Clifford, 14 Nev. 72; Lawrence v. S., 20 Tex. Ap. 536; Reed v. S., 8 Tex. Ap. 40; Neely v. S., 8 Tex. Ap. 64; Reg. v. Kerr, 8 C. & P. 176; Reg. v. Moore, L. & C. 1.

[2] Allen v. S., 91 Ala. 19.

[3] Ransom v. S., 22 Conn. 153.

[4] C. v. Titus, 116 Mass. 42; S. v. Arkle, 116 N. C. 1017.

[5] See cases *supra*, § 545.

[6] Griggs v. S., 58 Ala. 425; Rountree v. S., 58 Ala. 381.

[7] Smith v. S., 85 Ind. 553; S. v. Williams, 19 Mo. 389.

[8] S. v. Sherlock, 26 Tex. 106; Ridgeway v. S., 41 Tex. 231; Muldrew v.

and carry away, etc., is sufficient.[1] The necessary formalities of the indictment in this respect will be discussed in another section.[2] In proving criminal intent the prosecution must go further than to merely show a taking and an appropriation. Thus, where the evidence shows a trespass, but the circumstances do not indicate a felonious purpose, larceny is not established.[3] The question whether there was a felonious intent in the wrongful act is for the jury.[4] While some cases seem to require that the act must be clandestinely done, or accompanied with an effort of concealment in order to show fraudulent intent,[5] yet this is not the proper view. The fact that the property is taken openly and in the presence of others may be considered as tending to show want of criminal intent and as indicating some claim or belief of right,[6] but such conduct is not conclusive.[7] Subsequent acts of accused may be shown as throwing light on the intention with which the property was taken.[8] Any evidence tending to show that defendant was acting under supposed authority and in good faith may be received.[9] It is sufficient evidence of intent that the felonious taking is without color of right or excuse, and with the knowledge by the person taking that he has no authority.[10] But the mere fact of buying goods which are stolen, with notice of the

S., 12 Tex. Ap. 617; Tallant v. S., 14 Tex. Ap. 234; Peralto v. S., 17 Tex. Ap. 578.

[1] C. v. Butler, 144 Pa. St. 568; S. v. Hackett, 47 Minn. 425; Gandolpho v. S., 33 Ind. 439; S. v Jones, 41 La. An. 784.

[2] *Infra*, § 608.

[3] McCourt v. P., 64 N. Y. 583; Mason v. S., 32 Ark. 238; Winn v. S., 11 Tex. Ap. 304.

[4] P. v. Carabin, 14 Cal. 438; S. v. Watson, 7 S. C. 63; S. v. Gaither, 72 N. C. 458; Reg. v. Hore, 3 F. & F. 315.

[5] Long v. S., 11 Fla. 295; O'Bannon v. S., 76 Ga. 29; Stuckey v. S., 7 Tex. Ap. 174; Ainsworth v. S., 11 Tex. Ap. 339. And see cases in note 3, *supra*.

[6] 4 Bl. Com. 232; 3 Chit. Cr. L. 927; Hall v. C., 78 Va. 678; Johnson v. S., 73 Ala. 523; Causey v. S., 79 Ga. 564; S. v. Shores, 31 W. Va. 491; Littlejohn v. S., 59 Miss. 273; S. v. Fitzpatrick, 9 Houst. 385; McDaniel v. S., 33 Tex. 419; Gardiner v. S., 33 Tex. 692; Herber v. S., 7 Tex. 69; Seymore v. S., 12 Tex. Ap. 391.

[7] P. v. Hansen, 84 Cal. 291; Booth v. C., 4 Grat. 525; Vaughn v. C., 10 Grat. 758; S. v. Fisher, 70 N. C. 78; S. v. Powell, 103 N. C. 424; Barnes v. S., 103 Ala. 44; McMullen v. S., 53 Ala. 531. It is not essential to show an attempt to conceal: S. v. Hill, 114 N. C. 780.

[8] Quinn v. P., 123 Ill. 333; P. v. Hansen, 84 Cal. 291; Duckett v. S., 65 Ga. 369; S. v. Powell, 103 N. C. 424; S. v. Farrow, Phill. 161; Gardner v. S., 55 N. J. 17.

[9] S. v. Matthews, 20 Mo. 55; S. v. Gresser, 19 Mo. 247.

[10] S. v. Rivers, 60 Ia. 381.

fact, is not sufficient to show criminal intent.[1] The fact of voluntarily returning the property, or offering to do so, may be considered as tending to disprove felonious intent in the taking.[2] But the circumstances may rebut any presumption in defendant's favor from such fact.[3] And if larceny is committed in the taking, a return of the property or payment therefor will not purge the offense.[4] But in Texas, by statute, a voluntary return of the property within a reasonable time will reduce the punishment to that of a misdemeanor.[5] So in Michigan, restoration of or satisfaction for the property may be shown, in case of a first offense, to reduce it to a misdemeanor.[6] The general doctrines as to how criminal intent is to be disproven[7] are applicable here; for instance, intoxication such as to show that defendant was incapable of entertaining a specific criminal intent,[8] or kleptomania,[9] may be shown. The doctrine that a person taking provisions for the purpose of saving himself from starvation is acting under such legal necessity as to excuse the act is wholly without support in adjudications, and is mentioned by writers of text-books only to be condemned as unfounded in law or morals.[10]

§ 573. Connection with the offense; principal and accessory; receiver.— The general doctrines as to principal and accessory[11] are applicable here, except that, although petit larceny was deemed a felony at common law,[12] no accessories therein were recognized,[13] the crime being in this, as in some other

[1] Parchman v. S., 2 Tex. Ap. 228.

[2] Anderson v. S., 25 Tex. Ap. 593; Georgia v. Kepford, 45 Ia. 48.

[3] Stepp v. S., 31 Tex. Ap. 349; Harris v. S., 29 Tex. Ap. 101.

[4] S. v. Scott, 64 N. C. 586; Truslow v. S., 95 Tenn. 189; Trafton v. S., 5 Tex. Ap. 480.

[5] Owen v. S., 44 Tex. 248; Ingle v. S., 1 Tex. Ap. 307; Brill v. S., 1 Tex. Ap. 572; Bennett v. S., 17 Tex. Ap. 143; Bennett v. S., 28 Tex. Ap. 342. The return may be voluntary, though induced by fear of prosecution and punishment: Allen v. S., 12 Tex. Ap. 190; Bird v. S., 16 Tex. Ap. 528 (apparently overruling Stephenson v. S., 4 Tex. Ap. 591). If the return is only on detection it is not voluntary: Boze v. S., 31 Tex. Ap 347. The return must be of the property as taken, not in an altered form: Horseman v. S., 43 Tex. 353; Grant v. S., 2 Tex. Ap. 163. Where the indictment was for larceny of money, *held*, that a return of the pocket-book need not be considered: Wheeler v. S., 15 Tex. Ap. 607.

[6] P. Hubbard, 86 Mich. 440.

[7] *Supra*, ch. 6.

[8] Chatham v. S., 92 Ala. 47.

[9] Looney v. S., 10 Tex. Ap. 520; Harris v. S., 18 Tex. Ap. 287.

[10] 4 Bl. Com. 31; 1 Hale, P. C. 54, 565; 1 Hawk. P. C., ch. 33, § 20; *supra*, § 136.

[11] *Supra*, §§ 204–210.

[12] *Supra*, § 581.

[13] Ward v. P., 3 Hill (N. Y.), 395;

respects, like a misdemeanor, even where it is not made a misdemeanor by statute. A few illustrations of the application of the general principles on the subject may be mentioned here. One may be principal in the offense though he does not participate in the act, if present for the purpose of aiding and abetting,[1] or if he joins in carrying out the criminal plan, though not immediately present.[2] An employee who assists his employer in the wrongful taking, with knowledge of the purpose for which it is done, is liable as a principal.[3] To be a principal one must have taken the property or assisted in the taking,[4] and all persons who counsel, aid and abet, or advise, are equally guilty as accessories before the fact with those who actually commit the offense.[5] One who forms or combines in the general plan and assists in receiving and disposing of the property is a principal, though not present at the taking.[6] But if he merely encourages the general object and afterwards receives the property, he is guilty only as an accessory.[7] The receiver of stolen goods with knowledge that they are stolen is guilty of a substantive offense, to be hereafter discussed;[8] but he is not guilty of larceny, not having participated therein, although he had knowledge at the time of receiving the goods that they were stolen.[9] Nor in such cases is the receiver of stolen goods an accessory after the fact to the larceny.[10]

S. v. Barden, 1 Dev. 518; S. v. Stroud, 95 N. C. 626; S. v. Henderson, 35 La. An. 45; Lasington's Case, Cro. Eliz. 750; 1 Bish. Cr. L., § 680. And see *supra*, § 210.

1 C. v. Lucas, 2 Allen, 170; S. v. Wilson, 30 Conn. 500; Hogsertt v. S., 40 Miss. 522.

2 Wells v. S., 4 Tex. Ap. 20; Reg. v. Murphy, 6 Cox, 340.

3 Taylor v. S., 5 Tex. Ap. 529; Hannon v. S., 5 Tex. Ap. 549; Murphy v. S., 6 Tex. Ap. 42ι.

4 Wright v. S., 18 Tex. Ap. 358. If two are indicted as principals, one only may be convicted, it appearing that the other is accessory only: S. v. Clayton, 11 Rich. 581.

5 S. v. Gaston, 73 N. C. 93. There may be such guilt although the property is recovered before division is made and accused receives none of it: C. v. Hollister, 157 Pa. St. 13.

6 S. v. Honig, 78 Mo. 249; Watson v. S., 21 Tex. Ap. 598.

7 Vincent v. S., 9 Tex. Ap. 46.

8 *Infra*, § 713.

9 P. v. Maxwell, 24 Cal. 14; S. v. Calvin, 22 N. J. 207; Hall v. S., 3 Ohio St. 575; S. v. Empey, 79 Ia. 460; Cohea v. S., 9 Tex. Ap. 173; McAfee v. S., 14 Tex. Ap. 668; Clayton v. S., 15 Tex. Ap. 348; Prator v. S., 15 Tex. Ap. 363; Trimble v. S., 18 Tex. Ap. 632; Phillips v. S., 19 Tex. Ap. 158; Collins v. S., 24 Tex. Ap. 141; Boyd v. S., 24 Tex. Ap. 570; Buchanan v. S., 26 Tex. Ap. 52.

10 P. v. Stakem, 40 Cal. 599. And see full discussion of the question

VI. Compound Larcenies.

§ 574. Elements of aggravation.— Larceny is involved in other common-law crimes, such as robbery or burglary, which are elsewhere discussed, and the relation of the stealing to the higher offense is considered.[1] But by statutory provisions found in England and in most of the states, larceny, under certain specified circumstances of aggravation, is punishable to a greater extent than where such circumstances do not exist, and these statutory forms of larceny are designated as compound larceny as distinguished from simple larceny.[2] The circumstances of aggravation usually mentioned are the taking from the person, and the taking from a house, dwelling, building, store-house or other place specially mentioned. These aggravated larcenies are sometimes declared grand larceny without regard to the value of the property stolen, and in other statutes made punishable by heavier penalties than simple larceny.

§ 575. From the person.— To constitute larceny from the person the property must have been under the protection of the person.[3] The fact that the one from whom the property is taken is asleep does not prevent larceny being from the person.[4] To constitute this offense it is not essential that any violence be used, nor fraud. The taking of the property from the hand is enough, even if there is no resistance.[5] The offense is thus in some cases distinguished from robbery.[6] To constitute larceny from the person the article must be completely removed from the person and all connection with the person severed.[7] The offense is sometimes described by statutes so as to involve the idea of a secret taking without the owner's knowledge.[8] The offense of stealing from the person is an in-

[1] See as to robbery, § 466; and as to burglary, § 505. A larceny committed in burglary is not a simple but an aggravated larceny: Pitcher v. P., 16 Mich. 142.

[2] 4 Bl. Com. 239; 2 Bish. Cr. L., § 892.

[3] Reg. v. Hamilton, 8 C. & P. 49; Reg. v. Selway, 8 Cox, 235.

[4] Hall v. P., 39 Mich. 717; Nichols v. S., 28 Tex. Ap. 105. And see under the subject of receiving stolen goods, *infra*, § 713.

Reg. v. Hamilton, 8 C. & P. 49; Rex v. Thomas, Car. C. L. 295.

[5] C. v. Dimond, 3 Cush. 235; Johnson v. C., 24 Grat. 555; S. v. Chavis, 34 S. C. 132; Green v. S., 28 Tex. Ap. 493.

[6] Reg. v. Hughes, 2 C. & K. 214.

[7] Harrison v. P., 50 N. Y. 518; McLin v. S., 29 Tex. Ap. 171; Rex v. Thompson, 1 Moody, 78; Reg. v. Simpson, Dears. 421.

[8] S. v. Chavis, 34 S. C. 132; Powell

dependent substantive offense, distinct from that of larceny, and as such must be charged and proven,[1] and, as usually defined, it is a felony without regard to the value of the property stolen.[2] The allegations of the indictment must show not merely larceny, but the taking from the person by some of the means specified in the statute.[3] But it is sufficient, where the offense consists merely in the taking from the person, to say that the property was on the person[4] or was taken from the person,[5] as the statute may provide. The offense being distinct from that of larceny, it is not necessary to allege the felonious stealing, taking and carrying away as required in the common-law indictment for larceny, but it will be sufficient to charge the act as described in the statute.[6] The offense necessarily includes, however, as usually described, the offense of larceny,[7] and it is necessarily included in the offense of robbery.[8]

§ 576. **From the dwelling-house.**— The crime of larceny from a dwelling-house may be committed in any dwelling which would be so considered under the law with reference to burglary; that is, the term includes any building occupied to dwell and sleep in, or any apartment connected therewith under the same roof.[9] But perhaps it does not include buildings separate from the dwelling, although within the curtilage.[10] Property in the house is within its protection, although the owner is there, also, if he is asleep.[11] But money in the pocket of a person in the house is under the protection of the person and not of the house, and therefore the stealing thereof would not be larceny from the dwelling-house.[12] Clothing hanging on the railing of the outer edge of the piazza is not within the protection of the

v. S., 88 Ga. 32; or without resistance: Woodard v. S., 9 Tex. Ap. 412. In such case an indictment simply charging stealing and carrying away privately from the person is not sufficient: Kerry v. S., 17 Tex. Ap. 178.

[1] King v. S., 54 Ga. 184; McEntee v. S., 24 Wis. 43; Harris v. S., 17 Tex. Ap. 132; Gage v. S., 22 Tex. Ap. 123; Nichols v. S., 28 Tex. Ap. 105.

[2] Brown v. S., 34 Neb. 448.

[3] S. v. Lawrence, 20 Oreg. 236.

[4] C. v. Bonner, 97 Mass. 587.

[5] S. v. Lee Ping Bow, 10 Oreg. 27.

[6] Randall v. S., 53 N. J. 485; Powell v. S., 88 Ga. 32.

[7] Fanning v. S., 12 Lea, 651; S. v. Gleason, 56 Ia. 203; S. v. Taylor, 3 Oreg. 10.

[8] S. v. Graff, 66 Ia. 482.

[9] S. v. Clark, 89 Mo. 423.

[10] Rex v. Turner, 6 C. & P. 407.

[11] Reg. v. Hamilton, 8 C. & P. 49; Rex v. Thomas, Car. C. L. 295. But see Hall v. People, 39 Mich. 717.

[12] Rex v. Owen, 2 East. P. C. 645. And see Roberts v. S., 83 Ga. 369; C. v. Lester, 129 Mass. 101.

house in such sense that stealing thereof is larceny from the dwelling.[1] If the goods are in the protection of the house, the stealing of them by the owner or occupier of the house may be larceny in the dwelling-house,[2] and one who is stopping in the house by invitation may be guilty of larceny in the dwelling.[3] But where the statute provides a punishment for entering a dwelling and committing larceny, the entry must be with a criminal intent.[4] If the statutory offense is stealing in the dwelling-house, persons being therein and put in fear, it must appear that the persons were put in fear by the prisoner.[5] The indictment for the offense need not describe the particular articles; a general allegation is sufficient under statutory provisions.[6] But if the articles are particularly described as to ownership, the proof must correspond.[7] The offense includes a simple larceny.[8] The degree of the offense is not usually made to depend upon the value of the goods.[9]

§ 577. **From the house.**— Some statutes provide a punishment for larceny committed "from the house" or "in the house;"[10] and the term "house," as thus used, is not limited to a dwelling-house.[11] But where the statute refers to a house within the curtilage, the rule is different.[12] A tent is not a house within the meaning of such a statute.[13] It is sufficient if the property is within the house,[14] although it would seem that if it is personally under the control of the owner it is not in the protection of the house, but under the protection of the

1 Henry v. S., 39 Ala. 679. And see Martinez v. S., cited under the next section.

2 Rex v. Taylor, Russ. & Ry. 418; Rex v. Carroll, 1 Moody, 89; Reg. v. Bowden, 1 C. & K. 147.

3 Point v. S., 37 Ala. 148.

4 S. v. Chambers, 6 Ala. 855; Parks v. S., 66 Ga. 192.

5 Rex v. Ethrington, 2 East, P. C. 635.

6 Reg. v. Johnson, L. & C. 489.

7 Reg. v. Ashley, 1 C. & K. 198. Proof of taking of a portion of several articles charged will be sufficient: C. v. Byce, 8 Gray, 461.

8 Moore v. S., 40 Ala. 49; S. v. Mikesell, 70 Ia. 176.

9 S. v. Ramelsburg, 30 Mo. 26; S. v. Brown, 75 Mo. 317; S. v. Kennedy, 88 Mo. 341; S. v. Treadwell, 54 Kan. 513.

10 Stanley v. S., 58 Ga. 430.

11 Simmons v. S., 73 Ga. 609. The term "dwelling" sufficiently indicates a house: S. v. O'Neil, 21 Oreg. 170.

12 Inman v. S., 54 Ga. 219; Middleton v. S., 53 Ga. 248.

13 Callahan v. S., 41 Tex. 43.

14 Irvin v. S., 37 Tex. 412. It is not necessary that it belong to or be under the control of the owner of the house if the ownership of the article is charged as in another: Hill v. S., 41 Tex. 157.

person.[1] But if it is even temporarily out of the personal control of the owner, it is within the protection of the house.[2] If the stolen property is taken while hanging outside of the house, the larceny is not from the house.[3] The offense is one as to the property taken, rather than as to the building from which it is taken.[4] In the indictment, the house should be described by the name of the owner;[5] but possession and occupancy are sufficient to support such allegation.[6] In Texas the statute with reference to larceny from the house excepts cases of larceny by domestic servants employed therein, and such offense is simply theft.[7] But a workman hired for a special service, not having direct reference to the occupancy of the house, is not a domestic servant within this statutory provision.[8]

§ 578. **From a building, store-house, warehouse, vessel, etc.**— In order to constitute larceny from a building the goods must be under the protection of the building and not within the control of any one in the building.[9] But the fact that there is a watchman in the building to catch the thief will not prevent the larceny from being from the building rather than from the person.[10] Under the Massachusetts statute the building must be other than the building of defendant, and larceny committed from one's own building, or by the wife from the building of her husband, would not be within the statute.[11] An unfinished building which is so far completed as to be closed and locked is a building within such statute;[12] and a church is such building.[13] The term "refreshment saloon" does not necessarily imply a building, and the use of that description would not, therefore, show a case within the statute.[14] This offense includes simple larceny.[15] The value of the goods stolen need

[1] Roberts v. S., 83 Ga. 369. And see Rex v. Owen, 2 East, P. C. 645; C. v. Lester, 129 Mass. 101.

[2] Simmons v. S., 73 Ga. 609.

[3] Martinez v. S., 41 Tex. 126. And see Henry v. S., cited under the preceding section.

[4] Simmons v. S., 73 Ga. 609; Williams v. S., 46 Ga. 212.

[5] Lamkin v. S., 42 Tex. 415.

[6] Markham v. S., 25 Ga. 52.

[7] Taylor v. S., 42 Tex. 387; Wakefield v. S., 41 Tex. 556; Coleman v. S., 44 Tex. 109; Ullman v. S., 1 Tex. Ap. 220.

[8] Williams v. S., 41 Tex. 649; Richardson v. S., 43 Tex. 456.

[9] C. v. Lester, 129 Mass. 101. And see Roberts v. S., 83 Ga. 369; Rex v. Owen, 2 East, P. C. 645.

[10] C. v. Nott, 135 Mass. 269.

[11] C. v. Hartnett, 3 Gray, 450.

[12] Rex v. Worrall, 7 C. & P. 516.

[13] Rex v. Hickman, 2 East, P. C. 593.

[14] C. v. Mahar, 8 Gray, 469.

[15] C. v. Lavery, 101 Mass. 207.

not be alleged or proven;[1] but the ownership should be proved as alleged, and it should be shown that they were of some value.[2] A building used for business purposes only, is within the statute as to larceny from a warehouse;[3] and an inclosure partially covered over is a warehouse within such statute;[4] and so is a granary built and used for keeping farming utensils, etc.[5] The term necessarily involves the idea of an inclosure of some sort — some kind of a structural barrier to the ingress of the public; and a place to which the public has free access and used as a common passage-way about a depot is not a warehouse.[6] A "store-house" must be in use as such, and not simply built for that purpose, to come within that term in the statute.[7] To constitute a building used for manufacturing, the structure must be made use of in the process of the manufacture of goods.[8] The description of the kind of building should be proved as alleged.[9] Under the statute as to larceny from a car, making the offense grand larceny, the value of the property need not be proven;[10] but ownership of the car should be alleged.[11]

§ 579. **In night-time or day-time.**— The fact of stealing from a house in the night-time is sometimes made an aggravated form of the offense, and the circumstance as to the time affects only the degree of the punishment,[12] the act committed in the day-time being still the offense of larceny from a dwelling-house and punishable as such.[13] But by the Massachusetts statute the two offenses are so described that larceny from the house in the day-time is not an included offense in larceny from the house in the night-time, but the two are distinct and must be proven as alleged.[14]

[1] C. v. Sego, 125 Mass. 210.

[2] Hawkins v. S., 95 Ga. 458.

[3] Reg. v. Edmundson, 2 El. & El. 77.

[4] Bennett v. S., 52 Ala. 370; Hagan v. S., 52 Ala. 373.

[5] Ray v. C., 12 Bush, 397. But "warehouse" should not be construed as including "granary," but rather as a place for storing goods intended eventually for sale: S. v. Wilson, 47 N. H. 101. Store-house may include warehouse: Bailey v. S., 99 Ala. 143.

[6] Lynch v. S., 89 Ala. 18.

[7] Jefferson v. S., 100 Ala. 59. Larceny "from" a store-house is proved by showing larceny "in" such building: Bailey v. S., 99 Ala. 143.

[8] Rex. v. Dixon, Russ. & Ry. 53.

[9] Thompson v. S., 92 Ga. 448.

[10] S. v. Sharp, 106 Mo. 106.

[11] Cooper v. S., 89 Ga. 222.

[12] S. v. Elsham, 70 Ia. 531.

[13] S. v. Dawson, 17 Ia. 584.

[14] C. v. McLaughlin, 11 Cush. 598; Hopkins v. C., 3 Met. 460, 466.

§ 580. **Common thief.**— It seems that at common law one might be punished as a common thief, constant repetition of the crime being in itself an offense somewhat distinct from simple larceny and punishable more severely.[1] But it was said not to be sufficient to charge in a general way the crime of being a common thief without specifying the particular acts.[2] Under the statute imposing a special penalty upon one who should be for the third time convicted of larceny or receiving stolen goods, the penalty not being greater than the maximum penalty for grand larceny, however, it was held that the prescribed punishment could be inflicted when the facts authorizing it appeared on the trial, though not charged in the indictment, the statute not creating a distinct crime but only providing a special punishment.[3] A prior conviction can be proven for the purpose of showing a second or other repeated offense only by a judgment showing such conviction.[4] Prior larcenies committed at such time that a prosecution therefor as ordinary thefts would be barred cannot be shown to prove the crime in connection with an act which is within the statutory period.[5]

VII. VALUE AS DETERMINING PUNISHMENT; GRAND AND PETIT.

§ 581. **Felony.**— The common-law larceny is divided into grand and petit, depending upon the value of the property stolen.[6] According to an early English statute,[7] where the value of the property was over twelve pence the offense was grand larceny; when the value did not exceed twelve pence it was

[1] See *supra*, § 28.

[2] 2 Hale, P. C. 182; 2 Hawk. P. C., ch. 25, § 59; 1 Bish. Cr. Pr. 530. The indictment may charge a larceny and a former conviction for another larceny: S. v. Moore, 121 Mo. 514.

[3] S. v. Riley, 28 Ia. 547.

[4] S. v. Brown, 115 Mo. 409. And a material variance between the name used in such judgment and the name of defendant will exclude the judgment: S. v. Griffie, 118 Mo. 188.

[5] World v. S., 50 Md. 49. Bad reputation within a year may be shown by evidence which goes back beyond the statutory period, a continuance within the statutory period being shown: Ibid.

[6] The term includes both grand and petit: S. v. Keyser, 56 Vt. 622. The two divisions of the offense are not distinct crimes or degrees, but are distinguished only with reference to the punishment: S. v. Murray, 55 Ia. 530; S. v. Hessian, 58 Ia. 68; Ex parte Bell, 19 Fla. 608. Thus, one who is extradited for grand larceny may be tried for petit larceny: S. v. Walker, 119 Mo. 467.

[7] See *supra*, § 534.

petit.[1] But both grand and petit larcenies were felonies although the punishment differed, grand larceny being punishable by death, while to the offense of petit larceny was affixed some lesser punishment under various statutory provisions.[2] The punishment for larceny has been so universally regulated by statute in the United States that a further discussion as to whether the lower branch is a felony and as to the punishment imposed for the two branches respectively becomes necessary.

§ 582. **Some value essential.**— To sustain a conviction for larceny there must be evidence that the property taken had some value.[3] But it is not necessary to prove that the property was of value by direct evidence; the fact may be sufficiently established by inference; for instance, from the declarations or admissions of the defendant showing that he treated or dealt with the property as of value.[4] Any intrinsic value whatever is sufficient.[5] It is not necessary that the value be that of some particular coin, even the smallest.[6]

§ 583. **What essential for grand larceny.**— The importance of the question of value, however, is in the fact that at common law, and almost universally by statute, if the goods are of

[1] The value which marks the distinction between grand and petit is much higher as now fixed by statute in the various states. By English statute (7 and 8 Geo. 4, c. 29, § 2) all distinction between grand and petit larceny is now abolished: See 2 Russ. Cr. 1.

[2] 4 Bl. Com. 229, 236–239; 1 Bish. Cr. L., § 679; 1 Hale, P. C. 530; 2 East, P. C. 736; 2 Inst. 189. In Pennsylvania, by reason of peculiar colonial regulations, neither grand nor petit larceny was ever a felony: Lynch v. C., 88 Pa. St. 189. Under the statutes of the United States larceny is an infamous crime: Ex parte McClusky, 40 Fed. R. 71. On this question see, also, § 210.

[3] Collins v. P., 39 Ill. 233; C. v. Cahill, 12 Allen, 540; Whitehead v. S., 20 Fla. 841; S. v. Krieger, 68 Mo. 98; Radford v. S., 35 Tex. 15; Hall v. S., 15 Tex. Ap. 40; Sands v. S., 30 Tex. Ap. 578; Rex v. Phipoe, 2 East, P. C. 599. Property which the owner considers as of no value to him may still have actual value: Reg. v. Edwards, 13 Cox, 384. As to whether notes and bills not delivered or redeemed are to be deemed as of value, see *supra*, § 543.

[4] S. v. Harris, 64 N. C. 127; Vincent v. S., 3 Heisk. 120; Houston v. S., 13 Ark. 66. One who steals a bank note and passes it as genuine sufficiently admits thereby that it had some value: Cummings v. C., 2 Va. Cas. 128.

[5] S. v. Slack, 1 Bailey, 330. It is sufficient if the property be found to have been of some value to the owner at least: C. v. Riggs, 14 Gray, 376. The owner may state the value of the property to him as furnishing some evidence of its real value: Cohen v. S., 50 Ala. 108.

[6] Wolverton v. C., 75 Va. 909; Reg. v. Morris, 9 C. & P. 349. In general, as to value, see *supra*, § 543.

above a certain value the offense is grand larceny, while if their value does not exceed such amount it is petit larceny, the punishment in the two cases being different, the one usually a felony and the other a misdemeanor. It is therefore important to determine whether or not the value of the property is such as to make the offense grand larceny. There cannot be conviction of grand larceny without evidence of the value of the property,[1] and to warrant such conviction the evidence must satisfy the jury beyond a reasonable doubt that the value of the property was such as to constitute that degree of the offense.[2]

§ 584. **Aggregate value.**— Where there are two or more distinct larcenies they cannot be aggregated so as to make the value of the property stolen sufficient to constitute grand larceny, the value of the goods in each distinct larceny being insufficient for that purpose.[3] This is so, even if the goods belong to the same owner, where they are taken in distinct transactions.[4] But if, though the larceny is of different articles, they are taken in substantially the same transaction, their aggregate value may be considered in determining whether the offense is grand larceny.[5] Under a statute specifying larceny of money or goods and chattels as a distinct offense from that of the larceny of bank bills, notes, etc., it is held that where in one transaction goods and bank bills are stolen, the value of the two classes of property cannot be aggregated for the purpose of making the offense grand larceny.[6]

§ 585. **Value, how estimated.**— The basis for estimating the value of property stolen is the value of such property on the

[1] Stokes v. S., 58 Miss. 677; Moore v. S., 17 Tex. Ap. 176.

[2] S. v. Wood, 46 Ia. 116; S. v. McCarty, 73 Ia. 51.

[3] Monoughan v. P., 24 Ill. 340.

[4] Scarver v. S., 53 Miss. 407; Cody v. S., 31 Tex. Ap. 183; Lacey v. S., 22 Tex. Ap. 657.

[5] Rex v. Jones, 4 C. & P. 217. Where several trees are damaged in the same transaction their aggregate value may be considered in determining whether the damage is of the amount necessary to constitute an offense by statute: Reg. v. Shepherd, L. R. 1 C. C. 118. If two defendants are jointly indicted for larceny of property of such aggregate value as that the offense is grand larceny, it will be immaterial what portion in value was taken by each: Clay v. S., 40 Tex. 67. As to whether the indictment should state the separate or the aggregate value, see *infra*, § 586.

[6] Johnson v. S., 11 Ohio St. 324.

market and not its special value to the owner.[1] Where the property has no market value which would adequately represent its actual value, as, for instance, clothing which has been worn, the jury is to determine its fair and reasonable value.[2] For this purpose they may consider the value of the goods when new, allowing a reasonable deduction for the wear.[3] The price which such goods would bring on the market is not to be considered their value, for such price does not represent their actual worth.[4] The value is to be estimated as at the time of the taking; but as the taking may be deemed a continuing one so long as the thief exercises control over the property,[5] he cannot complain if its value is estimated as of the time and place of his disposal of it.[6] Where the property has been damaged or partially destroyed in the taking of it, its value is to be estimated at the inception of the taking. Thus, where a thief broke up a cast-iron balance wheel so as to make old iron out it, which he carried away, it was suggested that he was properly indicted and tried for the larceny of the balance wheel, and that it could not properly be held that he ought to have been charged only with the larceny of old iron.[7] Bank notes or coins, the value of which is fixed by law, are to be estimated at their face,[8] and this is true, of course, of federal treasury notes.[9] The value of a receipt or release is the sum of money represented as having been due to the owner as paid.[10] So a check is presumed to be of its face value.[11] Where an instru-

[1] S. v. Smith, 48 Ia. 595; S. v. Doepke, 68 Mo. 208; S. v. James, 58 N. H. 67; Cannon v. S., 18 Tex. Ap. 172; Martinez v. S., 16 Tex. Ap. 122.

[2] Cooksie v. S., 26 Tex. Ap. 72. "Brood sows" not having a market value, evidence of real value is admissible: S. v. Walker, 119 Mo. 467.

[3] Pratt v. S., 35 Ohio St. 514.

[4] Pratt v. S., 35 Ohio St. 514; Cooksie v. S., 26 Tex. Ap. 72.

[5] *Supra*, § 551.

[6] S. v. Brown, 55 Kan. 611.

[7] Gettinger v. S., 13 Neb. 308.

[8] Whalen v. C., 90 Va. 544. But in another case it is said that it cannot be presumed, without evidence, that a check has any value: Burrows v. S., 137 Ind. 474. It cannot be assumed that a railroad ticket charged to have been stolen had any value unless it is alleged that it was stamped, dated and signed: S. v. Holmes, 9 Wash. 528.

[9] Adams v. C., 23 Grat. 949; S. v. Cassel, Har. & G. 407; Grant v. S., 55 Ala. 201. And see Bagley v. S., 3 Tex. Ap. 163.

[10] Collins v. P., 39 Ill. 233; S. v. Henry, 24 Kan. 457; C. v. Williams, 9 Met. 273; Duvall v. S., 63 Ala. 12. But the value of a bank note may be shown to be less than its face: Broms v. C., 2 Duv. 351.

[11] C. v. Williams, 9 Met. 273. This

ment in writing is taken which is of value to the owner, though it is not an obligation for the payment of money,— for instance, where it is a soldier's discharge which is essential to enable him to draw a pension,— it is a thing of value, and the jury in determining the value may take into account its worth as a part of the documentary evidence necessary to obtain a right.[1]

§ 586. **Allegation and proof of value.**— The indictment should allege the value of the property stolen in order to show whether the offense is grand or petit larceny.[2] If, however, the charge is some form of aggravated larceny, in which the punishment does not depend upon the value of the property, allegation of the value is immaterial.[3] But some courts hold an allegation of value essential in all cases.[4] It is sufficient, where the charge is of the larceny of several articles, to allege the aggregate value.[5] But it is better to allege the value of each article.[6] If only the aggregate value is alleged, the value of the different articles, if they are of the same kind, may still be proven separately, and a conviction will be supported whether the proof shows that all the articles were stolen, or only a part of them.[7] And even if the articles are of different kinds, proof of the larceny of all of them, or of some of each

is sometimes provided by statute: S. v. Pierson, 59 Ia. 271.

[1] C. v. Lawless, 103 Mass. 425.

[2] Davis v. S., 40 Ga. 229; S. v. Pedigo, 71 Mo. 443; Pittman v. S., 14 Tex. Ap. 576; Reg. v. Gamble, 16 M. & W. 384. Uncertainty in the allegation of value will render the indictment invalid: Williams v. S., 44 Ala. 396; Smitherman v. S., 63 Ala. 24; S. v. Holmes, 9 Wash. 528. But such allegation is not a part of the description and a variance will not be fatal: C. v. Garland, 3 Met. (Ky.) 478. Allegation of value as so many dollars "current money" is sufficient: Gardner v. S., 25 Md. 146. So is an allegation of value in "dollars" alone: P. v. Winkler, 9 Cal. 234.

[3] Sheppard v. S., 42 Ala. 531; Shaw v. S., 23 Tex. Ap. 493; Bennett v. S., 16 Tex. Ap. 236; Lopez v. S., 20 Tex. 780. In such cases the description of the articles stolen as goods and chattels imports some value: Buntin v. S., 68 Ind. 38. That allegation of value is not necessary in charging horse-stealing or kindred offense, see *infra*, § 589. Nor is it necessary, usually, in other crimes involving personal property: S. v. Gillespie, 80 N. C. 396; Wilson v. S., 43 Neb. 745.

[4] C. v. Smith, 1 Mass. 245; C. v. Cahill, 12 Allen, 540; S. v. Goodrich, 46 N. H. 186; Wilson v. S., 1 Port. 118; P. v. Belcher, 58 Mich. 325.

[5] S. v. Mook, 40 Ohio St. 588; S. v. Brew, 4 Wash. 95; Thompson v. S., 43 Tex. 268.

[6] Meyer v. S., 4 Tex. Ap. 121; Doyle v. S., 4 Tex. Ap. 253.

[7] S. v. Mook, 40 Ohio St. 588; S. v. Buck, 46 Me. 531; S. v. Beatty, 90 Mo. 143.

kind, will warrant a conviction, although there is but an aggregate value alleged.[1] Or if the aggregate value of each of two or more classes is alleged, proof of the larceny of some of any class will be sufficient.[2] But proof of the larceny of some of several different articles of which an aggregate value only is given will not warrant a conviction, as it will not thereby appear that the articles shown to have been stolen had any value.[3] Such an objection may not be ground for arrest of judgment, even though it would be on a motion to quash.[4] In proving the value any evidence is competent from which the value may be inferred.[5] But witnesses called to testify as to the value must show that they possess knowledge of the value of such property.[6] If two persons are indicted together for stealing the same goods, one cannot be convicted of petit larceny and the other of grand larceny.[7]

§ 587. **Finding as to value.**— The value of the property as alleged determines whether the offense shall be tried as grand or petit larceny.[8] But there are not two degrees of the offense, the difference between the two forms being only as to the punishment,[9] and it is not necessary to expressly designate the offense as grand or petit larceny.[10] It is not necessary that the value of the property be proven as alleged; and if the proof shows the stealing of property of less than the maxim value for petit larceny, there may be a conviction for that grade of the offense, although grand larceny was charged.[11] And there may thus be a conviction for petit larceny under an indictment, although petit larceny is not an offense triable on indictment,

[1] S. v. Hood, 51 Me. 363; Clifton v. S., 5 Blackf. 224; C. v. Cahill, 12 Allen, 540; Jackson v. S., 69 Ala. 249.

[2] C. v. Sawtelle, 11 Cush. 142.

[3] Hope v. C., 9 Met. 134; S. v. Gerrish, 78 Me. 20; S. v. Brew, 4 Wash. 95.

[4] S. v. Murphy, 8 Blackf. 498.

[5] Saddler v. S., 20 Tex. Ap. 195.

[6] Engster v. S., 11 Neb. 539. Evidence of value by at least one witness shown to be competent to testify with reference thereto is necessary: Edmonds v. S., 42 Neb. 684.

[7] S. v. Wilson, 3 McCord, 187; S. v. Larumbo, Harper, 183.

[8] S. v. Church, 8 Ia. 252.

[9] S. v. Murray, 55 Ia. 530. And see *supra*, § 581.

[10] S. v. Powell, 28 La. An. 315; S. v. Lartigue, 29 La. An. 642.

[11] McCorkle v. S., 14 Ind. 39; S. v. Hessian, 58 Ia. 68. The jury may find defendant guilty of petit larceny, though the evidence shows the value to be such as to authorize a conviction for grand larceny: S. v. Bennett, 2 Brev. 575.

but cognizable only before a justice of the peace.[1] If the jury has a reasonable doubt as to whether the value of the property is such as to constitute grand larceny, they should convict only of petit larceny.[2] To warrant a judgment for grand larceny, the finding of value showing that grade of the offense must be definite.[3]

§ 588. **What sufficient finding.**— The verdict must either state the value of the property taken or find the prisoner guilty as charged, otherwise no judgment can be rendered thereon.[4] There is a conflict in the cases as to whether a general verdict without special finding of value is sufficient as to grand larceny. In some it is held that if the indictment charges the offense in such form as to show grand larceny, and a general verdict is returned of guilty, it is sufficient to support a conviction for grand larceny.[5] Others hold a finding essential to conviction of grand larceny.[6] In some states the jury are authorized to fix the punishment within the limit and under the circumstances specified by statute.[7] But, in general, the power to fix the punishment is with the judge.[8]

[1] S. v. Church, 8 Ia. 252; S. v. Stingley, 10 Ia. 488; S. v. Miller, 45 Minn. 521; S. v. Wood, 1 Mill Const. 29.

[2] S. v. Wood, 46 Ia. 116.

[3] McCormick v. S., 42 Neb. 866.

[4] S. v. Coon, 18 Minn. 518.

[5] C. v. Butler, 144 Pa. St. 568; Wilborn v. S., 8 Smed. & M. 345; Cook v. S., 49 Miss. 8; Jones v. S., 13 Ala. 153; S. v. Colwell, 43 Minn. 378; P. v. Whitely, 64 Cal. 211; Mason v. P., 2 Colo. 373; S. v. Bunten, 2 Nott & McC. 441; Howell v. S., 1 Oreg. 241; P. v. Gaugh, 2 Utah, 70. If the evidence of value is conflicting, defendant may request a special finding as to value: Mason v. P., 2 Colo. 373.

[6] Highland v. P., 2 Ill. 392; Collins v. P., 39 Ill. 233; Williams v. P., 44 Ill. 478; Ruth v. P., 99 Ill. 185; Ray v. S., 1 Greene (Ia.), 316; S. v. Redman, 17 Ia. 329; Shines v. S., 42 Miss. 321; Unger v. S., 42 Miss. 642; Miles v. S., 3 Tex. Ap. 58. If the jury finds only the aggregate value instead of the value of each article, it is an irregularity of which defendant cannot take advantage after the verdict is received: Case v. S., 26 Ala. 17. The finding of the larceny of so many dollars upon an indictment charging the larceny of so many dollars in bank-bills is sufficient: Hildreth v. P., 32 Ill. 36. A general verdict is not sufficient where part of the judgment may consist in damages to the injured party according to the value of the property taken: Locke v. S., 32 N. H. 106. Where a special penalty is imposed for the stealing of animals according to the number stolen, the verdict must show the number, and a general verdict will not be sufficient: S. v. Bunten, 2 Nott & McC. 441.

[7] Irwin v. S., 25 Tex. Ap. 558; P. v. Littlefield, 5 Cal. 355.

[8] Moss v. S., 42 Ala. 546.

§ 589. Cases where value immaterial; horse-stealing, etc. Some larcenies are punishable without regard to the value of the property, the kind of property taken or the circumstances under which it is taken being such as to justify the infliction of the higher punishment. In such cases it is not necessary that the indictment allege or that the jury find the value of the property stolen.[1] Horse-stealing is a crime thus usually punishable without regard to the value of the animal.[2] So cattle-stealing,[3] hog-stealing,[4] and larceny of any domestic animal,[5] are sometimes provided for by special statutes. But the stealing of an animal within such a statute means stealing the animal alive, and it does not apply to the larceny of the carcass of the animal, unless it was killed by the defendant with the intention of carrying it away and appropriating the body.[6] One who steals an animal described in such special statutes may, however, be prosecuted for simple larceny.[7] Unless the charge clearly appears to be under the special statute, even though it be for the stealing of a horse, it will be deemed to be for simple larceny;[8] and if the charge is of stealing a horse

[1] P. v. Townsley, 39 Cal. 405; McDaniels v. P., 118 Ill. 301; Wilson v. S., 43 Neb. 745; McDowell v. S., 61 Ala. 172; Adams v. S., 60 Ala. 52; Gregg v. S., 55 Ala. 116; Walker v. S., 50 Ark. 532; S. v. Daniels, 32 Mo. 558; Green v. S., 28 Tex. Ap. 493; Johnson v. S., 29 Tex. 492; S. v. Hill, 46 La. An. 736.

[2] Hoge v. P., 117 Ill. 35; Wells v. S., 11 Neb. 409; S. v. Small, 26 Kan. 209. If the verdict in such a case is for petit larceny, it will not be valid: S. v. Spurgin, 1 McCord, 252. Where the indictment charges in two counts larceny in general, and horse-stealing, punishment may be imposed for the higher offense: P. v. Morris, 80 Mich. 634. But where the allegation is of larceny in general, although the property is described as a horse, conviction can be had only for grand larceny when the proper value is shown: P. v. Martin, 91 Mich. 650. Horse-stealing has been made in some states punishable capitally: Wilcox v. S., 3 Heisk. 110; Turner v. S., 3 Heisk. 452; S. v. Putney, Phill. 543. The provisions as to horse-stealing making the offense of higher grade irrespective of value are applicable also to embezzlement: S. v. Small, 26 Kan. 209; but not, it is said, to conversion by bailee: S. v. Hayes, 13 Mont. 116.

[3] Johnson v. S., 58 Ga. 491; Adams v. S., 60 Ala. 52; Davis v. S., 40 Tex. 134.

[4] McDowell v. S., 61 Ala. 172; Walker v. S., 50 Ark. 532.

[5] T. v. Pendry, 9 Mont. 67.

[6] Hunt v. S., 55 Ala. 138; Golden v. S., 63 Miss. 466.

[7] Quinn v. P., 123 Ill. 333; Chiles v. C., 2 Va. Cas. 260. *Contra*, S. v. Ripley, 2 Brev. 300. The statute creating the special offense is not exclusive of the general offense: Kollenberger v. P., 9 Colo. 233; S. v. Snyder, 50 N. H. 150 (overruling, on this point, S. v. Nelson, 8 N. H. 163).

[8] P. v. Jones, 49 Mich. 591; P. v. Martin, 91 Mich. 650.

and other chattels, it will be presumed not to be for the aggravated offense.[1] Even where the nature of the property makes the case grand larceny without regard to value, it seems that it must appear the property was of some value.[2]

VIII. PROCEDURE.

§ 590. **Jurisdiction and venue.**— Questions relating to the jurisdiction and the venue in cases of goods brought into a county after being stolen in another county, or in another state, or in a foreign country, have already been discussed.[3] In the federal court the jurisdiction in larceny depends on the offense being committed at a place over which the United States has jurisdiction in some form. Under the judiciary act of 1790,[4] larceny was cognizable in the federal courts only when committed in a place under the sole and exclusive jurisdiction of the United States and not within the jurisdiction of any state.[5] But by a later act[6] larceny may be punished in the federal courts, though committed in a place not under the sole and exclusive jurisdiction of the United States, if it is within its admiralty jurisdiction.[7] As to the venue as between different counties, there is nothing peculiar in larceny as distinct from any other crime. The verdict of guilty as charged sufficiently shows the offense to have been committed in the county charged in the indictment.[8] If the indictment is repugnant or uncertain as to the venue, it will be bad.[9]

§ 591. **Indictment.**— Some forms of indictment will be given in another place.[10] The common-law indictment charges that defendant, at the time and place named, "feloniously did steal, take, and carry away [certain property described] of the goods and chattels of the said A. B." The statutes of the various

[1] S. v. Nelson, 8 N. H. 163; S. v. Snyder, 50 N. H. 150; Boody v. P., 43 Mich. 34; P. v. Seller, 58 Mich. 327. *Contra*, Williams v. Reg., 7 Q. B. 251.

[2] Lucas v. S., 96 Ala. 51. And see, in general, § 582, *supra*.

[3] See *supra*, §§ 552, 553. An accessory to the larceny can only be prosecuted where the original taking was committed unless he was also accessory to taking into another county: West v. S., 27 Tex. Ap. 472; West v. S., 28 Tex. Ap. 1.

[4] Ch. 9, § 16.

[5] U. S. v. Coombs, 12 Pet. 72; U. S. v. Davis, 5 Mason, 356.

[6] Act of 1825, ch. 65.

[7] U. S. v. Davis, 5 Mason, 356.

[8] P. v. Magallones, 15 Cal. 426.

[9] Cain v. S., 18 Tex. 391.

[10] *Infra*, § 610.

states, either by general provisions with reference to indictments, or by special provisions as to indictment for larceny, have to some extent changed the common-law requirements, and in particular instances it may be that the common-law indictment is not sufficient.[1] It may be necessary under such statutes to conclude "against the form of the statute" instead of "against the peace and dignity," etc.[2] The elements of the indictment will be considered in the following order: The description of the property, the act done, and the intent.

§ 592. **Description of the property.**— The description of the property is material, and must be proved as alleged.[3] Where the indictment charges the stealing of a black horse, it will not be supported by evidence of the stealing of a brown horse.[4] Even if the articles are described with greater particularity than necessary, some description being essential, that given must be proved, and the portion which is unnecessarily particular cannot be regarded as surplusage.[5] Thus, where a revolver was described as a "Smith & Weston" revolver, it was held that evidence of the stealing of a "Smith & Wesson" revolver was not sufficient;[6] so an indictment for stealing one pair of boots was held not to be supported by proof of the stealing of two boots, each being the right one of two different pairs;[7] and the proof of larceny of a pair of sheep-skin gloves was held not to support the allegation of the larceny of buckskin gloves.[8] But the particular description of the article in the indictment is not necessary. It may be described by the name usually applied to it.[9] Articles of clothing and house-

[1] Johnson v. P., 113 Ill. 99.

[2] S. v. Gray, 14 Rich. 174; S. v. Thomas, 14 Rich. 163; S. v. Wheeler, 15 Rich. 362. And see Chiles v. C., 2 Va. Cas. 260; S. v. Ripley, 2 Brev. 300.

[3] S. v. Noble, 15 Me. 476; S. v. Jackson, 30 Me. 29; S. v. Babb, 76 Mo. 501; Alkenbrack v. P., 1 Denio, 80.

[4] S. v. Jackson, 30 Me. 29. A description unnecessarily particular as to color and markings of an animal must be proven: Courtney v. S., 3 Tex. Ap. 257. But the color and other particulars need not be alleged: See *infra*, § 594.

[5] Alkenbrack v. P., 1 Denio, 80; Turner v. S., 3 Heisk. 452. If the indictment describes the animal as a "beef-steer" or a "work-steer," these particulars must be proven: Cameron v. S., 9 Tex. Ap. 332; Gray v. S., 11 Tex. Ap. 411.

[6] Morgan v. S., 61 Ind. 447.

[7] S. v. Harris, 3 Harr. 559.

[8] McGee v. S., 4 Tex. Ap. 625. Allegation of larceny of a woolen sheet is not supported by proof of larceny of a sheet partly of wool: Alkenbrack v. P., 1 Denio, 80.

[9] Dignowitty v. S., 17 Tex. 521. Where the article stolen was de-

hold goods may be described by number and kind.[1] A more particular description than is reasonably practicable is not required;[2] but there must be such a description numerically and specifically as to individualize the property with legal certainty, so that the jury can determine whether the property proved to have been stolen is the same as that described in the indictment.[3] Moreover, the description should be such as to show that the property is subject of larceny, enable the accused to make defense if he have any, and protect him from another prosecution for the same offense.[4] It will not constitute a variance that the indictment does not sufficiently describe some of the articles stolen if it is sufficient as to others, and the proof as to the part sufficiently described is such as to support a verdict.[5] Thus, if the description of ownership of the property is true only as to part of it, a proof as to that part will support a verdict.[6] If, however, the number is a part of the description as to each article or portion, it must be proven as alleged. Thus, where defendant was charged with stealing five certificates of shares of stock of a certain number, and the proof showed but one such certificate, and not a series of five, the variance was held fatal.[7]

§ 593. **Sufficiency of description in particular cases.**—A description of the property as "one book;"[8] or "one parcel of oats;"[9] or "twenty-three head of cattle;"[10] or "one bolt of cotton domestic;"[11] or a certain number of yards of cloth of a value named without further description;[12] or "eight cords of wood;"[13] or a part of an outstanding crop of corn;[14] or a

scribed as a gold watch, *held*, that proof of the stealing of a watch the case of which was partly gold, being such as is generally called gold by the public, was sufficient: Pfister v. S., 84 Ala. 432; Glover v S., 22 Fla. 493.

[1] Ware v. S., 2 Tex. Ap. 547.

[2] S. v. Fenn, 41 Conn. 590.

[3] S. v. Hoyer, 40 La. An. 744.

[4] S. v. Nipper, 95 N. C. 653; Barnes v. S., 40 Neb. 545; Glover v. S., 22 Fla. 493.

[5] C. v. Williams, 2 Cush. 582; C. v. Eastman, 2 Gray, 76; C. v. Johnson, 133 Pa. St. 293; S. v. Kreps, 8 Ala. 951; Reid v. S., 88 Ala. 36. *Contra*, S. v. Kersh, 1 Strobh. 352.

[6] S. v. Evans, 23 S. C. 209. Under an indictment for stealing two animals or articles, there may be a conviction on proof of stealing one of them: Alderson v. S., 2 Tex. Ap. 10; Swinney v. S., 8 Smed. & M. 576.

[7] P. v. Coon, 45 Cal. 672.

[8] Turner v. S., 102 Ind. 425.

[9] S. v. Brown, 1 Dev. 137.

[10] S. v. White, 129 Ind. 153.

[11] S. v. Odum, 11 Tex. 12.

[12] C. v. Campbell, 103 Mass. 436.

[13] S. v. Labauve, 46 La. An. 548.

[14] Harris v. S., 100 Ala. 129.

certain number of pounds of seed cotton of a specified value;[1] or a certain number of handkerchiefs, the proof showing the larceny of a number of patterns of new handkerchiefs in the piece;[2] or "a pair of pants;"[3] or "four pairs of shoes, four pairs of pants, one lot of jewelry, one lot of shirts,"[4] is sufficient. But "one case of merchandise" is not a sufficient description, at least unless there is some excuse for not giving a more particular one;[5] nor is "two ladies' walking jackets;"[6] nor is a description as a certain lot of dry goods obtained from a certain firm with which the defendant had many transactions, the particular lot not being described.[7] A description of the stolen property as "meat" is not sufficient;[8] but the description "one ham" is sufficient, the word "ham" having acquired a meaning which is universally understood.[9] A description of the property stolen as "six bottles of whiskey" is not supported by proof of the taking of a quantity of whiskey not in bottles; the term "bottle" cannot be taken as a measure of quantity.[10] An indictment for stealing a "plow" is not sustained by proof of stealing a plow-share only;[11] but where, under an indictment for stealing a "shovel-plow," it was proposed to prove the stealing of the iron part of such a plow, it was held that it should have been left to the jury whether the thing stolen was, according to common understanding, a shovel-plow as alleged.[12] An indictment for stealing a "bull-tongue" was held to sufficiently specify a peculiarly shaped plow-share usually known by that name.[13] The stealing of ingots of tin or iron may be charged as of so many pounds weight of tin or iron respectively.[14] The charge of theft of a "certain trunk or chest containing various articles of clothing, jewelry," etc., is insufficient as to the property contained in such trunk or chest;[15] and

[1] Borum v. S., 66 Ala. 468. "Two bales of cotton" is sufficient: Peters v. S., 100 Ala. 10.

[2] Rex v. Nibbs, 1 Moody, 25.

[3] S. v. Johnson, 30 La. An., part II, 904.

[4] S. v. Curtis, 44 La. An. 320.

[5] S. v. Dawes, 75 Me. 51.

[6] McCowan v. S., 58 Ark. 17.

[7] Redmond v. S., 35 Ohio St. 81.

[8] S. v. Morey, 2 Wis. 494; S. v. Patrick, 79 N. C. 655.

[9] Reg. v. Gallears, 2 C. & K. 981.

[10] C. v. Gavin, 121 Mass. 54.

[11] S. v. Cockfield, 15 Rich. 316.

[12] S. v. Sansom, 3 Brev. 5.

[13] S. v. Clark, 8 Ired. 226.

[14] Reg. v. Mansfield, Car. & M. 140. And see S. v. Horan, Phill. 571. An indictment charging larceny of "gold metal" of a certain value was held sufficient: U. S. v. Jones, 69 Fed. R. 973.

[15] Potter v. S., 39 Tex. 388.

it was so held also as to an indictment charging the stealing of a box containing watches and chains;[1] so an indictment charging the stealing of "a pocket-book and contents of the value," etc., does not charge the theft of the contents.[2] A description of the property stolen as a "cast-iron balance wheel" is proper, although, for the purpose of effecting the theft, the wheel has been broken into pieces and become old iron.[3]

§ 594. **Description of animals.**— It is sufficient in alleging the larceny of a domestic animal to name the kind of animal and the ownership. No special description of the particular animal aside from that of ownership is essential. Thus, the allegation that defendant feloniously took "a horse, the personal property of" a person named, was held sufficient.[4] It is not necessary to describe any particular brand on the animal, even though it is branded.[5] Where there are statutory provisions in regard to branding, the brand furnishes some evidence as to title.[6] The difficulties in regard to animals have arisen under statutes providing a special punishment for larcenies of particular animals named, and the particularity pursued in the statutes in the specification of the animals intended has led to corresponding technicality with reference to their description in indictments under such statutes, so that a minute accuracy of description has been required which was not necessary in the common-law indictment for larceny. Thus, where the statute as to horse-stealing specifies the larceny of "one horse, gelding, mare, colt, ass or mule," it has been held that the charge of the theft of a horse is not sustained by proof of the

[1] S. v. Derst, 10 Nev. 443.

[2] Johnson v. S., 32 Ark. 181.

[3] Gettinger v. S., 13 Neb. 308.

[4] McBride v. C., 13 Bush, 337. So held also where the description was "one mare:" S. v. Friend, 47 Minn. 449; "one mule:" Gabriel v. S., 40 Ala. 357; S. v. King, 31 La. An. 179; "one beef cattle:" Duval v. S., 8 Tex. Ap. 370; "one hog:" Grant v. S., 2 Tex. Ap. 163; S. v. Mansfield, 33 Tex. 129; P. v. Stanford, 64 Cal. 27; Matthews v. S., 24 Ark. 484; "three hogs about eleven months old," etc.: Barnes v. S., 40 Neb. 545. As to pigs, see Brown v. S., 44 Ga. 300. The animal may be said in the indictment to be of "the goods and chattels" of the owner: S. v. Gomer, 6 La. An. 311.

[5] Perry v. S., 37 Ark. 54. But if the brand be described it must be proved as alleged: Allen v. S., 8 Tex. Ap. 360.

[6] Robertson v. S., 1 Tex. Ap. 311; and the want of a brand may be shown as indicating that the taking was not with wrongful intent: Perry v. S., 37 Ark. 54.

theft of a mare,[1] nor by proof of the theft of a gelding.[2] So under such a statute the indictment for stealing a steer will not support a conviction on proof of stealing a bull;[3] but if such a statute mentions merely cattle or neat cattle, an indictment for stealing animals designated as "cattle," or for stealing "a cow" or "a steer," will be sufficient.[4] Indeed, in California, under a statute specifying among other animals "a cow, steer, bull, calf," it was held that an indictment for the larceny of "two head of cattle" was sufficient.[5] Under such a statute it is usually sufficient to charge the stealing of a hog without further specification.[6] On the contrary, in another case it is said that as the statute provides only for larceny of a hog, an indictment for stealing a pig will not come within the statute.[7] Under statutes not using the same particularity in describing the kinds of animals covered, the same particularity of description and proof is not essential. Thus, if the statute names adult animals only, the young are included under the same description;[8] but where the young are enumerated with the adult

[1] Banks v. S., 28 Tex. 644. And see Taylor v. S., 44 Ga. 263.

[2] Hooker v. S., 4 Ohio, 348; Turley v. S., 3 Humph. 323; S. v. Buckles, 26 Kan. 237; Swindel v. S., 32 Tex. 102; Gibbs v. S., 34 Tex. 134; Marshall v. S., 31 Tex. 471; Persons v. S., 3 Tex. Ap. 240; and *vice versa:* S. v. McDonald, 10 Mont. 21. So proof of the theft of a ridgling (a horse castrated on one side only) does not support the allegation of theft of a gelding: Brisco v. S., 4 Tex. Ap. 219. But this technical construction seems to have been changed in Texas by statute: Valesco v. S., 9 Tex. Ap. 76. Where the larceny of a horse or mule was made a capital offense, and a previous statute as to the larceny of a horse, mule, colt, etc., was to that extent repealed, *held,* that the larceny of a colt was not within the new statute, and was therefore punishable under the old: S. v. Major, 14 Rich. 76. In a statute specifying "horse, mare, gelding," etc., the term "horse" indicates a stallion: Turley v. S., 3 Humph. 323; Brisco v. S., 4 Tex. Ap. 219. If the statute requires a specification of the nature, character, sex, etc., the term "horse" is not sufficiently descriptive: Brown v. S., 86 Ga. 633.

[3] S. v. Royster, 65 N. C. 539.

[4] Hubotter v. S., 32 Tex. 479; S. v. Hoffman, 53 Kan. 700; S. v. Lawn, 80 Mo. 241: S. v. Crow, 107 Mo. 341; P. v. Littlefield, 5 Cal. 355. But "twenty-five head of cattle," held insufficient: S. v. Brookhouse, 10 Wash. 87. The term "cattle" under such a statute means domesticated animals of the bovine genus: MacIntosh v. S., 18 Tex. Ap. 284. But under such statute it must appear that the animals stolen were cattle, and that they were taken from the possession of someone: Castello v. S., 36 Tex. 324.

[5] P. v. Barnes, 65 Cal. 16.

[6] Grant v. S., 2 Tex. Ap. 163.

[7] S. v. McLain, 2 Brev. 443.

[8] Rex v. Welland, Russ. & Ry. 494; P. v. Soto, 49 Cal. 67.

they must be correctly described.[1] If the statute uses only the general names, without distinction of sex or age, then the general term will be sufficient in the indictment.[2] In an indictment for larceny under the common law, or under a general statute defining that offense and not in regard to specific animals, a general description of the kind of animal is sufficient. Thus, under an indictment for stealing a horse, proof of the theft of a mare is admissible;[3] so proof of larceny of a gelding may be introduced under the charge of stealing a horse;[4] so an indictment charging theft of "certain neat cattle, to wit, one beef," or "one head of neat cattle," has been held sufficient;[5] so the allegation of theft of a "cow" covers theft of a heifer;[6] so an indictment for stealing "one certain calf of the neat cattle kind" is sufficient;[7] but the description of the animal as "a yearling" is not sufficient, as it does not designate what kind of an animal was stolen.[8] The charge of stealing a hog is supported by proof of stealing a pig.[9] So proof of stealing hens supports a charge of stealing chickens.[10]

§ 595. **Written instruments, bills and notes.**— Where a written instrument is the subject of larceny, it may be described in the indictment by the term usually employed to describe it without stating its purport or giving a copy of it;[11] so in an indictment for the larceny of a railroad ticket, a particular description is not required;[12] so the description of a certain

[1] Rex v. Cook, 2 East, P. C. 616; Rex v. Loom, 1 Moody, 160.

[2] Watson v. S., 55 Ala. 150; S. v. Godet, 7 Ired. 210; P. v. Sensabaugh, 2 Utah, 473; S. v. Tootle, 2 Harr. 541; Reg. v. Aldridge, 4 Cox, 143; Rex v. Gillbrass, 7 C. & P. 444; Rex v. Stroud, 6 C. & P. 535; Reg. v. Spicer, 1 C. & K. 699; Reg. v. Jewett, 2 Cox, 227; Reg. v. McCulley, 2 Moody, 34; Reg. v. Strange, 1 Cox, 58.

[3] P. v. Pico, 62 Cal. 50; Baldwin v. P., 2 Ill. 304; Davis v. S., 23 Tex. Ap. 210; S. v. Gooch, 60 Ark. 218; but not proof as to a horse under a charge as to a mare: Thrasher v. S., 6 Blackf. 460.

[4] S. v. Donnegan, 34 Mo. 67; Halkem v. C., 2 Va. Cas. 4. An indictment charging larceny of "an animal of the horse species" is sufficient: Smythe v. S., 17 Tex. Ap. 244.

[5] S. v. Garrett, 34 Tex. 674; S. v. Murphy, 39 Tex. 46. An indictment charging larceny of "a beef" is sufficient: S. v. Baden, 42 La. An. 295; and under such indictment testimony showing theft of a cow is admissible: Smith v. S., 24 Tex. Ap. 290. "One beef steer" is a sufficient designation of the kind of animal: Short v. S., 36 Tex. 644; so is "one head of neat cattle:" S. v. Murphy, 39 Tex. 46.

[6] P. v. Soto, 49 Cal. 67.

[7] Grant v. S., 3 Tex. Ap. 1.

[8] Stollenwerk v. S., 55 Ala. 142.

[9] Washington v. S., 58 Ala. 355.

[10] S. v. Bassett, 34 La. An. 1108.

[11] S. v. Hall, 85 Mo. 669.

[12] S. v. Brin, 30 Minn. 522. But it

stated number of county warrants drawn by the order of the auditor, etc., on the treasury, etc., and stating the amounts for which they were drawn, was held sufficient.[1] Under statutes as to larceny of promissory notes, bills of exchange, etc., it is not necessary to describe the instrument stolen more particularly than in case of property, and the description of the instrument by its usual name, and the amount of the face thereof and its value, is sufficient.[2] The Pennsylvania cases seem to require a greater particularity of description, and hold that an indictment for larceny of "a certain promissory note of the value," etc., is not sufficient;[3] but, at any rate, the description need not give the particulars as to indorsements, etc., at least where the indictment alleges inability to do so.[4] Exact accuracy as to the name of the payee in a check has been held not necessary.[5] The allegation of stealing United States bonds was held not to be supported by evidence of the theft of a silver certificate,[6] and the allegation of larceny of pieces of printed paper "commonly called United States bonds, of the value of," etc., was held not sufficient under a statute providing a punishment for the stealing of such bonds, because it did not state that such pieces of paper were bonds or certificates, etc., within the language of the statute.[7] Where bonds are sufficiently described, the indictment for the larceny of coupons from such bonds will be sufficient.[8] For the purpose of showing the instrument to be an instrument of value, it is not necessary to specially set out the fact of liability thereunder, as

should be described as stamped, dated, signed, etc., so as to show it to have been duly issued and something of value: S. v. Holmes, 9 Wash. 528.

[1] Engleman v. S., 2 Ind. 91. But an indictment for larceny of "a certain writ of *fi. fa.* belonging to the superior court," or "a certain process of and belonging to the superior court," or "a certain record of and belonging to the superior court," the three descriptions being in three counts, was held too vague to authorize a conviction: S. v. McLeod, 5 Jones, 318.

[2] C. v. Brettun, 100. Mass. 206; S. v. Pierson, 59 Ia. 271; Du Bois v. S., 50 Ala. 139. "One paper purporting to be a check" is sufficient: Whalen v. C., 90 Va. 544.

[3] Stewart v. C., 4 S. & R. 194; C. v. Boyer, 1 Binn. 201.

[4] S. v. Fenn, 41 Conn. 590.

[5] P. v. Arras, 89 Cal. 223.

[6] Stewart v. S., 62 Md. 412.

[7] Kearney v. S., 48 Md. 16.

[8] S. v. Wade, 7 Baxt. 22. Proof of stealing an instrument not under seal will not support an indictment charging larceny of a bond: P. v. Wiley, 3 Hill, 194.

liability will appear from the nature of the instrument.[1] Instruments described as "bonds of the state," etc., are by that description designated as lawful and valid bonds.[2] Where the indictment alleges the value of a check, such allegation is to be taken as equivalent to an allegation that the instrument called for at least that amount of money.[3]

§ 596. **Bank-notes, treasury notes, etc.**—Larceny of bank-notes is punishable under a general statute with reference to stealing "promissory notes for the payment of money," but to bring a bank-bill within that description it is not sufficient to describe it as a bank-note of a certain named bank, but the indictment must show that it is a note for the payment of money.[4] While it is true of bank-bills as it is of promissory notes, as stated in the last section, that they need not be described with particularity, yet it has been held necessary to allege the number and value of each, and that the description of them as "sundry bank-bills," of an aggregate value named, is not sufficient.[5] In some cases it has been held that a description of bank-bills should specify the kind, number and denomination;[6] and if the description includes bills together with other property, in the alternative, it will be insufficient.[7] The modern statutes usually specify bank-bills or bank-notes as subjects of larceny, and it is not necessary, therefore, to describe them as promissory notes, nor as money.[8] It is not necessary

[1] S. v. Hickman, 8 N. J. 299; Phelps v. P., 72 N. Y. 334. But under statute of South Carolina it was held that even in case of bank-bills it was necessary to state a certain sum as due thereon: S. v. Thomas, 2 McCord, 527.

[2] S. v. Wade, 7 Baxt. 22.

[3] S. v. Pierson, 59 Ia. 271.

[4] C. v. Boyer, 1 Binn. 201. "A promissory note for the payment of money, commonly called a bank-note," *held* sufficient: S. v. Bond, 8 Ia. 540. But that a bank-bill should not be described as a promissory note, see Damewood v. S., 2 Miss. 262.

[5] Hamblett v. S., 18 N. H. 384. But this is sufficient in Massachusetts: C. v. Stebbins, 8 Gray, 492; C. v. Grimes, 10 Gray, 470; Larned v. C., 12 Met. 240; C. v. Collins, 138 Mass. 483. Where the indictment alleged the larceny of nine bank-notes amounting in the whole to the sum of £9 and of the value of £9, it was held that this was an allegation of the larceny of nine bank-notes for £1 each and was sufficient: Rex v. Johnson, 2 Russ. Cr. 110.

[6] Hamblett v. S., 18 N. H. 384; U. S. v. Barry, 4 Cranch, C. C. 606; T. v. Shipley, 4 Mont. 468; S. v. Oakley, 51 Ark. 112.

[7] Rhodus v. C., 2 Duv. 159; Lewis v. S., 3 Heisk. 333; S. v. Cason, 20 La. An. 48.

[8] S. v. Gorham, 55 N. H. 152. Bank-

that bank-bills be minutely described.[1] The description of the note by the bank issuing it, and the denomination, is sufficient.[2] Indeed, the weight of authority is that the name of the bank is not essential, the number, denomination and value being sufficient.[3] There is some discrepancy in the cases as to how United States treasury notes and national bank notes are to be described. In one case it was said that, under a statute with reference to the stealing of notes of any bank chartered by the United States, or by an individual state, the indictment must state by what authority the bank issuing the notes was chartered.[4] It has also been held that, under an indictment for taking money of a certain description designated as "lawful money of the United States," it was not proper to prove the taking of national bank notes.[5] An indictment for larceny of notes of the "national currency of the United States" was held sufficient under a statute which provided as to the larceny of "United States currency."[6] A description of such bills as "United States treasury notes," or as "United States promissory or bank-notes," has been held sufficient;[7] so the description of "bank-notes," or "currency notes commonly called

bill and bank-note are terms that may be used interchangeably: Roth v. S., 10 Tex. Ap. 27. They may be described as promissory notes, commonly called bank-notes: McLaughlin v. C., 4 Rawle, 464.

[1] Wilson v. S., 66 Ga. 591; P. v. Holbrook, 13 Johns. 90; S. v. Smart, 4 Rich. 356. Description in the language of the statute is sufficient: S. v. Cassel, 2 Har. & G. 407.

[2] Salisbury v. S., 6 Conn. 101; P. v. Holbrook, 13 Johns. 90; Crawford v. S., 2 Ind. 132. The proof must correspond to the allegations as to the bank issuing: Pomeroy v. C., 2 Va. Cas. 342.

[3] S. v. Stevens, 62 Me. 284; C. v. Richards, 1 Mass. 337; S. v. Mahanna, 48 N. H. 377; Hart v. S., 55 Ind. 599; Foster v. S., 71 Md. 553; Baldwin v. S., 1 Sneed, 411; Pyland v. S., 4 Sneed, 357; P. v. Kent, 1 Doug. 42; Carden v. S., 89 Ala. 130; S. v. Evans, 15 Rich. 31; C. v. Moseley, 2 Va. Cas. 154; Pomeroy v. C., 2 Va. Cas. 342; S. v. Anderson, 25 Minn. 66; S. v. Bond, 8 Ia. 540; S. v. Graham, 65 Ia. 617; Munson v. S., 4 Greene (Ia.), 483; U. S. v. McDaniel, 4 Cranch, C. C. 721; C. v. Grimes, 10 Gray, 470; Larned v. C., 12 Met. 240.

[4] U. S. v. Porte, 1 Cranch, C. C. 369.

[5] Hamilton v. S., 60 Ind. 193. And see S. v. Collins, 72 N. C. 144. A description of the bill stolen as "one ten-dollar United States national bank note of the value," etc., was held sufficient: Wells v. S., 4 Tex. Ap. 20.

[6] Dull v. C., 25 Grat. 965. So the description of "one twenty-dollar bill United States of America paper currency money of the value," etc., was held sufficient: Cook v. S., 4 Tex. Ap. 265.

[7] S. v. Thomason, 71 N. C. 146; Bell v. S., 41 Ga. 589.

greenbacks," is sufficient.[1] A gold certificate may properly be described as a United States treasury note.[2] These cases sufficiently indicate that a special description beyond what would be reasonably practicable in such a case is not required; but indictments sometimes excuse the want of greater particularity by alleging that the names of the banks issuing the notes are to the grand jury unknown.[3] Failure to specify the number and denomination may be excused in the same way;[4] so uncertainty of description as to whether money stolen is in bank-notes or coin may be excused,[5] or in treasury notes or national bank notes.[6] But where there is a description, the evidence must in some way identify the property stolen as that described.[7]

§ 597. **Money, coin.**— At common law coin should be specifically described by the number, denomination and value,[8] but this rule is not now observed, being changed either by statute or by the general tendency to more liberal construction of indictments, and it is almost universally held that the description of the kind of coin (that is, gold, silver or copper), and the value of the quantity stolen, is sufficient.[9] Indeed, the description of a certain sum of money has been held sufficient, there being a statutory provision authorizing such description;[10] but the allegation of the theft of so many "dollars"

[1] S. v. Hockenberry, 30 Ia. 504; Levy v. S., 79 Ala. 259; Statum v. S., 9 Tex. Ap. 273. And see S. v. Beebe, 17 Minn. 241.

[2] Randall v. S., 53 N. J. 485.

[3] C. v. Grimes, 10 Gray, 470.

[4] S. v. Hoppe, 39 Ia. 468; C. v. Gallagher, 126 Mass. 54; C. v. Griffiths, 126 Mass. 252.

[5] Haskins v. P., 16 N. Y. 344; Davis v. S., 32 Tex. Ap. 377.

[6] Duvall v. S., 63 Ala. 12. Under such an indictment the jury may acquit if the evidence shows that the grand jury knew a more particular description of the money, but not if it only appears that they could have ascertained the more particular description by reasonable diligence: Duvall v. S., 63 Ala. 12.

[7] Vale v. P., 161 Ill. 309, 43 N. E. R. 1091.

[8] Lord v. S., 20 N. H. 404; S. v. Murphy, 6 Ala. 845; Reg. v. Bond, 1 Den. 517; S. v. Hanshew, 3 Wash. 12.

[9] C. v. Gallagher, 16 Gray, 240; C. v. Sawtelle, 11 Cush. 142; C. v. Duffy, 11 Cush. 145; P. v. Green, 15 Cal. 512; P. v. Bogart, 36 Cal. 245; P. v. Ball, 14 Cal. 101; McKane v. S., 11 Ind. 195; S. v. Jackson, 26 W. Va. 250; Porter v. S., 26 Fla. 56; Bryant v. S., 16 Tex. Ap. 144; Bravo v. S., 20 Tex. Ap. 177; U. S. v. Kurtz, 4 Cranch, C. C. 674; U. S. v. Barry, 4 Cranch, C. C. 606. So the description of "a quantity of money of the value of seventy-seven dollars," etc., was held sufficient: S. v. Hanshew, 3 Wash. 12.

[10] Brown v. P., 29 Mich. 232; Hammond v. S., 121 Ind. 512; Graves v. S., 121 Ind. 357; S. v. Walker, 22 La. An. 425. So the description of a certain number of "dollars" in money, or "in lawful money of the United

is not sufficient.[1] The allegation of the larceny of so many "dollars in United States currency" has been held insufficient for not specifying the kind of currency.[2] In other cases it has been held that the description of "dollars in paper currency of the United States," or "national currency of the United States," was sufficient.[3] In the case of coins not legal tender, or securities, the value should be specifically alleged;[4] but where the property stolen is described as money, a special allegation of value is not necessary.[5] Insufficiency of description as to the kind of money and the denomination is excused by alleging that such description is to the grand jury unknown.[6] An indictment for theft of money will not cover theft of checks.[7]

§ 598. **Money not goods and chattels.**— Coin should not be described as "of the goods and chattels" of the owner,[8] but the description of the coin as "of the goods and chattels" may be omitted as surplusage if the balance of the description is sufficient.[9] Bank-bills are usually by statute made subject of larceny in analogy with bills and notes, and are therefore properly described as "of the goods and chattels."[10]

States," is held sufficient: Randall v. S., 132 Ind. 539; S. v. Freeman, 89 N. C. 469; Wofford v. S., 29 Tex. Ap. 536; S. v. Blanchard, 11 Wash. 116. But under the Texas statute defining money as used in such an indictment as meaning legal tender currency of the United States, the indictment charging the stealing of money is not supported by evidence that the money was a twenty-dollar bill of American money: Otero v. S., 30 Tex. Ap. 450.

1 Merwin v. P., 26 Mich. 298; Croker v. S., 47 Ala. 53; S. v. Longbottoms, 11 Humph. 39; Barton v. S., 29 Ark. 68; Lavarre v. S., 1 Tex. Ap. 685; Dukes v. S., 22 Tex. Ap. 192. *Contra*, S. v. Greene, 27 La. An. 598.

2 Leftwich v. C., 20 Grat. 716; Merrill v. S., 45 Miss. 657; Martinez v. S., 41 Tex. 164; Ridgeway v. S., 41 Tex. 231. An indictment should show the country of which the money is the currency: Boyle v. S., 37 Tex. 359; Williams v. S., 5 Tex. Ap. 116.

3 S. v. Ziord, 30 La. An., part II, 867; Du Bois v. S., 50 Ala. 139. "United States paper currency money" includes silver certificates and national bank notes: Kimbrough v. S., 28 Tex. Ap. 367.

4 C. v. Smith, 1 Mass. 245; P. v. Donald, 48 Mich. 491.

5 S. v. King, 37 La. An. 91. Evidence that the property stolen was "good and lawful money of the United States" is not ground for reversal if not objected to: Graves v. S., 121 Ind. 357.

6 Chisholm v. S., 45 Ala. 66.

7 Lancaster v. S., 9 Tex. Ap. 393.

8 S. v. Parker, 1 Houst. Cr. C. 9. The stealing of coin is an offense at common law: S. v. Evans, 7 Gill & J. 290. As to a similar question arising under the statute as to receiving stolen goods, see *infra*, § 718.

9 Eastman v. C., 4 Gray, 416; C. v. Moseley, 2 Va. Cas. 154; Reg. v. Radley, 2 C. & K. 974.

10 P. v. Holbrook, 13 Johns. 90; Boyd

§ 599. **Evidence of identity and value.**— Coin cannot be identified so strictly as other property, and such evidence as satisfies the jury that the coin stolen was the same as that described is sufficient.[1] The value of bank-bills is sufficiently shown by evidence that they were good money.[2]

§ 600. **"Personal property," "goods and chattels."** — The property need not be described as personal property if that fact appears from the description used.[3] It is usual to charge that the property described was "of the goods and chattels of" the person named as owner. Such description indicates ownership even though the property is not strictly within the common-law term of goods and chattels.[4] It is not necessary to use the term "personal" with "goods and chattels,"[5] and it is not necessary to use the term "goods and chattels" at all where the description sufficiently indicates that the thing stolen is of that character.[6]

§ 601. **Ownership.**— It is essential, as has already been shown,[7] that the property taken belong to another than the person charged with the wrongful taking. In order to make this essential fact appear, the ownership of the property charged to have been wrongfully taken must be alleged.[8] The description of the property as the goods and chattels of a person named is a sufficient allegation of ownership in such person;[9] and even if the property is not goods and chattels, but is subject of larceny, the ownership may nevertheless be sufficiently indicated by the description of the property as of the goods and chattels of a

v. C., 1 Rob. (Va.) 691. This is authorized at common law: Reg. v. Sadi, 2 East, P. C. 748.

[1] P. v. Linn, 23 Cal. 150; S. v. Freeman, 72 N. C. 521; Roberts v. S., 83 Ga. 369.

[2] S. v. Evans, 15 Rich. 31; Baldwin v. S., 1 Sneed, 411.

[3] Jones v. S., 51 Miss. 718; S. v. Gallinore, 7 Ired. 147.

[4] S. v. Bartlett, 55 Me. 200; P. v. Kent, 1 Doug. 42. The term "goods and articles" will include a horse: S. v. Ward, 49 Conn. 429.

[5] Choen v. S., 85 Ind. 209.

[6] S. v. Parker, 34 Ark. 158; S. v. Bayonne, 36 La. An. 761.

[7] See *supra*, § 547.

[8] P. v. Hanselman, 76 Cal. 460; S. v. McAloon, 40 Me. 133; Reg. v. Ward, 7 Cox, 421. The allegation of fraudulent taking, etc., from the possession of the person named, without the allegation of ownership in such person, is not sufficient: Maddox v. S., 14 Tex. Ap. 447; S. v. Ellis, 119 Mo. 437. But if the indictment describes the person from whose possession the property was taken as the owner thereof, that is sufficient: Mathews v. S., 17 Tex. Ap. 472.

[9] Garber v. S., 94 Ind. 219.

person named.[1] With reference to this requirement that the property shall appear to have belonged to another than the person wrongfully taking it, it has been said that ownership in a particular person is not material,[2] and that therefore under statutory provisions amendment of the indictment in this respect may be made by the trial court;[3] but description of the property by means of the ownership thereof is a proper means of designating the property charged to have been stolen, and in this respect it is generally regarded as very material, and therefore cannot be amended.[4] Without such allegation of ownership the description of the property is usually insufficient, and the indictment defective,[5] and the ownership must be proven as alleged.[6] A failure to aver the ownership should be explained,[7] as, for instance, by alleging the owner to be unknown to the grand jury.[8] The fact that the ownership was unknown to the jurors is in such a case a material allegation;[9] and if it appears that the name of the owner might have been discovered

[1] Eastman v. C., 4 Gray, 416.

[2] S. v. Bell, 65 N. C. 313.

[3] C. v. O'Brien, 2 Brews. 566; Baker v. S., 88 Wis. 140; S. v. Hanks, 39 La. An. 234; S. v. Harris, 42 La. An. 980; S. v. Ware, 44 La. An. 954; Reg. v. Fullarton, 6 Cox, 194; Reg. v. Pritchard, L. & C. 34. *Contra*, S. v. Van Cleve, 5 Wash. 642; Reg. v. Ward, 7 Cox, 421.

[4] S. v. Van Cleve, 5 Wash. 642.

[5] S. v. Van Cleve, 5 Wash. 642; Stone v. S., 12 Tex. Ap. 193; S. v. Sheppard, 33 La. An. 1216. Thus, the allegation that the property belonged to the estate of a deceased person is not sufficient: S. v. Woodley, 25 Ga. 235. The allegation of ownership giving the surname only of the alleged owner is not sufficient without the averment that the Christian name is unknown: Morningstar v. S., 52 Ala. 405.

[6] S. v. Dwyre, 2 Hill (S. C.), 287; S. v. Pitts, 12 S. C. 180; S. v. Washington, 15 Rich. 39; Hughes v. C., 17 Grat. 565; Jones v. C., 17 Grat. 563; King v. S., 44 Ind. 285; Bell v. S., 46 Ind. 453; Miller v. P., 13 Colo. 166; Clark v. S., 29 Tex. Ap. 437. An indictment for stealing a horse of A. cannot be sustained by proof of stealing a horse of B., unless the horse is otherwise so described as to be identified without regard to ownership: McBride v. C., 13 Bush, 337. It is not essential that proof of ownership be made by the testimony of the owner himself; the fact may be established by the testimony of others cognizant of the fact: Lawrence v. S., 4 Yerg. 145.

[7] Reed v. C., 7 Bush, 641; Brewer v. S., 18 Tex. Ap. 456.

[8] S. v. Bell, 65 N. C. 313; S. v. Polland, 53 Me. 124; S. v. Haddock, 2 Hayw. 162; C. v. O'Brien, 2 Brewster, 566; Thompson v. S., 9 Tex. Ap. 301; Mackey v. S., 20 Tex. Ap. 603; McVey v. S., 23 Tex. Ap. 659. An allegation that the animal taken was an estray sufficiently shows an unknown owner: S. v. Anderson, 34 Tex. 611. So, under allegation of unknown ownership, proof that the animal was an estray is sufficient: Wills v. S., 40 Tex. 69.

[9] Williamson v. S., 13 Tex. Ap. 514.

by the grand jury in the exercise of reasonable diligence, a conviction cannot be sustained.[1] In case of robbery or stealing from the person, ownership of the property taken is immaterial, the offense being one against the person rather than with reference to the property.[2] So, under a charge of horse-stealing as a specific crime, ownership of the animal is not an essential averment.[3]

§ 602. **Joint ownership; several owners.**— If the property is alleged to be that of an individual named, evidence that it belongs to that person and another or others jointly will not support the indictment.[4] An allegation of ownership in one person is not supported by evidence of ownership by two persons as partners.[5] An allegation of ownership in A. and B. will be supported by evidence of ownership by A. and B. as partners;[6] but allegation of ownership in a firm by the firm name only is sufficient.[7] An averment of ownership in two persons named is proper where the evidence supports the allegation;[8] but if the evidence shows that the ownership is only in one, the variance will be fatal;[9] so, under the allegation of joint ownership, proof of ownership of different portions of the

[1] Jorasco v. S., 6 Tex. Ap. 238; Atkinson v. S., 19 Tex. Ap. 462; Langham v. S., 26 Tex. Ap. 533; Swink v. S., 32 Tex. Ap. 530. But if the owner is charged to be unknown, the state is not bound to elect as between two or more possible owners, as shown by the evidence, there being but one act referred to: Black v. S., 83 Ala. 81.

[2] P. v. Watson, 72 Cal. 402.

[3] Halkem v. C., 2 Va. Cas. 4. So under a statute punishing the stealing or carrying away of corn, etc., from the land of another, it is not necessary to allege the ownership of the property taken: S. v. Schatz, 71 Mo. 502.

[4] McDowell v. S., 68 Miss. 348; S. v. London, 3 S. C. 230; S. v. Burgess, 74 N. C. 272; Brown v. S., 35 Tex. 689; S. v. Wilson, 6 Oreg. 428. A statute which authorizes ownership to be laid in one of the owners, naming him, "and another, or others, as the case may be," will cure such difficulty: C. v. Arrance, 5 Allen, 517; but will not authorize an indictment alleging the property to be in the person named, "and another, or others," such an allegation being indefinite as in the alterative: S. v. Harper, 64 N. C. 129.

[5] C. v. Trimmer, 1 Mass. 476; Hogg v. S., 3 Blackf. 326; S. v. Owens, 10 Rich. 169. To the contrary, under statutory provisions as to indictments, see S. v. Cunningham, 21 Ia. 433; S. v. Connor, 5 Coldw. 311.

[6] P. v. Goggins, 80 Cal. 229; P. v. Barnes, 65 Cal. 16. If the ownership is laid in a partnership, giving the full name of the members, it is necessary to prove the names as laid: Doan v. S., 26 Ind. 495.

[7] P. v. Ah Sing, 19 Cal. 598.

[8] S. v. Scripture, 42 N. H. 485; Dodd v. S., 10 Tex. Ap. 370.

[9] Parmer v S., 41 Ala. 416; Widner v. S., 25 Ind. 234.

property by the two persons named in severalty will constitute a fatal variance.[1] Allegation of ownership in the same count in A. and also in B. is fatal;[2] but it is proper to allege ownership of the same property in different persons in different counts, and if the evidence supports the allegation of one count it will authorize a conviction.[3] It is proper, however, to allege in one count the larceny of different articles belonging to different persons named, where they are taken in one transaction.[4] But it must appear that the articles were stolen at the same time, otherwise the indictment will be bad for duplicity.[5] Where the taking of articles is properly charged in one count as committed in the same transaction, there may be a conviction, although the evidence shows different transactions, as the validity of the indictment will not be affected by the evidence.[6]

§ **603. What sufficient ownership.**— It has already been shown that the requirement of ownership in cases of larceny is fulfilled by actual possession, and that the bailee or other person in possession of the property may be treated as owner, and the wrongful taking may be alleged as of his property;[7] therefore, proof of possession by the person alleged as owner is sufficient, although at the same time the evidence shows the real ownership to be in another.[8] It has been already shown, also, that ownership may be alleged in bailor, although the possession is in bailee,[9] and under somewhat analogous reasoning it has been held that where a draft forwarded by a county treasurer through various channels to be paid into the state treasury was stolen, the ownership might be alleged to be in the state, although the draft had never reached the custody of the state treasurer, and

[1] S. v. Ellison, 58 N. H. 325.

[2] Morton v. S., 1 Lea, 498.

[3] P. v. Connor, 17 Cal. 354; P. v. Thompson, 28 Cal. 214; Butler v. S., 91 Ala. 87; Mabry v. C., 2 Va. Cas. 396.

[4] S. v. Merrill, 44 N. H. 624; Fulmer v. C., 97 Pa. St, 503; Bushman v. C., 138 Mass. 507; S. v. Newton, 42 Vt. 537; S. v. Simons, 70 N. C. 336; Lowe v. S., 57 Ga. 171; P. v. Johnson, 81 Mich. 573; Hoiles v. U. S., 3 MacArthur, 370.

[5] Joslyn v. S., 128 Ind. 160. If the allegation shows that the different articles were taken on the same day it will be presumed that they were taken in the same transaction: Bushman v. C., 138 Mass. 507.

[6] Fulmer v. C., 97 Pa. St. 503. As to larceny of different articles in the same transaction, see, also, *supra*, § 551.

[7] See *supra*, § 546.

[8] Kennedy v. S., 31 Fla. 428; S. v. Somerville, 21 Me. 14.

[9] See *supra*, § 546.

also that the ownership might likewise be charged as in one of the officers through whose hands it should pass, who should have the custody of it at the time it was taken.[1] So in an indictment for the larceny of whiskey in a government warehouse, ownership may be laid in the person having the right to take the property on payment of the tax.[2] So where a piece of meat cut off for a customer was by the butcher laid on his counter, and payment therefor had been made by the customer, larceny of the meat before it was taken up by the purchaser was held properly charged as of the property of the purchaser.[3] Where the indictment alleges not only ownership, but the taking from the possession of the person thus named as owner, proof of taking from the possession of another who has temporary rightful possession will not support the allegation.[4]

§ **604. Ownership in corporation.**— Where ownership is laid in a corporation, the fact of incorporation should be alleged;[5] but by statute such allegation is sometimes made unnecessary.[6] The proof must correspond with the allegation as to the corporate name, and a variance will be fatal.[7] But proof of existence *de facto* is enough.[8] So if a corporation conducts its business in a name different from its corporate name, a crime as to the corporate property may be charged with an allegation of ownership of the property in the assumed name.[9] Allegation of ownership in a corporation, and taking thereof from possession of the receiver of such corporation, is proper.[10] After verdict it will be presumed that there was sufficient evidence of the corporate existence.[11] Where the property is that of an unincorporated company, it should be described as belonging

1 Phelps v. P., 72 N. Y. 334.

2 S. v. Harmon, 104 N. C. 792.

3 S. v. Robinson, 35 La. An. 964.

4 C. v. Williams, 1 Va. Cas. 14.

5 Wallace v. P., 63 Ill. 451; White v. S., 24 Tex. Ap. 231; Thurmond v. S., 30 Tex. Ap. 539; McCowan v. S., 58 Ark. 17.

6 S. v. Grant, 104 N. C. 908.

7 S. v. Sharp, 106 Mo. 106; White v. S., 24 Tex. Ap. 231. But proof of incorporation may be made by showing the business carried on in the corporate name. The certificate of incorporation need not be shown: Reg. v. Langton, 2 Q. B. D. 296.

8 S. v. Habib, 18 R. I. 558; Smith v. S., 28 Ind. 321; P. v. Barric, 49 Cal. 342. And as to a similar question in regard to forgery, see *infra*, § —.

9 Jackson v. S., 93 Ga. 165.

10 S. v. Coss, 12 Wash. 673. And though the receiver is one appointed by a federal court, the state court will have jurisdiction of the crime: Ibid.

11 Lithgow v. C., 2 Va. Cas. 297. Proof of the *de facto* existence of the cor-

to the persons composing the company.[1] Where the county is a municipal corporation for the purpose of holding property, ownership of the stolen property may be alleged in it rather than its officers.[2]

§ 605. **Effect of mistake in name.**— The Christian name of the owner should be alleged, and an allegation giving the initial or initials only of the Christian name or names is not sufficient;[3] but such an objection must be made to the indictment, for if it is not urged until after verdict it will be too late.[4] Under an indictment naming the owner by the initials only of his Christian name, evidence is admissible that he was thus generally known, and such evidence will prevent the defendant being entitled to an acquittal on account of variance.[5] Indeed, the owner may be described by the name under which he is generally known in his business, although such is not his real name.[6] The names alleged must be proven, and a variance will be fatal. Thus, where the ownership of the property was laid in "John Peter Sinish," while the proof showed that it belonged to "John Sinish," it was held that the evidence did not support the indictment.[7] It was so held also where the owner was named as "Gabriel Carter," while the proof showed his name to be "Carter Gabriel."[8] So held also where the owner was named in the indictment "J. W. Flannagan," while in the evidence he was referred to only as "Major Flannagan."[9] So held also where the owner was described by "N. J.," as the initials of his Christian name, while the evidence showed his initials to be "M. J."[10] Where the indictment charged the Christian name of the owner of the property to be "Elizabeth

poration is sufficient: S. v. Collens, 37 La. An. 607. If the corporation is foreign, it is not necessary to prove that it was legally doing business in the state: S. v. Hopkins, 56 Vt. 250.

1 Wallace v. P., 63 Ill. 451. And see *supra*, § 602.

2 P. v. Bennett, 37 N. Y. 117; S. v. Rollins, 28 Ind. 390; S. v. Gaffery, 12 La. An. 265.

3 S. v. Rook, 42 Kan. 419; Unger v. S., 42 Miss. 642.

4 S. v. Rook, 42 Kan. 419; S. v. Flack, 48 Kan. 146; Unger v. S., 42 Miss. 642; S. v. McMillan, 68 N. C. 440; S. v. Vanderlip, 4 La. An. 444.

5 Thompson v. S., 48 Ala. 165.

6 P. v. Leong Quong, 60 Cal. 107. And see Jackson v. S., 93 Ga. 165.

7 S. v. English, 67 Mo. 136.

8 Collins v. S., 43 Tex. 577. Where the indictment gives the Christian name and father's name, it will be sufficient, although the name by which the owner is known is the mother's name: Young v. S., 30 Tex. Ap. 308.

9 Perry v. S., 4 Tex. Ap. 566.

10 Willis v. S., 24 Tex. Ap. 487.

M.," while the evidence showed that the property belonged to "Betsy M.," it was held that the question whether the two forms of the name described the same person was for the jury.[1] Though the name given is not the real name, yet if it appears that the owner is as well known by that as the other the variance will be immaterial.[2] The general doctrine of *idem sonans* is applicable in indictments for this crime as in other cases.[3] Where the name is correctly recited in the indictment, but in another place incorrectly recited, the erroneous name may be treated as a merely clerical error.[4] If there is a total variance or failure of proof as to the ownership as alleged, the prosecution will not bar another prosecution for stealing the same property under a correct averment of the ownership.[5] Acquittal under a charge of ownership unknown, if properly made, will bar a prosecution for larceny of the same property described as that of a known owner.[6]

§ 606. Defective indictment cured by verdict.— As has been stated in the last section, a defect in the indictment as to the name of the owner will be cured if no objection is taken until after verdict. Other objections, as that the evidence shows the ownership in two persons, whereas the indictment lays ownership in only one,[7] or that the corporate existence is not sufficiently proven, where the ownership is laid in a corporation,[8] are also cured by verdict, and cannot be afterwards raised. Other objections to the description are similarly cured.[9] Objection that an indictment for the statutory offense of horse-

[1] S. v. Godet, 7 Ired. 210.

[2] C. v. Williams, 161 Mass. 442.

[3] Thus it was held that where the name in the indictment was "Anne Fooley," and the evidence showed the name of the owner to be "Anne Foley," there was not a variance: Underwood v. S., 72 Ala. 220. So "Johnson" and "Johnston" are not variant: Truslow v. S., 95 Tenn. 189. See Rex v. Sulls, 2 Leach, 861.

[4] Greeson v. S., 6 Miss. 33.

[5] S. v. Williams, 45 La. An. 936; Price v. S., 19 Ohio, 423; Reg. v. Green, Dears. & B. 113; unless it appears that the two names mean the same person: S. v. Risher, 1 Rich. 219. So, in the second indictment, the property may be described as that of an unknown owner: S. v. Birmingham, Busbee, 120; S. v. Revels, Busbee, 200. But in Georgia it is held that a misdescription of the property as to the owner will not prevent the prosecution being a bar to another: Buhler v. S., 64 Ga. 504; Goode v. S., 70 Ga. 752; Knox v. S., 89 Ga. 259.

[6] Fenton v. S., 33 Tex. Ap. 633.

[7] S. v. Burgess, 74 N. C. 272.

[8] Lithgow v. C., 2 Va. Cas. 297.

[9] S. v. Crow, 107 Mo. 341; P. v. Jim Ti, 32 Cal. 60; S. v. Gilbert, 13 Vt. 647; S. v. Derst, 10 Nev. 443.

stealing does not conclude "contrary to the form of the statute" cannot be raised after verdict.[1]

§ 607. Allegation of "stealing, taking, and carrying away." As has already been said,[2] the technical words for describing the act in the indictment are "take, steal, and carry away."[3] It has been held that the omission of the word "steal" is not necessarily a fatal defect, the allegation of the feloniously taking and carrying away being sufficient;[4] but where the indictment also omitted the word "away," as well as the word "steal," it was held to be fatally defective;[5] and even where the three verbs were used, "steal, take, and carry," it was held that the omission of "away" was fatal, as asportation is essential to the offense;[6] but under a statute in Texas, the taking away may be alleged generally without the technical words "carry away."[7] Where the statute uses the word "steal" alone in describing the offense, that word implies the taking and carrying away, and is sufficient in the indictment,[8] at least after verdict, the omission of the other words being deemed only a formal defect.[9] Under a Texas statute which requires allegation of taking from possession of the owner, and with intent to appropriate, the misspelling of "possession" and of "appropriate," so as to destroy the identity of the words, has been held fatal.[10] The indictment must state the facts in some form; thus, it has been held that an allegation that defendant "converted" with intent to steal was not sufficient.[11] But a superfluous allegation of an immaterial fact, as that defendant stole and carried away "and did kill" one beef ox, will not vitiate the indictment.[12] The manner of taking, as by a conspiracy to cheat at a game of cards, need not be alleged.[13]

[1] Chiles v. C., 2 Va. Cas. 260.

[2] See *supra*, § 548.

[3] The common-law form is sufficient to charge what was larceny at common law, although the statute makes other acts, such as wrongful conversion, also larceny: S. v. Friend, 47 Minn. 449.

[4] S. v. Lee Yan Yan, 10 Oreg. 365; Damewood v. S., 1 How. (Miss.) 262.

[5] Rountree v. S., 58 Ala. 381.

[6] C. v. Adams, 7 Gray, 43.

[7] Austen v. S., 42 Tex. 345.

[8] S. v. Mann, 25 Ohio St. 668; Beery v. U. S., 2 Colo. 186.

[9] Green v. C., 111 Mass. 417.

[10] S. v. Williamson, 43 Tex. 500; Jones v. S., 25 Tex. Ap. 621. Where intent to defraud and intent to appropriate are charged in the same indictment, it is not necessary to repeat "then and there" as to each intent: Harris v. S., 2 Tex. Ap. 102.

[11] P. v. Poggi, 19 Cal. 600.

[12] S. v. Johnson, 30 La. An., part 1, 305.

[13] S. v. Reis, 9 Wash. 329.

§ 608. Felonious intent.— A felonious intent is sufficiently alleged by charging the act to have been feloniously done,[1] and such allegation sufficiently indicates that the taking was unlawful.[2] At common law it is undoubtedly necessary to allege the act as felonious;[3] but under statutory definitions of larceny, the word "feloniously" may not be necessary if other words indicating the intent are used corresponding to the terms of the statute. Where the offense is a misdemeanor, the word "steal" sufficiently indicates that the intent was what at common law would be felonious.[4] In Texas the statute describing larceny requires a fraudulent taking, and the indictment must therefore charge the act to be fraudulent; charging it to be felonious is not sufficient.[5]

§ 609. As an included offense; joinder.—Larceny is included in the offense of robbery;[6] but it is not necessarily included in that of burglary.[7] The offense of larceny from the person differs from robbery only in the element of force and violence, or putting in fear;[8] and therefore there may be a conviction of larceny from the person, although the evidence shows such violence as to indicate robbery.[9] For a similar reason, acquittal of larceny from a dwelling-house in the night-time prevents a prosecution for robbery in the same transaction, as the offense of larceny is included in each.[10] Thus, also, a prior prosecution for larceny will be a bar to a prosecution of larceny from the person.[11] Under an indictment for larceny from the person there may be a conviction for larceny.[12] An indictment for larceny from a dwelling-house also includes simple larceny.[13] In a prose-

[1] P. v. Willet, 102 N. Y. 251; P. v. Brown, 27 Cal. 500.

[2] S. v. Jones, 7 Nev. 408; Barker v. C., 2 Va. Cas. 122; Reg. v. Butterworth, 12 Cox, 132.

[3] Smith v. S., 93 Ind. 67; P. v. Cheong Foon Ark, 61 Cal. 527.

[4] Gardiner v. S., 55 N. J. 17.

[5] Muldrew v. S., 12 Tex. Ap. 617 (overruling Mosquez v. S., 41 Tex. 226); Sloan v. S., 18 Tex. Ap. 225; Ortis v. S., 18 Tex. Ap. 282; Ware v. S., 19 Tex. Ap. 13; Spain v. S., 19 Tex. Ap. 469; McPherson v. S., 20 Tex. Ap. 194.

[6] P. v. Jones, 53 Cal. 58; Allen v. S., 58 Ala. 98; S. v. Keeland, 90 Mo. 337; *supra*, § 511. And there may be a conviction for larceny although the evidence is such as would have sustained a prosecution for robbery: Skipworth v. S., 8 Tex. Ap. 135.

[7] P. v. Parrow, 80 Mich. 567; P. v. Garnett, 29 Cal. 622. And see *supra*, § 511.

[8] S. v. Miller, 83 Ia. 291.

[9] S. v. Graff, 66 Ia. 482.

[10] S. v. Mikesell, 70 Ia. 176.

[11] S. v. Gleason, 56 Ia. 203.

[12] S. v. Taylor, 3 Oreg. 10; Fanning v. S., 12 Lea, 651.

[13] Moore v. S., 40 Ala. 49.

cution for grand larceny there may of course be a conviction for petit larceny.[1] These are not two degrees of crime, but only of punishment, and a conviction for petit larceny bars a subsequent prosecution for grand larceny.[2] If an indictment charges a compound larceny, there may be a conviction for simple larceny.[3] Larceny includes the crime of driving stock from its accustomed range without the owner's consent.[4] Under an indictment for the offense, there may be conviction for an attempt, although no taking or carrying away is shown.[5] The offense of receiving stolen goods is a distinct one from that of larceny, and under an indictment for larceny a conviction for receiving the stolen property cannot be had;[6] so the charge of larceny does not include embezzlement.[7] But although the offense of receiving stolen goods or that of embezzlement cannot be charged in the same count with larceny, yet as at common law different offenses may be charged in different counts of the same indictment, there will be no objection to thus charging the receiving of stolen goods,[8] or embezzlement,[9] together with larceny, in distinct counts, either where the common law remains unmodified in this respect, or where, although by stat-

[1] P. v. Jack, 76 Mich. 218.

[2] S. v. Murray, 55 Ia. 530. And see *supra*, § 581.

[3] Hall v. S., 7 Lea, 685.

[4] Counts v. S., 37 Tex. 593; Powell v. S., 7 Tex. Ap. 467; Turner v. S., 7 Tex. Ap. 596.

[5] Wolf v. S., 41 Ala. 412. And further as to attempts, see that subject, *supra*, § 229.

[6] Ross v. S., 1 Blackf. 390; Alexander v. S., 60 Miss. 953; S. v. Whitaker, 89 N. C. 472; S. v. Moultrie, 33 La. An. 1146; Gaither v. S., 21 Tex. Ap. 527; McCampbell v. S., 9 Tex. Ap. 124; Johnson v. S., 13 Tex. Ap. 378; Brown v. S., 15 Tex. Ap. 581 (overruling Parchman v. S., 2 Tex. Ap. 228; Vincent v. S., 10 Tex. Ap. 330). So, under indictment for receiving, there can be no conviction for theft: Gonzales v. S., 13 Tex. Ap. 48.

[7] C. v. Simpson, 9 Met. 138; P. v. De Coursey, 61 Cal. 134; Huntsman v. S., 12 Tex. Ap. 619 (overruling Whitworth v. S., 11 Tex. Ap. 414). Otherwise in Missouri by statute: S. v. Broderick, 70 Mo. 622; S. v. Owen, 78 Mo. 367.

[8] S. v. Stimpson, 45 Me. 608; C. v. O'Connell, 12 Allen, 451; S. v. Lawrence, 81 N. C. 522; S. v. Morrison, 85 N. C. 561; S. v. Baker, 70 N. C. 530; S. v. Carter, 113 N. C. 639; Redman v. S., 1 Blackf. 429; Maynard v. S., 14 Ind. 427; Janeway v. S., 1 Head, 130; Hampton v. S., 8 Humph. 69; Ayrs v. S., 5 Coldw. 26; Cook v. S., 16 La, 461; S. v. Posey, 7 Rich. 484; S. v. Blakesley, 43 Kan. 250; Reg. v. Ward, 2 F. & F. 18; Rex v. Wheeler, 7 C. & P. 170; Reg. v. Beeton, 2 C. & K. 960; Reg. v. Huntley, Bell, 238; Reg. v. Craddock, 2 Den. 31; Reg. v. Holman, L. & C. 177; Reg. v. Sarsfield, 6 Cox, 12.

[9] Murphy v. P., 104 Ill. 528, 4 Am. Cr. R. 323 and note.

ute different offenses cannot be charged in the same indictment, an exception is made in regard to this particular case. So, by statute, counts for larceny and burglary may be joined, even where the joinder of different offenses is prohibited by statute.[1] Of course, unless there is some statutory prohibition, distinct larcenies may be charged in separate counts of the same indictment.[2] Where joinder in different counts of larceny and of receiving the goods stolen is allowed, different defendants may be convicted under the same indictment, one for the larceny, and another for the receiving.[3]

§ **610. Form of indictment.**— The indictment for larceny in common use is modeled quite definitely after the form in Latin early used in England. It is applicable to all cases except those under special statutes; and even to those it may be applied with but slight change. It will not be necessary, therefore, to give many examples.

OF GOODS AND CHATTELS.

That A. B., at ——, on ——, one silver spoon of the value of five dollars, one hat of the value of one dollar, one gold watch of the value of fifty dollars, two oxen of the value of one hundred and eighty dollars, one horse of the value of one hundred dollars, one certain riding wagon of the value of ninety dollars, and one harness of the value of twenty dollars, of the goods and chattels of one C. D. [or stating the ownership of each article separately if they belong to different owners], then and there being found, feloniously did steal, take and carry away.[4]

[1] McCullough v. S., 132 Ind. 427.

[2] S. v. Lockwood, 58 Vt. 378.

[3] Rex v. Wheeler, 7 C. & P. 170.

[4] See S. v. Leavitt, 66 Me. 440; Bish. Direc. & F., § 582; 1 Whart. Prec. 415. "There being found" is omitted in late English precedents and many of the precedents in the various states: See 2 Archbold, Cr. Pl. & Pr. 354; Moore, Cr. L. 342; Maxwell, Cr. Pr. 376. Some forms, instead of simply "then and there being found," say, "then and there in the possession of said C. D. being found:" Lewis, Cr. Law, 660; Heard, Mass. Cr. L. 733. But this allegation as to possession is unnecessary: S. v. Leavitt, *supra*. While the old forms of indictment for larceny of living animals charge that accused "did take and lead away" in case of a horse, or "did take and drive away" in case of cattle, sheep, etc. (1 Hale, P. C. 504), instead of "did steal, take and carry away," as in case of other goods and chattels, yet this distinction is now wholly disregarded, and the general form is used in such cases. In none of the authorities cited in this note is any such variation recognized. That the animals are here described with sufficient definiteness, see *supra*, § 594.

OF MONEY; FROM THE PERSON.

That A. B., in the county aforesaid, on ——, sundry gold coins, current as money in this state, of the aggregate value of twenty-nine dollars, and sundry bank-bills usually known and described as national bank notes, of the value of one hundred and eighty dollars, of the money of C. D., then and there being upon the person of said C. D. [*or* then and there being from the person of said C. D.], feloniously did steal, take and carry away.[1]

OF PROMISSORY NOTE.

That A. B., in the county aforesaid, on ——, one promissory note of the value of three hundred dollars, and one piece of paper of the value of three hundred dollars [*or*, one paper purporting to be a check for the payment of one hundred and twenty-five dollars, of the value of one hundred and twenty-five dollars], of the goods and chattels of one C. D., feloniously did steal, take and carry away.[2]

§ 611. **Restitution of property.**— At common law a writ for the restitution of stolen property could be given only on an appeal of felony for the theft;[3] but by statute 21 Henry 8, chapter 11, a writ or order of restitution was authorized on conviction in criminal proceedings.[4] This statute, which is old

[1] That this is a sufficient description of money and bank-bills, see C. v. Sawtelle, 11 Cush. 142; C. v. Gallagher, 16 Gray, 240; S. v. Hoppe, 39 Ia. 468; S. v. Hockenberry, 30 Ia. 504; McEntee v. S., 24 Wis. 43. But such an allegation has been held insufficient in Hamblett v. S., 18 N. H. 384, in which it is said that the number of the coins or bills, and the value of each, should be stated. This particularity of description, where it is required, can be obviated by the allegation that the number and value of the particular coins or bills is to the grand jury unknown: C. v. Sawtelle, 11 Cush. 142. The indictment will not be bad for alleging that the coins or bills are "of the goods and chattels of, etc.," rather than "of the money of, etc.:" See *supra*, § 598. As to the method of alleging that the larceny is from the person so as to bring the case within a statute making that a form of compound larceny, see Whalen v. C., 90 Va. 544; 1 Whart. Prec. 442; Heard, Mass. Cr. L. 733.

[2] As to the promissory note, see C. v. Brettun, 100 Mass. 206. As to the check, see Whalen v. C., 90 Va. 544; S. v. Pierson, 59 Ia. 271. In the latter case the check is further described by giving the name of the signer and of the bank. At common law choses in action are properly described as "personal property" instead of "goods and chattels;" but the form here used is undoubtly sufficient in that respect and in accordance with present usage: See *supra*, § 595.

[3] Reg. v. London, L. R. 4 Q. B. 371.

[4] 2 Bish. Cr. Pr., §§ 755–763; Abbott, Cr. Brief, §§ 877–883; Am. & Eng. Ency. of Law, "Restitution;" 4 Bl. Com. 362; 2 Russ. Cr. 130; 1 Hale, P. C. 541; 1 Arch. Cr. Pr. & Pl. [192];

enough to be common law in this country, is generally superseded both in this country and in England by other statutory provisions,[1] under which the court on the conviction of the defendant may properly enter an order for the restitution to the owner of the property stolen.[2] But the court has no jurisdiction to render judgment against the prisoner, nor award execution in favor of the owner.[3] Before property can be thus ordered returned it must appear that it is stolen property, and the property involved in the larceny for which the defendant is on trial.[4] When restitution is to be a part of the judgment, the verdict should find what property was taken.[5] Restitution of the proceeds of the stolen property in the hands of the thief may be ordered if he has parted with the property itself.[6] The court has no authority to determine the right of a third person to the property, but can only make an order for its restoration to the person from whom it was stolen.[7] This procedure with reference to restitution does not affect

2 East, P. C. 787; 2 Hawk. P. C., ch. 23, §§ 49–57; 1 Rosc. Cr. Ev. 231.

1 In England the present statute on the subject is 24 and 25 Victoria, chapter 96, section 100, replacing 7 and 8 George 4, chapter 29, section 57. These statutes do not confer upon the court of Queen's Bench any authority to award a writ of restitution, except in case of a conviction before that court: Reg. v. London, L. R. 4 Q. B. 371. The order of restitution may be enforced by attachment for contempt: Reg. v. Wollez, 8 Cox, 337. Restitution is not to be made of bank-notes, negotiable securities, etc., which have passed into the hands of an innocent purchaser: Rex v. Stanton, 7 C. & P. 431; Chichester v. Hill, 15 Cox, 258. This is a general principle, without regard to statutory provisions: Saltus v. Everett, 20 Wend. 267; McMahon v. Sloan, 12 Pa. St. 229.

2 Lance v. Cowan, 1 Dana, 195; S. v. Williams, 61 Ia. 517.

3 C. v. Henley, 1 Va. Cas. 145.

4 Reg. v. Smith, 12 Cox, 597; Reg. v. Goldsmith, 12 Cox, 594; Reg. v. London, 27 L. J. M. C. 231; Josephs v. Atkins, 2 Stark. 76; Sullivan v. Robinson, 39 Ala. 613; Huntzinger v. C., 97 Pa. St. 336. Where there is a charge of larceny of money and a larger sum is found on the prisoner, but none of it is identified as that stolen, there is no right to retain therefrom the amount claimed as stolen: Ferguson v. U. S., 64 Fed. R. 88.

5 S. v. Somerville, 21 Me. 20.

6 Lance v. Cowan, 1 Dana, 195; Rex v. Powell, 7 C. & P. 640; Rex v. Rooney, 7 C. & P. 515. *Contra*, C. v. Boudrie, 4 Gray, 418.

7 S. v. Williams, 61 Ia. 517; Reg. v. London, E. B. & E. 509; but there are English cases which seem to intimate that the court may consider the rights of third persons: Reg. v. Macklin, 5 Cox, 216; Reg. v. Horan, 6 Ir. R. C. L. 293. Although, in England, anything stolen from the mails is charged as the property of the postmaster-general, he is not entitled to an order of restitution: Reg. v. Jones, 14 Cox, 528.

the owner's right to retake the property otherwise,[1] and he may of course follow it into the hands of an innocent purchaser;[2] but while the property is in the possession of the court through its officers, pending the trial of the case, no action can be maintained against them for its recovery.[3] If the defendant is acquitted, he is entitled to the return of the property which has been taken from him by the officers under the charge of larceny, and may maintain an action against the officer who fails to make such return, even though the property has been seized for his debts.[4] These provisions as to restitution of stolen property are not applicable in case of property obtained by false pretenses, except as they are made applicable by statutory provisions.[5] In such a case the purchaser from the wrong-doer gets good title, and therefore restitution as against him cannot be ordered.[6]

IX. EVIDENCE.

§ **612. Corpus delicti.**— To support a conviction there must be evidence that the property in question was actually stolen. Mere suspicious circumstances connected with the possession of the property by defendant, or opportunity on his part to commit the larceny, will not be sufficient.[7] In other words, there must be proof of a particular larceny.[8] The evidence of possession of stolen property, as will appear in a subsequent section, tends to connect defendant with the larceny when proven, but it does not establish the fact of larceny having been committed.[9] The question of the identification of the property

[1] Lance v. Cowan, 1 Dana, 195; Reifsnyder v. Lee, 44 Ia. 101; Scattergood v. Sylvester, 15 C. B. 506; Golightly v. Reynolds, Lofft, 88, 90.

[2] Bassett v. Spofford, 45 N. Y. 387; Barton v. Faherty, 3 Greene (Ia.), 327; Walker v. Matthews, 8 Q. B. D. 109; Binns v. Piggott, 9 C. & P. 208; Reg. v. Stancliffe, 11 Cox, 318; Reg. v. Wollez, 8 Cox, 337.

[3] Simpson v. St. John, 93 N. Y. 363; Weller v. Ely, 45 Conn. 547. But garnishment of the officer by the owner was sustained: Reifsnyder v. Lee, 44 Ia. 101.

[4] Fitzgerald v. Jordan, 11 Allen, 128. Thus, property taken from the prisoner on his arrest is not subject to levy: Commercial Exch. Bank v. McLeod, 65 Ia. 665.

[5] See *infra*, § 712.

[6] Rex v. Devaux, 2 East, P. C. 789, 839; Moyce v. Newington, 4 Q. B. D. 32.

[7] S. v. Furlong, 19 Me. 225; Tyner v. S., 5 Humph. 383; Burton v. March, 6 Jones, 409; Jorasco v. S., 8 Tex. Ap. 540.

[8] P. v. Williams, 57 Cal. 108.

[9] P. v. Williams, 57 Cal. 108. And see *infra*, § 616.

is not of any importance until the actual commission of the larceny is shown.[1] But the *corpus delicti* need not be shown by direct evidence; that is, there need not necessarily be proof of loss of property by theft, distinct from the facts showing that property found in the defendant's possession was wrongfully taken from the owner thereof.[2] Proof of the act is not necessary where the circumstances can only be explained by a felonious act.[3]

§ **613. Identification of property.**—For the purpose of connecting the defendant with the crime, the owner of the property stolen should be able to identify the property which it is charged the defendant took, with that stolen;[4] but identification by memory is not essential. The owner may for that purpose use a description in a written list of property,[5] and only such identification will be required as is reasonable, considering the nature of the property.[6] The defendant may be sufficiently connected with the larceny in other ways, although the stolen article may not be identified or even found.[7] In case of cattle or other animals, a brand or mark is often proven for the purpose of identification. In Texas, by statute, ownership cannot be established by proof of a mark or brand in such cases, unless such mark or brand has been recorded.[8]

1 S. v. McGowan, 1 S. C. 14.

2 Roberts v. S., 61 Ala. 401; Reg. v. Burton, Dears. 282; Reg. v. Mockford, 11 Cox, 16.

3 S. v. Rodman, 62 Ia. 456; Johnson v. S., 47 Ala. 62; Kemp v. S., 89 Ala. 52; Smiley v. S., 66 Ga. 754.

4 S. v. Furlong, 19 Me. 225.

5 S. v. Lull, 37 Me. 246.

6 S. v. Babb, 76 Mo. 501. So held as to money: Jenkins v. S., 62 Wis. 49; S. v. Hoppe, 39 Ia. 468; S. v. Buckley, 60 Ia. 471; S. v. Graham, 65 Ia. 617. And further, as to money, see note to § 616.

7 S. v. Kent, 65 N. C. 311.

8 S. v. Poag, 40 Tex. 151; Allen v. S., 42 Tex. 517; Wyers v. S., 21 Tex. Ap. 448; Romero v. S., 24 Tex. Ap. 130. But a witness may testify as to identity and ownership from brands or other marks, although unrecorded: Tittle v. S., 30 Tex. Ap. 597; Alexander v. S., 24 Tex. Ap. 126; Coffelt v. S., 19 Tex. Ap. 436; Poage v. S., 43 Tex. 454. The rule that the state must show a recorded brand applies only where the brand alone is relied upon as showing ownership: Hutto v. S., 7 Tex. Ap. 44; Fisher v. S., 4 Tex. Ap. 181; Wolf v. S., 4 Tex. Ap. 332. Although an indictment need not describe the brand, yet if the brand be described it must be proven in accordance with the allegation: Allen v. S., 8 Tex. Ap. 360; Sweat v. S., 4 Tex. Ap. 617. As to driving stock out of the county for sale without leaving on record a list of marks and brands, see Senterfit v. S., 41 Tex. 186.

§ 614. Identification of defendant; declarations; circumstantial evidence.— Aside from the effect of recent possession of the stolen property which will be considered in a subsequent section, the rules of evidence relating to the identification of the criminal in cases of larceny are not different from those applicable in other crimes; but a few illustrations of them may be here given. As to circumstantial evidence, it is essential in order to support a conviction that it shall be so conclusive in character as to prove beyond a reasonable doubt that the accused and no other person committed the offense charged.[1] But circumstantial evidence may be sufficient.[2] Acts or declarations of defendant may tend to identify him as the person who committed the crime. Thus, if it appears that defendant made statements leading to the discovery of the stolen property or produced the property, such a fact, without an explanation of how he became aware of its location, would tend to implicate him in the theft.[3] Contradictory statements with reference to facts tending to throw suspicion on defendant may be shown as indicating his guilt.[4] Admissions or acts of a third person tending to show him to have committed the larceny are not admissible in behalf of defendant, as they are hearsay evidence.[5] Bad character of others who might have committed the offense cannot be shown in defendant's behalf.[6]

[1] Kaiser v. S., 35 Neb. 704. Circumstantial evidence in particular cases held not sufficient to support a conviction: Hines v. S., 51 Ga. 301; S. v. McCarter, 72 N. C. 99; S. v. Wilkerson, 72 N. C. 376; Powers v. S., 16 Tex. 546. The court should instruct the jury as to the law of circumstantial evidence, if such evidence is relied on for conviction: Howell v. S., 16 Tex. Ap. 93; Bryant v. S., 16 Tex. Ap. 144; Allen v. S., 16 Tex. Ap. 237; Kenneda v. S., 16 Tex. Ap. 258; Ramirez v. S., 20 Tex. Ap. 133.

[2] S. v. Brady, 27 Ia. 126; Stevens v. S., 77 Ga. 310; Kemp v. S., 89 Ala. 52; S. v. Cameron, 40 Vt. 555.

[3] S. v. Lindsey, 78 N. C. 499; S. v. Clark, 4 Strobh. 311; Belote v. S., 36 Miss. 96; Hudson v. S., 9 Yerg. 407. But as tending to establish defendant's innocence it may be shown that he himself put the officer in pursuit of the stolen property: McIntosh v. S., 52 Ala. 355; Pinkard v. S., 30 Ga. 757.

[4] S. v. White, 89 N. C. 462; S. v. Cameron, 40 Vt. 555; White v. S., 11 Tex. 769. But false statements by the wife of the thief made with reference to the stolen property were held not sufficient to establish her guilt, there being no proof of participation in the crime itself: Porter v. S., 43 Tex. 367.

[5] C. v. Chabbock, 1 Mass. 144; Rhea v. S., 10 Yerg. 257; S. v. White, 68 N. C. 158.

[6] Bennett v. S., 52 Ala. 370.

§ 615. **Other crimes.**— Other distinct larcenies committed by the defendant cannot be shown for the purpose of identifying him as the one who committed the larceny in question;[1] but other crimes of the same character and forming a part of the same transaction may be shown.[2] Thus, where other property is stolen at the same time as the property in question, and is found with the property in question in possession of defendant, that fact may be shown as a part of the *res gestæ*, although such evidence might also establish an independent crime.[3] For the purpose of showing criminal intent, if the intent is in controversy, other criminal acts of the same character as the one charged may be proven.[4] Evidence of general bad character of defendant's family is of course not admissible.[5]

[1] P. v. Hartman, 62 Cal. 562; P. v. Tucker, 104 Cal. 440; S. v. Goetz, 34 Mo. 85; Miller v. C., 78 Ky. 15; S. v. Kelley, 65 Vt. 531; Barton v. S., 18 Ohio, 221; S. v. Wisdom, 8 Port. 511; Endaly v. S., 39 Ark. 278; Walker v. C., 1 Leigh, 628; S. v. Vinson, 63 N. C. 335; Gilbraith v. S., 41 Tex. 567; Kelley v. S., 18 Tex. Ap. 262; Williams v. S., 24 Tex. Ap. 412; Nixon v. S., 31 Tex. Ap. 205.

[2] Sartin v. S., 7 Lea, 679; Links v. S., 13 Lea, 701. Such testimony should not be received unless the court can plainly see the connection between the two offenses: S. v. Bates, 46 La. An. 849.

[3] P. v. Robles, 34 Cal. 591; P. v. Ross, 65 Cal. 104; P. v. Walker, 38 Mich. 156; Yarborough v. S., 41 Ala. 405; Griffin v. S., 86 Ga. 257; S. v. Ditton, 48 Ia. 677; S. v. Flynn, 124 Mo. 480; Speights v. S., 1 Tex. Ap. 551; Satterwhite v. S., 6 Tex. Ap. 609; Ivey v. S., 43 Tex. 425; Musgrave v. S., 28 Tex. Ap. 57. In the same way all the acts of defendant connected with the transaction may be shown, although they would tend to indicate an attempt to commit another felony: Burr v. C., 4 Grat. 534. Possession of other stolen property, together with that in question, may be shown as strengthening other inculpatory evidence: Webb v. S., 8 Tex. Ap. 115; at least where the other property tends to identify the property stolen: Tyler v. S., 13 Tex. Ap. 205. The object for which such evidence is admitted should be explained to the jury: Long v. S., 11 Tex. Ap. 381; Barnes v. S., 28 Tex. Ap. 29; Hanley v. S., 28 Tex. Ap. 375. But in general possession of other stolen property at the time or previously cannot be shown: Reg. v. Oddy, T. & M. 593; unless authorized by statute: Reg. v. Jones, 14 Cox, 3; Reg. v. Drage, 14 Cox, 83; unless its possession tends to connect defendant with the property which is in question; then possession may be shown, even though it tends to prove another crime: Reed v. S., 54 Ark. 621.

[4] Holmes v. S., 20 Tex. Ap. 509; P. v. Fehrenbach, 102 Cal. 394; P. v. Tomlinson, 102 Cal. 19; Copperman v. P., 56 N. Y. 591; Reg. v. Bleasdale, 2 C. & K. 765. For instance, it may be shown that defendant was connected with a band of thieves: Hinds v. S., 11 Tex. Ap. 238.

[5] McClure v. C., 81 Ky. 448.

§ 616. Recent possession of stolen goods.— The fact that the person charged with larceny is found in possession of the stolen goods soon after the commission of the larceny may be considered as tending to identify him as the person who committed the crime.[1] Such fact furnishes circumstantial evidence of guilt.[2] But this doctrine is one involving numerous explanations and qualifications as well as some conflict in the authorities, and must be discussed in various phases. In the first place such recent possession does not in itself prove any crime whatever, and the *corpus delicti* must be otherwise established.[3] Moreover, in order that recent possession of goods shall be admissible as against the defendant, the goods must be identified as those stolen.[4] But circumstantial evidence is admissible to show the defendant to have been in possession of the stolen goods.[5] In order that this recent possession shall be considered as any evidence whatever connecting the defendant with the crime, it must be personal, recent, unexplained, and such as to involve a conscious assertion of claim to the property.[6] These characteristics will be considered in subsequent sections; but if the evidence of recent possession is such as to make it admissible against defendant, it is still subject to explanation

[1] 2 Hale, P. C. 289; 2 Arch. Cr. Pr. & Pl. [369]; Roscoe, Crim. Ev. 912; 3 Greenl. Ev., §§ 31–33; 2 Bish. Crim. Proc., § 739; Whart. Crim. Ev., § 758; Best, Ev., §§ 211–214.

[2] Sullivan v. S., 18 Tex. Ap. 623; Hyden v. S., 31 Tex. Ap. 401; Baldwin v. S., 31 Tex. Ap. 589. And the court should instruct as to the weight of circumstantial evidence: Taylor v. S., 27 Tex. Ap. 463. The presumption is that the crime was committed in the jurisdiction where the goods are found: Simpson v. S., 4 Humph. 456. *Contra,* Williams v. S., 11 Tex. Ap. 275.

[3] S. v. Furlong, 19 Me. 225; Smathers v. S., 46 Ind. 447; S. v. Taylor, 25 Ia. 273; S. v. Tucker, 76 Ia. 232; Hunt v C., 13 Grat. 757; Garcia v. S., 26 Tex. 209. Further as to *corpus delicti,* see *supra,* § 612.

[4] S. v. Osborne, 45 Ia. 425; C. v. Slate, 11 Gray, 60; Garcia v. S., 26 Tex. 209; U. S. v. Candler, 65 Fed. R. 308. In case of money the identification need not be so complete; it may be shown that defendant had money after the crime and had had none before for some time: S. v. Bruce, 106 N. C. 792; Jenkins v. S., 62 Wis. 49; C. v. Montgomery, 11 Met. 534; Boston & W. R. Co. v. Dana, 1 Gray, 83, 102; S. v. Grebe, 17 Kan. 458. And see *supra,* § 613, and *infra,* § 619.

[5] Eckels v. S., 20 Ohio St. 508.

[6] Lehman v. S., 18 Tex. Ap. 174; Robinson v. S., 22 Tex. Ap. 129; Moreno v. S., 24 Tex. Ap. 401; Jackson v. S., 28 Tex. Ap. 143; Jackson v. S., 28 Tex. Ap. 370; Williamson v. S., 30 Tex. Ap. 330; Clark v. S., 30 Tex. Ap. 402; S. v. Scott, 109 Mo. 226; S. v. Castor, 93 Mo. 242.

by him, and this point will also demand further explanation. Before passing to a discussion of the effect of such evidence, it is proper to say that it is admissible, not only with reference to the charge of larceny, but in any case where defendant is found in possession of property which apparently could have come into his possession only by reason of his connection with a specific crime for which he is on trial, the *corpus delicti* of such crime having been otherwise proven.[1] Thus, recent possession of the fruits of the crime may be shown to establish murder accompanied with robbery,[2] or to show burglary[3] or arson.[4] Recent possession of a part of the stolen property may be considered as tending to show defendant guilty of stealing all.[5]

§ 617. Effect of such evidence; presumption; burden of proof.— The most general statement as to the effect of proof of recent possession by defendant of the stolen property is that it may be considered as evidence of his guilt of the crime charged.[6] The more common statement, however, is that such evidence is presumptive or *prima facie* evidence of guilt.[7] By saying that such evidence is presumptive or *prima facie* evidence of guilt, the courts usually mean that it will support a conviction in the absence of anything explaining or contradicting it;[8] but many courts refuse to give so great effect to such

[1] Knickerbocker v. P., 43 N. Y. 177.

[2] Williams v. C., 29 Pa. St. 102.

[3] See *supra*, § 514.

[4] S. v. Owens, 79 Mo. 619; S. v. Vatter, 71 Ia. 557.

[5] C. v. Millard, 1 Mass. 6; S. v. Owens, 79 Mo. 619; S. v. Beatty, 90 Mo. 143; Snowden v. S., 62 Miss. 100. But it is error to say that such evidence gives rise to the presumption of guilt as to all: Gonzales v. S., 18 Tex. Ap. 449.

[6] S. v. Williams, 2 Jones, 194; S. v. Shaw, 4 Jones, 430; Graves v. S., 12 Wis. 591; Matthews v. S., 61 Miss. 155; P. v. Fagan, 66 Cal. 534; S. v. En, 10 Nev. 277. That the production of the property, or pointing out its location, tends to connect defendant with the crime, see *supra*, § 614.

[7] S. v. Brady, 27 Ia. 126; S. v. Golden, 49 Ia. 48; Knickerbocker v. P., 43 N. Y. 177; S. v. Lawn, 80 Mo. 241; S. v. White, 126 Mo. 591; Young v. S., 24 Fla. 147; Unger v. S., 42 Miss. 642; Snowden v. S., 62 Miss. 100; Foster v. S., 52 Miss. 695; S. v. Bennet, 3 Brev. 514; S. v. Jones, 3 Dev. & B. 122; S. v. Smith, 2 Ired. 402; Tucker v. S., 57 Ga. 503; S. v. Turner, 65 N. C. 592; U. S. v. Jones, 31 Fed. R. 718; Reg. v. Langmead, L. & C. 427.

[8] C. v. Randall, 119 Mass. 107; C. v. Millard, 1 Mass. 6; Thompson v. S., 6 Neb. 102; S. v. Hessians, 50 Ia. 135; Johnson v. Miller, 63 Ia. 529; Jones v. P., 12 Ill. 259; Comfort v. P., 54 Ill. 404; Smith v. P., 103 Ill. 82; S. v. Hill, 65 Mo. 84; S. v. Creson, 38 Mo. 372; S. v. Bruin, 34 Mo. 537; S. v. Gray, 37 Mo. 463; S. v. Cassady, 12

evidence, and declare that it is not in itself *prima facie* or presumptive evidence of guilt, but that it is a circumstance only to be taken into account with other facts.[1] As to the effect of the evidence, a few courts say that if there is no evidence to explain or overcome the presumption arising therefrom, the jury ought to convict; that is, they regard the evidence as conclusive;[2] but this statement of the law seems entirely untenable, and is doubtless made through inadvertence. No evidence can be said to be conclusive.[3] Some courts say that the evidence of recent possession throws upon defendant the burden of explaining such possession consistently with his innocence,[4] and others say in a slightly different form that such

Kan. 550, 1 Am. Cr. R. 567, and note; S. v. Hoffman, 53 Kan. 700; Pennsylvania v. Myers, Addis. 320; Taliaferro v. C., 77 Va. 411; Belote v. S., 36 Miss. 96; Branson v. C., 92 Ky. 330; Tilly v. S., 21 Fla. 242; Robinson v. S., 22 Tex. Ap. 129; Emerson v. S., 33 Tex. Ap. 89.

1 P. v. Chambers, 18 Cal. 382; P. v. Ah Ki, 20 Cal. 177; P. v. Gassaway, 23 Cal. 51; P. v. Antonio, 27 Cal. 404; P. v. Brown, 48 Cal. 253; P. Swinford, 57 Cal. 86; Stuart v. P., 42 Mich. 255; Ryan v. S., 83 Wis. 486; Ingalls v. S., 48 Wis. 647; S. v. Reece, 27 W. Va. 375; Matthews v. S., 61 Miss. 155; Harper v. S., 71 Miss. 202; Conkwright v. P., 35 Ill. 204; S. v. Graves, 72 N. C. 482; Boykin v. S., 34 Ark. 448; S. v. Hale, — Oreg. —, 7 Pac. R. 523; S. v. Walters, 7 Wash. 246; Yates v. S., 37 Tex. 202; Barnes v. S., 43 Tex. 98; Thompson v. S., 43 Tex. 268; McCoy v. S., 44 Tex. 616; Foster v. S., 1 Tex. Ap. 363; Hernandez v. S., 9 Tex. Ap. 288; Dreyer v. S., 11 Tex. Ap. 503; Pettigrew v. S., 12 Tex. Ap. 225; Truax v. S., 12 Tex. Ap. 230. In Roberts v. S., 17 Tex. 82, the court overrules earlier cases on this subject and holds that the presumption if explained will support a conviction, and this doctrine seems to be followed in Robinson v. S., 22 Tex. Ap. 129; but in later cases the same court seems to re-affirm the earlier doctrine: Boyd v. S., 24 Tex. Ap. 570; Cooper v. S., 29 Tex. Ap. 8; and it is held error to say that proof of such recent possession is presumptive evidence of guilt; such an instruction is improper as being on the weight of the evidence: Lee v. S., 27 Tex. Ap. 475; Lockhart v. S., 29 Tex. Ap. 35. The court is not justified in saying that the fact is a strong circumstance tending to show guilt, as the court should not instruct as to the weight to be given to evidence: Denmark v. S., 58 Ark. 576.

2 Hughes v. S., 8 Humph. 75; Fields v. S., 6 Coldw. 524; S. v. Gray, 37 Mo. 463; S. v. Kelly, 73 Mo. 608; S. v. Owens, 79 Mo. 619; S. v. Phelps, 91 Mo. 478.

3 S. v. Jones, 33 Ia. 9; S. v. Jordan, 69 Ia. 506; S. v. Snell, 46 Wis. 524; P. v. Gutierrez, 74 Cal. 81; Fisher v. S., 46 Ala. 717; Curtis v. S., 6 Coldw. 9; Wilcox v. S., 3 Heisk. 110; Billard v. S., 30 Tex. 367. And see cases in note below, to the effect that the question is one of fact for the jury.

4 P. v. Kelly, 28 Cal. 423; P. v. Abbott, 101 Cal. 645; S. v. Weston, 9 Conn. 527; S. v. Kelly, 73 Mo. 608; Williams v. S., 30 Tex. Ap. 330; Mondragon v. S., 33 Tex. 481; S. v. Whitmer, 77 Ia. 557.

evidence throws upon defendant the burden of overcoming by other evidence the presumption arising therefrom,[1] and allow the defendant to show, as overcoming the presumption against him, not merely an explanation of his possession, but any fact tending to establish his innocence; such, for instance, as his good character or an *alibi*.[2] But a statement of the rule in any form which throws the burden of proof upon the defendant is objected to by other courts, which hold that the burden of proof does not shift,[3] and under this view it is not incumbent upon defendant to make out a case of innocence by overcoming the presumption of recent possession by a preponderance of evidence, but evidence for the defendant, whether consisting of an explanation of the recent possession, or other evidence tending to show his innocence, which raises a reasonable doubt of his guilt as against the evidence of recent possession, is sufficient.[4] The latter doctrine seems to be sounder in principle than that which requires the defendant in some form to overcome the presumption, and establish his innocence,[5] and this doctrine is supported by many cases in which it is said that the question whether the evidence of recent possession is sufficient to require a conviction is one for the jury.[6] The presumption from recent possession is one of fact, not of law.[7]

[1] Knickerbocker v. P., 43 N. Y. 177; Goldstein v. P., 82 N. Y. 231; Waters v. P., 104 Ill. 544; Sahlinger v. P., 102 Ill. 241; S. v. Raymond, 46 Conn. 345; S. v. Cassady, 12 Kan. 550; S. v. Turner, 65 N. C. 592; S. v. Daly, 37 La. An. 576; T. v. Casio, 1 Ariz. 485.

[2] Conkwright v. P., 35 Ill. 204; Clackner v. S., 33 Ind. 412; S. v. Kelly, 57 Ia. 644; S. v. Richart, 57 Ia. 245; S. v. Bruin, 34 Mo. 537; S. v. Williams, 54 Mo. 170; S. v. Sidney, 74 Mo. 390; S. v. Crank, 75 Mo. 406; S. v. North, 95 Mo. 615. To the contrary as to good character, see S. v. Hogard, 12 Minn. 293.

[3] S. v. Hodge, 50 N. H. 510; Stover v. P., 56 N. Y. 315; S. v. Merrick, 19 Me. 398; Robb v. S., 35 Neb. 285; Hoge v. P., 117 Ill. 35. It is error to make conviction depend upon the truth or falsity of the explanation rather than upon defendant's guilt: Pollard v. S., 33 Tex. Ap. 197.

[4] S. v. Richart, 57 Ia. 245; S. v. Emerson, 48 Ia. 172; S. v. Peterson, 67 Ia. 564; S. v. Kirkpatrick, 72 Ia. 500, 7 Am. Cr. R. 334, and note; S. v. Manley, 74 Ia. 561; Thompson v. P., 4 Neb. 524; Hoge v. P., 117 Ill. 35; P. v. Walters, 76 Mich. 195; S. v. Merrick, 19 Me. 398; Taylor v. S., 15 Tex. Ap. 356; Hays v. S., 30 Tex. Ap. 472.

[5] S. v. Hodge, 50 N. H. 510.

[6] P. v. Titherington, 59 Cal. 598; Hill v. S., 63 Ga. 578; Griffin v. S., 86 Ga. 257.

[7] S. v. Raymond, 46 Conn. 345; S. v. Hodge, 50 N. H. 510; Robb v. S., 35 Neb. 285; Young v. S., 24 Fla. 147; S. v. Heaton, 23 W. Va. 773; S. v. Hale, 12 Oreg. 352; Stover v. P., 56 N. Y. 315; Graves v. S., 12 Wis. 591;

§ 618. Sufficiency of explanation.— It is recent possession unexplained, that is, without circumstances appearing which indicate that such possession is consistent with defendant's innocence, which constitutes evidence against him. Thus, if it appears that the possession of defendant had its inception subsequently to the time of the commission of the crime, such explanation will obviate the effect of the possession as tending to show criminality.[1] As showing the nature of the possession, any explanation thereof made by the defendant is admissible in evidence either for or against him.[2] Thus, explanations made by defendant contemporaneously with or when first required to account for his possession of stolen property may be shown in his behalf,[3] and so may statements by defendant made when first arrested;[4] but in either event such declarations are not admissible in evidence unless possession and acts of ownership at the time they are made are first proved.[5] The declarations are to be shown in connection with the possession as explanatory of it, and as therefore a part of the *res gestæ;*[6] but it seems that declarations made on the first occasion for explanation may be shown although defendant had already parted with possession.[7] An explanation made by another at defend-

Crilley v. S., 20 Wis. 231; S. v. Kelly, 57 Ia. 644; Smith v. S., 58 Ind. 340; Bellamy v. S., 35 Fla. 242; Watkins v. S., 2 Tex. Ap. 73; Ayres v. S., 21 Tex. Ap. 399; Lockhart v. S., 29 Tex. Ap. 35.

[1] Head v. S., 25 Wis. 421; S. v. Jackson, 126 Mo. 521; Williams v. S., 11 Tex. Ap. 275; S. v. Humason, 5 Wash. 499. If the possession of defendant is traced to a finding of the stolen goods after the larceny, with no evidence that he placed the goods where found, this will not tend to show his guilt: S. v. Scott, 109 Mo. 226.

[2] Perry v. S., 41 Tex. 483; Ward v. S., 41 Tex. 611; Shackleford v. S., 2 Tex. Ap. 385; Eads v. S., 26 Tex. Ap. 69.

[3] Payne v. S., 57 Miss. 348; Walker v. S., 28 Ga. 254; and, much more, statements made by defendant before suspicion attached to him: Reg. v. Abraham, 2 C. & K. 550; but, contrary to what seems to be the almost universally accepted doctrine, it is said in one case that defendant cannot prove declarations made by him as to how the goods came into his possession: S. v. Slack, 1 Bailey, 330. Contemporaneous statements are more effectual than explanations made when called as a witness: S. v. Moore, 101 Mo. 316.

[4] Shackelford v. S., 43 Tex. 138; Darnell v. S., 43 Tex. 147; Castellow v. S., 15 Tex. Ap. 551.

[5] Cameron v. S., 44 Tex. 652; Childress v. S., 10 Tex. Ap. 698; Lewis v. S., 17 Tex. Ap. 140; Heskew v. S., 17 Tex. Ap. 161; Smith v. S., 103 Ala. 40.

[6] Walker v. S., 28 Ga. 254; Shackelford v. S., 43 Tex. 138.

[7] Hampton v. S., 5 Tex. Ap. 463; Anderson v. S., 11 Tex. Ap. 576;

ant's request is entitled to the same weight as though made by himself,[1] and what is said to defendant at the time of his acquiring possession may be shown by him in the same way as what is said by him.[2] It is plain that the prosecution may show, as against him, defendant's explanation with regard to his possession of the stolen property;[3] and it may thus be shown that the explanation given is contradictory,[4] or unreasonable or incredible;[5] or the prosecution may by other evidence show that the explanation is false,[6] and as indicating its falsity inconsistent circumstances may be proven;[7] but proof of the falsity of the explanation will not be sufficient in itself to sustain a conviction where the other evidence of guilt is insufficient.[8] The effect of the proof of recent possession may be overcome by proof of an open public purchase free from circumstances of suspicion,[9] or by proof of purchase from a real person named, or even from the thief without collusion;[10] but it seems that an explanation of purchase from a stranger is not sufficient to overcome the presumption of guilt from the recent possession.[11] If the explanation of defendant is reasonable and probable, the burden is on the prosecution to prove its falsity,[12]

Taylor v. S., 15 Tex. Ap. 356. Where the witnesses differed in their statements as to defendant's first explanation, *held*, that his statements on the following day might be shown in corroboration of what he claimed to be his first statements: Andrews v. S., 25 Tex. Ap. 339. Evidence that defendant, on first meeting the owner of property which defendant had sold, offered to pay for it, was held not admissible as an explanation: Brooks v. S., 26 Tex. Ap. 184.

[1] Windham v. S., 19 Tex. Ap. 413.

[2] S. v. Jordan, 69 Ia. 506; S. v. Kelly, 57 Ia. 644.

[3] S. v. Weaver, 104 N. C. 758.

[4] Reg. v. Dibley, 2 C. & K. 818.

[5] Reg. v. Exall, 4 F. & F. 922; Reg. v. Wilson, Dears. & B. 157.

[6] S. v. Hallet, 63 Ia. 259; S. v. Campbell, 108 Mo. 611.

[7] C. v. Grose, 99 Mass. 423; P. v. Cunningham, 66 Cal. 668.

[8] Norwood v. S., 20 Tex. Ap. 306.

[9] Jones v. P., 12 Ill. 259. In Texas proof of recent possession of stolen cattle is made *prima facie* evidence of guilt, unless defendant has a bill of sale for such cattle; but this presumption is not conclusive: Flores v. S., 13 Tex. Ap. 665; Gomez v. S., 15 Tex. Ap. 64; Schindler v. S., 15 Tex. Ap. 394. Defendant may thus show a purchase from one claiming to be agent of the owner of stray cattle, although he has no bill of sale: Smith v. S., 41 Tex. 168.

[10] S. v. Brown, 25 Ia. 561. *Contra*, S. v. Boone, 70 Mo. 649.

[11] S. v. Brown, 25 Ia. 561.

[12] Reg. v. Crowhurst, 1 C. & K. 370; Reg. v. Smith, 2 C. & K. 207; Garcia v. S., 26 Tex. 209; Irvine v. S., 13 Tex. Ap. 499; Harris v. S., 15 Tex. Ap. 411; Ross v. S., 16 Tex. Ap. 554; Schultz v. S., 20 Tex. Ap. 315; Brothers v. S., 22 Tex. Ap. 447; Clark v. S., 22 Tex. Ap.

which must be established beyond a reasonable doubt;[1] and if there is no evidence of its falsity, the evidence of recent possession must be regarded as overcome, and a conviction based on such evidence alone will not be warranted.[2] If defendant's explanation is unreasonable or improbable on the face of it, it is not incumbent upon the prosecution, in order to secure conviction, to assume the burden of showing the falsity of the explanation.[3] The question as to the sufficiency and credibility of the explanation is for the jury.[4]

§ 619. **When possession deemed sufficiently recent.**—It is not the possession of the stolen goods *at any time* after the commission of the crime that constitutes evidence of guilt, but it is the *recent* possession of such goods.[5] The possession is only evidence of guilt when it appears that the possessor could not well have come by such property except by stealing it.[6] What is recent possession will depend somewhat upon the nature of the property.[7] Thus, if the property is such as to pass readily from hand to hand, the possession, in order to be evidence of guilt, should be much more recent than if it is of a

599; Arispe v. S., 26 Tex. Ap. 581; Clark v. S., 27 Tex. Ap. 405; White v. S., 28 Tex. Ap. 71; Ewing v. S., 29 Tex. Ap. 434.

1 S. v. Kirkpatrick, 72 Ia. 500, 7 Am. Cr. R. 334 and note.

2 Johnson v. S., 12 Tex. Ap. 385; York v. S., 17 Tex. Ap. 441; Brothers v. S., 22 Tex. Ap. 447; Tarin v. S., 25 Tex. Ap. 360; Hyatt v. S., 32 Tex. Ap. 580; Bellamy v. S., 35 Fla. 242. When defendant has made a reasonable and probable statement with regard to his possession, he is entitled to have the law applicable thereto stated to the jury: Miller v. S., 18 Tex. Ap. 34; but he is not entitled to have the court say to the jury that they can acquit if the state fails to show defendant's explanation to be false, because there are usually other criminative facts besides the recent possession: Hart v. S., 22 Tex. Ap. 563.

3 Reg. v. Harmer, 3 Cox, 487; Reg. v. Crowhurst, 1 C. & K. 370; Reg. v. Smith, 2 C. & K. 207. But the evidence of possession may be considered for what it is worth, even if it is explained or though the explanation is unreasonable: Payne v. S., 21 Tex. Ap. 184.

4 P. v. Cline, 74 Cal. 575; Grentzinger v. S., 31 Neb. 460; Hays v. S., 30 Tex. Ap. 472; P. v. Walters, 76 Mich. 195; P. v. Hawksley, 82 Mich. 71; S. v. Kimble, 34 La. An. 392.

5 Warren v. S., 1 Greene (Ia.), 106; S. v. Wolff, 15 Mo. 168; S. v. Floyd, 15 Mo. 349; Shepherd v. S., 44 Ark. 39; Jones v. S., 26 Miss. 247; White v. S., 72 Ala. 195. And the court should describe the possession which may be taken into consideration as recent; but omission to do so will be immaterial where the fact that the possession was recent affirmatively appears: Young v. S., 95 Ga. 456.

6 Gregory v. Richards, 8 Jones, 410.

7 S. v. Floyd, 15 Mo. 349; Rex v. Partridge, 7 C. & P. 551.

class which circulates more slowly or is rarely transmitted;[1] and the evidence is strong or weak depending on the length of time which has elapsed and the character of the property.[2] In some cases the court has considered the length of time elapsing between the crime and the possession to have been so great, in view of the nature of the property, that it would not support a conviction based upon the evidence of possession alone.[3] In general, however, the length of time elapsing between the

[1] S. v. Walker, 41 Ia. 217; Jones v. S., 26 Miss. 247.

[2] Gablick v. P., 40 Mich. 292; S. v. Rights, 82 N. C. 675; Florez v. S., 26 Tex. Ap. 477. Thus, the possession of money recently stolen is usually of slight weight; yet, if it is of a kind rarely seen in circulation, the weight of the evidence is greatly increased: P. v. Getty, 49 Cal. 581. But recent possession of current money may nevertheless be sufficient evidence of guilt: Jenkins v. S., 62 Wis. 49; S. v. Bruce, 106 N. C. 792; S. v. Grebe, 17 Kan. 458; C. v. Montgomery, 11 Met. 534; Boston & W. R. Co. v. Dana, 1 Gray, 83, 102. And see *supra*, § 616.

[3] For instance, where the stolen goods, the nature of which is not stated, were found in defendant's possession sixteen months after the theft, the judge directed an acquittal: Anon., 2 C. & P. 459; and so where tools were found in defendant's possession three months after they were missed, an acquittal was likewise directed: Rex v. Adams, 3 C. & P. 600; and the same result was reached in a similar case where the possession was six or seven months after the theft: Reg. v. Cruttenden, 6 Jur. 267. Possession by a letter carrier of a bank-note some months after it had been lost in the mail was held not sufficient evidence: Reg. v. Smith, 3 F. & F. 123. Possession of a stolen horse six months after the commission of the crime was held not to constitute sufficient evidence to go to the jury: Reg. v. Cooper, 3 C. & K. 318. Where sheep were lost in September and found in defendant's possession in March following, *held*, that there was no case for the jury: Reg. v. Harris, 8 Cox, 333. And see, as holding that in particular cases the possession was too remote from the crime to support a conviction, S. v. Jennett, 88 N. C. 665; Jones v. S., 26 Miss. 247; S. v. Wallace, 47 Ia. 660; Beck v. S., 44 Tex. 430; Bragg v. S., 17 Tex. Ap. 219; Romero v. S., 25 Tex. Ap. 394. But where pieces of cloth were stolen and were found in the possession of defendant two months afterward, still in the same condition, it was held that the possession was sufficiently recent to call on the prisoner for an explanation: Rex v. Partridge, 7 C. & P. 551. So possession of stolen goods a day and a half after the theft without explanation was held sufficient to support a conviction: Brown v. S., 59 Ga. 456; and possession of a cow nearly ten months after she was last known to have been on the owner's ranch was held to raise a question for the jury: Willis v. S., 24 Tex. Ap. 586. And see Reg. v. Knight, L. & C. 378. Where defendant claims to have owned the property prior to the larceny, so that the question is one as to identity of the property, the interval between the crime and the possession will be immaterial: Reg. v. Evans, 2 Cox, 270.

crime and the possession goes only to the weight of the testimony, and is to be taken into consideration by the jury for that purpose,[1] and the sufficiency of the evidence is to be left to the jury under proper instructions.[2]

§ 620. **Possession exclusive.**— In order that the recent possession shall be evidence of guilt, it must be exclusive in the defendant; that is, it must be such as to indicate that the defendant and not some one else took the property. If the place where the property is found is such that others have access thereto as well as defendant, the property cannot be said to be in the exclusive possession of defendant, and the circumstance would not be evidence of his guilt.[3] Some cases sanction a broader rule in this respect, and allow the evidence to be considered although it appears that the goods are found in a place not exclusively occupied or controlled by defendant, the fact that other persons had access to the place weakening, but not destroying, the effect of the evidence;[4] but evidence of finding the property in a house belonging to and under the control of another, with whom defendant is acquainted, and where he has been staying, has been held not admissible.[5] Where two persons have such possession of property as implies control in them jointly, they may each be said to have exclusive possession;[6] and where there

[1] P. v. Weldon, 111 N. Y. 569; C. v. Montgomery, 11 Met. 534; S. v. Miller, 45 Minn. 521.

[2] S. v. Walker, 41 Ia. 217; Price v. C., 21 Grat. 846; Florez v. S., 26 Tex. Ap. 477.

[3] P. v. Hurley, 60 Cal. 74; Gablick v. P., 40 Mich. 292; S. v. Castor, 93 Mo. 242; Turbeville v. S., 42 Ind. 490; Casas v. S., 12 Tex. Ap. 59; Warren v. S., 1 Greene (Ia.), 106; Reg. v. Coots, 2 Cox, 188; evidence that defendant clandestinely visited the place where the goods are found is a circumstance only, and not sufficient alone to support a verdict: Smathers v. S., 46 Ind. 447; S. v. Rice, 83 N. C. 661; and the finding of the stolen property in defendant's place of business, there being other inmates of the place, will not alone be evidence of guilt unless it appears that he is the person who brought the property there: S. v. Griffin, 71 Ia. 372.

[4] C. v. Parmenter, 101 Mass. 211; Padfield v. P., 146 Ill. 660. Part of the stolen goods having been found in the exclusive possession of defendant, evidence that the remainder were found where defendant had an opportunity to conceal them is admissible: S. v. Phelps, 91 Mo. 478.

[5] P. v. Williams, 24 Mich. 156. But evidence that stolen cattle were found on the premises of defendant's father, where defendant made his home, was held proper to go to the jury: S. v. Van Winkle, 80 Ia. 15.

[6] S. v. Raymond, 46 Conn. 345. Thus, where property was found in a house occupied exclusively by defendant and his wife, it was held that such possession was evidence

is evidence tending to implicate two persons in the crime, evidence of recent possession by one is criminating against the other.[1] But possession by one defendant is not presumptive against another, even where they reside in the same house, if the latter is a lodger or hired man of the former, unless there is some further evidence to connect the latter with the possession of the property.[2] The question whether the property is in defendant's possession is for the jury.[3]

as against defendant: S. v. Johnson, 1 Winst., i, 238. Thus, also, where a stolen horse was found soon after the larceny, and being ridden by a companion of defendant, such fact was held a circumstance tending to prove defendant's guilt: S. v. Pennyman, 68 Ia. 216.

[1] S. v. Phelps, 91 Mo. 478; S. v. Wohlman, 34 Mo. 482.

[2] S. v. Wolff, 15 Mo. 168; Ivey v. S., 43 Tex. 425.

[3] S. v. Van Winkle, 80 Ia. 15; Gablick v. P., 40 Mich. 292; Gelvin v. S., 93 Ind. 550.

CHAPTER 27.

EMBEZZLEMENT.

I. NATURE OF THE OFFENSE.
II. BY SERVANT, CLERK, AGENT, ETC.
III. BY CARRIER OR OTHER BAILEE.
IV. BY PUBLIC OFFICER.
V. PROCEDURE.

I. NATURE OF THE OFFENSE.

§ 621. **What constitutes.**— In the discussion of larceny it has already appeared [1] that trespass is necessary to constitute that offense, and if the person who wrongfully converts a chattel already had possession of it before such conversion, the crime of larceny is not committed. In the same connection [2] it has been stated that custody by a servant is distinguishable from possession, and that the servant may be guilty of larceny of his master's property of which he has the custody at the time of the conversion to his own use. In regard to these cases of conversion by a servant, but more especially in regard to cases where the property comes into the hands of the servant for the master without having yet actually reached the master's possession, there was at common law much difficulty, and the various statutes passed from time to time providing for the punishment of embezzlement seem to have had their origin in a desire to extend by statute the scope of the crime of larceny in this direction.[3] The popular signification of the word "embezzle" seems originally to have been "to steal, pilfer or purloin," [4] and accordingly the statute of Elizabeth provides for the punishment of one who embezzles the king's army stores.[5] The original statute for the punishment of embezzlement covers the appropriation by servants of the property of their masters in violation of the trust and confidence reposed in them.[6] Subsequent English statutes extended the offense to

[1] *Supra*, §§ 549, 554.

[2] *Supra*, § 556.

[3] 3 Stephen's Hist. Cr. L. 151.

[4] Jacob, Law Dictionary, s. v. "Imbezzle."

[5] 31 Eliz., ch. 4; 1 Hawk. P. C., ch. 18, § 18.

[6] 21 Henry 8, ch. 7.

cover cases of misappropriation by servants of property received by them for their masters.[1] The English statutes and the statutes of the various states make prominent also the misappropriation of funds, although the statute of Henry likewise covered money as well as caskets, jewels, goods and chattels. In the United States another class of cases of breach of trust is made a distinct form of embezzlement, to wit: misappropriation of public funds by officers. This latter branch of embezzlement seems to be of recent origin. The English statutes above named have no reference to public officers.[2] At common law a public officer is subject to discretionary fine and imprisonment for this offense;[3] with us, however, it has, by statutes, become an important part of the law of embezzlement.

§ 622. **Definition.**— These offenses cannot be defined with the accuracy which is possible with reference to the ordinary common-law felonies. Being statutory in origin and regulated by statute in all the states, the definition must depend upon the terms of the particular statute in question.[4] The word "embezzle" in itself implies the wrongful appropriation by the defendant of the money or property of another to his own use.[5] The only general essential is the fraudulent conversion or misappropriation by the defendant of property received by him in some fiduciary capacity.[6] The difficult question as to what constitutes a conversion must be considered hereafter.

§ 623. **How distinguished from larceny.**— Cases which are not larceny because there is no trespass on the owner's possession have been considered under the head of larceny, and it there appeared that this was the distinguishing difference between the two offenses.[7] There are, however, two

[1] 39 Geo. 3, ch. 85; 7 and 8 Geo. 4, ch. 29, § 47; 24 and 25 Vict., ch. 96, § 68; 2 Russ. Cr. 167; 2 Bish. Cr. L., §§ 318–323. The statute of Geo. 3 is held not to be a part of the common law in this country: T. v. Maxwell, 2 N. Mex. 250.

[2] There are, of course, provisions in the English statutes for punishment of public servants for breaches of trust as to the public funds, but such offenses are not called embezzlement.

[3] 4 Bl. Com. 122; Hellings v. C., 5 Rawle, 63.

[4] S. v. Walton, 62 Me. 106; Ker v. P., 110 Ill. 627; S. v. Trolson, 21 Nev. 419, 9 Am. Cr. R. 243 and note; S. v. Wolff, 34 Lá. An. 1153; Note in 98 Am. Dec. 126.

[5] S. v. Wolff, 34 La. An. 1153.

[6] S. v. Walton, 62 Me. 106; S. v. Mason, 108 Ind. 48; 2 Bish. Cr. L., § 325.

[7] See *supra*, § 554; S. v. Baldwin, 70 Ia. 180.

classes of cases which are not larceny on account of the absence of the element of trespass. The first of these is where the wrong-doer is the servant of the owner, but the property has been received from another for the owner, and has not yet passed into such owner's actual possession. Thus, a clerk in a store who receives money for his employer, and at once converts it to his own use, is guilty of embezzlement and not larceny.[1] So where a servant, employed to haul his master's goods from the cars to the master's sheds, received the goods from the railroad company and sold them before he delivered them to the master, he was held to be guilty of embezzlement and not of theft.[2] Other pertinent illustrations with reference to this point are given in connection with the discussion of larceny;[3] but on the other hand, where the goods are in the possession of the master and the servant has the custody only, the offense is larceny and not embezzlement.[4] Thus, where the money is delivered to a servant to carry from the owner to another, the taking is larceny,[5] and in such case it is immaterial whether the felonious intent was formed by the servant before or after the receipt of the money.[6] The teller of a bank who at night opens the vault and takes money therefrom with intent to defraud the bank is guilty of larceny and not embezzle-

[1] C. v. Ryan, 155 Mass. 523. This case goes even further than the statement in the text would indicate. The clerk had put the money received into the cash register without registering it, and had withdrawn it a moment afterward and appropriated it to his own use, and the court decided that the question was whether the clerk had deposited the money in the cash register with the intention of abandoning his control over it and had subsequently formed the purpose of taking it. The early English cases relating to larceny by a servant are cited and considered.

[2] Cody v. S., 31 Tex. Ap. 183. Similar illustrations of the distinction between receiving goods from another for the master, and from the master to be delivered to another, are found in Rex v. Sullens, 1 Moody, 129; Reg. v. Betts, Bell, 90; Reg. v. Hawkins, 1 Den. 584. But where coal was received by the servant into the master's cart, it was held to have passed into the master's possession and that the taking thereof by the servant was not embezzlement: Reg. v. Reid, Dears. 257. And see Reg. v. Hayward, 1 C. & K. 518; Reg. v. Hawkins, 4 Cox, 224.

[3] See *supra*, § 556.

[4] Warmoth v. C., 81 Ky. 133; Cobletz v. S., 36 Tex. 353; Reg. v. Read, 3 Q. B. D. 131.

[5] C. v. Berry, 99 Mass. 428. But if the servant is intrusted with the expenditure of the money and misappropriates it the offense is not larceny: Reg. v. Goodenough, Dears. 210.

[6] C. v. O'Malley, 97 Mass. 584.

ment, for, having the keys and the right to access, the property is in his custody as servant, and it is by virtue of that relation that he wrongfully takes it,[1] and in such case it is not necessary that the money shall have been specially deposited with or intrusted to the officer.[2] The other class of cases where there is such absence of interference with possession as to make the act embezzlement instead of larceny includes cases in which property delivered by the owner to another for a purpose not involving transfer of title is by the person to whom it is delivered, in violation of such trust reposed in him, appropriated to his own use; and here it becomes important to know the intention with which the bailee received the property; for, if he intended from the first to apply it to his own use in violation of the trust, then his offense is larceny, because his fraudulent purpose prevents the possession which is give to him from being lawful;[3] but if the intention to misapp priate was formed after possession was lawfully received, then the wrongful act will be embezzlement and not larceny.[4]

§ 624. **Whether statute exclusive.**— The statutes in regard to embezzlement having been passed for the purpose of covering cases which were not punishable as larceny at common law, there has been a tendency to limit their application to cases not covered by the law of larceny,[5] and in construing the English statutes the courts seem to have considered that if the offense was larceny it could not be embezzlement, and *vice versa*.[6] But under the more liberal construction of these statutes which has generally prevailed in the United States, the weight

[1] C. v. Barry, 116 Mass. 1.

[2] S. v. Tuller, 34 Conn. 280.

[3] See *supra*, § 562.

[4] S. v. Stone, 68 Mo. 101; P. v. Salorse, 62 Cal. 139; C. v. O'Malley, 97 Mass. 584; Ennis v. S., 3 Greene (Ia.), 67; Moore v. U. S., 160 U. S. 268.

[5] Smith v. S., 28 Ind. 321; Quinn v. P., 123 Ill. 333; Kibs v. P., 81 Ill. 599; Wharton, Cr. L. (8th ed.), § 1050. Thus, where there are two different statutes relating to different forms of embezzlement, it has been said that they are to be so construed that the same act will not fall within both: S. v. Wingo, 89 Ind. 204; Pullam v. S., 78 Ala. 31. But this construction has not always prevailed, and in a New York case it is said that it is competent for the legislature, if it sees fit, to include in the new statute offenses punishable under a previous one: Bork v. P., 91 N. Y. 5.

[6] Rex v. Murray, 1 Moody, 276; Reg. v. Hawkins, 1 Den. 584; Rex v. Smith, Russ. & Ry. 267; 2 Russ. Cr. 180. To the same effect see C. v. King, 9 Cush. 284; C. v. Doherty, 127 Mass. 20.

of authority seems to be that the statutory offense of embezzlement is not necessarily limited to acts which would not be larceny, and, indeed, there seems no reason for considering the offenses exclusive, especially where the punishment for embezzlement is substantially the same as that for larceny; as the same act may constitute different offenses, and may be prosecuted as either at the election of the state.[1]

§ 625. **Whether embezzlement is a form of larceny.**— The language of the statutes in some instances is such as to indicate that the offense described is larceny. In other words, they seem to contemplate an extension of the crime of larceny to cover acts of embezzlement which without a statute would not be larceny;[2] but, notwithstanding language to this effect, it is uniformly held that there cannot be a conviction of embezzlement under an indictment, in the ordinary form, for larceny.[3] The offenses are distinct in that they possess different characteristics; and to warrant a conviction of embezzlement, an act constituting embezzlement within the language of the statute must be alleged.[4] However, by statute, a conviction of embezzlement under an indictment for larceny is sometimes allowed.[5]

[1] S. v. Shirer, 20 S. C. 392; S. v. Taberner, 14 R. I. 272; Lowenthal v. S., 32 Ala. 589; Planters' Ins. Co. v. Tuntstall, 72 Ala. 142; Ker v. P., 110 Ill. 627; 2 Bish. Cr. L., § 328.

[2] Rex v. Johnson, 3 Mau. & S. 539; S. v. Tracey, 73 Md. 447; S. v. Broderick, 70 Mo. 622; Terry v. S., 1 Wash. 277. Thus, it has been held in England that one who knowingly receives goods which have been embezzled is guilty of receiving stolen goods: Reg. v. Frampton, Dears. & B. 585. And to same effect see C. v. Leonard, 140 Mass. 473. But *contra*, on this point, see Leal v. S., 12 Tex. Ap. 279. But even where the statutory name is still larceny, it is not improper to describe the offense in the indictment as embezzlement: S. v. Sweet, 2 Oreg. 127.

[3] C. v. Simpson, 9 Met. 138; P. v. Allen, 5 Denio, 76; S. v. Mason, 108 Ind. 48; Fulton v. S., 13 Ark. 168. By Louisiana statute the crimes are distinct, and the requirements as to the indictment in case of larceny are not applicable in case of embezzlement: S. v. Fricker, 45 La. An. 646.

[4] C. v. King, 9 Cush. 284; C. v. O'Malley, 97 Mass. 584: C. v. Berry, 99 Mass. 428; C. v. Doherty, 127 Mass. 20. By a special statute it may be provided that proof of larceny will sustain a charge of embezzlement: S. v. Broderick, 70 Mo. 622; S. v. Poland, 33 La. An. 1161. But even under such a statute proof of embezzlement will not sustain a conviction for larceny: Reg. v. Gorbutt, Dears. & B. 166.

[5] Whitworth v. S., 11 Tex. Ap. 414; Reg. v. Rudge, 13 Cox, 17.

II. BY SERVANT, CLERK, AGENT, ETC.

§ 626. **Who deemed servant or clerk.**— As has already been suggested, the statutory offense of embezzlement had its origin in an attempt to provide a punishment for wrongful acts of servants with reference to their master's property, which did not come within the scope of larceny; and it will be necessary to consider who, under the statutes on the subject, comes within the definition of a servant or clerk, and afterwards who comes within the meaning of the other terms respectively which have been employed in defining the offense. As to the term "servant," it is said that it designates one who is directly answerable to and under the immediate direction and control of an employer in the discharge of his duties.[1] It seems that the term is not limited to general servants, but includes persons who act in that capacity occasionally or in one instance only.[2] Thus, a stage-driver employed to carry packages for his employer, incidentally to his employment as stage-driver, is a servant with reference to such packages.[3] But there must be some employment to constitute the relation of master and servant; one who acts for another on request without any obligation to do so does not become a servant so as to be guilty of embezzlement.[4] Exclusive employment by the prosecutor is, however, not important.[5] There may be employment in other capacities than

[1] Gravatt v. S., 25 Ohio St. 162. The cashier of a partnership bank is a servant or clerk: S. v. Yeiter, 54 Kan. 277.

[2] Reg. v. Hughes, 1 Moody, 370; Reg. v. Winnall, 5 Cox, 326; Reg. v. Tongue, Bell, 289; Reg. v. Hastie, L. & C. 269; Rex v. Spencer, Russ. & Ry. 299. Thus, where defendant was employed by a merchant to sweep out the store, etc., but not as clerk, and on a particular occasion was authorized to take merchandise and sell it at a neighboring town, and he converted the proceeds of such sale, *held*, that he was indictable for larceny as servant: S. v. Costin, 89 N. C. 511, 4 Am. Cr. R. 169, and note. One employed only on temporary occasions is, within the language of the English statute, "employed in the capacity of clerk or servant:" Reg. v. Woolley, 4 Cox, 251; Reg. v. Foulkes, L. R. 2 C. C. 150. One who assumes to act as agent, and is recognized as such, may commit the offense: S. v. Ezzard, 40 S. C. 312.

[3] P. v. Sherman, 10 Wend. 298. But in another case it is said that one cannot be convicted of embezzlement as servant who is not regularly in the employ of another, but who merely goes on errands for him occasionally: Johnson v. S., 9 Baxt. 279.

[4] Rex v. Freeman, 5 C. & P. 534; Rex v. Nettleton, 1 Moody, 259; Reg. v. Hoare, 1 F. & F. 647.

[5] Reg. v. Batty, 2 Moody, 257, Rex

that of servant, so that the person employed, though authorized to deal with his employer's property, is not a servant within the meaning of the embezzlement statutes.[1] One who receives material as a mechanic, to be worked upon, is not a servant.[2] One who acts as agent in the sale of goods or collection of debts on commission is not a servant or clerk within the language of the English statute.[3] But if the employee is to devote his entire time to the service of the employer, he is a clerk or a servant, even though his compensation is given in the way of commissions.[4] No abuse of confidence other than that resulting from the relation of servant is necessary.[5]

§ **627. Who deemed agent.**— The term "agent" as used in the statutes is broader than servant or clerk, and, if the indictment charges embezzlement by agent, it is not sustained by proof that defendant was a servant or a clerk.[6] Where the statute uses the term "agent" generally, it includes special as well as general agents, whether employed regularly or only for the single or special case, and it is immaterial whether there is remuneration or not.[7] But where there is an enumeration of certain classes of agents, such as bankers, brokers, attorneys,

v. Carr, Russ. & Ry. 198. A servant of partners is the servant of each: Rex v. Leech, 3 Stark. 70; Reg. v. Frankland, L. & C. 276. Where the servant was to account to one partner who was accountable to the partnership, it was held that he was properly described as the servant of such partner: Reg. v. White, 8 C. & P. 742. One may be a servant jointly of two or more companies: Reg. v. Bayley, Dears. & B. 121.

[1] Rex v. Hartley, Russ. & Ry. 139; Reg. v. Goodbody, 8 C. & P. 665; Reg. v. Walker, Dears. & B. 600; Reg. v. Barnes, 8 Cox, 129; Rex v. Burton, 1 Moody, 237. But one may be a servant although his rendering the service in question is optional with himself: Reg. v. Thomas, 6 Cox, 403. One who receives money as servant is to be deemed a servant with reference to the embezzlement of such money: Rex v. Beacall, 1 C. & P. 312; Rex v. Wellings, 1 C. & P. 454; Reg. v. Welch, 2 C. & K. 296; Ex parte Ricord, 11 Nev. 287.

[2] C. v. Young, 9 Gray, 5.

[3] Reg. v. Bowers, L. R. 1 C. C. 41; Reg. v. Negus, L. R. 2 C. C. 34; Reg. v. Mayle, 11 Cox, 150; Reg. v. May, L. & C. 13.

[4] Reg. v. Bailey, 12 Cox, 56. Even where he was not to give his entire time to one employer and was to be paid by commissions, it was held that there was such evidence of his being servant of the prosecutor as might go to the jury: Reg. v. Tite, L. & C. 29.

[5] S. v. Wilson, 101 N. C. 730.

[6] P. v. Allen, 5 Denio, 76.

[7] S. v. Barter, 58 N. H. 604. Thus, the manipulator of a pool to whom money is intrusted in that capacity is sufficiently an agent to be included within the statute of embezzlement: S. v. Shadd, 80 Mo. 358.

etc., and the words "other agent" follow such enumeration, these words are to be limited to agents of the classes named, and do not include an ordinary agent, not within any of such classes, to whom property is intrusted.[1] Under some statutes it is held that one who acts on commission, having therefore an interest in the money or property coming into his hands by virtue of his employment, is not an agent with reference to the proceeds of sales or the moneys collected;[2] but under other statutes there may be embezzlement in such cases if the property is not received by virtue of a distinct business such as that of attorney or factor.[3] Where the agent has no right to the goods or money intrusted to or received by him, he may be guilty of embezzlement although his compensation is in the form of a commission.[4] The question whether the agency still continued at the time of the receipt of the money is for the jury.[5]

§ 628. **For hire.**— Where the statute specifies agents, clerks, servants, or persons to whom property is intrusted for hire, it has been held that the limiting words "for hire" apply to agents, clerks, etc., as well as persons intrusted, and such element must be charged in the indictment.[6]

§ 629. **Trustees, attorneys, collectors, etc.**— There are classes of persons who receive money or property in a fiduciary capacity who still do not come under the designation of servant, clerk or agent. Thus, trustees of various kinds, brokers, etc., are held not to be included within the terms "agent or servant."[7] So it has been held that an attorney is not an agent in such sense as to be guilty of embezzlement under such provisions.[8] But it is held, on the other hand, that an attorney

[1] Reg. v. Portugal, 16 Q. B. D. 487.

[2] C. v. Libbey, 11 Met. 64; S. v. Kent, 22 Minn. 41.

[3] Campbell v. S., 35 Ohio St. 70.

[4] C. v. Smith, 129 Mass. 104.

[5] Thomas v. S., 33 Fla. 464.

[6] Terry v. S., 1 Wash. 277.

[7] Rex v. White, 4 C. & P. 46; Reg. v. Tatlock, 2 Q. B. D. 157; Reg. v. Gibbs, Dears. 445; Reg. v. Cosser, 13 Cox, 187. Thus, where a clerk deposited with his employer a sum of money as security for the faithful discharge of his duties, it was held that the employer was not guilty of embezzlement in failing to return the money, as the transaction gave rise to a debt and not to a bailment: Mulford v. P., 139 Ill. 586.

[8] Reg. v. Gibson, 8 Cox, 436; Reg. v. Cooper, L. R. 2 C. C. 123. Nor can a solicitor, to whom money is intrusted for investment, be convicted of embezzling such money

may be convicted as agent,[1] and in some of the states there are statutes especially applicable to attorneys.[2] Under such a statute, the relation of attorney and client must be directly charged.[3] The statute may also include collectors and other persons who receive money in that capacity;[4] but such a provision does not cover the case of a constable who receives money for property sold under execution.[5] There are sometimes special provisions applicable to trustees,[6] administrators[7] and guardians.[8]

§ **630. Custodian.**— To cover cases of trust where money or property has been left with a custodian to be invested or managed as may be directed there have been special statutes.[9] But such a statute does not cover the case of clerk, business manager or other employee who acts for the employer in such sense that money paid to him may be deemed to have been given into the possession of the employer. Thus, where one was authorized by the officers and members of a church to solicit and collect contributions therefor, it was held that he could not be convicted under such statute for embezzlement.[10] Such a statute applies only to persons to whom securities are intrusted in the exercise of their function or business.[11]

§ **631. Partnerships and associations.**— Where there is a right of ownership in the money or property, the case does not fall within the original idea of embezzlement. Thus, the misappropriation by a partner of partnership funds is not the crime of embezzlement.[12] But the mere fact that compensation is to be paid on the basis of a sharing in the profits does not constitute a partnership in this sense, and the employee may,

under the charge of misappropriating property received for safe custody: Reg. v. Newman, 8 Q. B. D. 706.

[1] P. v. Converse, 74 Mich. 478; In re Converse, 42 Fed. R. 217.

[2] Stoker v. P., 114 Ill. 320; S. v. Brooks, 85 Ia. 366; S. v. Belden, 35 La. An. 823.

[3] P. v. Tryon, 4 Mich. 665; Zink v. S., 34 Neb. 37.

[4] S. v. Brooks, 85 Ia. 366.

[5] Stoker v. P., 114 Ill. 320.

[6] Reg. v. Fletcher, L. & C. 180.

[7] S. v. Borowsky, 11 Nev. 119.

[8] Ex parte Blumer, 86 Pa. St. 371.

[9] Rex v. White, 4 C. & P. 46; Reg. v. Golde, 2 M. & Rob. 425; Reg. v. Christian, L. R. 2 C. C. 94; Reg. v. Fullagar, 14 Cox, 370.

[10] Shelburn v. C., 85 Ky. 173. And see Rex v. Burton, 1 Moody, 237.

[11] Rex v. Prince, 2 C. & P. 517.

[12] Gary v. Northwestern Masonic Aid Ass'n, 87 Ia. 25; Napoleon v. S., 3 Tex. Ap. 522. Though the partner is deemed for some purposes the agent of the other partners, he is not an agent within the terms of the statutes relating to embezzlement: S. v. Butman, 61 N. H. 511; S. v. Reddick, 2 S. Dak. 124.

notwithstanding such an arrangement, be liable for embezzlement of the funds received in pursuance of such employment.[1] The surviving partner, authorized by statute to settle the partnership affairs, is a person acting in a fiduciary capacity within the terms of some statutes relating to embezzlement.[2] In England there have been many cases relating to the officers of mutual benefit or friendly societies, and it has been held that where they were as members interested in the funds, they could not be convicted of embezzlement;[3] but where the person charged with embezzlement receives and holds money which he embezzles, not as a member of the society, but as servant of the trustees or other officers, he may be convicted notwithstanding his membership, the ownership of the money being laid in such trustees.[4] Under a statute providing for the punishment of a partner embezzling partnership funds, it has been held that a voluntary association for mutual improvement does not constitute a partnership within the meaning of such statute, there being no participation in profits possible, and therefore no partnership.[5] As to corporations it is immaterial, therefore, that the person charged with embezzlement of their funds is a member or has an interest, provided he has received the money by virtue of his employment, and not by virtue of his membership;[6] at least this is true where the statute in defining embezzlement does not in describing it make use of the term "property of another."[7]

§ 632. **Officers or agents of corporations.**— Some statutes in defining the offense mention, in addition to the agent, clerk or servant of any private person, the officer, agent or servant of any incorporated company,[8] but such terms are intended to

[1] C. v. Bennett, 118 Mass. 443; Reg. v. McDonald, L. & C. 85; Reg. v. Wortley, 2 Den. 333.

[2] S. v. Matthews, 129 Ind. 281.

[3] Reg. v. Bren, L. & C. 346; Reg. v. Marsh, 3 F. & F. 523; Reg. v. Tyree, L. R. 1 C. C. 177.

[4] Reg. v. Proud, L. & C. 97; Rex v. Hall, 1 Moody, 474; Reg. v. Miller, 2 Moody, 249; Reg. v. Woolley, 4 Cox, 251; Reg. v. Redford, 11 Cox, 367; Rex v. Jenson, 1 Moody, 434; Reg. v. Diprose, 11 Cox, 185. An unincorporated association having charitable features is not a partnership, and a member may be guilty of embezzlement of the funds thereof: Laycock v. S., 136 Ind. 217.

[5] Reg. v. Robson, 16 Q. B. D. 137.

[6] Reg. v. Atkinson, 2 Moody, 278.

[7] S. v. Kusnick, 45 Ohio St. 535; P. v. Mahlman, 82 Cal. 585.

[8] The treasurer of a railroad company is an officer thereof, and though he has control of its funds he may embezzle them without the consent

cover private corporations only and not public or municipal corporations.[1] Where the term employed was "corporation," it was held that the statute covered officers of a municipal corporation as well.[2] It has even been held that one employed by another who occupies a position as a public officer, in discharging the duties of the office, is not within the statute relating to agents, clerks, etc.;[3] but this is not in accordance with English cases which have held collectors of poor rates and assistant overseers to be servants of the overseers or guardians of the poor or the inhabitants of the parish.[4] The president and directors of a bank are included in the terms "cashier or other officer," but not in the terms "clerk, servant or agent."[5] A statute with reference to embezzlement by officers, etc., of an incorporated bank has been held applicable to national banks within the state,[6] but this point has also been decided the other way.[7] While the crime of embezzlement by officers or agents of a national bank is punishable under federal statute, yet there may be an embezzlement by such officer or agent of property of private persons in the possession of the bank which shall be punishable under the state law.[8] The fact that a national bank has no authority to take liens on personal property does not constitute a defense in a prosecution of the officer or agent of such a bank for embezzling such property.[9]

§ 633. **Persons under the age of sixteen years.**— In some statutes the definition of agent, clerk or servant expressly excludes persons under the age of sixteen years. But under such

of his employer, the directors being his employers in that sense: C. v. Tuckerman, 10 Gray, 173. Such statute covers a *de facto* officer: P. v. Leonard, 106 Cal. 302.

[1] Coats v. P., 22 N. Y. 245.

[2] S. v. Smith, 13 Kan. 274. And in the same state it is held that the term "agent" used generally in such a statute is applicable to officers or servants of the state: S. v. Bancroft, 22 Kan. 170. Where the statute referred to officers of a public or private corporation, *held*, that the selectmen of a county were included: S. v. Boody, 53 N. H. 610. The words "agent, clerk or officer" cover a municipal officer: S. v. Isensee, 12 Wash. 254.

[3] Coats v. P., 22 N. Y. 245.

[4] Reg. v. Adey, 1 Den. 571; Reg. v. Townsend, 2 C. & K. 168; Reg. v. Welch, 2 C. & K. 296; Reg. v. Carpenter, L. R. 1 C. C. 29; Rex v. Squire, Russ. & Ry. 349. But a bailiff of a county court was held not to be a servant of the high bailiff: Reg. v. Glover, L. & C. 466.

[5] C. v. Wyman, 8 Met. 247.

[6] C. v. Tenney, 97 Mass. 50; S. v. Fuller, 34 Conn. 280.

[7] C. v. Ketner, 92 Pa. St. 372.

[8] C. v. Tenney, 97 Mass. 50.

[9] Leonard v. S., 7 Tex. Ap. 417.

a statute it has been held that the language of the exception made it applicable to clerks, agents or servants of a private person or copartnership and not to officers, agents and clerks of an incorporated company.[1]

§ 634. **Property received by virtue of employment.**— It will be seen hereafter that in some states there are statutes broad enough to cover any case of misappropriation by persons to whom the property of another is intrusted; but the statutes which have been considered above, relating to agent, clerk or servant, evidently contemplate that the misappropriation is to be of something received in consequence of some employment instead of as bailee,[2] and is also to be of funds or property received by virtue of the employment.[3] Therefore, a servant is not guilty of embezzling money which he was not authorized to receive.[4] But the word "employment" is not to receive a strict construction in such cases, and if the receipt of the money is within the general scope of the agent's authority, he is to be held answerable therefor, although beyond the limits of express authority in a particular case;[5] and the money may be received by virtue of the employment, although the employer has only a temporary right thereto, and is not the ultimate owner.[6] If the money is received in the course of the employment, the crime of embezzlement of such money may be committed after the employment has terminated.[7] It is not neces-

[1] S. v. Goode, 68 Ia. 593.

[2] S. v. Foster, 37 Ia. 404, 1 Am. Cr. R. 146 and note.

[3] S. v. Johnson, 49 Ia. 141; S. v. Roubles, 43 La. An. 200; S. v. Johnson, 21 Tex. 775; Taylor v. S., 29 Tex. Ap. 466; Griffin v. S., 4 Tex. Ap. 390; Reg. v. Cullum, L. R. 2 C. C. 28. Even where the statute covers the case of one to whom "money shall have been delivered," such delivery must be by virtue of some trust or employment, and the statute does not cover a delivery by mistake: C. v. Hays, 14 Gray, 62. The indictment should allege receipt of the money or property by defendant as clerk or employee: Moore v. U. S., 160 U. S. 268.

[4] Rex v. Thorley, 1 Moody, 343; Rex v. Snowley, 4 C. & P. 390; Reg. v. Harris, Dears. 344; Reg. v. Arman, Dears. 575.

[5] Rex v. Beechey, Russ. & Ry. 319; Reg. v. Adey, 3 C. & K. 339; Rex v. Smith, Russ. & Ry. 516. Where an agent drew money without authority, though within the scope of his business, and appropriated it, he was held to have received it by virtue of his employment: Ex parte Hedley, 31 Cal. 108; P. v. Gallagher, 100 Cal. 466.

[6] Reg. v. Beaumont, Dears. 270; Reg. v. Thorpe, Dears. & B. 562; Reg. v. Gale, 2 Q. B. D. 141.

[7] Rex v. Lovell, 2 M. & Rob. 236; S. v. Jennings, 98 Mo. 493.

sary that at the time of the conversion the money be held by defendant by virtue of his employment.[1] Under some statutes it seems to be necessary to allege that the employee received the money from his employer.[2] Under statutes using language which makes the offense consist in misappropriating the money or property of any other person which shall have come into the custody of the employee by virtue of his employment, it is not necessary that the money shall have been received from some one other than the employer, "other person" being construed to mean some other person than the employee.[3] For the purpose of showing a fiduciary relation as to the money, the indictment must positively allege the money to be the property of the employer.[4] Where the property is not received by the defendant by virtue of the employment and as the property of the employer, the offense is not committed.[5] But it is not necessary that there be further possession or custody than that involved in the relation of employer and employee.[6] Thus, where a bank clerk, having access, by virtue of his employment, to the funds and securities of the bank in its vault, misappropriated such property, it was held that he was guilty of embezzlement.[7]

§ **635. Illegally received.** — The fact that the money or property is illegally received,[8] or received under an illegal em-

[1] Taylor v. S., 29 Tex. Ap. 466. A trustee holding property after the termination of the transaction in which it was intrusted to him may be guilty of embezzlement thereof: C. v. Butterick, 100 Mass. 1.

[2] P. v. Bailey, 23 Cal. 577. But even under such a statute it is not necessary that the money be received directly from the employer; it may be received from another servant: S. v. Fournier, 12 Mont. 235; and see Reg. v. Masters, 1 Den. 332; or it may be received by the party charged through his agent: S. v. Hinckley, 38 Me. 31.

[3] C. v. Stearns, 2 Met. 343; P. v. Hennessey, 15 Wend. 147; S. v. Porter, 26 Mo. 201; T. v. Maxwell, 2 N. Mex. 250; Fleener v. S., 58 Ark. 98.

[4] Rex v. McGregor, 3 Bos. & P. 106; Rex v. Beacall, 1 Moody, 15; Griffin v. S., 4 Tex. Ap. 390; Washington v. S., 72 Ala. 272; Ricord v. Central Pacific R. Co., 15 Nev. 167.

[5] Thus, a mail rider stealing money sent in a registered letter is not the agent of the person sending the letter so as to be punishable for embezzlement by an agent: Brewer v. S., 83 Ala. 113. So where a husband converted to his own use money deposited with the wife by a third person, *held*, that the husband was not guilty of embezzlement: Pullam v. S., 78 Ala. 31.

[6] S. v. Ezzard, 40 S. C. 312.

[7] Ker v. P., 110 Ill. 627.

[8] Thus, money received by virtue of a state appropriation was held subject of embezzlement, although the order therefor was improperly

ployment, will not render the embezzlement thereof any the less punishable.[1] So the fact that the money is received as officer of a club not organized according to law,[2] or as agent of a foreign corporation which has not filed its articles as required by state statute,[3] will not prevent the conversion thereof being punishable. But if the money or property is not that of another there can be no embezzlement. Thus, to receive wages which have been assigned by a transfer which is invalid, and has therefore not passed the right to them, is not criminal.[4]

§ 636. What property subject to embezzlement; value.— Where the statute as to embezzlement refers to "money or property," the term "property" means the same as it does under an indictment for larceny using the same term.[5] Indeed most of the cases relating to the question as to what is a subject of larceny would be applicable here.[6] But cases relating specially to embezzlement may properly be referred to in this connection. Where the statute includes in the enumeration of property subject to embezzlement "bank bills or notes," the word "notes" must be considered to mean bank notes, and not promissory notes.[7] A negotiable bond, bill, or note, which has not yet been put in circulation by the maker, may nevertheless be subject of embezzlement by one who converts it to his own use by putting it into circulation and obtaining a consideration therefor.[8] Shares of stock constitute property and

drawn by the governor instead of the state treasurer: P. v. Royce, 106 Cal. 173.

[1] C. v. Cooper, 130 Mass. 285; S. v. Tumey, 81 Ind. 559; Rex v. Beacall, 1 C. & P. 312; Rex v. Wellings, 1 C. & P. 454. So irregularity in the organization of a society will not prevent punishment of its servants for embezzlement: Reg. v. Miller, 2 Moody, 249; Reg. v. Stainer, L. R. 1 C. C. 230; Reg. v. Frankland, L. & C. 276; otherwise, if the organization is an unlawful combination: Reg. v. Hunt, 8 C. & P. 642.

[2] Reg. v. Tankard, 1 Q. B. D. (1894), 548.

[3] S. v. O'Brien, 94 Tenn. 79.

[4] S. v. Williamson, 118 Mo. 146; St. Clair v. S., 100 Ala. 61.

[5] S. v. Orwig, 24 Ia. 102. This case holds that bills of exchange are included under such a statute.

[6] See §§ 536–543, *supra*. A charge of embezzling money is not sustained by proof of embezzling a check without evidence that it had been converted into money: Reg. v. Keena, L. R. 1 C. C. 113.

[7] S. v. Stimson, 24 N. J. 9. Halves of bank-notes sent in a letter were held to be goods and chattels: Rex v. Mead, 4 C. & P. 535.

[8] S. v. White, 66 Wis. 343. So where defendant procured acceptance of bills which he was afterwards to sign as drawer, and which he subsequently negotiated, misappropriating the proceeds, *held*, that he was guilty of embezzling securi-

may be embezzled.[1] Where the statute includes the embezzlement of "any instrument being the act of another," it does not include a chattel mortgage executed by defendant himself.[2] There may be an embezzlement involved in the unauthorized assignment of an instrument held as agent or trustee, although the holder is unable by means of such assignment to convey a title to the property represented by such instrument.[3] Where the description of the offense is analogous to that of larceny, the statutes generally make use of the term "property of another."[4] As has already been explained, this means of another than the agent, clerk or servant who is charged with embezzlement.[5] Such a statutory definition prevents there being any embezzlement in the case of auctioneers or commission men who lawfully receive the proceeds of property sold and mingle them with their own, such proceeds not being the property of another because their duty is only to account, and not to turn over the identical funds received.[6] In order to show that the property is that of another, it is necessary to name the owner in the indictment.[7] In analogy with the rule in larceny it has been held necessary to allege that the property embezzled was of some value;[8] but these statutes as to embezzlement do not in all cases divide the offense as to the punishment into two degrees or branches, depending upon the value of the property.[9] Sometimes, however, the value is essential to determine the punishment, as in larceny, and must be alleged.[10]

ties: Reg. v. Bowerman, 1 Q. B. D. (1891), 112. But where the charge was of embezzling exchequer bills, it was held that bills not signed by a person duly authorized did not come within that description: Rex v. Aslett, Russ. & Ry. 67.

1 P. v. Williams, 60 Cal. 1.

2 S. v. Grisham, 90 Mo. 163.

3 C. v. Pratt, 137 Mass. 98.

4 Embezzlement cannot be predicated on a disposition of money which is the absolute property of accused, even though he fraudulently conceal it from his creditors: Parli v. Reed, 30 Kan. 534.

5 See § 634, *supra*.

6 C. v. Stearns, 2 Met. 343. See, also, *infra*, § 639.

7 S. v. Lyon, 45 N. J. 272.

8 S. v. Stimson, 24 N. J. 9.

9 P. v. Salorse, 62 Cal. 139; S. v. Weydeman, 3 Wash. 399.

10 P. v. Schultz, 85 Mich. 114; Grant v. S., 35 Fla. 581; Cooksie v. S., 26 Tex. Ap. 72; Aldrich v. S., 29 Tex. Ap. 394. Where the stealing of certain kinds of property is punishable as larceny without regard to value, the value is immaterial in a prosecution for embezzlement of such property: Washington v. S., 72 Ala. 272.

§ 637. **What acts sufficient.**—So long as the person intrusted with money or property acts with reference thereto in accordance with the terms of the trust, whether as servant, clerk, agent, or trustee, he evidently cannot be guilty of embezzlement. The question as to what acts shall be sufficient to show the commission of the crime is, in many classes of cases, one of great difficulty. Some of these classes must be discussed separately.

§ 638. **Conversion of property.**— With regard to property, not money, it is necessary that some adverse use or holding be shown depriving the owner of his property.[1] But there is no prescribed set of circumstances which will be necessary or sufficient to show a fraudulent conversion. The question is one of fact.[2] For instance, it was held sufficient evidence of the embezzlement of a piano that defendant sold it with that purpose and took a note for the proceeds in his own name.[3] So where one, pretending to have a customer for diamonds, procured diamonds from a broker with the agreement that he would return the proceeds of the sale or the diamonds if not sold, and, instead of doing so, pawned the diamonds, it was held that embezzlement was sufficiently established.[4] Where a clerk in charge of an elevator issued fictitious grain orders, and delivered grain upon such orders, appropriating the money paid therefor, he was held to be guilty of embezzlement.[5] But, in general, an agent authorized to sell is not guilty of embezzlement in selling, though he may be guilty with reference to the misappropriation of the proceeds.[6] Indeed, the fact of conversion alone does not establish embezzlement,[7] but the question

[1] Chaplin v. Lee, 18 Neb. 440.

[2] P. v. Dalton, 15 Wend. 581, where it is said that conversion of a letter containing money does not necessarily involve the opening of the letter and the extracting of the money therefrom.

[3] S. v. Adams, 108 Mo. 208.

[4] S. v. Samuels, 111 Mo. 566; S. v. Foley, 81 Ia. 36. So, in general, an agent receiving property for sale on commission is guilty of conversion in pledging it for money borrowed for his own use, with the intent to deprive the owner of his property: Morehouse v. S., 35 Neb. 643.

[5] Calkins v. S., 18 Ohio St. 366.

[6] P. v. Doane, 77 Cal. 560; Carter v. S., 53 Ga. 326; S. v. Wallick, 87 Ia. 369. Where, however, one authorized to sell bonds for a city delivered them to a broker for sale, directing the proceeds to be placed to his own or another's credit and not to the credit of the city, he was held guilty of conversion of the bonds: Bork v. P., 91 N. Y. 5.

[7] S. v. Wallick, 87 Ia. 369.

of authority and intent must also be considered.[1] The conversion necessary in embezzlement is the taking the property of another for the defendant's own purposes, knowing that such taking is without right, and without the consent of the owner, by concealment, such concealment implying an affirmative deception or preconceived and intentional fraud.[2] The fraudulent concealment alone under some statutes amounts to embezzlement where it is with intent to convert.[3] Refusal to account for the property on demand may be evidence of embezzlement,[4] but conversion may be otherwise shown than by demand and refusal. Demand is not essential where there has been an actual conversion.[5]

§ 639. **Conversion of money; demand and refusal.**— The most difficult question in determining whether there has been a conversion of money depends upon the determination as to whether the money has been in the custody of the servant, clerk, or agent for the master or employer, or whether the relation between the parties has been that of debtor and creditor. It is evident that the mere failure of one who ought to pay money to his creditor to do so does not constitute embezzlement, but is a mere breach of contract.[6] Thus, if one intrusted with property for sale, and who is to account for the proceeds thereof, but has the right to mingle such proceeds with his own money, and pay for the property under the terms of a contract with reference to the sale thereof, as is proper in the case of auctioneers and commission men, fails to account for such proceeds, he will not under the ordinary statutes relating to

[1] As to intent see *infra*, § 641.

[2] C. v. Tuckerman, 10 Gray, 173, 202; S. v. Pierce, 77 Ia. 245; Fleener v. S., 58 Ark. 98; P. v. O'Brien, 106 Cal. 104; S. v. Ezzard, 40 S. C. 312.

[3] Spaulding v. Cook, 48 Vt. 145; S. v. Goode, 68 Ia. 593. But where one who hauled bales of cotton for the owner of a gin mill marked one of the bales with his son's name, and took a receipt for it in that name, but afterward turned the receipt over to the owner on being questioned, *held*, that he was not guilty of fraudulent secreting with intent to convert: Penny v. S., 88 Ala. 105.

[4] S. v. Foley, 81 Ia. 36.

[5] C. v. Hussey, 111 Mass. 432; S. v. New, 22 Minn. 76.

[6] Keeller v. S., 4 Tex. Ap. 527; Reg. v. Barnes, 8 Cox, 129. But the fact that a party has given bond for the discharge of his duties as trustee will be no defense in a prosecution for embezzlement of trust funds: P. v. De Lay, 80 Cal. 52. The fact that the money has been paid over by a guaranty company will not prevent prosecution for the crime: Fleener v. S., 58 Ark. 98.

embezzlement be guilty of the crime.[1] In such cases the money received cannot be said to be that of another within the terms of the usual embezzlement statutes.[2] There may be special statutory provisions, however, which render a factor or commission merchant criminally liable for not accounting for the proceeds of sales of the principal's property on demand being made therefor.[3] The question whether he was acting as a broker in the transaction and therefore authorized to mix the proceeds with his own property and thus become a debtor, or whether he was merely agent for the transfer of the property and handing over the proceeds, is for the jury, and the fact that he gives his own notes to secure the payment of the proceeds is not conclusive.[4] An agent or the officer of a corporation may become liable for embezzlement, although as agent or officer he has authority to handle such funds in the course of his employment.[5] Thus, where the treasurer of a corporation had the right to pay the funds of the corporation into the bank to his account as treasurer, and to draw the same in the course of the business, it was held that he might be guilty of embezzlement of such funds, and did not occupy the relation of a mere debtor.[6] Where one intrusts money to another to be used or invested in a particular way, there may be embezzlement by misappropriation although the money was never to be returned to the owner.[7] In England the statutes applicable

[1] C. v. Stearns, 2 Met. 343. So held where the defendant was agent of the manufacturer of agricultural implements, and the contract authorized time settlements with the employer for the machinery sold: Miller v. S., 16 Neb. 179; S. v. Wallick, 87 Ia. 369. And see *supra*, § 636.

[2] C. v. Stearns, 2 Met. 343. So where defendant was furnished sewing machines for sale on terms requiring him to account in money or in notes payable to his principal, but by a subsequent contract he was authorized to trade machines for live-stock, and to convert the stock into money and account therefor, *held*, that the authority thus conferred changed the character of the contract, so that neither the stock taken nor the proceeds of such stock constituted the property of the principal, and there could be no embezzlement: Webb v. S., 8 Tex. Ap. 310.

[3] Wright v. P., 61 Ill. 382; Warriner v. P., 74 Ill. 346; C. v. Harris, 168 Pa. St. 619.

[4] C. v. Foster, 107 Mass. 221.

[5] C. v. Smith, 129 Mass. 104.

[6] C. v. Tuckerman, 10 Gray, 173. The mere fact that the money held by a bailee is deposited in bank, and the money drawn on that account is afterwards converted, will not prevent the act being embezzlement: C. v. Mead, 160 Mass. 319.

[7] Kribs v. P., 82 Ill. 425, 2 Am. Cr. R. 109, and note. A broker to whom money is sent to be invested in certain stocks on margin is guilty of

to such cases require, in order that the failure to use the money for the purpose intended shall be embezzlement, that there shall have been a direction in writing as to the use to be made of it.[1] Aside from a special duty with reference to funds received by an agent or trustee, the mere fact that he is intrusted with funds and fails to account for them, even where he has expended the money as his own, will not conclusively show embezzlement, but the question will be whether such disposition was with intention to defraud.[2] But if the failure to account for funds so received is found to have been fraudulent, there is sufficient ground for the conviction of embezzlement.[3] If one who has money for another has a lien thereon, as, for instance, for services as attorney, embezzlement will not be committed in failing to pay over the funds until there has been a settlement.[4] Mere proof of the receipt of funds and failure to account therefor is not, in general, sufficient to show embezzlement by an agent or servant; the fact of conversion must be proven.[5] Demand and refusal may be evidence of conversion.[6] But the fact may be shown otherwise than by demand and refusal.[7] The embezzlement is complete if the funds are by the agent turned into his own account with fraudulent intent,[8] the intent being the important element in such cases.[9]

§ 640. Failure to account or pay over.— In regard to money it is sometimes difficult to determine just when the embezzle-

embezzlement if he retains the money assuming the contract himself. The custom of assuming the contract by the broker is illegal: C. v. Cooper, 130 Mass. 285. And see Reg. v. Christian, L. R. 2 C. C. 94.

[1] Rex v. White, 4 C. & P. 46; Reg. v. Christian, L. R. 2 C. C. 94; Reg. v. Golde, 2 M. & Rob. 425.

[2] P. v. Galland, 55 Mich. 628; P. v. Hurst, 62 Mich. 276; P. v. Wadsworth, 63 Mich. 500; Fitzgerald v. S., 50 N. J. 475; P. v. Gale, 77 Cal. 120.

[3] P. v. De Lay, 80 Cal. 52; Fitzgerald v. S., 50 N. J. 475.

[4] Van Etten v. S., 24 Neb. 734. And further as to embezzlement by attorneys, see *supra*, § 629.

[5] S. v. Bryan, 40 Ia. 379; Thomas v. Dunaway, 30 Ill. 373; P. v. Wyman, 102 Cal. 552; P. v. Royce, 106 Cal. 173; Fleener v. S., 58 Ark. 98; S. v. O'Kean, 35 La. An. 901. And see *supra*, § 639.

[6] S. v. Bryan, 40 Ia. 379; S. v. Brooks, 85 Ia. 366.

[7] C. v. Tuckerman, 10 Gray, 173; C. v. Mead, 160 Mass. 319; S. v. Tompkins, 32 La. An. 620; S. v. Porter, 26 Mo. 201. See *supra*, § 638. It is not necessary to allege demand: S. v. Flournoy, 46 La. An. 1518. There may be conversion although the time for paying over has not arrived: P. v. Royce, 106 Cal. 173.

[8] C. v. Butterick, 100 Mass. 1.

[9] C. v. Este, 140 Mass. 279. But there must be an adverse holding or use: Ibid. And further on the subject of intent, see *infra*, § 641.

ment takes place. Under earlier English statutes it seems to have been held that a mere failure to pay over, where there had been no omission to enter up the amount received on the proper books, did not constitute an embezzlement.[1] Mere receipt, however, and a failure to account, where it appears to have been wilful, is sufficient to show embezzlement.[2] Entries on account books are not conclusive on the person making them, and may even be made for the purpose of covering up previous deficiencies without in themselves constituting embezzlement;[3] but if the agent, to cover up deficiencies on account of sums of money previously received, reports certain sums as unpaid which have in fact been received by him, he therein is guilty of embezzlement.[4] Books of account kept by defendant for his employer, or receipts given by him, are admissible to show the sums with which he is chargeable.[5] Where a clerk's accounts showed that on the morning of the day in question he had on hand a certain sum which in the evening he was unable to produce, there being no showing that the shortage had occurred previously, it was held that there might properly be a conviction for the embezzlement of the amount of the shortage without any evidence as to the persons from whom the money with which he had charged himself was received.[6] It has been thought in some cases necessary to point out the particular sum embezzled,[7] but it would seem by the later cases that a failure to pay over a portion of a general balance, as has already been indicated, would be sufficient.[8]

[1] Rex v. Hodgson, 3 C. & P. 422; Reg. v. Creed, 1 C. & K. 63. But a correct entry was held not to excuse a concealment and failure to pay over a portion of sums received: Reg. v. White, 8 C. & P. 742; Reg. v. Guelder, Bell, 284; Reg. v. Lister, Dears. & B. 118. It is not enough to prove the receipt of money not entered up unless there is also evidence of denial of receipt: Rex v. Jones, 7 C. & P. 833.

[2] Reg. v. Jackson, 1 C. & K. 384; Reg. v. Aston, 2 C. & K. 413; Rex v. Hall, Russ. & Ry. 463. Thus, where a servant, having received money in England, immediately went off to Ireland with it, it was held that the jury might infer an intent to embezzle: Rex v. Williams, 7 C. & P. 338.

[3] C. v. Este, 140 Mass. 279.

[4] Bowman v. Brown, 52 Ia. 437.

[5] P. v. Bidleman, 104 Cal. 608; P. v. Leonard, 106 Cal. 302; S. v. Reinhart, 26 Oreg. 466.

[6] Rex v. Grove, 7 C. & P. 635. And see Reg. v. Moah, Dears. 626.

[7] Reg. v. Chapman, 1 C. & K. 119; Reg. v. Wolstenholme, 11 Cox, 313; Rex v. Murray, 5 C. & P. 145.

[8] Rex v. Grove, 7 C. & P. 635; Reg. v. Moah, Dears. 626; Rex v. Hall, Russ. & Ry. 463.

While it may be that under some statutes a refusal to pay on demand is sufficient to constitute a conversion, the demand by another than the principal, on his behalf, will not be sufficient to make a failure to pay in response thereto embezzlement, unless the person making the demand has authority from the principal to make it.[1]

§ 641. **Intent necessary.**— The statutes frequently make intent to defraud an essential part of the offense, and in such case the use of the word "embezzle" alone without an allegation of such intent to defraud is not sufficient.[2] And aside from this statutory requirement it is essential that there be, as in other crimes, a criminal intent.[3] If the defendant has not concealed the receipt of the money, but has claimed in good faith to keep it under some right as against the owner, he is not guilty of embezzlement.[4] But where the statute makes a particular act embezzlement, such as the act of the officer of a bank in knowingly overdrawing his account, then knowingly doing the act is sufficient without regard to the intent with which it was done.[5] It is immaterial whether the intent to convert was formed before or after the receipt of the money.[6] So, where the officer of a bank was charged with wilfully misapplying the funds in certain speculations, it was held that defendant could not disprove such averment by showing that his actions were known to the president and some of the directors, and were sanctioned by them and were intended for the bank's benefit.[7] If there is a taking with wrongful intent, an intent to return or restore is immaterial.[8]

[1] P. v. Tomlinson, 66 Cal. 344.

[2] S. v. Lyon, 45 N. J. 272.

[3] U. S. v. Sander, 6 McLean, 598; Stallings v. S., 29 Tex. Ap. 220; C. v. Este, 140 Mass. 279. The doing of the wrongful, fraudulent and illegal act sufficiently shows the intent: U. S. v. Harper, 33 Fed. R. 471.

[4] Reg. v. Norman, Car. & M. 501. If defendant claims to have acted in the belief that he was authorized to use the money as he did, his acts inconsistent with such belief may be shown: P. v. Bidleman, 104 Cal. 608.

[5] S. v. Stimson, 24 N. J. 478.

[6] S. v. Findley, 101 Mo. 217.

[7] U. S. v. Taintor, 11 Blatch. 374.

[8] C. v. Tenney, 97 Mass. 50; S. v. Pratt, 98 Mo. 482; S. v. Trolson, 21 Nev. 419. And so it will be immaterial that defendant offered return or repayment before a prosecution was instituted: P. v. De Lay, 80 Cal. 52. But in England a disclosure seems to have been held material in a bankruptcy proceeding: Reg. v. Skeen, Bell, 97.

§ 642. **Other acts.**— For the purpose of showing intent it is proper to prove other acts of embezzlement similar to that charged.[1]

§ 643. **Without employer's consent.**— Statutes sometimes make it essential that the misappropriation shall have been without the consent of the owner, and under such a statute the want of consent should be charged;[2] but to prove want of consent it is not necessary to show dissent on the part of the owner.[3] In the case of an officer of a company, the phrase "without consent of the employer or master" would refer to the consent of the directors, and would be applicable even though the officer has exclusive control of the funds as to depositing and paying them out.[4] Without regard to any statutory provision the consent of the owner of the money or property would of course show absence of wrong;[5] but the master's consent involved in marking money to be paid by another to the servant in the usual course of business for the master would not be such consent as to prevent the wrongful taking being embezzlement, the consent involved being a consent to the lawful act and not to the conversion.[6]

III. By Carrier or Other Bailee.

§ 644. **Carrier liable.**— The rule has been already stated in connection with the subject of larceny, that a bailee or carrier is not guilty of that crime in appropriating the goods to his own use, in violation of the purposes with which they are delivered to him, unless, as in case of a carrier, there is a breaking of the package or some such act which may be deemed a renunciation of the bailment.[7] The offense of un-

[1] P. v. Gray, 66 Cal. 271; Stanley v. S., 88 Ala. 154; Lang v. S., 97 Ala. 41; P. v. Cobler, 108 Cal. 538; S. v. Lewis, 19 Oreg. 478; Reg. v. Proud, L. & C. 97; Reg. v. Richardson, 2 F. & F. 343.

[2] S. v. Foster, 11 Ia. 291. But where such a clause is used with reference to a conversion of goods, it may be applicable only where it is claimed that the goods were disposed of without the owner's consent, and not to a case of fraudulent conversion by defendant to his own use: Alderman v. S., 57 Ga. 367.

[3] P. v. Dalton, 15 Wend. 581.

[4] C. v. Tuckerman, 10 Gray, 173.

[5] Henderson v. S., 1 Tex. Ap. 432. Subsequent ratification of the act by the employer will not be a defense: S. v. Frisch, 45 La. An. 1283.

[6] Rex v. Headge, Russ. & Ry. 160; Rex v. Whittingham, 2 Leach, 912; Reg. v. Gill, Dears. 289.

[7] *Supra*, §§ 554, 555.

lawful conversion of property in such cases is by many statutes made the crime of embezzlement. Such statutes sometimes apply specially to common carriers, that is, those who receive goods to be carried for hire;[1] and such statutes may not extend to any other cases of bailment than those to a common carrier.[2] As to bailees in general, they are not included within a statute relating to embezzlement by agents, trustees, servants or clerks.[3] But the general statute may be broad enough to embrace all persons who are guilty of fraudulently securing or converting to their own use the money or property of others intrusted to them or placed in their hands to be carried or delivered;[4] and this may cover an ordinary bailment.[5] In such case the delivery may be constructive. For instance, where baggage checks were delivered, it was held to be such delivery of the baggage as to make a conversion of the baggage by means of possession of the checks, embezzlement.[6] Under statutes for the punishment of those who wrongfully convert property intrusted to them, a pledgee may be guilty of embezzlement.[7] So, one to whom implements are intrusted for sale may be guilty of embezzlement in converting them to his own use without the owner's consent.[8] But one to whom property is hired, or delivered under a conditional sale, is not guilty of embezzlement in selling the property in disregard of the limitations upon his rights therein.[9] Where the statute defining the offense of embezzlement by carrier or other bailee does not make demand an element of the crime, conviction may be had without proof of such demand.[10] The property must have come into the possession of defendant by virtue of the embezzlement,[11] and the indictment must show specifically what property is charged to have been converted,[12] and in what capacity the defendant received it.[13]

[1] White v. S., 20 Wis. 233; S. v. Stoller, 38 Ia. 321.

[2] S. v. Grisham, 90 Mo. 163.

[3] Hutchinson v. C., 82 Pa. St. 472. And see Reed v. S., 16 Tex. Ap. 586.

[4] Johnson v. C., 5 Bush, 430; Alderman v. S., 57 Ga. 367.

[5] S. v. Foster, 37 Ia. 404.

[6] P. v. Husband, 36 Mich. 306.

[7] C. v. Butterick, 100 Mass. 1; P. v. Husband, 36 Mich. 306.

[8] S. v. Leicham, 41 Wis. 565. And though in case the bailee may have authority to sell, the sale may be a conversion if with intent to misappropriate the proceeds: Epperson v. S., 22 Tex. Ap. 694.

[9] Watson v. S., 70 Ala. 13; Williams v. S., 25 Tex. Ap. 733.

[10] Wallis v. S., 54 Ark. 611.

[11] Gaddy v. S., 8 Tex. Ap. 127.

[12] P. v. Cohen, 8 Cal. 42.

[13] C. v. Concannon, 5 Allen, 502.

IV. By Public Officers.

§ 645. **Special statutory provisions.**— It has been generally assumed that the ordinary statutes as to embezzlement by agents, clerks and servants do not apply to public officers.[1] At any rate, the mere use of public funds by an officer for private gain is not an offense at common law.[2]

§ 646. **Who deemed public officer.**— A statute which provides for the punishment of embezzlement by any public officer who is a receiver of public money will embrace all officers of states, counties and other public corporations to whom money is intrusted by virtue of such office.[3] It is difficult to determine in all cases who is to be deemed a public officer. If the office is one involving the taking of an oath and the filing of a bond by the occupant, whether he be elective or not, such occupant is a public officer.[4] This general description would cover a state treasurer,[5] or his deputy,[6] or a deputy sheriff.[7] Where the statute specifies municipal officers, the treasurer of a school district is within its terms,[8] and a statute specifying officers appointed or elected by virtue of the constitution or any law of the state covers township trustees[9] or a city treasurer.[10] It has been held that a clerk of the board of county commissioners is within the statute "a clerk to a body corporate," the commissioners being a corporation.[11] A tax collector,[12] and a clerk of the administrator of city finance,[13] have been held to

[1] *Supra*, § 621.

[2] In re Breene, 14 Colo. 401. Perhaps there is at common law some punishment for the embezzlement of public funds; but where the statute provides a specific remedy, this remedy is exclusive of any other: Hellings v. C., 5 Rawle, 63.

[3] S. v. Boody, 53 N. H. 610.

[4] S. v. Walton, 62 Me. 106; P. v. Bedell, 2 Hill, 196. As to who is a public officer under federal statute, see U. S. v. Hartwell, 6 Wall. 385; but a general federal statute as to public officers does not cover an assignee in bankruptcy: U. S. v. Bixby, 10 Biss. C. C. 238.

[5] P. v. McKinney, 10 Mich. 54.

[6] S. v. Brandt, 41 Ia. 593. An assistant may be an officer, and not merely a servant or clerk of his superior officer: U. S. v. Bornemann, 36 Fed. R. 257.

[7] S. v. Brooks, 42 Tex. 62.

[8] C. v. Morrisey, 86 Pa. St. 416. So an officer employed by the state in the operation of its gas works was held to be within the terms of such a statute: Culp v. C., 109 Pa. St. 363.

[9] S. v. Cleveland, 80 Mo. 108.

[10] S. v. Krug, 12 Wash. 288.

[11] S. v. Denton, 74 Md. 517; Denton v. S., 77 Md. 527.

[12] Shivers v. S., 53 Ga. 149.

[13] S. v. Exnicios, 33 La. An. 253.

be public officers. By statute one may be guilty of such offense by aiding and abetting the officer, although not an officer himself.[1]

§ **647. De facto officer.**— One who acts *de facto* as a public officer cannot escape liability for embezzlement on the ground that he is not such officer *de jure*,[2] and it is immaterial that the officer has not taken the oath or given bond as required by law.[3] It is sufficient to allege that defendant was a public officer, stating the office, without alleging how he came into such office or that he was duly qualified.[4]

§ **648. Public funds.**— The money or property for which an officer may be held accountable under the statutes with reference to embezzlement by such officers must be the property of the state, county, city or other public corporation, and the ownership of the property must be alleged as in other cases.[5] But a city bond not yet issued may be property within the meaning of an embezzlement statute, although the city has not yet become liable thereon.[6] The money may be alleged to be that of a township, although the township does not by its own officers collect taxes and pay indebtedness, the money embezzled, however, being a part of a fund collected to pay township bonds;[7] but on the other hand, in such cases the township bonds may be charged to be the property of the county which has the custody thereof.[8] Where the fund embezzled belongs in part to the county and in part to the state, the taking of the whole may be charged as one embezzlement.[9] It is not necessary, however, to allege the source from which the em-

[1] Brown v. S., 18 Ohio St. 497.

[2] S. v. Goss, 69 Me. 22; Diggs v. S., 49 Ala. 311; S. v. Stone, 40 Ia. 547; S. v. Sellers, 7 Rich. 368; S. v. Maberry, 3 Strobh. 144.

[3] Fortenberry v. S., 56 Miss. 286; C. v. Logue, 160 Mass. 551. It is no defense to a deputy that the principal appointing him had never qualified: P. v. Cobler, 108 Cal. 538.

[4] S. v. Goss, 69 Me. 22; Rex v. Barrett, 6 C. & P. 124; Reg. v. Townsend, Car. & M. 178; 1 Whart. Prec. 460; 2 Arch. Crim. Pr. 462.

[5] Crane v. S., 26 Tex. Ap. 482; Alden v. S., 18 Fla. 187.

[6] S. v. White, 66 Wis. 343. Where a treasurer forwarded a county order to the auditor for credit, although he knew such order had been redeemed by his predecessor, *held*, that he was guilty of embezzlement: S. v. Baumhager, 28 Minn. 226.

[7] S. v. Clarkson, 59 Mo. 149.

[8] S. v. Cunningham, 51 Mo. 479.

[9] P. v. De La Guerra, 31 Cal. 416.

bezzled fund has been derived, nor to identify any precise sum,[1] nor need the indictment specially allege ownership in county or state or other municipality; it is sufficient to describe the fund as public moneys or funds in accordance with the language of the statute.[2] Money which an officer has received without any authority to receive it cannot be deemed public funds in his hands,[3] but it is not necessary that it be specially charged that the funds were received by the officer as such. The allegation that they were under his official control and custody is sufficient.[4] It is not necessary that the funds shall have actually come into the treasury in order to render the treasurer liable for embezzlement thereof, if they have come under the treasurer's control by virtue of his office.[5]

§ 649. **What constitutes conversion.**— Where the statute makes the offense consist in the failure of the officer to account for or pay over public funds received by him, it must appear that there was some failure to pay over or account where the officer was legally called upon to do so; for instance, where there is lawful occasion to pay, such as the termination of the term of office,[6] or lawful demand and a refusal.[7] Under some statutes failure to account or pay over when properly called on is essential to constitute the offense;[8] but there may be additional statutory provisions making the misuse of the public funds criminal without regard to whether there is any ultimate loss thereof or failure to account therefor when called on to do so.[9] It is not necessary, however, to allege the mode unless the

[1] S. v. Boody, 53 N. H. 610; S. v. Walton, 62 Me. 106; P. v. McKinney, 10 Mich. 54.

[2] S. v. Hays, 78 Mo. 600; S. v. Flint, 62 Mo. 393; S. v. Walton, 62 Me. 106.

[3] S. v. Newton, 26 Ohio St. 265. But it is sufficient that it is received on account of his office: Denton v. S., 77 Md. 527.

[4] P. v. McKinney, 10 Mich. 54; Bork v. P., 91 N. Y. 5.

[5] P. v. McKinney, 10 Mich. 54; S. v. Ring, 29 Minn. 78; P. v. Gray, 66 Cal. 271; P. v. Cobler, 108 Cal. 538; Robson v. S., 83 Ga. 166.

[6] Hemingway v. S., 68 Miss. 371; S. v. Hebel, 72 Ind. 361; S. v. Govan, 48 Ark. 76.

[7] S. v. Bryan, 40 Ia. 379; S. v. King, 81 Ia. 587; S. v. Cameron, 3 Heisk. 78; S. v. Munch, 22 Minn. 67; S. v. Leonard, 6 Coldw. 307.

[8] S. v. Brandt, 41 Ia. 593; Hale v. Richards, 80 Ia. 164; S. v. Parsons, 54 Ia. 405. But if embezzlement has been committed it is immaterial, in a prosecution therefor, that the loss has been made good by bondsmen: Robson v. S., 83 Ga. 166. And see Fleener v. S., 58 Ark. 98.

[9] S. v. Brandt. 41 Ia. 593; Comstock v. Gage, 91 Ill. 328; S. v. Krug, 12 Wash. 288; Reg. v. Moah, Dears. 626.

statute makes some act other than conversion punishable.[1] And the mere failure to make returns or account as required is sufficient.[2] A conversion need not be of the specific coins or bills received, but may be of money taken in exchange therefor.[3] There may be embezzlement in applying money received for public purposes to the extinguishment of a shortage in the officer's accounts, but this will not depend on a mere question of book-keeping, but on whether the money received was actually applied to public purposes or not.[4] The question may arise in such cases as to when the embezzlement actually took place, and the officer will not be estopped by his acts from showing that it really occurred prior to the statutory period of limitation for such prosecution, although at a settlement held within the statutory period he was able to satisfy the accounting officers that he had on hand the public funds required.[5] The books of a treasurer being public records are admissible to show the receipt of funds unaccounted for or a failure to account for funds received, and it will be immaterial whether the books are kept by the defendant or by his clerk or deputy, though of course entries on such books by others will not be conclusive.[6] The embezzlement may be committed by an accomplice or by allowing another to misappropriate to his own use funds in the custody of the officer.[7] If the act of the officer in the misuse of the public funds is unlawful, the intention with which the act was done will be immaterial. He is bound to know the law, and good faith or innocent motives will not serve as an excuse.[8] The indictment should charge the act as felonious, and an allegation of the act itself in the language of the statute without the usual averment of intent is not sufficient.[9]

[1] S. v. Clarkson, 59 Mo. 149.

[2] Britton v. S., 77 Ala. 202.

[3] P. v. Bringard, 39 Mich. 22.

[4] C. v. Este, 140 Mass. 279.

[5] S. v. Hutchinson, 60 Ia. 478. It is immaterial as tending to prove embezzlement at a given time that the officer had money on deposit in excess of the amount of the alleged embezzlement, where it does not appear that he did not misappropriate the particular money charged: Ida County v. Wood, 79 Ia. 148.

[6] Hemmingway v. S., 68 Miss. 371; P. v. McKinney, 10 Mich. 74.

[7] Brown v. S., 18 Ohio St. 497; Noble v. S., 59 Ala. 73.

[8] S. v. Manley, 107 Mo. 364; U. S. v. Adams, 2 Dak. 305.

[9] Stropes v. S., 120 Ind. 562.

V. PROCEDURE.

§ 650. **Venue.**— It often becomes a matter of great importance to determine where the offense is to be deemed to have been committed. It is of course committed wherever the wrongful conversion or failure to account takes place, but that is sometimes a question of much complication. It is in general proper to lay the venue in the county where the defendant receives the money or property which he subsequently fails to account for;[1] but if it appears that he has taken the property into another county before converting it, he cannot be convicted for embezzlement in the county where the property was received. In such case the question as to where the intent of wrongful conversion was first entertained may be material.[2] If, however, the crime charged consists in the failure to account, the venue should be laid in the county where defendant was under obligation to account, or declined to do so on proper demand.[3] One who is in another state may commit embezzlement in a county where he causes his employer to be defrauded by means of a check drawn upon him through a broker.[4] In case of embezzlement by a public officer, the crime will be taken to have been committed in the county of which he is an officer, unless the contrary affirmatively appears.[5] It will appear from the foregoing discussion that there may sometimes be an election in the prosecution to lay the offense either where the money or

[1] Ex parte Palmer, 86 Cal. 631; S. v. Small, 26 Kan. 209; Cole v. S., 16 Tex. Ap. 461; Reed v. S., 16 Tex. Ap. 586; Wallis v. S., 54 Ark. 611; Rex v. Hobson, Russ. & Ry. 56. But the indictment should allege the conversion as well as the receipt in that county: S. v. Mayberry, 9 Wash. 193. The delivery fixing the venue may be constructive; for instance, by delivery of checks for baggage: Cohen v. S., 20 Tex. Ap. 224.

[2] P. v. Murphy, 51 Cal. 376.

[3] S. v. Bailey, 50 Ohio St. 636; Campbell v. S., 35 Ohio St. 70; Brown v. S., 23 Tex. Ap. 214; Rex v. Taylor, 3 B. & P. 596; Reg. v. Murdock, 2 Den. 298. Thus, where an agent who had received moneys in another county wrote a letter to his employer intended to conceal the fact of the receipt of the money, it was held that the prosecution might be had in the county where such letter was received by the employer: Reg. v. Rogers, 3 Q. B. D. 28. But the mere fact of an admission of embezzlement being made in a different county than that where the money was received, or that where it should have been paid over, will not establish the venue in such county: Reg. v. Treadgold, 39 L. T. 291.

[4] Ex parte Hedley, 31 Cal. 108.

[5] Robson v. S., 83 Ga. 166.

property was received, or where there was a failure to account therefor;[1] but it would be manifestly unjust to allow the prosecution by a mere technicality to lay the venue in a county other than that in which some wrong was actually done.[2]

§ 651. **Time.**— The offense may perhaps be deemed a continuing one from the first wrongful act up to the final failure to account. Thus, where fraudulent checks were issued by the party to an accomplice and were cashed a few days afterwards, thus consummating the crime, it was held continuous from the first date to the last.[3] But even if deemed continuous, it is fully completed when there is a final conversion; and an indictment showing possession and concealment, on a certain date, of money embezzled and converted on a previous date, is not good as a charge of embezzlement on the latter date.[4] In general, it is sufficient to allege the embezzlement as of the date of failure to account on proper demand,[5] but it is not necessary to prove the crime as committed on the date alleged,[6] and the taking of separate sums at different times may be proven.[7]

§ 652. **Description of money or property.**— As a general proposition the money or property should be described with the same certainty as in an indictment for larceny,[8] and if there has been a change in form of the property between the time of receipt and the time of embezzlement, it should be described as of the form at the time of embezzlement.[9] In the case of money, unless there is a statutory provision to the contrary, there must be some description, just as in larceny.[10] But even aside from any special statute, it is not required that money be described with impracticable particularity, the exact sum and the exact specification of the bills or coins being in most cases impossible.[11] Where money is received by an officer or agent

[1] S. v. Bailey, 50 Ohio St. 636; Rex v. Hobson, Russ. & Ry. 56.

[2] S. v. Bailey, 50 Ohio St. 636.

[3] S. v. Cushing, 11 R. I. 313.

[4] S. v. Nute, 63 N. H. 79.

[5] Colvin v. S., 127 Ind. 403.

[6] S. v. Pratt, 98 Mo. 482; P. v. Bidleman, 104 Cal. 608; Reg. v. Welch, 2 C. & K. 296.

[7] S. v. Reinhart, 26 Oreg. 466; Reg. v. Proud, L. & C. 97.

[8] P. v. Cox, 40 Cal. 275; S. v. Edson, 10 La. Ann. 229; Grant v. S., 35 Fla. 581; Watson v. S. 64 Ga. 61.

[9] C. v. Merrifield, 4 Met. 468.

[10] S. v. Denton, 74 Md. 517; S. v. Thompson, 42 Ark. 517; S. v. Ward, 48 Ark. 36; Reside v. S., 10 Tex. Ap. 675; Gerard v. S., 10 Tex. Ap. 690; U. S. v. Greve, 65 Fed. R. 488.

[11] S. v. Thompson, 32 La. An. 796; Malcolmson v. S., 25 Tex. Ap. 267; Taylor v. S., 29 Tex. Ap. 466; Wallis v. S., 54 Ark. 611; U. S. v. Borne-

from various sources and through considerable periods of time, it is not required that the indictment specify with certainty the particular kind of funds wrongfully appropriated.[1] Therefore in a number of states special provisions are found relieving the prosecution from the necessity of alleging the kind or description of funds embezzled, and making it sufficient to charge simply the embezzlement of so much money.[2] If the money is described as currency of the United States, the court will take judicial notice of the value.[3] But value is not always material; and where it is not, no evidence of value is necessary if it appears that the article taken was of some value.[4] As to property other than money, it is evident that the description ought to be as specific as in case of larceny, except as the statute has prescribed a form.[5] Under an indictment for embezzlement of money it is not admissible to show embezzlement of a county order.[6] The description of the property as "a bond of the United States for the payment of money," and stating its value, is a sufficient description.[7]

§ 653. **Ownership of property.**— The ownership of the property embezzled should be alleged,[8] and a variance between allegations and proof in this respect will be fatal.[9] In case of ownership by partners it is not necessary to state their individual names;[10] but such names may be used.[11] If the owner-

mann, 36 Fed. R. 257; Rex v. Carson, Russ. & Ry. 303; Rex v. Grove, 1 Moody, 447.

[1] S. v. Smith, 13 Kan. 274; S. v. Carrick, 16 Nev. 120; Reg. v. Balls, L. R. 1 C. C. 328; Rex v. Tyers, Russ. & Ry. 402.

[2] C. v. Bennett, 118 Mass. 443; C. v. Pratt, 137 Mass. 98; P. v. Bringard, 39 Mich. 22; Huffman v. S., 89 Ala. 33; S. v. Pratt, 98 Mo. 482; P. v. Cobler, 108 Cal. 538; S. v. Fain, 106 N. C. 760; Lewis v. S., 28 Tex. Ap. 140. The defendant may be in such case entitled to a bill of particulars: Rex v. Hodgson, 3 C. & P. 422; C. v. Bennett, 118 Mass. 443.

[3] Gady v. S., 83 Ala. 51.

[4] S. v. Fain, 106 N. C. 760. And see § 636, *supra*.

[5] Mayo v. S., 30 Ala. 32. It is sufficient to follow the statutory language: S. v. Trolson, 21 Nev. 419.

[6] Goodhue v. P., 94 Ill. 37.

[7] C. v. Butterick, 100 Mass. 1.

[8] S. v. Nute, 63 N. H. 79; S. v. Roubles, 43 La. An. 200; S. v. Collins, 4 N. Dak. 433; Grant v. S., 35 Fla. 581.

[9] Livingston v. S., 16 Tex. Ap. 652; McCrary v. S., 81 Ga. 334.

[10] S. v. Mohr, 68 Mo. 303.

[11] Ker v. P., 110 Ill. 627. In England the statute authorizes the ownership to be laid in one of the partners named and others: Reg. v. Pritchard, L. & C. 34. If one of the partners is accountable to the others, the money may be alleged as his individually: Reg. v. White, 8 C. & P. 742.

ship is laid in a corporation, proof of *de facto* existence will be sufficient.[1]

§ 654. The relation under which the property is received. There must be some allegation of the character or capacity in which defendant received the money so as to show that he comes within the classes of persons who by statute may be guilty of the crime,[2] and the particular trust or relation under which it is charged the defendant received the property must be proved as laid.[3] But it is sufficient to allege the receipt of the money or property by defendant as agent or as bailee, or in some such general terms, without stating the particulars of the transaction or the relationship.[4] By some statutes it is specifically provided that it is sufficient to describe the fiduciary relation in the general terms of the statute.[5] It is not essential that the indictment use the particular words of the statute in describing the receipt of the money by defendant as agent, as bailee, etc., if the facts alleged show in what capacity it was received.[6] It seems that defendant should be advised by the indictment, however, from whom the money or property is charged to have been received by him.[7]

[1] P. v. Leonard, 106 Cal. 302; Fleener v. S., 58 Ark. 98. The objection that the indictment does not state whether or not the association named as owner is incorporated is a technical one, not to be raised after verdict: Laycock v. S., 136 Ind. 217.

[2] C. v. Smart, 6 Gray, 15; C. v. Wyman, 8 Met. 247. But it is sufficient that the indictment alleges that the money in question was delivered in trust and confidence to be held in defendant's custody until demand made, as this implies a bailment for safe keeping: C. v. Doherty, 127 Mass. 20.

[3] C. v. O'Keefe, 121 Mass. 59.

[4] P. v. Hill, 3 Utah, 334; S. v. Washington, 41 La. An. 778; S. v. Meyers, 68 Mo. 266; S. v. Jamison, 74 Ia. 602. *Contra*, S. v. Griffith, 45 Kan. 142; P. v. Cobler, 108 Cal. 538. If the statute is applicable to bailees under certain circumstances only, the circumstances necessary to bring the case within the statute must be alleged: P. v. Cohen, 8 Cal. 42; P. v. Peterson, 9 Cal. 313; but there is no such necessity where the statute applies to all bailees: P. v. Poggi, 19 Cal. 600. If the statute specifies carriers for hire, the allegation of the indictment must show delivery for that purpose: S. v. Mims, 26 Minn. 191; C. v. Williams, 3 Gray, 461. But the indictment should directly charge the receipt of the money: Grant v. S., 35 Fla. 581.

[5] Lycan v. P., 107 Ill. 423.

[6] P. v. Johnson, 71 Cal. 384; P. v. Neyce, 86 Cal. 393.

[7] S. v. Griffith, 45 Kan. 142; S. v. Combs, 47 Kan. 136; Gaddy v S., 8 Tex. Ap. 127.

§ 655. **Description of the act.**— Where the statute specifies in the alternative several things which shall constitute embezzlement, it is sufficient to allege embezzlement in one of the ways thus described,[1] or in both or all such ways.[2] In the absence of some special statutory provision the particular acts relied upon must be set out.[3] But the charge of embezzling and converting to defendant's own use, after the property has been sufficiently described, and it has been alleged to have come into the possession of defendant in such capacity as to make the conversion thereof embezzlement, is sufficient;[4] and indeed an allegation of fraudulent conversion alone has been held sufficient.[5] Where the offense consists in the overdrawing of his account by an officer, it is sufficient to allege such overdrawing without specifying the particular check by which the money was drawn, or the specific coin, etc., which were drawn.[6] In some states, the requisites of the indictment are regulated by statute.[7] Where the statute defines embezzlement as a form of larceny, the indictment should allege that the defendant "did feloniously steal, take and carry away" the property in the same way as in an indictment for larceny;[8] but where the offense is otherwise described by statute as a distinct crime, it is sufficient to allege the act as done unlawfully, fraudulently and feloniously,[9] or otherwise as the language of the statute may require.

§ 656. **Joinder of counts; duplicity.**— Under the common-law rules of procedure both embezzlement and larceny might be charged in different counts in the same indictment.[10] In such case the prosecution may elect upon which count to proceed.[11]

[1] S. v. Stimson, 24 N. J. 9.

[2] S. v. Dale, 8 Oreg. 229.

[3] C. v. Wyman, 8 Met. 247; McCann v. U. S., 2 Wyo. 267.

[4] Claassen v. U. S., 142 U. S. 140; S. v. Jamison, 74 Ia. 602.

[5] S. v. Munch, 22 Minn. 67; Hoyt v. S., 50 Ga. 313; Gibbs v. S., 41 Tex. 491.

[6] S. v. Stimson, 24 N. J. 478.

[7] C. v. Butterick, 100 Mass. 1; Lycan v. P., 107 Ill. 423; Ker v. P., 110 Ill. 627.

[8] C. v. Pratt, 132 Mass. 246; Heller v. P., 2 Colo. Ap. 459. It is not error to describe the offense as larceny, though the statute simply declares that the acts described shall be a felony: S. v. Isensee, 12 Wash. 254.

[9] S. v. Noland, 111 Mo. 473. "Embezzle and convert" is sufficient without an allegation of stealing, taking and carrying away: S. v. Reinhart, 26 Oreg. 466.

[10] Rex v. Johnson, 3 Mau. & S. 539; Reg. v. Holman, L. & C. 177; Rex v. Murray, 5 C. & P. 145; Mayo v. S., 30 Ala. 32.

[11] Reg. v. Holman, L. & C. 177.

And even where it is not admissible to thus charge different offenses in separate counts of the same indictment, a count charging larceny in an indictment for embezzlement may be dismissed, and the conviction for embezzlement will stand.[1] And in general, where the indictment sufficiently charges embezzlement, any additional language in the same count tending to show larceny may be treated as surplusage.[2] Separate embezzlements relating to different property may be prosecuted in separate counts although all the property is taken at one time.[3] But there may be one conversion of sums received at different times from different persons, and it is not necessary to describe them as separate offenses.[4] So where there are successive embezzlements in the case of one employment, and coming within the same general description, the prosecution will not be limited to a proof of one only under an indictment which in its terms is applicable to each.[5] But this doctrine would not apply to conversion of some particular articles of property, as in case of a bailment.[6] Where a public officer in one act takes public funds in his custody belonging in part to the state, and in part to the county, or township, or other municipal corporation, the entire transaction may be charged as one embezzlement, the property being described as one sum belonging to the different divisions of the government.[7]

§ **656a. Forms of indictment.**— The offense being entirely statutory and the statutes varying materially in several important respects, it will be impossible to do more than give examples of indictments which have been held sufficient under particular statutes, care being taken, however, to select those which present the features usually necessary.

[1] Heller v. P., 2 Colo. Ap. 459.

[2] S. v. Adams, 108 Mo. 208; S. v. Gilmore, 110 Mo. 1; S. v. Lanier, 89 N. C. 517; S. v. Harris, 106 N. C. 682.

[3] C. v. Butterick, 100 Mass. 1. And the prosecution cannot be required to elect: S. v. Bailey, 50 Ohio St. 636. See S. v. Rapley, 60 Ark. 13.

[4] Gravatt v. S., 25 Ohio St. 162; S. v. Reinhart, 26 Oreg. 466.

[5] Brown v. S., 18 Ohio St. 497; Ker v. P., 110 Ill. 627. By Wisconsin statute, any embezzlement committed within six months after the time fixed in the indictment may be proven: S. v. Cornhauser, 74 Wis. 42.

[6] Kribs v. P., 82 Ill. 425; Goodhue v. P., 94 Ill. 37.

[7] Brown v. S., 18 Ohio St. 497.

ENGLISH FORM.

That A. B., on ——, at ——, was clerk to one C. D., and being clerk as aforesaid did then and there by virtue of his said employment as such clerk as aforesaid receive and take into his possession, for and on account of the said C. D., divers, to wit, nine bank-notes for the payment of divers sums of money amounting in the whole to a certain sum of money, to wit, the sum of £9 of lawful money and of the value of £9 of lawful money; and the said A. B., having so received and taken into his possession the said bank-notes, for and on account of his employer, the said C. D., he, the said A. B., afterwards, to wit, on ——, in the county aforesaid, fraudulently and feloniously did embezzle and secrete the same. So the jurors aforesaid do say that he, the said A. B., on the said ——, at ——, in manner and form aforesaid, feloniously did steal, take and carry away the said bank-notes from his said employer, the said C. D., the said bank-notes being then and there the property of the said C. D., on whose account the same were received by and taken into the possession of him, the said A. B., being such clerk as aforesaid, and the several sums of money payable and secured thereby being then, to wit, at the time of the committing the felony aforesaid, to wit, on ——, due and unsatisfied to the said C. D., against the form of the statute and against the peace, etc.[1]

BY OFFICER OF A NATIONAL BANK.

That A. B., at ——, on ——, was the president of a certain national banking association, known as the Sixth National Bank of the city of New York, organized under the act of congress of June third, 1864 (ch. 106), and acting and carrying on a banking business in the city of New York, and being such president and officer of such bank aforesaid did then and there by virtue of his said office and employment, and while he was so employed and acting as such president as aforesaid, receive and take into his possession certain funds and credits, to wit: [certain bonds and obligations particularly described, to the value in all of $672,000] then and there being the property of the said association and which he held for and in the name and on account of the said association, and did then and there wilfully and unlawfully, and with intent to injure and defraud the said association, embezzle the said bonds and written obligations, and convert them to his own use.[2]

[1] This follows the indictments set out in Rex v. Johnson, 3 Mau. & S. 539; and a similar form is found in Rex v. Taylor, Russ. & Ry. 63.

[2] Claassen v. U. S., 142 U. S. 140.

UNDER MASSACHUSETTS STATUTE.

That A. B., on ——, at ——, being then and there the clerk, servant and agent of G. P. and E. W., said P. and W. then and there being copartners in business (the said A. B. not being then and there an apprentice to the said P. and W. or to either of them, and not being then and there a person under the age of sixteen years), did then and there, by virtue of his said employment, have, receive and take into his possession certain money to the amount and of the value of twenty-five thousand dollars, of the said P. and W. as such copartners, the said employers of the said A. B., and that the said A. B. the said money so by him had, received and possessed, then and there feloniously did embezzle and fraudulently convert to his own use, without the consent of his said employers, or either of them, whereby, and by force of the statute in such case made and provided, the said A. B. is deemed to have committed the crime of simple larceny. And so the jurors aforesaid, upon their oath aforesaid, do say that the said A. B. then and there, in manner and form aforesaid, the said money, of the property and moneys of the said P. and W., feloniously did steal, take and carry away, against, etc.[1]

OF CHATTELS.

That A. B., in the county aforesaid, on ——, being then and there the servant and agent of one P. F., and being over the age of sixteen years, did, by virtue of his said employment, have, receive and take into his possession and under his control one gold watch of the value of ninety-five dollars, the property of said P. F., his employer, and the said gold watch, without the consent of his said employer, did feloniously embezzle and fraudulently convert to his own use.[2]

[1] C. v. Bennett, 118 Mass. 443. This case is under a Massachusetts statute which provides that in a prosecution for embezzling bullion, money, notes, checks, etc., it shall be sufficient to allege generally in the indictment the embezzling or fraudulent conversion of money to a certain amount without specifying any particulars of such embezzlement. The statutory definition of the offense in Massachusetts excepts apprentices and persons under sixteen years of age, and this indictment negatives such exceptions. A form similar in this respect is given in P. v. Donald, 48 Mich. 491.

[2] See S. v. Foster, 37 Ia. 404. The statute under which this indictment was drawn limits the offense to persons over sixteen years of age. It also declares that any one who embezzles, etc., shall be guilty of larceny; but it will be noticed that this indictment does not charge the crime as larceny, as is done in the preceding form taken from the Massachusetts case, which is followed also in the Michigan case cited thereunder, although the statute in Iowa as in each of these states also declares the offense to be larceny.

OF A DEED OF MORTGAGE.

That one I. H., at Deadham, in the county of Norfolk, on ——, did deliver to A. B. a certain paper writing containing a conveyance of land, the same being then and there a deed of mortgage of certain land situate in Roxbury, in the county of Norfolk, before then made and executed by the said A. B. to one H. D., and delivered to said H. D. by said A. B., of the property, goods and chattels of the said H. D., and of the value of four hundred and fifty dollars, to be carried by the said A. B. to the said H. D., and to be delivered by the said A. B. to the said H. D. at Boston, in the county of Suffolk, the said paper writing being then and there the subject of larceny; and that the said A. B. did then and there take and receive into his possession the aforesaid paper writing so as aforesaid delivered to him by the said I. H. to be by him, the said A. B., carried and delivered as aforesaid; and that the said A. B. afterward, to wit, on ——, at Deadham, in the county of Norfolk, and before the said paper writing so delivered to him as aforesaid was by the said A. B. delivered to the said H. D. at Boston, in the county of Suffolk, feloniously did embezzle and fraudulently convert the same to his own use.[1]

BY PUBLIC OFFICER.

That A. B., on ——, in the county aforesaid, then and there being a public officer, to wit, the collector of taxes of the town of Minot, in said county, did, by virtue of his said office and whilst he was employed in said office, receive and have in his possession and under his control certain money to a large amount, to wit, to the amount of fifteen thousand dollars, and of the value of fifteen thousand dollars, of the property of the inhabitants of the town of Minot aforesaid, and then and there the money aforesaid did unlawfully embezzle and fraudulently convert to his own use; and so the jurors aforesaid, upon their oaths aforesaid, do say that the said A. B., in manner and form aforesaid, the aforesaid money of the property of the inhabitants of the town of Minot aforesaid feloniously did steal, take and carry away, against the peace, etc.[2]

[1] C. v. Concannon, 5 Allen, 502.

[2] S. v. Goss, 69 Me. 22. Where the town or city is deemed a corporation, the money in such a case as this would be charged as "of the property" of such town or city, and not as the property of the inhabitants thereof. In such case the indictment should allege that the town or city was a municipal corporation existing under the laws of the state, and, if incorporated by special statute, the statute should be properly referred to: See P. v. Potter, 35 Cal. 110. As illustrating the fact that the money need not be particularly described, see the form in P. v. McKinney, 10 Mich. 54, and also the form here given following this one.

BY PUBLIC OFFICER; ANOTHER FORM.

That A. B., in the county of ——, on ——, was then and there an officer of said county, a corporation duly organized and existing under the laws of this state, to wit, the treasurer of said county, duly elected and qualified and legally authorized and empowered to perform all the duties of said office; and that A. B., as such officer and treasurer of said county, was then and there intrusted with, and did then and there have in his possession and under his care by virtue of his said office, certain public moneys, to wit, the sum of sixty-seven thousand three hundred seventy-eight dollars and forty-two cents of the property and effects of said county, and of the value of sixty-seven thousand three hundred seventy-eight dollars and forty-two cents; and that the said A. B. did then and there unlawfully, fraudulently and feloniously embezzle and convert to his own use, without the assent of the said county or of any person thereunto authorized, all of the same public moneys aforesaid, with the custody and care of which he, the said A. B., was then and there so as aforesaid intrusted, and which he, the said A. B., did then and there have and hold by virtue of his said office of treasurer of said county.[1]

[1] S. v. Smith, 13 Kan. 274.

CHAPTER 28.

FALSE PRETENSES; CHEATS AND FRAUDS.

I. NATURE OF THE OFFENSES.
II. SUFFICIENCY OF THE FALSE PRETENSE.
III. CONNECTION BETWEEN THE FALSE PRETENSE AND THE WRONG DONE.
IV. INTENT AND KNOWLEDGE.
V. THE FRAUD PERPETRATED.
VI. INDICTMENT AND EVIDENCE.

I. NATURE OF THE OFFENSES.

§ 657. **General scope of this chapter.**— No other subject furnishes so good an example of the development of the law in the recognition of violations of good faith and fair dealing, not only as civil but also as criminal wrongs. From the common-law notion, that to constitute a cheat or false pretense there must be some false token, to the present notion embodied in many statutory forms, that any false representation of such nature that the opposite party might reasonably and in good faith rely thereon constitutes a crime if injury results from such reliance, there has been a long stride in advance. If it seems that frauds are multiplying, a full explanation of any such appearance is to be found in the tendency toward a vast increase of the business that is done on faith and credit, a tendency which the law supports, and to which it responds in holding the individual liable to a much higher degree than formerly for any violation of good faith. The great development through which this branch of law has passed renders a lucid discussion of it exceedingly difficult, not only by reason of the great complexity of the subject-matter covered, but also by reason of the fact that as to the same class of cases the tenor of the law has from time to time been changing.

§ 658. **General divisions.**— The subject is not capable of any very definite classification. If we had only the English statutes to deal with, the simplest arrangement would be to discuss under each statute the questions which have arisen. But the statutes in the various states do not show the same lines of division which appear in the English statutes, and therefore no such classification is feasible. The best that can be done is to consider briefly the earlier and simpler forms of cheating so far as they were recognized by common law or early English statute to be criminal, and then to consider with such minuteness as is practicable the general classes of false pretenses defined by various more recent statutes which cover and expand the earlier notions of the subject.

§ 659. **Distinguished from larceny.**— In discussing larceny it appeared that one who obtains title to property from the owner by means of false pretenses is not guilty of larceny, because he commits no trespass.[1] Therefore, if the intent of the owner is only to part with possession, and not with title to his property, the person who wrongfully obtains possession is not guilty of obtaining property by false pretenses,[2] while if the owner parts with his property not expecting to have it back again, and he is induced to do so by what constitutes false pretenses, there cannot be conviction for larceny.[3]

§ 660. **Cheat defined.**— It would not be worth while to try to reach any definite statement of what are criminal cheats at common law, not modified by statute. The whole fabric of the present law on the subject is built upon the interpretations of statutes passed from time to time, and a useful definition is thereby rendered impracticable. The general descriptions found in the books are rather, in each case, the author's conception of the policy of the statutes than any specific statement of principles of law outside of statutory provisions.[4] The older

[1] See *supra*, § 563.

[2] Reg. v. Kilham, L. R. 1 C. C. 261; S. v. Kube, 20 Wis. 217; Canter v. S., 7 Lea, 349; S. v. Vickery, 19 Tex. 326; Cline v. S., 43 Tex. 494; Curtis v. S., 31 Tex. Ap. 39.

[3] Reg. v. Thompson, L. & C. 233; Reg v. Barnes, 2 Den. 59; Reg. v. Green, Dears. 323. And see *supra*, § 560. But it has been held false pretenses to take from a child a gold coin for a small purchase and return only change for a similar silver coin, the child being ignorant of the real value of the coin: Jones v. S., — Ga. —, 25 S. E. R. 319. So some other forms of cheating by tricks, as, for instance, by concerted action of confederates, are held to be cheating by false pretenses, although analogous to tricks which are deemed within the scope of the crime of larceny: P. v. Watson, 75 Mich. 582; Jones v. S., 93 Ga. 547. By the language of the English statute a person charged with obtaining property by false pretenses cannot be convicted if the circumstances are such as to show larceny: Reg. v. Bulmer, L. & C. 476.

[4] For attempted definitions, see

definitions and cases required that the fraud be one affecting the public in general, and not merely one calculated to injure a particular person.[1] But this distinction is of no practical value in the interpretation of the modern statutes, which seem to be drawn for the punishment of frauds directed against individuals as well as for those calculated to affect the public in general.

§ **661. Cheating by false tokens.**—Under the common-law notion that, to be criminal, the fraud or cheat must be such as is likely to affect the public in general, it was necessary that some false symbol or token calculated to mislead any one to his injury, and not merely one person only, should be used.[2] And the earliest English statute on the subject embodies the same idea in using the terms "privy tokens and counterfeit letters."[3] Thus, to sell in the course of trade a spurious article for the genuine one, for instance, a copy of a picture with the painter's name imitated upon it for the genuine picture, is a cheat at common law;[4] so it is to pass a bank-bill which is not genuine, even though it has only the external appearance of a bank-bill, and would not be of legal effect if it were actually what in language it purports to be.[5] But the promissory note of an individual does not constitute a public token.[6] A private writing may, however, be a false token.[7] It is an in-

1 Hawk. P. C., ch. 71; 4 Bl. Com. 157; 3 Stephen, Hist. Cr. L. 161; 2 Russ. Cr. 275; 1 Bish. Cr. L., § 571; 2 Bish. Cr. L., § 143. The offense is limited to personal property: P. v. Cummins, — Cal. —, 46 Pac. R. 284.

[1] S. v. Justice, 2 Dev. 199; P. v. Miller, 14 Johns. 371; Rex v. Bower, Cowp. 323; Rex v. Lara, 2 East, P. C. 819; Rex v. Wheatley, 1 W. Bl. 273; Rex v. Dunnage, 2 Burr. 1130. See the definitions and explanations found in text-writers above referred to.

[2] P. v. Stone, 9 Wend. 182; Bickle's Ex'rs v. Fasig's Adm'r, 33 Pa. St. 463; C. v. Warren, 6 Mass. 72; Ranney v. P., 22 N. Y. 413; S. v. Burrows, 11 Ired. 477; Reg. v. Eagleton, Dears. 515.

[3] 33 Henry 8, ch. 1, § 1. And see references to text-writers as given above.

[4] Reg. v. Closs, Dears. & B. 460.

[5] S. v. Grooms, 5 Strobh. 158. This case was under a statute in the main analogous to the common law in its provisions. So if what purports to be a bill of a bank is of no validity because there is no such bank, the passing of the instrument with knowledge of its character is a cheat at common law: C. v. Speer, 2 Va. Cas. 65. Other cases of the passing of false or fraudulent notes will be found under the discussion of false pretenses, *infra*, § 675.

[6] S. v. Patillo, 4 Hawks, 348. So a fraudulent deed seems not to be a false token: S. v. Burrows, 11 Ired. 477.

[7] But it must be the writing of some person other than defendant: P. v. Gates, 13 Wend. 311. And see statute of Henry 8, cited above.

dictable offense to put false marks on barrels of bread denoting their weight.[1] A sale of barrels of crude turpentine with the representation that the contents are the same all through, the fact being that the interior is largely made up of chips, has been held to constitute cheating by false tokens.[2] Where persons were enabled to perpetrate a fraud by pretending to be, the one a merchant and the other a broker, and carrying on a pretended barter, it was held that the transaction constituted a common-law cheat.[3] The obtaining of property by mock auctions may constitute a cheat at common law.[4] And similarly it has been held that a false check purporting to be the genuine check of a substantial man of business, whereas it was known to be worthless by the person passing it, constituted a false token.[5] But a false affirmation as to name, and as to being the owner of a business establishment, thereby obtaining goods, was held not to be cheating by false tokens.[6] Defrauding by mere oral misrepresentations will not constitute cheating by false tokens.[7] But evidence of oral representations in connection with the false token is admissible to show its character.[8] It must of course appear that the false token was delivered to the person injured, and that he parted with his money or property in reliance thereon.[9]

§ **662. Swindling by gambling devices, etc.**— Analogous to cheating by false tokens are the crimes, recognized at common law and by statute, of cheating or swindling by means of various gambling devices.[10] Under such a statute, although the fraudulent use of cards may be one of the means enumerated,

[1] Resp. v. Powell, 1 Dall. 47.

[2] S. v. Jones, 70 N. C. 75.

[3] Rex v. Macarty, 2 East, P. C. 823.

[4] Ranney v. P., 22 N. Y. 413.

[5] Lesser v. P., 73 N. Y. 78; Rex v. Jackson, 3 Camp. 370. But see Rex v. Lara, 6 Term R. 565. As to checks and drafts without funds, see, also, *infra*, § 674.

[6] C. v. Warren, 6 Mass. 72.

[7] S. v. Delyon, 1 Bay, 353; Lucas v. Flinn, 35 Ia. 9; Reg. v. Jones, 1 Salk. 379. And the term "other fraudulent and swindling practices" used in a statute defining cheating by false tokens does not enlarge the offense so as to cover oral false representations: S. v. Sumner, 10 Vt. 587. Giving counterfeit money in making change is not cheating by a false token: S. v. Allred, 84 N. C. 749. But by modern statutes as to false pretenses oral representations may be sufficient: S. v. Reidel, 26 Ia. 430. And see *infra*, § 665.

[8] Wagoner v. S., 90 Ind. 504.

[9] Wagoner v. S., 90 Ind. 504. And further to the effect that the false pretense must be the occasion of injury, see *infra*, § 667.

[10] C. v. Ashton, 125 Mass. 384; P. v. Rose, 85 Cal. 378; P. v. Figerio, 107

the offense may be committed by other means of a similar nature.[1] If the trick, however, involves the obtaining possession, only, of the property, and afterwards wrongfully appropriating it,[2] or obtaining possession only with the preconceived intent to deprive the owner of it, then the offense is larceny and not cheating.[3] But the fact that the act may amount to larceny will not prevent conviction under the statute as to swindling.[4]

§ 663. **False packing.**— By statutes in some states the selling of goods by false sample,[5] or goods falsely packed, with intent to defraud,[6] is made criminal.

§ 663a. **Frauds on hotel-keepers.**— By statute it is made criminal to obtain accommodations at a hotel by a false show of baggage, or to fraudulently remove baggage on which the hotel-keeper has a lien,[7] and such a statute is constitutional.[8]

§ 664. **False personation.**— By statute in some states it is made criminal to obtain property by falsely personating another with intent to convert the property.[9] So, falsely pretending to be an officer having a warrant for the arrest of another and thereby extorting money from him constitutes a false pretense.[10] False personation in authenticating a conveyance for registration may be made criminal.[11]

§ 665. **False pretenses; general nature of the offense.**— The crime of obtaining money or property by false pretenses as now generally defined by statutes goes beyond the early statutory offense of cheating by false tokens in two respects: first, "the false pretense" is broader than "the false token," and includes mere oral representations; and secondly, the early

Cal. 151; Blemer v. P., 76 Ill. 265; Gray v. S., 32 Tex. Ap. 598; Reg. v. O'Connor, 15 Cox, 3.

[1] C. v. Ashton, 125 Mass. 384; S. v. Quinn, 47 Ia. 368. Cards are not necessarily a gambling device: S. v. Hardin, 1 Kan. 474.

[2] Rex v. Robson, Russ. & Ry. 413.

[3] Rex v. Marsh, 1 Leach, 345; Rex v. Watson, 2 East, P. C. 680; Rex v. Moore, 2 East, P. C. 679.

[4] P. v. Figerio, 107 Cal. 151.

[5] Cowles v. S., 50 Ala. 454.

[6] Jones v. S., 22 Tex. Ap. 680; Lidtke v. S., 27 Tex. Ap. 500; Anderson v. S., 30 Tex. Ap. 699.

[7] S. v. Kingsley, 108 Mo. 135; S. v. Yardley, 95 Tenn. 546.

[8] S. v. Benson, 28 Minn. 424; Atkins v. S., 95 Tenn. 474.

[9] Goodson v. S., 29 Fla. 511; U. S. v. Bradford, 53 Fed. R. 542; C. v. Meserve, 154 Mass. 64; S. v. Brown, 25 Ia. 561; S. v. Goble, 60 Ia. 447; Kirtley v. S., 38 Ark. 543.

[10] C. v. Henry, 22 Pa. St. 253; Perkins v. S., 67 Ind. 270. And see *infra*, § 914.

[11] Martin v. S., 1 Tex. Ap. 586.

statutes included only cases of obtaining money or chattels by means of the fraud, while the modern statutes include the obtaining of any kinds of valuable property, including the signature to an instrument.[1] The crime as now recognized involves (1) the use of false pretenses; (2) with knowledge of their falsity and intent to defraud; (3) the accomplishment of an actual fraud, and (4) such accomplishment by means of the false pretenses made use of for the purpose.[2] The offense consists in obtaining the money or property, not in making the pretense,[3] and it is no defense that the person defrauding is an infant. The fact that the contract is void as to the infant does not render the fraud less punishable.[4]

II. SUFFICIENCY OF THE FALSE PRETENSE.

§ 666. **False pretense; what constitutes.**— A false pretense has been defined as such a fraudulent representation of a fact, past or existing, by a person who knows it to be untrue, as is adapted to induce the person to whom it is made to part with something of value.[5] The knowledge of the untruth of the statement and the fact that valuable property is secured thereby are elements of the offense to be discussed further on. But the question now to be considered relates to the adaptability of the pretense to the object; for the term, as used in the statutes, is not construed in its lexicographic sense, but is to be given a legal and technical meaning.[6] It has already been seen that certain false tokens and false writings were recognized by the common law and by early statutes in England as sufficient, but the scope of the offense has been greatly expanded by modern statutes. It may be still be said in a general way that bald, naked falsehoods are not, in every case at least, sufficient to constitute false pretenses,[7] but the pretenses must be of some specious character such as that the party injured might

[1] P. v. Stone, 9 Wend. 182.

[2] S. v. Clark, 46 Kan. 65; S. v. Matthews, 44 Kan. 596; P. v. Wakely, 62 Mich. 297; Johnson v. S., 75 Ind. 553; P. v. Jordan, 66 Cal. 10; S. v. Phifer, 65 N. C. 321; Mathena v. S., 15 Tex. Ap. 473.

[3] C. v. Van Tuyl, 1 Met. (Ky.) 1.

[4] P. v. Kendall, 25 Wend. 399.

[5] Jackson v. P., 126 Ill. 139.

[6] McKenzie v. S., 11 Ark. 594.

[7] By the early English cases a bare naked lie was said not to be enough: Rex v. Lara, 6 Term R. 565. A distinction was also made between cheating by a tradesman, as a goldsmith, and a private person: Rex v. Bower, Cowp. 323.

reasonably rely thereon.[1] It is immaterial whether the representation is in the form of an oral or a written statement; or, indeed, whether any statement whatever is made, as the representation may be made by conduct as well as by words.[2] A false assumption is enough without any false declaration.[3] So falsely pretending, by wearing a cap or gown, to be an Oxford student, was held a sufficient false pretense in obtaining goods in that character to be criminal, though nothing was said on the subject;[4] so a workman in a tannery, who clandestinely removed skins of leather from the warehouse for the purpose of delivering them to the foreman, and securing pay therefor as for his own work, was held guilty of an attempt to obtain money by false pretenses.[5] So the act of a railroad employee in turning in a portion of the uniform belonging to another employee for the purpose of securing the wages due to such other employee was held to be criminal.[6] So where a workman in a coal mine changed the tokens attached to a coal-tub so as to get a credit to which another workman was entitled, the act was held to be a false pretense.[7] So sending a false voucher through various municipal offices for the purpose of securing money thereon is a false pretense, although no oral or

[1] S. v. Green, 7 Wis. 676; P. v. Baker, 96 N. Y. 340; Wallace v. S., 11 Lea, 542. Where a hotel-keeper falsely stated that a certain person had boarded with him, and thus induced another to board with him and advance money for his board, the false statement was held not to be criminal: Morgan v. S., 42 Ark. 131. But where defendant represented to prosecutor that he had cut for him a quantity of wood, such representation being false, and thereby obtained money, *held*, that the pretense was criminal: S. v. Eason, 86 N. C. 674. Further as to the point that a false pretense must be such as is calculated to deceive, see *infra*, § 687.

[2] C. v. Drew, 19 Pick. 179; C. v. Howe, 132 Mass. 250; P. v. Wasservogle, 77 Cal. 173; Roberts v. P., 9 Colo. 458; S. v. Mikle, 94 N. C. 843; Reg. v. Giles, L. & C. 502; Reg. v. Adamson, 1 C. & K. 192. A carrier obtaining the payment of his charges by pretending to have delivered goods and lost the receipt for them is guilty of the crime: Rex v. Airey, 2 East, P. C. 831.

[3] Rex v. Story, Russ. & Ry. 81; Jones v. S., — Ga. —, 25 S. E. R. 319. And further as to false pretenses, see *supra*, § 665.

[4] Rex v. Barnard, 7 C. & P. 784.

[5] Reg. v. Holloway, 2 C. & K. 942.

[6] Reg. v. Bull, 13 Cox, 608. It was held false pretenses for a railroad conductor to conspire with the timekeeper to return more time for the conductor than he was entitled to, for the fraudulent purpose of securing more pay: C. v. Hutton, 95 Ky. 302.

[7] Reg. v. Hunter, 10 Cox, 642.

written representations are made as to its validity.[1] If the false pretense consists in words which are indefinite and uncertain, the jury is to determine whether they were intended to and did convey a false impression, the circumstances surrounding the transaction being taken into account in determining that question.[2]

§ 667. **Relevancy of the pretense, continued.**— Before giving some of the more general headings under which false pretenses may be classified, it will be proper to collect into a miscellaneous catalogue, in addition to those given in the preceding section, some examples of what have been held to be criminal false pretenses, and the following may be enumerated: Obtaining goods under a treaty of marriage;[3] pretending to have been intrusted with a horse to be taken from Ireland to London, and to have run out of money by reason of detention by contrary winds;[4] getting goods to furnish a house by pretending to be a person of means;[5] getting fees as an attorney on the false representation of having performed services for another similar to those proposed to be performed for the prosecutor;[6] getting money in trust on the pretense of being a shop-keeper with whom prosecutrix might live until she got a situation;[7] pretending to be in business and in want of a clerk, and obtaining a deposit of money as security for prosecutor's honesty as such clerk;[8] pretending to be able to communicate with spirits of the dead,[9] or to be able to control the action of others by charms,[10] or to have cured disease by a particular remedy;[11] borrowing money on the representation that defendant's brother was to arrive with money to be used in

[1] P. v. The Court, 83 N. Y. 436. As to false accounts, see *infra*, § 674.

[2] S. v. Call, 48 N. H. 126.

[3] Anon., Lofft, 146.

[4] Rex v. Villeneuve, 2 East, P. C. 830.

[5] Reg. v. Howarth, 11 Cox, 588.

[6] Rex v. Asterley, 7 C. & P. 191.

[7] Reg. v. Fry, Dears. & B. 449.

[8] Reg. v. Crab, 11 Cox, 85. And see *infra*, § 676.

[9] Reg. v. Lawrence, 36 L. T. 404.

[10] Reg. v. Giles, L. & C. 502.

[11] Reg. v. Bloomfield, Car. & M. 537. Where defendant falsely pretended to be a physician and to have restored sight to a blind person, and to be able to eliminate a poison which he claimed to infect prosecutor's premises, and obtained money for doing so, *held*, that he was guilty of obtaining money by false pretenses: Bowen v. S., 9 Baxt. 45. Falsely pretending to be a witch doctor and to be able to destroy witches, and that the victim was possessed by witches which would kill him if not destroyed, *held* not criminal, being expressions of opinion only: S. v. Burnett, 119 Ind. 392.

the payment of the sum borrowed,[1] or on the representation that defendant had purchased a farm in the neighborhood;[2] obtaining property on pretense that defendant was a chaplain in the army;[3] pretending to be about to make a loan to another person and to be desirous of borrowing money in order to do so;[4] pretending to desire to purchase property so as to induce another purchaser to give more.[5] The characteristic of all these cases is that the pretense is not as to the essential fact but as to some collateral matter which tends, however, to enable the wrong-doer to accomplish his fraudulent purpose.[6] But it is possible that the misrepresentation be so remote, as compared with the wrong, that it cannot be deemed the cause thereof, and will therefore not be criminal. Thus, it was held that the false pretense to a parish officer as an excuse for not working that the person had no clothes was not criminal, although it induced the officer to give him clothes;[7] so held, also, as to a false pretense in connection with borrowing money as to the purpose for which the money was desired.[8] The pretense must be of some materiality; that is, such that, if the fact had been as represented, it would have been of some pecuniary advantage to the party defrauded.[9] To falsely represent, as a means of inducing a person to take a certificate of insurance, that the company has a large reserve fund is criminal.[10]

§ 668. Misrepresentation of fact.— It will appear by the discussion in the subsequent sections that the misrepresentation must be of a fact and not the statement of an opinion or

[1] S. v. Fooks, 65 Ia. 196. So a false pretense, for the purpose of borrowing money, that others had agreed to pay defendant's debts at a future time: S. v. Switser, 63 Vt. 604.

[2] S. v. Fooks, 65 Ia. 452.

[3] Thomas v. P., 34 N. Y. 351.

[4] S. v. Nichols, 1 Houst. Cr. C. 114.

[5] S. v. Rowley, 12 Conn. 101.

[6] False statements as to owning property which is offered for exchange, *held* criminal: S. v. Newell, 1 Mo. 248; false statements as to the purpose for which property is desired may constitute false pretenses: Reg. v. Archer, Dears. 449.

[7] Rex v. Wakeling, Russ. & Ry. 504.

[8] Reg. v. Johnston, 2 Moody, 254; Reg. v. Woodman, 14 Cox, 179. Using false pretenses to retain a position, with intent to abuse the facilities offered thereby to defraud, is not criminal: Watson v. S., 27 Ill. Ap. 493.

[9] P. v. McAllister, 49 Mich. 12. Thus, a false statement by a traveling man as to the standing of his house and the general cheapness of their prices is not criminal: P. v. Morphy, 100 Cal. 84.

[10] P. v. Shelters, 99 Mich. 333.

the making of a promise. It is proper, however, to collect in this section a few miscellaneous illustrations of what is deemed in general a matter of fact, the cases which distinguish fact from opinion and from promise being considered under those headings. One who represented that a certain bet had been made, and thereby induced another to pay the bet, was held guilty of making false pretenses;[1] so it was held criminal in the sale of cheese to pass off false "tasters" fraudulently pretending that they were extracted from the cheese offered.[2] One who falsely pretended that his wife had died, and thereby secured an allowance on that account from a benefit society, was held guilty of false pretenses;[3] so it has been held to be criminal to pretend to hold a ticket entitling one to fees whereas such ticket has been lawfully assigned;[4] or to sell baking powder under a spurious label;[5] or to pretend that the note to which the signature of another is obtained is only an order;[6] or to fraudulently use a false letter-head to obtain goods;[7] or to fraudulently point out a certain lot as the one corresponding with the description in a conveyance, and thereby effect a sale, whereas the lot described is a different one;[8] or to falsely represent that a house and shop had been built on certain land on which an advance of money is secured.[9] A person's intention may be a fact, and a false representation with reference thereto may be criminal.[10]

§ 669. **Distinguished from opinion.**— The principle is fully recognized that, to constitute a false pretense, the misrepresentation must be of a matter of fact, and not of a mere opinion.[11] Thus, it is said that a simple misrepresentation of the quality

[1] Young v. Rex, 3 Term R. 98.

[2] Reg. v. Goss, Bell, 208.

[3] Reg. v. Dent, 1 C. & K. 249.

[4] S. v. Hargrave, 103 N. C. 328.

[5] Reg. v. Smith, Dears. & B. 566.

[6] S. v. Joaquin, 43 Ia. 131; or to take advantage of an illiterate person to obtain his signature to a note for a larger amount than intended by him: Hill v. S., 1 Yerg. 76.

[7] Taylor v. C., 94 Ky. 281.

[8] S. v. McConkey, 49 Ia. 499. And held that it would be immaterial that the defendant was the owner of the lot fraudulently pointed out as well as of the one described: Ibid.

[9] Reg. v. Burgon, Dears. & B. 11.

[10] C. v. Walker, 108 Mass. 309. And see for cases as to obtaining credit, *infra*, §§ 678, 679.

[11] P. v. Jacobs, 35 Mich. 36; S. v. Webb, 26 Ia. 262; S. v. Hefner, 84 N. C. 751; S. v. Daniel, 114 N. C. 823. A statement that another was possessed of witches, which defendant could destroy, held to be a mere statement of opinion: S. v. Burnett, 119 Ind. 392.

of goods will not constitute a false pretense, provided the goods are in specie what they are represented to be;[1] but if the statement is not mere exaggerated praise or with reference to a matter of opinion, but a statement of a specific fact, it may constitute a false pretense. Thus, a representation that a chain is of gold of a known and definite quality, the fact that it is known not to be of that quality makes the representation a false pretense;[2] so where a package was sold as containing good tea, but the principal part of the contents was not tea at all, this was held not to be a mere expression of opinion, but a false pretense;[3] so a false representation as to the cause of lameness in sheep offered for sale, the statement being that it was due to certain specific injuries which had never been received, and was not due to disease, is sufficient to constitute a false pretense.[4] But statements that goods were of a certain grade,[5] and that a certain piece of land was well wooded and timbered,[6] were held to be statements of opinion only. A statement as to the value of a business and the price paid therefor may be a criminal false pretense.[7]

§ 670. Statements as to value, or indebtedness.— A representation as to value is to be deemed a matter of opinion, and therefore, though false, not a false pretense.[8] But false affir-

[1] Reg. v. Bryan, Dears. & B. 265, which was a case of false statement of the quality of spoons; so, where the representation was that certain plated goods were of the best silver plate, whereas the foundation was Britannia metal instead of nickel, and covered with a mere film of silver: Reg. v. Levine, 10 Cox, 374. So held, also, where a chain was pledged as gold, but proved to be a compound containing but a small quantity of gold: Reg. v. Lee, 8 Cox, 233.

[2] Reg. v. Ardley, L. R. 1 C. C. 301; Reg. v. Suter, 10 Cox, 577. So, where articles were pawned as silver when in fact they were of a composition, the attempt to secure money on them under such representation was held to be an attempt to obtain money by false pretenses: Reg. v. Roebuck, Dears. & B. 24; Reg. v. Ball, Car. & M. 249. But see Rex v. Bower, 1 Cowp. 323.

[3] Reg. v. Foster, 2 Q. B. D. 301. So held as to a sale of a barrel filled with chips and refuse covered with turpentine, for turpentine: S. v. Jones, 70 N. C. 75.

[4] P. v. Crissie, 4 Denio, 525.

[5] S. v. Young, 76 N. C. 258.

[6] S. v. Paul, 69 Me. 215.

[7] C. v. Blood, 141 Mass. 571.

[8] S. v. Paul, 69 Me. 215; S. v. Estes, 46 Me. 150; Reg. v. Williamson, 11 Cox, 328. However, false representations as to the market value of certain railroad bonds, and that banks would lend money on them to that amount, and that the railroad was in running order and paying expenses, were held indictable: P. v. Jordan, 66 Cal. 10.

mations as to the weight of goods sold, by which the purchaser is induced to pay for a larger quantity than is delivered, are indictable.[1] So where a sale was made of a herd of cattle at a distant place, the seller representing that, although some of the animals might have died or strayed, there was still at least a certain number, whereas the number was very much less by reason of a sale which had been made of a portion of the animals, it was held that the seller was guilty of false pretenses.[2] A misrepresentation as to indebtedness on account will not constitute a false pretense;[3] but where a false account is rendered, it may constitute a false pretense.[4]

§ 671. **Incumbrance on property.**— A false representation that property sold is unincumbered constitutes a false pretense.[5]

§ 672. **Fraudulent second sale.**— To fraudulently sell property a second time is made criminal by statute in some states.[6]

§ 673. **Misrepresentation of authority.**— One who procures money on the false representation that he has been sent for it by another is guilty of obtaining money under false pretenses.[7]

§ 674. **Checks, drafts, orders, or accounts.**— Assertions with reference to having funds at a bank, and obtaining money by checks on such funds which do not exist, constitute false pretenses.[8] Indeed, the mere offering of a check upon a bank constitutes a representation that the drawer has funds, or at

[1] Rex v. Reed, 7 C. & P. 848; Reg. v. Ridgway, 3 F. & F. 838; Reg. v. Lee, L. & C. 418; Reg. v. Sherwood, Dears. & B. 251; Reg. v. Ragg, Bell, 215; Reg. v. Eagleton, Dears. 515. But see Rex v. Wheatley, 1 W. Bl. 273; Rex v. Dunnage, 2 Burr. 1130.

[2] S. v. Jackson, 42 Kan. 448.

[3] Reg. v. Evans, L. & C. 252; Reg. v. Oates, Dears. 459.

[4] Rex v. Witchell, 2 East, P. C. 830; Reg. v. Leonard, 2 C. & K. 514.

[5] S. v. Munday, 78 N. C. 460; S. v. Butler, 47 Minn. 483; S. v. Dorr, 33 Me. 498. The fact that the incumbrance is recorded is immaterial: S. v. Hill, 72 Me. 238. *Contra*, C. v. Grady, 13 Bush. 285. But if the incumbrance is invalid as to the person to whom the representation is made, there is no fraud perpetrated, and therefore no criminality: S. v. Garris, 98 N. C. 733; S. v. Asher, 50 Ark. 427; Graves v. S., 31 Tex. Ap. 65.

[6] P. v. Garnett, 35 Cal. 470; S. v. Dozier, Dudley, 155.

[7] S. v. Dixon, 101 N. C. 741; P. v. Johnson, 12 Johns. 292; Reg. v. Davis, 11 Cox, 181; Reg. v. Burnsides, Bell, 282; Reg. v. Butcher, Bell, 6; Reg. v. Essex, Dears. & B. 371. But see Reg. v. Tully, 9 C. & P. 227. If there is lawful authority, a misappropriation will not constitute false pretenses: Reg. v. Richardson, 1 F. & F. 488. The use of a forged written order is more than mere false pretense: Rex v. Evans, 5 C. & P. 553.

[8] Smith v. P., 47 N. Y. 303; Lesser v. P., 73 N. Y. 78; S. v. Scott, 48 Mo. 422; S. v. Dennis, 80 Mo. 589; Casily v. S., 32 Ind. 62; P. v. Wasservogle,

least that the check will be paid, and if the drawer knows it will not be paid he is guilty of false pretenses.[1] If the goods are obtained on the mere promise to pay, the fact that a check is subsequently given for the amount without funds to meet it will not constitute the offense of obtaining property by false pretenses.[2] A false voucher may constitute a false pretense;[3] so may an order on a county officer which has been falsely obtained.[4] The presentation of a false claim or account to a public officer for payment constitutes a false pretense.[5]

§ 675. **Using false money, notes, or checks.**— The passing of counterfeit money is an offense in itself, and is perhaps not punishable as a false pretense.[6] But if the bill or coin does not really purport to be money, but is only in semblance of money, then the use of it might constitute the offense of false pretenses.[7] Undoubtedly the use of counterfeit money, whether coin or bank-bills, would in every instance be a false pretense unless it is punishable as a higher crime.[8] So it constitutes false pretenses to pass as of value a note of a bank which has failed, and with knowledge that the note will not be paid.[9] It has been said that it must be shown in such a case that the note

77 Cal. 173; P. v. Donaldson, 70 Cal. 116; S. v. Cadwell, 79 Ia. 473; Rex v. Parker, 7 C. & P. 825.

[1] C. v. Drew, 19 Pick. 179; Reg. v. Hazleton, L. R. 2 C. C. 134; Rex v. Jackson, 3 Camp. 370. But to present to the bank itself a check without funds to meet it is not a false pretense: C. v. Drew, 19 Pick. 179. And it is said that obtaining credit with one's own banker by drawing a bill on another which it is known will not be paid does not constitute the obtaining of money by false pretenses: Rex v. Wavell, 1 Moody, 224.

[2] S. v. Willard, 109 Mo. 242.

[3] Ochs v. P., 124 Ill. 399.

[4] S. v. Walton, 114 N. C. 783.

[5] P. v. Carolan, 71 Cal. 195; Hauck v. S., 45 Ohio St. 439; U. S. v. Route, 33 Fed. R. 246; U. S. v. Jones, 32 Fed. R. 482. There is a federal statute in relation to obtaining public money by altered or forged instruments: U. S. v. Reese, 4 Sawyer, 629.

[6] Roberts v. S., 2 Head, 501; Cheek v. S., 1 Coldw. 172.

[7] Roberts v. S., 2 Head, 501; C. v. Nason, 9 Gray, 125; Reg. v. Coulson, 1 Den. 592; Reg. v. Jessop, Dears. & B. 442; Rex v. Freeth, Russ. & Ry. 127.

[8] C. v. Hulbert, 12 Met. 446; S. v. Adams, 92 Ind. 116; Rex v. Freeth, Russ. & Ry. 127. To constitute the crime of advertising counterfeit money under statute, the scheme must be to sell or exchange counterfeit money or what purports to be such (green goods): P. v. Albow, 140 N. Y. 130.

[9] C. v. Stone, 4 Met. 43; Reg. v. Philpotts, 1 C. & K. 112; Reg. v. Evans, Bell, 187; Reg. v. Dowey, 11 Cox, 115; Reg. v. Murphy, 13 Cox, 298; Reg. v. Jarman, 14 Cox, 48.

was of no value.[1] But it is not necessary to prove that the bank is insolvent, and that no recovery on the note can be had against the stockholders; the material point is the worthlessness of the note as currency.[2] One who passes a promissory note or check with the representation that it is good and of the value stated on its face, while in fact it is worthless, is guilty of false pretenses.[3]

§ **676. Contract; warranty.**—It seems to have been once thought that there could be no prosecution for false pretenses where the prosecutor had relied on defendant's contract;[4] for, as will appear in a following section, a promise which is not performed does not usually constitute a false pretense. Thus, it has been held that there can be no prosecution for false pretenses where the purchase-price of property has been obtained by giving a warranty although the defendant may have had no title.[5] So if the contract is to deliver property of a certain description, and when delivered it turns out not to be of that description, this will not constitute a false pretense.[6] It is said that the promise that another will repay money borrowed will not constitute a false pretense even though known to be untrue and coupled with the assertion that the person referred to is indebted to the one making the promise;[7] and that the promise to give employment and obtaining money by such promise will not be criminal, although the person making it has no employment to give.[8] But it is said on the other hand, and with better reason, that the fact that money is procured by means of a promise does not negative criminal liability if the promise

[1] Rex v. Spencer, 3 C. & P. 420; Rex v. Flint, Russ. & Ry. 460.

[2] C. v. Stone, 4 Met. 43; Reg. v. Smith, 6 Cox, 314.

[3] Maley v. S., 31 Ind. 192; Reg. v. Martin, 5 Q. B. D. 34; Reg. v. Coulson, 1 Den. 592; Reg. v. Wickham, 10 A. & E. 34; Rex v. Cartwright, Russ. & Ry. 106; Reg. v. Hughes, 1 F. & F. 355; Prehm v. S., 22 Neb. 673. But it has been said that where a party sells a promissory note which he knows has been paid, but represents as still due according to its face, the offense is not indictable but a mere civil injury: Middleton v. S., Dudley, 275. So it is said that a promissory note is not a false token: P. v. Gibbs, 98 Cal. 661.

[4] Rex v. Codrington, 1 C. & P. 661; but this case is doubted in Reg. v. Kenrick, 5 Q. B. 49.

[5] S. v. Chunn, 19 Mo. 233; S. v. Butler, 47 Minn. 483; Fay v. C., 28 Grat. 912; Rex v. Codrington, 1 C. & P. 661.

[6] C. v. Haughey, 3 Met. (Ky.) 223.

[7] S. v. Magee, 11 Ind. 154.

[8] Ranney v. P., 22 N. Y. 413. See, also, *supra*, § 667.

is founded on a false statement;[1] for instance, that the person making the representation has a position which he can give to the one to whom the representation is made, and from whom money is secured on that account.[2] So where there is a warranty or contract, if there be also false representations of material facts, the transaction may constitute the offense of obtaining property by false pretenses.[3] In Alabama there is a statute making it criminal to obtain property with intent to defraud by entering into a contract to render any service and afterward, with like intent, refusing to perform such service.[4]

§ 677. False representations in sale of horse.— As illustrating the doctrine of the last paragraph to the effect that the warranty may be a false pretense, several cases may be cited relating to false statements in connection with the sale or exchange of horses. Thus, a false statement as to the identity of the animal may constitute a false pretense, even though the value of the two animals is substantially the same.[5] So it is a false pretense and not merely a statement of opinion to represent falsely that the animal is sound, healthy, kind, and the like.[6] Of course, in such cases the statement of commendation may be merely "dealer's talk;"[7] but if it is an affirmation of a fact, it may be a criminal pretense although it is also a commendation.[8] And the question whether or not the statement is one of fact or of mere opinion and commendation is for the jury.[9]

[1] Reg. v. Kenrick, 5 Q. B. 49; Reg. v. Garlick, 1 Den. 276; Reg. v. Abbott, 2 C. & K. 630. And for illustrations of obtaining money by a false contract, see S. v. Norman, 110 N. C. 484; S. v. Daggs, 106 Mo. 160.

[2] P. v. Winslow, 39 Mich. 505; S. v. Bayne, 88 Mo. 604.

[3] S. v. Butler, 47 Minn. 483; Jackson v. P., 126 Ill. 139; S. v. Wilkerson, 103 N. C. 337. And it makes no difference that the bill of sale conveying the property in connection with the warranty states that payment is made in consideration of the warranty alone, and not upon any verbal or other representations: Jackson v. P., 126 Ill. 139.

[4] Copeland v. S., 97 Ala. 30; Tennyson v. S., 97 Ala. 78.

[5] S. v. Mills, 17 Me. 211.

[6] Watson v. P., 87 N. Y. 561; Jackson v. P., 126 Ill. 139; S. v. Stanley, 64 Me. 157; C. v. Jackson, 132 Mass. 16; S. v. Burke, 108 N. C. 750; S. v. Mangum, 116 N. C. 998; Tatum v. S., 58 Ga. 408; Reg. v. Kenrick, 5 Q. B. 49. But if the defect is patent and is discovered by the buyer before the conclusion of the sale, the false representation will not be criminal: Rainey v. S., 94 Ga. 599. And on this point see *infra*, §§ 684–687.

[7] S. v. Holmes, 82 N. C. 607.

[8] Jackson v. P., 126 Ill. 139; S. v. Hefner, 84 N. C. 751; Parks v. S., 94 Ga. 601.

[9] C. v. Jackson, 132 Mass. 16.

§ 678. False promises; statement of fact as distinguished from promise.— A false statement in order to constitute a false pretense must be with reference to past or existing facts, and not a mere promise to do something in the future.[1] Although the person making the promise has no intention of performing it, and therefore so far as it implies an existing intention it is a false pretense of a fact, yet it is after all merely a false promise and does not constitute a false pretense.[2] However, there are cases in which, although the representation is only as to present intention in regard to a future transaction, it is held criminal.[3] But if there is a false representation as to an existing fact it may constitute a false pretense, although it is coupled with a false promise which assists in inducing the other party to part with his money or property.[4] And where the defendant said that he was prepared to pay a sum mentioned provided prosecutor would execute a note therefor, it was held that the representation implied a readiness and ability to pay, in the absence of which the representation constituted a false pretense.[5]

[1] Canter v. S., 7 Lea, 349; Moulden v. S., 5 Lea, 577; Dillingham v. S., 5 Ohio St. 280; S. v. Evers, 49 Mo. 542; S. v. De Lay, 93 Mo. 98; S. v. Kingsley, 108 Mo. 135; S. v. Petty, 119 Mo. 425; In re Snyder, 17 Kan. 542, 2 Am. Cr. R. 228; Morris v. P., 4 Colo. Ap. 136; Keller v. S., 51 Ind. 111; Strong v. S., 86 Ind. 208; S. v. Magee, 11 Ind. 154; C. v. Warren, 94 Ky. 615; Colly v. S., 55 Ala. 85; Ryan v. S., 45 Ga. 128; S. v. Haines, 23 S. C. 170; Burrow v. S., 12 Ark. 65; Scarlett v. S., 25 Fla. 717; Johnson v. S., 41 Tex. 65; Allen v. S., 16 Tex. Ap. 150; S. v. Colly, 39 La. An. 841. Where A. pretended that for a consideration he would tell B. where his animals had strayed, and was convicted for obtaining money under false pretenses, *held*, that the conviction would not stand, but that to sustain it there should have been an allegation and proof that A. pretended to know where the animals were: Rex v. Douglas, 1 Moody, 462.

[2] P. v. Blanchard, 90 N. Y. 314; C. v. Stevenson, 127 Mass. 446; C. v. Moore, 99 Pa. St. 570; S. v. De Lay, 93 Mo. 98; Rex v. Goodhall, Russ. & Ry. 461; Reg. v. Lee, L. & C. 309.

[3] S. v. Cowdin, 28 Kan. 269; S. v. Thaden, 43 Minn. 325; S. v. Dowe, 27 Ia. 273; S. v. Montgomery, 56 Ia. 195; C. v. Moore, 89 Ky. 542; S. v. Vorback, 66 Mo. 168; Reg. v. West, Dears. & B. 575; Reg. v. Jennison, L. & C. 157; Reg. v. Bates, 3 Cox, 201; Reg. v. Copeland, Car. & M. 516.

[4] Reg. v. Jones, 6 Cox, 467; Reg. v. Cooper, 2 Q. B. D. 510; Reg. v. Speed, 15 Cox, 24. But see Reg. v. Henshaw, L. & C. 444. Thus, where a party pretending to have come to pay a debt fraudulently procured a receipt therefor, without paying it or having any intention to pay it, *held*, that a crime was committed: S. v. Dowe, 27 Ia. 273. As to fraudulent purchase with intent not to pay, see next section.

[5] Reg. v. Gordon, 23 Q. B. D. 354.

§ 679. False statements of financial ability.— False pretenses as to financial ability made by a purchaser of goods for the purpose of obtaining credit are criminal.[1] It has been so held where the representations were merely of a general character with reference to the purchaser's circumstances.[2] At any rate, false representations as to the amount of indebtedness, as to the ownership of property, and as to its being unincumbered, may constitute false pretenses.[3] But where a defendant has had credit on the ground of ownership of property, a secret disposal of the property and a subsequent purchase by taking advantage of the same credit, without any further statement, has been held not to be criminal.[4] Of course the false representations in these cases, as in others, must not be mere statements of opinion; a statement as to solvency may be more than that.[5] So the statement must be something more than a mere promise; but if there is a false representation with reference to financial condition, it may constitute a false pretense even though coupled with a false promise;[6] and the fact that the promise is made with intent to carry it out will not render the false pretense any the less criminal.[7] Indeed, the actual financial ability of the party is immaterial if the statements on which credit is obtained are knowingly false.[8] False representations as to the ownership of personal property, made for the purpose of obtaining credit, are not merged in a mortgage given on such property as security for the debt, and may still be prosecuted as false pretenses.[9] In Massachusetts, if the

[1] C. v. Burdick, 2 Pa. St. 163; Rothschild v. S., 13 Lea, 294; S. v. Lichliter, 95 Mo. 402. The same principle applies where a bank secures a loan by representations of solvency: C. v. Schwartz, 92 Ky. 510. So where a party, for the purpose of inducing the sale of his own paper by the holder thereof at much less than its real value, falsely represented that he was insolvent, largely indebted, etc., *held*, that this was a false pretense: S. v. Tomlin, 29 N. J. 13. False representations as to another's solvency in order to induce a sale to him may be criminal: Haines v. T., 3 Wyo. 167.

[2] P. v. Haynes, 14 Wend. 546; S. C., 11 Wend. 557; C. v. Wallace, 114 Pa. St. 405.

[3] S. v. Pryor, 30 Ind. 350; S. v. Snyder, 66 Ind. 203; Smith v. S., 55 Miss. 513; S. v. Hill, 72 Me. 238.

[4] Blum v. S., 20 Tex. Ap. 578. So it is not criminal to fail to send in a new statement as promised and accept credit on the basis of the old one: Morris v. P., 4 Colo. Ap. 136.

[5] S. v. Tomlin, 29 N. J. 13.

[6] C. v. Wallace, 114 Pa. St. 405.

[7] S. v. Neimeier, 66 Ia. 634.

[8] C. v. Coe, 115 Mass. 481.

[9] C. v. Lee, 149 Mass. 179, 8 Am. Cr. R. 249, and note.

false pretense consists solely in the statement that defendant is able to pay, it must by statutory provision be in writing in order to be criminal.[1] In Colorado there is a statute making it criminal to induce a false statement to be made by a commercial agency and thereby procure goods.[2]

III. CONNECTION BETWEEN THE FALSE PRETENSE AND THE WRONG DONE.

§ 680. **Fraud accomplished.**— It must appear that there has been a fraud accomplished, that is, somebody has been injured.[3] It is the obtaining of the money or property that is the perpetration of the fraud, not the making of the false pretenses that constitutes the crime.[4] But of course the attempt may be committed, and, if such attempt is criminal under the laws of any particular state, may be punished, although the fraud is not consummated.[5] If fraud is perpetrated, it is not essential that actual loss shall follow to the person defrauded. Thus, it is immaterial that goods given in an exchange secured by false pretenses were equal in value to those obtained;[6] or, that if a loan is secured by false pretenses, defendant had the means to repay it.[7] But if the effect of the false representa-

[1] C. v. Coe, 115 Mass. 481.

[2] Morris v. P., 4 Colo. Ap. 136; Schayer v. P., 5 Colo. Ap. 75.

[3] Jones v. U. S., 5 Cranch, C. C. 647; S. v. Matthews, 44 Kan. 596; S. v. Clark, 46 Kan. 65; P. v. Wakeley, 62 Mich. 297. Therefore held that the issuance of fraudulent certificates for witness fees sold by a third person, and the proceeds of which never came into the hands of the party perpetrating the fraud, did not constitute the crime: Bracey v. S., 64 Miss. 26. To induce one whose money is in the possession of a bank to loan it to the bank is a sufficient "obtaining" on the part of the officers of the bank to constitute a crime if accomplished by false pretenses as to the bank's solvency: C. v. Schwartz, 92 Ky. 510.

[4] C. v. Van Tuyl, 1 Met. (Ky.) 1.

[5] C. v. Wilgus, 4 Pick. 177; Reg. v. Hensler, 11 Cox, 570; Reg. v. Keighley, Dears. & B. 145; Reg. v. Eagleton, Dears. 515.

[6] S. v. Dorr, 33 Me. 498; nor that goods given in exchange were equal in value to those which they were falsely represented to be: S. v. Mills, 17 Me. 211; Bartlett v. S., 28 Ohio St. 669.

[7] C. v. Coe, 115 Mass. 481; S. v. Thatcher, 35 N. J. 445. So it is immaterial, in a prosecution for obtaining goods by the assignment of a fictitious note and mortgage, that the defendant thereby rendered himself liable: T. v. Ely, 6 Dak. 128. Where the false pretense consisted in representations as to the ownership of a plantation for the purpose of obtaining credit, *held*, that evidence by defendant might be excluded as to the ownership of other property: Culver v. S., 86 Ga. 197.

tions is that defendant secures only that which is his legal right, he is not guilty of crime.[1]

§ 681. By means of the false pretense.— There must be a causal connection between the false pretense and the injury done.[2] If, for instance, the false pretense is made after the obtaining of possession of the goods, the crime of obtaining by false pretenses is not committed.[3] But if the property, though not in existence at the time the pretense is made, is afterward parted with on the strength thereof, it is sufficient.[4] If the person from whom the money or property is obtained knows the falsity of the pretenses, he is of course not defrauded thereby, and the crime is not committed.[5]

§ 682. Illegality of mutual purpose.— The fact that the person parting with his money or property knows that the other intends to commit a fraud upon a third person does not make him such *particeps criminis* as to prevent the act being punishable in the other party.[6] And it is likewise immaterial that the money or property is parted with for other illegal purposes.[7]

An offer to refund the money obtained is immaterial: Carlisle v. S., 77 Ala. 71. And of course it is immaterial that the property wrongfully obtained by the fraud is regained by the owner: Donahoe v. S., 59 Ark. 375.

[1] P. v. Thomas, 3 Hill, 169; C. v. McDuffy, 126 Mass. 467; S. v. Hurst, 11 W. Va. 54; P. v. Getchell, 6 Mich. 496.

[2] Thus, a false pretense that there is no lien on property delivered by defendant to prosecutor is not criminal if it does not appear that defendant represented himself to be the owner: Jenkins v. S., 97 Ala. 66.

[3] P. v. Haynes, 14 Wend. 546; S. v. Church, 43 Conn. 471; S. v. Willard, 109 Mo. 242; Reg. v. Brooks, 1 F. & F. 502. But it is not material that the goods are actually delivered to defendant before the representations are made, if they are delivered with intention to receive simltaneous payment, and not of giving credit, credit being given on account of the false pretenses then made: C. v. Devlin, 141 Mass. 423.

[4] Reg. v. Martin, L. R. 1 C. C. 56.

[5] Rainey v. S., 94 Ga. 599; Reg. v. Mills, Dears. & B. 205; Reg. v. Keighley, Dears. & B. 145; Reg. v. Hensler, 11 Cox, 570. And see *infra*, §§ 684, 687. But the fact that the party from whom the property is obtained laid a plan to entrap the prisoner into a commission of the offense will be no excuse: Rex v. Ady, 7 C. & P. 140. Knowledge on the part of county officers of the falsity of a claim against the county is not to be imputed to the county: Ochs v. P., 124 Ill. 399.

[6] P. v. Shaw, 57 Mich. 403; Casily v. S., 32 Ind. 62. But it is a defense that the party injured parted with his property with the criminal purpose of carrying out the fraud: S. v. Crowley, 41 Wis. 271.

[7] McCord v. P., 46 N. Y. 470; P. v. Martin, 102 Cal. 558; P. v. Watson,

§ 683. Made to or by agent or third person.— The fact that the false representation is made to an agent of the owner from whom the money or property is obtained will not prevent the punishment of the false pretense as made to him directly.[1] So a representation may be made by an agent of the person perpetrating the fraud;[2] or, in general, by any other intermediate party used as a means of conveying the false pretenses from the defendant to the person to be defrauded.[3] But if the connection between the fraudulent pretenses and the wrong done is not immediate, the crime is not committed.[4]

§ 684. Pretense relied upon.— It must be shown both by the allegations and the proof that the false pretense was relied upon by the person parting with his money or property as the inducement thereto.[5] It is not enough to allege the making of the false pretense and the obtaining of the property by the defendant, but it must be specifically charged that the other party was induced to part with his property by reason of such pretenses, being deceived thereby.[6] The connection between the false pretense and the wrong done must be so alleged that it may appear that the false pretense was the inducement to

75 Mich. 582. It is immaterial that the person defrauded has also made fraudulent representations which might be subject of indictment: C. v. Morrill, 8 Cush. 571.

1 C. v. Harley, 7 Met. 462; P. v. Wakely, 62 Mich. 297; S. v. Crowley, 39 N. J. 264; S. v. Crawley, 103 N. C. 353. But if the indictment alleges the representation as made to a person other than the one from whom the money or property is obtained, the fact of agency must be alleged: Jacobs v. S., 31 Neb. 33. Where the party defrauded is a corporation, the false representation may be alleged to have been made to it, and proved by evidence of its being made to an officer or agent: Roberts v. P., 9 Colo. 458.

2 C. v. Call, 21 Pick. 515; White v. S., 87 Ala. 24.

3 Reg. v. Moseley, L. & C. 92; Reg. v. Dent, 1 C. & K. 249; Reg. v. Kealey, 2 Den. 68.

4 Shaffer v. S., 82 Ind. 221; Reg. v. Watson, Dears. & B. 348; Reg. v. Gardner, Dears. & B. 40; Reg. v. Bryan, 2 F. & F. 567; Reg. v. Willot, 12 Cox, 68; Reg. v. Larner, 14 Cox, 497.

5 S. v. Metsch, 37 Kan. 222; S. v. Lewis, 26 Kan. 123; S. v. Palmer, 50 Kan. 318; S. v. Benson, 110 Mo. 18; S. v. Bonnell, 46 Mo. 395; Schleisinger v. S., 11 Ohio St. 669; S. v. Saunders, 63 Mo. 482; Bonnell v. S., 64 Ind. 498; Lutton v. S., 14 Tex. Ap. 518; Reg. v. Kelleher, 2 Ir. L. R. 11; Rex v. Dale, 7 C. & P. 352.

6 S. v. Philbrick, 31 Me. 401. In Massachusetts the indictment must charge that the person alleged to have been defrauded believed the pretenses to be true and was induced thereby to part with his property; but this form of allegation seems not to be required by the English precedents: C. v. Dunleay, 153 Mass. 330.

the action of the other party and in what way.[1] And it must appear that the person to whom the pretenses were made believed them to be true, otherwise he would not be defrauded thereby.[2] But in some states this strictness of requirement as to allegation and proof is not insisted upon, and it is held sufficient to allege that the property was obtained upon the strength of or by means of the pretenses,[3] and to prove that such pretenses induced the other party to part with his money or property otherwise than by the direct evidence of such party himself,[4] the question how the false pretense induced the prosecutor to part with his money or property, and whether he did so, being for the jury.[5]

§ 685. **Falsity of pretense; fraud perpetrated.**— No matter how fraudulent the purpose may be, the pretense must be actually false to constitute the crime.[6] Thus, if, though false when made, it becomes true before being acted upon, there is no crime.[7] So although there be a concealment of an incumbrance upon property, yet if such incumbrance is invalid as to the other party by reason of his want of notice thereof, the concealment is not criminal.[8]

§ 686. **Controlling cause.**— It is evident from the preceding discussion that the false pretense must be the controlling cause in inducing the person defrauded to part with his money or property.[9] But it is not necessary that the false pretense be the only cause. It is sufficient if it materially entered into the cause which induced the person to part with his property, that is, if the owner would not have parted with his property unless such pretense had been made.[10] Nor is it necessary that the

[1] P. v. Gates, 13 Wend. 311; Johnson v. S., 11 Ind. 481; S. v. Orvis, 13 Ind. 569; Cooke v. S., 83 Ind. 402; Jones v. S., 50 Ind. 473; Abbott v. S., 59 Ind. 70.

[2] Therasson v. P., 82 N. Y. 238; Clifford v. S., 56 Ind. 245; S. v. Evers, 49 Mo. 542; P. v. Mauritzen, 84 Cal. 37. And see *supra*, § 681.

[3] Norris v. S., 25 Ohio St. 217; S. v. Butler, 47 Minn. 483; S. v. McConkey, 49 Ia. 499; S. v. Neimeier, 66 Ia. 634; S. v. Hurst, 11 W. Va. 54.

[4] Therasson v. P., 82 N. Y. 238; C. v. Coe, 115 Mass. 481; S. v. Jordan, 34 La. An. 1219; P. v. Herrick, 13 Wend. 87; Jones v. U. S., 5 Cranch, C. C. 647.

[5] Thomas v. P., 34 N. Y. 351.

[6] P. v. Reynolds, 71 Mich. 343.

[7] In re Snyder, 17 Kan. 542.

[8] S. v. Garris, 98 N. C. 733; S. v. Asher, 50 Ark. 427; Graves v. S., 31 Tex. Ap. 65.

[9] P. v. Wakely, 62 Mich. 297; S. v. Green, 7 Wis. 676; Woodbury v. S., 69 Ala. 242.

[10] S. v. Thatcher, 35 N. J. 445; C. v.

false pretense shall have been the inducing cause as to the whole of the money or property obtained.[1]

§ 687. Want of prudence of person defrauded.— In some early cases in this country it was said that a mere cheat against which common prudence might have guarded would not constitute false pretenses.[2] And following this doctrine it has been said that the question whether the pretense was such as could not have been guarded against in the exercise of common sagacity and prudence is one for the court, and not for the jury.[3] But in more recent cases it is held that the fact that investigation and the exercise of ordinary prudence would have disclosed the falsity of the pretenses will not render them insufficient to support a conviction.[4] Indeed, it has been held that it is not necessary that the pretense be sufficient to deceive a person of ordinary prudence if it deceived the person defrauded, and that it is only a statement which is in itself absurd and incredible that will not support a conviction.[5] And the question whether

Drew, 19 Pick. 179; S. v. Hill, 72 Me. 238; P. v. Henssler, 48 Mich. 49; S. v. Fooks, 65 Ia. 196; In re Snyder, 17 Kan. 542; Wax v. S., 43 Neb. 18; Donohoe v. S., 59 Ark. 375; S. v. Knowlton, 11 Wash. 512; P. v. Haynes, 14 Wend. 546; S. C., 11 Wend. 557; Fay v. C., 28 Grat. 912; Smith v. S., 55 Miss. 513; S. v. Tessier, 32 La. An. 1227; Reg. v. Hewgill, Dears. 315; Reg. v. Lince, 28 L. T. 570.

[1] C. v. Lee, 149 Mass. 179; S. v. Bayne, 88 Mo. 604.

[2] P. v. Babcock, 7 Johns. 201; P. v. Williams, 4 Hill, 9; S. v. Estes, 46 Me. 150; S. v. De Hart, 6 Baxt. 222; Delaney v. S., 7 Baxt. 28; C. v. Grady, 13 Bush, 285, 2 Am. Cr. R. 105, and note; Buckalew v. S., 11 Tex. Ap. 352; S. v. Simson, 3 Hawks, 620; S. v. Stroll, 1 Rich. 244; Henshaw v. Bryant, 5 Ill. 97; Cowen v. P., 14 Ill. 348. The standard is to be an ordinary mind, not a prudent and cautious mind: Clifford v. S., 56 Ind. 245; Bonnell v. S., 64 Ind. 498; Miller v. S., 73 Ind. 88.

[3] S. v. Estes, 46 Me. 150; Smith v. P., 47 N. Y. 303; S. v. Burnett, 119 Ind. 392. But in Maine, at least, this doctrine has been abandoned, and it is held that the sufficiency of the pretenses is a question for the jury: S. v. Mayberry, 48 Me. 218.

[4] Watson v. P., 87 N. Y. 561; P. v. Phelps, 83 N. Y. 436; S. v. Mills, 17 Me. 211; C. v. Lee, 149 Mass. 179; Thomas v. P., 113 Ill. 531; Jenkins v. S., 97 Ala. 66.

[5] S. v. Vanderbilt, 27 N. J. 328. It is enough if surrounding circumstances give color to the statements so that the party defrauded had reason to believe them to be true: P. v. Henssler, 48 Mich. 49. Other cases holding it not to be necessary that the pretense be such as to deceive a person of ordinary prudence are the following: Bartlett v. S., 28 Ohio St. 669; In re Greenough, 31 Vt. 279; Johnson v. S., 36 Ark. 242; Colbert v. S., 1 Tex. Ap. 314; Reg. v. Woolley, 3 C. & K. 98. Therefore, although the deception practiced by defendant was successful only by reason of the weak credulity of the

the injured party relied upon the false pretense and was thereby defrauded is for the jury.[1]

IV. INTENT AND KNOWLEDGE.

§ 688. **Purpose to defraud.**— It must appear that the purpose with which the false pretense was made was to perpetrate the resulting fraud.[2] In other words, the intent to defraud is essential to the crime.[3] An indictment must therefore allege that the false pretenses were made "with intent to defraud."[4] The intent is not to be inferred merely from the acts alleged, but should be specifically charged.[5] As a matter of proof the intent may be inferred from the acts.[6]

§ 689. **Intent.**— The fraudulent intent must be shown.[7] And such intent is not to be presumed as a rule of law from the fact of making false pretenses.[8] Accordingly it is said in one case that the fact that defendant intended to replace the money obtained might be shown as a defense.[9] Thus, if the intent with which money is obtained is only to secure payment of a just debt, the act will not be criminal.[10] But the mere intention

person defrauded, that fact will constitute no defense: S. v. Fooks, 65 Ia. 196; Bowen v. S., 9 Baxt. 45.

[1] S. v. Knowlton, 11 Wash. 512. If he has knowledge that the pretense was false, the crime is not committed. See *supra*, §§ 681, 684.

[2] Bowler v. S., 41 Miss. 570; Reg. v. Stone, 1 F. & F. 311; Reg. v. Garrett, Dears. 232.

[3] Sharp v. S., 53 N. J. 511; S. v. Oakley, 103 N. C. 408. For instance, if questions are asked of one seeking to obtain goods on credit for the purpose of determining whether credit shall be extended, he must have knowledge of the purpose in order that his false answers to such questions shall constitute criminal false pretenses: P. v. McAllister, 49 Mich. 12.

[4] Reg. v. James, 12 Cox, 127. But it is not necessary to aver that the particular result which in fact followed was the one designed. Thus, if the false procuring of money as a loan is alleged, it is not necessary to specifically allege the intent to obtain it as a loan, since it is immaterial whether the design was to obtain it as a loan or for other fraudulent purposes: Todd v. S., 31 Ind. 514.

[5] Stringer v. S., 13 Tex. Ap. 520.

[6] C. v. Drew, 153 Mass. 588.

[7] P. v. Baker, 96 N. Y. 340; Carlisle v. S., 76 Ala. 75; S. v. Norton, 76 Mo. 180; Fay v. C., 28 Grat. 912, 3 Am. Cr. R. 85, and note.

[8] P. v. Baker, 96 N. Y. 340.

[9] P. v. Baker, 96 N. Y. 340.

[10] Rex v. Williams, 7 C. & P. 354. And see *supra*, § 680. But it is criminal to seek to secure what is believed to be a just claim against the government by affidavits of third persons which are known to be false: U. S. v. Jones, 32 Fed. R. 482.

to repay the money obtained by false pretenses will not relieve the one making them from criminal liability.[1]

§ 690. **Knowledge of falsity.**— It must appear that defendant had knowledge of the falsity of the statements made,[2] and such knowledge must be directly alleged,[3] unless the facts as stated show it to have been impossible that defendant did not know the falsity of his statements.[4] The usual method of alleging knowledge is that defendant "knowingly" made the false statements.[5] It is not enough to allege that the statements were "falsely and fraudulently" made;[6] or that they were made with intent to cheat and defraud.[7] It is sufficient, however, to charge the false statements to have been "designedly" made.[8]

§ 691. **Evidence of intent; other transactions.**— Knowledge of the falsity of the representations and intent to defraud thereby are to be proven in general in the same way as criminal intent in other cases.[9] The making of other false pretenses of a similar character may be shown as tending to indicate the fraudulent intent with which the pretenses in question were made.[10] Other representations than those charged, made with reference to the same transaction, cannot be shown to establish

[1] S. v. Hill, 72 Me. 238; Carlisle v. S., 77 Ala. 71; P. v. Wieger, 100 Cal. 352; Buntain v. S., 15 Tex. Ap. 515; Reg. v. Naylor, L. R. 1 C. C. 4.

[2] C. v. Devlin, 141 Mass. 423; S. v. Garris, 98 N. C. 733; S. v. Rivers, 58 Ia. 102; U. S. v. Route, 33 Fed. R. 246; Reg. v. Rymes, 3 C. & K. 327; Reg. v. Keighley, Dears. & B. 145.

[3] S. v. Smith, 8 Blackf. 489; Johnson v. S., 75 Ind. 553; P. v. Fitzgerald, 92 Mich. 328; P. v. Behee, 90 Mich. 356; S. v. Janson, 80 Mo. 97.

[4] S. v. Bradley, 68 Mo. 140; P. v. Fitzgerald, 92 Mich. 328.

[5] S. v. Blauvelt, 38 N. J. 306; Maranda v. S., 44 Tex. Ap. 442; Hirsch v. S., 1 Tex. Ap. 393.

[6] Reg. v. Henderson, Car. & M. 328.

[7] S. v. Blauvelt, 38 N. J. 306. But it is said in an English case that the omission of the word "knowingly" is not ground for arresting judgment: Reg. v. Bowen, 13 Q. B. 790.

[8] C. v. Hulbert, 12 Met. 446; S. v. Snyder, 66 Ind. 203.

[9] For the general law as to criminal intent, see *supra*, ch. 6.

[10] S. v. Rivers, 58 Ia. 102; Trogden v. C., 31 Grat. 862; S. v. Jackson, 112 Mo. 585; S. v. Walton, 114 N. C. 783; Reg. v. Francis, L. R. 2 C. C. 128. But see Reg. v. Holt, Bell, 280. So, where the intent charged was to defraud the public in general, evidence of other false pretenses of the same character as those described in the indictment were held admissible: Reg. v. Cooper, 1 Q. B. D. 19; Reg. v. Stenson, 12 Cox, 111. And other transactions may be shown for the purpose of establishing system and thereby showing guilty intent: Rafferty v. S., 91 Tenn. 655. Where

the falsity of the statements charged.[1] Nor can distinct offenses of the same kind be shown by evidence of the business in which accused is engaged and his manner of conducting it.[2]

V. THE FRAUD PERPETRATED.

§ 692. **What constitutes property.**— The earlier statutes have reference to the obtaining of money or property by false pretenses, and some question has occasionally arisen as to what is property in this connection; but this term is considered in the discussion of the subject of larceny,[3] and there need not be a further discussion here. For instance, dogs not being the subject of larceny are not chattels within the terms of the statute of George IV. as to false pretenses.[4] One who by false pretenses obtains board and lodging is not guilty of a criminal offense under a statute relating to the obtaining of "money, goods or other property."[5] The obtaining of property involves the obtaining either of the title thereto or the unqualified right of possession thereof.[6] To fraudulently obtain an indorsement of credit on a note is not a crime.[7] Nor does it constitute obtaining money by false pretenses to thus secure satisfaction of a debt, no money passing.[8]

§ 693. **Notes, checks and other instruments.**— There has been difficulty under some forms of statute in convicting for falsely obtaining notes or other instruments, because, just as in case of larceny, they have been held not to come under the designation of money or property.[9] This difficulty has been covered

statements are made on different occasions, it is a question for the jury whether they are so connected as to form one continuing representation: Reg. v. Welman, Dears. 188.

[1] S. v. Church, 43 Conn. 471.

[2] Jackson v. P., 126 Ill. 139. Where the false pretenses charged consisted in statements as to the character of a horse sold, *held*, that proof of similar false statements in other independent sales was not admissible: Jackson v. P., 18 Ill. Ap. 508.

[3] See *supra*, §§ 536, 543.

[4] Reg. v. Robinson, Bell, 34.

[5] S. v. Black, 75 Wis. 490. But by statute it is in some states made criminal to obtain entertainment at a hotel with intent not to pay therefor: Atkins v. S., 95 Tenn. 474; S. v. Yardley, 95 Tenn. 546. As to frauds on hotel-keepers, see *supra*, § 663*a*.

[6] S. v. Anderson, 47 Ia. 142.

[7] S. v. Moore, 15 Ia. 412.

[8] Jamison v. S., 37 Ark. 445.

[9] C. v. Swinney, 1 Va. Cas. 146, 151 note; Rex v. Hill, Russ. & Ry. 190. See, for instance, as to books of account, U. S. v. Carico, 2 Cranch, C. C. 446. But a railway ticket was held to be a chattel: Reg. v. Boulton, 2 C. & K. 917.

to some extent by the use in the English and American statutes of the term "valuable thing" or "valuable security," and the words "other effects" have been held to cover the same ground and to include a promissory note.[1] A note, bill or bond is a valuable security after its execution, even though it has not yet passed out of the hands of the person executing it. It is a valuable thing to the maker on account of the liability he incurs when it passes out of his hands;[2] but if the instrument obtained is of no validity and cannot in any way affect the signer, it does not come under the head of a valuable "thing" or "security."[3]

§ 694. **Obtaining signature.**— Even with the extension of meaning given to the term "valuable security," by which it covers instruments executed but not yet delivered, there are found to be cases which are not sufficiently covered by that term. For instance, it has been decided that to obtain an acceptance of a bill of exchange was not the obtaining of a valuable security from the acceptor.[4] To cover this difficulty statutes have been passed in England and in this country extending the crime of false pretenses to the obtaining of the signature to a written instrument, the false making of which would be forgery.[5] Under such a statute it is not necessary that the person whose signature has been obtained has been compelled to pay the instrument. Actual loss resulting therefrom is not essential.[6] But

[1] P. v. Stone, 9 Wend. 182; so under Texas statute: Baker v. S., 14 Tex. Ap. 332. It is a cheat to induce an illiterate person, by false representations and false reading, to sign a note for a different amount from that agreed upon: Hill v. S., 1 Yerg. 76.

[2] S. v. Thatcher, 35 N. J. 445; S. v. Newell, 1 Mo. 248; S. v. Porter, 75 Mo. 171; Tarbox v. S., 38 Ohio St. 581; P. v. Genung, 11 Wend. 18; Bork v. P., 91 N. Y. 5; Reg. v. Essex, Dears. & B. 371; Reg. v. Greenhalgh, 1 Dears. 267.

[3] Robinson v. S., 53 N. J. 41; S. v. Clay, 100 Mo. 571; Rex v. Yates, 1 Moody, 170.

[4] In re Payson, 23 Kan. 757; S. v. Switser, 63 Vt. 604; Reg. v. Danger, Dears. & B. 307.

[5] S. v. House, 55 Ia. 466; S. v. Joaquin, 43 Ia. 131; In re Payson, 23 Kan. 757; S. v. Switser, 63 Vt. 604.

[6] P. v. Stone, 9 Wend. 182; P. v. Genung, 11 Wend. 18; P. v. Gates, 13 Wend. 311; P. v. Crissie, 4 Denio, 525; S. v. Pryor, 30 Ind. 350. The fact that the defendant afterwards obtained money by means of the instrument to which the signature was secured may be alleged in the same indictment with the charging of obtaining the signature: C. v. Frey, 50 Pa. St. 245; Wallace v. S., 2 Lea, 29.

the instrument to which the signature is obtained must be one which on its face is valid or calculated to prejudice the party in his property. Thus, where a married woman's deed would be invalid without acknowledgment, it was held not criminal to fraudulently procure her signature to such an instrument without such acknowledgment.[1] But in general a signature to a deed or mortgage containing covenants sufficiently indicates a liability.[2] Furthermore, it must appear that the instrument to which the signature was obtained was delivered or parted with by the person signing. The instrument must be acquired or come into possession of by some person by means of the false pretenses.[3] But it is said that the allegation of obtaining the signature implies that the instrument was delivered by the party signing it.[4] The obtaining of the signature of a party is not in itself the obtaining of something of value under that language as found in the statutes, and if it is merely the means by which money or property is obtained, it is not the offense of obtaining a signature but is that of obtaining the money or property.[5] If the fraud is in obtaining the indorsement of another upon a note, it is the indorsement and not the amount of the note which should be charged as obtained.[6]

§ 695. **Obtaining charity.**—In an early New York case it was intimated that the false pretense of a beggar to obtain charity did not constitute a crime under these statutes.[7] But this seems not to have been the rule in England,[8] and it is not followed in this country; the doctrine recognized in other cases

[1] P. v. Galloway, 17 Wend. 540; S. v. Clay, 100 Mo. 571. And see discussion to the same effect in Robinson v. S., 53 N. J. 41.

[2] S. v. Butler, 47 Minn. 483; S. v. Jamison, 74 Ia. 613. It is not necessary to describe the property embraced in the mortgage: Fenton v. P., 4 Hill, 126. But the instrument should be so described as to bring it within the terms of the statute: S. v. Layman, 8 Blackf. 330. For instance, it is not necessary to allege that the instrument is one the false making of which would constitute forgery, if it is set out in full in the indictment: S. v. Switser, 63 Vt. 604. But to merely describe the instrument by name is not enough; the substance or tenor should be shown: Langford v. S., 45 Ala. 26.

[3] S. v. McGinnis, 71 Ia. 685; S. v. Clark, 72 Ia. 30; In re Payson, 23 Kan. 757.

[4] Fenton v. P., 4 Hill, 126; S. v. Switser, 63 Vt. 604.

[5] Kennedy v. S., 34 Ohio St. 310; Tarbox v. S., 38 Ohio St. 581.

[6] S. v. Blauvelt, 38 N. J. 306.

[7] P. v. Clough, 17 Wend. 351.

[8] Reg. v. Jones, 3 C. & K. 346.

being that one is none the less guilty of obtaining goods or money in such case by such pretenses because delivered from charitable, not from mercenary, considerations.[1]

VI. INDICTMENT AND EVIDENCE.

§ **696. Venue.**— The general proposition as to the venue is that it should be laid where the property is obtained by the false pretenses; and if the criminal obtains property in one county or state and takes it with him into another, he is not to be prosecuted in the latter.[2] It is the county or state in which the property is obtained and not the one in which the pretenses are made that fixes the venue,[3] for the offense is not complete until the obtaining of the property.[4] Thus, where by means of a letter sent into another state false pretenses are made, and, in response to such pretenses, money or property is delivered there to a carrier or into the mails for transmission to the defendant at the place of his residence, the offense is committed in the state where the letter is received and money or property delivered for transmission.[5] The fact that the

[1] C. v. Whitcomb, 107 Mass. 486; S. v. Matthews, 91 N. C. 635; Strong v. S., 86 Ind. 208. Where it was alleged that defendant, under false representations as to the happening of an accident, secured from one B., who had been deceived thereby, $5 of the money of the Detroit Stove Works, *held*, that the indictment was fatally defective in failing to allege any connection between B. and the stove works: P. v. Behee, 90 Mich. 356. But where it was alleged that the person from whom the money was obtained by the false representation was a member of a copartnership, and that it was the money of such copartnership which was obtained, *held*, that the indictment was sufficient: P. v. Fitzgerald, 92 Mich. 328.

[2] Reg. v. Stanbury, L. & C. 128. So where negotiable bills were obtained by false pretenses in Maryland, and the bills were then brought into the District of Columbia, *held*, that the defendant could not be prosecuted in the District of Columbia: U. S. v. Plympton, 4 Cranch, C. C. 309.

[3] S. v. House, 55 Ia. 466; Stewart v. Jessup, 51 Ind. 413; Sims v. S., 28 Tex. Ap. 447.

[4] Rex v. Buttery, 3 B. & C. 700.

[5] P. v. Adams, 3 Denio, 190; S. C., 1 N. Y. 173; Norris v. S., 25 Ohio St. 217, 2 Am. Cr. R. 85, and note; Connor v. S., 29 Fla. 455; Reg. v. Leech, Dears. 642. If the return is made by letter, the postoffice is deemed the agent of the defendant in receiving the letter where it is mailed: Reg. v. Jones, 1 Den. 551; C. v. Wood, 142 Mass. 459. So where, by false pretenses contained in a letter, goods were procured to be sent by carrier to a fictitious consignee in another state, and were there taken possession of by defendant, *held*, that the offense was committed where the goods were delivered to the carrier: C. v. Taylor, 105 Mass. 172. So where an order was transmitted through a

thing thus obtained consists in a draft or order on which the defendant obtains money in the state of his residence does not make that the place of obtaining the property, the crime consisting in such case of the obtaining of the original instrument and not of the cash thereon.[1] Under similar reasoning, where the defendant obtained money from a St. Louis bank on a draft drawn upon a party in New York who was the party defrauded, it was held that the offense was committed in New York, the St. Louis bank being merely the agent of defendant in procuring the money.[2] There are decisions in England not entirely harmonious with those just cited; for instance, where a manufacturer in England sent a letter containing false pretenses to a customer in France and received in response thereto, by mail, a draft on which he procured money at the place of his residence, it was held that the offense was committed in England.[3] It is immaterial where the property is situated in regard to which the false pretenses are made.[4]

§ 697. **Parties indictable; combination.**— False pretenses made by one of several persons in pursuance of an agreement are chargeable to all.[5] The false pretenses may be made by one in the presence of others acting in concert and all be liable.[6] Indeed, all who should participate in the proceeds of the crime committed in pursuance of their common purpose may be jointly indicted, although such proceeds are actually obtained by one of them in the absence of the others.[7] Where several combine to procure money or property by false pretenses, such combination of course constitutes a criminal conspiracy.[8]

salesman to his principal in another state and goods were shipped to defendant under such order, it was held that defendant's crime of false pretenses in connection with such order was committed where the goods were shipped: C. v. Karpowski, 167 Pa. St. 225.

[1] C. v. Wood, 142 Mass. 459.

[2] S. v. Shaeffer, 89 Mo. 271.

[3] Reg. v. Holmes, 12 Q. B. D. 23. And see Reg. v. Cooke, 1 F. & F. 64.

[4] C. v. Van Tuyl, 1 Met. (Ky.) 1.

[5] Cowen v. P., 14 Ill. 348; C. v. Harley, 7 Met. 462. A combination between attorney and client to enforce by legal process payment of sums known by them not to be due, but falsely represented to be due, may render both liable: Reg. v. Taylor, 15 Cox, 265; Reg. v. Taylor, 15 Cox, 268.

[6] Young v. Rex, 3 T. R. 98.

[7] Jones v. U. S., 5 Cranch, 647.

[8] P. v. Watson, 75 Mich. 582; C. v. Meserve, 154 Mass. 64. And see the chapter on Conspiracy.

§ 698. **The indictment; statutory form.**— All the elements necessary to constitute the crime should, in general, be charged in the indictment,[1] including the statement of the false pretenses used.[2] But in some states there are statutory provisions as to the indictment which relieve the prosecution from the necessity of making so full and explicit a statement as is required at common law.[3] Under such statutes it has been held not necessary to set out the false pretenses intended to be relied on, and that it is sufficient to allege in a general way the obtaining of the property with intent to cheat and defraud, etc.[4] But so far as such a statute authorizes an indictment which does not state the name of the person whose property is obtained, or description of the property or the means used, it is unconstitutional.[5]

§ 699. **Statement of the false pretenses.**— Aside from the statutory provisions referred to in the last section, it is necessary that the indictment particularly set forth the false pretenses used.[6] It is not sufficient to use the words of the statute.[7] And nothing will be supplied by intendment except what the words of the indictment themselves charge. For instance, a charge that the defendant presented a false writing will not imply that it was represented to be genuine; nor will the charge that defendant knew such writing to be false supply the omission.[8] Nor is it enough to allege the making of a false statement for the purpose of obtaining, etc., without allegation of the method pursued,[9] or the particulars in which the representation was false.[10] But it is sufficient to allege that the par-

[1] S. v. Dickson, 88 N. C. 643.

[2] P. v. Gates, 13 Wend. 311; C. v. Goddard, 4 Allen, 312; Glackan v. C., 3 Met. (Ky.) 232; S. v. Chapel, 117 Mo. 639.

[3] Jim v. S., 8 Humph. 603; O'Conner v. S., 30 Ala. 9.

[4] S. v. Blizzard, 70 Md. 385; S. v. Fancher, 71 Mo. 460; S. v. Porter, 75 Mo. 171; S. v. Morgan, 112 Mo. 202; S. v. Burke, 108 N. C. 750; S. v. Lewis, 41 La. An. 590.

[5] S. v. Reynolds, 106 Mo. 146; S. v. Terry, 109 Mo. 601; S. v. Benson, 110 Mo. 18; S. v. Cameron, 117 Mo. 371; S. v. Kain, 118 Mo. 5.

[6] U. S. v. Ross, Morris, 164; Rex v. Mason, 2 T. R. 581; Reg. v. Marsh, 1 Den. 505.

[7] P. v. McKenna, 81 Cal. 158.

[8] P. v. Gates, 13 Wend. 311.

[9] Higler v. P., 44 Mich. 299; S. v. Dyer, 41 Tex. 520; S. v. Cameron, 117 Mo. 371.

[10] S. v. Lambeth, 80 N. C. 393. But a failure to set out the particulars may be cured by verdict: Reg. v. Goldsmith, L. R. 2 C. C. 74.

ticular means are to the grand jury unknown.[1] If the means set out are such as might deceive, the question whether they did deceive and induce the parting with the property is a question of fact for the jury.[2] The particulars being set out must be proved as alleged, and a variance therein will be fatal.[3]

§ 700. **Setting out the words or instrument.**— It is not necessary to set out the exact words in which the false pretense was made;[4] but where the false pretense consists in the use of a false written instrument, the writing should be set out by its tenor and proved as laid.[5]

§ 701. **Several pretenses.**— The indictment may allege several false pretenses, and it is not necessary to prove all such pretenses, but it is sufficient that the evidence show some of them which are in themselves adequate to constitute a crime.[6] Nor is it necessary to set out in the indictment all the false pretenses used, provided those set out are sufficient and are proved.[7] If several false pretenses are set out, some of which are immaterial, and would not of themselves be sufficient, the court must instruct the jury upon which of the pretenses, if found to have been made, they may convict.[8]

§ 702. **Falsity of the pretenses.**— It is essential that the indictment falsify, by distinct and specific averments, the pretenses alleged.[9] Each pretense relied upon by the prosecution must be thus negatived.[10] It is not sufficient to negative the

[1] C. v. Ashton, 125 Mass. 384.

[2] Thomas v. P., 34 N. Y. 351; S. v. Call, 48 N. H. 126. And see *supra*, § 687.

[3] C. v. Jeffries, 7 Allen, 548; S. v. Metsch, 37 Kan. 222; S. v. Corbett, 1 Jones, 264; Keller v. S., 51 Ind. 111. Further, as to variance, see *infra*, § 710. A slight variance, the pretenses being substantially proved as alleged, will not defeat the prosecution: C. v. Karpowski, 167 Pa. St. 225.

[4] S. v. Call, 48 N. H. 126; S. v. Vanderbilt, 27 N. J. 328.

[5] Ferguson v. S., 25 Tex. Ap. 451; Langford v. S., 45 Ala. 26.

[6] S. v. Dunlap, 24 Me. 77; S. v. Mills, 17 Me. 211; C. v. Parmenter, 121 Mass. 354; C. v. Meserve, 154 Mass. 64; Webster v. P., 92 N. Y. 422; Todd v. S., 31 Ind. 514; Beasley v. S., 59 Ala. 20; Rex v. Hill, Russ. & Ry. 190; Rex v. Story, Russ. & Ry. 81; Rex v. Dale, 7 Car. & P. 352.

[7] Cowen v. P., 14 Ill. 348.

[8] P. v. Jacobs, 35 Mich. 36.

[9] S. v. Paul, 69 Me. 215; S. v. Peacock, 31 Mo. 413; P. v. Haynes, 11 Wend. 557; S. v. Smith, 8 Blackf. 489; P. v. Behee, 90 Mich. 356; S. v. Palmer, 50 Kan. 318; S. v. Pickett, 78 N. C. 458; S. v. Levi, 41 Tex. 563.

[10] P. v. Stone, 9 Wend. 182; P. v. Gates, 13 Wend. 311.

pretenses in a general way, but the particulars with reference to which such pretenses were untrue must be set out.[1]

§ **703. Intent.**— The offense is usually of such grade by the statute that it constitutes a felony, and the acts charged should be therefore described as "feloniously" done as in other felonies.[2] It seems that it is the obtaining and not the pretending that should be charged as felonious.[3] Intent to defraud should be alleged,[4] and it should be charged that the pretense was "designedly" made.[5] Where the statute allowed the intent to be alleged in the alternative, "to injure or defraud," it was held that the indictment charging "the intent to defraud" alone, was sufficient.[6]

§ **704. Person defrauded.**—Aside from any statutory provision in the matter, it is necessary that the indictment name the person defrauded.[7] And the person named as the one to whom the false pretenses were made must be the same person as the one from whom the property is alleged to have been obtained; that is to say, the making of the false pretenses is not punishable unless the goods were obtained by defendant and not by some one else.[8] But it is not necessary that the property pass directly to defendant. It is sufficient if it was delivered to another at his request and in payment of his debt.[9] And it is immaterial, if the property passes to the person making the false pretenses, whether it is obtained by him for his own

[1] S. v. Peacock, 31 Mo. 413; Dillingham v. S., 5 Ohio St. 280; Redmond v. S., 35 Ohio St. 81; S. v. Trisler, 49 Ohio St. 583; Keller v. S., 51 Ind. 111; Wills v. S., 24 Tex. Ap. 400. Insufficiency in this respect may be cured by verdict: Hamilton v. Reg., 9 Q. B. 271. Where the charge was that defendant pretended to have authority to collect money, and it was alleged in denial that he was not at any time authorized to collect any money, etc., by the person named, *held*, that this was sufficient: P. v. Fitzgerald, 92 Mich. 328.

[2] S. v. Tate, 6 Humph. 424; S. v. Small, 31 Tex. 184; S. v. Bryan, 112 N. C. 848; S. v. Caldwell, 112 N. C. 854; S. v. Wilson, 116 N. C. 979.

[3] Rex v. Walker, 6 C. & P. 657. Similarly it is held that it is not necessary to charge that defendant "knowingly and designedly" *pretended:* Rex v. Howorth, 3 Stark. 26.

[4] S. v. Daniels, 90 Ia. 491, 58 N. W. R. 891.

[5] S. v. Switser, 63 Vt. 604; S. v. Baggerly, 21 Tex. 757.

[6] White v. S., 86 Ala. 69.

[7] S. v. Woodson, 5 Humph. 55; Burd v. S., 39 Tex. 509. As to statutory provision in this respect, see *supra*, § 698.

[8] Reg. v. Martin, 1 F. & F. 501; Reg. v. Franklin, 4 F. & F. 94; Connor v. S., 29 Fla. 455.

[9] Sandy v. S., 60 Ala. 58.

benefit or that of another.[1] An indictment charging the false pretenses to have been made to one person and the deceit to have been practiced on another is bad.[2]

§ 705. **Corporation deemed person.**— Under the usual statutory description of the offense of obtaining property from a "person," a corporation is included in that term,[3] and the corporation may be considered a person as distinct from its officers in such sense that the latter may be guilty of obtaining by false pretenses the property of the corporation.[4]

§ 706. **How fraud effected; means.**— The indictment must allege that it was by reason of the false pretenses that the property was obtained.[5] Thus, if the allegation is of obtaining money from a bank by false representations made to N., it is defective without some statement of N.'s connection with the bank as agent or otherwise.[6] It is essential to allege that it was by means of the false pretenses that the delivery of the property to defendant was secured.[7] An allegation that defendant made certain false pretenses and requested the injured party in consideration thereof to pay to him the money in question sufficiently shows that defendant's purpose in making the false pretenses was to obtain such money.[8] It seems that the allegation, that by means of the false pretenses defendant obtained possession of the property from the injured party, is sufficient.[9] And the allegation that the injured party was induced by the false pretenses to part with his money, sufficiently shows that he relied on them.[10] A variance between

[1] C. v. Harley, 7 Met. 462.

[2] Rex v. Lara, 6 T. R. 565.

[3] Norris v. S., 25 Ohio St. 217.

[4] Ochs v. P., 124 Ill. 399.

[5] C. v. Strain, 10 Met. 521; Pendry v. S., 18 Fla. 191; Hightower v. S., 23 Tex. Ap. 451; Mathena v. S., 15 Tex. Ap. 473; Reg. v. Closs, Dears. & B. 460. The connection between the false pretenses and the obtaining of the property must be made to appear: Johnson v. S., 75 Ind. 553. And see *supra*, §§ 680, 687.

[6] Owens v. S., 83 Wis. 496. But where the false pretense was with reference to a request by a third person, it was held unnecessary to allege what the relation was between the third person and the one from whom the money was obtained: May v. S., 17 Tex. Ap. 213.

[7] C. v. Goddard, 4 Allen, 312; Ladd v. S., 17 Fla. 215; Arnold v. S., 11 Tex. Ap. 472; Erwin v. S., 11 Tex. Ap. 536; Epperson v. S., 42 Tex. 79.

[8] C. v. Howe, 132 Mass. 250.

[9] P. v. Cline, 44 Mich. 290.

[10] P. v. Jacobs, 35 Mich. 36; S. v. Bloodsworth, 25 Oreg. 83. An allegation of the pretense in regard to sale of property by defendant, and that the buyer bought the same and paid defendant therefor, sufficiently shows that defendant obtained the

the indictment and the evidence as to the means used will be fatal.[1]

§ 707. **Name of party defrauded; ownership of property.** The indictment must set out the name of the party defrauded as a means of identifying the offense charged.[2] For the same reason it is essential to charge the name of the owner of the property obtained.[3] And this rule is applicable even under statutes which relieve the prosecution from the necessity of charging the name of the person to be defrauded. The ownership of the property is as essential an allegation in false pretenses as it is in larceny.[4] It is necessary also that the ownership of the property be alleged as in the person charged to have been defrauded.[5] Statutes sometimes, however, relieve the prosecution from the necessity of proving the ownership as alleged where the description of the property is otherwise sufficient.[6]

§ 708. **Description of the property.**— The indictment must describe the property obtained with the same particularity as in larceny.[7] The same principles apply with reference to the description of money as in cases of larceny. A general allegation of the obtaining of a certain number of dollars in money

money: S. v. Knowlton, 11 Wash. 512.

[1] Baker v. S., 31 Ohio St. 314.

[2] S. v. Horn, 93 Mo. 190; S. v. McChesney, 90 Mo. 120.

[3] S. v. Lathrop, 15 Vt. 279; Ladd v. S., 17 Fla. 215; Leobold v. S., 33 Ind. 484; Halley v. S., 43 Ind. 509; Washington v. S., 41 Tex. 583; Reg. v. Martin, 8 A. & E. 481; Reg. v. Norton, 8 C. & P. 196; Reg. v. Parker, 3 Q. B. 292; White v. Reg., 13 Cox, 318.

[4] S. v. Blizzard, 70 Md. 385; Sill v. Reg., Dears. 132; S. C. (on error), 1 El. & B. 553.

[5] Thomson v. P., 24 Ill. 60; S. v. Smith, 8 Blackf. 489; Halley v. S., 43 Ind. 509. But here as in larceny cases, legal title need not be shown, but only a possessory right: Mack v. S., 63 Ala. 138; May v. S., 15 Tex. Ap. 430.

[6] Hennessy v. C., 88 Ky. 301. And see for a similar statute, Reg. v. Moss, Dears. & B. 104.

[7] S. v. Reese, 83 N. C. 637; S. v. Kube, 20 Wis. 217; Johnson v. S., 75 Ind. 553; Bonnell v. S., 64 Ind. 498; Smith v. S., 33 Ind. 159; Treadaway v. S., 37 Ark. 443; Jamison v. S., 37 Ark. 445. The ownership must be alleged: Mays v. S., 28 Tex. Ap. 484. And this is so even under a statute prescribing the form for such indictment: S. v. Crooker, 95 Mo. 389. It is sufficient to describe the property obtained as "a check and order for the payment of money of the value of," etc.: C. v. Coe, 115 Mass. 481. But on the contrary, *held*, that describing the instrument as a check, giving the bank and the amount, was not sufficient without showing the date, payor and payee: Bonnell v. S., 54 Ind. 498.

is sufficient.[1] And it is said that where the offense charged is in essence a fraud rather than a wrongful taking as in larceny, the description of the property, as a certain named sum of money of a kind and description to the grand jury unknown, is sufficient.[2] The evidence must show that the property obtained was that described in the indictment.[3]

§ 709. **Value.**— If the degree of the offense is not made to depend, as it is in larceny, upon the value of the goods obtained, it is not necessary to aver the value.[4] But if the statute makes the offense larceny, there is the same necessity for alleging value as there is in ordinary cases of larceny.[5] It is not essential that the value be proved as alleged; a variance in that respect will not be material.[6]

§ 710. **Variance.**— The effect of variance as to some particular allegations has already been considered. As a general proposition, the material averments must be proved as laid.[7] Thus, a material variance as to the false representations will be fatal,[8] and, in general, the transaction must be proved as al-

[1] C. v. Lincoln, 11 Allen. 233; S. v. Hurst, 11 W. Va. 54; S. v. Knowlton, 11 Wash. 512. But it is has been held otherwise in Smith v. S., 33 Ind. 159; S. v. Reese, 83 N. C. 637; Cain v. S., 58 Ark. 43. And see, in general, the discussion as to larceny, *supra*, §§ 596–598. A description of the money as "currency of the U. S." will cover national bank notes: Edwards v. S., 49 Ala. 334.

[2] P. v. Dimick, 107 N. Y. 13.

[3] Wilburn v. S., 60 Ark. 141.

[4] S. v. Gillespie, 80 N. C. 396; Oliver v. S., 37 Ala. 134; P. v. Millan, 106 Cal. 320.

[5] S. v. Porter, 75 Mo. 171; Jackson v. C., 86 Ky. 1; Wax v. S., 43 Neb. 18.

[6] C. v. Morrill, 8 Cush. 571; Hagerman v. S., 54 N. J. 104; Moore v. S., 20 Tex. Ap. 233.

[7] Jones v. S., 8 Tex. Ap. 648.

[8] Reg. v. Bulmer, L. & C. 476. The most pertinent illustrations of this proposition are those furnished by cases where the false pretense consists in the misrepresentation of the value of property and the proof does not correspond with the allegation as to what value the defendant placed upon the property. Such a variance has been held fatal: Todd v. S., 31 Ind. 514. So where it was alleged that defendant pretended that his debts did not exceed $300 while the proof showed that they did not exceed $400: C. v. Davidson, 1 Cush. 33. In P. v. Herrick, 13 Wend. 87, it is said that the variance in stating the amount which defendant alleged to be due him from a third person was immaterial if the actual amount of the indebtedness was such as to form a sufficient basis for the verdict; but this case is disapproved of in Todd v. S., 31 Ind. 514. Where the representation alleged was that defendant had $300 in bank, and the proof was that he said he had more than enough to pay a certain bill of that amount, *held*, that the proof was sufficient: C. v. Karpowski, 167 Pa. St. 225. So exact accuracy in stating the amount

leged. But a slight variance between the exact words and the false pretenses as laid and proved is not material if the effect would be substantially the same.[1] The description of the property must be proved as laid.[2] The evidence as to the false pretenses made must be limited to those alleged.[3]

§ 711. **Forms of indictment.**— The following illustrations of forms under various statutes will be found to cover the usual cases, and to give sufficient guidance by analogy for cases arising under any of the statutes:

BY COUNTERFEIT COIN.

That A. B., on ——, at ——, devising and intending by unlawful ways and means to obtain and get into his possession and hands the goods, merchandise, chattels, effects and personal property of the honest and good citizens of this commonwealth, and with intent then and there to cheat and defraud, did then and there unlawfully, knowingly and designedly falsely pretend and represent to one C. D. that a certain metallic medal and substance which he, the said A. B., then and there had, was a good and current gold coin, called an eagle, of the gold coin current in the commonwealth aforesaid by the laws and usages thereof, and was then and there of the value of ten dollars; and the said A. B. did then and there deliver said metallic medal and substance to the said C. D. as and for a good and current gold coin of the money current in said commonwealth, and of the value of ten dollars. And the said C. D., then and there believing the said false pretenses and representations so made as aforesaid by the said A. B., and being then and there deceived thereby, was then and there induced by reason of the false pretenses and representations so made as aforesaid to receive the said metallic medal and substance as and for a good and current gold coin current in said commonwealth by the laws and usages thereof, called an eagle; and was induced by the false pretenses and representations, so by the said A. B. then and there made as aforesaid, to deliver, and did then and there deliver to the said A. B., in exchange for said metallic medal and substance, sundry bank-bills current in said common-

of the note used as an instrument to defraud is not required: S. v. Bloodsworth, 25 Oreg. 83.

[1] S. v. Thatcher, 35 N. J. 445.

[2] Berrien v. S., 83 Ga. 331. But it is said that an attempt to obtain by fraud a check on which money could be obtained may be shown under an indictment charging an attempt to obtain money: S. v. Terry, 109 Mo. 601. Where the fraud consists of misdescribing property it may be described in the indictment as it was represented by defendant: P. v. Nesbitt, 102 Cal. 327.

[3] P. v. Gates, 13 Wend. 311.

wealth by the laws and usages thereof, amounting together to the sum of nine dollars, and then and there of the value of nine dollars, and sundry pieces of silver coin current in said commonwealth by the laws and usages thereof, amounting together to seventy cents, and then and there of the value of seventy cents, of the moneys of him, the said C. D. And the said A. B. did then and there unlawfully, knowingly and designedly receive and obtain the said moneys of the said C. D. by means of the false pretenses and representations aforesaid, and with intent then and there to cheat and defraud the said C. D. of the said moneys. Whereas, in truth and fact, the said metallic medal and substance was not then and there a good and current gold coin, called an eagle, of the gold coin current in said commonwealth by the laws and usages thereof, and was not then and there of the value of ten dollars, but was then and there of little value, to wit, of the value of five cents, all which he, the said A. B., then and there well knew.[1]

BY FALSELY REPRESENTING PROPERTY.

That A. B., on ——, at ——, contriving and intending, knowingly and designedly by false pretenses to cheat and defraud one J. L. of his money, goods, wares and merchandise and other things, did knowingly and designedly falsely pretend to said J. L. that a certain horse which he, the said A. B., then wished and offered to exchange with said J. L. for a certain colt and five dollars in money, was then and there a sound horse and was the horse called the "Charlie," the said horse called the "Charlie" being well known to said J. L., by true and correct representations which he had received, although he had not seen said horse called the "Charlie," by which false pretenses said A. B. then and there induced the said J. L. to exchange with and deliver to said A. B. his said colt and five dollars in money for said horse, falsely represented as aforesaid to be the "Charlie;" whereas, in truth and in fact, the said horse which said A. B. offered to and exchanged with said J. L., and which he represented as a sound horse and as the horse called the "Charlie," was not a sound horse and was not the horse called the "Charlie," but was a different horse and unsound and wholly worthless.[2]

[1] C. v. Nason, 9 Gray, 125. Probably the following very much shorter form, taken from that given in S. v. Boon, 4 Jones, 463, would be sufficient for such cases:

That A. B., at ——, on ——, knowingly and designedly by means of a certain false token, to wit, by means of a quarter of a dollar which the said A. B. well knew to be counterfeit, did then and there obtain from one C. D. one piece of gingerbread with intent to cheat and defraud the said C. D.

See Bishop, Direc. & F. 423, n. For a form where the false pretense consists in misrepresenting the amount due on a bill, see S. v. Hurst, 11 W. Va. 54, 3 Am. Cr. R. 100.

[2] S. v. Mills, 17 Me 211.

BY FALSE PERSONATION.

That A. B., on ——, at ——, with intent to cheat and defraud C. D. of his money, did unlawfully, knowingly and designedly falsely pretend and represent to E. F., a person who owed a sum to C. D., to wit, the sum of eleven dollars and sixty-three cents, that he, the said A. B., was an authorized collector and a servant of C. D.; that said C. D. had sent him, the said A. B., to collect and receive the sum of money so due and owed by E. F. to said C. D., and that said E. F., believing the false pretenses so made and being deceived thereby, was induced by reason of them to deliver, and did deliver to the said A. B., the sum of eleven dollars and sixty-three cents due and owing from him, the said E. F., to said C. D., of the proper money and effects of said E. F. due and owing to said C. D., and the said A. B. did receive and obtain the same by means of the false pretenses and representations and with the intent to cheat and defraud said E. F. and said C. D. of the same money and effects; whereas, in fact, the said A. B. was not an authorized collector and a servant of the said C. D., and the said C. D. had not employed and sent him and did not then and there employ and send him to collect and receive for him the sum so due from said E. F. to him, but had forbidden the said A. B. to collect and receive any sum or sums for him and had turned him, the said A. B., out of the employment of him, the said C. D. And so the jurors say that the said A. B., by means of the false pretenses and representations, unlawfully, knowingly and designedly did receive and obtain from E. F. the sum of eleven dollars and sixty-three cents, being the said money due and owing as aforesaid and effects of the proper money and effects of the said E. F. due, owing and payable to said C. D., with intent to defraud said C. D. of the same.[1]

BY MISREPRESENTING FINANCIAL STANDING.

That A. B., on ——, at ——, having applied to one C. D. to loan him, the said A. B., the sum of twenty-five dollars in money, and in order to induce the said C. D. to believe him, the said A. B., worthy of credit, and loan him, the said A. B., the said sum of money, to wit, twenty-five dollars in money, of the value of twenty-five dollars, with intent to cheat and defraud said C. D., he, the said A. B., did then and there designedly, falsely, fraudulently and feloniously represent and pretend to the said C. D. that he, the said A. B., was then and there engaged in store-keeping in ——; and he, the said C. D.,

[1] C. v. Call, 21 Pick. 515. For an indictment charging the obtaining from an express company of a package of money by false pretense that defendant was the husband of the woman to whom the package was addressed, see S. v. Kube, 20 Wis. 217.

believing and relying upon the said false pretenses and representations so made as aforesaid by the said A. B., and being then and there deceived thereby, and being then and there induced thereby, was induced to make said loan and to deliver, and did then and there deliver to the said A. B., the sum of twenty-five dollars of the moneys, goods and chattels of him, the said C. D. And the said A. B. did then and there designedly, knowingly, falsely, fraudulently and feloniously obtain from the said C. D., by means of the said false, fraudulent and felonious pretenses aforesaid, twenty-five dollars in money, of the value of twenty-five dollars, of the personal property, goods and chattels of him, the said C. D. Whereas, in truth and in fact, the said A. B. was not then and there, to wit, on ——, engaged as a store-keeper at ——, or at any other time or place, all of which the said A. B. then and there well knew, to the great damage and deception of the said C. D., and to the evil example of all others in like cases offending.[1]

OBTAINING SIGNATURE.

That A. B., on ——, at ——, did unlawfully, feloniously, designedly and with intent to defraud one S. S. represent and pretend to him, the said S. S., that a certain written instrument which he, the said A. B., then and there had prepared ready to be executed by him, the said S. S., was an order for a certain number of patent churns, it being then and there understood by and between the said A. B. and the said S. S. that he, the said S. S., should execute and deliver to him, the said A. B., such an order for patent churns, and by means of such false representations and pretense the said A. B. did then and there obtain the name and signature of the said S. S. to a certain written instrument, to wit, a promissory note of him, the said S. S., purporting to bear date of the day and year aforesaid, and to be given for the sum of one hundred and eighty dollars, payable sixty days after date to said A. B. or order, for value received, which said written instrument so signed by the said S. S. was then and there, by reason of said false representations and pretense, delivered by said S. S. to said A. B.; whereas, in truth and in fact, the said instrument so prepared and made ready for the signature of him, the said S. S., was not an order for a certain number of patent churns, which the said A. B. then and there well knew, and that the said A. B. then and there well knew that the said pretense and representations were false, and said representations and pretense were designedly then and there so made by him, the said A. B., with intent to defraud him, the said S. S.[2]

[1] Higler v. P., 44 Mich. 299. For a similar form, see S. v. Call, 48 N. H. 126.

[2] This follows a form found in S. v. Joaquin, 43 Ia. 131, with additional averments as to delivery held necessary in S. v. McGinnis, 71 Ia. 685.

§ **712. Restitution.**— The English practice as to restitution of the property in cases of larceny is not applicable, it seems, in prosecutions for obtaining money by false pretenses.[1] But there is a special English statute on the subject, and under this the court may order a restitution of the proceeds as well as of the property itself, provided the proceeds are still in the hands of defendant or his agent.[2] And it has even been held that under this statute the property may be restored although it has passed into the hands of an innocent purchaser.[3]

[1] Parker v. Patrick, 5 T. R. 175; Rex v. Devaux, 2 East, P. C. 789; 2 Bish. Cr. Pr. 198.

[2] Reg. v. Justices, 17 Q. B. D. 598; S. C., 18 Q. B. D. 314.

[3] Bentley v. Vilmont, 12 App. Cas. 471, overruling Moyce v. Newington, 4 Q. B. D. 32. And see Cundy v. Lindsay, 1 Q. B. D. 348; S. C., 2 Q. B. D. 96, and 3 App. Cas. 459.

CHAPTER 29.

RECEIVING STOLEN GOODS.

§ 713. Nature of the offense.—While one who knowingly receives stolen goods, or assists in concealing them for the purpose of aiding the thief to escape, would be at common law an accessory after the fact to the larceny,[1] statutes have been passed both in England and the various states of this Union making the act of knowingly buying, receiving or concealing stolen goods a substantive offense, and perhaps such statutes have superseded the common law, so that the receiver is not under any circumstances an accessory after the fact, and is only punishable by statute.[2] In early cases in this country the courts seem to have regarded these statutes as partial substitutes only for the common law, and to have held that, wherever the crime is not specifically described in such way as to make it a substantive offense under the statute, the common-law doctrine, that the accessory could only be convicted after conviction of the principal, is applicable;[3] but under the statutes making the receiver punishable as principal or for a substantive offense, it is wholly immaterial whether the thief has been tried and convicted or not.[4] The receiver is therefore indictable as for an independent crime, and not for the larceny,[5] and if the evidence shows him guilty of larceny,

1 Licette v. S., 75 Ga. 253. And see *supra*, § 209.

2 S. v. Calvin, 22 N. J. 207; Rex v. Morris, 2 East, P. C. 748.

3 C. v. Andrews, 3 Mass. 126; Licette v. S., 75 Ga. 253; S. v. Ives, 13 Ired. 338; S. v. Groff, 1 Murph. 270; S. v. Goode, 1 Hawks, 463. As to the provisions of early statutes, see S. v. Harkness, 1 Brev. 276; S. v. Minton, Phill. 196. But even though this be the correct rule, which is doubted, the objection that the principal has not been convicted is not available in arrest of judgment: Martin v. S., 95 Ga. 478.

4 S. v. S. L., 2 Tyler, 249; Redman v. S., 1 Blackf. 429; C. v. Frye, 1 Va. Cas. 19; Smith v. C., 10 Leigh, 695; S. v. Weston, 9 Conn. 527; S. v. McAloon, 40 Me. 133; Butler v. S., 3 McCord, 383; Swaggerty v. S., 9 Yerg. 338.

5 Bieber v. S., 45 Ga. 569; S. v. Hodges, 55 Md. 127; Brown v. S., 15 Tex. Ap. 581; Chandler v. S., 15 Tex. Ap. 587.

he should not be convicted under the charge of receiving stolen goods;[1] though it is said that a defendant may be guilty of receiving stolen goods although he participated with another in the larceny itself.[2] But some statutes make the receiver a principal in the larceny.[3] The statutes are sometimes broad enough to cover receiving of goods procured by embezzlement[4] or false pretenses[5] as well as those stolen; but they do not cover cases of receiving goods unlawfully obtained where the crime of larceny, embezzlement or false pretenses has not been committed.[6] The crime may be committed in receiving property procured by burglary or robbery as well as that procured by simple larceny.[7]

§ 714. **What acts sufficient.**— The buying, aiding and receiving constitute but one offense, and the proof of any of these acts is sufficient under the indictment charging all of them.[8] The retaining of the goods even for a moment, or allowing them to be placed in defendant's possession, constitutes a receiving;[9] and the receiving may be by a servant if with the knowledge and consent of the defendant;[10] and so the act may be com-

[1] S. v. Honig, 78 Mo. 249; Sartorious v. S., 24 Miss. 602; Reg. v. Kelly, 2 C. & K. 379; Reg. v. Coggins, 29 L. T. 469. But if the larceny and the receiving are charged in two counts, there may be a conviction for the receiving, although the evidence also shows the larceny: Reg. v. Hilton, Bell, 20. In such case if the offenses are by statute the same in degree and in punishment, there may be a general conviction under the two counts without an election between them: S. v. Speight, 69 N. C. 72; Campbell v. P., 109 Ill. 565. *Contra*, S. v. Larkin, 49 N. H. 39.

[2] Jenkins v. S., 62 Wis. 49.

[3] S. v. Ward, 49 Conn. 429; Price v. C., 21 Grat. 846.

[4] C. v. Leonard, 140 Mass. 473; Reg. v. Frampton, Dears. & B. 585. *Contra*, Leal v. S., 12 Tex. Ap. 279.

[5] Taylor v. Reg., 1 Q. B. D. (1895) 25.

[6] Reg. v. Wilson, 2 Moody, 52.

[7] S. v. Turner, 19 Ia. 144; S. v. Lane, 68 Ia. 384. The early South Carolina statute covered only goods taken in burglary or house-breaking: S. v. Sanford, 1 Nott & M. 512.

[8] Stevens v. C., 6 Met. 241; S. v. Nelson, 29 Me. 329; Huggins v. S., 41 Ala. 393.

[9] S. v. Scovel, 1 Mill, Const. 274; Leonardo v. T., 1 N. M. 291. One who acts as agent as between the thief and the owner for the purpose of restoring the goods and sharing in the part retained as a reward for the return of the property is a receiver: P. v. Wiley, 3 Hill (N. Y.), 195. As to sufficiency of the evidence in particular cases, see U. S. v. Montgomery, 3 Sawyer, 544; S. v. St. Clair, 17 Ia. 149.

[10] Reg. v. Parr, 2 M. & Rob. 346; Reg. v. Rogers, 37 L. J. M. C. 83. In such cases the servant, knowing the goods to be stolen, is also guilty of the crime: Cassels v. S., 4 Yerg. 149; Wright v. S., 5 Yerg. 154.

mitted jointly;[1] but when persons are jointly charged, a joint receipt must be proven.[2] It is not necessary that the goods come into the manual possession of the defendant, but if they are by his direction delivered to and disposed of by a servant, that is sufficient;[3] so if they come within the possession of defendant's wife with defendant's consent, it will constitute a receiving by him;[4] but a subsequent adoption by the husband of the wife's act will not render him guilty of a joint receiving.[5] The husband may be guilty in receiving property which his wife has voluntarily and without any constraint on his part obtained by larceny.[6] But the wife is not punishable for receiving from the husband.[7] To show the prisoner guilty of receiving, it must appear that in some of the ways designated he actually had the goods in his possession.[8] It is not necessary that any consideration pass between the receiver and the thief.[9] To constitute a concealing it is not necessary that defendant shall have aided in the actual hiding or secreting, but any act tending to assist the thief in converting the property to his own use and keeping it from the observation of the owner is sufficient.[10] An act done in order to hinder identification of the article stolen is sufficient,[11] but merely assisting the thief by giving him breakfast and feed for stolen animals, knowing them to be stolen, does not constitute a crime. The defendant must have assisted in hiding the property in order to elude pursuit or avoid discovery in order to make him guilty.[12]

§ 715. **What goods.**— It is essential that the goods which the defendant is charged with receiving shall be shown to be stolen goods,[13] and if, by the consent or direction of the owner, the goods are delivered to the receiver, the latter will not be guilty of receiving stolen goods even though he supposes

[1] Faunce v. P., 51 Ill. 311.

[2] Rex v. Messingham, 1 Moody, 257; Reg. v. Dovey, 4 Cox, 428.

[3] Reg. v. Miller, 6 Cox, 353; Reg. v. Smith, Dears. 494; S. v. St. Clair, 17 Ia. 149.

[4] Reg. v. Woodward, L. & C. 122.

[5] Reg. v. Dring, Dears. & B. 329.

[6] Reg. v. McAthey, L. & C. 250.

[7] Reg. v. Brooks, Dears. 184.

[8] Reg. v. Hill, 2 C. & K. 978; Reg. v. Wiley, 2 Den. 37.

[9] Hopkins v. P., 12 Wend. 76.

[10] P. v. Reynolds, 2 Mich. 422.

[11] S. v. Ward, 49 Conn. 429.

[12] Upton v. S., 5 Ia. 465.

[13] See *infra*, § 724, where the question as to evidence of the fact of the theft is considered.

he is receiving them from the thief.[1] Although the property has been altered in form, the receiving will be criminal if the property be described as in the condition it was in when received.[2] Indeed, if the property is still of the same species when received as when stolen, the indictment describing it as it was when stolen will be sufficient, although there has been some alteration before its receipt.[3] Where goods taken in distinct larcenies are received at one time, there is but one offense of receiving.[4] It has been said that under statutes providing for the punishment of the receiver of stolen goods and chattels there cannot be a conviction for receiving money or bank-bills;[5] and the same doctrine has been extended by the English judges to the receiver of stolen promissory notes on the theory that although by statute the stealing of promissory notes is made larceny, yet if the statute with reference to receiving stolen goods does not specifically include promissory notes, it cannot be enlarged to cover property not within the original meaning of those terms.[6] A contrary doctrine, however, was recognized by the judges a few years after in Ireland,[7] and has been followed in this country.[8]

§ **716. Guilty knowledge.**— The knowledge that the property has been stolen is an essential element in the offense of receiving or concealing such property,[9] and the burden is on the prosecution to show such knowledge, and not on the defendant

[1] Reg. v. Villensky, 2 Q. B. D. (1892) 597; Reg. v. Schmidt, L. R. 1 C. C. 15; Reg. v. Dolan, Dears. 436; Reg. v. Hancock, 38 L. T. 787.

[2] For instance, if the theft was of a live animal, and the receiving was of the flesh in the form of pork or mutton: Rex v. Cowell, 2 East, P. C. 617; Sands v. S., 30 Tex. Ap. 578. And see Reg. v. Robinson, 4 F. & F. 43.

[3] C. v. White, 123 Mass. 430.

[4] S. v. Nelson, 29 Me. 329. This would be otherwise under the charge of being accessory after the fact to the larcenies, in which case there would be a distinct offense as to each larceny: C. v. Andrews, 2 Mass. 409.

[5] S. v. Calvin, 22 N. J. 207; Rutherford v. C., 2 Va. Cas. 141; Rex v. Morris, 2 East, P. C. 748.

[6] Rex v. Gaze, Russ. & Ry. 384. But where stamped bank-notes had been retired and were being held for re-issue, an indictment for receiving them as stamped paper was supported: Rex v. Vyse, 1 Moody, 218.

[7] Rex v. Crone, Jebb, 47.

[8] Hall v. S., 3 Ohio St. 575. And see a discussion of the same question under larceny, *supra*, § 543.

[9] O'Connell v. S., 55 Ga. 191; S. v. Caveness, 78 N. C. 484; Wilson v. S., 12 Tex. Ap. 481; Rex v. Kernon, 2 Russ., Cr. 562; Reg. v. Wood, 1 F. & F. 497; Reg. v. Larkin, Dears. 365.

to show the want of it.[1] But it is not necessary to prove absolute knowledge of that fact, which would often be impossible. It is sufficient to show that the property was received by defendant believing it to have been stolen, that being the fact.[2] If the circumstances are such as to induce a man of ordinary observation to believe the property to have been stolen, that is sufficient.[3] That goods were received with such belief may appear from the circumstance that defendant paid much less for them than their real value,[4] although this is open to the objection, in case of goods not new, that it is difficult to determine their real value, and that a second-hand dealer buying goods, even if new, usually pays less than the value of new goods, because, in the nature of his business, he cannot sell even new goods for their price as new goods.[5] The fact of buying the property very much below its value is not conclusive proof of guilty knowledge, but only a circumstance tending to prove it.[6] The proof of previous good character is to be considered in determining the weight of such evidence.[7] The fact that defendant received the goods clandestinely, or immediately concealed them, will tend to show guilty knowledge.[8]

§ 717. **Intent.**— There must be a felonious intent,[9] and this felonious intent consists in the purpose of depriving the owner of the property,[10] or deriving gain from receiving or concealing the goods.[11] Consequently, if the goods are received with the owner's consent,[12] or with the honest purpose of restoring them

1 Reg. v. Davis, L. R. 1 C. C. 272; Reg. v. Harwood, 11 Cox, 388. Proof that defendant had a general knowledge of the circumstances under which the goods were taken is not enough, unless it satisfies the jury that he knew that the circumstances constituted larceny: Reg. v. Adams, 1 F. & F. 86.

2 Reg. v. White, 1 F. & F. 665.

3 Frank v. S., 67 Miss. 125; Collins v. S., 33 Ala. 434; Cobb v. S., 76 Ga. 664. As to proof of guilty knowledge in case of recent possession, see *infra*, § 726.

4 Jupitz v. P., 34 Ill. 516.

5 Andrews v. P., 60 Ill. 354.

6 P. v. Levison, 16 Cal. 98.

7 Jupitz v. P., 34 Ill. 516.

8 Isaacs v. P., 118 Ill. 538; Collins v. S., 33 Ala. 434; Murio v. S., 31 Tex. Ap. 210.

9 S. v. Caveness, 78 N. C. 484; P. v. Weldon, 111 N. Y. 569.

10 Rice v. S., 3 Heisk. 215; Hurell v. S., 5 Humph. 68. If the taking is not in collusion with the thief, or is in opposition to his wishes or intentions, it will not be a criminal receiving: Reg. v. Wade, 1 C. & K. 739.

11 Aldrich v. P., 101 Ill. 16; P. v. Avila, 43 Cal. 196.

12 Dodge v. Brittain, Meigs, 84. Guilty intent will be immaterial if the goods are in fact received from the owner: *Supra*, § 715.

to the owner without deriving any pecuniary advantage therefrom,[1] there will be no crime; but if the intent is to secure a reward by returning them, the crime is committed.[2] One who receives for the mere purpose of concealment, though without intent to derive any profit, is punishable,[3] and it is no excuse that they were received out of mere friendship for the thief;[4] or simply to assist the thief in getting away with them;[5] or even for the purpose of saving defendant himself from loss.[6] While the intent is material, it may be inferred from the guilty knowledge.[7]

§ 718. **Indictment; description of the property.**— The indictment for receiving stolen goods should describe the goods with the same accuracy as an indictment for larceny.[8] The general discussion of this subject under the head of larceny is pertinent in this connection.[9] A description of stolen money received which is not sufficient under the requirements as to an indictment for larceny will not be sufficient in the indictment for receiving.[10] The description of the stolen property by alleging the ownership thereof is subject to the same rules as in larceny,[11] and one from whom the property is wrongfully taken may be named as owner, although he is not the rightful owner.[12]

§ 719. **Description of the larceny.**— The indictment for receiving or concealing alone (not charging the larceny as a substantive offense) need not describe the stealing of the goods with the same technicality as would be necessary in an indictment for such larceny. It is sufficient to allege that the goods

1 Aldrich v. P., 101 Ill. 16.

2 S. v. Pardee, 37 Ohio St. 63; Baker v. S., 58 Ark. 513. That taking with intent to secure a reward for returning is larceny, see *supra*, § 567.

3 Rex v. Richardson, 6 C. & P. 335.

4 C. v. Bean, 117 Mass. 141.

5 S. v. Rushing, 69 N. C. 29.

6 Campbell v. P., 109 Ill. 565.

7 S. v. Turner, 19 Ia. 144; S. v. Lane, 68 Ia. 384; S. v. Smith, 88 Ia. 1.

8 Williams v. P., 101 Ill. 382. As to how the goods are to be described when they have been altered in form between the larceny and the receiving thereof, see *supra*, § 715.

9 See *supra*, § 592 *et seq.*

10 Baggett v. S., 69 Miss. 625; Burney v. S., 87 Ala. 80.

11 S. v. Tiedeman, 4 Strobh. 300; P. v. Ribolsi, 89 Cal. 492; O'Connell v. S., 55 Ga. 296. If property is alleged to be that of a corporation, proof of a *de facto* corporation is sufficient: Butler v. S., 35 Fla. 246.

12 C. v. Finn, 108 Mass. 466. And see *supra*, § 546. So ownership may be laid in the agent in possession when stolen: Arcia v. S., 28 Tex. Ap. 198.

were "then lately before stolen," and that the defendant knew them to have been stolen, without alleging technically the stealing, taking and carrying away.[1] Nor is it necessary to allege by whom the theft of the goods was committed, or that the name of the person committing the theft is unknown.[2] It seems that it is not necessary even to allege from whom the goods were received.[3] Neither is it required that the indictment state when and where the original larceny was committed.[4]

§ 720. **Jurisdiction and venue.**— It has been held in England that if the goods were stolen outside of the kingdom there could not be a guilty receiving of them in the kingdom.[5] In this country it has been held that it is immaterial that the goods were stolen outside of the state,[6] and there is sometimes a statutory provision to that effect.[7] The venue of the offense, if deemed a substantive one, is in the county where the goods are received;[8] but if it is accessorial in its

[1] C. v. Lakeman, 5 Gray, 82; S. v. McAloon, 40 Me. 133. And see Brothers v. S., 22 Tex. Ap. 447. Where the charge is of receiving goods obtained by false pretenses, it is not necessary to set out the false pretenses: Taylor v. Reg., 1 Q. B. D. (1895) 25.

[2] C. v. Slate, 11 Gray, 60; S. v. Hazard, 2 R. I. 474; Shriedly v. S., 23 Ohio St. 130; P. v. Ribolsi, 89 Cal. 492; S. v. Smith, 37 Mo. 58; Swaggerty v. S., 9 Yerg. 338; Hester v. S., 103 Ala. 83; P. v. Caswell, 21 Wend. 86; Rex v. Jervis, 6 C. & P. 156; Rex v. Thomas, 2 East, P. C. 605. It is said, however, that if the name of the thief be alleged it must be proven as laid: C. v. King, 9 Cush. 284; Rex v. Woolford, 1 M. & Rob. 384. *Contra*, P. v. Caswell, 21 Wend. 86. The fact that, in a separate indictment for the larceny, a different person is named as thief than the one named in the indictment for the receiving will be immaterial: C. v. Hill, 11 Cush. 137.

[3] Levi v. S., 14 Neb. 1; S. v. Moultree, 34 La. An. 489; Huggins v. S., 41 Ala. 393; 2 Bishop, Cr. Pr., § 983; Arch. Cr. Pr. & Pl. 474. *Contra*, S. v. Beatty, Phill. 52; S. v. Ives, 13 Ired. 338; U. S. v. De Bare, 6 Biss. 358. But where it was alleged that such person was unknown, whereas the fact was otherwise, there was held to be a fatal variance: Sault v. P., 3 Colo. Ap. 502.

[4] C. v. Sullivan, 136 Mass. 170; P. v. Goldberg, 39 Mich. 545; P. v. Smith, 94 Mich. 644; S. v. Crawford, 39 S. C. 343; Holford v. S., 2 Blackf. 103. The allegation that the goods were feloniously received sufficiently indicates that they were received from the thief: Kaufman v. S., 49 Ind. 248.

[5] Reg. v. De Bruiel, 11 Cox, 207.

[6] Holford v. S., 2 Blackf. 103; C. v. White, 123 Mass. 430.

[7] P. v. Goldberg, 39 Mich. 545.

[8] Campbell v. P., 109 Ill. 565; Roach v. S., 5 Coldw. 39; Licette v. S., 75 Ga. 253. One who receives under an arrangement that the goods shall be stolen in another county and shipped to him is triable in the county where

character by the statute, the venue is where the goods were stolen.[1]

§ 721. **Allegation of intent and knowledge.**— The necessity of knowledge and intent being alleged and proven has been sufficiently discussed in a preceding section.[2] As the substantive offense is statutory, the method of alleging the intent will depend somewhat on the language of the statute.[3] It is not necessary to allege that the felonious receiving was with intent to defraud the owner or any person,[4] and an allegation that defendant received the property well knowing that the same had been feloniously stolen, etc., is sufficient to charge knowledge.[5]

§ 722. **Joinder.**— Where the offense is considered an accessorial one, the offense of receiving may be charged, together with that of the larceny, in one count;[6] but even where the receiving is regarded as a substantive offense, it may be charged in an additional count of the indictment charging the larceny;[7] and under such an indictment, of which one count charges one defendant with larceny, and another charges a different defendant with receiving, there may be a conviction of the receiver without conviction of the person charged with the theft.[8] But it is said that if the transaction is so described in the indictment that the failure to prove the larceny shows that the goods received by the defendant charged with receiving were not stolen goods, then he should be acquitted also.[9] Where two are charged jointly with receiving, there may be a conviction of one alone;[10] but to warrant a conviction of two for joint re-

they are thus shipped: S. v. Habib, 18 R. I. 558.

[1] S. v. Ward, 49 Conn. 429.

[2] See *supra*, §§ 716, 717.

[3] P. v. Weldon, 111 N. Y. 569; S. v. Moultrie, 34 La. An. 489. Where "not having the intent to restore" is a part of the statutory definition, such intent must be negatived: Sellers v. S., 49 Ala. 357.

[4] S. v. Hartleb, 35 La. An. 1180. And further as to the requisite intent with reference to the owner, see *supra*, § 717.

[5] Huggins v. S., 41 Ala. 393.

[6] C. v. Adams, 7 Gray, 43. And if the count is not sufficient to charge the larceny it will not support a conviction for receiving: Ibid.

[7] S. v. Hazard, 2 R. I. 474; S. v. Laque, 37 La. An. 853; Reg. v. Reardon, L. R. 1 C. C. 31. And further, see a discussion of the same subject in connection with indictment for larceny, *supra*, § 609.

[8] C. v. Slate, 11 Gray, 60.

[9] C. v. King, 9 Cush. 284; C. v. Adams, 9 Gray, 43; S. v. Antoine, 42 La. An. 945.

[10] C. v. Slate, 11 Gray, 60; S. v. Smith, 37 Mo. 58.

ceiving, it must appear that the receiving was actually joint, and not by one from the other.[1] The same defendant may be charged in two counts with larceny and with receiving, but the count for receiving must be sufficient in itself;[2] and on such indictment a verdict of receiving, etc., is good as a general verdict on the second count.[3] Indeed, it is said that where the punishment for the theft and the receiving are the same, a general verdict on such indictment, not specifying which offense the conviction is for, will be sustained.[4]

§ 723. **Finding of value.**— Where the degree of punishment for the receiving is dependent upon the value of the goods received, the value must be alleged and proven just as in larceny,[5] but if by statute there is no division of the offense into degrees dependent upon the value of the goods, it is not necessary to allege nor find the value;[6] and in the latter case it is, of course, immaterial whether the evidence shows the receiving of all the goods charged to have been received or not.[7] Where the value is important, the values of goods received at several times in pursuance of one general plan may be aggregated.[8]

§ 724. **Evidence.**— Proof of the larceny of the goods alleged to have been received is essential to establish the *corpus delicti* of the crime of receiving, and therefore cannot be established by the uncorroborated confession of the accused.[9] Such larceny is to be established as if it was the crime charged.[10] The

[1] Rex v. Messingham, 1 Moody, 257; Reg. v. Dovey, 2 Den. 92.

[2] S. v. Phelps, 65 N. C. 451.

[3] Oxford v. S., 33 Ala. 416.

[4] Campbell v. P., 109 Ill. 565; S. v. Speight, 69 N. C. 72. *Contra*, S. v. Larkin, 49 N. H. 39.

[5] Sawyer v. P., 8 Ill. 53; Tobin v. P., 104 Ill. 565; Thompson v. P., 125 Ill. 256.

[6] Engster v. S., 11 Neb. 539; Sands v. S., 30 Tex. Ap. 578; P. v. Rice, 73 Cal. 220; P. v. Fitzpatrick, 80 Cal. 538.

[7] P. v. Fitzpatrick, 80 Cal. 538; C. v. Johnson, 133 Pa. St. 293.

[8] Levi v. S., 14 Neb. 1.

[9] Williams v. P., 101 Ill. 382.

[10] Reg. v. Blick, 4 C. & P. 377. Thus, admissions of guilt by the thief while in custody, made in the presence of the receiver, are evidence against the receiver: Reg. v. Cox, 1 F. & F. 90; and it is said that such a confession, though not made in the presence of the receiver, is admissible, there being nothing in it which charges the offense upon the receiver: S. v. Smith, 37 Mo. 58; Reilley v. S., 14 Ind. 217. But this is doubtful, and it has been decided, on the other hand, that the record of the conviction of the principal thief on his plea of guilty is not admissible as against the receiver: C. v. Elisha, 3 Gray, 460. Parol evidence of the trial and conviction of the principal thief will be sufficient unless objection is made

thief is a competent witness on behalf of the state as against the receiver,[1] but there should not be a conviction unless his evidence is corroborated.[2]

§ 725. **Recent possession.**— The recent possession of property stolen is evidence tending to show the guilty receipt of such property.[3] In view of what has been said under the head of larceny with reference to the finding of recently stolen goods in defendant's possession,[4] it is evident that such recent possession is evidence of the substantive crime of the guilty receipt only where the circumstances indicate that defendant was not the thief.[5] The rule that defective or insufficient explanations as to how the goods came into defendant's possession will not remove the inference of guilt derived therefrom is the same as in larceny.[6]

§ 726. **Guilty knowledge.**— The evidence of recent possession will warrant conviction for guilty receiving only where it appears also that defendant had knowledge that the goods had been stolen.[7] As bearing on the question of such knowledge, evidence of what was said by the party from whom the goods were received at the time of their receipt is admissible, and also any arrangement or understanding under which they

that it is not the best evidence: Martin v. S., 95 Ga. 478. Of course conversations between defendant and the thief before the commission of the offense relating to the proposed receiving may be shown: C. v. Jenkins, 10 Gray, 485.

[1] S. v. Coppenburg, 2 Strobh. 273.

[2] Reg. v. Robinson, 4 F. & F. 43. The mere fact of the finding of the goods on the prisoner's premises is not a sufficient corroboration in such case: Reg. v. Pratt, 4 F. & F. 315.

[3] Comfort v. P., 54 Ill. 404; Sahlinger v. P., 102 Ill. 241; Jenkins v. S., 62 Wis. 49; Boston & W. R. Co. v. Dana, 1 Gray, 83, 102; S. v. Grebe, 17 Kan. 458. So the fact that defendant produces or secures the return of stolen property tends to show his connection with the receiving: Reg. v. Hobson, Dears. 400. Circumstances showing that acts connected with the wrongful taking of the property were done on defendant's premises will tend to show a guilty receiving: C. v. Slate, 11 Gray, 60. If the defendant admits having bought the article which is found in his house, this constitutes evidence of the receipt without other evidence of possession by him: Reg. v. Matthews, 1 Den. 596.

[4] See *supra*, § 616.

[5] Sartorious v. S., 24 Miss. 602; Reg. v. Langmead, L. & C. 427.

[6] P. v. Harris, 93 Mich. 617; S. v. Mayer, 45 Ia. 698; Adams v. S., 52 Ala. 379. And as to the whole subject of the effect of recent possession, see the discussion under the head of larceny, *supra*, §§ 616–620.

[7] Tolliver v. S., 25 Tex. Ap. 600; Rex v. Densley, 6 C. & P. 399. Further as to knowledge, see *supra*, § 716.

were received.[1] As tending to show knowledge that the goods had been stolen, evidence of the previous receipt of other stolen goods with guilty knowledge is admissible.[2] In England it has been doubted whether the mere fact that defendant had previously received other stolen goods, without evidence that as to such other goods he had knowledge of their character, is admissible to show guilty knowledge in the receiving of the goods in question;[3] but a statute makes the finding of other stolen property in the possession of the person charged admissible in evidence.[4] So in this country it has been held that the mere fact of the previous receipt of stolen property, without evidence of guilty knowledge as to such property, does not raise the presumption of guilty knowledge in regard to the property in question,[5] and of course the subsequent receipt of stolen property does not tend to show guilty knowledge in the previous receiving.[6] Recent possession is corroborative evidence of the testimony of an accomplice with reference to the receiving with knowledge, whether the accomplice testifies to such possession or not.[7] Proof that the alleged thief had previously stolen other goods of the same kind is not admissible for any purpose under a prosecution for the illegal receiving.[8] Of course, whatever has been said about previous receipt of stolen goods is equally applicable to the receipt of other stolen goods at the same time as the goods in question.[9]

§ 727. Forms of indictment.—It is common to charge the receiving in the same indictment with a charge of larceny, either in a separate count or in the same count;[10] but it is not necessary to repeat here the count or portion of a count charging the larceny, the forms already given for that purpose being available here.[11]

[1] Durant v. P., 13 Mich. 351.

[2] Copperman v. P., 56 N. Y. 591; Shriedley v. S., 23 Ohio St. 130, 142; Devoto v. C., 3 Met. (Ky.) 142; S. v. Ditton, 48 Ia. 677; S. v. Habib, 18 R. I. 558; Reg. v. Nicholls, 1 F. & F. 51; Rex v. Dunn, 1 Moody, 146.

[3] Reg. v. Oddy, 2 Den. 264.

[4] But this statute does not extend to proof of the previous possession of stolen property: Reg. v. Carter, 12 Q. B. D. 522; Reg. v. Drage, 14 Cox, 83.

[5] S. v. Bulla, 89 Mo. 595.

[6] P. v. Willard, 92 Cal. 482.

[7] C. v. Savory, 10 Cush. 535.

[8] McIntire v. S., 10 Ind. 26.

[9] S. v. Jacob, 30 S. C. 131; Harwell v. S., 22 Tex. Ap. 251.

[10] C. v. Adams, 7 Gray, 43.

[11] For forms of indictment for larceny, see *supra*, § 610.

GENERAL FORM.

That A. B., on ——, in the county aforesaid, feloniously did receive, have and conceal [description of the property], of the goods and chattels of C. D., then lately before stolen, taken and carried away by a certain evil-disposed person; he, the said A. B., then well knowing the said goods and chattels to have been feloniously stolen.[1]

LARCENY AND RECEIVING JOINED.

That A. B., in the county of ——, on ——, three sleigh shaws of the goods and chattels of one T. G., and all of the value of thirty-seven dollars, then and there in the possession of said T. G. being found, feloniously did steal, take and carry away, against, etc. . . . And the jurors aforesaid, etc. . . . that C. D., in said county, afterwards, to wit, on the same day, the said goods and chattels of said T. G. aforesaid, so as aforesaid feloniously stolen, taken and carried away, feloniously did receive and have and did then and there aid in concealing the same; he, the said C. D., then and there well knowing the said goods and chattels to have been feloniously stolen, taken and carried away, against, etc.[2]

[1] See Archbold, Cr. Pr. & Pl. 474; C. v. Adams, 7 Gray, 43. "Feloniously stolen" as here employed is sufficient without saying also "taken and carried away:" C. v. Lakeman, 5 Gray, 82.

[2] See the form given in S. v. McAloon, 40 Me. 133; with a change in the second count as to the ownership of the property for the purpose of obviating the objection made to the indictment in that case.

CHAPTER 30.

OBTAINING PROPERTY BY THREATS; BLACKMAIL.

§ 728. **What constitutes.**— Elsewhere the offense of taking property from the presence of another by putting in fear is discussed under the head of robbery.[1] There is also a discussion elsewhere of the offense of extorting money by officers.[2] In each of these cases is present the element of securing property by some sort of fear, or, as is popularly said, by extortion. But the term "extortion" has been appropriated to the case of wrongfully obtaining property by an officer acting in some sort of assumed official capacity, and it cannot properly be used otherwise.[3] It has been suggested that obtaining money by threats such as would overcome the ordinary free will of a firm man might be punished at common law;[4] but in general the offense is regarded as statutory only. Statutes now universally recognize, however, as a crime the obtaining of money or property from another by threats of injury to the person, property or character. The offenses which are thus grouped together are statutory entirely, and it is necessary to consult the statutes of the various states in order to determine what constitutes the crime in any particular case. There are, however, certain well marked statutory forms which may be considered under general headings.

§ 729. **Sending threatening letters.**— The earliest English statutes on the subject (9 Geo. 1, ch. 22; amended by 27 Geo. 2, ch. 15) relate to the sending of anonymous threatening letters demanding money or property.[5] The usual statutes in regard

[1] See *supra*, § 468.

[2] See *infra*, § 914.

[3] 4 Bl. Com. 141; 2 Bishop, Cr. Law, 390. But statutes sometimes use the term "extortion" in the popular sense, and extend the crime to cover the obtaining of property by threats: P. v. Tonielli, 81 Cal. 275; P. v. Hughes, 137 N. Y 29. See, also, as giving this broader meaning to the term "extortion:" C. v. O'Brien, 12 Cush. 84, 90.

[4] Rex v. Southerton, 6 East, 126; 2 Russ. Cr. 706.

[5] 4 Bl. Com. 144; Rex v. Robinson, 2 East, P. C. 1110. A letter may be anonymous though from its contents the writer might be discovered: Rex

to threatening letters do not make it important that the writer conceals his identity, and it is generally criminal to send a letter maliciously threatening to do injury to the person or business of another with the intent to compel the person so threatened to do an act against his will.[1]

§ 730. Threats for the purpose of extortion.—A leading English statute (7 & 8 Geo. 4, ch. 29, sec. 8) makes it criminal to send a letter demanding, with menaces and without reasonable and probable cause, any money or property or threatening to accuse of crime.[2] A later English statute (24 & 25 Vict., ch. 96, sec. 45) is similar in its terms, making it an offense to demand money with menaces. Under this statute it is held that a threat to accuse of misconduct not amounting to a criminal offense might be sufficient;[3] and it is held to be a sufficient menace to threaten to expose infamous conduct on the part of a clergyman;[4] or to threaten to charge another with adultery.[5] So it is within the statute to threaten to accuse another of an abominable offense.[6] So a threat to set fire to property may be sufficient.[7] But the menace must be such as to produce in a reasonable mind some degree of alarm or bodily fear, and such alarm must be of such nature and extent as to unsettle the mind upon which it operates and take away that free, voluntary action which constitutes consent.[8] But this question is to be determined by the nature of the threat and not by the condition of the nerves of the party to whom it is addressed.[9] The menaces need not be of injury to the party

v. Wagstaff, Russ. & Ry. 398; but not if it plainly appears that the writer intended that it should be known by whom the letter was written: Rex v. Heming, 2 East, P. C. 1116. Whether or not the letter is a threatening one lies with the jury: Reg. v. Carruthers, 1 Cox, 138.

[1] S. v. Compton, 77 Wis. 460.

[2] Rex v. Pickford, 4 C. & P. 227; Rex v. Robinson, 2 M. & Rob. 14; Rex v. Edwards, 6 C. & P. 515.

[3] Reg. v. Tomlinson, 1 Q. B. D. (1895), 706.

[4] Reg. v. Miard, 1 Cox, 22.

[5] Reg. v. Chalmers, 16 L. T. 363.

[6] Reg. v. Redman, L. R. 1 C. C. 12; Reg. v. Cooper, 3 Cox, 547. To obtain money or property from a person by threatening to accuse of this crime is, in England, held to be robbery: See *supra*, § 470. But to threaten to charge with making overtures towards the commission of such offense is not sufficient: Rex v. Hickman, 1 Moody, 34; Reg. v. Middleditch, 1 Den. 92. And see Reg. v. Norton, 8 C. & P. 671.

[7] Reg. v. Taylor, 1 F. & F. 511.

[8] Reg. v. Walton, L. & C. 288. And see Rex v. Southerton, 6 East, 126.

[9] Reg. v. Smith, 1 Den. 510.

making them. If he seeks to secure money for preventing pretended injury threatened by another, he is also guilty.[1]

§ 731. **American statutes.**— In this country the statutes are usually broad enough in their terms to cover either written or oral threats, and to include the obtaining or attempting to obtain money or property or anything of value, or even the inducing of another to do any act against his will, by means of threatening prosecution or injury to the person, property or reputation.[2]

§ 732. **The threat.**— Although the modern statutes provide for the punishment of oral as well as written threats, it is essential that some threat be made, and it has been held that it is not sufficient if by gestures or signs, where the statute requires that it be verbal or in writing;[3] but it is not necessary that a letter be in the form of a threat if by its terms it fairly conveys that meaning.[4] Under most statutes it is the threatening which is material, and it is not essential to the crime that any money be actually extorted or advantage gained by means of the threat;[5] nor is it material whether the threat is with reference to something to be done by the accused or by another.[6]

§ 733. **Must be communicated.**— The threat must be made directly to, or in the presence of, the person against whom it is directed, or indirectly to him through another. If made to such third person without any purpose of having it communicated, it will not be criminal though it may be actually communicated to him.[7] If the charge is of sending threatening letters, it must appear that such letters were sent;[8] but the sending is completed when the letter is put in course of transmission by a method likely to result in its being received by

[1] Reg. v. Smith, 1 Den. 510; Reg. v. Yates, 6 Cox, 441.

[2] Elliott v. S., 36 Ohio St. 318; S. v. Ullman, 5 Minn. 13; Robinson v. C., 101 Mass. 27; Motsinger v. S., 123 Ind. 498; P. v. Tonielli, 81 Cal. 275; S. v. Morgan, 3 Heisk. 262; S. v. Young, 26 Ia. 122; S. v. Lewis, — Ia. —, 65 N. W. R. 295; S. v. Compton, 77 Wis. 460. In Texas it is within the statute to extort money, etc., by threatening to do any illegal act: Williams v. S., 13 Tex. Ap. 285.

[3] Robinson v. C., 101 Mass. 27.

[4] P. v. Thompson, 97 N. Y. 313.

[5] S. v. Bruce, 24 Me. 71; P. v. Tonielli, 81 Cal. 275; S. v. Young, 26 Ia. 122; S. v. Evans, 1 Houst. Cr. C. 97.

[6] P. v. Thompson, 97 N. Y. 313; S. v. Compton, 77 Wis. 460.

[7] S. v. Brownlee, 84 Ia. 473.

[8] Castle v. S., 23 Tex. Ap. 286; Landa v. S., 26 Tex. Ap. 580.

the party to whom it is intended, and it is not necessary that it be formally addressed to such party; but the indictment should allege the sending to be to the party threatened, and not to a third party employed as a medium for transmission.[1]

§ 734. The thing threatened; violence.— To compel the payment of money by threats of personal violence is criminal under all the statutes;[2] but a threat to arrest in a civil proceeding is not a threat of injury to the person.[3] It is sometimes made criminal to threaten personal violence to another. So far as such threats are in the nature of breaches of the peace, they are considered hereafter;[4] so far as they constitute assaults, they have already been considered.[5]

§ 735. Injury to business.— The statutes usually cover the case of a threat to unlawfully injure the business of another, as by threat of a boycott.[6]

§ 736. Injury to character.— The statutes cover also any threat to accuse another of an act which would bring him into disgrace or contempt.[7] It is not necessary that the matter threatened to be published be libelous.[8] Of course, a threat to accuse of a crime would therefore be within the statutes, and it is immaterial whether the threatened accusation be of a felony or a misdemeanor.[9]

§ 737. Threat to prosecute.— A threat of a legal prosecution is within the statutes, provided it is made for the purpose of compelling the person threatened to pay money; for, while it is to the public interest that crime should be prosecuted, it is directly contrary to such interest that the process of law shall be taken advantage of for private ends of gain or malice;

[1] Rex v. Wagstaff, Russ. & Ry. 398; Reg. v. Grimwade, 1 C. & K. 592; Rex v. Paddle, Russ. & Ry. 484; Reg. v. Williams, 1 Cox, 16; Reg. v. Jones, 2 C. & K. 398; Reg. v. Jones, 2 Cox, 434; Reg. v. Jones, 5 Cox, 226. Merely to show a letter to another which threatens to accuse him of a crime is not sufficient: Rex v. Mayor, 2 East, P. C. 1118. The carrier of such a letter, though privy to its contents, is not punishable as sender: Rex v. Hammond, 2 East, P. C. 1119. If the address is not accurate, the question whether the letter was intended for the one receiving it is for the jury: Reg. v. Carruthers, 1 Cox, 138.

[2] S. v. Hollyway, 41 Ia. 200; Reg. v. Murphy, 6 Cox, 340.

[3] C. v. Mosby, 163 Mass. 291.

[4] *Infra*, § 1017.

[5] *Supra*, ch. 17.

[6] P. v. Hughes, 137 N. Y. 29.

[7] Motsinger v. S., 123 Ind. 498, 8 Am. Cr. R. 110, and note; Kistler v. S., 54 Ind. 400; P. v. Tonielli, 81 Cal. 275.

[8] Reg. v. Coghlan, 4 F. & F. 316.

[9] S. v. Linthicum, 68 Mo. 66.

therefore it is immaterial whether the person threatened has been guilty of the crime with which it is proposed to charge him.[1] To threaten to accuse of a crime includes the threat to put in motion any preliminary means necessary to cause the prosecution of such crime;[2] and to threaten that a criminal prosecution will be commenced by another, in which the person making the threat will testify as a witness, is sufficient.[3] Where the threat is of a prosecution for a crime, it is immaterial whether the crime threatened is one involving disgrace.[4] In an early English case it was held that to threaten a proceeding to recover penalties for violation of the Stamp Act was criminal;[5] but to say to the maker of a note that he is liable for violating the revenue act by failing to stamp it and requesting payment of the note has been held not a threat to extort money.[6]

§ 738. **The advantage obtained.**— The intention, under the statutes, must be to extort money or some pecuniary advantage. The right to prosecute an appeal is property, so that a threat made to induce the dismissal of an appeal is a threat to extort property from another.[7] Many of the statutes, as already indicated,[8] make it criminal to threaten with intent to compel another to do an act against his will. Thus, it is criminal to threaten with a prosecution with intent to procure the signature of the person threatened to a deed against his will.[9] The act thus contemplated, however, is something not indifferent in itself, but of pecuniary loss or advantage to another.[10] But it is not necessary that the object sought to be obtained be a pecuniary advantage.[11]

[1] P. v. Whittemore, 102 Mich. 519; C. v. Buckley, 148 Mass. 27; Elliott v. S., 36 Ohio St. 318; S. v. Goodwin, 37 La. An. 713; S. v. Vaughan, 1 Bay, 282; Reg. v. Cracknell, 10 Cox, 408; Reg. v. Robertson, L. & C. 483; Rex v. Gardner, 1 C. & P. 479. The truth of the charge may be material in determining whether the intention of accusation was to extort money or merely to compound a felony: Reg. v. Richards, 11 Cox, 43.

[2] C. v. Murphy, 12 Allen, 449.

[3] P. v. Braman, 30 Mich. 460. But on this point the court was equally divided.

[4] Elliott v. S., 36 Ohio St. 318.

[5] Rex v. Southerton, 6 East, 126.

[6] Brabham v. S., 18 Ohio St. 485.

[7] P. v. Cadman, 57 Cal. 562. Under the English statutes it was a crime by menaces and threats to obtain valuable securities, and an obligation to pay might be a valuable security, though not in form a promissory note: Reg. v. John, 13 Cox, 100.

[8] *Supra*, § 731.

[9] P. v. Whittemore, 102 Mich. 519.

[10] S. v. Ullman, 5 Minn. 213.

[11] S. v. Young, 26 Ia. 122.

§ **739. Venue.**— Where the threats are made by letter the prosecution may be in the county where it is delivered in the course of the mail to the party threatened.[1] This was decided in the cases just cited, with reference to an offense under an English statute of sending threatening letters. Under the usual statutory provisions as to obtaining money by threat, etc., the venue would of course be where the threats were made and the property obtained.

§ **740. The indictment.**— It is sufficient to charge the offense with certainty to a common intent without alleging the particulars.[2] But it is not enough to merely aver that defendant threatened to accuse another of a crime.[3] If the offense to be charged consists in sending a threatening letter, the letter should be set out.[4] But it seems that where the statutory offense is that of threatening either verbally or in writing, it is not necessary to set out the writing by its tenor although the offense is charged to have been committed by means of a threatening letter.[5] Where the threats are verbal it is sufficient to set them forth in substance or effect.[6] It is not necessary to set out accurately the words used, nor to describe the offense threatened to be charged with the particularity which would be necessary in a prosecution for such offense.[7] If the threat is by letter which is set out and in unambiguous terms, it is for the court to say whether it constitutes a threat; but if the language is ambiguous it may be explained by extrinsic evidence, the question as to the meaning being for the jury.[8] It is not necessary to set out the explanatory facts which will give a criminal meaning to the letter, but they may be shown under an innuendo attributing to the terms of the letter the general meaning claimed for it.[9] The words used by defendant are not conclusive, but

[1] Rex v. Esser, 2 East, P. C. 1125; Rex v. Girdwood, 2 East, P. C. 1120.

[2] Elliott v. S., 36 Ohio St. 318.

[3] S. v. Robinson, 85 Me. 195.

[4] Rex v. Lloyd, 2 East, P. C. 1122.

[5] S. v. Stewart, 90 Mo. 507; S. v. Lewis, — Ia. —, 65 N. W. R. 295.

[6] C. v. Moulton, 108 Mass. 307; S. v. O'Mally, 48 Ia. 501.

[7] C. v. Goodwin, 122 Mass. 19; C. v. Philpot, 130 Mass. 59; C. v. Dorus, 108 Mass. 488; C. v. Carpenter, 108 Mass. 15; C. v. Bacon, 135 Mass. 521.

[8] S. v. Harper, 94 N. C. 936; S. v. Patterson, 68 Me. 473; Motsinger v. S., 123 Ind. 498; Reg. v. Smith, 2 C. & K. 882; Rex v. Boucher, 4 C. & P. 562; Rex v. Pickford, 4 C. & P. 227; Rex v. Tucker, 1 Moody, 134; Reg. v. Kain, 8 C. & P. 187.

[9] P. v. Tonielli, 81 Cal. 275; P. v. Choynski, 95 Cal. 640; S. v. Linthicum, 68 Mo. 66.

the intent to be conveyed may be shown by the circumstances.[1] In general, an indictment must show what injury was threatened or what criminal offense was threatened to be charged. The allegation of vague and indefinite threats is not sufficient.[2] And the allegations must be proved as made; thus, if the charge is of extortion by threats of criminal prosecution before a certain justice, evidence of threats to prosecute before another justice will not be admissible.[3] The indictment must show also by whom the unlawful demand was made and who was threatened.[4] The indictment may follow the statute and allege conjunctively the general forms in which, by the statute, the offense may be committed.[5] But it is not proper to charge separate acts of threatening in the same indictment.[6] If the statute requires that the act shall be done knowingly, it is not sufficient to charge that it was unlawfully done.[7]

§ 741. **Forms of indictment.**— Offenses of this character are entirely statutory, and forms which have been held sufficient under particular statutes can be looked upon only as illustrative.

THREATENING PERSONAL INJURY.

That A. B., at ——, on ——, feloniously and maliciously did threaten to shoot one G. P. then and there being, with intent then and there, by means of said threat, to compel the said G. P. to submit to his person being searched, the same being against the will of him, the said G. P.[8]

THREATENING TO ACCUSE OF CRIME.

That A. B. did at ——, on ——, maliciously and verbally threaten one H. K. to accuse said H. K. of having committed the crime of adultery with A. H., wife of N. H., with the view and with the intent to extort money from the said H. K.[9]

[1] C. v. Goodwin, 122 Mass. 19.

[2] P. v. Jones, 62 Mich. 304.

[3] Strange v. S., 33 Tex. Ap. 315.

[4] Rex v. Dunkley, 1 Moody, 90.

[5] S. v. Lewis, — Ia. —, 65 N. W. R. 295; U. S. v. Fero, 18 Fed. R. 901.

[6] Reg. v. Ward, 10 Cox, 42.

[7] Tynes v. S., 17 Tex. Ap. 123.

[8] S. v. Young, 26 Ia. 122. This does not charge pecuniary advantage intended to be secured, but is held sufficient under the Iowa statute, which is similar in this respect to statutes in many of the states.

[9] C. v. Moulton, 108 Mass. 307.

ANOTHER FORM OF THREATENING TO ACCUSE.

That A. B., at ——, on ——, unlawfully, wilfully and feloniously did accuse one S. W., then and there being, of the crime of maliciously procuring a barn of the value of four hundred and fifty dollars, the same being his own property, situate in ——, and insured against loss or damage by fire, to be burned, with the intent thereby to prejudice the insurer thereof, said crime being punishable by the laws of this state with imprisonment in the penitentiary, with the intent then and there by means of such unlawful accusation to extort and gain from the said S. W. certain money, to wit, the sum of five hundred dollars, of the amount and value of five hundred dollars, and certain chattels and valuable securities, to wit, certain promissory notes of the amount and value of three hundred dollars, said moneys, chattels and valuable securities being then and there the property of said S. W.[1]

THREATENING LETTER.

That A. B., at ——, on ——, with intent feloniously to extort money and property from one E. L., did then and there wilfully, unlawfully and feloniously send to said E. L. a certain letter in writing, the wording of which did express and imply and was adapted to imply a threat to impute to the said E. L. disgrace and to expose the same, which said letter and writing was then and there in the words and figures following, to wit: [Here the letter is set out.][2]

§ 742. **Evidence; other acts.**—Proof of other similar but disconnected crimes is not admissible,[3] unless perhaps it tends to show a general scheme or plan for extorting money.[4] If a conspiracy between defendants to carry on a general plan of extorting money appears, then similar acts by either defendant may be shown as against both.[5]

[1] Elliott v. S., 36 Ohio St. 318.

[2] P. v. Tonielli, 81 Cal. 275.

[3] C. v. White, 162 Mass. 403; Kistler v. S., 64 Ind. 371.

[4] Reg. v. Cooper, 3 Cox, 547.

[5] S. v. Lewis, — Ia. —, 65 N. W. R. 295.

2 VOLS

FOUNDATIONS OF CRIMINAL JUSTICE

A TREATISE

ON

THE CRIMINAL LAW

VOL. II

FOUNDATIONS OF CRIMINAL JUSTICE

FOUNDATIONS OF CRIMINAL JUSTICE

TREATISE
ON
THE CRIMINAL LAW

BY

EMLIN McCLAIN

with a new preface by

Alton R. Waldon, Jr.

VOL. II

AMS PRESS
NEW YORK, 1974

Library of Congress Cataloging in Publication Data

McClain, Emlin, 1851-1915.
A treatise on the criminal law as now administered in the United States.

(Foundations of criminal justice)
1. Criminal law—United States. 2. Criminal procedure—United States. I. Title. II. Series.
KF9219.M3 1974 345'.73'05 74-156026
ISBN 0-404-01927-X

mv 8/6/84

International Standard Book Number:
Complete Set: 0-404-01927-X
Volume II: 0-404-09167-9

Foundations of Criminal Justice Series
General Editors: Richard H. Ward and Austin Fowler,
John Jay College of Criminal Justice

Published in the United States by AMS Press, Inc.
56 E. 13th Street, New York, N.Y. 10003

Manufactured in the United States of America

A TREATISE

ON

THE CRIMINAL LAW

AS NOW ADMINISTERED IN THE
UNITED STATES

BY

EMLIN McCLAIN, A. M., LL. D.

Chancellor of the Law Department of the State University of Iowa

IN TWO VOLUMES

VOLUME II

CHICAGO
CALLAGHAN AND COMPANY
1897

ANALYSIS OF CONTENTS.

VOLUME II.

PART VII.

OFFENSES AGAINST PROPERTY (CONTINUED).

CHAPTER 31.

FORGERY AND COUNTERFEITING.

§ 743. General nature.

I. FORGERY.

744. Defined.
745. Written instruments.
746. Part false.
747. Classes of instruments.
748. Effect of statutes; felony or misdemeanor.
749. What instruments.
750. Public records or process; wills.
751. Bonds and deeds.
752. Notes, bills, checks and other instruments.
753. Undertakings, warrants, or orders for the payment of money or the delivery of goods.
754. Receipts.
755. Books of account.
756. Validity or legal effect of the writing.
757. Apparent legal efficacy.
758. Invalid instrument.
759. Invalid for lack of authority.
§ 760. Delivery not essential.
761. False signature; similarity not essential.
762. Unauthorized signature.
763. By procurement.
764. Fictitious name.
765. Alteration.
766. Intent to defraud.
767. Intent inferred.
768. Execution of the intent.
769. Fraudulent tendency of the act.
770. Person to be defrauded.
771. Name of person intended to be defrauded.
772. Existence of corporation.
773. Perpetration of fraud.

II. COUNTERFEITING.

774. What deemed counterfeit; similitude.
775. Foreign coin or notes.
776. Intent.

III. POSSESSION OF COUNTERFEITING TOOLS.

777. What criminal.
778. Of intent.
779. How charged.

IV. UTTERING, PASSING, OR HAVING IN POSSESSION.

§ 780. Offenses defined.
781. What constitutes an uttering.
782. Passing counterfeit money.
783. What constitutes a passing.
784. Having in possession.
785. What constitutes possession.
786. Possession with intent.
787. Representation of genuineness.
788. The intent.
789. Guilty knowledge.

V. PROCEDURE.

790. Jurisdiction of state and United States.
791. Venue.
792. Indictment.
793. Description of instrument.
794. Setting out the instrument.
795. Foreign language; translation.
796. Purport.
797. Immaterial matters.
798. Variance.
799. Name forged; *idem sonans*.
800. Statutory provisions as to indictment.
801. Allegations as to the act.
802. Allegation of intent; feloniously.
803. Different offenses; duplicity.
804. Form of indictment.

VI. EVIDENCE.

805. Production of instrument.
806. Comparison of handwriting.
807. Capacity of defendant and other matters.
808. Evidence of other crimes.
809. Inferences from the act or possession.
810. In cases of conspiracy.

CHAPTER 32.

MALICIOUS MISCHIEF; WILFUL TRESPASS.

§ 811. Nature of these crimes.
812. Malicious mischief by early statutes; Black Act.
§ 813. Distinguished from larceny.
814. Injuries to personal property.
815. Injuries to animals.
816. Altering brand, etc.
817. Injuries to machinery.
818. Injuries to vessels.
819. Injury to public property.
820. Forcible trespass.
821. Injury to buildings.
822. Hunting or fishing without permission.
823. Injuries to real property.
824. Trespass after warning, or when forbidden.
825. Offenses against possession.
826. The intent; malice.
827. Under claim of right.
828. Under claim of authority.
829. Malice against owner.
830. Indictment; ownership of property.
831. Other description.
832. The act, how charged.
833. As to intent.
834. Value of property.
835. Joinder.

CHAPTER 33.

FORCIBLE ENTRY AND DETAINER.

§ 836. Common-law offenses.
837. What constitutes forcible entry.
838. Forcible detainer.
839. Possession involved.
840. Description of premises.
841. Restitution.

CHAPTER 34.

FRAUDULENT CONVEYANCES; CONCEALMENT OF PROPERTY.

§ 842. General characteristics.
843. Concealing or disposing of property to defraud creditors.
844. Fraudulent conveyances.

§ 845. Fraud perpetrated.
846. Removal or disposal of property covered by chattel mortgage.
847. Consent of mortgagee.
§ 848. Selling or removing property subject to lien.
849. The intent.
850. Venue.
851. Indictment.

PART VIII.

OFFENSES AGAINST PUBLIC JUSTICE.

CHAPTER 35.

PERJURY.

I. What Constitutes.
§ 852. Definition.
853. Elements of the offense.
II. The Oath.
854. Essential.
855. Before authorized officer.
856. Acting officer.
857. State officer acting under federal statute.
III. In a Court Having Jurisdiction.
858. Jurisdiction essential.
IV. Where an Oath is Authorized.
859. Collateral proceedings in court.
860. Proceedings not in court.
V. Materiality.
861. Essential.
862. Collateral facts.
863. Illustrations.
864. As to credibility of witness.
865. Effect immaterial.
866. Materiality is for the court.
VI. Falsity.
867. Essential.
868. Statement of fact.
VII. Intent.
869. What essential.
870. Advice of counsel.
VIII. The Indictment.
871. Jurisdiction.
872. Requisites.
§ 873. The proceeding.
874. Description of the oath.
875. Authority of officer.
876. Jurisdiction of the court.
877. The matter falsely sworn.
878. Materiality.
879. Availability and effect.
880. The averment as to falsity.
881. Intent; knowledge.
882. Time and place.
883. Separate counts; several assignments.
884. Joinder of defendants.
885. Forms of indictment.
IX. The Evidence.
886. As to the proceedings or issue.
887. Administration of the oath.
888. The testimony or statement.
889. Materiality.
890. Wilful falsity.
891. Sufficiency of testimony; contradictory statements of accused.
892. One witness not sufficient.
X. Subornation; Attempt to Procure.
893. What constitutes.
894. Attempt to procure or incite.
895. Form of indictment.

CHAPTER 36.

BRIBERY.

§ 896. What constitutes.
897. Who subject to bribery.
898. Bribing witness.
899. Bribing jurors; embracery.

§ 900. Venue.
901. Indictment.
902. Forms of indictment.
903. Evidence.

CHAPTER 37.

OFFICIAL MISCONDUCT; EXTORTION.

§ 904. Usurpation.
905. Abuse of authority.
906. Misconduct.
907. Refusal to act.
908. Disregard of duty.
909. Neglect of duty.
910. Permitting a prisoner to escape.
911. Public contracts.
912. Who deemed officer.
913. Intent.
914. Extortion.
915. Indictment for misconduct or neglect.
916. Stating the office.
917. Alleging the intent.
918. Describing the act or omission.
919. Removal; penalty.

CHAPTER 38.

OBSTRUCTING JUSTICE.

I. In General.

§ 920. What constitutes.

II. Resisting an Officer.

§ 921. When criminal.
922. What officers; authority.
923. What constitutes resistance.
924. Intent; justifiable resistance.
925. Indictment.
926. Allegation of act.
927. Charging the intent.
928. Duplicity.
929. Evidence.

III. Breaking Jail; Escape; Rescue.

930. What criminal.
931. Legality of arrest or confinement.
932. Pound-breach.
933. Intent.
934. Indictment.
935. Practice.
936. Evidence.

IV. Tampering with a Witness.

937. Nature of the offense.

CHAPTER 39.

MISPRISION OF FELONY; COMPOUNDING OFFENSES.

§ 938. What constitutes misprision.
939. Compounding offenses.
940. Further as to the crime of compounding.

PART IX.

OFFENSES AGAINST THE ELECTIVE FRANCHISE.

CHAPTER 40.

VIOLATION OF ELECTION LAWS.

§ 941. Under statutes.
942. What deemed an election.
943. Illegal voting.
944. Disqualified voters.
§ 945. Crimes by election officers.
946. Interference with elections.
947. Improperly influencing voters.
948. Federal election laws.
949. Intent.
950. Indictment.
951. Evidence.

PART X.

OFFENSES AGAINST PUBLIC PEACE AND SECURITY.

CHAPTER 41.

CONSPIRACY; UNLAWFUL COMBINATION.

I. WHAT CONSTITUTES THE OFFENSE.

§ 952. General nature.
953. Definitions.
954. Purpose or means as criminal or unlawful.
955. Common-law conspiracy.
956. Conspiracies to commit a crime.
957. To charge with crime.
958. To slander.
959. To seduce female or entice to prostitution.
960. To defraud private persons.
961. To deprive of a right.
962. To injure the public.
963. In restraint of trade.
964. To defraud the government.
965. To overthrow the government.
966. Overt act.
967. Impossibility.
968. The combination.
969. Joining in the execution.
970. Liability of one for acts of all.
971. Intent.

II. PROCEDURE.

972. Jurisdiction and venue.
973. Limitation.
974. The indictment; allegation of wrongful purpose.
975. Setting out the unlawful means.
976. Bills of particulars.
977. Charging overt act.
978. Duplicity.
979. Merger.
980. Joinder of offenses.
981. Joinder of defendants.
982. The person to be injured.
983. Description of property.
984. Statutory language.
§ 985. Variance.
986. Form of indictment.
987. Punishment.

III. EVIDENCE.

988. Declarations and acts of co-conspirators.
989. Proof of the existence of the conspiracy.
990. Necessity of corroboration.

CHAPTER 42.

RIOT; UNLAWFUL ASSEMBLY.

I. IN GENERAL.

§ 991. Nature of offenses.

II. RIOT AND ROUT.

992. Definition.
993. Unlawfulness of act or manner.
994. Numbers of persons.
995. Participation.
996. Conviction of one alone.
997. Reading the riot act.
998. Indictment.
999. Forms of indictment.
1000. Description of property.
1001. Included crime.
1002. Punishment.

III. UNLAWFUL ASSEMBLY.

1003. Defined.
1004. Intent sufficient.
1005. Statutory definition.

CHAPTER 43.

AFFRAYS AND BREACHES OF THE PEACE.

I. AFFRAY.

§ 1006. Defined.
1007. Fighting by consent; mere words not enough.
1008. In a public place.
1009. Indictment.
1010. Conviction of joint offense.
1011. Included offense.

II. BREACH OF THE PEACE AND DISORDERLY CONDUCT.

§ 1012. What constitutes.
1013. Prize-fighting.
1014. Injuries to property.
1015. Shooting in streets or highways.
1016. Noise and disturbance.
1017. Threatening and insulting language.
1018. Disorderly persons; vagrants; drunkards.
1019. Public place.
1020. Disturbance of family or neighborhood.
1021. Method of charging offense.

III. DISTURBANCE OF MEETINGS.

1022. What constitutes.
1023. What deemed public meeting.
1024. Congregation assembled for worship.
1025. Disturbance of school.
1026. What deemed a disturbance.
1027. The intent.
1028. The indictment.

CHAPTER 44.

CARRYING CONCEALED WEAPONS.

§ 1029. At common law.
1030. Constitutionality of statutes.
1031. What made criminal.
1032. The intent.
1033. What weapons.
1034. Exceptions; apprehension of attack.
1035. On one's own premises.
1036. Travelers.
§ 1037. Officers.
1038. Indictment.
1039. Evidence.

CHAPTER 45.

LIBEL AND SLANDER.

§ 1040. Nature of the offenses.
1041. Definition.
1042. Common law or statutory.
1043. As against private individuals.
1044. As against a family or class or corporation.
1045. As against wife.
1046. As against the dead.
1047. As against public officers.
1048. As against government.
1049. Blasphemous or obscene publications.
1050. Freedom of the press.
1051. The truth as a defense.
1052. Privileged publications.
1053. Intent; malice.
1054. Mitigation.
1055. Publication.
1056. Liability for acts of servants or agents.
1057. Slander.
1058. Venue.
1059. Indictment.
1060. Colloquium and innuendo.
1061. Setting out the language.
1062. In foreign language.
1063. Whole publication.
1064. Indecent matter not set out.
1065. Alleging publication.
1066. Description of the person.
1067. Allegation of intent.
1068. Duplicity.
1069. Forms of indictment.
1070. Functions of court and jury.

PART XI.

OFFENSES AGAINST CONJUGAL AND PARENTAL RIGHTS.

CHAPTER 46.

BIGAMY.

§ 1071. Definition.
1072. What constitutes.
§ 1073. The second marriage.
1074. Validity of prior marriage.
1075. Prior marriage terminated by divorce.

§ 1076. Intent; belief as to death of former consort.
1077. Jurisdiction and venue.
1078. Limitation.
1079. Indictment.
1080. Negativing proviso.
1081. Allegation of intent.
1082. Evidence; proof of former marriage.
1083. Admissions of defendant.
1084. Evidence that former spouse is still living.
1085. Testimony of husband or wife.

CHAPTER 47.

ADULTERY.

§ 1086. What constitutes.
1087. Living in adultery; habitual intercourse.
1088. Validity of marriage.
1089. Presumption of continuance.
1090. Termination by divorce.
1091. Intent; knowledge.
1092. Mutual criminal intent.
§ 1093. Complaint of husband or wife.
1094. Indictment.
1095. Joinder; included offenses.
1096. Evidence as to the marriage.
1097. Proof of act.
1098. Proof of other acts.
1099. Competency of husband or wife as a witness.

CHAPTER 48.

ABDUCTION OF FEMALES.

§ 1100. In case of girls.
1101. From the custody of parent or guardian.
1102. Consent.
1103. What constitutes a taking.
1104. Purpose of the abduction.
1105. Knowledge as to age.
1106. Chastity of the female.
1106*a*. Abduction or enticement of woman; pimping or procuring.
1107. The indictment.
1108. Evidence.

PART XII.

OFFENSES AGAINST CHASTITY, DECENCY AND MORALITY.

CHAPTER 49.

SEDUCTION.

§ 1109. Classification of sexual crimes.
1110. Table of sexual crimes.
1111. What constitutes seduction.
1112. Seductive arts; promise of marriage.
1113. Prosecutrix unmarried and chaste.
1114. Indictment.
1115. Included offenses.
1116. Marriage a bar.
1117. Evidence in general.
1118. Evidence of chastity.
1119. Sufficiency of evidence; corroboration.

CHAPTER 50.

INCEST.

§ 1120. What constitutes.
1121. Mutuality.
1122. The act.
1123. Indictment.
1124. Evidence.

CHAPTER 51.

FORNICATION AND BASTARDY.

§ 1125. Fornication; when punishable.
1126. Bastardy.
1127. Jurisdiction and venue.
1128. Complaint.
1129. Evidence.

CHAPTER 52.

ILLICIT COHABITATION.

§ 1130. How far criminal.
1131. Intent; joint offenses.
1132. Other incidents of indictment and evidence.

CHAPTER 53.

PROSTITUTION AND LEWDNESS.

§ 1133. Prostitution and night-walking.
1134. Frequenting houses of ill-fame.
1135. Lewdness.
1136. Indecent exposure.

CHAPTER 54.

KEEPING DISORDERLY HOUSES.

§ 1137. What deemed criminal.
1138. Keeping houses of ill-fame.
1139. What deemed a house.
1140. What constitutes a keeping.
1141. Procuring or encouraging.
1142. Permitting the use or leasing for the purpose.
1143. Indictment.
1144. Forms of indictment.
1145. Evidence.

CHAPTER 55.

PROCURING ABORTION; CONCEALING BIRTH OF BASTARD.

§ 1146. Procuring abortion.
1147. Where death results.
1148. Attempting; advising.
1149. Consent; necessity.
1150. The indictment.
§ 1151. Evidence.
1152. Concealing birth of a bastard.

CHAPTER 56.

SODOMY.

§ 1153. What constitutes.
1154. Indictment.
1155. Evidence.

CHAPTER 57.

OBSCENITY AND INDECENCY.

§ 1156. Obscene language.
1157. Indecent exhibitions and prints.
1158. Indictment and evidence.

CHAPTER 58.

BLASPHEMY AND PROFANITY.

§ 1159. What constitutes.
1160. Indictment.

CHAPTER 59.

CRUELTY TO ANIMALS.

§ 1161. What punishable.
1162. What deemed animal.
1163. Intent.
1164. Indictment.

CHAPTER 60.

VIOLATION OF RIGHT OF SEPULTURE.

§ 1165. Failure to bury; preventing inquest.
1166. Disposal of dead bodies.
1167. Violation of graves.
1168. Desecration of cemeteries.

PART XIII.

OFFENSES AGAINST PUBLIC HEALTH AND GENERAL WELFARE.

CHAPTER 61.

PUBLIC NUISANCE.

§ 1169. What constitutes.
1170. Further as to what constitutes a nuisance.
1171. Whether public benefit a defense.
1172. Acts under public authority.
1173. Illegal continuance of use.
1174. Liability of owner or servant.
1175. Effect of contribution to the nuisance.
1176. Intent and knowledge.
1177. Venue.
1178. Indictment; charging public nature.
1179. Charging the act.
1180. Joinder of different acts; continuance.
1181. Description of locality.
1182. Abatement.
1183. Forms of indictment.

CHAPTER 62.

OFFENSES AS TO HIGHWAYS.

I. OBSTRUCTION OR NON-REPAIR OF HIGHWAYS.

§ 1184. Deemed a nuisance.
1185. Failure to open or repair.
1186. Obstruction; what constitutes.
1187. Obstruction by railroads.
1188. Continuance of obstruction.
1189. The intent.
1190. What deemed highway.
1191. Private ways.
1192. Streets, alleys and public places.
1193. Indictment.
1194. Title in defendant.

II. OBSTRUCTION OF NAVIGABLE RIVERS.

§ 1195. When criminal.

III. INTERFERENCE WITH THE OPERATION OF RAILROADS.

1196. What criminal.

IV. LAW OF THE ROAD.

1197. Turning to the right; bicycles.
1198. Racing on the highway.

CHAPTER 63.

VIOLATION OF LIQUOR LAWS.

I. GENERAL STATUTORY REGULATIONS; CONSTITUTIONALITY AND CONSTRUCTION OF STATUTES; CONCURRENT FEDERAL, STATE AND CITY REGULATIONS.

§ 1199. General character of statutory regulations.
1200. Constitutionality of liquor legislation.
1201. Federal constitution; fourteenth amendment.
1202. Regulation of commerce.
1203. Restriction of transportation into the state.
1204. Sale in original package.
1205. Effect of Wilson law.
1206. Under state constitutions.
1207. Due process of law; taking private property for public use.
1208. Jury trial.
1209. License; impairing obligation of contract.
1210. Local or special laws; local option.
1211. Uniformity of taxation.
1212. Conditions for granting license.
1213. Constitutional prohibition.

§ 1214. Sale by public agent.
1215. Constitutionality of provisions as to evidence.
1216. Construction of statutes.
1217. Concurrent effect of federal, state and city provisions.

II. WHAT DEEMED INTOXICATING LIQUOR.

1218. Law or fact; judicial notice.
1219. Mixed or compounded liquor.
1220. Particular classes of liquors.
1221. Other descriptions; "spirituous," "fermented," etc.
1222. Evidence as to character of liquor; knowledge by defendant.

III. SYSTEMS OF REGULATION; LICENSE; LOCAL OPTION.

1223. The license system.
1224. License not retroactive.
1225. Direct and collateral attack; appeal.
1226. Forfeiture or revocation.
1227. Not assignable; who protected by; agent or partner.
1228. Authority to issue, discretionary.
1229. Selling without license; allegation and proof of license.
1230. Carrying on the business without a license.
1231. Place of sale.
1232. Local option.

IV. ILLEGAL SELLING OR KEEPING FOR SALE.

1233. What deemed a sale.
1234. Consideration; barter or exchange.
1235. Giving; furnishing; disposing of.
1236. When sale complete; place of sale.
§ 1237. Liability for sales by servant.
1238. Sales by partner or wife.
1239. Liability of agent.
1240. Furnishing to members of club.
1241. Purchaser not punishable.
1242. Transporting.
1243. Unlawfully keeping for sale.
1244. The business of selling; being common seller.
1245. Retailing; wholesaling.
1246. Selling by small measure.
1247. To be drunk on the premises.
1248. Nuisance; keeping place for illegal sale.
1249. Charging and proving the nuisance.
1250. Regulations as to receipts, hour of closing, screens, etc.
1251. Intent.

V. SPECIAL EXCEPTIONS IN CASES OF PHYSICIANS, DRUGGISTS, PRODUCERS, ETC.

1252. Exceptions by statute; need not be negatived.
1253. Sales by physicians and druggists.
1254. Sales by producers or manufacturers.

VI. SPECIAL PROHIBITIONS.

1255. Provisions in general.
1256. Sales to prohibited persons.
1257. Intent or knowledge in such cases.
1258. Sale to minor or intoxicated person for another.
1259. Furnishing to minor or intoxicated person.
1260. Who deemed minor; allegation and proof of age.
1261. Consent of parent or guardian.
1262. Sales to habitual drunkard or intoxicated person.
1263. Sales to Indians.

§ 1264. Selling on Sundays or holidays.
1265. Selling on election day.
1266. Selling near churches, educational institutions, etc.

VII. The Procedure; Seizure; Indictment; Evidence.

1267. Seizure; property in liquors.
1268. Second offense.
1269. Venue.
1270. Indictment.
1271. Further as to description of the particular act.
1272. Time and place.
1273. Description of kind, quantity, price, etc.
1274. Name of purchaser.
1275. Joinder of offenses.
1276. Variance; election.
1277. Double punishment; included offenses; previous jeopardy.
1278. Negativing exceptions.
1279. Evidence.
1280. License as evidence.
1281. Burden of proof as to lawfulness of sales.

CHAPTER 64.

GAMING AND BETTING.

I. Gaming in General.

§ 1282. Introductory.
1283. Gaming in general.
1284. Statutory provisions.
1285. What deemed games.
1286. What deemed a wager.
1287. When offense complete.
1288. Aiding or procuring.
1289. Indictment in general.
1290. Names of parties.
1291. Charging the game played.
1292. The wager.
1293. Time and place.
1294. Joinder of defendants.
1295. Charging different offenses; duplicity.
1296. Evidence.

II. Betting.

§ 1297. In general; on horse-races.
1298. Betting on elections.
1299. Indictment; evidence.

III. Common Gambler.

1300. Who is.

IV. Gaming in Public Places.

1301. In general.
1302. The place.
1303. Further as to public place.
1304. Indictment and evidence.

V. Pool Selling.

1305. Statutory provisions.

VI. Keeping a Gaming House.

1306. What criminal.
1307. Place and time.
1308. The keeper.
1309. The indictment and evidence.

VII. Keeping and Exhibiting Gaming Devices and Tables.

1310. What constitutes.
1311. Procedure; indictment.
1312. Penalty; destruction of implements.

VIII. Allowing Games to be Played on the Premises.

1313. When criminal.

IX. Gaming by Minors.

1314. Permitting to game or to resort.

CHAPTER 65.

LOTTERIES.

§ 1315. Definition.
1316. Statutes.
1317. Constitutionality.
1318. Indictment.

CHAPTER 66.

VIOLATION OF SUNDAY LAWS.

§ 1319. Nature of regulations; constitutionality.
1320. What deemed Sunday.

§ 1321. Works of charity or necessity excepted.
1322. Sunday traveling.
1323. Operation of railroads or telegraph lines.
1324. Carrying on business.
1325. Sunday amusements.
1326. Indictment.

PART XIV.

OFFENSES UNDER FEDERAL REGULATIONS.

CHAPTER 67.

POSTAL CRIMES.

§ 1327. In general.
1328. Obstruction of mails.
1329. Robbery of the mails.
1330. Larceny or embezzlement by postal servants.
1331. Use of mails to defraud.
1332. Sending obscene matter through the mails.
1333. Defamatory or threatening matter.
1334. Lottery advertisements.
1335. Decoy letters.

CHAPTER 68.

REGULATIONS AS TO COMMERCE.

§ 1336. Discrimination.
1337. Unlawful combinations.
1338. Carriage of live-stock.
1338*a*. Trading with the Indians.

CHAPTER 69.

OFFENSES AGAINST BANKING ACT.

§ 1339. False entries.
1340. Embezzlement; misapplication of funds.

CHAPTER 70.

OFFENSES AGAINST NEUTRALITY, IMMIGRATION AND NATURALIZATION LAWS.

§ 1341. Violations of neutrality.
1342. Violence to foreign minister.
1343. Immigration laws; contract labor.
1344. Exclusion of Chinese.
1345. To whom applicable.
1346. Naturalization.

CHAPTER 71.

VIOLATION OF NAVIGATION LAWS.

§ 1347. What criminal.

CHAPTER 72.

VIOLATION OF PENSION LAWS.

§ 1348. What criminal.

CHAPTER 73.

VIOLATION OF REVENUE LAWS; MAKING FALSE CLAIMS.

§ 1349. Forfeiture of goods.
1350. Licenses and stamps.
1351. Customs duties.
1352. Presenting false claims.

CHAPTER 74.

VIOLATION OF LAND LAWS.

§ 1353. What punishable.

PART XV.

OFFENSES AGAINST SOVEREIGNTY.

CHAPTER 75.

TREASON.

§ 1354. History of the crime.
1355. Constitutional definitions.
1356. Statutory definitions.
§ 1357. Levying war; rendering aid and comfort.
1358. Overt act.

CHAPTER 76.

PIRACY.

§ 1359. Nature of the offense.

CRIMINAL LAW.

PART VII.

OFFENSES AGAINST PROPERTY (CONTINUED).

CHAPTER 31.

FORGERY AND COUNTERFEITING.

I. FORGERY.
II. COUNTERFEITING.
III. POSSESSION OF COUNTERFEITING TOOLS.
IV. UTTERING, PASSING, OR HAVING IN POSSESSION.
V. PROCEDURE.
VI. EVIDENCE.

§ 743. **General nature.**— The class of offenses of which forgery and counterfeiting are the principal examples, involving on the one hand the element of private fraud, and on the other that of general injury by reason of the doubt that is thereby thrown on public coins and documents and the instruments of commerce, may be here considered together, although the specific offenses are sometimes treated as distinct. Both forgery and counterfeiting were originally looked upon as offenses in derogation of the authority of the king, and as a species of treason or *laese-majesty*.[1] Indeed, counterfeiting is not found in the older English books as the name of a crime, but the offense is considered in connection with the statutes relating to the coin. Blackstone points out the inconsistency of classifying these offenses as treason, and suggests that they are better regarded as branches of the offense known to the civilians as *crimen falsi*, or, in general terms, fraud.[2] Forgery, however, was apparently not limited, even in the early law, to the false making of the king's seal or signature, or the otherwise falsifying of some public document, and it is pointed out that although

[1] 4 Bl. Com. 84, 89; 3 Stephen, Hist. Cr. L. 177.

[2] 4 Bl. Com. 89. And see 1 Stephen, Hist. Cr. L. 20.

the earliest recognized examples of forgery related to public documents and wills, yet that when occasion arose the courts treated other cases of falsification of instruments as constituting the offense.[1] It thus appears that primarily counterfeiting related to the coin, and forgery to public documents or other instruments; but the words "forgery" and "counterfeiting" were used quite indiscriminately in the earlier English statutes as they are in modern ones, and the tendency seems to be to extend the crime described as counterfeiting to include offenses relating to instruments issued by the government of a pecuniary nature, such as bonds, treasury notes, bank-notes, stamps, money orders, etc., although in many cases the instrument is such, by reason of its form, that the making of it could properly be described as forgery. The offenses of forgery and counterfeiting being of such an aggravated character, it is natural that acts intended to lead to their commission or connected therewith should be severely punished, although the higher crime is not actually involved. Thus, there are various offenses of uttering forged instruments, passing counterfeit coin, having in possession such coin with intent to pass, or even having in possession the implements or materials with which to commit the offenses with intent to commit them. The principal crimes of forgery and counterfeiting will be first considered, and then the minor offenses, while the peculiarities of jurisdiction, the indictment, and the evidence as to all will be discussed together at the end.

I. FORGERY.

§ 744. Defined.— It is difficult to give a more definite description of the offense than that found in Blackstone: "The fraudulent making or alteration of a writing to the prejudice of another man's right."[2] Some English judges have spoken of it as the making of a false instrument with intent to deceive,[3] but the deceit must involve danger of pecuniary loss, and it is suggested that the expression "with intent to de-

[1] 2 East, P. C. 852; 1 Hawk. P. C., ch. 70, §§ 1, 2. And see C. v. Searle, 2 Binney, 332; Rex v. Ward, 2 Ld. Ray. 1461.

[2] 4 Bl. Com. 247; U. S. v. Long, 30 Fed. R. 678; S. v. Flye, 26 Me. 312; Baldwin v. Weed, 17 Wend. 224, 229. See definitions collected in C. v. Ray, 3 Gray, 441; S. v. Fisher, 65 Mo. 437.

[3] 2 East, P. C. 853; Article, 30 Am. L. Rev. 500.

ceive in such a manner as to expose any person to loss or the risk of loss" would accurately express the idea.[1] In some cases a definition is adopted which gives prominence to the three elements of the offense substantially as follows: Falsely making or altering a writing, which is in such form as to be apparently of some legal efficacy, with intent to defraud.[2] If the party who commits the forgery effects his purpose of defrauding, the offense may also be false pretenses;[3] but the two offenses are distinct in that the forgery may be complete without any injury being accomplished,[4] while the crime of false pretenses in falsely using an instrument as that of another may be completed without the making or even passing of a forged instrument.[5] So, falsely personating another and signing his name to an instrument might be forgery, but the signature of another's name even without authority would not constitute the offense of falsely impersonating another as defined by statute.[6]

§ 745. **Written instruments.**— The forgery must be of some document or writing, and it has been said, therefore, that it would not constitute forgery to falsely paint an artist's name in the corner of a picture in order to pass it off as an original picture by that artist.[7] In general it is not merely the false signature, but the false making of an instrument, whether the falsity consists in a signature, an alteration of the instrument, or whatever it may be, which constitutes the crime; but the form of the statute may be such as to make the crime consist of the counterfeiting of the handwriting or signature, only.[8]

[1] 2 Stephen, Hist. Cr. L. 187.

[2] C. v. Beamish, 81 Pa. St. 389; S. v. Johnson, 26 Ia. 407; S. v. Thompson, 19 Ia. 299; S. v. Ford, 38 La. An. 797; Ames' Case, 2 Me. 365; C. v. Chandler, Thatch. Cr. Cas. 187; C. v. Ayer, 3 Cush. 150; Barnum v. S., 15 Ohio, 717; S. v. Holly, 2 Bay, 262; S. v. Smith, 8 Yerg. 150; Rex v. Jones, 2 East, P. C. 991.

[3] S. v. Farrell, 82 Ia. 553.

[4] See *infra*, § 760.

[5] Hoge v. First Nat. Bank, 18 Ill. Ap. 501; Rex v. Inder, 2 C. & K. 635; Reg. v. Smith, Dears. & B. 566. Attempting to obtain property by a forged instrument is not swindling but forgery: Mathews v. S., 33 Tex. 102. Passing a genuine bill as the bill of a fictitious person is the uttering of a fictitious bill: Reg. v. Nesbitt, 6 Cox, 320.

[6] P. v. Maurin, 77 Cal. 436.

[7] Reg. v. Closs, Dears. & B. 460. The making of a false diploma (Reg. v. Hodgson, Dears. & B. 3), or of a false label (Reg. v. Smith, Dears. & B. 566), has been held not to be forgery.

[8] Cohen v. P., 7 Colo. 274.

False printing as well as false writing may be forgery.[1] Thus, if an instrument is printed and has a printed signature, but its validity depends upon the written initials of some particular person being affixed to the printed signature, it is a subject of forgery.[2]

§ **746. Part false.**— To falsely make one of the signatures to an instrument,[3] or any material part of an instrument,[4] is forgery.

§ **747. Classes of instruments.**— The common law furnished a very indefinite description of the classes of instruments the false making of which might be punished as forgery, and it was therefore supplemented from time to time by legislation extending the offense to various instruments which had not before been definitely decided to be subject of forgery. It may be said in general that the tendency of this legislation has been to make the crime cover every sort of document which, if genuine, would be of legal effect.[5]

§ **748. Effect of statutes; felony or misdemeanor.**— The effect of the statutory definitions of forgery is not to repeal the common-law offense unless the statute covers the whole ground covered by the common law, and (except in states where common-law crimes are not recognized) cases not covered by the statute may still be punished by the common law.[6] Most of these statutes make the offense described therein a felony, but at common law it is a misdemeanor only.[7]

§ **749. What instruments.**— It would not be profitable to attempt to define just what instruments are subject of forgery, aside from statutory provision. Almost all indictments for the offense are under statutes, and it will be sufficient to discuss briefly the classes of instruments which, either by common law or statute, are within the scope of the offense, pointing out in particular instances the statutory terms where the decisions are made to depend on special provisions.

1 Benson v. McMahon, 127 U. S. 457; In re Benson, 34 Fed. R. 649.

2 S. v. Lee, 32 Kan. 360.

3 S. v. Davis, 69 N. C. 313.

4 P. v. Clements, 26 N. Y. 193.

5 See *infra*, § 756.

6 C. v. Ayer, 3 Cush. 150; S. v. Kimball, 50 Me. 409.

7 C. v. Duffy, 96 Pa. St. 506; Shuster v. C., 38 Pa. St. 206; S. v. Murphy, 17 R. I. 698; Cohen v. P., 7 Colo. 274; S. v. Williams, 86 N. C. 671; Martin v. S., 24 Tex. 62; U. S. v. McCarthy, 4 Cranch, C. C. 304. As to whether the indictment should charge the act as felonious, see *infra*, § 802.

§ 750. Public records or process; wills.— The earlier definitions of the common-law offense give prominence, as has already been suggested, to public records and wills as instruments with reference to which the offense may be committed, but they are usually also included in the statutory description. Thus, the statutes usually specify in detail the altering or falsifying of any public record or book belonging to a public office, etc.[1] It is forgery to alter a record of marriages, births and deaths.[2] A certified copy of a decree of divorce may be forged.[3] Falsely making or altering a process of court is made forgery by statute;[4] so it is forgery to falsely make a certificate of acknowledgment,[5] or an affidavit in a legal proceeding.[6] Forgery of wills was early recognized as a crime;[7] and it was held

[1] Ream v. C., 3 Serg. & R. 207; S. v. Granville, 45 Ohio St. 264; Loehr v. P., 132 Ill. 504; P. v. O'Brien, 96 Cal. 171; Turbeville v. S., 56 Miss. 793. Changing a chattel mortgage on file may constitute the crime of forging an instrument, although it is also the offense of altering a public record as described in another provision of the same statute: S. v. Adamson, 43 Minn. 196. A tax duplicate is not a public record: Smith v. S., 18 Ohio St. 420. Forging an office copy of the report of the accountant general of money paid into a bank, and also of a certificate of the bank cashier, was held forgery: Rex v. Gibson, 2 East, P. C. 899. Counterfeiting the certificate of a justice of the peace as to the presentation and destruction of gopher scalps, held forgery: S. v. Johnson, 26 Ia. 407. Forging a justice's docket entry is not criminal, where the statute refers only to forging the record of a court of record: S. v. Floyd, 1 Houst. Cr. C. 110.

[2] Reg. v. Bowen, 1 C. & K. 501. And it is immaterial that the marriage as to which the record is altered was void, or that the alteration, consisting in the false addition of the name of another witness, was immaterial: Reg. v. Asplin, 12 Cox, 391. But the forgery of a certificate of the parents of a minor consenting to the marriage of the minor is not within the statute: S. v. Rhine, 84 Ia. 169.

[3] Ex parte Finley, 66 Cal. 262. Aside from special statute, an engrossed copy of a legislative act is not subject of forgery: In re Corryell, 22 Cal. 178.

[4] Reg. v. Powner, 12 Cox, 235; Rex v. Harris, 6 C. & P. 129; Rex v. Graham, 2 East, P. C. 945. But a notice to produce is not process of the court: Reg. v. Castle, Dears. & B. 363. The English statute also makes it a felony to act or profess to act under any false color or pretense of a process of the court: Reg. v. Richmond, Bell, 142; Reg. v. Evans, Dears. & B. 236; Reg. v. Myott, 6 Cox, 406.

[5] Meserve v. C., 137 Mass. 109; P. v. Marion, 29 Mich. 31. But see Rogers v. S., 8 Tex. Ap. 401.

[6] Jacobs v. S., 61 Ala. 448; S. v. Kimball, 50 Me. 409; U. S. v. Spaulding, 3 Dak. 85; U. S. v. Hartman, 65 Fed. R. 490. But falsity of the matter in an affidavit will not constitute a forgery: U. S. v. Cameron, 3 Dak. 132; so held as to a false jurat to an affidavit: U. S. v. Moore, 60 Fed. R. 738.

[7] Rex v. Fitzgerald, 2 East, P. C.

to be immaterial that the supposed testator was living;[1] or that there was no such person as the one whose will the instrument purported to be.[2]

§ 751. **Bonds and deeds.**— A mortgage is a deed within the statutory description;[3] so is the release of a mortgage;[4] so at common law a power of attorney to transfer stock signed, sealed, and delivered was a deed.[5] An administrator's bond may be subject of forgery;[6] and so may a bail bond.[7] A certificate of city indebtedness is a bond under a statute as to forgery.[8]

§ 752. **Notes, bills, checks and other instruments.**— The statutory description of a note for the payment of money covers a due-bill.[9] The instrument may be described as a note, although the forgery consists in a false indorsement thereon, without which it would not be a valid instrument.[10] A bank-note or bill is a promissory note within the meaning of the statute;[11] and bank-bills or notes are within the statute although issued by an unchartered bank,[12] or by a foreign bank,[13] and whether current or in circulation in the state or not.[14] The false making of bank-notes is now usually covered by statutes

953; Rex v. Birch, 2 East, P. C. 980; Rex v. Rhodes, 1 Leach, 24; Reg. v. Barber, 1 C. & K. 442; Rex v. Buttery, Russ. & Ry. 342.

1 Rex v. Sterling, 2 East, P. C. 950; Rex v. Coogan, 2 East, P. C. 1001.

2 Reg. v. Avery, 8 C. & P. 596. But prior to the later statutes there could be no forgery of a will which was not attested by a sufficient number of witnesses: Rex v. Wall, 2 East, P. C. 953.

3 P. v. Wright, 9 Wend. 193.

4 Meserve v. C., 137 Mass. 109.

5 Rex v. Fauntleroy, 1 C. & P. 421; Reg v. Pringle, 2 Moody, 127. But a letter or order issued by a bishop certifying the admission of a person to be a deacon, with the episcopal seal affixed, was held not to be a deed, although to forge such an instrument would be a misdemeanor at common law: Reg. v. Morton, L. R. 2 C. C. 22.

6 Reg. v. Barber, 1 C. & K. 434.

7 Costley v. S., 14 Tex. Ap. 156; C. v. Linton, 2 Va. Cas. 476.

8 Bishop v. S., 55 Md. 138.

9 P. v. Finch, 5 Johns, 237. It is not necessary to allege that a bank-bill is for the payment of money, for the words are found in the statute covering bank-bills; the term itself imports a promise to pay money: Townsend v. P., 4 Ill. 326. But in England it was held that a promissory note for the payment of one guinea in cash or a Bank of England note was not a note for payment in money: Rex v. Wilcox, 2 Russ. Cr. 497.

10 C. v. Welch, 148 Mass. 296; C. v. Dallinger, 118 Mass. 439.

11 Stone v. S., 20 N. J. 401, 404.

12 U. S. v. Winslow, 2 Cranch, C. C. 47.

13 P. v. McDonnell, 80 Cal. 285; P. v. Marion, 29 Mich. 31; C. v. Hensley, 2 Va. Cas. 149.

14 Porter v. S., 17 Ind. 415. To come

as to counterfeiting, though by early English statutes it was a forgery.[1] The term "bill of exchange" covers a check.[2] The indorsement of a note is within the general terms of the statutory description although not specifically enumerated;[3] but the indorsement must have such relation to the instrument as to have some effect in the transfer of the property evidenced by the note.[4] The forgery of an acceptance of an order is criminal at common law.[5] Checks of canal commissioners payable at a future day were held to be securities for the payment of money within the statutory terms.[6] A United States treasury note is an instrument in writing.[7] The word "receipt" implies an instrument in writing.[8] Where the statute, after enumerating notes, bills, etc., specified "other instruments in writing," it was held that such language implied an unconditional obligation to pay; in other words, an instrument similar to the instruments previously enumerated.[9] But the language of the statutes does not usually require such narrow construction, and

within the English statute with regard to notes it was held not necessary that the instrument should be negotiable: Rex v. Box, Russ. & Ry. 300.

[1] Rex v. Elliott, 2 East, P. C. 951; Rex v. Bigg, 2 East, P. C. 882; Rex v. Treble, 2 Taunt. 328; Reg. v. Keith, Dears. 486; Reg. v. Rinaldi, L. & C. 330; Reg. v. Brackenridge, L. R. 1 C. C. 133. So the false making or second use of stamps was at one time punishable as forgery by the English statute, although it would not be within the description of counterfeiting: Rex v. Collicott, 4 Taunt. 300; Rex v. Smith, 5 C. & P. 107; Rex v. Field, 1 Leach, 383; Reg. v. Allday, 8 C. & P. 136.

[2] Hawthorn v. S., 56 Md. 530; Reg. v. Smith, 2 Moody, 295; Reg. v. Kinnear, 2 M. & Rob. 117. An order by a branch bank on the principal bank is a check: U. S. v. Shellmire, Baldw. 370; but a bank post-bill was held not to be a bill of exchange but properly described as a bank bill of exchange: Rex v. Birkett, Russ. & Ry. 251. A bill drawn by accused on himself, and by him accepted and indorsed, was held a bill of exchange; C. v. Butterick, 100 Mass. 12.

[3] Poage v. S., 3 Ohio St. 229; Cocke v. C., 13 Grat. 750; Powell v. C., 11 Grat. 822. See as to indorsement on a check: Reg. v. Wardell, 3 F. & F. 82; or a bill of exchange: Reg. v. Winterbottom, 2 C. & K. 37; or warrant on the treasury: U. S. v. Jolly, 37 Fed. R. 108. But proof of a forged indorsement on a genuine warrant will not support the charge of uttering a false and forged warrant: U. S. v. Albert, 45 Fed. R. 552.

[4] C. v. Spilman, 124 Mass. 327. Until the passage of recent English statutes the false indorsement of a warrant or order or letter of credit was not a forgery: Rex v. Arscott, 6 C. & P. 408; Reg. v. Wilton, 1 F. & F. 391.

[5] C. v. Ayer, 3 Cush. 150.

[6] Crofts v. P., 3 Ill. 442.

[7] Riggins v. S., 4 Kan. 173.

[8] S. v. Bibb, 68 Mo. 286; S. v. Fenly, 18 Mo. 445.

[9] Shirk v. P., 121 Ill. 61; Canadian Bank v. McCrea, 106 Ill. 281.

various instruments are covered which do not call for the payment of money, as, for instance, railway passes;[1] or a railway ticket;[2] or a theater ticket;[3] it being said in such cases that it is not necessary that the instrument fully state the nature of the contract, if it sufficiently imports an obligation on the part of the company to render a service.[4] An instrument which, if genuine, would effect the transfer of property is the subject of forgery;[5] and so a county warrant,[6] or a fictitious bill of costs,[7] or fee-bill[8] may be forged. A false application forwarded by an insurance agent for the purpose of procuring the commission which would be due thereon, if genuine, will constitute a forgery, although no policy is issued.[9] A teacher's certificate may be forged under a statute punishing the false making of any license or authority provided for by statute.[10] The false making of an affidavit may be forgery, as such an instrument constitutes a false writing.[11] So the making of a false certificate, or of a false claim,[12] may be criminal.[13] Statutes now use very broad and general language, such as "a writing which, if genuine, might apparently be of legal efficacy;"[14] or "to the prejudice of another's rights;"[15] or "creating a legal demand;"[16] or showing a "pecuniary obligation."[17] Under such general provisions any instrument on which, as the evidence shows, money might be obtained,[18] or by which another might be defrauded,[19] will be subject of forgery.

[1] S. v. Weaver, 94 N. C. 836; Reg. v. Boult, 2 C. & K. 604.

[2] C. v. Ray, 3 Gray, 441.

[3] In re Benson, 34 Fed. R. 659.

[4] C. v. Ray, 3 Gray, 441.

[5] Noakes v. P., 25 N. Y. 380; C. v. Wilson, 89 Ky. 157.

[6] S. v. Fenly, 18 Mo. 445.

[7] Luttrell v. S., 85 Tenn. 232.

[8] S. v. Haws, 98 Mo. 188.

[9] Fountain v. Smith, 70 Ia. 282.

[10] S. v. Grant, 74 Mo. 33; Maddox v. S., 87 Ga. 429.

[11] S. v. Kimball, 50 Me. 409; U. S. v. Spaulding, 3 Dak. 85. And see *supra*, § 750.

[12] S. v. Rhine, 84 Ia. 169. But a military land warrant was held not subject to forgery under federal statutes: U. S. v. Irwin, 5 McLean, 178.

[13] This will cover a bounty land warrant: U. S. v. Wilcox, 4 Blatch. 385; but not an export bond: U. S. v. Barney, 5 Blatch. 294.

[14] Smith v. S., 29 Fla. 408,— a case of an order drawn by a county board on its treasurer.

[15] S. v. Ward, 7 Baxt. 76.

[16] Horton v. S., 53 Ala. 488.

[17] Thus, a telegram announcing the death of a relative and directing money to be sent to a third party for forwarding the remains was held to be such an instrument within a statutory definition: Dooley v. S., 21 Tex. Ap. 549.

[18] S. v. Jefferson, 39 La. An. 331,— an instrument showing the performance of work.

[19] Billups v. S., 88 Ga. 27; Travis v.

§ 753. Undertakings, warrants, or orders for the payment of money or the delivery of goods.— Many cases decided chiefly under English statutes relate to obligations or orders for the payment of money, and to orders for the delivery of goods. They need be but briefly noticed. A note or due-bill, though indefinite as to the time of payment, was held to be an undertaking for the payment of money,[1] and instruments of guaranty were held to be covered by the same description.[2] A check is a warrant or order;[3] but a request to pay a third person money on account of the supposed writer is not within such description;[4] nor is an instrument professing to be a scrip certificate of a county.[5] An "order for the payment of money" covers a draft payable to bearer,[6] or a check on a bank,[7] or any assignable order.[8] The fact that the instrument is not addressed to any person does not render it the less an order.[9] An order for the payment of a sum in the bills of another person or of the drawee was held not specific enough to constitute an order either for money or for goods.[10] Under the English statute punishing the forgery of warrants or orders for the payment of money, it was held that the two terms were synonymous,[11] and covered a letter of credit,[12] a post-dated check,[13] or a bill of exchange or draft,[14] or any instrument directing the pay-

S., 83 Ga. 372; Rembert v. S., 53 Ala. 467. As to "other writings" or "other instruments," see U. S. v. Lawrence, 13 Blatch. 211.

[1] Reg. v. Anderson, 2 M. & Rob. 469; Reg. v. Chambers, L. R. 1 C. C. 341.

[2] Reg. v. Reed, 8 C. & P. 623; Reg. v. Joyce, L. & C. 576; Reg. v. Stone, 2 C. & K. 364; Reg. v. Coelho, 9 Cox, 8.

[3] Rex v. Crowther, 5 C. & P. 316. A pretended order from a seaman for payment of his wages was held to be a bill of exchange under the English statute: Rex v. McIntosh, 2 East, P. C. 942, 956.

[4] Reg. v. Roberts, Car. & M. 652; Reg. v. Curry, 2 Moody, 218; Reg. v. Thorn, Car. & M. 206; nor is a false authority to draw money within the description of an order: Reg. v. Dixon, 3 Cox, 289.

[5] Reg. v. West, 2 C. & K. 496.

[6] P. v. Brigham, 2 Mich. 550.

[7] P. v. Howell, 4 Johns. 296. An indictment charging a forged indorsement of an order for money which shows the instrument to be a check is sufficient to bring the case under a statute making it penal to utter a forged indorsement of a bill of exchange: P. v. Kemp, 76 Mich. 410.

[8] S. v. Lee, 32 Kan. 360.

[9] Powers v. S., 87 Ind. 97; S. v. Gullette, 121 Mo. 447; Noakes v. P., 25 N. Y. 380; Peete v. S., 2 Lea, 513; Alexander v. S., 28 Tex. Ap. 186; Reg. v. Hawkes, 2 Moody, 60.

[10] P. v. Farrington, 14 Johns. 348.

[11] Rex v. Mitchell, 2 East, P. C. 936.

[12] Reg. v. Raake, 8 C. & P. 626.

[13] Reg. v. Taylor, 1 C. & K. 213.

[14] Rex v. Willoughby, 2 East, P. C. 944. Where a check purported to be

ment of money by a third person,[1] and it was not necessary that the warrant or order be addressed to any particular person, as the direction might be supplied by extrinsic evidence;[2] nor that the name of the person to whom the money or property is to be delivered be stated;[3] and in such case it is immaterial that the instrument is uncertain as to the property to be delivered.[4] A postoffice money order was held to be both a warrant and an order for the payment of money;[5] but a mere direction to advance money for the supposed signer, or a request for money, was held not to be sufficient to come within the statute.[6] So an instrument which is necessary in order to secure the payment of money, but does not in itself call for such payment, is not within the statute.[7] A request to deliver property to a third person is within the statute as to forgery,[8] and it is not necessary that the supposed signer have any prop-

drawn on a bank where the person whose name was signed had funds but not subject to check, it was held that the instrument might be properly called a forged warrant, but not a forged order: Reg. v. Williams, 2 C. & K. 51.

[1] Reg. v. Smith, 1 C. & K. 700; Reg. v. Vivian, 1 C. & K. 719; Reg. v. McConnell, 1 C. & K. 371; Reg. v. Carter, 1 C. & K. 741; Reg. v. Harris, 1 C. & K. 179; Rex v. McIntosh, 2 East, P. C. 942; Reg. v. Autey, Dears. & B. 294; Reg. v. Dawson, 2 Den. 75; Reg. v. Lonsdale, 3 Cox, 222; Rex v. Bamfield, 1 Moody, 416.

[2] Reg. v. Rogers, 9 C. & P. 41; Reg. v. Pulbrook, 9 C. & P. 37; Rex v. Carney, 1 Moody, 351; Reg. v. Snelling, Dears. 219; Nelson v. S., 82 Ala. 44; S. v. Stephen, 45 La. An. 702. But see Rex v. Cullen, 5 C. & P. 116; Rex v. Clinch, 2 East, P. C. 938.

[3] S. v. Keeter, 80 N. C. 472; Hobbs v. S., 75 Ala. 1; Burke v. S., 66 Ga. 157; Thomas v. S., 59 Ga. 784; U. S. v. Book, 2 Cranch, C. C. 294; U. S. v. Brown, 3 Cranch, C. C. 268. But a bill drawn upon the treasurer of the navy to ——— or order, signed in the name of a navy surgeon, was held not sufficient, lacking the name of a payee: Rex v. Richards, Russ. & Ry. 193. And see Rex v. Ravenscroft, Russ. & Ry. 161; Reg. v. Ellis, 4 Cox, 258; Rex v. Randall, Russ. & Ry. 195.

[4] Burke v. S., 66 Ga. 157; Hobbs v. S., 75 Ala. 1; S. v. Keeler, 80 N. C. 472.

[5] Reg. v. Gilchrist, Car. & M. 224.

[6] Reg. v. Thorn, Car. & M. 206; Reg. v. Ellor, 2 East, P. C. 938. Otherwise under some statutes: Jones v. S., 50 Ala. 161; U. S. v. Green, 2 Cranch, C. C. 520. And see *infra*, § 756.

[7] Reg. v. Pilling, 1 F. & F. 324; Reg. v. Mitchell, 2 F. & F. 44.

[8] Chidester v. S., 25 Ohio St. 433; S. v. Cooper, 5 Day, 250; P. v. Shaw, 5 Johns. 236; Allen v. S., 74 Ala. 557; Hobbs v. S., 75 Ala. 1; Hale v. S., 1 Coldw. 167; S. v. Lane, 80 N. C. 407; Hendricks v. S., 26 Tex. Ap. 176; Rex v. Evans, 5 C. & P. 553; Reg. v. White, 9 C. & P. 282; Reg. v. James, 8 C. & P. 292; Rex v. Thomas, 7 C. & P. 851; Reg. v. Walters, Car. & M. 588; Rex v. Jones, 2 East, P. C. 941; Reg. v. Illidge, 2 C. & K. 871. It is immaterial that the payment is to

erty or funds in the hands of the drawee;[1] but a request to let the person have goods, for which the supposed drawer would see him paid, was held not a warrant or order for the delivery of goods.[2] A request for the delivery of goods, while not a warrant or order, was within the English statute.[3]

§ 754. **Receipts.**— The statutes uniformly include receipts in the enumeration of instruments which are subject of forgery.[4] A receipted bill for goods is a receipt within the statute;[5] so is a toll-gate ticket.[6] An entry on a bank book of the receipt of money is within the statute.[7] So where a banker's receipt for money deposited was forged and the money secured thereon, this was held to be within the statute.[8] The false entry of payment on a note in the payee's possession is a forgery, though unsigned.[9] The false making of a receipt may be a forgery although the intention and attempt is not to defraud the person whose receipt it purports to be, but others who are misled by the false payment of money. Thus, where one is entitled to reimbursement for money paid out, the falsifying of receipts for money claimed to have been thus paid out is criminal.[10] But

be for drawer's benefit: S. v. Nevins, 23 Vt. 519.

[1] C. v. Fisher, 17 Mass. 46; P. v. Way, 10 Cal. 336; Hoskins v. S., 11 Ga. 92; S. v. Leak, 80 N. C. 403. But it is otherwise under some statutes: S. v. Lamb, 65 N. C. 419; Walton v. S., 6 Yerg. 377.

[2] Rex v. Mitchell, 2 East, P. C. 936.

[3] Reg. v. Robson, 9 C. & P. 423; Reg. v. Williams, 2 Den. 61; Rex v. Cullen, 5 C. & P. 116.

[4] C. v. Talbot, 2 Allen, 161; S. v. Shelters, 51 Vt. 102; Rex v. Martin, 7 C. & P. 549; Reg. v. Boardman, 2 M. & Rob. 147. So the alteration of the date of a receipt is forgery: Allen v. S., 79 Ala. 34. False making of a receipt for a promissory note was held not within the terms of a statute, though it would be an offense at common law: S. v. Foster, 3 McCord, 442. An unsigned memorandum on the back of a note, showing money paid, was held not to be a receipt: S. v. Davis, 53 Ia. 252. A receipt is an instrument in writing: *Supra*, § 752.

[5] C. v. White, 145 Mass. 392.

[6] Reg. v. Fitch, L. & C. 159; but it is said that a railway ticket is not: Reg. v. Gooden, 11 Cox, 672. As to railway tickets, see *supra*, § 752.

[7] Rex v. Harrison, 2 East, P. C. 926; Reg. v. Smith, L. & C. 168.

[8] Reg. v. Atkinson, Car. & M. 325.

[9] Kegg v. S., 10 Ohio, 75. But it would seem that there must be some rule of law or agreement by which the indorsement of payment would have the force of a receipt to make the act criminal: S. v. Martin, 9 Humph. 55.

[10] C. v. Brown, 147 Mass. 585; Rex v. Martin, 7 C. & P. 549; Rex v. Thomas, 2 East, P. C. 934; Reg. v. Griffiths, Dears. & B. 548; Reg. v. Smith, L. & C. 168; Rex v. Jones, 2 East, P. C. 991. And see Rex v. Rice, 6 C. & P. 634; Rex v. Hope, 1 Moody, 414. It is not necessary to aver that there was a liability against which

where, by the rules of a society, members of one branch might be admitted into another upon showing full payment of dues in the branch from which they were admitted, it was held that the presentation of a false receipt for such dues was not forgery.[1] Falsifying receipts for goods as well as for money is within the statute.[2]

§ 755. **Books of account.**— Making a false entry in one's own books of account is not forgery, though the books might be admissible in evidence to prove the entries made therein;[3] and it seems that where an employee, for the purpose of covering up his embezzlement by presenting false slips, secures false entries in the books of the bank, he does not thereby commit forgery;[4] but it is said in another case that making false entries in the bank's books for the purpose of defrauding the bank is forgery;[5] and certainly the making of false entries by an agent in his principal's books for the purpose of showing himself to be accountable for a less sum than he is truly accountable for would be forgery.[6] The fraudulent alteration of an account stated would of course be forgery.[7]

§ 756. **Validity or legal effect of the writing.**—It is a general proposition of which there are numerous examples, that to be subject of forgery the writing must on its face be such as, if genuine, would be of some legal efficacy;[8] and the mere fact that it might have worked injury upon a person ignorant of the law, or might form a piece of evidence, if genuine, is not sufficient to make it the subject of forgery;[9] so an instrument which has never acquired any legal efficacy by being executed or issued cannot be the basis of a forged indorsement or ac-

the receipt purported to be given: Snell v. S., 2 Humph. 347.

1 Reg. v. French, L. R. 1 C. C. 217.

2 Reg. v. Fitchie, Dears. & B. 175; Reg. v. Pries, 6 Cox, 165; Reg. v. Meigh, 7 Cox, 401.

3 S. v. Young, 46 N. H. 266.

4 In re Tully, 20 Fed. R. 812. And see In re Winsor, 6 B. & S. 522.

5 C. v. Luberg, 94 Pa. St. 85.

6 Biles v. C., 32 Pa. St. 529.

7 Barnum v. S., 15 Ohio, 717.

8 P. v. Shall, 9 Cow. 778; Barnum v. S., 15 Ohio, 717; S. v. Evans, 15 Mont. 539. If the instrument does not, on its face, appear to be of such legal effect as to perpetrate an injury, the indictment must set out such extrinsic facts as are necessary for the purpose: Clarke v. S., 8 Ohio St. 630; P. v. Tomlinson, 35 Cal. 503; S. v. Briggs, 34 Vt. 501.

9 Roode v. S., 5 Neb. 174; S. v. Young, 46 N. H. 266; Brown v. P., 86 Ill. 239; S. v. Pierce, 8 Ia. 231; Reed v. S., 28 Ind. 396; Terry v. C., 87 Va. 672; Rex v. McIntosh, 2 East, P. C. 942.

ceptance. As the instrument is of no validity, the false writing thereon is of no legal effect.[1] And similarly, the fraudulent alteration of an incomplete note has been held not to be forgery.[2] A note payable to the maker's order is of no legal efficacy, and the alteration thereof by the maker before indorsement is not forgery;[3] but an alteration of a bill of exchange by the drawee after acceptance is forgery.[4] If, however, the instrument, though of no legal efficacy, may be made so by a holder of it, it may be subject of forgery.[5] On the other hand, if the legal efficacy of the instrument has been exhausted, it is not subject of forgery.[6] A mere recommendation or request for a favor is not an instrument importing such legal obligation that it is subject of forgery;[7] but in England it has been held that certificates of character or good conduct are such instruments as may be forged.[8] It is not necessary, however, that the instrument be one on which, if genuine, legal action might be maintained; if it is such as might be used as proof against the person by whom it purports to be executed, or in any other legal proceeding, it may be subject of forgery; and it was so held as to a receipt,[9] and also as to a marriage certificate.[10]

[1] Reg. v. Harper, 7 Q. B. D. 78; Reg. v. Mopsey, 11 Cox, 143; Reg. v. Butterwick, 2 M. & Rob. 196. Thus, for a private person to sign an instrument which could be of effect only when executed by a certain public officer was held not forgery: Rex v. Knight, 1 Salk. 375.

[2] S. v. Monnier, 8 Minn. 212; Reg. v. Turpin, 2 C. & K. 820; Rex v. Pateman, Russ. & Ry. 455; Rex v. Lyon, 2 East, P. C. 933.

[3] C. v. Dallinger, 118 Mass. 439. But falsely making and uttering a bill payable to the prisoner's own order, though not indorsed, was held criminal: Rex v. Birkett, Russ. & Ry. 86; Rex v. Wicks, Russ. & Ry. 149.

[4] P. v. Fitch, 1 Wend. 198. So, where a justice of the peace altered a writ issued by him after it had been served and returned, he was held guilty of forgery: C. v. Mycall, 2 Mass. 136.

[5] S. v. Mott, 16 Minn. 472.

[6] P. v. Fitch, 1 Wend. 198.

[7] Waterman v. P., 67 Ill. 91. And see *supra*, § 753. The false making of a statement that the supposed maker and the person who falsely makes the instrument are partners is not necessarily a forgery: Jackson v. Weisiger, 2 B. Mon. 214.

[8] Reg. v. Moah, Dears. & B. 550; Reg. v. Wilson, Dears. & B. 558; Reg. v. Toshack, 1 Den. 492; Reg. v. Mitchell, 2 F. & F. 44; Reg. v. Sharman, Dears. 285.

[9] S. v. Smith, 46 La. An. 1433. As to receipts, see, also, *supra*, § 754.

[10] S. v. Boasso, 38 La. An. 202. But *contra*, see Reg. v. Heywood, 2 C. & K. 352.

§ 757. Apparent legal efficacy.— It is, however, the apparent rather than the real legal efficacy of the instrument which is material, and the crime may be committed although there is some defect which would prevent the instrument from being effectual for the purpose for which it is apparently intended.[1] It is no defense that an inquiry into extrinsic facts,[2] or a careful scrutiny of it, would show that it is not effectual or genuine.[3] The question as to whether it is calculated to mislead is for the jury,[4] and the presumption is in favor of its validity.[5] It is not necessary that the instrument be such as to cause any injury to the party apparently affected thereby. It is enough that it be such as is calculated to expose another to loss or risk of loss. It is immaterial, therefore, that a forged deed purports to grant land to which the grantor named has no title;[6] and even although the person apparently bound by the instrument is not legally bound, yet as he may be put to the cost and risk of defending, he may be considered as the party defrauded.[7] While it was stated under an early Massachusetts statute, with reference to forging bank-notes, that the offense was not committed by making a note purporting to be signed by one who in fact never was the cashier of the bank,[8] yet, in general, it is not necessary that the person whose name is used as maker has any authority to execute the instrument.[9] The existence of the person or bank whose name is forged is immaterial.[10] Thus, it is immaterial in an indictment for making a false check that the person in whose name the check is drawn has no right to draw from the bank.[11] An order purporting to have been signed by the selectmen of a town is subject of forgery, without showing that the persons whose names were on the order were in fact such officers;[12] but on the other hand

[1] S. v. Fisher, 65 Mo. 437; S. v. Tompkins, 71 Mo. 613.

[2] S. v. Hilton, 35 Kan. 338, 8 Am. Cr. R. 261, and note; S. v. Pierce, 8 Ia. 231; S. v. Johnson, 26 Ia. 407; Reg. v. Pike, 2 Moody, 70.

[3] S. v. Robinson, 16 N. J. 507.

[4] Lemasters v. S., 95 Ind. 367.

[5] Bowles v. S., 37 Ohio St. 35.

[6] P. v. Van Alstine, 57 Mich. 69.

[7] Rounds v. S., 78 Me. 42.

[8] C. v. Boynton, 2 Mass. 77. To same effect with reference to an order for property: S. v. Cooper, 5 Day, 250.

[9] So with reference to names used as those of president and cashier on a bank-note: U. S. v. Turner, 7 Pet. 132; U. S. v. Brewster, 7 Pet. 164.

[10] U. S. v. Mitchell, Baldw. 366; S v. Pierce, 8 Ia. 231.

[11] C. v. Russell, 156 Mass. 196; Rex v. Lockett, 2 East, P. C. 940.

[12] S. v. Flye, 26 Me. 312.

the instrument must be of such form as to lead persons to believe that it was genuine, duly authorized and effectual.[1] If the instrument, however, if genuine, would be ineffectual only by reason of some condition not being complied with, upon which its validity depends, this would not render it the less subject of forgery.[2]

§ 758. **Invalid instrument.**— The false making of an instrument which is entirely without legal validity is not forgery.[3] Thus, it is said that there cannot be forgery of a bank-note for a less amount than bank-notes are authorized to be issued for.[4] But if such notes, although not authorized, are not expressly declared to be invalid, the act may be criminal, for they may be effectual as imposing an obligation, even though not authorized to circulate as money;[5] and the fact that an instrument is not in required legal form will not prevent its being subject of forgery where the statute does not make it wholly void.[6] It is not necessary that the instrument be shown to be perfect and effectual, but it is sufficient that it appears to be one which, if genuine, might have some legal effect.[7] So a false instru-

[1] Snow v. S., 14 Wis. 479; Rex v. Rushworth, Russ. & Ry. 317. And the false making of an order purporting to be made by a magistrate, to allow a burial at the expense of the county, was held criminal, although the name used was not that of any magistrate in the county: Rex v. Froud, Russ. & Ry. 389.

[2] C. v. Costello, 120 Mass. 358; P. v. Heed, 1 Idaho, N. S. 531; Rex v. Fawcett, 2 East, P. C. 862. For instance, if a certificate of indebtedness is transferable only by the holder in person, a false indorsement may be forgery, as the objection might be waived: Bishop v. S., 55 Md. 138.

[3] Where certificates of subscription to a corporation were falsely made, it was held that no crime was committed if the conditions imposed by charter as precedent to the right to issue such certificates had not been complied with: Manaway v. S., 44 Ala. 375. So it is not forgery to make a false certificate of a trade-mark if there is no valid trade-mark: U. S. v. Braun, 39 Fed. R. 775. But a pretended certificate of city indebtedness may be a forgery, though the city had no authority to issue such certificate: S. v. Eades, 68 Mo. 150.

[4] Rex v. Moffatt, 2 East, P. C. 954.

[5] S. v. Van Hart, 17 N. J. 327; Butler v. C., 12 Serg. & R. 237; Van Horne v. S., 5 Ark. 349.

[6] Rex v. Lyon, Russ. & Ry. 255. Where by statute a city warrant was not valid unless it showed the fund upon which it was drawn, a warrant not showing that fact was held not subject of forgery: Raymond v. P., 2 Colo. Ap. 329.

[7] Allgood v. S., 87 Ga. 668. So held as to an order signed by a married woman which would be good against her separate estate: Wilcoxson v. S., 60 Ga. 184. So held, also, as to a mortgage signed by a married man which would be effectual only when signed

ment purporting to be the deed of a man who is dead may be a forgery.[1] Under some statutes it has been held that if some extrinsic fact would be necessary to render the instrument effectual, if genuine, such fact must be alleged to show that the instrument might be capable of defrauding.[2] But by the weight of authority it is sufficient that the instrument appears to be one that might be good and effectual, if valid, though the circumstances which would render it effectual do not appear.[3] So an instrument which by law is required to be stamped may, though unstamped, be subject of forgery,[4] for the stamp might be subsequently affixed and the instrument rendered valid.[5] So an instrument purporting to be dated on Sunday,[6] or which appears to be void as against public policy,[7] may still be subject of forgery. But if the instrument appears to be one without legal efficacy, an allegation of the false making of it will not be sufficient to show forgery.[8]

§ 759. **Invalid for lack of authority.**— If the signature to or indorsement of an instrument is not that of one who is apparently authorized to sign or indorse it, the false making will

by himself and wife: P. v. Baker, 100 Cal. 188.

[1] Henderson v. S., 14 Tex. 503.

[2] Dixon v. S., 81 Ala. 61; S. v. Humphreys, 10 Humph. 442; Tait v. S., 3 Yerg. 449; S. v. Anderson, 30 La. An., Part I, 557. Making a false claim for money against a county where there was no indebtedness was held not to be forgery: S. v. Corfield, 46 Kan. 207. There must be both intention and power to defraud: Williams v. S., 90 Ala. 649.

[3] Smith v. S., 29 Fla. 408; P. v. Bibby, 91 Cal. 470; S. v. Wingard, 40 La. An. 733; S. v. Holley, 1 Brev. 35; Snell v. S., 2 Humph. 347; Kennedy v. S., 33 Tex. Ap. 183; Rex v. Gade, 2 East, P. C. 874; Reg. v. Vanderstein, 10 Cox, 146. If the instrument could in no way injuriously affect the party who, it is alleged, was intended to be defrauded, there cannot be a conviction for forgery: S. v. Dufour, 63 Ind. 567; Barnum v. S., 15 Ohio, 717.

[4] Laird v. S., 61 Md. 309; Cross v. P., 47 Ill. 152; S. v. Haynes, 6 Coldw. 550; P. v. Frank, 28 Cal. 507; S. v. Hill, 30 Wis. 416; Rex v. Hawkeswood, 2 East, P. C. 955; Rex v. Morton, 2 East, P. C. 955; Rex v. Reculist, 2 East, P. C. 956. *Contra*, John v. S., 23 Wis. 504.

[5] S. v. Young, 47 N. H. 402.

[6] Shaffer v. McCrackin, 90 Ia. 578.

[7] P. v. Munroe, 100 Cal. 664.

[8] Williams v. S., 51 Ga. 535; Cox v. S., 66 Miss. 14; Dixon v. S., 81 Ala. 61; S. v. Givens, 5 Ala. 747; S. v. Ward, 7 Baxt. 76; S. v. Corley, 4 Baxt. 410; Reed v. S., 28 Ind. 396; P. v. Stearns, 21 Wend. 409; Howell v. S., 37 Tex. 591. If the instrument does not on its face appear to be valuable or calculated to work a fraud, extrinsic facts must be averred to show a fraudulent tendency: P. v. Tomlinson, 35 Cal. 503; S. v. Murphy, 46 La. An. 415.

not be criminal;[1] but it is not necessary that the maker had the actual power or authority so long as the instrument on its face is such as to be likely to defraud those who act upon it as genuine.[2] Thus, while an order may be so entirely lacking in legal effect as not to be subject of forgery,[3] yet if the instrument is of doubtful legality, and by proper allegations its apparent validity may be shown, it is subject of forgery;[4] and in a number of cases orders which were indefinite and uncertain in terms have nevertheless been held to be so far legal that forgery thereof could be committed.[5]

§ 760. **Delivery not essential.**— It is the false making with intent to defraud, and not the act of defrauding, that constitutes the crime; therefore it is not necessary to allege or prove that the forged instrument was delivered to any one or in any way passed or uttered.[6]

§ 761. **False signature; similarity not essential.**— It is immaterial in what form the false signature is written,[7] and an imitation of an engraved signature would be forgery as fully as if the imitation were by writing.[8] So it is forgery to sign another's name by means of a mark.[9] The counterfeiting of another's handwriting may be forgery although not so skilfully done as to deceive those acquainted with the genuine signature.[10] It is not necessary that the false signature bear an exact resemblance to the genuine; it is sufficient if the in-

[1] Drake v. S., 19 Ohio St. 211; S. v. Wheeler, 19 Minn. 98.

[2] S. v. Eades, 68 Mo. 150.

[3] Bynam v. S., 17 Ohio St. 142; Anderson v. S., 20 Tex. Ap. 595, 598.

[4] Rollins v. S., 22 Tex. Ap. 548; Williams v. S., 24 Tex. Ap. 342; Baysinger v. S., 77 Ala. 63.

[5] S. v. Baumon, 52 Ia. 68; Evans v. S., 8 Ohio St. 196; P. v. d'Argencour, 95 N. Y. 624; Wright v. S., 79 Ala. 262; S. v. Schwartz, 64 Wis. 432; S. v. Coyle, 41 Wis. 267; Reddick v. S., 31 Tex. Ap. 587; Hendricks v. S., 26 Tex. Ap. 176; S. v. Ferguson, 35 La. An. 1042; S. v. Morgan, 35 La. An. 293. The name of the party to whom the order is addressed need not appear on the face of the instrument, but may be shown by extrinsic evidence: Reg. v. Snelling, Dears. 219. And see *supra*, § 753.

[6] C. v. Ladd, 15 Mass. 526; Hawkins v. S., 28 Fla. 363; Keeler v. S., 15 Tex. Ap. 111; Rex v. Crocker, Russ. & Ry. 97. And see *infra*, § 773.

[7] For instance, whether in Gothic or Roman characters: Duffin v. P., 107 Ill. 113.

[8] C. v. Ray, 3 Gray, 441.

[9] Rex v. Dunn, 2 East, P. C. 962.

[10] C. v. Stephenson, 11 Cush. 481; S. v. Cross, 101 N. C. 770. Want of similarity may be evidence of the absence of an intent to defraud, but not where the fraud has actually been committed: S. v. Cross, 101 N. C. 770.

strument is calculated to deceive.[1] But the name used, where the forgery is charged as consisting of the use of a false name, must be such as, if genuine, would be effectual to defraud; and where the name as signed would not bind the party who it is claimed was intended to be represented thereby, the act is not a forgery although the person signing may have intended to bind such person.[2] The similarity of the false instrument to a genuine one, which is necessary in counterfeiting, is not essential in forgery.[3]

§ 762. **Unauthorized signature.**— The essence of the wrongful act is the execution of the instrument with the intent that it shall be received as the act of another than the party signing it.[4] Thus, it is forgery for one to sign his own name to an instrument intending that it shall be taken as the name of another.[5] Where a bill was addressed to a person named at a certain address, and was accepted in that name without address, it was held that the fact that there was no person of the name at that address did not prove a forgery, the acceptance being by a person of the proper name.[6] But where one person purports to represent another and to make the instrument thereby binding on such other person and not on himself, the mere want of authority to bind the other will not render the instrument a forgery.[7] It is not enough that the signature

[1] Rex v. Elliott, 2 East, P. C. 951; Reg. v. Mahony, 6 Cox, 487; S. v. Dennett, 19 La. An. 395. The misspelling of the name of the signer will not prevent the act being forgery: S. v. Gryder, 44 La. An. 962; Peete v. S., 2 Lea, 513; S. v. Covington, 94 N. C. 913; Gooden v. S., 55 Ala. 178.

[2] Abbott v. S., 59 Ind. 70.

[3] S. v. Carr, 5 N. H. 367; P. v. Stewart, 4 Mich. 655; S. v. Gullette, 121 Mo. 447; U. S. v. Trout, 4 Biss. 105. See *infra*, § 774.

[4] C. v. Foster, 114 Mass. 311; and it is immaterial that defendant has previously used the same name for innocent purposes, if in the particular instance he uses it for fraudulent purposes: C. v. Costello, 120 Mass. 358.

[5] P. v. Peacock, 6 Cow. 72; Barfield v. S., 29 Ga. 127; U. S. v. Long, 30 Fed. R. 678; Mead v. Young, 4 Term R. 28. If a person gets another to accept a bill in his true name intending at the time to represent such name to be that of another for fraudulent purposes, it is forgery: Reg. v. Mitchell, 1 Den. 282. So if the address of the person whose name is signed is added or changed for the purpose of making it appear that the signature is that of another than the one who signs, the act is forgery: Reg. v. Blenkinsop, 2 C. & K. 531; Reg. v. Epps, 4 F. & F. 81.

[6] Rex v. Webb, Russ. & Ry. 405. And see Rex v. Story, Russ. & Ry. 81.

[7] S. v. Wilson, 28 Minn. 52; P. v. Bendit, — Cal. —, 43 Pac. R. 901,

implies an authority to act for the person whose name is used, which the defendant did not have. If the signature is known to have been made by him, it will not constitute forgery though he acted without authority in making it.[1] Nor will one who signs his own name as treasurer of a municipal corporation be guilty of forgery in doing so, even though he is not such officer.[2] But where an instrument is signed or issued in the name of another, and the handwriting of the person whose instrument it purports to be is disproved, it is not necessary to further prove by direct evidence that he did not authorize the execution of such instrument in his name by the person who executed it. Other circumstances may be sufficient to show that the act was with criminal intent.[3] Where one signs his own name, or that of another for whom he is authorized to act, to a false instrument, it is forgery.[4]

§ 763. **By procurement.**— While it seems that procuring the forgery of an instrument without being present at the execution does not constitute the offense of forgery, but is punishable only under statutes with reference to procuring the commission of offenses,[5] yet the crime may be committed through an innocent agent.[6] Thus, where a daughter was induced by another to sign her father's name to a note of hand, it was held a forgery on the part of the person procuring such signature, the daughter being innocent of any wrongful intent, and hav-

31 L. R. A. 831, and note; S. v. Taylor, 46 La. An. 1332; S. v. Lurch, 12 Oreg. 95; Rex v. Forbes, 7 C. & P. 224; Reg. v. Parish, 8 C. & P. 94; Reg. v. White, 2 C. & K. 404. Thus if, by reason of previous instruments executed in the name of another having been acknowledged by such person, an implied authority to sign such name has arisen, a subsequent use of the name in the same manner will not be a forgery: Reg. v. Beard, 8 C. & P. 143; so where implied authority is otherwise shown: Reg. v. Clifford, 2 C. & K. 202; Reg. v. Beardsall, 1 F. & F. 629; Reg. v. Smith, 3 F. & F. 504. But where a signature is proven not to be that of the person whose signature it purports to be, it is not necessary to go further and show that it was without the authority of some other person of the same name: Rex v. Hampton, 1 Moody, 255. Want of authority must, however, under the Texas statute, be alleged and proved: Shanks v. S., 25 Tex. Supp. 326. Where defendant admits the signature, the burden is on the prosecution to show that it was unauthorized: Romans v. S., 51 Ohio St. 528.

[1] C. v. Baldwin, 11 Gray, 197.

[2] P. v. Mann, 75 N. Y. 484.

[3] Reg. v. Hurley, 2 M. & Rob. 473.

[4] Hooper v. S., 30 Tex. Ap. 412; Moore v. C., 92 Ky. 630.

[5] Chidester v. S., 25 Ohio St. 433.

[6] C. v. Foster, 114 Mass. 311.

ing previously acted under her father's directions in executing a similar instrument.[1] But there is no reason why, if the offense is a felony, the procurer should not be guilty as accessory before the fact, even though the act is done by one who has guilty knowledge.[2] Forgery may be committed by procuring a party through fraud to sign his own name to a different instrument than that which he intends to sign.[3] But it is not forgery to induce a person, by misreading an instrument, to sign it when he would not have done so if it had been correctly read,[4] or to induce him by fraudulent representations to consent to an alteration in an instrument executed by him before it is delivered, that is, before it has become effective.[5]

§ **764. Fictitious name.**— It has already been said that the instrument must be one purporting to bind a person who, if the instrument were genuine, would be in some way bound thereby.[6] Thus, if the forgery is of an order purporting to bind a person having no authority to make such order, the crime is not committed.[7] And it has been accordingly held that one who, with intent to forge the check of a firm, signs a name which is not the firm name, does not commit forgery, but the statutory crime of making a note or check bearing a fictitious signature with intent to defraud.[8] It is the uttering and not the making of a fictitious instrument which such a statute makes punishable.[9] But on the other hand it seems to have been settled by a long line of decisions that where the person intended to be defrauded is not fictitious, the act may be forgery although the instrument is executed in the name of a fictitious person.[10] The instrument supposed to be forged must

[1] Gregory v. S., 26 Ohio St. 510.

[2] C. v. Ray, 3 Gray, 441.

[3] S. v. Shurtliff, 18 Me. 368. To procure a party to sign an antedated deed, with intent to defraud a prior grantee, is forgery: Reg. v. Ritson, L. R. 1 C. C. 200.

[4] C. v. Sankey, 22 Pa. St. 390; Douglass v. Matting, 29 Ia. 498; Wells v. S., 89 Ga. 788; Reg. v. Chadwick, 2 M. & Rob. 545; Reg. v. Collins, 2 M. & Rob. 461.

[5] S. v. Flanders, 38 N. H. 324.

[6] *Supra*, § 759.

[7] Rex v. Baker, 1 Moody, 231; Reg. v. Newton, 2 Moody, 59; Rex v. Williams, 2 East, P. C. 937.

[8] P. v. Elliott, 90 Cal. 586; P. v. Eppinger, 105 Cal. 36. There is such a statute in Georgia as to fictitious bills of exchange: Townsend v. S., 92 Ga. 732.

[9] Shirk v. P., 121 Ill. 61.

[10] P. v. Marion, 29 Mich. 31; C. v. Chandler, Thach. Cr. Cas. 187; S. v. Givens, 5 Ala. 747; Thompson v. S., 49 Ala. 16; Ex parte Hibbs, 26 Fed. R. 421; S. v. Wheeler, 20 Oreg. 192;

be a false instrument, and if it is understood to be the instrument of the one who signs it, his use of a fictitious name will not make it a forgery, the credit having been given to him without regard to the name.[1] On similar principles it is forgery to sign a dead man's name to an instrument with intent to defraud.[2] One who made a false power of attorney authorizing him to receive a seaman's wages, executing it in the name of a supposed child of the deceased seaman as administratrix, there being in fact no such child, was held guilty of forgery.[3]

§ 765. **Alteration.**— A fraudulent alteration equally with a false making or false signature will constitute forgery,[4] and this is so even though, by statute, alteration is expressly made criminal.[5] The instrument thus altered may be charged as forged.[6] So it is forgery to detach a condition from an instrument by which it is converted into an instrument of a different effect,[7] or to change or erase an indorsement.[8] Raising the amount mentioned in an instrument is a well-recognized form

S. v. Minton, 116 Mo. 605; S. v. Hahn, 38 La. An. 169; Rex v. Bolland, 2 East, P. C. 958; Rex v. Lewis, 2 East, P. C. 957; Rex v. Wilks, 2 East, P. C. 957; Rex v. Taylor, 2 East, P. C. 960; Rex v. Taft, 2 East, P. C. 959; Rex v. Marshall, Russ. & Ry. 75; Rex v. Parkes, 2 East, P. C. 963; Rex v. Whiley, Russ. & Ry. 90; Rex v. Peacock, Russ. & Ry. 278; Reg. v. Rogers, 8 C. & P. 629. And see article in 30 Am. L. Rev. 500. Evidence that no person of the character and address represented on the instrument is to be found is *prima facie* evidence of the non-existence of such person: P. v. Eppinger, 105 Cal. 36; Rex v. Backler, 5 C. & P. 118; Rex v. King, 5 C. & P. 123; Reg. v. Ashby, 2 F. & F. 560; Reg. v. White, 2 F. & F. 554. But the fact that a person uses another name than that by which he is generally known will not constitute forgery, unless it appears that such assumption was with the original purpose of committing the fraud involved in the use of the duplicate name: Reg. v. White, 5 Cox, 290; Rex v. Francis, Russ. & Ry. 209; Rex v. Bontien, Russ. & Ry. 260; Rex v. Aickles, 2 East, P. C. 968.

[1] Rex v. Dunn, 2 East, P. C. 961; Reg. v. Martin, 5 Q. B. D. 34.

[2] Henderson v. S., 14 Tex. 503; Brewer v. S., 32 Tex. Ap. 74; Billings v. S., 107 Ind. 54.

[3] Rex v. Lewis, 2 East, P. C. 957.

[4] S. v. Wooderd, 20 Ia. 541; Caulkins v. Whisler, 29 Ia. 495; U. S. v. Wood, 2 Cranch, C. C. 164; S. v. Waters, 1 Treadw. Const. 669; S. v. Floyd, 5 Strobh. 58; S. v. Kattlemann, 35 Mo. 105.

[5] Rex v. Teague, 2 East, P. C. 979.

[6] C. v. Woods, 10 Gray, 477; C. v. Boutwell, 129 Mass. 124; Stoughton v. S., 2 Ohio St. 563; S. v. Weaver, 13 Ired. 491; Rex v. Dawson, 2 East, P. C. 978. And see *infra*, § 801.

[7] S. v. Stratton, 27 Ia. 420.

[8] Garner v. S., 5 Lea, 213; S. v. McLeron, 1 Aik. 311; Rex v. Birkett, Russ. & Ry. 251; or to obliterate a release indorsed on the instrument: S. v. Thornburg, 6 Ired. 79.

of forgery.[1] Where one fills a blank in an instrument without authority to do so, he commits forgery;[2] equally so if, having authority to fill in a certain amount, he inserts a larger amount.[3] The alteration of a note by inserting, without authority, a rate of interest where a blank for the rate of interest has been left,[4] or a material change in the date of the instrument, will constitute forgery.[5] But the alteration, to constitute forgery, must be material;[6] and a harmless alteration,[7] or one which does not affect legal rights,[8] will not constitute a forgery. It is not necessary, however, that the alteration be such as that the instrument would, if genuine, be effective, but only that the instrument be given the general appearance of one which would be effectual if genuine.[9] Where the indictment charges the alteration as the means of committing forgery, the nature of the alteration must be stated so as to make it appear that it was material.[10] And it must also appear that the instrument altered was genuine.[11]

§ 766. **Intent to defraud.**— The intent to defraud is essential to constitute the crime of forgery.[12] And this intent must be alleged;[13] and the court should include that question in its

[1] C. v. Hide, 94 Ky. 517; Rex v. Dawson, 2 East, P. C. 978; Rex v. Elsworth, 2 East, P. C. 986; Reg. v. Vaughan, 8 C. & P. 276; Rex v. Post, Russ. & Ry. 101. And see Haynes v. S., 15 Ohio St. 455. But where pieces were cut from a bank-bill with the intention of inserting other pieces, thus raising the amount, *held*, that the crime of forgery had not yet been accomplished: C. v. Hayward, 10 Mass. 34.

[2] Flower v. Shaw, 2 C. & K. 703.

[3] Rex v. Hart, 7 C. & P. 652; Reg. v. Wilson, 2 C. & K. 527.

[4] Conger v. Crabtree, 88 Ia. 536.

[5] Allen v. S., 79 Ala. 34; S. v. Maxwell, 47 Ia. 454; Rex v. Atkinson, 7 C. & P. 669; Reg. v. Milton, 10 Cox, 364.

[6] S. v. Riebe, 27 Minn. 315; S. v. Bryant, 17 N. H. 323. But falsely putting a witness' name to a bond was held forgery, although it would be valid without being witnessed: S. v. Gherkin, 7 Ired. 206.

[7] Jackson v. S., 72 Ga. 28.

[8] S. v. Dorrance, 86 Ia. 428.

[9] Haynes v. S., 15 Ohio St. 455.

[10] Bittings v. S., 56 Ind. 101; Kahn v. S., 58 Ind. 168; S. v. Fisher, 58 Mo. 256; Mount v. C., 1 Duv. 90; S. v. Weaver, 13 Ired. 491. But the indictment may follow the statute in charging that defendant did falsely make, forge, alter and counterfeit, etc., without setting out the particular alteration relied upon: S. v. Flye, 26 Me. 312.

[11] Moore v. S., 33 Ga. 225. Thus, it must appear that the instrument had become effectual by being put into circulation: S. v. Greenlee, 1 Dev. 523. *Contra*, Rex v. Kinder, 2 East, P. C. 855.

[12] Pa. v. Misner, Addison, 44.

[13] S. v. Garrigan, 36 Kan. 322; S. v. Seran, 28 N. J. 519; Hooper v. S.,

instructions to the jury.[1] If the act is done under the mistaken belief of authority the crime is not committed.[2] The criminal intent must exist at the time the act is done; if the instrument is signed in good faith and afterwards used as that of another, the act is not forgery.[3] In prosecutions for uttering or passing forged instruments the knowledge of the character of the instrument is essential to the crime;[4] but the allegation of knowledge is not essential where the charge is that of forgery.[5] However, in cases of uttering, the intent to defraud as well as the knowledge of the falsity of the instrument is essential.[6] Knowledge that a deed of land is a forgery cannot be imputed to one by reason of constructive notice by a public record of the existence of a previous grant inconsistent with the one in question.[7]

§ 767. **Intent inferred.**— The intent to defraud may be inferred from the circumstances or the character of the act, if the perpetration of the fraud would be the natural result of the act done.[8] It is the making, etc., with a fraudulent intent, whereby another may be prejudiced, that constitutes forgery; and therefore the fact that defendant intended to secure a just claim,[9] or that he intended to take up the instrument at maturity and had the means to do so, and thus prevent injury,[10] or that he intended to devote the money procured by the forgery to such purpose as to prevent pecuniary injury to the per-

8 Humph. 93; Williams v. S., 9 Humph. 79; S. v. Jackson, 89 Mo. 561.

[1] S. v. Warren, 109 Mo. 430.

[2] Kotter v. P., 150 Ill. 441; Claibourne v. S., 51 Ark. 88; Montgomery v. S., 12 Tex. Ap. 323.

[3] C. v. Foster, 114 Mass. 311.

[4] S. v. Williams, 66 Ia. 573; S. v. Nicholson, 14 La. An. 785. And see *infra*, § 789.

[5] S. v. Cook, 52 Ind. 574; Reg. v. Bowen, 1 C. & K. 501.

[6] Couch v. S., 28 Ga. 367.

[7] Pearson v. S., 55 Ga. 659.

[8] S. v. Kimball, 50 Me. 409; Fletcher v. S., 49 Ind. 124: U. S. v. Brooks, 3 MacArthur, 315; Smith v. S., 29 Fla. 408; Phillips v. S., 6 Tex. Ap. 364. For instance, the presentation of a forged order to the partner of the person on whom it is drawn, and the delivery of goods by him thereunder, will show fraudulent intent, and will not constitute a variance: S. v. Hall, 108 N. C. 776. If a forged acceptance is knowingly uttered with intent that the bill be taken as a bill with a genuine acceptance, the intent to defraud the person to whom the bill is passed and also the person whose name is used is to be presumed: Reg. v. Cooke, 8 C. & P. 582.

[9] S. v. Wooderd, 20 Ia. 541; Bush v. S., 77 Ala. 83.

[10] C. v. Henry, 118 Mass. 460; Reg. v. Geach, 9 C. & P. 499.

son defrauded,[1] will not prevent the act being criminal. The false making, without the uttering, may be criminal, but the presumption of an intent to defraud does not arise from proof of that act alone. The possession of the forged instrument is evidence tending to prove a fraudulent intent, but is not conclusive.[2] Intoxication and insanity are defenses to the same extent only as in other cases where criminal intent is charged.[3]

§ 768. **Execution of the intent.**— At common law it was necessary to charge the intent to defraud some person or persons.[4] The act must be to the prejudice of somebody's rights or it will not constitute forgery;[5] and even though, as is stated in a following section,[6] it is no longer necessary to charge the intent to defraud a particular person, nevertheless there must be proof of the intent to defraud some one.[7] It is not necessary that the injury intended be pecuniary; it is sufficient that the intention be to deprive the other of a legal right.[8]

§ 769. **Fraudulent tendency of the act.**— It must appear either from the face of the instrument or from averments in the indictment that the act charged had a tendency to or was calculated to defraud.[9] But it is not necessary to show in what manner the act charged is to result in fraud; that is a matter of evidence.[10]

§ 770. **Person to be defrauded.**— In cases of forgery there are usually two persons who legally may be defrauded, the one

[1] Claiborne v. S., 51 Ark. 88.

[2] Fox v. P., 95 Ill. 71; Rex v. Crocker, Russ. & Ry. 97.

[3] P. v. Blake, 65 Cal. 275; U. S. v. Roudenbush, 1 Bald. 514.

[4] Drake v. S., 19 Ohio St. 211.

[5] Pauli v. C., 89 Pa. St. 432; Reg. v. Tylney, 1 Den. 319.

[6] See *infra*, § 771.

[7] Reg. v. Hodgson, Dears. & B. 3.

[8] So held under a charge of forging a deposition to prevent a decree of divorce being rendered: S. v. Kimball, 50 Me. 409. To make a forged order for a diploma may be criminal: Alexander v. S., 28 Tex. Ap. 186. A false entry in books made with intent to cover up a previous defalcation is sufficient as to the injury intended: Phelps v. P., 72 N. Y. 365. But the thing intended must be calculated to put the injured party in a worse condition than before: Colvin v. S., 11 Ind. 361.

[9] C. v. Hinds, 101 Mass. 209; C. v. Costello, 120 Mass. 358; C. v. Dunleay, 157 Mass. 386; P. v. Cady, 6 Hill, 490; Clark v. S., 8 Ohio St. 630; Yount v. S., 64 Ind. 443. And while it is not necessary to allege and prove intent to defraud a particular person, yet the intent and means of defrauding must be shown: Reg. v. Hodgson, Dears. & B. 3; Reg. v. Trenfield, 1 F. & F. 43.

[10] Mead v. S., 53 N. J. 601; S. v. Kimball, 50 Me. 409; S. v. Maxwell, 47 Ia. 454; Travis v. S., 83 Ga. 372; Rex v. Powell, 2 East, P. C. 976.

whose name is forged and the one to whom the forged instrument is to be passed. The intent alleged and proved may be as to the one or the other.[1] If money is obtained from the payee upon the instrument forged, it will sufficiently show intent to defraud such payee rather than the apparent maker.[2] The intent to defraud the apparent maker may be inferred even where there is such want of similitude that the maker would not be likely to pay the instrument.[3] On the other hand, where a forged check on one bank was presented to another to be cashed, it was held that the intent to defraud the latter was proven.[4] But where under statute a person was prosecuted for passing counterfeit gold dust, it was held that the requisite intent was intent to defraud the receiver.[5] Where the charge is of forging an auditor's warrant on the state treasurer, the intended fraud should be alleged as against the state.[6] It is immaterial that the person charged as intended to be defrauded is a servant only, if that fact is unknown to the defendant.[7] In an indictment for forging a transfer of shares of stock, the fraud may be alleged as upon the stockholder and the company.[8] Where the intent to defraud is alleged as against an individual, proof that the fraud will affect the firm of which he is a member is sufficient.[9]

§ 771. **Name of person intended to be defrauded.**— It seems that, aside from statute, it is necessary to allege the name of the person intended to be defrauded, or to state that his name is to the grand jurors unknown.[10] So in cases of uttering it has

[1] S. v. Cleaveland, 6 Nev. 181.

[2] Duffin v. P., 107 Ill. 113; Reg. v. Trenfield, 1 F. & F. 43.

[3] Rex v. Mazagora, Russ. & Ry. 291.

[4] Rex v. Crowther, 5 C. & P. 316.

[5] P. v. Sloper, 1 Ida. T. 183.

[6] Cunningham v. S., 49 Miss. 685. So a forged warrant on the treasurer of a school township should be alleged to have been with intent to defraud the board: Gregory v. S., 11 Ohio St. 329.

[7] C. v. Starr, 4 Allen, 301.

[8] Reg. v. Hotson, 2 C. & K. 777. And the register of shareholders in the company is evidence to show that the shareholder appearing therefrom to be the owner of the stock would be defrauded thereby: Reg. v. Nash, 2 Den. 493.

[9] S. v. Hastings, 53 N. H. 452; Reg. v. Hanson, Car. & M. 334. And where the indictment charged the forgery of the name of the firm with intent to defraud two persons named, and it did not appear that they composed the firm, the evidence was held insufficient: S. v. Harrison, 69 N. C. 143.

[10] Stone v. S., 20 N. J. 404; S. v. Weller, 20 N. J. 521. So held in case of counterfeiting: S. v. Odel, 3 Brev. 552; Cunningham v. S., 49 Miss. 685; Rex v. Rushworth, Russ. & Ry. 317.

been held necessary to allege the name of the person intended thereby to be defrauded.[1] But statutes relieving the prosecution from the necessity of proving the name of the person intended to be defrauded are so general that it may now be laid down as the rule that it is unnecessary to allege or prove that fact, a general intent to defraud being sufficient.[2]

§ 772. **Existence of corporation.**— Under the doctrine that it is necessary to allege and prove the name of the person to be defrauded, it has been held with some strictness that where the instrument purports to be the note or obligation of a bank or other corporation the corporate existence must be alleged and proved.[3] Under some statutes it is enough to allege that the instrument purported on its face to be the note of a bank, without alleging or proving the name of such bank.[4] Even

But to sustain the charge of intent to defraud a person named it is not necessary to prove that defendant had such person in mind. It is sufficient that the act would have defrauded him: U. S. v. Long, 30 Fed. R. 678. The charge of intent to defraud two or more persons is sustained by proof of intent to defraud one of them: Gates v. S., 71 Miss. 874; McDonnell v. S., 58 Ark. 242.

1 McClellan v. S., 32 Ark. 609; S. v. Murphy, 17 R. I. 698. *Contra*, S. v. Hart, 67 Ia. 142. An averment of passing to A. will not be supported by proof of passing to B. through A., an innocent agent: Rouse v. S., 4 Ga. 136.

2 McClure v. C., 86 Pa. St. 353; S. v. Kimball, 50 Me. 409; S. v. Keneston, 59 N. H. 36; S. v. Lurch, 12 Oreg. 104; Roush v. S., 34 Neb. 325; S. v. Hart, 67 Ia. 142; S. v. Maxwell, 47 Ia. 454; P. v. Van Alstine, 57 Mich. 69; S. v. Fisher, 65 Mo. 437; S. v. Warren, 109 Mo. 430; S. v. Gullette, 121 Mo. 447; P. v. Stearns, 23 Wend. 634; Noakes v. P., 25 N. Y. 380; P. v. D'Argencour, 95 N. Y. 624; Phillips v. S., 17 Ga. 459; Dukes v. S., 94 Ga. 393; U. S. v. Moses, 4 Wash. C. C. 726; U. S. v. Jolly, 37 Fed. R. 108; Reg. v. Marcus, 2 C. & K. 356. So held, also, in cases of uttering: S. v. Barrett, 8 Ia. 536; S. v. Hart, 67 Ia. 142; so also in passing counterfeit money: S. v. Morton, 8 Wis. 352. The law presumes the intent to be to defraud any one who may suffer a loss by receiving the false paper as genuine: U. S. v. Shellmire, 1 Baldw. 370.

3 S. v. Givens, 5 Ala. 747; Kennedy v. C., 2 Met. (Ky.) 36; S. v. Murphy, 17 R. I. 698; S. v. Morton, 8 Wis. 352; De Bow v. P., 1 Denio, 9. But held not necessary that the bank shall have actually commenced business, if it was in such condition that it might be prejudiced by the forged notes purporting to be issued by it: P. v. Peabody, 25 Wend. 472. Where the bank named was not within the state, *held*, that the indictment should aver its existence: S. v. Twitty, 2 Hawks, 248.

4 P. v. Peabody, 25 Wend. 472; Johnson v. S., 35 Ala. 370; U. S. v. Foye, 1 Curtis, 364. Under a statute punishing the forgery of any note, etc., it is sufficient to prove the forgery of the note of an unchartered bank: Murry v. C., 5 Leigh, 720.

where the existence of the bank must be alleged, evidence that notes of such bank are in general circulation has been held sufficient proof of such existence.[1] Under more recent statutory provisions, allegation or evidence of the incorporation or existence of the bank is unnecessary.[2]

§ 773. **Perpetration of fraud.**— It is not necessary that the fraud be effected in order to constitute the offense, if fraud was intended.[3] It is immaterial whether the expected advantage was to accrue to the forger himself or to another, or whether the purpose was successfully attained or not.[4] In case of uttering, it is necessary, aside from statute, to show the perpetration of the fraud.[5]

II. COUNTERFEITING.

§ 774. **What deemed counterfeit; similitude.**— Some degree of similitude is evidently essential to constitute counterfeiting as known at the common law, but in early English cases it was held that a stamping or impression was not required, and that to make a piece of metal resembling a common worn coin without any impression or stamping constituted counterfeiting.[6] It was said that it was a question of fact whether the coin made was in resemblance to the real coin.[7] It has also been held by the English court that to file off the edges of a genuine coin so as to remove the milling entirely, and then add a new milling, renders the coin false and counterfeit.[8] Under a statute punishing the possession or passing of

[1] C. v. Carey, 2 Pick. 47; Sasser v. S., 13 Ohio, 453, 486; P. v. Ah Sam, 41 Cal. 645; Reed v. S., 15 Ohio, 217; C. v. Smith, 6 Serg. & R. 568; Cady v. C.. 10 Grat. 776.

[2] Roush v. S., 34 Neb. 325; C. v. Smith, 6 Serg. & R. 568.

[3] Rex v. Ward, 2 East, P. C. 861; Dunn v. P., 4 Colo. 126; S. v. Phillips, 78 Mo. 49; S. v. Washington, 1 Bay, 120; S. v. Lurch, 12 Oreg. 99; nor that fraud was possible: Reg. v. Nash, 2 Den. 448. Thus, in case of forged papers to be used in making entry of goods at the custom-house, the existence of such goods need not be alleged: U. S. v. Lawrence, 13 Blatch. 211. The fact that the person whose name is fraudulently signed to the instrument pays it in order to condone the offense does not render the act less criminal: S. v. Tull, 119 Mo. 421. That the instrument need not have been passed, see *supra*, § 760.

[4] S. v. Cross, 101 N. C. 770.

[5] Reg. v. Boult, 2 C. & K. 604.

[6] Rex v. Welsh, 1 East, P. C. 87, 164; Rex v. Wilson, 1 Leach, 285.

[7] Rex v. Welsh, 1 East, P. C. 87, 164.

[8] Reg. v. Hermann, 4 Q. B. D. 284. (Three judges concurred and two dissented.)

counterfeit gold dust for the purpose of defrauding, it was said that the crime was established by proving that the dust was debased, though to an inconsiderable extent.[1] But to make a token which does not purport to be an imitation or in substitution for any known coin is not counterfeiting.[2] The resemblance, however, need not be exact; it is enough if the false coin would be likely to deceive one not an expert, but using ordinary caution.[3] Here the distinction between counterfeiting as a violation of the laws of the United States and the same act as a crime against state law[4] becomes apparent. The offense, so far as the United States is concerned, consists in making something in imitation of the coin, bills, bonds, etc., of the United States, and unless such imitation exists the offense against federal law is not committed, so that a similitude seems necessary;[5] and the making of an instrument like a United States bond and blank as to signature does not constitute an offense.[6] But it is not essential that the instrument should purport to be an obligation of the United States or have such similitude thereto as to deceive experts, if it is calculated to deceive a person of ordinary observation and care.[7] Under a statute prohibiting the counterfeiting or executing of any impression in the likeness of any obligation of the United States, the prohibited act is held criminal although the similitude between the impression and the original is not such that the

[1] P. v. Page, 1 Ida. N. S. 189.

[2] U. S. v. Bogart, 9 Ben. 314.

[3] U. S. v. Hopkins, 26 Fed. R. 443; U. S. v. Morrow, 4 Wash. C. C. 733; U. S. v. Burns, 5 McLean, 23; U. S. v. King, 5 McLean, 208; Clark v. S., 8 Ohio St. 630; Dement v. S., 2 Head, 505; S. v. Gutridge, 1 Bay, 285. Whether the imitation of minor coin shall be deemed counterfeiting under a particular statute will depend on the statutory language: U. S. v. Bicksler, 1 Mackey, 341. Under early English statutes, uttering or tendering counterfeit copper money was not indictable: Rex v. Cirwan, 1 East, P. C. 182.

[4] See *infra*, § 790.

[5] U. S. v. Stevens, 52 Fed. R. 120. And the question of similitude is for the jury: Id. See, also, S. v. Jones, 1 Bay, 207. The allegation that defendant made a "false, forged and counterfeited obligation of the United States," setting out the instrument, implies that there was a genuine instrument of which that set out was an imitation: U. S. v. Owens, 37 Fed. R. 112.

[6] U. S. v. Williams, 14 Fed. R. 550; U. S. v. Sprague, 48 Fed. R. 828.

[7] U. S. v. Sprague, 48 Fed. R. 828. But if the note has similitude to the obligations of the United States, it is immaterial that it is really the note of an insolvent state bank, and is therefore worthless: U. S. v. Stevens, 52 Fed. R. 120.

counterfeit is calculated to deceive the public.[1] And where coins had been produced which were capable of being treated as genuine, it was held that the crime of counterfeiting was complete although defendant intended to coat them with silver before putting them into circulation.[2] But under state statutes the offense is a species of fraud, and it is not necessary to allege that the counterfeit had any similitude to the current coin, or was of any value.[3] And it is counterfeiting to imitate any bank-notes which have had a legal existence although the bank which issued them no longer exists.[4] It is not necessary that the note purported to be of any actually existing bank, if the prosecution is for passing a false note.[5] But on the ground of fraud there can be no conviction for uttering and passing a bill which purports to be of a kind forbidden by statute, as everyone would be supposed to know that such a bill could not be lawfully received.[6] However, the question whether the offense consists in the imitation of a valid note or coin will depend on the form of the statute, and if its language relates to an instrument made in the similitude of a bill issued by a bank established by law, it will not cover a note which is not like any bank-note of a known bank, but a purely fictitious note.[7] Even under such statutory language it is not necessary that the bill bear similitude to any bill actually issued by the bank, if there be such bank having authority to issue bills.[8]

[1] Ex parte Holcomb, 2 Dill. 392. Fraudulently putting off a Confederate note for valid money does not constitute the offense of passing a note in imitation of a national bank note: U. S. v. Wilson, 44 Fed. R. 751. The penalty for violating the federal statute forbidding issuance of business cards in likeness of United States bonds or national bank notes is to be recovered in a *qui tam* action and not by indictment: U. S. v. Laescki, 29 Fed. R. 699.

[2] U. S. v. Abrams, 18 Fed. R. 823.

[3] S. v. Williams, 8 Ia. 533. If the statute prohibits the making of a counterfeit of current coin it must appear that the coin counterfeited is current: Nicholson v. S., 18 Ala. 529.

[4] White v. C., 4 Binn. 418.

[5] McCartney v. S., 3 Ind. 353.

[6] Gutchins v. P., 21 Ill. 642.

[7] C. v. Morse, 2 Mass. 138; S. v. McKenzie, 42 Me. 392. A statute punishing the passing of uncurrent and worthless bank-bills was held not to cover the passing of an instrument not purporting to be signed by the officers of the bank: C. v. Clancy, 7 Allen, 537.

[8] C. v. Smith, 7 Pick. 137; Trice v. S., 2 Head, 591. So held, also, under federal statute as to counterfeiting treasury notes: U. S. v. Owens, 37 Fed. R. 112. In forgery similitude is not necessary: See *supra*, § 761.

By an early English statute the coloring or gilding base coin to resemble coin of a higher value was criminal.[1] One who gilds false coin already made is guilty with those who make the coin.[2]

§ 775. **Foreign coin or notes.**— The states punish counterfeiting of the notes of foreign banks or the coin of a foreign country circulating as currency.[3] But a statute with reference to the counterfeiting of currency which is recognized by usage does not cover the case of coin issued in contravention of the laws of the United States, and therefore illegal.[4] Congress in the exercise of its power to define and punish offenses against the law of the United States may make the counterfeiting of the notes or coin of a foreign government criminal.[5] The court and jury will take notice without proof as to what coins are made current by act of congress, so that the counterfeiting of them is punishable by federal law;[6] and it is sufficient in an indictment to charge defendant with having passed counterfeit "dollars."[7]

§ 776. **Intent.**— If the statute forbids the making of counterfeit coin, the intent is immaterial.[8] The doctrine of intent in general in such cases will be found discussed elsewhere in this chapter.[9]

III. POSSESSION OF COUNTERFEITING TOOLS.

§ 777. **What criminal.**— At common law it is a misdemeanor to have tools for counterfeiting with intent to use them;[10] and at common law, or under statutes similar in effect,

[1] Rex v. Lavey, 1 East, P. C. 166; Rex v. Case, 1 East, P. C. 165; Reg. v. Turner, 2 Moody, 42.

[2] Rasnick v. C., 2 Va. Cas. 356.

[3] C. v. Delany, 1 Grant, 224; C. v. Stearns, 10 Met. 256. And see Reg. v. Roberts, Dears. 539. So a statute providing for the punishment of counterfeiting private trade-marks may cover trade-marks of a foreign merchant: S. v. Gibbs, 56 Mo. 133.

[4] C. v. Bond, 1 Gray, 564.

[5] U. S. v. White, 25 Fed. R. 716; U. S. v. White, 27 Fed. R. 200. But held that the Spanish head pistareen was not a coin made current by law in the United States, and was therefore not subject of counterfeiting: U. S. v. Gardner, 10 Pet. 618.

[6] U. S. v. Burns, 5 McLean, 23; U. S. v. King, 5 McLean, 208.

[7] Peek v. S., 2 Humph. 78.

[8] U. S. v. Russell, 22 Fed. R. 390. It is not necessary to charge the act as done with intent to defraud: U. S. v. Otey, 31 Fed. R. 68.

[9] *Supra*, § 766, and *infra*, § 788.

[10] Rex v. Sutton, 1 East, P. C. 172.

a collar of iron for marking the edges of the money,[1] and a press for coinage,[2] are held to be such tools. So a mold or puncheon containing the stamp of one side of a coin is such a tool, although it would be useless without the reverse.[3] It is not necessary that the defendant shall have been in a position to complete the offense of making counterfeit coin.[4] So by way of preparation for the commission of the offense, it is sufficient to constitute a crime under statute that a part of a plate has been engraved or a part of an impression has been made.[5] It seems that if the instrument is not capable of use in counterfeiting, as, for instance, a mold with no channel through which the metal can run,[6] the offense would not be committed. Nor does it constitute a crime to have in possession an implement such as a crucible which might be used in counterfeiting and also for lawful purposes.[7] Under a statute punishing the having in possession of any blank or unfinished bank-note, it is criminal to have such unfinished blanks, whether genuine or counterfeit.[8] But a federal statute relating to the having in possession of any plates engraved or transferred from those from which fractional currency has been printed does not apply to false or counterfeit plates.[9] By state statute it may be criminal to have tools for counterfeiting foreign coin or bank-bills.[10]

§ 778. **Of intent.**— To constitute the crime the possession of the tools must be for the purpose of making counterfeit money therewith.[11] It is immaterial whether the intention of the person in possession is to use the tools for his own benefit or that of another;[12] but it is not enough that the instruments are designed for counterfeiting; they must be in possession for that purpose.[13] However, the knowingly having in possession such tools has been held sufficient to warrant a conviction.[14] Where the statutory offense consists in having dies impressed with the

[1] Rex v. Moore, 2 C. & P. 235.

[2] Rex v. Bell, 1 East, P. C. 169.

[3] C. v. Kent, 6 Met. 221; Rex v. Lennard, 1 East, P. C. 170; Rex v. Ridgeley, 1 East, P. C. 171; Reg. v. Richmond, 1 C. & K. 240.

[4] Reg. v. Roberts, Dears. 539.

[5] P. v. D'Argencour, 95 N. Y. 624; Rex v. Foster, 7 C. & P. 495.

[6] Reg. v. MacMillan, 1 Cox, 41.

[7] S. v. Bowman, 6 Vt. 594.

[8] Stone v. S., 20 N. J. 401.

[9] U. S. v. Addatte, 6 Blatch. 132.

[10] P. v. McDonnell, 80 Cal. 285.

[11] S. v. Collins, 3 Hawks, 191; P. v. White, 34 Cal. 183.

[12] Sasser v. S., 13 Ohio, 453.

[13] C. v. Morse, 2 Mass. 128; P. v. Page, 1 Ida. T. 114.

[14] Reg. v. Harvey, L. R. 1 C. C. 284; Reg. v. Weeks, L. & C. 18.

resemblance of the coin, it is proper to negative lawful authority or excuse.[1] But if the statutory description is having in possession instruments designed for making counterfeit coin, it is not necessary to negative authority.[2]

§ 779. **How charged.**— The description of the material of which the tool is made is unnecessary;[3] but the kind of instrument should be described,[4] and the manner in which the instrument was to be used.[5] As to the coin to be counterfeited it is sufficient to allege that it was coin current by law and usage.[6]

IV. UTTERING, PASSING, OR HAVING IN POSSESSION.

§ 780. **Offenses defined.**— Uttering an instrument consists in the declaration that it is good, with an intention to pass, or an offer to pass it.[7] The two acts are distinct, and the passing may be punished as at common law, although not covered by the statute as to uttering.[8] So the offense of uttering and publishing as genuine is distinct from that of selling or bartering and disposing of.[9] So also the offense of selling spurious notes is different from that of passing, uttering and publishing such notes;[10] but the uttering and the putting off counterfeit coin as prohibited by statute are held not distinct offenses, but as together constituting only one act.[11] The offense of issuing false and unauthorized bank-bills was held not to be committed by exhibiting or paying out such a bill, as the offense intended was the issuance rather than the circulation of such bills.[12] The offense of uttering is distinct from that of forging.[13] The person who utters need not be the one who forges the instrument.[14] The uttering abroad, by which the instrument is put in circulation at home, is a crime.[15] Whether the crimes here referred

1 Reg. v. Harvey, L. R. 1 C. C. 284.

2 Harlan v. P., 1 Doug. 207.

3 Rex v. Oxford, Russ. & Ry. 382.

4 Chamberlain v. S., 5 Blackf. 573; Peoples v. S., 6 Blackf. 95; C. v. Scott, 1 Rob. 695.

5 Bell v. S., 10 Ark. 536.

6 Bradford v. S., 3 Humph. 369.

7 U. S. v. Mitchell, Bald. 366.

8 C. v. Searle, 2 Binn. 332.

9 Hutchins v. S., 13 Ohio, 198.

10 U. S. v. Nelson, 1 Abbott, C. C. 135.

11 McGregor v. S., 16 Ind. 9.

12 P. v. Wells, 8 Mich. 104.

13 Parker v. P., 97 Ill. 32; Ball v. S., 48 Ark. 94; Peterson v. S., 25 Tex. Ap. 70; Rex v. Reeves, 2 Leach, 808, 814. And a statute punishing the false making or altering does not cover a case of uttering: Hatch v. S., 8 Tex. Ap. 416.

14 S. v. Boasso, 38 La. An. 202.

15 Reg. v. Taylor, 4 F. & F. 511.

to can be charged in the same indictment will be discussed in a subsequent section.[1]

§ 781. **What constitutes an uttering.**— The offense of uttering is committed without any fraud being actually perpetrated; thus, one who presents a forged instrument to a bank to have it cashed is guilty of uttering although the bank does not accept it.[2] And it seems that it is not necessary that the instrument be exhibited with the purpose of securing money upon it, and that it is enough if it is shown with the intention of obtaining credit.[3] To use a forged instrument by pledging it is an uttering;[4] or to deliver it in a sealed letter to one supposed to be authorized to open and act upon it;[5] or to give it to another with intention that it shall be delivered to a third party;[6] or to deliver it even to one's own agent to be forwarded.[7] And the passing by an innocent agent will be criminal in the principal, though he may not know to whom the agent will pass it.[8] Thus, it seems that the mere exhibiting is sufficient, though no wrong is effected;[9] and it is not necessary that the instrument be directly calculated to defraud the person to whom it is given.[10] The recording of a forged deed is an uttering;[11] so is the attempting to raise money upon or make any other beneficial use of such an instrument.[12] The bringing of suit on a

[1] *Infra*, § 803.

[2] P. v. Brigham, 2 Mich. 550; P. v. Caton, 25 Mich. 388; Reg. v. Cooke, 8 C. & P. 582; Rex v. Arscott, 6 C. & P. 408; Reg. v. Radford, 1 C. & K. 707.

[3] S. v. Horner, 48 Mo. 520; Reg. v. Ion, 2 Den. 475. But to show an instrument, the uttering of which would be criminal, merely with an intent of raising a false idea of one's means, is not in itself an uttering, nor, after exhibiting it, to deposit it for safe keeping: Rex v. Shukard, Russ. & Ry. 200.

[4] Thurmond v. S., 25 Tex. Ap. 366.

[5] U. S. v. Carter, 2 Cranch, C. C. 243.

[6] Reg. v. Heywood, 2 C. & K. 352; Reg. v. Palmer, Russ. & Ry. 72.

[7] Rex v. Collicott, Russ. & Ry. 212.

[8] C. v. Hill, 11 Mass. 136.

[9] S. v. Hahn, 38 La. An. 169; Rex v. Martin, 7 C. & P. 549. So where the instrument was delivered to a detective the offense was held complete: Rex v. Holden, Russ. & Ry. 154.

[10] Reg. v. McConnell, 1 C. & K. 371; Reg. v. Fitchie, Dears. & B. 175. Thus, where, for the purpose of showing that a sum of money had been deposited by defendant as secretary for a society, he showed a bank book with a false entry, it was held that the offense was completed: Reg. v. Moody, L. & C. 173.

[11] P. v. Dane, 79 Mich. 361; P. v. Swetland, 77 Mich. 53; P. v. Baker, 100 Cal. 188; U. S. v. Brooks, 3 MacArthur, 315.

[12] P. v. Dane, 79 Mich. 361; Perkins v. P., 27 Mich. 386.

forged paper as counsel is an uttering, and criminal if done with knowledge of the forgery and intent to defraud.[1]

§ 782. **Passing counterfeit money.**— The offense of selling or otherwise disposing of false and counterfeit notes as described by statute is different from that of uttering the same;[2] and it is immaterial that the buyer was deceived also by misrepresentations as to the genuineness of the money.[3] The offense of passing or putting off counterfeit money consists in putting it into circulation rather than in the direct fraud involved, and is consummated by giving such money to a confederate for the purpose of uttering.[4] So an early English statute made the selling of counterfeit coin at a lower rate than its denomination would import an offense.[5] Under the federal statute, the passing of counterfeit coin is not a felony but a misdemeanor only.[6]

§ 783. **What constitutes a passing.**— The giving of counterfeit money in charity was not a passing under the early English statute, an attempt to defraud being essential.[7] But in the United States it has been held that the staking of counterfeit money at a gambling table is an attempt to utter, and losing it at play is a passing.[8] But it is also said that pledging a counterfeit note to be redeemed at a future day is not a passing.[9] Passing to one's own agent with intent to defraud the

[1] Chahoon v. C., 20 Grat. 733. Under a statute punishing the showing forth in evidence, it is necessary to prove such showing forth to have been in a judicial proceeding, and it is not necessary to allege in what proceeding the act was done: S. v. Stanton, 1 Ired. 424.

[2] Van Valkenburg v. S., 11 Ohio, 404.

[3] Leonard v. S., 29 Ohio St. 408.

[4] Rex v. Palmer, Russ. & Ry. 72. And where the defendant attempted to make a purchase with a counterfeit coin, and on being told that the coin was counterfeit left both the goods and coin, he was held guilty of "putting it off:" Reg. v. Welch, 2 Den. 78.

[5] Rex v. Hedges, 3 C. & P. 410; Rex v. Joyce, Car. C. L. 184. But where a bargain was made for the sale of counterfeit money, which was produced but complete transfer was prevented, *held*, that there was not a "putting off:" Rex v. Wooldridge, 1 East, P. C. 179.

[6] In re Wilson, 18 Fed. R. 33.

[7] Reg. v. Page, 8 C. & P. 122. But an indictment for uttering bad money by "ringing the changes" was held good without stating that it was uttered in payment, the words of the statute being in the disjunctive, "utter or tender in payment:" Rex v. Franks, 2 Leach, 644. The fact that the consideration for which the money is paid is illegal will not prevent the act being an uttering: Anon., 1 Cox, 250.

[8] S. v. Beeler, 1 Brev. 482.

[9] Gentry v. S., 3 Yerg. 451.

public is criminal.[1] Where, by statute, the offense consists in uttering counterfeit money with intent to defraud, the crime is sufficiently proved by showing a counterfeit note to have been uttered as true.[2]

§ 784. **Having in possession.**—English statutes have made the having counterfeit coin in possession with intent to utter criminal.[3] Such an offense as defined by statute is different from the crime of attempting to pass counterfeit money as genuine;[4] it is usually a misdemeanor only.[5] The statutes defining the offense usually describe it as consisting of the having in possession of current money.[6] The having in possession of several counterfeit bank-notes is only one offense although they are of different denominations and purport to be of different banks, and although the intent may be to pass to different persons.[7]

§ 785. **What constitutes possession.**—The possession may be sufficient although the counterfeit coin is deposited in a secret place, provided it is within the knowledge and control of the accused;[8] and even though acquired by the accused with the knowledge of the police and immediately afterwards seized so that there could not have been any opportunity for making a fraudulent use thereof.[9] If the offense is described by statute as consisting of knowingly having in possession with intent to pass some specified number of pieces of counterfeit coin, the simultaneous possession of that number must be shown.[10] There may be a joint possession where two or more persons are acting in concert in the having and intending to pass;[11] and the possession may be by an agent.[12]

[1] U. S. v. Morrow, 4 Wash. C. C. 733; U. S. v. Hinman, 1 Baldw. 292; C. v. Starr, 4 Allen, 301.

[2] U. S. v. Marcus, 53 Fed. R. 784.

[3] Rex v. Heath, Russ. & Ry. 184; Rex v. Stewart, Russ. & Ry. 288.

[4] Bevington v. S., 2 Ohio St. 161.

[5] U. S. v. Wright, 2 Cranch, C. C. 68; Perdue v. S., 2 Humph. 494; Quigley v. P., 3 Ill. 301; Rex v. Fuller, Russ. & Ry. 308. See Rex v. Parker, 1 Leach, 41.

[6] S. v. Keneston, 59 N. H. 36; S. v. Shelton, 7 Humph. 30; Clark v. C., 16 B. Mon. 206. It may, however, by statute be made criminal to have in possession unfinished forged bank-bills: P. v. Ah Sam, 41 Cal. 645.

[7] S. v. Benham, 7 Conn. 414.

[8] S. v. Washburn, 11 Ia. 245.

[9] P. v. McDonnell, 80 Cal. 285.

[10] S. v. Pepper, 11 Ia. 347; Edwards v. C., 19 Pick. 124; S. v. Bonney, 34 Me. 223; Scott v. C., 14 Grat. 687.

[11] Reg. v. Rogers, 2 Moody, 85.

[12] Reg. v. Williams, Car. & M. 259.

§ 786. Possession with intent.— The possession of counterfeit money is criminal only as coupled with some unlawful intent, and such intent must be established to make a *prima facie* case.[1] There are two classes of criminal possession as defined by statute, the one consisting in the having possession with intent to pass for the purpose of perpetrating a fraud, the other in having possession with intent to put into circulation, although no fraud upon the person to whom the counterfeit is passed is intended. The latter covers the case of those who deal in counterfeit money.[2] In the first class it is necessary to show that the intention was to pass the counterfeit as genuine or true.[3] But if the offense is made to consist simply in having in possession with intent to pass, the fraudulent purpose as to the one to whom the counterfeit is to be passed is immaterial.[4] It is not necessary that the intention be to pass within the state; at least this is true as to bills of a bank situated within the state, as the passing of counterfeits of its bills anywhere would tend to defraud it.[5] Continued possession of counterfeit money may be shown as tending to prove guilty knowledge;[6] and, in general, the intent may be inferred from the circumstances of the possession.[7] So evidence of a fraudulent sale is competent to support a charge of fraudulent possession.[8] Whether it is necessary to allege the criminal intention in such cases will depend on statute.[9]

§ 787. Representation of genuineness.— The offense of uttering involves a representation of the genuineness of the in-

[1] Brown v. P., 9 Ill. 439; Fergus v. S., 6 Yerg. 345; Owen v. S., 5 Sneed, 493.

[2] Bevington v. S., 2 Ohio St. 161; P. v. Stewart, 4 Mich. 655.

[3] P. v. Stewart, 4 Mich. 655; Gabe v. S., 6 Ark. 519.

[4] Hopkins v. C., 3 Met. 460, 464; C. v. Davis, 11 Gray, 4; Wilkinson v. S., 10 Ind. 372.

[5] C. v. Cone, 2 Mass. 132; Spence v. S., 8 Blackf. 281; Clark v. C., 16 B. Mon. 206.

[6] Harrison's Case, 2 Lewin, 118.

[7] S. v. Vincent, 91 Mo. 662; Reg. v. Jarvis, Dears. 552; Rex v. Fuller, Russ. & Ry. 308.

[8] U. S. v. Biebusch, 1 McCrary, 42. It is not necessary to prove the purpose of the possession if it appears that defendant knowingly had the counterfeit in possession and secretly kept it: Sasser v. S., 13 Ohio, 453.

[9] Sizemore v. S., 3 Head, 26. The indictment may follow the language of the statute and need not describe the elements of the crime of counterfeiting: Long v. S., 10 Tex. Ap. 186.

strument, and without that the offense is not committed, but the representation may be implied from the circumstances.[1]

§ 788. **The intent.**—There must be an intent to defraud by the deceit and falsity exercised in making the instrument appear genuine.[2] It is not necessary, however, that the intent be to defraud any particular person or corporation, and therefore the name of the person intended to be defrauded need not be alleged.[3] To exhibit an engraving of a forged note as a pattern or specimen of skill is not criminal.[4] So the accused may show that he received the counterfeit accidentally and in the usual course of business.[5] But as in other cases where criminal intent is necessary the intent may be inferred from the act.[6] There may be a joint uttering by which wrongful act and intent are combined so as to constitute the offense.[7]

[1] S. v. Calkins, 73 Ia. 128; S. v. Sherwood, 90 Ia. 550; Folden v. S., 13 Neb. 328; Smith v. S., 20 Neb. 284. Where a party executing a deed pretended to get his wife's signature thereto, but in fact procured his wife's name to be signed by his daughter, having the same name as his wife, and delivered the instrument to the mortgagee, he was held guilty of uttering a forged instrument: S. v. Farrell, 82 Ia. 553.

[2] U. S. v. King, 5 McLean, 208; Reg. v. Bradford, 2 F. & F. 859. Thus, where the forged instrument was presented to one who was acting in collusion with reference to the forgery in order that it might be protested, the act was held not to be criminal; and it was further held that if the protest and notice were only intended to induce the indorser whose name was forged to cover up the maker's guilt, no offense was committed: S. v. Redstrake, 39 N. J. 365. So where a forged diploma was exhibited to the public, it was held that there was no crime in such exhibition: Reg. v. Hodgson, Dears. & B. 3.

[3] S. v. Callendine, 8 Ia. 288; S. v. Barrett, 8 Ia. 536; Gentry v. S., 6 Ga. 503; Harrison v. S., 36 Ala. 248. But if the name of the person intended to be defrauded is alleged it must be proven: S. v. Newland, 7 Ia. 242. And in such case if a corporation is named as the person intended to be defrauded, proof of the existence of such corporation is necessary; but that fact may be shown by reputation: S. v. Newland, 7 Ia. 242; S. v. Barrett, 8 Ia. 536. In an old case it was said that in an indictment for putting off counterfeit money the names of the persons to whom it was put off should be set out: Anon., 1 East, P. C. 180. And it seems that under some statutory provisions it is still necessary to allege the name of the persons intended to be defrauded: Goodson v. S., 29 Fla. 511; Buckley v. S., 2 Greene (Ia.), 162. (But the later Iowa cases are *contra*. See above in this note.)

[4] Rex v. Harris, 7 C. & P. 428.

[5] U. S. v. Kenneally, 5 Biss. 122.

[6] Rex v. Shepherd, 2 East, P. C. 967; Reg. v. Hill, 8 C. & P. 274.

[7] Rex v. Harris, 7 C. & P. 416; Reg. v. Vanderstein, 10 Cox, 146; Rex v. Else, Russ. & Ry. 142; Reg. v. Gerrish, 2 M. & Rob. 219; Rex v. Skerritt, 2 C. & P. 427; Reg. v. Hurse, 2

§ **789. Guilty knowledge.**— As an element in the wrongful intent knowledge of the falsity of the instrument is necessary, and must be alleged and proven;[1] and the question whether such knowledge existed is necessarily one for the jury.[2] As proving guilty knowledge, the possession or uttering of other counterfeit coin may be shown.[3]

V. PROCEDURE.

§ **790. Jurisdiction of state and United States.**— The offenses relating to the coin were, before the organization of the federal government, punishable by the states, and the authority of the states in the matter continues unless taken away by the constitution of the United States and the statutes passed in pursuance thereof.[4] The constitution confers upon congress the power "to provide for the punishment of counterfeiting the securities and current coin of the United States;"[5] and under this authority statutes have been passed from time to time by congress. While congress may undoubtedly, in the legislation upon any subject confided to it, make its statutes exclusive of state regulations on the same subject, yet in its statutes relating to crimes it does not attempt to do so, but has specially enacted that such provisions shall not be held to take away or impair the jurisdiction of the courts of the several states under the laws thereof.[6] And although in another sec-

M. & Rob. 360. But to render two or more liable for the same act of uttering, it must appear that they were so near each other as that each could assist in the act: Reg. v. Jones, 9 C. & P. 761; Rex v. Manners, 7 C. & P. 801; Rex v. Seares, Russ. & Ry. 25; Reg. v. West, 2 Cox, 237.

[1] U. S. v. Carll, 105 U. S. 611; P. v. Mitchell, 92 Cal. 590; P. v. Smith, 103 Cal. 563; S. v. Williams, 66 Ia. 573; S. v. Morton, 8 Wis. 352; Wash v. C., 16 Grat. 530; Gates v. S., 71 Miss. 874; Elsey v. S., 47 Ark. 572; Powers v. S., 87 Ind. 97; S. v. Nicholson, 14 La. An. 785; Reg. v. Jones, 9 C. & P. 761; Reg. v. Page, 9 C. & P. 756. To charge with "knowingly uttering" is not enough; it must appear that defendant uttered with knowledge: S. v. Williams, 139 Ind. 43.

[2] Parker v. P., 97 Ill. 32; Carver v. P., 39 Mich. 786; Reg. v. Byrne, 6 Cox, 475.

[3] U. S. v. Burns, 5 McLean, 23; U. S. v. King, 5 McLean, 208; Reg. v. Forster, Dears. 456. But where the offense charged was uttering a counterfeit coin after a previous conviction, it was held that the previous conviction could not be put in evidence for the purpose of proving guilty knowledge: Reg. v. Goodwin, 10 Cox, 534.

[4] C. v. Fuller, 8 Met. 313.

[5] U. S. Const., art. 1, § 8.

[6] R. S., § 5328.

tion it is provided that the jurisdiction of the courts of the United States shall be exclusive with reference to all crimes and offenses cognizable under the authority of the United States,[1] this provision must be taken in conjunction with the other, and as not negativing the exception there made. It has accordingly been held in the federal courts and in the courts of many of the states that the counterfeiting even of United States coin or notes, and the uttering of such counterfeits, are punishable under state statutes as offenses in the nature of a fraud, although they are also punishable under the federal statutes.[2] This doctrine has not gone entirely unquestioned, but the cases to the contrary are few.[3] The general reservation to the states of the jurisdiction above referred to does not apply, however, to the punishment of offenses in connection with the national banks other than the counterfeiting of their bills, such, for instance, as embezzlement and the like; and in these cases it is held that the punishment provided by the federal statutes is exclusive of any power to punish by the states.[4] But where an offense under the national banking act is committed by forgery, the forgery is punishable under the state law.[5] Under the power to regulate commerce and to coin money, as well as that of punishing the offenses against the law of nations, congress may punish the counterfeiting of foreign coin.[6] But this authority does not exclude that of the states in the same mat-

[1] R. S., § 711.

[2] Fox v. S., 5 How. 410, 432; C. v. Fuller, 8 Met. 313; Dashing v. S., 78 Ind. 357; P. v. McDonnell, 80 Cal. 285; S. v. McPherson, 9 Ia. 53; Jett v. C., 18 Grat. 933; S. v. Pitman, 1 Brev. 32; S. v. Antonio, 3 Brev. 562; S. v. Tutt, 2 Bailey, 44; Chess v. S., 1 Blackf. 198; Sizemore v. S., 3 Head, 26; In re Truman, 44 Mo. 181; Martin v. S., 18 Tex. Ap. 224; Ex parte Geisler, 50 Fed. R. 411. The same principle is applicable to having in possession instruments used in counterfeiting coin: P. v. White, 34 Cal. 183; S. v. Brown, 2 Oreg. 221. So, if the act, while it may constitute a crime under the laws of the United States, is also a distinct offense under the laws of the state, the jurisdiction of the state courts to punish it is not precluded: Hoke v. P., 122 Ill. 511; C. v. Luberg, 94 Pa. St. 85.

[3] Mattison v. S., 3 Mo. 421; S. v. Brown, 2 Oreg. 221; Ex parte Houghton, 7 Fed. R. 657.

[4] C. v. Felton, 101 Mass. 204; C. v. Tenney, 97 Mass. 50; S. v. Tuller, 34 Conn. 280; Hoke v. P., 122 Ill. 511; P. v. Fonda, 62 Mich. 401.

[5] S. v. Cross, 101 N. C. 770. The forgery of a promissory note made payable at a national bank is not a crime against the United States: Cross v. North Carolina, 132 U. S. 131.

[6] U. S. v. Marigold, 9 How. 560; U. S. v. White, 27 Fed. R. 200.

ter.[1] It seems that one state has no authority to punish the offense of counterfeiting committed in another state.[2] But, on the other hand, it has been held that the offense of forging in another state titles to lands to be used for the purpose of committing a fraud within the state of the jurisdiction is punishable in the latter.[3] As the essence of the crime of forgery is the fraudulent intent, the crime may be considered as committed where the false making or alteration is effected; it is immaterial that the property to be affected is in another state.[4]

§ 791. **Venue.**— The crime of forgery may be punished in the county in which the forged instrument is uttered and published.[5] So there may be an uttering and publishing through the hands of an innocent agent, so as to constitute the offense where the agent acts, although the principal is in another county.[6] Under some statutes it has been held that putting a letter containing a forged instrument into the mail is an uttering where the letter is mailed, and the postmark is evidence thereof;[7] but it is not an uttering in the county of the person to whom it is addressed.[8] Under other statutes it is properly held that the uttering with intent to defraud is committed where the letter is received through the mail,[9] and not, even partially, in the county where the letter is mailed.[10] Possession or uttering is evidence of the commission of the crime of forgery in the same county.[11]

§ 792. **Indictment.**— The indictment should describe the instrument, the act of defendant which is complained of with reference thereto, and the fraudulent intent with which it was done.[12]

[1] Sutton v. S., 9 Ohio, 133; S. v. Antonio, 3 Brev. 562.

[2] S. v. Knight, 1 Taylor, 65.

[3] Hanks v. S., 13 Tex. Ap. 289.

[4] P. v. Flanders, 18 Johns. 164.

[5] McGuire v. S., 37 Ala. 161; Mason v. S., 32 Tex. Ap. 95.

[6] Bishop v. S., 30 Ala. 34; C. v. Hill, 11 Mass. 136.

[7] Perkins' Case, 2 Lewin, 150.

[8] U. S. v. Plympton, 4 Cranch, C. C. 309; U. S. v. Wright, 2 Cranch, C. C. 296.

[9] P. v. Rathbun, 21 Wend. 509.

[10] S. v. Hudson, 13 Mont. 112.

[11] S. v. Gullette, 121 Mo. 447; Bland v. P., 4 Ill. 364; S. v. Thompson, 19 Ia. 299; S. v. Blanchard, 74 Ia. 628; S. v. Poindexter, 23 W. Va. 805; S. v. Morgan, 2 Dev. & B. 348; Johnson v. S., 35 Ala. 370; U. S. v. Britton, 2 Mason, 464; Rex v. Pim, Russ. & Ry. 425. *Contra*, C. v. Parmenter, 5 Pick. 279.

[12] P. v. Wright, 9 Wend. 193; S. v. Stuart, 61 Ia. 203; Hughes v. C., 89 Ky. 227; Smith v. S., 29 Fla. 408; U. S. v. Moore, 60 Fed. R. 738.

§ 793. **Description of instrument.**— Some term descriptive of the general class of instruments subject to forgery to which the instrument in question belongs is common, and should be such as to indicate that the instrument is of that class. Thus, where the forgery of bank-bills is not provided for, the instrument, though a bank-bill, should be described as a promissory note to bring it within that description of the statute, and such a description will not constitute a variance.[1] But if the statute describes the two classes of instruments in the alternative, the distinction must be preserved in the indictment and the instrument accurately described in accordance therewith.[2] In general the description must be accurate, as will hereafter appear.[3] If the signature is forged, the instrument should not be described as one "signed by" the person whose name it bears, but "purporting to be signed" by such person.[4] If the indictment is for forging an instrument purporting to be the act of a firm, it should allege the partnership, and state the name of each member, or that the same is unknown.[5] It is not necessary to allege the money value of the instrument forged.[6] The same rules which are applicable to the description of an instrument in case of forgery are applicable also to a charge of passing a forged instrument.[7] But the contrary has been held on

[1] C. v. Woods, 10 Gray, 477. A genuine instrument with a forged indorsement should not be described as a false and forged instrument: U. S. v. Albert, 45 Fed. R. 552.

[2] C. v. Dole, 2 Allen, 165; S. v. Ward, 6 N. H. 529. Where the statute enumerated both bonds and writings obligatory, it was held that a description of the instrument as a bond and writing obligatory was not fatal, a part of the description being superfluous: Rex v. Dunnett, 2 East, P. C. 985. So an indictment may describe the instrument as a warrant and order where the statute mentions a warrant or order: S. v. Jones, 1 McMull. 236; S. v. Holley, 1 Brev. 35. It is not error to describe the instrument as "a certain bond" instead of "a certain paper writing purporting to be a bond:" S. v. McGardiner, 1 Ired. 27.

[3] See *infra*, § 798.

[4] Rex v. Carter, 2 East, P. C. 985. An indictment charging the forging and counterfeiting of a certain paper writing was held good: Duffin v. P., 107 Ill. 113.

[5] Labbaite v. S., 6 Tex. Ap. 483. But where the instrument purports to have been executed by an agent in the name of the principal, the indictment need not aver the agent's authority: Cross v. P., 47 Ill. 152.

[6] Chidester v. S., 25 Ohio St. 433.

[7] P. v. Wright, 9 Wend. 193; equally so where the charge is of having in possession: S. v. Callendine, 8 Ia. 288; Jones v. S., 11 Ind. 357.

the theory that the uttering and publishing is a distinct offense from the forgery itself.[1]

§ 794. **Setting out the instrument.**— As a general proposition the instrument must be set forth in the indictment.[2] This is called setting it forth by its tenor, and is essential unless some good reason be given for not doing so, such as that the instrument is lost or in the hands of defendant or otherwise not obtainable.[3] This general rule is applicable in case of passing or having in possession as well as in forgery.[4] Even where there is an excuse for not setting out the instrument by its tenor there must be some description which will reasonably identify it.[5] But such description need not be proved with the same accuracy as is required where the instrument is set out by its tenor.[6] No particular form of words need be used in setting forth the instrument;[7] it is sufficient to use the expression, "the tenor of which is as follows;"[8] but to say that the instrument is of the "purport and effect following" is not sufficient, even though a copy be correctly set out.[9] It is not proper, however, to incorporate the instrument into the indictment by sewing or pasting it upon the paper.[10] Where the offense charged is the alteration of a public book of record, it

[1] C. v. Ross, 2 Mass. 373.

[2] S. v. Atkins, 5 Blackf. 458; McMillen v. S., 5 Ohio, 268; S. v. Johnson, 26 Ia. 407; S. v. Dowden, 2 Dev. 443; Dana v. S., 2 Ohio St. 91; S. v. Houseal, 2 Brev. 219; S. v. Jones, 1 McMull, 236; Croxdale v. State, 1 Head, 139; S. v. Parker, 1 D. Chip. 298; S. v. Twitty, 2 Hawks, 248; S. v. Harris, 5 Ired. 287; Stephens v. S., Wright, 73; Thomas v. S., 18 Tex. Ap. 213; Smith v. S., 18 Tex. Ap. 399.

[3] P. v. Kingsley, 2 Cow. 522; P. v. Badgley, 16 Wend. 53; C. v. Houghton, 8 Mass. 107; S. v. Gustin, 5 N. J. 857; S. v. Callahan, 124 Ind. 364; Munson v. S., 79 Ind. 541; Armitage v. S., 13 Ind. 441; U. S. v. Howell, 64 Fed. R. 110. In setting out a receipt by its tenor it is not necessary to copy a bill of particulars to which it refers: Rex v. Testick, 2 East, P. C. 925.

[4] S. v. Callendine, 8 Ia. 288; Jones v. S., 11 Ind. 357; McMillen v. S., 5 Ohio, 269.

[5] Birdg v. S., 31 Ind. 88; S. v. Briggs, 34 Vt. 501; Roberts v. S., 72 Miss. 110; S. v. Stephen, 45 La. An. 702.

[6] C. v. Parmenter, 5 Pick. 279; P. v. Badgley, 16 Wend. 53; Rex v. May, 1 Dougl. 193.

[7] S. v. Johnson, 26 Ia. 407.

[8] Swain v. P., 5 Ill. 178; Rex v. Powell, 2 East, P. C. 976.

[9] S. v. Bonney, 34 Me. 383; S. v. Witham, 47 Me. 165; Dana v. S., 2 Ohio St. 91. But under a statute making technical errors immaterial, such a form of introducing the instrument was held sufficient: S. v. Johnson, 26 Ia. 407.

[10] U. S. v. Fisler, 4 Biss. 59; Rex v. Harris, 7 C. & P. 429.

is sufficient to describe the book by its usual name and allege where it is kept in its general use, so that it may be clearly identified.[1] The question of setting out the instrument by its tenor is entirely different from the question as to proof. Even though the instrument is destroyed or cannot be produced in evidence, it is proper to set it out by its tenor, if that be practicable.[2] Where the act charged is the alteration of an instrument, the prosecution may set out the instrument exactly as altered, or set it out as originally made and describe the alteration.[3]

§ 795. **Foreign language; translation.**— If the instrument is in a foreign language, it is not necessary to set it forth in such language, but the setting forth of the translation will be sufficient;[4] or both the original and the translation may be set out.[5]

§ 796. **Purport.**— Where it is impracticable to set out the instrument *in hæc verba*, its purport should be alleged so that the court may see that it is an instrument the false making of which will constitute a crime.[6] And so if the instrument set out does not on its face show that it is one of the instruments the false making or passing of which will be criminal, its purport must be explained so as to show that the offense has been committed.[7] But it is unnecessary to give the purport if the instrument, as set out with the names of the parties to it, shows upon its face that it is an instrument the false making of which is forgery.[8] It is immaterial what name is given to the instrument in the indictment, if its proper name and description ap-

[1] S. v. Granville, 45 Ohio St. 264.

[2] S. v. Potts, 9 N. J. 26; S. v. Gustin, 5 N. J. 857.

[3] S. v. Robinson, 16 N. J. 507; S. v. Bryant, 17 N. H. 323; Hawkins v. S., 28 Fla. 363; 2 East, P. C. 979; 3 Chitty, Cr. L. 469.

[4] P. v. Ah Woo, 28 Cal. 205.

[5] Duffin v. P., 107 Ill. 113; Rex v. Szudurskie, 1 Moody, 429; Rex v. Goldstein, Russ. & Ry. 473. But if the translation is defective the indictment will be insufficient: Rex v. Harris, 7 C. & P. 429; Rex v. Warshaner, 1 Moody, 466.

[6] Wallace v. P., 27 Ill. 45; S. v. Horan, 64 N. H. 548.

[7] C. v. Ray, 3 Gray, 441; Henry v. S., 35 Ohio St. 128; Carberry v. S., 11 Ohio St. 410; S. v. Cook, 52 Ind. 574; Fomby v. S., 87 Ala. 36; King v. S., 27 Tex. Ap. 567.

[8] C. v. Castles, 9 Gray, 123; P. v. Clements, 26 N. Y. 193; S. v. Bibb, 68 Mo. 286; S. v. Fenly, 18 Mo. 445; P. v. Todd, 77 Cal. 464; P. v. Tomlinson, 35 Cal. 503; Cross v. P., 47 Ill. 152; Smith v. S., 29 Fla. 408; S. v. Covington, 94 N. C. 913; Morris v. S., 17 Tex. Ap. 660.

pear from the instrument as set out.[1] But a variance between the purport and the tenor of the instrument will be fatal.[2] As some description is necessary, that portion of the purporting clause which is inconsistent with the tenor cannot be rejected as surplusage.[3] It is not a variance, however, to charge the forging of the name of one person to an instrument which purports to be signed by two.[4]

§ 797. **Immaterial matters.**— Even when it is necessary to set out the instrument by its tenor, it is only necessary to set out that part of it which forms the contract on which the forgery is based; thus, if the forged instrument purports to be a promissory note, the indorsement thereon, being in itself a separate contract and not a part of the note, need not be set out.[5] For the same reason it is unnecessary to set out any figures, words, or devices in the margin of the instrument which do not constitute an essential part thereof.[6] So the omission of the

[1] S. v. Crawford, 13 La. An. 300; U. S. v. Trout, 4 Biss. 105; U. S. v. Williams, 4 Biss. 302; U. S. v. Marcus, 53 Fed. R. 784; U. S. v. Bennett, 17 Blatch. 357.

[2] C. v. Ray, 3 Gray, 441; C. v. Lawless, 101 Mass. 32; S. v. Handy, 20 Me. 81; S. v. Shawley, 5 Hayw. 256; Roberts v. S., 2 Tex. Ap. 4; Westbrook v. S., 23 Tex. Ap. 401; Rex v. Gillchrist, 2 East, P. C. 982; Rex v. Jones, 2 East, P. C. 883; Rex v. Reading, 1 East, 180, n. But under a statute making any variance immaterial which does not affect the substantial rights of the defendant, a discrepancy between the tenor and the purporting clause will not vitiate the indictment: Myers v. S., 101 Ind. 379.

[3] C. v. Ray, 3 Gray, 441.

[4] S. v. Flora, 109 Mo. 293; Fogg v. S., 9 Yerg. 392.

[5] Miller v. P., 52 N. Y. 304; C. v. Ward, 2 Mass. 397; S. v. Yerger, 86 Mo. 33; S. v. Jackson, 90 Mo. 156; Perkins v. C., 7 Grat. 651; Labbaite v. S., 6 Tex. Ap. 257; Hennessey v. S., 23 Tex. Ap. 340. If the indorsement is forged it is to be set out as a distinct contract: C. v. Adams, 7 Met. 50. If the indorsement constitutes a part of the forgery, the indictment should so allege and the indorsement must then be set out: S. v. Handy, 20 Me. 81. Variance as to residence of drawee of a forged bill is immaterial: Trask v. P., 151 Ill. 523.

[6] C. v. Bailey, 1 Mass. 62; C. v. Henry, 118 Mass. 460; S. v. Carr, 5 N. H. 367; S. v. Robinson, 16 N. J. 507; S. v. Flye, 26 Me. 312; Langdale v. P., 100 Ill. 263; Buckland v. C., 8 Leigh, 732; Smith v. S., 29 Fla. 408; Burke v. S., 24 Tex. Ap. 326. Thus, it is not necessary to set out the number of a check: Cross v. P., 47 Ill. 152; C. v. Bailey, 1 Mass. 62: or the figures cut in a draft: White v. T., 1 Wash. 279; nor a notice required to be printed on the instrument, but no part of it: U. S. v. Marcus, 53 Fed. R. 784. It is not necessary to exhibit the seal of the treasury in an indictment for counterfeiting a treasury note: U. S. v. Bennett, 17 Blatch. 357. But the omission of a part of the date is fatal: C. v. Stevens, 1 Mass. 203. The omission of the name of the state in the margin of

proper revenue stamp has been held immaterial, although such stamp might be essential to authorize the introduction of the original in evidence.[1]

§ 798. **Variance.**— As a general proposition the evidence as to the nature of the instrument, whether it be the original itself or secondary evidence with reference thereto, must correspond with the description of the instrument in the indictment, and a variance will be fatal.[2] And this rule is applicable even where immaterial matter is included in the description or the copy of the instrument as set out.[3] This strict rule requires the proof to correspond with the instrument as set out by its tenor, even to the spelling of words and the initials of the names of the parties,[4] and is especially applicable to any variance in the amount stated.[5] But a mere misspelling of a word which does not make it another word is, by the weight of authority, immaterial.[6] And where the forged instrument is in such clumsy and unintelligible chirography as to be difficult to decipher, a doubtful variance even in the name will not be fatal.[7] It was so held also where there was an error in giving the abbreviations of certain Latin words on the seal affixed to the instrument which the pleader had attempted to set out.[8] It does not constitute a variance that the allegation is of the forgery of a note with two signatures, while the proof shows the forgery of one signature only.[9]

a bank-note is a material variance: C. v. Wilson, 2 Gray, 70.

[1] C. v. McKean, 98 Mass. 9; C. v. Hall, 97 Mass. 570; Miller v. P., 52 N. Y. 304.

[2] U. S. v. Hinman, 1 Bald. 292; S. v. Waters, 3 Brev. 507; S. v. Lytle, 64 N. C. 255; Ex parte Rogers, 10 Tex. Ap. 755. Thus, a variance as to the date will be fatal: C. v. Stow, 1 Mass. 54. It is not a variance that coins alleged to have been forged are described as fifty-cent pieces and twenty-five cent pieces, although they are described in the statute as half dollars and quarter dollars: U. S. v. Burns, 5 McLean, 23; U. S. v. King, 5 McLean, 208.

[3] S. v. Clark, 23 N. H. 429; S. v. Smith, 31 Mo. 120; Rooker v. S., 65 Ind. 86; McDonnell v. S., 58 Ark. 242.

[4] Brown v. P., 66 Ill. 344; S. v. Pease, 74 Ind. 263; S. v. Smith, 31 Mo. 120. It will not constitute a variance that in the instrument as set out an innuendo is incorporated in parentheses: Alexander v. S., 28 Tex. Ap. 186.

[5] Burress v. C., 27 Grat. 934; Shirley v. S., 1 Oreg. 269.

[6] Allgood v. S., 87 Ga. 668; U. S. v. Hinman, 1 Bald. 292; 1 Bishop, Cr. Proc., § 562.

[7] S. v. Gryder, 44 La. An. 962.

[8] U. S. v. Mason, 12 Blatch. 497. So where the discrepancy arose from the attempt to make a precise imitation of the name it was held immaterial: Mathena v. S., 20 Ark. 70.

[9] Duffin v. P., 107 Ill. 113; S. v. Cross, 101 N. C. 770. But the evi-

§ 799. Name forged; idem sonans.— In describing the person on whom the offense was committed, certainty to a common intent only is necessary, the name by which he is usually known being a sufficient description.[1] If the indictment sets out in full the name of the person whose name is alleged to be forged, while the instrument as set out by the tenor shows only the initials of his Christian name, the indictment should expressly allege that the two names as thus given represent the same person.[2] Without this such a variance would be fatal.[3] A variance between the name as given in the indictment and as shown by the evidence is material and will defeat the prosecution.[4] Thus, a variance between the evidence and the allegation as to the first name of the person whose name is charged to have been forged is material.[5] But where there was uncertainty in the name signed, and it appeared that the signature was an attempt to imitate the genuine signature, a discrepancy between the imitated signature and the real name was held not to be fatal.[6] The wrong spelling of a name is unimportant if the same sound is preserved.[7]

§ 800. Statutory provisions as to indictment.—To obviate the technical difficulties which may arise where the attempt is made to set the instrument out by its tenor, many statutes provide that it shall be sufficient to give the purport of the instrument only.[8] And under such provisions it is sufficient to

dence must show the forgery of the names alleged to have been forged and not of other names, the forgery of which is not charged: P. v. Marion, 28 Mich. 255.

1 Durham v. P., 5 Ill. 172; Rex v. Lovell, 2 East, P. C. 990.

2 Shinn v. S., 57 Ind. 144; S. v. Jones, 1 McMull. 236.

3 S. v. Houseal, 2 Brev. 219; English v. S., 30 Tex. Ap. 470. Further as to variance between the tenor and the purport as set out see the preceding section.

4 Jacobs v. S., 61 Ala. 448; McClellan v. S., 32 Ark. 609; Potter v. S., 9 Tex. Ap. 55; Murphy v. S., 6 Tex. Ap. 554.

5 Murphy v. S., 6 Tex. Ap. 554. But an allegation that a forged deed purported to be the deed of Abram Barnes was held to be supported by proof that the signature was A. Barnes: Ham v. S., 4 Tex. Ap. 645. Variance as to middle initial is immaterial: P. v. Smith, 103 Cal. 563.

6 S. v. Nichols, 38 Ia. 110.

7 S. v. Bean, 19 Vt. 530: S. v. Wheeler, 35 Vt. 261; Powers v. S., 87 Ind. 97; S. v. Collins, 115 N. C. 716; Parker v. P., 97 Ill. 32; S. v. Lane, 80 N. C. 407.

8 S. v. Hill, 30 Wis. 416; S. v. Henderson, 29 W. Va. 147; S. v. Clinton, 67 Mo. 380; McGuire v. S., 37 Ala. 161; S. v. Sherwood, 41 La. An. 316; Reg. v. Davies, 9 C. & P. 427; Reg. v. Collins, 2 M. & Rob. 461; Rex v. Burgiss, 7 C. & P. 490.

designate the instrument by any name by which it is usually described.[1] A description which would be sufficient in an indictment for larceny of the instrument is enough.[2] Under the usual statutory provision that a variance which is not prejudicial to the defendant shall not defeat the prosecution, it was held that a variance as to date which could not have misled the defendant was immaterial.[3]

§ 801. **Allegations as to the act.**— The indictment must allege the acts constituting the forgery, as that defendant signed the name of another person without authority, or procured some one to do so, or the like. The allegation that the accused "forged" the writing is merely a legal conclusion, and is not sufficient.[4] But under statutes in some states, a general allegation that defendant "forged," etc.,[5] or procured the forgery, or acted and assisted therein,[6] is sufficient. Where the forgery consists in altering, the indictment may charge the alteration, or simply charge the false making.[7] And similarly it has been held that under a statute for altering, corrupting, or defacing a public record, it was sufficient to allege that defendant "altered" or "corrupted," describing the record, without setting out the facts.[8] The charge of forging and counterfeiting is not repugnant.[9] Under an indictment charging defendant with the act, he may be convicted upon proof of procuring the act to be done by another in his presence.[10] In general the allegation as to the act done must be such as to connect it with the accomplishment of the fraud; for instance, if the charge is of forging a deed, it must appear that the party intended to be defrauded had some interest in the property;[11] or where the

[1] S. v. Clement, 42 La. An. 583; S. v. Pons, 28 La. An. 43; S. v. Nelson, 28 La. An. 46; Hughes v. C., 89 Ky. 227; P. v. Rynders, 12 Wend. 425.

[2] P. v. Stewart, 4 Mich. 655; Coleman v. C., 25 Grat. 865.

[3] S. v. Blanchard, 74 Ia. 628.

[4] C. v. Williams, 13 Bush, 267; Stowers v. C., 12 Bush, 342. The same rule is applicable to an allegation of uttering: C. v. Williams, 13 Bush, 267.

[5] Jones v. S., 50 Ala. 161; S. v. Maas, 37 La. An. 292.

[6] Huffman v. C., 6 Rand. 685; Brown v. C., 2 Leigh, 769.

[7] S. v. Weaver, 13 Ired. 491. And see *supra*, § 765. But to allege generally the alteration and defacing, without charging the acts done, is not sufficient: S. v. Knippa, 29 Tex. 295.

[8] Loehr v. P., 132 Ill. 504.

[9] Hobbs v. S., 9 Mo. 845; Mackey v. S., 3 Ohio St. 362, overruling Kirby v. S., 1 Ohio St. 185.

[10] Hughes v. C., 89 Ky. 227.

[11] P. v. Wright, 9 Wend. 193.

forgery charged is of an instrument transferring a note, the existence of the note must be shown.[1] The forging of a part of an instrument may properly be charged as the forgery of the whole instrument.[2]

§ **802. Allegation of intent; feloniously.**— The offense not being a felony at common law, it was not, and in general is not, necessary to allege that the act was feloniously done; the only object of such allegation being to show the criminal intent, which may be expressed in other words as the language of the statute may require.[3] But the intent to defraud must be expressed in some form.[4] While it is usual to charge the instrument as having been "falsely" made, that word is not essential.[5]

§ **803. Different offenses; duplicity.**— It seems to have been usual to charge in one count the forging and uttering of the forged instrument, and such an indictment, it has been held, does not charge two offenses so as to be obnoxious to the objection of duplicity.[6] So, under statutes which forbid more than one crime being charged in the same indictment, it is held that the forging and the uttering may be charged in separate counts.[7] But, notwithstanding these authorities, it is undoubtedly the correct view that the forging and uttering are distinct offenses, neither one being necessarily involved in the commission of the other.[8] And under this view, counts for forging and for uttering contained in the same indictment, though

[1] Simms v. S., 32 Tex. Ap. 277. And see Rex v. Wilcox, Russ. & Ry. 50.

[2] C. v. Butterick, 100 Mass. 12; P. v. Clements, 26 N. Y. 193; S. v. McGardiner, 1 Ired. 27; Ham v. S., 4 Tex. Ap. 645.

[3] S. v. Murphy, 17 R. I. 698; Cohen v. P., 7 Colo. 274; Miller v. P., 3 Ill. 233.

[4] P. v. Mitchell, 92 Cal. 590; Morris v. S., 17 Tex. Ap. 660.

[5] P. v. Mitchell, 92 Cal. 590; S. v. McKiernan, 17 Nev. 224. As to intent, see, also, *supra*, §§ 766, 776, 778, 783. As to knowledge, see § 789.

[6] Parker v. P., 97 Ill. 32; P. v. Altman, 147 N. Y. 473; In re Walsh, 37 Neb. 454; S. v. Rounds, 76 Me. 123; P. v. Frank, 28 Cal. 507; P. v. Leyshon, 108 Cal. 440; Gardner v. S., 96 Ala. 12.

[7] P. v. Adler, 140 N. Y. 331; P. v. Tower, 135 N. Y. 457; Parker v. P., 97 Ill. 32; S. v. Zimmerman, 47 Kan. 242; Chester v. S., 23 Tex. Ap. 577; S. v. Clement, 42 La. An. 583.

[8] Parker v. P., 97 Ill. 32; S. v. McCormack, 56 Ia. 585; Page v. C., 9 Leigh, 683; Mowbray v. C., 11 Leigh, 643; Scott v. C., 14 Grat. 687; Bell v. S., 57 Md. 108; Ball v. S, 48 Ark. 94; S. v. Snow, 30 La. An., Part I, 401; Hooper v. S., 30 Tex. Ap. 412; Crawford v. S., 31 Tex. Ap. 51.

they relate to the same instrument, are bad for duplicity.[1] Where, however, different acts, such as those of counterfeiting, passing, having in possession, etc., of counterfeit money, are enumerated in one section as constituting a crime with a single punishment, they may be charged conjunctively in one count without objection.[2] So the doing and procuring may be charged in the same count, being made criminal by the same section of the statute.[3] If a minor offense is charged and proved, there should be a conviction although the evidence shows a higher offense of the same character.[4] The forgery of different instruments cannot be charged in the same count,[5] even though the instruments are of the same character, and made and uttered at the same time.[6] If different acts to constitute an uttering are parts of the same transaction, the prosecutor need not elect as to which shall be relied on until the whole evidence is in.[7] The possession of different kinds of coin may be charged in different counts to meet the evidence.[8]

§ 804. **Form of indictment.**— So much depends upon the statutes describing the offense and also the general statutory provisions in each state as to indictments in general, that it is difficult to give any forms which can be relied on, but the following will suggest the allegations which are usual. Statutes making it unnecessary to allege the name of the person intended to be defrauded are now so nearly universal that it is not deemed necessary to include such an averment among the allegations. The pleader must consult the statutes of his own state as to details.

[1] S. v. McCormack, 56 Ia. 585.

[2] S. v. McPherson, 9 Ia. 53; S. v. Barrett, 8 Ia. 536; S. v. Myers, 10 Ia. 448; McGregor v. S., 16 Ind. 9; S. v. Murphy, 17 R. I. 698. Otherwise if the acts are by statute made distinct offenses: S. v. Wilkins, 17 Vt. 151.

[3] S. v. Morton, 27 Vt. 310; Rasnick v. C., 2 Va. Cas. 356; S. v. Houseal, 2 Brev. 219; or in different counts of the same indictment: U. S. v. King, 5 McLean, 208; U. S. v. Burns, 5 McLean, 23.

[4] Anon., Russ. & Ry. 378. So if the evidence proves the common-law offense, defendant may be convicted accordingly, although the statutory offense charged in the indictment is not made out: S. v. Lamb, 65 N. C. 419.

[5] P. v. Wright, 9 Wend. 193.

[6] Barton v. S., 23 Wis. 587. *Contra*, Rex v. Thomas, 2 East, P. C. 934.

[7] Rex v. Hart, 7 C. & P. 652.

[8] U. S. v. Howell, 65 Fed. R. 402.

FORGERY IN GENERAL.

That A. B., in ——, on ——, feloniously did falsely and fraudulently make and forge a certain [name the instrument according to the statutory description], in words and figures following, to wit: [here set out the instrument], with intent to defraud.

OF AN ORDER NOT SET OUT.

That A. B., in ——, on ——, feloniously did falsely and fraudulently make and forge a certain paper writing purporting to be an order signed by C. D. and directed to E. F., requesting the payment by said E. F. to said A. B. of the sum of —— dollars, and which said paper writing is lost and destroyed and a copy thereof cannot by the grand jury be set forth, which said paper writing was so feloniously, falsely and fraudulently made and forged with intent to defraud.

UTTERING.

That A. B., at ——, on ——, feloniously did utter and attempt to employ as true a certain [name the instrument, or say a certain paper writing], in words and figures as follows, to wit: [set out copy of the instrument or state that it is lost, or otherwise explain the inability to set it out], with intent to defraud, then and there well knowing that said [naming the instrument as above] was false and forged.[1]

VI. EVIDENCE.

§ 805. Production of instrument.— The best evidence of the forgery is the production of the instrument, and it must be produced or its absence accounted for;[2] thereupon the next best evidence is required.[3] In the absence of better evidence

[1] See S. v. Tingler, 32 W. Va. 546.

[2] C. v. Snell, 3 Mass. 82; S. v. Potts, 9 N. J. 26; P. v. Swetland, 77 Mich. 53; Kirk v. C., 9 Leigh, 627; Manaway v. S., 44 Ala. 375; Dovalina v. S., 14 Tex. Ap. 312; Rex v. Hunter, 3 C. & P. 591; Rex v. Hunter, 4 C. & P. 128. If the instrument is supposed to be in the control of defendant, notice must be given to defendant to produce it before secondary evidence is admissible: Rex v. Haworth, 4 C. & P. 254. By Michigan statute, where the instrument is shown to be in the defendant's control, notice to produce is not necessary in order to authorize the introduction of the record thereof: P. v. Swetland, 77 Mich. 53.

[3] U. S. v. Britton, 2 Mason, 464; Thompson v. S., 30 Ala. 28; S. v. Blodgett, 1 Root, 534; S. v. Ford, 2 Root, 93; Ross v. Bruce, 1 Day, 100; Pendleton v. C., 4 Leigh, 694; Reg. v. Hall, 12 Cox, 159.

the contents may be proved by the oral testimony of one who has seen it and can describe it, whether by reference to a copy or otherwise.[1] Nor is it necessary to have alleged in the indictment that the instrument is lost or cannot be produced in order to warrant the introduction of secondary evidence at the trial, when such fact appears.[2] The original is properly admitted in evidence, however badly written, if it is decipherable;[3] but where it is so faded as to be illegible, a photographic copy is admissible upon proof that it is an exact copy.[4]

§ 806. **Comparison of handwriting.**— It is not competent to introduce writing supported by evidence that it is the writing of defendant, but not admitted by him to be such, for the purpose of comparison with the signature alleged to be forged.[5] Nor is it proper to allow the prosecuting witness to write his name in the presence of the jury for the purpose of comparison with the signature alleged to be forged.[6] But there is no objection to a witness who attempts to describe the genuine signature of the person whose name is alleged to be forged, making in the presence of the jury the letters of such name for the purpose of illustrating how such party usually makes his signature.[7] An expert may not testify to a comparison previously made between the genuine writing of the person whose signature is claimed to be forged and the signature in question.[8] But an expert may testify as to the condition of an instrument with reference to whether it appears to have been traced or not;[9] and the jury may inspect the document with a magnifying-glass in order to understand its condition.[10] The jury may examine the whole instrument for the purpose of forming their own conclusion as to whether it was produced by one and the same hand,[11] and draw such inference as they may think warranted with reference to the order in which the different sig-

[1] C. v. Snell, 3 Mass. 82; C. v. Hutchinson, 1 Mass. 7. And it is not necessary that the witness testifying to the contents by examination be an expert: Duffin v. P., 107 Ill. 113.

[2] Mead v. S., 53 N. J. 601.

[3] Hager v. S., 71 Ga. 164.

[4] Duffin v. P., 107 Ill. 113.

[5] S. v. Henderson, 29 W. Va. 147; S. v. Ezekiel, 33 S. C. 115; S. v. Fritz, 23 La. An. 55; Reg. v. Aldridge, 3 F. & F. 781.

[6] S. v. Koontz, 31 W. Va. 127; S. v. Lurch, 12 Oreg. 99.

[7] S. v. Henderson, 29 W. Va. 147.

[8] P. v. Mitchell, 92 Cal. 590.

[9] Reg. v. Williams, 8 C. & P. 434.

[10] Hatch v. S., 6 Tex. Ap. 384.

[11] S. v. Scott, 45 Mo. 302.

natures were written and other matters.[1] The testimony of witnesses acquainted with the signatures of the president and cashier of a bank from having seen them on notes of such bank in circulation is sufficient to prove the falseness of the signatures on the bill claimed to be counterfeit.[2] These are but illustrations of the application of rules which prevail in civil as well as in criminal evidence, and it is not necessary to go at length into the proof of handwriting by comparison and similar questions.

§ 807. **Capacity of defendant and other matters.**— The mere ability to commit the act, as, for instance, skill in imitating peculiarities of signatures, cannot be shown;[3] but proof of the manner in which the defendant read the instrument to the witness to whom he offered it is admissible to show the intent;[4] and the fabrication of a deposition to prove the authenticity of an instrument may be shown as constituting an admission of its falsity.[5] Evidence of the pecuniary condition of the defendant at the time a receipt alleged to be forged purports to have been executed to him is admissible, to show that he was not able at that time to pay the sum appearing by the instrument to have been paid.[6]

§ 808. **Evidence of other crimes.**— It is not a violation of the general rule that on the trial of one offense proof of the commission of other offenses is not admissible, to allow proof, in a prosecution for forgery, of the commission of another forgery at or about the same time, such evidence being admissible to show the intent with which the act charged was committed.[7] But it would seem that such evidence should be limited to a case where the other transaction was with reference to paper of the identical character of that involved in the act charged, and that it must be shown that the other transaction constituted a crime, and the instrument referred to must be pro-

[1] C. v. Butterick, 100 Mass. 12.

[2] S. v. Carr, 5 N. H. 367; at least where the president and cashier are beyond the reach of a subpœna: S. v. McAllister, 24 Me. 139.

[3] S. v. Hopkins, 50 Vt. 316.

[4] Butler v. S., 22 Ala. 43.

[5] S. v. Williams, 27 Vt. 724.

[6] S. v. Henderson, 29 W. Va. 147.

[7] C. v. White, 145 Mass. 392, 7 Am. Cr. R. 192, and note; McDonald v. S., 83 Ala. 46; Francis v. S., 7 Tex. Ap. 501; Mason v. S., 31 Tex. Ap. 306. Proof of another forgery committed by defendant at the same time is admissible to identify the guilty party and the transaction: Cross v. P., 47 Ill. 152.

duced, or its absence accounted for.[1] Especially in cases of uttering forged instruments or passing counterfeit money is evidence of other acts of uttering and passing similar paper or money admissible to show guilty knowledge of the character of the instrument or money.[2] So in a charge for passing or having in possession counterfeit money, evidence of the possession about the same time of other counterfeit money is admissible.[3] It is evident that the other guilty act of possession must be nearly enough connected in point of time with the crime charged to warrant an inference by the jury that the intent in the two cases was the same; but it is said to be impracticable to lay down any general rule as to the necessary proximity in point of time.[4] If the transactions are not in any way connected, the evidence of another criminal act of the same character will not be admissible.[5] Admissions or confessions

[1] S. v. Saunders, 68 Ia. 370; S. v. Breckenridge, 67 Ia. 204; Rex v. Millard, Russ. & Ry. 245. It must be shown that the other instruments were forgeries: P. v. Altman, 147 N. Y. 473.

[2] P. v. Kemp, 76 Mich. 410; Foute v. S., 15 Lea, 712; Steele v. P., 45 Ill. 152; Langford v. S., 33 Fla. 233; Bishop v. S., 55 Md. 138; S. v. Cole, 19 Wis. 129; P. v. Stewart, 5 Mich. 243; U. S. v. Doebler, 1 Bald. 519; S. v. McAllister, 24 Me. 139; P. v. Frank, 28 Cal. 507; S. v. Tindal, 5 Harr. 488; C. v. Bigelow, 8 Met. 235; C. v. Price, 10 Gray, 472; C. v. Hall, 97 Mass. 570; S. v. Van Houton, 3 N. J. 672; S. v. Robinson, 16 N. J. 507; S. v. Houston, 1 Bailey, 300; Finn v. C., 5 Rand. 701; Martin v. C., 2 Leigh, 745; Hendrick v. C., 5 Leigh, 707; Ham v. S., 4 Tex. Ap. 645; Heard v. S., 9 Tex. Ap. 1; Reg. v. Salt, 3 F. & F. 834; Rex v. Ball, Russ. & Ry. 132; Rex v. Wylie, 1 N. R. 92; Reg. v. Green, 3 C. & K. 209; Reg. v. Colclough, L. R. 10 Ir. 241. Evidence of the admission of defendant of the embezzlement of other funds in a conversation in which he admitted passing the check in question was held admissible to show his intent in connection with the passing of the check: Strang v. S., 32 Tex. Ap. 219.

[3] C. v. Russell, 156 Mass. 196; P. v. Farrell, 30 Cal. 316; Rex v. Hough, Russ. & Ry. 120; Reg. v. Zeigert, 10 Cox, 555. So the possession of instruments for coining may be shown to prove guilty knowledge: S. v. Antonio, 3 Brev. 562.

[4] Reg. v. Salt, 3 F. & F. 834. Similar forgeries by defendant nine months after the one in question are not admissible: P. v. Baird, 104 Cal. 462.

[5] U. S. v. Roudenbush, 1 Bald. 514; Morris v. S., 16 Miss. 762; S. v. Odel, 3 Brev. 552; Rex v. Taverner, Car. C. L. 195; Reg. v. Moore, 1 F. & F. 73; and it is said that if a second uttering is the subject of a distinct indictment, it can be given in evidence to show guilty knowledge in the former uttering: Rex v. Smith, 2 C. & P. 633.

as to other criminal acts of the same character cannot be shown.[1]

§ 809. Inferences from the act or possession.— The fact that defendant intentionally derives a benefit from the use of the false instrument is admissible as showing his intent to defraud.[2] So the possession of a forged instrument is evidence that the party having it in possession is guilty of the forgery.[3] Such evidence is admissible on much the same principle as evidence of a recent possession of stolen property may be received as indicating guilt of the larceny;[4] and it may be shown in rebuttal that the possession was not exclusive.[5]

§ 810. In cases of conspiracy.— Where defendant is shown to have been connected with others in the transaction, evidence of criminal acts on the part of the others is admissible as though they had been done by defendant himself.[6]

[1] Fox v. P., 95 Ill. 71; S. v. Odel, 3 Brev. 552; Reg. v. Cooke, 8 C. & P. 586.

[2] Anson v. P., 148 Ill. 494; Timmons v. S., 80 Ga. 216; S. v. Patterson, 116 Mo. 505; Berrisford v. S., 66 Ga. 53; S. v. Lane, 80 N. C. 407; C. v. Hide, 94 Ky. 517; U. S. v. Brooks, 3 MacArthur, 315; Rex v. Shepherd, 2 East, P. C. 967; Reg. v. Johnson, 6 Cox, 18.

[3] C. v. Talbot, 2 Allen, 161; S. v. Haws, 98 Mo. 188; Hobbs v. S., 75 Ala. 1; S. v. Britt, 3 Dev. 122; Spencer v. C., 2 Leigh, 751; S. v. Outs, 30 La. An., Part II, 1155; Reg. v. James, 4 Cox, 90. But such possession or the uttering of the instrument does not raise a presumption that defendant forged it, but is simply evidence tending to prove the fact: Miller v. S., 51 Ind. 405.

[4] S. v. Allen, 116 Mo. 548.

[5] Pagaud v. S., 13 Miss. 491.

[6] Martin v. C., 2 Leigh, 745; U. S. v. Craig, 4 Wash. 729; S. v. Morton, 27 Vt. 310; S. v. Thaden, 43 Minn. 253.

CHAPTER 32.

MALICIOUS MISCHIEF; WILFUL TRESPASS.

§ 811. **Nature of these crimes.**— While it is said, as will appear in some of the following sections, that the malicious destruction of or injury to property was recognized at common law as a misdemeanor,[1] yet the cases are so entirely based upon statutes that any theoretical discussion of what might be criminal in this direction without a statute would be of no value. Inasmuch as the kind of property the injury of which would be criminal must therefore depend upon statutory description, and no uniform distinction as between what property shall and what shall not be the subject of the offense is maintained among the statutes, it will be useless to try to maintain any such distinction in this discussion. It will be found that injury to animals or personal property in general is frequently by statute included under the head of malicious mischief, although injuries to buildings and to trees are also included in that offense; while by other statutes the term "wilful trespass" or "forcible trespass" is used to include injuries to real property and to some extent to personal property. Forcible entry and detainer[2] is an offense with reference to real property only, and is susceptible of more accurate definition, but in many states the statutes with reference thereto are not criminal but provide a civil remedy only.

§ 812. **Malicious mischief by early statutes; Black Act.**— Some early English statutes provide for the punishment of various forms of malicious mischief, conspicuous among them being the so-called Black Act, which provided, among other things, for the punishment of the offense of setting fire to houses, hay, etc., the killing of cattle, the destroying of trees, etc.[3]

[1] C. v. Wing, 9 Pick. 1; S. v. Watts, 48 Ark. 56; Loomis v. Edgerton, 19 Wend. 419; P. v. Smith, 5 Cow. 258; Rivers v. S., 10 Tex. Ap. 177; Resp. v. Teischer, 1 Dall. 335. But see to the contrary, S. v. Beekman, 27 N. J. 124; S. v. Clark, 29 N. J. 96; Kilpatrick v. P., 5 Denio, 277.

[2] See the next chapter.

[3] 4 Bl. Com. 244; 2 East, P. C. 1036;

The Black Act is not in force in this country as a part of the common law and has not usually been re-enacted in that form.[1]

§ 813. Distinguished from larceny.— It has already been stated under the chapter relating to larceny[2] that to take and carry away trees, crops, etc., which are a part of the realty does not constitute larceny. Some statutes are evidently designed to obviate this objection and make punishable as malicious mischief the act of depriving the owner of such property.[3] To carry away the metal from a building or the like, which is likewise not larceny, is included within the statutes covering injuries to real property. But these acts will be properly considered hereafter in this chapter in sections relating to trespasses to realty.[4] The destruction of trees, crops, etc., which would also not be larceny for the additional reason that there is no taking and carrying away, are punishable under various statutes;[5] but to come within these statutes the property must be some sort of agricultural product or product of the soil,[6] and there must be a destruction total or partial; the mere carrying away will not be sufficient.[7]

§ 814. Injuries to personal property.— The statutes relating to malicious mischief are generally broad enough to cover all kinds of personal property, and under them it has been held criminal to maliciously or wantonly injure or destroy any personal property;[8] but under some statutes the offense of mali-

S. v. Sutcliffe, 4 Strobh. 372. And see C. v. Williams, 110 Mass. 401, and S. v. Clark, 29 N. J. 96, quoting Blackstone's definition.

[1] S. v. Campbell, T. U. P. Charl. 166. The so-called "Ku-Klux" laws, passed in some of the southern states soon after the rebellion, for the punishment of those who committed depredations while masked, somewhat resembled the English statute; especially in imposing a very heavy penalty: See Walpole v. S., 9 Baxt. 370.

[2] *Supra*, § 536.

[3] S. v. Luther, 8 R. I. 151; S. v. Malone, 46 Ark. 140.

[4] *Infra*, §§ 821–823. And see S. v. Stone, 30 N. J. 299.

[5] S. v. Purdie, 67 N. C. 326; Ex parte Eads, 17 Neb. 145; S. v. Priebnow, 14 Neb. 484; Rex v. Taylor, Russ. & Ry. 373.

[6] Murray v. S., 21 Tex. Ap. 620; Terry v. S., 25 Tex. Ap. 714.

[7] S. v. Cole, 90 Ind. 112. If the statute provides for punishing the destruction of plants, etc., the mere injury thereto from which death results will not be included: Reg. v. Boucher, 5 Jur. 709. To deaden a tree standing on public ground is indictable: C. v. Eckert, 2 Browne, 249.

[8] Loomis v. Edgerton, 19 Wend. 419; S. v. Webster, 17 N. H. 543; P. v. Olsen, 6 Utah, 284; Hannel v. S., 4 Ind. Ap. 485. It may be made criminal to deface or destroy a tombstone: S. v. Wilson, 94 N. C. 1015. It has been held not indictable to remove

cious mischief can only be committed as to the realty,[1] while other statutes have been held applicable to personal property only, and not to anything a part of the realty.[2] The destruction of a part of the property is sufficient to constitute the crime.[3]

§ 815. **Injuries to animals.**— The most common form of the offense of malicious mischief with reference to personal property is that involved in injuring, maiming or killing domestic animals of another.[4] The term "cattle," as used in such a statute, includes horses,[5] also asses[6] and swine.[7] The indictment must, however, specify the kind of animal.[8] There has been a diversity of opinion as to whether injuring or killing a dog is within statutes relating to malicious mischief. It has been held in a number of cases that the term "domestic animals" does not include a dog;[9] but there are other cases to the contrary.[10] To constitute an offense under these statutes it is not necessary to prove the use of any instrument to inflict the wound.[11] And it is not necessary that the animal be killed.[12] If the animal is killed the offense is committed though the act is unlawful aside from the result in the death of the animal, as, for instance, by setting fire to a stable in which cows are kept, the death of the animals resulting therefrom;[13] nor is it necessary that the injury be permanent;[14] but under

a corner-stone in a boundary line: S. v. Burroughs, 7 N. J. 426.

[1] Shell v. S., 6 Humph. 283; S. v. Wheeler, 3 Vt. 344.

[2] S. v. Helmes, 5 Ired. 364; C. v. Dougherty, 6 Gray, 349. A Georgia statute has been held applicable only to inanimate property, and not as covering animals of any kind: Patton v. S., 93 Ga. 111.

[3] C. v. Soule, 2 Met. 21.

[4] S. v. Alexander, 14 Rich. 247; P. v. Smith, 5 Cow. 258; Snap v. P., 19 Ill. 80; Resp. v. Teischer, 1 Dall. 335; S. v. Godfrey, 97 N. C. 507; S. v. Brigman, 94 N. C. 888; T. v. Crozier, 6 Dak. 8; S. v. Igo, 108 Mo. 568; Rivers v. S., 10 Tex. Ap. 177.

[5] S. v. Cliffton, 73 Ala. 473; Rex v. Patty, 2 East, P. C. 1074; Rex v. Moyle, 2 East, P. C. 1076.

[6] Reg. v. Whitney, 1 Moody, 3.

[7] Rex v. Chapple, Russ. & Ry. 77; S. v. Enslow, 10 Ia. 115. And see Rivers v. S., 10 Tex. Ap. 177, to the effect that an allegation of maliciously injuring a hog comes within the statutory provision as to swine. As to description of animals, see *infra*, § 831, n.

[8] Rex v. Chalkley, Russ. & Ry. 258.

[9] S. v. Harriman, 75 Me. 562; Davis v. C., 17 Grat. 617; U. S. v. Gideon, 1 Minn. 292.

[10] S. v. McDuffie, 34 N. H. 523; S. v. Latham, 13 Ired. 33; S. v. Sumner, 2 Ind. 377; Sosat v. S., 2 Ind. Ap. 586; Kinsman v. S., 77 Ind. 132.

[11] Reg. v. Bullock, L. R. 1 C. C. 115.

[12] Rex v. Owens, 1 Moody, 205.

[13] Rex v. Haughton, 5 C. & P. 559.

[14] Rex v. Haywood, 2 East, P. C.

an early English statute it was held not criminal to injure sheep by setting a dog upon them.[1] A form of injury which is sometimes specially prohibited is mixing poison with the feed of animals or putting out poison with the intention that it shall be taken by them and cause their destruction;[2] but it has been said that aside from statute, injury to animals, no matter how malicious, wanton or cruel, is not a crime at common law, being a mere civil trespass.[3] Accordingly it is said not to be indictable to shave the mane or crop the hair from the tail of another's horse,[4] but in other cases such an act has been held to constitute malicious mischief.[5] The question may become material whether at the time of the injury to the animal it was trespassing. Some statutes make that fact a defense where the premises are surrounded by a lawful fence;[6] and aside from statute the fact would have a bearing on the question of intent;[7] but the fact that the animal is trespassing is not in itself an excuse for injuring or killing it,[8] nor is it any defense that the animal is unlawfully at large.[9]

§ **816. Altering brand, etc.**— One form of injury to an owner of animals is by altering the brand or mark thereon, and this is sometimes prohibited by statute. But it must, of course, be wilful and with intent to injure or defraud the owner.[10] So it may be made criminal to unlawfully mark or brand the animal of another.[11] In Texas it is made criminal to drive cattle off their accustomed range.[12]

1076. But this will depend on the language of the statute: Reg. v. Jeans, 1 C. & K. 539.

[1] Rex v. Hughes, 2 C. & P. 420. But see Elmsley's Case, 1 Lewin, 126.

[2] S. v. La Bounty, 63 Vt. 374; P. v. Keeley, 81 Cal. 210; Rex v. Mogg, 4 C. & P. 364; Daniel v. Janes, 2 C. P. D. 351.

[3] S. v. Beekman, 27 N. J. 124; S. v. Allen, 72 N. C. 114; S. v. Manuel, 72 N. C. 201; S. v. Waters, 6 Jones, 276; S. v. Landreth, 2 Law Repos. 446.

[4] S. v. Smith, Cheves, 157.

[5] Boyd v. S., 2 Humph. 39; Oviatt v. S., 19 Ohio St. 573.

[6] Thomas v. S., 30 Ark. 433; Jones v. S., 3 Tex. Ap. 228; McMahan v. S., 29 Tex. Ap. 348; S. v. Godfrey, 97 N. C. 507. If it is made criminal to kill or abuse the animal of another in an inclosure not surrounded by a lawful fence, it is not sufficient to charge such an offense as committed in a field: S. v. Stanton, 66 N. C. 660.

[7] Gaskill v. S., 56 Ind. 550; Reedy v. S.. 22 Tex. Ap. 271.

[8] Sosat v. S., 2 Ind. Ap. 586; Thompson v. S., 67 Ala. 106.

[9] S. v. Brigman, 94 N. C. 888.

[10] S. v. Davis, 2 Ired. 153; S. v. O'Neal, 7 Ired. 251; West v. S., 32 Tex. 651.

[11] Murrah v. S., 51 Miss. 675; S. v. Nichols, 12 Rich. 672; Frierson v. Hewitt, 2 Hill (S. C.), 499.

[12] Darnell v. S., 43 Tex. 147; Smith

§ 817. Injuries to machinery.— In England statutes have been passed for the punishment of malicious injuries to machinery of various kinds, specially named, the occasion for the passage of such statutes evidently having been a malicious destruction of machinery by those who considered that its introduction was injurious to their employment. The cases are sufficiently referred to by citing them together in the note.[1] A similar statute as to maliciously cutting the cotton warp on looms in a factory is found in Delaware.[2]

§ 818. Injuries to vessels.— English statutes also especially provide for the punishment of malicious injury to vessels or to commerce.[3]

§ 819. Injury to public property.— Malicious injury to public property, such as bridges[4] and public buildings,[5] is made punishable by statute. It is also made criminal to cut down boundary-line trees[6] or tear down public notices.[7] Such statutes are sometimes passed with reference to injuring railroad property,[8] but these statutes usually apply to such property as pertains to or is connected with the operation of the road, not to such a structure as a fence.[9] Injuring toll-gates,[10] or dams,[11] or canal banks,[12] may be criminal.

§ 820. Forcible trespass.— In some states there are statutes for the punishment of trespass committed by force or violence, and these statutes relate to personal as well as to real prop-

v. S., 43 Tex. 433; Long v. S., 43 Tex. 467.

[1] Rex v. Mackerel, 4 C. & P. 448; Reg. v. Whittingham, 9 C. & P. 234; Reg. v. Norris, 9 C. & P. 241; Deac. Cr. L. 1517, 1518; Rex v. Hill, Russ. & Ry. 483; Rex v. Tracy, Russ. & Ry. 452; Reg. v. Smith, 6 Cox, 198; Rex v. Ashton, 2 B. & Ad. 750; Reg. v. Clegs, 3 Cox, 295; Rex v. Woodhead, 1 M. & Rob. 549; Rex v. Fidler, 4 C. & P. 449; Reg. v. Gray, L. & C. 365; Reg. v. Fisher, L. R. 1 C. C. 7.

[2] S. v. Hamilton, 1 Houst. Cr. C. 281.

[3] Rex v. De Londo, 2 East, P. C. 1098; Rex v. Bowyer, 4 C. & P. 559; Reg. v. McGregor, 1 C. & K. 429; Reg. v. Wallace, Car. & M. 200; Reg. v. Kohn, 4 F. & F. 68; Reg. v. Wallace, 2 Moody, 200; Rex v. Philp, 1 Moody, 263; Rex v. Hastings, 1 Moody, 82; Harrod v. Worship, 30 L. J. M. C. 165.

[4] O'Dea v. S., 16 Neb. 241.

[5] S. v. Costello, 62 Conn. 128; C. v. Horrigan, 2 Allen, 159.

[6] S. v. Malloy, 34 N. J. 410. As to removing land-marks which determine boundaries, see *supra*, § 45.

[7] Folwell v. S., 49 N. J. 31; Pennsylvania v. Gillespie, Add. 267; U. S. v. Buford, 8 Utah, 173; *supra*, § 45.

[8] Johnson v. S., 98 Ala. 57.

[9] S. v. Walsh, 43 Minn. 444. Obstruction to railways is, however, further considered: *Infra*, § 1196.

[10] Bock v. S., 50 Ind. 281; S. v. Walters, 64 Ind. 226.

[11] S. v. Weeks, 30 Me. 182.

[12] S. v. Bush, 29 Ind. 110.

erty.[1] To constitute the offense there must be actual employment of force, in excess of a bare civil trespass and more than mere threatening or abusive words. There must be a demonstration by means of weapons or other outward signs of violence, or by numbers such as is calculated to put the occupant of the premises or the person who is in possession of personal property in fear.[2] It is not a mere invasion of property that constitutes the offense,[3] and title to the property is immaterial.[4] There must be something which tends to or constitutes a breach of the peace.[5] A mere civil trespass without threats of violence or force is not sufficient to constitute the offense.[6] This offense as affecting real property is similar to that of forcible entry, to be considered in the next chapter.

§ 821. **Injury to buildings.**— Some statutes contain special provisions with reference to malicious injury to a dwelling-house or other buildings,[7] and such a statute covers injury to a church or other public building.[8] To defile a building with filth comes within such a statute.[9]

§ 822. **Hunting or fishing without permission.**— Some statutes contain special provisions with reference to trespass by hunting or fishing on another's land without permission.[10]

§ 823. **Injuries to real property.**— Merely to break and enter the close of another is a civil trespass only; but if such entry be attended by circumstances constituting a breach of the peace or malicious injury to the premises, it may be criminal at common law.[11] Statutes usually make it criminal to thus

[1] S. v. Gray, 109 N. C. 790; S. v. Barefoot, 89 N. C. 565.

[2] S. v. Covington, 70 N. C. 71; S. v. Widenhouse, 71 N. C. 279; S. v. King, 74 N. C. 177; S. v. Hinson, 83 N. C. 640; S. v. Lloyd, 85 N. C. 573; S. v. Barefoot, 89 N. C. 565; S. v. Gray, 109 N. C. 790.

[3] S. v. Mace, 65 N. C. 344.

[4] S. v. Laney, 87 N. C. 535.

[5] S. v. Laney, 87 N. C. 535; S. v. Jacobs, 94 N. C. 950.

[6] Temple v. S., 6 Baxt. 496; Temple v. S., 7 Baxt. 109; S. v. Mills, 104 N. C. 905.

[7] S. v. Hockenberry, 11 Ia. 269; S. v. Semotan, 85 Ia. 57; S. v. Whitener, 93 N. C. 798; S. v. McBeth, 49 Kan. 584; S. v. Wilson, 3 Mo. 125; S. v. Morris, 3 Mo. 127; S. v. Batchelder, 5 N. H. 549.

[8] S. v. Brant, 14 Ia. 180.

[9] C. v. Williams, 110 Mass. 401; Smith v. S., 63 Ga. 168.

[10] S. v. Turner, 60 Conn. 222; Winlock v. S., 121 Ind. 531; Wellington v. S., 52 Ark. 266; Holtzgraft v. S., 23 Tex. Ap. 404.

[11] Henderson v. C., 8 Grat. 708; C. v. Taylor, 5 Binn. 277. As to the offense of forcible trespass, see *supra*, § 820; as to forcible entry, see next chapter.

go upon another's premises and cut timber or trees.[1] To recklessly injure the shade trees in a highway in front of one's premises is a crime under a statute providing for the punishment of wrongful injuries to property.[2] So it is criminal under perhaps all the statutes to enter the premises of another and maliciously or wantonly destroy or tear down the fences.[3] Where the offense described is trespass to realty there must be something more than a mere removal of a chattel found on the premises.[4] So under a statute providing a punishment for destroying a pipe used as an aqueduct, injury to the pipe must be done while it constitutes an aqueduct.[5] And in general a statute with reference to injury to real or personal property will not cover a mere incorporeal right.[6] But taking ice from a pond found on another's land is a criminal trespass.[7] The fact that one's dog does damage within another's field does not constitute malicious injury,[8] though it may by statute be criminal to cause one's animals to go within the inclosed field of another.[9]

[1] Brown v. S., 100 Ala. 92. Carrying away is not necessary: Johnson v. S., 61 Ala. 9; and to carry away wood is not enough; there must be a cutting down of standing timber: S. v. McConkey, 20 Ia. 574. The crime may be committed by a tenant in possession if the act is without the landlord's authority: Derixson v. S., 65 Ind. 385. A crime may be committed in cutting and carrying away timber from school land, the title of which is still in the United States: Chalfont v. U. S., Morris, 214. Burning woodland of another is criminal: Phillips v. S., 19 Tex. 158.

[2] Daily v. S., 51 Ohio St. 348.

[3] Brazleton v. S., 66 Ala. 96; S. v. Hovis, 76 N. C. 117; S. v. Biggers, 108 N. C. 760; Dawson v. S., 52 Ind. 478; S. v. Hoover, 31 Ark. 676; C. v. Drass, 146 Pa. St. 55; Roberts v. S., 17 Tex. Ap. 148; Woodyard v. S., 19 Tex. Ap. 516. In case of joint owners of a fence it is not criminal for one to tear it down: Drees v. S., 37 Ark. 122; Hurlbut v. S., 12 Tex. Ap. 252. If one owner tears down a part of such fence and the other replaces such part, the first may then be guilty of tearing down the fence of another: Jamison v. S., 27 Tex. Ap. 442. Certainly it is not criminal to remove a partition fence which is wholly on the land of the person removing it: S. v. Watson, 86 N. C. 626. Mere posts set in the ground to prevent persons driving out of the highway across an adjoining field do not constitute a fence: S. v. Roberts, 101 N. C. 744. The mere taking down of a fence for more convenient passage, without exposing crops to depredation and the like, is not criminal: Hooks v. S., 25 Tex. Ap. 601.

[4] Bates v. S., 31 Ind. 72.

[5] S. v. Jones, 33 Vt. 443.

[6] Laws v. Eltringham, 8 Q. B. D. 283.

[7] S. v. Pottmeyer, 30 Ind. 287.

[8] Reg. v. Prestney, 3 Cox, 505.

[9] Cleveland v. S., 8 Tex. Ap. 44; Coggins v. S., 12 Tex. Ap. 109.

§ 824. Trespass after warning, or when forbidden.— Some statutes make it criminal to go upon another's premises after a warning not to do so, or when forbidden to do so, irrespective of any damage that may be done to the premises.[1]

§ 825. Offenses against possession.— The statutes as to criminal trespass are for the protection of the person in possession of the land, and not for the protection of the owner as distinct from the person in possession.[2] Thus, one may be guilty of a crime in pulling down a fence on premises to which he claims title if another is in peaceable possession;[3] but the owner entitled to possession cannot be prosecuted for acts committed on premises in the occupation of a mere trespasser or person without legal right;[4] and it is not competent for defendant to prove title in a person other than the complainant in possession. The question of title is not in issue.[5] Mere constructive possession is not enough. Thus, a tenant who has abandoned the premises has not such possession that he can maintain

[1] Ryan v. S., 5 Ind. Ap. 396. But the warning must be such as to constitute an actual notice: Owens v. S., 74 Ala. 401; and the entry must follow the warning. One already in possession, even though without right, cannot by a warning be rendered guilty of the crime: Goldsmith v. S., 86 Ala. 55. The warning should be by the person in possession: Matthews v. S., 81 Ala. 66; Sewell v. S., 82 Ala. 57; S. v. Lawson, 101 N. C. 717; S. v. Green, 35 S. C. 266. But where the statute refers to notice by the owner it is not necessary to aver that the owner himself was in possession: Beggs v. S., 122 Ind. 54. The term "premises," used in such a statute, means any real estate for the entry on which a civil action might be maintained, and includes an inclosed field though situate at a distance from the dwelling of the owner: Sandy v. S., 60 Ala. 18. But under such a statute a wharf was held not to be within the definition of "inclosed land:" Daniels v. S., 91 Ga. 1.

[2] S. v. Gurnee, 14 Kan. 111.

[3] Carter v. S., 18 Tex. Ap. 573; S. v. Marsh, 91 N. C. 632; Lawson v. S., 100 Ala. 7.

[4] S. v. Clark, 29 N. J. 96; Malone v. S., 11 Lea. 701; Windsor v. S., 13 Ind. 375. Verbal permission to plant a patch of turnips in defendant's field without consideration and without specifying any part of the field, *held* not to render defendant criminally liable for trespass in destroying the crop so planted: S. v. Gadsden, 20 S. C. 456.

[5] Knight v. S., 64 Miss. 802; S. v. Burns, 123 Ind. 437; Jenkins v. S., 7 Tex. Ap. 146. But title in a third person under whom defendant claims to have lawfully acted may be shown: S. v. Boyce, 109 N. C. 739; Ryan v. S., 5 Ind. Ap. 396. Where both parties are in possession claiming adversely, one cannot be convicted for criminal trespass with reference to such premises: White v. S., 14 Tex. Ap. 449.

a prosecution for going upon such land without his consent.[1] Nor is it trespass upon the improved land of another to destroy grain growing on land forming a portion of the public highway.[2] And one who has peaceably entered upon land and erected buildings thereon is not guilty of criminal trespass in tearing them down on discovering that the land belongs to another.[3] One who is a tenant in common in possession is not punishable for trespass;[4] nor is a tenant guilty of criminal trespass in removing from the premises crops in which, as a tenant, he has an interest, though the removal is without the consent of the landlord, who has title to and control of the crops.[5]

§ 826. **The intent; malice.**— The statutes usually employ terms indicating that wilfulness, maliciousness or wantonness in the act is essential to make it criminal, and something more than a mere intentional doing of that which is wrong must appear to warrant a conviction.[6] It is not enough that the act be voluntarily and knowingly done; there must be an evil purpose connected with it.[7] To constitute the offense of cutting down trees which are monuments of boundary, it must appear that the intent was to destroy a tree as constituting such monument; and the mere destruction of the tree without knowledge of its character would not be sufficient.[8] There must be the intent to maliciously injure or destroy the property; if the injury is the accidental result of an attempt to injure the person of another, the offense is not committed.[9] Therefore any evidence tending to show that the act was done without malicious intent is admissible.[10] Thus, if the act is in good faith under a

[1] Hester v. S., 67 Miss. 129.

[2] P. v. O'Brien, 60 Mich. 8.

[3] S. v. Reynolds, 95 N. C. 616.

[4] Mays v. S., 89 Ala. 37.

[5] Padgett v. S., 81 Ga. 466.

[6] C. v. Walden, 3 Cush. 558; C. v. Williams, 110 Mass. 401; Duncan v. S., 49 Miss. 331; Pippen v. S., 77 Ala. 81; Hampton v. S., 10 Lea, 639; Branch v. S., 41 Tex. 622; Browder v. S., 30 Tex. Ap. 614.

[7] Folwell v. S., 49 N. J. 31; C. v. Kneeland, 20 Pick. 206.

[8] S. v. Malloy, 34 N. J. 410.

[9] Reg. v. Pembliton, L. R. 2 C. C. 119. And see Reg. v. Latimer, 17 Q. B. D. 359. Where the death of an animal resulted from the administration of poisonous substances intended to improve his appearance, *held*, that no crime was committed: Rex v. Mogg, 4 C. & P. 364. Breaking down the bank of a fish-pond was held not criminal under an English statute providing for such an act, where it appeared that the object was to steal the fish and not to let them escape through the breach: Rex v. Ross, 2 East, P. C. 1067.

[10] S. v. Bush, 29 Ind. 110.

mistake of fact[1] or under compulsion,[2] no crime is committed. So to kill an animal to prevent its trespassing,[3] or to destroy other property in the attempt to protect the possession or enjoyment of one's own property,[4] is not criminal. But this matter must after all be determined largely by the language of the statute; and if the language is such as to make the doing of a particular act of injury criminal, it is not necessary to show maliciousness;[5] and in such cases the intentionally wrongful doing of the act is enough.[6] In such cases the wrongful intent may be sufficiently shown by the doing of the forbidden act without any claim of right or excuse;[7] and a mistake of fact as to the title of the property will not be a defense if defendant might have ascertained by the use of reasonable means that the property was not his own.[8] An offer to pay the damages will not be a defense.[9]

§ 827. **Under claim of right.**— From what has been said in the preceding section, it is evident that there is no criminal liability for the acts contemplated in this chapter where they are done in a *bona fide* exercise of a supposed right and without malicious purpose;[10] but if the right which is claimed is exercised maliciously for the purpose of intentionally injuring another, it will be no defense.[11] The determination of the ques-

1 Lossen v. S., 62 Ind. 437; Palmer v. S., 45 Ind. 388; S. v. Newkirk, 49 Mo. 84; S. v. Hanks, 66 N. C. 612.

2 Rex v. Crutchley, 5 C. & P. 133.

3 Wright v. S., 30 Ga. 325.

4 P. v. Kane, 131 N. Y. 111; S. C., 142 N. Y. 366.

5 Tatum v. S., 66 Ala. 465; Johnson v. S., 1 Ala. Sel. Cas. 72.

6 S. v. Doig, 2 Rich. 179; S. v. Council, 1 Overt. 305.

7 P. v. Stevens, 109 N. Y. 159; Knight v. S., 64 Miss. 802; Wallace v. S., 30 Tex. 758; Reg. v. Pembliton, L. R. 2 C. C. 119; Reg. v. Welch, 1 Q. B. D. 23. Under a statute forbidding injury to a toll-gate, malice need not be alleged: S. v. Walters, 64 Ind. 226. Where the killing of trespassing animals in inclosures not lawfully fenced was forbidden, it was held that if the killing was by carelessness, as by negligently firing a gun to frighten them, the carelessness would supply the wrongful intent: S. v. Barnard, 88 N. C. 661.

8 Clark v. S., 50 Ark. 570; S. v. Fisher, 109 N. C. 817.

9 S. v. Doig, 2 Rich. 179; Roe v. S., 82 Ala. 68.

10 Barlow v. S., 120 Ind. 56; Palmer v. S., 45 Ind. 388; Goforth v. S., 8 Humph. 37; Reg. v. Matthews, 14 Cox, 5; even though the claim is unfounded: S. v. Hanse, 71 N. C. 518. So professional advice may be shown to indicate good faith: Dawson v. S., 52 Ind. 478; but such advice is immaterial if defendant had no claim of right: Watson v. S., 63 Ala. 19. The question of good faith is for the jury: S. v. Luther, 8 R. I. 151.

11 Harris v. S., 73 Ga. 41; S. v. Howell, 107 N. C. 835; Rex v. Whateley, 4 M. & Rob. 431.

tion whether defendant acted under a *bona fide* claim of right may involve the title to the property.[1]

§ 828. Under claim of authority.— If the act is done under a good-faith belief of authority derived from one who might properly authorize the act it is not criminal;[2] so where the act of defendant in breaking the lock on a church door was done under a reasonable claim of right to do so as an officer of the church, he was held not punishable.[3] If one acts in good faith under supposed authority as an officer he is not punishable for malicious mischief or trespass;[4] but if the act of the officer is unlawful[5] or under process issued without jurisdiction he may be guilty of the crime.[6]

§ 829. Malice against owner.— Under some statutes it has been held that to constitute malicious mischief the injury done must be with malice towards the owner of the property and with the purpose of doing him an injury, and that mere malice towards an animal injured, or wantonness, is not sufficient.[7] This malice may, however, appear from the circumstances of the act.[8] In some cases it has been held that malice towards the owner is immaterial, and that it is the wilful or wanton injury of the animal which constitutes the crime.[9]

§ 830. Indictment; ownership of property.— In some statutes the offense is so described that the property must appear

[1] Bohannon v. S., 73 Ala. 47; S. v. Rising, 10 Nev. 97.

[2] S. v. Winslow, 95 N. C. 649; Reg. v. James, 8 C. & P. 131. But defendant relying on such authority must establish it: Ritter v. S., 33 Tex. 608. Even though defendant knew the title to be in dispute he cannot be held criminally liable for having acted under authority from one of the parties, having relied thereon in good faith: Lackey v. S., 14 Tex. Ap. 164.

[3] Woodward v. S., 33 Tex. Ap. 554.

[4] S. v. Lyle, 100 N. C. 497; Denny v. Thwaites, 2 Ex. D. 21; but not if the acts are malicious and with motives of ill-will though in the line of his duty: Lemasters v. S., 10 Ind. 391.

[5] S. v. Whitaker, 107 N. C. 802.

[6] S. v. Yarborough, 70 N. C. 250.

[7] S. v. Newby, 64 N. C. 23; S. v. Jackson, 12 Ired. 329; S. v. Robinson, 3 Dev. & B. 130; U. S. v. Gideon, 1 Minn. 292; S. v. Wilcox, 3 Yerg. 277; S. v. Pierce, 7 Ala. 728; Hobson v. S., 44 Ala. 380; Northcot v. S., 43 Ala. 330; P. v. Olsen, 6 Utah, 284; Rex v. Pearce, 2 East, P. C. 1072; Rex v. Shepherd, 2 East, P. C. 1073. The intent to injure the owner cannot be presumed from the mere fact of doing the injury: Newton v. S., 3 Tex. Ap. 245.

[8] S. v. Enslow, 10 Ia. 115; S. v. Linde, 54 Ia. 139; S. v. Williamson, 68 Ia. 351; P. v. Olsen, 6 Utah, 284; Hill v. S., 43 Ala. 335.

[9] Brown v. S., 26 Ohio St. 176; T. v. Crozier, 6 Dak. 8; Johnson v. S., 37 Ala. 457; Reg. v. Tivey, 1 C. & K. 704. See *infra*, § 1161.

to be that of some one other than the defendant, and in such cases the ownership should be alleged in order to show the necessary fact.[1] But aside from this there must of course be some description of the property, and it is usually held that the name of the owner must be particularly alleged,[2] or stated to be unknown.[3] The allegation as to ownership must be proven as alleged.[4] The ownership may of course be laid in the party in possession, though he be only bailee or agent or tenant.[5] It seems to have been held, however, in a few cases that where the injury alleged is to animals the name of the owner is not material in the description.[6] And where the charge was of injury to a designated public bridge it was held not necessary to aver ownership.[7]

§ 831. **Other description.**— It is usually deemed unnecessary to describe the property, if it be land, other than by the name of the owner and the locality, sufficiently to bring the offense within the jurisdiction of the court.[8] In other cases some description, such as "a fence" or "a saddle," should be given.[9]

[1] Ex parte Eads, 17 Neb. 145; S. v. Smith, 21 Tex. 748; Woodward v. S., 33 Tex. Ap. 554. But if the name of the owner is given it is not necessary to allege that the property did not belong to defendant: S. v. Purdie, 67 N. C. 326.

[2] Davis v. C., 30 Pa. St. 421; S. v. Jackson, 7 Ind. 270; Dorrell v. S., 80 Ind. 566; Rex v. Patrick, 2 East, P. C. 1059. Description of the land upon which trespass was committed as belonging to the estate and heirs of a person named, deceased, held sufficient: S. v. Paul, 81 Ia. 596.

[3] Moyer v. C., 7 Pa. St. 439; S. v. McConkey, 20 Ia. 574; Ostler v. S., 3 Ind. Ap. 122.

[4] S. v. Weeks, 30 Me. 182; Mayes v. S., 33 Tex. 340. But it has been said not to be essential to instruct the jury that such allegation must be proven beyond a reasonable doubt where they have been directed that they must be satisfied as to the ownership: S. v. Sears, Phill. 146; S. v. Knox, Phill. 312.

[5] Rex v. Woodward, 2 East, P. C. 563; Reg. v. Jones, 1 C. & K. 181; S. v. Whittier, 21 Me. 341.

[6] Davis v. C., 30 Pa. St. 421; S. v. Brocker, 32 Tex. 611; Smith v. S., 43 Tex. 433.

[7] Owens v. S., 52 Ala. 400.

[8] Newland v. S., 30 Ind. 111; Johnson v. S., 68 Ind. 43; P. v. O'Brien, 60 Mich. 8. But in one case it is stated that the description in the indictment as "the premises of," etc., was insufficient: S. v. French, 120 Ind. 229. Sometimes there is a description of the premises as "the homestead of," etc.: Ritter v. S., 33 Tex. 608; or as a place of a given name: Watson v. S., 63 Ala. 19.

[9] S. v. Smith, 7 Ind. Ap. 166; Hannel v. S., 4 Ind. Ap. 485. So a description of trees cut down as "ornamental and shade trees" was held sufficient: S. v. Priebnow, 14 Neb. 484. Under a statute punishing the shooting of a hog, etc., evidence is admissible to show the shooting of a sow: Shubrick v. S., 2 S. C. 21; but

But if it consists of a promissory note the indictment should state whether it was payable in money or property.[1]

§ 832. **The act, how charged.**— In general it is essential to state the kind and extent of the injury done, or the destruction of the property, as the case may be, in order to bring the act within the terms of the statute.[2] It is not sufficient to say that defendant "did wilfully injure," but the manner of the injury must be particularly shown.[3]

§ 833. **As to intent.**— Under statutes with reference to malicious mischief or malicious injury it is held necessary to charge the act as maliciously done;[4] but where the intentional doing of the act is all that is required by the statute it is not necessary to allege it to have been maliciously done.[5] In such cases, however, it is sometimes said to be necessary to charge the act as knowingly done.[6] It is not necessary to charge the act as unlawfully done where that fact appears from the other averments.[7] At common law, of course, it is necessary to charge the act as felonious, provided it is a felony;[8] but the averment that it was done with force and arms is wholly superfluous.[9] Where a particular intent, such as that of converting to the wrong-doer's own use, is specified, it must be charged.[10] Where the offense consists in entering without license the license should be negatived.[11]

proof of wilful killing of a gelding is not admissible under the allegation of the killing of a horse: Gholston v. S., 33 Tex. 342. Further, as to description of animals, see the same question under the head of larceny, *supra*, § 594.

[1] Birdg v. S., 31 Ind. 88.

[2] Brown v. S., 76 Ind. 85; S. v. Aydelott, 7 Blackf. 157.

[3] S. v. Costello, 62 Conn. 128. But in other cases it has been held sufficient to charge that defendant "did destroy and injure and cause to be destroyed and injured:" S. v. Slocum, 8 Blackf. 315; Boswell v. S., 8 Ind. 499.

[4] Boyd v. S., 2 Humph. 39; S. v. Jackson, 12 Ired. 329; Thompson v. S., 51 Miss. 353; Rex v. Lewis, 2 Russ. Cr. 1066.

[5] P. v. O'Brien, 60 Mich. 8.

[6] S. v. Stalls, 37 Tex. 440; S. v. Arnold, 39 Tex. 74; or "wilfully" if that is the word in the statute: Uecker v. S., 4 Tex. Ap. 234. But the allegation of guilty knowledge is unnecessary where the act is charged as wilful and malicious: C. v. Falvey, 108 Mass. 304.

[7] S. v. Maddox, 85 Ind. 585; S. v. Martin, 107 N. C. 904. On the other hand it was held unnecessary to charge the act as knowingly and wilfully done where it was averred as unlawful: S. v. Hartman, 8 Baxt. 384.

[8] Reg. v. Gray, 9 Cox, 417.

[9] Taylor v. S., 6 Humph. 285.

[10] McCord v. S., 79 Ala. 269.

[11] S. v. Bullard, 72 N. C. 445.

§ 834. Value of property.— It seems to have been thought necessary in some cases that the amount of the injury to the owner should be alleged.[1] At any rate this is necessary where the punishment is made to depend upon the amount of damage done;[2] and in such case the injury to the owner, and not merely the value of the property, should be stated.[3] But where the punishment does not depend upon the value, it has been held unnecessary that any finding of the value be made by the jury.[4] If an increased punishment is provided for where the damage is above a certain amount, it is unnecessary to allege value in order to secure conviction and a minimum punishment.[5] By statute the necessity of alleging value may be dispensed with entirely, even where the value determines the amount of the fine which may be imposed.[6]

§ 835. Joinder.— Injury to different animals at different times cannot be charged in the same count;[7] but injury at the same time to property of different owners may be charged as one offense.[8]

[1] S. v. Garner, 8 Porter, 447; S. v. Heath, 41 Tex. 426.

[2] S. v. Sparks, 60 Ind. 298. Under the English statutes, see Reg. v. Dodson, 9 A. & E. 704; Reg. v. Whiteman, Dears. 353; Reg. v. Williams, 9 Cox, 338; Reg. v. Thomas, 12 Cox, 54.

[3] S. v. Peden, 2 Blackf. 371; Harness v. S., 27 Ind. 425; Nicholson v. S., 3 Tex. Ap. 31. But, of course, if the property is destroyed, a statement of the value of such property is sufficient: S. v. Shadley, 16 Ind. 230. To charge the injury as being to the property instead of to the owner is not a material defect: Kinsman v. S., 77 Ind. 132; S. v. Pitzer, 62 Ind. 362.

[4] S. v. Gigher, 23 Ia. 318.

[5] C. v. Cox, 7 Allen, 577.

[6] Dorrell v. S., 80 Ind. 566.

[7] Burgess v. S., 44 Ala. 190.

[8] Smith v. S., 63 Ga. 168. An indictment for "cutting and removing" timber does not charge two offenses: U. S. v. Stone, 49 Fed. R. 848.

CHAPTER 33.

FORCIBLE ENTRY AND DETAINER.

§ 836. Common-law offenses.— The offense of violently taking or keeping possession of lands or tenements with menaces, force and arms and without authority of law[1] was indictable by the early common law.[2] But the whole matter has been regulated by statute in England from early times.[3] The early statutes are said to have been declaratory of the common law and in force in this country.[4] They did undoubtedly extend the law so as to make punishable the act of forcibly asserting even a legal right of possession as against one in the occupancy of the premises.[5] The statutes also provide for restitution, which is the feature of the proceeding regarded as of principal importance in this country; so that while in England the procedure was criminal, and in some of our states is still technically so,[6] yet at most with us it is partly civil and partly criminal, the provision for the fine rendering it a criminal proceeding,[7] while the provisions as to restitution are in the nature of a civil remedy.[8] In many of the states the criminal feature has been entirely abandoned and the action is deemed a civil one.[9]

§ 837. What constitutes forcible entry.— To constitute the offense of forcible entry there must be entry by actual force

[1] 4 Bl. Com. 128.

[2] C. v. Shattuck, 4 Cush. 141; Cruiser v. S., 18 N. J. 206; Rex v. Bathurst, Say. 225; Rex v. Wilson, 8 T. R. 357.

[3] See 5 Rich. 2, St. 1, ch. 8; 15 Rich. 2, ch. 2; 8 Henry 6, ch. 9; 31 Eliz., ch. 11; 21 James 1, ch. 15.

[4] S. v. Morgan, 59 N. H. 322.

[5] 4 Bl. Com. 148, and Hammond's note thereto; Newton v. Harland, 2 Scott, N. R. 474; Pollen v. Brewer, 7 C. B. (N. S.) 371; Turner v. Meymott, 1 Bing. 158; Beddall v. Maitland, 17 Ch. D. 174. And a contract by a tenant waiving his right to prosecute a criminal action for interference with his possession is not valid: Edwick v. Hawkes, 18 Ch. D. 199.

[6] C. v. Meyer, 2 Serg. & R. 453.

[7] S. v. Harvey, 3 N. H. 65; S. v. Lord, 5 N. H. 335.

[8] S. v. Harvey, 3 N. H. 65.

[9] S. v. Morgan, 59 N. H. 322; P. v. Runkle, 9 Johns. 147; P. v. Hickox, 3 Hill, 446; Covenhaven v. S., 1 N. J. 258. In New Jersey the civil remedy is deemed only a substitute for the English statutory provisions as to restitution, and the act is still punishable as a common-law offense: Cruiser v. S., 18 N. J. 206.

and violence against the person in possession, or with such numbers of persons and show of force as would be calculated to deter the rightful owner from maintaining his possession or making resistance.[1] But the entry must be "with a strong hand," and the ordinary allegation of trespass by force and arms is not sufficient.[2]

§ 838. **Forcible detainer.**— One of the early English statutes extended the remedy to cases where the entry was peaceable, but the detainer was by force.[3] The entry, however, must have been unlawful.[4] If the entry is rightful, even though it could not properly have been made with force, yet it may be maintained by force.[5] Although forcible entry and forcible detainer are therefore distinguished as different offenses, nevertheless, when relating to the same transaction, they may be charged in one count.[6]

§ 839. **Possession involved.**— Even though there is a right to possession, yet if the entry is made with force it will be criminal.[7] Thus, a prosecution may be maintained by a person who has been in possession of lands without title against the true owner for expelling complainant with a strong hand.[8] It is said that one having a right of entry may at common law use force, provided it does not amount to an actual breach of the peace, whereas one not having a right of entry is indictable if he enter with a strong hand under circumstances calculated to excite terror, although the force used does not amount to a breach of the peace.[9] One early case in this country confined the remedy to a case where there was lawful possession,

[1] C. v. Shattuck, 4 Cush. 141; Lissner v. S., 84 Ga. 669; Resp. v. Sloane, 2 Yeates, 229; S. v. Davis, 109 N. C. 809; S. v. Talbott, 97 N. C. 494; Brazee v. S., 9 Ind. Ap. 618; Rex v. Smyth, 5 C. & P. 201; Milner v. Maclean, 2 C. & P. 17. Acts which would induce force in resistance may be sufficient: Pennsylvania v. Robison, Addis. 14; but not a mere trivial trespass: Thompson v. C., 116 Pa. St. 155. Nor is a mere forcible attempt to enter sufficient: S. v. Bryant, 103 N. C. 436.

[2] C. v. Brown, 138 Pa. St. 447; S. v. Pearson, 2 N. H. 550.

[3] S. v. Morgan, 59 N. H. 322; P. v. Rickert, 8 Cow. 226.

[4] Rex v. Oakley, 4 B. & Ad. 307; Rex v. Wilson, 3 A. & E. 817.

[5] Vess v. S., 93 Ind. 211; C. v. Knarr, 135 Pa. St. 35.

[6] C. v. Rogers, 1 Serg. & R. 124; C. v. Miller, 107 Pa. St. 276.

[7] Pennsylvania v. Leach, Addis. 352; Reg. v. Studd, 14 L. T. 633.

[8] Beattie v. Mair, L. R. 10 Ir. 208; Rex v. Smyth, 5 C. & P. 201.

[9] S. v. Ross, 4 Jones, 315; S. v. Smith, 100 N. C. 466.

as under a lease not yet terminated;[1] but the weight of authority is to the effect that the legality of the right of possession is not involved and that actual peaceable possession is sufficient.[2] But mere constructive possession after the termination of actual occupation is not sufficient.[3] A possession which is not exclusive of that of the owner, but is simply the occupancy of the owner himself, is not sufficient.[4] Nor is a possession sufficient which is merely temporary, obtained under fraudulent pretense of title.[5]

§ 840. **Description of premises.**— It is not necessary that the description be perfect, as by courses and distances or the like, but a description which is sufficient in ejectment at common law will be enough.[6] The proof must correspond with the description given.[7]

§ 841. **Restitution.**— The statute of Henry VI.[8] provided for the making of restitution of possession by the magistrate authorized to proceed in the case, and a statute of Elizabeth[9] limited this right to cases where the wrong-doer had not been in possession for three years.[10] But three years' peaceable possession does not bar prosecution for the crime.[11] To entitle the complainant to restitution, the estate possessed by him should be set out.[12]

[1] P. v. Nelson, 13 Johns. 340.

[2] P. v. Leonard, 11 Johns. 504; Swails v. S., 4 Ind. 516; Reg. v. Child, 2 Cox, 102; Rex v. Williams, 9 B. & C. 549; Lows v. Telford, 1 App. Cas. 414.

[3] Pennsylvania v. Lemmon, Addis. 315.

[4] Allen v. England, 3 F. & F. 49.

[5] Collins v. Thomas, 1 F. & F. 416.

[6] Dean v. C., 3 Serg. & R. 418; Vanpool v. C., 13 Pa. St. 391.

[7] Ball v. S., 26 Ind. 155.

[8] 8 Henry 6, ch. 9.

[9] 31 Eliz., ch. 11.

[10] S. v. Morgan, 59 N. H. 322; C. v. Stoever, 1 Serg. & R. 480; C. v. Rogers, 1 Serg. & R. 124.

[11] Pennsylvania v. Robison, Addis. 14.

[12] Vanpool v. C., 13 Pa. St. 391; Burd v. C., 6 Serg. & R. 252; Torrence v. C., 9 Pa. St. 184; Reg. v. Bowser, 8 Dowl. P. C. 128; Rex v. Hoare, 6 Mau. & S. 266; Rex v. Dillon, 2 Chit. 314. Further as to the proceeding in regard to restitution, see Reg. v. Harland, 8 A. & E. 826; Rex v. Hake, 4 M. & R. 483; Rex v. Williams, 9 B. & C. 549.

CHAPTER 34.

FRAUDULENT CONVEYANCES; CONCEALMENT OF PROPERTY.

§ 842. **General characteristics.**— Forms of fraud consisting in putting property beyond the reach of creditors by means of concealment or fraudulent conveyances, or in defrauding purchasers by a second conveyance of property, or in defrauding chattel mortgagees or other lien-holders by concealing or removing property covered thereby, are recognized by statute, although they were not indictable at common law.

§ 843. **Concealing or disposing of property to defraud creditors.**— It is not a "secreting" to refuse to give up a watch which one is carrying on his person, when required to do so by an officer levying execution.[1] To constitute a secreting it is not necessary that the possession of the property be concealed from every one; thus, where a town officer was prosecuted for secreting the books of the town, it was held he committed the crime by refusing to give them up and denying their possession, although some of the citizens knew them to be in his possession.[2] The statutes against the secreting of property apply to those who assist the debtor in doing so as well as to the debtor himself. Thus, a mortgagee under a fraudulent mortgage may be guilty of the offense of concealing the property of the mortgagor even though the mortgage is recorded and the mortgagee has been garnished.[3] But one who buys or receives property without knowledge of any claim thereon, and then refuses to disclose the location of the property, is not criminally punishable.[4] The charge of removing property to a place unknown is not sufficient to show a violation of a statute prohibiting removal out of the county.[5] The charge of fraudulently receiving the property of a debtor to prevent its seizure for his debts is not sufficient under a statute forbidding the fraudulent receiving of a mortgage, pledge or conveyance, or a fraudulent

[1] P. v. Morrison, 13 Wend. 399.

[2] S. v. Williams, 30 Me. 484.

[3] S. v. Johnson, 33 N. H. 441.

[4] Thomas v. S., 92 Ala. 49.

[5] Thomas v. P., 19 Wend. 480.

concealment. In charging the offense of secreting goods for the purpose of avoiding the payment of debts and thereby defrauding creditors, it is not sufficient to follow the language of the statute, but the time, place and circumstances must be alleged and the names of the parties intended to be defrauded.[2]

§ 844. **Fraudulent conveyances.**— The conveyance of property with intent to defraud creditors may be made criminal, the intent being the essential element of the crime.[3] Such a statute is constitutional.[4] A conveyance such as is made criminal by the statute is void.[5] Another form of fraudulent conveyance sometimes made criminal is making a second deed without reciting or disclosing a former one to the same property,[6] or conveying land, knowing that it is incumbered, with intent to defraud.[7] But the giving of a mortgage upon land by one who has already conveyed his title to it is not the disposing of the land by fraudulent sale, after having once sold it, within statutory language.[8] It is sometimes provided that the act of a vendor of property disposed of by conditional sale in retaking it without refunding to the purchaser the amount paid by him is criminal.[9] But the usual recording acts furnish protection against subsequent conveyances, etc., and provisions for the punishment of such conveyances as criminal are not common. Another offense somewhat similar in character is that of the removal by the mortgagor of real property of buildings therefrom without obtaining the mortgagee's consent.[10] In any of these cases the description of the land involved should be sufficiently particular to identify it; a mere location of it, as within the county, not being sufficient.[11] The instrument by which the fraud was committed must also be described.[12] The intent to defraud may be alleged in the words of the statute

[1] S. v. Leslie, 16 N. H. 93.

[2] Hartmann v. C., 5 Pa. St. 60.

[3] Lillie v. McMillan, 52 Ia. 463; Davenport v. Cummings, 15 Ia. 219.

[4] Herold v. S., 21 Neb. 50.

[5] Davenport v. Cummings, 15 Ia. 219.

[6] S. v. Jones, 68 Mo. 197.

[7] S. v. Hunkins, 90 Wis. 264.

[8] P. v. Cox, 45 Cal. 342.

[9] Weil v. S., 46 Ohio St. 450.

[10] S. v. Decker, 52 Kan. 193.

[11] C. v. Brown, 15 Gray, 189. But it may be sufficient to describe the property generally as that mortgaged to a certain named party, giving the date of the mortgage and alleging that a more particular description cannot be given: C. v. Strangford, 112 Mass. 289.

[12] C. v. Brown, 15 Gray, 189.

without going into details so long as the act is sufficiently set out to show the particular transaction referred to.[1]

§ 845. **Fraud perpetrated.**— It is necessary to allege and prove that in some way the parties named as those intended to be defrauded were or could have been prejudiced by the act charged;[2] for instance, where the charge is of mortgaging property to defraud creditors, it must be averred that the property was not exempt from levy.[3] But it is not necessary to show that the creditor was in a position to seize the property at the time the fraudulent act is charged to have been done, and an immediate or prospective, absolute or contingent, right on the part of the creditor is sufficient.[4]

§ 846. **Removal or disposal of property covered by chattel mortgage.**— In various states there are statutes making it criminal to dispose of or to remove out of the state personal property which is covered by chattel mortgage without the written consent of the mortgagee.[5] And such a statute covers a transfer by exchange as well as a sale.[6] But where it is disposal which is prohibited, taking out of the state is not criminal.[7] Where the statute prohibits the disposal of personal property, having knowledge of any mortgage or lien thereon, without written consent, etc., or without paying the mortgage, it is criminal for the holder of a junior mortgage or lien to dispose of the property without such consent and without providing for the payment of the prior mortgage or lien.[8] It is immaterial that the defendant had no title to the property.[9] The mortgage must be valid at the time of the act complained of. If given by a minor and not ratified no offense is committed,[10] for the sale is a disaffirmance of the mortgage.[11] A mortgage on unplanted crops constitutes a valid and lawful claim thereon when planted;[12] and a mortgage on cows covers

[1] S. v. Miller, 98 Ind. 70.

[2] S. v. Chapman, 68 Me. 477; Day v. Lown, 51 Ia. 364; S. v. Robinson, 29 N. H. 274.

[3] S. v. Collins, 62 Vt. 195.

[4] S. v. Johnson, 33 N. H. 441.

[5] Conley v. S., 85 Ga. 348; Williams v. S., 27 Tex. Ap. 258; Moye v. S., 9 Tex. Ap. 88; S. v. Harberson, 43 Ark. 378; Cooper v. S., 37 Ark. 412.

[6] Johnson v. S., 69 Ala. 593.

[7] S. v. Rice, 43 S. C. 200; S. v. Julien, 48 Ia. 445.

[8] S. v. Reeder, 36 S. C. 497.

[9] S. v. Williams, 32 Minn. 537.

[10] S. v. Plaisted, 43 N. H. 413.

[11] Jones v. S., 31 Tex. Ap. 252.

[12] Varnum v. S., 78 Ala. 28; Hamilton v. S., 94 Ga. 770. *Contra*, Hardeman v. S., 16 Tex. Ap. 1. A cropper's right to his share may be mortgaged, and the sale of such interest may

their increase.[1] It is not usually criminal to purchase the mortgaged property from the mortgagor.[2] But some statutes are broad enough to cover the purchaser as well as the seller.[3]

§ 847. **Consent of mortgagee.**— While the statutes require the consent of the mortgagee to be in writing, yet a consent given before the execution of the mortgage may perhaps constitute a continuing consent and prevent an act done in accordance with such consent from being criminal. Such consent may lead the mortgagor to naturally suppose that he could rightfully do the act.[4] Where consent is given it does not constitute a waiver of the mortgagee's lien on the property.[5] Some statutes make it criminal to sell without the written consent of the mortgagee, or without informing the person to whom the sale is made that the property is mortgaged, and under such statutes compliance with one of the conditions is sufficient.[6]

§ 848. **Selling or removing property subject to lien.**— An offense analogous to that above described with reference to property covered by chattel mortgage is that provided for by some statutes of selling or removing property subject to a lien without satisfying the lien or obtaining consent of the lienholder, or giving previous notice of the intention to sell or remove. These statutes are applicable mainly to cases of landlords' liens.[7]

§ 849. **The intent.**— While it may be said that intent to defraud is material, yet it is the wrongful doing of the prohibited act which constitutes the crime, and therefore it is generally held that the intent to defraud may be inferred from the intentional making of the sale without consent, etc.;[8] and under this view it is not necessary to charge that the act was done with intent to defraud.[9] But it has been held that, where only

constitute a crime: Beard v. S., 43 Ark. 284.

[1] Dyer v. S., 88 Ala. 225.

[2] McDonald v. Norton, 72 Ia. 652. Therefore a subsequent mortgage on the same property by the mortgagor is not void: Tootle v. Taylor, 64 Ia. 629.

[3] S. v. Woods, 104 N. C. 898.

[4] Walker v. Camp, 69 Ia. 741.

[5] Oswald v. Hayes, 42 Ia. 104.

[6] C. v. Damon, 105 Mass. 580.

[7] Money v. S., 89 Ala. 110; Smith v. S., 84 Ala. 438; S. v. Turner, 106 N. C. 691; S. v. Smith, 106 N. C. 653; S. v. Williams, 106 N. C. 646; S. v. Johnson, 20 S. C. 387.

[8] C. v. Cutler, 153 Mass. 252; Beard v. S., 43 Ark. 284; S. v. Reeder, 36 S. C. 497.

[9] S. v. Hurds, 19 Neb. 316. *Contra,* Satchell v. S., 1 Tex. Ap. 438.

a part of the mortgaged property was disposed of, it is improper to charge that the intent will be presumed from wilfully and knowingly doing the prohibited act, inasmuch as in such cases the act would not naturally and necessarily result in injury to the mortgagee.[1] It is essential that there be knowledge of the existence of the mortgage or lien.[2]

§ 850. **Venue.**— Where the offense consists in removing property from the state it is one which cannot be committed wholly within the state, and therefore it falls within statutory provisions such as are found in Texas relative to the place of prosecuting crimes committed wholly or partly without the state and made punishable by law within it. Under such provisions the prosecution is to be had in the county where the defendant is found and not in the county from which the property was removed.[3] A prosecution for fraudulent sale of property under a lien should be commenced in the county where the sale was made.[4]

§ 851. **Indictment.**— The indictment need not set out the mortgage by its tenor, nor aver the amount of the indebtedness which it was given to secure, nor, in case of removal of the property, the value of the property;[5] and it is not necessary that it describe the property as it is described in the mortgage, if the description given is sufficient to identify the property.[6] In case of sale it must allege the value of the property at the time of sale in order to show that there was a wrong done to the mortgagee, and under a statute by which double damages are authorized to be given to the injured party, in order to show the amount of such damage.[7] The indictment should also show that the mortgage was valid, subsisting and unpaid at the time the act complained of was done,[8] the place of the wrongful act so as to show the venue,[9] and the name of the person to whom the property was sold or disposed of, where that is the wrong alleged;[10] and it should negative the written consent of the mortgagee, naming him.[11]

1 S. v. Manning, 107 N. C. 910.

2 Foster v. S., 88 Ala. 182.

3 Williams v. S., 27 Tex. Ap. 258.

4 Robberson v. S., 3 Tex. Ap. 502.

5 Wilson v. S., 43 Neb. 745.

6 Glass v. S., 23 Tex. Ap. 425. As to general requisites of the indictment, see S. v. Pickens, 79 N. C. 652.

7 S. v Ladd, 32 N. H. 110.

8 S. v. Gustafson, 50 Ia. 194; Satchell v. S., 1 Tex. Ap. 438.

9 S. v. Hinkle, 27 Kan. 308.

10 S. v. Hughes, 38 Neb. 366; Smith v. S., 26 Tex. Ap. 577; Alexander v. S., 27 Tex. Ap. 94; Armstrong v. S., 27 Tex. Ap. 462.

11 S. v. Hughes, 38 Neb. 366.

PART VIII.

OFFENSES AGAINST PUBLIC JUSTICE.

CHAPTER 35.

PERJURY.

I. What Constitutes.
II. The Oath.
III. In a Court Having Jurisdiction.
IV. Where an Oath is Authorized.
V. Materiality.
VI. Falsity.
VII. Intent.
VIII. The Indictment.
IX. The Evidence.
X. Subornation; Attempt to Procure.

I. What Constitutes.

§ 852. **Definition.**— Perjury is, in its essence, an attempt to subvert public justice by false swearing.[1] An early English statute on the subject[2] relates only to the perjury of a witness in giving his testimony, and therefore the crime under that statute and others similar to it in terms does not include such cases as false oath to an answer in chancery, or in swearing the peace against another, and the like.[3] But the common law seems to recognize a much broader scope for the offense.[4] As the definition is usually given, the crime consists in the taking of a wilful false oath in a judicial proceeding in regard to a matter or thing material to a point involved therein.[5] Doubt-

[1] S. v. Whittemore, 50 N. H. 245.

[2] 5 Eliz., ch. 9.

[3] Resp. v. Newell, 3 Yeates, 407; Rither's Case, Cro. Eliz. 148; Matthew's Case, 2 Leon. 201; Miller's Case, Yelv. 120; Agar's Case, Moore, 627.

[4] Resp. v. Newell, 3 Yeates, 407.

[5] C. v. Powell, 2 Met. (Ky) 10 Cothran v. S., 39 Miss. 541; Hood v. S., 44 Ala. 81; Rex v. Aylett, 1 T. R. 63. The definition from Hawkins is somewhat more elaborate: "A wilful false oath by one who, being lawfully required to depose the truth in any proceeding in a course of justice, swears absolutely in a matter of some consequence to the point in question, whether he be believed or not:" 1 Hawk. P. C., ch.

less this definition, as well as the others given in the note, is too restricted to cover the cases which are now by statute included in the crime. The offense is almost universally extended so as to include false swearing in any case where an oath is authorized by law.[1] Many cases of perjury under the statutory definitions do not relate to any judicial proceeding whatever, but it is impossible to form a definition which shall cover all cases, as statutes frequently make particular forms of false oath criminal without regard to or in addition to a general definition. By some statutes there is an offense of false swearing which covers cases outside of common-law perjury.[2] The cases just cited illustrate the fact that under such statutes the taking of a false oath may be criminal although not in any judicial proceeding, and in such cases it is evident that there is not the same requirement as to materiality as in cases arising in a judicial proceeding.[3] At common law, falsehood not strictly amounting to perjury may be an indictable misdemeanor.[4] The offense is a misdemeanor only, unless under the statutes it is made a felony.[5]

§ 853. **Elements of the offense.**— From the definition of the offense it will appear that the testimony or statement relied upon as constituting the perjury must be (1) under oath, (2) in a court having jurisdiction, or (3) under circumstances where the taking of an oath is authorized, (4) in a material respect,

69. Blackstone adopts Coke's definition as follows: "A crime committed when a wilful oath is administered in some judicial proceeding to a person who swears wilfully, absolutely and falsely in a matter material to the issue or point in question:" 4 Bl. Com. 137. Bishop's definition is, "The wilful giving under oath in a judicial proceeding or court of justice of false testimony material to the issue or point of inquiry:" 2 Bish. Cr. L., § 1015.

[1] C. v. Hughes, 5 Allen, 499; S. v. Byrd, 28 S. C. 18; U. S. v. Bedgood, 49 Fed. R. 54; U. S. v. Landsberg, 23 Fed. R. 585; U. S. v. Ambrose, 108 U. S. 336.

[2] C. v. Maynard, 91 Ky. 131; C. v. Scowden, 92 Ky. 120; C. v. Still, 83 Ky. 275; S. v. Runyan, 130 Ind. 208; S. v. Baker, 64 Vt. 355; Davidson v. S., 22 Tex. Ap. 372; Steber v. S., 23 Tex. Ap. 176; U. S. v. Dickey, Morris, 412; Rex v. Hodgkiss, L. R. 1 C. C. 212. Though a particular form of false swearing may be made a misdemeanor, it may also constitute perjury: P. v. Platt, 67 Cal. 21. Perjury is not contempt of court: S. v. Lazarus, 37 La. An. 401.

[3] S. v. Flagg, 25 Ind. 243. Further as to materiality, see *infra*, § 861.

[4] Ex parte Overton, 2 Rose, 257; Reg. v. Chapman, 2 C. & K. 846.

[5] Anon., R. M. Charlt. 228.

(5) false, and (6) wilfully and corruptly so. The discussion of the questions which arise may conveniently be arranged under these headings with the addition of matters pertaining to the indictment and the evidence. Subornation and attempts will be discussed under a concluding heading.

II. THE OATH.

§ 854. Essential.— It is absolutely essential to the offense that the testimony or statement relied on as constituting perjury was under an oath actually administered. Without this there can be no conviction for the offense.[1] It is not enough that the defendant made and subscribed in open court a false and corrupt oath;[2] but there must have been some oral form of oath or affirmation by the affiant recognizing the solemnity of the act, equal to the invocation of the Deity, and not a mere statement.[3] The usual form of charging the offense is to allege that defendant took his "corporal" oath to speak the truth, etc., but such an allegation is sufficiently proved by evidence that he assented by some corporal action, whether by kissing the testament, or holding up his hand, or in any other of the ways practiced to signify such assent.[4] If the false oath charged is a written statement sworn to by defendant, it is immaterial whether the oath was administered before or after the statement was reduced to writing and signed.[5]

[1] Case v. P., 76 N. Y. 242; O'Reilly v. P., 86 N. Y. 154; S. v. Divoll, 44 N. H. 140; P. v. Bartman, 81 Cal. 200.

[2] S. v. Divoll, 44 N. H. 140. One may "swear" who is not "sworn." If no oath is administered there is no perjury; U. S. v. McConaughey, 33 Fed. R. 168.

[3] O'Reilly v. P., 86 N. Y. 154.

[4] S. v. Norris, 9 N. H. 96; U. S. v. Baer, 18 Blatch. 493. The averment that the witness took his corporal oath is unnecessary, and proof of any method of assent used in the courts is sufficient: C. v. Reynolds, 89 Ky. 147. If the evidence shows that the oath was administered, the presumption is that it was rightfully done: S. v. Mace, 86 N. C. 668. A witness who takes an oath without objecting to the manner in which it is offered and swears falsely is guilty of perjury: S. v. Whisenhurst, 2 Hawks, 458.

[5] C. v. Sargent, 129 Mass. 115. Under a federal statute for the punishment of one who shall falsely "state" or "subscribe," etc., either form of falsification is sufficient: U. S. v. Neale, 14 Fed. R. 767. Making a mark in response to the direction "If you swear to this statement put your mark here," is sufficient under federal statute: U. S. v. Mallard, 40 Fed. R. 151.

Indeed, it is immaterial whether the writing was signed at all, the material point being that the statement was sworn to.[1]

§ 855. **Before authorized officer.**— It is essential to the offense that the oath shall have been administered by an officer authorized to do so.[2] Thus, if the person administering the oath as officer has not qualified to act as such,[3] or is not yet authorized to enter upon the discharge of his duties,[4] or is acting under an invalid appointment,[5] or after his authority to act has terminated,[6] or acts outside of the limits of the territory within which he has authority to act,[7] there can be no conviction for the false swearing. If a deputy is authorized to administer oaths, the oath before him will be effectual;[8] but the allegation must in such case charge the administration of the oath by the deputy and not by the principal.[9] Where the oath was administered by an assistant of the clerk of the court at his request, it was said that it would be presumed to have been done with the assent of the presiding judge, and therefore to have been properly administered.[10] But where it was charged that upon a coroner's inquest the oath was administered by a justice of the peace in the presence and by the direction of the coroner, it was held that the oath was insufficient, the justice having no jurisdiction to act in such a case.[11] If the oath is taken in a court having jurisdiction, it is sufficient if the officer acting is one of a class having *prima facie* authority; but if the oath is not in a judicial proceeding, but *ex parte*, the officer must be one authorized to administer such oath.[12]

§ 856. **Acting officer.**— It is not necessary, however, to prove the authority of the officer by producing his commission or cer-

[1] C. v. Carel, 105 Mass. 582.

[2] U. S. v. Curtis, 107 U. S. 671; U. S. v. Hall, 131 U. S. 50; Morrell v. P., 32 Ill. 499; Van Dusen v. P., 78 Ill. 645; S. v. Owen, 73 Mo. 440; U. S. v. Bedgood, 49 Fed. R. 54. For cases under English statutes, see Rex v. Hanks, 3 C. & P. 419; Reg. v. Stone, Dears. 251; Reg. v. Hallett, 2 Den. 237; Reg. v. Dunn, 12 Q. B. 1026. Where a register or receiver of the land office is authorized to take testimony, authority to administer an oath is implied: Peters v. U. S., 2 Okl. 116.

[3] Biggerstaff v. C., 11 Bush, 169.

[4] S. v. Phippen, 62 Ia. 54.

[5] Muir v. S., 8 Blackf. 154.

[6] S. v. Cannon, 79 Mo. 343.

[7] Van Dusen v. P., 78 Ill. 645.

[8] Warwick v. S., 25 Ohio St. 21; P. v. Waite, 102 Cal. 251.

[9] Hitesman v. S., 48 Ind. 473.

[10] Stephens v. S., 1 Swan, 157.

[11] S. v. Knight, 84 N. C. 789.

[12] S. v. Dreifus, 38 La. An. 877.

tificate of election or appointment; proof that when the oath was administered he was an acting officer is sufficient.[1] Indeed, it was said in one case that even though the officer had not been legally appointed, if he had openly and notoriously discharged the functions of his office and administered the oath in his official capacity it would be sufficient.[2] But the rule generally recognized is that the officer must be one authorized *de jure* and not merely *de facto*.[3] It is only when there has been originally a valid authority in the elective or appointing power, and the election or appointment is irregular, that the officer may be considered as authorized *de facto* although not strictly *de jure*. If the appointment was without authority from the beginning, the oath is not official and perjury cannot be predicated upon it.[4]

§ 857. **State officer acting under federal statute.**— The statutes of the United States authorize oaths in various cases to be taken before justices or notaries appointed under state authority, and under such statutes there may be a conviction in the federal court for perjury committed in swearing falsely before a state officer in a case where the oath is thus authorized.[5] But the case must be one in which authority is given by the federal statute to the state officer to administer such oaths.[6]

III. IN A COURT HAVING JURISDICTION.

§ 858. **Jurisdiction essential.**— False swearing in a proceeding in a court which has no jurisdiction thereof cannot constitute perjury.[7] There must be a tribunal so constituted as to be authorized to proceed in the case,[8] and a matter under investiga-

[1] Server v. S., 2 Blackf. 35; S. v. Gregory, 2 Murph. 69; Keator v. P., 32 Mich. 484; Reg. v. Newton, 1 C. & K. 469; Reg. v. Howard, 1 M. & Rob. 187; Rex v. Verelst, 3 Campb. 432.

[2] Izer v. S., 77 Md. 110.

[3] Staight v. S., 39 Ohio St. 496; Lambert v. P., 76 N. Y. 220.

[4] Lambert v. P., 76 N. Y. 220.

[5] U. S. v. Curtis, 107 U. S. 671; U. S. v. Bailey, 9 Pet. 238; U. S. v. Madison, 21 Fed. R. 628; U. S. v. Hearing, 26 Fed. R. 744; U. S. v. Boggs, 31 Fed. R. 337; U. S. v. Law, 50 Fed. R. 915.

[6] U. S. v. Curtis, 107 U. S. 671; U. S. v. Howard, 37 Fed. R. 666; U. S. v. Manion, 44 Fed. R. 800.

[7] S. v. Alexander, 4 Hawks, 182; S. v. Wyatt, 2 Hayw. 56; S. v. Whittemore, 50 N. H. 245; S. v. Furlong, 26 Me. 69; S. v. Hayward, 1 Nott & M. 546; S. v. McCroskey, 3 McCord, 308.

[8] P. v. Tracy, 9 Wend. 265; S. v. Peters, 57 Vt. 86; Reg. v. Lloyd, 19 Q. B. D. 213.

tion before such tribunal which it is authorized to investigate.[1] If the proceeding is void on its face there can be no perjury;[2] but mere irregularity will not constitute a defense.[3] Thus, if the proceeding in which the false oath was taken was criminal and commenced by warrant, it will not defeat the prosecution for perjury that such warrant was issued without complaint or affidavit.[4] But where the prosecution could only be on indictment found and the grand jury ignored the bill, it was held that the proceeding was so far without jurisdiction that false swearing in a motion to tax the costs could not be perjury.[5] If the objection to the jurisdiction is one based on the exemption of the person only and not on defect in the court, there will not be such want of jurisdiction as to constitute a defense for perjury committed.[6] If a preliminary examination is held before a magistrate not authorized to hold an examination for the crime charged, false swearing therein will not be punishable.[7] So it must appear that some charge had been made before the magistrate pending the investigation of which the false testimony was given;[8] and if the sworn information does not show the requisite statutory facts to authorize such prose-

[1] Pankey v. P., 2 Ill. 80; Mackin v. P., 115 Ill. 312; Reg. v. Ewington, Car. & M. 319. If the proceeding is based on an ordinance or other such municipal action, and the ordinance or action is void, there is no jurisdiction, and false swearing therein will not be perjury: S. v. Crumb, 68 Mo. 206; Buell v. S., 45 Ark. 336; Kerfoot v. C., 89 Ky. 174.

[2] Collins v. S., 78 Ala. 433.

[3] S. v. Lavalley, 9 Mo. 824; S. v. Ridley, 114 N. C. 827; Ryalls v. Reg., 11 Q. B. 781; Reg. v. Proud, L. R. 1 C. C. 71; Reg. v. Johnson, L. R. 2 C. C. 15. Thus, if the jurisdiction is improperly exercised by reason of non-residence, but such objection is not made, the court cannot be said to be without jurisdiction: P. v. McCaffrey, 75 Mich. 115; Walker v. Reg., 8 E. & B. 439. So if the information is defective, but might be made good by amendment, it is sufficient: Maynard v. P., 135 Ill. 416.

[4] S. v. Peters, 107 N. C. 876. So the fact that there was not a legal summons or information will be immaterial: Reg. v. Fletcher, L. R. 1 C. C. 320; Reg. v. Hughes, 4 Q. B. D. 614; Reg. v. Millard, Dears. 166; Reg. v. Berry, Bell, 46; Reg. v. Simmons, Bell, 168; Reg. v. Shaw, L. & C. 579. The test is whether the prosecution would bar another prosecution for the same offense: Anderson v. S., 24 Tex. Ap. 705.

[5] S. v. Gates, 107 N. C. 832

[6] Cordway v. S., 25 Tex. Ap. 405.

[7] S. v. Furlong, 26 Me. 69; S. v. Jenkins, 26 S. C. 121; S. v. Wymberly, 40 La. An. 460.

[8] Reg. v. Pearson, 8 C. & P. 119. But as an affidavit to hold to bail may be sworn to before the issuing of the writ of summons, an indictment for perjury committed in such an affidavit need not allege that there was an action pending: King v. Reg., 14 Q. B. 31.

cution there can be no perjury.[1] There must be a proceeding pending in which the false testimony is given,[2] and if it appears that jurisdiction thereof was not yet acquired,[3] or had already been lost,[4] there can be no perjury. But it is immeterial what the result of the proceeding may be.[5]

IV. WHERE AN OATH IS AUTHORIZED.

§ **859. Collateral proceedings in court.**— Under the statutes it is not necessary that the oath shall have been in a judicial proceeding;[6] but it must be one that is authorized by law or the taking of it will not be perjury.[7] Thus, false swearing in a bill or answer under oath in chancery, where a sworn bill or answer is not called for, is not perjury.[8] But perjury may be committed in the verification of a pleading where a sworn pleading is authorized by statute.[9] At various stages of a judicial proceeding affidavits may be appropriate for securing service by publication;[10] or to procure a writ of *habeas corpus;*[11] or to secure submission to arbitration;[12] or on a motion for continuance,[13] or other motion;[14] and false swearing in any such affidavit may be perjury. But, as will hereafter be shown, there must have been occasion for the use of such affidavit or it will not be deemed material.[15] False swear-

[1] Johnson v. S., 58 Ga. 397; Reg. v. Scotton, 5 Q. B. 493.

[2] S. v. Hanson, 39 Me. 337.

[3] S. v. Plummer, 50 Me. 217; Reg. v. Bishop, Car. & M. 302.

[4] As by failure to grant a continuance: S. v. Hall, 49 Me. 412. As to defeating the jurisdiction by unauthorized amendment as to parties: Reg. v. Pearce, 3 B. & S. 531.

[5] Reg. v. Bray, 9 Cox, 218.

[6] S. v. Dayton, 23 N. J. 49. And see *supra*, § 852.

[7] S. v. Mace, 76 Me. 64; S. v. McCarthy, 41 Minn. 59; Collins v. S., 33 Fla. 446; U. S. v. Babcock, 4 McLean, 113; U. S. v. Nickerson, 1 Sprague, 232; Overton v. Reg., 4 Q. B. 83; Lamden v. S., 5 Humph. 83.

[8] Silver v. S., 17 Ohio, 365; P. v. Gaige, 26 Mich. 30; Reg. v. Yates, Car. & M. 132.

[9] C. v. Kimball, 108 Mass. 473.

[10] S. v. Bunker, 38 Kan. 737.

[11] White v. S., 9 Miss. 149.

[12] S. v. Stephenson, 4 McCord, 165; or in submitting evidence to a board of arbitration: Reg. v. Vreones, 1 Q. B. D. (1891) 360.

[13] S. v. Johnson, 7 Blackf. 49; S. v. Shupe, 16 Ia. 36; Morrell v. P., 32 Ill. 499; Sanders v. P., 124 Ill. 218.

[14] P. v. Fox, 25 Mich. 492; Ryalls v. Reg., 11 Q. B. 781; Reg. v. Alsop, 11 Cox, 264. So an affidavit before a justice of the peace by defendant in an action on a note, to the effect that he never signed the note, was held sufficient as a plea, and subject of perjury: S. v. Roberts, 11 Humph. 539.

[15] Morrell v. P., 32 Ill. 499; *infra*, § 879.

ing of a juror on an examination touching his competency may constitute perjury, although no formal issue as to his competency has been raised.[1] A false oath made before a magistrate for the purpose of instituting a criminal prosecution, being in a matter authorized by law, is perjury;[2] so is false testimony in an investigation before a grand jury.[3] So, perjury may be committed in testifying in an investigation by a legislative body on a charge of bribery against one of its members;[4] or in a proceeding by a poor debtor to secure his discharge from imprisonment;[5] or in qualifying as surety on a bond authorized by law.[6] False swearing in a naturalization proceeding is perjury.[7] Other illustrations are given in the note.[8]

§ 860. **Proceedings not in court.**— The illustrations in the preceding section have related mainly to evidence by way of affidavits or otherwise used in some form in proceedings before a court; but affidavits are also sometimes authorized for other purposes than use before a court; thus, where the officers of a bank were required by statute to make report under oath, the making of a false report was held to be perjury, although such

[1] Hilliard v. S., 14 Lea, 648; S. v. Wall, 9 Yerg. 347.

[2] Langford v. S., 9 Tex. Ap. 283; Carpenter v. S., 4 How. (Miss.) 163; Pennaman v. S., 58 Ga. 336. But if the sworn accusation is deficient in the facts required by statute to give the tribunal jurisdiction, no perjury is committed: Johnson v. S., 58 Ga. 397. One who is examined before a magistrate as to whether there is cause for a complaint being filed cannot be prosecuted for perjury in swearing falsely, there being no proceeding pending: P. v. Titmus, 102 Mich. 318.

[3] S. v. McCormick, 52 Ind. 169; S. v. Offutt, 4 Blackf. 355; Pipes v. S., 26 Tex. Ap. 318; P. v. Young, 31 Cal. 563. And the testimony of a grand juror is competent to prove that such false evidence was given: P. v. Young, 31 Cal. 563.

[4] Ex parte McCarthy, 29 Cal. 395; or in proceedings before a court-martial (*semble*): Reg. v. Heane, 4 B. & S. 947.

[5] Arden v. S., 11 Conn. 408; C. v. Calvert, 1 Va. Cas. 181.

[6] T. v. Weller, 2 New Mex. 470; Ralfe v. U. S., 11 Biss. 88.

[7] Rump v. C., 30 Pa. St. 475; S. v. Whittemore, 50 N. H. 245; U. S. v. Jones, 14 Blatchf. 90; U. S. v. Grottkau, 30 Fed. R. 672; U. S. v. Lehman, 39 Fed. R. 49; U. S. v. Lehman, 39 Fed. R. 768.

[8] Special proceedings against an attorney: Rex v. Crossley, 7 Term R. 315. Proceedings before marine board: Reg. v. Tomlinson, L. R. 1 C. C. 49. Bastardy proceedings: Maynard v. P., 135 Ill. 416; Reg. v. Fletcher, L. R. 1 C. C. 320; Reg. v. Berry, Bell, 46; Reg. v. Cooke, 2 Den. 462; Reg. v. Hughes, Dears. & B. 188; Reg. v. Chugg, 11 Cox, 558. Coroner's inquest: Reg. v. Johnson, L. R. 2 C. C. 15.

report was not for use in any judicial proceeding.[1] So an affidavit may be required in connection with the filing for record of a chattel mortgage;[2] or in connection with the acknowledgment of a deed;[3] or in procuring a marriage license;[4] or in connection with public accounts;[5] or the return of property for taxation;[6] or in the payment of customs duties;[7] or in claiming exemption from military duties;[8] or in land claims or contests in a United States land office.[9]

V. MATERIALITY.

§ 861. **Essential.**— To constitute perjury the false statement under oath must be with reference to a material matter. If the false swearing is as a witness it must be as to some fact material to the issue in the case;[10] and the materiality of the testimony must appear either by direct allegation or from the other averments of the indictment;[11] and must be established by the evidence; it cannot be left to presumption or inference.[12] Where the statute extends the offense to other cases of false swearing than those in a judicial proceeding so as to cover in general false oaths in a matter where an oath is authorized by law, it is not necessary that the false statement under oath be with reference to an issue in a judicial proceeding;[13] but even in such cases some materiality to the subject in regard to which the false statement under oath is made must appear.[14] The mere

1 S. v. Dayton, 23 N. J. 49.

2 S. v. Collins, 62 Vt. 195. And see Reg. v. Hodgkiss, L. R. 1 C. C. 212.

3 Ex parte Carpenter, 64 Cal. 267.

4 Cell v. S., 20 Ohio St. 330; S. v. Floto, 81 Md. 600; Maybush v. C., 29 Grat. 857, 3 Am. Cr. R. 292; Rex v. Foster, Russ. & Ry. 459; Reg. v. Chapman, 2 C. & K. 846.

5 U. S. v. Ambrose, 108 U. S. 336; Vance v. S., 62 Miss. 137; O'Bryan v. S., 27 Tex. Ap. 339.

6 S. v. Smith, 43 Tex. 655; S. v. Cannon, 79 Mo. 343.

7 U. S. v. Barton, Gilp. 439.

8 U. S. v. Sonachall, 4 Biss. 425.

9 Caha v. U. S., 152 U. S. 211; U. S. v. Wood, 70 Fed. R. 485.

10 Pankey v. P., 2 Ill. 80; S. v. Hobbs, 40 N. H. 229; Plath v. Braunsdorff, 40 Wis. 107; S. v. Dodd, 3 Murphy, 226; S. v. Ammons, 3 Murphy, 123; S. v. Bailey, 34 Mo. 350; Hinch v. S., 2 Mo. 158; S. v. Hattaway, 2 Nott & M. 118; P. v. Perazzo, 64 Cal. 106; P. v. Ah Sing, 95 Cal. 657; White v. S., 9 Miss. 149; Nelson v. S., 47 Miss. 621; Miller v. S., 15 Fla. 577; U. S. v. Robinson, 4 Dak. 72.

11 S. v. Beard, 25 N. J. 384; S. v. Geer, 46 Kan. 529; S. v. Anderson, 103 Ind. 170; U. S. v. Robinson, 4 Dak. 72. And see as to the indictment, *infra*, § 878.

12 S. v. Aikens, 32 Ia. 403.

13 S. v. Byrd, 28 S. C. 18.

14 U. S. v. Shinn, 14 Fed. R. 447.

allegation of an intent to defraud by means of the false affidavit is not enough without showing that it might effect such result.[1] If the false statement in an affidavit is of a matter not necessary to be alleged for the purpose for which the affidavit is to be used, it will not be perjury.[2] Not only must the evidence be material with reference to the fact sought to be proved, but the fact must be material to the issues.[3]

§ 862. **Collateral facts.**— There may be perjury, however, in falsely swearing as to facts which are not immediately in issue, but which constitute material circumstances legitimately tending to prove or disprove facts which are in issue, or strengthen or weaken the testimony with reference to such facts.[4] So where the question is as to what testimony was given at a former trial, the statement of the witnesses with reference thereto is material, although the evidence referred to on the former trial was not material in that case.[5] A general inquisitorial investigation by a grand jury, directed to no specific end, does not constitute such a proceeding that false testimony therein will be perjury, as such testimony is not material to any particular issue.[6]

§ 863. **Illustrations.**— In general, a variance in the testimony of a witness as to the date of a circumstance connected with a criminal act will not serve as a basis for a prosecution for perjury.[7] But the date of particular circumstances may become material so that false swearing with reference thereto may be punishable.[8] The words "value received" not being material in a note, false testimony by a witness that he had

[1] S. v. Lamont, 2 Wis. 437; S. v. Collins, 62 Vt. 195. The fact that the affidavit may have some actual effect will not make it material if it is not legally material: Reg. v. Southwood, 1 F. & F. 356.

[2] Pollard v. P., 69 Ill. 148; Gibson v. S., 44 Ala. 17; Hood v. S., 44 Ala. 81; S. v. Helle, 2 Hill (S. C.), 290; U. S. v. Howard, 37 Fed. R. 666. Whether in an affidavit the description of the deponent at the commencement of it is to be deemed a material part, *quære:* Reg. v. Chapman, 2 C. & K. 846.

[3] S. v. Bailey, 34 Mo. 350.

[4] Dilcher v. S., 39 Ohio St. 130; S. v. Clogston, 63 Vt. 215; Mackin v. P., 115 Ill. 312; S. v. Day, 100 Mo. 242; S. v. Hunt, 137 Ind. 537; Williams v. S., 68 Ala. 551; Robinson v. S., 18 Fla. 898; Smith v. Deaver, 6 Jones, 563; U. S. v. Landsberg, 23 Fed. R. 585.

[5] S. v. Mooney, 65 Mo. 494.

[6] Banks v. S., 78 Ala. 14.

[7] Rhodes v. C., 78 Va. 692; U. S. v. Shinn, 14 Fed. R. 447.

[8] C. v. Monahan, 9 Gray, 119; Henderson v. P., 117 Ill. 265.

executed a note, but none with those words, was held not perjury.[1] False testimony tending to prove an *alibi* will be perjury.[2] False testimony as to matters of aggravation or mitigation in a criminal prosecution may be perjury.[3] Other illustrations of cases where testimony as to a collateral fact was held sufficient to constitute perjury are given in the note.[4]

§ 864. **As to credibility of witness.**— Testimony as to a fact which affects the credibility of other witnesses is material, and if false constitutes perjury.[5] And this is true as to false testimony given in answer to a question asked with a design to impair the credit of the witness himself.[6] Thus, it is perjury to testify falsely as to having previously made a different statement.[7] But it is said that if the witness' evidence in chief is immaterial, perjury cannot be predicated upon false testimony given on cross-examination as to matters affecting his credibility only.[8]

§ 865. **Effect immaterial.**— Perjury is in its essence an attempt to subvert public justice by false swearing, and it is immaterial that it has never become effective to accomplish its purpose. If made in an affidavit which was intended to be used and might have been used in a proceeding, it will constitute no defense that the affidavit was not used.[9] Neither is it

[1] P. v. McDermott, 8 Cal. 288.

[2] S. v. Gibbs, 10 Mont. 213.

[3] S. v. Keenan, 8 Rich. 456; Stephens v. S., 1 Swan, 157.

[4] Tuttle v. P., 36 N. Y. 431; S. v. Blize, 111 Mo. 464; Reg. v. Tyson, L. R. 1 C. C. 107; Reg. v. Mullany, L. & C. 593; Reg. v. Berry, Bell, 46. In a prosecution of a husband for assault upon his wife, false testimony as to adultery committed by the wife is not material, as it would not constitute a defense: Reg. v. Tate, 12 Cox, 7.

[5] Dilcher v. S., 39 Ohio St. 130; Washington v. S., 22 Tex. Ap. 26; and it will make no difference that such evidence is legally inadmissible for that purpose, and ought not to have been received: Reg. v. Gibbon, L. & C. 109.

[6] P. v. Courtney, 94 N. Y. 490; S. v. Strat, 1 Murphy, 124; Williams v. S., 28 Tex. Ap. 301; Reg. v. Overton, Car. & M. 655; Reg. v. Lavey, 3 C. & K. 26; Reg. v. Baker, 1 Q. B. D. (1895) 797.

[7] P. v. Barry, 63 Cal. 62; U. S. v. Hall, 44 Fed. R. 864.

[8] Stanley v. U. S., 1 Okl. 336.

[9] S. v. Whittemore, 50 N. H. 245; P. v. Naylor, 82 Cal. 607; U. S. v. Volz, 14 Blatch. 15; Rex v. White, M. & M. 271; Reg. v. Chapman, 2 C. & K. 846; Rex v. Crossley, 7 Term R. 315; Reg. v. Vreones, 1 Q. B. D. (1891) 360; nor that there was some informality about the affidavit which would have prevented its being used: Reg. v. Christian, Car. & M. 388; nor that the court refused to take jurisdiction under such affidavit: Stewart v. S., 22 Ohio St. 477.

any defense as to the giving of false testimony that such testimony would not alone have been effectual for the purpose for which it was offered.[1] If the oath was material when taken, the fact that some other circumstance has intervened or has not been shown, which renders the oath ineffectual for the purpose intended, does not affect its materiality;[2] it is enough that the evidence might, from some point of view or in some event, be material.[3] Neither is it of any consequence that the false testimony assigned as perjury was not legally admissible, if it was actually admitted.[4] Indeed, it is not a defense that the testimony was not received, if it was taken by proper authority with a view of its being introduced in the case.[5] So if the witness could have interposed an objection to being called to testify in the matter but waived it, perjury may be predicated upon his false answer.[6] Nor is it material that the witness was not competent to testify as to the facts sworn to.[7] It seems, however, that if the testimony is wholly incompetent and should not, under the law, be considered, it cannot constitute perjury.[8]

[1] S. v. Flagg, 27 Ind. 24; Galloway v. S., 29 Ind. 442; S. v. Norris, 9 N. H. 96; Dilcher v. S., 39 Ohio St. 130; Hoch v. P., 3 Mich. 552; nor that the jury did not give credit to the oath: Hampers' Case, 3 Leon. 230; nor that the testimony did not affect the result: Reg. v. Moreau, 11 Q. B. 1028.

[2] S. v. Dayton, 23 N. J. 49; Sanders v. P., 124 Ill. 218. Thus, the fact that the jury in the case in which the false testimony was given was not sworn does not prevent such testimony from being perjury: Smith v. S., 31 Tex. Ap. 315.

[3] P. v. Naylor, 82 Cal. 607; S. v. Wakefield, 73 Mo. 549; C. v. Grant, 116 Mass. 17; C. v. Pollard, 12 Met. 225; Wood v. P., 59 N. Y. 117; P. v. Hitchcock, 104 Cal. 482.

[4] Chamberlain v. P., 23 N. Y. 85; Cronk v. P., 131 Ill. 56; S. v. Molier, 1 Dev. 263; Reg. v. Gibbon, L. & C. 109; Reg. v. Philpotts, 3 C. & K. 135. The fact that a witness testifying before a grand jury was not properly sworn will not render false testimony as to what was testified to by such witness immaterial: Robertson v. S., 54 Ark. 604.

[5] S. v. Langley, 34 N. H. 529; Rex v. Hailey, 1 C. & P. 258; Reg. v. Christian, Car. & M. 388.

[6] P. v. Courtney, 94 N. Y. 490; Sanford v. Gaddis, 13 Ill. 329; Mackin v. P., 115 Ill. 312; Haley v. McPherson, 3 Humph. 104; Sharp v. Wilhite, 2 Humph. 434; S. v. Hawkins, 115 N. C. 712; S. v. Maxwell, 28 La. An. 361; Mattingly v. S., 8 Tex. Ap. 345; Pipes v. S., 26 Tex. Ap. 318.

[7] Montgomery v. S., 10 Ohio, 220; Rex v. Browne, 3 C. & P. 572.

[8] Crump v. C., 75 Va. 922; Warner v. Fowler, 8 Md. 25; S. v. Trask, 42 Vt. 152. Thus, it is said that a sworn answer denying a promise which is absolutely void by the statute of frauds cannot constitute perjury: Rex v. Dunston, Ry. & M. 109; Rex v. Benesech, Peaks' Add. Cas. 93; but where a statute authorizes the

§ 866. **Materiality is for the court.**— The question as to whether the alleged false oath was material to the issues in the case in which it was taken is for the court and not the jury;[1] but, like any other question of law, the materiality of the testimony may depend upon the facts, and in such a case it should be submitted to the jury on proper instructions.[2]

VI. FALSITY.

§ 867. **Essential.**—As will appear under the next subdivision the oath must be false in its intent, but it must also be false in fact; and the falsity of the statement relied on to constitute perjury is a material element of the crime.[3] As testimony must always be with reference to what the witness believes to be true, even though he testifies absolutely as to a fact, the falsity of the testimony consists in a statement which is contrary to the witness' knowledge and belief; and if the witness actually believes his statement to be true there is no falsity, however much he may be mistaken as to the truth of the matter testified to.[4] And accordingly it has been said that it is not necessary, in order to constitute perjury, that the facts testified to be untrue, if the witness swears to them without knowing or believing them to be true.[5] On the other hand, one may be convicted of

proof of an oral contract which is within the statute of frauds by the testimony of the party sought to be charged, his false testimony with reference thereto will be perjury: S. v. Voght, 27 Ia. 117.

[1] Gordon v. S., 48 N. J. 611; S. v. Williams. 30 Mo. 364; P. v. Lem You, 97 Cal. 224; Smith v. S., 27 Tex. Ap. 50; S. v. Spencer, 45 La. An. 1; Peters v. U. S., 2 Okl. 138; U. S. v. Singleton, 54 Fed. R. 488; Reg. v. Southwood, 1 F. & F. 356.

[2] Washington v. S., 23 Tex. Ap. 336; Foster v. S., 32 Tex. Ap. 39; Mackin v. P., 115 Ill. 312; Stanley v. U. S., 1 Okl. 336; Reg. v. Schlesinger, 10 Q. B. 670; Reg. v. Lavey, 3 C. & K. 26; Reg. v. Goddard, 2 F. & F. 361; 2 Bish. Cr. L., § 1039*a*.

[3] S. v. Tappan, 21 N. H. 56; Thomas v. S., 71 Ga. 252; S. v. Nickerson, 46 Ia. 447; C. v. Monahan, 9 Gray, 119; Urquhart v. S., 103 Ala. 90. The falsity of the testimony must therefore be charged in the indictment: See *infra*, § 880.

[4] C. v. Brady, 5 Gray, 78; Scott v. Cook, 1 Duv. 314; C. v. Cornish, 6 Binn. 249; S. v. Cockran, 1 Bailey, 50; Aguierre v. S., 31 Tex. Ap. 519; U. S. v. Shellmire, Bald. 370; Rex. v. Edwards, 3 Russ. Cr. 1.

[5] S. v. Cruikshank, 6 Blackf. 62; S. v. Gates, 17 N. H. 373; U. S. v. Atkins, Sprague, 558; but this proposition has been pronounced unsound as a legal definition of perjury, and it has been urged that there must be some fact falsely stated with knowledge of its falsity, before there can be perjury: U. S. v. Moore, 2 Lowell, 232.

perjury in falsely testifying as to what he believes, if he has not probable ground for such belief, and might by reasonable care have known the truth.[1] As the criminal falsity depends upon the intent of the person making the statement, it is for the jury to say what his meaning was in using the words charged.[2]

§ 868. **Statement of fact.**— It is nevertheless a false statement of fact which constitutes perjury; thus, perjury cannot be predicated upon a mere promissory oath;[3] but this is so self-evident that it is not necessary in general to instruct the jury to the effect that the false statement must relate to something past or present.[4] The testimony must be as to a fact distinguished from a conclusion or deduction.[5] For instance, perjury cannot be predicated upon an assertion involving the legal construction of a statute.[6] But a mere belief may be a subject of false testimony, the difficulty being, however, to prove the belief as alleged.[7] Thus, perjury may be committed in swearing to an account as just and true to affiant's best knowledge and belief,[8] or as to the value of property.[9]

VII. INTENT.

§ 869. **What essential.**— The usual definition of perjury involves the wilful and corrupt taking of a false oath.[10] Thus, it is proper to show by way of defense that the evidence was given under a mistake.[11] It is sufficient, however, that the false

[1] C. v. Cornish, 6 Binn. 249; Johnson v. P., 94 Ill. 505; S. v. Knox, Phill. 312; Rex v. Pedley, 1 Leach, 325.

[2] C. v. Butland, 119 Mass. 317; Hernandez v. S., 18 Tex. Ap. 134.

[3] U. S. v. Glover, 4 Cranch, C. C. 190.

[4] Kitchen v. S., 26 Tex. Ap. 165.

[5] S. v. Henderson, 90 Ind. 406; S. v. Marshall, 47 Mo. 378; S. v. Lloyd, 77 Wis. 630; Harp v. S., 59 Ark. 113. But if the falsity is as to the facts from which the deduction is made as well as the deduction itself, the statement may be perjury: Hoch v. P., 3 Mich. 552.

[6] S. v. Woolverton, 8 Blackf. 452; Rex v. Crespigny, 1 Esp. 280; Rex v. Pepys, Peake, 138.

[7] Reg. v. Schlesinger, 10 Q. B. 670; S. v. Hascall, 6 N. H. 352; Floyd v. S., 30 Ala. 511.

[8] Patrick v. Smoke, 3 Strobh. 147.

[9] C. v. Butland, 119 Mass. 317.

[10] Green v. S., 41 Ala. 419; Hood v. S., 44 Ala. 81; Coyne v. P., 124 Ill. 17; Hicks v. Rising, 24 Ill. 566; S. v. Higgins, 124 Mo. 640; Foster v. S., 32 Tex. Ap. 39.

[11] Hood v. S., 44 Ala. 81; Flemister v. S., 48 Ga. 170; Brookin v. S., 27 Tex. Ap. 701. In Texas, though the statute provides that the false testimony given through mistake or inadvertence is not perjury, it is not necessary in the indictment to negative the fact of its being thus made: Brown v. S., 9 Tex. Ap. 171.

testimony is wilfully given with intent that it shall be acted upon; further evidence of its being corruptly given is not necessary.[1] Where the false testimony is given in an affidavit it must appear that it was with intention that the affidavit should be used.[2] Substantial truth of a statement is all that is necessary to disprove the criminal intent.[3] The intoxication of defendant at the time the testimony was given may be shown to negative the intent;[4] but threats against the defendant previously made out of court to induce him to testify falsely will not serve as an excuse for such false testimony.[5]

§ 870. **Advice of counsel.**— It being material to determine whether the testimony as given was wilfully false, the fact that advice of counsel was taken in reference to the facts about which the testimony is given may be shown for the purpose of negativing the criminal intent.[6] But the advice of counsel based on an assumption of fact known by the witness to be false will not justify or excuse the false statement.[7]

VIII. THE INDICTMENT.

§ 871. **Jurisdiction.**— In accordance with general principles of the criminal law, which need not be here amplified, there can be no prosecution for perjury committed in a foreign state.[8] But it is said that any person making or knowingly using a false affidavit made abroad is guilty of a misdemeanor in attempting to pervert public justice.[9] Perjury committed in a judicial investigation under authority of acts of congress is an offense against the United States and exclusively cognizable in the federal courts.[10] The power to punish a witness for falsely testifying in a judicial proceeding inheres in the government in whose tribunal the proceeding is had.[11]

§ 872. **Requisites.**— In general the indictment must name the court and the parties to the action in which the false tes-

[1] S. v. Anderson, 92 Ia. 764, 60 N. W. R. 630; Morgan v. S., 63 Miss. 162.

[2] S. v. Smith, 3 Wash. 14.

[3] S. v. Lawson, 98 N. C. 759.

[4] Lyle v. S., 31 Tex. Ap. 103.

[5] Bain v. S., 67 Miss. 557.

[6] S. v. McKinney, 42 Ia. 205; Jesse v. S., 20 Ga. 156; U. S. v. Stanley, 6 McLean, 409.

[7] Barnett v. S., 89 Ala. 165.

[8] Musgrave v. Medex, 19 Ves. 652.

[9] Omealey v. Newel, 8 East, 364.

[10] Ex parte Bridges, 2 Woods, 428; P. v. Kelly, 38 Cal. 145.

[11] In re Loney, 134 U. S. 372.

timony is alleged to have been given, the officer by whom the oath was administered and state that he had authority so to do, set out the testimony alleged to be false, aver its materiality, and state that it was false and was wilfully and corruptly given.[1] As to these matters the common-law requirements are very strict and specific, as will hereafter appear under the discussion of the various requisites; and to obviate the necessity of this strictness, which is such as to frequently defeat the prosecution on purely technical grounds, statutes have been passed in many of the states prescribing what shall be sufficient in such an indictment. These statutes, as a rule, preserve the essential requisites as here enumerated, but allow them to be alleged more generally than is permitted according to common-law rules.[2] Some of these statutes are quite specific as to what is necessary to be alleged, making it sufficient that the indictment state the substance of the controversy or matter in respect to which the crime was committed, the authority of the officer to administer the oath, the testimony complained of and its falsity and materiality, without setting forth any part of the record or proceeding, or the commission or authority of the court or officer.[3] That the legislature has authority to thus regulate the form of the indictment cannot be questioned;[4] but these provisions as to the form of the indictment do not change the constituent elements of the offense, which must be proved as before;[5] and the facts must still be set forth with such particularity and certainty as to give the accused reasonable notice of what he is to defend himself against.[6] Practi-

[1] Lytle v. S., 31 Ohio St. 196; Perdue v. C., 96 Pa. St. 311; C. v. Kane, 92 Ky. 457; Lodge v. C., 2 Grat. 579; C. v. Stockley, 10 Leigh, 678; Cox v. S., 13 Tex. Ap. 479; S. v. Harlis, 33 La. An. 1172; Stanley v. U. S., 1 Okl. 336.

[2] S. v. Peters, 107 N. C. 876; S. v. Gates, 107 N. C. 832; S. v. Corson, 59 Me. 137; S. v. Camley, 67 Vt. 322; Flint v. P., 35 Mich. 491; Brown v. S., 47 Ala. 47; Barnett v. S., 89 Ala. 165; Walker v. S., 96 Ala. 53; S. v. Schill, 27 Ia. 263; S. v. Newton, 1 Greene (Ia.), 160; S. v. Foulks, 57 Mo. 461; Massie v. S., 5 Tex. Ap. 81; West v. S., 8 Tex. Ap. 119; Mattingly v. S., 8 Tex. Ap. 345; Fisher v. U. S., 1 Okl. 252.

[3] P. v. Phelps, 5 Wend. 9; Burk v. S., 81 Ind. 128; Halleck v. S., 11 Ohio, 400; S. v. Divoll, 44 N. H. 140.

[4] S. v. Moore, 104 N. C. 743; S. v. Peters, 107 N. C. 876.

[5] S. v. Peters, 107 N. C. 876; S. v. Corson, 59 Me. 137; S. v. Ah Lee, 18 Oreg. 540.

[6] Stofer v. S., 3 W. Va. 692; Davis v. S., 79 Ala. 20; S. v. Powell, 28 Tex. 626; Markham v. U. S., 160 U. S. 319.

cally the same result has been reached under the general provision that the indictment shall not be deemed insufficient by reason of any defect in matter of form which does not tend to the prejudice of the defendant.[1]

§ **873. The proceeding.**— The indictment must specify the court, tribunal, or officer in or before which the false testimony was given, in such way as to show jurisdiction, and if the tribunal is not a court of general jurisdiction, but having only a special power of inquiry, it must appear that it was legally constituted and authorized to act.[2] At common law, if the false testimony is given in a judicial proceeding, it is necessary to set forth the style of the court,[3] the pleadings, the proceedings and the evidence.[4] But under statutes it is sufficient to state the substance of the controversy upon which the false oath was taken.[5] Thus, if the proceeding in which the perjury is charged to have been committed was a criminal prosecution, it is not necessary to describe the crime charged in such prosecution with technical particularity.[6] The indictment should distinctly aver what was the subject of inquiry before the court, so that the materiality of the testimony may appear.[7] But under the usual statutory provisions the issue may be alleged in general terms,[8] and the substance only of the controversy need be set out.[9] Variance between the allegation and the proof as to the names of the parties to the proceeding will be fatal;[10] as will also a variance between the pleadings if set out and the proof thereof, although it may not have been

[1] P. v. Phelps, 5 Wend. 9; S. v. See, 4 Wash. 344.

[2] U. S. v. Wilcox, 4 Blatch. 391; Conner v. C., 2 Va. Cas. 30.

[3] S. v. Street, 1 Murph. 156.

[4] S. v. Stillman, 7 Coldw. 341; Reg. v. Gardiner, 8 C. & P. 737.

[5] S. v. Stillman, 7 Coldw. 341; Woods v. S., 14 Lea, 460; S. v. Hoyle, 6 Ired. 1; S. v. Bishop, 1 D. Chip. 120; Crusen v. S., 10 Ohio St. 258; C. v. Warden, 11 Met. 406; S. v. Oppenheimer, 41 Tex. 82; S. v. Witham, 6 Oreg. 366. Any mere vagueness or incompleteness of the description of the proceeding must be taken advantage of before trial and not in arrest of judgment: Pennaman v. S., 58 Ga. 336.

[6] C. v. Flynn, 3 Cush. 525; Kimmell v. P., 92 Ill. 457; Rex v. Dowlin, 5 Term R. 311.

[7] Conner v. C., 2 Va. Cas. 30; Perdue v. C., 96 Pa. St. 311; S. v. McCormick, 52 Ind. 169.

[8] Covey v. S., 23 Tex. Ap. 388; Peters v. U. S., 2 Okl. 138.

[9] S. v. Stillman, 7 Coldw. 341; Burk v. S., 81 Ind. 128; Flint v. P., 35 Mich. 491; S. v. Divoll, 44 N. H. 140.

[10] S. v. Green, 100 N. C. 547; S. v. Harvell, 4 Jones, 55; Rex v. Stoveld, 6 C. & P. 489.

necessary to set out the pleadings in describing the issue.[1] So where the proceeding in which the false testimony was charged to have been given was a criminal prosecution for selling a lottery ticket, and a copy of the ticket in Chinese characters was set out without translation, the indictment for perjury was held insufficient on a motion in arrest of judgment.[2] But where the perjury charged was in a prosecution for swindling a bank by means of a draft, and the draft was set out in the indictment for perjury, by way of inducement, a variance therefrom in the evidence was held immaterial.[3] So a variance as to the day of holding the court at which the perjury is charged as committed will be immaterial.[4] Under indictment charging the proceeding to have been before the sheriff, it was held not a variance to prove it to have been before the under-sheriff or secondary;[5] but under an indictment for perjury committed before A., proof of perjury committed before A. and T. was held fatally variant.[6]

§ 874. **Description of the oath.**—It is not necessary in the indictment for perjury to allege in what particular form the person charged was sworn; it is sufficient to allege that he was "duly sworn," or to use other words to the same general effect.[7] But any averment describing the manner in which the oath was administered is material and must be proved substantially as alleged, although a mere verbal variance will not be material.[8] It is sufficient to allege that the oath was taken before the officer, and it is not required that the indictment shall state that it was administered by him.[9] But it must distinctly appear that defendant was sworn;[10] and it is not enough to charge that in certain answers in the deposition he did "depose and swear."[11] The material fact is that he swore to the truth of

[1] S. v. Ammons, 3 Murphy, 123.

[2] P. v. Ah Sum, 92 Cal. 648.

[3] King v. S., 32 Tex. Ap. 463.

[4] S. v. Clark, 2 Tyler, 277.

[5] Reg. v. Dunn, 7 C. & P. 730; Reg. v. Schlesinger, 10 Q. B. 670.

[6] S. v. Mayson, 3 Brev. 284.

[7] Tuttle v. P., 36 N. Y. 431; S. v. Farrow, 10 Rich. 165; Dodge v. S., 24 N. J. 455; Jackson v. S., 15 Tex. Ap. 579; Beach v. S., 32 Tex. Ap. 240; Rex v. McCarther, Peake, 155; Rex v. Rowley, Ry. & M. 299; Reg. v. Southwood, 1 F. & F. 356.

[8] S. v. Gates, 17 N. H. 373; S. v. Davis, 69 N. C. 383; S. v. Porter, 2 Hill, 611.

[9] Campbell v. P., 8 Wend. 636; S. v. Ellison, 8 Blackf. 225.

[10] S. v. Hamilton, 7 Mo. 300.

[11] U. S. v. McConaughy, 33 Fed. R. 168; U. S. v. Henderson, 33 Fed. R. 170.

certain facts, not that he was sworn to make a written statement or that he was sworn to the truth of it, where such statement is the basis of the prosecution.[1] Irregularity in the venue or jurat of the affidavit on which the charge of perjury is based will be immaterial.[2]

§ 875. **Authority of officer.**— The indictment must aver that the oath was administered by or taken before some one having authority to administer the same;[3] and this may be done by setting out such facts as make it judicially appear that the officer had such authority and jurisdiction.[4] It must be alleged before whom the oath was taken, in order that the accused may inquire into the authority of the officer who administered it;[5] but an allegation that it was taken on the trial of the cause in a court named need not designate the officer who administered it.[6] The commission or other authority of the officer need not be specially alleged; it is sufficient to aver generally that he was authorized and duly qualified to act in that respect.[7] The court will take judicial notice of the authority of the proper officer to administer the oath.[8]

§ 876. **Jurisdiction of the court.**— Aside from statute it is necessary to allege in specific terms the nature of the court or tribunal before which the cause or inquiry was pending in which the false oath is alleged to have been taken.[9] If the case is one of special jurisdiction, the facts showing such jurisdiction in the court, tribunal or officer must be alleged.[10] But

[1] C. v. Hatfield, 107 Mass. 227; C. v. Carel, 105 Mass. 582.

[2] S. v. Hopper, 133 Ind. 460.

[3] S. v. Nickerson, 46 Ia. 447.

[4] S. v. Cunningham, 66 Ia. 94; S. v. Hopper, 133 Ind. 460; S. v. Green, 24 Ark. 591.

[5] Kerr v. P., 42 Ill. 307.

[6] S. v. Spencer, 6 Oreg. 152; S. v. O'Hagan, 38 Ia. 504; Keator v. P., 32 Mich. 484.

[7] Markham v. U. S., 160 U. S. 319; C. v. Hughes, 5 Allen, 499; C. v. Hatfield, 107 Mass. 227; S. v. Marshall, 47 Mo. 378; S. v. Keel, 54 Mo. 182; Johnson v. P., 94 Ill. 505; Stewart v. S., 6 Tex. Ap. 184; Bradberry v. S., 7 Tex. Ap. 375; St. Clair v. S., 11 Tex. Ap. 297; Rich v. U. S., 2 Okl. 146; Rex v. Callanan, 6 B. & C. 102. But under federal statute, *held*, that it was not sufficient to describe the officer as "a commissioner of the United States duly appointed," without averring how, or by whom, or under what statute or for what purpose he was appointed: U. S. v. Wilcox, 4 Blatch. 391.

[8] Babcock v. U. S., 34 Fed. R. 873; U. S. v. Lehman, 39 Fed. R. 49.

[9] S. v. Hamilton, 65 Mo. 667; Anderson v. S., 18 Tex. Ap. 17.

[10] For instance, in a case of false swearing before a register or receiver of the United States land office: Rich v. U. S., 1 Okl. 354. But where

under the statutes it is usually sufficient to aver generally the jurisdiction of the court, tribunal or officer without specifying the particulars of such jurisdiction.[1] And especially in a case of a court of general jurisdiction it is sufficient to show that the case is one over which the court might have had jurisdiction.[2] If the case was a criminal prosecution it need not be alleged whether jurisdiction was acquired by indictment or information.[3]

§ 877. **The matter falsely sworn.**— The indictment must set out the substance and effect of the testimony constituting the perjury;[4] and the fact that the evidence was given or the affidavit was made by the accused must be clearly charged;[5] but it is enough to say that the facts alleged were sworn to.[6] If the false swearing is in a written instrument, such as an affidavit, it is usual to set the instrument out by its tenor as well as by substance and effect, unless there is special statutory provision to the contrary. The precedents are not uniform in this respect, but the older ones set out the affidavit,[7] and in Indiana and Texas this is held essential.[8] A federal statute, following an English statute, makes it unnecessary to set out the instrument by its tenor in indictments in the federal courts.[9] Probably statutes in many of the states have the same effect. It is not necessary to set forth the whole instrument or the whole of the evidence in which the perjury was committed, but only so much as is necessary to show in what particular it

the false swearing was charged as before an election board, it was held sufficient to allege that such board was organized according to law without charging the manner of such organization: Johnson v. P., 94 Ill. 505. So where the charge was of perjury committed in a prosecution before a city court, it was held necessary to show that such court had jurisdiction to entertain and determine the proceeding: Franklin v. S., 91 Ga. 712.

1 C. v. Knight, 12 Mass. 273; C. v. Butland, 119 Mass. 317; Franklin v. S., 91 Ga. 712; S. v. Peters, 42 Tex. 7.

2 Eighmy v. P., 79 N. Y. 546; S. v. Newton, 1 Greene (Ia.), 160; Reg. v. Dunning, L. R. 1 C. C. 290.

3 Powers v. S., 17 Tex. Ap. 428; S. v. Wise, 3 Lea, 38; Steinston v. S., 6 Yerg. 530.

4 S. v. Groves, Busbee, 402.

5 Copeland v. S., 23 Miss. 257; Rex v. Stevens, 5 B. & C. 246.

6 Flint v. P., 35 Mich. 491.

7 2 Bish. Cr. Pr., § 915.

8 Coppack v. S., 36 Ind. 513; S. v. Blackstone, 74 Ind. 592; S. v. Umbdenstock, 43 Tex. 554; Rohrer v. S., 13 Tex. Ap. 163. For a form setting out the affidavit, see P. v. Sweetman, 3 Park. Cr. R. 358; and for a similar form omitting the affidavit, see S. v. Whittemore, 50 N. H. 245.

9 U. S. v. Walsh, 22 Fed. R. 644; U. S. v. Law, 50 Fed. R. 915.

was false, and if oral, only the substance of it.[1] The particulars set forth must, however, be substantially proven,[2] and a variance in a material matter, as, for instance, in a deed designated in such testimony or statement, will be fatal.[3] So if the false swearing was in an affidavit, a variance in the name under which the affidavit is sworn to, from that of defendant, will be fatal.[4]

§ 878. **Materiality.**— The materiality of the matter falsely sworn to must clearly appear; and it must appear, not only that the testimony was material to the question which the indictment states was raised, but also that that question was material under the issues.[5] If the testimony is alleged to have been material, and it may be seen from the proceeding as described that it was so, that will be sufficient.[6] In many cases it is stated as a rule that the general allegation of the materiality of the false testimony is sufficient without a particular

[1] P. v. Phelps, 5 Wend. 9; Campbell v. P., 8 Wend. 636; S. v. Neal, 42 Mo. 119; Rex v. Callanan, 6 B. & C. 102. Where the testimony of a witness was given in a foreign language but set out in a deposition in English, and subscribed and sworn to in this form, it was held sufficient to set it out in English: Reg. v. Thomas, 2 C. & K. 806.

[2] Berrian v. S., 22 N. J. 9. A charge of falsely swearing to one's qualification as an elector is not sustained by proof that the affiant has lost his right to vote: S. v. Houston, 103 N. C. 383.

[3] S. v. Frisby, 90 Mo. 530. So where the charge was of suing out a warrant for rent, *held*, that proof of suing out a warrant on some other ground constituted a variance: C. v. Hickman, 2 Va. Cas. 323.

[4] Tardy v. S., 4 Blackf. 152; Gandy v. S., 27 Neb. 707. But where the variance was evidently a mere clerical error, *held*, that it was immaterial: S. v. Raymond, 20 Ia. 582.

[5] P. v. Collier, 1 Mich. 137; S. v. Trask, 42 Vt. 152; S. v. Hobbs, 40 N. H. 229; Weathers v. S., 2 Blackf. 278; S. v. Flagg, 25 Ind. 243; S. v. Beard, 25 N. J. 384; P. v. Ross, 103 Cal. 425; Hembree v. S., 52 Ga. 242; S. v. Bowlus, 3 Heisk. 29; S. v. Hayward, 1 Nott & M. 546; C. v. Pickering, 8 Grat. 628; Donohoe v. S., 14 Tex. Ap. 638; Martin v. S., 33 Tex. Ap. 317; Buller v. S., 33 Tex. Ap. 551; Agar v. S., 29 Tex. Ap. 605; U. S. v. Bedgood, 49 Fed. R. 54; Rex v. Nicholl, 1 B. & Ad. 21; Reg. v. Bartholomew, 1 C. & K. 366; Reg. v. Cutts, 4 Cox, 435. It is sometimes said that the indictment must conclusively show that the testimony was material to the issue: S. v. Thrift, 30 Ind. 211; S. v. Chandler, 42 Vt. 446.

[6] Hoch v. P., 3 Mich. 552; Sanders v. P., 124 Ill. 218; Johnson v. P., 94 Ill. 505; C. v. Pollard, 12 Met. 225; Markham v. U. S., 160 U. S. 319. And it is not necessary in such a case, under the California code, to set out precisely the manner in which the testimony would affect the parties to the proceeding: P. v. Naylor, 82 Cal. 607; P. v. Ah Bean, 77 Cal. 12; P. v. Brilliant, 58 Cal. 214.

showing of how it was material.[1] At any rate, such a general averment is sufficient under some statutes, though it might not be at common law.[2] The ultimate fact of materiality, without the evidential or probative facts showing such materiality, is usually all that is required to be alleged;[3] though in some jurisdictions the general averment is not sufficient without the facts showing the materiality in some way appear.[4] If the materiality appear either by direct allegation or inferentially from the facts alleged, that is enough;[5] and there are numerous illustrations and applications of the proposition that an express allegation of materiality is not necessary where the facts alleged in themselves show the materiality.[6]

§ 879. **Availability and effect.**— As a part of the requirement in regard to materiality, it must appear by the allegations in the indictment that the false testimony was given in some cause, matter or proceeding before a court, tribunal, public of-

[1] Lea v. S., 64 Miss. 278; S. v. Davis, 69 N. C. 495; S. v. Mumford, 1 Dev. 519; Kimmel v. P., 92 Ill. 457; Gandy v. S., 23 Neb. 436; C. v. McCarty, 152 Mass. 577; Rich v. U. S., 1 Okl. 354; S. v. Maxwell, 28 La. An. 361; S. v. Gonsoulin, 42 La. An. 579; S. v. Jean, 42 La. An. 946; Washington v. S., 22 Tex. Ap. 26; Rex v. Dowlin, 5 Term R. 311; Reg. v. Bennett, 3 C. & K. 124; Reg. v. Gardiner, 8 C. & P. 737; Reg. v. Scott, 2 Q. B. D. 415; Reg. v. Smith, 1 F. & F. 98. A mere averment that it became material to ascertain the truth of the matter alleged to have been sworn to has been held not a sufficient averment of materiality: Reg. v. Goodfellow, Car. & M. 569.

[2] Lawson v. S., 3 Lea, 309.

[3] Tuttle v. P., 36 N. Y. 431.

[4] S. v. Keel, 54 Mo. 182; S. v. Holden, 48 Mo. 93; S. v. Shanks, 66 Mo. 560; U. S. v. Singleton, 54 Fed. R. 488. But of course if the substance of the false statement as charged plainly shows its materiality, this is sufficient without an express allegation: S. v. Marshall, 47 Mo. 378. It is said that when the proposition is laid down that the materiality may be generally alleged, that statement refers not to the materiality of the false testimony, which must, in every case, appear on the face of the charge, but only to the questions or issues to which the false testimony has reference: S. v. Holden, 48 Mo. 93.

[5] S. v. Beard, 25 N. J. 384; S. v. Cunningham, 66 Ia. 94; S. v. Madigan, 57 Minn. 425; Massie v. S., 5 Tex. Ap. 81; Mattingly v. S., 8 Tex. Ap. 345; Partain v. S., 22 Tex. Ap. 100; Rex v. McKeron, 5 Term R. 316; Rex v. Dunn, 1 D. & R. 10; Reg. v. Harvey, 8 Cox, 99.

[6] S. v. Hall, 7 Blackf. 25; S. v. Johnson, 7 Blackf. 49; Hendricks v. S., 26 Ind. 493; Galloway v. S., 29 Ind. 442; Burk v. S., 81 Ind. 128; S. v. Hopper, 133 Ind. 460; S. v. Biebusch, 32 Mo. 276; S. v. Cave, 81 Mo. 450; Lamden v. S., 5 Humph. 83; P. v. Kelly, 59 Cal. 372; Campbell v. P., 8 Wend. 636; S. v. Bunker, 38 Kan. 737; S. v. Nees, 47 Ark. 553; U. S. v. McHenry, 6 Blatch. 503.

ficer or body; that is, that it was a false oath taken under such circumstances as that an oath was authorized by law.[1] In the case of an affidavit it must appear that it was intended for use in, and was material to, some proceeding or inquiry in which such an affidavit would be admissible;[2] but it is not necessary to allege that the affidavit was actually used.[3]

§ 880. **The averment as to falsity.**— The indictment must expressly allege the falsity of the statement under oath relied on to constitute perjury, by negativing such statement.[4] If the statement was upon information and belief, while the indictment traverses in unqualified language the truth of the fact thus stated, perjury is not charged, because the fact might have been believed by the affiant to have been otherwise;[5] moreover, the statement may have been true as a matter of fact, and yet false according to the knowledge or belief of the defendant, and therefore have been perjury; so that it is not the absolute falsity of the statement itself as a statement of fact, but its falsity as the statement of the defendant, that is material. Therefore it is said that the indictment need not negative the truth of the statement itself.[6] But the indictment should clearly and distinctly aver that defendant swore falsely;[7] or use equivalent language. The falsity may be shown by a general averment of facts showing that such statement was necessarily false, and such general contradiction is sufficient where the falsity is thus made clearly to appear, although the identical statement is not in terms contradicted.[8] Where time, place or manner are involved in the alleged false statement, but not as material elements thereof, the assignment as to falsity should not be limited to such time, place or manner.[9] If

[1] S. v. Geer, 46 Kan. 529; S. v. Ayer, 40 Kan. 43; S. v. Smith, 40 Kan. 631; S. v. Simons, 30 Vt. 620; U. S. v. Wilcox, 4 Blatch. 391.

[2] S. v. Lloyd, 77 Wis. 630; P. v. Fox, 25 Mich. 492; Rex v. Foster, Russ. & Ry. 459.

[3] S. v. Hopper, 133 Ind. 460.

[4] C. v. Monahan, 9 Gray, 119; Gibson v. S., 44 Ala. 17; Henderson v. P., 117 Ill. 265.

[5] Lambert v. P., 76 N. Y. 220; Williams v. S., 7 Humph. 47; Leverette v. S., 32 Tex. Ap. 471; Rex v. Harris, 5 B. & Ald. 926.

[6] S. v. Cruikshank, 6 Blackf. 62; S. v. Gates, 17 N. H. 373.

[7] S. v. Nickerson, 46 Ia. 447; Maddox v. S., 28 Tex. Ap. 533; Reg. v. Oxley, 3 C. & K. 317.

[8] S. v. Voorhis, 52 N. J. 351; S. v. Smith, 63 Vt. 201; De Bernie v. S., 19 Ala. 23; Reg. v. London, 12 Cox, 50.

[9] Henderson v. P., 117 Ill. 265; S. v. Swaim, 97 N. C. 462; S. v. Ah Sam, 7 Oreg. 477; Harp v. S., 59 Ark. 113;

the indictment charges a false statement in a schedule in a bankruptcy proceeding, it should be alleged wherein such statement is false and incorrect.[1] But it is sufficient to allege that property was omitted, without setting out a full and particular account of the property of the petitioner.[2] The traverse of the statement alleged to have been false must be particular as to what the facts were;[3] and it is not enough to simply say that the statements were wilfully and deliberately made and were false to the knowledge of defendant;[4] but the indictment should continue, "whereas in truth and in fact," and then state what the facts were.[5] If a part only of the statement is charged to have been false, such part must be pointed out and its truth specifically denied.[6]

§ 881. **Intent; knowledge.**— In order to show that the false testimony was intentionally false it is usual and proper to allege that it was wilfully and corruptly given;[7] and the omission of such allegation is not cured by a general concluding clause in the indictment charging that defendant did wilfully and corruptly commit perjury.[8] The omission of "wilfully" has been held to render the indictment bad.[9] It seems that where the

Martinez v. S., 7 Tex. Ap. 394; Reg. v. Stolady, 1 F. & F. 518; Reg. v. Whitehouse, 3 Cox, 86; Reg. v. Burraston, 4 Jur. 697.

1 U. S. v. Morgan, Morris, 341. An indictment for false return of property for assessment should show that the property not returned was subject to assessment: S. v. Cunningham, 66 Ia. 94.

2 P. v. Phelps, 5 Wend. 9; U. S. v. Chapman, 3 McLean, 390; U. S. v. Deming, 4 McLean, 3.

3 S. v. Bixler, 62 Md. 354.

4 Gabrielsky v. S., 13 Tex. Ap. 428.

5 Turner v. S., 30 Tex. Ap. 691.

6 S. v. Mace, 76 Me. 64; Thomas v. S., 51 Ark. 138.

7 S. v. Davis, 84 N. C. 787; S. v. Bobbitt, 70 N. C. 81; Thomas v. C., 2 Rob. (Va.) 795; P. v. Ross, 103 Cal. 425; Rex v. Stevens, 5 B. & C. 246. In Florida it is said that the allegation should be that the oath taken was wilfully false: Robinson v. S., 18 Fla. 898; but the word "wilful" is not essential in an indictment for perjury at common law, though it may be under the statute, 5 Eliz., ch. 9: Rex v. Cox, 1 Leach, C. C. 71.

8 S. v. Morse, 90 Mo. 91; S. v. Day, 100 Mo. 242. Such concluding clause is surplusage: U. S. v. Wood, 44 Fed. R. 753; Ryalls v. Reg., 11 Q. B. 781; Reg. v. Hodgkiss, L. R. 1 C. C. 212.

9 S. v. Day, 100 Mo. 242; U. S. v. Edwards, 43 Fed. R. 67. But other words may supply the omission of "wilfully:" S. v. Spencer, 45 La. An. 1. In Texas, under statutory definition, it is held necessary to allege that the false statement was deliberately and wilfully made: S. v. Webb, 41 Tex. 67; S. v. Perry, 42 Tex. 238; Allen v. S., 42 Tex. 12; Smith v. S., 1 Tex. Ap. 620. But it is not necessary to charge that the false statement was not made through inad-

oath is charged as wilful it is not necessary to also charge that it was corrupt.[1] There are, as to this crime, no peculiar words of art essential, as in some felonies, to the description of the offense.[2] The indictment must also show knowledge on the part of the accused of the falsity of the statement at the time it was made, and it is not sufficient to merely negative the truth of the statement.[3] But the charge that the statement was wilfully false necessarily shows that it was knowingly false.[4] And the allegation that defendant did at a certain time testify to certain matters, "whereas he did know that they were false," sufficiently indicates such knowledge at the time the testimony was given.[5] But in a prosecution for perjury in swearing as an insolvent debtor to a schedule which omitted certain claims belonging to insolvent, it was held necessary to allege that at the time of taking the oath he knew and remembered that such claims were due and owing to him.[6]

§ 882. **Time and place.**— The indictment should allege, as in other cases, the time of the commission of the crime charged;[7] and it is said that if the indictment charges the perjury as of a wrong term of court the variance is fatal.[8] But as a general rule the date need not be proven as alleged,[9] unless the perjury was by means of an instrument set out by its tenor; in that

vertence or by mistake: Brown v. S., 9 Tex. Ap. 171.

1 S. v. Bixler, 62 Md. 354; U. S. v. Hearing, 26 Fed. R. 744.

2 Resp. v. Newell, 3 Yeates, 407.

3 S. v. Lea, 3 Ala. 602; S. v. Carland, 3 Dev. 114; S. v. Champion, 116 N. C. 987; Juaraqui v. S., 28 Tex. 625; S. v. Morse, 1 Greene (Ia.), 503.

4 Johnson v. P., 94 Ill. 505; S. v. Stein, 48 Minn. 466; S. v. Smith, 63 Vt. 201.

5 S. v. Wood, 17 Ia. 18; S. v. Lindenburg, 13 Tex. 27.

6 C. v. Cook, 1 Rob. (Va.) 729. Under the Iowa statute it is not necessary to allege that defendant knew the falsity of the matter sworn to, unless the assignment of perjury is upon the statement of the accused as to his belief: S. v. Raymond, 20 Ia. 582. In Oregon it is said that averment as to knowledge of the falsity of the matter is unnecessary, although such fact must be proven: S. v. Ah Lee, 18 Oreg. 540.

7 S. v. Fenlason, 79 Me. 117, 7 Am. Cr. R. 495 and note; Rhodes v. C., 78 Va. 692; U. S. v. Law, 50 Fed. R. 915; U. S. v. Bowman, 2 Wash. 328.

8 S. v. Lewis, 93 N. C. 381.

9 Richey v. C., 81 Ky. 524; C. v. Davis, 94 Ky. 612; Lucas v. S., 27 Tex. Ap. 322; U. S. v. Matthews, 68 Fed. R. 880; S. C., Matthews v. U. S., 161 U. S. 500. In such a prosecution time and place are sometimes material and necessary to be alleged with precision and sometimes not: Rex v. Aylett, 1 Term R. 63.

case the instrument as introduced in evidence must correspond in date with the copy set out.[1]

§ 883. **Separate counts; several assignments.**— Several charges of perjury may be made in different counts;[2] but if the statement is false in several particulars it is not necessary to embrace those particulars in separate counts, but they may be included in the same count.[3] Where falsity of the statement in several particulars is charged it is usual to assign the falsity of each, and proof of falsity as to any one particular assigned, if material, will be sufficient to warrant a conviction.[4] But if the entire matter alleged to have been falsely stated is set out in one averment the whole must be proved.[5] If one assignment is sufficient, an improper assignment in connection with it will not vitiate the indictment;[6] and such improper assignment will not be a ground for quashing the indictment, and can only be taken advantage of by excepting to the evidence introduced thereunder.[7] If the attention of the court is called, however, to the improper assignment, it should be withdrawn from the jury or it will not appear whether the verdict is on the proper or the improper assignment, and the conviction cannot be sustained.[8] Where there are several assignments the falsity of each should be specially alleged.[9]

§ 884. **Joinder of defendants.**— Perjury is a separate act in each person committing it, and two or more cannot be jointly charged with the crime.[10] But it is said that two persons may be charged in the same indictment, the one with perjury and the other with procuring the perjury to be committed.[11]

[1] Dill v. P., 9 Colo. 469; Matthews v. U. S., 161 U. S. 500.

[2] Ryalls v. Reg., 11 Q. B. 781; Castro v. Reg., 6 Ap. Cas. 229.

[3] S. v. Bishop, 1 D. Chip. 120; S. v. Bordeaux, 93 N. C. 560.

[4] C. v. Johns, 6 Gray, 274; Harris v. P., 64 N. Y. 148; S. v. Blaisdell, 59 N. H. 328; Smith v. S., 103 Ala. 57; Moore v. S., 32 Tex. Ap. 405; S. v. Day, 100 Mo. 242; Reg. v. Chapman, 2 C. & K. 846.

[5] S. v. Blaisdell, 59 N. H. 328; Rex v. Leefe, 2 Camp. 134.

[6] S. v. Smith, 63 Vt. 201.

[7] C. v. Sargent, 129 Mass. 115.

[8] Wood v. P., 59 N. Y. 117. If no evidençe is given as to one assignment, it is not competent for defendant to show that as to such assignment the testimony was true: Rex v. Hemp, 5 C. & P. 468.

[9] Gabrielsky v. S., 13 Tex. Ap. 428; Reg. v. Burraston, 4 Jur. 697.

[10] Rex v. Philips, 2 Stra. 921; Resp. v. Goss, 2 Yeates, 479.

[11] C. v. Devine, 155 Mass. 224. The correctness of this decision may be questioned. It is true that principal and accessory may be charged in

§ 885. **Forms of indictment.**— The common-law indictment for perjury is an exceedingly complicated instrument by reason of the difficulty of setting out the various essentials, especially the nature of the proceeding, the jurisdiction of the court, the administration of the oath, the testimony given, and its falsity. As already indicated, these requirements have been simplified in some states by express statutory provisions as to what shall be sufficient in an indictment for the crime, and in other states by general provisions as to sufficiency of indictments. The forms here given are suggestive only; they would probably be found good in most states, but it will be necessary in applying them to bear in mind the statutory provisions.

PERJURY IN PROOF OF ALIBI.

Heretofore, to wit, at the January term, A. D. 1896, of the district court of Johnson county, held on the 25th day of January, A. D. 1896, a certain indictment in which John Adams was charged with the crime of burglary in feloniously breaking and entering the dwelling-house of one Timothy Brown came on to be tried in due form of law and was then and there tried by a jury of such county in that behalf duly sworn, upon which said trial the said A. B. [defendant] appeared as a witness for and in behalf of the said John Adams, and was then and there duly sworn before the duly authorized clerk of said court, that the evidence which he, the said A. B., should give to the court there, and the said jury so sworn as aforesaid, touching the matter then in question in the trial of said indictment, should be the truth, the whole truth, and nothing but the truth; and on the said trial of said indictment it became material to inquire where the said John Adams was on the night of the fourteenth and fifteenth of December, A. D. 1895, at which time, as appeared from the evidence, said burglary charged in the indictment aforesaid was committed, and the said A. B. then and there feloniously, falsely, knowingly, maliciously, wilfully and corruptly testified in substance as follows, to wit: that between the hours of ten and twelve o'clock of said night, the said A. B. was in company with the said John Adams at the house of one Peter King, in the city of Iowa City, in said county of John-

the same indictment, but the crime of suborning perjury seems to be considered a distinct offense from that of perjury. Certainly there must be some crimes so individual in their nature that no accessory is possible. Could one who had never been married at all be convicted of bigamy because he had procured and induced a man already married to marry a second wife?

son, and that between the hours of twelve and four o'clock of said night, the said A. B. was in company with the said John Adams at the house of one William Jones, in said city of Iowa City; whereas, in truth and in fact, as the said A. B. well knew, the said John Adams was not at the house of the said Peter King between the hours of ten and twelve o'clock of said night, or during any portion of that time; and whereas, in truth and in fact, as the said A. B. well knew, the said John Adams was not at the house of the said William Jones between the hours of twelve and four o'clock of said night or during any portion of that time. Wherefore the grand jurors aforesaid, on their oath aforesaid, do say that the said A. B. did, in manner and form aforesaid, commit wilful and corrupt perjury.[1]

To illustrate the method of charging perjury in an oath not taken in a judicial proceeding, the following is presented:

PERJURY IN AFFIDAVIT FOR NATURALIZATION.

That A. B., on ——, at Hancock, in the county of Hillsborough aforesaid, giving his testimony in and by a certain affidavit by him subscribed as a witness relative to an application in writing thereafter to be made to the police court of the city of Nashua, in said county, to be admitted a citizen of the United States, by one B. C., an alien and a subject of Victoria, Queen of the United Kingdoms of Great Britain and Ireland, in his own proper person, on the said ——, at Hancock aforesaid, appeared and was then and there sworn as such witness for said B. C., and in support of said application by and before Joseph Davis, a justice of the peace within and for said county, then and there having lawful and competent power and authority to administer the said oath to the said A. B. in that behalf; and as such witness he, the said A. B., took his corporal oath concerning the matter set forth in said affidavit pertaining to said application, and that the facts therein stated and by him subscribed were true, which said oath the said justice of the peace then and there had sufficient and competent authority to administer to him, the said A. B., in that behalf; and the said A. B., being so sworn as aforesaid, did then and there in said affidavit feloniously, falsely, knowingly, maliciously, wilfully and corruptly depose and swear, among other things, in sub-

[1] The first part of this form, describing the proceeding, is based to some extent upon the case of Reg. v. Dunning, L. R. 1 C. C. 290, in which an indictment less specific than this was held sufficient under an English statute. See, also, Reg. v. Hughes, 1 C. & K. 519; Lavey v. Reg., 17 Q. B. 496. As to the allegation of the testimony and the falsity thereof, see S. v. Ah Lee, 18 Oreg. 540. As to the allegation in regard to the administration of the oath to defendant, see S. v. Divoll, 44 N. H. 140. As to the averment of materiality, see C. v. Kelly, 123 Mass. 417.

stance as follows, to wit: that B. C., meaning the said B. C. above mentioned, had resided within the limits and under the jurisdiction of the United States for five years then last past, and for one year then last past within the state of New Hampshire, and that during said period he had behaved himself as a man of good moral character, attached to the principles of the constitution of the United States and well disposed to the good order and happiness of the same, which said affidavit is in the words and figures following, to wit: [Copy of affidavit.] Whereas, in truth and in fact, as the said A. B. then well knew, the said B. C. had no residence within the limits and under the jurisdiction of the United States for five years then last past, and for one year last past within the state of New Hampshire; and whereas, in truth and in fact, as the said A. B. then well knew, the said B. C. during the same period had not behaved himself as a man of good moral character, attached to the principles of the constitution of the United States and well disposed to the good order and happiness of the same; and whereas the said affidavit was, as the said A. B. then well knew, in all respects utterly false and untrue at the time the said A. B. so made and swore to the same. And so the jurors aforesaid, upon their oath aforesaid, do say that the said A. B. did commit wilful and corrupt perjury.[1]

IX. THE EVIDENCE.

§ 886. As to the proceedings or issue.— The charge in connection with which the alleged false testimony was given should be definitely proved.[2] Such proof should properly be made by the production of the record of the action.[3] But if the proceed-

[1] The first part of this indictment follows substantially one given in S. v. Whittemore, 50 N. H. 245. The assignment of the statement in the affidavit and the falsity thereof is in accordance with an indictment in P. v. Sweetman, 3 Park. Cr. R. 358, though considerably abridged from the language there used. As to whether it is necessary to set out a copy of the affidavit, see *supra*, § 877.

[2] Reg. v. Carr, 10 Cox, 564.

[3] McMurry v. S., 6 Ala. 324; Smith v. S., 103 Ala. 57; Heflin v. S., 88 Ga. 151; Rex v. Ward, 6 C. & P. 366; Porter v. Cooper, 6 C. & P. 354. A transcript is not necessary, however, where the documents constituting the essential record are produced from the custody of the proper officer: Reg. v. Turner, 2 C. & K. 732; Reg. v. Newman, 3 C. & K. 240. If the proceeding was on indictment there should be formal proof of the commencement thereof by production of the summons, information, or the like: Reg. v. Hurrell, 3 F. & F. 271; Reg. v. Newall, 6 Cox, 21; but in a bastardy proceeding, *held*, that the summons was not essential, the evidence showing that the information was duly made: Reg. v. Smith, L. R. 1 C. C. 110; nor the original writ of summons in a civil action, copy thereof being produced, with other evidence of the proceeding:

ing was in the same court it will take notice of its own records.[1] The usual evidence under common-law procedure of the proceeding in the action is the *postea;* [2] and this is enough without showing the final judgment.[3] Proof of the final conviction or judgment in the proceeding is not material.[4]

§ 887. **Administration of the oath.**— The fact that defendant was sworn may be shown by proof of the signature, by handwriting or otherwise, to the oath, if subscribed, and the evidence of the officer administering it, or proof of his signature to the jurat.[5] The official character of the officer administering the oath may be established by parol evidence of his acting *de facto*.[6]

§ 888. **The testimony or statement.**— While it has been said that the whole of the testimony of the defendant in which the false statement is charged to have been made should be proved,[7] yet the rule as generally stated is that only so much of the testimony of the defendant as relates to the particular fact on which the perjury is assigned need be shown.[8] The evidence need not be limited to proof of the exact words; proof of the substance is sufficient.[9] Parol evidence is admissible as

Reg. v. Scott, 2 Q. B. D. 415. Other evidence of the information and summons may be received after notice to produce the original: Reg. v. Dillon, 14 Cox, 4; Reg. v. Newall, 6 Cox, 21.

1 U. S. v. Erskine, 4 Cranch, C. C. 299.

2 Resp. v. Goss, 2 Yeates, 479.

3 Anon., Bull. N. P. 243. Where the *postea* could not be drawn up because a rule for a new trial was pending, *held*, that the *nisi prius* record was sufficient: Rex v. Browne, 3 C. & P. 572.

4 Reg. v. Goodfellow, Car. & M. 569. Where it is proper to prove the final judgment it may be shown by the production of the book from the proper office: Reg. v. Gordon, Car. & M. 410.

5 C. v. Warden, 11 Met. 406; Van Dusen v. P., 78 Ill. 645; Rex v. Benson, 2 Camp. 508; Rex v. Spencer, 1 C. & P. 260. But the administration of the oath must be affirmatively proved. The presumption that the officer did his duty will not prevail over the presumption of innocence: Sloan v. S., 71 Miss. 459. However, the proof of the officer's signature to the jurat, in addition to proof of defendant's signature to the oath, is sufficient: S. v. Madigan, 57 Minn. 425; Rex v. Morris, 2 Burr. 1189. In a particular case, *held*, that the evidence of the identity of the defendant as the person swearing to the affidavit charged as constituting perjury was not sufficiently established: Reg. v. Barnes, 10 Cox, 539.

6 Woodson v. S., 24 Tex. Ap. 153. And see *supra*, § 856.

7 Rex v. Jones, Peake, 37; Rex v. Dowlin, Peake, 170. At any rate, proof of the whole testimony is admissible: Reg. v. Harrison, 9 Cox, 503.

8 U. S. v. Erskine, 4 Cranch, C. C. 299; Rex v. Rowley, Ry. & M. 299.

9 Taylor v. S., 48 Ala. 157.

to what the testimony was.[1] The stenographer who took down the evidence may prove what the evidence was by reference to his notes;[2] but the judge's notes of the evidence are not in themselves admissible.[3] To prove false testimony given before a grand jury, persons who were properly present in the grand jury room as officers or otherwise, and who were not as grand jurors subject to the oath of secrecy, may testify.[4] Indeed, even a grand juror who has been sworn to secrecy may properly be required to divulge such testimony.[5]

§ 889. **Materiality.**— The general doctrine as to the necessity of showing the materiality of the false statement has already been explained.[6] It is only necessary here to say that there must be some evidence that the statement was material;[7] and that the fact cannot be left to presumption or inference.[8] For the purpose of showing materiality, it may be proper to show what other testimony was given at the same time, and it will be no objection to doing so that the defendant charged with perjury was not present when such other testimony was given.[9]

§ 890. **Wilful falsity.**—The necessity of negativing the truth of the statement set out as constituting perjury has already been explained.[10] The whole *res gestæ* of the transaction as to which the testimony was given may be shown for the purpose or proving that this testimony as to some of the particulars was false.[11] The record of the trial upon which the perjury was alleged to have been committed is admissible as inducement, but cannot be considered for the purpose of establishing the falsity of the testimony; thus, where the perjury charged was in giving evidence in behalf of the prosecution of a criminal charge, it was held that the fact that the defendant in that trial was acquitted did not tend to show that the testimony

[1] P. v. Curtis, 50 Cal. 95; S. v. Gibbs, 10 Mont. 213.

[2] P. v. Lem You, 97 Cal. 224; S. v. Camley, 67 Vt. 322.

[3] Reg. v. Child, 5 Cox, 197; Reg. v. Morgan, 6 Cox, 107.

[4] Reg. v. Hughes, 1 C. & K. 519.

[5] Izer v. S., 77 Md. 110.

[6] *Supra*, §§ 861–866. And as to charging the materiality in the indictment, see *supra*, § 878.

[7] Lawrence v. S., 2 Tex. Ap. 479.

[8] S. v. Aikens, 32 Ia. 403; Nelson v. S., 32 Ark. 192; Brooks v. S., 29 Tex. Ap. 582.

[9] P. v. Lem You, 97 Cal. 224.

[10] See *supra*, § 880.

[11] Heflin v. S., 88 Ga. 151.

was false.[1] And evidence which might be admissible in the case in which the perjury is claimed to have been committed may not be admissible in the prosecution for perjury; for instance, where the perjury was in a criminal case, admissions of the accused in that case are not admissible to show the falsity of the testimony of the witness, though they were admissible to show defendant's guilt.[2] If the alleged perjury relates to a written instrument, the instrument should be produced in evidence or its absence accounted for.[3] Where the false statement consisted in false entries at the custom-house, made under oath in regard to the cost of imported goods, it was held that the falsity could be shown by documentary evidence and the correspondence of the accused without living witnesses.[4] As to whether the false evidence was wilfully and corruptly given, the accused may show that immediately after the transaction to which his evidence related he gave the same account as in his testimony in regard to what took place.[5] But in general the accused is not allowed to show statements made out of court

[1] Kitchen v. S., 26 Tex. Ap. 165; Hutcherson v. S., 33 Tex. Ap. 67; Hemphill v. S., 71 Miss. 877; Reavis v. S., — Wyo. —, 44 Pac. R. 62. But see U. S. v. Butler, 38 Fed. R. 498, a case in which defendant was accused of perjury committed in a prosecution against him for illegal sale of liquors and in which he testified (under statute allowing the defendant in a criminal case to be a witness in his own behalf) that he had not sold any liquor, and a judgment of acquittal was entered. Thereupon it was held that this result was conclusive as to the truth of such evidence and defendant could not be convicted of perjury. The judge disclaims putting this conclusion on the ground of a prior adjudication, but states a doctrine analogous thereto, to the effect that, where a question has once been inquired into, the result is conclusive of the subsequent question between the same parties; citing the case of Coffey v. U. S., 116 U. S. 436, in which it was held that after acquittal in a criminal prosecution by the United States for violation of the internal revenue law a civil suit could not be maintained for the forfeiture of property on account of such violation. But this result seems very questionable; the issues in the two cases are not the same, although they happen to involve incidentally the same question of fact. It would be a strange result if, where the defendant having made himself a witness secures his own acquittal by perjury, the state should thereby be cut off by that result from afterwards calling him to account for his false swearing.

[2] Reavis v. S., — Wyo. —, 44 Pac. R. 62; Brown v. S., 57 Miss. 424. *Contra*, Martin v. S., 33 Tex. Ap. 317.

[3] Reg. v. Elworthy, L. R. 1 C. C. 103; Reg. v. Milnes, 2 F. & F. 10.

[4] U. S. v. Wood, 14 Pet. 430.

[5] S. v. Curtis, 12 Ired. 270. *Contra*, S. v. Hunt, 137 Ind. 537.

corresponding with his testimony which is charged as false, without also showing that such statements were made before the intent to misrepresent the facts could have been formed.[1] This is in harmony with the general rule of evidence as to corroborating testimony of the witnesses where an attempt is made to impeach him.[2] For the purpose of proving the wilful falsity of defendant's testimony the prosecution may show that defendant had given expression to malice toward the person against whom the false evidence was given;[3] or that he endeavored to influence another person to give false testimony in the same case.[4] Proof of other perjury than that assigned in the indictment cannot be introduced; but if evidence thereof is legitimately brought out and relates to the subject-matter of the perjury charged, it may be considered in determining defendant's corrupt intent.[5] Where the perjury was committed in a divorce proceeding, the wife, party to such suit, is a competent witness against her husband prosecuted for perjury in testifying against her.[6] A witness may testify directly that the statement in question was false, if he states facts showing it to be so.[7]

§ 891. Sufficiency of testimony; contradictory statements of accused.— Proof that accused has given contradictory testimony under oath at a different time will not be sufficient to establish the falsity of the testimony charged as perjury, for this would leave simply one oath of the defendant as against another, and it would not appear that the testimony charged was false rather than the testimony contradictory thereof. The two statements will simply neutralize each other; there must be some corroboration of the contradictory testimony.[8]

[1] McCord v. S., 83 Ga. 521; S. v. Parish, 79 N. C. 610.

[2] 1 Greenl. Ev., § 469. And see Rex v. Parker, 3 Dougl. 242. It seems that accused may show that the testimony contrary to his own in the case in which the perjury is alleged to have been committed was false, as tending to prove the correctness of his own testimony, although such evidence is not directly corroborative of what he swore: S. v. Jones, 91 N. C. 629.

[3] Rex v. Munton, 3 C. & P. 491.

[4] Heflin v. S., 88 Ga. 151.

[5] S. v. Raymond, 20 Ia. 582.

[6] Dill v. P., 19 Colo. 469.

[7] Adams v. S., 93 Ga. 166.

[8] C. v. Parker, 2 Cush. 212; U. S. v. Mayer, Deady, 127; Freeman v. S., 19 Fla. 552; Schwartz v. C., 27 Grat. 1025; Dodge v. S., 24 N. J. 455; S. v. Buckley, 18 Oreg. 228; S. v. Williams, 30 Mo. 364; Brooks v. S., 29 Tex. Ap. 582; Waters v. S., 30 Tex. Ap. 284; Reg. v. Muscot, 10 Mod. 192; Reg. v.

Such corroboration, however, may be furnished by evidence *aliunde* tending to show the perjury independently of the declarations or testimony of the accused.[1]

§ 892. **One witness not sufficient.**— On a principle analogous to that stated in the last paragraph, it has been held at common law without controversy in the authorities that the testimony of one witness as to the falsity of the statement assigned as perjury is not sufficient, for under such circumstances the oath of the accused and the oath of the witness to its falsity counteract each other.[2] This doctrine has sometimes been stated in such language as to indicate that the testimony of two witnesses to the falsity of the oath was necessary to a conviction, but if such ever was the rule, it has been changed by the later decisions, and as now expressly recognized it is only that to warrant a conviction the testimony of one witness as to the falsity of the statement must be corroborated by other testimony or by circumstances which may be shown in evidence tending to prove such falsity.[3] This rule exists in Texas, and perhaps in other states, by statute requiring the falsity of the defendant's testimony to be shown by two credible witnesses, or one credible witness corroborated strongly by other evidence.[4] And under such statute a credible witness is one

Wheatland, 8 C. & P. 238; Reg. v. Hughes, 1 C. & K. 519; Reg. v. Braithwaite, 1 F. & F. 638; 2 Bish. Cr. Proc., § 927; 1 Greenl. Ev., § 259. The accused is not estopped from showing that his oath contradictory of that charged as perjury was false: S. v. J. B., 1 Tyler, 269.

[1] S. v. Buckley, 18 Oreg. 228. Such, for instance, as the books of account and papers relating to the same prosecution: U. S. v. Mayer, Deady, 127.

[2] Reg. v. Yates, Car. & M. 132; Reg. v. Boulter, 3 C. & K. 236; Reg. v. Webster, 1 F. & F. 515; Rex v. Lee, 3 Russ. Cr. 78; Champney's Case, 2 Lewin, 258; P. v. Davis, 61 Cal. 536.

[3] C. v. Parker, 2 Cush. 212; U. S. v. Wood, 14 Pet. 430; Crusen v. S., 10 Ohio St. 258; S. v. Heed, 57 Mo. 252; S. v. Jean, 42 La. An. 946; S. v. Peters, 107 N. C. 876; Crandall v. Dawson, 6 Ill. 556; Mackin v. P., 115 Ill. 312; S. v. Raymond, 20 Ia. 582; S. v. Gibbs, 10 Mont. 213; Gandy v. S., 27 Neb. 707; U. S. v. Hall, 44 Fed. R. 864; Reg. v. Boulter, 3 C. & K. 236; Reg. v. Webster, 1 F. & F. 515; Reg. v. Muscot, 10 Mod. 192. And the corroborating evidence must relate to the testimony adduced in support of the charge, and not to some distinct and immaterial matter: S. v. Buie, 43 Tex. 532.

[4] Maines v. S., 26 Tex. Ap. 14; Smith v. S., 22 Tex. Ap. 196. It is error under such statute to fail to instruct the jury accordingly: Gartman v. S., 16 Tex. Ap. 215; Washington v. S., 22 Tex. Ap. 26; Wilson v. S., 27 Tex. Ap. 47; Miller v. S., 27 Tex. Ap. 497; Brookin v. S., 27 Tex. Ap. 701; Grandison v. S., 29 Tex. Ap. 186; Aguierre v. S., 31 Tex. Ap. 519.

who, being competent to give evidence, is worthy of belief.[1] The corroboration required by the general rule may consist of statements made by accused contradictory of the statement which is charged as false;[2] though on this point there are authorities to the contrary.[3] One case has gone so far in mitigating the rule as to the corroboration required as to hold that the manner and nature of the testimony of the accused in his own behalf may be a sufficient corroboration to justify conviction on the testimony of one other witness.[4] And in another case it is said that circumstantial evidence is sufficient in corroboration, which is undoubtedly true.[5] But the circumstantial evidence which is relied on in corroboration must be such as to conclusively demonstrate defendant's guilt.[6] It is said in some cases that the corroborating evidence must be equivalent to the testimony of a second witness.[7] But under the cases already considered, it is evident that this is not the rule, and it is expressly negatived in other cases.[8] The corroboration may consist of documents, entries or other such matter which is competent as to the fact.[9] It must be substantial and not in some particular only;[10] but it need not go to the identical fact sworn to by the contradicting witness, if it is in itself contradictory of the truth of the statement of accused.[11] The evidence corroborating must relate to the same assignment of perjury; proof of one assignment is not corroborated by proof of another, even when all the perjuries as-

[1] Smith v. S., 22 Tex. Ap. 196; Wilson v. S., 27 Tex. Ap. 47; Kitchen v. S., 29 Tex. Ap. 45.

[2] Rex v. Mayhew, 6 C. & P. 315; S. v. Molier, 1 Dev. 263; S. v. Blize, 111 Mo. 464.

[3] Peterson v. S., 74 Ala. 34; Reg. v. Boulter, 3 C. & K. 236.

[4] S. v. Miller, 24 W. Va. 802.

[5] Hernandez v. S., 18 Tex. Ap. 134.

[6] Beach v. S., 32 Tex. Ap. 240. Purely circumstantial evidence without the testimony of one witness is under the Texas statute not sufficient: Waters v. S., 30 Tex. Ap. 284. And see P. v. Wells, 103 Cal. 631.

[7] McClerkin v. S., 20 Fla. 879; Reg. v. Parker, Car. & M. 639.

[8] S. v. Peters, 107 N. C. 876; Hendricks v. S., 26 Ind. 493; S. v. Jean, 42 La. An. 946; Rex v. Lee, 3 Russ. C. & M. 78.

[9] U. S. v. Wood, 14 Pet. 430.

[10] Reg. v. Yates, Car. & M. 132. One witness cannot corroborate himself: Gabrielsky v. S., 13 Tex. Ap. 428. Corroboration in a particular case held sufficient: Flemister v. S., 81 Ga. 768.

[11] C. v. Davis, 92 Ky. 460; Reg. v. Roberts, 2 C. & K. 607; Reg. v. Hare, 13 Cox, 174. As to sufficiency in particular cases, see S. v. Hawkins, 115 N. C. 712; P. v. Porter, 104 Cal. 415.

signed are committed at the same time and place.[1] The rule requiring two witnesses, or one witness corroborated by other evidence, is limited in reason and by weight of authority to the falsity of the oath; the giving of the testimony, or of the making of the statement charged as false, may be proven by one witness without corroboration.[2]

X. SUBORNATION; ATTEMPT TO PROCURE.

§ 893. **What constitutes.**— This offense, which is distinct from that of perjury,[3] is defined as that of procuring another to take a false oath amounting to perjury.[4] And the one who procures the perjury to be committed is an accessory before the fact to that crime.[5] It is essential that perjury be actually committed by the person suborned,[6] and if he is acquitted of perjury the person accused of subornation should be acquitted of that offense.[7] If the witness testifies truthfully the crime of subornation is not committed by the one who procures him to testify, although the person thus procuring knows that the testimony will be in fact false.[8] The accused must not only know the statements to be in fact false, but also that the witness knew them to be false.[9] It is also essential that the false

[1] Lea v. S., 64 Miss. 278; Williams v. C., 91 Pa. St. 493; 1 Greenl. Ev., § 257*a*.

[2] C. v. Pollard, 12 Met. 225; S. v. Wood, 17 Ia. 18; S. v. Hayward, 1 Nott & M. 546; U. S. v. Hall, 44 Fed. R. 864. *Contra*, S. v. Howard, 4 McCord, 159.

[3] The person committing the perjury is not an accomplice of the procurer, and his evidence need not be corroborated as that of an accomplice: U. S. v. Thompson, 31 Fed. R. 331.

[4] 1 Hawk. P. C., ch. 69, § 10; 2 Bish. Cr. L., § 1197. Bishop speaks of it as in its essence perjury, but this seems to be inaccurate. Some crimes may be committed by procurement, but to induce another to swear falsely is evidently not the same thing as the direct giving of false testimony, although it may be equally criminal in its nature. The rule that the perjury and the procuring may be charged in the same indictment (*supra*, § 884) may seem contrary to this view, but, even if well founded in reason, is perhaps not conclusive.

[5] C. v. Smith, 11 Allen, 243.

[6] U. S. v. Wilcox, 4 Blatch. 393; U. S. v. Evans, 19 Fed. R. 912. It is subornation of perjury in an attorney to procure false evidence, knowing it to be false, with the intention of deceiving the court: Beattie v. P., 33 Ill. Ap. 651.

[7] Maybush v. C., 29 Grat. 857, 3 Am. Cr. R. 292 and note.

[8] C. v. Douglass, 5 Met. 241; Coyne v. P., 124 Ill. 17.

[9] U. S. v. Evans, 19 Fed. R. 912; U. S. v. Dennee, 3 Woods, 39.

evidence as given be material and possess the other requisites of perjury; that is, it must be given for use under such circumstances as that it will constitute perjury, and must be so used;[1] but it is not necessary to allege that the perjury was committed by reason of and in consequence of the subornation of the accused.[2] It is enough to charge the perjury on the part of the person who falsely testified, and then allege that the accused did falsely and maliciously incite such person to commit perjury "in the manner and form aforesaid."[3] Though the technical requirements as to the indictment at common law are mitigated by statute, it must show the essential elements of the offense.[4] If the offense committed in a prosecution for a capital offense is more heavily punishable than in another case, the indictment should show the nature of the case in which the perjury was committed.[5]

§ 894. **Attempt to procure or incite.**— Although one who attempts to procure another to commit perjury does not actually commit it and is not technically guilty of subornation of perjury, he is, by both the common law and statute, guilty of a crime.[6] But under statutes which provide only for the punishment of subornation the attempt to suborn is not a crime.[7] Under a prosecution for the attempt it must be affirmatively alleged that the testimony attempted to be procured was material.[8] And the charge as to the false testimony attempted to be procured should be specific, definite and certain as in an indictment for perjury.[9] In this offense as in case of subornation it is essential that the party solicited to give the testimony shall know that the testimony which he is solicited to give would be false, so that if given it would have been perjury.[10] As to the procurement, it is not sufficient to show that the accused told the person solicited to give the testimony that

[1] Smith v. S., 125 Ind. 440; S. v. Geer, 46 Kan. 529; S. v. Leach, 27 Vt. 317; U. S. v. Wilcox, 4 Blatch. 393.

[2] S. v. Geer, 48 Kan. 752.

[3] C. v. Devine, 155 Mass. 224; Stewart v. S., 22 Ohio St. 477.

[4] Rivers v. S., 97 Ala. 72.

[5] Thompson v. S., 89 Wis. 253.

[6] 1 Hawk. P. C., ch. 69, § 10; 2 Bish. Cr. L., § 1197; Ex parte Overton, 2 Rose, 257.

[7] P. v. Thomas, 63 Cal. 482.

[8] S. v. Tappan, 58 N. H. 152; S. v. Joaquin, 69 Me. 218.

[9] Rivers v. S., 97 Ala. 72. But to the contrary it is said that the indictment need not particularly specify the perjury which the accused is charged with having attempted to suborn: S. v. Holding, 1 McCord, 31.

[10] Coyne v. P., 124 Ill. 17.

another would pay him therefor if he would so testify.[1] It is questioned whether a statute against attempting to procure another to commit perjury applies in a case where the perjury solicited was to be committed in another state.[2]

§ 895. **Form of indictment.**— The common-law form seems to be to charge the perjury as committed by the witness who swears falsely and then to charge the procurement of such perjury by the accused. It is believed that the following would be sufficient in most of the states:

Heretofore, to wit, at the January term, A. D. 1896, of the district court of Johnson county, held on the 25th day of January, A. D. 1896, a certain indictment in which John Adams was charged with the crime of burglary in feloniously breaking and entering the dwelling-house of one Timothy Brown, came on to be tried in due form of law and was then and there tried by a jury of such county in that behalf duly sworn, upon which said trial one Henry Wilson appeared as a witness for and in behalf of the said John Adams, and was then and there duly sworn before the duly authorized clerk of said court that the evidence which he, the said Henry Wilson, should give to the court there and the said jury so sworn as aforesaid, touching the matter then in question in the trial of said indictment, should be the truth, the whole truth, and nothing but the truth; and on the said trial of said indictment it became material to inquire where the said John Adams was on the night of the fourteenth and fifteenth of December, A. D. 1895, at which time, as appeared from the evidence, the said burglary charged in the indictment aforesaid was committed, and the said Henry Wilson then and there feloniously, falsely, knowingly, maliciously, wilfully and corruptly testified in substance as follows, to wit: That between the hours of ten and twelve o'clock of said night the said Henry Wilson was in company with the said John Adams at the house of one Peter King in the city of Iowa City in said county of Johnson; and that between the hours of twelve and four o'clock of said night the said Henry Wilson was in company with the said John Adams at the house of one William Jones in said city of Iowa City; whereas, in truth and in fact, as the said Henry Wilson then well knew, the said John Adams was not at the house of the said Peter King between the hours of ten and twelve o'clock of said night or during any portion of that time; and whereas, in truth and in fact, as the said Henry Wilson then well knew, the said John Adams was not at the house of the said William Jones between the hours of twelve and four o'clock of said night or during any portion of that time. And the said A. B.

[1] Watson v. S., 5 Tex. Ap. 11.

[2] Coyne v. P., 124 Ill. 17.

[defendant] did feloniously, wilfully and corruptly, knowing that the testimony so given by the said Henry Wilson as aforesaid was knowingly, wilfully and corruptly false as aforesaid, suborn, incite and procure the said Henry Wilson, being so sworn as aforesaid, to feloniously, knowingly, wilfully, corruptly and falsely testify as aforesaid; whereas, in truth and in fact, as both the said Henry Wilson and the said A. B. then well knew, the said John Adams was not at the house of the said Peter King between the hours of ten and twelve o'clock of said night or during any portion of that time; and whereas, in truth and in fact, as the said Henry Wilson and the said A. B. then well knew, the said John Adams was not at the house of the said William Jones between the hours of twelve and four o'clock of said night or during any portion of that time. Wherefore the grand jurors aforesaid, on their oath aforesaid, do say that the said A. B. did, in manner and form aforesaid, feloniously, wilfully and corruptly commit the crime of subornation of perjury.

CHAPTER 36.

BRIBERY.

§ 896. **What constitutes.**— Bribery is the receiving from or giving to another anything of value, or any valuable service, intended to influence him in the discharge of an official duty.[1] The mere attempt, also, to commit the crime by the offer of a bribe, though it be not accepted, is an indictable offense both by statute and common law.[2] The offense of the bribe-giver does not depend on the guilt of the taker, but is completed whether the officer bribed agrees or intends to carry out the purpose for which the bribe was given or not;[3] nor is it dependent on the fact that the officer to whom the bribe is offered has authority to do the act requested, or upon the fact that the act if done would be effectual and accomplish the object of the briber.[4] The crime of offering a bribe is complete without the tender or production of the money,[5] and the party who offers the bribe is guilty whether the money constituting the bribe comes from himself or another.[6] The bribe offered is sufficient although at the time it was not in existence or did not import value, so long as it would be of value when delivered, as stock in a railway company, to obtain the franchise of which the bribe is offered.[7] A police officer who accepts money for his promise not to arrest any one of a certain class of offenders

[1] 4 Bl. Com. 139; Dishon v. Smith, 10 Ia. 212.

[2] U. S. v. Worrall, 2 Dall. 384; S. v. Ellis, 33 N. J. 102. But an offer by a public officer to accept a bribe is not punishable as a crime under the laws of Texas; and this case holds that the gift must precede the act: Hutchinson v. S., 36 Tex. 293. The Texas courts also hold that where a jailer or other officer suggests his willingness to allow a prisoner to escape for a consideration, the prisoner is not guilty of bribery if he accepts the offer; thus making the guilt depend on the party originating it: O'Brien v. S., 6 Tex. Ap. 665; O'Brien v. S., 7 Tex. Ap. 181.

[3] C. v. Murray, 135 Mass. 530.

[4] S. v. Ellis, 33 N. J. 102.

[5] Jackson v. S., 43 Tex. 421; P. v. Ah Fook, 62 Cal. 493; Rex v. Cripland, 11 Mod. 387. Under the statute there is a distinction between "offering" and "promising:" S. v. Harker, 4 Harr. 559.

[6] P. v. Fong Ching, 78 Cal. 169.

[7] Watson v. S., 39 Ohio St. 123.

is guilty under a statute prohibiting the receiving of a bribe by any executive officer in a matter which "may be brought before him in his official capacity." It need not be shown that an offense was committed and that the officer failed to arrest.[1] Thus, it is not essential that one who attempts to secure an office by bribery should be eligible to the office. The gravamen of the offense is the bribery.[2] So it is an indictable offense at common law to offer a bribe to a justice of the peace, corruptly to decide a suit not then pending and which in fact was never instituted, although the bribe was not accepted.[3] So it is criminal for an officer to receive a consideration to use his position to secure the release of property from seizure.[4] Similarly a police officer is guilty of receiving a bribe if he allows a prisoner to escape for a consideration, although the arrest and custody are illegal.[5]

§ 897. **Who subject to bribery.**— Blackstone describes the offense of bribery as committed by judges or other persons concerned in the administration of justice.[6] Coke mentions bribery as committed only by men in judicial places.[7] The courts have enlarged the scope of the crime so that it includes other officers; thus, in England it has been held a misdemeanor to offer money to the first lord of the treasury to procure a patent for the reversion of the office of the clerk of the supreme court of Jamaica.[8] The later commentators, supported by the adjudged cases, maintain this broader doctrine without exception, that any attempt to influence the conduct of an officer, whether in the executive, legislative or judicial department of the government, by the offer of a reward or pecuniary consideration, is an indictable common-law misdemeanor.[9] It is sufficient that the officer is such *de facto*, although he has not

1 P. v. Markham, 64 Cal. 157.

2 S. v. Graham, 96 Mo. 120.

3 Barefield v. S., 14 Ala. 603.

4 S. v. Potts, 78 Ia. 656.

5 Mosely v. S., 25 Tex. Ap. 515.

6 4 Bl. Com. 139.

7 3 Inst. 145.

8 Rex v. Vaughan, 4 Burr. 2494. And see Rex v. Pollman, 2 Camp. 229; Rex v. Plympton, 2 Ld. Raym. 1377.

9 S. v. Ellis, 33 N. J. 102. A statute providing for the punishment of any person who executes the functions of a public office, when convicted of bribery, includes municipal officers, as aldermen, not state officers only: P. v. Jaehne, 103 N. Y. 182. The usual statutes as to bribery of public officers include a milk inspector: C. v. Lapham, 156 Mass. 480; or a member of the board of education: S. v. Womack, 4 Wash. 19. By statute, in Texas, it is a crime

qualified as directed by statute,[1] or although appointed under an unconstitutional statute.[2] In connection with elections there may be bribery of an officer or of a voter, but this matter will be considered in the chapter relating to elections.[3]

§ 898. **Bribing witness.**—While subornation of perjury is a distinct crime and treated separately under perjury, yet bribery is often resorted to as a means of inducing a witness to absent himself for the purpose of avoiding testifying in a case. It is not important whether he be a material witness, nor with what intent the bribe is offered, nor what is the nature of the case in which he is a witness; the mere fact of the attempt is sufficient.[4] It is not necessary, to render the act criminal, that the witness to whom the bribe is offered shall have been already subpœnaed, nor that the case be already pending in which it is supposed he may be a witness.[5] Other interference with witnesses may be punishable as an obstruction of justice.[6]

§ 899. **Bribing jurors; embracery.**—At common law there is an offense called embracery, the attempting to corruptly influence a juror.[7] Hawkins considers it simply a form of the general offense of maintenance.[8] According to a recent case it consists in practices tending to unduly influence the administration of justice by improperly working upon the minds of the jurors.[9] There must be something more than the forma-

to bribe an attorney as to the discharge of his duties: Reed v. S., 43 Tex. 319.

1 Florez v. S., 11 Tex. Ap. 102.

2 S. v. Gardner, 53 Ohio St. 145, 42 N. E. R. 999.

3 *Infra*, § 947.

4 S. v. Biebusch, 32 Mo. 276. A bribe to a witness to influence his testimony does not cover a case of one who seeks by the aid of gifts to induce a witness to tell the truth when he imagines the witness is prejudiced and intending to testify falsely against him: P. v. Fong Ching, 78 Cal. 169. As to subornation of perjury, see *supra*, § 893.

5 Jackson v. S., 43 Tex. 421; Scoggins v. S., 18 Tex. Ap. 298; Chrisman v. S., 18 Neb. 107. But under a charge of bribing a witness to disobey a subpœna it must be alleged that it was lawfully issued, and a suit was pending, and the names of the parties thereto must be alleged: Brown v. S., 13 Tex. Ap. 358; S. v. Hughes, 43 Tex. 518.

6 *Infra*, § 937.

7 4 Bl. Com. 140; 1 Hawk. P. C., ch. 85; 2 Bish. Cr. L., § 384; Stephen, Dig. Cr. L., art. 128.

8 1 Hawk. P. C., ch. 83, § 3.

9 S. v. Brown, 95 N. C. 685. In another case it is said to be an attempt by either party or a stranger to corrupt or influence a jury, or to incline them to favor one side by gifts or promises, threats or persuasions, or by instructing them in the cause, or any other way, except by opening and enforcing the evidence by counsel at the trial, whether the jurors give

tion of a corrupt purpose; there must be an attempt to carry it into effect.[1] But the statutes providing for the punishment of the attempt to corrupt a juror by offering him improper inducements to influence his decision supersede the common law and the early English statutes relating to embracery, so that under that name the crime is practically unknown with us, the offense which the statutes create being analogous to those of bribery and accepting bribes. Thus, it is criminal by statute for any person to give or offer to give to a juror, or for any juror to ask, receive or agree to receive, any bribe with the intention of influencing his vote;[2] and it is immaterial whether the attempt to bribe was successful.[3] Where the attempt to influence a juror is charged it must appear that the intent was to influence him as to the particular case named.[4]

§ 900. **Venue.**— Writing a letter in Philadelphia and putting it into the postoffice there, directed to an officer of the United States, proposing a bribe, and which reaches him in another state, is an offense completed in the district of Pennsylvania.[5]

§ 901. **Indictment.**— It is not essential to allege the specific value of the bribe offered;[6] nor need the indictment aver that the judgment of the officer bribed was influenced in relation to some matter then pending before him. It is enough to aver the corrupt intention so to influence him in any matter pending before him or which may by law be brought before him.[7] The word "bribe" has a legal and statutory significa-

a verdict or not, and whether the verdict be true or false: Gibbs v. Dewey, 5 Cow. 503; S. v. Sales, 2 Nev. 268. Embracery in itself is only an attempt, and therefore there cannot be a criminal attempt to commit it: S. v. Sales, 2 Nev. 268. These seem to be the only cases in the United States on the subject.

[1] S. v. Brown, 95 N. C. 685.

[2] P. v. Squires, 99 Cal. 327; Caruthers v. S., 74 Ala. 406; S. v. McCrystal, 43 La. An. 907.

[3] S. v. Sales, 2 Nev. 268.

[4] White v. S., 103 Ala. 72.

[5] U. S. v. Worrall, 2 Dall. 384.

[6] Watson v. S., 39 Ohio St. 123; C. v. Chapman, 1 Va. Cas. 138. But some positive offer of a bribe is necessary, and it is not enough to leave it merely conjectural, *e. g.*, that a present or a certain sum of money was offered: S. v. Stephenson, 83 Ind. 246. Where the charge is of furnishing money to bribe a witness it must be stated that the money was paid to the witness: S. v. Baller, 26 W. Va. 90.

[7] C. v. Lapham, 156 Mass. 480. Under a statute making it a crime to bribe any executive, legislative or judicial officer, an indictment for attempting to bribe a milk inspector which sets out all necessary facts in

tion, and is sufficient as a description of the act.[1] The object to be effected may be stated in a general way without stating the particular act sought to be secured.[2]

§ 902. Forms of indictment.—There is no very definite type of indictment for the different forms of bribery, but the following illustrations will be of assistance in forming indictments under the various statutes:

ATTEMPTING TO BRIBE CONSTABLE.

That on ——, one C. D. was duly elected, qualified, commissioned and acting constable in and for the township of ——, in the county of ——, in this state; and that on the day aforesaid one E. F., who was then and there a justice of the peace in and for said township, duly elected, commissioned and qualified, duly issued to said C. D., as such constable, a warrant under his hand and seal in the case of The State of —— v. G. H., then duly pending before said E. F., commanding said C. D., in the name of the state of ——, to immediately arrest said G. H., to answer in said cause, and duly placed said warrant in the hands of said C. D., to be by him served and executed according to law; and that A. B. [the defendant], well knowing the premises, and contriving and feloniously intending to pervert the due course of law and justice, and to prevent the said G. H. from being arrested and taken under and by virtue of the warrant aforesaid, afterwards, to wit, on the day and year aforesaid, in the county aforesaid, feloniously, wickedly and corruptly did offer to the said C. D., so being constable as aforesaid, and having in his custody and possession the said warrant so delivered to him to be executed as aforesaid, a large sum of money, to wit, the sum of ten dollars, if he, the said C. D., would refrain from executing the said warrant, and from taking and arresting the said G. H. under and by virtue of the same.[3]

BRIBERY OF JUSTICE OF THE PEACE.

That on ——, at ——, in said county, a certain cause in which said A. B. was plaintiff, and C. D. was defendant, was pending and undetermined before L. M., then and there being

relation to his official position is sufficient, though it does not set forth in terms that he was an executive officer: S. v. Pearce, 14 Fla. 153; S. v. Womack, 4 Wash. 19; P. v. Turnbull, 93 Cal. 630.

[1] C. v. Stephenson, 3 Met. (Ky.) 226.

[2] Reed v. S., 43 Tex. 319. Where an indictment charged a bribe to vote for a certain resolution, it is sufficient to designate the resolution by its title only: S. v. Smalls, 11 S. C. 262.

[3] This follows to some extent a form found in Gillett, Cr. L., 231, said to be based on Archbold's form.

a justice of the peace of the said county, duly elected, qualified, commissioned and sworn, and then and there acting as a justice of the peace in and for said county; and that the said A. B. [the defendant] then and there feloniously, wickedly and corruptly did give to the said L. M., a justice of the peace as aforesaid, a large sum of money, to wit, the sum of one hundred dollars in money, as a bribe, with intent thereby to influence the decision of the said L. M. as justice of the peace as aforesaid in the said cause then and there pending before him as aforesaid in his official capacity as such justice in favor of him, the said A. B.[1]

RECEIVING OF BRIBE.

That said A. B., on ——, in the county aforesaid, being then and there a ministerial officer, to wit, a city marshal of the city of Omaha, duly and legally appointed, confirmed, qualified and sworn to discharge the duties of that office, it being an office of importance and trust concerning the administration of public justice, law and order within said city, county and state, contriving and intending the powers and duties of his said office and the trust and confidence thereby reposed in him to violate, prostitute and betray, and contriving and intending then and there the powers and duties of his said office to discharge and perform with partiality and favor and contrary to law, then and there, with the intent aforesaid, unlawfully, knowingly, corruptly and feloniously did take, accept and receive from one B. C. a large sum of money, to wit, the sum of three hundred dollars in money and of the value of three hundred dollars, as a bribe and pecuniary reward offered and given by the said B. C. and by the said A. B. taken, accepted and received with the intent and purpose to induce him, the said A. B., in his office aforesaid, to permit, authorize and allow certain gamblers, to wit, C. H., S. B., H. K. and others to the grand jurors unknown, to keep, use and occupy within the corporate limits of said city of Omaha, in the county aforesaid, buildings and rooms for the purpose of and devoted to gambling, to there exhibit gaming tables, gaming establishments, gaming devices and other apparatus to win and gain money and to carry these on, conduct and prosecute the habit, practice and business of gambling, and to induce and influence him, the said A. B., then and there and thereafter not to arrest nor cause to be arrested the said gamblers, and to keep and protect them from arrest and punishment, and free, clear and

[1] This form, though shorter than the preceding, would doubtless be sufficient in most states. It is based on a form found in Moore, Cr. L., 466.

exempt from municipal and police molestation, interference or attack while engaged in the business, practice and profession of gambling as aforesaid in violation of law.[1]

BRIBING OF MILK INSPECTOR.

That C. D., on ——, in the county aforesaid, being a duly appointed inspector of milk in the city of Lowell in said county, took certain specimens of milk, then and there being in the custody and possession of one A. B., hereinafter named, with intent then and there of him, the said A. B., to sell and exchange the same; and that afterwards, to wit, on the day and year last mentioned, the said C. D., then and there being such inspector of milk as aforesaid, in the further performance and discharge of his duty as such inspector of milk, caused said specimens of milk so as aforesaid taken, being then and there in the custody and possession of the said A. B., with the intent then and there of him, the said A. B., to sell and exchange the same as aforesaid, to be analyzed or otherwise satisfactorily tested; that the said analysis and test showed that the said specimens of milk, so as aforesaid taken by the said C. D., being then and there in the custody and possession of the said A. B., with the intent then and there of him, the said A. B., to sell and exchange the same as aforesaid, were not of good standard quality, in violation of the laws as aforesaid then and there in force in relation to the inspection and sale of milk; and thereupon it became the further duty of the said C. D., as such inspector of milk, to record the result of said analysis and test, so as aforesaid made, and preserve the result of said analysis and test as evidence, and to institute a complaint for such violation as aforesaid of the provisions of the laws as aforesaid in respect to the inspection and sale of milk then and there in force in said commonwealth; and that the defendant, unlawfully, wickedly and corruptly devising, contriving and intending to tempt, seduce, bribe and corrupt the said C. D., then and there being an inspector of milk as aforesaid in, of and for said city of Lowell, duly appointed and qualified as such, and as such engaged then and there in inquiring into the quality and kinds of milk sold and exchanged, and the manner and methods of the sale and exchange of milk then and there being made in said city of Lowell, to prostitute and abuse his, the said C. D.'s, trust, and to violate his, the said C. D.'s, duty, as such inspector of milk as aforesaid, towards the good people of this commonwealth in the aforesaid matters and in other matters which might and would properly come before him, the said C. D., as such inspector of milk as aforesaid, he, the said A. B., on ——, at Lowell aforesaid, in the county aforesaid, did wick-

[1] See substantially this form in Guthrie v. S., 16 Neb. 667.

edly, wilfully, unlawfully and corruptly offer and give to the said C. D., then and there being an inspector of milk as aforesaid, a large sum of money, to wit, the sum of two hundred and fifty dollars, with intent thereby then and there wickedly, wilfully, unlawfully and corruptly to influence the act, opinion, decision and judgment of him, the said C. D., as such inspector of milk, in the discharge and performance of his duties as such inspector of milk, in favor of the said A. B.[1]

ATTEMPTING TO CORRUPT WITNESS.

That A. B., on ——, in the county aforesaid, being then and there charged with a criminal offense, and duly indicted under lawful authority by the grand jury of said county of the December term of the district court of said county in the year of ——, for the crime of cutting one C. D. with intent to kill him, the said C. D., in the county of ——, and state aforesaid, and he, the said A. B., being then and there held to bail under said charge, to appear at the February term of the said district court aforesaid, the said court having jurisdiction of the said offense, unlawfully did then and there attempt to corrupt and influence, and did corrupt and influence, one C. D., then and there being, by offering to and paying to him, the said C. D., the sum of fifty dollars, with the further offer and promise to the said C. D. of the further sum of money of five hundred and twenty-five dollars, to corruptly and unlawfully influence and procure him, the said C. D., to leave the said county of ——, and state aforesaid, and go beyond the jurisdiction and process of said district court, and secrete himself so that the said C. D. could not be obtained as a witness on the part of the state of ——, in the said action aforesaid, against the said A. B. aforesaid, the said C. D. being, as the said A. B. then well knew, then and there a very important witness in said action, to wit, the prosecuting witness in the said cause so pending as aforesaid against the said A. B.[2]

§ **903. Evidence.**— To prove the corrupt intent, other instances of bribery of the same character, indicating a general plan or purpose, may be shown.[3]

[1] This is taken from C. v. Lapham, 156 Mass. 480.

[2] For this indictment, see Chrisman v. S., 18 Neb. 107.

[3] Guthrie v. S., 16 Neb. 667. By statute, corroboration of the testimony of one witness is sometimes required: Russell v. C., 3 Bush, 469.

CHAPTER 37.

OFFICIAL MISCONDUCT; EXTORTION.

§ 904. **Usurpation.**— To falsely assume to be and to act as an officer,[1] or to act as such without authority,[2] or before giving a bond as required by law,[3] is criminal. But one who only assumes to be an officer without acting as such,[4] or who acts in good faith under color of right,[5] or being a detective serves a warrant of arrest without assuming to be other than a detective,[6] or being re-elected constable serves a warrant without requalifying,[7] is not guilty under the law.

§ 905. **Abuse of authority.**—An officer who with corrupt motive does an act beyond his lawful authority, assuming to act officially and under his official designation, in such a manner as is likely to deceive and mislead others, is guilty of malfeasance in office,[8] and it is unnecessary that any injurious effect results from his misconduct.[9] Under particular statutes which are found in many of the states it has been held criminal to issue a county warrant where no claim was filed,[10] or to let a contract on disadvantageous terms without advertising for bids,[11] it making no difference that such contract was illegal,[12]

[1] P. v. Cronin, 80 Mich. 646; C. v. Wolcott, 10 Cush. 61. It must appear that the assumption was false, with intent to defraud: U. S. v. Curtain, 43 Fed. R. 433. Extorting money by pretending to be an officer, *e. g.*, a military officer entitled to grant a discharge from service, is criminal: Serlested's Case, Latch, 202. So it is criminal to make use of pretended legal process to compel the payment of money: S. v. Shooter, 8 Rich. 72; and see Bloomfield v. Blake, 6 C. & P. 75. To act as grand juror without being selected was, in an old case, held to be a crime: Scarlet's Case, 12 Coke, 98.

[2] S. v. Bevans, 37 Ia. 178. So it was held that officers who had acted under authority of the Confederate government were civilly liable for their acts: Caperton v. Martin, 4 W. Va. 138, and other cases on pp. 173, 176, 203, 354 and 420 of same volume.

[3] U. S. v. Evans, 1 Cranch, C. C. 149.

[4] P. v. Cronin, 80 Mich. 646; C. v. Wolcott, 10 Cush. 61.

[5] Kreidler v. S., 24 Ohio St. 22.

[6] S. v. Withers, 7 Baxt. 16.

[7] S. v. Bates, 23 Ia. 96.

[8] S. v. Wedge, 24 Minn. 150.

[9] S. v. Glasgow, Cam. & N. 38.

[10] S. v. Pierce, 52 Kan. 521.

[11] S. v. Kern, 51 N. J. 259.

[12] Duty v. S., 9 Ind. Ap. 595.

or to issue a warrant upon a claim for an amount more than was due,[1] or to vote to allow such a claim,[2] or to allow one not due.[3]

§ 906. **Misconduct.**— Where a county attorney procures the discharge of a prisoner through the influence of his office he is guilty of malfeasance even though the writ is insufficient.[4] An officer who destroys a public document,[5] or abstracts legal papers and substitutes others with false returns thereon, is guilty of an indictable offense.[6] Where a public officer receives money for safe keeping, that being outside of his official duties, a conversion of it will not be punishable under a statute for official misconduct;[7] and under a similar statute it was held that embezzlement of property belonging to a private person was not included.[8] Demanding illegal fees may be misconduct under a statute making official misconduct a ground for removal.[9] Where an act acquires weight by reason of the office held by the person doing it that it would not otherwise have,[10] a falsification or misdoing is criminal. Consequently a false certificate as to official records,[11] or as to the amount of witness fees,[12] or a false statement to court by an official under color of his office,[13] is an indictable offense. Unnecessary cruelty or harshness in the treatment of persons under an officer's control is not to be tolerated,[14] and this even extends to a director of the poor who apprentices a child to a cruel and inhuman master.[15] An unlawful arrest may subject the officer to punishment for false imprisonment.[16] But the crime of false imprisonment is discussed elsewhere.[17]

§ 907. **Refusal to act.**—Where an officer has a duty to perform that is not discretionary, a refusal to act makes him lia-

1 S. v. Corning, 44 Kan. 442.

2 S. v. Spidle, 44 Kan. 439.

3 S. v. Crowley, 39 N. J. 264.

4 S. v. Wedge, 24 Minn. 150. See, also, C. v. Mycall, 2 Mass. 136.

5 P. v. Peck, 138 N. Y. 386.

6 Baldwin v. S., 11 Ohio St. 681.

7 S. v. Heath, 70 Mo. 565.

8 S. v. Connelly, 104 N. C. 794.

9 Brackenridge v. S., 27 Tex. Ap. 513.

10 S. v. Leach, 60 Me. 58.

11 S. v. Leach, 60 Me. 58.

12 Bracey v. S., 64 Miss. 17.

13 S. v. O'Gorman, 68 Mo. 179.

14 S. v. Hawkins, 77 N. C. 494; S. v. Yarborough, 77 N. C. 524; Sanders v. S., 55 Ala. 183.

15 C. v. Coyle, 160 Pa. St. 36.

16 P. v. Wheeler, 73 Cal. 252; Ex parte Morrill, 35 Fed. R. 261. To detain a prisoner after expiration of term of sentence is criminal: Knox v. S., 9 Baxt. 202.

17 *Supra*, §§ 485–492.

ble to indictment.[1] It follows that a justice of the peace is punishable for refusing to deliver a transcript of a judgment on tender of the fees,[2] and he may not refuse an adjournment in a proper case[3] or refuse to take an affidavit.[4] A sheriff must levy when he receives a proper writ,[5] it being his protection.[6]

§ 908. **Disregard of duty.**— A grand juror is indictable for rendering himself incapable of doing his duty by reason of intoxication;[7] but a statute punishing wilful failure or refusal to act, or neglect of duty by an officer, does not cover drunkenness.[8]

§ 909. **Neglect of duty.**— A public officer may not neglect a duty imposed by law;[9] nor will the fact that others have failed to do acts which alone will make the performed duty effective be a defense.[10] If it is not an absolute duty but a conditional one, dependent upon the honest exercise of judgment, the omission to perform is not an indictable offense *per se*.[11] In line with this doctrine the courts have held liable to indictment a road supervisor for failing to lay out a road,[12] but not for failing to keep a road in repair where it is impossible;[13] a commissioner of the poor who neglected his duty,[14] as in failing to supply food;[15] a clerk of the court who failed to publish a report as required by law;[16] a constable for failing to execute a valid process;[17] a justice of the peace for taking unreasonably small bail,[18] or failing to take active measures to suppress a riot;[19] an officer for failing to hand over the records to the proper officer as required by law,[20] or to pay over to his suc-

[1] Wilson v. C., 10 Serg. & R. 373; C. v. Genther, 17 Serg. & R. 135.

[2] Bailey v. C., 5 Rawle, 59; Wilson v. C., 10 Serg. & R. 373.

[3] P. v. Calhoun, 3 Wend. 420.

[4] P. v. Brooks, 1 Denio, 457.

[5] S. v. Ferguson, 76 N. C. 197.

[6] Buck v. C., 90 Pa. St. 110. But the officer may be liable civilly: S. v. Tatom, 69 N. C. 35.

[7] Pennsylvania v. Keffer, Addison, 290.

[8] Craig v. S., 31 Tex. Ap. 29.

[9] S. v. Williams, 12 Ired. 172; S. v. Woodbury, 35 N. H. 230; S. v. Hoit, 23 N. H. 355.

[10] S. v. Woodbury, 35 N. H. 230.

[11] S. v. Williams, 12 Ired. 172.

[12] C. v. Reiter, 78 Pa. St. 161.

[13] Moore v. S., 27 Tex. Ap. 439; Parker v. S., 29 Tex. Ap. 372.

[14] S. v. Hoit, 23 N. H. 355.

[15] S. v. West, 14 Lea, 38.

[16] Moose v. S., 49 Ark. 499.

[17] S. v. Ferguson, 76 N. C. 197.

[18] P. v. Coon, 15 Wend. 277; Resp. v. Burns, 1 Yeates, 370; but not for failure to deliver money in the absence of a demand: S. v. Coon, 14 Minn. 456.

[19] Resp. v. Montgomery, 1 Yeates, 419.

[20] Baysinger v. P., 115 Ill. 419.

cessor money coming into his hands by virtue of his office;[1] but a board of aldermen were held not liable for the failure of their properly constituted agents to remove a nuisance.[2]

§ **910. Permitting a prisoner to escape.**— It is criminal misconduct on the part of an officer lawfully having a prisoner in charge to wilfully permit him to escape.[3] It is not necessary to charge that the prisoner was held under a warrant if the offense for which he is alleged to have been held is one for which the arrest might be made without warrant.[4]

§ **911. Public contracts.** — In the public interest county officers are in some states prohibited from becoming interested in any sale to the county,[5] attorneys are prohibited from buying notes for the purpose of collection,[6] and public officers are punishable for becoming interested financially in public contracts.[7]

§ **912. Who deemed officer.**— Provisions as to official misconduct or neglect of duty apply to a deputy[8] or a *de facto* officer;[9] and one who assume the duties of an officer cannot dispute the validity of his appointment when prosecuted for misconduct;[10] nor can he set up invalidity of the writ under which he acted when charged with improper conduct or neglect thereunder.[11]

§ **913. Intent.**— To constitute criminal misconduct on the part of an officer there must be an intentional act,[12] unless the penalty be removal from office; in that case, as the object is to rid the public of an incompetent officer, intent may be imma-

[1] Johnson v. P., 123 Ill. 624. But in most states this is a form of embezzlement: See *supra*, §§ 645-649.

[2] S. v. Hall, 97 N. C. 474. So held also as to county commissioners: S. v. County Commissioners, 97 N. C. 388.

[3] C. v. Mitchell, 3 Bush, 30; S. v. Baldwin, 80 N. C. 390. And see *infra*, § 930.

[4] S. v. Sparks, 78 Ind. 166.

[5] Rigby v. S., 27 Tex. Ap. 55.

[6] P. v. Walbridge, 3 Wend. 120.

[7] Doll v. S., 45 Ohio St. 445.

[8] S. v. Berkshire, 2 Ind. 207. But under a statute imposing penalties on road supervisors for failing to perform their duties, it was held that street commissioners were not included: Graffins v. C., 3 Pen. & W. 502.

[9] S. v. Maberry, 3 Strobh. 144; S. v. Sellers, 7 Rich. 368; Diggs v. S., 49 Ala. 311; S. v. Goss, 69 Me. 22; 2 Hawk. P. C., ch. 19, §§ 23, 28.

[10] S. v. Sellers, 7 Rich. 368.

[11] Turner v. S., 5 Blackf. 254.

[12] S. v. Pinger, 57 Mo. 243; S. v. Kite, 81 Mo. 97; P. v. Ward, 85 Cal. 585; S. v. Smith, 18 N. H. 91; S. v. Miller, 100 N. C. 543; S. v. Buxton, 2 Swan, 57.

terial.[1] If the act be in its nature judicial, the officer can be called to account only by impeachment,[2] unless the misconduct is malicious, in which case it may be indictable;[3] that is, an officer who has a discretion is not liable for errors of judgment,[4] nor for ignorance of the law.[5] A ministerial officer, however, is presumed to know the law.[6] While the act must be knowingly done to constitute official misfeasance, yet it is knowledge of fact rather than of law which must be shown.[7] The nature of the act is often conclusive as to the intent;[8] thus, it is not necessary in charging a justice of the peace with refusing to give a copy of proceedings had before him to allege that he corruptly so refused.[9] So where a particular act or neglect is made criminal, corrupt intent need not be shown.[10] While the presumption of innocence will prevail against circumstances of mere suspicion, it may be overcome by proof of delinquencies of a similar nature.[11]

§ 914. **Extortion.**— This offense consists in the taking by color of office of money or other thing of value that is not due, before it is due, or more than is due.[12] The crime is a species of malfeasance in office. In order that improper influences shall not be brought to bear upon officers with reference to their action, the compensation therefor is fixed by law;[13] and

1 S. v. Leach, 60 Me. 58.

2 Brodie v. Rutledge, 2 Bay, 69; S. v. O'Driscoll, 3 Brev. 526.

3 S. v. Hastings, 38 Neb. 584; S. v. Ross, 4 Ind. 541; P. v. Coon, 15 Wend. 277.

4 C. v. Thompson, 126 Pa. St. 614.

5 S. v. Reeves, 15 Kan. 396.

6 P. v. Burns, 75 Cal. 627; P. v. Brooks, 1 Denio, 457. He will not be protected against mistake of law, even by reliance on the opinion of the attorney-general: Dodd v. S., 18 Ind. 56.

7 P. v. Burns, 75 Cal. 627.

8 French v. White, 4 W. Va. 170; S. v. Morse, 52 Ia. 509.

9 Wilson v. C., 10 Serg. & R. 373.

10 S. v. Hatch, 116 N. C. 1003.

11 Bottomley v. U. S., 1 Story, 135.

12 P. v. Whaley, 6 Cow. 661; Williams v. S., 2 Sneed, 159; C. v. Saulsbury, 152 Pa. St. 554; S. v. Cansler, 75 N. C. 442; U. S. v. Deaver, 14 Fed. R. 595; U. S. v. Waitz, 3 Sawy. 473; 4 Bl. Com. 141; Stephen, Dig. Cr. L., art. 119; 1 Bish. Cr. L., § 573. As to obtaining money by threats, sometimes called in general extortion, see *supra*, § 728 *et seq.* In 2 Bish. Cr. L., § 390, the definition is made broad enough to cover demanding as well as receiving. This is in accordance with the statutory definition found in Texas and perhaps in other states: Brackenridge v. S., 27 Tex. Ap. 513; but the common-law definitions, as given in the cases already cited in this note, seem uniformly to contemplate the receipt and not merely the demanding. The offense is one at common law as well as by statute: S. v. Jones, 71 Miss. 872.

13 P. v. Kalloch, 60 Cal. 116.

a contract for higher fees than allowed by law will not be enforced,[1] nor will an officer be allowed to recover as *quantum meruit* a larger amount than allowed by law.[2] But for extra services not required by law it seems that the officer may charge an additional compensation.[3] Where the statutory offense is committed by unlawful demand, the filing of a claim before the county board for an allowance of fees payable by the county is a sufficient demand to constitute the crime if the fees are not due.[4] Where the crime consists in unlawfully receiving, it is immaterial whether the money or property extorted is received as fees or to defendant's use, and it is sufficient to allege that it was extorted by color of office.[5] The thing exacted must be something of value.[6] As to the act, it is sufficient to constitute the crime that the officer exacts a greater fee than the law allows,[7] or a fee for services not performed,[8] or where no fee is allowed by law for the services rendered.[9] So it is criminal to extort a fee before the officer is entitled to receive it.[10] Thus, if the officer exacts a sum of money as his fees for charges, the lawful amount of which cannot be determined until an adjudication is made by the court, the demand thereof being enforced by the refusal to perform an official duty unless such charges are paid, he is guilty of extortion.[11] Where, however, the service to be rendered is definite, statutes usually authorize the officer to require his fees in advance.[12] The act of issuing or levying an execution for an amount in excess of that which may lawfully be collected is criminal;[13] and the return of the officer as

[1] Gilman v. Des Moines Valley R. Co., 40 Ia. 200. Even if the fees contracted for are less than those allowed by law it seems that the contract would be invalid: Ibid.

[2] Smith v. McLaughlin, 77 Ill. 596.

[3] S. v. Bauer, 1 N. Dak. 273; C. v. Shed, 1 Mass. 227; Ferkle v. P., 16 Ill. Ap. 310.

[4] Brackenridge v. S., 27 Tex. Ap. 513.

[5] P. v. Whaley, 6 Cow. 661. But to receive money for a party to the case to be paid with the view of securing a settlement is not extortion in the officer: White v. S., 56 Ga. 385.

[6] C. v. Cony, 2 Mass. 523.

[7] Ferkle v. P., 16 Ill. Ap. 310.

[8] S. v. Burton, 3 Ind. 93. Where a fee is allowed to a county judge for the trial of a case, it is criminal for him to claim such fee where the case is dismissed: Brackenridge v. S., 27 Tex. Ap. 513.

[9] S. v. Merritt, 5 Sneed, 67. *Contra*, under Texas statute, Smith v. S., 10 Tex. Ap. 413; S. v. Smythe, 33 Tex. 546.

[10] C. v. Bagley, 7 Pick. 279; Lane v. S., 47 N. J. 362.

[11] S. v. Vasel, 47 Mo. 416.

[12] Wilson v. C., 10 Serg. & R. 373.

[13] S. v. Lawrence, 45 Mo. 492; Seany v. S., 6 Blackf. 403; Williams v. S., 2 Sneed, 159.

to the amount collected under the execution will not be conclusive as to the fact.[1] The negotiation by an officer for a bribe for the omission of duty will not constitute extortion, though it will, of course, be punishable under statutes as to bribery.[2] Any officer, whether federal, state, municipal or judicial, and every person occupying an official or *quasi*-official position, may be guilty of the offense.[3] Thus, in England, a church warden[4] and a collector of post-horse duty[5] have been held punishable for extortion. So an attorney as an official of the court may be guilty of extortion.[6] The offense may be committed by a collector of tolls,[7] and a pound-keeper.[8] The officer may be *de facto* or *de jure*,[9] but he must have acted in an official capacity,[10] and the indictment must allege that he was an officer, designating his office.[11] The indictment should charge not only the taking of unlawful fees, but the facts showing the fees to be unlawful.[12] It should state what was demanded and received, and that nothing was due or what was due,[13] and that the officer exacted an amount in excess of what was due;[14] and it must be charged that what was received was for official services.[15] As to the intent, the statute should be limited to cases where there is a purpose to extort, and it may be shown by way of defense that the officer had ground to believe and did believe that he was justified in taking the fees received.[16] Therefore, the indictment should allege and prove that the officer acted knowingly and corruptly.[17] It is not necessary, however, that the indictment charge the extortion to have been wilful, where it otherwise appears that it was intentional.[18]

[1] Williams v. S., 2 Sneed, 159.

[2] S. v. Pierce, 76 Ia. 189.

[3] C. v. Saulsbury, 152 Pa. St. 554.

[4] Rex v. Eyres, 1 Sid. 307.

[5] Rex v. Higgins, 4 C. & P. 247.

[6] Adams v. Savage, Holt, 179; Troy's Case, 1 Mod. 5.

[7] C. v. Carmalt, 2 Binn. 235.

[8] S. v. Critchett, 1 Lea, 271.

[9] C. v. Saulsbury, 152 Pa. St. 554.

[10] Collier v. S., 55 Ala. 125.

[11] T. v. McElroy, 1 Mont. T. 86.

[12] S. v. Maires, 33 N. J. 142; Halsey v. S., 4 N. J. 324; C. v. Saulsbury, 152 Pa. St. 554.

[13] S. v. Coggswell, 3 Blackf. 54.

[14] S. v. Stotts, 5 Blackf. 460.

[15] S. v. Oden, 10 Ind. Ap. 136, 9 Am. Cr. R. 295, and note.

[16] S. v. Cutter, 36 N. J. 125; Leeman v. S., 35 Ark. 438.

[17] Triplett v. Munter, 50 Cal. 644. Evidence that the whole amount of the fee-bill was less than the amount authorized by law is admissible to negative the criminal intent as to one item of excessive charge: Cleaveland v. S., 34 Ala. 254.

[18] S. v. Cansler, 75 N. C. 442.

§ 915. Indictment for misconduct or neglect.— It is necessary to set out the duty of the officer which has been violated;[1] and for this purpose the facts or circumstances giving rise to the duty should be alleged;[2] but it is not necessary to allege the circumstances with great particularity.[3] If the officer has an option between two methods of performing a duty, each must be negatived;[4] or if there is a condition upon which the duty depends, the performance of the condition must be alleged.[5] If the duty is one imposed generally, it is not necessary to specifically allege such duty.[6] In general it is said that to show official misconduct it is necessary to charge such misconduct as would constitute a breach of the official bond.[7] As indicating what is necessary in particular instances to show criminality on the part of the officer, it has been held that in charging a false return on a writ the indictment must state wherein the return was false;[8] and that in charging a justice with taking too small bail the insufficiency must appear.[9]

§ 916. Stating the office.— The indictment should allege what office defendant held,[10] and that he acted under color of his office.[11] If the act is one that may be done by an acting officer or one assuming the office, it will be unnecessary to charge the fact of election or appointment and qualification;[12] and even if such an allegation is made it is sufficient to put it in general terms.[13] If, however, the act is such that it would be of no force unless by a properly elected or appointed officer, the facts showing him qualified to act must be stated.[14]

1 S. v. Hageman, 13 N. J. 314; S. v. Fishblate, 83 N. C. 654; S. v. Com'rs of Wayne Co., 97 N. C. 388.

2 S. v. Winright, 12 Mo. 410; Hall v. P., 90 N. Y. 498; S. v. Boyles, 7 Blackf. 90; S. v. Hunter, 8 Blackf. 212.

3 Baysinger v. P., 115 Ill. 419; P. v. Burns, 75 Cal. 627. After verdict the general allegation of disregard of duty will be sufficient: S. v. Hoit, 23 N. H. 355.

4 S. v. Longley, 10 Ind. 482; S. v. Daniels, 44 N. H. 383; S. v. Fitts, 44 N. H. 621. Matters of defense need not be negatived: S. v. Harsh, 6 Blackf. 346.

5 P. v. Adsit, 2 Hill, 619; S. v. Bailey, 21 N. H. 185; S. v. Demerritt, 64 N. H. 313; S. v. Sanders, 2 Ind. 578; S. v. Hall, 97 N. C. 474.

6 S. v. Miller, 100 N. C. 543.

7 Lathrop v. S., 6 Blackf. 502.

8 Tibballs v. S., 5 Wis. 596.

9 P. v. Coon, 15 Wend. 277.

10 S. v. Lubin, 42 La. An. 79.

11 S. v. Pritchard, 107 N. C. 921; S. v. Kite, 81 Mo. 97.

12 S. v. Hoit, 23 N. H. 355; P. v. Coon, 15 Wend. 277.

13 Wilson v. C., 10 Serg. & R. 373.

14 C. v. Rupp, 9 Watts, 114; Edge v. C., 7 Pa. St. 275.

§ 917. Alleging the intent.— If the breach of duty charged is in the discharge of a judicial office, it is not sufficient to allege the wrongful act as wilfully and knowingly done in the words of the statute, but it must be charged as malicious, corrupt and partial.[1] And in any case if it is sought to charge culpable neglect of duty the indictment must allege the neglect as intentional and corrupt.[2] If fraud is charged it is not necessary to allege the intent to defraud any particular person.[3]

§ 918. Describing the act or omission.— In general, the neglect or misconduct must be definitely specified; thus, in the charge against road overseers for not opening a road as required, there must be a description of the road.[4]

§ 919. Removal; penalty.— A statute providing for removal of an officer for misconduct is not penal;[5] and if the recovery of a penalty is provided for, the proceedings should be by civil action and not by indictment.[6]

[1] S. v. Pinger, 57 Mo. 243; P. v. Ward, 85 Cal. 585; P. v. Coon, 15 Wend. 277; S. v. Gardner, 2 Mo. 23; S. v. Hein, 50 Mo. 362; S. v. Odell, 8 Blackf. 396.

[2] S. v. Buxton, 2 Swan, 57; S. v. Kite, 81 Mo. 97; S. v. Hoit, 23 N. H. 355; S. v. Miller, 100 N. C. 543; S. v. Yarborough, 77 N. C. 524. But the charge need not be that the act was "knowingly" done if it is one forbidden by statute: S. v. Jones, 71 Miss. 872.

[3] S. v. Morse, 52 Ia. 509.

[4] Hardemann v. S., 25 Tex. 179; S. v. Hail, 21 Tex. 587. In an indictment for cruelty to paupers their names must be stated or charged as unknown: S. v. Hawkins, 77 N. C. 494. If the indictment is for making a fraudulent claim, it must be stated to whom the claim was presented: U. S. v. Wallace, 40 Fed. R. 144. But in charging a justice of the peace with misconduct at a particular trial, it is not essential to state the names of the persons tried: S. v. Foy, 93 N. C. 744. In charging failure to return a writ or warrant the writ or warrant must be set out: S. v. Smith, 5 Blackf. 327; but it is not necessary to set out the proceedings preliminary to the writ or warrant: Stewart v. S., 4 Blackf. 171. If it is a warrant, however, it must be shown to have been issued in the name of the state: Floyd v. S., 12 Ark. 43.

[5] S. v. Leach, 60 Me. 58.

[6] S. v. Snuggs, 85 N. C. 541.

CHAPTER 38.

OBSTRUCTING JUSTICE.

I. In General.
II. Resisting an Officer.
III. Breaking Jail; Escape; Rescue.
IV. Tampering with a Witness.

I. In Generai

§ 920. **What constitutes.**— A number of somewhat specific offenses, such as resisting an officer, breaking jail and tampering with witnesses, will be considered under sub-headings of this chapter; but aside from these it is, in general, criminal to obstruct the administration of justice; for instance, by destroying a dead body to prevent an inquest, the case being one in which an inquest may properly be held;[1] by wilfully attempting to destroy public records,[2] or carrying away such records;[3] or by harboring a criminal fleeing from justice;[4] or by refusing as a county jailer to deliver over prisoners when served with a proper order;[5] or by fraudulently causing another to be falsely convicted of a criminal charge in order to get him out of the way;[6] or by advising resistance to an officer;[7] or by obtaining a judicial writ and keeping it for the purpose of impeding the official action of a public officer;[8] or in general by obstructing an officer in the execution of his office.[9] There can be no obstruction of justice, however, without knowledge that justice is being administered.[10]

1 Reg. v. Stephenson, 13 Q. B. D. 331; Reg. v. Price, 12 Q. B. D. 247.

2 U. S. v. De Groat, 30 Fed. R. 64.

3 P. v. Bussey, 82 Mich. 49.

4 Hallett v. S., 29 Ohio St. 168; U. S. v. O'Brian, 3 Dill. 381. As to this, see the discussion of accessory after the fact, *supra*, § 209, and of misprision, *infra*, § 938.

5 U. S. v. Martin, 17 Fed. R. 150.

6 U. S. v. Kindred, 4 Hughes, 493.

7 S. v. Caldwell, 2 Tyler, 212.

8 S. v. Lovett, 3 Vt. 110. In Texas malicious prosecution is made criminal: Dempsey v. S., 27 Tex. Ap. 269; Johnson v. S., 32 Tex. Ap. 58.

9 So held in case of a contempt of a justice of the peace though not amounting to a breach of the peace: Brooker v. C., 12 Serg. & R. 175. Bribery may be punished as a contempt: In re Brule, 71 Fed. R. 943.

10 Pettibone v. U. S., 148 U. S. 197.

II. RESISTING AN OFFICER.

§ 921. **When criminal.**— Resisting an officer who is acting legally in the performance of his duty is in general a crime, though in some courts and under some statutes there has been a tendency to restrict the offense to cases of resisting arrest or the service of a process.[1] The resistance of an officer usually constitutes a common-law assault.[2]

§ 922. **What officers; authority.**— There are cases where a private person is authorized to make arrest, and in such a case resistance to the arrest after the purpose is made known to the one to be arrested will be unlawful;[3] but in general, in order that the resistance to an officer shall be criminal, the officer must be acting within his jurisdiction,[4] and at the proper time,[5] and under a lawful warrant or process.[6] Resistance to an officer attempting to act without a warrant, except in those cases where he is authorized to so act, will be lawful;[7] but even in such cases if the resistance is with undue violence the person resisting may be guilty of assault, or manslaughter, or even murder.[8] The resistance may be criminal though the person to be arrested is not guilty,[9] or is misdescribed in the warrant,[10] or though the warrant is irregular,[11] provided it is one the magistrate has a right to issue,[12] and it is duly issued,[13] and is fair upon its face.[14] To be valid on its face the warrant should

[1] Maverty v. S., 10 Lea, 729; S. v. Putnam, 35 Ia. 561; Broxton v. S., 9 Tex. Ap. 97; McGrew v. S., 17 Tex. Ap. 613; U. S. v. Lukins, 3 Wash. 335.

[2] U. S. v. Doyle, 6 Sawy. 612.

[3] Brooks v. C., 61 Pa. St. 352. As to homicide in resisting arrest, see *supra*, §§ 328, 340.

[4] S. v. Scammon, 22 N. H. 44; Reg. v. Cumpton, 5 Q. B. D. 341; Rex v. Osmer, 5 East, 304; Ferrar's Case, Foster, 313.

[5] Byrant v. S., 16 Neb. 651; Reg. v. Marsden, L. R. 1 C. C. 131.

[6] C. v. Foster, 1 Mass. 488; S. v. Martin, 105 Mass. 178; S. v. Boynton, 75 Ia. 753; Reg. v. Prebble, 1 F. & F. 325.

[7] Bowers v. P., 17 Ill. 373; S. v. Lovell, 23 Ia. 304; Reg. v. Sanders, L. R. 1 C. C. 75.

[8] S. v. Johnson, 76 Mo. 121; Roberts v. S., 14 Mo. 138; Reg. v. Mabel, 9 C. & P. 474. And see *supra*, § 340.

[9] S. v. Garrett, 80 Ia. 589; S. v. Bates, 23 Ia. 96.

[10] S. v. Dula, 100 N. C. 423.

[11] Nolty v. S., 17 Wis. 668; Faris v. S., 3 Ohio St. 159; S. v. Weed, 21 N. H. 262; S. v. Cassady, 52 N. H. 500; S. v. Cassidy, 4 S. Dak. 58.

[12] S. v. Foster, 10 Ia. 435.

[13] S. v. Brown, 6 Wash. 609.

[14] S. v. Cassady, 52 N. H. 500; S. v. Weed, 21 N. H. 262; S. v. McNally, 34 Me. 210; P. v. Cooper, 13 Wend. 379; U. S. v. Tinklepaugh, 3 Blatch. 425.

have the seal of the magistrate or officer issuing it, provided he have a seal.[1] But not only must the warrant be fair upon its face, it must have been issued by an officer having jurisdiction of the offense and of the person against whom it is issued.[2] If, for instance, an affidavit is necessary to give the officer jurisdiction who issued the warrant, it is not sufficient that it be fair upon its face if no affidavit was actually filed.[3] But some courts hold that even knowledge on the part of the officer that the warrant is issued without jurisdiction will not deprive him of the protection of the warrant, provided it be apparently regular.[4] The authority of the officer depends upon the warrant and not upon facts which may afterwards occur; so that the legality of the officer's action cannot be affected by an improper return made by him,[5] nor by his failure to subsequently lodge a complaint,[6] or by the fact that the warrant is subsequently set aside;[7] and the protection of the officer depends upon his warrant and not upon the good faith with which he acts.[8] The protection given to an officer extends to a deputy,[9] a bailiff,[10] a special officer,[11] and a *de facto* officer.[12] And it is immaterial that the person acting as a *de facto* officer is constitutionally incapacitated from holding office.[13] Indeed, the protection which the law gives to official action so as to make resistance unlawful extends to a custodian with whom property is left,[14] a receiver,[15] and a road supervisor;[16] but not to an in-

[1] S. v. Curtis, 1 Hayw. 471.

[2] Grumon v. Raymond, 1 Conn. 40; Tracey v. Williams, 4 Conn. 107; S. v. Leach, 7 Conn. 452; Nichols v. Thomas, 4 Mass. 232; 1 East, P. C. 309.

[3] Housh v. P., 75 Ill. 487.

[4] P. v. Warren, 5 Hill, 440.

[5] S. v. Moore, 39 Conn. 244; S. v. Fifield, 18 N. H. 34.

[6] C. v. Tobin, 108 Mass. 426.

[7] C. v. Roark, 8 Cush. 210.

[8] C. v. Newton, 123 Mass. 420.

[9] S. v. Moore, 39 Conn. 244; U. S. v. Tinklepaugh, 3 Blatch. 425. But resisting one who is deputized by a justice of the peace to serve process in a particular instance does not constitute the offense of hindering an officer in the execution of his office: S. v. McOmber, 6 Vt. 215.

[10] U. S. v. Terry, 41 Fed. R. 771.

[11] S. v. Buchanan, 17 Vt. 573; S. v. Oliver, 2 Houst. 585; Andrews v. S., 78 Ala. 483; S. v. Armistead, 106 N. C. 639.

[12] C. v. Kane, 108 Mass. 423; C. v. Tobin, 108 Mass. 426; P. v. Hopson, 1 Denio, 574; S. v. Dierberger, 90 Mo. 369; Floyd v. S., 79 Ala. 39.

[13] Heath v. S., 36 Ala. 273.

[14] U. S. v. McDonald, 8 Biss. 439.

[15] S. v. Rivers, 66 Ia. 653.

[16] Hendershot v. S., 44 Ohio St. 208; Woodworth v. S., 26 Ohio St. 196. *Contra*, S. v. Putnam, 35 Ia. 561; Maverty v. S., 10 Lea, 729.

spector or other custom-house officer acting beyond his authority;[1] nor a member of the Indian police of the United States.[2]

§ **923. What constitutes resistance.**— Any obstruction to a lawful process, civil or criminal,[3] whether it be by omission or commission, is indictable.[4] Thus, attempting to prevent a bailiff from removing a person from court;[5] or an assault and battery upon,[6] or an obstruction of, the officer by persons not concerned in the proceeding or matter in which he is acting;[7] or combining to oppose the execution of a warrant;[8] or assailing an officer's assistants;[9] or snatching the warrant from the officer's hands;[10] or arresting the officer while acting within the scope of his duty;[11] or obstructing an officer in the charge of goods seized;[12] or by disturbance and breach of the peace preventing the sale of goods under execution,[13] will constitute resistance. The person is not in duty bound to produce property on the demand of the officer,[14] and mere vague threats without intention of carrying them into execution will not constitute the crime;[15] nor will mere refusal to give information to an officer when asked for it.[16] Resistance implies force, and a mere trespass after levy, without violence, is not criminal.[17] But by statute it may be criminal to interfere with the custody of the officer after levy.[18]

§ **924. Intent; justifiable resistance.**— The officer cannot be required to determine subtle questions of property,[19] and if there is reasonable ground of belief that the property belongs to the debtor the real owner is not justified in resisting,[20] unless the officer acts in bad faith.[21] But the wrongful intent is an

[1] C. v. King, 1 Whart. 448; C. v. Gillam, 8 Serg. & R. 50; U. S. v. Baird, 48 Fed. R. 554.

[2] U. S. v. Mullin, 71 Fed. R. 682.

[3] U. S. v. McDonald, 8 Biss. 439.

[4] S. v. Hailey, 2 Strobh. 73.

[5] U. S. v. Terry, 41 Fed. R. 771.

[6] S. v. Webster, 39 N. H. 96.

[7] Roddy v. Finnegan, 43 Md. 490.

[8] U. S. v. O'Neale, 2 Cranch, C. C. 183.

[9] S. v. Emery, 65 Vt. 464.

[10] King v. S., 89 Ala. 43.

[11] Anon., 1 East, P. C. 305.

[12] U. S. v. McDonald, 8 Biss. 439.

[13] S. v. Morrison, 46 Kan. 679.

[14] Crumpton v. Newman, 12 Ala. 199.

[15] S. v. Welch, 37 Wis. 196.

[16] Reg. v. Green, 8 Cox, 441.

[17] Farris v. S., 14 Lea, 295; Davis v. S., 76 Ga. 721.

[18] S. v. Cassidy, 4 S. Dak. 58.

[19] S. v. Fifield, 18 N. H. 34; S. v. Downer, 8 Vt. 424. *Contra*, C. v. Kennard, 8 Pick. 132.

[20] Faris v. S., 3 Ohio St. 159; S. v. Richardson, 38 N. H. 208.

[21] U. S. v. McDonald, 8 Biss. 439.

essential element of the crime of resistance, and if the officer is acting unlawfully and without authority, resistance will not be criminal.[1] The courts do not all agree, however, that it is lawful to resist by force an unwarranted act of the officer not involving the security of the person.[2] And at any rate the resistance must be reasonable and not to the extent of a breach of the peace.[3] It is of course essential to the crime that the person resisting had knowledge of the official character of the person resisted.[4] But intent may be presumed from the commission of a criminal act amounting to resistance, even though there was no specific intent to resist.[5] If there is knowledge of the official character, and that the act is done under a warrant, it is no excuse for resistance that the warrant is not exhibited.[6] And even in the absence of knowledge of official character it will not be excusable homicide to take the life of the officer unless it is necessary for self-defense.[7]

§ 925. **Indictment.**—It should be alleged that the warrant or process under which the officer was acting was issued out of a court having jurisdiction;[8] and if the court is one of limited jurisdiction, the facts showing jurisdiction should be stated.[9] It must also appear that the process was such as to give the officer authority.[10] In some cases it has been held that the general allegation of this fact is sufficient;[11] other cases hold it necessary to describe the process particularly,[12] or set it out in general terms;[13] and even that it must be set out in order that

[1] P. v. Hopson, 1 Denio, 574; P. v. Hubbard, 24 Wend. 369; Agee v. S., 64 Ind. 340; Smith v. P., 99 Ill. 445; C. v. Eyre, 1 Serg. & R. 347; U. S. v Terry, 42 Fed. R. 317; Rex v. Mitton, 3 C. & P. 31.

[2] Smith v. P., 99 Ill. 445.

[3] C. v. Kennard, 8 Pick. 132; P. v. Cooper, 13 Wend. 379.

[4] P. v. Durfee, 62 Mich. 487; S. v. Garrett, 80 Ia. 589; S. v. Grant, 76 Mo. 236; S. v. Hayes, 89 Mo. 262.

[5] U. S. v. Keen, 5 Mason, 453. The crime of assault upon a constable in the execution of his duty may be committed without knowledge that he was in the execution of his duty if he was actually assaulted: Reg. v. Forbes, 10 Cox, 362.

[6] S. v. Dula, 100 N. C. 423.

[7] S. v. Underwood, 75 Mo. 230.

[8] S. v. Beasom, 40 N. H. 367; U. S. v. Tinklepaugh, 3 Blatch. 425.

[9] Cantrill v. P., 8 Ill. 356; S. v. Tuell, 6 Blackf. 344.

[10] Hill v. S., 43 Tex. 329; Pierce v. S., 17 Tex. Ap. 232.

[11] McQuoid v. P., 8 Ill. 76; Bowers v. P., 17 Ill. 373; S. v. Hailey, 2 Strobh. 73; S. v. Moore, 39 Conn. 244; S. v. Hayes, 24 Mo. 358; S. v. Perkins, 43 La. An. 186; S. v. Flagg, 50 N. H. 321; S. v. Roberts, 52 N. H. 492; S. v. Cassady, 52 N. H. 500; Slicker v. S., 13 Ark. 397.

[12] S. v. Hailey, 2 Strobh. 73.

[13] S. v. Roberts, 52 N. H. 492; Slicker v. S., 13 Ark. 397.

the court may determine whether it is valid on its face.[1] It must be alleged that the officer was acting within his jurisdiction,[2] and that he had authority to act;[3] but it is not necessary to allege that he was duly and legally appointed.[4] It must appear that the officer was in the discharge of his official functions;[5] for instance, that he was acting under process which he was authorized to serve.[6] But it is not necessary to state from whom or how the warrant was received;[7] nor is it necessary to allege that the officer had the warrant in his possession at the time of the resistance.[8] The mere statement that the officer was in the due and legal performance of his duty is not enough without showing what he was doing.[9] It is generally presumed that the officer acted properly,[10] and the manner of execution of the process need not be alleged,[11] but it must appear what official duty the officer was performing.[12]

§ 926. **Allegation of act.**— The mode of obstruction should be alleged;[13] that is, the facts should be made to appear.[14] The obstruction charged must be proven.[15] The particulars as to the name of the person to be arrested under the process need

[1] S. v. Henderson, 15 Mo. 486; S. v. Downer, 8 Vt. 424; S. v. Burt, 25 Vt. 373; S. v. Shaw, 3 Ired. 20.

[2] S. v. Scammon, 22 N. H. 44; Rex v. Osmer, 5 East, 304.

[3] S. v. Dickerson, 24 Mo. 365; S. v. Downer, 8 Vt. 424; S. v. Burt, 25 Vt. 373; S. v. Hooker, 17 Vt. 658; S. v. Hailey, 2 Strobh. 73; U. S. v. Tinklepaugh, 3 Blatch. 425.

[4] S. v. Cassady, 52 N. H. 500; S. v. Roberts, 52 N. H. 492.

[5] U. S. v. Beale, 4 Cranch, C. C. 313.

[6] Cantril v. P., 8 Ill. 356; Bowers v. P., 17 Ill. 373; S. v. Hooker, 17 Vt. 658. But the offense of assaulting an officer in the discharge of his official duty may be charged without any allegation that he either had or was attempting to serve process at the time of the assault: P. v. Nash, 1 Idaho, 206.

[7] S. v. Estis, 70 Mo. 427; S. v. Hooker, 17 Vt. 658; Blake v. U. S., 71 Fed. R. 286.

[8] S. v. Estis, 70 Mo. 427.

[9] S. v. Flagg, 50 N. H. 321; S. v. Johnson, 42 La. An. 559.

[10] S. v. Freeman, 8 Ia. 428; S. v. Hooker, 17 Vt. 658.

[11] S. v. Fifield, 18 N. H. 34; S. v. Downer, 8 Vt. 429; Lamberton v. S., 11 Ohio, 282; U. S. v. Batchelder, 2 Gall. 15.

[12] S. v. Maloney, 12 R. I. 251.

[13] S. v. Maloney, 12 R. I. 251; S. v. Hailey, 2 Strobh. 73; S. v. Downer, 8 Vt. 424; S. v. Burt, 25 Vt. 373. But to the effect that a general allegation as to the act of defendant is sufficient, see McQuoid v. P., 8 Ill. 74; S. v. Fifield, 18 N. H. 34; U. S. v. Batchelder, 2 Gall. 15.

[14] Lamberton v. S., 11 Ohio, 282; U. S. v. Smith, 1 Dill. 212; Reg. v. Sherlock, L. R. 1 C. C. 20.

[15] Jones v. S., 60 Ala. 99. But proof of assault and battery sufficiently supports a charge of resistance: S. v. Gilbert, 21 Ind. 474.

not be alleged;[1] nor as to the fact of the return of the writ;[2] and it is sufficient to state facts such as will show that the action of the officer was authorized.[3] It is usually held sufficient that the indictment follows the language of the statute.[4]

§ 927. **Charging the intent.**— The indictment must state that defendant had knowledge that the person arrested was an officer,[5] and failure to so state may be taken advantage of even after verdict in arrest of judgment.[6] Such terms as "wilfully, knowingly and designedly" sufficiently charge the intent.[7]

§ 928. **Duplicity.**— The indictment may without duplicity charge defendant with assaulting and beating the officer as well as obstructing him in the discharge of his duty.[8] And in general the different forms in which the offense may be committed may be charged conjunctively.[9]

§ 929. **Evidence.**— Proof that the officer is one *de facto* is sufficient,[10] without evidence of his official appointment.[11] In regard to whether the offense was committed for which the offender was being arrested, the record of his conviction is conclusive;[12] but acquittal does not prove the arrest to have been illegal.[13] The proceedings resulting in the issuance of the warrant need not be shown,[14] for the burden is on the defense to show the illegality of the warrant,[15] and there may be a conviction even without proof that the officer had a warrant,[16] and he is presumed to be acting within his authority.[17] Knowledge of the officer's character may be shown by proof of personal

[1] S. v. Dunn, 109 N. C. 839; S. v. Garrett, 80 Ia. 589.

[2] S. v. Fifield, 18 N. H. 34.

[3] S. v. Hooker, 17 Vt. 658.

[4] S. v. Perkins, 43 La. An. 186; S. v. Fifield, 18 N. H. 34; U. S. v. Batchelder, 2 Gall. 15.

[5] C. v. Israel, 4 Leigh, 675; S. v. Smith, 11 Oreg. 205; S. v. Downer, 8 Vt. 424; S. v. Burt, 25 Vt. 373; S. v. Deniston, 6 Blackf. 277; S. v. Maloney, 12 R. I. 251; Blake v. U. S., 71 Fed. R. 286; U. S. v. Tinklepaugh, 3 Blatch. 425.

[6] S. v. Carpenter, 54 Vt. 551. But see C. v. Caldwell, 14 Mass. 330.

[7] C. v. Kirby, 2 Cush. 577. But if, by statute, it is not required that the act be knowingly done, such an allegation is unnecessary in the indictment: S. v. Perkins, 43 La. An. 186.

[8] S. v. Hailey, 2 Strobh. 73.

[9] S. v. Smith, 24 Tex. 285.

[10] C. v. Kane, 108 Mass. 423; C. v. Tobin, 108 Mass. 426.

[11] S. v. Holcomb, 86 Mo. 371.

[12] C. v. Feldman, 131 Mass. 588.

[13] C. v. Coughlin, 123 Mass. 436; Montgomery v. Sutton, 67 Ia. 497.

[14] Reg. v. Davis, 8 Cox, 486.

[15] Kernan v. S., 11 Ind. 471. But see U. S. v. Batchelder, 2 Gall. 15.

[16] P. v. Nash, 1 Idaho, 206.

[17] S. v. Freeman, 8 Ia. 428.

acquaintance on the part of the defendant.[1] By way of proving lawful resistance defendant may show that the property being levied upon was not the property of the defendant in the execution,[2] but not that there was connivance between the plaintiff and defendant in the execution to cheat him out of his property.[3]

III. BREAKING JAIL; ESCAPE; RESCUE.

§ **930. What criminal.**— One who is in lawful confinement or lawful custody of an officer is guilty of a crime in escaping from such confinement or custody.[4] An officer who wilfully or negligently allows a prisoner to escape,[5] or any party who assists in the escape,[6] or the prisoner who escapes, is guilty of a crime.[7] It is unnecessary that there be force used in the accomplishment of the escape.[8] A prisoner who escapes through the negligence of an officer is himself guilty,[9] even though he walks away without being interfered with.[10] But there must be an actual escape in order to render one who attempts to assist liable.[11] A rescue is assisting a prisoner to escape by force with knowledge of the fact that he is lawfully under arrest.[12]

1 C. v. Sawyer, 142 Mass. 530.

2 Oliver v. S., 17 Ark. 508.

3 S. v. Buchanan, 17 Vt. 573.

4 S. v. Brown, 82 N. C. 585; C. v. Farrell, 5 Allen, 130. The offense is a misdemeanor: S. v. Murray, 15 Me. 100; C. v. Morihan, 4 Allen, 585. A statute providing a punishment for an escape from the penitentiary to be imposed otherwise than as a result of a criminal prosecution, held unconstitutional: S. v. Lewin, 53 Kan. 679. Under a statute authorizing the hiring out of convicts, an escape from the person to whom the convict is hired may be criminal: Carter v. S., 29 Tex. Ap. 5. So there may be a crime in escaping from one who has become bail: Smith v. S., 81 Ala. 74. Under statute, escape from jail may be a different offense from that of escape from an officer: Mason v. S., 7 Tex. Ap. 623.

5 Smith v. S., 76 Ala. 79; Meehan v. S., 46 N. J. 355. And see *supra*, § 910.

6 P. v. Tompkins, 9 Johns, 70; Ash v. S., 81 Ala. 76; Williams v. S., 24 Tex. Ap. 17.

7 Ex parte Clifford, 29 Ind. 106; White v. S., 13 Tex. 133.

8 C. v. Farrell, 5 Allen, 130; S. v. Doud, 7 Conn. 384; Hobert's Case, Cro. Car. 209; 4 Bl. Com. 129; 2 Hawk. P. C., ch. 18, § 1.

9 Butler v. Washburn, 25 N. H. 251.

10 Floyd v. S., 79 Ala. 39.

11 Hughes v. S., 6 Ark. 131; Hurst v. S., 79 Ala. 55. But the offense of attempting to assist a prisoner to escape may be punishable by statute: Poncio v. S., 28 Tex. Ap. 104; Ash v. S., 81 Ala. 76; Simmons v. S., 88 Ga. 169.

12 4 Bl. Com. 131. By the Georgia statute a rescue is committed when the prisoner is taken out of confinement or custody without any effort on his part: Robinson v. S., 82 Ga. 535.

§ **931. Legality of arrest or confinement.**— It is not criminal to escape from unlawful imprisonment,[1] nor to assist another to make such escape.[2] A prisoner who breaks out of a jail where he is unlawfully confined is not guilty of a crime, because as to him the building is not a jail;[3] but the lawfulness of the imprisonment does not depend upon the actual guilt or innocence of the prisoner.[4] If the arrest and confinement are lawful the prisoner should not escape whether he is guilty or innocent;[5] even a right to release on *habeas corpus* will not justify breaking jail.[6] And danger of injury to the health due to the lack of sanitary provisions in the jail will only justify a reasonable effort to secure relief and not a breaking out.[7] A mere informality or irregularity in the commitment will not justify an escape,[8] such a case being different from one where the arrest or confinement are wholly without authority.[9] A proper *mittimus* makes the imprisonment lawful.[10] Non-payment of costs may be made the ground of imprisonment, and if so, it may be criminal to escape before they are paid.[11]

§ **932. Pound-breach.**— An offense analogous to that of rescue is pound-breach, the offense of releasing distrained animals which have been lawfully impounded; or *rescous*, the offense of releasing such animals on the way to the pound.[12]

§ **933. Intent.**— The intent is a necessary element of the crimes here considered,[13] and must be present when the act is committed;[14] but it may be inferred from the nature of the thing done.[15] If the officer allowing a prisoner to escape is not aware that he is a prisoner so that there is an official duty to perform with reference to him,[16] there will be no criminality,

[1] S. v. Leach, 7 Conn. 452; Housh v. P., 75 Ill. 487; S. v. Beebe, 13 Kan. 589; S. v. Jones, 78 N. C. 420.

[2] P. v. Ah Teung, 92 Cal. 421; Hillian v. S., 50 Ark. 523.

[3] S. v. Leach, 7 Conn. 452.

[4] S. v. Lewis, 19 Kan. 260; S. v. Bates, 23 Ia. 96; Holland v. S., 60 Miss. 939; C. v. Miller, 2 Ashmead, 61.

[5] C. v. Morihan, 4 Allen, 585; S. v. Murray, 15 Me. 100.

[6] S. v. Murray, 15 Me. 100.

[7] S. v. Davis, 14 Nev. 439.

[8] S. v. James, 37 Conn. 355; S Murray, 15 Me. 100.

[9] Goodwin v. Griffis, 88 N. Y. 629; Dunford v. Weaver, 84 N. Y. 445; 2 Bish. Cr. L., § 1094.

[10] C. v. Miller, 2 Ashmead, 61; S. v. Hollon, 22 Kan. 580. It may depend upon the authority of the jailer: C. v. Barker, 133 Mass. 399.

[11] Riley v. S., 16 Conn. 47.

[12] [illegible] v. Young, 18 N. H. 543; S. v. B[illegible]ett, 42 N. H. 466; C. v. Beale, 5 [illegible]k. 514; 3 Bl. Com. 146; 2 Hawk. C., ch. 10, § 56.

[13] Meehan v. S., 46 N. J. 355.

[14] Riley v. S., 16 Conn. 47.

[15] Randall v. S., 53 N. J. 488; P. v. Rose, 12 Johns. 339.

[16] S. v. Fry, 40 Kan. 311; S. v. Law-

but the officer cannot excuse himself for mere irregularity in the writ or proceeding.[1]

§ 934. **Indictment.**— In some states it is held necessary to set out the crime for which the prisoner was confined,[2] and the order of court under which he was confined;[3] but a general allegation of the charge under which he was confined is sufficient;[4] and indeed, there is good authority to the effect that it is not necessary to charge the facts as to the cause of the arrest,[5] nor as to the nature of the crime,[6] nor that the indictment was valid.[7] It is necessary to allege the acts done by way of assistance where that is the offense charged.[8] Where the offense is that of furnishing implements to be used in making the escape, the indictment should state what the implements were,[9] and that they were useful for that purpose.[10] The indictment should also allege intent or knowledge.[11] But to charge the act as unlawful and negligently or forcibly done is usually sufficient.[12] To charge an officer with aiding, assisting and suffering a prisoner to escape is not objectionable on the ground of duplicity, as the charges as to aiding and assisting are surplusage.[13]

§ 935. **Practice.**— Where the prisoner under arrest is guilty of the offense of escape he should be tried for the crime for which he was arrested first,[14] and the trial for escape or jail-breach should come after the sentence for the original offense is served.[15] The additional sentence will therefore follow after the original sentence.[16]

rence, 43 Kan. 125; S. v. Errickson, 32 N. J. 421.

1 Martin v. S., 32 Ark. 124; S. v. Garrett, 82 N. C. 580.

2 P. v. Hamaker, 92 Mich. 11; Kyle v. S., 10 Ala. 236; S. v. Hilton, 26 Mo. 199; S. v. Jones, 78 N. C. 420.

3 S. v. Dunn, 25 N. J. 214; Martin v. S., 32 Ark. 124.

4 S. v. Ritchie, 107 N. C. 857.

5 S. v. Hedrick, 35 Tex. 485.

6 S. v. Addcock, 65 Mo. 590; S. v. Johnson, 93 Mo. 73.

7 Gunyon v. S., 68 Ind. 79.

8 C. v. Filburn, 119 Mass. 297; C. v. Malloy, 119 Mass. 347.

9 Hurst v. S., 79 Ala. 55.

10 Ramsey v. S., 43 Ala. 404.

11 C. v. Filburn, 119 Mass. 297; Walker v. S., 91 Ala. 32; S. v. Hilton, 26 Mo. 199. *Contra*, P. v. Murray, 57 Mich. 396. It need not be alleged that the rescuer knew the prisoner to be committed on a charge of felony: Wilson v. S., 61 Ala. 151.

12 S. v. McLain, 104 N. C. 894; S. v. Ritchie, 107 N. C. 857; C. v. Malloy, 119 Mass. 347. It is not necessary to charge jail-breaking as done wilfully and by force: Loggins v. S., 32 Tex. Ap. 358.

13 Clemons v. S., 4 Lea, 23.

14 S. v. Cuthbert, T. U. P. Charl. 13.

15 S. v. Jolly, 96 Mo. 435; Ex parte Meyers, 44 Mo. 279.

16 Ex parte Clifford, 29 Ind. 106.

§ 936. **Evidence.**— It must be shown in behalf of the prosecution that the prisoner was in legal custody,[1] which may be done by transcript of the judgment.[2] If an officer is prosecuted for negligently permitting a prisoner to escape he must show that he used due care.[3] Where the charge is of assisting a prisoner while attempting to escape, it may be shown that the accused held one of the officer's *posse*, although his name is not set out in the indictment.[4]

IV. TAMPERING WITH A WITNESS.

§ 937. **Nature of the offense.**— The crime of bribing a witness has already been considered,[5] but it is an offense also at common law to induce, solicit or persuade a witness not to appear as such,[6] or to hinder or prevent or attempt to prevent his attendance before a court of justice;[7] or to procure false evidence, as, for instance, an affidavit of one not qualified to testify.[8] It is immaterial that the subpœna for the witness has not yet been issued.[9] It is not necessary to allege the date of the subpœna nor that the witness' evidence would be material;[10] nor that there was a cause pending requiring his attendance.[11] It is not sufficient, however, to merely allege the endeavor to influence or obstruct the administration of justice by means of a threatening letter.[12] Where the means of influencing the action of a witness is charged to have been by an assault, it is not sufficient to show an assault committed after the testimony was given, as such a wrong would not impede the course of justice.[13] In such a case the assault must have some relation to the fact of the person assailed being a witness.[14]

1 P. v. Johnson, 110 N. Y. 134.

2 Sanford v. S., 11 Ark. 328.

3 S. v. Lewis, 113 N. C. 622.

4 Perry v. S., 63 Ga. 402.

5 *Supra*, § 898. To support a charge of furnishing money to bribe a witness it must appear that the money was paid to the witness: S. v. Baller, 26 W. Va. 90.

6 S. v. Ames, 64 Me. 386; Perrow v. S., 67 Miss. 365.

7 C. v. Reynolds, 14 Gray, 87; S. v. Keyes, 8 Vt. 57; S. v. Holt, 84 Me. 509.

8 P. v. Brown, 74 Cal. 306.

9 S. v. Keyes, 8 Vt. 57. One who appears voluntarily is a witness for this purpose: S. v. Tisdale, 41 La. An. 338.

10 C. v. Reynolds, 14 Gray, 87.

11 S. v. Holt, 84 Me. 509.

12 U. S. v. Armstrong, 59 Fed. R. 568.

13 U. S. v. Thomas, 47 Fed. R. 807.

14 U. S. v. Kee, 39 Fed. R. 603.

CHAPTER 39.

MISPRISION OF FELONY; COMPOUNDING OFFENSES.

§ 938. **What constitutes misprision.**— It has already appeared that one who assists a felon to escape with knowledge of the commission of the felony is, at common law, deemed guilty as an accessory after the fact,[1] but it has also appeared that one who in no way participates in procuring, planning or committing the crime or in assisting the criminal is not guilty of such crime either as principal or accessory, though he may have been cognizant of the purpose to commit it and may have taken no steps to prevent it.[2] However, at common law, it is criminal to conceal the commission of a felony with knowledge thereof, although without assistance therein such as to constitute guilt as accessory after the fact.[3] In some states the offense is recognized by statute.[4] But the whole doctrine of guilt by misprision, like that of the guilt involved in being accessory after the fact, has become practically obsolete, and perhaps not a single case can be cited in which punishment for such connection with a felony has been inflicted in the United States. If such criminal liability is recognized in any form it is by statute making particular acts of that character substantive offenses rather than by the preservation of the common-law doctrine of misprision of felony.

§ 939. **Compounding offenses.**— Whatever may have been the common law of England on the subject, it is well settled in the United States, as has already appeared, that a civil remedy in behalf of the injured party is not denied by reason of the fact that the wrong involves also a crime; nor is it even suspended until the crime has been prosecuted;[5] there-

[1] See *supra*, § 209.

[2] Connaughty v. S., 1 Wis. 159; S. v. Hildreth, 9 Ired. 440; Carroll v. S., 45 Ark. 539. And see *supra*, §§ 194, 209.

[3] 4 Bl. Com. 119–121; 1 Hawk. P. C., ch. 59; Stephen, Dig. Cr. L., art. 157; 1 Bish. Cr. L., §§ 716–722; S. v. Hann, 40 N. J. 228.

[4] S. v. Hann, 40 N. J. 228.

[5] *Supra*, § 11.

fore the person injured may settle with the wrong-doer the civil injury committed, and such settlement will not be unlawful or criminal;[1] but if the person injured receives anything of value in consideration of agreeing to stifle criminal proceedings he puts himself in a position to hinder the administration of justice, and his act in thus agreeing not to prosecute may constitute the crime of compounding a criminal offense.[2] But it is uncertain whether at common law it is criminal to compound a misdemeanor. The law seems to favor, rather than discourage, the adjustment of controversies which do not affect the public, and this distinction is suggested in some of the cases;[3] but in other cases it is held that it is illegal to compromise even a misdemeanor.[4] This question has usually arisen, however, in civil cases wherein the validity of a contract made in consideration of the stifling of a prosecution for a criminal offense has arisen, the general proposition being that, if the compounding be criminal, any contract made in whole or in part in consideration of such compounding is invalid and not enforceable.[5] So it is equally unlawful to lend money for the purpose of enabling another to compound an offense, and the money so loaned cannot be recovered back.[6] By some statutes the compromise of a prosecution for a minor offense may be lawfully made by approval of court;[7] but after conviction there can be

[1] Burnham v. Holt, 14 N. H. 367; Reg. v. Hardey, 14 Q. B. 529. And see Deere v. Wolff, 65 Ia. 32. But it will be criminal to compound the offense under the pretense of only receiving satisfaction for the civil wrong: S. v. Duhammel, 2 Harr. 532.

[2] 4 Bl. Com. 133; 1 Hawk. P. C., ch. 59; 1 Bish. Cr. L., §§ 709–715*a*. The early form of the offense seems to have been that of taking back the goods in larceny or robbery with an agreement not to prosecute. This is called "theftbote," and is something more than misprision of the felony: 3 Inst. 134.

[3] Keir v. Leeman, 6 Q. B. 308; Johnson v. Ogilby, 3 P. Wms. 277; Rex v. Crisp, 1 B. & A. 282; Stancel v. S., 50 Ga. 152; Goolsby v. Bush, 53 Ga. 353; Dodson v. McCauley, 62 Ga. 130.

[4] Partridge v. Hood, 120 Mass. 403; Jones v. Rice, 18 Pick. 440.

[5] Plumer v. Smith, 5 N. H. 553; Bowen v. Buck, 28 Vt. 308; Baird v. Boehner, 77 Ia. 622; Smith v. Steely, 80 Ia. 738; Allison v. Hess, 28 Ia. 388; Peed v. McKee, 42 Ia. 689; Friend v. Miller, 52 Kan. 139; Springfield F. & M. Ins. Co. v. Hull, 51 Ohio St. 270.

[6] Plumer v. Smith, 5 N. H. 553.

[7] Pearce v. Wilson, 111 Pa. St. 14; Geier v. Shade, 109 Pa. St. 180; S. v. Hunter, 14 La. An. 71; Reg. v. Lovett, 11 Cox, 602; Rex v. Gotley, Russ. & Ry. 84. But this is discretionary with the court: McDaniel v. S., 27 Ga. 197. In Kentucky something in the nature of a compounding is authorized by the provision that in certain offenses the penalty may be

no remission of the penalty on account of any compounding or compromise with the compounder.[1]

§ 940. Further as to the crime of compounding.— There are but few illustrations of the crime of compounding a felony. It seems that it is immaterial whether any offense was actually committed, such as is charged to have been compounded, the mere agreement to stifle a prosecution being in itself a wrong which the law punishes.[2] Therefore the acquittal of the person charged with the crime which it is claimed was compounded is immaterial.[3] Neither is it necessary to allege that the defendant actually desisted from the prosecution in consideration of his agreement;[4] indeed, the offense of compounding may be committed by a person other than the one injured by the crime.[5] It is the receiving of anything of value in consideration for an agreement not to prosecute which is criminal, and the offense may therefore be committed by receiving a note, even though such a note is never collected nor collectible.[6] Knowledge of the commission of the crime must be alleged and proven in a prosecution for compounding.[7] It is sufficient to charge in general terms the commission of an offense by one party, and knowledge thereof by the defendant, and the receipt by him of some consideration to compound or conceal it or abstain from the prosecution thereof.[8] The person who pays the consideration for the agreement to stifle prosecution is not an accomplice in the crime of compounding, and therefore his testimony does not require corroboration.[9]

reduced one-half upon confession of judgment: Sneed v. C., 6 Dana, 338. By English statute it was criminal to take money under pretense of helping a man to goods stolen from him: Rex v. Ledbitter, 1 Moody, 76; Reg. v. Pascoe, 2 C. & K. 927.

[1] P. v. Bishop, 5 Wend. 111; Bury v. Levy, 1 W. Bl. 443.

[2] Fribly v. S., 42 Ohio St. 205; Smith v. Steely, 80 Ia. 738; Reg. v. Best, 9 C. & P. 368.

[3] P. v. Buckland, 13 Wend. 592.

[4] Reg. v. Burgess, 16 Q. B. D. 141; Rex v. Stone, 4 C. & P. 379; Reg. v. Daly, 9 C. & P. 342.

[5] S. v. Ruthven, 58 Ia. 121; Reg. v. Burgess, 16 Q. B. D. 141.

[6] C. v. Pease, 16 Mass. 91.

[7] S. v. Henning, 33 Ind. 189.

[8] Watt v. S., 97 Ala. 72; P. v. Bryon, 103 Cal. 675. If the date of the alleged felony is stated as subsequent to the date of the alleged compounding, the indictment is invalid: S. v. Dandy, 1 Brev. 395.

[9] Ash v. S., 81 Ala. 76.

PART IX.

OFFENSES AGAINST THE ELECTIVE FRANCHISE.

CHAPTER 40.

VIOLATION OF ELECTION LAWS.

§ 941. **Under statutes.**— While various acts concerning elections have been held to be offenses at common law as tending to disturb the due regulation and domestic order of the state,[1] yet indictments for offenses of this character are almost uniformly drawn under some statutory enactment.

§ 942. **What deemed an election.**— To subject a person to punishment for having illegally voted, the election must be legal and valid;[2] but a mere irregularity as to holding the election will not prevent violation of the election laws with reference thereto being punished. It must appear that the election was one authorized by law and duly called by the proper officers;[3] but mere irregularities in the manner of holding it are no defense,[4] and if the election is held under color of law that is sufficient.[5] Only such elections as are contemplated by the statute punishing offenses thereat are to be deemed within its provisions;[6] but within this scope may be a town meeting,[7] a school election,[8] a municipal election,[9] or an election to determine whether intoxicating liquors shall be sold under a local-option law.[10] But under particular statutes municipal elections and local-option elections have been held not included.[11]

[1] Mason v. S., 55 Ark. 529; C. v. McHale, 97 Pa. St. 397; C. v. Silsbee, 9 Mass. 417; S. v. Philbrick, 84 Me. 562. *Contra*, S. v. Liston, 9 Humph. 603.

[2] Ex parte Rodriguez, 39 Tex. 705.

[3] C. v. Shaw, 7 Met. 52; S. v. Williams, 25 Me. 561.

[4] S. v. Cohoon, 12 Ired. 178.

[5] Hall v. P., 90 N. Y. 498. So held with reference to the offense of carrying weapons on election day: Cooper v. S., 25 Tex. Ap. 530.

[6] C. v. Howe, 144 Mass. 144.

[7] S. v. Marshall, 45 N. H. 281.

[8] S. v. Philbrick, 84 Me. 562.

[9] C. v. Duff, 87 Ky. 586.

[10] Gandy v. S., 82 Ala. 61.

[11] S. v. Liston, 9 Humph. 603; C. v. Howe, 144 Mass. 144.

§ 943. Illegal voting.— Where the offense is that of illegal voting, one who hands his vote to the proper officer and whose name is announced and registered by the clerk has voted, even though the ballot is not deposited in the box.[1] It is usually criminal to vote at any other place than the one at which the person is entitled to vote;[2] but under a statute punishing voting out of the county, city or town of the voter's residence, it is not sufficient to show a vote cast in the wrong precinct of the town in which the voter resides.[3] It is criminal to vote under the name of another;[4] also, to vote more than once at the same election.[5] This seems to be so without statute.[6] And it is immaterial in such case that the first vote was illegal and should not be counted,[7] or that the second ballot was not for the offices voted for in the first ballot.[8] Under some statutes registration is essential as a condition of the right to vote, and the making of a false oath as to the voter's qualifications in order to secure registration is a crime.[9] Attempting to vote unlawfully is also criminal in some states,[10] but in other states the crime is committed only when the unlawful vote is cast.[11] It may be made criminal to advise unlawful voting, and this will be deemed a substantive offense and not accessorial.[12]

§ 944. Disqualified voters.— Statutes make it criminal for one who is not qualified to vote; for instance, one who is not naturalized,[13] or who is a minor.[14] And statutes usually disqualify one who has been convicted of an offense and not pardoned; and such a one casting a vote commits a crime;[15] and it is no excuse that he has forgotten the fact or has been advised that there is no record of such conviction,[16] for he is presumed to know the

[1] Steinwehr v. S., 5 Sneed, 586.

[2] S. v. Minnick, 15 Ia. 123.

[3] Nettles v. S., 49 Ala. 35.

[4] U. S. v. Watkinds, 6 Fed. R. 152.

[5] Wilson v. S., 52 Ala. 299; S. v. Bailey, 21 Me. 62.

[6] S. v. Philbrick, 84 Me. 562; C. v. Silsbee, 9 Mass. 417.

[7] S. v. Perkins, 42 Vt. 399.

[8] S. v. Welch, 21 Minn. 22.

[9] S. v. Houston, 103 N. C. 383; U. S. v. Jacques, 55 Fed. R. 53. And see U. S. v. Burley, 14 Blatch. 91.

[10] S. v. Moore, 27 N. J. 105; U. S. v. Seaman, 23 Fed. R. 882.

[11] Dennis v. S., 17 Fla. 389; U. S. v. Watkinds, 6 Fed. R. 152; U. S. v. Trainor, 36 Fed. R. 176.

[12] U. S. v. Carroll, 32 Fed. R. 775.

[13] S. v. Cloksey, 5 Sneed, 482; U. S. v. Burley, 14 Blatch. 91.

[14] Gordon v. S., 52 Ala. 308; Carter v. S., 55 Ala. 181.

[15] Thompson v. S., 26 Tex. Ap. 94; Burkett v. McCarty, 10 Bush, 758.

[16] Gandy v. S., 82 Ala. 61.

facts.[1] But the disqualification does not attach until judgment has been rendered on a conviction.[2] The question whether there is such guilt as to disqualify must be determined judicially, and not by means of a test oath administered by the election officers.[3]

§ 945. Crimes by election officers.— The election officers have certain duties to perform which they may not wilfully and knowingly disregard, but mistakes or unintentional errors will not make them criminally liable.[4] But where the refusal to receive a vote is with wrongful animus and intent, the fact that it is based on a pretended view of the law which justifies it will not be a defense.[5] They may not wilfully and fraudulently refuse to receive a ballot tendered them by a person qualified to vote;[6] nor may they wilfully and knowingly receive illegal votes.[7] If a question of fact is left to the officer to be decided in determining whether a voter is qualified, he will not be criminally responsible for receiving illegal votes by reason of an error of judgment.[8] Officers may be guilty of a crime also in altering a ballot in such way as will destroy its effectiveness in any particularity.[9] Duties as to registration are imposed upon election officers, and a violation of these duties is criminal.[10] The election officers have also certain duties to perform with reference to entries upon poll-books, keeping a tally-list, etc., a violation of which may be criminal.[11] A slight departure from directory provisions may not be criminal,[12] but the intent of the officer will be immaterial if the plain provisions of the law are violated.[13] There can be no punishment, however, with reference to an act not pertaining to the duty

[1] Thompson v. S., 26 Tex. Ap. 94.

[2] S. v. Houston, 103 N. C. 383. But it has been held that it may be made the duty of the election officer to pass on the question whether the voter is disqualified by reason of having made bets upon the result: Byrne v. S., 12 Wis. 519.

[3] Burkett v. McCarty, 10 Bush, 758.

[4] S. v. Bush, 47 Kan. 201; Byrne v. S., 12 Wis. 519; U. S. v. Dwyer, 56 Fed. R. 464; U. S. v. Kelsey, 42 Fed. R. 882.

[5] U. S. v. Foster, 6 Fed. R. 247.

[6] S. v. Tuibell, 26 Ind. 264.

[7] C. v. Gray, 2 Duv. 373; U. S. v. Doherty, 25 Fed. R. 28; U. S. v. Eagan, 30 Fed. R. 495.

[8] Byrne v. S., 12 Wis. 519.

[9] C. v. McGurty, 145 Mass. 257.

[10] U. S. v. Molloy, 31 Fed. R. 19.

[11] Ex parte Coy, 127 U. S. 731; Van Buren v. U. S., 36 Fed. R. 77; U. S. v. Bader, 16 Fed. R. 116; C. v. Duff, 87 Ky. 586.

[12] S. v. Bush, 47 Kan. 201.

[13] S. v. Bush, 45 Kan. 138.

of the particular officer in question; thus, a clerk of election is not punishable for making a false certificate where the duty of making the certificate is not imposed on the clerk.[1]

§ 946. Interference with elections.— Persons who are neither voters nor officers may be guilty of violating the election laws by tampering with the registration lists,[2] or by hindering, preventing or intimidating voters from exercising their right.[3] So where the voter is entitled to be present at the counting of the votes it may be criminal to interfere with such presence.[4] So an attempt to interfere with the right of others in voting may be criminal.[5] It may be criminal also to unlawfully seize and carry away ballot-boxes,[6] or to destroy them.[7] So intimidating judges of election,[8] or interfering with officers who have duties to perform in connection with the election, may be criminal.[9] A conspiracy to unlawfully influence the result of an election is, of course, criminal.[10] And so it is criminal to procure another to fraudulently register or vote.[11] There are statutes specially intended to preserve the peace and quiet on election day without regard to whether the acts prohibited have any direct influence upon the election; thus, it is in some states made criminal to carry weapons on that day,[12] or to keep open any place for the sale of liquor, although such sale would be legal on other days.[13]

§ 947. Improperly influencing voters.— The very purpose for which elections are held makes it improper that the action of the voters should be determined by any other influences than those which relate to the public welfare; therefore it is made criminal to treat electors for the purpose of obtaining their votes,[14] or to bribe an elector by paying or promising to him or

[1] U. S. v. Green, 33 Fed. R. 619.

[2] U. S. v. Eagan, 30 Fed. R. 498; U. S. v. O'Connor, 31 Fed. R. 449; U. S. v. Mullaney, 32 Fed. R. 370.

[3] U. S. v. Belvin, 46 Fed. R. 381; U. S. v. Guion, 37 Fed. R. 263; U. S. v. Goldman, 3 Woods, 187; U. S. v. Cahill, 3 McCrary, 200.

[4] U. S. v. Badinelli, 37 Fed. R. 138.

[5] S. v. Hardy, 47 N. H. 538; Randolph v. C., 6 Serg. & R. 398; C. v. Clark, 6 Grat. 675.

[6] Connors v. U. S., 158 U. S. 408.

[7] Mason v. S., 55 Ark. 529; Ex parte Brown, 97 Cal. 83; C. v. Ryan, 157 Mass. 403.

[8] Resp. v. Gibbs, 3 Yeates, 429.

[9] U. S. v. Taylor, 57 Fed. R. 391; U. S. v. Wardell, 49 Fed. R. 914.

[10] Moschell v. S., 53 N. J. 498.

[11] U. S. v. Brown, 58 Fed. R. 558.

[12] Cooper v. S., 26 Tex. Ap. 575.

[13] See the chapter on intoxicating liquors, *infra*, ch. 63.

[14] S. v. Darnal, 1 Humph. 290; S. v. Shaw, 8 Humph. 32; S. v. Pearis, 35 W. Va. 320.

to any other person a sum of money, or to give or offer to give other pecuniary inducements for voting or forbearing to vote,[1] or for an elector to receive such bribe;[2] and it seems that this is an offense at common law.[3] Trading votes is indictable if the agreement is carried out.[4] While the law thus attempts to prevent unlawful influences it does not forbid the use of every honorable means of persuasion and reasoning which are intended calmly to influence the mind of the voter in the proper exercise of his privilege.[5] There may, indeed, be improper inducements offered to a body of electors, such as a proposition on the part of the officer to return to the treasury, if elected, a part or all of the compensation authorized by law for the office.[6] But it is not improper to offer to the electors as an inducement a general public advantage which will result from their voting in favor of a particular proposition; thus, where the question of the location of the county seat is submitted to vote, it is not improper to offer in behalf of one location the dedication of public grounds or the occupation of public buildings as an inducement for locating at that place.[7] Betting on elections is made criminal by statutes as to gaming and betting,[8] as well as by election laws.

§ **948. Federal election laws.**— Under the federal constitution the qualification of electors is left to be determined by the states, except in so far as the provisions of the fifteenth amendment forbidding discrimination on account of race, color, etc., constitute a limitation upon that power.[9] The right to vote is not a privilege or immunity which by the fourteenth amendment cannot be impaired by state regulation.[10] But as to elections at which a representative or delegate in congress is to

[1] S. v. Jackson, 73 Me. 91; S. v. Purdy, 36 Wis. 213; C. v. Stephenson, 3 Met. (Ky.) 226; Rex v. Plympton, 2 Ld. Raym. 1377; Rex v. Cripland, 11 Mod. 387.

[2] Russell v. C., 3 Bush, 469.

[3] S. v. Ames, 64 Me. 386; S. v. Jackson, 73 Me. 91; Resp. v. Ray, 3 Yeates, 65; Rex v. Pitt, 3 Burr. 1335; Rex v. Plympton, 2 Ld. Raym. 1377.

[4] C. v. Callaghan, 2 Va. Cas. 460.

[5] Williams v. C., 91 Pa. St. 493.

[6] Carrothers v. Russell, 53 Ia. 346; S. v. Church, 5 Oreg. 375.

[7] Hall v. Marshall, 80 Ky. 552; Dishon v. Smith, 10 Ia. 212; Hawes v. Miller, 56 Ia. 395.

[8] See *infra*, ch. 64.

[9] U. S. v. Reese, 92 U. S. 214; U. S. v. Crosby, 1 Hughes, 448; U. S. v. Anthony, 11 Blatch. 200; Anthony v. Halderman, 7 Kan. 50.

[10] Minor v. Happersett, 21 Wall. 162; U. S. v. Anthony, 11 Blatch. 200.

be chosen, congress has the power to legislate;[1] and accordingly there are specific provisions in the federal statutes for the punishment of interference with such elections and the rights of the voters thereat, as specific crimes against the federal government.[2] And under these statutory provisions it has been held criminal for an election officer to neglect or violate his duty as to the poll-books, tally-sheets, etc.;[3] or to forge or tamper with the returns;[4] or for any one to unlawfully secure the registration of names of persons not entitled to vote,[5] or to interfere with the exercise of their right on the part of those entitled to vote.[6] In pursuance of this authority on the part of congress to regulate elections for representatives and delegates in congress, congress has, instead of adopting a uniform system of election laws applicable to such elections, made use of the state laws and provided for the punishment by the federal government of the violation of such state regulations; and it has been held constitutional for the federal government to thus punish state election officers for the violation of the provisions of state statutes where a congressman is to be elected at the same election as state officers;[7] but this federal regulation is only applicable to state elections at which a congressman is thus to be chosen.[8]

[1] U. S. Const., art. 1, § 4.

[2] R. S., §§ 5511–5515.

[3] Ex parte Coy, 127 U. S. 731; U. S. v. Eagan, 30 Fed. R. 495. But it must be charged that the act or omission was knowingly done on the part of the officer: U. S. v. Kelsey, 42 Fed. R. 882.

[4] Van Buren v. U. S., 36 Fed. R. 77.

[5] U. S. v. O'Connor, 31 Fed. R. 449.

[6] U. S. v. Beloni, 46 Fed. R. 381; U. S. v. Guion, 37 Fed. R. 263. The federal statutes do not cover the case of attempt except where the attempt is to vote in the name of another: U. S. v. Trainor, 36 Fed. R. 176; but they do cover advising a violation of the statutes, and said advising is not an accessorial but a substantive offense: U. S. v. Carroll, 32 Fed. R. 775. Other cases of prosecution under the federal statutes are cited in the preceding sections of this chapter.

[7] Ex parte Seebold, 100 U. S. 317; Ex parte Clark, 100 U. S. 399; U. S. v. Given, 17 Int. Rev. Rec. 189 and 195, 25 Fed. Cas. 1324 and 1328.

[8] U. S. v. Gitma, 3 Hughes, 549; U. S. v. Nicholson, 3 Wood, 215; Mason v. S., 55 Ark. 529. A governor of a state in certifying the result of an election for a member of congress under a state statute is not an election officer punishable under the federal statutes: U. S. v. Clayton, 2 Dill. 219. The state courts have jurisdiction of a prosecution for illegal voting for electors of president and vice-president and may punish therefor without federal interference even though a congressman was voted for at the same election: In re Green, 134 U. S. 377.

§ 949. **Intent.**— The criminal intent is essential.[1] Usually violations of such laws are punishable only as they involve a corrupt intent, and an honest belief that the act is lawful, though due to a mistake of fact, for instance, as to whether the voter is a minor, will prevent illegal voting being punishable.[2] So under a charge of voting twice it may be shown that the accused was so intoxicated that he had no knowledge of what he was doing.[3] But the fact of a previous conviction of a felony constituting a disqualification must be presumed to be known to the person disqualified, and he cannot claim to have acted under a mistake of fact in illegally voting.[4] Nor will it be any defense that accused took legal advice as to his right to vote when that right depends simply upon a fact;[5] and the fact of having taken the advice of others not learned in the law will constitute no defense whatever.[6] But if the facts as to qualification are submitted to the judges of election and the voter is allowed to cast his ballot, he cannot be convicted for doing so although not entitled to vote.[7] In general, a mistake of law,[8] such as the belief on the part of a woman that under the constitution of the United States she is entitled to vote, will not constitute a defense.[9] And indeed, the criminal intent may be presumed in some cases from the nature of the act where it is a plain violation of the law.[10] An election officer who acts *bona fide*, though in a mistaken exercise of his judgment, is not punishable.[11]

§ 950. **Indictment.**— Sometimes it is said that an indictment in the language of the statute is sufficient, but it may be necessary to allege the particular circumstances in order to advise defendant of the charge against him.[12] To charge simply

[1] S. v. Tuibell, 26 Ind. 264; Austin v. S., 71 Ga. 595; U. S. v. Wright, 16 Fed. R. 112. Intent is essential though not made so by the statute: C. v. Shaw, 7 Met. 52. The necessity of intent appears also with reference to specific forms of violation in the preceding sections of this chapter.

[2] Gordon v. S., 52 Ala. 308; Carter v. S., 55 Ala. 181.

[3] P. v. Harris, 29 Cal. 678.

[4] Thompson v. S., 26 Tex. Ap. 94; Gandy v. S., 86 Ala. 20.

[5] Gandy v. S., 82 Ala. 61.

[6] S. v. Sheeley, 15 Ia. 404; S. v. Hart, 6 Jones, 389; S. v. Boyett, 10 Ired. 336.

[7] S. v. Pearson, 97 N. C. 434.

[8] S. v. Macomber, 7 R. I. 349; McGuire v. S., 7 Humph. 54.

[9] U. S. v. Anthony, 11 Blatch. 200.

[10] S. v. Bush, 45 Kan. 138.

[11] Byrne v. S., 12 Wis. 519.

[12] P. v. Neil, 91 Cal. 465; U. S. v. Hirschfield, 13 Blatch. 330; U. S. v. Wardell, 49 Fed. R. 914.

fraudulent voting is not sufficient.[1] As a general proposition, therefore, it may be stated that the facts should be alleged,[2] and for failure to do so the indictment is vulnerable to demurrer;[3] but in various cases indictments which state little more than the general charge in the language of the statute have been upheld.[4] In charging bribery of an elector the indictment should state that an election of the qualified voters of a particular ward or precinct, describing it, was held to select certain named officers, and that the accused attempted to influence a certain named and qualified voter in such ward or precinct to give his vote thereat by offering and paying him a certain sum of money or other valuable consideration, as the case may be.[5] In other cases the election should be named,[6] and the purpose for which it was held;[7] but it is not necessary

[1] P. v. McKenna, 81 Cal. 158.

[2] Randolph v. C., 6 Serg. & R. 398; C. v. Clark, 6 Grat. 675; U. S. v. McCabe, 58 Fed. R. 557; U. S. v. Brown, 58 Fed. R. 558; U. S. v. Wardell, 49 Fed. R. 914; S. v. Moore, 27 N. J. 105; P. v. Standish, 6 Park. Cr. 111; S. v. Tweed, 27 N. J. 111; Gallagher v. S., 10 Tex. Ap. 469; Pearce v. S., 1 Sneed, 63; Quinn v. S., 35 Ind. 485. *Contra*, S. v. Douglass, 7 Ia. 413; C. v. Shaw, 7 Met. 52; S. v. Marshall, 45 N. H. 281; U. S. v. Quinn, 18 Blatch. 48.

[3] S. v. Bruce, 5 Oreg. 68.

[4] Thus, it has been held sufficient to charge a judge with altering a ballot: C. v. McGurty, 145 Mass. 257; or to charge that defendant was a minor and voted: Gordon v. S., 52 Ala. 308. And see S. v. Welch, 21 Minn. 22. But it is not enough to charge defendant with being an alien and having voted: U. S. v. Hirschfield, 13 Blatch. 330; nor to charge the preventing of another from voting without setting out the facts: S. v. Hardy, 47 N. H. 538. In charging defendant with advising fraudulent registration it is not necessary to set out the particular words of advice used: U. S. v. Brown, 58 Fed. R. 558. So in charging a conspiracy to prevent voting it is not necessary to set out the particular acts showing the conspiracy: U. S. v. Goldman, 3 Woods, 187.

[5] S. v. Jackson, 73 Me. 91; C. v. Selby, 87 Ky. 594; P. v. Purley, 2 Cal. 564; Old v. C., 18 Grat. 915; Newell v. C., 2 Wash. (Va.) 88; S. v. McCrystal, 43 La. An. 907. The following indictment was held sufficient: "That said A. B., on ——, in the county aforesaid, bribed C. D. to vote at the August election, 1859, with money and property of value of five dollars, and for said bribe he did vote for J. B. for governor of Kentucky, A. A. for lieutenant governor of Kentucky, T. P. for auditor of Kentucky, and L. M. for congress:" C. v. Stephenson, 3 Met. (Ky.) 226. An indictment charging generally that defendant hindered a certain person from voting, without setting forth the acts and method, is too indefinite: U. S. v. Belvin, 46 Fed. R. 381.

[6] Lane v. S., 39 Ohio St. 312; U. S. v. Cahill, 3 McCrary, 200; U. S. v. Seaman, 23 Fed. R. 882.

[7] Tipton v. S., 27 Ind. 492; Bellair v. S., 6 Blackf. 104; Carter v. S., 55 Ala. 181.

to go into great particularity in this respect, and it is sufficient to charge that the election was duly holden,[1] mentioning the candidates,[2] the specific authority for the election,[3] and that the officers were the proper and legal ones.[4] The place of holding the election should be charged.[5] In charging false swearing in connection with an election it must appear that the act was done where an oath was required by law,[6] and to a person authorized to take a statement under oath.[7] But it has been held that a charge of false swearing as to elections cannot be sustained where there is no charge of having illegally voted.[8] The allegation of intent is an essential one,[9] but this is properly charged by the statement that the act was done wilfully[10] or illegally.[11] In charging a person with voting in the name of another it is necessary to allege that he knowingly so voted.[12] Several acts which are made by the indictment to constitute the offense may be charged jointly in one count.[13] Officers who have distinct and several duties to perform cannot be jointly indicted.[14]

§ 951. Evidence.— The burden of proof to show the violation of the law is, of course, on the prosecution; but presumptions may arise from the evidence which the defendant must overcome; for instance, where it is shown that defendant was

[1] S. v. Marshall, 45 N. H. 281; S. v. Boyington, 56 Me. 512. But it is not enough to state that it was a certain corporation election at a place and date stated: Lane v. S., 39 Ohio St. 312.

[2] S. v. Bailey, 21 Me. 62; Gallagher v. S., 10 Tex. Ap. 469; S. v. Minnick, 15 Ia. 123; Wilson v. S., 52 Ala. 299.

[3] Gallagher v. S., 10 Tex. Ap. 469.

[4] S. v. Douglass, 7 Ia. 413. Where certain persons were alleged to have been officers it is sufficient to charge that they were legal officers: S. v. Randles, 7 Humph. 9. Where illegality is charged as to one officer it is not necessary to make allegations as to the acts of the other officers: C. v. Gray, 2 Duv. 373.

[5] U. S. v. McCabe, 58 Fed. R. 557; U. S. v. Brown, 58 Fed. R. 558; S. v. Fitzpatrick, 4 R. I. 269. And see U. S. v. Doherty, 25 Fed. R. 28; U. S. v. Johnson, 2 Sawy. 482.

[6] Dennis v. S., 17 Fla. 389.

[7] U. S. v. Jacques, 55 Fed. R. 53.

[8] Humphreys v. S., 17 Fla. 381.

[9] U. S. v. Taylor, 57 Fed. R. 391; C. v. Shaw, 7 Met. 52. And see S. v. Bush, 45 Kan. 138. And see *supra*, § 949.

[10] U. S. v. Dwyer, 56 Fed. R. 464; or wilfully and unlawfully: S. v. Moore, 27 N. J. 105.

[11] S. v. Haynorth, 3 Sneed, 64.

[12] U. S. v. Watkinds, 6 Fed. R. 152.

[13] Connors v. U. S., 158 U. S. 408. Placing a number of forged names on the registration list at the same time and place constitutes but one offense: U. S. v. Eagan, 30 Fed. R. 498.

[14] U. S. v. Davis, 33 Fed. R. 621.

a resident of another state until within a recent period.[1] In proving the fact of registration or voting, the records of the proceedings at the registration office or at the polls are the best evidence.[2] Under an indictment for altering a ballot, the ballot cast, which has been preserved under order of court, is the best evidence;[3] but where the statute directs the officer to preserve the ballots in packages unopened for a certain time and then destroy them, if there is no contest, the court has no authority in a criminal prosecution to compel the production of such ballots, and in such a case secondary evidence is admissible;[4] and, of course, where the ballots have been destroyed pursuant to law, secondary evidence is admissible.[5] A statute which requires one offender against the election laws to testify against another, protecting him, however, against self-crimination by a provision that such testimony shall not be used in any prosecution against him, and that such witness shall not thereafter be liable to prosecution or punishment for the offense with reference to which he testifies, is constitutional.[6] One who, in a prosecution for improperly writing names on the registration book, testifies in his own behalf that he did not write them, may, on cross-examination, be compelled to write the same names on a paper in the presence of the jury, this being a legitimate cross-examination and not a violation of the privilege of the witness not to furnish evidence against himself, such privilege having been waived by testifying.[7] Questions of evidence relating to particular offenses have been considered in preceding sections.

[1] C. v. Bradford, 9 Met. 268; or where it appears that defendant is unknown where he voted and his family resides elsewhere: Ibid.; but if it is charged that due and diligent inquiry has been made for the defendant without his being found in the ward or precinct, that fact does not in itself show the commission of an offense in his having voted there: Southworth v. U. S., 19 Court of Cl. 278.

[2] S. v. Bailey, 21 Me. 62. A poll-list is the best evidence of who voted: Wilson v. S., 52 Ala. 299; but the list must be properly authenticated: Hunter v. S., 55 Ala. 76.

[3] C. v. Ryan, 157 Mass. 403.

[4] Ex parte Brown, 97 Cal. 83.

[5] C. v. Ryan, 157 Mass. 403.

[6] Ex parte Cohen, 104 Cal. 524. And see on the question whether such a provision is a sufficient protection of the constitutional right not to be a witness against one's self, Brown v. Walker, 161 U. S. 591.

[7] U. S. v. Mullaney, 32 Fed. R. 370.

PART X.

OFFENSES AGAINST PUBLIC PEACE AND SECURITY.

CHAPTER 41.

CONSPIRACY; UNLAWFUL COMBINATION.

I. What Constitutes the Offense.
II. Procedure.
III. Evidence.

I. What Constitutes the Offense.

§ 952. **General nature.**— The law regards the act of unlawful combination and confederacy as dangerous to the public peace and welfare, and makes such combination and confederacy punishable criminally as a wrong distinct from that which was sought to be accomplished.[1] The punishment for the conspiracy may be more severe than that provided for the commission of the wrong intended.[2]

§ 953. **Definitions.**—According to the usual definition, which is satisfactory as far as a definition can go, a conspiracy is a combination of two or more persons by concerted action to accomplish a criminal or unlawful purpose, or some purpose not in itself criminal by criminal or unlawful means.[3] The English cases have been summarized as indicating three divisions of the crime; first, where the thing to be attained is in itself a crime; second, where the object is lawful, but the means to be resorted to are unlawful; third, where the object is to do an injury to a third party of such nature that, if inflicted by one person, it

[1] U. S. v. Cassidy, 67 Fed. R. 698.

[2] Clune v. U. S., 159 U. S. 590.

[3] Pettibone v. U. S., 148 U. S. 197; U. S. v. Cassidy, 67 Fed. R. 698; S. v. Rowley, 12 Conn. 101; S. v. Mayberry, 48 Me. 218; C. v. Hunt, 4 Met. 111; Smith v. P., 25 Ill. 17; Spies v. P., 122 Ill. 1; Alderman v. P., 4 Mich. 414; S. v. Burnham, 15 N. H. 396; S. v. Potter, 28 Ia. 554; S. v. Stevens, 30 Ia. 391; S. v. Jones, 13 Ia. 269; Wilson v. C., 96 Pa. St. 56; S. v. Buchanan, 5 Har. & J. 317; Rex v. Seward, 1 Ad. & El. 706.

would be a civil wrong only and not a crime.[1] But this classification will not cover all cases, and it will be necessary to discuss the elements of the crime more specifically.

§ 954. **Purpose or means as criminal or unlawful.**— The early common-law definitions, as well as the provisions of the earliest English statute on the subject, were very restricted in their scope and indicate that the combinations aimed at were mainly those involving the malicious procuring of a false indictment against an innocent man.[2] A few of the early decisions in this country restricted the offense to cases where the purpose to be accomplished or the means employed involved a crime.[3] But as will be seen in succeeding paragraphs, the cases now uniformly recognize as criminal many combinations having a purpose, or involving the use of means, not criminal but wrongful.[4] How far the courts shall go in thus making punishable combinations to do acts which are merely unlawful and not criminal has been a question of much discussion, but the scope of the crime has been enlarged from time to time, and just what will constitute a punishable conspiracy must be determined by the precedents in particular classes of cases.[5] It seems, however, that the crime has not been extended to cover combinations to do any possible wrong; for instance, a conspiracy to commit a mere civil trespass is not criminal.[6] And of course a combination to do an act not wrongful in itself, or in the means to be used, and not injurious to the public, is not criminal; for instance, a combination to assist a father to secure the custody of his child.[7]

§ 955. **Common-law conspiracy.**— Although both in England and in this country there are statutes defining conspiracies in general, and also making particular forms of combinations

[1] Reg. v. Parnell (No. 3), 14 Cox, 508.

[2] 3 Inst. 143; 4 Bl. Com. 136; 33 Edw. I, Stat. 2.

[3] S. v. Rickey, 9 N. J. 293; P. v. Richards, 1 Mich. 216; Alderman v. P., 4 Mich. 414; Lambert v. P., 9 Cowan, 578.

[4] S. v. Rowley, 12 Conn. 101; Smith v. P., 25 Ill. 17; S. v. Buchanan, 5 Har. & J. 317; C. v. Hunt, 4 Met. 111; S. v. Burnham, 15 N. H. 396; Rex v. Mawbey, 6 Term R. 619; Reg. v. Best, 2 Ld. Raym. 1167; Rex v. Kinnersley, 1 Strange, 193; Rex v. Timberly, 1 Sid. 68; 1 Hawk. P. C., ch. 72, § 2.

[5] 3 Chit. Cr. Law, 1199; Archbold, Crim. Plead. 617; P. v. Richards, 1 Mich. 216.

[6] S. v. Straw, 42 N. H. 393; S. v. Clary, 64 Me. 369.

[7] C. v. Myers, 146 Pa. St. 24.

criminal as conspiracies, yet these statutes are deemed not to abrogate the common law as to conspiracies unless plainly so intended, and common-law conspiracies are therefore, as a rule, still punishable in the various states.[1] For instance, the statutes of the United States on the subject do not create any new offense but merely recognize the crime as known at the common law.[2]

§ 956. **Conspiracies to commit a crime.**— As to a confederation for the purpose of committing a crime there is no doubt about the criminality at common law.[3] It matters not whether the offense is one created by statute or existing at the common law.[4] And conspiracies to commit two or more crimes may be treated as one conspiracy.[5] But a conspiracy to do a lawful act for the purpose of enabling one of the conspirators to commit a crime is not criminal unless it appears that it was for the purpose of aiding and abetting in the commission of such crime.[6] By federal statute it is expressly made criminal to conspire to commit any offense against the United States.[7]

§ 957. **To charge with crime.**— It is criminal to conspire to charge another with a crime, even though it does not appear that the purpose was to procure legal process to be issued;[8] and it is also immaterial in such case whether the object

[1] S. v. Norton, 23 N. J. 33; C. v. Hunt, 4 Met. 111; S. v. Burnham, 15 N. H. 396; S. v. Pulle, 12 Minn. 164; Wilson v. C., 96 Pa. St. 56.

[2] U. S. v. McCord, 72 Fed. R. 159.

[3] Hazen v. C., 23 Pa. St. 355; Twitchell v. C., 9 Pa. St. 211; C. v. Myers, 146 Pa. St. 24; C. v. Kingsbury, 5 Mass. 106; S. v. Buchanan, 5 Har. & J. 317; P. v. Mather, 4 Wend. 229; S. v. Shooter, 8 Rich. 72. So held in case of robbery: P. v. Richards, 67 Cal. 412; and larceny: Browder v. S., 102 Ala. 164; and assault and battery: C. v. Putnam, 29 Pa. St. 296; and assault with intent to inflict great bodily injury: S. v. Ormiston, 66 Ia. 143. But a conspiracy to pervert the due course of justice by means of perjury committed by each of the conspirators is not a combination for the purpose of committing a felony, the perversion of the course of justice not being a felony: S. v. McKinstry, 50 Ind. 465.

[4] Hazen v. C., 23 Pa. St. 355; Reg. v. Bunn, 12 Cox, 316; Reg. v. Thompson, 16 Q. B. 832.

[5] Ochs v. P., 25 Ill. Ap. 379; S. v. Sterling, 34 Ia. 443.

[6] C. v. Barnes, 132 Mass. 242.

[7] R. S., § 5440; U. S. v. Wootten, 29 Fed. R. 702; U. S. v. Thompson, 29 Fed. R. 86; U. S. v. Stevens, 44 Fed. R. 132; U. S. v. Newton, 48 Fed. R. 218; U. S. v. Cassidy, 67 Fed. R. 698; Pettibone v. U. S., 148 U. S. 197; U. S. v. Wilson, 60 Fed. R. 890; U. S. v. Van Leuven, 62 Fed. R. 62. And it is immaterial that the defendants have never been indicted for the offense itself: U. S. v. De Grieff, 16 Blatch. 20.

[8] C. v. Tibbetts, 2 Mass. 536.

be to pervert justice or to obtain money or property by means of a criminal charge, whether false or true.[1]

§ 958. To slander.— It is likewise criminal to conspire to cause another to be suspected of a crime, and to this extent, at least, it is criminal to conspire to slander another.[2] But to conspire to injure the character of a married woman by procuring a decree of divorce against her on the ground of adultery is not criminal where no unlawful means are used and the only wrong involved is a false representation to her for the purpose of procuring her acceptance of notice that the divorce is sought on other grounds, she not being able to read.[3] It was held criminal, however, to falsely make it appear that a person was married, so as to prevent him from contracting another marriage.[4]

§ 959. To seduce female or entice to prostitution.— Pertinent examples of cases where the conspiracy will be criminal though the purpose is only unlawful and not criminal are furnished by conspiracies to seduce a female, which are uniformly held punishable, although seduction may not be criminal by the state statute.[5] So it is criminal to conspire to solicit, persuade or procure a female (at least if a minor) to become a prostitute.[6] And it is even held criminal to conspire to entice away or assist an infant daughter to escape from her parents with a view to a marriage against the parents' will.[7] But an agreement to commit adultery or fornication or any like offense entered into between the parties contemplating the commission of such offense is not criminal conspiracy, for if it were so in

[1] Johnson v. S., 26 N. J. 313; P. v. Richards, 1 Mich. 216; Reg. v. Best, 1 Salk. 174; Rex v. Spragg, 2 Burr. 993. So where persons conspired to induce another to violate the law in order that they might make profit out of his fears of prosecution, *held*, that the conspiracy was criminal regardless of whether the act of defendants was in itself illegal: P. v. Saunders, 25 Mich. 119.

[2] S. v. Hickling, 41 N. J. 208; S. v. Rowley, 12 Conn. 101; Reg. v. Best, 2 Ld. Raym. 1167.

[3] S. v. Stevens, 30 Ia. 391.

[4] C. v. Waterman, 122 Mass. 43.

[5] Smith v. P., 25 Ill. 17; Anderson v. C., 5 Rand. 627; Rex v. Grey, 1 East, P. C. 460. It is a misdemeanor to conspire by fraudulent representations to procure a young girl to have illicit carnal connection with a man: Reg. v. Mears, 2 Den. 79.

[6] Reg. v. Mears, 2 Den. 79; Reg. v. Howell, 4 F. & F. 160; Rex v. De la Val, 3 Burr. 1434. So it is criminal to conspire to accomplish illicit carnal connection with a female by means of a sham marriage: S. v. Murphy, 6 Ala. 765.

[7] Mifflin v. C., 5 Watts & S. 461.

such cases there would be involved in the same act the two offenses of the conspiracy and the act itself.[1]

§ 960. **To defraud private persons.**— Where the conspiracy is to defraud by means of false pretenses such as constitute a crime, it is of course criminal.[2] But whether it is a conspiracy to combine in order to defraud another of his money by means which are wrongful but not criminal is a question on which the authorities differ, the difference depending upon the conflict of views already discussed in a preceding section, as to whether intent to do a wrongful act not criminal may be a conspiracy. The weight of authority, however, is to the effect that such a conspiracy may be criminal.[3] So a conspiracy by one partner with others to cheat and defraud a copartner is criminal;[4] so is a conspiracy between bidders at an auction either to keep down or to raise the price at which the property shall be sold.[5] But there must be some illegal means agreed upon tending to the accomplishment of the object.[6] Under a statute providing for the offense of a conspiracy to injure the person, character, business or property of another, the injury contemplated is one against the property itself and not merely a deprivation of the property.[7]

§ 961. **To deprive of a right.**— By federal statute it is made criminal to conspire to injure, oppress, threaten or intimidate any citizen in the free exercise of any right or privilege secured by the constitution and laws of the United States.[8] And this

[1] Shannon v. C., 14 Pa. St. 226.

[2] P. v. Clark, 10 Mich. 310; S. v. Roberts, 34 Me. 320; S. v. Mayberry, 48 Me. 218; C. v. Eastman, 1 Cush. 189; C. v. Meserve, 154 Mass. 64; Thomas v. P., 113 Ill. 531; Ochs v. P., 124 Ill. 399; Johnson v. P., 22 Ill. 314; Musgrave v. S., 133 Ind. 297.

[3] S. v. Buchanan, 5 Har. & J. 317; C. v. Ward, 1 Mass. 473; Twitchell v. C., 9 Pa. St. 211; Ellzey v. S., 57 Miss. 827; S. v. Younger, 1 Dev. 357; Rex v. Hollingberry, 4 B. & C. 329; Reg. v. Kenrick, 5 Q. B. 49: Rex v. Robinson, 2 East, P. C. 1010; Rex v. Rispal, 1 W. Bl. 368; Rex v. Mackarty, 2 Ld. Raym. 1179; Reg. v. Carlisle, Dears. 337; Reg. v. Whitehouse, 6 Cox, 38; Reg. v. Orman, 14 Cox, C. C. 381; Reg. v. Taylor (No. 1), 15 Cox, 265; Reg. v. Taylor (No. 2), 15 Cox, 268. *Contra*, S. v. Rickey, 9 N. J. 293; Alderman v. P., 4 Mich. 414.

[4] S. v. Cole, 39 N. J. 324; Reg. v. Warburton, L. R. 1 C. C. 274.

[5] Levi v. Levi, 6 C. & P. 239; Reg. v. Lewis, 11 Cox, 484.

[6] C. v. Prius, 9 Gray, 127; S. v. Parker, 43 N. H. 83.

[7] S. v. Hewett, 31 Me. 396; S. v. Clary, 64 Me. 369.

[8] R. S., § 5508; U. S. v. Lancaster, 44 Fed. R. 896; U. S. v. Mitchell, 1 Hughes, 439; U. S. v. Butler, 1 Hughes, 457. It must appear that the right is one derived from the laws of the

statute has been held applicable to a conspiracy to deprive a settler on public lands of a residence thereon such would entitle him to acquire the same;[1] or to deprive a prisoner in the custody of the United States marshal of his privileges under the constitution and laws;[2] or to secure the violation of an injunction procured by a party in the federal court;[3] or to hinder an officer who is a citizen of the United States in the discharge of his duty.[4] The federal statute also provides that any felony or misdemeanor committed in the violation of the section just referred to shall be punished.[5] And under this provision the crime of murdering a revenue officer in a conspiracy to prevent his discharging his duties,[6] or the agent of a party who has secured an injunction in enforcing the same, is punishable.[7] But the federal statutes do not apply to acts committed within a state not relating to the operation of the federal government.[8]

§ 962. **To injure the public.**— A conspiracy to cheat and defraud the public or a large body of persons, as, for instance, a municipal corporation, is a crime *per se*, although the purpose is not a criminal one nor the means to be employed unlawful.[9] And under this doctrine it has been held criminal to conspire to cause a false public record of a marriage to be made;[10] or to influence by unlawful means the action of a school trustee in the appointment of a teacher;[11] or to unlawfully take from an

United States and not from state authority: U. S. v. Cruikshank, 92 U. S. 542. The statute has no application to aliens: Baldwin v. Franks, 120 U. S. 678.

[1] U. S. v. Waddell, 16 Fed. R. 221.

[2] U. S. v. Logan, 45 Fed. R. 872; s. c., Logan v. U. S., 144 U. S. 263. So it is criminal to conspire to oppress or intimidate or injure any private citizen for informing a marshal of the violation of internal revenue laws: In re Quarles, 158 U. S. 532.

[3] U. S. v. Lancaster, 44 Fed. R. 885.

[4] U. S. v. Patrick, 54 Fed. R. 338. But it must appear that the officer against whom the conspiracy was directed was a citizen, so as to bring the case within the language of the statute: U. S. v. Patrick, 53 Fed. R. 356.

[5] R. S., § 5509.

[6] U. S. v. Patrick, 54 Fed. R. 338; U. S. v. Logan, 45 Fed. R. 872.

[7] U. S. v. Lancaster, 44 Fed. R. 896.

[8] Baldwin v. Franks, 120 U. S. 678. The provision as to preventing witnesses from attending court does not apply to witnesses called to testify before a commissioner: Todd v. U. S., 158 U. S. 278.

[9] S. v. Young, 37 N. J. 184; S. v. Cardoza, 11 S. C. 195; S. v. Trammell, 2 Ired. 379; C. v. Carlisle, Bright. 36; Rex v. Starling, 1 Sid. 174; Rex v. Norris, 2 Keny. 300.

[10] C. v. Waterman, 122 Mass. 43.

[11] Shircliff v. S., 96 Ind. 369.

officer goods levied on;[1] or to put in circulation forged notes purporting to be the genuine notes of a bank of another state;[2] or to bring about a change in the form of government by the use of force if necessary;[3] or to defraud an incorporated bank, such bank being deemed a public institution;[4] or to unlawfully obtain money from a county, it being immaterial in such cases that the falsity of the claim against the county was known to the officers.[5] But it is said not to be a crime to conspire to throw the burden of maintaining a pauper upon another parish.[6] It is criminal to conspire to obtain money as a reward for appointment to an office under government.[7] It is a fraud on the public, and therefore indictable, to conspire to issue fabricated shares in a stock company;[8] or to raise the price of public funds on a particular day by false rumors;[9] or to induce the taking of shares in a worthless company by means of circulating a false prospectus;[10] or to cause the price of a particular stock to be falsely quoted;[11] or to fix the price of a commodity for general sale.[12] It is made criminal to conspire to hinder the execution of a law of the United States.[13]

§ **963. In restraint of trade.**— Combinations of workmen for the purpose of controlling employers in the conduct of their business have two aspects: first, that of an injury to the individual employer or employee, and second, that of an injury to the public; but these two phases are so combined in the cases that it is impossible to make any clear distinction on this basis. The cases which have arisen have uniformly involved combinations which, while they might affect an individual only in a particular instance, were directed against persons in general coming within the general scope of business or employment attempted to be regulated, and therefore all of them have been

[1] S. v. Harris, 38 Ia. 242.

[2] Clary v. C., 4 Pa. St. 210.

[3] Spies v. P., 122 Ill. 1.

[4] S. v. Norton, 23 N. J. 33, overruling S. v. Rickey, 9 N. J. 293.

[5] Ochs v. P., 124 Ill. 399.

[6] Rex v. Seward, 1 A. & E. 706.

[7] Rex v. Pollman, 2 Camp. 229.

[8] Rex v. Mott, 2 C. & P. 521.

[9] Rex v. De Berenger, 3 Maule & S. 68.

[10] Reg. v. Gurney, 11 Cox, 414; Reg. v. Esdaile, 1 F. & F. 213; Reg. v. Burch, 4 F. & F. 407.

[11] Reg. v. Aspinwall, 2 Q. B. D. 48.

[12] Rex v. Norris, 2 Keny. 300.

[13] In re Grand Jury, 26 Fed. R. 749; In re Baldwin, 27 Fed. R. 187. But R. S., § 5336, applies only to conspiracy against the government of the United States and not merely to a violation of its laws: Baldwin v. Franks, 120 U. S. 678.

cases affecting the public in general. An agreement between workmen not to work for any person who should employ journeymen or others not members of a particular society is not criminal, as each individual workman has a right to determine for whom he shall work, and if the object is only to build up the society to which the individuals belong there is nothing criminal either in the purpose or the means.[1] But if the object is by some form of oppression other than the mere refusal to work, as by preventing the public generally from dealing with an employer who does not comply with the requirements of the association, or by inducing employees who are already bound to render service to such employer to break their contracts, or by intimidation and threats of violence to prevent workmen from accepting employment from such employer, then there is such unlawfulness in the purpose and the means as to render the combination criminal.[2] But even where the purposes or means are such as would not be criminal in an individual, yet the combination may be criminal as an interference with trade.[3] In many of the states statutes have been passed regulating combinations in restraint of trade, and making conspiracies of that kind criminal even though they would not be só at common law.[4] There are provisions in the federal statutes against combinations to regulate prices or create a monopoly or trust in restraint of trade;[5] and these provisions are applicable as against combinations of workmen as well as of

[1] C. v. Hunt, 4 Met. 111.

[2] C. v. Hunt, 4 Met. 111; C. v. Dyer, 128 Mass. 70; S. v. Donaldson, 32 N. J. 151; Charge to Grand Jury, 62 Fed. R. 828; U. S. v. Debs, 63 Fed. R. 436; Arthur v. Oakes, 63 Fed. R. 310, 9 Am. Cr. R. 169, and note. So held in cases of boycotting: S. v. Stewart, 59 Vt. 273; Crump v. C., 84 Va. 927; and picketing: Vegelahn v. Guntner, — Mass. —, 44 N. E. R. 1077. It is unlawful for workmen to combine and quit work to compel their employer to withdraw from his relations with a third party for the purpose of injuring such third party: U. S. v. Cassidy, 67 Fed. R. 698.

[3] P. v. Fisher, 14 Wend. 9; Rex v. Bykerdyke, 1 M. & Rob. 179; Reg. v. Hewitt, 5 Cox, 162.

[4] S. v. Glidden, 55 Conn. 46; P. v. Fisher, 14 Wend. 9: P. v. Sheldon, 139 N. Y. 251; S. v. Phipps, 50 Kan. 609; P. v. Petheram, 64 Mich. 252. As to English statutes on the subject, see Reg. v. Duffield, 5 Cox, 404; Reg. v. Shepherd, 11 Cox, 325; Reg. v. Bunn, 12 Cox, 316; Reg. v. Bauld, 13 Cox, 282.

[5] In re Greene, 52 Fed. R. 104; U. S. v. Nelson, 52 Fed. R. 646; U. S. v. Greenhut, 50 Fed. R. 469; In re Corning, 51 Fed. R. 205; In re Terrell, 51 Fed. R. 213; U. S. v. Patterson, 59 Fed. R. 280.

capitalists.[1] But these provisions are applicable only to monopolies in international and interstate commerce and not to a monopoly in the manufacture of a particular commodity.[2]

§ 964. **To defraud the government.**— The federal statute already referred to,[3] punishing conspiracies to commit an offense against the United States, also includes a conspiracy to defraud the United States, and such a combination is criminal.[4]

§ 965. **To overthrow the government.**— A conspiracy to bring about a revolution in government, by peaceful means if possible, but by force if necessary, is criminal.[5]

§ 966. **Overt act.**— The definition of conspiracy has already indicated that the crime consists in the unlawful combination and not in what is done toward carrying out such combination, and the crime is completed when the conspiracy is entered into although no act done in pursuance thereof is committed.[6] Thus, in case of a conspiracy to obtain money by false pretenses, it is not necessary to show that any money was obtained or that any one was defrauded.[7] A conspiracy to do an unlawful act is a separate and distinct offense from that of the act itself, and is to be governed in its prosecution by the provisions

[1] U. S. v. Workingmen's Amalgamated Council, 54 Fed. R. 994; U. S. v. Elliott, 64 Fed. R. 27; U. S. v. Debs, 64 Fed. R. 724.

[2] U. S. v. E. C. Knight Co., 156 U. S. 1; s. c., 60 Fed. R. 306.

[3] R. S., § 5440. See *supra*, § 956.

[4] U. S. v. Owen, 32 Fed. R. 534; U. S. v. Adler, 49 Fed. R. 736; In re Benson, 58 Fed. R. 962; U. S. v. Thompson, 29 Fed. R. 86. There is a special provision as to a conspiracy to defraud the revenue: U. S. v. Rindskopf, 6 Biss. 259.

[5] Spies v. P., 122 Ill. 1, 253. United States Revised Statutes, section 5336, applies to conspiracies to overthrow the government and not merely to those for violating its laws: Baldwin v. Franks, 120 U. S. 678.

[6] C. v. Judd, 2 Mass. 329; C. v. Tibbetts, 2 Mass. 536; C. v. Warren, 6 Mass. 74; Heine v. C., 91 Pa. St. 145; P. v. Mather, 4 Wend. 229; Collins v. C., 3 Serg. & R. 220; P. v. Clark, 10 Mich. 310; P. v. Richards, 1 Mich. 216; S. v. Pulle, 12 Minn. 164; S. v. Rickey, 9 N. J. 293; S. v. Buchanan, 5 Har. & J. 317; McDonald v. P., 126 Ill. 150; S. v. Savoye, 48 Ia. 562; S. v. Ormiston, 66 Ia. 143; Landringham v. S., 49 Ind. 186; Musgrave v. S., 133 Ind. 297; S. v. Cawood, 2 Stew. 360; Johnson v. S., 3 Tex. Ap. 590; U. S. v. Lancaster, 44 Fed. R. 896; U. S. v. Newton, 52 Fed. R. 275; Rex v. Best, 6 Mod. 185; Rex v. Edwards, 8 Mod. 320; O'Connell v. Reg., 11 Cl. & F. 155. Overt acts may be charged in the indictment, but they are so charged by way of aggravation or to show the intent with which the combination was formed, rather than as an integral part of the crime of conspiracy: See *infra*, § 977.

[7] C. v. Davis, 9 Mass. 415; S. v. Bruner, 135 Ind. 419; Collins v. C., 3 Serg. & R. 220; Isaacs v. S., 48 Miss. 234.

relating to conspiracies and not those relating to the specific offense.[1] If the charge is of a conspiracy to defraud, no act need be alleged; but if it is of an attempt to defraud, there must be proof of some act which constituted an attempt.[2] However, in some states there are statutes requiring, either as to the offense in general, or as to particular forms of the offense, that an overt act shall have been committed in pursuance of the conspiracy.[3] The federal statute also requires an overt act.[4] But proof of a single overt act is sufficient, and several overt acts will not constitute more than one offense where they are done under a continuous agreement or combination.[5] Indeed, it is not necessary that the overt act be the completed purpose intended to be accomplished by the combination,[6] and it may be done outside the jurisdiction of the court in which the conspiracy is prosecuted.[7]

§ 967. **Impossibility.**— From the principle stated in the preceding section that the conspiracy is completed when the combination is formed, it is apparent that the impossibility of carrying out the object of the conspiracy will not prevent punishment for the conspiracy itself.[8] Thus, one who enters into a conspiracy for the commission of a crime may be punished therefor, although he himself could not commit the crime.[9]

§ 968. **The combination.**— To constitute conspiracy there must be a guilty combination of two or more;[10] and as the husband and wife are deemed but one person in regard to a joint offense, they cannot be charged with conspiracy for a combina-

1 C. v. McHale, 97 Pa. St. 397.

2 U. S. v. Ulrici, 3 Dill. 532.

3 Wood v. S., 47 N. J. 180; S. v. Norton, 23 N. J. 33; New York Penal Code, § 171. But even where an overt act is required by the statute it is not necessary to show a complete execution of the conspiracy, but any act done in carrying out the agreement is sufficient: S. v. Hickling, 41 N. J. 208.

4 R. S., § 5440; U. S. v. Reichert, 32 Fed. R. 142; U. S. v. Milner, 36 Fed. R. 890; U. S. v. Wootten, 29 Fed. R. 702; U. S. v. Thompson, 29 Fed. R. 86; U. S. v. Cassidy, 67 Fed. R. 698; U. S. v. McCord, 72 Fed. R. 159.

5 U. S. v. Howell, 56 Fed. R. 21; U. S. v. Cassidy, 67 Fed. R. 698; U. S. v. Debs, 65 Fed. R. 210.

6 U. S. v. Wilson, 60 Fed. R. 890.

7 Dealy v. U. S., 152 U. S. 539.

8 Ochs v. P., 124 Ill. 399; S. v. Ripley, 31 Me. 386; S. v. Bartlett, 30 Me. 132; Reg. v. Whitchurch, 24 Q. B. D. 420, 8 Am. Cr. R. 1 and note.

9 U. S. v. Stevens, 44 Fed. R. 132; U. S. v. Martin, 4 Cliff. 156.

10 Evans v. P., 90 Ill. 384; Mulcahy v. Reg., L. R. 3 H. L. 306.

tion entered into between them only.[1] There must be something of active participation more than mere cognizance of fraudulent or illegal action or intention on the part of others.[2] And if the acts of one of the parties, though imprudent and improper, are not done with intent to commit or assist the other in committing the wrong contemplated, and the subsequent wrong is not done in pursuance of any previous understanding or advice or direction, there is no conspiracy.[3] But an agreement in terms is not essential; it is enough that there is in fact a joint assent, and this may be inferred from circumstances.[4] It is sufficient if two or more persons in any manner, or through any contrivance, positively or tacitly come to a mutual understanding to accomplish a common unlawful design.[5] The agreement of those who conspire is an act in advancement of the intention which each of them has conceived in his mind.[6] The mere fact of giving to another something capable of improper use will not constitute a conspiracy with reference to such improper use on the part of the other.[7] It is not necessary that defendant should have had knowledge of the transaction, provided he was aware of the result intended and concurred in furthering it even without particular benefit to himself.[8] But if there is no participation in the unlawful design or the unlawful means there is no criminality.[9] It is not necessary that express agreement be shown if it appears that the parties by their acts pursued the same object by the same means, their acts being calculated jointly to produce the result.[10] On the other hand, if there is a common design the use of different means will not prevent the persons conspiring from being guilty of criminal conspiracy.[11] But there must be a

[1] P. v. Mather, 4 Wend. 229; P. v. Miller, 82 Cal. 107.

[2] Evans v. P., 90 Ill. 384; U. S. v. Lancaster, 44 Fed. R. 896. The person charged must incite, procure, encourage or assist in the wrong contemplated: U. S. v. Johnson, 26 Fed. R. 682; U. S. v. Newton, 52 Fed. R. 275; Reg. v. Boulton, 12 Cox, 87.

[3] Evans v. P., 90 Ill. 384.

[4] Spies v. P., 122 Ill. 1; Ochs v. P., 124 Ill. 399.

[5] U. S. v. Cassidy, 67 Fed. R. 698.

[6] Mulcahy v. Reg., L. R. 3 H. L. 306.

[7] S. v. Trice, 88 N. C. 627.

[8] Reg. v. Estaile, 1 F. & F. 213; Reg. v. Timothy, 1 F. & F. 39.

[9] Reg. v. Barry, 4 F. & F. 389; Reg. v. Read, 6 Cox, 134.

[10] Reg. v. Murphy, 8 C. & P. 297.

[11] U. S. v. Cole, 5 McLean, 513; Reg. v. Banks, 12 Cox, 393.

combination or pre-arranged plan. Mere concurrence of action is not enough.[1]

§ 969. **Joining in the execution.**— Where persons join in the execution of a wrong it is not necessary to prove any previous plan amongst them against the person intended to be injured, but their joint execution will render them liable for conspiracy, although their original purpose was a lawful one.[2] So one person who joins in carrying out a conspiracy already entered into by others becomes a party thereto and equally guilty with the other conspirators.[3] On the other hand, it is not necessary that it be within the contemplation of the parties combining that the act be carried out by all of them;[4] if they all combine to bring about the common object, by means of wrongful acts perpetrated by some of them, they are all guilty.[5] If the conspiracy contemplates a wrongful act in relation to a future contingency, one conspirator will not be liable for acts done by another when the contingency happens, unless the crime and intention continue to that time.[6]

§ 970. **Liability of one for acts of all.**— The general doctrine is that where two or more combine to commit a crime, each is liable for the acts of others done in carrying out the general design,[7] even though such specific acts were not agreed upon, if within the general scope of the common plan.[8] But there is no such liability for acts done by others outside the scope of the general plan and not assented to.[9] This whole question of liability for subsequent acts is, however, outside of the scope of the present discussion. It is fully treated elsewhere.[10]

§ 971. **Intent.**— There must be a criminal intent in conspiracy, which involves knowledge;[11] and the doctrine that

[1] U. S. v. Barrett, 65 Fed. R. 62.

[2] Lowery v. S., 30 Tex. 402.

[3] P. v. Mather, 4 Wend. 229; Spies v. P., 122 Ill. 1; Lamar v. S., 63 Miss. 265; S. v. Dyer, 67 Vt. 690; U. S. v. Babcock, 3 Dillon, 581; U. S. v. Cassidy, 67 Fed. R. 698.

[4] Ochs v. P., 124 Ill. 399; U. S. v. Newton, 52 Fed. Rep. 275; U. S. v. Johnson, 26 Fed. Rep. 682; Reg. v. Murphy, 8 C. & P. 297.

[5] C. v. Waterman, 122 Mass. 43; C. v. Eberle, 3 Serg. & R. 9; Brennan v. P., 15 Ill. 511; Hardin v. S., 4 Tex. Ap. 355; U. S. v. Smith, 1 Dill. 212.

[6] Reg. v. Banks, 12 Cox, 393.

[7] Spies v. P., 122 Ill. 1; S. v. McCahill, 72 Ia. 111.

[8] Spies v. P., 122 Ill. 1; Lamb v. P., 96 Ill. 73; Hamilton v. P., 113 Ill. 34.

[9] Lamb v. P., 96 Ill. 73; Pettibone v. U. S., 148 U. S. 197.

[10] *Supra*, § 195.

[11] P. v. Powell, 63 N. Y. 88.

ignorance of law is no defense in a prosecution for its violation is not applicable to a conspiracy to obstruct the administration of justice, as without a knowledge that justice was being administered there could be no intention to obstruct it.[1] The criminal guilt in conspiracy resides in the intention of the parties to the agreement construed in connection with the purpose contemplated, and the mere fact that the conspiracy has for its object the committing of an act which may be unlawful, followed by the committing of such act, does not constitute the crime of conspiracy unless it is found that the parties were connected by a criminal intent, and this question of intent is for the jury.[2] The intent must be a corrupt one, and it is not sufficient that it be merely to do an act which is illegal.[3] However, where defendant was indicted for conspiracy to produce a false certificate in evidence, it was held unnecessary to allege that defendant knew at the time of the conspiracy that the contents of the certificate were false, it being sufficient that he agreed with others to certify the fact as true without knowing it to be so.[4] A mere feigned assent to the conspiracy will not make one guilty;[5] nor will there be any guilt where the act agreed to be done is in the exercise of a legal right.[6] The fact that the party injured by a conspiracy to defraud was at the time engaged in an attempt to defraud some one else will not make the conspiracy less criminal.[7] But where the person defrauded paid over the money of which he was deprived in the furtherance of a supposed criminal enterprise, it was held that those who combined to obtain the money from him were not punishable, he being a *particeps criminis*.[8] So assent to the thing sought to be accomplished given by the person injured, with a view to his own advantage, will prevent the combination from being criminal.[9]

[1] Pettibone v. U. S., 148 U. S. 197.

[2] P. v. Flack, 125 N. Y. 324. Motive may be shown as tending to prove intent: U. S. v. Babcock, 3 Dillon, 581.

[3] Wood v. S., 47 N. J. 461.

[4] Rex v. Mawbey, 6 Term R. 619.

[5] Woodworth v. S., 20 Tex. Ap. 375.

[6] S. v. Flynn, 28 Ia. 26.

[7] Reg. v. Hudson, Bell, 263.

[8] S. v. Crowley, 41 Wis. 271.

[9] S. v. Crane, 54 Kan. 251.

II. PROCEDURE.

§ **972. Jurisdiction and venue.**— The venue of the offense is either where the conspiracy is formed or where the overt act thereunder is done, the crime being presumed to continue down to the time of the act, and to exist at that time and place.[1] But acts done elsewhere than in the jurisdiction cannot be shown.[2] It is immaterial that one of the conspirators resides in another state; he is answerable for the conspiracy where the overt act is committed.[3] It seems also that the offense is punishable where the conspiracy is entered into, although it contemplates the doing of a wrongful act elsewhere.[4]

§ **973. Limitation.**— The conspiracy being complete when the crime is entered into, the statute of limitations as against the prosecution therefor begins to run from that time;[5] and the fact that the overt acts upon which the proof of the conspiracy rests are, as distinct offenses, barred by the statute, does not necessarily constitute a bar to the conspiracy, the overt acts being merely evidence to show the existence of the conspiracy.[6] Under the federal statute requiring an overt act to constitute the crime of conspiracy, the period of the statute commences to run with the first overt act;[7] and it is not permissible, in order to avoid the statute of limitations, to consider subsequent acts in pursuance of the same combination as a new conspiracy; even the bringing in of a new party to the combination will not constitute a new conspiracy.[8]

§ **974. The indictment; allegation of wrongful purpose.** Where the criminality of the combination consists in the wrongfulness of the purpose sought to be accomplished, it should

[1] P. v. Mather, 4 Wend. 229; U. S. v. Newton, 52 Fed. R. 275; Rex v. Brisac, 4 East, 164.

[2] Reg. v. Boulton, 12 Cox, 88; U. S. v. Newton, 52 Fed. R. 275.

[3] C. v. Gillespie, 7 Serg. & R. 469. Indeed, it is immaterial whether any of the defendants reside in the jurisdiction where the act is done: U. S. v. Newton, 52 Fed. R. 275.

[4] In re Wolf, 27 Fed. R. 606; Bloomer v. S., 48 Md. 521.

[5] C. v. Bartilson, 85 Pa. St. 482. But it is said, on the contrary, that the prosecution for the conspiracy is not barred until the expiration of the statutory period after the last overt act in pursuance of the conspiracy is done, this perhaps being on the principle that the agreement is constructively attached to the act done in pursuance of it: Ochs v. P., 124 Ill. 399.

[6] C. v. Bartilson, 85 Pa. St. 482.

[7] U. S. v. Owen, 32 Fed. R. 534; U. S. v. Dennee, 3 Woods, 47.

[8] U. S. v. McCord, 72 Fed. R. 159.

clearly appear from the indictment that the purpose was illegal.[1] It must appear that the agreement was to do an unlawful act;[2] and the evidence must be limited to the specific wrong alleged to have been intended.[3] If the wrongful act charged to have been intended is a crime, it is said in some cases that it should be described with the same particularity as in a prosecution for the crime itself.[4] But by the weight of authority it is sufficient to describe the crime intended by the proper name or term by which it is usually known.[5] It will clearly be impossible to designate with exactness the crime intended which may never have been committed.[6] On the other hand, the allegation should be specific enough to point out the particular crime as distinct from general crimes of the same character, so that the defendant may know with what he is charged.[7] The combination to commit a particular wrong must appear by direct averments, and not merely by intendment.[8]

§ 975. **Setting out the unlawful means.**— Where the indictment charges the object of the conspiracy in such way as to show it to be criminal, it is unnecessary to allege specifically the means by which such object was to be accomplished.[9] But where the criminality of the conspiracy consists in the unlawfulness of the means intended to be used, the means must be distinctly set out.[10] There is some doubt under the authorities to which of these classes of cases a conspiracy to cheat and defraud or to obtain money by false pretenses belongs. It has

[1] S. v. Hewett, 31 Me. 396.

[2] C. v. Wallace, 16 Gray, 221; S. v. Stevens, 30 Ia. 391; U. S. v. Walsh, 5 Dillon, 58; U. S. v. Watson, 17 Fed. R. 145.

[3] McDonald v. P., 126 Ill. 150.

[4] Landringham v. S., 49 Ind. 186; Scudder v. S., 62 Ind. 13; Smith v. S., 93 Ind. 67.

[5] S. v. Potter, 28 Ia. 554; S. v. Savoye, 48 Ia. 562; P. v. Dyer, 79 Mich. 480; Reinhold v. S., 130 Ind. 467.

[6] C. v. McKisson, 8 Serg. & R. 420; C. v. Gillespie, 7 Serg. & R. 469; Dealy v. U. S., 152 U. S. 539.

[7] Hartmann v. C., 5 Pa. St. 60.

[8] S. v. Jones, 13 Ia. 269.

[9] Lambert v. P., 9 Cow. 578; S. v. Ripley, 31 Me. 386; P. v. Mather, 4 Wend. 229; P. v. Arnold, 46 Mich. 268; S. v. Crowley, 41 Wis. 271; S. v. Grant, 86 Ia. 216; S. v. Ormiston, 66 Ia. 143. Where defendant was charged with interfering "by force and intimidation" with the employment of another, the means were held to be sufficiently stated: C. v. Dyer, 128 Mass. 70.

[10] S. v. Mayberry, 48 Me. 218; C. v. Hunt, 4 Met. 111; Alderman v. P., 4 Mich. 414; Smith v. P., 25 Ill. 17; S. v. Stevens, 30 Ia. 391; S. v. Jones, 13 Ia. 269; Pettibone v. U. S., 148 U. S. 193.

been held that, in charging the conspiracy to obtain money or goods by false pretenses, it is sufficient to follow the words of the statute, without setting out the particular false pretense relied upon.[1] And likewise it is said that, where the allegation is of a conspiracy to cheat and defraud, the means need not be set out.[2] It is urged that, if the wrongful act is not done, it is impossible to specify definitely the means, and that if it is done the overt act itself may be alleged, but will constitute evidence only of the means intended to be used, or of the character of the conspiracy.[3] On the other hand, it has been urged that, as it is not criminal to cheat and defraud, these terms not being limited to criminal acts, the means employed constitute the criminal element in the conspiracy and should be specifically set forth.[4] The cases which hold that the means to be used to defraud need not be set out seem to be based on Reg. v. Gill, cited above, which has been strongly dissented from both in England and in the United States.[5]

§ 976. **Bills of particulars.**— The indefiniteness allowed by some English cases, as shown in the preceding paragraph, led to the introduction of a rule in accordance with which the court would require the prosecution to furnish a bill of particulars of the means relied upon, where the defendant demanded it, if the indictment was in a general form;[6] and the prosecution was limited thereupon to the transactions thus specified.[7]

[1] Thomas v. P., 113 Ill. 531, 5 Am. Cr. R. 127, and note; McDonald v. P., 126 Ill. 150; Ochs v. P., 124 Ill. 399; P. v. Clark, 10 Mich. 310; S. v. Parker, 43 N. H. 83. This seems to be on the theory that cheating by false pretenses being criminal in itself, the means need not be specifically set out: P. v. Clark, and Thomas v. P., *supra.*

[2] S. v. Young, 37 N. J. 184; S. v. Brady, 107 N. C. 822; Rex v. Eccles, 1 Leach, 274; Reg. v. Gompertz, 9 Q. B. 824; Rex v. Gill, 2 Barn. & Ald. 204; Reg. v. Yates, 6 Cox, 441; Latham v. Reg., 5 B. & S. 635; Taylor v. Reg., 1 Q. B. D. (1895) 25.

[3] S. v. Brady, 107 N. C. 822; S. v. Cardoza, 11 S. C. 195.

[4] C. v. Eastman, 1 Cush. 189; C. v. Wallace, 16 Gray, 221; C. v. Meserve, 154 Mass. 64; Alderman v. P., 4 Mich. 414; P. v. Barkelow, 37 Mich. 455; P. v. Arnold, 46 Mich. 268; S. v. Parker, 43 N. H. 83; S. v. Jones, 13 Ia. 269; S. v. Roberts, 34 Me. 320; Reg. v. Peck, 9 A. & E. 686; Reg. v. King, 7 Q. B. 782.

[5] C. v. Wallace, 16 Gray, 221; Sydserff v. Reg., 11 Q. B. 249.

[6] Rex v. Hamilton, 7 C. & P. 448; Reg. v. Rycroft, 6 Cox, 76; Reg. v. Esdaile, 1 F. & F. 213; C. v. Meserve, 154 Mass. 64.

[7] McDonald v. P., 126 Ill. 150.

But proof of any of the means alleged is sufficient, and it is not necessary to prove all.[1]

§ 977. **Charging overt act.**— From what has already been said in regard to an overt act, it is plain that it is not necessary to charge anything as done in pursuance of the conspiracy except where by statute an overt act is required.[2] If the indictment alleges substantially the facts necessary to show a conspiracy, no act done or injury suffered in consequence thereof need be charged.[3] Although, as will be seen hereafter, the conspirators are each chargeable with whatever is done by any of them in pursuance of the common design,[4] yet the wrong done must be in the carrying out of the conspiracy and must be so charged;[5] and the allegation of wrongful acts will not show the crime of conspiracy where the combination to do such wrongful acts or make use of them as a means does not appear.[6] However, it is a recognized form of charging the crime to allege that defendants conspired to do a certain wrong and then set out the overt acts done in pursuance thereof, thus showing the unlawful act done or means used; and this is regarded as a sufficient charge of conspiring to do such unlawful act or use such unlawful means.[7] But it is immaterial that the overt act as charged constituted an independent crime, even a crime of a higher grade than the conspiracy; for the charge in such form is not considered as a charge of the crime involved in the act done, but of the crime of conspiracy involved in the agreement to do the act.[8] In such cases the allegation of the act done is to be regarded rather as matter of aggravation than as matter of substance.[9] It is not essential, therefore, to conviction that the

[1] C. v. Meserve, 154 Mass. 64.

[2] *Supra*, § 966.

[3] C. v. Fuller, 132 Mass. 563; State v. Straw, 42 N. H. 393; P. v. Richards, 1 Mich. 216.

[4] *Infra*, § 988. And this is true even though the acts done by the several conspirators separately constitute distinct offenses: C. v. O'Brien, 12 Cush. 84.

[5] C. v. Shedd, 7 Cush. 514.

[6] C. v. Hunt, 4 Met. 111; S. v. Rickey, 9 N. J. 293; P. v. Clark, 10 Mich. 310; S. v. Swain, 68 Mo. 605.

[7] Dealy v. U. S., 152 U. S. 539; C. v. Foering, Brightly, 315.

[8] S. v. Bradley, 48 Conn. 535; S. v. Mayberry, 48 Me. 218; S. v. Murray, 15 Me. 100; S. v. Ormiston, 66 Ia. 143; C. v. McHale, 97 Pa. St. 397; C. v. Delany, 1 Grant, 224; U. S. v. Gardner, 42 Fed. R. 829; Wright v. Reg., 14 Q. B. 148; Reg. v. Esdaile, 1 F. & F. 213.

[9] S. v. Murray, 15 Me. 100; C. v. Ward, 92 Ky. 158; U. S. v. Dennee, 3 Woods, 47; U. S. v. Gardner, 42 Fed. R. 829.

overt act be proven, provided enough be established to show the conspiracy charged;[1] and more than one overt act may be charged,[2] and other overt acts than those charged may be proven.[3] But it is not admissible to show a specific overt act whölly independent of the acts charged and having no relation thereto except in being the act of the same persons.[4] Where the statute makes the unlawful malicious combination to injure the business of another criminal, the means or overt acts employed are properly set out as showing the malice.[5]

§ 978. **Duplicity.**— The charge of conspiracy to commit more than one offense is not bad for duplicity, the conspiracy being single.[6] Neither does it constitute duplicity that, under the federal statute which provides an additional punishment in a particular form of conspiracy for the commission of a crime in pursuance thereof, the commission of such crime is also charged.[7]

§ 979. **Merger.**— At common law conspiracy was a misdemeanor, and the rule of procedure as to misdemeanors being that different crimes of that grade might be charged in the same indictment, it was said that, where a misdemeanor was committed in pursuance of the conspiracy, such conspiracy was not merged in the misdemeanor, while it was merged if the crime subsequently committed was a felony.[8] The decided weight of the more recent cases is in support of the proposition that the conspiracy is not merged in the subsequent commission of the contemplated offense, even though it be a felony.[9]

§ 980. **Joinder of offenses.**— On the principle stated in the preceding paragraph, it is held proper to join a count for a misdemeanor committed in pursuance of the conspiracy with a count for the conspiracy itself;[10] and of course the same

1 C. v. Judd, 2 Mass. 329.

2 McDonald v. P., 126 Ill. 150.

3 S. v. Young, 37 N. J. 184.

4 McDonald v. P., 126 Ill. 150.

5 P. v. Petheram, 64 Mich. 252.

6 Noyes v. S., 41 N. J. 418; S. v. Grant, 86 Ia. 216; O'Connell v. Reg., 11 Cl. & F. 155.

7 U. S. v. Lancaster, 44 Fed. R. 885.

8 P. v. Richards, 1 Mich. 216; P. v. Mather, 4 Wend. 265; S. v. Noyes, 25 Vt. 415; C. v. Delany, 1 Grant, 224; Fitzgerald v. S., 14 Mo. 413; C. v. Kingsbury, 5 Mass. 106. In Arkansas this is the rule by statute: Elsey v. S., 47 Ark. 572.

9 Johnson v. S., 26 N. J. 313; S. v. Wilson, 30 Conn. 500; S. v. Grant, 86 Ia. 216; P. v. Petheram, 64 Mich. 252; U. S. v. Gardner, 42 Fed. R. 829; Reg. v. Button, 11 Q. B. 929.

10 Thomas v. P., 113 Ill. 531.

conspiracy may be charged in different counts in different forms.[1]

§ **981. Joinder of defendants.**— As a conspiracy necessarily involves guilt on the part of two or more persons,[2] if two are indicted for the crime an acquittal of one is necessarily an acquittal of the other.[3] So the entry of a *nol. pros.* as to one prevents further proceedings as against the other.[4] If one of several defendants is acquitted, the record of his acquittal is admissible in evidence in favor of another of the defendants subsequently tried.[5] But one of the conspirators may be indicted separately;[6] or if two or more are indicted a separate trial may be granted to one;[7] and judgment may be rendered as against the one first tried, notwithstanding the possibility that the others charged with the same conspiracy may be acquitted.[8] If where two or more are tried together a ground for new trial is shown as to one, the new trial must be granted as to all.[9] The strictness of procedure in the case of principal and accessory requiring that the accessory shall not be punished unless the principal is convicted is not applicable, however, to conspiracy cases; and one conspirator may be convicted although the other has died, so that a conviction will be impossible.[10] If the defendant is indicted for conspiring with other parties to the grand jury unknown, a failure to convict another will have no effect in regard to the conviction of the one charged.[11] And under the charge against one defendant of conspiring with others named, there may be a conviction on a proof of conspiracy with any of the others named, without proof of such conspiracy participated in by all of them.[12] So, if several are indicted jointly, two or more may be convicted.[13]

[1] Reg. v. Gompertz, 9 Q. B. 824.

[2] U. S. v. Cole, 3 McLean, 513.

[3] S. v. Tom, 2 Dev. 569; O'Connell v. Reg., 11 Cl. & F. 155; Reg. v. Manning, 12 Q. B. D. 241.

[4] S. v. Jackson, 7 S. C. 283.

[5] Paul v. S., 12 Tex. Ap. 346.

[6] P. v. Richards, 67 Cal. 412; C. v. Demain, Brightly, 441; Heine v. C., 91 Pa. St. 145; U. S. v. Miller, 3 Hughes, 553.

[7] S. v. Buchanan, 5 Har. & J. 500; S. v. Brien, 32 N. J. 414; Reg. v. Ahearne, 6 Cox, 6.

[8] Reg. v. Ahearne, 6 Cox, 6.

[9] Reg. v. Gompertz, 9 Q. B. 824.

[10] Rex v. Nicholls, 13 East, 412, n.; Reg. v. Henrick, 5 Q. B. 49.

[11] P. v. Mather, 4 Wend. 229; C. v. Edwards, 135 Pa. St. 474.

[12] S. v. Adams, 1 Houst. Cr. C. 361; Woodworth v. S., 20 Tex. Ap. 375; Reg. v. Thompson, 16 Q. B. 832.

[13] O'Connell v. Reg., 11 Cl. & F. 155.

§ 982. **The person to be injured.**— Where the charge is of a conspiracy to defraud in general, it is not necessary to specifically allege the name of the person or persons intended to be defrauded. It is enough to charge the intent to defraud persons of a particular class or description.[1] But if the conspiracy charged is to defraud a particular person, he should be named.[2] And the proof must correspond to the allegation in this respect.[3] If the charge is of a conspiracy to defraud the public generally, proof of an intent to defraud a particular person will constitute a variance.[4] But it is not necessary to allege the name of all persons intended to be injured; it is sufficient to state the names of some and that the names of others are to the grand jurors unknown.[5]

§ 983. **Description of property.**— Where the intent alleged as involved in the conspiracy is to deprive another of property by a certain means stated, the property should be in some way specified.[6] But it is not essential that the conspiracy have reference to any particular property.[7]

§ 984. **Statutory language.**— Where the statute defining the particular kind of conspiracy which is sought to be charged is specific as to what constitutes the crime, the indictment may follow the language of the statute;[8] but if the language of the statute is general, as it usually is, in defining conspiracy, it is not sufficient to follow the words of the statute.[9] And a statute prescribing the form of indictment which does not advise the defendant as to the facts relied on to constitute the offense is unconstitutional.[10]

§ 985. **Variance.**— The conspiracy and its object must be proven as alleged;[11] but certainty to a common intent is all that is required.[12]

[1] C. v. Judd, 2 Mass. 329; P. v. Arnold, 46 Mich. 268; Rex v. Bykerdyke, 1 M. & Rob. 179; Reg. v. Steel, Car. & M. 337; Reg. v. Peck, 9 A. & E. 686; Rex v. De Berenger, 3 Maule & S. 68; Reg. v. King, 7 Q. B. 782.

[2] Reg. v. Parker, 3 Q. B. 292; King v. Reg., 7 Q. B. 795; Sydserff v. Reg., 11 Q. B. 245; Reg. v. Bullock, Dears. 653; U. S. v. Gardner, 42 Fed. R. 829.

[3] Reg. v. Dean, 4 Jur. 364.

[4] C. v. Kellogg, 7 Cush. 473.

[5] S. v. Grant, 86 Ia. 216.

[6] S. v. Rochforde, 52 Mo. 199; Rex v. Richardson, 1 M. & Rob. 402.

[7] Reg. v. Blake, 6 Q. B. 126; Reg. v. Gompertz, 9 Q. B. 824.

[8] Cole v. P., 84 Ill. 216; Reg. v. Rowlands, 17 Q. B. 671.

[9] U. S. v. Cruikshank, 92 U. S. 542; In re Benson, 58 Fed. Rep. 965; Reg. v. Peck, 9 A. & E. 686.

[10] Landringham v. S., 49 Ind. 186.

[11] Evans v. P., 90 Ill. 384; McDonald v. P., 126 Ill. 150.

[12] U. S. v. Stevens, 44 Fed. R. 132.

§ 986. Form of indictment.—There are no special words or terms of art regarded as indispensable in an indictment for conspiracy, and the form varies so much with the circumstances of the case that it is impracticable to present in a few examples the details which may be necessary to fit every occasion. The forms presented may serve as types, however, and to that extent will be useful. It is to be noticed that the averment of an overt act, as has been already explained, is unnecessary, though common. Such a form of averment is introduced in one of the following examples and would be proper in any of them, while, on the other hand, it is not essential in the one in which it is used.

TO COMMIT A CRIME.

That the said A. B. and C. D., on the —— day of ——, in the county aforesaid, did unlawfully conspire and agree together to commit the crime of robbery, to wit, by then and there assaulting one John Jones, and putting him, the said John Jones, in bodily fear; and did then and there from the person and against the will of him, the said John Jones, by means of the said assault and putting him in fear as aforesaid, feloniously, forcibly and by violence, steal, take and carry away one gold watch of the value of twenty-five dollars, the property of the said John Jones.

TO FALSELY CHARGE WITH A CRIME.

That the said A. B., C. D., E. F. and G. H., on the —— day of ——, in the county aforesaid, did among themselves unlawfully conspire, combine, confederate and agree to extort, obtain and procure of and from one W. P. large sums of money and a large amount of property for their own use, and, in order to extort, obtain and procure the same, did corruptly and unlawfully conspire and agree together falsely to charge and cause to have feloniously charged the said W. P., before one of the justices of the peace of said county, on and by the oath of the said A. B., with the crime of rape committed on the person of the said A. B., and to procure the issuing of a warrant thereupon by said justice of the peace for the arrest of said W. P. upon the said charge aforesaid, and when the said W. P. should be so arrested, and under duress of imprisonment, to extort, obtain and procure from the said W. P. said money and property by offering to receive the same for the suppression and compromise of the said charge, and for the liberation of the said W. P. from arrest and imprisonment under said warrant.[1]

[1] This is based in the main on the first count of the indictment in Johnson v. S., 26 N. J. 313.

TO DEFRAUD.

That the said A. B., C. D. and E. F., on the —— day of ——, in the county aforesaid, wickedly and injuriously devising and intending one J. C. to defraud and cheat of his goods and property, did then and there feloniously and fraudulently conspire, combine, confederate and agree together among themselves to get and obtain knowingly and designedly by false pretenses of the said J. C. one horse of the value of six hundred dollars, the property of him, the said J. C., with the intent then and there to cheat and defraud the said J. C. of said horse.[1]

TO BOYCOTT.

That said A. B., on the —— day of ——, in the county aforesaid, with C. D., E. F., and other persons to the said grand jurors unknown, did unlawfully combine, conspire, confederate and agree together to prevent, hinder and deter by violence, threats and intimidations the Ryegate Granite Works, a corporation then and there being and existing by law, from retaining and taking into its employment J. O., W. G., and others to the said grand jurors unknown, then and there being, as laborers in the labor and occupation of granite cutting, to the great damage of the said Ryegate Granite Works and the said J. O. and W. G.[2]

§ 987. **Punishment.**—Where the punishment to be inflicted is not fixed in any way by statute, but is left, as at common law, for the court to determine, it is said that it should not be greater than that provided for the offense which the conspirators combined to commit.[3] And as conspiracy is at common

[1] This is a form of indictment sustained in Johnson v. P., 22 Ill. 314. It was urged as an objection that it did not specify with sufficient definiteness the crime intended to be committed or the means intended to be used, but the court say that the very nature of the offense would as a general thing render it impossible for the prosecutor to ascertain and prove the means agreed to be employed. Perhaps the indictment in this form would not be held sufficient in states where it is required that the offense intended to be committed shall be described with the same particularity as in an indictment for such offense itself, but under the decisions in many of the states it would unquestionably be sufficient. An indictment for conspiracy to procure by false pretenses, false representations, and other fraudulent means, a female named to have illicit carnal connection with a man named, drawn in the same concise language as the indictment here set out, was held sufficient in Smith v. P., 25 Ill. 17.

[2] This is substantially based on the first count in the indictment set out in S. v. Stewart, 59 Vt. 273.

[3] Hartmann v. C., 5 Pa. St. 60; Williams v. C., 34 Pa. St. 178. See *supra*, § 952.

law a misdemeanor only, the punishment should, aside from statutory provision, be only that for a misdemeanor.[1]

III. EVIDENCE.

§ 988. Declarations and acts of co-conspirators.— The rules of evidence relating in the prosecution of any crime to the weight to be given to the admissions of a co-conspirator and the necessity for corroboration are not for discussion here; for they have no peculiar connection with a prosecution for conspiracy. But as applied in prosecutions for the crime of conspiracy some statement of them is proper in this chapter. One of these rules finding particular application in this connection is that the declarations of one of the conspirators in furtherance of the common design may be shown against the others, the fact of conspiracy having been established.[2] And as such declarations may tend to show the object of the conspiracy, they are admissible even as against one who was not a party to it at the time they were made, but afterwards engaged therein.[3] The same rule applicable to declarations is recognized as to acts of co-conspirators.[4] As to other acts or declarations it is immaterial that they were not done or made in the presence of the conspirator against whom they are sought to be proven.[5] This rule, allowing proof of other acts and declarations, is liberally applied in cases of insurrectionary conspiracies so as to allow public addresses, printed matter, and everything relating to the carrying out of the conspiracy, to be shown as against any one of the conspirators.[6] Transactions

[1] S. v. Jackson, 82 N. C. 565; S. v. Dyer, 67 Vt. 690; Bannon v. U. S., 156 U. S. 464.

[2] Wilson v. P., 94 Ill. 299; Spies v. P., 122 Ill. 1; Seville v. S., 49 Ohio St. 117; P. v. Geiger, 49 Cal. 643; S. v. Simons, 4 Strobh. 266; C. v. O'Brien, 140 Pa. St. 555; Gill v. S., 59 Ark. 422; P. v. Trim, 39 Cal. 75; S. v. Banks, 40 La. An. 736; S. v. Ford, 37 La. An. 443; Cohea v. S., 11 Tex. Ap. 153; U. S. v. Graff, 14 Blatchf. 381; U. S. v. Lancaster, 44 Fed. R. 896; U. S. v. Cassidy, 67 Fed. R. 698; Rex v. Salter, 5 Esp. 225. Acts and declarations of those not joined in the prosecution may be shown, if done or made in carrying out the conspiracy: Clune v. U. S., 159 U. S. 590.

[3] Sands v. C., 21 Grat. 871; U. S. v. Logan, 45 Fed. R. 872.

[4] U. S. v. Lancaster, 44 Fed. R. 896; U. S. v. Cassidy, 67 Fed. R. 698; Reg. v. Desmond, 11 Cox, 146; Reg. v. Blake, 6 Q. B. 126; Reg. v. Esdaile, 1 F. & F. 213.

[5] P. v. McKane, 143 N. Y. 455; S. v. Anderson, 92 N. C. 732; S. v. Cardoza, 11 S. C. 195; U. S. v. Logan, 45 Fed. R. 872.

[6] Spies v. P., 122 Ill. 1; Reg. v. Vin-

other than those involved in the crime charged, for instance, the defrauding of other persons than those named in the indictment, by similar means, may be shown.[1] The introduction of proof of declarations or acts of co-conspirators must be limited, however, to those made during the existence of the conspiracy. Declarations made by one of the conspirators before the formation of the conspiracy are not admissible as against the others;[2] nor are those made after the conspiracy is ended.[3] The general proposition is that the declaration, to be admissible as above indicated, must have been made while the person making it was himself a co-conspirator with the defendant.[4]

§ 989. Proof of the existence of the conspiracy.— From what has been said in the preceding paragraph it is evident that acts and declarations of another are admissible as against defendant on the theory that such other person is a co-conspirator, only when that fact is established; but while it is usual to first introduce the evidence of the conspiracy before the proof of such acts or declarations is offered, yet the order of introduction of the evidence is in the discretion of the court, and in such discretion the acts or declarations may be received subject to the production of subsequent proof of the conspiracy which will make them available as against the defendant.[5] But the fact of the conspiracy must be established by sufficient evidence to make out a *prima facie* case in order to justify the jury in considering the acts and declarations. The conspiracy itself cannot be shown by proof of acts of the alleged conspirators taken separately.[6] Nevertheless, as the conspiracy

cent, 9 C. & P. 275; Reg. v. Shellard, 9 C. & P. 277; Reg. v. Duffield, 5 Cox, 404; Rex v. Hunt, 3 B. & A. 566.

[1] Reg. v. Stenson, 12 Cox, 111; Reg. v. Whitehouse, 6 Cox, 38; Rex v. Roberts, 1 Campb. 399; Reinhold v. S., 130 Ind. 467.

[2] Wilson v. P., 94 Ill. 299; Cox v. S., 8 Tex. Ap. 254.

[3] Danville Bank v. Waddill's Adm'r, 31 Grat. 469; Logan v. U. S., 144 U. S. 263; S. v. Dean, 13 Ired. 63; Snowden v. S., 7 Baxt. 482; Ricks v. S., 19 Tex. Ap. 308; Reg. v. Blake, 6 Q. B. 126.

[4] Sands v. C., 21 Grat. 871.

[5] Spies v. P., 122 Ill. 1; S. v. Cardoza, 11 S. C. 195; Bloomer v. S., 48 Md. 521; Devore v. T., 2 Okl. 562; Queen's Case, 2 Brod. & Bing. 302. The defendant can be sufficiently protected by instructions to the jury to disregard such acts and declarations unless the conspiracy is proved: Loggins v. S., 12 Tex. Ap. 65. Conspiracy may be shown, even when not charged as a substantive offense, for the purpose of connecting defendant as accessory before the fact to the completed offense charged: Spies v. P., 122 Ill. 1.

[6] Shields v. McKee, 11 Ill. Ap. 188;

itself may be made out by circumstantial evidence,[1] proof of the carrying out of the general plan by those charged, and the committing of acts connected with the accomplishment of such plan, may show the conspiracy without proof of intimacy, private meetings, consultations, etc.[2] The vital element is the fraudulent and corrupt combination, which must be proved either by direct evidence or through the explanation of such circumstances as necessarily tend to show it.[3]

§ 990. **Necessity of corroboration.**— The general rule that one is not to be convicted of a crime on the confessions or declarations of an accomplice without corroboration is applicable where, as against defendant, it is sought to establish a conspiracy by proof of such confessions or declarations on the part of a co-conspirator.[4]

Danville Bank v. Waddill's Adm'r, 31 Grat. 469.

[1] S. v. Sterling, 34 Ia. 443; U. S. v. Barrett, 65 Fed. R. 62.

[2] C. v. Warren, 6 Mass. 74; Ochs v. P., 124 Ill. 399; Spies v. P., 122 Ill. 1; S. v. Sterling, 34 Ia. 443; C. v. Eberle, 3 Serg. & R. 9; Reg. v. Brittain, 3 Cox, 77; Rex v. Ferguson, 2 Stark. 489.

[3] C. v. Ridgway, 2 Ashm. 247; Nail v. S., 70 Miss. 32; Reg. v. Taylor, 25 L. T. 75.

[4] U. S. v. Lancaster, 44 Fed. R. 896; U. S. v. Logan, 45 Fed. R. 872; U. S. v. Howell, 56 Fed. R. 21; U. S. v. Cole, 5 McLean, 513.

CHAPTER 42.

RIOT; UNLAWFUL ASSEMBLY.

I. In General.
II. Riot and Rout.
III. Unlawful Assembly.

I. In General.

§ 991. **Nature of offenses.**— These offenses are alike in that they involve the element of public disturbance by reason of combination, and require that three or more participate.[1] Affray is a similar crime, elsewhere discussed, which may be committed by two.[2] Other disturbances, not involving the element of combination, are discussed under another chapter relating to the breaches of the peace.

II. Riot and Rout.

§ 992. **Definition.**— The definition given by Hawkins is the one which has been most frequently quoted: "A riot seems to be a tumultuous disturbance of the peace by three or more per-

[1] Blackstone's discussion is instructive here: "Riots, routs and unlawful assemblies must have three persons at least to constitute them. An unlawful assembly is when three or more do assemble themselves together to do an unlawful act; as, to pull down inclosures; to destroy a warren or the game therein; and part without doing it or making any motion towards it. A rout is where three or more meet to do an unlawful act upon a common quarrel; as, forcibly breaking down fences upon a right claimed of common, or of way; and make some advances toward it. A riot is where three or more actually do an unlawful act of violence, either with or without a common cause or quarrel; as, if they beat a man; or hunt and kill game in another's park, chase, warren, or liberty; or do any other unlawful act with force and violence; or even do a lawful act; as, removing a nuisance in a violent and tumultuous manner." 4 Bl. Com. 146. For rout, which need not be further discussed, as it has received but slight practical recognition in this country, see, also, S. v. Sumner, 2 Speers, 599; 2 Bish. Cr. L., § 1183; 1 Hawk. P. C., ch. 65, § 8. The term "routously," as well as "riotously," is used in indictments for riot (see S. v. Boies, 34 Me. 235; S. v. Russell, 45 N. H. 83); but in the forms hereafter given (*infra*, § 999), based on those cases, it is omitted as wholly useless.

[2] See *infra*, § 1006.

sons assembled together of their own authority, with the intent mutually to assist one another against any one who shall oppose them in the execution of some enterprise of a private nature, and who afterwards actually execute the same in a violent and turbulent manner to the terror of the people, whether the act intended were of itself lawful or unlawful."[1] Statutory definitions usually embody substantially the common-law notion, save that the element of unlawfulness in the assembling is usually omitted, it being sufficient that the persons assembled, whether with lawful intentions or not, shall proceed to do an unlawful act of violence, or any act in a violent and tumultuous manner.[2]

§ 993. **Unlawfulness of act or manner.**— Some form of violence seems an essential element of the crime of riot,[3] and it was at common law usual to charge the act as accompanied with terror to the people in general.[4] But this allegation is only necessary where the gist of the offense consists in the terror of the public by the conduct of the parties,[5] and not where an act of violence is charged.[6] There are many illustra-

[1] 1 Hawk. P. C., ch. 65, § 1; 1 Russ. Cr. L. 266. This has been expressed in somewhat more modern language, as follows: "A riot is a tumultuous disturbance of the peace by three or more persons assembled together of their own authority with the intent mutually to assist each other against any who shall oppose them, and putting their design into execution in a terrifying and violent manner, whether the object was lawful or not:" S. v. Connolly, 3 Rich. 337. The essence of Hawkins' definition is repeated in an abbreviated form in S. v. Cole, 2 McCord, 117. Bishop's definition is probably theoretically sufficient. It is certainly concise: "A riot is such disorderly conduct in three or more assembled persons, mutually accomplishing an object, as is calculated to terrify others:" 2 Bish. Cr. L., § 1143.

[2] Dougherty v. P., 5 Ill. 179; Logg v. P., 92 Ill. 598; Davenport v. S., 38 Ga. 184; Rachels v. S., 51 Ga. 374; Stafford v. S., 93 Ga. 207; Blackwell v. S., 30 Tex. Ap. 672; U. S. v. McFarland, 1 Cranch, C. C. 140; U. S. v. Dunn, 1 Cranch, C. C. 165. It is sufficient if the facts shown constitute an attempt to commit an act of violence, which, if completed, would be an indictable offense: S. v. York, 70 N. C. 66. But in an earlier case in the same state it was said that, if the assembly is lawful, the subsequent ill-conduct on the part of the persons assembled will not make them rioters: S. v. Stalcup, 1 Ired. 30.

[3] S. v. Russell, 45 N. H. 83; Scott v. U. S., Morris, 142.

[4] S. v. Voshall, 4 Ind. 589; Rex v. Cox, 4 C. & P. 538; Rex v. Hughes, 4 C. & P. 273; 2 Bish. Cr. Pr., § 997.

[5] S. v. Whitesides, 1 Swan, 88.

[6] C. v. Runnells, 10 Mass. 518; Thayer v. S., 11 Ind. 287. It seems that if any one person is terrified this is sufficient to substantiate such a charge in the indictment: Reg. v. Langford, Car. & M. 602. But where

tions of riot where the violence is toward one individual only or one family. Thus, where three persons using threatening language toward an individual proceeded to destroy or injure his property, it was held that the acts were sufficient to constitute a riot.[1] Under an English statute the tumultuous assembling of persons to demolish a house, with acts amounting to the beginning of such demolition, constitutes a riot.[2] But the offense may be committed without violence threatened toward any particular individual. Violently breaking into a public meeting with loud noise and shouts is sufficient.[3] The use of force, or the threat to use it, need not necessarily be noisy, boisterous or tumultuous if the intent and power exist.[4] While political demonstrations are proper, a tumultuous assembly for the purpose of violence to an individual or class of individuals or destruction of their property will be criminal.[5] Assembling in a tumultuous manner to oppose the course of justice or to raise opposition to the government is a riot;[6] so is the assembling for an unlawful act or in a way to disturb the peace at an unseasonable time.[7] It is not necessary that any unlawful act be done or threatened; the manner of doing a lawful act may be so tumultuous and riotous as to constitute a crime.[8] The crime may consist in the nature of the act done in view of the time and place of doing it. Thus, attending a place of worship, and laughing and talking there in such manner as to show an intention and determination to resist by force any effort to remove the intruders, may constitute a riot.[9]

the indictment alleged the assembling in a violent and tumultuous manner, etc., near the dwelling-house of A. B., with the use of opprobious epithets towards A. B. and his wife, that the indictment for riot was not sufficient, it not appearing that A. B. and his wife were in the house: S. v. Hathcock, 7 Ired. 52.

1 S. v. Jackson, 1 Speers, 13; S. v. Alexander, 7 Rich. 5; Sanders v. S., 60 Ga. 126. So held where the rioters went to the house of another and assaulted and beat him: Bolden v. S., 64 Ga. 361.

2 Reg. v. Langford, Car. & M. 602; Reg. v. Harris, Car. & M. 661; Reg. v. Howell, 9 C. & P. 437; Rex v. Thomas, 4 C. & P. 237; Rex v. Price, 5 C. & P. 510; Rex v. Batt, 6 C. & P. 329. There seems to be a similar statute in Virginia: Samanni v. C., 16 Grat. 543.

3 C. v. Runnels, 10 Mass. 518.

4 P. v. O'Loughlin, 3 Utah, 133.

5 S. v. Russell, 45 N. H. 83.

6 Pennsylvania v. Morrison, Addison, 274; S. v. Boies, 34 Me. 235.

7 Pennsylvania v. Cribs, Addison, 277.

8 Kiphart v. S., 42 Ind. 273; S. v. Dillard, 5 Blackf. 365; S. v. Brooks, 1 Hill (S. C.), 361.

9 C. v. Dupuy, Brightly, 44. But it

By an Indiana statute, known as the "White Cap Act," it is made criminal to combine together for the purpose of doing an unlawful act in the night-time, while wearing white cap masks, etc.;[1] but under a statute for the punishment of committing an unlawful act in a riotous manner, it is not sufficient merely to prove a riotous assembling, but there must be an act, or an attempt to commit an act, which is in itself unlawful.[2]

§ 994. **Numbers of persons.**— The definition of riot at common law, as already given, involves the assembling of three or more persons,[3] but statutes in some states make the assembling and riotous proceeding by two or more sufficient.[4]

§ 995. **Participation.**— There must be the intent on the part of those assembled to participate in threatened violence or tumult,[5] presence alone not being sufficient;[6] and even the fact of subsequent participation by those assembled will not necessarily constitute a riot, if there was not an intention in assembling to proceed riotously;[7] but the intent may be inferred from the circumstances.[8] All who are present intending to aid and abet will be guilty, although the riotous acts are done by only one,[9] the question whether those present were encouraging and taking part in the general design being for the jury.[10] Indeed, those who take part in the general design and plan may be guilty, though not present when the acts of violence are actually committed.[11]

is said that "being concerned in a row" is not indictable: S. v. Ridgley, 10 La. An. 302.

[1] Hobbs v. S., 133 Ind. 404.

[2] Smith v. S., 14 Mo. 147.

[3] *Supra*, § 992; Maxwell v. Carlile, 1 McCord, 534; S. v. Calder, 2 McCord, 462.

[4] Prince v. S., 30 Ga. 27; Stafford v. S., 93 Ga. 207; Dougherty v. P., 5 Ill. 179; Logg v. P., 92 Ill. 598; S. v. Sumner, 2 Speers, 599.

[5] S. v. Kempf, 26 Mo. 429; Sloan v. S., 9 Ind. 565.

[6] Nicholson's Case, 1 Lewin, 300; Reg. v. Atkinson, 11 Cox, 330. But the acts may be proven first before connecting the others present with them: Reg. v. Cooper, 1 Russ., C. & M. 405.

[7] S. v. Kempf, 26 Mo. 429.

[8] Pennsylvania v. Cribs, Addison, 277; U. S. v. Stockwell, 4 Cranch, C. C. 671; U. S. v. Fenwick, 4 Cranch, C. C. 675.

[9] S. v. Straw, 33 Me. 554; Williams v. S., 9 Mo. 268; Newby v. T., 1 Oreg. 163; Reg. v. Howell, 9 C. & P. 437; Rex v. Hunt, 1 Russ., C. & M. 388. As to liability of those participating for other injuries done, see *supra*, § 197.

[10] Reg. v. Harris, Car. & M. 661.

[11] Reg. v. Simpson, Car. & M. 669; Reg. v. Sharpe, 3 Cox, 228; Reg. v. Howell, 9 C. & P. 437.

§ **996. Conviction of one alone.**— One alone cannot be convicted under a charge of riot, unless it is shown that others were engaged in the unlawful act;[1] but even if three or more be indicted, it is not necessary to prove three of them guilty, if the charge is of acting with others described as unknown, and it appears that three or more were engaged in the unlawful proceeding.[2] As in other cases it seems to be necessary, however, where the averment is that the other rioters are to the grand jurors unknown, to prove that fact.[3] And the fact that others engaged in the riot, or the result as between the defendant and those so engaged, is immaterial.[4] As in the case of conspiracy, it is not necessary that others be convicted before one defendant who is proved guilty of the offense is sentenced.[5]

§ **997. Reading the riot act.**— There are provisions in England, and in various states, by which magistrates are required to go before the rioters and command them to disperse, reading the statute provided in such cases, after which a continuance in the riot constitutes a much more serious offense.[6] But such a proceeding on the part of the magistrate is not necessary to render the rioters guilty of the common-law offense.[7]

§ **998. Indictment.**— It is sufficient to allege that defendants riotously, etc., assembled to disturb the peace of the state, and being so assembled did commit a specifically named act of violence, without setting out that they had assembled to do the particular act which they did do.[8] But the allegation of un-

[1] Pennsylvania v. Craig, Addison, 190; Hardebeck v. S., 10 Ind. 459; Turpin v. S., 4 Blackf. 72.

[2] C. v. Berry, 5 Gray, 93; S. v. Brazil, Rice, 257; S. v. Blair, 13 Rich. 93; S. v. Eagan, 10 La. An. 698.

[3] S. v. Calder, 2 McCord, 462. But in another case it is said that a charge that some of the rioters are unknown is a negative averment which need not be proven, the *onus* of disproving it being on the defendant: S. v. Blair, 13 Rich. 93.

[4] Whitley v. S., 66 Ga. 656.

[5] S. v. Bailey, 3 Blackf. 209; Rex v. Scott, 3 Burr. 1262. As to conspiracy, see *supra*, § 981.

[6] Rex v. James, 5 C. & P. 153; Rex v. Woolcock, 5 C. & P. 516; Rex v. Childe, 4 C. & P. 442; Rex v. Kennett, 5 C. & P. 282, n.; Reg. v. Neale, 9 C. & P. 431; Rex v. Fursey, 6 C. & P. 81.

[7] S. v. Russell, 45 N. H. 83; C. v. Runnels, 10 Mass. 518; Rex v. Fursey, 6 C. & P. 81. As to the protection given to the magistrates and peace officers and the authority which they may exercise in calling for assistance under the English statute, see Rex v. Pinney, 5 C. & P. 254; Rex v. Kennett, 5 C. & P. 282, n.; Reg. v. Phelps, Car. & M. 180; Reg. v. Brown, Car. & M. 314.

[8] S. v. Russell, 45 N. H. 83; Bonneville v. S., 53 Wis. 680.

lawful assembling is essential, the mere charge that they riotously and violently did some act not being sufficient.[1] Where the charge was riotously disturbing, etc., a justice's court then and there held, etc., it was considered unnecessary to set out what case was being tried, or that the justice was lawfully holding court, or that he was lawfully authorized or appointed to hold such court.[2] Although some state statutes seem to provide a summary remedy, a defendant should not be tried and convicted without an indictment setting forth the nature and cause of the accusation.[3]

§ 999. **Forms of indictment.**— The following illustrations will sufficiently indicate the method in which the elements of the offense are usually charged:

BREAKING UP A COURT.

The said A. B., together with divers other persons to the number of ten, who are to the grand jurors unknown, on the —— day of ——, in the county aforesaid, with force and arms did unlawfully and riotously, and in a violent and tumultuous manner, assemble to disturb the peace of the state; and being so then and there assembled, did unlawfully, riotously and in a violent and tumultuous manner, then and there disturb, obstruct, enter and break up a justice's court, then and there held before Joseph Barrett, one of the justices of the peace within and for the county aforesaid, to the terror and disturbance of others of the good people of the state.[4]

TO MAKE AN ASSAULT.

That A. B., C. D., E. F. and G. H., on the —— day of ——, in the county aforesaid, with force and arms did unlawfully and riotously assemble and gather together to disturb the peace of the state; and being then and there so assembled and gathered together, in and upon one F. J. unlawfully and riotously did make an assault, and him, the said F. J., did then and there unlawfully and riotously beat, wound and ill-treat, so that his life was thereby greatly endangered, and other

[1] C. v. Gibney, 2 Allen, 150; Reg. v. Soley, 2 Salk. 594. There must be not only an unlawful act done but an unlawful assembly of two or more persons: Blackwell v. S., 30 Tex. Ap. 672.

[2] S. v. Boies, 34 Me. 235.

[3] Mackaboy v. C., 2 Va. Cas. 268.

[4] This follows substantially a count which was held sufficient in S. v. Boies, 34 Me. 235. As to the forms of averment which may properly be used, see, also, U. S. v. Fenwick, 4 Cranch, C. C. 675.

wrongs then and there unlawfully and riotously did commit, to the great damage of him, the said F. J., and to the great terror of the people.[1]

TO THREATEN INJURY.

That said A. B., C. D. and E. F., on the —— day of ——, in the said county, did then and there in a riotous, tumultuous and violent manner assemble themselves together, and then and there in a riotous, tumultuous and violent manner, having then and there the present ability so to do, did unlawfully attempt to commit a violent injury on the person of one Richard Roe, by then and there violently threatening to beat, cut and shoot the said Richard Roe.[2]

§ **1000. Description of property.**— If an indictment charges the pulling down of a dwelling-house as an unlawful act done, it should set forth whose house it was;[3] and where riot and forcible trespass is charged, the premises should be described as in the possession of the occupant, rather than in that of the owner.[4] Parol evidence of possession is sufficient.[5]

§ **1001. Included crime.**— It seems to be permissible in some states, under a single count charging a riot and assault and battery, to convict the defendants, or one of them, for assault, or assault and battery alone;[6] but it is more in accordance with the general rule against charging more than one crime in a single count to hold, as some cases do, that a conviction for assault and battery cannot be had under an indictment for riot, the two offenses being distinct, and the one not necessarily included in the other, the charge of assault and battery included in the count charging a riot being construed as a part of the charge of riot.[7] Of course, at common law, where different misdemeanors might be charged in different counts, there would be no objection to charging riot in one count and an assault and battery in another.[8]

[1] This is based upon an indictment held sufficient in S. v. Russell, 45 N. H. 83.

[2] This was held sufficient in S. v. Acra, 2 Ind. Ap. 384, 28 N. E. R. 570.

[3] S. v. Martin, 3 Murph. 533.

[4] S. v. Wilson, 1 Ired. 32.

[5] S. v. Wilson, 1 Ired. 32; S. v. Bennett, 4 Dev. & B. 43.

[6] Shouse v. C., 5 Pa. St. 83; White v. P., 32 N. Y. 465; C. v. Hall, 142 Mass. 454; S. v. Ham, 54 Me. 194.

[7] Freeland v. P., 16 Ill. 380; Furgeson v. P., 90 Ill. 510; S. v. Russell, 45 N. H. 83; Pennsylvania v. Craig, Addison, 190.

[8] Rex v. Fieldhouse, Cowp. 325.

§ **1002. Punishment.**— The offense at common law is a misdemeanor, not in its nature infamous;[1] but it is to be properly classed as a high misdemeanor where such classification of crimes is recognized.[2]

III. Unlawful Assembly.

§ **1003. Defined.**— The nature of this offense is explained as being the assembling of three or more persons with a purpose, which, if carried out, would constitute a riot; but Hawkins, who thus defines it, continues by saying that any meeting whatsoever, of great numbers of people, with such circumstances of terror as cannot but endanger the public peace, and arouse fears and jealousies among the king's subjects, seems properly to be called an unlawful assembly.[3] Thus, it is said that an assembly of a number of persons, which, from its general appearance and accompanying circumstances, is calculated to excite terror, alarm and consternation, is criminal and unlawful;[4] but if the assembly is for a lawful purpose and with no intention of carrying it out unlawfully, even though there is knowledge on the part of those assembled that they will be opposed, and with reason to suppose that a breach of the peace might be committed by those opposing, it will not be an unlawful assembly.[5] Although a person is justified in arming himself and his friends for the defense of his house against those threatening to make an unlawful entry, he cannot thus assemble his friends to prevent trespass on his premises.[6] The owner of a building has no authority to enter the same as against another lawfully in possession thereof, and an assembling to do so would be unlawful.[7]

§ **1004. Intent sufficient.**— The intent is the essence of the offense, which may be proved by a consideration of the time, place and circumstances of the act and speech of those assem-

[1] Clellans v. C., 8 Pa. St. 223. And see U. S. v. McFarlane, 1 Cranch, C. C. 163.

[2] S. v. Furlong, 26 Me. 69.

[3] 1 Hawk. P. C., ch. 65, § 9. For Blackstone's definition, see *supra*, § 991, n. See, also, Reg. v. Graham, 16 Cox, 420; 2 Bish. Cr. L., § 1256.

[4] Rex v. Hunt, 1 Russ. Cr. 388; Rex v. Hunt, 3 Barn. & Ald. 566; Reg. v. Vincent, 9 C. & P. 91; Reg. v. Neale, 9 C. & P. 431.

[5] Beatty v. Gillbanks, 9 Q. B. D. 308.

[6] Rex v. Bishop of Bangor, 1 Russ. Cr. 274; 1 Hawk. P. C., ch. 65, § 10.

[7] Meese v. S., 15 Neb. 558.

bled.[1] The assembling is unlawful without regard to the subsequent commission of a riot or any unlawful act.[2] If an injury is done to a building or other property, there may be an offense distinct from that of unlawful assembling.[3]

§ **1005. Statutory definition.**— A New York statute provides that whenever three or more persons, being assembled, attempt or threaten any act tending towards a breach of the peace, or an injury to the person or property, or any unlawful act, such an assembly is unlawful; and under this it was held that a meeting at which speeches were made denouncing and threatening with death officers who had enforced the law against anarchists, and calling upon other persons to arm and resist the authority, the other persons of the assembly concurring in the views thus expressed, was an unlawful assembly.[4]

[1] Dutcher v. S., 16 Neb. 30.

[2] Rex v. Birt, 5 C. & P. 154; Rex v. Woolcock, 5 C. & P. 516; Reg. v. McNaughten, 14 Cox, 576.

[3] S. v. Johnson, 89 Ia. 594.

[4] P. v. Most, 128 N. Y. 108.

CHAPTER 43.

AFFRAYS AND BREACHES OF THE PEACE.

I. AFFRAY.
II. BREACH OF THE PEACE AND DISORDERLY CONDUCT.
III. DISTURBANCE OF MEETINGS.

I. AFFRAY.

§ 1006. Defined.— The fighting of two or more persons in some public place, to the terror of the people, constitutes an affray.[1]

§ 1007. Fighting by consent; mere words not enough.— The fighting must be by mutual consent,[2] and the mere fact that two parties are found fighting together raises no presumption that such fighting was by agreement.[3] But one who aids, assists and abets is guilty as principal, although he was not himself engaged in the fight.[4] The fact that defendant acted in self-defense would undoubtedly be a justification as against the charge of an affray;[5] but if, after retreating, he returns and fights voluntarily, he is guilty.[6] Mere words are not enough to constitute an affray;[7] but if the parties use abusive and insulting language, and commit acts tending to violence, and this is done in a public place, it may amount to an affray.[8]

[1] 4 Bl. Com. 145. Blackstone continues: "For if the fighting be in private, it is no affray. but an assault." And the feature of the offense as causing terror to the people is also emphasized by Hawkins, 2 P. C., ch. 63. For definition of the offense, see, also, 1 Russ. Cr. 291; 1 Bish. Cr. L., § 535; 2 id., § 1; Simpson v. S., 5 Yerg. 356; Pollock v. S., 32 Tex. Ap. 29.

[2] Klum v. S., 1 Blackf. 377: Metcalf v. P., 2 Colo. Ap. 262. In this an affray differs from an assault and battery: Duncan v. C., 6 Dana, 295.

[3] Klum v. S., 1 Blackf. 377. Evidence of previous fighting between the parties, and threats on the part of one of them to injure the other, is not admissible without some proof connecting the former encounter and threats with the affray: Skains v. S., 21 Ala. 218.

[4] Hawkins v. S., 13 Ga. 322; Curlin v. S., 4 Yerg. 143.

[5] Hunter v. S., 62 Miss. 540.

[6] S. v. Downing, 74 N. C. 184.

[7] Hawkins v. S., 13 Ga. 322; O'Neill v. S., 16 Ala. 65; 1 Hawk. P. C., ch. 63, § 2. But a challenge to fight a duel is punishable: See *infra*, § 324.

[8] Hawkins v. S., 13 Ga. 322.

And if one person, by such abusive language toward another as is calculated and intended to bring on a fight, induces the other to strike him, he is guilty of an affray, though he does not return the blow.[1]

§ **1008. In a public place.**— It must be alleged and proved that the fighting was in some public place in order to constitute an affray.[2] It is not enough to allege that the fighting took place in a town[3] or in a highway,[4] but it seems that the indictment need not set forth a description of the place if it avers that the fighting was in a public place.[5] It seems, also, that it is not necessary that the place be public ground in order to constitute it a public place. Thus, it was said that an inclosed lot ninety feet from a street and visible from the street was a public place.[6] But, on the other hand, the mere presence of another person or persons at the fight does not make the place a public one, and it was held that a field surrounded by a forest situated a mile from any highway was private in its character, though others were present.[7]

§ **1009. Indictment.**— A general allegation of fighting in a public place is not sufficient. It is necessary to show between whom the fighting took place;[8] but it is said to be sufficient to allege that defendants did make an affray by fighting,[9] or did unlawfully and wilfully fight together, the time and place being designated;[10] and under such an indictment those charged may be convicted, although they did not fight against each other, but in common against a person not named.[11]

§ **1010. Conviction of joint offense.**— This is an offense requiring the participation of more than one, and therefore if two are indicted they must be tried together, and a successful

[1] S. v. Fanning, 94 N. C. 940; S. v. Perry, 5 Jones, 9; S. v. Sumner, 5 Strobh. 53. *Contra*, O'Neill v. S., 16 Ala. 65.

[2] S. v. Sumner, 5 Strobh. 53; S. v. Weekly, 29 Ind. 206; Reg. v. O'Neill, 6 Ir. R. C. L. 1.

[3] S. v. Heflin, 8 Humph. 84.

[4] S. v. Weekly, 29 Ind. 206.

[5] S. v. Baker, 83 N. C. 649.

[6] Carwile v. S., 35 Ala. 392.

[7] Taylor v. S., 22 Ala. 15.

[8] S. v. Vanloan, 8 Ind. 182; S. v. Woody, 2 Jones, 335.

[9] S. v. Benthal, 5 Humph. 519; S. v. Priddy, 4 Humph. 428.

[10] S. v. Billingsly, 43 Tex. 93. And in another case it is said to be sufficient to charge that defendants, being unlawfully assembled together, did then and there make an affray, to the great terror of the, etc.: S. v. Washington, 19 Tex. 128.

[11] Thompson v. S., 70 Ala. 26.

defense of one will operate as an acquittal of both;[1] but if more than two are jointly indicted, the acquittal of one will not prevent the conviction of the others.[2] One alone may be indicted, tried and convicted, although others are not convicted.[3]

§ **1011. Included offense.**— Under an indictment for an affray there may be conviction for assault and battery.[4] So if there has been conviction for assault and battery, that will not bar a subsequent prosecution for an affray.[5]

II. BREACH OF THE PEACE AND DISORDERLY CONDUCT.

§ **1012. What constitutes.**— The term "breach of the peace" is a very general one, including riots, unlawful assemblies and affrays;[6] but aside from these offenses, which are specific crimes in themselves, statutes usually describe breaches of the peace so as to cover tumultuous and offensive carriage, quarreling, challenging, fighting, etc. An offense as thus defined may be committed without commission of an assault and battery or other crime,[7] but of course an assault and battery or other such offense may also constitute a breach of the peace.[8] Something will depend also on the time and place, and disregard of the Sunday laws may be a breach of the peace when it disturbs the quiet to which citizens are entitled in the enjoyment of the day.[9]

§ **1013. Prize-fighting.**— A mere sparring match does not constitute a breach of the peace,[10] but such pugilistic exercises may be abused and carried beyond the limits of healthful and lawful exercise and sport and may thus become a breach of the peace, or even degenerate into a prize-fight.[11] To constitute a crime it must appear that the parties fought together[12]

[1] Hawkins v. S., 13 Ga. 322. *Contra,* Cash v. S., 2 Overt. 198.

[2] McClellan v. S., 53 Ala. 640.

[3] S. v. Wilson, Phil. 238.

[4] Thompson v. S., 70 Ala. 26; McClellan v. S., 53 Ala. 640; S. v. Allen, 4 Hawks, 356. But it is said the assault and battery must be separately charged: C. v. Perdue, 2 Va. Cas. 227. At any rate, to support a conviction for assault and battery, the indictment must contain all the substantive allegations necessary to charge that crime: Childs v. S., 15 Ark. 204.

[5] S. v. Albertson, 113 N. C. 633.

[6] 4 Bl. Com. 142.

[7] S. v. Farrall, 29 Conn. 72.

[8] S. v. Barrows, 57 Vt. 576.

[9] C. v. Jeandell, 2 Grant, 506.

[10] Reg. v. Young, 10 Cox, 371; Reg. v. Orton, 39 L. T. 292; S. v. Olympic Club, 46 La. An. 935.

[11] S. v. Burnham, 56 Vt. 445; Seville v. S., 49 Ohio St. 117.

[12] Sullivan v. S., 67 Miss. 346.

with intent to inflict on each other some degree of bodily harm and with expectation of reward to be gained thereby.[1] Consent of the parties engaged will not prevent such a fight from being a breach of the peace.[2] Prize-fights are illegal, and all persons engaging in them, or aiding and abetting therein, are punishable by the common law.[3] Indeed it was once said that all persons present as spectators, intending that there should be a breach of the peace, were punishable as principals,[4] but subsequently by a divided court it was held in England that presence alone was not enough to show criminality in such cases.[5] By statute, prize-fighting is usually expressly prohibited,[6] and it is even made criminal for inhabitants of a state, by previous agreement, to leave the state and engage in a fight outside of its limits.[7] To charge an offense under the statutes it is generally sufficient to follow the statutory language without stating the particulars,[8] but the facts must be sufficiently set out to bring the case within the statutory definition.[9]

§ **1014. Injuries to property.**— An injury to a dwelling-house, calculated to put the inmates thereof in fear, is plainly a breach of the peace without regard to any statute,[10] and the fact that defendant had the right to enter into the premises will be immaterial;[11] but the offenses of forcible trespass upon property and forcible entry and detainer have been discussed elsewhere.[12]

§ **1015. Shooting in streets or highways.**— By reason of the danger to the public involved therein, it is a breach of the peace to shoot in or across the public street or highway.[13] Else-

1 P. v. Taylor, 96 Mich. 576.

2 S. v. Burnham, 56 Vt. 445; Reg. v. Young, 10 Cox, 371.

3 Reg. v. Brown, 1 Car. & M. 314; Reg. v. Young, 10 Cox, 371.

4 Rex v. Perkins, 4 C. & P. 537.

5 Reg. v. Coney, 8 Q. B. D. 534.

6 C. v. Welsh, 7 Gray, 324; Sullivan v. S., 67 Miss. 346; P. v. Taylor, 96 Mich. 576.

7 C. v. Barrett, 108 Mass. 302.

8 C. v. Welsh, 7 Gray, 324; P. v. Taylor, 96 Mich. 576.

9 Sullivan v. S., 67 Miss. 346; Seville v. S., 49 Ohio St. 117.

10 S. v. Wilson, 3 Mo. 91; S. v. Batchelder, 5 N. H. 549; C. v. Taylor, 5 Binn. 277; Harding's Case, 1 Me. 22.

11 C. v. Haley, 4 Allen, 318. But an abusive entering a house for the purpose of taking one's own property is not a breach of the peace: Pennsylvania v. Kerr, Addison, 324.

12 *Supra*, §§ 820 and 836–841.

13 P. v. Bartz, 53 Mich. 493; Woods v. S., 67 Miss. 575; S. v. Hogan, 31 Mo. 340.

where will be found a particular discussion of the offenses relating to highways.[1]

§ **1016. Noise and disturbance.**— Making a noise, brawl or tumult to the disturbance of the public is an offense;[2] but every noise, even though unusual, is not a breach of the peace, and it has been held that a charivari is not necessarily a breach of the peace unless so conducted as to be an annoyance to somebody.[3] But the question whether there is a disturbance of the public peace will not depend on whether particular persons were disturbed.[4] While it may be necessary to aver that the noise, etc., was to the disturbance of all good citizens,[5] yet proof that it was of such nature as to tend to annoy all good citizens, and to the actual annoyance of some, is sufficient.[6]

§ **1017. Threatening and insulting language.**— Threatening and insulting language, calculated to cause a breach of the peace, is punishable, even though no actual violence results, and this is true whether the language be addressed to one individual or to many.[7] So loud shouting in the streets may be a breach of the peace.[8] In some states there are statutes against using abusive language intended or naturally calculated to provoke an assault,[9] or obscene or licentious language in the presence of a female,[10] or in the presence of children,[11] or in the

[1] *Infra*, ch. 62.

[2] S. v. Perkins, 42 N. H. 464.

[3] St. Charles v. Meyer, 58 Mo. 86.

[4] St. Charles v. Meyer, 58 Mo. 86; S. v. White, 64 N. H. 48; C. v. Harris, 101 Mass. 29. One who is not himself "in the peace" cannot complain that he is disturbed: S. v. Lunn, 49 Mo. 90.

[5] C. v. Smith, 6 Cush. 80.

[6] C. v. Oaks, 113 Mass. 8.

[7] S. v. Warner, 34 Conn. 276; S. v. Benedict, 11 Vt. 236; C. v. Foley, 99 Mass. 497; Hearn v. S., 34 Ark. 550; Embry v. C., 79 Ky. 439. Where the use of language is complained of on the ground that it was intended and calculated to incite others to break the peace, it must appear that it was uttered in the presence of those intended to be influenced thereby: Ex parte Kearny, 55 Cal. 212. Mere quarrelsome words are not, however, sufficient: S. v. Taylor, 3 Sneed, 662; Carr v. Conyers, 84 Ga. 287. In Texas, by statute, seriously threatening to kill is criminal: Longley v. S., 43 Tex. 490; Sively v. S., 44 Tex. 274; Buie v. S., 1 Tex. Ap. 58; March v. S., 3 Tex. Ap. 107; Pickens v. S., 9 Tex. Ap. 270.

[8] P. v. Johnson, 86 Mich. 175.

[9] Peters v. S., 66 Wis. 339; Stener v. S., 59 Wis. 472; Foreman v. S., 31 Tex. Ap. 477; Moore v. S., 50 Ark. 25; Porter v. S., 86 Ga. 362; Newton v. S., 94 Ga. 593.

[10] S. v. Coffing, 3 Ind. Ap. 304; McVay v. S., 100 Ala. 110; Weaver v. S., 79 Ala. 279; Henderson v. S., 63 Ala. 193; Benson v. S., 68 Ala. 544.

[11] Ex parte Foley, 62 Cal. 508.

dwelling-house of another.[1] Mere personal abuse, however, does not necessarily bring the case within these statutory provisions.[2] Whether the language is abusive, insulting or obscene is for the jury.[3] If, however, the language alleged is not in its nature within the provisions of the statute, and there is no averment indicating any other meaning than that appearing on its face, the information may be quashed.[4]

§ **1018. Disorderly persons; vagrants; drunkards.**—Vagrants may be bound over to keep the peace, but aside from that, an act of vagrancy is perhaps not criminal;[5] but persons who are idle and disorderly may by statute be subjected to punishment.[6] The criminality in such cases depends on the habitual character of the improper conduct.[7] A more general form of statutory provision is that for the punishment of drunkenness.[8] It is not usual that intoxication in itself is made criminal,[9] but the criminality generally depends upon its being habitual and public; thus, it is held that a single act of drunkenness, though open, public and notorious, is not indictable.[10] The offense as usually described involves, therefore, the character of being a common drunkard,[11] which term, it is said, implies the element of publicity.[12] The indictment should charge the offense as a continuing one, and, if it is so charged, it is not necessary to prove intoxication on each of the days included within the period described.[13] If the offense is that of being found intoxicated, the indictment must use the word "found," and a charge of being intoxicated and drunk will not be sufficient.[14] Usually the offense consists in being found intoxicated

[1] Quin v. S., 65 Miss. 479; Brooks v. S., 67 Miss. 577; Weaver v. S., 79 Ala. 279; Bragg v. S., 69 Ala. 204. And held that the "curtilage" specified in the statute included the yard or space used in connection with the dwelling: Ivey v. S., 61 Ala. 58.

[2] Brook v. S., 67 Miss. 577.

[3] Weaver v. S., 79 Ala. 279.

[4] S. v. Coffing, 3 Ind. Ap. 304.

[5] *Supra*, § 61.

[6] C. v. Doherty, 137 Mass. 245. As to keeping a house resorted to by disorderly persons, see *infra*, § 1137.

[7] C. v. Sullivan, 5 Allen, 511.

[8] 4 Bl. Com. 64; S. v. Garrett, 80 Ia. 589.

[9] But under one statute it was held optional with the grand jurors to present for a single act of drunkenness: S. v. Smith, 3 Heisk. 465.

[10] Hutchison v. S., 5 Humph. 141; Hill v. P., 20 N. Y. 363.

[11] S. v. Otis, 42 N. H. 71.

[12] C. v. Whitney, 5 Gray, 85.

[13] C. v. McNamee, 112 Mass. 285. If the charge is of drunkenness on a specified day, and on divers other days and times not named, it is a charge of one act of drunkenness only: C. v. Foley, 99 Mass. 499; Hutchison v. S., 5 Humph. 141.

[14] S. v. Bromley, 25 Conn. 6.

in some public place so as to be open and notorious.[1] If the statute specifies the public places referred to by it, the indictment must particularly allege the intoxication to have been in one of such places.[2] Indeed, the indictment should specify the place in order to show that it is a public place within the statutory definition.[3] If the intoxication is of the character and in a place such as is contemplated by statute, it is immaterial whether the accused disturbed the public peace and good order.[4] In general, it is sufficient to charge the offense in accordance with the statutory description.[5] Drunkenness, to come within the ordinary statutory description, must be caused by the excessive use of intoxicating liquors, not by chloroform or narcotics.[6] The intoxication contemplated is voluntary intoxication,[7] but not necessarily intentional.[8] Under some statutes the defendant escapes punishment if he discloses the person from whom the liquor was obtained.[9]

§ **1019. Public place.**— Many of the statutes with regard to noisy or disorderly conduct make it punishable only when committed in some public place,[10] and to fulfill this description it is not sufficient that the act be done openly and in the presence of other persons.[11] Where the term "public place" is used in connection with street, alley, etc., it means a public place within

[1] S. v. Locker, 50 N. J. 512; S. v. Waller, 3 Murph. 229.

[2] S. v. McLoon, 78 Me. 420.

[3] Rosenstein v. S., 9 Ind. Ap. 290; S. v. Welch, 88 Ind. 308.

[4] C. v. Conley, 1 Allen, 6; C. v. Boon, 2 Gray, 74.

[5] Alexander v. Card, 3 R. I. 145; C. v. Miller, 8 Gray, 487; C. v. Boon, 2 Gray, 74.

[6] C. v. Whitney, 11 Cush. 477. It is not necessary that the statute otherwise define the word "drunk:" S. v. Brown, 38 Kan. 390; Evans v. S., 59 Ind. 563. As to the meaning of the terms "drunk" and "intoxicated," see S. v. Kelley, 47 Vt. 294; S. v. Huxford, 47 Ia. 16; S. v. Pierce, 65 Ia. 85.

[7] C. v. Hughes, 133 Mass. 496; S. v. Brown, 38 Kan. 390, 8 Am. Cr. R. 165. But see S. v. Sevier, 117 Ind. 338.

[8] S. v. White, 64 Vt. 372.

[9] In re Irish, 64 Vt. 376.

[10] But the offense of using vulgar or profane language in the presence of children, etc., need not be committed in a public place: Ex parte Foley, 62 Cal. 508; nor need the offense of being publicly intoxicated be in a public place; one may be publicly drunk in a private place: S. v. McNinch, 87 N. C. 567. If the offense is charged as committed in a school-house, described as a public place, it will be inferred that there were persons there assembled: Parsons v. S., 33 Tex. Ap. 540.

[11] S. v. Kennison, 55 N. H. 242; S. v. Sowers, 52 Ind. 311. A grand-jury room is a public place: Murchison v. S., 24 Tex. Ap. 8; but not a guest's room at a hotel: Bordeaux v. S., 31 Tex. Ap. 37.

the compact part of a town and not merely a public highway.[1] In general it is sufficient to charge the offense as committed in a public street.[2] If the statute specifies "highway," it will not cover an act done on the track of a railway.[3]

§ 1020. **Disturbance of family or neighborhood.**— Special protection is sometimes by statute extended to a family or neighborhood as against loud or indecent language and disorderly conduct, but language addressed to one person in particular does not come within such statutory prohibition,[4] nor does such offense include a disturbance of an assembly.[5]

§ 1021. **Method of charging offense.**— Where the words of the statute specify sufficiently the acts contemplated thereby so as to advise the defendant as to the nature of the crime with which he is charged, it is sufficient to follow the words of the statute;[6] but where the statute does not define the offense, but only provides a punishment for it, allowing the definition to be determined by the common law, the use of the words of the statute is not sufficient.[7] In a charge for inciting to a breach of the peace, it is not necessary to set out the particular words and gestures used,[8] it being a sufficient designation of the offense to name the person to whom the language was addressed;[9] and even if the indictment does specify the words used, evidence of other abusive words on the same occasion may be introduced.[10] The name of the person to whom, or in whose presence, abusive language is charged to have been used with intent to provoke an assault should be alleged.[11] The place is

[1] S. v. Stevens, 36 N. H. 59.

[2] S. v. Waggoner, 52 Ind. 481; S. v. Moriarty, 74 Ind. 103; Rosenstein v. S., 9 Ind. Ap. 290.

[3] Comer v. S., 62 Ala. 320.

[4] S. v. Schlottman, 52 Mo. 164; S. v. Fogerson, 29 Mo. 416. *Infra*, § 1156.

[5] S. v. Hughes, 82 Mo. 86.

[6] Bassette v. S., 51 N. J. 502; S. v. Rollins, 55 N. H. 101; S. v. Craddock, 44 Kan. 489; Weaver v. S., 79 Ala. 279. Where the statute made it an offense to use opprobrious words "of or to" another, and the charge was of using such words "of and to" a person named, *held*, that proof of using such words of, but not to, such person, was sufficient: Lecroy v. S., 89 Ga. 335.

[7] S. v. Peirce, 43 N. H. 273; Finch v. S., 64 Miss. 461. A charge that defendant did "revel," etc., was held sufficiently definite: Began's Petition, 12 R. I. 309.

[8] Stuckmyer v. S., 29 Ind. 20.

[9] Moore v. S., 50 Ark. 25; Foreman v. S., 31 Tex. Ap. 477.

[10] Porter v. S., 86 Ga. 362; Benson v. S., 68 Ala. 544. But to the contrary, see S. v. Burrell, 86 Ind. 313; Stener v. S., 59 Wis. 472.

[11] S. v. Clark, 31 Minn. 207; Peters v. S., 66 Wis. 339.

so far essential that a variance with reference thereto will be fatal.[1] Under a statute punishing the use of profane and vulgar language in a public place, it was held sufficient to charge that defendant "used profane and vulgar language on [a day named] and on divers other days in a public street and in the presence and hearing of divers persons then and there assembled, and then and there repeated the same, to the evil example and common nuisance of all," etc.[2] But where the charge was of behaving in a noisy, disorderly and indecent manner, without specifications, it was held insufficient.[3]

III. DISTURBANCE OF MEETINGS.

§ 1022. **What constitutes.**— The disturbance of any assembly of the people or public officers for a lawful purpose being conducted in an orderly manner is a public wrong punishable at common law,[4] and within the same category disturbance of public worship is an act tending to destroy the public morals and to cause a breach of the peace.[5] A breach of the peace in open court is a direct disturbance and palpable contempt of the authority of the court.[6]

§ 1023. **What deemed public meeting.**— Under a statute punishing the disturbing of any school or other assembly of people met for a lawful purpose, it was held that the disturbance of a temperance meeting was punishable.[7] The statutes include any lawful disturbance or interruption of an assembly of people, authorized under the general constitutional assurance of the right to meet and consult upon the common good, and perhaps extends to other assemblages for lawful purposes.[8]

§ 1024. **Congregation assembled for worship.**— Statutes use various terms in defining the offense of disturbing a religious meeting, but the particular terms used seem to be immaterial. An ordinary Sunday-school, where the Bible and re-

[1] Quin v. S., 65 Miss. 479.

[2] S. v. Brewington, 84 N. C. 783.

[3] S. v. Fiske, 18 R. I. 416.

[4] Campbell v. C., 59 Pa. St. 266. A statute for the punishment of persons who shall disturb any religious society when meeting together for public worship is sufficiently definite: S. v. Stuth, 11 Wash. 423.

[5] U. S. v. Aubrey, 1 Cranch, C. C. 185; U. S. v. Brooks, 4 Cranch, C. C. 427; S. v. Jasper, 4 Dev. 323.

[6] Ex parte Terry, 128 U. S. 289.

[7] C. v. Porter, 1 Gray, 476; S. v. Norris, 59 N. H. 536.

[8] C. v. Porter, 1 Gray, 476.

ligious precepts are taught, is held to be a religious assembly;[1] but where the statute distinctly specifies assemblages for religious worship, assemblages for conducting a Sunday-school, an assemblage for transacting business pertaining to religious worship or the Sunday-school, etc., the charge of disturbing a congregation assembled for religious worship will not be sustained by proof of disturbing a Sunday-school;[2] nor, under such statute, will proof that a congregation assembled for business purposes was opened with religious exercises bring it within the description of a congregation assembled for worship.[3] The statute as to disturbance of a congregation met for worship does not apply to any assemblage of people, except when congregated in a regular place of worship, or place set apart for such purpose; it will not cover an assembly in a public street.[4] But the method of worship is immaterial, the protection of the statute being extended to all, irrespective of creed, opinion or mode of worship; and it was therefore held that a meeting of the Salvation Army came within the protection of the statute.[5] To constitute an assembly for divine worship, some considerable number of people must be collected at or about the time when worship is to commence in the place where it is to be celebrated;[6] but the protection continues until the assembly is dispersed, and is not limited to the time of actual service;[7] and even where the church authorities assembled after the close of religious services for the purpose of the trial of a member, it was held that disorderly conduct was punishable as the disturbance of public worship.[8] But there can be no disturbance of a religious congregation committed after the congregation has dispersed.[9] The question whether the assembly is one for religious worship,[10] or whether such assemblage still continues

[1] Martin v. S., 6 Baxt. 234. But a meeting for the enjoyment of the Christmas festival, although intended especially for the Sunday school scholars and teachers, was held not to be within the statute: Layne v. S., 4 Lea, 199.

[2] Hubbard v. S., 32 Tex. Ap. 389.

[3] Wood v. S., 11 Tex. Ap. 318.

[4] S. v. Schlieneman, 64 Mo. 386.

[5] Hull v. S., 120 Ind. 153.

[6] S. v. Bryson, 82 N. C. 576.

[7] S. v. Lusk, 68 Ind. 264; S. v. Ramsay, 78 N. C. 448; Williams v. S., 3 Sneed, 313; C. v. Jennings 3 Grat. 624; Lancaster v. S., 53 Ala. 398; Kinney v. S., 38 Ala. 224; Dawson v. S., 7 Tex. Ap. 59.

[8] Hollingsworth v. S., 5 Sneed, 518.

[9] S. v. Jones, 53 Mo. 486; S. v. Edwards, 32 Mo. 548.

[10] S. v. Norris, 59 N. H. 536.

and is in existence at the time of the disturbance complained of,[1] is for the jury.

§ **1025. Disturbance of school.**— A statute providing for punishment of disturbing a school does not cover an assembly for culture and improvement without the element of master and pupil and the usual organization,[2] but it does include any school for the purpose of instruction regularly established and in operation, whether public or private.[3] To take possession of the school-house, when the pupils are not assembled, and prevent the use of the building for the assembling of the school, is not a disturbance or interruption of the school.[4]

§ **1026. What deemed a disturbance.**—Irreverent and unbecoming conduct, such as to embarrass and annoy the minister, will be sufficient to constitute a disturbance of public worship.[5] So one who engages voluntarily in a fight at the church door,[6] or goes out and employs loud and profane language, such as to be heard through the church, is guilty of a disturbance.[7] Engaging in violent and insulting discourse, on being given leave to speak by a member of the assembly, may constitute a disturbance;[8] and so it may be a disturbance to interrupt the services by speaking in regard to the expulsion of a member after being directed by the minister to stop;[9] but it is not a disturbance to remonstrate, with those assembled for worship, against their use of a church edifice on the ground that they have no right thereto.[10] It is not necessary that the acts complained of entirely prevent the progress and objects

[1] S. v. Snyder, 14 Ind. 429.

[2] S. v. Gager, 28 Conn. 232.

[3] S. v. Leighton, 35 Me. 195.

[4] S. v. Spray, 113 N. C. 686.

[5] Friedlander v. S., 7 Tex. Ap. 204. So held as to cracking and eating of nuts: Hunt v. S., 3 Tex. Ap. 116. But where the information charged disturbance by loud and vociferous exclamations and swearing, *held*, that evidence of laughing and talking was not sufficient to warrant a conviction: Lyons v. S., 25 Tex. Ap. 403.

[6] Wright v. S., 8 Lea, 563. Where the fight was not near enough to be heard by the congregation in the church where assembled, but it was announced to them that there was a fight in progress, whereupon they came out, it was held that the crime of disturbing worship was not committed: S. v. Kirby, 108 N. C. 772. Conviction for assault and battery will not bar a prosecution for disturbance by assault and battery and profane swearing, as the latter is sufficient in itself: Smith v. S., 67 Miss. 116.

[7] McIlroy v. S., 25 Tex. 507.

[8] Lancaster v. S., 53 Ala. 398.

[9] S. v. Ramsay, 78 N. C. 448.

[10] Morris v. S., 84 Ala. 457.

of the meeting;[1] nor is it necessary that the whole congregation be disturbed, the disturbance of one or a few is sufficient;[2] and an allegation that certain persons named were disturbed is surplusage and need not be proved as laid.[3] Evidence of particular persons, who were present, that they were not disturbed is immaterial;[4] and it is not competent for a witness to testify that the manner of the defendant was not such as was calculated to disturb the congregation where the words used directly appear.[5] But a witness may properly testify that the parties complained of were trying to fight,[6] or caused general confusion, excitement and disturbance.[7]

§ 1027. **The intent.**— The intent is of the essence of the offense, and if the disturbance is not wilful, but the result of acting in good faith for a proper purpose, it is not criminal;[8] but the unlawful intent may be inferred from doing and persisting in acts which are the primary cause of a disturbance.[9] Under the Texas statute it is necessary that the congregation be conducting itself in a lawful manner;[10] but the fact that the accused believed the congregation were not conducting themselves in a lawful manner, because they were trespassing on the right of another congregation, will not be a defense.[11] As bearing on the intent, the fact of similar previous acts of disturbance, or similar acts of disturbance committed by others, without objection, is not admissible.[12]

§ 1028. **The indictment.**— In general the manner of disturbance should be alleged,[13] but it is not necessary to allege in

1 Brown v. S., 46 Ala. 175.

2 Cockreham v. S., 7 Humph. 11; McIlroy v. S., 25 Tex. 507.

3 Hull v. S., 120 Ind. 153.

4 Holt v. S., 1 Baxt. 192.

5 Calvert v. S., 14 Tex. Ap. 154.

6 Reeves v. S., 96 Ala. 33.

7 Lewis v. S., 33 Tex. Ap. 618.

8 Richardson v. S., 5 Tex. Ap. 470; S. v. Linkhaw, 69 N. C. 215; S. v. Jacobs, 103 N. C. 397; Bays v. S., 6 Neb. 167. The evidence must show that the acts complained of were wilful, malicious and contemptuous: S. v. Jones, 53 Mo. 486. Mere mischievous or heedless conduct is not enough: Brown v. S., 46 Ala. 175.

9 West v. S., 9 Humph. 65; Salter v. S., 99 Ala. 207; Johnson v. S., 92 Ala. 82. This last case practically overrules Harrison v. S., 37 Ala. 154, in which it was held that mere recklessness or carelessness leading to a disturbance would not be punishable. A charge of doing acts directly constituting a disturbance is sufficient to show that the acts were wilful: S. v. Stuth, 11 Wash. 423.

10 Nash v. S., 32 Tex. Ap. 368; Morgan v. S., 32 Tex. Ap. 413.

11 Dorn v. S., 4 Tex. Ap. 67.

12 Harrison v. S., 37 Ala. 154.

13 Jones v. S., 28 Neb. 495; S. v. Butcher, 79 Ia. 110; S. v. Fiske, 18

detail the words used [1] nor the acts done; [2] neither is it necessary to state the object for which the meeting was held,[3] nor the denomination of the religious society.[4] Generally it is held sufficient to follow the words of the statute.[5] It is not necessary to allege the locality, other than to bring the offense within the jurisdiction of the court,[6] but the disturbance must be so alleged as to show that it was sufficiently near the meeting to disturb it.[7] Acts of disturbance at another time than that relied upon cannot be shown.[8]

R. I., 416. It is sufficient to allege the disturbance to have been "by cursing and quarreling and fighting and discharging a loaded pistol, and by boisterous conduct, and by otherwise indecently acting:" Huffman v. S., 95 Ga. 469.

1 S. v. Ratliff, 10 Ark. 530.

2 S. v. Hinson, 31 Ark. 638. But a variance in proof from the method of disturbance alleged will be fatal: S. v. Sherrill, 1 Jones, 508.

3 Howard v. S., 87 Ind. 68. Proof of an assemblage for a protracted meeting will sustain an allegation that the people disturbed were assembled for religious worship: S. v. Yarborough, 19 Tex. 161.

4 Tate v. S., 6 Blackf. 110.

5 Howard v. S., 87 Ind. 68; Riggs v. S., 7 Lea, 475; Jones v. S., 28 Neb. 495; Kindred v. S., 33 Tex. 67; Copping v. S., 7 Tex. Ap. 61; S. v. Horn, 19 Ark. 578; Hicks v. S., 60 Ga. 464.

6 S. v. Smith, 5 Harr. 490; Corley v. S., 3 Tex. Ap. 412.

7 S. v. Doty, 5 Coldw. 33.

8 Brown v. S., 46 Ala. 175.

CHAPTER 44.

CARRYING CONCEALED WEAPONS.

§ **1029. At common law.**— In 1328 an English statute was passed making it a misdemeanor for any one to go or ride anywhere armed by night or day, except the king and his ministers or servants;[1] but this statute was held to be simply declaratory of the common law.[2] Thus, the crime of carrying weapons without lawful occasion or excuse may be regarded as a part of the common law derived from England,[3] but it rests now entirely upon statutory provisions.

§ **1030. Constitutionality of statutes.**— The provision of the second amendment to the constitution of the United States, that, "A well-regulated militia being necessary to the security of a free state, the right of the people to keep and bear arms shall not be infringed," applies only to the federal government, and does not in any manner restrain the power of the states to regulate the bearing of arms, or prohibit it altogether when it would endanger the public safety.[4] So a provision in the bill of rights in a state constitution saving the rights of citizens to bear arms in defense of themselves and the state is not contravened by an act prohibiting the carrying of concealed weapons.[5] In general such statutes are constitutional.[6] The constitu-

[1] 2 Edw. 3, ch. 3 (statute of Northampton).

[2] Knights' Case, 3 Mod. 117.

[3] S. v. Huntly, 3 Ired. 418.

[4] U. S. v. Cruikshank, 92 U. S. 542; Presser v. Illinois, 116 U. S. 252; Fife v. S., 31 Ark. 455; S. v. Buzzard, 4 Ark. 18; S. v. Shelby, 90 Mo. 302; S. v. Wilforth, 74 Mo. 528; Andrews v. S., 3 Heisk. 165; Aymette v. S., 2 Humph. 154; Nunn v. S., 1 Ga. 243; S. v. Reid, 1 Ala. 612; S. v. Mitchell, 3 Blackf. 229; S. v. Jumel, 13 La. An. 399; S. v. Chandler, 5 La. An. 489; S. v. Smith, 11 La. An. 633; S. v. Workman, 35 W. Va. 367. The constitutional guaranty of the right of the people to bear arms without infringement, with a grant to the general assembly of power to describe the manner in which arms may be borne, does not prohibit legislation making it penal to bear arms in the presence of a court: Hill v. S., 53 Ga. 472.

[5] Wright v. C., 77 Pa. St. 470; S. v. Wilburn, 7 Baxt. 57; S. v. Speller, 86 N. C. 697.

[6] Miller v. Texas, 153 U. S. 535; Haile v. S., 38 Ark. 564. Sale of pistols may be prohibited: Dabbs v. S., 39 Ark. 353.

tional provisions as to the right to bear arms relate to the arms of warfare which the subject may keep and use for purposes of training and defense, and not to such other weapons as are employed in riots and disorders;[1] but an act providing for the forfeiture of the weapons upon a conviction for carrying weapons contrary to statute is unconstitutional.[2]

§ 1031. **What made criminal.**— The statutes usually limit the offense as defined to cases of carrying weapons concealed, and one who carries a pistol in an open manner, and so plainly and fully exposed to view that any person coming in contact with him in the usual and ordinary associations of life can see that it is a pistol, does not violate the statute;[3] but the weapon may be considered "concealed" if persons near enough otherwise to see it in ordinary intercourse cannot see it; and this is a question for the jury.[4] If the weapon be carried concealed but for a moment, the law is violated.[5] It matters not how the weapon is concealed.[6] It is a violation of the provisions of a statute punishing the carrying of a deadly weapon concealed "about" the person to carry such a weapon concealed in a basket[7] or satchel.[8] So carrying a pistol in a holster is a violation of the statute against carrying weapons;[9] but carrying a pistol in a wagon is not a carrying about the person.[10] So one who merely picks up a pistol, and in a few minutes lays it down again, is not guilty of carrying about his person.[11] In Massachusetts it is made criminal to have concealed weapons when arrested for another offense.[12]

[1] English v. S., 35 Tex. 473; Cockrum v. S., 24 Tex. 394; for instance, "brass knuckles:" Bell v. S., 89 Ala. 61; Harris v. S., 22 Tex. Ap. 677.

[2] Jennings v. S., 5 Tex. Ap. 298; Leatherwood v. S., 6 Tex. Ap. 244.

[3] Smith v. S., 96 Ala. 66; Stockdale v. S., 32 Ga. 225; Killet v. S., 32 Ga. 292.

[4] Street v. S., 67 Ala. 87; Owen v. S., 31 Ala. 387; Jones v. S., 51 Ala. 16; S. v. Johnson, 16 S. C. 187; S. v. Lilly, 116 N. C. 1049; Sutton v. S., 12 Fla. 135; S. v. Bias, 37 La. An. 259.

[5] Brinson v. S., 75 Ga. 882.

[6] S. v. Judy, 60 Ind. 138.

[7] S. v. McManus, 89 N. C. 555; Diffey v. S., 86 Ala. 66; Boles v. S., 86 Ga. 255, 8 Am. Cr. R. 126, and note.

[8] Warren v. S., 94 Ala. 79.

[9] Barton v. S., 7 Baxt. 105; Lewis v. S., 2 Tex. Ap. 26.

[10] Cathey v. S., 23 Tex. Ap. 492. To constitute a carrying about the person the pistol must be so connected with the person of defendant as to go with his movements: Ladd v. S., 92 Ala. 58.

[11] Brooks v. S., 15 Tex. Ap. 88.

[12] C. v. Doherty, 103 Mass. 443; C. v. O'Connor, 7 Allen, 583.

§ 1032. The intent.— Different views are entertained as to the element of intent involved in the crime. Some courts hold the intent not to be an ingredient of the crime and immaterial, as the statute makes the act, and not the intent, criminal;[1] and though, no doubt, evidence that the weapon was carried through restraint or in ignorance of its real character might be shown in defense, yet, where the statute does not make the crime consist in wilfully carrying the weapon, it is not necessary to negative possible excuses, and evidence of the carrying alone will warrant a conviction.[2] It is not admissible to prove, in behalf of defendant, that he was advised by a third person to carry a weapon.[3] Nevertheless, criminal intent is essential as in other crimes, and may be negatived in the same way;[4] and it may be shown that the weapon is being carried, not as a weapon, but merely as a piece of property, for instance from a place of purchase or repair,[5] or for the purpose of returning it to its owner,[6] or by reason of its having been found.[7] But it is said that one who carries a weapon for the purpose of trading it off is in violation of the law.[8] The fact that a party was engaged to play a part in a school exhibition in which a pistol was to be used was held not an excuse where it appeared that he carried it on a different day and used it in a personal difficulty.[9] So, where it was claimed that the weapon was being carried to the purchaser, evidence that it was subsequently in defendant's possession was held admissible.[10] And where it was claimed that the weapon was broken and inefficient and was being taken for repair, the act of carrying was held criminal, it appearing that it was used for the purpose of making a hostile demonstration.[11] The statutes provide certain excuses, as will appear in the following sections. In general,

[1] Strahan v. S., 68 Miss. 347; Walls v. S., 7 Blackf. 572; Cutsinger v. C., 7 Bush, 392.

[2] S. v. Williams, 70 Ia. 52.

[3] Berney v. S., 69 Ala. 233; Coffee v. S., 4 Lea, 245; Hopkins v. C., 3 Bush, 480.

[4] Polk v. S., 62 Ala. 237; Shorter v. S., 63 Ala. 129; Hardin v. S., 63 Ala. 38. The conflict in the decisions as to whether want of criminal intent will be a defense for violating a statutory regulation has already been discussed: *Supra*, § 128.

[5] Pressler v. S., 19 Tex. Ap. 52; S. v. Gilbert, 87 N. C. 527.

[6] S. v. Brodnax, 91 N. C. 543.

[7] Mangum v. S., 15 Tex. Ap. 362.

[8] S. v. Dixon, 114 N. C. 850 (overruling S. v. Harrison, 93 N. C. 605).

[9] Preston v. S., 63 Ala. 127.

[10] Upton v. S., 33 Tex. Ap. 231.

[11] Crawford v. S., 94 Ga. 772.

other excuses for carrying a weapon are not allowed to be shown;[1] but there are other cases which seem to recognize the doctrine that special emergencies, not provided for by statute, may constitute an excuse for the act.[2]

§ **1033. What weapons.**— In a charge of carrying a concealed pistol it is not necessary to allege and prove that it was loaded;[3] but the weapon must be such that it may be effective as a pistol.[4] If, however, it is capable of being discharged by striking the hammer with a knife or other instrument it may be within the statute, although the main spring of the lock is broken.[5] So it may be criminal to carry the pieces of a pistol which may readily be put together so as to make an effective weapon, though as carried they are separate and incapable of immediate use.[6] An exception of "horsemen's pistols" may cover an "army repeater," it being carried by a person of the same class of persons who were in the habit of carrying "horsemen's pistols" at the time of the enactment of the statute and in the same manner.[7] Under statutes making it criminal to carry bowie knives or other deadly weapons, one may be punished for carrying a butcher knife;[8] but a statute specifying bowie knives, pistols and dirks does not cover a razor as a dangerous weapon, it not being sold on the market as a weapon.[9] A statute prohibiting the carrying of knives in form, shape or use resembling bowie knives is not void for indefiniteness.[10]

§ **1034. Exceptions; apprehension of attack.**— Under a statutory exemption of persons threatened with or having good reason to apprehend an attack, it is not an excuse that there has been a conditional threat of violence unaccompanied with any act or conduct on the part of the person making the threat evincing a design to carry it out. The apprehension must be justified by facts and circumstances such as will show the jury that it was well founded;[11] but it is not necessary that

[1] Alexander v. S., 27 Tex. Ap. 533.

[2] Strickland v. S., 33 Tex. Ap. 559; Barkley v. S., 28 Tex. Ap. 99.

[3] S. v. Duzan, 6 Blackf. 31; S. v. Wardlaw, 43 Ark. 73.

[4] Evins v. S., 46 Ala. 88; Cook v. S., 11 Tex. Ap. 19.

[5] Williams v. S., 61 Ga. 417; Redus v. S., 82 Ala. 53; Atwood v. S., 53 Ala. 508.

[6] Hutchinson v. S., 62 Ala. 3.

[7] Puryear v. S., 44 Ga. 221.

[8] S. v. Erwin, 91 N. C. 545.

[9] S. v. Nelson, 38 La. An. 942.

[10] Haynes v. S., 5 Humph. 120; Sears v. S., 33 Ala. 347.

[11] S. v. Barnett, 34 W. Va. 74; Collier v. S., 68 Ala. 499; Baker v. S., 49 Ala. 350; Smith v. S., 69 Ind. 140; O'Neal v. S., 32 Tex. Ap. 42.

the threatened attack be one which is to be anticipated at a particular time. A person in danger may carry arms when he has reasonable grounds to believe that his person or the person of some member of his family will be in immediate danger of violence at the hands of another.[1] Under statutes, however, which make no exception on account of apprehension of attack, it is no defense against a charge of carrying concealed weapons that one's life is believed to be in danger.[2]

§ **1035. On one's own premises.**— Some statutes permit one to carry a concealed weapon on his own premises. A laborer on the land of another is not within such exception;[3] nor is one upon his own premises when in fact he has leased the premises to another without reservation of authority to enter thereon.[4] The common stairway or halls of a building, occupied by offices of different persons, are not within the description of one's "own property."[5] So one engaged in supervising the erection of a building for another is not on his own premises.[6] Under a statute not making such an exception, it is no defense that the weapon was carried within the curtilage of defendant's abode.[7]

§ **1036. Travelers.**— Some statutes permit travelers to carry concealed weapons, and one who is going from home to a point far enough distant to be beyond the circle of his neighbors and not within the routine of his daily business is a traveler or upon a journey within the meaning of such an exception.[8] So one returning to his permanent home from a temporary residence is a traveler;[9] but one is not a traveler in going from his residence to his county seat in the usual method of making such a

[1] Suddith v. S., 70 Miss. 250; Bailey v. C., 11 Bush, 688; Maupin v. S., 89 Tenn. 367; Short v. S., 25 Tex. Ap. 379.

[2] Livingstone v. S., 3 Tex. Ap. 74; Chatteaux v. S., 52 Ala. 388; S. v. Speller, 86 N. C. 697.

[3] S. v. Terry, 93 N. C. 585.

[4] Zallner v. S., 15 Tex. Ap. 23. The premises must be those in some way occupied by the accused: Brannon v. S., 23 Tex. Ap. 428; but the portion of the highway adjoining one's premises may be deemed a part thereof: S. v. Hewell, 90 N. C. 705; Lemmons v. S., 56 Ark. 559.

[5] Clark v. S., 49 Ark. 174.

[6] Kinkead v. S., 45 Ark. 336.

[7] Harman v. S., 69 Ala. 248; Dycus v. S., 6 Lea, 584; Carroll v. S., 28 Ark. 99; Titus v. S., 42 Tex. 578.

[8] Davis v. S., 45 Ark. 359; Hathcote v. S., 55 Ark. 181; Wilson v. S., 68 Ala. 41; Lockett v. S., 47 Ala. 42; Burst v. S., 89 Ind. 133; McGuirk v. S., 64 Miss. 209.

[9] Campbell v. S., 28 Tex. Ap. 44.

journey.[1] The privilege commences when the person is setting out on his journey and continues until he reaches the end thereof.[2] A mail carrier is not within the exception,[3] unless while going from one route to another.[4] The traveling may be for business, pleasure or health;[5] for instance, one may be traveling while in pursuit of a fugitive from justice,[6] but a fugitive fleeing from the officers of the law to evade arrest cannot be deemed a person traveling.[7] If, while on one's journey, he departs from his general purpose, to visit saloons, gambling houses and so on, he cannot during that time be deemed a person traveling.[8]

§ **1037. Officers.**— The statutes recognize the propriety of certain officers carrying weapons while engaged in the discharge of an official duty. Thus, a deputy marshal is within such exception,[9] but not private detectives and tax collectors.[10] Perhaps the belief in good faith that one is an officer and as such entitled to carry a weapon may be considered an excuse, although his warrant of appointment as officer is void;[11] but one who knows that his right to act as an officer has not been perfected by qualifying in pursuance of his appointment cannot claim such exemption.[12] In general, the exception in behalf of an officer only applies while he is in the discharge of his duty.[13]

§ **1038. Indictment.**— In general, it is sufficient to charge the offense in the words of the statute, and it is not necessary to allege that the defendant was in the habit of carrying concealed weapons or that the act was done with an unlawful purpose;[14] but it should be alleged and proven that accused

1 Carr v. S., 34 Ark. 448.

2 Coker v. S., 63 Ala. 95; McGuirk v. S., 64 Miss. 209.

3 S. v. Barnett, 34 W. Va. 74.

4 Lott v. S., 122 Ind. 393.

5 Burst v. S., 89 Ind. 133.

6 Haywood v. S., 66 Miss. 402; Rice v. S., 10 Tex. Ap. 288.

7 Shelton v. S., 27 Tex. Ap. 443.

8 Stilly v. S., 27 Tex. Ap. 445; Ratigan v. S., 33 Tex. Ap. 301.

9 In re Lee, 46 Fed. R. 59.

10 Horn v. S., 6 Lea, 335; Gayle v. S., 4 Lea, 466.

11 Blair v. S., 26 Tex. Ap. 387; Rainey v. S., 8 Tex. Ap. 62.

12 Ringer v. S., 33 Tex. Ap. 180.

13 West v. S., 26 Tex. Ap. 99; Love v. S., 32 Tex. Ap. 85; Brewer v. S., 6 Baxt. 446; Miller v. S., 6 Baxt. 449; Reach v. S., 94 Ala. 113; Bell v. S., 100 Ala. 78. If the exception depends on being engaged in executing criminal process, the officer must introduce the process in evidence or a certified copy thereof if obtainable: Beasley v. S., 5 Lea, 705; Carmichael v. S., 11 Tex. Ap. 27.

14 S. v. Swope, 20 Ind. 106.

does not belong to any of the classes of persons exempted from the provisions of the statute.[1]

§ **1039. Evidence.**— Until evidence is introduced as to the fact of carrying a weapon concealed it is not necessary for defendant to give any explanation as to his possession thereof.[2] Possession, however, is by some statutes made *prima facie* evidence of concealment;[3] but on the production of evidence that the weapon was carried outside the clothing and uncovered the presumption of concealment is rebutted.[4] Where the claim on the part of the defendant is that he was an officer, his statements at the time of exhibiting his weapon that he was such officer are admissible as a part of the *res gestæ*, and not being contradicted constitute a defense.[5] The act of carrying is deemed continuous, and it is therefore not necessary that the evidence shall relate to the same moment of time.[6] The proof must correspond to the allegation as to the description of weapon carried, but the term "brass knucks" being one descriptive of a kind of weapon rather than of the material used, the proof may show the carrying of such an instrument made of lead instead of brass.[7] An indictment for carrying two weapons concealed is sufficiently sustained by proof of the carrying of one of them.[8]

[1] P. v. Pendleton, 79 Mich. 317; S. v. Duke, 42 Tex. 455; Young v. S., 42 Tex. 462; Smith v. S., 42 Tex. 464; Summerlin v. S., 3 Tex. Ap. 444; S. v. Clayton, 43 Tex. 410. *Contra*, C. v. McClanahan, 2 Met. (Ky.) 8.

[2] Ridenour v. S., 65 Ind. 411.

[3] S. v. McManus, 89 N. C. 555; S. v. Woodfin, 87 N. C. 526; S. v. Hayne, 88 N. C. 625.

[4] S. v. Roten, 86 N. C. 701.

[5] Irvine v. S., 18 Tex. Ap. 51. So a statement as to the intended use of the weapon made at the time of borrowing it is admissible: Wilson v. S., 33 Ark. 557.

[6] Dean v. S., 98 Ala. 71.

[7] Patterson v. S., 3 Lea, 575.

[8] C. v. Howard, 3 Met. (Ky.) 407.

CHAPTER 45.

LIBEL AND SLANDER.

§ **1040. Nature of the offenses.**— The criminality of libel is made to depend upon the tendency of the publication of defamatory matter, by writing, printing, signs or pictures, to cause a breach of the peace.[1] It is assumed that spoken words alone will not have so great a tendency, and therefore slander is not, in general, made criminal. This distinction seems arbitrary, and has, to some extent, been obliterated by statute in a few of the states making slander punishable in particular cases,[2] but in the main it is preserved as a fundamental distinction in the law of criminal defamation.[3] A civil action for damages for the same libel is no bar to a criminal prosecution therefor.[4]

§ **1041. Definition.**—It is difficult to give a definition of libel which shall suggest the different forms which it may take, but Blackstone's definition will serve the purpose of a short description to be explained by illustrations. It is, in substance, a malicious defamation of any person made public by either printing, writing, signs or pictures, in order to provoke him to wrath or expose him to public hatred, contempt and ridicule.[5]

§ **1042. Common law or statutory.**— Libel is an offense at common law.[6] There are various statutory definitions in the

[1] 1 Hawk. P. C., ch. 73, § 3; 4 Bl. Com. 150; Case De Libellis Famosis, 5 Coke, 125; Moody v. S., 94 Ala. 42; Reg. v. Lord Mayor, 16 Q. B. D. 772; Reg. v. Holbrook, 4 Q. B. D. 42, 46.

[2] See *infra*, § 1057.

[3] 1 Bish. Cr. L., §§ 470, 540, 591.

[4] Foster v. C., 8 Watts & S. 77.

[5] 4 Bl. Com. 150. And see, for a fuller definition, the following: "A libel is a malicious publication in printing, writing, signs or pictures, imputing to another something which has a tendency to injure his reputation, to disgrace or degrade him in society, and lower him in the esteem and the opinion of all, or to bring him into public hatred, contempt or ridicule:" S. v. Jeandell, 5 Harr. 475. Bishop's definition is concise, but perhaps too broad to represent the law as it actually stands. It is as follows: "A libel is any representation in writing, or by pictures, effigies, or the like, calculated to create disturbances of the peace, to corrupt the public morals, or to lead to any act which, when done, is indictable:" 2 Bish. Cr. L., § 907.

[6] S. v. Burnham, 9 N. H. 34; C. v. Chap, 4 Mass. 163; C. v. Blanding, 3

different states, but frequently these are merely a designation of the offense as it existed at common law. The English statute on the subject has been held not to be a definition but a description only, providing a punishment for what is criminal by the common law.[1]

§ 1043. As against private individuals.— Words which impute to another any act, the tendency of which is to disgrace him or deprive him of the confidence and good will of society, or lessen its esteem for him, are libelous *per se*.[2] It is not necessary that the publication impute a crime.[3] Thus, a publication is libelous which charges another with corruption[4] or misconduct as a juror in reaching a verdict by a game;[5] or with having been ejected from a house of ill-fame;[6] or with being a scoundrel;[7] or with having had his house searched for stolen property;[8] or with having, as a political worker, aimed to secure doubtful pension grants and *anti*-convict-labor bills to catch votes.[9] But a newspaper article commenting on the attitude of a person named in not contributing to a fund was held not to be libelous, as it did not impute to him any moral delinquency or conduct unfitting him for general society, or expose

Pick. 304; C. v. Chapman, 13 Met. 68; S. v. Avery, 7 Conn. 266; P. v. Croswell, 3 Johns. Cas. 337.

[1] Reg. v. Munslow, 1 Q. B. D. (1895) 758. The statutory definition of criminal libel in Iowa is used also in defining what libels are actionable: Stewart v. Pierce, — Ia. —, 61 N. W. R. 388.

[2] S. v. Smily, 37 Ohio St. 30; S. v. Schmitt, 49 N. J. 579; P. v. Jackman, 96 Mich. 269; C. v. Wright, 1 Cush. 46; Hartford v. S., 96 Ind. 461; S. v. Spear, 13 R. I. 324. Thus, it is libelous to charge one with having been pardoned from the penitentiary: S. v. Brady, 44 Kan. 435. To write a letter in the name of another, using language such as is calculated to subject the supposed writer to public hatred and contempt, is libelous: S. v. Hollon, 12 Lea, 482.

[3] Hartford v. S., 96 Ind. 461; S. v. Spear, 13 R. I. 324; S. v. Henderson, 1 Rich. 179. It was held libelous to charge one with having entertained (knowingly) a discreditable person: Gregory v. Reg., 15 Q. B. 957.

[4] Hartford v. S., 96 Ind. 461.

[5] C. v. Wright, 1 Cush. 46.

[6] P. v. Jackman, 96 Mich. 269.

[7] Crowe v. P., 92 Ill. 231; Woody v. S., 16 Tex. Ap. 252.

[8] S. v. Smily, 37 Ohio St. 30.

[9] S. v. Schmitt, 49 N. J. 579. So, a newspaper article charging a real-estate agent with discriminating against negroes and advising such persons not to patronize him, but to leave "the old skunk to himself to stink himself to death," was held libelous: Pledger v. S., 77 Ga. 242. A newspaper article reporting the filing of an information for assault and battery characterized the act as "brutal;" *held*, that this was sufficient to degrade and disgrace the party charged, and therefore libelous: C. v. Keenan, 67 Pa. St. 203.

him to ridicule or contempt.[1] It is a libel to send to another through the mail an envelope bearing an address thereon in large letters "Bad debt collection agency."[2] So also there may be a publication as to another's property which will expose him to hatred, contempt or ridicule, and therefore be libelous.[3]

§ **1044. As against a family or class or corporation.**— A libel need not be on a particular person, but may be upon a family or class of persons, if the tendency of the publication is to stir up riot and disorder and incite to a breach of the peace.[4] Therefore it was held to be a criminal libel to publish that "Gov. Harvey pardoned his own brother out of the penitentiary," although there might be more than one brother.[5] So there may a libel on a corporation.[6]

§ **1045. As against wife.**— A husband is not indictable for defaming his wife,[7] and it has been so held in England notwithstanding the married woman's property act.[8]

§ **1046. As against the dead.**—The publication of a libel on the character of a dead person in pursuance of a malicious purpose to vilify the memory of the deceased, with a view to injure his relatives, may, it seems, be criminal;[9] but to falsely and maliciously announce the death of a person with intent to annoy and harass him and his family does not constitute a libel.[10]

§ **1047. As against public officers.**— The publication of a charge against a public officer, imputing to him dishonesty and corruption in the discharge of his official duty, is libelous.[11]

§ **1048. As against government.**— In England publications inveighing against the government, tending to degrade and vilify it and promote discontent and insurrection, have been held libelous,[12] but the doctrine of freedom of the press has been so

[1] P. v. Jerome, 1 Mich. 142.

[2] S. v. Armstrong, 106 Mo. 395.

[3] S. v. Mason, 26 Oreg. 273.

[4] S. v. Brady, 44 Kan. 435; Palmer v. Concord, 48 N. H. 211; Rex v. Williams, 5 B. & Ald. 595.

[5] S. v. Brady, 44 Kan. 435.

[6] S. v. Boogher, 3 Mo. Ap. 442.

[7] S. v. Edens, 95 N. C. 693.

[8] Reg. v. Lord Mayor, 16 Q. B. D. 772.

[9] C. v. Clap, 4 Mass. 163; Rex v. Topham, 4 T. R. 126; Reg. v. Labouchere, 12 Q. B. D. 320; Steven, Dig. Cr. L. 267; 1 Hawk. P. C., ch. 73, § 1; Case De Libellis Famosis, 5 Coke, 125; 2 Bish. Cr. L., § 939.

[10] S. v. Riggs, 22 Vt. 321.

[11] C. v. Damon, 136 Mass. 441; C. v. Child, 13 Pick. 198; S. v. Mott, 45 N. J. 494.

[12] Rex v. Pain, Comb. 358; Rex v. Woodfall, Lofft, 776; Reg. v. Collins, 9 Car. & P. 456; Reg. v. Lovett, 9

much more fully recognized with us than in England that there has been little, if any, occasion to entertain prosecutions for this branch of the offense. In an early case in this country it was said that the publication of an article in a newspaper inveighing against the constitution and form of government of the United States would be criminal or not according to the intent with which it was published.[1] But evidently a libel on the federal government could not be an offense under the laws of a state; and while doubtless such an offense against the United States might be prescribed by statute, if so circumscribed as not to interfere with constitutional limitations, yet, aside from statute, there can be no such offense punished in the federal courts, because they have no jurisdiction of common-law crimes.[2]

§ **1049. Blasphemous or obscene publications.**— It has been held in England that publications which reflect on the Christian religion or on virtue and morality, or tend to disturb the civil order of society, are libelous.[3] The decision in most of these cases is simply that blasphemy and obscenity are punishable at common law; and the cases in this country[4] are to the same effect, and can hardly be considered to support the proposition that such cases are within the scope of libel. These offenses are not within the usual definitions of libel at common law,[5] nor within the statutory definitions as found in most of the states. They are made criminal, if at all, as distinct offenses, and will be discussed elsewhere.[6]

§ **1050. Freedom of the press.**— The constitutional guaranties as to freedom of the press found in the federal and state constitutions include freedom from censorship as to what shall be published and also, probably, protection against legal cen-

Car. & P. 462; Rex v. Lambert, 2 Camp. 398; Reg. v. Sullivan, 11 Cox, 44. Publications tending to degrade and defame persons in stations of power and dignity in foreign countries may be treated as libels on the ground that they tend to involve the country in disputes or warfare: Rex v. Gordon, 1 Russ. Cr. 247.

[1] Resp. v. Dennie, 4 Yeates, 267.

[2] U. S. v. Hudson, 7 Cranch, 32.

[3] Rex v. Curl, 2 Stra. 788; Rex v. Wilkes, 4 Burr. 2527; Rex v. Carlile, 3 B. & Ald. 161; Rex v. Waddington, 1 B. & C. 26; Dugdale v. Reg., 1 El. & B. 435; Rex v. Williams, 26 Howell, St. Tr. 656; Reg. v. Gathercole, 2 Lewin, 237; Reg. v. Hetherington, 5 Jur. 529.

[4] C. v. Holmes, 17 Mass. 336; C. v. Sharpless, 2 Serg. & R. 91; Bell v. S., 1 Swan, 42.

[5] *Supra*, § 1041.

[6] *Infra*, § 1156, and § 1159.

sure and punishment for any publication, provided it is not so far injurious to public morals or to private reputation as to be deemed criminal by the common-law standards, by which defamatory publications were judged when this freedom was made a constitutional right.[1] As understood in England, freedom of the press involved perhaps only freedom from censorship, the liability for the publication, when made, being determined by the rules of law applicable to civil and criminal libel.[2] The question of freedom of the press becomes, therefore, one as to the extent to which publications are to be deemed privileged for the public good, notwithstanding injury resulting therefrom to individuals or to the government.

§ 1051. The truth as a defense.— The common-law rule in regard to criminal libel differs from that as to a civil action for damages for a libel in that, in the criminal prosecution, the truth of the defamatory matter constitutes no defense,[3] and in England until the passage of Lord Campbell's Act[4] it was immaterial whether the defendant had knowledge of the untruth of the libel, though that fact might be weighed in affixing the punishment.[5] Therefore, the truth of the matter spoken is not at common law admissible on behalf of defendant, except in cases of privilege to be hereafter considered.[6] In most of the states of the Union there are either constitutional or statutory provisions entitling the defendant in the criminal prosecution to introduce evidence of the truth of the publication, and in some states the truth is made a justification without regard to the motive or purpose with which the publication is made.[7]

[1] Cooley, Const. Lim. (6th ed.) 510.

[2] 4 Bl. Com. 151; De Lolme, Const. of Eng., ch. 12, p. 199.

[3] 1 Hawk. P. C., ch. 73, § 6; Case De Libellis Famosis, 5 Coke, 125; Rex v. Burdett, 4 B. & Ald. 95.

[4] 6 & 7 Vic., ch. 96, § 6. In seditious libel the truth is still not a defense: Reg. v. Duffy, 2 Cox, 45.

[5] Boaler v. Reg., 21 Q. B. D. 284.

[6] C. v. Clap, 4 Mass. 163; C. v. Blanding, 3 Pick. 304; S. v. Lehre, 2 Treadw. Const. 809; Rex v. Wright, 8 Term R. 293; Rex v. Creevey, 1 Maule & S. 273.

[7] Hartford v. S., 96 Ind. 461; S. v. Bush, 122 Ind. 42; S. v. Hosmer, 85 Mo. 553; Johnson v. S., 31 Tex. Ap. 464. In Kansas the constitutional provision is that, if it shall appear that the matter was published for justifiable ends, the accused shall be acquitted. And it has been held that a statute requiring that the publication shall have been with good motives and for justifiable ends is unconstitutional. in so far as it relates to the motive: S. v. Verry, 36 Kan. 416; S. v. Wait, 44 Kan. 310.

Under such provision in Missouri, it is said that the burden of proving the truth of the defamatory matter is on the defendant;[1] but in Indiana it is held that defendant is not required to prove the truth of the publication, but if from all the evidence a reasonable doubt arises in the minds of the jury as to the truth of the publication, defendant is entitled to the benefit of the doubt.[2] The usual form of constitution or statutory provision, however, is that the truth may be given in evidence and will constitute a defense if it appears that it was published with good motives and for justifiable ends; and under such provisions the question becomes one of privilege, that is, whether the circumstances were such as to make the publication proper,[3] and it is for defendant to allege and prove that the case is one of privilege.[4] But the justification on the ground of truth of the matter published and the existence of a lawful occasion must be as broad as the libel. It is not sufficient to show that part of the libel is true.[5] Where the truth is relied on, the proof must be by direct evidence, and not by rumor or report, however strong it may be by reason of repetition and continuance.[6] And according to the Massachusetts practice the prosecution is entitled to a bill of particulars setting forth the facts relied upon by defendant to sustain his libelous charges.[7]

§ **1052. Privileged publications.**— It is undoubtedly the law as to criminal libels, as it is in civil actions for libel, that some publications are privileged and are not to be deemed libelous, no matter what may be their nature. Thus, a petition to the king,[8] or to parliament, or to a committee thereof, or any articles of peace exhibited to justices of the peace, or any other proceedings in the regular course of justice, cannot be deemed

[1] S. v. Hosmer, 85 Mo. 553.

[2] S. v. Bush, 122 Ind. 42. And to same effect, see McArthur v. S., 59 Ark. 431.

[3] As to privilege, see *infra*, § 1052.

[4] C. v. Bonner, 9 Met. 410; S. v. Conable, 81 Ia. 60.

[5] S. v. Burnham, 9 N. H. 34; Melton v. S., 3 Humph. 388; Reg. v. Newman, 1 El. & Bl. 268. This rule is the same as in civil cases: Skinner v. Power, 1 Wend. 451; Stow v. Converse, 4 Conn. 17; Roberts v. Brown, 10 Bing. 519. Where the charge was of robbery it was held that proof of cheating was not admissible in defense: S. v. Verry, 36 Kan. 416.

[6] C. v. Snelling, 15 Pick. 337; C. v. Place, 153 Pa. St. 314; S. v. White, 7 Ired. 180; Rex v. Holt, 5 Term R. 436; Reg. v. Newman, 1 El. & Bl. 268.

[7] C. v. Snelling, 15 Pick. 321.

[8] Case of the Seven Bishops, 12 Howell's St. Tr. 183.

libelous.[1] In general, all judicial proceedings are privileged in this sense,[2] but the privilege extends only to such statements as are pertinent to the issue, and will not cover irrelevant matter inserted falsely, maliciously and wilfully.[3] Publication of legislative or judicial proceedings is also privileged if confined to a true and honest statement of what has actually taken place.[4] The privilege does not extend to a comment on the proceedings or the action of an attorney therein.[5] So, as the public good requires the truth to be published in regard to the action of public officers and the fitness of persons who are seeking office for the positions of trust which they hold or aspire to, a publication of the truth as to them will be privileged; but the privilege extends only so far as the public interest demands such publications, and if charges are made with a purpose of causing injury to the individual, rather than of affording proper information or protection to the public, the matter will be libelous, even though the person as to whom it is published is a public officer.[6] An attorney at law is not, however, a public officer in such sense that publications in regard to his conduct are to be deemed privileged.[7] The discussion in this section has been with reference to matters which, though true, would be libelous in a criminal sense were it not for the justifiable ends involved in the publication. But the doctrine of privilege extends further, to the protection of false defamatory statements made, under some circumstances, in good faith, believing them to be true.[8] In these cases something more than the fact that the publication is in the public interest is required. If there is malice or ill-will the publication will be libelous, even though there is a lawful occasion and probable cause to believe the statement to be true.[9] And if the statements are made as of defendant's own knowledge and are false, the fact

[1] 1 Hawk. P. C., ch. 73, § 8.

[2] Lindsey v. S., 18 Tex. Ap. 280.

[3] Gilbert v. P., 1 Denio, 41; C. v. Clap, 4 Mass. 168.

[4] S. v. Wait, 44 Kan. 310; Rex v. Wright, 8 Term R. 293; Wason v. Walter, L. R. 4 Q. B. 73. The last case disapproves Rex v. Lord Abingdon, 1 Esp. 226, and Rex v. Creevey, 1 Maule & S. 273, except so far as they indicate that the publication of a single speech, made for the purpose of injury, may be libelous.

[5] S. v. Wait, 44 Kan. 310.

[6] C. v. Wardwell, 136 Mass. 164; Vallery v. S., 42 Neb. 123.

[7] S. v. Wait, 44 Kan. 310.

[8] S. v. Balch, 31 Kan. 465.

[9] S. v. Burnham, 9 N. H. 34.

that the person of whom they are made is a candidate for public office will be no defense.[1]

§ 1053. **Intent; malice.**— While a criminal intent is essential in this as in other crimes, yet, as in other crimes, the intent is to be inferred from the doing of the unlawful act, and malice, as the term is generally used in connection with libel, means nothing more than this.[2] But under a statute providing that, if the truth is shown, malice must be proved in order to render the publication libelous, the intent becomes material,[3] and must be proved beyond a reasonable doubt.[4] Where proof of actual malice becomes essential, other publications so connected in point of time and subject-matter with the publication charged to be libelous as to throw light on the intent with which that publication was made, and indicating a persistent disposition to bring the person defamed into public contempt, hatred or ridicule, may be proved, whether they constitute a distinct criminal libel or not.[5] For the same purpose other parts of the same publication not set out in the indictment may be read,[6] and other motives than those of the public good may be shown.[7]

§ 1054. **Mitigation.**— In the second preceding section the admissibility of evidence of the truth of the defamatory matter was considered, but it may be proper here to add, that even though good motive and justifiable ends are required by the constitutional or statutory provisions to make out, with evidence of the truth of the defamatory matter, a good defense, nevertheless, by most of these provisions, the truth is directly made admissible in evidence, and, doubtless, even where the good motive or justifiable end is not shown, may be considered by way of mitigation.[8] Evidence of the publication of a re-

[1] S. v. Schmitt, 49 N. J. 579; Briggs v. Garrett, 111 Pa. St. 404.

[2] Reg. v. Munslow, 1 Q. B. D. (1895) 758; Rex v. Shipley, 4 Doug. 73; C. v. Snelling, 15 Pick. 337; C. v. Blanding, 3 Pick. 304; C. v. Bonner, 9 Met. 410; S. v. Mason, 26 Oreg. 273. It is not a defense to show that the publication was in defendant's paper without his consent or knowledge, unless it also appears that there was no negligence or want of care on his part: S. v. Mason, 26 Oreg. 273.

[3] C. v. Damon, 136 Mass. 441.

[4] Beal v. S., 99 Ala. 234.

[5] C. v. Damon, 136 Mass. 441; Eldrige v. S., 27 Fla. 162; S. v. Conable, 81 Ia. 60; C. v. Place, 153 Pa. St. 314; Rex v. Pearce, Peake, 75.

[6] S. v. Conable, 81 Ia. 60; Rex v. Lambert, 2 Campb. 398; and papers may be read which are referred to in the publication in question: Rex v. Slaney, 5 C. & P. 213.

[7] S. v. Conable, 81 Ia. 60.

[8] The truth in mitigation goes to

traction or apology is allowed in Massachusetts in mitigation of sentence, but is not admissible on the trial.[1] So affidavits may be introduced in mitigation of sentence showing belief on reasonable grounds of the truth of the charge.[2] The feelings of the person about whom the defamatory matter is published are not involved in the prosecution, and, therefore, evidence of what he said as to the charge, showing that he treated it lightly, is not competent.[3] Neither, on the other hand, is the bad character of the prosecuting witness material. In a civil case bad character of plaintiff may be shown simply on the question of damages.[4]

§ 1055. **Publication.**— In a civil action for damages for libel, some publication of the matter to others than the one about whom the defamatory matter is published is essential, for without such proof no damage is shown. But as the essential element in criminal libel, as against a private person, is the tendency to provoke a breach of the peace, the publication is sufficient to complete the crime when the libelous matter is published to the person defamed, and therefore proof of transmission of such matter to him in a sealed letter by mail is sufficient,[5] or its communication to him in any other manner.[6] It is said that if the publication relied on is to the party defamed, the indictment must expressly allege that it was made with an intent to provoke a breach of the peace, although such

the court only, if the power to sentence is in the court, but to the jury if it has power to fix the punishment: C. v. Morris, 1 Va. Cas. 176.

[1] C. v. Morgan, 107 Mass. 199.

[2] Rex v. Halpin, 4 Man. & Ry. 8; Reg. v. Newman, 1 El. & Bl. 268. So as to provocation: Hartford v. S., 96 Ind. 461. Attempt to justify by proving the truth of the charge is inconsistent with a confession of falsity and an attempt to excuse by proof of rumors: S. v. Mills, 116 N. C. 1051.

[3] C. v. Morgan, 107 Mass. 199.

[4] C. v. Snelling, 15 Pick. 337.

[5] Hodges v. S., 5 Humph. 112; S. v. Barnes, 32 Me. 530; S. v. Hollon, 12 Lea, 482; Reg. v. Adams, 22 Q. B. D. 66. This proposition is controverted, however, in S. v. Syphrett, 27 S. C. 29, where it is held that even though the person to whom the letter is addressed, being unable to read, has it read to him by his wife, the publication is not sufficient; but this result seems to be reached upon the reasoning in civil cases, which, as indicated in the text, is not applicable in a criminal prosecution. But it is said that if the intent is to injure one in his profession, publication to him alone will not be sufficient: Rex v. Wegener, 2 Stark. 245. Mailing a sealed letter libelous in its nature is a criminal attempt: Hodges v. S., 5 Humph. 112.

[6] Haase v. S., 53 N. J. 34; Phillips v. Jansen, 2 Esp. 624.

an allegation is not deemed necessary where the publication is to third persons.[1] In one case it was urged that there was no publication by defendant in speaking slanderous words of another in his wife's presence, but the court held otherwise.[2] It has also been held to be a publication for a third person to communicate to husband or wife a libel concerning the other.[3] To constitute a publication it is not necessary that the defendant shall have himself written or published in writing or printing the defamatory matter, if he communicates it for publication to a newspaper and it is there published, especially if he afterwards indorses the publication as made and adopts it as his own.[4] So where one employed a collection agency with knowledge of its method of doing business by sending through the mail, to the debtors, envelopes having indorsed thereon in large letters "Bad debt collection agency," he was held guilty of publication of the defamatory matter thus circulated.[5] Publication is complete when a letter containing libelous matter is given to a clerk to copy, and is copied by him.[6] It is no defense that the publication in writing of oral defamation is at the request of the person defamed.[7]

§ **1056. Liability for acts of servants or agents.**—In criminal libel as in civil, one is held responsible for a publication or distribution of defamatory matter by his agents or servants regularly employed in the prosecution of his business, although without his actual knowledge.[8] At any rate if defendant,

[1] S. v. Syphrett, 27 S. C. 29; Reg. v. Wegener, 2 Stark. 245. *Contra*, Reg. v. Brooke, 7 Cox, 251. See *infra*, § 1067.

[2] S. v. Shoemaker, 101 N. C. 690. In a civil case it is said that for a husband to communicate a libel or a slanderous statement concerning a third person to his wife does not constitute a publication: Wennhak v. Morgan, 20 Q. B. D. 635; Sesler v. Montgomery, 78 Cal. 486 (on rehearing, overruling the opinion of the court on the first hearing reported in 19 Pac. R. 686); Townshend, Slander and Libel, 153. That a husband is not guilty of libel in publishing defamatory matter concerning his wife, see *supra*, § 1045.

[3] Schenck v. Schenck, 20 N. J. 208; Wenman v. Ash, 13 C. B. 836.

[4] Clay v. P., 86 Ill. 147; S. v. Osborn, 54 Kan. 473; Reg. v. Cooper, 8 Q. B. 533. But merely to communicate the statement to a person known to be a newspaper reporter is not enough: S. v. Osborn, 54 Kan. 473. If the jury finds the defendant guilty of publication that is sufficient, whatever may be their finding as to whether defendant wrote, composed or printed the matter: C. v. Morgan, 107 Mass. 199.

[5] S. v. Armstrong, 106 Mo. 395.

[6] S. v. McIntire, 115 N. C. 769.

[7] Vallery v. S., 42 Neb. 123.

[8] Reg. v. Holbrook, 4 Q. B. D. 42, 47.

either through negligence or failure to use due care and precaution in the management of his business, allows the publication of libelous matter, he is guilty although not cognizant of the actual matter published. And a proprietor or publisher is *prima facie* liable for his servant's acts.[1] But under a statute which provides that when the truth is shown actual malice must be proved in order to make the publication libelous, defendant must be convicted of actual knowledge.[2] The mere fact of want of knowledge in such a case is not material unless it is also shown that by reason of absence, sickness or otherwise, notwithstanding due precaution on his part, the publication was made.[3] In Nebraska it is a felony to publish libelous matter in a newspaper of general circulation, but otherwise only a misdemeanor, and if it appears that the paper was of circulation in one county only, the offense is of the lower grade, though it is not necessary in order to establish a general circulation that it appear that the paper is circulated outside of the state, nor in all the counties of the state.[4]

§ **1057. Slander.**— In early cases in which it was sought to punish for oral defamation, the judges hesitated to declare positively that under no circumstances would slanderous words be deemed criminal, and in some cases it was suggested that charging a magistrate in the discharge of his duties with ignorance, incompetence or corruption might be punishable criminally;[5] but it was finally settled that slander is not criminal at common law,[6] although it has still been doubted whether good reason for this distinction between oral and written def-

When the proprietor or publisher of a newspaper containing libelous matter, being a competent witness under a statute authorizing defendant in a criminal case to testify, refuses to testify or to state the real author, he is to be considered the author himself or he may be punished for contempt: Pledger v. S., 77 Ga. 242.

[1] Rex v. Almon, 5 Burr. 2686; Rex v. Walter, 3 Esp. 21; Rex v. Alexander, Moody & M. 437; S. v. Mason, 26 Oreg. 273. But such presumption may be rebutted: Rex v. Gutch, Moody & M. 433.

[2] C. v. Damon, 136 Mass. 441.

[3] C. v. Morgan, 107 Mass. 199.

[4] Koen v. S., 35 Neb. 676.

[5] Rex v. Darby, 3 Mod. 139; Reg. v. Langly, 2 Ld. Raym. 1029. And see Rex v. Spiller, 2 Show. 207; Rex v. Benfield, 2 Burr. 980.

[6] Reg. v. Wrightson, 11 Mod. 166; Rex v. Pocock, 2 Stra. 1157; Rex v. Weltje, 2 Camp. 142; Ex parte Chapman, 4 A. & E. 773; Ex parte Duke of Marlborough, 5 Q. B. 955.

amation can be given.[1] There is no question that as a rule of common law the same doctrine prevails uniformly in the United States;[2] but in some states statutes have been passed making the speaking of words imputing unchastity to a virtuous woman criminal.[3] In construing the North Carolina statute, which uses the term "innocent woman," it is held that "innocent" means virtuous and chaste, and that a woman who has once been unchaste may, by subsequent propriety of life, become an "innocent woman" within the language of the statute;[4] also that an "innocent woman" is one who has not had illicit sexual intercourse with a man.[5] And the mere imputation of impurity not amounting to actual unchastity will not be criminal.[6] Under these statutes it is said in North Carolina that the indictment need not state the circumstances under which, or the words by which, the imputation of unchastity is made;[7] but in Texas it is held that the words or acts should be at least substantially set forth, and it should appear that the words were uttered in the presence of some one,[8] and the words as set forth must be proved.[9] The language as charged must be such as to show directly an imputation of want of chastity, and the name of the person with reference to whom the charge is made.[10] If the language charged is ambiguous, the meaning should be made clear by innuendo,[11] and testimony explaining the facts and circumstances surrounding the parties at the time

[1] Thorley v. Lord Kelly, 4 Taunt. 355.

[2] S. v. Wakefield, 8 Mo. Ap. 11; S. v. Grigg, 104 N. C. 882.

[3] It seems that in Alabama it is criminal to verbally accuse another of a felony, such, for instance, as bribery: Booker v. S., 100 Ala. 30.

[4] S. v. Grigg, 104 N. C. 882.

[5] S. v. Davis, 92 N. C. 764; S. v. Brown, 100 N. C. 519; S. v. Malloy, 115 N. C. 737. It matters not that she has been caught in the attempt to have such intercourse, if it has not taken place: S. v. Hinson, 103 N. C. 374.

[6] S. v. Moody, 98 N. C. 671.

[7] S. v. McIntosh, 92 N. C. 794; S. v. Haddock, 109 N. C. 873.

[8] McMahon v. S., 13 Tex. Ap. 220; Hammers v. S., 13 Tex. Ap. 344; Wiseman v. S., 14 Tex. Ap. 74; Conlee v. S., 14 Tex. Ap. 222; Berry v. S., 27 Tex. Ap. 483; Rogers v. S., 30 Tex. Ap. 462.

[9] Stichtd v. S., 25 Tex. Ap. 420; Conlee v. S., 14 Tex. Ap. 222; Berry v. S., 27 Tex. Ap. 483. While it is not necessary for the indictment to mention the name of more than one person in whose presence the slander was uttered, yet, when the names of two or more persons are alleged, the allegation must be proven, the names being descriptive of the offense: Neely v. S., 32 Tex. Ap. 370.

[10] Neely v. S., 32 Tex. Ap. 370.

[11] Riddle v. S., 30 Tex. Ap. 425; Rogers v. S., 30 Tex. Ap. 432.

is admissible, but not what the witness understood by it.[1] Malice on the part of the accused against the woman spoken of is not essential.[2] The Texas statute provides that the truth of the charge shall be a defense,[3] and that on this issue the general reputation of the woman for chastity may be inquired into, and if such reputation is shown to have been bad, defendant is entitled to an acquittal.[4] It is also competent for defendant to prove that the woman was unchaste, this fact, as well as the false charge made with reference to her, being in issue.[5] The burden of proof, as to the chastity of prosecutrix, is not on the defendant, for whatever presumption of chastity may exist will not prevail as against the presumption of innocence.[6]

§ **1058. Venue.**—The crime is committed where the publication is made;[7] but if the publication is in a newspaper intended for circulation, it may be deemed made in each county into which it is sent, even though printed in another state.[8] The delivery of a sealed letter at the post-office, addressed to the person to whom the libelous contents are intended to be communicated, is deemed a publication, and the offense may be prosecuted where the letter is thus mailed.[9]

§ **1059. Indictment.**—In order to properly charge the offense, the indictment should allege the publication of the libelous matter, with such additional facts as may be necessary to show the intent of the language used concerning a person named, and such facts as show him to be the person referred to injuriously in the matter published.[10]

§ **1060. Colloquium and innuendo.**—It is sometimes necessary to allege extrinsic facts in order to show the defamatory

[1] Dickson v. S., 34 Tex. Ap. 1.

[2] Haley v. S., 63 Ala. 83.

[3] Wagner v. S., 17 Tex. Ap. 554; Wood v. S., 32 Tex. Ap. 476.

[4] Crane v. S., 30 Tex. Ap. 464; Duke v. S., 19 Tex. Ap. 14; Shaw v. S., 28 Tex. Ap. 236. But in North Carolina a prevalent report of unchastity cannot be shown: S. v. Hinson, 103 N. C. 374.

[5] Wood v. S., 32 Tex. Ap. 476; McMahon v. S., 13 Tex. Ap. 220.

[6] S. v. McDaniel, 84 N. C. 803; McArthur v. S., 59 Ark. 431. As to a similar question in cases of seduction, see *infra*, § 1118.

[7] Rex v. Burdett, 4 B. & Ald. 95. In this case it is said that if the writing with intent to publish is done in one county and the publication is made in another, the offense may be punished in either.

[8] C. v. Blanding, 3 Pick. 304.

[9] Mills v. S., 18 Neb. 575; Rex v. Burdett, 4 B. & Ald. 95.

[10] S. v. Corbett, 12 R. I. 288; Gregory v. Reg., 15 Q. B. 957.

meaning in which the words were used and their applicability to the person as to whom they are charged to have been used. This matter should be averred in traversable form and is called the inducement. The colloquium is the averment that the defamatory words were used "of and concerning" the person as to whom they are alleged to have been used and "of and concerning" the facts alleged as inducement. The innuendo is an allegation of the meaning, either as to the sense in which the words were used, or the person with reference to whom they were used, and connects the introductory matter and colloquia with the particular words laid, showing their identity and drawing what is then the legal inference from the whole indictment, that such was, under the circumstances thus set out, the meaning of the words used.[1] These terms are also in use with reference to the declaration in a civil action for slander or libel.[2] If the language used is not libelous on its face, but possesses a latent meaning which renders it libelous, such meaning must be explicitly set forth by way of averment or colloquium so as to make it appear from the face of the indictment that the matter is libelous,[3] and these averments must be made in traversable form as independent averments of fact, and not merely as recitals.[4] The jury are to understand the words used according to their general meaning; but if there are extrinsic facts showing a defamatory meaning not appearing on the face of the words used, such facts must be alleged and connected by colloquium with the words charged,[5] and the introductory statement of such facts must be proved, as well as the publication and libelous meaning.[6] If, however, the words in themselves fairly suggest facts sufficient to connect the defamatory meaning with the party against whom the libel is directed, so that the words as used will be libelous under the facts so suggested, the colloquium is unnecessary and the innuendo may carry out the meaning suggested by the words themselves;[7] even in such

[1] C. v. Child, 13 Pick. 198; S. v. Schmitt, 49 N. J. 579.

[2] Carter v. Andrews, 16 Pick. 1, 6.

[3] S. v. Henderson, 1 Rich. 179; S. v. Spear, 13 R. I. 324; P. v. Collins, 102 Cal. 345; S. v. Osborn, 54 Kan. 473.

[4] C. v. Child, 13 Pick. 198; S. v Atkins, 42 Vt. 252; S. v. Schmitt, 49 N. J. 579; S. v. Aler, 39 W. Va. 549.

[5] C. v. Child, 13 Pick. 198; S. v. Mott, 45 N. J. 494; S. v. White, 6 Ired. 418.

[6] S. v. Perrin, 2 Brev. 474.

[7] S. v. Mott, 45 N. J. 494; C. v. Keenan, 67 Pa. St. 203; Hoare v. Sil-

case, however, the meaning contended for should be set forth by innuendo, connecting such meaning with the person against whom the libel is directed.[1] But the innuendo will not sustain the indictment, if the words as charged, or as helped out by the introductory averments of specific facts, do not support the meaning which the innuendo attributes to them.[2] However, if the innuendo goes beyond the meaning that the words will bear, either of themselves or as helped out by introductory averments, it may be rejected as surplusage, and if the other allegations convey in themselves a libelous meaning the indictment will be sufficient.[3]

§ **1061. Setting out the language.**— The indictment should set forth the literal language of the libel according to its tenor; to give the substance is not sufficient.[4] Indeed, it has been held that if the averment is that the matter set out is in substance that published, the indictment will be defective, even though the words are in fact set out by their tenor, on the ground that the averment, as to the substance, cannot be rejected as surplusage.[5] But in other cases with more liberality of construction the use of the expression "in substance"[6] or "that is to say"[7] is held immaterial where the words are in fact set out. Pasting into the indictment the libelous matter clipped from a newspaper in which the publication was made is a proper method of setting out the language.[8]

verlock, 12 Q. B. 624. A witness may testify that from the facts set out he understood the publication to refer to the person about whom the words are charged to have been published: S. v. Mason, 26 Oreg. 273.

[1] S. v. Carr, 37 Kan. 421; S. v. Schmitt, 49 N. J. 580; Berry v. S., 27 Tex. Ap. 483; Riddle v. S., 30 Tex. Ap. 425; Rogers v. S., 30 Tex. Ap. 462.

[2] S. v. Mott, 45 N. J. 494. The object of the innuendo is simply to show the application of the language used to particular persons and things. It does not obviate the necessity of setting out extrinsic facts: S. v. Atkins, 42 Vt. 252; S. v. Aler, 39 W. Va. 549.

[3] S. v. Mott, 45 N. J. 494; S. v. Schmitt, 49 N. J. 579; C. v. Keenan, 67 Pa. St. 203; C. v. Snelling, 15 Pick. 321.

[4] S. v. Townsend, 86 N. C. 676; C. v. Sweney, 10 Serg. & R. 173; S. v. Brownlow, 7 Humph. 63; C. v. Tarbox, 1 Cush. 66; S. v. Bildstein, 44 La. An. 778; Coulson v. S., 16 Tex. Ap. 189.

[5] C. v. Sweney, 10 Serg. & R. 173. "To the purport and effect" is not enough, even when quotation marks are used: C. v. Wright, 1 Cush. 46.

[6] S. v. Smith, 7 Lea, 249.

[7] Bonney v. S., 2 Idaho, 1015.

[8] S. v. Bildstein, 44 La. An. 778.

§ 1062. In foreign language.— The general rule in setting out by its tenor an instrument in a foreign language is to give a copy of the original and add a translation,[1] but it is said that in such cases an averment of the substance is sufficient.[2]

§ 1063. Whole publication.— It is not necessary to set out the whole of the book, pamphlet, article or other publication containing the defamatory matter, but it is sufficient to set out the portion thereof relied upon as defamatory.[3]

§ 1064. Indecent matter not set out.— It is a sufficient reason for not incorporating the actual language used into the indictment that it is so obscene and indecent that it would not be proper to preserve it on the records of the court, the excuse for not setting out the language being stated in the indictment.[4]

§ 1065. Alleging publication.— In a recent New York case it has been held that it is not sufficient to allege simply that defendant, at a time and place designated, wrongfully, unlawfully and maliciously *published* of and concerning, etc., for such an averment does not state in a plain and concise manner the act constituting the crime. The manner of publication ought to be set out.[5] It seems, however, that an averment that defendant caused to be printed and published the defamatory matter is sufficient without an allegation as to the method and form of publication.[6] If the libelous matter consists in putting up a defamatory representation it must be alleged as to whom such publication is made and the caricature, or whatever it may be, is exhibited; and where the averment was that the defendant set up in public a board on which was a painting or picture of a human head, etc., etc., it was held that proof that the representation referred to was inscribed or cut in the board

[1] Rex v. Peltier, 28 How. St. Tr. 529; 1 Bish. Cr. Pr., § 564.

[2] S. v. Willers, 27 La. An. 246; P. v. Ah Woo, 28 Cal. 205. See Haase v. S., 53 N. J. 34.

[3] S. v. Barnes, 32 Me. 530. As to introducing in evidence other portions of the same publication, see *supra*, § 1053.

[4] C. v. Holmes, 17 Mass. 336; C. v. Tarbox, 1 Cush. 66; McNair v. P., 89 Ill. 441; P. v. Girardin, 1 Mich. 90. But *contra*, see Reg. v. Bradlaugh, 2 Q. B. D. 569. *Infra*, § 1158.

[5] P. v. Stark, 13 N. Y. 538.

[6] Tracy v. C., 87 Ky. 578. It is not necessary to specifically allege publication in a newspaper, that form of publication being the one intended, where the averments indicate the fact: Rattray v. S., 61 Miss. 377. Matter in a foreign language may be alleged to have been "published:" Haase v. S., 53 N. J. 34.

by means of some instrument, but not painted upon it, constituted a fatal variance.[1]

§ 1066. **Description of the person.**— Where the libel consists in the defamation of an individual, there must be, of course, a statement as to who was intended to be defamed, but there need not be a correspondence between the name used in the libel and that stated in the indictment, provided there are averments connecting the words of the indictment with the person against whom the libel is alleged to have been published.[2]

§ 1067. **Allegation of intent.**—It is not usual to employ any particular form of allegation as to the intent, it not even being necessary, though usual, to allege the act as malicious, provided it is charged as unlawful;[3] but some form of averring the wrongfulness of the act would seem to be essential.[4] Where the indictment alleged that accused wilfully and maliciously libeled and defamed, etc., it was held not essential to charge that the matter complained of was wilfully and maliciously published.[5] It is certainly not necessary in general to charge that the publication was with intent to provoke a breach of the peace, but it has been held that where the publication is by letter sent to the person defamed it is essential that there be such averment.[6] In an English case, however, such an averment, even under these circumstances, has been held unnecessary.[7]

§ 1068. **Duplicity.**— Where the statute does not allow two or more different offenses to be charged in the same indictment, it is not permissible to allege two or more different and distinct defamations of the same person.[8] But there is no objection to alleging the publication of libelous matter as made concerning different persons named, the publication being a single wrongful act.[9]

[1] S. v. Powers, 12 Ired. 5.

[2] Hartford v. S., 96 Ind. 461. Unnecessary description of the person libeled, as that she was "the only daughter of," etc., need not be proved: S. v. Perrin, 3 Brev. 152.

[3] Reg. v. Munslow, 1 Q. B. D. (1895) 758.

[4] Webber v. S., 10 Mo. 4.

[5] S. v. Armstrong, 106 Mo. 395.

[6] S. v. Syphrett, 27 S. C. 29; Reg. v. Wegener, 2 Stark. 245.

[7] Reg. v. Brooke, 7 Cox, 251.

[8] P. v. Jackman, 96 Mich. 269.

[9] Tracy v. C., 87 Ky. 578.

§ 1069. Forms of indictment.— The common-law forms which have been followed in many of the cases in this country are unnecessarily prolix. On the other hand, some forms which have been held sufficient under statutory provisions of particular states would not be safe guides elsewhere. It is believed that the following forms are sufficient in the states where the common law still prevails:

AGAINST A PRIVATE PERSON.

That said A. B., on the —— day of ——, in the county aforesaid, maliciously contriving to injure, aggrieve, vilify, scandalize and defame the good name, fame and reputation of one A. E., and intending as much as in him lay to bring the said A. E. into contempt, hatred, infamy and disgrace, did compose, print and publish in a certain newspaper called The New England Galaxy and Masonic Magazine, whereof the said A. B. was editor and publisher, a certain false, scandalous and malicious libel, and did cause and procure to be published in said newspaper the said certain false, scandalous and malicious libel of and concerning the said A. E., and of and concerning the conduct of the said A. E. as a parent, and of and concerning the manner of treatment by said A. E. of his, the said A. E.'s, daughter, in which said malicious, false and scandalous libel is contained, among other things, certain false, scandalous and malicious words according to the tenor and effect following, that is to say: "We in this part of the Union boast much of our skill in music, but a few of us who have been in Europe are unwilling to see this divine art treated with such little respect as to witness the total want of taste, expression and feeling in our musical friends. We should no longer award the palm to those (meaning, among others, the said daughter of said A. E.) who by incessant drilling under a cruel and heartless master (meaning said A. E.) have attained a rapidity of fingering which serves only to astonish for a moment, but which produces no effect upon the feelings except pity for the almost lifeless automaton (meaning the said daughter of said A. E.), whose haggard cheeks and feeble frame evince the daily drudgery to which she (meaning the said daughter of said A. E.) has been subjected by threats, promises and flattery; a feeling which is not alleviated by the smallest ray of kindness or affection in the parent (meaning said A. E.), who (meaning said A. E.) sacrifices all the future prospects of a child's (meaning the said daughter of said A. E.) happiness at the altar of ambition. A virtuous and enlightened community should frown indignation and contempt upon the tyrant (meaning said A. E.)," to the great damage of said A. E., to the pernicious example of all others in like case offending, and against the peace of said commonwealth.[1]

EXCUSE FOR NOT SETTING OUT.

Instead of setting out the libelous matter, an excuse therefor may be given as follows:

Which said printed book is so lewd, wicked and obscene that the same would be an offense to the court here, and improper to be placed upon the records thereof; wherefore the jurors aforesaid do not set forth the same in this indictment.[2]

BY LETTER.

That said A. B., on the —— day of ——, in the county aforesaid, unlawfully, wickedly and maliciously intending to injure, vilify and prejudice one G. M., and one S. M., the wife of said G. M., and to injure their good name, and the good name of each of them, and to bring them, and each of them, into contempt, did then and there unlawfully, maliciously and wickedly write and publish a certain false and malicious libel in the form of a letter directed to one G. W., by delivering the same and by causing the same to be delivered to said G. W., which said letter, as delivered and caused to be delivered as aforesaid, contained divers false, scandalous and malicious matters of and concerning said G. M. and his said wife, S. M., according to the tenor and effect following: (Setting out the letter with innuendoes.)[3]

BY CARICATURE OR EFFIGY.

That B. F. P., the defendant, contriving, and unlawfully, wickedly and maliciously intending to hurt, injure, vilify and prejudice one S. F., and to deprive him of his good name, etc., and to bring him into great contempt, etc., on the —— day of ——, with force and arms in the county aforesaid, did publish and exhibit, and cause and procure to be published and exhib-

[1] This is taken in substance from C. v. Buckingham, 2 Wheeler, Cr. C. 181. It is modified, however, by the omission of the averment in that case that the person of whom the libel was published was the Russian consul, which was wholly immaterial to the charge, and also by changing the averment as to the words used, so as to show that they are set out by their tenor and effect in order to correspond with the requirement announced in C. v. Wright, 1 Cush. 46, in which case it was held that the precedents commonly in use in Massachusetts allowing the setting out of the matter according to its purport were erroneous.

[2] C. v. Holmes, 17 Mass. 336.

[3] This averment follows with some modifications the indictment in part set out in Melton v. S., 3 Humph. 388.

ited, in a certain public place in the county aforesaid, a certain wicked, libelous and scandalous painting and picture on a board or plank, meaning by said board or plank a pillory representing the head of a man (thereby meaning the head of the said S. F.) with a picture, likeness and representation of a human ear thereon (meaning thereby the ear of the said S. F.) with an iron nail driven into the said painted representation and likeness of an ear (meaning thereby to represent an ear of the said S. F. nailed to the pillory for the crime of perjury), from which said nail driven into said painting or likeness of an ear was suspended, and caused and procured to be suspended, by him, the said B. F. P., a pair of shears (thereby, to wit, by said board, paint, nails and shears meaning to indicate and represent that the ears of the said S. F. should be nailed to the pillory or whipping-post and be cut off for the crime of perjury).[1]

ON GOVERNMENT.

Although of little practical importance, because in this country there are no prosecutions for such offenses, yet as a form often quoted and approved by text-writers the following is given in the original language:

"That the said John Horne, being a wicked, malicious, seditious and ill-disposed person, and being greatly disaffected to our said present Sovereign Lord the King, and to his administration of the government of this kingdom, and the dominions thereunto belonging, and wickedly, maliciously and seditiously intending, devising and contriving to stir up and excite discontent and seditions among his Majesty's subjects, and to alienate and withdraw the affection, fidelity and allegiance of his said Majesty's subjects from his said Majesty, and to insinuate and cause it to be believed that divers of his Majesty's innocent and deserving subjects had been inhumanly murdered by his Majesty's troops in the province, colony or plantation of the Massachusetts Bay in New England, in America, belonging to the crown of Great Britain, and unlawfully and wickedly to seduce and encourage his said Majesty's subjects in the said province, colony or plantation to resist and oppose his Majesty's government, on the 8th day of June, in the fifteenth year of the reign of our present Sovereign Lord George the Third, by the grace of God of Great Britain, France and Ireland, King, Defender of the Faith, etc., with force and arms at London aforesaid, in the parish of St. Mary le Bow, in

[1] This follows with slight changes the form given in S. v. Powers, 12 Ired. 5. The conviction in that case was reversed because the evidence showed that the representation was inscribed upon the plank instead of being painted, the court intimating that a more general description would have been sufficient.

the ward of Cheap, wickedly, maliciously and seditiously did write and publish, and cause and procure to be written and published, a certain, false, wicked, malicious, scandalous and seditious libel of and concerning his said Majesty's government and the employment of his troops, according to the tenor and effect following: — "King's Arms Tavern, Cornhill, June 7, 1775. At a special meeting this day of several members of the Constitutional Society, during an adjournment, a gentleman proposed that a subscription should be immediately entered into (by such of the members present who might approve the purpose), for raising the sum of £100 to be applied to the relief of the widows, orphans and aged parents of our beloved American fellow subjects, who, faithful to the character of Englishmen, preferring death to slavery, were, for that reason only, inhumanly murdered by the King's (meaning his said Majesty's) troops, at or near Lexington, Concord, in the province of Massachusetts (meaning the said province, colony or plantation of Massachusetts Bay in New England in America), on the 19th of last April, which sum being immediately collected, it was thereupon resolved that Mr. Horne (meaning himself, the said John Horne) do pay to-morrow into the hands of Messrs. Brownes and Collinson, on the account of Dr. Franklin, the said sum of £100, and that Dr. Franklin be requested to apply the same to the above-mentioned purpose. John Horne." (meaning himself, the said John Horne) in contempt of our said Lord the King, in open violation of the laws of this kingdom, to the evil and pernicious example of all others in the like case offending, and also against the peace of our said present Sovereign Lord the King, his Crown and Dignity.[1]

§ **1070. Functions of court and jury.**— The question whether the defamatory matter was published, and whether it was of and concerning the person named in the indictment, is for the jury,[2] and according to the practice in other criminal cases it would be the province of the jury also to determine ultimately whether the matter was defamatory, this question involving the intent of the defendant.[3] In England an anomalous practice was introduced by the judges of submitting to the jury only the fact of the publication and the truth of the innuendoes making the defamatory matter applicable to the person named, and reserving for the court the construction of the language

[1] This is the first count in the indictment in Rex v. Horne, 2 Cowp. 672. It is repeated in the report of the same case on writ of error in Parliament, 7 Bro. P. C. 543.

[2] P. v. McDowell, 71 Cal. 194; S. v. Schmitt, 49 N. J. 579.

[3] S. v. White, 6 Ired. 418; P. v. McDowell, 71 Cal. 194; S. v. Schmitt, 49 N. J. 579.

used as to whether or not it was libelous.[1] But there was a conflict of authority as to the correctness of this practice.[2] The adoption of this method of procedure in political prosecutions created great popular opposition and was the occasion of the passage of the "Fox Libel Act,"[3] which provided that the case should be submitted to the jury under the instructions of the court as to the law as in other cases. All this statute does is to prevent the question being left to the jury in the narrow way which some courts had previously recognized as proper. The judge still remains the judge of the law as in other criminal prosecutions, but under his instructions the whole case is to be submitted to the jury as in other cases.[4] It was undoubtedly the agitation in England of this question relating to the freedom of the press which led to the insertion in the early constitutions of the various states of similar provisions,[5] and to the passage of statutes of the same nature. Under these constitutional and statutory provisions it is usually held that the court has the same authority in prosecutions for libel, as in other prosecutions, to determine questions of law relating to the admission of testimony and other matters preliminary to the final submission, and to instruct the jury respecting their legitimate province in the decision of the case and the principles of law applicable to it.[6] Therefore, errors of law committed by the court in the trial of the case are ground for reversal as in other criminal cases.[7] The jury then render a

[1] Rex v. Withers, 3 Term R. 428; Rex v. Dean of St. Asaph, 3 Term R. 428, n.; Rex v. Shipley, 4 Doug. 73. This doctrine was sanctioned in some early cases in this country: P. v. Croswell, 3 Johns. Cas. 337; Whart. St. Tr. 688.

[2] Rex v. Holt, 5 Term R. 436; Rex v. Woodfall, 5 Burr. 2661.

[3] 32 Geo. 3, ch. 60. See Cooley, Const. Lim. (6th ed.) 564.

[4] Rex v. Burdett, 4 B. & Ald. 95.

[5] The provision in the constitution of Pennsylvania, adopted in 1790, was that the jury should determine the law and fact in prosecutions for libel under the direction of the court as in other cases. The adoption of this constitution preceded by two years the passage of the "Fox Libel Act" in England, but the bill had been pending for some years in parliament and the language of the Pennsylvania constitution was probably borrowed from it. Provisions are found in nearly all the state constitutions to the same effect, although different forms have been used.

[6] Drake v. S., 53 N. J. 23; S. v. Jay, 34 N. J. 368; S. v. Syphrett, 27 S. C. 29; S. v. Rice, 56 Ia. 431; Montgomery v. S., 11 Ohio, 424; S. v. Allen, 1 McCord, 525.

[7] S. v. Rice, 56 Ia. 431; S. v. Syphrett, 27 S. C. 29.

general verdict on the whole matter.[1] Under the constitutional provisions found in some states, however, to the effect that the jury, under the direction of the court, shall determine the law and the facts, it has been held that the jury are the judges of the law in a peculiar sense not recognized in other criminal cases, and are not bound to follow the instructions of the court,[2] and therefore arguments to the jury as to the law of the case are proper.[3]

[1] S. v. Lehre, 2 Brev. 446; S. v. Goold, 62 Me. 509.

[2] S. v. Armstrong, 106 Mo. 395 (overruling S. v. Hosmer, 85 Mo. 553, in which it had been held that the court should instruct the jury as to the law as in other cases). This is not the result reached under the Iowa statute which uses much the same language: S. v. Rice, 56 Ia. 431.

[3] S. v. Verry, 36 Kan. 416. Counsel may therefore read to the jury the law as stated in books of recognized authority, and it is error for the court to deny this right: S. v. Whitmore, 53 Kan. 343.

PART XI.

OFFENSES AGAINST CONJUGAL AND PARENTAL RIGHTS.

CHAPTER 46.

BIGAMY.

§ **1071. Definition.**— The offense of having a plurality of wives is properly styled polygamy, but in common parlance, as well as in many of the statutes, it is designated as bigamy, although the term "bigamy" once had a different meaning, that of second marriage whether the first consort was alive or not.[1] The offense was not distinctly recognized as a temporal crime until the statute of James I. passed in 1604,[2] although it was taken cognizance of by the spiritual courts. As this antedated the first English settlement in America, it would doubtless be common law here were it not that it is in its terms limited to England and Wales. In all the states the offense rests entirely upon statutory provisions. Some statutes create an analogous offense, that of knowingly marrying the wife of another.[3]

§ **1072. What constitutes.**— The essential elements of the crime are (1) a marriage after (2) a prior valid marriage not dissolved either by death of the spouse or by decree of divorce and (3) with criminal intent. Lewdness is not an element,[4] but of course cohabitation under the second marriage may be adultery.[5] One who is present at the bigamous marriage aiding and abetting is guilty as principal in the second degree.[6]

[1] 1 East, P. C. 464; 1 Hawk. P. C., ch. 43; 4 Bl. Com. 163.

[2] 1 James I, ch. 11. This statute was expressly adopted in Maryland: U. S. v. Jernegan, 4 Cranch, C. C. 1; Bish. Stat. Crimes, § 580.

[3] Arnold v. S., 53 Ga. 574.

[4] S. v. Nadal, 69 Ia. 478.

[5] Owens v. S., 94 Ala. 97; Hildreth v. S., 19 Tex. Ap. 195.

[6] Boggus v. S., 34 Ga. 275.

§ 1073. The second marriage.— The essence of the offense is in the fact of marriage itself during the existence of a previous marriage, and not the unlawful cohabitation or sexual intercourse.[1] Some statutes, however, make the continuing to cohabit under the bigamous marriage criminal, but even in such case sexual intercourse is immaterial, the cohabiting implying living together as husband and wife ordinarily do.[2] Such statutes make cohabitation, in pursuance of a bigamous marriage, criminal, although such marriage is contracted in another state, and the act of marrying bigamously cannot therefore be punished.[3] So there may be a prosecution for continuing to cohabit under the illegal marriage, although a prosecution for the bigamy in the marriage itself is barred.[4] The fact that the marriage charged as bigamous is invalid on another ground than that of the previous marriage will not prevent the offense being complete and punishable.[5] Thus, if the second marriage is between persons within a prohibited degree of relationship, the offense of bigamy is nevertheless committed.[6]

§ 1074. Validity of prior marriage.— The fact that the prior marriage was absolutely void will be a complete defense in prosecution for bigamy for a subsequent marriage.[7] It was therefore held under the English statute, declaring a marriage

[1] Nelms v. S., 84 Ga. 466; S. v. Patterson, 25 Ired. 346; Gise v. C., 81 Pa. St. 428; Beggs v. S., 55 Ala. 108; Scoggins v. S., 32 Ark. 205.

[2] Cannon v. U. S., 116 U. S. 55; C. v. Lucas, 158 Mass. 81.

[3] Tucker v. P., 117 Ill. 88; S. v. Sloan, 55 Ia. 217; S. v. Nadal, 69 Ia. 478; S. v. Johnson, 12 Minn. 476. But it must be alleged that the second marriage was unlawful in the state where it was had: S. v. Palmer, 18 Vt. 570. The law of another state as to the validity of marriages is presumed, in the absence of a showing to the contrary, to be the same as that of the state where the trial is had: S. v. Nadal, 69 Ia. 478; Johnson v. S., 60 Ark. 308. The Texas statute seems to limit the crime to a second marriage within the state: La Rose v. S., 29 Tex. Ap. 215.

[4] S. v. Sloan, 55 Ia. 217. In Tennessee, continuing to cohabit under a void marriage is a distinct crime: Finney v. S., 3 Head, 544. And see La Rose v. S., *supra*.

[5] Reg. v. Brawn, 1 C. & K. 144; Reg. v. Orgill, 9 C. & P. 80.

[6] P. v. Brown, 34 Mich. 339; Reg. v. Allen, L. R. 1 C. C. 367. So it is immaterial that in the second marriage the parties do not contract under their real names: Rex v. Allison, Russ. & Ry. 109; Rex v. Edwards, Russ. & Ry. 283; Rex v. Penson, 5 C. & P. 412; Reg. v. Rea, L. R. 1 C. C. 365.

[7] P. v. McQuaid, 85 Mich. 123; Sunderland's Case, 2 Lewin, 109.

with the deceased's wife's sister to be invalid, that a subsequent marriage would not constitute bigamy.[1] But the fact that residents of a state, where marriage between them would be illegal, go to another state where such marriage is legal and there contract marriage, does not render the marriage thus contracted illegal in the state of their residence, so that a subsequent marriage between one of them and another person will not be bigamy.[2] If the solemnization of the first marriage is not such as renders it lawful, then a subsequent marriage by one of the parties will not be bigamous,[3] unless there has been such subsequent cohabitation as to constitute a valid marriage;[4] but usually statutes regulating the form of marriage do not render a marriage not in accordance with that form invalid, but only provide a punishment for not complying with the statute, and in such case, unless the statute expressly makes the irregular marriage invalid, although the first marriage is not in compliance with statutory provisions, a subsequent marriage by one of the parties will be criminal.[5] Evidence that the parties lived together and held themselves out as husband and wife, and had children, is in some states enough to prove the prior marriage.[6] If the first marriage is *prima facie* valid it is sufficient.[7] So if the previous marriage was voidable because one

[1] Reg. v. Chadwick, 11 Q. B. 173. This would doubtless be so in any case where the first marriage was within degrees of relationship prohibited by statute; but in South Car olina it has been held that the relationship of nephew and aunt was not such that a marriage between them was unlawful, and therefore a subsequent marriage between the nephew and another, the first marriage still subsisting, would be bigamy: S. v. Barefoot, 2 Rich. 209.

[2] C. v. Lane, 113 Mass. 458. And see C. v. Graham, 157 Mass. 73. Further on this point, see *infra*, § 1088.

[3] Weinberg v. S., 25 Wis. 370; P. v. McQuaid, 85 Mich. 123.

[4] P. v. McQuaid, 85 Mich. 123; Kopke v. P., 43 Mich. 41.

[5] Carmichael v. S., 12 Ohio St. 533; Robinson v. C., 6 Bush, 309; S. v. Parker, 106 N. C. 711.

[6] S. v. Gonce, 79 Mo. 600, 4 Am. Cr. R. 68, and note. It is said that evidence that the parties cohabited and spoke of each other as husband and wife is not enough without proof of a contract of marriage *per verba de præsenti:* Hiler v. P., 156 Ill. 511.

[7] Murphy v. S., 50 Ga. 150; S. v. Abbey, 29 Vt. 60; Foster v. S., 31 Tex. Ap. 409; Taylor v. S., 52 Miss. 84, 2 Am. Cr. R. 13, and note. In England irregularity as to the publication of bans and as to marriage in a licensed chapel will not render the marriage so far invalid as to prevent a prosecution for bigamy on a subsequent marriage: Rex v. Hind, Russ. & Ry. 253; Rex v. Tibshels, 1 B. & Ad. 190; Rex v. Wroxton, 4 B. & Ad. 640; Rex v. St. John Delpike,

of the parties was under the age when consent to a valid marriage can be given, a subsequent marriage will nevertheless be bigamous, unless the prior marriage was avoided by the party entitled to avoid it.[1] A second marriage, however, by the party under the age of consent at the time of the prior marriage, the second marriage being entered into before the first marriage has become binding, will constitute an annulment of the first marriage, and therefore will not be bigamous.[2] The fact that one of the parties to the prior marriage was a minor and that the consent of parents to the marriage was not obtained will not render it invalid.[3] Fraud in the prior marriage will not render it invalid, where the parties who purported to enter into it live together afterwards as husband and wife. The fact that the husband intended not to be bound is not available to him as a defense in a subsequent prosecution for bigamy.[4] Neither will it be any defense to the husband for bigamy that the prior marriage was only entered into by him to avoid a prosecution for seduction, it being provided by statute that such a prosecution shall be dismissed on the marriage of the parties.[5] The prior marriage which is relied upon as subsisting at the time of the alleged bigamous marriage may be shown by way of defense to have been void by reason of a previous marital relation still subsisting on the part of one of the parties thereto; so that if the first marriage relation, which renders the second one invalid, does not still subsist at the time of the third marriage, which is the basis of the prosecution for bigamy, there can be no conviction.[6] But if the circumstances are such as to give rise to a presumption that the first marriage relation was no longer existing at the time the second was entered into, a prosecution for a third marriage

2 B. & Ad. 226; Reg. v. Cresswell, 1 Q. B. D. 446; Reg. v. Bowen, 2 C. & K. 227; Reg. v. Tilson, 1 F. & F. 54; Reg. v. Hawes, 1 Den. 270.

[1] P. v. Slack, 15 Mich. 193; P. v. Beevers, 99 Cal. 286; Beggs v. S., 55 Ala. 108; Cooley v. S., 55 Ala. 162; Walls v. S., 32 Ark. 565. But where the prior marriage in such case would be valid only by reason of cohabitation after reaching the age of consent, there can be no conviction for bigamy in a subsequent marriage unless such cohabitation appears: P. v. Bennett, 39 Mich. 208.

[2] Shafher v. S., 20 Ohio, 1.

[3] Rex v. Birmingham, 8 B. & C. 29; Reg. v. Clark, 2 Cox, 183; Rex v. Jacobs, 1 Moody, 140.

[4] Hayes v. P., 25 N. Y. 390.

[5] Medrano v. S., 32 Tex. Ap. 214.

[6] C. v. McGrath, 140 Mass. 296; Halbrook v. S., 34 Ark. 511; Reg. v. Wilson, 3 F. & F. 119.

as bigamous on account of the subsistence of the second may be sustained.[1]

§ 1075. **Prior marriage terminated by divorce.**— If it appears that the prior marriage was terminated by a valid divorce, of course the second marriage will not be criminal, but the divorce must antedate the second marriage.[2] In some states there are provisions by which the party for whose fault the divorce is granted is prohibited from marrying, and a subsequent marriage by such party is declared bigamous, although as to the other party to the prior marriage it is dissolved. And it is said that a divorce granted in another state where the court had no jurisdiction of the party who is subsequently prosecuted for bigamy in marrying again will not constitute a defense as to him, the state not being bound to recognize decisions of another state having only jurisdiction to determine the *status* of its citizens, without personal jurisdiction having been obtained in that state of the other party to the marriage.[3] But as a general proposition a divorce which is valid as to one of the parties to the marriage contract terminates the marriage as to both of them, even though the court does not have personal jurisdiction of the other party, the decree being deemed *in rem*, and, if valid where rendered, entitled to recognition everywhere.[4] Moreover, although the statute of a state where a divorce is granted renders the party for whose fault it is granted incapable of subsequent marriage, such subsequent marriage will not be bigamous even in that state, unless the statute specially so provides.[5] Certainly it will not be bigamy for such party to marry again in another state, unless such marriage in another state is contracted for the purpose of avoiding the laws of the state of his residence, in which case such remarriage is declared criminal.[6] A divorce which is entirely invalid by reason of want of jurisdiction of the case in the court in which it is rendered will not be a defense to a prosecution for bigamy in a subsequent marriage;[7] and a decree of divorce is not conclu-

[1] Gibson v. S., 38 Miss. 313.

[2] Baker v. P., 2 Hill, 325.

[3] P. v. Faber, 92 N. Y. 146.

[4] P. v. Baker, 76 N. Y. 78.

[5] C. v. Richardson, 126 Mass. 34.

[6] C. v. Lane, 113 Mass. 458.

[7] Tucker v. P., 122 Ill. 583; Van Fossen v. S., 37 Ohio St. 317; P. v. Dawell, 25 Mich. 247; Davis v. C., 13 Bush, 318.

sive evidence by way of defense, for its validity may be impeached as having been obtained by fraud.[1]

§ 1076. Intent; belief as to death of former consort.— While criminal intent is an essential element of this crime, as of every other,[2] yet the intent involved in doing an act prohibited by law is all that is necessary to render a second marriage criminal. Thus, a religious belief that polygamy is right will be no defense for a second marriage which is contrary to law;[3] nor will it be a defense that the accused believed that by reason of the continued absence of the first consort the prior marriage was void, such a belief being merely a mistake of law;[4] nor will the fact that accused acted under reputable legal advice in contracting the second marriage be of any avail;[5] nor will ignorance of the invalidity of a prior decree of divorce be a defense.[6] No other intent is necessary than that which must be inferred from the second marriage, knowing the first consort to be living, or not having a reasonable belief of his death.[7] Provision is made in the statutes by which absence of the consort for some specified time, without knowledge on the part of the accused that such consort was still living, shall be a defense to a prosecution for bigamy based on a second marriage, even if it appears afterwards in fact that such consort was still alive when the second marriage was contracted, and therefore that the former marriage relation still existed, and the second marriage was invalid. Under such a provision it has been held in some cases that only the actual expiration of the time fixed by statute, after the former consort was last known by the accused to have been alive, and a belief that the consort was actually dead, will constitute a defense; or, in other words, that

[1] Duchess of Kingston's Case, 1 East, P. C. 468.

[2] As to mistake in general, see *supra*, § 133.

[3] Reynolds v. U. S., 98 U. S. 145; Church of Jesus Christ v. U. S., 136 U. S. 1; U. S. v. Reynolds, 1 Utah, 226. The federal statute punishing polygamy in the territories is not void as a law respecting the establishment of religion or forbidding the free exercise thereof: Davis v. Beason, 133 U. S. 333.

[4] Medrano v. S., 32 Tex. Ap. 214.

[5] S. v. Hughes, 58 Ia. 165.

[6] S. v. Armington, 25 Minn. 29; Davis v. C., 13 Bush, 318. It is said, however, that a *bona fide* belief that a divorce had been obtained by the other party to the first marriage, in another state, would be a defense, but only where grounded on careful inquiry and reasonable cause: Squire v. S., 46 Ind. 459.

[7] Dotson v. S., 62 Ala. 141.

no belief of the death of the former consort will be a defense unless it is based upon the length of absence and want of knowledge specified by the statute.[1] But it seems unreasonable to deny to the accused in a prosecution of this kind the benefit of a defense founded on an honest mistake of fact; and while, doubtless, it is competent for the legislature to throw upon one who desires to prosecute a business which is subject to legislative regulation the obligation of ascertaining at his peril that the circumstances are such as justify him in prosecuting such business,[2] yet legislation in regard to marriage ought not, unless the language of the statute absolutely requires it, to be so construed as to throw this burden on one who enters into a marriage which, under the circumstances believed by him in good faith to exist, would be lawful;[3] and there is some authority for saying that a good-faith belief on the part of the accused that the former consort was dead at the time the second marriage was entered into will constitute a defense, although the statutory period of absence has not elapsed.[4] Some support to this last proposition may be found in the decision of the Indiana court that *bona fide* belief of the procurement by the prior consort of a divorce in another state would constitute a defense,[5] and in the decision of the Georgia court that, where the prosecution is for marrying the wife of another, it must appear that accused knew at the time of such marriage that the woman was another's wife.[6] It has also been said that the law presumes against the commission of crime, and that where, in a prosecution for bigamy, it appears that the accused has married even within a year after the former consort was last heard of, it is incumbent upon the prosecution to prove that the first consort was still alive at the time of the second marriage.[7] Under the English statute, if the ac-

[1] C. v. Mash, 7 Met. 472; C. v. Hayden, 163 Mass. 453; Jones v. S., 67 Ala. 84; S. v. Barrow, 31 La. An. 691.

[2] See *supra*, § 134.

[3] 1 Bish. Cr. L., § 303*a*, ¶¶ 13–16, in note.

[4] Reg. v. Tolson, 23 Q. B. D. 168. This case, however, was decided by a court almost equally divided. The previous English cases on the subject were contradictory. In some it has been held that a good-faith belief without the lapse of the statutory period was a defense: Reg. v. Moore, 13 Cox, 544; Reg. v. Horton, 11 Cox, 670; while the contrary conclusion was reached in Reg. v. Bennett, 14 Cox, 45; Reg. v. Gibbons, 12 Cox, 237.

[5] Squire v. S., 46 Ind. 459.

[6] Arnold v. S., 53 Ga. 574.

[7] Rex v. Twyning, 2 B. & Ald. 386.

cused has married only after the lapse of the statutory period of absence of the first consort, it is for the prosecution to show that such marriage was with knowledge that the previous consort was still alive,[1] and that a finding by the jury that the accused might have known by inquiry that the former consort was alive would not justify a conviction.[2] Also, it is suggested that the true construction of the statute is that accused must have been ignorant during the whole of the statutory period that the former consort was alive.[3]

§ **1077. Jurisdiction and venue.**—The crime is committed where the second marriage takes place, and therefore the second marriage must be within the state where the offense is prosecuted, unless there is some statute which makes it a crime to continue to cohabit in the state under a bigamous marriage celebrated elsewhere.[4] But if there is such a statute, then the continuing to cohabit may be punished as bigamy, although the bigamous marriage itself was in another state.[5] Likewise, as between different counties in the same state, the venue will be in the county where the marriage takes place;[6] but here, also, if the continuing to cohabit is made criminal, as distinct from the marriage itself, there may be a prosecution in any county where there is cohabitation.[7] It is sometimes provided in regard to this offense that defendant may be prosecuted in any county in which he is apprehended.[8] There is such a provision in the English statute;[9] but in states where

[1] Reg. v. Curgerwen, L. R. 1 C. C. 1; Reg. v. Heaton, 3 F. & F. 819; Reg. v. Jones, 21 L. T. 396. In another case it is said that whether evidence on the part of the prosecution to show such knowledge is necessary will depend on the particular facts of each case: Reg. v. Ellis, 1 F. & F. 309; and whether accused knew that the former consort was still alive is a question for the jury: Reg. v. Dane, 1 F. & F. 323; Reg. v. Cross, 1 F. & F. 510.

[2] Reg. v. Jones, Car. & M. 614; Reg. v. Briggs, Dears. & B. 98.

[3] S. v. Williams, 20 Ia. 98.

[4] Johnson v. C., 86 Ky. 122; S. v. Barnett, 83 N. C. 615.

[5] S. v. Sloan, 55 Ia. 217; S. v. Nadal, 69 Ia. 478; *supra*, § 1073.

[6] Williams v. S., 44 Ala. 24; Beggs v. S., 55 Ala. 108; Scoggins v. S., 32 Ark. 205.

[7] S. v. Hughes, 58 Ia. 165; Finney v. S., 3 Head, 544. In such a prosecution, evidence of the bigamous marriage in another county is proper to fix the nature of the subsequent cohabitation: S. v. Hughes, 58 Ia. 165.

[8] S. v. Sweetsir, 53 Me. 438; S. v. Griswold, 53 Mo. 181.

[9] Rex v. Gordon, Russ. & Ry. 48; Rex v. Fraser, 1 Moody, 407; Reg. v. Smith, 1 F. & F. 36; Reg. v. Whiley, 1 C. & K. 150; Reg. v. Topping, Dears. 647.

the constitution requires that the trial shall be had in the county where the offense is committed, a statute authorizing trial in the county where the defendant is apprehended is unconstitutional.[1]

§ **1078. Limitation.**— As the offense is committed and complete when the second marriage is entered into, the statute of limitations commences to run at that time whether the offense be defined as having two wives at the same time, or as marrying another wife during the life of the former.[2] If the statute makes continuance of cohabitation under the bigamous marriage criminal, there may be a prosecution for such cohabitation, although the prosecution for the bigamous marriage itself is barred.[3]

§ **1079. Indictment.**— As to the bigamous marriage, the facts are to be alleged according to general principles of pleading. The name of the second wife should be given, and a variance therein will be fatal, unless she was generally known by the name given.[4] The exact locality of the second marriage is, of course, immaterial, provided the evidence of place is such as to establish the venue and bring it within the jurisdiction of the court.[5] Beyond this it is usually held sufficient to allege a former marriage, and that the first wife was living when the second marriage took place;[6] and the time and place of the first marriage and the name of the first wife need not be specifically alleged;[7] and an error in the name of the first wife will be immaterial;[8] but there are cases holding that the time and place of the first marriage and the name of the first wife or husband, as the case may be, must be averred as other facts.[9] It is not

[1] S. v. Cutshall, 110 N. C. 538; S. v. Smiley, 98 Mo. 605; Walls v. S., 32 Ark. 565.

[2] Gise v. C., 81 Pa. St. 428.

[3] S. v. Sloan, 55 Ia. 217.

[4] S. v. Davis, 109 N. C. 780; Robinson v. C., 88 Ky. 386; U. S. v. Miles, 2 Utah, 19; s. c., 103 U. S. 304; Rex v. Deeley, 4 C. & P. 579.

[5] P. v. Calder, 30 Mich. 85; S. v. Nadal, 69 Ia. 478.

[6] Kopke v. P., 43 Mich. 41; S. v. Hughes, 58 Ia. 165; S. v. Armington, 25 Minn. 29; Hiler v. P., 156 Ill. 511.

[7] Hutchins v. S., 28 Ind. 34; S. v. Bray, 13 Ired. 289; S. v. Davis, 109 N. C. 780; P. v. Giesea, 61 Cal. 53; Watson v. S., 13 Tex. Ap. 76.

[8] S. v. Armington, 25 Minn. 29.

[9] S. v. La Bore, 26 Vt. 765; Davis v. C., 13 Bush, 318 (overruling C. v. Whaley, 6 Bush, 266); Bish. Stat. Crimes, § 602. A variance as to the date of the first marriage will be immaterial: Faustre v. C., 92 Ky. 34. The averment that the name of the first wife is to the grand jury unknown is sufficient: Nelms v. S., 84 Ga. 466.

necessary to negative a divorce, or otherwise allege that the first marriage was still subsisting;[1] nor to allege specifically that the first marriage was lawful.[2]

§ 1080. **Negativing proviso.**— The usual proviso that a certain number of years' absence of the first consort, unheard of, will be a defense, need not be negatived by the prosecution, but must be relied on by the defendant.[3]

§ 1081. **Allegation of intent.**— The indictment should charge the second marriage as being unlawful[4] or felonious, if the statute makes the offense a felony;[5] but if it is by statute a misdemeanor it should not be described as felonious.[6]

§ 1082. **Evidence; proof of former marriage.**— The former marriage must be established.[7] A certificate thereof, with evidence identifying the parties, is sufficient proof.[8] Identification may be by a photographic likeness of the former spouse shown to the witness present at the first marriage in order to prove the identity of such spouse with the person mentioned in the marriage certificate.[9] But a marriage may be proved otherwise than by a certificate or official register thereof.[10] The testimony of a witness who was present and saw the marriage celebrated is sufficient.[11] Where the prior marriage relied upon was in another state or country, it must be proved

[1] S. v. Norman, 2 Dev. 222; Murray v. Reg., 7 Q. B. 700. So, on the other hand, the averment of the existence of a former marriage relation was held sufficient without an averment that the lawful wife was still living: S. v. Hughes, 58 Ia. 165.

[2] Kopke v. P., 43 Mich. 41; S. v. Hughes, 58 Ia. 165. *Contra*, King v. S., 40 Ga. 244.

[3] Kopke v. P., 43 Mich. 41; Stanglein v. S., 17 Ohio St. 453; Fleming v. P., 27 N. Y. 329; Barber v. S., 50 Md. 161; S. v. Abbey, 29 Vt. 60; S. v. Williams, 20 Ia. 98; Reg. v. Cullen, 9 C. & P. 681. *Contra*, King v. S., 40 Ga. 244.

[4] Parker v. S., 77 Ala. 47.

[5] Kopke v. P., 43 Mich. 41.

[6] S. v. Darrah, 1 Houst. Cr. C. 112.

[7] Arnold v. S., 53 Ga. 574.

[8] Reg. v. Hawes, 1 Den. 270. The authority of the officer or the clerical character of the minister may be shown by parol: C. v. Hayden, 163 Mass. 453. But the certificate of marriage in a foreign country to be admissible in evidence must be duly proved or authenticated: S. v. Horn, 43 Vt. 20; Faustre v. C., 92 Ky. 34.

[9] Reg. v. Tolson, 4 F. & F. 103. Identity of names and residence held sufficient to show on behalf of defendant that a record of divorce related to the prior marriage alleged in the indictment: C. v. Lucas, 158 Mass. 81.

[10] Moore v. C., 9 Leigh, 639; Sayer v. Glossop, 2 C. & K. 694.

[11] S. v. Williams, 20 Ia. 98; S. v. Hughes, 58 Ia. 165; S. v. McCance, 110 Mo. 398; C. v. Dill, 156 Mass. 226; Reg. v. Manwaring, Dears. & B. 132. Thus, the party to the bigamous

satisfactorily that a valid marriage did take place there,[1] and it has been said that persons who were present will not be competent to testify as to what the law of the place was, so as to show the validity of such marriage according to the law of that place.[2] But the later and controlling decisions in England and the United States are to the effect that proof of a marriage in fact celebrated in another state, followed by cohabitation, will be sufficient proof of the validity of the marriage without evidence as to the law of the place where the marriage was celebrated, nothing appearing to cast discredit on the proceeding.[3] It is even said that such a marriage may be proved by the admissions of defendant, without evidence of cohabitation;[4] but the admission must show the state in which the marriage took place in conformity with the allegation of the indictment.[5]

§ **1083. Admissions of defendant.**— The prior marriage may be proved by the admission of the accused without the production of the record or a witness present at the marriage,[6] but the jury must be satisfied that the admission of the marriage involved an admission of its validity.[7] The rule has more frequently, however, been stated as being to the effect that declarations or admissions of accused as to the prior marriage, and proof of cohabitation, are sufficient evidence thereof.[8]

marriage may testify thereto: C. v. Hayden, 163 Mass. 453.

[1] Oneale v. C., 17 Grat. 582.

[2] Reg. v. Povey, Dears. 32; Reg. v. Savage, 13 Cox, 178.

[3] Dale v. S., 88 Ga. 552; S. v. Wylde, 110 N. C. 500; Miles v. U. S., 103 U. S. 304; Bird v. C., 21 Grat. 800; Reg. v. Griffin, L. R. 4 Ir. 497; Reg. v. Newton, 2 M. & Rob. 503; S. C., S. N. Reg. v. Simmonsto, 1 C. & K. 164; 1 Bish. Mar. & Div. (ed. 1891), § 1115; Whart. Cr. Ev., § 169. And see *supra*, § 1073, n.

[4] S. v. Wylde, 110 N. C. 500.

[5] Tucker v. P., 117 Ill. 88.

[6] Oneale v. C., 17 Grat. 583; S. v. Armington, 25 Minn. 29; S. v. Johnson, 12 Minn. 476; C. v. Hayden, 163 Mass. 453; Squire v. S., 46 Ind. 459; Crane v. S., 94 Tenn. 86, 98; Williams v. S., 54 Ala. 131; Parker v. S., 77 Ala. 47; S. v. Wylde, 110 N. C. 500; U. S. v. Miles, 2 Utah, 19; S. C., Miles v. U. S., 103 U. S. 304. It was doubted in the earlier English cases whether acknowledgment alone would be sufficient: Rex v. Truman, 1 East, P. C. 470; Reg. v. Flaherty, 2 C. & K. 782.

[7] Williams v. S., 54 Ala. 131; U. S. v. Miles, 2 Utah, 19; S. C., Miles v. U. S., 103 U. S. 304. The fact that defendant, when expostulated with in regard to his second marriage, on the ground that his former wife was still living, was silent and did not deny the fact, is competent evidence against him in the nature of an admission: S. v. Plym, 43 Minn. 385.

[8] Wolverton v. S., 16 Ohio, 173; S. v. Hilton, 3 Rich. 434; S. v. Britton,

Proof of the mere fact of cohabitation will not be sufficient, but that fact coupled with the holding out of the other party to the supposed marriage as husband or wife is evidence of marriage, though it does not constitute a marriage,[1] and it is for the jury to say whether such evidence shows an actual marriage.[2] Such evidence may properly be held to throw the burden on defendant to rebut the presumption.[3] General reputation alone is insufficient, but taken in connection with cohabitation and admissions it may make out a *prima facie* case.[4]

§ **1084. Evidence that former spouse still living.**— The fact that the former spouse is still alive may be established by circumstantial evidence.[5] It has been said that there is a presumption, after proof that the former spouse was alive at a date prior to the second marriage, that such life continued until the second marriage, there being no evidence to the contrary.[6] This presumption, however, is one of fact and not of law, and of varying strength according to the circumstances. It must be considered by the jury in connection with the length of time intervening, the age and health of the person, and other circumstances affecting the probability of the continuance of life.[7] The fact of the former spouse being alive at the time of the second marriage must be proved beyond a reasonable doubt.[8] As against the presumption of the continu-

4 McCord, 256; Warner v. C., 2 Va. Cas. 95; Langtry v. S., 30 Ala. 536; S. v. Seals, 16 Ind. 352; C. v. Murtagh, 1 Ashmead, 272; Halbrook v. S., 34 Ark. 511; C. v. Jackson, 11 Bush, 679; Rex v. Truman, 1 East, P. C. 470. There is some authority to the contrary proposition, that the marriage cannot be established by admissions and declarations: S. v. Roswell, 6 Conn. 446; P. v. Humphrey, 7 Johns. 314.

[1] S. v. Cooper, 103 Mo. 266; Dumas v. S., 14 Tex. Ap. 464.

[2] C. v. Jackson, 11 Bush, 679.

[3] S. v. Nadal, 69 Ia. 478.

[4] Dumas v. S., 14 Tex. Ap. 464.

[5] Parker v. S., 77 Ala. 47; Crane v. S., 94 Tenn. 86, 98. A decree of divorce between accused and his former wife after the alleged bigamous marriage, giving her the custody of a child, *held prima facie* evidence that she was alive when the second marriage was contracted: S. v. Ashley, 37 Ark. 403. The fact that the former wife, at the time of marriage to defendant, bore the name of another man, and had a child who called him father, does not make it necessary for the prosecution to prove the death of such person, as it does not show a marriage to him: Simon v. S., 31 Tex. Ap. 186.

[6] Parker v. S., 77 Ala. 47; Gorman v. S., 23 Tex. 646.

[7] S. v. Plym, 43 Minn. 385; Squire v. S., 46 Ind. 459; Reg. v. Lumley, L. R. 1 C. C. 196; Reg. v. Jones, 11 Q. B. 118.

[8] Squire v. S., 46 Ind. 459.

ance of life, there is the presumption of innocence,[1] and therefore it is more reasonable to say that there is no presumption either way, but that the question is one for the jury solely as a matter of fact.[2] Thus, where defendant seeks to show that the alleged prior marriage was void because of a still earlier marriage then subsisting, he may prove that the spouse of the earlier marriage was alive at a time prior to the marriage which he claims was void, but the ultimate question as to whether or not this evidence makes out a defense is for the jury.[3]

§ 1085. **Testimony of husband or wife.**— Bigamy is not such a wrong or injury to the wife on the part of the husband as to make her testimony with reference to her marriage to him, or as to his admissions thereof, competent in a prosecution against him for bigamy in a subsequent marriage, under a statute authorizing the wife to testify against her husband in case of personal wrongs or injuries to her.[4] But for the purpose of showing that such wife was not really the wife of defendant she may be asked if she was not the person to whom defendant was married at a certain time, for the purpose of showing, in connection with other evidence, that defendant was at that time already married, and that the witness was therefore not incompetent to testify against him.[5] The woman with whom the bigamous marriage is charged to have been contracted is, of course, a competent witness as to such marriage,[6] provided it has been established by other evidence to the satisfaction of the court that the first marriage was valid; but while the validity of the first marriage is in controversy the wife of the second marriage is incompetent to testify.[7]

[1] Rex v. Twyning, 2 B. & Ald. 386.

[2] C. v. McGrath, 140 Mass. 296; Reg. v. Willshire, 6 Q. B. D. 366. In one case it is said that proof of the mere fact that the former spouse was alive three years before the second marriage was not sufficient to support a conviction: P. v. Feilen, 58 Cal. 218.

[3] C. v. McGrath, 140 Mass. 296; Reg. v. Willshire, 6 Q. B. D. 366.

[4] Bassett v. U. S., 137 U. S. 496; P. v. Quanstrom, 93 Mich. 254; Hiler v. P., 156 Ill. 511; Boyd v. S., 33 Tex. Ap. 470. And see to the same effect, S. v. McDavid, 15 La. An. 403; S. v. Patterson, 2 Ired. 346; Williams v. S., 44 Ala. 24; S. v. McCance, 110 Mo. 398; S. v. Sloan, 55 Ia. 217; S. v. Hughes, 58 Ia. 165. And see *infra*, §§ 1099, 1124.

[5] Slater v. S., 92 Ala. 68. But as to this, *quære:* Peat's Case, 2 Lewin, 111.

[6] C. v. Hayden, 163 Mass. 453.

[7] Miles v. U. S., 103 U. S. 304.

CHAPTER 47.

ADULTERY.

§ **1086. What constitutes.**— At common law the act of illicit sexual intercourse between persons one or both of whom were married was not punishable as a crime.[1] The term, however, was in use in England, prior to the settlement of this country, in two senses: in the ecclesiastical courts it was recognized as a ground of divorce consisting in the fact that a married person had illicit intercourse with another than the lawful husband or wife, while in the common-law courts as a basis of a civil right of action it consisted only in a man having criminal conversation with a married woman, thus introducing the danger of spurious issue of the marriage, and furnishing the husband a cause of action.[2] Statutes for the punishment of adultery as a crime were passed in some of the American colonies before independence, and such statutes are now general; but where they do not define the offense, but merely name it, leaving the definition to be determined from the common law, difficulty arises in determining which of the two meanings of the term already in use in England should be recognized. In some cases it has been held that the offense consists in a man having illicit intercourse with another man's wife;[3] while in other cases the ecclesiastical definition of the term is recognized, and the crime is held to consist in a person who is married having sexual intercourse with one who is not the lawful husband or wife.[4] But where the offense is defined

[1] C. v. Call, 21 Pick. 509; S. v. Marvin, 35 N. H. 22; S. v. Cooper, 16 Vt. 551; S. v. Lash, 16 N. J. 380; S. v. Gray, 37 N. J. 368; Ex parte Thomas, 103 Cal. 497; S. v. Brunson, 2 Bailey, 149; Anderson v. C., 5 Rand. 627; C. v. Isaacs, 5 Rand. 634. But adultery has sometimes been held to be a misdemeanor without statute: U. S. v. Clapox, 35 Fed. R. 575.

[2] 3 Bl. Com. 139; 4 Bl. Com. 65; S. v. Lash, 16 N. J. 380; C. v. Call, 21 Pick. 509.

[3] S. v. Lash, 16 N. J. 380; S. v. Wallace, 9 N. H. 515; S. v. Taylor, 58 N. H. 331; Hood v. S., 56 Ind. 263; S. v. Pearce, 2 Blackf. 318; S. v. Armstrong, 4 Minn. 335.

[4] C. v. Call, 21 Pick. 509; Helfrich v. C., 33 Pa. St. 68; S. v. Fellows, 50 Wis. 65; Miner v. P., 58 Ill. 59; S. v. Hinton, 6 Ala. 864; Hull v. Hull, 2 Strobh. Eq. 174.

by statute, the latter of these two meanings is the one generally recognized.[1] Although by this definition an unmarried man having intercourse with a married woman would not be guilty of adultery,[2] yet by statute this also is made criminal by additional provisions.[3] So it is sometimes specifically defined as adultery for a married man to have connection with an unmarried woman.[4] Most statutory definitions are now broad enough to make illicit sexual intercourse constitute adultery where either or both of the parties thereto are married persons.[5] What constitutes carnal knowledge of a woman is the same in adultery as in rape; at any rate proof of emission is unnecessary, it being unnecessary in rape.[6]

§ 1087. **Living in adultery; habitual intercourse.**—In some states illicit intercourse, to which a married person is a party, is made criminal by statute only when it is continuous in character, and it is then designated as "living in adultery," or by like terms. To constitute this offense, which may be committed by a married and an unmarried person, or by two married persons not husband and wife, there must be something more than mere criminal intimacy. One act, or even several acts, not in pursuance of a general illicit relation will not be enough.[7] But it is not necessary that the relation continue for any definite length of time; it may be sufficient that it is for a day only if it is with an intention of continuance.[8] Repeated acts of intercourse in pursuance of a general agreement of habitual surrender on the part of the female are sufficient, although the parties do not exclusively "live together."[9] But

[1] Holdren v. S., 29 Ohio St. 651. By federal statute intended to reach those who practice polygamy in the territories, if the woman is married, both are gulty of adultery, but if she is single, the man alone is guilty: In re Nielsen, 131 U. S. 176.

[2] Resp. v. Roberts, 2 Dallas, 124; Morrissett v. C., 6 Grat. 673.

[3] C. v. Elwell, 2 Met. 190; C. v. Reardon, 6 Cush. 78.

[4] In a prosecution under such statute the indictment must allege that the woman was unmarried: S. v. Searle, 56 Vt. 516.

[5] S. v. Hinton, 6 Ala. 864. And see Hull v. Hull, 2 Strobh. Eq. 174.

[6] C. v. Hussey, — Mass. —, 32 N. E. R. 362; C. v. Squires, 97 Mass. 59; Noble v. S., 22 Ohio St. 541. But as to the evidence, see *infra*, § 1097.

[7] Smith v. S., 39 Ala. 554; Quartemas v. S., 48 Ala. 269; Wright v. S., 5 Blackf. 358; S. v. Gartrell, 14 Ind. 280; McLeland v. S., 25 Ga. 477.

[8] Hall v. S., 53 Ala. 463.

[9] S. v. Jolly, 3 Dev. & B. 110; Collins v. S., 14 Ala. 608; Bodiford v. S., 86 Ala. 67; Smith v. S., 86 Ala. 57; Walker v. S., 104 Ala. 56.

under some statutes it is held that to constitute a "living together" in adultery the parties must actually dwell together.[1] Indeed, some statutes require that the living together shall be open and notorious, as of husband and wife.[2] By some statutes habitual illicit intercourse on the part of a married person constitutes adultery, even though it does not amount to a living in adultery.[3] But the illicit intercourse must be habitual, and not merely occasional.[4] This form of the offense is different from the other and must be proved as alleged.[5]

§ **1088. Validity of marriage.**— As there can be no such crime unless at least one of the parties is married,[6] the validity of the marriage may be a question in issue, and it is essential to the crime that the marriage be one which is deemed valid in the state in which the crime is prosecuted.[7] Thus, it has been held if a divorce is granted under a statute prohibiting a marriage between the guilty party and the paramour on account of the connection with whom the divorce is granted, a subsequent marriage between the guilty party and the paramour in another state for the purpose of evading the laws of the state where the divorce is granted will not be recognized as valid in the latter, and the person thus married cannot subsequently be guilty of adultery.[8] But the guilty party to the divorce does

[1] Bird v. S., 27 Tex. Ap. 635; Richardson v. S., 37 Tex. Ap. 346.

[2] Miner v. P., 58 Ill. 59; Carotti v. S., 42 Miss. 334; P. v. Gates, 46 Cal. 52.

[3] Swancoat v. S., 4 Tex. Ap. 105; Parks v. S., 4 Tex. Ap. 134; S. v. Carroll, 30 S. C. 85.

[4] S. v. Carroll, 30 S. C. 85; Granberry v. S., 61 Miss. 440; Collum v. S., 10 Tex. Ap. 708.

[5] Randle v. S., 12 Tex. Ap. 250; Burns v. S., 12 Tex. Ap. 394; Mitten v. S., 24 Tex. Ap. 346; Bird v. S., 27 Tex. Ap. 635. But it is held that both forms may be charged in one count: Heath v. S., 91 Ga. 126.

[6] The offense as between persons, neither of whom is married, if any, is fornication: Banks v. S., 96 Ala. 41. And see *infra*, § 1125. Therefore, if there is failure to prove that one of the parties is married, there may be conviction for fornication: *Infra*, § 1095. In some states the statutes provide a punishment for adultery and fornication, without distinction: Wasden v. S., 18 Ga. 264; S. v. Lyerly, 7 Jones, 158; though it seems that if the charge is that the crime was committed by a male defendant with an unmarried woman, evidence of its commission with a married woman constitutes a variance: Williams v. S., 86 Ga. 548; Bigby v. S., 44 Ga. 344.

[7] Marriages are in some states invalid if between white and colored persons; so cohabitation of such persons, even under the form of marriage, will be criminal: See *infra*, § 1130.

[8] Pennegar v. S., 87 Tenn. 244. And see *supra*, § 1074.

not commit adultery in remarrying and living with the second wife, even though such marriage may be void; for when contracting the second marriage he is not a married person by reason of the prior marriage which has been dissolved.[1] There must be proof of the actual, not merely of the reputed, marriage.[2] In civil cases, presumptive, as distinguished from direct, evidence of marriage is *prima facie* sufficient; for instance, evidence that a man and woman cohabit and speak of each other as husband and wife; but in a criminal prosecution involving the validity of the marriage, the fact of the marriage must be proven directly and not made out by mere presumption.[3] It is said, however, that general reputation is competent evidence, but not alone sufficient.[4] Where the crime charged consists in the defendant living as husband or wife with another under a marriage which is claimed to be void by reason of such other person having a living husband or wife under a previous marriage, the defendant may show the invalidity of such previous marriage by proving that the person with whom it was contracted was already married to another, such marriage relation continuing undissolved.[5]

§ **1089. Presumption of continuance.**— The marriage state, however, being shown to have existed, the presumption is that it continues until dissolved by death or divorce, and the burden is upon the accused to prove such dissolution.[6] The common-law presumption of death after continued absence of the husband or wife for seven years without being heard from may be shown as proving the termination of the marriage;[7] but such presumption may be overcome by evidence, and it is not necessary to show that the husband knew of the wife's continued existence.[8] It has already appeared in connection with the discussion of bigamy that a second marriage, though invalid by reason of a continuance of a prior marriage, will not constitute bigamy if there has been absence of the former spouse unheard of for some period fixed by statute; and the same exception will doubtless be applicable to defeat a prosecution for adultery

[1] S. v. Weatherby, 43 Me. 258; C. v. Putnam, 1 Pick. 136.

[2] Miner v. P., 58 Ill. 59.

[3] Green v. S., 21 Fla. 403.

[4] U. S. v. Higgerson, 46 Fed. R. 750.

[5] Banks v. S., 96 Ala. 41.

[6] P. v. Stokes, 71 Cal. 263; Cameron v. S., 14 Ala. 546.

[7] P. v. Stokes, 71 Cal. 263.

[8] P. v. Stokes, 71 Cal. 263.

on account of living with such second wife; but the exception is not available, it is said, to a husband who has abandoned his wife and left her beyond sea.[1] But where, in a prosecution for adultery, it is claimed that the defendant is not legally married because of invalidity of a supposed marriage relation with one having a former spouse living, the termination of such other marriage will not be made out by presumption from the absence of the former spouse, for such a presumption is not enough to overcome the presumption of innocence.[2]

§ **1090. Termination by divorce.**— The question whether the accused is married or not may depend on the validity of a divorce which as he claims has extinguished a previously existing marriage relation. It may be provided by statute that a sentence of imprisonment for life shall dissolve the marriage of the person sentenced without any judgment of divorce or other legal process, and such a dissolution will prevent a party to such marriage from being afterwards guilty of adultery. Such a dissolution of the marriage tie is not void as a legislative divorce in states where such divorces are forbidden by the constitution.[3] An order for a judgment of divorce without an entry thereof does not terminate the marriage, and even though the judgment is entered as of the date of the finding and order it does not take effect from that date so as to render an intervening marriage by one of the parties legal and support a charge against him of adultery in subsequent illicit connections.[4] If a decree of divorce is void for want of jurisdiction, the marriage still continues so as to support a conviction for adultery.[5] So where a husband procured a divorce and remarried, but subsequently the decree was set aside and declared void on the ground that it was procured by fraud, it was held that such divorce was no defense in a prosecution for adultery in cohabiting with the second wife.[6]

§ **1091. Intent; knowledge.**— In accordance with the general proposition that criminal intent is necessary to constitute a crime, it has been held that where a woman supposes herself

[1] C. v. Johnson, 10 Allen, 196.

[2] S. v. Henke, 58 Ia. 457; Williams v. S., 86 Ga. 548.

[3] S. v. Duket, 90 Wis. 272, 31 L. R. A. 515, and note.

[4] S. v. Eaton, 85 Wis. 587.

[5] S. v. Fleak, 54 Ia. 429.

[6] S. v. Whitcomb, 52 Ia. 85.

legally married she is not guilty of adultery in living with her supposed husband, though as a matter of fact the marriage is invalid by reason of a former continuing marriage relation on his part.[1] On the other hand, there are numerous cases to the effect that criminal intent or knowledge of the facts which will render the act criminal is not essential in a prosecution for this crime.[2] And certainly a mere mistake of law as to the validity of a former marriage, there being no mistake of fact, will not constitute an excuse.[3] So it is said that while a defendant accused of adultery committed by living in assumed marriage with one whose husband or wife has been absent unheard of for seven years cannot be convicted, yet if the absence has been less than seven years there may be a conviction, although the defendant in good faith believed the prior marriage to have been terminated.[4]

§ 1092. **Mutual criminal intent.**— The question has been raised whether the crime of adultery does not involve mutual criminality, and it has been urged that where the connection has been had by violence and against the woman's will so that the crime amounts to rape, a conviction for adultery on the part of the man cannot be sustained; but this view is not indorsed by the courts, and so far as the man is concerned the act may be both adultery and rape.[5] So where the charge is of incestuous adultery it is not necessary to show a common knowledge of the relationship, but it is sufficient to show a knowledge of the relationship on the part of the person charged.[6]

§ 1093. **Complaint of husband or wife.**— Some statutes provide that the prosecution for this offense shall be had only at

[1] Banks v. S., 96 Ala. 41; Vaughan v. S., 83 Ala. 55.

[2] C. v. Elwell, 2 Met. 190. It is not for the state to prove a guilty intent. If defendant relies on want of knowledge that the other party was married, the fact must be made out: S. v. Cody, 111 N. C. 725.

[3] S. v. Goodenow, 65 Me. 30; Owens v. S., 94 Ala. 97. Thus, if a divorce from a former marriage is invalid by reason of fraud, a subsequent marriage of one of the parties will be adulterous when the decree of divorce is set aside, although the other party to the second marriage believed the decree to be invalid: S. v. Whitcomb, 52 Ia. 85.

[4] C. v. Webster, 6 Allen, 591.

[5] C. v. Bakeman, 131 Mass. 577; S. v. Henderson, 84 Ia. 161; S. v. Sanders, 30 Ia. 582; S. v. Donovan, 61 Ia. 278. And see *infra*, § 1121. So the same offense may constitute adultery and incest: Cook v. S., 11 Ga. 53.

[6] Morgan v. S., 11 Ala. 289.

the instance of the husband or wife of the married party to the crime. Such provisions seem to indicate that the offense is regarded as one against the husband or wife rather than against society in general.[1] The right to prosecute as complaining witness is not perhaps limited to the husband or wife, but such husband or wife should institute the proceedings.[2] Inasmuch as the proceeding can be instituted under such statutory provisions only by the husband or wife, such party may withdraw them after they are instituted and the prosecution cannot properly proceed further.[3] But the proceeding being properly commenced, it may be continued without further co-operation on the part of the husband or wife.[4] It is a sufficient commencement of the prosecution by the husband or wife that such party institutes the proceedings before an examining magistrate in which the defendant is held to answer, without appearing before the grand jury or otherwise in the further prosecution of the case.[5] It is not essential that the name of the husband or wife be indorsed on the indictment as private prosecutor.[6] It is not, however, a sufficient commencement of the prosecution that the husband or wife appears before the grand jury in response to a subpœna, supposing such appearance and testimony to be required.[7] In case of a prosecution of an unmarried person for the crime, the husband or wife of the married party is the proper person to commence the prosecution under such statutory provision.[8] It is not necessary to aver in the indictment that the prosecution is commenced by the husband or wife.[9] The fact that the prosecution is com-

[1] S. v. Bennett, 31 Ia. 24; S. v. Hazen, 39 Ia. 648. Nevertheless, the crime is a public offense in such sense that to break and enter a dwelling by night to commit it is burglary: S. v. Corliss, 85 Ia. 18. *Contra*, under the definition of burglary in the Wisconsin statute: S. v. Goodrich, 84 Wis. 359. And see *supra*, § 220. Nor will the fact that before the commencement of the prosecution the husband or wife of the defendant has obtained a divorce prevent the case being prosecuted on complaint: S. v. Russell, 90 Ia. 569.

[2] P. v. Davis, 52 Mich. 569; Bayliss v. P., 46 Mich. 221.

[3] P. v. Dalrymple, 55 Mich. 519.

[4] S. v. Baldy, 17 Ia. 39.

[5] S. v. Dingee, 17 Ia. 232.

[6] S. v. Briggs, 68 Ia. 416.

[7] S. v. Donovan, 61 Ia. 278; S. v. Stout, 71 Ia. 343.

[8] Bayliss v. P., 46 Mich. 221; S. v. Wilson, 22 Ia. 364; Bush v. Workman, 64 Ia. 205; S. v. Mahan, 81 Ia. 121.

[9] S. v. Brecht, 41 Minn. 50; S. v. Maas, 83 Ia. 469. If the indictment does not show that complaint is by

menced by the husband or wife, when required by statutory provisions, is so far an essential element of the crime that it must be proved by the state;[1] and the averment of the fact in the indictment, if made, is not conclusive or even presumptive evidence thereof.[2] It is to be determined by the jury as any other question of fact, and not by the court upon a motion to dismiss the prosecution.[3] But it is not a fact which must be established beyond a reasonable doubt.[4] The offense of adultery is not condoned, like that of seduction, by a subsequent intermarriage of the guilty parties.[5]

§ **1094. Indictment.**—In general the offense is to be described in accordance with the language of the statute.[6] It is necessary, of course, in some form to charge that one of the parties was married,[7] but the charge of committing adultery is said to imply that fact without particular allegation.[8] And the allegation that the woman with whom the connection was had was the wife of another person, naming him, is sufficient showing that the parties between whom the connection was had were not husband and wife;[9] but it must appear in some way that they were not husband and wife.[10] The word "adultery"

the husband or wife, it will not be presumed that defendant is married unless that fact appears on the face of the indictment, and therefore the objection cannot be raised by demurrer, but only as a matter of defense: S. v. Mahan, 81 Ia. 121.

[1] S. v. Briggs, 68 Ia. 416.

[2] S. v. Roth, 17 Ia. 336; S. v. Henke, 58 Ia. 457.

[3] S. v. Briggs, 68 Ia. 416.

[4] S. v. Donovan, 61 Ia. 278. Failure to instruct the jury as to the necessity of proof of this fact is not error where no instruction is asked, and the fact appears without dispute: S. v. Hazen, 39 Ia. 648.

[5] Fox v. S., 3 Tex. Ap. 329.

[6] Lord v. S., 17 Neb. 526; S. v. Stubbs, 108 N. C. 774; S. v. Tally, 74 N. C. 322.

[7] Tucker v. S., 35 Tex. 113; T. v. Whitcomb, 1 Mont. 358; Miner v. P., 58 Ill. 59.

[8] S. v. Hinton, 6 Ala. 864; S. v. Lashley, 84 N. C. 754.

[9] C. v. Reardon, 6 Cush. 78; S. v. Parker, 57 N. H. 123. So the allegation that defendant had a wife then living, naming her, sufficiently negatives his being the husband of the woman with whom he is charged to have had connection: Helfrich v. C., 33 Pa. St. 68. Where the charge is of having carnal knowledge of a woman, the wife of a person named, it is not necessary to especially aver that the husband of such woman was still living: S. v. Parker, 57 N. H. 123.

[10] Moore v. C., 6 Met. 243. A charge of adultery in connection with a charge of begetting a bastard child sufficiently indicates that the parties were not husband and wife: Gorman v. C., 124 Pa. St. 536.

also implies carnal knowledge without further specification. Where the offense may consist in connection between a married man and a woman not his wife, whether married or single, it is unnecessary to allege the state of the woman in this respect.[2] The indictment need not allege the sex of the parties, nor charge that they were of different sexes, inasmuch as the charge of adultery or the facts constituting adultery necessarily implies that fact.[3] Nor need it be alleged to whom the married party is married.[4] It has been said to be necessary to charge the name of the person with whom the adultery was committed,[5] but this is doubtful, and it is suggested that it would be scandalous to thus ascribe a crime to a person having no opportunity to defend himself.[6] At any rate it is sufficient to charge the name of the person with whom the adultery was committed as to the grand jurors unknown, if that is the fact.[7] In general it is not necessary to lay the offense with a *continuando*, as one act is sufficient.[8] But, where the statutory offense charged was of wantonly cohabiting with a woman in a state of adultery, it was held proper to allege it as a continuing offense and committed between certain times named, and that proof of cohabitation during any portion of the time would establish the commission of the offense.[9] So, under the federal statute for the punishment of cohabitation with more than one woman (passed for the suppression of polygamy in the territories), there can be but one punishment for one continuous unlawful cohabitation.[10]

1 Helfrich v. C., 33 Pa. St. 68.

2 C. v. Thompson, 2 Cush. 551.

3 McLeod v. S., 35 Ala. 395; S. v. Dunn, 26 Ark. 34; Hildreth v. S., 19 Tex. Ap. 195; S. v. Lashley, 84 N. C. 754.

4 Hildreth v. S., 19 Tex. Ap. 195; Collum v. S., 10 Tex. Ap. 708; Moore v. C., 6 Met. 243. And see the forms of indictment in C. v. Thompson, 2 Cush. 551; S. v. Hutchinson, 36 Me. 261.

5 S. v. Vittum, 9 N. H. 519.

6 This suggeston is made in connection with a charge of adultery as a ground for divorce: Farr v. Farr, 34 Miss. 597. But in such cases it is usual to name the other guilty party as co-respondent: Wood v. Wood, 2 Paige, 108; Church v. Church, 3 Mass. 157. In Vermont it is not necessary to set out the offense with particularity in this respect, but the court may require additional specifications to be furnished when the reasons are shown for so doing: S. v. Bridgman, 49 Vt. 202.

7 C. v. Thompson, 2 Cush. 551.

8 S. v. Glaze, 9 Ala. 283; Swancoat v. S., 4 Tex. Ap. 105.

9 S. v. Way, 5 Neb. 283.

10 Ex parte Snow, 120 U. S. 274; In re Nielsen, 131 U. S. 176.

§ 1095. Joinder; included offenses.—The two parties to the crime, where both are by statute guilty, may be jointly indicted.[1] But it is better to indict them separately.[2] If indicted and tried jointly an acquittal of one will necessarily acquit the other.[3] But the fact that one of the parties thus jointly indicted is not arrested or brought to trial with the other will not preclude the other being put on trial or found guilty.[4] But two cannot be jointly indicted for living in a state of adultery where they are not charged with living with each other.[5] Though the offenses of adultery and fornication are sometimes described in the same section of the statute, yet they are usually distinct offenses, and therefore on an indictment for adultery there cannot be a conviction, if the evidence shows that the parties were unmarried.[6] Under other statutes, however, there may be an indictment for fornication and adultery charged in one count, and the jury may find defendant guilty of fornication without adultery.[7] Fornication may be deemed an included offense in adultery.[8] In such case it is proper to charge the jury in a prosecution for adultery with reference both to adultery and fornication.[9] As a single act constitutes adultery, it is not proper to charge several acts in the indictment, even though committed with the same person.[10] But the allegation of other acts committed on divers other days may be rejected as surplusage.[11] Bigamy may constitute adultery.[12]

§ 1096. Evidence as to the marriage.—In order to show that one of the parties is married, record evidence of the marriage is not necessary. The fact may be established by parol testimony,[13] or by proof of admissions of the defend-

[1] S. v. Bartlett, 53 Me. 446; C. v. Elwell, 2 Met. 190.

[2] S. v. Dingee, 17 Ia. 232.

[3] S. v. Mainor, 6 Ired. 340; S. v. Rinehart, 106 N. C. 787.

[4] S. v. Carroll, 30 S. C. 85; S. v. Lyerly, 7 Jones, 158.

[5] Maull v. S., 37 Ala. 160.

[6] Smitherman v. S., 27 Ala. 23.

[7] S. v. Cowell, 4 Ired. 231.

[8] Resp. v. Roberts, 2 Dall. 124; Gorman v. C., 124 Pa. St. 536.

[9] Kelley v. S., 33 Tex. Ap. 579.

[10] C. v. Fuller, 163 Mass. 499.

[11] S. v. Briggs, 68 Ia. 416. If but one act is charged, and evidence as to different acts is introduced, the prosecution may withdraw evidence as to all other acts but one, and thus cure the error: S. v. Donovan, 61 Ia. 278.

[12] *Supra*, § 1072.

[13] S. v. Wilson, 22 Ia. 364. While a certificate of foreign marriage will

ant.[1] So a marriage contract signed by the parties is admissible.[2] But reputation is not sufficient.[3] While evidence of words of present consent without official solemnization may be sufficient,[4] yet where the witness of such fact is the wife of defendant her admissions contradicting her testimony may be proved.[5]

§ **1097. Proof of act.**— The fact of illicit connection between a man and a woman is one which from its nature can very rarely be directly proved, and direct evidence of it is not necessary to support a conviction.[6] It may be inferred from circumstances, such as the fact of a man and woman, not husband and wife, occupying the same bed;[7] or that they lived together for some months in the same room;[8] or that the woman has, while separated from her husband, given birth to children who have been treated as his own by the man charged with her.[9] In corroboration, other evidence of bad character of the woman for chastity may be shown;[10] but evidence of birth of a child by the woman is alone not competent;[11] nor are admissions of the woman with whom defendant is charged to have committed the crime.[12] The fact that defendant does not call his partner in the alleged crime to testify for him is not a fact to be viewed with suspicion as an indication of guilt.[13] Mere suspicions and jealousies and neighborhood rumors are not admissible to sustain an indictment.[14] One credible wit-

not be admissible as a record or an independent declaration of an officiating minister, it is admissible as part of the *res gestæ* in corroboration of the testimony of a party who was present: S. v. Behrman, 114 N. C. 797.

[1] S. v. Medbury, 8 R. I. 543; S. v. Sanders, 30 Ia. 582; S. v. Behrman, 114 N. C. 797; Cameron v. S., 14 Ala. 546; Boger v. S., 19 Tex. Ap. 91.

[2] S. v. Behrman, 114 N. C. 797.

[3] Buchanan v. S., 55 Ala. 154.

[4] Buchanan v. S., 55 Ala. 154.

[5] Bailey v. S., 36 Neb. 808.

[6] Lawson v. S., 20 Ala. 65; S. v. Eliason, 91 N. C. 564; S. v. Dixon, 104 N. C. 704.

[7] C. v. Mosier, 135 Pa. St. 221; S. v. Poteet, 8 Ired. 23; though it is said that this would not be conclusive: S. v. Way, 6 Vt. 311; Blackham v. S., 36 Ala. 295. Being found in the same room is not sufficient: S. v. Waller, 80 N. C. 401.

[8] Richardson v. S., 34 Tex. 142.

[9] S. v. Chancy, 110 N. C. 507.

[10] Blackham v. S., 36 Ala. 295; Cox v. S., 99 Ala. 162; Hall v. S., 88 Ala. 236; C. v. Gray, 129 Mass. 474.

[11] C. v. O'Connor, 107 Mass. 219.

[12] S. v. McGuire, 50 Ia. 153.

[13] P. v. Hendrickson, 53 Mich. 525.

[14] S. v. Crowley, 13 Ala. 172; Belcher v. S., 8 Humph. 62.

ness is sufficient to prove the crime; corroboration is not required.[1]

§ 1098. **Proof of other acts.**—While one act may constitute the crime, yet, as the offense is one difficult of exact proof, other acts of illicit intercourse between the same parties may be shown for the purpose of indicating the nature of the relation of the parties which is claimed to have been adulterous. Thus, proof of indecent or improper familiarity prior to the time when the adultery is charged to have been committed,[2] or subsequent thereto,[3] is admissible. And improper conduct, though not such as to be criminal, may thus be proved.[4] So if the offense is by statute continuous in its nature, and the period during which it is charged to have continued is fixed in the indictment, evidence of improper acts between the parties anterior to such time may be admitted in corroboration of the testimony as to later acts, but not as a basis for conviction under the indictment.[5] So evidence of distincts acts so long before the finding of the indictment that a conviction therefor would be barred may be shown as tending to prove subsequent adulterous connection.[6] The presumption in civil cases that criminal intercourse once established continues while the parties live under the same roof is not applicable in a criminal prosecution.[7]

§ 1099. **Competency of husband or wife as a witness.**—Where the wife is made a competent witness against her husband as to an offense committed by him against her, it becomes a question whether the offense of adultery is one of that character. Some courts hold that she is a competent witness in such a case.[8] But in other cases it is held that such a statutory provision is to be construed as merely embodying the

[1] C. v. Cregor, 7 Grat. 591.

[2] McLeod v. S., 35 Ala. 395; Lawson v. S., 20 Ala. 65; Bodiford v. S., 86 Ala. 67; S. v. Kemp, 87 N. C. 538; S. v. Pippin. 88 N. C. 646; S. v. Guest, 100 N. C. 410.

[3] Cole v. S., 6 Baxt. 239, 243; S. v. Bridgman, 49 Vt. 202; S. v. Way, 5 Neb. 283.

[4] Alsabrooks v. S., 52 Ala. 24; S. v. Stubbs, 108 N. C. 774.

[5] Brevaldo v. S., 21 Fla. 789; Alsabrooks v. S., 52 Ala. 24.

[6] S. v. Potter, 52 Vt. 33; S. v. Briggs, 68 Ia. 416.

[7] Carotti v. S., 42 Miss. 334.

[8] S. v. Bennett, 31 Ia. 24; S. v. Hazen, 39 Ia. 648; S. v. Vollander, 57 Minn. 225; Lord v. S., 17 Neb. 526; Bailey v. S., 36 Neb. 808.

common-law rule by which a wife is a competent witness against her husband in a criminal case only when the crime is one against her person.[1] Of course the party with whom the accused is alleged to have committed the offense is a competent witness.[2]

[1] S. v. Armstrong, 4 Minn. 335; McLean v. S., 32 Tex. Ap. 521; Compton v. S., 13 Tex. Ap. 271 (overruling Morrill v. S., 5 Tex. Ap. 447; Roland v. S., 9 Tex. Ap. 277). And see Overton v. S., 43 Tex. 616; *supra*, § 1085, and *infra*, § 1124. And this rule is even extended to render the husband of the woman with whom the adultery is claimed to have been committed incompetent to testify against the man charged separately with the offense: Howard v. S., 94 Ga. 587. But after the female has pleaded guilty, her husband is a competent witness against the other defendant: S. v. Guest, 100 N. C. 410. The incompetency of the husband continues after the granting of a divorce to him: S. v. Jolly, 3 Dev. & B. 110. The incompetency of the husband or wife, however, does not extend so far as to prevent the giving of evidence with reference to circumstances not directly criminating, but which may, in connection with other facts, tend to criminate: S. v. Bridgman, 49 Vt. 202.

[2] S. v. Crowley, 13 Ala. 172.

CHAPTER 48.

ABDUCTION OF FEMALES.

§ **1100. In case of girls.**— There have been various statutes in England punishing forcible abduction and marriage of females;[1] but the offense covered by the early statutes involved the motive of lucre.[2] The wrong involved in this crime is apparently to some extent the deprivation of the parent or guardian of the proper control of a minor child, and in England it is criminal at the present time to entice, or to take or detain by force, a child under fourteen years of age, from its parent or guardian;[3] but the statutes in this country usually relate to the abduction of female children under some specified age from the custody of their parents, guardians, or those having the legal right to control them, for the purposes of prostitution or defilement.[4] The offense consists in the taking away for the prohibited purpose, and therefore the crime is committed in the county where the defendant makes advances to the girl, urging her to go away with him, whether the unlawful purpose with which the girl was taken away was carried out in that county or not.[5] An analogous offense is that of defiling a female child, committed by one to whom the custody of such child has been intrusted.[6]

§ **1101. From the custody of parent or guardian.**— The offense may be committed by taking from the custody of the

[1] 4 Bl. Com. 208; 1 Hawk. P. C., § 1; 1 Hale, P. C. 660; Stephen, Dig. Cr. L., art. 261.

[2] Reg. v. Barratt, 9 C. & P. 387.

[3] Stephen, Dig. Cr. L., art. 263.

[4] S. v. Tidwell, 5 Strobh. 1; S. v. Sullivan, 85 N. C. 506; P. v. Chu Quong, 15 Cal. 332. It is also usually made criminal to entice, or take by force, a virtuous female to a house of prostitution: See *infra*, § 1106*a*.

[5] S. v. Johnson, 115 Mo. 480.

[6] S. v. Jones, 16 Kan. 608; S. v. Arnold, 55 Mo. 89; S. v. Buster, 90 Mo. 514. And the statute of Missouri has been extended to cover the case of an employer of a female servant: S. v. Young, 99 Mo. 284; S. v. Strattman, 100 Mo. 540; S. v. Terry, 106 Mo. 209; S. v. Rogers, 108 Mo. 202. In Ohio the statute covers the relation of teacher and pupil: Brown v. S., 38 Ohio St. 374.

mother, although the father may be living and have the better right to such custody, and may have given his consent to the taking;[1] and the guardian mentioned by the statute is the person who is guardian in fact of the child, though he may not be legally appointed.[2] But the person having a mere temporary charge, as a schoolmaster, is not intended. It is enough, however, that the person is one who, by permission of the parents, if living, is intrusted with the custody of the child as an actual member of the family.[3] So the master by whom a female child is employed may be the person from whose custody she is taken, although she has parents.[4] The female may be in the control of a parent or guardian, so that the crime may be committed although she is temporarily absent from her home, even in another state;[5] and in such case the person who detains her for the purpose of concubinage without the consent of the parent or guardian is guilty of the crime in the state where such detention takes place.[6]

§ **1102. Consent.**— As usually defined, the offense involves want of consent of the parent or guardian or person from whose custody the child is taken,[7] but consent of the female herself is immaterial.[8] No matter how willingly she may go, the crime is committed if she is enticed to go without the consent of her

[1] P. v. Fowler, 88 Cal. 136. And see Reg. v. Burrell, L. & C. 354.

[2] P. v. Carrier, 46 Mich. 442.

[3] S. v. Ruhl, 8 Ia. 447.

[4] Reg. v. Miller, 13 Cox, 179.

[5] Reg. v. Mycock, 12 Cox, 28; S. v. Gordon, 46 N. J. 432; S. v. Round, 82 Mo. 679. So even where the girl was away from home without her father's consent, leading a dissolute and immoral life, the defendant was held guilty in persuading her to go to a house of ill-fame: P. v. Cook, 61 Cal. 478. But under the English statute one who finds a girl in the street and induces her to go with him is not guilty of taking her from the possession of her father: Reg. v. Green, 3 F. & F. 274; Reg. v. Hibbert, L. R. 1 C. C. 184.

[6] S. v. Gordon, 46 N. J. 432.

[7] Reg. v. Primelt, 1 F. & F. 50. Under some statutes, however, want of consent of the parent need not be alleged, though perhaps consent may be shown by way of defense: S. v. Jamison, 38 Minn. 21; S. v. Chisenhall, 106 N. C. 676. On the question of consent of the parents it has been held admissible to show that the child had, with their knowledge, been an inmate of a bawdy-house: Brown v. S., 72 Md. 477.

[8] Scruggs v. S., 90 Tenn. 81; Tucker v. S., 8 Lea, 633. But in the crime of kidnapping want of consent of the person taken is essential, even though a special punishment is provided for the kidnapping of a female under fifteen years of age: Castillo v. S., 29 Tex. Ap. 127. A conviction for the abduction will bar a prosecution for kidnapping: Mason v. S., 29 Tex. Ap. 24.

legal custodian, and it is not necessary, therefore, that the taking be with force or violence.[1]

§ 1103. What constitutes a taking.— To induce a female by solicitations and presents to leave her home and go with defendant is a sufficient taking;[2] any representation or suggestion designed to induce the female to go is enough; an open solicitation is not necessary.[3] If the female leaves the control of her parents by reason of persuasions or inducement held out by defendant, he is guilty, though the particular act of leaving home was voluntary on the part of the female, and not by his immediate direction.[4] So, where it appears that defendant assisted the girl in escaping from her home and eloped with her, he was held guilty, although she herself had proposed his rendering such assistance.[5] But if the girl acts of her own free will and without any inducement or assistance of the defendant, he is not criminally liable for the taking.[6]

§ 1104. Purpose of the abduction.— According to most of the statutes the abduction, in order to constitute a crime, must be for the purpose of prostitution or concubinage. If the prohibited purpose is that of prostitution, it is not sufficient to show an intent on the part of the defendant to have connection with the girl by himself alone. Prostitution implies indiscriminate sexual intercourse.[7] If the crime under the statute is that of abduction for the purposes of concubinage, it is not necessary that the intent shall be that the connection shall last for any particular or considerable period of time. It is enough that

[1] P. v. Demousset, 71 Cal. 611; P. v. Marshall, 59 Cal. 386; S. v. Keith, 47 Minn. 559; S. v. Jamison, 38 Minn. 21; Reg. v. Frazer, 8 Cox, 446; Reg. v. Mankletow, Dears. 159 (explaining Reg. v. Meadows, 1 C. & K. 399).

[2] S. v. Johnson, 115 Mo. 480.

[3] P. v. Carrier, 46 Mich. 442.

[4] Reg. v. Robb, 4 F. & F. 59; Reg. v. Olifier, 10 Cox, 402; Reg. v. Kipps, 4 Cox, 167; Reg. v. Mankletow, Dears. 159. Indeed, it was held criminal to quit a parent's house with the girl even in consequence of a proposition emanating from the girl herself: Reg. v. Biswell, 2 Cox, 279.

[5] Reg. v. Robins, 1 C. & K. 456. For other cases under the English statutes, see Reg. v. Hopkins, Car. & M. 254; Reg. v. Baillie, 8 Cox, 238.

[6] Jenkins v. S., 15 Lea, 674; S. v. Gibson, 111 Mo. 92; Reg. v. Handley, 1 F. & F. 648; Reg. v. Miller, 13 Cox, 179; Reg. v. Burrell, L. & C. 354; Reg. v. Meadows, 1 C. & K. 399.

[7] S. v. Brow, 64 N. H. 577; S. v. Stoyell, 54 Me. 24; C. v. Cook, 12 Met. 93; S. v. Ruhl, 8 Ia. 447. Nor is the crime committed by taking the girl in order that a third person may have connection with her on one occasion: Haygood v. S., 98 Ala. 61.

the intent is to enter without limit as to time or place upon a continuous relation of sexual intercourse.[1] It is not necessary that it appear that a course of cohabitation was intended; intent to cohabit for a single night is said to be sufficient.[2] And it need not be shown that the defendant's intent was to keep the girl away from her home permanently.[3] A statute covering both prostitution and concubinage covers all cases where the intent is for illicit intercourse of whatever nature and for whatever length of time.[4] But cohabitation as man and wife will not constitute concubinage if in pursuance of a valid common-law marriage, although on account of the minority of the girl and the refusal of consent of the parents a license for the marriage could not be procured.[5] The unlawful purpose must be established by evidence.[6] For the purpose of showing the intent in the taking, subsequent sexual intercourse of the defendant with the girl may be shown;[7] but proof of one act of sexual intercourse will not be sufficient in itself to establish the intent.[8] Proof of previous sexual intercourse between the parties will not be sufficient alone to show the criminal purpose in the taking.[9] If the charge is of abducting for purpose of prostitution, the knowledge on the part of the person abducting of the bad character of the house to which the girl is taken will be admissible to show the purpose;[10] and even the general bad reputation of the place may be shown without direct proof of knowledge thereof as tending to show the defendant's intent.[11] But the fact that the girl is brought to a house of prostitution will not in itself be conclusive evidence that the keeper of the house is guilty of enticing or detaining her for that purpose.[12] In general, some improper motive in the abduction must be shown in order that it shall be criminal.[13]

§ **1105. Knowledge as to age.**— Where the criminality depends upon the age of the girl, a mistake on the part of the

[1] Henderson v. P., 124 Ill. 607.

[2] S. v. Feasel, 74 Mo. 524; S. v. Gibson, 111 Mo. 92. Further, as to cohabitation, see *infra*, § 1130.

[3] Reg. v. Timmins, Bell, 276.

[4] P. v. Bristol, 23 Mich. 118; P. v. Cummons, 56 Mich. 544.

[5] S. v. Bittick, 103 Mo. 183.

[6] S. v. Jamison, 38 Minn. 21.

[7] S. v. Johnson, 115 Mo. 480.

[8] U. S. v. Zes Cloya, 35 Fed. R. 493.

[9] S. v. Jamison, 38 Minn. 21.

[10] S. v. Chisenhall, 106 N. C. 676.

[11] S. v. Chisenhall, 106 N. C. 676.

[12] Brown v. S., 72 Md. 468.

[13] Reg. v. Tinkler, 1 F. & F. 513.

defendant as to her age, and a *bona fide* belief that she is over the age specified by the statute, will be immaterial.[1]

§ 1106. Chastity of the female.— From the previous discussion of the nature of the offense it is evident that the character of the female for chastity is immaterial.[2]

§ 1106a. Abduction or enticement of women; pimping or procuring.— There is a New York statute prohibiting the "taking a woman against her will for the purpose of marriage or to be defiled," and in other states there are analogous statutes punishing abduction for purposes of prostitution or concubinage. It is a taking within such a statute if the woman is induced to go by deceit or false pretenses without the use of actual physical force.[3] There must be proof of some means to take or entice her against her will;[4] but the fact that she is by reason of insanity incapable of dissenting will not be a defense in a prosecution for such taking.[5] Enticing a woman to a house of prostitution or detaining her therein is usually made criminal.[6] Such offense of detention is not committed by one who has illicit intercourse with a member of his own family in the house of his residence.[7] The purpose must be that of prostitution, that is, of having common, indiscriminate, meretricous commerce, and the purpose on the part of the abductor to himself only have intercourse with the female is not sufficient to constitute the crime.[8] The offense is usually described in a way to limit it to the abduction of females of previously chaste character,[9] and in such case the chastity must

[1] P. v. Dolan, 96 Cal. 315; P. v. Fowler, 88 Cal. 136; S. v. Ruhl, 8 Ia. 447; S. v. Newton, 44 Ia. 45; S. v. Johnson, 115 Mo. 480; Reg. v. Prince, L. R. 2 C. C. 154; Reg. v. Robins, 1 C. & K. 456; Reg. v. Olifier, 10 Cox, 402; Reg. v. Booth, 12 Cox, 321; Reg. v. Mycock, 12 Cox, 28. And see *supra*, § 134.

[2] P. v. Demousset, 71 Cal. 611; P. v. Dolan, 96 Cal. 315; S. v. Gibson, 111 Mo. 92; S. v. Johnson, 115 Mo. 480; Brown v. S., 72 Md. 477.

[3] Schnicker v. P., 88 N. Y. 192; Beyer v. P., 86 N. Y. 369. But though it is not essential there be such force as in rape, the act must be against the will: Pollard v. S., 2 Ia. 567.

[4] P. v. Plath, 100 N. Y. 590.

[5] Higgins v. C., 94 Ky. 54.

[6] S. v. Terrill, 76 Ia. 149. But the offenses of enticing and detaining are distinct: Ibid.

[7] Bunfill v. P., 154 Ill. 640.

[8] Miller v. P., 121 Ind. 294. Therefore an indictment charging the purpose to have been to unlawfully and feloniously prostitute the female and have carnal intercourse with her was held not sufficient, not being equivalent to the statutory definition, "for the purpose of prostitution:" Ibid. And see *infra*, § 1133.

[9] Nichols v. S., 127 Ind. 406. Where the statute described the offense of

be proved affirmatively, not merely by the presumption of chastity.[1] Where the statutory description is of the offense of abduction for the purpose of concubinage, a taking away for the purpose of one act of sexual intercourse is not enough.[2] To constitute a house of ill-fame under the statute as to enticing, the place must be one resorted to for that purpose; the case of enticing to other houses for purposes of prostitution being a distinct offense;[3] but it is not necessary that the house shall have already been used for that purpose if it is prepared and intended therefor.[4] The indictment should state the particular house or place to which the woman was enticed.[5] There is a federal statute prohibiting the importation of females for purposes of prostitution, and under such statute it is sufficient to state the fact of importation and in general the purpose, without allegation of the specific facts nor the place.[6] Analogous to the offense of enticing is that recognized by statute in some states, of procuring a female to have illicit carnal connection with a man,[7] or of being a pimp.[8] A "pimp" or "bawd" is a person who procures opportunities for illicit sexual intercourse for others,[9] the former term being usually applied, it is believed, to a man, the latter to a woman. "Procuring" does not include seduction.[10] If several acts are described as constituting the offense of being a pimp they may be charged conjunctively in one count.[11]

soliciting a female to enter a house of ill-fame for the purpose of becoming a prostitute, it was held that the crime was not committed by soliciting a prostitute to abandon one house of that character and become an inmate of another; P. v. Cook, 96 Mich. 368.

1 C. v. Whittaker, 131 Mass. 224. But, aside from this question, it is not proper for defendant in a prosecution of this kind to prove specific acts of unchastity with other men on the part of the female: Cargill v. C., 93 Ky. 578.

2 S. v. Wilkinson, 121 Mo. 485; S. v. Gibson, 108 Mo. 575. A charge against three men of taking a female for the purpose of concubinage by having intercourse with them charges no offense, as the female could not be the concubine of all three: S. v. Gibson, 111 Mo. 92.

3 S. v. McCrum, 38 Minn. 154.

4 P. v. Cook, 96 Mich. 368.

5 Nichols v. S., 127 Ind. 406.

6 U. S. v. Pagliano, 53 Fed. R. 1001.

7 P. v. Roderigas, 49 Cal. 9.

8 Fahnestock v. S., 102 Ind. 156.

9 Dyer v. Morris, 4 Mo. 214. Therefore it is erroneous to define the word "pimp" as designating a man who has intercourse with a lewd woman, who takes care of and supports him: P. v. Gastro, 75 Mich. 127.

10 P. v. Roderigas, 49 Cal. 9.

11 Fahnestock v. S., 102 Ind. 156.

§ **1107. The indictment.**— The indictment must state the name of the parent or guardian from whose custody the girl is charged to have been abducted.[3] But it need not allege the means by which the abduction was effected.[2] Where two different purposes, to wit, prostitution and concubinage, are mentioned by statute, the indictment must specify which one is intended to be charged, as the offenses are to be deemed distinct.[3] The charge of enticing away two girls by the same act is not improper as charging two offenses.[4] It would not be profitable to set out forms of the indictment, inasmuch as the elements of the offense differ so entirely under different statutes, but cases cited in the note furnish illustrations.[5]

§ **1108. Evidence.**— It was early held that though in general the wife was not a competent witness for or against her husband, yet, where the crime of abduction and forcible marriage had been committed, she was a competent witness against her husband, even though the marriage might be valid.[6] In some states corroboration of the testimony of the female is required in such cases,[7] while other statutes do not include this offense among those in which corroboration of the testimony of the female is necessary.[8]

[1] Jones v. S., 16 Lea, 466. *Contra*, S. v. Keith, 47 Minn. 559.

[2] S. v. George, 93 N. C. 567; S. v. Keith, 47 Minn. 559.

[3] S. v. Goodwin, 33 Kan. 538.

[4] P. v. Milne, 60 Cal. 71.

[5] S. v. Jamison, 38 Minn. 21; S. v. Keith, 47 Minn. 559; S. v. Johnson, 115 Mo. 480.

[6] 1 Bl. Com. 443; 4 Bl. Com. 209; 1 East, P. C. 454; Rex v. Wakefield, 2 Lewin, 279.

[7] S. v. Keith, 47 Minn. 559.

[8] S. v. Stone, 106 Mo. 1.

PART XII.

OFFENSES AGAINST CHASTITY, DECENCY AND MORALITY.

CHAPTER 49.

SEDUCTION.

§ **1109. Classification of sexual crimes.**— While sexual intercourse between a man and a woman who are not married to each other is unlawful it is not in all states made criminal.[1] The crimes growing out of sexual relations which are almost universally punishable in the various states are those involving some element of aggravation; such as rape, where the act is by force; bigamy, where it is a violation of marital rights; and seduction, where the element of artifice or false promises is involved. There are other crimes of a similar character, where the element of aggravation is the publicity of the act and the resulting tendency to corrupt the public morals or shock the public taste, such as prostitution, lewdness, obscenity and the kindred offense of keeping houses of prostitution. The accompanying table will serve to classify the various crimes of this character with reference to their principal characteristics.

[1] Simple fornication is, however, in some states punishable by statute: See *supra*, § 1086; *infra*, § 1125.

§ 1110. Table of sexual crimes.—

1. Sexual connection between man and woman not lawfully married.
   - Single act criminal.
     - Criminal in man only.
       - Rape.
         - Without actual consent of female.
           - Resistance overcome.
           - By fraud (probably).
           - By taking advantage of insensibility.
         - With actual consent, but where there is not capacity to give valid consent.
           - By reason of imbecility.
           - By reason of not having attained age of consent.
       - Seduction, the consent of a chaste, unmarried woman being procured by artifice or a false promise.
     - Criminal in either sex (statutory).
       - Incest, between persons within specified degrees of relationship.
       - Adultery, where one party or both are married.
       - Fornication (not made criminal in all states, except as it is continued, or public).
   - Criminal by reason of publicity or repetition.
     - Prostitution. (To which are closely allied the crimes of keeping house of ill-fame, or frequenting such house, or leasing premises for such purpose.)
     - Lewdness.
2. Illegal marriages.
   - Within prohibited degree of relationship (constituting incest).
   - Plural marriages (constituting bigamy).
3. Criminal acts allied to sexual crimes but not involving connection with opposite sex.
   - Sodomy.
   - Obscene exposure of person.
   - Obscene publications.

§ 1111. What constitutes seduction.— Under a statute in England antedating the settlement of this country, the taking a girl under sixteen years of age out of the possession or custody of her parent or guardian was punishable, with an additional penalty for defiling her, or, without the consent of her parents, contracting marriage with her.[1] But this statute is in the main similar to the earlier statutes which have been the basis of the statutes in the United States relating to the abduction of girls.[2] Aside from this there is no basis in the common law or in the English statutes which form a part of the common law for us, for the offense of seduction as defined by the various state statutes.[3] In South Carolina the English statute is declared to be in force.[4] In general, as defined by the state statutes, the offense consists in seducing and debauching an unmarried female of previously chaste character. To seduce means to corrupt or draw aside from the path of virtue, while debauching implies carnal knowledge.[5]

§ 1112. Seductive arts; promise of marriage.— Where the statute does not specially define the means which shall be sufficient to constitute the crime there must be some artifice, promise, flattery or the like, by means of which the intercourse is secured, in order to constitute a seduction.[6] There must be something more than the mere appeal to lust, passion or cupidity.[7] But the exact manner or kind of seductive arts cannot be defined; every case must depend upon its own peculiar circumstances, together with the conditions in life, advantages, age and intelligence of the parties.[8] So where it appeared that prosecutrix was of tender years and under the protection of

1 4 & 5 Phil. & M., ch. 8 (1557).

2 *Supra*, § 1100.

3 C. v. Cook, 12 Met. 93; P. v. Rodrigas, 49 Cal. 9; Anderson v. C., 5 Rand. 627; S. v. Sullivan, 85 N. C. 506; Rex v. Marriot, 4 Mod. 144.

4 S. v. Findlay, 2 Bay, 418; s. c., S. v. Findley, 1 Brev. 107. The fourth section of the English act which was applied in this case is not limited in application to a female possessing lands or goods, or an heiress or heiress apparent: Ibid.

5 S. v. Reeves, 97 Mo. 668, 8 Am. Cr. R. 698, and note; Wood v. Mathews, 47 Ia. 409; Putman v. S., 29 Tex. Ap. 454.

6 S. v. Crawford, 34 Ia. 40; S. v. Bollerman, 92 Ia. 460, 61 N. W. R. 183.

7 S. v. Fitzgerald, 63 Ia. 268; Putman v. S., 29 Tex. Ap. 454.

8 S. v. Higdon, 32 Ia. 262. But in a particular case held that allegations in the indictment as to representations that the act was innocent with promise of presents, etc., were sufficient: S. v. Fitzgerald, 63 Ia. 268. And see S. v. Carter, 8 Wash. 272.

defendant, it was held that the circumstances themselves would tend to make out a case of seduction.[1] A promise of marriage is sufficient to constitute the element of enticement and false promise essential to the crime.[2] By some statutes promise of marriage is alone mentioned as the means;[3] but even where there is a promise of marriage, intercourse must have been brought about by means thereof and the influence thereby obtained, and not by a mere appeal to the passions; in other words, there must have been the element of seduction.[4] It is not material how long a time has elapsed after the promise of marriage before the intercourse if such promise was relied upon by the prosecutrix.[5] Even a conditional promise to marry, dependent upon the ability of the parties to support themselves,[6] or upon permission to have intercourse,[7] or in case of pregnancy,[8] has been held sufficient. Nor is it necessary that the prosecutrix shall have accepted the promise of marriage, and entered into a reciprocal promise, as that fact may be inferred from her consent to the act.[9] It is not necessary that the promise of marriage be one binding upon the proposer,[10] or that the promise shall have been made in good faith;[11] for instance, though the promiser is already a married man he may be guilty of seduction under promise of marriage.[12] But if the prosecutrix knew that the defendant was married at the

[1] Lybarger v. S., 2 Wash. 552.

[2] S. v. Heatherton, 60 Ia. 175; S. v. Reeves, 97 Mo. 668; Boyce v. P., 55 N. Y. 644; Wilson v. S., 58 Ga. 328; Putman v. S., 29 Tex. Ap. 454.

[3] S. v. Primm, 98 Mo. 368; S. v. Ferguson, 107 N. C. 841; Putman v. S., 29 Tex. Ap. 454.

[4] S. v. Reeves, 97 Mo. 668; O'Neill v. S., 85 Ga. 383; Putman v. S., 29 Tex. Ap. 454. But in an earlier Georgia case, it was said that to establish sexual intercourse with a virtuous woman pending an engagement of marriage might be seduction, though consent was obtained without other persuasion than that implied in proposing the intercourse and repeating the promise: Wilson v. S., 58 Ga. 328. And to the same effect, see S. v. Eckler, 106 Mo. 585.

[5] Armstrong v. P., 70 N. Y. 38. Nor is it necessary that the promise be renewed at the time of the act (S. v. Brassfield, 81 Mo. 151), though such repetition may imply persuasion: McTyier v. S., 91 Ga. 254.

[6] Armstrong v. P., 70 N. Y. 38.

[7] Boyce v. P., 55 N. Y. 644; S. v. Thornton, 108 Mo. 640.

[8] P. v. Van Alstyne, 144 N. Y. 361; S. v. Cochran, 10 Wash. 562.

[9] Kenyon v. P., 26 N. Y. 203; S. v. Eckler, 106 Mo. 585.

[10] Callahan v. S., 63 Ind. 198.

[11] P. v. Samonset, 97 Cal. 448; S. v. Prizer, 49 Ia. 531. Even if the promise is made directly for the purpose of securing intercourse, it may be sufficient: S. v. Knutson, 91 Ia. 549.

[12] S. v. Bryan, 34 Kan. 63.

time of the intercourse, such knowledge would of course show that the promise was not relied on, and therefore that there was no seduction.[1] So while the fact that defendant was already engaged to be married to another will not prevent the prosecutrix relying upon his promise of marriage to her as constituting seduction, yet such fact may have a bearing on the question as to whether she yielded her virtue on account of the promise.[2]

§ 1113. Prosecutrix unmarried and chaste.—Even without express statutory provision the crime can only be committed as to an unmarried female of previously chaste character, the term "seduction" implying as much;[3] and the fact that prosecutrix was unmarried at the time of the alleged seduction must be shown.[4] Most statutes specifically define the offense, however, as committed only with a woman who is unmarried and chaste, and under such statutes the chastity of the female must appear.[5] But it is the fact of chastity, and not defendant's belief with reference thereto, that is material. If prosecutrix was, in fact, unchaste, his belief that she was chaste would not justify a conviction.[6] As to what constitutes chastity the courts are not entirely agreed. It has been held that, as a legal definition, an unmarried woman is chaste if she has never had sexual intercourse with a man, and that it is not for the jury to determine that she is unchaste otherwise than by this test.[7] But other courts hold that by the term "chaste" something more is meant than that the woman has not had illicit intercourse,

[1] Norton v. S., 72 Miss. 128; Wood v. S., 48 Ga. 192. So if the false promise was extraordinary, and such as the defendant was known to be incapable of performing, that fact should be considered in determining whether the prosecutrix relied thereon: S. v. Groome, 10 Ia. 308.

[2] S. v. Brown, 86 Ia. 121.

[3] Norton v. S., 72 Miss. 128. And see *infra*, § 1118. Thus, previous chastity is essential without express provision: P. v. Brewer, 27 Mich. 134; Ferguson v. S., 71 Miss. 805.

[4] S. v. Wheeler, 108 Mo. 658; P. v. Krusick, 93 Cal. 74; S. v. Carr, 60 Ia. 453.

[5] Norton v. S., 72 Miss. 128; Brock v. S., 95 Ga. 474; S. v. Patterson, 88 Mo. 88; Polk v. S., 40 Ark. 482; Luckie v. S., 33 Tex. Ap. 562. Previously chaste character is not essential in a civil action by a parent for seduction of his minor daughter: Updegraff v. Bennett, 8 Ia. 72.

[6] Barker v. C., 90 Va. 820.

[7] O'Neill v. S., 85 Ga. 383; S. v. Crowell, 116 N. C. 1052. An instruction that lewd and immodest acts and deportment would show want of chastity was held unnecessary: P. v. Samonset, 97 Cal. 448.

and that her character for chastity and purity of heart and feeling may be successfully impeached without any actual sexual intercourse being shown, obscenity of language, indecency of conduct, or undue familiarity with men being sufficient to warrant the jury in finding that she was of unchaste character.[1] However, impropriety of conduct on a previous occasion may not be inconsistent with a chaste character.[2] The question of chastity is one of character and not of reputation;[3] and want of it is not shown by proof of the general bad reputation of the house at which prosecutrix resided, but only by proof of particular acts.[4] A chaste character, though lost by illicit sexual intercourse, may be regained by repentance and reformation, so that the crime of seduction may be committed in leading such woman for a second time from the path of virtue;[5] but the mere lapse of time between previous unchastity and the act in question will not in itself show a re-establishment of a chaste character.[6] Although the previous illicit intercourse was with defendant, a character for chastity may be regained by breaking off such intercourse and reforming, so that subsequent intercourse between the parties may constitute seduction.[7] So, a previous seduction by defendant, under promise of marriage, will not prevent a renewal of the intercourse under a new promise from being punishable as seduction.[8]

§ **1114. Indictment.**— It is not necessary in the indictment to allege the particular means employed;[9] it is enough to

[1] Andre v. S., 5 Ia. 389; Boak v. S., 5 Ia. 430; S. v. Standley, 76 Ia. 215; S. v. Bell, 49 Ia. 440; Wood v. S., 48 Ga. 192. But an instruction as to the fact of proof of improper liberties allowed to others than defendant prior to the act charged was held misleading in not defining the meaning of such term: S. v. Carr, 60 Ia. 453.

[2] S. v. Brinkhaus, 34 Minn. 285.

[3] Andre v. S., 5 Ia. 389; Boak v. S., 5 Ia. 430; S. v. Wells, 48 Ia. 671; S. v. Higdon, 32 Ia. 262.

[4] Barker v. C., 90 Va. 820; *infra*, § 1118.

[5] S. v. Carron, 18 Ia. 372; S. v. Knutson, 91 Ia. 549; Wilson v. S., 73 Ala. 527; Williams v. S., 3 Ind. Ap. 350. Thus, evidence of improper conduct on the part of the female some years before the act relied on as seduction was held properly excluded: S. v. Dunn, 53 Ia. 526.

[6] P. v. Squires, 49 Mich. 487; S. v. Primm, 98 Mo. 368.

[7] S. v. Timmins, 4 Minn. 325; S. v. Moore, 78 Ia. 494; S. v. Gnagy, 84 Ia. 177; S. v. Brassfield, 81 Mo. 151; Kelly v. S., 33 Tex. Ap. 31.

[8] P. v. Millspaugh, 11 Mich. 278. As to presumption and proof with reference to chastity, see *infra*, § 1118.

[9] Wilson v. S., 73 Ala. 527; S. v. Curran, 51 Ia. 112; S. v. Conkright, 58 Ia. 338.

charge that the seduction was under promise of marriage.[1] Indeed, it is said that a general averment of the seduction will be sufficient without alleging the agreement to marry.[2] Nor is it essential, it is said, where the allegation is of seduction under promise of marriage, to aver that the woman was single,[3] nor that she was of previously chaste character, as such fact will be presumed.[4] But in reason it would seem that if the statute defining the offense requires that the woman be unmarried and of previously chaste character, these elements of the crime should be distinctly alleged.[5] The indictment need not specify whether the accused was single or married;[6] nor need it charge that the seduction was of a woman, that fact being presumed from the use of the name indicating a person.[7] The exact time of the seduction is not material.[8] From the preceding discussion it is evident that no form of indictment which could be relied on in all the states can very well be given, the form depending so entirely upon the language of the statute. It will certainly be sufficient in any case to charge the facts which under the statute constitute the offense, but it is essential that the indictment directly charge the seduction of the person with whom the crime was committed.[9]

§ **1115. Included offenses.**—Where fornication is a crime it is necessarily included in the charge of seduction, and there may therefore be a conviction for fornication although the seduction is not shown.[10] So there may be a conviction for adultery, or adultery and fornication, under the charge of seduction.[11] But the crime of rape is not included; and if the evidence shows that the connection was had by force and against the will, there should be no conviction either for seduction or for rape,[12]

[1] S. v. Abrisch, 41 Minn. 41.

[2] S. v. Primm, 98 Mo. 368.

[3] Norton v. S., 72 Miss. 128. It is sufficient that the fact appears generally from the allegations of the indictment: Ferguson v. S., 71 Miss. 805.

[4] Ferguson v. S., 71 Miss. 805; P. v. Brewer, 27 Mich. 134.

[5] West v. S., 1 Wis. 209; S. v. Gates, 27 Minn. 52; S. v. Wenz, 41 Minn. 196; S. v. Framness, 43 Minn. 490; Mesa v. S., 17 Tex. Ap. 395.

[6] Luckie v. S., 33 Tex. Ap. 562. And see *supra*, § 1112.

[7] S. v. Hemm, 82 Ia. 609.

[8] S. v. McClintic, 73 Ia. 663.

[9] S. v. Marshall, 121 Mo. 476.

[10] Dinkey v. C., 17 Pa. St. 126; Hopper v. S., 54 Ga. 389.

[11] Wood v. S., 48 Ga. 192.

[12] P. v. [illegible] Fore, 64 Mich. 693; S. v. Lewis, 48 [illegible]78; S. v. Horton, 100 N. C. 443.

and the court should instruct the jury that if there was no consent the crime of seduction cannot be found.[1] Indeed, it has been said that the crime of seduction cannot be committed with a female under the age of consent, as in that case the offense would be rape.[2]

§ **1116. Marriage a bar.**— It is sometimes provided by statute that the marriage of the parties, even after commencement of the prosecution, shall constitute a bar to further proceedings, and such marriage is encouraged by the law,[3] and will constitute a defense though entered into by defendant merely for the sake of escaping punishment.[4] A marriage thus contracted cannot be deemed invalid because entered into under duress.[5] Under such a statute an offer of defendant to marry the prosecutrix is not a bar to the prosecution and is immaterial.[6] But the fact of such an offer may be shown as bearing upon the question as to whether the woman was really seduced, or may be considered by the court in fixing the punishment.[7] In Texas, however, an offer on the part of defendant in good faith to marry the prosecutrix will defeat the prosecution, and all that is required is a submission to the marriage rite; it is not necessary that the court believe that defendant intends in good faith to live with the female as his wife.[8]

§ **1117. Evidence in general.**— The testimony of the prosecutrix as to the arts, false promises, etc., must be clear and definite. There should not be any strained construction put upon her language in order to sustain a conviction. It is to be expected that she should, as far as possible, shield herself and cast the blame on the defendant.[9] If her age is material she

[1] P. v. De Fore, 64 Mich. 693; Croghan v. S., 22 Wis. 444. It is improper for counsel, without any evidence that the connection was by force, to comment upon the extreme improbability of conception taking place if the intercourse was by force: S. v. Lingle, 128 Mo. 528.

[2] S. v. Carter, 8 Wash. 272. And see *supra*, § 442 *et seq.*

[3] Armstrong v. Lester, 43 Ia. 159.

[4] S. v. Otis, 135 Ind. 267.

[5] Medrano v. S., 32 Tex. Ap. 214.

[6] S. v. Brandenburg, 118 Mo. 181; S. v. Mackey, 82 Ia. 393.

[7] S. v. Thompson, 79 Ia. 703. Evidence that the prosecutrix offered to settle the case for a sum of money is not admissible: S. v. Deitrick, 51 Ia. 467. No other compromise than that of marriage between the parties will bar prosecution: Barker v. C., 90 Va. 820.

[8] Wright v. S., 31 Tex. Ap. 354.

[9] S. v. Haven, 43 Ia. 181.

may be permitted to testify with reference thereto.[1] It is not necessary that the state show affirmatively defendant's age.[2] It must, of course, appear in some way that the parties were not married to each other, but that fact is, without doubt, sufficiently shown by the evidence proving the other elements of the crime. However, the fact that prior to the day set for the marriage between the parties, and when no marriage was contemplated, defendant introduced the woman as his wife, and registered her name as such at the hotel and occupied the same room with her, was held not to show such mutual assumption of marital rights as to constitute a valid marriage which would be a defense to the prosecution.[3] Prosecutrix may testify that her consent was by reason of defendant's promise of marriage.[4] The relations between the parties both before and after the alleged seduction may be shown.[5] Acts subsequent to the alleged seduction are to be considered in determining whether the criminal intent existed at the first act,[6] and as bearing on the previous character of the prosecutrix.[7] To prove a promise of marriage the conduct of the parties both before and after the seduction is admissible as bearing on that question.[8] The fact that prosecutrix was, during the time of defendant's attentions to her, keeping company with another man may be shown as tending to disprove her claim that defendant had promised to marry her.[9] In regard to the fact of the connection at a particular time, the ordinary period of gestation may be shown to furnish the basis for an inference as to the time when a child born on a certain date was begotten.[10] In seduction cases it has been held proper to exhibit to the jury a child claimed to have been conceived at the time of the con-

[1] S. v. Cougot, 121 Mo. 458; S. v. McClain, 49 Kan. 730.

[2] Kenyon v. P., 26 N. Y. 203.

[3] P. v. Lehman, 104 Cal. 631.

[4] S. v. Brinkhaus, 34 Minn. 285; Ferguson v. S., 71 Miss. 805. *Contra*, Wilson v. S., 73 Ala. 527.

[5] P. v. Hubbard, 92 Mich. 322; Ferguson v. S., 71 Miss. 805. Previous conviction of defendant on a charge of bastardy brought by the same complainant cannot be shown: S. v. Wenz, 41 Minn. 196.

[6] S. v. Mackey, 82 Ia. 393.

[7] Ferguson v. S., 71 Miss. 805.

[8] S. v. Curran, 51 Ia. 112; S. v. Bell, 79 Ia. 117; McTyier v. S., 91 Ga. 254. But a witness will not be allowed to testify that defendant acted towards prosecutrix as a suitor, such a statement being of a conclusion only: Carney v. S., 79 Ala. 14.

[9] S. v. Baldoser, 88 Ia. 55.

[10] S. v. Richards, 72 Ia. 17.

nection in question, as tending by resemblance to the defendant to identify him as the party with whom the connection was had.[1] In one case, however, such exhibition was held to have been erroneous and to require a reversal.[2]

§ 1118. **Evidence of chastity.**— The weight of authority is to the effect that the chastity of the prosecutrix will be presumed and that no direct evidence thereof need be introduced, but that it is for defendant to show the want of chastity as a defense;[3] and this fact the defendant must establish by a preponderance of evidence.[4] According to this view the defendant has the burden of proof to show unchastity.[5] But according to other cases the presumption of chastity continues only until there is evidence of want of chastity.[6] The claim that this presumption of chastity is in conflict with the presumption of defendant's innocence is disallowed by the courts taking this view, it being said that his presumption of innocence of the fact is not inconsistent with the presumption of the rectitude of the woman's character,[7] and that it is not necessary to charge that if there is a reasonable doubt of defendant's guilt on all the evidence, including that as to want of chastity, the jury should acquit, but that they may properly be told that if want of chastity has not been shown by preponderance of evidence the jury should find that she was chaste.[8] But the correctness of this reasoning is denied by other courts, which hold that the chastity of the prosecutrix is an essential element of the crime, and therefore the burden of proving chastity is upon the state,[9] and that if such proof is made by the prosecutrix her tes-

[1] S. v. Horton, 100 N. C. 443. This was held admissible in case of a child two years old: S. v. Smith, 54 Ia. 104; but not in case of a child three months old, it being held that any resemblance in so young a child would be too indefinite and uncertain to be reliable evidence: S. v. Danforth, 48 Ia. 43 (explaining S. v. Hummel, 39 Ia. 478). It is not error to allow prosecutrix to testify that at a certain date after the alleged seduction she gave birth to a child; Cunningham v. S., 73 Ala. 51; and that the child with her is such child: S. v. Clemons, 78 Ia. 123.

[2] S. v. Carter, 8 Wash. 272. And see Robnett v. P., 16 Ill. Ap. 299.

[3] Ferguson v. S., 71 Miss. 805; McTyier v. S., 91 Ga. 254; Barker v. C., 90 Va. 820; S. v. Thornton, 108 Mo. 640; Polk v. S., 40 Ark. 482.

[4] Andre v. S., 5 Ia. 389; S. v. Wells, 48 Ia. 671; S. v. Higdon, 32 Ia. 262; S. v. Brown, 86 Ia. 121.

[5] S. v. Hemm, 82 Ia. 609; S. v. Bell, 79 Ia. 117; S. v. McClintic, 73 Ia. 663.

[6] P. v. Squires, 49 Mich. 487; Munkers v. S., 87 Ala. 94.

[7] Andre v. S., 5 Ia. 389.

[8] S. v. Hemm, 82 Ia. 609.

[9] Oliver v. C., 101 Pa. St. 215; C. v.

timony must be corroborated.[1] The defendant can show unchastity only by particular acts[2] and not by proof of general reputation.[3] But in rebuttal of evidence of specific acts of unchastity the prosecution may show the general reputation for chastity.[4] To show unchastity, evidence of any former act of illicit intercourse on the part of prosecutrix is admissible;[5] also evidence that before the seduction she was often out late at night.[6] While evidence of improper language and conduct is admissible to indicate want of chastity,[7] yet it must be nearly enough connected with the time of the offense to indicate unchastity at that time.[8] The question of chastity being directly in issue, the prosecutrix may, on cross-examination, be asked as to matters which would tend to show want of chastity previous to the seduction.[9] The evidence as to chastity must be strictly confined to the time immediately prior to the alleged seduction,[10] and evidence of improper conduct after the time of the seduction should be excluded.[11]

§ **1119. Sufficiency of evidence; corroboration.**— What has already been said in regard to the sufficiency of evidence in a prosecution for rape, and as to the necessity of corroboration of the prosecutrix in such case,[12] is applicable also in a prosecution for seduction,[13] and by statute such corroboration is required in most of the states. The corroboration should extend to the inducement held out, such as promise of mar-

Whittaker, 131 Mass. 224; Zabriskie v. S., 43 N. J. 640; S. v. Wenz, 41 Minn. 196; S. v. McCaskey, 104 Mo. 644; P. v. Krusick, 93 Cal. 74. And on a similar question, see *supra*, § 1057.

1 S. v. Lockerby, 50 Minn. 363. As to whether corroboration of the testimony of prosecutrix is necessary, see next section.

2 Polk v. S., 30 Ark. 482; S. v. Bowman, 45 Ia. 418; *supra*, § 1113.

3 Kenyon v. P., 26 N. Y. 203; S. v. Prizer, 49 Ia. 531; S. v. Shean, 32 Ia. 88; McTyier v. S., 91 Ga. 254; Lewis v. S., 89 Ga. 396. It is not competent to prove that the mother of prosecutrix with whom she was living, being a minor, kept a house of ill-fame: Kenyon v. P., 26 N. Y. 203.

4 P. v. Samonset, 97 Cal. 448; S. v. Clark, 9 Oreg. 466; S. v. Brandenburg, 118 Mo. 181; S. v. Prizer, 49 Ia. 531; S. v. Shean, 32 Ia. 88; S. v. Lenihan, 88 Ia. 670.

5 P. v. Clark, 33 Mich. 112.

6 S. v. Clemons, 78 Ia. 123.

7 *Supra*, § 1113.

8 S. v. Hemm, 82 Ia. 609.

9 S. v. Sutherland, 30 Ia. 570.

10 S. v. Gnagy, 84 Ia. 177; S. v. Deitrick, 51 Ia. 467.

11 Mann v. S., 34 Ga. 1; S. v. Wells, 48 Ia. 671.

12 *Supra*, § 458.

13 Cooper v. S., 90 Ala. 641.

riage, as well as to the fact of sexual intercourse.[1] Under the New York statute it is held that there need not be corroboration as to the previous chaste character of the female,[2] and corroboration to this extent is sufficient under the Iowa statute, which requires that the testimony of the injured party must be corroborated by other evidence tending to connect defendant with the commission of the offense.[3] Under such statutes corroborative evidence of the fact of courtship and the circumstances attending the seduction, such as that the parties kept company and acted as lovers usually do, is sufficient.[4] But mere proof of acquaintance and opportunity are not sufficient; the corroboration must be such as to connect defendant with the commission of the offense.[5] The court is to determine whether the evidence is corroborative, and the jury is to pass upon the credibility of it.[6] In general, it is said that the corroboration need not be direct and positive, or such as is sufficient to convict independently of the evidence of the prosecutrix, but all that is required is that such circumstances be shown as tend to support the testimony of prosecutrix and satisfy the jury that she is worthy of credit.[7] In some states the requirements as to corroboration are more strict, and it is necessary that the prosecutrix be supported as to all the elements of the crime, including the element of previous chastity.[8] Some statutes require the corroboration which is necessary in perjury.[9] Evidently no fact which is proved only by the tes-

1 S. v. Ferguson, 107 N. C. 841; Ferguson v. S., 71 Miss. 805.

2 Kenyon v. P., 26 N. Y. 203; Armstrong v. P., 70 N. Y. 38; P. v. Plath, 100 N. Y. 590.

3 S. v. Wells, 48 Ia. 671.

4 S. v. Wells, 48 Ia. 671; S. v. Curran, 51 Ia. 112; S. v. Richards, 72 Ia. 17; S. v. McClintic, 73 Ia. 663; S. v. Gnagy, 84 Ia. 177; S. v. Smith, 84 Ia. 522; S. v. Baldoser, 88 Ia. 55; Stevenson v. Belknap, 6 Ia. 97; Cunningham v. S., 73 Ala. 51; Wilson v. S., 73 Ala. 527; Munkers v. S., 87 Ala. 94; S. v. Wheeler, 108 Mo. 658; Wright v. S., 31 Tex. Ap. 354. Letters written by defendant to prosecutrix in connection with other facts showing intimacy were held to be properly admitted as corroborative evidence: S. v. Bell, 79 Ia. 117.

5 S. v. Painter, 50 Ia. 317; S. v. Smith, 54 Ia. 743; S. v. Araah, 55 Ia. 258.

6 S. v. Bell, 49 Ia. 440. Corroboration in particular cases held sufficient: S. v. Shean, 32 Ia. 88; S. v. Fitzgerald, 63 Ia. 268; S. v. Standley, 76 Ia. 215.

7 Wright v. S., 31 Tex. Ap. 354.

8 Zabriskie v. S., 43 N. J. 640.

9 S. v. Reeves, 97 Mo. 668; S. v. Wheeler, 108 Mo. 658; La Rosae v. S., 132 Ind. 219.

timony of the prosecutrix can serve as corroboration of her evidence.[1] Thus, the fact that prosecuting witness made preparations for marriage with defendant as testified to by her does not furnish the necessary corroboration.[2]

[1] S. v. Enke, 85 Ia. 35; S. v. Kingsley, 39 Ia. 439; S. v. McCaskey, 104 Mo. 644.

[2] S. v. Lenihan, 88 Ia. 670. Nor is that fact as testified to by another than prosecutrix admissible where the purpose of the preparation is known only by hearsay: Cooper v. S., 90 Ala. 641.

CHAPTER 50.

INCEST.

§ 1120. What constitutes.— Incest is defined as the carnal copulation of a man and woman related to each other in any of the degrees within which marriage is prohibited by law.[1] At common law this offense, like that of adultery, was punishable only in the ecclesiastical courts.[2] The degrees of relationship which render persons incompetent to marry are determined by statute, and, inasmuch as these statutory provisions are not uniform, it has been held necessary in charging the offense to specify that the parties were not married to each other, inasmuch as the marriage of persons within the degree of relationship specified by the state statute might be valid if elsewhere contracted.[3] The relationships specified by statute include those by illegitimate as well as legitimate kinship;[4] also relations of the half blood as well as of the whole blood.[5] By statute, relationship by affinity as well as by consanguinity is usually included, so that connection with a sister-in-law is criminal.[6] But it seems that where the relationship is by marriage, it must appear that the marriage still exists; thus, where the crime is charged as committed with a step-daughter, it must appear that the mother is still alive and the wife of the defendant.[7]

[1] S. v. Herges, 55 Minn. 464.

[2] S. v. Keesler, 78 N. C. 469; 4 Bl. Com. 604. A prosecution under special statutory provision concerning incestuous marriage was held to be a criminal proceeding: Atty. Gen. v. Broaddus, 6 Munf. 116.

[3] In this case the parties were first cousins: S. v. Fritts, 48 Ark. 66.

[4] P. v. Lake, 110 N. Y. 61; P. v. Jenness, 5 Mich. 305; S. v. Schaunhurst, 34 Ia. 547; Baker v. S., 30 Ala. 521. Where the indictment charged the offense as committed with a "legitimate" daughter of defendant, it was held that proof of the marriage of the parents was necessary to support the indictment: S. v. Roswell, 6 Conn. 446.

[5] P. v. Jenness, 5 Mich. 305; Shelly v. S., 95 Tenn. 152; S. v. Reedy, 44 Kan. 190; Simon v. S., 31 Tex. Ap. 186; T. v. Corbett, 3 Mont. 50.

[6] Stewart v. S., 39 Ohio St. 152.

[7] Noble v. S., 22 Ohio St. 541; Johnson v. S., 20 Tex. Ap. 609; McGrew v. S., 13 Tex. Ap. 340. An early Virginia statute made marriage with a brother's widow a crime: C. v. Perryman, 2 Leigh, 717.

Relationship by affinity exists only between one spouse and the blood relations of the other, and does not include relations of the other spouse by affinity only; thus, a husband is not related by affinity to his wife's brother's wife.[1]

§ **1121. Mutuality.**— There is a well-marked conflict in the cases as to whether the offense involves mutual criminality of the parties to the intercourse, or whether there may be criminality in one party to the relation, although by reason of want of knowledge of the relationship or lack of consent to the act, as, for instance, where it is by force, the other party is not guilty of incest. In many cases it has been held that the crime is committed by the male, although as to the female the connection is by force and against the will, and therefore constitutes rape;[2] or where, by reason of want of knowledge of the relationship, there is no criminality in the female.[3] A similar question has been discussed in the chapter on adultery.[4] By perhaps the weight of authority it is held, however, that the crime involves mutual consent to the illicit relation.[5] Under this doctrine there cannot, of course, be any conviction of one party without the guilt of the other is proved;[6] but it does not follow that the parties must be jointly indicted; one may be indicted alone and convicted,[7] and counts for incest and rape may be joined.[8] The question whether consent of both parties is necessary arises also in determining whether corroboration

[1] Chinn v. S., 47 Ohio St. 575.

[2] S. v. Chambers, 87 Ia. 1; P. v. Gleason, 99 Cal. 359; C. v. Bakeman, 131 Mass. 577; P. v. Barnes, 2 Idaho, 148; Mercer v. S., 17 Tex. Ap. 452.

[3] S. v. Ellis, 74 Mo. 384.

[4] *Supra*, §§ 1092, 1095.

[5] Baumer v. S., 49 Ind. 544; S. v. Wentler, 76 Wis. 89; P. v. Jenness, 5 Mich. 305; Delany v. P., 10 Mich. 241; P. v. Skutt, 96 Mich. 449; Yeoman v. S., 21 Neb. 171; P. v. Harriden, 1 Park. Cr. 344; Noble v. S., 22 Ohio St. 541; S. v. Jarvis, 20 Oreg. 437; S. v. Thomas, 53 Ia. 214; P. v. Patterson, 102 Cal. 239. Thus, if the female is under the age of consent, the offense may be rape, but cannot be incest: De Groat v. P., 39 Mich. 124. So, where the offense was described by statute as consisting in a connection between brother and sister over sixteen years of age, it was held that each must be over that age: U. S. v. Hiler, Morris, 330. But there may be, even in incest, some amount of force or power exerted resulting from the age, relationship and circumstances of the parties, not sufficient, however, to constitute rape: Raiford v. S., 68 Ga. 672.

[6] P. v. Jenness, 5 Mich. 305; De Groat v. P., 39 Mich. 124; Baumer v. S., 49 Ind. 544.

[7] P. v. Patterson, 102 Cal. 239; Yeoman v. S., 21 Neb. 171; Powers v. S., 44 Ga. 209.

[8] Porath v. S., 90 Wis. 527.

of the testimony of the other party to the connection is required; for if the connection must be voluntary, then the other party is an accomplice, whose evidence must be corroborated.[1] Even though the crime may be committed without the consent of the other party, yet, if it appears that such party did consent, she is an accomplice, and her evidence requires corroboration.[2]

§ **1122. The act.**— To prove incest committed by sexual intercourse the same proof of penetration is necessary as in case of rape, and also of emission if that is necessary to the commission of rape.[3] But by some statutes a marriage within the prohibited degrees constitutes the offense without regard to carnal knowledge.[4] The attempt is sometimes made criminal.[5]

§ **1123. Indictment.**— As one act of intercourse is sufficient to constitute the offense it is not proper to charge the crime as a continuous one.[6] Knowledge of the relationship must be alleged.[7] The relationship may be charged by describing the connection as had with a daughter, without otherwise specifying the particulars of such relationship.[8] If the offense charged is that of incestuous marriage, it is sufficient to charge that the defendant did incestuously intermarry with another, without an allegation that the other party did intermarry with him.[9] Under a statute making incest to consist in adultery or fornication with another person related within the prohibited de-

[1] S. v. Jarvis, 18 Oreg. 360. *Contra*, holding that no corroboration is required even though the other party consented: Whittaker v. C., 95 Ky. 632. Without deciding that corroboration was necessary, it was held the province of the jury to say what weight should be given to the testimony introduced as corroborating: S. v. Moore, 81 Ia. 578.

[2] Shelly v. S., 95 Tenn. 152; Mercer v. S., 17 Tex. Ap. 452; Blanchette v. S., 29 Tex. Ap. 46; Tipton v. S., 30 Tex. Ap. 530; Schoenfeldt v. S., 30 Tex. Ap. 695.

[3] Noble v. S., 22 Ohio St. 541. As to rape, see § 450.

[4] S. v. Schaunhurst, 34 Ia. 547; S. v. Lawrence, 19 Neb. 307. Under such a definition proof of marriage or cohabitation is sufficient: Simon v. S., 31 Tex. Ap. 186.

[5] P. v. Gleason, 99 Cal. 359. But an attempt to contract an incestuous marriage involves more than mere preparation for such marriage: P. v. Murray, 14 Cal. 159.

[6] Barnhouse v. S., 31 Ohio St. 39.

[7] Williams v. S., 2 Ind. 439. *Contra*, S. v. Bullinger, 54 Mo. 142.

[8] Hicks v. P., 10 Mich. 395; Bergen v. P., 17 Ill. 426; Hintz v. S., 58 Wis. 493.

[9] Hutchins v. C., 2 Va. Cas. 331. The fact of marriage between persons of a prohibited degree of relationship constitutes the offense, and it is not necessary to use the exact word in the indictment: S. v. Herges, 55 Minn. 464.

grees, it was held necessary to allege the facts showing whether the offense was committed by adultery or by fornication;[1] but, on the other hand, it was held, under a similar statute, that a conviction would not be set aside on the ground that it appeared that accused was a married man, though the charge was of incest committed by fornication.[2]

§ **1124. Evidence.**— To prove the illicit connection previous acts of sexual intercourse between the parties may be shown;[3] but previous guilty relations of the female with other men is no defense.[4] Where the offense is charged as consisting in a marriage within prohibited degrees of relationship, the registry of marriages is sufficient evidence of the fact.[5] The relationship of the parties may be established by admissions and declarations of the defendant.[6] Relation may also be proved by reputation.[7] Incest committed by a married man has been held an offense committed against the wife in such sense that her evidence is admissible as against him.[8]

1 Martin v. S., 58 Ark. 3.

2 P. v. Cease, 80 Mich. 576.

3 P. v. Skutt, 95 Mich. 449; P. v. Cease, 80 Mich. 576; P. v. Patterson, 102 Cal. 239; C. v. Bell, 166 Pa. St. 405; Lefforge v. S., 129 Ind. 551; Burnett v. S., 32 Tex. Ap. 86.

4 S. v. Winningham, 124 Mo. 423. Evidence for the prosecution that, by consent of the father, his daughter had been living in a house of ill-fame was held improperly admitted as tending to the prejudice of defendant: P. v. Benoit, 97 Cal. 249.

5 S. v. Schaunhurst, 34 Ia. 547.

6 Bergen v. P., 17 Ill. 426; Morgan v. S., 11 Ala. 289; P. v. Harriden, 1 Park. Cr. 344. The fact of an incestuous marriage may be established in the same way: S. v. Schaunhurst, 34 Ia. 547.

7 Ewell v. S., 6 Yerg. 363.

8 S. v. Chambers, 87 Ia. 1. *Contra*, Compton v. S., 13 Tex. Ap. 271. For analogous cases under bigamy and adultery, see *supra*, §§ 1085, 1099.

CHAPTER 51.

FORNICATION AND BASTARDY.

§ **1125. Fornication; when punishable.**— Illicit carnal intercourse is in general not punishable criminally except as some circumstance of aggravation taken account of by the law accompanies it and makes of it some one of the recognized sexual crimes.[1] If fornication is punishable at all it is an included offense in adultery, seduction and like crimes.[2]

§ **1126. Bastardy.**— By early English statutes the begetting of a bastard child was made criminal in the father, and a specific punishment for having such a child was visited upon the mother.[3] Probably at common law it is a misdemeanor to beget a bastard child,[4] and the crime is complete when the child is begotten.[5] In some states bastardy is, together with fornication, punishable criminally, and in such states the birth of the child is immaterial, being merely evidence of the bastardy.[6] In perhaps all the states are statutory provisions by which the father may be compelled to furnish support for the child or pay the expenses incident to its birth,[7] the object of the proceedings with reference to such support being to indemnify the town or county for the possible charge of the child as well as to afford it support.[8] The statutes frequently provide for a proceeding dual in its nature; civil so far as it relates to holding the father liable for the support of the child, and criminal in that a fine may be imposed.[9] But with reference to the proceeding to compel the payment

[1] C. v. Isaacs, 5 Rand. 634; C. v. Jones, 2 Grat. 555; Pollard v. Lyon, 91 U. S. 225; S. v. Foster, 31 Tex. 578; S. v. Smith, 32 Tex. 167; *supra*, § 1109.

[2] Gorman v. C., 124 Pa. St. 536.

[3] 4 Bl. Com. 65.

[4] S. v. Phelps, 9 Md. 21; Coleman v. Frum, 4 Ill. 377.

[5] S. v. Wynne, 116 N. C. 981; Sheay v. S., 74 Md. 52.

[6] Gorman v. C., 124 Pa. St. 536.

[7] S. v. Such, 53 N. J. 351; Hauskins v. P., 82 Ill. 193; Robinson v. S., 128 Ind. 397; Cross v. P., 10 Mich. 24.

[8] Castles v. Welch, 63 N. H. 369.

[9] Bond v. S., 34 Fla. 45; S. v. Cagle, 114 N. C. 835. The commencement of the proceedings is frequently as in criminal cases: Castles v. Welch, 63 N. H. 369; S. v. Green, 71 N. C. 172; S. v. Ritchie, 107 N. C. 857.

of support the case is usually considered as a civil one.[1] Thus, it is not necessary to conclude the complaint "against the statute in such case made and provided."[2] In general the procedure is that in a civil case;[3] therefore the rules of evidence applicable are those of civil cases,[4] and it is not necessary to make out defendant's guilt beyond reasonable doubt, a preponderance of evidence being sufficient;[5] but on the other hand, imprisonment to compel the payment of the fine or allowance is not unconstitutional as imprisonment for debt.[6] So it has been held that in such a case the state is allowed peremptory challenges as in criminal cases,[7] the writ of error is to be as in criminal cases,[8] and the verdict is conclusive as to both elements of the wrong.[9]

§ **1127. Jurisdiction and venue..**— As the offense of bastardy is complete when the child is begotten, it is immaterial that the birth was out of the state;[10] but by some statutes the proceedings must be where the child was born.[11]

§ **1128. Complaint.**— Where the proceeding is for maintenance of the child and not otherwise, it is necessary to allege the sex of the child by way of description.[12]

§ **1129. Evidence.**— The prosecution must show that the parties are not married to each other; and indeed, to prove fornication as distinct from adultery, must show that neither is a married person.[13] But the offense of bastardy is not inconsistent with that of adultery.[14] It may be inferred that the woman was unmarried if it appears that the defendant was

[1] S. v. Edwards, 110 N. C. 511; Jerdee v. S., 36 Wis. 170.

[2] C. v. Moore, 3 Pick. 194; Wilbur v. Crane, 13 Pick. 284; S. v. Peeples, 108 N. C. 768.

[3] Mann v. P., 35 Ill. 467; P. v. Starr, 50 Ill. 52; McCoy v. P., 71 Ill. 111; S. v. McGlothlen, 56 Ia. 544; S. v. Johnson, 89 Ia. 1; Powell v. S., 96 Ind. 108; S. v. Klitzke, 46 Minn. 343; S. v. McIntosh, 64 N. C. 607.

[4] E. N. E. v. S., 25 Fla. 268.

[5] Mann v. P., 35 Ill. 467; Lewis v. P., 82 Ill. 104; Cox v. P., 109 Ill. 457; Semon v. P., 42 Mich. 141. *Contra*, Van Tassel v. S., 59 Wis. 351.

[6] S. v. Giles, 103 N. C. 391; S. v. Wynne, 116 N. C. 981; S. v. Palin, 63 N. C. 471; S. v. Brewer, 38 S. C. 263.

[7] C. v. Addis, 1 Browne, 285.

[8] C. v. Immell, 6 Binn. 403.

[9] C. v. Gurley, 45 Pa. St. 392.

[10] Sheay v. S., 74 Md. 52.

[11] S. v. Woodson, 99 Ala. 201. In Pennsylvania it is optional to proceed in the county of the birth or in the county of the commission of the act: Heikes v. C., 26 Pa. St. 513.

[12] C. v. Pintard, 1 Browne, 59; Simmons v. C., 1 Rawle, 142.

[13] Wells v. S., 9 Tex. Ap. 160.

[14] Reg. v. Collingwood, 12 Q. B. 681; Rex v. Luffe, 8 East, 193.

paying attentions to her with a view of marriage.[1] Prior acts of illicit intercourse may be shown for the purpose of establishing the relations existing between the parties.[2] For the purpose of impeaching the testimony of prosecutrix as to the paternity of the child, it may be shown that she had intercourse with another man at a time such as that, in the course of nature, the intercourse may have resulted in the birth of the child;[3] and that fact may be shown by the person with whom it is claimed such intercourse was had.[4] But one who is called to testify to such illegitimate intercourse may decline to answer on the ground that his answer may expose him to prosecution.[5] It is not essential that it should appear that the period of gestation was of usual length if the evidence of paternity is otherwise sufficient.[6] While the presumption is that a child born in wedlock is legitimate, such presumption is not conclusive and may be rebutted by circumstances showing that the husband could not have been the father; and the mother is a competent witness to prove such non-access, as she is not in such case testifying for or against her husband.[7] According to the weight of authority the child may be exhibited to the jury, and they may consider its resemblance to the putative father or the contrary, as bearing on the question of paternity;[8] but some cases have held the exhibition of the child to the jury to be improper.[9] The color of the child cannot be depended upon as conclusive to overthrow other evidence of paternity.[10] The fact that the mother has named the child after the putative father cannot be shown.[11]

[1] Durham v. P., 49 Ill. 233; Cook v. P., 51 Ill. 143.

[2] Ramey v. S., 127 Ind. 243; Holcomb v. P., 79 Ill. 409; S. v. Smith, 47 Minn. 475; Baker v. S., 69 Wis. 32; S. v. Wheeler, 104 N. C. 893.

[3] Gaunt v. S., 52 N. J. 178; Goodwine v. S., 5 Ind. Ap. 63.

[4] P. v. Kaminsky, 73 Mich. 637.

[5] Stevens v. S., 50 Kan. 712.

[6] Cook v. P., 51 Ill. 143.

[7] S. v. McDowell, 101 N. C. 734.

[8] Gaunt v. S., 50 N. J. 490; S. v. Smith, 54 Ia. 104; S. v. Woodruff, 67 N. C. 89; Finnegan v. Dugan, 14 Allen, 197. In Iowa it was held that any fancied resemblance in the case of an infant three months old would be too unreliable to be considered, and therefore that it was error to have exhibited such a child to the jury: S. v. Danforth, 48 Ia. 43. But in Risk v. S., 19 Ind. 152, a child of that age was exhibited to the jury and no objection was raised. Further see *supra*, § 1117.

[9] Robnett v. P., 16 Ill. Ap. 299; S. v. Carter, 8 Wash. 272.

[10] West v. S., 84 Ga. 527.

[11] Corcoran v. P., 27 Ill. Ap. 638.

CHAPTER 52.

ILLICIT COHABITATION.

§ **1130. How far criminal.**— Statutes in the various states contain provisions, by no means uniform and yet quite similar, for the punishment of cohabiting as husband and wife without being married, or of lewd and lascivious cohabitation. To constitute the former, it is essential that the parties shall have lived together in the same house, deporting themselves as husband and wife usually do, though it is not necessary that they shall have asserted the existence of marriage between them or have held each other out as husband and wife.[1] To constitute lewd and lascivious cohabitation, the relation must be so far open as to offend public decency, cause scandal or tend to corrupt public morals;[2] though it is said that it is not necessary that the cohabitation be notorious.[3] Where the statute provides for distinct offenses of living together in fornication and habitual carnal intercourse, it is necessary to specify which offense is intended.[4] Mere sexual intercourse, even between parties living in the same house, is not sufficient to constitute the offense of cohabitation as husband and wife;[5] nor is the assumption of the marital relation for one occasion only sufficient; cohabitation implies a dwelling together for some period of time.[6]

§ **1131. Intent — Joint offenses.**— It seems that the intent is immaterial if the act is such as is prohibited; thus, where a

[1] Sullivan v. S., 32 Ark. 187; Kinard v. S., 57 Miss. 132.

[2] Pinson v. S., 28 Fla. 735; Luster v. S., 23 Fla. 339.

[3] S. v. Cagle, 2 Humph. 414.

[4] Powell v. S., 12 Tex. Ap. 238; Jones v. S., 29 Tex. Ap. 347.

[5] Taylor v. S., 36 Ark. 84. But it is not necessary to instruct the jury that the parties must, as to both bed and board, live together as husband and wife: Bush v. S., 37 Ark. 215.

[6] C. v. Calef, 10 Mass. 153; Turney v. S., 60 Ark. 259; Luster v. S., 23 Fla. 339; S. v. Crowner, 56 Mo. 147. Mere evidence of fornication or adultery is not sufficient: Jones v. C., 80 Va. 18. It seems that the term "living together" implies such continuous relation at the place of defendant's residence and not at any place where in pursuance of his business he may spend a portion of each night: Thomas v. S., 28 Tex. Ap. 300.

marriage of a white person with a black person is prohibited, the cohabitation under such a marriage will be criminal,[1] even though it has been in pursuance of legal advice.[2] So if the cohabitation is between one against whom a divorce has been granted for his own fault in a state where that fact is a bar to another marriage and a woman with whom he has attempted to contract marriage in violation of such prohibition, it will be criminal.[3] But if the marriage is illegal only by reason of omission of some formal requirement, cohabitation thereunder will not constitute this offense. There must be more than cohabitation under mistaken but honest belief that there is a legal marriage.[4] The same principle was held applicable to the act of living together under a marriage contracted after one of the parties had been divorced in another state, in a proceeding valid in the state where rendered, though void in the state where the parties subsequently cohabited.[5] The offense is a joint one, and both parties thereto must be guilty in order to warrant the conviction of either;[6] and accordingly it has been held that the indictment must charge the cohabitation in such form as to show that it was lewd and lascivious as to both or it will not be good as to either,[7] but it is not necessary that the parties be jointly indicted.[8]

§ 1132. Other incidents of indictment and evidence.— It is usually sufficient to charge the crime in the words of the

[1] **Miscegenation.**— In some states there are special statutes prohibiting marriage between white persons and persons of color, and therefore cohabitation between such persons is criminal: S. v. Fore, 1 Ired. 378; Linton v. S., 88 Ala. 216; Mulling v. S., 74 Ga. 10; Frasher v. S., 3 Tex. Ap. 263; S. v. Kennedy, 76 N. C. 251; Kinney v. C., 30 Grat. 858; S. v. Tutty, 41 Fed. R. 753. Such statutes are constitutional: Green v. S., 58 Ala. 190; Frasher v. S., 3 Tex. Ap. 263; even as applied to a marriage contracted in another state where it is valid: S. v. Bell, 7 Baxt. 9. *Contra*, S. v. Ross, 76 N. C. 242.

[2] Hoover v. S., 59 Ala. 57; Green v. S., 59 Ala. 68.

[3] Hood v. S., 56 Ind. 263. But the living together of such parties does not constitute lewd and lascivious behavior: C. v. Hunt, 4 Cush. 49.

[4] C. v. Munson, 127 Mass. 459.

[5] Schoudel v. S., 57 N. J. 209, 30 Atl. R. 598.

[6] Delany v. P., 10 Mich. 241. *Contra*, S. v. Cutshall, 109 N. C. 764.

[7] Delany v. P., 10 Mich. 241; S. v. Foster, 21 W. Va. 767. To charge both jointly with living together in an open state of fornication, that being the language of the statute, held sufficient: King v. P., 7 Colo. 224.

[8] Scott v. C., 77 Va. 344; S. v. Foster, 21 W. Va. 767; S. v. Cox, 2 Taylor, 165.

statute, and therefore it is not necessary to allege that the parties were not married to one another or that the woman was not a married woman, there being no such description of the offense in the statute.[1] The fact that the woman was married, so that the offense is adultery and not fornication, must appear by way of defense.[2] But under other statutes the fact that the parties were not married to each other must be shown;[3] but that fact may appear, without specific allegation, from the other facts stated in the indictment.[4] It is not necessary to specifically charge the cohabitation as constituting fornication if the facts alleged sufficiently show the commission of that offense,[5] but it must appear that the parties cohabited together or with each other.[6] The single state is presumed until the contrary is shown, and therefore evidence that the parties were not married to each other is not required in the first instance from the prosecution.[7] The evidence of the intercourse may be circumstantial,[8] but proof that the parties lived together in the same house but in different rooms is not sufficient;[9] nor is the general reputation in the neighborhood admissible to prove the fact of cohabitation.[10]

[1] S. v. Stephens, 63 Ind. 542. **Form:** The following has been held sufficient under a statute which practically embodies the common-law definition: That the defendants "did wilfully and unlawfully commit divers acts of public and notorious indecency and open lewdness, grossly scandalous and tending to debauch the morals and manners of the people of this state, by then and there wilfully and unlawfully living and cohabiting together as husband and wife, he, the said —— ——, and she, the said —— ——, not being then married to each other:" Schoudel v. S., 57 N. J. 209, 30 Atl. R. 598.

[2] S. v. Gooch, 7 Blackf. 468.

[3] P. v. Colton, 2 Utah, 457; Stebbins v. S., 31 Tex. Ap. 294.

[4] S. v. Clark, 54 N. H. 456; Lawson v. S., 20 Ala. 65. So the fact that the parties are of different sexes may sufficiently appear without direct allegation: S. v. Fore, 1 Ired. 378.

[5] S. v. Chandler, 96 Ind. 591.

[6] S. v. Foster, 26 W. Va. 272. A charge that two defendants named did "then and there unlawfully live together in an open state of fornication" is held sufficient to charge a joint offense: King v. P., 7 Colo. 224.

[7] S. v. McDuffie, 107 N. C. 885; Gaunt v. S., 50 N. J. 490. *Contra*, Hopper v. S., 19 Ark. 143.

[8] Pinson v. S., 28 Fla. 735; C. v. Dill, 156 Mass. 226; Van Dolsen v. S., 1 Ind. Ap. 108.

[9] Smelser v. S., 31 Tex. 95.

[10] Overstreet v. S., 3 How. (Miss.) 328.

CHAPTER 53.

PROSTITUTION AND LEWDNESS.

§ **1133. Prostitution and night-walking.**— Mere association with persons reputed to be prostitutes and thieves is not in itself an act to be made the subject of criminal punishment; there must be some purpose in the association which is dangerous to the public welfare and safety.[1] The term "night-walker," used in this connection, covers the case of a woman strolling the streets at night for the unlawful purpose of picking up men for lewdness whether for gain or not,[2] and it is not necessary to give a more specific description of the offense in the indictment than that the defendant is a common night-walker.[3] As to prostitution, it is not enough to charge that defendant was a female prostitute without alleging facts to show that she was such.[4] Where it appeared that defendants lived by themselves, had no occupation, were frequently on the streets at night and solicited passing men and retired with them, it was held that the evidence sufficiently showed that they were common prostitutes;[5] but the fact is not to be made out by general reputation or evidence of the bad character of associates, but by proof of particular acts.[6] A prostitute is a woman who engages in indiscriminate sexual commerce with men,[7] but it is

[1] St. Louis v. Fitz, 53 Mo. 582. And in general, see *supra*, § 25. An ordinance may be valid punishing any lewd woman having the reputation of a prostitute who shall be found employed as a beer carrier in a saloon. Such ordinance contemplates a case where the woman is principal as well as where she is employee: S. v. Canton, 43 Mo. 48.

[2] Stokes v. S., 92 Ala. 73; Williams v. S., 98 Ala. 52.

[3] S. v. Russell, 14 R. I. 506. But it is said not to be sufficient to charge that fact without an averment of an unlawful motive or purpose: Thomas v. S., 55 Ala. 260.

[4] Delano v. S., 66 Ind. 348.

[5] Peabody v. S., 72 Miss. 104.

[6] Arnold v. S., 28 Tex. Ap. 480.

[7] Osborn v. S., 52 Ind. 526; Miller v. S., 121 Ind. 294; Fahnestock v. S., 102 Ind. 156; Springer v. S., 16 Tex. Ap. 591. The mercenary element is sometimes specifically embodied in the definition: S. v. Stoyell, 54 Me. 24; C. v. Cook, 12 Met. 93. But that prostitution need not necessarily be for hire, see S. v. Smith, 29 Minn. 193; S. v. Clark, 78 Ia. 492.

for the jury to say what acts are, under the circumstances, sufficient to render a person a prostitute.[1]

§ 1134. Frequenting houses of ill-fame.— It is sometimes made criminal by statute to frequent a house of ill-fame, but it must appear that there is something more than merely living in such house.[2] However, it is said that knowledge of the character of the house frequented is not essential to be charged,[3] and that the crime may be committed without proof of lewdness.[4]

§ 1135. Lewdness.— The offense of lewd and lascivious cohabitation has already been considered,[5] but there is a somewhat different offense described as open and lascivious lewdness or by like terms which involves the openness and publicity of the act itself as distinct from a secret act.[6] The offense is not necessarily a joint one, as one party only may be guilty therein;[7] and even though two are charged therewith as joint offenders so that the guilt of one is inconsistent with the innocence of the other, yet the testimony may be sufficient to convict one and not the other, and the conviction of one may be good.[8] In general, the indictment may charge the offense in the language of the statute.[9] It should aver that the acts were openly and publicly committed,[10] and that the parties were not married to each other.[11] The evidence may be circumstantial,[12] but the crime cannot be made out by general reputation.[13]

[1] S. v. Rice, 56 Ia. 431.

[2] P. v. Ah Ho, 1 Ida. (N. S.) 691.

[3] S. v. Richards, 76 Wis. 354.

[4] Weideman v. S., 4 Ind. Ap. 397.

[5] *Supra*, § 1130.

[6] C. v. Catlin, 1 Mass. 8; C. v. Wardell, 128 Mass. 52; S. v. Juneau, 88 Wis. 180; S. v. Marvin, 12 Ia. 499; S. v. Kirkpatrick, 63 Ia. 554; S. v. Brunson, 2 Bailey, 149; Reg. v. Elliott, L. & C. 103.

[7] S. v. Caldwell, 8 Baxt. 576. But see *supra*, § 1131.

[8] S. v. Miller, 81 Ia. 72.

[9] C. v. Parker, 4 Allen, 313.

[10] S. v. Moore, 1 Swan, 136.

[11] S. v. Clinch, 8 Ia. 401; Crouse v. S., 16 Ark. 566. Where a woman having been divorced for her fault married again out of the state and returned, *held*, that though the marriage was void, she was not guilty of "lascivious behavior:" C. v. Hunt, 4 Cush. 49. An indictment charging that defendants at a certain place and time were guilty of open and gross lewdness and lascivious behavior and were then and there guilty of open and notorious acts of public indecency grossly scandalous by then and there lewdly and lasciviously abiding and cohabiting with each other, was held sufficient: S. v. Osborne, 69 Mo. 143.

[12] Peak v. S., 10 Humph. 98.

[13] Buttram v. S., 4 Coldw. 171. Evidence of acts proved at a trial on a former indictment for the same offense is admissible: Mynatt v. S., 8 Lea, 47.

§ 1136. Indecent exposure.—The statutes usually provide a punishment for obscene and indecent exhibition or exposure of the person, meaning thereby an exposure of those parts of the person which are commonly considered as private, and which custom and decency require should be covered and kept concealed from public sight.[1] Thus, bathing in public view without covering may be punishable as indecency.[2] It is also criminal as indecent exposure for a man, soliciting sexual intercourse without her consent, to indecently exhibit his person to a woman.[3] The exposure must be intentional and not merely accidental,[4] but evidence of other similar acts is admissible to show that the act was designedly done; and an indecent proposal to a woman in whose presence the exposure is made may be shown for the same purpose.[5] Under the language of some of the statutes the exposure must be public, and it is not sufficient that it is seen by one person only and capable of being seen by only one person; but it may be public if seen by only one, provided others are in such situation as that it might be seen by them.[6] Other statutes, however, make such exposure punishable if in a public place, without regard to the number of persons who see it.[7] A place where persons are in the habit of going, although it is not in sight of the public way or not a place to which they have a right to go, may still be a public place within the English statute as to indecent exposure.[8] It is sufficient if the place be made public by the assemblage of persons so that the act is done where a number of persons may

[1] Tucker v. S., 28 Tex. Ap. 541; Ardery v. S., 56 Ind. 328.

[2] Rex v. Crunden, 2 Camp. 89; Reg. v. Reed, 11 Cox, 689.

[3] Fowler v. S., 5 Day, 81; S. v. Millard, 18 Vt. 574.

[4] Van Houten v. S., 46 N. J. 16.

[5] S. v. Stice, 88 Ia. 27.

[6] Reg. v. Farrell, 9 Cox. 446; Reg. v. Webb, 2 C. & K. 933.

[7] S. v. Roper, 1 Dev. & B. 208; S. v. Hazle, 20 Ark. 157; Reg. v. Holmes, Dears. 207; Reg. v. Harris, L. R. 1 C. C. 282; Reg. v. Orchard, 3 Cox, 248. It may be sufficient to charge in the indictment the exposure of the person upon the public highway, without alleging the act as open and notorious: S. v. Rose, 32 Mo. 560; but such an indictment is not supported by evidence showing the act to have been done in a place near the highway and in full view of it: Reg. v. Farrell, 9 Cox, 446. Under a Texas statute it is held that the publicity contemplated has reference to persons who may witness the act rather than to the locality: Mofflt v. S., 43 Tex. 346.

[8] Reg. v. Wellard, 14 Q. B. D. 63. It seems that the offense is indictable if committed before divers subjects, even if the place is not public: Ibid.

be offended by it and see it.[1] A shop or other building which is the private property of the owner is not a public place, although he has invited a number of persons thereto and such persons have assembled there in pursuance of the invitation.[2] The language of the statute is a sufficient guide in charging this offense.[3] It is not necessary to call it a common nuisance.[4] The averment that the act was "in the sight and view" of a person named does not mean that he actually saw it, but only that he might have seen it.[5]

[1] Van Houten v. S., 41 N. J. 16; Reg. v. Thallman, L. & C. 326; Reg. v. Mallam, 33 L. J. M. C. 58.

[2] Lorimer v. S., 76 Ind. 495.

[3] S. v. Griffin, 43 Tex. 538. **Form:** It has been held sufficient to allege that defendant, "devising and intending the morals of the people of this commonwealth to debauch and corrupt," on ——, at ——, "in a certain public building there situate, in presence of divers citizens of said commonwealth then and there being, and within sight and view of the said citizens in and about said public building then and there passing and repassing, unlawfully, scandalously and wantonly did expose to the view of said persons present and so passing and repassing as aforesaid the body and person of him, the said defendant, naked and uncovered, for the space of one hour, to the manifest corruption of public morals and manners, and against the peace of said commonwealth, and the form of the statute in such case made and provided:" C. v. Haynes, 2 Gray, 72.

[4] C. v. Haynes, 2 Gray, 72; Reg. v. Holmes, Dears. 207.

[5] Reg. v. Webb, 1 Den. 338.

CHAPTER 54.

KEEPING DISORDERLY HOUSES.

§ **1137. What deemed criminal.**—At common law it is a crime to keep a disorderly house,[1] that is, any house in which illegal practices are habitually carried on or to which people promiscuously resort for purposes injurious to the public morals.[2] If the complaint is that the house is habitually used for the purpose of carrying on illegal practices, it must appear that such practices are contrary to law, though they may be either *mala in se* or *mala prohibita*.[3] Indeed, it has been said that a place kept for the purpose of carrying on an unlawful business, and resorted to for that purpose, is a nuisance whether the acts there done are themselves punishable as crimes or not; thus, a place where pools are sold on horse races, or gambling in stocks, grain, etc., is carried on, may be deemed a disorderly house, although such betting or gambling may not be criminal, the betting or gambling contract being, however, illegal.[4] But a place in which a lawful business is carried on, such as a ten-pin alley, which is not forbidden by statute, will not be a disorderly house unless conducted in a disorderly manner.[5] So a house may be disorderly on account of being the cause of disturbance to others, even though the acts done are not in themselves unlawful, as, for instance, where a licensed tippling house is so conducted as to constitute a nuisance.[6] A house where evil-

[1] S. v. Bailey, 21 N. H. 343; Smith v. C., 6 B. Mon. 21; Wilson v. C., 12 B. Mon. 2; C. v. Stewart, 1 Serg. & R. 342; U. S. v. Dixon, 4 Cranch, C. C. 107; U. S. v. Gray, 2 Cranch, C. C. 675; Rex v. Higginson, 2 Burr. 1232; 4 Bl. Com. 167.

[2] Haring v. S., 51 N. J. 386; S. v. Williams, 30 N. J. 102; U. S. v. Coulter, 1 Cranch, C. C. 203; U. S. v. Lindsay, 1 Cranch, C. C. 245.

[3] S. v. Williams, 30 N. J. 102; Meyer v. S., 42 N. J. 145.

[4] McClean v. S., 49 N. J. 471; S. v. Lovell, 39 N. J. 463; Cheek v. C., 79 Ky. 359; Kneffler v. C., 94 Ky. 359; U. S. v. Milburn, 4 Cranch, C. C. 719. But *contra*, held that an office for the sale of lottery tickets was not a common nuisance, although by statute lotteries were declared nuisances: P. v. Jackson, 3 Denio, 101.

[5] S. v. Hall, 32 N. J. 158.

[6] S. v. Mullikin, 8 Blackf. 260; S. v. Bertheol, 6 Blackf. 474; Bloomhuff v. S., 8 Blackf. 205.

disposed persons come together and, at unseemly hours, tipple, curse, swear, quarrel, and otherwise misbehave, to the disturbance of the public, is a disorderly house;[1] but it is immaterial that the disturbance occurs on the street or highway outside of the house if it is the character of the house which causes it by attracting disorderly persons.[2] To constitute a disorderly house of this character it is necessary that it be to the disturbance of others, that is, the public;[3] and it is not necessary that the place have a bad reputation if the fact of disturbance of the public is shown.[4] This form of the offense is necessarily a continuing one, and is not shown by one instance of riot or disorder.[5] But the house may be so far disorderly as to be a nuisance though it is kept for but a single day.[6] The question whether the keeper of a house has committed, or allowed to be committed on his premises, illegal acts so far continuous in their character as to constitute a nuisance is for the jury, and the court cannot, as a matter of law, determine how many repetitions of the illegal acts will constitute the offense.[7] A house may also be disorderly by reason of being a place of resort for disorderly characters, even though there is not such noise or disturbance as to be offensive to the public.[8] The nuisance involved in keeping such a house consists in the danger of causing injury to the public, due to the character of the

[1] S. v. Bailey, 21 N. H. 343; C. v. Stewart, 1 Serg. & R. 342; Haring v. S., 51 N. J. 386; Price v. S., 96 Ala. 1; S. v. Buckley, 5 Harr. 508; S. v. Palmer, 4 Mo. 453.

[2] S. v. Webb, 25 Ia. 235; S. v. Pierce, 65 Ia. 85; Cable v. S., 8 Blackf. 531. But where the disorderly conduct was more than one-half mile from the house, though it resulted from the drinking of liquor purchased at the house, it was held that the house was not a nuisance: S. v. Dieffenbach, 47 Ia. 638.

[3] Hunter v. C., 2 Serg. & R. 298; S. v. Pierce, 65 Ia. 85; S. v. Dean, 44 Ia. 648; S. v. Odell, 42 Ia. 75; S. v. Alderman, 40 Ia. 375; S. v. Wright, 6 Jones, 25; Palfus v. S., 36 Ga. 280. However it is immaterial whether few or many persons are in fact disturbed if the house is so situated and conducted that it is a public nuisance: S. v. Robertson, 86 N. C. 628.

[4] S. v. Maxwell, 33 Conn. 259. As to whether in a charge for keeping a house of ill-fame it must appear that the house is of bad reputation, see *infra*, § 1138.

[5] Overman v. S., 88 Ind. 6; S. v. Dean, 44 Ia. 648.

[6] S. v. Reckards, 21 Minn. 47; S. v. Pierce, 65 Ia. 85.

[7] Brown v. S., 49 N. J. 61.

[8] C. v. Cobb, 120 Mass. 356; Lord v. S., 16 N. H. 325; S. v. Williams, 30 N. J. 102; U. S. v. Elder, 4 Cranch, C. C. 507; U. S. v. Columbus, 5 Cranch, C. C. 304.

persons resorting to it,[1] and not the fact that it actually does disturb the public.[2] If the house is kept for a lawful purpose and in a lawful manner, the fact that disorderly persons, such as prostitutes and vagabonds, resort thereto, will not make the keeping a crime.[3] Some statutes expressly make criminal the keeping of a house to which vagrants and vagabonds resort.[4] To constitute this offense it is not essential that the house be kept for gain or lucre, although that circumstance is usually charged in the indictment.[5] Various classes of houses, more specifically described, are declared nuisances by statute, such as houses where intoxicating liquors are illegally sold,[6] gambling houses,[7] and houses of ill-fame.[8] The specific offenses of keeping gambling houses and houses for the illegal sale of intoxicating liquors are discussed elsewhere,[9] and that of keeping a house of ill-fame is more fully considered in the following section.

§ **1138. Keeping houses of ill-fame.**— A house of ill-fame within statutory definition is a bawdy-house; that is, a house resorted to by persons of both sexes for lewdness and prostitution, and lewdness within this definition means the unlawful indulgence of the animal desires.[10] It is not necessary that the

[1] S. v. Bailey, 21 N. H. 343; S. v. Main, 31 Conn. 572; Thatcher v. S., 48 Ark. 60.

[2] Beard v. S., 71 Md. 275, 8 Am. Cr. R. 173, and note.

[3] McElhany v. S., 12 Tex. Ap. 231; Harmes v. S., 26 Tex. Ap. 190.

[4] Johnson v. S., 28 Tex. Ap. 562. But the terms "prostitute" and "vagabond" are not synonymous: Springer v. S., 16 Tex. Ap. 591. Some statutes declare prostitutes and professional gamblers to be vagrants, but such persons are not necessarily vagabonds: Johnson v. S., 28 Tex. Ap. 562. Keepers of bawdy-houses, though described as disorderly persons, are also punishable specifically as keepers of such houses: P. v. Gustin, 57 Mich. 407; Ex parte Birchfield, 52 Ala. 377. A vagrant may be such although he is not under the necessity of laboring and supporting himself or following any business or vocation: C. v. Brown, 141 Mass. 78. Idle and disorderly persons, rogues and vagrants and incorrigible rogues are all deemed offenders against the good order of society and punishable as such at common law: 4 Bl. Com. 169.

[5] S. v. Bailey, 21 N. H. 343; S. v. Porter, 38 Ark. 637. And see *infra*, § 1140.

[6] Delaney v. S., 51 N. J. 37; Henry v. C., 9 B. Mon. 361.

[7] U. S. v. Ismenard, 1 Cranch, C. C. 150; S. v. Doon, R. M. Charl. 1; Rex v. Rogier, 1 B. & C. 272.

[8] S. v. Holmes, 56 Ia. 588; S. v. Odell, 42 Ia. 75; S. v. Alderman, 40 Ia. 375.

[9] *Infra*, §§ 1248, 1306.

[10] S. v. Toombs, 79 Ia. 741; S. v. Lee, 80 Ia. 75.

reputation of the house be bad if it is kept for this purpose;[1] and it is not essential that the disorderly conduct of the frequenters of the house should be perceptible from the exterior.[2] The offense is in this respect distinctive from that of keeping a nuisance;[3] and therefore it is not necessary that the place be used habitually or for any length of time for the prohibited purpose in order to constitute the offense.[4] It is not unconstitutional, however, to provide a punishment for the keeping of a house reputed to be a bawdy-house, the object being to prevent the assembly of disorderly persons which a house of such character is likely to cause.[5] So it may be made criminal to keep a house used as a place of resort where lewd women are employed to draw custom, dance or for purposes of prostitution.[6] To constitute such offense it must appear that the keeper had knowledge of the acts and doings of the women employed.[7] The intent in keeping a house need not be particularly alleged or proved, as it may be implied from the act.[8] The fact of keeping a house to which men resort for purposes of prostitution, and that frequent acts of prostitution are there committed, and that the house has that reputation, is sufficient to constitute the keeping of a house of ill-fame, though it is not shown that any women other than defendant engaged in prostitution in the house.[9] But although the question is for the jury whether the house is of ill-fame, yet it is said not to be error for the court to state that the occupation of a house by one woman and the frequenting of the same by one man for the purpose of prostitution and illicit intercourse between them at the house are sufficient to make it a house of ill-fame, assignation or pros-

[1] S. v. Boardman, 64 Me. 523; Henson v. S., 62 Md. 231; S. v. Lee, 80 Ia. 75; King v. P., 83 N. Y. 587; S. v. Maxwell, 33 Conn. 259.

[2] Herzinger v. S., 70 Md. 278; Reg. v. Rice, L. R. 1 C. C. 21; 1 Hawk. P. C., ch. 75, § 1.

[3] King v. P., 83 N. Y. 587; P. v. Pinkerton, 79 Mich. 110; C. v. Lavonsair, 132 Mass. 1; C. v. Lambert, 12 Allen, 177; S. v. Calley, 104 N. C. 858.

[4] S. v. Lee, 80 Ia. 75.

[5] S. v. Main, 31 Conn. 572.

[6] S. v. Brown, 7 Wash. 10.

[7] Johnson v. S., 32 Tex. Ap. 504; though the reputation of the women employed may sufficiently show knowledge on the part of the keeper: Ibid.; S. v. Schaffer, 74 Ia. 704. So where the offense is keeping a place to which girls under a specified age resort for the purpose of illicit intercourse, knowledge of the age may be inferred from the personal appearance of the girls: Hermann v. S., 73 Wis. 248.

[8] C. v. Shea, 150 Mass. 314.

[9] P. v. Mallette, 79 Mich. 600.

titution within the language of the statute;[1] but one act of illicit intercourse in the house is not sufficient to make it a house of ill-fame,[2] though proof of one such act coupled with circumstantial evidence may be sufficient to justify the jury in finding that it was kept for that purpose.[3] That the house was "resorted to" requires further evidence than of one act.[4] One may be guilty of keeping a lewd house if his wife or daughter practices therein open and notorious lewdness with his knowledge and without his dissent.[5] Punishment for the offense of keeping a house of ill-fame may be delegated to the city instead of being provided for by state statute.[6]

§ **1139. What deemed a house.**— Under the charge of keeping a disorderly house it is sufficient to show the use of only one room in the house for the illegal purpose;[7] but it is not sufficient to use the word "tenement" in such an indictment, as a tenement may mean something other than a building.[8] A woman, though only a lodger and having but a single room, may be convicted of keeping a house of ill-fame if she uses her room for that purpose.[9] The word "house" does not necessarily imply a dwelling-house, but is any building kept and used for the illegal purpose.[10] So a boat,[11] or a canvas tent,[12] may be a house within the statutory meaning.

[1] Fahnestock v. S., 102 Ind. 156.

[2] P. v. Gastro, 75 Mich. 127; Fahnestock v. S., 102 Ind. 156. And see *supra*, § 1133.

[3] S. v. Garing, 74 Me. 152.

[4] S. v. Garing, 74 Me. 152; C. v. Lambert, 12 Allen, 177. Under the English statute providing for the punishment of any person who induces or knowingly suffers a girl under sixteen years of age to resort to or be in or upon his premises for the purpose of being carnally known, etc., it is held to be immaterial that the girl thus suffered to be upon the premises is the daughter of defendant: Reg. v. Webster, 16 Q. B. D. 134.

[5] Scarborough v. S., 46 Ga. 26. But to the contrary see S. v. Calley, 104 N. C. 858. And it is said that one woman cannot be convicted for keeping a bawdy-house merely because, living by herself, she habitually admits one or many men to illicit intercourse with her: S. v. Evans, 5 Ired. 603.

[6] P. v. Buchanan, 1 Ida. (N. S.) 681; P. v. Ah Ho, 1 Ida. (N. S.) 691.

[7] S. v. Garity, 46 N. H. 61; S. v. Main, 31 Conn. 572; C. v. Donovan, 16 Gray, 18; C. v. Bulman, 118 Mass. 456.

[8] C. v. Wise, 110 Mass. 181. Further as to the use of the term "tenement," see *infra*, § 1181.

[9] P. v. Buchanan, 1 Ida. (N. S.) 681. And see cases cited in preceding section.

[10] S. v. Powers, 36 Conn. 77.

[11] S. v. Mullen, 35 Ia. 199.

[12] Killman v. S., 2 Tex. Ap. 222.

§ 1140. What constitutes a keeping.— Mere proof of residing in the house,[1] or as owner of the house leasing it to a tenant, spending a part of the time therein, does not constitute one the keeper of such house;[2] but evidence that he carried on the business, for instance, by making entries on the books of account and by being instrumental in bringing women to the house, will show the fact of such keeping.[3] The mere fact of letting rooms to prostitutes for prostitution, or knowingly permitting them to be used and resorted to for that purpose, the occupants being merely boarders or lodgers, may constitute a keeping.[4] But one who merely occupies a room in a disorderly house is not liable as keeper unless she is the proprietress.[5] One who is the owner of the land and buildings and occupies the establishment in which the nuisance is maintained is guilty as keeper.[6] Exercising such control over it as men usually have over their own houses will authorize the jury to find that defendant kept the house.[7] While knowledge of the character is essential to show criminality on the part of the keeper and that with such knowledge he permitted the improper use,[8] yet such knowledge and assent may be inferred by the jury from the publicity of the lewd conduct carried on there and the reputation of the house as known to him as well as his personal conduct.[9] But the fact of being a keeper cannot be proved by general reputation and rumor.[10] To constitute a keeping it is not necessary to show that the place was kept for the improper purpose for lucre or gain.[11]

§ 1141. Procuring or encouraging.— Any one who procures, aids, abets or encourages the keeping of a house of ill-fame is guilty as principal, there being no accessories in

[1] Toney v. S., 60 Ala. 97.

[2] S. v. Pearsall, 43 Ia. 630.

[3] C. v. Clark, 145 Mass. 251; Sullivan v. S., 75 Wis. 650.

[4] S. v. Smith, 15 R. I. 24.

[5] Moore v. S., 4 Tex. Ap. 127. In Texas the statute provides for the punishment of "owner, lessee or tenant:" Lamar v. S., 30 Tex. Ap. 693. And see *supra*, § 1138.

[6] C. v. Collins, 16 Gray, 29.

[7] S. v. Wells, 46 Ia. 662.

[8] S. v. Stafford, 67 Me. 125.

[9] S. v. Wells, 46 Ia. 662.

[10] S. v. Hand, 7 Ia. 411; Allen v. S., 15 Tex. Ap. 320. Such testimony is not only insufficient but inadmissible: Burton v. S., 16 Tex. Ap. 156.

[11] C. v. Wood, 97 Mass. 225. See C. v. Ashley, 2 Gray, 356; S. v. Nixon, 18 Vt. 70; S. v. Porter, 38 Ark. 637. And see *supra*, § 1137, as to the same point with reference to other disorderly houses. As to whether prostitution involves the element of gain or lucre, see *supra*, § 1133.

misdemeanor;[1] and it is immaterial whether he has the power to suppress it.[2] Thus, the owner of a house, and even one who procures the letting of it to the keeper for improper use, may be indicted as keeper if the act was with knowledge of the purpose;[3] but the landlord of a house occupied by a tenant as a house of ill-fame is not liable as an aider or abettor simply because he has not remonstrated with the tenant and taken advantage of a provision for terminating the lease on failure to pay rent, after knowledge of the improper use, he having retained no control over the premises under the lease.[4] The offense of being a procurer for such house is considered elsewhere.[5]

§ 1142. Permitting the use or leasing for the purpose.— The statutes usually specially provide for the punishment of any owner of premises who permits the same to be used as a house of ill-fame or leases the premises to be used for that purpose. The keeping and the permitting to be kept are, under such statute, separate offenses, and cannot be charged in one count.[6] On the other hand, under the charge of permitting, it may be proved that the premises were leased to the tenant for the improper purpose and used for that purpose, even though the leasing for such purpose is a distinct offense; the difference between the two offenses apparently being that the leasing may be criminal although the premises are not used for the improper purpose.[7] It constitutes a permitting that the owner

[1] C. v. Gannett, 1 Allen, 7; S. v. Engeman, 54 N. J. 247; S. v. McGregor, 41 N. H. 407; Ross v. C., 2 B. Mon. 417; Harlow v. C., 11 Bush, 610; Clifton v. S., 53 Ga. 241. Thus, one who leases a house for the improper purpose with knowledge of the contemplated use may be guilty as principal: C. v. Harrington, 3 Pick. 26; and it is sufficient to charge that the owner leased the house knowing that the lessee intended to use it for the purpose of prostitution, and that it was so used: Harlow v. C., 11 Bush, 610. But on the contrary, it has been held that something more must be charged than the mere knowledge of the intended use, and that the indictment in such case should particularly allege the keeping and maintaining: S. v. Wheatley, 4 Lea, 230.

[2] S. v. Engeman. 54 N. J. 257.

[3] Troutman v. S., 49 N. J. 33; P. v. Erwin, 4 Denio, 129 (explaining Brockway v. P., 2 Hill, 558, in which it was held that the owner letting his house for purposes of prostitution was not guilty of the statutory offense of procuring or encouraging the keeping of such house).

[4] S. v. Williams, 30 N. J. 102. And see cases cited in next section.

[5] See *supra*, § 1106*a*.

[6] C. v. Bartley, 138 Mass. 181.

[7] S. v. Shanahan, 54 N. H. 437.

who has charge of the house, with knowledge of its illegal use, remains passive and fails to interfere or prevent such use.[1] The improper use must be knowingly permitted,[2] and it seems that something more than mere inactivity should be shown.[3] An indictment charging simply a suffering and permitting is not sufficient, in that it does not charge either the keeping or leasing, or that the house was within the occupancy and control of the defendant.[4] Mere failure to retake possession under a provision of the lease authorizing him to do so will not render the owner liable for an illegal use by the tenant not contemplated when the lease was made.[5] In charging the offense of leasing for the improper purpose, it must appear that the defendant had knowledge of the purpose or permitted the continuance of the lease after being informed of such purpose.[6] It is not sufficient to prove merely that the lessee was of low repute, and that prostitutes had been seen in the house.[7] The offense is not a continuing one and should be charged as on a certain day, and the party to whom the house is let should be named or alleged as unknown;[8] but, of course, the date of the lease is immaterial as in other cases.[9] The various acts described by the statute providing for the punishment of leasing a house for such purposes constitute but one offense and may be charged conjunctively in one indictment,[10] and proof of one of the illegal uses charged will be sufficient.[11]

§ **1143. Indictment.**— In charging the general offense of keeping a disorderly house it appears that the particular acts showing it to have been disorderly must be alleged, as by charging that the accused procured, permitted, etc., persons of evil fame, etc., to frequent and come together in his house, and to then and there remain, drinking, tippling and misbehaving themselves, etc.[12] In some cases even less than this has been

[1] T. v. Stone, 2 Dak. 155.

[2] Drake v. S., 14 Neb. 535. So if the offense consists in leasing, it must appear that there was knowledge of the contemplated use when the lease was made: Crofton v. S., 25 Ohio St. 249.

[3] Abrahams v. S., 4 Ia. 541; S. v. Abrahams, 6 Ia. 117.

[4] Taylor v. C., 1 Duv. 160.

[5] Crofton v. S., 25 Ohio St. 249; S. v. Williams, 30 N. J. 102; *infra*, § 1248.

[6] S. v. Leach, 50 Mo. 535.

[7] P. v. Saunders, 29 Mich. 269.

[8] C. v. Moore, 11 Cush. 600.

[9] C. v. Harrington, 3 Pick. 26.

[10] S. v. Abrahams, 6 Ia. 117.

[11] C. v. Kimball, 7 Gray, 328.

[12] C. v. Stewart, 1 Serg. & R. 342; S. v. Towler, 13 R. I. 661; Frederick v.

held sufficient;[1] but generally it is required that the particular manner in which the house is disorderly shall be stated.[2] This is particularly necessary where the acts charged would or would not be criminal, depending on the circumstances of locality, time, etc.[3] But if particular acts are by statute punishable, as, for instance, the keeping of a bawdy-house, it is sufficient to charge the offense in the language of the statute.[4] In charging locality it is not necessary to be more specific than to charge the county,[5] or perhaps in some states the city or town,[6] but not the particular location as to street, etc.[7] Where the charge is simply of keeping a disorderly house, without regard to particular statutory specifications, the indictment must allege, as in other cases of nuisance, that the acts were to the common nuisance of the people of the state, etc.;[8] but where the charge is of some specific statutory offense, the allegation that the act was "to the common nuisance" is unnecessary.[9]

C., 4 B. Mon. 7; S. v. Flynn, 35 Tex. 354. It is not necessary to charge the improper *use* by defendant; the crime consists in the keeping for improper use by any one: C. v. Kimball, 7 Gray, 328. But it must be charged that defendant permitted, etc. Stephanes v. S., 21 Tex. 206.

[1] S. v. Dame, 60 N. H. 479; Shilling v. S., 5 Ind. 443.

[2] Leary v. S., 39 Ind. 544; Hosea v. S., 47 Ind. 180.

[3] S. v. Haines, 30 Me. 65; S. v. Dame, 60 N. H. 479.

[4] C. v. Ashley, 2 Gray, 356; C. v. Edds, 14 Gray, 406; C. v. Kelly, 12 Gray, 175; Betts v. S., 93 Ind. 375; S. v. Homer, 40 Me. 438; S. v. Osgood, 85 Me. 288; S. v. Haines, 30 Me. 65; Brown v. S., 2 Tex. Ap. 189; Killman v. S., 2 Tex. Ap. 222. If the statutory description is that of a house of ill-fame resorted to for purposes of prostitution or lewdness, such a charge is sufficient: S. v. Toombs, 79 Ia. 741; Jordan v. S., 60 Ga. 656. Indeed, it was held unnecessary to charge the purpose for which the house was resorted to: Clifton v. S., 53 Ga. 241. If the indictment charges the keeping and also solicitation to lewdness and prostitution, the latter part of the charge may be treated as surplusage: S. v. Schaffer, 74 Ia. 704. In general, as to requisites of an indictment for nuisance in keeping a disorderly house, see Hickey v. S., 53 Ala. 514; Lowe v. S., 4 Tex. Ap. 34; Lasindo v. S., 2 Tex. Ap. 59.

[5] S. v. Shaw, 35 Ia. 575; Handy v. S., 63 Miss. 207.

[6] Jenks v. S., 17 Wis. 665; S. v. Nixon, 18 Vt. 70.

[7] S. v. Stevens, 40 Me. 559; S. v. Hendricks, 15 Mont. 194. Therefore, if the charge is of keeping during a certain time a house of ill-fame at a certain town, it is error to admit proof of keeping such a house during such time at more than one place in the town: S. v. Plant, 67 Vt. 454.

[8] S. v. Haines, 30 Me. 65.

[9] S. v. Stevens, 40 Me. 559; S. v. Wilson, 93 N. C. 608; Mains v. S., 42 Ind. 327. It will not invalidate the indictment, however, that the act charged is designated as a nuisance, though it falls within some express statutory prohibition: S. v. Shaw, 35 Ia. 575.

The offense of keeping a disorderly house is a continuous one, and is distinct from the individual acts which may tend to show such offense.[1]

§ 1144. Forms of indictment.— The following forms will sufficiently suggest the method of charging these offenses, but in their application the particular features of each statute must be considered and the forms adapted thereto:

FOR KEEPING DISORDERLY HOUSE.

That A. B., at ——, on ——, and on divers other days and times between that date and the finding of this indictment, unlawfully did keep and maintain a common, ill-governed and disorderly house, and in the said house, for his own gain and lucre, certain evil-disposed persons, as well men as women, of evil fame, manner and conversation, then and on said other days and times there unlawfully and willingly did cause and procure to frequent and come together, and the said men and women in the said house at unlawful times, as well in the night as in the day, on the days and times aforesaid, there to be and remain drinking, tippling, cursing, swearing, quarreling and otherwise misbehaving themselves, unlawfully did permit and suffer, to the great injury and common nuisance of all the peaceable citizens of said state there residing, inhabiting and passing.[2]

FOR KEEPING HOUSE OF ILL-FAME.

That A. B., on —— and on divers days and times between that date and the finding of this indictment, kept a house of ill-fame at ——, for the sake of lucre, whereby divers unlawful assemblies, riots, violations of the peace of the state and lewd offenses in the same house at such times as well in the night as in the day were committed, to the great damage and common nuisance of all the citizens of the state, against good morals, etc.[3]

[1] Meyer v. S., 41 N. J. 6. Therefore one conviction bars a prosecution for a similar offense on a prior date: Freeman v. S., 119 Ind. 501; unless the first indictment has carved out a particular time as that during which the offense was committed, and the second prosecution is for a time prior thereto: Huffman v. S., 23 Tex. Ap. 491. Indeed, it is said by way of *dictum* that in different counts the offenses may be charged as committed on each different day during which the house was kept, and a conviction may be had on each count on the same trial: Hall v. S., 32 Tex. Ap. 474.

[2] This is substantially the form sustained in S. v. Bailey, 21 N. H. 343; Smith v. C., 6 B. Mon. 21; C. v. Stewart, 1 Serg. & R. 342; Thatcher v. S., 48 Ark. 60.

[3] Jennings v. C., 17 Pick. 80.

ANOTHER FORM.

That A. B. and C. B., in the county aforesaid, on —— and on divers other times and days between said date and the finding of this indictment, and continuously from said —— to the date of finding this indictment, did keep and still continue to keep a house of ill-fame for the purpose of prostitution and lewdness, and did then and there permit divers persons of both sexes in said house to commit fornication and adultery to the distubance of others and to the common nuisance of all the good people of the state.[1]

§ **1145. Evidence.**— While it is the general character of the house which is in issue, and the proof of one illegal act will not be sufficient to show the house to have been a disorderly one, yet proof of one particular unlawful act may be admissible as going to show, with other evidence, that the house was disorderly.[2] General disorderly conduct may be shown, such as quarreling, fighting or breaking in and out of the place by the frequenters of the house.[3] But the opinion of a witness that the house as kept is a nuisance is not competent.[4] In determining whether the house was a nuisance the particular acts testified to and their probable result, rather than the testimony of particular witnesses as to whether they were annoyed, is the proper evidence.[5] With special reference to houses of ill-fame it is said that the conversation of the inmates of the house may be shown as indicating its character;[6] and further as showing the character of the house, it is competent to prove the bad reputation of its occupants or those who visit it;[7] but as to whether evidence of the bad reputation of the house itself can be given there is a conflict in the authorities, it being held by

[1] S. v. Alderman, 40 Ia. 375.

[2] Mahalovitch v. S., 54 Ga. 217. The nuisance must be shown as an existing fact, and it is not sufficient alone to prove the reputation of the house: S. v. Foley, 45 N. H. 466.

[3] C. v. O'Brien, 8 Gray, 487.

[4] Smith v. C., 6 B. Mon. 21.

[5] Garrison v. S., 14 Ind. 287.

[6] C. v. Kimball, 7 Gray, 328; S. v. Toombs, 79 Ia. 741; but not, of course, conversation of persons who have left the house, such conversation not being in the presence of the keeper or inmates: C. v. Harwood, 4 Gray, 41.

[7] C. v. Kimball, 7 Gray, 328; S. v. McGregor, 41 N. H. 407; S. v. Boardman, 64 Me. 523; Herzinger v. S., 70 Md. 278; Beard v. S., 71 Md. 275; Handy v. S., 63 Miss. 207; King v. S., 17 Fla. 183; S. v. Schaffer, 74 Ia. 704; S. v. McDowell, Dudley, 346; Winslow v. S., 5 Ind. Ap. 306; Sylvester v. S., 42 Tex. 496; U. S. v. Stevens, 4 Cranch, C. C. 341; U. S. v. McDowell, 4 Cranch, C. C. 423; but not the bad character of defendant: U. S. v. Nailor, 4 Cranch, C. C. 372.

perhaps the weight of authority that evidence of the general reputation of the house is not admissible,[1] while other cases hold that evidence that the general reputation of the house in the community is that it is kept for public prostitution is admissible.[2] Particular acts of disorderly conduct committed by the occupants or frequenters of the house, either within the house[3] or of the occupants of the house committed elsewhere,[4] are admissible.

[1] S. v. Boardman, 64 Me. 523; Handy v. S., 63 Miss. 207; Henson v. S., 62 Md. 231; U. S. v. Jourdine, 4 Cranch, C. C. 338.

[2] S. v. McDowell, Dudley, 346; King v. S., 17 Fla. 183; S. v. Mack, 41 La. An. 1079; T. v. Chartrand, 1 Dak. T. 379; T. v. Stone, 2 Dak. 155; Cook v. S., 22 Tex. Ap. 511; Morris v. S., 38 Tex. 603.

[3] S. v. McGregor, 41 N. H. 407; S. v. Garing, 75 Me. 591.

[4] Beard v. S., 71 Md. 275.

CHAPTER 55.

PROCURING ABORTION; CONCEALING BIRTH OF BASTARD.

§ **1146. Procuring abortion.**— The miscarriage of a pregnant woman consists in the premature explosion of the ovum or fetus, or of the living child,[1] and to produce such miscarriage is to procure an abortion.[2] At common law the procuring of an abortion is not criminal as against the mother unless it is without her consent, in which case it is an aggravated assault;[3] but to cause the death of the child after it has quickened is criminal, though it is not homicide.[4] But in some states it is held that procuring an abortion is criminal whether the child was quick or not.[5] A woman is said to be quick with child when she has conceived, but she is with quick child, or the child is quick, when the mother has felt the child alive and quick within; that is, at whatever time the fetus may have a separate existence.[6] By statutes, both in England and the United States, the procuring of an abortion is now criminal whether the child is quick or not, there being, however, in some states, a heavier penalty if the offense is committed after quickening.[7] To procure an abortion within the statutory definition implies intention to produce that effect, and one who by violence, but without any purpose to cause such result, does an injury to a pregnant woman producing miscarriage, is not punishable for the crime of producing abortion.[8]

[1] Smith v. S., 33 Me. 48.

[2] Mills v. C., 13 Pa. St. 631; Abrams v. Foshee, 3 Ia. 274. The word "abortion" is properly used in connection with the woman and not the embyro of the child: Mills v. C., 13 Pa. St. 631.

[3] C. v. Parker, 9 Met. 263; S. v. Cooper, 22 N. J. 52; Abrams v. Foshee, 3 Ia. 274; Hatfield v. Gano, 15 Ia. 177.

[4] C. v. Parker, 9 Met. 263; S. v. Cooper, 22 N. J. 52; Mitchell v. C., 78 Ky. 204; Smith v. S., 33 Me. 48; 3 Inst. 50; *supra*, § 294.

[5] Mills v. C., 13 Pa. St. 631; C. v. Demain, Bright, 441; S. v. Slagle, 83 N. C. 630.

[6] Goldsmiths' Case, 3 Camp. 76; Reg. v. Wycherley, 8 C. & P. 262; Rex v. Phillips, 3 Camp. 77.

[7] S. v. Cooper, 22 N. J. 52.

[8] Slattery v. P., 76 Ill. 217.

§ 1147. Where death results.— Under the ordinary provisions the offense is committed without regard to the death either of the woman or of the child, though such circumstances may constitute an aggravation.[1] If the death of the child results after birth by reason of the premature birth or injury before birth, such death constitutes a homicide, and is criminal or not, depending on the circumstances.[2] If the death of the woman is caused by an unlawful attempt to procure abortion, the crime will be at least manslaughter,[3] and it is immaterial whether the woman is quick with child or not.[4] But where the procuring of the abortion is a felony, the death resulting therefrom will be murder in the second degree.[5] In some states the act of cansing the death of a woman in an attempt to procure an abortion upon her is made a distinct offense, and, if so, it should be thus charged, and not charged in the form of an indictment for homicide.[6] Under an indictment for such offense there may be a conviction for procuring an abortion,[7] or for attempting to procure it.[8] But it is not competent to make the attempt to procure an abortion manslaughter where neither the death of the child nor the death of the mother is a necessary element of the crime.[9]

§ 1148. Attempting; advising.— At common law it is a misdemeanor to administer a noxious drug to a woman with the intent to produce an abortion.[10] There are various statutory provisions relating to the attempt to procure, or the administration of drugs, etc., or the use of instruments, with intent to procure, or the advising of a woman to take such drug

[1] S. v. Gedicke, 43 N. J. 86; C. v. Thompson, 108 Mass. 461.

[2] *Supra*, §§ 294, 347.

[3] S. v. McNab, 20 N. H. 160; *supra*, § 327.

[4] Yundt v. P., 65 Ill. 372; Peoples v. C., 87 Ky. 487. In an attempt causing death the crime will be manslaughter whether the woman was pregnant or not: Reg. v. Gaylor, Dears. & B. 288.

[5] S. v. Moore, 25 Ia. 128; S. v. McNab, 20 N. H. 160; C. v. Parker, 9 Met. 263; *supra*, § 327.

[6] C. v. Jackson, 15 Gray, 187; Montgomery v. S., 80 Ind. 338; Traylor v. S., 101 Ind. 65.

[7] P. v. Jackson, 3 Hill, 92.

[8] C. v. Adams, 127 Mass. 15.

[9] S. v. Young, 55 Kan. 349.

[10] S. v. Slagle, 82 N. C. 653; Holliday v. P., 9 Ill. 111. By an Arkansas statute it is a felony to give to a pregnant woman drugs for the procuring of an abortion before the period of quickening. If this element is not charged in the indictment the conviction may be for the common-law misdemeanor: S. v. Reed, 45 Ark. 333.

or use such instruments with intent to procure an abortion. Under such statutes it is immaterial to charge an assault, but the charge of an assault will not prevent the indictment being sufficient if the statutory crime is charged;[1] nor will the fact that the evidence shows an actual miscarriage to have been procured prevent a conviction for administering a drug with intent.[2] Under these statutes the crime may be committed during any portion of the period of gestation.[3] The several acts or means by which the abortion was attempted to be procured may be charged conjunctively in one count,[4] the object being the same and both forms of the charge being included in the same statutory provisions.[5] The English statute provides a punishment for administering or causing to be taken any "noxious thing" with intent to produce a miscarriage, and it has been held that if the substance in the quantity taken is not calculated to produce the result intended, the crime is not committed;[6] but that the question whether in the quantity taken it was dangerous was for the jury.[7] So under a statute prohibiting the furnishing of any article or thing to a pregnant woman designed and intended for procuring an abortion, it was held that the sale of an ordinary English catheter manufactured for a lawful purpose would not be criminal, although the sale was with the intention that it should be used in an attempt to procure an abortion.[8] Under American statutes as to administering "any poison, drug, medicine or noxious thing," it is not necessary that the drug as administered be capable of producing the result if it is noxious or harmful and given with that intent.[9] Indeed, it is said not to be material to either allege or prove that the thing administered was in fact poisonous or noxious, or that it would tend to produce the result intended and desired, the intent on the part of defendant being the essence of the crime.[10] In defining the word "poison" as used

[1] Hatchard v. S., 79 Wis. 357.

[2] Dougherty v. P., 1 Colo. 514.

[3] Wilson v. S., 2 Ohio St. 319.

[4] P. v. Davis, 56 N. Y. 95; C. v. Brown, 14 Gray, 419.

[5] C. v. Brown, 14 Gray, 419. And it is immaterial that the indictment also alleges the death of the woman as caused thereby: Ibid.

[6] Reg. v. Perry, 2 Cox, 223; Reg. v. Isaacs, L. & C. 220.

[7] Reg. v. Cramp, 5 Q. B. D. 307; Reg. v. Hollis, 28 L. T. 455.

[8] S. v. Forsythe, 78 Ia. 595.

[9] S. v. Gedicke, 43 N. J. 86.

[10] C. v. Morrison, 16 Gray, 224; Dougherty v. P., 1 Colo. 514; S. v. Owens, 22 Minn. 238; S. v. Fitzgerald, 49 Ia. 260.

in such a statute it is said that it includes all substances which operate in any way calculated to superinduce a miscarriage or make it possible,[1] and it seems that the name or nature of the drug, etc., need not be specified if the statutory description is used.[2] It is not necessary that the attempt should have the result intended in order to constitute the crime of prescribing "any drug, etc.," with intent to procure abortion;[3] nor will it disprove such crime as charged that the abortion was in fact caused by some other means;[4] nor is it necessary to allege and prove that the woman was in fact pregnant, or that defendant knew or believed her to be so.[5] The early English statute on the subject related only to the administering or causing to be administered;[6] but under statute making it criminal to administer or advise to be taken, etc., it was held not essential that the drug be actually taken, as the act of defendant in advising it would be sufficient to constitute the crime.[7] So if the abortion is in fact procured, the one who advises it would be an accomplice, but if not he would be punishable as principal for an attempt.[8] Under the New York statute, however, it is held that one who advises is guilty only where the advice is acted upon.[9] Even under the English statute if the advice be given and followed the one who advises may be punished for the offense of causing to be taken;[10] and under a still more recent English statute for the punishment of supplying any noxious thing with intent that it shall be employed for the purpose, it is not necessary that the intention of employing it should exist in the mind of any other person than the person supplying it.[11]

[1] Dougherty v. P., 1 Colo. 514; P. v Carmichael, 5 Mich. 10.

[2] Dougherty v. P., 1 Colo. 514; S. v. Reed, 45 Ark. 333; S. v. Van Houten, 37 Mo. 357; S. v. Vawter, 7 Blackf. 592.

[3] S. v. Owens, 22 Minn. 238; Dougherty v. P., 1 Colo. 514.

[4] S. v. Morrow, 40 S. C. 221.

[5] C. v. Tibbetts, 157 Mass. 519; C. v. Taylor, 132 Mass. 261; C. v. Follansbee, 155 Mass. 274; Reg. v. Goodchild, 2 C. & K. 293; Reg. v. Titley, 14 Cox, 502. *Contra*, Rex v. Scudder, 1 Moody, 216. Much less is it necessary that the child be quick: C. v. Wood, 11 Gray, 85; S. v. Fitzgerald, 49 Ia. 260; but under the New Jersey statute it was held necessary that the woman be pregnant, though actual knowledge of that fact on the part of the defendant need not be alleged or proved further than as implied in an intent to procure a miscarriage: Powe v. S., 48 N. J. 34.

[6] Rex v. Cadman, 1 Moody, 114.

[7] S. v. Murphy, 27 N. J. 112.

[8] Willingham v. S., 33 Tex. Ap. 98.

[9] P. v. Phelps, 133 N. Y. 267.

[10] Reg. v. Farrow, Dears. & B. 164; Reg. v. Wilson, Dears. & B. 127.

[11] Reg. v. Hillman, L. & C. 343.

So under the Maryland statute one was held guilty "of causing to be used" who sent by mail a letter to a pregnant woman accompanying it with a bottle of medicine, with directions for its use, and naming other means to be employed.[1] The act of sending through the mails medicines, articles, etc., designed or intended for the prevention of conception or for the procuring of abortion, or advertisements of such things, is punishable as a crime against the federal postal laws, which must be limited in their operation, however, to the protection of the mails.[2]

§ **1149. Consent; necessity.**— The consent of the woman is no defense to the crime, the malice necessary to constitute the offense being merely the absence of lawful justification.[3] Some statutes contain an exception of cases where the abortion is necessary to save the life of the woman, and in some cases it is held that such exception must be negatived in the indictment.[4] Other cases, however, hold that the exception need not be negatived in the indictment, but is a matter of defense.[5]

§ **1150. The indictment.**— In general, as in other offenses of this description, it is sufficient to follow the words of the statute,[6] and it is held not to be necessary to allege the kind of

[1] Jones v. S., 70 Md. 326.

[2] U. S. v. Bott, 11 Blatchf. 346. Further as to the use of the mails for such purposes, see *infra*, ch. 67.

[3] C. v. Wood, 11 Gray, 85. Therefore the charge of assault connected with the act is unnecessary and superfluous: C. v. Snow, 116 Mass. 47. An infant is incapable of consenting to the procurement of an abortion: White v. Murtland, 71 Ill. 250.

[4] Moody v. S., 17 Ohio St. 111; S. v. Stokes, 54 Vt. 179. And the allegation must be as broad as the statute and negative the necessity for procuring the miscarriage, and not merely the necessity for using the means made use of: Bassett v. S., 41 Ind. 303. But it is not necessary to negative the statutory provision as to the act being upon the advice of two physicians, as that is only a matter of evidence bearing on the question of necessity: Moody v. S., 17 Ohio St. 111.

[5] S. v. Rupe, 41 Tex. 33; C. v. Wood, 11 Gray, 85. At least this is true where the statute does not specifically make an exception and the necessity is relied on generally as a common-law defense: S. v. Wood, 53 N. H. 484.

[6] C. v. Corkin. 136 Mass. 429. **Form:** The said A. B., in ——, on ——, did wilfully, knowingly, unlawfully and feloniously give and administer to M. B., a woman who was then and there pregnant and in a family way, and who had been so about three months, a certain deleterious drug, potion and medicine, which said M. B. took inwardly — the said drug, potion and medicine is unknown to the said grand jury — with intent to, and did thereby, by giving and administering to her as aforesaid, cause her, the said M. B., to abort and miscarry and bring forth many months before her time:" Mitchell v. C., 78 Ky. 204.

drug or instrument used.[1] At any rate it is sufficient to allege the use of a certain drug or a certain instrument, the name and a more particular description of which are to the grand jurors unknown.[2] Several different means may be charged and a conviction had upon the proof of any one of them.[3] If the indictment charges an attempt and the use of means, etc., it is not necessary that it specifically allege the intent.[4] In an indictment for making public by printing or writing, etc., information as to where advice may be obtained for the purpose of procuring a miscarriage, it was held necessary to allege the manner in which the printing and writing were made public.[5] Cases furnishing illustrations as to the form of indictment held sufficient under particular statutes are cited in the note.[6] The offense is complete where the medicine is administered, and the venue may be laid in that county, although the miscarriage occurs in another county.[7] If the offense is that of advising or procuring a drug to be taken, the state where the woman was when the advice was given may take jurisdiction, although the defendant was in another state and sent the advice and the medicine by mail.[8]

§ **1151. Evidence.**— Circumstantial evidence is sufficient, and it is not necessary to show that it was impossible for the crime to have been committed by another than the defendant.[9] The fact of pregnancy by illicit intercourse may be shown,[10] and the fact that at the time of the act the woman was an inmate of a house of ill-fame.[11] Evidence of different attempts at about the same time to produce a miscarriage on the same woman are admissible as parts of the same transaction.[12] The intent is sufficiently established by proving the act and the occasion for it.[13] The declarations of the woman indicating present pain at the time of the abortion are admissible.[14] The woman upon

[1] S. v. Vawter, 7 Blackf. 592; Watson v. S., 9 Tex. Ap. 237; Cave v. S., 33 Tex. Ap. 335.

[2] C. v. Corkin, 136 Mass. 429; C. v. Thompson, 159 Mass. 56; Baker v. P., 105 Ill. 452.

[3] Scott v. P., 141 Ill. 195.

[4] Scott v. P., 141 Ill. 195.

[5] S. v. Fiske, 66 Vt. 434.

[6] C. v. Thompson, 108 Mass. 461; Baker v. P., 105 Ill. 452; Dougherty v. P., 1 Colo. 514.

[7] S. v. Hollenbeck, 36 Ia. 112.

[8] S. v. Morrow, 40 S. C. 221.

[9] C. v. Leach, 156 Mass. 99.

[10] P. v. Josselyn, 39 Cal. 393; Scott v. P., 141 Ill. 195.

[11] Hays v. S., 40 Md. 633.

[12] Scott v. P., 141 Ill. 195.

[13] S. v. Montgomery, 71 Ia. 630.

[14] C. v. Leach, 156 Mass. 99.

whom the attempt is made with her consent is not an accomplice in such sense that her testimony requires corroboration;[1] but the woman may be an accomplice in such sense that her admissions or declarations are admissible against the defendant as those of a confederate.[2]

§ **1152. Concealing birth of a bastard.**— There are statutes in some of the states punishing the concealment on the part of the mother of the birth or death of a bastard child, the object of such statutes doubtless being to cover cases where it appears that the bastard was born, but it cannot be shown whether it was born dead or alive, and therefore the crime of child-murder cannot be established.[3] The concealment need not be from all persons, but it is sufficient if the woman does anything to prevent the fact being generally known with the purpose of concealment and the quieting of investigation.[4] These statutes relate to the concealment of the birth only where the child is dead,[5] and the indictment must expressly allege that the child was dead at the time of the concealment,[6] and the concealment as shown must be in connection with the birth and death of the child.[7] The concealment must be with intent to prevent

[1] C. v. Wood, 11 Gray, 85; C. v. Follansbee, 155 Mass. 274; Dunn v. P., 29 N. Y. 523; S. v. Owens, 22 Minn. 238; Willingham v. S., 33 Tex. Ap. 98; Watson v. S., 9 Tex. Ap. 237. And see *supra*, § 199. *Contra*, P. v. Josselyn, 39 Cal. 393, holding, however, that the corroboration need not extend to the particular method employed but only to the general intent of defendant.

[2] P. v. Davis, 56 N. Y. 95; P. v. Murphy, 101 N. Y. 126, overruling P. v. Vedder, 98 N. Y. 630.

[3] C v. Clark, 2 Ashmead, 105; Pennsylvania v. McKee, Addison, 1; S. v. Kirby, 57 Me. 30; S. v. Ihrig, 106 Mo. 267; Sullivan v. S., 36 Ark. 64; Dunn v. S., 57 Ark. 560; Reg. v. Morris, 3 Cox, 489.

[4] S. v. Hill, 58 N. H. 475. As to what is sufficient concealment under the English statute, see Rex v. Cornwall, Russ. & Ry. 336; Reg. v. Turner, 8 C. & P. 755; Reg. v. Coxhead, 1 C. & K. 623; Reg. v. Sleep, 9 Cox, 559; Rex v. Snell, 2 M. & Rob. 44; Reg. v. Perry, Dears, 471; Reg. v. Goldthorpe, Car. & M. 335; Reg. v. Farnham, 1 Cox, 349; Reg. v. Goode, 6 Cox, 318; Reg. v. Hounsell, 2 M. & Rob. 292; Reg. v. Brown, L. R. 1 C. C. 244; Reg. v. Cook, 21 L. T. 216; Reg. v. Opic, 8 Cox, 332; Reg. v. George, 11 Cox, 41.

[5] Pennsylvania v. McKee, Addison, 1; Reg. v. May, 10 Cox, 448; Reg. v. Bell, 8 Ir. R. C. L. 541.

[6] Douglass v. C., 8 Watts, 535; Boyles v. C., 2 Serg. & R. 40. But it is not necessary to state whether the child died before, at, or after, its birth: Reg. v. Coxhead, 1 C. & K. 623. In an English case it is said that the dead body must be found and identified: Reg. v. Williams, 11 Cox, 684.

[7] C. v. Clark, 2 Ashmead, 105; S. v. Kirby, 57 Me. 30.

the fact of birth and death being known;[1] but if the act of disposing of the body is such as to lead to that result, it is not necessary to allege or prove any specific intent.[2] The indictment must allege facts showing the commission of the act and not simply the legal conclusion that accused concealed the birth of the child by secreting it so that it might not be known whether or not it had been born alive.[3] But the means by which the mother endeavored to effect the concealment need not be alleged.[4] The mother alone can be guilty as principal in the offense,[5] but she may commit it through an accomplice,[6] and the accomplice may be guilty of aiding and abetting, if that is made criminal by the statute.[7] The English cases differ as to what is a "child" within the meaning of the statute, it having been held that it must appear that the child had gone such a time in its mother's womb that it would in the ordinary course of things when born have a fair chance of living, and that under seven months it may fairly be presumed that it would not be born alive;[8] while in another case it is held that it was properly left to the jury to say whether, even though the child had not gone seven months, it had so far matured as to become a child or was only a fetus or the unformed subject of a premature miscarriage.[9]

[1] Reg. v. Clarke, 4 F. & F. 1040; Rex v. Higley, 4 C. & P. 366; Reg. v. Bate, 11 Cox, 686; Reg. v. Morris, 3 Cox, 489.

[2] S. v. White, 76 Mo. 96; S. v. Ihrig, 106 Mo. 267.

[3] Foster v. C., 12 Bush, 373.

[4] Boyles v. C., 2 Serg. & R. 40.

[5] Reg. v. Wright, 9 C. & P. 754.

[6] Rex v. Douglas, 7 C. & P. 644.

[7] Reg. v. Skelton, 3 C. & K. 119; Reg. v. Bird, 2 C. & K. 817.

[8] Reg. v. Berriman, 6 Cox, 388.

[9] Reg. v. Hewitt, 4 F. & F. 1101. In another case it was said that a fœtus no bigger than a man's finger, but having the shape of a child, was a child: Reg. v. Colmer, 9 Cox, 506.

CHAPTER 56.

SODOMY.

§ **1153. What constitutes.**— This offense is sufficiently described by calling it, with Blackstone, the crime against nature, committed either with a human being or a beast.[1] A fowl has been thought not to come within the term "beast" in this definition; at any rate it was held that where the fowl was so small that entrance of the male organ into its private parts was impossible and they were torn in the attempt, the crime was not committed,[2] but the criminal attempt to commit may be with a fowl.[3] The act must be in that part where sodomy is usually committed; the act in a child's mouth does not constitute the offense.[4] No doubt the requirement as to penetration and emission is the same as in rape.[5] If the act is between human beings, each is guilty if both consent,[6] but consent of

[1] 4 Bl. Com. 215; C. v. Dill, 160 Mass. 536. Webster defines it as "carnal copulation in a manner against nature; buggery." Under the Texas statute requiring that offenses to be punishable must be expressly defined by statute, it was held that a definition of the offense as "the abominable and detestable crime against nature committed with mankind or beast," was not sufficiently definite: Fennell v. S., 32 Tex. 378; Frazier v. S., 39 Tex. 390. But this is not the rule elsewhere, and it is no longer the rule in Texas, and the statutory description as the crime against nature is sufficient: S. v. Williams, 34 La. An. 87; Cross v. S., 17 Tex. Ap. 476. In states where common-law crimes are not recognized, and there is no statute as to this offense, it is of course not punishable: Estes v. Carter, 10 Ia. 400; Melvin v. Weiant, 36 Ohio St. 184; Davis v. Brown, 27 Ohio St. 326; S. v. Place, 5 Wash. 773.

[2] Rex v. Mulreaty, 1 Russ. Cr. 699.

[3] Reg. v. Brown, 24 Q. B. D. 357.

[4] Rex v. Jacobs, Russ. & Ry. 331; Prindle v. S., 31 Tex. Ap. 551.

[5] C. v. Thomas, 1 Va. Cas. 307; Pennsylvania v. Sullivan, Add. 143; Comstock v. S., 14 Neb. 205; Hodges v. S., 94 Ga. 593; Rex v. Reekspear, 1 Moody. 342; Rex v. Cozins, 6 C. & P. 351. Some cases hold that, aside from statutory provisions, emission must be shown: P. v. Hodgkin, 94 Mich. 27; S. v. Gray, 8 Jones, 170; Williams v. S., 14 Ohio, 222; Rex v. Duffin, 1 East, P. C. 365; 2 Bish. Cr. L., § 1127. Penetration may, however, be proved by circumstantial evidence: Collins v. S., 73 Ga. 76; Cross v. S., 17 Tex. Ap. 476.

[6] Reg. v. Allen, 2 C. & K. 869; 4 Bl. Com. 216.

one is immaterial as to the guilt of the other.[1] The attempt may be punishable,[2] and a conviction therefor may be had under an indictment charging the offense.[3] So an assault to commit the offense may be punished as an indecent assault, but not where the other party assents,[4] unless such consent is given in ignorance of the nature of the act.[5]

§ **1154. Indictment.**— An indictment which charges that defendant "did unlawfully and feloniously commit a certain unnatural and lascivious act" with a person named,[6] or "did feloniously, etc., commit the infamous crime against nature" with, etc.,[7] is sufficient. But it is not enough to simply follow the general language of the statute without charging the act.[8] It is not sufficient to say that defendants did commit together "divers lewd, beastly, unnatural and sodomitical practices."[9] The offense may be charged as committed with a certain person named without otherwise alleging that it was committed with a human being as distinguished from an animal,[10] or with a "bitch"[11] or with a "mare, the same being a beast."[12]

[1] Reg. v. Jellyman, 8 C. & P. 604.

[2] Reg. v. Eaton, 8 C. & P. 417; or an assault with intent to commit: Davis v. S., 3 Har. & J. 154; S. v. Place, 5 Wash. 773.

[3] S. v. Frank, 103 Mo. 120.

[4] Reg. v. Wollaston, 12 Cox, 180.

[5] Reg. v. Lock, L. R. 2 C. C. 10; Mascolo v. Montesanto, 61 Conn. 50.

[6] C. v. Dill, 160 Mass. 536.

[7] P. v. Williams, 59 Cal. 397; S. v. Chandonette, 10 Mont. 280; S. v. Williams, 34 La. An. 87. **Form:** The common-law indictment, as given in 1 Archb. Cr. Pr. & Pl. 309, is as follows: "That A. B., at ——, on ——, in and upon one C. D., feloniously did make an assault, and then feloniously, wickedly and against the order of nature had a venerial affair with the said C. D., and then feloniously did know the said C. D., and then feloniously, wickedly and against the order of nature with the said C. D. did commit and perpetrate the abominable crime of buggery." But the allegation in this indictment that defendant had a "venerial affair," etc., is not essential: Lambertson v. P., 5 Park. Cr. 200.

[8] S. v. Campbell, 29 Tex. 44. **Form:** But in that state the following was held sufficient: "Did then and there unlawfully and wilfully commit with a mare, the same being a beast, the abominable and detestable crime against nature, by then and there having carnal connection with said beast, and did then and there commit the crime of sodomy with said beast:" Cross v. S., 17 Tex. Ap. 476. The attempt to commit was held sufficiently charged as follows: "That before the finding of this indictment A. B., against the order of nature, attempted to carnally know a certain beast, to wit, a mare:" Bradford v. S., 104 Ala. 68.

[9] Reg. v. Rowed, 3 Q. B. 180.

[10] P. v. Moore, 103 Cal. 508.

[11] Reg. v. Allen, 1 C. & K. 495.

[12] Cross v. S., 17 Tex. Ap. 476.

§ 1155. Evidence.— It is not competent to show a general disposition or inclination to commit such offenses.[1] The crime is one, like rape, easy to charge and difficult to disprove; and therefore the accusation should be clearly made out to warrant conviction,[2] especially if a considerable period of time has elapsed before complaint is made by the injured party.[3] The fact only of such complaint, and not the particulars of it, may be shown.[4] A consenting party is an accomplice, whose evidence must be corroborated.[5]

[1] Rex v. Cole, 1 Russ. Cr. 700.

[2] 4 Bl. Com. 215; P. v. Moore, 103 Cal. 508. As to rape, see *supra*, § 458.

[3] Reg. v. Robins, 1 Cox, 114.

[4] S. v. Gruso, 28 La. An. 952.

[5] Medis v. S., 27 Tex. Ap. 194; Reg. v. Jellyman, 8 C. & P. 604. And see C. v. Snow, 111 Mass. 411.

CHAPTER 57.

OBSCENITY AND INDECENCY.

§ **1156. Obscene language.**— Indecent and obscene publications are at common law punishable in some cases as libels,[1] but they are more conveniently and consistently discussed as constituting a distinct offense. Aside from any statute, the utterance of obscene words in public, being a gross violation of public decency and good morals, is indictable.[2] The offense is usually defined by statute, and particular forms of obscenity are specified, such as sending indecent letters to women,[3] or using obscene language in the presence of females.[4] In construing the language of a publication charged as obscene, it is the province of the court to determine whether or not it is so; but the question whether it was designed in making such publication to corrupt the morals of youth is to be submitted to the jury, as that question involves the intention of the person using the language, and not the meaning of the language used.[5] Statutes sometimes provide for the seizure and destruction of an indecent publication.[6]

§ **1157. Indecent exhibitions and prints.**— The offense of indecent exposure of the person has already been considered,[7] but statutes relating to that form of indecency are applicable

[1] *Supra*, § 1049.

[2] Bell v. S., 1 Swan, 42; S. v. Appling, 25 Mo. 315; S. v. Toole, 106 N. C. 736.

[3] Larison v. S., 49 N. J. 256. The offense of sending is completed when defendant puts the communication in the course of transmission intending it to reach the woman, although it may not be by direct means; the course pursued, however, being one likely to produce the result intended, and the result being actually accomplished by the means used: Ibid.

[4] The offense may be committed though the presence of a female is not known to the person using the language: Thomas v. S., 92 Ala. 85. To address a person as a "son of a bitch" is not the use of obscene lauguage under such a statute: Shields v. S., 89 Ga. 549. And see *supra*, § 341. It is sometimes made criminal to use obscene language near the dwelling of another: Mullens v. S., 82 Ala. 42; *Supra* § 1020.

[5] Smith v. S., 24 Tex. Ap. 1.

[6] Reg. v. Hicklin, L. R. 3 Q. B. 360; Ex parte Bradlaugh, 3 Q. B. D. 509.

[7] *Supra*, § 1136.

to the human body and not to representations thereof.[1] While in general the exhibition of an indecent or lewd picture may be a public nuisance,[2] yet it may be punishable by statute without regard to its being a nuisance, but as an offense against public morals.[3] Public indecency may be criminal aside from statute;[4] but a statute for the punishment of public indecency does not cover the use of obscene words unless specially included, and applies rather to exhibitions of lewd pictures or exposure of the person or monsters or the like; acts which have a direct bearing on public morals.[5] The procuring of indecent prints with intent to publish them may be criminal, but preserving and keeping them in possession with such intent is not, as the latter does not involve any criminal act.[6] To constitute a publication of a lewd picture it is not necessary that it be exhibited in a public place or to sundry persons; any exhibition is in itself a publication and an offense;[7] and the publication of a book introduced in evidence in a trial in which it was charged as obscene, such publication being made in connection with a report of the trial, was held not privileged but indictable, without regard to the motives of the person making such publication.[8] A picture is to be deemed lewd and indecent which tends to debauch and corrupt and to rouse in the minds of persons who see it inordinate and lustful desires;[9] and the only method of deciding as to the obscenity of such a representation is by reference to the representation itself. Not the fact of nudity, but the intent of the picture to rouse in the spectator impure imaginations, and to deprave and corrupt, is the test, and it is immaterial what are the other inci-

[1] Tucker v. S., 28 Tex. Ap. 541; although under an English statute relating to obscene exhibitions, an obscene exposure of the person to spectators who had paid admission to view such exhibition was held to be criminal: Reg. v. Saunders, 1 Q. B. D. 15. An indecent exhibition may be criminal as a nuisance although not lewd; thus, the exposure as an advertisement of the picture of a man naked to his waist, and covered with an eruption of sores, was held to be criminal, although not immoral, and made with an innocent motive: Reg. v. Grey, 4 F. & F. 73.

[2] Reg. v. Grey, 4 F. & F. 73. So a ribald song may constitute a nuisance: S. v. Toole, 106 N. C. 736.

[3] C. v. Sharpless, 2 Serg. & R. 91.

[4] S. v. Appling, 25 Mo. 315.

[5] McJunkins v. S., 10 Ind. 140.

[6] Dugdale v. Reg., 1 El. & Bl. 435.

[7] C. v. Sharpless, 2 Serg. & R. 91; Rex v. Curl, 2 Strange, 788; Reg. v. Carlile, 1 Cox, 229.

[8] Steele v. Brannan, L. R. 7 C. P. 261.

[9] C. v. Sharpless, 2 Serg. & R. 91.

dents and qualities of the picture if they are merely accessory to this primary object.[1]

§ **1158. Indictment and evidence.**— The indictment should set out the exact language of the publication, provided it is within the power of the prosecution to do so, unless it is too gross and indecent to be placed upon the records, the excuse for not setting out the exact language being in such case stated.[2] Even if the matter is not set out by reason of its indecency, it must be stated in what the indecency consists.[3] Particularly must the publication be so identified by its title or otherwise that defendant cannot be subjected to a second prosecution for the same offense.[4] If the charge is of indecent exhibitions or representations, it is not necessary to particularly describe them, but general language setting out their obscene character will be sufficient.[5] The manner of publication or distribution must be stated.[6] Where the intent is not a part of the statutory definition of the offense it is not necessary to specifically aver or prove it.[7] The proof must correspond with the allegation,[8] and the evidence must identify the particular act complained of.[9] Other acts of indecent publication or exhibition cannot be proven as affecting the charge in question;[10] and where the charge was of sending an indecent letter to a female, it was held incompetent to introduce evidence of an indecent criminal act toward another female.[11]

1 P. v. Muller, 96 N. Y. 408.

2 McNair v. P., 89 Ill. 441; C. v. Tarbox, 1 Cush. 66; C. v. Holmes, 17 Mass. 336; S. v. Smith, 17 R. I. 415; S. v. Brown, 27 Vt. 619; P. v. Girardin, 1 Mich. 90; Reyes v. S., 34 Fla. 181. As to a similar question in libel, see *supra*, § 1064.

3 Reyes v. S., 34 Fla. 181; Jennings v. S., 16 Ind. 335; S. v. Hayward, 83 Mo. 299; S. v. Hansen, 23 Tex. 232. And see Bradlaugh v. Reg., 3 Q. B. D. 607.

4 C. v. Wright, 139 Mass. 382.

5 Barker v. C., 19 Pa. St. 412; S. v. Pennington, 5 Lea, 506; C. v. Dejardin, 126 Mass. 46.

6 S. v. Smith, 17 R. I. 415.

7 S. v. Smith, 17 R. I. 415; Reg. v. Hicklin, L. R. 3 Q. B. 360.

8 Thus, an allegation of printing and publishing pictures of naked girls is not sustained by proof of printing and publishing pictures of girls naked to the waist: C. v. Dejardin, 126 Mass. 46.

9 Rex v. Rosenstein, 2 C. & P. 414.

10 Montross v. S., 72 Ga. 261.

11 Larison v. S., 49 N. J. 256.

CHAPTER 58.

BLASPHEMY AND PROFANITY.

§ 1159. **What constitutes.**—Christianity is recognized by the common law as the prevailing religion, and profanity and blasphemy committed in maliciously exposing the doctrines of Christianity to ridicule and contempt in scurrilous and opprobrious language, or speaking profanely of God, Christ, the Holy Spirit or the Holy Scriptures, is criminal both at common law and by statutes as found in most of the states.[1] Thus, it is blasphemy to use words concerning God calculated and designed to impair and destroy the reverence, respect and confidence due him, with an impious purpose to derogate from the divine majesty and to alienate the minds and manner of others from the reverence of God, wilfully and maliciously and not in honest and fair discussion for the purpose of discovering the truth, or in a sincere and simple avowal of a disbelief in the attributes and character of a Supreme Being on proper occasions.[2] In determining whether the language is criminal, all the facts and circumstances under which it was used and its connections will be taken into account in ascertaining the purpose of the use of the language.[3] Statutes for the punishment of wilful blasphemy consisting in denying the existence of God, the cursing or contumaciously reproaching God, his creation, etc., are not a violation of the constitutional provisions as to freedom of religion.[4] An offense of a less degree of criminality

[1] Updegraph v. C., 11 Serg. & R. 394; S. v. Chandler, 2 Harr. 553; Vidal v. Girard's Ex'rs, 2 How. 127, 198; P. v. Ruggles, 8 Johns. 290; Taylor's Case, 1 Vent. 293; Rex v. Woolston, 2 Strange, 834; Rex v. Waddington, 1 B. & C. 26; 4 Bl. Com. 59. In a prosecution for the publication of Payne's "Age of Reason," it was held criminal to defame Christianity in general: Rex v. Williams, 26 Howell's St. Tr. 656.

[2] C. v. Kneeland, 20 Pick. 206. Thus, it was held criminal to say in a debating club that "the Holy Scriptures are a mere fable, a contradiction; and, although they contain a number of good things, yet they contain a great many lies:" Updegraph v. C., 11 Serg. & R. 394.

[3] C. v. Kneeland, 20 Pick. 206.

[4] C. v. Kneeland, 20 Pick. 206; S. v. Chandler, 2 Harr. 553.

than that of blasphemy is that of profane swearing, which is punishable by statute both in England and the United States.[1] The use of profane language is a constituent of a disorderly house.[2] But while profanity in itself is sometimes made criminal,[3] it is usually punishable only as constituting a nuisance, and its criminality in this respect will depend upon repetition and publicity so that it should become an annoyance and inconvenience to people in general.[4] A single act of profane swearing is generally not indictable as a nuisance;[5] but where there was continued and public use of profane oaths frequently and boisterously repeated, though on a single occasion and but for the space of five minutes, it was held that there was an indictable nuisance.[6]

§ **1160. Indictment.**— Some cases require that the language charged as constituting the blasphemy or profanity shall be set out in the indictment.[7] On the other hand it has been held not necessary to recite the language.[8] Where the words are so set out it is not necessary to allege that they were used profanely.[9] In charging the profanity as constituting a nuisance it should be alleged that the swearing was in the presence and hearing of citizens and to their annoyance.[10]

[1] 4 Bl. Com. 59; S. v. Kirby, 1 Murphy, 254; Bodenhamer v. S., 60 Ark. 10.

[2] C. v. Murray, 14 Gray, 397; *supra*, § 1137.

[3] Bodenhamer v. S., 60 Ark. 10.

[4] S. v. Jones, 9 Ired. 38; Goree v. S., 71 Ala. 7; Young v. S., 10 Lea, 165; C. v. Linn, 158 Pa. St. 22, 22 L. R. A. 353, and note; S. v. Kirby, 1 Murphy, 254; S. v. Ellar, 1 Dev. 267; S. v. Baldwin, 1 Dev. & B. 195; S. v. Barham, 79 N. C. 646; S. v. Graham, 3 Sneed, 134.

[5] Gaines v. S., 7 Lea, 410.

[6] S. v. Chrisp, 85 N. C. 528.

[7] Updegraph v. C., 11 Serg. & R. 394; Walton v. S., 64 Miss. 207. And it is sufficient to prove the words substantially as charged: Updegraph v. C., 11 Serg. & R. 394.

[8] Ex parte Foley, 62 Cal. 508; Bodenhamer v. S., 60 Ark. 10. It is certainly not required to set out the whole conversation: S. v. Steele, 3 Heisk. 135; and an indictment charging that defendant "did profanely curse," without setting forth the language used, was held sufficient after verdict: S. v. Freeman, 63 Vt. 496.

[9] Taney v. S., 9 Ind. Ap. 46.

[10] Young v. S., 10 Lea, 165: C. v. Linn, 158 Pa. St. 22; S. v. Kirby, 1 Murphy, 254.

CHAPTER 59.

CRUELTY TO ANIMALS.

§ **1161. What punishable.**— In the discussion of malicious mischief something has already been said as to injuries to animals,[1] but the offense there described involves injury to the owner as in the case of any other trespass to property. However, by statutes in most of the states it is made criminal to cruelly beat, wound, mutilate or kill an animal, such statutes being intended to prevent wanton cruelty or ill-treatment of the animal without regard to the ownership; so that the offense may be committed whether the animal belongs to the person who ill-treats it or to another.[2] Therefore an acquittal of the offense of killing an animal with the intent to injure the owner will not prevent a prosecution under the charge of wanton killing.[3] A distinction is made by some statutes between cruelly beating, wounding, etc., and unnecessary cruelty in failing to provide food, drink or shelter.[4] Cruelly driving, etc., is by some statutes made a particular form of the offense.[5] To cause the cruel injury of one animal by another, as in cock-fighting[6] or dog-fighting,[7] is punishable under these statutes. So it is criminal to cause a bagged fox to be turned loose for the purpose of hunting it with dogs.[8] But in a shooting match to wound pigeons set loose from a trap, if they are immediately killed upon discovery of their wounded condition, is not criminal.[9] Under a statute for the punishment for killing or maiming, there is no criminal liability for the mere

[1] *Supra*, § 815.

[2] S. v. Avery, 44 N. H. 392; S. v. Hambleton, 22 Mo. 452; C. v. Lufkin, 7 Allen, 579; Ex parte Phillips, 33 Tex. Ap. 126. And see *supra*, § 829.

[3] Irvin v. S., 7 Tex. Ap. 78.

[4] C. v. Whitman, 118 Mass. 458; C. v. Curry, 150 Mass. 509; C. v. Edmands, 162 Mass. 517.

[5] McKinne v. S., 81 Ga. 164.

[6] This was an offense at common law, being barbarous and cruel sport, leading to disorder and danger: C. v. Tilton, 8 Met. 232.

[7] C. v. Thornton, 113 Mass. 457.

[8] C. v. Turner, 145 Mass. 296.

[9] C. v. Lewis, 140 Pa. St. 261.

shooting of an animal, the owner being remanded to his civil remedy.[1] Under such a statute the word "maim" means to cripple, and does not necessarily imply that the animal is deprived of a part of its body.[2] By federal statute it is made a crime to confine animals in transit from one state to another for more than twenty-eight consecutive hours without unloading for rest, food and water, and such a statute is within the power of congress with reference to interstate commerce.[3] One company is not liable for the default of a connecting carrier in this respect, except that it is chargeable with notice of the time during which the animals have been confined when they come into its possession.[4]

§ **1162. What deemed animal.**— Various terms are used in the statute as designating the kind of animal referred to, such as "domestic animal," "dumb animal," etc., or particularly describing the class of animals. Under these terms a mule is a "domestic animal,"[5] and a horse comes within the term "cattle;"[6] but a tame buffalo is not "cattle."[7] A dog is a "dumb animal."[8] The term "domestic animal" covers pet birds or birds kept in a state of captivity and trained as decoy birds for the purpose of bird catching,[9] but it does not include a lizard or chameleon.[10]

§ **1163. Intent.**— It has already been said that malice as against the owner of the animal is not material.[11] As to the criminal intent, it is sufficient that there is a violation of the statute, as, for instance, the provision punishing the unnecessary failure to provide food, water or shelter, and intentional cruelty is not an element of the offense.[12] So it is no defense to an indictment for knowingly and intentionally overdriving a horse that there was no specific intent to inflict injury or

[1] Bailey v. S., 65 Ga. 410. But under a statute making it an offense to "wound" an animal, there may be an indictment for "shooting:" S. v. Butts, 92 N. C. 784.

[2] Turman v. S., 4 Tex. Ap. 586.

[3] U. S. v. Boston & Albany R. Co., 15 Fed. R. 209. See *infra* § 1338.

[4] U. S. v. Louisville & Nashville R. Co., 18 Fed. R. 480.

[5] S. v. Gould, 26 W. Va. 258.

[6] S. v. Hambleton, 22 Mo. 452.

[7] S. v. Crenshaw, 22 Mo. 457.

[8] McDaniel v. S., 5 Tex. Ap. 475.

[9] Colam v. Pagett, 12 Q. B. D. 66.

[10] In re Racey, 49 Alb. L. J. 252 (a case before the police judge of Montreal, Canada).

[11] *Supra*, § 1161.

[12] C. v. Curry, 150 Mass. 509; C. v. Edmands, 162 Mass. 517; C. v. Whitman, 118 Mass. 458.

torture.[1] But where the charge is of killing, wounding, mutilating, etc., it is a defense that the act is done, not out of cruelty, but for the purpose of protecting one's own property, such as crops or animals, against animals about to cause injury thereto, other means of protection not being available or effectual.[2] So if the charge is of wilful and wanton killing of an animal there cannot be a conviction for killing an animal in the protection of one's own.[3] It is not sufficient that the killing was unlawful.[4] The right to protect one's property against trespassing animals is recognized by some statutes.[5] According to some provisions it is the "needlessly" torturing or mutilating which is punished.[6] One is not criminally liable for cruelty in the punishment of an animal for the purpose of discipline, if in good faith and with proper motives.[7]

§ 1164. **Indictment.**— These statutory offenses may properly be charged in the language of the statute[8] without specially alleging the mode or circumstances of killing, wounding or otherwise injuring.[9] But the language used must be such as to bring the case within the statute.[10] The act should be charged as wilful or malicious and unlawful in accordance with the statutory language.[11] It is not necessary to allege further that the act was knowingly or intentionally done,[12] or that it was done out

[1] C. v. Wood, 111 Mass. 408.

[2] Stephens v. S., 65 Miss. 329, 8 Am. Cr. R. 157, and note; Farmer v. S., 21 Tex. Ap. 423.

[3] Thomas v. S., 14 Tex. Ap. 200; Lane v. S., 16 Tex. Ap. 172.

[4] Jones v. S., 9 Tex. Ap. 178. But where a minor was prosecuted for wantonly killing a dog, evidence of instructions from his father to do so should the animal be again found in mischief on the premises was held not material: McDaniel v. S., 5 Tex. Ap. 475.

[5] Davis v. S., 12 Tex. Ap. 11; Payne v. S., 17 Tex. Ap. 40; McRay v. S., 18 Tex. Ap. 331; Chappell v. S., 35 Ark. 345; Murphy v. S., 62 Miss. 97; Ashworth v. S., 63 Ala. 120. And see *supra*, § 826. Tender of compensation to the owner is admissible on the question of wantonness: Lott v. S., 9 Tex. Ap. 206.

[6] Grise v. S., 37 Ark. 456; Hodge v. S., 11 Lea, 528; Hunt v. S., 3 Ind. Ap. 383; S. v. Porter, 112 N. C. 887.

[7] S. v. Avery, 44 N. H. 392.

[8] C. v. Brooks, 9 Gray, 299; C. v. Flannigan, 137 Mass. 560.

[9] C. v. Sowle, 9 Gray, 304; S. v. Goss, 74 Mo. 592; S. v. Hambleton, 22 Mo. 452; S. v. Greenlees, 41 Ark. 353. But if the charge is of wounding and killing, proof of wounding without killing will not be sufficient: Reid v. S., 8 Tex. Ap. 430.

[10] S. v. Watkins, 101 N. C. 702. The word "beat" has a sufficiently definite meaning to be used in the indictment: C. v. McClellan, 101 Mass. 34.

[11] C. v. Brooks, 9 Gray, 299; S. v. Allison, 90 N. C. 733.

[12] C. v. Flannigan, 137 Mass. 560.

of a spirit of revenge or wanton cruelty.[1] Inasmuch as the offense consists in the cruelty with reference to the animal, and not in any injury to the owner, it is not necessary that the name of the owner be alleged or that the animal be described except by its general species.[2] But if the allegation of ownership is made, it should be proved.[3] Where by the statute several different acts are named as constituting the offense, they may be joined conjunctively in one count.[4]

[1] Rembert v. S., 56 Miss. 280.

[2] C. v. Whitman, 118 Mass. 458; Grise v. S., 37 Ark. 456; Turman v. S., 4 Tex. Ap. 586. *Contra*, S. v. Deal, 92 N. C. 802.

[3] Bass v. S., 63 Ala. 108; McLaurine v. S., 28 Tex. Ap. 530.

[4] S. v. Bosworth, 54 Conn. 1; S. v. Harris, 11 Ia. 414. Even though they cannot be properly joined, allegations as to the others may be regarded as surplusage and the indictment upheld: S. v. Gould, 26 W. Va. 258.

CHAPTER 60.

VIOLATION OF RIGHT OF SEPULTURE.

§ 1165. **Failure to bury; preventing inquest.**— It is the duty of a person in whose house a death occurs, unless some one else is charged with such duty, to attend to the proper burial of the body, and for that purpose to carry it decently covered to a place of burial;[1] and to cast a dead body into a river without the rites of Christian sepulture is indictable as an offense against common decency.[2] It is the duty of a parent to bury the body of a deceased child; but he is not criminally punishable for not providing for such burial, even though a nuisance may be occasioned by allowing the body to remain unburied, if he has not the means to provide therefor.[3] If the case of death is one in which a coroner's inquest should be held, it is indictable to bury the body before such inquest.[4] It is also criminal to obstruct or prevent a burial or interfere with a burial service.[5] The matter of burials is one that may properly be placed under the control of a board of health, and it may be a proper regulation by such board that no one but a licensed undertaker shall be allowed to remove bodies from the place of death for burial.[6]

§ 1166. **Disposal of dead bodies.**— It is an indictable offense at common law to take a dead body and dispose of it for profit for the purpose of dissection.[7] So it was held criminal for one charged with the disposal of the body of an executed convict to sell it for dissection in the absence of any order made in the sentence to that effect.[8] There are in England, and many of the states, statutes by which the bodies of persons who are

[1] Reg. v. Stewart, 12 A. & E. 773.

[2] Kanavan's Case, 1 Me. 226.

[3] Reg. v. Vann, 2 Den. 325. And it was held that although the poor-law authorities offered a loan to defray such expenses, the parent was not under obligation to accept such loan and obligate himself to repay it: Ibid.

[4] Anon., 7 Mod. 10; Reg. v. Clerk, 1 Salk. 377; Reg. v. Stephenson, 13 Q. B. D. 331; Reg. v. Price, 12 Q. B. D. 247; Stephen, Dig. Cr. L., art. 175.

[5] Rex v. Cheere, 4 B. & C. 902.

[6] C. v. Goodrich, 13 Allen, 546.

[7] Rex v. Lynn, 2 Term R. 733; Rex v. Gilles, Russ. & Ry. 367, n.

[8] Rex v. Cundick, 1 Dow. & Ry. (N. P.) 13.

executed, or who die while in the custody of the public authorities, as in prisons, poor-houses or asylums, may be disposed of for scientific purposes, with the usual provision, however, that such disposal of the body shall not be made if relatives claim it or require that it shall be buried. Under such a statute it was held that if a person charged with the disposal of such a body, by misrepresentations induced the relatives to believe that it was already buried, and thus prevented their requiring that it should be buried as they might do under the statute, he was not guilty of a crime in afterwards disposing of it in accordance with the provisions of the law.[1] A person cannot have a lien on a body for debts of the deceased such as will justify him in refusing to deliver the body up to those entitled thereto for the purpose of burial.[2]

§ **1167. Violation of graves.**— The digging up and removing of a dead body after interment is an offense at common law,[3] and it matters not if the motive be a pious one, as, for instance, to take the body of a relative from a dissenter's burying ground and inter it in a church yard.[4] So it was held criminal at common law to exhume bodies in the course of an excavation made for business purposes, though the burial ground had been for some time disused.[5] The matter of removal of bodies once buried is usually regulated by statute,[6] and the intent with which the removal is made may be material in determining the criminal liability.[7] Such statutes usually relate to and cover unauthorized removals;[8] and if a removal is under public authority, whether it is caused for a legitimate end or not, if it is upon *bona fide* information sufficient to call for action by the public authorities, it will not be criminal, even though the proceeding is not regular.[9] The statutory provisions are usually specially directed against the removal of a dead body for the purpose of sale.[10] Evidence that a body

[1] Reg. v. Feist, Dears. & B. 590.

[2] Reg. v. Fox, 2 Q. B. 658; Reg. v. Scott, 2 Q. B. 659. As to larceny of dead bodies, see *supra*, § 542.

[3] C. v. Cooley, 10 Pick. 37.

[4] Reg. v. Sharpe, Dears. & B. 160.

[5] Reg. v. Jacobson, 14 Cox, 522.

[6] C. v. Loring, 8 Pick. 369.

[7] C. v. Slack, 19 Pick. 304.

[8] McNamee v. P., 31 Mich. 473.

[9] P. v. Fitzgerald, 105 N. Y. 146.

[10] By the Indiana statute the offense consists in the removal of a dead body without the consent of the deceased person given in his life-time, or of the near relatives of the deceased given after his death: S. v. McClure, 4 Blackf. 328; Tate v. S., 6 Blackf. 110. One may be guilty of the offense, though not present, if

is disinterred secretly during the night-time and is concealed tends to show that the disinterment was for an unlawful purpose.[1] The fact that a person has made arrangements with outside parties for the delivery of dead bodies to a medical institution is not sufficient in itself to show that he contemplated an unlawful delivery.[2]

§ 1168. **Desecration of cemeteries.**— At common law the defacing of a tomb or monument to the dead is criminal.[3] Where there was a provision by statute against desecrating graves, it was held that the crime might be committed by the owner of land on which an interment had been made, not constituting a public cemetery, if he had expressly or by implication consented to such interment;[4] but the ordinary statutes as to desecration of cemeteries apply only to such burying places as are established according to law.[5] However, it seems that the establishment of the place as a burial ground may be established by the user for that purpose by others than the owner of the fee,[6] and that the subsequent disuse will not authorize the owner of the fee to make other use of the premises.[7] Nor is the owner of lots in a cemetery entitled to use them for any other purpose than for burial.[8] By statute, the cutting down of trees or shrubs, the removal of fences, etc., in or about a cemetery, is criminal;[9] and under such a statute the removal of a fence may be punished, even though the fence had already fallen into decay and the person removing it had furnished better protection to the cemetery by inclosing it with another field.[10]

near enough to render assistance with the intention of doing so: Tate v. S., 6 Blackf. 110.

1 S. v. Pugsley, 75 Ia. 742.

2 Schnieder v. S., 40 Ohio St. 336.

3 3 Inst. 202.

4 S. v. Wilson, 94 N. C. 1015.

5 Winters v. S., 9 Ind. 172.

6 C. v. Viall, 2 Allen, 512; Lay v. S., 12 Ind. Ap. 362.

7 C. v. Wellington, 7 Allen, 299.

8 C. v. Wellington, 7 Allen, 299.

9 Phillips v. S., 29 Tex. 226; Lay v. S., 12 Ind. Ap. 362.

10 Phillips v. S., 29 Tex. 226. **Form:** The following was held a sufficient indictment for removing a fence: That A. B., on ——, did wrongfully destroy and remove the fence from around a certain graveyard near the town of ——, in said county, which said fence was placed around said graveyard for its protection and inclosure: Phillips v. S., 29 Tex. 226. And in the same case the following Massachusetts precedent is quoted: That A. B., on ——, at ——, in said county, one willow tree of the value of five dollars, of the property of one J. W., placed within the limits of a certain cemetery there situate, unlawfully, wilfully and maliciously did deface, injure and destroy.

PART XIII.

OFFENSES AGAINST PUBLIC HEALTH AND GENERAL WELFARE.

CHAPTER 61.

PUBLIC NUISANCE.

§ **1169. What constitutes.**— A common nuisance punishable criminally, as distinct from a private nuisance which is a ground for civil action for damages by the party injured, consists either in doing a thing which tends to the annoyance of the public, or neglecting to do a thing which the common good requires.[1] Where the civil code defines a nuisance as "whatever is injurious to the health, or indecent, or offensive to the senses, or an obstruction to the free use of property so as to essentially interfere with the comfortable enjoyment of life or property," such definition is applicable as defining a public nuisance under the criminal code when the act affects the public.[2] So a definition of nuisance in the criminal code is applicable in determining what are private nuisances when only particular individuals are affected thereby.[3] Some annoyances to the public which are deemed public nuisances are also punishable under specific statutes, such as keeping disorderly houses,[4] obscenity and indecency,[5] blasphemy and profanity,[6] the obstruction of highways,[7] and the keeping of places for the illegal sale of intoxicating liquors,[8] and common gambling.[9] An enumeration of

[1] 1 Hawk. P. C., ch. 75, §§ 1, 2; 3 Bl. Com. 216; 4 ibid. 167. This definition is too general to be of much value. Indeed, it is quite impossible to frame a short definition which shall clearly draw the line between what is and what is not indictable as a nuisance: See 1 Bish. Cr. L., § 1072; S. v. Baldwin, 1 Dev. & B. 195.

[2] Hackney v. S., 8 Ind. 494.

[3] S. v. Close, 35 Ia. 570; S. v. Kaster, 35 Ia. 221.

[4] *Supra*, § 1137.

[5] *Supra*, § 1157.

[6] *Supra*, § 1159.

[7] *Infra*, § 1184.

[8] *Infra*, § 1248.

[9] *Infra*, § 1306.

all the specific injuries which may be punishable as nuisances would be impracticable. It is sufficient here to indicate what forms of nuisance are deemed sufficiently public to be punishable criminally, and it is to be noticed that some things which would not, under any circumstances, be a ground for civil action may be deemed so far detrimental to the public as to be considered common nuisances; thus, the offense of being a common scold or a common barrator is recognized as criminal at common law, both in England and in the United States.[1] Other offensive and injurious acts which may be the ground for civil action for damages by a private party are punishable as public nuisances only when they interfere with the people in general in the enjoyment of a public right, such as the use of a highway[2] or a public stream,[3] or the right to pure air, which may be corrupted by noxious gases or odors so as to render it unwholesome and offensive to the people in general.[4] If the act complained of interferes with public rights, such as the use of a highway or public stream, it is immaterial how many persons are affected thereby, and proof of injury to one is sufficient.[5] So if the act is by statute made a common nuisance *per se*, it is not necessary to prove the annoyance to any number of people.[6] But where the complaint is of annoyance to the public by noxious odors, it must appear that such annoyance is to persons who rightfully pass and repass within the radius of such odors, or who reside sufficiently near to the source thereof to be injuriously affected;[7] and evidence that a single person living in the vicinity was annoyed is insuffi-

[1] *Supra*, §§ 26, 27. But the punishment by the ducking stool, which was formerly inflicted in England for being a common scold, has become obsolete and is not applicable in this country, even though not expressly abolished by statute: James v. C., 12 Serg. & R. 220.

[2] S. v. Close, 35 Ia. 570. For instance, the exposing the dead body of an infant near a highway so as to shock and disgust passers-by and outrage public decency: Reg. v. Clark, 15 Cox, 171. So it may be a nuisance to place spring-guns in a shop beside the highway so as to endanger the public in passing: S. v. Moore, 31 Conn. 479. Further as to danger to the public, see next section.

[3] S. v. Smith, 82 Ia. 423. In general, as to obstruction of highways or rivers, see *infra*, ch. 62.

[4] S. v. Close, 35 Ia. 570.

[5] S. v. Wolf, 112 N. C. 889; S. v. Smith, 82 Ia. 423; C. v. Hopkins, 133 Mass. 381.

[6] C. v. Buxton, 10 Gray, 9.

[7] S. v. Houck, 73 Ind. 37; Hackney v. S., 8 Ind. 494; Lippman v. South Bend, 84 Ind. 276; C. v. Webb, 6 Rand. 726.

cient.[1] The power to declare and abate nuisances is frequently given to municipal corporations, but such authority does not supersede the authority of the state with reference thereto.[2]

§ 1170. Further as to what constitutes a nuisance.— Any act which essentially interferes with the comfortable enjoyment of life or property, if it affects the public, is a public nuisance.[3] Thus, it is a nuisance to sell unwholesome provisions not fit to be eaten by man,[4] or to contaminate the water in a well,[5] or to supply to the citizens of a city unwholesome and poisonous water.[6] A public nuisance may be created by a mill-dam which causes the accumulation of decaying matter, rendering the air noxious and unwholesome,[7] or causes the water of the stream to overflow adjoining land, rendering it marshy and thereby corrupting and infecting the air.[8] A slaughter-house or a place where the carcasses of animals are accumulated, whereby the air is rendered noisome and offensive, is a nuisance.[9] So it is nuisance to keep a piggery in a city, which occasions

[1] S. v. Wolf, 112 N. C. 889.

[2] S. v. Wilson, 43 N. H. 415. And this authority, while it may be exercised to prevent the setting up of an obnoxious business within the city limits or portions thereof, will not extend to the abatement of a business already established unless it is a nuisance in fact: Wreford v. P., 14 Mich. 41. And see *supra*, § 66.

[3] S. v. Taylor, 29 Ind. 517.

[4] S. v. Smith, 3 Hawks, 378; S. v. Buckman, 8 N. H. 203.

[5] As by putting a dead animal into it: S. v. Buckman, 8 N. H. 203.

[6] Stein v. S., 37 Ala. 123. So it was held to constitute a nuisance to urinate in a spring near a public highway from which travelers were accustomed to drink: S. v. Taylor, 29 Ind. 517. And see *supra*, § 30.

[7] P. v. Townsend, 3 Hill, 479; Douglass v. S., 4 Wis. 387; S. v. Lord, 16 N. H. 357; S. v. Holman, 104 N. C. 861. And the long-continued existence of the mill-dam or the pond created thereby does not prevent the owner from being punishable for the nuisance caused: S. v. Rankin, 3 S. C. 438.

[8] S. v. Close, 35 Ia. 570. But the maintaining of a mill-dam will not be a nuisance if the smells and noxious vapors arising therefrom are of the same extent and nature as those that would arise from the river in its natural course: Beach v. P., 11 Mich. 106. Nor will the dam be a nuisance if the overflow and collection of water in pools is caused by the acts of others without the aid of the dam; as, for instance, by increased cultivation or ditching, bringing in an accumulation of silt which chokes the channel: S. v. Rankin, 3 S. C. 438. The erection of the frame of a mill-dam, which, if completed, would cause the water to accumulate in ponds, does not in itself constitute a nuisance: S. v. Suttle, 115 N. C. 784.

[9] S. v. Woodbury, 67 Vt. 602; Seacord v. P., 121 Ill. 623. And it is not necessary that the odors be injurious to the public health if they are offensive to the senses: S. v. Woodbury, 67 Vt. 602.

noxious exhalations and offensive smells.[1] A house may be a nuisance from being kept in a negligent and filthy state.[2] The keeping of gunpowder in large quantities in a city near to the dwelling of citizens or the highway is not *per se* a nuisance, but it may become such if improvidently, carelessly and unsuitably kept so as to cause danger to the public.[3] Indeed, in an English case, it was held to be a nuisance to keep large quantities of wood naptha in a warehouse in the business part of a city, no matter how carefully protected, the risk of ignition from outside being sufficient to render it dangerous.[4] A city ordinance making it a nuisance to keep a stallion within the city limits for service is invalid, such keeping not being a nuisance *per se*. In such a case, only the improper method of conducting the business would be punishable.[5]

§ **1171. Whether public benefit a defense.**— In considering whether certain acts constitute a public nuisance, the court will not weigh benefits to determine whether they are equal to the inconvenience and annoyance caused; for if it could do so, the citizens residing in the neighborhood of the nuisance would be subjected to a servitude to other localities without compensation, a servitude, therefore, not voluntarily assumed or legally imposed on them;[6] but works of public improvement authorized by the legislature which must, in their nature, necessarily cause some annoyance and unhealthiness in the neighborhood, are not to be deemed nuisances;[7] nor are acts of municipal officers in burning bedding, etc., during a small-pox epidemic, for the preservation of the public health, though

[1] C. v. Van Sickle, Bright. 69; C. v. Perry, 139 Mass. 198; S. v. Payson, 37 Me. 361; S. v. Kaster, 35 Ia. 221. Evidence of noise made by the animals at night constituting an annoyance to persons living in the city may be received as part of the facts connected with the nuisance: S. v. Kaster, 35 Ia. 221. The question whether such place is a nuisance is one of degree to be decided by the jury: C. v. Perry, 139 Mass. 198.

[2] S. v. Purse, 4 McCord, 472.

[3] P. v. Sands, 1 Johns. 78; S. v. Paggett, 8 Wash. 579; Rex v. Taylor, 2 Strange, 1167.

[4] Reg. v. Lister, Dears. & B. 209. That anything dangerous to the public may be a nuisance, see S. v. Moore, 31 Conn. 479, a case of a spring-gun, cited in the preceding note.

[5] Ex parte Robinson, 30 Tex. Ap. 493.

[6] Seacord v. P., 121 Ill. 623; S. v. Kaster, 35 Ia. 221; C. v. Van Sickle, Bright. 69; Att'y-Gen'l v. Leeds, 39 L. J. 254; Rex v. Ward, 4 A. & E. 384 (overruling Rex v. Russell, 6 B. & C. 566). And see *infra*, § 1195.

[7] C. v. Reed, 34 Pa. St. 275.

noxious vapors may be thus created.[1] Something must depend on the character of the business and the location and surroundings. While the right to pure air is in one sense an absolute one, yet in another sense it is relative, and people who live in great cities sustained by manufacturing enterprises must necessarily be subject to many annoyances and discomforts by reason of smoke, dust and noise, more or less disagreeable, produced by the enterprises which support the city.[2]

§ **1172. Acts under public authority.**— It is sometimes provided by statute that the place and manner of carrying on certain businesses in the city shall be regulated by the city council, but the licenses thus granted will not exempt the licensee from the penalty attaching to the maintaining of a public nuisance; such a license will only abrogate the common law to the extent of protecting the licensee so long as he carries on the business in a lawful manner, that is, by methods the least likely to cause injury to the public, and with the use of the greatest skill, care and diligence.[3] And the fact that the city authorities do not assign a place for the carrying on of such business under authority given them to do so does not excuse the carrying on of the business in a way that is unlawful.[4] But it is error to exclude evidence offered by defendant that he was carrying on his business under the permission and inspection of the health department.[5] Parties who act under legislative authority which provides for the construction of a canal are not liable to prosecution for an act done in pursuance of their authority unless done in a wanton manner;[6] nor will a municipal corporation be indictable for failing to remove a nuisance caused by an act done under legislative authority, although they are vested with the power to abate nuisances.[7]

§ **1173. Illegal continuance of use.**— It seems to have been thought at one time that if a business, when established, was lawful in view of existing circumstances, such as that there were no houses in such proximity to the place of business that the residents therein would be annoyed, that fact might be

[1] S. v. Knoxville, 12 Lea, 146.

[2] C. v. Miller, 139 Pa. St. 77; Huckenstine's Appeal, 70 Pa. St. 102; P. v. Rosenberg, 138 N. Y. 410.

[3] Garrett v. S., 49 N. J. 94; C. v. Kidder, 107 Mass. 188.

[4] S. v. Hart, 34 Me. 36.

[5] P. v. Rosenberg, 138 N. Y. 410.

[6] Butler v. S., 6 Ind. 165.

[7] P. v. Albany, 11 Wend. 539.

shown as against a prosecution for the annoyance suffered by people living in houses subsequently built nearer to such place of business;[1] but this is not the recognized rule, and the fact that when the business was established there were no houses in the neighborhood does not give a right to continue to conduct the business after the neighborhood becomes settled. There is no prescription in favor of a nuisance.[2] So the fact that the business was at one time adjudged not to be a nuisance will not bar a subsequent prosecution for causing a nuisance thereby.[3] Nor in a prosecution against the lessee of a canal for a nuisance created in maintaining it will it be any defense that the lessee maintained it as it had previously been maintained by the city from whom he has leased it.[4]

§ **1174. Liability of owner or servant.**— To charge one with maintaining a nuisance it is necessary to prove some act done by him with reference thereto; the mere fact that he owns the place on or in which the nuisance is maintained does not necessarily render him guilty of the offense of maintaining;[5] and a landlord who innocently makes a lease of premises and reserves no control thereof cannot be convicted on a charge of permitting the building to be used for such purpose.[6] But the offense may be committed by a person who is not in control if he leases the premises to be used for the illegal purpose, or, after having knowledge of such use, allows the tenant to remain when he might be ejected.[7] One may be liable for maintaining a nuisance whether he be sole or joint owner, or if he have care and control only. But as against the injury which might result from an abatement of the nuisance the owner's rights will be protected if he is innocent.[8] The employee may be indicted as principal if, being in charge and control and in the absence of the proprietor, he keeps and

[1] Ellis v. S., 7 Blackf. 534; Rex v. Cross, 2 C. & P. 483.

[2] Douglass v. S., 4 Wis. 387; C. v. Upton, 6 Gray, 473; S. v. Franklin Falls Co., 49 N. H. 240; P. v. Cunningham, 1 Denio, 524; P. v. Detroit Lead Works, 82 Mich. 471; C. v. Van Sickle, Bright. 69.

[3] P. v. Townsend, 3 Hill (N. Y.), 479.

[4] Delaware Division Canal Co. v. C., 60 Pa. St. 367.

[5] Bruce v. S., 87 Ind. 450.

[6] C. v. Wentworth, 146 Mass. 36.

[7] S. v. Frazier, 79 Me. 95. And see, for discussion of this question with reference to disorderly houses, *supra*, §§ 1140–1142.

[8] S. v. Haines, 30 Me. 65.

maintains the premises as a nuisance.[1] So a party who is the agent of a company may be guilty of maintaining a nuisance in the conduct of the business, even though his employment does not consist in managing the particular part of the business which causes the nuisance, if he, by virtue of his employment, exercises influence in such management and encourages and permits the acts causing the nuisance.[2] But an employee or servant cannot be indicted as principal unless he has some control independently of the proprietor or employer.[3]

§ 1175. **Effect of contribution to the nuisance.**— One who contributes to the contamination of water in a stream is guilty of the nuisance caused thereby;[4] but the defendant can only be held liable for the consequences which his act produces, and the nuisance complained of must be the natural and direct result of his act.[5] The fact that the parties complaining have indirectly assisted in the maintaining of the nuisance by employing defendant in his business and furnishing some of the material used by him therein will not be a defense to the complaint of nuisance in carrying on such business.[6]

§ 1176. **Intent and knowledge.**— In a prosecution for maintaining a nuisance the intent of the defendant is immaterial; the question is only whether his acts or conduct have caused the annoyance of the people which is complained of.[7] And knowledge of the fact that the premises maintained by defendant were a nuisance is also immaterial.[8] It is no defense that accused was pecuniarily unable to abate the nuisance.[9] The exercise of ordinary care or the performance of the act or duty with the best of motives and in the best manner known to ac-

[1] C. v. Brady, 147 Mass. 583; C. v. Merriam, 148 Mass. 425; C. v. Roberts, 132 Mass. 267; C. v. Kimball, 105 Mass. 465; S. v. Bell, 5 Port. 365. And see *supra*, §§ 189–192.

[2] C. v. Mann, 4 Gray, 213.

[3] C. v. Churchill, 136 Mass. 148.

[4] S. v. Smith, 82 Ia. 423; Douglass v. S., 4 Wis. 387.

[5] Gay v. S., 90 Tenn. 645.

[6] Seacord v. P., 121 Ill. 623.

[7] Seacord v. P., 121 Ill. 623. But where the complaint was of furnishing to the inhabitants of a city unwholesome water, it was held that the charge should have been that it was knowingly or intentionally done: Stein v. S., 37 Ala. 123.

[8] S. v. Ryan, 81 Me. 107. But it is said that knowledge of the facts or conditions constituting the nuisance must be imputable to the person sought to be charged: Nicholson v. P., 29 Ill. Ap. 57. And see S. v. McMahon, 14 R. I. 285.

[9] Baltimore & Yorktown Turnpike Road Co. v. S., 63 Md. 573.

cused will not relieve him from liability for his acts, if injury results to the public therefrom.[1]

§ **1177. Venue.**— It is the place where the nuisance is caused, and not the place where the act is done causing the nuisance, that determines the venue. Thus, if a nuisance is created in one county by reason of the backing up of water in a stream by a dam, it is immaterial whether the dam causing the nuisance is in such county.[2] And where offensive matter is discharged into a stream in one county which renders impure the waters of such stream as it flows through another county, the offense is one partly committed in each county.[3]

§ **1178. Indictment; charging public nature.**— At common law it is usual to allege that the acts complained of were "to the common nuisance of all the citizens of the state there residing, inhabiting and passing," or to use other language indicating the public nature of the injury;[4] but where the statute defines the offense, making certain acts nuisances *per se*, and not using the words "to the common nuisance," etc., or equivalent language, it is not necessary to charge in the indictment that the acts complained of were to the common nuisance.[5] If, however, the acts described in the statute are defined and punished as a common nuisance, it is necessary in some way to allege that defendant kept a common nuisance, and it is not sufficient to simply charge the facts specified by the statute.[6]

§ **1179. Charging the act.**— The facts set out must show that the nuisance has been maintained; it is not enough to allege facts which may or may not constitute a nuisance, according to circumstances.[7] But where the statute specifies what

[1] S. v. Portland, 74 Me. 268; Seacord v. P., 121 Ill. 623; S. v. Boll, 59 Mo. 321; Moses v. S., 58 Ind. 185.

[2] S. v. Lord, 16 N. H. 357.

[3] S. v. Smith, 82 Ia. 423.

[4] S. v. Bailey, 21 N. H. 343; C. v. Faris, 5 Rand. 691; C. v. Sweeney, 131 Mass. 579; C. v. Kimball, 7 Gray, 328; Mains v. S., 42 Ind. 327; C. v. Mohn, 52 Pa. St. 243. Where a statute defined a public nuisance as one "to the injury of any part of the citizens of this state," it was held sufficient to charge the act complained of as an "injury to divers citizens near said nuisance," without alleging it to be an injury to all citizens: Moses v. S., 58 Ind. 185. See forms of indictment, *infra*, § 1183.

[5] C. v. Parker, 4 Allen, 313; C. v. Howe, 13 Gray, 26; C. v. Goulding, 135 Mass. 552; S. v. Noyes, 30 N. H. 279.

[6] C. v. Davis, 11 Gray, 48.

[7] Morris & Essex R. Co. v. S., 36 N. J. 553.

shall be a nuisance, it is *prima facie* sufficient to charge the act in the words of the statute without any allegation of special circumstances to show wherein the injury consists.[1] If, however, it appears from the statute itself that the matter complained of is to be deemed a nuisance only when offensive to the public, then the circumstances showing it to be a nuisance must be stated.[2] It is not essential to use the ordinary words "kept and maintained," or "created and maintained," but any words which sufficiently describe an act, the commission of which will constitute a nuisance, are sufficient.[3]

§ 1180. Joinder of different acts; continuance.— Where the statute enumerates in the alternative various acts as constituting a nuisance, it is not objectionable to charge all of them conjunctively as creating one nuisance, for the nuisance may be single, notwithstanding it is created by various acts.[4] While it is usual to charge the creating and maintaining in one count,[5] a continuance is not essential[6] unless an abatement is sought, when a continuance to the time of finding the indictment should be alleged.[7] But it is said that the creating and continuing the nuisance are distinct offenses, not to be charged in a single count.[8]

§ 1181. Description of locality.— No more particular description of the locality than to show the venue is necessary when the abatement of the nuisance is not an essential part of the judgment, but may or may not be ordered at the discretion of the court.[9] Nor is a description of a particular locality necessary if the order is to be to the defendant himself to abate the nuisance.[10] But if the necessary result will be an order to an officer to abate the nuisance, the particular locality must be

[1] Seacord v. P., 121 Ill. 623.

[2] P. v. Rosenberg, 138 N. Y. 410.

[3] S. v. Noyes, 30 N. H. 279.

[4] S. v. Spurbeck, 44 Ia. 667; S. v. Hart, 34 Me. 36. And see Bish. Direc. & F., § 776. Whether a particular form as alleged must be proved, or whether some other analogous form of nuisance may be shown under the indictment, *quære:* P. v. Townsend, 3 Hill, 479.

[5] See forms *infra*, § 1183.

[6] S. v. Schilling, 14 Ia. 455; C. v. Gallagher, 1 Allen, 592.

[7] *Infra*, § 1182.

[8] Burke v. P., 23 Ill. Ap. 36; Hoadley v. P., 23 Ill. Ap. 39.

[9] C. v. Rumford Chemical Works, 16 Gray, 231; C. v. Tolman, 149 Mass. 229; C. v. Logan, 12 Gray, 136; Howard v. S., 6 Ind. 444; S. v. Lang, 63 Me. 215; S. v. Cox, 82 Me. 417; S. v. Sturdivant, 21 Me. 9; Jenks v. S., 17 Wis. 665; Seacord v. P., 121 Ill. 623.

[10] Kern v. S., 7 Ohio St. 411.

so described as to enable the officer to execute the order.[1] Where the statute describes the offense as keeping a "tenement," the use of that word in the description of the place is sufficient.[2] A tenement is one room or a suite of rooms occupied by a person who does not occupy the entire building in which they are situated,[3] and proof of the keeping of any part or parts of the suite of rooms as a nuisance is sufficient.[4] But the whole building may be alleged to have been kept and used as a nuisance, although only part of it was in fact so used, if the defendant occupied the whole of it.[5] The floor in which the tenement is situated and the street on which it fronts is a sufficient description if the building in which it is contained is accurately described, even though there are other rooms on the same floor and fronting on the same street.[6] But where a particular description is used, no evidence is admissible of a nuisance at any other place than that described.[7] So if the charge is that the nuisance was located near the residences of certain persons named, this is a matter of description and must be proved as laid.[8]

§ **1182. Abatement.**— The right of a private party to abate by his own act a nuisance injurious to him, provided he can do so without riot or other breach of the peace, is recognized at common law,[9] and is not taken away by statutory provisions for the abatement of nuisances by process of law.[10] So a traveler along a high road has a right to abate a toll-gate on a part

1 Wood v. S., 5 Ind. 433; S. v. Sturdivant, 21 Me. 9.

2 C. v. Skelley, 10 Gray, 464.

3 C. v. Clynes, 150 Mass. 71.

4 C. v. Buckley, 147 Mass. 581. But if the allegation is that defendant permitted a tenement *and* building to be used for illegal purposes, it is not sufficient to prove that he permitted such use of a tenement consisting of only a part of a building: C. v. Bossidy, 112 Mass. 277.

5 C. v. Shattuck, 14 Gray, 23; C. v. Logan, 12 Gray, 136; otherwise if defendant does not keep or occupy the whole building, but only a tenement or shop therein: C. v. McCaughey, 9 Gray, 296.

6 C. v. Hill, 14 Gray, 24.

7 S. v. Lashus, 67 Me. 564.

8 Dennis v. S., 91 Ind. 291. An allegation that the nuisance was situated in a certain named borough was held enough to show that it was in the neighborhood of dwellings: Delaware Division Canal Co. v. C., 60 Pa. St. 367.

9 3 Bl. Com. 5.

10 S. v. Moffett, 1 Greene (Ia.), 247. Thus, a dog that persistently assails people passing along a public road is a nuisance, and may be killed by any person so assailed: Nehr v. S., 35 Neb. 638.

of the road which has been left out of repair for a considerable time.[1] But to show want of malice in abating what defendant has considered a public nuisance he must introduce evidence to show that there was a general expression of opinion in the community to the effect that the thing abated was a nuisance, and that he had been advised of his legal right to abate it; his own mere testimony that there was such a general opinion is not competent.[2] At common law the court may properly, in connection with the judgment in a criminal prosecution for maintaining a nuisance, order the abatement thereof by defendant himself,[3] and such an order for abatement by defendant is necessary in some states to support the further order that in the event of his failure to do so the abatement shall be made by an officer;[4] and a general order to defendant to abate will be effectual, although the specific order for abatement by an officer is not authorized.[5] An order of abatement by defendant may be enforced by attachment for contempt,[6] and by committing defendant until the order is complied with.[7] But to justify an order for abatement, either by the defendant or an officer, it must appear that the nuisance has been continued up to the time of judgment.[8] Punishment for a nuisance may, however, be imposed although it has been discontinued.[9] If the nuisance consists in the manner in which the building or structure has been kept or used, the abatement should be of the improper use, and not of the building or structure itself;[10] but the owner cannot complain that he will be injured by an order for the abatement of a nuisance maintained by a tenant or occupant.[11] The proceeding under an indictment for a nuisance will not be postponed to await the trial of an injunction proceeding for an abatement of the same nuisance.[12]

[1] S. v. Flannagan, 67 Ind. 140.

[2] C. v. Tolman, 149 Mass. 229.

[3] P. v. Vanderbilt, 28 N. Y. 396.

[4] Barclay v. C., 25 Pa. St. 503; Campbell v. S., 16 Ala. 144.

[5] C. v. Alden, 143 Mass. 113.

[6] Schultz v. S., 32 Ohio St. 276.

[7] Taggart v. C., 21 Pa. St. 527.

[8] S. v. Hull, 21 Me. 84; Miller v. S., 3 Ohio St. 475.

[9] S. v. Noyes, 30 N. H. 279.

[10] Bloomhuff v. S., 8 Blackf. 205; Barclay v. C., 25 Pa. St. 503; S. v. Kaster, 35 Ia. 221.

[11] Delaware Division Canal Co. v. C., 60 Pa. St. 367; Chute v. S., 19 Minn. 271. But of course the statute will not be construed as involving an injury to the innocent owner on account of the wrongful acts of an occupant where such construction is not required: S. v. Paggett, 8 Wash. 579.

[12] Taylor v. C., 29 Grat. 780.

§ 1183. Forms of indictment.— It would be impracticable to give illustrations for all the various classes of indictments which must be drawn under the general head of nuisances, but a few will sufficiently indicate the general plan to be pursued. In most cases the statutes will furnish important assistance in determining what should be alleged.

GENERAL FORM; OFFENSIVE TRADE.

That A. B., on ——, and on divers other days and times between that day and the day of the finding of this indictment, near unto the dwelling-houses of divers citizens of this state, and also near unto a certain public and common highway in the county aforesaid, unlawfully and injuriously did kill and cause to be killed a great number of cattle, to wit, one hundred horned cattle, and the excrements, blood, entrails and other filth coming from the said cattle did then and on the said other days and times cause and permit to lie, be and remain near to the said public and common highway for a long space of time, to wit, for the space of one week; whereby divers noisome and unwholesome smells from the said excrements, blood, entrails and other filth, then and on the said other days and times did arise, so that the air was then and on the said other days and times greatly corrupted and infected, to the great damage and common nuisance, not only of the said citizens near the same place being and residing, but also of all the citizens of the state going and returning, passing and repassing, along and over the said public and common highway.[1]

NOXIOUS MANUFACTORY.

That A. B., on ——, in ——, near certain public highways and private dwelling-houses, did set up and maintain certain furnaces, boilers, stills, retorts and other apparatus for refining and preparing for sale and use petroleum and other oils, and on that day and divers other days between it and the day of the finding of this indictment, unlawfully and injuriously caused to be heated and boiled in said boilers, and other vessels and apparatus, large quantities of petroleum and other oils, and mixed them with other substances, and shook and agitated them in the process of refining and preparing them for sale and use, and thereby then and there caused to be emitted noisome and unwholesome substances, smokes, smells and stenches, which then and there filled and impregnated, and continue to

[1] This is an adaptation of the general form given in 2 Arch. Cr. Pr. & Pl. 607. And see, also, 2 Whart. Pr. & Pl. 674; C. v. Brown, 13 Met. 365. If it is desired that the court shall order an abatement of the nuisance, a particular description of the premises should be given: See *supra*, § 1177.

fill and impregnate, the earth and air so as to render the earth and air corrupt, offensive, uncomfortable and unwholesome, to the great damage and common nuisance of all the citizens of the state there inhabiting, being and residing, and going and returning over the said highways.[1]

MAINTAINING AN OFFENSIVE SLAUGHTER-HOUSE.

That A. B., on ——, in said county and near the city of ——, and at divers other times before said day and the finding of this indictment, at and near the dwelling-houses of divers citizens of said place and county, did unlawfully maintain and cause and procure to be maintained a slaughter-house for the purpose of slaughtering cattle and boiling the entrails and offal of the said cattle; and the said A. B. did then and there, and on divers other days and times before the commencement of this action, unlawfully kill and slaughter cattle and boil the entrails and offal, and cause and procure the slaughtered cattle and the entrails and offal of the same to be boiled, to the injury of divers citizens near said slaughter-house as aforesaid; by reason whereof divers noisome, offensive and unwholesome smokes, smells and stinks during the time aforesaid were from them emitted, so that the air then and there was filled and impregnated with said smokes, smells and stinks, and made offensive, uncomfortable and unwholesome to the citizens near said slaughter-house.[2]

MAINTAINING AN OFFENSIVE PIGGERY.

That A. B., on ——, at ——, near a certain public street and common highway there and near the dwelling-houses of divers citizens of the state there situate and being, unlawfully and injuriously did make, erect, set up, continue and use, and did cause and procure to be made, erected, set up, continued and used, a certain inclosure, pen and lot of ground in which he did then and there and does still unlawfully and injuriously keep and confine certain hogs, to wit, twelve hogs; and then and there did and still does feed and cause to be fed the said hogs, with offal, slops and decayed feed, and then and there unlawfully and injuriously did and does still retain and cause to be retained within the said inclosure, pen and lot of ground, the excrements, decayed feed, slops and other filth resulting from the said keeping and feeding of said hogs; which said employment and use of said inclosure, pen and lot of ground for said purpose, and permitting of said excrements, decayed feed, slops and filth to remain upon and within said inclosure, then and there did and still does occasion noxious

[1] See C. v. Kidder, 107 Mass. 188.

[2] This follows an information set out in Moses v. S., 58 Ind. 185.

exhalations and offensive and unwholesome smells so that the air then and there was and still is greatly corrupted and infected thereby, and other annoyances becoming and being dangerous to the health, comfort and property of the citizens of the state residing in that immediate neighborhood and to the health and comfort of the people of the state there passing, repassing, being and residing, and a common and public nuisance to said people.[1]

IMPROPERLY MAINTAINING A MILL-DAM.

That A. B., at and within said county, on ——, being possessed of a certain mill-dam and mill, with their appurtenances, situate near and adjacent to a common highway and public road and the dwelling-houses of divers persons and citizens of said county, did at the time aforesaid and on divers other days and times between that day and the finding of this indictment, unlawfully and injuriously cause and permit the waters of said mill-dam to overflow the adjacent lands as well of others as his own, by means whereof the water of said mill-dam or pond was rendered impure, corrupt and unwholesome, and the land overflowed as aforesaid by the means aforesaid was rendered and kept marshy and filled with noxious weeds and putrid vegetation and corrupt, impure and unwholesome water, whereby the air became corrupt and infected, to the injury and prejudice and to the great damage and common nuisance of all the citizens of the state there being and residing and passing and repassing.[2]

KEEPING DANGEROUS SUBSTANCES.

That said A. B., heretofore, to wit, on ——, in ——, unlawfully, knowingly and wilfully did deposit and caused to be deposited in a certain warehouse and premises of him, the said A. B., and near to divers streets and common highways there, and also to divers dwelling-houses of the citizens of the state, divers large and excessive quantities of a certain dangerous, ignitible and explosive fluid called wood naptha, to wit, ten thousand gallons of said fluid; and from the day and year aforesaid until the day of the finding of this indictment, there unlawfully, knowingly and wilfully did keep in the said warehouse and premises and near to the streets, highways and dwelling-houses aforesaid, the said fluid in such large, excess-

[1] See S. v. Kaster, 35 Ia. 221; S. v. Payson, 37 Me. 361. And see, for a simple but less comprehensive form, C. v. Perry, 139 Mass. 198.

[2] See S. v. Close, 35 Ia. 570; Stephen v. C., 2 Leigh, 759. The conclusion is made more in accordance with general form than that found in the Iowa case.

ive and dangerous quantities as aforesaid; by reason of which said premises the said citizens of the state during the time aforesaid passing and proceeding in, over and along the said streets and highways, and residing and being near to the said warehouse and premises, were in great danger and peril of their lives and property, and were kept in great alarm, fear and terror, and were greatly impeded, disturbed and incommoded in the performance of their lawful occupation, and prevented and deterred from using the said streets and highways and from passing and repassing in, over and along the same, as otherwise and but for the premises aforesaid they could, might and should have done, to the common nuisance of the citizens of the state and the endangerment of their lives and property.[1]

CREATING A PUBLIC DISTURBANCE.

That A. B., on ——, at ——, was a disturber and breaker of the peace of said state, and did in and near to one of the public streets of said town utter loud exclamations and cries, and did then and thereby draw together a number of persons, to the great disturbance, damage and common nuisance of all the citizens of said state then and their inhabiting, being and residing.[2]

[1] This is modeled on the indictment in Reg. v. Lister, Dears. & B. 209.

[2] C. v. Oaks, 113 Mass. 8. And see C. v. Smith, 6 Cush. 80.

CHAPTER 62.

OFFENSES AS TO HIGHWAYS.

I. OBSTRUCTION OR NON-REPAIR OF HIGHWAYS.	III. INTERFERENCE WITH OPERATION OF RAILROADS.
II. OBSTRUCTION OF NAVIGABLE RIVERS.	IV. LAW OF THE ROAD.

I. OBSTRUCTION OR NON-REPAIR OF HIGHWAYS.

§ 1184. **Deemed a nuisance.**— A form of the general crime of public nuisance is that of the obstruction of a highway,[1] or failure on the part of the person or corporation charged with such duty to keep the same in repair.[2] Thus, it is criminal to drive a carriage over the streets of a populous city in such a manner as to endanger the lives of the inhabitants,[3] or to run a traction engine bearing unusually large loads, back and forth, several times a day, over an ordinary country highway, to the inconvenience and danger of travelers and to the damage of the road and bridges.[4] The placing of spring-guns so as to cause actual danger to passers-by in the street, constituting an annoyance to the public of a real and substantial nature, is criminal.[5] It constitutes a nuisance to place goods in a public street for the purpose of sale by an auctioneer,[6] or to place a fruit stall upon the sidewalk, even though by permission of the owner of the adjoining premises.[7] Indeed, one carrying on a business adjoining the street which calls for an assemblage of large numbers of carts and drays in the street is indictable for a nuisance in thus causing an obstruction, even though the vehicles belong to other parties.[8] Nevertheless, some obstruc-

[1] S. v. Miskimmons, 2 Ind. 440; S. v. Berdetta, 73 Ind. 185.

[2] S. v. Rye, 35 N. H. 368; C. v. Central Bridge Corp., 12 Cush. 242. It is immaterial to the offense of erecting a nuisance in the highway that there has been no notice to remove it; the statutory provision for a fine for not removing after notice being cumulative: Kelly v. C., 11 Serg. & R. 345; 4 Bl. Com. 167.

[3] U. S. v. Hart, Pet. C. C. 390.

[4] C. v. Allen, 148 Pa. St. 358.

[5] S. v. Moore, 31 Conn. 479.

[6] C. v. Passmore, 1 Serg. & R. 217; C. v. Milliman, 13 Serg. & R. 403.

[7] C. v. Wentworth, Bright. 318.

[8] P. v. Cunningham, 1 Denio, 524.

tion of a highway is incident to the public use thereof, and may be so far recognized as a convenience to the public as to be lawful.[1] The question whether the thing complained of is an obstruction to the highway is a question for the jury;[2] but they are to take into account not merely the actual interference with the use of the surface, but the rights of the public in the street both above and below the surface.[3] The offense consists in the interference with the rights of the public; therefore it is not criminal to obstruct a highway which, by reason of natural obstacles, cannot be used by the public.[4] But the fact that the highway is impassable in one portion thereof will not excuse obstructions placed therein at a place where it is passable;[5] and the crime of obstruction may be committed although the obstacle does not entirely prevent the use of the highway and is even in the non-used portion thereof, for the rights of the public are not to be encroached upon.[6] To constitute a nuisance the way which is obstructed must be public and not merely private, even though it may be open to general use.[7] But a turnpike constructed by a company under a public charter for public use is a public highway, although it is to some extent within private control.[8] At common law, and under many of the statutes, the proceeding for obstructing a highway is the ordinary criminal proceeding for the crime of nuisance;[9] although cumulative remedies are sometimes also provided for.[10] So there may be the usual proceeding for abatement,[11] but other methods of securing the removal of the obstruction are sometimes authorized.[12] The right of a private individual whose use of the highway is interfered with to abate the nuisance seems to be the same as exists with reference to

[1] C. v. Hauck, 103 Pa. St. 536; S. v. Louisville, etc. R. Co., 86 Ind. 114.

[2] P. v. Carpenter, 1 Mich. 273.

[3] Bybee v. S., 94 Ind. 443.

[4] S. v. Shinkle, 40 Ia. 131.

[5] S. v. McGee, 40 Ia. 595.

[6] C. v. King, 13 Met. 115.

[7] U. S. v. Schwartz, 4 Cranch, C. C. 160; S. v. Price, 21 Md. 449; P. v. Jackson, 7 Mich. 432.

[8] C. v. Wilkinson, 16 Pick. 175; Northern Central R. Co. v. C., 90 Pa. St. 300.

[9] S. v. Cotton, 29 Minn. 187; S. v. Galvin, 27 Minn. 16; S. v. Brown, 16 Conn. 54.

[10] St. Louis, A. & T. R. Co. v. S., 52 Ark. 51; S. v. Galvin, 27 Minn. 16. The statutory remedy does not exclude the common-law proceeding: *Infra*, § 1195, n. Sometimes a special remedy is exclusive: S. v. Hayden, 32 Wis. 663; S. v. Smith, 54 Vt. 403.

[11] Matthews v. S., 25 Ohio St. 536.

[12] S. v. Berry, 12 Ia. 58.

other nuisances;[1] but a private individual is not justified in removing or abating summarily an erection put up by the authority of law, on the ground that the conditions upon which it was allowed have not been complied with, and an obstruction has thereby been caused to public travel, unless he shows that he has suffered peculiar injury necessitating immediate action.[2] The general discussion of the law of nuisances found in the preceding chapter should be borne in mind in considering the questions discussed in this chapter, and the general propositions announced in this section will be found further illustrated by the discussion in the following sections.

§ **1185. Failure to open or repair.**— At common law in England, the duty to keep highways in repair devolved upon some individual or parish, and a breach of such duty was subject to indictment.[3] In the United States the statutes usually provide for public officers whose duty it shall be to see to the opening and repair of highways, and a failure on their part to perform their duty subjects them to a similar proceeding.[4] But to subject such a person to punishment as such officer for failure of duty it must appear that the duties of the office have devolved upon him.[5] If there is anything which by statute is made a condition precedent to the existence of the duty on the part of the officer, the averment and proof must be such as to show the duty to have become complete.[6] So it may be punishable on the part of citizens who are required by statute to render service in the opening or repair of highways, that they have failed to do so upon proper demand and notice.[7] The fact that by

[1] S. v. Anthoine, 40 Me. 435; S. v. Smith, 52 Wis. 134; C. v. Ruddle, 142 Pa. St. 144; S. v. Brumfield, 83 Ind. 136., Dimmett v. Eskridge, 6 Munf. 308. And see *supra*, § 1182.

[2] C. v. Tolman, 149 Mass. 229.

[3] 4 Bl. Com. 167.

[4] Edge v. C., 7 Pa. St. 275; S. v. Hogg, 5 Ind. 515.

[5] But acting as such officer is sufficient to render him liable: S. v. Stroope, 20 Ark. 202; S. v. Moore, 23 Ark. 550. And the right of the appointing power to make the appointment cannot be questioned if he has acted *de facto*: Read v. C., 3 Bibb, 484.

[6] S. v. Hageman, 13 N. J. 314; C. v. Thompson, 4 Bibb, 230. But evidence that the road district is in debt will not be admissible as showing excuse, inasmuch as, notwithstanding that fact, it might be practicable for the officer to discharge his duty: C. v. Johnson, 134 Pa. St. 635.

[7] S. v. Pool, 106 N. C. 698; Bennett v. S., 26 Tex. Ap. 671; Ford v. S., 51 Ark. 103.

statute it is an offense on the part of the abutting property owner to obstruct the highway will not relieve the officer from liability in failing to remove the obstruction and keep the highway in proper condition.[1] The duty of seeing to the repair of streets in cities or incorporate towns usually devolves on an officer different from the one who is charged with the duty of repairing highways outside of corporate limits.[2] Where the duty of maintaining a highway rests upon private parties, as, for instance, where a turnpike is constructed by a private corporation under public authority, the failure to keep it in repair to the injury of the public is criminal.[3] Indeed, if by the charter of the company a turnpike is required to be kept in a particular condition, failure to comply will be an indictable offense.[4] In some of the New England states and perhaps elsewhere municipal corporations may be proceeded against by indictment for failure to keep the public highways within their limits in repair,[5] notwithstanding there may be a civil liability.[6] To fix a liability for breach of duty in keeping a highway in proper condition, it may not be necessary to show that it is absolutely unsafe if it appears that it is kept in a state which renders the use thereof by the public inconvenient.[7] Neither will it be any defense that there is another road available to the public, as it may be the duty of the corporation to maintain both of them.[8] Nor is it any defense that another corporation fails to repair a portion of the same highway, without which the portion which is charged as defective as against the defendant would be of no use; each corporation is to be liable for the breach of its own duty.[9] In such a proceeding against a municipal corporation, it is not a defense that the highway is open and in proper repair at the time of the indictment; the corporation may still be subject to at least a nominal fine for

[1] S. v. Moore, 23 Ark. 550. See, also, C. v. Boston, 97 Mass. 555.

[2] S. v. Jones, 18 Tex. 874.

[3] P. v. Cooper, 6 Hill, 516; Simpson v. S., 10 Yerg. 525; New York & G. L. R. Co. v. S., 50 N. J. 303. Nor is this liability abrogated by a statute imposing a special penalty to be enforced by civil process: Susquehanna Turnpike Co. v. P., 15 Wend. 267.

[4] S. v. Godwinsville Road Co., 49 N. J. 266.

[5] C. v. Boston, 97 Mass. 555; S. v. Milo, 32 Me. 57.

[6] S. v. Madison, 63 Me. 546.

[7] C. v. Taunton, 16 Gray, 228.

[8] S. v. Fryeburg, 15 Me. 405.

[9] C. v. Deerfield, 6 Allen, 449.

its neglect of duty.[1] In determining whether there is a duty to open or repair a particular way, the question whether it is a public highway is material, but this point will be discussed in a subsequent section.[2] Under statutes providing for the indictment of a town for failing to construct and open a public way, and also for failure to keep the way in repair, there may be a liability for unreasonable delay in taking steps to raise and put in repair a road laid out by the proper authorities.[3] The allegations of the indictment must conform to the facts, and there cannot be a conviction for failing to construct and open a newly-laid out road under a charge for neglecting to repair a road already in existence.[4] And the state of the road complained of, as that it was bad or needed making, or was not passable, etc., should be alleged.[5] By some statutes a punishment is imposed for defacing a highway; that is, by making an improper change therein, inconsistent with the plan under which it has been constructed.[6] There are usually provisions requiring road officers to put up sign boards and mile posts, and a failure to do so may be indictable.[7] So it may be made criminal to deface or destroy a mile post or sign board erected by a public officer or by private enterprise.[8]

§ **1186. Obstruction; what constitutes.**—The placing of any obstruction upon a highway and the keeping of it therein for any considerable space of time is an obstruction of the highway and a nuisance,[9] and it is not essential that the obstruction or erection complained of be across the traveled part of the way, but any obstruction which renders the way less commodious is a nuisance.[10] So an obstruction may be a nuisance though it is on the part of the way not actually maintained in condition for travel or at the unused side of the way.[11] It is enough that the public are materially inconvenienced in

[1] S. v. Fryeburg, 15 Me. 405.

[2] *Infra*, § 1190.

[3] S. v. Landaff, 22 N. H. 588.

[4] Walpole v. S., 16 N. H. 157; S. v. Canterbury, 28 N. H. 195. So failure to construct a bridge cannot be shown under a charge for failure to repair or make a highway: S. v. Canterbury, 28 N. H. 195.

[5] S. v. Canterbury, 28 N. H. 195. For a form of information charging failure to keep a highway in repair which was held sufficient, see S. v. Raymond, 27 N. H. 388.

[6] S. v. Hunter, 68 Ia. 447.

[7] S. v. Nicholson, 2 Murphy, 135; S. v. Mathis, 30 Tex. 506.

[8] Pullum v. S., 88 Ala. 190.

[9] C. v. King, 13 Met. 115.

[10] S. v. Merrit, 35 Conn. 314.

[11] C. v. King, 13 Met. 115.

passing to and fro and that the obstruction is protracted unreasonably, and not merely temporarily and from necessity.[1] Thus, it is an obstruction that the steps of a building project into the highway,[2] or that goods or stalls for the sale of goods are kept or set up upon a portion of the highway, although passage is not entirely obstructed thereby.[3] An obstruction includes any object which unnecessarily impedes or incommodes the lawful use of the highway by the people;[4] but the question as to whether a particular use of the highway constitutes a nuisance must depend somewhat on circumstances, and the fact that the obstruction in question is useful to the public and recognized as a public convenience may render it lawful.[5] In determining this question the amount of travel and the use to which the highway is put and its location may be considered and its condition as compared with that of other similar ordinary roads.[6] So it may not constitute a nuisance *per se* to keep a market cart standing in a street for an hour or so at a time, it appearing that there is no prevention of the ordinary passing and repassing by vehicles and foot passengers.[7] Of course, an obstruction is not criminal if it is erected by virtue of lawful authority;[8] but if a permanent obstruction is placed in the streets without lawful authority it is no justification that its erection is beneficial to the public.[9] The obstruction may be indirect, as by damming a stream and causing it to overflow the highway or render a ford impassable.[10] So filling up a high-

[1] P. v. Cunningham, 1 Denio, 524; Clift v. S., 6 Ind. Ap. 199.

[2] C. v. Blaisdell, 107 Mass. 234.

[3] C. v. Wentworth, Bright. 318; C. v. Passmore, 1 Serg. & R. 217; C. v. Milliman, 13 Serg. & R. 403. So scales erected in a public street for private business may be removed by order of the council: Emerson v. Babcock, 66 Ia. 257. When the space in front of lots in a city is granted to the owners of the lots for certain purposes enumerated in the dedication, the use thereof for any other purpose may be an obstruction: P. v. Carpenter, 1 Mich. 273.

[4] S. v. Leaver, 62 Wis. 387. But by the Wisconsin statute there is a distinction between obstruction and encroachment: S. v. Pomeroy, 73 Wis. 664.

[5] C. v. Hauck, 103 Pa. St. 536. Thus, the placing of a railing around a public square with gates at convenient intervals may be proper if under public authority, and not indictable as a nuisance: S. v. Commissioners, 3 Hill (S. C.), 149.

[6] C. v. Taunton, 16 Gray, 228.

[7] S. v. Edens, 85 N. C. 522.

[8] Baker v. S., 27 Ind. 485; Neaderhouser v. S., 28 Ind. 257.

[9] See *infra*, § 1195.

[10] S. v. Smith, 54 Vt. 403; Prim v. S., 36 Ala. 244; S. v. Phipps, 4 Ind. 515; Dimmett v. Eskridge, 6 Munf. 308.

way or taking a part therefrom so as to reduce the grade may be criminal.[1]

§ 1187. **Obstruction by railroads.**— In the absence of statutory authority it is criminal for a railway company to obstruct a highway by the laying of its tracks across such highway, either below or above grade;[2] but statutory provision is usually made, either in the charter of such company or by general statute applicable to them, by which they are allowed to lay their tracks across highways, being charged with the duty of leaving the highway in good condition after the crossing is made, and the temporary obstruction to the highway due to the construction of a track will not be an indictable nuisance.[3] If the company fails to put the highway in good condition after the laying of its track, it may be indicted for a nuisance although the track was laid under lawful authority.[4] Where the railroad crosses an ordinary highway the company is not bound to construct the bridges made necessary to the full width of the highway; the question will only be whether the railroad unnecessarily impedes the usefulness of the highway.[5] But a street railway must be kept in such condition to its entire width that it shall not obstruct travel either across or along it, otherwise it will constitute a nuisance.[6] A railway being constructed across a highway under proper authority does not constitute a nuisance though the use of it to some extent obstructs traffic, if all reasonable care is used to render the traffic as safe and convenient as practicable;[7] but an unnecessary obstruction, as by leaving a hand-car stand on the track at a crossing, may be punishable as a nuisance.[8] So it may be a

[1] S. v. Peckard, 5 Harr. 500; C. v. Ruddle, 142 Pa. St. 144.

[2] St. Louis, A. & T. R. Co. v. S., 52 Ark. 51.

[3] S. v. Portland, S. & P. R. Co., 58 Me. 46; S. v. Chicago, B. & P. R. Co., 63 Ia. 508. But if a railway is constructed across the highway without authority, the obstruction resulting from the process of construction is a nuisance: C. v. Vermont & M. R. Corp., 4 Gray, 22.

[4] S. v. Monongahela R. Co., 37 W. Va. 108; S. v. Ohio River R. Co., 38 W. Va. 242. In restoring the highway the company may use planks, but must keep the plank crossing in good condition: S. v. Roanoke R. & L. Co., 109 N. C. 860.

[5] P. v. New York, N. H. & H. R. Co., 89 N. Y. 266.

[6] Memphis P. P. & B. R. Co. v. S., 87 Tenn. 746.

[7] S. v. Louisville, N. A. & C. R. Co., 86 Ind. 114.

[8] Cincinnati R. Co. v. C., 80 Ky. 137. And see S. v. Chicago, M. & St. P. R. Co., 77 Ia. 442.

nuisance to cross the highway with trains running at full speed without warning.[1] But there are usually statutory regulations as to how long trains shall be allowed to stand on the track at street crossings,[2] and a violation of such regulations by the servants of the company will render the company liable, no matter how much care has been exercised by the company itself in instructing its employees to conform to the regulations.[3]

§ 1188. **Continuance of obstruction.**— Where an obstruction has been placed in a highway by a previous owner and the grantee maintains it or allows the highway to be out of repair by reason of such obstruction, the grantee may be liable for the nuisance;[4] but the original proprietor will not be liable for the nuisance as existing after his ownership or control has terminated unless he has participated in some way in the additional obstruction.[5] Under some statutes the offense of continuing a nuisance is distinct from that of erecting or causing it,[6] and merely to allow an obstruction to remain will not be criminal on the part of one who did not originally cause it,[7] at least until after notice to remove the obstruction.[8] So it is not a nuisance to fail to remove a fence where a newly-established highway is laid out until after reasonable notice requiring its removal.[9]

§ 1189. **The intent.**— Intent to obstruct is not a material part of the crime of obstructing, and is only of importance in determining whether the act was wilful or merely accidental.[10] Thus, it is no defense that the accused had permission from an

[1] Louisville, C. & L. R. Co. v. C., 80 Ky. 143.

[2] S. v. Malone, 8 Ind. Ap. 8.

[3] C. v. New York, N. H. & H. R. Co., 112 Mass. 412. But it has been held that the superintendent of a railroad company cannot be convicted for wilfully obstructing the public road by cars placed therein by employees in violation of his positive instructions: Gude v. S., 76 Ala. 100.

[4] New York & G. L. R. Co. v. S., 50 N. J. 303; S. v. Troy & Boston R. Co., 57 Vt. 144; S. v. Yarrell, 12 Ired. 130; S. v. Willis, Busbee, 223.

[5] Watson v. S., 25 Tex. Ap. 651. The owner of premises may be liable for obstruction of the highway caused by a contractor in building a house on such premises if it appears that he has any control over the work: Sanders v. S., 18 Ark. 198.

[6] S. v. Brown, 16 Conn. 54; Lowe v. P., 28 Ill. 518; P. v. Young, 72 Ill. 411; Hoadley v. P., 23 Ill. Ap. 39.

[7] S. v. Pollok, 4 Ired. 303; S. v. Hunter, 5 Ired. 369; Freeman v. S., 6 Porter, 372.

[8] Sweeney v. P., 28 Ill. 208.

[9] S. v. Ratliff, 32 Ia. 189; Rankin v. S., 25 Tex. Ap. 694.

[10] S. v. Gould, 40 Ia. 372. The indictment need not, therefore, allege

unauthorized officer;[1] nor that he honestly believed the obstruction to be on his own land.[2] But some statutes define the crime as that of wilfully or knowingly obstructing,[3] and in such case wilfulness must be proved; it cannot be presumed.[4] To prove a wilful obstruction it is not enough to show that it was voluntary or intentional; but wilfulness implies disregard of law, and therefore one who acts in good faith and under permission from the proper authorities, although erroneously given, is not punishable criminally.[5] But if defendant relies on a discontinuance of the road by the county authorities which was in fact without jurisdiction, he must be presumed to have known of the want of jurisdiction, and an obstruction placed and maintained by him in such highway in opposition to the command of the authorities to remove it will be criminal.[6] At common law there is said to be an implied license on the part of the public, when the highway becomes impassable, to drive over the adjoining land, and this privilege is not to be deemed a taking of land for public use without compensation, but is acquired by the public in connection with the acquisition of the highway itself.[7] But this principle will not justify one who finds a city street impassable in driving upon the sidewalk contrary to law, and obstructing the use of such sidewalk by pedestrians, for whom it is specially set apart.[8]

§ **1190. What deemed highway.**— To support a conviction either for obstructing or for failing to keep in repair, it must appear that the road in question was a public highway.[9] If the road has been laid out without authority there can be no conviction.[10] Nor is it sufficient that it is a highway on paper merely, not having been laid out on the ground and no steps

the act to have been knowingly and wilfully done: S. v. Chesapeake & Ohio R. Co., 24 W. Va. 809.

1 Nichols v. S., 89 Ind. 298.

2 C. v. Dicken, 145 Pa. St. 453.

3 Wyman v. S., 13 Wis. 663; Prim v. S., 36 Ala. 244; Dimmett v. Eskridge, 6 Munf. 308; Shubert v. S., 16 Tex. Ap. 645; Trice v. S., 17 Tex. Ap. 43. Under such a statute the indictment must allege the *scienter:* Bailey v. C., 78 Va. 19.

4 Brinkoeter v. S., 14 Tex. Ap. 67.

5 S. v. Preston, 34 Wis. 675.

6 S. v. Castle, 44 Wis. 670.

7 Campbell v. Race, 7 Cush. 408.

8 S. v. Brown, 109 N. C. 802.

9 S. v. Moore, 23 Ark. 550.

10 Clark v. C., 33 Pa. St. 112; Ward v. S., 12 Lea, 469; Laroe v. S., 30 Tex. Ap. 374.

having been taken to open it.[1] So if a highway is impassable by reason of natural obstacles and cannot be used, there is no crime committed in obstructing it.[2] So, also, if the road has been discontinued by lawful authority, there can be no crime in a public officer failing to keep it in repair;[3] and there may be an abandonment by lapse of time and the action of adjoining land-owners in fencing in the land, obliterating the road so that it is not capable of identification, so that the officer is not bound to repair it.[4] But mere failure to use a portion of a public highway properly established will not be a defense for placing an obstruction therein.[5] Usually land does not become a public highway until it is acquired by the public authorities in a legal manner, or a dedication has been made by the owner, or there has been actual user by the public for a sufficiently long period to show a prescription.[6] The use, in order to give rise to a prescriptive right, must be adverse to the rights of the owner of the land;[7] and such use must not only be with the knowledge of the owner, but with his consent, express or implied.[8] Where a dedication is relied on there must also be

[1] C. v. Noxon, 121 Mass. 42; Jackson v. P., 9 Mich. 111; Bailey v. C., 78 Va. 19; Day v. S., 14 Tex. Ap. 26.

[2] S. v. Shinkle, 40 Ia. 131. But if duly laid out, the fact that it is not yet traveled will be no defense: Harrow v. S., 1 Greene (Ia.), 439. Nor will it be any defense that another portion of the road is impassable if that portion obstructed is capable of use: S. v. McGee, 40 Ia. 595. Of course it is no excuse that others have made similar obstructions at other points on the same road: Henline v. P., 81 Ill. 269.

[3] S. v. Broyles, 1 Bailey, 134; S. v. Chappell, 2 Hill (S. C.), 391.

[4] Howell v. S., 29 Tex. Ap. 592.

[5] Elkins v. S., 2 Humph. 543.

[6] P. v. Jones, 6 Mich. 176; Mauck v. S., 66 Ind. 177. If, however, there has been a dedication on a condition subsequent, the mere breach of the condition will not excuse the owner in obstructing the road as dedicated: C. v. Smyth, 14 Gray, 33. The question as to whether the facts show the existence of a highway is for the jury: Zimmerman v. S., 4 Ind. Ap. 583.

[7] S. v. Stewart, 91 N. C. 566. Use of a highway for the prescriptive period without obstruction will cut off the right to revive an obstruction previously existing: C. v. Belding, 13 Met. 10. Prescription does not run against the public by mere failure to take steps to remove the encroachment: S. v. Wertzel, 62 Wis. 184.

[8] Sullivan v. S., 52 Ind. 309. Consent and user may be shown to prove a highway: S. v. Robinson, 28 Ia. 514. Use with assent may show a dedication without proof of its continuance for the period of prescription: S. v. Wilson, 42 Me. 9. But an indefinite use of a wide extent of open land will not establish a prescriptive highway: Friel v. P., 4 Colo. Ap. 259.

an acceptance by the public, either through the proper officers,[1] or by public use.[2] Long-continued use and recognition may be shown as proving the existence of the highway without any official action.[3] In a criminal prosecution for the obstruction of a highway the proceedings of the public authorities laying it out cannot be collaterally questioned on account of irregularities.[4] But if the proceeding was entirely without jurisdiction, that fact may be shown.[5]

§ **1191. Private ways.**— There may be roads used more or less by all persons who desire to pass over them which have not been so far dedicated or accepted as to become highways in such sense as to render an obstruction thereof criminal;[6] but in some states the statutes provide for what are called private or neighborhood roads, and to obstruct or fail to repair a road of this character is as much a crime as though it were a highroad.[7] Turnpikes, although controlled by private corporations, are nevertheless public highways; and an obstruction thereof is criminal.[8]

§ **1192. Streets, alleys and public places.**— A public street in a city or town is a highway within the statutes as to obstruction of highways;[9] but an alley not connecting public streets, and existing merely for the convenience of the lot-

[1] Mansair v. S., 60 Ind. 357; S. v. Paine Lumber Co., 84 Wis. 205; P. v. Beaubien, 2 Doug. 256. Public use without acceptance may not be enough to render a town liable for non-repair: S. v. Wilson, 42 Me. 9. Where a town is laid out by public statute, and its streets are declared to be public highways, acceptance by the public is unnecessary: C. v. McNaugher, 131 Pa. St. 55.

[2] P. v. Loehfelm, 102 N. Y. 1; S. v. Central R. Co., 32 N. J. 220; S. v. Proctor, 90 Mo. 334.

[3] C. v. Abney, 4 T. B. Mon. 477; S. v. Sartor, 2 Strobh. 60; C. v. Marshall, 137 Pa. St. 170; Michel v. S., 12 Tex. Ap. 108; Berry v. S., 12 Tex. Ap. 249; Hall v. S., 13 Tex. Ap. 269.

[4] S. v. Smith, 100 N. C. 550; C. v. Ditto, Hard. 450.

[5] S. v. Logue, 73 Wis. 598.

[6] S. v. McDaniel, 8 Jones, 284; U. S. v. Schwartz, 4 Cranch, C. C. 160; S. v. Price, 21 Md. 449; P. v. Jackson, 7 Mich. 432.

[7] Ex parte Withers, 3 Brev. 83; S. v. Mobley, 1 McMull. 44; S. v. Duncan, 1 McCord, 404; S. v. Floyd, 39 S. C. 23; Anderson v. S., 10 Humph. 119. A private road or path under this nomenclature is distinguished from a private way, the latter being not public in any sense: S. v. Floyd, 39 S. C. 23.

[8] C. v. Wilkinson, 16 Pick. 175; Northern Central R. Co. v. C., 90 Pa. St. 300.

[9] S. v. Mathis, 21 Ind. 277; S. v. Beeman, 35 Me. 242; C. v. Gowen, 7 Mass. 378; C. v. Boston, B. & G. R. Co., 135 Mass. 550.

owners, is not to be deemed a public highway.[1] Statutes specially referring to the obstruction of streets in a particular manner may appear by their provisions not to be applicable to all highways in a city, but only to the streets in the thickly-settled parts thereof.[2] Public squares and grounds used as means of access to public buildings may be deemed substantially public highways with reference to their obstruction, and may, in an indictment for obstruction, be described as public highways.[3]

§ 1193. **Indictment.**— There must be a description of the highway the obstruction or non-repair of which is complained of, and it is said that this description must be sufficiently definite, by naming the road or otherwise, to indicate what highway is intended.[4] An error in the description, so long as the identity of the road is established, will not vitiate a conviction.[5] It is sufficient to use any name by which the highway is generally known.[6] It is not necessary, although it is quite common, to state the termini of the highway.[7] Indeed, some cases would indicate that no other description than that the highway is in a certain county, town or city, as the case may be, is necessary.[8] It is not necessary to state how the road in question became a public highway; the allegation that it is such is sufficient.[9] At any rate, a general description of the road, with a particular description of the part obstructed, is sufficient.[10] The locality of the obstruction itself, not being material to the offense provided it is within the jurisdiction of

[1] P. v. Jackson, 7 Mich. 432; Bagley v. P., 43 Mich. 355.

[2] S. v. Hall, 22 N. H. 384.

[3] S. v. Long, 94 N. C. 896; S. v. Eastman, 109 N. C. 785; S. v. Atkinson, 24 Vt. 448; C. v. Rush, 14 Pa. St. 186; S. v. Commissioners, 3 Hill (S. C.), 149.

[4] S. v. Withrow, 47 Ark. 551; S. v. Lemay, 13 Ark. 405; S. v. Crumpler, 88 N. C. 647; S. v. Stewart, 66 Ind. 555; Alexander v. S., 16 Ala. 661; Nichols v. S., 89 Ind. 298. Where there are by statute different classes of roads, a mistake in naming the kind of road will constitute a fatal variance: S. v. Snyder, 25 Ia. 208.

[5] Harrow v. S., 1 Greene (Ia.), 439.

[6] Patton v. S., 50 Ark. 53.

[7] S. v. Harsh, 6 Blackf. 346; S. v. Hume, 12 Oreg. 133. But if the termini are stated they must be proved as alleged: S. v. Northumberland, 46 N. H. 156; Martin v. P., 23 Ill. 395; Houston v. P., 63 Ill. 185.

[8] C. v. Hall, 15 Mass. 240; C. v. Allen, 11 Met. 403.

[9] S. v. Madison, 63 Me. 546; Tate v. S., 5 Blackf. 73; Nichols v. S., 89 Ind. 298.

[10] P. v. Young, 72 Ill. 411; Martin v P., 23 Ill. 395.

the court, need not be proved as charged.[1] It is sufficient to allege the obstruction itself in general terms, as that it was by an embankment, a ditch, a fence, etc.;[2] but different forms of obstruction must not be alleged in the alternative.[3] The charge must show that the ditch, or other obstruction complained of, was in, across or upon the highway.[4] As in the case of other offenses, the particular day of the obstruction is immaterial.[5] If an abatement of the nuisance is sought it must be charged as continuing.[6] If the particular form of obstruction complained of is one specially prohibited by statute, it is not necessary to employ the usual allegation that the use of the highway for public travel was thereby obstructed.[7]

§ **1194. Title in defendant.**— In an ordinary case the fact that defendant has title to the *locus in quo* could, of course, be shown as negativing the existence of a public highway; but in Wisconsin there is a special provision by which, when the prosecution is before a justice of the peace, the defendant claiming title must set it up in writing, and the prosecution will then be transferred to a court of record.[8]

II. OBSTRUCTION OF NAVIGABLE RIVERS.

§ **1195. When criminal.**— The erection of bridges over or dam in a navigable stream so as to obstruct the navigation thereof is a crime at common law;[9] but by statute some forms of obstruction may be authorized, and if so, such obstruction

[1] S. v. Godfrey, 12 Me. 361; S. v. Buxton, 31 Ind. 67; Matthews v. S., 25 Ohio St. 536.

[2] S. v. Day, 52 Ind. 483; Thompson v. S., 20 Ala. 54.

[3] Johnson v. S., 32 Ala. 583. Nor is it sufficient to say that the obstruction was by a "number of sheds" without stating the number or otherwise specifying them: C. v. Hall, 15 Mass. 240.

[4] S. v. Baker, 58 Ind. 417.

[5] S. v. Forrest, 30 Tex. 503.

[6] Wroe v. S., 8 Md. 416.

[7] C. v. Derby, 162 Mass. 183; Matthews v. S., 25 Ohio St. 536.

[8] S. v. Doane, 14 Wis. 483; S. v. Huck, 29 Wis. 202; S. v. Blonien, 36 Wis. 303.

[9] S. v. Narrow's Island Club, 100 N. C. 477. A remedy for such obstruction given by statute does not take away the common-law remedy by indictment for a nuisance: Renwick v. Morris, 7 Hill (N. Y.), 575; Rex v. Stanton, 2 Show. 30; *supra*, § 1184. An owner of a vessel sunk by accident in a navigable river is not indictable for failure to remove it: Rex v. Watts, 2 Esp. 675.

will not be criminal, unless it unreasonably interferes with navigation.[1] Even streams not technically navigable, but which are used for floating logs, rafts, etc., may be so far public in their use that an obstruction thereof will be criminal.[2] So it is said that at common law it is a nuisance to obstruct the passage of fish in a non-navigable stream, but there may be statutory provisions warranting obstruction.[3] Obstruction of a harbor[4] or a landing[5] is also indictable. The erection of buildings or the making of deposits on the shore of a navigable stream, or of a harbor between its high and low water mark, not interfering with the navigation, is not a nuisance,[6] for an owner has the right to make reasonable use of the bank; but this does not authorize the forming of a pool for rafts by damming the stream, no such exception being made by the statute.[7] The act of congress[8] prohibiting obstruction of navigable streams is directed toward casting into or constructing upon the bed thereof anything creating an obstruction more or less permanent in character, and does not apply to the floating of logs or rafts which may temporarily obstruct the surface of a stream.[9] In charging the obstruction the indictment should allege the name of the river, and that at the place where the obstruction is complained of it is navigable and a common highway, etc., and should state the place where the obstruction is situated, and that it hinders the use of the stream by the public as a highway.[10] If the statute prohibits certain forms of obstruction the intent is imma-

[1] S. v. Freeport, 43 Me. 198; S. v. Godfrey, 12 Me. 361; Ensworth v. C., 52 Pa. St. 320; Renwick v. Morris, 7 Hill (N. Y.), 575. Whether the obstruction is unreasonable is for the jury: Reg. v. Betts, 16 Q. B. 1022; or for the court if the proceeding is in equity: Pennsylvania v. Wheeling, etc. Bridge Co., 13 How. 518.

[2] Gerrish v. Brown, 51 Me. 256. A stream is to be deemed navigable if so used and recognized: S. v. Thompson, 2 Strobh. 12.

[3] C. v. Chapin, 5 Pick. 199.

[4] Rex v. Tindall, 6 A. & E. 143; S. v. Wilson, 42 Me. 9.

[5] S. v. Graham, 15 Rich. 310.

[6] Zug v. C., 70 Pa. St. 138. Between high and low water marks both the abutting owner and the public have some rights: S. v. Wilson, 42 Me. 9. But the rights of the owner may be defined and limited by legislation: C. v. Alger, 7 Cush. 53.

[7] C. v. Church, 1 Pa. St. 105.

[8] September 19, 1890, ch. 907, § 6; 26 Stat. at Large, 453.

[9] U. S. v. Marthinson, 58 Fed. R. 765; U. S. v. Burns, 54 Fed. R. 351.

[10] Cox v. S., 2 Blackf. 193. The particular place of obstruction should be stated: U. S. v. Burns, 54 Fed. R. 351.

terial.[1] It is immaterial that the erection complained of would be beneficial to the public.[2]

III. INTERFERENCE WITH THE OPERATION OF RAILROADS.

§ **1196. What criminal.**— Railroads are in one sense public highways, and the obstruction or interference with the operation thereof is by statute made criminal;[3] and such statutes are usually applicable to any railroad, whether duly chartered as such or not,[4] and whether or not the company has lawfully secured the right of way;[5] and to street railways as well as those operated by steam.[6] It is not necessary to allege that the railroad company is a corporation or a carrier or that its railroad is used for travel.[7] It is not essential that the obstruction actually obstructed and hindered trains;[8] nor, indeed, that it was calculated to do so, if it was placed on the track for that purpose.[9] But the act complained of must be one calculated to obstruct the operation of the road in a way that would be dangerous, and therefore it was held that the act of pulling a cord used as a signal to stop the train, with the purpose of doing so, although unlawfully done without authority, was not criminal within the meaning of the statute.[10] But under the English statute it is held to be an "obstructing" to stop a train by signals without authority.[11] If the statute provides for the placing of obstructions on the railroad wilfully and maliciously so as to endanger life, the obstruction must be one

[1] S. v. White Oaks River Corp., 111 N. C. 661. In such a case it is not necessary to say that the obstruction was to the common nuisance, etc.: C. v. Knowlton, 2 Mass. 530.

[2] P. v. Vanderbilt, 28 N. Y. 396; P. v. St. Louis, 10 Ill. 351; Resp. v. Caldwell, 1 Dall. 150; Pennsylvania v. Wheeling Bridge Co., 13 How. 518; Rex v. Ward, 4 A. & E. 384 (overruling Rex v. Russell, 6 B. & C. 566).

[3] Weinecke v. S., 34 Neb. 314; Mitchell v. S., 94 Ala. 68; S. v. Oliver, 55 Kan. 711.

[4] Hodge v. S., 82 Ga. 643.

[5] S. v. Hessenkamp, 17 Ia. 25.

[6] C. v. Hicks, 7 Allen, 573; C. v. Temple, 16 Gray, 69.

[7] S. v. Wentworth, 37 N. H. 196.

[8] S. v. Clemens, 38 Ia. 257; S. v. Kilty, 28 Minn. 421.

[9] Riley v. S., 95 Ind. 446. Under a statute prohibiting the placing of obstructions on a track, whereby cars are thrown off, it was held not criminal to so place an obstruction as to throw off a hand-car, the statute not specially mentioning hand-cars: Harris v. S., 14 Lea, 485.

[10] C. v. Killian, 109 Mass. 345.

[11] Reg. v. Hadfield, L. R. 1 C. C. 253; Reg. v. Hardy, L. R. 1 C. C. 278.

calculated to cause that result.[1] Such a statute relates to endangering the lives of persons working or traveling on the railroad, and does not extend to an act directed especially against an individual employee by which the lives of travelers generally are not endangered;[2] but it is not essential that the defendant intended to take life, if the act is wilful and malicious and actually does endanger life.[3] Malice will be implied from the intentional doing of the act,[4] even though the specific intent to derail the train or imperil the lives of passengers is not shown;[5] for instance, where, after obstructing a track, the engineer of the approaching train was warned thereof.[6] The charge of wilfully and maliciously obstructing a street railway is established by proving the wilful intent on the part of a person whose vehicle is on the track of a street railway to follow his own convenience to the disregard of others, although there is no specific intention shown to injure the company.[7] Of the same character as the statutes just described are those which make it criminal to throw missiles at a railway car or locomotive in motion, or in use for transportation although temporarily stopped.[8]

IV. LAW OF THE ROAD.

§ 1197. Turning to the right; bicycles.— The general statutory provision in the United States with reference to the use of highways is that a person driving a carriage or other vehicle and meeting a person like himself traveling shall turn to the right of the traveled portion of the road, and it may be an offense not to do so whether the party who fails to drive to the right leaves sufficient room for the person meeting him or not, and contributory negligence on the part of the other person is not material.[9] The center of the traveled part of the road means

[1] Bullion v. S., 7 Tex. Ap. 462; McCarty v. S., 37 Miss. 411.

[2] P. v. Dunkel, 39 Mich. 255.

[3] S. v. Beckman, 57 N. H. 174.

[4] S. v. Hessenkamp, 17 Ia. 25. But the presumption of wilfulness is not conclusive: Allison v. S., 42 Ind. 354.

[5] Clifton v. S., 73 Ala. 473.

[6] S. v. Johns, 124 Mo. 379; Crawford v. S., 15 Lea, 343. To constitute the crime of attempting to wreck a train, it must appear, if no wreck ensued, that there was an intent or purpose to wreck: Nowell v. S., 94 Ga. 588.

[7] C. v. Hicks, 7 Allen, 573; C. v. Temple, 16 Gray, 69.

[8] S. v. Boyd, 86 N. C. 634.

[9] C. v. Allen, 11 Met. 403.

the center of the part which is worked, whether it is in the center or at one side of the highway.[1] A statute of this kind relating to carriages or vehicles applies to a bicycle.[2] This rule as to turning to the right is applicable not only to public highways, but to any road which is generally used by the public.[3] It is usually made criminal to ride or drive a horse or other animal upon a sidewalk, and such a statute is applicable to bicycles, as it is intended to cover the driving of a vehicle over the sidewalk, and there is no reason for a distinction between a bicycle and any other vehicle.[4]

§ **1198. Racing on the highway.**— It is usually made criminal to race along a public highway, as such an act involves danger to property and person.[5] To constitute racing it should appear that two persons engaged therein, and that they competed with each other in the speed of their animals.[6] It is not necessary, however, that any bet be made, or that a determinate distance be run, or that judges be appointed.[7]

[1] Clark v. C., 4 Pick. 125.

[2] S. v. Collins, 16 R. I. 371; C. v. Forrest, 170 Pa. St. 40.

[3] C. v. Gammons, 23 Pick. 201.

[4] C. v. Forrest, 170 Pa. St. 40. And see *supra*, § 1189.

[5] Robb v. S., 52 Ind. 216; Watson v. S., 3 Ind. 123; S. v. Burgett, 1 Ind. 479; Thrasher v. S., 6 Blackf. 460. It seems this would be so at common law: S. v. Ellis, 6 Baxt. 549.

[6] S. v. Catchings, 43 Tex. 654.

[7] Watson v. S., 3 Ind. 123.

CHAPTER 63.

VIOLATION OF LIQUOR LAWS.

I. General Statutory Regulations; Constitutionality and Construction of Statutes; Concurrent Federal, State and City Regulations.
II. What Deemed Intoxicating Liquor.
III. Systems of Regulation; License; Local Option.
IV. Illegal Selling or Keeping for Sale.
V. Special Exceptions in Cases of Physicians, Druggists, Producers, etc.
VI. Special Prohibitions.
VII. The Procedure; Indictment; Evidence.

I. General Statutory Regulations; Constitutionality and Construction of Statutes; Concurrent Federal, State and City Regulations.

§ 1199. General character of statutory regulations.— Aside from statutory provision there is no crime involved in the sale of intoxicating liquors except that of so conducting the business as to render the place where sales are made a public nuisance.[1] In general, in the absence of statute, intoxicating liquors may be dealt with as other articles of commerce.[2] From early times in England there have been statutes regulating the selling of intoxicating liquors,[3] and these statutes have been the basis of legislation in the United States. But this legislation has in recent years taken on such a multiplicity of forms that it is extremely difficult to cover it by any general discussion. The most common method of regulation is that of

[1] Stephens v. Watson, 1 Salk. 45. And see Rex v. Faulkner, 1 Saund. 249; s. c., 2 Keb. 506; Rex v. Edwards, 3 Salk. 27; Rex v. Marriot, 4 Mod. 144; Rex v. Ivyes, 2 Show. 468; *supra*, §§ 1137, 1169.

[2] C. v. McDonough, 13 Allen, 581; S. v. Fay, 44 N. J. 474. As to property in liquors, see *infra*, § 1267.

[3] The earliest English statute seems to be that of 11 Henry VII, ch. 2 (1494), which authorized the denial of the right to keep an ale-house. But the statute to which our present regulations are more immediately traceable is that of 5 & 6 Edward VI, ch. 25 (1552), which restricted the keeping of ale and tippling-houses to those to whom a license should be granted.

requiring a license to engage in the business, with restrictions, more or less specific, as to who shall receive such licenses, coupled with statutes more or less definite in their provisions by which licenses shall be denied in particular localities. There are also local-option laws by which municipalities and districts of the state, more or less extended, may vote that licenses shall not be issued, or, as against general prohibition, may authorize licenses; and in some states, finally, there are provisions, either in the statutes or in the constitution, prohibiting entirely the sale of intoxicating liquors except for some specified purposes. By way of further regulation there are generally statutory provisions prohibiting sales to particular classes of persons, on particular days, by particular methods, etc., etc. Legislation as to the sale of intoxicating liquors is, however, civil as well as criminal, extending to the regulation of recovery of damages by the relatives of persons to whom liquor is improperly sold, the declaring of contracts for the sale of liquor invalid, the recovery of money paid for liquors illegally sold, and finally, provisions for proceedings in equity by the citizen for the abatement of places where liquors are illegally sold, as nuisances, the noticeable feature of such proceedings being that the necessity of a jury trial is obviated. There are also statutory provisions as to the seizure and destruction of liquors kept for improper sale, involving the employment of the search-warrant. The discussion in this chapter will, however, be limited to the violations of liquor laws which are criminal.

§ 1200. **Constitutionality of liquor legislation.**— In discussing the police power it has already been pointed out that the regulation of the sale of liquors is justified in the interest of public health and public morals.[1] That the state may, in the exercise of its police power, regulate the mode, manner and circumstances under which the liquor traffic may be conducted, and surround the right to pursue it with such restrictions and limitations as the legislature may deem proper, is unquestionable.[2] A discussion of the constitutional questions involved in

[1] *Supra*, § 29.

[2] Giozza v. Tiernan, 148 U. S. 657; Miller v. Ammon, 145 U. S. 421; Crowley v. Christensen, 137 U. S. 86; S. v. Hodgson, 66 Vt. 134; Bostwick v. S., 47 Ark. 126; In re Hoover, 30 Fed. R. 51.

the exercise of this general power is not properly within the scope of this chapter, but it will be necessary to discuss some of the specific objections which have been made to liquor legislation under the federal and state constitutions in order to determine to what extent criminal provisions may be valid.

§ **1201. Federal constitution; fourteenth amendment.**— There is nothing in the fourteenth amendment to the federal constitution which restricts a state, in the exercise of police power, from regulating the traffic in intoxicating liquors;[1] for instance, the right to sell liquors is not one of the privileges and immunities of a citizen of the United States which, by that amendment, the states are forbidden to impair.[2] Nor is it a denial to the citizens of another state of the privileges and immunities granted to its own citizens for the state to restrict the issuance of licenses to sell, to those who are citizens of the state.[3] Notwithstanding the fact that liquor legislation may result in greatly diminishing in value or directly destroying the property in liquors which are kept for sale, and of property or premises devoted to the manufacture or sale of liquors, and may prohibit the pursuit of a calling which had prior to such legislation been recognized as legitimate, nevertheless, such legislation, even though no compensation is provided for the loss thus entailed, is not invalid as depriving persons of their property without due process of law or as taking property for public use without compensation, for all property is owned and all business is conducted subject to the exercise of legitimate police power on the part of the states, and the prohibition of the business does not constitute the taking of anything for the public use.[4] Furthermore, the statutes found in some of the states which provide that the unlawful selling or keeping for sale shall be a nuisance, abatable in an equitable proceeding without jury trial, the decree of the court being enforcible by punishment for contempt, does not constitute a denial of due process of law, the proceeding in

1 Bartemeyer v. Iowa, 18 Wall. 129; Beer Co. v. Massachusetts, 97 U. S. 25; Foster v. Kansas, 112 U. S. 201; Prohibitory Amendment Cases, 24 Kan. 700.

2 Bartemeyer v. Iowa, 18 Wall. 129; In re Hoover, 30 Fed. R. 51; S. v. Brennan, 2 S. Dak. 384; Bell v. S., 28 Tex. Ap. 96; S. v. Gray, 61 Conn. 39.

3 Kohn v. Melcher, 29 Fed. R. 433.

4 Mugler v. Kansas, 123 U. S. 623; Kidd v. Pearson, 128 U. S. 1; Kaufman v. Dostal, 73 Ia. 691.

equity to abate a nuisance in this method having been a recognized form of procedure at the time of the adoption of the fourteenth amendment.[1]

§ 1202. **Regulation of commerce.**— It has already been pointed out that a discrimination by a state statute between the right to sell property brought from another state and that produced or owned in the state itself will be unconstitutional;[2] and it would seem that some of the regulations found in the laws of the different states discriminating in favor of liquors manufactured within the state, or manufactured from fruit or grain grown in the state, or imposing heavier burdens on the sale of foreign liquors than those imposed on liquors of domestic manufacture, or exempting from the operation of a general tax wine or cider manufactured from grapes or apples grown within the state, or beer manufactured in the state, would be unconstitutional as an interference with the power of congress to regulate commerce between the states.[3] While there have been state decisions to the contrary,[4] and the questions arising out of these provisions have not been fully passed upon by the supreme court of the United States, yet there can be little doubt that all such distinctions based on the place of manufacture or ownership are invalid. There is nothing, however, in the federal constitution limiting the right of the state to prohibit the manufacture of intoxicating liquors for export; interstate commerce cannot begin until after the article is manufactured.[5] It should be stated, however, with reference to statutes which make exceptions or discriminations in behalf of liquors manufactured in the state or manufactured from the

[1] Mugler v. Kansas, 123 U. S. 623; Kidd v. Pearson, 128 U. S. 1; Eilenbecker v. District Court, 134 U. S. 31; Littleton v. Fritz, 65 Ia. 488.

[2] *Supra*, § 44.

[3] Walling v. Michigan, 116 U. S. 446; Tiernan v. Rinker, 102 U. S. 123; Webber v. Virginia, 103 U. S. 344; S. v. Deschamp, 53 Ark. 490; S. v. Marsh, 37 Ark. 356; Powell v. S., 69 Ala. 10; McCreary v. S., 73 Ala. 480.

[4] McGuire v. S., 42 Ohio St. 530; S. v. Stucker, 58 Ia. 496; P. v. Walling, 53 Mich. 264 (reversed on appeal: 116 U. S. 446). So it has been held that the state may prohibit or restrict the sale of liquors within its territory, although the United States has a treaty with a foreign nation providing for the admission of the wines of such country into the United States: S. v. Peckham, 3 R. I. 289; Charleston v. Ahrens, 4 Strobh. 241.

[5] Kidd v. Pearson, 128 U. S. 1; Pearson v. International Distillery Co., 72 Ia. 348. But in Rhode Island the statute does not forbid sale for export: Hanley v. Powers, 11 R. I. 82.

products of the state that their unconstitutionality in this respect will not necessarily render them invalid *in toto*, but the invalidity may extend no further than to the portion which provides for the improper discrimination.[1]

§ 1203. Restriction of transportation into the state.—For the purpose of preventing the procuring of liquor for illegal sale by those not authorize to sell, some statutes make criminal the transportation of liquors by railroads, except such liquors as are consigned to persons having a permit to sell for authorized purposes. But such a statute is unconstitutional as an attempt to regulate commerce between the states, it being held that although in the exercise of its police power the state may, for the protection of person and property within the state, exclude from transportation articles generally recognized as dangerous or injurious, it cannot, by simply declaring to be injurious a kind of property previously generally recognized as legitimate, make the transportation thereof from another state unlawful, such a regulation not being deemed properly within the scope of the police power.[2]

§ 1204. Sale in original package.—Following an early decision to the effect that the right to import involves the right of the importer to sell the imported article in the form in which it is imported,[3] it has been held that police regulations of the state with reference to the sale of intoxicating liquors are not applicable to their sale within the state by the person who brings them into the state, in the form in which they are thus brought into the state as articles of interstate commerce; that is, in the so-called "original package."[4] To exempt the sale of liquors within a state, in violation of its police regula-

[1] Tiernan v. Rinker, 102 U. S. 123; S. v. Deschamp, 53 Ark. 490; S. v. Marsh, 37 Ark. 356. See, also, C. v. Gagne, 153 Mass. 205; C. v. Kimball, 24 Pick. 359; S. v. Gurney, 37 Me. 149; S. v. Kibling, 63 Vt. 636; S. v. Amery, 12 R. I. 64.

[2] Bowman v. C. & N. W. R. Co., 125 U. S. 465; Ex parte Loeb, 72 Fed. R. 657. And see S. v. Stilsing, 52 N. J. 517. Further as to regulations regarding transportation, see *infra*, § 1242.

[3] Brown v. Maryland, 12 Wheat. 419.

[4] Leisy v. Hardin, 135 U. S. 100; Lyng v. Michigan, 135 U. S. 161; S. v. Burns, 82 Me. 558; S. v. Winters, 44 Kan. 723: S. v. Pfleajor, 81 Ia. 759; S. v. Coonan, 82 Ia. 400: In re Beine, 42 Fed. R. 545. And see *supra*, § 76. But sales in the original package to minors or habitual drunkards may be within proper police regulations and criminal: C. v. Zelt, 138 Pa. St. 615.

tions, from the penalties attaching thereto by such regulations, it must appear, therefore, that the sale is by the importer, or his agent, in the original package, of liquor brought into the state from another state or foreign country, and in such manner as not to constitute the place of sale a public nuisance.[1] The supreme court of the United States has not given any definite test for determining what is an original package within this rule, and some difficulty has arisen in the state courts over that question. It has been defined as a package of such form and size as is used by producers or shippers for the purpose of securing both convenience in handling and security in transportation of merchandise between dealers in actual commerce, and may include any form of receptacle holding a fixed quantity, either with or without subdivisions; or if, for purpose of sale, the package contains smaller packages to be sold separately, then the term "original package" is applicable to the larger package in which shipment is made, and which must be opened and its contents disposed of in smaller packages in the process of sale, and not to the smaller packages themselves.[2]

§ **1205. Effect of Wilson law.**— Soon after the announcement by the supreme court of the United States of the rule stated in the preceding section, congress passed an act known

[1] S. v. Chapman, 1 S. Dak. 414; S. v. Robinson, 49 Me. 285; License Cases, 5 How. (U. S.) 504. And see *infra*, § 1278.

[2] C. v. Schollenberger, 156 Pa. St. 201; C. v. Swihart, 138 Pa. St. 629; Keith v. S., 91 Ala. 2; Harrison v. S., 91 Ala. 62; Haley v. S., 42 Neb. 556; S. v. Chapman, 1 S. Dak. 414; Smith v. S., 54 Ark. 248; In re Harmon, 43 Fed. R. 372. And it seems to be immaterial that the top of the box in which bottles, separately wrapped and each marked "original package," are shipped, is open; but if the boxes are furnished by the carrier and fastened to the car so as to virtually become a part thereof, the bottles separately wrapped and directed are the original packages: Keith v. S., 91 Ala. 2; and this is so if the bottles thus separately wrapped and directed were by the carrier, without the knowledge of the consignee, put into boxes for the purpose of transportation: Tinker v. S., 96 Ala. 115. But in Iowa it is held that after liquors are put up in bottles, sealed, labeled and packed, and for mere convenience in shipment such bottles are put together in boxes or barrels, the separate bottles, and not the box or barrel, constitutes the original package: S. v. Coonan, 82 Ia. 400; S. v. Miller, 86 Ia. 638. But if the purchaser is permitted to open the bottle upon the premises and furnished with facilities for drinking the contents there, the bottle being retained by the seller, this does not constitute a sale in the original package: Hopkins v. Lewis, 84 Ia. 690.

as the "Wilson law,"[1] which provides that intoxicating liquors brought into any state shall be subject to the laws enacted in the exercise of its police power "to the same extent and in the same manner as though such liquors had been produced in such state, and shall not be exempt therefrom by reason of being introduced therein in original package or otherwise." This statute is not unconstitutional as a delegation of legislative authority to the states,[2] and is applicable to liquors already in the state at the time the act was passed so as to subject them to state regulations.[3] The effect of the "Wilson law" was not merely to authorize further legislation by the states but to remove the obstacles found in the interstate commerce provision of the federal constitution to the enforcement of existing state statutes of that character, and such statutes became applicable to liquor brought into the state without re-enactment,[4] for the state statutes were not invalid *in toto* on account of their interference with interstate commerce, but only so far as their provisions had that effect.[5] But even the Wilson law does not remove the objection to a state statute which prohibits the *bringing* of liquor *into* the state, and therefore the South Carolina dispensary act, by which it is attempted to prevent any importation of liquor whatever, except by the state itself, is in that respect unconstitutional as an interference with interstate commerce.[6]

§ **1206. Under state constitutions.**— Many objections to the various liquor laws have been raised under state constitutions, but, in general, such statutes have been declared valid.[7] Where they have been overturned it has usually been on account of some failure to comply with constitutional provisions

[1] Act of August 8, 1890, ch. 728, 26 Stat. at Large, 313.

[2] In re Spickler, 43 Fed. R. 653.

[3] Tinker v. S., 90 Ala. 638.

[4] In re Rahrer, 140 U. S. 545; In re Van Vliet, 43 Fed. R. 761; C. v. Calhane, 154 Mass. 115; S. v. Fraser, 1 N. Dak. 425.

[5] See *supra*, § 1202.

[6] Ex parte Edgerton, 59 Fed. R. 115; In re Langford, 57 Fed. R. 570; Ex parte Jervey, 66 Fed. R. 957. And see *infra*, § 1214.

[7] Lodano v. S., 25 Ala. 64; Perdue v. Ellis, 18 Ga. 586; Schwuchow v. Chicago, 68 Ill. 444; Streeter v. P., 69 Ill. 595; Dennehy v. Chicago, 120 Ill. 627; Jones v. P., 14 Ill. 196; Kettering v. Jacksonville, 50 Ill. 39; Timm v. Harrison, 109 Ill. 593; Santo v. S., 2 Ia. 165; McLane v. Bonn, 70 Ia. 752; Keller v. S., 11 Md. 525; P. v. Gallagher, 4 Mich. 244; C. v. Blackington, 24 Pick. 352; Lincoln v. Smith, 27 Vt. 328; Gill v. Parker, 31 Vt. 610; Bell v. S., 28 Tex. Ap. 96.

as to the enactment of statutes.[1] Sometimes particular provisions for the enforcement of the law render it unconstitutional, such as a provision for unreasonable searches and seizures,[2] or because imposing excessive fines or cruel and unusual punishments.[3]

§ 1207. Due process of law; taking private property for public use.— It has already been stated that such statutes are not unconstitutional on these grounds under the fourteenth amendment to the federal constitution,[4] but similar provisions existed in the state constitutions before the adoption of the fourteenth amendment, and under them some difference of opinion arose among the state courts as to the validity of such statutes, and in some cases they were held unconstitutional as in violation of such restrictions, especially as applied to liquors already owned prior to the passage of the statute.[5] The weight of authority, however, is distinctly against all such objections.[6] Questions have also arisen as to whether the procedure provided in these statutes is due process of law, but in general they have been sustained in this respect.[7]

§ 1208. Jury trial.— It has already been stated that an equitable proceeding for abating the illegal sale or keeping for

[1] Geebrick v. S., 5 Ia. 491; S. v. Weir, 33 Ia. 134; Koehler v. Hill, 60 Ia. 543; S. v. Baum, 33 La. An. 981; In re Hauck, 70 Mich. 396; S. v. Wright, 14 Oreg. 365; Cowley v. Rushville, 60 Ind. 327; S. v. Campbell, 50 Kan. 433. But see Adler v. S., 55 Ala. 16; Watson v. S., 55 Ala. 158; Parkinson v. S., 14 Md. 184; S. v. Becker, 3 S. Dak. 29.

[2] Fisher v. McGirr, 1 Gray, 1; Hibbard v. P., 4 Mich. 125; S. v. Snow, 3 R. I. 64; Baldwin v. Smith, 82 Ill. 162; Greene v. James, 2 Curt. 187.

[3] Robison v. Miner, 68 Mich. 549; Luton v. Circuit Judge, 69 Mich. 610. But *contra* see S. v. Becker, 3 S. Dak. 29; C. v. Hitchings, 5 Gray, 482; Pervear v. Massachusetts, 5 Wall. 475; O'Neil v. Vermont, 144 U. S. 323; *supra*, § 80.

[4] *Supra*, § 1201.

[5] Wynehamer v. P., 13 N. Y. 378; Beebe v. S., 6 Ind. 501; Herman v. S., 8 Ind. 545. And see McLane v. Leicht, 69 Ia. 401; Bartemeyer v. Iowa, 18 Wall. 129; Beer Co. v. Massachusetts, 97 U. S. 25.

[6] S. v. Snow, 3 R. I. 64; S. v. Paul, 5 R. I. 185; S. v. Keeran, 5 R. I. 497; McLane v. Bonn, 70 Ia. 752; Kaufman v. Dostal, 73 Ia. 691; Dickinson v. Heeb Brewing Co., 73 Ia. 705; Drake v. Kaiser, 73 Ia. 703; Drake v. Jordan, 73 Ia. 707; S. v. Barringer, 110 N. C. 525; Stickrod v. C., 86 Ky. 285; P. v. Hawley, 3 Mich. 330; Heck v. S., 44 Ohio St. 536; Ex parte Lynn, 19 Tex. Ap. 293; Steele v. S., 19 Tex. Ap. 425.

[7] As to proceeding by affidavit, see S. v. Whisner, 35 Kan. 271; In re Dougherty, 27 Vt. 325; S. v. Conlin, 27 Vt. 318. As a proceeding for seizure is *in rem*, it may be valid without jury trial: Lincoln v. Smith, 27 Vt. 328; S. v. Smith, 55 Vt. 82; S. v. O'Neil, 58 Vt. 140.

sale, as a nuisance, with punishment by proceedings for contempt for failure to obey the order of abatement in such case, is due process of law under the fourteenth amendment to the federal constitution, notwithstanding the accused does not have a jury trial.[1] Under provisions in state constitutions guaranteeing the right of trial by jury in criminal prosecutions, it is likewise held that an equitable proceeding which does not involve jury trial is sufficient.[2]

§ 1209. **License; impairing obligation of contract.**—Where a license law has been in force, the question may arise as to whether any statute imposing additional regulations or preventing the carrying on of the business by the person holding the license is unconstitutional as impairing the obligations of a contract; but it is held that a license is not a contract, and that the person who pursues his business under it does so subject to the police power of the state, just as any other business is carried on, and therefore if a prohibitory law is passed it takes effect with reference to those sellers having licenses as well as others;[3] and additional burdens or requirements may be imposed on those holding licenses.[4]

§ 1210. **Local or special laws; local option.**—There are various statutory provisions as to sales in particular localities, such as within a certain distance from educational institutions, or a church, or within a certain distance of a city; and also provisions as to licensing sales in cities of a certain size. Such

[1] *Supra*, § 1201.

[2] Littleton v. Fritz, 65 Ia. 48; Martin v. Blattner, 68 Ia. 286, 6 Am. Cr. R. 148, and note; S. v. Jordan, 72 Ia. 377; Carleton v. Rugg, 149 Mass. 550; S. v. Aiken, 42 S. C. 222; Ex parte Keeler, — S. C. —, 23 S. E. R. 865. The provision in the federal constitution requiring trial by jury is not applicable to the states but only to proceedings in the federal courts: Eilenbecker v. District Court, 134 U. S. 31.

[3] Prohibitory Amendment Cases, 24 Kan. 700; Calder v. Kurby, 5 Gray, 597; C. v. Brennan, 103 Mass. 70; Freleigh v. S., 8 Mo. 606; S. v. Barringer, 110 N. C. 525; Schwuchow v. Chicago, 68 Ill. 444; Columbus City v. Cutcomp, 61 Ia. 672; S. v. Holmes, 38 N. H. 225; Fell v. S., 42 Md. 71; Brown v. S., 82 Ga. 224; S. v. Fairfield, 37 Me. 517; S. v. Horton, 21 Oreg. 83; Robertson v. S., 12 Tex. Ap. 541; Weil v. Calhoun, 25 Fed. R. 865. But it is said that a law which repeals the provisions for license should not, unless required by its specific terms, be construed as annulling unexpired licenses: Hirn v. S., 1 Ohio St. 15. As to the effect of a United States retailer's license, see *infra*, § 1217.

[4] C. v. Donahue, 149 Pa. St. 104; State v. Isabel, 40 La. An. 340.

statutes, although to some extent local or special, are not unconstitutional.[1] A local-option statute is not unconstitutional as being a statute not uniform in its operation, nor as a delegation of legislative power to the people of a particular locality.[2]

§ 1211. **Uniformity of taxation.**— Licenses for the sale of liquors are imposed for the purpose of raising taxes as well as by way of regulation, but the regulation feature is usually deemed the principal one, and therefore the imposition of a license is not taxation in such sense that it must be uniform.[3] It is neither necessary that the license be at the same rate as licenses imposed on other forms of business, nor that it be uniform as to all dealers or all localities.[4]

[1] Streeter v. P., 69 Ill. 595; Dorman v. S., 34 Ala. 216; Ex parte McClain, 61 Cal. 436; S. v. Berlin, 21 S. C. 292; S. v. Muse, 4 Dev. & B. 319; Howell v. S., 71 Ga. 224; S. v. Rauscher, 1 Lea, 96; S. v. Shroeder, 51 Ia. 197; Centerville v. Miller, 51 Ia. 712; Toledo v. Edens, 59 Ia. 352; Hunzinger v. S., 39 Neb. 653. A special provision in the charter of an agricultural society prohibiting sales within a certain distance of its grounds during the time of a fair, except by persons regularly located in business, was held constitutional: S. v. Stovall, 103 N. C. 416. A statute applicable to a county or city of a certain population is not a special statute because at the time it is passed there is but one county or city in the state having such population: Hunzinger v. S., 39 Neb. 653.

[2] S. v. Common Pleas of Morris Co., 36 N. J. 72; S. v. Circuit Court, 50 N. J. 585; Rice v. Foster, 4 Harr. 479; S. v. Pond, 93 Mo. 606; S. v. Moore, 107 Mo. 78; Locke's Appeal, 72 Pa. St. 491; S. v. Parker, 26 Vt. 357; S. v. Noyes, 30 N. H. 279; S. v. Wilcox, 42 Conn. 364; C. v. Bennett, 108 Mass. 27; C. v. Dean, 110 Mass. 357; P. v. Collins, 3 Mich. 343; Feek v. Bloomingdale, 82 Mich. 393; Groesch v. S., 42 Ind. 547; Fell v. S., 42 Md. 71; S. v. Strauss, 49 Md. 288; Savage v. C., 84 Va. 619; Anderson v. C., 13 Bush, 485; Lemon v. Peyton, 64 Miss. 161; Schulherr v. Bordeaux, 64 Miss. 59; S. v. Cooke, 24 Minn. 247; Gordon v. S., 46 Ohio St. 607; Caldwell v. Barrett, 73 Ga. 604; Boyd v. Bryant, 35 Ark. 69; T. v. O'Connor, 5 Dak. 397; S. v. Bott, 31 La. An. 663; Trammell v. Bradley, 37 Ark. 374; Weil v. Calhoun, 25 Fed. R. 865. But a provision that the taking effect of the statute is to depend on a vote of the people of the state is unconstitutional; as, however, in this case the statute was regularly enacted, it was held that only the provision for submission was unconstitutional, and the statute went into effect without such vote: Santo v. S., 2 Ia. 165. In a subsequent Iowa case it was held that an act to license and regulate the sale of liquor which was to go into effect only in the counties where it was adopted by a popular vote was unconstitutional: Geebrick v. S., 5 Ia. 491; but see the explanation of this case given in Dalby v. Wolf, 14 Ia. 228. See, also, Maize v. S., 4 Ind. 342; Meshmeier v. S., 11 Ind. 482.

[3] Pleuler v. S., 11 Neb. 547; S. v. Hudson, 78 Mo. 302; Ex parte Hurl, 49 Cal. 557; Fahey v. S., 27 Tex. Ap. 146.

[4] Dennehy v. Chicago, 120 Ill. 627;

§ 1212. Conditions for granting license.—It is not unconstitutional to impose conditions on the granting of a license, such as that the licensee shall have a good moral character, shall not have been engaged in illegal selling, etc., etc.[1] Under some constitutions, however, it is not permitted to grant a license for the sale of intoxicating liquors, and the question then arises whether a tax on such sale is valid. For the purpose of taxation no assumption can be made that the business is illegal, the only question being as to its existence; and as the levying of a tax grants no privilege, it is not necessarily a license, nor does it become a license because one of its objects is police regulation;[2] nor is it improper to provide for the enforcement of the payment of the tax by a criminal proceeding.[3] But where the legislation went further and provided that both the payment of a tax and the giving of a bond should be conditions precedent to engaging in the business, the provisions of the statute were held to constitute in effect a license law.[4] The result of the cases seems to be that a statute establishing conditions which must be met before there is a right to engage in the business is in effect a license law and

Timm v. Harrison, 109 Ill. 593; U. S. Distillery Co. v. Chicago, 112 Ill. 19; Kaliski v. Grady, 25 La. An. 576; S. v. Rolle, 30 La. An., Part II, 991.

[1] C. v. Blackington, 24 Pick. 352; In re Ruth, 32 Ia. 250; Rohrbacher v. Jackson, 51 Miss. 735; P. v. Brown, 85 Mich. 119; S. v. Brown, 19 Fla. 563. But where the qualifications are fixed by state statute it is said that the municipal authorities acting under such statute cannot arbitrarily discriminate between individuals on account of personal fitness, no such discretion having been given: Ex parte Theisen, 30 Fla. 529. So it is not a valid exercise of power by the city to limit the granting of licenses to certain portions of the city to be designated by the mayor: S. v. Kantler, 33 Minn. 69.

[2] Youngblood v. Sexton, 32 Mich. 406; Adler v. Whitbeck, 44 Ohio St. 539; Pleuler v. S., 11 Neb. 547.

[3] P. v. Walling, 53 Mich. 264.

[4] S. v. Hipp, 38 Ohio St. 199. In Ohio, where a license law is unconstitutional, it was provided as a part of the taxing law that no person should engage in selling liquors upon land not owned by him without first getting the written consent of the owner, and it was objected that this was in effect a license law discriminating between land owners and those not owning land in regard to the privilege of selling liquors. This provision was at first thought to be constitutional: S. v. Frame, 39 Ohio St. 399; later it was held unconstitutional: Butzman v. Whitbeck, 42 Ohio St. 223; S. v. Sinks, 42 Ohio St. 345; but in still later cases the court seems to have returned to its first holding: Adler v. Whitbeck, 44 Ohio St. 539; Anderson v. Brewster, 44 Ohio St. 576.

not a tax, but that a requirement that the tax must be paid in advance is merely a taxing provision and does not render the statute unconstitutional as being a license law.[1]

§ 1213. Constitutional prohibition.— In some states the principle of prohibition as a method of regulating the sale of liquors is embodied in the constitution itself, with authority to the legislature to provide means for enforcing the regulation. Under such a provision the legislature may carry out the constitutional prohibition by statutes providing different means for accomplishing the object.[2] But a constitutional prohibition will not be self-executing, and until the legislature provides means for its execution, a previous license law is not to be deemed repealed.[3] Such a constitutional provision does not deprive the legislature of the power which it previously had to pass a prohibitory law.[4] Where the constitution authorizes the legislature to regulate or prohibit the sale, it limits the power which the legislature otherwise would have had to exercise authority with respect to the subject other than by regulation or prohibition of the sale, and under such constitutional provision a statute punishing the keeping for sale is not valid.[5]

§ 1214. Sale by public agent.— In a few states the plan has been tried of prohibiting all sales by private parties, and vesting the right to sell for proper purposes in some public officer or agent who shall have no direct personal interest in the business.[6] In South Carolina a recent statute vests in the state the entire and exclusive right to bring into the state and keep or sell intoxicating liquors. As to its interference with interstate commerce, this act has already been mentioned;[7] as to its constitutionality in other respects, the views of the supreme court of the state have not been uniform. At first it was held that the act was unconstitutional upon various grounds, the principal of which were that it abridges the individual rights of the citizens to engage in the business, and is not a police regulation.[8] But

[1] Fahey v. S., 27 Tex. Ap. 146.

[2] S. v. Becker, 3 S. Dak. 29.

[3] S. v. Swan, 1 N. Dak. 5.

[4] S. v. Kane, 15 R. I. 395.

[5] S. v. Gilman, 33 W. Va. 146.

[6] Lauten v. Rowan, 59 N. H. 215; S. v. Parks, 29 Vt. 70; Street v. Hall, 29 Vt. 165; Atkins v. Randolph, 31 Vt. 226; S. v. Fisher, 35 Vt. 584; Baldwin v. Coburn, 39 Vt. 441; S. v. Bartlett, 43 Vt. 86.

[7] *Supra*, § 1205.

[8] S. v. Jacobs, 41 S. C. 220; Ex parte Brunson, 41 S. C. 501. And see In re Langford, 57 Fed. R. 570.

in the later cases the constitutionality of the act has been upheld as a police regulation.[1] In each of the principal cases the supreme court has been divided.

§ 1215. Constitutionality of provisions as to evidence.— The difficulty of securing a conviction under the liquor laws by reason of subterfuges resorted to in carrying on the business has led to the adoption in various states of special rules affecting the evidence in such prosecutions. The constitutionality of these special provisions has been frequently called in question, but in a general way these statutes have been upheld, although they place burdens upon the defendant which he is not compelled to bear in other prosecutions, if they leave him a fair opportunity for defense. Thus, it is held that the legislature may make admissible certain classes of hearsay evidence, or provide that upon proof of certain suspicious circumstances a presumption shall arise that defendant is guilty, thereby throwing upon him the burden of overcoming such a presumption. Thus, the fact of delivery, or possession, or drinking upon the premises, may be made *prima facie* evidence of guilt.[2] It is constitutional to make the general reputation of the place admissible evidence to prove the illegal character of the business done there sufficient to warrant a conviction, and so long as the discretion of the jury in weighing such evidence is not interfered with, this is constitutional.[3] But if the statute leaves to the jury no discretion, but attempts to make the bad reputation of the place exclusive evidence of defendant's guilt, it will be unconstitutional as interfering with due process of law.[4] It is competent for the legislature to throw upon defendant the burden of showing that he is duly licensed to make sales.[5] So it is constitutional to throw upon the physician who prescribes

[1] S. v. Aiken, 42 S. C. 222; Ex parte Keeler, — S. C. —, 23 S. E. R. 865; S. v. Porterfield, — S. C. —, 25 S. E. R. 39; S. v. Pickett, — S. C. —, 25 S. E. R. 46. And see *supra*, § 76, n.

[2] C. v. Williams, 6 Gray, 1; C. v. Wallace, 7 Gray, 222; S. v. Hurley, 54 Me. 562; Auburn v. Merchant, 103 N. Y. 143; Santo v. S., 2 Ia. 165.

[3] S. v. Wilson, 15 R. I. 180; S. v. Waldron, 16 R. I. 191.

[4] S. v. Beswick, 13 R. I. 211; S. v. Kartz, 13 R. I. 528. But in Connecticut a similar statute was given a somewhat different interpretation and was upheld: S. v. Morgan, 40 Conn. 44; S. v. Thomas, 47 Conn. 546.

[5] C. v. Tuttle, 12 Cush. 502; S. v. Higgins, 13 R. I. 330; S. v. Mellor, 13 R. I. 666; S. v. Buckley, 40 Conn. 246; Mugler v. Kansas, 123 U. S. 623. And see *infra*, § 1281.

intoxicating liquors as a medicine, the burden of showing that the patient needed the liquor for that purpose.[1]

§ 1216. **Construction of statutes.**— The only question of any special interest arising in the construction of liquor laws is as to the effect of the adoption in successive statutes of conflicting methods of dealing with the subject. Thus, a local-option statute may succeed a licensing statute, and, of course, if it permits the sale in localities, the restrictions of the licensing statute may thereby be removed; while, on the other hand, if under the local-option statute sales in particular districts are prohibited which before might have been made under the licensing statute, the penalties of the license statute may still be enforced as an additional method of punishment. It is impossible to discuss the questions which have arisen in particular cases, as they involve the provisions of special statutes, but the cases cited in the note are in point on the general question.[2] So it was held that a provision prohibiting sales to minors was repealed by a local-option law abolishing entirely the license system and substituting stringent prohibition.[3] In general it may be stated that regulations not inconsistent with each other may be enforced, although they are not parts of the same system, but seek to obtain the object of regulation by different means;[4] but if the different systems are wholly distinct and apparently intended to be exclusive, there cannot be prosecution under both systems.[5] Where there is a state regulation and also a power of regulation given to cities, the question may arise as to whether the regulations by ordinances

[1] C. v. Minor, 88 Ky. 422.

[2] Robertson v. S., 5 Tex. Ap. 155; Boone v. S., 12 Tex. Ap. 184; S. v. Turner, 18 S. C. 103; Kohlbrunner v. S., 67 Miss. 368; Boswell v. S., 70 Miss. 395; Butler v. S., 25 Fla. 347; S. v. Smiley, 101 N. C. 709; S. v. Martin, 3 Heisk. 487; Garner v. S., 8 Blackf. 568; Baird v. S., 52 Ark. 326; Blackwell v. S., 45 Ark. 90; Mazzia v. S., 51 Ark. 177; S. v. Orton, 41 Ark. 305; S. v. Cathey, 41 Ark. 308; C. v. Weller, 14 Bush, 218; C. v. Brennan, 103 Mass. 70; S. v. Benjamin, 2 Oreg. 125.

[3] S. v. Yewell, 63 Md. 120; T. v. Pratt, 6 Dak. 483. Where permits are required, the same act of illegal selling may be punishable as a sale without a permit or under general provision for illegal selling or keeping for sale, which is applicable equally to those who have permits: S. v. Waynick, 45 Ia. 516; S. v. Douglass, 73 Ia. 279. As to punishment of the same act under several statutes, see, also, *infra*, § 1217.

[4] S. v. Deaton, 101 N. C. 728; S. v. Cain, 8 W. Va. 720; Teague v. S., 39 Miss. 516; New v. S., 34 Tex. 100.

[5] Butler v. S., 25 Fla. 347.

are exclusive of the state legislation or concurrent with it; this will depend upon the language of the statute, for if the delegation of power to the city is to make additional regulations, the state law will be enforced in the city;[1] but if the power of regulation is placed exclusively in the city, the state statutes will be inoperative as to such city so far as sales are authorized under city ordinances;[2] although, if a sale is not authorized under a city ordinance, there may be punishment under the state law as well.[3] If the provisions of the ordinance are inconsistent with the state law and beyond the authority of the city they will, of course, be void.[4] The adoption of local option in a particular locality may suspend in that locality the general state law.[5] If, as between two statutes, the later one repeals the former by implication, it will prevent prosecutions for offenses already committed under the former statute unless there is some form of saving clause.[6] Where, by local option, the provisions of the general liquor law are suspended and not repealed, a person may be convicted after such suspension for violation of the law committed before the adoption of local option.[7] Indeed, any superseding statute which leaves the prior statute in force for some purposes will leave in existence all the laws relating to the enforcement of the prior act.[8]

[1] Ambrose v. S., 6 Ind. 351; Sloan v. S., 8 Blackf. 361; Gardner v. P., 20 Ill. 430; Corbett v. T., 1 Wash. T. 431; Sanders v. S., 34 Neb. 872; S. v. Harris, 50 Minn. 128; Hill v. Dalton, 72 Ga. 314; Angerhoffer v. S., 15 Tex. Ap. 613.

[2] C. v. Luck, 2 B. Mon. 296; S. v. Wheeler, 27 Minn. 76; Phillips v. Tecumseh, 5 Neb. 312; Hetzer v. P., 4 Colo. 45; Craddock v. S., 18 Tex. Ap. 567. As to the question of construction, see Woodward v. Turnbull, 4 Ill. 1.

[3] S. v. Pfeifer, 26 Minn. 175; S. v. Fleckenstein, 26 Minn. 177; S. v. Langdon, 29 Minn. 393; S. v. Langdon, 31 Minn. 316.

[4] Adams v. Albany, 29 Ga. 56; S. v. Winkelmeier, 35 Mo. 103.

[5] P. v. Murphy, 93 Mich. 41; C. v. Mueller, 81 Pa. St. 127. And see Barnes v. S., 49 Ala. 342.

[6] Halfin v. S., 5 Tex. Ap. 212; Boone v. S., 12 Tex. Ap. 184; Freese v. S., 14 Tex. Ap. 31; Prather v. S., 14 Tex. Ap. 453; Dawson v. S., 25 Tex. Ap. 670. By special provision the repeal of prohibition in a county may not have the effect of releasing offenders who have violated the prohibitory law while in force: Ezzell v. S., 29 Tex. Ap. 521. On the other hand, a conviction for illegal sales is good although after the offense and before the trial a law was passed authorizing such sales: Acree v. C., 13 Bush, 353.

[7] P. v. Wade, 101 Mich. 89; Winterton v. S., 65 Miss. 238.

[8] Sanders v. C., 117 Pa. St. 293; S. v. Funk, 27 Minn. 318.

§ 1217. Concurrent effect of federal, state and city provisions.— By the federal statute providing for the raising of internal revenue, retail liquor dealers are required to pay a license, but the possession of such license does not exempt the holder from the operation of state laws regulating or even prohibiting the sale of liquors, the federal statute being the means only of raising revenue and not a police regulation,[1] which would be beyond the power of congress. There are also federal statutes passed in the exercise of the power to regulate commerce with Indian tribes, prohibiting the introduction of spirituous liquor into the Indian country;[2] and the payment of a revenue tax for a license to sell liquors in a particular district does not authorize the seller to introduce such liquors into the Indian country, although it is within such district.[3] Furthermore, in the exercise of the power of the federal government to legislate for the territory of Alaska, the importation of liquor into that territory, or the sale of liquor therein, is prohibited.[4] As pointed out in the preceding section, there may be difficulty in determining whether a state statute regulating the sale of liquors continues in force in a city which, under authority given to it, passes ordinances respecting the same matter. In general, the power given to a city will not be deemed exclusive, but must be exercised in subordination to the general laws of the state.[5] Yet the city may impose addi-

[1] McGuire v. C., 3 Wall. 387; Pervear v. C., 5 Wall. 475; C. v. Thornilley, 6 Allen, 445; C. v. O'Donnell, 8 Allen, 548; C. v. Sanborn, 116 Mass. 61; S. v. Delano, 54 Me. 501; S. v. Lillard, 78 Mo. 136; Pierson v. S., 39 Ark. 219; S. v. McCleary, 17 Ia. 44; S. v. Carney, 20 Ia. 82; S. v. Stutz, 20 Ia. 488; S. v. Baughman, 20 Ia. 497; S. v. Downs, 116 N. C. 1064; S. v. Hazell, 100 N. C. 471; S. v. Joyner, 81 N. C. 534; In re Jordan, 49 Fed. R. 238. The holder of a government license has no right to sell liquors on a steamboat plying on a navigable river without complying with the state laws: Boyd v. S., 12 Lea, 687; C. v. Sheckels, 78 Va. 36. The federal courts have no jurisdiction of a violation of a state law by the holder of a federal license: C. v. Casey, 12 Allen, 214. As to the effect of a federal license as evidence of illegal selling or keeping for sale, see *infra*, § 1280.

[2] In re Boyd, 49 Fed. R. 48; U. S. v. Carr, 2 Mont. T. 234. This does not, however, prevent transportation of liquors through the Indian country; U. S. v. Twenty-nine Gallons of Whiskey, 45 Fed. R. 847. As to regulation of sales to Indians, see *infra*, § 1263.

[3] U. S. v. Forty-three Gallons of Whiskey, 108 U. S. 491.

[4] Nelson v. U. S., 30 Fed. R. 112; U. S. v. Warwick, 51 Fed. R. 280; In re Moore, 66 Fed. R. 947.

[5] S. v. Harper, 58 Mo. 530; Sweet v. Wabash, 41 Ind. 7; Loeb v. Attica, 82 Ind. 175; S. v. Peterson, 38

tional restrictions.[1] In the general power given to a city to restrict, suppress or prohibit the sale of liquor, it may pass an ordinance licensing such sale, that being a partial prohibition.[2] Where the city is authorized to make additional regulations the dealer must comply with both the general law and the city regulations, and the compliance with either one will not prevent his punishment under the other.[3] The same act may be punishable in as many prosecutions as there are jurisdictions, the laws of which are violated by such act.[4] The general subject of the exercise by the city of police power under delegation from the state has, however, been discussed elsewhere.[5]

II. WHAT DEEMED INTOXICATING LIQUOR.

§ 1218. Law or fact; judicial notice.— It is often a matter of controversy as to whether a particular liquor is within the terms of the statute regulating the sale of liquors. The stat-

Minn. 143; S. v. Fisher, 33 Wis. 154; S. v. Chase, 33 La. An. 287; S. v. Harper, 42 La. An. 312; Ex parte Ginnochio, 30 Tex. Ap. 584.

[1] Dennehy v. Chicago, 120 Ill. 627; Morris v. Rome, 10 Ga. 532; Columbus City v. Cutcomp, 61 Ia. 672; P. v. Townsey, 5 Denio, 70. Where the power of the city is only to regulate in general conformity with the state law, it cannot impose restrictions which will be unreasonable upon persons authorized to sell under the laws of the state: Ward v. Greeneville, 8 Baxt. 228; Grills v. Jonesboro, 8 Baxt. 247; but a reasonable regulation may be proper: Ex parte Wolf, 14 Neb. 24.

[2] Emporia v. Volmer, 12 Kan. 622; St. Louis v. S., 2 Mo. 113; Keokuk v. Dressel, 47 Ia. 597. But a power to regulate does not in itself imply power to license: S. v. Fay, 44 N. J. 474; Burlington v. Bumgardner, 42 Ia. 673. The power to license may be conferred by statute upon a city: S. v. Columbia, 17 S. C. 80.

[3] Elk Point v. Vaughn, 1 Dak. 108; S. v. Sherman, 50 Mo. 265; S. v. Harper, 58 Mo. 530; Harrison v. S., 9 Mo. 526; Ex parte Lawrence, 69 Cal. 608; Paton v. P., 1 Colo. 77; S. v. Mancke, 18 S. C. 81; S. v. Propst, 87 N. C. 560; Parsley v. Hutchins, 2 Jones, 159; Furman v. Knapp, 19 Johns. 248; S. v. Estabrook, 6 Ala. 653. In Georgia it is held that a county or state license will protect the dealer against a city ordinance passed in pursuance of authority given after the county or state license was granted: Mayor of Rome v. Lumpkin, 5 Ga. 447; Chastain v. Calhoun, 29 Ga. 333; and to same effect see Ex parte Schmitker, 6 Neb. 108. But where the ordinance was passed after but in pursuance of authority given before the license was granted, the dealer must take out both licenses: Cuthbert v. Conly, 32 Ga. 211. That the license is not, however, a contract which is to be protected against subsequent legislation, see *supra*, § 1209; McKinney v. Salem, 77 Ind. 213.

[4] Elk Point v. Vaughn, 1 Dak. 108; Thon v. C., 31 Grat. 887; S. v. Stevens, 114 N. C. 873. And see *infra*, § 1277.

[5] See *supra*, §§ 62–69.

utes frequently name particular kinds of liquor, and, in that case, if the liquor in question is charged to have been one of such particular kinds named, there is merely a question of fact as to whether it is of that kind; and any question as to its intoxicating character is immaterial, it being deemed intoxicating because named by statute.[1] So if by statute the percentage of alcohol which will render a liquor intoxicating is fixed, the only question for the jury is whether or not it contains that percentage of alcohol, its intoxicating character being immaterial.[2] But if the liquor sold is not specially named in the statute, the question whether it comes under general terms used in the statute, such as "intoxicating," "spirituous," "vinous," "malt," "fermented," etc., is in its nature a question of fact, and some courts would always leave it to the jury under general instructions as to what constitutes a liquor of the kind which the statute describes.[3] But many courts consider that it is not a question of fact whether certain well-known liquors are intoxicating, but that the court can take judicial notice that whisky, ale, wine, lager beer and other such liquors are intoxicating, leaving to the jury only the question of whether the liquor sold was one of these particular kinds of liquor as charged.[4] In accordance with this view

[1] S. v. Curley, 33 Ia. 359; Worley v. Spurgeon, 38 Ia. 465; S. v. Thornton, 63 N. H. 114; S. v. Spaulding, 61 Vt. 505; C. v. Dean, 14 Gray, 99; C. v. Curran, 119 Mass. 206; Kettering v. Jacksonville, 50 Ill. 39.

[2] C. v. Brelsford, 161 Mass. 61; S. v. McKenna, 16 R. I. 398; P. v. Ingraham, 100 Mich. 530.

[3] S. v. Starr, 67 Me. 242, 2 Am. Cr. R. 390; S. v. Stewart, 31 Me. 515; S. v. McCafferty, 63 Me. 223; S. v. Wall, 34 Me. 165; S. v. Page, 66 Me. 418; S. v. Biddle, 54 N. H. 379, 1 Am. Cr. R. 490; S. v. Lowry, 74 N. C. 121; Bach v. S., 8 Mo. 497; C. v. Reyburg, 122 Pa. St. 299; C. v. Blos, 116 Mass. 56. In S. v. Biddle, *supra*, the court says: "If the legislature had intended absolutely to prohibit the sale of ale, leaving no question as to its intoxicating qualities to be settled by anybody, it was easy for them to have said so in a single word. What they did was to prohibit the sale of intoxicating liquors, leaving it to be determined in some way by the tribunal charged with administering the law whether the particular case comes within the prohibition." Again, "If it were known with absolute certainty that all fermented ale and cider invariably produce intoxication, it would still remain *a fact* that they are intoxicating liquors, just as much as though the matter were in dispute and the evidence conflicting."

[4] Fenton v. S., 100 Ind. 598; Eagan v. S., 53 Ind. 162; S. v. Jones, 3 Ind. Ap. 121; Klare v. S., 43 Ind. 483; Schlicht v. S., 56 Ind. 173; S. v. Schaefer, 44 Kan. 90; Briffitt v. S., 58 Wis. 39; S. v. Tisdale, 54 Minn. 105; S. v. Packer, 80 N. C. 439; Frese v. S., 23 Fla. 267; Adler v. S., 55 Ala.

some courts have held that the term "beer" necessarily indicates a malt liquor within statutory terms.[1] Other courts refuse to give the term so definite a meaning, holding that it properly includes liquors which are not produced by the use of malt, but would consider lager beer, ale, porter, etc., to be malt liquors.[2] As to liquors having names the meaning of which is not definitely fixed by usage, the question whether or not they are within the statutory description must be left to the jury.[3] If there is no doubt as to whether the name of the liquor sold indicates a liquor which comes within the statutory description, the question should be left to the jury as to whether or not the liquor was of that description.[4] It is to be borne in mind, however, that the name which is given to the liquor charged to have been sold is only presumptive of its character, and that it is still open for the jury to determine whether it actually was of that character if there is any conflict in the evidence on that question.[5]

§ 1219. **Mixed or compounded liquor.**— Where the statutory description is simply "intoxicating liquor," it will include any liquor the active principle of which is alcohol, and which

16; Watson v. S., 55 Ala. 158; Freiberg v. S., 94 Ala. 91. Thus, it has been held that to charge the sale of whisky is a sufficient charge of the sale of intoxicating liquor: Schlicht v. S., 56 Ind. 173; also that proof of the sale of gin would justify an inference by the jury that the liquor was intoxicating without evidence to that effect: C. v. Peckham, 2 Gray, 514. So it has been held that ale is a "strong and spirituous liquor:" Nevin v. Ladue, 3 Denio, 437. The following cases, while not discussing the doctrine of judicial notice, necessarily proceed upon the principle that the court may know as matter of law whether liquors of certain descriptions are or are not intoxicating, spirituous, malt, etc.: Caswell v. S., 2 Humph. 402; Fritz v. S., 1 Baxt. 15; S. v. Moore, 5 Blackf. 118; Welsh v. S., 126 Ind. 71; S. v. Thompson, 20 W. Va. 674; S. v. Haymond, 20 W. Va. 18; S. v. Oliver, 26 W. Va. 422.

[1] S. v. May, 52 Kan. 53; U. S. v. Ducournau, 54 Fed. R. 138; S. v. Tisdale, 54 Minn. 105. Where beer is named in the statute it is for defendant to prove that a liquor sold under that name is not intoxicating: S. v. Cloughly, 73 Ia. 626; Milwaukee Malt Extract Co. v. Chicago, R. I. & P. R. Co., 73 Ia. 98. And see *infra*, § 1220.

[2] Netso v. S., 24 Fla. 363; S. v. Sioux Falls Brewing Co., 5 S. D. 39; S. v. Beswick, 13 R. I. 211; S. v. Rush, 13 R. I. 198; S. v. Goyette, 11 R. I. 592. Proof of the sale of lager beer is sufficient without showing that it contains the percentage of alcohol specified by statute: C. v. Snow, 133 Mass. 575.

[3] Williams v. S., 35 Ark. 430; S. v. May, 52 Kan. 53; Intoxicating Liquor Cases, 25 Kan. 751; S. v. Scott, 116 N. C. 1012.

[4] Brown v. Piper, 91 U. S. 37.

[5] S. v. May, 52 Kan. 53; S. v. Tisdale, 54 Minn. 105.

is commonly used as a beverage, and in fact intoxicates those who drink it in sufficient quantities.[1] Of course any liquor into the composition of which alcohol in any of its forms enters so far as to render it intoxicating is an intoxicating liquor, provided it is used as a beverage, though, as suggested in the preceding section, the percentage of alcohol necessary to render the liquor intoxicating may be fixed by statute, in which case the question is only as to percentage and not as to effect. It is not enough, however, that the liquor contains alcohol unless it is in such quantities as to cause intoxication.[2] The mere fact that a preparation not usually used as a beverage contains sufficient alcohol to make it intoxicating if drunk will not bring it within the term "intoxicating liquor."[3] Thus, medical preparations frequently contain sufficient alcohol to render them intoxicating if used as a beverage, but this will not bring them within the scope of the statutes as to intoxicating liquors if they are usually sold as medicines.[4] If, however, the medical substance, such as drugs, barks, seeds, or the like, is put into the liquor merely for the purpose of evading the statute and selling it really for use as a beverage, but under the name of medicine, its sale will be within the restrictions of the statute as to liquors.[5]

[1] S. v. Giersch, 98 N. C. 720; S. v. Biddle, 54 N. H. 379; Commissioners v. Taylor, 21 N. Y. 173; S. v. Colwell, 3 R. I. 284. Thus, proof of the sale of a "whisky cocktail" was held sufficient to support a charge of the sale of whisky: Galloway v. S., 23 Tex. Ap. 398.

[2] C. v. Blos, 116 Mass. 56. Under the Iowa statute which names alcohol as an intoxicating liquor it is said that the sale of any liquor containing alcohol, no matter in what degree of dilution, is covered: S. v. Intoxicating Liquors, 76 Ia. 243; S. v. Yager, 72 Ia. 421.

[3] Intoxicating Liquor Cases, 25 Kan. 751; Russell v. Sloan, 33 Vt. 656; C. v. Ramsdell, 130 Mass. 68.

[4] Carl v. S., 87 Ala. 17, 8 Am. Cr. R. 404, and note; Carl v. S., 89 Ala. 93; King v. S., 58 Miss. 737; U. S. v. Stubblefield, 40 Fed. R. 454. But where the statute specifically named "mixed liquor, of which a part is spirituous and intoxicating," it was held that a medicine, a part of which was intoxicating liquor, was included: S. v. Gray, 61 Conn. 39.

[5] King v. S., 58 Miss. 737; Davis v. S., 50 Ark. 17; S. v. Neese, 38 S. C. 261; S. v. Laffer, 38 Ia. 422; S. v. Lillard, 78 Mo. 136; S. v. Wilson, 80 Mo. 303; Wall v. S., 78 Ala. 417; S. v. Bennett, 3 Harr. 565; U. S. v. Wilson, 69 Fed. R. 144. The question whether defendant sold the liquor as a medicine, or whether it was generally sold as a medicine, is immaterial; if the liquor was in fact intoxicating, and purchased as a beverage, the sale will be within the statute: C. v. Hallett, 103 Mass. 452; King v. S., 66 Miss. 502. On proof of a sale, and that the article sold was intoxicating, a *prima facie* case is

§ 1220. Particular classes of liquors.— It has already been stated that the court will take judicial notice that liquors known by certain well-known names are intoxicating liquors.[1] Thus, whisky,[2] brandy,[3] rum,[4] gin,[5] ale[6] and wine[7] are intoxicating. Lager beer is a term usually considered as indicating an intoxicating liquor.[8] As to the general term "beer," the weight of authority seems to be that it also indicates an intoxicating liquor, the burden being on the defendant to show that the liquor in question known by that name was not intoxicating.[9] Alcohol is an intoxicating liquor,[10] but not a vinous or spirituous liquor.[11] Lager beer is not a spirituous liquor.[12] But in another case it is said that the term "spirituous liquor" includes fermented liquors as well as distilled liquors.[13] Cider, when shown to be intoxicating, is within the statutes,[14] but it will not be presumed to be intoxicating, unless specially named in the statute, and its character as intoxicating liquor must be alleged and proved.[15]

made, and it then devolves upon the seller to show that the article was a medicine and not a liquor: King v. S., 66 Miss. 502.

[1] *Supra*, § 1218.

[2] Carmon v. S., 18 Ind. 450; Schlicht v. S., 56 Ind. 173; Frese v. S., 23 Fla. 267.

[3] Fenton v. S., 100 Ind. 598; S. v. Wadsworth, 30 Conn. 55; S. v. Tisdale, 54 Minn. 105.

[4] S. v. Wadsworth, 30 Conn. 55.

[5] S. v. Wadsworth, 30 Conn. 55; S. v. Peckham, 2 Gray, 514.

[6] Nevin v. Ladue, 3 Denio, 437.

[7] S. v. Packer, 80 N. C. 439; Wolf v. S., 59 Ark. 297.

[8] S. v. Rush, 13 R. I. 198. And see *supra*, § 1218.

[9] Myers v. S., 93 Ind. 251 (overruling earlier cases in the same state); Welsh v. S., 126 Ind. 71; Briffitt v. S., 58 Wis. 39; S. v. Jenkins, 32 Kan. 477; S. v. Teissedre, 30 Kan. 476, 479, 484; Markle v. Akron, 14 Ohio, 587; S. v. Dick, 47 Minn. 375; P. v. Hawley, 3 Mich. 330; S. v. Cloughly, 73 Ia. 626; Milwaukee Malt Co. v. Chicago, R. I. & P. R. Co., 73 Ia. 98. *Contra*, S. v. Beswick, 13 R. I. 211; Hansberg v. P., 120 Ill. 21 (but see Monroe v. P., 113 Ill. 670); C. v. Hardiman, 9 Gray, 136; Bell v. S., 91 Ga. 227.

[10] Snider v. S., 81 Ga. 753; Winn v. S., 43 Ark. 151. And see S. v. Martin, 34 Ark. 340; S. v. Witt, 39 Ark. 216.

[11] Lemly v. S., 70 Miss. 241.

[12] So held under federal statute prohibiting the introduction of spirituous liquors or wine into the Indian country: Sarlls v. U. S., 152 U. S. 570. But to the contrary, see U. S. v. Ellis, 51 Fed. R. 808.

[13] S. v. Giersch, 98 N. C. 720.

[14] S. v. Hutchinson, 72 Ia. 561.

[15] C. v. Chappel, 116 Mass. 7; S. v. Biddle, 54 N. H. 379; S. v. Oliver, 26 W. Va. 422. It is said in one case, however, that hard cider may be presumed to be intoxicating: S. v. Schaefer, 44 Kan. 90. Some statutes contain provisions as to cider: S. v. Preston, 48 Vt. 12; Shaw v. Carpenter, 54 Vt. 155; S. v. Roach, 75 Me. 123; S. v. McNamara, 69 Me. 133;

§ 1221. Other descriptions; "spirituous," "fermented," etc.— Something has been said in the preceding section as to whether certain liquors are within the term "spirituous." All spirituous, vinous and malt liquors are within the general description of intoxicating liquors,[1] but the general term "intoxicating liquors" is not limited to those which are spirituous, vinous or malt.[2] So it is said that wine,[3] beer,[4] ale,[5] porter[6] and cider[7] are not spirituous. Vinous liquor is within the term "intoxicating liquor."[8] Doubtless a liquor might be spirituous, that is, containing the product of the still, and yet so diluted as not to be intoxicating.[9] Fermented liquors are usually named by the statute and therefore included without regard to whether they are intoxicating or spirituous.[10] Under the term "ardent" liquors is included bitters or cordials containing a considerable percentage of alcohol.[11] Vinous liquor is a liquor made from the juice of grapes,[12] and if specially mentioned by statute need not be intoxicating to be within the statutory regulation.[13] The term "liquor" as used in these statutes seems not to have any very definite meaning. It is not necessarily intoxicating,[14] but has been held to include champagne wine.[15]

§ 1222. Evidence as to character of liquor; knowledge by defendant.— Where the question is whether certain liquor

Guptill v. Richardson, 62 Me. 257; C. v. Dean, 14 Gray, 99.

[1] Bell v. S., 91 Ga. 227.

[2] McDuffy v. S., 87 Ga. 687; Weisbrodt v. S., 50 Ohio St. 192; Allred v. S., 89 Ala. 112.

[3] Caswell v. S., 2 Humph. 402; Fritz v. S., 1 Baxt. 15 (overruling S. v. Sharrer, 2 Coldw. 323); S. v. Moore, 5 Blackf. 118.

[4] S. v. Thompson, 20 W. Va. 674; Fritz v. S., 1 Baxt. 15. And see cases in preceding section.

[5] Walker v. Prescott, 44 N. H. 512; S. v. Adams, 51 N. H. 568.

[6] S. v. Adams, 51 N. H. 568.

[7] S. v. Adams, 51 N. H. 568.

[8] Hatfield v. C., 120 Pa. St. 395. As to what constitutes intoxication, see *infra*, § 1262.

[9] In general, see Merkle v. S., 37 Ala. 139; C. v. White, 10 Metc. 14; C. v. Bathrick, 6 Cush. 247; and cases as to alcohol cited in § 1219, *supra*.

[10] S. v. Volmer, 6 Kan. 371; Merkle v. S., 37 Ala. 139. Fermented cider is a fermented liquor: P. v. Foster, 64 Mich. 715; Eureka Vinegar Co. v. Gazette Printing Co., 23 Fed. R. 570. Rum is not a fermented but a spirituous liquor: C. v. Jordan, 18 Pick. 28.

[11] Gostorf v. S., 39 Ark. 450. And see Brock v. C., 6 Leigh, 634.

[12] Adler v. S., 55 Ala. 16.

[13] Hatfield v. C., 120 Pa. St. 395.

[14] Ward v. S., 48 Ind. 293.

[15] Keizer v. Randleman. 5 Jones, 478.

was intoxicating, it is competent to prove that fact by the effect of the use thereof,[1] or by the opinions of witnesses, although not experts, who have had personal experience or observation such as to enable them to form a correct opinion.[2] It is not necessary that the witness be able to swear absolutely as to the nature of the liquor.[3] A general opinion to the effect that the liquor is intoxicating is sufficient if the jury believes therefrom that it is so.[4] The character of the liquor sold may be proved by circumstantial evidence without direct testimony.[5] Knowledge by the defendant as to the character of the liquor, either as to what it is or whether it is intoxicating, is wholly immaterial;[6] so when one sells a liquor purporting to be a medicine, but which is in fact intoxicating, ignorance of this quality on the part of the seller will not be a defense; he is bound, at his peril, to ascertain and know the nature of the article sold.[7] As to some forms of violation of liquor laws, no doubt the intent is material; for instance, where the offense charged is that of keeping with intent to sell illegally;[8] but in such case the intent refers to the purpose of selling, not to the knowledge of the nature of the liquor.[9]

[1] Carl v. S., 87 Ala. 17, 8 Am. Cr. R. 404, and note; Tharpe v. S., 89 Ga. 748. Evidence that other witnesses who had drank the liquor were not affected by it is admissible: Knowles v. S., 80 Ala. 9. It is not for the court to say that the fact that a person was made drunk by the use of the liquor is proof of its being intoxicating liquor, as this is upon the weight of evidence, which is for the jury: Fairly v. S., 63 Miss. 333.

[2] Carl v. S., *supra;* C. v. Timothy, 8 Gray, 480.

[3] C. v. Aaron, 114 Mass. 255; C. v. Dowdican, 114 Mass. 257; C. v. Powderly, 148 Mass. 457; S. v. Miller, 53 Ia. 84.

[4] C. v. Leo, 110 Mass. 414; C. v. Gavin, 160 Mass. 523; C. v. Gourdier, 14 Gray, 390.

[5] Dant v. S., 83 Ind. 60. Further as to evidence of sale, see *infra,* § 1233.

[6] C. v. Boynton, 2 Allen, 160; C. v. Daly, 148 Mass. 428; S. v. Moulton, 52 Kan. 69. For instance, if defendant has kept and sold a kind of beer which he supposes not to contain sufficient alcohol to render it intoxicating, his mistake in that respect, though honest, would constitute no defense: C. v. Savery, 145 Mass. 212; C. v. O'Kean, 152 Mass. 584. Nor will it be a defense against a statute providing for the sale of lager beer that the accused did not know that the substance sold was lager beer: S. v. Tomasi, 67 Vt. 312.

[7] King v. S., 66 Miss. 502; Farrell v. S., 32 Ohio St. 456. On the general subject of mistake in regard to a business which is subject to statutory regulation, see *supra,* § 128.

[8] *Infra,* § 1243.

[9] C. v. Goodman, 97 Mass. 117.

III. Systems of Regulation; License; Local Option.

§ **1223. The license system.**— There are not distinct systems under which the privilege of selling intoxicating liquors is granted or restricted, for licensing is a limited prohibition, and prohibition is not, in any case, so absolute that permission to sell for some purposes and under some circumstances is not granted; and local option is only a method of determining how and to what extent permission shall be granted or denied in particular localities. Nevertheless, where the general principle of regulation is that permission to sell as a beverage shall be granted only on conditions which are uniform, the system may be called a license system; while if the privilege of selling is to be granted or refused in particular localities, depending upon the action of the public authorities, or of the voters in those localities, the system may be called one of local option. In general terms "a license is permission granted by some competent authority to do an act which without such permission would be illegal." [1] In states having so-called prohibitory laws intending to prevent entirely the sale as a beverage and permit sales only for other purposes, the authority to sell is usually called a permit.[2] This distinction between licenses and permits is maintained even where the license system prevails.[3] A license is an exception, and the party relying upon it must bring himself strictly within the terms of the law. It must usually be in writing.[4] The statutes generally provide what are the essentials of the license.[5] It must be issued by the proper authority,[6] and after compliance with preliminary re-

[1] S. v. Hipp, 38 Ohio St. 199, 226.

[2] The permit holder must exercise due diligence and act in good faith in determining whether a person buying intends to use the liquor for a lawful purpose: S. v. Blair, 72 Ia. 591; S. v. Aulman, 76 Ia. 624. Sales without a permit, even in good faith and for proper purposes, will be criminal: S. v. Benadom, 79 Ia. 90.

[3] Moore v. P., 109 Ill. 499.

[4] Oral permission to sell, granted by a person having the power to issue a written license, is not sufficient: Lawrence v. Gracy, 11 Johns. 179.

[5] If it is required that the license specify the room where the liquor is to be sold, a failure to comply with this requirement will render it invalid: C. v. McCormick, 150 Mass. 270; C. v. Cauley, 150 Mass. 272; C. v. Merriam, 136 Mass. 433. Of course if there is no such requirement in the statute such a specification is unnecessary: C. v. Stratton, 150 Mass. 188. In one case it is held that such a statutory provision is directory only: Goforth v. S., 60 Miss. 756.

[6] If the commissioner who issues the license is not authorized, the li-

quirements.[1] Any material failure to comply with the requirements of the statute will render the license invalid and leave the holder without protection for sales made under it.[2] The giving of a bond is usually required, conditioned that the person receiving the license shall not violate any of the provisions of the statute with reference to sales made under such license.[3] The bond is given to secure observance of the law by the person to whom the license is granted, and is forfeited upon a violation by him, and not merely upon his failure to pay the penalties and costs imposed.[4] But compliance with all the con-

cense will be no protection: Cronin v. Stoddard, 97 N. Y. 271. The signature of the authorized officer may be by *fac-simile* stamp or by an authorized agent: Swarth v. P., 109 Ill. 621.

[1] C. v. Welch, 144 Mass. 356; C. v. Pillsbury, 12 Gray, 127; S. v. Shaw, 32 Me. 570; S. v. Fisher, 33 Wis. 154. And see Crutz v. S., 4 Ind. 385; Ex parte Bell, 24 Tex. Ap. 428. So held where the required petition of the majority of the legal voters was not obtained: House v. S., 41 Miss. 737; Ex parte Cox, 19 Ark. 688. But where the requisite number of signers was afterwards obtained, it was held that the proceeding, although irregular, was not invalid: S. v. Jefferson Co., 20 Fla. 425. The license may be invalid for defects in the required affidavit of the applicant: Russel v. S., 77 Ala. 89; or for failure to make the payment required by statute: Townsend v. S., 2 Blackf. 151; or because it authorizes sales within a prohibited distance of a public school: C. v. Whelan, 134 Mass. 206; C. v. Heaganey, 137 Mass. 574; or because the applicant is disqualified to receive a license: S. v. Mancke, 18 S. C. 81; P. v. Davis, 36 N. Y. 77. So if the license authorized by statute is for one year a license for a shorter time will be invalid: Gurley v. S., 65 Ga. 157. So if the notice necessary to authorize the action of the public authorities in issuing the license has not been given, the license issued will be deemed invalid, even in a collateral proceeding: Zielke v. S., 42 Neb. 750. Irregularity in the license, by which it limits the purpose for which sale may be made further than required by statute, will not render it invalid as to the purposes recited: S. v. Emerson, 16 N. H. 87.

[2] S. v. Fisher, 33 Wis. 154; S. v. Moore, 1 Jones, 276. Honest belief in the validity of the license will be no protection: S. v. Mullenhoff, 74 Ia. 271.

[3] Providence v. Bligh, 10 R. I. 208. Failure to insert the name of the officer to whom the bond is executed will not invalidate it: Tripp v. Norton, 10 R. I. 125. Liability on the bond will not be avoided by showing that the sale complained of as a violation of such bond was made to a police officer sent as a detective to ascertain whether illegal sales were being made: Tripp v. Flanigan, 10 R. I. 128. Defect in justification of the sureties will not relieve them from liability: P. v. Laning, 73 Mich. 284. It may be provided that the sureties shall be liable to pay any judgment rendered against their principals; the sureties will not have the right in such case to relitigate the question of breach of the bond: Ibid.

[4] Lightner v. C., 31 Pa. St. 341. Liability on the bond is not termi-

ditions necessary to entitle the applicant to a license will not be a protection if the license has not in fact been issued, and a mere order for the license is not enough.[1] The licensee is usually required to perform certain conditions in connection with his enjoyment of the privilege, such as making reports, etc., and these conditions must be substantially complied with.[2] It is evident that under the strictness of construction which is applied to license laws there can be no implied licenses; for instance, payment of a fine imposed for selling without a license does not operate as a license for future sales;[3] and the fact that sales in particular localities can be made only in pursuance of license does not imply that sales outside of such localities are authorized without a license.[4] So a statute authorizing a license to sell for certain specified purposes impliedly prohibits sales for other purposes.[5]

§ **1224. License not retroactive.**— Sales which have been made on the strength of an order for a license are not validated after a license has been issued, for it relates only to future sales;[6]

nated by the imprisonment of the principal for failure to pay the fine imposed: Brown v. C., 114 Pa. St. 335. The bond will not cover violations of a subsequent statute with reference to sales, nor those already committed under a prior statute, unless the act under which the bond was given refers to such prior statute: Crawley v. C., 123 Pa. St. 275.

[1] C. v. Spring, 19 Pick. 396; S. v. Bach, 36 Minn. 234; Houser v. S., 18 Ind. 106; Schlicht v. S., 31 Ind. 246; Wiles v. S., 33 Ind. 306. It has been held, however, that the mere fact that the licensee has not received his license, being entitled to it, will not destroy his protection: Drapert v. S., 14 Ind. 123; also that if the license is wrongfully withheld, sales pending an appeal to secure it will be lawful: Padgett v. S., 93 Ind. 396. Certainly where all the conditions entitling the party to a license have not been performed, he will not be protected: S. v. Gray, 39 Me. 353; Brown v. S., 27 Tex. 335. But mere failure of the clerk to issue a license which has been granted will not render sales made in good faith criminal: S. v. White, 23 Ark. 275.

[2] Barnard v. Houghton, 34 Vt. 264. But *held* that failure of a permit holder to make reports, and selling at illegal profit, would not render him liable to punishment for sales thereunder otherwise lawful: S. v. Von Haltschuherr, 72 Ia. 541.

[3] S. v. McBride, 4 McCord, 332. It is no justification that officials allow a person to carry on the business, collecting money from him therefor, without his complying with the law: Hanlon v. S., 51 Ark. 186.

[4] S. v. Cofield, 22 S. C. 301. And in general, prohibiting the right to do certain things does not imply the right to do other things not mentioned: Moog v. Hannon's Adm'r, 93 Ala. 503; C. v. Matthews, 129 Mass. 485.

[5] S. v. Perkins, 26 N. H. 9.

[6] S. v. Hughes, 24 Mo. 147; Edwards v. S., 22 Ark. 253; Wilson v.

and dating a license back will not validate sales made before its actual issuance.[1] If the power which grants the license has authority to pardon past offenses, the granting of an antedated license may be a waiver of liability for sales already made.[2]

§ 1225. **Direct and collateral attack; appeal.**— If a license is granted by a tribunal, whether a court or a special tribunal, having power to do so, it cannot be collaterally attacked, but must be questioned, if at all, upon appeal. Such a license is valid until the tribunal granting it has been reversed, and sales under it before that time are lawful, provided, of course, the tribunal had authority to grant it.[3] But the question whether the tribunal had jurisdiction to grant the license is open to investigation by collateral attack, and if it can be shown that any of the preliminary steps required by the statute were omitted, the license is void and will afford no protection.[4] If, however, the defect complained of is as to a matter which was necessarily determined by the tribunal issuing the license, the question cannot be raised by a collateral attack, but only directly.[5] If the license is granted contrary to the state law, while it may be no protection against a criminal prosecution, it may estop the city granting it from insisting upon a penalty for illegal sales made in accordance with it.[6]

S., 35 Ark. 414; Bolduc v. Randall, 107 Mass. 121.

[1] Dudley v. S., 91 Ind. 312; Keiser v. S., 78 Ind. 430; S. v. Wilcox, 66 Ind. 557 (overruling earlier cases in the same state); Brown v. S., 27 Tex. 335; C. v. Welch, 144 Mass. 356; Reese v. Alanta, 63 Ga. 344. So one who sells after the expiration of his license cannot defend on the ground that he was induced to believe that his license would be renewed and that it was customary to date licenses back: S. v. Brady, 14 R. I. 508.

[2] Charleston v. Corleis, 2 Bailey, 186; Charleston v. Schmidt, 11 Rich. 343.

[3] Padgett v. S., 93 Ind. 396. It may be that by statute sales pending an appeal are illegal: Molihan v. S., 30 Ind. 266; Young v. S., 34 Ind. 46.

[4] Thus, where a bond was not first executed as required: S. v. Fisher, 33 Wis. 154; C. v. Welch, 144 Mass. 356. So where the building was within the prohibited distance of a public school: C. v. Whelan, 134 Mass. 206; C. v. Heaganey, 137 Mass. 574. So where a license was improperly granted to a non-resident: P. v. Davis, 36 N. Y. 77; or without the required recommendation of the board of commissioners: S. v. Moore, 1 Jones, 276.

[5] Goff v. Fowler, 3 Pick. 300; Hornaday v. S., 43 Ind. 306; S. v. Evans, 83 Mo. 319; C. v. Graves, 18 B. Mon. 33; S. v. Brandon, 28 Ark. 410; Blackwell v. S., 36 Ark. 178.

[6] Genoa v. Van Alstine, 108 Ill. 555; Martel v. East St. Louis, 94 Ill. 67.

§ 1226. Forfeiture or revocation.— It may be provided that a license shall be revoked on account of the licensee becoming a citizen of another state,[1] or on account of violation of its terms by illegal sales.[2] Usually, however, the forfeiture for improper conduct is to be enforced by revocation after conviction for the illegal selling, or in a proceeding in which there is an opportunity to be heard and a judgment rendered;[3] but it may not be essential that all the formalities of a trial be provided for and observed.[4] The revocation does not, in itself, constitute a punishment.[5] A proceeding for revocation is not a criminal proceeding nor a proceeding which may deprive the licensee of property.[6] Sometimes where the granting of a license is left as a matter of discretion to the tribunal, the revocation is left equally within its discretion.[7] Revocation may result from a repeal of the law under which the license was granted;[8] but the presumption will be against the intent to repeal a privilege already granted for the term during which it has been granted, unless the provisions of the statute are plain.[9] It is always understood that a license is subject to the general law existing at the time it was granted.[10]

§ 1227. Not assignable; who protected by; agent or partner.— A license confers a personal privilege not assignable by the licensee.[11] Therefore, one who has purchased the business

[1] Krant v. S., 47 Ind. 519.

[2] Illegal selling may be by the agent as well as by the principal: P. v. Meyers, 95 N. Y. 223; S. v. Beloit, 74 Wis. 267.

[3] C. v. Moylan, 119 Mass. 109; C. v. Kiley, 150 Mass. 325; S. v. Lamos, 26 Me. 258; Plummer v. C., 1 Bush, 26; S. v. Plunket, 1 Ired. 115; S. v. Tomah, 80 Wis. 198.

[4] C. v. Hamer, 128 Mass. 76.

[5] S. v. Harris, 50 Minn. 128.

[6] S. v. Schmidtz, 65 Ia. 556.

[7] Downs v. S., 19 Md. 571; Neuman v. S., 76 Wis. 112. Where the tribunal was authorized to revoke the license for cause, it was held that a conviction in another court of illegal selling was sufficient cause: Davis v. C., 75 Va. 944.

[8] S. v. Mullenhoff, 74 Ia. 271; S. v. Holmes, 38 N. H. 225; C. v. Sellers, 130 Pa. St. 32; Brown v. S., 82 Ga. 224; Robertson v. S., 12 Tex. Ap. 541. The license gives no vested right: See *supra*, § 1209.

[9] Watts v. C., 78 Ky. 329; Hirn v. S., 1 Ohio St. 15; S. v. Andrews, 26 Mo. 171; S. v. Andrews, 28 Mo. 14; Swarth v. P., 109 Ill. 621.

[10] Lambert v. S., 8 Mo. 492; Baldwin v. Smith, 82 Ill. 162. And see Schwuchow v. Chicago, 68 Ill. 444; O'Flinn v. S., 66 Miss. 7. The right conferred by a city charter to grant licenses is subject to the general law of the state: Louisville v. Kean, 18 B. Mon. 9. And see *supra*, § 1217.

[11] Godfrey v. S., 5 Blackf. 151; S. v. Hadlock, 43 Me. 282; C. v. Bryan, 9

of a licensed saloon-keeper has no protection from the license,[1] and the executor or administrator of one deceased holding a license cannot carry on the business thereunder.[2] But one holding a license may carry on the licensed business through an agent, and such agent is protected by his principal's license.[3] The agent's authority, however, comes only from the principal, and he becomes liable to punishment for violation of the statute if he makes sales which his principal has no right to make;[4] for instance, at a place where the principal has no right to sell.[5] If the principal moves from the state and thereby disqualifies himself from acting under the license, his agent will no longer be protected in making sales.[6] Obviously, where agency is a mere pretense to cover up what is in fact a trans-

Dana, 310; Algier v. Weston, 14 Johns. 231; Lewis v. U. S., 1 Morris, 199.

[1] Heath v. S., 105 Ind. 342; S. v. Lydick, 11 Neb. 366.

[2] U. S. v. Overton, 2 Cranch, C. C. 42; In re Blumenthal, 125 Pa. St. 412; P. v. Syks, 96 Mich. 452. It does not follow that the personal representative or assignee in insolvency cannot dispose of the stock of liquors in other ways than by carrying on the business: Williams v. Troop, 17 Wis. 463; Gignoux v. Bilbruck, 63 N. H. 22.

[3] Runyon v. S., 52 Ind. 320; Pickens v. S., 20 Ind. 116; Barnes v. C., 2 Dana, 388. Thus, a privilege of selling given to a producer or manufacturer may be exercised through an agent, who will be protected: C. v. Mahoney, 152 Mass. 493; S. v. Hart, 107 N. C. 796; Jeffries v. S., 52 Ark. 420. In Kentucky it seems to have been held that under the supervision of a person holding a license one may carry on the business in his own behalf, and not merely as agent of the licensee: Duncan v. C., 2 B. Mon. 281. This was the case of a tavern license, and perhaps distinguishable in that way from other cases; at any rate the doctrine does not extend to the case where the person licensed does not exercise supervision over the person making the sale: C. v. Branamon, 8 B. Mon. 374. As to liability of employer and employee respectively, see *infra*, §§ 1237, 1239.

[4] P. v. Metzger, 95 Mich. 121.

[5] P. v. Lester, 80 Mich. 643; C. v. Holstine, 132 Pa. St. 357; S. v. Copp, 34 Kan. 522; Peitz v. S., 68 Wis. 538. But agents may solicit orders and enter into contracts to sell at places where their principals have no license to make sales, the sale being deemed made where the title passes and where the principal has a license, and not where the contract of sale is made: Haug v. Gillett, 14 Kan. 140; Garbracht v. C., 96 Pa. St. 449. And see *infra*, § 1236.

[6] Krant v. S., 47 Ind. 519; Keiser v. S., 58 Ind. 379. But absence in the war was held not such a change of residence as to forfeit the right under a license, and the agent was held to be still protected thereby: Pickens v. S., 20 Ind. 116; S. v. McNeeley, 1 Winst. 234. Removal to another county in the same state was held not to affect the agent's right to sell at the licensed place, there being no requirement that the licensee should be a resident of the county: Thompson v. S., 37 Ala. 15.

fer of the business, the purchaser of the business, pretending to act as agent, is not protected.[1] As a partner is agent of the firm, a license issued to a firm will protect any one of the partners; but a license to one member of a partnership does not confer authority upon the other members to make sales, for they are agents of the firm and not of the licensed member.[2] So where one holding an individual license forms a partnership with another person, the latter is not entitled to sell;[3] but if a license is issued to a firm, one of the members who succeeds to the business of the firm may continue to sell under the partnership license.[4] This would seem to be reasonable, inasmuch as a license to a firm is evidently a license to each member of the firm.

§ **1228. Authority to issue discretionary.**— A statute requiring that sales shall be made only by persons having licenses is a means of regulation and not merely a means of taxation; therefore the statutes usually provide that the license may be granted or refused at the discretion of the licensing power,[5] and there is usually no appeal from the decision of the tribunal vested with the discretion;[6] nevertheless, if the refusal

[1] Heath v. S., 105 Ind. 342; Keiser v. S., 58 Ind. 379.

[2] Shaw v. S., 56 Ind. 188. And see Burke v. S., 72 Ind. 392; Wharton v. King, 69 Ala. 365; Long v. S., 27 Ala. 32. *Contra*, Barnes v. C., 2 Dana, 388. Where the statutes require that a person who has a right to sell shall be a registered pharmacist, or act under the supervision of such a pharmacist, the partner of a registered pharmacist has not the right to make sales while acting not under the supervision of the partner: S. v. Mullenhoff, 74 Ia. 271.

[3] C. v. Hall, 8 Grat. 588.

[4] U. S. v. Glab, 99 U. S. 225; U. S. v. Davis, 37 Fed. R. 468; S. v. Gerhardt, 3 Jones, 178.

[5] Pierce v. C., 10 Bush, 6; Nepp v. C., 2 Duv. 546; Ex parte Yeager, 11 Grat. 655; French v. Noel, 22 Grat. 454; Ailstock v. Page, 77 Va. 386; Hein v. Smith, 13 W. Va. 358; Attorney General v. Justices of Guilford, 5 Ired. 315; Muller v. Buncombe County Commissioners, 89 N. C. 171; Ex parte Whittington, 34 Ark. 394; Ex parte Levy, 43 Ark. 42; S. v. Cass County Commissioners, 12 Neb. 54; S. v. Board of Commissioners, 45 Ind. 501; S. v. Holt County Court, 39 Mo. 521; Perry v. Salt Lake City, 7 Utah, 143; U. S. v. Commissioners, 6 Mackey, 409. But by some statutes no discretion is given to the officers authorized to issue a license and they must do so on compliance with the statute: S. v. Justices, etc., 15 Ga. 408; Miller v. Wade, 58 Ind. 91; McLeod v. Scott, 21 Oreg. 94; Dougherty v. C., 14 B. Mon. 239.

[6] French v. Noel, 22 Grat. 454; Pierce v. C., 10 Bush, 6; Toole's Appeal, 90 Pa. St. 376. And see In re Berg, 139 Pa. St. 354; Leister's Appeal, — Pa. St. —, 11 Atl. R. 387; Hein v. Smith, 13 W. Va. 358. But

to grant a license is arbitrary and without reason, a writ of *mandamus* will lie to compel the licensing power to grant it.[1] The officers who corruptly grant or withhold a license in violation of duty are criminally liable for official misconduct.[2] The validity of a license when issued without authority may be tested by *quo warranto*.[3] But even if the applicant for a license is wrongfully denied the privilege asked, or the law is such that it is impossible to comply with the requirements for a license, the inability to secure authority to sell will be no defense for sales made without such authority.[4]

§ 1229. Selling without license; allegation and proof of license.— The general subject of illegal sales will be discussed in subsequent sections;[5] it is only necessary here to suggest that, in general, a sale without the license required is punishable, and one who undertakes to sell or carry on the business of selling must have the authority which the law demands.[6] So if a license authorizes sales for certain purposes and prohibits other sales, a sale for an unauthorized purpose is punishable as though no license had been issued for any purpose;[7] and it is so where the regulations as to the methods in which the business under the license is to be carried on are violated.[8] But it

in some states an appeal is allowed: Ex parte Dunn, 14 Ind. 122; S. v. Board of Commissioners, 45 Ind. 501; Groscop v. Rainier, 111 Ind. 361; Lydick v. Korner, 13 Neb. 10; Ex parte Lester, 77 Va. 663; Lester v. Price, 83 Va. 648.

[1] Zanone v. Mound City, 103 Ill. 552; Sparrow's Petition, 138 Pa. St. 116; In re Prospect Brewing Co., 127 Pa. St. 523.

[2] Attorney General v. Justices etc., 5 Ired. 315; S. v. Kite, 81 Mo 97; Rex v. Holland, 1 T. R. 692; P. v. Norton, 7 Barb. (N. Y.) 477.

[3] Swarth v. P., 109 Ill. 621.

[4] Wrongful refusal to grant: S. v. Cron, 23 Minn. 140; Charleston v. Hollenback, 3 Strobh. 355; S. v. Downer, 21 Wis. 274; S. v. Jamison, 23 Mo. 330; Deitz v. City of Central, 1 Colo. 323; Brock v. S., 65 Ga. 437; Roberts v. S., 26 Fla. 360; C. v. Blackington, 24 Pick. 352; Curry v. S., 28 Tex. Ap. 477; Kadgihn v. Bloomington, 58 Ill. 229; Kansas City v. Flanders, 71 Mo. 281. Impossibility of obtaining: S. v. Tucker, 45 Ark. 55; Erb v. S., 35 Ark. 631; S. v. Brown, 41 La. An. 771; S. v. McNeary, 88 Mo. 143; Welsh v. S., 126 Ind. 71; Indianapolis v. Fairchild, 1 Ind. 315; S. v. Graeter, 6 Blackf. 105; Reese v. Atlanta, 63 Ga. 344; S. v. Kantler, 33 Minn. 69.

[5] *Infra*, §§ 1233–1240.

[6] S. v. Thornburg, 16 S. C. 482; Keller v. S., 11 Md. 525; Chew v. S., 43 Ark. 361.

[7] S. v. Keen, 34 Me. 500; C. v. Barnes, 138 Mass. 511; C. v. Chadwick, 142 Mass. 595; C. v. Davis, 121 Mass. 352.

[8] C. v. Salmon, 136 Mass. 431; Thomasson v. S., 15 Ind. 449. So, where a statute required licensed tavern-keepers to conduct their busi-

is said that a Sunday sale must be punished as such and not as a sale without license, although the license forbids sales on Sunday;[1] and on the other hand there are some violations which can only be committed by licensed dealers.[2] Where the statute authorizes a city to vote on the question of whether liquor shall be licensed or not and the vote is in the negative, one selling liquor within such city should be indicted for the offense of selling after a vote against license and not for the offense of selling without a license.[3] The courts are hopelessly in conflict, however, in their decisions as to which party must raise and establish the fact of license or want of it. This conflict is doubtless due to some extent to difference in the language of the statutes, and to some extent to difference of view as to the nature of a license, but it will be impossible to particularize in this respect, and all that can be said is that in many cases it is held necessary for the prosecution to allege that the sale or the carrying on of the business, as the case may be, was without a license,[4] although this allegation may be in general terms.[5] Thus, it is sufficient to say that the sale was made without authority, or in violation of law,[6] and it is

ness in a particular way, it was held that a tavern-keeper having a license, but violating the provisions as to the method of conducting his business, was punishable as for selling without a license: S. v. Heise, 7 Rich. 518. But failure to make reports as required will not subject a permit-holder to punishment for sales otherwise legal: S. v. Von Haltschuherr, 72 Ia. 541.

[1] S. v. Thomasson, 19 Ind. 99.

[2] Brubaker v. S., 89 Ind. 577.

[3] S. v. Hanley, 25 Minn. 429.

[4] C. v. Hampton, 3 Grat. 590; S. v. Simons, 17 N. H. 83; Burke v. S., 52 Ind. 461; Howe v. S., 10 Ind. 423; Neales v. S., 10 Mo. 498; Berning v. S., 51 Ark. 550; S. v. Horan, 25 Tex. Sup. 271. If a valid license may be obtained in different ways, or from different tribunals, or for different purposes, it is necessary to negative a license obtained in any manner, or from any tribunal, or for any purpose: C. v. Roberts, 1 Cush. 505; Meier v. S., 57 Ind. 386; O'Brien v. S., 63 Ind. 242; S. v. Webster, 10 N. J. 293; S. v. Sutton, 25 Mo. 300; S. v. Haden, 15 Mo. 447. But if it is illegal to sell at all without some form of a license, a general negative of the possession of license is sufficient: S. v. Wishon, 15 Mo. 503.

[5] S. v. Tall, 56 Wis. 577; S. v. Barker, 3 R. I. 280; S. v. Johnson, 3 R. I. 94; C. v. Turner, 4 B. Mon. 4; S. v. Clark, 23 Vt. 293; C. v. Hatcher, 6 Grat. 667.

[6] C. v. Stowell, 9 Met. 569; C. v. Dunn, 14 Gray, 401; C. v. Byrnes, 126 Mass. 248; C. v. Intoxicating Liquors, 110 Mass. 416; C. v. Burke, 121 Mass. 39; S. v. Connelly, 63 Me. 212; S. v. Lang, 63 Me. 215. It is not necessary to negative the authority in the language of the statute: S. v. Keen, 34 Me. 500; S. v. Buckner, 52 Ind. 278. It may even be sufficient to negative the authority inferen-

said that the want of authority must be proved by the prosecution, notwithstanding the rule that where negative averments have reference to some personal qualification peculiar to defendant, or the proof thereof depends upon some written document committed to the sole custody of the accused, or where the negative averment is peculiarly within his knowledge, the burden of establishing the defense is on the person who relies upon it.[1] On the other hand, there are many cases in which it is held that the indictment need not allege, and, of course, the prosecution need not prove, that defendant has no license or other authority, and that such license or authority, if it exists, must be shown in defense.[2]

§ **1230. Carrying on the business without a license.**—The earliest forms of licenses were those required for keeping taverns or tippling-houses where liquors were sold;[3] and a license to keep a tavern was under such regulations held to imply a license to retail intoxicating liquors to be drunk there.[4] The

tially: Webster v. S., 7 Dana, 215; Boyle v. C., 14 Grat. 674; Sires v. S., 73 Wis. 251. If a license is only required under certain circumstances, a general negative of license is not sufficient without showing that the sale was one not legal without a license: C. v. Dean, 21 Pick. 334. But if the statute covers every sale, a general negative of authority under such statute is sufficient: C. v. Gilland, 9 Gray, 3; and it is not necessary to negative all the possible cases in which it would be lawful for one to sell: C. v. Brusie, 145 Mass. 117. A general negative of any legal appointment or authority covers every case under which the sale of liquor is lawful, whether by special authority or where the statute does not require license for all sales: C. v. Lafontaine, 3 Gray, 479. Where negation of authority is necessary, it is not enough to say that the act was "unlawfully" done: C. v. Crossley, 162 Mass. 515. Where two are jointly indicted, a general negative of license without specifying that neither is licensed is sufficient: C. v. Tower, 8 Met. 527. In general, see also *infra*, § 1270.

[1] Berning v. S., 51 Ark. 550. But, on the contrary, it is held that such negative averment need not be proved: Fairly v. S., 63 Miss. 333. See *infra*, § 1281.

[2] C. v. Allen, 15 B. Mon. 1; C. v. Harvey, 16 B. Mon. 1; S. v. Sorrell, 98 N. C. 738; S. v. Emery, 98 N. C. 668; P. v. Curtis, 95 Mich. 212; S. v. Beneke, 9 Ia. 203; S. v. Collins, 11 Ia. 141; S. v. Jordan, 39 Ia. 387; S. v. Devers, 38 Ark. 517; *supra*, § 1215.

[3] Bonner v. Welborn, 7 Ga. 296; S. v. Prettyman, 3 Harr. 570. A specific sale need not be alleged: P. v. Telford, 56 Mich. 541; P. v. Breidenstein, 65 Mich. 65. A license for retailing is sometimes required where carried on in connection with other business: Curd v. C., 14 B. Mon. 386; S. v. Cahen, 35 Md. 236; S. v. Sies, 30 La. An., Part II, 918. Further as to retailing, see *infra*, § 1245.

[4] S. v. Chamblyss, 1 Cheves, 220; Hirn v. S., 1 Ohio St. 15; C. v. Kamp, 14 B. Mon. 385. *Contra*, Page v. S., 11 Ala. 849; Braswell v. C., 5 Bush, 544.

offense of keeping a dram-shop without license is a different one from that of retailing without having paid a special tax required therefor.[1] Statutes of this kind imply something more than a single sale or single act of manufacture, as the case may be.[2] This subject is, however, more fully discussed hereafter in considering the offense of keeping a place for the illegal sale of liquors constituting a nuisance.[3]

§ **1231. Place of sale.**— A license for selling or keeping for sale usually restricts the licensee as to the place where sales may be made or the business carried on, so that under particular licenses such acts elsewhere than at the place specified will be criminal.[4] In determining what shall be regarded as one place, something will depend upon the character of the license and the language of the statute under which it is issued; but commonly two buildings are not one place, although they may be on the same lot,[5] or close together, even with internal connections;[6] on the other hand, two bars in connecting rooms in a single building may constitute one place if the whole building is under the control of one person.[7] Where two or more rooms are connected by archways, or even by doors, there being a bar in each room, one license is usually regarded as sufficient.[8] A brewer's license will only protect sales made at

[1] Volmer v. S., 34 Ark. 487.

[2] Johnson v. S., 44 Ala. 414.

[3] *Infra*, § 1248.

[4] S. v. Prettyman, 3 Harr. 570; S. v. Walker, 16 Me. 241; S. v. Hughes, 24 Mo. 147; Zinner v. C., — Pa. St. —, 14 Atl. R. 431; Wason v. Severance, 2 N. H. 501; S. v. Moody, 95 N. C. 656.

[5] C. v. Estabrook, 10 Pick. 293.

[6] S. v. Fredericks, 16 Mo. 382.

[7] Gray v. C., 9 Dana, 300. But this would not always be so: Sanders v. Elberton, 50 Ga. 178; P. v. Hughes, 97 Mich. 543. Where a saloon is connected with a restaurant by a swinging door through which patrons go in and out, this is an open saloon, whether the front door is open or not: P. v. Cummerford, 58 Mich. 328. So where a restaurant and saloon are kept in the same building with an internal connection they may constitute one establishment: S. v. Clark, 28 N. H. 176. Two rooms, one over the other, controlled by the same owner may be considered as one establishment, unless it appears that the room above is not used as an appendage to the one below: Brown v. S., 27 Ala. 47. Where the statute provides that no licenses shall be granted to be exercised in any dwelling-house, a license to sell in a house partly occupied by the licensee as a dwelling-house is void, whether the two parts are connected by an inside door or not: C. v. McCormick, 150 Mass. 270. Further as to connection between bar and other place of business, see *infra*, §§ 1264, 1265.

[8] Hochstadler v. S., 73 Ala. 24; St. Louis v. Gerardi, 90 Mo. 640. The question whether two bars are one and the same stand so as to be covered by one license is a question of fact: S. v. Fredericks, 16 Mo. 382.

the brewery, and will confer no right to sell kegs of beer away from the premises, either by agent or otherwise.[1] In subsequent sections limitations on the right to sell in particular localities are discussed.[2]

§ **1232. Local option.**— Where the right to sell depends upon the adoption of a regulation in some particular locality, such as a county, township, city or district, the adoption by the county of the provisions of the law will be applicable over the entire territory, including cities and districts therein;[3] but a failure to so adopt will not prevent adoption of such provisions in a township, city or district which is authorized to act independently.[4] Where a district has adopted local option, and subsequently a new district of the same character is created out of a portion of it, the local-option provision continues in force in the new district without independent adoption.[5] There are usually conditions upon which the action of any particular locality in adopting or repealing local-option provisions must be based, and if these conditions are not complied with the attempt to adopt or repeal will be nugatory.[6] Sometimes, however, the terms of the statute are such that the tribunal authorized to act in determining whether local option shall go into effect must pass upon the sufficiency of the previous steps, and if so, its determination cannot be subsequently questioned for the purpose of nullifying its action.[7] There must be a determination by the proper authority that the provision was adopted; that fact cannot be proved *aliunde;*[8] but if no particular method of proclaiming the result is provided, the fact of adoption is all that is necessary to be shown.[9] An

1 Peitz v. S., 68 Wis. 538.

2 *Infra,* § 1266.

3 Tatum v. S., 79 Ga. 176.

4 Ex parte Cox, 28 Tex. Ap. 537. So it was held that where local option had been adopted in a county it might subsequently be repealed in a smaller district, although not repealed in the county: Whisenhunt v. S., 18 Tex. Ap. 491.

5 Higgins v. S., 64 Md. 419.

6 Prather v. S., 12 Tex. Ap. 401; Akin v. S., 14 Tex. Ap. 142; McMillan v. S., 18 Tex. Ap. 375; Smith v. S., 19 Tex. Ap. 444; Carnes v. S., 23 Tex. Ap. 449; P. v. Murphy, 93 Mich. 41. But where the prerequisite is a certain publication, it is held that the failure to make entry of the fact of publication will not defeat the subsequent proceedings, as such fact might be proved otherwise: Ezzell v. S., 29 Tex. Ap. 521.

7 Conrad v. S., 70 Miss. 733; S. v. Emery, 98 N. C. 768; S. v. Cooper, 101 N. C. 684; S. v. Dugan, 110 Mo. 138; Young v. C., 14 Bush, 161.

8 McDonald v. S., 68 Miss. 728.

9 Mackin v. S., 62 Md. 244; P. v. Adams, 95 Mich. 541.

indictment based on local-option provisions should allege that they have been adopted and gone into effect.[1] Where the defense in a prosecution for selling is the adoption of a local-option provision authorizing such sale, the fact of such adoption must be shown by defendant.[2] The adoption of the provision must be in accordance with the terms of the statute authorizing such adoption, and if it provides for a submission of the question as to "sale," the adoption of a provision as to "sale, gift or exchange" will be invalid.[3] Statutes sometimes provide that the court shall take judicial notice of the result of an election on the submission of the question of local option, and in such case it is not necessary to allege that the election was held and the result thereof;[4] but in the absence of some such provision judicial notice cannot be taken of such fact.[5]

IV. Illegal Selling or Keeping for Sale.

§ **1233. What deemed a sale.**— As the statutes usually provide for the punishment of selling intoxicating liquors, except as duly authorized, and also provide special punishments for sales in particular classes of cases, such as to minors, etc., it becomes important to determine what is a sale, and the question has been found not to be free from difficulty. The word "sell" is to be construed, however, according to the settled rules of law, there being no special definition of the term by statute.[6] The question has often arisen whether one who procures liquor for another is punishable as a seller, and it has usually been held that he is not if he has no interest in the sale, but acts only as the agent or friend of the purchaser.[7] Nor is such an

[1] West v. S., 70 Miss. 598; S. v. Dugan, 110 Mo. 138; P. v. Adams, 95 Mich. 541; S. v. Chambers, 93 N. C. 600.

[2] Donaldson v. S., 15 Tex. Ap. 25.

[3] Steele v. S., 19 Tex. Ap. 425; Ninenger v. S., 25 Tex. Ap. 449; Croom v. S., 25 Tex. Ap. 556.

[4] S. v. Bertrand, 72 Miss. 516.

[5] Whitman v. S., 80 Md. 410.

[6] Siegel v. P., 106 Ill. 89. In Massachusetts delivery is made *prima facie* evidence of a sale, except when the delivery is in or from a dwelling-house: C. v. Dobbyn, 14 Gray, 44; C. v. Taylor, 113 Mass. 4.

[7] Campbell v. S., 79 Ala. 271; Morgan v. S., 81 Ala. 72; Du Bois v. S., 87 Ala. 101; S. v. Taylor, 89 N. C. 577; S. v. Thomas, 13 W. Va. 848; Anderson v. S., 32 Fla. 242; Johnson v. S., 63 Miss. 228. One cannot be convicted under a penal statute of this kind for doing an act which merely contravenes the policy thereof: Young v. S., 58 Ala. 358. This rule is applicable to procuring liquor for a minor, where sales to minors are prohibited: Bryant v. S., 82 Ala. 51. But to purchase liquor with money furnished by a minor,

act a giving away or otherwise disposing of intoxicating liquor under statutory prohibitions;[1] but such act may constitute a furnishing.[2] However, one who ostensibly procures liquor for another, but makes the transaction merely a subterfuge to cover an illegal sale of liquor by himself, is guilty of selling;[3] and one who receives money and delivers liquor therefor may be treated as the seller, no other person filling that character in the transaction being pointed out by the evidence.[4] Difficulty has also arisen out of cases where, even though there is no intermediate agent, the person charged with selling has not dealt personally with the buyer. But it is not essential to the sale that the liquor be asked for and handed to the person who asks for it;[5] and where it appears that one person put down money in the defendant's presence and took away a bottle of liquor belonging to defendant without his objection, the fact of a sale is sufficiently shown.[6] So the fact that the liquor is left where the purchaser can find it, and the latter leaves money in its place, is sufficient to sustain a verdict for unlawful selling.[7]

and give it to him, has been held a sale to the minor: Burnett v. S., 92 Ga. 474. And for a dealer to give liquor to a minor or intoxicated person on payment therefor by another is criminal: S. v. Best, 108 N. C. 747; Foster v. S., 45 Ark. 361; S. v. Hubbard, 60 Ia. 466; Walton v. S., 62 Ala. 197. At any rate, such act would be a "furnishing" to the minor within statutory provisions: P. v. Neumann, 85 Mich. 98. And as to this matter, see, also, *infra*, § 1259. A purchaser is not guilty of any crime: See *infra*, § 1241.

[1] Morgan v. S., 81 Ala. 72.

[2] S. v. Hassett, 64 Vt. 46; S. v. Deusting, 33 Minn. 102.

[3] White v. S., 93 Ga. 47. So the procurer is guilty as seller if he has a pecuniary interest in the sale whether he is a partner of the seller or not: Phillips v. S., 95 Ga. 478. So a storekeeper who does not keep liquor, but makes himself an agent and carrier to procure it for and distribute it among his customers, violates the statute as to selling: S. v. Buck, 37 Vt. 657.

[4] Paschal v. S., 84 Ga. 326; Grant v. S., 87 Ga. 265.

[5] Kimball v. P., 20 Ill. 348.

[6] McClure v. S., 43 Ark. 75; Liles v. S., 43 Ark. 95. And see S. v. McMinn, 83 N. C. 668.

[7] Stultz v. S., 96 Ind. 456. So evidence showing that the purchaser had entered defendant's place of business and put a piece of money in a drawer, at the same time calling for whisky, and that such drawer was returned with the whisky in it, is sufficient even though the purchaser who testifies to the transaction did not see who supplied the whisky: Showalter v. S., 84 Ind. 562. A sale may be sufficiently proved by the call for liquor, the subsequent delivery, and the placing of an apparently satisfactory consideration within reach of the seller: S. v. Wiggin, 20 N. H. 449. So where witness testified that he came into defendant's barber shop and asked if he

§ 1234. Consideration; barter or exchange.— A sale is not implied from the mere fact of furnishing liquor to another, even by a dealer, nothing being said about payment and no payment being made;[1] but where a person calls for liquor at a usual place of sale and it is delivered to him, this is sufficient evidence of a sale though no money is paid and no directions given as to charging.[2] An understanding between the parties that the liquor shall be settled for at a future time is sufficient,[3] and it is not material that under the provisions of the statute no action to recover the price could be maintained.[4] The consideration for a sale may be credit given on an indebtedness,[5] or the use of property.[6] The fact that other property besides liquor is given for the money paid will not be material if the liquor is in part consideration for such payment.[7] Where liquor is exchanged or bartered for other property,[8] or is delivered with an agreement that it shall be returned in kind, the transaction does not constitute a sale.[9] The statutes usu-

had any whisky, and on defendant's saying "no, but that there was some in a box which belonged to some one else," witness said he would take a drink, which he did without saying anything, as he had done on previous occasions, the evidence was held sufficient: Roberson v. S., 100 Ala. 37. But where it appeared that witness entered defendant's room attached to his grocery, and there found in a box a bottle of whisky from which he took a drink, laid down ten cents and departed, there being no evidence that defendant knew of it or received the money, *held*, that the evidence did not support a conviction: S. v. Ferrell, 22 W. Va. 759. And it is not a selling or giving away to simply hand over to another liquor purchased for the latter by a third person as agent and temporarily left in defendant's possession: Amos v. S., 73 Ala. 498.

[1] Keiser v. S., 82 Ind. 379. So where defendant took some whisky from his wagon and gave it to several persons, saying that he had some for his friends but not for sale, and the drinkers threw money upon the wagon seat about equivalent to the price of the liquor furnished, but it did not appear whether he took it, *held*, that a verdict for defendant was improperly set aside: S. v. Cooper, 26 W. Va. 338. As to gifts see next section.

[2] Hill v. S., 37 Ark. 395. And see C. v. Reichart, 108 Mass. 482. Even though the seller, after delivering the liquor, informs the purchaser that he need not pay for it, this is not conclusive against a sale; the jury is to determine whether at the time of delivery it was intended as a sale: S. v. Greenleaf, 31 Me. 517; S. v. Simons, 17 N. H. 83.

[3] S. v. Gerber, 80 Mo. 94.

[4] C. v. Burns, 8 Gray, 482.

[5] S. v. Poteet, 86 N. C. 612.

[6] Paschal v. S., 84 Ga. 326.

[7] C. v. Thayer, 8 Met. 525; Marcus v. S., 89 Ala. 23; Archer v. S., 45 Md. 33; Looney v. S., 43 Ark. 389.

[8] Stevenson v. S., 65 Ind. 409.

[9] Coker v. S., 91 Ala. 92; Gillan v.

ally make the exchange or barter criminal as well as the sale, and under such a provision it is not necessary to allege the value of the bartered article; the burden is upon defendant to show that it had no value.[1] It is a sale and not a barter to give liquor in exchange for pool checks, chips or tickets which have been previously sold.[2]

§ 1235. **Giving; furnishing; disposing of.**— To cover cases where there is neither an exchange nor a barter the statutes usually contain provisions in regard to giving, but in most of the statutes these provisions cover only giving in consideration of the purchase of other property,[3] or as a shift or device in evasion of the law against selling.[4] Generally the mere giving as an act of hospitality is not criminal.[5] Even where the statute makes it criminal to give or furnish liquor to another on Sunday,[6] or to a minor or person in the habit of becoming intoxicated,[7] it is not criminal to thus furnish liquor to another, not in the way of business, but at a private house, by way of hospitality. But on this qnestion there are analogous cases the other way, for instance, as to giving on election day, which may very reasonably be deemed in contravention of the policy as well as the language of the statute.[8] If it is intended to show a giving within the prohibition of the statute the act should be so charged, and not as a sale, the offenses being distinct.[9] A giving away or a delivery for optional purchase may be punished as "furnishing" within the language of some statutes, although it is without consideration.[10] By some statutes

S., 47 Ark. 555; Robinson v. S., 59 Ark. 341; but such a transaction may be a transfer within statutory pro visions: C. v. Abrams, 150 Mass. 393.

[1] Forkner v. S., 95 Ind. 406.

[2] Billingsley v. S., 96 Ala. 114; S. v. Horacek, 41 Kan. 87; U. S. v. Wittig, 2 Low. 466. *Contra*, Massey v. S., 74 Ind. 368.

[3] S. v. Finan, 10 Ia. 19.

[4] Kober v. S., 10 Ohio St. 444; S. v. Hutchins, 74 Ia. 20: S. v. Ball, 27 Neb. 601; Wendt v. S., 32 Neb. 182; P. v. Sweetser, 1 Dak. 295; S. v. Standish, 37 Kan. 643.

[5] Reynolds v. S., 73 Ala. 3; S. v. Jones, 39 Vt. 370; S. v. Ball, 27 Neb. 601.

[6] C. v. Carey, 151 Pa. St. 368; C. v. Heckler, 168 Pa. St. 575.

[7] Albrecht v. P., 78 Ill. 510, 2 Am. Cr. R. 401; Cruse v. Aden, 127 Ill. 231.

[8] Cearfoss v. S., 42 Md. 403, 1 Am. Cr. R. 460; Baker v. S., 2 Ind. Ap. 517. So, giving to an intoxicated person has been held criminal, under a statute forbidding sales to such persons: Dahmer v. S., 56 Miss. 787.

[9] Williams v. S., 91 Ala. 14; Humpeler v. P., 92 Ill. 400; Birr v. P., 113 Ill. 645; Wood v. S., 1 Oreg. 223. So, evidence of a sale will not sustain a charge of giving away: Harvey v. S., 80 Ind. 142; Kurz v. S., 79 Ind. 481.

[10] S. v. Deusting, 33 Minn. 102; S. v.

the "transferring or disposing" of intoxicating liquors otherwise than by law is prohibited.[1]

§ 1236. **When sale complete; place of sale.**— The mere executory agreement to sell does not constitute a sale, but actual delivery must be proved,[2] and the sale is to be deemed made at the place of delivery.[3] The place of sale is determined by the same rules as in a civil case; it is the place where title passes,[4] and it is not necessarily the place from which the liquor is shipped.[5] Thus, if an order is taken in one county by the agent of a dealer in another county, and the liquor is shipped by the principal to the agent, who makes delivery and collects payment, the sale is in the county where delivery is made;[6] but if the agent forwards an order which is subject to the approval of his principal and the order is accepted and the liquor shipped to the purchaser by a common carrier, the place of sale is the place where the liquor is thus delivered to the carrier. If the principal is authorized to sell at that place, the transaction is not criminal, either on the part of the seller or his agent;[7] and it does not affect the case that the agent afterwards collects payment at the place where the order is taken.[8] By the weight of authority this rule is applicable also

Freeman, 27 Vt. 520; S. v. Hassett, 64 Vt. 46; S. v. Comings, 28 Vt. 508.

[1] Roberson v. S., 100 Ala. 37; C. v. Abrams, 150 Mass. 393.

[2] Riley v. S., 43 Miss. 397.

[3] Doster v. S., 93 Ga. 43.

[4] C. v. Eggleston, 128 Mass. 408.

[5] C. v. Burgett, 136 Mass. 450.

[6] C. v. Shurn, 145 Mass. 150; C. v. Holstine, 132 Pa. St. 357; Bagby v. S., 82 Ga. 786; S. v. Swift, 35 W. Va. 542; U. S. v. Cline, 26 Fed. R. 515. So if one sends orders to a liquor dealer in another county and receives the packages and delivers them to the parties ordering, he is guilty of selling where the delivery is made: Bryant v. S., 89 Tenn. 581; Berger v. S., 50 Ark. 20; Yowell v. S., 41 Ark. 355; Blackwell v. S., 42 Ark. 275.

[7] Fuller v. Leet, 59 N. H. 163; Corning v. Abbott, 54 N. H. 469; Pearson v. S., 66 Miss. 510; Brechwald v. P., 21 Ill. Ap. 213; Newman v. S., 88 Ala. 115; Dunn v. S., 82 Ga. 27; S. v. Colby, 92 Ia. 463, 61 N. W. Rep. 187. Of course the rule is the same if the order is taken by the seller in person in a county other than that of his place of business, and is filled by delivery to a carrier at his place of business: Herron v. S., 51 Ark. 133. Indeed there may be a sufficient setting apart at the place of business in response to an order to constitute a delivery there to the purchaser and fix that as the place of sale, although the seller is to transport the liquor in his own wagons to the buyer in another county: C. v. Hess, 148 Pa. St. 98.

[8] Sarbecker v. S., 65 Wis. 171; Pearson v. S., 66 Miss. 510; S. v. Hughes, 22 W. Va. 743.

to cases where the shipment is by express, C. O. D., either on an order received through an agent or directly from the purchaser, and such a sale is to be deemed made at the place where the liquor is delivered to the carrier, the provision as to collection amounting only to the retention of a lien for the price.[1] There are cases, however, holding that where the liquor is shipped C. O. D., the seller makes the carrier his agent, and the sale is therefore complete where the liquor is delivered by the express company to the buyer and payment is collected.[2]

§ 1237. **Liability for sales by servant.**— In general, an illegal sale made by an agent or servant is a sale by the principal or master for which the latter is punishable.[3] There could be no question as to liability in such a case if the particular sale was directed by the employer, or made by his servant in his presence so that his authority might be implied.[4] Sometimes it is expressly provided by statute that there shall be a liability for sales made by an agent, clerk or servant, but such a statute probably imposes no greater liability than would be implied without it, and simply renders the principal responsible for acts done for him by another,[5] unless, perhaps, it raises a *prima facie* liability for sales made by clerks or servants in the course of their employment.[6] Even if this be true, the fact of such a sale is merely evidence from which the jury may infer the guilt of the employer, and does not raise a presumption that the sale was by the employer's authority so as to absolutely fix his liability.[7] There is a well-marked conflict in the authorities as to the employer's liability for sales made by a clerk or servant in the general course of his employment but without the express authority of the employer. The general

[1] C. v. Fleming, 130 Pa. St. 138; S. v. Flanagan, 38 W. Va. 53; S. v. Carl, 43 Ark. 353; Herron v. S., 51 Ark 133.

[2] S. v. O'Neil, 58 Vt. 140; S. v. Goss, 59 Vt. 266; Crabb v. S., 88 Ga. 584.

[3] McCutcheon v. P., 69 Ill. 601; Carey v. S., 83 Ind. 597; Schmidt v. S., 14 Mo. 137; S. v. Dow, 21 Vt. 484. As to charging sale by agent, see *infra*, § 1271.

[4] Forrester v. S., 63 Ga. 349; Johnson v. S., 83 Ga. 553.

[5] S. v. Brown, 31 Me. 520; S. v. Stewart, 31 Me. 515; S. v. Intoxicating Liquors, 50 Me. 506; Hanson v. S., 43 Ind. 550.

[6] S. v. Wentworth, 65 Me. 234.

[7] C. v. Briant, 142 Mass. 463; C. v. Stevenson, 142 Mass. 466; C. v. Hurley, 160 Mass. 10. The *prima facie* case may be overcome by showing that the sale was made against the employer's positive orders, given in good faith: S. v. McCance, 110 Mo. 398; S. v. Weber, 111 Mo. 204.

rule in criminal law, as has already been shown, is that the master or employer is not criminally liable for the acts of his servant or agent not done by his authority, though within the scope of the employment,[1] and accordingly many courts have held that in case of illegal sale of liquor by a clerk or servant the direct authority or consent of the employer must be proved in order to fix criminal liability upon him.[2] But in accordance with the principle heretofore discussed by which one who carries on a business which is subject to statutory regulation is held accountable for any violation of the provisions of the statute in the conduct of such business without regard to his knowledge of or consent to such violation,[3] it has been held by many courts that an employer carrying on the business of selling liquor is responsible criminally for violations of the statute by his employees in conducting such business, even though such violation is contrary to his express directions;[4] and this doctrine is especially insisted on where the illegality consists in the method of doing the business and not in the business itself; for instance, where, in the course of carrying on a lawful business of selling, the clerk or servant sells to a minor or an intoxicated person, even though directly forbidden by his em-

[1] *Supra*, § 188.

[2] P. v. Hughes, 86 Mich. 180; P. v. Parks, 49 Mich. 333; C. v. Wachendorf. 141 Mass. 270; Lauer v. S., 24 Ind. 131; Lathrope v. S., 51 Ind. 192; S. v. Mahoney, 23 Minn. 181; Goods v. S., 3 Greene (Ia.), 566; Cloud v. S., 36 Ark. 151; Gaiocchio v. S., 9 Tex. Ap. 387. And see *supra*, § 189. One keeping intoxicating liquors for sale for prohibited purposes will not be guilty of the crime of nuisance on account of illegal sales made by a clerk without his knowledge or authority: S. v. Hayes, 67 Ia. 27. The question whether the illegal sale by a servant was under the authority and with the consent of the master is for the jury under all the circumstances: C. v. Honle, 147 Mass. 380; Neideiser v. S., 6 Baxt. 499. Of course, if the sale is by one who is not authorized to act for the employer at all in making sales, the employer will not be liable if the act is without his consent: S. v. Summey, 1 Winst. 108; Minden v. Silverstien, 36 La. An. 912; Perkins v. S., 92 Ala. 66. In determining whether the person selling was servant of defendant it is competent to prove that about the time of the sale defendant was in the business of selling: S. v. Bonney, 39 N. H. 206.

[3] *Supra*, §§ 128, 134.

[4] Mullinix v. P., 76 Ill. 211; Noecker v. P., 91 Ill. 494; S. v. Priester, 43 Minn. 373; Riley v. S., 43 Miss. 397; U. S. v. White, 42 Fed. R. 138. In one case it is said that any person having an interest in liquor illegally sold may be convicted for such sale, although not in his presence or with his knowledge: Gathings v. S., 44 Miss. 343. A sale by the person in charge is enough to render the proprietor liable: O'Flinn v. S., 66 Miss. 7.

ployer to make such sales.[1] And this doctrine is recognized in such cases even by courts which hold that the general liability for illegal selling cannot be fixed upon the principal by an unauthorized act of his agent or servant.[2]

§ 1238. **Sales by partner or wife.**— The general principles discussed in the preceding section are applicable to sales by a partner, and it has accordingly been held that one partner may be convicted upon a sale of liquor by his associate, although without his consent and in his absence.[3] A husband is not responsible for acts of his wife not committed in his presence or by his command or consent,[4] but for her act done in his presence he is presumed to be liable.[5] For her acts not in his presence he may be liable if done as his agent.[6] On the principle that the husband is responsible for the use of the premises on which his wife resides with him, he may be criminally liable for the illegal business of selling liquor carried on there, although it is without his consent and against his remonstrances.[7]

§ 1239. **Liability of agent.**— Offenses against the liquor laws being misdemeanors, all who aid or assist in their commis-

[1] Carroll v. S., 63 Md. 551, S. v. Kittelle, 110 N. C. 560; Mogler v. S., 47 Ark. 109; S. v. Denoon, 31 W. Va. 122; Loeb v. S., 75 Ga. 258; Fahey v. S., 62 Miss. 402. And see cases cited *supra*, § 189; but *contra*, even in these cases, see P. v. Hughes, 86 Mich. 180; S. v. Findley, 45 Ia. 435; Johnson v. S., 83 Ga. 553; Cloud v. S., 36 Ark. 151.

[2] Thus, in Massachusetts, the employer is held liable for the unauthorized act of his servant in putting up curtains or shutters in violation of the statutory regulations: C. v. Kelley, 140 Mass. 441; and for sales to minors: C. v. Emmons, 98 Mass. 6; otherwise if the servant acts in good faith, believing the person not to be a minor: C. v. Stevens, 153 Mass. 421. And see *infra*, § 1257. And in Michigan it is held that the employer is liable for the unlawful sale by his servant on Sunday, though made without authority: P. v. Roby, 52 Mich. 577; P. v. Blake, 52 Mich. 566. At any rate there is a presumptive liability in such case, and want of consent, express or implied, on the part of the defendant, should be shown if relied on: Sanders v. S., 74 Ga. 82.

[3] Whiton v. S., 37 Miss. 379; Sellers v. S., 98 Ala. 72; Segars v. S., 88 Ala. 144; Robinson v. S., 38 Ark. 641; Waller v. S., 38 Ark. 656. *Contra*, Acree v. C., 13 Bush, 353.

[4] Pennybaker v. S., 2 Blackf. 484.

[5] Geuing v. S., 1 McCord, 573; Hensley v. S., 52 Ala. 10. But this presumed liability for the acts of the wife done in the husband's presence does not apply to acts of a concubine: U. S. v. Bonham, 31 Fed. R. 808.

[6] C. v. Lafayette, 148 Mass. 130.

[7] S. v. McDaniel, 1 Houst. Cr. Cas. 506. And see *supra*, § 148.

sion are liable as principals;[1] but one who, as agent or servant of another, does the act which is forbidden is, of course, criminally liable therefor under the general rule of criminal liability.[2] There must be some participation in or connection with the unlawful act,[3] but any form of aiding or assisting is sufficient.[4] A mere volunteer who, without any compensation, assists in making sales is criminally liable therefor.[5] It has already been stated that if the principal has a license, his agent selling within the terms of such license and the law is protected;[6] if, however, the employer is not licensed, then both employer and servant are criminally liable for sales which the servant makes.[7] Without regard to the liability of the principal, the agent is liable for illegal sales made by him, notwithstanding the general proposition that a sale by an agent is deemed the act of the principal.[8] Even where the offense consists in carrying on the business illegally, as without a wholesaler's license,[9] or so as to constitute a nuisance,[10] or in illegally keeping for sale,[11] or selling to be drunk on the premises,[12] or

[1] C. v. Ahearn, 160 Mass. 300. Persons may thus be jointly liable who are not partners: Janks v. S., 29 Tex. Ap. 233.

[2] *Supra*, § 190. A command of the employer will be no defense, even in the case of a minor, unless he is of such tender years as to be legally incapable of committing a crime: Cagle v. S., 87 Ala. 93.

[3] Zeller v. S., 46 Ind. 304.

[4] S. v. Murdoch, 71 Me. 454; Johnson v. P., 83 Ill. 431; C. v. Ahearn, 160 Mass. 300. Although the wife owns the store in which liquors are sold in violation of law by a clerk, the husband may be guilty if he controls and manages the store: Faircloth v. S., 73 Ga. 426. A storekeeper, who, while not keeping liquors for sale, makes himself an agent and carrier to procure it for division and distribution, is guilty of illegal selling: S. v. Buck, 37 Vt. 657.

[5] S. v. Finan, 10 Ia. 19; S. v. Herselus, 86 Ia. 214; Beck v. S., 69 Miss. 217; S. v. Bugbee, 22 Vt. 32; Cagle v. S., 87 Ala. 93.

[6] *Supra*, § 1227.

[7] S. v. Keith, 37 Ark. 96; Johnson v. S., 37 Ark. 98; Lane v. S., 37 Ark. 272; Thompson v. S., 5 Humph. 137; Sellers v. S., 98 Ala. 72; S. v. Chastain, 19 Oreg. 176; Tardiff v. S., 23 Tex. 169. But where the indictment is for being a dealer, evidence that the defendant was a clerk will not be admissible: Archer v. S., 10 Tex. Ap. 482.

[8] S. v. Haines, 35 N. H. 207; S. v. Kriechbaum, 81 Ia. 633. Certainly a bartender is liable when he does all the acts constituting the sale in the absence of his employer: C. v. Sinclair, 138 Mass. 493. If the statutory offense of acting as agent in such sales is charged, the name of the principal should be stated: S. v. Higgins, 53 Vt. 191.

[9] Abel v. S., 90 Ala. 631.

[10] S. v. Stucker, 33 Ia. 395; S. v. Hoxsie, 15 R. I. 1; C. v. Dowling, 114 Mass. 259; S. v. Sullivan, 83 Me. 417.

[11] S. v. McGuire, 64 N. H. 529.

[12] C. v. Hadley, 11 Met. 66.

keeping open a saloon on election day,[1] or on Sunday,[2] the agent who thus carries it on illegally is punishable as well as the principal.[3] But under some statutes it is held that a servant is not liable for keeping a nuisance where all his acts in connection therewith are done under the direct control and supervision of his master, and he does not himself have at any time control of the premises.[4]

§ 1240. **Furnishing to members of club.**— Where liquor is procured out of a common fund and distributed to those contributing to the fund, the question arises as to whether the person thus making distribution is guilty of selling, or whether the corporation, if there be one, such as a club, by which the liquors are bought for supplying its members, is carrying on an illegal business, or a business requiring a license. It is said that one who procures liquor upon the inducement of several, members of a common party, for their common refreshment, all contributing with him to the expense, is not a seller;[5] but there is great diversity of opinion among the courts as to the legal *status* of clubs with reference to the furnishing of liquor, due perhaps to the variety of methods in which it has been sought to thus evade the restrictions of the law. Where liquors are purchased by a club and left with its steward for sale to members at a price that will practically reimbu se the club for the cost of the liquor, such selling has been held to be a retailing which is criminal without license,[6] and the steward has been held punishable for such a transaction as a selling.[7] It

[1] Janks v. S., 29 Tex. Ap. 233.

[2] Blahut v. S., 34 Ark. 447.

[3] Some courts, however, have considered that the defendant is not punishable as seller when he is acting for a principal: S. v. Intoxicating Liquors, 63 Me. 121; S. v. Gravelin, 16 R. I. 407.

[4] C. v. Churchill, 136 Mass. 148; C. v. Galligan, 144 Mass. 171; S. v. Gravelin, 16 R. I. 407. *Contra*, S. v. Sullivan, 83 Me. 417.

[5] Hogg v. P., 15 Ill. Ap. 288; Graff v. Evans. 8 Q. B. D. 373. *Contra*, Hunter v. S., 60 Ark. 312. As to procuring for others, see *supra*, § 1233.

[6] S. v. Essex Club, 53 N. J. 99; S. v. Boston Club, 45 La. An. 585; P. v. Soule, 74 Mich. 250. A corporation may be a person in such sense as to be amenable to the penalty for unlawful sale of intoxicating liquors, and punishable for the acts of its officers supplying liquors to those participating in a picnic under its auspices: Stewart v. Waterloo Turn Verein, 71 Ia. 226.

[7] S. v. Neis, 108 N. C. 787; S. v. Lockyear, 95 N. C. 633; S. v. Horacek, 41 Kan. 87; Kentucky Club v. Louisville, 92 Ky. 309; S. v. Mercer, 32 Ia. 405; Cantril v. Sainer, 59 Ia. 26. When liquor belonging to a club is separated from the bulk and payment is made therefor, the sale is complete and the law regulating

need not be shown that the sole purpose of the club was to sell and distribute intoxicating liquors; it is sufficient that that was one of the purposes for which the place was kept;[1] and it is wholly immaterial that no actual profit accrues to the club from the transaction.[2] It does not vary the case that the club sells chips or checks to its members, each chip representing a drink or glass of liquor, and delivers the liquor on return of the chips;[3] or that it sells to its members tickets entitling the holder at a picnic of the association to a glass of beer or other refreshment, or to participate in some amusement at his option; the association in that case is, nevertheless, a dealer in malt liquor.[4] Of course, there is no question but that if the club or association is a mere pretense for evading the law by a person whose business is to sell liquor, he is punishable notwithstanding the method thus resorted to.[5] Some statutes expressly prohibit the keeping and distribution of liquor by clubs to their members.[6] There are many well-considered cases, however, which hold that a *bona fide* club organized with a limited membership, supplying to its members liquors at prices simply reimbursing it the expense of the liquor furnished, is not a seller or retailer of liquor within statutory provisions.[7]

§ **1241. Purchaser not punishable.**—The intoxicating liquor laws are directed against the selling, giving, furnishing, etc., of intoxicating liquors, and not against the purchase of them.

sales is violated. P. v. Andrews, 115 N. Y. 427, 8 Am. Cr. R. 410, and note.

[1] C. v. Jacobs, 152 Mass. 276.

[2] S. v. Easton Social, etc. Club, 73 Md. 97. Such violation of law on the part of the club is an abuse of its corporate powers, such as to constitute a cause of forfeiture: Ibid.

[3] S. v. Horacek, 41 Kan. 87; U. S. v. Wittig, 2 Low. 466; S. v. Mercer, 32 Ia. 405; Cantril v. Sainer, 59 Ia. 26.

[4] U. S. v. Giller, 54 Fed. R. 656. And see C. v. Loesch, 153 Pa. St. 502.

[5] Rickart v. P., 79 Ill. 85, 2 Am. Cr. R. 385, and note; C. v. Ryan, 152 Mass. 283; C. v. Ewig, 145 Mass. 119; C. v. Smith, 102 Mass. 144; C. v. Tierney, 148 Pa. St. 552; C. v. Loesch, 153 Pa. St. 502; S. v. Bacon Club, 44 Mo. Ap. 86.

[6] C. v. Baker, 152 Mass. 337; Chesapeake Club v. S., 63 Md. 446; S. v. Standish, 37 Kan. 643.

[7] C. v. Pomphret, 137 Mass. 564; P. v. Adelphi Club, 149 N. Y. 5, 31 L. R. A. 510, and note; Seim v. S., 55 Md. 566, 39 Am. R. 419; S. v. St. Louis Club, 125 Mo. 308. Such a club is not required to procure a license as a retail dealer: Tennessee Club v. Dwyer, 11 Lea, 452, 47 Am. R. 298; Piedmont Club v. C., 87 Va. 540; S. v. McMaster, 35 S. C. 1; S. v. Austin Club, — Tex. Ap. —, 33 S. W. R. 113; Koenig v. S., 33 Tex. Ap. 367; Barden v. Montana Club, 10 Mont. 330. The question whether the club exists *bona fide* or whether it is a mere means of evasion of the liquor law is a question of fact: C. v. Smith, 102 Mass. 144.

Even where the statute provides a punishment for selling or tippling an intoxicating beverage in certain localities, a purchaser in such locality is not punishable.[1] In general a purchaser of liquor sold in violation of law is not a participant with the seller in the commission of a crime and is not guilty thereof as accomplice or otherwise;[2] therefore he need not be corroborated as an accomplice; nor can the purchaser object to testifying as a witness with reference to purchases made by him on the ground that such testimony might tend to criminate him.[3] It has already been said that one who procures liquor for another, having no interest in the transaction except as he may be jointly interested in the purchase, is not guilty of selling.[4]

§ 1242. **Transporting.**— For the purpose of making the regulations as to sale more effectual, some statutes provide a punishment for transporting liquor intended for illegal sale. It has already been shown that such regulations are unconstitutional as far as they relate to interstate commerce,[5] but they are valid as a police regulation with reference to transportation between points in the same state. The fact that the liquors have been lawfully sold in another place where the sale is lawful does not render the transportation and delivery of such liquors lawful in a place where the sale is illegal, if the person transporting has reasonable ground to believe that the liquor he is carrying is intended for illegal purposes.[6] To show that the liquors transported are for an unlawful purpose it may be shown that the premises to which they are being carried have recently been used for illegal sales;[7] but knowledge of the intoxicating character of the liquors,[8] and no doubt of the illegal

[1] Harney v. S., 8 Lea, 113 (explaining S. v. Bonner, 2 Head, 135).

[2] S. v. Cullins, 53 Kan. 100; C. v. Willard, 22 Pick. 476; S. v. Rand, 51 N. H. 361; S. v. Teahan, 50 Conn. 92; S. v. Baden, 37 Minn. 212; Wakeman v. Chambers, 69 Ia. 169; S. v. Miller, 26 W. Va. 106; Anderson v. S., 32 Fla. 242. And see *supra*, § 199. So under a statute prohibiting sales to minors, a purchase by a minor, or by an adult for a minor, is not criminal: Bryant v. S., 82 Ala. 51. And see *infra*, § 1259.

[3] C. v. Gould, 158 Mass. 499; Page v. S., 11 Lea, 202. Nor is it proper to refer to the fact that the witness testifies to purchasing liquor as discrediting his testimony: P. v. Kahler, 93 Mich. 625. A detective who purchases is not incompetent to testify; the fact goes only to his credibility: S. v. Baden, 37 Minn. 212. And see *supra*, § 117.

[4] *Supra*, § 1233; Anderson v. S., 32 Fla. 242.

[5] *Supra*, § 1202.

[6] C. v. McLaughlin, 108 Mass. 477.

[7] C. v. Kenney, 115 Mass. 149.

[8] S. v. McDonough, 84 Me. 488.

purpose for which they are intended, unless the statute prohibits transportation except under specific circumstances, must be alleged. The officers or agents of the company engaging in the illegal transportation are personally punishable if they have reasonable cause to believe that the liquor is intended for illegal sale.[1] In charging illegal transportation the places between which the liquor was transported should be alleged in order to identify the offense.[2] At least the towns or particular localities in which, or to and from which, the liquors were conveyed should be stated, the naming of the county not being sufficient;[3] but an allegation of transportation from place to place within the city named is sufficiently definite.[4]

§ **1243. Unlawfully keeping for sale.**— As a further security against violation of the provisions as to unlawfully selling, it is usual to provide that the keeping of liquor with the intent to sell it in violation of law shall be, in itself, a crime; and such a regulation is proper, though in general the mere possession of instruments of crime is not such an overt act as to be punishable at common law.[5] To constitute guilt in keeping for illegal sale it is not necessary that defendant shall have owned the liquor; if he is acting for another he may be punished;[6] and it is not necessary to allege in the indictment the name of the person by whom such liquors are intended to be illegally sold.[7] But the intent to illegally sell must be an intent on the part of the owner who has a right to sell,[8] and the ownership is therefore an essential fact.[9] It is not essential that the liquors be kept with the intent to illegally sell them at the place where they are thus kept; an intent to thus sell them elsewhere within the state will be sufficient.[10] Perhaps the mere fact of possession does not raise a presumption that

[1] C. v. Brown, 154 Mass. 55.

[2] S. v. Lashus, 79 Me. 541.

[3] C. v. Hutchinson, 6 Allen, 595; C. v. Reily, 9 Gray, 1.

[4] C. v. Hutchinson, 6 Allen, 595.

[5] S. v. Wheeler, 62 Vt. 439.

[6] C. v. O'Reilley, 116 Mass. 15.

[7] S. v. Kaler, 56 Me. 88.

[8] S. v. Miller, 48 Me. 576. A charge that defendant "kept with intent to sell" shows a "keeping for sale:" C. v. Sprague, 128 Mass. 75.

[9] This was a case, however, for the forfeiture of liquors kept for illegal sale: S. v. Intoxicating Liquors, 63 Me. 121. The liquor may be subject to forfeiture if kept by any one for illegal sale: S. v. Miller, 48 Me. 576; S. v. Learned, 47 Me. 426.

[10] S. v. Viers, 82 Ia. 397; C. v. Gillon, 148 Mass. 15; C. v. Intoxicating Liquors, 116 Mass. 24. Indeed, it is said that it may be criminal to keep for illegal sale in another state: S. v. Guinness, 16 R. I. 401. *Contra*, Barnett v. S., 36 Me. 198.

liquors are kept with intent to sell them in violation of law;[1] but it may be provided by statute that such possession by a person not legally authorized to make sales, and not in a private dwelling-house, is presumptive evidence of keeping for illegal sale.[2] So intent to sell illegally may be presumed from proof of illegal sales, although the person keeping has a permit to sell for lawful purposes.[3] Where the statute punishes the "exposing and keeping for sale illegally," it is not necessary to prove that the liquors were exposed or offered publicly; a proof of the keeping is sufficient.[4] The keeping for sale is not a continuing offense in the sense that it requires a repetition or frequency, as in the case of nuisances; any keeping for any period of time is sufficient.[5] Some circumstances attending the keeping indicating that it was kept for sale must appear;[6] but evidence of a bar kept by the owner a short distance away, used for selling, is sufficient.[7] For the same purpose the fact of an unusual number of persons resorting to the place, their conduct and appearance in coming away intoxicated, or language when leaving, may be proved.[8] So it may be shown that furniture, utensils, etc., were found upon the premises, inconsistent with the presumption of keeping for family use;[9] or that there were bottles, glasses and other implements about the premises such as are used in connection

[1] C. v. Canny, 158 Mass. 210.

[2] S. v. Shank, 74 Ia. 649; s. c., 79 Ia. 47; S. v. Farley, 87 Ia. 22; Lincoln v. Smith, 27 Vt. 328; *infra*, § 1249. But a conviction under other statutory provisions for keeping a nuisance under the liquor laws is not conclusive as to the intent to unlawfully sell: S. v. McGill, 65 Vt. 547. If a license provides where liquors may be sold or kept. a keeping elsewhere will be criminal: C. v. Welch, 147 Mass. 374.

[3] S. v. Sartori, 55 Ia. 340; C. v. Intoxicating Liquors, 116 Mass. 21.

[4] C. v. Atkins, 136 Mass. 160; C. v. Henderson, 140 Mass. 303; C. v. Tay, 146 Mass. 146. And one sale may be sufficient evidence that the liquor was kept and exposed for sale: C. v. Hoar, 121 Mass. 375.

[5] C. v. Cleary, 105 Mass. 384; C. v. Coolidge, 138 Mass. 193.

[6] C. v. Intoxicating Liquors, 105 Mass. 595; C. v. Intoxicating Liquors, 116 Mass. 21.

[7] C. v. Intoxicating Liquors, 116 Mass. 24; C. v. Shea, 160 Mass. 6; C. v. Moore, 157 Mass. 324. Evidence of finding of liquors in any part of a building (C. v. Hurley, 158 Mass. 159), or on adjoining premises frequently visited by defendant, a seller, is admissible: C. v. Murphy, 153 Mass. 290. So the finding of liquor on the premises soon after the time of the alleged illegal keeping is admissible: C. v. Neylon, 159 Mass. 541.

[8] C. v. Berry, 109 Mass. 366; C. v. Carney, 108 Mass. 417; C. v. Kennedy, 97 Mass. 224; C. v. Blood, 11 Gray, 74.

[9] C. v. Levy, 126 Mass. 240.

with sales;[1] or that jugs were carried from defendant's premises to places where liquor was sold, and that employees of defendant ran away from the place where liquors were kept, carrying such jugs, when a search was being made.[2] So the finding of other liquors on the premises kept in the way in which liquors are usually kept for sale may be shown;[3] but proof of an actual sale or offer to sell is not necessary, as the jury may find the intention from all the circumstances,[4] including admissions of defendant.[5] The crime of keeping liquor for illegal sale is not, like the keeping of a place for illegal selling, a local offense; the liquor may be kept anywhere, or carried about.[6]

§ 1244. **The business of selling; being common seller.**— Under some statutes a punishment is imposed upon one engaged in the occupation or business of selling without a license, although selling alone without a license is not criminal. To engage in the business implies occupying the time or attention or labor with the selling of liquor for the purpose of a livelihood or profit. A single act will not show the engaging in or carrying on the business, yet a series of sales might do so.[7] Whether or not one who sells at different times is engaged in the occupation of selling is a question for the jury.[8] So under the charge of keeping a hotel without a license,[9] or keeping a grocery for the retail of ardent spirits without a license, it is necessary to show that defendant engaged in the business;[10] and where the crime is that of selling or retailing, a single act constitutes the offense.[11] Some statutes require that a "com-

[1] C. v. McHugh, 147 Mass. 401; C. v. McKenna, 158 Mass. 207; C. v. Canny, 158 Mass. 210; C. v. McManus, 161 Mass. 64; C. v. Martin, 162 Mass. 402.

[2] C. v. Ham, 150 Mass. 122; C. v. Kane, 150 Mass. 294; C. v. Daily, 133 Mass. 577; *infra*, § 1249.

[3] C. v. McKenna, 158 Mass. 207; C. v. Canny, 158 Mass. 210; C. v. McManus, 161 Mass. 64; C. v. Martin, 162 Mass. 402; C. v. Kyne, 162 Mass. 146.

[4] S. v. McGlynn, 34 N. H. 422.

[5] S. v. McGlynn, 34 N. H. 422; C. v. Kyne, 162 Mass. 146.

[6] C. v. Kern, 147 Mass. 595.

[7] Abel v. S., 90 Ala. 631; Lemons v. S., 50 Ala. 130; Mansfield v. S., 17 Tex. Ap. 468; Halfin v. S., 18 Tex. Ap. 410; La Norris v. S., 13 Tex. Ap. 33; Merritt v. S., 19 Tex. Ap. 435.

[8] McReynolds v. S., 26 Tex. Ap. 372.

[9] Pettibone v. S., 19 Ala. 586.

[10] Hensley v. S., 6 Ark. 252.

[11] P. v. Kropp, 52 Mich. 582; S. v. Paddock, 24 Vt. 312; S. v. Chandler, 15 Vt. 425; S. v. Cassety, 1 Rich. 90; S. v. Glasgow, Dudley, 40; Lewis v. C., 90 Va. 843; Woody v. S., 32 Ga. 595; Dansey v. S., 23 Fla. 316.

mon seller" shall have a license and comply with statutory regulations. To constitute a common seller it is necessary that selling be his customary and ordinary business.[1] Proof of three sales is sufficient to raise a presumption that the seller is a common seller;[2] but it is not necessary that such sales be proved by direct evidence.[3] Indeed, circumstantial evidence may be sufficient without positive proof of any particular sales,[4] as proof of finding decanters, glasses and other appliances;[5] but the evidence must be such as to warrant the jury in finding that defendant was a seller, and not merely that he had a place fitted up for the purpose of sale.[6] The offense is not the same as that of keeping a tippling-house, the element of repetition being essential to constitute a common seller, while the keeping of a building or place for sale is essential to constitute a keeper.[7] So a violation of other statutory regulations does not constitute one a common seller without a license; he should be punished for the failure to comply with the statutory requirements under which he purports to act.[8] Being a common seller without a license is a continuing offense,[9] in which time is material and must be proved as laid.[10] It is not a local offense, and the place need not be alleged or proved except to bring the case within the jurisdiction of the court.[11]

§ 1245. **Retailing; wholesaling.**— Some statutes require that retailers shall have a license,[12] and under them it becomes necessary to determine what is a retailing. Where the liquor is separated from a larger quantity in a cask for the purchaser, the sale is at retail,[13] and certainly sales in quantities less than a quart and sales of liquor to be drank on the premises consti-

[1] S. v. O'Connor, 49 Me. 594.

[2] C. v. Dady, 7 Allen, 531; C. v. Clark, 14 Gray, 367; C. v. Tubbs, 1 Cush. 2; S. v. Day, 37 Me. 244; S. v. Williams, 6 R. I. 207. The three distinct sales may be on the same day or the same evening to the same person: C. v. Parley, 2 Cush. 559; C. v. Rumrill, 1 Gray, 388. Under a statutory regulation as to a "seller," not using the word "common," it was held that proof of one sale was sufficient: C. v. Thurlow, 24 Pick. 374.

[3] C. v. Clark, 14 Gray, 368; C. v. Dady, 7 Allen, 531.

[4] C. v. Van Stone, 97 Mass. 548; S. v. O'Connor, 49 Me. 594. On the other hand, proof of three sales is not conclusive: S. v. O'Connor, 49 Me. 594; S. v. Day, 37 Me. 244.

[5] C. v. Lamere, 11 Gray, 319.

[6] C. v. Tubbs, 1 Cush. 2.

[7] S. v. Inness, 53 Me. 536.

[8] S. v. Burr, 10 Me. 438; S. v. Savage, 48 N. H. 484.

[9] S. v. Ingalls, 59 N. H. 88.

[10] S. v. Small, 80 Me. 452.

[11] C. v. Clapp, 5 Gray, 97.

[12] Dyer v. S., 1 Meigs, 237.

[13] Tripp v. Hennessy, 10 R. I. 129.

tute the seller a retailer.[1] Sometimes the statutes provide that sales of less than a specified quantity shall be retail sales, and in such a case it is sufficient to charge a selling by retail without averring the quantity to be less than that specified by statute.[2] The federal statutes require retail dealers to take out a United States license, and under that provision it is held necessary that to be a retailer the dealer must have had an intent to sell the liquor at retail and carried it out by one or more acts; it is not enough that he has dispensed the liquor as an act of kindness or accommodation, even for money, if there has been no intention to retail.[3] One who sells a medicinal preparation knowing that it contains an intoxicating quality, and for use as a beverage, or with knowledge that it was purchased to be used as a beverage, is a retail dealer.[4] To constitute a retailing one sale may be sufficient, but not to constitute a carrying on of the business of retailing;[5] and certainly not where the sale is not in pursuance of any business or employment, but is merely an individual matter.[6] The statutes sometimes require that wholesalers shall pay a license tax, this provision being, however, for the purpose of revenue rather than for the purpose of regulation. To constitute one a wholesale dealer within such statute it is not enough to show sales by the quart, even though not to be drunk on the premises.[7] A general

[1] Lillensteine v. S., 46 Ala. 48. Sometimes sales by "merchants" are allowed, although tippling-shops are prohibited: Cole v. C., 8 Dana, 31; C. v. McGeorge, 9 B. Mon. 3.

[2] C. v. Eaton, 9 Pick. 165; Reiser v. S., 79 Ga. 326. Where the legislature authorized the city council to regulate the retail of spirituous liquors, *held*, that the passage of an ordinance that one who sells in a less quantity than twenty gallons shall be a retailer was not valid, as that was too great a quantity to be considered a sale by retail: Harris v. Livingstone, 28 Ala. 577.

[3] U. S. v. Bonham, 31 Fed. R. 808. Selling an occasional drink of spirituous liquor out of a barrel not in a bar-room, where there is no intention to defraud the revenue, is not criminal under the federal statute: U. S. v. Jackson, 1 Hughes, 531. But a physician who prescribes and furnishes liquor to his patients is a retailer: U. S. v. Smith, 45 Fed. R. 115.

[4] U. S. v. Starnes, 37 Fed. R. 665; otherwise if the preparation, though containing spirituous liquor, is sold *bona fide* as a medicine and not as a beverage: U. S. v. Calhoun, 39 Fed R. 604.

[5] Lawson v. S., 55 Ala. 118.

[6] Bryant v. S., 46 Ala. 302; Moore v. S., 16 Ala. 411. So the gratuitous distribution of ardent spirits at a public gaming table does not constitute the proprietor a retailer: U. S. v. Mickle, 1 Cranch, C. C. 268.

[7] S. v. Lowenhaught, 11 Lea, 13; S. v. Tarver, 11 Lea, 658; Webb v. S., 11 Lea, 662; Webb v. Baird, 11 Lea, 667.

merchant selling by the quart or gallon, even though the liquor is not to be drunk upon the premises, is not a wholesaler.[1] The wholesaler may or may not be subject to other regulations as to selling liquor, depending on the language of the statutes.[2]

§ **1246. Selling by small measure.**— Analogous to retailing, for which a license must be procured, is the selling by small measure, designated by some statutes as requiring a license. Where the statute specifies the quantity, the sale of which amount or less shall come within its provisions, it is the amount sold for the use of one individual which determines the character of the sale, and not the aggregate amount of sales for several persons, though bought and paid for by one of them.[3] But the amount sold to one individual at one time is to be counted as one quantity, although it is delivered in several packages; thus, where three pint bottles of beer were disposed of at one sale, it was held not to be a sale of a quart or less.[4] If a sale is made of a quantity, only a part of which is delivered, the residue remaining in the vendor's barrel not measured out, this is a sale of the part delivered only.[5] So, where the agreement was to deliver to the purchaser from time to time spirits in quantities less than a quart, as they should be called for, the purchaser to take on the whole a quart in quantity, to be paid for when the whole was delivered, it was held that this was a violation of the statute prohibiting the sale of liquors in quantities of less than a quart without a license.[6] But where the whole quantity was separated and kept for the buyer in a vessel to be taken away in portions as called for, it was held that the sale was of such entire quantity.[7] There is conflict in the decisions as to how a sale in small quantities may be alleged. Where the statute specifies that the sale of a quantity less than a specified amount shall be deemed a sale by small measure, some courts have held that the charge of a sale of a quantity less than the amount specified is not sufficient without negativing the fact that the sale was of the specified quantity or more; that is, that the allega-

Sometimes sales of more than a quart are to be deemed as wholesale, but there is no definite meaning which can be given to the term "wholesale dealer" aside from statute: Dennehey v. Chicago, 120 Ill. 627.

[1] Espy v. S., 47 Ala. 533.

[2] S. v. Benz, 41 Minn. 30.

[3] Weireter v. S., 69 Ind. 269; Klein v. S., 76 Ind. 333.

[4] Olmstead v. S., 90 Ala. 634.

[5] Thomas v. S., 37 Miss. 353.

[6] S. v. Kirkham, 1 Ired. 384.

[7] S. v. Bell, 2 Jones, 337; Dobson v. S., 57 Ind. 69.

tion of the sale of a pint or gill will not be sufficient to charge the sale of less quantity than a quart, unless it is also alleged that the quantity sold was less than a quart; the argument being that there is a sale of less quantity involved in a sale of the larger.[1] There is, however, authority the other way.[2] If the offense of selling in small measure is properly charged, it is not necessary that the proof show the sale of the exact quantity charged, but it is enough that the sale shown is of a quantity which brings the case within the statutory prohibition.[3]

§ **1247. To be drunk on the premises.**— In statutes regulating the retailing or the selling in small measure, there are usually regulations also as to selling liquor to be drunk on the premises.[4] The offense is complete without the actual drinking of the liquor on the premises, provided it is sold to be drunk there.[5] Where the provision is against permitting to be drunk on the premises, the place where the liquor is to be drunk must be one over which the seller has the legal right to exercise authority or control;[6] but if the prohibition is against selling to

[1] C. v. Odlin, 23 Pick. 275; S. v. Fanning, 38 Mo. 409; Wood v. S., 21 Ind. 276; Arbintrode v. S., 67 Ind. 267 (overruling Reams v. S., 23 Ind. 111; McCool v. S., 23 Ind. 127; Willard v. S., 4 Ind. 407); Grupe v. S., 67 Ind. 327; Swigart v. S., 67 Ind. 601. It is sufficient, however, to allege that the sale was of "one-half pint of intoxicating liquor, the same being less quantity than a quart:" Quinn v. S., 123 Ind. 59; or of "less than a quart, to wit, one gill:" Mullen v. S., 96 Ind. 304; Walter v. S., 105 Ind. 589. So where the charge was that defendant without a license was the retailer of spirituous liquors in less quantity than twenty-eight gallons (that being the amount specified by statute as determining whether the sale was at retail), and did sell and retail two quarts of spirituous liquor, this was held sufficient as indicating that the sale was of a less quantity than twenty-eight gallons: Goodhue v. C., 5 Met. 553.

[2] S. v. Wyman, 42 Minn. 182; S. v. Lavake, 26 Minn. 526.

[3] Klein v. S., 76 Ind. 333; Buell v. S., 72 Ind. 523. And see *infra*, § 1273.

[4] This is a distinct offense, however, from that of selling in small measure, and both elements need not be alleged: S. v. Corll, 73 Ind. 535 (overruling S. v. Zeitler, 63 Ind. 441). Another form of the provision is prohibiting to be sold in a quart or greater quantity to be drunk at the place where sold: Sanderlin v. S., 2 Humph. 315.

[5] C. v. Luddy, 143 Mass. 563; Rater v. S., 49 Ind. 507. It is sufficient to allege that it was "sold to be drunk on the premises:" Picket v. S., 22 Ohio St. 405; Werneke v. S., 49 Ind. 202; Vanderwood v. S., 50 Ind. 26; Bilbro v. S., 7 Humph. 534. But it is not sufficient to charge that it was sold and drunk on the premises: S. v. Freeman, 6 Blackf. 248.

[6] Downman v. S., 14 Ala. 342; Swan v. S., 11 Ala. 594. And the same construction applies where the prohibition is against the sale of liquor to be drunk in defendant's house, out-house, etc.: Plunkett v. S., 69

be drunk "on or about the premises," this embraces places over which the seller has no legal right to exercise authority, but which are so near to his premises and so situated in relation thereto that they are within the mischief intended to be remedied;[1] even under such a provision, however, it has been held that a sale in a public alley out of sight of but adjoining to the seller's premises, though not connecting with them, was not sufficient.[2] The place of drinking may be "on or about" defendant's premises, although it is in a place not leased by him and belonging to another, if it appears from all the circumstances that it was under his control, and that he permitted the drinking there.[3] Other statutes, broader still, cover the drinking in a public street or alley adjoining the place where the liquor is sold.[4] It seems that "the premises" are the premises where the liquor is sold, whether they belong to the seller or he is carrying on business there or not.[5] Sometimes the prohibition is in regard to selling to be drunk in the building or any place appurtenant thereto, and in such case the place appurtenant need not be a part of the premises, but may be some convenient place where customers are in the habit of going with the knowledge and consent of the seller.[6] The intention of the seller as to where the liquor sold by him was to be drunk may be shown by all the circumstances,[7] and it is not material that it appear that he knew the exact spot or that he consented that it should be drunk there, as long as the circumstances show that he connived at and took no means to prevent such drinking.[8] Indeed, it is proper to charge that it was the seller's duty to prevent the liquor being drunk on or about his premises, and that if it was drunk there, even though

Ind. 68. And see Blough v. S., 121 Ind. 355.

[1] Daly v. S., 33 Ala. 431; Patterson v. S., 36 Ala. 297.

[2] Daly v. S., 33 Ala. 431. And see Easterling v. S., 30 Ala. 46.

[3] Stone v. S., 30 Ind. 115. Some statutes include an adjoining place of public resort: Aultfather v. S., 4 Ohio St. 467. A street may be a public resort: Bandalow v. P., 90 Ill. 218.

[4] Bandalow v. P., 90 Ill. 218. And drinking in a public street adjoining defendant's premises may be a drinking about the premises: Whaley v. S., 87 Ala. 83; Brown v. S., 31 Ala. 353.

[5] Pearce v. S., 40 Ala. 720; Powell v. S., 63 Ala. 177. It is otherwise if the statute says "to be drunk on *his* premises:" S. v. Woolsey, 92 Ind. 131.

[6] Stout v. S., 93 Ind. 150; Shields v. S., 95 Ind. 299; Stockwell v. S., 85 Ind. 522.

[7] O'Connor v. S., 45 Ind. 347.

[8] Rater v. S., 49 Ind. 507.

without his knowledge and against his caution to the contrary, he would be liable.[1]

§ 1248. Nuisance; keeping place for illegal sale.— Under the head of nuisance it has already appeared that it is a well-recognized form of that offense to keep a disorderly tippling-house,[2] and statutes usually specify such a crime in connection with the illegal sale of liquors.[3] Some statutes refer specially to the keeping of a tippling-house, which is a place where liquors are sold to be drunk on the premises.[4] But the statutes usually go further than this, and make it an offense to keep a place for the illegal sale of intoxicating liquors,[5] and declare the building or place where liquor is illegally sold, or kept with intent to sell, to be a nuisance,[6] and the offense of keeping such a place is distinct from that of illegally selling or illegally keeping for sale.[7] But to constitute a nuisance the place must

[1] Christian v. S., 40 Ala. 376; Jones v. S., 96 Ala. 56. But to prove the offense on the part of a druggist who may properly sell, but not to be drunk on the premises, it must be shown that such drinking was with his assent: S. v. McAdoo, 80 Mo. 216.

[2] *Supra,* § 1169; S. v. Thornton, Busbee, 252; S. v. Burchinal, 4 Harr. 572.

[3] S. v. Chapman, 1 S. Dak. 414; Burrell v. S., 129 Ind. 290.

[4] S. v. McNamara, 69 Me. 133; Koop v. P., 47 Ill. 327; Thomason v. S., 92 Ga. 456. Sale as a beverage does not imply drinking on the premises, but includes sales for drinking either at the place or elsewhere, and is distinct, therefore, from a sale for tippling purposes: S. v. Roach, 75 Me. 123. Selling by the quart to be drunk in the house where the sale is made does not constitute keeping a tippling-house: Moore v. S., 9 Yerg. 353.

[5] S. v. Fraser, 1 N. Dak. 425. And within such statutes a hotel is a place: C. v. Purcell, 154 Mass. 388. So a dwelling-house is a "place of public resort" for a sale of liquor if it is frequented by the public for that purpose with the same freedom that men exercise in going to ordinary public resorts for drinking purposes: S. v. Spaulding, 61 Vt. 505. So a dwelling-house may be a liquor-shop: Wooster v. S., 6 Baxt. 533; Koop v. P., 47 Ill. 327. To charge the keeping of a bar-room within such a statute it should be alleged to have been used as a place of resort: S. v. Stone, 54 Vt. 550. A public bar may be defined by the court, the word being sufficiently precise in its meaning to admit of such definition: C. v. Rogers, 135 Mass. 536. The word "appurtenant," in describing the place or building, is used to indicate connection with other premises used by the same occupant, and its construction is a matter of law: S. v. Kelleher, 81 Me. 346. To constitute the keeping of a house for illegal sale it is sufficient that a part only is used for that purpose, if the whole house is under the control of the defendant: C. v. Rooney, 142 Mass. 474.

[6] S. v. Dugan, 52 Kan. 23.

[7] S. v. Harris, 64 Ia. 287; S. v. Howorth, 70 Ia. 157; S. v. Jangraw, 61 Vt. 39; S. v. Reno, 41 Kan. 674;

be kept and used for illegal sale or illegal keeping for sale,[1] and must be one frequented by persons desiring to procure intoxicating liquors.[2] The presence of the liquor in the building is essential.[3] It is not necessary, however, that the intent be to sell in and from the building where kept, but the keeping for illegal sale elsewhere within the state will be sufficient to constitute the place a nuisance.[4] The language of these statutes usually implies habitual action on the part of the keeper,[5] but the offense is not necessarily a continuing one extending over a period of time; if at any one time the place is kept for a purpose forbidden by law, the crime is complete.[6] On the other hand, one sale is not enough to show that the place is kept as a nuisance; there must be some succession or series of sales or other illegal acts.[7] But evidence of more than one sale would be sufficient to go to the jury as tending to show that the place was kept for the purpose of making illegal sales.[8] One may be guilty of keeping a nuisance who has the control, care or management of the place where illegal sales

Robinson v. C., 6 Dana, 287; S. v. Gumber, 37 Wis. 298. Punishment for keeping a nuisance may be inflicted after the place has been abated as a nuisance or has ceased to be maintained for that purpose: Clinton v. S., 33 Ohio St. 27. So it does not constitute double punishment that the same person is punished for individual sales and also for keeping a nuisance: Oshe v. S., 37 Ohio St. 494.

[1] C. v. Carolin, 2 Allen, 169.

[2] S. v. Harris, 64 Ia. 287. But it must appear that there was use of the premises by defendant for the purpose: S. v. Dodge, 78 Me. 439.

[3] S. v. Hass, 22 Ia. 193; S. v. Harris, 27 Ia. 429; S. v. Tierney, 74 Ia. 237; S. v. Shank, 79 Ia. 47.

[4] S. v. Viers, 82 Ia. 397. It is the keeping of the place rather than the doing of the acts which constitutes the offense: S. v. Price, 75 Ia. 243. It is not necessary that the sale of liquors be the main purpose of the place complained of, but it is enough that liquor selling is one of the incidents or subordinate purposes: S. v. Hoxsie, 15 R. I. 1.

[5] S. v. Stanley, 84 Me. 555; Hinton v. C., 7 Dana, 216.

[6] C. v. Kerrissey, 141 Mass. 110; Kroer v. P., 78 Ill. 294; Borschenious v. P., 41 Ill. 236; S. v. Johnson, 65 Me. 362. It is not necessary that the nuisance should continue up to or exist at the time of the indictment: S. v. Schilling, 14 Ia. 455.

[7] Miller v. S., 3 Ohio St. 475; C. v. Hayes, 150 Mass. 506; C. v. Patterson, 138 Mass. 498; S. v. Fay, 44 N. J. 474; S. v. Hoxsie, 15 R. I. 1; Dunnaway v. S., 9 Yerg. 350. *Contra*, S. v. Reyelts, 74 Ia. 499.

[8] C. v. McNeff, 145 Mass. 406. And evidence of other sales than those charged in the indictment, and to any persons whatever, will be admissible: S. v. Conner, 30 Ohio St. 405. Evidence of two sales during the time specified may be sufficient: C. v. Buckley, 148 Mass. 27. But illegal sales on two different occasions do not, as a matter of law, show the keeping of a nuisance: S. v. Stan-

are made, though he is not the owner of the premises.[1] On the other hand, the owner may be guilty of keeping a nuisance, although he does not himself intend to make illegal sales there, if he knowingly permits another to keep liquor there for illegal purposes;[2] but it must appear that after becoming aware of the illegal use of the premises he did some act or made some declaration affirmatively assenting thereto.[3] A colorable lease of the premises to a barkeeper will not protect the owner if it appears that he still retains control.[4] The liability of a servant for the illegal keeping and use of the premises under the immediate direction and control of his employer has already been considered.[5] The purpose of the keeping must be illegal; that is, the place must be kept for the purpose of illegal sales, or illegally keeping for sale.[6] But it is immaterial whether the illegal selling or keeping is entirely without authority, or in a manner or for a purpose in violation of authority given to sell or keep for sale.[7] The intent of the keeper of the place or the good faith with which he keeps it will be immaterial if the place is kept by him for purposes not authorized by the statute.[8]

§ **1249. Charging and proving the nuisance.**— It is not necessary to charge the particular forms of illegal sales;[9] nor is it necessary to allege the names of the parties to whom the illegal sales were made; the gist of the offense is the keeping of the place.[10] The keeping of a nuisance may be proved by evidence showing that the place was resorted to by disorderly

ley, 84 Me. 555. Nor will evidence of two sales at the place show that the keeping or selling was with the owner's consent: Lucker v. C., 4 Bush, 440.

[1] Schultz v. S., 32 Ohio St. 276; S. v. Hadlock, 43 Me. 282.

[2] C. v. Reed, 162 Mass. 215; C. v. Lynch, 160 Mass. 298; C. v. Churchill, 136 Mass. 148.

[3] S. v. Ballingall, 42 Ia. 87. A landlord is not bound to interfere with and invoke the law against a tenant who, having leased the premises for a lawful purpose, makes unlawful use thereof: Crocker v. S., 49 Ark. 60. And see *supra*, §§ 1142, 1174.

[4] C. v. Locke, 148 Mass. 125.

[5] *Supra*, § 1239.

[6] S. v. Johnson, 61 Ia. 504: S. v. Wacker, 71 Wis. 672.

[7] S. v. Webber, 76 Ia. 686; S. v. Waynick, 45 Ia. 516. It is not necessary to allege that the accused was licensed: Joseph v. S., 42 Ind. 370. Nor, on the other hand, will a license protect accused for sales illegally made or for disturbances caused in the keeping of the licensed premises: C. v. Murray, 138 Mass. 508.

[8] S. v. Mullenhoff, 74 Ia. 271; S. v. Crabtree, 27 Mo. 232.

[9] Kern v. S., 7 Ohio St. 411. And see Miller v. S., 3 Ohio St. 475.

[10] S. v. Lang, 63 Me. 215; C. v. Purdy, 147 Mass. 29. No allegation of selling is necessary: S. v. Dorr, 82 Me. 157. It is enough to charge the keep-

persons who created there disturbance and noise annoying to others, and to that end evidence is admissible to show the actions and appearance of persons immediately after going from the place indicating that they were intoxicated;[1] and the evidence may extend to the conduct of persons frequenting the immediate locality.[2] But evidence of disturbance and noise at a considerable distance from the premises, and not in the presence of defendant or his family or employees, is not admissible.[3] It may also be shown that at the place in question kept under the control of defendant, bottles, glasses and other appurtenances or implements usually used in drinking places were found.[4] It seems that evidence as to the general reputation of the place is not admissible.[5] Proof of the manufacture, sale, or keeping with intent to sell, in violation of law, is presumptive proof of a nuisance;[6] and the record of a previous conviction for keeping the same house for illegal purposes is admissible to prove the use, nature or character of the house.[7] Where, by statute, the finding of liquor in the possession of the accused in any other place than his private dwelling-house is presumptive evidence that such liquor is illegally kept for sale, such proof of finding will also be evidence of a nuisance committed by keeping with intent to sell.[8] So if it appears that accused illegally kept for sale and sold intoxicating liquors at his place of business, the finding of such liquors on other premises where he resided is admissible to show that the lat-

ing of "a certain nuisance, to wit, a tenement used for the illegal sale of intoxicating liquors:" C. v. Quinlan, 153 Mass. 483; S. v. Schilling, 14 Ia. 455. But it is not enough to charge that defendant "kept a tippling-house by retailing spirituous liquors:" Our v. C., 9 Dana, 30; Woods v. C., 1 B. Mon. 74; Bush v. Republic, 1 Tex. 455.

[1] S. v. Pierce, 65 Ia. 85; C. v. Meaney, 151 Mass. 55; C. v. Finnerty, 148 Mass. 162.

[2] C. v. Wallace, 143 Mass. 88.

[3] C. v. Davenport, 2 Allen, 299.

[4] S. v. Hoxsie, 15 R. I. 1; S. v. Wambold, 74 Ia. 605; Brown v. S., 49 N. J. 61; C. v. Boyle, 145 Mass. 373; C. v. Locke, 145 Mass. 401; C. v. Sullivan, 156 Mass. 229. And see *supra*, § 1243.

[5] C. v. Eagan, 151 Mass. 45. And see *infra*, § 1279. But the notoriously bad or intemperate character of the persons visiting the place may be shown: S. v. Hoxsie, 15 R. I. 1.

[6] S. v. Guisenhause, 20 Ia. 227; S. v. Baughman, 20 Ia. 497; S. v. Freeman, 27 Ia. 333; C. v. Carney, 152 Mass. 566; S. v. Beaumier, 87 Me. 214.

[7] S. v. Hall, 79 Me. 501. But conviction of defendant for keeping another house is not admissible: Ibid.

[8] S. v. Norton, 41 Ia. 430; *supra*, § 1243.

ter place was kept as a nuisance.[1] The keeping of the premises may be abated as any other nuisance,[2] but such abatement should be of the nuisance caused by the illegal use of the premises and not by destruction of the building itself.[3] If no special provision is made for the punishment of this form of nuisance it may be punished as provided by statute with reference to other nuisances.[4]

§ **1250. Regulations as to receipts, hour of closing, screens, etc.**— Some special regulations as to the method of conducting the business must still be mentioned. It is provided, for instance, in at least one state that the person holding a license must keep posted a receipt showing that he has paid his license tax,[5] and the federal statutes as to retailers require a like posting of the internal revenue tax receipt. The effect of the posting of this internal tax receipt as evidence that the business of selling liquor is being carried on will hereafter be considered.[6] So it may be required that saloons be closed between certain hours.[7] By way of preventing concealment of illegal selling, it is provided in some of the states that the windows of the place where liquor is sold shall not be obstructed by screens, shutters or otherwise. This is a proper police regulation and is constitutional,[8] and may properly be enforced as to windows opening on private grounds as well as those opening on the public thoroughfare.[9] It is immaterial whether the blinds or screens which are required by such statute to be removed were affixed to the windows before the enactment of the statute or afterwards.[10] These statutes may

[1] S. v. Illsley, 81 Ia. 49. So where it appears that defendant kept liquor on adjoining premises, and that it was carried to the place charged to have been a nuisance, and that persons resorted to the latter for the purpose of drinking, the fact of keeping the liquor on the adjoining premises may be shown: C. v. Lyons, 160 Mass. 174; C. v. Vahey, 151 Mass. 57.

[2] S. v. Adams, 81 Ia. 593.

[3] S. v. Paul, 5 R. I. 185; S. v. Keeran, 5 R. I. 497. A private individual would not be authorized to abate a nuisance, except so far as it actually obstructs him in the exercise of his rights: Ibid.

[4] S. v. McGrew, 11 Ia. 112; S. v. Collins, 11 Ia. 141; S. v. Schilling, 14 Ia. 455; S. v. Little, 42 Ia. 51; S. v. Dean, 44 Ia. 648.

[5] P. v. Paquin, 74 Mich. 34.

[6] *Infra*, § 1280.

[7] P. v. James, 100 Mich. 522. As to closing on Sundays, holidays and election days, see *infra*, §§ 1264, 1265.

[8] S. v. Doyle, 15 R. I. 325.

[9] C. v. Brothers, 158 Mass. 200.

[10] C. v. Sawtelle, 150 Mass. 320; C. v. Kane, 143 Mass. 92.

apply to internal screens or partitions as well as to obstructions in the windows, but they ought not to be considered as applicable to permanent partitions between rooms necessarily divided, where partitions are for the purpose of enabling the occupant to rent a portion of his premises for another purpose,[1] or where the license recognizes the existence of two rooms in the premises occupied by the licensee.[2] Whether any particular obstruction which is not total in its character materially interferes with the view of the interior of the premises is a question for the jury.[3] These regulations apply not only to the times when the place is legally and actually open but to all times.[4]

§ **1251. Intent.**—The question as to the extent to which knowledge and intent are essential to constitute the offense provided for by the various liquor laws has already been discussed under different sections of this chapter,[5] and will be further considered with reference to sales to minors and intoxicated persons in a subsequent section.[6] Evidence as bearing on the intent will be spoken of under the sections relating to evidence.[7] Little is left to be said in this section except to state the general proposition that the intent with which the prohibited act is done is immaterial in determining its criminality. The person making a sale or carrying on the business which comes within statutory regulation is bound to know whether or not his acts are contrary to the law.[8] Even where by statute the intent is made material, the question is not one of good conduct and uprightness in the transaction of the business, but whether the defendant intended to do the act under circumstances prohibited by law.[9] Thus, if the statute prohibits sales by an innkeeper except to guests, the innkeeper is bound to know, at his peril, whether the person to whom

[1] S. v. Andrews, 82 Tex. 73.

[2] C. v. Barnes, 140 Mass. 447.

[3] C. v. McDonnough, 150 Mass. 504.

[4] C. v. Casey, 134 Mass. 194.

[5] *Supra*, §§ 1222, 1237.

[6] *Infra*, § 1257.

[7] *Infra*, § 1279.

[8] C. v. Sinclair, 138 Mass. 493; C. v. Holstine, 132 Pa. St. 357; S. v. Downs, 116 N. C. 1064; S. v. Chastain, 19 Oreg. 176; McMillan v. S., 18 Tex. Ap. 375. And see *supra*, § 128. But in an action for a penalty imposed for retailing, it appearing that defendant had apparently acted ignorantly and not wilfully, the court refused to set aside a verdict for defendant, saying that it was a hard action: Gilbert v. Hendricks, 2 Brev. 161.

[9] U. S. v. White, 42 Fed. R. 138.

the sale is made is a guest or not.[1] If a sale is made which is within the statutory prohibition, it is immaterial that the purpose of the purchaser was to use the liquor for external application only;[2] it is immaterial, also, that the defendant was entrapped into making the sale by a detective.[3] As intent is not material, it is not necessary to charge that the act complained of was wilfully done.[4]

V. SPECIAL EXCEPTIONS IN CASES OF PHYSICIANS, DRUGGISTS, PRODUCERS, ETC.

§ 1252. Exceptions by statute; need not be negatived.— While it has been said in some cases that the law will make the necessary exceptions to the rigid provisions of the statutes as to sales of liquors so as to exclude cases that are not within the mischief intended to be remedied by the statute, such as sales for medicinal or sacramental purposes,[5] yet the weight of authority is probably to the contrary, and it is quite positively declared in many cases that unless an exception is made by statute none can be made by the courts, even though the act complained of was for the humane purpose of alleviating suffering, and not such as would seem to be within the policy of the statutory regulations.[6] Even statutory provisions authorizing sales by physicians and druggists, or sales for authorized purposes, are to be looked upon as matter of defense which the accused must establish, and which the prosecution need not negative in the indictment, unless the exception is embodied in the statutory definition of the offense,[7] or, as is said, in the en-

[1] C. v. Barnes, 138 Mass. 511. Whether under a statute requiring that the sale of liquor shall be only in connection with furnishing food and shelter, the person who orders liquor with a small amount of food is a *bona fide* guest or not, is for the jury: C. v. Hagan, 140 Mass. 289.

[2] S. v. Brown, 31 Me. 522.

[3] P. v. Curtis, 95 Mich. 212. And in general see *supra*, § 118.

[4] S. v. Abbott, 31 N. H. 434. And further as to charging the intent in the indictment, see *infra*, § 1270.

[5] Donnell v. S., 2 Ind. 658; Thomason v. S., 15 Ind. 449; Ball v. S., 50 Ind. 595; Hooper v. S., 56 Ind. 153; Elrod v. S., 72 Ind. 292; Payne v. S., 74 Ind. 203; Nixon v. S., 76 Ind. 524; S. v. Larrimore, 19 Mo. 391; S. v. Wray, 72 N. C. 253.

[6] S. v. Gummer, 22 Wis. 441; C. v. Kimball, 24 Pick. 366; S. v. Brown, 31 Me. 522; S. v. Woodward, 34 Me. 293; Thomason v. S., 70 Ala. 20; Carl v. S., 89 Ala. 93; S. v. Wool, 86 N. C. 708; Gault v. S., 34 Ga. 533; Noecker v. P., 91 Ill. 468.

[7] Metzker v. P., 14 Ill. 101; C. v. Hill, 5 Grat. 682; S. v. Downs, 116

acting clause.[1] This conclusion, however, is not reached by all the courts, and it has sometimes been held that where the statute contains provisions exempting druggists and physicians from its operation, the indictment should negative the fact that the person making the sale complained of was a druggist or physician or within other such provision.[2]

§ **1253. Sales by physicians and druggists.**— On the principle stated in the preceding section that exceptions are not to be made to the liquor laws save as therein provided, a sale of liquor by a physician or druggist, even in good faith, to one purchasing for use as a medicine, is not lawful, except as the provisions of the statute in regard to such cases are complied with;[3] but the administering of spirituous liquors by a physician to a patient is not, in itself, a sale within the meaning of such statutes in regard to a sale of liquor.[4] Where the statute authorizes liquor to be furnished by a regular practicing physician who in good faith prescribes the same as medicine to his patient, a druggist may sell upon a prescription given by the physician.[5] Generally, however, the statutes authorize

N. C. 1064; S. v. Jaques, 68 Mo. 260; S. v. Moore, 107 Mo. 78; Surratt v. S., 45 Miss. 601. Sale in original package need not be negatived, though such sale would be lawful: S. v. Robinson, 49 Me. 285; *supra*, § 1204. And see *infra*, § 1278.

[1] Baeumel v. S., 26 Fla. 71. So as to an exception of domestic wine: S. v. Stapp, 29 Ia. 551; S. v. Curley, 33 Ia. 359; S. v. Miller, 53 Ia. 84. But in another case it is said that the rule as to negativing an exception is to depend upon its nature and not upon the place in the statute where it is made: S. v. O'Donnell, 10 R. I. 472.

[2] P. v. Haas, 79 Mich. 499; P. v. Decarie, 80 Mich. 578; S. v. McBride, 64 Mo. 364; S. v. Starney, 71 N. C. 202; Kinser v. S., 9 Ind. 543; S. v. Scarlett, 38 Ark. 563; Thompson v. S., 37 Ark. 408. Objection on this ground should be taken by motion to quash and not afterwards: P. v. Drennan, 86 Mich. 445. Where the complaint was for keeping a saloon open after legal hours, it was held not necessary to aver that the place kept open was not a drug-store, the name of the place as stated in the indictment being sufficient to negative the exception referred to: P. v. Robbins, 70 Mich. 130; P. v. Sullivan, 83 Mich. 355. If it appears that defendant was a druggist, and it is charged that he had not paid the tax and filed a bond as required, the burden of showing such facts is on the prosecution: P. v. Beach, 93 Mich. 25. *Contra*, C. v. Perry, 148 Mass. 160.

[3] Carson v. S., 69 Ala. 235; Barton v. S., 99 Ind. 89; Wright v. P., 101 Ill. 126; Newman v. S., 7 Lea, 617; Woods v. S., 36 Ark. 36; S. v. McBrayer, 98 N. C. 619; U. S. v. Smith, 45 Fed. R. 115.

[4] Schaffner v. S., 8 Ohio St. 642.

[5] C. v. Reynolds, 89 Ky. 147. *Contra*, under statute requiring practicing physicians to file an affidavit, etc.: Battle v. S., 51 Ark. 97.

druggists to sell on physicians' prescriptions for medicinal purposes; but even then the sale must be for a proper purpose or on the reasonable belief that it is for a proper purpose.[1] So where physicians are authorized to sell for medicinal purposes, it is essential that the person to whom the liquor is sold be a *bona fide* patient in course of treatment, and if the sale is merely in evasion of the law as to selling for a beverage the physician will be liable.[2] Where the statute specifies that sales by druggists may be made on physicians' prescriptions, it is necessary that the prescription have all the requisites indicated by statute.[3] If a statute specifies that such sales may be made on "the requisition of a physician for medicinal purposes," a verbal or written request by the physician will be sufficient.[4] It is sometimes provided that there must be a separate prescription for each sale.[5] Where the statute authorizes sales by druggists on the physician's prescription, it seems that one who is both a physician and a druggist cannot sell on his own prescription.[6] Statutes uniformly make some provision for sales for mechanical, medicinal, sacramental and other proper purposes, but they do not agree as to the method in which such sales shall be made. Generally druggists are authorized to sell for those purposes, sometimes without special permit or license, except such druggist's license as may be required of them to carry on the general business,[7] while in other states a special license or permit in addition to the druggist's

[1] C. v. Gould, 158 Mass. 499; P. v. Safford, 5 Denio, 112. But all that is required of the physician is that after reasonable investigation he shall believe in good faith that his patient needs the liquor as a medicine before he prescribes it: C. v. Minor, 88 Ky. 422.

[2] Redding v. S., 91 Ga. 231; S. v. Atkinson, 33 S. C. 100.

[3] S. v. Tetrick, 34 W. Va. 137; S. v. Cox, 23 W. Va. 797.

[4] Bain v. S., 61 Ala. 75.

[5] Carrington v. C., 78 Ky. 83. And whether a sale of the quantity authorized by a prescription in portions on different occasions, instead of the whole quantity at once, will be illegal, will depend on the circumstances of the case as bearing on the question of good faith: S. v. May, 33 S. C. 39. Even where the statute does not require a separate prescription for each sale, a written prescription directing a repetition of the medicine as needed will not cover more than one sale: Edwards v. S., 121 Ind. 450.

[6] S. v. Anderson, 81 Mo. 78; Brinson v. S., 89 Ala. 105. *Contra,* Boone v. S., 10 Tex. Ap. 418.

[7] S. v. Cox, 23 W. Va. 797; Harper v. S., 3 Lea, 211; Jones v. S., 68 Ala. 559; Brooks v. S., 55 Miss. 445; S. v. Mercer, 58 Ia. 182.

license is necessary.[1] And under the right thus given to druggists to sell they may sell to other druggists for purposes of compounding and manufacturing incident to the druggist's business;[2] but they cannot sell to an ordinary purchaser separately the ingredients of which a medical preparation is composed, one of them being intoxicating liquor, leaving to the purchaser to do the compounding.[3] A druggist will usually be protected in sales made for proper purposes if good faith has been used and the sale is made in the belief that the purchaser intends to use the liquor for the purpose for which he pretends to buy it. He is not required to investigate the truth of the purchaser's statements, even though the purchaser be a stranger to him;[4] but for illegal selling, even though having a license or permit, he will be punishable as other sellers without authority.[5] The question is one of good faith,[6] and if the sale by the druggist is without knowledge or belief on his part that the liquor is to be used for the proper purpose for which it is ostensibly sold,[7] or artfully sold to evade the law as to selling for a beverage,[8] or without ordinary caution and diligence in ascertaining for what purpose the liquor is wanted,[9] the druggist will be punishable for illegal selling. While the general question is whether the intent is to violate the law,[10] and the druggist is not bound to ascertain at his peril for what use the liquor is bought,[11] yet

[1] S. v. Gray, 61 Conn. 39; Brown v. S., 9 Neb. 189; S. v. Bissell, 67 Ia. 616. Where it is required that the druggist be a registered pharmacist, it is no defense for one who is not registered that the sales were made by a clerk who was duly registered: S. v. Norton. 67 Ia. 641.

[2] Dennehy v. Chicago, 120 Ill. 627; Wood v. Smith, 23 Vt. 706.

[3] S. v. Hall, 79 Me. 501; S. v. Brown, 60 N. H. 205.

[4] P. v. Hinchman, 75 Mich. 587.

[5] Baeumel v. S., 26 Fla. 71; S. v. Harris, 64 Ia. 287; S. v. Knowles, 57 Ia. 669; S. v. Salts, 77 Ia. 193. See *supra*, § 1229.

[6] U. S. v. White, 42 Fed. R. 138; Zapf v. S., 11 Ind. Ap. 360; S. v. Tanner, 50 Kan. 365.

[7] Leppert v. S., 7 Ind. 300; McGuire v. S., 37 Miss. 369.

[8] S. v. Harris, 64 Ia. 287; S. v. Knowles, 57 Ia. 669.

[9] Davis v. S., 93 Ga. 45; S. v. Cummins, 76 Ia. 133. The kind and quantity of liquor kept by the druggist may be considered in determining the intent with which it is kept: S. v. Shank, 74 Ia. 649. Evidence of other sales may be received as bearing on the intent: Dobson v. S., 5 Lea, 271; S. v. Elliott, 45 Kan. 525. The burden of showing good faith is on the seller: Miles v. S., 5 W. Va. 524; Haynie v. S., 32 Miss. 400. Proof of the justification devolves upon the druggist: Hines v. S., 93 Ga. 187. And see *infra*, § 1281.

[10] Hottendorf v. S., 89 Ind. 282.

[11] S. v. Mitchell, 28 Mo. 562.

the burden of proof is on the defendant to show that the sale was within the specifications of the statute; that is, that the conditions of the statute had been complied with.[1] Thus, a pharmacist may be guilty of keeping a nuisance under a statute declaring a place kept for the illegal sale of liquor to be a nuisance,[2] or for selling to be drunk on the premises,[3] even though he has a permit as a pharmacist. Where the statute provides for sales by pharmacists on written applications, or prescriptions of a physician, the pharmacist must determine from all the circumstances whether the purchase is in good faith for proper purposes.[4]

§ 1254. **Sales by producers or manufacturers.**— Some statutes exempt from the provisions of the law as to sales the producer or manufacturer and sometimes the product of domestic fruit, etc.[5] The constitutionality of these statutes has already been discussed.[6] The statutes frequently limit the right of retail sales on the part of the manufacturer or producer to his own premises,[7] and a sale at some distance from the place of manufacture, though on land belonging to the manufacturer, will not be lawful as at the place of manufacture;[8] nor if the producer has two or more houses will sales at each of them be deemed sales on the premises; but the right to sell will be limited to the place of production.[9] Where the exemption was of sale of cider by the maker thereof, it was held to be applicable to cider manufactured from fruit raised by others as well as by the manufacturer;[10] but a provision in behalf of persons making wine from grapes or berries of their own growing will not extend to cover such liquors made from wild berries.[11] Where

[1] C. v. Perry, 148 Mass. 160.

[2] S. v. Mullenhoff, 74 Ia. 271; S. v. Salts, 77 Ia. 193.

[3] C. v. Mandeville, 142 Mass. 469.

[4] S. v. Aulman, 76 Ia. 624; S. v. Thompson, 74 Ia. 119; S. v. Huff, 76 Ia. 200.

[5] As to alleging and proving this exception, see *supra*, § 1252.

[6] *Supra*, § 1202.

[7] S. v. Jaeger, 63 Mo. 403.

[8] S. v. Hazell, 100 N. C. 471; S. v. Whissenhunt, 98 N. C. 682. Sometimes a distiller's license gives him the right to sell at a single place within the county, and that place need not be the place of manufacture: Britton v. C., 105 Pa. St. 311.

[9] S. v. Wyl, 55 Mo. 67.

[10] C. v. Mahoney, 152 Mass. 493. The exemption protects sales by servants or agents of the manufacturer as well as those made by the manufacturer personally: Ibid.; S. v. Hart, 107 N. C. 796; Jeffries v. S., 52 Ark. 420.

[11] Galloway v. S., 60 Ark. 362. A provision as to "grapes or berries"

manufacturers are permitted to sell at the place of manufacture, they are thereby relieved from the requirement to have a license as retailers or dram-shop keepers.[1] Sometimes the manufacturer's right to sell is limited to a considerable quantity, or to such a package as liquor is usually put up in by manufacturers.[2] A manufacturer is not a wholesale dealer within statutes as to taxation.[3] It may be required, however, of manufacturers that they shall obtain license, but such provisions are usually applicable to sales as merchants and not as manufacturers.[4]

VI. Special Prohibitions.

§ 1255. Provisions in general.— It is generally provided that sales shall not be made to certain classes of persons, such as minors, drunkards, Indians, etc., and in certain localities, such as within a specified distance of an educational institution, or on special days, such as Sundays, holidays, and election days. Regulations like this are in the proper exercise of the police power,[5] and are not unconstitutional because lacking uniformity in their application.[6] Thus, it has been provided that sales shall not be made to females in any wine-room kept in connection with a saloon,[7] or in any place where women are employed or led to assemble for the purpose of business therein carried on,[8] or in any restaurant or refreshment saloon,[9] or in any place of amusement or apartment opening into the same.[10] There have also been special provisions as to sales within a specified distance of a certain factory,[11] or a certain railroad in the process of construction.[12] But it will be necessary to discuss some classes of exceptions separately.

will not cover peaches, though grown by the manufacturer: Ibid.

[1] S. v. Hart, 107 N. C. 796; Jeffries v. S., 52 Ark. 420.

[2] S. v. Schroeder, 43 Minn. 231; Tipton v. P., 156 Ill. 241.

[3] Taylor v. Vincent, 12 Lea, 282 (explaining Webb v. S., 11 Lea, 362; Webb v. Baird, 11 Lea, 667).

[4] Lawson v. C., 14 B. Mon. 225; S. v. Stiefel, 74 Md. 546.

[5] *Supra*, § 39. It may be forbidden to allow minors to play pool in saloons where even non-intoxicating liquors are sold as beverages: Snow v. S., 50 Ark. 557.

[6] *Supra*, §§ 77, 1211.

[7] Walker v. P., 5 Colo. Ap. 37.

[8] S. v. Marion, 14 Mont. 458.

[9] S. v. Hogan, 30 N. H. 268.

[10] S. v. White, 7 Baxt. 158.

[11] Ashurst v. S., 79 Ala. 276; Barnes v. S., 49 Ala. 342.

[12] S. v. Hampton, 77 N. C. 526.

§ 1256. Sales to prohibited persons.— Under statutes prohibiting sales to minors or persons in the habit of becoming intoxicated, it is immaterial what the purpose of the sale may be, or whether it is within the evils intended to be remedied; the statutory regulations must be complied with. Thus, it is no defense in making such a sale not in accordance with the law that it is for medicinal purposes.[1] And it is generally immaterial whether the seller is authorized to sell for lawful purposes or not.[2] Some courts have, however, construed exceptions into the statutes with reference to sales to minors, just as they have into the other statutory provisions prohibiting sales,[3] and have held that such sales if for medicinal purposes,[4] or in large quantity when the general statutes prohibit only sales in small quantity without a license, are not criminal.[5] These special restrictions, being in the nature of proper police regulations, are applicable to sales in the original package, although such sales may otherwise be legal.[6] As the purpose of these statutes is to prevent the evil effects which would result to the persons of the particular classes intended and others by reason of their drinking intoxicating liquor, it has generally been held criminal to procure and furnish liquor to such persons, even though the person furnishing is not a seller, but an agent for the buyer.[7] This is not in accordance with the weight of authority as to what constitutes a sale for other purposes, as stated in a preceding section,[8] where it is said that to thus furnish is not to sell. And indeed one court has held that thus to furnish liquor to a minor is not criminal, inasmuch as there is no crime involved in the purchase by the minor, and therefore not in a purchase through an agent.[9] The liability of a

[1] S. v. McBrayer, 98 N. C. 619. Thus, in charging sale by a druggist to a person in the habit of getting intoxicated, it is not necessary to allege that the liquor was sold to be used as a beverage: P. v. Hamilton, 101 Mich. 87.

[2] Altenburg v. C., 126 Pa. St. 602; Johnson v. P., 83 Ill. 431; Fitzenrider v. S., 30 Ind. 338; Johnson v. S., 74 Ind. 197; S. v. Gowgill, 75 Ind. 599; S. v. Hamilton, 75 Ind. 238.

[3] See *supra*, § 1252.

[4] Payne v. S., 74 Ind. 203.

[5] Brutton v. S., 4 Ind. 601; Brosee v. S., 5 Ind. 75; Cool v. S., 16 Ind. 355; Manvelle v. S., 58 Ind. 63; S. v. Zeitler, 63 Ind. 441; Arbintrode v. S., 67 Ind. 267; Grupe v. S., 67 Ind. 327; Maxwell v. S., 27 Ala. 660.

[6] C. v. Zelt, 138 Pa. St. 615.

[7] Burnett v. S., 92 Ga. 474; S. v. Best, 108 N. C. 747; Walton v. S., 62 Ala. 197; Foster v. S., 45 Ark. 361; S. v. Hubbard, 60 Ia. 466.

[8] *Supra*, § 1233.

[9] Bryant v. S., 82 Ala. 51.

dealer for sales made by his employees to a minor or intoxicated person without his knowledge or consent has been already discussed under the general subject of liability for acts of servants or agents in making illegal sales.[1] Illegal selling to such person is not a continuing offense,[2] but each such separate sale is a distinct crime.[3] Neither is such a sale in any sense a local crime, and it is therefore not necessary to specify the particular place where it was made or bring it within the terms of the seller's license.[4] The punishment for this special class of illegal sales may be different from that for illegal selling in general.[5]

§ **1257. Intent or knowledge in such cases.**— The difficulty which has already appeared under a variety of forms as to whether there is criminal liability for acts such as are prohibited by statute, but done in good faith and without knowledge of the particular circumstances which make the act criminal,[6] also arises here and there in the same diversity in the views of the courts that has already been noticed. Many courts hold that the seller must act at his peril in this respect as in others, and must know absolutely whether the person to whom a sale is made is one under such disability of minority or of character as to habitual intoxication that sale to him is prohibited, and the good faith of the transaction or the lack of knowledge, or even of any circumstances to put the seller on inquiry as to the disability, will be no defense.[7] But there is perhaps an equal weight of authority for the proposition that intent is essential in this as in other offenses, and that if without knowledge and without negligence a sale is made to a person who is under disability in this respect, the

1 *Supra*, § 1237.

2 P. v. Hamilton, 101 Mich. 87.

3 S. v. Blahut, 48 Ark. 34.

4 S. v. Boggess, 36 W. Va. 713.

5 S. v. Douglass, 73 Ia. 279; Baer v. C., 10 Bush, 8.

6 *Supra*, §§ 128, 134, 1222, 1251, 1253.

7 C. v. Gould, 158 Mass. 499; C. v. Stevens, 155 Mass. 291; C. v. Julius, 143 Mass. 132; C. v. Emmons, 98 Mass. 6; C. v. Zelt, 138 Pa. St. 615; McCutcheon v. P., 69 Ill. 601; Mapes v. P., 69 Ill. 523; Farmer v. P., 77 Ill. 322; Gallagher v. P., 29 Ill. Ap. 401; Flynn v. Galesburg, 12 Ill. Ap. 200; Jamison v. Burton, 43 Ia. 282; Dudley v. Sautbine, 49 Ia. 650; S. v. Ward, 75 Ia. 637; S. v. Thompson, 74 Ia. 119; S. v. Hartfiel, 24 Wis. 60; S. v. Heck, 23 Minn. 549; Ulrich v. C., 6 Bush, 400; Hill v. S., 62 Ala. 168; S. v. Cain, 9 W. Va. 559; S. v. Gilmore, 9 W. Va. 641; S. v. Farr, 34 W. Va. 84; Redmond v. S., 36 Ark. 58; Crampton v. S., 37 Ark. 108; Pounders v. S., 37 Ark. 399.

seller will be excused.[1] Some statutes define the offense so as to make knowledge essential, and under them the indictment must allege such knowledge.[2] But where knowledge is not required by the statutory definition, the prosecution is not required to allege want of knowledge even in those states where want of knowledge would be a defense;[3] that fact being an excuse which the defendant must establish, and the burden being upon him to show that he had not such knowledge, and that the circumstances were not such as to put him upon inquiry.[4] Thus, he may show that the appearance of the person to whom the sale was made was not such as to indicate that he was a minor.[5] The mere statement by the minor that he is of age will not be sufficient to show due diligence on the part of the seller.[6] Evidence of the general reputation of the party to whom the liquor is sold as being a habitual drunkard is admissible for the purpose of proving knowledge of the fact on the part of defendant.[7] Under this general view the question whether defendant had knowledge of the age or habits of the person to whom sale was made is for the jury.[8]

[1] Miller v. S., 5 Ohio St. 275; Crabtree v. S., 30 Ohio St. 382; Faulks v. P., 39 Mich. 200; Adler v. S., 55 Ala. 16; S. v. Kalb, 14 Ind. 403; Robinius v. S., 63 Ind. 235; Robinius v. S., 67 Ind. 94; Swigart v. S., 99 Ind. 111; Hunter v. S., 101 Ind. 241.

[2] C. v. Bell, 14 Bush, 433; Hunter v. S., 18 Tex. Ap. 444; Williams v. S., 23 Tex. Ap. 70; Koblenschlag v. S., 23 Tex. Ap. 264.

[3] C. v. Sellers, 130 Pa. St. 32; Ward v. S., 48 Ind. 289; Werneke v. S., 50 Ind. 22; Berry v. S., 67 Ind. 222; Payne v. S., 74 Ind. 203; S. v. Baer, 37 W. Va. 1.

[4] Burnett v. S., 92 Ga. 474; Farbach v. S., 24 Ind. 77; Goetz v. S., 41 Ind. 162; Williams v. S., 48 Ind. 306; Farrell v. S., 45 Ind. 371; Ferrell v. S., 48 Ind. 118; Brown v. S., 24 Ind. 113; Kreamer v. S., 106 Ind. 192; Mulreed v. S., 107 Ind. 62; Fehn v. S., 3 Ind. Ap. 568; Solomon v. S., 71 Miss. 567.

[5] S. v. Kalb, 14 Ind. 403. Where the offense consists in knowingly selling, evidence that a minor generally circulated the report that he was of age is admissible in behalf of defendant: Pressler v. S., 13 Tex. Ap. 95. Of course, where want of knowledge is no defense, evidence that the minor appeared to be of full age is immaterial.

[6] Harkey v. S., 89 Ga. 478.

[7] Adams v. S., 25 Ohio St. 584; Atkins v. S., 60 Ala. 45. But it is said that evidence that the intemperate habits of such person were generally known in the community is irrelevant, as that would not justify the inference that they were known to the defendant: Stanley v. S., 26 Ala. 26.

[8] Elam v. S., 25 Ala. 53. The defendant must show that he used special diligence and made honest inquiry: Reich v. S., 63 Ga. 616.

§ 1258. Sale to minor or intoxicated person for another.— Under statutes making it criminal to sell to minors, the question has arisen whether a sale to a minor for the use of an adult is criminal. Certainly, if the minor does not disclose the fact of his agency, the sale is unlawful.[1] Some statutes forbid the sale to a minor, whether for his own use or for the use of another, and no question of agency can therefore be raised.[2] Aside from statutory provision it is, by the weight of authority, not criminal to sell and deliver to a minor liquor bought by him as agent for and to be delivered to a third person to whom the sale might lawfully be made;[3] and it is generally held that a sale in good faith to a minor for a third person on the representation made by the minor, believed on reasonable investigation by the seller to be true, that the liquor is purchased as agent for the third person, will not be illegal.[4] But undoubtedly where the sale is directly to a minor or intoxicated person it will be criminal, although the liquor is to be drunk by another; thus, where a sale was made to an intoxicated person of liquor to be furnished by the seller to a prostitute, it was held that the sale was criminal.[5]

§ 1259. Furnishing to minor or intoxicated person.— The statutory provisions as to sales to minors or intoxicated persons are usually broad enough to include not merely a technical sale, but also a furnishing or giving,[6] and it is therefore immaterial whether the liquor is paid for by the minor or by a third person;[7] and the same rule is applicable to sales to intoxicated

[1] C. v. Gormley, 133 Mass. 580; Ritcher v. S., 63 Miss. 304; Neely v. S., 60 Ark. 66; Siceluff v. S., 52 Ark. 56.

[2] C. v. O'Leary, 143 Mass. 95; C. v. Murphy, 155 Mass. 284; Sumner v. S., 4 Ind. Ap. 403.

[3] C. v. Lattinville, 120 Mass. 385; S. v. Walker, 103 N. C. 413; Wallace v. S., 54 Ark. 542; Waldstien v. S., 29 Tex. Ap. 82. But a later Texas case is to the contrary: Yakel v. S., 30 Tex. Ap. 391. And also see P. v. Garrett, 68 Mich. 487, 8 Am. Cr. R. 399, and note.

[4] Monaghan v. S., 66 Miss. 513; Holmes v. S., 88 Ind. 145. But it is held in some cases that the seller must act at his peril and will be protected only where the liquor is actually delivered by the minor to a third person and not used by himself: Dixon v. S., 89 Ga. 785.

[5] Schullherr v. S., 68 Miss. 227.

[6] Dahmer v. S., 56 Miss. 787; C. v. Davis, 12 Bush, 240. The ownership of the liquor furnished is immaterial; it is the voluntary delivery into the possession of a minor or person of known intemperate habits, with or without anything being given in consideration, which is punishable: Hill v. S., 62 Ala. 168.

[7] S. v. Best, 108 N. C. 747; S. v.

persons. Thus, the seller is liable if he furnishes liquor to one to whom the sale may properly be made, but with the known purpose on the part of such person to have a part of it drunk by a minor or intoxicated person in the seller's presence by way of treating;[1] and it makes no difference that the money with which the purchase is made is furnished by the minor or intoxicated person;[2] and if the seller knew that the liquor or a part of it was for the consumption of a minor or intoxicated person he is guilty.[3] But of course, if the sale is to an adult who purchases for a minor not present, though with the minor's money, while the sale is to the minor through such agent, yet the seller is not liable for selling to a minor.[4] In some cases, however, it has been held that a sale of liquor to an adult, though it is known to be procured for a minor or intoxicated person for drinking, even in the presence of the seller, is not a sale to a minor or intoxicated person and is therefore not criminal.[5]

§ 1260. Who deemed minor; allegation and proof of age.— The question of minority is one of age, not of disability. Thus, although the civil disabilities of a person under the age of minority have been removed,[6] or the minor is carrying on business for himself,[7] nevertheless the sale will be illegal. The fact of minority must be averred in order to show the act to be criminal.[8] The age may be proved by the testimony of the minor himself based on reputation in his family;[9] or by testi-

Munson, 25 Ohio St. 381; P. v. Neumann, 85 Mich. 98.

[1] Page v. S., 84 Ala. 446; Walton v. S., 62 Ala. 197; S. v. Hubbard, 60 Ia. 466.

[2] Liles v. S., 88 Ala. 139; S. v. Scoggins, 107 N. C. 959. It is even said that an adult, who with the minor's money buys liquor for the minor, is an aider and procurer of the sale to a minor and punishable: Foster v. S., 45 Ark. 361.

[3] Hunter v. S., 101 Ind. 241.

[4] Gillan v. S., 47 Ark. 555.

[5] Siegel v. P., 106 Ill. 89; Birr v. P., 113 Ill. 645; Bryant v. S., 82 Ala. 51; Ward v. S., 45 Ark. 351. And see *supra*, § 1233. Whether the sale is to an adult or to a minor may be a question of fact on the evidence: Edgar v. S., 45 Ark. 356. It is immaterial that the minor furnishes the money for the purchase if that fact is not known to the seller: Siegel v. P., 106 Ill. 89.

[6] Coker v. S., 91 Ala. 92.

[7] Pounders v. S., 37 Ark. 399.

[8] C. v. Fowler, 145 Mass. 398. Where the statute prohibited selling to any white person under the age of twenty-one years. etc., it was held necessary to aver in the indictment that the minor was a white person: C. v. Ewing, 7 Bush, 105.

[9] S. v. Best, 108 N. C. 747; Edgar v. S., 37 Ark. 219; Pounders v. S., 37

mony of witnesses that it was reasonably apparent to observation that the purchaser was not of age,[1] or by the general opinion of persons acquainted with the minor.[2]

§ 1261. **Consent of parent or guardian.**— The statutes usually make an exception to the prohibition as to sales to minors in case of written consent to such sale given by the parent or guardian of the minor, but such exception is strictly construed, and no consent save that which comes within the terms of the statute will constitute an excuse.[3] It will not excuse a sale to a minor without the written consent required, that he has no parent or guardian by whom consent might be given.[4] The written authority must be special for each sale; a general permit or license extended to a dealer to sell to a minor without limitation as to time or quantity will not be sufficient.[5] As the description of the offense itself is usually that the sale is without the written consent, etc., it is necessary to allege the sale to have been without such consent in order to charge the crime; but such want of written consent may be alleged in the general terms of the statute.[6] The negation must, however, be broad enough to cover in itself written consent which would be valid; thus, it is not sufficient to negative the consent of the father or the mother where consent of either parent would be sufficient;[7] likewise, it is not sufficient to negative the consent

Ark. 399. Where the statute prohibited sale of liquor to a free person of color, it was held competent to prove the status of the person to whom liquor was sold by evidence of hearsay or general reputation: Tucker v. S., 24 Ala. 77.

[1] Walker v. S., 25 Tex. Ap. 448; Garner v. S., 28 Tex. Ap. 561.

[2] C. v. O'Brien, 134 Mass. 198. The testimony of the father, or other party having opportunity to know, that the purchaser "will be twenty-one next August," *held* sufficient evidence that he was not twenty-one at the time of the sale: Dolke v. S., 99 Ind. 229 (overruling Meyer v. S., 50 Ind. 18).

[3] Adler v. S., 55 Ala. 16; S. v. Lawrence, 97 N. C. 492; Blahut v. S., 54 Ark. 538; S. v. Coenan, 48 Ia. 567; S. v. Clottu, 33 Ind. 409. And the exception of written consent may be by statute taken away entirely: Grepel v. S., 32 Ohio St. 167. It is no defense that the sale was with the oral consent of the parent, afterwards reduced to writing: Hill v. S., 37 Ark. 395.

[4] Blair v. S., 81 Ga. 628.

[5] Gill v. S., 86 Ga. 751; Dixon v. S., 86 Ga. 754. *Contra*, Mascowitz v. S., 49 Ark. 170.

[6] Freiberg v. S., 94 Ala. 91; Parkinson v. S., 14 Md. 184; S. v. Allen, 12 Ind. Ap. 528; Mogler v. S., 47 Ark. 109; Weed v. S., 55 Ala. 13; Marshall v. S., 49 Ala. 21.

[7] Newman v. S., 63 Ga. 533; Lantznester v. S., 19 Tex. Ap. 320. But an indictment negativing the consent of the mother is sufficient if the

of the guardian only;[1] nor is it proper to allege that the sale was without the written consent *and* request, when a written consent *or* request would be sufficient under the statute.[2] Since the fact of the giving of written consent is peculiarly within the defendant's knowledge, the burden of proving it is upon defendant,[3] and the prosecution makes a *prima facie* case by proving the sale without any evidence as to the want of such consent.[4]

§ 1262. Sale to habitual drunkard or intoxicated person. The statutes are not uniform in defining the offense of selling to drunkards or intoxicated persons. If the statutory prohibition is as to sales to drunkards or persons in the habit of becoming intoxicated or of known intemperate habits, it will be sufficient to show that the buyer was in the habit of using liquor intemperately;[5] and proof of a particular number of intoxications within a given time cannot be declared sufficient by the court as a matter of law to establish the fact; the question is one for the jury.[6] Witnesses may properly testify, however, that they frequently have seen the person to whom the sale is charged to have been made, under the influence of liquor.[7] But a person who is in the habit of drinking is not necessarily in the habit of getting intoxicated.[8] It is sufficient to show that such person has been intoxicated frequently and has thereby acquired an involuntary tendency to become intoxicated.[9] The person to whom the sale was made is competent to testify as to his intemperate habits,[10] and all persons having sufficient knowledge of his general character are competent to testify as to whether he was or was not generally known as a person of intemperate habits.[11] If it is sought

proof shows the death of the father and that there is no guardian: Reich v. S., 63 Ga. 616.

[1] S. v. Emerick, 35 Ark. 324.

[2] C. v. Hadcraft, 6 Bush, 91.

[3] Reynolds v. S., 32 Tex. Ap. 36.

[4] Birr v. P., 113 Ill. 645; Monroe v. P., 113 Ill. 670; Harbaugh v. Monmouth, 74 Ill. 367; Farrall v. S., 32 Ala. 557; Freiberg v. S., 94 Ala. 91; Ridling v. S., 56 Ga. 601; Edgar v. S., 37 Ark. 219; Pounders v. S., 37 Ark. 399.

[5] Mapes v. P., 69 Ill. 523.

[6] Kamman v. P., 24 Ill. Ap. 388.

[7] S. v. Pratt, 34 Vt. 323; Mapes v. P., 69 Ill. 523. Evidence of five occasions of intoxication is sufficient evidence to go to the jury on that question: Gallagher v. P., 120 Ill. 179.

[8] Mullinix v. P., 76 Ill. 211.

[9] Murphy v. P., 90 Ill. 59. But it is not essential to show beyond a reasonable doubt that he is constantly or usually intoxicated: Ibid.

[10] Tatum v. S., 63 Ala. 147.

[11] Tatum v. S., 63 Ala. 147.

to prove that the sale was to an intoxicated person, it is not necessary to prove that such person was drunk at the very moment of the sale; if it appears that he was drunk shortly before the sale it is sufficient.[1] But if the charge is of a sale to a person in the habit of getting intoxicated, it must appear that he had that habit at the time the sale was made.[2] Some statutes make the offense to consist in selling to a habitual drunkard after notice in writing that he is such.[3] A person is drunk in the legal sense when he is so far under the influence of intoxicating liquor that his passions are visibly excited and his judgment impaired.[4]

§ **1263. Sales to Indians.**— The federal statutes and the statutes of some states prohibit the sales of intoxicating liquors to Indians,[5] and such a provision in a state statute is not in conflict with the federal statutes on the same subject; it is a proper exercise of police power.[6] But the federal courts have exclusive jurisdiction of the violation of the federal statutes, no matter where the sale may be made.[7] Such a state statute is applicable to Indians as a class, regardless of their citizenship or tribal relations;[8] but the federal statutes relate only to Indians who are under the charge of an Indian superintendent or agent.[9]

[1] Kammann v. P., 124 Ill. 481.

[2] Zeizer v. S., 47 Ind. 129; Wiedemann v. P., 92 Ill. 314; Dolan v. S., 122 Ind. 141.

[3] Dolan v. S., 122 Ind. 141; S. v. Smith, 122 Ind. 178. If the statute prohibits sales by hotel-keeper, merchant, grocer, etc., to any person after notice not to sell to such person, the fact of notice and that the defendant was one of the classes of persons named in the statute must be alleged: S. v. Heitsch, 29 Minn. 134.

[4] S. v. Pierce, 65 Ia. 85. And see S. v. Huxford, 47 Ia. 16. Drunkenness has the same significance as intoxication: Smith v. Bigelow, 19 Ia. 459.

[5] U. S. v. Winslow, 3 Saw. 337; U. S. v. Flynn, 1 Dill. 451; Bruguier v. U. S., 1 Dak. 5; P. v. Bray, 105 Cal. 344.

[6] T. v. Guyot, 9 Mont. 46.

[7] U. S. v. Burdick, 1 Dak. 142. Sales by an Indian to an Indian within an Indian reservation are not prohibited: Ibid.; U. S. v. Winslow, 3 Saw. 337.

[8] P. v. Bray, 105 Cal. 344.

[9] U. S. v. Burdick, 1 Dak. 142; U. S. v. Flynn, 1 Dill. 451. The fact that the Indian has received allotted land and taken an oath of allegiance to the United States and become a citizen is not sufficient to show that he is not within the control of an Indian agent if he has not been released by the government from the charge, supervision and control of such agent: Renfrow v. U. S., 3 Okl. 161.

§ 1264. Selling on Sundays or holidays.— There are usually statutory provisions as to sales on Sunday or on a legal holiday or on an election day;[1] and a provision as to Sunday selling is not unconstitutional as an interference with religious freedom.[2] A day set apart by recommendation of the governor or president as a day of fasting, prayer or thanksgiving, whether it be a regular thanksgiving day or a different day designated for a special reason, may be by statute a public holiday.[3] But a declaration by statute that bills and notes shall not be presented for acceptance or payment, etc., on a particular day does not make it a legal holiday for every purpose, and therefore does not bring it within the provisions of statutes as to selling liquor on holidays.[4] In general, a license to sell does not authorize sales on Sunday in violation of the general Sunday statutes;[5] but where there are statutes prohibiting sales on Sunday it is immaterial whether the seller has a license or permit or not,[6] unless, of course, the statute as to Sunday sales relates specifically to particular classes of persons, such as licensed dealers or tavern-keepers.[7] If the general statutes relating to sales of liquor apply only to sales of certain small quantities, then a statute as to sales on Sunday will be limited in its application to sales of like quantities;[8] but under other forms of the statute sales in any quantity are illegal.[9] In general, that will constitute a sale, furnishing, giving, etc., upon Sunday which would constitute such acts within statutes regulating sales on other days.[10] Where the sale is one which would be unlawful on any day, for instance, by an un-

[1] S. v. Sinnott, 15 Neb. 472; Martin v. S., 30 Neb. 507; S. v. Peterson, 38 Minn. 143. A sale between Saturday midnight and dawn of Sunday morning is a sale on the night of Sunday within the statutory meaning: Kroer v. P., 78 Ill. 294. And see cases cited in the next section, where it is said that the statute as to selling or keeping open upon an election day extends to all portions of the twenty-four hours within which the election is held.

[2] S. v. Ambs, 20 Mo. 214.

[3] P. v. Ackerman, 80 Mich. 588.

[4] Ruge v. S., 62 Ind. 388; S. v. Atkinson, 139 Ind. 426.

[5] Omit v. C., 21 Pa. St. 426.

[6] Meyer v. S., 50 Ind. 18; Stein v. S., 50 Ind. 21; Lehritter v. S., 42 Ind. 383; S. v. Edlavitch, 77 Md. 144; S. v. Heckler, 81 Mo. 417.

[7] Bode v. S., 7 Gill, 326; Jensen v. S., 60 Wis. 577.

[8] Schlict v. S., 31 Ind. 246; Morris v. S., 47 Ind. 503; Beardsley v. S., 49 Ind. 240.

[9] S. v. Eskridge, 1 Swan, 413.

[10] *Supra*, §§ 1233–1235.

licensed dealer, it may be prosecuted under the general statute as an illegal selling, although it is made on Sunday and would be also punishable under the Sunday statute;[1] but if a dealer has authority to sell on other days, and the sale is illegal only because made on Sunday, he should be proceeded against under the Sunday statute and not for selling without a license.[2] Sometimes the statutes relate only to *selling* on Sunday,[3] but where they provide for selling or keeping open a place for sale, these are two distinct offenses for which separate convictions may be had, even though there is only proof of one particular sale.[4] It is sufficient to constitute a keeping open that a place for selling was open for that purpose, without regard to whether any sales were actually made,[5] or whether the liquor sold was drunk on the premises.[6] Neither is it necessary to allege or prove that the keeping open of the place was a nuisance or hurtful to the neighborhood or to the encouragement of idleness, gaming, etc.[7] Generally the purpose for which the place is open is held to be immaterial, and an opening on Sunday for any kind of business,[8] or even for cleaning out the place,[9] or for the purpose of drying fruit,[10] or in order that the bartender may help himself to a drink,[11] is criminal. If the sale of liquor is carried on in the same place as other business, it is unlawful to keep the place open for the transaction of the other business although no sale of liquor is contemplated;[12] as, for instance, where a restaurant and a bar-room are connected by internal connections, the keeping open of the restaurant, through which access may be had to the bar-room, is unlawful,[13] and it is immaterial that the internal connection

[1] C. v. Harrison, 11 Gray, 310. So if a license expressly forbids Sunday selling, a sale on Sunday, even by a licensed dealer, may be prosecuted as a sale without license: C. v. Hoyer, 125 Mass. 209.

[2] C. v. Naylor, 34 Pa. St. 86. And see *supra*, § 1229.

[3] S. v. Fearson, 2 Md. 310; Lincolnton v. McCarter, Busbee, 429.

[4] S. v. Ambs, 20 Mo. 214.

[5] Hall v. S., 3 Ga. 18; Koop v. P., 47 Ill. 327. But it is said to be essential that the keeping open be for tippling purposes: Patten v. Centralia, 47 Ill. 370.

[6] Harris v. P., 1 Colo. Ap. 289.

[7] Hall v. S., 3 Ga. 18; Fant v. P., 45 Ill. 259.

[8] P. v. Minter, 59 Mich. 557.

[9] P. v. Roby, 52 Mich. 577.

[10] Klug v. S., 77 Ga. 734.

[11] P. v. Crowley, 90 Mich. 366.

[12] McNeill v. S., 92 Tenn. 719.

[13] Cooper v. S., 88 Ga. 441; Harmon v. S., 92 Ga. 455; P. v. Higgins, 56 Mich. 159; P. v. Beller, 73 Mich. 640; P. v. Ringsted, 90 Mich. 371. Al-

is apparently shut off on Sunday by curtains or otherwise, provided there is in fact a means of access to the bar-room.[1] It is not necessary that the place for selling be kept open in the same manner as on week days; it is enough that it is so kept that access may be had thereto and liquor there obtained, whether by one door or by another, and whether the door is kept open or is opened upon application for admittance.[2] Thus, if a part of a tippling-house is used as a bed-room, the keeping open on Sunday of a door from such bed-room into the saloon is a violation of the law;[3] but to open the door in response to a knock of an officer to allow him to search for a person is not an opening on Sunday, though a crowd follows him into the bar.[4] In general, however, the intent is immaterial, the question simply being whether the place is kept open either by the proprietor or those having charge of the place under his authority.[5] It is sufficient to show a sale on any Sunday within the period covered by the prosecution without regard to the particular date named in the indictment.[6] It is not necessary to allege the particular location of the place kept open further than to bring it within the jurisdiction of the court.[7]

§ **1265. Selling on election day.**—Where a statute prohibits selling or keeping open on election day, such prohibition applies to the whole day of twenty-four hours on which the election is held, without regard to the hours of the day during which the polls are by law required to be kept open.[8] A permission

though a restaurant may be permitted to serve meals on Sunday, yet the keeping open of a saloon may be criminal, although it is kept open for the furnishing of meals, if it furnishes liquor at the same time: Lynch v. P., 16 Mich. 472.

[1] Hussey v. S., 69 Ga. 54; P. v. Hughes, 90 Mich. 368.

[2] Kroer v. P., 78 Ill. 294.

[3] Harvey v. S., 65 Ga. 568.

[4] Miller v. S., 68 Miss. 533.

[5] P. v. Blake, 52 Mich. 566.

[6] Koop v. P., 47 Ill. 327; Lucas v. S., 92 Ga. 454. The fact that the day of the month named falls on a week-day is immaterial if the charge is of keeping open on Sunday: Marquardt v. S., 52 Ark. 269; Megowan v. C., 2 Met. (Ky.) 3. The rule requiring the date of the commission of the offense to be charged is applicable as in other offenses unless there is some statutory provision on the subject: Effinger v. S., 47 Ind. 235. But usually the statutory provisions are such that a charge of a sale on Sunday is sufficient without allegation of date: P. v. Wheeler, 96 Mich. 1.

[7] P. v. Ringsted, 90 Mich. 371; Megowan v. C., 2 Met. (Ky.) 3.

[8] Schuck v. S., 50 Ohio St. 493; C. v. Murphy, 95 Ky. 38; Kane v. C., 89 Pa. St. 522; Janks v. S., 29 Tex. Ap. 233; Jones v. S., 32 Tex. Ap. 533; Lawrence v. S., 7 Tex. Ap. 192.

of the judges of election to sell or keep open either during the hours of election or after the closing of the polls will be no defense.[1] But when the statute prohibits selling during a public election, a charge of selling on and during an election day will not be good.[2] It is immaterial that the act of selling or giving away liquor on election day has no reference to the election itself, no exceptions being made by the statute.[3] In case of keeping open a saloon, it is immaterial that other commodities are kept there for sale.[4] The statutes are usually broad enough to cover any election, whether state, county or municipal, general or special. Thus, an election held in pursuance of an act allowing cities to vote on the question of water-works is a municipal election;[5] and where the general statute regulates primary as well as general elections, a primary election may be within the provisions as to selling or keeping open on election day.[6] The validity of a special election cannot be called in question in a prosecution for selling on the day it is held, on the ground that it was irregularly called.[7] So if a special election is held in one ward, a sale in the city, though outside of such ward, is unlawful under a statute prohibiting the sale of liquor upon the day of any election in the "city where the same may be holden."[8] Where the statute referred only to election day, it was held that the day of the election of a school director was not included.[9] It is necessary to allege positively the holding of the election on the day when the sale or act of keeping open is charged,[10] and it is said that it must also be alleged what the election was for, not merely that an election was held;[11] but it is generally held sufficient to allege that de-

[1] English v. S., 7 Tex. Ap. 171; Jones v. S., 32 Tex. Ap. 533.

[2] S. v. Starney, 71 N. C. 202.

[3] Wolf v. S., 59 Ark. 297.

[4] Haines v. S., 7 Tex. Ap. 30; Croell v. S., 25 Tex. Ap. 596. And see cases cited in preceding section as to keeping open on Sunday.

[5] S. v. Kidd, 74 Ind. 554.

[6] S. v. Hirsch, 125 Ind. 207.

[7] Janks v. S., 29 Tex. Ap. 233; Geib v. S., 31 Tex. Ap. 514.

[8] Qualter v. S., 120 Ind. 92. But where the statute prohibits selling by any person during the day on which any election is held in his voting precinct, it is necessary in charging such selling to allege that the election was being held in his, the defendant's, voting precinct, and there cannot be any conviction for selling in another precinct during a special election held there: Smith v. S., 18 Tex. Ap. 454.

[9] Stout v. S., 43 Ark. 413.

[10] S. v. Weaver, 83 Ind. 542.

[11] Hoskey v. S., 9 Tex. Ap. 202.

fendant did sell or did keep open a place for the sale of liquor on a certain named day being an election day,[1] or simply on election day,[2] and that such election was held by lawful authority in case it is a special election.[3]

§ 1266. Selling near churches, educational institutions, etc.— In some states there are statutory provisions against the sale of liquor within specified distances of churches,[4] school-houses,[5] or institutions of learning.[6] The prohibition with reference to a church is not applicable to a building used primarily for educational purposes, in which religious services are held on suitable occasions and at stated intervals.[7] But where the statute has special reference to a particular church, it will be immaterial that the church has been discontinued, inasmuch as the protection may be considered to have been for the benefit of the people living within the specified territory as well as for the benefit of the church itself.[8] In measuring distance it should be estimated in a straight line from any part of the building or place in which the liquor is sold to any part of the school or other building with reference to which the prohibition is sought

[1] S. v. Powell, 3 Lea, 164.

[2] S. v. Irvine, 3 Heisk. 155.

[3] Janks v. S., 29 Tex. Ap. 233; Geib v. S., 31 Tex. Ap. 514. **Form**: Under the Texas statute it has been held sufficient to allege that the defendant sold or gave away the liquor, as the case may be, during a certain day, "being an election day in which an election was then and there being held under and by lawful authority for the purpose of voting for presidential electors, congressmen, state, district, county and precinct officers, the same being a general election," and this will doubtless be sufficient in any state: Borches v. S., 33 Tex. Ap. 96.

[4] S. v. Sowers, 111 N. C. 685.

[5] In re Liquor Locations, 13 R. I. 733. The Massachusetts statute prohibits the granting of a license to sell within four hundred feet of a school-house situated on the same street: C. v. Jenkins, 137 Mass. 572; and such prohibition extends to that distance from a school-house on the same thoroughfare though it has different names in its different parts: C. v. McDonald, 160 Mass. 528. The boarding up of the entrance or windows fronting on the street in question is not material: C. v. Whelan, 134 Mass. 206.

[6] It is immaterial whether the institution is a private one or is supported out of the public school fund: Tillery v. S., 10 Lea, 35. And the prohibition applies to the time when the institution is not in operation by reason of vacation as well as to other times: Ibid. But under the Arkansas statute the provision does not apply to common schools: Blackwell v. S., 36 Ark. 178. If the prohibition is as to a certain distance from an incorporated school, the fact of incorporation is material: Brewer v. S., 7 Lea, 682.

[7] S. v. Midgett, 85 N. C. 538.

[8] S. v. Eaves, 106 N. C. 752.

to be applied.[1] Such prohibitions even as applicable to fair grounds during the time that a fair is held there are not unconstitutional, persons engaged in regular business within the prohibited territory not being forbidden to transact such business.[2] It appears that sales by druggists and for excepted purposes may be made within the protected territory, even without particular provision therefor.[3] The indictment should specifically show that the sale was within the prescribed territory.[4] It is not necessary to designate the institution, nor the beverage sold,[5] nor give the name of the person to whom the sale was made, nor negative exceptions in the statute.[6]

VII. THE PROCEDURE; SEIZURE; INDICTMENT; EVIDENCE.

§ **1267. Seizure; property in liquors.**— In many of the states it is provided that liquor kept for illegal sale may be seized under search-warrant and on condemnation destroyed. Such a proceeding is not a criminal proceeding against any individual, and an individual becomes a party only by a voluntary appearance.[7] A discussion of the peculiarities of such proceeding would not be germane to criminal law, but in the note cases referring thereto are collected.[8] To render liquors sub-

[1] In re Liquor Locations, 13 R. I. 733.

[2] S. v. Stovall, 103 N. C. 416.

[3] Henwood v. S., 41 Miss. 579. But *held* that a manufacturer could not sell within the prohibited territory, though in wholesale packages, if for consumption: S. v. Tarver, 11 Lea, 658.

[4] Ragan v. S., 67 Miss. 332. Where the charge was of selling within the prescribed distance of "church and schools," *held*, that it was not sufficiently definite: Gazola v. S., 45 Ark. 458.

[5] S. v. Odam, 2 Lea, 220. The indictment need not describe the church, for instance, by the exact words used in the statute: Block v. S., 66 Ala. 493.

[6] S. v. Staley, 3 Lea, 565. In general as to indictment, see *infra*, §§ 1270–1274.

[7] S. v. U. S. Express Co., 70 Ia. 271. But the proceeding is criminal in its nature, and it is said that one who has himself made a party as a claimant to the liquor has the rights of the defendant in a criminal prosecution; for instance, a verdict in his favor should not be set aside upon motion in arrest of judgment: S. v. Harris, 40 Ia. 95. The process for search and seizure does not authorize search and seizure against the person, but only as to a place named: S. v. Therrien, 86 Me. 425. The appearance of the claimant and presentation of his claim cures all defects in the notice on which the search-warrant is issued so far as he is concerned: C. v. Intoxicating Liquors, 146 Mass. 509.

[8] S. v. Intoxicating Liquors, 44 Vt. 208; S. v. Intoxicating Liquors, 58 Vt. 594; S. v. Whalen, 85 Me. 469; S.

ject to seizure and confiscation, it must appear that they were kept to be illegally sold; the mere fact of finding liquors is not sufficient.[1] But it is not necessary that the liquors were kept to be sold at the house where they are found or on the premises; the unlawful keeping for sale may be for sale in any place where such selling would be unlawful.[2] The intent to sell in violation of law must be by the person having the right to sell; that is, the owner.[3] Under statutory provision for the seizure and destruction of liquor found in the possession of a carrier for illegal transportation, it is immaterial whether the officers of the carrying corporation know the character of the property and the use to which it is to be put; it is their duty to know whether the goods received for transportation are such as the law authorizes to be sold.[4] Liquors seized under the provisions of statute cannot be taken from the officer upon replevin, for they are in the custody of the law;[5] but intoxicating liquors are property, although their sale may be forbidden and they are kept for an unlawful purpose, and they may therefore be attached for debt,[6] and the stealing of them may

v. Riley, 86 Me. 144; C. v. Intoxicating Liquors, 135 Mass. 519; S. v. Thompson, 44 Ia. 399; Weir v. Allen, 47 Ia. 482. As to sufficiency of description of the place to be searched, see C. v. Intoxicating Liquors, 146 Mass. 509; S. v. Thompson, 44 Ia. 399. Some statutes provide that no warrant shall be issued for searching a dwelling-house, except under specific circumstances: S. v. Whalen, 85 Me. 469; Sanders v. S., 2 Ia. 230, 277. As to making complaint against the person by the officer seizing the liquor, see S. v. Intoxicating Liquor, 58 Vt. 594; Fenner v. S., 3 R. I. 107.

[1] C. v. Intoxicating Liquors, 105 Mass. 595; C. v. Intoxicating Liquors, 116 Mass. 21; C. v. Intoxicating Liquors, 116 Mass. 24; Darst v. P., 51 Ill. 286; S. v. Harris, 38 Ia. 136. And the information should charge some specific person as owner or keeper with the illegal intent, and the evidence should show the keeping by the person thus specified with such intent: S. v. Intoxicating Liquors, 64 Ia. 300; or the name of the person may be described as unknown: C. v. Intoxicating Liquors, 116 Mass. 24. Liquors owned and kept by and in possession of a corporation, and intended by its directors to be sold lawfully in its business, but which are by its manager intended to be and are unlawfully sold, without the knowledge and consent of the directors, are subject to forfeiture under a complaint of keeping with intent to sell by such manager: C. v. Intoxicating Liquors, 163 Mass. 42.

[2] C. v. Intoxicating Liquors, 116 Mass. 24. But the fact of selling is not material: C. v. Intoxicating Liquors, 142 Mass. 470.

[3] S. v. Intoxicating Liquors, 63 Me. 121.

[4] S. v. U. S. Express Co., 70 Ia. 271.

[5] Funk v. Israel, 5 Ia. 438; S. v. Harris, 38 Ia. 242; Weir v. Allen, 47 Ia. 482; Fries v. Porch, 49 Ia. 351.

[6] Tucker v. Adams, 63 N. H. 361; S. v. Johnson, 33 N. H. 441; Fuller v. Bean, 30 N. H. 181.

constitute larceny.[1] If the liquor is owned for a lawful purpose, it may be recovered by replevin from one who has unlawfully taken it.[2]

§ 1268. **Second offense.**— It is frequently provided by statute that the second or subsequent offense under these statutes shall be more severely punished. A second violation means a violation of the law after conviction for a prior offense of the same character.[3] All the acts of illegal selling before the first conviction constitute but one offense;[4] at any rate, there must be evidence of a prior conviction before there can be conviction of a second offense.[5] But under charge of a second offense there may be conviction of a first offense.[6] A second offense does not necessarily consist in the same form of violation of the statute, but if the statute prohibits the selling, furnishing or giving away, a conviction for selling is available to double the penalty if there is a subsequent conviction for furnishing.[7]

§ 1269. **Venue.**— The venue must, of course, be proved as in any other crime. If the charge is of selling, it must appear that the sale was made in the county of the prosecution;[8] but the question as to whether the place of sale is to be deemed the place where the order is taken or where the order is filled has already been discussed.[9]

§ 1270. **Indictment.**— These offenses being statutory, the general rule is applicable that an indictment or information is sufficient which follows the language of the statute or ordinance under which the offense is charged.[10] Nevertheless, it is essential that the act charged as constituting the crime be so designated by time, place and other characteristics as that defendant may know for what he is prosecuted and be enabled to prepare his defense,[11] and the indictment must be broad

[1] S. v. May, 20 Ia. 305.

[2] Harrison v. Nichols, 31 Vt. 709.

[3] C. v. Welsh, 2 Va. Cas. 57.

[4] U. S. v. Gordon, 1 Cranch, C. C. 58.

[5] S. v. Haynes, 35 Vt. 570; Walters v. S., 5 Ia. 507; S. v. Leis, 11 Ia. 416.

[6] S. v. Ensley, 10 Ia. 149; S. v. Gaffeny, 66 Ia. 262.

[7] S. v. Haynes, 36 Vt. 667; S. v. Sawyer, 67 Vt. 239.

[8] Rice v. P., 38 Ill. 435; S. v. Williams, 3 Hill (S. C.), 91. A statute as to the venue of public offenses committed within five hundred yards of the boundary line of the county is applicable to violations of the liquor law: S. v. Rockwell, 82 Ia. 429.

[9] *Supra*, § 1237.

[10] C. v. Wood, 4 Gray, 11; Skinner v. S., 120 Ind. 127; S. v. Hoard, 123 Ind. 34; Mankato v. Arnold, 36 Minn. 62; S. v. Adams, 16 Ark. 497.

[11] Arrington v. C., 87 Va. 96; Burch v. Republic, 1 Tex. 608; S. v. Cox, 29

enough to bring the case within the statute.[1] But in some cases it has been held sufficient to aver generally that the act was in violation of law.[2] The allegation that the act was contrary to law is said not to be sufficient, however, if it may or may not be criminal, depending on circumstances; in that event, the circumstances showing it to be criminal must be pleaded.[3] But if all acts of a particular character are illegal, for instance, sales without license, then it is enough to say that the sale was without a license or was unlawful, or use other such general language negativing the lawfulness of the act;[4] though in most cases the indictments of this character are supported under some general statutory provision as to what shall be a sufficient charge in prosecutions under the liquor law.[5] The necessity

Mo. 475; S. v. Steedman, 8 Rich. 312; C. v. White, 18 B. Mon. 492; Smith v. S., 32 Neb. 105; S. v. Pischel, 16 Neb. 490; S. v. Burchard, 4 S. Dak. 548. It is not sufficient to charge that defendant wrongfully failed and omitted to close and keep closed a saloon without stating that he owned it or had control of it: S. v. Gluck, 41 Minn. 553. It is not enough to charge that defendant *is* the keeper of a saloon in which intoxicating liquors *are* kept for sale, etc., without charging that such circumstances existed at the time of the commission of the offense: Sikes v. S., 67 Ala. 77. In some states the court may require specifications of the particulars of the offense if deemed necessary, to advise the defendant as to the act charged: S. v. Bacon, 41 Vt. 526; S. v. Tracey, 12 R. I. 216.

1 Woodworth v. S., 4 Ohio St. 487. Thus, an indictment for selling by wholesale without paying a special tax prescribed is defective if it fails to charge that the defendant is a liquor dealer and to state whether the special tax was a state or county tax: S. v. Martin, 34 Ark. 340. If the statute prohibits sales by any hotel-keeper, merchant, grocer, etc., to any person after notice not to sell to such person, it must be charged that defendant is one of the classes of sellers specified in the statute: S. v. Heitsch, 29 Minn. 134.

2 S. v. Smith, 35 Tex. 132; S. v. Allen, 32 Ia. 248. It has been held sufficient to say that it was in violation of a particular section of the state statutes: Oshe v. S., 37 Ohio St. 494; S. v. Freeman, 27 Ia. 333.

3 C. v. Intoxicating Liquors, 138 Mass. 506; C. v. Hickey, 126 Mass. 250; Crone v. S., 49 Ind. 538. In charging the keeping of a place for illegal sale or keeping for sale, it is not necessary to negative the circumstances under which selling or keeping would be legal; the general allegation of keeping for an illegal purpose is sufficient: C. v. Bennett, 108 Mass. 27.

4 S. v. Young, 5 Coldw. 51; S. v. Mooty, 3 Hill (S. C.), 187; Howell v. S., 4 Ind. Ap. 148. But it seems that to say that a sale charged was unlawful is not enough, without showing how it was unlawful; as, for instance, whether by a person not having any license: C. v. Crossley, 162 Mass. 515; C. v. Byrnes, 126 Mass. 248.

5 Bogan v. S., 84 Ala. 449; Cost v.

of negativing the license is considered elsewhere.[1] If the sale would be unlawful whether defendant had a license or not, it is not necessary to charge that the sale was by a person having a license.[2] As it is the prohibited doing of the act which is criminal without regard to the particular intent, it is not necessary to charge that the act was wilfully done.[3] Cases as to sufficiency of indictments under particular statutes are cited in the note.[4] Some statutes make particular provisions as to who may make complaint, and how it shall be made, but these are so far special that they cannot be discussed generally.[5]

§ 1271. Further as to description of the particular act.— Where the statutory crime may be committed in different forms, as by selling or giving away, etc.,[6] or selling to minors or to be drunk on the premises, it is said not to be necessary to specify the particular form in which the statute has been violated.[7] Thus, under statutory provisions as to indictment in liquor cases there may be a conviction, either for violation of a general statute as to sales, or of some particular prohibition of the statute;[8] but if the statute provides for distinct offenses, the charge must be specific as to which offense is committed, otherwise it would be objectionable on the

S., 96 Ala. 60; Olmstead v. S., 89 Ala. 16; West v. S., 70 Miss. 598; White v. S., 11 Tex. Ap. 476. If the statute prohibits the issuing of a license for selling for any other purpose than certain purposes named, it is sufficient to allege that the sale was for other purposes than those named: S. v. Perkins, 26 N. H. 9.

1 *Supra*, §§ 1229, 1252; *infra*, §§ 1278, 1281.

2 C. v. O'Brien, 134 Mass. 198.

3 S. v. Abbott, 31 N. H. 434. And see *supra*, § 1251.

4 S. v. Benjamin, 49 Vt. 101; S. v. Paige, 50 Vt. 445; Cearfoss, v. S. 42 Md. 403; S. v. Church, 4 W. Va. 745; S. v. Chapman, 25 W. Va. 408; Johnson v. S., 60 Ga. 634; Herine v. C., 13 Bush, 295; Hainline v. C., 13 Bush, 350; Morrison v. C., 7 Dana, 218; Powell v. S., 69 Ala. 10; Boon v. S., 69 Ala. 226; McPherson v. S., 54 Ala. 221; S. v. Marcus, 20 Ark. 201.

5 C. v. Murphy, 147 Mass. 577; S. v. Brooks, 33 Kan. 708; McCullough v. C., 67 Pa. St. 30.

6 Devine v. S., 4 Ia. 443.

7 Kern v. S., 7 Ohio St. 411; S. v. Fant, 2 La. An. 837; S. v. Bogan, 2 La. An. 838. So, where the statute forbids the keeping of a grog-shop or place used for the sale or keeping of intoxicating liquors or otherwise maintaining a nuisance in connection with the sale of liquor, it is sufficient to follow the statutory language and to charge the offense as committed in each of those methods, and proof of its commission in any one mode will be sufficient: S. v. Plastridge, 6 R. I. 76. But the requisite circumstances, as that the sale was to a person named who was a minor, or the like, must be alleged: Myers v. P., 67 Ill. 503.

8 Olmstead v. S., 89 Ala. 16.

ground of duplicity.[1] The cases do not entirely agree as to the particularity with which the crime is to be described, and some of the questions involved will be considered in succeeding paragraphs. In charging the unlawful keeping for sale, it is usually considered sufficient to state the time when and the place where and the person believed to be guilty thereof.[2] To charge the offense of illegally carrying on the business, it may be sufficient to show that for a continuous period defendant was a seller, etc., without using the words "common seller."[3] To charge the maintaining of a nuisance it is sufficient to say that defendant kept, used and maintained a certain building and place, etc.[4] In charging an illegal sale it is usually sufficient to say that defendant "sold,"[5] and it is not necessary to set out a technical contract.[6] But in other cases it is said that where the charge is of a particular sale and not of carrying on a business or selling in general, there should be a specification of some particular act of selling,[7] and that an allegation of selling *or* giving away is too indefinite.[8] A sale made by an agent may be charged as made by the principal.[9]

[1] Miller v. S., 5 How. (Miss.) 250; S. v. Apperger, 80 Mo. 173; S. v. White, 31 Kan. 342. But, as above indicated, if the statute describes but one offense, though it may be committed in different forms, it is not objectionable to charge the different forms in one indictment: Jillard v. C., 26 Pa. St. 169; S. v. Fant, 2 La. An. 837; S. v. Bogan, 2 La. An. 838; S. v. Plastridge, 6 R. I. 76; Vaughn v. S., 5 Ia. 369; S. v. Becker, 20 Ia. 438; S. v. Baughman, 20 Ia. 497; S. v. Brown, 36 Vt. 560.

[2] S. v. Brennan, 2 S. Dak. 384; Vaughn v. S., 5 Ia. 369. It is not a material defect that the indictment charges the keeping "for the purpose of sale," instead of "with intent to sell," in the language of the statute: S. v. Mohr, 53 Ia. 261.

[3] C. v. Leonard, 8 Met. 529.

[4] S. v. Price, 75 Ia. 243; C. v. Sampson, 113 Mass. 191. It is sufficient under some statutes to charge defendant with keeping a tippling-house: C. v. Riley, 14 Bush, 44. And to say that he kept a certain grog-shop and tippling-shop is sufficient, it appearing that the two are, under the statute, the same thing: S. v. Tracey, 12 R. I. 216.

[5] Foreman v. Hunter, 59 Ia. 550. This case, however, was under special statutory provision as to sufficiency of an indictment or information under the liquor laws.

[6] C. v. Buck, 12 Met. 524. The averment that defendant was a retailer, etc., to a certain named person, sufficiently imports a sale: C. v. Kimball, 7 Met. 304.

[7] P. v. Heffron, 53 Mich. 527; P. v. Minnock, 52 Mich. 628; Alexander v. S., 29 Tex. 495.

[8] Raisler v. S., 55 Ala. 64; Thompson v. S., 37 Ark. 408. So it is too indefinite to say that defendant sold whisky *or* brandy, but it may be sufficient to charge that he sold whisky *and* brandy: Thompson v. S., 37 Ark. 408.

[9] S. v. McCance, 110 Mo. 398; O'Bryan v. S., 48 Ark. 42.

§ **1272. Time and place.**— Aside from statutory provisions it is of course necessary that the time be alleged,[1] but it is not essential to prove the time as charged.[2] The offense of keeping for sale may be charged with a *continuando*,[3] but even in that case it is not necessary to prove the keeping within the time fixed, but any other date may be proved within the period of limitation.[4] As to place, it is sufficient as in ordinary cases to charge the offense as committed at a place within the jurisdiction of the court; as, for instance, in the county, without more particular specification.[5] But if the charge is of illegally keeping,[6] or selling to be drunk on the premises, it is said that the place must be particularly described,[7] and if the illegality of the sale depends upon its having been made within a particular portion of the county, such as a certain township or city, the sale must be charged as within such locality.[8] If the offense charged is of keeping a nuisance, it is also said to be unnecessary to allege the particular locality.[9] But if an order of abate-

[1] S. v. O'Keefe, 41 Vt. 691; S. v. Kennedy, 36 Vt. 563; S. v. Havey, 58 N. H. 377. The allegation of time, by some statutes, need not be made where time is immaterial: Brown v. S., 16 Neb. 658.

[2] U. S. v. Burch, 1 Cranch, C. C. 36; U. S. v. Birch, 1 Cranch, C. C. 571; S. v. Layton, 25 Ia. 193; S. v. Johnson, 69 Ia. 623; S. v. Reyelts, 74 Ia. 499; S. v. Whipple, 57 Vt. 637. Even though the charge is of selling upon a certain day and upon divers other times, it is sufficient as it states but one offense: South v. C., 79 Ky. 493; S. v. Whipple, 57 Vt. 637. If the charge is of selling on Sunday, the prosecution being for violation of the general law and not the Sunday statute, it is not necessary to prove the sale to have been on Sunday: P. v. Krank, 110 N. Y. 488; S. v. Fletcher, 13 R. I. 522. It is, of course, necessary that the evidence shall show the offense to have been committed before the finding of the indictment: White v. S., 93 Ga. 47; and at a time after the passage of the statute making it illegal: S. v. Jacobs, 75 Ia. 247. Even if the date is not material, yet the court may, in its discretion, refuse to allow evidence of a sale at a date so remote from the date alleged as to prejudice the defendant in his defense: S. v. Rundlett, 33 N. H. 70.

[3] C. v. Chisholm, 103 Mass. 213. It is improper, however, to charge the selling with a *continuando:* S. v. Pischel, 16 Neb. 490.

[4] S. v. Havey, 58 N. H. 377.

[5] S. v. Jaques, 68 Mo. 260; C. v. Taylor, 113 Mass. 1; S. v. Hickok, 90 Wis. 161; S. v. Cottrill, 31 W. Va. 162; P. v. Sweetser, 1 Dak. 308. *Contra*, Grimme v. C., 5 B. Mon. 263.

[6] S. v. Kelleher, 81 Me. 346; and proved as laid: Ibid.

[7] Arrington v. C., 87 Va. 96; C. v. Head, 11 Grat. 819. But a charge of selling to be drunk in several different named places on the premises is not bad: Leary v. S., 39 Ind. 360.

[8] Seifried v. C., 101 Pa. St. 200; Legori v. S., 8 Sm. & M. 697; Botto v. S., 26 Miss. 108; Young v. C., 14 Bush, 161.

[9] Kern v. S., 7 Ohio St. 411; S. v.

ment is desired, the premises must be particularly described as in other cases of nuisance where such relief is asked.[1] If the particular locality is specified it must be proved as alleged, although a particular description might not have been essential.[2] Even where the locality must be particularly stated, no very minute description is essential.[3] It is not necessary that the particular sale should be so described as to time and place as that it could be pleaded in bar of another indictment for the same offense, because defendant will be protected against a second prosecution for any sale to which the evidence of the first prosecution related.[4]

§ **1273. Description of kind, quantity, price, etc.**— Where the statute provides what kind of liquor shall come within its provisions, such as intoxicating liquor, spirituous liquor, malt liquor, etc., a description of the liquor as "intoxicating," "spirituous," "malt," or otherwise, in accordance with the statutory specification, is sufficient without an allegation of the particular kind of liquor of the specified class which is charged to have been sold;[5] or the indictment may charge the sale of a particular

Jacobs, 75 Ia. 247; S. v. Lang, 63 Me. 215. But where the punishment for keeping a saloon in a disorderly manner as a public nuisance is forfeiture of the license, the place in which the liquor is sold and for which the license to sell is granted must be specifically stated: Davis v. S., 52 Ind. 488.

1 S. v. Waltz, 74 Ia. 610; Hagan v. S., 4 Kan. 89. And see *supra*, § 1181.

2 S. v. Crogan, 8 Ia. 523. And see S. v. Verden, 24 Ia. 126, where the court was equally divided. See, also, S. v. Gurlagh, 76 Ia. 141.

3 S. v. Crogan, 8 Ia. 523; S. v. Kreig, 13 Ia. 462; West v. Columbus, 20 Kan. 633; Conley v. S., 5 W. Va. 522.

4 Olmstead v. S., 92 Ala. 64.

5 C. v. Odlin, 23 Pick. 275; C. v. Conant, 6 Gray, 482; S. v. Blaisdell, 33 N. H. 388; S. v. Dorr, 82 Me. 341; S. v. Wyman, 80 Me. 117; S. v. Reynolds, 47 Vt. 297; S. v. McGinnis, 30 Minn. 52; Zarresselier v. P., 17 Ill. 101; S. v. Whalen, 54 Ia. 753; S. v. Graeter, 6 Blackf. 105; S. v. Mullinix, 6 Blackf. 554; Josephdaffer v. S., 32 Ind. 402; Connell v. S., 46 Ind. 446; Hooper v. S., 56 Ind. 153; Wills v. S., 69 Ind. 286; Plunkett v. S., 69 Ind. 68; Callahan v. S., 2 Ind. Ap. 417; S. v. Packer, 80 N. C. 439; S. v. Downs, 116 N. C. 1064; Williams v. S., 89 Ga. 483; P. v. Sweetser, 1 Dak. 308; Frisbie v. S., 1 Oreg. 248; S. v. Witt, 39 Ark. 216; U. S. v. Gordon, 1 Cranch, C. C. 58. But the evidence should be more specific and show the particular kind of liquor: Houser v. S., 18 Ind. 106. It is said in one case that where the statute enumerates particular kinds and adds, "or other ardent spirits," it is not enough to charge the sale of ardent spirits without specifying the particular kind: S. v. Fox, 16 N. J. 162. In Kansas the statute specially provides that it is not necessary to state the kind of liquor: S. v. Whisner, 35 Kan. 271; and such a statute is constitutional: S. v. Sterns, 28 Kan. 154.

kind which is expressly included within the different classes as named by the statute, or which the court may know judicially is a kind coming within the general description.[1] So an indictment may charge the sale conjunctively of two or more different kinds of liquor which belong to the classes of liquors the sale of which is prohibited.[2] It would seem that an indictment charging disjunctively a sale of two different classes of liquor mentioned by the statute would be bad for uncertainty; as, for instance, where the charge is of selling "spirituous or intoxicating liquors;"[3] but there are decisions to the effect that a disjunctive charge of the sale of the classes of liquors enumerated by the statute will be sufficient.[4] It is also decided in accordance with general principles that if an indictment does specify the particular kind it must be proved as alleged, although a particular description was not necessary,[5] but there is authority to the contrary on this proposition also.[6] It is not necessary to allege the quantity, nor prove the exact quantity if specified;[7] and even where the statute makes it criminal to

[1] Thus, it is sufficient to charge the sale of brandy, whisky or other liquor which is known to be intoxicating liquor, where the statute uses the general term "intoxicating liquor:" S. v. Dengolensky, 82 Mo. 44; S. v. Jones, 3 Ind. Ap. 121; *supra*, § 1218. Under a charge of selling whisky, evidence may be introduced of sale of a liquor containing whisky, though it is mixed with water and sugar, and it is not necessary to charge such sale as a mixed liquor, although the statute specially refers to mixed liquors: C. v. White, 10 Met. 14; C. v. Morgan, 149 Mass. 314. And see *supra*, § 1219.

[2] P. v. Adams, 17 Wend. 475; S. v. Cottle, 15 Me. 473. Such an indictment charges but one offense, and is not, therefore, objectionable on the ground of duplicity: S. v. Whitted, 3 Ala. 102; and will be supported by proof of the sale of any one of the kinds enumerated. Indeed, where the statute specifies different classes of liquor, the sale of any one of which is criminal, different classes may be charged to have been sold: S. v. Rogers, 39 Mo. 431.

[3] C. v. Grey, 2 Gray, 501.

[4] Morgan v. C., 7 Grat. 592; Thomas v. C., 90 Va. 92; Cunningham v. S., 5 W. Va. 508; Bridges v. S., 37 Ark. 224; Brantley v. S., 91 Ala. 47.

[5] S. v. Hesner, 55 Ia. 494; Brantley v. S., 91 Ala. 47; C. v. Luscomb, 130 Mass. 42.

[6] Frisbie v. S., 1 Oreg. 248.

[7] C. v. Odlin, 23 Pick. 275; C. v. Buck, 12 Met. 524; C. v. Conant, 6 Gray, 482; C. v. Dillane, 11 Gray, 67; S. v. Moore, 14 N. H. 451; S. v. Rust, 35 N. H. 438; S. v. Connell, 38 N. H. 81; S. v. King, 37 Ia. 462; Block v. S., 66 Ala. 493; Bruguier v. U. S., 1 Dak. T. 5; S. v. Tisdale, 54 Minn. 105; Plunkett v. S., 69 Ind. 68; S. v. Kuhn, 24 La. An. 474; White v. S., 11 Tex. Ap. 476. If the sale of less than a specified quantity is necessary to constitute the crime, quantity must be alleged: Brutton v. S., 4 Ind. 601; Cool v. S., 16 Ind. 355; Manvelle v. S., 58 Ind. 63.

sell less than a certain quantity, it is only necessary to allege a sale of such less quantity, and the proof need not correspond with the particular quantity specified if it brings the case within the statute.[1] It is unnecessary to allege the price or compensation for which the liquor was sold or furnished;[2] or that the liquor was to be used as a beverage, in the absence of such description of the offense in the statute.[3] But if the offense as described consists in selling as a beverage, that fact must be alleged, and it will not be enough to allege that the sale was wilfully and maliciously made.[4]

§ **1274. Name of purchaser.**— By many courts it has been held that in charging illegal selling in any form it is unnecessary to state the name of the person to whom the sale was made;[5] but many other courts have held that necessary particu-

[1] S. v. Robinson, 39 Me. 150; S. v. Crowell, 30 Me. 115; S. v. Shaw, 2 Dev. 198; Redding v. C., 3 B. Mon. 339; Askill v. C., 3 B. Mon. 342. It was said in one case, however, that the charge of selling "any quantity less than one quart," following the exact language of the statute, was too indefinite: Bridgeford v. Lexington, 7 B. Mon. 47.

[2] S. v. Downer, 21 Wis. 274; S. v. Pischel, 16 Neb. 490; S. v. King, 37 Ia. 462; S. v. Ladd, 15 Mo. 430 (overruling Austin v. S., 10 Mo. 591); S. v. Miller, 24 Mo. 532; Williams v. S., 89 Ga. 483; S. v. Hines, 13 R. I. 10. *Contra*, Divine v. S., 4 Ind. 240; Segur v. S., 6 Ind. 451; Leary v. S., 39 Ind. 360.

[3] S. v. Carpenter, 20 Ind. 219.

[4] S. v. Hafsoos, 1 S. Dak. 382. Charging the sale "as a beverage" is sufficient under a statute making it criminal to sell "to be used as a beverage:" P. v. Hinchman, 75 Mich. 587.

[5] P. v. Adams, 17 Wend. 475; S. v. Munger, 15 Vt. 290; Cannady v. P., 17 Ill. 158; Rice v. P., 38 Ill. 435; S. v. Bielby, 21 Wis. 204; S. v. Gummer, 22 Wis. 441; S. v. Becker, 20 Ia. 438; S. v. King, 37 Ia. 462; S. v. Ladd, 15 Mo. 430; S. v. Miller, 24 Mo. 532; S. v. Spain, 29 Mo. 415; S. v. Fanning, 38 Mo. 359; S. v. Melton, 38 Mo. 368; S. v. Rogers, 39 Mo. 431; S. v. Jaques, 68 Mo. 260 (overruling Neales v. S., 10 Mo. 498; Austin v. S., 10 Mo. 591); S. v. Whisner, 35 Kan. 271; S. v. Moseli, 49 Kan. 142; P. v. Sweetser, 1 Dak. 308; S. v. Muse, 4 Dev. & B. 319; Riley v. S., 43 Miss. 397; Williams v. S., 89 Ga. 483; S. v. Chisnell, 36 W. Va. 659; Dansey v. S., 23 Fla. 316; S. v. Parnell, 16 Ark. 506; McCuen v. S., 19 Ark. 630; McCuen v. S., 19 Ark. 636; Johnson v. S., 40 Ark. 453; S. v. Bailey, 43 Ark. 150; U. S. v. Gordon, 1 Cranch, C. C. 58. So held as to an indictment for selling in violation of the Sunday law: S. v. Hickerson, 3 Heisk. 375; and for carrying on the business without a license: Lea v. S., 64 Miss. 201; Jordan v. S., 22 Fla. 528; S. v. Brown, 41 La. An. 771; Mansfield v. S., 17 Tex. Ap. 468; S. v. Heldt, 41 Tex. 220; S. v. Kuhn, 24 La. An. 474; and for maintaining a nuisance: S. v. Jordan, 39 Ia. 387; S. v. Doyle, 15 R. I. 527; and for selling as a druggist: S. v. Ferrell, 30 W. Va. 683; and for selling without a federal license: S. v. Warwick, 51 Fed. R. 280. In one case it is said that if the name of the

larity in describing the offense requires that the indictment shall state the name of the person to whom the illegal sale is made,[1] or that the name of such person is to the grand jury unknown.[2] An indictment for sale to two or more is good, as a sale may be made to two or more jointly;[3] and indeed, the charge of a sale to two may be supported by proof of a sale to any one of the persons named.[4] Charge of sale to a person named may be supported by evidence of a sale to his agent without naming the agent.[5] So a sale to one who is in fact an agent but who does not disclose his agency may be charged as made to him, and proof that he bought as agent only will not constitute a variance;[6] but if the sale is to an agent for a disclosed principal, the sale should be charged as made to the principal and not to the agent.[7]

§ **1275. Joinder of offenses.**—Where a statute prescribes different acts as constituting the offense, such as selling, giving, furnishing, or the like, such different acts may be charged con-

party to whom the sale is made is alleged, the proof must correspond: S. v. Hays, 36 Mo. 80. And see *infra*, § 1276.

[1] C. v. Shearman, 11 Cush. 546; S. v. Schmail, 25 Minn. 368; S. v. Pischel, 16 Neb. 490; Martin v. S., 30 Neb. 507; Martin v. S., 30 Neb. 421; S. v. Starney, 71 N. C. 202; S. v. Doyle, 11 R. I. 574; Wilson v. C., 14 Bush, 159; Dorman v. S., 34 Ala. 216; S. v. Walker, 3 Harr. 547; S. v. Allen, 32 Ia. 491; Dixon v. S., 21 Tex. Ap. 517; Martin v. S., 31 Tex. Ap. 27. So held as to sales to minors: Myers v. P., 67 Ill. 503; and as to sales by a druggist under statute requiring that druggists shall sell only by prescription setting forth the name of the person for whom the prescription is given: S. v. Martin, 108 Mo. 117. A statute authorizing the omission of the name of the person to whom the sale is made is unconstitutional: McLaughlin v. S., 45 Ind. 338. But the omission to name the person to whom the liquor is sold is merely a formal defect which must be raised before trial: Green v. C., 111 Mass. 417. The name of the person to whom the sale was made must be proved as alleged: C. v. Shearman, 11 Cush. 546.

[2] Gordon v. S., 46 Ohio St. 607; Hulstead v. C., 5 Leigh, 724; Capritz v. S., 1 Md. 569; S. v. Faucett, 4 Dev. & B. 107; S. v. Carter, 7 Humph. 157; S. v. Bodeckar, 11 Wash. 417. If the allegation is of sale to a person named and divers other persons whose names are unknown, proof of sale to any other person than the person named is proper: S. v. Wolff, 46 Mo. 584; Moore v. S., 79 Ga. 498; Dukes v. S., 79 Ga. 795; Hall v. S., 87 Ga. 233.

[3] S. v. King, 37 Ia. 462.

[4] S. v. Johnson, 69 Ia. 623; Hall v. S., 87 Ga. 233; Dukes v. S., 79 Ga. 795. *Contra*, Brown v. S., 48 Ind. 38.

[5] Hall v. S., 86 Ga. 233.

[6] C. v. Kimball, 7 Met. 308; C. v. McGuire, 11 Gray, 460; C. v. Fowler, 145 Mass. 398; S. v. Wentworth, 35 N. H. 442.

[7] C. v. Remby, 2 Gray, 508.

junctively in the same indictment without objection for duplicity;[1] but under the general rules of procedure in criminal cases, it is not proper to charge in one count different violations of the liquor laws which are by the statute distinct offenses, such as unlawful selling and unlawful keeping open.[2] Separate offenses of the same class, different only in degree of punishment, may, however, be united in the same indictment in different counts.[3] This is a matter of general procedure and depends largely upon the statutes of the particular states. It is usually permitted by special legislation applicable to liquor cases to join different offenses of the same character in different counts;[4] but the separate counts should show distinct offenses, and not offenses any one of which may be proved by the evidence applicable to others.[5] The first and second or second and third offenses cannot be charged in the same indictment.[6] In the same count a charge of sale to two persons may be made, as such an act is possible;[7] but retailing to two distinct persons at the same time and place constitutes two distinct offenses which should not be charged in one count.[8] Two persons may together commit one offense and may therefore be

[1] S. v. Schweiter, 27 Kan. 499; S. v. Kerr, 3 N. Dak. 523. So, if the crime consists in bringing intoxicating liquors into a place with certain specified intents, the bringing with all such different intents may be charged conjunctively: C. v. Igo, 158 Mass. 199. If the charge is of keeping a nuisance, all the methods of keeping the house constituting a nuisance under the statute may be charged: S. v. Lang, 63 Me. 215; S. v. Stanley, 84 Me. 555. An indictment charging defendant with having sold without having filed a bond, paid a tax and posted a receipt as required by law charges but one offense: P. v. Wade, 101 Mich. 89.

[2] Hudson v. Geary, 4 R. I. 485; P. v. Keefer, 97 Mich. 15.

[3] Tillery v. S., 10 Lea, 35.

[4] C. v. Porter, 4 Gray, 426; Gitchell v. P., 146 Ill. 175; Walters v. S., 5 Ia. 507; Jackson v. Boyd, 53 Ia. 536; S. v. McLaughlin, 47 Kan. 143; S. v. McAdoo, 80 Mo. 216; S. v. Gluck, 49 Kan. 533. If on an information before a justice different offenses are charged, one of which is triable before him and the other is not, he may proceed as to the charge of which he has jurisdiction: S. v. Peck, 32 Vt. 172. Illegal sales may be charged in conjunction with the charge of being a common seller or of maintaining a nuisance: C. v. Porter, 4 Gray, 426; Gitchell v. P., 146 Ill. 75.

[5] S. v. Von Haltschuherr, 72 Ia. 541.

[6] S. v. Leis, 11 Ia. 416. And see *supra*, § 1268.

[7] Peer's Case, 5 Grat. 674; Gordon v. S., 46 Ohio St. 607. See preceding section.

[8] C. v. Dove, 2 Va. Cas. 26. However, if liquor is furnished in answer to one call therefor and by a single act, there is but one sale and one

indicted together,[1] and there may be a conviction of one only.[2] If there is a joint conviction the punishment should be imposed severally.[3]

§ **1276. Variance; election.**— It has already appeared that the particular time charged for the unlawful sale or other violation of the law is, in general, immaterial,[4] and therefore the evidence need not be limited to the time thus alleged, and proof of any sale within the statutory period of limitation and before the commencement of the prosecution may be made;[5] and there may therefore be evidence of distinct sales introduced under an indictment charging one sale, inasmuch as the verdict can be but for one offense, and the defendant will be protected against being again put on trial for any offense which might have been proved under the charge.[6] So it is not necessary to prove the exact quantity of liquor as alleged so long as the quantity proved comes within the terms of the statute.[7] If several different sales are charged in different counts which are allowed to be joined, there may be proof of as many sales as there are counts;[8] but it is said that evidence is not admissible of a greater number of sales than there are counts in the charge.[9] Also, if the offense charged is a continuing one, such as maintaining a nuisance or carrying on an illegal business, proof of different sales is admissible.[10] But some cases hold that if but one illegal sale is charged, evidence of distinct sales should not

penalty incurred, though it may be drunk by more than one person: S. v. Barron, 37 Vt. 57.

1 Lemons v. S., 50 Ala. 130; S. v. Caswell, 2 Humph. 399; C. v. Sloan, 4 Cush. 52.

2 S. v. Simmons, 66 N. C. 622.

3 P. v. Walbaum, 1 Dak. 308; C. v. Harris, 7 Grat. 600.

4 *Supra*, § 1272.

5 C. v. Carroll, 15 Gray, 409; Koch v. C., 32 Ohio St. 353; Miazza v. S., 36 Miss. 613; Loftus v. C., 3 Grat. 631. Thus, it is said that on an appeal from a conviction before a justice of the peace, the court may hear evidence of another sale than that which was attempted to be proved before the justice: S. v. Remelee, 35 Vt. 562. But in Kansas it is held that a sale not covered by the affidavit on which the prosecuting officer has based his information cannot be shown: S. v. Nulty, 47 Kan. 259; S. v. Brooks, 33 Kan. 708.

6 C. v. Carroll, 15 Gray, 409; Fitzpatrick v. S., 37 Ark. 373. And see next section.

7 S. v. Cooper, 16 Mo. 551. And see *supra*, § 1273.

8 S. v. Smith, 22 Vt. 74; S. v. Croteau, 23 Vt. 14; S. v. Malling, 11 Ia. 239.

9 Hodgman v. P., 4 Denio, 235.

10 S. v. Estlinbaum, 47 Kan. 291; S. v. Lund, 49 Kan. 209.

be admitted,[1] or at least that the prosecution must elect upon what particular sale it relies.[2] Other courts, however, refuse to require an election, and will allow a conviction on evidence relating to different sales, upon proof of any one sale, under a charge of one sale.[3] The evidence must, however, correspond to the charge, and if the indictment is for unlawfully keeping liquors on the premises, proof of having such liquors upon the person, that being a distinct offense, will constitute a variance,[4] and proof of a sale to B. is not admissible under a charge of a sale to A.[5] Of course, no matter how indefinite the charge may be allowed to be under statutory provisions, or under liberality of construction by the courts, the evidence must be specific as to the particular act.[6]

§ **1277. Double punishment; included offenses; previous jeopardy.**— Where the statute defines distinct crimes[7] there may be a double punishment for the same act as constituting distinct offenses.[8] Thus, sales which are criminal in themselves may also be punished as constituting a nuisance,[9] or may be used in evidence as showing the same party to have been a common seller and punishable as such.[10] So criminal proceedings for illegal selling or keeping for sale will not prevent proceedings to condemn the liquors themselves,[11] or a civil action for violation of the seller's bond.[12] To state the same principle

[1] Ware v. S., 71 Miss. 204. *Contra*, S. v. Smith, 22 Vt. 74; S. v. Croteau, 23 Vt. 14.

[2] S. v. Lund, 49 Kan. 209; S. v. Crimmins, 31 Kan. 376; S. v. Chisnell, 36 W. Va. 659; Murphy v. S., 9 Lea, 373; S. v. Von Haltschuherr, 72 Ia. 541. In Michigan the prosecution may be required to elect as between different counts: P. v. Keefer, 97 Mich. 15.

[3] Osgood v. P., 39 N. Y. 449; Sanders v. S., 88 Ga. 254; Elam v. S., 26 Ala. 48. At any rate it is not error to fail to require an election, unless the defendant has asked it: Koch v. S., 32 Ohio St. 353.

[4] S. v. Therrien, 86 Me. 425.

[5] C. v. Taggart, 8 Grat. 697. And see *supra*, § 1274.

[6] S. v. Burgess, 4 Ind. 606.

[7] See *supra*, § 1271.

[8] S. v. Sonnerkalb, 2 Nott & M., 280.

[9] S. v. Lincoln, 50 Vt. 644; S. v. Waynick, 45 Ia. 516.

[10] S. v. Johnson, 3 R. I. 94; S. v. Coombs, 32 Me. 529; S. v. Maher, 35 Me. 225. But without regard to these decisions it is said in a later case that the offense of being a common seller includes that of making actual sales: S. v. Day, 37 Me. 244.

[11] Sanders v. S., 2 Ia. 230.

[12] S. v. Adams, 20 Ia. 486; S. v. Stutz, 20 Ia. 488. It is not unconstitutional to punish criminally and also to annul the license held by the party making the illegal sales on account of such sales: C. v. Brothers, 158 Mass. 200.

and course of reasoning in another form, a previous conviction for illegal selling will not bar a prosecution for keeping a nuisance proved by evidence of the same sales, or *vice versa*.[1] So keeping a nuisance and being a common seller are offenses which may be proved by evidence of the same sales, and a prosecution for one will not bar a prosecution for the other.[2] A similar principle is applicable to the offenses of selling without a license and selling to a minor without the consent of the parent;[3] of selling and keeping for sale;[4] of selling without a license and selling on Sunday,[5] and in similar cases. But in so far as the same evidence would sustain the two indictments, while the second will not be barred by the first, yet an acquittal in the first in regard to sales within a particular time may be introduced in evidence for the defendant in the second prosecution to show that he was not guilty of such illegal selling, a judgment on a particular point being conclusive in relation to such point as between the parties, though the subject-matter of the two suits may be different.[6] While in general there should be but one conviction for maintaining a nuisance during any period which is covered by one indictment therefor, yet if there has been a change of statute so that the offense of keeping a nuisance prior to that time is different from keeping after that time, there may be two indictments for such separate offenses.[7] But if the offense is that of selling, each sale constituting a distinct crime, the fact that on one prosecution the witness testifies as to several sales will not prevent some of the same sales being proved under a subsequent prosecution, as there may be as many distinct or successive prosecutions as there are distinct sales.[8] Also the same act may constitute an offense in violation of the state statutes and also in violation of a city ordinance, and the prosecution for one will not bar a prosecution for the other.[9]

[1] C. v. Brelsford, 161 Mass. 61; C. v. McCabe, 163 Mass. 98; C. v. McCabe, 163 Mass. 400; S. v. Lincoln, 50 Vt. 644; S. v. Wheeler, 62 Vt. 439; S. v. Jangraw, 61 Vt. 39; S. v. Graham, 73 Ia. 553.

[2] C. v. Bubser, 14 Gray, 83; S. v. Coombs, 32 Me. 529; S. v. Maher, 35 Me. 225.

[3] Ruble v. S., 51 Ark. 170; Blair v. S., 81 Ga. 629.

[4] S. v. Head, 3 R. I. 135.

[5] Arrington v. C., 87 Va. 96.

[6] S. v. Dewey, 65 Vt. 196.

[7] S. v. Webber, 76 Ia. 686.

[8] S. v. Small, 31 Mo. 197. And see *supra*, §§ 1272, 1275.

[9] S. v. Stevens, 114 N. C. 873. And see *supra*, § 1217.

§ **1278. Negativing exceptions.**— The method of charging a sale without a license or without authority has already been considered,[1] and it has also been said that if there is a proviso or exemption in a different section of the statute making sales criminal, it is not necessary to negative such exemption, that being a matter of defense;[2] but it is proper to further illustrate here the general proposition that it is not incumbent on the prosecution to negative the exceptions created by separate statutory provisions; thus, the authority under a constitutional provision to sell in the original package is a matter of defense which need not be negatived, and it is for the defendant to prove by way of defense that the sale was of that character.[3] So it is as to an exception of wine of domestic production.[4] Nor, in a charge of keeping for illegal sale, is it for the prosecution to negative the fact that the liquor was for sale in other states.[5] So if the sale would be illegal under the state statute unless made under a state license, it is not necessary to allege that the sale did not take place in the state.[6]

§ **1279. Evidence.**— Many questions of evidence have been already considered in this chapter and but little remains for discussion here. In proving the selling, as well as the keeping with intent to sell or keeping a place for illegal sale, evidence of the surroundings of the premises of defendant in which it is claimed the crime was committed is admissible; as, for instance, to show the presence of the usual furniture and implements or utensils used in the sale of liquor, and it is immaterial that the evidence does not show the selling or keeping of the kind of liquor sought to be proved.[7] So evidence of an attempt to

[1] *Supra*, §§ 1229, 1270. As to proving the exception, see *infra*, § 1281.

[2] *Supra*, § 1252.

[3] C. v. Waters, 11 Gray, 81; C. v. Gagne, 153 Mass. 205. And to the same effect, where the exemption in regard to sales in original packages is by statute, see S. v. Robinson, 39 Me. 150: S. v. Becker, 20 Ia. 438; *supra*, § 1204.

[4] S. v. Stapp, 29 Ia. 551; S. v. Curley, 33 Ia. 359; S. v. Miller, 53 Ia. 84.

[5] S. v. Perkins, 63 N. H. 368.

[6] S. v. Tamler, 19 Oreg. 528.

[7] S. v. Gorman, 58 N. H. 77; S. v. Shaw, 58 N. H. 73; C. v. Intoxicating Liquors, 150 Mass. 164; C. v. Brothers, 158 Mass. 200; C. v. McNeese, 156 Mass. 231; S. v. Burroughs, 72 Me. 479; P. v. Hicks, 79 Mich. 457. And see *supra*, §§ 1243, 1244, 1249. A witness may be asked whether he purchased such liquor of defendant and whether he knows of defendant selling such liquor to others, and as to what defendant's business was: S. v. Roben, 39 Ia. 424.

secrete or destroy liquor on the premises for the purpose of preventing its being found by officers is admissible.[1] By some statutes the reputation of the place is admissible in determining whether it is kept as a nuisance,[2] but aside from statute such general reputation is not admissible.[3] And on the other hand, defendant's reputation for carrying on the business in a lawful manner and the reputation of his place of business are not admissible in defense under a charge of a specific violation of law as to the methods of doing business, such as a sale to a minor; for the rule that defendant may put in evidence his general good reputation in regard to the elements of character involved in the commission of the crime does not apply to acts not involving moral turpitude but constituting merely *mala prohibita*.[4] Evidence of the receipt of liquor by the defendant about the time of the illegal selling charged is admissible.[5] To prove the proprietorship of defendant, where that is involved in the offense charged, acts of the defendant in managing and taking care of the premises are admissible.[6] The question has sometimes been raised as to the admissibility of evidence of facts obtained by officers making unlawful searches or otherwise acting improperly, but it has been held that such evidence is admissible notwithstanding the improper means by which the knowledge has been secured.[7]

§ **1280. License as evidence.**— The fact of procuring a United States license to sell spirituous liquor is evidence that liquor sold by defendant was believed by him to be of that character, in contradiction to his claim that it was not intoxicating,[8] or in general to show his preparation and intention to sell such liquor;[9] and the fact of having such license may be proved by other evidence than the license itself; for instance,

[1] C. v. Sullivan, 156 Mass. 487; C. v. Hurley, 153 Mass. 159.

[2] S. v. Kingston, 5 R. I. 297. And see *supra*, § 1249. As to the constitutionality of such provisions, see *supra*, § 1215.

[3] C. v. Eagan, 151 Mass. 45.

[4] C. v. Nagle, 157 Mass. 554.

[5] Fossdahl v. S., 89 Wis. 482; Klepfler v. S., 121 Ind. 491.

[6] C. v. Mead, 153 Mass. 284; S. v. Wilson, 5 R. I. 291; S. v. Knott, 5 R. I. 293; Needham v. S., 19 Tex. 332; P. v. Kridler, 80 Mich. 592.

[7] C. v. Welsh, 1 Allen, 1; C. v. Intoxicating Liquors, 4 Allen, 593; C. v. Murphy, 155 Mass. 284; C. v. Hurley, 158 Mass. 159; C. v. Brelsford, 161 Mass. 61; P. v. Murphy, 93 Mich. 41. And see *supra*, §§ 117, 118.

[8] P. v. Ingraham, 100 Mich. 530; S. v. Schultz, 79 Ia. 478.

[9] C. v. Keenan, 11 Allen, 262; C. v. Uhrig, 146 Mass. 132.

by a certified copy of the collector's record, or by other evidence of such license having been issued.[1] Admissions of the defendant that he has such license, [2] or the fact of having such a license hung up on the premises,[3] may be proved. It has been held, however, that having a United States license is not a circumstance tending to show a violation of the state law, unless it is expressly made so by statute.[4] And at any rate, the possession of a license is not conclusive evidence of violation of the state law.[5] The returns of a pharmacist made in accordance with law showing sales made by him may be introduced in evidence against him without proof of his signature thereto.[6]

§ **1281. Burden of proof as to lawfulness of sales.**— Where the sales of liquor are proven, but defendant claims that they were made under such circumstances as to be lawful, the burden of proof is upon him to show that fact;[7] and if defendant claims that sales on his premises were without his knowledge or approval, he has the burden of establishing that fact.[8] So if defendant claims that the sales were made under a license, he has the burden of proving that fact,[9] and that the sales were such as were authorized by his license.[10] So if the defendant relies on the fact of authority received by vote of the municipality

[1] S. v. Gorham, 65 Me. 270; S. v. Wiggin, 72 Me. 425. Extrinsic evidence is admissible to connect the premises named in the license with those in which the sale is claimed to have been made: S. v. Hall, 79 Me. 501.

[2] C. v. Cameron, 141 Mass. 83.

[3] C. v. Brown, 124 Mass. 318.

[4] S. v. Stutz, 20 Ia. 488.

[5] C. v. Keenan, 11 Allen, 262; S. v. Gorham, 65 Me. 270; S. v. Intoxicating Liquors, 80 Me. 57.

[6] S. v. Thompson, 74 Ia. 119.

[7] S. v. Cloughly, 73 Ia. 626; S. v. Kriechbaum, 81 Ia. 633; S. v. Becker, 20 Ia. 438; Morel v. S., 89 Ind. 275; S. v. Edwards, 60 Mo. 490. Thus, if it is claimed that a sale was by an innkeeper to a guest, and therefore lawful, that fact must be shown by defendant: C. v. Molter, 142 Mass. 533. As to whether the indictment should negative exceptions, see *supra*, § 1252.

[8] U. S. v. Sykes, 58 Fed. R. 1000.

[9] Noecker v. P., 91 Ill. 468; C. v. Belou, 115 Mass. 139; S. v. Woodward, 34 Me. 293; S. v. Hadlock, 43 Me. 282; S. v. Crowell, 25 Me. 171; S. v. Nulty, 57 Vt. 543; S. v. Lipscomb, 52 Mo. 32; Sharp v. S., 17 Ga. 290; Haskill v. C., 3 B. Mon. 342; Easterling v. S., 35 Miss. 210; Pond v. S., 47 Miss. 39; Fairly v. S., 63 Miss. 333; Thomas v. S., 37 Miss. 353; S. v. Crow, 53 Kan. 662; S. v. Morrison, 3 Dev. 299; Flower v. S., 39 Ark. 209. And see *supra*, §§ 1215, 1229.

[10] C. v. Rafferty, 133 Mass. 574; C. v. Towle, 138 Mass. 490.

to makes sales, that fact must be established by him.[1] Even in states where it is held that the prosecution must allege that the sale is without a license, it has been held that the burden of proving a license is on the defendant.[2] In other states it is held that aside from some statutory provision the burden is on the prosecution to prove its allegation that a sale was without a license.[3] If a license issued by a public tribunal is shown, it is presumed to be valid, and the burden is on the prosecution to show its invalidity.[4]

[1] C. v. Kennedy, 108 Mass. 292; C. v. Dean, 110 Mass. 357; C. v. Babcock, 110 Mass. 107; S. v. Shaw, 35 N. H. 217; S. v. McGlynn, 34 N. H. 422.

[2] S. v. Foster, 23 N. H. 348; S. v. Perkins, 53 N. H. 435; S. v. Keggon, 55 N. H. 19; Fairly v. S., 63 Miss. 333; Shearer v. S., 7 Blackf. 99. And see *supra*, § 1229.

[3] C. v. Thurlow, 24 Pick. 374; C. v. Kimball, 7 Met. 304; Hepler v. S., 58 Wis. 46; S. v. Nye, 32 Kan. 201; S. v. Kuhuke, 26 Kan. 405; Wells v. S., 18 Tex. Ap. 417. But this is changed in Massachusetts by statute: C. v. Lahy, 8 Gray, 459; C. v. Kelly, 10 Cush. 69. This statutory provision does not extend to prosecutions for keeping a nuisance: C. v. Lahy, 8 Gray, 459; nor does it extend to cases where the charge is of making sales which are unlawful without regard to a license, and the prosecution must prove that the sales were of that character: C. v. Livermore, 2 Allen, 292; C. v. Dean, 110 Mass. 357.

[4] S. v. Kuhuke, 26 Kan. 405.

CHAPTER 64.

GAMING AND BETTING.

I. GAMING IN GENERAL.
II. BETTING.
III. BEING A COMMON GAMBLER.
IV. GAMING IN PUBLIC PLACES.
V. POOL SELLING.
VI. KEEPING GAMING HOUSE.
VII. KEEPING OR EXHIBITING GAMING TABLE OR DEVICE.
VIII. ALLOWING GAMES TO BE PLAYED ON THE PREMISES.
IX. GAMING BY MINORS.

I. GAMING IN GENERAL.

§ 1282. **Introductory.**— This whole subject is practically statutory, though at common law the keeping of a gaming house was punishable as a nuisance.[1] But it is deemed advisable to discuss that subject in this chapter in connection with the other crimes involving the element of gaming. It will not be practicable to refer particularly to the terms of different statutes, and only their general scope and application can be considered; but these statutes fall under different general headings, which it will be convenient to discuss separately, even though they to some extent run into each other and this method of treatment may involve some repetition. Statutes regulating or prohibiting lotteries are analogous to those in relation to gaming, but that subject will be considered separately in the succeeding chapter.

§ 1283. **Gaming in general.**— Aside from statute gaming and betting are not criminal offenses.[2] Under the ordinary statutes prohibiting or providing for the licensing of gaming, it may be defined to be a hazarding of anything of value upon a game; that is, playing a game for a wager;[3] while betting

[1] *Supra*, §§ 1169, 1170.

[2] S. v. Hawkins, 15 Ark. 259; U. S. v. Willis, 1 Cranch, C. C. 511; S. v. Cotton, 6 Tex. 425; Remmington v. S., 1 Oreg. 281.

[3] Williams v. Warsaw, 60 Ind. 457; C. v. Taylor, 14 Gray, 26. Any action depending on the chance of a game is within the statute: S. v. Leighton, 23 N. H. 167; Sigel v. Jebb, 3 Stark. 1. Gaming embraces pooling schemes and other forms of betting on games: P. v. Weithoff, 51 Mich. 203. Some statutes of this character are declared to be remedial rather than penal: Seal v. S., 13 Sm. & M. 286; Cain v. S., 13 Sm. & M. 456; on the other hand, see McGowan v. S., 9 Yerg. 184. Gaming is playing for a wager and not simply deriving a profit from furnishing facilities for playing games not for money: P. v. Carroll, 80 Cal. 153.

is the staking of a valuable thing upon a chance or contingency.[1] Betting is, however, under the usual statutes, a distinct offense,[2] but it is also the gist of the offense of gaming.[3] Special statutes sometimes make the playing of games unlawful, even when unaccompanied by betting, but they are usually limited in their application to particular times, such as Sunday, or particular places, such as public places.[4] Generally, in order that there may be an offense, there must be a wager;[5] on the other hand, a wager in the absence of a game lacks an essential element of gaming.[6] To constitute a bet there must be a chance or uncertainty, and so a bet on a rule of play is not sufficient.[7] The game may be either one of chance or one of skill.[8]

§ **1284. Statutory provisions.**— The statutes against gaming are not usually so worded as to restrict their application to games specially mentioned, but usually cover all those at which money or property is lost or won.[9] But the language of the

[1] Parsons v. S., 2 Ind. 499; Hizer v. S., 12 Ind. 330. A mere agreement to pay the purchase price of an article bought if a certain event happens, otherwise not, is said not to be a wager: Wagner v. S., 63 Ind. 250. "The legal definition of the term 'bet' is a mutual agreement and tender of a gift or something valuable, which is to belong to one or the other of the contending parties according to the result of a trial of skill or chance, or both combined:" Long v. S., 22 Tex. Ap. 194.

[2] Myers v. S., 3 Sneed, 98; Parsons v. S., 2 Ind. 499; Hizer v. S., 12 Ind. 330; S. v. Lovell, 39 N. J. 463.

[3] Fagan v. S., 21 Ark. 390. To play for the use of the table has been held lawful, as the winner makes no profit, which is the essence of gaming: Blewett v. S., 34 Miss. 606. But see *infra*, § 1286.

[4] Harris v. S., 31 Ala. 362; s. c., 33 Ala. 373. So it is made criminal to carry on a shooting match within two hundred yards of a public road: Myers v. S., 3 Sneed, 98; and see *infra*, §§ 1301–1303; or to engage in horse-racing on a public road: S. v. Fiddler, 7 Humph. 501; and see *supra*, § 1198.

[5] S. v. Quaid, 43 La. An. 1076; S. v. Leicht, 17 Ia. 28; Tuttle v. S., 1 Tex. Ap. 364; Whitney v. S., 10 Tex. Ap. 377; S. v. Smitherman, 1 Ired. 14; S. v. Gupton, 8 Ired. 271. Proof that a person played "pin pool," and that the rules of the game required a bet, will sustain conviction: Cohen v. S., 17 Tex. 142.

[6] S. v. Henderson, 47 Ind. 127; S. v. Smith, 1 Meigs, 98. Betting on a horse-race is not gaming: C. v. Shelton, 8 Grat. 592; S. v. Lemon, 46 Mo. 375; but betting on a cock-fight is: Bagley v. S., 1 Humph. 485; and so is selling prize candy packages: Eubanks v. S., 3 Heisk. 488.

[7] Pope v. St. Leger, 1 Salk. 344. Thus, where the dealer and exhibitor of a gaming bank bet A. that the latter had made a bad bet, it was held that there could not be a conviction of the dealer on the charge of betting at a gaming bank: Askey v. S., 20 Tex. Ap. 443.

[8] S. v. Miller, 53 Ia. 154; S. v. Black, 94 N. C. 809.

[9] Vicaro v. C., 5 Dana, 504; P. v. Carroll, 80 Cal. 153; Miller v. S., 48 Ala. 122; Smith v. S., 17 Tex. 191; S. v. Gitt Lee, 6 Oreg. 425. *Contra*, S. v. Mann, 2 Oreg. 238.

statute must govern,[1] and so where games of chance alone are prohibited betting on a game of skill is not an offense;[2] nor can "backgammon" be included under the term "cards or dice."[3] The name of the game is, however, immaterial; the law cannot be evaded by playing the same game under a new name.[4] Even where the game played is different from the prohibited game but of kindred nature, the statutory name has often been held to include both; so the term "billiards" has been held to include pool;[5] "cards" to include faro;[6] "faro" to include "thimbles;"[7] but throwing dice for money is not raffling.[8] Where the statute names special games, following with a general term such as "or other devices,"[9] "or other games,"[10] "or any banking game,"[11] or other like terms, any game similar to those mentioned is usually deemed to be included.

§ **1285. What deemed games.**— The game is usually immaterial so long as there is a wager connected with it, and the term has therefore been held to include bagatelle,[12] base ball,[13] billiards,[14] cards,[15] dice throwing,[16] dominoes,[17] equality,[18] faro,[19]

[1] Smoot v. S., 18 Ind. 18; S. v. Blair, 41 Tex. 30.

[2] S. v. King, 113 N. C. 631; S. v. Gupton, 8 Ired. 271; S. v. Jackson, 39 Mo. 420. A horse-race is not a game of hazard or skill: S. v. Rorie, 23 Ark. 726. The court will not take judicial notice that a game of chance can be played with cards: S. v. Taylor, 111 N. C. 680.

[3] Wetmore v. S., 55 Ala. 198.

[4] P. v. Carroll, 80 Cal. 153; Smith v. S., 17 Tex. 191.

[5] Sikes v. S., 67 Ala. 77. *Contra*, Squier v. S., 66 Ind. 317.

[6] Gibboney v. C., 14 Grat. 582.

[7] S. v. Red, 7 Rich. 8.

[8] Darling Jones v. S., 26 Ala. 155.

[9] U. S. v. Speeden, 1 Cranch, C. C. 535.

[10] Miller v. S., 48 Ala. 122; Smith v. S., 17 Tex. 191.

[11] P. v. Carroll, 80 Cal. 153; Randolph v. S., 9 Tex. 521.

[12] Neal v. C., 22 Grat. 917.

[13] Mace v. S., 58 Ark. 79; P. v. Weithoff, 51 Mich. 203.

[14] S. v. Book, 41 Ia. 550; S. v. Miller, 53 Ia. 154; S. v. Bishel, 39 Ia. 42; Sikes v. S., 67 Ala. 77. But see S. v. Mosely, 14 Ala. 390; S. v. Allaire, 14 Ala. 435; Owens v. S., 52 Ala. 213; Clark v. S., 49 Ala. 37. The indictment should show that the billiard table was used as a gambling device: S. v. Bristow, 41 Tex. 146.

[15] P. v. Carroll, 80 Cal. 153; Miller v. S., 48 Ala. 122; Smith v. S., 17 Tex. 191; S. v. Brannen, 8 Jones, 208; Bachellor v. S., 10 Tex. 258. It is said that betting at cards is not punishable: Remmington v. S., 1 Oreg. 281; but the same court holds a pack of cards to be a gambling device: Frisbie v. S., 1 Oreg. 264.

[16] S. v. De Boy, 117 N. C. 702; McDaniel v. C., 6 Bush, 326; Darling Jones v. S., 26 Ala. 155; Miller v. S., 48 Ala. 122. But see Whitney v. S., 10 Tex. Ap. 377.

[17] Harris v. S., 31 Ala. 362; s. c., 33 Ala. 373.

[18] U. S. v. Speeden, 1 Cranch, C. C. 535.

[19] Gibboney v. C., 14 Grat. 582; S. v. Burton, 25 Tex. 420; Ritte v. C., 18

keno,[1] monte,[2] nine pins,[3] ten pins,[4] pico,[5] poker,[6] pin pool,[7] pool,[8] French pool,[9] ramps,[10] rondo[11] and roulette.[12] Some things which are not usually called games, but which involve the element of chance, come within the statutes prohibiting gaming; for instance, cock-fighting,[13] horse-racing,[14] dealing in options or futures,[15] gift enterprises[16] and raffles.[17] So wagering money upon the result of a shooting match has been held indictable as gaming.[18]

§ **1286. What deemed a wager.**— The stake must be something of value,[19] but the amount is immaterial;[20] and so it is held sufficient if cigars, beer or other treats,[21] or even the use of the table on which the game is played,[22] is to be paid for by the

B. Mon. 35; Ashlock v. C., 7 B. Mon. 44; S. v. Holland, 22 Ark. 242; P. v. Ah Own, 85 Cal. 580.

1 Brown v. S., 40 Ga. 689; New Orleans v. Miller, 7 La. An. 651; Eslava v. S., 44 Ala. 406.

2 Wardlow v. S., 18 Tex. Ap. 356; McKissick v. S., 2 Tex. 356; P. v. Saviers, 14 Cal. 29.

3 Bass v. S., 37 Ala. 469.

4 Walker v. S., 2 Swan, 287; but not if there is no wager: S. v. Gupton, 8 Ired. 271.

5 Euper v. S., 35 Ark. 629.

6 S. v. Wade, 43 Ark. 77; S. v. Gitt Lee, 6 Oreg. 425; Nuckolls v. C., 32 Grat. 884. *Contra*, S. v. Mann, 2 Oreg. 238; Ransom v. S., 26 Fla. 364.

7 Cohen v. S., 17 Tex. 142; S. v. Book, 41 Ia. 550; S. v. Miller, 53 Ia. 154. *Contra*, S. v. Quaid, 43 La. An. 1076.

8 Tuttle v. S., 1 Tex. Ap. 364; S. v. Kelly, 24 Tex. 182; S. v. Jackson, 39 Mo. 420; Rodgers v. S., 26 Ala. 76. But see S. v. Mosely, 14 Ala. 390; S. v. Allaire, 14 Ala. 435; Chiles v. S., 1 Tex. Ap. 27.

9 C. v. Simonds, 79 Ky. 618.

10 Bryan v. S., 26 Ala. 65.

11 S. v. Mann, 13 Tex. 61; Barker v. S., 12 Tex. 273; but it is not a banking game: S. v. Hawkins, 15 Ark. 259.

12 Ritte v. C., 18 B. Mon. 35.

13 Bagley v. S., 1 Humph. 485; Johnson v. S., 4 Sneed, 614.

14 Cheesum v. S., 8 Blackf. 332; P. v. Weithoff, 51 Mich. 203; S. v. Shaw, 39 Minn. 153. *Contra*, C. v. Shelton, 8 Grat. 592; S. v. Lemon, 46 Mo. 375.

15 Fortenbury v. S., 47 Ark. 188.

16 Bell v. S., 5 Sneed, 507.

17 S. v. De Boy, 117 N. C. 702; Long v. S., 22 Tex. Ap. 194. *Contra*, Norton v. S., 15 Ark. 71. And see *infra*, § 1315.

18 Myers v. S., 3 Sneed, 98.

19 Carr v. S., 50 Ind. 178.

20 The legislature sometimes regulates the amount: C. v. Garland, 5 Rand. 652; Long v. S., 22 Tex. Ap. 194.

21 S. v. Wade, 43 Ark. 77; S. v. Bishel, 39 Ia. 42; S. v. Maurer, 7 Ia. 406; S. v. Cooster, 10 Ia. 453; S. v. Leicht, 17 Ia. 28; Bachellor v. S., 10 Tex. 258; Brown v. S., 49 N. J. 61; McDaniel v. C., 6 Bush, 326; Hitchins v. P., 39 N. Y. 454.

22 S. v. Book, 41 Ia. 550; S. v. Miller, 53 Ia. 154; S. v. Bishel, 39 Ia. 42; Alexander v. S., 99 Ind. 450; Hamilton v. S., 75 Ind. 586; S. v. Leighton, 23 N. H. 167; C. v. Taylor, 14 Gray, 26; Sigel v. Jebb, 3 Stark. 1. Playing for the "rub" is an offense: Mount v. S., 7 Ind. 654. But to the contrary it is said that playing for

loser. The intrinsic value of the stake is immaterial if it represents or is convertible into something of value, as checks, chips or the like.[1] But the party betting must stake something, and where one bets chips used in the game, paying nothing for them, he cannot be convicted of gaming, for he has nothing at stake.[2] The wager must be a thing hazarded, and so a prize offered for the winner in a feat of skill is not a wager.[3] It is not necessary that the stake be "put up;"[4] nor indeed that there be any definite agreement to pay the amount of the wager, it being understood and expected that it shall be paid.[5]

§ 1287. **When offense complete.**— The offense of gaming is complete when the stake or wager is put up or the offer to bet accepted,[6] but mere scoring or practice on a billiard table is not enough, for there must be at least the beginning of a game.[7] The offense, even when described as that of gaming, is not a continuing one, but may be committed by one act of the kind.[8]

§ 1288. **Aiding or procuring.**—The offense may be committed by procurement through the act of another;[9] so where one stakes money on a game played by others, he may be guilty of gaming, the players being considered the agents of those who bet;[10] but the actual players who do not bet are not usually deemed guilty.[11] One who encourages gaming may be guilty thereof as principal in the misdemeanor.[12]

§ 1289. **Indictment in general.**— It is usually sufficient, as in other statutory offenses, to follow the descriptive words used

the use of the table is not gambling, for the winner makes no profit: Blewett v. S., 34 Miss. 606; S. v. Hall, 32 N. J. 158; Clark v. S., 49 Ala. 37; Owens v. S., 52 Ala. 213.

1 Gibbons v. P., 33 Ill. 442; Porter v. S., 51 Ga. 300; Walton v. S., 14 Tex. 381.

2 Fagan v. S., 21 Ark. 390.

3 Delier v. Plymouth Co. Ag'l Soc., 57 Ia. 481. And see *infra*, § 1297.

4 Alexander v. S., 99 Ind. 450.

5 The game was for treats, but it was agreed that it should be voluntary, no one being bound to treat unless he chose: Walker v. S., 2 Swan, 287.

6 S. v. Welch, 7 Port. 463.

7 Sikes v. S., 67 Ala. 77.

8 Cameron v. S., 15 Ala. 383; Swallow v. S., 20 Ala. 30.

9 Williams v. S., 20 Miss. 58.

10 Parmer v. S., 91 Ga. 152; P. v. Weithoff, 51 Mich. 203. A person who bets at a game of faro dealt by another plays faro: S. v. McDaniel, 20 Oreg. 523.

11 S. v. Smitherman, 1 Ired. 14; S. v. Gupton, 8 Ired. 271; Strawhern v. S., 37 Miss. 422. But to the contrary, it was held that where a party played a game, knowing that others were betting thereon, he was guilty of gaming: Smith v. S., 5 Humph. 163.

12 Fugate v. S., 2 Humph. 397; Howlett v. S., 5 Yerg. 144.

in the statute,[1] but the indictment must be sufficiently specific to bring the acts within the statutory description,[2] and it must not be indefinite or uncertain.[3] If the charge is of one form of the offense, there cannot, of course, be a conviction for another form which is by statute made a distinct crime.[4]

§ **1290. Names of parties.**— By many courts it has been held that the indictment must name the parties playing,[5] or allege that their names are to the grand jurors unknown.[6] In other courts, however, it has been held that the names of the parties playing need not be alleged.[7] If, however, the names are alleged, it seems that they must be proved in accordance with the allegation although such allegation was unnecessary.[8] It need not be charged that defendant played with or bet with another person.[9] A charge that certain parties played and bet with each other is sustained by proof that they all bet against the dealer.[10] The allegation that defendant won a

[1] S. v. Light, 17 Oreg. 358; Wingard v. S., 13 Ga. 396; S. v. Grider, 18 Ark. 297; Spratt v. S., 8 Mo. 247; Burnett v. S., 30 Ala. 19; P. v. Gossett, 93 Cal. 641. If the statute specifies a trotting race or a running race, the indictment must say which: Stearns v. S., 81 Md. 341.

[2] S. v. Norwood, 94 N. C. 935; S. v. Stillwell, 16 Kan. 24.

[3] C. v. Perrigo, 3 Met. (Ky.) 5.

[4] Chambers v. S., 77 Ala. 80; Nairn v. S., 18 Tex. Ap. 260; Averheart v. S., 30 Tex. Ap. 651.

[5] S. v. Irvin, 5 Blackf. 343; Butler v. S., 5 Blackf. 280; Ball v. S., 7 Blackf. 242; Parrott v. S., 10 Ark. 574; Moffit v. S., 11 Ark. 169; Jester v. S., 14 Ark. 552; Groner v. S., 6 Fla. 39; Davis v. S., 7 Ohio, 204; Shook v. S., 25 Tex. Ap. 345; Davis v. S., 22 Ga. 101. It must be plainly alleged with whom the bet was made, whether with a player or outsider: S. v. Stallings, 3 Ind. 531.

[6] S. v. Maxwell, 5 Blackf. 230; Drew v. S., 10 Ark. 82; Barkman v. S., 13 Ark. 703; Orr v. S., 18 Ark. 540; S. v. Dole, 3 Blackf. 294; S. v. Ross, 7 Blackf. 322; Webster v. S., 8 Blackf. 400; Johnston v. S., 15 Miss. 58; S. v. Prescott, 33 N. H. 212; S. v. Trotter, 5 Yerg. 184; S. v. Ake, 9 Tex. 322.

[7] S. v. Light, 17 Oreg. 358; Roberts v. S., 32 Ohio St. 171; Carper v. S., 27 Ohio St. 572; Goodman v. S., 41 Ark. 228; Sharp v. S., 28 Fla. 357; Johnson v. S., 36 Tex. 198; Hinton v. S., 68 Ga. 322. So where the charge is dealing the game of monte: P. v. Saviers, 14 Cal. 29; Green v. P., 21 Ill. 125.

[8] Hany v. S., 9 Ark. 193.

[9] Day v. S., 27 Tex. Ap. 143.

[10] Archer v. S., 69 Ga. 767. A charge that three persons played jointly is not proved by evidence that two played together and that the other played with another person: Lindsey v. S., 48 Ala. 169. An allegation that two persons named bet on an election was held to charge that they bet with each other: S. v. Griggs, 34 W. Va. 78. And see *infra*, § 1294. It is unnecessary to state with whom the bet was made or the amount: S. v. Bridges, 24 Mo. 353.

wager of another is equivalent to alleging a bet with such person.[1]

§ 1291. Charging the game played.— The courts have usually held that it is unnecessary to name in the indictment the game played,[2] but the nature of the game should be stated.[3] Where the statute prohibits certain games and others of like kind, it is necessary to charge one of the prohibited games or to show that the game played is of like kind with those prohibited.[4] To name the game as one of those expressly prohibited is sufficient.[5] Under some statutes it may not be necessary to state the name of the game at all;[6] nor, indeed, to allege that the game was actually played.[7] But under other statutes the fact that the game was actually played is material.[8] The prosecution will not be compelled to elect on which game it will proceed where the evidence tends to establish different

[1] S. v. Little, 6 Blackf. 267.

[2] Dean v. Tennessee, Mart. & Y. 127; S. v. McBride, 8 Humph. 65; S. v. Maxwell, 5 Blackf. 230; Drew v. S., 10 Ark. 82; Barkman v. S., 13 Ark. 703; Orr v. S., 18 Ark. 540; Green v. P., 21 Ill. 125; S. v. Dole, 3 Blackf. 294; S. v. Ross, 7 Blackf. 322; Webster v. S., 8 Blackf. 400; Romp v. S., 3 Greene (Ia.), 276; Johnston v. S., 15 Miss. 58; S. v. Prescott, 33 N. H. 212; S. v. Trotter, 5 Yerg. 184; S. v. Ake, 9 Tex. 322; S. v. Gitt Lee, 6 Oreg. 425; S. v. Bougher, 3 Blackf. 307. *Contra*, S. v. Jeffrey, 33 Ark. 136. It is not necessary to charge in an indictment for keeping a common gaming house that any particular game was played, but, having so charged, it is necessary to prove it: Dudney v. S., 22 Ark. 251.

[3] S. v. Gitt Lee, 6 Oreg. 425; Webster v. S., 8 Blackf. 400. The facts of the transaction should be given: Burch v. Republic, 1 Tex. 608; Lewellen v. S., 18 Tex. 538; S. v. Catchings, 43 Tex. 654; Dixon v. S., 21 Tex. Ap. 517. An indictment for playing a "game of cards" sufficiently charges playing a game *with* cards: S. v. Shult, 41 Tex. 548.

[4] Booth v. S., 26 Tex. 203; S. v. Blair, 41 Tex. 30; S. v. Grider, 18 Ark. 297. When an indictment charges unlawful playing at a game of cards in a public place, and the evidence shows the game to have been "monte," it will not sustain conviction under a statute providing different penalties for "playing with cards" and for "monte:" Averheart v. S., 30 Tex. Ap. 651. An information charging that the defendant "did play cards for money" is not a sufficient allegation that there was a "gambling device" or a game played by means of a "gambling device:" S. v. Stillwell, 16 Kan. 24. An indictment for betting money upon a certain game known as "pool" is not sufficient without charging that the betting was on a gaming table or bank or a gambling device: Tate v. S., 21 Tex. 202.

[5] S. v. Mann, 13 Tex. 61; Warren v. S., 18 Ark. 195; P. v. Beatty, 14 Cal. 566; McKissick v. S., 2 Tex. 356; Wingard v. S., 13 Ga. 396; Short v. S., 23 Tex. Ap. 312.

[6] S. v. Grace, 21 Ark. 227.

[7] Rosson v. S., 92 Ala. 76.

[8] Smith v. S., 63 Ala. 55; Johnson v. S., 75 Ala. 7; Dreyfus v. S., 83 Ala. 54; Tolbert v. S., 87 Ala. 27; Dobkins v. S., 2 Humph. 424.

games within the terms of the statute.[1] If the proof shows a game essentially different from the one charged, the variance will be fatal,[2] but, if the game charged and the game proved are practically the same, a conviction will be proper.[3]

§ 1292. **The wager.**— Where the statute prohibits the playing of a game, it is not necessary to allege that defendant bet on the game;[4] but if the statute is against gaming, a bet or wager must be alleged.[5] It is usually sufficient that the bet or wager be alleged without a statement that it is a thing of value,[6] or the amount thereof;[7] and so it is not necessary to charge what the bet or wager was.[8] If the indictment is under a statute for playing at a certain game of cards on which money was bet, it is not necessary to allege that defendant bet or that he knew money was bet.[9] Courts will take judicial notice that money is a thing of value, and so the charge that money was bet sufficiently charges the betting of a thing of value within the statute.[10] So an averment that United States fractional currency was bet is equivalent to an averment that money was bet;[11] but an indictment for betting money is not sustained by proof of betting property;[12] nor will proof of winning a note for five dollars sustain a charge of winning "five dollars."[13]

[1] Hinton v. S., 68 Ga. 322.

[2] Bartender v. S., 51 Ind. 73; S. v. Grider, 18 Ark. 297.

[3] Flynn v. S., 34 Ark. 441.

[4] Stockden v. S., 18 Ark. 186.

[5] Rosson v. S., 92 Ala. 76; S. v. Stillwell, 16 Kan. 24.

[6] Long v. S., 22 Tex. Ap. 194; Hinton v. S., 68 Ga. 322; Jacobson v. S., 55 Ala. 151; Mitchell v. S., 55 Ala. 160. A charge in an indictment that defendant bet a certain "valuable thing" is too vague; it must describe the valuable thing: Anthony v. S., 4 Humph. 83; and so the words "goods, wares and merchandise" do not describe the wager with sufficient certainty: S. v. Kilgore, 6 Humph. 44.

[7] Collins v. S., 70 Ala. 19; Dean v. Tennessee, Mart. & Y. 127; S. v. McBride, 8 Humph. 65; S. v. Bridges, 24 Mo. 353; nor is it necessary to prove it if alleged: Medlock v. S., 18 Ark. 363; Parsons v. S., 2 Ind. 499; C. v. McAtee, 8 Dana, 28; C. v. Garland, 3 Met. (Ky.) 478. And it is not necessary to prove the exact denomination of the coin bet: S. v. Douglas, 1 Mo. 374.

[8] Harrison v. S., 15 Tex. 239. It is not necessary to prove the amount lost as alleged: Parsons v. S., 2 Ind. 499.

[9] Reeves v. S., 9 Tex. 447; S. v. Ward, 9 Tex. 370.

[10] Grant v. S., 89 Ga. 393.

[11] Collins v. S., 70 Ala. 19. Nickels staked on a game need not be proved to be of value: Mallory v. S., 62 Ga. 164. A charge of winning a large sum of money, to wit, $1, therefore is a sufficient allegation that money was bet: Graham v. S., 1 Ark. 171.

[12] Horton v. S., 13 Ark. 62; Tate v. S., 5 Blackf. 174; Hale v. S., 8 Tex. 171.

[13] Tate v. S., 5 Blackf. 174.

§ 1293. **Time and place.**—No particular time need be alleged,[1] and it is enough to prove that the offense was committed before the finding of the indictment and within the period of the statute of limitations.[2] Under a charge of one particular offense the prosecution may introduce evidence of any offense within the description of the indictment,[3] and one prosecution under such an indictment does not confer immunity for all offenses which might have been proved under such an indictment, or of which evidence was introduced.[4] It is not necessary to locate the offense with reference to any particular house, whether of defendant or another.[5] If, however, the particular place is described the evidence must correspond.[6]

§ 1294. **Joinder of defendants.**— Two or more defendants may be charged in one indictment;[7] but it must appear that they played together.[8] If more than one is indicted, one or more may be convicted without the conviction of others.[9]

§ 1295. **Charging different offenses; duplicity.**— Charging conjunctively all the acts which by statute are specified as constituting the offense is not improper;[10] and so it has been held that a count for gaming and a count for keeping a gambling house may be properly joined;[11] or a count for exhibiting and another for playing, and a third for suffering to be played;[12] oı one for gaming and one for keeping a gaming table.[13] Where the statute is against gaming, an indictment for gaming and

[1] Word v. C., 3 Leigh, 743.

[2] C. v. Hyde, Thach. Cr. Cas. 19; Chapman v. S., 18 Ga. 736; S. v. Agudo, 5 La. An. 185; Ramey v. S., 14 Tex. 409; Anthony v. S., 4 Humph. 83; S. v. Marchant, 15 R. I. 539.

[3] Pope v. S., 63 Miss. 53.

[4] Pope v. S., 63 Miss. 53.

[5] Word v. C., 3 Leigh, 743; Sublett v. S., 9 Tex. 53; Rosson v. S., 92 Ala. 76. Having described the place the indictment need not describe the room: P. v. Saviers, 14 Cal. 29; S. v. Atkins, 1 Ala. 180.

[6] C. v. Butts, 2 Va. Cas. 18.

[7] Johnson v. S., 13 Ark. 684.

[8] Galbreath v. S., 36 Tex. 200; Herron v. S., 36 Tex. 285; S. v. Roderica, 35 Tex. 507. If A. and B. are jointly indicted and tried for gaming, the evidence showing that they played at different times, and that the other was not present when either played, no conviction can be had: Elliott v. S., 26 Ala. 78. If it is intended to charge them with distinct offenses that fact must definitely appear: S. v. Homan, 41 Tex. 155; Parker v. S., 26 Tex. 204. And see *supra*, § 1290.

[9] Covy v. S., 4 Port. 186; Ward v. S., 22 Ala. 16; Brown v. S., 5 Yerg. 367.

[10] P. v. Gosset, 93 Cal. 641.

[11] Wheeler v. S., 42 Md. 563.

[12] C. v. McGuire, 1 Va. Cas. 119.

[13] Whitfield v. S., 4 Ark. 171.

keeping is bad for duplicity;[1] so is one for gaming and permitting,[2] or for betting and holding stakes.[3]

§ **1296. Evidence.**— To show that the playing was for stakes it is competent to prove that money was seen on the table where defendant and others were playing cards,[4] and it is sufficient *prima facie* evidence of guilt if it appears that defendant was present in the room where gaming was going on and fled on the entrance of an officer.[5] Proof of playing supports a charge of being present at the game,[6] and testimony that defendant won implies that the money was paid.[7] As the mere throwing of dice or playing of cards may not be criminal, evidence that there was betting or a wager is material.[8] If guilt depends on ownership or control of the building in which the game is carried on, such fact will not be presumed from having a store in a part of the building.[9] Statements of a player, during or immediately after the close of the game, that he has lost a certain sum thereon may be shown as part of the *res gestæ*.[10] A witness cannot testify that defendant kept a gaming house, but may only tell the facts from which such an inference may be drawn.[11] Expert witnesses are not competent to testify as to what the game consists in,[12] but one who has played the game may tell what he knows of it.[13] A participant in the unlawful game is an accomplice whose evidence requires corroboration,[14] but one who simply advises is not an accomplice,[15] nor is one who plays without betting.[16]

1 S. v. Howe, 1 Rich. 260.

2 S. v. Fant, 2 Brev. 487.

3 S. v. Bridges, 24 Mo. 353.

4 Rice v. S., 10 Tex. 545. But see Orr v. S., 26 Fla. 520; Tatum v. S., 33 Fla. 311.

5 S. v. Boyer, 79 Ia. 330. And so where the officers found defendant walking about in a room that they had to break into where gaming implements were found between the ceiling and floor above, and the officers heard some one running up the stairs, *held*, that the evidence was sufficient to warrant conviction: C. v. Warren, 161 Mass. 281.

6 C. v. Hogarty, 141 Mass. 106. Evidence that other persons played or bet is relevant as showing that there was some one present to bet with, and some game on which to bet: Thompson v. S., 99 Ala. 173.

7 Branscum v. S., 7 Ind. 593.

8 Whitney v. S., 10 Tex. Ap. 377; Oder v. S., 26 Fla. 520.

9 Holtzclow v. S., 26 Tex. 682.

10 Glover v. S., 89 Ga. 391.

11 Wheeler v. S., 42 Md. 563. He may, however, state generally that about the time charged he had seen accused conducting a game of faro: S. v. Wilson, 9 Wash. 16.

12 P. v. Carroll, 80 Cal. 153.

13 Nuckolls v. C., 32 Grat. 884.

14 Davidson v. S., 33 Ala. 350. *Contra*, C. v. Bossie, — Ky. —, 37 S. W. R. 844; *supra*, § 199.

15 Smith v. S., 37 Ala. 472.

16 Bass v. S., 37 Ala. 469.

II. BETTING.

§ 1297. In general; on horse-races.—As already indicated,[1] betting, being a form of gaming, is criminal only as made so by statute.[2] Many forms of betting are, indeed, punishable as gaming,[3] but some forms are specially mentioned by statute as criminal and must be considered. Horse-racing for money is generally within the statute as to gaming;[4] but to offer a premium to the owner of the winning horse in a race is not the staking of a bet, for there is no hazarding of money on the result of the contest;[5] neither is the racing of horses for a prize or premium offered by a third person to be deemed gambling.[6] The general prohibition of betting on horse-races applies to all horse-races no matter where run,[7] and is therefore applicable to a race to be run out of the state.[8] But if the offense charged is of keeping a house for pool selling or otherwise betting or gambling, or permitting betting or gambling therein, the act of betting or gambling by placing money in a pool room on a horse-race in another state is consummated where the money is thus placed or the bet made, and not where the defendant negotiates for the transmission of the bet on a race out of the state.[9] In some states betting or pool selling with reference to races run on a licensed track are excepted from the statutory prohibition.[10] In many states, however, all pooling schemes are forbidden by statute.[11]

§ 1298. Betting on elections.—There are usually express provisions against election bets, but such betting is not gam-

[1] *Supra*, § 1283.

[2] Smoot v. S., 18 Ind. 18.

[3] *Supra*, § 1283. *Contra*, C. v. Shelton, 8 Grat. 592; S. v. Rorie, 23 Ark. 726. For instance, it is said not to be within the statute as to games of chance: Harless v. U. S., Morris, 169; nor is it a gambling device: S. v. Lemon, 46 Mo. 375.

[4] Cheesum v. S., 8 Blackf. 332; P. v. Weithoff, 51 Mich. 203. And see *supra*, § 1285.

[5] Delier v. Plymouth Co. Ag'l Soc'y, 57 Ia. 481.

[6] Harris v. White, 81 N. Y. 532; Misner v. Knapp, 13 Oreg. 135; Porter v. Day, 71 Wis. 296; Alvord v. Smith, 63 Ind. 58. *Contra*, Comly v. Hillegass, 94 Pa. St. 132; Bronson Ag'l, etc. Ass'n v. Ramsdell, 24 Mich. 441.

[7] S. v. Lovell, 39 N. J. 463.

[8] Stearns v. S., 81 Md. 341; Lacey v. Palmer, — Va. —, 24 S. E. R. 930; Williams v. S., 92 Tenn. 275.

[9] Lescallett v. C.. 89 Va. 878.

[10] S. v. Posey, 1 Humph. 384; S. v. Blackburn, 2 Coldw. 235; Huff v. S., 2 Swan, 279; S. v. Fiddler, 7 Humph. 501; but not otherwise: Williams v. S., 92 Tenn. 275.

[11] C. v. Simonds, 79 Ky. 618. And see *infra*, § 1305.

ing,[1] although it may be a violation of the statute against betting upon a game or wager.[2] The object of some of the statutes is to protect the ballot from any undue influence resulting from an effort which may be made because of the bet,[3] and such a provision is applicable to a bet on the vote of a precinct,[4] or on the election of a candidate,[5] or upon the result of the presidential election;[6] but not to a bet, made after the conclusion of the election, as to the result,[7] nor upon the result of an election in another state.[8] But under other statutes the gist of the offense is the bet, and therefore a bet made after the election is over,[9] or a bet on the election in another state,[10] is indictable.

§ 1299. **Indictment; evidence.**— The general discussion in preceding sections[11] of indictments in cases of gambling covers sufficiently the ordinary cases where betting is alleged, but there are some peculiarities to be noticed in regard to betting upon an election. Such an offense must be charged with some accuracy; thus, an indictment for betting on the state election for presidential electors is not supported by proof of a bet that the state would vote for a certain presidential candidate.[12] As to the time, it should be alleged as in other cases, but not necessarily with exactness.[13] But if the indictment alleges the winning of money by betting on an election, it is held that the date must be alleged as subsequent to that of the election referred to.[14] If the bet is charged to have been made as to the success of a particular candidate, it is necessary to aver that he was a candidate at the election.[15]

[1] S. v. Henderson, 47 Ind. 127; S. v. Smith, 1 Meigs, 98.

[2] Parsons v. S., 2 Ind. 499; Hizer v. S., 12 Ind. 330.

[3] C. v. Kirk, 4 B. Mon. 1.

[4] C. v. Kennedy, 15 B. Mon. 531.

[5] C. v. Pash, 9 Dana, 31.

[6] Quarles v. S., 5 Humph. 560.

[7] S. v. Mahan, 2 Ala. 340; S. v. McLelland, 4 Sneed, 437.

[8] S. v. McLelland, 4 Sneed, 437. Thus, if the statute is against laying a wager on the result of any public election held within the state, it will not apply to a bet upon the result of the presidential election: Covington v. S., 28 Tex. Ap. 225.

[9] Miller v. S., 33 Miss. 356.

[10] Sharkey v. S., 33 Miss. 353.

[11] *Supra*, §§ 1289–1295.

[12] Gamble v. S., 35 Miss. 222. But in another case it is said that a charge of betting on the election of a certain person as president is well laid though electors only are selected: Porter v. S., 5 Sneed, 358.

[13] Lewellen v. S., 18 Tex. 538; Gamble v. S., 35 Miss. 222.

[14] S. v. Windell, 60 Ind. 300. Of course if the charge is of betting on the result of an election, the date may be fixed either before or after the election, as the bet may be made before the event or afterwards as to its result: Miller v. S., 33 Miss. 356.

[15] S. v. Cross, 2 Humph. 301; C. v. Shouse, 16 B. Mon. 325.

III. Common Gambler.

§ **1300. Who is.**— A person who makes a business of gambling or habitually engages in gaming is a common gambler,[1] and under some statutes is subject to severe punishment; but the term "common gambler" has no absolute and definite meaning, being used to define certain specific acts; for instance, the keeping open of any place, or the exhibiting of any device for gaming, may be made by statute to constitute the offense of being a common gambler.[2] So it may be provided that every person guilty of playing faro, or banking for others to do so, shall be a common gambler, and proof of one such act is sufficient to establish the offense.[3] But according to the usual employment of the term, the person charged must have actually engaged in playing,[4] or there must have been an apparent intent to play.[5] Proof of the mere reputation of being a common gambler is not sufficient to constitute the offense.[6] But the defendant is not entitled to a bill of particulars as to the acts relied upon as making him a common gambler.[7]

IV. Gaming in Public Places.

§ **1301. In general.**— Some statutes make it a distinct offense to play cards, dice or other enumerated games in public places.[8] These statutes do not imply that the playing of such games is in itself illegal, but only that it is against public policy to allow them to be played in public places, because likely to produce a disturbance.[9] Some statutes, however, limit the offense to betting on games or playing for money in such places.[10] The publicity being the essence of the offense, it is not necessary that

[1] Howard v. S., 64 Ind. 516.

[2] P. v. Sponsler, 1 Dak. 277.

[3] S. v. Melville, 11 R. I. 417. And see S. v. Carr, 6 Oreg. 133.

[4] Bowe v. S., 25 Ind. 415.

[5] Howard v. S., 64 Ind. 516.

[6] C. v. Hopkins, 2 Dana, 418.

[7] C. v. Moore, 2 Dana, 202.

[8] Roquemore v. S., 19 Ala. 528; Flake v. S., 19 Ala. 551; Rodgers v. S., 26 Ala. 76; Dreyfus v. S., 83 Ala. 54; S. v. Robinson, 40 S. C. 553; S. v. Langford, 3 Ired. 354.

[9] S. v. Brast, 31 W. Va. 380. Therefore it is immaterial whether there is betting or not: C. v. Terry, 2 Va. Cas. 77; Bosshard v. S., 25 Tex. Supp. 207.

[10] Ansley v. S., 36 Ark. 67. In Texas it seems that the offense is made out on proof of playing without evidence that anything was bet, but that defendant may negative guilt by showing that nothing was bet on the game: Wilcox v. S., 26 Tex. 145.

the indictment show that defendant played with any one.[1] The offense of gaming and that of playing in a public place are usually so connected that a prosecution under one statutory provision will bar a prosecution under the other.[2] So also, if defendant is charged with playing at a public place and also with betting, he cannot be convicted for playing alone, as the indictment amounts to a charge of betting;[3] and an indictment for playing a game at which a bet was made charges gaming and not simply playing.[4]

§ 1302. **The place.**— Statutes usually enumerate certain places where gaming is specially prohibited; such as taverns,[5] retail liquor houses,[6] and the like;[7] and it is not necessary in such cases to allege that the place is public, it being sufficient to show that it is of the statutory description. But where the statute relates to a public place it must be alleged and proved that the place is public.[8] Where the designation of the place is particular, such as tavern, retail liquor shop and the like, it covers all parts of the building or premises used for the purpose, and the playing in any room in such building or in any part of the premises, so far as they are thus occupied or used, is criminal, whether the room be public or not;[9] but if the description is general, as that of a public place, it will not include rooms occupied by others in the same building not public in their nature,[10] and not so connected with the public place as to

[1] Coggins v. S., 7 Port. 263. And see *supra*, § 1290.

[2] Fiddler v. S., 7 Humph. 508.

[3] Clayborne v. S., 103 Ala. 53.

[4] Johnson v. S., 75 Ala. 7.

[5] C. v. Terry, 2 Va. Cas. 77; Linkous v. C., 9 Leigh, 608.

[6] Coggins v. S., 7 Port. 263; Napier v. S., 50 Ala. 168; Ray v. S., 50 Ala. 172; Early v. S., 23 Tex. Ap. 364; S. v. Hox, 3 Dev. 116; Cole v. S., 9 Tex. 42; Royal v. S., 9 Tex. 449; Comer v. S., 26 Tex. Ap. 509. An indictment for playing at a dram-shop or grocery is not void for uncertainty, the word "grocery" not being used in the statute: Ballentine v. S., 48 Ark. 45.

[7] C. v. Wilson, 9 Leigh, 648. A navigable river is not, in Alabama, a highway within the statute against gaming on the highway: Glass v. S., 30 Ala. 529.

[8] S. v. Fuller, 31 Tex. 559; Elsberry v. S., 41 Tex. 158; Wallace v. S., 12 Tex. Ap. 479; Dailey v. S., 27 Tex. Ap. 569.

[9] Records v. S., 4 Harr. 554; Bryan v. S., 28 Ala. 65; Smith v. S., 22 Ala. 54; Ray v. S., 50 Ala. 172; Foster v. S., 84 Ala. 451; McCalman v. S., 96 Ala. 98; Russell v. S., 72 Ala. 222; S. v. Hox, 3 Dev. 116; Cole v. S., 9 Tex. 42; Stebbins v. S., 22 Tex. Ap. 32; Early v. S., 23 Tex. Ap. 364.

[10] S. v. Black, 9 Ired. 378; Dale v. S., 27 Ala. 31; Watson v. S., 13 Tex. Ap. 160; Johnson v. S., 36 Tex. 198; Galbreath v. S., 36 Tex. 200.

be a part of it.[1] But in any event the statutory provision does not extend beyond the prohibited building and appurtenances of the place designated or the place charged to be public, and therefore will not include outbuildings on the same lot,[2] or offices or shops in the same building not used for the specific purpose.[3] Sometimes the statute specially refers to outhouses, by which term is meant any house standing out and apart from a dwelling or business house,[4] and therefore it includes a still-house,[5] or unoccupied store.[6] As part of a public place it must be some place where people may and do go, though only occasionally,[7] or to which more than the players resort at a particular time.[8] A person playing must know what places are within the statutory prohibition.[9]

§ **1303. Further as to public place.**— Where the specific terms used in the statute are followed by general words, such as "or other public place," these terms are not to be considered as including the places already specifically mentioned.[10] The general term does not imply ownership by the public,[11] nor is it confined to places devoted solely to public use.[12] It implies a place where the public commonly resort or people have the privilege of going at pleasure.[13] The fact that the place is one designed primarily for private use, and kept locked so that no one can enter but by permission, will not show that it is not a public place if it appears that those who desire to play are admitted.[14] It is sufficient that it is a place resorted to for the prohibited purpose for the time being only,[15] as distinguished from a private place or one where there is no general invita-

[1] Pickens v. S., 100 Ala. 127; S. v. Hawkins, 91 N. C. 626; Winters v. S., 33 Tex. Ap. 395; Jackson v. S., 16 Tex. Ap. 373; Bowman v. S., 16 Tex. Ap. 513.

[2] C. v. Sanders, 5 Leigh, 751.

[3] Purcell v. C., 14 Grat. 679; S. v. Keisler, 6 Jones, 73. An indictment need not specify the place as one of a particular kind described by statute if it comes within the general description of a public place: Rosson v. S., 92 Ala. 76.

[4] Wheelock v. S., 15 Tex. 260.

[5] S. v. Faulkner, 2 McCord, 438.

[6] Swallow v. S,, 20 Ala. 30.

[7] Downey v. S., 90 Ala. 644.

[8] S. v. Norton, 19 Tex. 102. So where two or three persons went to an outhouse and played, held not sufficient: Cain v. S., 30 Ala. 534; Wheelock v. S., 15 Tex. 260.

[9] Johnson v. S., 75 Ala. 7.

[10] Windham v. S., 26 Ala. 69.

[11] Shihagan v. S., 9 Tex. 430; Lockhart v. S., 10 Tex. 275.

[12] Parker v. S., 26 Tex. 204.

[13] S. v. Brast, 31 W. Va. 380; Walker v. C., 2 Va. Cas. 515.

[14] Smith v. S., 52 Ala. 384.

[15] Campbell v. S., 17 Ala. 369.

tion to enter, and therefore a place where players assemble by invitation only is not included.[1] Thus, a club-room, to which only the club members and invited visitors are admitted, is not a public place.[2] A school-house is a public place within statutory description as well when the school is not in session as when it is.[3] It must appear that at the time complained of the place was a public place.[4] Whether any specific house or place is public within the statute is a question of law, if the char acter of the place is undisputed;[5] but whether the place comes within the general statutory description of a public place is a question of fact for the jury.[6] Under the circumstances of particular cases the following places have been held to be public, to wit: a ferry-boat,[7] a steam-boat,[8] a jury-room,[9] a barn near a tavern on muster day,[10] an infirmary,[11] a place so near the highway that the playing can be seen therefrom,[12] a public road,[13] a path used by children going to school.[14] Rooms in the rear of or over public places have been held so far connected therewith as to constitute a part of the place where occupied by the same parties as the public place itself.[15] Other cases in which places more or less public have been held not within the statute are cited in the note.[16]

1 Roquemore v. S., 19 Ala. 528; Coleman v. S., 20 Ala. 51; Clarke v. S., 12 Ala. 492; Sherrod v. S., 25 Ala. 78.

2 Grant v. S., 33 Tex. Ap. 527; Koenig v. S., 33 Tex. Ap. 367.

3 Cole v. S., 28 Tex. Ap. 536. *Contra*, McDaniels v. S., 35 Ala. 390.

4 Lynn v. S., 27 Tex. Ap. 590; Logan v. S., 24 Ala. 182.

5 Shihagan v. S., 9 Tex. 430; Skinner v. S., 87 Ala. 105.

6 Shihagan v. S., 9 Tex. 430; Cherry v. S., 30 Tex. 439; S. v. Alvey, 26 Tex. 155; Lowrie v. S., 43 Tex. 602; Fossett v. S., 18 Tex. Ap. 330.

7 Dickey v. S., 68 Ala. 508.

8 Coleman v. S., 13 Ala. 602.

9 Wilcox v. S., 26 Tex. 145.

10 Farmer v. C., 8 Leigh, 741.

11 Flake v. S., 19 Ala. 551.

12 Smith v. S., 23 Ala. 39; Henderson v. S., 59 Ala. 89.

13 Mills v. S., 20 Ala. 86.

14 Henderson v. S., 59 Ala. 89.

15 Moore v. S., 30 Ala. 550; Arnold v. S., 29 Ala. 46; Wilson v. S., 31 Ala. 371; Huffman v. S., 30 Ala. 532; s. c., 29 Ala. 40; Bentley v. S., 32 Ala. 596; Burnett v. S., 30 Ala. 19; Roquemore v. S., 19 Ala. 528; Skinner v. S., 30 Ala. 524; Redditt v. S., 17 Tex. 610.

16 So held as to a woods, brush or hollow: Bledsoe v. S., 21 Tex. 223; Bythwood v. S., 20 Ala. 47; Smith v. S., 23 Ala. 39; C. v. Vandine, 6 Grat. 689; a livery-stable: Metzer v. S., 31 Tex. Ap. 11; a sleeping room over a dance hall: Skinner v. S., 87 Ala. 105; a store house or office after public hours: C. v. Feazle, 8 Grat. 585; McCauley v. S., 26 Ala. 135; Smith v. S., 37 Ala. 472; Clarke v. S., 12 Ala. 492; Sherrod v. S., 25 Ala. 78.

§ **1304. Indictment and evidence.**— Where the charge is of playing in a public place, the place must be thus described,[1] for the name of the place itself is not enough.[2] Under some statutes designating particular places and "other public places," the general allegation that the place is public is sufficient;[3] but under others the generic term must be also stated,[4] unless facts showing the publicity are set out.[5] So, where the place is named and described as a public place, the allegation is sufficient[6] without adding the owner's name.[7] The place of playing is material if the charge is of playing in a public place, and if the statute specifies a public house or premises appurtenant thereto, the charge of playing on premises appurtenant is not supported by proof of playing in the house itself.[8]

V. POOL SELLING.

§ **1305. Statutory provisions.**— The business of pool selling is a species of gaming prohibited by special statutes in many of the states.[9] A pool is the money paid in by those buying a right in it, which is to go to the winner according to the agreement or scheme under which the money is paid;[10] and the seller is the person who manipulates the scheme and buys and sells

[1] Tolbert v. S., 87 Ala. 27; Robert v. C., 10 Leigh, 686; Bishop v. C., 13 Grat. 785; Jackson v. S., 16 Tex. Ap. 3; Bowman v. S., 16 Tex. Ap. 513; Jnihagan v. S., 9 Tex. 430.

[2] Bacchus v. S., 18 Tex. Ap. 15; Fossett v. S., 16 Tex. Ap. 375; Tummins v. S., 18 Tex. Ap. 13.

[3] Wortham v. C., 5 Rand. 669; Roquemore v. S., 19 Ala. 528; Flake v. S., 19 Ala. 551; Rodgers v. S., 26 Ala. 76.

[4] S. v. Barns, 25 Tex. 654; Millican v. S., 25 Tex. 664; S. v. Jurgins, 31 Tex. 588.

[5] S. v. Fuller, 31 Tex. 559; Elsberry v. S., 41 Tex. 158; Wallace v. S., 12 Tex. Ap. 479; Metzer v. S., 31 Tex. Ap. 11; Weiss v. S., 16 Tex. Ap. 431.

[6] Bosshard v. S., 25 Tex. Supp. 207; S. v. Lopez, 18 Tex. 33; Sheppard v. S., 1 Tex. Ap. 304.

[7] Prior v. S., 4 Tex. 383; Wilson v. S., 5 Tex. 21.

[8] Ballew v. S., 26 Tex. Ap. 483. It seems that proof of playing in a "public highway" does not sustain a charge of playing "in a public place:" Bush v. S., 18 Ala. 415.

[9] But pool selling is also within the usual statutes as to gaming, and may be punishable thereunder, although not covered by special statute: Swigart v. P., 154 Ill. 284. And see *supra*, § 1297. Although the business is illegal, the crime of embezzlement may be committed by the agent who receives the money, in appropriating it to his own use: S. v. Shadd, 80 Mo. 358. But see Lanahan v. Pattison, 1 Flip. 410, where it is held that a due-bill for the purchase price of lottery tickets sold contrary to law cannot be collected.

[10] C. v. Watson, 154 Mass. 135.

chances, or records or registers bets.[1] To regulate the bets and sell pools are parts of the same offense.[2] It makes no difference that the race on which the pool is made is outside the state,[3] nor that the seller claims to be only an agent to transfer wagers or results for a principal out of the state.[4] The indictment need not charge the names of the persons with whom the transaction was had.[5]

VI. KEEPING A GAMING HOUSE.

§ **1306. What criminal.**— At common law the keeping of a gaming house is held to be a nuisance,[6] because it has a tendency to bring together disorderly persons, promote immorality and lead to breaches of the peace.[7] In charging the common-law offense it is unnecessary either to allege or prove the names of the players or that there was gambling in fact,[8] it being sufficient that the house is kept for that purpose, thus creating a nuisance. An ordinance regulating gambling houses will not abrogate the common law in this respect where the ordinance does not fully cover the common-law offense.[9] But if by statute some games are made unlawful and others are licensed, games which are not mentioned will be considered lawful, the common law being superseded by such a statute.[10] The statutes on the subject are usually directed to the prevention of the evil of gaming and not for the suppression of the nuisance incident thereto.[11] The gaming need not have been

[1] C. v. Clancy, 154 Mass. 128; C. v. Swain, 160 Mass. 354; S. v. Howard, 9 Ind. Ap. 635; C. v. Ferry, 146 Mass. 203; C. v. Moody, 143 Mass. 177.

[2] C. v. Ferry, 146 Mass. 203. That the books, etc., are gaming devices, see *infra*, § 1310.

[3] Edwards v. S., 8 Lea, 411. And see *supra*, § 1297.

[4] P. v. Weithoff, 93 Mich. 631; Ransome v. S., 91 Tenn. 716.

[5] C. v. Swain, 160 Mass. 354.

[6] T. v. Sponsler, 1 Dak. 277; S. v. Layman, 5 Harr. 510; P. v. Jackson, 3 Denio, 101; Lord v. S., 16 N. H. 325; S. v. Crammey, 17 Minn. 72; U. S. v. Ismenard, 1 Cranch, C. C. 150; U. S. v. Milburn, 4 Cranch, C. C. 719; Rex v. Higginson, 2 Burr. 1232; Rex v. Rogier, 1 B. & C. 272. And see *supra*, § 1169.

[7] P. v. Jackson, 3 Denio, 101; Lord v. S., 16 N. H. 325; S. v. Savannah, T. U. P. Charl. 235. The offense is committed in causing and procuring many persons to resort to game for the defendant's profit, directly or indirectly: S. v. Layman, 5 Harr. 510.

[8] S. v. Prescott, 33 N. H. 212; S. v. Crammey, 17 Minn. 72.

[9] U. S. v. Holly, 3 Cranch, C. C. 656.

[10] P. v. Goldman, 1 Idaho, 714.

[11] S. v. Crogan, 8 Ia. 523; New Orleans v. Miller, 7 La. An. 651. Habit-

actually commenced or carried on if the place is fitted out for the purpose and with the intent prohibited by statute.[1] As the crime consists in keeping for gaming purposes, the game contemplated must be one having a hazard,[2] which may be money,[3] treats,[4] or the use of the table or room,[5] or anything of value.[6]

§ **1307. Place and time.**— Any place fitted up for the purpose and with the intention that it shall be used for gaming is a gambling house,[7] and it is unnecessary that this be the principal business,[8] or even that the game itself is played in the room if the betting is done there.[9] It matters not that the place is a sleeping-room,[10] and it is not essential that every person who desires shall have access to it,[11] it being sufficient that every person is admitted who desires to play and is vouched for by some one known to the keeper. Keeping a gambling house is not a continuing offense, and therefore the keeping for

ual use of a house for such purpose makes it a disorderly house: Brown v. S., 49 N. J. 61.

[1] Robbins v. P., 95 Ill. 175; S. v. Staker, 3 Ind. 570; S. v. Pancake, 74 Ind. 15; S. v. Miller, 5 Blackf. 502; McAlpin v. S., 3 Ind. 567.

[2] P. v. Sergeant, 8 Cow. 139; New Orleans v. Miller, 7 La. An. 651; S. v. Markham, 15 La. An. 498. It need not be a game of chance: S. v. Black, 94 N. C. 809. Whether it is a game of chance is for the jury: Glascock v. S., 10 Mo. 508. It is not necessary to charge that any particular game was played, but having so charged it is necessary to prove as charged: Dudney v. S., 22 Ark. 251. The sum lost or won need not be particularly specified: C. v. Crupper, 3 Dana. 466.

[3] Robbins v. P., 95 Ill. 175.

[4] S. v. Eaton, 85 Me. 237; S. v. Maurer, 7 Ia. 406; S. v. Cooster, 10 Ia. 453; S. v. Leicht, 17 Ia. 28; S. v. Bishel, 39 Ia. 42.

[5] S. v. Book, 41 Ia. 550. *Contra*, Harbaugh v. P., 40 Ill. 294; P. v. Sergeant, 8 Cow. 139. And see *supra*, § 1286.

[6] Lord v. S., 16 N. H. 325.

[7] Robbins v. P., 95 Ill. 175; S. v. Carpenter, 60 Conn. 97. The place must be resorted to for illegal gaming: C. v. Stahl, 7 Allen, 304; however, actual resorting to the premises is not necessary to constitute a keeping of a house for the purpose of betting with persons resorting thereto, but it is necessary to the offense of keeping a house to which persons resort for betting: Reg. v. Brown, 1 Q. B. D. (1895) 119. To prove the keeping of a house for the purpose of betting, receipt of telegrams at such house relating to bets, and conversations therein as to the same matter, may be shown, though the bets are actually made elsewhere: Ibid.; Reg. v. Worton, 1 Q. B. D. (1895) 227.

[8] S. v. Eaton, 85 Me. 237; Hitchins v. P., 39 N. Y. 454.

[9] P. v. Weithoff, 51 Mich. 203.

[10] S. v. Black, 94 N. C. 809.

[11] Lockhart v. S., 10 Tex. 275; Rice v. S., 10 Tex. 545.

one day,[1] or even the allowing to play but once, is enough.[2] If the offense is the keeping of such house without a license, the taking out of a license will be no excuse for the offense as already committed.[3]

§ **1308. The keeper.**— Under some statutes the keeper or person within the scope of the law must be the owner of the place,[4] but under others he may be a lessee,[5] or a person in charge of the place,[6] or a servant.[7] The lessor may be guilty although the place is kept by another;[8] but it must appear that he had knowledge of the prohibited purpose.[9] To render one guilty as keeper he must knowingly permit the playing;[10] that is, he must knowingly[11] keep the place for the prohibited purpose.[12] One who takes a percentage for the use of his rooms is guilty of keeping.[13]

§ **1309. The indictment and evidence.**— The indictment need not charge that the keeping was for gain or reward,[14] nor

[1] S. v. Pancake, 74 Ind. 15; S. v. Crogan, 8 Ia. 523; Buck v. S., 1 Ohio St. 62.

[2] S. v. Cooster, 10 Ia. 453; Hitchins v. P., 39 N. Y. 454; S. v. Markham, 15 La. An. 498.

[3] S. v. Raymond, 12 Mont. 226.

[4] Poteete v. S., 72 Ala. 558.

[5] Poteete v. S., 72 Ala. 558. It may be made criminal for the officers of an agricultural society to lease a portion of the grounds for the purpose of gaming: S. v. Darroch, 12 Ind. Ap. 527.

[6] Stevens v. P., 67 Ill. 587; S. v. Raymond, 12 Mont. 226; Chase v. P., 2 Colo. 509. But one may be guilty of permitting the playing of games in a public place without being the keeper of a gambling house: S. v. Currier, 23 Me. 43.

[7] Wooten v. S., 24 Fla. 335.

[8] S. v. Ebert, 40 Mo. 186; Voght v. S., 124 Ind. 358; Rodifer v. S., 74 Ind. 21; C. v. Dean, 1 Pick. 387; C. v. Bolkom, 3 Pick. 289. And see *supra*, §§ 1140-1142, 1174, 1248.

[9] Harris v. S., 5 Tex. 11.

[10] C. v. Crupper, 3 Dana, 466. If a table is ordinarily used for proper purposes it must appear that the keeper had knowledge of improper use; but such knowledge may be inferred in the absence of proof of want of knowledge: Yepperson v. S., 39 Tex. 48.

[11] S. v. Carpenter, 60 Conn. 97; Padgett v. S., 68 Ind. 46; S. v. Currier, 23 Me. 43; S. v. Cooster, 10 Ia. 453. An indictment for "unlawfully and knowingly" keeping is sufficient: S. v. Crowder, 39 Tex. 47. The lessor must have direct knowledge: S. v. Ebert, 40 Mo. 186. General reputation of the place held sufficient to give the lessor knowledge: Voght v. S., 124 Ind. 358; but not when lessor lives at a distance: Rodifer v. S., 74 Ind. 21; C. v. Dean, 1 Pick. 386. But see C. v. Bolkom, 3 Pick. 280.

[12] Stoltz v. P., 5 Ill. 168. The fact that defendant dealt the cards at a house where faro was played held *prima facie* evidence that he was the keeper: U. S. v. Miller, 4 Cranch, C. C. 104.

[13] Ransom v. S., 26 Fla. 364.

[14] C. v. Colton, 8 Gray, 488.

state who played,[1] nor that the house was his house.[2] Neither is it necessary to charge that a particular game was played; but if the offense is so charged it must be proved.[3] The indictment need not describe the house other than to state the location so as to bring it within the jurisdiction of the court.[4] A charge of permitting sufficiently shows knowledge.[5] The keeping and permitting may be charged in the same count as constituting the offense, without duplicity.[6] Circumstantial evidence may be sufficient to sustain a conviction.[7] Evidence that for previous years the house was used for proper purposes will be no excuse.[8] It need not be shown that the house was actually used for gaming if it appears that it was kept by defendant with that intention.[9] A witness should not be allowed to testify that it was so kept, as that is a question for the jury.[10] By statute, the finding of gaming implements, devices or appurtenances may be made *prima facie* evidence that the house is kept for such purposes, and such a statute will not be unconstitutional.[11]

VII. KEEPING AND EXHIBITING GAMING DEVICES OR TABLES.

§ 1310. What constitutes.— Some statutes provide for the offense of keeping and exhibiting gaming tables or devices as distinct from the offense of gaming.[12] Such statutes are usually

[1] S. v. Noland, 29 Ind. 212; S. v. Prescott, 33 N. H. 212; Chase v. P., 2 Colo. 509.

[2] S. v. Hubbard, 3 Ind. 530.

[3] Dudney v. S., 22 Ark. 251.

[4] Dohme v. S., 68 Ga. 339; S. v. Prescott, 33 N. H. 212. In charging such offense it is not necessary to say that the defendant "then and there" did the acts complained of: S. v. Marchant, 15 R. I. 539.

[5] S. v. Kaufman, 59 Ia. 273; S. v. Cure, 7 Ia. 479. It would be better to charge that the house was under the control of defendant: S. v. Middleton, 11 Ia. 246.

[6] Davis v. S., 100 Ind. 154; S. v. Cooster, 10 Ia. 453.

[7] S. v. Worth, R. M. Charl. 5.

[8] Scott v. S., 29 Ga. 263.

[9] Chase v. P., 2 Colo. 509; S. v. Miller, 5 Blackf. 502.

[10] Wheeler v. S., 42 Md. 563.

[11] Wooten v. S., 24 Fla. 335; Houston v. S., 24 Fla. 356.

[12] Setting up a gaming table is an entire offense, and inducing others to bet upon it a distinct one, but where both are perpetrated at the same time there is but one offense: Hinkle v. C., 4 Dana, 518; S. v. Pate, 67 Mo. 488. A charge of frequenting and keeping a gaming table charges but one offense, that of keeping: T. v. Copeley, 1 N. Mex. 571. On the other hand it is said that keeping a faro bank and betting on the same are offenses which may properly be joined: S. v. Holland, 22 Ark. 242. Merely betting at faro is not carrying on the game: Ex parte Ah Yem, 53 Cal. 246. But where a party is indicted under the charge of playing and conducting a game as owner,

so worded as to prohibit the keeping of certain devices by name; such as devices for playing faro,[1] keno,[2] banking games,[3] etc., and they then add, in general terms, "games of like nature."[4] But such general term includes only devices of like nature as those enumerated.[5] A table on which poker is played,[6] or dice

he may be convicted of playing at another's game: P. v. Ah Own, 85 Cal. 580. In Maryland the keeper of a faro table to be within the act must be a tavern-keeper or a retailer of spirituous liquors: U. S. v. Lefevre, 1 Cranch, C. C. 244.

[1] S. v. Holland, 22 Ark. 242; C. v. Monarch, 6 Bush, 301; Brown v. S., 10 Ark. 607; S. v. Whitworth, 8 Port. 434. Counts for exhibiting and betting may be joined: S. v. Holland, 22 Ark. 242.

[2] Hazen v. S., 18 Fla. 184; Trimble v. S., 27 Ark. 355; Portis v. S., 27 Ark. 360; Miller v. S., 48 Ala. 122.

[3] Parker v. S., 13 Tex. Ap. 213; Buford v. C., 14 B. Mon. 24. A pool table may be a gaming table, but it is not a "banking device" within the statutory prohibition: Webb v. S., 17 Tex. Ap. 205.

[4] They may thus cover a billiard table kept for hire: Holt v. C., 2 Bush, 33; C. v. Kinsley, 133 Mass. 578; Blanton v. S., 5 Blackf. 560; a bowling alley: S. v. Howery, 41 Tex. 506; or a crap table: Bell v. S., 32 Tex. Ap. 187. Shuffle board is a game of skill and the keeping of the table is not indictable: S. v. Bishop, 8 Ired. 266. Pico is within the mischief intended: Euper v. S., 35 Ark. 629. Tables for draw poker are included: Wren v. S., 70 Ala. 1; also pool tables: S. v. Kelly, 24 Tex. 182; Webb v. S., 17 Tex. Ap. 205; a "stock clock:" S. v. Grimes, 49 Minn. 443; haphazard: C. v. Wyatt, 6 Rand. 693; C. v. Fraize, 5 Bush, 325; a ten-pin alley or grand raffle: Stearnes v. S., 21 Tex. 692; an apparatus for drawing lots: Lowry v. S., 1 Mo. 518. "Any kind of a gaming table or gambling device for the purpose of playing any game of chance for money," etc., includes cards: Eubanks v. S., 5 Mo. 450; S. v. Herryford, 19 Mo. 377. But see S. v. Gilmore, 98 Mo. 206. A crack in the floor may constitute a gaming device: S. v. Flack, 24 Mo. 378. A horse-race is not a device: S. v. Hayden, 31 Mo. 35; but black-boards, sheets, manifold books and policy slips for placing bets on horse-races may be: C. v. Adams, 160 Mass. 310; S. v. Shaw, 39 Minn. 153; but see *contra*, P. v. Weithoff, 93 Mich. 631. The statute does not include selling pools on a horse-race: James v. S., 63 Md. 242. Game cocks are not implements for gambling within the statute: Coolidge v. Choate, 11 Met. 79. It is not necessary to describe the "gambling device;" it is sufficient to allege the time, place and person to whom exhibited and that the name is unknown: Pemberton v. S., 85 Ind. 507.

[5] S. v. Bryant, 90 Mo. 534; Huff v. C., 14 Grat. 648. The question of "like character" is one of law, but the question whether a particular table is of the species is one of fact: Mims v. S., 88 Ga. 458. Keeping a policy shop is not within an ordinance forbidding the keeping of any rolly-pooly, keno or faro table or other instrument or device for the purpose of gaming: Marquis v. Chicago, 27 Ill. Ap. 251. But a statute simply prohibiting generally the keeping of all gaming devices has been held void for uncertainty: S. v. Mann, 2 Oreg. 238.

[6] Lyle v. S., 30 Tex. Ap. 118.

are thrown,[1] is not a gaming device; nor are ordinary playing cards a gaming device in this sense.[2] By some statutes it is necessary that the keeping be for "hire, gain or reward," and without that element the offense is not committed.[3] The evil aimed at is that of gaming;[4] but the crime is complete if the table or device is shown to have been kept for the purpose, although there is no proof of actual playing.[5] It is not necessary that the keeper himself shall play;[6] and he may either be owner, agent or servant.[7] The keeper of a pool table will not be punishable unless he knew or could by reasonable diligence have known that the table was used for gaming purposes.[8] Of course, the fact that he is licensed to keep such table or device will be an excuse,[9] unless the provisions of the license are vio-

1 Chappell v. S., 27 Tex. Ap. 310.

2 S. v. Gilmore, 98 Mo. 206, 8 Am. Cr. R. 312.

3 P. v. Weithoff, 100 Mich. 393.

4 Wolz v. S., 33 Tex. 331. The statute was intended to suppress contrivances used for gambling purposes, and not those ordinarily used for amusement, although money may be lost and won: Ritte v. C., 18 B. Mon. 35. An essential of the device is that it is kept for the purpose that the keeper gain money: Pratt v. S., 19 Ohio St. 270. The keeper himself must bet: Sumner v. S., 74 Ind. 52. A bet of checks is enough: Ashlock v. C., 7 B. Mon. 44.

5 S. v. Thomas, 50 Ind. 292; App v. S., 90 Ind. 73. It is not necessary to charge that the game was for money: S. v. Ellis, 4 Mo. 474; S. v. Flack, 24 Mo. 378. Nor is it necessary to prove any money was bet: S. v. Fulton, 19 Mo. 680. It need not be proved that a thing of value was bet: Simms v. S., 60 Ga. 145. It is not necessary to charge the "unlawful and wilful keeping:" S. v. Howe, 100 N. C. 449; nor to state how much money was lost and won: Montee v. C., 3 J. J. Marsh. 132; nor to charge in the indictment that the place was kept for play or that it took place: Needham v. S., 1 Tex. 139. It is not enough that the game is merely permitted: Ervine v. C., 5 Dana, 216. A table accessible to any one who may choose to play on it is a public one, for the keeping of which without a license defendant is liable, though no charge was made for playing, it being understood that the loser was to treat from the bar: Schmetzer v. S., 63 Md. 420.

6 C. v. Burns, 4 J. J. Marsh. 177.

7 U. S. v. Conner, 1 Cranch, C. C. 102. He may be a servant: Trimble v. S., 27 Ark. 355; Portis v. S., 27 Ark. 360. An incorporated club may be guilty under the act: Germania v. S., 7 Md. 1. A party who has a room where the game is played and keeps the cards is guilty: Miller v. S., 48 Ala. 122. One who sets up a billiard table and rents it to another is liable: U. S. v. Duval, 2 Cranch, C. C. 42. One who operates for another on a salary a gaming device is guilty, though he has no interest in the affair further than his salary: Atkins v. S., 95 Tenn. 474.

8 Smith v. S., 28 Tex. Ap. 102.

9 Harris v. S., 9 Tex. Ap. 308; Houghton v. S., 41 Tex. 136; S. v. Johnson, 41 Tex. 504; Overby v. S., 18 Fla. 178. In Arkansas it seems

lated.[1] The payment of a tax upon a table or other such property will not justify its use as a gaming device.[2] The offense is not a continuing one, and a single act is sufficient.[3] It is immaterial under these provisions whether the place be public or private,[4] and therefore the indictment need not describe the building, and need only state the place with sufficient definiteness to show the jurisdiction.[5]

§ **1311. Procedure; indictment.**— It is usually sufficient to charge the offense in the language of the statute, where the statute specifies certain things as gambling devices.[6] In general, if the indictment states that the device was for the purpose of gaming it is sufficient whether the game is mentioned or not.[7]

§ **1312. Penalty; destruction of implements.**— Sometimes the penalty imposed is enforceable in an action *qui tam;*[8] sometimes the statutes have imposed disqualification for voting or holding office as a penalty.[9] It is usual to provide for the seizure and destruction of the implements used,[10] and to warrant such destruction it is not necessary to prove guilty knowledge on the part of the owner.[11] After seizure the implements are in the custody of the court and cannot be recovered by action,[12]

necessary to prove that the party has refused to pay his tax: Mayers v. S., 8 Ark. 222.

[1] Reeves v. S., 12 Tex. Ap. 199. A municipal license issued without authority will be no protection: Schuster v. S., 48 Ala. 199; S. v. Caldwell, 3 La. An. 435.

[2] S. v. Doon, R. M. Charl. 1.

[3] App v. S., 90 Ind. 73.

[4] Lowry v. S., 1 Mo. 518; S. v. Horan, 11 Tex. 144.

[5] App v. S., 90 Ind. 73.

[6] C. v. Monarch, 6 Bush, 301; S. v. Whitworth, 8 Port. 434; Brown v. S., 10 Ark. 607; S. v. Holland, 22 Ark. 242. And in Texas it seems necessary to also state that the device was kept for the purpose of gaming: Kramer v. S., 18 Tex. Ap. 13; Doyle v. S., 19 Tex. Ap. 410.

[7] Bibb v. S., 84 Ala. 13; Toney v. S., 61 Ala. 1; Frisbie v. S., 1 Oreg. 264; Simms v. S., 60 Ga. 145; Longworth v. S., 41 Tex. 508; S. v. Howery, 41 Tex. 506; Parker v. S., 13 Tex. Ap. 213. The game of keno not being specifically named in the statute, the court will not take judicial notice of its character: C. v. Monarch, 6 Bush, 298. An information which did not charge the keeping of a gambling game, held defective: S. v. Davis, 20 La. An. 354.

[8] S. v. Fillyaw, 3 Ala. 735. But even where a portion of the penalty goes to the informer an indictment may be proper: U. S. v. Evans, 4 Cranch, C. C. 105.

[9] Harper v. C., 93 Ky. 290.

[10] Willis v. Warren, 1 Hilt. 590; P. v. Sponsler, 1 Dak. 277.

[11] C. v. Gaming Implements, 155 Mass. 165.

[12] Willis v. Warren, 1 Hilt. 590.

and the possession of the officer is presumed to be rightful.[1] But the power of the court over the implements ends with the pronouncing of final judgment, and any order it may make with reference to their disposition should be made before or in connection with such final judgment.[2]

VIII. Allowing Games to be Played on the Premises.

§ **1313. When criminal.**— The offense of allowing or permitting gaming upon one's own premises is specially provided for by some statutes in order to discourage gaming.[3] The crime is distinct from that of keeping a house or shop or other place resorted to for the purpose of gaming.[4] Guilty knowledge is a necessary element of the crime, and the usual charge is that the defendant knowingly permitted.[5] But it is presumed that the occupant of the house has knowledge of games carried on therein.[6] It is the duty of the owner to protect his premises against illegal use.[7] As these provisions are directed against the evil of gaming, they apply to all games, such, for instance, as games with cards;[8] or other forms of games of chance,[9] or, indeed, any kind of game which comes within the statutory prohibition of gaming,[10] unless, of course, some special forms of

1 Way v. T., 1 Wash. 415.

2 S. v. Robbins, 124 Ind. 308.

3 C. v. Lampton, 4 Bibb, 261; S. v. Scaggs, 33 Mo. 92; Foster v. T., 1 Wash. 411; Jacobi v. S., 59 Ala. 71; Stoltz v. P., 5 Ill. 168. In Texas there is no such offense: S. v. Bullion, 42 Tex. 77. The permitting and encouraging of gaming in this manner is indictable under statutes as to gaming: Fugate v. S., 2 Humph. 397.

4 S. v. Currier, 23 Me. 43.

5 S. v. Mathis, 3 Ark. 84; Marston v. C., 18 B. Mon. 485; Harris v. S., 5 Tex. 11; S. v. Middleton, 11 Ia. 246. An indictment cannot be sustained when it appears that the gaming was carried on in a tavern without the tavern-keeper's knowledge, in a room which he had leased for a bedroom: C. v. Watson, 2 Duv. 408.

6 Robinson v. S., 24 Tex. 152; Mount v. S., 7 Sm. & M. 277. It is no defense to a prosecution of a licensed retailer for allowing gaming that the room where it was done was leased by him to another person, unless he satisfies the jury that he let it for a lawful purpose: Campbell v. S., 55 Ala. 89.

7 Roberts v. C., 11 B. Mon. 3. But of course ownership or control of the premises must be shown: Biles v. S., 25 Tex. Ap. 441.

8 S. v. Lewis, 12 Wis. 434; Horan v. S., 24 Tex. 161; Kimbrough v. S., 25 Tex. Ap. 397; S. v. Gilmore, 98 Mo. 206, 8 Am. Cr. R. 312.

9 C. v. Branham, 3 Bush, 1; C. v. Price, 8 Leigh, 757; C. v. Goding, 3 Met. 130; Marston v. C., 18 B. Mon. 485.

10 Wortham v. S.. 59 Miss. 179; Ward v. S., 17 Ohio St. 32.

games may be excepted from the statute,[1] and it seems unnecessary that the game shall have been actually played.[2] But perhaps it is necessary that there shall be more than one instance of playing to constitute the crime.[3] This form of statutory provision, unlike that previously discussed in regard to gaming in public places,[4] does not imply publicity of the place, so that it may be committed in a private house.[5] The highway in front of a person's house is not a part of his premises, in such a way as to make him liable for allowing others to play games therein.[6] Some statutes of this nature limit the offense to permitting gaming in a public house, such as a tavern or retail liquor house.[7] The offense is one committed by the person having control of the place, and therefore it may be committed by the managers of a social club,[8] or by a lessor who has some control of the premises,[9] but not by a lessor retaining no control,[10] nor by an interloper having no right on the premises.[11] The charge of keeping the house where play was permitted sufficiently shows occupancy.[12] It is unnecessary in an indictment to state the names of the persons playing.[13] The indictment must specify with some certainty the offense.[14] Thus, if it charges the renting of certain rooms to two persons for card playing, while the proof shows that they were rented to one alone, there should be an acquittal;[15] and an indictment for permitting playing of cards in a saloon is not supported by evidence that the playing was in a disconnected room over the saloon.[16]

1 Stith v. S., 13 Ark. 680; S. v. Stillwell, 20 Ark. 96.

2 Ward v. P., 23 Ill. Ap. 510.

3 Armstrong v. S., 4 Blackf. 247.

4 *Supra*, § 1301.

5 S. v. Brice, 2 Brev. 66. Under statutes applicable to a steamboat in rivers of the state, a charge of permitting in a steamboat navigating Mobile river is not proved by evidence of playing in Mobile bay: Johnson v. S., 74 Ala. 337.

6 Perez v. S., 48 Ala. 356.

7 C. v. Price, 8 Leigh, 757; C. v. Bolkom, 3 Pick. 281; Farmer v. S., 45 Ark. 95; Ballentine v. S. 48 Ark. 45. In charging an offense under such a statute, the house must be particularly described, so as to bring it within the provision: S. v. Mansker, 36 Tex. 364.

8 Jacobi v. S., 59 Ala. 71.

9 Kimbrough v. S., 25 Tex. Ap. 397.

10 Diebel v. S., 68 Miss. 725.

11 Calvert v. C., 5 B. Mon. 264.

12 Stoltz v. P., 5 Ill. 168.

13 Foster v. T., 1 Wash. 411; Romp v. S., 3 Greene (Ia.), 276; Horan v. S., 24 Tex. 161; Clark v. S., 19 Ala. 552. *Contra*, Ball v. S., 7 Blackf. 242; Sowle v. S., 11 Ind. 492. And see *supra*, § 1209.

14 C. v. Perrigo, 3 Metc. (Ky.) 5.

15 Cronin v. S., 30 Tex. Ap. 278.

16 O'Brien v. S., 10 Tex. Ap. 544.

IX. GAMING BY MINORS.

§ 1314. Permitting to game or to resort.— In a number of the states persons who keep billiard or pool or other gaming tables are prohibited from allowing minors to play thereat or even to resort to places where such gaming is carried on.[1] The place must be a public one;[2] but it is not necessary, according to some statutes, that the minor shall actually engage in betting or gaming, the allowing him to play games without betting in such a place being prohibited.[3] Some statutes are so framed as to be only applicable to promoting gaming by minors, the intent being to keep minors from the gaming table, and under such a statute the word "bet" implies the wager of money or thing of value.[4] If the statute prohibits the allowing of minors to congregate in such places, it must be shown, to constitute the offense, that two or more minors came together in such a place, for congregation implies joint action or co-operation.[5] Sometimes it is the allowing of minors to play in or frequent such places without the consent of parent or guardian which is prohibited.[6] There is here the same conflict as elsewhere in regard to whether want of knowledge of the age of the minor will constitute a defense, some cases holding that the persons who conduct such establishments must know at their peril whether those resorting to them are of age,[7] while the contrary is also maintained.[8] So it is held that the keeper of a place of the kind will be liable for the unauthorized act of his servant in charge in permitting a minor to resort thereto, although without his knowledge and against his directions;[9] but there are also cases to the contrary in regard to analogous offenses of illegal sales of liquors to minors and the like.[10] In

[1] See *supra*, § 59.

[2] Manheim v. S., 66 Ind. 65; S. v. Dupies, 91 Ind. 233. But to constitute a saloon within such statute it is not necessary that intoxicating liquors be sold. The sale of other liquors or refreshments may constitute the place a saloon as distinct from a dram-shop: Snow v. S., 50 Ark. 557.

[3] Bond v. S., 52 Ind. 457; S. v. Ward, 57 Ind. 537; Ready v. S., 62 Ind. 1; Green v. C., 5 Bush, 327.

[4] Martin v. S., 71 Miss. 87.

[5] Powell v. S., 62 Ind. 531.

[6] C. v. Emmons, 98 Mass. 6; Green v. C., 5 Bush, 327; Conyers v. S., 50 Ga. 103; Kiley v. S., 120 Ind. 65.

[7] C. v. Emmons, 98 Mass. 6; S. v. Probasco, 62 Ia. 400.

[8] Stern v. S., 53 Ga. 229. And see *supra*, §§ 128, 1257.

[9] S. v. Probasco, 62 Ia. 400.

[10] See *supra*, § 1237, where cases on both sides are collected.

determining the age of the person claimed to have been a minor, his appearance on the stand as a witness may be considered by the jury.[1] The indictment should show that a game was played, and, if it charges playing by the minor, with whom it was played.[2] The game played must be correctly stated;[3] and though it is not necessary to negative the exception in the statute as to playing in a private house, yet the act charged should be alleged to have been illegal.[4]

[1] C. v. Emmons, 98 Mass. 6. But the jury may take into account such appearance in determining whether accused believed the person to be of age: Bird v. S., 104 Ind. 384; Robinius v. S., 63 Ind. 235.

[2] Alexander v. S., 48 Ind. 394; Donniger v. S., 52 Ind. 326; Zook v. S., 47 Ind. 463. If the allegation is that the minor played with persons to the grand jurors unknown, proof of playing with one person constitutes a variance: Moore v. S., 65 Ind. 213.

[3] Squier v. S., 66 Ind. 317.

[4] S. v. Dupies, 91 Ind. 233; Alexander v. S., 48 Ind. 394.

CHAPTER 65.

LOTTERIES.

§ **1315. Definition.**— A lottery is a scheme for the distribution of property by lot or chance among persons who have paid or agreed to pay a valuable consideration for the privilege of participating in such scheme.[1] In some cases the element of consideration has been left out of the definition,[2] but where the point has been raised, it has always been held to be an essential ingredient of the offense.[3] The crime of conducting a lottery is similar to that of gaming, and in fact a lottery is a species of gaming.[4] The evil which the law is designed to remedy is much the same as in gaming, being the excitement of an inordinate desire for gain, leading to an arousing of the baser passions and tending to mendicancy and idleness.[5] In applying the law the courts have taken this as the evil to be rem-

[1] S. v. Moren, 48 Minn. 555; S. v. Clarke, 33 N. H. 329; P. v. Art Union, 7 N. Y. 240; P. v. Art Union, 13 Barb. 577; Bennett v. Art Union, 5 Sandf. 614; Hull v. Ruggles, 56 N. Y. 424; Wooden v. Shotwell, 23 N. J. 465; Ballock v. S., 73 Md. 1; S. v. Boneil, 42 La. An. 1110. A lottery is a game in which a price is paid for a chance for a prize: C. v. Sullivan, 146 Mass. 142.

[2] S. v. Kansas Merc. Ass'n, 45 Kan. 351; S. v. Shorts, 32 N. J. 398; S. v. Lovell, 39 N. J. 458; Randle v. S., 42 Tex. 580. And see the definitions in Webster's dictionary and Bouvier's law dictionary. The consideration may be money or anything of value: Hudelson v. S., 94 Ind. 426.

[3] Hull v. Ruggles, 56 N. Y. 424; Wilkinson v. Gill, 10 Hun, 156; Governor v. Art Union, 7 N. Y. 228; Buckalew v. S., 62 Ala. 334; Yellowstone Kit v. S., 88 Ala. 196; S. v. Bryant, 74 N. C. 207; C. v. Wright, 137 Mass. 250; S. v. Clarke, 33 N. H. 329; S. v. Shorts, 32 N. J. 398; S. v. Mumford, 73 Mo. 647; Thomas v. P., 59 Ill. 160; U. S. v. Olney, 1 Deady, 461. The gratuitous distribution of business cards entitling the holders each to a chance in a drawing of a piano has been held not to be a lottery or gift enterprise, there being no valuable consideration paid for the chance to participate: Cross v. P., 18 Colo. 321.

[4] Thomas v. P., 59 Ill. 160; Eubanks v. S., 3 Heisk. 488; Bell v. S., 5 Sneed, 507; and as to gift enterprises, see *supra*, § 1285. But statutes as to particular gaming devices are not necessarily applicable to lotteries: Marquis v. Chicago, 27 Ill. Ap. 251; Buckalew v. S., 62 Ala. 334; Eslava v. S., 44 Ala. 406.

[5] Yellowstone Kit v. S., 88 Ala. 196; Johnson v. S., 83 Ala. 65.

edied,[1] and uncertain or doubtful terms have been construed with this object in mind.[2] While as a matter of fact many lotteries have been established and conducted for the purpose of raising funds for charitable or other laudable enterprises, yet the purpose to which the proceeds of the lottery are to be devoted is immaterial in determining whether it is criminal in its character.[3] As a rule lottery schemes have no distinct names, as have many of the well-known games, but some schemes or devices having distinct names have been held to be lotteries, such as playing policy,[4] raffles,[5] pools, as on horse-races,[6] gift enterprises,[7] and any scheme for the sale of goods or merchandise whereby a prize is given to some buyer to be determined by lot or chance.[8] These schemes are so various that it is difficult to cover them even by a general description; but in most of them the chance to secure something of value by lot, usually evidenced by a ticket, is given as an additional inducement to the purchasers of goods of a particular description or of a specified value.[9] So a sale of public bonds with a bonus to some of the purchasers depending upon the turn of a wheel of fortune

[1] Ehrgott v. New York, 96 N. Y. 264.

[2] S. v. Moren, 48 Minn. 555; Boyd v. S., 53 Ala. 601.

[3] Thomas v. P., 59 Ill. 160.

[4] P. v. Elliott, 74 Mich. 264; P. v. Hess, 85 Mich. 128; S. v. Carpenter, 60 Conn. 97; S. v. Kansas Merc. Ass'n, 45 Kan. 351.

[5] S. v. Overton, 16 Nev. 136. *Contra*, S. v. Pinchback, 2 Mill Const. 128. Raffling is gaming: S. v. De Boy, 117 N. C. 702; Long v. S., 22 Tex. Ap. 194. *Contra*, Norton v. S., 15 Ark. 71. And see *supra*, § 1285; C. v. Garland, 5 Rand. 652. Raffling may be lawful where properly licensed: Hawkins v. S., 33 Ala. 433.

[6] S. v. Lovell, 39 N. J. 458. But pool selling is not included in "lotteries for a drawing or disposing of money or any property whatever:" P. v. Reilly, 50 Mich. 384.

[7] Long v. S., 73 Md. 527; S. v. Bryant, 74 N. C. 207; Randle v. S., 42 Tex. 580. A gift enterprise is said to be a scheme for the division or distribution of certain articles of property to be determined by chance: Lohman v. S., 81 Ind. 15.

[8] So held as to prize candy packages: Holoman v. S., 2 Tex. Ap. 610; S. v. Lumsden, 89 N. C. 572; and the sale of keys, one of which will open a box containing a prize: Davenport v. Ottawa, 54 Kan. 711; and as to sale of tickets to an entertainment where those who attend are entitled to participate in the distribution of prizes: Thomas v. P., 59 Ill. 160; S. v. Overton, 16 Nev. 136.

[9] Dunn v. P., 40 Ill. 465; S. v. Mumford, 73 Mo. 647; U. S. v. Olney, 1 Abb. (U. S.) 275. So where a number of persons agreed to pay one dollar each week into a common fund from which a suit of clothes should be purchased each week for one of the number, determined by lot, until all were supplied, *held*, that the enterprise was a lottery: S. v. Moren, 48 Minn. 555.

constitutes a lottery scheme.[1] By the federal statutes regulating the use of the United States mails, it is made criminal to send through the mails any circulars or advertisements or even a newspaper containing an advertisement of a lottery scheme, but this matter will be discussed under the head of the postal laws.[2]

§ **1316. Statutes.**— Keeping or operating a lottery is not an offense at common law, and it is not punishable as a nuisance as is the keeping of a gaming house.[3] So far as such acts are criminal at all they are made so by statute, and the offenses thus created vary according to the wording of the various statutes.[4] Such statutes are applicable within the jurisdiction of the state to both domestic and foreign lotteries.[5] An exception is sometimes made, however, as to lotteries authorized by law, meaning those authorized by the law of the state and not those authorized by foreign law.[6] Under the statutes of most of the states it is unlawful to operate or conduct a lottery, or to aid and assist it by selling tickets,[7] advertising it,[8] or promoting it in any manner.[9] Where lotteries are thus forbidden, a contract which contemplates the establishment or conducting of a lottery is void, and no relief can be had for breach thereof.[10]

§ **1317. Constitutionality.**— Lotteries are so far questionable as to their effect upon the public morals that they come within the power of police regulation of the states, and may therefore be prohibited even though a grant or charter to carry on such an enterprise is thereby impaired or practically destroyed, for the business, like any other, is subject to proper police regulation.[11] But the state cannot in the exercise of its

[1] Ballock v. S., 73 Md. 1; Horner v. U. S., 147 U. S. 449.

[2] *Infra*, § 1334.

[3] P. v. Jackson, 3 Denio, 101.

[4] Boyd v. S., 61 Ala. 177; Marks v. S., 45 Ala. 38; S. v. Randle, 41 Tex. 292.

[5] S. v. Moore, 63 N. H. 9; S. v. Sykes, 28 Conn. 225.

[6] P. v. Sturdevant, 23 Wend. 418; C. v. Dana, 2 Met. 329.

[7] C. v. Gillespie, 7 Serg. & R. 469.

[8] S. v. Willis, 78 Me. 70; Lohman v. S., 81 Ind. 15; C. v. Clapp, 5 Pick. 41; S. v. Kaub, 90 Mo. 196; Louisville Courier-Journal v. C., 92 Ky. 22; S. v. Sykes, 28 Conn. 225.

[9] C. v. Horton, 2 Gray, 69.

[10] Lanahan v. Pattison, 1 Flip. 410. But one who embezzles from a pool on a horse race may be punished criminally: S. v. Shadd, 80 Mo. 358.

[11] Stone v. Mississippi, 101 U. S. 814; Moore v. S., 48 Miss. 147; P. v. Noelke, 94 N. Y. 137. *Contra*, Kellum v. S., 66 Ind. 588. And see *supra*, § 75. As

police power prohibit enterprises into which no element of chance enters,[1] and it has been held unconstitutional to prohibit the use of the prize system among shopkeepers.[2] Congress cannot, of course, legislate directly as to lotteries, as that would be the exercise of a police power not given to it; but as the regulation of the mails is entirely within the province of the federal government, statutes have been passed forbidding their use for the dissemination of matter of this character, and such statutes are entirely within the scope of congressional powers.[3]

§ **1318. The indictment.**— As in other statutory offenses it is usually held sufficient to follow the words of the statute,[4] and it is enough to charge the conducting of a lottery without describing the offense more particularly.[5] It is unnecessary to state the purpose of the lottery.[6] If the ticket is set out in the indictment and shows the nature of the scheme to be such as to constitute a lottery, the charge is in this respect sufficient.[7] An indictment for advertising a lottery which sets out a copy of the indictment, showing the nature of the scheme and other facts making the advertisement criminal, is sufficient.[8] There is some diversity in the decisions as to indictments for the sale of lottery tickets in regard to the necessity of setting out copies of tickets, describing the subject-matter of the lottery, the name of the owner, the place of the drawing, etc.; but as these matters must depend largely upon the

to the constitutionality of particular lottery statutes, see Broadbent v. S., 7 Md. 416; S. v. Overton, 16 Nev. 136; S. v. Phalen, 3 Harr. 441.

1 Long v. S., 74 Md. 565.

2 P. v. Gillson, 109 N. Y. 389.

3 In re Rapier, 143 U. S. 110; Horner v. U. S., 143 U. S. 207. And see *infra*, § 1334.

4 C. v. Harris, 13 Allen, 534; France v. S., 6 Baxt. 478.

5 C. v. Harris, 13 Allen, 534. It is sufficient to charge the selling of tickets for a lottery called a raffle: S. v. Kennon, 21 Mo. 262; or the setting up of a lottery without legislative authority: Salomon v. S., 27 Ala. 26; or to charge the setting up of a lottery for the purpose of disposing of money, "a more particular description of which is unknown:" P. v. Taylor, 3 Denio, 91. For other cases as to sufficiency of indictment see Boullemet v. S., 28 Ala. 83; S. v. Sykes, 28 Conn. 225; C. v. Eaton, 15 Pick. 273; C. v. Horton, 2 Gray, 69; S. v. Follet, 6 N. H. 53. Usually a violation of the statutes as to lotteries is indictable, but not always: Swan v. S., 29 Ga. 616.

6 France v. S., 6 Baxt. 478; Charles v. P., 1 N. Y. 180. *Contra*, P. v. Payne, 3 Denio, 88.

7 C. v. Thacher, 97 Mass. 583.

8 S. v. Willis, 78 Me. 70; S. v. Kaub, 90 Mo. 196.

statutory language, it is sufficient to give the cases in a note.[1] The indictment may charge the sending out of a number of circulars,[2] or the sale of several tickets sold at once,[3] or the publication of an advertisement stating both the place of sale of tickets and the place of drawing,[4] without ground of objection as to duplicity.

[1] P. v. Noelke, 94 N. Y. 137; P. v. Taylor, 3 Denio, 99; S. v. Willis, 78 Me. 70; S. v. Ochsner, 9 Mo. Ap. 216; C. v. Bierman, 13 Bush, 345; Whitney v. S., 10 Ind. 404; France v. S., 6 Baxt. 478; C. v. Horton, 2 Gray, 69; C. v. Sheedy, 159 Mass. 55; C. v. Clapp, 5 Pick. 41; S. v. Shorts, 32 N. J. 398; Markle v. S., 3 Ind. 535.

[2] U. S. v. Patty, 9 Biss. 429, 2 Fed. R. 664.

[3] Fontaine v. S., 6 Baxt. 514.

[4] Lohman v. S., 81 Ind. 15.

CHAPTER 66.

VIOLATION OF SUNDAY LAWS.

§ 1319. **Nature of regulations; constitutionality.**— From very early times there have been statutory regulations as to the observance of the Sabbath,[1] and it may be safely said that, aside from any express statutory provision, a breach of the Sabbath is a misdemeanor, but it is not a breach of the peace if without noise or disturbance to the public.[2] A Sunday law is purely a police regulation, and therefore is not in violation of the provisions in the federal and state constitutions as to the establishment of religion or prohibiting the free exercise thereof.[3] Such statutes have probably been passed in all the states, and in none of them have they been held unconstitutional as interfering with religious freedom;[4] nor are such statutes uncon-

[1] The earliest recognition of the Christian Sabbath as a civil institution seems to have been in the edict of Constantine the Great (A. D. 221), decreeing a rest on that day from all labor except agricultural pursuits. In England regulations as to the observance of the Sabbath are found from the time of King Alfred to the present, an enumeration of which would be of no advantage; but see references to the subject in 2 Inst. 264; 4 Bl. Com. 69; Drury v. De Fontaine, 1 Taunt. 131; Reg. v. Cleworth, 4 B. & S. 927.

[2] C. v. Eyre, 1 Serg. & R. 347.

[3] Ex parte Burke, 59 Cal. 6; P. v. Bellet, 99 Mich. 151; Judefind v. S., 78 Md. 510; 1 Dill. Mun. Corp., § 397; Cooley's Const. Lim. 584, 725.

[4] C. v. Wolf, 3 Serg. & R. 48; Updegraph v. C., 11 Serg. & R. 394; Specht v. C., 8 Pa. St. 312; Johnston v. C., 22 Pa. St. 102; Society v. C., 52 Pa. St. 125; Story v. Elliot, 8 Cow. 27; Neuendorff v. Duryea, 69 N. Y. 557; Lindenmuller v. P., 33 Barb. 548; C. v. Colton, 8 Gray, 488; C. v. Has, 122 Mass. 40; C. v. Dextra, 143 Mass. 28; Warner v. Smith, 8 Conn. 14; S. v. Noyes, 47 Me. 189; Thorpe v. Rutland & B. R. Co., 27 Vt. 140; Bloom v. Richards, 2 Ohio St. 387; Voglesong v. S., 9 Ind. 112; S. v. Ambs, 20 Mo. 214; Charleston v. Benjamin, 2 Strobh. 508; Karwisch v. Atlanta, 44 Ga. 404; P. v. Griffin, 1 Ida. (N. S.) 476; Gunn v. S., 89 Ga. 341; Shover v. S., 7 Ark. 259; Lewis v. S., 21 Ark. 209; Gabel v. Houston, 29 Tex. 335; Sunday Law Cases, 30 Tex. 521; Ex parte Sundstrom, 25 Tex. Ap. 133; Usener v. S., 8 Tex. Ap. 177; In re King, 46 Fed. R. 905. In California there has been some objection as to the validity of such statutes, but they are now upheld: Ex parte Burke, 59 Cal. 6; Ex parte Koser, 60 Cal. 177; Ex parte Andrews, 18 Cal. 678; Ex parte Bird, 19 Cal. 130. *Contra,* Ex parte Newman, 9 Cal. 502. The following cases are to

stitutional as depriving a subject of his liberty or property without due process of law, or denying him equal protection of the law.[1] But a statute prohibiting special occupations on Sunday which are no more objectionable than others which are permitted is unconstitutional, for it amounts to special legislation and is an interference with liberty and rights of property.[2] Sunday laws are not unconstitutional as applied to those who conscientiously observe the seventh day of the week,[3] but it is usual to make an exception in the statute so that it shall not apply to such persons. Such exception, however, is not available to one who does not observe the seventh day of the week, even though he may believe that it is the day which ought to be observed;[4] nor does such exception authorize one who does not observe the seventh day to trade on Sunday with those who do.[5] While it is the general public welfare which is consulted in passing these statutes, yet it is not merely anything which constitutes an annoyance to the public that is a breach thereof and punishable, but any act in violation is a crime.[6]

§ **1320. What deemed Sunday.**— In general all parts of the twenty-four hours from midnight on Saturday until midnight on Sunday are covered by the statutes as to Sunday observance;[7] but in some states it has been held that the statute relates to the solar day only, while in others the day begins on midnight of Saturday and ends at sundown on Sunday, and in still others the evening of Sunday, but of course not the evening preceding it, is included.[8]

some extent exceptional, but do not contravene the general power of the state to pass such statutes: S. v. Brooksbank, 6 Ired. 73; S. v. Williams, 4 Ired. 400; S. v. Schnierle, 5 Rich. 299; Ward v. Green, 11 Conn. 455.

[1] P. v. Bellet, 99 Mich. 151.

[2] Eden v. P., 161 Ill. 296; S. v. Granneman, — Mo. —, 33 S. W. R. 784; Ex parte Jentzsch, 112 Cal. 468, 44 Pac. R. 803. *Contra*, P. v. Havnor, 149 N. Y. 195. And see *supra*, § 77. The cases here cited relate to keeping open barber-shops on Sunday. But a statute making it unlawful "to open on Sunday for the purpose of trade or sale of goods, etc., any shop, store, building, or place of business whatever," does not include a barber-shop: S. v. Krech, 10 Wash. 166.

[3] C. v. Wolf, 3 Serg. & R. 48; C. v. Starr, 144 Mass. 359; C. v. Has, 122 Mass. 40; Scales v. S., 47 Ark. 476.

[4] Liberman v. S., 26 Neb. 464.

[5] Ex parte Sundstrom, 25 Tex. Ap. 133.

[6] Parker v. S., 16 Lea, 476; Gunter v. S., 1 Lea, 129.

[7] As to closing saloons on Sunday, see *supra*, § 1264.

[8] S. v. Green, 37 Mo. 466; Fox v. Abel, 2 Conn. 541; Finn v. Donahue,

§ 1321. Works of charity or necessity excepted.— The statutes uniformly contain some exception as to works of necessity or charity, and in general a question as to whether a particular act complained of was within the exception is for the jury;[1] but the necessity which will excuse must be a real, not a fancied one.[2] In applying these exceptions there is some diversity in the result as to particular classes of cases. There are many illustrations of the general proposition that work of necessity includes such as is essential to avoid considerable pecuniary loss which would result if it was not done; such, for instance, as the harvesting of crops which would probably be destroyed by delay, there having been no negligence in not securing them sooner,[3] or the turning of malt which would otherwise be damaged,[4] or the operating of an ice factory, it appearing that to close it over Sunday would cause a delay of a day or more in getting it again into operation,[5] or the boiling down of maple sap which would be lost if not thus attended to,[6] or the shoeing of horses on Sunday to enable a stage company to carry the mails on Monday morning in accordance with a contract.[7] So feeding of stock on Sunday is a matter of necessity.[8] On the other hand, the mere fact that pecuniary loss will result does not in itself show that the work is one of necessity. Thus, it is held not lawful to clean a wheel-pit on Sunday for the purpose of avoiding the necessity of stopping the mill on a week day;[9] nor to gather sea-weed which would otherwise have been washed away by the next tide.[10] The mere fact that work can be more conveniently done on Sunday will not bring it within the exception.[11] Some occupations must be

35 Conn. 216; Bryant v. Biddeford, 39 Me. 193; C. v. Newton, 8 Pick. 234.

1 S. v. Knight, 29 W. Va. 340; C. v. Josselyn, 97 Mass. 411; Edgerton v. S., 67 Ind. 588; C. v. Gillespie, 146 Pa. St. 546.

2 Johnson v. Irasburgh, 47 Vt. 28.

3 Turner v. S., 67 Ind. 595; Wilkinson v. S., 59 Ind. 416; S. v. Goff, 20 Ark. 289; Reg. v. Cleworth, 4 B. & S. 927.

4 Crocket v. S., 33 Ind. 416.

5 Hennersdorf v. S., 25 Tex. Ap. 597. Whether or not the pumping of an oil well on Sunday is a work of necessity is a question of fact: C. v. Gillespie, 146 Pa. St. 546.

6 Morris v. S., 31 Ind. 189. So hauling to market watermelons which would otherwise have spoiled was held lawful: Wilkinson v. S., 59 Ind. 416.

7 Nelson v. S., 25 Tex. Ap. 599.

8 Edgerton v. S., 67 Ind. 588.

9 McGrath v. Merwin, 112 Mass. 467.

10 C. v. Sampson, 97 Mass. 407.

11 Cleary v. S., 56 Ark. 124. It may be a work of necessity, however, to repair the highway on Sunday: Flagg v. Millbury, 4 Cush. 243.

pursued on Sunday out of regard to the health and general comfort of the public dependent on such services, which cannot be performed on week days, so as to avoid the necessity of Sunday labor therein; thus, it may be necessary to carry on the business of selling medicines or drugs on Sunday,[1] or that of furnishing water or supplying milk to customers; but as to whether the business of baking can properly be carried on upon Sunday there seems to be doubt.[2] The sale of cigars and tobacco is not necessary on Sunday,[3] nor, it seems, is it necessary for a barber to shave customers on that day,[4] or for a newsdealer to sell newspapers.[5]

§ 1322. **Sunday traveling.**— Much conflict has arisen in determining whether traveling on Sunday is a work of necessity or charity such as to take it out of the Sunday statutes. In general, traveling on matters of business comes within the prohibition unless it is for necessity or charity.[6] But if the traveling becomes necessary by reason of sickness or accident,[7] or is for the purpose of attending worship,[8] it may be proper.

[1] But this will not cover the sale of tobacco and cigars though by a druggist: C. v. Marzynski, 149 Mass. 68; or liquors: Elkin v. S., 63 Miss. 129. The question whether Florida water is a medicine or not so that the sale thereof on Sunday at a drug store may be proper, see Todd v. S., 30 Tex. Ap. 667. Alcohol is within the statute relating to the sale of goods, wares and merchandise at retail on Sunday: Bridges v. S., 37 Ark. 224; Hall v. S., 3 Ga. 18. But an innkeeper authorized to sell liquor may properly sell on Sunday: Hall v. S., 4 Harr. 132. And see Omit v. C., 21 Pa. St. 426; Atkinson v. Sellers, 5 C. B. (N. S.) 442

[2] Rex v. Cox, 2 Burr. 785; Rex v. Younger, 5 T. R. 449. But one who sells bread and groceries is not within the statutory exception as to bakers: C. v. Crowley, 145 Mass. 430.

[3] Mueller v. S., 76 Ind. 310; Friedeborn v. C., 113 Pa. St. 242. But it may be proper for a tavern-keeper in the course of his business to sell cigars to guests: Carver v. S., 69 Ind. 61.

[4] C. v. Waldman, 140 Pa. St. 89; Ungericht v. S., 119 Ind. 379; C. v. Jacobus, 1 Leg. Gaz. R. 491, 15 Cent. L. J. 145; S. v. Frederick, 45 Ark. 347; C. v. Dextra, 143 Mass. 28; Phillips v. Innes, 4 Cl. & F. 234. But barbering on Sunday is not a nuisance: S. v. Lorry, 7 Baxt. 95.

[5] C. v. Dale, 144 Mass. 363. In Pennsylvania it has been held that issuing, publishing and circulating a newspaper on Sunday is a worldly employment within the language of the Sunday statute: C. v. Matthews, 152 Pa. St. 166; and a contract as to advertising in a Sunday newspaper is void: Smith v. Wilcox, 24 N. Y. 353; Handy v. St. Paul Globe Pub. Co., 41 Minn. 188.

[6] Holcomb v. Danby, 51 Vt. 428; Johnson v. Irasburgh, 47 Vt. 28; Jones v. Andover, 10 Allen, 18; Connolly v. Boston, 117 Mass. 64; C. v. Knox, 6 Mass. 76.

[7] Gorman v. Lowell, 117 Mass. 65; Crosman v. Lynn, 121 Mass. 301.

[8] C. v. Nesbit, 34 Pa. St. 398; Feital v. Middlesex R. Co., 109 Mass. 398.

Carrying pleasure seekers to a picnic is not a work of necessity or charity.[1] Where one engaged in furnishing accommodations for travelers does so on Sunday in good faith to a person representing that he needs the accommodation for a proper purpose he is not punishable.[2] In some of the New England states it has been held that inasmuch as traveling on Sunday is unlawful, there can be no recovery by a passenger against a carrier or against the persons chargeable with the care of the highway for injuries received on Sunday;[3] but there is a great preponderance of authority in favor of the proposition that the illegality of the business in which the traveler is engaged will be no defense to his action for damages on account of an injury received.[4]

§ **1323. Operation of railroads or telegraph lines.**— It was at one time held that the operation of street railways for the carriage of passengers was a violation of the Sunday statutes;[5] but at the present day the operation of railroads for the purpose of transporting passengers, and also for the carriage of goods which would be materially injured by delay, is regarded as proper.[6] But as to the general freight business of a railroad there seems no reason why it should be admitted within the statutory exception as to necessity or charity, and some courts have therefore held such operation to be unlawful.[7] In some states there are express statutory regulations as to operation of Sunday trains,[8] and such a statute is not unconstitutional as an interference with interstate commerce.[9] The transmission of ordinary telegraph messages cannot be regarded as a work of

[1] Dougan v. S., 125 Ind. 130.

[2] Myers v. S., 1 Conn. 502; Shover v. S., 7 Ark. 259; Brittin v. S., 10 Ark. 299; Taylor v. Humphries, 17 C. B. (N. S.) 539.

[3] Bosworth v. Swansey, 10 Met. 363; Jones v. Andover, 10 Allen, 18.

[4] Philadelphia, etc. R. Co. v. Philadelphia, etc. Tow Boat Co., 23 How. 209; Sutton v. Wauwatosa, 29 Wis. 21; Dutton v. Weare, 17 N. H. 34; Cooley, Torts, 156; 2 Dillon, Municipal Corp., § 1020, n.

[5] C. v. Jeandell, 2 Grant, 506. And to the same effect as to omnibuses, see Johnston v. C., 22 Pa. St. 102.

[6] C. v. Louisville, etc. R. Co., 80 Ky. 291; Augusta R. Co. v. Renz, 55 Ga. 126; Phil. etc. R. Co. v. Lehman, 56 Md. 209.

[7] Sparhawk v. Union Passenger R. Co., 54 Pa. St. 401; S. v. Baltimore & Ohio R. Co.. 15 W. Va. 362; S. v. Norfolk & W. R. Co., 33 W. Va. 440. See, also, as to transportation by canal, Scully v. C., 35 Pa. St. 511.

[8] Jackson v. S., 88 Ga. 787; McNealy v. S., 94 Ga. 592; Heard v. S., 92 Ga. 477; C. v. Nesbit, 34 Pa. St. 398.

[9] Hennington v. Georgia, 163 U. S. 299.

necessity, but if a necessity is shown the contract to send the message will be legal.[1]

§ 1324. **Carrying on business.**— In general the carrying on of ordinary traffic with the public is within the prohibition of the Sunday laws, and not within the exception as to necessity or charity.[2] So the execution and delivery of a promissory note is prohibited.[3] Statutes sometimes specifically prohibit the keeping open of a store on Sunday, and the offense may be committed by leaving the door only partly open or by opening it for one who knocks for admission.[4] It is not sufficient, however, to constitute a violation of the law that the door is kept open without traffic.[5] Perhaps a single sale may not constitute a keeping open within such a statute.[6] Sometimes the offense as to carrying on business is limited to that of pursuing one's ordinary vocation, and under such a statute it may not be criminal to do business such as one is not in the habit of doing on other days.[7]

§ 1325. **Sunday amusements.**— To sell tickets on Sunday for an entertainment to be given in a public theater on that day has been held criminal under the ordinary statutes on this subject,[8] and the playing of baseball has been held to fall within the definition of "sporting" prohibited by a Sunday statute.[9] Fishing on Sunday is usually within the statutory prohibition even though it be within a private pond.[10] Playing at cards or dice is of course not business or labor,[11] neither is it within the prohibition of exhibiting plays or games, etc.[12]

[1] Western U. Tel. Co. v. Yopst, 118 Ind. 248.

[2] C. v. Nagle, 117 Mass. 142. A butcher shop is a store within statutory provisions as to keeping open a store on Sunday: Petty v. S., 58 Ark. 1.

[3] Allen v. Deming, 14 N. H. 133; Sanders v. Johnson, 29 Ga. 526; Reynolds v. Stevenson, 4 Ind. 619; Wetzler v. S., 18 Ind. 416; Carver v. S., 69 Ind. 61; Hoacek v. Keobler, 5 Neb. 355; Hellams v. Abercrombie, 15 S. C. 110.

[4] C. v. Lynch, 8 Gray, 384; Seel'g v. S., 43 Ark. 96. As to keeping open liquor shops on Sunday see *supra*, § 1264.

[5] Snider v. S., 59 Ala. 64.

[6] Dixon v. S., 76 Ala. 89.

[7] Foltz v. S., 33 Ind. 215; Eitel v. S., 33 Ind. 201; Wetzler v. S., 18 Ind. 416; Scarfe v. Morgan, 4 M. & W. 270; Drury v. Defontaine, 1 Taunt. 131.

[8] Quarles v. S., 55 Ark. 10.

[9] S. v. O'Rourk, 35 Neb. 614.

[10] P. v. Moses, 140 N. Y. 214 (overruling P. v. Dennin, 35 Hun, 327, which held ball playing to be lawful if not so conducted as to constitute a disturbance).

[11] S. v. Conger, 14 Ind. 396.

[12] Rucker v. S., 67 Miss. 328.

§ 1326. **Indictment.**— It is usually sufficient to charge the violation of the Sunday laws in accordance with the general language of the statute,[1] though there should be reasonable particularity as to the transaction complained of.[2] It is not necessary to specifically charge the criminal intent.[3] The indictment should show that the offense was committed on some Sunday, though the particular Sunday is not material;[4] but the allegation must be particular as to Sunday, and if the charge is that the offense was committed on a certain day which is in fact Sunday, that will not be sufficient unless it is charged to have been on Sunday, for otherwise the act may be proved on any day within the statutory period of limitations.[5] The particular part of the day on which the act was done is immaterial, it being sufficient that it was upon Sunday.[6] The place need not be further stated than to bring it within the jurisdiction of the court.[7] While it is necessary to show in some form that the act was unlawful,[8] yet the unlawful purpose may be alleged generally if the exception of necessity or charity is negatived.[9] The act need not be alleged as within the usual vocation of defendant, under a statute using that form of prohibition, if it is such an act as the court can judicially take notice of as an ordinary occupation.[10]

[1] Cleary v. S., 56 Ark. 124.

[2] C. v. Shannihan, 145 Mass. 99; C. v. De Voe, 159 Mass. 101; Mosely v. S., 18 Tex. Ap. 311; S. v. Anderson, 30 Ark. 131. If the charge is of trading on Sunday, it is not necessary to name the person with whom defendant is charged to have traded: S. v. Meyer, 1 Spears, 305.

[3] Brittin v. S., 10 Ark. 299.

[4] C. v. Gelbert, 170 Pa. St. 426; Robinson v. S., 38 Ark. 548; Jackson v. S., 88 Ga. 787; Frasier v. S., 5 Mo. 536; Pancake v. S., 81 Ind. 93. And if the act is charged as committed on Sunday, it will be immaterial that the wrong day of the month is stated: S. v. Drake, 64 N. C. 589; Roy v. S., 91 Ind. 417; S. v. Eskridge, 1 Swan, 413.

[5] S. v. Saurbaugh, 122 Ind. 208; Gilbert v. S., 81 Ind. 565; S. v. Brunker, 46 Conn. 327.

[6] C. v. Messenger, 4 Mass. 462; P. v. Maguire, 26 Cal. 635.

[7] C. v. Phelps, 170 Pa. St. 430.

[8] C. v. Collins, 2 Cush. 556.

[9] C. v. Wright, 12 Allen, 187; Louisville & N. R. Co. v. C., 92 Ky. 114.

[10] Eitel v. S., 33 Ind. 701; McCarthy v. S., 56 Ind. 203.

PART XIV.

OFFENSES UNDER FEDERAL REGULATIONS.

CHAPTER 67.

POSTAL CRIMES.

§ **1327. In general.**— In the exercise of its power to establish post-offices and post-roads,[1] congress has passed statutes making it criminal to interfere with or obstruct the transmission and delivery of mail matter either on the part of those who interfere with the proper officers in the discharge of their duties or those who as officers neglect to discharge their proper functions or violate the trust reposed in them. These offenses will be considered in subsequent sections, but it may be here suggested that, apart from the embezzlement of the mail on the part of a postal clerk or employee, there is a special crime of embezzling funds of the United States on the part of a postmaster or his assistant.[2] The sale and use of stamps by postmasters is expressly regulated by statute, and it is made unlawful to dispose thereof except by sale for cash at their face value to another person as purchaser.[3] There are also regulations as to the franking privilege, and violation thereof may be criminal.[4] An offense against the postal laws may be committed by forging an indorsement on a postoffice money order with intent to defraud.[5] In the exercise of the authority to regulate the postal business it has been made criminal to establish any private express for the conveyance or delivery of

[1] U. S. Const., art. 1, § 8.

[2] U. S. v. Norton, 91 U. S. 566; Faust v. U. S., 163 U. S. 452; U. S. v. Woodruff, 68 Fed. R. 536.

[3] U. S. v. Douglass, 33 Fed. R. 381. And to make an offer of a contract to a postmaster for the purchase of stamps on credit is criminal, although the compensation to him may not be greater than he is entitled to for a cash sale: In re Palliser, 136 U. S. 257.

[4] Dewee's Case, Chase Dec. 531.

[5] U. S. v. Morris, 16 Blatch. 133.

letters by regular trips or at stated periods over any post route established by law,[1] and the streets of a city may be in this sense a post route.[2] In addition to the regulations intended to secure the safe and proper transportation of the mails, there are statutes for the protection of the public against the transmission through the mails of matter which shall tend to corrupt the public morals, such as obscene letters or publications, or which will promote business which is against public policy, such as lottery schemes, or which may be made use of for fraudulent purposes, such as schemes to defraud, but these various regulations must be separately considered.

§ 1328. **Obstruction of mails.**— In general any act which obstructs or retards the transmission or passage of the mails is criminal. Thus, it has been held to be a crime for one to assault a postmaster in the postoffice so as to cause a delay in the transmission of mail in the office.[3] But before one can be convicted of thus obstructing the mail by reason of a quarrel with the postmaster, it must appear that the accused had knowledge that his acts would have that effect and so intended.[4] So a toll-gate keeper who obstructs the passage of a wagon carrying the mail for the purpose of compelling payment of toll is guilty of obstructing the mails;[5] and one is guilty of a crime who, having a lien upon horses for their keeping, enforces the same in such manner as to stop the mail by preventing their use in drawing the stage-coach in which it is being carried.[6] It seems from these illustrations that to constitute the crime of obstructing the mails it is not necessary that there be any intent to accomplish that result; it is enough if such result follows as a natural consequence from the act done. Thus, where boys placed obstructions on the track of an electric railway whereon United States mails were carried, and by so doing delayed the mail and forced it to be carried in another way, they were held guilty of the crime of obstructing the mails;[7] and one who in attempting to secure his own

[1] U. S. v. United States Express Co., 5 Biss. 91.

[2] U. S. v. Easson, 18 Fed. R. 590.

[3] U. S. v. Claypool, 14 Fed. R. 127.

[4] U. S. v. Woodward, 44 Fed. R. 592.

[5] U. S. v. Sears, 55 Fed. R. 268.

[6] U. S. v. Barney, 3 Hughes, 545. But such offense is not committed unless the mail is *in transitu*, and the horses thus seized are employed in transporting it: U. S. v. McCracken, 3 Hughes, 544.

[7] U. S. v. Thomas, 55 Fed. R. 380.

transportation on a railway train resists the conductor in the discharge of his duties with reference to causing a mail-car to be detached and forwarded is guilty of obstructing the mail.[1] A similar principle is applied in cases where strikers attempt to interfere with the operations of a railroad by obstructing trains which are carrying mails, and such an act is held to be criminal even though the strikers expressly avoid any interference with the mails and are willing that the mail-cars be separated from the balance of the train and carried without delay; for it is said that a mail train is a train as usually and regularly made up, including not merely a mail-car but such other cars as are usually drawn in such a train, and to interfere with the passage of a portion of such train is an obstruction of the whole train.[2] Knowledge on the part of the persons obstructing the trains that they are carrying United States mail is not essential to be shown, for the law makes all railroads postal routes, and it is within every one's knowledge that nearly all passenger trains carry mail, and therefore one obstructing the operation of such a train must be presumed to have intended the natural consequence of his act.[3]

§ **1329. Robbery of the mails.**— The federal statutes make it a felony to rob a carrier of the mails.[4] The offense may be aggravated by being committed by the use of a dangerous weapon,[5] and it is complete wherever the mail or any part thereof is taken violently from the possession of the carrier against his will, by force or by putting him in fear.[6] So it is a crime to forcibly break into or attempt to break into any post-office or building used in whole or part as a postoffice with intent to commit larceny or other depredation.[7]

[1] U. S. v. Kane, 19 Fed. R. 42.

[2] U. S. v. Clark, 23 Int. Rev. Rec. 306; U. S. v. Cassidy, 67 Fed. R. 698. The railroad company is not bound under its obligations to the federal government to run special trains for the carrying of mails when the movement of its regular trains for that purpose is prevented: In re Grand Jury, 62 Fed. R. 834.

[3] U. S. v. Cassidy, 67 Fed. R. 698; U. S. v. Debs, 65 Fed. R. 210; U. S. v. Kirby, 7 Wall. 482.

[4] Harrison v. U. S., 163 U. S. 140.

[5] U. S. v. Reeves, 38 Fed. R. 404.

[6] U. S. v. Reeves, 38 Fed. R. 404. It is also criminal to attempt to rob the mails by assaulting the person having custody thereof, an attempt implying an endeavor carried beyond mere preparation: Ibid. An aider or abettor may be guilty of the crime whether he enters the car or place where the mail is being carried or kept or not: Ibid.

[7] U. S. v. Campbell, 16 Fed. R. 233.

§ 1330. Larceny or embezzlement by postal servants.— The federal statutes provide for two distinct offenses by those in charge of the mails; the one consists in the secreting, embezzlement or destruction of mail matter without regard to its containing any article of value, the other in the embezzlement by such person of any letter or package containing an article of value.[1] There has been some difficulty in determining what is mail matter under these provisions, it being held in a few cases that a decoy letter addressed to a fictitious person or place and not intended to be delivered was not subject of larceny or embezzlement;[2] but the weight of authority is to the effect that intention on the part of the postal authorities who have caused the letter or package to be placed in the mail to intercept it before it is delivered or before it has passed through the usual channels for delivery will not prevent its being mail matter covered by the statute as to embezzlement.[3] As to who

[1] U. S. v. Lacher, 134 U. S. 624; Beery v. U. S., 2 Colo. 186; U. S. v. Wight, 38 Fed. R. 106; U. S. v. Byrne, 44 Fed. R. 188; U. S. v. Davis, 33 Fed. R. 865; Rosecrans v. U. S., — U. S. —, 17 S. C. R. 302. The only offense actually punishable under the R. S., § 5467, is that of stealing articles contained in the mail intrusted to him. The offense of embezzling, secreting, etc., as to the mail matter is within the provisions of the R. S., § 3891: U. S. v. Hartley, 42 Fed. R. 835; U. S. v. Gruver, 35 Fed. R. 59; U. S. v. Long, 4 Woods, 454. But it is not objectionable to charge the embezzlement of a letter and the stealing of its contents: U. S. v. Byrne, 44 Fed. R. 188. It is not essential that the letter be stolen from a bag or an article from the letter: U. S. v. Pelletreau, 14 Blatch. 126. The penalty prescribed in the last clause of the United States Revised Statutes, section 5469, applies also to the preceding clause, including a prohibition of an employee stealing a letter from a postal clerk: U. S. v. Falkenhainer, 21 Fed. R. 624. It is criminal to receive property knowing it to have been stolen from the mail: U. S. v. Thomas, 69 Fed. R. 588.

[2] U. S. v. Matthews, 35 Fed. R. 890; U. S. v. Denicke, 35 Fed. R. 407; U. S. v. Rapp, 30 Fed. R. 818; U. S. v. Whittier, 5 Dill. 35.

[3] U. S. v. Wight, 38 Fed. R. 106; U. S. v. Dorsey, 40 Fed. R. 752; U. S. v. Bethea, 44 Fed. R. 802. And see Walster v. U. S., 42 Fed. R. 891, and to same effect, Reg. v. Young, 2 C. & K. 466 (overruling Reg. v. Gardner, 1 C. & K. 628). And see Reg. v. Shepherd, Dears. 606; Reg. v. Rathbone, Car. & M. 220. Also see *infra*, section 1335, where the whole subject of decoy letters is fully considered. The term "branch post-office," employed in section 5467 of the Revised Statutes with reference to secreting or destroying letters, etc., includes every place within such office where letters are kept in the regular course of business: Goode v. U. S., 159 U. S. 663. And the term "mail," as used in section 5469 relative to robbing the mails, may mean either the whole body of matter transported by the postal agents or any letter or pack-

is to be deemed a postoffice employee or mail agent within the terms of the federal statutes, it is held that one who is in the postal service and receives for mailing a letter which he fails to mail may be guilty of embezzlement in stealing the contents.[1] The fact that the mail matter stolen is by the law unmailable will constitute no excuse for the crime;[2] nor is it any defense that an employee who takes money out of a letter does so with the hope and expectation of returning it, and does return it, the object of the statute being to prevent and punish any interference with the contents of a letter in the custody of the employee.[3] One who induces a servant of the postoffice to

age forming a component part of it: U. S. v. Inabnet, 41 Fed. R. 130. In England under analogous statutes some question has arisen as to what is a post-letter, and it is held that after the letter is placed in the custody of the person authorized to receive letters for the mail it is a post-letter, although not yet stamped and put into the letter-box: Rex v. Pearson, 4 C. & P. 572; Reg. v. Rogers, 5 Cox, 293; but that a letter-carrier to whom money is given to procure a money order is not guilty of stealing a post-letter in appropriating such money: Reg. v. Glass, 2 C. & K. 395. Where money was pinned inside an unsealed letter for the payment of postage and dropped into a letter-box, it was held that a servant stealing such letter was punishable for stealing a post-letter containing money: Reg. v. Mence, Car. & M. 234. But the theft of a letter containing money given to a servant at an inn to post was held not to be within the statute as to the theft of a post-letter: Reg. v. Harley, 1 C. & K. 89. To constitute larceny by a postal servant it is not necessary that the money contained in the letter be appropriated, or indeed that there be any knowledge that the letter contains money; and if the letter is destroyed or concealed in order to prevent detection of mistake in not properly forwarding or delivering, the crime is committed: Reg. v. Wynn, 2 C. & K. 859; Reg. v. Poynton, L. & C. 247.

1 U. S. v. Hamilton, 11 Biss. 85. Under the English statutes it has been held that one employed by the postmaster personally to carry mail, and whose salary was reimbursed by the postoffice department, was an employee: Rex v. Salisbury, 5 C. & P. 155; and that even one engaged in gratuitously assisting the postmaster at his request in the handling of the mail was criminally liable as an employee for stealing letters: Reg. v. Reason, Dears. 226; proof of appointment being unnecessary: Rex v. Rees, 6 C. & P. 606. But if the mail matter does not come into the hands of accused as a postal employee, he will not be liable under the statute as to embezzlement or larceny of letters by such employees: Reg. v. Glass, 2 C. & K. 395; Rex v. Pearson, 4 C. & P. 572. But see Reg. v. Bickerstaff, 2 C. & K. 761.

2 Beery v. U. S., 2 Colo. 186; U. S. v. Randall, Deady, 524.

3 U. S. v. Thompson, 29 Fed. R. 706. Therefore it is not necessary to allege that the act was done with a fraudulent intent: U. S. v. Atkinson, 34 Fed. R. 316. In a prosecution for stealing letters from the mail

intercept and not forward a letter which is in the course of transmission is guilty of larceny either as principal or as accessory before the fact to the larceny committed by the servant, and in either view may be convicted on a charge of stealing the letter.[1] The indictment must show that the letter or package stolen was a part of the mail;[2] but it is not necessary to allege that the letter or package had not been delivered or that it was intended to be conveyed by mail;[3] and it is sufficient to allege generally that defendant was a person employed in one of the departments of the postoffice establishment of the United States, and that the letter embezzled or stolen contained a bank-note, check or other such thing, without particularly describing it.[4] No averment of the ownership of the money or article taken need be made,[5] although ownership may properly be laid in the person to whom the letter was addressed.[6] In an indictment for detaining mail it is sufficient to allege, in the words of the statute, that the letter described was unlawfully detained, stating the time, with intent to prevent its arrival and delivery. It is not necessary to charge that such letter was knowingly and wilfully detained.[7]

committed by a boy under twelve years of age, it was left to the jury to say whether he took them with criminal intent or from a spirit of boyish mischief: U. S. v. Wilson, 44 Fed. R. 593. To constitute the crime of stealing from the mail there must be an intent to steal at the time the mail matter is taken: U. S. v. Inabnet, 41 Fed. R. 130.

[1] Reg. v. James, 24 Q. B. D. 439.

[2] Farnum v. U. S., 1 Colo. 309.

[3] In re Wight, 134 U. S. 136; U. S. v. Wight, 38 Fed. R. 106. If it is averred that the letter was intended to be conveyed by post, it is not necessary to designate the place to which it was to be conveyed: U. S. v. Okie, 5 Blatch. 516; but if the *termini* between which the letter was intended to be sent by post are stated, the allegation must be proved as laid: U. S. v. Foye, 1 Curt. 364.

[4] U. S. v. Patterson, 6 McLean, 466; U. S. v. Clark, Crabbe, 584.

[5] U. S. v. Okie, 5 Blatch. 516.

[6] U. S. v. Jackson, 29 Fed. R. 503; U. S. v. Jones, 31 Fed. R. 718; U. S. v. Jones, 31 Fed. R. 725. It is not necessary to state the value of the packet or thing alleged to have been taken: Jones v. U. S., 27 Fed. R. 447. If the check alleged to have been taken is accurately described as it was at the time it was stolen, subsequent indorsements or alterations will be immaterial: U. S. v. Jones, 31 Fed. R. 718.

[7] U. S. v. Holmes, 40 Fed. R. 750; U. S. v. Hilbury, 29 Fed. R. 705. The statute as to detaining or opening covers a package as well as a letter: U. S. v. Blackman, 17 Fed. R. 837. Simply to open a letter without authority is not larceny under the English statute: Reg. v. Godfrey, 8 C. & P. 563. It is not larceny from the mails to take a letter after it has been delivered to the person to whom it is addressed: U. S. v. Safford, 66

§ 1331. Use of mails to defraud.— By the postal laws[1] it is made criminal to use the United States mails for the purpose of perpetrating frauds, the offense described involving the devising or intending to devise a scheme or artifice to defraud, the opening or intending to open correspondence or communication with some other person or inciting such person to open correspondence by means of the postoffice department with the one devising the scheme, and in pursuance of the scheme putting a letter or packet in the mail or taking one out.[2] It is not essential that fraud be actually perpetrated,[3] nor is it necessary that the accused be the originator of the fraudulent scheme, nor that the letter be deposited by him, if deposited under his direction.[4] Under this statute it has been held criminal to send through the mail circulars for the purpose of inducing the purchase of counterfeit money, without regard to an intention to defraud the persons solicited to purchase;[5] or to send out circulars for the ostensible purpose of securing agents with the intention of inducing them to advance money for canvassing outfits for which no returns are to be made;[6] or to defraud by sending mail orders for goods with the intention not to pay for them when received;[7] but there must be at the

Fed. R. 942. By state statute it may be criminal to read and make known the contents of a letter opened without authority: S. v. Bagwell, 107 N. C. 859.

[1] U. S. Rev. Stat., § 5480.

[2] U. S. v. Wootten, 29 Fed. R. 702. The punishment is by imprisonment in the state penitentiary, and the crime is therefore infamous: Stokes v. U. S., 60 Fed. R. 597. By the statute as amended by act of March 2, 1889, chapter 393, the matter improper to be sent by mail includes everything designed to defraud by representations as to the past and present and suggestions and promises as to the future: Durland v. U. S., 161 U. S. 306.

[3] Weeber v. U. S., 62 Fed. R. 740; U. S. v. Mitchell, 36 Fed. R. 492; Durland v. U. S., 161 U. S. 306; nor that the statements contained in letters deposited in furtherance of the scheme be false: U. S. v. Hoeflinger, 33 Fed. R. 469.

[4] U. S. v. Flemming, 18 Fed. R. 907.

[5] Streep v. U. S., 160 U. S. 128; U. S. v. Jones, 20 Blatch. 235.

[6] U. S. v. Stickle, 15 Fed. R. 798; U. S. v. Finney, 45 Fed. R. 41.

[7] U. S. v. Watson, 35 Fed. R. 358. So held as to mail orders for securing the insertion of advertisements in newspapers on a promise to pay the bills therefor when rendered, but with intention not to do so: U. S. v. Staples, 45 Fed. R. 195. So a scheme to sell an organ worth $150 for $33, warranted for ten years, the money to be refunded at any time within three years if the instrument was returned as not satisfactory, it appearing that there was no intention to carry out the promises in this respect, was held to be fraudulent: U. S. v. Beatty, 60 Fed. R. 740.

time of the mailing of the letter the intent not to pay for the goods.[1] It must be shown that in sending out circulars making certain statements which it was claimed were with intent to defraud, defendant intended to defraud every person sending money in response to such circulars.[2] But merely to falsely state in a letter that money is inclosed therein and to inclose worthless slips of paper in place of such money is not within the terms of the statute.[3] To constitute a crime under this provision it must appear that the fraudulent scheme included the intended use of the United States mail in its execution,[4] and the motive must be one of gain on the part of the accused.[5] The intent to defraud must be specifically charged and not left to implication;[6] but evidence of the mailing of similar letters is admissible on the question of intent.[7] Defendant's intent is to be determined by inference from all the facts and circumstances.[8] If the scheme be adapted in its plan to work a fraud upon others and defendant knew that the representation therein contained and calculated to deceive was not true, or if he did not believe that it was true, the intent is sufficiently made out.[9] The scheme must be stated with some particularity.[10] The names and addresses of persons to whom the letters are sent and the names of the persons intended to be defrauded may be alleged as unknown to the grand jury if such be the fact.[11] Each letter mailed or received in carrying out the fraudulent scheme is a distinct offense.[12]

[1] U. S. v. Wootten, 29 Fed. R. 702.

[2] U. S. v. Staples, 45 Fed. R. 195.

[3] U. S. v. Owens, 17 Fed. R. 72.

[4] U. S. v. Harris, 68 Fed. R. 347; U. S. v. Long, 68 Fed. R. 348.

[5] U. S. v. Beach, 71 Fed. R. 160.

[6] U. S. v. Smith, 45 Fed. R. 561.

[7] U. S. v. Watson, 35 Fed. R. 358.

[8] U. S. v. Finney, 45 Fed. R. 41.

[9] U. S. v. Ried, 42 Fed. R. 134. Evidence as to defendant's knowledge and experience in financial schemes and as to previous attacks upon the honesty of the scheme in question is admissible as tending to show whether defendant was himself deceived and acted in good faith: U. S. v. Durland, 65 Fed. R. 408.

[10] U. S. v. Beatty, 60 Fed. R. 740. The charge of an unexecuted scheme to defraud is not a sufficient allegation that defendant was engaged in the unlawful business so as to bring the assumption and use of, and request to be addressed by, a fictitious name within the scope of the section above referred to: U. S. v. Smith, 45 Fed. R. 561.

[11] Durland v. U. S., 161 U. S. 306.

[12] In re Henry, 123 U. S. 372. But by express provision of the statute three distinct offenses may be charged in one indictment or information; a single sentence, however, being rendered thereon: Ibid.; U. S. v. Martin, 28 Fed. R. 812.

§ 1332. Sending obscene matter through the mails.— By several statutes the mailing of obscene or indecent matter has been prohibited.[1] Such provisions are not unconstitutional as interfering with freedom of speech and of the press.[2] Prior to the amendment of September 26, 1888, there was a doubt as to whether the statute applied to sealed letters not showing in any way on the envelope or wrapper that the contents were objectionable;[3] but since the amendment of 1888 it is settled that a sealed letter without indication of the nature of its contents is within the terms of the statute,[4] the statute forbidding any one to open any sealed letter not addressed to himself being a sufficient protection to private correspondence.[5] The test of obscenity, within the meaning of the statutory provision against the use of the mails for the circulation of obscene matter, is whether the matter is calculated to deprave and corrupt the minds of those whose minds are open to such immoral influences by exciting lustful and sensual desires.[6] It is imma-

[1] For instance, there are statutes making it criminal to send through the mail any article designed or intended for the prevention of conception or the procuring of an abortion: U. S. v. Bott, 11 Blatch. 346; U. S. v. Kaltmeyer, 16 Fed. R. 760; Bates v. U. S., 10 Biss. 70. There is a statute as to taking obscene publications from the mails for the purpose of circulating or disposing of them: U. S. v. Chase, 27 Fed. R. 807. The provision under which most of the prosecutions have been had is that found in United States Revised Statutes, section 3893, as amended by act of July 12, 1886, chapter 186, and act of September 26, 1888, chapter 1039.

[2] Harman v. U. S., 50 Fed. R. 921; U. S. v. Harmon, 45 Fed. R. 414; U. S. v. Bennett, 16 Blatch. 338.

[3] As holding that such letters were not within the terms of the statute, see U. S. v. Loftis, 8 Saw. 194; U. S. v. Comerford, 25 Fed. R. 902; U. S. v. Huggett, 40 Fed. R. 636; U. S. v. Mathias, 36 Fed. R. 892. *Contra*, U. S. v. Gaylord, 17 Fed. R. 438; U. S. v. Hanover, 17 Fed. R. 444; U. S. v. Britton, 17 Fed. R. 731; U. S. v. Morris, 18 Fed. R. 900; U. S. v. Thomas, 27 Fed. R. 682. This question was settled by the supreme court of the United States holding a sealed letter not to be covered by the statute: U. S. v. Chase, 135 U. S. 255.

[4] Andrews v. U. S., 162 U. S. 420; Grimm v. U. S., 156 U. S. 604; In re Wahll, 42 Fed. R. 822; U. S. v. Martin, 50 Fed. R. 918; U. S. v. Gaylord, 50 Fed. R. 410; U. S. v. Andrews, 58 Fed. R. 861; U. S. v. Nathan, 61 Fed. R. 936; U. S. v. Ling, 61 Fed. R. 1001. But even under the amendment the courts did not all agree to this result until the question was finally settled by the supreme court: U. S. v. Wilson, 58 Fed. R. 768; U. S. v. Jarvis, 59 Fed. R. 357; U. S. v. Warner, 59 Fed. R. 355.

[5] U. S. v. Martin, 50 Fed. R. 918.

[6] U. S. v. Bennett, 16 Blatch. 338; U. S. v. Slenker, 32 Fed. R. 691; U. S. v. Clarke, 38 Fed. R. 732; U. S. v. Harmon, 45 Fed. R. 414; U. S. v. Durant, 46 Fed. R. 753; Dunlop v. U. S., — U. S. —, 17 S. C. R. 375.

terial that the matter is such as may properly be used in a medical treatise; if intended for general circulation, and not suitable for such purpose, it may be within the statute.[1] Even since the amendment of September 26, 1888, already referred to, the word "indecent," used in the section of the statute, applies only to publications, not to letters, and therefore an indecent letter which is not obscene, lewd, or lascivious, is not within the terms of the statute;[2] but a letter from a man to an unmarried woman proposing a clandestine trip, necessarily implying illicit intercourse, is an obscene letter, and the sending of it is within the statute.[3] In determining the character of the letter or publication the effect of the whole as taken together may be considered, whether produced by single passages or by many passages or portions.[4] The mailing of a paper containing a single obscene article among others not objectionable is within the statute.[5] The statute does not cover matter which is coarse and vulgar and grossly libelous, if it is not calculated to excite lascivious thoughts or impure desires.[6] The question whether or not the particular letter or publication is obscene, lewd, or lascivious, is for the jury, and not a matter of law for the court.[7] The offense is complete when the letter is mailed, and the indictment need not allege that it reached the person to whom it was sent, or conveyed the objectionable information.[8] The motive with which the letter or

The terms used in the statute have the same meaning as are given to them at common law in prosecutions for obscene libel: U. S. v. Clarke, 38 Fed. R. 500; "lascivious" is synonymous with "lewd:" U. S. v. Clarke, 38 Fed. R. 732.

[1] U. S. v. Chesman, 19 Fed. R. 497; U. S. v. Smith, 45 Fed. R. 476. If claimed that the communication is privileged, as by a physician to a patient, the relation of the parties must appear: U. S. v. Smith, 45 Fed. R. 476. It is not necessary in the indictment to negative a proper occasion for sending such matter: U. S. v. Clarke, 38 Fed. R. 500.

[2] U. S. v. Clark, 43 Fed. R. 574.

[3] U. S. v. Martin, 50 Fed. R. 918. "Obscene," within the meaning of the statute, is that which is offensive to chastity and modesty: Ibid.

[4] U. S. v. Clarke, 38 Fed. R. 732; U. S. v. Davis, 38 Fed. R. 326.

[5] U. S. v. Harman, 38 Fed. R. 827.

[6] Swearingen v. U. S., 161 U. S. 446; U. S. v. Males, 51 Fed. R. 41; U. S. v. Wightman, 29 Fed. R. 636.

[7] U. S. v. Clarke, 38 Fed. R. 500; U. S. v. Davis, 38 Fed. R. 326. But it is proper, of course, for the court to construe the document and to decide whether a verdict establishing its obscenity would be set aside as against evidence and reason: U. S. v. Smith, 45 Fed. R. 476.

[8] U. S. v. Grimm, 45 Fed. R. 558. Therefore an indictment which charges that letters addressed to H. H. and W. W. were intended to

publication is mailed is immaterial,[1] provided the defendant had knowledge of its character.[2] If the letter or publication on its face appears to be harmless, the prosecution is entitled to allege and prove that it was in fact of an objectionable character; as, for instance, that it gave information concerning obscene pictures or literature, and was sent for that purpose.[3] The indictment for sending an obscene letter or publication through the mails need not set forth in language the matter objected to, provided the letter or publication is otherwise identified so that defendant may know what is intended;[4] but there should be some description to identify the matter.[5] The fact that the objectionable matter is sent in response to an inquiry made by a detective will not constitute a defense.[6]

§ 1333. **Defamatory or threatening matter.**— There are statutory provisions prescribing a punishment for sending through the mails any matter upon the envelope or wrapper of which, or any postal card upon which, any delineations or language of an indecent, defamatory or threatening character are written or printed,[7] and under these provisions it is held criminal to send through the mails a postal card demanding payment of a

and did convey information to R. M. as to where obscene pictures could be obtained, etc., is not defective: U. S. v. Grimm, 50 Fed. R. 528.

[1] U. S. v. Harmon, 45 Fed. R. 414.

[2] U. S. v. Bebout, 28 Fed. R. 522; U. S. v. Slenker, 32 Fed. R. 691; U. S. v. Clark, 37 Fed. R. 106. "Knowingly depositing" is sufficient to show knowledge of the character of the letter or publication: U. S. v Nathan, 61 Fed. R. 936; U. S. v. Bennett, 16 Blatch. 338.

[3] U. S. v. Grimm, 50 Fed. R. 528. And the indictment may further aver that the defendant had in his possession a large number of obscene pictures, and that the letters charged were written and deposited in the mail with intention to give information concerning such pictures, and did in fact convey such information: Ibid.; Grimm v. U. S., 156 U. S. 504. While the indictment would doubtless be sufficient if it used the language of the statute, yet if it sets out the letter referred to, which does not appear on its face to be objectionable, it must also set out other extrinsic facts showing its objectionable character: U. S. v. Grimm, 45 Fed. R. 558.

[4] Grimm v. U. S., 156 U. S. 604; Rosen v. U. S., 161 U. S. 29; Dunlop v. U. S., — U. S. —, 17 S. C. R. 375; U. S. v. Bennett, 16 Blatch. 338; Bates v. U. S., 10 Biss. 70; In re Wahll, 42 Fed. R. 822.

[5] U. S. v. Harmon, 34 Fed. R. 872; U. S. v. Fuller, 72 Fed. R. 771. Notice of where an article for the prevention of conception may be obtained should be set out unless it is so obscene as to be unfit to go upon the records: U. S. v. Kaltmeyer, 16 Fed. R. 760.

[6] Grimm v. U. S., 156 U. S. 604. And see *infra*, § 1335.

[7] Act of September 26, 1888, ch. 1039, 25 Stat. at Large, 496.

debt and stating that if not paid at once it will be placed with a lawyer for collection,[1] or like threatening or defamatory matter in regard to the non-payment of an alleged debt.[2] So to mail a letter in an envelope on which is printed in large letters words indicating that it is sent by a collection agency is criminal.[3]

§ **1334. Lottery advertisements.**— By several statutes it is criminal to send through the mails any letter, postal card or circular concerning any lottery or similar enterprise, or any newspaper or circular containing any advertisement of any such enterprise.[4] Such statutes are constitutional.[5] To constitute a lottery or gift enterprise within the language of the statute it is sufficient that the element of lot or chance is involved; thus, government bonds which give to the purchaser any chance of receiving in addition to the principal and interest a prize to be determined by lot constitutes a lottery scheme.[6] So where the value of bonds in an investment company depends upon their numbers, indicating the order in which they are purchased, the scheme is a lottery scheme within the statute.[7] So a scheme of insurance whereby an impossible guarantee is made has been held a lottery scheme.[8] So a scheme for increasing the circulation of a newspaper whereby all paid-up subscribers receive tickets, to the holders of which prizes are

[1] U. S. v. Bayle, 40 Fed. R. 664.

[2] U. S. v. Smith, 69 Fed. R. 971; U. S. v. Simmons, 61 Fed. R. 640.

[3] U. S. v. Brown, 43 Fed. R. 135. The objectionable character of the letter may consist in a distinctively colored envelope indicating it to be a dunning letter: U. S. v. Dodge, 70 Fed. R. 235. But the statute does not apply to a printed paper which, though not inclosed in an envelope, is folded and thus sent through the mails: U. S. v. Gee, 45 Fed. R. 194. A postal card containing a notice of rent being due and unpaid, with the statement that if not paid by a certain date the matter will be placed in the hands of an officer, *held* not to come within the statute: U. S. v. Elliott, 51 Fed. R. 807.

[4] The latest statute is the act of September 19, 1890, chapter 908, 26 Statutes at Large, 465.

[5] In re Rapier, 143 U. S. 110; Horner v. U. S., 143 U. S. 207. While the charter of a lottery corporation may be protected as a contract, the subject-matter of the corporation is within the regulation of the state: New Orleans v. Houston, 119 U. S. 265. That in the exercise of its police power the state may prohibit the lottery business, although such prohibition interferes with the exercise by a corporation of the powers granted by its charter, see *supra*, § 75.

[6] Horner v. U. S., 147 U. S. 449; U. S. v. Politzer, 59 Fed. R. 273.

[7] MacDonald v. U. S., 63 Fed. R. 426; U. S. v. McDonald, 59 Fed. R. 563.

[8] U. S. v. Fulkerson, 74 Fed. R. 619.

distributed in accordance with a drawing of tickets from a box, is a lottery scheme.[1] And in general it is said that the word "lottery" embraces the element of procuring through lot or chance, by the investment of money or something of value, some greater amount of money or thing of greater value.[2] A lottery ticket, with a schedule of drawing on the back, is a circular concerning a lottery within the language of the statute.[3] The statute applies to the advertiser or promoter and is not violated by one who as a prospective purchaser of a ticket writes to the manager of a lottery;[4] but such a letter may be returned to the sender under other provisions.[5] By the statute such matter is unmailable,[6] and the crime is complete, therefore, when such mail matter is placed in the mail-box.[7] Therefore such offense can be tried in the district in which the matter is mailed, and statutory provision for trying it elsewhere is unconstitutional.[8] But the offense of causing the prohibited matter to be delivered by mail is committed where delivery by mail is made and may be tried there.[9] The fact that the prohibited matter is mailed in response to a decoy letter,[10] or that it is addressed to a fictitious person and delivered to an officer,[11] will not constitute an excuse.[12] The indictment must set out with particularity the scheme in the carrying out of which the matter complained of was deposited in the mail.[13] Evidence outside the mail matter itself may be introduced by the prosecution to show that the business advertised was in fact a lottery.[14]

§ **1335. Decoy letters.**— The question whether it constitutes a defense in a prosecution for crime that the act is done in pursuance of a solicitation of or opportunity offered by an officer

1 U. S. v. Wallis, 58 Fed. R. 942.

2 U. S. v. Wallis, 58 Fed. R. 942. And as to lotteries in general, see *supra*, § 1315.

3 U. S. v. Clark, 22 Fed. R. 708.

4 U. S. v. Mason, 22 Fed. R. 707.

5 U. S. Rev. Stat., §§ 3929, 4041; Dauphin v. Key, 4 MacAr. 203.

6 U. S. v. Zeisler, 30 Fed. R. 499.

7 U. S. v. Lynch, 49 Fed. R. 851.

8 U. S. v. Conrad, 59 Fed. R. 458.

9 Horner v. U. S., 143 U. S. 570; U. S. v. Horner, 44 Fed. R. 677; U. S. v. Conrad, 59 Fed. R. 458. Merely to send to the postoffice, however, a letter which is not actually placed in the mail does not constitute the offense: U. S. v. Dauphin, 20 Fed. R. 625.

10 U. S. v. Moore, 19 Fed. R. 39.

11 U. S. v. Duff, 19 Blatch. 9.

12 See next section.

13 U. S. v. MacDonald, 65 Fed. R. 486. In the earlier cases it was held sufficient to charge that the matter was concerning a lottery and to promote and aid the same: U. S. v. Conrad, 59 Fed. R. 458. And see U. S. v. Bailey, 47 Fed. R. 117.

14 McDonald v. U. S., 63 Fed. R. 426.

who acts for the purpose of detecting and arresting the defendant for the commission of such crime has already been discussed.[1] In connection with prosecutions for violation of the postal laws, the question has often arisen as to whether the fact that the act charged was committed with reference to decoy letters that were put in the mail simply for the purpose of being placed in the hands of an employee who should wrongfully take them, or unmailable matter which is sent in consequence of a fictitious letter calling for such matter, is a defense. In a few cases it has been held that the fact that sending unmailable matter was in response to a fictitious inquiry may be shown;[2] but these cases are discredited by others, in which it is held that a letter placed in the mail, addressed to a fictitious person and not intended to be delivered, is still mail matter, and the taking of it by an employee may be embezzlement or larceny from the mails.[3] A postoffice inspector who has carried on correspondence with defendant in order to convict him of crime in the use of the United States mails is not an accomplice in the commission of such crime whose testimony requires corroboration; he is not to be considered as one who induces to the commission of crime, but simply as a detective seeking to ascertain whether the defendant was engaged in acts which are criminal.[4] Nor will the fact that the inspector resorts to decoy letters in order to detect the mailing of improper matter operate to discredit his testimony.[5] An inspector who opens a letter bearing a fictitious address, sent in response to a decoy letter, is not guilty of an offense under the statute with reference to opening letters.[6]

[1] *Supra*, §§ 117, 118.

[2] U. S. v. Whittier, 5 Dill. 35; U. S. v. Adams, 59 Fed. R. 674. But on this exact point, see, to the contrary, U. S. v. Moore, 19 Fed. R. 39; U. S. v. Duff, 19 Blatch. 9; U. S. v. Bott, 11 Blatch. 346; Bates v. U. S., 10 Fed. R. 92.

[3] U. S. v. Bethea, 44 Fed. R. 802; U. S. v. Wight, 38 Fed. R. 106; U. S. v. Dorsey, 40 Fed. R. 752; Walster v. U. S., 42 Fed. R. 891; U. S. v. Foye, 1 Curt. 364; U. S. v. Cottingham, 2 Blatch. 470. *Contra*, U. S. v. Matthews, 35 Fed. R. 890; U. S. v. Denicke, 35 Fed. R. 407. The English cases accord with the weight of authority in the courts of the United States: Reg. v. Young, 2 C. & K. 466 (overruling Reg. v. Gardner, 1 C. & K. 628); Reg. v. Rathbone, Car. & M. 220. But see *contra*, Reg. v. Shepherd, Dears. 606.

[4] Grimm v. U. S., 156 U. S. 604; Goode v. U. S., 159 U. S. 663; Montgomery v. U. S., 162 U. S. 410; Andrews v. U. S., 162 U. S. 420.

[5] U. S. v. Slenker, 32 Fed. R. 691.

[6] Andrews v. U. S., 162 U. S. 420.

CHAPTER 68.

REGULATIONS AS TO COMMERCE.

§ **1336. Discrimination.**— The federal statute for the regulation of interstate commerce [1] relates to carriers engaged in transportation of passengers or freight from one state to another, whether the particular carrier in question operates a line extending into or through more than one state or not,[2] and prohibits undue preferences by receiving greater or less compensation from one shipper than from another for whom like service is rendered,[3] or charging more for a short haul than for a long haul in the same direction and under similar circumstances.[4] Free passes, except under specified circumstances, are prohibited,[5] but it must appear that the pass has been used, not merely that it has been issued.[6] While an agent may be liable for making unjust discriminations, as by issuing a free pass in a case where it is not authorized by law,[7] yet a mere collecting agent, having nothing to do with fixing rates, is not indictable for collecting a greater rate for a short than for a long haul.[8]

§ **1337. Unlawful combinations.**— A federal statute [9] provides for the punishment of combinations in restraint of commerce among the states, and confers jurisdiction on the federal courts to restrain violations of the act, which restraint may be

[1] Act of February 4, 1887, ch. 104; 24 Stat. at Large, 397, with amendments.

[2] In re Grand Jury, 62 Fed. R. 834.

[3] U. S. v. Hanley, 71 Fed. R. 672. But it is not enough to charge the giving of a rebate to one shipper unless it is stated also that a like rebate was refused to other shippers: Ibid. In determining whether preferences have been given, a joint rate and the local rate should not be compared: Ibid.

[4] U. S. v. Mellen, 53 Fed. R. 229. But in comparing rates for long and short hauls it is not proper to make a joint rate the basis of comparison with a local rate: Ibid.

[5] In re Charge to Grand Jury, 66 Fed. R. 148.

[6] In re Huntington, 68 Fed. R. 881.

[7] In re Charge to Grand Jury, 66 Fed. R. 146.

[8] U. S. v. Mellen, 53 Fed. R. 229.

[9] Act of July 2, 1890, ch. 647; 26 Stat. at Large, 209.

by injunction.[1] The injunction may be enforced by information to punish a violation thereof, and may be thus enforced as against a party not specifically named in the bill nor served with subpœna, if the injunction order has been served on him as one of the unknown defendants referred to in the bill.[2] This statute is applicable to a combination whose professed object is to resist the operation of railroads, the lines of which extend from one state into another, until such roads accede to certain demands made upon them, whether such demands are in themselves reasonable or unreasonable.[3] But the statute does not cover the case of a purchase of stock in a manufacturing company for the purpose of acquiring control of the business of manufacturing a certain article.[4]

1338. Carriage of live-stock.— In further exercise of the constitutional power to regulate commerce among the states, congress has made regulations as to the transportation of live-stock being carried from one state into or through another, by which such animals are not to be confined for more than twenty-eight consecutive hours without unloading for rest, water and feeding,[5] and such a statute is within the power of congress on the subject.[6] One connecting carrier is not liable for the default of a preceding carrier except as it may be chargeable with notice of the time during which the animals have been confined before coming into its possession.[7]

§ 1338a. Trading with the Indians.— There are some federal regulations as to trading with Indians without a license.[8]

[1] U. S. v. Agler, 62 Fed. R. 824; and such provision is constitutional: U. S. v. Elliott, 64 Fed. R. 27.

[2] U. S. v. Agler, 62 Fed. R. 824; U. S. v. Elliott, 64 Fed. R. 27.

[3] U. S. v. Elliott, 62 Fed. R. 801. And see *supra*, § 963.

[4] U. S. v. E. C. Knight Co., 156 U. S. 1; U. S. v. E. C. Knight Co., 60 Fed. R. 934.

[5] Newport N. & M. V. Co. v. U. S., 61 Fed. R. 488.

[6] U. S. v. Boston & Albany R. Co., 15 Fed. R. 209.

[7] U. S. v. Louisville & Nashville R. Co., 18 Fed. R. 480. This statute has already been mentioned under the head of cruelty to animals, *supra*, § 1161.

[8] U. S. v. Certain Property, 1 Ariz. 31. As to sale of liquor to Indians, see *supra*, § 1263. As to what is deemed Indian country, see American Fur Co. v. U. S., 2 Pet. 358; Ex parte Crow Dog, 109 U. S. 556; Bates v. Clark, 95 U. S. 204.

CHAPTER 69.

OFFENSES AGAINST BANKING ACT.

§ 1339. **False entries.**— Under the statutes relating to the organization and control of the national banks, it is criminal for any officer to make false entries in the books, reports or statements of such bank with intent to deceive or mislead its own officers or the officers of the government with reference to the condition of the bank.[1] Thus, it is criminal to make such false entry with intent to deceive a director or officer of the bank,[2] or the controller of the currency;[3] and it is immaterial that the officer making such false entry or report does it through a clerk and without actual knowledge of its falsity, the matter being one about which it is his duty to have knowledge and make proper statements.[4] But as the sole duty of bank directors in regard to reports to the controller is to attest them by their signatures, and any change in the report by a director would be a mere spoliation thereof, such directors cannot be held criminally liable for false statements made in such report.[5] It is not necessary to allege that the reports were transmitted to the controller or were published; it is the act of making false entries which is criminal.[6] Nor is it necessary that the false entries be acted on, or that they actually deceive or mislead the officer to whom they are made.[7] But to come within the statute the entries must be wilfully and intentionally false, and not merely erroneous by reason of clerical mistakes.[8] In charging the in-

[1] U. S. v. Harper, 33 Fed. R. 471; U. S. v. Crecilius, 34 Fed. R. 30. This offense is exclusively within the jurisdiction of the federal courts: In re Eno, 54 Fed. R. 669.

[2] U. S. v. Means, 42 Fed. R. 599.

[3] U. S. v. French, 57 Fed. R. 382. But if the charge is of making false entries in a report to the controller with intent to deceive its directors, it is not sufficient to prove intent to deceive other persons: U. S. v. Allen, 47 Fed. R. 696.

[4] U. S. v. Allen, 47 Fed. R. 696.

[5] U. S. v. Potter, 56 Fed. R. 83.

[6] U. S. v. Potter, 56 Fed. R. 83.

[7] U. S. v. Means, 42 Fed. R. 599; U. S. v. Graves, 53 Fed. R. 634. But if the officers alleged to have been deceived were accomplices in making the false entries, it seems that the act would not be criminal: U. S. v. Means, 42 Fed. R. 599.

[8] U. S. v. Allen, 47 Fed. R. 696; U. S. v. Graves, 53 Fed. R. 634. In determining the guilt of the officer

tent to defraud by such false entries it may be alleged that they were made with intent to injure and defraud the banking association and persons to the grand jurors unknown.[1] It is sufficient to charge that defendant knowingly, wilfully and unlawfully made false entries, etc., setting out the report and stating the particulars of its falsity.[2] The indictment need not describe the report with technical accuracy.[3] One may be guilty as aider and abettor or procurer who assists in or induces the making of the false entries, or indeed in other violations of the national banking act, although he is not an officer of the bank.[4]

§ **1340. Embezzlement; misapplication of funds.**— The banking act provides for the punishment of embezzlement and wilful misapplication of the moneys, etc., of such a bank, and these are distinct offenses though they may be joined in one indictment in separate counts.[5] To constitute the offense of embezzlement under this statute it must appear that the funds of the bank came lawfully into the possession of the defendant and that while so held by him were converted to his own use with intent to defraud the bank.[6] Misapplication of funds by the president may consist in permitting overdrafts without any reasonable ground to believe that the money can be repaid, intending thereby to injure and defraud the bank.[7] It is a crime under the banking act to certify a check drawn by one not having on deposit sufficient money to meet the same.[8]

charged with making false entries the jury should consider his relation to the bank and whether he had any motive for the act, together with circumstances such as may have induced him to do it, and evidence of his good character may be sufficient to resolve any doubt as to fraudulent intent in his favor: U. S. v. Allen, 47 Fed. R. 696.

[1] U. S. v. Potter, 56 Fed. R. 97; Potter v. U. S., 155 U. S. 438; U. S. v. Britton, 107 U. S. 655.

[2] U. S. v. Hughitt, 45 Fed. R. 47.

[3] Cochran v. U. S., 157 U. S. 286.

[4] Coffin v. U. S., 162 U. S. 664; Coffin v. U. S., 156 U. S. 432; U. S. v. French, 57 Fed. R. 382.

[5] U. S. v. Cadwallader, 59 Fed. R. 677.

[6] U. S. v. Harper, 33 Fed. R. 471. And as to embezzlement, see further, *supra*, § 621 et seq.

[7] Coffin v. U. S., 162 U. S. 664. For other instances of misapplication of funds see Batchelor v. U. S., 156 U. S. 426; Coffin v. U. S., 156 U. S. 432; U. S. v. Britton, 107 U. S. 655; and for cases of aiding and abetting in such misapplication of funds, see Evans v. U. S., 153 U. S. 584; Claassen v. U. S., 142 U. S. 140; U. S. v. Northway, 120 U. S. 327.

[8] U. S. v. Potter, 56 Fed. R. 83.

CHAPTER 70.

OFFENSES AGAINST THE NEUTRALITY, IMMIGRATION AND NATURALIZATION LAWS.

§ 1341. **Violations of neutrality.**— There are strict statutory provisions against organizing or fitting out military or naval expeditions against a foreign state with whom the United States may be at peace,[1] and these provisions cover the case of an expedition composed of men who, in pursuance of a common plan, leave the United States unarmed, but after reaching the high seas are supplied with arms brought for them on the same vessel or otherwise, and organize and drill as a military force to carry on operations against a foreign friendly power.[2] And the captain of a vessel who knowingly allows persons who have taken passage on his vessel to be thus supplied with arms and organized is guilty of an offense.[3] But the statute does not forbid the shipping of arms or ammunition or military equipments to a foreign country, nor forbid individuals singly or in unarmed associations from leaving the United States for the purpose of joining in military operations which are being carried on in other countries.[4] Mere words will not constitute the offense under the statute, nor the procuring of means with the mere intent to use them on the occurrence of a contingency, there being no overt act.[5]

§ 1342. **Violence to foreign minister.**— By an early statute, which is still continued in force,[6] it is made criminal to assault or offer violence to the person of a public minister in violation of

[1] U. S. Rev. Stat., §§ 5281–5291.

[2] Wiborg v. U. S., 163 U. S. 632.

[3] U. S. v. Hughes, 70 Fed. R. 972; s. c., 75 Fed. R. 267; U. S. v. Rand, 17 Fed. R. 142. The military character of such an expedition may be determined by the designation of officers or leaders, the organization of the men in regiments or companies and the purchase of military stores, but no particular number of men is necessary, nor is it necessary that the expedition should actually set out: U. S. v. Ybanez, 53 Fed. R. 536.

[4] U. S. v. Pena, 69 Fed. R. 983; U. S. v. Trumbull, 48 Fed. R. 99.

[5] U. S. v. Lumsden, 1 Bond, 5.

[6] U. S. Rev. Stat., § 4062.

the law of nations. Where the violence consisted in firing at the minister's house, it was held essential that the defendant should be shown to have known that fact.[1] But where the assault was on a public minister personally, knowledge of his official character was said to be immaterial.[2] A case under this statute was held not to be one affecting an ambassador or other public minister in such sense as to give rise to the question whether the supreme court of the United States had original jurisdiction thereof.[3]

§ **1343. Immigration laws; contract labor.**— There are provisions against bringing into the country alien immigrants who are under contract to perform labor, and authorizing the secretary of the treasury, in case he shall be satisfied that an immigrant has been allowed to land contrary to such prohibition, to cause him, within one year, to be taken into custody and returned to the country whence he came, at the expense of the owner of the importing vessel or the person contracting for his services.[4] One who, though of foreign birth, has been a resident of the United States without naturalization, is not an alien immigrant within the meaning of this provision.[5] In applying the provision as to the return of an immigrant who has been brought in contrary to this statute, the decision of the secretary of the treasury as to whether or not the immigrant is a prohibited person is conclusive and will not be reviewed by the courts.[6] In determining whether the immigrant is under "contract," that term is to be construed as meaning an enforcible contract, express or implied.[7] The statute applies to the case of an under coachmen, as he is within the terms of the statute "a personal or domestic servant;"[8] but it does not cover an alien who comes as a chemist on a sugar plantation, his expenses being paid by his employer.[9] To ren-

[1] U. S. v. Hand, 2 Wash. C. C. 435.

[2] U. S. v. Little, 2 Wash. C. C. 159; U. S. v. Ortega, 4 Wash. C. C. 531; U. S. v. Benner, Baldw. 234.

[3] U. S. v. Ortega, 11 Wheat. 467.

[4] Act of October 19, 1888, chapter 1210, 25 Stat. at Large, 566, which supersedes other statutory provisions on the subject.

[5] In re Panzara, 51 Fed. R. 275.

[6] In re Howard, 63 Fed. R. 263. Under previous statutes there have been similar rulings: In re Didfirri, 48 Fed. R. 168; In re Lifieri, 52 Fed. R. 293.

[7] U. S. v. Edgar, 45 Fed. R. 44.

[8] In re Howard, 63 Fed. R 263.

[9] U. S. v. Laws, 163 U. S. 258. As to what is a new industry within the exception of the statute as to

der the master of a vessel liable for landing or permitting to land any such alien immigrant, the burden is on the prosecution to show that the act was knowingly or unlawfully permitted.[1] The district courts have concurrent jurisdiction with the circuit courts of suits for penalties under this statutory provision.[2]

§ 1344. Exclusion of Chinese.— Statutes have been passed to exclude from the country Chinese laborers, and even to expel those who were in the country at the time of the passage of such act for failure to comply with certain regulations as to registration, and these statutory provisions have been held to be constitutional, it being within the province of the federal government to regulate intercourse with foreign nations in this respect.[3] The expulsion from the country provided for by these statutes is not in the nature of punishment for crime, and therefore does not involve the usual requirements as to criminal procedure.[4] While executive or subordinate officials cannot be given authority to subject persons to infamous punishment or confiscation of property without a trial, yet detention or temporary confinement may be authorized upon the action of such officials as a part of the means necessary to give effect to the act.[5] The action of the treasury officials in the enforcement of such a statute may be made conclusive;[6] but such officials do not have final jurisdiction to determine that a person of Chinese

importation of laborers under contract, see U. S. v. Bromley, 58 Fed. R. 554.

[1] U. S. v. Spruth, 71 Fed. R. 678 (distinguishing Warren v. U. S., 58 Fed. R. 559).

[2] U. S. v. Whitcomb Metal Bedstead Co., 45 Fed. R. 89.

[3] Chae Chan Ping v. U. S., 130 U. S. 581; Fong Yue Ting v. U. S., 149 U. S. 698; Lem Moon Sing v. U. S., 158 U. S. 538.

[4] U. S. v. Wong Sing, 51 Fed. R. 79; In re Ng Loy Hoe, 53 Fed. R. 914; U. S. v. Hing Quong Chow, 53 Fed. R. 233; In re Sing Lee, 54 Fed. R. 334. An amendment to the first act extended the time of registration with an exception as to persons who had been convicted of felony: U. S. v. Chew Cheong, 61 Fed. R. 200.

[5] Wong Wing v. U. S., 163 U. S. 228; U. S. v. Wong Sing, 51 Fed. R. 79; In re Ah Yuk, 53 Fed. R. 781. There was some difficult under the first act in regard to funds to defray the expense of deportation, but the subsequent act made an appropriation of such funds, and it was held that a district judge called upon to act in such a case by issuing a warrant of arrest would not be justified in refusing to do so on account of there being no such funds available: U. S. v. Chum Shang Yuen, 57 Fed. R. 588; In re Lintner, 57 Fed. R. 587.

[6] Nishimura Ekiu v. U. S., 142 U. S. 651; U. S. v. Jung Ah Lung, 124 U. S. 621.

descent is not a citizen of the United States, where he claims the right to admission on that ground, and the question of citizenship may be passed on by a court on writ of *habeas corpus.*[1] Statutes as to deportation provide that a Chinaman found not entitled to remain in the United States shall be returned to the country whence he came, which will be that in which his residence was prior to coming into the United States — not necessarily China.[2] In a prosecution for aiding or abetting the landing in the United States from any vessel of any Chinese person not lawfully entitled to enter, it must appear that the Chinese person was one prohibited from landing, and that he was brought on the same vessel from which he landed, on a voyage terminating at the time of the landing.[3]

§ **1345. To whom applicable.**— The statutes are applicable to Chinese laborers and not to merchants, and it is provided that the character of one claiming to be a merchant must be established by a certificate of the representative of the United States in China, and without such certificate one is not entitled to admission as merchant no matter what other evidence he may have as to his character.[4] But such provisions as to a certificate are not applicable to one who claims the right to return to this country or remain in the country on account of having previously been established here as a merchant, and the fact of such character may be shown by other evidence.[5] The statutes require that to have been a merchant the person seeking to return on that ground must have conducted business in his own name and his interest in the business must have been real, and if the business was a partnership business his name must have appeared in the partnership articles, although

[1] In re Tom Yum, 64 Fed. R. 485. But the finding of a commissioner on a question of fact affecting the right of a Chinaman to remain in the country will not be disturbed on appeal unless clearly against the weight of evidence: U. S. v. Chung Fung Sun, 63 Fed. R. 361.

[2] Wan Shing v. U. S., 140 U. S. 424; U. S. v. Don On, 49 Fed. R. 569; In re Leo Hem Bow, 47 Fed. R. 302; In re Mah Wong Gee, 47 Fed. R. 433; U. S. v. Chong Sam, 47 Fed. R. 878. But where the Chinaman has been a sojourner in the country through which he has come on returning from China he should be sent back to China: U. S. v. Ah Toy, 47 Fed. R. 305.

[3] U. S. v. Trumbull, 46 Fed. R. 755.

[4] In re Wo Tai Li, 48 Fed. R. 668.

[5] Lau Ow Bew v. U. S., 144 U. S. 47; U. S. v. Lee Hoy, 48 Fed. R. 825; but see In re Yee Lung, 61 Fed. R. 641.

it is not necessary that it shall have appeared in the firm designation.[1] The term "laborer" in the exclusion act has the same meaning as in the treaty with China, in which the language used was broad enough to include gamblers and high-binders.[2] A restaurant proprietor who keeps a place for serving meals and prepares the material for such meals is a laborer and not a merchant.[3] So one who has been serving a term of imprisonment at hard labor is a laborer, although he may previously have been a merchant.[4] A temporary absence from the United States with intent to return will not forfeit a residence already acquired.[5]

§ **1346. Naturalization.**— Some offenses are provided for in connection with naturalization laws, such as taking a false oath[6] or presenting a false and fraudulent certificate.[7] The United States may sue in the federal courts for the cancellation of a certificate or decree of naturalization which has been obtained by fraud even in a state court.[8] It is criminal to sell a certificate of naturalization to a person to whom it is not issued, and it is immaterial that the certificate thus offered to be sold is fraudulent, provided it is apparently valid.[9]

[1] Lee Kan v. U. S., 62 Fed. R. 914; In re Quan Gin, 61 Fed. R. 395. Absence for even six years while retaining an interest in firm business and receiving a share of the profits continues a commercial domicile in the United States and prevents being sent back under the exclusion act: U. S. v. Chin Quong Look, 52 Fed. R. 203.

[2] U. S. v. Ah Fawn, 57 Fed. R. 591.

[3] In re Ah Yow, 59 Fed. R. 561.

[4] U. S. v. Wong Ah Hung, 62 Fed. R. 1005. A woman married according to Chinese law to a Chinaman then in the United States, being brought to the United States by direction of her husband, both acting in good faith, is entitled to land: In re Lum Ling Ying, 59 Fed. R. 682.

[5] U. S. v. Lee Yung, 63 Fed. R. 520.

[6] U. S. v. Lehman, 39 Fed. R. 768.

[7] U. S. v. Lehman, 39 Fed. R. 768.

[8] U. S. v. Norsch, 42 Fed. R. 417.

[9] U. S. v. Raggazzini, 50 Fed. R. 923.

CHAPTER 71.

VIOLATION OF NAVIGATION LAWS.

§ 1347. **What criminal.**—The navigation laws of the United States provide for the punishment of an officer for beating or ill-treating one of the crew, and any one is an officer under this statute who by authority exercises the function of control over the actions of the crew or any part of it.[1] It is also criminal to harbor and secrete deserting seamen;[2] but such statute does not apply to the harboring or secreting of a person employed or engaged to serve on a vessel not belonging to a citizen of the United States.[3] It is criminal to destroy a vessel with the intent to defraud underwriters.[4] For the purpose of preventing introduction of disease from foreign countries, there are regulations requiring a vessel bound for the United States to procure in the port of departure for the United States, from the United States consul there, a bill of health, the port of departure, in this sense, being not necessarily the last port at which the ship stops while bound for the United States, but the port from which she clears.[5] The United States, in the exercise of its admiralty and maritime jurisdiction, provides for the punishment of various crimes on the high seas and navigable waters of the United States, such as that of murder, manslaughter, and the like.[6] Crimes thus provided for are not essentially different from like crimes committed elsewhere, and need not be here specially discussed. For the purpose of having the coasting trade carried on by vessels of this country, it is made criminal to transport merchandise between ports of the United States on foreign vessels; but such statute is not violated by shipping goods from a port of this country to a

[1] U. S. v. Trice, 30 Fed. R. 490. It is also criminal in an officer to force a mariner on shore: U. S. v. Ruggles, 5 Mason, 192.

[2] U. S. v. Grant, 55 Fed. R. 414. Deserting seamen may be arrested and returned to the master: Robertson v. Baldwin, — U. S. —, 17 S. C. R. 326.

[3] Grant v. U. S., 58 Fed. R. 694.

[4] U. S. v. Johns, 1 Wash. C. C. 363.

[5] U. S. v. The Dago, 61 Fed. R. 986.

[6] U. S. v. Beacham, 29 Fed. R. 284.

foreign port in a foreign vessel and afterwards forwarding them by another foreign vessel to another port of the United States, although this was the intention from the outset.[1] State statutes as to pilotage,[2] boarding vessels before being made fast to the wharf,[3] and the like, are so far peculiar in their nature that a general discussion of them is not practicable.

[1] U. S. v. Two Hundred and Fifty Kegs of Nails, 61 Fed. R. 410.

[2] C. v. Ricketson, 5 Met. 412.

[3] C. v. Kennedy, 160 Mass. 312.

CHAPTER 72.

VIOLATION OF PENSION LAWS.

§ 1348. **What criminal.**— There are provisions against making a false certificate in support of an application for a pension,[1] or a false affidavit.[2] So one who makes a false deposition to enable another to obtain a penson is punishable.[3] It is also an offense for a member of the board of examining surgeons to receive a bribe.[4] For the protection of the pensioner it is made criminal to wrongfully withhold from such a person a pension due him;[5] further it is made criminal to charge a pensioner for services in securing a pension more than a sum fixed by law.[6] It is also made criminal to receive any compensation for procuring a pension claim before it is allowed.[7]

1 U. S. v. Kessel, 62 Fed. R. 57.

2 U. S. v. Van Leuven, 62 Fed. R. 69; U. S. v. Adler, 49 Fed. R. 733. And the latter crime may be committed though the affidavit is made before the proper officer, as the provision applies also to the offense of using a genuine instrument knowing it to be false, with intent to defraud the United States: U. S. v. Cowdy, 87 Fed. R. 332.

3 U. S. v. Rhodes, 30 Fed. R. 431.

4 U. S. v. Kessel, 62 Fed. R. 57; U. S. v. Van Leuven, 62 Fed. R. 62.

5 Ballew v. U. S., 160 U. S. 187; U. S. v. Scott, 25 Fed. R. 470.

6 Frisbie v. U. S., 157 U. S. 160; U. S. v. Van Vliet, 23 Fed. R. 35; U. S. v. Hague, 22 Fed. R. 706; U. S. v. Mathews, 23 Fed. R. 74. One who as attorney fills out the vouchers necessary to obtain the first payment of pension money is within the terms of the statute making it a misdemeanor for a person instrumental in prosecuting the claim to retain a greater compensation than allowed by law: U. S. v. Reynolds, 48 Fed. R. 721. It is not necessary to specify in what way the accused was instrumental in obtaining a pension: U. S. v. Reynolds, 48 Fed. R. 215.

7 U. S. v. Van Leuven, 62 Fed. R. 52.

CHAPTER 73.

VIOLATION OF REVENUE LAWS; MAKING FALSE CLAIMS.

§ **1349. Forfeiture of goods.**— There are provisions for the forfeiture of property on which a required revenue tax is not paid, or property used in the attempt to evade the payment of revenue duties on other property.[1] Proceedings for forfeiture are not strictly criminal cases if it is not sought to impose fine or imprisonment,[2] and the forfeiture of the property will not constitute a bar to a criminal prosecution of the person for violation of the law, the proceedings for forfeiture being *in rem.*[3]

§ **1350. Licenses and stamps.**— It is criminal to carry on some forms of business without a federal license, such, for instance, as to retail spirituous or fermented liquors.[4] To protect the United States in the collection of internal revenue tax it is made criminal to use cases or packages previously in-

[1] Gregory v. U. S., 17 Blatch. 325; U. S. v. Two Horses, 9 Ben. 529. But condemnation of the property itself on which the tax is payable will not be conclusive in a proceeding for the condemnation of other property claimed to have been fraudulently used in the attempt to evade such tax: U. S. v. Two Horses, 9 Ben. 529. To warrant a forfeiture, evidence of intent to defraud must be introduced: U. S. v. Fourteen Packages of Whisky, 66 Fed. R. 984. Where the information charging the facts relied on to support a forfeiture is vague, the claimant of the property may be entitled to a bill of particulars: U. S. v. Two Hundred Bushels of Corn, 9 Ben. 186.

[2] Coffee v. U. S., 116 U. S. 427.

[3] U. S. v. Three Copper Stills, 47 Fed. R. 495. But in a suit on a distiller's bond the dismissal of the indictments for the violations sought to be recovered for on the bond and compromise of the claim will constitute a bar: U. S. v. Chouteau, 102 U. S. 603.

[4] U. S. v. Rennecke, 28 Fed. R. 847; U. S. v. Smith, 27 Fed. R. 854. And see *supra*, § 1245. Where a brewer's license was issued to a firm, and during the year one partner bought out the other and continued the business for the rest of the year, *held*, that there was no violation of the law: U. S. v. Glab, 1 McCrary, 166. It is made criminal to ship spirituous or fermented liquors or wines under any other name than that known to the trade as designating the kind or quality thereof, and such provision is not unconstitutional: U. S. v. Loeb, 49 Fed. R. 636.

spected for the sale of spirits, for spirits of a different quality from those contained in them at the time of the inspection, but to constitute the offense it must appear that the change was brought about by filling with other spirits or the withdrawal of the original contents or part thereof.[1] It is criminal to change or alter the marks and stamps used in connection with the collection of the internal revenue,[2] or to remove canceled or used stamps without their being destroyed or defaced, or to have canceled stamps in possession with a fraudulent purpose.[3]

§ **1351. Customs duties.**— The offense of smuggling, that is, importing goods which are subject to the payment of an import duty without payment of such duty, is punishable under the federal statutes.[4] Possession of smuggled goods is *prima facie* evidence of guilt, which must be overcome by the defendant.[5] It is a crime to make false and fraudulent entry of goods by means of false affidavits, statements or otherwise;[6] but the violation of the customs laws is punishable also by a forfeiture of the goods unlawfully brought in or some portion thereof, or an increased duty,[7] or of the vessel in which the goods are unlawfully imported; but the vessel is not to be held liable for a penalty imposed on its mate.[8] Under provisions by which bonded freight is allowed to pass through the United States in transit between two places in the British provinces, there is no punishment for breaking open a bonded car, although there

[1] U. S. v. Bardenheier, 49 Fed. R. 846.

[2] U. S. v. Bardenheier, 49 Fed. R. 846.

[3] U. S. v. Spiegel, 116 U. S. 270; U. S. v. Loup, 1 McCrary, 168.

[4] U. S. v. Thomas, 2 Abb. (U. S.) 114; The Missouri, 4 Ben. 410. The indictment must charge facts which render the alleged importation unlawful: U. S. v. Thomas, 2 Abb. (U. S.) 114.

[5] U. S. v. Fraser, 42 Fed. R. 140. An indictment charging that defendant smuggled and clandestinely introduced into the United States, etc., without paying or accounting for such duty, etc., sufficiently charges that defendant knew that the duty on the smuggled goods had not been paid: U. S. v. Dunbar, 60 Fed. R. 75; Dunbar v. U. S., 156 U. S. 185.

[6] U. S. v. Cutajar, 60 Fed. R. 744.

[7] Pings v. U. S., 72 Fed. R. 260; U. S. v. Lot of Jewelry, 59 Fed. R. 684; U. S. v. York Street, etc. Co., 17 Blatch. 138. The burden of proof is on the United States to show individual fraud on the part of the importer: U. S. v. One Hundred and Twenty-nine Bales of Merchandise, 46 Fed. R. 468; although where there is probable cause for seizure, it is provided that the burden is upon the claimant of the goods: U. S. v. Lot of Jewelry, 59 Fed. R. 684.

[8] The C. G. White v. U. S., 64 Fed. R. 579.

is such provision as to a car passing from a port of entry of the United States to another place therein.[1]

§ 1352. **Presenting false claims.**— Under various chapters of the revised statutes there are special penalties provided for presenting false affidavits, certificates, etc., but there are also general provisions as to presenting false claims for payment in the civil, military or naval service or otherwise.[2] One who presents what purports to be an affidavit in support of a fraudulent claim is estopped to deny that the document was not an affidavit when presented in evidence against him.[3]

[1] U. S. v. Durwood, 49 Fed. R. 446.

[2] U. S. v. Ingraham, 49 Fed. R. 155; U. S. v. Strobach, 48 Fed. R. 902; U. S. v. Bowen, 3 MacAr. 64; U. S. v. Moore, 3 MacAr. 226; U. S. v. Ambrose, 2 Fed. R. 764; U. S. v. Goggin, 3 Fed. R. 492; U. S. v. Bittinger, 21 Int. Rev. Rec. 342; U. S. v. Miskell, 15 Fed. R. 369; U. S. v. Rhodes, 30 Fed. R. 431; U. S. v. Reichert, 32 Fed. R. 142; U. S. v. Jones, 32 Fed. R. 482; U. S. v. Route, 33 Fed. R. 246.

[3] Ingraham v. U. S., 155 U. S. 434.

CHAPTER 74.

VIOLATION OF LAND LAWS.

§ **1353. What punishable.**— To protect the property of the United States it is made criminal to cut or remove timber from lands open to private entry with intent to use it for any other than United States naval purposes;[1] or to cut timber from mineral lands, the intent in such case being immaterial.[2]

[1] U. S. v. Garretson, 42 Fed. R. 22.

[2] U. S. v. Reder, 69 Fed. R. 965. And see Maskill v. S., 8 Blackf. 299.

PART XV.

OFFENSES AGAINST SOVEREIGNTY.

CHAPTER 75.

TREASON.

§ 1354. **History of the crime.**—While the general conception of the crime of treason as involving the violation of the duty of allegiance owed by an inferior to a superior seems to have been early recognized in the English law, yet there had been so much uncertainty as to the particular classes of acts which should be deemed a violation of such duty as to be criminal, and so great a tendency to punish political enemies by conviction for merely constructive treason, that the statute of Edward 3, in which treason was carefully defined, was regarded long after as one of the most important statutes in English history.[1] This statute defined both high and petit treason, giving definite form to each, and in the definition of high treason used language which is employed in the constitution of the United States in defining the crime; but levying war and lending aid and comfort were by that statute only one of the many forms of high treason. The other forms there defined have been eliminated by our constitutional provisions, and though they are the basis for a large part of the discussion of the crime in the English books are of no significance for us.[2] These authors consider quite fully the theory of allegiance, a matter which was of considerable importance under the early law when the duty of an inferior to his superior was deemed a personal one, but under the modern notion, by which the scope of law is territorial rather than personal, this doctrine of allegiance has

[1] 25 Edward 3, St. 5, ch. 2 (A. D. 1350). And see Coke's commentaries thereon, 3 Inst. 1.

[2] For the English authorities, see 3 Inst. 1; 1 Hale, P. C. 58; 1 Hawk. P. C., ch. 17, § 1; 1 Bl. Com. 75; Foster, 183; Stephen's Digest Cr. L., ch. 6, and note thereto; 2 Stephen's History Cr. L. 241. And see 2 Bish. Cr. L., § 1202.

become of little significance. Except as the international law recognizes the doctrine of exterritoriality, all persons within the territorial limits of a sovereign state owe allegiance to the sovereign power and may be guilty of treason. Undoubtedly also the subjects of a sovereign state may be guilty of treason by acts done outside of its territory. But these questions have not been very fully discussed by the American courts. Their elaboration may for the present be left for writers on international law.[1] The whole conception of the relation between sovereign and subject has been changed by the substitution of the conception of the people instead of a ruler as sovereign, and accordingly our notions of treason have changed more in substance than any change in the particular language used with reference to the crime would indicate.[2] By the statute of Edward 3, above referred to, petit treason was defined as "First, where a servant kills his master; secondly, where a wife kills her husband; thirdly, where an ecclesiastical man, secular or religious, kills his prelate to whom he owes obedience;"[3] but these acts by the present law, both in England and the United States, are simply murder, and the term "petit treason" has entirely lost its significance.[4]

§ **1355. Constitutional definitions.**— The fact that in England there had been much difficulty, not only before the statute of Edward 3, but afterwards, in determining what was high treason, and that prosecutions for the crime had been used as instruments of political oppression, led the framers of the federal constitution to incorporate therein a definition taken from the statute of Edward 3, but embodying only one of the forms of the crime defined by that statute, to wit: "Treason against the United States shall consist only in levying war against them, or adhering to their enemies, giving

[1] 2 Kent Com. 39; Whart. Conf. of L., §§ 2-4, 902-920; 4 Bl. Com. 74. And in general as to the theory of allegiance in the United States, see Carlisle v. U. S., 16 Wall. 147; Inglis v. Sailor's Snug Harbor, 3 Pet. 99, 155; Jackson v. Goodell, 20 Johns. 188; Wallace v. Harmstad, 44 Pa. St. 492, 501; S. v. Hunt, 2 Hill (S. C.), 1; also Rex v. Delamotte, 1 East, P. C. 53.

[2] Note to 4 Bl. Com., ch. 6, page 119, Hammond's edition.

[3] 3 Inst. 19; 1 Hawk. P. C., ch. 32, § 1.

[4] 3 Stephen, Hist. Cr. L. 34; 1 Bish. Cr. L., § 611. As petit treason has never been recognized in the United States, a statute providing that the punishment for the crime shall be as for murder in the second degree is without effect: S. v. Bilansky, 3 Minn. 246.

them aid and comfort."[1] Similar definitions are found in the constitutions of the various states.[2] The incorporation into state constitutions and criminal codes of definitions of the crime indicate a general assumption that there may be treason against a state, and there are examples of prosecutions for treason in state courts.[3] It is entirely possible that the same act may constitute treason against a state and also against the United States and be punishable as a crime by each, but no such question has ever been discussed in the courts of last resort.[4]

§ 1356. **Statutory definitions.**— The crime of treason is defined by federal statutes in accordance with the language of the constitution, and the punishment is fixed, which is to be death, or imprisonment at hard labor and fine, at the discretion of the court, the imprisonment, however, to be not less than five years and the fine not less than $10,000. The penalty of disqualification for holding office is also added.[5] Similar definitions are found in state statutes; but the prosecutions for treason under either the federal or state provisions have been so few that little light on the construction of these statutes is to be derived from adjudication.[6] In the following sections the doctrine of the cases so far as they have been officially reported will be briefly stated. Some crimes similar in their nature to treason are also defined by statute, such as misprision of treason, inciting or encouraging insurrection, seditious conspiracy, and the like, but there are no adjudications of any significance under these provisions.[7] In England, various crimes which would by early law have been treason are

[1] U. S. Const., art. 3, § 3.

[2] It seems that no such provision is found in any of the state constitutions adopted prior to the federal constitution.

[3] For instance, the trial of Dorr in 1844 before the supreme court of Rhode Island under an indictment for treason against that state, in consequence of which he was convicted and sentenced; and the trial of John Brown in 1859 on charge of treason against Virginia under an indictment also alleging murder and incitement of insurrection among the slaves, under which he was found guilty and hung.

[4] Treason against the United States by furnishing aid to its enemies does not constitute treason against the state of which the person furnishing such aid is a citizen: P. v. Lynch, 11 Johns. 549.

[5] U. S. Rev. Stat., §§ 5331, 5332.

[6] A list of all the trials for treason in the federal or state courts is given in 46 Albany L. J. 345.

[7] U. S. Rev. Stat., §§ 5333–5338.

now defined by statute as treason-felony, for instance, concealing treasure trove.[1]

§ 1357. Levying war; rendering aid and comfort.— It is suggested that to levy war means to raise, create, make or carry on war, and for this purpose it must appear that a state of war exists.[2] To conspire to levy war and to actually levy war are distinct offenses.[3] But if a state of war exists, all who participate therein in any way are guilty of the act of levying war.[4] Intent is essential, but duress will not excuse unless it involves danger to life; threat of destruction of property will not suffice.[5] It has been said in England, and the view receives some support in this country, that combining to secure by intimidation or violence the repeal of a law, or to oppose and prevent by force and terror the execution of a law, is the act of levying war.[6] But the conspiracy and insurrection connected with it must be to effect something of a public nature, to overthrow the government or to nullify some law of the United States and to totally hinder its execution or compel its repeal.[7] Perhaps in case of rebellion there can be no such offense as adhering to the enemies of the government, giving them aid and comfort, as rebels, being citizens, are not enemies; but aid rendered to the rebellion may sustain a conviction for levying war, to constitute which there must be an assemblage of people with force and arms to overthrow the government or resist the laws.[8]

1 Reg. v. Thomas, L. & C. 313; Reg. v. Toole, 10 Cox, 75.

2 Opinion of Chief Justice Marshall in the trial of Aaron Burr, 4 Cranch (Appendix), 470. The trial of Burr is not here fully reported, but as privately reported by Coombs is given in Federal Cases, 14692*a*–14694*a*.

3 Ex parte Bollman, 4 Cranch, 75.

4 Ex parte Bollman, 4 Cranch, 75; U. S. v. Greathouse, 2 Abb. (U. S.) 364. And see Reg. v. Frost, 9 C. & P. 129; Rex v. Stone, 6 T. R. 527; Reg. v. Brittain, 3 Cox, 77; Reg. v. Meaney, 10 Cox, 506; Rex v. McGrowther, 1 East, P. C. 71; Rex v. Gordon, 1 East, P. C. 71.

5 U. S. v. Hodges, 2 Wheeler, Cr. C. 477; 1 East, P. C. 71.

6 U. S. v. Mitchell, 2 Dall. 348. And see Reg. v. Gallagher, 15 Cox, 291; Rex v. Gordon, 2 Doug. 590. The open and active opposition of a number of persons to the execution of a law of the United States if of such a formidable nature as to constitute a defiance for the time being of the authority of the government may constitute an insurrection even though not accompanied by bloodshed, nor of such magnitude as to render success probable: In re Charge to Grand Jury, 62 Fed. R. 828.

7 U. S. v. Hanway, 2 Wall. Jr. 139; U. S. v. Hoxie, 1 Paine, 265.

8 U. S. v. Greathouse, 2 Abb. (U. S.) 364. It is said that the bombard-

§ **1358. Overt act.**— As indicated in the preceding section, there must be some act of war or of giving aid and comfort.[1] The constitution requires[2] that there must be two witnesses to the same overt act unless the crime is confessed in open court, and this rule is adopted from England.[3]

ment of Fort Sumter was the beginning of the war of the Rebellion, and one who adhered to the government after that event was not guilty of treason whatever may have been his acts before that time: Culliton v. U. S., 5 Ct. of Cl. 627.

[1] See, also, Mulcahy v. Reg., L. R. 3 H. L. 306; Reg. v. Oxford, 9 C. & P. 525; Reg. v. McCafferty, 10 Cox, 603. The prisoner is not bound to show the object or meaning of his acts; the offense must be made out by the prosecution: Reg. v. Frost, 9 C. & P. 129. It is an overt act to procure provisions for or attempt to furnish them to the enemy, but not to set out with the intention of procuring such provisions: U. S. v. Pryor, 3 Wash. C. C. 234. So it is treason during a state of war to release prisoners: U. S. v. Hodges, 2 Wheeler, Cr. C. 477; or to send intelligence to the enemy: Rex v. Stone, 6 T. R. 527.

[2] U. S. Const., art. 3, § 3.

[3] Reg. v. McCafferty, 10 Cox, 603; Rex v. Jellias, 1 East, P. C. 130. And see Rex v. Gahagan, 1 East, P. C. 129; Rex v. Horne Tooke, 1 East, P. C. 60, 69.

CHAPTER 76.

PIRACY.

§ 1359. **Nature of the offense.**— In England piracy has been spoken of as a form of treason if committed by a subject against the king's ships in time of war,[1] but in general it is an offense committed on the high seas similar to that of robbery or other felonious depredation on land, and is a crime against the law of nations, punishable, however, by any sovereignty by which the guilty party may be seized and put on trial.[2] The offense as a crime against the United States is considerably enlarged by statute and made to cover acts which might not have been piracy at common law.[3] It did not constitute piracy, under the act of 1790, that a crime of this nature was committed on board of a vessel of a foreign state by a person not a citizen of the United States.[4] Acts of those who do not acknowledge allegiance to any government whatever, and commit piratical acts on the high seas, are, however, punishable by the United States without regard to the portion of the sea where they are committed.[5] Persons who act on the high seas under the assumed authority of a government to which bel-

[1] Rex v. Evans, 1 East, P. C. 80; 1 Hawk. P. C., ch. 32, § 1. And see U. S. Rev. Stat., § 5373.

[2] U. S. Const., art. 1, § 8; U. S. Rev. Stat., §§ 5368–5373; 2 Whart. Cr. L., § 1860; 2 Bish. Cr. L., § 1058; 4 Bl. Com. 72; Stephen, Dig. Cr. L., art. 104; U. S. v. Baker, 5 Blatch. 6. The federal statutes refer to the law of nations for a definition of piracy, and this is sufficient: U. S. v. Smith, 5 Wheat. 153 and note. The definition given by Blackstone, taken from Hawkins, is as follows: "The offense of piracy at common law consisted in committing those acts of robbery and depredation upon the high seas which if committed upon land would have amounted to felony there:" 4 Bl. Com. 72. This definition is quoted in Dole v. New England Mut. M. Ins. Co., 2 Cliff. 394, 415; U. S. v. Tully, 1 Gall. 247. Pirates may be lawfully captured on the ocean by the public or private ships of every nation: The Marianna Flora, 11 Wheat. 1.

[3] See U. S. Rev. Stat., *supra;* U. S. v. Jones, 3 Wash. C. C. 228.

[4] U. S. v. Palmer, 3 Wheat. 610; U. S. v. Kessler, Baldw. 15.

[5] U. S. v. Pirates, 5 Wheat. 184; U. S. v. Klintock, 5 Wheat. 144; U. S. v. Furlong, 5 Wheat. 184. So the courts of the United States may take cognizance of piracy on board an American ship although committed on the

ligerent rights have not been accorded by any recognized government will be treated as pirates;[1] but if a recognized state of belligerency between two opposing powers exists, the United States government will not treat those who act under one of such powers as pirates, although the power under which they act has not been recognized by it as an independent state.[2] All who confederate or conspire with sea robbers or pirates are guilty of the crime committed;[3] but in order to effect all the officers and crew with guilt, the original voyage must have been undertaken with piratical design and participated in by all of them, otherwise those are alone guilty who actively cooperate in the crime.[4] The intent must be felonious, but it is not necessary that personal violence shall have been used or contemplated.[5] Intent alone is, however, not sufficient; there must be an overt act.[6]

sea adjacent to foreign territory and within the three-mile limit: U. S. v. Ross, 1 Gall. 624. So mutiny on a ship of the United States is punishable in the federal courts although defendant is a foreigner: U. S. v. Peterson, 1 Woodb. & M. 305.

1 The Ambrose Light, 25 Fed. R. 408; U. S. v. Klintock, 5 Wheat. 144; The Magellan Pirates, 1 Spinks' Eccl. & Adm. 81.

2 The Josefa Segunda, 5 Wheat. 338; U. S. v. Palmer, 3 Wheat. 610. As to proving commission from foreign government, see The Estrella, 4 Wheat. 298; U. S. v. Pirates, 5 Wheat. 184; The Santissima Trinidad, 7 Wheat. 283; U. S. v. Reyburn, 6 Pet. 352. A commission from a recognized belligerent will protect against a prosecution for piracy, even in the courts of the enemy: U. S. v. Baker, 5 Blatch. 6.

3 U. S. v. Howard, 3 Wash. C. C. 340.

4 U. S. v. Gibert, 2 Sumn. 19; U. S. v. Jones, 3 Wash. C. C. 209.

5 U. S. v. Tully, 1 Gall. 247; U. S. v. Jones. 3 Wash. C. C. 228; U. S. v. Brig Malek Adhel, 2 How. 210.

6 The City of Mexico, 28 Fed. R. 148.

TABLE OF CASES.

In this table, as throughout the book, the words "United States," "State," "Commonwealth," "People," and "Territory," used in the titles of cases, are abbreviated to "U. S.," "S.," "C.," "P.," and "T.," respectively, and the individual names in the titles of such cases are placed first in this table. Where the names of cities occur in the titles of cases, whether as "City of —," or "Mayor of —," or "City Council of —," the name of the city only is used. References are to sections, which are numbered continuously throughout the two volumes, §§ 1-742 being in Vol. I, and §§ 743-1359 in Vol. II.

Aaron, C. v., 114 Mass. 255. § 1222.
v. S., 37 Ala. 106. § 373*a*.
v. S., 39 Ala. 684. § 552.
v. S., 40 Ala. 307. § 98.
v. S., 31 Ga. 167. §§ 126, 300.
S. v., 4 N. J. 231. §§ 150, 152.
Abarr, S. v., 39 Ia. 185. §§ 307, 335.
Abbey, S. v., 29 Vt. 60. §§ 1074, 1080.
Abbot, P. v., 19 Wend. 192. § 460.
Abbott v. C., 8 Watts, 517. § 97.
C. v., 130 Mass. 472. §§ 404, 417.
v. P., 86 N. Y. 460. § 307.
P. v., 53 Cal. 284. § 569.
P. v., 101 Cal. 645. § 617.
P. v., 97 Mich. 484. § 454, 460.
Reg. v., 2 C. & K. 630. § 676.
v. S., 59 Ind. 70. §§ 684, 761.
S. v., 16 N. H. 507. §§ 494, 505.
S. v., 31 N. H. 434. §§ 1251, 1270.
S. v., 8 W. Va. 741. §§ 306, 307, 412.
Abel v. S., 90 Ala. 631. §§ 1239, 1244.
Abernethy v. C., 101 Pa. St. 322. §§ 359, 419.
Abingdon, Rex v., 1 Esp. 226. § 1052.
Able v. C., 5 Bush, 698. § 204.
Abney, C. v., 4 T. B. Mon. 477. § 1190.
Abraham, Reg. v., 2 C. & K. 550. § 618.
Abrahams, C. v., 156 Mass. 57. § 66.
v. S., 4 Ia. 541. § 1142.
S. v., 6 Ia. 117. § 1142.
Abram, S. v., 10 Ala. 928. § 434.
Abrams, C. v., 150 Mass. 392. §§ 1234, 1235.
v. Foshee, 3 Ia. 274. §§ 294, 1146.
U. S. v., 18 Fed. R. 823. § 774.
Abrisch, S. v., 41 Minn. 41. § 1114.
Absence, S. v., 4 Port. 397. § 437.
Achey v. S., 64 Ind. 56. § 343.
Acker, In re, 66 Fed. R. 290. § 9.
v. C., 94 Pa. St. 284. § 468.
Ackerman, P. v., 80 Mich. 588. §§ 190, 1264.
Ackles, S. v., 8 Wash. 462. §§ 265, 271.
Acra, S. v., 2 Ind. Ap. 384. § 999.
Acree v. C., 13 Bush, 353. §§ 101, 1216, 1238.
Acuff, S. v., 6 Mo. 54. § 106.
Adams v. Albany, 29 Ga. 56. § 1216.
v. Barrett, 5 Ga. 404. §§ 11, 18.
v. C., 23 Grat. 949. § 585.
C. v., 7 Gray, 43. §§ 548, 607, 722, 727.
C. v., 114 Mass. 323. §§ 123, 240.
C. v., 127 Mass. 15. §§ 212, 1147.
C. v., 160 Mass. 310. § 1310.
C. v., 7 Met. 50. § 797.
v. P., 47 Ill. 376. §§ 309, 389, 425.
v. P., 109 Ill. 444. §§ 325, 330.
P. v., 3 Denio, 190; 1 N. Y. 173. §§ 207, 211, 696.
P. v., 52 Mich. 105. § 245.
P. v., 17 Wend. 475. §§ 1273, 1274.
Reg. v., 1 Den. 38. § 563.
Reg. v., 1 F. & F. 86. § 716.
Reg. v., 22 Q. B. D. 66. § 1055.
Rex v., 3 C. & P. 600. § 619.
Rex v., Russ. & Ry. 225. §§ 546, 563.
v. Savage, Holt, 179. § 914.
v. S., 52 Ala. 379. § 725.
v. S., 55 Ala. 143. § 511.
v. S., 60 Ala. 52. § 589.
v. S., 62 Ala. 177. § 529.
v. S., 28 Fla. 511. § 333.
v. S., 34 Fla. 185. § 411.
v. S., 72 Ga. 85. § 298.
v. S., 93 Ga. 166. § 890.
v. S., 65 Ind. 565. §§ 200, 208.
v. S., 45 N. J. 448. §§ 546, 547, 564.
v. S., 25 Ohio St. 584. § 1257.
S. v., 16 Ark. 497. § 1270.
S. v., 1 Houst. Cr. C. 361. § 981.
S. v., 92 Ind. 116. § 675.
S. v., 20 Ia. 486. § 1277.
S. v., 78 Ia. 292. §§ 267, 339.
S. v., 81 Ia. 593. § 1249.
S. v., 16 Me. 67. § 85.
S. v., 76 Mo. 355. §§ 152, 419.
S. v., 108 Mo. 208. §§ 638, 656.
S. v., 51 N. H. 568. § 1221.
U. S. v., 2 Dak. 305. §§ 128, 649.
U. S. v., 59 Fed. R. 674. § 1335.
v. Waggoner, 33 Ind. 531. § 249.
Adamson, Reg. v., 1 C. & K. 192. § 666.
S. v., 43 Minn. 196. § 750.
Addatte, U. S. v., 6 Blatch. 132. § 777.

Addcock, S. v., 65 Mo. 590. § 934.
Addington, S. v., 77 Mo. 110. § 34.
Addis, C. v., 1 Browne, 285. § 1126.
Rex v., 6 C. & P. 388. § 340.
Adell v. S., 34 Ind. 543. §§ 266, 268.
Adelphi Club, P. v., 149 N. Y. 5. § 1240.
Aden, Reg. v., 12 Cox, 512. § 554.
Adey, Reg. v., 3 C. & K. 339. § 634.
Reg v., 1 Den. 571. § 632.
Adkinson v. S., 5 Baxt. 569. § 502.
Adler, P. v., 140 N. Y. 331. § 803.
v. S., 55 Ala. 16. §§ 1206, 1218, 1221, 1257, 1261.
U. S. v., 49 Fed. R. 733. § 1348.
U. S. v., 49 Fed. R. 736. § 964.
v. Whitbeck, 44 Ohio St. 589. § 1212.
Adsit, P. v., 2 Hill, 619. § 915.
Adwards, P. v., 5 Mich. 22. § 227.
Adwell v. C., 17 B. Mon. 310. § 426.
Ady, Rex v., 7 C. & P. 140. § 681.
Agar's Case, Sir F. Moore, 627. § 852.
Agar v. S., 29 Tex. Ap. 608. § 878.
Agee v. S., 64 Ind. 340. § 924.
S. v., 83 Ala. 110. § 44.
S. v., 68 Mo., 264. § 255.
Agitone v. S., 41 Tex. 501. § 275.
Agler, U. S. v., 62 Fed. R. 874. § 1337.
Agudo, S. v., 5 La. An. 185. § 1293.
Aguierre v. S., 31 Tex. Ap. 519. § 892.
Aguila, S. v., 14 Mo. 130. §§ 524, 531.
Ahearn, C. v., 160 Mass. 300. §§ 195, 210, 1239.
Ahearne, Reg. v., 6 Cox, 6. § 981.
Ah Bean, P. v., 77 Cal. 12. § 878.
Ah Cha, Ex parte, 40 Cal. 426. §§ 271, 280.
Ah Chew, S. v., 16 Nev. 50. § 29.
Ah Chong, In re, 6 Saw. 451. § 46.
Ah Choy, P. v., 1 Ida. (N. S.) 317. §§ 361, 420.
Ah Fat, P. v., 48 Cal. 61. §§ 214, 292.
Ah Fawn, U. S. v., 57 Fed. R. 591. § 1345.
Ah Fook, P. v., 62 Cal. 493. § 896.
P. v., 64 Cal. 380. § 409.
Ah Fung, P. v., 16 Cal., 137. § 396.
Ah Gee Yung, P. v., 86 Cal. 144. § 333.
Ah Ho, P. v., 1 Ida. (N. S.) 691. §§ 212, 1134, 1139.
Ah Hop, P. v., 1 Ida. (N. S.) 698. § 212.
Ah Jim, S. v., 9 Mont. 167. § 78.
Ah Jow, In re, 29 Fed. R. 181. § 62.
Ah Ki, P. v., 20 Cal. 177. § 617.
Ah Kong, P. v., 49 Cal. 6. § 346.
Ah Lee, P. v., 60 Cal. 85. § 359.
S. v., 7 Oreg. 237. §§ 391, 430.
S. v., 8 Oreg. 214. §§ 332, 431.
S. v., 18 Oreg. 540. §§ 872, 881, 885.
Ah Lim v. T., 1 Wash. 156. § 29.
Ah Loi, S. v., 5 Nev. 99. § 473.
Ah Luck, P. v., 62 Cal. 503. § 293.
Ah Mook, S. v., 12 Nev. 369. § 358.
Ah Own, P. v., 85 Cal. 580. §§ 1285, 1310.
Ah Ping, P. v., 27 Cal. 489. § 194.
Ah Sam, P. v., 41 Cal. 645. §§ 772, 784.
S. v., 7 Nev. 127. § 511.
S. v., 7 Oreg. 477. § 880.
Ah Sing, P. v., 19 Cal. 598. § 602.
P. v., 95 Cal. 654. § 474.
P. v., 95 Cal. 657. § 861.
Ah Sum, P. v., 92 Cal. 648. § 873.
Ah Teung, P. v., 92 Cal. 421. § 931.
Ah Toy, U. S. v., 47 Fed. R. 305. § 1344.
Ah Woo, P. v., 28 Cal. 205. §§ 795, 1062.
Ah Ye, P. v., 31 Cal. 451. § 509.
Ah Yek, P. v., 29 Cal. 575. §§ 449, 452.
Ah Yem, P. v., 53 Cal. 246. § 1310.
Ah Yow, In re, 59 Fed. R. 561. § 15.
Ah Yuk, In re, 53 Fed. R. 781. § 1344.
Aickles, Rex v., 2 East, P. C. 675. § 560.
Rex v., 2 East, P. C. 968. § 764.
Aiken v. S., 10 Tex. Ap. 610. § 325.
S. v., 42 S. C. 222. §§ 29, 76, 1208, 1214.
Aikens, S. v., 32 Ia. 403. §§ 861, 889.
Aikin v. S., 35 Ala. 399. §§ 386, 420.
v. S., 58 Ark. 544. § 310.
Ailstock, C. v., 3 Grat. 650. § 381.
v. Page, 77 Va. 386. § 1228.
Ainsworth v. S., 8 Tex. Ap. 532. § 316.
v. S., 11 Tex. Ap. 339. § 572.
v. S., 29 Tex. Ap. 599. § 334.
Airey, Rex v., 2 East, P. C. 831. § 666.
Ake v. S., 30 Tex. 466. §§ 322, 353.
v. S., 31 Tex. 416. §§ 365, 420.
v. S., 6 Tex. Ap. 398. § 153.
S. v., 9 Tex. 322. §§ 1290, 1291.
Akin v. S., 14 Tex. Ap. 142. § 1232.
Albany, P. v., 11 Wend. 539. §§ 183, 1172.
Albert, U. S. v., 45 Fed. R. 552. §§ 752, 793.
Albertson, S. v., 113 N. C. 633. § 1011.
Alberty v. U. S., 162 U. S. 499. §§ 313, 421.
Albow, P. v., 140 N. Y. 130. § 675.
Albrecht v. P., 78 Ill. 510. § 1235.
Albritton v. S., 32 Fla. 358. § 204.
Alcott v. S., 8 Blackf. 6. § 82.
Alden, C. v., 143 Mass. 113. § 1180.
v. S., 18 Fla. 187. § 648.
Alderman v. P., 4 Mich. 414. §§ 953, 954, 960, 975.
v. S., 57 Ga. 367. §§ 643, 644.
S. v., 40 Ia. 375. §§ 1137, 1144.
Alderson v. S., 2 Tex. Ap. 10. § 592.
Aldrich v. P., 101 Ill. 16. § 717.
v. S., 29 Tex. Ap. 394. § 636.
v. Wright, 53 N. H. 398. §§ 142, 299, 538.
Aldridge, Reg. v., 4 Cox, 143. § 594.
Reg. v., 3 F. & F. 781. § 806.
v. S., 88 Ala. 113. § 508.
Aldrige v. S., 59 Miss. 250. § 267.
Aleck, S. v., 41 La. An. 83. §§ 124, 268.
Aler, S. v., 39 W. Va. 549. § 1060.
Alexander v. Blodgett, 44 Vt. 476. § 462.
v. Card, 3 R. I. 145. § 1018.
v. C., 90 Va. 809. § 551.
Rex v., Moody & M. 37. § 1056.
v. S., 16 Ala. 661. § 1193.
v. S., 3 Heisk. 475. § 377.
v. S., 48 Ind. 394. §§ 59, 1314.
v. S., 99 Ind. 450. § 1286.
v. S., 60 Miss. 953. § 609.
v. S., 29 Tex. 495. § 1271.
v. S., 9 Tex. Ap. 48. § 546.
v. S., 17 Tex. Ap. 614. § 333.

Alexander v. S., 24 Tex. Ap. 126. §§ 546, 613.
v. S., 27 Tex. Ap. 94. § 851.
v. S., 27 Tex. Ap. 533. § 1032.
v. S., 28 Tex. Ap. 186. §§ 753, 768, 798.
v. S., 31 Tex. Ap. 359. § 506.
S. v., 4 Hawks, 182. § 858.
S. v., 66 Mo. 148. §§ 307, 316.
S. v., 74 N. C. 232. § 548.
S. v., 7 Rich. 5. § 993.
S. v., 14 Rich. 247. § 815.
S. v., 30 S. C. 74. §§ 157, 178, 326, 333.
v. U. S., 138 U. S. 353. § 412.
Alfele v. Wright, 17 Ohio St. 238. § 550.
Alford v. S., 8 Tex. Ap. 545. §§ 340, 347.
v. S., 31 Tex. Ap. 299. § 47.
Alfred v. S., 33 Ga. 303. § 332.
v. S., 37 Miss. 296. § 341.
S. v., 44 La. An. 582. § 257.
Alger, C. v., 7 Cush. 53. § 1195.
Algier v. Weston, 14 Johns. 231. § 1227.
Alibez, P. v., 49 Cal. 452. § 375.
Alison, Reg. v., 8 C. & P. 418. § 290.
Alivtre, P. v., 55 Cal. 263. § 307.
Alkenbrack v. P., 1 Denio, 80. § 592.
Allaire, S. v., 14 Ala. 435. §§ 96, 1285.
Allday, Reg. v., 8 C. & P. 136. § 752.
Allen, C. v., 15 B. Mon. 1. § 1229.
C. v., 11 Met. 403. §§ 1193, 1197.
C. v., 135 Pa. St. 483. § 459.
C. v., 148 Pa. St. 358. § 1184.
v. Deming, 14 N. H. 133. § 1324.
v. England, 3 F. & F. 49. § 839.
v. P., 82 Ill. 610. § 257.
P. v., 5 Denio, 76. §§ 625, 627.
Reg. v., 1 C. & K. 495. § 1154.
Reg. v., 9 C. & P. 31. § 450.
Reg. v., 9 C. & P. 521. § 452.
Reg. v., 1 Den. 364. § 1153.
Reg. v., L. R. 1 C. C. 367. § 1073.
Reg. v., 17 L. T. (N. S.) 222. § 328.
Rex v., 7 C. & P. 153. § 351.
v. S., 40 Ala. 334. §§ 118, 501.
v. S., 52 Ala. 391. § 267.
v. S., 58 Ala. 98. § 609.
v. S., 74 Ala. 557. § 753.
v. S., 79 Ala. 34. §§ 754, 765.
v. S., 87 Ala. 107. §§ 451, 457.
v. S., 91 Ala. 19. § 571.
v. S., 4 Baxt. 21. § 260.
v. S., 28 Ga. 395. § 257.
v. S., 51 Ga. 264. § 61.
v. S., 74 Ga. 769. § 203.
v. S., 12 Lea, 424. § 506.
v. S., Mart. & Y. 294. § 393.
v. S., 66 Miss. 385. § 309.
v. S., 10 Ohio St. 287. §§ 13, 520, 521.
v. S., 42 Tex. 12. § 881.
v. S., 42 Tex. 517. § 613.
v. S., 8 Tex. Ap. 360. §§ 594, 613.
v. S., 12 Tex. Ap. 190. § 572.
v. S., 15 Tex. Ap. 320. § 1140.
v. S., 16 Tex. Ap. 150. § 678
v. S., 16 Tex. Ap. 237. § 614.
v. S., 17 Tex. Ap. 637. § 303.
Allen v. S., 24 Tex. Ap. 216. § 309.
v. S., 5 Wis. 329. § 91.
v. S., 85 Wis. 22. § 362.
S. v., 47 Conn. 121. § 198.
S. v., 4 Hawks, 356. § 1011.
S. v., 32 Ia. 248. § 1270.
S. v., 32 Ia. 491. § 1274.
S. v., 12 Ind. Ap. 528. § 1261.
S. v., 37 La. An. 685. § 214
S. v., 1 McCord, 525. § 1070.
S. v., 116 Mo. 548. § 809.
S. v., 72 N. C. 114. § 815.
S. v., 103 N. C. 433. § 546.
S. v., 30 Tex. 59. § 240.
S. v., 5 Yerg. 453. § 339.
v. U. S., 157 U. S. 675. §§ 302, 309, 342.
U. S. v., 47 Fed. R. 696. § 1339.
v. Wyckoff, 48 N. J. 90. § 46.
Alley, S. v., 68 Mo. 124. § 304.
Allgood v. S., 87 Ga. 668. §§ 758, 798.
Allison, In re, 13 Colo. 525. § 477.
v. C., 99 Pa. St. 17. §§ 426, 429.
v. Farmers' Bank, 6 Rand. 204. § 11.
v. Hess, 28 Ia. 388. § 959.
Rex v., Russ. & Ry. 109. § 1073.
v. S., 42 Ind. 354. § 1196.
v. S., 14 Tex. Ap. 122. § 199.
S. v., 90 N. C. 733. § 1164.
v. U. S., 160 U. S. 203. § 303.
Allred v. S., 89 Ala. 112. § 1221.
S. v., 84 N. C. 749. § 661.
Allsup v. S., 5 Lea, 362. § 365.
Almon, Rex v., 5 Burr. 2686. §§ 188, 1056.
Alsabrooks v. S., 52 Ala. 24. § 1098.
Alsey v. S., 39 Ala. 664. § 553.
Alsop, Reg. v., 11 Cox, 264. § 859.
Alston v. S., 63 Ala. 178. § 404.
Altenburg v. C., 126 Pa. St. 602. § 1256.
Altman, P. v., 147 N. Y. 473. §§ 803, 808.
Alvey, S. v., 26 Tex. 155. § 1303.
Alviso, P. v., 55 Cal. 230. § 396.
Alvord v. Smith, 63 Ind. 58. § 1297.
Ambler, S. v., 56 Vt. 672. § 520.
Ambrose v. S., 6 Ind. 351. § 1216.
U. S. v., 108 U. S. 336. §§ 852, 860.
Ambrose Light, U. S. v., 25 Fed. R. 408. §§ 123, 1359.
Ambs, S. v., 20 Mo. 214. §§ 1264, 1319.
Amedy, U. S. v., 11 Wheat. 392. §§ 110, 522.
American Express Co. v. P., 133 Ill. 649. § 46.
American Fur Co. v. U. S., 2 Pet. 358. § 1338*a*.
Amery, S. v., 12 R. I. 64. § 1202.
Ames's Case, 2 Me. 365. § 744.
Ames, S. v., 64 Me. 386. §§ 220, 937, 947.
Amey, Rex v., Russ. & Ry. 500. § 255.
Ammons, S. v., 3 Murph. 123. §§ 861, 873.
Amos v. S., 73 Ala. 498. § 1233.
Reg. v., 2 Den. 55. § 520.
Amsden, U. S. v., 6 Fed. R. 819. § 54.
Anable v. C., 24 Grat. 563. § 563.
Anderson v. Brewster, 44 Ohio St. 576. § 1212.
v. C., 13 Bush, 485. § 1210.

Anderson v. C., 5 Rand. 627. §§ 959, 1086, 1111.
P. v., 39 Cal. 703. § 307.
P. v., 44 Cal. 65. § 305.
P. v., 80 Cal. 205. § 473.
P. v., 14 Johns. 294. § 571.
Reg. v., 2 M. & Rob. 469. § 753.
Rex v., 1 Russ. Cr. 731. § 339.
v. Savannah, 69 Ga. 472. § 29.
v. S., 48 Ala. 665. § 508.
v. S., 79 Ala. 5. §§ 408, 419, 426.
v. S., 5 Ark. 444. § 384.
v. S., 34 Ark. 257. § 452.
v. S., 6 Baxt. 608. § 245.
v. S., 43 Conn. 514. §§ 157, 360.
v. S., 32 Fla. 242. §§ 1233, 1241.
v. S., 42 Ga. 9. § 164.
v. S., 63 Ga. 675. § 216.
v. S., 3 Heisk. 86. § 332.
v. S., 10 Humph. 119. § 1191.
v. S., 26 Neb. 387. § 353.
v. S., 22 Ohio St. 305. § 189.
v. S., 31 Tex. 440. § 365.
v. S., 1 Tex. Ap. 730. § 275.
v. S., 11 Tex. Ap. 576. § 618.
v. S., 15 Tex. Ap. 447. §§ 330, 391.
v. S., 16 Tex. Ap. 132. § 260.
v. S., 17 Tex. Ap. 305. § 494.
v. S., 18 Tex. Ap. 17. § 876.
v. S., 20 Tex. Ap. 595. § 759.
v. S., 24 Tex. Ap. 705. § 858.
v. S., 25 Tex. Ap. 593. § 572.
v. S., 30 Tex. Ap. 699. § 663.
S. v., 30 Ark. 131. § 1326.
S. v., 1 Hill (S. C.), 327. § 298.
S. v., 1 Houst. Cr. C. 38. § 336.
S. v., 103 Ind. 170. § 861.
S. v., 47 Ia. 142. § 692.
S. v., 92 Ia. 764, 60 N. W. R. 630. § 869.
S. v., 30 La. An. 557. § 758.
S. v., 25 Minn. 66. §§ 569, 596.
S. v., 81 Mo. 78. § 1253.
S. v., 86 Mo. 309. § 309.
S. v., 89 Mo. 312. § 309.
S. v., 98 Mo. 461. §§ 365, 380, 391.
S. v., 92 N. C. 732. § 988.
S. v., 104 N. C. 771. § 51.
S. v., 4 Nev. 265. §§ 377, 413.
S. v., 40 N. J. 224. § 92.
S. v., 10 Oreg. 448. § 421.
S. v., 2 Overt. 6. § 329.
S. v., 34 Tex. 611. § 601.
Andre v. S., 5 Ia. 389. §§ 1113, 1118.
Andrews, Ex parte, 18 Cal. 678. § 1319.
C. v., 2 Mass. 14. § 553.
C. v., 2 Mass. 409. § 715.
C. v., 3 Mass. 126. §§ 215, 713.
v. P., 60 Ill. 354. § 716.
P. v., 115 N. Y. 427. § 1240.
Reg. v., Car. & M. 121. § 505.
Rex v., 2 M. & Rob. 37. § 211.
v. S., 78 Ala. 483. § 922.
v. S., 21 Fla. 598. § 395.
v. S., 3 Heisk. 165. § 1030.
v. S., 13 Tex. Ap. 343. § 255.
v. S., 25 Tex. Ap. 339. § 618.
Andrews, S. v., 84 Ia. 88. § 361.
S. v., 26 Mo. 171. § 1226.
S. v., 28 Mo. 14. §§ 75, 78, 100, 1226.
S. v., 82 Tex. 73. § 1250.
v. U. S., 2 Story, 202. § 83.
v. U. S., 162 U. S. 420. §§ 118, 133, 1335.
U. S. v., 58 Fed. R. 861. § 135.
Androscoggin, etc. Co. v. Bethel S. Mill Co., 64 Me. 441. § 184.
Androscoggin R. Co., S. v., 76 Me. 41 §§ 5, 7.
Angel v. C., 2 Va. Cas. 228. § 546.
v. C., 2 Va. Cas. 231. § 435.
S. v., 7 Ired. 27. § 373.
S. v., 42 Kan. 216. § 485.
Angell v. S., 36 Tex. 542. § 328.
Angelo v. P., 96 Ill. 209. §§ 149, 152.
Angerhoffer v. S., 15 Tex. Ap. 613. § 1216.
Angus v. S., 29 Tex. Ap. 52. §§ 391, 418.
Ann v. S., 11 Humph. 158. § 325.
Ann, The, 1 Gallis. 61. § 132.
Anone, S. v., 2 Nott & M. 27. § 118.
Anonymous, Bull. N. P. 243. § 886.
2 C. & P. 459. § 619.
1 Cox, 250. § 783.
5 Cox, 279. § 130.
1 East, P. C. 180. § 788.
1 East, P. C. 261. § 348.
1 East, P. C. 305. § 923.
2 East, P. C. 556. § 548.
2 East, P. C. 559. § 145.
2 Lewin, 48. § 246.
Lofft, 146. § 667.
Lofft, 272. § 252.
7 Mod. 10. § 1165.
12 Mod. 559. § 180.
R. M. Charlt. 228. § 852.
1 Russ. Cr. 932. § 458.
Russ. & Ry. 378. § 803.
Anschicks v. S., 6 Tex. Ap. 524. § 440.
Anselm, S. v., 43 La. An. 195. § 504.
Ansley v. S., 36 Ark. 67. § 1301.
Anson v. P., 148 Ill. 494. § 809.
Anthoine, S. v., 40 Me. 435. § 1184.
Anthony v. Halderman, 7 Kan. 50. § 948.
P. v., 56 Cal. 397. § 409.
v. S., 29 Ala. 27. §§ 227, 228, 378.
v. S., 4 Humph. 83. §§ 1292, 1293.
v. S., Meigs, 265. §§ 357, 358.
v. S., 13 Sm. & M. 263. § 274.
S. v., 7 Ired. 234. § 478.
U. S. v., 11 Blatch. 200. §§ 135, 948–9.
Antoine, S. v., 42 La. An. 945. § 722.
Antonio, P. v., 27 Cal. 404. § 617.
S. v., 3 Brev. 562. §§ 790, 808.
App v. S., 90 Ind. 73. § 1310.
Apperger, S. v., 80 Mo. 173. § 1271.
Applegarth, S. v., 81 Md. 293. § 44.
Aplin, P. v., 86 Mich. 393. § 497.
Appling, S. v., 25 Mo. 315. §§ 12, 1156–7.
Araah, S. v., 55 Ia. 258. § 1119.
Arbintrode v. S., 67 Ind. 267. §§ 1246, 1256.
Arbuckle v. S., 32 Ind. 34. § 82.
Archer, Reg. v., Dears. 449. § 667.
Reg. v., 1 Fost. & F. 361. § 347.
Rex v., 1 Moody, 143. § 145.

Archer v. S., 69 Ga. 767. § 1290.
v. S., 45 Md. 33. § 1234.
v. S., 10 Tex. Ap. 482. § 1239.
S. v., 54 N. H. 465. §§ 173, 229, 454.
S. v., 34 Tex. 646. § 271.
Arcia v. S., 28 Tex. Ap. 198. §§ 546, 718.
Ardaga, P. v., 51 Cal. 371. § 458.
Arden v. S., 11 Conn. 408. § 859.
S. v., 1 Bay, 487. §§ 204, 392.
Ardery v. S., 56 Ind. 328. §§ 13, 1136.
Ardley, Reg. v., L. R. 1 C. C. 301. § 669.
Arensberg, P. v., 103 N. Y. 388. § 34.
P. v., 105 N. Y. 123. § 34.
Ariel, S. v., 38 S. C. 221. §§ 316, 333.
Aris, Rex v., 6 C. & P. 348. § 520.
Arispe v. S., 26 Tex. Ap. 581. § 618.
Arkle, S. v., 116 N. C. 1017. § 571.
Arlin, S. v., 39 N. H. 179. § 101.
Arman, Reg. v., Dears. 575. § 634.
Armington, S. v., 25 Minn. 29. §§ 133, 1076, 1079, 1083.
Armistead, S. v., 106 N. C. 639. § 922.
Armitage v. S., 13 Ind. 441. § 794.
Armour v. S., 3 Humph. 379. § 498.
Armstrong v. Lester, 43 Ia. 159. § 1116.
v. P., 70 N. Y. 38. §§ 1112, 1119.
P. v., 73 Mich. 288. §§ 65, 66.
v. S., 4 Blackf. 247. § 1313.
v. S., 27 Fla. 366. § 179.
v. S., 30 Fla. 170. §§ 169, 173, 179.
v. S., 27 Tex. Ap. 462. § 851.
v. S., 33 Tex. Ap. 417. § 216.
S. v., 4 Minn. 335. §§ 1086, 1099.
S. v., 106 Mo. 395. §§ 1043, 1070.
U. S. v., 2 Curt. 446. §§ 333, 346, 369.
U. S. v., 59 Fed. Rep. 568. § 937.
Arnold v. C., 80 Ky. 300. § 9.
C. v., 83 Ky. 1. § 390.
P. v., 15 Cal. 476. §§ 307, 316.
P. v., 46 Mich. 268. §§ 975, 982.
v. S., 29 Ala. 46. § 1303.
v. S., 53 Ga. 574. §§ 1071, 1076, 1082.
v. S., 52 Ind. 281. § 481.
v. S., 11 Tex. Ap. 472. § 706.
v. S., 28 Tex. Ap. 480. § 1133.
S. v., 13 Ired. 184. §§ 153, 427.
S. v., 55 Mo. 89. § 1100.
S. v., 107 N. C. 861. § 382.
S. v., 39 Tex. 74. § 833.
Arp v. S., 97 Ala. 5. § 137.
Arrance, C. v., 5 Allen, 517. §§ 546, 602.
Arras, P. v., 89 Cal. 223. § 595.
Arrington v. C., 87 Va. 96. §§ 1270, 1272, 1277.
Arscott, Rex v., 6 C. & P. 408. §§ 752, 781.
Art Union, P. v., 13 Barb. 577. § 1315.
P. v., 7 N. Y. 240. § 1315.
Arthur v. Oaks, 63 Fed. R. 310. § 963.
P. v., 93 Cal. 536. § 514.
Arto v. S., 19 Tex. Ap. 126. § 306.
Asbill, In re, 104 Cal. 205. § 46.
Ash v. P., 11 Mich. 347. § 69.
v. S., 81 Ala. 76. §§ 199, 200, 930, 940.
v. S., 56 Ga. 583. § 268.
Ashby, Reg. v., 2 F. & F. 560. § 764.
Asher, Ex parte, 23 Tex. Ap. 662. § 44.
S. v., 50 Ark. 427. §§ 671, 685.
v. Texas, 128 U. S. 129. § 44.
Ashford v. S., 36 Neb. 38. §§ 504, 505.
Ashley, C. v., 2 Gray, 356. §§ 1140, 1143.
Reg. v., 1 C. & K. 198. § 576.
S. v., 37 Ark. 403. § 1084.
S. v., Dudley, 188. § 12.
Ashlock v. C., 7 B. Mon. 44. §§ 1285, 1310.
Ashman, Reg. v., 1 F. & F. 88. § 256.
Ashton's Case, 2 Lewin, 147. §§ 426, 431.
Ashton v. S., 68 Ga. 25. § 494.
C. v., 125 Mass. 384. §§ 662, 699.
Rex v., 2 B. & Ad. 750. § 817.
Ashurst v. S., 79 Ala. 276. § 1255.
Ashwell, Reg. v., 16 Q. B. D. 190. §§ 554, 561.
Ashworth v. S., 63 Ala. 120. § 1163.
v. S., 31 Tex. Ap. 419. § 471.
Askew v. S., 94 Ala. 4. § 306.
Askey v. S., 20 Tex. Ap. 443. § 1283.
Askill v. C., 3 B. Mon. 342. § 1273.
Aslesen, S. v., 50 Minn. 5. § 34.
Aslett, Rex v., Russ. & Ry. 67. §§ 543, 636.
Aspinall, Reg. v., 13 Cox, 563. § 962.
Asplin, Reg. v., 12 Cox, 391. § 750.
Asterley, Rex v., 7 C. & P. 191. § 667.
Astley, Rex v., 2 East, P. C. 729. § 470.
Aston, Reg. v., 2 C. & K. 413. § 640.
Atchison v. Everitt, Cowp. 382. § 7.
S. v., 3 Lea, 729. § 183.
Athea, Rex v., 1 Moody, 329. § 508.
Athens Armory, U. S. v., 2 Abb. C. C. 129. § 84.
Atherton, S. v., 50 Ia. 189. §§ 448, 454, 463.
Atkins, C. v., 136 Mass. 160. § 1243.
v. Randolph, 31 Vt. 226. § 1214.
v. S., 60 Ala. 45. § 1257.
v. S., 16 Ark. 568. §§ 307, 339, 342.
v. S., 95 Tenn. 474. §§ 210, 663*a*, 692, 1310.
v. S., 11 Tex. Ap. 8. § 255.
S. v., 1 Ala. 180. § 1293.
S. v., 5 Blackf. 458. § 794.
S. v., 42 Vt. 252. § 1060.
U. S. v., 1 Sprague, 558. § 867.
Atkinson, Reg. v., Car. & M. 325. § 754.
Reg. v., Car. & M. 525. § 546.
Reg. v., 11 Cox, 330. § 995.
Reg. v., 2 Moody, 278. § 631.
Rex v., 7 C. & P. 669. § 765.
Rex v., Russ. & Ry. 104. § 256.
v. Sellers, 5 C. B. (N. S.) 442. § 1321.
v. S., 19 Tex. Ap. 462. § 601.
S. v., 139 Ind. 426. § 1264.
S. v., 33 S. C. 100. § 1253.
S. v., 40 S. C. 363. §§ 212, 408, 409.
S. v., 24 Vt. 448. § 1192.
U. S. v., 34 Fed. R. 316. § 1330.
Atkyns, Rex v., 3 Burr. 1706. § 16.
Atteberry v. S., 33 Tex. Ap. 88. § 233.
Atterberry v. S., 56 Ark. 515. § 205.
v. S., 19 Tex. Ap. 401. § 563.
Attoo v. C., 2 Va. Cas. 382. § 96.

Attorney-General v. Broaddus, 6 Munf. 116. § 1120.
v. Justices, 5 Ired. 315. § 1228.
v. Leeds, 39 L. J. 254. § 1171.
v. Riddle, 2 Cromp. & J. 493. § 194.
Atwood v. S., 53 Ala. 508. § 1033.
Aubrey, U. S. v., 1 Cranch, C. C. 185. § 1022.
Auburn v. Merchant, 103 N. Y. 143. § 1215.
Aucarola, U. S. v., 17 Blatch. 423. § 490.
Audley's Case, 3 How. St. Tr. 401. § 449.
Auffmordt, U. S. v., 122 U. S. 197. § 102.
Aulger v. P., 34 Ill. 486. § 324.
Augusta R. Co. v. Renz, 55 Ga. 126. § 1323.
Aulman, S. v., 76 Ia. 624. §§ 1223, 1253.
Aultfather v. S., 4 Ohio St. 467. § 1247.
Austen v. S., 42 Tex. 345. § 607.
Austin v. S., 14 Ark. 556. § 418.
v. S., 71 Ga. 595. § 949.
v. S., 10 Mo. 591. §§ 1273, 1274.
S. v., 114 N. C. 855. § 66.
Austin Club, S. v., — Tex. —, 33 S. W. R. 113. § 1240.
Austine v. P., 51 Ill. 236. § 461.
v. P., 110 Ill. 248. §§ 440, 457.
Autey, Reg. v., Dears. & B. 294. § 753.
Averheart v. S., 30 Tex. Ap. 651. §§ 1289, 1291.
Avery, Reg. v., Bell, 150. § 558.
Reg. v., 8 C. & P. 596. § 750.
S. v., 7 Conn. 266. §§ 118, 220, 1042.
S. v., 113 Mo. 475. § 290.
S. v., 64 N. C. 608. § 341.
S. v., 109 N. C. 798. § 520.
S. v., 44 N. H. 392. §§ 160, 1161, 1163.
Avila, P. v., 43 Cal. 196. § 717.
Aydelott, S. v., 7 Blackf. 157. § 832.
Ayer, C. v., 3 Cush. 150. §§ 95, 744, 748, 752.
S. v., 40 Kan. 43. § 879.
S. v., 23 N. H. 301. §§ 506, 511, 546.
Ayers v. S., 60 Miss. 709. § 142.
v. Watson, 132 U. S. 394. § 431.
Ayes, Rex v., Russ. & Ry. 166. § 339.
Aylett, Rex v., 1 T. R. 63. §§ 852, 882.
Aymette v. S., 2 Humph. 154. § 1030.
Ayres v. S., 21 Tex. Ap. 399. § 617.
Ayrs v. S., 5 Coldw. 26. § 609.
Azzopardi, Reg. v., 1 C. & K. 203. § 369.

Babb v. S., 8 Tex. Ap. 173. § 316.
v. S., 12 Tex. Ap. 491. § 334.
S. v., 76 Mo. 501. §§ 514, 592, 613.
Babcock, C. v., 110 Mass. 107. § 1281.
v. P., 13 Colo. 515. §§ 311, 353.
P. v., 7 Johns. 201. § 687.
S. v., 51 Vt. 570. § 522.
v. U. S., 34 Fed. R. 873. § 875.
U. S. v., 3 Dill. 581. §§ 969, 971.
U. S. v., 4 McLean, 113. § 859.
Baca, T. v., 2 N. Mex. 183. § 5.
Bacchus v. S., 18 Tex. Ap. 15. § 1304.
Baccigalupo v. C., 33 Grat. 807. §§ 178, 179.
Bach v. S., 8 Mo. 497. § 1218.
Bach, S. v., 36 Minn. 234. § 1223.
Bachellor v. S., 10 Tex. 258. §§ 1285, 1286.
Backarow, S. v., 38 La. An. 316. § 489.
Backler, Rex v., 5 C. & P. 118. § 764.
Bacon's Case, 1 Lev. 146. § 263.
Bacon, C. v., 135 Mass. 521. § 740.
S. v., 41 Vt. 526. § 1270.
Bacon Club, S. v., 44 Mo. Ap. 86. § 1240.
Badcock, Rex v., Russ. & Ry. 249. § 204.
Baden, S. v., 42 La. An. 295. § 594.
S. v., 37 Minn. 212. § 1241.
Bader, U. S. v., 4 Woods, 189; 16 Fed. R. 116. § 945.
Badgley, P. v., 16 Wend. 53. § 794.
Badinelli, U. S. v., 37 Fed. R. 138. § 946.
Baer v. C., 10 Bush, 8. § 1256.
S. v., 37 W. Va. 1. § 1257.
U. S. v., 18 Blatch. 493. § 854.
Baeumel v. S., 26 Fla. 71. §§ 1252, 1253.
Bagan, S. v., 41 Minn. 285. §§ 441, 454, 463.
Bagby v. S., 82 Ga. 786. § 1236.
Baggerly, S. v., 21 Tex. 757. § 703.
Baggett v. S., 69 Miss. 625. § 718.
Bagley, C. v., 7 Pick. 279. §§ 132, 914.
v. P., 43 Mich. 355. § 1192.
v. S., 1 Humph. 485. §§ 1283, 1285.
v. S., 3 Tex. Ap. 163. § 585.
Bagwell, S. v., 107 N. C. 859. § 1330.
Bailey v. C., 11 Bush, 688. §§ 82, 1034.
v. C., 5 Rawle, 59. § 907.
v. C., 78 Va. 19. §§ 1189, 1190.
v. C., 82 Va. 107. § 440.
C. v., 1 Mass. 62. § 797.
P. v., 23 Cal. 577. § 634.
Reg. v., 2 Cox, 311. § 533.
Reg. v., 12 Cox, 56. § 626.
Reg. v., Dears. 244. § 516.
Reg. v., L. R. 1 C. C. 347. §§ 543, 566.
Rex v., 1 Moody, 23. §§ 494, 495.
Rex v., Russ. & Ry. 341. § 503.
v. S., 58 Ala. 414. § 561.
v. S., 99 Ala. 143. § 578.
v. S., 65 Ga. 410. § 1161.
v. S., 70 Ga. 617. § 303.
v. S., 52 Ind. 462. § 571.
v. S., 36 Neb. 808. §§ 1096, 1099.
v. S., 18 Tex. Ap. 426. § 557.
v. S., 20 Tex. Ap. 68. § 546.
S. v., 43 Ark. 150. § 1274.
S. v., 3 Blackf. 209. § 996.
S. v., 10 Conn. 144. § 497.
S. v., 21 Me. 62. §§ 943, 950, 951.
S. v., 21 Mo. 484. § 268.
S. v., 34 Mo. 350. § 861.
S. v., 21 N. H. 185. §§ 915, 1137.
S. v., 21 N. H. 343. §§ 1137, 1144, 1178.
S. v., 50 Ohio St. 636. §§ 650, 656.
U. S. v., 9 Pet. 238. § 857.
U. S. v., 47 Fed. R. 117. § 1334.
Baillie, Reg. v., 8 Cox, 238. § 1103.
Bain, Ex parte, 121 U. S. 1. § 20.
Reg. v., L. & C. 129. §§ 223, 229.
v. S., 61 Ala. 75. § 1253.
v. S., 67 Miss. 557. §§ 137, 869.
Bains v. The James, Baldw. 544. § 12.
Baird v. Boehner, 77 Ia. 622. § 939.

Baird, P. v., 104 Cal. 462. § 808.
v. S., 52 Ark. 326. § 1216.
U. S. v., 48 Fed. R. 554. § 922.
Bakeman, C. v., 131 Mass. 577. §§ 1092, 1121.
Baker v. C., 93 Ky. 302. § 311.
C. v., 152 Mass. 337. § 1240.
C. v., 155 Mass. 287. § 117.
v. P., 2 Hill (N. Y.), 325. § 1075.
v. P., 49 Ill. 308. § 267.
v. P., 105 Ill. 452. § 1150.
P. v., 100 Cal. 188. §§ 758, 781.
P. v., 76 N. Y. 78. § 1075.
P. v., 96 N. Y. 340. §§ 125, 666, 689.
Reg. v., 1 C. & K. 254. § 233.
Reg. v., 3 Cox, 581. § 499.
Reg. v., 1 Q. B. D. (1895) 797. § 864.
Rex v. 2 East, P. C. 702. § 469.
Rex v., 1 Moody, 231. § 764.
Rex v., 2 M. & Rob. 53. § 425.
v. S., 30 Ala. 521. § 1120.
v. S., 49 Ala. 350. § 1034.
v. S., 81 Ala. 38. § 309.
v. S., 4 Ark. 56. § 434.
v. S., 58 Ark. 513. §§ 567, 717.
v. S., 17 Fla. 406. § 565.
v. S., 27 Ind. 485. § 1186.
v. S., 134 Ind. 657. § 268.
v. S., 2 Ind. Ap. 517. § 1235.
v. S., 53 N. J. 45. § 26.
v. S., 12 Ohio St. 214. § 200.
v. S., 29 Ohio St. 184. § 571.
v. S., 31 Ohio St. 314. § 706.
v. S., 4 Tex. Ap. 223. § 390.
v. S., 7 Tex. Ap. 612. § 203.
v. S., 14 Tex. Ap. 332. § 693.
v. S., 54 Wis. 368. § 42.
v. S., 69 Wis. 32. § 1129.
v. S., 88 Wis. 140. § 601.
S. v., 58 Ind. 417. § 1193.
S. v., 1 Jones, 267. § 381.
S. v., 30 La. An., Pt. II, 1134. § 413.
S. v., 71 Mo. 475. § 189.
S. v., 110 Mo. 7. §§ 147. 435.
S. v., 13 Mont. 160. § 367.
S. v., 63 N. C. 276. §§ 377, 392.
S. v., 65 N. C. 332. § 235.
S. v., 70 N. C. 530. § 609.
S. v., 83 N. C. 649. § 1008.
S. v., 64 Vt. 355. § 852.
U. S. v., 5 Blatch. 6. § 1359.
Balch, S. v., 31 Kan. 465. § 1052.
Baldock, Reg. v., 2 Cox, 55. § 520.
Baldoser, S. v., 88 Ia. 55. §§ 1117, 1119.
Baldridge, S. v., 105 Mo. 319. § 271.
U. S. v., 11 Fed. R. 552. § 123.
Baldwin, In re, 27 Fed. R. 187. § 962.
v. Coburn, 39 Vt. 441. § 1214.
C. v., 11 Gray, 197. § 762.
C. v., 149 Pa. St. 305. § 58.
v. Franks, 120 U. S. 678. §§ 83, 961, 962, 965.
v. P., 2 Ill. 304. § 594.
Rex v., 3 Camp. 265. § 216.
v. Smith, 82 Ill. 162. §§ 1206, 1226.
v. S., 12 Mo. 223. § 158.
v. S., 11 Ohio St. 681. § 906.
Baldwin v. S., 1 Sneed, 411. §§ 596, 599.
v. S., 15 Tex. Ap. 275. § 448.
v. S., 31 Tex. Ap. 589. § 616.
S. v., 45 Conn. 134. § 96.
S. v., 1 Dev. & B. 195. §§ 1159, 1169.
S. v., 70 Ia. 180. § 623.
S. v., 79 Ia. 714. §§ 361, 365.
S. v., 36 Kan. 1. § 354.
S. v., 80 N. C. 390. § 910.
v. Weed, 17 Wend. 224. § 744.
Baldy, S. v., 17 Ia. 39. § 1093.
Balencia, P. v., 21 Cal. 544. § 162.
Bales v. S., 63 Ala. 30. § 172.
v. S., 3 W. Va. 685. § 542.
Ball v. C., 81 Ky. 662. § 175.
P. v., 14 Cal. 101. § 597.
Reg. v., Car. & M. 249. §§ 223, 669.
Rex v., 1 Moody, 30. § 518.
Rex v., 1 Moody, 330. § 328.
Rex v., Russ. & Ry. 132. § 808.
v. S., 48 Ark. 94. §§ 780, 803.
v. S., 7 Blackf. 242. §§ 1290, 1313.
v. S., 26 Ind. 155. § 840.
v. S., 50 Ind. 595. §§ 128, 1252.
S. v., 27 Mo. 324. § 390.
S. v., 27 Neb. 601. § 1235.
v. U. S., 140 U. S. 118. § 376.
U. S. v., 163 U. S. 662. §§ 381, 407.
Ballard v. S., 19 Neb. 609. § 179.
v. S., 43 Ohio St. 340. §§ 328, 340.
S. v., 97 N. C. 443. § 536.
Ballentine v. S., 48 Ark. 45. §§ 1302, 1313.
Baller, S. v., 26 W. Va. 90. §§ 220, 901, 937.
Ballew v. Alexander, 6 Humph. 433. § 11.
v. S., 26 Tex. Ap. 483. § 1304.
v. U. S., 160 U. S. 187. § 1348.
Ballingall, S. v., 42 Ia. 87. § 1248.
Ballock v. S., 73 Md. 1. § 1315.
Ballou, C. v., 124 Mass. 26. § 94.
v. S., 87 Ala. 144. § 44.
Balls, Reg. v., L. R. 1 C. C. 328. § 652.
Baltimore, etc. R. Co. v. S., 63 Md. 573. § 1176.
S. v., 15 W. Va. 362. §§ 180, 181, 183, 184, 1323.
Baltrip v. S., 30 Tex. Ap. 545. §§ 311, 359.
Bamfield, Rex v., 1 Moody, 416. § 753.
Bancroft, S. v., 22 Kan. 170. §§ 110, 632.
S. v., 10 N. H. 105. § 504.
Bandalow v. P., 90 Ill. 218. § 1247.
Bang v. S., 60 Miss. 571. § 305.
Bangor, S. v., 30 Me. 341. § 5.
Banister, S. v., 35 S. C. 290. §§ 426, 430.
Bank of S. C., S. v., 12 Rich. 609. § 96.
Banks, In re, — Kan. —, 42 Pac. R. 693. § 60.
Reg. v., 8 C. & P. 574. § 349.
Reg. v., 12 Cox, 393. §§ 968. 969.
Rex v., Russ. & Ry. 441. § 554.
v. S., 72 Ala. 522. § 404.
v. S., 78 Ala. 14. § 862.
v. S., 96 Ala. 41. §§ 1087, 1088, 1091.
v. S., 28 Tex. 644. § 594.
v. S., 24 Tex. Ap. 559. § 353.
S. v., 48 Ind. 197. § 558.
S. v., 40 La. An. 736. § 988.

Baunen, Reg. v., 1 C. & K. 295. §§ 118, 187, 201.
Bannigan, T. v., 1 Dak. 432. §§ 343, 361, 382.
Bannon v. S., 49 Ark. 167. § 77.
v. U. S., 156 U. S. 464. §§ 20, 987.
Bantley, S. v., 44 Conn. 537. § 292.
Baptiste v. S., 5 Blackf. 283. § 54.
Barada v. S., 13 Mo. 94. § 191.
Barbee, S. v., 92 N. C. 820. § 161.
Barber, Minnesota v., 136 U. S. 313. § 35.
Reg. v., 1 C. & K. 434. § 751.
Reg. v., 1 C. & K. 442. § 750.
v. S., 78 Ala. 19. § 506.
v. S., 13 Fla. 675. § 487.
v. S., 50 Md. 161. § 1080.
Barberi, P. v., — N. Y. —, 43 N. E. R. 635. § 365.
Barbier v. Connolly, 113 U. S. 27. § 39.
Barclay v. C., 25 Pa. St. 503. § 1182.
Barcus v. S., 49 Miss. 17. § 323.
Bard v. S., 55 Ga. 319. § 271.
Barden v. Montana Club, 10 Mont. 330. § 1240.
S. v., 1 Dev. 518. § 573.
Bardenheier, U. S. v., 49 Fed. R. 846. § 1350.
Bardetta, S. v., 73 Ind. 185. § 15.
Barefield v. S., 14 Ala. 603. § 896.
Barefoot, S. v., 89 N. C. 565. § 820.
S. v., 2 Rich. 209. § 1074.
Barfield v. S., 29 Ga. 127. § 762.
S. v., 7 Ired. 299. § 342.
S. v., 8 Ired. 344. § 307.
Barham, S. v., 82 Mo. 67. § 421.
S. v., 79 N. C. 646. § 1159.
Barkelow, P. v., 37 Mich. 455. § 975.
Barker v. C., 19 Pa. St. 412. § 1158.
v. C., 90 Va. 820. §§ 1113, 1116, 1118.
v. C., 2 Va. Cas. 122. § 608.
C. v., 133 Mass. 399. § 931.
v. P., 20 Johns. 457. § 20.
Rex v., 3 C. & P. 589. § 460.
v. S., 12 Tex. 273. § 1285.
S. v., 64 Mo. 282. § 511.
S. v., 28 Ohio St. 583. § 327.
S. v., 3 R. I. 280. § 1229.
Barkhamsted v. Parsons, 3 Conn. 1. § 211.
Barkley v. S., 28 Tex. Ap. 99. § 1032.
Barkman v. S., 13 Ark. 703. §§ 1290, 1291.
Barlow, C. v., 4 Mass. 439. §§ 18, 210, 221, 263.
v. S., 120 Ind. 56. § 827.
Barnaby v. S., 21 Ind. 450. § 76.
U. S. v., 51 Fed. R. 20. §§ 235, 268.
Barnard v. C., 94 Ky. 285. § 462.
v. Houghton, 34 Vt. 264. § 1223.
Rex v., 7 Car. & P. 784. § 666.
S. v., 88 N. C. 661. § 826.
Barnards v. S., 88 Tenn. 183. §§ 303, 304.
Barnes v. C., 2 Dana, 388. § 1227.
C. v., 132 Mass. 242. § 956.
C. v., 138 Mass. 511. §§ 1229, 1251.
C. v., 140 Mass. 447. § 1250.
Barnes, P. v., 65 Cal. 16. §§ 594, 602.
P. v., 2 Ida. 148. § 1121.
Reg. v., 8 Cox, 129. §§ 626, 639.
Reg. v., 10 Cox, 539. § 887.
Reg. v., 2 Den. 59. §§ 563, 659.
Reg. v., L. R. 1 C. C. 45. § 556.
v. S., 49 Ala. 342. §§ 1216, 1255.
v. S., 88 Ala. 204. §§ 460, 461.
v. S., 103 Ala. 44. §§ 565, 572.
v. S., 19 Conn. 398. §§ 128, 188, 189.
v. S., 40 Neb. 545. §§ 548, 564, 592, 594.
v. S., 43 Tex. 98. § 617.
v. S., 9 Tex. Ap. 128. § 473.
v. S., 28 Tex. Ap. 29. § 615.
S. v., 34 La. An. 395. § 292.
S. v., 32 Me. 530. § 1055.
S. v., 24 Oreg. 366. § 46.
v. Ward, 9 C. B. 392. § 420.
Barnett v. P., 54 Ill. 325. § 390.
Reg. v., 2 C. & K. 594. §§ 197, 484.
v. S., 83 Ala. 40. §§ 455, 456.
v. S., 89 Ala. 165. §§ 114, 870, 872.
v. S., 100 Ind. 171. § 308.
v. S., 36 Me. 198. § 1243.
v. S., 38 Ohio St. 7. § 497.
S. v., 83 N. C. 615. § 1077.
S. v., 34 W. Va. 74. §§ 1034, 1036.
Barney, C. v., 10 Cush. 478. §§ 497, 518, 527.
C. v., 10 Cush. 480. § 519.
v. P., 22 Ill. 160. §§ 455, 457.
U. S. v., 5 Blatch. 294. §§ 14, 752.
U. S. v., 3 Hughes, 545. § 1328.
Barnhart, P. v., 59 Cal. 381. §§ 504, 512.
Barnhouse v. S., 31 Ohio St. 39. § 1123.
Barns, S. v., 25 Tex. 654. § 1304.
Barnum v. S., 15 Ohio, 717. §§ 744, 755, 756, 758.
Barnwell, S. v., 80 N. C. 466. § 330.
Baron v. P., 1 Park. Cr. 246. § 211.
Barr v. Moore, 87 Pa. St. 385. § 111.
v. P., 113 Ill. 471. § 463.
v. S., 45 Neb. 458. § 304.
S. v., 11 Wash. 481. §§ 142, 325.
U. S. v., 4 Saw. 254. § 101.
Barrackmore, S. v., 47 Ia. 684. § 565.
Barratt, Reg. v., 9 Car. & P. 387. § 1100.
Reg. v., L. R. 2 C. C. 81. § 448.
Barretry, Case of, 8 Co. 36*b*. § 27.
Barrett, C. v., 108 Mass. 302. §§ 324, 1013.
Reg. v., 2 C. & K. 343. § 379.
Rex v., 6 C. & P. 124. § 647.
S. v., 8 Ia. 536. §§ 771, 788, 803.
S. v., 40 Minn. 77. §§ 196, 291.
S. v., 42 N. H. 466. §§ 52, 932.
U. S. v., 65 Fed. R. 62. §§ 968, 989.
Barric, P. v., 49 Cal. 342. §§ 117, 604.
Barringer, S. v., 110 N. C. 525. §§ 1207, 1209.
Barron, S. v., 37 Vt. 57. § 1275.
Barronet, In re, 1 El. & B. 1. § 132.
Barrow, Reg. v., L. R. 1 C. C. 156. § 446.
S. v., 31 La. An. 691. § 1076.
Barrows, S. v., 57 Vt. 576. § 1012.
Barry, C. v., 115 Mass. 146. § 148.
C. v., 116 Mass. 1. § 623.
C. v., 124 Mass. 325. §§ 560, 562.

Barry, C. v., 125 Mass. 390. § 548.
P. v., 31 Cal. 357. § 418.
P. v., 63 Cal. 62. § 864.
P. v., 94 Cal. 481. § 503.
Reg. v., 4 F. & F. 389. § 968.
U. S. v., 4 Cranch, C. C. 606. §§ 596, 597.
Bartemeyer v. Iowa, 18 Wall. 129. §§ 29, 1201, 1207.
Bartender v. S., 51 Ind. 73. § 1291.
Barter, S. v., 58 N. H. 604. §§ 84, 627.
Bartholomew, Reg. v., 1 C. & K. 366. § 878.
Bartilson, C. v., 85 Pa. St. 482. § 973.
Bartle, U. S. v., 1 Cranch, C. C. 236. § 245.
Bartlett v. Brown, 6 R. I. 37. § 536.
P. v., 14 Cal. 651. § 324.
v. S., 28 Ohio St. 669. §§ 680, 687.
v. S., 21 Tex. Ap. 500. § 274.
S. v., 30 Me. 132. § 967.
S. v., 53 Me. 446. § 1095.
S. v., 55 Me. 200. § 600.
S. v., 43 N. H. 224. §§ 175, 179.
S. v., 11 Vt. 650. § 553.
S. v., 43 Vt. 86. § 1214.
Bartley, C. v., 138 Mass. 181. § 1142.
S. v., 34 La. An. 147. § 377.
Bartman, P. v., 81 Cal. 200. § 854.
Barton v. Faherty, 3 G. Gr. (Ia.) 327. § 611.
Reg. v., 3 Cox, 275. § 157.
v. S., 29 Ark. 68. § 597.
v. S., 7 Baxt. 105. § 1031.
v. S., 99 Ind. 89. §§ 128, 1253.
v. S., 18 Ohio, 221. § 615.
v. S., 23 Wis. 587. § 803.
U. S. v., Gilpin, 439. § 860.
Bartz, P. v., 53 Mich. 493. § 1015.
Baskett, S. v., 111 Mo. 271. § 451.
Bass v. S., 37 Ala. 469. §§ 1285, 1296.
Rex v., 2 East, P. C. 566. § 556.
v. S., 63 Ala. 108. § 1164.
v. S., 1 Lea, 444. § 500.
v. S., 16 Tex. Ap. 62. § 448.
Bassell, P. v., 59 Mich. 104. § 93.
Basserman, S. v., 54 Conn. 88. § 187.
Bassett v. Spofford, 45 N. Y. 387. § 611.
v. S., 41 Ind. 303. § 1149.
S. v., 34 La. An. 1108. § 594.
v. U. S., 137 U. S. 496. § 1085.
Bassette v. S., 51 N. J. 502. § 1021.
Basye v. S., 45 Neb. 261. § 307.
Batchelder, P. v., 27 Cal. 69. § 142.
S. v., 5 N. H. 549. §§ 821, 1014.
U. S. v., 2 Gallis. 15. §§ 925, 926, 929.
Batchelor v. U. S., 156 U. S. 426 § 1340.
Bate, Reg. v., 11 Cox, 686. § 1152.
Bates' Case, 55 N. H. 325. § 9.
Bates v. Clark, 95 U. S. 204. § 1338*a*.
Reg. v., 3 Cox, 201. § 678.
v. S., 31 Ind. 72. § 823.
S. v., 23 Ia. 96. §§ 904, 922, 931.
S. v., 46 La. An. 849. § 615.
v. U. S., 10 Biss. 70. § 1332.
v. U. S., 10 Fed. R. 92. § 1335.
Bateswell, S. v., 105 Mo. 609. § 241.
Bathrick, C. v., 6 Cush. 247. § 1221.
Bathurst, Rex v., Say. 225. § 836.
Batstone, Reg. v., 10 Cox, 20. § 523.
Batt. Rex v., 6 C. & P. 329. § 993.
Batten v. S., 80 Ind. 394. §§ 139, 304, 306, 400, 421.
Batterson v. S., 63 Ind. 531. § 453.
Battle v. S., 51 Ark. 97. § 1253.
v. S., 74 Ga. 101. § 431.
v. S., 92 Ga. 465. § 339.
v. S., 4 Tex. Ap. 595. § 466.
Batty, Reg. v., 2 Moody, 257. § 626.
Bauer v. S., 25 Ohio St. 70. § 499.
Baughman, S. v., 20 Ia. 497. §§ 1217, 1249, 1271.
Bauld, Reg. v., 13 Cox, 282. § 963.
Baum, S. v., 33 La. An. 981. § 1206.
Baumer v. S., 49 Ind. 544. § 1121.
Baumhager v. S., 28 Minn. 226. § 648.
Baumon, S. v., 52 Ia. 68. § 759.
Baur. S. v., 1 N. D. 273. § 914.
Bautsch v. S., 27 Tex. Ap. 342. § 6.
Bawden, P. v., 90 Cal. 195. § 363.
Baxter v. P., 8 Ill. 368. §§ 214, 217.
Bayle, U. S. v., 40 Fed. R. 664. § 1333.
Bayley, Reg. v., Dears. & B. 121. § 626.
Bayliss v. P., 46 Mich. 221. § 1093.
Bayne, S. v., 88 Mo. 604. §§ 676, 686.
Bayonne, S. v., 36 La. An. 761. § 600.
Bays v. S., 6 Neb. 167. § 1027.
Baysinger v. P., 115 Ill. 419. §§ 909, 915.
v. S., 77 Ala. 63. § 759.
Beacall, Rex v., 1 C. & P. 312. §§ 626, 635.
Rex v., 1 Moody, 15. § 634.
Beach v. Hancock, 27 N. H. 223. § 233.
v. P., 11 Mich. 106. § 1170.
P. v., 93 Mich. 25. § 1252.
v. S., 32 Tex. Ap. 240. §§ 874, 892.
U. S. v., 71 Fed. R. 160. § 1331.
Beacham, U. S. v., 29 Fed. R. 284. § 1347.
Beadon, S. v., 17 S. C. 55. § 260.
Beal v. S., 99 Ala. 234. § 1053.
v. S., 15 Ind. 378. § 553.
S. v., 75 Me. 289. § 46.
S. v., 37 Ohio St. 108. §§ 226, 506.
Beale, C. v., 5 Pick. 514. § 932.
Reg. v., L. R. 1 C. C. 10. §§ 444, 464.
U. S. v., 4 Cranch, C. C. 313. § 925.
Beall v. S., 53 Ala. 460. § 508.
v. S., 4 Blackf. 107. § 44.
Bealoba, P. v., 17 Cal. 389. §§ 353, 355, 356, 357, 358, 359.
Beals, C. v., 133 Mass. 396. § 140.
Beam, P. v., 66 Cal. 394. § 272.
Beaman, C. v., 8 Gray, 497. §§ 541, 552.
Reg. v., Car. & M. 595. § 556.
Beamish, C. v., 81 Pa. St. 389. §§ 110, 744.
Bean, C. v., 117 Mass. 141. § 717.
C. v., 148 Mass. 172. § 34.
v. P., 124 Ill. 576. § 455.
v. S., 17 Tex. Ap. 60. §§ 204, 373, 374, 382.
v. S., 25 Tex. Ap. 346. § 389.
S. v., 36 N. H. 122. § 260.
S. v., 19 Vt. 530. § 799.
Beard, Reg. v., 8 C. & P. 143. § 762.
v. S., 43 Ark. 284. §§ 846, 849.
v. S., 71 Md. 275. §§ 1137, 1145.
v. S., 74 Md. 130. §§ 95, 96.
S. v., 25 N. J. 384. §§ 861, 878.

Beard v. U. S., 158 U. S. 550. § 311.
Bearden v. S., 95 Ga. 459. § 499.
Beardsall, Reg. v., 1 F. & F. 629. § 762.
Beardsley v. S., 49 Ind. 240. § 1264.
Bearse, C. v., 108 Mass. 487. § 236.
C. v., 132 Mass. 542. § 39.
Bearss, P. v., 10 Cal. 68. §§ 215, 216.
Beasley v. S., 18 Ala. 535. § 268.
v. S., 50 Ala. 149. § 159.
v. S., 59 Ala. 20. § 701.
v. S., 138 Ind. 552. § 558.
v. S., 5 Lea, 705. § 1037.
S. v., 5 Mo. 91. § 106.
Beasom, S. v., 40 N. H. 367. § 925.
Beattie v. Mair, L. R. 10 Ir. 208. § 839.
v. P., 33 Ill. Ap. 651. § 893.
Beatty v. Gillbanks, 9 Q. B. D. 308. § 1003.
P. v., 14 Cal. 566. § 1291.
v. S., 61 Miss. 18. § 569.
S. v., 90 Mo. 143. §§ 586, 616.
S. v., Phil. 52. § 719.
U. S. v., 60 Fed. R. 740. § 1331.
Beaty v. S., 30 Tex. Ap. 677. § 338.
U. S. v., Hemp. 487. § 83.
Beaubien, P. v., 2 Doug. 256. § 1190.
Beauchamp v. S., 6 Blackf. 299. §§ 332, 338, 345.
Beaudet, S. v., 53 Conn. 536. § 404.
Beaumier, S. v., 87 Me. 214. § 1249.
Beaumont, Reg. v., Dears. 270. § 634.
Beaver, P. v., 49 Cal. 57. § 514.
Beavers v. S., 103 Ala. 36. § 419.
v. S., 58 Ind. 530. §§ 377, 382, 395.
v. S., 14 Tex. Ap. 541. §§ 541, 548.
Bebout, U. S. v., 28 Fed. R. 522. § 1332.
Becht, S. v., 23 Minn. 411. § 9.
Beck, P. v., 21 Cal. 385. § 474.
v. S., 76 Ga. 452. §§ 159, 160.
v. S., 72 Ind. 250. § 9.
v. S., 69 Miss. 217. § 1239.
v. S., 44 Tex. 430. § 619.
Becker, S. v., 20 Ia. 438. §§ 1271, 1274, 1278, 1281.
S. v., 3 S. D. 29. §§ 1206, 1213.
Beckett, Rex v., 1 M. & Rob. 526. § 256.
Beckham v. S., 100 Ala. 15. § 571.
Beckman, S. v., 57 N. H. 174. § 1196.
S. v., 58 N. H. 399. § 45.
Beckwith v. P., 26 Ill. 500. § 271.
P. v., 103 N. Y. 360. §§ 342, 359.
Beckworth, S. v., 68 Mo. 82. § 509.
Becomb, Pennsylvania v., Addison, 386. § 538.
Bedard, S. v., 65 Vt. 278. § 455.
Beddall v. Maitland, 17 Ch. D. 174. § 836.
Bedell, Ex parte, 20 Mo. Ap. 125. § 80.
P. v., 2 Hill (N. Y.), 196. § 646.
v. S., 50 Miss. 492. §§ 271, 278.
S. v., 65 Vt. 541. § 520.
Bedgood v. S., 115 Ind. 275. § 460.
U. S. v., 49 Fed. R. 54. §§ 852, 855, 878.
Bedingfield, Reg. v., 14 Cox, 341. § 414.
Beebe v. S., 6 Ind. 501. §§ 29, 1207.
S. v., 13 Kan. 589. § 931.
S. v., 17 Minn. 241. §§ 196, 217, 596.
Beebe, U. S. v., 2 Dak. 292. § 420.
Beecham, Reg. v., 6 Cox, 181. § 543.
Beechey, Rex v., Russ. & Ry. 319. § 634.
Beekman, S. v., 27 N. J. 124. §§ 811, 815.
Beeler, S. v., 1 Brev. 482. § 783.
Beeman, S. v., 35 Me. 242. § 1192.
Beer Co. v. Massachusetts, 97 U. S. 25. §§ 29, 75, 1201, 1207.
Beerman, U. S. v., 5 Cranch, C. C. 412. § 551.
Beers v. S., 24 Neb. 614. §§ 353, 358.
Beery v. U. S., 2 Colo. 186. §§ 12, 542, 607, 1330.
Beeton, Reg. v., 2 C. & K. 960. § 609.
Beets v. S., Meigs, 106. §§ 196, 291, 429.
Beevers, P. v., 99 Cal. 286. § 1074.
Began's Petition, 12 R. I. 309. § 1021.
Beggs v. S., 55 Ala. 108. §§ 1073, 1074, 1077.
v. S., 122 Ind. 54. § 824.
Behan v. P., 17 N. Y. 516. § 8.
Behee, P. v., 90 Mich. 356. §§ 690, 695, 702.
Behimer, S. v., 20 Ohio St. 572. § 390.
Behm, S. v., 72 Ia. 533. § 286.
Behrman, S. v., 114 N. C. 797. § 1096.
Behymer v. S., 95 Ind. 140. § 271.
Beine, In re, 42 Fed. R. 545. § 1204.
Beiser v. S., 79 Ga. 326. § 1245.
Bejarnao v. S., 6 Tex. Ap. 265. § 412.
Belcher, P. v., 58 Mich. 325. § 586.
v. S., 8 Humph. 62. § 1097.
Belden, P. v., 37 Cal. 51. § 556.
S. v., 35 La. An. 823. § 629.
S. v., 33 Wis. 120. § 390.
Belding, C. v., 13 Met. 10. § 1190.
Belencia, P. v., 21 Cal. 544. § 359.
Belk v. P., 125 Ill. 584. §§ 130, 292.
S. v., 76 N. C. 10. § 260.
Belknap v. Milliken, 23 Me. 381. § 11.
Bell, Ex parte, 19 Fla. 608. § 581.
Ex parte, 24 Tex. Ap. 428. § 1223.
Ex parte, 32 Tex. Ap. 308. §§ 65, 66.
C. v., 14 Bush, 433. § 1257.
C. v., 164 Pa. St. 517. § 396.
C. v., 166 Pa. St. 405. § 1124.
v. Hansley, 3 Jones, 131. § 249.
P. v., 49 Cal. 485. §§ 159, 178, 400.
Reg. v., 8 Ir. R. C. L. 541. § 1152.
Rex v., 1 East, P. C. 169. § 777.
v. S., 48 Ala. 684. § 511.
v. S., 89 Ala. 61. § 1030.
v. S., 100 Ala. 78. § 1037.
v. S., 10 Ark. 536. § 779.
v. S., 4 Baxt. 426. § 537.
v. S., 41 Ga. 589. § 596.
v. S., 91 Ga. 227. §§ 1220, 1221.
v. S., 92 Ga. 49. §§ 145, 148.
v. S., 46 Ind. 453. § 601.
v. S., 57 Md. 108. § 803.
v. S., 72 Miss. 507. § 426.
v. S., 5 Sneed, 507. §§ 1285, 1315.
v. S., 1 Swan, 42. §§ 1049, 1156.
v. S., 1 Tex. Ap. 598. § 476.
v. S., 7 Tex. Ap. 25. § 550.
v. S., 17 Tex. Ap. 538. § 311.

Bell v. S., 18 Tex. Ap. 53. § 255.
v. S., 20 Tex. Ap. 445. § 306.
v. S., 28 Tex. Ap. 96. §§ 1201, 1206.
v. S., 32 Tex. Ap. 187. § 1310.
v. S., 20 Wis. 599. § 495.
S. v., 7 Baxt. 9. § 1131.
S. v., 29 Ia. 316. § 507.
S. v., 49 Ia. 440. §§ 1113, 1119.
S. v., 79 Ia. 117. §§ 1117, 1118, 1119.
S. v., 2 Jones, 337. § 1246.
S. v., 65 N. C. 313. § 601.
S. v., 5 Port. 365. § 1174.
T. v., 5 Mont. 562. § 481.
v. Troy, 35 Ala. 184. § 11.
Bellair v. S., 6 Blackf. 104. § 950.
Bellamy v. S., 35 Fla. 242. §§ 617, 618.
Beller, P. v., 73 Mich. 640. § 1264.
Bellet, P. v., 99 Mich. 151. § 1319.
Bellinger v. S., 92 Ala. 86. § 566.
Beloit, S. v., 74 Wis. 267. § 1226.
Belon, C. v., 115 Mass. 139. § 1281.
Belote v. S., 36 Miss. 96. §§ 614, 617.
Belstead, Rex v., Russ. & Ry. 411. § 546.
Beltram v. S., 9 Tex. Ap. 280. § 332.
Belvin, U. S. v., 46 Fed. R. 381. §§ 946, 948, 950.
Bemis, P. v., 51 Mich. 422. § 377.
Bemmerley, P. v., 87 Cal. 117. § 429.
Bemmerly, P. v., 98 Cal. 299. § 178.
Ben v. S., 37 Ala. 103. §§ 423, 427.
Benadom, S. v., 79 Ia. 90. § 1223.
Benavides v. S., 31 Tex. 580. § 426.
Bendit, P. v., — Cal. —, 43 Pac. R. 901. 762.
Benedict v. S., 14 Wis. 423. § 419.
S. v., 11 Vt. 236. §§ 233, 1017.
Beneke, S. v., 9 Ia. 203. § 1229.
Benesech, Rex v., Peake Ad. Cas. 93. § 865.
Benevides v. S., 14 Tex. Ap. 378. § 391.
Benfield, Rex v., 2 Bur. 980. §§ 252, 1057.
Benge v. C., 92 Ky. 1. § 213.
Reg. v., 4 F. & F. 504. § 130.
Benham v. S., 1 Ia. 542. § 253.
S. v., 7 Conn. 414. § 784.
S. v., 23 Ia. 154. § 351.
Benjamin, S. v., 2 Oreg. 125. § 1216.
S. v., 49 Vt. 101. § 1270.
Benner, U. S. v., Baldw. 234. §§ 235, 1342.
Bennefield v. S., 80 Ga. 107. § 58.
Bennet v. S., 26 Tex. Ap. 671. § 1185.
S. v., 3 Brev. 514. § 617.
Bennett v. Art Union, 5 Sandf. 614. § 1315.
C. v., 108 Mass. 27. §§ 1210, 1270.
C. v., 118 Mass. 443. §§ 631, 652, 656a.
P. v., 39 Mich. 208. § 1074.
P. v., 37 N. Y. 117. §§ 546, 604.
P. v., 49 N. Y. 137. §§ 123, 396.
P. v., 4 Paige, 282. § 9.
Reg. v., Bell, 1. § 188.
Reg. v., 4 F. & F. 1105. §§ 238, 249, 256.
Reg. v., 14 Cox, 45. § 1076.
Rex v., Russ. & Ry. 289. § 497.
Bennett v. S., 52 Ala. 370. §§ 578, 614.
v. S., Mart. & Y. 133. § 159.
v. S., 12 Tex. Ap. 15. § 315.
v. S., 16 Tex. Ap. 236. § 586.
v. S., 17 Tex. Ap. 143. § 572.
v. S., 28 Tex. Ap. 342. § 572.
v. S., 32 Tex. Ap. 216. § 546.
v. S., 57 Wis. 69. § 156.
S. v., 2 Brev. 575. § 587.
S. v., 4 Dev. & B. 43. § 1000.
S. v., 3 Harr. 565. § 1219.
S. v., 14 Ia. 479. § 553.
S. v., 31 Ia. 24. §§ 1093, 1099.
U. S. v., 16 Blatch. 338. § 1332.
U. S. v., 17 Blatch. 357. §§ 796, 797.
Benoit, P. v., 97 Cal. 249. § 1124.
Benson, In re, 34 Fed. R. 649. §§ 745, 752.
In re, 58 Fed. R. 962. §§ 964, 984.
v. McMahon, 127 U. S. 457. § 745.
v. Mfg. Co., 9 Met. 562. § 184.
P. v., 6 Cal. 221. §§ 458, 460.
Rex v., 2 Camp. 508. § 887.
v. S., 68 Ala. 544. §§ 1017, 1021.
v. S., 5 Minn. 19. §§ 13, 105.
S. v., 28 Minn. 424. § 663a.
S. v., 110 Mo. 18. §§ 684, 698.
U. S. v., 31 Fed. R. 896. § 87.
Benstine v. S., 2 Lea, 169. § 455.
Benthal, S. v., 5 Humph. 519. § 1009.
Benthall, S. v., 82 N. C. 664. § 466.
Bentley, P. v., 75 Cal. 407. § 271.
v. S., 32 Ala. 596. § 1303.
v. Vilmont, 12 Ap. Cas. 471. § 712.
Benton v. C., 89 Va. 570. §§ 18, 505.
S. v., 18 N. H. 47. § 82.
Benz, S. v., 41 Minn. 30. § 1245.
Berdetta, S. v., 73 Ind. 185. §§ 15, 1184.
Berg, In re, 139 Pa. St. 354. § 1228.
v. S., 2 Tex. Ap. 148. §§ 550, 562.
Bergemann v. Backer, 157 U. S. 655. § 361.
Bergen v. P., 17 Ill. 426. §§ 1123, 1124.
Berger v. S., 50 Ark. 20. § 1236.
Bergin, In re, 31 Wis. 383. § 4.
v. S., 31 Ohio St. 111. § 101.
Berkley, S. v., 109 Mo. 665. § 338.
Berkshire, S. v., 2 Ind. 207. §§ 111, 190, 912.
Berlin, P. v., 9 Utah, 383. § 560.
S. v., 21 S. C., 292. § 1210.
Bernadotte, Reg. v., 11 Cox, 316. §§ 426, 429.
Bernard, Reg. v., 1 F. & F. 240. §§ 117, 194, 196.
Berney v. S., 69 Ala. 233. § 1032.
Berning v. S., 51 Ark. 550. § 1229.
S. v., 91 Mo. 82. § 271.
Berrian v. S., 22 N. J. 9. § 877.
Berrien v. S., 83 Ga. 381. § 710.
Berriman, Reg. v., 6 Cox, 388. § 1152.
Berrisford v. S., 66 Ga. 53. § 809.
Berritt, S. v., 17 N. H. 268. § 271.
Berry, C. v., 5 Gray, 93. § 996.
C. v., 99 Mass. 428. §§ 556, 623, 625.
C. v., 109 Mass. 366. § 1243.
Reg. v., Bell, 46. §§ 858, 859, 863.

Berry, Reg. v., Bell, 95. § 558.
Reg. v., 1 Q. B. D. 447. §§ 155, 166.
v. S., 67 Ind. 222. § 1257.
v. S., 31 Ohio St. 219. § 567.
v. S., 4 Tex. Ap. 492. §§ 206, 211.
v. S., 8 Tex. Ap. 515. § 391.
v. S., 12 Tex. Ap. 249. § 1190.
v. S., 27 Tex. Ap. 483. §§ 1057, 1060.
v. S., 30 Tex. Ap. 423. § 259.
S. v., 12 Ia. 58. § 1184.
Berryman, S. v., 8 Nev. 262. §§ 536, 537.
Bertheol, S. v., 6 Blackf. 474. §§ 15, 1137.
Bertrand, S. v., 3 Oreg. 61. § 316.
S. v., 72 Miss. 516. §§ 1232, 1239.
Berzaman, S. v., 10 Wash. 277. § 462.
Best, P. v., 39 Cal. 690. § 158.
Reg. v., 9 C. & P. 368. § 940.
Reg. v., 2 Ld. Raym. 1167, 1 Salk. 174. §§ 954, 957, 958.
Rex v., 6 Mod. 185. § 966.
S. v., 108 N. C. 747. §§ 1233, 1256, 1259, 1260.
Beswick, S. v., 13 R. I. 211. §§ 1215, 1218, 1220.
Bethea, U. S. v., 44 Fed. R. 802. §§ 1330, 1335.
Bethel v. C., 80 Ky. 526. § 454.
Bethune v. S., 48 Ga. 505. § 499.
Bethurum, Ex parte, 66 Mo. 545. § 78.
Betsall, S. v., 11 W. Va. 703. § 508.
Bettis v. Taylor, 8 Port. 564. § 83.
Betton, C. v., 5 Cush. 427. § 523.
Betts v. Armstead, 20 Q. B. D. 771. § 128.
Reg. v., Bell, 90. §§ 556, 623.
Reg. v., 16 Q. B. 1022. § 1195.
v. S., 66 Ga. 508. § 421.
v. S., 93 Ind. 375. § 1143.
Bevans, S. v., 37 Ia. 178. § 904.
U. S. v., 3 Wheat. 336. § 14.
Beverley's Case, 4 Co. 123*b*. § 154.
Bevington v. S., 2 Ohio St. 161. §§ 784, 786.
Beyer v. P., 86 N. Y. 369. §§ 448, 1106*a*.
U. S. v., 31 Fed. R. 35. § 246.
Bezek, C. v., 168 Pa. St. 603. §§ 178, 421.
Bezy, P. v., 67 Cal. 223. § 423.
P. v., 73 Cal. 186. § 359.
Bias, S. v., 37 La. An. 259. § 1031.
Bibb v. S., 84 Ala. 13. § 1311.
v. S., 94 Ala. 31. § 146.
S. v., 68 Mo. 286. §§ 752, 796.
Bibby, P. v., 91 Cal. 470. § 758.
Bibithe's Case, 4 Co. 43, 1 Hale, P. C. 437. § 208.
Bickerstaff, Reg. v., 2 C. & K. 761. § 1330.
Bickle's Ex'r v. Fasig's Adm'r, 33 Pa. St. 463. § 661.
Bicksler, U. S. v., 1 Mackey, 341. § 774.
Biddle, C. v., 139 Pa. St. 605. § 41.
S. v., 54 N. H. 379. §§ 1218, 1219, 1220.
Bidleman, P. v., 104 Cal. 608. §§ 640, 641, 651.
Bieber v. S., 45 Ga. 569. § 713.
Biebusch, S. v., 32 Mo. 276. §§ 878, 898.
U. S. v., 1 McCrary, 42. § 786.
Bielby, S. v., 21 Wis. 204. § 1274.
Bielfus, P. v., 59 Mich. 576. § 514.
Bierman, C. v., 13 Bush, 345. § 1318.
Bigby v. S., 44 Ga. 344. § 1088.
Bigelow, C. v., 8 Met. 235. § 808.
Bigg, Rex v., 2 East, P. C. 882. § 752.
Biggers, S. v., 108 N. C. 760. § 823.
Biggerstaff v. C., 11 Bush, 169. § 855.
Biggins, P. v., 65 Cal. 564. § 338.
Biggs v. S., 29 Ga. 723. §§ 267, 299.
Bigham v. S., 31 Tex. Ap. 244. §§ 494, 509.
Bigler, P. v., 5 Cal. 23. § 214.
Bilansky v. S., 3 Minn. 427. § 362.
S. v., 3 Minn. 246. §§ 89, 1354.
Bilbo v. S., 7 Humph. 534. § 1247.
Bildstein, S. v., 44 La. An. 778. § 1061.
Biles v. C., 32 Pa. St. 529. § 755.
v. S., 25 Tex. Ap. 441. § 1313.
S. v., 6 Wash. 186. § 518.
Bill, S. v., 6 Jones, 34. § 515.
Billard v. S., 30 Tex. 367. § 617.
Billings v. S., 52 Ark. 303. § 418.
v. S., 107 Ind. 54. § 764.
S. v., 81 Ia. 99. § 401.
Billingslea v. S., 68 Ala. 486. § 417.
Billingsley v. S., 96 Ala. 114. § 1234.
Billingsly, S. v., 43 Tex. 93. § 1009.
Billups v. S., 88 Ga. 27. § 752.
Binder, S. v., 38 Mo 450. § 63.
Binfield v. S., 15 Neb. 484. § 307.
Bingham v. S., 6 Tex. Ap. 169. §§ 275, 307.
Bingley, Rex v., 5 C. & P. 602. § 472.
Rex v., Russ. & Ry. 446. § 195.
Bininger, In re, 7 Blatchf. 262. § 120.
Binns v. Pigot, 9 C. & P. 208. § 611.
v. S., 46 Ind. 311. § 428.
v. S., 57 Ind. 46. §§ 416, 424.
v. S., 66 Ind. 428. §§ 358, 416.
Birch, Reg. v., 2 C. & K. 193. § 484.
Rex v., 2 East, P. C. 980. § 750.
U. S. v., 1 Cranch, C. C. 571. § 1272.
Birchall, Reg. v., 4 F. & F. 1087. §§ 349, 351.
Birchfield, Ex parte, 52 Ala. 377. § 1137.
Bird, Ex parte, 19 Cal. 130. § 1319.
v. C., 21 Grat. 800. § 1082.
Reg. v., 2 C. & K. 817. §§ 195, 1152.
Reg. v., 9 C. & P. 44. §§ 500, 509.
Reg. v., 12 Cox, 257. § 560.
v. S., 18 Fla. 493. § 382.
v. S., 55 Ga. 317. § 338.
v. S., 104 Ind. 384. § 1314.
v. S., 16 Tex. Ap. 528. § 572.
v. S., 27 Tex. Ap. 635. § 1087.
Birdg v. S., 31 Ind. 88. §§ 794, 831.
Birdseye, Rex v., 4 C. & P. 386. § 551.
Birdwell, S. v., 36 La. An. 859. §§ 303, 418.
Birkett, Rex v., Russ. & Ry. 86. § 756.
Rex v., Russ. & Ry. 251. §§ 752, 765.
Birmingham, Reg. v., 9 C. & P. 469. §§ 180, 182.
Rex v., 8 B. & C. 29. § 1074.
S. v., Busb. 120. § 605.

Birney v. S., 8 Ohio. 230. § 128.
Birr v. P., 113 Ill. 645. §§ 1235, 1259, 1261.
Birt, Rex v., 5 C. & P. 154. § 1004.
Bishel, S. v., 39 Ind. 421. §§ 1285, 1286, 1306.
Bishop of Bangor, Rex v., 1 Russ. Cr. 274. § 1003.
Bishop v. C., 13 Grat. 785. § 1304.
P. v., 5 Wend. 111. §§ 247, 939.
Reg. v., Car. & M. 302. § 858.
Reg. v., 5 Q. B. D. 259. § 128.
v. S., 30 Ala. 34. § 791.
v. S., 86 Ga. 329. § 232.
v. S., 55 Md. 138. §§ 751, 757, 808.
S. v., 7 Conn. 181. §§ 4, 5.
S. v., 1 D. Chip. 120. §§ 873, 883.
S. v., 8 Ired. 266. § 1310.
S. v., 73 N. C. 44. § 404.
S. v., 51 Vt. 287. § 499.
Biss, Reg. v., 8 C. & P. 773. § 373*a*.
Bissell v. Gold, 1 Wend. 210. § 235.
S. v., 67 Ia. 616. § 1253.
Biswell, Reg. v., 2 Cox, 279. § 1103.
Bitancourt, P. v., 74 Cal. 188. § 508.
Bitman, S. v., 13 Ia. 485. §§ 242, 252.
Bittick v. S., 40 Tex. 117. §§ 260, 268.
S. v., 103 Mo. 183. § 1104.
Bittings v. S., 56 Ind. 101. § 765.
Bittle v. S., 78 Md. 526. § 228.
Bivens v. S., 11 Ark. 455. § 332.
Bixby, U. S. v., 10 Biss. 238. § 646.
Bixler, S. v., 62 Md. 354. §§ 880, 881.
Black, In re, 52 Kan. 64. § 512.
v. S., 83 Ala. 61. § 601.
v. S., 2 Md. 376. § 520.
v. S., 8 Tex. Ap. 329. § 267.
v. S., 9 Tex. Ap. 328. § 267.
v. S., 18 Tex. Ap. 124. § 505.
S. v., 9 Ired. 378. § 1302.
S. v., 42 La. An. 861. §§ 419, 426, 428.
S. v., 63 Me. 210. § 443.
S. v., 94 N. C. 809. §§ 1283, 1306, 1307.
S. v., 109 N. C. 856. § 245.
S. v., 1 Wins. (N. C.) 266. § 243.
S. v., 75 Wis. 490. §§ 90, 692.
Blackburn, C. v., 1 Duv. 4. § 221.
v. S., 98 Ala. 63. § 426.
v. S., 22 Ohio St. 102. §§ 444, 450.
v. S., 23 Ohio St. 146. §§ 156, 205, 290, 291, 401.
v. S., 50 Ohio St. 428. § 28.
v. S., 39 Tex. 153. § 255.
v. S., 44 Tex. 457. § 546.
S. v., 2 Coldw. 235. § 1297.
Blackford v. S., 11 Ohio St. 327. § 499.
Blackham, Rex v., 2 East, P. C. 711. § 470.
v. S., 36 Ala. 295. § 1097.
Blackington, C. v., 24 Pick. 352. §§ 1206, 1212, 1228.
Blackman v. S., 98 Ala. 77. § 566.
S. v., 35 La. An. 483. § 213.
U. S. v., 17 Fed. R. 837. 1330.
Blackson, Rex v., 8 C. & P. 43. § 212.
Blackstone, S. v., 74 Ind. 592. § 877.
Blackwell v. S., 36 Ark. 178. §§ 1225, 1266.
v. S., 42 Ark. 275. § 1236.
v. S., 45 Ark. 90. § 1216.
v. S., 30 Tex. Ap. 416. § 260.
v. S., 30 Tex. Ap. 672. §§ 992, 998.
v. S., 33 Tex. Ap. 278. § 271.
S. v., 9 Ala. 79. § 232.
Blahut v. S., 34 Ark. 447. § 1239.
v. S., 54 Ark. 538. § 1261.
S. v., 48 Ark. 34. § 1256.
Blain v. S., 24 Tex. Ap. 626. § 195.
v. S., 30 Tex. Ap. 702. § 197.
v. S., 33 Tex. Ap. 236. § 196.
Blair v. Cuming County, 111 U. S. 363. § 40.
v. S., 81 Ga. 628. § 1261.
v. S., 81 Ga. 629. § 1277.
v. S., 26 Tex. Ap. 387. § 1037.
S. v., 72 Ia. 591. § 1223.
S. v., 13 Rich. 93. § 996.
S. v., 41 Tex. 30. §§ 1284, 1291.
Blaisdell, C. v., 107 Mass. 234. § 1186.
S. v., 33 N. H. 388. § 1273.
S. v., 59 N. H. 328. §§ 390, 883.
Blake v. Barnard, 9 C. & P. 626. § 233.
P. v., 65 Cal. 275. §§ 159, 767.
P. v., 52 Mich. 566. §§ 1237, 1264.
Reg. v., 6 Q. B. 126. §§ 983, 988.
S. v., 39 Me. 322. §§ 269, 452, 466.
v. U. S., 71 Fed. R. 286. §§ 925, 927.
Blakely v. S., 24 Tex. Ap. 616. § 209.
Blakeney, S. v., 33 S. C. 111. § 381.
Blakesley, S. v., 43 Kan. 250. § 609.
Blan, S. v., 69 Mo. 317. §§ 213, 377, 381.
Blanchard, P. v., 90 N. Y. 314. § 678.
v. S., 3 Ind. Ap. 395. § 48.
S. v., 74 Ia. 628. §§ 791, 800.
S. v., 11 Wash. 116. § 597.
Blanchette v. S., 29 Tex. Ap. 46. § 1121.
Bland v. P., 4 Ill. 364. § 791.
v. S., 18 Tex. Ap. 12. § 557.
S. v., 97 N. C. 438. § 298.
Blanding, C. v., 3 Pick. 304. §§ 118, 1042, 1051, 1053, 1058.
Blanton v. S., 5 Blackf. 560. § 1310.
v. S., 1 Wash. 265. § 383.
Blassingame v. Glaves, 6 B. Mon. 38. § 11.
Blauvelt, S. v., 38 N. J. 306. §§ 690, 694.
Bleasdale, Reg. v., 2 C. & K. 765. §§ 187, 551, 615.
Bledsoe v. S., 10 Mo. 388. § 87.
v. S., 21 Tex. 223. § 1303.
Blemer v. P., 76 Ill. 265. § 662.
Blenkinsop, Reg. v., 2 C. & K. 531. § 762.
Blewett v. Smith, 74 Mo. 404. § 5.
v. S., 34 Miss. 606. §§ 1283, 1286.
Blick, Rex v., 4 C. & P. 377. §§ 536, 724.
Blige v. S., 20 Fla. 742. § 257.
Bliss, C. v., 1 Mass. 32. § 11.
Bliven, P. v., 112 N. Y. 79. § 217.
Blize, S. v., 111 Mo. 464. §§ 863, 892.
Blizzard, S. v., 70 Md. 385. §§ 698, 707.
Block v. S., 66 Ala. 493. §§ 1266, 1273.
v. S., 14 Ind. 425. § 53.
U. S. v., 4 Saw. 211. § 20.

Blocker v. S., 27 Tex. Ap. 16. § 391.
Blodgett, C. v., 12 Met. 56. §§ 115, 486.
S. v., 1 Root, 534. § 805.
Bloedow, S. v., 45 Wis. 279. §§ 124, 274.
Blonien, S. v., 36 Wis. 303. § 1193.
Blood, C. v., 11 Gray, 74. § 1243.
C. v., 141 Mass. 571. § 669.
Bloodsworth, S. v., 25 Oreg. 83. §§ 706, 710.
Bloodworth v. S., 6 Baxt. 614. § 446.
Bloom v. Richards, 2 Ohio St. 387. § 1319.
Bloomer v. S., 48 Md. 521. §§ 972, 989.
v. S., 3 Sneed, 66. §§ 232, 252.
Bloomfield v. Blake, 6 C. & P. 75. § 904.
Reg. v., Car. & M. 537. § 667.
v. Trimble, 54 Ia. 399. § 69.
Bloomhuff v. S., 8 Blackf. 205. §§ 1137, 1182.
Blos, C. v., 116 Mass. 56. §§ 1218, 1219.
Blough v. S., 121 Ind. 355. § 1247.
Blount, S. v., 85 Mo. 543. § 46.
Blue Mountain Joe, P. v., 129 Ill. 370. § 36.
Blum v. S., 20 Tex. Ap. 578. § 679.
Blunt v. C., 4 Leigh, 689. § 560.
S. v., 91 Mo. 503. § 339.
S. v., 110 Mo. 322. § 370.
Blumenthal, In re, 125 Pa. St. 412. § 1227.
Blumer, Ex parte, 86 Pa. St. 371. § 629.
Blyth, S. v., 1 Bay, 166. § 247.
Boak v. S., 5 Ia. 430. § 1113.
Boaler v. Reg., 21 Q. B. D. 284. § 1051.
Boardman v. Gore, 15 Mass. 331. § 11.
Reg. v., 2 M. & Rob. 147. § 754.
S. v., 64 Me. 523. §§ 1138, 1145.
Board of Com'rs, S. v., 45 Ind. 501. § 1228.
Boasso, S. v., 38 La. An. 202. §§ 756, 780.
Boatwright v. S., 89 Ga. 140. §§ 304, 309, 332.
Bobbitt, S. v., 70 N. C. 71. § 881.
Bock v. S., 50 Ind. 281. § 819.
Boddie v. S., 52 Ala. 395. §§ 458, 460.
Bode v. S., 7 Gill, 326. § 1264.
v. S., 6 Tex. Ap. 424. § 303.
Bodeckar v. S., 11 Wash. 417. § 1274.
Boden, Reg. v., 1 C. & K. 395. § 479.
Bodenhamer v. S., 60 Ark. 10. §§ 1159, 1160.
Bodiford v. S., 86 Ala. 67. §§ 1087, 1098.
Boes v. S., 125 Ind. 205. § 492.
Boetcher v. Staples, 27 Minn. 308. § 11.
Bogan v. S., 84 Ala. 449. § 1270.
S. v., 2 La. An. 838. § 1271.
Bogart, P. v., 36 Cal. 245. § 597.
U. S. v., 9 Ben. 314. § 774.
Boger v. S., 19 Tex. Ap. 91. § 1096.
Boggess, S. v., 36 W. Va. 713. § 1256.
Boggs v. C., 76 Va. 989. § 46.
U. S. v., 31 Fed. R. 337. § 857.
Boggus v. S., 34 Ga. 275. § 1072.
Bogue, S. v., 52 Kan. 79. § 217.
Bohan, S. v., 15 Kan. 407. § 425.
S. v., 19 Kan. 28. § 306.
Bohanan v. S., 15 Neb. 209. § 365.
v. S., 18 Neb. 57. § 330.
Bohannon v. C., 8 Bush, 481. §§ 301, 303.
v. S., 73 Ala. 47. § 827.
v. S., 14 Tex. Ap. 271. §§ 322, 374.
Boice, S. v., 1 Houst. Cr. C. 355. § 365.
Boies, S. v., 34 Me. 235. §§ 991, 993, 998, 999.
Bolander, S. v., 71 Ia. 706. § 571.
Bolanger, P. v., 71 Cal. 17. § 117.
Bolden v. S., 64 Ga. 361. § 993.
Bolding v. S., 23 Tex. Ap. 172. §§ 242, 271.
Bolduc v. Randall, 107 Mass. 121. § 1224.
Bolen v. S., 26 Ohio St. 371. § 125.
Boles v. S., 58 Ark. 35. § 481.
v. S., 86 Ga. 255. § 1031.
v. S., 18 Tex. Ap. 422. § 232.
Bolkom, C. v., 3 Pick. 281. §§ 1308, 1313.
Boll, S. v., 59 Mo. 321. §§ 15, 1176.
Bolland, Rex v., 2 East. P. C. 958. § 764.
Bollerman, S. v., 92 Ia. 460, 61 N. W. R. 183. § 1112.
Bolling v. S., 54 Ark. 588. §§ 157, 158, 168, 169, 173, 178, 418.
Bollman, Ex parte, 4 Cranch, 75. § 1357.
Bolzer v. P., 129 Ill. 112. §§ 162, 330, 331, 342.
Bond, C. v., 1 Gray, 564. § 775.
Reg. v., 1 Den. 517. § 597.
v. S., 21 Fla. 738. § 307.
v. S., 34 Fla. 45. § 1126.
v. S., 52 Ind. 457. §§ 59, 1314.
v. S., 23 Ohio St. 349. § 178.
v. S., 20 Tex. Ap. 421. § 468.
v. S., 23 Tex. Ap. 180. § 565.
S. v., 8 Ia. 540. §§ 565, 596.
Bonds v. S., Mart. & Y. 143. § 166.
S. v., 2 Nev. 265. §§ 300, 316, 333.
Bone v. S., 86 Ga. 108. § 296.
Boneil, S. v., 42 La. An. 1110. § 1315.
Bonfanti v. S., 2 Minn. 123. §§ 178, 274.
Bonham v. S., 65 Ala. 456. § 550.
U. S. v., 31 Fed. R. 808. §§ 1238, 1245.
Bonilla, P. v., 38 Cal. 699. § 382.
Bonker v. P., 37 Mich. 4. § 410.
Bonnard v. S., 25 Tex. Ap. 173. §§ 339, 342.
Bonnell v. S., 64 Ind. 498. §§ 684, 687, 708.
S. v., 46 Mo. 395. § 684.
Bonner, C. v., 97 Mass. 587. § 575.
C. v., 9 Met. 410. §§ 1051, 1053.
Rex v., 6 C. & P. 386. § 426.
v. S., 97 Ala. 47. § 235.
v. S., 65 Miss. 293. §§ 439, 442, 443.
v. S., 29 Tex. Ap. 223. § 338.
S. v., 2 Head, 135. §§ 199, 1241.
v. Welborn, 7 Ga. 296. § 1230.
Bonneville v. S., 53 Wis. 680. § 998.
Bonney v. S., 2 Ida. 1015. § 1061.
S. v., 34 Me. 223. § 785.
S. v., 34 Me. 383. § 794.
S. v., 39 N. H. 206. § 1237.
Bonsell v. U. S., 1 Greene (Ia.), 111. § 214.
Bonsor, S. v., 49 Kan. 758. § 461.

Bontien, Rex v., Russ. & Ry. 260. § 764.
Boody v. Keating, 4 Me. 164. § 11.
v. P., 43 Mich. 34. § 589.
S. v., 53 N. H. 610. §§ 632, 646, 648.
Boogher, S. v., 71 Mo. 631. § 101.
S. v., 3 Mo. Ap. 422. § 1044.
Book, S. v., 41 Ia. 550. §§ 1285, 1286, 1306.
U. S. v., 2 Cranch, C. C. 294. § 753.
Booker, Reg. v., 2 Cox, 272. §§ 145, 150.
v. S., 100 Ala. 30. § 1057.
Boon, C. v., 2 Gray, 74. § 1018.
v. S., 69 Ala. 226. § 1270.
S. v., 13 Ired. 244. §§ 463, 500, 501.
S. v., 4 Jones, 463. § 711.
S. v., 82 N. C. 637. § 342.
Boone v. S., 31 Tex. 557. § 241.
v. S., 10 Tex. Ap. 418. § 1253.
v. S., 12 Tex. Ap. 184. § 1216.
S. v., 70 Mo. 649. § 618.
Boose v. S., 10 Ohio St. 575. § 479.
Booth v. C., 4 Grat. 425. § 572.
v. S., 4 Conn. 65. § 72.
v. S., 26 Tex. 203. § 1291.
Reg. v., 12 Cox, 321. § 1105.
Boothe v. S., 4 Tex. Ap. 202. § 404.
Boot, C. v., Thach. (Mass.) Cr. 390. § 324.
Borches v. S., 33 Tex. Ap. 96. § 1265.
Borda, P. v., 105 Cal. 636. § 30.
Bordeaux v. S., 31 Tex. Ap. 37. § 1019.
S. v., 93 N. C. 530. §§ 560, 883.
Boren v. S., 32 Tex. Ap. 637. § 367.
Borgetto, P. v., 99 Mich. 336. §§ 173, 4[illegible].
Bork v. P., 91 N. Y. 5. §§ 89, 624, 638, 648, 693.
Bornemann, U. S. v., 36 Fed. R. 257. §§ 646, 652.
Borowsky, S. v., 11 Nev. 119. § 629.
Borschenious v. P., 41 Ill. 236. § 1248.
Borum v. S., 66 Ala. 468. § 593.
Bossie, C. v., — Ky. —, 37 S. W. R. 844. § 1296.
Bosshard v. S., 25 Tex. Sup. 207. §§ 1301, 1304.
Bossidy, C. v., 112 Mass. 277. § 1181.
Bostic v. S., 94 Ala. 45. § 313.
Boston, C. v., 97 Mass. 555. §§ 183, 1185.
Boston, etc. R. Co., C. v., 11 Cush. 512. §§ 78, 181, 288.
C. v., 121 Mass. 36. §§ 83, 288.
C. v., 129 Mass. 500. § 288.
C. v., 134 Mass. 211. §§ 184, 288.
C. v., 135 Mass. 550. § 1192.
v. S., 32 N. H. 215. §§ 40, 180, 288.
S. v., 80 Me. 430. § 288.
U. S. v., 15 Fed. R. 209. §§ 1161, 1338.
Boston & Worcester R. R. v. Dana, 1 Gray, 83. §§ 11, 616, 619, 725.
Boston Club, S. v., 45 La. An. 585. § 1240.
Bostwick v. S., 47 Ark. 126. § 1200.
Boswell, Ex parte, 86 Cal. 232. § 63.
v. C., 20 Grat. 860. §§ 178, 179.
v. S., 63 Ala. 307. §§ 158, 178, 179.
v. S., 92 Ga. 581. § 514.
v. S., 8 Ind. 499. § 832.
Boswell v. S., 70 Miss. 395. § 1216.
Bosworth, S. v., 54 Conn. 1. § 1164.
v. Swansey, 10 Met. 363. § 1322.
Botsch v. S., 43 Neb. 501. § 265.
Bott, S. v., 31 La. An. 663. § 1210.
U. S. v., 11 Blatch. 346. §§ 1148, 1332, 1335.
Botto v. S., 26 Miss. 108. § 1272.
Bottomley v. U. S., 1 Story, 135. § 913.
Boucher, Reg. v., 5 Jur. 709. § 813.
Rex v., 4 C. & P. 562. § 740.
Boudrie, C. v., 4 Gray, 418. § 611.
Bougher, S. v., 3 Blackf. 307. § 1291.
Boulden v. S., 102 Ala. 78. §§ 358, 426, 429.
Bouldin v. S., 8 Tex. Ap. 332. § 403.
Boullemet v. S., 28 Ala. 83. § 1318.
Boulo v. S., 49 Ala. 22. § 61.
Boult, Reg. v., 2 C. & K. 604. §§ 752, 773.
Boulter, Reg. v., 3 C. & K. 236. § 892.
Boulton, Reg. v., 12 Cox, 87. §§ 968, 972.
Reg. v., 1 Den. 508, 2 C. & K. 917. §§ 543, 693.
Rex v., 5 C. & P. 537. § 546.
Bourne, Rex v., 5 C. & P. 120. § 348.
Boutwell, C. v., 129 Mass. 124. § 765.
Bovard v. S., 30 Miss. 600. § 158.
Bowden, Reg. v., 1 C. & K. 147. § 576.
v. S., 2 Tex. Ap. 56. § 260.
Bowe v. S., 25 Ind. 415. § 1300.
Bowen, Ex parte, 25 Fla. 214. § 215.
v. Buck, 28 Vt. 308. § 939.
C. v., 13 Mass. 356. §§ 200, 221, 290.
P. v., 49 Cal. 654. § 463.
Reg. v., 1 C. & K. 501. §§ 750, 766.
Reg. v., 2 C. & K. 227. § 1074.
Reg. v., Car. & M. 149. § 195.
Reg. v., 13 Q. B. 790. § 690.
v. S., 9 Baxt. 45. §§ 665, 667, 687.
v. S., 25 Fla. 645. § 216.
S. v., 16 Kan. 475. §§ 369, 370, 381.
U. S. v., 4 Cranch, C. C. 604. § 500.
U. S. v., 3 MacAr. 64. § 1352.
Bower, Rex v., Cowp. 323. §§ 660, 666, 669.
v. S., 5 Mo. 364. §§ 358, 361.
Bowerman, Reg. v. (1891), 1 Q. B. D. 112. § 636.
Bowers v. P., 17 Ill. 373. §§ 922, 925.
Reg. v., L. R. 1 C. C. 41. § 626.
v. S., 24 Tex. Ap. 542. § 196.
S. v., 35 S. C. 262. § 220.
Bowler v. S., 41 Miss. 570. § 688.
Bowles v. S., 58 Ala. 335. §§ 292, 307.
v. S., 37 Ohio St. 35. § 757.
Bowling v. S., 13 Tex. Ap. 338. § 557.
S. v., 10 Humph. 52. § 271.
Bowlus, S. v., 3 Heisk. 29. § 878.
Bowman v. Brown, 52 Ia. 437. § 640.
v. Chicago & N. W. R. Co., 125 U. S. 465. §§ 35, 76, 1203.
P. v., 81 Cal. 566. § 359.
v. S., 16 Tex. Ap. 513. §§ 1302, 1304.
S. v., 45 Ia. 418. § 1118.
S. v., 80 N. C. 432. § 421.

Bowman, S. v., 6 Vt. 594. § 777.
U. S. v., 2 Wash. 328. § 882.
Bowser, Reg. v., 8 D. P. C. 128. § 841.
S. v., 42 La. An. 936. § 307.
Bowyer, Rex v., 4 C. & P. 559. § 818.
Box, Reg. v., 9 C. & P. 126. §§ 560, 562.
Rex v., Russ. & Ry. 300. § 752.
Boyce v. P., 55 N. Y. 644. § 1112.
Rex v., 1 Moody, 29. § 256.
S. v., 109 N. C. 739. § 825.
Boyd, In re, 49 Fed. R. 48. § 1217.
v. Alabama, 94 U. S. 645. § 75.
v. Bryant, 35 Ark. 69. § 1210.
v. C., 1 Rob. (Va.) 691. § 598.
v. S., 53 Ala. 601. § 1315.
v. S., 61 Ala. 177. § 1316.
v. S., 88 Ala. 169. § 242.
v. S., 7 Coldw. 69. § 353.
v. S., 17 Ga. 194. §§ 215, 328, 385.
v. S., 2 Humph. 39. §§ 815, 833.
v. S., 12 Lea, 687. § 1217.
v. S., 14 Lea, 161. §§ 373*a*, 401, 407.
v. S., 18 Tex. Ap. 339. § 565.
v. S., 24 Tex. Ap. 570. §§ 569, 573, 617.
v. S., 33 Tex. Ap. 470. § 1085.
S. v., 36 Minn. 538. § 571.
S. v., 86 N. C. 634. § 1196.
v. U. S., 142 U. S. 450. §§ 196, 418.
U. S. v., 45 Fed. R. 851. §§ 15, 196, 206, 285, 321, 332.
Boyden, S. v., 13 Ired. 505. § 274.
Boyer, C. v., 1 Binn. 201. §§ 543, 595, 596.
S. v., 79 Ia. 330. § 1296.
v. Sweet, 4 Ill. 120. § 12.
Boyett v. S., 2 Tex. Ap. 93. §§ 337, 342.
S. v., 10 Ired. 336. § 949.
Boyington, S. v., 56 Me. 512. § 950.
Boykin v. S., 34 Ark. 443. § 617.
Boyle v. C., 14 Grat. 674. § 1229.
C. v., 145 Mass. 373. § 1249.
v. S., 97 Ind. 322, 105 Ind. 469. §§ 428, 429, 431.
v. S., 37 Tex. 359. § 597.
v. S., 57 Wis. 472. §§ 325, 368.
v. S., 61 Wis. 440. §§ 160, 331, 417.
S. v., 28 Ia. 522. §§ 361, 390.
S. v., 10 Kan. 113. § 101.
S. v., 13 R. I. 537. § 145.
Boyles v. C., 2 Serg. & R. 40. § 1152.
S. v., 7 Blackf. 90. § 915.
Boynton, C. v., 2 Allen, 160. § 1222.
C. v., 12 Cush. 499. §§ 32, 124.
C. v., 2 Mass. 77. § 757.
C. v., 116 Mass. 343. § 199.
S. v., 75 Ia. 753. §§ 240, 252, 922.
Boze v. S., 31 Tex. Ap. 347. § 572.
Brabham v. S., 18 Ohio St. 485. §§ 85, 737.
S. v., 108 N. C. 793. § 421.
Brabston v. S., 68 Miss. 208. § 196.
Bracco, S. v., 103 N. C. 349. § 44.
Braceville Coal Co. v. P., 147 Ill. 66. § 55.
Bracey v. S., 64 Miss. 17. § 906.
v. S., 64 Miss. 26. § 680.
Bracken v. S., 29 Tex. Ap. 362. § 339.
Brackenridge, Reg. v., L. R. 1 C. C. 133. § 752.
v. S., 27 Tex. Ap. 513. §§ 906, 914.
Bradberry v. S., 7 Tex. Ap. 375. § 875.
v. S., 22 Tex. Ap. 273. §§ 232, 266.
Braden, S. v., 2 Tenn. 68. § 549.
Bradford, C. v., 9 Met. 268. §§ 110, 114, 132, 951.
Reg. v., 2 F. & F. 859. § 788.
v. S., 104 Ala. 68. § 1154.
v. S., 3 Humph. 369. § 779.
v. S., 6 Lea, 634. § 537.
S. v., 33 La. An. 921. § 383.
U. S. v., 53 Fed. R. 542. § 664.
Bradlaugh, Ex parte, 3 Q. B. D. 509. § 1156.
v. Reg., 3 Q. B. D. 607. § 1158.
Reg. v., 2 Q. B. D. 569. § 1064.
Bradley v. P., 8 Colo. 599. §§ 82, 105, 128.
v. S., 103 Ala. 29. § 473.
v. S., 32 Ark. 704. § 463.
v. S., 31 Ind. 492. §§ 156, 315.
v. S., 68 Mo. 140. § 690.
v. S., 10 Sm. & M. 618. § 279.
v. S., Walk. (Miss.) 156. § 243.
S. v., 48 Conn. 535. § 977.
S. v., 1 Houst. Cr. C. 164. § 529.
S. v., 6 La. An. 555. § 303.
S. v., 34 S. C. 136. § 426.
S. v., 34 Tex. 95. § 262.
S. v., 64 Vt. 466. §§ 401, 419.
S. v., 67 Vt. 465. §§ 390, 400, 417.
Bradshaw v. C., 10 Bush, 576. § 412.
Reg. v., 14 Cox, 83. § 347.
Brady, C. v., 5 Gray, 78. § 867.
C. v., 147 Mass. 583. §§ 190, 1174.
P. v., 72 Cal. 490. §§ 429, 431.
P. v., 90 Mich. 459. § 36.
S. v., 41 Conn. 588. § 63.
S. v., 27 Ia. 126. §§ 614, 617.
S. v., 44 Kan. 435. §§ 1043, 1044.
S. v., 39 La. An. 687. § 268.
S. v., 107 N. C. 822. § 975.
S. v., 14 R. I. 508. § 1224.
S. v., 14 Vt. 353. § 505.
Bragg v. S., 69 Ala. 204. § 1017.
v. S., 17 Tex. Ap. 219. § 619.
S. v., 86 N. C. 687. §§ 536, 537.
Brailey, C. v., 134 Mass. 527. § 529.
Brain, Rex v., 6 C. & P. 349. § 294.
Braithwaite, Reg. v., 1 F. & F. 638. § 891.
Brakefield v. S., 1 Sneed, 214. § 426.
Braman, P. v., 30 Mich. 460. § 737.
Bramley, Rex v., L. & C. 21. § 560.
Rex v., Russ. & Ry. 478. § 546.
Branamon, C. v., 8 B. Mon. 374. § 1227.
Branch v. S., 41 Tex. 622. § 826.
v. S., 15 Tex. Ap. 96. §§ 306, 307.
Brandenburg, S. v., 118 Mo. 181. §§ 1116, 1118.
Brandon, S. v., 28 Ark. 410. § 1225.
S. v., 8 Jones, 463. §§ 157, 325, 420, 424.
Brandt v. C., 94 Pa. St. 290. §§ 217, 218.
S. v., 41 Ia. 593. §§ 108, 646, 649.

Branham, C. v., 3 Bush, 1. § 1313.
C. v., 8 Bush, 387. § 332.
S. v., 13 S. C. 389. § 504.
Brannan, S. v., 3 Nev. 238. § 228.
Brannen, S. v., 8 Jones, 208. § 1285.
Brannigan v. P., 3 Utah, 488. §§ 382, 391.
Brannon v. S., 23 Tex. Ap. 428. § 1035.
Bransby, P. v., 32 N. Y. 525. §§ 232, 249, 441, 463, 464.
Branscum v. S., 7 Ind. 593. § 1296.
Branson v. C., 92 Ky. 330. § 617.
Bransteller, S. v., 65 Mo. 149. § 338.
Brant, S. v., 14 Ia. 180. § 821.
Brantley v. S., 91 Ala. 47. § 1273.
S. v., 84 N. C. 766. § 416.
Brasier, Rex v., 1 East, P. C. 443. § 456.
Brass v. Stoeser, 153 U. S. 391. § 40.
Brassfield v. S., 55 Ark. 556. §§ 326, 376, 381.
S. v., 81 Mo. 151. §§ 1112, 1113.
Brast, S. v., 31 W. Va. 380. §§ 1301, 1303.
Braswell v. C., 5 Bush, 544. § 1230.
Bratton v. S., 10 Humph. 103. § 357.
Brauer v. S., 25 Wis. 413. § 450.
Braun, U. S. v., 39 Fed. R. 775. § 758.
Bravo v. S., 20 Tex. Ap. 177. § 597.
v. S., 20 Tex. Ap. 188. § 504.
Brawn, Reg. v., 1 C. & K. 144. §§ 200, 1073.
Bray, P. v., 105 Cal. 344. §§ 77, 1263.
Reg. v., 9 Cox, 218. § 858.
Reg. v., 15 Cox, 197. § 260.
v. S., 41 Tex. 203. § 564.
S. v., 13 Ired. 289. § 1079.
Brazee v. S., 9 Ind. Ap. 618. § 837.
Brazier, Rex v., Russ. & Ry. 337. § 555.
Brazil, S. v., Rice, 257. § 996.
Brazleton v. S., 66 Ala. 96. § 823.
Brazzil v. S., 28 Tex. Ap. 584. §§ 309, 310.
Brecht, S. v., 41 Minn. 50. § 1093.
Brechwald v. P., 21 Ill. Ap. 213. § 1236.
Breckenridge, S. v., 67 Ia. 204. § 808.
Bredin, C. v., 165 Pa. St. 224. § 183.
Breedlove v. S., 26 Tex. Ap. 445. § 341.
Breene, In re, 14 Colo. 401. §§ 12, 645.
Breese v. S., 12 Ohio St. 146. §§ 206, 511.
Breidenstein, P. v., 65 Mich. 65. § 1230.
Brelsford, C. v., 161 Mass. 61. §§ 1218, 1277, 1279.
Bren, Reg. v., L. & C. 346. § 631.
Brennan, C. v., 103 Mass. 70. §§ 1209, 1216.
v. P., 15 Ill. 511. §§ 196, 291, 321, 390, 969.
S. v., 2 S. D. 384. §§ 29, 1201, 1271.
v. Titusville, 153 U. S. 289. § 44.
Brennon v. S., 25 Ind. 403. §§ 469, 471.
Brettel, Reg. v., Car. & M. 609. § 551.
Brettun, C. v., 100 Mass. 206. §§ 543, 595, 610.
Brevaldo v. S., 21 Fla. 789. § 1098.
Brew, S. v., 4 Wash. 95. § 586.
Brewer, P. v., 27 Mich. 134. §§ 1113, 1114.
v. S., 83 Ala. 113. § 634.
v. S., 6 Baxt. 446. § 1037.
v. S., 7 Lea, 682. § 1266.
Brewer v. S., 18 Tex. Ap. 456. § 601.
v. S., 32 Tex. Ap. 74. § 764.
S. v., 53 Ia. 735. § 480.
S. v., 22 La. An. 273. § 99.
S. v., 8 Mo. 373. § 85.
S. v., 109 Mo. 648. § 195.
S. v., 38 S. C. 263. § 1126.
U. S. v., 139 U. S. 278. § 83.
Brewington, S. v., 84 N. C. 783. § 1021.
Brewster, U. S. v., 7 Pet. 164. § 757.
Breyessee, C. v., 160 Pa. St. 451. § 323.
Briant, C. v., 142 Mass. 463. §§ 189, 1237.
Brice, Rex v., Russ. & Ry. 450. §§ 500, 503.
S. v., 2 Brev. 66. § 1313.
Bridgeford v. Lexington, 7 B. Mon. 47. § 1273.
Bridges, Ex parte, 2 Woods, 428. § 871.
P. v., 142 Ill. 30. § 46.
v. S., 37 Ark. 224. §§ 1273, 1321.
S. v., 24 Mo. 353. §§ 1290, 1295.
S. v., 1 Murph. 134. § 437.
Bridgman, S. v., 49 Vt. 202. §§ 1094, 1098, 1099.
Brien, S. v., 32 N. J. 414. § 981.
Briffitt v. S., 58 Wis. 39. §§ 1218, 1220.
Brig Malek Adhel, U. S. v., 2 How. 210. § 1359.
Briggs v. Garrett, 111 Pa. St. 404. § 1052.
Reg. v., Dears. & B., 98. § 1076.
Reg. v., 1 Moody, 318. §§ 256, 268.
v. S., 6 Tex. Ap. 144. § 257.
v. S., 20 Tex. Ap. 106. § 546.
S. v., 68 Ia. 416. §§ 1093, 1095, 1098.
S. v., 3 Ired. 357. § 245.
S. v., 34 Vt. 501. §§ 756, 794.
Brigham, P. v., 2 Mich. 550. §§ 753, 781.
Bright, S. v., 38 La. An. 1. §§ 6, 63.
Brightwell v. S., 41 Ga. 482. § 525.
Brigman, S. v., 94 N. C. 888. § 815.
Briley, S. v., 8 Port. 472. §§ 432, 434.
Brill v. S., 1 Tex. Ap. 572. § 572.
Brilliant, P. v., 58 Cal. 214. § 878.
Brimilow, Reg. v., 9 C. & P. 366. § 449.
Brimmer v. Rebman, 138 U. S. 78. § 35.
Brin, S. v., 30 Minn. 522. § 595.
Bringard, P. v., 39 Mich. 22. §§ 625, 649, 652.
Brinkhaus, S. v., 34 Minn. 285. §§ 1113, 1117.
Brinkley v. S., 89 Ala. 34. § 309.
v. S., 58 Ga. 296. §§ 156, 171.
Brinkoeter v. S., 14 Tex. Ap. 67. § 1189.
Brinson v. S., 89 Ala. 105. § 1253.
v. S., 75 Ga. 882. § 1031.
Brinton, C. v., 132 Pa. St. 69. § 44.
Brinyea, S. v., 5 Ala. 241. § 177.
Brisac, Rex v., 4 East, 164. §§ 187, 211, 972.
Brisco v. S., 4 Tex. Ap. 219. § 594.
Briscoe, S. v., 30 La. An., Pt. I, 433. § 333.
Bristol, P. v., 23 Mich. 118. § 1104.
Bristow v. C., 15 Grat. 634. § 329.
S. v., 41 Tex. 146. § 1285.
Britt v. S., 7 Humph. 45. § 470.

Britt, S. v., 3 Dev. 122. § 809.
Brittain, Reg. v., 3 Cox, 77. §§ 989, 1357.
S. v., 89 N. C. 481. § 333.
Brittin v. S., 10 Ark. 299. §§ 1322, 1326.
Britton v. C., 105 Pa. St. 311. § 1254.
v. S., 77 Ala. 202. § 649.
S. v., 4 McCord, 256. § 1083.
U. S. v., 17 Fed. R. 731. § 1332.
U. S. v., 2 Mason, 464. §§ 791, 805.
U. S. v., 107 U. S. 655. §§ 1339, 1340.
U. S. v., 108 U. S. 199. § 14.
Broadbent v. S., 7 Md. 416. § 1317.
Broadwell v. Conger, 2 N. J. 210. § 84.
Brock v. C., 92 Ky. 183. § 425.
v. C., 6 Leigh, 634. § 1221.
v. S., 26 Ala. 104. § 533.
v. S., 65 Ga. 437. § 1228.
v. S., 95 Ga. 474. § 1113.
Brocker, S. v., 32 Tex. 611. § 830.
Brockett, Reg. v., 4 Cox, 274. § 556.
Brockway, C. v., 150 Mass. 322. §§ 210, 215.
v. P., 2 Hill (N. Y.), 558. § 1141.
Broderick, S. v., 59 Mo. 318. §§ 468, 469.
S. v., 70 Mo. 622. §§ 609, 625.
Brodie v. Rutledge, 2 Bay, 69. § 913.
Brodnax, S. v., 91 N. C. 543. § 1032.
S. v., Phill. 41. § 339.
Bromiley, U. S. v., 58 Fed. R. 554. § 1343.
Bromley v. P., 150 Ill. 297. § 504.
S. v., 25 Conn. 6. § 1018.
Broms v. C., 2 Duv. 351. § 585.
Bronson v. S., 2 Tex. Ap. 46. § 260.
Bronson Agl. Ass'n v. Ramsdell, 24 Mich. 441. § 1297.
Brooke, Reg. v., 7 Cox. 251. §§ 1055, 1067.
Brooker v. C., 12 Serg. & R. 175. §§ 9, 920.
Brookes, Reg. v., Car. & M. 544. § 508.
Brookhouse, S. v., 10 Wash. 87. § 594.
Brookin v. S., 27 Tex. Ap. 701. §§ 869, 892.
Brooks v. C., 61 Pa. St. 352. §§ 139, 348, 922.
C. v., 1 Duv. 150. § 468.
C. v., 109 Mass. 355. § 71.
v. P., 14 Colo. 413. § 83.
v. P., 49 N. Y. 436. § 473.
P. v., 1 Denio, 457. §§ 132, 907, 913.
P. v., 101 Mich. 98. § 46.
Reg. v., Dears. 184. §§ 145, 714.
Reg. v., 1 F. & F. 502. § 681.
Rex v., 4 C. & P. 131. § 538.
v. S., 88 Ala. 122. § 36.
v. S., 5 Baxt. 607. § 546.
v. S., 3 Humph. 24. § 389.
v. S., 90 Ind. 428. § 329.
v. S., 65 Miss. 445. § 1253.
v. S., 67 Miss. 577. § 1017.
v. S., 35 Ohio St. 46. §§ 545, 571.
v. S., 15 Tex. Ap. 88. § 1031.
v. S., 26 Tex. Ap. 184. §§ 552, 618.
v. S., 29 Tex. Ap. 582. §§ 889, 891.
S. v., 4 Conn. 446. § 499.
S. v., 1 Hill (S. C.), 361. § 993.
S. v., 85 Ia. 366. §§ 629, 639.
Brooks, S. v., 33 Kan. 708. §§ 1270, 1276.
S. v., 99 Mo. 137. § 308.
S. v., 76 N. C. 1. § 463.
U. S. v., 4 Cranch, C. C. 427. § 1022.
U. S. v., 3 MacAr. 315. §§ 767, 781, 809.
Brooksbank, S. v., 6 Ired. 73. § 1319.
Brosee v. S., 5 Ind. 75. § 1256.
Brosnahan, In re, 18 Fed. R. 62. § 33.
Brothers, C. v., 158 Mass. 200. §§ 1250, 1277, 1279.
v. S., 22 Tex. Ap. 447. §§ 618, 719.
Brotherton v. P., 75 N. Y. 159. §§ 175, 179, 426, 428.
Brow, C. v., 9 Gray, 299. § 1164.
S. v., 64 N. H. 577. § 1104.
Browder v. S., 102 Ala. 164. § 956.
v. S., 30 Tex. Ap. 614. § 826.
Brown, Ex parte, 65 Ala. 446. §§ 338, 342.
Ex parte, 97 Cal. 83. §§ 946, 951.
Ex parte, 40 Fed. R. 81. §§ 263, 265, 271, 274.
In re, 32 Cal. 48. § 364.
v. C., 14 Bush, 398. § 173.
v. C., 2 Leigh, 769. § 801.
v. C., 8 Mass. 59 § 84.
v. C., 73 Pa. St. 321. § 425.
v. C., 76 Pa. St. 319. § 411.
v. C., 114 Pa. St. 335. § 1223.
v. C., 86 Va. 466. §§ 305, 310, 311, 336.
v. C., 90 Va. 671. §§ 329, 332.
v. C., 2 Va. Cas. 516. § 324.
C. v., 14 Gray, 419. § 1148.
C. v., 15 Gray, 189. § 844.
C. v., 4 Mass. 580. §§ 555, 556.
C. v., 121 Mass. 69. § 140.
C. v., 124 Mass. 318. § 1280.
C. v., 141 Mass. 78. § 1137.
C. v., 147 Mass. 585. § 754.
C. v., 154 Mass. 55. § 1242.
C. v., 13 Met. 365. § 1183.
C. v., 138 Pa. St. 447. § 837.
C. v., 3 Rawle, 207. §§ 494, 506.
v. Maryland, 12 Wheat. 419. §§ 35, 76, 1204.
v. P., 20 Colo. 161. § 556.
v. P., 9 Ill. 439. § 786.
v. P., 66 Ill. 344. § 798.
v. P., 86 Ill. 239. § 756.
v. P., 29 Mich. 232. § 597.
v. P., 36 Mich. 203. § 440.
P. v., 27 Cal. 500. § 608.
P. v., 47 Cal. 447. § 440.
P. v., 48 Cal. 253. § 617.
P. v., 59 Cal. 345. § 328.
P. v., 74 Cal. 306. §§ 124, 937.
P. v., 105 Cal. 66. § 566.
P. v., 34 Mich. 339. § 1073.
P. v., 85 Mich. 119. § 1212.
v. Perkins, 1 Allen, 89. § 194.
v. Piper, 91 U. S. 37. § 1218.
Reg. v., Car. & M. 314. §§ 997, 1013.
Reg. v., Dears. 616. § 562.
Reg. v., 3 F. & F. 821. § 524.
Reg. v., L. R. 1 C. C. 244. § 1152.

Brown, Reg. v., 1 Q. B. D. (1895) 119. § 1307.
Reg. v., 10 Q. B. D. 381. § 226.
Reg. v., 24 Q. B. D. 357. §§ 226, 1153.
Rex v., 1 East, P. C. 231, 245, 274. §§ 339, 347.
Rex v., 2 East, P. C. 487. § 500.
Rex v., 2 East, P. C. 493. § 498.
Rex v., 2 East, P. C. 501. § 491.
Rex v., 2 East, P. C. 731. § 470.
v. S., 27 Ala. 47. § 1231.
v. S., 31 Ala. 353. § 1247.
v. S., 46 Ala. 175. §§ 1026, 1027, 1028.
v. S., 47 Ala. 47. § 872.
v. S., 52 Ala. 345. §§ 520, 525.
v. S., 55 Ala. 123. § 502.
v. S., 74 Ala. 42. § 241.
v. S., 74 Ala. 478. § 425.
v. S., 79 Ala. 51. § 125.
v. S., 83 Ala. 33. § 316.
v. S., 100 Ala. 92. § 823.
v. S., 10 Ark. 607. §§ 1310, 1311.
v. S., 28 Ark. 126. § 479.
v. S., 55 Ark. 593. §§ 307, 312.
v. S., 6 Baxt. 422. §§ 443, 464.
v. S., 18 Fla. 472. § 380.
v. S., 28 Ga. 199. §§ 197, 204, 208, 368.
v. S., 40 Ga. 689. § 1285.
v. S., 44 Ga. 300. § 594.
v. S., 55 Ga. 169. § 275.
v. S., 58 Ga. 212. §§ 257, 267, 309.
v. S., 59 Ga. 456. §§ 504, 619.
v. S., 61 Ga. 311. § 514.
v. S., 76 Ga. 623. § 450.
v. S., 82 Ga. 224. §§ 1209, 1226.
v. S., 86 Ga. 633. § 594.
v. S., 95 Ga. 481. §§ 224, 225.
v. S., 24 Ind. 113. § 1257.
v. S., 48 Ind. 38. § 1274.
v. S., 76 Ind. 85. § 832.
v. S., 2 Lea, 158. § 61.
v. S., 41 La. An. 345. § 434.
v. S., 72 Md. 468. § 1104.
v. S., 72 Md. 477. §§ 1102, 1106.
v. S., 32 Miss. 433. § 426.
v. S., 57 Miss. 424. § 890.
v. S., 72 Miss. 997. §§ 452, 460.
v. S., 9 Neb. 189. § 1253.
v. S., 16 Neb. 658. § 1272.
v. S., 33 Neb. 354. § 484.
v. S., 34 Neb. 448. § 575.
v. S., 49 N. J. 61. §§ 1137, 1249, 1286, 1306.
v. S., 18 Ohio St. 497. §§ 217, 646, 649, 656.
v. S., 26 Ohio St. 176. § 829.
v. S., 38 Ohio St. 374. § 1100.
v. S., 27 Tex. 335. §§ 1223, 1224.
v. S., 35 Tex. 689. § 602.
v. S., 38 Tex. 482. § 292.
v. S., 2 Tex. Ap. 189. § 1143.
v. S., 4 Tex. Ap. 275. § 333.
v. S., 7 Tex. Ap. 569. § 223.
v. S., 9 Tex. Ap. 171. §§ 869, 881.
v. S., 13 Tex. Ap. 358. § 898.
v. S., 15 Tex. Ap. 581. §§ 609, 713.
v. S., 16 Tex. Ap. 197. § 252.
Brown v. S., 23 Tex. Ap. 214. § 650.
v. S., 26 Tex. Ap. 540. § 41.
v. S., 27 Tex. Ap. 330. § 463.
v. S., 5 Yerg. 367. § 1294.
S. v., 9 Baxt. 53. § 539.
S. v., 16 Conn. 54. §§ 1184, 1188.
S. v., 1 Dev. 137. § 593.
S. v., 19 Fla. 563. § 1212.
S. v., 1 Hayw. 100. § 553.
S. v., 1 Houst. Cr. C. 539. § 347.
S. v., 25 Ia. 561. §§ 217, 551, 562, 618, 664.
S. v., 67 Ia. 289. § 332.
S. v., 86 Ia. 121. §§ 1112, 1118.
S. v., 21 Kan. 38. §§ 217, 361, 383, 404.
S. v., 22 Kan. 222. § 307.
S. v., 38 Kan. 390. §§ 128, 163, 1018.
S. v., 54 Kan. 71. § 455.
S. v., 55 Kan. 611. § 585.
S. v., 55 Kan. 766. § 460.
S. v., 21 La. An. 347. §§ 268, 281.
S. v., 40 La. An. 725. § 391.
S. v., 41 La. An. 345. § 257.
S. v., 41 La. An. 410. § 391.
S. v., 41 La. An. 771. §§ 1228, 1274.
S. v., 31 Me. 520. §§ 187, 1237.
S. v., 31 Me. 522. §§ 1251, 1252.
S. v., 41 Minn. 319. §§ 333, 358, 359.
S. v., 60 Mo. 141. §§ 221, 263.
S. v., 63 Mo. 439. §§ 307, 308, 419.
S. v., 73 Mo. 631. § 511.
S. v., 75 Mo. 317. § 576.
S. v., 104 Mo. 365. §§ 476, 479, 480.
S. v., 115 Mo. 409. § 530.
S. v., 8 Nev. 208. § 552.
S. v., 60 N. H. 205. § 1253.
S. v., 82 N. C. 585. § 930.
S. v., 95 N. C. 685. §§ 224, 228, 899.
S. v., 100 N. C. 519. § 1057.
S. v., 109 N. C. 802. § 1189.
S. v., 113 N. C. 645. §§ 472, 480, 483.
S. v., 2 Oreg. 221. § 790.
S. v., 7 Oreg. 186. § 355.
S. v., 34 S. C. 41. § 316.
S. v., 27 Vt. 619. § 1158.
S. v., 36 Vt. 560. § 1271.
S. v., 49 Vt. 437. §§ 191, 195.
S. v., 6 Wash. 609. § 922.
S. v., 7 Wash. 10. § 1138.
v. Swineford, 44 Wis. 282. § 11.
v. U. S., 113 U. S. 568. § 86.
v. U. S., 159 U. S. 100. § 340.
U. S. v., 3 Cranch, C. C. 268. § 753.
U. S. v., 43 Fed. R. 135. § 1333.
U. S. v., 58 Fed. R. 558. §§ 946, 950.
v. Walker, 161 U. S. 591. § 951.
Brown, etc. Co., S. v., 18 R. I. 16. § 55.
Browne, Rex v., 3 C. & P. 572. §§ 865, 886.
Brownell v. Pacific R. Co., 47 Mo. 239. § 425.
v. P., 38 Mich. 732. § 307.
Browning v. S., 2 Tex. Ap. 47. § 260.
Brownlee, S. v., 84 Ia. 473. §§ 201, 733.
Brownlow, S. v., 7 Humph. 63. § 1061.
Broxton v. S., 9 Tex. Ap. 97. § 921.

Broyles, S. v., 1 Bailey, 134. § 1190.
Brubaker v. S., 89 Ind. 577. § 1229.
Bruce, Reg. v., 2 Cox, 262. § 285.
v. S., 87 Ind. 450. § 1174.
S. v., 24 Me. 71. § 732.
S. v., 5 Oreg. 68. § 950.
S. v., 106 N. C. 792. §§ 616, 619.
Bruggy, P. v., 93 Cal. 476. § 338.
Bruguier v. U. S., 1 Dak. T. 5. § 1263, 1273.
Bruin, S. v., 34 Mo. 537. § 617.
Brule, In re, 71 Fed. R. 943. §§ 9, 920.
Bruley v. Rose, 57 Ia. 657. § 546.
Brumby, Rex v., 3 C. & K. 315. § 536.
Brumfiel, S. v., 83 Ind. 136. § 1184.
Bruner v. S., 58 Ind. 159. § 368.
S. v., 135 Ind. 419. §§ 83, 966.
Brunet v. S., 12 Tex. Ap. 521. § 307.
Brunker, S. v., 46 Conn. 327. § 1326.
Brunneto, S. v., 13 La. An. 45. § 425.
Brunson, Ex parte, 41 S. C. 501. § 1214.
S. v., 2 Bailey, 149. §§ 1086, 1135.
Brunswick, Rex v., 1 Moody, 26. § 546.
Brusie, C. v., 145 Mass. 117. § 1229.
Brutton v. S., 4 Ind. 601. §§ 1256, 1273.
Bryan, C. v., 9 Dana, 310. § 1227.
Reg. v., Dears. & B. 265. § 669.
Reg. v., 2 F. & F. 567. § 683.
v. S., 26 Ala. 65. §§ 1285, 1302.
v. S., 36 Ala. 270. § 373*a*.
v. S., 19 Fla. 864. § 380.
v. S., 62 Ga. 179. § 514.
S. v., 40 Ia. 379. §§ 639, 649.
S. v., 34 Kan. 63. § 1112.
S. v., 112 N. C. 848. § 703.
Bryant v. Biddeford, 39 Me. 193. § 1320.
v. S., 46 Ala. 302. § 1245.
v. S., 82 Ala. 51. §§ 1233, 1241, 1256, 1259.
v. S., 41 Ark. 359. § 262.
v. S., 7 Baxt. 67. § 333.
v. S., 60 Ga. 358. § 497.
v. S., 80 Ga. 272. § 426.
v. S., 16 Neb. 651. § 922.
v. S., 89 Tenn. 581. § 1236.
v. S., 16 Tex. Ap. 144. §§ 597, 614.
v. S., 25 Tex. Ap. 751. § 566.
S. v., 55 Mo. 75. § 307.
S. v., 90 Mo. 534. §§ 90, 1310.
S. v., 102 Mo. 24. § 309.
S. v., 17 N. H. 323. §§ 765, 794.
S. v., 74 N. C. 124. § 559.
S. v., 74 N. C. 207. § 1315.
S. v., 103 N. C. 436. § 837.
S. v., 111 N. C. 693. § 45.
S. v., 9 Rich. 113. § 552.
Bryon, P. v., 103 Cal. 675. § 940.
Bryson, S. v., 81 N. C. 595. §§ 113, 135.
S. v., 82 N. C. 576. § 1024.
S. v., 1 Winst. ii, 86. § 246.
Bubb, Reg. v., 4 Cox, 455. § 286.
Bubser, C. v., 14 Gray, 83. § 1277.
Bubster v. S., 33 Neb. 663. § 557.
Buchanan, P. v., 1 Ida. (N. S.) 681. § 1138–9.
v. S., 55 Ala. 154. § 1096.
v. S., 24 Ga. 282. § 368.
v. S., 24 Tex. Ap. 195. §§ 494, 504.
v. S., 26 Tex. Ap. 52. § 573.
Buchanan, S. v., 5 Har. & J. 317. §§ 953, 954, 956, 960, 966.
S. v., 5 Har. & J. 500. § 981.
S. v., 1 Houst. Cr. C. 79. § 338.
S. v., 17 Vt. 573. §§ 142, 922, 929.
Bucher v. C., 103 Pa. St. 528. § 49.
Buck v. C., 90 Pa. St. 110. § 907.
C. v., 12 Met. 524. §§ 1271, 1273.
v. S., 1 Ohio St. 62. § 1307.
S. v., 46 Me. 531. § 586.
S. v., 108 Mo. 622. § 42.
S. v., 37 Vt. 657. §§ 1233, 1239.
Buckalew v. S., 62 Ala. 334. § 1315.
v. S., 11 Tex. Ap. 352. § 687.
Buckhannon v. C., 86 Ky. 110. § 162.
Buckingham, C. v., 2 Wheeler, Cr. C. 181. § 1069.
Buckland v. C., 8 Leigh, 732. § 797.
P. v., 13 Wend. 592. §§ 218, 940.
Buckles, S. v., 26 Kan. 237. § 594.
Buckley, C. v., 147 Mass. 581. § 1181.
C. v., 148 Mass. 27. §§ 529, 737, 1248.
Reg. v., 13 Cox, 293. § 413.
v. S., 2 Greene (Ia.), 162. § 788.
S. v., 40 Conn. 246. § 1215.
S. v., 2 Harr. 552. § 243.
S. v., 5 Harr. 508. § 1137.
S. v., 60 Ia. 471. § 613.
S. v., 18 Oreg. 228. § 891.
Buckman, S. v., 8 N. H. 203. § 1170.
Buckmaster, Reg. v., 20 Q. B. D. 182. § 560.
Buckner v. Beck, Dudley, 168. § 247.
v. C., 14 Bush, 601. §§ 4, 389.
S. v., 52 Ind. 278. § 1229.
Budd v. New York, 143 U. S. 517. § 40.
Buel v. P., 78 N. Y. 492. § 355.
Buell v. S., 45 Ark. 336. § 858.
v. S., 72 Ind. 523. § 1246.
Buelna, P. v., 81 Cal. 135. §§ 546, 571.
Buford v. C., 14 B. Mon. 24. §§ 18, 1310.
U. S. v., 8 Utah, 173. §§ 45, 819.
Bugbee, S. v., 22 Vt. 32. § 1239.
Buhler v. S., 64 Ga. 504. § 605.
Buie v. S., 1 Tex. Ap. 58. § 1017.
S. v., 43 Tex. 532. § 892.
Bull v. C., 14 Grat. 613. § 426.
Reg. v., 9 C. & P. 22. §§ 303, 410.
Reg. v., 13 Cox, 608. § 666.
Reg. v., 2 F. & F. 201. § 287.
v. S., 80 Ga. 704. § 58.
Bulla, S. v., 89 Mo. 595. § 726.
Bullard, S. v., 72 N. C. 445. § 833.
Buller v. S., 33 Tex. Ap. 551. § 878.
Bulling, S. v., 105 Mo. 204. §§ 341, 365.
Bullinger, S. v., 54 Mo. 142. § 1123.
Bullion, Reg. v., Dears. 653. § 982.
Reg. v., L. R. 1 C. C. 115. § 815.
v. S., 7 Tex. Ap. 462. § 1196.
S. v., 42 Tex. 77. § 1313.
Bullock, S. v., 13 Ala. 413. § 161.
Bulman, C. v., 118 Mass. 456. § 1139.
Bulmer, Reg. v., L. & C. 476. §§ 659, 710.
Bunce, Reg. v., 1 F. & F. 523. § 562.
Bunfill v. P., 154 Ill. 640. § 1106*a*.
Bunkall, Reg. v., 9 Cox, 419. § 554.
Bunker, S. v., 38 Kan. 737. §§ 859, 878.
Bunn, Reg. v., 12 Cox, 316. §§ 956, 963.

Buntain v. S., 15 Tex. Ap. 485. § 502.
v. S., 15 Tex. Ap. 515. § 689.
Bunten, S. v., 2 Nott & M. 441. § 588.
Buntin v. S., 68 Ind. 38. §§ 228, 228a, 269, 586.
Burch, Reg. v., 4 F. & F. 407. § 962.
v. Republic, 1 Tex. 608. §§ 1270, 1291.
U. S. v., 1 Cranch, C. C. 36. § 1272.
Burchard, S. v., 4 S. Dak. 548. § 1270.
Burchinal, S. v., 4 Harr. 572. § 1248.
Burd v. C., 6 Serg. & R. 252. § 841.
v. S., 39 Tex. 509. § 704.
Burden v. P., 26 Mich. 162. § 336.
Burdett, Rex v., 4 B. & Ald. 95. §§ 118, 1051, 1058, 1070.
Burdick, C. v., 2 Pa. St. 163. § 679.
U. S. v., 1 Dak. 142. § 1263.
Burgdorf, S. v., 53 Mo. 65. § 440.
Burge, S. v., 7 Ia. 255. § 47.
Burger v. S., 83 Ala. 36. § 546.
Burgess, P. v., 35 Cal. 115. § 504.
Reg. v., L. & C. 258. §§ 274, 290.
Reg. v., L. & C. 299. § 546.
Reg. v., 16 Q. B. D. 141. § 940.
v. Salmon, 97 U. S. 381. § 78.
v. S., 44 Ala. 190. § 835.
v. S., 93 Ga. 304. § 419.
S. v., 4 Ind. 606. § 1276.
S. v., 78 Mo. 234. § 365.
S. v., 74 N. C. 272. §§ 602, 606.
Burgett, C. v., 136 Mass. 450. § 1236.
S. v., 1 Ind. 479. § 1198.
Burgiss, Rex v., 7 C. & P. 490. § 800.
Burgon, Reg. v., Dears. & B. 11. § 668.
Burguier v. U. S., 1 Dak. T. 5. § 18.
Burk, C. v., 11 Gray, 437. § 145.
v. S., 81 Ind. 128. §§ 872, 873, 878.
v. S., 8 Tex. Ap. 336. § 450.
S. v., 89 Mo. 635. § 271.
Burke, Ex parte, 59 Cal. 6. § 1319.
C. v., 105 Mass. 376. §§ 438, 445.
C. v., 114 Mass. 261. § 190.
C. v., 121 Mass. 39. § 1229.
v. P., 148 Ill. 70. § 481.
v. P., 23 Ill. Ap. 36. § 1180.
P. v., 11 Wend. 129. § 553.
v. S., 66 Ga. 157. § 753.
v. S., 74 Ga. 372. § 468.
v. S., 52 Ind. 461. § 1229.
v. S., 72 Ind. 392. § 1227.
v. S., 5 Tex. Ap. 74. §§ 505, 506, 513.
v. S., 24 Tex. Ap. 326. § 797.
S. v., 54 N. H. 92. § 377.
S. v., 73 N. C. 83. §§ 468, 478.
S. v., 82 N. C. 551. § 245.
S. v., 108 N. C. 750. §§ 677, 698.
S. v., 15 R. I. 324. § 189.
v. T., 2 Okl. 499. § 9.
Burkett v. McCarty, 10 Bush, 758. § 944.
Burkhard v. S., 18 Tex. Ap. 599. § 162.
Burley, U. S. v., 14 Blatch. 91. §§ 943, 944.
Burlington v. Beasley, 94 U. S. 310. § 40.
v. Bumgardner, 42 Ia. 673. §§ 69, 1217.
C. v., 136 Mass. 435. § 58.
Burnett v. S., 30 Ala. 19. §§ 1289, 1303.
v. S., 92 Ga. 474. §§ 1233, 1256, 1257.
v. S., 14 Lea, 439. §§ 292, 330.
v. S., 32 Tex. Ap. 86. § 1124.
S. v., 119 Ind. 392. §§ 667, 669, 687.
S. v., 77 Mo. 570. § 5.
Burney v. S., 87 Ala. 80. § 718.
v. S., 21 Tex. Ap. 565. § 463.
Burnham v. Holt, 14 N. H. 367. § 939.
v. S., 43 Tex. 322. § 353.
S. v., 9 N. H. 34. §§ 95, 1042, 1051, 1052.
S. v., 15 N. H. 396. §§ 953, 954, 955.
S. v., 56 Vt. 445. §§ 249, 1013.
Burns v. C., 3 Met. (Ky.) 13. § 274.
v. C., 129 Pa. St. 138. § 485.
C. v., 8 Gray, 482. § 1234.
C. v., 4 J. J. Marsh. 177. § 1310.
v. P., 1 Park. Cr. 182. § 389.
P. v., 63 Cal. 614. § 509.
P. v., 75 Cal. 627. §§ 128, 913, 915.
Respublica v., 1 Yeates, 370. § 909.
v. S., 49 Ala. 370. § 307.
v. S., 61 Ga. 192. § 414.
v. S., 89 Ga. 527. § 137.
v. S., 5 Ind. Ap. 385. § 45.
v. S., 35 Tex. 724. § 557.
v. S., 12 Tex. Ap. 269. § 482.
v. S., 12 Tex. Ap. 391. § 1087.
S. v., 8 Ala. 313. § 271.
S. v., 123 Ind. 427. § 825.
S. v., 30 La. An., Pt. I, 679. § 307.
S. v., 82 Me. 558. § 1204.
S. v., 33 Mo. 483. § 430.
U. S. v., 54 Fed. R. 351. § 1195.
U. S. v., 5 McLean, 23. §§ 774, 775, 789, 798, 803.
Burnsides, Reg. v., Bell, 282. § 673.
Burr v. C., 4 Grat. 534. § 615.
S. v., 10 Me. 438. § 1244.
U. S. v., 2 Robertson, 481. § 14.
Burraston, Reg v., 4 Jur. 697. §§ 880, 883.
Burrell, Reg. v., L. & C. 354. §§ 1101, 1103.
v. S., 129 Ind. 290. § 1248.
v. S., 18 Tex. 713. §§ 194, 425.
S. v., 86 Ind. 313. § 1021.
Burress v. C., 27 Grat. 934. § 798.
Burroughs, S. v., 72 Me. 479. § 1279.
S. v., 7 N. J. 426. §§ 16, 814.
U. S. v., 3 McLean, 405. § 546.
Burrow v. S., 12 Ark. 65. § 678.
Burrows, Rex v., 1 Moody, 274. § 496.
Rex v., Russ. & Ry. 519. § 450.
v. S., 137 Ind. 474. § 585.
S. v., 1 Houst. Cr. C. 74. § 529.
S. v., 11 Ired. 477. § 661.
Burst v. S., 89 Ind. 133. § 1036.
Burt, P. v., 51 Mich. 199. § 340.
S. v., 41 La. An. 787. § 431.
S. v., 64 N. C. 619. § 536.
S. v., 25 Vt. 373. §§ 925, 926, 927.
Burton v. March, 6 Jones, 409. § 612.
Reg. v., Dears. 282. §§ 396, 612.
Reg. v., 3 F. & F. 772. § 156.
Rex v., 1 Moody, 237. §§ 626, 630.

Burton v. S., 92 Ga. 449. § 389.
v. S., 3 Tex. Ap. 408. § 257.
v. S., 16 Tex. Ap. 156. § 1140.
S. v., 1 Houst. Cr. C. 363. § 450.
S. v., 3 Ind. 93. § 914.
S. v., 25 Tex. 420. § 1285.
Bury v. Levy, 1 W. Bl. 443. § 939.
Bush v. C., 78 Ky. 268. § 292.
C. v., 112 Mass. 280. § 139.
v. P., 10 Colo. 566. §§ 140, 309, 313.
P. v., 65 Cal. 129. § 309.
P. v., 4 Hill (N. Y.), 133. §§ 220, 228.
v. Republic, 1 Tex. 455. § 1249.
Rex v., Russ. & Ry. 372. § 214.
v. S., 18 Ala. 415. § 1304.
v. S., 77 Ala. 83. § 767.
v. S., 37 Ark. 215. § 1130.
v. S., 65 Ga. 658. § 505.
S. v., 29 Ind. 110. §§ 819, 826.
S. v., 122 Ind. 42. § 1051.
S. v., 45 Kan. 138. §§ 945, 949, 950.
S. v., 47 Kan. 201. § 945.
v. Workman, 64 Ia. 205. § 1093.
Bushman v. C., 138 Mass. 507. § 602.
Bushton, P. v., 80 Cal. 160. §§ 133, 333.
Bussell, P. v., 59 Mich. 104. § 92.
Bussey, P. v., 82 Mich. 149. § 920.
v. S., 71 Ga. 100. § 470.
Buster v. Newkirk, 20 Johns. 75. § 538.
v. S., 42 Tex. 315. § 363.
S. v., 90 Mo. 514. § 1100.
Buswell, S. v., 40 Neb. 158. § 36.
Butcher, Reg. v., Bell, 6. §§ 187, 673.
S. v., 79 Ia. 110. § 1028.
Butland, C. v., 119 Mass. 317. §§ 867, 868, 876.
Butler v. C., 2 Duv. 435. §§ 194, 291.
v. C., 12 Serg. & R. 237. § 758.
v. C., 81 Va. 159. § 508.
C. v., 1 Allen, 4. § 145.
C. v., 144 Pa. St. 568. §§ 572, 588.
v. Goreley, 146 U. S. 303. § 104.
v. P., 4 Denio, 68. §§ 504, 513.
v. P., 125 Ill. 641. § 196.
P. v., 8 Cal. 435. §§ 338, 423.
P. v., 3 Cow. 347. § 28.
P. v., 16 Johns. 203. § 523.
Rex v., 6 C. & P. 368. §§ 221, 462.
v. Ricker, 6 Me. 268. § 84.
v. S., 22 Ala. 43. § 807.
v. S., 91 Ala. 87. § 602.
v. S., 5 Blackf. 280. §§ 343, 1290.
v. S., 25 Fla. 347. § 1216.
v. S., 35 Fla. 246. § 718.
v. S., 92 Ga. 601. § 300.
v. S., 6 Ind. 165. § 1172.
v. S., 3 McCord, 383. § 713.
S. v., 47 Minn. 483. §§ 671, 676, 684, 694.
S. v., 67 Mo. 59. § 553.
S. v., 65 N. C. 309. § 548.
S. v., 21 S. C. 353. § 564.
S. v., 8 Wash. 194. § 220.
U. S. v., 38 Fed. R. 498. § 890.
U. S. v., 1 Hughes, 457. § 961.
v. Washburn, 25 N. H. 251. § 930.
Butman, S. v., 42 N. H. 490. §§ 271, 278.
S. v., 61 N. H. 511. §§ 630, 631.
Butterfield, Reg. v., 1 Cox, 39. § 209.
Butterick, C. v., 100 Mass. 1. §§ 634, 639, 644, 652, 655, 656.
C. v., 100 Mass. 12. §§ 752, 801, 806.
Butterwick, Reg. v., 2 M. & Rob. 196. § 756.
Butterworth, Reg. v., 12 Cox, 132. § 608.
Rex v., Russ. & Ry. 520. § 511.
Buttery, Rex v., 3 B. & C. 700. § 696.
Rex v., Russ. & Ry. 342. § 750.
Button, P. v., 106 Cal. 628. § 310.
Reg. v., 8 C. & P. 660. §§ 124, 236.
Reg. v., 11 Q. B. 929. §§ 22, 979.
Buttram v. S., 4 Coldw. 171. § 1135.
Butts, C. v., 2 Va. Cas. 18. § 1293.
S. v., 92 N. C. 784. § 1161.
S. v., 3 S. Dak. 577. § 132.
Butzman v. Whitbeck, 42 Ohio St. 223. § 1212.
Buxton, C. v., 10 Gray, 9. § 1169.
S. v., 31 Ind. 67. § 1193.
S. v., 2 Swan, 57. §§ 913, 917.
Buzzard, S. v., 4 Ark. 18. § 1030.
Buzzell, C. v., 16 Pick. 153. § 524.
S. v., 59 N. H. 65. § 213.
Bybee v. S., 94 Ind. 443. § 1184.
v. S., 4 Tex. Ap. 505. § 211.
Byce, C. v., 8 Gray, 461. § 576.
Byerly, C. v., 2 Brewst. 566. § 543.
Byers, S. v., 100 N. C. 512. § 333.
U. S. v., 4 Cranch, C. C. 171. § 543.
Bykerdyke, Rex v., 1 M. & Rob. 179. §§ 963, 982.
Bynam v. S., 17 Ohio St. 142. § 759.
Byrd v. C., 89 Va. 536. § 303.
S. v., 28 S. C. 18. §§ 852, 861.
Byrne, Reg. v., 6 Cox, 475. § 789.
v. S., 12 Wis. 519. §§ 135, 944, 945, 949.
S. v., 45 Conn. 273. § 522.
v. Stewart, 3 Desau. 466. § 78.
U. S. v., 44 Fed. R. 188. § 1330.
Byrnes, C. v., 126 Mass. 248. §§ 1229, 1270.
C. v., 158 Mass. 172. § 34.
P. v., 30 Cal. 206. § 391.
Bythwood v. S., 20 Ala. 47. § 1303.

Cabbage, Rex v., Russ. & Ry. 292. § 568.
Cabbell v. S., 46 Ala. 195. §§ 194, 265.
Cable v. S., 8 Blackf. 531. § 1137.
S. v., 117 Mo. 380. § 310.
Caddle, S. v., 35 W. Va. 73. §§ 565, 568.
Cadman, P. v., 57 Cal. 562. § 738.
Rex v., 1 Moody, 114. §§ 227, 1148.
Cadwallader, U. S. v., 59 Fed. R. 677. § 1340.
Cadwell, S. v., 79 Ia. 432. § 42.
S. v., 79 Ia. 473. § 674.
Cady v. C., 10 Grat. 776. § 772.
P. v., 6 Hill (N. Y.), 490. § 769.
Caesar, S. v., 9 Ired. 391. § 339.
Cagle v. S., 87 Ala. 93. § 1239.
S. v., 2 Humph. 414. § 1130.
S. v., 114 N. C. 835. § 1126.

Caha v. U. S., 152 U. S. 211. § 860.
Cahen, S. v., 35 Md. 236. § 1230.
Cahill, C. v., 12 Allen, 540. §§ 481, 582, 586.
U. S. v., 3 McCr. 200. §§ 946, 950.
Cain, Reg. v., Car. & M. 309. § 546.
v. S., 30 Ala. 534. § 1302.
v. S., 58 Ark. 43. § 708.
v. S., 13 Sm. & M. 456. § 1283.
v. S., 18 Tex. 391. § 590.
v. S., 20 Tex. 355. § 86.
S. v., 8 W. Va. 720. § 1216.
S. v., 9 W. Va. 559. § 1257.
S. v., 20 W. Va. 679. §§ 305, 306, 310, 410.
Calder v. Bull, 3 Dall. 386. § 78.
v. Kurby, 5 Gray, 597. § 1209.
P. v., 30 Mich. 85. § 1079.
S. v., 2 McCord, 462. §§ 994, 996.
Caldwell v. Barrett, 73 Ga. 604. § 1210.
v. Bridal, 48 Ia. 15. § 56.
C. v., 14 Mass. 330. § 927.
Respublica v., 1 Dall. 150. § 1195.
v. S., 55 Ala. 133. § 78.
v. S., 41 Tex. 86. § 298.
v. S., 28 Tex. Ap. 566. § 381.
S. v., 8 Baxt. 576. § 1135.
S. v., 3 La. An. 435. § 1310.
S. v., 112 N. C. 854. § 703.
S. v., 115 N. C. 794. §§ 369, 426.
S. v., 2 Tyler, 212. § 920.
Calef, C. v., 10 Mass. 153. § 1130.
Calfield's Case, 1 Rol. 189. § 298.
Calhane, C. v., 154 Mass. 115. § 1205.
Calhoun, P. v., 3 Wend. 420. § 907.
S. v., 72 Ia. 432. §§ 474, 478.
U. S. v., 39 Fed. R. 604. § 1245.
Calkins v. S., 14 Ohio St. 222. §§ 96, 101.
v. S., 18 Ohio St. 366. § 638.
S. v., 73 Ia. 128. § 787.
Call, C. v., 21 Pick. 509. § 1086.
C. v., 21 Pick. 515. §§ 683, 711.
P. v., 1 Denio, 120. §§ 556, 570.
S. v., 48 N. H. 126. §§ 666, 699, 700, 711.
Callaghan, C. v., 2 Va. Cas. 460. § 947.
Callahan v. S., 63 Ind. 198. § 1112.
v. S., 2 Ind. Ap. 417. § 1273.
v. S., 21 Ohio St. 306. § 126.
v. S., 41 Tex. 43. § 577.
v. S., 30 Tex. Ap. 275. § 334.
S. v., 124 Ind. 364. § 794.
Callan, Rex v., Russ. & Ry. 157. § 500.
v. Wilson, 127 U. S. 540. § 6.
Callanan, Rex v., 6 B. & C. 102. §§ 875, 877.
Callendine, S. v., 8 Ia. 288. §§ 788, 793, 794.
Calley, S. v., 104 N. C. 858. § 1138.
Calligan, S. v., 17 N. H. 253. § 278.
Calloway v. S., 7 Tex. Ap. 585. § 546.
Calvert v. C., 5 B. Mon. 264. § 1313.
C. v., 1 Va. Cas. 181. § 859.
v. S., 14 Tex. Ap. 154. § 1026.
Calvert's Lessee v. Eden, 2 Har. & McH. 335. § 12.
Calvin, S. v., 22 N. J. 207. §§ 209, 543, 573, 713, 715.
Cameron, C. v., 141 Mass. 83. § 1280.
v. S., 14 Ala. 546. §§ 1089, 1096.
v. S., 15 Ala. 383. § 1287.
v. S., 44 Tex. 652. § 618.
v. S., 9 Tex. Ap. 332. § 592.
S. v., 3 Heisk. 78. § 649.
S. v., 117 Mo. 371. §§ 698, 699.
S. v., 40 Vt. 555. §§ 614, 649.
U. S. v., 3 Dak. 132. § 750.
Camfield, Rex v., 1 Moody, 42. § 508.
Camley, S. v., 67 Vt. 322. §§ 872, 888.
Camp, P. v., 56 Mich. 548. § 562.
P. v., 139 N. Y. 87. § 491.
v. S., 3 Ga. 417. § 460.
v. S., 25 Ga. 689. § 384.
Campbell v. C., 88 Ky. 402. §§ 313, 337.
v. C., 59 Pa. St. 266. § 1022.
v. C., 84 Pa. St. 187. §§ 117, 214, 217, 377, 416.
C. v., 7 Allen, 541. § 196.
C. v., 103 Mass. 436. § 593.
Pennsylvania v., Addis. 232. §§ 549, 550.
v. P., 16 Ill. 17. §§ 295, 306, 307.
v. P., 109 Ill. 565. §§ 713, 717, 720, 722.
v. P., 34 Mich. 351. § 454.
v. P., — Ill. —, 42 N. E. R. 13. § 396.
v. P., 8 Wend. 636. §§ 874, 877, 878.
P. v., 40 Cal. 129. § 362.
P. v., 59 Cal. 243. §§ 303, 386.
P. v., 4 Park. Cr. 386. § 539.
v. Phelps, 17 Mass. 244. § 111.
v. Race, 7 Cush. 408. § 1189.
v. Rankins, 11 Me. 103. § 489.
Reg. v., 11 Cox, 323. § 351.
Reg. v., 1 C. & K. 82. § 373*a*.
Rex v., 1 Moody, 179. § 560.
v. S., 16 Ala. 144. § 1182.
v. S., 17 Ala. 369. § 1303.
v. S., 23 Ala. 44. § 408.
v. S., 46 Ala. 116. § 29.
v. S., 55 Ala. 89. § 1313.
v. S., 79 Ala. 271. § 1233.
v. S., 38 Ark. 498. § 307.
v. S., 11 Ga. 353. § 425.
v. S., 48 Ga. 353. § 487.
v. S., 35 Ohio St. 70. §§ 102, 546, 627, 650.
v. S., 9 Tex. Ap. 147. § 268.
v. S., 15 Tex. Ap. 506. § 353.
v. S., 28 Tex. Ap. 44. § 1036.
S. v., 50 Kan. 433. § 1206.
S. v., 108 Mo. 611. §§ 564, 618.
S. v., 64 N. H. 402. § 33.
S. v., 103 N. C. 344. § 543.
S. v., 107 N. C. 948. § 309.
S. v., 35 S. C. 28. § 419.
S. v., T. U. P. Charl. 166. § 812.
S. v., 29 Tex. 44. § 1154.
U. S. v., 16 Fed. R. 233. § 1329.
Camplin, Reg. v., 1 C. & K. 746. § 438.
v. S., 1 Tex. Ap. 108. § 565.
Canada, S. v., 68 Ia. 397. § 463.

Canadian Bank v. McCrea, 106 Ill. 281. § 752.
Candler, U. S. v., 65 Fed. R. 308. § 616.
Cannady v. P., 17 Ill. 158. § 1274.
Canney, S. v., 19 N. H. 135. § 499.
Cannon v. P., 141 Ill. 270. § 400.
P. v., 139 N. Y. 32. § 47.
Rex v., Russ. & Ry. 146. § 470.
v. S., 57 Miss. 147. § 330.
v. S., 18 Tex. Ap. 172. § 585.
S. v., 79 Mo. 343. §§ 855, 860.
v. U. S., 116 U. S. 55. § 1073.
Canny, C. v., 158 Mass. 210. § 1243.
Cansler, S. v., 75 N. C. 442. § 914.
Canter v. S., 7 Lea, 349. §§ 659, 678.
Canterbury, S. v., 28 N. H. 195. § 1185.
Cantieny, S. v., 34 Minn. 1. §§ 141, 430.
Canton, S. v., 43 Mo. 48. § 1133.
Cantril v. Sainer, 59 Ia. 26. § 1240.
Cantrill v. P., 8 Ill. 356. § 925.
Cantwell v. P., 138 Ill. 602. § 560.
Caperton v. Martin, 4 W. Va. 138. § 904.
Capritz v. S., 1 Md. 569. § 1274.
Carabin, P. v., 14 Cal. 438. §§ 562, 572.
Caradice, Rex v., Russ. & Ry. 205. § 538.
Carberry v. S., 11 Ohio St. 410. § 796.
Carden v. S., 89 Ala. 130. § 596.
Cardoza, S. v., 11 S. C. 195. §§ 962, 975, 988, 989.
Carel, C. v., 105 Mass. 582. §§ 854, 874.
Carey, C. v., 2 Brews. 404. § 302.
C. v., 12 Cush. 246. §§ 308, 340, 425.
C. v., 151 Pa. St. 368. § 1235.
C. v., 2 Pick. 47. § 772.
v. S., 83 Ind. 597. §§ 187, 1237.
S. v., 4 Wash. 424. § 36.
Cargill v. C., 93 Ky. 578. § 1106*a*.
v. S., 8 Tex. 41. § 487.
Carico v. C., 7 Bush, 124. § 307.
U. S. v., 2 Cranch, C. C. 446. § 693.
Carkhuff, P. v., 24 Cal. 640. § 424.
Carl v. S., 87 Ala. 17. §§ 1219, 1222.
v. S., 89 Ala. 93. §§ 1219, 1252.
S. v., 43 Ark. 353. § 1236.
Carland, S. v., 3 Dev. 114. § 881.
Carleton v. Rugg, 149 Mass. 550. § 1208.
Carlile v. Maxwell, 1 McCord, 534. § 994.
Reg. v., 1 Cox, 229. § 1157.
Rex v., 3 B. & Ald. 161. § 1049.
Carlisle, C. v., Bright. 36. § 962.
Reg. v., Dears. 337. § 960.
v. S., 76 Ala. 75. § 689.
v. S., 77 Ala. 71. §§ 680, 689.
v. S., 31 Tex. Ap. 537. § 211.
v. U. S., 16 Wall. 147. § 1364.
Carll, U. S. v., 105 U. S. 611. § 789.
Carlton v. P., 150 Ill. 181. § 533.
P. v., 57 Cal. 83. § 424.
S. v., 48 Vt. 636. § 414.
Carmalt, C. v., 2 Binn. 235. § 914.
Carmichael, P. v., 5 Mich. 10. §§ 122, 227, 1148.
v. S., 12 Ohio St. 553. § 1074.
v. S., 11 Tex. Ap. 27. § 1037.
Carmisales v. S., 11 Tex. Ap. 474. § 553.
Carmon v. S., 18 Ind. 450. § 1220.
Carmouche v. Bouis, 6 La. An. 96. § 299.
Carnes v. S., 23 Tex. Ap. 449. § 1232.
Carney, C. v., 108 Mass. 417. § 1243.
C. v., 152 Mass. 566. § 1249.
Rex v., Moody, 351. § 753.
v. S., 79 Ala. 14. § 1117.
v. S., 84 Ala. 7. § 58.
S. v., 20 Ia. 82. § 1217.
Carolan, P. v., 71 Cal. 195. § 674.
Carolin, C. v., 2 Allen. 169. § 1248.
Carotti v. S., 42 Miss. 334. §§ 1087, 1098.
Carpenter, Ex parte, 64 Cal. 267. § 860.
C. v., 108 Mass. 15. § 740.
v. Pennsylvania, 17 How. 456. § 78.
P. v., 1 Mich. 273. §§ 1184, 1186.
P. v., 102 N. Y. 238. § 157.
Reg. v., L. R. 1 C. C. 29. § 632.
v. S., 4 How. (Miss.) 163. § 859.
S. v., 60 Conn. 97. §§ 15, 62, 66, 1307, 1308, 1315.
S. v., 1 Houst. 367. §§ 500, 505.
S. v., 23 Ia. 506. § 280.
S. v., 20 Ind. 219. § 1273.
S. v., 54 Vt. 551. § 927.
Carper v. S., 27 Ohio St. 572. § 1290.
Carr v. Congers, 84 Ga. 287. § 1017.
Reg. v., 10 Cox, 564. § 886.
Rex v., 8 C. & P. 163, n. § 351.
Rex v., Russ. & Ry. 198. § 626.
Rex v., Russ. & Ry. 377. § 258.
v. S., 34 Ark. 448. § 1036.
v. S., 43 Ark. 99. §§ 298, 413.
v. S., 50 Ind. 178. § 1286.
v. S., 135 Ind. 1. § 236.
v. S., 23 Neb. 749. § 322.
v. S., 9 Tex. Ap. 463. § 535.
v. S., 24 Tex. Ap. 562. §§ 150, 152.
S. v., 43 Ia. 418. §§ 469, 470, 473, 543.
S. v., 60 Ia. 453. § 1113.
S. v., 37 Kan. 421. § 1060.
S. v., 5 N. H. 367. §§ 761, 797, 806.
S. v., 6 Oreg. 133. § 1300.
S. v., 53 Vt. 37. § 358.
U. S. v., 2 Mont. T. 234. § 1217.
U. S. v., 1 Woods, 480. §§ 136, 297*a*, 303.
Carrell, Rex v., 2 East, P. C. 506. § 494.
Carrick, S. v., 16 Nev. 120. § 652.
Carrier, P. v., 46 Mich. 442. §§ 1101, 1103.
S. v., 5 Day, 131. § 499.
Carrington v. C., 78 Ky. 83. § 1253.
Carroll v. C., 84 Pa. St. 107. § 416.
C. v., 15 Gray, 409. § 1276.
P. v., 80 Cal. 153. §§ 1283, 1284, 1285, 1296.
P. v., 54 Mich. 334. § 514.
Rex v., 1 Moody, 89. § 576.
v. S., 28 Ark. 99. § 1035.
v. S., 45 Ark. 539. §§ 209, 938.
v. S., 63 Md. 551. §§ 189, 1237.
v. S., 24 Tex. Ap. 366. § 463.
S. v., 85 Ia. 1. § 526.
S. v., 31 La. An. 860. § 420.
S. v., 13 Mont. 246. § 505.
S. v., 30 S. C. 85. §§ 1087, 1095.

Carroll, S. v., 67 Vt. 477. § 455.
U. S. v., 32 Fed. R. 775. §§ 943, 948.
Carron, S. v., 18 Ia. 372. § 1113.
Carrothers v. Russell, 53 Ia. 346. § 947.
Carruthers, Reg. v., 1 Cox, 138. §§ 729, 733.
v. S., 74 Ala. 406. § 899.
Carson, C. v., 166 Pa. St. 179. §§ 504, 510, 511.
Rex v., Russ. & Ry. 303. § 652.
v. S., 69 Ala. 235. § 1253.
v. S., 80 Ga. 170. § 321.
S. v., 115 N. C. 743. § 409.
S. v., 36 S. C. 524. § 195.
Carter v. Andrews, 16 Pick. 1. § 1060.
C. v., 94 Ky. 527. §§ 200, 205.
C. v., 132 Mass. 12. § 33.
Reg. v., 12 Q. B. D. 522. § 726.
Reg. v., 1 C. & K. 173. § 499.
Reg. v., 1 C. & K. 741. § 753.
Rex v., 2 East, P. C. 985. § 793.
v. S., 55 Ala. 181. §§ 944, 949, 950.
v. S., 68 Ala. 96. § 500.
v. S., 82 Ala. 13. § 311.
v. S., 87 Ala. 113. §§ 232, 239.
v. S., 22 Fla. 553. § 358.
v. S., 35 Ga. 263. § 463.
v. S., 53 Ga. 326. § 638.
v. S., 12 Tex. 500. § 159.
v. S., 8 Tex. Ap. 372. § 303.
v. S., 18 Tex. Ap. 573. § 825.
v. S., 28 Tex. Ap. 355. § 274.
v. S., 29 Tex. Ap. 5. § 930.
v. S., 30 Tex. Ap. 551. §§ 298, 309, 339, 348, 391.
S. v., 1 Houst. Cr. C. 402. §§ 501, 505.
S. v., 7 Humph. 157. § 1274.
S. v., 45 La. An. 1326. § 307.
S. v., 98 Mo. 176. § 161.
S. v., 72 N. C. 99. § 614.
S. v., 76 N. C. 20. § 338.
S. v., 113 N. C. 639. § 609.
S. v., 27 N. J. 499. § 369.
S. v., 8 Wash. 272. §§ 1112, 1115, 1117, 1129.
U. S. v., 2 Cranch, C. C. 243. § 781.
Cartwright v. Green, 2 Leach, 952. § 545.
Rex v., Russ. & Ry. 106. § 675.
v. S., 8 Lea, 376. § 162.
v. S., 14 Tex. Ap. 486. § 309.
v. S., 16 Tex. Ap. 473. § 315.
Caruthers v. S., 74 Ala. 406. § 899.
v. S., 13 Tex. Ap. 339. § 274.
Carver v. P., 39 Mich. 786. § 789.
v. S., 69 Ind. 61. §§ 1321, 1324.
S. v., 22 Oreg. 602. § 359.
v. U. S., 160 U. S. 553. § 426.
v. U. S., — U. S. —, 17 S. C. R. 228. § 431.
Carwile v. S., 35 Ala. 392. § 1008.
Casados, S. v., 1 Nott & McC. 91. § 543.
Casas v. S., 12 Tex. Ap. 59. § 620.
Casat v. S., 40 Ark. 511. §§ 156, 178.
Casavant, S. v., 64 Vt. 405. § 546.
Case v. P., 76 N. Y. 242. § 854.
Reg. v., 1 Den. 580. §§ 249, 446, 462.
Case, Rex v., 1 East, P. C. 165. § 774.
v. S., 26 Ala. 17. §§ 556, 588.
v. S., 12 Tex. Ap. 228. § 546.
S. v., 53 Mo. 246. § 41.
Casey, C. v., 12 Allen, 214. § 1217.
C. v., 11 Cush. 417. § 429.
C. v., 134 Mass. 194. § 1250.
P. v., 72 N. Y. 393. §§ 252, 257, 262.
Casford, S. v., 76 Ia. 330. §§ 442, 452.
Cash v. S., 2 Overt. 198. § 1010.
S. v., 38 Kan. 50. § 500.
Casily v. S., 32 Ind. 62. §§ 674, 682.
Casio, T. v., 1 Ariz. 485. § 617.
Cason, S. v., 20 La. An. 48. § 596.
Caspar, Reg. v., 9 C. & P. 289. § 212.
Cass, S. v., 41 Tex. 552. § 255.
Cass Co. Com'rs, S. v., 12 Neb. 54. § 1228.
Cassady, S. v., 12 Kan. 550. §§ 214, 617.
S. v., 52 N. H. 500. §§ 922, 925.
Cassel, S. v., 2 Har. & G. 407. §§ 585, 596.
Cassels v. S., 4 Yerg. 149. § 714.
Casser, Reg. v., 13 Cox, 187. § 554.
Cassety, S. v., 1 Rich. 90. § 1244.
Cassidy, S. v., 85 Ia. 145. §§ 457, 458.
S. v., 4 S. Dak. 58. §§ 922, 923.
U. S. v., 67 Fed. R. 698. §§ 952, 953, 956, 963, 966, 968, 969, 988, 1328.
Casteel, S. v., 53 Mo. 124. §§ 546, 571.
Castello v. S., 36 Tex. 324. § 594.
S. v., 62 Ia. 404. §§ 292, 332.
Castellow v. S., 15 Tex. Ap. 551. § 618.
Castenada v. S., 11 Tex. Ap. 390. § 505.
Castillo v. S., 29 Tex. Ap. 127. § 1102.
v. S., 31 Tex. Ap. 145. § 455.
Castle, Reg. v., Dears. & B. 363. § 750.
v. S., 23 Tex. Ap. 286. § 733.
S. v., 44 Wis. 670. § 1189.
Castles, C. v., 9 Gray, 123. § 796.
v. Welch, 63 N. H. 369. § 1126.
Castor, S. v., 93 Mo. 242. §§ 616, 620.
Castro v. Reg., 6 App. Cas. 229. § 883.
Caswell, P. v., 21 Wend. 96. § 719.
v. S., 2 Humph. 402. §§ 1218, 1221.
S. v., 2 Humph. 399. § 1275.
Catchings, S. v., 43 Tex. 654. §§ 1198, 1291.
Cate v. S., 3 Sneed, 120. § 92.
S. v., 58 N. H. 240. § 39.
Cates v. S., 50 Ala. 166. § 343.
Cathcart v. C., 37 Pa. St. 108. §§ 377, 386.
Catherall, Reg. v., 13 Cox, 109. § 454.
Cathey v. S., 23 Tex. Ap. 492. § 1031.
S. v., 41 Ark. 308. § 1216.
Catlin, C. v., 1 Mass. 8. § 1135.
Cato v. S., 4 Tex. Ap. 87. § 232.
Caton, P. v., 25 Mich. 388. 781.
Reg. v., 12 Cox, 624. §§ 197, 208.
Cauley, C. v., 150 Mass. 272. § 1223.
Caulkins v. Whisler, 29 Ia. 495. § 765.
Causey v. S., 79 Ga. 564. § 572.
Cavaness v. S., 43 Ark. 331. § 396.
Cave v. S., 33 Tex. Ap. 335. § 1150.
S. v., 81 Mo. 450. § 878.
Cavendish, Reg. v., 8 Ir. R. C. L. 178. §§ 300, 316.

Caveness, S. v., 78 N. C. 484. §§ 716, 717.
Cavey, C. v., 97 Mass. 541. § 46.
Cawood, S. v., 2 Stew. 360. § 966.
Cearfoos v. S., 42 Md. 403. §§ 83, 1235, 1270.
Cease, P. v., 80 Mich. 576. §§ 1123, 1124.
Cell v. S., 20 Ohio St. 330. § 860.
Center, S. v., 35 Vt. 378. §§ 347, 426.
Centerville v. Miller, 51 Ia. 712. § 1210.
v. Miller, 57 Ia. 56. § 69.
Central Bridge, C. v., 12 Cush. 242. §§ 182, 1184.
Central Bridge Co. v. Butler, 2 Gray, 130. § 175.
Central R. Co., S. v., 32 N. J. 220. § 1190.
Certain Property, U. S. v., 1 Ariz. 31. § 1338*a*.
C. G. White, The, v. U. S., 64 Fed. R. 579. § 1351.
Chabbock, C. v., 1 Mass. 144. § 614.
Chace, C. v., 9 Pick. 15. § 538.
Chadbourne, S. v., 74 Me. 506. §§ 83, 102.
Chadwick, C. v., 142 Mass. 595. § 1229.
P. v., 7 Utah, 134. §§ 203, 209.
Reg. v., 2 M. & Rob. 545. § 763.
Reg. v., 11 Q. B. 173. § 1074.
Chae Chan Ping v. U. S., 130 U. S. 581. § 1344.
Chahoon v. C., 20 Grat. 733. § 781.
Chaims, S. v., 25 Oreg. 221. § 463.
Chalfont v. U. S., Morris, 214. § 823.
Chalkley, Rex v., Russ. & Ry. 258. § 815.
Chalkling, Rex v., Russ. & Ry. 334. § 496.
Chalmers, Reg. v., 16 L. T. (N. S.) 363. § 730.
Chamberlain v. P., 23 N. Y. 85. § 865.
Reg. v., 10 Cox, 486. § 287.
v. S., 5 Blackf. 573. § 779.
v. S., 2 Tex. Ap. 451. § 260.
Chambers, P. v., 18 Cal. 382. § 617.
Reg. v., L. R. 1 C. C. 341. § 753.
v. S., 77 Ala. 80. § 1289.
v. S., 62 Miss. 108. § 565.
v. S., 25 Tex. 307. § 82.
S. v., 6 Ala. 855. § 576.
S. v., 87 Ia. 1. §§ 1121, 1124.
S. v., 87 Mo. 406. § 428.
S. v., 93 N. C. 600. §§ 39, 1232.
S. v., 22 W. Va. 779. §§ 535, 548.
Chamblyss, S. v., 1 Cheves, 220. § 1230.
Champer v. S., 14 Ohio St. 437. § 249.
Champion, S. v., 116 N. C. 987. § 881.
Champlin. Reg. v., 1 C. & K. 746. § 445.
Champney's Case, 2 Lewin, 258. § 892.
Chancy, S. v., 110 N. C. 507. § 1097.
Chandler, In re, 45 La. An. 696. § 166.
Chandler, C. v., Thacher, Crim. Cas. 187. §§ 744, 764.
Reg. v., Dears. 453. § 286.
v. S., 15 Tex. Ap. 587. § 713.
S. v., 2 Harr. 553. § 1159.
S. v., 96 Ind. 591. § 1131.
S. v., 5 La. An. 489. §§ 304, 1030.
Chandler, S. v., 24 Mo. 371. § 268.
S. v., 15 Vt. 425. § 1244.
S. v., 42 Vt. 446. § 878.
Chandonette, S. v., 10 Mont. 280. § 1154.
Chanet v. Parker, 1 Mill. 333. § 210.
Chap, C. v., 4 Mass. 163. § 1042.
Chapel, S. v., 117 Mo. 639. § 698.
Chapin, C. v., 5 Pick. 199. § 1195.
S. v., 17 Ark. 561. § 211.
Chaplin v. Lee, 18 Neb. 440. § 638.
Chapman, Ex parte, 4 A. & E. 773. § 1057.
C. v., 11 Cush. 422. §§ 205, 213, 377, 380.
C. v., 13 Met. 68. §§ 12, 1042.
C. v., 1 Va. Cas. 138. § 901.
v. P., 39 Mich. 357. § 381.
P. v., 62 Mich. 280. § 449.
Reg. v., 1 C. & K. 119. § 640.
Reg. v., 2 C. & K. 846. §§ 221, 852, 860, 861, 865, 883.
Reg. v., 8 C. & P. 558. § 410.
v. S., 78 Ala. 463. § 232.
v. S., 18 Ga. 736. § 1293.
v. S., 16 Tex. Ap. 76. § 82.
S. v., 88 Ia. 254. § 440.
S. v., 33 Kan. 134. § 83.
S. v., 68 Me. 477. § 845.
S. v., 6 Nev. 320. § 217.
S. v., 1 S. Dak. 414. §§ 1204, 1248.
S. v., 25 W. Va. 408. § 1270.
U. S. v., 3 McLean, 390. § 880.
Chappel, C. v., 116 Mass. 7. § 1220.
Chappell v. S., 52 Ala. 359. §§ 468, 479.
v. S., 35 Ark. 345. § 1163.
v. S., 27 Tex. Ap. 310. § 1310.
S. v., 2 Hill, 391. § 1190.
Chapple, Reg. v., 9 C. & P. 355. § 209.
Rex v., Russ. & Ry. 77. § 815.
Chard, Rex v., Russ. & Ry. 488. § 543.
Charge to Grand Jury, In re, 62 Fed. R. 828. §§ 963, 1357.
In re, 66 Fed. R. 146. § 1336.
Chariton v. Barber, 54 Ia. 360. § 69.
Charles v. P., 1 N. Y. 180. § 1318.
v. S., 11 Ark. 389. § 442.
Charleston v. Ahrens, 4 Strobh. 241. § 1202.
v. Benjamin, 2 Strobh. 508. § 1319.
v. Corleis, 2 Bailey, 186. § 1224.
v. Hollenback, 3 Strobh. 355. § 1228.
v. Schmidt, 11 Rich. 343. § 1224.
Charlewood, Rex v., 2 East, P. C. 689. §§ 555, 569.
Chartrand, T. v., 1 Dak. 379. § 1145.
Chase v P., 2 Colo. 509. §§ 1308, 1309.
v. P., 40 Ill. 352. § 179.
v. S., 46 Miss. 683. §§ 307, 423.
v. S., 50 Wis. 510. § 382.
S. v., 33 La. An. 287. § 1217.
U. S. v., 27 Fed. R. 807. § 1332.
U. S. v., 135 U. S. 255. § 1332.
Chastain v. Calhoun, 29 Ga. 333. § 1217.
S. v., 19 Oreg. 176. §§ 190, 1239, 1251.
Chatham v. S., 92 Ala. 47. §§ 161, 572.
Chathams, C. v., 50 Pa. St. 181. § 554.

Chatteaux v. S., 52 Ala. 388. § 1034.
Chavez, P. v., 103 Cal. 407. § 454.
Chavis, S. v., 80 N. C. 353. § 308.
S. v., 34 S. C. 132. § 575.
Cheafor, Reg. v., 2 Den. 367. § 538.
Cheatham v. S., 59 Ala. 40. § 525.
Cheek v. C., 79 Ky. 359. § 1137.
v. S., 1 Coldw. 172. § 675.
v. S., 35 Ind. 492. §§ 416, 424.
v. S., 4 Tex. Ap. 444. §§ 302, 390.
Cheere, Rex v., 4 B. & C. 902. §§ 241, 1165.
Cheeseman, Reg. v., L. & C. 140. § 223.
Rex v., 7 C. & P. 455. § 348.
Cheesum v. S., 8 Blackf. 332. §§ 1285, 1297.
Cheezem v. S., 2 Ind. 149. § 96.
Cheney, C. v., 114 Mass. 281. § 148.
Cheong Foon Ark, P. v., 61 Cal. 527. § 608.
Cherokee v. Fox, 34 Kan. 16. § 44.
Cherry, Rex v., 2 East, P. C. 556. § 548.
v. S., 30 Tex. 439. § 1303.
S. v., 11 Ired. 475. § 233.
S. v., 3 Murph. 7. § 376.
S. v., 63 N. C. 439. § 519.
S. v., 1 Swan, 160. § 454.
Chesapeake Club v. S., 63 Md. 446. § 1240.
Chesapeake & O. R. Co., S. v., 24 W. Va. 809. § 1189.
Chesman, U. S. v., 19 Fed. R. 497. § 332.
Chess v. S., 1 Blackf. 198. § 790.
Chester v. S., 23 Tex. Ap. 577. § 803.
Cheverton, Reg. v., 2 F. & F. 833. § 398.
Chew v. S., 43 Ark. 361. § 1229.
Chew Cheong, U. S. v., 61 Fed. R. 200. § 1344.
Chew Muck You, S. v., 20 Oreg. 215. § 554.
Chicago, B. & P. R. Co., S. v., 63 Ia. 508. § 1187.
Chicago, B. & Q. R. Co. v. Iowa, 94 U. S. 155. § 40.
Chicago, M. & St. P. R. Co. v. Minnesota, 134 U. S. 418. § 40.
S. v., 77 Ia. 442. § 1187.
Chichester v. Hill, 15 Cox, 258. § 611.
Chick v. S., 7 Humph. 161. §§ 434, 436, 436*a*.
Chidester v. S., 25 Ohio St. 433. §§ 753, 763, 793.
Child, C. v., 13 Pick. 198. §§ 1047, 1060.
Reg. v., 2 Cox, 102. § 839.
Reg. v., 5 Cox, 197. § 888.
Reg. v., L. R. 1 C. C. 307. § 523.
S. v., 42 Kan. 611. § 269.
Childe, Rex v., 4 C. & P. 442. § 997.
Childers v. S., 33 Tex. Ap. 509. § 339.
Childress v. S., 86 Ala. 77. § 524.
v. S., 10 Tex. Ap. 698. § 618.
Childs v. S., 15 Ark. 204. §§ 253, 1011.
Chiles v. C., 2 Va. Cas. 260. §§ 589, 591, 606.
v. Drake, 2 Met. (Ky.) 146. § 11.
v. S., 1 Tex. Ap. 27. § 1285.
Chilvers v. P., 11 Mich. 43. § 69.
Chinault, S. v., 55 Kan. 326. §§ 122, 269.
Ching Gang, S. v., 16 Nev. 62. § 29.
Chin Quong Look, 52 Fed. R. 203. § 1345.
Chin Hane, P. v., 108 Cal. 597. §§ 416, 421.
Chinn v. S., 47 Ohio St. 575. § 1120.
Chiovaro, C. v., 129 Mass. 489. § 212.
Chipchase, Rex v., 2 East, P. C. 567. § 556.
Chisenhall, S. v., 106 N. C. 676. §§ 1102, 1104.
Chisholm, C. v., 103 Mass. 213. § 1272.
v. S., 45 Ala. 66. § 597.
Chisnell, S. v., 36 W. Va. 659. §§ 1274, 1276.
Chitten, S. v., 2 Dev. 49. § 216.
Chivarrio v. S., 15 Tex. Ap. 330. § 375.
Choen v. S., 85 Ind. 209. §§ 511, 600.
Choice v. S., 31 Ga. 424. §§ 159, 173, 391.
Choiser, P. v., 10 Cal. 310. § 377.
Chong Sam, U. S. v., 47 Fed. R. 878. § 1344.
Chouteau, U. S. v., 102 U. S. 603. § 1349.
Chowne v. Baylis, 31 Beav. 351. § 11.
Choynski, P. v., 95 Cal. 640. § 740.
Chrisman v. S., 54 Ark. 283. §§ 161, 275, 332.
v. S., 18 Neb. 107. §§ 898, 902.
Chrisp, S. v., 85 N. C. 528. § 1159.
Christian v. C., 23 Grat. 954. § 452.
Reg. v., Car. & M. 388. § 865.
Reg. v., L. R. 2 C. C. 94. §§ 630, 639.
v. S., 40 Ala. 376. § 1247.
v. S., 96 Ala. 89. § 267.
S. v., 30 La. An., Pt. I, 367. § 511.
S. v., 44 La. An. 950. § 307.
S. v., 66 Mo. 138. §§ 309, 324, 342.
Christie, Rex v., Car. C. L. 232. § 426.
Christman, S. v., 67 Ind. 328. § 93.
Christmas, S. v., 6 Jones, 471. § 170.
S. v., 101 N. C. 749. § 477.
Christopher, Reg. v., Bell, C. C. 27. § 571.
Chrystal v. C., 9 Bush, 669. § 351.
Chuey Ying Git, P. v., 100 Cal. 437. § 472.
Chugg, Reg. v., 11 Cox, 558. § 859.
Chum Shang Yuen, U. S. v., 57 Fed. R. 588. § 1344.
Chumley v. S., 28 Tex. Ap. 87. § 203.
S. v., 67 Mo. 41. § 268.
Chung Fung Sun, U. S. v., 63 Fed. R. 261. § 1344.
Chunn, S. v., 19 Mo. 233. § 676.
Chu Quong, P. v., 15 Cal. 332. §§ 489, 1100.
Church v. Church, 3 Mass. 157. § 1094.
C. v., 1 Pa. St. 105. § 1195.
S. v., 43 Conn. 471. §§ 681, 691.
S. v., 8 Ia. 252. § 587.
S. v., 63 N. C. 15. § 232.
S. v., 5 Oreg. 375. § 947.
S. v., 4 W. Va. 745. § 1270.
Church of Jesus Christ v. U. S., 136 U. S. 1. § 1076.
Churchill, C. v., 136 Mass. 148. §§ 190, 1174, 1239, 1248.
C. v., 2 Met. 118. § 102.
Chute v. S., 19 Minn. 271. § 1182.
Cincinnati R. v. C., 80 Ky. 137. § 1187.

Circuit Court, S. v., 50 N. J. 585. § 1210.
Cirwan's Case, 1 East, P. C. 182. § 774.
City Council, S. v., 42 S. C. 222. §§ 29, 76, 1208, 1214.
City of Mexico, The, 28 Fed. R. 148. § 1359.
Civil Rights Cases, 109 U. S. 3. § 54.
Claasen, In re, 140 U. S. 200. § 20.
Claassen v. U. S., 142 U. S. 140. §§ 655, 656a, 1340.
Clackner v. S., 33 Ind. 412. § 617.
Claiborne v. S., 51 Ark. 88. §§ 766, 767.
S. v., Meigs, 331. § 54.
Clair, S. v., 84 Me. 248. § 278.
Claire, S. v., 41 La. An. 191. § 418.
S. v., 84 Me. 248. § 278.
Clampitt v. S., 9 Tex. Ap. 27. § 418.
Clancy, C. v., 7 Allen, 537. § 774.
C. v., 154 Mass. 128. § 1305.
Clanton v. S., 20 Tex. Ap. 615. § 341.
Clap, C. v., 4 Mass. 163. §§ 1046, 1051, 1052.
Clapox, U. S. v., 35 Fed. R. 575. § 1086.
Clapp, C. v., 5 Gray, 97. § 1244.
C. v., 5 Pick. 41. §§ 1316, 1318.
Clare v. P., 9 Colo. 122. § 409.
Clarence, Reg. v., 22 Q. B. D. 23. §§ 238, 243, 249.
C. v., 5 Pick. 41. §§ 1316, 1318.
Clark, In re, 9 Wend. 212. §§ 4, 5, 17.
v. C., 16 B. Mon. 206. §§ 784, 786.
v. C., 33 Pa. St. 112. § 1190.
v. C., 4 Pick. 125. § 1197.
v. C., 90 Va. 360. §§ 292, 311, 410.
C. v., 2 Ashm. 105. § 1152.
C. v., 6 Grat. 675. §§ 228, 946, 950.
C. v., 14 Gray, 367. § 1244.
C. v., 145 Mass. 251. § 1140.
C. v., 2 Met. 23. § 142.
P. v., 84 Cal. 573. § 142.
P. v., 106 Cal. 32. § 473.
P. v., 10 Mich. 310. §§ 960, 966, 975, 977.
P. v., 33 Mich. 112. § 1118.
P. v., 7 N. Y. 385. §§ 329, 357, 358.
v. Reg., 14 Q. B. D. 92. § 123.
Reg. v., 2 Cox, 183. § 1074.
Reg. v., 6 Cox, 210. § 28.
Reg. v., 15 Cox, 171. § 1169.
Rex v., Russ. & Ry. 181. § 543.
Rex v., Russ. & Ry. 358. § 373a.
v. S., 19 Ala. 552. § 1313.
v. S., 49 Ala. 37. §§ 1285, 1286.
v. S., 49 Ark. 174. § 1035.
v. S., 50 Ark. 570. §§ 135, 826.
v. S., 84 Ga. 577. § 232.
v. S., 8 Humph. 671. § 357.
v. S., 8 Ohio St. 630. §§ 769, 774.
v. S., 86 Tenn. 511. § 226.
v. S., 19 Tex. Ap. 495. § 323.
v. S., 22 Tex. Ap. 599. § 618.
v. S., 23 Tex. Ap. 612. §§ 546, 552.
v. S., 27 Tex. Ap. 405. §§ 553, 618.
v. S., 28 Tex. Ap. 189. § 477.
v. S., 29 Tex. Ap. 437. § 601.
v. S., 30 Tex. Ap. 402. § 616.
v. S., 69 Wis. 203. § 499.
Clark, S. v., 69 Ia. 196. §§ 390, 435.
S. v., 69 Ia. 294. §§ 455, 456.
S. v., 72 Ia. 30. § 694.
S. v., 78 Ia. 492. § 1133.
S. v., 8 Ired. 226. § 593.
S. v., 7 Jones, 167. § 518.
S. v., 46 Kan. 65. §§ 665, 680.
S. v., 46 La. An. 704. § 391.
S. v., 31 Minn. 207. § 1021.
S. v., 89 Mo. 423. § 576.
S. v., 23 N. H. 429. § 798.
S. v., 28 N. H. 176. §§ 63, 66, 68, 1231.
S. v., 54 N. H. 456. § 1132.
S. v., 29 N. J. 96. §§ 82, 811, 812, 825.
S. v., 9 Oreg. 466. § 1118.
S. v., 4 Strobh. 311. § 614.
S. v., 2 Tyler, 277. § 873.
S. v., 23 Vt. 293. § 1229.
S. v., 42 Vt. 629. § 500.
U. S. v., Crabbe, 584. § 1330.
U. S. v., 22 Fed. R. 708. § 1334.
U. S. v., 31 Fed. R. 710. § 297a.
U. S. v., 37 Fed. R. 106. § 1332.
U. S. v., 43 Fed. R. 574. § 1332.
U. S. v., 23 Int. Rev. Rec. 306. § 1328.
Clarke, Ex parte, 100 U. S. 399. § 948.
v. C., 25 Grat. 908. §§ 493, 500–1, 514.
Reg. v., 1 C. & K. 421. § 509.
Reg. v., Dears. 397. § 446.
Reg. v., 2 F. & F. 2. § 424.
Reg. v., 4 F. & F. 1040. § 1152.
Rex v., 2 Stark. 241. §§ 455, 459, 460.
v. S., 12 Ala. 492. § 1303.
v. S., 12 Ga. 350. § 271.
v. S., 35 Ga. 75. § 333.
v. S., 89 Ga. 768. § 245.
v. S., 23 Miss. 261. § 78.
v. S., 8 Ohio St. 630. §§ 756, 769, 774.
S. v., 33 N. H. 329. §§ 82, 204, 1315.
S. v., 54 Mo. 17. § 89.
v. T., 1 Wash. T. 68. §§ 257, 262.
U. S. v., 2 Cranch, C. C. 158. § 159.
U. S. v., 38 Fed. R. 500. § 1332.
U. S. v., 38 Fed. R. 732. § 1332.
Clarkson, S. v., 59 Mo. 149. §§ 648, 649.
Clary v. C., 4 Pa. St. 210. § 962.
v. S., 33 Ark. 561. § 468.
S. v., 64 Me. 369. §§ 954, 960.
Claude, S. v., 35 La. An. 71. § 307.
Clay v. P., 86 Ill. 147. § 1055.
Reg. v., 5 Cox, 146. § 460.
Rex v., Russ. & Ry. 387. § 541.
v. S., 40 Tex. 67. § 584.
S. v., 12 La. An. 431. § 523.
S. v., 100 Mo. 571. §§ 693, 694.
Clayborne v. S., 103 Ala. 53. § 1301.
Clayburn, Rex v., Russ. & Ry. 360. § 497.
Claypool, U. S. v., 14 Fed. R. 127. § 1328.
Clayton, Reg. v., 1 C. & K. 128. §§ 200, 210.
v. S., 15 Tex. Ap. 348. §§ 557, 573.
S. v., 100 Mo. 516. §§ 221, 252, 268.
S. v., 11 Rich. 581. § 573.
S. v., 43 Tex. 410. § 1038.
U. S. v., 2 Dill. 219. §§ 85, 948.
Cleary, C. v., 105 Mass. 384. § 1243.
Reg. v., 2 F. & F. 850. §§ 323, 426.

Cleary v. S., 56 Ark. 124. §§ 1321, 1326.
Cleaveland v. S., 34 Ala. 254. § 914.
S. v., 6 Nev. 181. § 770.
Cleaver, Resp. v., 4 Yeates, 69. § 107.
Clegs, Reg. v., 3 Cox, 295. § 817.
Clellans v. C., 8 Pa. St. 223. § 1002.
Clem v. S., 33 Ind. 418. § 205.
v. S., 42 Ind. 420. § 375.
Clemens, S. v., 38 Ia. 257. § 1196.
Clement, S. v., 42 La. An. 583. §§ 800, 803.
Clements, P. v., 68 Mich. 655. § 142.
P. v., 26 N. Y. 193. §§ 746, 796, 801.
v. S., 50 Ala. 117. §§ 298, 329, 333.
v. S., 84 Ga. 660. § 474.
S. v., 32 Me. 279. § 142.
Clemons v. S., 4 Lea, 23. § 934.
v. S., 92 Tenn. 282. § 473.
S. v., 51 Ia. 274. § 391.
S. v., 78 Ia. 123. §§ 1117, 1118.
Clendon, Rex v., 2 Ld. Raym. 1572. § 252.
Clerk, Reg. v., 1 Salk. 377. § 1165.
Cleveland v. S., 86 Ala. 1. §§ 162, 316, 358.
v. S., 8 Tex. Ap. 44. § 823.
S. v., 58 Me. 564. §§ 361, 362.
S. v., 80 Mo. 108. §§ 90, 103, 646.
Clew, U. S. v., 4 Wash. C. C. 700. § 556.
Clewes, Rex v., 4 C. & P. 221. § 416.
Cleworth, Reg. v., 4 B. & S. 927. §§ 1319, 1321.
Click v. S., 3 Tex. 282. §§ 485, 489.
Clifford, Ex parte, 29 Ind. 106. §§ 930, 935.
C. v., 8 Cush. 215. §§ 471, 473.
Reg. v., 2 C. & K. 202. §§ 187, 762.
v. S., 56 Ind. 245. §§ 684, 687.
v. S., 58 Wis. 477. §§ 139, 141, 308, 309, 332.
S. v., 14 Nev. 72. § 571.
Clift v. S., 5 Blackf. 224. § 586.
v. S., 6 Ind. Ap. 199. § 1186.
Clifton v. S., 73 Ala. 473. §§ 815, 1196.
v. S., 26 Fla. 523. § 505.
v. S., 53 Ga. 241. §§ 1141, 1143.
S. v., 30 La. An., Pt. II, 951. § 508.
Clinch, Rex v., 2 East, P. C. 938. § 753.
S. v., 8 Ia. 401. § 1135.
Cline, P. v., 74 Cal. 575. § 618.
P. v., 44 Mich. 290. § 706.
v. S., 43 Tex. 494. § 659.
U. S. v., 26 Fed. R. 515. § 1236.
Clinger, S. v., 43 Mo. 127. § 178.
Clinton, Reg. v., Ir. L. R. 4 C. L. 6. § 536.
v. S., 33 Ohio St. 27. § 1248.
S. v., 67 Mo. 380. § 800.
Clintsman v. Northrup, 8 Cow. 45. § 35.
Cliver v. S., 45 N. J. 46. §§ 249, 443.
Clogston, S. v., 63 Vt. 215. § 862.
Cloksey, S. v., 5 Sneed, 482. § 944.
Clore v. S., 26 Tex. Ap. 624. § 162.
Close, S. v., 35 Ia. 570. §§ 1169, 1170, 1183.
Closs, Reg. v., Dears. & B. 460. §§ 661, 706, 745.
Clottu, S. v., 33 Ind. 409. §§ 74, 1261.
Cloud v. S., 36 Ark. 151. § 1237.
v. S., 81 Ga. 444. § 299.
Clough, P. v., 17 Wend. 351. § 695.
v. S., 7 Neb. 320. §§ 416, 417.
Cloughly, S. v., 73 Ia. 626. §§ 1220, 1281.
Cluck v. S., 40 Ind. 263. § 160.
Cluderoy, Reg. v., 2 C. & K. 907. § 227.
Clune v. U. S., 159 U. S. 590. §§ 952, 988.
Clynes, C. v., 150 Mass. 71. § 1181.
Coates, Rex v., 6 C. & P. 394. § 256.
v. S., 50 Ark. 330. §§ 178, 440, 442.
v. S., 2 Tex. Ap. 16. § 441.
v. S., 31 Tex. Ap. 257. §§ 504, 557.
Coats v. P., 22 N. Y. 245. § 632.
Cobb, C. v., 120 Mass. 356. § 1137.
v. S., 76 Ga. 664. § 716.
U. S. v., 43 Fed. R. 570. § 20.
Cobbs, S. v., 7 La. An. 107. § 389.
Cobden, Reg. v., 3 F. & F. 833. § 515.
Cobia v. S., 16 Ala. 781. § 362.
Cobler, P. v., 108 Cal. 538. §§ 642, 647, 648, 652, 654.
Cobletz v. S., 36 Tex. 353. § 623.
Coburn, C. v., 132 Mass. 555. § 288.
Cochran, P. v., 61 Cal. 548. § 303.
v. S., 91 Ga. 763. § 490.
v. S., 28 Tex. Ap. 422. § 339.
S. v., 10 Wash. 562. § 1112.
v. U. S., 157 U. S. 286. § 1339.
Cochrane v. S., 6 Md. 400. § 523.
Cockburn, Reg. v., 3 Cox, 543. § 464.
Cocke v. C., 13 Grat. 750. § 752.
Cocker v. S., 20 Ark. 53. § 307.
S. v., 3 Harr. 554. § 511.
Cockerell v. S., 32 Tex. Ap. 585. § 414.
Cockfield, S. v., 15 Rich. 316. § 593.
Cockran, S. v., 1 Bailey, 50. § 867.
Cockreham v. S., 7 Humph. 11. § 1026.
Cockrill v. C., 95 Ky. 22. §§ 304, 305, 311.
Cockrum v. S., 24 Tex. 394. §§ 78, 332, 1030.
Codrington, Rex v., 1 C. & P. 661. § 676.
Cody v. S., 31 Tex. Ap. 183. §§ 584, 623.
S. v., 111 N. C. 725. § 1091.
S. v., 18 Oreg. 506. § 435.
S. v., 1 Wins., i, 197. § 505.
Coe, C. v., 115 Mass. 481. §§ 679, 680, 684, 708.
S. v., 72 Me. 456. § 192.
Coelho, Reg. v., 9 Cox, 8. § 753.
Coenan, S. v., 48 Ia. 567. § 1261.
Coffee, C. v., 9 Gray, 139. § 542.
v. S., 4 Lea, 245. § 1032.
Coffelt v. S., 19 Tex. Ap. 436. § 613.
v. S., 27 Tex. Ap. 608. § 481.
Coffey, S. v., 41 Tex. 46. § 255.
v. U. S., 116 U. S. 427. § 1349.
v. U. S., 116 U. S. 436. § 890.
Coffin v. U. S., 156 U. S. 432. §§ 213, 228, 1339, 1340.
v. U. S., 162 U. S. 664. §§ 1339, 1340.
Coffing, S. v., 3 Ind. Ap. 304. § 1017.
Coffman v. C., 10 Bush, 495. § 292.
P. v., 24 Cal. 230. §§ 177, 178.
Cofield, S. v., 22 S. C. 301. § 1223.

Coggins, Reg. v., 29 L. T. 469. § 713.
v. S., 7 Port. 263. §§ 1301, 1302.
v. S., 12 Tex. Ap. 109. § 823.
Coggswell, S. v., 3 Blackf. 54. § 914.
Coghill v. S., 37 Ind. 111. § 92.
Coghlan, Reg. v., 4 F. & F. 316. § 736.
Cognovitch, S. v., 34 La. An. 529. § 256.
Cohea v. S., 9 Tex. Ap. 173. § 573.
v. S., 11 Tex. Ap. 153. § 988.
Cohen, Ex parte, 104 Cal. 524. § 951.
C. v., 120 Mass. 198. § 212.
v. P., 7 Colo. 274. §§ 745, 748, 802.
P. v., 8 Cal. 42. §§ 644, 654.
Reg. v., 11 Cox, 99. § 147.
Reg. v., 2 Den. 249. § 560.
v. S., 50 Ala. 108. § 582.
v. S., 17 Tex. 142. §§ 1283, 1285.
v. S., 20 Tex. Ap. 224. § 650.
Cohn, S. v., 9 Nev. 179. § 533.
Cohoon, S. v., 12 Ired. 178. § 942.
Cokely v. S., 4 Ia. 477. §§ 245, 268, 280.
Coker v. S., 63 Ala. 95. § 1036.
v. S., 91 Ala. 92. §§ 1234, 1260.
v. S., 20 Ark. 53. § 308.
Colam v. Pagett, 12 Q. B. D. 66. § 1162.
Colbath v. S., 2 Tex. Ap. 391. §§ 162, 362.
Colbert v. S., 91 Ga. 705. § 500.
v. S., 1 Tex. Ap. 314. § 687.
Colby, S. v., 92 Ia. 463, 61 N. W. R. 187. § 1236.
Colclough, Reg. v., L. R. 10 Ir. 241. § 808.
Coldwell v. S., 59 Tenn. 429. § 562.
Cole v. P., 84 Ill. 216. § 984.
P. v., 43 N. Y. 508. § 558.
P. v., 4 Park. Cr. 35. §§ 139, 342.
Reg. v., 3 Cox, 340. § 562.
Rex v., 1 Russ. Cr. 700. § 1155.
v. S., 10 Ark. 318. §§ 268, 275.
v. S., 59 Ark. 50. § 400.
v. S., 6 Baxt. 239. § 1098.
v. S., 9 Tex. 42. § 1302.
v. S., 16 Tex. Ap. 461. § 650.
v. S., 28 Tex. Ap. 536. § 1303.
S. v., 90 Ind. 112. § 813.
S. v., 63 Ia. 695. § 417.
S. v., 2 McCord, 1. §§ 93, 96.
S. v., 2 McCord, 117. § 992.
S. v., 39 N. J. 324. § 960.
S. v., 19 Wis. 129. § 808.
v. Tucker, 6 Tex. 266. § 11.
U. S. v., 5 McLean, 513. §§ 968, 981, 990.
Colee v. S., 75 Ind. 511. § 160.
Coleman v. C., 25 Grat. 865. § 800.
C. v., 157 Mass. 460. § 33.
v. Frum, 4 Ill. 377. § 1126.
P. v., 4 Cal. 46. § 46.
v. S., 13 Ala. 602. § 1303.
v. S., 20 Ala. 51. § 1303.
v. S., 26 Fla. 61. § 409.
v. S., 28 Ga. 78. § 241.
v. S., 44 Tex. 109. § 577.
v. S., 2 Tex. Ap. 512. § 509.
v. S., 26 Tex. Ap. 252. § 505.
v. S., 26 Tex. Ap. 673. § 5.
Coleman, S. v., 27 La. An. 691. §§ 173, 174, 178.
S. v., 5 Port. 32. § 208.
S. v., 6 S. C. 185. § 333.
S. v., 17 S. C. 473. § 381.
S. v., 20 S. C. 441. §§ 167, 178.
Collberg, C. v., 119 Mass. 350. § 249.
Collens, S. v., 37 La. An. 607. § 604.
Collett, Rex v., Russ. & Ry. 498. § 495.
Colley, Reg. v., 2 M. & Rob. 475. § 520.
Collicott, Rex v., Russ. & Ry. 212, 4 Taunt. 300. §§ 752, 781.
Collier, P. v., 1 Mich. 137. § 878.
v. S., 55 Ala. 125. § 914.
v. S., 68 Ala. 499. § 1034.
v. S., 69 Ala. 247. § 368.
v. S., 13 Ark. 676. § 424.
v. S., 20 Ark. 36. § 429.
v. S., 39 Ga. 31. § 275.
Collings, Reg. v., 9 C. & P. 456. § 1048.
Collingwood, Reg. v., 12 Q. B. 681. § 1129.
Collins v. C., 3 Serg. & R. 220. § 966.
C. v., 12 Allen, 181. §§ 556, 562.
C. v., 2 Cush. 556. § 1326.
C. v., 16 Gray, 29. § 1140.
C. v., 138 Mass. 483. § 596.
v. P., 39 Ill. 233. §§ 480, 543, 582, 585, 588.
P. v., 53 Cal. 185. 501.
P. v., 102 Cal. 345. § 1060.
P. v., 3 Mich. 343. § 1210.
Reg. v., L. & C. 471. §§ 224, 226.
Reg. v., 2 M. & Rob. 461. §§ 763, 800.
v. S., 14 Ala. 608. § 1087.
v. S., 33 Ala. 434. § 716.
v. S., 70 Ala. 19. § 1292.
v. S., 78 Ala. 433. § 858.
v. S., 33 Fla. 429. § 42.
v. S., 33 Fla. 446. § 859.
v. S., 73 Ga. 76. § 1153.
v. S., 88 Ga. 347. § 213.
v. S., 3 Heisk. 14. §§ 227, 236.
v. S., 15 Lea, 68. § 563.
v. S., 43 Tex. 577. § 605.
v. S., 20 Tex. Ap. 197. § 509.
v. S., 24 Tex. Ap. 141. § 573.
S. v., 3 Hawks, 191. § 778.
S. v., 11 Ia. 141. §§ 1229, 1249.
S. v., 32 Ia. 36. § 307.
S. v., 1 McCord, 355. § 17.
S. v., 81 Mo. 652, 86 Mo. 245. § 365.
S. v., 72 N. C. 144. § 596.
S. v., 115 N. C. 716. § 799.
S. v., 4 N. Dak. 433. § 653.
S. v., 16 R. I. 371. § 1197.
S. v., 62 Vt. 195. §§ 845, 860, 861.
v. Thomas, 1 F. & F. 416. § 839.
Collison, P. v., 85 Mich. 105. § 46.
Rex v., 4 C. & P. 565. § 197.
Collum v. S., 10 Tex. Ap. 708. §§ 1087, 1094.
Colly v. S., 55 Ala. 85. § 678.
S. v., 39 La. An. 841. § 678.
Collyer, S. v., 17 Nev. 275. §§ 268, 271.
Colman v. S., 26 Tex. Ap. 252. § 505.
Colmer, Reg. v., 9 Cox, 506. § 1152.

Colt, P. v., 3 Hill (N. Y.), 432. § 377.
Colter, S. v., 6 R. I. 195. § 511.
Colton, C. v., 8 Gray, 488. §§ 54, 1309, 1319.
P. v., 2 Utah, 457. § 1132.
Columbia, S. v., 17 S. C. 80. § 1217.
Columbus v. Cutcomp, 61 Ia. 672. §§ 6, 75, 1209, 1217.
U. S. v., 5 Cranch, C. C. 304. § 1137.
Colvin v. S., 11 Ind. 361. § 768.
v. S., 127 Ind. 403. § 651.
Colwell, S. v., 43 Minn. 378. § 588.
S. v., 3 R. I. 284. § 1219.
Combs v. C., 93 Ky. 313. § 526.
v. S., 75 Ind. 215. § 423.
S. v., 47 Kan. 136. § 654.
Comer, Rex v., 1 Leach, 36. § 511.
v. S., 62 Ala. 320. § 1019.
v. S., 26 Tex. Ap. 509. § 1302.
Comerford, U. S. v., 25 Fed. R. 902. § 1332.
Comfort v. P., 54 Ill. 404. §§ 617, 725.
Comings, S. v., 28 Vt. 508. § 1235.
Comly v. Hillegass, 94 Pa. St. 132. § 1297.
Commander v. S., 60 Ala. 1. § 417.
Commercial Exch. Bank v. McLeod, 65 Ia. 665. § 611.
Commissioners, S. v., 3 Hill (S. C.), 149. §§ 1186, 1192.
v. Taylor, 21 N. Y. 173. § 1219.
U. S. v., 6 Mackey, 409. § 1228.
Common Pleas of Morris Co., S. v., 36 N. J. 72. § 1210.
Compagnie Generale Transatlantique, P. v., 107 U. S. 59. § 35.
Compton, Rex v., 3 C. & P. 418. § 511.
Rex v., 7 C. & P. 139. § 502.
v. S., 13 Tex. Ap. 271. §§ 1099, 1124.
S. v., 77 Wis. 460. §§ 729, 731, 732.
Comstock v. Gage, 91 Ill. 328. § 649.
P. v., 49 Mich. 330. § 279
v. S., 14 Neb. 205. §§ 450, 459, 1153.
S. v., 46 Ia. 265. §§ 217, 458.
Conable, S. v., 81 Ia. 60. §§ 1051, 1053.
Conahan, S. v., 10 Wash. 268. § 316.
Conant, C. v., 6 Gray, 482. § 1273.
Concannon, C. v., 5 Allen, 502. §§ 543, 644, 656*a*.
Conde, Reg. v., 10 Cox, 547. §§ 286, 349.
v. S., — Tex. Ap. —, 34 S. W. R. 286. § 396.
Cone, C. v., 2 Mass. 132. § 786.
S. v., 1 Jones, 18. § 455.
Coney, Reg. v., 8 Q. B. D. 534. §§ 196, 249, 1013.
v. S., 2 Tex. Ap. 62. § 260.
Congdon, P. v., 77 Mich. 351. § 485.
Conger v. Crabtree, 88 Ia. 536. § 765.
S. v., 14 Ind. 396. § 1325.
Congleton, P. v., 44 Cal. 92. §§ 257, 260, 271.
Conkling, S. v., 19 Cal. 501. § 102.
Conkright, S. v., 58 Ia. 338. § 1114.
Conkwright v. P., 35 Ill. 204. § 617.
Conlee v. S., 14 Tex. Ap. 222. § 1057.
S. v., 25 Ia. 237. § 21.
Conley, C. v., 1 Allen, 6. § 1018.
v. S., 85 Ga. 348. § 846.
Conley v. S., 5 W. Va. 522. § 1272.
S. v., 39 Me. 78. §§ 320, 365, 380, 381.
T. v., 2 Wyo. 324. § 212.
Conlin, S. v., 27 Vt. 318. § 1207.
Conlon, S. v., 65 Conn. 478. § 44.
Conn v. P., 116 Ill. 458. §§ 275, 276, 325.
Connaghan v. P., 88 Ill. 460. §§ 267, 303.
Connaughty v. S., 1 Wis. 159. §§ 194, 291, 938.
Connell v. S., 46 Ind. 446. § 1273.
v. S., 2 Tex. Ap. 422. §§ 547, 552.
S. v., 38 N. H. 81. § 1273.
Connelly, S. v., 63 Me. 212. § 1229.
S. v., 104 N. C. 794. § 906.
Conner v. C., 13 Bush, 714. § 389.
v. C., 2 Va. Cas. 30. § 873.
Rex v., 7 C. & P. 438. § 347.
v. S., 25 Ga. 515. § 200.
v. S., 14 Mo. 561. § 502.
v. S., 4 Yerg. 136. §§ 139, 333, 342.
S. v., 107 N. C. 931. §§ 46, 190.
S. v., 30 Ohio St. 405. § 1248.
U. S. v., 1 Cranch, C. C. 102. § 1310.
Conners v. S., 45 N. J. 340. § 499.
v. S., 47 Wis. 523. § 441.
Connolly v. Boston, 117 Mass. 64. § 1323.
S. v., 3 Rich. 337. § 992.
Connor v. P., 18 Colo. 373. § 118.
P. v., 17 Cal. 354. § 602.
P. v., 126 N. Y. 278. § 440.
Reg. v., 2 Cox, 65. §§ 518, 526, 529.
v. S., 29 Fla. 455. §§ 696, 704.
v. S., 24 Tex. Ap. 245. §§ 546, 557.
S. v., 5 Coldw. 311. § 602.
S. v., 59 Ia. 357. § 278.
S. v., 7 La. An. 379. § 90.
Connors v. S., 45 N. J. 211. § 268.
v. U. S., 158 U. S. 408. §§ 946, 950.
Conolly's Case, 2 Lewin, 229. § 145.
Conolly v. P., 4 Ill. 474. §§ 269, 281.
Conrad v. S., 70 Miss. 733. § 1232.
T. v., 1 Dak. 363. §§ 255, 262, 271.
U. S. v., 59 Fed. R. 458. § 1334.
Conroy, P. v., 97 N. Y. 62. §§ 123, 359, 361.
Converse, In re, 42 Fed. R. 217. § 629.
P. v., 74 Mich. 478. § 629.
Conway, S. v., 18 Mo. 321. § 571.
Cony, C. v., 2 Mass. 523. § 914.
Conyers v. S., 50 Ga. 103. §§ 59, 1314.
Coogan, Rex v., 2 East, P. C. 1001. § 750.
Cook, C. v., 12 Met. 93. §§ 1104, 1111, 1133.
C. v., 1 Rob. (Va.) 729. § 881.
v. Ellis, 6 Hill (N. Y.), 466. § 11.
v. Hart, 146 U. S. 183. § 118.
v. P., 51 Ill. 143. § 1129.
P. v., 61 Cal. 478. § 1101.
P. v., 39 Mich. 236. §§ 140, 292.
P. v., 96 Mich. 368. § 1106*a*.
Reg. v., 21 L. T. 216. § 1152.
Rex v., 2 East, P. C. 616. § 594.
v. S., 11 Ga. 53. § 1092.
v. S., 77 Ga. 96. § 329.
v. S., 16 Lea, 461. § 609.

Cook v. S., 49 Miss. 8. § 588.
v. S., 72 Miss. 517. § 381.
v. S., 4 Tex. Ap. 265. § 596.
v. S., 11 Tex. Ap. 19. § 1033.
v. S., 14 Tex. Ap. 96. § 199.
v. S., 22 Tex. Ap. 511. § 1145.
S. v., 52 Ind. 574. §§ 766, 796.
S. v., 65 Ia. 560. § 460.
S. v., 92 Ia. 483, 61 N. W. R. 185. §§ 455, 458.
S. v., 20 La. An. 145. §§ 476, 482.
S. v., 42 La. An. 85. § 436.
S. v., Phill. 535. § 295.
v. U. S., 138 U. S. 157. § 78.
Cooke, Reg. v., 8 C. & P. 582. §§ 767, 781.
Reg. v., 8 C. & P. 586. § 808.
Reg. v., 2 Den. 462. § 859.
Reg. v., 1 F. & F. 64. § 696.
Reg. v., L. R. 1 C. C. 295. § 556.
v. S., 83 Ind. 402. § 684.
S. v., 24 Minn. 247. § 1210.
Cooksie v. S., 26 Tex. Ap. 72. §§ 585, 636.
Cool v. S., 16 Ind. 355. §§ 1256, 1273.
Cooley, C. v., 6 Gray, 350. § 241.
C. v., 10 Pick. 37. §§ 95, 1167.
v. S., 55 Ala. 162. § 1074.
v. S., 88 Tenn. 250. §§ 273, 274.
Coolidge v. Choate, 11 Met. 79. § 1310.
C. v., 138 Mass. 193. § 1243.
U. S. v., 1 Wheat. 415. § 14.
Coombes v. S., 17 Tex. Ap. 258. § 548.
Coombs, S. v., 32 Me. 529. § 1277.
S. v., 55 Me. 477. §§ 550, 562, 570.
U. S. v., 12 Pet. 72. § 590.
Coon, P. v., 45 Cal. 672. § 592.
P. v., 15 Wend. 277. §§ 909, 913, 915, 916, 917.
S. v., 14 Minn. 456. § 909.
S. v., 18 Minn. 518. § 588.
Coonan, S. v., 82 Ia. 400. § 1204.
Cooper's Case, Cro. Car. 544. §§ 299, 312.
Cooper, C. v., 5 Allen, 495. §§ 426, 431.
C. v., 130 Mass. 285. § 635.
v. Johnson, 81 Mo. 483. § 194.
P. v., 6 Hill (N. Y.), 516. § 1185.
P. v., 13 Wend. 379. §§ 922, 924.
Reg. v., 3 C. & K. 318. § 619.
Reg. v., 3 Cox, 547. §§ 730, 741.
Reg. v., 1 Den. 459. § 58.
Reg. v., L. R. 2 C. C. 123. § 629.
Reg. v., 2 Q. B. D. 510. § 678.
Reg. v., 1 Russ. Cr. 405. § 995.
Reg. v., 1 Q. B. D. 19. § 691.
Reg. v., 8 Q. B. 533. § 1055.
Rex v., 5 C. & P. 535. §§ 200, 521.
v. S., 87 Ala. 135. § 514.
v. S., 90 Ala. 641. § 1119.
v. S., 37 Ark. 412. § 846.
v. S., 88 Ga. 441. § 1264.
v. S., 89 Ga. 222. § 578.
v. S., 22 Tex. Ap. 419. § 448.
v. S., 25 Tex. Ap. 530. § 942.
v. S., 26 Tex. Ap. 575. § 946.
v. S., 29 Tex. Ap. 8. § 617.
Cooper, S. v., 5 Blackf. 258. § 54.
S. v., 5 Day, 250. §§ 753, 757.
S. v., 32 La. An. 1084. § 307.
S. v., 16 Mo. 551. § 1276.
S. v., 71 Mo. 436. § 336.
S. v., 103 Mo. 266. § 1083.
S. v., 101 N. C. 684. § 1232.
S. v., 22 N. J. 52. § 1146.
S. v., 16 Vt. 551. §§ 505, 1086.
S. v., 26 W. Va. 338. § 1234.
v. Witham, Lev. 247. § 11.
Cooster, S. v., 10 Ia. 453. §§ 1286, 1306, 1307, 1308, 1309.
Coots, Reg. v., 2 Cox, 188. §§ 514, 620.
Copeland, Reg. v., Car. & M. 516. § 678.
v. S., 97 Ala. 30. § 676.
v. S., 7 Humph. 479. §§ 306, 342.
v. S., 23 Miss. 257. § 876.
S. v., 86 N. C. 691. § 550.
Copeley, T. v., 1 N. M. 571. § 1310.
Copenhaven v. S., 15 Ga. 264. § 511.
Copp, S. v., 34 Kan. 522. § 1227.
Coppack v. S., 36 Ind. 513. § 877.
Coppenburg, S. v., 2 Strobh. 273. § 724.
Copperman v. P., 56 N. Y. 591. §§ 615, 726.
Copping v. S., 7 Tex. Ap. 61. § 1028.
Corbett, S. v., 1 Jones, 264. §§ 292, 699.
S. v., 12 R. I. 288. § 1059.
v. T., 1 Wash. T. 431. § 1216.
T. v., 3 Mont. 50. § 1120.
Corcoran v. P., 27 Ill. Ap. 638. § 1129.
Cordell v. S., 22 Ind. 1. § 380.
Cordway v. S., 25 Tex. Ap. 405. § 858.
Core v. James, L. R. 7 Q. B. 135. § 128.
Corfield, S. v., 46 Kan. 207. § 758.
Corkin, C. v., 136 Mass. 429. § 1150.
Corley v. S., 95 Ga. 465. § 271.
v. S., 3 Tex. Ap. 412. § 1028.
S. v., 4 Baxt. 410. § 758.
Corliss, S. v., 85 Ia. 18. §§ 505, 1093.
Corll, S. v., 73 Ind. 535. § 1247.
Corneille v. S., 16 Ind. 232. § 263.
Cornelison v. C., 84 Ky. 583. § 255.
Cornelius v. C., 15 B. Mon. 539. § 307.
v. S., 13 Tex. Ap. 349. §§ 449, 452.
Cornell, P. v., 16 Cal. 187. § 18.
v. S., 6 Lea, 624. § 242.
U. S. v., 2 Mason, 91. § 329.
Cornhauser, S. v., 74 Wis. 42. § 656.
Corning, In re, 51 Fed. R. 205. § 963.
v. Abbott, 54 N. H. 469. § 1236.
S. v., 44 Kan. 442. § 905.
Cornish, C. v., 6 Binn. 249. § 867.
Reg. v., Dears. 425. § 555.
Cornwall, Rex v., Russ. & Ry. 336. § 1152.
Cornwell v. S., Mart. & Y. 147. §§ 159, 160.
Corryell, In re, 22 Cal. 178. § 750.
Corson, S. v., 59 Me. 137. § 872.
Corwin v. Walton, 18 Mo. 71. § 11.
Cory, Reg. v., 10 Cox, 23. § 538.
Cosgrove, S. v., 42 La. An. 753. § 303.
Coss, S. v., 12 Wash. 673. §§ 546, 604.
Cossell, S. v., 2 Har. & G. 407. § 596.
Cosser, Reg. v., 13 Cox, 187. § 629.

Cost v. S., 96 Ala. 60. § 1270.
Costello, C. v., 120 Mass. 358. §§ 757, 762, 769.
P. v., 15 Cal. 350. § 411.
S. v., 62 Conn. 128. §§ 819, 832.
Costen, S. v., 1 Houst. Cr. C. 340. § 339.
Costin, S. v., 89 N. C. 511. § 626.
Costley, C. v., 118 Mass. 1. §§ 292, 377, 378, 395.
v. S., 48 Md. 175. § 417.
v. S., 14 Tex. Ap. 156. § 751.
Cotesworth, Reg. v., 6 Mod. 172. § 235.
Cothran v. S., 39 Miss. 541. § 852.
Cotta, P. v., 49 Cal. 166. §§ 195, 358.
Cotteral, P. v., 18 Johns. 115. § 526.
Cottingham, U. S. v., 2 Blatch. 470. § 1335.
Cottle, S. v., 15 Me. 473. § 1273.
Cotton, Reg. v., 12 Cox, 400. § 418.
v. S., 31 Miss. 504. §§ 303, 339.
v. S., 4 Tex. 260. § 246.
S. v., 29 Minn. 187. § 1184.
S. v., 6 Tex. 425. § 1283.
Cottrill, S. v., 31 W. Va. 162. § 1272.
Couch v. S., 28 Ga. 367. § 766.
Coughlin, C. v., 14 Gray, 389. § 145.
C. v., 123 Mass. 436. § 929.
Cougot, S. v., 121 Mo. 458. § 1117.
Couk, T. v., 2 Dak. 188. § 413.
Coulson, Reg. v., 1 Den. 592. § 675.
v. S., 16 Tex. Ap. 189. § 1061.
Coulter, U. S. v., 1 Cranch, C. C. 203. § 1137.
Council, S. v., 1 Overt. 305. § 826.
Counts v. S., 37 Tex. 593. § 609.
County, Rex v., 2 Russ. Cr. 230. § 195.
County Com'rs, S. v., 97 N. C. 388. §§ 909, 915.
Courier, P. v., 79 Mich. 366. §§ 450, 451, 452, 454, 463, 464.
Court, The, P. v., 83 N. Y. 436. § 666.
Courtenay, Reg. v., 5 Cox, 218. § 508.
Courtney, P. v., 31 Hun, 199, 94 N. Y. 490. §§ 864, 865.
v. S., 3 Tex. Ap. 257. § 592.
v. S., 13 Tex. Ap. 502. § 274.
Cousins, C. v., 2 Leigh, 708. § 552.
Covenhaven v. S., 1 N. J. 258. § 836.
Covey v. S., 23 Tex. Ap. 388. § 873.
Covington v. S., 28 Tex. Ap. 225. § 1298.
S. v., 2 Bailey, 569. § 118.
S. v., 70 N. C. 71. § 820.
S. v., 94 N. C. 913. §§ 761, 796.
Covy v. S., 4 Port. 186. § 1294.
Cowan, S. v., 7 Ired. 239. §§ 478, 480.
Coward v. S., 6 Tex. Ap. 59. § 416.
Cowdin, S. v., 28 Kan. 269. § 678.
Cowell, Rex v., 2 East, P. C. 617. § 715.
S. v., 4 Ired. 231. § 1095.
S. v., 12 Nev. 337. § 506.
Cowen v. P., 14 Ill. 348. §§ 687, 697, 701.
Cowles, P. v., 4 Keyes, 38. § 9.
v. S., 50 Ala. 454. § 663.
Cowley v. P., 83 N. Y. 464. §§ 58, 180.
v. Rushville, 60 Ind. 327. § 1206.
v. S., 10 Lea, 282. § 239.
Cox, Ex parte, 19 Ark. 688. § 1223.
Cox, Ex parte, 28 Tex. Ap. 537. § 1232.
C. v., 7 Allen, 577. § 834.
v. P., 82 Ill. 191. § 220.
v. P., 109 Ill. 457. § 1126.
v. P., 80 N. Y. 500. §§ 355, 361.
P. v., 40 Cal. 275. § 652.
P. v., 45 Cal. 342. § 844.
Reg. v., 1 C. & K. 494. § 540.
Reg. v., 3 Cox, 58. § 258.
Reg. v., 1 F. & F. 90. § 724.
Rex v., 2 Burr. 785. § 1321.
Rex v., 4 C. & P. 538. 993.
Rex v., Russ. & Ry. 362. § 256.
Rex v., 1 Leach, 71. § 881.
v. S., 99 Ala. 162. § 1097.
v. S., 3 Blackf. 193. §§ 115, 1195.
v. S., 66 Miss. 14. § 758.
v. S., 43 Tex. 101. § 546.
v. S., 5 Tex. Ap. 493. § 353.
v. S., 8 Tex. Ap. 254. §§ 412, 988.
v. S., 13 Tex. Ap. 479. § 872.
S. v., 88 Ind. 254. § 182.
S. v., 82 Me. 417. § 1181.
S. v., 29 Mo. 475. § 1270.
S. v., 65 Mo. 29. §§ 194, 205.
S. v., 110 N. C. 503. § 333.
S. v., 2 Taylor, 165. § 1131.
S. v., 23 W. Va. 797. § 1253.
Coxhead, Reg. v., 1 C. & K. 623. § 1152.
Coxwell v. S., 66 Ga. 309. § 417.
Coy, Ex parte, 127 U. S. 731. § 945.
In re, 31 Fed. R. 794. § 84.
C. v., 157 Mass. 200. §§ 380, 388.
S. v., 2 Aikens, 181. §§ 79, 271.
Coyle, C. v., 160 Pa. St. 36. § 906.
S. v., 41 Wis. 267. § 759.
Coyne v. P., 124 Ill. 17. §§ 869, 893, 894.
Cozins, Rex v., 6 C. & P. 351. §§ 450, 1153.
Cozlett's Case, 2 East, P. C. 556. § 548.
Cozzens, S. v., 42 La. An. 1069. § 70.
Crab, Reg. v., 11 Cox, 85. § 667.
Crabb v. S., 88 Ga. 584. § 1236.
Crabtree v. S., 1 Lea, 267. § 303.
v. S., 30 Ohio St. 382. §§ 128, 1257.
S. v., 27 Mo. 232. § 1248.
Cracknell, Reg. v., 10 Cox, 408. § 737.
Craddock, Reg. v., 2 Den. 31. § 609.
v. S., 18 Tex. Ap. 567. § 1216.
S. v., 44 Kan. 489. § 1021.
Craemer, S. v., 12 Wash. 217. § 408.
Craft v. C., 81 Ky. 250. § 431.
v. S., 3 Kan. 450. §§ 353, 358, 391.
S. v., 72 Mo. 456. §§ 126, 224.
Craig, Pennsylvania v., Addis. 190. §§ 996, 1001.
v. S., 18 Tex. Ap. 321. § 464.
v. S., 30 Tex. Ap. 619. § 414.
v. S., 31 Tex. Ap. 29. § 908.
S. v., 23 Ind. 185. § 91.
S. v., 80 Me. 85. §§ 46, 85.
U. S. v., 4 Wash. C. C. 729. § 810.
Craige, S. v., 89 N. C. 475. § 548.
Cram, S. v., 84 Me. 271. § 20.
Crammey, S. v., 17 Minn. 72. § 1306.
Cramp, Reg. v., 5 Q. B. D. 307. § 1148.
Crampton v. S., 37 Ark. 108. § 1257.

Crandall v. Dawson, 6 Ill. 556. § 892.
v. S., 10 Conn. 339. § 46.
v. S., 28 Ohio St. 479. § 44.
Crane, C. v., 158 Mass. 218. § 34.
C. v., 162 Mass. 506. § 34.
v. S., 94 Tenn. 86. §§ 1083, 1084.
v. S., 41 Tex. 494. § 267.
v. S., 26 Tex. Ap. 482. § 648.
v. S., 30 Tex. Ap. 464. § 1057.
S. v., 54 Kan. 251. § 971.
S. v., 95 N. C. 619. § 311.
U. S. v., 4 McLean, 317. § 215.
Crank, S. v., 2 Bailey, 66. §§ 215, 216.
S. v., 75 Mo. 406. § 617.
Cranor v. S., 39 Ind. 64. § 13.
Craton, S. v., 6 Ired. 164. §§ 332, 340, 347, 345.
Crawford v. P., 12 Colo. 290. § 345.
v. S., 44 Ala. 382. § 499.
v. S., 12 Ga. 142. § 391.
v. S., 94 Ga. 772. § 1032.
v. S., 2 Ind. 112. § 53.
v. S., 2 Ind. 132. § 596.
v. S., 15 Lea, 343. § 1196.
v. S., Minor, 143. § 84.
v. S., 31 Tex. Ap. 51. § 803.
S. v., 2 Dev. 425. § 435.
S. v., 34 Ia. 40. § 1112.
S. v., 11 Kan. 32. §§ 101, 179, 320.
S. v., 13 La. An. 300. § 796.
S. v., 99 Mo. 74. § 533.
S. v., 115 Mo. 620. § 414.
S. v., 33 S. C. 330. § 511.
S. v., 39 S. C. 343. § 719.
Crawley v. C., 123 Pa. St. 275. § 1223.
S. v., 103 N. C. 353. § 683.
Creadon, C. v., 162 Mass. 466. § 454.
Crecilius, U. S. v., 34 Fed. R. 30. § 1339.
Creditor, S. v., 44 Kan. 565. § 36.
Creed, C. v., 8 Gray, 387. §§ 226, 228, 266, 268, 270.
Reg. v., 1 C. & K. 63. § 640.
Creek v. S., 24 Ind. 151. §§ 306, 368.
Creevey, Rex v., 1 Mau. & S. 273. §§ 1051, 1052.
Cregor, C. v., 7 Grat. 591. § 1097.
Crenshaw, P. v., 46 Cal. 65. § 214.
S. v., 45 La. An. 496. § 511.
S. v., 22 Mo. 457. § 1162.
Creson, S. v., 38 Mo. 372. § 617.
Crespigny, Rex v., 1 Esp. 280. § 868.
Crespin, Reg. v., 11 Q. B. 913. § 252.
Cresswell, Reg. v., 1 Q. B. D. 446. § 1074.
Creswell v. S., 14 Tex. Ap. 1. § 307.
Crews v. P., 120 Ill. 317. § 316.
P. v., 102 Cal. 174. § 426.
v. S., 3 Coldw. 350. §§ 468, 474.
Cribbs, Pennsylvania v., Addis. 277. §§ 993, 995.
Crick, Reg. v., 1 F. & F. 519. § 287.
Crilley v. S., 20 Wis. 231. § 617.
Crimmins, S. v., 31 Kan. 376. § 1276.
Cripland, Rex v., 11 Mod. 387. §§ 896, 947.
Crisham, Reg. v., Car. & M. 187. § 449.
Crisp, Rex v., 1 B. & Ald. 282. § 932.
S. v., 126 Mo. 605. § 173.
Crissie, P. v., 4 Denio, 525. §§ 669, 694.
Critchett, S. v., 1 Lea, 271. § 914.
Crocheron v. S., 86 Ala. 64. § 556.
Crocker, Rex v., Russ. & Ry. 97. §§ 760, 767.
v. S., 49 Ark. 60. § 1248.
Crocket v. S., 33 Ind. 416. § 1321.
Crockett, Rex v., 4 C. & P., 544. § 426.
v. S., 49 Ga. 185. § 455.
v. S., 5 Tex. Ap. 526. § 546.
Croell v. S., 25 Tex. Ap. 596. § 1265.
Croft, S. v., 15 Tex. 575. § 268.
Crofton v. S., 79 Ga. 584. § 554.
v. S., 25 Ohio St. 249. § 1142.
Crofts v. P., 3 Ill. 442. § 752.
Crogan, S. v., 8 Ia. 523. §§ 1272, 1306, 1307.
Croghan v. S., 22 Wis. 444. § 1115.
Croker v. S., 47 Ala. 53. § 597.
Cromley, C. v., 1 Ashm. 179. §§ 92, 93.
Cron, S. v., 23 Minn. 140. § 1228.
Crone, Rex v., Jebb, 47. § 715.
v. S., 49 Ind. 538. § 1270.
Cronin v. P., 82 N. Y. 318. § 66.
P. v., 34 Cal. 191. § 377.
P. v., 80 Mich. 646. § 904.
v. S., 30 Tex. Ap. 278. § 1313.
S. v., 64 Conn. 293. § 426.
v. Stoddard, 97 N. Y. 271. § 1223.
Cronk v. P., 131 Ill. 56. § 865.
Crook, Reg. v., 1 F. & F. 521. § 287.
Crooker, S. v., 95 Mo. 389. § 708.
Crookham v. S., 5 W. Va. 510. § 404.
Croom v S., 71 Ala. 14. § 548.
v. S., 85 Ga. 718. § 328.
v. S., 25 Tex. Ap. 556. § 1232.
Crosby v. Hawthorne, 25 Ala. 221. § 84.
v. Leng, 12 East, 409. § 11.
v. P., 137 Ill. 325. §§ 123, 161.
U. S. v., 1 Hughes, 448. § 948.
Crosman v. Lynn, 121 Mass. 301. § 1322.
Cross v. Guthery, 2 Root, 90. § 11.
v. North Carolina, 132 U. S. 131. § 790.
v. P., 18 Colo. 321. § 1315.
v. P., 47 Ill. 152. §§ 199, 758, 793, 796, 797, 808.
v. P., 10 Mich. 24. § 1126.
Reg. v., 1 F. & F. 510. § 1076.
Rex v., 2 C. & P. 483. § 1173.
v. S., 68 Ala. 476. § 332.
v. S., 138 Ind. 254. § 461.
v. S., 17 Tex. Ap. 476. §§ 1153, 1154.
v. S., 55 Wis. 261. §§ 160, 257, 274.
S. v., 2 Humph. 301. § 1299.
S. v., 12 Ia. 66. §§ 440, 454, 455, 463.
S. v., 68 Ia. 180. § 354.
S. v., 4 Jones, 421. § 96.
S. v., 27 Mo. 332. § 162.
S. v., 101 N. C. 770. §§ 761, 773, 790, 798.
U. S. v., 1 MacAr. 149. § 18.
Crosset, S. v., 81 N. C. 579. §§ 113, 135.
Crossley, C. v., 162 Mass. 515. § 1270.
Rex v., 7 T. R. 315. §§ 859, 865.
Crossmire, C. v., 156 Pa. St. 304. § 420.
Crosswell v. P., 13 Mich. 427. §§ 448, 464.

Croswell, P. v., 3 Johns. Cas. 337. §§ 1042, 1070.
Croteau, S. v., 23 Vt. 14. § 1276.
Crouse v. S., 16 Ark. 566. § 1135.
Crow v. S., 41 Tex. 468. §§ 232, 233.
v. S., 33 Tex. Ap. 264. § 409.
S. v., 1 Ired. 375. § 232.
S. v., 53 Kan. 662. § 1281.
S. v., 107 Mo. 341. §§ 594, 606.
Crow Dog, Ex parte, 109 U. S. 556. § 1338*a*.
U. S. v., 3 Dak. 106. §§ 139, 316, 332.
Crowder v. S., 8 Lea, 669. § 267.
S. v., 39 Tex. 47. § 1308.
Crowe v. P., 92 Ill. 231. § 1043.
Crowell, C. v., 156 Mass. 215. § 44.
v. Merrick, 19 Me. 392. § 11.
S. v., 25 Me. 171. § 1281.
S. v., 30 Me. 115. § 1273.
S. v., 116 N. C. 1052. § 1113.
Crowey, P. v., 56 Cal. 36. § 332.
Crowhurst, Reg. v., 1 C. & K. 370. § 618.
Crowley v. Christensen, 137 U. S. 86. § 1200.
v. C., 11 Met. 575. § 511.
C. v., 145 Mass. 430. § 1321.
P. v., 100 Cal. 478. § 505.
P. v., 90 Mich. 366. § 1264.
P. v., 102 N. Y. 234. § 450.
S. v., 13 Ala. 172. §§ 1097, 1099.
S. v., 33 La. An. 782. § 416.
S. v., 60 Me. 103. § 83.
S. v., 39 N. J. 264. §§ 84, 683, 905.
S. v., 41 Wis. 271. §§ 682, 971, 975.
Crowner, S. v., 56 Mo. 147. § 1130.
Crowther, Rex v., 5 C. & P. 316. §§ 753, 770.
Croxdale v. S., 1 Head, 139. § 794.
Crozier, S. v., 12 Nev. 300. § 382.
T. v., 6 Dak. 8. §§ 815, 829.
Cruger, P. v., 102 N. Y. 510. §§ 562. 569.
Cruikshank, S. v., 6 Blackf. 62. §§ 867, 880.
U. S. v., 92 U. S. 254. §§ 542, 961, 984, 1030.
Cruiser v. S., 18 N. J. 206. §§ 5, 836.
Crum v. S., 64 Miss. 1. § 292.
Crumb, S. v., 68 Mo. 206. § 858.
Crumbley v. S., 61 Ga. 582. § 233.
Crumes v. S., 28 Tex. Ap. 516. § 281.
Crummey, S. v., 17 Minn. 72. § 12.
Crump v. C., 75 Va. 922. § 865.
v. C., 84 Va. 927. § 963.
Rex v., 1 C. & P. 658. § 566.
Crumpler, S. v., 88 N. C. 647. § 1193.
Crumpton v. Newman, 12 Ala. 199. § 923.
Reg. v., Car. & M. 597. § 348.
Crunden, Rex v., 2 Camp. 89. § 1136.
Crupper, C. v., 3 Dana, 466. §§ 1306, 1308.
Cruse v. Aden, 121 Ill. 231. § 1235.
Reg. v., 8 C. & P. 541. §§ 161, 195, 274.
Crusen v. S., 10 Ohio St. 258. §§ 873, 892.
Crutcher v. Kentucky, 141 U. S. 47. § 44.
Crutchley, Rex v., 5 C. & P. 133. §§ 137, 826.
Cruttenden, Reg. v., 6 Jur. 267. § 619.
Crutz v. S., 4 Ind. 385. § 1223.
Cryer, Reg. v., Dears. & B. 324. § 552.
S. v., 20 Ark. 64. § 272.
Cudd v. S., 28 Tex. Ap. 124. § 381.
Cuddihi, P. v., 54 Cal. 53. § 279.
Cuddy, Reg. v., 1 C. & K. 210. §§ 205, 324.
Culkin, Rex v., 5 C. & P. 121. § 378.
Cullen, Reg. v., 9 C. & P. 681. § 1080.
Rex v., 5 C. & P. 116. § 753.
v. S., 42 Conn. 55. § 93.
Culler, S. v., 82 Mo. 623. § 309.
Cullins, C. v., 1 Mass. 116. §§ 546, 553.
S. v., 53 Kan. 100. §§ 199, 1241.
Culliton v. U. S., 5 Ct. of Cl. 627. § 1357.
Cullum, Reg. v., L. R. 2 C. C. 28. § 634.
Culp v. C., 109 Pa. St. 363. § 646.
v. S., 1 Port. 33. § 543.
Culver v. S., 86 Ga. 197. § 680.
Cumberland, etc. Co. v. Portland, 56 Me. 77. § 184.
Cummerford, P. v., 58 Mich. 328. § 1231.
Cummings v. C., 2 Va. Cas. 128. §§ 543, 582.
v. Missouri, 4 Wall. 277. §§ 78, 79.
P. v., — Cal. —, 46 Pac. R. 284. § 660.
v. S., 1 Harr. & J. 340. § 553.
S. v., 33 Conn. 260. §§ 553, 571.
S. v., 5 La. An. 330. § 381.
S. v., 36 Mo. 263. § 38.
Cummins, P. v., 47 Mich. 334. § 156.
v. S., 12 Tex. Ap. 121. § 553.
S. v., 76 Ia. 133. § 1253.
Cummons, P. v., 56 Mich. 544. § 1104.
Cumpton, Reg. v., 5 Q. B. D. 341. § 922.
Cundick, Rex v., Dow. & R., N. P. 13. § 1166.
Cundy v. Lindsay, 3 App. Cas. 459. § 712.
Cunningham, C. v., 13 Mass. 245. § 251.
P. v., 66 Cal. 668. § 618.
P. v., 1 Denio, 524. §§ 1173, 1184, 1186.
v. S., 73 Ala. 51. §§ 1117, 1119.
v. S., 49 Miss. 685. §§ 222, 265, 770, 771.
v. S., 56 Miss. 269. §§ 157, 158, 179.
v. S., 17 Tex. Ap. 89. § 365.
v. S., 27 Tex. Ap. 479. § 569.
v. S., 5 W. Va. 508. § 1273.
S. v., 21 Ia. 433. § 602.
S. v., 66 Ia. 94. §§ 875, 878, 880.
S. v., 51 Mo. 479. § 648.
S. v., 100 Mo. 382. §§ 439, 448.
S. v., 2 Speers, 246. § 324.
Curd v. C., 14 B. Mon. 386. § 1230.
Cure, S. v., 7 Ia. 479. § 1309.
Curgerwen, Reg. v., L. R. 1 C. C. 1. § 1076.
Curkendall v. P., 36 Mich. 309. §§ 498, 519.
Curl, Rex v., 2 Stra. 788. §§ 1049, 1157.
Curley, S. v., 33 Ia. 359. §§ 1218, 1278.

Curlin v. S., 4 Yerg. 143. §§ 210, 1007.
Curran's Case, 7 Grat. 619. § 525.
Curran, C. v., 119 Mass. 206. § 1218.
Rex v., 3 C. & P. 397. § 328.
S. v., 51 Ia. 112. §§ 1114, 1117, 1119.
Currier, S. v., 23 Me. 43. §§ 1308, 1313.
Curry v. C., 2 Bush, 67. § 162.
C. v., 150 Mass. 509. §§ 160, 1161, 1163.
Reg. v., 2 Moody, 218. § 753.
v. S., 4 Neb. 545. § 274.
v. S., 5 Neb. 412. §§ 87, 272.
v. S., 4 Tex. Ap. 574. § 462.
v. S., 28 Tex. Ap. 477. § 1228.
S. v., 1 Jones, 280. § 339.
Curtain, U. S. v., 43 Fed. R. 433. § 904.
Curtis, Ex parte, 106 U. S. 371. § 74.
C. v., 9 Allen, 266. §§ 66, 130.
v. P., 2 Ill. 285. § 279.
P. v., 50 Cal. 95. § 888.
P. v., 76 Cal. 57. § 511.
P. v., 52 Mich. 616. §§ 140, 309, 332, 343, 419.
P. v., 95 Mich. 212. §§ 1229, 1251,
v. S., 26 Ark. 439. § 362.
v. S., 6 Coldw. 9. § 617.
v. S., 31 Tex. Ap. 39. § 659.
S. v., 1 Hayw. 471. § 922.
S. v., 12 Ired. 270. § 890.
S. v., 30 La. An., Pt. II, 814. § 510.
S. v., 44 La. An. 320. § 593.
S. v., 70 Mo. 594. §§ 353, 358, 424.
U. S. v., 107 U. S. 671. §§ 855, 857.
Curvan, Rex v., 1 Moody, 132. § 340.
Cushing, S. v., 29 Mo. 215. § 359.
S. v., 11 R. I. 313. § 651.
Custer, S. v., 65 N. C. 339. § 61.
Cutajar, U. S. v., 60 Fed. R. 744. § 1351.
Cuthbert v. Conly, 32 Ga. 211. § 1217.
S. v., T. U. P. Charl. 13. § 935.
Cutler, C. v., 153 Mass. 252. § 849.
C. v., 156 Mass. 52. § 66.
v. S., 59 Ind. 300. § 232.
Cutshall, S. v., 109 N. C. 764. § 1131.
S. v., 110 N. C. 538. § 1077.
Cutsinger v. C., 7 Bush, 392. § 1032.
Cutter, S. v., 36 N. J. 125. §§ 124, 128, 132, 914.
Cutts, Reg. v., 4 Cox, 435. § 878.
Czizek, S. v., 38 Minn. 192. § 122.

Dabbs v. S., 39 Ark. 353. § 1030.
Dade, Rex v., 1 Moody, 307. § 195.
Dady, C. v., 7 Allen, 531. § 1244.
Daggett v. S., 4 Conn. 60. §§ 84, 85.
Daggs, S. v., 106 Mo. 160. § 676.
Dago, The, U. S. v., 61 Fed. R. 986. § 1347.
Dahmer v. S., 56 Miss. 787. §§ 1235, 1259.
Dailey, C. v., 110 Mass. 503. § 495.
v. S., 27 Tex. Ap. 569. § 1302.
Daily, C. v., 133 Mass. 577. § 1243.
v. New York, etc. R. Co., 32 Conn. 356. § 425.
v. S., 51 Ohio St. 348. § 823.
Dains v. S., 2 Humph. 438. §§ 357, 359.
Dalby v. Wolf, 14 Ia. 228. § 1210.
Dale, C. v., 144 Mass. 363. § 1321.
Dale, Reg. v., 6 Cox, 14. § 227.
Rex v., 7 C. & P. 352. §§ 684, 701.
v. S., 27 Ala. 31. § 1302.
v. S., 88 Ga. 552. § 1082.
v. S., 32 Tex. Ap. 78. § 548.
v. S., 10 Yerg. 550. § 356.
S. v., 108 Mo. 205. § 358.
S. v., 8 Oreg. 229. §§ 554, 655.
Daley, S. v., 29 Conn. 272. § 96.
S. v., 41 Vt. 564. §§ 268, 279.
S. v., 53 Vt. 442. § 565.
Dallinger, C. v., 118 Mass. 439. §§ 752, 756.
Dalloway, Reg. v., 2 Cox, 273. § 351.
Dalrymple, P. v., 55 Mich. 519. § 1093.
Dalton, P. v., 15 Wend. 581. §§ 638, 643.
S. v., 27 Mo. 13. § 213.
S. v., 106 Mo. 463. §§ 443, 450.
Daly, C. v., 148 Mass. 428. § 1222.
Reg. v., 9 C. & P. 342. § 940.
v. S., 33 Ala. 431. § 1247.
S. v., 37 La. An. 576. § 617.
Dame, S. v., 11 N. H. 271. § 260.
S. v., 60 N. H. 479. § 1143.
Damewood v. S., 2 Miss. 262. §§ 543, 596, 607.
Damon, C. v., 105 Mass. 580. § 847.
C. v., 136 Mass. 441. §§ 1047, 1053, 1056.
Dan, S. v., 18 Nev. 345. § 494.
Dana, C. v., 2 Met. 329. § 1316.
v. S., 2 Ohio St. 91. § 794.
Danby, S. v., 1 Houst. Cr. C. 166. § 177.
Dancy, S. v., 83 N. C. 608. § 464.
Dandy, S. v., 1 Brev. 395. § 940.
Dane, P. v., 79 Mich. 361. § 781.
P. v., 81 Mich. 36. § 78.
Reg. v., 1 F. & F. 323. § 1076.
Danenhoffer v. S., 69 Ind. 295. § 242.
Danforth, S. v., 3 Conn. 112. §§ 12, 19, 279.
S. v., 48 Ia. 43. §§ 1117, 1129.
D'Angelo, S. v., 9 La. An. 46. § 418.
Danger, Reg. v., Dears. & B. 307. § 694.
Daniel v. Janes, 2 C. P. D. 351. § 815.
v. S., 10 Lea, 261. § 246.
S. v., 31 La. An. 91. § 426.
S. v., 87 N. C. 507. § 460.
S. v., 114 N. C. 823. § 669.
Daniels v. S., 91 Ga. 1. § 824.
v. S., 4 Tex. Ap. 429. § 274.
S. v., 90 Ia. 491. § 703.
S. v., 32 Mo. 558. §§ 551, 589.
S. v., 44 N. H. 383. § 915.
Dann, P. v., 53 Mich. 490. § 142.
Dannelly, Rex v., Russ. & Ry. 310. § 501.
Danner v. S., 54 Ala. 127. § 509.
Dansey v. S., 23 Fla. 316. §§ 1244, 1274.
Dant, Reg. v., 10 Cox, 102. § 351.
v. S., 83 Ind. 60. § 1222.
Danville Bank v. Adm'r, 31 Grat. 469. §§ 988, 989.
Darby, Rex v., 3 Mod. 139. § 1057.
D'Argencour, P. v., 95 N. Y. 624. §§ 123, 759, 771, 777.
Darling Jones v. S., 26 Ala. 155. §§ 1284, 1285.

Darnal, S. v., 1 Humph. 290. § 947.
Darnell v. S., 43 Tex. 147. §§ 618, 816.
v. S., 24 Tex. Ap. 6. § 166.
Darrah, S. v., 1 Houst. Cr. C. 112. § 1081.
Darroch, S. v., 12 Ind. Ap. 527. § 1308.
Darry v. P., 10 N. Y. 120. §§ 320, 321, 350, 358.
Darst v. P., 51 Ill. 286. § 1267.
Dart, S. v., 29 Conn. 153. § 402.
Dartnell, Reg. v., 20 L. T. 1020. § 554.
Dashing v. S., 78 Ind. 357. § 790.
Dauphin v. Key, 4 MacAr. 203. § 1334.
U. S. v., 20 Fed. R. 625. § 1334.
Davenport v. Bird, 34 Ia. 524. § **6**.
v. C., 1 Leigh, 588. § 489.
C. v., 2 Allen, 299. § 1249.
v. Cummings, 15 Ia. 219. § **844**.
v. Kelley, 7 Ia. 102. § 71.
v. Ottawa, 54 Kan. 711. § **1315**.
v. S., 38 Ga. 184. § 992.
S. v., 38 S. C. 348. § 570.
David, S. v., 4 Jones, 353. § 193.
Davidson, C. v., 1 Cush. 33. § **710**.
v. P., 4 Colo. 145. § 307.
P. v., 5 Cal. 133. § 214.
v. S., 33 Ala. 350. § 1296.
v. S., 135 Ind. 254. § 400.
v. S., 77 Md. 388. § 38.
v. S., 22 Tex. Ap. 372. § 852.
S. v., 38 Mo. 374. §§ 468, 474.
S. v., 95 Mo. 155. §§ 309, 339.
S. v., 30 Vt. 377. §§ 414, 476.
Davies, Reg. v., 9 C. & P. 427. § 800.
Reg. v., 1 F. & F. 69. §§ 156, 526.
Davis v. Beason, 133 U. S. 333. § 1076.
v. Brown, 27 Ohio St. 326. § 1153.
v. C., 13 Bush, 318. §§ 1075, 1076, 1079.
v. C., 17 Grat. 617. § 815.
v. C., 95 Ky. 19. §§ 404, 425.
v. C., 30 Pa. St. 421. § 830.
v. C., 75 Va. 944. § 1226.
C. v., 12 Bush, 240. §§ 84, **1259**.
C. v., 11 Gray, 4. § 786.
C. v., 11 Gray, 48. §§ 91, **1178**.
C. v., 92 Ky. 460. § 892.
C. v., 94 Ky. 612. § 882.
C. v., 9 Mass. 415. § 966.
C. v., 121 Mass. 352. § **1229**.
C. v., 140 Mass. 485. § 66.
C. v., 162 Mass. 510. § 70.
C. v., 11 Pick. 432. § 27.
v. P., 19 Ill. 74. § 373*a*.
v. P., 114 Ill. 86. §§ 338, **423**.
P. v., 61 Cal. 536. § 892.
P. v., 73 Cal. 355. §§ 377, **382**.
P. v., 97 Cal. 194. §§ 546, 557.
P. v., 52 Mich. 569. § 1093.
P. v., 36 N. Y. 77. §§ 1223, 1225.
P. v., 56 N. Y. 95. §§ 425, 1148, 1151.
P. v., 8 Utah, 412. § 382.
Reg. v., 3 C. & K. 328. § **166**.
Reg. v., 6 Cox, 367. § 503.
Reg. v., 8 Cox, 486. § 929.
Reg. v., 11 Cox, 181. § 673.
Reg. v., 14 Cox, 563. § 159.
Reg. v., 15 Cox, 174. § 292.
Davis, Reg. v., Dears. 640. § 561.
Reg. v., L. R. 1 C. C. 272. § **716**.
Rex v., 7 C. & P. 785. § 340.
Rex v., 2 East, P. C. 499. § **494**.
Rex v., 2 East, P. C. 593. § 536.
Rex v., Russ. & Ry. 113. § 204.
Rex v., Russ. & Ry. 322. § **497**.
Rex v., Russ. & Ry. 499. § 503.
v. S., 17 Ala. 415. § 546.
v. S., 52 Ala. 357. §§ 525, 529.
v. S., 54 Ala. 88. § 509.
v. S., 68 Ala. 58. § 50.
v. S., 79 Ala. 20. § 872.
v. S., 87 Ala. 10. §§ 221, 222, **516**.
v. S., 92 Ala. 20. §§ 144, 309.
v. S., 45 Ark. 359. § 1036.
v. S., 50 Ark. 17. § 1219.
v. S., 3 Coldw. 77. § 504.
v. S., 35 Fla. 614. § 269.
v. S., 22 Ga. 101. § 1290.
v. S., 40 Ga. 229. § 586.
v. S., 76 Ga. 16. § 514.
v. S., 76 Ga. 721. § 923.
v. S., 79 Ga. 767. § 257.
v. S., 93 Ga. 45. § 1253.
v. S., 3 Har. & J. 154. §§ 263, **1153**.
v. S., 52 Ind. 488. § 1272.
v. S., 100 Ind. 154. § 1309.
v. S., 10 Lea, 707. § 548.
v. S., 39 Md. 355. §§ 361, 389.
v. S., 31 Neb. 240. § 443.
v. S., 31 Neb. 247. § 464.
v. S., 77 N. C. 483. § 404.
v. S., 7 Ohio, 204. § 1290.
v. S., 15 Ohio, 72. § 145.
v. S., 19 Ohio St. 270. § 85.
v. S., 25 Ohio St. 369. §§ 162, **333**.
v. S., 38 Ohio St. 505. § 508.
v. S., 40 Tex. 134. § 589.
v. S., 42 Tex. 226. §§ 443, 449, **452**.
v. S., 43 Tex. 189. § 450.
v. S., 3 Tex. Ap. 91. § 213.
v. S., 6 Tex. Ap. 133. § 242.
v. S., 6 Tex. Ap. 166. § 40.
v. S., 12 Tex. Ap. 11. § 1163.
v. S., 15 Tex. Ap. 475. § 265.
v. S., 20 Tex. Ap. 302. § 271.
v. S., 22 Tex. Ap. 45. § 435.
v. S., 23 Tex. Ap. 210. § 594.
v. S., 32 Tex. Ap. 377. § 596.
S. v., 1 Hill (S. C.), 46. § 235.
S. v., 1 Houst. Cr. C. 13. § **339**.
S. v., 41 Ia. 311. § 384.
S. v., 53 Ia. 252. § 754.
S. v., 1 Ired. 125. §§ 231, 232.
S. v., 2 Ired. 153. § 816.
S. v., 7 Jones, 52. § 246.
S. v., 22 La. An. 77. §§ 12, 536.
S. v., 29 Mo. 391. §§ 205, 213, **269**.
S. v., 70 Mo. 467. § 58.
S. v., 121 Mo. 404. § 269.
S. v., 14 Nev. 439. § 931.
S. v., 38 N. J. 176. § 566.
S. v., 69 N. C. 313. § 746.
S. v., 69 N. C. 383. § 874.
S. v., 69 N. C. 495. § 878.
S. v., 84 N. C. 787. § 881.

Davis, S. v., 87 N. C. 514. § 291.
S. v., 92 N. C. 764. § 1057.
S. v., 109 N. C. 780. § 1079.
S. v., 109 N. C. 809. § 827.
S. v., 14 R. I. 281. § 209.
v. Texas, 139 U. S. 651. § 77.
v. U. S., 160 U. S. 469. §§ 175, 179.
U. S. v., 33 Fed. R. 621. § 950.
U. S. v., 33 Fed. R. 865. § 1330.
U. S. v., 37 Fed. R. 468. § 1227.
U. S. v., 38 Fed. R. 326. § 1332.
U. S. v., 5 Mason, 356. §§ 543, 590.
v. Utah, 151 U. S. 262. § 361.
Davison v. P., 90 Ill. 221. §§ 121, 411.
v. S., 12 Tex. Ap. 214. § 563.
Dawell, P. v., 25 Mich. 247. § 1075.
Dawes, S. v., 75 Me. 51. § 593.
Dawkes v. Coveneigh, Style, 346. § 11.
Dawkins v. S., 58 Ala. 376. § 443.
Dawson, Reg. v., 2 Den. 75. § 753.
Rex v., 2 East, P. C. 978. § 765.
Rex v., 3 Stark. 62. § 454.
v. S., 29 Ark. 116. §§ 442, 451.
v. S., 52 Ind. 478. §§ 823. 827.
v. S., 7 Tex. Ap. 59. § 1024.
v. S., 25 Tex. Ap. 670. § 216.
v. S., 32 Tex. Ap. 535. § 515.
S. v., 2 Bay, 360. § 188.
S. v., 17 Ia. 584. § 579.
Day v. Lown, 51 Ia. 364. § 845.
Reg. v., 9 C. & P. 722. §§ 249, 440.
v. S., 14 Tex. Ap. 26. § 1190.
v. S., 27 Tex. Ap. 143. § 1290.
S. v., 52 Ind. 483. § 1193.
S. v., 37 Me. 244. §§ 1244, 1277.
S. v., 100 Mo. 242. §§ 862, 881, 883.
S. v., 4 Wash. 104. §§ 374, 380, 381.
Dayton, S. v., 23 N. J. 49. §§ 859, 860, 865.
Deal v. S., 140 Ind. 354. § 310.
S. v., 64 N. C. 270. §§ 113, 565.
S. v., 92 N. C. 802. § 1164.
Dealy v. U. S., 152 U. S. 539. §§ 966, 974, 977.
Dean v. C., 32 Grat. 912. §§ 408, 409.
v. C., 3 Serg. & R. 418. § 840.
C. v., 14 Gray, 99. §§ 1218, 1220.
C. v., 110 Mass. 357. §§ 1210, 1281.
C. v., 1 Pick. 387. § 1308.
C. v., 21 Pick. 334. § 1229.
Reg. v., 4 Jur. 364. § 982.
v. S., 89 Ala. 46. § 242.
v. S., 98 Ala. 71. § 1039.
v. S., Mart. & Y. 127. §§ 1291, 1292.
S. v., 44 Ia. 648. §§ 1137, 1249.
S. v., 49 Ia. 73. § 571.
S. v., 13 Ired. 63. § 988.
Dearborn, S. v., 15 Me. 402. § 142.
S. v., 54 Me. 442. §§ 248, 252.
Dearing, S. v., 65 Mo. 530. § 160.
De Arman v. S., 71 Ala. 351. §§ 305, 308.
v. S., 77 Ala. 10. § 308.
Deaton, S. v., 101 N. C. 728. § 1216.
Deaver, U. S. v., 14 Fed. R. 595. § 914.
Deaves, Reg. v., 11 Cox, 227. § 571.
De Banks, Reg. v., 13 Q. B. D. 29. § 554.
De Bare, U. S. v., 6 Biss. 358. § 719.
Debbs v. S., 43 Tex. 650. § 544.
Deberenger, Rex v., 3 Mau. & S. 67. §§ 962, 982.
De Bernie v. S., 19 Ala. 23. § 880.
Debney v. S., 45 Neb. 856. § 376.
De Bow v. P., 1 Denio, 9. § 772.
De Boy, S. v., 117 N. C. 702. §§ 1285, 1315.
De Bruhl, S. v., 10 Rich. 23. § 523.
De Bruiel, Reg. v., 11 Cox, 207. §§ 553, 720.
Debs, U. S. v., 63 Fed. R. 436. § 963.
U. S. v., 64 Fed. R. 724. § 963.
U. S. v., 65 Fed. R. 210. §§ 966, 1328.
Decarie, P. v., 80 Mich. 578. § 1252.
Decker, S. v., 52 Kan. 193. § 844.
Decklotts, S. v., 19 Ia. 447. §§ 321, 329, 336, 365.
De Coursey, P. v., 61 Cal. 134. § 609.
Dedieu v. P., 22 N. Y. 178. § 532.
Dee v. S., 68 Mass. 601. § 36.
Deeley, Rex v., 4 C. & P. 579. § 1079.
Deere v. Wolff, 65 Ia. 32. § 939.
Deerfield, C. v., 6 Allen, 449. § 1185.
Defoor, P. v., 100 Cal. 150. § 271.
Deford v. S., 30 Md. 179. § 351.
De Fore, P. v., 64 Mich. 693. § 1115.
Defrese v. S., 3 Heisk. 53. § 560.
De Grieff, U. S. v., 16 Blatch. 20. § 956.
De Groat v. P., 39 Mich. 124. § 1121.
U. S. v., 30 Fed. R. 764. §§ 14, 15, 920.
De Hart, S. v., 6 Baxt. 222. § 687.
Deitrick, S. v., 51 Ia. 467. §§ 1116, 1118.
Deitz v. Central City, 1 Colo. 323. §§ 63, 68, 1228.
P. v., 86 Mich. 419. §§ 307, 410.
Dejardin, C. v., 126 Mass. 46. § 1158.
Dejarnette v. C., 75 Va. 867. §§ 158, 333.
De La Cour Soto, P. v., 63 Cal. 165. §§ 361. 386.
Delafoile v. S., 54 N. J. 381. § 241.
De La Guerra, P. v., 31 Cal. 416. § 648.
Delamotte, Rex v., 1 East, P. C. 53. § 1354.
Delaney v. S., 7 Baxt. 28. § 687.
v. S., 51 N. J. 37. § 1137.
S. v., 28 La. An. 431. § 271.
Delano v. Goodwin, 48 N. H. 203. § 125.
v. S., 66 Ind. 348. § 1133.
S. v., 54 Me. 501. § 1217.
Delany, C. v., 1 Grant, 224. §§ 775, 977, 979.
v. P., 10 Mich. 241. §§ 1121, 1131.
v. S., 41 Tex. 601. § 526.
Delaval, Rex v., 3 Bur. 1434. § 959.
Delaware Division Canal v. C., 60 Pa. St. 367. §§ 183, 190, 1173, 1181, 1182.
Delay, P. v., 80 Cal. 52. §§ 639, 641.
S. v., 93 Mo. 98. § 678.
De Leon, P. v., 109 N. Y. 226. § 489.
Delier v. Plymouth Ag'l Soc., 57 Ia. 481. §§ 1286, 1297.
Delk v. S., 64 Miss. 77. §§ 548, 568.
De Londo, Rex v., 2 East, P. C. 1098. § 818.

De Longchamps, Resp. v., 1 Dall. 111. § 235.
De Los Angeles, P. v., 61 Cal. 188. §§ 299, 440.
Delyon, S. v., 1 Bay, 353. § 661.
Demain, C. v., Brightly, 441. §§ 981, 1146.
Demarchi, U. S. v., 5 Blatch. 84. § 376.
Demareste, S. v., 41 La. An. 617. § 303.
Dement v. S., 2 Head, 505. § 774.
Demerritt, S. v., 64 N. H. 313. § 915.
Deming, U. S. v., 4 McLean, 3. § 880.
Demousset, P. v., 71 Cal. 611. §§ 1102, 1106.
Dempsey v. P., 47 Ill. 323. § 217.
v. S., 27 Tex. Ap. 269. § 920.
Demuth, C. v., 12 Serg. & R. 389. § 180.
Dengolensky, S. v., 82 Mo. 44. § 1273.
Denicke, U. S. v., 35 Fed. R. 407. §§ 1330, 1335.
Deniston, S. v., 6 Blackf. 277. § 927.
Denkins, S. v., 24 La. An. 29. § 241.
Denman v. S., 15 Neb. 138. § 292.
Denmark v. S., 58 Ark. 576. § 617.
Denmour, Reg. v., 8 Cox, 440. § 554.
Dennee, U. S. v., 3 Woods, 39. § 893.
U. S. v., 3 Woods, 47. §§ 973, 977.
Dennehy v. Chicago, 120 Ill. 627. §§ 1206, 1211, 1217, 1245, 1253.
Dennett, S. v., 19 La. An. 395. § 761.
Dennie, Resp. v., 4 Yeates, 267. § 1048.
Dennin, P. v., 35 Hun, 327. § 1325.
S. v., 32 Vt. 158. § 523.
Dennis, C. v., 105 Mass. 162. §§ 221, 290.
v. P., 27 Mich. 151. § 500.
P. v., 39 Cal. 625. § 417.
v. S., 5 Ark. 230. § 449.
v. S., 17 Fla. 389. §§ 943, 950.
v. S., 91 Ind. 291. § 1181.
S. v., 80 Mo. 589. § 674.
Dennison v. S., 13 Ind. 510. §§ 336, 345.
S. v., 44 La. An. 135. § 358.
S. v., 108 Mo. 541. § 267.
Denny v. Thwaites, 2 Ex. D. 21. § 828.
Denoon, S. v., 31 W. Va. 122. §§ 189, 1237.
Densley, Rex v. 6 C. & P. 399. § 726.
Densmore, C. v., 12 Allen, 535. § 424.
Dent, Reg. v., 1 C. & K. 249. §§ 668, 683.
S. v., 6 S. C., 383. § 395.
S. v., 25 W. Va. 1. § 36.
v. West Virginia, 129 U. S. 114. § 36.
Denton v. S, 77 Md. 527. §§ 646, 648.
v. S., 1 Swan, 278. §§ 414, 415.
S. v., 74 Md. 517. §§ 646, 652.
Depass, S. v., 45 La. An. 1151. § 307.
Depuy, C. v., 148 Pa. St. 201. § 539.
De Rance, S. v., 34 La. An. 186. § 177.
Derby, C. v., 163 Mass. 183. § 1193.
Dering, S. v., 84 Wis. 585. §§ 65, 66, 77.
Derixson v. S., 65 Ind. 385. §§ 132, 823.
Derst, S. v., 10 Nev. 443. §§ 593, 606.
Deschamp, S. v., 53 Ark. 490. § 1202.
Deschamps, S. v., 42 La. An. 567. §§ 332, 411.
Desmarteau, C. v., 16 Gray, 1. §§ 353, 356, 361.
Des Moines v. Hillis, 55 Ia. 643. § 62.
Desmond, C. v., 123 Mass. 407. § 101.
Reg. v., 11 Cox, 146. § 988.
Detroit Lead Works, P. v., 82 Mich. 471. §§ 63, 183, 1173.
Detroit, etc. R. Co., P. v., 79 Mich. 471. § 40.
Deusting, S. v., 33 Minn. 102. §§ 1233, 1235.
Devaux, Rex v., 2 East, P. C. 789. §§ 611, 712.
Devers, S. v., 38 Ark. 517. § 1229.
Devine, C. v., 155 Mass. 224. §§ 884, 893.
P. v., 59 Cal. 630. §§ 222, 273.
P. v., 95 Cal. 227. § 565.
v. S., 4 Ia. 443. § 1271.
Devlin, C. v., 141 Mass. 423. §§ 681, 690.
Devoe v. C., 3 Met. 316. §§ 499, 506.
C. v., 159 Mass. 101. § 1326.
Devore v. T., 2 Okl. 562. §§ 560, 989.
Devoto v. C., 3 Met. (Ky.) 417. § 726.
De Walt, U. S. v., 128 U. S. 393. § 20.
Dewee's Case, Chase, Dec. 531. § 1327.
Dewer, S. v., 65 N. C. 572. § 18.
Dewey, P. v., 2 Ida. 79. § 414.
S. v., 65 Vt. 196. § 1277.
De Winton, P. v., — Cal. —, 45 Pac. R. 708. § 521.
Dewitt, C. v., 10 Mass. 154. § 552.
De Witt, S. v., 32 Mo. 571. § 565.
Dextra, C. v., 143 Mass. 28. §§ 1319, 1321.
Dias v. S., 7 Blackf. 20. §§ 373*a*, 380, 384.
Dibley, Reg. v., 2 C. & K. 818. § 618.
Dibney v. S., 45 Neb. 856. § 369.
Dibrell v. S., 3 Tex. Ap. 456. § 463.
Dick v. S., 53 Miss. 384. § 525.
v. S., 3 Ohio St. 89. § 362.
S. v., 47 Minn. 375. § 1220.
Dicken, C. v., 145 Pa. St. 453. § 1189.
Reg. v., 14 Cox, 8. § 442.
Dickerson v. C., 2 Bush, 1. §§ 271, 281.
S. v., 24 Mo. 365. § 925.
S. v., 98 N. C. 708. § 242.
Dickey v. S., 68 Ala. 508. § 1303.
U. S. v., Morris, 412. § 852.
Dickinson v. Barber, 9 Mass. 225. § 111.
v. Heeb Brewing Co., 73 Ia. 705. § 1207.
Rex v., Russ. & Ry. 420. § 566.
v. S., 70 Ind. 247. §§ 228, 228*a*.
S. v., 41 Wis. 299. § 425.
U. S. v., Hempst. 1. § 440.
Dicks, Rex. v., 1 Russ. Cr. 19. § 147.
Dickson v. S., 88 N. C. 643. § 698.
v. S., 39 Ohio St. 73. § 307.
v. S., 34 Tex. Ap. 1. § 1057.
S. v., 78 Mo. 438. §§ 396, 421.
S. v., 75 N. C. 275. § 311.
Didfirri, In re, 48 Fed. R. 168. § 1343.
Diebel v. S, 68 Miss. 725. § 1313.
Dieffenbach, S. v., 47 Ia. 638. § 1137.
Dierberger, S. v., 90 Mo. 369. § 922.
S. v., 96 Mo. 666. § 298.
Diffey v. S., 86 Ala. 66. § 1031.
Digby v. P., 113 Ill. 123. § 426.

Diggs v. S., 49 Ala. 311. §§ 647, 912.
Dignowitty v. S., 17 Tex. 521. §§ 535, 562, 568, 592.
Dilcher v. S., 39 Ohio St. 130. §§ 862, 864, 865.
Dilger v. C., 88 Ky. 550. §§ 298, 328.
Dill, C. v., 156 Mass. 226. §§ 1082, 1132.
C. v., 160 Mass. 536. §§ 1153, 1154.
v. P., 19 Colo. 469. §§ 882, 890.
v. S., 25 Ala. 15. §§ 299, 304, 309.
v. S., 1 Tex. Ap. 278. § 377.
v. S., 6 Tex. Ap. 113. § 470.
S. v., 75 N. C. 57. § 543.
Dillahunt, S. v., 3 Harr. 551. § 159.
Dillane, C. v., 11 Gray, 67. § 1273.
Dillard, S. v., 5 Blackf. 365. § 993.
Dillin v. P., 8 Mich. 357. § 417.
Dillingham v. S., 5 Ohio St. 280. §§ 678, 702.
Dillon, P. v., 8 Utah, 92. § 175.
Reg. v., 14 Cox, 4. § 886.
Rex v., 2 Chit. 314. § 841.
v. S., 9 Ind. 408. § 386.
S. v., 74 Ia. 653. § 330.
Dilworth, Reg. v., 2 M. & Rob. 531. § 236.
Dimmett v. Eskridge, 6 Munf. 308. §§ 1184, 1186, 1189.
Dimick, P. v., 107 N. Y. 13. § 708.
Dimond, C. v., 3 Cush. 235. § 575.
Dineen, S. v., 10 Minn. 407. §§ 240, 257.
Dingee, S. v., 17 Ia. 232. §§ 1093, 1095.
Dingler, Rex v., 1 East, P. C. 356. § 426.
Dinkey v. C., 17 Pa. St. 126. § 1115.
Diprose, Reg. v., 11 Cox, 185. § 631.
Dishon v. Smith, 10 Ia. 212. §§ 896, 947.
Ditto, C. v., Hard. 450. § 1190.
Ditton, S. v., 48 Ia. 677. §§ 615, 726.
Divine v. S., 4 Ind. 240. 1273.
Divoll, S. v., 44 N. H. 140. §§ 854, 872, 873, 885.
Dixon, Reg. v., 3 Cox, 289. § 753.
Reg. v., 11 Cox, 341. § 167.
Reg. v., Dears. 580. § 571.
Rex v., Russ. & Ry. 53, 1 East, P. C. 313. §§ 298, 578.
Rex v., 3 Mau. & S. 11. §§ 130, 188.
v. S., 76 Ala. 89. § 1324.
v. S., 81 Ala. 61. § 758.
v. S., 13 Fla. 636. §§ 333, 419.
v. S., 86 Ga. 754. § 1261.
v. S., 89 Ga. 785. § 1258.
v. S., 21 Tex. Ap. 517. §§ 1274, 1291.
S. v., 101 N. C. 741. § 673.
S. v., 104 N. C. 704. § 1097.
S. v., 114 N. C. 850. § 1032.
U. S. v., 4 Cranch, C. C. 107. § 1137.
Doan v. S., 26 Ind. 495. §§ 213, 214, 217, 602.
Doane, P. v., 77 Cal. 560. § 638.
S. v., 14 Wis. 483. § 1194.
Dobard, S. v., 45 La. An. 1412. § 66.
Dobbs, Rex v., 2 East, P. C. 513. § 506.
Dobbyn, C. v., 14 Gray, 44. § 1233.
Dobkins v. S., 2 Humph. 424. § 1291.
Dobson v. S., 57 Ind. 69. § 1246.
Dobson v. S., 5 Lea, 271. § 1253.
S. v., 3 Harr. 563. § 543.
Dodd v. Hamilton, 2 Tayl. 31. § 557.
v. S., 18 Ind. 56. §§ 114, 913.
v. S., 10 Tex. Ap. 370. § 602.
S. v., 3 Murph. 226. § 861.
Dodel, P. v., 77 Cal. 293. §§ 232, 257.
Dodge v. Brittain, Meigs, 84. §§ 118, 717.
v. S., 24 N. J. 455. §§ 874, 891.
S. v., 78 Me. 439. § 1248.
U. S. v., 70 Fed. R. 235. § 1333.
Dodson v. McCauley, 62 Ga. 130. § 939.
Reg. v., 9 A. & E. 704. § 834.
S. v., 4 Oreg. 64. § 307.
Doe v. Avaline, 8 Ind. 6. § 84.
P. v., 1 Mich. 451. § 361.
S. v., 79 Ind. 9. § 539.
Doebler, U. S. v., 1 Baldw. 519. § 808.
Doepke, S. v., 68 Mo. 208. §§ 542, 585.
Doherty, C. v., 10 Cush. 52. §§ 228, 509.
C. v., 103 Mass. 443. § 1031.
C. v., 127 Mass. 20. §§ 624, 625, 654.
C. v., 137 Mass. 245. § 1018.
Reg. v., 16 Cox, 306. §§ 162, 331.
v. S., 84 Wis. 152. §§ 332, 348.
S. v., 2 Overt. 80. § 150.
U. S. v., 25 Fed. R. 28. §§ 945, 950.
Dohme v. S., 68 Ga. 339. § 1309.
Dohring, P. v., 59 N. Y. 374. § 440.
Doig, S. v., 2 Rich. 179. § 826.
Dolan v. P., 64 N. Y. 485. §§ 355, 361.
P. v., 9 Cal. 576. § 389.
P. v., 96 Cal. 315. §§ 1105, 1106.
Reg. v., Dears. 436. § 715.
v. S., 81 Ala. 11. § 303.
v. S., 122 Ind. 141. § 1262.
Dole, C. v., 2 Allen, 165. § 793.
v. New England M. M. Ins. Co., 2 Cliff. 394. § 1359.
S. v., 3 Blackf. 294. §§ 1290, 1291.
Doles v. S., 97 Ind. 555. §§ 414, 430.
Dolke v. S., 99 Ind. 229. § 1260.
Doll v. S., 45 Ohio St. 445. § 911.
Domingus v. S., 94 Ala. 9. § 329.
Donahoe v. S., 59 Ark. 375. § 680.
S. v., 78 Ia. 486. §§ 315, 316.
Donahue, C. v., 148 Mass. 529. § 142.
C. v., 149 Pa. St. 104. § 1209.
Donald, P. v., 48 Mich. 491. §§ 597, 636a.
Donaldson v. C., 95 Pa. St. 21. § 410.
P. v., 70 Cal. 116. § 674.
v. S., 10 Tex. Ap. 307. § 238.
v. S., 15 Tex. Ap. 25. § 1232.
S. v., 32 N. J. 151. § 963.
Donelon, S. v., 45 La. An. 744. § 411.
Don Moran v. P., 25 Mich. 356. § 448.
Donnally, Rex v., 2 East, P. C. 713. § 470.
Donnegan, S. v., 34 Mo. 67. § 594.
Donnell v. S., 2 Ind. 658. § 1252.
Donnelly v. S., 26 N. J. 463. §§ 357, 358, 377, 425, 426, 430, 431.
v. S., 26 N. J. 601. §§ 358, 427.
Donnevan, Rex v., 2 W. Bl. 682. § 518.
Donniger v. S., 52 Ind. 326. §§ 59, 1314.
Donohoe v. S., 59 Ark. 375. § 680.
v. S., 14 Tex. Ap. 638. § 878.
Donohoo v. S., 36 Ala. 281. §§ 500, 503.

Don On. U. S. v., 49 Fed. R. 569. § 1344.
Donovan, C. v., 16 Gray, 18. § 1139.
Reg. v., 4 Cox, 400. § 222.
S. v., 1 Houst. Cr. C. 43. § 538.
S. v., 61 Ia. 278. §§ 1092, 1093, 1095.
S. v., 61 Ia. 369. § 463.
Donyes, S. v., 14 Mont. 70. § 245.
Doody, Reg. v., 6 Cox, 463. §§ 161, 290.
Dooley v. S., 21 Tex. Ap. 549. § 752.
S. v., 89 Ia. 584. §§ 388, 411, 418.
S. v., 64 Mo. 146. § 511.
S. v., 121 Mo. 591. § 269.
T. v., 4 Mont. 295. § 271.
Doolittle v. S., 93 Ind. 272. § 123.
Doon. S. v., R. M. Charl. 1. §§ 1137, 1310.
Doran v. S., 7 Tex. Ap. 385. § 363.
Dorman v. S., 34 Ala. 216. §§ 1210, 1274.
Dorn v. S., 4 Tex. Ap. 67. § 1027.
Dorr, S. v., 33 Me. 498. §§ 671, 680.
S. v., 82 Me. 157. § 1249.
S. v., 82 Me. 341. § 1273.
Dorrance, S. v., 86 Ia. 428. § 765.
Dorrell v. S., 80 Ind. 566. §§ 830, 834.
Dorsey v. S., 1 Tex. Ap. 33. § 460.
U. S. v., 40 Fed. R. 752. §§ 1330, 1335.
Dorus, C. v., 108 Mass. 488. § 740.
Doss v. S., 21 Tex. Ap. 505. § 548.
Dossett, Reg. v., 2 C. & K. 306. § 533.
v. U. S., 3 Okl. 591. § 409.
Doster v. S., 93 Ga. 43. § 1236.
Dotson v. S., 62 Ala. 141. § 1076.
v. S., 51 Ark. 119. § 554.
Doty, S. v., 5 Coldw. 33. § 1028.
S. v., 5 Oreg. 491. §§ 267. 268.
Doud, S. v., 7 Conn. 384. § 930.
Dougan v. S., 125 Ind. 130. § 1322.
Dougherty, In re, 27 Vt. 325. § 1207.
v. C., 14 B. Mon. 239. § 1228.
C. v., 107 Mass. 243. § 143.
v. P., 1 Colo. 514. §§ 236, 1148, 1150.
v. P., 5 Ill. 179. §§ 992, 994.
Douglas, Rex v., 7 C. & P. 644. § 1152.
Rex v., 1 Moody, 462. § 678.
S. v., 17 Me. 193. § 552.
Douglass v. C., 2 Rawle, 262. §§ 72, 84.
v. C., 8 Watts. 535. § 1152.
C. v., 5 Met. 241. § 893.
v. Matting, 29 Ia. 498. § 763.
P. v., 87 Cal. 281. § 309.
v. S., 72 Ind. 385. § 93.
v. S., 8 Tex. Ap. 520. § 365.
v. S., 26 Tex. Ap. 109. §§ 268, 377.
v. S., 4 Wis. 387. §§ 1170, 1173, 1175.
S. v., 7 Ia. 413. § 950.
S. v., 73 Ia. 279. §§ 1216, 1256.
S. v., 34 La. An. 523. § 206.
S. v., 1 Mo. 374. § 1292.
S. v., 28 W, Va. 297. §§ 320, 321.
U. S. v., 2 Blatch. 207. §§ 213, 218.
U. S. v., 33 Fed. R. 381. § 1327.
Dovalina v. S., 14 Tex. Ap. 312. § 805.
Dove, C. v., 2 Va. Cas. 26. § 1275.
v. S., 37 Ark. 261. § 566.
v. S., 3 Heisk. 348. §§ 156, 178, 179.
Dover v. S., 75 Ala. 40. § 362.
Dovey, Reg. v., 4 Cox, 428. § 714.
Reg. v., 2 Den. 92. § 722.
Dow, C. v., 10 Met. 382. § 100.
v. S., 12 Tex. Ap. 343. § 569.
S. v., 21 Vt. 484. § 1237.
Dowd. S. v., 19 Conn. 388. §§ 359, 361, 362.
Dowden, S. v., 2 Dev. 443. § 794.
Dowdican, C. v., 114 Mass. 257. § 1222.
Dowe, S. v., 27 Ia. 273. § 678.
Dowell, S. v., 106 N. C. 722. §§ 187, 449, 463.
Dowers, S. v., 45 N. H. 543. § 25.
Dowey, Reg. v., 11 Cox, 115. §§ 187, 675.
Dowlen v. S., 14 Tex. Ap. 61. § 242.
Dowlin, Rex v., Peake, 170. § 888.
Rex v., 5 T. R. 311. §§ 873, 878.
Dowling, C. v., 114 Mass. 259. §§ 190, 1239.
Downer, S. v., 8 Vt. 424. §§ 142, 924, 925, 926, 927.
S. v., 21 Wis. 274. §§ 1228, 1273.
Downes, Reg. v., 1 Q. B. D. 8. § 286.
Downey v. S., 90 Ala. 644. § 1302.
Downham, S. v., 1 Houst. Cr. C. 45. § 342.
Downing, C. v., 4 Gray, 29. § 117.
v. S., 66 Ga. 160. § 35.
S. v., 74 N. C. 184. § 1007.
Downman v. S., 14 Ala. 342. § 1247.
Downs, P. v., 123 N. Y. 558. § 316.
v. S., 19 Md. 571. § 1226.
S. v., 91 Mo. 19. §§ 326, 368.
S. v., 59 N. H. 320. § 519.
S. v., 116 N. C. 1064. §§ 114, 1217, 1251, 1252, 1273.
Dowsell, Rex v., 6 C. & P. 398. § 195.
Doyal v. S., 70 Ga. 134. § 307.
Doyell, P. v., 48 Cal. 85. §§ 336, 365.
Doyle, Rex v., 1 Leach, 67. § 394.
v. S., 4 Tex. Ap. 253. § 586.
v. S., 19 Tex. Ap. 410. § 1311.
S. v., 107 Mo. 36. §§ 123, 274.
S. v., 11 R. I. 574. § 1274.
S. v., 15 R. I. 325. § 1250.
S. v., 15 R. I. 527. § 1274.
U. S. v., 6 Saw. 612. § 921.
Dozier v. S., 26 Ga. 156. §§ 321, 391.
S. v., Dudley, 155. § 672.
S. v., 73 N. C. 117. § 499.
Drage, Reg. v., 14 Cox, 83. §§ 615, 726.
Drake, C. v., 124 Mass. 21. § 199.
v. Jordan, 73 Ia. 707. § 1207.
v. Kaiser, 73 Ia. 703. § 1207.
v. S., 75 Ga. 413. §§ 307, 405.
v. S., 14 Neb. 535. § 1142.
v. S., 53 N. J. 23. § 1070.
v. S., 19 Ohio St. 211. §§ 759, 768.
v. S., 25 Tex. Ap. 293. § 429.
S. v., 64 N. C. 589. § 1326.
Draper v. S., 4 Baxt. 246. § 303.
S. v., 1 Houst. Cr. C. 291. § 155.
S. v., 1 Houst. Cr. C. 531. § 338.
S. v., 65 Mo. 335. § 427.
Drapert v. S., 14 Ind. 123. § 1223.

Drass, C. v., 146 Pa. St. 55. § 823.
Drees v. S., 37 Ark. 122. § 823.
Dreessen v. S., 38 Neb. 375. §§ 396, 402, 409.
Dreifus, S. v., 38 La. An. 877. § 855.
Drennan v. P., 10 Mich. 169. §§ 18, 141.
P. v., 86 Mich. 445. § 1252.
Drew, C. v., 3 Cush. 279. § 190.
C. v., 4 Mass. 391. §§ 142, 197, 328, 333, 340, 347.
C. v., 153 Mass. 588. § 688.
C. v., 19 Pick. 179. §§ 666, 674, 686.
v. S., 10 Ark. 82. §§ 1290, 1291.
U. S. v., 5 Mason, 28. § 159.
Dreyer v. S., 11 Tex. Ap. 503. §§ 546, 617.
v. S., 11 Tex. Ap. 631. § 565.
Dreyfus v. S., 83 Ala. 54. §§ 1291, 1301.
Dring, Reg. v., Dears. & B. 329. § 714.
Driscoll v. C., 93 Ky. 393. § 36.
Reg. v., Car. & M. 214. § 246.
Drum, C. v., 58 Pa. St. 9. §§ 139, 302, 308, 311, 316, 329, 332, 336.
Drummond, Rex v., 1 East, P. C. 353, n. § 431.
Drury v. Defontaine, 1 Taunt. 131, §§ 1319, 1324.
Drye v. S., 14 Tex. Ap. 185. § 377.
Duane, C. v., 1 Binn. 601. § 96.
C. v., 98 Mass. 1. § 70.
Dubarry, S. v., 44 La. An. 1117. §§ 65, 71.
Du Bois v. S., 51 Ala. 139. §§ 595, 597.
v. S., 87 Ala. 101. § 1233.
Dubose v. S., 10 Tex. Ap. 230. § 404.
v. S., 13 Tex. Ap. 418. § 362.
Dubuque v. Stout, 32 Ia. 80. § 70.
Ducher v. S., 18 Ohio, 308. §§ 495, 502.
Duchess of Kingston's Case, 1 East, P. C. 468. § 1075.
Ducker, S. v., 8 Oreg. 394. § 561.
Duckett v. S., 65 Ga. 369. § 572.
v. S., 93 Ga. 415. § 211.
Duckworth, Reg. v., 2 Q. B. D. (1892) 83. §§ 223, 226, 232, 258.
Ducournau, U. S. v., 54 Fed. R. 138. § 1218.
Dudley, C. v., 6 Leigh, 613. § 324.
Reg. v., 14 Q. B. D. 273. § 137.
v. Sautbine, 49 Ia. 650. §§ 128, 1257.
v. S., 91 Ind. 312. § 1224.
Dudley, etc. Banking Co. v. Spittle, 1 Johns. & H. 14. § 11.
Dudney v. S., 22 Ark. 251. §§ 1291, 1306, 1309.
Duebbe v. S., 1 Tex. Ap. 159. § 325.
Duff, C. v., 87 Ky. 586. §§ 92, 942, 945.
U. S. v., 19 Blatch. 9. §§ 1334, 1335.
Duffield, Reg. v., 5 Cox, 404. §§ 963, 988.
Duffin v. P., 107 Ill. 113. §§ 761, 770, 793, 795, 798, 805.
Rex v., 1 East, P. C. 365. § 1153.
Rex v., Russ. & Ry. 365. § 269.
Duffy, C. v., 11 Cush. 145. § 597.
C. v., 96 Pa. St. 506. § 748.
v. P., 6 Hill, 75. § 58.
v. P., 26 N. Y. 588. § 197.
Duffy, Reg. v., 2 Cox, 45. § 1051.
S. v., 124 Mo. 1. § 449.
S. v., 128 Mo. 549. § 460.
U. S. v., 1 Cranch, C. C. 164. § 546.
Dufour, S. v., 63 Ind. 567. § 758.
S. v., 31 La. An. 804. §§ 420, 421.
Dugan, S. v., 1 Houst. Cr. C. 563. §§ 142, 323, 333.
S. v., 52 Kan. 23. § 1248.
S. v., 110 Mo. 138. § 1232.
Dugdale v. Reg., 1 El. & B. 435. §§ 1049, 1157.
Dugle v. S., 100 Ind. 259. § 520.
Duhammel, S. v., 2 Harr. 532. § 939.
Duke v. S., 19 Tex. Ap. 14. § 1057.
S. v., 42 Tex. 455. § 1038.
Dukes v. S., 14 Fla. 499. §§ 333, 359.
v. S., 79 Ga. 795. § 1274.
v. S., 94 Ga. 393. § 771.
v. S., 11 Ind. 557. §§ 307, 380, 382, 400.
v. S., 22 Tex. Ap. 192. §§ 547, 548, 597.
Duket, S. v., 90 Wis. 272. § 1090.
Dula v. S., 8 Yerg. 510. § 370.
S. v., 100 N. C. 423. §§ 922, 924.
S. v., Phill. 211. § 413.
Duling v. Johnson, 32 Ind. 155. § 425.
Dull v. C., 25 Grat. 965. § 596.
Dumar, P. v., 106 N. Y. 502. § 563.
Dumas v. S., 62 Ga. 58. §§ 195, 291, 426.
v. S., 63 Ga. 600. §§ 373, 374, 420.
v. S., 14 Tex. Ap. 464. § 1083.
Dumphey, S. v., 4 Minn. 438. §§ 307, 361.
Dunan, C. v., 128 Mass. 422. §§ 400, 424.
Dunaway v. P., 110 Ill. 333. §§ 123, 276, 325.
Dunbar v. U. S., 156 U. S. 185. § 1351.
U. S. v., 60 Fed. R. 75. § 1351.
Duncan v. C., 2 B. Mon. 281. § 1227.
v. C., 6 Dana, 295. §§ 249, 1007.
v. C., 85 Ky. 614. § 509.
C. v., 91 Ky. 592. § 259.
v. Missouri, 152 U. S. 377. §§ 77, 78.
v. S., 88 Ala. 31. § 416.
v. S., 29 Fla. 439. §§ 520, 527, 529.
v. S., 84 Ind. 204. §§ 139, 304.
v. S., 49 Miss. 431. § 826.
S. v., 6 Ired. 236. § 216.
S. v., 1 McCord, 404. § 1191.
S. v., 116 Mo. 288. §§ 391, 412.
S. v., 7 Wash. 336. § 214.
T. v., 5 Mont. 478. § 509.
Dunford v. Weaver, 84 N. Y. 445. § 931.
Dungey, Reg. v., 4 F. & F. 99. §§ 238, 454.
Dunham v. S., 9 Tex. Ap. 330. § 511.
Dunkel, P. v., 39 Mich. 255. § 1196.
Dunkley, Rex v., 1 Moody, 90. § 740.
S. v., 3 Ired. 116. § 361.
Dunlap, S. v., 24 Me. 77. § 701.
Dunleay, C. v., 153 Mass. 330. § 684.
C. v., 157 Mass. 386. § 769.
Dunlop v. U. S., — U. S. —, 17 S. C. R. 375. § 1332.
Dunman v. S., 1 Tex. Ap. 593. § 195.
Dunn, Ex parte, 14 Ind. 122. § 1228.
C. v., 14 Gray, 401. § 1229.

Dunn v. P., 4 Colo. 126. §§ 202, 773.
v. P., 40 Ill. 465. § 1315.
v. P., 109 Ill. 635. §§ 156, 160, 202.
v. P., 29 N. Y. 523. §§ 199, 1151.
P. v., 1 Ida. T. 75. § 391.
Reg. v., 7 C. & P. 730. § 873.
Reg. v., 12 Q. B. D. 1026. § 855.
Rex v., 1 Dow. & R., N. P. 10. § 878.
Rex v., 2 East, P. C. 961. §§ 761, 764.
Rex v., 1 Moody, 146. § 726.
v. S., 2 Ark. 229. § 416.
v. S., 57 Ark. 560. § 1152.
v. S., 82 Ga. 27. § 1236.
S. v., 26 Ark. 34. § 1094.
S. v., 53 Ia. 526. § 1113.
S. v., 41 La. An. 610. § 390.
S. v., 18 Mo. 419. §§ 345, 358, 359.
S. v., 80 Mo. 681. § 342.
S. v., 25 N. J. 214. § 934.
S. v., 109 N. C. 839. § 926.
U. S. v., 1 Cranch, C. C. 165. § 992.
Dunnage, Rex v., 2 Burr. 1130. §§ 660, 670.
Dunnaway v. S., 9 Yerg. 350. § 1248.
Dunnellan v. C., 7 Bush, 676. § 332.
Dunnett, Rex v., 2 East, P. C. 985. § 793.
Dunning, Reg. v., L. R. 1 C. C. 290. §§ 876, 885.
S. v., 83 Me. 178. § 46.
Dunston, Rex v., Ry. & M., N. P. 109. § 865.
Dupies, S. v., 91 Ind. 233. §§ 59, 1314.
Dupont, S. v., 2 McCord, 334. § 324.
Dupree, P. v., 98 Mich. 26. §§ 496, 500, 504.
v. S., 33 Ala. 380. §§ 303, 307.
Dupuy, C. v., Brightly, N. P. 44. § 993.
Duran v. S., 14 Tex. Ap. 195. § 355.
Durand v. P., 47 Mich. 332. § 281.
Durant v. P., 13 Mich. 351. § 726.
U. S. v., 46 Fed. R. 753. § 1332.
Duren v. S., 15 Tex. Ap. 624. § 546.
Durfee, P. v., 62 Mich. 487. §§ 157, 924.
Durham v. P., 5 Ill. 172. § 799.
v. P., 49 Ill. 233. § 1129.
v. S., 70 Ga. 264. § 323.
S. v., 72 N. C., 447. § 22.
Durkee, U. S. v., 1 McAl. 196. §§ 566, 568.
Durland v. U. S., 161 U. S. 306. § 1331.
U. S. v., 65 Fed. R. 408. § 1331.
Durr v. Howard, 6 Ark. 461. § 251.
Durrett v. S., 62 Ala. 434. § 565.
Durwood, U. S. v., 49 Fed. R. 446. § 1351.
Dutcher v. S., 16 Neb. 30. § 1004.
Dutton v. Weare, 17 N. H. 34. § 1322.
Duty v. S., 9 Ind. Ap. 595. § 905.
Duval v. S., 8 Tex. Ap. 370. § 594.
U. S. v., 2 Cranch, C. C. 42. § 1310.
Duvall v. S., 63 Ala. 12. §§ 585, 596.
S. v., 26 Wis. 415. § 358.
Duzan, S. v., 6 Blackf. 31. § 1033.
Dwenger, T. v., 2 N. M. 73. § 216.
Dwerryhouse, Reg. v., 2 Cox, 446. § 166.
Dwyer v. S., 12 Tex. Ap. 535. § 377.
U. S. v., 56 Fed. R. 464. §§ 945, 950.
Dwyre, S. v., 2 Hill (S. C.), 287. § 601.
Dycus v. S., 6 Lea, 584. § 1035.
Dyer v. Morris, 4 Mo. 214. § 1106*a*.
C. v., 128 Mass. 70. §§ 963, 975.
P. v., 79 Mich. 480. § 974.
Rex v., 2 East, P. C. 767. § 209.
v. S., 88 Ala. 225. § 846.
v. S., Meigs, 237. § 1245.
S. v., 59 Me. 303. § 147.
S. v., 41 Tex. 520. § 699.
S. v., 67 Vt. 690. §§ 969, 987.
Dyson, Rex v., Russ. & Ry. 523. §§ 205, 290.
Rex v., 1 Stark. 246. § 255.
v. S., 26 Miss. 362. § 306.
v. S., 14 Tex. Ap. 454. § 313.

E. N. E. v. S., 25 Fla. 268. § 1126.
Eades, S. v., 68 Mo. 150. §§ 758, 759.
Eads, Ex parte, 17 Neb. 145. §§ 813, 830.
v. S., 26 Tex. Ap. 69. § 618.
Eagan, C. v., 103 Mass. 71. §§ 145, 147.
C. v., 151 Mass. 45. §§ 1249, 1279.
v. S., 53 Ind. 162. § 1218.
S. v., 10 La. An. 698. § 996.
U. S. v., 30 Fed. R. 495. §§ 945, 948.
U. S. v., 30 Fed. R. 498. §§ 946, 950.
Eagle, Reg. v., 2 F. & F. 827. § 345.
Eagleton, Reg. v., Dears. 515. §§ 223, 661, 670, 680.
Eanes v. S., 10 Tex. Ap. 421. § 341.
Earhart v. C., 9 Leigh, 671. § 520.
Earle, C. v., 1 Whart. 525. § 362.
Early v. C., 86 Va. 921. § 521.
v. S., 9 Tex. Ap. 476. § 416.
v. S., 23 Tex. Ap. 364. § 1302.
Earnest, S. v., 70 Mo. 520. § 355.
S. v., 98 N. C. 740. § 251.
Earnhardt, S. v., 107 N. C. 789. §§ 64, 66.
Eason v. S., 6 Baxt. 431. § 392.
S. v., 86 N. C. 674. § 666.
Easson, U. S. v., 18 Fed. R. 590. § 1327.
Eastall, Rex v., 2 Russ. Cr. 291. § 546.
Easterling v. S., 30 Ala. 46. § 1247.
v. S., 35 Miss. 210. § 1281.
Eastern R. Co., C. v., 5 Gray, 473. § 288.
Eastman v. C., 4 Gray, 416. §§ 598, 601.
C. v., 1 Cush. 189. §§ 960, 975.
C. v., 2 Gray, 76. § 592.
P. v., 77 Cal. 171. § 565.
v. S., 109 Ind. 278. § 36.
S. v., 109 N. C. 785. § 1192.
Easton Social, etc. Club, S. v., 73 Md. 97. § 1240.
Eaton, C. v., 9 Pick. 165. § 1245.
C. v., 15 Pick. 273. §§ 511, 1318.
Reg. v., 8 C. & P. 417. § 1153.
Reg. v., 2 Den. 274. § 195.
S. v., 3 Harr. 554. § 505.
S. v., 85 Me. 237. §§ 1306, 1307.
S. v., 75 Mo. 586. § 410.
S. v., 85 Wis. 587. § 1090.
U. S. v., 144 U. S. 677. §§ 4, 14, 34.
Eaves, S. v., 106 N. C. 752. § 1266.
Eberle, C. v., 3 Serg. & R. 9. §§ 969, 989.
Eberling v. S., 136 Ind. 117. § 490.
Ebert, S. v., 40 Mo. 186. § 1308.

Eccles, Rex v., 1 Leach, 274. § 975.
Eckart, In re, 85 Wis. 681. § 362.
Eckels v. S., 20 Ohio St. 508. §§ 548, 616.
Eckert, C. v., 2 Browne, 249. § 813.
Eckler, S. v., 106 Mo. 585. § 1112.
E. C. Knight Co. U. S. v., 60 Fed. R. 934. § 1337.
U. S. v., 156 U. S. 1, 60 Fed. R. 306. §§ 963, 1337.
Eddings, S. v., 71 Mo. 545. § 160.
Eddon, S. v., 8 Wash. 292. §§ 423, 431.
Edds, C. v., 14 Gray, 406. § 1143.
Eden v. P., 161 Ill. 296, 43 N. E. R. 1108. §§ 55, 77, 1319.
Edens, S. v., 85 N. C. 522. § 1186.
S. v., 95 N. C. 693. §§ 243, 1045.
Edgar v. S., 37 Ark. 219. §§ 1260, 1261.
v. S., 45 Ark. 356. § 1259.
U. S. v., 45 Fed. R. 44. § 1343.
Edge v. C., 7 Pa. St. 275. §§ 916, 1185.
Edgell, Reg. v., 11 Cox, 132. § 518.
Edgerton, Ex parte, 59 Fed. R. 115. §§ 29, 76, 1205.
v. S., 67 Ind. 588. § 1321.
Edlavitch, S. v., 77 Md. 144. § 1264.
Edmands, C. v., 162 Mass. 517. §§ 1161, 1163.
Edmeads, Rex v., 3 C. & P. 390. § 198.
Edmonds v. S., 70 Ala. 8. §§ 535, 548.
v. S., 34 Ark. 720. §§ 373a, 377, 415.
v. S., 42 Neb. 684. § 586.
Edmondson v. S., 41 Tex. 496. § 381.
Edmonson, T. v., 4 Mont. 141. § 316.
Edmundson, Reg. v., 2 El. & El. 77. § 578.
S. v., 64 Mo. 398. § 380.
Edson, S. v., 10 La. An. 229. § 652.
Edwards v. C., 19 Pick. 124. § 785.
C. v., 135 Pa. St. 474. § 981.
P. v., 41 Cal. 640. § 307.
P. v., 59 Cal. 359. § 508.
P. v., 93 Mich. 636. § 516.
Reg. v., 8 C. & P. 611. § 286.
Reg. v., 1 Cox, 32. § 479.
Reg. v., 12 Cox, 230. § 413.
Reg. v., 13 Cox, 384. §§ 540, 544, 582.
Rex v., 5 C. & P. 518. § 470.
Rex v., 6 C. & P. 515. § 730.
Rex v., 6 C. & P. 521. § 484.
Rex v., 8 Mod. 320. § 966.
Rex v., 3 Russ. Cr. 1. § 867.
Rex v., Russ. & Ry. 283. § 1073.
Rex v., Russ. & Ry. 497. § 541.
Rex v., 3 Salk. 27. § 1199.
v. S., 49 Ala. 334. § 708.
v. S., 22 Ark. 253. § 1224.
v. S., 25 Ark. 444. § 382.
v. S., 27 Ark. 493. §§ 145, 377.
v. S., 80 Ga. 127. § 209.
v. S., 121 Ind. 450. § 1253.
v. S., 8 Lea, 411. § 1305.
v. S., 47 Miss. 581. § 303.
v. S., 5 Tex. Ap. 593. § 246.
v. S., 29 Tex. Ap. 452. § 553.
S. v., 34 La. An. 1012. § 419.
Edwards, S. v., 86 Me. 102. § 40.
S. v., 32 Mo. 548. § 1024.
S. v., 36 Mo. 394. § 558.
S. v., 60 Mo. 490. § 1281.
S. v., 70 Mo. 480. § 368.
S. v., 71 Mo. 312. § 325.
S. v., 109 Mo. 315. §§ 499, 514.
S. v., 86 N. C. 666. § 546.
S. v., 110 N. C. 511. § 1126.
S. v., 112 N. C. 901. §§ 309, 310.
U. S. v., 43 Fed. R. 67. § 881.
Edwick v. Hawkes, 18 Ch. D. 199. § 836.
Effinger v. S., 47 Ind. 235. § 1264.
Egan, T. v., 3 Dak. 119. § 330.
Egerton, Rex v., Russ. & Ry. 375. § 470.
Eggington, Rex v., 2 East, P. C. 494, 666. §§ 496, 557.
Egginton, Rex v., Bos. & P. 508. § 118.
Eggleston, C. v., 128 Mass. 408. §§ 187, 211, 1236.
Ehrgott v. New York City, 96 N. Y. 264. § 1315.
Eichelberger, C. v., 119 Pa. St. 254. §§ 543, 560, 563.
Eichenberg, C. v., 14 Pa. St. 158. § 44.
Eighmy v. P., 79 N. Y. 546. § 876.
Eight Hour Law, In re, — Colo. —, 39 Pac. R. 328. § 55.
Eiland v. S., 52 Ala. 322. §§ 302, 303, 307, 309, 332.
Eilenbecker v. District Court, 134 U. S. 31. §§ 1201, 1208.
Eitel v. S., 33 Ind. 201. §§ 1324, 1326.
Elam v. Rawson, 21 Ga. 139. § 83.
v. S., 25 Ala. 53. § 1257.
v. S., 26 Ala. 48. § 1276.
Elder, P. v., 100 Mich. 515. § 195.
S. v., 21 La. An. 157. § 521.
U. S. v., 4 Cranch, C. C. 507. § 1137.
Eldershaw, Rex v., 3 C. & P. 396. §§ 226, 465.
Eldridge v. S., 27 Fla. 162. § 1053.
Eliason, S. v., 91 N. C. 564. § 1097.
Elick, S. v., 7 Jones, 58. § 463.
Elisha, C. v., 3 Gray, 460. § 724.
Elizando v. S., 31 Tex. Ap. 237. § 397.
Elkin v. S., 63 Miss. 129. § 1321.
Elkins v. S., 2 Humph. 543. § 1190.
S. v., 63 Mo. 159. §§ 307, 419.
S. v., 101 Mo. 344. § 428.
Elk Point v. Vaughn, 1 Dak. 108. § 1217.
Ellar, S. v., 1 Dev. 267. § 1159.
Ellick, S. v., 1 Winst. ii, 56. § 316.
Elliot, Reg. v., L. & C. 103. § 1135.
S. v., 11 N. H. 540. § 142.
Elliott v. C., 12 Bush, 176. § 563.
C. v., 2 Mass. 372. §§ 11, 247.
P. v., 80 Cal. 296. § 333.
P. v., 90 Cal. 586. § 764.
P. v., 74 Mich. 264. § 1315.
Rex v., 2 East, P. C. 951. §§ 752, 761.
v. S., 26 Ala. 78. § 1294.
v. S., 46 Ga. 159. § 274.
v. S., 36 Ohio St. 318. §§ 731, 737, 740, 741.
S. v., 7 Blackf. 280. § 252.
S. v., 45 Ia. 486. § 307.

Elliott, S. v., 45 Kan. 525. § 1253.
S. v., 98 Mo. 150. § 348.
U. S. v., 51 Fed. R. 807. § 1333.
U. S. v., 62 Fed. R. 801. § 1337.
U. S. v., 64 Fed. R. 27. §§ 963, 1337.
Ellis, C. v., 158 Mass. 555. § 44.
C. v., 160 Mass. 165. § 58.
Reg. v., 2 C. & K. 470. § 378.
Reg. v., 4 Cox, 258. § 753.
Reg. v., 1 F. & F. 309. § 1076.
v. S., 76 Ala. 90. § 546.
v. S., 7 Blackf. 534. § 1173.
v. S., 25 Fla. 702. § 455.
v. S., 30 Tex. Ap. 601. §§ 153, 322.
v. S., 33 Tex. Ap. 86. §§ 171, 173.
S. v., 6 Baxt. 549. § 1198.
S. v., 3 Conn. 185. § 553.
S. v., 12 La. An. 390. § 205.
S. v., 4 Mo. 474. § 1310.
S. v., 74 Mo. 207. §§ 336, 338, 342, 345, 358, 366, 1121.
S. v., 119 Mo. 437. § 601.
S. v., 33 N. J. 102. §§ 896, 897.
S. v., 101 N. C. 765. § 420.
U. S. v., 51 Fed. R. 808. §§ 84, 1220.
Ellison, Rex v., 1 Moody, 336. § 520.
v. S., 12 Tex. Ap. 557. § 391.
S. v., 8 Blackf. 225. § 874.
S. v., 58 N. H. 325. § 602.
Elliston v. S., 10 Tex. Ap. 361. § 391.
Ellor, Reg. v., 2 East, P. C. 938. § 753.
Ellzey v. S., 57 Miss. 827. § 960.
Elmore, S. v., 44 Tex. 102. § 252.
Elmsley's Case, 1 Lewin, 126. § 815.
Elmstead, Rex v., 2 Russ. Cr. 128. § 470.
Elrod v. S., 72 Ind. 292. § 1252.
Elsberry v. S., 52 Ala. 8. § 190.
v. S., 41 Tex. 158. §§ 1302, 1304.
Elschlep v. S., 11 Tex. Ap. 301. § 452.
Else, Rex v., Russ. & Ry. 142. § 788.
Elsey v. S., 47 Ark. 572. §§ 789, 979.
Elsham, S. v., 70 Ia. 531. § 579.
Elsmore v. St. Briavels, 8 B. & C. 461. § 518.
Elsworth, Rex v., 2 East, P. C. 986. § 765.
Elwell, C. v., 2 Met. 190. §§ 134, 1086, 1091, 1095.
Elworthy, Reg. v., L. R. 1 C. C. 103. § 890.
Ely, S. v., 35 La. An. 895. § 505.
T. v., 6 Dak. 128. § 680.
Embry v. C., 79 Ky. 439. § 1017.
Emerick, S. v., 35 Ark. 324. § 1261.
Emerson v. Babcock, 66 Ia. 257. § 1186.
v. S., 33 Tex. Ap. 89. § 617.
S. v., 48 Ia. 172. § 617.
S. v., 72 Me. 455. § 192.
S. v., 16 N. H. 87. § 1223.
S. v., 53 N. H. 619. § 520.
Emert v. Missouri, 156 U. S. 296. § 44.
S. v., 103 Mo. 241. § 44.
Emery, S. v., 78 Mo. 77. § 350.
S. v., 98 N. C. 668. § 1229.
S. v., 98 N. C. 768. § 1232.
S. v., 65 Vt. 464. § 923.
Emmerson v. Annison, 1 Mod. 89. § 537.
Emmonds v. S., 87 Ala. 12. § 508.
Emmons, C. v., 98 Mass. 6. §§ 128, 1237, 1257, 1314.
P. v., 61 Cal. 487. § 256.
S. v., 72 Ia. 265. §§ 499, 508.
Empey, S. v., 79 Ia. 460. § 573.
Emporia v. Volmer, 12 Kan. 622. § 1272.
En, S. v., 10 Nev. 277. § 617.
Endaly v. S., 39 Ark. 278. § 615.
Engeman, S. v., 54 N. J. 247. § 1141.
England, Reg. v., 1 C. & K. 533. § 518.
S. v., 8 Jones, 399. §§ 554, 571.
Engleman v. S., 2 Ind. 91. § 595.
English v. S., 35 Tex. 473. § 1030.
v. S., 7 Tex. Ap. 171. § 1265.
v. S., 30 Tex. Ap. 470. § 799.
S. v., 67 Mo. 136. § 605.
S. v., 14 Mont. 399. § 551.
Engster v. S., 11 Neb. 539. §§ 586, 723.
Enke, S. v., 85 Ia. 35. § 1119.
Ennis v. S., 3 Greene (Ia.), 67. §§ 569, 623.
Eno, In re, 54 Fed. R. 669. § 1339.
Enoch, P. v., 13 Wend. 159. § 361.
Rex v., 5 C. & P. 539. § 294.
Enright v. P., 155 Ill. 32. § 304.
S. v., 90 Ia. 520. § 448.
Ensley, S. v., 10 Ia. 149. § 1268.
Enslow, S. v., 10 Ia. 115. §§ 815, 829.
Ensworth v. C., 52 Pa. St. 320. § 1195.
Enterprise, The, 1 Paine, 32. § 83.
Epperson v. S., 42 Tex. 79. § 706.
v. S., 22 Tex. Ap. 694. § 644.
S. v., 27 Mo. 255. §§ 232, 259.
Eppinger, P. v., 105 Cal. 36. § 764.
Epps, Reg. v., 4 F. & F. 81. § 762.
v. S., 102 Ind. 539. § 370.
Erb v. S., 35 Ark. 631. § 1228.
Erickson, S. v., 45 Wis. 86. § 454.
Ernest v. S., 20 Fla. 383. § 358.
Errickson, S. v., 32 N. J. 421. § 933.
Errington's Case, 2 Lewin, 148. § 426.
2 Lewin, 217. § 325.
Erskine v. C., 8 Grat. 624. §§ 520, 521.
U. S. v., 4 Cranch, C. C. 299. §§ 886, 888.
Ervine v. C., 5 Dana, 216. § 1310.
Erwin, P. v., 4 Denio, 129. §§ 200, 210, 1141.
v. S., 29 Ohio St. 186. §§ 311, 332, 336.
v. S., 11 Tex. Ap. 536. § 706.
S. v., 91 N. C. 545. § 1033.
Escanaba Co. v. Chicago, 107 U. S. 678. § 76.
Escareno v. S., 16 Tex. Ap. 85. § 342.
Eschbach, S. v., 13 Mont. 399. § 259.
Esdaile, Reg. v., 1 F. & F. 213. §§ 962, 968, 976, 977, 988.
Eskridge, S. v., 1 Swan, 413. §§ 1264, 1326.
Eslava v. S., 44 Ala. 406. §§ 1285, 1315.
Esop, Rex v., 7 C. & P. 456. § 132.
Espy v. S., 47 Ala. 533. § 1245.
Esser, Rex v., 2 East, P. C. 1125. § 739.
Essex, Reg. v., Dears. & B. 371. §§ 563, 673, 693.

Essex Club, S. v., 53 N. J. 99. § 1240.
Essex Co., C. v., 13 Gray, 239. § 5.
Estabrook, C. v., 10 Pick. 293. § 1231.
  S. v., 6 Ala. 653. § 1217.
Este, C. v., 140 Mass. 279. §§ 639, 640, 641, 649.
Estell v. S., 51 N. J. 182. § 347.
Estep v. C., 86 Ky. 39. §§ 311, 313.
Estes v. Carter, 10 Ia. 400. §§ 13, 15, 1153.
  v. S., 55 Ga. 31. §§ 160, 162, 360.
  S. v., 46 Me. 150. §§ 670, 687.
Estis, S. v., 70 Mo. 427. §§ 260, 925.
Estlinbaum, S. v., 47 Kan. 291. § 1276.
Estrada, P. v., 53 Cal. 600. § 466.
Estrado, P. v., 49 Cal. 171. § 345.
Estrella, The, 4 Wheat. 298. § 1359.
Ethrington, Rex v., 2 East, P. C., 635. § 576.
Etter, P. v., 81 Mich. 570. § 461.
Ettinger v. C., 98 Pa. St. 338. § 416.
Eubanks v. S., 3 Heisk. 488. §§ 1283, 1315.
  v. S., 5 Mo. 450. § 1310.
  S. v., 41 Tex. 291. § 252.
Euper v. S., 35 Ark. 629. §§ 1285, 1310.
Eureka Vinegar Co. v. Gazette Ptg. Co., 35 Fed. R. 570. § 1221.
European, etc. R. Co., S. v., 67 Me. 479. § 288.
Euzebe, S. v., 42 La. An. 727. § 414.
Evan, C. v., 13 Serg. & R. 426. § 8.
Evans, C. v., 132 Mass. 11. §§ 33, 128.
  C. v., 16 Pick. 448. § 91.
  v. Evans, 1 Hag. Con. 35. § 396.
  v. P., 90 Ill. 384. §§ 968, 985.
  v. P., 12 Mich. 27. §§ 373*a*, 381.
  v. P., 49 N. Y. 86. §§ 294, 327.
  Reg. v., Bell, 187. § 675.
  Reg. v., Car. & M. 298. § 499.
  Reg. v., Car. & M. 632. §§ 556, 562.
  Reg. v., 8 C. & P. 765. § 373*a*.
  Reg. v., 2 Cox, 270. § 619.
  Reg. v., Dears. & B. 236. § 750.
  Reg. v., L. & C. 252. § 670.
  Rex v., 5 C. & P. 553. §§ 673, 753.
  Rex v., 1 East, P. C. 80. § 1359.
  Rex v., Russ. Cr. 676. § 284.
  v. S., 62 Ala. 6. § 417.
  v. S., 80 Ala. 4. § 469.
  v. S., 58 Ark. 47. §§ 377, 414.
  v. S., 33 Ga. 4. §§ 308, 389.
  v. S., 1 Humph. 394. § 268.
  v. S., 44 Miss. 762. §§ 303, 304.
  v. S., 52 N. J. 261. § 443.
  v. S., 8 Ohio St. 196. § 759.
  v. S., 25 Tex. 304. § 252.
  v. S., 6 Tex. Ap. 513. § 365.
  v. S., 13 Tex. Ap. 225. § 391.
  v. S., 15 Tex. Ap. 31. § 565.
  S. v., 7 Gill & J. 290. § 598.
  S. v., 1 Hayw. 281. § 435.
  S. v., 1 Houst. Cr. C. 97. § 732.
  S. v., 5 Ired. 603. § 1138.
  S. v., 39 La. An. 912. § 274.
  S. v., 65 Mo. 574. §§ 123, 303, 332, 353.
Evans, S. v., 83 Mo. 319. § 1225.
  S. v., 124 Mo. 397. §§ 309, 333, 426.
  S. v., 128 Mo. 406. § 309.
  S. v., 15 Mont. 539. § 756.
  S. v., 15 Rich. 31. §§ 596, 599.
  S. v., 23 S. C. 209. § 592.
  S. v., 33 W. Va. 417. §§ 305, 306, 307.
  T. v., 2 Ida. 634. § 46.
  v. U. S., 153 U. S. 584. §§ 124, 1340.
  U. S. v., 1 Cranch, C. C. 149. § 904.
  U. S. v., 4 Cranch, C. C. 105. § 1312.
  U. S. v., 19 Fed. R. 912. § 893.
Everage, S. v., 23 La. An. 120. § 546.
Everett v. S., 33 Fla. 661. § 212.
  v. S., 62 Ga. 65. §§ 400, 419.
  v. S., 30 Tex. Ap. 682. §§ 305, 417.
Evers, Ex parte, 29 Tex. Ap. 539. §§ 86, 159, 160, 162.
  v. S., 31 Tex. Ap. 318. §§ 159, 341.
  S. v., 49 Mo. 542. §§ 678, 684.
Eversole v. C., 95 Ky. 623. § 311.
Everson, C. v., 140 Mass. 292. § 132.
Evins v. S., 46 Ala. 88. § 1033.
Ewell v. S., 6 Yerg. 363. § 1124.
Ewer, P. v., 141 N. Y. 129. § 59.
Ewig, C. v., 145 Mass. 119. § 1240.
Ewing, C. v., 7 Bush, 105. § 1260.
  v. S., 4 Tex. Ap. 417. § 274.
  v. S., 29 Tex. Ap. 434. § 618.
Ewington, Reg. v., Car. & M. 319. § 858.
Exall, Reg. v., 4 F. & F. 922. §§ 514, 618.
Exnicios, S. v., 33 La. An. 253. § 646.
Eyler v. S., 71 Ind. 49. § 455.
Eyre, C. v., 1 Serg. & R. 347. §§ 232, 924, 1319.
  Reg. v., 2 F. & F. 579. § 456.
Eyres, Rex v., 1 Sid. 307. § 914.
Ezekiel, S. v., 33 S. C. 115. § 806.
Ezeta, In re, 60 Fed. R. 672. § 474.
Ezzard, S. v., 40 S. C. 312. §§ 626, 634, 638.
Ezzell v. S., 29 Tex. Ap. 521. §§ 1216, 1232.

Faber, P. v., 92 N. Y. 146. § 1075.
Fagan, P. v., 66 Cal. 534. § 617.
  v. S., 21 Ark. 390. §§ 1283, 1286.
  v. S., 47 N. J. 175. § 83.
  S. v., 22 La. An. 545. § 86.
Fagent, Rex v., 7 C. & P. 238. §§ 426, 429.
Fager v. S., 22 Neb. 332. § 458.
Fagg v. S., 50 Ark. 506. § 391.
Fahey v. S., 62 Miss. 402. § 1237.
  v. S., 27 Tex. Ap. 146. §§ 1211, 1212.
Fahnestock v. S., 23 Ind. 231. §§ 139, 358, 373, 399, 423, 424.
  v. S., 102 Ind. 156. §§ 1106*a*, 1138.
Faile, S. v., 43 S. C. 52. §§ 307, 425.
Fain v. C., 78 Ky. 183. § 305.
  S. v., 106 N. C. 760. § 652.
Fairbanks v. Antrim, 2 N. H. 105. § 84.
  P. v., 7 Utah, 3. § 267.
Fairchild, P. v., 48 Mich. 31. §§ 518, 521.
Faircloth v. S., 73 Ga. 426. § 1230.

Fairclough, S. v., 29 Conn. 47. § 555.
Fairfield, S. v., 37 Me. 517. §§ 75, 1209.
Fairlamb, S. v., 121 Mo. 137. §§ 356, 358, 367, 382.
Fairly v. S., 63 Miss. 333. §§ 1222, 1229, 1281.
Fairy v. S., 18 Tex. Ap. 314. § 546.
Falkenhainer, U. S. v., 21 Fed. R. 624. § 1330.
Falkenham, S. v., 73 Md. 463. § 89.
Falkingham, Reg. v., L. R. 1 C. C. 222. § 58.
Falks v. P., 39 Mich. 200. § 128.
Fallon, Reg. v., L. & C. 217. § 214.
Fallows, Rex v., 5 C. & P. 508. § 474.
Falvey, C. v., 108 Mass. 304. § 833.
v. S., 85 Ga. 157. § 514.
Fancher, S. v., 71 Mo. 460. § 698.
Fann, S. v., 65 N. C. 317. § 554.
Fanning v. S., 66 Ga. 167. § 469.
v. S., 12 Lea, 651. §§ 575, 609.
S. v., 38 Mo. 359. § 1274.
S. v., 38 Mo. 409. § 1246.
S. v., 94 N. C. 940. § 1007.
Fanshawe, P. v., 137 N. Y. 68. § 526.
Fant v. P., 45 Ill. 259. § 1264.
S. v., 2 Brev. 487. § 1295.
S. v., 2 La. An. 837. § 1271.
Farbach v. S., 24 Ind. 77. § 1257.
Faris, C. v., 5 Rand. 691. § 1178.
v. S., 3 Ohio St. 159. §§ 922, 924.
Farley, Ex parte, 40 Fed. R. 66. § 86.
S. v., 87 Ia. 22. § 1243.
Farmer v. C., 8 Leigh, 741. § 1303.
v. P., 77 Ill. 322. § 1257.
P. v., 77 Cal. 1. §§ 426, 428.
v. S., 45 Ark. 95. § 1313.
v. S., 91 Ga. 720. § 299.
v. S., 21 Tex. Ap. 423. § 1163.
S. v., 4 Ired. 224. §§ 442, 452.
S. v., 49 Wis. 459. § 41.
Farnborough, Reg. v., 2 Q. B. D. (1895) 484. §§ 123, 564.
Farnham, Reg. v., 1 Cox, 349. § 1152.
U. S. v., 2 Blatch. 528. §§ 347, 351.
Farnsworth v. Montana, 129 U. S. 104. § 20.
T. v., 5 Mont. 303. §§ 20, 44.
Farnum, C. v., 114 Mass. 267. § 44.
v. U. S., 1 Colo. 309. §§ 542, 1330.
Farr v. Farr, 34 Miss. 597. § 1094.
S. v., 33 Ia. 553. § 194.
S. v., 34 W. Va. 84. §§ 128, 1257.
Farrall v. S., 32 Ala. 557. § 1261.
S. v., 29 Conn. 72. § 1012.
Farrand, S. v., 8 N. J. 333. § 105.
Farrar, S. v., 41 N. H. 53. § 490.
Farrel, Rex v., 2 East, P. C. 557. § 471.
Farrell, C. v., 5 Allen, 130. §§ 12, 930.
v. P., 16 Ill. 506. §§ 560, 563.
P. v., 30 Cal. 316. §§ 117, 808.
P. v., 31 Cal. 576. § 166.
Reg. v., 9 Cox, 446. § 1136.
Rex v., 1 Leach, 322, n. § 548.
v. S., 45 Ind. 371. § 1257.
v. S., 54 N. J. 416. §§ 443, 464.
v. S., 54 N. J. 421. § 87.
Farrell v. S., 32 Ohio St. 456. §§ 128, 1222.
S. v., 82 Ia. 553. §§ 744, 787.
S. v., 23 Mo. Ap. 176. § 46.
Farren, C. v., 9 Allen, 489. § 128.
Farrer v. S., 2 Ohio St. 54. § 156.
v. S., 42 Tex. 265. § 330.
Farrier, S. v., 1 Hawks, 487. § 324.
Farrington, P. v., 14 Johns. 348. § 753.
Rex v., Russ. & Ry. 207. § 526.
Farris v. C., 14 Bush, 362. §§ 303, 332.
v. S., 14 Lea. 295. § 923.
v. S., 26 Tex. Ap. 105. § 476.
Farrow, Reg. v., Dears. & B. 164. § 1148.
S. v., Phill. 161. § 572.
S. v., 10 Rich. 165. § 874.
Fastbinder v. S., 42 Ohio St. 341. § 275.
Faucett, S. v., 4 Dev. & B. 107. § 1274.
Faulkener, S. v., 2 McCord, 438. § 1302.
Faulkner, Reg. v., 13 Cox, 550. § 526.
Rex v., 1 Saund. 249, 2 Keb. 506. § 1199.
S. v., 32 La. An. 725. § 551.
U. S. v., 35 Fed. R. 730. §§ 158, 179.
Faulks v. P., 39 Mich. 200. § 1257.
Faunce v. P., 51 Ill. 311. § 714.
Fauntleroy, Rex v., 1 C. & P. 421. § 751.
Faust v. U. S., 163 U. S. 452. § 1327.
Faustre v. C., 92 Ky. 34. §§ 1079, 1082.
Fawcett, Rex v., 2 East, P. C. 862. § 757.
Fay v. C., 28 Grat. 912. §§ 563, 676, 686, 689.
v. Parker, 53 N. H. 342. § 11.
S. v., 44 N. J. 474. §§ 69, 1199, 1217, 1248.
Fayette v. Shafroth, 25 Mo. 445. § 62.
Feamster, S. v., 12 Wash. 461. § 268.
Fearson, S. v., 2 Md. 310. § 1264.
Feasel v. S., 74 Mo. 524. § 1104.
Featherstone, Reg. v., Dears. 369. § 558.
Feazle, C. v., 8 Grat. 585. § 1303.
Fee, S. v., 19 Wis. 562. § 274.
Feek v. Bloomingdale, 82 Mich. 393. § 1210.
Feeney, C. v., 13 Allen, 560. § 145.
Fehn v. S., 3 Ind. Ap. 568. § 1257.
Fehrenbach, P. v., 102 Cal. 394. §§ 560, 615.
Feilen, P. v., 58 Cal. 218. § 1084.
Feist, Reg. v., Dears. & B. 590. § 1166.
Feital v. Middlesex R., 109 Mass. 398. § 1322.
Felder v. S., 23 Tex. Ap. 477. § 431.
Feldman, C. v., 131 Mass. 588. § 929.
Felker v. S., 54 Ark. 489. §§ 222, 228, 269, 309.
Fell, Rex v., 1 Salk. 272. § 111.
v. S., 42 Md. 71. §§ 1209, 1210.
Fellows, S. v., 50 Wis. 65. § 1086.
Felter v. S., 9 Yerg. 397. § 562.
S. v., 32 Ia. 49. § 178.
Felton, C. v., 101 Mass. 204. § 790.
v. S., 139 Ind. 531. § 448.
Fenlason, S. v., 79 Me. 117. § 882.
Fenly, S. v., 18 Mo. 445. §§ 752, 796.
Fenn, S. v., 41 Conn. 590. §§ 560, 592, 595.
Fennell v. S., 32 Tex. 378. § 1153.

Fenner v. S., 3 R. I. 107. § 1267.
Fenno, C. v., 125 Mass. 387. §§ 257, 270.
Fenton, C. v., 139 Mass. 195. § 70.
v. P., 4 Hill (N. Y.), 126. § 694.
v. S., 100 Ind. 598. §§ 1218, 1220.
v. S., 33 Tex. Ap. 633. § 605.
Fenwick, U. S. v., 4 Cranch, C. C. 675. §§ 995, 999.
Ferens v. O'Brien, 11 Q. B. D. 21. §§ 536, 548.
Fergus v. S., 6 Yerg, 345. § 786.
Ferguson, Reg. v., Dears. 427. § 484.
Rex v., 2 Stark. 489. § 989.
v. S., 32 Ga. 658. § 476.
v. S., 49 Ind. 33. § 343.
v. S., 71 Miss. 805. §§ **1113**, **1114**, 1117, 1118, 1119.
v. S., 4 Tex. Ap. 156. § 260.
v. S., 6 Tex. Ap. 504. § 275.
v. S., 25 Tex. Ap. 451. § 700.
S. v., 2 Hill (S. C.), 619. §§ 325, 342.
S. v., 35 La. An. 1042. § 759.
S. v., 2 McMul. 502. § 571.
S. v., 9 Nev. 106. § 303.
S. v., 33 N. H. 424. § 63.
S. v., 76 N. C. 197. §§ 907, 909.
S. v., 107 N. C. 841. §§ 1112, 1119.
v. U. S., 64 Fed. R. 88. § 611.
Ferkle v. P., 16 Ill. Ap. 310. § 914.
Fernald, S. v., 88 Ia. 553. § 448.
Fernandez v. S., 4 Tex. Ap. 419. § 411.
Fero, U. S. v., 18 Fed. R. 901. § 740.
Ferrar's Case, Foster, 313. § 922.
Ferrell v. S., 48 Ind. 118. § 1257.
v. S., 2 Lea, 25. § 271.
v. S., 43 Tex. 503. § 161.
S. v., 22 W. Va. 759. § 1233.
S. v., 30 W. Va. 683. § 1274.
Ferrett v. Atwill, 1 Blatch. 151. § 83.
Ferrigan, C. v., 44 Pa. St. 386. §§ 307, 416, 418.
Ferrill v. C., 1 Duv. 153. § 552.
Ferris, P. v., 55 Cal. 588. § 162.
Ferry, C. v., 146 Mass. 203. § 1305.
Fertilizer Co. v. S., 24 Ohio St. 611. §§ 180, 181.
Fetterer, S. v., 65 Conn. 287. § 44.
Fick, P. v., 89 Cal. 144. §§ 487, 489.
Ficklen v. Shelby Co. Taxing Dist., 145 U. S. 1. § 44.
Fiddler v. S., 7 Humph. 508. § 1301.
S. v., 7 Humph. 501. §§ 1283, 1297.
Fidler, Rex v., 4 C. & P. 449. § 817.
Field, Rex v., Leach, 383. § 752.
v. S., 50 Ind. 15. § 277.
v. S., 57 Miss. 474. § 415.
S. v., 14 Me. 244. §§ 303, 307.
S. v., 49 Mo. 270. § 181.
Fielden v. Illinois, 143 U. S. 452. § 77.
Fieldhouse, Rex v., Cowp. 325. § 1001.
Fielding, S. v., 32 Me. 585. § 452.
Fields, C. v., 4 Leigh, 648. § 463.
v. S., 47 Ala. 603. § 307.
v. S., 52 Ala. 348. § 365.
v. S., 6 Coldw. 524. §§ 565, 617.
v. S., 134 Ind. 46. §§ 302, 306, 315.
Fields, S. v., — Ia. —, 62 N. W. R. **653**. § 42.
Fife v. S., 31 Ark. 455. § 1030.
S. v., 2 Bailey, 337. § 536.
Fifield, S. v., 18 N. H. 34. §§ 142, **922**, 924, 925, 926.
Figerio, P. v., 107 Cal. 151. § 662.
Filburn, C. v., 119 Mass. 297. § 934.
Filkins v. P., 69 N. Y. 101. §§ 125, **142**, 280.
Fillyaw, S. v., 3 Ala. 735. § 1312.
Finan, S. v., 10 Ia. 19. §§ 1235, **1239**.
Finch v. C., 14 Grat. 643. § 500.
P. v., 5 Johns. 237. § 752.
Rex v., 1 Moody, 418. § 536.
v. S., 81 Ala. 41. § 311.
v. S., 64 Miss. 461. § 1021.
Findlay, S. v., 2 Bay, 418. § 1111.
Findley v. Bear, 8 Serg. & R. 571. § **539**.
v. S., 5 Blackf. 576. § 409.
S. v., 1 Brev. 107. § 1111.
S. v., 101 Mo. 217. § 641.
Fine, P. v., 53 Cal. 263. § 271.
Finley, Ex parte, 66 Cal. 262. § **750**.
P. v., 38 Mich. 482. § 157.
Finn v. C., 5 Rand. 701. § 808.
C. v., 108 Mass. 466. § 718.
v. Donahue, 35 Conn. 216. § 1320.
v. S., 5 Ind. 400. § 353.
Finnegan v. Dugan, 14 Allen, 197. § 1129.
Finnerty, C. v., 148 Mass. 162. § 1249.
Finney, Reg. v., 12 Cox, 625. § 350.
v. S., 3 Head, 544. §§ 1073, 1077.
U. S. v., 45 Fed. R. 41. § 1331.
Fire Creek Coal & Coke Co., S. v., 33 W. Va. 188. § 55.
First Congregational Church v. Muscatine, 2 Ia. 69. § 9.
First Nat. Bank, S. v., 2 S. D. 568. §§ **42**, 53, 180.
Firth, Reg. v., L. R. 1 C. C. 172. §§ **542**, 548, 551.
Fischer v. Hayes, 6 Fed. R. 63. § **9**.
Fish, P. v., 125 N. Y. 136. § 333.
S. v., 27 N. J. 323. § 521.
Fishback v. S., 131 Ind. 304. § 9.
Fishblate, S. v., 83 N. C. 654. § **915**.
Fisher v. C., 1 Bush, 211. § 551.
C. v., 17 Mass. 46. § 753.
C. v., 138 Mass. 504. § 190.
v. McGirr, 1 Gray, 1. § 1206.
v. P., 23 Ill. 283. § 174.
P. v., 51 Cal. 319. § 521.
P. v., 14 Wend. 9. § 963.
Reg. v., 8 C. & P. 182. §§ 341, **343**, 345.
Reg. v., 3 Cox, 68. § 212.
Reg. v., L. R. 1 C. C. 7. § 817.
v. S., 43 Ala. 17. §§ 497, 500.
v. S., 46 Ala. 717. §§ 511, **617**.
v. S., 64 Ind. 435. § 159.
v. S., 77 Ind. 42. § 418.
v. S., 10 Lea, 151. §§ 292, **357**.
v. S., 33 Tex. 792. § 551.
v. S., 4 Tex. Ap. 181. § **613**.
v. S., 30 Tex. Ap. 502. §§ **167**, **174**, **178**.

Fisher, S. v., 33 La. An. 1344. § 307.
S. v., 52 Mo. 174. § 39.
S. v., 58 Mo. 256. § 765.
S. v., 65 Mo. 437. §§ 744, 757, 771.
S. v., 70 N. C. 78. § 572.
S. v., 109 N. C. 817. § 826.
S. v., 35 Vt. 584. § 1214.
S. v., 33 Wis. 154. §§ 1217, 1223, 1225.
v. U. S., 1 Okl. 252. § 872.
Fisk v. S., 9 Neb. 62. § 458.
Fiske, Ex parte, 72 Cal. 125. §§ 62, 71, 77.
S. v., 63 Conn. 388 §§ 161, 265, 274.
S. v., 18 R. I. 416. §§ 1021, 1028.
S. v., 66 Vt. 434. § 1109.
Fisler, U. S. v., 4 Biss. 59. § 794.
Fissington v. Hutchinson, 15 L. T. 390. § 11.
Fitch, P. v., 1 Wend. 198. § 756.
Reg. v., Dears. & B. 87. § 558.
Reg. v., L. & C. 159. § 754.
Fitchburg R. Co., C. v., 10 Allen, 189. § 288.
C. v., 126 Mass. 472. § 288.
Fitchie, Reg. v., Dears. & B. 175. §§ 754, 781.
Fitchpatrick, P. v., 106 Cal. 286. § 304.
Fitts, S. v., 44 N. H. 621. § 915.
Fitzenrider v. S., 30 Ind. 238. § 1256.
Fitzgerald v. Jordan, 11 Allen, 128. § 611.
v. P., 37 N. Y. 413. § 361.
P. v., 92 Mich. 328. §§ 690, 695, 702.
P. v., 105 N. Y. 146. § 1167.
Rex v., 2 East, P. C. 953. § 750.
v. S., 15 Lea, 99. § 308.
v. S., 14 Mo. 413. § 979.
v. S., 11 Neb. 577. § 426.
v. S., 50 N. J. 475. § 639.
S. v., 49 Ia. 260. §§ 145, 1148.
S. v., 63 Ia. 268. §§ 1112, 1119.
Fitzhue v. S., 13 Lea, 258. § 307.
v. S., 2 Oreg. 227. § 425.
Fitzpatrick v. C., 81 Ky. 357. § 156.
v. P., 98 Ill. 269. § 463.
P. v., 80 Cal. 538. § 723.
v. S., 37 Ark. 238. § 343.
v. S., 37 Ark. 373. § 1276.
S. v., 9 Houst. 385. §§ 546, 547, 572.
S. v., 4 R. I. 269. § 950.
Fitzporter, S. v., 93 Mo. 390. § 327.
Fitzsimmons, S. v., 63 Ia. 656. § 348.
Fitzsimon, S. v., 18 R. I. 236. § 511.
Fixmer v. P., 153 Ill. 123. § 217.
Fizell v. S., 25 Wis. 364. § 464.
Flack, P. v., 125 N. Y. 324. § 971.
S. v., 48 Kan. 146. § 605.
S. v., 24 Mo. 378. § 1310.
Flagg, C. v., 135 Mass. 545. § 220.
v. Millbury, 4 Cush. 243. § 1321.
S. v., 25 Ind. 243. §§ 852, 878.
S. v., 27 Ind. 24. § 865.
S. v., 50 N. H. 321. § 925.
Flahave, P. v., 58 Cal. 249. §§ 304, 316.
Flaherty, In re, 105 Cal. 558. § 62.
C. v., 140 Mass. 454. § 145.
Flaherty, Reg. v., 2 C. & K. 782. § 1083.
Flake v. S., 19 Ala. 551. §§ 1301, 1303, 1304.
Flanagan, C. v., 7 W. & S. 415. §§ 355, 361.
v. P., 52 N. Y. 467. § 156.
P. v., 60 Cal. 2. § 299.
Reg. v., 10 Cox, 561. § 556.
v. S., 46 Ala. 703. §§ 338, 416.
S. v., 38 W. Va. 53. § 1236.
Flanders, P. v., 18 Johns. 164. § 790.
S. v., 38 N. H. 324. § 763.
Flanegan v. S., 64 Ga. 52. § 412.
Flanigan v. P., 86 N. Y. 554. §§ 160, 162.
Flannagan, Rex v., Russ. & Ry. 187. § 494.
S. v., 67 Ind. 140. § 1182.
S. v., 26 W. Va. 116. § 396.
Flannelly, C. v., 15 Gray, 195. § 12.
Flannigan, C. v., 137 Mass. 560. § 1164.
S. v., 6 Md. 167. § 390.
Flatman, Reg. v., 14 Cox, 396. § 558.
Flattery, Reg. v., 2 Q. B. D. 410. § 446.
Fleak, S. v., 54 Ia. 429. § 1090.
Fleckenstein, S. v., 26 Minn. 177. § 1216.
Fleener v. S., 58 Ark. 98. §§ 634, 638, 639, 649, 653.
Fleet v. Hegeman, 14 Wend. 42. § 538.
Fleetwood v. C., 80 Ky 1. § 328.
Fleming, C. v., 130 Pa. St. 138. § 1236.
v. P., 27 N. Y. 329. § 1080.
P. v., 94 Cal. 308. § 463.
v. S., 136 Ind. 149. § 560.
v. S., 60 Miss. 434. § 363.
S. v., 107 N. C. 905. §§ 96, 500, 512.
Flemister v. S., 48 Ga. 170. § 869.
v. S., 81 Ga. 768. § 892.
Flemming, S. v., 66 Me. 142. § 77.
U. S. v., 18 Fed. R. 907. § 1331.
Fletcher v. Peck, 6 Cranch, 87. § 78.
v. P., 52 Ill. 395. § 487.
v. P., 117 Ill. 184. §§ 352, 363.
Reg. v., Bell, 63. §§ 438, 448.
Reg. v., 2 C. & K. 215. § 524.
Reg. v., L. R. 1 C. C. 39. § 448.
Reg. v., L. R. 1 C. C. 320. §§ 447, 858, 859.
Reg. v., L. & C. 180. § 629.
Rex v., 4 C. & P. 545. § 555.
v. S., 49 Ind. 124. § 767.
v. S., 10 Lea, 338. §§ 497, 513.
v. S., 16 Tex. Ap. 635. § 564.
S. v., 5 N. H. 257. § 12.
S. v., 24 Oreg. 295. §§ 404, 407, 426.
S. v., 1 R. I. 193. § 96.
S. v., 13 R. I. 522. § 1272.
Flinn, In re, 57 Fed. R. 496. § 44.
Flint v. P., 35 Mich. 491. §§ 872, 873, 877.
Rex v., Russ. & Ry. 460. § 675.
S. v., 63 Conn. 248. § 63.
S. v., 62 Mo. 393. § 648.
Flora, S. v., 109 Mo. 293. § 796.
Florenza, S. v., 28 La. An. 945. § 377.
Flores v. S., 13 Tex. Ap. 665. § 618.
Florez v. S., 11 Tex. Ap. 102. § 897.
v. S., 26 Tex. Ap. 477. § 619.

Floto, S. v., 81 Md. 600. § 860.
Flournoy v. S., 16 Tex. 31. § 257.
 v. S., 25 Tex. Ap. 244. § 232.
 v. S., 46 La. An. 1518. § 639.
Flower v. Shaw, 2 C. & K. 703. § 765.
 v. S., 39 Ark. 209. § 1281.
Flowers, Reg. v., 16 Q. B. D. 643. § 561.
 T. v., 2 Mont. 531. § 12.
Floyd v. S., 30 Ala. 511. § 868.
 v. S., 79 Ala. 39. §§ 922, 930.
 v. S., 82 Ala. 16. § 309.
 v. S., 12 Ark. 43. §§ 486, 487, 918.
 v. S., 36 Ga. 91. § 246.
 v. S., 3 Heisk. 342. § 332.
 v. S., 29 Tex. Ap. 349. §§ 194, 255.
 S. v., 1 Houst. Cr. C. 110. § 750.
 S. v., 6 Jones, 392. § 339.
 S. v., 15 Mo. 349. § 619.
 S. v., 39 S. C. 23. § 1191.
 S. v., 5 Strobh. 58. § 765.
Flye, S. v., 26 Me. 312. §§ 175, 444, 744, 757, 765, 797.
Flynn, C. v., 3 Cush. 525. § 873.
 v. Galesburg, 12 Ill. Ap. 200. § 1257.
 P. v., 73 Cal. 511. § 515.
 P. v., 96 Mich. 276. § 455.
 P. v., 7 Utah, 378. § 566.
 v. S., 34 Ark. 441. § 1291.
 v. S., 8 Tex. Ap. 368. § 260.
 S. v., 28 Ia. 26. § 971.
 S. v., 124 Mo. 480. § 615.
 S. v., 35 Tex. 354. § 1143.
 U. S. v., 1 Dill. 451. § 1263.
Foering, C. v., Bright. 315. § 977.
Fogerson, S. v., 29 Mo. 416. § 1020.
Fogerty, C. v., 8 Gray, 489. §§ 449, 452, 453.
Fogg v. S., 9 Yerg. 392. § 796.
Folden v. S., 13 Neb. 328. § 787.
Foley, Ex parte, 62 Cal. 508. §§ 1017, 1019, 1160.
 C. v., 99 Mass. 497. §§ 26, 1017.
 C. v., 99 Mass. 499. § 1018.
 Reg. v., 17 Cox, 142. § 537.
 v. S., 9 Ind. 363. § 271.
 S. v., 81 Ia. 36. § 638.
 S. v., 45 N. H. 466. § 1145.
Folkes, Reg. v., 2 M. & Rob. 460. §§ 454, 462.
 Rex v., 1 Moody, 354. § 449.
 v. S., 63 Miss. 81. § 44.
Follansbee, C. v., 155 Mass. 274. §§ 1148, 1151.
Follet, S. v., 6 N. H. 53. § 1318.
Foltz v. S., 33 Ind. 215. § 1324.
Folwell v. S., 49 N. J. 31. §§ 819, 826.
Fomby v. S., 87 Ala. 36. § 796.
Fonda, P. v., 62 Mich. 401. § 790.
Fondren v. S., 16 Tex. Ap. 48. § 259.
Fong Ching, P. v., 78 Cal. 169. §§ 896, 898.
Fong Yue Ting v. U. S., 149 U. S. 698. §§ 79, 1344.
Fontaine v. S., 6 Baxt. 514. § 1318.
Fontenette, S. v., 38 La. An. 61. § 462.
Fonville v. S., 91 Ala. 39. §§ 160, 413.
Fooks, S. v., 65 Ia. 196. §§ 667, 686, 687.
 S. v., 65 Ia. 452. § 667.
Foote v. P., 56 N. Y. 321. §§ 12, 21.
 v. S., 59 Md. 264. § 80.
Foot You, S. v., 24 Oreg. 61. §§ 428, 429.
Forbes, Reg. v., 10 Cox, 362. § 924.
 Rex v., 7 C. & P. 224. § 762.
 U. S. v., Crabbe, 558. § 159.
Forcier, S. v., 65 N. H. 42. § 36.
Ford, C. v., 5 Gray, 475. § 139.
 Rex v., Russ. & Ry. 329. § 328.
 v. S., 71 Ala. 385. §§ 173, 179.
 v. S., 34 Ark. 649. § 421.
 v. S., 51 Ark. 103. § 1185.
 v. S., 12 Md. 514. § 362.
 S. v., 30 La. An., Pt. I, 311. § 511.
 S. v., 37 La. An. 443. §§ 307, 988.
 S. v., 38 La. An. 797. § 744.
 S. v., 70 Mo. 469. § 5.
 S. v., 2 Root, 93. § 805.
 U. S. v., 50 Fed. R. 467. § 34.
Forde v. Skinner, 4 C. & P. 239. § 235.
Fore, S. v., 1 Ired. 378. §§ 1131, 1132.
Foreman v. Hunter, 59 Ia. 550. § 1271.
 v. S., 31 Tex. 477. §§ 1017, 1021.
Foren, P. v., 25 Cal. 361. § 357.
Forkener v. S., 95 Ind. 406. § 1234.
Forney, P. v., 81 Cal. 118. § 232.
 S. v., 24 La. An. 191. § 334.
Forrest, C. v., 170 Pa. St. 40. § 1197.
 v. S., 13 Lea, 103. § 375.
 v. S., 3 Tex. Ap. 232. § 257.
 S. v., 30 Tex. 503. § 1193.
Forrester, Reg. v., 4 F. & F. 857. § 426.
 v. S., 63 Ga. 349. § 1237.
Forsgate, Rex v., 1 Leach, 463. § 546.
Forshner, S. v., 43 N. H. 89. § 460.
Forster, Reg. v., Dears. 456. § 789.
Forsythe, S. v., 78 Ia. 595. § 1148.
 S. v., 89 Mo. 667. § 142.
Fort v. S., 82 Ala. 50. § 567.
 v. S., 92 Ga. 8. § 41.
Fortenberry v. S., 55 Miss. 403. § 303.
 v. S., 56 Miss. 286. § 647.
Fortenbury v. S., 47 Ark. 188. § 1285.
Forty-three Gallons of Whiskey, U. S. v., 108 U. S. 491. § 1217.
Foss, P. v., 80 Mich. 559. §§ 142. 245.
Fossdahl v. S., 89 Wis. 482. § 1279.
Fossett v. S., 16 Tex. Ap. 375. § 1304.
 v. S., 18 Tex. Ap. 330. § 1303.
Foster v. C., 12 Bush. 373. § 1152.
 v. C., 8 Watts & S. 77. §§ 9, 11, 1040.
 C. v., 1 Mass. 488. § 922.
 C. v., 107 Mass. 221. § 639.
 C. v., 114 Mass. 311. §§ 762, 763, 766.
 v. Kansas, 112 U. S. 201. §§ 29, 1201.
 v. P., 1 Colo. 293. §§ 82, 435, 437.
 v. P., 50 N. Y. 598. §§ 326, 432, 434.
 P. v., 64 Mich. 715. § 1221.
 Reg. v., 2 Q. B. D. 301. § 669.
 Rex v., 6 C. & P. 325. § 414.
 Rex v., 7 C. & P. 495. § 777.
 Rex v., Russ. & Ry. 459. §§ 860, 879.
 v. S., 84 Ala. 451. § 1302.
 v. S., 88 Ala. 182. § 849.
 v. S., 45 Ark. 361. §§ 1233, 1256, 1259.
 v. S., 71 Md. 553. § 596.
 v. S., 52 Miss. 695. § 617.

Foster v. S., 1 Tex. Ap. 363. § 617.
v. S., 8 Tex. Ap. 248. § 414.
v. S., 11 Tex. Ap. 105. § 311.
v. S., 31 Tex. Ap. 409. § 1074.
v. S., 32 Tex. Ap. 39. §§ 866, 869.
S. v., 10 Ia. 435. § 922.
S. v., 11 Ia. 291. § 643.
S. v., 37 Ia. 404. §§ 634, 644, 656a.
S. v., 7 La. An. 525. § 389.
S. v., 36 La. An. 857. § 363.
S. v., 3 McCord, 442. § 754.
S. v., 61 Mo. 549. §§ 353, 359.
S. v., 23 N. H. 348. §§ 188, 1281.
S. v., 31 Tex. 578. § 1125.
S. v., 21 W. Va. 767. § 1131.
S. v., 26 W. Va. 272. § 1132.
v. T., 1 Wash. 411. § 1313.
v. Tucker, 3 Me. 458. § 11.
U. S. v., 6 Fed. R. 247. § 945.
Foulkes, Reg. v., L. R. 2 C. C. 150. § 626.
S. v., 57 Mo. 461. § 872.
Fountain v. Smith, 70 Ia. 282. § 752.
Fourcade, S. v., 45 La. An. 717. § 6.
Fournier, S. v., 12 Mont. 235. § 634.
Fourteen Pkgs. Whiskey, U. S. v., 66 Fed. R. 984. § 1349.
Foute v. S., 15 Lea, 712. § 808.
Fouts v. S., 4 Greene (Ia.), 500. §§ 353, 359, 361.
v. S., 8 Ohio St. 98. §§ 320, 326, 361, 383, 388.
Fowler, C. v., 145 Mass. 398. §§ 1260, 1274.
P. v., 88 Cal. 136. §§ 84, 1101, 1105.
v. S., 100 Ala. 96. § 546.
v. S., 5 Day, 81. § 1136.
v. S., 3 Heisk. 154. § 252.
S. v., 52 Ia. 103. §§ 150, 316.
Fox v. Abel, 2 Conn. 541. § 1320.
C. v., 7 Gray, 585. §§ 292, 325, 332, 377.
v. P., 95 Ill. 71. §§ 767, 808.
P. v., 25 Mich. 492. §§ 859, 879.
Reg. v., 2 Q. B. 658. § 1166.
Reg. v., 19 W. R. 109. § 220.
v. S., 5 How. (Miss.) 410. § 790.
v. S., 3 Tex. Ap. 329. § 1093.
S. v., 80 Ia. 312. §§ 505, 506, 508.
S. v., 94 N. C. 928. § 210.
S. v., 16 N. J. 152. §§ 187, 1273.
S. v., 25 N. J. 566. § 377.
v. T., 2 Wash. T. 297. § 36.
U. S. v., 95 U. S. 670. § 78.
Foxby, Reg. v., 6 Mod. 11. § 26.
Foy, P. v., 138 N. Y. 664. § 157.
S. v., 82 N. C. 679. § 536.
S. v., 98 N. C. 744. § 918.
Foye, U. S. v., 1 Curt. 364. §§ 772, 1330, 1335.
Frahm, S. v., 73 Ia. 355. §§ 504, 514.
Fraize, C. v., 5 Bush, 325. § 1310.
Frame, S. v., 4 Harr. 569. § 550.
S. v., 39 Ohio St. 399. § 1212.
Framness, S. v., 43 Minn. 490. § 1114.
Frampton, Reg. v., 2 C. & K. 47. § 517.
Reg. v., Dears. & B. 585. §§ 625, 713.
France v. S., 6 Baxt. 478. § 1318.
S. v., 76 Mo. 681. §§ 341, 383.
Frances, Reg. v., 4 Cox, 57. § 172.
S. v., 36 La. An. 336. § 274.
Francis, P. v., 38 Cal. 183. § 169.
Reg. v., L. R. 2 C. C. 128. § 691.
Rex v., Russ. & Ry. 209. § 764.
v. S., 7 Tex. Ap. 501. § 808.
Francisco v. S., 24 N. J. 30. §§ 253, 487.
Franco v. S., 42 Tex. 276. § 506.
Frank, P. v., 28 Cal. 507. §§ 803, 808, 758.
v. S., 27 Ala. 37. § 323.
v. S., 39 Miss. 705. §§ 500, 514.
v. S., 67 Miss. 125. § 716.
v. S., 30 Tex. Ap. 381. § 563.
S. v., 41 La. An. 596. § 494.
S. v., 103 Mo. 120. §§ 229, 1153.
Frankland, Reg. v., L. & C. 276. §§ 626, 628, 635.
Franklin v. C., 92 Ky. 612. § 416.
Reg. v., 15 Cox, 163. § 347.
Reg. v., 4 F. & F. 94. § 704.
v. S., 29 Ala. 14. §§ 303, 307.
v. S., 5 Baxt. 613. § 395.
v. S., 69 Ga. 36. §§ 406, 420.
v. S., 91 Ga. 712. § 876.
v. S., 27 Tex. Ap. 136. § 141.
v. S., 30 Tex. Ap. 628. §§ 309, 339.
S. v., 36 Tex. 155. § 257.
T. v., 2 N. M. 307. § 160.
Franklin Falls Co., S. v., 49 N. H. 240. §§ 46, 102, 1173.
Franks, Rex v., 2 Leach, 644. § 783.
S. v., 64 Ia. 39. §§ 499, 516.
Franz, Reg. v., 2 F. & F. 580. § 408.
Fraser, Rex v., 1 Moody, 407. § 1077.
Rex v., 1 Moody, 419. § 255.
v. S., 55 Ga. 325. §§ 416, 418, 420.
S. v., 1 N. D. 425. §§ 1205, 1248.
U. S. v., 42 Fed. R. 140. § 1351.
Frasher v. S., 3 Tex. Ap. 263. § 1131.
Frasier v. S., 5 Mo. 536. § 1326.
Fray, Rex v., 1 East, P. C. 236. § 347.
Frazer, Reg. v., 8 Cox, 446. § 1102.
Frazier v. S., 85 Ala. 17. § 560.
v. S., 135 Ind. 38. § 514.
v. S., 39 Tex. 390. § 1153.
v. S., 18 Tex. Ap. 434. § 557.
S. v., 1 Houst. Cr. C. 176. §§ 414, 429, 430.
S. v., 79 Me. 95. § 1174.
S. v., 53 Kan. 87. §§ 228, 454, 466.
S. v., 54 Kan. 719. § 454.
Frederick v. C., 4 B. Mon. 7. § 1143.
S. v., 45 Ark. 347. § 1321.
S. v., 85 Mo. 145. § 217.
Fredericks, P. v., 106 Cal. 554. § 421.
S. v., 16 Mo. 382. § 1231.
Freel, P. v., 48 Cal. 436. § 336.
v. S., 21 Ark. 212. §§ 145, 204, 208.
v. S., 125 Ind 166. § 266.
Freeland v. P., 16 Ill. 380. § 1001.
P. v., 6 Cal. 96. § 373a.
Freels, S. v., 3 Humph. 228. § 268.
Freeman v. P., 4 Denio, 9. §§ 166, 169.
P. v., 1 Ida. (N. S.) 322. § 536.

Freeman, Rex v., 5 C. & P. 534. § 626.
v. S., 19 Fla. 552. § 891.
v. S., 70 Ga. 736. § 338.
v. S., 119 Ind. 501. § 1143.
v. S., 6 Port. 372. § 1188.
S. v., 6 Blackf. 248. § 1247.
S. v., 8 Ia. 428. §§ 925, 929.
S. v., 27 Ia. 333. §§ 1249, 1270.
S. v., 72 N. C. 521. § 599.
S. v., 89 N. C. 469. § 597.
S. v., 100 N. C. 429. §§ 455, 456, 460.
S. v., 38 N. H. 426. § 38.
S. v., 1 Speers, 57. §§ 378, 425.
S. v., 27 Vt. 520. § 1235.
S. v., 63 Vt. 496. § 1160.
U. S. v., 4 Mason, 505. § 325.
Freeport, S. v., 43 Me. 198. §§ 183, 1195.
Freese v. S., 14 Tex. Ap. 31. § 1216.
Freeth, Rex v., Russ. & Ry. 127. § 675.
Freiberg v. S., 94 Ala. 91. §§ 1218, 1261.
Freleigh v. S., 8 Mo. 606. §§ 75, 1209.
French v. Noel, 22 Grat. 454. § 1228.
P. v., 102 N. Y. 583. §§ 4, 18.
Reg. v., 14 Cox, 328. § 389.
Reg. v., L. R. 1 C. C. 217. § 754.
Rex v., Russ. & Ry. 491. § 495.
v. S., 85 Wis. 400. § 166.
S. v., 120 Ind. 229. § 831.
U. S. v., 57 Fed. R. 382. § 1337.
v. White, 4 W. Va. 170. § 913.
Frese v. S., 23 Fla. 267. §§ 1218, 1220.
Fretwell, Reg. v., 9 Cox, 152. §§ 207, 327.
Reg. v., L. & C. 443. § 276.
Frey, C. v., 50 Pa. St. 245. § 694.
Fribly v. S., 42 Ohio St. 205. § 940.
Fricker, S. v., 45 La. An. 646. § 625.
Frieberg, S. v., 49 Ohio St. 585. § 30.
Friedeborn v. C., 113 Pa. St. 242. § 1321.
Friederich v. P., 147 Ill. 310. § 265.
Friedlander v. S., 7 Tex. Ap. 204. § 1026.
Friel v. P., 4 Colo. Ap. 259. § 1190.
Friend v. Miller, 52 Kan. 139. § 939.
Rex v., Russ. & Ry. 20. §§ 130, 286, 248.
S. v., 47 Minn. 449. §§ 594, 607.
Frierson v. Hewett, 2 Hill (S. C.), 499. § 816.
Friery v. P., 2 Keyes, 424. § 160.
Fries v. Porch, 49 Ia. 351. § 1267.
Frigerio, P. v., 107 Cal. 151. § 662.
Frisbie v. S., 1 Oreg. 248. § 1273.
v. S., 1 Oreg. 264. §§ 1285, 1311.
v. U. S., 157 U. S. 160. § 1348.
Frisby, S. v., 90 Mo. 530. § 877.
Frisch, S. v., 45 La. An. 1283. § 643.
Fritchler, S. v., 54 Mo. 424. § 564.
Fritts, S. v., 48 Ark. 66. § 1120.
Fritz v. S., 1 Baxt. 15. §§ 1218, 1221.
S. v., 23 La. An. 55. § 806.
Frorer v. P., 141 Ill. 171. § 55.
Frost, C. v., 5 Mass. 53. §§ 53, 190.
Reg. v., 9 C. & P. 129. §§ 1357, 1358.
S. v., 1 Brev. 385. § 247.
Froud, Rex v., Russ. & Ry. 389. § 757.
Frowen, Reg. v., 4 Cox, 266. § 508.
Fry, Reg. v., Dears. & B. 449. § 667.
Rex v., Russ. & Ry. 482. § 543.
Fry v. S., 81 Ga. 645. § 338.
v. S., 63 Ind. 552. § 44.
S. v., 40 Kan. 311. § 933.
Frye, C. v., 1 Va. Cas. 19. § 713.
Fryeburg, S. v., 15 Me. 405. § 1185.
Fuentes, S. v., 5 La. An. 427. § 338.
Fugate v. S., 2 Humph. 397. §§ 1288, 1313.
Fulcher v. S., 41 Tex. 233. § 463.
v. S., 28 Tex. Ap. 465. § 414.
v. S., 32 Tex. Ap. 621. § 561.
v. S., 33 Tex. Ap. 22. § 389.
Fulford v. S., 50 Ga. 591. § 268.
Fulgham v. S., 46 Ala. 143. § 243.
Fulkerson, S. v., Phill. 233. § 323.
U. S. v., 74 Fed. R. 619. § 1334.
Fullagar, Reg. v., 14 Cox, 370. § 630.
Fullarton, Reg. v., 6 Cox, 194. § 601.
Fuller v. Bean, 30 N. H. 181. § 1267.
v. Chicago & N. W. R. Co., 31 Ia. 187. § 40.
v. Chicago & N. W. R. Co., 17 Wall. 560. § 40.
C. v., 132 Mass. 563. § 977.
C. v., 163 Mass. 499. § 1095.
C. v., 8 Met. 313. § 790.
v. Leet, 59 N. H. 163. § 1236.
P. v., 2 Park. Cr. 16. §§ 347, 351.
Rex v., Russ. & Ry. 308. §§ 784, 786.
Rex v., Russ. & Ry. 408. § 470.
v. S., 48 Ala. 273. §§ 494, 514.
v. S., 30 Tex. Ap. 559. §§ 302, 305, 365, 390.
S. v., 34 Conn. 280. § 632.
S. v., 96 Mo. 165. § 298.
S. v., 114 N. C. 885. § 359.
S. v., 31 Tex. 559. §§ 1302, 1304.
U. S. v., 72 Fed. R. 771. § 1332.
Fulmer v. C., 97 Pa. St. 503. § 602.
Fulton v. S., 13 Ark. 168. §§ 569, 625.
S. v., 19 Mo. 680. § 1310.
Funk v. Israel, 5 Ia. 438. § 1267.
S. v., 27 Minn. 318. § 1216.
Furbush, S. v., 72 Me. 493. § 44.
Furgeson v. Earl of Kinnoull, 9 Cl. & F. 251. § 120.
v. P., 90 Ill. 510. § 1001.
Furley v. Chicago, M. & St. P. R Co., 90 Ia. 146. § 128.
Furlong, S. v., 19 Me. 225. §§ 612, 613, 616.
S. v., 26 Me. 69. §§ 858, 1002.
U. S. v., 5 Wheat. 184. § 1359.
Furman v. Knapp, 19 Johns. 248. § 1217.
P. v., 85 Mich. 110. § 94.
Furnish v. C., 14 Bush, 180. §§ 235, 253.
Furnival, Rex v., Russ. & Ry. 445. § 506.
Fursey, Rex v., 6 C. & P. 81. §§ 997.
Fussell v. S., 94 Ga. 78. § 309.
S. v., 45 Ark. 65. § 36.

Gabe v. S., 6 Ark. 519. § 786.
Gabel v. Houston, 29 Tex. 335. § 1319.
Gable, C. v., 7 Serg. & R. 423. §§ 109, 368.
Gablick v. P., 40 Mich. 292. §§ 619, 620.
Gabriel v. S., 40 Ala. 357. § 594.

Gabrielsky v. S., 13 Tex. Ap. 428. §§ 880, 883, 892.
Gaby, Rex v., Russ. & Ry. 178. § 546.
Gaddy v. S., 8 Tex. Ap. 127. §§ 644, 654.
Gade, Rex v., 2 Leach, 732, 2 East, P. C. 874. § 758.
Gadsby, U. S. v., 1 Cranch, C. C. 55. § 7.
Gadsden, S. v., 20 S. C. 456. § 825.
Gadson v. S., 36 Tex. 350. § 546.
Gadway, P. v., 61 Mich. 285. § 85.
Gady v. S., 83 Ala. 51. § 652.
Gaffeny, S. v., 66 Ia. 262. § 1268.
Gaffery, S. v., 12 La. An. 265. § 604.
Gage, P. v., 62 Mich. 271. § 456.
v. Shelton, 3 Rich. 242. § 521.
v. S., 22 Tex. 123. §§ 553, 575.
Gager, S. v., 28 Conn. 232. § 1025.
Gagne, C. v., 153 Mass. 205. §§ 1202, 1278.
Gahagan, Rex v., 1 East, P. C. 129. § 1358.
Gaige, P. v., 26 Mich. 30. § 859.
Gailor, S. v., 71 N. C. 88. § 529.
Gaines v. S., 7 Lea, 410. § 1159.
v. S., 4 Tex. Ap. 330. § 546.
Gainus, S. v., 86 N. C. 632. § 268.
Gaiocchio v. S., 9 Tex. Ap. 387. § 1237.
Gaitan v. S., 11 Tex. Ap. 544. §§ 322, 344.
Gaither v. S., 21 Tex. Ap. 527. § 609.
S. v., 72 N. C. 458. § 572.
Galavan, C. v., 9 Allen, 271. § 236.
Galbreath v. S., 36 Tex. 200. §§ 1294, 1302.
Gale, P. v., 77 Cal. 120. § 639.
Reg. v., 2 Q. B. D. 141. § 634.
Gallagher, C. v., 1 Allen, 592. § 1180.
C. v., 16 Gray, 240. §§ 597, 610.
C. v., 126 Mass. 54. § 596.
C. v., 6 Met. 565. §§ 256, 478.
v. P., 29 Ill. Ap. 401. § 1257.
v. P., 120 Ill. 179. § 1262.
P. v., 100 Cal. 466. § 634.
P. v., 4 Mich. 244. § 1206.
Reg. v., 15 Cox, 291. § 1357.
v. S., 3 Minn. 270. §§ 139, 246, 311.
v. S., 10 Tex. Ap. 469. § 950.
U. S. v., 2 Paine, 447. § 260.
Galland, P. v., 55 Mich. 628. § 639.
Gallears, Reg. v., 2 C. & K. 981. § 593.
Reg. v., 1 Den. 501. § 538.
Gallery v. S., 92 Ga. 463. §§ 274, 275.
Galligan, C. v., 144 Mass. 171. § 190.
Gallinore, S. v., 7 Ired. 147. § 600.
Galloway, P. v., 17 Wend. 540. § 694.
v. S., 60 Ark. 362. § 1254.
v. S., 29 Ind. 442. §§ 865, 878.
v. S., 23 Tex. Ap. 398. § 1219.
Galvin v. S., 6 Coldw. 283. §§ 340, 341.
S. v., 27 Minn. 16. § 1184.
Gamble, Reg. v., 10 Cox, 545. § 226.
Reg. v., 16 M. & W. 384. § 586.
v. S., 35 Miss. 222. § 1299.
S. v., 119 Mo. 427. § 241.
Gaming Implements, C. v., 155 Mass. 165. § 1312.
Gamlen, Reg. v., 1 F. & F. 90. § 161.
Gammons, C. v., 23 Pick. 201. § 1197.
Gandolpho v. S., 33 Ind. 439. § 572.
Gandy v. S., 82 Ala. 61. §§ 942, 944, 949.
v. S., 86 Ala. 20. § 949.
v. S., 23 Neb. 436. § 878.
v. S., 27 Neb. 707. §§ 877, 892.
Gannett, C. v., 1 Allen, 7. § 1141.
Gannon, C. v., 97 Mass. 547. §§ 145, 148.
v. P., 127 Ill. 507. § 390.
Garber v. S., 4 Coldw. 161. § 413.
v. S., 94 Ind. 219. § 601.
Garbracht v. C., 96 Pa. St. 449. § 1227.
Garbutt, P. v., 17 Mich. 9. §§ 179, 307, 320.
Garcia v. S., 26 Tex. 209. §§ 557, 616, 618.
v. S., 19 Tex. Ap. 389. § 257.
Gardenheir v. S., 6 Tex. 348. § 271.
Gardiner, Reg. v., 8 C. & P. 737. §§ 873, 878.
v. S., 55 N. J. 17. § 608.
v. S., 33 Tex. 692. § 572.
Gardner, C. v., 11 Gray, 438. §§ 78, 91, 353, 361.
C. v., 133 Pa. St. 284. § 44.
v. P., 4 Ill. 83. §§ 414, 419.
v. P., 20 Ill. 430. § 1216.
v. P., 62 N. Y. 299. § 132.
P. v., 98 Cal. 127. §§ 453, 454, 462.
P. v., 2 Johns. 477. § 553.
P. v., 144 N. Y. 119. §§ 226, 405.
Reg. v., 1 C. & K. 628. §§ 557, 1330, 1335.
Reg. v., Dears. & B. 40. § 683.
Reg. v., 1 F. & F. 669. § 289.
Reg. v., L. & C. 243. § 566.
Rex v., 1 C. & P. 479. §§ 470, 737.
Rex v., 1 Moody, 390. § 255.
v. S., 96 Ala. 12. §§ 169, 803.
v. S., 4 Ind. 632. § 242.
v. S., 25 Md. 146. § 586.
v. S., 55 N. J. 17. § 572.
S. v., 1 Houst. Cr. C. 146. § 365.
S. v., 2 Mo. 23. § 917.
S. v., 5 Nev. 377. § 112.
S. v., 53 Ohio St. 145. § 897.
U. S. v., 42 Fed. R. 829. §§ 977, 979, 982.
U. S. v., 10 Pet. 618. § 775.
Garfield v. S., 74 Ind. 60. § 543.
Garibaldi, S. v., 44 La. An. 809. §§ 62, 65, 71.
Garing, S. v., 74 Me. 152. § 1138.
S. v., 75 Me. 591. § 1145.
Garity, S. v., 46 N. H. 61. § 1139.
Garland, Ex parte, 4 Wall. 333. §§ 78, 79.
C. v., 3 Met. (Ky.) 478. §§ 586, 1292.
C. v., 5 Rand. 652. §§ 1286, 1315.
Garlick, Reg. v., 1 Den. 276. § 676.
Garlitz v. S., 71 Md. 293. §§ 359, 365.
Garner, Reg. v., 4 F. & F. 346. § 418.
v. S., 8 Blackf. 568. § 1216.
v. S., 28 Fla. 113. § 307.
v. S., 5 Lea, 213. § 765.
v. S., 36 Tex. 693. § 546.

Garner v. S., 28 Tex. Ap. 561. § 1260.
v. S., 31 Tex. Ap. 22. § 503.
S. v., 8 Port. 447. § 834.
Garnet v. S., 1 Tex. Ap. 605. §§ 227, 236.
Garnett, P. v., 29 Cal. 622. § 609.
P. v., 35 Cal. 470. § 672.
Garnham, Reg. v., 8 Cox, 451. § 538.
Garraud, S. v., 5 Oreg. 216. §§ 353, 426.
Garretson, U. S. v., 42 Fed. R. 22. §§ 83, 1353.
Garrett, P. v., 68 Mich. 487. § 1258.
Reg. v., Dears. 232. §§ 211, 688.
v. S., 89 Ga. 446. § 265.
v. S., 49 N. J. 94. §§ 115, 1172.
S. v., 80 Ia. 589. §§ 922, 924, 926, 1018.
S. v., 82 N. C. 580. § 933.
S. v., 34 Tex. 674. § 594.
Garris v. S., 35 Ga. 247. § 548.
S. v., 98 N. C. 733. §§ 671, 685, 690.
Garrison v. P., 6 Neb. 274. §§ 438, 458, 463.
v. S., 14 Ind. 287. § 1145.
S. v., 52 Kan. 180. § 499.
Garrity v. P., 70 Ill. 83. § 281.
v. P., 107 Ill. 162. § 514.
Gartman v. S., 16 Tex. Ap. 215. § 892.
Gartrell, S. v., 14 Ind. 280. § 1087.
Garvey's Case, 7 Colo. 384. §§ 320, 361.
Garvey v. C., 8 Gray, 382. § 28.
S. v., 11 Minn. 154. §§ 161, 267.
Garvigan, S. v., 36 Kan. 322. § 766.
Gary v. Masonic Aid Ass'n, 87 Ia. 25. § 631.
Garza v. S., 11 Tex. Ap. 345. §§ 274, 275.
Gascoigne, Rex v., 2 East, P. C. 709. § 469.
Gaskill v. S., 56 Ind. 550. § 815.
Gaskins, S. v., 93 N. C. 547. § 339.
Gassaway, P. v., 23 Cal. 51. § 617.
P. v., 28 Cal. 404. § 205.
Gassert, S. v., 65 Mo. 352. § 368.
Gaster, S. v., 45 La. An. 636. §§ 13, 15.
Gaston, S. v., 73 N. C. 93. § 573.
Gastro, P. v., 75 Mich. 127. §§ 1106*a*, 1138.
Gates, P. v., 46 Cal. 52. § 1087.
P. v., 13 Wend. 311. §§ 661, 684, 694, 698, 699, 702, 710.
P. v., 15 Wend. 159. § 529.
v. S., 71 Miss. 874. §§ 771, 789.
S. v., 17 N. H. 373. §§ 867, 874, 880.
S. v., 27 Minn. 52. § 1114.
S. v., 107 N. C. 832. §§ 858, 872.
Gatewood, P. v., 20 Cal. 147. § 139.
Gathercole, Reg. v., 2 Lewin, 237. § 1049.
Gathings v. S., 44 Miss. 343. § 1237.
Gatlin v. S., 5 Tex. Ap. 531. § 332.
Gatton v. C., R. I. & P. R. Co., — Ia. —, 63 N. W. R. 589. § 14.
Gaugh, P. v., 2 Utah, 70. § 588.
Gaul, S. v., 50 Conn. 578. §§ 438, 442.
Gault v. S., 34 Ga. 533. § 1252.
Gaunt v. S., 50 N. J. 490. §§ 1129, 1132.
v. S., 52 N. J. 178. § 1129.
S. v., 13 Oreg. 115. § 13.
Gavin, C. v., 121 Mass. 54. § 593.
C. v., 160 Mass. 523. § 1222.
Gay, Rex v., 7 C. & P. 230. § 429.
v. S., 90 Tenn. 645. § 1175.
S. v., 10 Mo. 440. § 191.
T. v., 2 Dak. T. 125. §§ 316, 333.
Gayle v. S., 4 Lea, 466. § 1037.
Gaylor, Reg. v., Dears. & B. 288. §§ 200, 208, 347, 1147.
Gaylord, U. S. v., 17 Fed. R. 438. § 1332.
U. S. v., 50 Fed. R. 410. § 1332.
Gaze, Rex v., Russ. & Ry. 384. § 715.
Gazell, S. v., 30 Mo. 92. § 548.
Gazley v. S., 17 Tex. Ap. 267. § 455.
Gazola v. S., 45 Ark. 458. § 1266.
Geach, Reg. v., 9 C. & P. 499. § 767.
Gedicke, S. v., 43 N. J. 86. § 1147.
Gee, S. v., 85 Mo. 647. § 342.
U. S. v., 45 Fed. R. 194. § 1333.
Geebrick v. S., 5 Ia. 491. §§ 1206, 1210.
Geer v. Connecticut, 161 U. S. 519. § 46.
S. v., 61 Conn. 144. § 46.
S. v., 46 Kan. 529. §§ 861, 879, 893.
S. v., 48 Kan. 752. § 893.
Geering, Reg. v., 18 L. J. M. C. 215. § 418.
Gee Woo v. S., 36 Neb. 241. § 36.
Gehrke v. S., 13 Tex. 568. §§ 173, 353, 361.
Geib v. S., 31 Tex. Ap. 514. § 1265.
Geier v. Shade, 109 Pa. St. 180. § 939.
Geiger, P. v., 49 Cal. 643. §§ 988, 1195.
Geisler, Ex parte, 50 Fed. R. 411. § 790.
Gelbert, C. v., 170 Pa. St. 426. § 1326.
Gelvin v. S., 93 Ind. 550. § 620.
Genesee General Sessions, P. v., 13 Johns. 85. § 11.
Genkinger v. C., 32 Pa. St. 99. § 96.
Genoa v. Van Alstine, 108 Ill. 555. § 1225.
Genther, C. v., 17 Serg. & R. 135. § 907.
Gentile v. S., 29 Ind. 409. § 46.
Gentry v. S., 6 Ga. 503. § 788.
v. S., 3 Yerg. 451. § 783.
Genung, P. v., 11 Wend. 18. §§ 543, 693, 694.
George, Reg. v., 11 Cox, 41. § 1152.
v. S., 11 Tex. Ap. 95. § 255.
S. v., 93 N. C. 567. § 1107.
Georgia v. Kepford, 45 Ia. 48. § 572.
Gerard v. S., 10 Tex. Ap. 690. § 652.
Gerber, S. v., 80 Mo. 94. § 1234.
Gerhardt, S. v., 3 Jones, 178. § 1227.
Gerkin, S. v., 1 Ired. 121. § 435.
Germaine, P. v., 101 Mich. 485. § 410.
German, S. v., 54 Mo. 526. § 397.
Germania v. S., 7 Md. 1. § 1310.
Gerrish v. Brown, 51 Me. 256. § 1195.
Reg. v., 2 M. & Rob. 219. § 788.
S. v., 78 Me. 20. § 586.
Gessert, S. v., 21 Minn. 369. §§ 369, 376.
Getchell, C. v., 16 Pick. 452. § 102.
P. v., 6 Mich. 496. § 680.
Gettinger v. S., 13 Neb. 308. §§ 548, 565, 585, 593.
Getty, P. v., 49 Cal. 581. § 619.
Geuing v. S., 1 McCord, 573. § 1238.
Gherkin, S. v., 7 Ired. 206. § 765.
Gholston v. S., 33 Tex. 342. § 831.
Giacamella, P. v., 71 Cal. 48. § 520.

Giancoli, P. v., 74 Cal. 642. § 311.
Gibbon's Case, Foster, 107. § 503.
Gibbon, Reg. v., L. & C. 109. §§ 864, 865.
Gibboney v. C., 14 Grat. 582. §§ 1284, 1285.
Gibbons v. Ogden, 9 Wheat. 1. § 35.
v. P., 33 Ill. 442. § 1286.
Rex v., 2 East, P. C. 490. § 503.
Rex v., Russ. & Ry. 442. § 494.
S. v., 4 N. J. 40. § 324.
Gibbs v. Dewey, 5 Cow. 503. § 899.
P. v., 98 Cal. 661. § 675.
Reg. v., Dears. 445. § 629.
Resp. v., 3 Yeates, 429. § 946.
v. S., 34 Tex. 134. § 594.
v. S., 41 Tex. 491. § 655.
S. v., 56 Mo. 133. § 775.
S. v., 10 Mont. 213. §§ 863, 888, 892.
S. v., 115 N. C. 700. § 44.
Gibert, U. S. v., 2 Sumner, 19. § 1359.
Giblin, P. v., 115 N. Y. 196. §§ 355, 361.
Gibney, C. v., 2 Allen, 150. § 998.
Gibson v. C., 2 Va. Cas. 111. §§ 378, 426.
C. v., 2 Va. Cas. 70. § 382.
v. Mississippi, 162 U. S. 565. § 78.
P. v., 17 Cal. 283. §§ 346, 358, 359.
P. v., 106 Cal. 458. § 400.
P. v., 58 Mich. 368. § 504.
Reg. v., 8 Cox, 436. § 629.
Rex v., 2 East, P. C. 508. § 496.
Rex v., 2 East, P. C. 899. § 750.
v. S., 44 Ala. 17. §§ 861, 880.
v. S., 89 Ala. 121. §§ 196, 316.
v. S., 91 Ala. 64. § 309.
v. S., 35 Ga. 224. § 107.
v. S., 38 Ga. 571. §§ 83, 223.
v. S., 54 Md. 447. § 519.
v. S., 38 Miss. 313. § 1074.
v. S., 17 Tex. Ap. 574. § 452.
v. S., 23 Tex. Ap. 414. § 341.
S. v., 36 Ind. 389. § 57.
S. v., 10 Ired. 214. § 246.
S. v., 108 Mo. 575. § 1106*a*.
S. v., 111 Mo. 92. §§ 1103, 1104, 1106, 1106*a*.
Giddins, Reg. v., Car. & M. 634. § 477.
Gideon, U. S. v., 1 Minn. 292. §§ 815, 829.
Gier, P. v., 53 Cal. 629. § 466.
Giersch, S. v., 98 N. C. 720. §§ 1219, 1220.
Giesca, P. v., 61 Cal. 53. § 1079.
Gigher, S. v., 23 Ia. 318. § 834.
Gignoux v. Bilbruck, 63 N. H. 22. § 1227.
Gilbert, C. v., 160 Mass. 157. § 46.
v. Hendricks, 2 Brev. 161. § 1251.
v. P., 1 Denio, 41. § 1252.
Reg. v., 1 C. & K. 84. § 497.
Rex v., 1 Moody, 185. § 560.
v. S., 65 Ga. 449. § 511.
v. S., 81 Ind. 565. § 1326.
v. S., 87 N. C. 527. § 1032.
S. v., 21 Ind. 474. § 926.
S. v., 13 Vt. 647. § 606.
Gilbraith v. S., 41 Tex. 567. § 615.
Gilchrist, Reg. v., Car. & M. 224. §§ 543, 753.
S. v., 113 N. C. 673. § 362.
Gilcrease v. S., 33 Tex. Ap. 619. § 309.
Gile, S. v., 8 Wash. 12. §§ 287, 368, 428.
Giles, Reg. v., L. & C. 502. §§ 666, 667.
Rex v., 1 Moody, 166. § 187.
S. v., 125 Ind. 124. § 89.
S. v., 103 N. C. 391. § 1126.
Gill v. Bright, 6 T. B. Mon. 130. § 556.
v. Parker, 31 Vt. 610. § 1206.
P. v., 6 Cal. 637. §§ 369, 376.
P. v., 7 Cal. 356. § 101.
Reg. v., Dears. 289. § 643.
Rex v., 2 B. & Ald. 204. § 975.
v. S., 59 Ark. 422. § 988.
v. S., 86 Ga. 751. § 1261.
Gillam, C. v., 8 Serg. & R. 50. § 922.
Gillan v. S., 47 Ark. 555. §§ 1234, 1259.
Gilland, C. v., 9 Gray, 3. § 1229.
Gillbrass, Rex v., 7 C. & P. 444. § 594.
Gillchrist, Rex v., 2 East, P. C. 982. § 796.
Gilleland v. S., 44 Tex. 356. § 309.
Giller, U. S. v., 54 Fed. R. 656. § 1240.
Gilles, Rex v., Russ. & Ry. 367, n. § 1166.
Gillespie, C. v., 146 Pa. St. 546. § 1321.
C. v., 7 Serg. & R. 469. §§ 187, 211, 972, 974, 1316.
Pennsylvania v., Addis. 267. § 819.
v. S., 9 Ind. 380. § 271.
v. S., 13 Tex. Ap. 415. § 274.
S. v., 80 N. C. 96. §§ 586, 709.
Gillet v. Mason, 7 Johns. 16. § 538.
Gillett, S. v., 56 Ia. 459. §§ 265, 280.
S. v., 92 Ia. 527. § 499.
Gilliam v. S., 71 Ala. 10. § 50.
Gillick, S. v., 7 Ia. 287. §§ 332, 357, 359, 426.
Gillikin, S. v., 114 N. C. 832. § 45.
Gillings, Reg. v., 1 F. & F. 36. § 562.
Gillis, P. v., 6 Utah, 84. § 548.
Gillon, C. v., 2 Allen, 502. § 110.
C. v., 148 Mass. 15. § 1243.
Gillow, Rex v., 1 Moody, 85. § 280.
Gillson, P. v., 109 N. Y. 389. § 1317.
Gillum v. S., 62 Miss. 547. § 416.
Gilly v. S., 15 Tex. Ap. 287. § 391.
Gilman v. Des M. Valley R. Co., 40 Ia. 200. § 914.
S. v., 51 Me. 206. § 420.
S. v., 69 Me. 163. §§ 142, 275, 276, 323, 332.
S. v., 33 W. Va. 146. § 1213.
Gilmore, P. v., 4 Cal. 376. § 390.
v. S., 99 Ala. 154. § 509.
S. v., 95 Mo. 554. § 309.
S. v., 98 Mo. 206. §§ 1310, 1313.
S. v., 110 Mo. 1. § 656.
S. v., 24 N. H. 461. § 288.
S. v., 9 W. Va. 641. § 1257.
Gilstrap, Ex parte, 14 Tex. Ap. 240. § 404.
Gimson v. Woodfull, 2 C. & P. 41. § 11.
Ginnochio, Ex parte, 30 Tex. Ap. 584. § 1217.
Ginns, S. v., 1 Nott & M. 583. § 498.

Giozza v. Tiernan, 148 U. S. 657. §§ 74, 1200.
Girard, P. v., 145 N. Y. 105. § 33.
Girardin, P. v., 1 Mich. 90. §§ 1064, 1158.
Girdwood, Rex v., 2 East, P. C. 1120. § 739.
Girr, P. v., 53 Cal. 629. § 466.
Gise v. C., 81 Pa. St. 428. §§ 1073, 1078.
Gitchell v. P., 146 Ill. 175. § 1275.
Gitma, U. S. v., 3 Hughes, 549. § 948.
Gitt Lee, S. v., 6 Oreg. 425. §§ 1284, 1285, 1291.
Given, U. S. v., 17 Int. Rev. Rec. 189, 195, § 948.
Givens v. C., 29 Grat. 830. § 443.
v. S., 32 Tex. Ap. 457. § 552.
S. v., 5 Ala. 747. §§ 758, 764, 772.
Glab, U. S. v., 1 McCrary, 166. § 1350.
U. S. v., 99 U. S. 225. § 1227.
Glackan v. C., 3 Met. (Ky.) 232. § 698.
Gladden v. S., 12 Fla. 562. § 306.
v. S., 13 Fla. 623. § 333.
Gladson, S. v., 57 Minn. 385. § 40.
Glascock v. S., 10 Mo. 508. § 1306.
Glasgow, S. v., Cam. & N. 38. § 905.
S. v., Dudley, 40. § 1244.
Glass, Reg. v., 2 C. & K. 395. §§ 554, 1330.
v. S., 30 Ala. 529. § 1302.
v. S., 23 Tex. Ap. 425. § 851.
S. v., 5 Oreg. 73. § 402.
Glaze, S. v., 9 Ala. 283. § 1094.
Gleason, P. v., 99 Cal. 359. §§ 1121, 1122.
S. v., 56 Ia. 203. §§ 575, 609.
Glein, S. v., 17 Mont. 17. § 218.
Glenn, P. v., 10 Cal. 32. §§ 425, 429.
Glidden, S. v., 55 Conn. 46. § 963.
Glory v. S., 13 Ark. 236. § 411.
Gloucester, C. v., 110 Mass. 491. § 183.
Glover v. C., 86 Va. 382. §§ 222, 223, 224, 454, 463, 464.
C. v., 111 Mass. 395. §§ 196, 212, 218, 504.
P. v., 71 Mich. 303. § 460.
Reg. v., L. & C. 466. § 632.
v. S., 22 Fla. 493. § 592.
v. S., 89 Ga. 391. § 1296.
v. S., 33 Tex. Ap. 224. § 313.
S. v., 27 S. C. 602. §§ 232, 266, 272.
U. S. v., 4 Cranch, C. C. 190. § 868.
Glovery, S. v., 10 Nev. 24. § 265.
Gluck, S. v., 49 Kan. 533. § 1275.
S. v., 41 Minn. 553. § 1270.
Glyde, Reg. v., L. R. 1 C. C. 139. § 571.
Gnagy, S. v., 84 Ia. 177. §§ 1113, 1118, 1119.
Gnosil, Rex v., 1 C. & P. 304. § 469.
Goaler v. S., 5 Baxt. 678. § 391.
Goble, S. v., 60 Ia. 447. § 664.
Goddard, C. v., 4 Allen, 312. §§ 698, 706.
Reg. v., 15 Cox, 7. § 426.
Reg. v., 2 F. & F. 361. § 866.
S. v., 69 Me. 181. §§ 18, 252.
Godet, S. v., 7 Ired. 210. §§ 594, 605.
Godfrey v. P., 63 N. Y. 207. § 435.
Reg. v., 8 C. & P. 563. §§ 568, 1330.
Reg. v., Dears. & B. 426. § 543.
v. S., 31 Ala. 323. §§ 149, 150, 152.
Godfrey v. S., 5 Blackf. 151. § 1227.
S. v., 12 Me. 361. §§ 1193, 1195.
S. v., 97 N. C. 507. § 815.
S. v., 17 Oreg. 300. §§ 232, 257, 259, 454.
Goding, C. v., 3 Met. 130. § 1313.
Godwinsville Road Co., S. v., 49 N. J. 266. § 1185.
Goersen v. C., 99 Pa. St. 388. §§ 377, 401, 418.
Goetz v. S., 41 Ind. 162. § 1257.
S. v., 34 Mo. 85. § 615.
Goff v. Anderson, 91 Ky. 303. § 294.
v. Fowler, 3 Pick. 300. § 1225.
v. Prime, 26 Ind. 196. § 208.
S. v., 20 Ark. 289. § 1321.
Goforth v. S., 8 Humph. 37. § 827.
v. S., 60 Miss. 756. § 1223.
Gogerly, Rex v., Russ. & Ry. 343. § 206.
Goggin, U. S. v., 3 Fed. R. 492. § 1352.
Goggins, P. v., 80 Cal. 229. §§ 13, 602.
Goin, S. v., 9 Humph. 175. § 150.
Goins v. S., 46 Ohio St. 457. §§ 195, 216.
Gold v. Bissell, 1 Wend. 210. § 235.
Goldberg, P. v., 39 Mich. 545. §§ 719, 720.
Golde, Reg. v., 2 M. & Rob. 425. §§ 630, 639.
Golden, P. v., 62 Cal. 542. §§ 432, 434.
v. S., 25 Ga. 527. §§ 162, 339.
v. S., 63 Miss. 466. § 589.
v. S., 18 Tex. Ap. 637. § 476.
S. v., 49 Ia. 48. §§ 506, 508, 514, 617.
S. v., 11 Wash. 422. § 214.
Golding v. S., 26 Fla. 530. § 365.
v. S., 31 Fla. 262. § 390.
Goldman, P. v., 1 Ida. (N. S.) 714. § 1306.
U. S. v., 3 Woods, 187. §§ 946, 950.
Goldsmith's Case, 3 Camp. 76. § 1146.
Goldsmith, Reg. v., 12 Cox, 594. § 611.
Reg. v., L. R. 2 C. C. 74. § 699.
v. S., 86 Ala. 55. § 824.
Goldstein v. P., 82 N. Y. 231. §§ 147, 617.
Rex v., Russ. & Ry. 473. § 795.
Goldston, S. v., 103 N. C. 323. § 466.
Goldthorpe, Reg. v., Car. & M. 335. § 1152.
Golightly v. Reynolds, Lofft, 88. § 611.
Golliher v. C., 2 Duv. 163. §§ 161, 325.
Gomer, S. v., 6 La. An. 311. § 594.
Gomez v. S., 15 Tex. Ap. 64. § 618.
v. S., 15 Tex. Ap. 327. § 330.
Gompertz, Reg. v., 9 Q. B. 824. §§ 975, 980, 981, 983.
Gonce, S. v., 79 Mo. 600. § 1074.
Gonsoulin, S. v., 42 La. An. 579. § 878.
Gonzales, P. v., 71 Cal. 569. §§ 139, 303, 308, 309.
v. S., 31 Tex. 495. § 307.
v. S., 5 Tex. Ap. 534. § 377.
v. S., 13 Tex. Ap. 48. § 609.
v. S., 18 Tex. Ap. 449. § 616.
v. S., 19 Tex. Ap. 394. § 355.
v. S., 28 Tex. Ap. 130. § 309.
v. S., 32 Tex. Ap. 611. § 458.
Gooch, Reg. v., 8 C. & P. 293. § 536.
v. S., 60 Ark. 5. § 564.

Gooch, S. v., 60 Ark. 218. § 594.
S. v., 7 Blackf. 468. § 1132.
S. v., 105 Mo. 392. § 195.
S. v., 94 N. C. 987. § 339.
Good, Reg. v., 1 C. & K. 185. § 145.
v. S., 61 Ind. 69. § 28.
Goodall, Reg. v., 2 Cox, 41. § 226.
v. S., 1 Oreg. 333. §§ 303, 316, 431.
Goodbody, Reg. v., 8 C. & P. 665. §§ 556, 626.
Goodchild, Reg. v., 2 C. & K. 293. §§ 226, 1148.
Goode, Reg. v., 7 A. & E. 536. § 166.
Reg. v., Car. & M. 582. § 556.
Reg. v., 6 Cox, 318. § 1152.
v. S., 70 Ga. 752. § 605.
S. v., 1 Hawks, 463. § 713.
S. v., 68 Ia. 593. §§ 633, 638.
v. U. S., 159 U. S. 663. §§ 118, 1330, 1335.
Gooden, Reg. v., 11 Cox, 672. § 754.
v. S., 55 Ala. 178. § 761.
Goodenough, Reg. v., Dears. 210. § 623.
Goodenow, S. v., 65 Me. 30. §§ 114, 132, 1091.
Goodfellow, Reg. v., Car. & M. 569. §§ 878, 886.
Goodhall, Reg. v., 1 Den. 187. § 226.
Rex v., Russ. & Ry. 461. § 678.
Goodhue v. C., 5 Met. 553. § 1246.
v. P., 94 Ill. 37. §§ 652, 656.
Gooding, U. S. v., 12 Wheat. 460. §§ 199, 210, 215.
Goodman, C. v., 97 Mass. 117. § 1222.
v. S., 41 Ark. 228. § 1290.
v. S., 4 Tex. Ap. 349. §§ 141, 340.
Goodnow, C. v., 117 Mass. 114. § 63.
Goodrich, C. v., 13 Allen, 546. §§ 73, 1165.
v. P., 19 N. Y. 574. § 32.
S. v., 46 N. H. 186. § 586.
S. v., 84 Wis. 359. §§ 220, 1093.
Goodrum v. S., 60 Ga. 509. § 238.
Goods v. S., 3 Greene (Ia.), 566. § 1237.
Goodson v. S., 29 Fla. 511. §§ 664, 788.
Goodwill, S. v., 33 W. Va. 179. § 55.
Goodwin, C. v., 3 Cush. 154. § 245.
C. v., 122 Mass. 19. §§ 110, 121, 740.
v. Griffis, 88 N. Y. 629. § 931.
Reg. v., 10 Cox, 534. § 789.
v. S., 102 Ala. 87. § 311.
v. S., 96 Ind. 550. § 419.
S. v., 33 Kan. 538. § 1107.
S. v., 37 La. An. 713. § 737.
Goodwine v. S., 5 Ind. Ap. 63. § 1129.
Goodwyn v. S., 4 Sm. & M. 520. § 378.
Goold, S. v. 62 Me. 509. § 1070.
Goolsby v. Bush, 53 Ga. 353. § 939.
Gorbutt, Reg. v., Dears. & B. 166. § 625.
Gordon, C. v., 159 Mass. 8. § 33.
v. P., 44 Mich. 485. §§ 91, 92, 93.
v. P., 33 N. Y. 501. § 409.
P. v., 70 Cal. 467. § 443.
P. v., 99 Cal. 227. § 271.
P. v., 103 Cal. 568. §§ 265, 271.
P. v., 81 Mich. 306. § 66.
Reg. v., Car. & M. 410. § 886.
Gordon, Reg. v., 23 Q. B. D. 354. § 678.
Rex v., 2 Doug. 590. § 1357.
Rex v., 1 East, P. C. 71. § 1357.
Rex v., 1 East, P. C. 312, 352. §§ 214, 328.
Rex v., 1 East, P. C. 315. § 328.
Rex v., 1 Russ. Cr. 247, n. § 1048.
Rex v., Russ. & Ry. 48. § 1077.
v. S., 52 Ala. 308. §§ 944, 949, 950.
v. S., 93 Ga. 531. § 449.
v. S., 48 N. J. 611. § 866.
v. S., 46 Ohio St. 607. §§ 1210, 1274, 1275.
v. S., 23 Tex. Ap. 219. § 268.
S. v., 3 Ia. 410. § 389.
S. v., 46 N. J. 432. § 1101.
U. S. v., 1 Cranch, C. C. 58. §§ 1268, 1273, 1274.
Gore's Case, 9 Co. 81. § 323.
Goree v. S., 71 Ala. 7. § 1159.
Gorham, C. v., 99 Mass. 420. § 110.
S. v., 65 Me. 270. § 1280.
S. v., 55 N. H. 152. §§ 205, 231, 233, 468, 469, 473, 483, 546, 596.
S. v., 115 N. C. 721. § 44.
Gorman v. C., 124 Pa. St. 536. §§ 1094, 1125, 1126.
v. Lowell, 117 Mass. 65. § 1322.
v. S., 23 Tex. 646. § 1084.
S. v., 58 N. H. 77. § 1279.
S. v., 2 Nott & M. 90. § 562.
Gormley, C. v., 133 Mass. 580. §§ 147, 1258.
Goshen v. Croxton, 34 Ind. 239. § 6.
Goshen, etc. Turnpike R., P. v., 11 Wend. 597. § 5.
Goslaw, P. v., 73 Cal. 323. § 359.
Gosnell v. S., 52 Ark. 228. § 36.
Goss, Reg. v., Bell, 208. § 668.
Resp. v., 2 Yeates, 479. §§ 884, 886.
S. v., 69 Me. 22. §§ 647, 656a, 912.
S. v., 74 Mo. 592. § 1164.
S. v., 59 Vt. 266. § 1236.
Gossett, P. v., 93 Cal. 641. §§ 1289, 1295.
Gostorf v. S., 39 Ark. 450. § 1221.
Gotley, Rex v., Russ. & Ry. 84. § 939.
Gould, C. v., 158 Mass. 499. §§ 1241, 1253, 1257.
S. v., 40 Ia. 372. § 1189.
S. v., 90 N. C. 658. § 377.
S. v., 26 W. Va. 258. §§ 1162, 1164.
Goulding, C. v., 135 Mass. 552. § 1174.
Goulette, P. v., 82 Mich. 36. §§ 460, 463.
Gourdier, C. v., 14 Gray, 390. § 1222.
Gourko v. U. S., 153 U. S. 183. §§ 309, 342.
Govan, S. v., 48 Ark. 76. § 649.
Governor v. Art Union, 7 N. Y. 228. § 1315.
Gowdy, U. S. v., 37 Fed. R. 332. § 1348.
Gowen, C. v., 7 Mass. 378. § 1192.
Rex v., 2 East, P. C. 1027. § 521.
Gowgill, S. v., 75 Ind. 599. § 1256.
Goyette, S. v., 11 R. I. 592. § 1218.
Grace, Ex parte, 12 Ia. 208. § 9.
S. v., 21 Ark. 227. § 1291.

Grady, C. v., 13 Bush, 285. §§ 671, 687.
v. S., 11 Ga. 253. § 220.
S. v., 34 Conn. 118. §§ 100, 211.
Graeter, S. v., 6 Blackf. 105. §§ 1228, 1273.
Graff v. Evans, 8 Q. B. D. 373. § 1240.
S. v., 66 Ia. 482. §§ 484, 575, 609.
U. S. v., 14 Blatch. 381. § 988.
Graffins v. C., 3 Pen. & W. 502. § 912.
Grafton Bank v. Flanders, 4 N. H. 239. § 11.
Graham v. C., 16 B. Mon. 587. §§ 174, 178.
C. v., 157 Mass. 73. § 1074.
P. v., 21 Cal. 261. § 455.
Reg. v., 16 Cox, 420. § 1003.
Rex v., 2 East, P. C. 945. § 750.
v. S., 40 Ala. 659. § 523.
v. S., 1 Ark. 171. § 1292.
v. S., 71 Miss. 208. § 44.
v. S., 29 Tex. Ap. 31. § 328.
S. v., 51 Ia. 72. § 271.
S. v., 61 Ia. 608. § 307.
S. v., 65 Ia. 617. §§ 596, 613.
S. v., 73 Ia. 553. § 1277.
S. v., 96 Mo. 120. § 896.
S. v., 74 N. C. 646. § 405.
S. v., 15 Rich. 310. § 1195.
S. v., 3 Sneed, 134. § 1159.
Grainger v. S., 5 Yerg. 459. § 306.
Grandberry v. S., 61 Miss. 440. § 1087.
Grandison v. S., 29 Tex. Ap. 186. § 892.
Grand Jury, In re, 26 Fed. R. 749. § 962,
In re, 62 Fed. R. 834. §§ 1328, 1336.
Grand Trunk Ry., S. v., 58 Me. 176. §§ 5, 288.
S. v., 59 Me. 189. § 5.
S. v., 60 Me. 145. § 288.
Granneman, S. v., — Mo. —, 33 S. W. R. 784. §§ 55, 77, 1319.
Grant, C. v., 116 Mass. 17. § 865.
Reg. v., 4 F. & F. 322. § 522.
v. S., 55 Ala. 201. § 585.
v. S., 97 Ala. 35. § 409.
v. S., 35 Fla. 581. §§ 636, 652, 653, 654.
v. S., 87 Ga. 265. § 1233.
v. S., 89 Ga. 393. § 1292.
v. S., 2 Tex. Ap. 163. §§ 572, 592, 594.
v. S., 3 Tex. Ap. 1. § 594.
v. S., 33 Tex. Ap. 527. § 1303.
S. v., 86 Ia. 216. §§ 975, 978, 979, 982.
S. v., 74 Mo. 33. § 752.
S. v., 76 Mo. 236. §§ 90, 552, 924.
S. v., 79 Mo. 113. § 419.
S. v., 104 N. C. 908. § 604.
S. v., 7 Oreg. 414. § 389.
v. U. S., 58 Fed. R. 694. § 1347.
U. S. v., 55 Fed. R. 414. § 1347.
Granville, S. v., 45 Ohio St. 264. §§ 750, 794.
Gravatt v. S., 25 Ohio St. 162. §§ 626, 656.
Gravelin, S. v., 16 R. I. 407. §§ 190, 1239.
Gravely v. C., 86 Va. 396. § 514.
v. S., 45 Neb. 878. § 417.
Graves, C. v., 18 B. Mon. 33. § 1225.
Graves, C. v., 97 Mass. 114. § 117.
C. v., 155 Mass. 163. §§ 28, 78.
v. S., 63 Ala. 134. § 508.
v. S., 121 Ind. 357. § 597.
v. S., 45 N. J. 347. § 361.
v. S., 14 Tex. Ap. 113. § 423.
v. S., 31 Tex. Ap. 65. §§ 671, 685.
v. S., 12 Wis. 591. § 617.
S. v., 72 N. C. 482. § 617.
U. S. v., 53 Fed. R. 634. § 1339.
Gravett v. S., 74 Ga. 191. § 490.
Graviotte, S. v., 22 La. An. 587. § 167.
Gray v. C., 9 Dana, 300. § 1231.
C. v., 2 Duv. 373. §§ 945, 950.
C. v., 129 Mass. 474. § 1097.
C. v., 150 Mass. 327. §§ 128, 187, 188.
v. Connecticut, 159 U. S. 74. § 38.
v. Coombs, 7 J. J. Marsh. 478. § 142.
P. v., 66 Cal. 271. §§ 642, 648.
Reg. v., 9 Cox, 417. § 833.
Reg. v., 4 F. & F. 1098. § 351.
Reg. v., 4 F. & F. 1102. § 522.
Reg. v., L. & C. 365. § 817.
Rex v., 7 C. & P. 164. § 449.
v. S., 63 Ala. 66. § 267.
v. S., 4 Baxt. 331. § 365.
v. S., 11 Tex. Ap. 411. § 592.
v. S., 24 Tex. Ap. 611. § 209.
v. S., 32 Tex. Ap. 598. § 662.
S. v., 61 Conn. 39. §§ 1201, 1219, 1253.
S. v., 8 Jones, 170. §§ 450, 1153.
S. v., 55 Kan. 135. §§ 198, 217.
S. v., 39 Me. 353. § 1223.
S. v., 37 Mo. 463. § 617.
S. v., 37 N. J. 368. § 1086.
S. v., 106 N. C. 734. § 548.
S. v., 109 N. C., 790. § 820.
S. v., 14 Rich. 174. § 591.
U. S. v., 2 Cranch, C. C. 675. § 1137.
Grayor, S. v., 89 Mo. 600. § 343.
Grayson v. S., 37 Tex. 228. § 239.
Grear, S. v., 28 Minn. 426. § 161.
S. v., 29 Minn. 221. § 178.
Great North of Eng. Ry., Reg. v., 9 Q. B. 315. § 183.
Great Works Milling & Mfg. Co., S. v., 20 Me. 41. §§ 180, 183.
Greathouse U. S. v., 2 Abb. (U. S.) 364. § 1357.
Grebe, S. v., 17 Kan. 458. §§ 616, 619, 725.
Green, In re, 134 U. S. 377. § 948.
v. C., 12 Allen, 155. § 361.
v. C., 5 Bush, 327. §§ 59, 1314.
v. C., 111 Mass. 417. §§ 607, 1274.
v. C., 83 Pa. St. 75. § 365.
C. v., 1 Ashm. 289. §§ 292, 357, 359.
C. v., 163 Mass. 103. § 128.
C. v., 2 Pick. 380. §§ 226, 465.
v. P., 3 Colo. 68. §§ 12, 221, 263.
v. P., 21 Ill. 125. §§ 1290, 1291.
P. v., 15 Cal. 512. § 597.
P. v., 1 Denio, 614. § 428.
Reg. v., 3 C. & K. 209. § 808.
Reg. v., 8 Cox, 441. § 923.
Reg. v., Dears. & B. 113. §§ 546, 605.

Green, Reg. v., Dears. 323. §§ 563, 659.
Reg. v., 3 F. & F. 274. § 1101.
Rex v., 7 C. & P. 156. § 351.
v. S., 41 Ala. 419. § 869.
v. S., 58 Ala. 190. §§ 54, 1131.
v. S., 59 Ala. 68. § 1131.
v. S., 66 Ala. 40. §§ 369, 370.
v. S., 68 Ala. 539. §§ 500.
v. S., 69 Ala. 6. § 307.
v. S., 98 Ala. 14. § 358.
v. S., 38 Ark. 304. § 416.
v. S., 45 Ark. 281. § 342.
v. S., 51 Ark. 189. §§ 196, 209, 358.
v. S., 56 Ark. 386. § 499.
v. S., 21 Fla. 403. § 1088.
v. S., 23 Miss. 509. § 466.
v. S., 28 Miss. 687. §§ 302, 332, 333.
v. S., 55 Miss. 454. § 363.
v. S., 67 Miss. 356. § 463.
v. S., 13 Mo. 382. §§ 199, 206, 329, 431.
v. S., 88 Tenn. 634. § 166.
v. S., 12 Tex. Ap. 445. § 391.
v. S., 28 Tex. Ap. 493. §§ 575, 589.
S. v., 24 Ark. 592. § 875.
S. v., 35 Conn. 203. § 416.
S. v., 1 Houst. Cr. C. 217. §§ 358, 418.
S. v., 7 Ired. 39. §§ 432, 434, 436.
S. v., 7 La. An. 518. § 323.
S. v., 36 La. An. 99. § 274.
S. v., 42 La. An. 644. § 382.
S. v., 46 La. An. 1522. § 307.
S. v., 37 Mo. 466. § 1320.
S. v., 66 Mo. 631. §§ 18, 327, 354, 385.
S. v., 87 Mo. 583. §§ 89, 92.
S. v., 111 Mo. 585. § 378.
S. v., 15 Mont. 424. § 505.
S. v., 71 N. C. 172. § 1126.
S. v., 81 N. C. 560. § 548.
S. v., 100 N. C. 547. § 873.
S. v., 27 Neb. 64. § 44.
S. v., 35 S. C. 266. § 824.
S. v., 7 Wis. 676. §§ 666, 686.
U. S. v., 2 Cranch, C C. 520. § 753.
U. S. v., 33 Fed. R. 619. § 945.
Greenacre, Rex v., 8 C. & P. 35. §§ 209, 333.
Greene, In re, 52 Fed. R. 104. §§ 14, 15, 963.
C. v., 111 Mass. 392. § 547.
v. James, 2 Curt. 187. § 1206.
S. v., 27 La. An. 598. § 597.
Greenfield v. P., 85 N. Y. 75. §§ 404, 405, 421.
Greenhalgh, Reg. v., Dears. 267. § 693.
S. v., 24 Mo. 373. § 257.
Greenhut, U. S. v., 50 Fed. R. 469. § 963.
Greening, P. v., 102 Cal. 384. §§ 118, 526.
Greenleaf, S. v., 31 Me. 517. § 1234.
Greenlee v. S., 4 Tex. Ap. 345. § 466.
S. v., 1 Dev. 523. § 765.
Greenlees, S. v., 41 Ark. 353. § 1164.
Greenough, In re, 31 Vt. 279. § 687.
Greensburgh v. Corwin, 58 Ind. 518. § 6.
Greenwade, S. v., 72 Mo. 298. § 196.
Greenwood, Reg. v., 2 C. & K. 339. § 484.
Reg. v., 2 Den. 453. §§ 195, 210.
Greer v. S., 3 Baxt. 321. §§ 361, 390.
v. S., 50 Ind. 267. §§ 271, 442, 443, 444.
v. S., 22 Tex. 588. §§ 96, 102.
S. v., 11 Wash. 244. § 391.
S. v., 22 W. Va. 800. § 313.
Greeson v. S., 5 How. (Miss.) 33. §§ 543, 605.
Gregg v. S., 55 Ala. 116. §§ 536, 589.
Gregor, S. v., 21 La. An. 473. § 412.
Gregory v. Reg., 15 Q. B. 957. §§ 1043, 1059.
Reg. v., 2 F. & F. 153. § 351.
Reg. v., L. R. 1 C. C. 77. § 207.
v. Richards, 8 Jones, 410. § 619.
v. S., 11 Ohio St. 329. § 770.
v. S., 26 Ohio St. 510. § 763.
S. v., 33 La. An. 737. § 520.
S. v., 83 Mo. 123. § 36.
S. v., 2 Murph. 69. § 856.
v. U. S., 17 Blatch. 325. § 1349.
Greiner, U. S. v., 4 Phila. 396. § 137.
Grentzinger v. S., 31 Neb. 460. § 618.
Grepel v. S., 32 Ohio St. 167. § 1261.
Gress, P. v., 107 Cal. 461. § 424.
Gresser, S. v., 19 Mo. 247. §§ 122, 572.
Greta v. S., 9 Tex. Ap. 429. § 391.
v. S., 10 Tex. Ap. 36. § 248.
Greve, U. S. v., 65 Fed. R. 488. § 652.
Grey, C. v., 2 Gray, 501. § 1273.
Reg. v., 4 F. & F. 73. § 1157.
Rex v., 1 East, P. C. 460. § 959.
Grider, S. v., 18 Ark. 297. §§ 1289, 1291.
Griffie, S. v., 118 Mo. 188. § 580.
Griffin, P. v., 19 Cal. 578. § 504.
P. v., 1 Ida. 476. § 1319.
P. v., 77 Mich. 585. §§ 496, 507.
Reg. v., 11 Cox, 402. § 348.
Reg. v., L. R. 4 Ir. 497. § 1082.
v. S., 39 Ala. 541. § 96.
v. S., 76 Ala. 29. § 456.
v. S., 90 Ala. 596. § 419.
v. S., 26 Ga. 493. § 223.
v. S., 86 Ga. 257. §§ 514, 615, 617.
v. S., 34 Ohio St. 299. §§ 82, 505.
v. S., 4 Tex. Ap. 390. § 634.
v. S., 12 Tex. Ap. 423. § 260.
S. v., 3 Harr. 539. § 489.
S. v., 71 Ia. 372. § 620.
S. v., 43 Tex. 538. § 1136.
Griffis, S. v., 3 Ired. 504. § 241.
Griffith v. S., 90 Ala. 583. §§ 200, 217, 375, 396.
v. S., 37 Ark. 324. § 431.
S. v., 45 Kan. 142. § 654.
Griffiths, C. v., 126 Mass. 252. § 596.
Reg. v., 8 C. & P. 248. § 280.
Reg. v., Dears. & B. 548. § 754.
Grigg, S. v., 104 N. C. 882. § 1087.
Griggs v. S., 58 Ala. 425. §§ 545, 571.
S. v., 34 W. Va. 78. § 1290.
Grills v. Jonesboro, 8 Baxt. 247. § 1217.
Grimes, C. v., 10 Gray, 470. § 596.
Rex v., 2 East, P. C. 647. § 543.
v. S., 63 Ala. 166. § 521.
v. S., 77 Ga. 762. § 500.

Grimes v. S., 25 Tex. Ap. 584. § 504.
S. v., 49 Minn. 443. § 1310.
Grimm v. U. S., 156 U. S. 604. §§ 118, 1332, 1335.
U. S. v., 45 Fed. R. 558. § 1332.
U. S. v., 50 Fed. R. 528. § 1332.
Grimme v. C., 5 B. Mon. 263. § 1272.
Grimwade, Reg. v., 1 C. & K. 592. § 733.
Grinden, S. v., 91 Ia. 505. § 292.
Grinder v. S., 2 Tex. 338. § 12.
Grise v. S., 37 Ark. 456. §§ 1163, 1164.
Grisham, S. v., 1 Hayw. 12. § 511.
S. v., 90 Mo. 163. §§ 90, 636, 644.
Grissom v. S., 62 Miss. 167. § 156.
v. S., 8 Tex. Ap. 386. § 307.
Griswold, P. v., 64 Mich. 722. § 558.
S. v., 67 Conn. 290. § 405.
S. v., 53 Mo. 181. § 1077.
Groesch v. S., 42 Ind. 547. § 1210.
Groff, S. v., 1 Murph. 270. §§ 215, 713.
Grogan v. S., 63 Miss. 147. § 269.
Groner v. S., 6 Fla. 39. § 1290.
Groning, S. v., 33 Kan. 18. § 500.
Groombridge, Rex v., 7 C. & P. 582. § 465.
Groome, S. v., 10 Ia. 308. § 1112.
Grooms, S. v., 5 Strobh. 158. § 661.
Groscop v. Rainier, 111 Ind. 361. § 1228.
Grose, C. v., 99 Mass. 423. § 618.
Grossheim, S. v., 79 Ia. 75. §§ 458, 464.
Grote, S. v., 109 Mo. 345. § 351.
Grottkau, U. S. v., 30 Fed. R. 672. § 859.
Grounsell, Rex v., 7 C. & P. 788. § 377.
Grout, Rex v., 6 C. & P. 629. § 351.
Grove, Rex v., 1 Moody, 447; 7 C. & P. 635. §§ 640, 652.
S. v., 77 Wis. 448. §§ 5, 21.
Grover, C. v., 16 Gray, 602. § 101.
Groves v. S., 6 Blackf. 489. § 53.
S. v., Bush. 402. § 877.
S. v., 15 R. I. 208. § 33.
Grubb, S. v., 55 Kan. 678. § 450.
Gruber v. S., 3 W. Va. 699. § 164.
Grumon v. Raymond, 1 Conn. 40. § 922.
Grunson v. S., 89 Ind. 533. § 560.
Grupe v. S., 67 Ind. 327. §§ 1246, 1256.
Gruso, S. v., 28 La. An. 952. § 1155.
Gruver, U. S. v., 35 Fed. R. 59. § 1330.
Gryder, S. v., 44 La. An. 962. §§ 761, 798.
Guagando v. S., 41 Tex. 626. § 166.
Guance, P. v., 57 Cal. 154. § 353.
Gude v. S., 76 Ala. 100. § 1187.
Guedel v. P., 43 Ill. 226. § 377.
Guelder, Reg. v., Bell, 284. § 640.
Guengerich v. Smith, 36 Ia. 587. § 11.
Guernsey, Reg. v., 1 F. & F. 394. § 566.
Guest v. S., 19 Ark. 405. § 437.
v. S., 24 Tex. Ap. 235. § 569.
S. v., 6 Ala. 778. § 487.
S. v., 100 N. C. 410. §§ 1098, 1099.
Guetig v. S., 63 Ind. 278. § 164.
v. S., 66 Ind. 94. §§ 157, 179.
Guffee v. S., 8 Tex. Ap. 187. § 353.
Guice v. S., 60 Miss. 714. § 308.
Guidice, S. v., 73 Cal. 226. § 262.
Guild, S. v., 10 N. J. 163. §§ 150, 152.
Guillory, S. v., 42 La. An. 581. § 389.
Guion, U. S. v., 37 Fed. R. 263. §§ 946, 948.
Guinness, S. v., 16 R. I. 401. § 1243.
Guisenhause, S. v., 20 Ia. 227. § 1249.
Guiteau's Case, 10 Fed. R. 161. §§ 120, 157, 179, 369.
Guiteau, U. S. v., 1 Mackey, 498. §§ 157, 168, 172, 369.
Gullette, S. v., 121 Mo. 447. §§ 753, 761, 771, 791.
Gumber, S. v., 37 Wis. 298. §§ 93, 96, 1248.
Gummell, S. v., 22 Minn. 51. § 271.
Gummer, S. v., 22 Wis. 441. §§ 1252, 1274.
Gunn v. S., 89 Ga. 341. § 1319.
Gunter v. S., 83 Ala. 96. § 179.
v. S., 1 Lea, 129. § 1319.
S. v., 116 N. C. 1068. § 255.
Gunther, U. S. v., 5 Dak. 234. §§ 435, 436.
Gunyon v. S., 68 Ind. 79. § 934.
Guptill v. Richardson, 62 Me. 257. § 1220.
Gupton, S. v., 8 Ired. 271. §§ 1283, 1284, 1285, 1288.
Gurlagh, S. v., 76 Ia. 141. § 1272.
Gurley, C. v., 45 Pa. St. 392. § 1126.
v. S., 65 Ga. 157. § 1223.
Gurney, Reg. v., 11 Cox, 414. § 962.
S. v., 37 Me. 149. § 1202.
Gurnee, S. v., 14 Kan. 111. §§ 210, 825.
Gustafson, S. v., 50 Ia. 194. § 851.
Gustin, P. v., 57 Mich. 407. §§ 92, 1137.
S. v., 5 N. J. 857. § 794.
Gut v. Minnesota, 9 Wall. 35. § 78.
S. v., 13 Minn. 341. §§ 78, 156, 158, 162, 178, 295, 297*a*, 337.
Gutch, Rex v., Moody & M. 433. §§ 188, 1056.
Gutchins v. P., 21 Ill. 642. § 774.
Guthrie, Reg. v., L. R. 1 C. C. 241. §§ 454, 462.
v. S., 16 Neb. 667. §§ 902, 903.
Gutierrez, Ex parte, 45 Cal. 429. § 28.
P. v., 74 Cal. 81. § 617.
v. S., 44 Tex. 587. § 452.
Gutridge, S. v., 1 Bay, 285. § 774.
Guttridges, Reg. v., 9 C. & P. 471. § 456.
Gutzweller v. P., 14 Ill. 142. § 38.
Guy's Case, 2 East, P. C. 748. § 543.
Guy v. Baltimore, 100 U. S. 434. §§ 44, 77.
S. v., 69 Mo. 430. §§ 307, 419, 423.
Guyer v. Reg., 23 Q. B. D. 100. § 46.
Guynes v. S., 25 Tex. Ap. 584. § 504.
Guyot, T. v., 9 Mont. 46. § 1263.

Haas, P. v., 79 Mich. 499. § 1252.
Haase v. S., 53 N. J. 34. §§ 1055, 1062, 1065.
Habib, S. v., 18 R. I. 558. §§ 604, 720, 726.
Hackett v. C., 15 Pa. St. 95. § 221.
C. v., 2 Allen, 136. §§ 292, 414.
S. v., 47 Minn. 425. §§ 511, 572.
Hackney v. S., 8 Ind. 494. §§ 13, 88, 1169.
Hadcraft, C. v., 6 Bush, 91. § 1261.

Hadden v. P., 25 N. Y. 373. §§ 200, 489.
Haddock, S. v., 2 Hayw. 162. § 601.
S. v., 109 N. C. 873. § 1057.
Haden, S. v., 15 Mo. 447. § 1229.
Hadfield, Reg. v., L. R. 1 C. C. 253. § 1196.
Hadley, C. v., 11 Met. 66. § 1239.
Hadlock, S. v., 43 Me. 282. §§ 1227, 1248, 1281.
Hafsoos, S. v., 1 S. D. 382. § 1273.
Hagan, C. v., 140 Mass. 289. § 1251.
Reg. v., 8 C. & P. 167. § 328.
Reg. v., 12 Cox, 357. § 417.
v. S., 52 Ala. 373. § 578.
v. S., 5 Baxt. 615. § 170.
v. S., 4 Kan. 89. § 1272.
v. S., 10 Ohio St. 459. §§ 200, 208, 361, 368, 383.
S. v., 45 La. An. 839. § 256.
Hageman, S. v., 13 N. J. 314. §§ 915, 1185.
Hagenlock, C. v., 140 Mass. 125. §§ 161, 232.
Hager v. S., 71 Ga. 164. § 805.
Hagerman v. S., 54 N. J. 104. § 709.
S. v., 47 Ia. 151. §§ 455, 458, 463.
Haggerty, P. v., 46 Cal. 354. § 523.
Hague v. S., 34 Miss. 616. § 333.
U. S. v., 22 Fed. R. 706. § 1348.
Hahn, S. v., 38 La. An. 169. §§ 764, 781.
Haigh, Reg. v., 7 Cox, 403. § 554.
Hail, S. v., 21 Tex. 587. § 918.
Haile v. S., 11 Humph. 154. § 160.
v. S., 1 Swan, 248. § 411.
v. S., 38 Ark. 564. § 1030.
Hailey, Rex v., 1 C. & P. 258. § 865.
S. v., 2 Strobh. 73. §§ 923, 925, 926, 928.
Haines, Reg. v., 2 C. & K. 368. §§ 349, 351.
Rex v., Russ. & Ry. 450. § 500.
v. S., 7 Tex. Ap. 30. § 1265.
S. v., 30 Me. 65. §§ 1143, 1174.
S. v., 35 N. H. 207. §§ 145, 1239.
S. v., 23 S. C. 170. § 678.
v. T., 3 Wyo. 167. § 679.
Hainline v. C., 13 Bush, 350. § 1270.
Hair, S. v., 37 Minn. 351. § 128.
Hairston v. S., 54 Miss. 689. § 245.
Hake, Rex v., 4 M. & Rob. 483. § 841.
Halbert v. S., 3 Tex. Ap. 656. § 358.
Halbrook v. S., 34 Ark. 511. §§ 1074, 1083.
Hale, Reg. v., 2 C. & K. 326. § 255.
v. Richards, 80 Ia. 164. § 649.
v. S., 1 Coldw. 167. § 755.
v. S., 15 Conn. 242. § 97.
v. S., 72 Miss. 140. §§ 410, 419.
v. S., 8 Tex. 171. § 1292.
S. v., 15 Mo. 606. § 36.
S. v., 12 Oreg. 352. § 617.
S. v., — Oreg. —, 7 Pac. R. 523. § 617.
Haley, C. v., 4 Allen, 318. § 1014.
v. McPherson, 3 Humph. 104. § 865.
v. S., 63 Ala. 83. § 1057.
v. S., 49 Ark. 147. §§ 484, 563.
v. S., 42 Neb. 556. § 1204.
Halfin v. S., 5 Tex. Ap. 212. § 1216.
v. S., 18 Tex. Ap. 410. § 1244.
Halford, Reg. v., 11 Cox, 88. § 565.
S. v., 104 N. C. 874. §§ 96, 505.
Halkem v. C., 2 Va. Cas. 4. §§ 594, 601.
Hall's Case, 3 Grat. 593. §§ 511, 514.
Hall v. C., 94 Ky. 322. § 311.
v. C., 78 Va. 678. § 572.
v. C., 89 Va. 171. § 426.
C. v., 8 Grat. 588. § 1227.
C. v., 15 Mass. 240. § 1193.
C. v., 97 Mass. 570. §§ 797, 808.
C. v., 128 Mass. 410. § 46.
C. v., 142 Mass. 454. § 1001.
v. Cranford, 5 Jones, 3. § 520.
v. De Cuir, 95 U. S. 485. § 54.
v. Marshall, 80 Ky. 552. § 947.
v. P., 39 Mich. 717. §§ 575, 576.
v. P., 43 Mich. 417. § 504.
v. P., 47 Mich. 636. §§ 460, 463.
v. P., 90 N. Y. 498. §§ 915, 942.
P. v., 94 Cal. 595. § 505.
P. v., 48 Mich. 482. § 396.
Reg. v., 2 C. & K. 947. § 567.
Reg. v., 12 Cox, 159. § 805.
Rex v., 3 C. & P. 409. §§ 135, 479.
Rex v., 1 Moody, 474. § 631.
Rex v., Russ. & Ry. 355. § 500.
Rex v., Russ. & Ry. 463. § 640.
v. S., 40 Ala. 698. §§ 359, 362, 414.
v. S., 53 Ala. 463. § 1087.
v. S., 88 Ala. 236. § 1097.
v. S., 100 Ala. 86. § 58.
v. S., 6 Baxt. 522. § 560.
v. S., 31 Fla. 176. § 362.
v. S., 3 Ga. 18. §§ 1264, 1321.
v. S., 65 Ga. 36. § 421.
v. S., 87 Ga. 233. § 1274.
v. S., 4 Harr. 132. § 1321.
v. S., 132 Ind. 317. §§ 236, 414.
v. S., 3 Lea, 552. § 533.
v. S., 7 Lea, 685. § 609.
v. S., 40 Neb. 320. §§ 442, 466.
v. S., 20 Ohio, 8. §§ 83, 103.
v. S., 3 Ohio St. 575. §§ 543, 573, 715.
v. S., 15 Tex. 40. § 582.
v. S., 41 Tex. 287. § 548.
v. S., 13 Tex. Ap. 269. § 1190.
v. S., 16 Tex. Ap. 6. § 255.
v. S., 22 Tex. Ap. 632. § 546.
v. S., 31 Tex. Ap. 565. § 275.
v. S., 32 Tex. Ap. 474. § 1143.
v. S., 48 Wis. 688. § 509.
S. v., 7 Blackf. 25. § 878.
S. v., 5 Harr. 492. §§ 536, 537.
S. v., 72 Ia. 525. § 54.
S. v., 76 Ia. 85. §§ 560, 563.
S. v., 49 Me. 412. § 858.
S. v., 79 Me. 501. §§ 1249, 1253, 1280.
S. v., 85 Mo. 669. § 595.
S. v., 9 Nev. 58. § 303.
S. v., 22 N. H. 384. § 1192.
S. v., 32 N. J. 158. §§ 1137, 1286.
S. v., 97 N. C. 474. §§ 909, 915.
S. v., 108 N. C. 776. § 767.
S. v., 114 N. C. 909. § 369.

Hall v. U. S., 150 U. S. 76. § 418.
U. S. v., 44 Fed. R. 864. §§ 864, 892.
U. S. v., 98 U. S. 343. § 14.
U. S. v., 131 U. S. 50. § 855.
Halleck v. S., 11 Ohio, 400. § 872.
Hallet, S. v., 63 Ia. 259. § 618.
Hallett, C. v., 103 Mass. 452. § 1219.
Reg. v., 9 C. & P. 748. §§ 440, 463.
Reg. v., 2 Den. 237. § 855.
v. S., 29 Ohio St. 168. §§ 105, 920.
Halley v. S., 43 Ind. 509. § 707.
Hallinger v. Davis, 146 U. S. 314. § 364.
Hallock, S. v., 14 Nev. 202. § 100.
Halloway, Rex v., 1 C. & P. 127. §§ 541, 552.
Halpin, Rex v., 4 Man. & Ry. 8. § 1054.
Halsell v. S., 29 Tex. Ap. 22. § 256.
Halsey v. S., 4 N. J. 324. § 914.
Halsted v. S., 41 N. J. 552. §§ 124, 128, 135.
Ham, C. v., 150 Mass. 122. § 1243.
C. v., 156 Mass. 485. § 58.
v. S., 4 Tex. Ap. 645. §§ 799, 801, 808.
S. v., 54 Me. 194. § 1001.
Hamaker, P. v., 92 Mich. 11. § 934.
Hambleton, S. v., 22 Mo. 452. §§ 12, 1161, 1162, 1164.
Hamblett v. S., 18 N. H. 384. §§ 596, 610.
Hambright, S. v., 111 N. C. 707. § 292.
Hamby v. S., 36 Tex. 523. § 359.
Hamer, C. v., 128 Mass. 76. § 1226.
Hamilton, C. v., 15 Gray, 480. § 520.
v. P., 113 Ill. 34. §§ 196, 257, 268, 270, 970.
P. v., 62 Cal. 377. § 178.
P. v., 101 Mich. 87. § 1256.
v. Reg., 9 Q. B. 271. § 702.
Reg. v., 8 C. & P. 49. §§ 575, 576.
Rex v., 7 C. & P. 448. § 976.
v. S., 94 Ga. 770. § 846.
v. S., 36 Ind. 280. §§ 226, 266.
v. S., 60 Ind. 193. § 596.
v. S., 75 Ind. 586. § 1286.
v. S., 35 Mo. 214. § 568.
v. S., 11 Ohio, 435. § 553.
v. S., 11 Tex. Ap. 116. §§ 501, 506, 513.
v. S., 26 Tex. Ap. 206. § 508.
S. v., 1 Houst. Cr. C. 281. § 817.
S. v., 75 Ind. 238. § 1256.
S. v., 7 Miss. 300. § 874.
S. v., 65 Mo. 667. § 876.
S. v., 13 Nev. 386. §§ 206, 211.
U. S. v., 11 Biss. 85. § 1330.
Hamilton Mfg. Co., C. v., 120 Mass. 383. §§ 55, 59, 73.
Hamlin, S. v., 47 Conn. 95. §§ 217, 218.
Hammers v. S., 13 Tex. Ap. 344. § 1057.
Hammil v. S., 90 Ala. 577. § 426.
Hammon, Rex v., 4 Taunt. 304. §§ 535, 556.
Hammond, Rex v., 2 East, P. C. 1119. § 733.
v. S., 121 Ind. 512. § 597.
v. S., 39 Neb. 252. §§ 440, 458.
S. v., 40 Minn. 43. § 62.
S. v., 35 Wis. 315. § 355.
Hammons v. S., 29 Tex. Ap. 445. § 506.
Hamper's Case, 3 Leon. 230. § 865.
Hampton, C. v., 3 Grat. 590. § 1229.
P. v., 144 N. Y. 639. § 409.
Rex v., 1 Moody, 255. § 762.
v. S., 45 Ala. 82. § 333.
v. S., 8 Humph. 69. § 609.
v. S., 10 Lea, 639. § 826.
v. S., 5 Tex. Ap. 463. § 618.
S. v., 63 N. C. 13. § 232.
S. v., 77 N. C. 526. § 1255.
Hancock, P. v., 7 Utah, 170. §§ 376, 418.
Reg. v., 38 L. T. (N. S.) 787. § 715.
Rex v., Russ. & Ry. 170. § 497.
Hand, S. v., 7 Ia. 411. § 1140.
U. S. v., 2 Wash. C. C. 435. §§ 231, 232, 235, 1342.
Handley, P. v., 100 Cal. 370. § 529.
P. v., 93 Mich. 46. §§ 518, 532.
Reg. v., 13 Cox, 79. §§ 286, 294.
Reg. v., 1 F. & F. 648. § 1103.
v. S., 96 Ala. 48. § 298.
S. v., 46 Mo. 416. § 160.
Hands, Reg. v., 16 Cox, 188, 8 Am. Cr. R. 469. § 560.
Handy v. St. Paul Globe Pub. Co., 41 Minn. 188. § 1321.
v. S., 63 Miss. 207. §§ 1143, 1145.
S. v., 4 Harr. 566. § 151.
S. v., 20 Me. 81. §§ 796, 797.
Haney, C. v., 127 Mass. 455. §§ 426, 429.
v. S., 34 Ark. 263. §§ 377, 378.
S. v., 67 N. C. 467. § 381.
Hang Tong, S. v., 115 Mo. 389. § 269.
Hanks, Rex v., 3 C. & P. 419. § 855.
v. S., 13 Tex. Ap. 289. § 790.
S. v., 39 La. An. 234. § 601.
S. v., 66 N. C. 612. § 826.
Hanley v. Powers, 11 R. I. 82. § 1202.
v. S., 28 Tex. Ap. 375. § 615.
S. v., 25 Minn. 429. § 1229.
U. S. v., 71 Fed. R. 672. § 1336.
Hanlon v. S., 51 Ark. 186. § 1223.
S. v., 62 Vt. 334. § 466.
Hann, S. v., 40 N. J. 228. §§ 209, 938.
Hanna v. P., 19 Mich. 316. § 454.
S. v., 84 Ind. 183. § 43.
T. v., 5 Mont. 248. § 410.
Hannahan v. S., 7 Tex. Ap. 664. §§ 78, 546.
Hannel v. S., 4 Ind. Ap. 485. §§ 814, 831.
Hannibal v. Guyott, 18 Mo. 515. §§ 38, 63, 102.
Hannon v. S., 5 Tex. Ap. 549. § 573.
v. S., 70 Wis. 448. § 455.
Hanoff v. S., 37 Ohio St. 178. § 217.
Hanover, U. S. v., 17 Fed. R. 444. § 1332.
Hanrahan v. P., 91 Ill. 142. § 274.
P. v., 75 Mich. 611. §§ 6, 66, 92, 94.
Hansberg v. P., 120 Ill. 21. § 1220.
Hanse, S. v., 71 N. C. 518. § 827.
Hansell, Reg. v., 3 Cox, 597. § 215.
Hanselman, P. v., 76 Cal. 460. §§ 118, 557, 600.
Hansen, P. v., 84 Cal. 291. § 572.

Hansen, S. v., 25 Oreg. 391. §§ 177, 178, 359.
S. v., 23 Tex. 232. § 1158.
Hansford v. S., 54 Ga. 55. § 250.
Hanshew, S. v., 3 Wash. 12. § 597.
Hanson, Reg. v., 2 C. & K. 912. § 236.
Reg. v., Car. & M. 334. § 770.
v. S., 43 Ind. 550. § 1237.
v. S., 43 Ohio St. 376. § 469.
S. v., 39 Me. 337. § 858.
Hanway, U. S. v., 2 Wall. Jr. 139. § 1357.
Hany v. S., 9 Ark. 193. § 1290.
Hapgood, Reg. v., L. R. 1 C. C. 221. §§ 229, 454.
Harbaugh v. Monmouth, 74 Ill. 367. § 1261.
v. P., 40 Ill. 294. § 1306.
Harberger v. S., 4 Tex. Ap. 26. § 536.
Harberson, S. v., 43 Ark. 378. § 846.
Hardebeck v. S., 10 Ind. 459. § 996.
Hardeman v. S., 25 Tex. 179. § 918.
v. S., 12 Tex. Ap. 207. § 548.
v. S., 16 Tex. Ap. 1. § 846.
Hardey, Reg. v., 14 Q. B. 529. § 939.
Hardie, S. v., 47 Ia. 647. §§ 130, 351.
Hardiman, C. v., 9 Gray, 136. §§ 409, 1220.
Hardin v. S., 63 Ala. 38. § 1032.
v. S., 4 Tex. Ap. 355. §§ 381, 969.
S. v., 1 Kan. 474. § 662.
Harding's Case, 1 Me. 22. § 1014.
Harding, Rex v., Russ. & Ry. 125. § 556.
v. P., 10 Colo. 387. §§ 36, 83, 124.
Hardison, S. v., 75 N. C. 203. § 546.
Hardister, S. v., 38 Ark. 605. § 287.
Hardtke v. S., 67 Wis. 552. § 450.
Hardwick v. S., 6 Lea, 103. § 464.
Hardy v. C., 17 Grat. 592. § 484.
v. Merrill, 56 N. H. 227. § 173.
Reg. v., L. R. 1 C. C. 278. § 1196.
v. S., 31 Tex. Ap. 289. § 419.
S. v., 47 N. H. 538. §§ 946, 950.
Hare, Reg. v., 13 Cox, 174. § 892.
Hargett, S. v., 65 N. C. 669. § 332.
Hargrave, S. v., 65 N. C. 466. § 450.
S. v., 103 N. C. 328. § 668.
Haring v. S., 51 N. J. 386. § 1137.
Harker, S. v., 4 Harr. 559. § 896.
Harkey v. S., 89 Ga. 478. § 1257.
Harkins v. S., 6 Tex. Ap. 452. § 488.
Harkness, S. v., 1 Brev. 276. § 713.
Harlan v. P., 1 Doug. 207. § 778.
v. S., 134 Ind. 399. § 509*a*.
Harland, Reg. v., 8 A. & E. 826. § 841.
Harless v. U. S., Morris, 169. § 1297.
Harley, C. v., 7 Met. 462. §§ 206, 683, 697, 704.
C. v., 7 Met. 506. § 122.
Reg. v., 1 C. & K. 89. § 1330.
Rex v., 4 C. & P. 369. § 227.
Harlis, S. v., 33 La. An. 1172. § 872.
Harlow v. C., 11 Bush, 610. § 1141.
S. v., 21 Mo. 446. § 160.
Harman v. Chicago, 147 U. S. 396. § 76.
v. C., 12 Serg. & R. 69. §§ 452, 454.
C. v., 4 Pa. St. 269. § 399.
v. S., 69 Ala. 248. § 1035.
S. v., 78 N. C. 515. § 312.
Harman v. U. S., 50 Fed. R. 921. § 1332.
U. S. v., 38 Fed. R. 827. § 1332.
Harmel, C. v., 166 Pa. St. 89. § 44.
Harmer, Reg. v., 3 Cox, 487. § 61.
Harmes v. S., 26 Tex. Ap. 190. § 1137.
Harmon, In re, 43 Fed. R. 372. § 1204.
v. S., 92 Ga. 455. § 1264.
S. v., 104 N. C. 792. § 603.
U. S. v., 34 Fed. R. 872. § 1332.
U. S. v., 45 Fed. R. 414. § 1332.
Harmwood, Rex v., 1 East, P. C. 411. §§ 22, 454.
Harnden, C. v., 19 Pick. 482. §§ 44, 123.
Harness v. S., 27 Ind. 425. § 834.
Harney, C. v., 10 Met. 422. § 521.
v. S., 8 Lea, 113. §§ 199, 1241.
S. v., 101 Mo. 470. §§ 220, 463.
Harp v. S., 59 Ark. 113. §§ 868, 880.
Harper v. C., 93 Ky. 290. § 1312.
P. v., 83 Mich. 273. § 391.
Reg. v., 7 Q. B. D. 78. § 756.
v. S., 3 Lea, 211. § 1253.
v. S., 71 Miss. 202. § 617.
S. v., 42 La. An. 312. § 1217.
S. v., 58 Mo. 530. § 1217.
S. v., 69 Mo. 425. § 257.
S. v., 64 N. C. 129. § 602.
S. v., 94 N. C. 936. § 740.
S. v., 35 Ohio St. 78. § 425.
U. S. v., 33 Fed. R. 471. §§ 641, 1339, 1340.
Harr, S. v., 38 W. Va. 58. § 256.
Harrel v. S., 39 Miss. 702. § 209.
Harrell v. S., 75 Ga. 842. § 276.
v. S., 13 Tex. Ap. 374. §§ 274, 280.
Harriden, P. v., 1 Park. Cr. 344. §§ 1121, 1124.
Harrigan, S. v., 9 Houst. 369. §§ 169, 303.
Harriman, S. v., 75 Me. 562. §§ 539, 815.
Harrington, C. v., 130 Mass. 35. § 28.
C. v., 3 Pick. 26. §§ 210, 213, 1141, 1142.
v. Miles, 11 Kan. 480. § 539.
Reg. v., 5 Cox, 231. § 196.
Reg. v., 10 Cox, 370. § 341.
v. S., 36 Ala. 236. §§ 118, 201.
v. S., 83 Ala. 9. § 368.
S. v., 9 Nev. 91. § 385.
Harris, C. v., 13 Allen, 534. § 1318.
C. v., 7 Grat. 600. § 1275.
C. v., 11 Gray, 310. § 1264.
C. v., 101 Mass. 29. § 1016.
C. v., 131 Mass. 336. § 460.
C. v., 168 Pa. St. 619. § 639.
v. Livingstone, 28 Ala. 577. § 1245.
v. P., 1 Colo. Ap. 289. § 1264.
v. P., 64 N. Y. 148. § 883.
P. v., 29 Cal. 678. §§ 161, 949.
P. v., 93 Mich. 617. § 725.
P. v., 95 Mich. 87. § 307.
Reg. v., 1 C. & K. 179. § 753.
Reg. v., Car. & M. 661, n. §§ 993, 995.
Reg. v., 8 Cox, 333. § 619.
Reg. v., 15 Cox, 75. § 523.
Reg. v., Dears. 344. § 634.
Reg. v., 4 F. & F. 342. § 533.

Harris, Reg. v., L. R. 1 C. C. 282. § 1136.
Rex v., 5 B. & Ald. 926. § 880.
Rex v., 5 C. & P. 159. § 258.
Rex v., 6 C. & P. 129. § 750.
Rex v., 7 C. & P. 416. § 788.
Rex v., 7 C. & P. 428. §§ 112, 788.
Rex v., 7 C. & P. 429. §§ 794, 795.
Rex v., 7 C. & P. 446. § 256.
Rex v., 2 East, P. C. 498. § 494.
Rex v., 2 East, P. C. 1023. § 521.
v. S., 31 Ala. 362. §§ 1283. 1285.
v. S., 33 Ala. 373. §§ 1283, 1285.
v. S., 60 Ala. 50. § 536.
v. S., 96 Ala. 24. §§ 311, 316, 413.
v. S., 100 Ala. 129. § 593.
v. S., 34 Ark. 469. §§ 162, 307, 337.
v. S., 36 Ark. 127. § 365.
v. S., 58 Ga. 332. § 324.
v. S., 73 Ga. 41. § 827.
v. S., 81 Ga. 758. §§ 562, 563.
v. S., 7 Lea, 124. § 203.
v. S., 14 Lea, 485. § 1196.
v. S., 47 Miss. 318. § 303.
v. S., 61 Miss. 304. §§ 509, 514.
v. S. 71 Miss. 462. § 243.
v. S., 5 Tex. 11. §§ 1308, 1313.
v. S., 2 Tex. Ap. 102. § 607.
v. S., 8 Tex. Ap. 90. §§ 322, 365.
v. S., 9 Tex. Ap. 308. § 1310.
v. S., 15 Tex. Ap. 411. § 618.
v. S., 15 Tex. Ap. 629. § 198.
v. S., 17 Tex. Ap. 132. § 575.
v. S., 17 Tex. Ap. 177. § 565.
v. S., 18 Tex. Ap. 287. § 572.
v. S., 20 Tex. Ap. 652. § 505.
v. S., 22 Tex. Ap. 677. § 1030.
v. S., 28 Tex. Ap. 308. § 396.
v. S., 29 Tex. Ap. 101. §§ 548, 572.
v. S., 30 Tex. Ap. 549. § 397.
S. v., 3 Harr. 559. § 592.
S. v., 11 Ia. 414. § 1164.
S. v., 27 Ia. 429. § 1248.
S. v., 36 Ia. 136. § 1267.
S. v., 38 Ia. 242. §§ 546, 962, 1267.
S. v., 40 Ia. 95. § 1267.
S. v., 64 Ia. 287. §§ 1248, 1253.
S. v., 5 Ired. 287. § 794.
S. v., 1 Jones, 190. § 306.
S. v., 8 Jones, 136. §§ 155, 166.
S. v., 42 La. An. 980. § 601.
S. v., 45 La. An. 842. §§ 307. 414.
S. v., 50 Minn. 128. §§ 1216, 1226.
S. v., 59 Mo. 550. §§ 303, 307.
S. v., 76 Mo. 361. § 358.
S. v., 12 Nev. 414. §§ 353, 356.
S. v., 63 N. C. 1. §§ 292, 330.
S. v., 64 N. C. 127. § 582.
S. v., 106 N. C. 682. § 656.
U. S. v., 68 Fed. R. 347. § 1331.
v. White, 81 N. Y. 532. § 1297.
Harrison's Case, 2 Lewin, 118. § 786.
Harrison v. C., 79 Va. 374. §§ 307, 309.
C. v., 11 Gray, 310. § 1264.
v. Nichols, 31 Vt. 709. § 1267.
v. P., 50 N. Y. 518. §§ 548, 575.
Reg. v., 9 Cox. 503. § 888.
Reg. v., 12 Cox, 19. § 558.
Harrison, Rex v., 2 East, P. C. 559. § 558.
Rex v., 2 East, P. C. 926. § 754.
v. S., 24 Ala. 67. §§ 142, 303, 325, 340.
v. S., 36 Ala. 248. § 788.
v. S., 37 Ala. 154. § 1027.
v. S., 79 Ala. 29. § 419.
v. S., 91 Ala. 62. § 1204.
v. S., 102 Ala. 170. § 36.
v. S., 2 Coldw. 232. §§ 268, 270.
v. S., 4 Coldw. 195. § 268.
v. S., 74 Ga. 801. § 494.
v. S., 9 Mo. 526. § 1217.
v. S., 15 Tex. 239. § 1292.
v. S., 6 Tex. Ap. 42. § 409.
v. S., 9 Tex. Ap. 407. § 409.
v. S., 10 Tex. Ap. 93. § 262.
v. S., 20 Tex. Ap. 387. § 414.
S. v., 5 Jones, 115. §§ 309. 403.
S. v., 30 La. An., Pt. 2, 1329. § 434.
S. v., 69 N. C. 143. § 770.
S. v., 93 N. C. 605. § 1032.
S. v., 66 Vt. 523. § 514.
S. v., 36 W. Va. 729. §§ 157, 158, 166.
v. U. S., 163 U. S. 140. § 1329.
Harrod v. Worship, 30 L. J. M. C. 165. § 818.
S. v., 102 Mo. 590. §§ 305, 307, 419.
Harrow v. S., 1 Greene (Ia.), 439. §§ 1190, 1193.
Harsh, S. v., 6 Blackf. 346. §§ 915, 1193.
Hart v. C., 85 Ky. 77. §§ 298, 300, 307.
C. v., 2 Brews. 546. §§ 160, 162.
C. v., 6 J. J. Marsh. 119. § 324.
P. v., 10 Utah, 204. § 514.
Rex. v., 6 C. & P. 106. §§ 543, 547, 549.
Rex v., 7 C. & P. 652. §§ 765, 803.
v. S., 55 Ind. 599. § 596.
v. S., 57 Ind. 102. § 564.
v. S., 29 Ohio St. 666. § 46.
v. S., 15 Tex. Ap. 202. § 405.
v. S., 22 Tex. Ap. 563. § 618.
S. v., 67 Ia. 142. § 771.
S. v., 6 Jones, 389. § 949.
S. v., 33 Kan. 218. § 390.
S. v., 34 Me. 36. §§ 1172, 1180.
S. v., 107 N. C. 796. §§ 1227, 1254.
U. S. v., Pet. C. C. 390. § 1184.
Hartfiel. S. v., 24 Wis. 60. §§ 128, 1257.
Hartford v. S., 96 Ind. 461. §§ 13, 1043, 1051, 1054, 1066.
Hartigan, S. v., 32 Vt. 607. § 463.
Hartleb, S. v., 35 La. An. 1180. § 721.
Hartley, Rex v., Russ. & Ry. 139. § 626.
U. S. v., 42 Fed. R. 835. § 1330.
Hartman v. Aveline, 63 Ind. 344. § 369.
P. v., 62 Cal. 562. § 615.
P. v., 103 Cal. 242. § 460.
S. v., 8 Baxt. 384. § 833.
S. v., 41 Tex. 562. § 252.
U. S. v., 65 Fed. R. 490. § 750.
Hartmann v. C., 5 Pa. St. 60. §§ 843, 974, 987.
Hartnett, C. v., 3 Gray, 450. §§ 558, 578.
Hartshorn v. S., 29 Ohio St. 635. §§ 212, 218.

Hartung v. P., 22 N. Y. 95. §§ 78, 96, 97.
v. P., 26 N. Y. 167. §§ 78, 96.
v. P., 28 N. Y. 400. §§ 78, 92, 96.
Hartwell, C. v., 128 Mass. 415. § 379.
U. S. v., 6 Wall. 385. § 646.
Harty v. S., 3 Blackf. 386. §§ 215, 217.
Hartzell, S. v., 58 Ia. 520. § 391.
Harvell, S. v., 4 Jones, 55. § 873.
Harvey v. C., 23 Grat. 941. § 538.
C. v., 16 B. Mon. 1. § 1229.
Reg. v., 9 C. & P. 353. § 556.
Reg. v., 8 Cox, 99. § 878.
Reg. v., L. R. 1 C. C. 284. § 778.
Rex v., 2 East, P. C. 669. § 560.
v. S., 53 Ark. 425. §§ 438, 445, 505, 506.
v. S., 65 Ga. 568. § 1264.
v. S., 67 Ga. 639. § 529.
v. S., 80 Ind. 142. § 1235.
S. v., 3 N. H. 65. § 836.
Harvick v. S., 49 Ark. 514. § 506.
Harwell v. S., 22 Tex. Ap. 251. § 726.
Harwood, C. v., 4 Gray, 41. § 1145.
Reg. v., 11 Cox, 388. § 716.
S. v., 104 N. C. 724. § 51.
Has, C. v., 122 Mass. 40. §§ 120, 1319.
Hascall, S. v., 6 N. H. 352. § 868.
Haskell, C. v., 140 Mass. 128. § 410.
Haskill v. C., 3 B. Mon. 342. § 1281.
Haskins v. P., 16 N. Y. 344. §§ 509*a*, 552, 596.
Hass, S. v., 22 Ia. 193. § 1248.
Hassall, Reg. v., 8 Cox, 491. § 554.
Hassett, S. v., 64 Vt. 46. §§ 1233, 1235.
Hastie, Reg. v., L. & C. 269. § 626.
Hastings, Rex v., 1 Moody, 82. § 818.
S. v., 38 Neb. 584. § 913.
S. v., 53 N. H. 452. § 770.
Hatch v. S., 6 Tex. Ap. 384. § 806.
v. S., 8 Tex. Ap. 416. § 780.
S. v., 116 N. C. 1003. § 913.
Hatchard v. S., 79 Wis. 357. §§ 347, 1148.
Hatcher, C. v., 6 Grat. 667. § 1229.
v. S., 18 Ga. 460. § 267.
Hatchett v. C., 75 Va. 925. § 216.
Hately v. S., 15 Ga. 346. § 204.
Hatfield v. C., 120 Pa. St. 395. § 1221.
C. v., 107 Mass. 227. §§ 874, 875.
v. Gano, 15 Ia. 177. § 1146.
S. v., 75 Ia. 592. § 458.
Hathaway v. S., 32 Fla. 56. §§ 305, 313.
S. v., 106 Mo. 236. § 36.
S. v., 115 Mo. 36. §§ 36, 77.
Hathcock, S. v., 7 Ired. 52. § 993.
Hathcote v. S., 55 Ark. 181. § 1036.
Hattaway, S. v., 2 Nott & M. 118. § 861.
Hatton v. S., 31 Tex. Ap. 586. § 266.
Hatwood v. S., 18 Ind. 492. § 54.
Hauck, In re, 70 Mich. 396. § 1206.
C. v., 103 Pa. St. 536. §§ 1184, 1186.
v. S., 45 Ohio St. 439. § 674.
Haug v. Gillett, 14 Kan. 140. §§ 5, 1227.
Haughey, C. v., 3 Met. (Ky.), 223. § 676.
Haughton, Rex v., 5 C. & P. 555. §§ 520, 815.
Haukey, U. S. v., 2 Cranch, C. C. 65. § 553.
Haun, P. v., 44 Cal. 96. §§ 353, 361.
Haunstine v. S., 31 Neb. 112. § 375.
Hauskins v. P., 82 Ill. 193. § 1126.
Haven, S. v., 43 Ia. 181. § 1117.
Havercamp, S. v., 54 Ia. 350. § 339.
Havey, S. v., 58 N. H. 377. § 1272.
Havnor, P. v., 149 N. Y. 195. §§ 55, 77, 1319.
Hawes v. Miller, 56 Ia. 395. § 947.
P. v., 98 Cal. 648. § 426.
Reg. v., 1 Den. 270. §§ 1074, 1082.
Hawkes, Reg. v., 2 Moody, 60. § 753.
Hakeswood, Rex v., 2 East, P. C. 955. § 758.
Hawkins, C. v., 11 Bush, 603. § 434.
C. v., 3 Gray, 463. §§ 162, 332, 333, 343, 344.
C. v., 157 Mass. 551. § 259.
P. v., 109 N. Y. 408. § 358.
Reg. v., 4 Cox, 224. §§ 556, 623.
Reg. v., 1 Den. 584. §§ 556, 623, 624.
Rex v., 3 C. & P. 392. §§ 197, 476.
Rex v., 2 East, P. C. 501. § 508.
v. S., 33 Ala. 433. § 1315.
v. S., 28 Fla. 363. §§ 760, 794.
v. S., 13 Ga. 322. §§ 1007, 1010.
v. S., 25 Ga. 207. § 338.
v. S., 95 Ga. 458. § 578.
v. S., 136 Ind. 630. § 440.
S. v., 15 Ark. 259. §§ 1283, 1285.
S. v., 77 N. C. 494. §§ 906, 918.
S. v., 91 N. C. 626. § 1302.
S. v., 115 N. C. 712. §§ 865, 892.
S. v., 8 Port. 461. §§ 548, 568.
Hawksley, P. v., 82 Mich. 71. § 618.
Hawley v. Bennett, 4 Paige, Ch. 162. § 9.
v. C., 75 Va. 847. § 384.
P. v., 3 Mich. 330. §§ 1207, 1220.
S. v., 63 Conn. 47. § 404.
Haworth, Rex v., 4 C. & P. 254. § 805.
Haws, S. v., 98 Mo. 188. §§ 752, 809.
S. v., 41 Tex. 161. § 47.
Hawthorn v. P., 109 Ill. 302. §§ 42, 77.
v. S., 56 Md. 530. § 752.
S. v., 9 Mo. 385. § 75.
Hawthorne v. S., 58 Miss. 778. §§ 332, 333.
v. S., 61 Miss. 749. § 307.
Hay, S. v., 29 Me. 457. § 66.
Hayden, C. v., 150 Mass. 332. §§ 520, 532.
C. v., 163 Mass. 453. §§ 1076, 1082, 1083, 1085.
v. S., 4 Blackf. 546. § 139.
S. v., 45 Ia. 11. §§ 511, 513.
S. v., 31 Mo. 35. § 1310.
S. v., 83 Mo. 198. § 307.
S. v., 51 Vt. 296. §§ 172, 173.
S. v., 32 Wis. 663. § 1184.
Haydon, Rex v., 7 C. & P. 445. § 556.
Hayes, Ex parte, 98 Cal. 555. §§ 55, 63, 77.
C. v., 145 Mass. 289. § 189.
C. v., 150 Mass. 506. § 1248.
v. Missouri, 120 U. S. 68. § 78.
v. P., 25 N. Y. 390. § 1074.

Hayes, P. v., 140 N. Y. 484. § 78.
v. S., 55 Ind. 99. § 91.
v. S., 15 Lea, 64. §§ 228, 231, 265, 269.
v. S., 14 Tex. Ap. 330. § 334.
S. v., 67 Ia. 27. §§ 189, 1237.
S. v., 24 Mo. 358. § 925.
S. v., 78 Mo. 307. §§ 223, 224, 521, 524.
S. v., 89 Mo. 262. § 924.
S. v., 105 Mo. 76. § 501.
S. v., 13 Mont. 116. § 589.
S. v., 111 N. C. 727. §§ 554, 562.
Haygood v. S., 98 Ala. 61. § 1104.
Haymond, S. v., 20 W. Va. 18. § 1218.
Hayne, S. v., 88 N. C. 625. § 1039.
Haynes' Case, 12 Co. 113. §§ 542, 546.
Haynes, C. v., 2 Gray, 72. § 1136.
C. v., 107 Mass. 194. § 110.
P. v., 11 Wend. 557, 14 Wend. 546. §§ 679, 681, 686, 702.
Reg. v., 1 F. & F. 666. § 157.
v. S., 17 Ga. 465. §§ 311, 417.
v. S., 5 Humph. 120. § 1033.
v. S., 15 Ohio St. 455. § 765.
v. S., 2 Tex. Ap. 84. § 260.
S. v., 6 Coldw. 550. § 758.
S. v., 66 Me. 307. §§ 190, 521.
S. v., 35 Vt. 570. § 1268.
S. v., 36 Vt. 667. § 1268.
Haynie v. S., 32 Miss. 400. § 1253.
Haynorth, S. v., 3 Sneed. 64. § 950.
Hays, Ex parte, 25 Fla. 279. § 215.
C. v., 14 Gray, 62. § 634.
v. P., 1 Hill (N. Y.), 351. §§ 232, 249, 443, 464.
v. S., 55 Ind. 99. § 91.
v. S., 77 Ind. 450. §§ 139, 271, 304.
v. S., 40 Md. 633. § 1151.
v. S., 57 Miss. 783. § 452.
v. S., 13 Mo. 246. § 190.
v. S., 30 Tex. Ap. 472. §§ 514, 617, 618.
S. v., 22 La. An. 39. § 168.
S. v., 23 Mo. 287. §§ 123, 307, 332, 421.
S. v., 36 Mo. 80. § 1274.
S. v., 67 Mo. 692. § 259.
S. v., 78 Mo. 600. §§ 90, 103, 648.
S. v., 41 Tex. 526. § 252.
Hayward, C. v., 10 Mass. 34. § 765.
Reg. v., 1 C. & K. 518. §§ 556, 623.
Rex v., 6 C. & P. 157. §§ 343, 426.
S. v., 83 Mo. 299. § 1158.
S. v., 1 Nott & M. 546. §§ 858, 878, 892.
Haywood, Rex v., 2 East, P. C. 1076. § 815.
v. S., 41 Ark. 479. § 538.
v. S., 66 Miss. 402. § 1036.
S. v., Phill. 376. §§ 156, 300, 333.
Hazard, S. v., 2 R. I. 474. §§ 719, 722.
Hazell, Reg. v., 11 Cox. 597. § 559.
S. v., 100 N. C. 471. §§ 1217, 1254.
...ton, Reg. v., L. R. 2 C. C. 134. § 674.
...od, C. v., 84 Ky. 681. § 539.
... 23 Pa. St. 355. § 956.

Hazen, P. v., 121 N. Y. 313. § 46.
v. S., 18 Fla. 184. § 1310.
S. v., 39 Ia. 648. §§ 1093, 1099.
Hazle, S. v., 20 Ark. 157. § 1136.
Head, C. v., 11 Grat. 819. § 1272.
v. Manufacturing Co., 113 U. S. 9. § 40.
v. Martin, 85 Ky. 480. § 298.
Reg. v., 1 F. & F. 350. § 538.
S. v., 3 R. I. 135. § 1277.
Headge, Rex v., Russ. & Ry. 160. § 643.
Heaganey v. C., 137 Mass. 574. §§ 1223, 1225.
Heald v. S., 36 Me. 62. § 96.
Health Department v. Rector, 145 N. Y. 32. § 30.
Heane, Reg. v., 4 B. & S. 947. § 859.
Heard v. S., 81 Ala. 55. § 521.
v. S., 92 Ga. 477. § 1323.
v. S., 9 Tex. Ap. 1. §§ 203, 808.
Hearing, U. S. v., 26 Fed. R. 744. §§ 857, 881.
Hearn v. S., 34 Ark. 550. § 1017.
v. S., 25 Tex. 336. § 82.
Heath, In re, 144 U. S. 92. §§ 20, 102.
v. C., 1 Rob. (Va.) 735. § 411.
C. v., 11 Gray, 303. §§ 174, 175, 179.
Reg. v., 2 Moody, 33. §§ 543, 556.
Rex v., Russ. & Ry. 184. § 784.
v. S., 36 Ala. 273. § 922.
v. S., 91 Ga. 126. § 1087.
v. S., 105 Ind. 342. § 1227.
v. S., 7 Tex. Ap. 464. § 565.
S. v., 70 Mo. 565. § 906.
S. v., 41 Tex. 426. § 834.
Heatherton, S. v., 60 Ia. 175. § 1112.
Heaton, Reg. v., 3 F. & F. 819. § 1076.
S. v., 77 N. C. 505. §§ 112, 123.
S. v., 23 W. Va. 773. § 617.
Hebel, S. v., 72 Ind. 361. § 649.
Heck v. S., 44 Ohio St. 536. §§ 39, 1207.
S. v., 23 Minn. 549. §§ 128, 1257.
Heckler, C. v., 168 Pa. St. 575. § 1235.
S. v., 81 Mo. 417. § 1264.
Hecox, S. v., 83 Mo. 531. §§ 497, 498, 499, 500, 501, 511, 548.
Hedderich v. S., 101 Ind. 564. §§ 15, 74, 105.
Hedges, Rex v., 3 C. & P. 410. § 782.
Rex v., 1 Leach, 201. § 536.
Hedley, Ex parte, 31 Cal. 108. §§ 634, 650.
Hedrick, S. v., 95 N. C. 624. § 241.
S. v., 35 Tex. 485. § 934.
Heed, P. v., 1 Ida. (N. S.) 531. § 757.
v. S., 25 Wis. 421. § 618.
S. v., 57 Mo. 252. § 892.
Heeson, Reg. v., 14 Cox, 14. § 418.
Heffren v. C., 4 Met. (Ky.) 5. § 324.
Heffron, C. v., 102 Mass. 148. § 148.
P. v., 53 Mich. 527. § 1271.
Heflin v. S., 88 Ga. 151. §§ 886, 890.
S. v., 8 Humph. 84. § 1008.
Hefner, S. v., 84 N. C. 751. §§ 669, 677.
Hehir, Reg. v., 29 Ir. L. T. 323. § 561.
Heidenhain, S. v., 42 La. An. 483. §§ 66, 70.

Heikes v. C., 26 Pa. St. 513. § 1127.
Heilman v. C., 84 Ky. 457. § 449.
Heims, Rex v., 7 C. & P. 312. § 328.
Hein v. Smith, 13 W. Va. 358. § 1228.
S. v., 50 Mo. 362. § 917.
Heine v. C., 91 Pa. St. 145. §§ 966, 981.
Heinemann, S. v., 80 Wis. 253. § 36.
Heinssen v. S., 14 Colo. 228. §§ 63, 102.
Heise, S. v., 7 Rich. 518. § 1229.
Heisembrittle v. Charleston, 2 McMul. 233. § 29.
Heitsch, S. v., 29 Minn. 134. §§ 1262, 1270.
Heldt, S. v., 41 Tex. 220. § 1274.
Helfrich v. C., 33 Pa. St. 68. §§ 1086, 1094.
Hellams v. Abercrombie, 15 S. C. 110. § 1324.
Helle, S. v., 2 Hill (S. C.), 290. § 861.
Heller v. P., 2 Colo. Ap. 459. §§ 655, 656.
Hellings v. C., 5 Rawle, 63. §§ 8, 621, 645.
Helm v. S., 67 Miss. 562. § 308.
S. v., 92 Ia. 540. §§ 307, 390, 423.
Helmes, S. v., 5 Ired. 364. § 814.
Helvin, S. v., 65 Ia. 289. § 481.
Hemanus v. S., 7 Tex. Ap. 372. § 462.
Hembree v. S., 52 Ga. 242. § 878.
Heming, Rex v., 2 East, P. C. 1116. § 729.
Hemingway v. S., 68 Miss. 371. § 649.
Hemm, S. v., 82 Ia. 609. §§ 1114, 1118.
Hemmaker v. S., 12 Mo. 453. § 553.
Hemmings, Reg. v., 4 F. & F. 50. § 479.
Hemp, Rex v., 5 C. & P. 468. § 883.
Hemphill v. S., 71 Miss. 877. § 890.
Hems, Rex v., 7 C. & P. 312. § 328.
Hench, Rex v., Russ. & Ry. 163. § 558.
Hendershot v. S., 44 Ohio St. 208. § 922.
Henderson v. C., 8 Grat. 708. § 823.
C. v., 140 Mass. 303. § 1243.
v. P., 117 Ill. 265. §§ 863, 880.
v. P., 124 Ill. 607. §§ 125, 1114.
P. v., 28 Cal. 465. § 307.
Reg. v., Car. & M. 328. § 690.
Reg. v., 11 Cox, 593. § 554.
v. S., 59 Ala. 89. § 1303.
v. S., 63 Ala. 193. § 1017.
v. S., 70 Ala. 29. §§ 275, 509, 514.
v. S., 77 Ala. 77. § 303.
v. S., 98 Ala. 35. § 347.
v. S., 50 Ind. 234. § 44.
v. S., 12 Tex. 525. § 274.
v. S., 14 Tex. 503. §§ 758, 764.
v. S., 1 Tex. Ap. 432. § 643.
S. v., 2 Dev. & B. 543. § 393.
S. v., 47 Ind. 127. §§ 1283, 1298.
S. v., 90 Ind. 406. § 868.
S. v., 84 Ia. 161. § 1092.
S. v., 13 La. An. 489. § 96.
S. v., 35 La. An. 45. § 573.
S. v., 15 Mo. 486. § 925.
S. v., 24 Oreg. 100. §§ 339, 412.
S. v., 1 Rich. 179. §§ 1043, 1060.
S. v., 29 W. Va. 147. §§ 800, 806, 807.
U. S. v., 33 Fed. R. 170. § 874.
Hendrick v. C., 5 Leigh, 707. § 808.
Reg. v., 5 Q. B. 49. § 981.
Hendricks v. S., 26 Ind. 493. §§ 878, 892.
v. S., 26 Tex. Ap. 176. §§ 753, 759.
S. v., 32 Kan. 559. §§ 145, 146.
S. v., 15 Mont. 194. § 1143.
Hendrickson v. C., 85 Ky. 281. §§ 284, 286.
v. Kingsbury, 21 Ia. 379. § 11.
P. v., 53 Mich. 525. § 1097.
Hendrix v. S., 50 Ala. 148. § 245.
Hendry, S. v., 10 La. An. 207. § 200.
Henessy v. S., 23 Tex. Ap. 340. § 797.
Henfield's Case, Whar. St. Tr. 49. § 14.
Henke, S. v., 58 Ia. 457. §§ 1089, 1093.
Henley, C. v., 1 Va. Cas. 145. § 611.
S. v., 30 Mo. 509. §§ 89, 506, 511.
Henline v. P., 81 Ill. 269. § 1190.
Hennah, Reg. v., 13 Cox, 547. § 236.
Hennersdorf v. S., 25 Tex. Ap. 597. § 1321.
Hennessey, P. v., 15 Wend. 147. § 634.
S. v., 23 Ohio St. 339. § 551.
Hennessy v. C., 88 Ky. 301. § 707.
Henning, S. v., 33 Ind. 189. § 940.
Hennington v. Georgia, 163 U. S. 299. §§ 40, 1323.
Henrie v. S., 41 Tex. 573. § 382.
Henry, In re, 123 U. S. 372. § 1331.
v. C., 9 B. Mon. 361. § 1137.
C. v., 2 Brewst. 556. § 543.
C. v., 118 Mass. 460. §§ 767, 797.
C. v., 22 Pa. St. 253. § 664.
v. S., 33 Ala. 389. § 382.
v. S., 39 Ala. 679. § 576.
v. S., 79 Ala. 43. §§ 309, 413.
v. S., 7 Coldw. 331. § 553.
v. S., 18 Ohio, 32. §§ 232, 266.
v. S., 35 Ohio St. 128. § 796.
v. S., 9 Tex. Ap. 358. § 565.
S. v., 9 Ired. 463. § 501.
S. v., 5 Jones, 65. § 460.
S. v., 24 Kan. 457. § 585.
U. S. v., 4 Wash. C. C. 428. § 199.
Henshall's Case, 2 Lewin, 135. § 256.
Henshaw v. Bryant, 5 Ill. 97. § 687.
Reg. v., L. & C. 444. § 678.
Hensler, Reg. v., 11 Cox, 570. §§ 223, 680, 681.
Hensley, C. v., 2 Va. Cas. 149. § 752.
v. S., 52 Ala. 10. § 1238.
v. S., 6 Ark. 252. § 1244.
v. S., 9 Humph. 242. § 533.
S. v., 94 N. C. 1021. § 308.
Henson v. S., 62 Md. 231. §§ 1138, 1145.
Henssler, P. v., 48 Mich. 49. § 686.
Henwood v. S., 41 Miss. 579. § 1266.
Hepburn's Case, 3 Bland, 114. § 11.
Hepler v. S., 58 Wis. 46. § 1281.
Herber v. S., 7 Tex. 69. § 572.
Herbert, P. v., 61 Cal. 544. § 303.
Herdina, S. v., 25 Minn. 161. §§ 140, 196.
Herges, S. v., 55 Minn. 464. §§ 1120, 1123.
Herine v. C., 13 Bush, 295. § 1270.
Herman v. S., 8 Ind. 545. §§ 29, 1207.
S. v., 117 Mo. 629. § 208.
Hermann, Reg. v., 4 Q. B. D. 284. § 774.
v. S., 73 Wis. 248. § 1138.

Hernandez v. S., 9 Tex. Ap. 286. § 617.
v. S., 18 Tex. Ap. 134. §§ 867, 892.
v. S., 20 Tex. Ap. 151. § 569.
v. S., 32 Tex. Ap. 271. § 268.
Herold v. S., 21 Neb. 50. § 844.
S. v., 9 Kan. 194. § 110.
Herrell, S. v., 97 Mo. 105. §§ 309, 341, 357, 382.
Herrick, C. v., 6 Cush. 465. § 93.
P. v., 13 Wend. 87. §§ 123, 684, 710.
Herrin v. S., 33 Tex. 638. § 358.
Herring v. S., 3 Tex. Ap. 108. §§ 488, 492.
Herrington, S. v., 21 Ark. 195. § 241.
Herriott, S. v., 1 McMul. 126. § 324.
Herron v. S., 51 Ark. 133. § 1236.
v. S., 93 Ga. 554. § 373*a*.
v. S., 36 Tex. 285. § 1294.
S. v., 12 Mont. 230. § 257.
Herryford, S. v., 19 Mo. 377. § 1310.
Herselus, S. v., 86 Ia. 214. § 1239.
Hersey, C. v., 2 Allen, 173. §§ 124, 383.
Hertzog, S. v., 41 La. An. 775. §§ 257, 259, 434.
Herzinger v. S., 70 Md. 278. §§ 1138, 1145.
Herzog, S. v., 25 Minn. 490. § 93.
Heskew v. S., 17 Tex. Ap. 161. § 618.
v. S., 18 Tex. Ap. 275. § 565.
Hesner, S. v., 55 Ia. 494. § 1273.
Hess, C. v., 148 Pa. St. 98. § 1236.
P. v., 85 Mich. 128. § 1315.
v. S., 45 N. J. 445. §§ 115, 124.
Hesseltine, Reg. v., 12 Cox, 404. §§ 522, 533.
Hessenkamp, S. v., 17 Ia. 25. §§ 384, 1196.
Hessian, S. v., 58 Ia. 68. §§ 217, 581, 587.
Hessians, S. v., 50 Ia. 135. § 617.
Hester v. C., 85 Pa. St. 139. § 416.
v. S., 103 Ala. 83. § 719.
v. S., 17 Ga. 130. §§ 520, 523.
v. S., 67 Miss. 129. § 825.
Hetherington, Reg. v., 5 Jur. 529. § 1049.
Hetzer v. P., 4 Colo. 45. § 1216.
Heuchert, S. v., 42 La. An. 270. § 6.
Hewell, S. v., 90 N. C. 705. § 1035.
Hewett, S. v., 31 Me. 396. §§ 960, 974.
Reg. v., 4 F. & F. 1101. § 1152.
Hewgill, Reg. v., Dears. 315. § 686.
Hewitt, Reg. v., 5 Cox, 162. § 963.
v. S., 15 Tex. Ap. 80. § 466.
Hewlett, Reg. v., 1 F. & F. 91. §§ 267, 276, 302.
Hey, Reg. v., 2 C. & K. 983. § 554.
Heygood v. S., 59 Ala. 49. § 546.
Heyward, S. v., 2 Nott & M. 312. § 476.
Heywood, Reg. v., 2 C. & K. 352. §§ 756, 781.
T. v., 2 Wash. T. 180. § 551.
Hibbard v. P., 4 Mich. 125. § 1206.
Hibbert, Reg. v., L. R. 1 C. C. 184. § 1101.
Hibbs, Ex parte, 26 Fed. R. 421. § 764.
Hickam, S. v., 95 Mo. 322. §§ 139, 140, 197.
Hickerson, S. v., 3 Heisk. 375. § 1274.
Hickey, Ex parte, 4 Sm. & M. 751. §§ 4, 9.
C. v., 126 Mass. 250. § 1270.
v. S., 53 Ala. 514. § 1143.
Hickland v. S., 8 Ark. 365. § 54.
Hicklin, Reg. v., L. R. 3 Q. B. 360. §§ 120, 1156, 1158.
Hickling, S. v., 41 N. J. 208. §§ 958, 966.
Hickman, C. v., 2 Va. Cas. 323. § 877.
Rex v., 5 C. & P. 151. § 285.
Rex v., 2 East, P. C. 593. § 578.
Rex v., 2 East, P. C. 728. § 470.
Rex v., 1 Moody, 34. §§ 220, 730.
S. v., 8 N. J. 299. §§ 543, 595.
Hickock, S. v., 90 Wis. 161. § 1272.
Hickory v. U. S., 160 U. S. 408. § 421.
Hickox, P. v., 3 Hill (N. Y.), 446. § 836.
Hicks v. C., 86 Va. 223. §§ 222, 224, 225, 227.
C. v., 7 Allen, 573. §§ 110, 121, 1196.
v. P., 10 Mich. 395. § 1123.
P. v., 66 Cal. 103. § 473.
P. v., 79 Mich. 457. § 1279.
P. v., 98 Mich. 86. § 456.
Reg. v., 2 M. & Rob. 302. §§ 373*a*, 389.
v. Rising, 24 Ill. 566. § 869.
v. S., 25 Fla. 535. §§ 359, 391.
v. S., 60 Ga. 464. § 1028.
v. S., 51 Ind. 407. §§ 299, 300.
S. v., 27 Mo. 588. §§ 307, 359.
v. U. S., 150 U. S. 442. § 200.
Hide, C. v., 94 Ky. 517. §§ 765, 809.
Hierb, Polk Co. v., 37 Ia. 361. § 5.
Higdon, S. v., 32 Ia. 262. §§ 1112, 1113, 1118.
Higgerson, U. S. v., 46 Fed. R. 750. § 1088.
Higginbotham v. S., 50 Ala. 133. §§ 257, 262.
v. S., 23 Tex. 574. § 232.
Higgins v. Butcher, Yelv. 89. § 11.
v. C., 94 Ky. 54. §§ 489, 1106*a*.
P. v., 56 Mich. 159. § 1264.
Rex v., 4 C. & P. 247. § 914.
v. S., 64 Md. 419. § 1232.
S. v., 88 Mo. 354. § 548.
S. v., 124 Mo. 640. § 869.
S. v., 13 R. I. 330. §§ 667, 1215.
S. v., 53 Vt. 191. § 1239.
Higginson, Reg. v., 1 C. & K. 129. § 156.
Rex v., 2 Burr. 1232. §§ 1137, 1306.
Higgs, Reg. v., 2 C. & K. 322. § 496.
High v. S., 26 Tex. Ap. 545. §§ 311, 396, 434.
Highland v. P., 2 Ill. 392. § 588.
Hightower v. S., 23 Tex. Ap. 451. § 706.
Higler v. P., 44 Mich. 299. §§ 699, 711.
Higley, Rex v., 4 C. & P. 366. § 1152.
Hilands v. C., 114 Pa. St. 372. § 389.
Hilbury, U. S. v., 29 Fed. R. 705. § 1330.
Hild v. S., 67 Ala. 39. § 500.
Hildebrand v. P., 56 N. Y. 394. § 560.
Hildreth v. P., 32 Ill. 36. §§ 543, 588.
v. S., 19 Tex. Ap. 195. §§ 1072, 1094.
S. v., 9 Ired. 429. § 333.
S. v., 9 Ired. 440. §§ 194, 938.

Hiler v. P., 156 Ill. 511. §§ 1074, 1079, 1085.
U. S. v., Morris. 330. § 1121.
Hill v. C., 2 Grat. 594. §§ 333, **426.**
v. C., 98 Pa. St. 192. § 519.
C. v., 11 Cush. 137. § 719.
C. v., 5 Grat. 682. § 1252.
C. v., 14 Gray, 24. § 1181.
C. v., 11 Mass. 136. §§ 187, 207, 211, 781, 791.
C. v., 14 Mass. 207. § 155.
C. v., 145 Mass. 305. §§ 125, 148.
v. Dalton, 72 Ga. 314. § 1216.
v. P., 1 Colo. T. 436. §§ 359, 361.
v. P., 20 N. Y. 363. § 1018.
P. v., 3 Utah, 334. §§ 82, 654.
Reg. v., 2 C. & K. 978. § 714.
Reg. v., 8 C. & P. 274. § 788.
Reg. v., 2 M. & Rob. 458. § 499.
Rex v., 1 East, P. C. 439. § 450.
Rex v., Russ. & Ry. 190. §§ 693, 701.
Rex v., Russ. & Ry. 483. § 817.
v. S., 43 Ala. 335. § 829.
v. S., 62 Ala. 168. §§ 1257, 1259.
v. S., 37 Ark. 395. §§ 1234, 1261.
v. S., 41 Ga. 484. §§ 332, 431.
v. S., 53 Ga. 125. § 221.
v. S., 53 Ga. 472. § 1030.
v. S., 63 Ga. 578. §§ 123, 150, 240, 617.
v. S., 72 Ga. 131. § 363.
v. S., 1 Head, 454. § 546.
v. S., 3 Heisk. 317. § 452.
v. S., 5 Lea, 725. § 455.
v. S., 42 Neb. 503. §§ 159, 213, 382, 474.
v. S., 41 Tex. 157. § 577.
v. S., 43 Tex. 329. § 925.
v. S., 5 Tex. Ap. 2. § 341.
v. S., 11 Tex. Ap. 456. §§ 345, 348.
v. S., 57 Wis. 377. §§ 554, 563, 569.
v. S., 1 Yerg. 76. §§ 668, 693.
S. v., 4 Dev. & B. 491. §§ 309, 310.
S. v., 2 Hill (S. C.), 607. § 455.
S. v., 1 Houst. Cr. C. 421. §§ 509, 543.
S. v., 46 La. An. 27. § 178.
S. v., 46 La. An. 736. § 589.
S. v., 55 Me. 365. § 526.
S. v., 72 Me. 238. §§ 671, 679, 686, 689.
S. v., 65 Mo. 84. § 617.
S. v., 69 Mo. 451. § 365.
S. v., 58 N. H. 475. § 1152.
S. v., 114 N. C. 780. § 572.
S. v., 19 S. C. 435. § 553.
S. v., 30 Wis. 416. §§ 758, 800.
U. S. v., 120 U. S. 169. § 86.
Hillhouse, P. v., 80 Mich. 580. § 565.
Hillian v. S., 50 Ark. 523. § 931.
Hilliard, C. v., 2 Gray, 294. § 344.
v. S., 14 Lea, 648. § 859.
v. S., 17 Tex. Ap. 210. § 257.
Hillman, Reg. v., L. & C. 343. § 1148.
Hilmes v. Stroebel, 59 Wis. 74. § 194.
Hiltabiddle v. S., 35 Ohio St. 52. §§ **449**, 450.
Hilton's Case, 2 Lewin, 214. § **286.**
Hilton, Reg. v., Bell, 20. § 713.
S. v., 35 Kan. 338. § 757.
S. v., 26 Mo. 199. § 934.
S. v., 32 N. H. 285. § 260.
S. v., 3 Rich. 434. § 1083.
Hinch v. S., 25 Ga. 699. §§ 305, 315, **339.**
v. S., 2 Mo. 158. § 861.
Hinchman, P. v., 75 Mich. 587. §§ 1253, 1273.
Hinckley, S. v., 38 Me. 21. §§ 187, **634.**
Hind, Reg. v., Bell, 253. § 425.
Rex v., Russ. & Ry. 253. § 1074.
Hindmarsh, Rex v., 2 Leach, 569. § **396.**
Hinds, C. v., 101 Mass. 209. § 769.
v. S., 11 Tex. Ap. 238. § 615.
Hines v. S., 51 Ga. 301. § 614.
v. S., 93 Ga. 187. § 1253.
v. S., 8 Humph. 597. § 361.
v. S., 3 Tex. Ap. 483. § 268.
S. v., 13 R. I. 10. § 1273.
Hing, S. v., 16 Nev. 307. § 361.
Hing Quong Chow, U. S. v., 53 **Fed. R.** 233. § 1344.
Hinkle v. C., 4 Dana, 518. § 1310.
v. S., 127 Ind. 490. § 242.
S. v., 27 Kan. 308. § 851.
Hinman v. Taylor, 2 Conn. 357. § 5.
U. S. v., Baldw. 292. §§ 783, 798.
Hinson, S. v., 31 Ark. 638. § 1028.
S. v., 83 N. C. 640. § 820.
S. v., 103 N. C. 374. § 1057.
Hinton v. C., 7 Dana, 216. § 1248.
v. S., 68 Ga. 322. §§ 1290, 1291, 1292.
v. S., 24 Tex. 454. §§ 306, 336.
S. v., 6 Ala. 864. §§ 1086, 1094.
Hintz v. S., 58 Wis. 493. § 1123.
Hipes v. S., 73 Ind. 39. § 188.
Hipp v. S., 5 Blackf. 149. § 188.
S. v., 38 Ohio St. 199. §§ 1212, 1223.
Hirn v. S., 1 Ohio St. 15. §§ 38, 75, 78, 1209, 1226, 1230.
Hirsch v. S., 1 Tex. Ap. 393. § 690.
S. v., 125 Ind. 207. § 1265.
Hirschburg v. P., 6 Colo. 145. § 93.
Hirschfield, U. S. v., 13 Blatch. 330. § 950.
Hislop, P. v., 77 N. Y. 331. § 8.
Hitchcock, P. v., 104 Cal. 482. § 865.
Hitchings, C. v., 5 Gray, 482. § 1206.
v. P., 39 N. Y. 454. §§ 1286, 1307.
Hite v. S., 9 Yerg. 197. §§ 546, 549.
Hitesman v. S., 48 Ind. 473. § 855.
Hittner v. S., 19 Ind. 48. §§ 310, 421.
Hizer v. S., 12 Ind. 330. §§ 1283, 1298.
Ho Ah Kow v. Nunan, 5 Saw. 552. § 80.
Hoacek v. Koebler, 5 Neb. 355. § 1324.
Hoadley v. P., 23 Ill. Ap. 39. §§ 1180, 1188.
Hoar, C. v., 121 Mass. 375. § 1243.
Hoard, S. v., 123 Ind. 34. § 1270.
Hoare, Reg. v., 1 F. & F. 647. §§ 554, 626.
Rex v., 6 Mau. & S. 266. § 841.
v. Silverlock, 12 Q. B. 624. § 1060.
Hobbs, C. v. 140 Mass. 443. § 236.

Hobbs v. S., 75 Ala. 1. §§ 753, 809.
v. S., 133 Ind. 404. § 993.
v. S., 9 Mo. 845. § 801.
v. S., 44 Tex. 353. §§ 511, 512.
v. S., 16 Tex. Ap. 517. § 267.
S. v., 33 La. An. 226. § 381.
S. v., 40 N. H. 229. §§ 861, 878.
S. v., 37 W. Va. 812. §§ 333, 359.
Hobert's Case, Cro. Car. 209. §§ 930, 939.
Hobgood, S. v., 46 La. An. 835. § 473.
Hobson, P. v., 48 Mich. 27. § 99.
Reg. v., Dears. 400. § 725.
Rex v., Russ. & Ry. 56. § 650.
v. S., 44 Ala. 380. § 829.
Hoch v. P., 3 Mich. 552. §§ 865, 868, 878.
Hochstadler v. S., 73 Ala. 24. § 1231.
Hockenberry, S. v., 11 Ia. 269. § 820.
S. v., 30 Ia. 504. §§ 596, 610.
Hockett, S. v., 70 Ia. 442. §§ 332, 335, 338, 341, 358, 363.
Hodge v. S., 97 Ala. 37. §§ 405, 416.
v. S., 98 Ala. 10. § 408.
v. S., 26 Fla. 11. §§ 177, 179, 380, 419.
v. S., 82 Ga. 643. § 1196.
v. S., 11 Lea, 528. § 1163.
S. v., 50 N. H. 510. § 617.
Hodges' Case, 2 Lewin, 227. § 409.
Hodges, Ex parte, 87 Cal. 162. § 65.
P. v., 27 Cal. 340. § 211.
Reg. v., 8 C. & P. 195. § 164.
Rex v., Moody & M. 341. § 536.
v. S., 94 Ga. 593. § 1153.
v. S., 5 Humph. 112. § 1055.
v. S., 3 Tex. Ap. 470. § 274.
S. v., 55 Md. 127. § 713.
U. S. v., 2 Wheeler, Cr. C. 477. §§ 1357, 1358.
Hodgkin, P. v., 94 Mich. 27. §§ 450, 1153.
Hodgkins v. S., 89 Ga. 761. § 241.
Hodgkiss, Reg. v., L. R. 1 C. C. 212. §§ 852, 860, 881.
Hodgman v. P., 4 Denio, 235. § 1276.
Hodgson, Reg. v., Russ. & Ry. 211. § 460.
Reg. v., Dears. & B. 3. §§ 745, 768, 769, 788.
Rex v., 3 C. & P. 422. §§ 640, 652.
S. v., 66 Vt. 134. § 1200.
Hoeflinger, U. S. v., 33 Fed. R. 469. § 1331.
Hoffman v. S., 88 Wis. 166. § 355.
S. v., 78 Mo. 256. § 257.
S. v., 53 Kan. 700. §§ 594, 617.
Hofner v. S., 94 Ind. 84. § 189.
Hogan, Reg. v., 2 Den. 277. § 58.
v. S., 61 Ga. 43. § 275.
v. S., 13 Tex. Ap. 319. § 408.
v. S., 30 Wis. 428. §§ 361, 362.
v. S., 36 Wis. 226. § 365.
S. v., 31 Mo. 340. § 1015.
S. v., 30 N. H. 268. § 1255.
Hogard, S. v., 12 Minn. 293. § 617.
Hogarty, C. v., 141 Mass. 106. § 1296.
Hoge v. First Nat. Bank, 18 Ill. Ap. 501. § 744.
Hoge v. P., 117 Ill. 35. §§ 589, 617.
Hogg v. P., 15 Ill. Ap. 288. § 1240.
Reg. v., 2 M. & Rob. 380. § 373*a*.
v. S., 3 Blackf. 326. § 602.
S. v., 5 Ind. 515. § 1185.
Hogsertt v. S., 40 Miss. 522. § 573.
Hogue, S. v., 6 Jones, 381. §§ 307, 332, 423.
Hoiles v. U. S., 3 MacAr. 370. §§ 551, 602.
Hoin, P. v., 62 Cal. 120. § 157.
Hoit, S. v., 23 N. H. 355. §§ 909, 915, 916, 917.
Hoke v. P., 122 Ill. 511. § 790.
Holbrook, C. v., 10 Allen. 200. § 29.
P. v., 13 Johns. 90. §§ 596, 598.
Reg. v., 3 Q. B. D. 60, 4 Q. B. D. 42. §§ 188, 1040, 1056.
Holcomb, Ex parte, 2 Dill. 392. § 774.
v. Danby, 51 Vt. 428. § 1322.
v. P., 79 Ill. 409. § 1129.
v. S., 41 Tex. 125. § 173.
S. v., 68 Ia. 107. § 66.
S. v., 86 Mo. 340. § 929.
Holden v. Minnesota, 137 U. S. 483. § 78.
Reg. v., 8 C. & P. 606. § 410.
Rex v., Russ. & Ry. 154. § 781.
v. S., 1 Tex. Ap. 225. § 391.
S. v., 48 Mo. 93. § 878.
Holder, C. v., 9 Gray, 7. § 553.
v. S., 5 Ga. 441. § 391.
S. v., 81 N. C. 527. § 539.
Holding, S. v., 1 McCord, 31. § 894.
Holdren v. S., 29 Ohio St. 651. § 1086.
Holebrook v. S., — Ala. —, 18 S. R. 109. § 554.
Holford v. S., 2 Blackf. 103. §§ 719, 720.
Holland, C. v., 1 Duv. 182. §§ 295, 479.
Reg. v., 10 Cox, 478. § 443.
Reg. v., 2 M. & Rob. 351. § 292.
Rex v., 1 T. R. 692. § 1228.
v. S., 12 Fla. 117. § 342.
v. S., 60 Miss. 939. § 931.
S. v., 22 Ark. 242. §§ 1285, 1310, 1311.
U. S. v., 3 Cranch, C. C. 254. §§ 205, 210.
Hollenbeck, S. v., 36 Ia. 112. § 1150.
Hollenscheit, S. v., 61 Mo. 302. § 205.
Holler v. S., 37 Ind. 57. § 307.
Holley v. S., 75 Ala. 14. §§ 306, 334.
S. v., 1 Brev. 35. §§ 758, 793.
Holliday v. P., 9 Ill. 111. § 1148.
Hollingberry, Rex v., 4 B. & C. 329. § 960.
Hollingsworth v. S., 5 Sneed, 518. § 1024.
Hollis v. Davis, 56 N. H. 74. § 11.
Reg. v., 28 L. T. 455. §§ 200, 1148.
v. S., 27 Fla. 387. § 440.
S. v., 1 Houst. Cr. C. 24. § 303.
Hollister v. C., 60 Pa. St. 103. §§ 499, 511.
C. v., 157 Pa. St. 13. §§ 117, 201, 572.
Hollohan v. S., 32 Md. 399. § 281.
Hollon, S. v., 22 Kan. 580. § 931.
S. v., 12 Lea, 482. §§ 1043, 1055.
Holloway v. C., 11 Bush, 344. §§ 305, 311, 314.

Holloway v. Reg., 17 Q. B. 317. § 215.
Reg. v., 2 C. & K. 942. § 566.
Reg. v., 1 Den. 370, 2 C. & K. 942. §§ 223, 566.
Hollwedell, Ex parte. 74 Mo. 395. §§ 4, 6.
Holly v. S., 54 Ala. 235. §§ 535, 536, 537.
v. S., 10 Humph. 141. § 339.
S. v., 2 Bay, 262. § 744.
U. S. v., 3 Cranch, C. C. 656. § 1306.
Hollyway, S. v., 41 Ia. 200. §§ 479, 734.
Hollywood v. P., 3 Keyes, 55. §§ 126, 239, 276.
Holman, Reg. v., L. & C. 177. §§ 656, 659.
S. v., 3 McCord, 306. § 90.
S. v., 104 N. C. 861. § 1170.
Holme, S. v., 54 Mo. 153. §§ 359, 365.
Holmes v. C., 25 Pa. St. 221. § 215.
C. v., 17 Mass. 336. §§ 1049, 1064, 1069. 1158.
C. v., 157 Mass, 233. §§ 377, 417.
Reg. v., Dears. 207. § 1136.
Reg. v., 12 Q. B.D. 23. § 696.
Reg. v., L. R. 1 C. C. 334. § 460.
v. S., 23 Ala. 17. § 302.
v. S., 88 Ala. 26. § 338.
v. S., 100 Ala. 80. §§ 311, 316, 418.
v. S., 88 Ind. 145. § 1258.
v. S., 11 Tex. Ap. 223. §§ 334, 391.
v. S., 20 Tex. Ap. 509. § 615.
S. v., 56 Ia. 558. § 1137.
S. v., 38 N. H. 225. §§ 38, 1209, 1226.
S. v., 82 N. C. 607. § 677.
S. v., 9 Wash. 528. §§ 585, 586, 595.
S. v., 12 Wash. 169. § 343.
U. S. v., 1 Cliff. 98. § 168.
U. S. v., 40 Fed. R. 750. § 1330.
U. S. v., 1 Wall. Jr. 1. § 137.
Holoman v. S.. 2 Tex. Ap. 610. § 1315.
Holsey v. S., 24 Tex. Ap. 35. § 564.
Holst v. S., 23 Tex. Ap. 1. § 455.
Holstine, C. v.. 132 Pa. St. 357. §§ 128, 1227, 1236, 1251.
Holt v. C., 2 Bush, 33. § 1310.
C. v., 146 Mass. 38. § 33.
Reg. v., Bell, 280. § 691.
Rex v., 7 C. & P. 518. §§ 276, 323.
Rex v., 5 T. R. 436. §§ 1051, 1070.
v. S., 1 Baxt. 192. § 1026.
v. S., 9 Tex. Ap. 571. §§ 303, 404.
S. v., 84 Me. 509. § 937.
Holt Co. Court, S. v., 39 Mo. 521. § 1228.
Holton v. S., 28 Fla. 303. §§ 443, 451.
Holtz v S., 76 Wis. 99. § 195.
Holtzclaw v. S., 26 Tex. 682. § 1296.
Holtzgraft v. S., 23 Tex. Ap. 404. § 823.
Holtzhauer, U. S. v., 40 Fed. R. 76. §§ 347, 349.
Homan, S. v., 41 Tex. 155. § 1294.
Homberg v. S., 12 Tex. Ap. 1. § 391.
Homer v. C., 106 Pa. St. 221. § 92.
C. v., 153 Mass. 343. § 78.
C. v., 5 Met. 555. § 82.
S. v., 40 Me. 438. § 1143.
Homes, S. v., 17 Mo. 379. § 565.
Honeycutt v. S., 8 Baxt. 371. § 420.
Hong Ah Duck, P. v., 61 Cal. 387. §§ 316, 377.
Hong Shen, Ex parte, 98 Cal. 681. § 63.
Honig, S. v., 78 Mo. 249. §§ 573, 713.
Honle, C. v., 147 Mass. 380. § 1237.
Honnicutt v. S., 20 Tex. Ap. 632. §§ 304, 410.
Honshell, P. v., 10 Cal. 83. § 142.
Hood, Rex v., 1 Moody, 281. § 340.
v. S., 44 Ala. 81. §§ 852, 861, 869.
v. S., 56 Ind. 263. §§ 13, 1086, 1131.
S. v., 51 Me. 363. § 586.
Hooghkerk, P. v., 96 N. Y. 149. § 197.
Hooker v. C., 13 Grat. 763. § 518.
v. S., 4 Ohio, 348. § 594.
S. v., 17 Vt. 658. §§ 925, 926.
Hooks v. S.. 99 Ala. 166. § 341.
v. S., 25 Tex. Ap. 601. § 823.
Hooper v. California, 155 U. S. 648. § 41.
v. S., 8 Humph. 93. § 766.
v. S., 56 Ind. 153. §§ 1252, 1273.
v. S., 29 Tex. Ap. 614. § 274.
v. S., 30 Tex. Ap. 412. §§ 762, 803.
S. v., 1 Houst. Cr. C. 17. § 51.
S. v., 82 N. C. 663. § 466.
Hoover, In re, 30 Fed. R. 51. §§ 1200, 1201.
v. S., 59 Ala. 57. § 1131.
S. v., 31 Ark. 676. § 823.
S. v., 107 N. C. 795. § 51.
Hope v. C., 9 Met. 134. § 586.
C. v., 22 Pick. 1. § 511.
P. v., 62 Cal. 291. § 516.
Rex v., 1 Moody, 414. § 754.
S. v., 15 Ind. 474. § 89.
Hopkins v. C.. 3 Bush, 480. § 1032.
v. C., 3 Met. 460. §§ 579, 786.
v. C., 50 Pa. St. 9. §§ 123, 357, 418, 419.
C. v., 2 Dana, 418. §§ 25, 1300.
C. v., 133 Mass. 381. § 1169.
v. Lewis, 84 Ia. 690. § 1204.
v. P., 12 Wend. 76. § 714.
Reg. v., Car. & M. 254. § 1103.
Reg. v., 8 C. & P. 591. § 396.
S. v., 15 S. C. 153. § 333.
S. v., 50 Vt. 316. § 807.
S. v., 56 Vt. 250. §§ 554, 604.
U. S. v., 26 Fed. R. 443. § 774.
Hopkinson v. P., 18 Ill. 264. § 274.
Hopkirk. S. v., 84 Mo. 278. § 355.
Hopley, Reg. v., 2 F. & F. 202. § 348.
Hoppe, S. v., 39 Ia. 468. §§ 596, 610, 613.
Hopper v. S., 19 Ark. 143. § 1132.
v. S., 54 Ga. 389. § 1115.
S. v., 133 Ind. 460. §§ 874, 875, 878, 879.
S. v., 71 Mo. 425. § 355.
Hopson, P. v., 1 Denio, 574. §§ 922, 924.
Hopt v. P., 104 U. S. 631. § 162.
v. Utah, 110 U. S. 574. §§ 78, 391.
Horacek, S. v., 41 Kan. 87. §§ 1234, 1240.
Horan, Reg. v., 6 Ir. R. C. L. 293. § 611.
v. S., 24 Tex. 161. § 1313.
S. v., 64 N. H. 548. § 796.
S. v., Phill. 571. § 593.
S. v., 11 Tex. 144. § 1310.
S. v., 25 Tex. Sup. 271. § 1229.
Hord, S. v., 8 S. C. 84. §§ 18, 263, 279.

Hore, Reg. v., 3 F. & F. 315. § 572.
Horn v. S., 98 Ala. 23. § 271.
v. S., 6 Lea, 335. § 1037.
S. v., 19 Ark. 578. § 1028.
S. v., 93 Mo. 190. § 707.
S. v., 116 N. C. 1037. § 342.
S. v., 43 Vt. 20. § 1082.
Hornaday v. S., 43 Ind. 306. § 1225.
Hornbeck v. S., 35 Ohio St. 277. §§ 456, 459.
v. S., 10 Tex. Ap. 408. § 563.
Hornby, Reg. v., 1 C. & K. 305. § 195.
Horne, Rex v., 2 Cowp. 672. § 1069.
v. S., 1 Kan. 42. § 409.
S. v., 9 Kan. 119. §§ 303, 306.
S. v., 92 N. C. 805. § 232.
S. v., 115 N. C. 739. § 62.
Horne Tooke, Rex v., 1 East, P. C. 60. § 1358.
Horner, Rex v., 1 Leach, 270. § 562.
v. S., 1 Oreg. 268. § 83.
S. v., 48 Mo. 520. § 781.
v. U. S., 143 U. S. 207. §§ 1317, 1334.
v. U. S., 143 U. S. 570. § 1334.
v. U. S., 147 U. S. 449. §§ 1315, 1334.
U. S. v., 44 Fed. R. 677. 1334.
Hornsby v. S., 94 Ala. 55. §§ 332, 335, 365, 377, 416.
Horrigan, C. v., 2 Allen, 159. § 819.
Horseman v. S., 43 Tex. 353. § 572.
Horsey, Reg. v., 3 F. & F. 287. § 289.
Horton, C. v., 2 Gray, 69. §§ 1316, 1318.
P. v., 4 Mich. 67. § 341.
Reg. v., 11 Cox, 670. § 1076.
v. S., 53 Ala. 488. § 752.
v. S., 60 Ala. 72. § 520.
v. S., 13 Ark. 62. § 1292.
S. v., 100 N. C. 443. §§ 1115, 1117.
S. v., 21 Oreg. 83. § 1209.
Hosea v. S., 47 Ind. 180. § 1143.
Hoskey v. S., 9 Tex. Ap. 202. § 1265.
Hoskins v. S., 11 Ga. 92. § 753.
v. Tarrence, 5 Blackf. 417. § 536.
Hoss v. S., 18 Ind. 349. § 336.
Hosmer, S. v., 81 Me. 506. § 41.
S. v., 85 Mo. 553. §§ 1051, 1070.
Hotson, Reg. v., 2 C. & K. 777. § 770.
Hottendorf v. S., 89 Ind. 282. § 1253.
Houck, S. v., 73 Ind. 37. § 1169.
Hough, Rex v., Russ. & Ry. 120. § 808.
Houghten, S. v., 65 Vt. 328. § 46.
Houghton, Ex parte, 7 Fed. R. 657. § 790.
C. v., 8 Mass. 107. § 794.
v. S., 41 Tex. 136. § 1310.
Hounsell, Reg. v., 2 M. & Rob. 292. § 1152.
House v. S., 41 Miss. 757. § 1223.
v. S., 9 Tex. Ap. 53. § 463.
v. S., 9 Tex. Ap. 567. § 463.
v. S., 16 Tex. Ap. 25. § 200.
S. v., 55 Ia. 466. §§ 694, 696.
S. v., 65 N. C. 315. § 538.
Houseal, S. v., 2 Brev. 219. §§ 794, 799, 803.
Houser v. S., 58 Ga. 78. § 509.
v. S., 18 Ind. 106. §§ 1223, 1273.
House Bill, In re, — Colo. —, 39 Pac. R. 431. § 55.
Housh v. P., 75 Ill. 487. §§ 922, 931.
Houston, In re, 47 Fed. R. 539. § 44.
v. C., 87 Va. 257. §§ 15, 468, 470, 480, 483.
v. P., 63 Ill. 185. § 1193.
v. S., 13 Ark. 66. § 582.
v. S., 24 Fla. 356. § 1309.
v. S., 38 Ga. 165. §§ 495, 508.
S. v., 1 Bailey, 300. § 808.
S. v., 19 Mo. 211. § 214.
S. v., 103 N. C. 383. §§ 877, 943, 944.
S. v., 29 S. C. 108. § 147.
Houx, S. v., 109 Mo. 654. §§ 442, 443, 451.
Hover, S. v., 58 Vt. 496. § 41.
Hovis, S. v., 76 N. C. 117. § 823.
Howard, In re, 63 Fed. R. 263. § 1343.
C. v., 3 Met. (Ky.) 407. § 1039.
P. v., 50 Mich. 239. § 190.
P. v., 73 Mich. 10. § 516.
Rex v., 1 M. & Rob. 187. § 856.
v. S., 34 Ark. 433. § 325.
v. S., 94 Ga. 587. § 1099.
v. S., 5 Ind. 183. § 96.
v. S., 6 Ind. 444. § 1181.
v. S., 64 Ind. 516. § 1300.
v. S., 67 Ind. 401. §§ 13, 232, 235, 252, 266.
v. S., 87 Ind. 68. § 1028.
v. S., 11 Ohio St. 328. § 452.
v. S., 8 Tex. Ap. 53. § 413.
v. S., 18 Tex. Ap. 348. § 257.
v. S., 23 Tex. Ap. 265. § 341.
v. S., 25 Tex. Ap. 602. § 565.
v. S., 25 Tex. Ap. 686. § 325.
S. v., 6 Conn. 475. § 19.
S. v., 9 Ind. Ap. 635. § 1305.
S. v., 14 Kan. 173. § 304.
S. v., 4 McCord, 159. § 892.
S. v., 72 Me. 459. § 85.
S. v., 118 Mo. 127. § 363.
S. v., 82 N. C. 623. § 416.
S. v., 112 N. C. 859. § 195.
S. v., 32 Vt. 380. § 413.
U. S. v., 37 Fed. R. 666. §§ 857, 861.
U. S. v., 3 Wash. C. C. 340. § 1359.
Howarth, Reg. v., 11 Cox, 588. § 667.
Rex v., 1 Moody, 207. § 255.
Howe, Ex parte, 26 Oreg. 181. § 5.
C. v., 13 Gray, 26. § 1178.
C. v., 132 Mass. 250. §§ 666, 706.
C. v., 144 Mass. 144. § 942.
v. S., 10 Ind. 423. § 1229.
S. v., 100 N. C. 449. § 1310.
S. v., 1 Rich. 260. § 1295.
Howell v. C., 5 Grat. 664. § 523.
P. v., 4 Johns. 296. § 753.
Reg. v., 1 C. & K. 689. § 426.
Reg. v., 9 C. & P. 437. §§ 196, 993, 995.
Reg. v., 1 Den. 1. § 426.
Reg. v., 4 F. & F. 160. § 959.
Rex v., 7 C. & P. 325. § 555.
v. S., 79 Ala. 283. § 309.
v. S., 5 Ga. 48. § 267.
v. S., 71 Ga. 224. § 1210.

Howell v. S., 4 Ind. Ap. 148. § 1270.
v. S., 1 Oreg. 241. § 588.
v. S., 37 Tex. 591. § 758.
v. S., 16 Tex. Ap. 93. § 614.
v. S., 29 Tex. Ap. 592. § 1190.
S. v., Ga. Dec., Pt. I, 158. §§ 269, 274.
S. v., 9 Ired. 485. § 342.
S. v., 107 N. C. 835. § 827.
U. S. v., 56 Fed. R. 21. §§ 966, 990.
U. S. v., 64 Fed. R. 110. § 794.
U. S. v., 65 Fed. R. 402. § 803.
Howerton, S. v., 58 Mo. 581. §§ 472, 481.
Howery, S. v., 41 Tex. 506. §§ 1210, 1311.
Howes, C. v., 15 Pick. 231. § 5.
Howlett v. S., 5 Yerg. 144. § 1288.
Howorth, Rex v., 3 Stark. 26. § 703.
S. v., 70 Ia. 157. § 1248.
Howser v. C., 51 Pa. St. 332. §§ 411, 416.
v. S., 58 Ga. 78. §§ 504, 514.
Hox, S. v., 3 Dev. 116. § 1302.
Hoxie, U. S. v., 1 Paine, 265. § 1357.
Hoxsie, S. v., 15 R. I. 1. §§ 190, 1239, 1248, 1249.
Hoyer, C. v., 125 Mass. 209. § 1264.
S. v., 40 La. An. 744. § 592.
Hoyle, S. v., 6 Ired. 1. § 873.
Hoyt v. S., 50 Ga. 313. §§ 554, 655.
S. v., 46 Conn. 330. § 178.
S. v., 47 Conn. 518. §§ 170, 171, 419.
S. v., 13 Minn. 132. §§ 142, 332, 336, 337, 338, 380, 421.
Hubbard v. Briggs, 31 N. Y. 518. § 431.
P. v., 86 Mich. 440. § 572.
P. v., 92 Mich. 322. § 1117.
P. v., 24 Wend. 369. § 924.
Reg. v., 14 Cox, 565. § 426.
v. S., 2 Tex. Ap. 506. §§ 96, 97.
v. S., 32 Tex. Ap. 389. § 1024.
S. v., 60 Ia. 466. §§ 1233, 1256, 1259.
S. v., 3 Ind. 530. § 1309.
Hubbs, S. v., 58 Ind. 415. § 232.
Hubby v. S., 8 Tex. Ap. 597. § 365.
Huber v. S., 25 Ind. 175. § 91.
v. S., 57 Ind. 341. § 560.
v. S., 126 Ind. 185. § 440.
Hubotter v. S., 32 Tex. 479. § 594.
Hubson, Rex v., 1 East, P. C. 258. § 289.
Huck, S. v., 29 Wis. 202. § 1194.
Hucks, Rex v., 1 Stark. 521. § 430.
Huckenstine's Appeal, 70 Pa. St. 102. § 1171.
Hudelson v. S., 94 Ind. 426. § 1315.
Hudgins v. S., 2 Ga. 173. § 144.
v. S., 61 Ga. 182. § 265.
Hudson, C. v., 97 Mass. 565. § 416.
v. Geary, 4 R. I. 485. § 1275.
Reg. v., Bell, 263. § 971.
v. S., 61 Ala. 333. § 533.
v. S., 3 Coldw. 355. § 427.
v. S., 6 Tex. Ap. 565. §§ 307, 341.
v. S., 9 Tex. Ap. 151. § 551.
v. S., 28 Tex. Ap. 323. § 416.
v. S., 9 Yerg. 407. § 614.
Hudson, S. v., 59 Mo. 135. § 308.
S. v., 78 Mo. 302. § 1211.
S. v., 13 Mont. 112. § 791.
U. S. v., 7 Cranch. 32. §§ 9, 14, 1048.
Huff v. C., 14 Grat. 648. § 1310.
v. S., 2 Swan, 279. § 1297.
S. v., 76 Ia. 200. § 1253.
S. v., 11 Nev. 17. § 293.
Huffman v. C., 6 Rand. 685. § 801.
v. S., 29 Ala. 40. §§ 84, 1303.
v. S., 30 Ala. 532. § 1303.
v. S., 89 Ala. 33. § 652.
v. S., 95 Ga. 469. § 1028.
v. S., 23 Tex. Ap. 491. § 1143.
Huffschmidt, S. v., 47 Mo. 73. §§ 12, 102.
Huggett, U. S. v., 40 Fed. R. 636. §§ 83, 1332.
Huggins, Rex v., 2 Ld. Raym. 1574. § 188.
v. S., 41 Ala. 393. §§ 714, 719, 721.
Hughes v. C., 17 Grat. 565. § 601.
v. C., 89 Ky. 227. §§ 792, 800, 801.
C. v., 5 Allen, 499. §§ 852, 875.
C. v., 133 Mass. 496. §§ 28, 1018.
P. v., 29 Cal. 257. § 522.
P. v., 86 Mich. 180. §§ 189, 1237.
P. v., 90 Mich. 368. § 1264.
P. v., 97 Mich. 543. § 1231.
P. v., 137 N. Y. 29. §§ 18, 728, 735.
Reg. v., Bell, 242. § 215.
Reg. v., 1 C. & K. 519. §§ 885, 888, 891.
Reg. v., 2 C. & K. 214. §§ 469, 575.
Reg. v., Car. & M. 593. § 546.
Reg. v., 9 C. & P. 752. § 450.
Reg. v., Dears. & B. 188. § 859.
Reg. v., Dears. & B. 248. §§ 349, 351.
Reg. v., 1 F. & F. 355. § 675.
Reg. v., 1 Moody. 370. § 626.
Reg. v., 4 Q. B. D. 614. § 858.
Rex v., 2 C. & P. 420. § 815.
Rex v., 4 C. & P. 373. § 993.
Rex v., 5 C. & P. 126. § 268.
Rex v., 2 East, P. C. 491. § 500.
Rex v., 2 Lewin, 229. § 147.
v. S., 12 Ala. 458. §§ 214, 263.
v. S., 6 Ark. 131. § 930.
v. S., 8 Humph. 75. § 617.
v. S., 29 Tex. Ap. 565. § 391.
S. v., 58 Ia. 165. §§ 1076, 1077, 1079, 1082, 1085.
S. v., 24 Mo. 147. §§ 1224, 1231.
S. v., 76 Mo. 323. §§ 228, 228*a*.
S. v., 82 Mo. 86. § 1020.
S. v., 38 Neb. 366. § 851.
S. v., 16 R. I. 403. §§ 87, 128.
S. v., 43 Tex. 518. § 898.
S. v., 22 W. Va. 743. § 1236.
U. S. v., 70 Fed. R. 972, 75 Fed. R. 267. § 1341.
Hughey v. S., 47 Ala. 97. § 303.
Hughitt, U. S. v., 45 Fed. R. 47. § 1339.
Hulbert, C. v., 12 Met. 446. §§ 675, 690.
Huling v. S., 17 Ohio St. 583. §§ 196, 420.
Hull v. Hull, 2 Strobh. Eq. 174. § 1086.
v. Ruggles, 56 N. Y. 424. § 1315.
v. S., 79 Ala. 32. §§ 260, 303.

Hull v. S., 120 Ind. 153. §§ 1024, 1026.
v. S., 6 Lea. 249. § 365.
v. S., 22 Wis. 580. § 441.
S. v., 34 Conn. 132. § 242.
S. v., 83 Ia. 112. § 523.
S. v., 21 Me. 84. § 1182.
Hulstead v. C., 5 Leigh, 724. § 1274.
Humason, S. v., 5 Wash. 499. § 618.
Hume, S. v., 12 Oreg. 133. § 1193.
Hummel, S. v., 39 Ia. 478. § 1117.
Humpeler v. P., 92 Ill. 400. § 1235.
Humphrey, P. v., 7 Johns. 314. § 1083.
S. v., 32 Vt. 569. § 562.
Humphreys v. S., 17 Fla. 381. § 950.
S. v., 10 Humph. 442. § 758.
Humphries, C. v., 7 Mass. 242. § 468.
v. Johnson, 20 Ind. 190. § 11.
Hundley, S. v., 46 Mo. 414. § 160.
Hundson's Case, 2 East, P. C. 611. § 538.
Hungate v. P., 7 Ill. Ap. 101. §§ 271, 274.
Hungerford, Rex v., 2 East, P. C. 518. § 511.
Hunkins, S. v., 90 Wis. 264. § 844.
Hunnicutt v. S., 20 Tex. Ap. 632. § 410.
Hunt, Ex parte, 28 Tex. Ap. 361. § 78.
v. C., 13 Grat. 757. §§ 571, 616.
C. v., 4 Cush. 49. §§ 1131, 1135.
C. v., 4 Met. 111. §§ 953, 954, 955, 963, 975, 977.
Reg. v., 8 C. & P. 642. §§ 542, 635.
Reg. v., 2 Cox, 239. § 426.
Reg. v., 8 Cox, 495. § 563.
Rex v., 3 B. & Ald. 566 §§ 988, 1003.
Rex v., 1 Moody, 93. § 259.
Rex v., 1 Russ. Cr. 388. §§ 995, 1003.
v. S., 55 Ala. 138. § 589.
v. S., 3 Ind. Ap. 383. § 1163.
v. S., 72 Miss. 413. § 302.
v. S., 3 Tex. Ap. 116. § 1026.
v. S., 6 Tex. Ap. 663. § 257.
v. S., 7 Tex. Ap. 212. § 409.
v. S., 33 Tex. Ap. 93. § 47.
v. S., 33 Tex. Ap. 252. § 169.
S. v., 2 Hill (S. C.), 1. § 1354.
S. v., 137 Ind. 537. §§ 862, 890.
S. v., 45 Ia. 673. § 548.
Hunter v. C., 2 Serg. & R. 298. § 1137.
Reg. v., 10 Cox, 642. § 666.
Rex v., 3 C. & P. 591. § 805.
Rex v., 4 C. & P. 128 § 805.
v. S., 55 Ala. 76. § 951.
v. S., 60 Ark. 312. § 1240.
v. S., 29 Fla. 486. § 463.
v. S., 43 Ga. 483. § 416.
v. S., 29 Ind. 80. § 509.
v. S., 101 Ind. 241. §§ 128, 1257, 1259.
v. S., 62 Miss. 540. §§ 301, 1007.
v. S., 40 N. J. 495. §§ 369, 377, 381, 413.
v. S., 8 Tex. Ap. 75. § 373*a*.
v. S., 18 Tex. Ap. 444. § 1257.
v. S., 30 Tex. Ap. 314. § 382.
S. v., 8 Blackf. 212. § 915.
S. v., 68 Ia. 447. § 1185.
S. v., 5 Ired. 369. § 1188.
S. v., 50 Kan. 302. § 552.
Hunter, S. v., 14 La. An. 71. § 939.
S. v., 42 La. An. 814. § 383.
S. v., 106 N. C. 796. § 62.
S. v., 44 Tex. 94. §§ 255, 260.
Huntington, In re, 68 Fed. R. 881. § 1336.
v. Cheesbro, 57 Ind. 74. § 69.
Huntley, C. v., 156 Mass. 236. § 34.
Reg. v., Bell. 238. § 609.
S. v., 3 Ired. 418. § 1029.
S. v., 25 Oreg. 349. §§ 500, 503.
Huntsman v. S., 12 Tex. Ap. 619. §§ 554, 609.
Huntzinger v. C., 97 Pa. St. 336. § 611.
Hunzinger v. S., 39 Neb. 653. § 1210.
Hupp, S. v., 31 W. Va. 355. §§ 508, 511.
Hurd v. P., 25 Mich. 405. §§ 332, 338, 343, 410.
Hurds, S. v., 19 Neb. 316. § 849.
Hurell v. S., 5 Humph. 68. § 717.
Hurford v. S., 91 Tenn. 669. § 44.
Hurl, Ex parte, 49 Cal. 557. § 1211.
Hurlbut v. S., 12 Tex. Ap. 252. § 823.
Hurley, C. v., 99 Mass. 433. §§ 200, 250.
C. v., 158 Mass. 159. §§ 1243, 1279.
C. v., 160 Mass. 10. § 1237.
P. v., 8 Cal. 390. §§ 167, 306.
P. v., 60 Cal. 74. § 620.
Reg. v., 2 M. & Rob. 473. § 762.
v. S., 30 Tex. Ap. 333. § 539.
S. v., 1 Houst. Cr. C. 28. §§ 159, 179.
S. v., 54 Me. 562. § 1215.
Hurrell, Reg. v., 3 F. & F. 271. § 886.
Hurse, Reg. v., 2 M. & Rob. 360. §§ 195, 205, 788.
Hurst, P. v., 62 Mich. 276. § 639.
v. S., 79 Ala. 55. §§ 930, 934.
S. v., 11 W. Va. 54. §§ 680, 684, 708, 711.
Hurt v. S., 55 Ala. 214. § 509.
v. S., 26 Ind. 106. § 552.
v. S., 25 Miss. 378. § 390.
S. v., 7 Mo. 321. § 18.
Hurtado, P. v., 63 Cal. 288. § 418.
Husband, P. v., 36 Mich. 306. § 644.
Hussey, C. v., 111 Mass. 432. § 638.
C. v., — Mass. —, 32 N. E. R. 362. § 1086.
v. S., 87 Ala. 121. § 426.
v. S., 69 Ga. 54. § 1264.
S. v., 7 Ia. 409. § 452.
Huston v. P., 121 Ill. 497. § 447.
v. S., 13 Tex. Ap. 595. § 50.
Hutcherson v. S., 33 Tex. Ap. 67. § 890.
Hutchins v. C., 2 Va. Cas. 331. § 1123.
v. S., 28 Ind. 34. § 1079.
v. S., 13 Ohio, 198. § 780.
S. v., 74 Ia. 20. § 1235.
Hutchinson v. C., 82 Pa. St. 472. §§ 123, 554, 644.
C. v., 6 Allen, 595. § 1242.
C. v., 1 Mass. 7. § 805.
v. Merchants', etc. Bank, 41 Pa. St. 42. § 11.
Reg. v., 9 Cox, 555. §§ 188, 291.
Rex v., 2 B. & C. 608, n. § 425.
Rex v., Russ. & Ry. 412. § 546.
v. S., 62 Ala. 3. § 1033.

Hutchinson v. S., 36 Tex. 293. § 896.
S. v., 60 Ia. 478. § 649.
S. v., 72 Ia. 561. § 1220.
S. v., 36 Me. 261. § 1094.
S. v., 111 Mo. 257. §§ 496, 504, 509, 511.
S. v., 7 Nev. 53. § 391.
Hutchison v. S., 5 Humph. 141. § 1018.
Huting, S. v., 21 Mo. 464. § 158.
Hutto v. S., 7 Tex. Ap. 44. § 613.
Hutton, C. v., 95 Ky. 302. § 666.
v. S., 23 Tex. Ap. 386. § 242.
Huxford, S. v., 47 Ia. 16. §§ 1018, 1262.
Huxley, Reg. v., Car. & M. 596. §§ 269, 270, 480.
Hyams, Rex v., 7 C. & P. 441. § 500.
Hyatt v. S., 32 Tex. Ap. 580. § 618.
Hyde, C. v., Thach. Cr. Cas. 19. § 1293.
S. v., 29 Conn. 564. § 142.
Hyden v. S., 31 Tex. Ap. 401. § 616.
Hymer, S. v., 15 Nev. 49. § 419.
Hyndman, P. v., 99 Cal. 1. §§ 361, 377, 419.

Ida County v. Wood, 79 Ia. 148. § 649.
Igo, C. v., 158 Mass. 199. § 1275.
S. v., 108 Mo. 568. § 815.
Ihrig, S. v., 160 Mo. 267. § 1152.
Illidge, Reg. v., 2 C. & K. 871. § 753.
Illies v. Knight, 3 Tex. 312. § 17.
Illinois C. R. Co. v. Illinois, 163 U. S. 142. § 40.
Illsley, S. v., 81 Ia. 49. § 1249.
Immell, C. v., 6 Binn. 403. § 1126.
Inabnet, U. S., 41 Fed. R. 130. § 1330.
Independence v. Noland, 21 Mo. 394. § 63.
Inder, Rex v., 2 C. & K. 635. § 744.
Indianapolis v. Fairchild, 1 Ind. 315. § 1228.
Ingalls v. S., 48 Wis. 647. §§ 28, 160, 617.
S. v., 59 N. H. 88. § 1244.
Ingersoll v. S., 11 Ind. 464. § 104.
S. v., 17 Wis. 631. §§ 78, 93, 96.
Ingle v. S., 1 Tex. Ap. 307. § 572.
Inglis v. Sailors' Snug Harbor, 3 Pet. 99. § 1354.
Ingold, S. v., 4 Jones, 216. § 310.
Ingraham, P. v., 100 Mich. 530. §§ 1218, 1280.
v. U. S., 155 U. S. 434. § 1352.
U. S. v., 49 Fed. R. 155. § 1352.
Ingram v. S., 67 Ala. 67. § 311.
v. S., 62 Miss. 142. § 304.
Inhabitants, Rex v., 1 Stra. 631. § 149.
Inhabitants of Hudson Co., S. v., 30 N. J. 137. § 182.
Inhabitants of Madison, S. v., 63 Me. 546. § 182.
Inman v. S., 54 Ga. 219. § 577.
Inness, S. v., 53 Me. 536. § 1244.
Inskeep v. S., 35 Ohio St. 482. § 166.
S. v., 49 Ohio St. 228. § 252.
Instan, Reg. v., 1 Q. B. D. (1893) 450. § 286.
Intoxicating Liquor Cases, 25 Kan. 751. §§ 1218, 1219.
Intoxicating Liquors, C. v., 4 Allen, 593. § 1279.
C. v., 105 Mass. 595. §§ 1243, 1267.
C. v., 110 Mass. 416. § 1229.
C. v., 115 Mass. 153. § 75.
C. v., 116 Mass. 21. §§ 1243, 1267.
C. v., 116 Mass. 24. §§ 1243, 1267.
C. v., 135 Mass. 519. § 1267.
C. v., 138 Mass. 506. § 1270.
C. v., 142 Mass. 470. § 1267.
C. v., 146 Mass. 509. § 1267.
C. v., 150 Mass. 164. § 1279.
C. v., 163 Mass. 42. § 1267.
S. v., 64 Ia. 300. § 1267.
S. v., 76 Ia. 243. § 1219.
S. v., 50 Me. 506. § 1237.
S. v., 63 Me. 121. §§ 1239, 1243, 1267.
S. v., 68 Me. 187. § 90.
S. v., 80 Me. 57. § 1280.
S. v., 44 Vt. 208. § 1267.
S. v., 58 Vt. 594. § 1267.
Inwood v. S., 42 Ohio St. 186. § 5.
Ion, Reg. v., 2 Den. 475. § 781.
Irby v. S., 25 Tex. Ap. 203. § 426.
v. S., 32 Ga. 496. §§ 151, 368.
Irish, In re, 64 Vt. 376. § 1018.
Irrisistible, The, 7 Wheat. 551. § 96.
Irvin v. S., 19 Fla. 872. § 359.
v. S., 37 Tex. 412. § 577.
v. S., 7 Tex. Ap. 78. § 1161.
S. v., 5 Blackf. 343. § 1290.
Irvine v. S., 13 Tex. Ap. 499. § 618.
v. S., 18 Tex. Ap. 51. § 1039.
S. v., 3 Heisk. 155. § 1265.
Irving, P. v., 95 N. Y. 541. § 257.
v. S., 9 Tex. Ap. 66. § 462.
Irwin v. S., 43 Tex. 236. § 303.
v. S., 25 Tex. Ap. 558. § 588.
U. S. v., 5 McLean, 178. §§ 91, 752.
Isaac, Rex v., 2 East, P. C., 1031. § 521.
Isaacs, C. v., 5 Rand. 634. §§ 1086, 1125.
v. P., 118 Ill. 538. § 716.
Reg. v., L. & C. 220. § 1148.
Rex v., 1 Russ. Cr. 63. § 194.
v. S., 48 Miss. 234. § 966.
v. S., 25 Tex. 174. §§ 139, 332.
Isabel, S. v., 40 La. An. 340. § 1209.
Isensee, S. v., 12 Wash. 254. §§ 632, 655.
Isham v. S., 38 Ala. 213. §§ 133, 389.
Ismenard, U. S. v., 1 Cranch, C. C. 150. §§ 1137, 1306.
Isom v. S., 83 Ga. 378. § 271.
Israel, C. v., 4 Leigh, 675. § 927.
Ives, S. v., 13 Ired. 338. §§ 713, 719.
Ivey v. S., 12 Ala. 276. § 324.
v. S., 61 Ala. 58. § 1017.
v. S., 43 Tex. 425. §§ 615, 620.
Ivyes, Rex v., 2 Show. 468. § 1199.
Izer v. S., 77 Md. 110. §§ 856, 888.

J. B., S. v., 1 Tyler, 269. § 891.
Jack, P. v., 76 Mich. 218. §§ 557, 609.
Jackman, P. v., 96 Mich. 269. §§ 1043, 1068.
Jacks v. Bell, 3 C. & P. 316. § 11.

Jackson, Ex parte, 45 Ark. 158. § 25.
v. Boyd, 53 Ia. 536. § 1275.
v. C., 19 Grat. 656. § 426.
v. C., 86 Ky. 1. § 709.
C. v., 11 Bush, 679. § 1083.
C. v., 15 Gray, 187. § 1147.
C. v., 132 Mass. 16. § 677.
v. Goodell, 20 Johns. 188. § 1354.
v. P., 18 Ill. 269. § 376.
v. P., 18 Ill. Ap. 508. § 691.
v. P., 126 Ill. 139. §§ 666, 676, 677, 691.
v. P., 9 Mich. 111. § 1190.
P. v., 3 Denio, 101. §§ 1137, 1306, 1316.
P. v., 3 Hill (N. Y.), 92. § 1147.
P. v., 7 Mich. 432. §§ 1184, 1191, 1192.
P. v., 111 N. Y. 362. § 406.
P. v., 3 Park. Cr. 391. §§ 453, 460.
Reg. v., 1 C. & K. 384. § 640.
Reg. v., 7 Cox, 357. § 196.
Reg. v., 9 Cox, 505. § 554.
Reg. v., 2 Moody, 32. § 556.
Reg. v., 1 Q. B. D. (1891) 671. § 243.
Rex v., 3 Camp. 370. §§ 661, 674.
Rex v., 1 East, P. C., Addenda, XXI. § 470.
Rex v., 1 Moody, 119. § 563.
Rex v., Russ. & Ry. 47. § 446.
v. S., 69 Ala. 249. § 586.
v. S., 74 Ala. 26. § 392.
v. S., 77 Ala. 18. §§ 338, 423.
v. S., 81 Ala. 33. § 309.
v. S., 91 Ala. 55. § 228.
v. S., 94 Ala. 85. §§ 139, 275, 303.
v. S., 102 Ala. 167. §§ 495, 505.
v. S., 6 Baxt. 452. §§ 303, 306.
v. S., 45 Ga. 198. § 338.
v. S., 51 Ga. 402. § 274.
v. S., 72 Ga. 28. § 765.
v. S., 76 Ga. 473. § 298.
v. S., 88 Ga. 784. § 391.
v. S., 88 Ga. 787. §§ 1323, 1326.
v. S., 91 Ga. 271. § 299.
v. S., 91 Ga. 322. § 235.
v. S., 93 Ga. 165. §§ 604, 605.
v. S., 46 La. An. 547. § 443.
v. S., 66 Miss. 89. § 298.
v. S., 49 N. J. 252. § 18.
v. S., 11 Ohio St. 104. § 536.
v. S., 39 Ohio St. 37. § 377.
v. S., 25 Tex. Sup. 229. § 262.
v. S., 43 Tex. 421. §§ 896, 898.
v. S., 7 Tex. Ap. 363. § 557.
v. S., 15 Tex. Ap. 84. § 315.
v. S., 15 Tex. Ap. 579. § 874.
v. S., 16 Tex. Ap. 373. §§ 1302, 1304.
v. S., 20 Tex. Ap. 190. § 194.
v. S., 25 Tex. Ap. 314. § 382.
v. S., 28 Tex. Ap. 143. § 616.
v. S., 28 Tex. Ap. 370. §§ 514, 616.
v. S., 29 Tex. Ap. 458. §§ 396, 397, 398.
v. S., 55 Wis. 589. § 508.
S. v., 1 Houst. 561. § 546.
S. v., 7 Ind. 270. § 830.
S. v., 12 Ired. 329. §§ 829, 832.
S. v., 42 Kan. 448. § 670.
Jackson, S. v., 12 La. An. 679. §§ 307, 423.
S. v., 33 La. An. 1087. § 303.
S. v., 37 La. An. 768. § 268.
S. v., 37 La. An. 896. § 303.
S. v., 43 La. An. 183. § 268.
S. v., 44 La. An. 160. §§ 303, 306.
S. v., 30 Me. 129. § 592.
S. v., 73 Me. 91. §§ 16, 947, 950.
S. v., 17 Mo. 544. §§ 248, 414.
S. v., 39 Mo. 420. §§ 1284, 1285.
S. v., 80 Mo. 175. § 57.
S. v., 89 Mo. 561. § 766.
S. v., 90 Mo. 156. § 797.
S. v., 99 Mo. 60. § 362.
S. v., 105 Mo. 196. § 78.
S. v., 112 Mo. 585. § 691.
S. v., 126 Mo. 521. § 618.
S. v., 65 N. C. 305. § 548.
S. v., 82 N. C. 565. § 987.
S. v., 7 S. C. 283. § 981.
S. v., 32 S. C. 27. § 306.
S. v., 1 Speers, 13. § 993.
S. v., 26 W. Va. 250. § 597.
U. S. v., 1 Hughes, 531. § 1245.
U. S. v., 29 Fed. R. 503. § 1330.
v. Weisiger, 2 B. Mon. 214. § 756.
Jacob, S. v., 30 S. C. 131. § 726.
Jacobi v. S., 59 Ala. 71. § 1313.
Jacobs, C. v., 9 Allen, 274. §§ 226, 489.
C. v., 152 Mass. 276. § 1240.
P. v., 35 Mich. 36. §§ 669, 701, 706.
Rex v., 1 Moody, 140. § 1074.
Rex v., Russ. & Ry. 331. § 1153.
v. S., 61 Ala. 448. §§ 750, 799.
v. S., 31 Neb. 33. § 683.
S. v., 75 Ia. 247. § 1272.
S. v., 94 N. C. 950. § 820.
S. v., 103 N. C. 397. § 1027.
S. v., 28 S. C. 29. § 310.
S. v., 41 S. C. 220. §§ 29, 76, 1214.
Jacobson, Reg. v., 14 Cox, C. C. 522. § 1167.
v. S., 55 Ala. 151. § 1292.
Jacobus, C. v., 1 Leg. Gaz. Rep. 491. § 1321.
Jacques v. P., 66 Ill. 84. § 463.
U. S. v., 55 Fed. Rep. 53. §§ 943, 950.
Jaeger, S. v., 63 Mo. 403. §§ 85, 1254.
Jaehne, In re, 35 Fed. Rep. 357. § 78.
P. v., 103 N. Y. 182. §§ 94, 897.
v. New York, 128 U. S. 189. § 78.
Jailer, U. S. v., 2 Abb. (U. S.) 265. § 298.
Jake, S. v., 1 Wins. No. 2, 80. § 498.
Jambor v. S., 75 Wis. 664. § 223.
James v. Campbell, 5 C. & P. 372. § 239.
v. C., 12 Serg. & R. 220. §§ 12, 26, 1169.
C. v., 1 Pick. 375. § 555.
P. v., 100 Mich. 522. § 1250.
Reg. v., 1 C. & K. 530. §§ 226, 233, 258.
Reg. v., 8 C. & P. 131. § 828.
Reg. v., 8 C. & P. 292. § 753.
Reg. v., 4 Cox, 90. § 809.

James, Reg. v., 12 Cox, 127. § 688.
Reg. v., 24 Q. B. D. 439. § 1330.
Rex v., 5 C. & P. 153. § 997.
v. S., 53 Ala. 380. § 474.
v. S., 63 Md. 242. § 1310.
S. v., 37 Conn. 355. § 931.
S. v., 63 Mo. 570. §§ 42, 128, 188.
S. v., 58 N. H. 67. §§ 543, 585.
Jamison v. Burton, 43 Ia. 282. §§ 128, 1257.
v. P., 145 Ill. 357. § 173.
v. S., 37 Ark. 445. §§ 692, 708.
v. S., 27 Tex. Ap. 442. § 823.
S. v., 74 Ia. 602. §§ 654, 655.
S. v., 74 Ia. 613. § 694.
S. v., 38 Minn. 21. §§ 1102, 1104, 1107.
S. v., 23 Mo. 330. § 1228.
Jane v. C., 3 Met. (Ky.) 18. §§ 377, 378.
Janeway v. S., 1 Head, 130. § 609.
Jangraw, S. v., 61 Vt. 39. §§ 1248, 1277.
Janks v. S., 29 Tex. Ap. 233. §§ 1239, 1265.
Jansen, S. v., 22 Kan. 498. §§ 118, 501.
Janson, Reg. v., 4 Cox, 82. § 562.
S. v., 80 Mo. 97. § 690.
Janvier, S. v., 37 La. An. 645. § 303.
Janzen v. P., — Ill. —, 42 N. E. R. 862. § 461.
Jaques S. v., 68 Mo. 260. §§ 1252, 1272, 1274.
Jaquith v. Royce, 42 Ia. 406. § 6.
Jarman, Reg. v., 14 Cox, 48. § 675.
Jarnigan v. S., 6 Tex. Ap. 465. § 232.
Jarrald, Reg. v., L. & C. 301. § 516.
Jarrell v. S., 58 Ind. 293. § 278.
Jarvis, Reg. v., Dears. 552. § 786.
Rex. v., 2 M. & Rob. 40. §§ 209, 276.
Rex. v., 1 Moody, 7. § 508.
S. v., 21 Ia. 44. §§ 271, 274.
S. v., 63 N. C. 556. § 556.
S. v., 18 Oreg. 360. § 1121.
S. v., 20 Oreg. 437. § 1121.
U. S. v., 59 Fed. R. 357. § 1332.
Jasper, S. v., 4 Dev. 323. § 1022.
Jaurez, P. v., 28 Cal. 380. § 568.
Jay, S. v., 34 N. J. 368. § 1070.
Jean. S. v., 42 La. An. 946. §§ 878, 892.
Jeandell, C. v., 2 Grant, 506. §§ 1012, 1323.
S. v., 5 Harr. 475. § 1041.
Jeans, Reg. v., 1 C. & K. 539. § 815.
Jeff v. S., 39 Miss. 593. §§ 273, 275.
Jefferson, P. v., 52 Cal. 452. §§ 504, 512.
v. S., 100 Ala. 59. § 578.
S. v., 6 Ired. 305. § 460.
S. v., 39 La. An. 331. § 752.
S. v., 77 Mo. 136. § 425.
U. S. v., 60 Fed. R. 736. § 55.
Jefferson Co., S. v., 20 Fla. 425. § 1223.
Jeffrey, S. v., 33 Ark. 136. § 1291.
Jeffries, C. v., 7 Allen, 548. § 699.
Reg. v., 3 Cox, 85. § 204.
v. S., 52 Ark. 420. §§ 1227, 1254.
v. S., 9 Tex. Ap. 598. § 161.
Jellias, Rex v., 1 East, P. C. 130. § 1358.
Jellyman, Reg. v., 8 C. & P. 604. §§ 199, 1153, 1155.
Jemmerson v. S., 80 Ga. 111. § 58.
Jenkins, C. v., 10 Gray, 485. § 724.
C. v., 137 Mass. 572. § 1266.
P. v., 16 Cal. 431. § 506.
Reg. v., 9 C. & P. 38. § 555.
Reg. v., L. R. 1 C. C. 187. § 426.
Rex v., Russ. & Ry. 244. §§ 496, 508.
v. S., 82 Ala. 25. § 347.
v. S., 97 Ala. 66. §§ 681, 687.
v. S., 53 Ga. 33. § 526.
v. S., 92 Ga. 470. § 267.
v. S., 93 Ga. 1. § 160.
v. S., 15 Lea, 674. § 1103.
v. S., 1 Tex. Ap. 346. § 439.
v. S., 7 Tex. Ap. 146. § 825.
v. S., 30 Tex. Ap. 379. § 257.
v. S., 62 Wis. 49. §§ 556, 613, 616, 619, 713, 725.
S. v., 120 Ind. 268. § 274.
S. v., 5 Jones, 430. § 494.
S. v., 32 Kan. 477. § 1220.
S. v., 78 N. C. 478. § 546.
S. v., 14 Rich. 215. §§ 377, 385.
S. v., 26 S. C. 121. § 858.
S. v., 90 Tenn. 580. § 48.
S. v., 2 Tyler, 377. § 571.
Jenks, Rex v., 2 East, P. C. 514. § 509.
v. S., 17 Wis. 665. §§ 143, 1181.
Jenness, P. v., 5 Mich. 305. §§ 455, 461, 1120, 1121.
Jennett, S. v., 88 N. C. 665. § 619.
Jennings' Case, 2 Lewin, 130. § 256.
Jennings v. C., 17 Pick. 80. §§ 95, 1144.
C. v., 3 Grat. 624. § 1024.
C. v., 105 Mass. 586. § 511.
Reg. v., Dears. & B. 447. § 546.
Rex v., 4 C. & P. 249. § 450.
v. S., 16 Ind. 335. §§ 13, 1158.
v. S., 9 Mo. 852. §§ 257, 269.
v. S., 5 Tex. Ap. 298. § 1030.
v. S., 7 Tex. Ap. 350. § 368.
S. v., 79 Ia. 513. §§ 509, 514.
S. v., 18 Mo. 435. § 358.
S. v., 98 Mo. 493. § 634.
S. v., 104 N. C. 774. § 255.
Jennison, Reg. v., L. & C. 157. § 678.
Jensen v. S., 60 Wis. 577. § 1264.
Jenson, Rex v., 1 Moody, 434. § 631.
Jentzsch, Ex parte, 112 Cal. 468. §§ 55, 77, 1319.
Jerdee v. S., 36 Wis. 170. § 1126.
Jernegan, U. S. v., 4 Cranch, C. C. 1. § 1071.
Jerome, P. v., 1 Mich. 142. § 1043.
Jerry v. S., 1 Blackf. 395. § 373.
Jersey, P. v., 18 Cal. 337. § 562.
Jervey, Ex parte, 66 Fed. R. 957. §§ 29, 76, 1205.
Jervis, Rex v., 6 C. & P. 156. § 719.
Jesse v. S., 20 Ga. 156. § 870.
v. S., 28 Miss. 100. §§ 382, 526.
Jester v. S., 14 Ark. 552. § 1290.
Jessop, Reg. v., Dears. & B. 442. § 675.
Jett v. C., 18 Grat. 933. § 790.

Jewett, Reg. v., 2 Cox, 227. § 594.
Jillard v. C., 26 Pa. St. 169. § 1271.
Jim v. S., 15 Ga. 535. § 301.
v. S., 5 Humph. 145. § 409.
v. S., 8 Humph. 603. § 698.
v. S., 3 Mo. 108. §§ 12, 100.
S. v., 1 Dev. 142. § 452.
S. v., 8 Jones, 459. § 519.
v. T., 1 Wash. 76. § 295.
Jim Ti, P. v., 32 Cal. 60. § 606.
Jinks v. S., 5 Tex. Ap. 68. § 546.
Joaquin, S. v., 43 Ia. 131. §§ 668, 694, 711.
S. v., 69 Me. 218. §§ 226, 894.
Jobling, Rex v., Russ. & Ry. 525. § 508.
Jochinsky, P. v., 106 Cal. 638. §§ 509*a*, 514.
Joe v. S., 6 Fla. 591. § 396.
Joeckel, S. v., 44 Mo. 234. § 359.
Johanneson, U. S. v., 35 Fed. R. 411. § 20.
John, Reg. v., 13 Cox, 100. §§ 145, 738.
Rex v., 1 East, P. C. 357. §§ 426, 430.
Rex v., 7 C. & P. 324. § 543.
v. S., 23 Wis. 504. § 758.
S. v., 8 Ired. 330. §§ 160, 341.
S. v., 5 Jones, 163. § 469.
Johns, C. v., 6 Gray, 274. § 883.
S. v., 32 La. An. 812. § 272.
S. v., 124 Mo. 379. § 1196.
U. S. v., 1 Wash. C. C. 363. § 1347.
Johnson v. C., 5 Bush, 430. § 644.
v. C., 24 Grat. 555. § 575.
v. C., 29 Grat. 796. § 194.
v. C., 81 Ky. 325. § 396.
v. C., 86 Ky. 122. § 1077.
v. C., 87 Ky. 189. § 508.
v. C., 24 Pa. St. 386. § 362.
C. v., 10 Allen, 196. § 1089.
C. v., 162 Mass. 596. § 58.
C. v., 133 Pa. St. 293. §§ 592, 723.
C. v., 134 Pa. St. 635. § 1185.
C. v., 162 Pa. St. 63. § 403.
v. Irasburgh, 47 Vt. 28. §§ 1321, 1322.
v. Miller, 63 Ia. 529. § 617.
v. Ogilby, 3 P. Wms. 277. § 939.
v. Patterson, 14 Conn. 1. § 142.
v. P., 22 Ill. 314. §§ 960, 986.
v. P., 83 Ill. 431. §§ 1239, 1256.
v. P., 94 Ill. 505. §§ 867, 875, 876, 878, 881.
v. P., 113 Ill. 99. §§ 535, 550, 554, 562, 591.
v. P., 123 Ill. 624. §§ 89, 909.
v. P., 55 N. Y. 512. § 28.
P. v., 71 Cal. 384. § 654.
P. v., 91 Cal. 265. § 560.
P. v., 106 Cal. 289. § 460.
P. v., 12 Johns. 292. § 673.
P. v., 81 Mich. 573. § 602.
P. v., 86 Mich. 175. § 1017.
P. v., 110 N. Y. 134. §§ 355, 936.
P. v., 139 N. Y. 358. §§ 411, 416.
Reg. v., Car. & M. 218. §§ 118, 201, 501.
Reg. v., 6 Cox, 18. § 809.
Johnson, Reg. v., Dears. & B. 340. § 546.
Reg. v., 2 Den. 310. § 560.
Reg. v., L. & C. 489. §§ 228, 228*a*, 576.
Reg. v., L. & C. 632. §§ 444, 462, 464.
Reg. v., L. R. 2 C. C. 15. §§ 858, 859.
Rex v., 2 East, P. C. 488. § 500.
Rex v., 3 Mau. & S. 539, 556. §§ 625, 656, 656*a*.
Rex v., 2 Russ. Cr. 110. § 596.
v. S., 1 Ala. Sel. Cas. 72. § 826.
v. S., 17 Ala. 618. §§ 362, 426, 427.
v. S., 32 Ala. 583. § 1193.
v. S., 35 Ala. 363. § 257.
v. S., 35 Ala. 370. §§ 772, 791.
v. S., 37 Ala. 457. § 829.
v. S., 44 Ala. 414. § 1230.
v. S., 47 Ala. 62. § 612.
v. S., 61 Ala. 9. § 823.
v. S., 69 Ala. 253. § 309.
v. S., 69 Ala. 593. § 846.
v. S., 73 Ala. 483. § 508.
v. S., 73 Ala. 523. § 572.
v. S., 74 Ala. 537. § 1313.
v. S., 75 Ala. 7. §§ 1291, 1301, 1302.
v. S., 83 Ala. 65. § 1315.
v. S., 92 Ala. 82. § 1027.
v. S., 94 Ala. 35. §§ 347, 351.
v. S., 98 Ala. 57. § 819.
v. S., 100 Ala. 55. § 546.
v. S., 102 Ala. 1. §§ 338, 426, 427.
v. S., 13 Ark. 684. § 1294.
v. S., 29 Ark. 31. § 390.
v. S., 32 Ark. 181. § 593.
v. S., 36 Ark. 242. § 687.
v. S., 37 Ark. 98. § 1239.
v. S., 40 Ark. 453. § 1274.
v. S., 58 Ark. 57. §§ 303, 310.
v. S., 60 Ark. 308. § 1073.
v. S., 9 Baxt. 279. § 626.
v. S., 14 Ga. 55. § 265.
v. S., 26 Ga. 611. § 257.
v. S., 30 Ga. 426. § 267.
v. S., 48 Ga. 116. § 518.
v. S., 58 Ga. 397. §§ 858, 859.
v. S., 58 Ga. 491. § 589.
v. S., 60 Ga. 634. § 1270.
v. S., 62 Ga. 299. § 752.
v. S., 72 Ga. 679. § 304.
v. S., 83 Ga. 553. § 1237.
v. S., 88 Ga. 203. § 411.
v. S., 92 Ga. 36. §§ 273, 276.
v. S., 2 Ind. 652. § 199.
v. S., 11 Ind. 481. § 684.
v. S., 68 Ind. 43. § 831.
v. S., 74 Ind. 197. § 1256.
v. S., 75 Ind. 553. §§ 665, 690, 706, 708.
v. S., 47 Miss. 671. § 552.
v. S., 54 Miss. 430. § 307.
v. S., 63 Miss. 228. §§ 83, 1233.
v. S., 63 Miss. 313. § 424.
v. S., 66 Miss. 189. § 307.
v. S., 27 Neb. 687. §§ 225, 463.
v. S., 26 N. J. 313. §§ 957, 979, 983, 986.
v. S., 29 N. J. 453. § 22.

Johnson v. S., 17 Ohio, 593. § 456.
v. S., 11 Ohio St. 324. § 584.
v. S., 4 Sneed, 614. § 1285.
v. S., 17 Tex. 515. §§ 235, 271.
v. S., 26 Tex. 117. § 255.
v. S., 27 Tex. 758. § 303.
v. S., 29 Tex. 492. § 589.
v. S., 30 Tex. 748. § 330.
v. S., 35 Tex. 198. §§ 1290, 1302.
v. S., 36 Tex. 375. § 544.
v. S., 39 Tex. 393. § 557.
v. S., 41 Tex. 65. § 678.
v. S., 41 Tex. 608. § 565.
v. S., 43 Tex. 576. §§ 225, 232.
v. S., 1 Tex. Ap. 130. § 268.
v. S., 3 Tex. Ap. 590. §§ 118, 966.
v. S., 4 Tex. Ap. 268. § 385.
v. S., 4 Tex. Ap. 594. § 546.
v. S., 4 Tex. Ap. 598. § 274.
v. S., 5 Tex. Ap. 43. § 255.
v. S., 7 Tex. Ap. 210. § 259.
v. S., 10 Tex. Ap. 571. § 178.
v. S., 12 Tex. Ap. 385. § 618.
v. S., 13 Tex. Ap. 378. § 609.
v. S., 18 Tex. Ap. 385. § 409.
v. S., 20 Tex. Ap. 609. § 1120.
v. S., 26 Tex. Ap. 631. §§ 309, 310.
v. S., 27 Tex. Ap. 163. § 450.
v. S., 28 Tex. Ap. 562. § 1137.
v. S., 30 Tex. Ap. 419. §§ 362, 415.
v. S., 31 Tex. Ap. 464. § 1051.
v. S., 32 Tex. Ap. 58. § 920.
v. S., 32 Tex. Ap. 504. § 1138.
S. v., 38 Ark. 568. § 553.
S. v., 7 Blackf. 49. §§ 859, 878.
S. v., 40 Conn. 136. §§ 162, 331, 360.
S. v., 41 Conn. 584. §§ 162, 331, 360.
S. v., 3 Hill (S. C.), 1. § 551.
S. v., 102 Ind. 247. § 368.
S. v., 8 Ia. 525. §§ 353, 358, 361.
S. v., 19 Ia. 230. §§ 223, 523.
S. v., 26 Ia. 407. §§ 744, 750, 757, 794.
S. v., 49 Ia. 141. § 634.
S. v., 61 Ia. 504. § 1248.
S. v., 69 Ia. 623. §§ 1272, 1274.
S. v., 72 Ia. 393. § 355.
S. v., 89 Ia. 1. § 1126.
S. v., 89 Ia. 594. § 1004.
S. v., 1 Ired. 354. §§ 331, 342.
S. v., 2 Jones, 247. § 418.
S. v., 3 Jones, 266. § 333.
S. v., 10 La. An. 456. § 420.
S. v., 30 La. An., Pt. I, 305. § 607.
S. v., 30 La. An., Pt. II, 904. § 593.
S. v., 30 La. An., Pt. II, 921. §§ 363, 404.
S. v., 31 La. An. 368. § 404.
S. v., 35 La. An. 968. § 414.
S. v., 38 La. An. 686. § 515.
S. v., 41 La. An. 1076. § 430.
S. v., 42 La. An. 559. § 925.
S. v., 65 Me. 362. § 1248.
S. v., 12 Minn. 476. §§ 1073, 1083.
S. v., 43 Minn. 350. § 41.
S. v., 76 Mo. 121. §§ 308, 309, 311, 328, 410, 426, 922.
Johnson, S. v., 81 Mo. 60. § 271.
S. v., 93 Mo. 73. §§ 518, 934.
S. v., 115 Mo. 480. §§ 1100, 1103, 1104, 1105, 1106, 1107.
S. v., 118 Mo. 491. §§ 426, 430.
S. v., 129 Mo. 26. § 271.
S. v., 9 Nev. 175. § 279.
S. v., 33 N. H. 441. §§ 843, 845, 1267.
S. v., 67 N. C. 55. § 452.
S. v., 75 N. C. 174. § 246.
S. v., 100 N. C. 494. § 443.
S. v., 114 N. C. 846. § 72.
S. v., 3 N. D. 150. § 271.
S. v., 2 Oreg. 115. § 553.
S. v., 7 Oreg. 210. § 196.
S. v., Phill. 140. § 478.
S. v., 3 R. I. 94. §§ 1229, 1277.
S. v., 16 S. C. 187. § 1031.
S. v., 20 S. C. 387. § 848.
S. v., 21 Tex. 775. § 634.
S. v., 41 Tex. 504. § 1310.
S. v., 28 Vt. 512. § 460.
S. v., 1 Wins., No. 1, 238. § 620.
T. v., 9 Mont. 21. § 359.
v. U. S., 157 U. S. 320. § 416.
U. S. v., 2 Cranch, C. C. 21. § 494.
U. S. v., 26 Fed. R. 682. §§ 968, 969.
U. S. v., 2 Sawy. 482. § 950.
Johnston's Case, 5 Grat. 660. §§ 139, 338, 339, 342.
Johnston v. C., 22 Pa. St. 102. §§ 1319, 1323.
v. C., 85 Pa. St. 54. § 501.
Reg. v., 2 Moody, 254. § 667.
v. S., 100 Ala. 32. § 539.
v. S., 15 Miss. 58. §§ 1290, 1291.
v. S., 7 Mo. 183. § 18.
v. S., 25 Tex. Ap. 731. § 535.
S. v., 76 N. C. 209. § 464.
S. v., 11 Tex. 22. § 268.
U. S. v., 124 U. S. 236. § 86.
Joice v. S., 53 Ga. 50. §§ 463, 466.
Joiner v. S., 62 Ga. 560. § 440.
Jolly v. S., 94 Ala. 19. § 196.
S. v., 3 Dev. & B. 110. §§ 1087, 1099.
S. v., 96 Mo. 435. § 935.
U. S. v., 37 Fed. R. 108. §§ 752, 771.
Jonathan, S. v., 3 N. H. 65. § 145.
Jones, Ex parte, 31 Tex. Ap. 422. §§ 341, 365.
v. Andover, 10 Allen, 18. § 1322.
v. Clay, 1 Bos. & P. 191. § 11.
v. C., 17 Grat. 563. § 601.
v. C., 31 Grat. 830. § 265.
v. C., 75 Pa. St. 403. §§ 162, 360.
v. C., 1 Rob. (Va.) 748. § 486.
v. C., 80 Va. 18. § 1130.
v. C., 86 Va. 661. § 78.
C. v., 10 Bush, 725. § 324.
C. v., 2 Grat. 555. § 1125.
C. v., 1 Leigh. 598. §§ 353, 354, 356.
v. Estis, 2 Johns. 375. § 84.
v. Hungerford, 4 Gill & J. 402. § 520.
v. Jones, 71 Cal. 89. § 546.
v. Leonard, 50 Ia. 106. § 369.
v. P., 6 Colo. 452. § 307.

Jones v. P., 12 Ill. 259. §§ 617, 618.
v. P., 14 Ill. 196. § 1206.
P. v., 53 Cal. 58. § 609.
P. v., 63 Cal. 168. § 160.
P. v., 6 Mich. 176. § 1190.
P. v., 46 Mich. 441. § 226.
P. v., 49 Mich. 591. § 589.
P. v., 62 Mich. 304. § 740.
Reg. v., 1 C. & K. 181. § 830.
Reg. v., 1 C. & K. 303. § 520.
Reg. v., 2 C. & K. 236. § 568.
Reg. v., 2 C. & K. 398. § 733.
Reg. v., 3 C. & K. 346. § 695.
Reg. v., Car. & M. 611. §§ 556, 562.
Reg. v., Car. & M. 614. § 1076.
Reg. v., 9 C. & P. 761. §§ 205, 788, 789.
Reg. v., 2 Cox, 434. § 733.
Reg. v., 3 Cox, 441. § 256.
Reg. v., 5 Cox, 226. § 733.
Reg. v., 6 Cox, 467. § 678.
Reg. v., 11 Cox, 393. § 488.
Reg. v., 11 Cox, 544. § 349.
Reg. v., 12 Cox, 628. § 351.
Reg. v., 14 Cox, 3. § 615.
Reg. v., 14 Cox, 528. § 611.
Reg. v., Dears. & B. 655. § 536.
Reg. v., 1 Den. 551. § 696.
Reg. v., 21 L. T. 396. § 1076.
Reg. v., 4 L. T. (N. S.) 154. § 447.
Reg. v., 11 Q. B. D. 118. § 1084.
Reg. v., 1 Salk. 379. §§ 16, 661.
Rex v., 4 C. & P. 217. § 584.
Rex v., 7 C. & P. 151. § 555.
Rex v., 7 C. & P. 833. § 640.
Rex v., 2 East, P. C. 504. § 495.
Rex v., 2 East, P. C. 883. § 796.
Rex v., 2 East, P. C. 941. § 753.
Rex v., 2 East, P. C. 991. §§ 744, 754.
Rex v., 1 Leach, 139. § 470.
Rex v., Peake, 37. § 888.
v. Rice, 18 Pick. 440. § 939.
v. S., 13 Ala. 153. §§ 169, 588.
v. S., 50 Ala. 161. §§ 753, 801.
v. S., 51 Ala. 16. § 1031.
v. S., 60 Ala. 99. § 926.
v. S., 67 Ala. 84. § 1076.
v. S., 68 Ala. 559. § 1253.
v. S., 76 Ala. 8. § 419.
v. S., 90 Ala. 628. §§ 311, 358.
v. S., 96 Ala. 56. § 1247.
v. S., 103 Ala. 1. §§ 125, 413.
v. S., 58 Ark. 390. §§ 214, 395.
v. S., 18 Fla. 889. § 509.
v. S., 29 Ga. 594. §§ 162, 329, 391.
v. S., 63 Ga. 141. § 504.
v. S., 63 Ga. 395. § 533.
v. S., 64 Ga. 697. § 216.
v. S., 65 Ga. 147. § 373a.
v. S., 65 Ga. 621. § 377.
v. S., 75 Ga. 825. § 495.
v. S., 93 Ga. 547. § 659.
v. S., — Ga. —, 25 S. E. R. 319. §§ 560, 659, 666.
v. S., 11 Ind. 357. § 793.
v. S., 35 Ind. 122. § 380.
v. S., 50 Ind. 473. § 684.
Jones v. S., 53 Ind. 235. § 552.
v. S., 59 Ind. 229. §§ 13, 554.
v. S., 71 Ind. 66. §§ 414, 426, 427, 428, 429, 430.
v. S., 16 Lea, 466. § 1107.
v. S., 70 Md. 326. § 1148.
v. S., 26 Miss. 247. § 619.
v. S., 51 Miss. 718. § 600.
v. S., 57 Miss. 684. § 419.
v. S., 70 Miss. 401. § 431.
v. S., 28 Neb. 495. § 1028.
v. S., 11 N. H. 269. § 506.
v. S., 51 Ohio St. 331. § 326,
v. S., 11 Sm. & M. 315. § 276.
v. S., 13 Tex. 168. §§ 365. 390.
v. S., 3 Tex. Ap. 228. § 815.
v. S., 4 Tex. Ap. 436. § 420.
v. S., 5 Tex. Ap. 397. § 334.
v. S., 8 Tex. Ap. 648. § 710.
v. S., 9 Tex. Ap. 178. § 1163.
v. S., 10 Tex. Ap. 552. § 448.
v. S., 18 Tex. Ap. 485. § 463.
v. S., 20 Tex. Ap. 665. § 801.
v. S., 22 Tex. Ap. 680. § 663.
v. S., 25 Tex. Ap. 621. § 607.
v. S., 28 Tex. Ap. 42. § 557.
v. S., 29 Tex. Ap. 338. § 353.
v. S., 29 Tex. Ap. 347. § 1130.
v. S., 31 Tex. Ap. 177. § 409.
v. S., 31 Tex. Ap. 252. § 846.
v. S., 32 Tex. Ap. 533. § 1265.
v. S., 33 Tex. Ap. 492. §§ 241, 341.
S. v., 1 Bay, 207. § 774.
S. v., 2 Dev. & B. 544. § 565.
S. v., 3 Dev. & B. 122. § 617.
S. v., 1 Houst. Cr. C. 21. § 353.
S. v., 3 Ind. Ap. 121. §§ 1218, 1273.
S. v., 10 Ia. 206. § 505.
S. v., 13 Ia. 269. §§ 953, 974, 975.
S. v., 33 Ia. 9. § 617.
S. v., 64 Ia. 349. § 332.
S. v., 70 Ia. 505. § 435.
S. v., 89 Ia. 182. §§ 302, 308, 310, 311.
S. v., 9 Ired. 38. § 1159.
S. v., 16 Kan. 608. § 1100.
S. v., 41 Kan. 309. § 407.
S. v., 38 La. An. 792. §§ 370, 426.
S. v., 39 La. An. 935. § 449.
S. v., 41 La. An. 784. § 572.
S. v., 45 La. An. 1454. § 382.
S. v., 1 McMul. 236. §§ 793, 794, 799.
S. v., 73 Me. 280. § 251.
S. v., 71 Miss. 872. §§ 914, 917.
S. v., 20 Mo. 58. §§ 345, 361, 380.
S. v., 53 Mo. 486. §§ 1024, 1027.
S. v., 64 Mo. 391. § 358.
S. v., 68 Mo. 197. § 844.
S. v., 106 Mo. 302. § 524.
S. v., 7 Nev. 408. § 608.
S. v., 50 N. H. 369. §§ 157, 165, 361.
S. v., 65 N. C. 395. § 548.
S. v., 70 N. C. 75. §§ 661, 669.
S. v., 78 N. C. 420. §§ 931, 934.
S. v., 83 N. C. 605. § 449.
S. v., 91 N. C. 629. § 890.
S. v., 95 N. C. 588. § 242.

Jones, S. v., 18 Oreg. 256. § 36.
S. v., 29 S. C. 201. §§ 306, 333.
S. v., 18 Tex. 874. § 1185.
S. v., 33 Vt. 443. § 823.
S. v., 39 Vt. 370. § 1235.
S. v., 20 W. Va. 764. §§ 267, 316.
v. U. S., 5 Cranch, C. C. 647. §§ 680, 684, 697.
v. U. S., 27 Fed. R. 447. § 1330.
U. S. v., 14 Blatch. 90. § 859.
U. S. v., 20 Blatch. 235. § 1331.
U. S. v., 31 Fed. R. 718. §§ 617, 1330.
U. S. v., 31 Fed. R. 725. § 1330.
U. S. v., 32 Fed. R. 482. §§ 674, 689, 1352.
U. S. v., 69 Fed. R. 973. § 593.
U. S. v., 3 Wash. C. C. 209. §§ 468, 1359.
U. S. v., 3 Wash. C. C. 220. § 194.
U. S. v., 3 Wash. C. C. 228. § 1359.
Jorasco v. S., 6 Tex. Ap. 238. § 601.
v. S., 8 Tex. Ap. 540. § 612.
Jordan, In re, 49 Fed. R. 238. § 1217.
v. Circuit Ct., 69 Ia. 177. § 9.
C. v., 18 Pick. 28. § 1221.
P. v., 66 Cal. 10. §§ 665, 670.
Reg. v., 9 C. & P. 118. §§ 449, 450.
Rex v., 7 C. & P. 432. § 206.
v. S., 79 Ala. 9. §§ 194, 292, 333, 419.
v. S., 81 Ala. 20. §§ 199, 291, 431.
v. S., 82 Ala. 1. § 195.
v. S., 22 Fla. 528. § 1274.
v. S., 22 Ga. 545. § 390.
v. S., 38 Ga. 585. § 101.
v. S., 56 Ga. 92. § 214.
v. S., 60 Ga. 656. § 1143.
v. S., 11 Tex. Ap. 435. § 304.
S. v., 39 Ia. 387. §§ 1229, 1274.
S. v., 69 Ia. 506. §§ 617, 618.
S. v., 72 Ia. 377. § 1208.
S. v., 87 Ia. 86. § 504.
S. v., 34 La. An. 1219. § 684.
S. v., 39 La. An. 340. § 510.
S. v., 19 Mo. 212. § 268.
S. v., 75 N. C. 27. § 221.
Jose, U. S. v., 63 Fed. R. 951. § 9.
Josefa Segunda, The, 5 Wheat. 338. § 1359.
Joseph v. S., 42 Ind. 370. § 1248.
Josephdaffer v. S., 32 Ind. 402. § 1273.
Josephs v. Atkins, 2 Stark. 76. § 611.
Joslyn v. S., 128 Ind. 160. § 602.
Josselyn, C. v., 97 Mass. 411. § 1321.
P. v., 39 Cal. 393. § 1151.
Josslyn v. C., 6 Met. 236. §§ 509, 511.
Jourdine, U. S. v., 4 Cranch, C. C. 338. § 1145.
Journey v. S., 1 Mo. 428. § 12.
Joy v. S., 14 Ind. 139. § 377.
Joyce, Reg. v., L. & C. 576. § 753.
Rex v., Carr. C. L. 184. § 782.
Joyner, S. v., 81 N. C. 534. § 1217.
Jowers, S. v., 11 Ired. 555. § 241.
Juaraqui v. S., 28 Tex. 625. § 881.
Juarez, P. v., 28 Cal. 380. § 568.
Judd, C. v., 2 Mass. 329. §§ 33, 966, 977, 982.
P. v., 10 Cal. 313. § 380.
Judd, Rex v., 2 East, P. C. 1018. § 520.
Judefind v. S., 78 Md. 510. § 1319.
Judge v. S., 58 Ala. 406. § 339.
Judges, P. v., 13 Johns. 85. § 247.
Judy, S. v., 60 Ind. 138. § 1031.
Julien, S. v., 48 Ia. 445. § 846.
Julius, C. v., 143 Mass. 132. § 1257.
Julow, S. v., 129 Mo. 163. § 55.
Jumel, S. v., 13 La. An. 399. § 1030.
Jumpertz v. P., 21 Ill. 375. §§ 401, 407.
Juneau, S. v., 88 Wis. 180. §§ 456, 1135.
Jung Ah Lung, U. S. v., 124 U. S. 621. § 1344.
Junkin, C. v., 170 Pa. St. 194. § 42.
Jupitz v. P., 34 Ill. 516. § 716.
Jurgins, S. v., 31 Tex. 588. § 1304.
Justice v. S., 99 Ala. 180. § 426.
S. v., 2 Dev. 199. § 660.
Justices v. P., 90 N. Y. 12. § 560.
Reg. v., 17 Q. B. D. 598; 18 Q. B. D. 314. § 712.
Reg. v., 24 Q. B. D. 181. § 48.
S. v., 15 Ga. 408. § 1228.
Justus, S. v., 11 Oreg. 178. 407.

Kadgihn v. Bloomington, 58 Ill. 229. § 1228.
Kaelin v. C., 84 Ky. 354. § 382.
Kahlenbeck v. S., 119 Ind. 118. § 413.
Kahler, P. v., 93 Mich. 625. § 1241.
Kahn v. S., 58 Ind. 168. § 765.
Kain, Reg. v., 8 C. & P. 187. § 740.
v. S., 8 Ohio St. 306. §§ 361, 383.
S. v., 118 Mo. 5. § 698.
Kaiser v. S., 35 Neb. 704. § 614.
S. v., 124 Mo. 651. § 412.
Kalb, S. v., 14 Ind. 403. § 1257.
Kaler, S. v., 56 Me. 88. § 1243.
Kaliski v. Grady, 25 La. An. 576. § 1211.
Kalloch, P. v., 60 Cal. 116. § 914.
Kaltmeyer, U. S. v., 16 Fed. R. 760. § 1332.
Kaminsky, P. v., 73 Mich. 637. § 1129.
Kamman v. P., 24 Ill. Ap. 388. § 1262.
Kammann v. P., 124 Ill. 481. § 1262.
Kamp, C. v., 14 B. Mon. 385. § 1230.
Kanavan's Case, 1 Me. 226. § 1165.
Kane v. C., 89 Pa. St. 522. § 1265.
v. C., 109 Pa. St. 541. § 424.
C. v., 92 Ky. 457. § 872.
C. v., 108 Mass. 423. §§ 922, 929.
C. v., 143 Mass. 92. § 1250.
C. v., 150 Mass. 294. § 1243.
v. P., 8 Wend. 203. § 180.
P. v., 131 N. Y. 111; 142 N. Y. 366. §§ 138, 142, 826.
S. v., 33 La. An. 1269. §§ 376, 546.
S. v., 15 R. I. 395. § 1213.
S. v., 63 Wis. 260. §§ 499, 509, 513.
U. S. v., 19 Fed. R. 42. § 1328.
Kansas Ass'n, S. v., 45 Kan. 351. § 1315.
Kansas (City of) v. Corrigan, 86 Mo. 67. § 62.
v. White, 69 Mo. 26. § 62.
Kansas City v. Clark, 68 Mo. 588. §§ 6, 96.
v. Flanders, 71 Mo. 281. § 1228.

Kansas City, etc. R. Co., S. v., 32 Fed. R. 722. § 7.
Kantler, S. v., 33 Minn. 69. §§ 1212, 1228.
Karpowski, C. v., 167 Pa. St. 225. §§ 696, 699, 710.
Karr v. S., 100 Ala. 4. § 307.
Kartz, S. v., 13 R. I. 528. § 1215.
Karwisch v. Atlanta, 44 Ga. 404. § 1319.
Kaspar, S. v., 5 Wash. 174. § 554.
Kaster, S. v., 35 Ia. 221. §§ 1169, 1170, 1171, 1182, 1183.
Kattleman, S. v., 35 Mo. 105. § 765.
Kaub, S. v., 90 Mo. 196. §§ 1316, 1318.
Kaufman v. Dostal, 73 Ia. 691. §§ 1201, 1207.
v. S., 49 Ind. 248. § 719.
S. v., 59 Ia. 273. § 1309.
Kay, Reg. v., Dears. & B. 231. § 546.
v. S., 40 Tex. 29. § 565.
Kealey, Reg. v., 2 Den. 68. § 683.
Kearley, S. v., 26 Kan. 77. §§ 342, 358.
Kearney v. S., 48 Md. 16. § 595.
Kearny, Ex parte, 55 Cal. 212. § 1017.
Keasling, S. v., 74 Ia. 528. §§ 274, 278, 357, 361, 365.
Keator v. P., 32 Mich. 484. §§ 856, 875.
Kee v. S., 28 Ark. 155. § 292.
U. S. v., 39 Fed. R. 603. § 937.
Keefe v. P., 40 N. Y. 348. §§ 326, 365, 367.
v. S., 19 Ark. 190. § 232.
S. v., 54 Kan. 197. § 307.
Keefer, P. v., 65 Cal. 232. §§ 214, 390.
P. v., 97 Mich. 15. §§ 1275, 1276.
Keel, S. v., 54 Mo. 182. §§ 875, 878.
Keeland, S. v., 90 Mo. 337. § 609.
Keele, S. v., 105 Mo. 38. § 268.
Keeler, Ex parte, — S. C. —, 23 S. E. R. 865. §§ 1208, 1214.
v. S., 15 Tex. Ap. 111. § 760.
S. v., 28 Ia. 551. § 396.
Keeley, P. v., 81 Cal. 210. §§ 236, 815.
Keeller v. S., 4 Tex. Ap. 527. § 639.
Keely v. S., 14 Ind. 36. § 568.
Keen, S. v., 34 Me. 500. §§ 128, 1229.
S. v., 10 Wash. 93. § 462.
U. S. v., 5 Mason, 453. § 924.
Keena, Reg. v., L. R. 1 C. C. 113. § 636.
S. v., 63 Conn. 329. § 529.
Keenan v. C., 44 Pa. St. 55. §§ 162, 357, 358, 365.
C. v., 11 Allen, 262. § 1280.
C. v., 67 Pa. St. 203. §§ 1043, 1060.
v. S., 8 Wis. 132. § 368.
S. v., 57 Conn. 286. § 5.
S. v., 8 Rich. 456. § 863.
Keene, S. v., 50 Mo. 357. § 307.
Keener v. S., 18 Ga. 194. §§ 304, 307.
Keeney, Ex parte, 84 Cal. 304. § 63.
Keeper of Prison, C. v., 2 Ashm. 227. §§ 353, 354.
Keeran, S. v., 5 R. I. 497. §§ 1207, 1249.
Keesler, S. v., 78 N. C. 469. § 1120.
Keeter, S. v., 80 N. C. 472. § 753.
Keeton v. C., 92 Ky. 522. §§ 161, 477, 479.
Keffer, Pennsylvania v. Addison, 290. § 908.
Kegan, S. v., 62 Ia. 106. §§ 480, 483.
Kegg v. S., 10 Ohio, 75. § 754.
Keggon, S. v., 55 N. H. 19. § 1281.
Kehoe v. C., 85 Pa. St. 127. §§ 359, 419, 426.
Keighley, Reg. v., Dears. & B. 145. §§ 680, 681, 690.
Keil, Ex parte, 85 Cal. 309. § 489.
Keir v. Leeman, 6 Q. B. 308. § 939.
P. v., 78 Mich. 98. § 71.
Keiser v. S., 58 Ind. 379. § 1227.
v. S., 78 Ind. 430. §§ 94, 1224.
v. S., 82 Ind. 379. § 1234.
Keisler, S. v., 6 Jones, 73. § 1302.
Keith, C. v., 8 Met. 531. § 18.
Reg. v., Dears. 486. § 752.
v. S., 91 Ala. 2. § 1204.
v. S., 97 Ala. 32. § 316.
v. S., 33 Tex. Ap. 341. § 150.
S. v., 37 Ark. 96. § 1239.
S. v., 47 Minn. 559. §§ 1102, 1107, 1108.
S. v., 63 N. C. 140. § 78.
Keithler v. S., 10 Sm. & M. 192. § 200.
Keizer v. Randleman, 5 Jones, 478. § 1221.
Keley v. S., 12 Tex. Ap. 245. § 257.
Kelleher, Reg. v., 2 Ir. L. R. 11. § 684.
S. v., 81 Me. 346. §§ 1248, 1272.
Kellenbeck v. S., 10 Md. 431. § 530.
Keller v. S., 51 Ind. 111. §§ 678, 699, 702.
v. S., 11 Md. 525. §§ 1206, 1229.
v. S., 12 Md. 322. §§ 96, 97.
U. S. v., 19 Fed. R. 633. §§ 347, 351.
Kelley, C. v., 123 Mass. 417. § 885.
C. v., 140 Mass. 441. § 1237.
v. S., 53 Ind. 311. § 292.
v. S., 18 Tex. Ap. 262. § 615.
v. S., 31 Tex. Ap. 211. § 515.
v. S., 31 Tex. Ap. 216. § 159.
v. S., 32 Tex. Ap. 579. § 1095.
S. v., 47 Vt. 294. § 1018.
S. v., 65 Vt. 531. § 615.
Kelliher, C. v., 12 Allen, 480. § 93.
Kellner, S. v., 22 Neb. 668. § 48.
Kellogg, C. v., 7 Cush. 473. § 982.
v. S., 26 Ohio St. 15. § 563.
Kellum v. S., 66 Ind. 588. §§ 75, 1317.
Kelly, In re, 46 Fed. R. 653. § 489.
v. C., 1 Grant, 484. §§ 162, 355, 359, 360, 365.
v. C., 11 Serg. & R. 345. §§ 95, 1184.
C. v., 10 Cush. 69. § 1281.
C. v., 12 Gray, 175. § 1143.
C. v., 163 Mass. 169. § 34.
v. P., 115 Ill. 583. § 28.
v. P., 132 Ill. 363. § 263.
P. v., 6 Cal. 210. §§ 293, 376.
P. v., 28 Cal. 423. § 617.
P. v., 38 Cal. 145. § 871.
P. v., 59 Cal. 372. § 878.
Reg. v., 2 C. & K. 379. §§ 206, 713.
Reg. v., 2 C. & K. 814. § 341.
Reg. v., 2 Cox, 171. § 195.
Rex v., 1 Moody, 113. § 377.

Kelly, Rex v., Russ. & Ry. 421. § 204.
v. S., 72 Ala. 244. § 509.
v. S., 7 Baxt. 323. § 551.
v. S., 68 Miss. 343. §§ 332, 339.
v. S., 3 Sm. & M. 518. § 160.
v. S., 33 Tex. Ap. 31. § 1113.
S. v., 57 Ia. 644. §§ 617, 618.
S. v., 74 Ia. 589. § 145.
S. v., 73 Mo. 608. § 617.
S. v., 24 Tex. 182. §§ 1285, 1310.
v. U. S., 27 Fed. R. 616. § 426.
Kelose v. S., 47 Ala. 573. § 416.
Kelsey v. S., 62 Ga. 558. § 454.
S. v., 89 Mo. 623. §§ 42, 90, 105.
U. S. v., 42 Fed. R. 882. §§ 945, 948.
Kelsoe, S. v., 76 Mo. 505. § 511.
Kemmler, In re, 136 U. S. 436. § 80.
P. v., 119 N. Y. 580. § 80.
Kemp v. C., 80 Va. 443. § 194.
P. v., 76 Mich. 410. §§ 753, 808.
v. S., 89 Ala. 52. §§ 548, 612, 614.
v. S., 11 Humph. 320. § 118.
v. S., 25 Tex. Ap. 589. § 255.
S. v., 87 N. C. 38. § 1098.
Kempf, S. v., 26 Mo. 429. § 995.
Kenard, C. v., 8 Pick. 133. § 924.
Kendall, C. v., 144 Mass. 357. § 102.
P. v., 25 Wend. 399. §§ 151, 665.
Reg. v., 12 Cox, 598. § 546.
v. S., 65 Ala. 492. § 362.
v. S., 8 Tex. Ap. 569. §§ 305, 311.
S. v., 73 Ia. 255. § 454.
Kendrick v. S., 55 Miss. 436. §§ 306, 409, 421.
Keneston, S. v., 59 N. H. 36. §§ 771, 784.
Kennade, S. v., 121 Mo. 405. §§ 307, 411, 423.
Kennard, C. v., 8 Pick. 132. § 142.
Kenneally, U. S. v., 5 Biss. 122. § 788.
Kenneda v. S., 16 Tex. Ap. 258. § 614.
Kennedy v. C., 14 Bush. 340. § 303.
v. C., 2 Met. (Ky.) 36. § 772.
C. v., 15 B. Mon. 531. § 1298.
C. v., 97 Mass. 224. § 1243.
C. v., 108 Mass. 292. § 1281.
C. v., 119 Mass. 211. § 148.
C. v., 160 Mass. 312. § 1347.
v. P., 40 Ill. 488. § 334.
v. P., 44 Ill. 283. § 457.
v. P., 122 Ill. 649. §§ 232, 262, 266.
v. P., 39 N. Y. 245. §§ 361, 416.
v. S., 85 Ala. 326. §§ 342, 431.
v. S., 15 Fla. 635. §§ 263, 279.
v. S., 31 Fla. 428. §§ 546, 603.
v. S., 81 Ind. 379. § 495.
v. S., 34 Ohio St. 310. § 694.
v. S., 33 Tex. Ap. 183. § 758.
S. v., 88 Mo. 341. §§ 511, 576.
S. v., 76 N. C. 251. § 1131.
S. v., 91 N. C. 572. § 311.
S. v., 36 Vt. 563. § 1272.
Kennett, Rex v., 5 C. & P. 282. § 997.
Kenney, C. v., 115 Mass. 149. § 1242.
v. S., 5 R. I. 385. § 252.
S. v., 101 Mo. 160. § 500.
Kennison, S. v., 55 N. H. 242. § 1019.
Kennon, S. v., 21 Mo. 262. § 1318.
Kenny v. P., 31 N. Y. 330. §§ 159, 162.
Reg. v., 2 Q. B. D. 307. § 558.
Kenrick, Reg. v., 5 Q. B. 49. §§ 676, 677, 960.
Kent, C. v., 6 Met. 221. § 777.
v. P., 8 Colo. 563. §§ 4, 333.
P. v., 1 Doug. 42. §§ 596, 600.
v. S., 8 Blackf. 163. § 83.
v. S., 84 Ga. 438. § 500.
S. v., 22 Minn. 41. § 627.
S. v., 65 N. C. 311. §§ 78, 613.
S. v., 4 N. D. 577. § 217.
Kentucky Club v. Louisville, 92 Ky. 309. § 1240.
Kenyon v. P., 26 N. Y. 203. §§ 1112, 1117, 1118, 1119.
v. S., 31 Tex. Ap. 13. § 53.
Keokuk v. Dressel, 47 Ia. 597. § 1217.
v. Scroggs, 39 Ia. 447. § 62.
Ker v. Illinois, 119 U. S. 436. § 118.
v. P., 110 Ill. 627. §§ 622, 634, 653, 655-6.
Kerby, S. v., 110 N. C. 558. § 58.
Kerfoot v. C., 89 Ky. 174. § 858.
Kern, C. v., 147 Mass. 595. § 1243.
P. v., 61 Cal. 244. § 417.
v. S., 7 Ohio St. 411. §§ 1181, 1249, 1271, 1272.
S. v., 51 N. J. 259. § 905.
Kernaghan, P. v., 72 Cal. 609. § 336.
Kernan v. S., 11 Ind. 471. § 929.
Kernon, Rex v., 2 Russ. Cr. 562. § 716.
Kerr v. P., 42 Ill. 307. § 875.
Pennsylvania v., Addison, 324. § 1014.
Reg. v., 8 C. & P. 176. § 571.
S., v., 3 N. D. 523. § 1275.
Kerrains v. P., 60 N. Y. 221. § 142.
Kerrigan, P. v., 73 Cal. 222. § 157.
P. v., 147 N. Y. 210. § 365.
Kerrissey, C. v., 141 Mass. 110. § 1248.
Kerry v. S., 17 Tex. Ap. 178. § 575.
Kersh, S. v., 1 Strobh. 352. § 592.
Kerwhacker v. Cleveland, etc. R. Co., 3 Ohio St. 172. § 12.
Kessal, Rex v., 1 C. & P. 437. §§ 339, 342.
Kessel, U. S. v., 62 Fed. R. 57. § 1348.
Kessler v. C., 12 Bush, 18. § 449.
S. v., 78 N. C. 469. § 1120.
U. S. v., Ba'dw. 15. § 1359.
Ketner, C. v., 92 Pa. St. 372. § 632.
Kettering v. Jacksonville, 50 Ill. 39. §§ 1206, 1218.
Keuhn, P. v., 93 Mich. 619. § 247.
Kew, Reg. v., 12 Cox, 355. § 349.
Key v. S., 12 Tex. Ap. 506. §§ 257, 260.
v. Vattier, 1 Ohio, 132. § 13.
Keyes, S. v., 8 Vt. 57. § 937.
T. v., 5 Dak. 244. §§ 464, 465, 466.
Keyn, Reg. v., L. R. 2 Ex. 63. § 369.
Keyser, S. v., 56 Vt. 622. § 581.
Kibler, P. v., 106 N. Y. 321. § 128.
Kibling, S. v., 63 Vt. 636. §§ 96, 1202.
Kibs v. P., 81 Ill. 599. §§ 554, 624.
Kidd v. Pearson, 128 U. S. 1. §§ 1201, 1202.
v. S., 83 Ala. 58. § 552.

Kidd, S. v., 74 Ind. 554. §§ 103, 1265.
Kidder, C. v., 107 Mass. 188. §§ 1172, 1183.
Kief v. S., 10 Tex. Ap. 286. § 233.
S. v., 12 Mont. 92. § 553.
Kierman, U. S. v., 3 Cranch, C. C. 435. § 232.
Kiley, C. v., 150 Mass. 325. § 1226.
v. S., 120 Ind. 65. §§ 59, 1314.
Kilgore v. S., 74 Ala. 1. § 392.
S. v., 6 Humph. 44. § 1292.
S. v., 70 Mo. 546. §§ 354, 359, 426.
Kilham, Reg. v., L. R. 1 C. C. 261. § 659.
Kilkelly v. S., 43 Wis. 604. § 274.
Killett v. S., 32 Ga. 292. § 1031.
Killian, C. v., 109 Mass. 345. § 1196.
Killins v. S., 28 Fla. 313. § 411.
Killman v. S., 2 Tex. Ap. 222. §§ 1139, 1143.
Kilpatrick v. C., 31 Pa. St. 198. §§ 332, 343, 359, 426.
v. P., 5 Denio, 277. § 811.
Kilty, S. v., 28 Minn. 421. § 1196.
Kilvington, P. v., 104 Cal. 86. § 298.
Kimball, C. v., 7 Gray, 328. §§ 1142, 1143, 1145, 1178.
C. v., 105 Mass. 465. § 1174.
C. v., 108 Mass. 473. § 859.
C. v., 7 Met. 304. §§ 1271, 1281.
C. v., 7 Met. 308. § 1274.
C. v., 21 Pick. 373. §§ 91, 96.
C. v., 24 Pick. 359. § 1202.
C. v., 24 Pick. 366. § 1252.
v. Davis, 19 Wend. 437. § 431.
v. P., 20 Ill. 348. § 1233.
S. v., 50 Me. 409. §§ 123, 748, 750, 752, 767, 768, 769, 771.
Kimble v. S., 12 Tex. Ap. 420. § 470.
S. v., 34 La. An. 392. § 618.
Kimbrough v. S., 25 Tex. Ap. 397. § 1313.
v. S., 28 Tex. Ap. 367. § 597.
Kimmel v. P., 92 Ill. 457. §§ 873, 878.
Kimmerling, S. v., 124 Ind. 382. § 487.
Kimmish v. Ball, 129 U. S. 217. §§ 56, 76, 77.
Kinard v. S., 57 Miss. 132. § 1130.
Kinder, Rex v., 2 East, P. C. 855. § 765.
Kindle, S. v., 47 Ohio St. 358. § 429.
Kindra, P. v., 102 Mich. 147. § 410.
Kindred v. S., 33 Tex. 67. § 1028.
U. S. v., 4 Hughes, 493. § 920.
King, C. v., 9 Cush. 284. §§ 556, 624, 625, 719, 722.
C. v., 13 Met. 115. §§ 95, 1184, 1186.
C. v., 1 Whart. 448. §§ 35, 188, 922.
v. P., 7 Colo. 224. §§ 1131, 1332.
v. P., 83 N. Y. 587. § 1138.
P. v., 27 Cal. 507. §§ 162, 377, 388.
P. v., 110 N. Y. 418. § 54.
v. Reg., 7 Q. B. 795. § 982.
v. Reg., 14 Q. B. 31. § 858.
Reg. v., 7 A. & E. 782. § 975.
Reg. v., 4 F. & F. 493. § 546.
Reg. v., 7 Q. B. 782. § 982.
Rex v., 5 C. & P. 123. § 764.
Rex v., Russ. & Ry. 332. § 200.
v. S., 71 Ala. 1. § 391.
King v. S., 89 Ala. 43. § 923.
v. S., 90 Ala. 612. §§ 161, 162, 307.
v. S., 55 Ark. 604. § 312.
v. S., 17 Fla. 183. § 1145.
v. S., 21 Ga. 220. §§ 265, 274.
v. S., 40 Ga. 244. §§ 1079, 1080.
v. S., 54 Ga. 184. § 575.
v. S., 5 How. (Miss.) 730. § 389.
v. S., 44 Ind. 285. § 546.
v. S., 58 Miss. 737. § 1219.
v. S., 65 Miss. 576. § 307.
v. S., 66 Miss. 502. §§ 1219, 1222.
v. S., 91 Tenn. 617. § 179.
v. S., 4 Tex. Ap. 54. § 275.
v. S., 9 Tex. Ap. 515. § 307.
v. S., 13 Tex. Ap. 277. §§ 303, 405.
v. S., 22 Tex. Ap. 650. §§ 445, 446.
v. S., 27 Tex. Ap. 567. § 796.
v. S., 32 Tex. Ap. 463. § 873.
S. v., 37 Ia. 462. §§ 6, 62, 63, 1273, 1274.
S. v., 81 Ia. 587. § 649.
S. v., 12 La. An. 593. §§ 86, 96, 97.
S. v., 31 La. An. 179. § 594.
S. v., 37 La. An. 91. § 597.
S. v., 111 Mo. 576. § 271.
S. v., 9 Mont. 445. § 212.
S. v., 74 N. C. 177. § 820.
S. v., 86 N. C. 603. § 123.
S. v., 98 N. C. 648. § 537.
S. v., 113 N. C. 631. § 1284.
U. S. v., 34 Fed. R. 302. §§ 15, 162, 310, 412.
U. S. v., 5 McLean, 208. §§ 774, 775, 788, 789, 798, 803.
Kingen v. S., 45 Ind. 518. § 302.
Kingsbury, C. v., 5 Mass. 106. §§ 956, 979.
Kingsley, P. v., 2 Cow. 522. § 794.
S. v., 39 Ia. 439. § 1119.
S. v., 108 Mo. 135. §§ 663*a*, 678.
Kingston, S. v., 5 R. I. 297. § 1279.
Kinkead v. S., 45 Ark. 536. § 1035.
Kinnear, Reg. v., 2 M. & Rob. 117. § 752.
Kinnersley v. Orpe, 2 Doug. 517. § 564.
Kinney v. C., 30 Grat. 858. § 1131.
v. P., 108 Ill. 519. §§ 306, 308, 339.
v. S., 38 Ala. 224. § 1024.
S. v., 44 Conn. 153. § 455.
S. v., 34 Minn. 311. § 244.
Kinser v. S., 9 Ind. 543. § 1252.
Kinsley, C. v., 133 Mass. 578. §§ 75, 1310.
Kinsman v. S., 77 Ind. 132. §§ 815, 834.
Kiphart v. S., 42 Ind. 273. § 993.
Kipps, Reg. v., 4 Cox, 167. § 1103.
Kirbie v. S., 5 Tex. Ap. 60. § 487.
Kirby, C. v., 2 Cush. 577. § 927.
v. S., 1 Ohio St. 185. § 801.
v. S., 23 Tex. Ap. 13. § 195.
v. S., 7 Yerg. 258. § 362.
v. S., 9 Yerg. 383. § 424.
S. v., 57 Me. 30. § 1152.
S. v., 115 Mo. 440. § 49.
S. v., 1 Murph. 254. §§ 1159, 1160.
S. v., 108 N. C. 772. § 1026.
U. S. v., 7 Wall. 482. § 1328.
Kirk v. C., 9 Leigh, 627. § 805.

Kirk, C. v., 4 B. Mon. 1. § 1298.
S. v., 10 Oreg. 505. § 213.
Kirkham, Reg. v., 8 C. & P. 115. §§ 333, 342.
S. v., 1 Ired. 384. § 1246.
Kirkland, S. v., 14 Rich. 230. § 391.
Kirkpatrick, S. v., 63 Ia. 554. § 1135.
S. v., 72 Ia. 500. §§ 617, 618.
Kirksey v. Fike, 29 Ala. 206. § 547.
Kirkwood, Rex v., 1 Moody, 304. § 195.
Kirland v. S., 43 Ind. 146. § 235.
Kirtley v. S., 38 Ark. 543. § 664.
Kiser v. S., 89 Ga. 421. § 87.
Kistler v. S., 54 Ind. 400. § 736.
v. S., 64 Ind. 371. § 741.
Kit v. S., 11 Humph. 167. §§ 474, 475.
Kitchen, Rex v., Russ. & Ry. 95. § 256.
v. S., 26 Tex. Ap. 165. §§ 868, 890.
v. S., 29 Tex. Ap. 45. § 892.
Kitchens v. S., 80 Ga. 810. § 434.
Kite v. C., 11 Met. 581. § 511.
S. v., 81 Mo. 97. §§ 112, 913, 916, 917, 1228.
Kittelle, S. v., 110 N. C. 560. §§ 189, 1237.
Klare v. S., 43 Ind. 483. § 1218.
Kleiforth v. S., 88 Wis. 163. § 504.
Klein v. P., 113 Ill. 596. § 469.
v. S., 76 Ind. 333. § 1246.
v. S., 9 Ind. Ap. 365. § 232.
Klepfler v. S., 121 Ind. 491. § 1279.
Kline, S. v., 54 Ia. 183. § 416.
Klinger, S. v., 43 Mo. 127. § 178.
Klintock, U. S. v., 5 Wheat. 144. § 1359.
Klitzke, S. v., 46 Minn. 343. § 1126.
Klopfer v. Bromme, 26 Wis. 372. § 11.
Kloss, S. v., 117 Mo. 591. § 342.
Klug v. S., 77 Ga. 734. § 1264.
Klum v. S., 1 Blackf. 377. § 1007.
Kluseman, S. v., 53 Minn. 541. § 151.
Knapp, C. v., 10 Pick. 477. §§ 212, 216.
P. v., 71 Cal. 1. § 333.
P. v., 1 Edm. Sel. Cas. 177. § 431.
P. v., 26 Mich. 112. §§ 197, 425, 426, 427, 431.
S. v., 6 Conn. 415. § 19.
S. v., 45 N. H. 148. §§ 455, 460, 461.
Knarr, C. v., 135 Pa. St. 35. § 838.
Kneeland, C. v., 20 Pick. 206. §§ 826, 1159.
Kneffler v. C., 94 Ky. 359. § 1137.
Knewland, Rex v., 2 East, P. C. 732. § 470.
Knickerbocker v. P., 43 N. Y. 177. §§ 514, 616, 617.
Knight's Case, 3 Mod. 117. § 1029.
Knight, C. v., 12 Mass. 273. § 876.
Reg. v., 12 Cox, 102. § 571.
Reg. v., L. & C. 378. § 619.
Rex v., 1 C. & P. 116, n. § 145.
Rex v., 2 East, P. C. 510. § 507.
Rex v., 1 Salk. 375. § 756.
v. S., 64 Miss. 802. §§ 825, 826.
S. v., 3 S. Dak. 509. § 9.
S. v., 43 Me. 11. §§ 123, 333.
S. v., 84 N. C. 789. § 855.
S. v., Taylor, 65. § 790.
S. v., 29 W. Va. 340. § 1321.
Knight Co., U. S. v., see E. C. Knight Co.
Knights, Reg. v., 2 F. & F. 46. § 286.
Knippa, S. v., 29 Tex. 295. § 801.
Knock, Reg. v., 14 Cox, 1. § 300.
Knott, S. v., 5 R. I. 293. § 1279.
Knouse, S. v., 29 Ia. 118. §§ 361, 390.
Knowles v. S., 80 Ala. 9. § 1222.
S. v., 57 Ia. 669. § 1253.
U. S. v., 4 Sawy. 517. § 286.
Knowlton, C. v., 2 Mass. 530. § 1195.
S. v., 11 Wash. 512. §§ 686, 687, 706, 708.
Knox, C. v., 6 Mass. 76. §§ 115, 1322.
v. S., 9 Baxt. 202. § 906.
v. S., 89 Ga. 259. § 605.
S. v., Phill. 312. §§ 830, 867.
Knoxville, S. v., 12 Lea, 146. § 1171.
Knutson v. S., 14 Tex. Ap. 570. § 564.
S. v., 91 Ia. 549. §§ 1112, 1113.
Kober v. S., 10 Ohio St. 444. § 1235.
Koblenschlag v. S., 23 Tex. Ap. 264. § 1257.
Koch v. S., 32 Ohio St. 353. § 1276.
S. v., 4 Harr. 570. § 546.
Koehler v. Hill, 60 Ia. 543. § 1206.
Koenig v. S., 33 Tex. Ap. 367. §§ 1240, 1303.
Koen v. S., 35 Neb. 676. § 1056.
Koerner v. S., 98 Ind. 7. § 417.
Koetting v. S., 88 Wis. 502. § 42.
Kohl v. Lehlbach, 160 U. S. 293. § 361.
Kohlbrunner v. S., 67 Miss. 368. § 1216.
Kohn v. Melcher, 29 Fed. R. 433. § 1201.
Reg. v., 4 F. & F. 68. § 818.
Kohnstamm, U. S. v., 5 Blatch. 222. § 101.
Kollenberger v. P., 9 Colo. 233. §§ 94, 541, 589.
Koontz, S. v., 31 W. Va. 127. § 806.
Koop v. P., 47 Ill. 327. §§ 1248, 1264.
Kopke v. P., 43 Mich. 41. §§ 1074, 1079, 1080, 1081.
Koppersmith v. S., 51 Ala. 6. § 72.
Koser, Ex parte, 60 Cal. 177. § 1319.
Koshland, S. v., 25 Oreg. 178. § 49.
Koster v. P., 8 Mich. 431. §§ 499, 513.
Kotovsky, S. v., 74 Mo. 247. §§ 156, 343, 358, 365.
Kotter v. P., 150 Ill. 441. § 766.
Kouns v. S., 3 Tex. Ap. 13. § 257.
Kramer v. S., 18 Tex. Ap. 13. § 1311.
Krank, P. v., 110 N. Y. 488. §§ 92, 1272.
Krant v. S., 47 Ind. 519. §§ 1226, 1227.
Krause v. C., 93 Pa. St. 418. § 554.
Krchnavy v. S., 43 Neb. 337. § 265.
Kreamer v. S., 106 Ind. 192. § 1257.
Krebs v. S., 3 Tex. Ap. 348. §§ 362, 425.
v. S., 8 Tex. Ap. 1. § 429.
Krech, S. v., 10 Wash. 166. § 1319.
Kreidler v. S., 24 Ohio St. 22. § 904.
Kreig, S. v., 13 Ia. 462. § 1272.
Kreps, S. v., 8 Ala. 951. § 592.
Kribs v. P., 82 Ill. 425. §§ 639, 656.
Krider, S. v., 78 N. C. 481. § 538.
Kridler, P. v., 80 Mich. 592. § 1279.
Kriechbaum, S. v., 81 Ia. 633. §§ 1239, 1281.

40

Krieger, S. v., 68 Mo. 98. § 582.
Kriel v. C., 5 Bush, 362. §§ 162, 179, 332.
Kring v. Missouri, 107 U. S. 221. §§ 78, 390.
S. v., 11 Mo. Ap. 92. § 390.
Kroer v. P., 78 Ill. 294. §§ 1248, 1264.
Kropp, P. v., 52 Mich. 582. § 1244.
Kroscher, S. v., 24 Wis. 64. § 529.
Krug, S. v., 12 Wash. 288. §§ 646, 649.
Kruget v. S., 1 Neb. 365. §§ 271, 279.
Krum v. S., 19 Neb. 728. § 463.
Krusick, P. v., 93 Cal. 74. §§ 1113, 1118.
Kuback, Ex parte, 85 Cal. 274. §§ 55, 77.
Kube, S. v., 20 Wis. 217. §§ 659, 708, 711.
Kuhn, S. v., 24 La. An. 474. §§ 1273, 1274.
Kuhuke, S. v., 26 Kan. 405. § 1281.
Kunkle v. S., 32 Ind. 220. §§ 142, 226, 266.
Kurtz, U. S. v., 4 Cranch, C. C. 674. § 597.
Kurz v. S., 79 Ind. 488. § 1235.
Kusnick, S. v., 45 Ohio St. 535. §§ 191, 631.
Kye, S. v., 46 La. An. 424. § 255.
Kyle v. S., 10 Ala. 236. § 934.
Kyne, C. v., 162 Mass. 146. § 1243.
S. v., 86 Ia. 616. § 454.

Labauve, S. v., 46 La. An. 548. § 593.
Labbaite v. S., 6 Tex. Ap. 257. § 797.
v. S., 6 Tex. Ap. 483. § 793.
La Bore, S. v., 26 Vt. 765. § 1079.
Labouchere, Reg. v., 12 Q. B. D. 320. § 1046.
La Bounty, S. v., 63 Vt. 374. § 815.
Labuzan, S. v., 37 La. An. 489. § 303.
Lacefield v. S., 34 Ark. 275. §§ 268, 276.
Lacey, Ex parte, 108 Cal. 326. § 66.
v. Palmer, — Va. —, 24 S. E. R. 930. § 1297.
v. S., 22 Tex. Ap. 657. § 584.
S. v., 111 Mo. 513. § 443.
Lacher, U. S. v., 134 U. S. 624. §§ 83, 93, 106, 1330.
Lackey v. S., 14 Tex. Ap. 164. § 828.
S. v., 2 Ind. 285. § 97.
Lacy v. S., 45 Ala. 80. § 455.
v. S., 7 Tex. Ap. 403. § 298.
v. S., 15 Wis. 13. §§ 524, 531.
Lad, Rex v., 1 Leach, 96. § 380.
Ladd, C. v., 15 Mass. 526. § 760.
v. S., 92 Ala. 58. § 1031.
v. S., 17 Fla. 215. §§ 706, 707.
S. v., 15 Mo. 430. §§ 1273, 1274.
S. v., 32 N. H. 110. § 851.
S. v., 2 Swan, 225. § 256.
Ladue, S. v., 3 Denio, 437. § 1220.
Laescki, U. S. v., 29 Fed. R. 699. § 774.
Lafayette, C. v., 148 Mass. 130. §§ 194, 1238.
Laffer, S. v., 38 Ia. 422. § 1219.
Lafontaine, C. v., 3 Gray, 479. § 1229.
Lahy, S. v., 65 Mo. 217. § 381.
Lair v. Killmer, 25 N. J. 522. § 83.
Laird v. S., 61 Md. 309. § 758.
Lake, P v., 110 N. Y. 61. § 1120.
Lakeman, C. v., 4 Cush. 597. § 245.
C. v., 5 Gray, 82. §§ 719, 727.
Laky, C. v., 8 Gray, 459. § 1281.
Lallement, Reg. v., 6 Cox, 204. § 276.
Lamar v. S., 63 Miss. 265. § 969.
v. S., 30 Tex. Ap. 693. § 1140.
Lamb, C. v., 1 Gray, 493. § 527.
v. P., 96 Ill. 73. §§ 197, 970.
P. v., 17 Cal. 323. § 309.
P. v., 2 Keyes, 360. §§ 303, 304.
v. S., 40 Neb. 312. § 571.
S. v., 65 N. C. 419. §§ 753, 803.
Lambert, C. v., 12 Allen, 177. § 1138.
C. v., 9 Leigh, 603. § 324.
v. P., 7 Cow. 166; 9 Cow. 578. §§ 954, 975, 978.
v. P., 76 N. Y. 220. §§ 856, 880.
Rex v., 2 Camp. 398. §§ 1048, 1053.
v. S., 8 Mo. 492. § 1226.
S. v., 9 Nev. 321. § 551.
S. v., 93 N. C. 618. § 404.
Lamberton v. S., 11 Ohio, 282. §§ 925, 926.
Lambertson v. P., 5 Park. Cr. R. 200. § 1154.
Lambeth v. S., 23 Miss. 322. § 431.
S. v., 80 N. C. 393. § 699.
Lambright v. S., 34 Fla. 564. § 414.
Lamden v. S., 5 Humph. 83. §§ 859, 878.
Lamere, C. v., 11 Gray, 319. § 1244.
Lamkin v. S., 42 Tex. 415. § 577.
Lamon, S. v., 3 Hawks, 175. § 376.
Lamont, S. v., 2 Wis. 437. § 861.
Lamos, S. v., 26 Me. 258. § 1226.
Lamphere, In re, 61 Mich. 105. § 13.
Lamphier v. S., 70 Ind. 317. § 558.
Lampkin v. S., 87 Ga. 516. § 478.
Lampton, C. v., 4 Bibb, 261. § 1313.
Lanagan, P. v., 81 Cal. 142. §§ 427, 428.
Lanahan v. C., 84 Pa. St. 80. § 359.
v. Pattison, 1 Flip. 410. §§ 1305, 1316.
Lancaster v. S., 53 Ala. 398. §§ 1024, 1026.
v. S., 2 Lea, 575. § 161.
v. S., 9 Tex. Ap. 393. § 597.
S. v., 63 N. H. 267. §§ 38, 44, 77.
U. S. v., 44 Fed. R. 885. §§ 9, 961, 978.
U. S. v., 44 Fed. R. 896. §§ 961, 966, 968, 988, 990.
Lance v. Cowan, 1 Dana, 195. § 611.
Landa v. S., 26 Tex. Ap. 580. § 733.
Landaff, S. v., 22 N. H. 588. § 1185.
Lander v. S., 12 Tex. 462. § 303.
Landgraf, S. v., 95 Mo. 97. § 292.
Landin v. S., 10 Tex. Ap. 63. § 564.
Landman, P. v., 103 Cal. 577. §§ 265, 274.
Landreth, S. v., 2 Car. Law Repos. 446. § 815.
Landringham v. S., 49 Ind. 186. §§ 480, 966, 974, 984.
Landsberg, U. S. v., 23 Fed. R. 585. §§ 852, 862.

Lane, Ex parte, 76 Cal. 587. § 223.
In re, 135 U. S. 443. § 452.
v. C., 59 Pa. St. 371. § 362.
C. v., 113 Mass. 458. §§ 1074, 1075.
v. P., 10 Ill. 305. § 571.
P. v., 100 Cal. 379. § 411.
P. v., 101 Cal. 513. §§ 169, 172, 203, 416.
P. v., 49 Mich. 340. § 397.
v. S., 85 Ala. 11. § 279.
v. S., 37 Ark. 272. § 1239.
v. S., 47 N. J. 362. § 914.
v. S., 39 Ohio St. 312. § 950.
v. S., 16 Tex. Ap. 172. §§ 123, 1163.
S. v., 68 Ia. 384. §§ 713, 717.
S. v., 4 Ired. 113. § 342.
S. v., 64 Mo. 319. §§ 353, 365.
S. v., 80 N. C. 407. §§ 753, 799, 809.
Laney, S. v., 87 N. C. 535. § 820.
Lang v. S., 84 Ala. 1. §§ 307, 358.
v. S., 97 Ala. 41. § 642.
S. v., 63 Me. 215. §§ 1181, 1229, 1249, 1272, 1275.
S. v., 65 N. H. 284. § 278.
Langan v. S., 27 Tex. Ap. 498. § 463.
Langcake, Resp. v., 1 Yeates, 415. §§ 330, 425, 435.
Langdale v. P., 100 Ill. 263. § 797.
Langdon, S. v., 29 Minn. 393. § 1216.
S. v., 31 Minn. 316. § 1216.
Lange v. S., 95 Ind. 114. § 257.
Langford, In re, 57 Fed. R. 570. §§ 29, 76, 1205, 1214.
Reg. v., Car. & M. 602. § 993.
v. S., 45 Ala. 26. §§ 694, 700.
v. S., 33 Fla. 233. § 808.
v. S., 8 Tex. 115. § 546.
v. S., 9 Tex. Ap. 283. § 859.
S. v., 1 Dev. 253. § 498.
S. v., 3 Ired. 354. § 1301.
S. v., 45 La. An. 1177. §§ 455, 466.
Langham v. S., 26 Tex. Ap. 533. § 601.
Langhorne v. Robinson, 20 Grat. 661. § 70.
Langley, Reg. v., 2 Ld. Raym. 1029. § 1057.
S. v., 34 N. H. 529. § 865.
Langmead, Reg. v., L. & C. 427. §§ 617, 725.
Langston v. S., 96 Ala. 44. § 536.
S. v., 45 La. An. 1182. § 256.
Langton, P. v., 67 Cal. 427. §§ 162, 331.
Reg. v., 2 Q. B. D. 296. § 604.
Langtry v. S., 30 Ala. 536. § 1083.
Lanier, S. v., 89 N. C. 517. § 656.
Laning, P. v., 73 Mich. 284. § 1223.
Lannan, C. v., 153 Mass. 287. §§ 556, 560.
Lannon, T. v., 9 Mont. 1. § 45.
La Norris v. S., 13 Tex. Ap. 33. § 1244.
Lantry, U. S. v., 30 Fed. R. 232. § 504.
Lantznester v. S., 19 Tex. Ap. 320. § 1261.
Lapage, S. v., 57 N. H. 245. § 411.
Lapham, C. v., 156 Mass. 480. §§ 897, 901, 902.
Lapier, Rex v., 2 East, P. C. 557. §§ 469, 471.
Lapoint, U. S. v., 1 Morris, 146. § 487.
Laque, S. v., 37 La. An. 853. § 722.
S. v., 41 La. An. 1070. § 404.
Lara, Rex v., 2 East, P. C. 810; 6 T. R. 565. §§ 660, 666, 704.
Largent, S. v., 9 Wash. 691. § 271.
Larison v. S., 49 N. J. 256. §§ 1156, 1158.
Larkin, Reg. v., Dears. 365. § 716.
S. v., 11 Nev. 314. § 416.
S. v., 49 N. H. 39. §§ 204, 713, 716, 722.
Larned v. C., 12 Met. 240. §§ 499, 506, 509, 513, 596.
Larner, Reg. v., 14 Cox, 497. § 683.
Laroe v. S., 30 Tex. Ap. 374. § 1190.
Larrimore, S. v., 19 Mo. 391. § 1252.
Larson, S. v., 85 Ia. 659. §§ 551, 565, 569.
Lartigue, S. v., 29 La. An. 642. § 587.
Larumbo, S. v., Harper, 183. § 586.
La Rosae v. S., 132 Ind. 219. § 1119.
La Rose v. S., 29 Tex. Ap. 215. § 1073.
Lash, S. v., 16 N. J. 380. § 1086.
Lashley, S. v., 84 N. C. 754. § 1094.
Lashus, S. v., 67 Me. 564. § 1181.
S. v., 79 Me. 541. § 1242.
Lasindo v. S., 2 Tex. Ap. 59. § 1143.
Lasington's Case, Cro. Eliz. 750. § 573.
Lasure v. S., 19 Ohio St. 43. § 13.
Latham v. Reg., 5 B. & S. 635. § 975.
S. v., 13 Ired. 33. §§ 539, 815.
Lathrop v. S., 6 Blackf. 502. § 915.
S. v., 15 Vt. 279. § 707.
Lathrope v. S., 51 Ind. 192. § 1237.
Latimer, Reg. v., 17 Q. B. D. 359. §§ 126, 259, 826.
Lattinville, C. v., 120 Mass. 385. § 1258.
Lau Ow Bew v. U. S., 144 U. S. 47. § 1345.
Lauer v. S., 24 Ind. 131. §§ 189, 1237.
Laugher, Reg. v., 2 C. & K. 225. § 145.
Laughlin v. C., 13 Bush, 261. § 97.
v. S., 18 Ohio, 99. § 456.
S. v., 8 Jones, 455. § 519.
Lauglin, S. v., 8 Jones, 354. § 521.
Lauten v. Rowan, 59 N. H. 215. § 1214.
Lautenschlager, S. v., 22 Minn. 514. §§ 123, 333.
Lavake, S. v., 26 Minn. 526. § 1246.
Lavalley, S. v., 9 Mo. 824. § 858.
Lavarre v. S., 1 Tex. Ap. 685. § 597.
Lavender v. S., 60 Ala. 60. § 546.
Lavery, C. v., 101 Mass. 207. § 578.
Lavey v. Reg., 17 Q. B. 496. § 885.
Reg. v., 3 C. & K. 26. §§ 864, 866.
Rex v., 1 East, P. C. 166. § 774.
Lavina v. S., 63 Ga. 513. § 486.
Lavonsair, C. v., 132 Mass. 1. § 1138.
Law v. C., 75 Va. 885. §§ 150, 152.
Reg. v., 2 F. & F. 836. § 167.
U. S. v., 50 Fed. R. 915. §§ 857, 877, 882.
Lawes, Reg. v., 1 C. & K. 62. § 509.
Lawless, C. v., 101 Mass. 32. § 796.
C. v., 103 Mass. 425. §§ 546, 570, 585.
Lawlor, S. v., 28 Minn. 216. § 416.
Lawn, S. v., 18 Mo. 241. §§ 594, 617.

Lawrence, Ex parte, 69 Cal. 608. § 1217.
v. C., 30 Grat. 845. §§ 443, 451.
v. Gracy, 11 Johns. 179. § 1223.
P. v., 21 Cal. 368. § 431.
P. v., 137 N. Y. 517. § 562.
Reg. v., 36 L. T. 404. § 667.
Rex v., 4 C. & P. 231. §§ 500, 502.
v. S., 84 Ala. 424. § 275.
v. S., 1 Humph. 228. § 545.
v. S., 2 Tex. Ap. 479. § 889.
v. S., 7 Tex. Ap. 192. § 1265.
v. S., 20 Tex. Ap. 536. § 571.
v. S., 4 Yerg. 145. § 601.
S. v., 43 Kan. 125. § 933.
S. v., 57 Me. 574. §§ 158, 164, 178.
S. v., 45 Mo. 492. § 914.
S. v., 19 Neb. 307. § 1122.
S. v., 81 N. C. 522. § 609.
S. v., 97 N. C. 492. § 1261.
S. v., 20 Oreg. 236. § 575.
U. S. v., 13 Blatch. 211. §§ 752, 773.
U. S. v., 4 Cranch, C. C. 514. § 174.
Lawry, S. v., 4 Nev. 161. § 267.
Laws v. Eltringham, 8 Q. B. D. 283. § 823.
v. S., 26 Tex. Ap. 643. §§ 299, 504.
U. S. v., 163 U. S. 258. § 1343.
Lawson v. C., 14 B. Mon. 225. § 1254.
v. S., 20 Ala. 65. §§ 1097, 1098, 1132.
v. S., 55 Ala. 118. § 1245.
v. S., 100 Ala. 7. § 825.
v. S., 3 Lea, 309. § 878.
v. S., 13 Tex. Ap. 83. § 255.
v. S., 17 Tex. Ap. 292. § 455.
v. S., 62 Miss. 556. § 257.
S. v., 98 N. C. 759. § 869.
S. v., 101 N. C. 717. § 824.
Lawton v. Steele, 152 U. S. 133. §§ 45, 46.
Lay v. S., 12 Ind. Ap. 362. § 1168.
S. v., 93 Ind. 341. § 377.
Laycock v. S., 136 Ind. 217. §§ 631, 653.
Laydon v. S., 52 Ind. 459. § 395.
Layman, S. v., 8 Blackf. 330. § 694.
S. v., 5 Harr. 510. § 1306.
Layne v. S., 4 Lea, 199. § 1024.
Layton, Reg. v., 4 Cox, 149. §§ 158, 172, 175, 178.
S. v., 25 Ia. 193. § 1272.
Lazarus, S. v., 37 La. An. 401. § 852.
S. v., 1 Treadw. 34. § 245.
Lazier v. C., 10 Grat. 708. § 377.
Lea v. S., 64 Miss. 201. § 1274.
v. S., 64 Miss. 278. §§ 878, 892.
S. v., 3 Ala. 602. § 881.
Leabo, S. v., 84 Mo. 168. § 417.
Leach, C. v., 156 Mass. 99. § 1151.
Pennsylvania v., Addison, 352. § 839.
S. v., 7 Conn. 452. §§ 922, 931.
S. v., 60 Me. 58. §§ 5, 906, 913, 919.
S. v., 50 Mo. 535. § 1142.
S. v., 27 Vt. 317. § 893.
Leache v. S., 22 Tex. Ap. 279. §§ 169, 175.
Leak, S. v., 80 N. C. 403. § 753.
S. v., Phill. 450. § 332.
Leal v. S., 12 Tex. Ap. 279. §§ 625, 713.
Learnard, S. v., 41 Vt. 585. §§ 150, 187.
Learned, S. v., 47 Me. 426. §§ 124, 1243.
Leary, P. v., 105 Cal. 486. §§ 156, 363.
v. S., 39 Ind. 360. §§ 1272, 1273.
v. S., 39 Ind. 544. § 1143.
S. v., 88 N. C. 615. § 278.
Leathers, U. S. v., 6 Sawy. 17. § 128.
Leatherwood v. S., 6 Tex. Ap. 244. § 1030.
Leaver, S. v., 62 Wis. 387. § 1186.
Leavitt, S. v., 66 Me. 440. §§ 546, 610.
Le Blanc, S. v., 1 Treadw. 354. § 450.
Le Blanch, S. v., 31 N. J. 82. § 553.
Le Bris, U. S. v., 121 U. S. 278. §§ 93, 102.
Lecroy v. S., 89 Ga. 335. § 1021.
Ledbetter v. S., 61 Miss. 22. § 420.
v. S., 26 Tex. Ap. 22. §§ 142, 338.
v. S., 33 Tex. Ap. 400. § 446.
Ledbitter, Rex v., 1 Moody, 76. § 939.
Leddington, Reg. v., 9 C. & P. 79. §§ 207, 290.
Ledford, S. v., 67 N. C. 60. § 564.
Ledger, Reg. v., 2 F. & F. 857. § 349.
Ledgerwood v. S., 134 Ind. 81. §§ 13, 15.
Ledley v. S., 4 Ind. 580. § 447.
Lee, In re, 46 Fed. R. 59. § 1037.
C. v., 149 Mass. 179. §§ 679, 686, 687.
P. v., 17 Cal. 76. § 426.
Reg. v., 8 Cox, 233. § 669.
Reg. v., 4 F. & F. 63. § 195.
Reg. v., L. & C. 309. § 678.
Reg. v., L. & C. 418. §§ 670, 678.
Rex v., 6 C. & P. 536. § 209.
Rex v., 3 Russ. Cr. 78. § 892.
v. Risdon, 7 Taunt. 188. §§ 536, 537.
v. S., 92 Ala. 15. §§ 144, 312.
v. S., 1 Coldw. 62. §§ 325, 368.
v. S., 56 Ga. 477. § 506.
v. S., 64 Ga. 203. § 553.
v. S., 27 Tex. Ap. 475. § 617.
v. S., 74 Wis. 45. § 455.
S. v., 1 Houst. Cr. C. 335. § 509.
S. v., 80 Ia. 75. § 1138.
S. v., 91 Ia. 499. §§ 216, 479.
S. v., 32 Kan. 360. §§ 745, 753.
S. v., 113 N. C. 681. § 44.
Lee Hoy, U. S. v., 48 Fed. R. 825. § 1345.
Lee Kan v. U. S., 62 Fed. R. 914. § 1345.
Lee Kong, P. v., 95 Cal. 666. §§ 226, 266, 454.
Lee Mut. Fire Ins. Co. v. S., 60 Miss. 395. § 41.
Lee Ping Bow, S. v., 10 Oreg. 27. § 575.
Lee Save Bo, P. v., 72 Cal. 623. § 426.
Lee Wah, P. v., 71 Cal. 80. § 36.
Lee Yan Yan, S. v., 10 Oreg. 365. § 607.
Lee Yung, U. S. v., 63 Fed. R. 520. § 1345.
Leech, Reg. v., Dears. 642. § 696.
Rex v., 3 Stark. 70. § 626.
Leedy, S. v., 95 Mo. 76. § 494.
Leefe, Rex v., 2 Camp. 134. § 883.
Leehman, S. v., 2 S. Dak. 171. §§ 156, 168, 173.
Leeman v. S., 35 Ark. 438. § 914.

Leep v. St. Louis, etc. R. Co., 58 Ark. 407. § 55.
Leeper, S. v., 70 Ia. 748. § 365.
Lefevre v. S., 1 Cranch, C. C. 244. § 1310.
Lefforge v. S., 129 Ind. 551. § 1124.
Leftwich v. C., 20 Grat. 716. §§ 563, 597.
C. v., 5 Rand. 657. § 96.
Leggett, Reg. v., 8 C. & P. 191. §§ 348, 351.
Legori v. S., 8 Sm. & M. 697. § 1272.
Lehigh Co. v. Schock, 113 Pa. St. 373. §§ 4, 17.
Lehigh Valley R. Co., C. v., 165 Pa. St. 162. § 180.
Lehman v. S., 18 Tex. Ap. 174. § 616.
U. S. v., 39 Fed. R. 49. §§ 859, 875.
U. S. v., 39 Fed. R. 768. §§ 859, 1346.
Lehmann, P. v., 104 Cal. 631. § 1117.
Lehre, S. v., 2 Brev. 446; 2 Tread. Const. 809. §§ 1051, 1070.
Lehritter v. S., 42 Ind. 383. § 1264.
Leiber v. C., 9 Bush, 11. § 427.
Leicham, S. v., 41 Wis. 565. § 644.
Leicht, S. v., 17 Ia. 28. §§ 1283, 1286, 1306.
Leigh v. P., 113 Ill. 372. § 431.
Reg. v., 4 F. & F. 915. § 167.
Rex v., 1 Leach, 52. § 543.
Rex v., 2 East, P. C. 694. § 569.
Leighton, S. v., 56 Ia. 595. § 480.
S. v., 35 Me. 195. § 1025.
S. v., 23 N. H. 167. §§ 1283, 1286.
U. S. v., 3 Dak. 29. § 303.
Leis, S. v., 11 Ia. 416. §§ 1268, 1275.
Leister's Appeal, — Pa. —, 11 Atl. R. 387. § 1228.
Leisy v. Hardin, 135 U. S. 100. §§ 76, 1204.
Leith, P. v., 52 Cal. 251. § 196.
Leloup v. Mobile, 127 U. S. 640. § 44.
Lem Moon Sing v. U. S., 158 U. S. 538. § 1344.
Lem You, P. v., 97 Cal. 224. §§ 866, 888, 889.
Lemasters v. S., 10 Ind. 391. § 828.
v. S., 95 Ind. 367. § 757.
Lemay, S. v., 13 Ark. 405. § 1193.
Lemly v. S., 70 Miss. 241. § 1220.
Lemmon, Pennsylvania v., Addis. 315. § 839.
Lemmons v. S., 56 Ark. 559. § 1035.
Lemon v. Peyton, 64 Miss. 161. § 1210.
S. v., 46 Mo. 375. §§ 1283, 1285, 1297.
Lemons v. S., 50 Ala. 130. §§ 1244, 1275.
Lenhart v. S., 33 Tex. Ap. 504. §§ 150, 495.
Lenihan, S. v., 88 Ia. 670. §§ 1118, 1119.
Lennard, Rex v., 1 East, P. C. 170. § 777.
Lennox, P. v., 67 Cal. 113. § 364.
Lenon, P. v., 79 Cal. 625. § 447.
Lentz, S. v., 45 Minn. 177. §§ 401, 416.
Leo, C. v., 110 Mass. 414. § 1222.
Leo Hem Bow, In re, 47 Fed. R. 302. § 1344.
Leobold v. S., 33 Ind. 484. § 707.
Leonard, C. v., 140 Mass. 473. §§ 625, 713.
C. v., 8 Met. 529. § 1271.
P. v., 103 Cal. 200. § 43.
P. v., 106 Cal. 302. §§ 632, 640, 653.
P. v., 11 Johns. 504. § 839.
Reg. v., 2 C. & K. 514. § 670.
v. S., 66 Ala. 461. § 309.
v. S., 96 Ala. 108. § 525.
v. S., 29 Ohio St. 408. § 782.
v. S., 7 Tex. Ap. 417. § 632.
v. S., 20 Tex. Ap. 442. § 468.
S. v., 6 Coldw. 307. § 649.
S. v., 6 La. An 420. § 338.
S. v., 22 Mo. 449. § 256.
v. T., 2 Wash. T. 381. §§ 383, 404.
Leonardi, P. v., 143 N. Y. 360. § 162.
Leonardo v. T., 1 N. M. 291. § 714.
Leong Quong, P. v., 60 Cal. 107. § 605.
Leoni v. S., 44 Ala. 110. §§ 438, 458.
Leopold v. P., 140 Ill. 552. § 9.
Leppard, Reg. v., 4 F. & F. 51. § 556.
Leppert v. S., 7 Ind. 300. § 1253.
Lescallet v. C., 89 Va. 878. § 1297.
Leschi v. T., 1 Wash. T. 13. §§ 361, 362.
Lesley, Reg. v., Bell, 220. § 487.
Leslie v. S., 35 Fla. 171. §§ 495, 514.
S. v., 16 N. H. 93. § 843.
Lesser v. P., 73 N. Y. 78. §§ 661, 674.
Lessing, S. v., 16 Minn. 75. § 361.
Lesslie v. S., 18 Ohio St. 390. § 390.
Lester, Ex parte, 77 Va. 663. § 1228.
C. v., 129 Mass. 101. §§ 576, 577, 578.
C. v., 2 Va. Cas. 198. §§ 433, 436.
P. v., 80 Mich. 643. § 1227.
v. Price, 83 Va. 648. § 1228.
v. S., 9 Mo. 658. §§ 293, 378, 381.
Levelle, S. v., 34 S. C. 120. §§ 290, 332, 338.
Levells v. S., 32 Ark. 585. § 311.
Leverette v. S., 32 Tex. Ap. 471. § 880.
Levi v. Levi, 6 C. & P. 239. § 960.
v. S., 14 Neb. 1. §§ 471, 719, 723.
S. v., 41 Tex. 563. § 702.
Levigne, S. v., 17 Nev. 435. §§ 332, 339.
Levine, Reg. v., 10 Cox, 374. § 669.
Levison, P. v., 16 Cal. 98. § 716.
v. S., 54 Ala. 520. § 362.
Levy, Ex parte, 43 Ark. 42. § 1228.
C. v., 126 Mass. 240. § 1243.
v. P., 80 N. Y. 327. §§ 216, 518, 521.
v. S., 79 Ala. 259. §§ 560, 596.
v. S., 28 Tex. Ap. 203. §§ 307, 341, 405.
S. v., 23 Minn. 104. § 571.
Lewallen v. S., 6 Tex. Ap. 475. § 307.
v. S., 33 Tex. Ap. 412. § 463.
Lewellen v. S., 18 Tex. 538. §§ 1291, 1299.
Lewin, S. v., 53 Kan. 679. § 930.
Lewis v. C., 90 Va. 843. § 1244.
C. v., 140 Pa. St. 261. § 1161.
Pennsylvania v., Addis. 279. § 365.
v. P., 82 Ill. 104. § 1126.
P. v., 36 Cal. 531. §§ 159, 400.
Reg. v., 1 C. & K. 419. § 249.
Reg. v., 9 C. & P. 523. §§ 223, 226.

Lewis, Reg. v., 11 Cox. 484. § 960.
Reg. v., Dears. & B. 182. § 369.
Rex v., 2 C. & P. 628. §§ 500, 501.
Rex v., 6 C. & P. 161. § 227.
Rex v., 2 East, P. C. 957. § 764.
Rex v., 2 Russ. Cr. 1066. § 833.
v. S., 30 Ala. 54. § 446.
v. S., 35 Ala. 380. §§ 223, 463.
v. S., 51 Ala. 1. §§ 307, 308.
v. S., 88 Ala. 11. §§ 309, 316.
v. S., 96 Ala. 6. § 125.
v. S., 21 Ark. 209. § 1319.
v. S., 16 Conn. 32. § 504.
v. S., 33 Ga. 131. § 253.
v. S., 72 Ga. 164. § 325.
v. S., 89 Ga. 396. § 1118.
v. S., 3 Head, 127. § 95.
v. S., 3 Heisk. 333. § 596.
v. S., 9 Sm. & M. 115. § 426.
v. S., 2 Tex. Ap. 26. § 1031.
v. S., 15 Tex. Ap. 647. §§ 322, 329.
v. S., 17 Tex. Ap. 140. § 618.
v. S., 18 Tex. Ap. 116. § 267.
v. S., 28 Tex. Ap. 140. § 652.
v. S., 29 Tex. Ap. 201. § 330.
v. S., 33 Tex. Ap. 618. § 1026.
S. v., 134 Ind. 250. § 46.
S. v., 48 Ia. 578. § 1115.
S. v., — Ia. —, 65 N. W. R. 295. §§ 731, 740, 741.
S. v., 19 Kan. 260. § 931.
S. v., 26 Kan. 123. § 684.
S. v., 41 La. An. 590. § 698.
S. v., 20 Mo. 333. § 178.
S. v., 74 Mo. 222. §§ 358, 365.
S. v., 118 Mo. 79. § 309.
S. v., 93 N. C. 581. § 882.
S. v., 113 N. C. 622. § 936.
S. v., 19 Oreg. 478. § 642.
S. v., 10 Rich. 20. § 520.
S. v., 12 Wis. 434. § 1313.
v. U. S., 1 Morris, 199. § 1227.
U. S. v., 36 Fed. R. 449. § 257.
Leyba, P. v., 74 Cal. 407. § 257.
Leyshon, P. v., 108 Cal. 440. § 803.
Libbey, C. v., 11 Met. 64. § 627.
Libby, U. S. v., 1 Woodb. & M. 221. § 207.
Libellis Famosis, Case de, 5 Co. 125*a*. §§ 1040, 1046, 1051.
Liberman v. S., 26 Neb. 464. § 1319.
License Cases, 5 How. (U. S.) 504. § 1204.
License Tax Cases, 5 Wall. 462. § 29.
Licette v. S., 75 Ga. 253. §§ 713. 720.
Lichliter, S. v., 95 Mo. 402. §§ 187, 679.
Lidtke v. S., 27 Tex. Ap. 500. § 663.
Lifieri, In re, 52 Fed. R. 293. § 1343.
Light, S. v., 17 Oreg. 358. §§ 1289, 1290.
Lightfoot v. C., 80 Ky. 516. § 204.
v. S., 20 Tex. Ap. 77. § 398.
Lightner v. C., 31 Pa. St. 341. § 1223.
Liles v. S., 30 Ala. 24. § 420.
v. S., 88 Ala. 139. § 1259.
v. S., 43 Ark. 95. § 1233.
S. v., 78 N. C. 496. § 536.
Lillard, S. v., 59 Ia. 479. § 552.
S. v., 78 Mo. 136. §§ 1217, 1219.
Lillensteine v. S., 46 Ala. 48. § 1245.
v. S., 46 Ala. 498. § 29.
Lilley, P. v., 43 Mich. 521. §§ 224, 226, 232.
Lillie v. McMillan, 52 Ia. 463. § 844.
Lilly v. P., 148 Ill. 467. § 158.
P. v., 38 Mich. 270. § 312.
v. S., 20 Tex. Ap. 1. § 142.
S. v., 116 N. C. 1049. § 1031.
Limas, S. v., 26 Ohio St. 400. § 539.
Linbeck v. S., 1 Wash. 336. § 506.
Lince, Reg. v., 28 L. T. 570. § 686.
Lincoln, C. v., 11 Allen, 233. § 708.
v. Smith, 27 Vt. 328. §§ 1206–7, 1243.
S. v., 50 Vt. 644. § 1277.
S. v., 17 Wis. 579. § 373*a*.
Lincolnton v. McCarter, Busbee, 429. § 1264.
Linde, S. v., 54 Ia. 139. § 829.
Lindenburg, S. v., 13 Tex. 27. § 881.
Lindenmuller v. P., 33 Barb. 548. § 1319.
Lindenthall, S. v., 5 Rich. 237. § 560.
Lindsay v. Cundy, 1 Q. B. D. 48; 2 Q. B. D. 96. § 712.
v. S., 36 Tex. Ap. 337. § 391.
S. v., 34 Ark. 372. § 63.
U. S. v., 1 Cranch, C. C. 245. § 1137.
Lindsey v. S., 48 Ala. 169. § 1290.
v. S., 18 Tex. Ap. 280. § 1052.
S. v., 78 N. C. 499. § 614.
Lines, Reg. v., 1 C. & K. 393. § 450.
Ling, U. S. v., 61 Fed. R. 1001. § 1332.
Lingle, S. v., 128 Mo. 528. § 1115.
Lingo v. S., 29 Ga. 470. §§ 307, 309.
Linkhaw, S. v., 69 N. C. 215. § 1027.
Linkous v. C., 9 Leigh, 608. § 1302.
Links v. S., 13 Lea, 701. § 615.
Linn, C. v., 158 Pa. St. 22. §§ 1159, 1160.
P. v., 23 Cal. 150. § 599.
Linney, S. v., 52 Mo. 40. § 140.
Linthicum, S. v., 68 Mo. 66. §§ 736, 740.
Lintner, In re, 57 Fed. R. 587. § 1344.
Linton, C. v., 2 Va. Cas. 205. § 369.
C. v., 2 Va. Cas. 476. § 751.
v. S., 88 Ala. 216. § 1131.
Lippman v. South Bend, 84 Ind. 276. § 1169.
Lipscomb, S. v., 52 Mo. 32. § 1281.
Liquor Locations, In re, 13 R. I. 733. § 1266.
Lissner v. S., 84 Ga. 669. § 837.
List v. C., 118 Pa. St. 322. §§ 41, 43.
S. v., 1 Houst. Cr. C. 133. § 340.
Lister, Reg. v., Dears. & B. 118. § 640.
Reg. v., Dears. & B. 209. §§ 1170, 1183.
v. S., 3 Tex. Ap. 17. § 316.
Liston, S. v., 9 Humph. 603. §§ 941, 942.
Lithgo, Rex v., Russ. & Ry. 357. § 496.
Lithgow v. C., 2 Va. Cas. 297. §§ 604, 606.
Littell v. S., 133 Ind. 577. § 377.
S. v., 45 La. An. 655. §§ 213, 217.
Little v. C., 25 Grat. 921. § 414.
Reg. v., 10 Cox, 559. § 558.
v. S., 6 Baxt. 491. § 307.
S. v., 6 Blackf. 267. § 1290.

Little, S. v., 42 Ia. 51. § 1249.
S. v., 67 Mo. 624. § 452.
S. v., 76 Mo. 52. § 36.
U. S. v., 2 Wash. C. C. 159. § 1342.
Littlefield, P. v., 5 Cal. 355. §§ 588, 594.
v. S., 42 Neb. 223. § 33.
S. v., 93 N. C. 614. § 78.
Littlejohn v. S., 59 Miss. 273. § 572.
S. v., 33 S. C. 599. § 306.
Littleton v. Fritz, 65 Ia. 488. §§ 1201, 1208.
v. S., 20 Tex. Ap. 168. § 546.
Livermore, C. v., 2 Allen, 292. § 1281.
S. v., 44 N. H. 386. § 520.
Livingston v. C., 14 Grat. 592. §§ 292, 361, 376, 415.
v. S., 16 Tex. Ap. 652. § 653.
Livingstone v. S., 3 Tex. Ap. 74. § 1034.
Lloyd, Reg. v., 19 Q. B. D. 213. § 858.
Rex v., 4 C. & P. 233. § 425.
Rex v., 7 C. & P. 318. §§ 451, 463.
Rex v., 2 East, P. C. 1122. § 740.
S. v., 2 Ind. 659. § 96.
S. v., 85 N. C. 573. § 820.
S. v., 77 Wis. 630. §§ 868, 879.
U. S. v., 4 Cranch. C. C. 468. § 279.
Loakman v. S., 32 Tex. Ap. 563. § 511.
Lochte, S. v., 45 La. An. 1405. § 64.
Lock, Reg. v., L. R. 2 C. C. 10. §§ 238, 249, 1153.
Locke's Appeal, 72 Pa. St. 491. § 1210.
Locke, C. v., 148 Mass. 125. § 1248.
v. New Orleans, 4 Wall. 172. § 78.
v. S., 32 N. H. 106. § 588.
Locker, S. v., 50 N. J. 512. § 1018.
Lockerby, S. v., 50 Minn. 363. § 1118.
Lockett, Rex v., 2 East, P. C. 940. § 757.
v. S., 47 Ala. 42. § 1036.
v. S., 63 Ala. 5. §§ 526, 529, 533.
Lockhardt, C. v., 144 Mass. 132. § 33.
Lockhart v. S., 10 Tex. 275. §§ 1303, 1307.
v. S., 29 Tex. Ap. 35. § 617.
S. v., 24 Ga. 420. § 505.
Lockwood, C. v., 109 Mass. 323. § 110.
P. v., 6 Cal. 205. § 373*a*.
v. S., 1 Tex. Ap. 749. § 279.
S. v., Kirby, 106. § 19.
S. v., 119 Mo. 463. § 349.
S. v., 58 Vt. 378. § 609.
Lockyear, S. v., 95 N. C. 633. § 1240.
Lodano v. S., 25 Ala. 64. § 1206.
Lodge v. C., 2 Grat. 579. § 872.
S. v., 9 Houst. 542. § 431.
Loeb, Ex parte, 72 Fed. R. 657. §§ 76, 1203.
v. Attica, 82 Ind. 175. § 1217.
v. S., 75 Ga. 258. § 1237.
U. S. v., 49 Fed. R. 636. § 1350.
Loeffner v. S., 10 Ohio St. 598. §§ 156, 174, 178, 361, 383.
Loehfelm, P. v., 102 N. Y. 1. § 1190.
Loehr v. P., 132 Ill. 504. §§ 750, 801.
Loesch, C. v., 153 Pa. St. 502. § 1240.
Loftis, U. S. v., 8 Saw. 194. § 1332.
Lofton v. Vogles, 17 Ind. 105. § 11.
Loftus v. C., 3 Grat. 631. § 1276.
Logan v. Austin, 1 Stew. 476. § 249.
C. v., 12 Gray, 136. § 1181.
v. S., 24 Ala. 182. § 1303.
v. S., 9 Humph. 24. § 426.
v. S., 2 Lea, 222. § 274.
v. S., 17 Tex. Ap. 50. §§ 307, 309.
v. U. S., 144 U. S. 263. §§ 54, 961, 988.
U. S. v., 45 Fed. R. 872. §§ 961, 988, 990.
Logg v. P., 92 Ill. 598. §§ 992, 994.
Loggins v. S., 8 Tex. Ap. 434. § 420.
v. S., 12 Tex. Ap. 65. § 989.
v. S., 32 Tex. Ap. 358. § 934.
Logue v. C., 38 Pa. St. 265. § 304.
C. v., 160 Mass. 551. § 647.
S. v., 73 Wis. 598. § 1190.
Lohman v. S., 81 Ind. 15. §§ 1315, 1316, 1318.
Lombard, P. v., 17 Cal. 316. §§ 303, 307.
London, Reg. v., 12 Cox, 50. § 880.
Reg. v., E., B. & E. 509. § 611.
Reg. v., 27 L. J. M. C. 231. § 611.
Reg. v., L R. 4 Q. B. 371. § 611.
S. v., 3 S. C. 230. § 602.
Loney, In re, 134 U. S. 372. § 871.
S. v., 82 Mo. 82. § 102.
Long v. P., 102 Ill. 331. § 271.
P. v., 39 Cal. 694. § 353.
P. v., 43 Cal. 444. § 510.
P. v., 50 Mich. 249. §§ 114, 547.
Rex v., 4 C. & P. 398. §§ 287, 407.
Rex v., 4 C. & P. 423. § 287.
v. Rodgers, 17 Ala. 540. § 235.
v. S., 27 Ala. 32. § 1227.
v. S., 11 Fla. 295. §§ 565, 572.
v. S., 12 Ga. 293. §§ 470, 478.
v. S., 38 Ga. 491. § 164.
v. S., 46 Ind. 582. § 277.
v. S., 73 Md. 527. § 1315.
v. S., 74 Md. 565. § 1317.
v. S., 52 Miss. 23. §§ 306, 330.
v. S., 1 Swan, 287. § 209.
v. S., 34 Tex. 566. § 279.
v. S., 43 Tex. 467. § 816.
v. S., 6 Tex. Ap. 643. § 50.
v. S., 10 Tex. Ap. 186. § 786.
v. S., 11 Tex. Ap. 381. § 615.
v. S., 22 Tex. Ap. 194. §§ 1283, 1285, 1286, 1292, 1315.
S. v., 94 N. C. 896. § 1192.
S. v., 48 Ohio St. 509. § 82.
U. S. v., 30 Fed. R. 678. §§ 744, 762, 771.
U. S. v., 68 Fed. R. 348. § 1331.
U. S. v., 4 Woods, 454. § 1330.
Long Island R. Co., P. v., 134 N. Y. 506. § 21.
Longbottom, Reg. v., 3 Cox, 439. § 349.
Longbottoms, S. v., 11 Humph. 39. §§ 543, 597.
Longden, Rex v., Russ. & Ry. 228. § 298.
Longley v. S., 43 Tex. 490. § 1017.
S. v., 10 Ind. 482. § 915.
Longstreeth, Rex v., 1 Moody, 137. § 558.

Longworth v. S., 41 Tex. 508. § 1311.
Lonon, S. v., 19 Ark. 577. § 252.
Lonsdale, Reg. v., 3 Cox, 222. § 753.
Reg. v., 4 F. & F. 56. § 551.
Look, C. v., 108 Mass. 452. § 46.
Loom, Rex v., 1 Moody, 160. § 594.
Loomis v. Edgerton, 19 Wend. 419. §§ 811, 814.
v. P., 67 N. Y. 322. §§ 562, 563.
P. v., 4 Denio, 380. § 543.
S. v., 115 Mo. 307. § 55.
Looney v. S., 43 Ark. 389. § 1234.
v. S., 10 Tex. Ap. 520. § 572.
Loose, Reg. v., Bell, 259. § 546.
Lopez v. S., 20 Tex. 780. § 586.
S. v., 15 Nev. 407. § 358.
S. v., 18 Tex. 33. § 1304.
Lord v. S., 17 Neb. 526. §§ 1094, 1099.
v. S., 16 N. H. 325. §§ 1137, 1306.
v. S., 20 N. 404. § 597.
S. v., 5 N. H. 335. § 836.
S. v., 16 N. H. 357. §§ 1170, 1177.
Lord Mayor, Reg. v., 16 Q. B. 772. §§ 1040, 1045.
Lord Ossulston, Rex v., 2 Stra. 1107. § 9.
Lorimer v. S., 76 Ind. 495. § 1136.
Loring, C. v., 8 Pick. 369. §§ 84, 1167.
Lorry S v., 7 Baxt. 95. § 1321.
Lorton v. S., 7 Mo. 55. § 551.
Lorway v. Lousada, 1 Low. 77. § 826.
Lose v. S., 72 Ind. 285. § 45.
Lot of Jewelry, U. S. v., 59 Fed. R. 684. § 1351.
Lott v. S., 122 Ind. 393. § 1036.
v. S., 9 Tex. Ap. 206. § 1163.
v. S., 17 Tex. Ap. 598. § 502.
v. S., 20 Tex. Ap. 230. § 548.
Loughridge, P. v., 1 Neb. 11. § 553.
Louisville v. Kean, 18 B. Mon. 9. § 1226.
Louisville, etc. R. Co. v. C., 92 Ky. 114. § 1326.
v. C., 80 Ky. 143. § 1187.
C. v., 80 Ky. 291. § 1323.
v. Mississippi, 133 U. S. 587. §§ 40, 54.
S. v., 86 Ind. 114. §§ 183, 1184, 1187.
U. S. v., 18 Fed. R. 480. §§ 1161, 1338.
Louisville Courier Journal Co. v. C., 92 Ky. 22. § 1316.
Loup, U. S. v., 1 McCrary, 168. § 1350.
Loutnan v. C., 79 W. Va. 196. § 74.
Love v. P., 160 Ill. 501. §§ 118, 501.
v. S., 78 Ga. 66. § 547.
v. S., 15 Tex. Ap. 563. § 557.
v. S., 31 Tex. Ap. 469. § 36.
v. S., 32 Tex. Ap. 85. § 1037.
S. v., 1 Bay, 167. § 421.
Lovegrove v. S., 31 Tex. Ap. 491. §§ 170, 178.
Lovelady v. S., 14 Tex. Ap. 545. § 396.
v. S., 17 Tex. Ap. 286. § 396.
Lovell, Reg. v., 8 Q. B. D. 185. § 559.
Rex v., 2 East, P. C. 990. § 799.
Rex v., 2 M. & Rob. 236. §§ 266, 634.
S. v., 23 Ia. 304. §§ 83, 84, 922.
Lovell, S. v., 39 N. J. 458. § 1315.
S. v., 39 N. J. 463. §§ 1137, 1283, 1297.
Lovett, Reg. v., 9 C. & P. 462. § 1048.
Reg. v., 11 Cox, 602. § 939.
v. S., 30 Fla. 142. §§ 305, 321, 358, 391.
v. S., 33 Fla. 389. § 78.
S. v., 3 Vt. 110. § 920.
Low v. Rees Ptg. Co., 41 Neb. 127. § 55.
Reg. v., 10 Cox, 168. § 556.
Lowder v. S., 63 Ala. 143. § 501.
Lowe v. P., 28 Ill. 518. § 1188.
Reg. v., 3 C. & K. 123. §§ 350, 351.
v. S., 57 Ga. 171. § 602.
v. S., 14 Lea, 204. § 506.
v. S., 4 Tex. Ap. 34. § 1143.
v. S., 11 Tex. Ap. 253. § 546.
Lowenhaught, S. v., 11 Lea, 13. § 1245.
Lowenthal v. S., 32 Ala. 589. § 624.
Lowery, C. v., 149 Mass. 67. § 511.
v. S., 72 Ga. 649. § 203.
v. S., 30 Tex. 402. § 969.
Lowndes, P. v., 130 N. Y. 455. § 46.
Lowrie, Reg. v., L. R. 1 C. C. 61. § 543.
v. S., 43 Tex. 602. § 1303.
Lowry, C. v., 158 Mass. 18. § 501.
v. S., 1 Mo. 518. § 1310.
S. v., 33 La. An. 1224. § 256.
Lows v. Telford, 1 Ap. Cas. 414. § 839.
Loyd v. S., 45 Ga. 57. §§ 156, 212.
v. S., 19 Tex. Ap. 321. § 110.
S. v., 2 Ind. 659. § 96.
Luberg, C. v., 94 Pa. St. 85. §§ 755, 790.
Lubin, S. v., 42 La. An. 79. § 916.
Luby v. C., 12 Bush, 1. § 314.
Lucas, C. v., 2 Allen, 170. §§ 206, 573.
C. v., 158 Mass. 81. §§ 1073, 1082.
v. Flinn, 35 Ia. 9. § 661.
v. S., 62 Ala. 26. § 552.
v. S., 96 Ala. 51. § 589.
v. S., 92 Ga. 454. § 1264.
v. S., 71 Miss. 471. § 389.
v. S., 19 Tex. Ap. 79. § 396.
v. S., 27 Tex. Ap. 322. § 882.
v. S., 33 Tex. Ap. 290. § 566.
S. v., 55 Ia. 321. § 197.
S. v., 57 Ia. 501. § 196.
S. v., 24 Oreg. 168. § 554.
Luck, C. v., 2 B. Mon. 296. § 1216.
Reg. v., 3 F. & F. 483. § 194.
v. S., 96 Ind. 16. § 368.
Lucker v. C., 4 Bush, 440. § 1248.
Luckie v. S., 33 Tex. Ap. 562. §§ 1113, 1114.
Luckinbell v. S., 52 Ark. 45. § 314.
Luckis, C. v., 99 Mass. 431. § 548.
Lucy, S. v., 41 Minn. 60. § 195.
Luddy, C. v., 143 Mass. 563. § 1247.
Luera v. S., 12 Tex. Ap. 257. § 309.
Luffe, Rex v., 8 East, 193. § 1129.
Lufkin, C. v., 7 Allen, 579. § 1161.
Lujano v. S., 32 Tex. Ap. 414. § 450.
Lukins, U. S. v., 3 Wash. C. C. 335. § 921.
Lull, S. v., 37 Me. 246. § 613.
Lum v. S., 11 Tex. Ap. 483. § 345.
Lum Ling Ying, 59 Fed. R. 682. § 1345.

Lumley, Reg. v., L. R. 1 C. C. 196. § 1084.
Lumsden, S. v., 89 N. C. 572. § 1315.
U. S. v., 1 Bond, 5. § 1341.
Lund, S. v., 49 Kan. 209. § 1276.
Lundy v. S., 60 Ga. 143. § 548.
v. S., 71 Ga. 360. § 514.
Lunn, S. v., 49 Mo. 90. § 1016.
Lunning v. S., 9 Ind. 309. § 96.
Lunny, Reg. v., 6 Cox, 477. § 414.
Lunsford, S. v., 81 N. C. 528. § 488.
Lunt, U. S. v., Sprague, 311. § 260.
Lurch, S. v., 12 Oreg. 95. § 762.
S. v., 12 Oreg. 99. §§ 773, 806.
S. v., 12 Oreg. 104. § 771.
Luscomb, C. v., 130 Mass. 42. § 1273.
Lusk v. S., 64 Miss. 845. § 526.
S. v., 68 Ind. 264. § 1024.
Luster v. S., 23 Fla. 339. § 1130.
Luther, S. v., 8 R. I. 151. §§ 813, 827.
Luton v. Circuit Judge, 69 Mich. 610. § 1206.
Lutteral v. Ryenell, 1 Mod. 282. § 11.
Lutterloh, S. v., 22 Tex. 210. §§ 252, 260.
Lutton, C. v., 157 Mass. 392. § 34.
v. S., 14 Tex. Ap. 518. § 684.
Luttrell v. S., 85 Tenn. 232. § 752.
Lutz v. C., 29 Pa. St. 441. § 381.
Lybarger v. S., 2 Wash. 552. § 1112.
Lycan v. P., 107 Ill. 423. §§ 654, 655.
Lydick v. Korner, 13 Neb. 10. § 1228.
S. v., 11 Neb. 366. § 1227.
Lyerly, S. v., 7 Jones, 158. §§ 1088, 1095.
Lyle v. S., 30 Tex. Ap. 118. § 1310.
v. S., 31 Tex. Ap. 103. §§ 161, 162, 869.
S. v., 100 N. C., 497. § 828.
Lymburn, S. v., 1 Brev. 397. § 250.
Lynch v. C., 77 Pa. St. 205. §§ 178, 341, 342, 345.
v. C., 88 Pa. St. 189. §§ 18, 581.
C. v., 8 Gray, 384. § 1324.
C. v., 160 Mass. 298. § 1248.
v. P., 16 Mich. 472. § 1264.
P. v., 101 Cal. 229. § 246.
P. v., 11 Johns. 549. § 1355.
P. v., 29 Mich. 274. § 440.
Rex v., 5 C. & P. 324. § 338.
v. S., 89 Ala. 18. § 578.
S. v., 20 Oreg. 389. §§ 269, 279.
U. S. v., 49 Fed. R. 851. § 1334.
Lyng v. Michigan, 135 U. S. 161. §§ 76, 1204.
Lynn, Ex parte, 19 Tex. Ap. 293. § 1207.
C. v., 123 Mass. 218. § 142.
Rex v., 2 Term R. 733. § 1166.
v. S., 27 Tex. Ap. 590. § 1303.
v. S., 33 Tex. Ap. 153. § 66.
Lyon, P. v., 99 N. Y. 210. §§ 18, 187, 207.
Rex v., 2 East, P. C. 933. § 756.
Rex v., Russ. & Ry. 255. § 758.
v. S., 61 Ala. 224. § 569.
v. S., 22 Ga. 399. § 325.
S. v., 45 N. J. 272. §§ 636, 641.
Lyons, C. v., 160 Mass. 174. § 1249.
v. P., 68 Ill. 271. §§ 499, 500, 511, 513.
Lyons, Reg. v., Bell, 38. § 523.
Rex v., 2 East, P. C. 497. § 494.
v. S., 25 Tex. Ap. 403. § 1026.
Lytle v. S., 31 Ohio St. 196. § 872.
S. v., 64 N. C. 255. § 798.

Maas, S. v., 83 Ia. 469. § 1093.
S. v. 37 La. An. 292. § 801.
Mabbett, Reg. v., 5 Cox, 339. § 286.
Mabel, Reg. v., 9 C. & P. 474. § 922.
Maberry, S. v., 3 Strob. 144. §§ 647, 912.
Mabrey, S. v., 64 N. C. 592. § 243.
Mabry v. C., 2 Va. Cas. 396. § 602.
McAdams v. S., 25 Ark. 405. §§ 320, 321, 329, 332, 361.
v. S., 8 Lea, 456. § 557.
McAdoo, S. v., 80 Mo. 216. §§ 1247, 1275.
McAdory v. S., 62 Ala. 154. § 533.
McAfee, C. v., 108 Mass. 458. §§ 243, 348, 377.
v. S., 31 Ga. 411. § 246.
v. S., 14 Tex. Ap. 668. § 573.
S. v., 107 N. C. 812. § 232.
McAllister, In re, 51 Fed. R. 282. §§ 34, 76.
P. v., 49 Mich. 12. §§ 667, 688.
v. S., 17 Ala. 434. § 169.
v. S., 72 Md. 390. § 34.
S. v., 24 Me. 139. 806, 808.
v. T., 1 Wash. 360. § 339.
McAloon, S. v., 40 Me. 133. §§ 601, 713, 719, 727.
McAlpin v. S., 3 Ind. 567. § 1306.
McAndrews, T. v., 3 Mont. 158. §§ 326, 333.
McArthur v. S., 59 Ark. 431. §§ 1051, 1057.
McAtee, C. v., 8 Dana, 28. § 1292.
McAthey, Reg. v., L. & C. 250. § 714.
McBeth v. S., 50 Miss. 81. § 292.
S. v., 49 Kan. 584. § 821.
McBirnie, Pennsylvania v., Addis. 28. § 265.
McBrayer, S. v., 98 N. C. 619. §§ 137, 1253, 1256.
McBride v. C., 13 Bush, 337. §§ 594, 601.
v. S., 7 Ark. 374. § 271.
S. v., 8 Humph. 65. §§ 1291, 1292.
S. v., 4 McCord, 332. § 1223.
S. v., 64 Mo. 364. § 1252.
McBryde, S. v., 97 N. C. 393. § 123.
McCabe, C. v., 163 Mass. 98. § 1277.
C. v., 163 Mass. 400. § 1277.
U. S. v., 58 Fed. R. 557. § 950.
McCafferty, C. v., 145 Mass. 384. § 66.
Reg. v., 10 Cox, 603. § 1358.
S. v., 63 Me. 223. § 1218.
McCaffrey, P. v., 75 Mich. 115. § 858.
S. v., 63 Ia. 479. § 440.
McCahill, S. v., 72 Ia. 111. § 970.
McCall v. California, 136 U. S. 104. § 44.
S. v., 4 Ala. 643. §§ 493, 500, 503.
McCallough v. C., 67 Pa. St. 30. § 1270.
McCalman v. S., 96 Ala. 98. § 1302.
McCalmen v. S., 77 Ind. 250. § 101.
McCampbell v. S., 9 Tex. Ap. 124. § 609.

McCance, S. v., 110 Mo. 398. §§ 1082, 1085, 1237, 1271.
McCann, P. v., 16 N. Y. 58. § 179.
S. v., 19 Mo. 249. §§ 545, 571.
v. U. S., 2 Wyo. 267. § 655.
McCannon, S. v., 51 Mo. 160. § 431.
McCants, S. v., 1 Spears, 384. §§ 162, 331, 343, 344.
McCarney v. P., 83 N. Y. 408. § 206.
McCarter, S. v., 98 N. C. 637. §§ 526, 529.
McCartey, S. v., 17 Minn. 76. §§ 556, 558.
McCarther, Rex v., Peake, 155. § 874.
McCarthy, Ex parte, 29 Cal. 395. § 859.
Ex parte, 72 Cal. 384. § 61.
v. S., 56 Ind. 203. § 1326.
S. v., 43 La. An. 541. § 423.
S. v., 41 Minn. 59. § 859.
U. S. v., 4 Cranch, C. C. 304. § 748.
McCartney v. S., 3 Ind. 353. § 774.
McCarty, C. v., 152 Mass. 577. § 878.
Resp. v., 2 Dall. 86. § 137.
v. S., 44 Ind. 214. §§ 215, 217.
v. S., 127 Ind. 223. § 481.
v. S., 26 Miss. 299. § 199.
v. S., 37 Miss. 411. § 1196.
S. v., 73 Ia. 51. § 583.
McCaskey, S. v., 104 Mo. 644. §§ 1118, 1119.
McCaughey, C. v., 9 Gray, 296. § 1181.
McCauley v S., 26 Ala. 135. § 1303.
v. U. S., Morris, 486. § 364.
McChesney, S. v., 90 Mo. 120. § 907.
McClain, Ex parte, 61 Cal. 436. § 1210.
S. v., 49 Kan. 730. § 1117.
McClaine v. T., 1 Wash. 345. § 518.
McClanahan, C. v., 2 Met. (Ky.) 8. § 1038.
McClean v. S., 49 N. J. 471. § 1137.
McCleary, S. v., 17 Ia. 44. § 1217.
McClellan, C. v., 101 Mass. 34. § 1164.
v. S., 53 Ala. 640. §§ 1010, 1011.
v. S., 32 Ark. 609. §§ 771, 799.
McClelland v. Kay, 14 B. Mon. 103. § 142.
McClerkin v. S., 20 Fla. 879. § 892.
McClintic, S. v., 73 Ia. 663. §§ 1114, 1118, 1119.
McClintock, S. v., 8 Ia. 203. § 250.
McCluer, S. v., 5 Nev. 132. §§ 316, 346.
McClung, S. v., 35 W. Va. 280. § 511.
McClure v. C., 81 Ky. 448. § 615.
v. C., 86 Pa. St. 353. § 771.
v. S., 43 Ark. 75. § 1233.
S. v., 4 Blackf. 328. § 1167.
S. v., 25 Mo. 338. § 78.
McClusky, Ex parte, 40 Fed. R. 71. §§ 20, 581.
McCollum, S. v., 119 Mo. 469. § 303.
McCombs v. S., 8 Ohio St. 643. §§ 455, 460.
McConaughy, U. S. v., 33 Fed. R. 168. §§ 854, 874.
McConkey v. C., 101 Pa. St. 416. § 416.
S. v., 20 Ia. 574. §§ 823, 830.
S. v., 49 Ia. 499. §§ 668, 684.
McConnell, Reg. v., 1 C. & K. 371. §§ 753, 781.
McConnell v. S., 13 Tex. Ap. 390. § 357.
McCook v. S., 91 Ga. 740. § 163.
McCool v. S., 23 Ind. 127. § 1246.
McCord v. P., 46 N. Y. 470. §§ 202, 682.
P. v., 76 Mich. 200. §§ 500, 501.
v. S., 79 Ala. 269. § 833.
v. S., 83 Ga. 521. § 890.
S. v., 8 Kan. 232. § 390.
U. S. v., 72 Fed. R. 159. §§ 955, 966, 973.
McCorkle v. S., 14 Ind. 39. § 587.
McCormac, S. v., 116 N. C. 1033. § 358.
McCormack v. S., 102 Ala. 156. §§ 126, 152, 269, 274, 276, 316.
S. v., 56 Ia. 585. § 803.
S. v., 8 Oreg. 236. § 551.
McCormick, C. v., 150 Mass. 270. §§ 1223, 1231.
v. S., 42 Neb. 866. § 587.
v. S., 26 Tex. Ap. 678. § 470.
S. v., 52 Ind. 169. §§ 859, 873.
S. v., 27 Ia. 402. §§ 359, 361, 383.
McCourt v. P., 64 N. Y. 583. §§ 112, 572.
McCowan v. S., 58 Ark. 17. §§ 593, 604.
McCoy v. P., 71 Ill. 111. § 1126.
v. S., 8 Ark. 451. §§ 142, 274.
v. S., 52 Ga. 287. § 214.
v. S., 25 Tex. 33. §§ 322, 330.
v. S., 44 Tex. 616. § 617.
S. v., 29 La. An. 593. § 307.
S. v., 42 La. An. 228. § 552.
S. v., 34 Mo. 531. § 174.
S. v., 89 N. C. 466. §§ 547, 550.
S. v., 115 N. C. 1059. § 63.
McCracken v. S., 27 Ind. 491. § 37.
v. S., 71 Md. 150. § 89.
U. S. v., 3 Hughes, 544. § 1328.
McCrary v. S., 81 Ga. 334. § 653.
McCready v. Virginia, 94 U. S. 391. § 46.
McCreary v. S., 73 Ala. 480. § 1202.
McCrillis v. S., 69 Ind. 159. § 495.
McCroskey v. S., 2 Coldw. 178. § 271.
S. v., 3 McCord, 308. § 858.
McCrum, S. v., 38 Minn. 154. § 1106a.
McCrystol, S. v., 43 La. An. 907. §§ 84, 899, 950.
McCue v. C., 78 Pa. St. 185. §§ 359, 416.
McCuen v. S., 19 Ark. 630. §§ 101, 1274.
v. S., 19 Ark. 636. § 1274.
McCulley, Reg. v., 2 Moody, 34. § 594.
v. S., 62 Ind. 428. § 235.
McCulloch, C. v., 15 Mass. 227. § 27.
v. S., 48 Ind. 109. § 396.
McCullough v. Brown, 41 S. C. 220. § 1214.
v. C., 67 Pa. St. 30. § 1270.
v. S., 132 Ind. 427. § 609.
v. S., 24 Tex. Ap. 128. § 266.
McCune, S. v., 5 R. I. 60. § 469.
McCutcheon v. P., 69 Ill. 601. §§ 128, 1237, 1257.
McDade v. P., 29 Mich. 50. §§ 220, 225.
v. S., 27 Tex. Ap. 641. § 303.
McDaniel's Case, Foster, 121. § 118.
McDaniel v. C., 6 Bush, 326. §§ 1285, 1286.
v. C., 77 Va. 281. §§ 329, 365.
v. S., 35 Ala. 390. § 1303.

McDaniel v. S., 76 Ala. 1. § 316.
v. S., 97 Ala. 14. § 311.
v. S., 27 Ga. 197. § 939.
v. S., 8 Sm. & M. 401. §§ 426, 468, 568.
v. S., 33 Tex. 419. § 572.
v. S., 5 Tex. Ap. 475. §§ 1162, 1163.
S. v., 1 Houst. Cr. C. 506. § 1238.
S. v., 8 Jones, 284. § 1191.
S. v., 45 La. An. 686. § 268.
S. v., 94 Mo. 301. §§ 365, 377.
S. v., 84 N. C. 803. § 1057.
S. v., 115 N. C. 807. § 162.
S. v., 20 Oreg. 523. § 1288.
S. v., 41 Tex. 229. § 215.
S. v., 1 Winst. 1, 249. §§ 224, 505, 506.
U. S. v., 4 Cranch, C. C. 721. § 596.
McDaniels v. P., 118 Ill. 301. §§ 543, 589.
P. v., 1 Park. Cr. R. 198. § 470.
McDavid, S. v., 15 La. An. 403. § 1085.
McDermott, P. v., 8 Cal. 288. § 863.
v. S., 89 Ind. 187. § 306.
v. S., 13 Ohio St. 332. § 460.
McDevitt, S. v., 69 Ia. 549. §§ 454, 462.
McDonald v. C., 86 Ky. 10. § 520.
C. v., 5 Cush. 365. §§ 226, 228.
C. v., 110 Mass. 405. § 440.
C. v., 160 Mass. 528. § 1266.
v. Norton, 72 Ia. 652. § 846.
v. P., 47 Ill. 533. § 522.
v. P., 126 Ill. 150. §§ 966, 974, 975, 976, 977, 985.
P. v., 2 Ida. 14. §§ 320, 321.
P. v., 9 Mich. 150. §§ 249, 443, 452, 454, 464, 467.
P. v., 43 N. Y. 61. § 556.
Reg. v., L. & C. 85. § 631.
Reg. v., 15 Q. B. D. 323. § 554.
v. S., 83 Ala. 46. § 808.
v. S., 68 Miss. 728. § 1232.
v. S., 89 Tenn. 161. § 302
S. v., 4 Jones, 19. § 325.
S. v., 20 Minn. 136. § 96.
S. v., 67 Mo. 13. §§ 260, 309.
S. v., 10 Mont. 21. § 594.
S. v., 9 W. Va. 456. § 510.
v. U. S., 63 Fed. R. 426. § 1334.
U. S. v., 8 Biss. 439. §§ 922, 923, 924.
U. S. v., 59 Fed. R. 563. § 1334.
U. S. v., 65 Fed. R. 486. § 1334.
McDonel v. S., 90 Ind. 320. § 322.
McDonell, P. v., 47 Cal. 134. § 178.
McDonnell, C. v., 157 Mass. 407. § 34.
P. v., 80 Cal. 285. §§ 223, 752, 777, 785, 790.
P. v., 92 N. Y. 657. § 389.
v. S., 81 Ala. 279. § 38.
v. S., 58 Ark. 242. §§ 771, 798.
S. v., 32 Vt. 491. §§ 329, 332, 339.
McDonnough, C. v., 150 Mass. 504. § 1250.
McDonough, C. v., 13 Allen, 581. §§ 78, 96, 98, 1199.
S. v., 84 Me. 488. § 1242.
McDougal v. S., 88 Ind. 24. § 320.
S. v., 20 Wis. 482. § 554.
McDowell, C. v., 1 Browne (Pa.), 359. § 543.
P. v., 71 Cal. 194. § 1070.
v. S., 61 Ala. 172. § 589.
v. S., 68 Miss. 348. § 602.
S. v., Dudley, 346. § 1145.
S. v., 1 Hawks, 449. § 474.
S. v., 101 N. C. 734. § 1129.
U. S. v., 4 Cranch, C. C. 423. § 1145.
McDuffie, S. v., 34 N. H. 523. §§ 539, 815.
S. v., 107 N. C. 885. § 1132.
McDuffy, C. v., 126 Mass. 467. § 680.
v. S., 87 Ga. 687. § 1221.
McElhaney v. S., 12 Tex. Ap. 231. § 1137.
McElhiney v. C., 22 Pa. St. 365. § 8.
McElreath v. S., 55 Ga. 562. § 499.
McElroy v. S., 14 Tex. Ap. 235. § 382.
T. v., 1 Mont. T. 86. § 914.
McElvaine v. Brush, 142 U. S. 155. §§ 77, 80.
McEntee v. S., 24 Wis. 43. §§ 481, 575, 610.
McEwan, U. S. v., 44 Fed. R. 594. § 255.
McFadden, P. v., 65 Cal. 445. § 274.
McFall, Pennsylvania v., Addis. 255. § 162.
McFarland v. S., 4 Kan. 68. § 553.
S. v., 49 Ia. 99. § 511.
U. S. v., 1 Cranch, C. C. 140. §§ 123, 992.
McFarlane, U. S. v., 1 Cranch, C. C. 163. § 1002.
McGahey, S. v., 3 N. D. 293. § 410.
McGardiner, S. v., 1 Ired. 27. §§ 793, 801.
McGarren, P. v., 17 Wend. 460. § 545.
McGary v. P., 45 N. Y. 153. §§ 518, 529.
McGavaran, Reg. v., 6 Cox, 64. § 238.
McGee, P. v., 1 Denio, 19. § 456.
v. S., 8 Mo. 495. §§ 361, 362.
v. S., 4 Tex. Ap. 625. § 592.
v. S., 21 Tex. Ap. 670. §§ 455, 463.
S. v., 40 Ia. 595. §§ 1184, 1190.
McGehee v. S., 62 Miss. 772. § 276.
McGill, S. v., 65 Vt. 547. § 1243.
U. S. v., 1 Wash. C. C. 463. § 369.
McGilver, P. v., 67 Cal. 55. § 508.
McGinnes, Reg. v., 11 Cox, 391. § 145.
McGinnis v. S., 31 Ga. 236. § 411.
S. v., 71 Ia. 685. §§ 694, 712.
S. v., 30 Minn. 52. § 1273.
S. v., 76 Mo. 326. § 365.
McGlothlen, S. v., 56 Ia. 544. § 1126.
McGlue, U. S. v., 1 Curtis, 1. §§ 159, 174, 332.
McGlynn, S. v., 34 N. H. 422. §§ 1243, 1281.
McGonigal, S. v., 5 Harr. 510. § 159.
McGorty, C. v., 114 Mass. 299. § 514.
McGovern, C. v., 10 Allen. 193. § 489.
McGowan v. S., 9 Yerg. 184. § 1283.
S. v., 1 S. C. 14. § 612.
McGrath, C. v., 140 Mass. 296. §§ 1074, 1084.
v. Merwin, 112 Mass. 467. § 1321.
Reg. v., 14 Cox, 598. §§ 521, 524.

McGrath, Reg. v., L. R. 1 C. C. 205. § 559.
S. v., 73 Mo. 181. § 189.
McGreer, S. v., 13 S. C. 464. § 246.
McGregor, Reg. v., 1 C. & K. 429. § 818.
Rex v., 3 Bos. & P. 106. § 634.
v. S., 16 Ind. 9. §§ 780, 803.
v. S., 4 Tex. Ap. 599. § 255.
S. v., 41 N. H. 407. §§ 205, 1141, 1145.
McGrew v. Cato, Minor, 8. § 11.
P. v., 77 Cal. 570. § 487.
v. S., 13 Tex. Ap. 340. § 1120.
v. S., 17 Tex. Ap. 613. § 921.
v. S., 31 Tex. Ap. 336. § 546.
S. v., 11 Ia. 112. § 1249.
McGrowther, Rex v., 1 East, P. C. 71. §§ 137, 1357.
McGuff v. S., 88 Ala. 147. §§ 443, 458, 459.
McGuffie v. S., 17 Ga. 497. § 339.
McGuire, C. v., 11 Gray, 460. § 1274.
C. v., 1 Va. Cas. 119. § 1295.
v. Massachusetts, 3 Wall. 387. §§ 29, 1217.
v. S., 37 Ala. 161. §§ 791, 800.
v. S., 7 Humph. 54. § 949.
v. S., 50 Ind. 284. § 271.
v. S., 37 Miss. 369. § 1253.
v. S., 42 Ohio St. 530. §§ 104, 1202.
S. v., 50 Ia. 153. § 1097.
S. v., 87 Ia. 142. § 278.
S. v., 64 N. H. 529. §§ 190, 1239.
McGuirk, C. v., 78 Pa. St. 298. § 92.
v. S., 64 Miss. 209. § 1036.
McGurk, U. S. v., 1 Cranch, C. C. 71. § 425.
McGurty, C. v., 145 Mass. 257. §§ 945, 950.
McHale, C. v., 97 Pa. St. 397. §§ 16, 941, 966, 971.
McHenry, U. S. v., 6 Blatch. 503. § 878.
McHugh, C. v., 147 Mass. 401. § 1243.
S. v., 31 Ala. 318. § 429.
McIlroy v. S., 25 Tex. 507. § 1026.
McIntire v. S., 10 Ind. 26. § 726.
S. v., 66 Ia. 339. § 463.
S. v., 115 N. C. 769. § 1055.
McIntosh, Rex v., 2 East, P. C. 942. §§ 753, 756.
v. S., 52 Ala. 355. § 614.
v. S., 18 Tex. Ap. 284. § 594.
S. v., 64 N. C. 607. § 1126.
S. v., 92 N. C. 794. § 1057.
S. v., 40 S. C. 349. §§ 312, 316.
McInturf v. S., 20 Tex. Ap. 335. § 78.
McJunkins v. S., 10 Ind. 140. § 1157.
McKale, Reg. v., L. R. 1 C. C. 125. § 560.
McKane, P. v., 143 N. Y. 455. § 988.
v. S., 11 Ind. 195. § 597.
McKay, P. v., 46 Mich. 439. § 244.
v. S., 44 Tex. 43. § 232.
McKean, C. v., 98 Mass. 9. § 797.
S. v., 36 Ia. 343. § 117.
McKee, Pennsylvania v., Addis. 1. § 1152.
v. P., 32 N. Y. 239. § 101.
McKee v. P., 36 N. Y. 113. § 359.
McKeen v. S., 7 Tex. Ap. 631. § 206.
McKeever, Reg. v., 5 Ir. R. C. L. 86. § 520.
McKenna, C. v., 158 Mass. 207. § 1243.
P. v., 81 Cal. 158. §§ 699, 950.
v. S., 61 Miss. 589. § 316.
S. v., 16 R. I. 398. § 1218.
McKensie v. S., 42 Ga. 334. §§ 174, 175.
McKenzie v. S., 11 Ark. 594. § 666.
v. S., 26 Ark. 334. § 329.
S. v., 42 Me. 392. § 774.
McKeone v. P., 6 Colo. 346. § 307.
McKeron, Rex v., 5 Term R. 316. § 878.
McKettrick, S. v., 14 S. C. 346. §§ 252, 260.
McKibbin v. S., 40 Ark. 480. § 128.
McKie, C. v., 1 Gray, 61. §§ 139, 179, 316.
McKiernan, S. v., 17 Nev. 224. § 802.
McKinley, S. v., 82 Ia. 445. §§ 245, 246.
McKinne v. S., 81 Ga. 164. § 1161.
McKinney, P. v., 10 Mich. 54. §§ 646, 648, 649, 656*a*.
P. v., 10 Mich. 74. § 649.
v. Salem, 77 Ind. 213. § 1217.
v. S., 8 Tex. Ap. 626. § 338.
S. v., 42 Ia. 205. § 870.
S. v., 111 N. C. 683. § 391.
McKinny v. S., 29 Fla. 565. §§ 443, 449, 464, 465.
McKinstry, S. v., 50 Ind. 465. § 956.
McKinzie, S. v., 102 Mo. 620. §§ 332, 368.
McKissick v. S., 2 Tex. 356. §§ 1285, 1291.
McKisson, C. v., 8 Serg. & R. 420. § 974.
McLain, S. v., 2 Brev. 443. § 594.
S. v., 104 N. C. 894. § 934.
McLane v. Bonn, 70 Ia. 752. §§ 1206, 1207.
v. Leicht, 69 Ia. 401. § 1207.
v. S., 4 Ga. 335. § 528.
S. v., 15 Nev. 345. § 377.
McLaughlin v. C., 4 Rawle, 464. § 596.
C. v., 5 Allen, 507. § 240.
C. v., 11 Cush. 598. § 579.
C. v., 12 Cush. 615. §§ 267, 276.
C. v., 105 Mass. 460. § 228.
C. v., 108 Mass. 477. § 1242.
v. S., 45 Ind. 338. § 1274.
v. S., 10 Tex. Ap. 340. §§ 353, 391.
S. v., 44 Ia. 82. §§ 458, 459.
S. v., 47 Kan. 143. § 1275.
McLaurine v. S., 28 Tex. Ap. 530. § 1164.
McLean, P. v., 71 Mich. 309. § 460.
v. S., 16 Ala. 672. § 426.
v. S., 4 Ga. 335. § 528.
v. S., 8 Mo. 153. § 430.
v. S., 32 Tex. Ap. 521. § 1099.
McLeland v. S., 25 Ga. 477. § 1087.
McLelland, S. v., 4 Sneed, 437. § 1298.
McLeod, P. v., 1 Hill (N. Y.), 377. § 115.
v. Scott, 21 Oreg. 94. § 1228.
v. S., 35 Ala. 395. §§ 1094, 1098.
S. v., 5 Jones, 318. § 595.
McLeran, S. v., 1 Aikens, 311. § 765.
McLin v. S., 29 Tex. Ap. 171. § 575.
McLoon, S. v., 78 Me. 420. § 1018.

McLoughlin, Reg. v., 8 C. & P. 635. § 256.
McMahan v. S., 29 Tex. Ap. 348. § 815.
S. v., 103 N. C. 379. § 328.
McMahon v. Sloan, 12 Pa. St. 229. § 611.
v. S., 1 Tex. Ap. 102. § 557.
v. S., 13 Tex. Ap. 220. § 1057.
v. S., 16 Tex. Ap. 357. § 275.
S. v., 53 Conn. 407. § 85.
S. v., 14 R. I. 285. § 1176.
McMakin, Reg. v., Russ. & Ry. 333, n. § 209.
McManus v. C., 91 Pa. St. 57. § 416.
C. v., 161 Mass. 64. § 1243.
v. S., 36 Ala. 285. §§ 368, 421.
S. v., 89 N. C. 555. §§ 1031, 1039.
McMaster, S. v., 35 S. C. 1. § 1240.
McMath v. S., 55 Ga. 303. §§ 443, 450, 452, 455.
McMillan, Reg. v., 1 Cox, 41. § 777.
v. S., 35 Ga. 54. § 329.
v. S., 18 Tex. Ap. 375. §§ 1232, 1251.
S. v., 68 N. C. 440. § 605.
McMillen v. S., 13 Mo. 30. § 417.
v. S., 5 Ohio, 268. § 794.
McMinn, S. v., 83 N. C. 668. § 1233.
McMullen v. S., 53 Ala. 531. § 572.
McMurrin v. Rigby, 80 Ia. 322. § 455.
McMurry v. S., 6 Ala. 324. § 886.
McNab, S. v., 20 N. H. 160. §§ 327, 1147.
McNaghten's Case, 10 Cl. & F. 200. §§ 132, 156, 158, 172, 174, 178.
McNair v. P., 89 Ill. 441. §§ 1064, 1158.
v. S., 53 Ala. 453. §§ 439, 451.
McNally, S. v., 34 Me. 210. § 922.
S. v., 87 Mo. 644. § 307.
McNamara, S. v., 69 Me. 133. §§ 1220, 1248.
McNamee, C. v., 112 Mass. 285. § 1018.
v. P., 31 Mich. 473. §§ 12, 1167.
Rex v., 1 Moody, 368. § 556.
v. S., 34 Neb. 288. § 292.
McNaugher, C. v., 131 Pa. St. 55. § 1190.
McNaughten, Reg. v., 14 Cox, 576. §§ 196, 291, 1004.
McNealy v. S., 17 Fla. 198. § 550.
v. S., 94 Ga. 592. § 1323.
McNeary, S. v., 88 Mo. 143. § 1228.
McNeeley, S. v., 1 Winst. Eq. 234. § 1227.
McNeely, S. v., 34 La. An. 1022. § 307.
McNeese, C. v., 156 Mass. 231. § 1279.
McNeill v. S., 102 Ala. 121. §§ 341, 342, 343.
v. S., 92 Tenn. 719. § 1264.
S. v., 92 N. C. 812. § 338.
McNeff, C. v., 145 Mass. 406. § 1248.
McNinch, S. v., 87 N. C. 567. § 1019.
S. v., 90 N. C. 695. § 241.
McNish v. S., 88 Ga. 499. § 556.
McNulty, Ex parte, 77 Cal. 164. §§ 36, 85.
P. v., 93 Cal. 427. §§ 101, 374.
McOmber, S. v., 6 Vt. 215. § 922.
McPhail v. S., 9 Tex. Ap. 164. §§ 548, 564.
McPhane, Reg. v., Car. & M. 212. § 205.
McPherson, Reg. v., Dears. & B. 197. §§ 226, 228, 506.
v. S., 54 Ala. 221. § 1270.
McPherson v. S., 29 Ark. 225. §§ 311, 389.
v. S., 22 Ga. 478. §§ 299, 428.
v. S., 20 Tex. Ap. 194. § 608.
v. S., 9 Yerg. 279. §§ 362, 431.
S. v., 9 Ia. 53. §§ 790, 803.
S. v., 70 N. C. 239. § 502.
T. v., 6 Dak. 27. § 89.
McPike, C. v., 3 Cush. 181. §§ 292, 400, 414.
McQuaid, P. v., 85 Mich. 123. § 1074.
McQueen v. S., 94 Ala. 50. § 426.
v. S., 103 Ala. 12. §§ 309, 329, 426.
v. S., 1 Lea. 285. § 365.
McQuirk v. S., 84 Ala. 435. § 460.
McQuoid v. P., 8 Ill. 76. §§ 925, 926.
McRae v. S., 71 Ga. 96. § 412.
S. v., 111 N. C. 665. §§ 546, 560.
McRay v. S., 18 Tex. Ap. 331. § 1163.
McReynolds v. S., 26 Tex. Ap. 372. § 1244.
McRoberts, C. v., 4 Blackf. 178. § 492.
McRue, Reg. v., 8 C. & P. 641. § 450.
McSpatton v. S., 30 Tex. Ap. 616. § 309.
McTigue v. S., 4 Baxt. 313. § 482.
McTyier v. S., 91 Ga. 254. §§ 1112, 1117, 1118.
McVay v. S., 100 Ala. 110. § 1017.
McVey v. S., 23 Tex. Ap. 659. § 601.
McWhirt's Case, 3 Grat. 594. § 343.
McWhorter, P. v., 93 Mich. 641. § 461.
Macard, P. v., 73 Mich. 15. §§ 137, 309.
Macarty, Rex v., 2 East, P. C. 823. § 661.
Macauley, Rex v., 1 Leach, 287. § 469.
Macdaniel, Rex v., 1 East, P. C. 333. § 283.
Mace v. S., 58 Ark. 79. § 1285.
S. v., 76 Me. 64. §§ 859, 880.
S. v., 65 N. C. 344. § 820.
S. v., 86 N. C. 668. § 854.
Mack v. S., 63 Ala. 138. § 707.
v. S., 63 Ga. 693. § 338.
S. v., 41 La. An. 1079. §§ 64, 66, 1145.
S. v., 20 Oreg. 234. § 504.
Mackaboy v. C., 2 Va. Cas. 268. § 998.
Mackaley's Case, Cro. Jac. 279. § 840.
Mackalley's Case, 9 Co. 65, 298. § 504.
Mackarty, Rex v., 2 Ld. Raym. 1179. § 960.
Mackay, Reg. v., 11 Cox, 148. § 426.
Mackerel, Rex v., 4 C. & P. 448. § 817.
Mackey v. P., 2 Colo. 13. § 12.
v. S., 3 Ohio St. 362. § 801.
v. S., 13 Tex. Ap. 360. § 345.
v. S., 20 Tex. Ap. 603. § 601.
S. v., 82 Ia. 393. §§ 1116, 1117.
T. v., 8 Mont. 168. § 45.
Mackin v. P., 115 Ill. 312. §§ 858, 862, 865, 866, 892.
v. S., 62 Md. 244. § 1232.
v. U. S., 117 U. S. 348. § 19.
Mackinley, P. v., 9 Cal. 250. § 543.
Macklin, Reg. v., 5 Cox, 216. § 611.
Macleod, Reg. v., 12 Cox, 534. § 287.
Macloon, C. v., 101 Mass. 1. §§ 286, 369, 377.

Macomber, C. v., 3 Mass. 254. §§ 83, 210.
S. v., 7 R. I. 349. § 949.
Maconnehey v. S., 5 Ohio St. 77. § 159.
Madan, C. v., 102 Mass. 1. § 416.
Madden v. S., 1 Kan. 340. § 332.
v. S., 1 Tex. Ap. 204. § 562.
S. v., 81 Mo. 421. § 57.
Maddox v. S., 87 Ga. 429. § 752.
v. S., 14 Tex. Ap. 447. § 601.
v. S., 28 Tex. Ap. 533. § 880.
S. v., 85 Ind. 585. § 833.
Madge, Reg. v., 9 C. & P. 29. § 553.
Madigan, S. v., 57 Minn. 425. §§ 878, 887.
Madison v. S., 16 Tex. Ap. 435. § 548.
S. v., 63 Me. 546. §§ 1185, 1193.
U. S. v., 21 Fed. R. 628. § 857.
Madox, Rex v., Russ. & Ry. 92. § 555.
Ma Foo, S. v., 110 Mo. 7. § 435.
Magallones, P. v., 15 Cal. 426. § 590.
Magdalene College Case, 11 Co. 66. § 82.
Magee v. P., 139 Ill. 138. § 514.
S. v., 11 Ind. 154. §§ 676, 678.
Magellan Pirates, The, 1 Spinks, Eccl. & Adm. 81. § 1359.
Magner v. P., 97 Ill. 320. § 46.
Magoon, S. v., 50 Vt. 333. § 410.
S. v., 61 Vt. 45. § 18.
Maguire, In re, 57 Cal. 604. §§ 55, 77.
P. v., 26 Cal. 635. § 1326.
v. S., 47 Md. 485. § 28.
S. v., 113 Mo. 670. §§ 271, 274.
Mahalovitch v. S., 54 Ga. 217. § 1145.
Mahan, S. v., 2 Ala. 340. § 1298.
S. v., 81 Ia. 121. § 1093.
Mahanna, S. v., 48 N. H. 377. § 596.
Mahar, C. v., 8 Gray, 469. § 578.
C. v., 16 Pick. 120. § 529.
Maher v. P., 10 Mich. 212. §§ 123, 274, 337, 338, 343, 410.
S. v., 35 Me. 225. § 1277.
Mahlman, P. v., 82 Cal. 585. §§ 13, 631.
Mahn, S. v., 25 Kan. 182. §§ 164, 332.
Mahon v. Justice, 127 U. S. 700. § 118.
Mahoney, C. v., 152 Mass. 493. §§ 1227, 1254.
v. S., 33 Tex. Ap. 388. § 566.
S. v., 23 Minn. 181. §§ 189, 1237.
Mahony, Reg. v., 6 Cox, 487. § 761.
Mah Wong Gee, In re, 47 Fed. R. 433. § 1344.
Maier, Ex parte, 103 Cal. 476. § 46.
S. v., 36 W. Va. 757. §§ 158, 173.
Maile v. C., 9 Leigh, 661. § 382.
Main, S. v., 31 Conn. 572. §§ 107, 1137, 1138, 1139.
Maine v. P., 9 Hun, 113. § 431.
Maine Cent. R. Co., S. v., 60 Me. 490. § 288.
S. v., 76 Me. 357. § 288.
S. v., 77 Me. 244. § 288.
S. v., 77 Me. 538. § 288.
S. v., 81 Me. 84. § 184.
Maines v. S., 26 Tex. Ap. 14. § 892.
Mainey, S. v., 65 Ind. 404. § 132.
Mainor, S. v., 6 Ired. 340. § 1095.
Mains v. S., 42 Ind. 327. §§ 1143, 1178.
Maires, S. v., 33 N. J. 142. § 914.
Mairs, S. v., 1 N. J. 335. § 12.
Maize v. S., 4 Ind. 342. § 1210.
Major, Rex v., 2 East, P. C. 1118. § 733.
S. v., 14 Rich. 76. § 594.
Makely, C. v., 131 Mass. 421. §§ 521, 522.
Malce v. S., 33 Tex. Ap. 14. § 417.
Malcolm, S. v., 8 Ia. 413. §§ 226, 232, 268.
Malcolmson v. S., 25 Tex. Ap. 267. § 652.
Males, U. S. v., 51 Fed. R. 41. § 1332.
Maley v. S., 31 Ind. 192. § 675.
Mallain, Reg. v., 33 L. J. M. C. 58. § 1136.
Mallard, U. S. v., 40 Fed. R. 151. § 854.
Mallette, P. v., 79 Mich. 600. §§ 8, 1138.
Malling, S. v., 11 Ia. 239. § 1276.
Mallinson, Rex v., 2 Burr. 679. § 538.
Mallory v. S., 62 Ga. 164. § 1292.
Malloy, C. v., 119 Mass. 347. § 934.
S. v., 34 N. J. 410. §§ 121, 123, 819, 826.
S. v., 115 N. C. 737. § 1057.
Malone v. C., 91 Ky. 307. § 489.
v. S., 8 Ga. 408. § 420.
v. S., 49 Ga. 210. § 338.
v. S., 14 Ind. 219. § 53.
v. S., 11 Lea, 701. § 825.
S. v., 46 Ark. 140. § 813.
S. v., 8 Ind. Ap. 8. § 1187.
U. S. v., 20 Blatch. 137. § 128.
Maloney, P. v., 1 Park. Cr. 593. § 539.
Reg. v., 9 Cox, 6. § 392.
S. v., R. M. Charl. 84. § 511.
S. v., 12 R. I. 251. §§ 925, 926, 927.
Maloy, S. v., 44 Ia. 104. § 196.
Manahan, P. v., 32 Cal. 68. § 461.
Manaway v. S., 44 Ala. 375. §§ 758, 805.
Manchester v. Massachusetts, 139 U. S. 240. §§ 14, 46.
Mancke, S. v., 18 S. C. 81. §§ 1217, 1223.
Mandeville, C. v., 142 Mass. 469. § 1253.
Maner v. S., 8 Tex. Ap. 361. § 488.
Mangan v. S., 76 Ala. 60. § 50.
Mangham v. S., 87 Ga. 549. § 514.
Mangum v. S., 15 Tex. Ap. 362. § 1032.
S. v., 116 N. C. 998. § 677.
Manheim v. S., 66 Ind. 65. § 1314.
Manigault v. S., 53 Ga. 113. § 271.
Manion, U. S. v., 44 Fed. R. 800. § 857.
Mankato v. Arnold, 36 Minn. 62. § 1270.
Mankletow, Reg. v., Dears. 159. §§ 1102, 1103.
Manley, S. v., 74 Ia. 561. § 617.
S. v., 107 Mo. 364. § 649.
Manly v. S., 7 Md. 135. § 272.
Manluff, S. v., 1 Houst. Cr. C. 208. §§ 505, 506.
Mann, C. v., 4 Gray, 213. §§ 190, 1174.
C. v., 116 Mass. 58. § 139.
v. P., 35 Ill. 467. § 1126.
P. v., 75 N. Y. 484. § 762.
v. S., 34 Ga. 1. § 1118.
S. v., 25 Ohio St. 668. § 607.
S. v., 2 Oreg. 238. §§ 1284, 1285, 1310.
S. v., 13 Tex. 61. §§ 1285, 1291.
v. Trabue, 1 Mo. 709. § 11.

Manners, Rex v., 7 C. & P. 801. §§ 205, 788.
Mannessier, S. v., 32 La. An. 1308. § 64.
Manning's Case, T. Raym. 212. § 341.
Manning, In re, 44 Fed. R. 275. § 9.
Reg. v., 2 C. & K. 886. §§ 146, 200, 217.
Reg. v., Dears. 21. §§ 200, 567.
Reg. v., L. R. 1 C. C. 338. § 520.
Reg. v., 12 Q. B. D. 241. § 981.
S. v., 107 N. C. 910. § 849.
Mansair v. S., 60 Ind. 357. § 1190.
Mansfield, Reg. v., Car. & M. 140. § 593.
v. S., 17 Tex. Ap. 468. § 1274.
S. v., 33 Tex. 129. § 594.
Mansker, S. v., 36 Tex. 364. § 1313.
Manson v. S., 24 Ohio St. 590. § 556.
Manuel, S. v., 4 Dev. & B. 20. § 54.
S. v., 72 N. C. 201. § 815.
Manvelle v. S., 58 Ind. 63. §§ 1256, 1273.
Manville v. Felter, 19 Kan. 253. § 8.
Manwaring, Reg. v., Dears. & B. 132. § 1082.
Mapes v. P., 69 Ill. 523. §§ 1257, 1262.
Marable v. S., 89 Ga. 425. § 416.
Maranda v. S., 44 Tex. Ap. 442. § 690.
Marble, P. v., 38 Mich. 117. § 411.
v. S., 13 Ind. 362. § 53.
March, P. v., 6 Cal. 543. §§ 169, 333, 392.
Reg. v., 1 C. & K. 496. § 237.
Rex v., 1 Moody, 182. § 521.
v. S., 3 Tex. Ap. 107. § 1017.
v. Walker, 48 Tex. 372. § 316.
Marchand, C. v., 155 Mass. 8. § 28.
Marchant, S. v., 15 R. I. 539. §§ 190, 1293, 1309.
Marcks, S. v., 3 N. Dak. 532. § 271.
Marcus, Reg. v., 2 C. & K. 356. § 771.
v. S., 89 Ala. 23. § 1234.
v. S., 26 Ind. 101. § 556.
S. v., 20 Ark. 201. § 1270.
U. S. v., 53 Fed. R. 784. §§ 783, 796, 797.
Margetts, Rex v., 2 Leach, 930. § 508.
Maria v. S., 28 Tex. 698. §§ 339, 391.
Marianna Flora, The, 11 Wheat. 1. § 1359.
Marigold, U. S. v., 9 How. (U. S.) 560. § 790.
Maring, P. v., 3 Keyes, 374. § 76.
Marion, P. v., 28 Mich. 255. § 798.
P. v., 29 Mich. 31. §§ 750, 752, 764.
S. v., 14 Mont. 458. § 1255.
Markham v. Cob, Latch, 144. § 11.
P. v., 64 Cal. 157. § 896.
v. S., 25 Ga. 52. § 577.
S. v., 15 La. An. 498. §§ 1306, 1307.
v. U. S., 160 U. S. 319. §§ 872, 875, 878.
Markle v. S., 3 Ind. 535. § 1318.
v. Akron, 14 Ohio, 587. § 1220.
Marks v. Borum, 57 Tenn. 87. § 299.
C. v., 4 Leigh, 658. § 504.
v. S., 45 Ala. 38. § 1316.
v. S., 71 Mass. 206. § 45.
Markuss, Reg. v., 4 F. & F. 356. § 287.
Marlborough, Ex parte, 5 Q. B. 955. § 1057.
Marler v. S., 67 Ala. 55. §§ 416, 418.
S. v., 68 Ala. 580. § 416.
Marmet v. S., 45 Ohio St. 63. §§ 39, 77.
Marnoch v. S., 7 Tex. Ap. 269. §§ 305, 417.
Marquardt v. S., 52 Ark. 269. § 1264.
Marquis v. Chicago, 27 Ill. Ap. 251. §§ 1310, 1315.
Marquis, P. v., 15 Cal. 38. § 362.
Marriott, Reg. v., 8 C. & P. 425. §§ 349, 351.
Rex v., 4 Mod. 144. §§ 1111, 1199.
Marsden, Reg. v., L. R. 1 C. C. 131. § 922.
Reg. v., 2 Q. B. D. (1891) 149. § 450.
Marsh v. Loader, 14 C. B. (N.S.) 535. § 149.
Reg. v., 3 Cox, 571. § 228.
Reg. v., 1 Den. 505. § 699.
Reg. v., 3 F. & F. 523. §§ 554, 631.
Rex v., 1 Leach, 345. § 662.
S. v., 37 Ark. 356. § 1202.
S. v., 36 N. H. 196. §§ 114, 132.
S. v., 91 N. C. 632. § 825.
Marshall v. Chicago, etc. R. Co., 48 Ill. 475. § 425.
v. C., 5 Grat. 663. §§ 256, 265.
C. v., 137 Pa. St. 170. § 1190.
C. v., 11 Pick. 350. §§ 96, 101.
P. v., 59 Cal. 386. § 1102.
Rex v., Russ. & Ry. 75. § 764.
v. S., 49 Ala. 21. § 1261.
v. S., 32 Fla. 462. § 353.
v. S., 59 Ga. 154. § 162.
v. S., 94 Ga. 589. § 500.
v. S., 123 Ind. 128. § 228.
v. S., 31 Tex. 471. §§ 557, 594.
v. S., 33 Tex. 664. § 363.
v. S., 4 Tex. Ap. 549. § 535.
v. S., 13 Tex. Ap. 492. § 260.
S. v., 14 Ala. 411. §§ 265, 273.
S. v., 47 Mo. 378. §§ 868, 875, 878.
S. v., 121 Mo. 476. § 1114.
S. v., 45 N. H. 281. §§ 942, 950.
S. v., 64 N. H. 579. § 34.
S. v., Phill. 49. § 455.
S. v., 13 Tex. 58. § 539.
Marshalltown v. Blum, 58 Ia. 184. §§ 44, 77.
Marsteller, S. v., 84 N. C. 726. § 245.
Marston v. C., 18 B. Mon. 485. § 1313.
Martel v. East St. Louis, 94 Ill. 67. § 1225.
Martha v. S., 26 Ala. 72. § 529.
Marthinson, U. S. v., 58 Fed. R. 765. § 1195.
Martin v. Blattner, 68 Ia. 286. § 1208.
v. C., 93 Ky. 189. § 416.
v. C., 2 Leigh, 745. §§ 808, 810.
C. v., 17 Mass. 359. §§ 84, 478.
C. v., 125 Mass. 394. § 377.
C. v., 130 Mass. 465. § 83.
C. v., 162 Mass. 402. § 1243.
v. P., 23 Ill. 395. § 1193.
P. v., 102 Cal. 558. § 682.
P. v., 91 Mich. 650. § 589.
Reg. v., 8 Ad. & El. 481. § 707.
Reg. v., 9 C. & P. 213. §§ 444, 462, 464.
Reg. v., 9 C. & P. 215. §§ 221, 249.

Martin, Reg. v., 11 Cox, 136. § 351.
Reg. v., 1 F. & F. 501. § 704.
Reg. v., 5 Q. B. D. 34. §§ 675, 764.
Reg. v., 8 Q. B. D. 54. § 256.
Reg. v., L. R. 1 C. C. 56. § 681.
Rex v., 3 C. & P. 211. § 351.
Rex v., 5 C. & P. 128. § 377.
Rex v., 6 C. & P. 562. § 460.
Rex v., 7 C. & P. 549. §§ 754, 781.
Rex v., 2 East, P. C. 618. § 540.
Rex v., Russ. & Ry. 108. § 494.
v. S., 28 Ala. 71. § 522.
v. S., 89 Ala. 115. §§ 196, 328.
v. S., 90 Ala. 602. §§ 150, 153.
v. S., 32 Ark. 124. §§ 933, 934.
v. S., 58 Ark. 3. § 1123.
v. S., 6 Baxt. 234. § 1024.
v. S., 25 Ga. 494. § 392.
v. S., 95 Ga. 478. §§ 713, 724.
v. S., 71 Miss. 87. § 1314.
v. S., 30 Neb. 421. § 1274.
v. S., 30 Neb. 507. §§ 189, 1264, 1274.
v. S., 24 Tex. 62. §§ 110, 748.
v. S., 40 Tex. 19. § 268.
v. S., 1 Tex. Ap. 525. §§ 500, 509.
v. S., 1 Tex. Ap. 586. § 664.
v. S., 9 Tex. Ap. 293. § 535.
v. S., 18 Tex. Ap. 224. § 790.
v. S., 31 Tex. Ap. 27. § 1274.
v. S., 33 Tex. Ap. 317. §§ 878, 890.
S. v., 34 Ark. 340. §§ 1220, 1270.
S. v., 3 Heisk. 487. § 1216.
S. v., 9 Humph. 55. § 754.
S. v., 2 Ired. 101. §§ 308, 410.
S. v., 105 Mass. 178. § 922.
S. v., 28 Mo. 530. §§ 546, 571.
S. v., 74 Mo. 547. § 418.
S. v., 76 Mo. 337. § 511.
S. v., 108 Mo. 117. § 1274.
S. v., 124 Mo. 514. §§ 332, 338, 414.
S. v., 3 Murph. 533. § 1000.
S. v., 82 N. C. 672. § 551.
S. v., 85 N. C. 508. § 232.
S. v., 107 N. C. 904. § 853.
S. v., 30 Wis. 216. §§ 144, 303, 390, 431.
U. S. v., 4 Cliff. 156. § 967.
U. S. v., 17 Fed. R. 150. § 920.
U. S. v., 28 Fed. R. 812. § 1331.
U. S. v., 50 Fed. R. 918. § 1332.
Martindale v. S., 19 Tex. Ap. 333. § 548.
Martinez v. S., 41 Tex. 126. § 577.
v. S., 41 Tex. 164. § 597.
v. S., 7 Tex. Ap. 394. § 880.
v. S., 16 Tex. Ap. 122. §§ 571, 585.
Marts v. S., 26 Ohio St. 162. § 307.
Marvin v. S., 19 Ind. 181. § 13.
S. v., 12 Ia. 499. § 1135.
S. v., 35 N. H. 22. § 1086.
Marx, P. v., 99 N. Y. 377. § 34.
Mary v. S., 24 Ark. 44. § 523.
Marzynski, C. v., 149 Mass. 68. § 1321.
Mascolo v. Montesanto, 61 Conn. 50. § 1153.
Mascowitz v. S., 49 Ark. 170. § 1261.
Mash, C. v., 7 Met. 472. §§ 123, 133, 1076.
Mask v. S., 32 Miss. 405. § 392.
v. S., 36 Miss. 77. § 332.
Maskill v. S., 8 Blackf. 299. § 1353.
Mason, In re, 43 Fed. R. 510. § 9.
C. v., 105 Mass. 163. §§ 546, 567.
v. P., 2 Colo. 373. § 588.
v. P., 26 N. Y. 200. §§ 495, 505.
Rex v., 1 East, P. C. 239. § 342.
Rex v., Russ. & Ry. 419. § 469.
Rex v., 2 Term R. 581. § 699.
v. S., 42 Ala. 532. § 515.
v. S., 32 Ark. 238. § 572.
v. S., 55 Ark. 529. §§ 941, 946, 948.
v. S., 7 Tex. Ap. 623. § 930.
v. S., 29 Tex. Ap. 24. § 1102.
v. S., 31 Tex. Ap. 306. § 808.
v. S., 32 Tex. Ap. 95. § 791.
S. v., 108 Ind. 48. §§ 622, 625.
S. v., 42 La. An. 714. § 436.
S. v., 26 Oreg. 273. §§ 188, 1043, 1053, 1056, 1060.
U. S. v., 12 Blatch. 497. § 798.
U. S. v., 22 Fed. R. 707. § 1334.
Massage, S. v., 65 N. C. 480. § 339.
Massey v. S., 74 Ind. 368. § 1234.
v. S., 31 Tex. Ap. 371. §§ 451, 454.
S. v., 86 N. C. 658. § 463.
S. v., 103 N. C. 356. § 96.
Massie v. S., 5 Tex. Ap. 81. §§ 872, 878.
Masters, Reg. v., 1 Den. 332. § 634.
Mastin, Rex v., 6 C. & P. 396. §§ 196, 351.
Mathena v. S., 20 Ark. 70. § 798.
v. S., 15 Tex. Ap. 473. §§ 665, 706.
Mather, P. v., 4 Wend. 229. §§ 211, 956, 966, 968, 969, 972, 975, 979, 981.
S. v., N. Chip. 32. § 504.
Mathes, S. v., 90 Mo. 571. § 431.
Mathews v. S., 19 Neb. 330. §§ 440, 458.
v. S., 33 Tex. 102. § 744.
v. S., 17 Tex. Ap. 472. § 601.
S. v., 14 Mo. 133. § 101.
S. v., 44 Mo. 523. § 43.
S. v., 98 Mo. 125. § 411.
U. S. v., 23 Fed. R. 74. § 1348.
Mathias, U. S. v., 36 Fed. R. 892. § 1332.
Mathis, S. v., 3 Ark. 84. § 1313.
S. v., 21 Ind. 277. § 1192.
S. v., 30 Tex. 506. § 1185.
Mattheson, Reg. v., 5 Cox, 276. § 554.
Matthews' Case, 2 Leon. 201. § 852.
Matthews, C. v., 89 Ky. 287. §§ 426, 428.
C. v., 122 Mass. 60. § 70.
C. v., 129 Mass. 485. § 1223.
C. v., 152 Pa. St. 166. § 1321.
Reg. v., 14 Cox, 5. § 827.
Reg. v., 1 Den. 596. §§ 145, 725.
Reg. v., 28 L. T. 645. §§ 562, 569.
v. S., 55 Ala. 65. § 509.
v. S., 81 Ala. 66. § 824.
v. S., 24 Ark. 484. § 594.
v. S., 61 Miss. 155. § 617.
v. S., 4 Ohio St. 539. §§ 479, 483.
v. S., 25 Ohio St. 536. §§ 1184, 1193.
S. v., 129 Ind. 281. § 631.
S. v., 44 Kan. 596. §§ 665, 680.
S. v., 38 La. An. 795. § 292.

Matthews, S. v., 20 Mo. 55. § 572.
S. v., 37 N. H. 450. § 9.
S. v., 76 N. C. 41. § 509.
S. v., 78 N. C. 523. §§ 307, 308.
S. v., 91 N. C. 635. § 695.
S. v., 87 Tenn. 689. § 553.
v. U. S., 161 U. S. 500. § 882.
U. S. v., 35 Fed. R. 890. §§ 1330, 1335.
U. S. v., 68 Fed. R. 880. § 882.
Mattingly v. S., 8 Tex. Ap. 345. §§ 865, 872, 878.
Mattison v. S., 3 Mo. 421. § 790.
Mattox v. U. S., 146 U. S. 140. §§ 425, 431.
v. U. S., 156 U. S. 237. §§ 425, 431.
Mauck v. S., 66 Ind 177. § 1190.
Maull v. S., 37 Ala. 160. § 1095.
Maupin v. S., 89 Tenn. 367. § 1034.
Maurer, S. v., 7 Ia. 406. §§ 1286, 1306.
Maurin, P. v., 77 Cal. 436. § 744.
Mauritzen, P. v., 84 Cal. 37. § 684.
Maverty v. S., 10 Lea, 729. §§ 921, 922.
Mawbey, Rex v., 6 T. R. 619. §§ 954, 971.
Mawgridge, Reg. v., J. Kel. 119. §§ 309, 321.
Max, Ex parte, 44 Cal. 579. § 280.
Maxwell v. Carlile, 1 McCord, 534. § 994.
P. v., 24 Cal. 14. § 573.
v. S., 27 Ala. 660. § 1256.
v. S., 89 Ala. 150. §§ 164, 178, 179.
v. S., 68 Miss. 339. § 530.
S. v., 5 Blackf. 230. §§ 1290, 1291.
S. v., 33 Conn. 259. §§ 1137, 1138.
S. v., 42 Ia. 208. § 511.
S. v., 47 Ia. 454. §§ 765, 769, 771.
S. v., 28 La. An. 361. §§ 865, 878.
T. v., 2 N. M. 250. §§ 621, 634.
Maxent, S. v., 10 La. An. 743. § 204.
May v. P., 8 Colo. 210. § 307.
Reg. v., 10 Cox, 448. § 1152.
Reg. v., L. & C. 13. § 626.
Rex v., 1 Doug. 193. § 794.
v. S., 85 Ala. 14. § 529.
v. S., 6 Tex. Ap. 191. § 246.
v. S., 15 Tex. Ap. 430. § 707.
v. S., 17 Tex. Ap. 213. § 706.
v. S., 23 Tex. Ap. 146. § 311.
S v., 20 Ia. 305. §§ 542, 1267.
S. v., 52 Kan. 53. § 1218.
S. v., 42 La. An. 82. § 454.
S. v., 33 S. C. 39. § 1253.
Mayberry, S. v., 48 Me. 218. §§ 687, 953, 960, 975, 977.
S. v., 9 Wash. 193. § 650.
Maybush v. C., 29 Grat. 857. §§ 860, 893.
Mayer, S. v., 45 Ia. 698. § 725.
U. S. v., Deady, 127. § 891.
Mayers, Reg. v., 12 Cox, 311. § 445.
v. S., 8 Ark. 222. § 1310.
Mayes v. P., 106 Ill. 306. §§ 322, 325, 378.
P. v., 66 Cal. 597. §§ 455, 458.
v. S., 33 Tex. 340. § 830.
Mayfield v. S., 44 Tex. 59. §§ 266, 268.
S. v., 66 Mo. 125. §§ 293, 381.
Mayhew, Rex v., 6 C. & P. 315. § 892.
Mayhew v. Wardly, 14 C. B. (N. S.) 550. § 195.
Mayle, Reg. v., 11 Cox, 150. § 626.
Maynard, C. v., 91 Ky. 131. § 852.
v. P., 135 Ill. 416. §§ 858, 859.
Rex v., 2 East, P. C. 501. § 495.
v. S., 14 Ind. 427. § 609.
Mayo v. S., 30 Ala. 32. §§ 652, 656.
v. S., 43 Ohio St. 567. §§ 485, 491.
v. S., 7 Tex. Ap. 342. § 443.
v. Wilson, 1 N. H. 53. § 105.
Mayor, Ex parte, 90 Ala. 516. § 69.
Mays v. S., 89 Ala. 37. § 825.
v. S., 28 Tex. Ap. 484. § 708.
Mayson, S. v., 3 Brev. 284. § 873.
Mazagora, Rex v., Russ. & Ry. 291. § 770.
Mazzia v. S., 51 Ark. 177. § 1216.
Mead, C. v., 10 Allen, 398. § 152.
C. v., 12 Gray, 167. § 307.
C. v., 153 Mass. 284. § 1279.
C. v., 160 Mass. 319. § 639.
Rex v., 2 B. & C. 605. § 425.
Rex v., 4 C. & P. 535. §§ 543, 636.
v. S., 25 Neb. 444. §§ 535, 565.
v. S., 53 N. J. 601. §§ 769, 805.
v. Young, 4 Term R. 28. § 762.
Meader, S. v., 62 Vt. 458. § 96.
Meadows, Reg. v., 1 C. & K. 399. §§ 1102, 1103.
S. v., 18 W. Va. 658. §§ 276, 280.
S. v., 22 W. Va. 766. § 510.
Meagher, U. S. v., 37 Fed. R. 875. §§ 161, 285, 320, 321, 349, 389.
Meakim, P. v., 133 N. Y. 214. § 21.
Meakin, Rex v., 7 C. & P. 297. § 161.
Meal, Reg. v., 3 Cox, 70. § 503.
Meaney, C. v., 151 Mass. 55. § 1249.
Reg. v., 10 Cox, 506. § 1357.
Means v. S., 10 Tex. Ap. 16. § 414.
U. S. v., 42 Fed. R. 599. § 1339.
Mears v. C., 2 Grant. 385. §§ 271, 466.
Reg. v., 2 Den. 79. § 959.
Meche, S. v., 42 La. An. 273. § 505.
Mecum, S. v., — Ia. —, 64 N. W. R. 286. § 509.
Medbury, S. v., 3 R. I. 138. § 46.
S. v., 8 R. I. 543. § 1096.
Medical Society, S. v., 32 Minn. 324. § 36.
Medis v. S., 27 Tex. Ap. 194. § 1155.
Medland, Reg. v., 5 Cox, 292. § 566.
Medley, In re, 134 U. S. 160. § 78.
Rex v., 6 C. & P. 292. § 130.
Medlicott, S. v., 9 Kan. 257. § 426.
Medlin, S. v., 1 Wins. 99. § 144.
Medlock v. S., 18 Ark. 363. § 1292.
Medrano v. S., 32 Tex. Ap. 214. §§ 132, 1074, 1076, 1116.
Meehan v. S., 46 N. J. 355. §§ 128, 930, 933.
Meeks v. S., 51 Ga. 429. § 275.
Meerchouse, S. v., 34 Mo. 344. § 494.
Meese v. S., 15 Neb. 558. § 1003.
Megowan v. C., 2 Met. (Ky.) 3. § 1264.
Megson, Reg. v., 9 C. & P. 418. § 426.
Reg. v., 9 C. & P. 420. §§ 455, 456.
Meier v. S., 57 Ind. 386. § 1229.

Meier v. S., 10 Tex. Ap. 39. § 260.
Meigh, Reg. v., 7 Cox, 401. § 754.
Meinhart, S. v., 73 Mo. 562. §§ 443, 464.
Meister v. P., 31 Mich. 99. § 218.
Mellen, U. S. v., 53 Fed. R. 229. § 1336.
Mellon, P. v., 40 Cal. 648. § 552.
Mellor, S. v., 13 R. I. 666. § 1215.
Melton v. S., 43 Ark. 367. § 194.
v. S., 3 Humph. 388. §§ 1051, 1069.
v. S., 24 Tex. Ap. 47. § 341.
v. S., 24 Tex. Ap. 287. § 500.
v. S., 30 Tex. Ap. 273. § 257.
S. v., 38 Mo. 368. § 1274.
S. v., 102 Mo. 683. §§ 140, 271.
S. v., 117 Mo. 618. § 18.
Melville, S. v., 11 R. I. 417. § 1300.
Melvin v. Weiant, 36 Ohio St. 184. § 1153.
Memphis, P., P. & B. R. Co. v. S., 87 Tenn. 746. § 1187.
Memphis, etc. R. Co., U. S. v., 6 Fed. R. 237. § 183.
Mence, Reg. v., Car. & M. 234. § 1330.
Mendez v. S., 29 Tex. Ap. 608. § 355.
Mendiola v. S., 18 Tex. Ap. 462. § 175.
Mendum v. C., 6 Rand. 704. § 408.
Menear v. S., 30 Tex. Ap. 475. § 481.
Mercer, Reg. v., 6 Jur. 243. § 455.
v. S., 17 Ga. 146. § 159.
v. S., 17 Tex. Ap. 452. § 1121.
S. v., 32 Ia. 405. § 1240.
S. v., 58 Ia. 182. § 1253.
Mercersmith v. S., 8 Tex. Ap. 211. § 197.
Meredith v. C., 18 B. Mon. 49. § 302.
Reg. v., 8 C. & P. 589. §§ 221, 241, 249.
Rex v., Russ. & Ry. 46. § 130.
v. S., 60 Ala. 441. § 274.
Merkle v. S., 37 Ala. 139. § 1221.
Merkley, S. v., 74 Ia. 695. §§ 237, 286.
Merriam, C. v., 136 Mass. 433. § 1223.
C. v., 148 Mass. 425. § 1174.
C. v., 14 Pick. 518. § 461.
Merrick v. S., 63 Ind. 327. § 374.
S. v., 19 Me. 398. § 617.
Merrifield, C. v., 4 Met. 468. § 652.
Merrill, C. v., 14 Gray, 415. § 451.
v. S., 45 Miss. 651. § 597.
S. v., 37 Me. 329. § 39.
S. v., 44 N. H. 624. § 602.
Merriman v. S., 6 Blackf. 449. § 53.
Merrit, S. v., 35 Conn. 314. § 1186.
Merritt v. S., 19 Tex. Ap. 435. § 1244.
S. v., Phill. 134. §§ 239, 250, 252.
S. v., 5 Sneed, 67. § 914.
Merriweather v. S., 33 Tex. 789. § 546.
Merry v. Green, 7 M. & W. 623. § 545.
Merwin v. P., 26 Mich. 298. § 597.
Mesa, P. v., 93 Cal. 580. §§ 458, 466.
v. S., 17 Tex. Ap. 395. § 1114.
Mesca, Resp. v., 1 Dall. 73. § 12.
Meserve v. C., 137 Mass. 109. §§ 750, 751.
C. v., 154 Mass. 64. §§ 664, 697, 701, 960, 975, 976.
Meshmeier v. S., 11 Ind. 482. §§ 104, 1210.
Messenger, C. v., 4 Mass. 462. § 1326.
v. S., 25 Neb. 674. § 54.
Messersmith, P. v., 61 Cal. 246. §§ 167, 178.
Messinger, C. v., 1 Binn. 273. § 107.
Messingham, Rex v., 1 Moody, 257. §§ 714, 722.
Metcalf v. P., 2 Colo. Ap. 262. § 1007.
Rex v., 1 Moody, 433. §§ 543, 556.
Methard v. S., 19 Ohio St. 363. § 514.
Metsch, S. v., 37 Kan. 222. §§ 681, 699.
Metzer v. S., 31 Tex. Ap. 11. §§ 1303, 1304.
Metzger, P. v., 95 Mich. 121. § 1227.
Metzker v. P., 14 Ill. 101. § 1252.
Meuly v. S., 26 Tex. Ap. 274. §§ 309, 311, 315, 342, 345.
Mewherter, S. v., 46 Ia. 88. § 365.
Meyer, C. v., 2 Serg. & R. 453. § 836.
v. S., 50 Ind. 18. §§ 1260, 1264.
v. S., 41 N. J. 6; 42 N. J. 145. §§ 1137, 1143.
v. S., 4 Tex. Ap. 121. § 586.
S. v., 1 Speers, 305. § 1326.
S. v., 58 Vt. 457. § 391.
Meyers, Ex parte, 44 Mo. 279. §§ 13, 935.
v. Baker, 120 Ill. 567. § 39.
v. C., 83 Pa. St. 131. §§ 162, 178.
P. v., 75 Cal. 383. § 548.
P. v., 95 N. Y. 223. § 1226.
S. v., 68 Mo. 266. § 654.
S. v., 99 Mo. 107. §§ 355, 361, 384.
S. v., 46 Neb. 152. § 456.
Miard, Reg. v., 1 Cox, 22. § 730.
Miazza v. S., 36 Miss. 613. § 1276.
Michael, Reg. v., 9 C. & P. 356. §§ 187, 388.
Micheaux v. S., 30 Tex. Ap. 660. § 567.
Michel v. S., 12 Tex. Ap. 108. § 1190.
Mickle, U. S. v., 1 Cranch, C. C. 268. § 1245.
Middleditch, Reg. v., 1 Den. 92. § 730.
Middleham, S. v., 62 Ia. 150. §§ 307, 410.
Middleship, Reg. v., 5 Cox, 275. § 286.
Middleton, Reg. v. L. R. 2 C. C. 38. § 561.
v. S., Dudley, 275. § 675.
v. S., 53 Ga. 248. § 577.
S. v., 11 Ia. 246. §§ 1309, 1313.
Midgett, S. v., 85 N. C. 538. § 1266.
Midland Ins. Co. v. Smith, 6 Q. B. D. 561. § 11.
Mifflin v. C., 5 Watts & S. 461. § 959.
Mikesell, S. v., 70 Ia. 176. §§ 576, 609.
Mikle, S. v., 81 N. C. 552. § 420.
S. v., 94 N. C. 843. § 666.
Milan v. S., 24 Ark. 346. §§ 269, 279.
Milburn, U. S. v., 4 Cranch, C. C. 719. §§ 1137, 1306.
Miles, P. v., 55 Cal. 207. § 354.
P. v., 143 N. Y. 383. § 168.
Reg. v., 6 Jur. 243. § 238.
v. S., 40 Ala. 39. § 101.
v. S., 1 Tex. Ap. 510. § 565.
v. S., 3 Tex. Ap. 58. § 588.
v. S., 18 Tex. Ap. 156. § 342.
v. S., 23 Tex. Ap. 410. § 255.
v. S., 5 W. Va. 524. § 1253.

Miles v. U. S., 103 U. S. 304. §§ 1079, 1082, 1083, 1085.
U. S. v., 2 Utah, 19. §§ 1079, 1083.
Milholland, S. v., 89 Ia. 5. §§ 123, 152.
Millain, S. v., 3 Nev. 409. § 361.
Millan, P. v., 106 Cal. 320. § 709.
Millard, C. v., 1 Mass. 6. §§ 514, 616, 617.
Reg. v., Dears. 166. § 858.
Rex v., Russ. & Ry. 245. § 808.
S. v., 18 Vt. 574. § 1136.
Miller's Case, Yelv. 120. § 852.
Miller v. Ammon, 145 U. S. 421. § 1200.
v. C., 8 Gray, 484. § 1018.
v. C., 78 Ky. 15. §§ 560, 615.
v. C., 89 Ky. 653. § 307.
C. v., 2 Ashm. 61. § 931.
C. v., 107 Pa. St. 276. § 838.
C. v., 131 Pa. St. 118. §§ 33, 34.
C. v., 139 Pa. St. 77. § 1171.
C. v., 1 Va. Cas. 310. § 361.
v. Dayton, 57 Ia. 423. § 196.
v. Jones, 80 Ala. 89. § 69.
v. P., 4 Colo. 182. § 564.
v. P., 13 Colo. 166. § 601.
v. P., 3 Ill. 233. § 802.
v. P., 39 Ill. 457. § 476.
v. P., 52 N. Y. 304. § 797.
P. v., 12 Cal. 291. § 389.
P. v., 82 Cal. 107. §§ 15, 145, 968.
P. v., 14 Johns. 371. § 660.
P. v., 49 Mich. 23. § 308.
P. v., 88 Mich. 383. § 46.
P. v., 91 Mich. 639. §§ 265, 280.
P. v., 96 Mich. 119. §§ 444, 454.
Reg. v., 6 Cox, 353. § 714.
Reg. v., 13 Cox, 179. §§ 1101, 1103.
Reg. v., 2 Moody, 249. §§ 631, 635.
v. S., 48 Ala. 122. §§ 1284, 1285, 1310.
v. S., 54 Ala. 155. § 358.
v. S., 77 Ala. 41. § 500.
v. S., 6 Baxt. 449. § 1037.
v. S., 15 Fla. 577. § 861.
v. S., 58 Ga. 200. §§ 18, 229.
v. S., 5 How. (Miss.) 250. § 1271.
v. S., 37 Ind. 432. § 332.
v. S., 51 Ind. 405. § 809.
v. S., 73 Ind. 88. § 687.
v. S., 74 Ind. 1. § 312.
v. S., 121 Ind. 294. §§ 1106a, 1133.
v. S., 33 Miss. 356. §§ 1298, 1299.
v. S., 68 Miss. 221. § 416.
v. S., 68 Miss. 533. § 1264.
v. S., 16 Neb. 179. § 639.
v. S., 3 Ohio St. 475. §§ 1182, 1248, 1249.
v. S., 5 Ohio St. 275. §§ 128, 1257.
v. S., 18 Tex. Ap. 34. § 618.
v. S., 18 Tex. Ap. 232. § 421.
v. S., 27 Tex. Ap. 497. § 892.
v. S., 28 Tex. Ap. 445. § 505.
v. S., 32 Tex. Ap. 319. §§ 328, 342.
v. S., 25 Wis. 384. §§ 146, 147, 196, 212, 425.
S. v., 5 Blackf. 502. §§ 1306, 1309.
S. v., 9 Houst. 564. §§ 333, 395, 397, 400, 416.
S. v., 27 Ind. 15. §§ 252, 274.
Miller, S. v., 58 Ind. 399. § 96.
S. v., 98 Ind. 70. § 844.
S. v., 140 Ind. 168. § 49.
S. v., 53 Ia. 84. §§ 1222, 1252, 1278.
S. v., 53 Ia. 154. §§ 1283, 1285, 1286.
S. v., 81 Ia. 72. § 1135.
S. v., 83 Ia. 291. §§ 469, 609.
S. v., 86 Ia. 638. § 1204.
S. v., 35 Kan. 328. § 420.
S. v., 53 Kan. 324. § 469.
S. v., 41 La. An. 53. §§ 62, 70.
S. v., 42 La. An. 1186. § 442.
S. v., 45 La. An. 1170. § 512.
S. v., 48 Me. 576. § 1243.
S. v., 45 Minn. 521. §§ 587, 619.
S. v., 24 Mo. 532. §§ 1273, 1274.
S. v., 50 Mo. 129. § 75.
S. v., 111 Mo. 542. §§ 156, 157, 243, 443.
S. v., 100 N. C. 543. §§ 913, 915, 917.
S. v., 112 N. C. 878. § 339.
S. v., 12 Vt. 437. § 142.
S. v., 3 Wash. 131. §§ 504, 508.
S. v., 24 W. Va. 802. § 892.
S. v., 26 W. Va. 106. § 1241.
v. Texas, 153 U. S. 535. §§ 77, 1030.
U. S. v., 4 Cranch, C. C. 104. § 1308.
U. S. v., 3 Hughes, 553. § 981.
v. Wade, 58 Ind. 91. § 1228.
Millett v. P., 117 Ill. 294. § 55.
Millican v. S., 25 Tex. 664. § 1304.
S. v., 15 La. An. 557. § 520.
Milliman, C. v., 13 Serg. & R. 403. §§ 1184, 1186.
Millner v. S., 15 Lea, 179. § 543.
Mills, In re, 135 U. S. 263. § 20.
v. C., 13 Pa. St. 631. § 1146.
C. v., 157 Mass. 405. § 34.
P. v., 17 Cal. 276. § 443.
P. v., 98 N. Y. 176. §§ 156, 162.
Reg. v., Dears. & B. 205. § 681.
v. S. 20 Ala. 86. § 1303.
v. S., 52 Ind. 187. § 454.
v. S., 18 Neb. 575. § 1058.
v. S., 13 Tex. Ap. 487. § 265.
S. v., 17 Me. 211. §§ 677, 680, 687, 701, 711.
S. v., 104 N. C. 905. § 820.
S. v., 116 N. C. 1051. § 1054.
U. S. v., 7 Pet. 138. § 200.
Millspaugh, P. v., 11 Mich. 278. § 1113.
Milne, P. v., 60 Cal. 71. § 1107.
Milner v. Maclean, 2 C. & P. 17. § 837.
U. S. v., 36 Fed. R. 890. § 966.
Milnes, Reg. v., 2 F. & F. 10. § 890.
Milo, S. v., 32 Me. 57. § 1185.
Milrainey v. S., 33 Tex. Ap. 577. § 309.
Milsaps, S. v., 82 N. C. 549. § 232.
Milton, Reg. v., 10 Cox, 364. § 765.
v. S., 6 Neb. 136. §§ 333, 353, 358, 365.
v. S., 23 Tex. Ap. 204. § 463.
Milwaukee Malt Co. v. Chicago, R. I. & P. R. Co., 73 Ia. 98. §§ 1218, 1220.
Mimms v. S., 16 Ohio St. 221. §§ 408, 416.
Mims v. S., 88 Ga. 458. § 1310.
S. v., 26 Minn. 191. § 654.

Minaghan v. S., 77 Wis. 643. §§ 267, 339.
Minden v. Silverstein, 36 La. An. 912. § 1237.
Miner v. P., 58 Ill. 59. §§ 1086, 1087, 1088, 1094.
Mingo, U. S. v., 2 Curt. 1. § 339.
Mink, C. v., 123 Mass. 422. § 290.
Minniard v. C., 87 Ky. 213. § 328.
Minnick, S. v., 15 Ia. 123. §§ 943, 950.
Minnock, P. v., 52 Mich. 628. § 1271.
Minor, In re, 69 Fed. R. 233. § 76.
C. v., 88 Ky. 422. §§ 1215, 1253.
v. Happersett, 21 Wall. 162. § 948.
v. S., 58 Ga. 551. § 200.
Minter, P. v., 59 Mich. 557. § 1264.
v. S., 26 Tex. Ap. 217. § 548.
Minton v. C., 79 Ky. 461. § 302.
S. v., 116 Mo. 605. § 764.
S. v., Phill. 196. § 713.
Miskell, U. S. v., 15 Fed. R. 369. § 1352.
Miskimmons, S. v., 2 Ind. 440. §§ 8, 1184.
Misner v. Knapp, 13 Oreg. 135. § 1297.
Pennsylvania v., Addis. 44. § 766.
Missouri, The, 4 Ben. 410. § 1351.
Mitchell v. C., 33 Grat. 845. §§ 195, 291.
v. C., 78 Ky. 204. §§ 1146, 1150.
v. C., 88 Ky. 349. §§ 496, 498, 509.
C. v., 3 Bush, 30. § 910.
v. Mims, 8 Tex. 6. § 11.
P. v., 92 Cal. 590. §§ 789, 802, 806.
P. v., 100 Cal. 328. § 404.
Reg. v., 3 C. & K. 181. § 484.
Reg. v., 1 Den. 282, n. § 762.
Reg. v., 2 F. & F. 44. §§ 753, 756.
Rex v., 2 East, P. C. 936. § 753.
v. S., 55 Ala. 160. § 1292.
v. S., 60 Ala. 26. § 391.
v. S., 94 Ala. 68. § 1196.
v. S., 12 Ark. 50. § 487.
v. S., 22 Ga. 211. §§ 308, 309.
v. S., 41 Ga. 527. § 303.
v. S., 92 Tenn. 668. § 562.
v. S., 1 Tex. Ap. 194. § 382.
v. S., 32 Tex. Ap. 479. § 505.
v. S., 5 Yerg. 340; 8 Yerg. 514. §§ 333, 361.
S. v., 3 Blackf. 229. § 1030.
S. v., 68 Ia. 116. §§ 455, 458.
S. v., 5 Ired. 350. § 523.
S. v., 54 Kan. 516. § 454.
S. v., 41 La. An. 1073. §§ 303, 308.
S. v., 28 Mo. 562. § 1253.
S. v., 64 Mo. 191. § 359.
S. v., 89 N. C. 521. § 463.
S. v., 3 S. D. 223. § 9.
U. S. v., Baldw. 366. §§ 757, 780.
U. S. v., 2 Dall. 348. § 1357.
U. S. v., Hughes, 439. § 961.
U. S. v., 36 Fed. R. 492. §§ 83, 1331.
v. Work, 13 R. I. 645. § 460.
Mitchum v. S., 45 Ala. 29. § 544.
v. S., 11 Ga. 615. §§ 395, 414.
Mitten v. S., 24 Tex. Ap. 346. § 1087.
Mitton, Rex v., 3 C. & P. 31. § 924.
Mix, S. v., 15 Mo. 153. §§ 195, 196.
Mize, P. v., 80 Cal. 41. § 274.
v. S., 36 Ark. 653. § 303.
Moah, Reg. v., Dears. 626. §§ 640, 649.
Reg. v., Dears. & B. 550. § 756.
Moan, P. v., 65 Cal. 532. §§ 162, 292.
Mobile, etc. R. Co. v. S., 29 Ala. 573. § 89.
Mobley v. S., 46 Miss. 501. § 452.
S. v., 1 McMul. 44. § 1191.
Mockabee v. C., 78 Ky. 380. § 328.
Mockford, Reg. v., 11 Cox, 16. § 612.
Moeck v. P., 100 Ill. 242. § 425.
Moelchen, S. v., 53 Ia. 310. §§ 416, 417.
Moffat's Case, 2 East, P. C. 954. § 758.
Moffett, S. v., 1 Greene (Ia.), 247. § 1182.
Moffit v. S., 43 Tex. 346. § 1136.
Moffitt v. S., 11 Ark. 169. § 1290.
Mogg, Rex v., 4 C. & P. 364. §§ 815, 826.
Mogler v. S., 47 Ark. 109. §§ 1237, 1261.
Mohn, C. v., 52 Pa. St. 243. §§ 12, 26, 1178.
S. v., 25 Kan. 182. § 164.
Mohr, S. v., 53 Ia. 261. § 1271.
S. v., 68 Mo. 303. § 653.
Moland, Reg. v., 2 Moody, 276. § 206.
Mole, Reg. v., 1 C. & K. 417. § 571.
Molette v. S., 49 Ala. 18. § 435.
Molier, S. v., 1 Dev. 263. §§ 865, 892.
Molihan v. S., 30 Ind. 266. § 1225.
Molloy, U. S. v., 31 Fed. R. 19. § 945.
Molter, C. v., 142 Mass. 533. § 1281.
Molton v. S., — Ala. —, 16 So. R. 795 § 548.
Monaghan v. S., 66 Miss. 513. § 1258.
Monahan, C. v., 9 Gray, 119. §§ 863, 867, 880.
Monarch, C. v., 6 Bush, 298. § 1311.
C. v., 6 Bush, 301. §§ 1310, 1311.
Monday v. S., 32 Ga. 672. § 275.
Mondragon v. S., 33 Tex. 481. § 617.
Money v. S., 89 Ala. 110. § 848.
Monnier, S. v., 8 Minn. 212. § 756.
Monongahela R. Co., S. v., 37 W. Va. 108. § 1187.
Monoughan v. P., 24 Ill. 340. § 584.
Monroe v. P., 113 Ill. 670. §§ 1220, 1261.
v. S., 5 Ga. 85. §§ 307, 414.
v. S., 71 Miss. 196. § 455.
Montag v. P., 141 Ill. 75. §§ 167, 174, 179, 413.
Montague v. S., 17 Fla. 662. § 449.
Montee v. C., 33 J. J. Marsh. 132. § 1310.
Montgomery v. C., 88 Ky. 509. § 169.
C. v., 11 Met. 534. §§ 616, 619.
Resp. v., 1 Yeates, 419. § 909.
v. S., 80 Ind. 338. §§ 425, 427, 428, 1147.
v. S., 10 Ohio 220. § 865.
v. S., 11 Ohio, 424. §§ 368, 426, 429, 430, 1070.
v. S., 2 Tex. Ap. 618. §§ 96, 97.
v. S., 4 Tex. Ap. 140. § 268.
v. S., 12 Tex. Ap. 323. § 766.
S. v., 7 Baxt. 162. § 269.
S. v., 56 Ia. 195. § 678.
S. v., 65 Ia. 483. § 246.
S. v., 71 Ia. 630. § 1151.
S. v., 79 Ia. 737. §§ 448, 458, 459.
S. v., 63 Mo. 296. § 224.
S. v., 91 Mo. 52. §§ 126, 276.

Montgomery, S. v., 98 Mo. 399. § 362.
S. v., 109 Mo. 645. §§ 223, 281, 465, 468.
v. Sutton, 67 Ia. 497. § 929.
v. U. S., 162 U. S. 410. §§ 118, 1335.
U. S. v., 3 Sawy. 544. § 714.
Montross v. S., 72 Ga. 261. § 1158.
Moody v. C., 4 Met. (Ky.) 1. § 324.
C. v., 143 Mass. 177. § 1305.
v. P., 20 Ill. 315. § 489.
Reg. v., L. & C. 173. § 781.
v. S., 94 Ala. 42. § 1040.
v. S., 6 Coldw. 299. § 196.
v. S., 16 Tex. Ap. 252. § 1043.
v. S., 30 Tex. Ap. 422. § 334.
v. S., 17 Ohio St. 111. § 1149.
S. v., 95 N. C. 656. § 1231.
S. v., 98 N. C. 671. § 1057.
Moog v. Hannon's Adm'r, 93 Ala. 503. § 1223.
Mook, S. v., 40 Ohio St. 588. § 586.
Moon v. S., 68 Ga. 687. §§ 330, 332.
S. v., 41 Wis. 684. § 557.
Mooney, Reg. v., 5 Cox, 318. § 426.
v. S., 33 Ala. 419. §§ 161, 246, 267.
v. S., 29 Tex. Ap. 257. §§ 438, 439, 443, 446.
S. v., 65 Mo. 494. § 862.
S. v., Phill. 434. § 232.
Moore, Ex parte, 30 Ind. 197. §§ 336, 343.
In re, 66 Fed. R. 947. § 1217.
v. C., 92 Ky. 630. §§ 169, 175, 762.
v. C., 9 Leigh, 639. § 1082.
v. C., 6 Met. 243. § 1094.
v. C., 8 Pa. St. 260. § 543.
C. v., 11 Cush. 600. § 1142.
C. v., 2 Dana, 202. § 1300.
C. v., 89 Ky. 542. § 678.
C. v., 130 Mass. 45. § 509.
C. v., 157 Mass. 324. § 1243.
C. v., 52 Pa. St. 243. § 12.
C. v., 99 Pa. St. 570. § 678.
C. v., 3 Pick. 194. § 1126.
v. Missouri, 159 U. S. 673. §§ 28, 512.
v. P., 109 Ill. 499. § 1223.
v. P., 146 Ill. 600. § 278.
v. P., 26 Ill. Ap. 137. § 262.
v. P., 47 Mich. 639. § 496.
P. v., 8 Cal. 90. § 358.
P. v., 103 Cal. 508. §§ 1154, 1155.
Reg. v., 3 C. & K. 319. § 161.
Reg. v., 13 Cox, 544. § 1076.
Reg. v., 1 F. & F. 73. § 808.
Reg. v., L. & C. 1. § 571.
Rex v., 3 B. & Ad. 184. § 123.
Rex v., 2 C. & P. 235. § 777.
Rex v., 2 East, P. C. 679. § 662.
Rex v., 1 Leach, 335. § 469.
v. S., 12 Ala. 764. § 427.
v. S., 16 Ala. 411. § 1245.
v. S., 18 Ala. 532. §§ 274, 275.
v. S., 30 Ala. 550. § 1303.
v. S., 40 Ala. 49. §§ 101, 576, 609.
v. S., 50 Ark. 25. §§ 1017, 1021.
v. S., 33 Ga. 225. § 765.
v. S., 79 Ga. 498. § 1274.
Moore v. S., 65 Ind. 213. § 1314.
v. S., 48 Miss. 147. §§ 75, 1317.
v. S., 55 Miss. 432. § 552.
v. S., 43 N. J. 203. § 78.
v. S., 2 Ohio St. 500. § 420.
v. S., 17 Ohio St. 521. §§ 442, 449.
v. S., 31 Tex. 572. § 322.
v. S., 4 Tex. Ap. 127. § 1140.
v. S., 8 Tex. Ap. 496. § 546.
v. S., 15 Tex. Ap. 1. §§ 307, 391.
v. S., 17 Tex. Ap. 176. § 583.
v. S., 20 Tex. Ap. 233. § 709.
v. S., 20 Tex. Ap. 275. § 464.
v. S., 26 Tex. Ap. 322. §§ 274, 337, 339.
v. S., 27 Tex. Ap. 439. § 909.
v. S., 31 Tex. Ap. 234. § 265.
v. S., 32 Tex. Ap. 405. § 883.
v. S., 33 Tex. Ap. 306. § 271.
v. S., 33 Tex. Ap. 351. § 341.
v. S., 79 Wis. 546. § 463.
v. S., 9 Yerg. 353. § 1248.
S. v., 23 Ark. 550. §§ 1185, 1190.
S. v., 5 Blackf. 118. §§ 1218, 1221.
S. v., 31 Conn. 479. §§ 142, 299, 1169, 1170, 1184.
S. v., 39 Conn. 244. §§ 922, 925.
S. v., 15 Ia. 412. § 692.
S. v., 25 Ia. 128. §§ 325, 327, 335, 1147.
S. v., 78 Ia. 494. § 1113.
S. v., 81 Ia. 578. §§ 458, 1121.
S. v., 11 Ired. 70. § 537.
S. v., 1 Jones, 276. §§ 1223, 1225.
S. v., 65 Mo. 606. §§ 128, 259.
S. v., 66 Mo. 372. § 543.
S. v., 101 Mo. 316. §§ 546, 618.
S. v., 107 Mo. 78. §§ 1210, 1252.
S. v., 117 Mo. 395. § 500.
S. v., 121 Mo. 514. §§ 28, 580.
S. v., 12 N. H. 42. §§ 123, 500, 501, 511.
S. v., 14 N. H. 451. § 1273.
S. v., 26 N. H. 448. §§ 12, 211.
S. v., 63 N. H. 9. § 1316.
S. v., 27 N. J. 105. §§ 943, 950.
S. v., 69 N. C. 267. §§ 343, 345.
S. v., 82 N. C. 659. § 466.
S. v., 104 N. C. 714. § 50.
S. v., 104 N. C. 743. §§ 377, 872.
S. v., 1 Swan, 136. § 1135.
v. U. S., 160 U. S. 268. §§ 554, 623, 632.
U. S. v., 19 Fed. R. 39. §§ 1334, 1335.
U. S. v., 60 Fed. R. 738. §§ 750, 792.
U. S. v., 3 MacAr. 226. § 1352.
U. S. v., 2 Low. 232. § 867.
v. Watts, Beech. Bre. 42. § 564.
Moore's Lessee v. Pearce, 2 Har. & McH. 241. § 12.
Moorman, P. v., 86 Mich. 433. § 36.
Moose v. S., 49 Ark. 499. § 909.
Mooty, S. v., 3 Hill (S. C.), 187. § 1270.
Mopsey, Reg. v., 11 Cox, 143. § 756.
Mora v. P., 19 Colo. 255. § 425.
Morain v. Devlin, 132 Mass. 87. § 111.
Moran, P. v., 123 N. Y. 254. § 226.
S. v., 7 Ia. 236. § 362.

Moran, S. v., 46 Kan. 318. §§ 265, 271.
Morby, Reg. v., 8 Q. B. D. 571. § 286.
Mordecai, S. v., 68 N. C. 207. §§ 497, 501.
Morea, S. v., 2 Ala. 275. § 292.
Morean, Reg. v., 11 Q. B. 1028. § 865.
Morehead v. S., 9 Humph. 635. § 549.
Morehouse v. S., 35 Neb. 643. § 638.
Morel v. S., 89 Ind. 275. § 1281.
Morelock v. S., 90 Tenn. 528. § 431.
Moren, S. v., 48 Minn. 555. § 1315.
Moreno v. S., 24 Tex. Ap. 401. § 616.
Morey, S. v., 25 Oreg. 241. §§ 307, 358.
S. v., 2 Wis. 494. § 593.
Morgan v. C., 14 Bush, 106. §§ 404, 421.
v. C., 7 Grat. 592. § 1273.
C. v., 11 Bush, 601. § 276.
C. v., 107 Mass. 199. §§ 188, 1054, 1055, 1056.
C. v., 149 Mass. 314. § 1273.
v. Nolte, 37 Ohio St. 23. §§ 25, 66.
Reg. v., 6 Cox, 107. § 888.
Reg. v., Dears. 395. § 560.
v. S., 11 Ala. 289. §§ 1092, 1124.
v. S., 33 Ala. 413. § 275.
v. S., 81 Ala. 72. § 1233.
v. S., 42 Ark. 131. § 666.
v. S., 63 Ga. 307. § 495.
v. S., 31 Ind. 198. § 426.
v. S., 61 Ind. 447. § 592.
v. S., 63 Miss. 162. § 869.
v. S., 13 Sm. & M. 242. §§ 276, 323.
v. S., 3 Sneed, 475. § 306.
v. S., 16 Tex. Ap. 593. §§ 292, 333.
v. S., 25 Tex. Ap. 513. § 514.
v. S., 32 Tex. Ap. 413. § 1027.
S. v., 40 Conn. 44. § 1215.
S. v., 2 Dev. & B. 348. § 791.
S. v., 3 Heisk. 262. § 731.
S. v., 3 Ired. 186. §§ 232, 267, 299.
S. v., 35 La. An. 293. § 759.
S. v., 112 Mo. 202. § 698.
S. v., 59 N. H. 322. §§ 836, 838, 841.
S. v., 85 N. C. 581. § 381.
S. v., 95 N. C. 641. § 400.
S. v., 98 N. C. 641. §§ 520, 523.
S. v., 2 S. D. 32. § 42.
S. v., 40 S. C. 345. §§ 162, 300.
S. v., 35 W. Va. 260. § 416.
U. S. v., Morris. 341. § 880.
Moriarty, C. v., 135 Mass. 540. § 508.
v. S., 62 Miss. 654. § 303.
S. v., 74 Ind. 103. § 1019.
Morihan, C. v., 4 Allen, 585. §§ 930, 931.
Morine, P. v., 61 Cal. 367. § 303.
Morino, P. v., 85 Cal. 515. § 569.
Morissey v. P., 11 Mich. 327. §§ 552, 553.
Morman v. S., 24 Miss. 54. § 278.
Morningstar, C. v., 144 Pa. St. 103. § 41.
v. S., 52 Ala. 405. §§ 516, 601.
v. S., 55 Ala. 148. § 565.
v. S., 59 Ala. 30. § 565.
Morphin, S. v., 37 Mo. 373. § 551.
Morphy, P. v., 100 Cal. 84. § 667.
S. v., 33 Ia. 270. §§ 292, 365.
Morrell v. P., 32 Ill. 499. §§ 855, 859.
Morrill, Ex parte, 35 Fed. R. 261. § 906.
Morrill, C. v., 8 Cush. 571. §§ 682, 709.
v. S., 5 Tex. Ap. 447. § 1099.
v. S., 38 Wis. 428. § 44.
S. v., 68 Vt. 60. § 553.
Morris's Case, 2 East, P. C., 748. § 543.
Morris, C. v., 1 Va. Cas. 176. § 1054.
v. P., 4 Colo. Ap. 136. §§ 678, 679.
P. v., 80 Mich. 634. § 589.
v. Rome. 10 Ga. 532. § 1217.
Reg. v., 9 C. & P. 349. §§ 543, 582.
Reg. v., 3 Cox, 489. § 1152.
Rex v., 2 Burr. 1189 § 887.
Rex v., 2 East, P. C. 748. §§ 209, 713, 715.
Rex v., 2 Leach, 1096. § 212.
Rex v., Russ. & Ry. 270. § 145.
v. S., 84 Ala. 457. § 1026.
v. S., 97 Ala. 82. § 484.
v. S., 31 Ind. 189. § 1321.
v. S., 47 Ind. 503. § 1264.
v. S., 16 Miss. 762. § 808.
v. S., 38 Tex. 603. § 1145.
v. S., 62 Tex. 728. § 78.
v. S., 13 Tex. Ap. 65. § 281.
v. S., 17 Tex. Ap. 660. §§ 796, 802.
S. v., 47 Conn. 179. § 504.
S. v., 3 Hawks, 388. § 250.
S. v., 27 La. An. 480. § 511.
S. v., 3 Mo. 127. § 821.
S. v., 77 N. C. 512. § 75.
S. v., 84 N. C. 756. § 416.
U. S. v., 16 Blatch. 133. § 1327.
U. S. v., 18 Fed. R. 900. § 1332.
Morris & Essex R. Co., S. v., 23 N. J. 360. §§ 180, 183, 187.
v. S., 36 N. J. 553. § 1179.
Morris's Lessee v. Vanderen, 1 Dall. 64. § 12.
Morrisette v. S., 77 Ala. 71. § 565.
Morrisey, C. v., 86 Pa. St. 416. § 646.
Morrison v. C., 7 Dana, 218. § 1270.
C. v., 16 Gray, 224. §§ 122, 1148.
Pennsylvania v., Addis. 274. § 993.
P. v., 1 Park. Cr. R. 625. § 440.
P. v., 13 Wend. 399. § 843.
Reg. v., Bell, 158. § 543.
Rex v., 8 C. & P. 22. § 420.
v. S., 84 Ala. 405. § 162.
v. S., 17 Tex. Ap. 34. § 569.
S. v., 3 Dev. 299. § 1281.
S. v., 46 Kan. 679. § 923.
S. v., 104 Mo. 638. § 368.
S. v., 85 N. C. 561. § 609.
Morrissett v. C., 6 Grat. 673. § 1086.
Morrissey, C. v., 157 Mass. 471. § 29.
S. v., 22 Ia. 158. § 508.
S. v., 70 Me. 401. §§ 373a, 377.
Morrow, S. v., 26 Mo. 131. §§ 75, 96.
S. v., 40 S. C. 221. §§ 1148, 1150.
U. S. v., 4 Wash. C. C. 733. § 774.
Morse, C. v., 2 Mass. 128. § 778.
C. v., 2 Mass. 138. § 774.
C. v., 14 Mass. 217. § 546.
S. v., 1 Greene (Ia.), 503. § 881.
S. v., 52 Ia. 509. §§ 913, 917.
S. v., 90 Mo. 91. § 881.
Mortimer, P. v., 48 Mich. 37. § 157.

Morton, Reg. v., L. R. 2 C. C. 22. § 751.
Rex v., 2 East, P. C. 955. § 758.
v. Skinner, 48 Ind. 123. § 17.
v. S., 1 Lea, 498. § 602.
S. v., 27 Vt. 310. §§ 803, 810.
S. v., 8 Wis. 352. §§ 771, 772, 789.
Mosby, C. v., 163 Mass. 291. § 734.
Moschell v. S., 53 N. J. 498. § 946.
Mose v. S., 36 Ala. 211. §§ 397, 408.
Moseli, S. v., 49 Kan. 142. § 1274.
Moseley, C. v., 2 Va. Cas. 154. §§ 596, 598.
Reg. v., L. & C. 92. § 683.
v. S., 42 Tex. 78. § 546.
Mosely v. S., 9 Tex. Ap. 137. § 466.
v. S., 18 Tex. Ap. 311. § 1326.
v. S., 25 Tex. Ap. 515. § 896.
S. v., 14 Ala. 390. § 1285.
S. v., 42 La. An. 975. §§ 256, 257.
Moses, P. v., 140 N. Y. 214. § 1325.
v. S., 58 Ind. 185. §§ 1176, 1178, 1183.
v. S., 65 Miss. 56. § 41.
S. v., 2 Dev. 452. § 380.
U. S. v., 4 Wash. C. C. 726. § 771.
Mosher, S. v., 78 Ia. 321. § 36.
Mosier, C. v., 135 Pa. St. 221. § 1097.
Mosler, C. v., 4 Pa. St. 264. §§ 157, 342.
Mosley, Rex v., 1 Moody, 98. §§ 380, 426.
Mosquez v. S., 41 Tex. 226. § 608.
Moss, Reg. v., Dears. & B. 104. § 707.
v. S., 42 Ala. 546. § 588.
Most, P. v., 128 N. Y. 108. § 1005.
Reg. v., 7 Q. B. D. 244. §§ 196, 200.
Motsinger v. S., 123 Ind. 498. §§ 731, 736, 740.
Mott, C. v., 21 Pick. 492. § 102.
Rex v., 2 C. & P. 521. § 962.
v. S., 29 Ark. 147. § 529.
S. v., 16 Minn. 472. § 756.
S. v., 45 N. J. 494. §§ 1047, 1060.
Moulden v. S., 5 Lea, 577. § 678.
Moulton, C. v., 108 Mass. 307. §§ 740, 741.
S. v., 52 Kan. 69. § 1222.
S. v., 48 N. H. 485. § 88.
U. S. v., 5 Mason, 537. § 543.
Moultrie, S. v., 33 La. An. 1146. § 609.
S. v., 34 La. An. 489. §§ 519, 719, 721.
Mount v. C., 1 Duv. 90. § 765.
v. S., 7 Ind. 654. § 1286.
v. S., 7 Sm. & M. 277. § 1313.
Mountford, Rex v., 7 C. & P. 242. § 225.
Mount Pleasant v. Breeze, 11 Ia. 399. § 69.
Mowbray v. C., 11 Leigh, 643. § 803.
Mowry, S. v., 37 Kan. 369. §§ 141, 156, 157, 162.
Moxley, S. v., 115 Mo. 644. § 365.
Moyce v. Newington, 4 Q. B. D. 32. §§ 611, 712.
Moye v. S., 65 Ga. 754. § 557.
v. S., 9 Tex. Ap. 88. § 846.
Moyer v. C., 7 Pa. St. 439. § 830.
Moylan, C. v., 119 Mass. 109. § 1226.
Moyle, Rex v., 2 East, P. C. 1076. § 815.
Moynihan v. S., 70 Ind. 126. § 355.
Mucklow, Rex v., 1 Moody, 160. § 569.
Mueller, C. v., 81 Pa. St. 127. § 1216.
v. S., 76 Ind. 310. § 1321.
S. v., 85 Wis. 203. §§ 452, 454.
Mugler v. Kansas, 123 U. S. 623. §§ 29, 77, 1201, 1215.
Muir v. S., 8 Blackf. 154. § 855.
Mulcahy v. Reg., L. R. 3 H. L. 306. §§ 968, 1358.
Muldrew v. S., 12 Tex. Ap. 617. § 572.
Mulford v. P., 139 Ill. 586. § 629.
Mulkern, S. v., 85 Me. 106. § 455.
Mulkey, P. v., 65 Cal. 501. § 505.
Mullaly v. P., 86 N. Y. 365. § 539.
Mullaney, U. S. v., 32 Fed. R. 370. §§ 946, 951.
Mullany, Reg. v., L. & C. 593. § 863.
Mullen v. S., 96 Ind. 304. § 1246.
S. v., 30 Ia. 203. § 546.
S. v., 35 Ia. 199. § 1139.
S. v., 14 La. An. 570. §§ 12, 161, 303, 304.
Mullens v. S., 82 Ala. 42. § 1156.
Mullenhoff, S. v., 74 Ia. 271. §§ 1223, 1226, 1227, 1248, 1253.
Muller v. Buncombe Co. Com'rs, 89 N. C. 171. § 1228.
P. v., 96 N. Y. 408. §§ 128, 1157.
Mulligan v. S., 25 Tex. Ap. 199. § 520.
Mullikin, S. v., 8 Blackf. 260. §§ 8, 12, 1137.
Mullin v. S., 37 Tex. 337. § 564.
U. S. v., 71 Fed. R. 682. § 922.
Mulling v. S., 74 Ga. 10. § 1131.
Mullinix v. P., 76 Ill. 211. §§ 1237, 1262.
v. S., 43 Ind. 511. § 97.
S. v., 6 Blackf. 554. § 1273.
Mullins v. Collins, L. R. 9 Q. B. 292. § 189.
v. S., 37 Tex. 337. § 125.
Mulreaty, Rex v., 1 Russ. Cr. 697. § 1153.
Mulreed v. S., 107 Ind. 62. § 1257.
Mumford, S. v., 1 Dev. 519. § 878.
S. v., 73 Mo. 647. § 1315.
Munch, S. v., 22 Minn. 67. §§ 649, 655.
Munco, S. v., 12 La. An. 625. §§ 273, 274.
Munday v. C., 81 Ky. 233. § 315.
v. Maiden, 33 L. T. 377. § 255.
Reg. v., 2 F. & F. 170. § 209.
Rex v. 2 East. P. C. 594. § 560.
S. v., 78 N. C. 460. § 671.
Munger, S. v., 15 Vt. 290. § 1274.
Municipality v. Wheeler, 10 La. An. 745. § 78.
Munkers v. S., 87 Ala. 94. §§ 1118, 1119.
Munn v. Illinois, 94 U. S. 113. § 40.
P. v., 65 Cal. 211. § 332.
Munroe, P. v., 100 Cal. 664. § 758.
Munsey, C. v., 112 Mass. 287. § 145.
Munslow, Reg. v., 1 Q. B. D. (1895) 758. §§ 1042, 1053, 1067.
Munson, C. v., 127 Mass. 459. § 1131.
Reg. v., 2 Cox, 186. § 520.
v. S., 4 Greene (Ia.), 483. § 596.
v. S., 79 Ind. 541. § 794.
S. v., 25 Ohio St. 381. § 1259.

Munton, Rex v., 3 C. & P. 491. § 890.
Murat, P. v., 45 Cal. 281. § 280.
Murback, P. v., 64 Cal. 369. § 338.
Murchison v. S., 24 Tex. Ap. 8. § 1019.
Murdoch, S. v., 35 La. An. 729. § 271.
S. v., 71 Me. 454. §§ 210, 454, 1239.
Murdock, Reg. v., 2 Den. 298. § 650.
v. S., 65 Ala. 520. §§ 248, 252.
Murdy, S. v., 81 Ia. 603. § 302.
Murio v. S., 31 Tex. Ap. 210. § 716.
Murphey v. S., 43 Neb. 34. §§ 265, 268, 280.
Murphy, In re, 109 Ill. 31. § 121.
v. C., 92 Ky. 485. §§ 169, 170.
C. v., 2 Allen, 163. § 454.
C. v., 12 Allen, 449. § 737.
C. v., 11 Cush. 472. § 374.
C. v., 2 Gray, 510. § 145.
C. v., 95 Ky. 38. § 1265.
C. v., 145 Mass. 250. § 190.
C. v., 147 Mass. 577. § 1270.
C. v., 153 Mass. 290. § 1243.
C. v., 155 Mass. 284. §§ 1258, 1279.
v. Hobbs, 7 Colo. 541. § 11.
v. P., 9 Colo. 435. §§ 332, 338, 368.
v. P., 37 Ill. 447. § 333.
v. P., 90 Ill. 59. § 1262.
v. P., 104 Ill. 528. §§ 546, 563, 609.
v. P., 120 Ill. 234. § 560.
v. P., 63 N. Y. 590. §§ 416, 420.
P. v., 39 Cal. 52. § 386.
P. v., 47 Cal. 103. § 548.
P. v., 93 Mich. 41. §§ 1216, 1232, 1279.
P. v., 101 N. Y. 126. § 1151.
Reg. v., 8 C. & P. 297. §§ 959, 968.
Reg. v., 6 Cox, 340. §§ 206, 573, 734.
Reg. v., 13 Cox, 298. § 675.
Rex v., 6 C. & P. 103. §§ 196, 208.
v. S., 37 Ala. 142. § 308.
v. S., 50 Ga. 150. § 1074.
v. S., 31 Ind. 511. §§ 332, 336.
v. S., 120 Ind. 115. §§ 249, 464.
v. S., 9 Lea, 373. § 1276.
v. S., 62 Miss. 97. § 1163.
v. S., 6 Tex. Ap. 420. § 573.
v. S., 6 Tex. Ap. 554. § 799.
v. S., 86 Wis. 626. § 514.
S. v., 6 Ala. 765. §§ 446, 959.
S. v., 6 Ala. 845. § 597.
S. v., 8 Blackf. 498. §§ 538, 586.
S. v., 21 Ind. 441. § 271.
S. v., 35 La. An. 622. § 269.
S. v., 46 La. An. 415. § 758.
S. v., 61 Me. 56. §§ 337, 339.
S. v., 27 N. J. 112. §§ 106, 220, 1148.
S. v., 17 R. I. 698. §§ 18, 748, 771, 772, 802, 803.
S. v., 39 Tex. 46. § 594.
U. S. v., 4 Cranch, C. C. 681. § 546.
U. S. v., MacAr. & M. 375. § 560.
Murrah v. S., 51 Miss. 652. § 47.
v. S., 51 Miss. 675. § 816.
S. v., 25 Tex. 759. §§ 255, 260.
Murray v. C., 79 Pa. St. 311. §§ 304, 305, 359.
C. v., 2 Ashm. 41. §§ 359, 425, 426, 430, 431.
Murray, C. v., 14 Gray, 397. § 1159.
C. v., 135 Mass. 530. § 896.
C. v., 138 Mass. 508. § 1248.
P. v., 8 Cal. 519. § 509.
P. v., 10 Cal. 309. §§ 307, 386.
P. v., 14 Cal. 159. §§ 225, 1122.
P. v., 67 Cal. 103. § 509.
P. v., 57 Mich. 396. § 934.
v. Reg., 7 Q. B. 700. § 1079.
Reg. v., 5 Cox, 509. § 351.
Rex v., 5 C. & P. 145. §§ 640, 656.
Rex v., 1 Moody, 276. § 624.
v. S., 48 Ala. 675. §§ 506, 508, 511.
v. S., 85 Ga. 378. § 337.
v. S., 1 Tex. Ap. 417. §§ 333, 342.
v. S., 21 Tex. Ap. 620. §§ 86, 813.
S. v., 55 Ia. 530. §§ 581, 587, 609.
S. v., 15 Me. 100. §§ 930, 931, 977.
S. v., 126 Mo. 526. § 195.
S. v., 126 Mo. 611. § 420.
S. v., 63 N. C. 31. § 460.
S. v., 11 Oreg. 413. § 156.
Murrow, Reg. v., 1 Moody, 456. § 256.
Murry v. C., 5 Leigh, 720. § 772.
Murtagh, C. v., 1 Ashm. 272. § 1083.
Murton, Reg. v., 3 F. & F. 492. § 292.
Muscoe v. C., 86 Va. 443. § 328.
v. C., 87 Va. 460. § 419.
Muscot, Reg. v., 10 Mod. 192. §§ 891, 892.
Muse, S. v., 4 Dev. & B. 319. §§ 1210, 1274.
Musgang, S. v., 51 Minn. 556. § 543.
Musgrave v. Medex, 19 Ves. 652. § 871.
v. S., 133 Ind. 297. §§ 960, 966.
v. S., 28 Tex. Ap. 57. § 615.
Musquez v. S., 41 Tex. 226. § 548.
Mutchler, In re, 55 Kan. 164. § 566.
Mutters, Reg. v., L. & C. 511. § 558.
Mycall, C. v., 2 Mass. 136. §§ 756, 906.
Mycock, Reg. v., 12 Cox, 28. §§ 1101, 1105.
Myerfield, S. v., Phill. 108. § 232.
Myers v. C., 90 Va. 705. § 333.
C. v., 146 Pa. St. 24. §§ 485, 954, 956.
Pennsylvania v., Addis. 320. § 617.
v. P., 26 Ill. 173. § 552.
v. P., 67 Ill. 503. § 1271.
P. v., 20 Cal. 76. § 529.
P. v., 20 Cal. 518. §§ 178, 179.
v. S., 62 Ala. 599. §§ 139, 303, 307, 416, 417.
v. S., 84 Ala. 11. § 452.
v. S., 1 Conn. 502. §§ 128, 1322.
v. S., 92 Ind. 390. §§ 28, 92.
v. S., 93 Ind. 251. § 1220.
v. S., 101 Ind. 379. § 796.
v. S., 121 Ind. 15. § 252.
v. S., 3 Sneed, 98. §§ 1282, 1285.
v. S., 33 Tex. 525. § 303.
v. S., 7 Tex. Ap. 640. § 409.
S. v., 10 Ia. 448. § 803.
S. v., 19 Ia. 517. §§ 130, 203, 232, 239.
S. v., 54 Kan. 206. § 42.
S. v., 82 Mo. 558. § 546.
S. v., 12 Wash. 77. § 404.

Myers, U. S. v., 1 Cranch, C. C. 310. § 232.
Mynatt v. S., 8 Lea, 47. § 1135.
Myott, Reg. v., 6 Cox, 406. § 750.

Nabors v. S., 82 Ala. 8. § 519.
Nadal, S. v., 69 Ia. 478. §§ 1072, 1073, 1077, 1079, 1083.
Nagle, C. v., 117 Mass. 142. § 1324.
  C. v., 157 Mass. 554. § 1279.
Nail v. S., 70 Miss. 32. § 989.
Nailor's Case, Foster, 278. §§ 139, 303.
Nailor, U. S. v., 4 Cranch, C. C. 372. § 1145.
Nairn v. S., 18 Tex. Ap. 260. § 1289.
Nalley v. S., 28 Tex. Ap. 387. § 391.
  v. S., 30 Tex. Ap. 456. §§ 304, 311.
Nancy v. S., 6 Ala. 483. § 271.
Napier v. S., 50 Ala. 168. § 1302.
Napoleon v. S., 3 Tex. Ap. 522. § 631.
Narrows Island Club, S. v., 100 N. C. 477. § 1195.
Nash, P. v., 1 Ida. 206. §§ 925, 929.
  v. Primm, 1 Mo. 178. § 11.
  Reg. v., 2 Den. 448. § 773.
  Reg. v., 2 Den. 493. § 770.
  Rex v., 2 East, P. C. 1021. § 520.
  v. S., 2 Greene (Ia.), 286. §§ 370, 380.
  v. S., 2 Tex. Ap. 362. §§ 241, 268.
  v. S., 20 Tex. Ap. 384. § 503.
  v. S., 32 Tex. Ap. 368. § 1027.
  S. v., 7 Ia. 347. §§ 421, 425, 426.
  S. v., 86 N. C. 650. §§ 239, 252.
  S. v., 88 N. C. 618. § 239.
  S. v., 109 N. C. 824. §§ 256, 446, 464.
Nashville, etc. R. Co. v. Alabama, 128 U. S. 96. § 38.
Nason, C. v., 9 Gray, 125. §§ 675, 711.
Natal, S. v., 41 La. An. 887. § 71.
Nathan, U. S. v., 61 Fed. R. 936. § 1332.
Nattrass, Reg. v., 15 Cox, 73. § 523.
Naylor, C. v., 34 Pa. St. 86. § 1264.
  P. v., 82 Cal. 607. §§ 865, 878.
  Reg. v., L. R. 1 C. C. 4. § 689.
Neaderhouser v. S., 28 Ind. 257. § 1186.
Neagle, In re, 135 U. S. 1. § 313.
Neal v. C., 22 Grat. 917. § 1285.
  C. v., 10 Mass. 152. § 145.
  v. S., 53 Ala. 465. § 509.
  v. S., 54 Ga. 281. § 242.
  S. v., 37 Me. 468. § 274.
  S. v., 42 Mo. 119. § 877.
  S. v., 27 N. H. 131. § 191.
Neale, Reg. v., 1 C. & K. 591. § 442.
  Reg. v., 9 C. & P. 431. §§ 997, 1003.
  U. S. v., 14 Fed. R. 767. § 854.
Neales v. S., 10 Mo. 498. §§ 1229, 1274.
Needham v. S., 1 Tex. 139. § 1310.
  v. S., 19 Tex. 332. § 1279.
Neel v. S., 33 Tex. Ap. 408. § 554.
Neeley, S. v., 20 Ia. 108. §§ 139, 303, 304, 309, 382.
Neely v. S., 60 Ark. 66. § 1258.
  v. S., 8 Tex. Ap. 64. §§ 133, 571.
  v. S., 32 Tex. Ap. 370. § 1057.
  S. v., 74 N. C. 425. § 463.
Nees, S. v., 47 Ark. 553. § 878.
Neese, S. v., 38 S. C. 261. § 1219.
Neff, S. v., 58 Ind. 516. § 242.
Negus, Reg. v., L. R. 2 C. C. 34. § 626.
Nehr v. S., 35 Neb. 638. § 1182.
Neideiser v. S., 6 Baxt. 499. § 1237.
Neiderluck v. S., 23 Tex. Ap. 38. §§ 501, 509.
Neil, P. v., 91 Cal. 465. § 950.
Neill, Ex parte, 32 Tex. Ap. 275. §§ 65, 66.
Neilson v. Garza, 2 Woods, 287. § 35.
Neimeier, S. v., 66 Ia. 634. §§ 679, 684.
Neis, S. v., 108 N. C. 787. § 1240.
Nelms v. S., 84 Ga. 466. §§ 1073, 1079.
  v. S., 13 Sm. & M. 500. § 451.
Nelson v. P., 23 N. Y. 293. §§ 257, 271.
  P. v., 56 Cal. 77. §§ 484, 546.
  P. v., 13 Johns. 340. § 839.
  v. S., 82 Ala. 44. § 753.
  v. S., 97 Ala. 79. § 36.
  v. S., 32 Ark. 192. § 889.
  v. S., 6 Baxt. 418. § 351.
  v. S., 32 Fla. 244. § 362.
  v. S., 7 Humph. 541. §§ 426, 427.
  v. S., 2 Ind. 249. § 271.
  v. S., 47 Miss. 621. § 861.
  v. S., 33 Neb. 528. § 298.
  v. S., 2 Swan, 237. § 391.
  v. S., 1 Tex. Ap. 41. § 380.
  v. S., 2 Tex. Ap. 227. § 260.
  v. S., 25 Tex. Ap. 599. § 1321.
  S. v., 28 La. An. 46. § 800.
  S. v., 38 La. An. 942. § 1033.
  S. v., 29 Me. 329. §§ 28, 147, 714, 715.
  S. v., 98 Mo. 414. § 195.
  S. v., 101 Mo. 464. § 342.
  S. v., 118 Mo. 124. § 391.
  S. v., 11 Nev. 334. § 473.
  S. v., 8 N. H. 163. § 589.
  S. v., 28 S. C. 16. § 536.
  v. U. S., 30 Fed. R. 112. § 1217.
  U. S. v., 1 Abb. (U. S.) 135. § 780.
  U. S. v., 52 Fed. R. 646. § 963.
Nepp v. C., 2 Duv. 546. § 1228.
Nesbit, C. v., 34 Pa. St. 398. §§ 1322, 1323.
Nesbitt, P. v., 102 Cal. 327. § 710.
  Reg. v., 6 Cox, 320. § 744.
Netso v. S., 24 Fla. 363. § 1218.
Nett, S. v., 50 Wis. 524. § 307.
Nettlebush, S. v., 20 Ia. 257. § 429.
Nettles, Ex parte, 58 Ala. 268. § 342.
  v. S., 49 Ala. 35. § 943.
Nettleton, Rex v., 1 Moody, 259. § 626.
Neubrandt v. S., 53 Wis. 89. § 514.
Neuendorff v. Duryea, 69 N. Y. 557. § 1319.
Neuman v. S., 76 Wis. 112. § 1226.
Neumann, P. v., 85 Mich. 98. §§ 1233, 1259.
Neuner, S. v., 49 Conn. 232. § 110.
Nevada v. Hutchins, 59 Ia. 506. § 69.
Neverson, U. S. v., 1 Mackey, 152. §§ 419, 421.
Neville, S. v., 6 Jones, 423. § 341.
Nevin v. Ladue, 3 Denio, 437. §§ 1218, 1220.
Nevins, S. v., 23 Vt. 519. § 753.

Nevling v. C., 98 Pa. St. 322. §§ 162, 360.
New v. S., 34 Tex. 100. § 1216.
S. v., 22 Minn. 76. § 638.
New Hampton v. Conroy, 56 Ia. 498. § 69.
New Orleans v. Houston, 119 U. S. 265. § 1334.
v. Miller, 7 La. An. 651. §§ 1285, 1306.
v. Steamship Co., 20 Wall. 387. § 9.
New York & G. S. R. Co. v. S., 50 N. J. 303. §§ 1185, 1188.
New York, etc. R., C. v., 112 Mass. 412. § 1187.
P. v., 89 N. Y. 266. § 1187.
Newall, Reg. v., 6 Cox, 21. § 886.
Newbegin, S. v., 25 Me. 500. § 500.
Newberry, P. v., 20 Cal. 439. § 208.
S. v., 26 Ia. 467. §§ 124, 269, 274, 382.
S. v., 43 Mo. 429. § 58.
Newboult, Reg. v., L. R. 1 C. C. 344. § 526.
Newby, S. v., 64 N. C. 23. § 829.
v. T., 1 Oreg. 163. § 995.
Newcomb v. S., 37 Miss. 383. §§ 174, 307, 377, 413.
S. v., 1 Houst. Cr. C. 66. § 303.
Newell v. C., 2 Wash. (Va.) 88. § 950.
C. v., 5 Gray, 76. § 5.
C. v., 7 Mass. 245. §§ 18, 432, 433, 505.
Resp. v., 3 Yeates, 407. §§ 83, 852, 881.
S. v., 1 Mo. 248. §§ 667, 693.
Newill, Rex v., 1 Moody, 458. § 526.
Newkirk, S. v., 49 Mo. 84. § 826.
Newland, Reg. v., 2 Cox, 283. § 552.
v. S., 30 Ind. 111. § 831.
S. v., 7 Ia. 242. § 788.
S. v., 27 Kan. 764. § 139.
Newman, Ex parte, 9 Cal. 502. § 1319.
v. Jones, 17 Q. B. D. 132. § 189.
Reg. v., 3 C. & K. 240. § 886.
Reg. v., 1 El. & B. 268. §§ 1051, 1054.
Reg. v., 8 Q. B. D. 706. § 629.
v. S., 88 Ala. 115. § 1236.
v. S., 63 Ga. 533. § 1261.
v. S., 7 Lea, 617. § 1253.
S. v., 9 Nev. 48. §§ 548, 553.
Newport N. & M. V. Co. v. U. S., 61 Fed. R. 488. § 1338.
Newton, C. v., 123 Mass. 420. § 922.
C. v., 8 Pick. 234. § 1320.
v. Harland, 2 Scott, N. R. 474. § 836.
Reg. v., 1 C. & K. 469. § 856.
Reg. v., 1 F. & F. 641. § 425.
Reg. v., 2 Moody, 59. § 764.
Reg. v., 2 M. & Rob. 503. § 1082.
v. S., 92 Ala. 33. § 275.
v. S., 94 Ga. 593. § 1017.
v. S., 3 Tex. Ap. 245. § 829.
S. v., 1 Greene (Ia.), 160. §§ 872, 876.
S. v., 59 Ind. 173. §§ 100, 104.
S. v., 44 Ia. 45. §§ 134, 443, 444, 451, 464, 1105.
S. v., 4 Nev. 410. § 332.
S. v., 50 N. J. 534. § 34.
Newton, S. v., 26 Ohio St. 265. § 648.
S. v., 42 Vt. 537. § 602.
U. S. v., 48 Fed. R. 218; 52 Fed. R. 275. §§ 956, 966, 968, 969, 972.
Newton Mfg. Co. v. White, 63 Ga. 697. § 113.
Neyce, P. v., 86 Cal. 393. § 654.
Neyland v. S., 13 Tex. Ap. 536. § 391.
Neylon, C. v., 159 Mass. 541. § 1243.
Nezzell, Reg. v., 3 C. & K. 150. § 195.
Ng Loy Hoe, In re, 53 Fed. R. 914. § 1344.
Nibbs, Rex v., 1 Moody, 25. § 593.
Nichol, Rex v., Russ. & Ry. 130. §§ 238, 462.
Nicholas, Reg. v., 2 C. & K. 246. § 456.
v. S., 23 Tex. Ap. 317. § 442.
Nicholl, Rex. v., 1 B. & Ad. 21. § 878.
Nicholls, Reg. v., 2 Cox, 182. §§ 229, 454.
Reg. v., 13 Cox, 75. § 286.
Reg. v., 1 F. & F. 51. § 726.
Rex v., 13 East, 412, n. § 981.
v. S., 68 Wis. 416. §§ 15, 501.
Nichols, In re, 48 Fed. R. 164. § 44.
v. C., 11 Bush, 575. §§ 329, 330, 338, 403.
v. C., 78 Ky. 180. § 551.
C. v., 10 Allen, 199. § 128.
C. v., 114 Mass. 285. § 461.
C. v., 10 Met. 259. § 188.
v. P., 17 N. Y. 114. § 555.
v. S., 89 Ind. 298. §§ 115, 1189, 1193.
v. S., 127 Ind. 406. § 1106*a*.
v. S., 46 Miss. 284. § 377.
v. S., 8 Ohio St. 435. §§ 160, 161, 259.
v. S., 24 Tex. Ap. 137. § 332.
v. S., 28 Tex. Ap. 105. §§ 553, 569, 575.
v. S., 35 Wis. 308. §§ 18, 217.
S. v., 8 Conn. 496. §§ 278, 279.
S. v., 1 Houst. Cr. C. 114. § 667.
S. v., 38 Ia. 110. § 799.
S. v., 12 Rich. 672. § 816.
v. Thomas, 4 Mass. 232. § 922.
Nicholson's Case, 1 Lewin, 300. § 995.
Nicholson v. P., 29 Ill. Ap. 57. § 1176.
Rex v., 1 East, P. C. 346. § 382.
Rex v., 2 East, P. C. 669. § 560.
v. S., 18 Ala. 529. § 774.
v. S., 100 Ala. 132. § 36.
v. S., 9 Baxt. 258. § 221.
v. S., 3 Tex. Ap. 31. § 834.
S. v., 14 La. An. 785. §§ 766, 789.
S. v., 2 Murph. 135. § 1185.
U. S. v., 3 Woods, 215. § 948.
Nickerson, C. v., 5 Allen, 518. §§ 190, 197, 485, 486, 489, 490.
S. v., 46 Ia. 447. §§ 867, 875, 880.
U. S. v., 1 Sprague, 232. § 859.
Nickleson, S. v., 45 La. An. 1172. §§ 150, 530.
Nickless, Reg. v., 8 C. & P. 757. § 197.
Nicolas, Reg. v., 6 Cox, 120. § 426.
Nielsen, In re, 131 U. S. 176. §§ 1086, 1094.
Niland v. S., 19 Tex. Ap. 166. § 341.

Niles, S. v., 47 Vt. 82. §§ 440, 455.
Ninenger v. S., 25 Tex. Ap. 449. § 1232.
Nipper, S. v., 95 N. C. 653. § 592.
Nishimura Ekiu v. U. S., 142 U. S. 651. § 1344.
Nixon v. P., 3 Ill. 267. § 279.
Rex v., 7 C. & P. 442. § 499.
v. S., 76 Ind. 524. § 1252.
v. S., 31 Tex. Ap. 205. § 615.
S. v., 32 Kan. 205. §§ 156, 179.
S. v., 18 Vt. 70. §§ 1140, 1143.
Noakes v. P., 25 N. Y. 380. §§ 752, 753, 771.
Reg. v., 4 F. & F. 920. § 287.
Noble v. S., 59 Ala. 73. § 649.
v. S., 22 Ohio St. 541. §§ 1086, 1120, 1121, 1122.
S. v., 15 Me. 476. § 592.
Noblett, S. v., 2 Jones, 418. § 377.
Nocton, S. v., 121 Mo. 537. § 426.
Noecker v. P., 91 Ill. 468. §§ 1252, 1281.
v. P., 91 Ill. 494. § 1237.
Noelke, P. v., 94 N. Y. 137. §§ 117, 1317, 1318.
Noftsinger v. S., 7 Tex. Ap. 301. §§ 194, 421.
Nolan, P. v., 22 Mich. 229. §§ 500, 518.
S. v., 92 Ia. 491, 61 N. W. R. 181. § 431.
S. v., 48 Kan. 723. § 525.
S. v., 37 Minn. 16. § 82.
S. v., 15 R. I. 529. § 20.
v. Traber, 49 Md. 460. § 147.
Noland v. S., 19 Ohio, 131. § 218.
S. v., 29 Ind. 212. § 1309.
S. v., 111 Mo. 473. § 655.
Noles v. S., 24 Ala. 672. §§ 252, 361.
v. S., 26 Ala. 31. §§ 340, 416.
Nolty v. S., 17 Wis. 668. § 922.
Noon, Reg. v., 6 Cox, 137. § 338.
Nordstrom, S. v., 7 Wash. 506. § 405.
Norfolk & W. R. Co. v. Pennsylvania, 136 U. S. 114. § 44.
S. v., 33 W. Va. 440. § 1323.
Norman, Reg. v., Car. & M. 501. § 641.
v. S., 26 Tex. Ap. 221. § 341.
S. v., 2 Dev. 222. § 1079.
S. v., 110 N. C. 484. § 676.
Norris, Reg. v., 9 C. & P. 241. § 817.
Rex v., 2 Keny. 300. § 962.
Rex v., Russ. & Ry. 69. § 497.
v. S., 16 Ala. 776. § 173.
v. S., 50 Ala. 126. § 509.
v. S., 87 Ala. 85. § 463.
v. S., 33 Miss. 373. § 553.
v. S., 25 Ohio St. 217. §§ 105, 684, 696, 705.
S. v., 9 N. H. 96. §§ 854, 865.
S. v., 59 N. H. 536. §§ 1023, 1024.
Norsch, U. S. v., 42 Fed. R. 417. § 1346.
North v. P., 139 Ill. 81. §§ 425, 427, 429.
Reg. v., 8 Cox, 43. § 560.
Rex v., 2 East, P. C. 1021. § 520.
S. v., 27 Mo. 464. § 44.
S. v., 95 Mo. 615. § 617.
Northcot v. S., 43 Ala. 330. § 829.
Northern Cent. Ry. v. C., 90 Pa. St. 300. §§ 183, 1184, 1191.
Northern Pac. Exp. Co., S. v., 58 Minn. 403. § 46.
Northumberland, S. v., 46 N. H. 156. § 1193.
Northway, U. S. v., 120 U. S. 327. § 1340.
Norton v. Ladd, 5 N. H. 203. § 538.
v. P., 8 Cow. 137. §§ 200, 546.
P. v., 7 Barb. 477. § 1228.
Reg. v., 8 C. & P. 196. § 707.
Reg. v., 8 C. & P. 671. § 730.
v. S., 15 Ark. 71. §§ 1285, 1315.
v. S., 98 Ind. 347. § 368.
v. S., 72 Miss. 128. §§ 1112, 1113, 1114.
v. S., 14 Tex. 387. § 255.
S. v., 41 Ia. 430. § 1249.
S. v., 67 Ia. 641. § 1253.
S. v., 2 Ired. 40. § 32.
S. v., 76 Mo. 180. §§ 122, 689.
S. v., 23 N. J. 33. §§ 95, 955, 962, 966.
S. v., 19 Tex. 102. § 1302.
U. S. v., 91 U. S. 566. § 1327.
Norvell v. S., 50 Ala. 174. § 112.
Norwood v. S., 20 Tex. Ap. 306. § 618.
S. v., 94 N. C. 935. § 1289.
S. v., 115 N. C. 789. §§ 332, 333.
Nott, C. v., 135 Mass. 269. § 578.
Nowacryk v. P., 139 Ill. 336. §§ 352, 363.
Nowell v. S., 94 Ga. 588. § 1196.
S. v., 60 N. H. 199. § 213.
Noxon, C. v., 121 Mass. 42. § 1190.
Noyes v. S., 41 N. J. 418. §§ 211, 978.
S. v., 30 N. H. 279. §§ 25, 62, 66, 77, 1178, 1179, 1182, 1210.
S. v., 47 Me. 189. § 1319.
S. v., 25 Vt. 415. § 979.
Nuckolls v. C., 32 Grat. 884. §§ 1285, 1296.
Nueslein, S. v., 25 Mo. 111. §§ 275, 345, 355.
Nugent v. S., 18 Ala. 521. §§ 450, 460.
S. v., 71 Mo. 136. § 419.
Nulty, S. v., 47 Kan. 259. § 1276.
S. v., 57 Vt. 543. § 1281.
Nunn v. S., 1 Ga. 243. § 1030.
Nute, S. v., 63 N. H. 79. §§ 651, 653.
Nuthill v. S., 11 Humph. 247. § 204.
Nutzel v. S., 60 Ga. 264. § 548.
Nye v. P., 35 Mich. 16. §§ 197, 322, 336.
S. v., 32 Kan. 201. § 1281.

Oakley, Rex v., 4 B. & Ad. 307. § 838.
S. v., 51 Ark. 112. § 596.
S. v., 103 N. C. 408. § 688.
Oaks, C. v., 113 Mass. 8. §§ 1016, 1183.
Oates, Reg. v., Dears. 459. § 670.
O'Bannon v. S., 76 Ga. 29. § 572.
Ober, C. v., 12 Cush. 493. § 44.
O'Blenis v. S., 47 N. J. 279. § 460.
O'Blennis v. S., 12 Mo. 311. § 191.
O'Brian, Reg. v., 2 C. & K. 115. § 377.
U. S. v., 3 Dill. 381. § 920.
O'Brien v. C., 89 Ky. 354. §§ 391, 416.
C. v., 2 Brews. 566. § 601.

O'Brien, C. v., 12 Cush. 84. §§ 728, 977.
C. v., 8 Gray, 487. § 1145.
C. v., 134 Mass. 198. §§ 1260, 1270.
C. v., 140 Pa. St. 555. § 988.
P. v., 64 Cal. 53. § 28.
P. v., 106 Cal. 104. § 638.
P. v., 60 Mich. 8. §§ 825, 831, 833.
P. v., 92 Mich. 17. § 414.
Reg. v., 4 Cox, 398. § 503.
v. S., 63 Ind. 242. § 1229.
v. S., 6 Tex. Ap. 665. § 896.
v. S., 7 Tex. Ap. 181. § 896.
v. S., 10 Tex. Ap. 544. § 1313.
v. S., 27 Tex. Ap. 448. § 509.
S. v., 81 Ia. 88. §§ 292, 325.
S. v., 81 Ia. 93. § 500.
S. v., 32 N. J. 169. §§ 349, 350.
S. v., 2 Root, 516. § 520.
S. v., 94 Tenn. 79. § 635.
O'Bryan v. S., 48 Ark. 42. § 1237.
v. S., 27 Tex. Ap. 339. § 860.
O'Callaghan, P. v., 2 Ida. 143. § 361.
Ocean Ins. Co. v. Fields, 2 Story, 59. § 11.
Ochs v. P., 124 Ill. 399. §§ 94, 674, 681, 705, 960, 962, 967, 968, 969, 973, 975, 989.
v. P., 25 Ill. Ap. 379. § 956.
Ochsner, S. v., 9 Mo. Ap. 216. § 1318.
O'Connell, C. v., 12 Allen, 451. § 609.
v. P., 87 N. Y. 377. §§ 175, 179.
v. Reg., 11 Cl. & F. 155. §§ 966, 978, 981.
v. S., 55 Ga. 191. § 716.
v. S., 55 Ga. 296. § 718.
v. S., 6 Minn. 279. § 89.
v. S., 18 Tex. 343. §§ 376, 391.
S. v., 26 Ind. 266. § 520.
O'Conner, C. v., 107 Mass. 219. § 1097.
Reg. v., 15 Cox, 3. § 662.
O'Connor, C. v., 7 Allen, 583. § 1031.
v. S., 30 Ala. 9. § 698.
v. S., 9 Fla. 215. § 392.
v. S., 64 Ga. 125. § 347.
v. S., 45 Ind. 347. § 1247.
v. S., 105 Mo. 121. § 479.
S. v., 13 La. An. 486. § 96.
S. v., 49 Me. 594. § 1244.
S. v., 58 Minn. 193. §§ 128, 189.
S. v., 31 Mo. 389. § 303.
S. v., 11 Nev. 416. § 279.
T. v., 5 Dak. 397. § 1210.
U. S. v., 31 Fed. R. 449. §§ 946, 948.
Odam, S. v., 2 Lea, 220. § 1266.
Oddy, Reg. v., 2 Den. 264. § 726.
Reg. v., T. & M. 593. § 615.
O'Dea v. S., 16 Neb. 241. § 819.
Odel, S. v., 3 Brev. 552. §§ 771, 808.
Odell, P. v., 1 Dak. 189. §§ 271, 279.
S. v., 8 Blackf. 396. § 917.
S. v., 42 Ia. 75. § 1137.
Oden, S. v., 10 Ind. Ap. 136. § 914.
Oder v. C., 80 Ky. 32. § 303.
v. S., 26 Fla. 520. § 1296.
Odgers, Reg. v., 2 M. & Rob. 479. § 280.
Odle v. S., 13 Tex. Ap. 612. § 476.
Odlin, C. v., 23 Pick. 275. §§ 1246, 1273.
O'Donnell, C. v., 8 Allen, 548. § 1217.
C. v., 150 Mass. 502. § 251.
S. v., 10 R. I. 472. § 1252.
O'Driscoll, S. v., 3 Brev. 526. § 913.
Odum, S. v., 11 Tex. 12. § 593.
Offord, Rex v., 5 C. & P. 168. § 156.
Offutt, S. v., 4 Blackf. 355. § 859.
O'Flaherty, S. v., 7 Nev. 153. §§ 266, 273.
O'Flinn v. S., 66 Miss. 7. §§ 1226, 1237.
Ogden v. S., 15 Tex. Ap. 454. § 374.
v. S., 12 Wis. 532. §§ 216, 218.
Ogle v. S., 16 Tex. Ap. 361. § 199.
Oglesby v. S., 39 Tex. 53. § 487.
Ogletree v. S., 28 Ala. 693. §§ 265, 274.
O'Gorman, S. v., 68 Mo. 179. § 906.
O'Grady v. S., 36 Neb. 320. § 161.
O'Hagan, S. v., 38 Ia. 504. § 875.
O'Hara, C. v., 10 Gray. 469. § 546.
S. v., 92 Mo. 59. §§ 330, 365.
O'Herrin v. S., 14 Ind. 420. § 160.
Ohio River R. Co., S. v., 38 W. Va. 242. § 1187.
O'Kean, C. v., 152 Mass. 584. § 1222.
S. v., 35 La. An. 901. § 639.
O'Keefe, C. v., 121 Mass. 59. § 654.
S. v., 41 Vt. 691. § 1272.
O'Keife v. S., 24 Ohio St. 175. § 90.
O'Kelley v. T., 1 Oreg. 51. § 386.
Okie, U. S. v., 5 Blatch. 516. § 1330.
Olcott v. S., 8 Blackf. 6. § 82.
Old v. C., 18 Grat. 915. § 950.
Oldham, Reg. v., 2 Den. 472. § 516.
Olds v. S., 97 Ala. 81. §§ 500, 503.
S. v., 18 Oreg. 440. § 332.
S. v., 19 Oreg. 397. § 359.
O'Leary, C. v., 143 Mass. 95. § 1258.
Oleson v. S., 11 Neb. 276. §§ 440, 44 455, 456, 458.
Olifier, Reg. v., 10 Cox, 402. §§ 110 1105.
Olive v. C., 5 Bush, 376. §§ 123, 505.
v. S., 11 Neb. 1. § 403.
Oliver v. C., 101 Pa. St. 215. § 1118.
Reg. v., Bell, 287. § 262.
Rex v., 2 Russ. Cr. 122. § 560.
v. S., 16 Ala. 587. § 304.
v. S., 17 Ala. 587. §§ 304, 332, 36 426.
v. S., 37 Ala. 134. § 709.
v. S., 17 Ark. 508. § 929.
v. S., 33 Tex. Ap. 541. § 533.
S. v., 2 Houst. 585. §§ 328, 922.
S. v., 55 Kan. 711. § 1196.
S. v., 43 La. An. 1003. § 419.
S. v., 70 N. C. 60. § 243.
S. v., 12 Wash. 547. § 96.
S. v., 26 W. Va. 422. §§ 1218, 12
Ollinger, U. S. v., 55 Fed. R. 959. §
Olmstead, P. v., 30 Mich. 431. §§ 4 428.
v. S., 89 Ala. 16. §§ 1270, 1271.
v. S., 90 Ala. 634. § 1246.
v. S., 92 Ala. 64. § 1272.
Olney, U. S. v., 1 Abb. (U. S.) 275. § 13
U. S. v., 1 Deady, 461. § 1315.
O'Loughlin, P. v., 3 Utah, 133. § 993

Olsen, P. v., 80 Cal. 122. §§ 196, 197, 326.
P. v., 6 Utah, 284. §§ 195, 814, 829.
Olwell, P. v., 28 Cal. 456. §§ 164, 390.
Olympic Club, S. v., 46 La. An. 935. § 1013.
O'Malley, C. v., 97 Mass. 584. §§ 556, 623, 625.
O'Mally, S. v., 48 Ia. 501. § 740.
O'Mara v. C., 75 Pa. St. 424. §§ 333, 411.
O'Mealy v. Newell, 8 East, 364. § 871.
O'Meara v. S., 17 Ohio St. 516. §§ 442, 449, 467.
Omit v. C., 21 Pa. St. 426. §§ 1264, 1321.
O'Neal v. S., 14 Tex. Ap. 582. § 199.
v. S., 32 Tex. Ap. 42. § 1034.
S. v., 1 Houst. Cr. C. 58. §§ 195, 339.
S. v., 7 Ired. 251. § 816.
Oneale v. C., 17 Grat. 582. §§ 1082, 1083.
U. S. v., 2 Cranch, C. C. 183. § 923.
Oneby, Rex v., 2 Stra. 766. §§ 309, 321, 333, 338, 343, 345.
One Hundred and Twenty-nine Bales of Merchandise, U. S. v., 46 Fed. R. 468. § 1351.
O'Neil, P. v., 48 Cal. 257. § 466.
P. v., 109 N. Y. 251. § 78.
S. v., 21 Oreg. 170. § 577.
S. v., 58 Vt. 140. §§ 80, 1207, 1236.
v. Vermont, 144 U. S. 323. §§ 80, 1206.
O'Neill, Reg. v., 6 Ir. R. C. L. 1. § 1008.
v. S., 16 Ala. 65. § 1007.
v. S., 85 Ga. 383. §§ 1112, 1113.
O'Niel, S. v., 1 Houst. Cr. C. 468. § 365.
S. v., 23 Ia. 272. § 381.
Opelousas v. Giron, 46 La. An. 1364. § 6.
Opie, Reg. v., 8 Cox, 332. § 1152.
Opinion of Judges, 3 Binn. 595. § 12.
Oppenheimer, S. v. 41 Tex. 82. § 873.
Orchard, Reg. v., 3 Cox, 248. § 1136.
Reg. v., 8 C. & P. 558, n. § 410.
Ordway, C. v., 12 Cush. 270. § 235.
O'Reilley, C. v., 116 Mass. 15. § 1243.
v. P., 86 N. Y. 154. § 854.
O'Reilly, S. v., 126 Mo. 597. §§ 162, 360, 406.
Organ v. S., 56 Ark. 267. § 46.
Orgill, Reg. v., 9 C. & P. 80. § 1073.
Orman, Reg. v., 14 Cox, 381. § 960.
v. S., 22 Tex. Ap. 604. § 341.
Ormiston, S. v., 66 Ia. 143. §§ 956, 966, 975, 977.
O'Rourke v. S., 8 Tex. Ap. 70. § 452.
S. v., 35 Neb. 614. § 1325.
Orr v. S., 18 Ark. 540. §§ 1290, 1291.
Orrell v. P., 94 Ill. 456. § 497.
S. v., 1 Dev. 139. § 293.
Ortega, U. S. v., 4 Wash. C. C. 531. §§ 235, 1342.
U. S. v., 11 Wheat. 467. § 1342.
Ortis v. S., 18 Tex. Ap. 282. § 608.
Ortiz v. S., 30 Fla. 256. § 418.
Orton, Reg. v., 39 L. T. (N. S.) 292. § 1013.
v. S., 4 Greene (Ia.), 140. § 271.
S. v., 41 Ark. 305. § 1216.
Ortwein v. C., 76 Pa. St. 414. § 178.
Orvis, S. v., 13 Ind. 569. § 684.
Orwig, S. v., 24 Ia. 102. § 636.
Osborn v. S., 52 Ind. 526. § 1133.
S. v., 54 Kan. 473. §§ 1055, 1060.
Osborne, Reg. v., Car. & M. 622. § 455.
v. S., 23 Tex. Ap. 431. §§ 354, 356.
S. v., 28 Ia. 9. § 557.
S. v., 45 Ia. 425. § 616.
S. v., 69 Mo. 143. § 1135.
Osgood v. P., 39 N. Y. 449. § 1276.
S. v., 85 Me. 288. § 1143.
Oshe v. S., 37 Ohio St. 494. §§ 1248, 1270.
Oskins, S. v., 28 Ind. 364. § 13.
Osman, Reg. v., 15 Cox, 1. § 426.
Osmer, Rex v., 5 East, 304. §§ 241, 922, 925.
Osmund, P. v., 138 N. Y. 80. § 341.
Ostler v. S., 3 Ind. Ap. 122. § 830.
Ostrander, S. v., 18 Ia. 435. § 332.
S. v., 30 Mo. 13. § 389.
O'Sullivan, P. v., 104 N. Y. 481. §§ 455, 461.
Oswald v. Hayes, 42 Ia. 104. § 847.
Otero v. S., 30 Tex. Ap. 450. §§ 557, 597.
Otey, U. S. v., 31 Fed. R. 68. § 776.
Otis, S. v., 135 Ind. 267. § 1116.
S. v., 42 N. H. 71. § 1018.
Our v. C., 9 Dana, 30. § 1249.
Outerbridge, S. v., 82 N. C. 617. § 376.
U. S. v., 5 Saw. 620. §§ 303, 353.
Outeveras, P. v., 48 Cal. 19. § 217.
Outlaw v. S., 35 Tex. 481. § 462.
S. v., 72 N. C. 598. § 494.
Outs, S. v., 30 La. An., Pt. II, 1155. § 809.
Overby v. S., 18 Fla. 178. § 1310.
Overman v. S., 88 Ind. 6. § 1137.
Overstreet v. S., 46 Ala. 30. § 526.
v. S., 3 How. (Miss.) 328. § 1132.
Overton, Ex parte, 2 Rose, 257. §§ 852, 894.
Reg. v., Car. & M. 655. § 864.
v. S., 43 Tex. 616. § 1099.
S. v., 16 Nev. 136. §§ 1315, 1317.
S. v., 24 N. J. 435. § 143.
U. S. v., 2 Cranch, C. C. 42. § 1227.
Oviatt v. S., 19 Ohio St. 573. § 815.
Owen, Rex v., 4 C. & P. 236. § 150.
Rex v., 2 East, P. C. 645. §§ 576, 577, 578.
Rex v., 1 Moody, 96. § 206.
v. S., 6 Humph. 330. § 546.
v. S., 5 Sneed, 493. § 786.
v. S., 44 Tex. 248. § 572.
S. v., 31 Ala. 387. § 1031.
S. v., 73 Mo. 440. § 855.
S. v., 78 Mo. 367. § 609.
S. v., 1 Murph. 452. §§ 377, 380, 382.
U. S. v., 32 Fed. R. 534. §§ 964, 973.
Owens, Rex v., 1 Moody, 205. § 815.
v. S., 52 Ala. 213. §§ 1285, 1286.
v. S., 52 Ala. 400. § 830.
v. S., 74 Ala. 401. § 824.
v. S., 94 Ala. 97. §§ 1072, 1091.
v. S., 19 Tex. Ap. 242. § 110.
v. S., 83 Wis. 496. § 706.
S. v., 1 Houst. Cr. C. 72. § 51.
S. v., 22 Minn. 238. §§ 199, 1148, 1151.

Owens, S. v., 79 Mo. 619. §§ 511, 514, 616, 617.
S. v., 10 Rich. 169. § 602.
U. S. v., 17 Fed. R. 72. § 1331.
U. S. v., 37 Fed. R. 112. § 774.
Owsley, S. v., 102 Mo. 678. § 463.
S. v., 111 Mo. 450. § 514.
Oxenham, Reg. v., 13 Cox, 349. § 554.
Oxford, Reg. v., 6 C. & P. 525. §§ 156, 233, 268, 1358.
Rex v., Russ. & Ry. 382. § 779.
v. S., 33 Ala. 416. § 722.
Oxley, Reg. v., 3 C. & K. 317. § 880.

Pace v. Alabama, 106 U. S. 583. §§ 54, 77.
v. S., 69 Ala. 231. §§ 54, 77.
Pacific Junction v. Dyer, 64 Ia. 38. §§ 44, 77.
Packard, Reg. v., Car. & M. 236. § 289.
Packer v. P., 8 Colo. 361. §§ 100, 101.
S. v., 80 N. C. 439. §§ 1218, 1220, 1273.
Packwood, S. v., 26 Mo. 340. § 365.
Paddle, Rex v., Russ. & Ry. 484. § 733.
Paddock, S. v., 24 Vt. 312. § 1244.
Padfield v. P., 146 Ill. 660. § 620.
Padgett v. S., 81 Ga. 466. § 825.
v. S., 68 Ind. 46. § 1308.
v. S., 93 Ind. 396. §§ 1223, 1225.
S. v., 18 S. C. 317. § 50.
Pagand v. S., 13 Miss. 491. § 809.
Pagano, S. v., 7 Wash. 549. § 409.
Page v. Camp, Kirby, 7. § 803.
v. C., 26 Grat. 943. § 519.
P. v., 1 Ida. 114. § 778.
P. v., 1 Ida. (N. S.) 189. § 774.
Reg. v., 8 C. & P. 122. § 783.
Reg. v., 9 C. & P. 756. § 789.
v. S., 11 Ala. 849. § 1230.
v. S., 61 Ala. 16. § 373*a*.
v. S., 69 Ala. 229. § 309.
v. S., 84 Ala. 446. § 1259.
v. S., 11 Lea, 202. § 1241.
S. v., 66 Me. 418. § 1218.
Pagels, S. v., 92 Mo. 300. § 157.
Paggett, S. v., 8 Wash. 579. §§ 1170, 1182.
Pagliano, U. S. v., 53 Fed. R. 1001. § 1106*a*.
Paice, Reg. v., 1 C. & K. 73. § 524.
Paige, S. v., 50 Vt. 445. § 1270.
Pain v. Boughtwood, 24 Q. B. D. 353. § 128.
Rex v.. Comb. 358. § 1048.
Paine, Rex v., 7 C. & P. 135. § 496.
v. S., 89 Ala. 26. § 524.
Paine Lumber Co., S. v., 84 Wis. 205. § 1190.
Painter v. P., 147 Ill. 444. §§ 405, 417, 423.
v. S., 26 Tex. Ap. 454. § 500.
S. v., 50 Ia. 317. § 1119.
S. v., 67 Mo. 84. § 257.
Palfus v. S., 36 Ga. 280. § 1137.
Palin v. S., 38 Neb. 862. § 461.
S. v., 63 N. C. 471. § 1126.
Palliser, In re, 136 U. S. 257. § 1327.
Pallister, P. v., 138 N. Y. 601. §§ 316, 411.
Palmer, Ex parte, 86 Cal. 631. § 650.
C. v., 134 Mass. 537. § 66.
v. Concord, 48 N. H. 211. § 1044.
v. P., 5 Hill (N. Y.), 427. § 28.
v. P., 138 Ill. 356. § 374.
v. P., 10 Wend. 165. § 547.
P. v., 96 Mich. 580. § 307.
P. v., 109 N. Y. 110. § 396.
Rex v., 2 East, P. C. 586. § 554.
Rex v., Russ. & Ry. 72. §§ 781, 782.
v. S., 7 Coldw. 82. § 497.
v. S., 45 Ind. 388. §§ 826, 827.
v. S., 39 Ohio St. 236. § 33.
S. v., 50 Kan. 318. §§ 684, 702.
S. v., 4 Mo. 453. § 1137.
S. v., 88 Mo. 568. § 139.
S. v., 18 Vt. 570. § 1073.
U. S. v., 3 Wheat. 610. § 1359.
Palmore v. S., 29 Ark. 248. §§ 307, 332, 353.
Pamperin, S. v., 42 Minn. 320. §§ 66, 69.
Pancake v. S., 81 Ind. 93. § 1326.
S. v., 74 Ind. 15. §§ 1306, 1307.
Pankey v. P., 2 Ill. 80. §§ 858, 861.
S. v., 104 N. C. 840. § 342.
Panton v. P., 114 Ill. 505. § 306.
Panzara, In re, 51 Fed. R. 275. § 1343.
Pape, P. v., 66 Cal. 366. § 259.
Paquin, P. v., 74 Mich. 34. § 1250.
Parchman v. S., 2 Tex. Ap. 228. §§ 572, 609.
Pardee, S. v., 37 Ohio St. 63. § 717.
Pardue v. S., 4 Baxt. 10. § 505.
Parfait, Rex v., 1 East, P. C. 416. § 484.
Parfitt, Reg. v., 8 C. & P. 288. § 512.
Pargeter, Reg. v., 3 Cox, 191. § 379.
Parish, Reg. v., 8 C. & P. 94. § 762.
S. v., 79 N. C. 610. § 890.
S. v., 104 N. C. 679. § 461.
Park, C. v., 1 Gray, 553. §§ 187, 188.
P. v., 41 N. Y. 21. § 18.
Parker, C. v., 4 Allen, 313. §§ 1135, 1178.
C. v., 2 Cush. 212. §§ 891, 892.
C. v., 9 Met. 263. §§ 1146, 1147.
C. v., 146 Pa. St. 343. § 454.
C. v., 2 Pick. 550. § 370.
v. Patrick, 5 T. R. 175. § 712.
v. P., 97 Ill. 32. §§ 780, 789, 799, 803.
v. P., 111 Ill. 581. §§ 45, 46.
P. v., 91 Cal. 91. § 508.
P. v., 4 Johns. 424. § 498.
Reg. v., Car. & M. 639. § 892.
Reg. v., 9 C. & P. 45. § 523.
Reg. v., 3 Q. B. 292. §§ 707, 982.
Rex v., 7 C. & P. 825. § 674.
Rex v., 3 Doug. 242. § 890.
Rex v., 1 Leach, 41. § 784.
v. S., 77 Ala. 47. §§ 1081, 1083, 1084.
v. S., 88 Ala. 4. § 310.
v. S., 136 Ind. 284. §§ 414, 419.
v. S., 16 Lea, 476. § 1319.
v. S., 55 Miss. 414. § 306.
v. S., 4 Ohio St. 563. § 213.
v. S., 26 Tex. 204. §§ 1294, 1303.

Parker v. S., 31 Tex. 132. § 313.
v. S., 9 Tex. Ap. 351. § 481.
v. S., 13 Tex. Ap. 213. §§ 1310, 1311.
v. S., 18 Tex. Ap. 72. § 311.
v. S., 20 Tex. Ap. 451. § 150.
v. S., 22 Tex. Ap. 105. § 311.
v. S., 29 Tex. Ap. 372. § 909.
S. v., 34 Ark. 158. §§ 537, 600.
S. v., 1 D. Chip. 298. § 794.
S. v., 1 Houst. Cr. C. 9. § 598.
S. v., 7 La. An. 84. § 420.
S. v., 42 La. An. 972. § 268.
S. v., 96 Mo. 382. §§ 309, 428.
S. v., 106 Mo. 217. §§ 306, 309.
S. v., 16 Nev. 79. § 508.
S. v., 65 N. C. 453. § 377.
S. v., 75 N. C. 249. § 235.
S. v., 91 N. C. 650. § 12.
S. v., 106 N. C. 711. § 1074.
S. v., 43 N. H. 83. §§ 960, 975.
S. v., 57 N. H. 123. § 1094.
S. v., 26 Vt. 357. §§ 1206, 1210.
Parkerson, S. v., 1 Strob. 169. § 149.
Parkes, Rex v., 2 East, P. C. 963. § 764.
Parkin, Rex v., 1 Moody, 45. § 552.
Parkinson v. P., 135 Ill. 401. § 461.
v. S., 14 Md. 184. §§ 84, 1206, 1261.
v. U. S., 121 U. S. 281. § 20.
Parks, P. v., 49 Mich. 333. §§ 188, 1237.
Rex v., 2 East, P. C. 671. § 563.
v. S., 66 Ga. 192. § 576.
v. S., 94 Ga. 601. § 677.
v. S., 3 Ohio St. 101. § 362.
v. S., 4 Tex. Ap. 134. § 1087.
v. S., 29 Tex. Ap. 597. § 565.
S. v., 29 Vt. 70. § 1214.
Parli v. Reed, 30 Kan. 534. § 636.
Parmelee, S. v., 9 Conn. 259. § 279.
Parmenter, C. v., 101 Mass. 211. § 620.
C. v., 121 Mass. 354. § 701.
C. v., 5 Pick. 279. §§ 791, 794.
Parmer v. S., 41 Ala. 416. § 602.
v. S., 91 Ga. 152. § 1288.
Parnell, Reg. v., 14 Cox, 508. § 953.
S. v., 16 Ark. 506. § 1274.
Parr, C. v., 5 Watts & S. 345. § 22.
Reg. v., 2 M. & Rob. 346. 714.
Parrish v. S., 18 Neb. 405. § 345.
v. S., 32 Tex. Ap. 583. § 245.
Parrott, Rex v., 6 C. & P. 402. § 520.
v. S., 10 Ark. 574. § 1290.
Parrow, P. v., 80 Mich. 567. §§ 511, 609.
Parshall, P. v., 6 Park. C. R. 129. § 489.
Parsley v. Hutchins, 2 Jones, 159. § 1217.
Parsons v. C., 78 Ky. 102. § 303.
v. S., 21 Ala. 300. § 292.
v. S., 81 Ala. 577. §§ 157, 165, 173, 178, 179.
v. S., 2 Ind. 499. §§ 1283, 1292, 1298.
v. S., 33 Tex. Ap. 540. § 1019.
S. v., 54 Ia. 405. § 649.
S. v., 124 Mo. 436. § 44.
Partain v. S., 22 Tex. Ap. 100. § 878.
Partlow, S. v., 90 Mo. 608. §§ 309, 310, 339.
S. v., 91 N. C. 550. § 39.
Partridge v. Hood, 120 Mass. 403. § 939.
P. v., 86 Mich. 243. § 443.
Partridge, Rex v., 7 C. & P. 551. § 619.
Paschal v. S., 84 Ga. 326. §§ 1233, 1234.
Pascoe, Reg. v., 2 C. & K. 927. § 939.
Pash, C. v., 9 Dana, 31. § 1298.
Passaic, etc. Soc., S. v., 54 N. J. 260. § 183.
Passey, Rex v., 7 C. & P. 282. §§ 195, 206.
Passmore, C. v., 1 Serg. & R. 217. §§ 1184, 1186.
v. S., 29 Tex. Ap. 241. § 463.
U. S. v., 4 Dall. 372. § 96.
Patch, C. v., 97 Mass. 221. § 66.
Pate v. S., 94 Ala. 14. §§ 416, 419.
S. v., 67 Mo. 488. § 1310.
Pateman, Rex v., Russ. & Ry. 455. § 756.
Paterno, S. v., 43 La. An. 514. § 307.
Patience, Rex v., 7 C. & P. 775. § 340.
Patillo, S. v., 4 Hawks, 348. § 661.
Paton v. P., 1 Colo. 77. §§ 63, 1217.
Patrick, C. v., 80 Ky. 605. § 199.
v. P., 132 Ill. 529. §§ 224, 225.
Rex v., 2 East, P. C. 1059. § 830.
v. Smoke, 3 Strob. 147. § 868.
S. v., 3 Jones, 443. § 424.
S. v., 107 Mo. 147. §§ 451, 455, 457.
S. v., 79 N. C. 655. § 593.
U. S. v., 53 Fed. R. 356. §§ 561, 961.
U. S. v., 54 Fed. R. 338. § 961.
Pattee, C. v., 12 Cush. 501. § 98.
Patten v. Centralia, 47 Ill. 370. § 1264.
v. P., 18 Mich. 314. §§ 139, 140, 304, 339.
Patterson, C. v., 138 Mass. 498. § 1248.
v. Kentucky, 97 U. S. 501. §§ 35, 75.
P. v., 102 Cal. 239. §§ 1121, 1124.
v. S., 36 Ala. 297. § 1247.
v. S., 91 Ala. 58. § 241.
v. S., 85 Ga. 131. §§ 123, 275.
v. S., 66 Ind. 185. § 339.
v. S., 3 Lea, 575. § 1039.
S. v., 2 Ired. 346. §§ 1073, 1085.
S. v., 52 Kan. 335. § 217.
S. v., 42 La. An. 934. § 480.
S. v., 68 Me. 473. § 740.
S. v., 73 Mo. 695. §§ 380, 398.
S. v., 88 Mo. 88. § 1113.
S. v., 116 Mo. 505. §§ 123, 809.
S. v., 45 Vt. 308. §§ 123, 144, 316, 333, 429, 431.
U. S. v., 59 Fed. R. 280. § 963.
U. S. v., 6 McLean, 466. § 1330.
Patton v. Freeman, Coxe, 113. § 11.
v. S., 50 Ark. 53. § 1193.
v. S., 93 Ga. 111. § 814.
S. v., 4 Ired. 16. § 184.
S. v., 12 La. An. 288. § 391.
S. v., 115 N. C. 753. § 255.
Patty, Rex v., 2 East, P. C. 1074. § 815.
U. S. v., 9 Biss. 429. § 1318.
Patza, S. v., 3 La. An. 512. § 416.
Paul, C. v., 148 Pa. St. 559. §§ 34, 76.
Reg. v., 25 Q. B. D. 202. § 456.
v. S., 65 Ga. 152. § 420.
v. S., 12 Tex. Ap. 346. § 981.

Paul, S. v., 81 Ia. 596. § 830.
S. v., 69 Me. 215. §§ 669, 670, 702.
S. v., 5 R. I. 185. §§ 1207, 1249.
v. Virginia, 8 Wall. 168. § 43.
Pauli v. C., 89 Pa. St. 432. § 768.
Paulin v. S., 21 Tex. Ap. 436. § 341.
Paulk, S. v., 18 S. C. 514. §§ 160, 177, 178, 179.
Paxton, S. v., 126 Mo. 500. § 308.
Payne v. C., 1 Met. (Ky.) 370. §§ 303, 307, 391.
v. P., 6 Johns. 103. § 543.
P. v., 8 Cal. 341. §§ 142, 299.
P. v., 3 Denio, 88. § 1318.
Rex v., 4 C. & P. 558. § 256.
v. S., 60 Ala. 80. § 303.
v. S., 74 Ind. 203. §§ 1252, 1256, 1257.
v. S., 57 Miss. 348. § 618.
v. S., 5 Tex. Ap. 35. § 268.
v. S., 17 Tex. Ap. 40. § 1163.
v. S., 21 Tex. Ap. 184. § 618.
S. v., 86 N. C. 609. § 178.
S. v., 1 Swan, 383. § 209.
S. v., 10 Wash. 545. §§ 333, 420.
Payson, In re, 23 Kan. 757. § 694.
S. v., 37 Me. 361. §§ 1170, 1183.
Payton, S. v., 90 Mo. 220. §§ 217, 354, 377.
Peabody, P. v., 25 Wend. 472. § 772.
v. S., 72 Miss. 104. § 1133.
Peace, Rex v., 3 B. & Ald. 579. § 252.
S. v., 1 Jones, 251. § 426.
Peachie v. S., 63 Ind. 399. § 13.
Peacock, P. v., 6 Cow. 72. § 762.
Rex v., Russ. & Ry. 278. § 764.
S. v., 31 Mo. 413. § 702.
S. v., 40 Ohio St. 333. § 144.
Peak v. S., 10 Humph. 98. § 1135.
v. S., 50 N. J. 179. § 426.
Pear, Rex v., 2 East, P. C. 685. § 562.
Pearce, Reg. v., 3 B. & S. 531. § 858.
Reg. v., 9 C. & P. 667. § 168.
Rex v., 2 East, P. C. 603. § 546.
Rex v., 2 East, P. C. 1072. § 829.
Rex v., Peake (N. P.). 75. § 1053.
v. S., 40 Ala. 720. § 1247.
v. S., 1 Sneed, 63. § 950.
S. v., 2 Blackf. 318. § 1086.
S. v., 14 Fla. 153. § 901.
S. v., 56 Minn. 226. §§ 199, 425, 431.
S. v., 15 Nev. 188. § 307.
v. Wilson, 111 Pa. St. 14. § 939.
Pearis, S. v., 35 W. Va. 320. § 947.
Pearsall, S. v., 43 Ia. 630. § 1140.
Pearson's Case, 2 Lewin, 144. § 160.
2 Lewin, 216. § 341.
Pearson v. Int. Dist. Co., 72 Ia. 348. § 1202.
Reg. v., 8 C. & P. 119. § 858.
Rex v., 4 C. & P. 572. § 1330.
v. S., 55 Ga. 659. § 766.
v. S., 66 Miss. 510. § 1236.
S. v., 97 N. C. 434. § 949.
S. v., 2 N. H. 550. § 837.
Pease, C. v., 16 Mass. 91. § 940.
v. S., 94 Ga. 615. § 563.
Pease v. S., 13 Tex. Ap. 18. § 305.
S. v., 74 Ind. 263. § 798.
Peat's Case, 2 Lewin, 111. § 1085.
Peat, Rex v., 2 East, P. C. 557. § 471.
Peck, P. v., 138 N. Y. 386. § 906.
Reg. v., 9 A. & E. 686. §§ 975, 982, 984.
v. S., 5 Tex. Ap. 611. § 303.
v. S., 9 Tex. Ap. 70. § 565.
S. v., 25 Ohio St. 26. § 50.
S. v., 32 Vt. 172. § 1275.
Peckard, S. v., 5 Harr. 500. § 1186.
Peckham, C. v., 2 Gray, 514. §§ 1218, 1220.
S. v., 3 R. I. 289. § 1202.
Peden v. S., 61 Miss. 267. § 196.
S. v., 2 Blackf. 371. § 834.
Pederson v. S., 21 Tex. Ap. 485. § 255.
Pedigo, S. v., 71 Mo. 443. § 586.
Pedley, Rex v., 1 Leach, 325. § 867.
Peed v. McKee, 42 Ia. 689. § 939.
Peek v. S., 2 Humph. 78. § 775.
Peel, Reg. v., 2 F. & F. 21. § 426.
Peel Splint Coal Co., S. v., 36 W. Va. 802. § 55.
Peeler v. S., 3 Tex. Ap. 533. § 200.
Peeples, S. v., 108 N. C. 768. § 1126.
Peer's Case, 5 Grat. 674. § 1275.
Peer v. Humphrey, 2 A. & E. 495. § 11.
Peete v. S., 2 Lea, 513. §§ 753, 761.
Pefferling v. S., 40 Tex. 486. §§ 455, 459.
Peffers, S. v., 80 Ia. 580. § 358.
Peirce, S. v., 43 N. H. 273. § 1021.
Peitz v. S., 68 Wis. 538. §§ 1227, 1231.
Pelfryman, Rex v., 2 East, P. C. 783. § 478.
Pelham, Reg. v., 8 Q. B. 959. § 130.
Pelletreau, U. S. v., 14 Blatch. 126. § 1330.
Pells v. S., 20 Fla. 774. § 508.
Peltier's Case, 28 How. St. Tr. 529. § 1062.
Pemberton, C. v., 118 Mass. 36. §§ 18, 355.
v. S., 85 Ind. 507. § 1310.
S. v., 30 Mo. 376. § 373*a*.
Pembliton, Reg. v., L. R. 2 C. C. 119. § 826.
Pence v. S., 110 Ind. 95. § 568.
Pendergrass, S. v., 2 Dev. & B. 365. § 242.
Pendleton v. C., 4 Leigh, 694. § 805.
P. v., 79 Mich. 317. § 1038.
v. S., 6 Ark. 509. § 54.
Pendry v. S., 18 Fla. 191. § 706.
S. v., 9 Mont. 67. § 589.
Penland v. S., 19 Tex. Ap. 365. § 303.
Pennaman v. S., 58 Ga. 336. §§ 859, 873.
Pennegar v. S., 87 Tenn. 244. § 1088.
Pennington, S. v., 5 Lea, 506. § 1158.
S. v., 124 Mo. 388. § 265.
Pennock, C. v., 3 Serg. & R. 199. § 494.
Pennsylvania, U. S. v., 69 Fed. R. 983. § 1341.
Pennsylvania R. Co., C. v., 117 Pa. St. 637. § 182.
Penny v. S., 88 Ala. 105. § 638.

Pennybaker v. S., 2 Blackf. 484. §§ 194, 1238.
Pennyman, S. v., 68 Ia. 216. § 620.
Penrod v. P., 89 Ill. 150. § 373a.
Penson, Rex v., 5 C. & P. 412. § 1073.
Peoples v. C., 87 Ky. 487. §§ 289, 325, 327, 347, 426, 1147.
v. S., 6 Blackf. 95. § 779.
Pepper, S. v., 11 Ia. 347. § 785.
Pepys, Rex v., Peake, 138. § 868.
Peralto v. S., 17 Tex. Ap. 578. § 572.
Perazzo, P. v., 64 Cal. 106. § 861.
Perdue v. C., 96 Pa. St. 311. §§ 872, 873.
C. v., 2 Va. Cas. 227. § 1011.
v. Ellis, 18 Ga. 586. § 1206.
P. v., 49 Cal. 425. § 309.
v. S., 2 Humph. 494. § 784.
Perez v. S., 48 Ala. 356. § 1313.
v. S., 8 Tex. Ap. 610. § 78.
Peri v. P., 65 Ill. 17. §§ 329, 332, 334.
Perigo, S. v., 70 Ia. 657. § 383.
Perini, P. v., 94 Cal. 573. § 556.
Perkes, Rex v., 1 C. & P. 300. § 500.
Perkin's Case, 2 Lewin, 150. § 791.
Perkins v. C., 7 Grat. 651. § 797.
v. P., 27 Mich. 386. § 781.
Reg. v., 9 C. & P. 395. §§ 426, 431.
Reg. v., 2 Den. 459. § 209.
Rex v., 4 C. & P. 537. §§ 196, 1013.
v. S., 60 Ala. 7. § 420.
v. S., 92 Ala. 66. § 1237.
v. S., 65 Ind. 317. § 563.
v. S., 67 Ind. 270. § 664.
v. S., 78 Wis. 551. § 339.
S. v., 6 Blackf. 20. § 324.
S. v., 43 La. An. 186. §§ 925, 926, 927.
S. v., 26 N. H. 9. §§ 1223, 1270.
S. v., 42 N. H. 464. § 1016.
S. v., 53 N. H. 435. § 1281.
S. v., 63 N. H. 368. § 1278.
S. v., 42 Vt. 399. § 913.
Perley, C. v., 2 Cush. 559. § 1244.
S. v., 86 Me. 427. § 472.
Perrigo, C. v., 3 Met. (Ky.) 5. §§ 1289, 1313.
Perrin v. C., 87 Va. 554. § 571.
S. v., 2 Brev. 474. §§ 1060, 1066.
Perris, C. v., 108 Mass. 1. § 495.
Perrow v. S., 67 Miss. 365. § 937.
Perry v. C., 3 Grat. 632. § 78.
C. v., 139 Mass. 198. §§ 1170, 1183.
C. v., 148 Mass. 160. §§ 1252, 1253.
C. v., 155 Mass. 117. § 55.
v. P., 14 Ill. 496. §§ 276, 279.
Reg. v., 1 C. & K. 725. § 543.
Reg. v., 2 Cox, 223. § 1148.
Reg. v., Dears. 471. § 1152.
v. Salt Lake City, 7 Utah, 143. § 1228.
v. S., 43 Ala. 21. § 336.
v. S., 87 Ala. 30. §§ 78, 164.
v. S., 37 Ark. 54. § 594.
v. S., 63 Ga. 402. § 936.
S. v., 5 Jones, 9. § 1007.
v. S., 44 Neb. 414. § 557.
v. S., 41 Tex. 483. § 618.
v. S., 44 Tex. 473. § 333.
Perry v. S., 4 Tex. Ap. 566. § 605.
S. v., 42 Tex. 238. § 881.
Perryman, C. v., 2 Leigh, 717. § 1120.
v. S., 36 Tex. 321. § 374.
Persons v. S., 90 Tenn. 291. § 401.
v. S., 3 Tex. Ap. 240. § 594.
Pervear v. Massachusetts, 5 Wall. 475. §§ 80, 1206, 1217.
Petch, Reg. v., 14 Cox, 17. §§ 537, 557.
Peter, S. v., 8 Jones, 19. § 455.
S. v., 14 La. An. 521. § 455.
Peters, Ex parte, 2 McCrary, 403. § 511.
C. v., 12 Met. 387. § 14.
Reg. v., 1 C. & K. 245. § 571.
v. S., 100 Ala. 10. § 593.
v. S., 67 Ga. 29. § 396.
v. S., 33 Tex. Ap. 170. § 500.
v. S., 66 Wis. 339. §§ 1017, 1021.
S. v., 56 Ia. 263. § 454.
S. v., 37 La. An. 730. § 83.
S. v., 107 N. C. 876. §§ 858, 872, 892.
S. v., 42 Tex. 7. § 876.
S. v., 57 Vt. 86. § 858.
v. U. S., 2 Okl. 116. § 855.
v. U. S., 2 Okl. 138. §§ 863, 873.
Peterson, P. v., 9 Cal. 313. § 654.
v. S., 74 Ala. 34. § 892.
v. S., 47 Ga. 524. § 377.
v. S., 12 Tex. Ap. 650. §§ 377, 389.
v. S., 14 Tex. Ap. 162. § 463.
v. S., 25 Tex. Ap. 70. § 780.
S. v., 67 Ia. 564. § 617.
S. v., 41 La. An. 85. § 304.
S. v., 38 Minn. 143. §§ 1217, 1264.
S. v., 41 Vt. 504. § 17.
Petheram. P. v., 64 Mich. 252. §§ 110, 963, 977, 979.
Petre v. S., 35 N. J. 64. § 546.
Pettes v. C., 126 Mass. 242. §§ 212, 217.
C. v., 114 Mass. 307. § 211.
Pettibone v. S., 19 Ala. 586. § 1244.
v. U. S.. 148 U. S. 197. §§ 920, 953, 956, 970, 971, 975.
Pettigrew v. S., 12 Tex. Ap. 225. §§ 154, 617.
Pettingill v. Rideout, 6 N. H. 454. § 11.
Pettis, S. v., 63 Me. 124. § 546.
Pettit, P. v., 3 Johns. 511. §§ 263, 268.
v. S., 28 Tex. Ap. 240. § 133.
Petty v. S., 58 Ark. 1. § 1324.
v. S., 6 Baxt. 610. § 332.
S. v., 119 Mo. 425. § 678.
Pfeifer, S. v., 26 Minn. 175. § 1216.
Pfister v. S., 84 Ala. 432. § 592.
Pfleajor, S. v., 81 Ia. 759. § 1204.
Phalen, S. v., 3 Harr. 441. § 1317.
Pharr v. S., 7 Tex. Ap. 472. § 355.
v. S., 9 Tex. Ap. 129. § 414.
v. S., 10 Tex. Ap. 485. § 390.
Phelan, S. v., 65 Mo. 547. §§ 256, 268.
Phelps, C. v., 170 Pa. St. 430. § 1326.
v. P., 55 Ill. 334. §§ 554, 562.
v. P., 72 N. Y. 334. §§ 546, 556, 595, 603.
v. P., 72 N. Y. 365. § 768.
P. v., 83 N. Y. 436. § 687.
P. v., 133 N. Y. 267. § 1148.

Phelps v., 5 Wend. 9. §§ 872, 877, 880.
v. Racey, 60 N. Y. 10. § 46.
Reg. v., Car. & M. 180. §§ 340, 389, 997.
v. S., 15 Tex. Ap. 45. § 357.
S. v., 9 Md. 21. § 1126.
S. v., 91 Mo. 478. §§ 617, 620.
S. v., 65 N. C. 451. § 722.
Phetheon, Reg. v., 9 C. & P. 552. § 566.
Phifer, S. v., 65 N. C. 321. § 665.
Philadelphia, etc. R. Co. v. Lehman, 56 Md. 209. § 1323.
Philadelphia, etc. R. Co. v. Philadelphia, etc. Tow Boat Co., 23 How. 209. § 1322.
Philbrick, S. v., 31 Me. 401. § 684.
S. v., 84 Me. 562. §§ 941, 942, 943.
U. S. v., 120 U. S. 52. §§ 60, 86, 102.
Philips v. C., 2 Duv. 328. §§ 303, 311, 314.
Reg. v., 8 C. & P. 736. §§ 226, 449, 465.
Rex v., 2 Stra. 921. § 884.
Philley, S. v., 67 Ind. 304. § 235.
Phillips, Ex parte, 33 Tex. Ap. 126. § 1161.
C. v., 16 Mass. 423. § 215.
C. v., 162 Mass. 504. § 444.
C. v., 11 Pick. 27. §§ 78, 83, 93.
v. Innes, 4 Cl. & F. 234. § 1321.
v. Jansen, 2 Esp. 624. § 1055.
v. P., 95 Ga. 478. § 1233.
Reg. v., 3 Cox, 225. § 271.
Rex v., 3 Camp. 77. § 1146.
Rex v., 2 East, P. C. 662. § 566.
v. S., 68 Ala. 469. § 292.
v. S., 36 Ark. 282. § 281.
v. S., 17 Ga. 459. § 771.
v. S., 29 Ga. 105. § 533.
v. S., 66 Ga. 755. § 267.
v. S., 9 Humph. 245. §§ 455, 456.
v. S., 85 Tenn. 551. § 546.
v. S., 19 Tex. 158. §§ 573, 823.
v. S., 29 Tex. 226. § 1168.
v. S., 6 Tex. Ap. 364. § 767.
v. S., 26 Tex. Ap. 228. §§ 198, 206, 214.
S. v., 24 Mo. 475. § 101.
S. v., 78 Mo. 49. § 773.
S. v., 117 Mo. 389. §§ 203, 208, 391.
S. v., 104 N. C. 786. § 257.
v. Tecumseh, 5 Neb. 312. § 1216.
Phillpot, Reg. v., Dears. 179. § 130.
Philp, Rex v., 1 Moody, 263. § 818.
Philpot v. C., 86 Ky. 595. § 257.
C. v., 130 Mass. 59. § 740.
Philpotts, Reg. v., 1 C. & K. 112. § 675.
Reg. v., 3 C. & K. 135. § 865.
Phipoe, Rex v., 2 East, P. C. 599. §§ 543, 582.
Phippen, S. v., 62 Ia. 54. § 855.
Phipps, P. v., 39 Cal. 333. § 409.
S. v., 4 Ind. 515. § 1186.
S. v., 50 Kan. 609. § 963.
Pickens v. S., 100 Ala. 127. § 1302.
v. S., 20 Ind. 116. § 1227.
v. S., 61 Miss. 52. § 342.
v. S., 9 Tex. Ap. 270. § 1017.
Pickens v. S., 13 Tex. Ap. 353. § 277.
v. S., 31 Tex. Ap. 554. § 341.
S. v., 79 N. C. 652. § 851.
Pickering, C. v., 8 Grat. 628. § 878.
Picket v. S., 22 Ohio St. 405. § 1247.
Pickett v. S., 60 Ala. 77. § 509.
v. S., 12 Tex. Ap. 86. § 334.
S. v., 11 Nev. 255. §§ 249, 443, 464.
S. v., 78 N. C. 458. § 702.
S. v., — S. C. —, 25 S. E. R. 46. § 1214,
v. U. S., 1 Ida. (N. S.) 523. § 376.
Pickford, Rex v., 4 C. & P. 227. §§ 730, 740.
Pico, P. v., 62 Cal. 50. §§ 171, 594.
Piedmont Club v. C., 87 Va. 540. § 1240.
Pierce's Case, 16 Me. 255. § 83.
Pierce v. Carskadon, 16 Wall. 234. § 78.
v. C., 10 Bush, 6. § 1228.
C. v., 138 Mass. 165. §§ 130, 237, 249, 287, 351.
v. S., 53 Ga. 365. §§ 159, 169.
v. S., 75 Ind. 199. § 278.
v. S., 63 Md. 592. § 34.
v. S., 13 N. H. 536. §§ 76, 82.
v. S., 17 Tex. Ap. 232. § 925.
v. S., 21 Tex. Ap. 540. § 257.
v. S., 21 Tex. Ap. 669. § 378.
S. v., 7 Ala. 728. § 829.
S. v., 8 Ia. 231. §§ 756, 757.
S. v., 65 Ia. 85. §§ 1018, 1137, 1249, 1262.
S. v., 76 Ia. 189. § 914.
S. v., 77 Ia. 245. § 638.
S. v., 52 Kan. 521. § 905.
v. U. S., 160 U. S. 355. § 377.
Pierson v. P., 79 N. Y. 424. §§ 416, 418.
P. v., 2 Ida. 71. §§ 308, 313, 314.
v. Post, 3 Caines, 175. § 538.
v. S., 99 Ala. 148. §§ 196, 391.
v. S., 39 Ark. 219. § 1217.
S. v., 44 Ark. 265. § 444.
S. v., 59 Ia. 271. §§ 585, 595, 610.
Pigg v. S., 43 Tex. 108. § 557.
Pigman v. S., 14 Ohio, 555. § 161.
Pike v. Hanson, 9 N. H. 491. § 488.
Reg. v., 2 Moody, 70. § 757.
Rex v., 3 C. & P. 598. § 431.
v. S., 8 Lea, 577. § 520.
S. v., 49 N. H. 399. §§ 159, 165, 173, 319, 321, 355, 361.
Pile, S. v., 5 Ala. 72. § 265.
Pilkington, S. v., 92 Ia. 92. § 463.
Pilling, Reg. v., 1 F. & F. 324. § 753.
Pillsbury, C. v., 12 Gray, 127. § 1223.
Pim, Rex v., Russ. & Ry. 425. § 791.
Pinchback, S. v., 2 Mill (Const.), 128. § 1315.
Pinckard v. S., 62 Ala. 167. § 536.
Pinckford v. S., 13 Tex. Ap. 468. § 416.
Pinder v. S., 27 Fla. 370. §§ 126, 300, 305, 306, 391.
Pines v. S., 50 Ala. 153. § 500.
Pinger, S. v., 57 Mo. 243. §§ 913, 917.
Pings v. U. S., 72 Fed. R. 260. § 1351.
Pinkard v. S., 30 Ga. 757. §§ 224, 614.
Pinkerton, P. v., 79 Mich. 110. § 1138.

Pinney, Rex v., 5 C. & P. 254. § 997.
Pinson v. S., 28 Fla. 735. §§ 1130, 1132.
v. S., 23 Tex. 579. §§ 257, 260.
Pintard, C. v., 1 Browne, 59. § 1128.
Piper, C. v., 120 Mass. 185. §§ 400, 407.
Pipes, C. v., 158 Pa. St. 25. § 299.
v. S., 26 Tex. Ap. 318. §§ 859, 865.
Pippen v. S., 77 Ala. 81. § 826.
Pippin, S. v., 88 N. C. 646. § 1098.
Pirates, U. S. v., 5 Wheat. 184. §§ 110, 1359.
Pirtle v. S., 9 Humph. 663. § 162.
Piscataqua Bank v. Turnley, 1 Miles, 312. § 11.
Pischel, S. v., 16 Neb. 490. §§ 1270, 1272, 1273, 1274.
Pitcher v. P., 16 Mich. 142. §§ 497, 513, 574.
Pitman, Rex v., 2 C. & P. 423. § 548.
v. S., 22 Ark. 354. § 412.
S. v., 1 Brev. 32. § 790.
Pitt, Rex v., 3 Burr. 1335. § 947.
Pittman v. S., 25 Fla. 648. §§ 257, 271.
v. S., 92 Ga. 480. § 307.
v. S., 14 Tex. Ap. 576. § 586.
Pitts, Reg. v., Car. & M. 284. § 284.
v. S., 43 Miss. 482. § 396.
v. S., 3 Tex. Ap. 210. §§ 562, 569.
v. S., 5 Tex. Ap. 122. § 563.
v. S., 29 Tex. Ap. 374. § 341.
S. v., 12 S. C., 180. § 601.
Pittsburgh, etc. Ry. v. C., 101 Pa. St. 192. §§ 8, 183.
Pitzer, S. v., 62 Ind. 362. § 834.
Place, C. v., 153 Pa. St. 314. §§ 1051, 1053.
S. v., 5 Wash. 773. § 1153.
Plaisted, C. v., 148 Mass. 375. §§ 44, 62, 69.
S. v., 43 N. H. 413. § 846.
Plake v. S., 121 Ind. 433. §§ 179, 383.
Plant, S. v., 67 Vt. 454. § 1143.
Planters' Ins. Co. v. Tuntstall, 72 Ala. 142. § 624.
Plasters v. S., 1 Tex. Ap. 673. § 307.
Plastridge, S. v., 6 R. I. 76. § 1271.
Plath v. Braunsdorff, 40 Wis. 107. § 861.
P. v., 100 N. Y. 590. §§ 1106a, 1119.
Platt, P. v., 67 Cal. 21. § 852.
Pleasant v. S., 13 Ark. 360. §§ 448, 460.
v. S., 15 Ark. 624. § 460.
Pledger v. S., 77 Ga. 242. §§ 1043, 1056.
Pleuler v. S., 11 Neb. 547. §§ 1211, 1212.
Pliemling v. S., 46 Wis. 516. § 326.
Plumbly v. C., 2 Met. 413. § 28.
Plumer v. Smith, 5 N. H. 553. § 939.
Plumley v. Massachusetts, 155 U. S. 461. § 34.
Plummer v. C., 1 Bush, 26. § 1226.
Reg. v., 1 C. & K. 600. § 286.
v. S., 135 Ind. 308. §§ 298, 304.
v. S., 6 Mo. 231. § 389.
v. S., 4 Tex. Ap. 310. §§ 126, 298, 300.
S. v., 50 Me. 217. § 858.
Plunket, S. v., 1 Ired. 115. § 1226.
Plunkett v. S., 69 Ind. 68. §§ 1247, 1273.
S. v., 18 N. J. 5. § 63.
Plym, S. v., 43 Minn. 385. §§ 1083, 1084.
Plympton, Rex v., 2 Ld. Raym. 1377. §§ 897, 947.
U. S. v., 4 Cranch, C. C. 309. §§ 696, 791.
Poag, S. v., 40 Tex. 151. § 613.
Poage v. S., 3 Ohio St. 229. § 752.
v. S., 43 Tex. 454. § 613.
Pocock, Reg. v., 17 Q. B. 34. § 350.
Rex v., 2 Stra. 1157. § 1057.
Poe v. S., 87 Ala. 65. §§ 306, 311.
v. S., 10 Lea, 673. § 408.
Poggi, P. v., 19 Cal. 600. §§ 555, 607, 654.
Pogue v. S., 12 Tex. Ap. 283. § 409.
Poindexter v. C., 33 Grat. 766. § 411.
S. v., 23 W. Va. 805. § 791.
Point v. S., 37 Ala. 148. § 576.
Pointer v. U. S., 151 U. S. 396. § 416.
Poland, S. v., 33 La. An. 1161. § 625.
Polin v. S., 14 Neb. 540. §§ 407, 416.
Polite, S. v., 33 La. An. 1016. § 376.
Politzer, U. S. v., 59 Fed. R. 273. § 1334.
Polk v. S., 62 Ala. 237. § 1032.
v. S., 36 Ark. 117. § 203.
v. S., 40 Ark. 482. §§ 1113, 1118.
v. S., 19 Ind. 170. § 179.
v. S., 30 Tex. Ap. 657. § 309.
Polk County v. Hierb, 37 Ia. 361. § 5.
Polland, S. v., 53 Me. 124. § 601.
Pollard, C. v., 12 Met. 225. §§ 865, 878, 892.
v. Lyon, 91 U. S. 225. § 1125.
v. P., 69 Ill. 148. § 861.
v. S., 2 Ia. 567. §§ 448, 1106a.
v. S., 33 Tex. Ap. 197. § 617.
Pollen v. Brewer, 7 C. B. (N. S.) 371. § 836.
Pollman, Rex v., 2 Camp. 229. §§ 897, 962.
Pollock v. S., 32 Tex. Ap. 29. § 1006.
Pollok, S. v., 4 Ired. 303. § 1188.
Polly, Reg. v., 1 C. & K. 77. § 510.
Polson v. S., 137 Ind. 519. §§ 454, 459.
Polsten v. S., 14 Mo. 463. § 523.
Polwart, Reg. v., 1 Q. B. 818. § 296.
Pomeroy v. C., 2 Va. Cas. 342. §§ 543, 596.
C. v., 117 Mass. 143. §§ 169, 175, 179.
v. S., 94 Ind. 96. § 446.
S. v., 73 Wis. 664. § 1186.
Pomphret, C. v., 137 Mass. 564. § 1240.
Poncio v. S., 28 Tex. Ap. 104. § 930.
Pond v. P., 8 Mich. 150. §§ 144, 299, 302, 304, 312.
v. S., 47 Miss. 39. § 1281.
S. v., 93 Mo. 606. § 1210.
Pons, S. v., 28 La. An. 43. § 800.
Pontius v. P., 82 N. Y. 339. § 279.
Pook, Reg. v., 13 Cox, 172, n. § 413.
Pool, P. v., 27 Cal. 572. §§ 328, 358, 411.
v. S., 87 Ga. 526. § 325.
S. v., 106 N. C. 698. § 1185.
Poole, Reg. v., Dears. & B. 345. § 567.
v. S., 2 Baxt. 288. § 382.
Pope, C. v., 3 Dana, 418. § 324.
v. St. Leger, 1 Salk. 344. § 1283.
v. S., 63 Miss. 53. § 1293.
S. v., 9 S. C. 273. § 520.
Porath v. S., 90 Wis. 527. §§ 461, 1121.

Porte, U. S. v., 1 Cranch, C. C. 369. § 596.
Porter, C. v., 1 Gray, 476. §§ 39, 1023.
C. v., 4 Gray, 426. § 1275.
v. Cooper, 6 C. & P. 354. § **886.**
v. Day, 71 Wis. 296. § **1297.**
P. v., 104 Cal. 415. § 892.
Reg. v., 12 Cox, 444. § **328.**
Reg. v., L. & C. 394. § **130.**
v. S., 57 Ark. 267. § **362.**
v. S., 26 Fla. 56. § **597.**
v. S., 51 Ga. 300. § 1286.
v. S., 86 Ga. 362. §§ **1017, 1021.**
v. S., 17 Ind. 415. § 752.
v. S., Mart. & Y. 226. § **545.**
v. S., 57 Miss. 300. § 266.
v. S., 5 Sneed, 358. § **1299.**
v. S., 43 Tex. 367. § 614.
v. S., 23 Tex. Ap. 295. § 569.
v. S., 33 Tex. Ap. 385. § 462.
S. v., 38 Ark. 637. §§ 1137, 1140.
S. v., 2 Hill (S. C.), 611. § **874.**
S. v., 34 Ia. 131. § 316.
S. v., 26 Mo. 201. §§ 634, 639.
S. v., 75 Mo. 171. §§ 693, 698, 709.
S. v., 90 N. C. 719. § 519.
S. v., 101 N. C. 713. § 257.
S. v., 112 N. C. 887. § 1163.
S. v., 25 W. Va. 685. § 563.
Porterfield, S. v., — S. C. —, 25 S. E. R. 39. § 1214.
Portis v. S., 27 Ark. 360. § 1310.
Portland, S. v., 74 Me. 268. §§ 183, **1176.**
Portland S. & P. R. Co., S. v., 58 Me. 46. § 1187.
Portugal, Reg. v., 16 Q. B. D. 487. § **627.**
Portwood v. S., 29 Tex. 47. § 505.
Posey, C. v., 4 Call, 109. § 518.
S. v., 1 Humph. 384. § **1297.**
S. v., 7 Rich. 484. § 609.
Post, Rex v., Russ. & Ry. 101. § **765.**
v. S., 10 Tex. Ap. 598. § 203.
Postal, S. v., 83 Ia. 460. § 278.
Postal Tel. Cable Co. v. Charleston, 153 U. S. 692. § 44.
Poston v. S., 12 Tex. Ap. 408. § **209.**
Poteet, S. v., 8 Ired. 23. § 1097.
S. v., 86 N. C. 612. § 1234.
Poteete v. S., 72 Ala. 558. § 1308.
v. S., 9 Baxt. 261. § 340.
Potter, P. v., 35 Cal. 110. § 656*a*.
P. v., 5 Mich. 1. §§ 123, 333, 353, 411.
Reg. v., 2 Den. 235. § **499.**
v. S., 42 Ark. 29. § 78.
v. S., 39 Tex. 388. § 593.
v. S., 9 Tex. Ap. 55. § **799.**
S. v., 28 Ia. 554. §§ 953, 974.
S. v., 13 Kan. 414. §§ 305, **423.**
S. v., 42 Vt. 495. § 145.
S. v., 52 Vt. 33. § 1098.
T. v., 1 Ariz. 421. §§ **440, 441.**
v. U. S., 155 U. S. 438. §§ 121, 1339.
U. S. v., 56 Fed. R. 83. §§ 1339, 1340.
U. S. v., 56 Fed. R. 97. § 1339.
Pottmeyer, S. v., 30 Ind. 287. § 823.
S. v., 33 Ind. 402. § 536.
Potts, Rex v., Russ. & Ry. 353. §§ 200, 205.
Potts, S. v., 78 Ia. 656. § 896.
S. v., 9 N. J. 26. §§ 794, 805.
S. v., 75 N. C. 129. § 494.
S. v., 100 N. C. 457. §§ 157, **159, 164,** 173, 175, 178.
Poulton, Rex v., 5 C. & P. 329. §§ **294,** 373*a*.
Pound v. S., 43 Ga. 88. § 307.
Pounders v. S., 37 Ark. 399. §§ **1257, 1260,** 1261.
Pounds v. S., 95 Ga. 475. § 440.
Povey, Reg. v., Dears. 32. § 1082.
Powderly, C. v., 148 Mass. 457. § **1222.**
Powe v. S., 48 N. J. 34. § 1148.
Powell v. C., 11 Grat. 822. § 752.
v. C., 114 Pa. St. 265. § 34.
C. v., 2 Met. (Ky.) 10. § 852.
v. Pennsylvania, 127 U. S. 678. § **34.**
P. v., 87 Cal. 348. § 333.
P. v., 63 N. Y. 88. §§ 128, 971.
Reg. v., 2 Den. 403. § 543.
Resp. v., 1 Dall. 47. § 661.
Rex v., 7 C. & P. 640. § 611.
Rex v., 2 East, P. C. 976. §§ **769, 794.**
v. S., 19 Ala. 577. § 307.
v. S., 52 Ala. 1. § 307.
v. S., 63 Ala. 177. § 1247.
v. S., 69 Ala. 10. §§ 1202, **1270.**
v. S., 34 Ark. 693. § 556.
v. S., 88 Ga. 32. § 575.
v. S., 62 Ind. 531. § 1314.
v. S., 96 Ind. 108. § 1126.
v. S., 67 Miss. 119. §§ 325, **416.**
v. S., 7 Tex. Ap. 467. § 609.
v. S., 12 Tex. Ap. 238. § 1130.
v. S., 13 Tex. Ap. 244. §§ 292, **416.**
S. v., 28 La. An. 315. § 587.
S. v., 3 Lea. 164. § 1265.
S. v., 94 N. C. 965. §§ 505, **506.**
S. v., 103 N. C. 424. § 572.
S. v., 106 N. C. 635. § 466.
S. v., 28 Tex. 626. § 872.
Powels, Rex v., 4 C. & P. 571. § **227.**
Power, C. v., 7 Met. 596. §§ 133, **143.**
Powers, P. v., 6 N. Y. 50. § 28.
v. S., 44 Ga. 209. § 1121.
v. S., 80 Ind. 77. § 380.
v. S., 87 Ind. 97. §§ 753, 789, **799.**
v. S., 87 Ind. 144. §§ 101, 389.
v. S., 16 Tex. 546. § 614.
v. S., 17 Tex. Ap. 428. § 876.
S. v., 36 Conn. 77. § 1139.
S. v., 12 Ired. 5. §§ 1065, 1069.
Powner, Reg. v., 12 Cox, 235. § 750.
Poyer v. Desplaines, 20 Ill. Ap. 30. § 66
Poynier, S. v., 36 La. An. 572. § 206.
Poynton, Reg. v., L. & C. 247. §§ 548, 1330.
Poyser, Reg. v., 2 Den. 233. § **555.**
Prather v. S., 12 Tex. Ap. 401. § **1232.**
v. S., 14 Tex. Ap. 453. § 1216.
Pratley, Rex v., 5 C. & P. 533. § **555.**
Prator v. S., 15 Tex. Ap. 363. § **573.**
Pratt, In re, 19 Colo. 138. § 18.
C. v., 126 Mass. 462. § 148.
C. v., 132 Mass. 246. § 655.
C. v., 137 Mass. 98. §§ **636, 652.**

Pratt, Reg. v., Dears. 360. § 547.
Reg. v., 4 F. & F. 315. § 724.
Rex v., 1 Moody, 250. § 560.
v. S., 49 Ark. 179. § 232.
v. S., 51 Ark. 167. § 454.
v. S., 19 Ohio St. 270. § 1310.
v. S., 19 Ohio St. 277. § 460.
v. S., 35 Ohio St. 514. §§ 546, 585.
S. v., 1 Houst. Cr. C. 249. §§ 177, 341.
S. v., 20 Ia. 267. §§ 548, 571.
S. v., 98 Mo. 482. §§ 641, 651, 652.
S. v., 88 N. C. 639. § 391.
S. v., 34 Vt. 323. § 1262.
T. v., 6 Dak. 483. § 1216.
Prebble, Reg. v., 1 F. & F. 325. § 922.
Prehm v. S., 22 Neb. 673. § 675.
Preisker v. P., 47 Ill. 382. § 462.
Prell v. McDonald, 7 Kan. 426. § 12.
Presbury, S. v., 13 Mo. 342. § 191.
Prescott, S. v., 33 N. H. 212. §§ 1290, 1291, 1306, 1309.
President of O. & M. R. Co., S. v., 23 Ind. 362. § 181.
Preslar, S. v., 3 Jones, 421. § 286.
Presnell, S. v., 12 Ired. 103. § 128.
Presser v. Illinois, 116 U. S. 252. § 1030.
v. S., 77 Ind. 274. § 310.
Pressler v. S., 13 Tex. Ap. 95. § 1257.
v. S., 19 Tex. Ap. 52. § 1032.
Pressly, S. v., 90 N. C. 730. § 495.
Prestney, Reg. v., 3 Cox, 505. § 823.
Preston, Reg. v., 2 Den. 353. § 571.
v. S., 63 Ala. 127. § 1032.
v. S., 25 Miss. 383. §§ 336, 338.
v. S., 4 Tex. Ap. 186. § 420.
S. v., 48 Vt. 12. § 1220.
S. v., 34 Wis. 675. § 1189.
Prestwood v. S., 87 Ala. 147. § 50.
Prettyman, S. v., 3 Harr. 570. §§ 1230, 1231.
Preuit v. P., 5 Neb. 377. § 365.
Prewitt v. S., 51 Ala. 33. § 242.
Price v. C., 21 Grat. 846. §§ 619, 713.
v. C., 33 Grat. 819. § 389.
C. v., 10 Gray, 472. § 808.
C. v., 8 Leigh, 757. § 1313.
v. P., 109 Ill. 109. §§ 117, 505.
v. P., 131 Ill. 223. § 303.
P. v., 74 Mich. 37. § 190.
Reg. v., 8 C. & P. 282. § 255.
Reg. v., 9 C. & P. 729. § 520.
Reg. v., 12 Q. B. D. 247. §§ 920, 1165.
Rex v., 5 C. & P. 510. § 993.
Rex v., 8 C. & P. 19. § 145.
v. S., 96 Ala. 1. § 1137.
v. S., 67 Ga. 723. § 61.
v. S., 72 Ga. 441. §§ 413, 426.
v. S., 36 Miss. 531. § 275.
v. S., 19 Ohio, 423. § 605.
v. S., 18 Tex. Ap. 474. § 299.
v. S., 22 Tex. Ap. 110. § 268.
S. v., 75 Ia. 243. §§ 1248, 1271.
S. v., 55 Kan. 606. § 552.
S. v., 6 La. An. 691. § 425.
S. v., 21 Md. 449. §§ 1184, 1191.
Price, S. v., 11 N. J. 203. § 519.
Priddy, S. v., 4 Humph. 428. § 1009
Pridgen v. S., 31 Tex. 420. § 307.
Priebnow, S. v., 14 Neb. 484. §§ 813, 831.
Pries, Reg. v., 6 Cox, 165. § 754.
Priester, S. v., 43 Minn. 373. § 63.
Priestley, S. v., 74 Mo. 24. §§ 462, 463.
Prim v. S., 36 Ala. 244. §§ 1186, 1189.
v. S., 32 Tex. 158. § 548.
Primelt, Reg. v., 1 F. & F. 50. § 1102.
Primm, S. v., 98 Mo. 368. §§ 1112, 1113, 1114.
Primus v. S., 2 Tex. Ap. 369. § 353.
Prince, Ex parte, 27 Fla. 196. § 543.
Reg. v., 11 Cox, 145. § 558.
Reg. v., L. R. 1 C. C. 150. § 563.
Reg. v., L. R. 2 C. C. 154. §§ 134, 451, 1105.
Rex v., 2 C. & P. 517. § 630.
v. S., 35 Ala. 367. § 265.
v. S., 30 Ga. 27. § 994.
v. S., 44 Tex. 480. § 514.
S. v., 42 La. An. 817. §§ 536, 537.
Prindeville v. P., 42 Ill. 217. § 454.
Prindle v. S., 31 Tex. Ap. 551. § 1153.
Pringle, Reg. v., 9 C. & P. 408. § 751.
Prior v. S., 41 Ga. 155. § 275.
v. S., 4 Tex. 383. § 1304.
Pritchard, Reg. v., L. & C. 34. §§ 601, 653.
S. v., 107 N. C. 921. § 916.
Pritchett v. S., 22 Ala. 39. § 307.
v. S., 92 Ga. 33. §§ 500, 514.
v. S., 92 Ga. 65. § 328.
v. S., 2 Sneed, 285. § 546.
Prius, C. v., 9 Gray, 127. § 960.
Privett, Reg. v., 2 C. & K. 114. § 556.
Prizer, S. v., 49 Ia. 531. §§ 1112, 1118.
Probasco, S. v., 62 Ia. 400. §§ 59, 1314.
Probert, Rex v., 2 East, P. C. 1030. § 521.
Proctor, S. v., 90 Mo. 334. §§ 101, 1190.
Prohibitory Amendment Cases, 24 Kan. 700. §§ 92, 1201, 1209.
Proper v. S., 85 Wis. 615. §§ 443, 455, 461.
Proprietors N. B. Bridge, C. v., 2 Gray, 339. §§ 183, 184.
Propst, S. v., 87 N. C. 560. § 1217.
Prospect Brewing Co., In re, 127 Pa. St. 523. § 1228.
Prosser, Rex v., 2 East, P. C. 502. § 495.
Proud, Reg. v., L. R. 1 C. C. 71. § 858.
Reg. v., L. & C. 77. §§ 631, 642, 651.
Providence v. Bligh, 10 R. I. 208. § 1223.
Prowes, Rex v., 1 Moody, 349. § 553.
Pruitt v. S., 20 Tex. Ap. 129. § 274.
Pryor v. C., 2 Dana, 298. § 543.
S. v., 30 Ind. 350. §§ 679, 694.
U. S. v., 3 Wash. C. C. 234. § 1358.
Puckering, Rex v., 1 Moody, 242. § 541.
Puckett, C. v., 92 Ky. 206. § 47.
Pugh v. S., 2 Tex. Ap. 539. § 260.
S. v., 7 Jones, 61. § 150.
S. v., 101 N. C. 737. § 241.
Pugsley, S. v., 75 Ia. 742. §§ 217, 1167.
Pulbrook, Reg. v., 9 C. & P. 37. § 753.
Pulham, Reg. v., 9 C. & P. 280. § 215.

Pullam v. S., 78 Ala. 31. §§ 624, 634.
Pulle, S. v., 12 Minn. 164. §§ 13, 955, 966.
Pulliam v. S., 88 Ala. 1. §§ 419, 426, 427.
Pullum v. S., 88 Ala. 190. § 1185.
Punshon, S. v., 124 Mo. 448. §§ 391, 424.
Purcell v. C., 14 Grat. 679. § 1302.
C. v., 154 Mass. 388. § 1248.
Purdie, S. v., 67 N. C. 326. §§ 813, 830.
Purdy, C. v., 147 Mass. 29. § 1249.
S. v., 36 Wis. 213. § 947.
Purley, P. v., 2 Cal. 564. § 950.
Purse, S. v., 4 McCord, 472. § 1170.
Purtell v. S., 43 Tex. 483. § 548.
Puryear v. S., 44 Ga. 221. § 1033.
v. S., 28 Tex. Ap. 73. § 396.
Putman v. S., 29 Tex. Ap. 454. §§ 1111, 1112.
Putnam, C. v., 4 Gray, 16. § 188.
C. v., 29 Pa. St. 296. § 956.
C. v., 1 Pick. 136. § 1088.
S. v., 35 Ia. 561. §§ 921, 922.
S. v., 38 Me. 296. § 128.
S. v., 18 S. C. 175. § 205.
Putney, S. v., Phill. 543. § 589.
Pybass, S. v., 4 Humph. 441. § 215.
Pyland v. S., 4 Sneed, 357. §§ 545, 596.
v. S., 33 Tex. Ap. 382. § 508.

Quaid, S. v., 43 La. An. 1076. §§ 1283, 1285.
Quail, Reg. v., 4 F. & F. 1076. § 200.
Qualter, Reg. v., 6 Cox, 357. § 426.
v. S., 120 Ind. 92. § 1265.
Quan Gin, In re, 61 Fed. R. 395. § 1345.
Quanstrom, P. v., 93 Mich. 254. § 1085.
Quarles, In re, 158 U. S. 532. § 961.
v. S., 55 Ark. 10. § 1325.
v. S., 5 Humph. 560. § 1298.
v. S., 1 Sneed, 407. § 336.
Quartemas v. S., 48 Ala. 269. § 1087.
Queen's Case, 2 Brod. & Bing. 302. § 989.
Quesenberry v. S., 3 Stew. & P. 308. § 307.
Quick, S. v., 15 Rich. 342. § 425.
Quigg, P. v., 59 N. Y. 83. § 94.
Quigley v. Aurora, 50 Ind. 28. § 6.
v. P., 3 Ill. 301. § 784.
Quimby v. Blackey, 63 N. H. 77. § 11.
Quin v. S., 65 Miss. 479. §§ 1017, 1021.
S. v., 3 Brev. 515. § 246.
Quincy, P. v., 8 Cal. 89. § 391.
Quinlan, C. v., 153 Mass. 483. § 1249.
Quinn v. P., 123 Ill. 333. §§ 546, 562, 572, 589, 624.
P. v., 18 Cal. 122. § 101.
v. S., 35 Ind. 485. § 950.
v. S., 123 Ind. 59. § 1246.
S. v., 47 Ia. 368. § 662.
U. S. v., 18 Blatch. 48. § 950.
Quitzow v. S., 1 Tex. Ap. 47. §§ 549, 551.
v. S., 1 Tex. Ap. 65. §§ 535, 569.

Raake, Reg. v., 8 C. & P. 626. § 753.
Racey, In re, 49 Alb. L. J. 252. § 1162.
Rachels v. S., 51 Ga. 374. § 992.
Radford, Reg. v., 1 C. & K. 707. § 781.
Radford v. S., 35 Tex. 15. § 582.
v. S., 33 Tex. Ap. 520. § 425.
Radley, Reg. v., 2 C. & K. 974. § 598.
Reg. v., 1 Den. 453. § 543.
Rae, P. v., 66 Cal. 423. § 560.
Rafferty, C. v., 133 Mass. 574. § 1281.
v. P., 69 Ill. 111. § 340.
v. P., 72 Ill. 37. §§ 328, 340, 342.
v. S., 91 Tenn. 655. §§ 18, 691.
Raffety's Case, 2 Lewin, 271. § 476.
Ragan v. S., 67 Miss. 332. § 1266.
Ragazzini, U. S. v., 50 Fed. R. 923. § 1346.
Ragg, Reg. v., Bell, 215. § 670.
Ragland, S. v., 31 W. Va. 453. § 36.
Ragsdale, U. S. v., Hemp. 497. § 83.
Raher, P. v., 92 Mich. 165. §§ 276, 280.
Rahrer, In re, 140 U. S. 545. §§ 104, 1205.
Raiford v. S., 59 Ala. 106. §§ 199, 217.
v. S., 68 Ga. 672. § 1121.
Railing v. C., 110 Pa. St. 109. § 425.
C. v., 113 Pa. St. 37. §§ 89, 327.
Railroad, S. v., 52 N. H. 528. § 288.
S. v., 58 N. H. 198. § 288.
S. v., 58 N. H. 510. § 288.
S. v., 59 N. H. 85. § 40.
Railroad Cars, U. S. v., 1 Abb. C. C. 196. § 113.
Railroad Co. v. Fuller, 17 Wall. 560. § 40.
S. v., 86 Ind. 114. § 78.
Railway Co. v. Hauks, 78 Tex. 300. § 539.
Rainey v. S., 94 Ga. 599. §§ 677, 681.
v. S., 8 Tex. Ap. 62. § 1037.
Rains v. S., 7 Tex. Ap. 588. § 557.
Rainsbarger, S. v., 71 Ia. 746. § 332.
Raischke, P. v., 83 Cal. 501. § 562.
Raisler v. S., 55 Ala. 64. § 1271.
Ralfe v. U. S., 11 Biss. 88. § 859.
Ramelsburg, S. v., 30 Mo. 26. § 576.
Ramey v. S., 127 Ind. 243. § 1129.
v. S., 14 Tex. 409. § 1293.
Ramirez v. S., 20 Tex. Ap. 133. § 614.
Ramsdell. C. v., 130 Mass. 68. § 1219.
Ramsay, S. v. 78 N. C. 448. §§ 1024, 1026.
U. S. v., Hemp. 481. § 83.
Ramsey v. Foy, 10 Ind. 493. § 83.
v. P., 142 Ill. 380. § 55.
v. S., 43 Ala. 404. § 934.
S. v., 5 Jones, 195. § 339.
S. v., 82 Mo. 133. §§ 160, 380.
Rand v. C., 9 Grat. 738. §§ 28, 78.
C. v., 7 Met. 475. §§ 543, 552, 553.
S. v., 33 N. H. 216. §§ 217, 495.
S. v., 51 N. H. 361. §§ 199, 1241.
U. S. v., 17 Fed. R. 142. § 1341.
Randall, C. v., 4 Gray, 36. §§ 123, 242.
C. v., 119 Mass. 107. § 617.
Rex v., Russ. & Ry. 195. § 753.
v. S., 132 Ind. 539. § 597.
v. S., 53 N. J. 485. §§ 575, 596.
v. S., 53 N. J. 488. § 933.
U. S. v., Deady, 524. § 1330.
Randle v. S., 49 Ala. 14. § 565.
v. S., 12 Tex. Ap. 250. § 1087.
v. S., 42 Tex. 580. § 1315.

Randle, S. v., 41 Tex. 292. § 1316.
Randles, S. v., 7 Humph. 9. § 950.
Randolph v. C., 6 Serg. & R. 398. §§ 220, 224, 946, 950.
C. v., 146 Pa. St. 83. §§ 16, 220.
P. v., 2 Park. Cr. 174. § 449.
v. S., 9 Tex. 521. §§ 83, 1284.
S. v., 1 Mo. Ap. 15. § 46.
Rankin, Rex v., Russ. & Ry. 43. § 339.
v. S., 25 Tex. Ap. 694. § 1188.
S. v., 3 S. C. 438. § 1170.
Ranney v. P., 22 N. Y. 413. §§ 661, 676.
Ransell, S. v., 41 Conn. 433. § 58.
Ransford, Reg. v., 13 Cox, 9. § 220.
Ransom v. S., 22 Conn. 153. § 571.
v. S., 26 Fla. 364. §§ 1285, 1308.
Ransome v. S., 91 Tenn. 716. § 1305.
Rapier, In re, 143 U. S. 110. §§ 1317, 1334.
Rapley, S. v., 60 Ark. 13. § 656.
Rapp v. C., 14 B. Mon. 614. §§ 267, 274, 304, 307, 338.
U. S. v., 30 Fed. R. 818. § 1330.
Rasberry v. S., 1 Tex. Ap. 664. §§ 241, 260.
Raschke, P. v., 73 Cal. 378. §§ 560, 564.
Rash v. S., 61 Ala. 89. § 400.
S. v., 12 Ired. 382. § 417.
Rasnick v. C., 2 Va. Cas. 356. §§ 774, 803.
Ratcliffe, Reg. v., 10 Q. B. D. 74. § 442.
Ratekin v. S., 26 Ohio St. 420. § 497.
Rater v. S., 49 Ind. 507. § 1247.
Rathbone, Reg. v., Car. & M. 220. §§ 557, 1330, 1335.
Rathbun, P. v., 21 Wend. 509. §§ 211, 791.
Ratigan v. S., 33 Tex. Ap. 301. § 1036.
Ratliff, S. v., 10 Ark. 530. § 1028.
S. v., 32 Ia. 189. § 1188.
Rattray v. S., 61 Miss. 377. § 1065.
Ratzky v. P., 29 N. Y. 124. §§ 78, 101.
Rau v. P., 63 N. Y. 277. § 90.
Rauscher, S. v., 1 Lea, 96. § 1210.
Ravara, U. S. v., 2 Dall. 297. § 14.
Raven, Rex v., J. Kel. 24. § 549.
Ravenscroft, Rex v., Russ. & Ry. 161. § 753.
Rawles, S. v., 65 N. C. 334. §§ 195, 232.
Rawlins, Rex v., 7 C. & P. 150. § 508.
Rex v., 2 East, P. C. 617. § 548.
Rawson v. S., 19 Conn. 292. §§ 83, 84.
Ray v. C., 12 Bush, 397. § 578.
C. v., 3 Gray, 441. §§ 210, 744, 752, 761, 763, 796.
Resp. v., 3 Yeates, 65. § 947.
v. S., 66 Ala. 281. § 501.
v. S., 15 Ga. 223. § 368.
v. S., 1 Greene (Ia.), 316. § 588.
v. S., 13 Tex. Ap. 51. § 565.
S. v., 50 Ala. 172. § 1302.
S. v., 109 N. C. 736. § 44.
Rayantis, S. v., 55 Minn. 126. § 70.
Rayland, S. v., 31 W. Va. 453. § 36.
Raymond, C. v., 97 Mass. 567. §§ 32, 128.
v. P., 2 Colo. Ap. 329. § 758.
P. v., 96 N. Y. 38. § 78.
Raymond, S. v., 46 Conn. 345. §§ 617, 620.
S. v., 20 Ia. 582. §§ 877, 881, 890, 892.
S. v., 12 Mont. 226. §§ 1307, 1308.
S. v., 11 Nev. 98. §§ 323, 353.
S. v., 27 N. H. 388. § 1185.
Rea, Reg. v., L. R. 1 C. C. 365. § 1073.
v. S., 8 Lea, 356. § 409.
Reach v. S., 94 Ala. 113. § 1037.
Read v. C., 3 Bibb, 484. § 1185.
v. C., 22 Grat. 924. §§ 274, 330.
Reg. v., 2 C. & K. 957. §§ 249, 464.
Reg. v., 6 Cox, 134. § 968.
Reg. v., 3 Q. B. D. 131. § 623.
Reader, Rex v., 4 C. & P. 245. §§ 520, 530.
Reading, Rex v., 1 East, 180. § 796.
Ready v. S., 62 Ind. 1. §§ 59, 1314.
S. v., 44 Kan. 697. § 480.
Reagan v. S., 28 Tex. Ap. 227. §§ 161, 451.
Real v. P., 42 N. Y. 270. §§ 159, 169, 380.
Ream v. C., 3 Serg. & R. 207. § 750.
Reams v. S., 23 Ind. 111. § 1246.
Reane, Rex v., 2 East, P. C. 734. § 470.
Reany, Reg. v., Dears. & B. 151. § 426.
Rearden, Reg. v., 4 F. & F. 76. §§ 461, 515.
Reardon, C. v., 6 Cush. 78. §§ 1086, 1094.
Reg. v., L. R. 1 C. C. 31. § 722.
Reason, Reg. v., Dears. 226. § 1330.
Reavis v. S., — Wyo. —, 44 Pac. R. 62. § 890.
S. v., 113 N. C. 677. § 232.
Reckards, S. v., 21 Minn. 47. § 1137.
Records, S. v., 4 Harr. 554. § 1302.
Rector, P. v., 19 Wend. 569. § 347.
v. S., 6 Ark. 187. § 251.
Reculist, Rex v., 2 East, P. C. 956. § 758.
Red, S. v., 7 Rich. 8. § 1284.
Redd v. S., 68 Ala. 492. § 419.
v. S., 69 Ala. 255. § 378.
Reddick v. S., 25 Fla. 112. § 373*a*.
v. S., 31 Tex. Ap. 587. § 759.
S. v., 2 S. D. 124. § 630.
Redding v. C., 3 B. Mon. 339. § 1273.
v. S., 91 Ga. 231. § 1253.
Redditt v. S., 17 Tex. 610. § 1303.
Redemeier, S. v., 71 Wis. 173. § 178.
Reder, U. S. v., 69 Fed. R. 965. § 1353.
Redfield, S. v., 73 Ia. 643. §§ 265, 280.
Redford, Reg. v., 11 Cox, 367. § 631.
Redgate v. Haynes, 1 Q. B. D. 89. § 188.
Redman, Reg. v., L. R. 1 C. C. 12. § 730.
v. S., 36 Ark. 58. § 128.
v. S., 1 Blackf. 429. §§ 609, 713.
v. S., 28 Ind. 205. § 141.
S. v., 17 Ia. 329. § 588.
Redmond v. S., 36 Ark. 58. §§ 128, 1257.
v. S., 35 Ohio St. 81. §§ 593, 702.
Redstrake, S. v., 39 N. J. 365. § 788.
Redus v. P., 10 Colo. 208. § 361.
v. S., 32 Ala. 53. § 1033.
Reece, S. v., 27 W. Va. 375. §§ 508, 617.
Reed v. C., 7 Bush, 641. § 601.
C. v., 162 Mass. 215. § 1248.

Reed, C. v., 34 Pa. St. 275. § 1171.
Reg. v., Car. & M. 306. §§ 135, 571.
Reg. v., 8 C. & P. 623. § 753.
Reg. v., 11 Cox, 689. § 1136.
Reg. v., Dears. 257. § 556.
Rex v., 7 C. & P. 848. § 670.
v. S., 16 Ark. 499. § 373a.
v. S., 54 Ark. 621. § 615.
v. S., 8 Ind. 200. § 382.
v. S., 28 Ind. 396. §§ 756, 758.
v. S., 62 Miss. 405. § 267.
v. S., 15 Ohio, 217. § 772.
v. S., 43 Tex. 319. §§ 897, 901.
v. S., 8 Tex. Ap. 40. § 571.
v. S., 9 Tex. Ap. 317. §§ 299, 338.
v. S., 11 Tex. Ap. 509. § 299.
v. S., 11 Tex. Ap. 587. § 195.
v. S., 14 Tex. Ap. 662. §§ 503, 509, 510.
v. S., 16 Tex. Ap. 586. §§ 644, 650.
S. v., 45 Ark. 333. § 1148.
S. v., 53 Kan. 767. §§ 304, 416, 426, 430.
S. v., 41 La. An. 581. § 166.
S. v., 62 Me. 129. § 421.
S. v., 12 Md. 263. § 376.
S. v., 85 Mo. 194. § 209.
S. v., 117 Mo. 604. §§ 358, 567.
S. v., 39 Vt. 417. § 460.
S. v., 40 Vt. 603. § 272.
Reeder, S. v., 36 S. C. 497. §§ 846, 849.
Reedy v. S., 22 Tex. Ap. 271. § 815.
S. v., 44 Kan. 190. § 1120.
Reekspear, Rex v., 1 Moody, 342. §§ 450, 1153.
Rees, Rex v., 6 C. & P. 606. § 1330.
Rex v., 7 C. & P. 568. § 508.
v. S., 7 Ga. 373. § 411.
Reese v. Atlanta, 63 Ga. 344. §§ 1224, 1228.
v. S., 73 Ala. 18. § 50.
v. S., 90 Ala. 624. §§ 338, 373a.
S. v., 83 N. C. 637. § 708.
U. S. v., 4 Saw. 629. § 674.
U. S. v., 92 U. S. 214. § 948.
Reeves, Reg. v., 5 Jur. (N. S.) 617. § 554.
Rex v.. 2 Leach, 808. § 780.
v. S., 96 Ala. 33. § 1026.
v. S., 7 Tex. Ap. 276. § 505.
v. S., 9 Tex. 447. § 1292.
v. S., 12 Tex. Ap. 199. § 1310.
S. v., 15 Kan 396. § 913.
S. v., 97 Mo. 668. §§ 18, 1111–2, 1119.
U. S. v., 38 Fed. R. 404. § 1329.
Regan, Reg. v., 4 Cox, 335. §§ 526, 533.
Reich v. S., 63 Ga. 616. §§ 1257, 1261.
Reichart, C. v., 108 Mass. 482. § 1234.
Reichert, U. S. v., 32 Fed. R. 142. §§ 966, 1352.
Reid, Reg. v., Dears. 257. § 623.
Reg. v., 2 Den. 88. § 484.
v. S., 88 Ala. 36. § 592.
v. S., 50 Ga. 556. § 346.
v. S., 71 Ga. 865. § 246.
v. S., 8 Tex. Ap. 430. § 1169.
S. v., 1 Ala. 612. § 1030.
S. v., 20 Ia. 413. §§ 494, 500, 514.
Reid, S. v., 125 Mo. 43. § 42.
Reidel, S. v., 26 Ia. 430. § 661.
Reifsnyder v. Lee, 44 Ia. 101. § 611.
Reiley, S. v., 75 Mo. 521. § 189.
Reilley v. S., 14 Ind. 217. § 724.
U. S. v., 20 Fed. R. 46. § 20.
Reilly, P. v., 50 Mich. 384. §§ 85, 1315.
Reily, C. v., 9 Gray, 1. § 1242.
Reinhart, S. v., 26 Oreg. 466. §§ 640, 651, 655, 656.
Reinhold v. S., 130 Ind. 467. §§ 509, 974, 988.
Reis, S. v., 9 Wash. 329. § 607.
Reisinger, U. S. v., 128 U. S. 398. § 101.
Reiter, C. v., 78 Pa. St. 161. § 909.
Rembert v. S., 53 Ala. 467. § 752.
v. S., 56 Miss. 280. § 1164.
Remby, C. v., 2 Gray, 508. § 1274.
Remelee, S. v., 35 Vt. 562. § 1276.
Remmington v. S., 1 Oreg. 281. §§ 83, 1283, 1285.
Remnant, Rex v., Russ. & Ry. 136. § 546.
Reneau v. S., 2 Lea, 720. § 298.
Renfrow, S. v., 111 Mo. 589. § 323.
v. U. S., 3 Okl. 161. § 1263.
Rennecke, U. S. v., 28 Fed. R. 847. § 1350.
Reno, S. v., 41 Kan. 674. § 1248.
Renshaw, Reg. v., 2 Cox, 385. §§ 58, 237.
Renwick v. Morris, 7 Hill (N. Y.), 575. § 1195.
Reonnals, S. v., 14 La. An. 278. § 553.
Reside v. S., 10 Tex. Ap. 675. § 652.
Revel v. S., 26 Ga. 275. §§ 321, 418, 421.
Revels v. S., 33 Fla. 308. § 274.
S. v., Busb. 200. § 605.
Rexroth v. Coon, 15 R. I. 35. § 538.
Reyburg, C. v., 122 Pa. St. 299. § 1218.
Reyburn, U. S. v., 6 Pet. 352. § 1359.
Reyelts, S. v., 74 Ia. 499. §§ 1248, 1272.
Reyes v. S., 34 Fla. 181. § 1158.
v. S., 10 Tex. Ap. 1. § 382.
Reynolds, Ex parte, 87 Ala. 138. § 69.
v. C., 93 Pa. St. 458. § 46.
C. v., 14 Gray, 87. § 937.
C. v., 89 Ky. 147. §§ 854, 1253.
C. v., 120 Mass. 190. § 123.
C. v., 122 Mass. 454. §§ 494, 504, 513.
P. v., 2 Mich. 422. § 714.
P. v., 71 Mich. 343. § 685.
v. S., 73 Ala. 3. § 1235.
v. S., 34 Fla. 175. §§ 389, 390.
v. S., 1 Ga. 222. §§ 389, 412.
v. S., 27 Neb. 90. § 441.
v. S., 11 Tex. 120. § 271.
v. S., 4 Tex. Ap. 327. § 257.
v. S., 14 Tex. Ap. 427. § 391.
v. S., 32 Tex. Ap. 36. § 1261.
S. v., 42 Kan. 320. §§ 287, 347.
S. v., 106 Mo. 146. § 698.
S. v., 126 Mo. 516. § 271.
S. v., 14 Mont. 383. § 77.
S. v., 95 N. C. 616. § 825.
S. v., 47 Vt. 297. § 1273.
v. Stevenson, 4 Ind. 619. § 1324.
v. U. S., 98 U. S. 145. §§ 120, 1076.

Reynolds, U. S. v., 48 Fed. R. 215. § 1348.
U. S. v., 48 Fed. R. 721. § 1348.
U. S. v., 1 Utah, 226. § 1076.
Rhea v. S., 30 Tex. Ap. 483. §§ 440, 455.
v. S., 10 Yerg. 257. §§ 404, 614.
Rhine, S. v., 84 Ia. 169. §§ 750, 752.
Rhodes v. C., 73 Va. 692. §§ 863, 882.
Rex v., 1 Leach, 24. § 750.
v. S., 1 Coldw. 350. §§ 249, 443, 464.
S. v., 1 Houst. Cr. C. 476. §§ 305, 337, 358, 365.
S. v., 48 Ia. 702. § 511.
S. v., 111 N. C. 647. §§ 532, 533.
S. v., Phill. 453. § 243.
U. S. v., 30 Fed. R. 431. §§ 1348, 1352.
Rhodus v. C., 2 Duv. 159. § 596.
Ribolsi, P. v., 89 Cal. 492. §§ 718, 719.
Rice v. C., 3 Bush, 14. §§ 263, 279.
C. v., 9 Met. 253. § 71.
v. Foster, 4 Harr. 479. § 1210.
v. P., 38 Ill. 435. §§ 1269, 1274.
v. P., 15 Mich. 9. §§ 268, 274.
P. v., 73 Cal. 220. § 723.
Reg. v., Bell, 87. § 536.
Reg. v., L. R. 1 C. C. 21. § 1138.
Rex v., 6 C. & P. 634. § 754.
Rex v., 3 East, 581. § 324.
v. S., 35 Fla. 236. §§ 447, 460.
v. S., 3 Heisk. 215. § 717.
v. S., 3 Kan. 141. §§ 82, 87.
v. S., 8 Mo. 561. §§ 36, 287.
v. S., 10 Tex. 545. §§ 1296, 1307.
v. S., 10 Tex. Ap. 288. § 1036.
S. v., 56 Ia. 431. §§ 1070, 1133.
S. v., 83 N. C. 661. § 620.
S. v., 43 S. C. 200. § 846.
Rich v. U. S., 1 Okl. 354. §§ 876, 878.
v. U. S., 2 Okl. 146. § 875.
Richards v. C., 13 Grat. 803. § 562.
C. v., 1 Mass. 337. § 596.
P. v., 67 Cal. 412. §§ 956, 981.
P. v., 1 Mich. 216. §§ 954, 957, 966, 977, 979.
P. v., 108 N. Y. 137. § 499.
Reg. v., 1 C. & K. 532. § 567.
Reg. v., 11 Cox, 43. § 737.
Reg. v., 1 F. & F. 87. §§ 167, 172.
Reg. v., 2 Q. B. D. 311. § 209.
Resp. v., 1 Yeates, 480. § 89.
Rex v., Russ. & Ry. 28. § 536.
Rex v., Russ. & Ry. 193. § 753.
v. S., 36 Neb. 17. § 455.
S. v., 39 Conn. 591. § 154.
S. v., 33 Ia. 420. § 455.
S. v., 72 Ia. 17. §§ 1117, 1119.
S. v., 32 W. Va. 348. § 44.
S. v., 76 Wis. 354. § 1134.
Richardson, C. v., 126 Mass. 34. § 1075.
Reg. v., 1 F. & F. 488. §§ 560, 673.
Reg. v., 2 F. & F. 343. § 642.
Rex v., 6 C. & P. 335. §§ 499, 717.
Rex v., 1 M. & Rob. 402. § 983.
v. S., 54 Ala. 158. § 454.
v. S., 3 Coldw. 122. § 101.
v. S., 34 Tex. 142. § 1097.
v. S., 37 Tex. 346. § 1087.
v. S., 43 Tex. 456. § 577.
Richardson v. S., 5 Tex. Ap. 470. § 1027.
v. S., 9 Tex. Ap. 612. § 316.
v. S., 28 Tex. Ap. 216. § 341.
v. S., 32 Tex. Ap. 524. § 316.
S. v., 45 La. An. 692. § 511.
S. v., 38 N. H. 208. §§ 142, 924.
U. S. v., 5 Cranch, C. C. 348. § 232.
Richart, S. v., 57 Ia. 245. § 617.
Richels v. S., 1 Sneed, 606. §§ 232, 239.
Richey v. C., 81 Ky. 524. § 882.
Richie v. S., 58 Ind. 355. §§ 238, 239, 454.
Richmond, P. v., 29 Cal. 414. § 151.
Reg. v., Bell, 142. § 750.
Reg. v., 1 C. & K. 240. § 777.
Reg. v., 29 L. T. 408. § 554.
S. v., 42 La. An. 299. § 373*a*.
Rickart v. P., 79 Ill. 85. § 1240.
Ricker, S. v., 29 Me. 84. §§ 215, 217, 218.
Rickert, P. v., 8 Cow. 226. § 838.
Ricketson, C. v., 5 Met. 412. § 1347.
Ricketts, Rex v., 3 Camp. 68. § 255.
U. S. v., 1 Cranch, C. C. 164. § 250.
Rickey, S. v., 9 N. J. 293. §§ 954, 960, 962, 966, 977.
Rickman, Rex v., 2 East, P. C. 1034. § 529.
Ricks v. S., 19 Tex. Ap. 308. § 988.
S. v., 32 La. An. 1098. § 307.
Ricord, Ex parte, 11 Nev. 287. § 626.
v. Central Pac. R. Co., 15 Nev. 167. § 634.
Riddle, Att'y-Gen'l v., 2 Cr. & J. 493. § 194.
v. S., 49 Ala. 389. §§ 241, 246.
v. S., 3 Heisk. 401. § 382.
v. S., 30 Tex. Ap. 425. §§ 1057, 1060.
S. v., 20 Kan. 711. § 307.
Ridenour v. S., 65 Ind. 411. § 1039.
v. S., 38 Ohio St. 272. §§ 123, 269.
Rider, S. v., 90 Mo. 54. §§ 309, 428.
Ridgeley, Rex v., 1 East, P. C. 171. § 777.
Ridgeway v. S., 41 Tex. 231. §§ 572, 597.
U. S. v., 31 Fed. R. 144. § 175.
Ridgley, S. v., 10 La. An. 302. § 993.
Ridgway, C. v., 2 Ashm. 247. § 989.
Reg. v., 3 F. & F. 838. § 670.
Ridley, Rex v., 2 Camp. 650. § 130.
S. v., 48 Ia. 370. §§ 511, 513.
S. v., 114 N. C. 827. § 858.
Ridling v. S., 56 Ga. 601. § 1261.
Ridout v. S., 6 Tex. Ap. 249. §§ 238, 255.
Riebe, S. v., 27 Minn. 315. § 765.
Ried, U. S. v., 42 Fed. R. 134. § 1331.
Rigby v. S., 27 Tex. Ap. 55. § 911.
Rigg, S. v., 10 Nev. 284. §§ 226, 233, 238, 266, 279.
Riggins v. S., 4 Kan. 173. § 752.
Riggs, C. v., 14 Gray, 376. § 582.
v. S., 7 Lea, 475. § 1028.
v. S., 26 Miss. 51. § 381.
v. S., 30 Miss. 635. §§ 342, 389.
S. v., 1 Houst. Cr. C. 120. § 439.
S. v., 22 Vt. 321. § 1046.
Rights, S. v., 82 N. C. 675. § 619.
Riley's Case, 2 Pick. 172. § 78.
Riley v. C., 94 Ky. 266. §§ 307, 311.
C. v., 14 Bush, 44. § 1271.

Riley, P. v., 75 Cal. 98. § 475.
Reg. v., Dears. 149. § 570.
Reg. v., 18 Q. B. D. 481. § 460.
v. S., 16 Conn. 47. §§ 931, 933.
v. S., 9 Humph. 646. §§ 354, 369, 370.
v. S., 95 Ind. 446. § 1196.
v. S., 43 Miss. 397. §§ 1236, 1237, 1274.
v. S., 20 Tex. Ap. 100. § 409.
S. v., 28 Ia. 547. § 580.
S. v., 42 La. An. 995. § 412.
S. v., 86 Me. 144. § 1267.
Rinaldi, Reg. v., L. & C. 330. § 752.
Rindskopf, U. S. v., 6 Biss. 259. § 964.
Rinehart, S. v., 75 N. C. 58. § 385.
S. v., 106 N. C. 787. § 1035.
Ring, S. v., 29 Minn. 78. § 648.
Ringer v. S., 33 Tex. Ap. 180. § 1037.
Ringsted, P. v., 90 Mich. 371. § 1264.
Riojas v. S., 8 Tex. Ap. 49. § 564.
Ripley, S. v., 2 Brev. 300. §§ 589, 591.
S. v., 31 Me. 386. §§ 967, 975.
Rippy v. S., 2 Head, 217. §§ 303, 306.
Risby v. S., 17 Tex. Ap. 517. § 313.
Risher, S. v., 1 Rich. 219. § 605.
Rising, S. v., 10 Nev. 97. § 827.
Risk v. S., 19 Ind. 152. § 1129.
Rispal, Rex v., 1 W. Bl. 368. § 960.
Ritcher v. S., 63 Miss. 304. § 1258.
v. S., 38 Tex. 643. § 544.
Ritchey v. S., 7 Blackf. 168. § 528.
Ritchie v. P., 155 Ill. 98. §§ 55, 77.
S. v., 107 N. C. 857. §§ 934, 1126.
Rither's Case, Cro. Eliz. 148. § 852.
Ritson, Reg. v., L. R. 1 C. C. 200. § 763.
Ritte v. C., 18 B. Mon. 35. §§ 1285, 1310.
Ritter v. S., 33 Tex. 608. §§ 828, 831.
Ritzman v. P., 110 Ill. 362. §§ 196, 377.
Rivers v. S., 97 Ala. 72. §§ 893, 894.
v. S., 10 Tex. Ap. 177. §§ 811, 815.
S. v., 58 Ia. 102. §§ 690, 691.
S. v., 60 Ia. 381. §§ 546, 548, 572.
S. v., 66 Ia. 653. § 922.
S. v., 68 Ia. 611. §§ 495, 514.
Rives v. S., 74 Ga. 375. § 262.
Rix v. S., 33 Tex. Ap. 353. § 214.
Roach v. P., 77 Ill. 25. § 305.
P. v., 17 Cal. 298. § 412.
v. S., 5 Coldw. 39. § 720.
v. S., 34 Ga. 78. §§ 309, 381.
v. S., 8 Tex. Ap. 478. § 361.
S. v., 75 Me. 123. §§ 1220, 1248.
Roadley, Reg. v., 14 Cox, 463. § 464.
Roane, S. v., 2 Dev. 58. §§ 298, 305, 308.
Roanoke Co., S. v., 109 N. C. 860. § 1187.
Roark, C. v., 8 Cush. 210. § 922.
Robb, Reg. v., 4 F. & F. 59. § 1103.
v. S., 52 Ind. 216. § 1198.
v. S., 35 Neb. 285. § 617.
Robberson v. S., 3 Tex. Ap. 502. § 850.
Robbins v. P., 95 Ill. 175. §§ 1306, 1307.
P. v., 70 Mich. 130. § 1252.
v. Shelby Co. Taxing Dist., 120 U. S. 489. § 44.
v. S., 20 Ala. 36. § 248.
v. S., 8 Ohio St. 131. §§ 326, 353, 354, 361, 425, 426.
v. S., 33 Tex. Ap. 573. § 209.
Robbins, S. v., 124 Ind. 308. § 1311.
Roben, S. v., 39 Ia. 424. § 1279.
Roberson v. S., 100 Ala. 37. §§ 1233, 1235.
v. S., 53 Ark. 516. § 309.
v. S., 15 Tex. Ap. 317. § 252.
Robert v. C., 10 Leigh, 686. § 1304.
Roberts v. Brown, 10 Bing. 519. § 1051.
v. C., 11 B. Mon. 3. § 1313.
C. v., 1 Cush. 505. § 1229.
C. v., 108 Mass. 296. §§ 205, 377, 426.
C. v., 132 Mass. 267. § 1174.
v. Mason, 10 Ohio St. 277. § 11.
v. P., 9 Colo. 558. §§ 666, 683.
v. P., 19 Mich. 401. §§ 159, 161, 1234.
Reg. v., 2 C. & K. 607. § 892.
Reg. v., Car. & M. 652. § 753.
Reg. v., 3 Cox, 74. § 556.
Reg. v., Dears. 539. §§ 775, 777.
Resp. v., 2 Dall. 124. §§ 1086, 1095.
Rex v., 1 Camp. 399. § 988.
Rex v., 7 C. & P. 485. § 546.
Rex v., 2 East, P. C. 487. § 503.
v. S., 61 Ala. 401. § 612.
v. S., 68 Ala. 156. § 307.
v. S., 7 Coldw. 359. §§ 521, 522.
v. S., 26 Fla. 360. § 1228.
v. S., 3 Ga. 310. § 158.
v. S., 65 Ga. 430. § 303.
v. S., 83 Ga. 369. §§ 576, 577, 578, 599.
v. S., 2 Head, 501. § 675.
v. S., 14 Mo. 138. §§ 142, 328, 340, 922.
v. S., 55 Miss. 421. § 511.
v. S, 72 Miss. 110. § 794.
v. S., 32 Ohio St. 171. § 1290.
v. S., 2 Tex. Ap. 4. § 796.
v. S., 5 Tex. Ap. 141. § 428.
v. S., 17 Tex. Ap. 82. § 617.
v. S., 17 Tex. Ap. 148. § 823.
v. S., 21 Tex. Ap. 460. § 569.
v. S., 30 Tex. Ap. 291. §§ 309, 310.
S. v., 1 Hawks, 349. § 339.
S. v., 11 Humph. 539. § 859.
S. v., 34 Me. 320. §§ 960, 975.
S. v., 15 Mo. 28. § 328.
S. v., 52 N. H. 492. § 925.
S. v., 59 N. H. 256. § 46.
S. v., 101 N. C. 744. § 823.
Robertson, In re, 156 U. S. 183. § 361.
v. Baldwin, — U. S. —, 17 S. C. R. 326. § 1347.
C. v., 162 Mass. 90. §§ 377, 380, 381, 388, 406.
Pennsylvania v., Addis. 246. § 295.
P. v., 67 Cal. 646. § 310.
Reg. v., L. & C. 483. § 737.
v. S., 54 Ark. 604. § 865.
v. S., 2 Lea, 239. §§ 130, 351.
v. S., 1 Tex. Ap. 311. § 594.
v. S., 5 Tex. Ap. 155. § 1216.
v. S., 12 Tex. Ap. 541. §§ 1209, 1226.
v. S., 30 Tex. Ap. 498. § 463.
S. v., 30 La. An., Pt. I, 340. § 380.
S. v., 38 La. An. 618. § 455.
S. v., 86 N. C. 628. § 1137.
Robinius v. S., 63 Ind. 235. §§ 128, 1257, 1314.
v. S., 67 Ind. 94. § 1257.

Robins, Reg. v., 1 C. & K. 456. §§ 1103, 1105.
Reg. v., 1 Cox, 114. § 1155.
Reg. v., Dears. 418. § 558.
Reg. 2 M. & Rob. 512. § 460.
v. S., 9 Tex. Ap. 666. § 349.
Robinson, Ex parte, 29 Tex. Ap. 186. § 35.
Ex parte, 30 Tex. Ap. 493. §§ 65, 66, 1170.
v. C., 16 B. Mon. 609. §§ 271, 274.
v. C., 6 Bush, 309. § 1074.
v. C., 6 Dana, 287. § 1248.
v. C., 88 Ky. 386. § 1079.
v. C., 101 Mass. 27. §§ 731, 732.
v. Culp, 3 Brev. 302. § 11.
P. v., 17 Cal. 363. § 376.
Reg. v., Bell, 34. §§ 539, 692.
Reg. v., 4 F. & F. 43. §§ 715, 724.
Rex v., 2 East, P. C. 1010. § 960.
Rex v., 2 East, P. C. 1110. § 729.
Rex v., 2 M. & Rob. 14. § 730.
Rex v., 1 Moody, 327. § 500.
v. S., 52 Ala. 587. § 509.
v. S., 38 Ark. 548. § 1326.
v. S., 38 Ark. 641. § 1238.
v. S., 59 Ark. 341. § 1234.
v. S., 1 Coldw. 120. §§ 549, 556.
v. S., 18 Fla. 898. §§ 862, 881.
v. S., 1 Ga. 563. § 546.
v. S., 82 Ga. 535. § 930.
v. S., 128 Ind. 397. § 1126.
v. S., 53 Md. 151. § 507.
v. S., 53 N. J. 41. §§ 693, 694.
v. S., 24 Tex. 152. § 1313.
v. S., 31 Tex. 170. § 232.
v. S., 11 Tex. Ap. 403. § 545.
v. S., 16 Tex. Ap. 347. § 333.
v. S., 22 Tex. Ap. 129. §§ 616, 617.
S. v., 3 Dev. & B. 130. § 829.
S. v., 28 Ia. 514. § 1190.
S. v., 29 La. An. 364. § 480.
S. v., 35 La. An. 964. § 602.
S. v., 33 Me. 564. §§ 82, 87.
S. v., 39 Me. 150. §§ 1273, 1278.
S. v., 49 Me. 285. §§ 1204, 1252.
S. v., 85 Me. 195. § 740.
S. v., 55 Minn. 169. § 188.
S. v., 73 Mo. 306. § 358.
S. v., 29 N. H. 274. § 845.
S. v., 16 N. J. 507. §§ 757, 794, 797, 808.
S. v., 35 N. J. 71. § 504.
S. v., 31 S. C. 453. § 271.
S. v., 35 S. C. 340. § 515.
S. v., 40 S. C. 553. § 1301.
S. v., 12 Wash. 349. §§ 208, 389.
S. v., 12 Wash. 491. § 412.
S. v., 20 W. Va. 713. §§ 159, 162, 360.
U. S. v., 4 Dak. 72. § 861.
Robison v. Miner, 68 Mich. 549. § 1206.
Pennsylvania v., Addis. 14. §§ 837, 841.
Robles, P. v., 34 Cal. 591. § 615.
Robnett v. P., 16 Ill. Ap. 299. §§ 1117, 1129.
Robson, Reg. v., 9 C. & P. 423. § 753.
Reg. v., L. & C. 93. § 554.
Reg. v., 16 Q. B. D. 137. §§ 631, 662.
Rex v., Russ. & Ry. 413. § 662.
v. S., 83 Ga. 166. §§ 648, 649, 650.
Roby, C. v., 12 Pick. 496. § 22.
P. v., 52 Mich. 577. §§ 128, 1237, 1264.
Roche v. S., 34 Ga. 78. § 381.
Rochforde, S. v., 52 Mo. 199. § 983.
Rockmore v. S., 93 Ga. 123. § 343.
Rockwell, P. v., 39 Mich. 503. § 285.
S. v., 82 Ia. 429. § 1269.
Roddy v. Finnegan, 43 Md. 490. § 923.
Roden, Reg. v., 12 Cox, 630. § 418.
v. S., 97 Ala. 54. § 311.
Roderica, S. v., 35 Tex. 507. § 1294.
Roderick, Rex v., 7 C. & P. 795. § 221.
Roderigas, P. v., 49 Cal. 9. §§ 1106*a*, 1111.
S. v., 7 Nev. 328. § 273.
Rodgers v. Kline, 56 Miss. 808. § 111.
v. P., 86 N. Y. 360. § 495.
v. S., 26 Ala. 76. §§ 1285, 1301, 1304.
v. S., 50 Ala. 102. § 377.
v. S., 30 Tex. Ap. 510. §§ 443, 450.
U. S. v., 1 Mackey, 419. § 560.
U. S. v., 150 U. S. 249. § 14.
Rodifer v. S., 74 Ind. 21. § 1308.
Rodman, S. v., 62 Ia. 456. § 612.
S. v., 58 Minn. 393. § 46.
Rodriguez, Ex parte, 39 Tex. 705. § 942.
v. S., 8 Tex. Ap. 129. §§ 267, 304.
Rodway, Reg. v., 9 C. & P. 784. § 560.
Roe, Reg. v., 11 Cox, 554. § 538.
v. S., 82 Ala. 68. § 826.
S. v., 12 Vt. 93. § 529.
Roebuck, Reg. v., Dears. & B. 24. § 669.
Rogers, Ex parte, 10 Tex. Ap. 655. § 793.
v. C., 5 Serg. & R. 463. §§ 226, 269.
C. v., 135 Mass. 536. § 1248.
C. v., 7 Met. 500. §§ 20, 133, 157, 158.
C. v., 1 Serg. & R. 124. §§ 838, 841.
v. P., 9 Colo. 450. §§ 63, 64.
P. v., 18 N. Y. 9. §§ 160, 162.
Reg. v., 8 C. & P. 629. § 764.
Reg. v., 9 C. & P. 41. § 753.
Reg. v., 5 Cox, 293. § 1330.
Reg. v., 37 L. J. M. C. 83. § 714.
Reg. v., L. R. 1 C. C. 136. § 552.
Reg. v., 2 Moody, 85. § 785.
Reg. v., 3 Q. B. D. 28. § 650.
Rex v., 2 East, P. C. 506. § 495.
v. S., 62 Ala. 170. § 305.
v. S., 60 Ark. 76. § 292.
v. S., 1 Tex. Ap. 187. § 460.
v. S., 8 Tex. Ap. 401. § 750.
v. S., 26 Tex. Ap. 404. §§ 522, 529.
v. S., 30 Tex. Ap. 462. §§ 1057, 1060.
S. v., 18 Kan. 78. §§ 309, 310.
S. v., 54 Kan. 683. § 499.
S. v., 39 Mo. 431. §§ 1273, 1274.
S. v., 108 Mo. 202. §§ 448, 1100.
v. Winch, 76 Ia. 546. § 458.
Rogier, Rex v., 1 B. & C. 272. §§ 1137, 1306.
Rohfrischt, S. v., 12 La. An. 382. §§ 521, 533.

Rohrbacher v. Jackson, 51 Miss. 735. § 1212.
Rohrer v. S., 13 Tex. Ap. 163. § 877.
Roland v. S., 9 Tex. Ap. 277. § 1099.
Rolland v. C., 82 Pa. St. 306. §§ 89, 108, 501.
v. C., 85 Pa. St. 66. §§ 12, 500, 504.
Rolle, S. v., 30 La. An., Pt. II, 991. § 1211.
Roller, S. v., 77 Mo. 120. § 93.
Rollins v. S., 98 Ala. 79. § 546.
v. S., 62 Ind. 46. § 252.
v. S., 22 Tex. Ap. 548. § 759.
S. v., 28 Ind. 390. § 604.
S. v., 8 N. H. 550. §§ 12, 102, 489, 490.
S. v., 55 N. H. 101. § 1021.
S. v., 113 N. C. 722. §§ 298, 307.
Roman v. S., 41 Wis. 312. § 342.
Romans v. S., 51 Ohio St. 528. § 762.
Rome v. Lumpkin, 5 Ga. 447. § 1217.
Romero v. S., 24 Tex. Ap. 130. § 613.
v. S., 25 Tex. Ap. 394. § 619.
Romine, T. v., 2 N. M. 114. §§ 359, 362.
Romp v. S., 3 G. Gr. (Ia.) 276. §§ 1291, 1313.
Roode v. S., 5 Neb. 174. § 756.
Rook, S. v., 42 Kan. 419. § 605.
Rooker v. S., 65 Ind. 86. § 798.
Rooney, C. v., 142 Mass. 474. § 1248.
Rex v., 7 C. & P. 515. § 611.
Rex v., 7 C. & P. 517. § 477.
Roosnell, C. v., 143 Mass. 32. §§ 443, 463–4.
Roper, S. v., 3 Dev. 473. § 571.
S. v., 1 Dev. & B. 208. § 1136.
S. v., 88 N. C. 656. § 520.
Roquemore v. S., 19 Ala. 528. §§ 1301, 1303, 1304.
Rorie, S. v., 23 Ark. 726. §§ 1284, 1297.
Rose, P. v., 85 Cal. 378. § 662
P. v., 12 Johns. 339. § 933.
Reg. v., 15 Cox, 540. § 313.
v. S., 19 Tex. Ap. 470. § 110.
S. v., 32 Mo. 560. §§ 12, 1136.
Rosecrans v. U. S., — U. S. —, 17 S. C. R. 302. § 1330.
Rosen v. U. S., 161 U. S. 29. §§ 123, 1332.
Rosenberg, P. v., 138 N. Y. 410. §§ 1171, 1172, 1179.
Reg. v., 1 C. & K. 233. § 558.
Rosenstein, Rex v., 2 C. & P. 414. § 1158.
v. S., 9 Ind. Ap. 290. §§ 1018, 1019.
Rosinski, Rex v., 1 Moody, 19. § 238.
Ross's Case, 2 Pick. 165. §§ 28, 78.
Ross v. Bruce, 1 Day, 100. § 805.
v. C., 2 B. Mon. 417. § 1141.
C. v., 2 Mass. 373. § 793.
v. P., 5 Hill (N. Y.), 294. § 563.
P. v., 65 Cal. 104. § 615.
P. v., 103 Cal. 425. §§ 878, 881.
Rex v., 2 East, P. C. 1067. § 826.
v. S., 62 Ala. 224. § 239.
v. S., 1 Blackf. 390. § 609.
v. S., 15 Fla. 55. § 489.
v. S., 59 Ga. 248. § 338.
v. S., 10 Tex. Ap. 455. §§ 142, 340.
v. S., 16 Tex. Ap. 554. §§ 502, 618.
S. v., 7 Blackf. 322. §§ 1290, 1291.
Ross, S. v., 4 Ind. 541. § 913.
S. v., 21 Ia. 467. § 118.
S. v., 4 Jones, 315. § 839.
S. v., 32 La. An. 854. § 392.
S. v., 25 Mo. 426. § 124.
S. v., 29 Mo. 32. §§ 213, 390.
S. v., 49 Mo. 416. § 101.
S. v., 76 N. C. 242. § 1131.
U. S. v., 1 Gall. 624. §§ 196, 291, 321, 1359.
U. S. v., Morris, 164. § 699.
Rosson v. S., 92 Ala. 76. §§ 1291, 1292, 1293, 1302.
Roswell, S. v., 6 Conn. 446. §§ 1083, 1120.
Roten v. S., 31 Fla. 514. §§ 328, 430.
S. v., 86 N. C. 701. § 1039.
Roth v. S., 51 Ohio St. 209. § 46.
v. S., 10 Tex. Ap. 27. §§ 552, 596.
S. v., 17 Ia. 336. § 1093.
Rothschild v. S., 13 Lea, 294. § 679.
v. S., 7 Tex. Ap. 519. § 373*a*.
Roubles, S. v., 43 La. An. 200. §§ 634, 653.
Rouch, S. v., 47 Ohio St. 478. §§ 6, 18.
Roudenbush, U. S. v., 1 Baldw. 514. §§ 161, 767, 808.
Rough, Rex v., 2 East, P. C. 607. § 538.
Rouland v. S., 55 Ala. 210. § 509.
Round, S. v., 82 Mo. 679. § 1101.
Rounds v. S., 78 Me. 42. § 757.
S. v., 76 Me. 123. § 803.
Rountree v. S., 58 Ala. 381. §§ 545, 548, 571, 607.
v. S., 10 Tex. Ap. 110. §§ 194, 291.
v. U. S., 1 Pinn. 59. § 260.
Rourke, C. v., 10 Cush. 397. §§ 542, 546.
Rex v., Russ. & Ry. 386. § 499.
Rouse v. S., 4 Ga. 136. § 771.
Roush v. S., 34 Neb. 325. §§ 771, 772.
Route, U. S. v., 33 Fed. R. 246. §§ 674, 690, 1352.
Rover, S. v., 10 Nev. 388. § 362.
Row, S. v., 81 Ia. 138. § 296.
Rowan v. S., 30 Wis. 129. § 368.
Rowe, Reg. v., Bell, 93. § 546.
S. v., 98 N. C. 629. § 501.
Rowed, Reg. v., 3 Q. B. 180. § 1154.
Rowlands, Reg. v., 2 Den. 364. § 984.
Rowley, Rex v., Ry. & M. (N. P.) 299. §§ 874, 888.
S. v., 12 Conn. 101. §§ 667, 953, 954, 958.
Roy, C. v., 140 Mass. 432. § 70.
S. v., 91 Ind. 417. § 1326.
v. S., 2 Kan. 405. § 389.
Royal, P. v., 53 Cal. 62. § 451.
v. S., 9 Tex. 449. § 1302.
Royall v. Thomas, 28 Grat. 130. § 324.
U. S. v., 3 Cranch, C. C. 620. § 26.
Royce, P. v., 106 Cal. 173. §§ 635, 639.
Rex v., 4 Burr, 2073. §§ 83, 205.
Royster, S. v., 65 N. C. 539. § 594.
Rozelle, In re, 57 Fed. R. 155. § 44.
P. v., 78 Cal. 84. §§ 217, 218.
Rubin, C. v., 165 Mass. 453. §§ 569, 570.
Ruble v. S., 51 Ark. 170. § 1277.
Ruby v. S., 7 Mo. 206. § 257.
S. v., 61 Ia. 86. § 504.

Ruby, S. v., 68 Me. 543. §§ 212, 218.
Rucker v. S., 95 Ga. 465. § 554.
v. S., 67 Miss. 328. § 1325.
v. S., 7 Tex. Ap. 549. §§ 194, 375.
S. v., 93 Mo. 88. § 200.
Ruddle, C. v., 142 Pa. St. 144. §§ 1184, 1186.
Rudge, Reg. v., 13 Cox, 17. § 625.
Rudick, Reg. v., 8 C. & P. 237. § 473.
Rudland, Reg. v., 4 F. & F. 495. § 440.
Rufer v. S., 25 Ohio St. 464. §§ 383, 416,
Ruge v. S., 62 Ind. 388. §§ 103, 1264.
Rugg, Reg. v., 12 Cox, 16. § 286.
Ruggles, C. v., 6 Allen. 588. § 239.
v. Illinois, 108 U. S. 526. § 40.
P. v., 8 Johns. 290. § 1159.
U. S. v., 5 Mason, 192. § 1347.
Ruhl, S. v., 8 Ia. 447. §§ 1101, 1104, 1105.
Ruloff v. P., 18 N. Y. 179. § 396.
v. P., 45 N. Y. 213. §§ 196, 357, 408.
Rumbo v. S., 28 Tex. Ap. 30. § 569.
Rumford Chemical Works, C. v., 16 Gray, 231. §§ 12, 1181.
Rump v. C., 30 Pa. St. 475. § 859.
Rumrill, C. v., 1 Gray, 388. § 1244.
Rundle, Reg. v., Dears. 482. § 130.
Rundlett, S. v., 33 N. H. 70. § 1272.
Runkle, P. v., 9 Johns. 147. § 836.
Runnels, C. v., 10 Mass. 518. §§ 993, 997.
Runyan v. S., 57 Ind. 80. § 311.
S. v., 130 Ind. 208. § 852.
Runyon v. S., 52 Ind. 320. § 1227.
Rupe, S. v., 41 Tex. 33. § 1149.
Rupp, C. v., 9 Watts, 114. § 916.
Rush, C. v., 14 Pa. St. 186. § 1192.
S. v., 13 R. I. 198. §§ 1218, 1220.
Rushing, S. v., 69 N. C. 29. § 717.
Rushworth, Rex v., Russ. & Ry. 317. §§ 757, 771.
Russell v. C., 5 Bush, 469. §§ 903, 947.
v. C., 78 Va. 400. § 408.
C. v., 156 Mass. 196. §§ 757, 808.
C. v., 162 Mass. 520. § 34.
P. v., 81 Cal. 616. § 520.
Reg. v., C. & M. 541. § 523.
Rex v., 6 B. & C. 566. §§ 1171, 1195.
Rex v., 1 Moody, 356. §§ 207, 290.
Rex v., 1 Moody, 377. § 500.
v. Sloan, 33 Vt. 656. § 1219.
v. S., 33 Ala. 366. § 394.
v. S., 72 Ala. 222. § 1302.
v. S., 77 Ala. 89. § 1223.
v. S., 11 Tex. Ap. 288. §§ 307, 423.
S. v., 90 Ia. 493. § 515.
S. v., 90 Ia. 569. § 1093.
S. v., 13 Mont. 164. § 426.
S. v., 91 N. C. 624. § 257.
S. v., 45 N. H. 83. §§ 991, 993, 997, 998, 999, 1001.
S. v., 14 R. I. 506. § 1133.
U. S. v., 22 Fed. R. 390. § 776.
Russen, Reg. v., 1 East, P. C. 438. § 450.
Russett, Reg. v., 2 Q. B. D. (1892) 312. §§ 560, 563.
Rust, Rex v., 1 Moody, 183. § 503.
v. S., 31 Tex. Ap. 75. § 511.
S. v., 35 N. H. 438. § 1273.
Ruth, In re, 32 Ia. 250. § 1212.
v. P., 99 Ill. 185. § 588.
S. v., 21 Kan. 583. § 447.
Rutherford v. C., 13 Bush, 608. § 391.
v. C., 2 Va. Cas. 141. § 715.
v. S., 11 Lea, 31. § 373*a*.
v. S., 13 Tex. Ap. 92. §§ 239, 252.
v. S., 15 Tex. Ap. 236. § 338.
v. S., 16 Tex. Ap. 649. § 391.
S. v., 1 Hawks. 457. §§ 298, 305, 308.
Ruthven, S. v., 58 Ia. 121. § 940.
Rutledge v. S., 88 Ala. 85. §§ 303, 307.
Ryalls v. Reg., 11 Q. B. 781. §§ 858, 859, 881, 883.
Ryan, C. v., 134 Mass. 223. § 402.
C. v., 152 Mass. 283. § 1240.
C. v., 155 Mass. 523. §§ 556, 623.
C. v., 157 Mass. 403. §§ 946, 951.
Reg. v., 2 M. & Rob. 213. § 276.
Rex v., 7 C. & P. 854. § 260.
v. S., 100 Ala. 105. § 418.
v. S., 45 Ga. 128. § 678.
v. S., 52 Ind. 167. § 252.
v. S., 5 Ind. Ap. 396. §§ 824, 825.
v. S., 83 Wis. 486. §§ 514, 617.
S. v., 30 La. An., Pt. II, 1176. § 307.
S. v., 81 Me. 107. §§ 132, 1176.
S. v., 13 Minn. 370. § 78.
S. v., 12 Nev. 401. § 566.
Rycroft, Reg. v., 6 Cox, 76. § 976.
Rye v. S., 8 Tex. Ap. 153. § 295.
S. v., 35 N. H. 368. § 1184.
Ryland, P. v., 97 N. Y. 126. §§ 147, 200.
Reg. v., 11 Cox, 101. § 454.
Reg. v., L. R. 1 C. C. 99. § 237.
Rymes, Reg. v., 3 C. & K. 327. § 690.
Rynders, P. v., 12 Wend. 425. § 800.

S. L., S. v., 2 Tyler, 249. § 713.
S. S., S. v., 1 Tyler, 180. § 324.
Saddler v. S., 12 Tex. Ap. 194. § 463.
v. S., 20 Tex. Ap. 195. § 586.
Sadi, Rex v., 2 East, P. C. 748. § 598.
Sadler, Rex v., 2 Chitty, 519. § 538.
Safford, P. v., 5 Denio, 112. §§ 8, 93, 1253.
U. S. v., 66 Fed. R. 942. § 1330.
Sage v. S., 127 Ind. 15. §§ 78, 96.
Sahlinger v. P., 102 Ill. 241. §§ 617, 725.
St. Asaph, Dean of, Rex v., 3 Term R. 428, n. § 1070.
St. Charles v. Meyer, 58 Mo. 86. § 1016.
v. Nolle, 51 Mo. 122. § 70.
St. Clair, P. v., 38 Cal. 137. § 495.
P. v., 56 Cal. 406. § 509.
v. S., 100 Ala. 61. § 635.
v. S., 11 Tex. Ap. 297. § 875.
S. v., 17 Ia. 149. § 714.
S. v., 16 Nev. 207. § 391.
v. U. S., 154 U. S. 134. §§ 362, 376, 382, 396, 420.
St. Geme, S. v., 31 La. An. 302. § 305.
St. George, Reg. v., 9 C. & P. 483. §§ 223, 226, 233, 271.
St. John Delpike, Rex v., 2 B. & Ad. 226. § 1074.

St. Louis v. Boffinger, 19 Mo. 13. §§ 62, 67.
v. Cafferata, 24 Mo. 94. § 63.
v. Fitz, 53 Mo. 582. §§ 25, 1133.
v. Foster, 52 Mo. 513. § 93.
v. Gerardi, 90 Mo. 640. § 1231.
v. Green, 70 Mo. 562. § 70.
v. Jackson, 25 Mo. 37. § 71.
v. McCoy, 18 Mo. 238. §§ 62, 67.
P. v., 10 Ill. 351. § 1195.
v. Siegrist, 46 Mo. 593. § 38.
v. S., 2 Mo. 113. § 1217.
v. S., 8 Neb. 405. § 416.
v. Sternberg, 69 Mo. 289. § 73.
St. Louis Club, S. v., 125 Mo. 308. § 1240.
St. Louis, A. & T. R. Co. v. S., 52 Ark. 51. §§ 1184, 1187.
St. Paul v. Hennessy, 38 Minn. 94. § 72.
Sales, S. v., 2 Nev. 268. § 899.
Salisbury, Rex v., 5 C. & P. 155. § 1330.
v. S., 6 Conn. 101. § 596.
Sally v. S., 39 Ala. 691. § 543.
Salmon, C. v., 136 Mass. 431. § 1229.
Reg. v., 6 Q. B. D. 79. § 351.
Rex v., Russ. & Ry. 26. §§ 523, 526.
Salomon v. S., 27 Ala. 26. § 1318.
Salorse, P. v., 62 Cal. 139. §§ 623, 636.
Salt, Reg. v., 3 F. & F. 834. § 808.
Salter, Rex v., 5 Esp. 225. § 988.
v. S., 99 Ala. 207. § 1027.
Salts, S. v., 77 Ia. 193. § 1253.
Saltus v. Everett, 20 Wend. 267. § 611.
Salyards, C. v., 158 Pa. St. 501. § 418.
Sam, S. v., 1 Winst. 300. §§ 449, 465.
Samanni v. C., 16 Grat. 543. § 993.
Samonset, P. v., 97 Cal. 448. §§ 1112, 1113, 1118.
Samora v. S., 4 Tex. Ap. 508. § 546.
Sampson v. C., 5 Watts & S. 385. §§ 212, 519.
C. v., 97 Mass. 407. § 1321.
C. v., 113 Mass. 191. § 1271.
S. v., 12 S. C. 567. §§ 498, 499.
Samuel, S. v., 3 Jones, 74. § 341.
Samuels, S. v., 111 Mo. 566. § 638.
Sanborn, C. v., 116 Mass. 61. § 1217.
Sanchez v. P., 22 N. Y. 147. §§ 341, 380.
P. v., 24 Cal. 17. §§ 339, 356, 358, 426.
Sander, U. S. v., 6 McLean, 598. § 641.
Sanderlin v. S., 2 Humph. 315. § 1247.
Sanders, In re, 52 Fed. R. 802. § 76.
v. C., 117 Pa. St. 293. §§ 101, 1216.
v. C., 118 Pa. St. 293. § 1216.
C. v., 5 Leigh, 751. § 1302.
v. Elberton, 50 Ga. 178. § 1231.
v. Johnson, 29 Ga. 526. § 1324.
v. P., 124 Ill. 218. §§ 859, 865, 878.
Reg. v., 9 C. & P. 79. § 499.
Reg. v., L. R. 1 C. C. 75. § 922.
v. S., 55 Ala. 183. § 906.
v. S., 18 Ark. 198. § 1188.
v. S., 60 Ga. 126. § 993.
v. S., 74 Ga. 82. § 1237.
v. S., 86 Ga. 717. § 554.
v. S., 88 Ga. 254. § 1276.
v. S., 77 Ind. 227. § 101.
Sanders v. S., 85 Ind. 318. § 12.
v. S., 94 Ind. 147. § 160.
v. S., 2 Ia. 230. §§ 1267, 1277.
v. S., 34 Neb. 872. § 1216.
v. S., 41 Tex. 306. § 391.
v. S., 18 Tex. Ap. 372. § 364.
S. v., 30 Ia. 582. §§ 1092, 1096.
S. v., 2 Ind. 578. § 915.
S. v., 76 Mo. 35. § 411.
Sands v. C., 21 Grat. 871. § 988.
P. v., 1 Johns. 78. § 1170.
v. S., 80 Ala. 201. § 529.
v. S., 30 Tex. Ap. 578. §§ 582, 715, 723.
Sandy v. S., 60 Ala. 18. § 824.
v. S., 60 Ala. 58. § 704.
S. v., 3 Ired. 570. §§ 518, 520, 523.
Sandys, Reg. v., Car. & M. 345. § 378.
Sanford v. Gaddis, 13 Ill. 329. § 865.
P. v., 43 Cal. 29. § 381.
v. S., 11 Ark. 328. § 936.
v. S., 12 Tex. Ap. 196. § 462.
S. v., 124 Mo. 484. § 459.
S. v., 1 Nott & M. 512. § 713.
Sankey, C. v., 22 Pa. St. 390. § 763.
Sansbury v. S., 4 Tex. Ap. 99. § 543.
Sansom, S. v., 3 Brev. 5. § 593.
Santissima Trinidad, The, 7 Wheat. 283. § 1359.
Santo v. S., 2 Ia. 165. §§ 1206, 1210, 1215.
Sarah v. S., 18 Ark. 114. § 136.
Sarbecker v. S., 65 Wis. 171. § 1236.
Sargent, C. v., 129 Mass. 115. §§ 854, 883.
Sarlls v. U. S., 152 U. S. 570. § 1220.
Sarradat, S. v., 46 La. An. 700. § 71.
Sarsfield, Reg. v., 6 Cox, 12. § 609.
Sartin v. S., 7 Lea, 679. § 615.
Sartor, S. v., 2 Strob. 60. § 1190.
Sartori, S. v., 55 Ia. 340. § 1243.
Sartorious v. S., 24 Miss. 602. §§ 713, 725.
Sasser v. S., 13 Ohio, 453. §§ 195, 772, 778, 786.
Satchell v. S., 1 Tex. Ap. 438. §§ 849, 851.
Satchwell, Reg. v., L. R. 2 C. C. 21. § 520.
Satterwhite v. S., 6 Tex. Ap. 609. § 615.
Saulsbury, C. v., 152 Pa. St. 554. § 914.
Sault v. P., 3 Colo. Ap. 502. § 719.
Saunders v. P., 38 Mich. 218. § 118.
P. v., 25 Mich. 119. § 957.
P. v., 29 Mich. 269. § 1142.
Reg. v., 8 C. & P. 265. §§ 249, 446.
Reg. v., 1 Q. B. D. 15. § 1157.
Rex v., 7 C. & P. 277. § 286.
S. v., 68 Ia. 370. § 808.
S. v., 19 Kan. 127. § 46.
S. v., 63 Mo. 482. § 684.
Saurbaugh, S. v., 122 Ind. 208. § 1326.
Savage v. C., 84 Va. 619. § 1210.
Reg. v., 13 Cox, 178. § 1082.
v. S., 18 Fla. 909. §§ 323, 357.
S. v., 32 Me. 583. §§ 499, 511.
S. v., 48 N. H. 484. § 1244.
Savannah, S. v., T. U. P. Charl. 235. §§ 17, 1306.
Savercool, P. v., 81 Cal. 650. §§ 259, 260.
Savery, C. v., 145 Mass. 212. § 1222.

Saviers, P. v., 14 Cal. 29. §§ 1285, 1290, 1293.
Savory, C. v., 10 Cush. 535. § 726.
Savoye, S. v., 48 Ia. 562. §§ 966, 974.
Saward, Reg. v., 5 Cox, 295. § 554.
Sawtelle, C. v., 11 Cush. 142. §§ 586, 597, 610.
C. v., 150 Mass. 320. § 1250.
S. v., 66 N. H. 488. § 212.
Sawyer, In re, 124 U. S. 200. § 78.
C. v., 142 Mass. 530. § 929.
v. P., 8 Ill. 53. § 723.
v. P., 91 N. Y. 667. § 139.
Rex v., 2 C. & K. 101. § 374.
Rex v., 1 Russ. Cr. 670. §§ 200, 291.
v. S., 35 Ind. 80. § 341.
S. v., 67 Vt. 239. § 1268.
Sawyers v. S., 15 Lea, 694. § 404.
Sayer v. Glossop, 2 C. & K. 694. § 1082.
Saylor, S. v., 6 Lea, 586. § 271.
Sayres v. C., 88 Pa. St. 291. § 417.
Scaggs v. S., 8 Sm. & M. 722. § 414.
S. v., 33 Mo. 92. § 1313.
Scaife, Rex v., 2 Lewin, 150. § 425.
Scales v. S., 96 Ala. 69. §§ 302, 342, 426.
v. S., 47 Ark. 476. § 1319.
v. S., 7 Tex. Ap. 361. §§ 206, 211.
Scammon, S. v., 22 N. H. 44. §§ 922, 925.
Scannel, C. v., 11 Cush. 547. §§ 442, 449, 452.
Scannell, S. v., 39 Me. 68. § 279.
Scarborough v. S., 46 Ga. 26. § 1138.
Scarfe v. Morgan, 4 M. & W. 270. § 1324.
Scarlet's Case, 12 Co. 98. § 904.
Scarlett v. S., 25 Fla. 717. § 678.
S. v., 38 Ark. 563. § 1252.
Scarver v. S., 53 Miss. 407. § 584.
Scates, S. v., 5 Jones, 420. § 292.
Scattergood v. Sylvester, 15 C. B. 506. § 611.
Schaefer v. S., 93 Ga. 177. § 397.
S. v., 44 Kan. 90. §§ 1218, 1220.
Schaffer v. S., 22 Neb. 557. § 320.
S. v., 74 Ia. 704. §§ 1138, 1143, 1145.
Schaffner v. S., 8 Ohio St. 642. § 1253.
Schaller v. S., 14 Mo. 502. § 159.
Schamberger v. S., 68 Ala. 543. § 536.
Schatz, S. v., 71 Mo. 502. § 601.
Schaunhurst, S. v., 34 Ia. 547. §§ 1120, 1122, 1124.
Schayer v. P., 5 Colo. Ap. 75. § 679.
Schechter, In re, 63 Fed. R. 695. § 44.
Scheele, S. v., 57 Conn. 307. §§ 144, 308.
Schele, S. v., 52 Ia. 608. § 271.
Schenault v. S., 10 Tex. Ap. 410. § 255.
Schenck, P. v., 2 Johns. 479. § 553.
v. Schenck, 20 N. J. 208. § 1055.
Schieneman, S. v., 64 Mo. 386. § 1024.
Schill, S. v., 27 Ia. 263. § 872.
Schilling, S. v., 14 Ia. 455. §§ 1180, 1248, 1249.
Schindler v. S., 15 Tex. Ap. 394. § 618.
Schingen, S. v., 20 Wis. 74. §§ 161, 556.
Schleagel, S. v., 50 Kan. 325. §§ 271, 275.
Schlect v. S., 75 Wis. 486. § 368.
Schleisinger v. S., 11 Ohio St. 669. § 684.
Schlemmer, S. v., 42 La. An. 1166. § 30.
Schlencker v. S., 9 Neb. 241. § 162.
v. S., 9 Neb. 300. §§ 333, 353, 359, 365.
Schlesinger, Reg. v., 10 Q. B. 670. §§ 866, 868, 873.
Schlicht v. S., 31 Ind. 246. §§ 1223, 1264.
v. S., 56 Ind. 173. §§ 1218, 1220.
Schloss, S. v., 93 Mo. 361. §§ 257, 268.
Schlottman, S. v., 52 Mo. 164. § 1020.
Schmail, S. v., 25 Minn. 368. § 1274.
Schmetzer v. S., 63 Md. 420. § 1310.
Schmidt, P. v., 63 Cal. 28. § 382.
Reg. v., L. R. 1 C. C. 15. § 715.
v. S., 78 Ind. 41. §§ 32, 128.
v. S., 14 Mo. 137. §§ 189, 1237.
S. v., 34 Kan. 399. § 101.
Schmidtz, S. v., 65 Ia. 556. § 1226.
Schmitker, Ex parte, 6 Neb. 108. § 1217.
Schmitt, S. v., 49 N. J. 579. §§ 1043, 1052, 1060, 1070.
Schmous, C. v., 162 Pa. St. 326. § 410.
Schneider v. S., 40 Ohio St. 336. §§ 128, 1167.
Schnicker v. P., 88 N. Y. 192. § 1106*a*.
Schnierle, S. v., 5 Rich. 299. § 1319.
Schoenfeldt v. S., 30 Tex. Ap. 695. § 1121.
Schoenwald, S. v., 31 Mo. 147. §§ 120, 121, 321, 391.
Schollenberger, C. v., 156 Pa. St. 201. §§ 34, 128, 1204.
Schoudel v. S., 57 N. J. 209. §§ 1131, 1132.
Schreiber, S. v., 41 Kan. 307. § 271.
Schroeder, S. v., 43 Minn. 231. § 1254.
Schryver, P. v., 42 N. Y. 1. § 316.
Schuchardt, S. v., 42 La. An. 49. § 72.
Schuchmann, S. v., — Mo. —, 33 S. W. R. 35. § 499.
Schuck v. S., 50 Ohio St. 493. § 1265.
Schulherr v. Bordeaux, 64 Miss. 59. § 1210.
Schullherr v. S., 68 Miss. 227. § 1258.
Schultz, P. v., 85 Mich. 114. § 636.
v. S., 32 Ohio St. 276. §§ 1182, 1248.
v. S., 20 Tex. Ap. 308. § 557.
v. S., 20 Tex. Ap. 315. § 618.
v. S., 30 Tex. Ap. 94. § 566.
S. v., 79 Ia. 478. § 1280.
S. v., 11 Mont. 429. § 36.
Schulz, S. v., 55 Ia. 628. § 287.
Schusler v. S., 29 Ind. 394. § 409.
Schuster v. S., 48 Ala. 199. § 1310.
Schuyler, P. v., 6 Cow. 572. § 558.
Schwartz v. C., 27 Grat. 1025. § 891.
C. v., 92 Ky. 510. §§ 679, 680.
P. v., 32 Cal. 160. §§ 214, 217, 522.
S. v., 64 Wis. 432. § 759.
U. S. v., 4 Cranch, C. C. 160. §§ 1184, 1191.
Schwarzschild, S. v., 83 Me. 261. § 41.
Schweiter, S. v., 27 Kan. 499. § 1275.
Schweitzer, S. v., 57 Conn. 532. § 58.
Schwuchow v. Chicago, 68 Ill. 444. §§ 1206, 1209, 1226.
Scofield, Rex v., 2 East, P. C. 1028. § 521.

Scoggins, P. v., 37 Cal. 676. §§ 303, 304, 307.
v. S., 32 Ark. 205. §§ 1073, 1077.
v. S., 18 Tex. Ap. 298. § 898.
S. v., 107 N. C. 959. §§ 128, 187, 189, 1259.
Scott v. C., 14 Grat. 687. §§ 785, 803.
v. C., 4 Met. (Ky.) 227. § 157.
v. C., 6 Serg. & R. 224. § 279.
v. C., 77 Va. 344. § 1131.
v. C., 2 Va. Cas. 54. § 96.
C. v., 1 Rob. (Va.) 695. § 779.
v. Cook, 1 Duv. 314. § 867.
v. Harbor, 18 Cal. 705. § 548.
v. P., 141 Ill. 195. §§ 1150, 1151.
P. v., 32 Cal. 200. § 529.
P. v., 74 Cal. 94. § 509*a*.
P. v., 6 Mich. 287. § 274.
Reg. v., 2 Q. B. D. 415. §§ 878, 886.
Reg. v., 2 Q. B. D. 659. § 1166.
Rex v., 3 Burr. 1262. § 996.
Rex v., Russ. & Ry. 13. § 546.
v. Shepherd, 2 W. Bl. 892. § 239.
v. S., 37 Ala. 117. §§ 325, 392.
v. S., 48 Ala. 420. §§ 455, 456.
v. S., 49 Ark. 156. §§ 239, 276.
v. S., 29 Ga. 263. § 1309.
v. S., 56 Miss. 287. §§ 303, 403.
v. S., 60 Miss. 268. § 389.
v. S., 62 Miss. 781. § 494.
v. S., 12 Tex. Ap. 31. § 160.
v. S., 31 Tex. Ap. 405. § 377.
S. v., 1 Hawks, 24. § 169.
S. v., 4 Ired. 409. § 339.
S. v., 12 La. An. 274. §§ 292, 426.
S. v., 38 La. An. 387. §§ 257, 382.
S. v., 41 Minn. 365. § 308.
S. v., 45 Mo. 302. § 806.
S. v., 48 Mo. 422. §§ 122, 123, 674.
S. v., 109 Mo. 226. §§ 505, 514, 616, 617, 618.
S. v., 64 N. C. 586. § 572.
S. v., 72 N. C. 461. § 466.
S. v., 116 N. C. 1012. § 1218.
S. v., 15 S. C. 434. § 272.
S. v., 24 Vt. 127. § 389.
S. v., 36 W. Va. 704. § 342.
v. U. S., Morris, 142. § 993.
U. S. v., 25 Fed. R. 470. § 1348.
Scotton, Reg. v., 5 Q. B. 493. § 858.
Scougal, S. v., 3 S. Dak. 55. § 42.
Scovel, S. v., 1 Mill (Const.), 274. § 714.
Scowden, C. v., 92 Ky. 120. § 852.
Scripture, S. v., 42 N. H. 485. §§ 500, 508, 602.
Scroggins, U. S. v., Hemp. 478. § 432.
Scruggs v. S., 90 Tenn. 81. § 1102.
Scudder, Rex v., 1 Moody, 216. § 1148.
v. S., 62 Ind. 13. § 974.
Scully v. C., 35 Pa. St. 511. § 1323.
Rex v., 1 C. & P. 319. § 142.
Scutt v. C., 2 Va. Cas. 54. § 96.
Seacord v. P., 121 Ill. 623. §§ 1170, 1171, 1175, 1176, 1179, 1181.
v. P., 22 Ill. Ap. 279. § 130.
Seagler, S. v., 1 Rich. 30. § 548.
Seal v. S., 13 Sm. & M. 286. § 1283.
Seals v. S., 3 Baxt. 459. §§ 337, 341.
S. v., 16 Ind. 352. § 1083.
Seaman, U. S. v., 23 Fed. R. 882. §§ 945, 950.
Seany v. S., 6 Blackf. 403. § 914.
Searing, Rex v., Russ. & Ry. 350. § 538.
Searle, C. v., 2 Binn. 332. §§ 743, 780.
v. S., 56 Vt. 516. § 1086.
Sears v. S., 33 Ala. 347. § 1033.
S. v., 86 Mo. 169. §§ 122, 232, 239, 266.
S. v., Phill. 146. § 830.
U. S. v., 55 Fed. R. 268. § 1328.
Seay, S. v., 3 Stew. 123. § 552.
Sebastian, S. v., 81 Mo. 514. § 257.
Seborn v. S., 51 Ga. 164. § 274.
Security Bank, S. v., 2 S. D. 538. § 180.
See, S. v., 4 Wash. 344. § 872.
Seelig v. S., 43 Ark. 96. § 1324.
Sefton, Rex v., Russ. & Ry. 202. § 496.
Segars v. S., 88 Ala. 144. § 1238.
Sego, C. v., 125 Mass. 210. § 578.
Segur v. S., 6 Ind. 451. § 1273.
Seibright v. S., 2 W. Va. 591. § 124.
Seifried v. C., 101 Pa. St. 200. § 1272.
Seiler v. P., 77 N. Y. 411. § 147.
Seiley, S. v., 41 La. An. 141. § 430.
Seim v. S., 55 Md. 566. § 1240.
Seitz v. S., 23 Ala. 42. § 275.
Selby, C. v., 87 Ky. 954. § 950.
Self, Rex v., 1 East, P. C. 226. § 349.
v. S., 28 Tex. Ap. 398. § 409.
S. v., 1 Bay, 242. § 556.
Selfridge, C. v., Whart. Hom. 417. §§ 139, 303, 306, 309.
Seling v. S., 18 Neb. 548. § 512.
Seller, P. v., 58 Mich. 327. § 589.
Sellers, C. v., 130 Pa. St. 32. §§ 1226, 1257.
Rex v., Car. C. L. 233. § 427.
v. S., 49 Ala. 357. § 721.
v. S., 98 Ala. 72. §§ 1238, 1239.
S. v., 7 Rich. 368. §§ 647, 912.
Sellis, Rex v., 7 C. & P. 850. § 294.
Selten, Reg. v., 11 Cox, C. C. 674. § 342.
Selvidge v. S., 30 Tex. 60. § 206.
Selway, Reg. v., 8 Cox, 235. § 575.
Semon v. P., 42 Mich. 141. § 1126.
Semotan, S. v., 85 Ia. 57. § 821.
Semple, Rex v., 2 East, P. C. 691. § 562.
Senior, Rex v., 1 Lewin, 183. § 294.
Sensabaugh, P. v., 2 Utah, 473. § 594.
Senterfit v. S., 41 Tex. 186. § 613.
Seran, S. v., 28 N. J. 519. §§ 218, 766.
Sergeant, P. v., 8 Cow. 139. § 1306.
Serlested's Case, Latch, 202. § 904.
Serne, Reg. v., 16 Cox, 311. § 326.
Server v. S., 2 Blackf. 35. § 856.
Sesler v. Montgomery, 78 Cal. 486. § 1055.
Sevailles, T. v., 1 N. M. 119. § 275.
Seven Bishops, Case of the, 12 How. St. Tr. 183. § 1052.
Sevier v. Justices, Peck, 334. § 17.
v. S., 117 Ind. 338. § 1018.
Seville v. S., 49 Ohio St. 117. §§ 988, 1013.

Seward, Rex v., 1 A. & E. 706. §§ 953, 962.
Sewell v. S., 82 Ala. 57. § 824.
S. v., 45 Ark. 387. § 40.
S. v., 3 Jones, 245. §§ 159, 169.
Seymore v. S., 12 Tex. Ap. 391. § 572.
Seymour v. S., 15 Ind. 288. §§ 468, 469.
S. v., 1 Houst. Cr. C. 508. § 265.
S. v., 36 Me. 225. §§ 504, 513.
Shackelford v. S., 43 Tex. Ap. 138. § 618.
U. S. v., 3 Cranch, C. C. 178. § 324.
Shackleford v. S., 79 Ala. 26. §§ 228, 418.
v. S., 2 Tex. Ap. 385. § 618.
Shadbolt, Rex v., 5 C. & P. 504. § 280.
Shadd, S. v., 80 Mo. 358. §§ 627, 1305, 1316.
Shade, S. v., 115 N. C. 757. § 255.
Shadley, S. v., 16 Ind. 230. § 834.
Shaeffer, S. v., 89 Mo. 271. § 696.
Shaffer v. McCrackin, 90 Ia. 578. § 758.
v. S., 82 Ind. 221. § 683.
v. S., 22 Neb. 557. § 383.
S. v., 21 Ia. 486. § 101.
S. v., 59 Ia. 290. §§ 511, 514.
Shaffner v. C., 72 Pa. St. 60. § 418.
Shafher v. S., 20 Ohio, 1. § 1074.
Shainwold, P. v., 51 Cal. 468. §§ 529, 533.
Shall, P. v., 9 Cow. 778. § 756.
Shanahan, S. v., 54 N. H. 437. § 1142.
Shank, S. v., 74 Ia. 649. §§ 1243, 1253.
S. v., 79 Ia. 47. §§ 1243, 1248.
Shanks v. S., 25 Tex. Supp. 326. § 762.
S. v., 66 Me. 560. § 878.
Shannahan v. C., 8 Bush, 463. § 162.
Shannihan, C. v., 145 Mass. 99. § 1326.
Shannon v. C., 14 Pa. St. 226. §§ 224, 959.
v. P., 5 Mich. 71. § 217.
S. v., 36 Ohio St. 423. § 46.
Shapleigh, S. v., 27 Mo. 344. § 76.
Sharkey v. S., 33 Miss. 353. § 1298.
Sharman, Reg. v., Dears. 285. § 756.
Sharp v. P., 29 Ill. 464. § 265.
v. S., 28 Fla. 357. § 1290.
v. S., 17 Ga. 290. § 1281.
v. S., 53 N. J. 511. § 688.
v. S., 19 Ohio, 379. §§ 140, 246, 274.
v. S., 6 Tex. Ap. 650. § 195.
v. S., 15 Tex. Ap. 171. §§ 447, 448, 461.
v. S., 29 Tex. Ap. 211. § 194.
S. v., 71 Mo. 218. § 357.
S. v., 106 Mo. 106. §§ 578, 604.
v. Wilhite, 2 Humph. 434. § 865.
Sharpe, Reg. v., 3 Cox, 288. § 995.
Reg. v., Dears. & B. 160. § 1167.
v. S., 17 Tex. Ap. 486. §§ 330, 382.
Sharpless, C. v., 2 Serg. & R. 91. §§ 1049, 1157.
Rex v., 2 East, P. C. 675. § 560.
Sharrer, S. v., 2 Coldw. 323. § 1221.
Shartzer v. S., 63 Md. 149. § 460.
Sharwin, Rex v., 1 East, P. C. 341. § 377.
Shattuck, C. v., 4 Cush. 141. §§ 836, 837.
C. v., 14 Gray, 23. § 1181.
Shaughnessy, P. v., 89 Mich. 130. § 499.
Shaw's Case, 1 East, P. C. 351. § 216.
Shaw v. Carpenter, 54 Vt. 155. § 1220.
C. v., 4 Allen, 308. §§ 542, 548.
C. v., 7 Met. 52. §§ 124, 942, 949, 950.
P. v., 5 Johns. 236. § 753.
P. v., 57 Mich. 403. §§ 559, 682.
Reg. v., L. & C. 579. § 858.
Rex v., 6 C. & P. 372. § 339.
v. S., 18 Ala. 547. §§ 266, 268.
v. S., 60 Ga. 246. §§ 392, 420.
v. S., 56 Ind. 188. § 1227.
v. S., 23 Tex. Ap. 493. § 586.
v. S., 28 Tex. Ap. 236. § 1057.
S. v., 2 Dev. 198. § 1273.
S. v., 8 Humph. 32. § 947.
S. v., 3 Ired. 20. § 925.
S. v., 4 Jones, 430. § 617.
S. v., 35 Ia. 575. § 1143.
S. v., 31 Me. 523. §§ 498, 519.
S. v., 32 Me. 570. § 1223.
S. v., 39 Minn. 153. §§ 1285, 1310.
S. v., 35 N. H. 217. § 1281.
S. v., 58 N. H. 73. § 1279.
Shawley, S. v., 5 Hayw. 256. § 796.
Shay v. P., 22 N. Y. 317. § 18.
v. P., 4 Park. Cr. R. 353. § 385.
S. v., 30 La. An., Pt. I, 114. § 377.
Shea, C. v., 150 Mass. 314. § 1138.
C. v., 160 Mass. 6. § 1243.
P. v., 8 Cal. 358. § 413.
P. v., 147 N. Y. 78. § 418.
Shean, S. v., 32 Ia. 88. §§ 1118, 1119.
Shear, S. v., 51 Wis. 460. § 454.
Sheard, Rex v., 7 C. & P. 846. § 256.
Shearer v. S., 7 Blackf. 99. § 1281.
Shearman, C. v., 11 Cush. 546. § 1274.
Sheay v. S., 74 Md. 52. §§ 1126, 1127.
Sheckels, C. v., 78 Va. 36. § 1217.
Shed, C. v., 1 Mass. 227. § 914.
Shedd, C. v., 7 Cush. 514. § 977.
Shee, S. v., 13 R. I. 535. § 145.
Sheedy, C. v., 159 Mass. 55. § 1318.
Sheele, S. v., 57 Conn. 307. § 144.
Sheeley, S. v., 15 Ia. 404. §§ 114, 949.
Sheerin, S. v., 12 Mont. 539. §§ 266, 268.
Sheffield, In re, 64 Fed. R. 833. § 44.
v. S., 1 Tex. Ap. 640. § 279.
Shelburn v. C., 85 Ky. 173. § 630.
Shelby, S. v., 90 Mo. 302. §§ 23, 1030.
Sheldon, P. v., 139 N. Y. 251. § 963.
Shell v. S., 88 Ala. 14. §§ 425, 431.
v. S., 6 Humph. 283. § 814.
Shellard, Reg. v., 9 C. & P. 277. § 988.
Shelledy, S. v., 8 Ia. 477. §§ 196, 326, 335, 349.
Shellmire, U. S. v., Baldw. 370. §§ 752, 771, 867.
Shelly v. S., 95 Tenn. 152. §§ 1120, 1121.
Shelters, P. v., 99 Mich. 333. § 667.
S. v., 51 Vt. 102. § 754.
Shelton v. C., 89 Va. 450. §§ 504, 513.
C. v., 8 Grat. 592. §§ 1283, 1285, 1297.
v. S., 34 Tex. 662. § 359.
v. S., 27 Tex. Ap. 443. § 1036.
S. v., 7 Humph. 30. § 784.
S. v., 2 Jones, 360. § 427.

Shelton, S. v., 64 Ia. 333. §§ 361, 383, 388, 419.
Shepard, S. v., 10 Ia. 126. §§ 233, 271.
Shepardson, P. v., 48 Cal. 189. §§ 209, 217, 476.
Shepheard v. Whitaker, L. R. 10 C. P. 502. § 111.
Shepherd v. P., 72 Ill. 480. § 373a.
v. P., 19 N. Y. 537. §§ 518, 521.
v. P., 25 N. Y. 406. §§ 78, 92.
Reg. v., 9 Cox, 123. § 286.
Reg. v., 11 Cox, 325. § 963.
Reg. v., Dears. 606. §§ 557, 1330, 1335.
Reg. v., L. R. 1 C. C. 118. § 584.
Rex v., 2 East, P. C. 967. §§ 788, 809.
Rex v., 2 East, P. C. 1073. § 829.
v. S., 44 Ark. 39. § 619.
v. S., 42 Tex. 501. § 511.
Sheppard, Reg. v., 9 C. & P. 121. §§ 195, 558.
Reg. v., 11 Cox, 302. § 524.
v. S., 42 Ala. 531. § 586.
v. S., 1 Tex. Ap. 304. § 1304.
v. S., 17 Tex. Ap. 74. § 294.
S. v., 33 La. An. 1216. §§ 536, 601.
Sherar v. S., 30 Tex. Ap. 349. § 322.
Sheriff, C. v., 16 Serg. & R. 304. § 215.
Sherlock, Reg. v., L. R. 1 C. C. 20. § 926.
S. v., 26 Tex. 106. § 572.
Sherman, P. v., 133 N. Y. 349. § 554.
P. v., 10 Wend. 298. § 626.
S. v., 50 Mo. 265. § 1217.
Shermer, S. v., 55 Mo. 83. §§ 562, 569.
Sherrill, S. v., 1 Jones, 508. § 1028.
Sherrington, Rex v., 1 Leach, 513. § 546.
Sherrod v. S., 25 Ala. 78. § 1303.
Sherwin v. P., 69 Ill. 55. §§ 457, 460.
Sherwood, Ex parte, 29 Tex. Ap. 334. § 340.
Reg. v., Dears. & B. 251. § 670.
v. S., 41 La. An. 316. § 800.
S. v., 90 Ia. 550. § 787.
Shettleworth, S. v., 18 Minn. 208. § 455.
Shickle, Reg. v., L. R. 1 C. C. 158. § 538.
Shields v. McKee, 11 Ill. Ap. 188. § 989.
v. S., 104 Ala. 35. § 405.
v. S., 89 Ga. 549. §§ 341, 1156.
v. S., 95 Ind. 299. § 1247.
v. S., 32 Tex. Ap. 498. §§ 460, 462, 463.
S. v., 45 Conn. 256. §§ 440, 447.
S. v., 110 N. C. 497. § 257.
Shiff v. S., 84 Ala. 454. § 44.
Shihagan v. S., 9 Tex. 430. §§ 1303, 1304.
Shilling v. S., 5 Ind. 443. § 1143.
Shines v. S., 42 Miss. 321. § 588.
Shinkle, S. v., 40 Ia. 131. §§ 1184, 1190.
Shinn v. C., 32 Grat. 899. § 554.
v. S., 57 Ind. 144. § 799.
v. S., 64 Ind. 13. § 469.
v. S., 68 Ind. 423. §§ 123, 252.
U. S. v., 14 Fed. R. 447. §§ 861, 863.
Shipley, Rex v., 4 Doug. 73. §§ 1053, 1070.
T. v., 4 Mont. 468. § 596.
Shipman, S. v., 81 N. C. 513. §§ 232, 233.
Shippey, S. v., 10 Minn. 223. §§ 156, 306, 325, 338.
Shipply v. P., 86 N. Y. 375. §§ 559, 560.
Shircliff v. S., 96 Ind. 369. § 962.
Shirer, S. v., 20 S. C. 392. §§ 554, 624.
Shirk v. P., 121 Ill. 61. §§ 90, 752, 764.
Shirley, C. v., 152 Pa. St. 170. § 34.
v. S., 1 Oreg. 269. § 798.
S. v., 64 N. C. 610. § 332.
Shivers v. S., 53 Ga. 149. § 646.
Shoaf, S. v., 68 N. C. 375. § 560.
Shock, S. v., 68 Mo. 552. § 355.
Shoemaker v. S., 12 Ohio, 43. § 358.
S. v., 20 N. J. 153. §§ 5, 91.
S. v., 101 N. C. 690. § 1055.
Shook v. S., 25 Tex. Ap. 345. 1290.
Shooter, S. v., 8 Rich. 72. §§ 904, 956.
Shores, S. v., 31 W. Va. 491. §§ 162, 565, 572.
Short v. Baker, 22 Ind. 148. § 11.
v. S., 63 Ind. 376. § 509.
v. S., 36 Tex. 644. § 594.
v. S., 15 Tex. Ap. 370. § 315.
v. S., 23 Tex. Ap. 312. § 1291.
v. S., 25 Tex. Ap. 379. § 1034.
v. S., 7 Yerg. 510. § 346.
S. v., 54 Ia. 392. §§ 495, 510.
Shorter v. P., 2 N. Y. 193. §§ 139, 302, 304, 306, 311.
v. S., 63 Ala. 129. § 1032.
Shorts, S. v., 32 N. J. 398. §§ 1315, 1318.
Shott, Reg. v., 3 C. & K. 206. § 442.
Shotwell v. S., 43 Ark. 345. § 510.
Shoultz, S. v., 25 Mo. 128. §§ 306, 359.
Shouse v. C., 5 Pa. St. 83. § 1001.
C. v., 16 B. Mon. 325. § 1299.
Shover v. S., 7 Ark. 259. §§ 1319, 1322.
Showalter v. S., 84 Ind. 562. § 1233.
Showers, S. v., 34 Kan. 269. § 101.
Shreves, S. v., 81 Ia. 615. § 303.
Shriedley v. S., 23 Ohio St. 130. §§ 471, 719, 726.
Shrivers v. S., 7 Tex. Ap. 450. § 420.
Shroeder, S. v., 51 Ia. 197. §§ 39, 1210.
Shropshire v. S., 69 Ga. 273. § 514.
Shroyer, S. v., 104 Mo. 441. § 463.
Shubert v. S., 16 Tex. Ap. 645. § 1189.
v. S., 20 Tex. Ap. 320. § 552.
Shubrick v. S., 2 S. C. 21. § 831.
Shufflin v. P., 62 N. Y. 229. § 341.
Shukard, Rex v., Russ. & Ry. 200. § 781.
Shuler, P. v., 28 Cal. 490. §§ 468, 473.
v. S., 23 Tex. Ap. 182. § 514.
S. v., 19 S. C. 140. § 536.
Shult, S. v., 41 Tex. 548. § 1291.
Shults v. S., 37 Neb. 481. § 173.
U. S. v., 6 McLean, 121. § 156.
Shultz, P. v., — Mich. —, 38 N. W. R. 868. § 565.
v. S., 13 Tex. 401. §§ 169, 409.
Shupe, S. v., 16 Ia. 36. § 859.
Shurn, C. v., 145 Mass. 150. § 1236.
Shurtliff, S. v., 18 Me. 368. § 763.
Shuster v. C., 38 Pa. St. 206. § 748.
Siberry v. S., 133 Ind. 677. § 405.
Sic, In re, 73 Cal. 142. § 63.
Siceluff v. S., 52 Ark. 56. § 1258.

Siddon, Att'y Gen'l v., 1 Cr. & J. 220. § 188.
Sidney, S. v., 74 Mo. 390. § 617.
Siebert v. P., 143 Ill. 571. §§ 401, 405, 416.
Siebold, Ex parte, 100 U. S. 371. § 948.
Siefried v. C., 101 Pa. St. 200. § 94.
Siegel v. P., 106 Ill. 89. §§ 1233, 1259.
Sies, S. v., 30 La. An., Pt. II, 918. § 1230.
Sifred v. C., 104 Pa. St. 179. § 92.
Sigel v. Jebb, 3 Stark. 1. §§ 1283, 1286.
Sigg, S. v., 86 Ia. 746. § 454.
Sigler v. S., 9 Tex. Ap. 427. § 565.
Sikes v. S., 67 Ala. 77. §§ 1270, 1284, 1285, 1287.
Silgar v. P., 107 Ill. 563. §§ 338, 339.
Sill v. Reg., Dears. 132, 1 El. & B. 553. § 707.
Silsbee, C. v., 9 Mass. 417. §§ 21, 941, 943.
Silver v. S., 17 Ohio, 365. § 859.
Silvus v. S., 22 Ohio St. 90. § 316.
Simmerman v. S., 16 Neb. 615. § 328.
Simmonds, Rex v., 1 Moody, 408. § 552.
Simmons v. C., 5 Binn. 617. § 553.
v. C., 1 Rawle, 142. § 1128.
Reg. v., Bell, 168. § 858.
v. S., 32 Fla. 387. § 382.
v. S., 4 Ga. 465. § 216.
v. S., 73 Ga. 609. § 577.
v. S., 88 Ga. 169. § 930.
S. v., 3 Ala. 497. § 435.
S. v., 6 Jones, 21. §§ 196, 291.
S. v., 66 N. C. 622. § 1275.
U. S. v., 61 Fed. R. 640. § 1333.
Simmonsto, Reg. v., 1 C. & K. 164. § 1082.
Simms v. Bean, 10 La. An. 346. § 83.
v. S., 60 Ga. 145. §§ 1310, 1311.
v. S., 2 Tex. Ap. 110. § 505.
v. S., 10 Tex. Ap. 131. § 212.
v. S., 32 Tex. Ap. 277. § 801.
S. v., 68 Mo. 305. § 158.
S. v., 71 Mo. 538. § 158.
U. S. v., 1 Cranch, 252. § 7.
U. S. v., 4 Cranch, C. C. 618. § 469.
Simon v. S., 31 Tex. Ap. 186. §§ 1084, 1120, 1122.
S. v., 50 Mo. 370. § 426.
Simonds, C. v., 79 Ky. 618. §§ 1285, 1297.
Simons v. P., 150 Ill. 66. § 426.
P. v., 60 Cal. 72. § 310.
Rex v., 2 East, P. C. 712. § 479.
Rex v., 2 East, P. C. 731. § 470.
S. v., 17 N. H. 83. §§ 1229, 1234.
S. v., 70 N. C. 336. § 602.
S. v., 4 Strob. 266. § 988.
S. v., 30 Vt. 620. § 879.
Simpson, C. v., 9 Met. 138. §§ 552, 609, 625.
P. v., 50 Cal. 304. §§ 521, 523.
P. v., 48 Mich. 474. §§ 426, 429.
Reg. v., Car. & M. 669. § 995.
Reg. v., 2 Cox, 235. § 558.
Reg. v., Dears. 421. §§ 548, 575.
Rex v., 1 Lewin, 172. § 287.
v. St. John, 93 N. Y. 363. § 611.
v. S., 59 Ala. 1. §§ 123, 142, 275, 325.
Simpson v. S., 56 Ark. 8. § 362.
v. S., 92 Ga. 41. §§ 251, 369.
v. S., 4 Humph. 456. §§ 553, 616.
v. S., 10 Tex. Ap. 681. § 543.
v. S., 5 Yerg. 356. § 1006.
v. S., 10 Yerg. 525. § 1185.
Sims, In re, 54 Kan. 1. § 9.
v. S., 136 Ind. 358. § 500.
v. S., 9 Tex. Ap. 586. § 304.
v. S., 28 Tex. Ap. 447. § 696.
S. v., 2 Bailey, 29. §§ 215, 216.
S. v., 3 Strob. 137. § 233.
Simson, S. v., 3 Hawks, 620. § 687.
Sinclair, C. v., 138 Mass. 493. §§ 190, 1239, 1251.
Reg. v., 13 Cox, 28. §§ 238, 249, 256.
Sindram v. P., 88 N. Y. 196. § 359.
Singer v. S., 72 Md. 464. § 38.
Sing Lee, In re, 54 Fed. R. 334. § 1344.
Singleton v. S., 1 Tex. Ap. 501. §§ 330, 354.
U. S. v., 54 Fed. R. 488. §§ 866, 878.
Sinks, S. v., 42 Ohio St. 345. § 1212.
Sinnott, S. v., 15 Neb. 472. § 1264.
Sipple v. S., 46 N. J. 197. §§ 223, 224.
Sires v. S., 73 Wis. 251. § 1229.
Sisson, S. v., 3 Brev. 58. § 332.
Sioux Falls Brewing Co., S. v., 5 S. D. 39. § 1218.
Sively v. S., 44 Tex. 274. § 1017.
Sizemore v. S., 3 Head, 26. §§ 786, 790.
S. v., 7 Jones, 206. §§ 338, 345.
Skaggs v. S., 31 Tex. Ap. 563. § 307.
Skains v. S., 21 Ala. 218. § 1007.
Skeen, Reg. v., Bell, 97. § 641.
Skeet, Reg. v., 4 F. & F. 931. §§ 96, 196, 347.
Skelley, C. v., 10 Gray, 464. § 1181.
Skelton, Reg. v., 3 C. & K. 119. § 1152.
Skerrit, Rex v., 2 C. & P. 427. §§ 195, 788.
Skidmore v. S., 2 Tex. Ap. 20. § 255.
S. v., 87 N. C. 509. § 239.
Skinner v. Power, 1 Wend. 451. § 1051.
v. S., 30 Ala. 524. § 1303.
v. S., 87 Ala. 105. § 1303.
v. S., 120 Ind. 127. § 1270.
v. S., 28 Neb. 814. §§ 462, 463.
Skipworth v. S., 8 Tex. Ap. 135. §§ 557, 609.
Skutt, P. v., 96 Mich. 449. §§ 1121, 1124.
Slack, C. v., 19 Pick. 304. § 1167.
P. v., 15 Mich. 193. § 1074.
P. v., 90 Mich. 448. § 351.
S. v., 1 Bailey, 330. §§ 582, 618.
Slagle, S. v., 82 N. C. 653. § 1148.
S. v., 83 N. C. 630. §§ 378, 1146.
Slaney, Rex v., 5 C. & P. 213. § 1053.
Slate, C. v., 11 Gray, 60. §§ 616, 719, 722, 725.
Slater v. S., 92 Ala. 68. § 1085.
Slatterly v. P., 58 N. Y. 354. § 379.
Slattery, C. v., 147 Mass. 423. § 441.
v. P., 76 Ill. 217. §§ 124, 1146.
v. S., 41 Tex. 619. § 434.
Slaughter House Cases, 16 Wall. 36. § 39.

Slaughter v. C., 13 Grat. 767. § 46.
v. P., 2 Doug. 334, n. §§ 4, 63, 69.
v. S., 6 Humph. 410. § 390.
v. S., 24 Tex. 410. § 362.
S. v., 70 Mo. 484. § 102.
Sleep, Reg. v., 9 Cox, 559. § 1152.
Slenker, U. S. v., 32 Fed. R. 691. §§ 1332, 1335.
Slicker v. S., 13 Ark. 397. § 925.
Sligh, P. v., 48 Mich, 54. § 209.
Sloan, C. v., 4 Cush. 52. § 1275.
P. v., 2 Utah, 326. § 96.
v. S., 8 Blackf. 361. § 1216.
v. S., 8 Ind. 312. § 188.
v. S., 9 Ind. 565. § 995.
v. S., 71 Miss. 459. § 887.
v. S., 18 Tex. Ap. 225. § 608.
S. v., 55 Ia. 217. §§ 1073, 1077, 1078, 1085.
S. v., 47 Mo. 604. §§ 139, 304, 307, 326, 368, 423.
Sloane, Resp. v., 2 Yeates, 229. § 837.
Slocum, S. v., 8 Blackf. 315. § 832.
Slomer v. P., 25 Ill. 70. § 487.
Sloper, P. v., 1 Ida. 183. § 770.
Slowly, Reg. v., 12 Cox, 269. § 560.
Slusser v. S., 71 Ind. 280. § 252.
Small v. C., 91 Pa. St. 304. §§ 345, 426.
v. S., 18 Tex. Ap. 336. § 565.
S. v., 26 Kan. 209. §§ 589, 649.
S. v., 80 Me. 452. § 1244.
S. v., 31 Mo. 197. § 1277.
S. v., 31 Tex. 184. § 703.
U. S. v., 2 Curt. 241. § 257.
Smalls, S. v., 11 S. C. 262. § 901.
S. v., 17 S. C. 62. §§ 271, 272.
Smallwood, S. v., 75 N. C. 106. § 410.
Smart, C. v., 6 Gray, 15. § 654.
S. v., 4 Rich. 356. § 596.
Smathers v. S., 46 Ind. 447. §§ 616, 620.
Smedley v. S., 30 Tex. 214. § 473.
Smelser v. S., 31 Tex. 95. § 1132.
Smiley v. S., 66 Ga. 754. § 612.
S. v., 98 Mo. 605. § 1077.
S. v., 101 N. C. 709. § 1216.
U. S. v., 6 Saw. 640. § 544.
Smily, S. v., 37 Ohio St. 30. § 1043.
Smith, In re, 54 Kan. 702. § 61.
v. Alabama, 124 U. S. 465. § 38.
v. Bigelow, 19 Ia. 459. § 1262.
v. C., 6 B. Mon. 121. §§ 1137, 1144, 1145.
v. C., 14 Bush, 31. § 536.
v. C., 1 Duv. 224. §§ 157, 162, 332.
v. C., 21 Grat. 809. §§ 377, 397, 398.
v. C., 10 Leigh, 695. § 713.
v. C., 54 Pa. St. 209. §§ 220, 225.
v. C., 100 Pa. St. 324. §§ 239, 240.
C. v., 11 Allen. 243. § 893.
C. v., 6 Cush. 80. §§ 1016, 1083.
C. v., 1 Mass. 245. §§ 586, 597.
C. v., 102 Mass. 144. § 1240.
C. v., 103 Mass. 444. § 128.
C. v., 119 Mass. 305. § 150.
C. v., 129 Mass. 104. §§ 542, 627, 639.
C. v., 141 Mass. 135. § 33.
C. v., 151 Mass. 491. § 520.
Smith, C. v., 7 Pick. 137. § 774.
C. v., 6 Serg. & R. 568. § 772.
v. Deaver, 6 Jones, 563. § 862.
v. Forehand, 100 Mass. 136. § 539.
v. McLaughlin, 77 Ill. 596. § 914.
v. Maryland, 18 How. 71. § 46.
v. P., 1 Colo. 121. §§ 195, 326.
v. P., 25 Ill. 17. §§ 953, 954, 959, 975, 986.
v. P., 99 Ill. 445. § 924.
v. P., 103 Ill. 82. § 617.
v. P., 115 Ill. 17. §§ 494, 495, 514.
v. P., 142 Ill. 117. § 333.
v. P., 47 N. Y. 303. §§ 87, 674, 687.
v. P., 53 N. Y. 111. § 562.
P. v., 15 Cal. 408. § 548.
P. v., 26 Cal. 665. § 413.
P. v., 31 Cal. 466. § 170.
P. v., 57 Cal. 130. § 169.
P. v., 79 Cal. 554. § 514.
P. v., 86 Cal. 238. § 505.
P. v., 103 Cal. 563. §§ 789, 799.
P. v., 106 Cal. 73. § 411.
P. v., 5 Cow. 258. §§ 811, 815.
P. v., 94 Mich. 644. § 719.
P. v., — Mich. —, 66 N. W. R. 382. § 30.
P. v., 69 N. Y. 175. § 92.
P. v., 104 N. Y. 491. § 430.
Reg. v., 1 C. & K. 423. § 556.
Reg. v., 1 C. & K. 700. § 753.
Reg. v., 2 C. & K. 207. § 618.
Reg. v., 2 C. & K. 882. § 740.
Reg. v., 8 C. & P. 153. § 237.
Reg. v., 8 C. & P. 160. § 342.
Reg. v., 8 C. & P. 173. § 256.
Reg. v., 6 Cox, 198. § 817.
Reg. v., 6 Cox, 314. § 675.
Reg. v., 11 Cox, 210. § 379.
Reg. v., 12 Cox, 597. § 611.
Reg. v., 14 Cox, 398. § 130.
Reg. v., Dears. 494. § 714.
Reg. v., Dears. 559. § 276.
Reg. v., Dears. 561. § 543.
Reg. v., Dears. & B. 566. §§ 668, 744, 745.
Reg. v., 1 Den. 510. § 730.
Reg. v., 2 Den. 449. §§ 547, 549.
Reg. v., 1 F. & F. 36. § 1077.
Reg. v., 1 F. & F. 98. § 878.
Reg. v., 3 F. & F. 123. § 619.
Reg. v., 3 F. & F. 504. § 762.
Reg. v., 4 F. & F. 1066. § 338.
Reg. v., L. & C. 168. § 754.
Reg. v., L. & C. 607. §§ 286, 429.
Reg. v., L. R. 1 C. C. 110. § 886.
Reg. v., L. R. 1 C. C. 266. § 209.
Reg. v., 2 Moody, 295. § 752.
Rex v., 2 C. & P. 449. §§ 130, 237, 286.
Rex v., 2 C. & P. 633. § 808.
Rex v., 4 C. & P. 569. § 526.
Rex v., 5 C. & P. 107. § 752.
Rex v., 6 C. & P. 151. § 373*a*.
Rex v., 7 C. & P. 147. § 546.
Rex v., 2 East, P. C. 497. § 494.
Rex v., 2 East, P. C. 783. § 480.

Smith, Rex v., 1 Leach, 288. § 216.
Rex v., 1 Moody, 178. § 500.
Rex v., 1 Moody, 473. § 554.
Rex v., 1 M. & Rob. 256. § 494.
Rex v., Ry. & M. 295. § 552.
Rex v., 1 Russ. Cr. 749. § 298.
Rex v., Russ. & Ry. 267. § 624.
Rex v., Russ. & Ry. 417. § 504.
Rex v., Russ. & Ry. 516. § 634.
v. Shultz, 2 Ill. 490. §§ 564, 569.
v. Seward, 3 Pa. St. 342. § 10.
v. Smith, 34 Tenn. 472. § 17.
v. S., 22 Ala. 54. § 1302.
v. S., 23 Ala. 39. § 1303.
v. S., 37 Ala. 472. §§ 1296, 1303.
v. S., 39 Ala. 554. § 1087.
v. S., 47 Ala. 540. § 455.
v. S., 52 Ala. 384. § 1303.
v. S., 55 Ala. 59. § 553.
v. S., 63 Ala. 55. § 1291.
v. S., 68 Ala. 424. §§ 337, 353.
v. S., 76 Ala. 79. § 930.
v. S., 81 Ala. 74. § 930.
v. S., 82 Ala. 40. § 10.
v. S., 83 Ala. 26. §§ 278, 336.
v. S., 84 Ala. 438. § 848.
v. S., 86 Ala. 28. §§ 267, 316.
v. S., 86 Ala. 57. § 1087.
v. S., 88 Ala. 23. §§ 196, 274.
v. S., 88 Ala. 73. §§ 207, 307, 339, 344, 411.
v. S., 92 Ala. 30. § 275.
v. S., 96 Ala. 66. § 1031.
v. S., 103 Ala. 4. §§ 338, 365.
v. S., 103 Ala. 40. §§ 571, 618.
v. S., 103 Ala. 57. §§ 883, 886.
v. S., 37 Ark. 274. § 214.
v. S., 50 Ark. 545. § 292.
v. S., 54 Ark. 248. § 1204.
v. S., 55 Ark. 259. §§ 157, 158.
v. S., 59 Ark. 132. §§ 306, 389.
v. S., 50 Conn. 193. § 361.
v. S., 25 Fla. 517. §§ 303, 306.
v. S., 29 Fla. 408. §§ 752, 758, 767, 792, 796, 797.
v. S., 46 Ga. 298. § 203.
v. S., 49 Ga. 482. § 338.
v. S., 52 Ga. 88. § 274.
v. S., 62 Ga. 663. §§ 504, 514.
v. S., 63 Ga. 168. §§ 821, 835.
v. S., 64 Ga. 605. 527.
v. S., 73 Ga. 31. § 339.
v. S., 77 Ga. 705. § 455.
v. S., 5 Humph. 163. § 1288.
v. S., 7 Humph. 43. §§ 485, 488.
v. S., 9 Humph. 9. §§ 426, 430.
v. S., 28 Ind. 321. §§ 82, 556, 604, 624.
v. S., 33 Ind. 159. § 708.
v. S., 58 Ind. 340. § 617.
v. S., 69 Ind. 140. § 1034.
v. S., 85 Ind. 553. § 571.
v. S., 93 Ind. 67. §§ 608, 974.
v. S., 125 Ind. 440. § 893.
v. S., 1 Kan. 365. § 361.
v. S., 8 Lea, 402. § 246.
v. S., 33 Me. 48. §§ 327, 1146
Smith v. S., 45 Md. 49. § 96.
v. S., 39 Miss. 521. § 232.
v. S., 55 Miss. 513. §§ 679, 686.
v. S., 67 Miss. 116. § 1026.
v. S., 14 Mo. 147. §§ 12, 993.
v. S., 4 Neb. 277. § 162.
v. S., 20 Neb. 284. § 787.
v. S., 32 Neb. 105. § 1270.
v. S., 34 Neb. 689. § 280.
v. S., 12 Ohio St. 466. §§ 13, 15, 221, 249, 443, 464.
v. S., 18 Ohio St. 420. § 750.
v. S., 1 Stew. 506. § 324.
v. S., 90 Tenn. 575. § 48.
v. S., 17 Tex. 191. §§ 1284, 1285.
v. S., 41 Tex. 168. § 618.
v. S., 42 Tex. 444. § 565.
v. S., 42 Tex. 464. § 1038.
v. S., 43 Tex. 433. §§ 816, 830.
v. S., 43 Tex. 643. §§ 380, 400.
v. S., 1 Tex. Ap. 620. § 881.
v. S., 7 Tex. Ap. 383. § 546.
v. S., 7 Tex. Ap. 414. § 359.
v. S., 9 Tex. Ap. 315. § 260.
v. S., 10 Tex. Ap. 413. § 914.
v. S., 13 Tex. Ap. 507. § 199.
v. S., 15 Tex. Ap. 139. § 391.
v. S., 15 Tex. Ap. 338. § 304.
v. S., 18 Tex. Ap. 69. § 41.
v. S., 18 Tex. Ap. 399. § 794.
v. S., 18 Tex. Ap. 454. § 1265.
v. S., 19 Tex. Ap. 95. § 178.
v. S., 19 Tex. Ap. 444. § 1232.
v. S., 22 Tex. Ap. 196. § 892.
v. S., 22 Tex. Ap. 316. § 169.
v. S., 22 Tex. Ap. 350. §§ 503, 511.
v. S., 23 Tex. Ap. 357. §§ 194, 526.
v. S., 24 Tex. Ap. 1. § 1156.
v. S., 24 Tex. Ap. 290. § 594.
v. S., 26 Tex. Ap. 577. § 851.
v. S., 27 Tex. Ap. 50. § 866.
v. S., 28 Tex. Ap. 102. § 1310.
v. S., 28 Tex. Ap. 309. § 409.
v. S., 31 Tex. Ap. 14. § 355.
v. S., 31 Tex. Ap. 33. § 274.
v. S., 31 Tex. Ap. 315. § 865.
v. S., 63 Wis. 453. §§ 489, 491.
S. v., 2 Bay, 62. § 248.
S. v., 5 Blackf. 327. § 918.
S. v., 8 Blackf. 489. §§ 690, 702, 707.
S. v., 1 Cheves, 157. § 815.
S. v., 7 Conn. 428. § 19.
S. v., 38 Conn. 397. § 103.
S. v., 49 Conn. 376. §§ 160, 162, 331, 358, 407.
S. v., 3 Dev. & B. 117. § 325.
S. v., 5 Harr. 490. § 1028.
S. v., 3 Hawks, 378. § 1170.
S. v., 3 Heisk. 465. § 1018.
S. v., 2 Humph. 457. § 233.
S. v., 122 Ind. 178. § 1262.
S. v., 7 Ind. Ap. 166. § 831.
S. v., 28 Ia. 565. § 520.
S. v., 46 Ia. 670. § 58.
S. v., 48 Ia. 595. § 585.
S. v., 54 Ia. 104. §§ 1117, 1129.
S. v., 54 Ia. 743. § 1119.

Smith, S. v., 73 Ia. 32. § 292.
S. v., 82 Ia. 423. §§ 1169, 1175, 1177.
S. v., 84 Ia. 522. § 1119.
S. v., 88 Ia. 1. § 717.
S. v., 2 Ired. 402. § 617.
S. v., 13 Kan. 274. §§ 82, 87, 632, 652, 656*a*.
S. v., 40 Kan. 631. § 879.
S. v., 11 La. An. 633. § 1030.
S. v., 41 La. An. 791. § 268.
S. v., 46 La. An. 1433. § 756.
S. v., 7 Lea, 249. § 1061.
S. v., 32 Me. 369. §§ 18, 377.
S. v., 65 Me. 257. §§ 286, 349, 379, 388.
S. v., 1 Meigs, 98. §§ 1283, 1298.
S. v., 29 Minn. 193. § 1133.
S. v., 47 Minn. 475. § 1129.
S. v., 56 Minn. 78. § 391.
S. v., 58 Minn. 35. § 31.
S. v., 31 Mo. 120. § 798.
S. v., 37 Mo. 58. §§ 719, 722, 724.
S. v., 53 Mo. 267. § 165.
S. v., 66 Mo. 61. § 552.
S. v., 66 Mo. 92. §§ 287, 379.
S. v., 80 Mo. 516. §§ 268, 439.
S. v., 114 Mo. 406. §§ 298, 300, 412.
S. v., 119 Mo. 439. § 480.
S. v., 12 Mont. 378. § 267.
S. v., 10 Nev. 106. §§ 292, 310.
S. v., 18 N. H. 91. § 913.
S. v., 77 N. C. 488. § 333.
S. v., 93 N. C. 516. § 123.
S. v., 100 N. C. 466. § 839.
S. v., 100 N. C. 550. § 1190.
S. v., 103 N. C. 403. § 64.
S. v., 106 N. C. 653. § 848.
S. v., 2 N. D. 515. § 511.
S. v., 11 Oreg. 205. § 927.
S. v., Phill. 302. § 443.
S. v., Phill. 340. § 377.
S. v., 10 R. I. 258. §§ 128, 188.
S. v., 15 R. I. 24. § 1140.
S. v., 17 R. I. 415. § 1158.
S. v., 10 Rich. 341. § 338.
S. v., 12 Rich. 430. § 307.
S. v., 2 Strobh. 77. §§ 320, 322, 323, 330.
S. v., 21 Tex. 748. § 830.
S. v., 24 Tex. 285. § 928.
S. v., 32 Tex. 167. § 1125.
S. v., 35 Tex. 132. § 1270.
S. v., 43 Tex. 655. § 860.
S. v., 22 Vt. 74. § 1276.
S. v., 43 Vt. 324. § 454.
S. v., 54 Vt. 403. §§ 1184, 1186.
S. v., 55 Vt. 82. § 1207.
S. v., 61 Vt. 346. § 46.
S. v., 63 Vt. 201. §§ 880, 881, 883.
S. v., 3 Wash. 14. § 869.
S. v., 9 Wash. 248. § 562.
S. v., 9 Wash. 341. § 396.
S. v., 52 Wis. 134. § 1184.
S. v., 8 Yerg. 150. § 744.
v. Steely, 80 Ia. 738. §§ 939, 940.
v. U. S., 161 U. S. 85. § 307.
U. S. v., 1 Dill. 212. §§ 926, 969.
Smith, U. S. v., 27 Fed. R. 854. § 1350.
U. S. v., 40 Fed. R. 755. § 20.
U. S. v., 45 Fed. R. 115. §§ 1245, 1253.
U. S. v., 45 Fed. R. 476. § 1332.
U. S. v., 45 Fed. R. 561. § 1331.
U. S. v., 69 Fed. R. 971. § 1333.
U. S. v., 5 Wheat. 153. § 1359.
v. Weaver, 2 Hayw. 108. § 11.
v. Wilcox, 24 N. Y. 353. § 1321.
Smitherman v. S., 27 Ala. 23. § 1095.
v. S., 63 Ala. 24. § 586.
S. v., 1 Ired. 14. §§ 1283, 1288.
Smoke v. S., 87 Ala. 143. § 529.
Smoot v. S., 18 Ind. 18. §§ 1284, 1297.
Smurr v. S., 88 Ind. 504. § 160.
Smyth, C. v. 14 Gray, 33. § 1190.
Rex v., 5 C. & P. 201. §§ 495, 837, 839.
S. v., 14 R. I. 100. § 33.
Smythe, S. v., 33 Tex. 546. § 914.
v. S., 17 Tex. Ap. 244. § 594.
Snap v. P., 19 Ill. 80. § 815.
Sneed v. C., 6 Dana, 338. § 939.
S. v., 25 Tex. Supp. 66. § 78.
Sneff, S. v., 22 Neb. 481. § 501.
Snell, C. v., 3 Mass. 82. § 805.
Rex v., 2 M. & Rob. 44. § 1152.
v. S., 50 Ga. 219. § 554.
v. S., 2 Humph. 347. §§ 754, 758.
S. v., 78 Mo. 240. §§ 342, 380.
S. v., 46 Wis. 524. § 617.
Snelling, C. v., 15 Pick. 321. §§ 1051, 1060.
C. v., 15 Pick. 337. §§ 1051, 1053, 1054.
Reg. v., Dears. 219. §§ 753, 759.
v. S., 87 Ga. 50. § 328.
Snider v. S., 59 Ala. 64. § 1324.
v. S., 81 Ga. 753. § 1220.
Snoddy, S. v., 128 Mo. 523. § 44.
Snow, Ex parte, 120 U. S. 274. § 1094.
C. v., 111 Mass. 411. § 1155.
C. v., 116 Mass. 47. § 1149.
C. v., 133 Mass. 575. § 1218.
Rex v., 1 East, P. C. 244. § 339.
v. S., 54 Ala. 138. § 511.
v. S., 50 Ark. 557. §§ 1255, 1314.
v. S., 14 Wis. 479. § 757.
S. v. 30 La. An., Pt. I, 401. § 803.
S. v., 3 R. I. 64. §§ 1206, 1207.
S. v., 41 Tex. 596. § 252.
Snowden v. S., 7 Baxt. 482. § 988.
v. S., 62 Miss. 100. § 617.
v. S., 12 Tex. Ap. 105. § 242.
Snowley, Rex v., 4 C. & P. 390. § 634.
Snuggs, S. v., 85 N. C. 541. § 919.
Snyder, In re, 17 Kan. 542. §§ 678, 685, 686.
v. P., 26 Mich. 106. § 521.
P. v., 75 Cal. 323. § 452.
v. S., 59 Ind. 105. §§ 361, 378, 420.
S. v., 14 Ind. 429. § 1024.
S. v., 66 Ind. 203. §§ 679, 690.
S. v., 25 Ia. 208. § 1193.
S. v., 50 N. H. 150. § 589.
U. S. v., 14 Fed. R. 554. § 210.

Soares, Rex v., 2 East, P. C. 974. §§ 200, 204. 788.
Society, etc. v. C., 52 Pa. St. 125. § 1319.
Soley, Reg. v., 2 Salk. 594. § 998.
Solomon v. S., 71 Miss. 567. § 1257.
Solomons, S. v., 3 Hill (S. C.), 96. § 83.
Somerton, Rex v., 7 B. & C. 463. § 556.
Somerville, S. v., 21 Me. 14. §§ 546, 552, 603.
S. v., 21 Me. 20. § 611.
Sonachall, U. S. v., 4 Biss. 425. § 860.
Sonnerkalb, S. v., 2 Nott & M. 280. § 1277.
Sonnier, S. v., 38 La. An. 962. § 269.
Soon Hing v. Crowley, 113 U. S. 703. § 39.
Soper, S. v., 16 Me. 293. § 203.
Sopher, S. v., 70 Ia. 494. § 358.
Sorenson, S. v., 32 Minn. 118. § 304.
Sorrell, S. v.. 98 N. C. 738. § 1229.
Sosat v. S., 2 Ind. Ap. 586. §§ 92, 815.
Soto, P. v., 49 Cal. 67. §§ 84, 594.
P. v., 53 Cal. 415. § 506.
Souey v. S., 13 Lea, 472. § 315.
Soule, C. v., 2 Met. 21. § 814.
P. v., 74 Mich. 250. § 1240.
v. S., 71 Ga. 267. § 554.
South v. C., 79 Ky. 493. § 1272.
S. v., 28 N. J. 28. § 566.
Souther v. S.. 18 Tex. Ap. 352. § 245.
Southerton, Rex v., 6 East, 126. §§ 728, 730, 737.
Southey, Reg. v., 4 F. & F. 864. § 166.
Southwood, Reg. v., 1 F. & F. 356. §§ 861, 866, 874.
Southworth v. S., 5 Conn. 325. § 19.
v. U. S., 19 Court of Cl. 278. § 951.
Sovereign v. S.. 4 Ohio St. 489. § 13.
Sowers, S. v., 52 Ind. 311. § 1019.
S. v., 111 N. C. 685. § 1266.
Sowle, C. v., 9 Gray, 304. § 1164.
v. S., 11 Ind. 492. § 1313.
Sowls, S. v., Phill. 151. §§ 468, 479.
Spain v. S., 59 Miss. 19. § 363.
v. S., 19 Tex. Ap. 469. § 608.
S. v., 29 Mo. 415. § 1274.
Spalding, P. v., 10 Paige Ch. 284. § 9.
Spangler, S. v., 40 Ia. 365. § 336.
Spanner, Reg. v., 12 Cox, 155. § 223.
Sparf v. U. S., 156 U. S. 51. § 391.
Sparhawk v. Union Passenger R. Co., 54 Pa. St. 401. § 1323.
Sparks v. C., 3 Bush, 111. §§ 347, 351.
v. C., 89 Ky. 644. § 311.
S. v., 60 Ind. 298. § 834.
S. v., 78 Ind. 166. § 910.
Sparrow's Petition, 138 Pa. St. 116. § 1228.
Spaulding v. Cook, 48 Vt. 145. § 638.
S. v.. 61 Vt. 505. §§ 1218, 1248.
U. S. v., 3 Dak. 85. §§ 750, 752.
Spear, C. v., 143 Mass. 172. § 33.
v. S., 16 Tex. Ap. 98. § 398.
S. v., 13 R. I. 324. §§ 1043, 1060.
Spearman v. S., 23 Tex. Ap. 224. §§ 267, 278.
Spears, S. v., 46 La. An. 1524. § 310.
Specht v. C., 8 Pa. St. 312. §§ 120, 1319.
Speed, Reg. v., 15 Cox, 24. § 678.
Speeden, U. S. v., 1 Cranch, C. C. 535. §§ 1284, 1285.
Speer, C. v., 2 Va. Cas. 65. § 661.
v. S., 60 Ga. 381. § 454.
Speiden v. S., 3 Tex. Ap. 156. §§ 118, 501.
Speight, S. v., 69 N. C. 72. §§ 713, 722.
Speights v. S., 1 Tex. Ap. 551. § 615.
Spell, S. v., 38 La. An. 20. § 307.
Speller, S. v., 86 N. C. 697. §§ 1030, 1034.
Spence v. S., 8 Blackf. 281. § 786.
v. S., 15 Lea, 539. §§ 159, 167.
Spencer v. C., 2 Leigh, 751. § 809.
Reg. v., 10 Cox, 525. § 287.
Reg. v., Dears. & B. 131. § 520.
Rex v., 3 C. & P. 420. § 675.
Rex v., 2 East, P. C. 712. § 479.
Rex v., Russ. & Ry. 299. § 626.
v. S., 13 Ohio, 401. §§ 508, 509.
S. v., 45 La. An. 1. §§ 866, 881.
S. v., 21 N. J. 196. §§ 157, 158, 169, 177.
S. v., 6 Oreg. 152. § 875.
Spendlove, S. v., 44 Kan. 1. § 307.
Speyer, S. v., 67 Vt. 502. § 30.
Spicer, Reg. v., 1 C. & K. 699. § 594.
Spickler, In re, 43 Fed. R. 653. § 1205.
Spidle, S. v., 44 Kan. 439. § 905.
Spiegel, U. S. v., 116 U. S. 270. § 1350.
Spies v. P., 122 Ill. 1. §§ 121, 196, 200, 206, 214, 217, 329, 357, 953, 962, 965, 968, 969, 970, 988, 989.
Spigner v. S., 103 Ala. 30. § 241.
Spiller, Rex v., 5 C. & P. 333. §§ 130, 287, 377.
Rex v., 2 Show. 207. § 1057.
Spilling, Reg. v., 2 M. & Rob. 107. § 287.
Spilman, C. v., 124 Mass. 327. § 752.
Spilsbury, Rex v., 7 C. & P. 187. § 426.
Spivey v. S., 26 Ala. 90. § 565.
v. S., 58 Miss. 858. § 417.
v. S., 30 Tex. Ap. 343. §§ 271, 391.
Sponsler, P. v., 1 Dak. 277. §§ 1300, 1306, 1312.
Spooner, Reg. v., 6 Cox, 392. § 256.
Spragg, Rex v., 2 Burr. 993. § 957.
Sprague v. Birdsal, 2 Cow. 419. § 84.
C. v., 128 Mass. 75. § 1243.
U. S. v., 48 Fed. R. 828. § 774.
Spratt v. S., 8 Mo. 247. § 1289.
Spray, S. v., 113 N. C. 686. § 1025.
Sprigs v. S., 2 Ind. 75. § 97.
Spring, C. v.. 19 Pick. 396. § 1223.
Springer v. S., 16 Tex. Ap. 591. §§ 1133, 1137.
Springfield v. S.. 96 Ala. 81. §§ 162, 303.
Springfield F. & M. Ins. Co. v. Hull, 51 Ohio St. 270. § 939.
Spruill v. S., 10 Tex. Ap. 695. §§ 546, 557.
Spruth, U. S. v., 71 Fed. R. 678. § 1343.
Spurbeck, S. v., 44 Ia. 667. § 1180.
Spurgin, S. v., 1 McCord, 252. § 589.
Squaires, S. v., 2 Nev. 226. § 196.
Squier v. S., 66 Ind. 317. §§ 1284, 1314.
Squire, C. v., 1 Met. 258. § 520.
Rex v., 1 Russ. Cr. 80. § 286.

Squire, Rex v., Russ. & Ry. 349. § 632.
v. S., 87 Ala. 114. § 311.
v. S., 46 Ind. 459. §§ 133, 1076, 1083, 1084.
Squires, C. v., 97 Mass. 59. § 1086.
P. v., 99 Cal. 327. § 899.
P. v., 49 Mich. 487. §§ 1113, 1118.
S. v., 26 Ia. 340. § 78.
S. v., 11 N. H. 37. § 511.
Staaden v. P., 82 Ill. 432. § 522.
Stabler v. C., 95 Pa. St. 318. §§ 220, 225.
Stackhouse, S. v., 24 Kan. 445. § 417.
Stacy, S. v., 103 Mo. 11. § 217.
Staeger v. C., 103 Pa. St. 469. § 520.
Stafford, C. v., 12 Cush. 619. § 376.
v. S., 55 Ga. 592. § 416.
v. S., 93 Ga. 207. §§ 992, 994.
S. v., 67 Me. 125. § 1140.
S. v., 113 N. C. 635. § 242.
Stagner v. S., 9 Tex. Ap. 440. § 414.
Stahl, C. v., 7 Allen, 304. § 1307.
Staight v. S., 39 Ohio St. 496. § 856.
Stainer, Reg. v., L. R. 1 C. C. 230. § 635.
Stair, S. v., 87 Mo. 268. §§ 405, 420.
Stakem, P. v., 40 Cal. 599. §§ 552, 573.
Staker, S. v., 3 Ind. 570. § 1306.
Stalcup, S. v., 1 Ired. 30. § 992.
Staley, S. v., 3 Lea, 565. § 1266.
Stallings v. S., 29 Tex. Ap. 220. § 641.
S. v., 3 Ind. 531. § 1290.
Stallion, Rex v., 1 Moody, 398. §§ 520, 523.
Stalls, S. v., 37 Tex. 440. § 833.
Stamper v. C., 7 Bush, 612. §§ 199, 200.
Stanbury, Reg. v., L. & C. 128. § 696.
Stancel v. S., 50 Ga. 152. § 939.
Stancliffe, Reg. v., 11 Cox, 318. § 611.
Standish, P. v., 6 Park. Cr. 111. § 950.
S. v., 37 Kan. 643. §§ 1235, 1240.
Standley, Rex v., Russ. & Ry. 305. § 195.
S. v., 76 Ia. 215. §§ 1113, 1119.
Stanfield v. S., 43 Tex. 167. § 255.
Stanford, P. v., 64 Cal. 27. § 594.
Stanglein v. S., 17 Ohio St. 453. § 1080.
Stanley v. C., 86 Ky. 440. § 304.
P. v., 47 Cal. 113. §§ 28, 203.
v. S., 26 Ala. 26. § 1257.
v. S., 88 Ala. 154. § 642.
v. S., 58 Ga. 430. § 577.
v. S., 24 Ohio St. 166. § 553.
v. S., 14 Tex. Ap. 315. § 353.
S. v., 33 Ia. 526. §§ 361, 374, 383, 388.
S. v., 48 Ia. 221. §§ 217, 546.
S. v., 64 Me. 157. § 677.
S. v., 84 Me. 555. §§ 1248, 1275.
v. U. S., 1 Okl. 336. §§ 864, 866, 872.
U. S. v., 6 McLean, 409. § 870.
Stanton, P. v., 106 Cal. 139. § 256.
Reg. v., 1 C. & K. 415. §§ 446, 451, 462, 463.
Rex v., 7 C. & P. 431. § 611.
Rex v., 2 Show. 30. § 1195.
S. v., 37 Conn. 421. § 128.
S. v., 1 Ired. 424. § 781.
S. v., 66 N. C. 660. § 815.
Staples, P. v., 91 Cal. 23. § 553.
v. S., 14 Tex. Ap. 136. § 487.
Staples, U. S. v., 45 Fed. R. 195. § 1331.
Stapleton, P. v., 2 Ida. 49. § 505.
Stapp v. S., 3 Tex. Ap. 138. § 274.
S. v., 29 Ia. 551. §§ 1252, 1278.
Starck v. S., 63 Ind. 285. § 571.
Starin v. P., 45 N. Y. 333. § 215.
Stark, P. v., 136 N. Y. 538. § 1065.
S. v., 1 Strohb. 479. § 179.
Starke v. S., 81 Ga. 593. § 418.
Starkey v. P., 17 Ill. 17. § 426.
Starkie v. C., 7 Leigh, 752. § 562.
Starks v. S., 7 Baxt. 64. § 256.
Starling, Rex v., 1 Sid. 174. § 962.
S. v., 6 Jones, 366. § 174.
Startup, S. v., 39 N. J. 423. §§ 21, 124, 128, 135.
Starnes, U. S. v., 37 Fed. R. 665. § 1245.
Starney, S. v., 71 N. C. 202. §§ 1252, 1265, 1274.
Starr, C. v., 4 Allen, 301. §§ 770, 783.
C. v., 144 Mass. 359. § 1319.
P. v., 50 Ill. 52. § 1126.
S. v., 67 Me. 242. § 1218.
S. v., 38 Mo. 270. §§ 309, 359.
v. U. S., 153 U. S. 614. §§ 298, 304.
U. S. v., 1 Hemp. 469. § 83.
Staten v. S., 30 Miss. 619. §§ 299, 313.
Staton, S. v., 88 N. C. 654. § 464.
Statum v. S., 9 Tex. Ap. 273. § 596.
Steadman v. S., 81 Ga. 736. § 506.
Stearnes v. S., 21 Tex. Ap. 692. § 1310.
Stearns, C. v., 2 Met. 343. §§ 634, 636, 639.
C. v., 10 Met. 256. § 775.
P. v., 21 Wend. 409. § 758.
P. v., 23 Wend. 634. § 771.
v. S., 81 Md. 341. §§ 1289, 1297.
S. v., 31 N. H. 106. § 5.
Stebbins, C. v., 8 Gray, 492. §§ 543, 565, 596.
v. S., 22 Tex. Ap. 32. § 1302.
v. S., 31 Tex. Ap. 294. § 1132.
Steber v. S., 23 Tex. Ap. 176. § 852.
Stedman, S. v., 7 Port. 495. § 271.
Steedman v. S., 11 Ohio, 82. § 42.
S. v., 8 Rich. 312. § 1270.
Steel, Reg. v., Car. & M. 337. § 982.
v. S., 26 Ind. 82. § 83.
Steele v. Brannan, L. R. 7 C. P. 261. § 1157.
v. P., 45 Ill. 152. § 808.
Reg. v., 12 Cox, 168. § 426.
v. S., 61 Ala. 213. § 414.
v. S., 83 Ala. 20. § 307.
v. S., 33 Fla. 348. § 307.
v. S., 19 Tex. Ap. 425. §§ 1207, 1232.
S. v., 3 Heisk. 135. § 1160.
S. v., 106 N. C. 766. § 244.
Steer, Reg. v., 2 C. & K. 988. §§ 558, 560.
Reg. v., 6 Mod. 183. § 538.
Steffy v. P., 130 Ill. 98. §§ 267, 275, 338.
Stegall v. S., 32 Tex. Ap. 100. § 568.
Steimling, C. v., 156 Pa. St. 400. § 536.
Stein v. S., 37 Ala. 123. §§ 1170, 1176.
v. S., 50 Ind. 21. § 1264.
S. v., 48 Minn. 466. § 881.

Steinke v. S., 33 Tex. Ap. 65. § 460.
Steinston v. S., 6 Yerg. 530. § 876.
Steinwehr v. S., 5 Sneed, 586. § 943.
Stener v. S., 59 Wis. 472. §§ 1017, 1021.
Stenson, Reg. v., 12 Cox, 111. §§ 691, 988.
Stephanes v. S., 21 Tex. 206. § 1143.
Stephen v. C., 2 Leigh, 759. § 1183.
v. S., 40 Ala. 67. § 101.
S. v., 45 La. An. 702. §§ 753, 794.
Stephens v. Myers, 4 C. & P. 349. § 232.
v. P., 19 N. Y. 549. §§ 404, 420.
Reg. v., L. R. 1 Q. B. 702. § 188.
v. S., 11 Ga. 225. § 455.
v. S., 107 Ind. 185. § 13.
v. S., 14 Ohio, 386. § 191.
v. S., 42 Ohio St. 150. §§ 191, 196, 206, 354.
v. S., 65 Miss. 329. § 1163.
v. S., 1 Swan, 157. §§ 855, 863.
v. S., Wright, 73. § 794.
S. v., 63 Ind. 542. § 1132.
S. v., 32 Tex. 155. § 547.
U. S. v., 12 Fed. R. 52. § 225.
v. Watson, 1 Salk. 45. § 1199.
Stephenson, C. v., 11 Cush. 481. § 761.
C. v., 3 Met. (Ky.) 226. §§ 901, 947, 950.
C. v., 8 Pick. 354. § 500.
Reg. v., 13 Q. B. D. 331. §§ 920, 1165.
v. S., 4 Tex. Ap. 591. § 572.
v. S., 33 Tex. Ap. 162. § 257.
S. v., 83 Ind. 246. § 901.
S. v., 4 McCord, 165. § 859.
Stepp v. S., 31 Tex. Ap. 349. §§ 571, 572.
Sterling, Rex v., 2 East, P. C. 950. § 750.
S. v., 34 Ia. 443. §§ 956, 989.
Stern v. S., 53 Ga. 229. §§ 59, 128, 1314.
Sternes, Ex parte, 82 Cal. 245. § 487.
Sterns, S. v., 28 Kan. 154. § 1273.
Sterrett, S. v., 80 Ia. 609. §§ 305, 332.
Sterritt, S. v., 19 Oreg. 352. § 56.
Stevens, In re, 52 Kan. 56. § 18.
v. C., 4 Leigh, 683. § 518.
C. v., 1 Mass. 203. § 797.
C. v., 10 Mass. 181. §§ 187, 194, 205.
C. v., 153 Mass. 421. §§ 188, 189, 1237.
C. v., 155 Mass. 291. § 1257.
C. v., 6 Met. 241. §§ 28, 714.
v. Dimond, 6 N. H. 330. § 7.
v. P., 1 Hill (N. Y.), 261. § 28.
v. P., 67 Ill. 587. § 1308.
P. v., 109 N. Y. 159. §§ 128, 826.
P. v., 13 Wend. 341. § 8.
Rex v., 5 B. & C. 246. § 881.
v. S., 77 Ga. 310. § 614.
v. S., 31 Ind. 485. § 156.
v. S., 50 Kan. 712. § 1129.
v. S., 19 Neb. 647. §§ 468, 484, 570.
v. S., 91 Tenn. 726. § 278.
v. S., 1 Tex. Ap. 591. § 246.
v. S., 27 Tex. Ap. 461. § 257.
S. v., 30 Ia. 391. §§ 953, 958, 974, 975.
S. v., 40 Me. 559. § 1143.
S. v., 62 Me. 284. § 596.
S. v., 36 N. H. 59. §§ 260, 1019.
Stevens, S. v., 114 N. C. 873. §§ 1217, 1277.
U. S. v., 4 Cranch, C. C. 341. § 1145.
U. S. v., 44 Fed. R. 132. §§ 956, 967, 985.
U. S. v., 52 Fed. R. 120. § 774.
Stevenson v. Belknap, 6 Ia. 97. § 1119.
C. v., 127 Mass. 446. § 678.
C. v., 142 Mass. 466. §§ 189, 1237.
P. v., 9 Cal. 273. § 377.
v. S., 5 Baxt. 681. § 505.
v. S., 69 Ga. 68. § 414.
v. S., 65 Ind. 409. §§ 189, 1234.
S. v., 52 Ia. 701. § 49.
v. U. S., 162 U. S., 313. § 391.
Stewart v. C., 4 Serg. & R. 194. § 595.
v. C., 10 Watts, 306. § 83.
C. v., 159 Mass. 113. § 34.
C. v., 1 Serg. & R. 342. §§ 1137, 1143, 1144.
v. Jessup, 51 Ind. 413. § 696.
P. v., 28 Cal. 395. § 307.
P. v., 90 Cal. 212. § 458.
P. v., 97 Cal. 238. §§ 455, 463.
P. v., 4 Mich. 655. §§ 761, 786, 800.
P. v., 5 Mich. 243. § 808.
P. v., 44 Mich. 484. §§ 506, 511.
v. Pierce, — Ia. —, 61 N. W. R. 388. § 1042.
Reg. v., 12 A. & E. 773. § 1165.
Rex v., Russ. & Ry. 288. § 784.
Rex v., Russ. & Ry. 363. § 204.
v. S., 78 Ala. 436. § 338.
v. S., 4 Blackf. 171. §§ 181, 918.
v. S., 66 Ga. 90. § 267.
v. S., 2 Lea, 598. § 426.
v. S., 62 Md. 412. § 595.
v. S., 1 Ohio St. 66. §§ 139, 309.
v. S., 15 Ohio St. 155. § 390.
v. S., 22 Ohio St. 477. §§ 865, 893.
v. S., 39 Ohio St. 152. § 1120.
v. S., 6 Tex. Ap. 184. § 875.
S. v., 6 Conn. 47. §§ 498, 519, 520.
S. v., 66 Ind. 555. § 1193.
S. v., 45 La. An. 1164. § 307.
S. v., 31 Me. 515. §§ 1218, 1237.
S. v., 29 Mo. 419. §§ 123, 275.
S. v., 90 Mo. 507. § 740.
S. v., 9 Nev. 120. § 303.
S. v., 91 N. C. 566. § 1190.
S. v., 26 S. C. 125. § 376.
S. v., 59 Vt. 273. §§ 963, 986.
v. Waterloo Turn Verein, 71 Ia. 226. §§ 183, 1240.
Stice, S. v., 88 Ia. 27. §§ 461, 1136.
Stichtd v. S., 25 Tex. Ap. 420. § 1057.
Stickle, U. S. v., 15 Fed. R. 798. § 1331.
Stickman, P. v., 34 Cal. 242. § 494.
Stickney, S. v., 53 Kan. 308. §§ 118, 501.
Stickrod v. C., 86 Ky. 285. § 1207.
Stiefel, S. v., 74 Md. 546. § 1254.
Stiles v. S., 57 Ga. 183. § 308.
Still, C. v., 83 Ky. 275. § 852.
Stillman, S. v., 7 Coldw. 341. § 873.
Stillwell, S. v., 20 Ark. 96. § 1313.
S. v., 16 Kan. 24. §§ 1289, 1291, 1292.
Stilly v. S., 27 Tex. Ap. 445. § 1036.

Stilsing, S. v., 52 N. J. 517. § 1203.
Stimpson, S. v., 45 Me. 608. § 609.
Stimson, S. v., 24 N. J. 9. §§ 90, 105, 636, 655.
S. v., 24 N. J. 478. §§ 87, 128, 641, 655.
Stingley, S. v., 10 Ia. 488. § 587.
Stinson v. P., 43 Ill. 397. §§ 552, 560.
S. v., 124 Mo. 447. § 468.
Stipp v. S., 11 Ind. 62. §§ 206, 208.
Stirman v. S., 21 Tex. 734. § 93.
Stit v. S., 91 Ala. 10. §§ 316, 411, 419.
Stites, P. v., 75 Cal. 570. § 223.
Stith v. S., 13 Ark. 680. § 1313.
Stock, P. v., 1 Ida. 218. § 307.
Rex v., Russ. & Ry. 185. §§ 494, 496.
Rex v., 1 Moody, 87. § 562.
Stockdale v. S., 32 Ga. 225. § 1031.
Stockden v. S., 18 Ark. 186. § 1292.
Stocking v. S., 7 Ind. 326. § 398.
Stockley, C. v., 10 Leigh, 678. § 872.
Stockton v. S., 25 Tex. 772. § 139.
S. v., 61 Mo. 382. §§ 138, 299, 306.
Stockwell v. S., 85 Ind. 522. § 1247.
U. S. v., 4 Cranch, C. C. 671. § 995.
Stoddard, C. v., 9 Allen, 280. §§ 58, 237.
Stodder, C. v., 2 Cush. 562. §§ 69, 70.
Stoever, C. v., 1 Serg. & R. 480. § 841.
Stofer v. S., 3 W. Va. 692. § 872.
Stoffel, S. v., 48 Kan. 364. § 478.
Stoffer v. S., 15 Ohio St. 47. § 310.
Stoke, S. v., 80 Ia. 68. § 245.
Stokely v. S., 24 Tex. Ap. 509. § 569.
S. v., 16 Minn. 282. §§ 332, 365.
Stoker v. P., 114 Ill. 320. § 629.
Stokes v. N. Y. Corp., 14 Wend. 87. § 38.
v. P., 53 N. Y. 164. §§ 307, 316, 333, 359.
P. v., 71 Cal. 263. § 1089.
Reg. v., 2 C. & K. 536. § 378.
Reg. v., 3 C. & K. 185. § 179.
v. S., 92 Ala. 73. § 1133.
v. S., 84 Ga. 258. §§ 506, 509, 514.
v. S., 58 Miss. 677. § 583.
S. v., 54 Vt. 179. § 1149.
v. U. S., 60 Fed. R. 597. § 1331.
Stolady, Reg. v., 1 F. & F. 518. § 880.
Stollenwerk v. S., 55 Ala. 142. § 594.
Stoller, S. v., 38 Ia. 321. § 644.
Stoltz v. P., 5 Ill. 168. §§ 1308, 1313.
Stone, C. v., 4 Met. 43. § 675.
v. Marsh, 6 B. & C. 551. § 11.
v. Mississippi, 101 U. S. 814. §§ 23, 75, 1317.
v. P., 3 Ill. 326. § 380.
P. v., 16 Cal. 369. §§ 547, 565.
P. v., 82 Cal. 36. §§ 142, 309.
P. v., 9 Wend. 182. §§ 661, 665, 693, 694, 702.
Reg. v., 2 C. & K. 364. § 753.
Reg. v., Dears. 251. § 855.
Reg. v., 1 F. & F. 311. § 688.
Rex v., 4 C. & P. 379. § 940.
Rex v., 6 Term R. 527. §§ 1357, 1358.
v. S., 63 Ala. 115. §§ 500, 501.
v. S., 56 Ark. 345. § 241.
v. S., 4 Humph. 26. § 418.
Stone v. S., 30 Ind. 115. § 1247.
v. S., 12 Mo. 400. § 44.
v. S., 20 N. J. 401, 404. §§ 752, 771.
v. S., 12 Tex. Ap. 193. § 601.
S. v., 40 Ia. 547. § 647.
S. v., 46 La. An. 147. §§ 33, 66, 69.
S. v., 68 Mo. 101. §§ 569, 623.
S. v., 106 Mo. 1. § 1108.
S. v., 30 N. J. 299. § 813.
S. v., 54 Vt. 550. § 1248.
S. v., 43 Wis. 481. § 96.
T. v., 2 Dak. 155. §§ 1142, 1145.
v. Trust Co., 116 U. S. 307. § 40.
U. S. v., 49 Fed. R. 848. § 835.
Stonecifer, P. v., 6 Cal. 405. §§ 306, 309, 316, 411.
Stoneham v. C., 86 Va. 523. §§ 305, 311, 312.
Stoneman v. C., 25 Grat. 887. § 306.
Stoops v. C., 7 Serg. & R. 491. § 215.
Pennsylvania v., Addis. 381. § 429.
Storey v. S., 71 Ala. 329. §§ 298, 362.
Storkey, S. v., 63 N. C. 7. § 442.
Storr, Rex v., 3 Burr. 1698. § 16.
Story v. Elliot, 8 Cow. 27. § 1319.
v. Hammond, 4 Ohio, 376. § 11.
Rex v., Russ. & Ry. 81. §§ 666, 701, 762.
v. S., 99 Ind. 413. §§ 309, 405.
v. S., 68 Miss. 609. § 416.
Stotts, S. v., 5 Blackf. 460. § 914.
Stough v. S., 88 Ala. 234. § 36.
Stoughton v. S., 2 Ohio St. 563. § 765.
Stout v. C., 11 Serg. & R. 177. § 466.
v. S., 43 Ark. 413. § 1265.
v. S., 93 Ind. 150. §§ 190, 1247.
v. S., 76 Md. 317. § 370.
S. v., 71 Ia. 343. § 1093.
S. v., 49 Ohio St. 270. § 279.
v. Wren, 1 Hawks, 420. § 249.
Stovall, S. v., 103 N. C. 416. §§ 1210, 1266.
Stoveld, Rex v., 6 C. & P. 489. § 873.
Stover v. P., 56 N. Y. 315. § 617.
Stow, C. v., 1 Mass. 54. § 798.
v. Converse, 4 Conn. 17. § 1051.
Stowell, C. v., 9 Met. 569. § 1229.
S. v., 60 Ia. 535. § 458.
Stowers v. C., 12 Bush, 342. § 801.
Stoyell, S. v., 54 Me. 24. §§ 1104, 1133.
Straesser, P. v., 153 Pa. St. 451. § 307.
Strahan v. S., 68 Miss. 347. §§ 128, 1032.
Strain, C. v., 10 Met. 521. § 706.
Strang v. P., 24 Mich. 1. §§ 440, 460.
v. S., 32 Tex. Ap. 219. § 808.
Strange, Reg. v., 1 Cox, 58. § 594.
v. S., 33 Tex. Ap. 315. § 740.
Strangford, C. v., 112 Mass. 289. § 844.
Strat, S. v., 1 Murph. 124. § 864.
Strattman, S. v., 100 Mo. 540. § 1100.
Stratton v. C., 10 Met. 217. § 26.
C. v., 114 Mass. 303. §§ 124, 236.
C. v., 150 Mass. 188. § 1223.
v. S., 45 Ind. 468. §§ 45, 210, 213.
S. v., 27 Ia. 420. § 765.
Strauder, S. v., 11 W. Va. 745. § 179.
Strauss, S. v., 49 Md. 288. § 1210.

Straw, S. v., 53 Me. 554. § 995.
S. v., 42 N. H. 393. §§ 954, 977.
Strawhern v. S., 37 Miss. 422. § 1288.
Strawn v. S., 14 Ark. 541. § 437.
Streep v. U. S., 160 U. S. 128. § 1331.
Street v. Hall, 29 Vt. 165. § 1214.
v. S., 67 Ala. 87. § 1031.
S. v., 1 Murph. 156. § 873.
Streeter v. P., 69 Ill. 595. §§ 1206, 1210.
Strickland v. S., 19 Tex. Ap. 518. § 381.
v. S., 33 Tex. Ap. 559. § 1032.
S. v., 2 Nott & M. 181. § 324.
Stringer, Reg. v., 1 C. & K. 188; 2 Moody, 261. § 470.
v. S., 13 Tex. Ap. 520. § 688.
Strobach, U. S. v., 48 Fed. R. 902. § 1352.
Stroll, S. v., 1 Rich. 244. § 687.
Stroner, Reg. v., 1 C. & K. 650. § 410.
Strong, P. v., 30 Cal. 151. § 409.
P. v., 46 Cal. 302. § 548.
v. S., 1 Blackf. 193. § 78.
v. S., 86 Ind. 208. §§ 678, 695.
Stroope, S. v., 20 Ark. 202. § 1185.
Stropes v. S., 120 Ind. 562. § 649.
Stroud, Reg. v., 1 C. & K. 187. § 373*a*.
Rex v., 6 C. & P. 535. § 594.
S. v., 95 N. C. 626. § 573.
Struble. S. v., 71 Ia. 11. § 512.
Struckman v. S., 7 Tex. Ap. 581. § 409.
Strupney, C. v., 105 Mass. 588. § 500.
Stuart v. P., 42 Mich. 255. § 617.
v. S., 1 Baxt. 178. § 179.
S. v., 61 Ia. 203. § 792.
Stubblefield, U. S. v., 40 Fed. R. 454. § 1219.
Stubbs, S. v., 108 N. C. 774. § 1094.
Stubenvoll, P. v., 62 Mich. 329. § 351.
Stucker, S. v., 33 Ia. 395. § 1239.
S. v., 58 Ia. 496. § 1202.
Stuckey v. S., 7 Tex. Ap. 174. § 572.
Stuckmeyer v. S., 29 Ind. 20. § 1021.
Studd. Reg. v., 14 L. T. 633. § 839.
Studstill v. S., 7 Ga. 2. §§ 216, 376.
Stultz v. S., 96 Ind. 456. § 1233.
Sturdevant, P. v., 23 Wend. 418. § 1316.
Sturdivant, S. v., 21 Me. 9. § 1181.
Sturtevant v. C., 158 Mass. 598. §§ 28, 80.
Sturtivant, C. v., 117 Mass. 122. §§ 400, 411.
Stuth, S. v., 11 Wash. 423. §§ 1022, 1027.
Stutson, S. v., Kirby, 52. § 195.
Stutz, S. v., 20 Ia. 488. §§ 1217, 1277, 1280.
Sublett v. S., 9 Tex. 53. § 1293.
Such, S. v., 53 N. J. 351. § 1126.
Suddith v. S., 70 Miss. 250. § 1034.
Sufferin, S. v., 6 Wash. 107. § 499.
Sugland, C. v., 4 Gray, 7. §§ 442, 452.
Sullens, Rex v., 1 Moody, 129. §§ 556, 623.
Sullivan v. C., 93 Pa. St. 284. §§ 353, 407, 426.
C. v., 5 Allen, 511. § 1018.
C. v., 6 Gray, 477. § 443.
C. v., 104 Mass. 552. § 546.
C. v., 136 Mass. 170. § 719.
C. v., 146 Mass. 142. § 1315.
Sullivan, C. v., 150 Mass. 315. § 96.
C. v., 156 Mass. 229. § 1249.
C. v., 156 Mass. 487. § 1279.
C. v., 13 Phila. 410. § 430.
Pennsylvania v., Addis. 143. §§ 450, 1153.
P. v., 83 Mich. 355. § 1252.
P. v., 7 N. Y. 396. § 343.
Reg. v., Car. & M. 209. § 265.
Reg. v., 11 Cox, 44, § 1048.
Rex v., 7 C. & P. 641. § 351.
v. Robinson, 39 Ala. 613. § 611.
v. S., 102 Ala. 135. §§ 311, 332, 428.
v. S., 32 Ark. 187. § 1130.
v. S., 36 Ark. 64. § 1152.
v. S., 52 Ind. 309. § 1190.
v. S., 67 Miss. 346. § 1013.
v. S., 5 Stew. & P. 175. § 521.
v. S., 13 Tex. Ap. 462. § 503.
v. S., 18 Tex. Ap. 623. § 616.
v. S., 31 Tex. Ap. 486. §§ 267, 275.
v. S., 75 Wis. 650. § 1140.
S. v., 51 Ia. 142. §§ 332, 429.
S. v., 83 Me. 417. §§ 190, 1239.
S. v., 85 N. C. 506. §§ 1100, 1111.
S. v., 14 Rich. 281. § 78.
S. v., 43 S. C. 205. §§ 307, 400.
Sullivant v. S., 8 Ark. 400. § 466.
Sulls, Rex v., 2 Leach. 861. § 605.
Summerfield, S. v., 107 N. C. 895. § 71.
Summerlin v. S., 3 Tex. Ap. 444. § 1038.
Summers v. S., 5 Tex. Ap. 365. § 353.
S. v., 36 S. C. 479. § 316.
Summey, S. v., 1 Winst. 108. § 1237.
Sumner v. P., 29 N. Y. 337. § 53.
v. S., 74 Ind. 52. § 1310.
v. S., 4 Ind. Ap. 463. § 1258.
S. v., 2 Ind. 377. §§ 539, 815.
S. v., 2 Speers, 599. §§ 991, 994.
S. v., 5 Strobh. 53. §§ 1007, 1008.
S. v., 10 Vt. 587. § 661.
Sunday Law Cases, 30 Tex. 521. § 1319.
Sunderland's Case, 2 Lewin, 109. § 1074.
Sundheimer, S. v., 93 Mo. 311. § 381.
Sundstrom, Ex parte, 25 Tex. Ap. 133. § 1319.
Surber v. S., 99 Ind. 71. § 368.
Surratt v. S., 45 Miss. 601. § 1252.
Susquehanna Road v. P., 15 Wend. 267. §§ 8, 183, 1185.
Sutcliffe v. S., 18 Ohio, 469. § 347.
S. v., 4 Strobh. 372. § 812.
Suter, Reg. v., 10 Cox, 577. § 669.
Sutherland, S. v., 30 Ia. 570. § 1118.
Suttle, S. v., 115 N. C. 784. § 1170.
Sutton v. Johnson, 62 Ill. 209. § 463.
v. P., 145 Ill. 279. §§ 438, 441, 455, 457.
Reg. v., 8 C. & P. 291. § 541.
Rex v., 1 East, P. C. 172. § 777.
v. S., 12 Fla. 135. § 1031.
v. S., 9 Ohio, 133. § 790.
v. S., 16 Tex. Ap. 490. §§ 206, 211.
S. v., 4 Gill, 494. § 454.
S. v., 116 Ind. 527. §§ 491, 492.
S. v., 25 Mo. 300. § 1229.
S. v., 100 N. C. 474. § 96.
v. Wauwatosa, 29 Wis. 21. § 1322.

Swafford, S. v., 3 Lea, 162. § 482.
Swaggerty v. S., 9 Yerg. 338. §§ 713, 719.
Swails v. S., 4 Ind. 516. § 839.
S. v., 8 Ind. 524. §§ 232, 266.
Swain, C. v., 160 Mass. 354. § 1305.
v. P., 5 Ill. 178. § 794.
S. v., 68 Mo. 605. §§ 355, 365, 413, 977.
Swaine, S. v., 97 N. C. 462. § 880.
Swallow, Rex v., 2 Russ. Cr. 9. § 501.
v. S., 20 Ala. 30. §§ 1287, 1302.
Swalm, P. v., 80 Cal. 46. §§ 546, 558.
Swan v. S., 11 Ala. 594. § 1247.
v. S., 4 Humph. 136. §§ 162, 358.
S. v., 1 N. D. 5. § 1213.
Swancoat v. S., 4 Tex. Ap. 105. §§ 1087, 1094.
Swann, S. v., 65 N. C. 330. §§ 257, 263, 279.
Swarth v. P., 109 Ill. 621. §§ 62, 63, 77, 1225, 1226, 1228.
Swasey, P. v., 6 Utah, 93. § 47.
Swatkins, Rex v., 4 C. & P. 548. § 520.
Swayze, S. v., 32 La. An., Pt. II, 1323. § 333.
S. v., 11 Oreg. 357. § 565.
Swearingen v. U. S., 161 U. S. 446. § 1332.
Sweat v. S., 4 Tex. Ap. 617. § 613.
S. v., 16 S. C. 624. § 78.
Sweeden v. S., 19 Ark. 205. § 271.
Sweeney, C. v., 131 Mass. 579. § 1178.
v. P., 28 Ill. 208. § 1188.
v. S., 35 Ark. 585. § 326.
Sweenie, Reg. v., 8 Cox, 223. § 446.
Sweet v. Wabash, 41 Ind. 7. § 1217.
S. v., 2 Oreg. 127. § 625.
Sweetman, P. v., 3 Park. Cr. 350. §§ 877, 885.
Sweetser, P. v., 1 Dak. 295. § 1235.
P. v., 1 Dak. 308. §§ 1272, 1273, 1274.
Sweetsir, S. v., 53 Me. 438. § 1077.
Sweney, C. v., 10 Serg. & R. 173. § 1061.
Swetland, P. v., 77 Mich. 53. §§ 410, 781, 805.
Swett, S. v., 87 Me. 99. §§ 46, 128.
Swift, P. v., 66 Cal. 348. § 391.
S. v., 57 Conn. 496. §§ 156, 426, 430.
S. v., 14 La. An. 827. § 303.
S. v., 35 W. Va. 542. § 1236.
Swift Run Gap Turnpike, C. v., 2 Va. Cas. 361. §§ 180, 184.
Swigart v. P., 154 Ill. 284. § 1305.
v. S., 67 Ind. 601. § 1246.
v. S., 99 Ind. 111. § 1257.
Swihart, C. v., 138 Pa. St. 629. § 1204.
Swindall, Reg. v., 2 C. & K. 230. §§ 196, 349, 351.
Reg. v., 2 Cox, 141. § 349.
Swindel v. S., 32 Tex. 102. § 594.
Swindle v. S., 2 Yerg. 581. § 118.
Swinford, P. v., 57 Cal. 86. § 617.
Swink v. S., 32 Tex. Ap. 530. §§ 546, 557, 601.
Swinney, C. v., 1 Va. Cas. 146. § 693.
v. S., 14 Ind. 315. § 53.
Swinney v. S., 8 Sm. & M. 576. § 592.
Swisher v. C., 26 Grat. 963. § 426.
Switser S. v., 63 Vt. 604. §§ 667, 694, 703.
Swope, S. v., 20 Ind. 106. § 1038.
Sydney v. S., 3 Humph. 478. § 444.
Sydserff v. Reg., 11 Q. B. 245. §§ 975, 982.
Sykes v. P., 127 Ill. 117. §§ 49, 94, 128.
S. v., 28 Conn. 225. §§ 1316, 1318.
U. S. v., 58 Fed. R. 1000. §§ 200, 210, 1281.
Syks, P. v., 96 Mich. 452. § 1227.
Sylvester, C. v., 13 Allen, 247. § 54.
v. S., 71 Ala. 17. § 332.
v. S., 72 Ala. 201. §§ 332, 390.
v. S., 42 Tex. 496. § 1145.
Syphrett, S. v., 27 S. C. 29. §§ 1055, 1067, 1070.
Szudurskie, Rex v., 1 Moody, 429. § 795.

Taber v. Hutson, 5 Ind. 322. § 11.
v. Jenny, 1 Sprague, 315. § 538.
Taberner, S. v., 14 R. I. 272. §§ 554, 624.
Tabler v. S., 34 Ohio St. 127. § 147.
Tachanatah, S. v., 64 N. C. 614. § 320.
Tackett, S. v., 1 Hawks. 210. § 307.
Tafoya, T. v., 2 N. M. 191. § 5.
Taft, Rex v., 2 East, P. C. 959. § 764.
Taggart v. C., 21 Pa. St. 527. § 1182.
C. v., 8 Grat. 697. § 1276.
P. v., 43 Cal. 81. § 504.
Rex v., 1 C. & P. 201. § 216.
Taing, P. v., 53 Cal. 602. § 303.
Taintor, U. S. v., 11 Blatch. 374. §§ 123, 641.
Tait v. S., 3 Yerg. 449. § 758.
Talbert, S. v., 41 S. C. 526. §§ 412, 414, 429.
Talbot, C. v., 2 Allen, 161. §§ 754, 809.
S. v., 97 N. C. 494. § 837.
Talfourd, Reg. v., 6 Cox, 333. § 194.
Taliaferro v. C., 77 Va. 411. §§ 514, 617.
Tall, S. v., 56 Wis. 577. § 1229.
Tallant v. S., 14 Tex. Ap. 234. § 572.
Tally, S. v., 102 Ala. 25. §§ 125, 199, 200 206.
S. v., 74 N. C. 322. § 1094.
Talmage, S. v., 107 Mo. 543. §§ 309, 310, 332, 342, 389, 391.
Tamkin, P. v., 62 Cal. 468. § 303.
Tamler, S. v., 19 Oreg. 528. § 1278.
Taney v. S., 9 Ind. Ap. 46. § 1160.
Tankard, Reg. v., 1 Q. B. D. (1894) 548. § 635.
Tanner v. C., 14 Grat. 635. § 545.
P. v., 128 N. Y. 416. § 82.
v. S., 92 Ala. 1. § 198.
S. v., 50 Kan. 365. § 1253.
Taplin, Rex v., 2 East, P. C. 712. § 470.
Tappan, S. v., 21 N. H. 56. § 867.
S. v., 58 N. H. 152. § 894.
Tarbox, C. v., 1 Cush. 66. §§ 1061, 1064, 1158.
v. S., 38 Ohio St. 581. §§ 693, 694.
Tardiff v. S., 23 Tex. 169. § 1239.
Tardy v. S., 4 Blackf. 152. § 877.
Tarin v. S., 25 Tex. Ap. 360. § 618.
Tarpley v. P., 42 Ill. 340. § 280.
v. S., 79 Ala. 271. § 51.

Tarpley v. S., 42 Ill. 340. § 280.
Tarr, S. v., 28 Ia. 397. §§ 439, 440, 448, 455.
Tarter, S. v., 26 Oreg. 38. § 307.
Tartt v. S., 86 Ala. 26. § 51.
Tarver v. S., 43 Ala. 354. §§ 231, 232, 275.
v. S., 95 Ga. 222. § 514.
S. v., 11 Lea, 658. §§ 1245, 1266.
Tate, Reg. v., 12 Cox, 7. § 863.
v. S., 5 Blackf. 73. § 1193.
v. S., 5 Blackf. 174. § 1292.
v. S., 6 Blackf. 110. §§ 206, 1028, 1167.
v. S., 46 Ga. 148. § 339.
v. S., 21 Tex. 202. § 1291.
S. v., 6 Humph. 424. § 703.
Tatlock, Reg. v., 2 Q. B. D. 157. § 629.
Tatom, S. v., 69 N. C. 35. § 907.
Tatro, S. v., 50 Vt. 483. § 162.
Tattan v. Great W. R. Co., 2 El. & El. 844. § 10.
Tatum v. S., 63 Ala. 147. § 1262.
v. S., 66 Ala. 465. § 826.
v. S., 33 Fla. 311. § 1296.
v. S., 58 Ga. 408. § 677.
v. S., 59 Ga. 638. § 275.
v. S., 79 Ga. 176. § 1232.
Taugher, P. v., 102 Mich. 598. § 569.
Taunton, C. v., 16 Gray, 228. §§ 1185, 1186.
Taverner, Rex v., Car. C. L. 195. § 808.
Tay, C. v., 146 Mass. 146. § 1243.
Tayler, S. v., 13 R. I. 541. § 538.
Taylor's Case, 1 Vent. 293. § 1159.
Taylor, Ex parte, 87 Cal. 91. § 63.
v. C., 3 Bush, 508. § 281.
v. C., 1 Duv. 160. § 1142.
v. C., 20 Grat. 825. § 452.
v. C., 29 Grat. 780. 1182.
v. C., 94 Ky. 281. § 668.
v. C., 109 Pa. St. 262. § 158.
C. v., 5 Binn. 277. §§ 823, 1014.
C. v., 14 Gray, 26. §§ 1283, 1286.
C. v., 105 Mass. 172. § 696.
C. v., 113 Mass. 1. § 1272.
C. v., 113 Mass. 4. § 1233.
C. v., 132 Mass. 261. § 1148.
v. Humphries, 17 C. B. (N. S.) 539. § 1322.
v. Newman, 4 B. & S. 89. § 564.
P. v., 3 Denio, 91. § 1318.
P. v., 3 Denio, 99. § 1318.
P. v., 2 Mich. 250. §§ 497, 519.
P. v., 96 Mich. 576. § 1013.
P. v., 138 N. Y. 398. §§ 156, 158, 167.
v. Reg., 1 Q. B. D. (1895) 25. §§ 713, 719, 975.
Reg. v., 1 C. & K. 213. § 753.
Reg. v., 9 C. & P. 672. § 351.
Reg. v., 3 Cox, 84. § 426.
Reg. v., 5 Cox, 136. § 533.
Reg. v., 12 Cox, 627. § 558.
Reg. v., 15 Cox, 265. §§ 697, 960.
Reg. v., 15 Cox, 268. §§ 697, 960.
Reg. v., 1 F. & F. 511. §§ 523, 730.
Reg. v., 4 F. & F. 511. § 780.
Reg. v., L. R. 1 C. C. 194. § 262.
Reg. v., L. R. 2 C. C. 147. § 196.
Taylor, Reg. v., 25 L. T. 75. §§ 225, 989.
Rex v., 3 Bos. & P. 596. §§ 650, 656*a*.
Rex v., 5 Burr. 2793. § 339.
Rex v., 2 East, P. C. 960. § 764.
Rex v., 2 East, P. C. 1020. § 523.
Rex v., 2 Lewin, 215. § 335.
Rex v., Russ. & Ry. 373. § 813.
Rex v., Russ. & Ry. 418. § 576.
Rex v., 2 Stra. 1167. § 1170.
v. Reynolds, 92 Cal. 573. § 6.
v. S., 22 Ala. 15. § 1008.
v. S., 48 Ala. 157. § 888.
v. S., 48 Ala. 180. §§ 303, 315.
v. S., 59 Ala. 19. § 61.
v. S., 100 Ala. 68. § 61.
v. S., 36 Ark. 84. § 1130.
v. S., 7 Blackf. 93. § 96.
v. S., 44 Ga. 263. § 594.
v. S., 50 Ga. 79. §§ 451, 463.
v. S., 6 Humph. 285. § 833.
v. S., 130 Ind. 66. § 481.
v. S., 6 Lea, 234. § 259.
v. S., 11 Lea, 708. § 361.
v. S., 52 Miss. 84. § 1074.
v. S., 35 Tex. 97. § 398.
v. S., 42 Tex. 387. § 577.
v. S., 3 Tex. Ap. 387. § 357.
v. S., 5 Tex. Ap. 529. § 573.
v. S., 7 Tex. Ap. 659. § 565.
v. S., 9 Tex. Ap. 100. §§ 196, 291.
v. S., 12 Tex. Ap. 489. § 564.
v. S., 15 Tex. Ap. 356. §§ 617, 618.
v S., 18 Tex. Ap. 489. § 557.
v. S., 22 Tex. Ap. 529. § 463.
v. S., 23 Tex. Ap. 639. §§ 503, 509.
v. S., 25 Tex. Ap. 96. § 554.
v. S., 27 Tex. Ap. 463. § 616.
v. S., 29 Tex. Ap. 466. §§ 634, 652.
v. S., 32 Tex. Ap. 110. §§ 560, 563.
v. S., 35 Wis. 298. § 39.
S. v., 3 Brev. 243. § 324.
S. v., 1 Houst. Cr. C. 436. § 396.
S. v., 29 Ind. 517. § 1170.
S. v., 25 Ia. 273. §§ 571, 616.
S. v., 20 Kan. 643. § 142.
S. v., 35 La. An. 834. § 437.
S. v., 46 La. An. 1332. § 762.
S. v., 2 McCord, 483. § 93.
S. v., 45 Me. 322. §§ 519, 523.
S. v., 21 Mo. 477. § 376.
S. v., 126 Mo. 531. §§ 358, 377.
S. v., 58 N. H. 331. § 1086.
S. v., 27 N. J. 117. § 538.
S. v., 82 N. C. 554. § 245.
S. v., 89 N. C. 577. § 1233.
S. v., 111 N. C. 680. § 1284.
S. v., 3 Oreg. 10. §§ 575, 609.
S. v., 3 Sneed, 662. § 1017.
v. U. S.. 3 How. 197. § 83.
U. S. v., 4 Cranch, C. C. 338. § 425.
U. S. v., 3 Fed. R. 563. § 54.
U. S. v., 57 Fed. R. 391. §§ 946, 950.
U. S. v., 1 Hughes, 514. § 14.
U. S. v., 5 McLean, 242. §§ 128, 351.
v. Vincent, 12 Lea, 282. § 1254.

Tazwell, S. v., 30 La. An., Pt. II, 884. § 200.
Teague, Rex v., Russ. & Ry. 33; 2 East, P. C. 979. § 765.
v. S., 39 Miss. 516. § 1216.
v. S., 25 Tex. Ap. 577. § 128.
Teahan, S. v., 50 Conn. 92. § 1241.
Teal v. S., 22 Ga. 75. § 306.
Teeter, S. v., 69 Ia. 717. §§ 123, 506, 508.
Teipner, S. v., 36 Minn. 535. § 459.
Teischer, Resp. v., 1 Dall. 335. §§ 811, 815.
Teissedre, S. v., 30 Kan. 476. § 1220.
Telford, P. v., 56 Mich. 541. § 1230.
Tempe v. S., 40 Ala. 350. §§ 101, 373a.
Temple, C. v., 14 Gray, 69. §§ 121, 1196.
v. S., 6 Baxt. 496. § 820.
v. S., 7 Baxt. 109. § 820.
Ten Elshof, P. v., 92 Mich. 167. §§ 461, 464.
Tennery, S. v., 9 Ia. 436. § 529.
Tennessee Club v. Dwyer, 11 Lea, 452. § 1240.
Tenney, C. v., 97 Mass. 50. §§ 632, 641, 790.
Tennyson v. S., 91 Ala. 78. § 676.
Tenorio, T. v., 1 N. M. 279. § 377.
Terrell, In re, 51 Fed. R. 213. § 963.
v. C., 13 Bush, 246. § 310.
v. S., 86 Tenn. 523. §§ 432, 433, 435.
S. v., 12 Rich. 321. §§ 404, 425, 427.
Terrill v. S., 74 Wis. 278. §§ 159, 326.
S. v., 76 Ia. 149. § 1106a.
Terry, Ex parte, 128 U. S. 289. § 1022.
v. C., 87 Va. 672. § 756.
C. v., 2 Va. Cas. 77. §§ 1301, 1302.
v. S., 13 Ind. 70. §§ 471, 480, 481, 483.
v. S., 25 Tex. Ap. 714. § 813.
v. S., 1 Wash. 277. §§ 625, 628.
S. v., 4 Dev. & B. 152. § 452.
S. v., 106 Mo. 209. § 1100.
S. v., 109 Mo. 601. §§ 698, 710.
S. v., 93 N. C. 585. § 1035.
U. S. v., 41 Fed. R. 771. §§ 922, 923.
U. S. v., 42 Fed. R. 317. §§ 147, 924.
Tesney v. S., 77 Ala. 33. §§ 309, 332.
Tessier, S. v., 32 La. An. 1227. § 686.
Testerman, S. v., 68 Mo. 408. §§ 212, 365, 381.
Testick, Rex v., 2 East, P. C. 925. § 794.
Tetrick, S. v., 34 W. Va. 137. § 1253.
Tewksbury, C. v., 11 Met. 55. § 45.
Thacher, C. v., 97 Mass. 583. § 1318.
Thaden, S. v., 43 Minn. 253. §§ 203, 810.
S. v., 43 Minn. 325. § 678.
Thallman, Reg. v., L. & C. 326. § 1136.
Thalls v. S., 21 Ohio St. 233. § 508.
Tharp v. C., 3 Met. (Ky.) 411. § 18.
U. S. v., 5 Cranch, C. C. 390. § 279.
Tharpe v. S., 89 Ga. 748. § 1222.
v. S., 13 Lea, 138. § 196.
Thatcher v. S., 48 Ark. 60. §§ 1137, 1144.
S. v., 35 N. J. 445. §§ 84, 543, 680, 686, 693, 710.
Thawley, S. v., 4 Harr. 562. §§ 307, 423.
Thayer, C. v., 8 Met. 525. § 1234.
v. S., 11 Ind. 287. § 993.
Theison, Ex parte, 30 Fla. 529. § 1212.
Therasson v. P., 82 N. Y. 238. § 684.
Therrien, S. v., 86 Me. 425. §§ 1267, 1276.
Thiede v. Utah, 159 U. S. 510. § 417.
Thomas, Ex parte, 103 Cal. 497. § 1086.
In re, 53 Kan. 659. § 63.
v. C., 2 Leigh, 741. § 489.
v. C., 2 Rob. (Va.) 795. § 881.
v. C., 90 Va. 92. § 1273.
C. v., 1 Va. Cas. 307. §§ 450, 1153.
v. Dunaway, 30 Ill. 373. § 639.
v. P., 2 Colo. Ap. 513. § 350.
v. P., 59 Ill. 160. § 1315.
v. P., 113 Ill. 531. §§ 687, 960, 975, 980.
v. P., 39 Mich. 309. § 410.
v. P., 34 N. J. 351. §§ 667, 684, 699.
v. P., 67 N. Y. 218. § 307.
v. P., 19 Wend. 480. § 843.
P. v., 63 Cal. 482. § 894.
P. v., 3 Hill (N. Y.), 169. § 680.
Reg. v., 2 C. & K. 806. § 877.
Reg. v., 9 C. & P. 741. § 560.
Reg. v., 6 Cox, 403. § 626.
Reg. v., 12 Cox, 54. § 834.
Reg. v., L. & C. 313. § 1356.
Rex v., Car. C. L. 295. § 575.
Rex v., 4 C. & P. 237. § 993.
Rex v., 7 C. & P. 817. §§ 162, 339.
Rex v., 7 C. & P. 851. § 753.
Rex v., 1 East, P. C. 417. § 484.
Rex v., 2 East, P. C. 605. § 719.
Rex v., 2 East, P. C. 934. §§ 754, 803.
v. S., 55 Ala. 260. § 1133.
v. S., 91 Ala. 34. §§ 469, 470.
v. S., 92 Ala. 49. § 843.
v. S., 92 Ala. 85. § 1156.
v. S., 97 Ala. 3. §§ 495, 499.
v. S., 30 Ark. 433. § 815.
v. S., 43 Ark. 149. § 205.
v. S., 51 Ark. 138. § 880.
v. S., 33 Fla. 464. § 627.
v. S., 27 Ga. 287. § 414.
v. S., 38 Ga. 117. § 368.
v. S., 59 Ga. 784. § 753.
v. S., 67 Ga. 460. § 405.
v. S., 71 Ga. 44. § 381.
v. S., 71 Ga. 252. § 867.
v. S., 91 Ga. 204. §§ 274, 328.
v. S., 5 How. (Miss.) 20. § 504.
v. S., 37 Miss. 353. §§ 1246, 1281.
v. S., 61 Miss. 60. § 308.
v. S., 41 Tex. 27. § 530.
v. S., 11 Tex. Ap. 315. § 303.
v. S., 14 Tex. Ap. 200. § 1163.
v. S., 16 Tex. Ap. 535. § 463.
v. S., 18 Tex. Ap. 213. § 794.
v. S., 28 Tex. Ap. 300. § 1130.
S. v., 47 Conn. 546. § 1215.
S. v., 29 Ind. 109. § 82.
S. v., 50 Ind. 292. § 1310.
S. v., 53 Ia. 214. § 1121.
S. v., 29 La. An. 601. § 382.
S. v., 2 McCord, 527. § 595.
S. v., 14 Rich. 163. § 591.
S. v., 13 W. Va. 848. § 1233.
v. Thomas, 51 Ill. 162. § 558.

Thomas, U. S. v., 2 Abb. (U. S.) 114. § 1351.
U. S. v., 27 Fed. R. 682. § 1332.
U. S. v., 47 Fed. R. 807. § 937.
U. S. v., 55 Fed. R. 380. § 1328.
U. S. v., 69 Fed. R. 588. § 1330.
U. S. v., 4 N. B. R. 370. § 1351.
Thomason v. S., 70 Ala. 20. § 1252.
v. S., 92 Ga. 456. § 1248.
S. v., 1 Jones, 274. § 431.
S. v., 71 N. C. 146. § 596.
Thomasson v. S., 22 Ga. 499. § 546.
v. S., 15 Ind. 449. §§ 29, 1229, 1252.
S. v., 19 Ind. 99. § 1229.
U. S. v., 4 Biss. 99. § 128.
Thompson, In re, 117 Mo. 83. § 61.
v. C., 1 Met. (Ky.) 13. §§ 200, 291.
v. C., 116 Pa. St. 155. § 837.
v. C., 2 Va. Cas. 135. § 546.
C. v., 4 Bibb, 230. § 1185.
C. v., 2 Cush. 551. § 1094.
C. v., 6 Mass. 134. §§ 287, 325.
C. v., 108 Mass. 461. §§ 1147, 1150.
C. v., 116 Mass. 346. § 467.
C. v., 159 Mass. 56. §§ 426, 1150.
C. v., 12 Met. 231. § 72.
C. v., 126 Pa. St. 614. § 913.
v. P., 125 Ill. 256. § 723.
v. P., 4 Neb. 524. §§ 535, 564, 617.
P. v., 28 Cal. 214. § 602.
P. v., 34 Cal. 671. § 547.
P. v., 97 N. Y. 313. § 732.
Reg. v., 2 Cox, 445. § 504.
Reg. v., 9 Cox, 244. § 562.
Reg. v., 11 Cox. 362. §§ 195, 516.
Reg. v., 1 Den. 549. § 558.
Reg. v., L. & C. 233. §§ 563, 659.
Reg. v., 16 Q. B. 832. §§ 956, 981.
Rex v., 2 East, P. C. 498. § 494.
Rex v., 2 East, P. C. 515. § 505.
Rex v., 1 Moody, 78. §§ 548, 575.
Rex v., 1 Moody, 80. § 340.
Rex v., 1 Moody, 139. § 377.
v. S., 20 Ala. 54. § 1193.
v. S., 25 Ala. 41. § 250.
v. S., 30 Ala. 28. § 805.
v. S., 37 Ala. 15. § 1227.
v. S., 48 Ala. 165. § 605.
v. S., 49 Ala. 16. § 764.
v. S., 67 Ala. 106. § 815.
v. S., 70 Ala. 26. §§ 1009, 1011.
v. S., 94 Ala. 535. § 548.
v. S., 99 Ala. 173. § 1296.
v. S., 26 Ark. 323. § 362.
v. S., 37 Ark. 408. §§ 1252, 1271.
v. S., 60 Ark. 59. § 544.
v. S., 24 Ga. 297. §§ 368, 425.
v. S., 55 Ga. 47. §§ 306, 338, 416.
v. S., 92 Ga. 448. § 578.
v. S., 5 Humph. 137. § 1239.
v. S., 18 Ind. 386. §§ 118, 501.
v. S., 51 Miss. 353. § 833.
v. S., 6 Neb. 102. § 617.
v. S., 44 Neb. 366. § 440.
v. S., 36 Tex. 326. § 382.
v. S., 43 Tex. 268. §§ 586, 617.
v. S., 43 Tex. 583. §§ 451, 462.
Thompson v. S., 9 Tex. Ap. 301. § 601.
v. S., 17 Tex. Ap. 253. § 44.
v. S., 26 Tex. Ap. 94. §§ 135, 944, 949.
v. S., 30 Tex. Ap. 325. § 410.
v. S., 33 Tex. Ap. 472. §§ 440, 452, 455.
v. S., 89 Wis. 253. § 893.
S. v., 42 Ark. 517. § 652.
S. v., 9 Ia. 188. §§ 139, 302, 303, 306, 311.
S. v., 19 Ia. 299. §§ 744, 791.
S. v., 31 Ia. 393. § 361.
S. v., 44 Ia. 399. § 1267.
S. v., 71 Ia. 503. § 142.
S. v., 74 Ia. 119. §§ 1253, 1257, 1280.
S. v., 79 Ia. 703. § 1116.
S. v., 2 Kan. 432. § 77.
S. v., 32 La. An. 796. § 652.
S. v., 45 La. An. 969. §§ 310, 311, 314.
S. v., 30 Mo. 470. § 257.
S. v., 83 Mo. 257. § 309.
S. v., 12 Nev. 140. §§ 160, 382.
S. v., 20 N. H. 250. § 260.
S. v., 93 N. C. 537. § 536.
S. v., 95 N. C. 596. § 565.
S. v., 97 N. C. 496. §§ 526, 529.
S. v., R. M. Charl. 80. § 511.
S. v., 2 Strob. 12. § 1195.
S. v., 20 W. Va. 674. §§ 1218, 1221.
U. S. v., 29 Fed. R. 86. §§ 956, 964, 966.
U. S. v., 29 Fed. R. 706. § 1330.
U. S. v., 31 Fed. R. 331. § 893.
Thomson v. P., 24 Ill. 60. § 707.
Rex v., 2 Russ. Cr. 328. § 552.
Thon v. C., 31 Grat. 887. § 1217.
Thorley, Rex v., 1 Moody, 343. § 634.
v. Lord Kelly, 4 Taunt. 355. § 1057.
Thorn, Reg. v., Car. & M. 206. § 753.
Thornburg, S. v., 6 Ired. 79. § 765.
S. v., 16 S. C. 482. § 1229.
Thorne, S. v., 81 N. C. 555. § 530.
v. Turck, 94 N. Y. 90. § 549.
Thorniley, C. v., 6 Allen, 445. § 1217.
Thornton, C. v., 113 Mass. 457. § 1161.
S. v., Busbee, 252. § 1248.
S. v., 26 Ia. 79. § 217.
S. v., 108 Mo. 640. §§ 1112, 1118.
S. v., 63 N. H. 114. §§ 102, 1218.
S. v., 56 Vt. 35. § 520.
Thorpe, Reg. v., Dears. & B. 62. § 634.
Rex v., 1 Leach, 396, n. § 1319.
v. Rutland, etc. R., 27 Vt. 140. § 1319.
Thrasher v. S., 6 Blackf. 460. §§ 594, 1198.
Three Copper Stills, U. S. v., 47 Fed. R. 495. § 1349.
Thrift, S. v., 30 Ind. 211. § 878.
Thristle, Reg. v., 2 C. & K. 842. § 554.
Thumm v. S., 24 Tex. Ap. 667. § 309.
Thurborn, Reg. v., 1 Den. 387. § 571.
Thurlow, C. v., 24 Pick. 374. §§ 1244, 1281.
Thurman, S. v., 66 Ia. 693. § 382.
Thurmond v. S., 25 Tex. Ap. 366. § 781.
v. S., 30 Tex. Ap. 539. § 604.
Thurston v. S., 3 Coldw. 115. § 82.

Thurston, S. v., 2 McMul. 382. § 555.
Tibballs v. S., 5 Wis. 596. § 915.
Tibbets, S. v., 36 Me. 553. § 92.
Tibbetts, C. v., 2 Mass. 536. §§ 957, 966.
C. v., 157 Mass. 519. § 1148.
Tibshelf, Rex v., 1 B. & Ad. 190. § 1074.
Tice, S. v., 90 Mo. 112. § 152.
Tickle v. S., 6 Tex. Ap. 623. § 338.
Tickner, Rex v., 1 East. P. C. 398. § 435.
Tidwell v. S., 70 Ala. 33. §§ 160, 292, 303, 360.
S. v., 43 Ark. 71. § 260.
S. v., 5 Strobh. 1. § 1100.
Tiedeman, S. v., 4 Strobh. 300. § 718.
Tiernan v. Rinker, 102 U. S. 123. § 1202.
Tierney, C. v., 148 Pa. St. 552. § 1240.
S. v., 74 Ia. 237. § 1248.
Tilghman, S. v., 11 Ired. 513. § 426.
Till, S. v., 1 Houst. Cr. C. 233. § 365.
Tillery v. S., 10 Lea, 35. §§ 1266, 1275.
v. S., 24 Tex. Ap. 251. §§ 306, 315.
S. v., 1 Nott & M. 9. § 543.
Tilly v. S., 21 Fla. 242. § 617.
S. v., 3 Ired. 424. §§ 307, 423.
Tilson, Reg. v., 1 F. & F. 54. § 1074.
Tilton, C. v., 8 Met. 232. § 1161.
S. v., 63 Ia. 117. § 514.
Timberly, Rex v., 1 Sid. 68. § 954.
Timm v. Harrison, 109 Ill. 593. §§ 1206, 1211.
Timmins, Reg. v., Bell, 276. § 1104.
Rex v., 7 C. & P. 499. §§ 351, 415.
S. v., 4 Minn. 325. § 1113.
Timmons v. S., 80 Ga. 216. § 809.
v. S., 34 Ohio St. 426. § 500.
Timothy, C. v., 8 Gray, 480. § 1222.
Reg. v., 1 F. & F. 39. § 968.
Tinckler, Rex v., 1 East, P. C. 354. § 426.
Tindal, S. v., 5 Harr. 488. § 808.
Tindall, Rex v., 6 A. & E. 143. § 1195.
Tiner v. S., 44 Tex. 128. § 302.
Tingler, S. v., 32 W. Va. 546. § 804.
Tinker v. S., 90 Ala. 638. § 1205.
v. S., 96 Ala. 115. § 1204.
Tinklepaugh, U. S. v., 3 Blatch. 425. §§ 922, 925, 927.
Tinkler, Reg. v., 1 F. & F. 513. § 1104.
Tinney v. S., 24 Tex. Ap. 112. § 546.
Tippin, Reg. v., Car. & M. 545. § 546.
Tippins v. S., 14 Ga. 492. § 553.
Tipton v. Norman, 72 Mo. 380. § 64.
v. P., 156 Ill. 241. § 1254.
v. S., 27 Ind. 492. § 950.
v. S., 30 Tex. Ap. 530. § 1121.
Tisdale, S. v., 41 La. An. 338. § 937.
S. v., 54 Minn. 105. §§ 1218, 1220, 1273.
Tite, Reg. v., L. & C. 29. § 626.
Titherington, P. v., 59 Cal. 598. § 617.
Titley, Reg. v., 14 Cox, 502. § 1148.
Titmus, P. v., 102 Mich. 318. § 859.
Tittle v. S., 30 Tex. Ap. 597. § 613.
Titus, C. v., 116 Mass. 42. § 571.
v. S., 7 Baxt. 132. § 460.
v. S., 49 N. J. 36. §§ 326, 355, 361, 390.
v. S., 42 Tex. 578. § 1035.
Tivey, Reg. v., 1 C. & K. 704. § 829.
Tivnon, C. v., 8 Gray, 375. § 516.
Tobin, C. v., 2 Brews. 570. § 547.
C. v., 108 Mass. 426. §§ 922, 929.
v. P., 104 Ill. 565. § 723.
Todd, P. v., 77 Cal. 464. § 796.
P. v., 61 Mich. 234. § 58.
Rex v., 1 Leach, 357, n. § 546.
v. S., 31 Ind. 514. §§ 688, 701, 710.
v. S., 30 Tex. Ap. 667. § 1321.
v. U. S., 158 U. S. 278. §§ 83, 961.
Tolbert v. S., 87 Ala. 27. §§ 1291, 1304.
v. S., 71 Miss. 179. § 328.
Toledo v. Edens, 59 Iowa, 352. § 1210.
Tolfree, Rex v., 1 Moody, 243. § 558.
Tollett, Reg. v., Car. & M. 112. § 558.
Tolliver v. S., 25 Tex. Ap. 600. § 726.
Tolman, C. v., 149 Mass. 229. §§ 1181, 1182, 1184.
Tolson, Reg. v., 4 F. & F. 103. § 1082.
Reg. v., 23 Q. B. D. 168. §§ 133, 1076.
U. S. v., 1 Cranch, C. C. 269. § 553.
Tom, S. v., 2 Dev. 569. § 981.
S. v., 2 Jones, 414. §§ 452, 466.
Tom Yum, In re, 64 Fed. R. 485. § 1344.
Tomah, S. v., 80 Wis. 198. § 1226.
Tomasi, S. v., 67 Vt. 312. §§ 128, 1222.
Tombeckbee Bank, S. v., 1 Stew. 347. § 96.
Tomlin, S. v., 29 N. J. 13. § 679.
Tomlinson, P. v., 35 Cal. 503. §§ 756, 758, 796.
P. v., 66 Cal. 344. §§ 13, 640.
P. v., 102 Cal. 19. §§ 560, 615.
Reg. v., L. R. 1 C. C. 49. § 859.
Reg. v., 1 Q. B. D. (1895) 706. § 730.
Rex v., 6 C. & P. 370. § 380.
S. v., 11 Ia. 401. § 455.
Thompkins, P. v., 9 Johns. 70. § 930.
S. v., 32 La. An. 620. § 639.
S. v., 71 Mo. 613. § 757.
Toney v. S., 60 Ala. 97. § 1140.
v. S., 61 Ala. 1. § 1311.
S. v., 15 S. C. 409. § 152.
Tongue, Reg. v., Bell, 289. § 626.
Tonielli, P. v., 81 Cal. 275. §§ 728, 731, 732, 736, 740, 741.
Tonkinson, Reg. v., 14 Cox, 603. § 554.
Toole's Appeal, 90 Pa. St. 376. § 1228.
Toole, Reg. v., 10 Cox, 75. § 1356.
S. v., 29 Conn. 342. § 518.
S. v., 106 N. C. 736. §§ 1156, 1157.
Toombs, S. v., 79 Ia. 741. §§ 1138, 1143, 1145.
Tooney v. S., 5 Tex. Ap. 163. §§ 354, 356.
v. S., 8 Tex. Ap. 452. §§ 415, 420.
Tootle, S. v., 2 Harr. 541. § 594.
v. Taylor, 64 Ia. 629. § 846.
Topeka, S. v., 36 Kan. 76. § 66.
Topham, Rex v., 4 Term R. 126. § 1046.
Topolanek v. S., 40 Tex. 160. §§ 455, 458.
Topping, Reg. v., Dears. 647. § 1077.
Torpey, Reg. v., 12 Cox, 45. §§ 146, 147.
Torrence v. C., 9 Pa. St. 184. § 841.
Torres v. S., 33 Tex. Ap. 125. § 554.

Toshack, Reg. v., 1 Den. 492. § 756.
Tottenham, Rex v., 7 C. & P. 237. § 520.
Toullet v. S., 100 Ala. 72. §§ 443, 463, 466.
Tower, C. v., 8 Met. 527. § 1229.
P. v., 135 N. Y. 457. § 803.
S. v., 84 Me. 444. § 46.
Towers, Reg. v., 12 Cox, 530. § 284.
Towle, C. v., 138 Mass. 490. § 1281.
Towler, S. v., 13 R. I. 661. § 1143.
Town, S. v., Wright, 75. § 333.
Townley, Reg. v., 3 F. & F. 839. § 158.
Reg. v., L. R. 1 C. C. 315. §§ 537, 538.
Townsend v. P., 4 Ill. 326. § 752.
P. v., 3 Hill (N. Y.), 479. §§ 149, 192, 1170, 1173, 1180.
Reg. v., Car. & M. 178. § 647.
Reg. v., 2 C. & K. 168. § 632.
v. S., 2 Blackf. 151. § 1223.
v. S., 92 Ga. 732. § 764.
S. v., 1 Houst. Cr. C. 337. § 380.
S. v., 66 Ia. 741. §§ 332, 357, 361, 383.
S. v., 86 N. C. 676. § 1061.
Townsey, P. v., 5 Denio, 70. § 1217.
Townsley, P. v., 39 Cal. 405. § 589.
Tracey, P. v., 9 Wend. 265. § 858.
S. v., 73 Md. 447. § 625.
S. v., 12 R. I. 216. §§ 1270, 1271.
Tracy v. C., 87 Ky. 578. §§ 1065, 1068.
v. P., 97 Ill. 101. § 426.
Rex v., Russ. & Ry. 452. § 817.
v. Williams, 4 Conn. 107. § 922.
Trafton v. S., 5 Tex. Ap. 480. § 572.
Trainer, Reg. v., 4 F. & F. 105. § 351.
Trainor, U. S. v., 36 Fed. R. 176. §§ 943, 948.
Trammell v. Bradley, 37 Ark. 374. § 1210.
S. v., 2 Ired. 379. § 962.
S. v., 40 S. C. 331. §§ 309, 311.
Trapp, S. v., 17 S. C. 467. § 495.
Trapshaw, Rex v., 2 East, P. C. 506. § 495.
Trask v. P., 151 Ill. 523. § 797.
S. v., 42 Vt. 152. §§ 865, 878.
Traube v. S., 56 Miss. 153. § 392.
Travers, P. v., 88 Cal. 233. § 178.
Traverse v. S., 61 Wis. 144. § 416.
Travis, P. v., 56 Cal. 251. § 307.
v. S., 83 Ga. 372. §§ 752, 769, 772.
Traylor v. S., 101 Ind. 65. § 1147.
Treadaway v. S., 37 Ark. 443. § 708.
Treadgold, Reg. v., 39 L. T. 291. § 650.
Treadwell v. S., 16 Tex. Ap. 560. § 292.
S. v., 54 Kan. 513. §§ 512, 576.
Trebilcock, Reg. v., Dears. & B. 453. § 566.
Treble, Rex v., 2 Taunt. 328. § 752.
Treeve, Rex v., 2 East, P. C. 821. § 130
Trefethen, C. v., 157 Mass. 180. § 401.
Trenfield, Reg. v., 1 F. & F. 43. §§ 769, 770.
Trevinio v. S., 27 Tex. Ap. 372. § 275.
Trexler v. S., 19 Ala. 21. § 268.
Trice v. S., 2 Head, 591. § 774.
v. S., 17 Tex. Ap. 43. § 1189.
S. v., 88 N. C. 627. § 968.
Trice, U. S. v., 30 Fed. R. 490. § 1347.
Trilloe, Reg. v., Car. & M. 650. § 294.
Trim v. C., 18 Grat. 983. § 206.
P. v., 39 Cal. 75. §§ 204, 988.
Trimble v. C., 78 Ky. 176. §§ 289, 389.
v. S., 27 Ark. 355. § 1310.
v. S., 16 Tex. Ap. 115. § 473.
v. S., 18 Tex. Ap. 632. § 573.
v. S., 33 Tex. Ap. 397. § 546.
S. v., 2 Ind. 655. § 97.
Trimmer, C. v., 1 Mass. 476. §§ 145, 500, 602.
Triplett v. Munter, 50 Cal. 644. § 914.
S. v., 52 Kan. 678. §§ 233, 271.
Tripp v. Flanigan, 10 R. I. 128. § 1223.
v. Hennessy, 10 R. I. 129. § 1245.
v. Norton, 10 R. I. 125. § 1223.
Trissler, S. v., 49 Ohio St. 583. § 702.
Trivas, S. v., 32 La. An. 1086. § 333.
Trogdon v. C., 31 Grat. 862. § 691.
v. S., 133 Ind. 1. § 305.
Trolson, S. v., 21 Nev. 419. §§ 622, 641, 652.
Trotter, S. v., 5 Yerg. 184. §§ 1290, 1291.
Trout, U. S. v., 4 Biss. 105. §§ 761, 796.
Troutman v. S., 49 N. J. 33. §§ 200, 1141.
Trowter, Rex v., 1 East, P. C., 356. § 429.
Troy's Case, 1 Mod. 5. § 914.
Troy, P. v., 96 Mich. 530. § 280.
Troy & Boston R. Co., S. v., 57 Vt. 144. § 1188.
Truax v. S., 12 Tex. Ap. 230. § 617.
True v. C., 90 Ky. 651. § 194.
Truitt v. S., 8 Tex. Ap. 148. § 206.
Truelock, S. v., 46 Ind. 289. § 252.
Truman, In re, 44 Mo. 181. § 790.
Rex v., 1 East, P. C. 470. § 1083.
Trumble v. S., 25 Tex. Ap. 631. §§ 307, 391.
Trumbull, U. S. v., 46 Fed. R. 755. § 1344.
U. S. v., 48 Fed. R. 99. § 1341.
Truslow v. S., 95 Tenn. 189. §§ 554, 566, 572, 605.
Tryon, C. v., 99 Mass. 442. § 148.
P. v., 4 Mich. 665. § 629.
S. v., 39 Conn. 183. § 62.
Tubbs, C. v., 1 Cush. 2. § 1244.
Tuberville v. Savage, 1 Mod. 3. § 232.
v. S., 40 Ala. 715. § 276.
Tucker v. Adams, 63 N. H. 361. § 1267.
C. v., 110 Mass. 403. § 523.
v. P., 117 Ill. 88. §§ 1073, 1082.
v. P., 122 Ill. 583. § 1075.
P. v., 104 Cal. 440. § 615.
Rex v., 1 Moody, 134. § 740.
v. S., 24 Ala. 77. § 1260.
v. S., 57 Ga. 241. § 617.
v. S., 57 Ga. 503. § 617.
v. S., 3 Heisk. 484. § 484.
v. S., 8 Lea, 633. § 1102.
v. S., 35 Tex. 113. § 1094.
v. S., 28 Tex. Ap. 541. §§ 1136, 1157.
S. v., 45 Ark. 55. § 1228.
S. v., 76 Ia. 232. § 616.
S. v., 84 Mo. 23. § 522.
Tuckerman, C. v., 10 Gray, 173. §§ 123, 632, 638, 639, 643.

Tuckwell, Reg. v., Car. & M. 215. §§ 200, 558.
Tuell, S. v., 6 Blackf. 344. § 925.
Tuibell, S. v., 26 Ind. 264. §§ 945, 949.
Tull, S. v., 119 Mo. 421. § 773.
Tuller v. S., 8 Tex. Ap. 501. § 521.
S. v., 34 Conn. 280. §§ 104, 623, 790.
Tully, In re, 20 Fed. R. 812. § 755.
v. C., 11 Bush, 154. §§ 209, 216.
v. C., 13 Bush, 142. § 211.
v. C., 4 Met. 357. § 510.
v. P., 6 Mich. 273. § 362.
v. P., 67 N. Y. 15. §§ 435, 436*a*.
Reg. v., 9 C. & P. 227. § 673.
S. v., 4 Ired. 424. § 330.
U. S. v., 1 Gallis. 247. § 1359.
Tumey, S. v., 81 Ind. 559. § 635.
Tummins v. S., 18 Tex. Ap. 13. § 1304.
Tunnard, Rex v., 2 East, P. C. 687. § 562.
Tunnell, T. v., 4 Mont. 148. § 316.
Turbeville v. S., 42 Ind. 490. § 620.
v. S., 56 Miss. 793. § 750.
Turley, P. v., 50 Cal. 469. § 338.
v. S., 3 Humph. 323. § 594.
U. S. v., 4 Cranch, C. C. 334. § 268.
Turlington, S. v., 102 Mo. 642. §§ 157, 298, 385, 426.
Turman v. S., 4 Tex. Ap. 586. §§ 1161, 1164.
Turnbull, P. v., 93 Cal. 630. § 901.
Turner v. C., 89 Ky. 78. §§ 303, 308, 314.
C. v., 4 B. Mon. 4. § 1229.
C. v., 1 Cush. 493. § 63.
C. v., 145 Mass. 296. § 1161.
v. Maryland, 107 U. S. 38. § 35.
v. Meymott, 1 Bing. 158. § 836.
P. v., 65 Cal. 540. § 260.
Reg. v., 2 C. & K. 732. § 886.
Reg. v., 8 C. & P. 755. § 1152.
Reg. v., 4 F. & F. 339. § 194.
Reg. v., 2 Moody, 42. § 774.
Rex v., 6 C. & P. 407. § 576.
Rex v., 2 East, P. C. 492. § 495.
Rex v., 1 Moody, 347. § 216.
v. S., 40 Ala. 21. § 78.
v. S., 97 Ala. 57. §§ 196, 377.
v. S., 5 Blackf. 254. § 912.
v. S., 70 Ga. 765. § 416.
v. S., 3 Heisk. 452. §§ 589, 592.
v. S., 67 Ind. 595. § 1321.
v. S., 102 Ind. 425. § 593.
v. S., 1 Ohio St. 422. §§ 105, 468, 474, 480, 543.
v. S., 89 Tenn. 547. § 429.
v. S., 7 Tex. Ap. 596. § 609.
v. S., 16 Tex. Ap. 378. §§ 144, 333.
v. S., 20 Tex. Ap. 56. § 197.
v. S., 30 Tex. Ap. 691. § 880.
S. v., 60 Conn. 222. § 822.
S. v., 1 Houst. Cr. C. 76. § 460.
S. v., 19 Ia. 144. §§ 713, 717.
S. v., 65 N. C. 592. § 617.
S. v., 66 N. C. 618. §§ 538, 540.
S. v., 106 N. C. 691. § 848.
S. v., 18 S. C. 103. § 1216.
S. v., 29 S. C. 34. § 307.
S. v., 10 Wash. 94. § 554.
Turner, U. S. v., 7 Pet. 132. § 757.
Turney v. S., 60 Ark. 259. § 1130.
v. S., 8 Sm. & M. 104. § 460.
S. v., 77 Ia. 269. § 511.
Turns v. C., 6 Met. 224. § 388.
Turpin, Reg. v., 2 C. & K. 820. § 756.
v. S., 4 Blackf. 72. § 996.
v. S., 55 Md. 462. § 303.
S. v., 77 N. C. 473. § 307.
Turton, Reg. v., 6 Cox, 385. § 166.
Tuton v. S., 4 Tex. Ap. 472. § 96.
Tutt, S. v., 2 Bailey, 44. § 790.
Tuttle, C. v., 12 Cush. 502. § 1215.
v. P., 36 N. Y. 431. §§ 863, 874, 878.
v. S., 4 Conn. 68. § 72.
v. S. 1 Tex. Ap. 364. §§ 1283, 1285.
Tutty, S. v., 41 Fed. R. 753. § 1131.
Tweed, S. v., 27 N. J. 111. § 950.
Tweedy v. S., 5 Ia. 433. § 311.
S. v., 11 Ia. 350. §§ 390, 391, 429.
S. v., 115 N. C. 704. § 66.
Twenty-nine Gallons of Whisky, U. S. v., 45 Fed. R. 847. § 1217.
Twist, Reg. v., 29 L. T. 546. § 560.
Twitchell v. C., 9 Pa. St. 211. §§ 956, 960.
Twitty, S. v., 2 Hawks, 248. §§ 772, 794.
S. v., 1 Hayw. 102. § 498.
Twogood, S. v., 7 Ia. 252. §§ 15, 235, 253.
Two Horses, U. S. v., 9 Ben. 529. § 1349.
Two Hundred Bushels of Corn, U. S. v., 9 Ben. 186. § 1349.
Two Hundred and Fifty Kegs of Nails, U. S. v., 61 Fed. R. 410. § 1347.
Twose, Reg. v., 14 Cox, 327. § 113.
Twyning, Rex v., 2 B. & Ald. 386. §§ 1076, 1084.
Tye, Rex v., Russ. & Ry. 345. § 378.
Tyers, Rex v., Russ. & Ry. 402. § 652.
Tyler v. P., Beech. Bre. 293. § 571.
v. P., 8 Mich. 320. §§ 369, 553.
P. v., 35 Cal. 553. § 454.
P. v., 36 Cal. 522. §§ 102, 460, 461.
P. v., 7 Mich. 161. § 82.
Reg. v., 8 C. & P. 616. §§ 137, 215, 321.
v. S., 13 Tex. Ap. 205. § 615.
Tylney, Reg. v., 1 Den. 319. § 768.
Tyner v. S., 5 Humph. 383. § 612.
Tynes v. S., 17 Tex. Ap. 123. § 740.
Tyra v. C., 2 Met. (Ky.) 1. §§ 159, 256, 259.
Tyree, Reg. v., L. R. 1 C. C. 177. § 631.
Tyrrell, S. v., 98 Mo. 354. §§ 508, 509.
Tyson, Reg. v., L. R. 1 C. C. 107. § 863.
S. v., 111 N. C. 687. § 71.
Tytus, S. v., 98 N. C. 705. § 509.

Udderzook v. C., 76 Pa. St. 340. §§ 398, 406.
Uecker v. S., 4 Tex. Ap. 234. § 833.
Uhl v. C., 6 Grat. 706. § 224.
Uhrig, C. v., 146 Mass. 132. § 1280.
Ullman v. S., 1 Tex. Ap. 220. § 577.
S. v., 5 Minn. 13. §§ 731, 738.
Ulrich v. C., 6 Bush, 400. § 1257.
Ulrici, U. S. v., 3 Dill. 532. § 966.
Umble, S. v., 115 Mo. 452. §§ 203, 426.

Umdenstock, S. v., 43 Tex. 554. § 877.
Umfried, S. v., 76 Mo. 404. §§ 144, 304, 338.
Umphrey v. S., 63 Ind. 223. § 566.
Underwood v. S., 72 Ala. 220. § 605.
v. S., 25 Tex. Supp. 389. §§ 301, 303.
S. v., 49 Me. 181. § 553.
S. v., 57 Mo. 40. §§ 359, 365.
S. v., 75 Mo. 230. § 924.
Unger v. S., 42 Miss. 642. §§ 588, 605, 617.
Ungericht v. S., 119 Ind. 379. § 1321.
Union Pac. R. Co. v. Proctor, 12 Colo. 194. §§ 5, 78.
Unis v. Charlton's Adm'r, 12 Grat. 484. § 431.
United States Distilling Co. v. Chicago, 112 Ill. 19. § 1211.
United States Ex. Co. S. v., 70 Ia. 271. § 1267.
U. S. v., 5 Biss. 91. § 1327.
Upchurch, S. v., 9 Ired. 454. § 520.
Updegraff v. Bennett, 8 Ia. 72. § 1113.
Updegraph v. C., 11 Serg. & R. 394. §§ 1159, 1160, 1319.
Uprichard, C. v., 3 Gray, 434. § 553.
Upstone v. P., 109 Ill. 169. §§ 159, 160, 162, 163, 331, 333.
Upton, C. v., 6 Gray, 473. § 1173.
v. S., 5 Ia. 465. § 714.
v. S., 33 Tex. Ap. 231. § 1032.
S. v., 1 Dev. 513. § 392.
S. v., 20 Mo. 397. § 362.
Urias, P. v., 12 Cal. 325. § 382.
Urquhart v. S., 103 Ala. 90. § 867.
Urquidas, P. v., 96 Cal. 239. § 505.
Usener v. S., 8 Tex. Ap. 177. § 1319.
Usselton v. P., 149 Ill. 612. §§ 204, 217.
Utzman v. S., 32 Tex. Ap. 426. § 416.

Vahey, C. v., 151 Mass. 57. § 1249.
Vaiden v. C., 12 Grat. 717. § 309.
Vail, S. v., 57 Ia. 103. § 6.
Valdez, T. v., 1 N. M. 548. § 251.
Vale v. P., 161 Ill. 309. § 596.
Valencia, P. v., 43 Cal. 552. §§ 212, 217, 218.
Valesco v. S., 9 Tex. Ap. 76. § 594.
Vallery v. S., 42 Neb. 123. §§ 1052, 1055.
Valwell, S. v., 66 Vt. 558. §§ 205, 515.
Vamplew, Reg. v., 3 F. & F. 520. § 150.
Van Alstine, P. v., 57 Mich. 69. §§ 757, 771.
Van Alstyne, P. v., 144 N. Y. 361. § 1112.
Van Blarcum, P. v., 2 Johns. 105. § 518.
Van Buren v. U. S., 36 Fed. R. 77. §§ 945, 948.
Van Butchell, Rex v., 3 C. & P. 629. §§ 287, 426.
Van Cleve, S. v., 5 Wash. 642. § 601.
Van Deleer, P. v., 53 Cal. 147. § 236.
Van Dolsen v. S., 1 Ind. Ap. 108. § 1132.
Van Doran, S. v., 109 N. C. 864. § 36.
Van Dusen v. P., 78 Ill. 645. §§ 855, 887.
Van Duzer v. Howe, 21 N. Y. 531. § 11.
Van Elten v. S., 24 Neb. 734. § 639.
Van Fossen v. S., 37 Ohio St. 317. § 1075.
Van Hagen, Ex parte, 25 Ohio St. 426. § 94.
Van Hart, S. v., 17 N. J. 327. § 758.
Van Horne v. S., 5 Ark. 349. § 758.
Van Houten v. S., 46 N. J. 16. §§ 123, 1136.
S. v., 37 Mo. 357. § 1148.
Van Houton, S. v., 3 N. J. 672. § 808.
Van Leuven, U. S. v., 62 Fed. R. 52. § 1348.
U. S. v., 62 Fed. R. 62. §§ 956, 1348.
U. S. v., 62 Fed. R. 69. § 1348.
Van Meter v. P., 60 Ill. 168. §§ 4, 17.
Van Ness v. Pacard, 2 Pet. 137. § 12.
Van Schaack, C. v., 16 Mass. 105. § 523.
Van Sickle, C. v., Bright. 69. §§ 1170, 1171, 1173.
Van Stone, C. v., 97 Mass. 548. § 1244.
Van Stralen, S. v., 45 Wis. 437. § 96.
Van Tassel v. S., 59 Wis. 351. § 1126.
Van Tuyl, C. v., 1 Met. (Ky.) 1. §§ 665, 680, 696.
Van Vliet, In re, 43 Fed. R. 761. § 1205.
S. v., 92 Ia. 76. §§ 92, 93.
U. S. v., 23 Fed. R. 35. § 1348.
Van Walker v. S., 33 Tex. Ap. 359. § 500.
Van Winkle, S. v., 80 Ia. 15. § 620.
Van Zant, S. v., 71 Mo. 541. § 269.
Vance v. C., 2 Va. Cas. 132. § 169.
P. v., 21 Cal. 400. § 382.
v. S., 62 Miss. 137. § 860.
S. v., 17 Ia. 138. §§ 130, 336.
S. v, 32 La. An. 1177. § 303.
Vanderbilt, P. v., 28 N. Y. 396. §§ 1182, 1195.
S. v., 27 N. J. 328. §§ 687, 700.
Vandercomb, Rex v., 2 East, P. C. 514, 517. §§ 505, 506.
Vanderlip, S. v., 4 La. An. 444. § 605.
Vandermark v. P., 47 Ill. 122. §§ 267, 276.
Vanderpool v. S., 34 Ark. 174. § 487.
Vandersluis, S. v., 42 Minn. 129. § 36.
Vanderstein, Reg. v., 10 Cox, 146. §§ 758, 788.
Vanderwood v. S., 50 Ind. 26. § 1247.
Vandine, C. v., 6 Grat. 689. § 1303.
Vanloan, S. v., 8 Ind. 182. § 1009.
Vann, Reg. v., 2 Den. 325. §§ 136, 1165.
v. S., 83 Ga. 44. § 333.
S. v., 82 N. C. 631. § 169.
S. v., 84 N. C. 722. § 166.
Vannoy, S. v., 65 N. C. 532. § 232.
Vanpool v. C., 13 Pa. St. 391. §§ 840, 841.
Vansant, S. v., 80 Mo. 67. §§ 428, 431.
Vanvalkenburg v. S., 11 Ohio, 404. § 782.
Varas v. S., 41 Tex. 527. § 565.
Varnedoe v. S., 75 Ga. 181. § 430.
Varnell v. S., 26 Tex. Ap. 56. §§ 308, 309.
Varner v. S., 72 Ga. 745. § 557.
Varnum v. S., 78 Ala. 28. § 846.
Vasel, S. v., 47 Mo. 416. §§ 132, 914.
Vasquez, P. v., 49 Cal. 560. § 196.
Vass v. C., 3 Leigh, 786. § 426.

Vasser v. S., 55 Ala. 264. §§ 439, 442, 443.
Vatter, S. v., 71 Ia. 557. §§ 533, 616.
Vaughan v. C., 86 Ky. 431. § 426.
v. C., 85 Va. 671. § 416.
C. v., 9 Cush. 594. § 416.
Reg. v., 8 C. & P. 276. § 765.
Rex v., 4 Burr. 2494. § 897.
v. S., 83 Ala. 55. § 1091.
v. S., 128 Ind. 14. § 274.
v. S., 3 Sm. & M. 553. § 232.
S. v., 1 Bay, 282. § 737.
Vaughn v. C., 10 Grat. 758. §§ 560, 572.
v. S., 88 Ga. 731. § 307.
v. S., 5 Ia. 369. § 1271.
Vawter, S. v., 7 Blackf. 592. §§ 1148, 1150.
Veal v. S., 8 Tex. Ap. 474. §§ 78, 238.
Veatch v. S., 60 Ind. 291. § 390.
Vedder, P. v., 98 N. Y. 630. § 1151.
Vegelahn v. Guntner, — Mass. —, 44 N. E. R. 1077. § 963.
Veitch, U. S. v., 1 Cranch, C. C. 115. §§ 425, 426, 428.
Vela v. S., 33 Tex. Ap. 322. § 320.
Verdegreen, P. v., 106 Cal. 211. § 443.
Verden, S. v., 24 Ia. 126. § 1272.
Verelst, Rex v., 3 Camp. 432. § 856.
Vermont Cent. R., S. v., 27 Vt. 103. § 183.
S. v., 28 Vt. 583. § 185.
Vermont R. Co., C. v., 4 Gray, 22. §§ 183, 1187.
Verrill, S. v., 54 Me. 408. §§ 353, 361, 362, 377.
Verry, S. v., 36 Kan. 416. §§ 1051, 1070.
Vess v. S., 93 Ind. 211. § 838.
Viall, C. v., 2 Allen, 512. § 1168.
Vicaro v. C., 5 Dana, 504. § 1284.
Vice, P. v., 21 Cal. 344. § 473.
Vickery, S. v., 19 Tex. 326. §§ 563, 659.
U. S. v., 1 Har. & J. 427. § 108.
Vidal v. Girard's Ex'rs, 2 How. (U. S.) 127. § 1159.
Vierra, P. v., 52 Cal. 451. § 260.
Viers, S. v., 82 Ia. 397. §§ 1243, 1248.
Vieth, C. v., 155 Mass. 442. §§ 33, 188.
Villeneuve, Rex v., 2 East, P. C. 830. § 667.
Villensky, Reg. v., 2 Q. B. D. (1892) 597. § 715.
Vincent, Ex parte, 26 Ala. 145. § 494.
Reg. v., 3 C. & K. 246. § 546.
Reg. v., 9 C. & P. 91. § 1003.
Reg. v., 9 C. & P. 275. § 988.
v. S., 3 Heisk. 120. § 582.
v. S., 9 Tex. Ap. 46. § 573.
v. S., 9 Tex. Ap. 303. § 565.
v. S., 10 Tex. Ap. 330. § 609.
S. v., 24 Ia. 570. § 399.
S. v., 91 Mo. 662. § 786.
Vines, S. v., 1 Houst. Cr. C. 424. § 303.
S. v., 93 N. C. 493. § 351.
Vinsant, S. v., 49 Ia. 241. §§ 452, 454.
Vinson, S. v., 63 N. C. 335. § 615.
Virgil v. S., 63 Miss. 317. § 391.
Virt, S. v., 3 Ind. 447. § 8.
Vittum, S. v., 9 N. H. 519. § 1094.
Vivian, Reg. v., 1 C. & K. 719. § 753.
Voght v. S., 124 Ind. 358. § 1308.
S. v., 27 Ia. 117. § 865.
Voglesong v. S., 9 Ind. 112. § 1319.
Voight, S. v., 90 N. C. 741. § 123.
v. Wright, 141 U. S. 62. § 35.
Vollander, S. v., 57 Minn. 225. § 1099.
Vollmer v. S., 24 Neb. 838. §§ 322, 333, 345.
Volmer v. S., 34 Ark. 487. §§ 101, 1230.
S. v., 6 Kan. 371. § 1221.
S. v., 6 Kan. 379. §§ 5, 28.
Volz, U. S. v., 14 Blatch. 15. § 865.
Von Haltschuherr, S. v., 72 Ia. 541. §§ 1223, 1229, 1275, 1276.
Von Pollnitz v. S., 92 Ga. 16. §§ 400, 414.
Von Sachs, S. v., 45 La. An. 1416. § 73.
Voorhees, In re, 32 N. J. 141. § 4.
Voorhis, S. v., 52 N. J. 351. § 880.
Vorback, S. v., 66 Mo. 168. § 678.
Vorey, S. v., 41 Minn. 134. §§ 448, 452.
Vosburg, S. v., 111 N. C. 718. § 536.
Vosburgh v. S., 82 Wis. 168. § 280.
Voshall, S. v., 4 Ind. 589. § 993.
Vowels, S. v., 4 Oreg. 9. §§ 324, 432.
Vreones, Reg. v., 1 Q. B. D. (1891) 360. § 859.
Vrooman, C. v., 164 Pa. St. 306. §§ 29, 41.
Vyse, Reg. v., 3 F. & F. 247. § 167.
Rex v., 1 Moody, 218. §§ 543, 715.

Wachendorf, C. v., 141 Mass. 270. §§ 189, 1237.
Wacker, S. v., 71 Wis. 672. §§ 12, 85, 1248.
Waddell v. S., 1 Tex. Ap. 720. § 246.
U. S. v., 16 Fed. R. 221. § 961.
Waddington, Rex v., 1 B. & C. 26. §§ 1049, 1159.
Rex v., 2 East, P. C. 513. § 504.
Wade, P. v., 101 Mich. 89. §§ 1216, 1275.
Reg. v., 1 C. & K. 739. § 717.
Reg. v., 11 Cox, 549. § 565.
v. S., 40 Ala. 74. § 101.
v. S., 94 Ala. 109. § 10.
v. S., 71 Ind. 535. §§ 205, 213.
v. S., 23 Tex. Ap. 308. § 374.
S. v., 43 Ark. 77. §§ 1285, 1286.
S. v., 7 Baxt. 22. § 595.
Wadlington v. S., 19 Tex. Ap. 266. §§ 338, 417.
Wadsworth, P. v., 63 Mich. 500. § 639.
S. v., 30 Conn. 55. § 1220.
Waggoner, S. v., 52 Ind. 481. § 1019.
Wagner v. Bissell, 3 Ia. 396. § 12.
P. v., 86 Mich. 594. § 49.
v. S., 63 Ind. 250. § 1283.
v. S., 43 Neb. 1. §§ 196, 210.
v. S., 17 Tex. Ap. 554. § 1057.
S. v., 78 Mo. 644. §§ 353, 354.
S. v., 118 Mo. 626. § 550.
Wagoner v. S., 90 Ind. 504. §§ 93, 661.
v. S., 5 Lea, 352. § 449.
Wagstaff, Rex v., Russ. & Ry. 398. §§ 729, 733.

Wagstaff v. Schippel, 27 Kan. 450. § 112.
Wagstaffe, Reg. v., 10 Cox, 530. § 286.
Wagster, S. v., 75 Mo. 107. § 187.
Wahll, In re, 42 Fed. R. 822. § 1332.
Waidley v. S., 34 Neb. 250. § 564.
Wainright, S. v., 60 Ark. 280. § 45.
Wainwright, Reg. v., 13 Cox, 171. § **413**.
Wait v. S., 99 Ala. 164. § 498.
S. v., 44 Kan. 310. §§ 1051, 1052.
Waite, P. v., 102 Cal. 251. § 855.
Reg. v., 2 Q. B. D. (1892) 600. § **449**.
Waitz, U. S. v., 3 Sawy. 473. § 914.
Wakefield, Rex v., 2 Lewin, 279. § 1108.
v. S., 41 Tex. 556. § 577.
S. v., 73 Mo. 549. § 865.
S. v., 8 Mo. Ap. 11. § 1057.
Wakeling, Rex v., Russ. & Ry. 504. § **667**.
Wakeley, P. v., 62 Mich. 297. §§ 665, 680, 683, 686.
Wakeman v. Chambers, 69 Ia. **169**. §§ 199, 1241.
Walbaum, P. v., 1 Dak. 308. § 1275.
Walbridge, P. v., 6 Cow. 512; 3 Wend. 120. §§ 37, 911.
Walden, C. v., 3 Cush. 558. § 826.
Waldman, C. v., 140 Pa. St. 89. § 1321.
Waldron, S. v., 16 R. I. 191. § 1215.
Waldstein v. S., 29 Tex. Ap. 82. §§ 128, 1258.
Walker v. Camp, 69 Ia. 741. § 847.
v. C., 28 Grat. 969. § 514.
v. C., 1 Leigh, 628. § 615.
v. C., 8 Leigh, 743. § 556.
v. C., 2 Va. Cas. 515. § 1303.
C. v., 108 Mass. 309. § 668.
v. Matthews, 8 Q. B. D. 109. § **611**.
v. P., 5 Colo. Ap. 37. § 1255.
v. P., 88 N. Y. 81. §§ 157, 179.
P. v., 38 Mich. 156. §§ 161, 615.
v. Prescott, 44 N. H. 512. § 1221.
v. Reg., 8 El. & Bl. 439. § 858.
Reg. v., Dears. 358. § 255.
Reg. v., Dears. & B. 600. § 626.
Reg. v., L. R. 10 Q. B. 355. § 21.
Reg. v., 2 M. & Rob. 212. §§ 455, 456.
Rex v., 3 Camp. 264. § 214.
Rex v., 1 C. & P. 320. §§ 349, **351**.
Rex v., 6 C. & P. 657. § 703.
Rex v., 1 Moody, 155. § 543.
v. S., 52 Ala. 376. § 500.
v. S., 63 Ala. 49. § 500.
v. S., 73 Ala. 17. § 260.
v. S., 91 Ala. 32. § 934.
v. S., 91 Ala. 76. §§ 157, 162.
v. S., 96 Ala. 53. § 872.
v. S., 97 Ala. 85. §§ 511, 515.
v. S., 104 Ala. 56. § 1087.
v. S., 50 Ark. 532. § 589.
v. S., 34 Fla. 167. § 380.
v. S., 28 Ga. 254. § 618.
v. S., 63 Ga. 150. § 416.
v. S., 8 Ind. 290. §§ 126, 332.
v. S., 2 Swan, 287. §§ 1285, 1286.
v. S., 6 Tex. Ap. 576. § 404.
v. S, 7 Tex. Ap. 627. § 275.
v. S., 9 Tex. Ap. 38. § 516.
Walker v. S., 13 Tex. Ap. 618. § 392.
v. S., 14 Tex. Ap. 609. §§ 381, **396**, 398.
v. S., 25 Tex. Ap. 448. § 1260.
v. S., 29 Tex. Ap. 621. § 206.
S. v., 41 Ia. 217. § 619.
S. v., 3 Harr. 547. § 1274.
S. v., 36 Kan. 297. § 57.
S. v., 22 La. An. 425. § 597.
S. v., 37 La. An. 560. § 325.
S. v., 16 Me. 241. §§ 190, 1231.
S. v., 77 Me. 488. § 412.
S. v., 98 Mo. 95. § 359.
S. v., 119 Mo. 467. §§ 581, 585.
S. v., 103 N. C. 413. § 1258.
Wall, Ex parte, 107 U. S. 265. § 9.
Rex v., 2 East, P. C. 953. § 750.
v. S., 78 Ala. 417. § 1219.
v. S., 23 Ind. 150. §§ 13, 91, 271.
v. S., 51 Ind. 453. §§ 301, 304, **306**, 310, 382.
v. S., 18 Tex. 682. §§ 78, 96, 338, **361**.
S. v., 34 Me. 165. § 1218.
S. v., 9 Yerg. 347. § 859.
Wallace, C. v., 7 Gray, 222. § 1215.
C. v., 16 Gray, 221. §§ 974, 975.
C. v., 114 Pa. St. 405. § 679.
C. v., 108 Mass. 12. § 213.
C. v., 143 Mass. 88. § 1249.
v. Georgia, etc. R. Co., 94 Ga. **732**. § 55.
v. Harmstad, 44 Pa. St. 492. § **1354**.
v. P., 27 Ill. 45. § 796.
v. P., 63 Ill. 451. § 604.
P. v., 9 Cal. 30. §§ 293, 377, 385.
Reg. v., Car. & M. 200. § 818.
Reg. v., 2 Moody, 200. § 818.
v. S., 54 Ark. 542. § 1258.
v. S., 2 Lea, 29. § 694.
v. S., 11 Lea, 542. § 666.
v. S., 30 Tex. 758. § 826.
v. S., 7 Tex. Ap. 570. § 409.
v. S., 10 Tex. Ap. 255. § 294.
v. S., 12 Tex. Ap. 479. §§ 1302, **1304**.
v. S, 20 Tex. Ap. 360. § 328.
S. v., 47 Ia. 660. § 619.
S. v., 9 N. H. 515. § 1086.
v. U. S., 162 U. S. 466. §§ 306, 307, 339.
U. S. v., 40 Fed. R. 144. § 918.
v. Young, 5 T. B. Mon. 155. § 520.
Wallick, S. v., 87 Ia. 369. §§ 638, 639.
Waller, Reg. v., 10 Cox, 360. §§ 554, 562.
v. S., 40 Ala. 325. §§ 439, 447, 450.
v. S., 89 Ala. 79. § 309.
v. S., 38 Ark. 656. § 1238.
S. v., 43 Ark. 381. § 18.
S. v., 88 Mo. 402. § 380.
S. v., 3 Murph. 229. § 1018.
S. v., 80 N. C. 401. § 1097.
Walling v. Michigan, 116 U. S. **446**. §§ 44, 1202.
P. v., 53 Mich. 264. §§ 1202, 1212.
v. S., 7 Tex. Ap. 625. § 452.
Wallis v. Mease, 3 Binn. 546. § **538**.
Reg. v., 3 Cox, 67. § 548.
Reg. v., 1 Salk. 334. § 291.

Wallis v. S., 54 Ark. 611. §§ 644, 650, 652.
U. S. v., 58 Fed. R. 942. § 1334.
Walls v. S., 90 Ala. 618. § 274.
v. S., 32 Ark. 565. §§ 1074, 1077.
v. S., 7 Blackf. 572. §§ 128, 1032.
Walpole v. S., 9 Baxt. 370. § 812.
v. S., 16 N. H. 157. § 1185.
Walsh, In re, 37 Neb. 454. § 803.
P. v., 43 Cal. 447. § 144.
Rex v., 1 Moody, 14. § 548.
Rex v., Russ. & Ry. 215. § 543.
S. v., 43 Minn., 444. § 819.
U. S. v., 5 Dill. 58. §§ 14, 974.
U. S. v., 22 Fed. R. 644. § 877.
Walster v. U. S., 42 Fed. R. 891. §§ 1330, 1335.
Walston v. C., 16 B. Mon. 15. § 425.
v. S., 54 Ga. 242. § 363.
Walter v. P., 32 N. Y. 147. §§ 174, 332.
P. v., 1 Ida. (N. S.) 386. §§ 158, 175, 178, 360.
Rex v., 3 Esp. 21. § 1056.
v. S., 105 Ind. 589. § 1246.
Walters v. C., 44 Pa. St. 135. § 368.
P. v., 98 Cal. 138. §§ 417, 418.
P. v., 76 Mich. 195. §§ 617, 618.
Reg. v., Car. & M. 164. § 347.
Reg. v., Car. & M. 588. § 753.
Rex v., 1 Moody, 13. § 497.
v. S., 52 Ga. 574. § 61.
v. S., 5 Ia. 507. §§ 1268, 1275.
v. S., 17 Tex. Ap. 226. § 560.
S. v., 64 Ind. 226. §§ 128, 819, 826.
S. v., 45 Ia. 389. §§ 461, 463.
S. v., 97 N. C. 489. § 108.
S. v., 7 Wash. 246. § 617.
Waltham, Reg. v., 3 Cox, 442. § 256.
Walton, Reg. v., L. & C. 288. § 730.
v. S., 62 Ala. 197. §§ 84, 1233, 1256, 1259.
v. S., 64 Miss. 207. § 1160.
v. S., 14 Tex. 381. § 1286.
v. S., 12 Tex. Ap. 117. § 61.
v. S., 29 Tex. Ap. 163. §§ 439, 451, 463, 505.
v. S., 6 Yerg. 377. § 753.
S. v., 62 Me. 106. §§ 622, 646, 648.
S. v., 114 N. C. 783. §§ 674, 691.
Waltz, S. v., 74 Ia. 610. § 1272.
Wambold, S. v., 74 Ia. 605. § 1249.
Wan Shing v. U. S., 140 U. S. 424. § 1344.
War, P. v., 20 Cal. 117. § 18.
Warburton, Reg. v., L. R. 1 C. C. 274. § 960.
Ward v. C., 14 Bush, 233. § 479.
C. v., 92 Ky. 158. § 977.
C. v., 1 Mass. 473. § 960.
C. v., 2 Mass. 397. § 797.
v. Green, 11 Conn. 455. § 1319.
v. Greenville, 8 Baxt. 228. § 1217.
v. Maryland, 12 Wall. 418. §§ 44, 79.
v. P., 3 Hill (N. Y.), 395; 6 Hill (N. Y.), 144. §§ 210, 536, 546, 573.
v. P., 23 Ill. Ap. 510. § 1313.
Ward, P. v., 85 Cal. 585. §§ 200, 913, **917.**
P. v., 105 Cal. 335. §§ 169, 178.
Reg. v., 7 Cox, 421. § 601.
Reg. v., 10 Cox, 42. § 740.
Reg. v., 2 F. & F. 18. § 609.
Rex v., 4 A. & E. 384. §§ 1171, 1195.
Rex v., 6 C. & P. 366. § 886.
Rex v., 2 Ld. Raym. 1461. §§ **743,** 773.
v. S., 22 Ala. 16. § 1294.
v. S., 48 Ala. 161. § 539.
v. S., 50 Ala. 120. § 499.
v. S., 96 Ala. 100. § 164.
v. S., 45 Ark. 351. § 1259.
v. S., 8 Blackf. 101. §§ 425, 429.
v. S., 49 Conn. 429. §§ 600, 713, 714, 720.
v. S., 56 Ga. 408. §§ 256, 262.
v. S., 48 Ind. 289. § 1257.
v. S., 48 Ind. 293. § 1221.
v. S., 12 Lea, 469. § 1190.
v. S., 70 Miss. 245. § 51.
v. S., 17 Ohio St. 32. § 1313.
v. S., 41 Tex. 611. § 618.
v. S., 30 Tex. Ap. 687. § 305.
S. v., 48 Ark. 36. § 652.
S. v., 7 Baxt. 76. §§ 752, 758.
S. v., 43 Conn. 489. § 502.
S. v., 5 Harr. 496. § 332.
S. v., 57 Ind. 537. §§ 59, 1314.
S. v., 73 Ia. 532. § 460.
S. v., 75 Ia. 637. § 1257.
S. v., 35 Minn. 182. §§ 449, 452.
S. v., 74 Mo. 253. §§ 164, 167.
S. v., 6 N. H. 529. § 793.
S. v., 103 N. C. 419. § 515.
S. v., 9 Tex. 370. § 1292.
S. v., 61 Vt. 153. § 533.
Wardell, C. v., 128 Mass. 52. § 1135.
Reg. v., 3 F. & F. 82. § 752.
U. S. v., 49 Fed. R. 914. §§ 946, 950.
Warden, C. v., 11 Met. 406. §§ 873, 887.
P. v., 144 N. Y. 529. § 38.
v. S., 60 Miss. 638. § 568.
v. S., 24 Ohio St. 143. §§ 204, 213, 218.
Wardlaw, S. v., 43 Ark. 73. § 1033.
Wardlow v. S., 18 Tex. Ap. 356. § 1285.
Wardroper, Reg. v., Bell, 249. § 145.
Wardwell, C. v., 136 Mass. 164. § 1052.
Ware, In re, 53 Fed. R. 783. § 76.
v. S., 67 Ga. 349. § 463.
v. S., 71 Miss. 204. § 1276.
v. S., 2 Tex. Ap. 547. § 592.
v. S., 19 Tex. Ap. 13. § 608.
S. v., 10 Ala. 814. § 568.
S. v., 44 La. An. 954. § 601.
Wareham v. S., 25 Ohio St. 601. § 323.
Warford, S. v., 106 Mo. 55. §§ 500, 514.
Waring v. Mayor, 8 Wall. 110. § 76.
Warman, Reg. v., 2 C. & K. 195. § 377.
Warmoth v. C., 81 Ky. 133. § 623.
Warner v. C., 1 Pa. St. 154. §§ 83, 85, 543.
v. C., 2 Va. Cas. 95. § 1083.
v. Fowler, 8 Md. 25. § 865.
v. Smith, 8 Conn. 14. § 1319.

Warner v. S., 54 Ark. 660. §§ 443, 452.
v. S., 56 N. J. 686. § 162.
S. v., 34 Conn. 276. § 1017.
S. v., 14 Ind. 572. § 511.
S. v., 25 Ia. 200. § 463.
S. v., 74 Mo. 83. § 452.
U. S. v., 59 Fed. R. 355. § 1332.
U. S. v., 4 McLean, 463. § 351.
Warren v. C., 37 Pa. St. 45. §§ 162, 359.
C. v., 94 Ky. 615. § 678.
C. v., 6 Mass. 72. § 661.
C. v., 6 Mass. 74. §§ 966, 989.
C. v., 160 Mass. 533. §§ 33, 34, 128.
C. v., 161 Mass. 281. § 1296.
P. v., 5 Hill (N. Y.), 440. § 922.
Reg. v., 10 Cox, 359. § 554.
Rex v., Russ. & Ry. 47. § 130.
v. S., 94 Ala. 79. § 1031.
v. S., 18 Ark. 195. § 1291.
v. S., 4 Coldw. 130. §§ 321, 325.
v S., 1 Greene (Ia.), 106. §§ 538, 619, 620.
v. S., 33 Tex. 517. § 232.
v. S., 9 Tex. Ap. 619. § 412.
v. S., 31 Tex. Ap. 573. § 307.
S. v., 33 Me. 30. § 518.
S. v., 77 Md. 121. § 551.
S. v., 109 Mo. 430. §§ 766, 771.
S. v., 113 N. C. 683. § 60.
S. v., 14 Tex. 406. § 324.
v. U. S., 58 Fed. R. 559. § 1343.
Warrick, Ex parte, 73 Ala. 57. § 338.
Warriner v. P., 74 Ill. 346. § 639.
Warshauer, Rex v., 1 Moody, 466. § 795.
Warwick v. S., 25 Ohio St. 21. § 855.
U. S. v., 51 Fed. R. 280. §§ 1217, 1274.
Wasden v. S., 18 Ga. 264. § 1088.
Wash v. C., 16 Grat. 530. § 789.
v. S., 14 Sm. & M. 120. § 454.
Washburn, S. v., 11 Ia. 245. § 785.
Washington v. P., 72 Ala. 272. §§ 634, 636.
v. S., 53 Ala. 29. § 276.
v. S., 58 Ala. 355. § 594.
v. S., 60 Ala. 10. §§ 320, 325.
v. S., 68 Ala. 85. § 520.
v. S., 72 Ala. 272. § 634.
v. S., 75 Ala. 582. § 78.
v. S., 82 Ala. 31. § 497.
v. S., 36 Ga. 222. §§ 196, 213, 391.
v. S., 68 Ga. 570. §§ 205, 291.
v. S., 41 Tex. 583. § 707.
v. S., 1 Tex. Ap. 647. §§ 328, 391.
v. S., 8 Tex. Ap. 377. § 420.
v. S., 16 Tex. Ap. 376. § 194.
v. S., 17 Tex. Ap. 197. § 509.
v. S., 17 Tex. Ap. 376. § 194.
v. S., 19 Tex. Ap. 521. § 414.
v. S., 22 Tex. Ap. 26. §§ 864, 878, 892.
v. S., 23 Tex. Ap. 336. § 866.
v. S., 25 Tex. Ap. 387. §§ 353, 355.
S. v., 1 Bay, 120. § 773.
S. v., 33 La. An. 1473. § 212.
S. v., 41 La. An. 778. § 654.
S. v., 15 Rich. 39. § 601.
Washington, S. v., 26 S. C. 604. § 536.
S. v., 19 Tex. 128. § 1009.
Wason v. Severance, 2 N. H. 501. § 1231.
v. Walter, L. R. 4 Q. B. 73. § 1052.
Wasservogle, P. v., 77 Cal. 173. §§ 666, 674.
Waterhouse v. S., 21 Tex. Ap. 663. § 501.
Waterman, C. v., 122 Mass. 43. §§ 120, 958, 962, 969.
v. P., 67 Ill. 91. § 756.
v. S., 13 Fla. 683. § 487.
Waters, C. v., 11 Gray, 81. § 1278.
v. P., 104 Ill. 544. § 617.
Reg. v., 2 C. & K. 864. §§ 286, 373*a*.
Rex v., 6 C. & P. 328. § 286.
Rex v., 7 C. & P. 250. § 378.
Rex v., 1 Moody, 457. § 373*a*.
v. S., 53 Ga. 567. § 504.
v. S., 30 Tex. Ap. 284. §§ 891, 892.
S. v., 3 Brev. 507. § 798.
S. v., 6 Jones, 276. § 815.
S. v., 39 Me. 54. § 279.
S. v., 1 Treadw. Const. 669. § 765.
Watkinds, U. S. v., 6 Fed. R. 152. §§ 943, 950.
Watkins, Reg. v., Car. & M. 264. § 511.
v. S., 89 Ala. 82. § 312.
v. S., 60 Miss. 323. § 558.
v. S., 2 Tex. Ap. 73. § 617.
S. v., 4 Humph. 256. § 489.
S. v., 27 Ia. 415. §§ 361, 383.
S. v., 11 Nev. 30. § 500.
S. v., 101 N. C. 702. § 1164.
Watson v. Carr, 1 Lewin, 6. § 25.
v. C., 85 Va. 867. § 359.
C. v., 2 Duv. 408. § 1313.
C. v., 154 Mass. 135. § 1305.
v. Mercer, 8 Pet. 88. § 78.
v. P., 87 N. Y. 561. §§ 677, 687.
P. v., 72 Cal. 402. § 601.
P. v., 75 Mich. 582. §§ 659, 682, 697.
P. v., 41 N. H. 533. § 562.
Reg. v., Dears. & B. 348. § 683.
Rex v., 2 East, P. C. 680. § 662.
v. S., 55 Ala. 150. § 594.
v. S., 55 Ala. 158. §§ 1206, 1218.
v. S., 63 Ala. 19. §§ 827, 831.
v. S., 70 Ala. 13. § 644.
v. S., 82 Ala. 10. § 365.
v. S., 64 Ga. 61. § 652.
v. S., 27 Ill. Ap. 493. § 667.
v. S., 3 Ind. 123. § 1198.
v. S., 36 Miss. 593. § 553.
v. S., 5 Mo. 497. § 389.
v. S., 39 Ohio St. 123. §§ 896, 901.
v. S., 5 Tex. Ap. 11. § 894.
v. S., 9 Tex. Ap. 237. §§ 1150, 1151.
v. S., 13 Tex. Ap. 76. § 1079.
v. S., 13 Tex. Ap. 160. § 1302.
v. S., 21 Tex. Ap. 598. § 573.
v. S., 25 Tex. Ap. 651. § 1188.
v. S., 28 Tex. Ap. 34. § 213.
v. S., 2 Wash. 504. § 265.
S. v., 70 Ala. 13. § 644.
S. v., 4 Ind. 595. § 42.
S. v., 81 Ia. 380. §§ 458, 459.
S. v., 36 La. An. 148. § 307.

Watson, S. v. 41 La. An. 598. § **436**.
S. v., 63 Me. 128. § 526.
S. v., 41 N. H. 533. § 562.
S. v., 86 N. C. 626. § 823.
S. v., 7 S. C. 63. § 572.
U. S. v., 17 Fed. R. 145. § **974**.
U. S. v., 35 Fed. R. 358. § **1331**.
Watt v. S., 97 Ala. 72. § 940.
v. S., 61 Ga. 66. § 520.
Watts v. C., 78 Ky. 329. § 1226.
C. v., 4 Leigh, 672. § 444.
Reg. v., Dears. 326. § 543.
Reg. v., 2 Den. 14. § 546.
Rex v., 2 Esp. 675. § 1195.
v. S., 6 Tex. Ap. 263. § 546.
v. S., 30 Tex. Ap. 533. §§ 223, **275**.
v. S., 5 W. Va 532. §§ 197, 265.
S. v., 48 Ark. 56. § 811.
Wandby, Reg. v., 2 Q. B. D. (1895) 482. §§ 210, 437.
Wavell, Rex v., 1 Moody, 224. § 674.
Wax v. S., 43 Neb. 18. §§ 686, 709.
Way, P. v., 10 Cal. 336. § 753.
S. v., 5 Neb. 283. §§ 1094, 1098.
S. v., 6 Vt. 311. § 1097.
v. T., 1 Wash. 415. § 1312.
Waybright v. S., 56 Ind. 122. § 421.
Waynick, S. v., 45 Ia. 516. §§ 1216, 1248, 1277.
Wealand, Reg. v., 20 Q. B. D. 827. § 456.
Weatherby, S. v., 43 Me. 258. § 1088.
Weatherford v. S., 31 Tex. Ap. 530. § 1388.
Weathers v. S., 2 Blackf. 278. § 878.
Weaver v. P., 132 Ill. 536. §§ 123, 275, 276.
v. S., 77 Ala. 26. §§ 569. 571.
v. S., 79 Ala. 279. §§ 1017, 1021.
v. S., 89 Ga. 639. § 44.
v. S., 24 Ohio St. 584. § 316.
v. S., 24 Tex. 387. § 257.
v. S., 19 Tex. Ap. 547. § 299.
S. v., Busbee, 9. § 489.
S. v., 83 Ind. 542. § 1265.
S. v., 13 Ired. 491. §§ 765, 801.
S. v., 94 N. C. 836. § 752.
S. v., 104 N. C. 758. §§ 551, 618.
v. Ward, Hob. 134. § 111.
Webb v. Baird, 11 Lea, 667. §§ 1245, 1254.
C. v., 6 Rand. 726. § 1169.
Reg. v., 5 Cox, 154. § 558.
Reg. v., 2 C. & K. 933. § 1136.
Rex v., Russ. & Ry. 405. § 762.
Rex v., Moody, 431. §§ 549, 567.
Rex v., 1 M. & Rob. 405. §§ 287, 377.
v S., 52 Ala. 422. §§ 508, 509.
v. S., 100 Ala. 47. § 332.
v. S., 11 Lea, 662. §§ 1245, 1254.
v. S., 5 Tex. Ap. 596. § 158.
v. S., 8 Tex. Ap. 115. § 615.
v. S., 8 Tex. Ap. 310. § 639.
v. S., 9 Tex. Ap. 490. § 178.
v. S., 17 Tex. Ap. 205. § 1310.
S. v., 25 Ia. 235. § 1137.
S. v., 26 Ia. 262. § 669.
S. v., 87 N. C. 558. § 550.
Webb, S. v., 41 Tex. 67. § 881.
Webber v. S., 10 Mo. 4. § 1067.
S. v., 76 Ia. 686. §§ 1248, 1277.
S. v., 107 N. C. 962. § 66.
v. Virginia, 103 U. S. 344. §§ **44**, 1202.
Weber, P. v., 66 Cal. 391. § 195.
S. v., 111 Mo. 204. § 1237.
Webster v. C., 80 Va. 598. § 508.
C. v., 6 Allen, 591. § 1091.
C. v., 5 Cush. 295. §§ 123, 284, **320**, **321**, **332**, **333**, **397**, **398**, **399**, **409**, 422.
v. P., 92 N. Y. 422. § 701.
P. v., 139 N. Y. 73. § 406.
Reg. v., 1 F. & F. 515. § 892.
Reg. v., L. & C. 77. § 546.
Reg. v., 16 Q. B. D. 134. § 1138.
v. S., 8 Blackf. 400. §§ 1290, **1291**.
v. S., 7 Dana, 215. § 1229.
v. S., 9 Tex. Ap. 75. § 509.
S. v., 17 N. H. 543. § 814.
S. v., 39 N. H. 96. § 923.
S. v., 10 N. J. 293. § 1229.
Wedge v. S., 7 Lea, 687. § 557.
S. v., 24 Minn. 150. §§ 905, **906**.
Weeber v. U. S., 62 Fed. R. 740. § **1331**.
Weed v. S., 55 Ala. 13. § 1261.
S. v., 21 N. H. 262. § 922.
Weekly, S. v., 29 Ind. 206. § 1008.
Weeks, Reg. v., L. & C. 18. § 778.
v. S., 79 Ga. 36. § 332.
S. v., 1 Dev. 135. § 245.
S. v., 30 Me. 182. §§ 819, 830.
Weese, S. v., 53 Ia. 92. § 362.
Wegener, Rex v., 2 Stark. 245. §§ **118**, 1055, 1067.
Weideman v. S., 4 Ind. Ap. 397. § **1134**.
Weighorst v. S., 7 Md. 442. § 365.
Weil v. Calhoun, 25 Fed. R. 865. §§ 1209, 1210.
v. S., 46 Ohio St. 450. § 844.
Weinberg v. S., 25 Wis. 370. § 1074.
Weinecke v. S., 34 Neb. 314. § 1196.
Weir v. Allen, 47 Ia. 482. § 1267.
S. v., 33 Ia. 134. § 1206.
Weireter v. S., 69 Ind. 269. § 1246.
Weisbrodt v. S., 50 Ohio St. 192. § 1221.
Weiss, C. v., 139 Pa. St. 247. § 128.
v. S., 16 Tex. Ap. 431. § 1304.
Weithoff, P. v., 51 Mich. 203. §§ 1283, 1285, 1288, 1297, 1305, 1307, 1310.
P. v., 93 Mich. 631. § 1310.
P. v., 100 Mich. 393. § 1310.
Welbourn, Rex v., 1 East, P. C. 358. §§ 426, 430.
Welch, C. v., 2 Dana, 330. § 96.
C. v., 144 Mass. 356. §§ 1223, **1224**, 1225.
C. v., 147 Mass. 374. § 1243.
C. v., 148 Mass. 296. § 752.
P. v., 49 Cal. 174. §§ 363, 391.
Reg. v., 2 C. & K. 296. §§ 626, 632, **651**.
Reg. v., 2 Den. 78. § 782.
Reg. v., 1 Q. B. D. 23. § 826.
S. v., 36 Conn. 215. § 63.

Welch, S. v., 88 Ind. 308. § 1018.
S. v., 21 Minn. 22. §§ 128, 160, 943, 950.
S. v., 28 Mo. 600. § 45.
S. v., 73 Mo. 284. §§ 132, 135.
S. v., 66 N. H. 178. § 46.
S. v., 7 Port. 463. § 1287.
S. v., 36 W. Va. 690. §§ 162, 359, 405.
S. v., 37 Wis. 196. § 923.
v. Ware, 32 Mich. 77. § 157.
Weldon, P. v., 111 N. Y. 569. §§ 619, 717, 721.
v. S., 32 Ind. 81. § 456.
S. v., 70 Mo. 572. § 28.
Welland, Rex v., Russ. & Ry. 494. § 594.
Wellar v. P., 30 Mich. 16. §§ 307, 322, 332, 347, 410, 417.
Wellard, Reg. v., 14 Q. B. D. 63. § 1136.
Weller, C. v., 14 Bush, 218. § 1216.
v. Ely, 45 Conn. 547. § 611.
S. v., 20 N. J. 521. §§ 122, 771.
T. v., 2 N. M. 470. § 859.
Wellings, Rex v., 1 C. & P. 454. §§ 626, 635.
Wellington, C. v., 7 Allen, 299. § 1168.
v. S., 52 Ark. 266. § 822.
Wellman, S. v., 34 Minn. 221. § 542.
Wellock v. Constantine, 2 H. & C. 146. § 11.
Wells v. Abrahams, L. R. 7 Q. B. 554. § 11.
P. v., 103 Cal. 631. § 892.
P. v., 8 Mich. 104. § 780.
Reg. v., 1 F. & F. 109. § 554.
v. S., 89 Ga. 788. § 763.
v. S., 11 Neb. 409. § 589.
v. S., 4 Tex. Ap. 20. §§ 573, 596.
v. S., 9 Tex. Ap. 160. § 1129.
v. S., 18 Tex. Ap. 417. § 1281.
S. v., 46 Ia. 662. § 1140.
S. v., 48 Ia. 671. §§ 1113, 1118, 1119.
S. v., 61 Ia. 629. §§ 354, 383.
S. v., 70 Mo. 635. § 128.
S. v., 1 N. J. 424. §§ 139, 308.
v. Weston, 22 Mo. 384. § 70.
Welman, Reg. v., Dears. 188. § 691.
Welsh, C. v., 1 Allen, 1. § 1279.
C. v., 7 Gray, 324. § 1013.
C. v., 2 Va. Cas. 57. § 1268.
Reg. v., 11 Cox, 336. § 338.
Rex v., 1 East, P. C. 87. § 774.
v. S., 97 Ala. 1. § 421.
v. S., 126 Ind. 71. §§ 1218, 1220, 1228.
v. S., 3 Tex. Ap. 413. § 206.
S. v., 73 Ia. 106. § 271.
Weltje, Rex v., 2 Camp. 142. § 1057.
Welton v. Missouri, 91 U. S. 275. § 44.
S. v., 55 Mo. 288. § 44.
Wendt v. S., 32 Neb. 182. § 1235.
Wenman v. Ash, 13 C. B. 836. § 1055.
Wenmouth, Reg. v., 8 Cox, 348. §§ 496, 505.
Wennhak v. Morgan, 20 Q. B. D. 635. § 1055.
Wensell, S. v., 98 Mo. 137. § 426.
Wentler, S. v., 76 Wis. 89. §§ 444, 1121.
Wentworth, C. v., Bright. 318. §§ 1184, 1186.
C. v., 118 Mass. 441. §§ 29, 128.
C. v., 146 Mass. 36. § 1174.
S. v., 65 Me. 234. §§ 189, 1237.
S. v., 35 N. H. 442. § 1274.
S. v., 37 N. H. 196. § 1196.
Wenz v. S., 1 Tex. Ap. 36. § 161.
S. v., 41 Minn. 196. §§ 1114, 1117, 1118.
Werley v. S., 11 Humph. 171. § 435.
Werneke v. S., 49 Ind. 202. § 1247.
v. S., 50 Ind. 22. § 1257.
Werner v. S., 44 Ark. 122. § 242.
Wernwag, S. v., 116 N. C. 1061. § 71.
Wertzel, S. v., 62 Wis. 184. § 1190.
Wesley v. S., 61 Ala. 282. § 481.
v. S., 65 Ga. 731. § 450.
v. S., 37 Miss. 327. §§ 303, 307.
Wessel, P. v., 98 Cal. 352. § 452.
West v. Columbus, 20 Kan. 633. § 1272.
v. P., 137 Ill. 189. § 43.
P. v., 49 Cal. 610. §§ 316, 346.
P. v., 106 N. Y. 293. § 128.
Reg. v., 2 C. & K. 496. § 753.
Reg. v., 2 C. & K. 784. § 294.
Reg. v., Dears. 402. §§ 545, 571.
Reg. v., Dears. & B. 109. § 543.
Reg. v., Dears. & B. 575. § 678.
v. S., 76 Ala. 98. §§ 404, 409.
v. S., 84 Ga. 527. § 1129.
v. S., 9 Humph. 65. § 1027.
v. S., 48 Ind. 483. § 380.
v. S., 59 Ind. 113. §§ 139, 140, 304.
v. S., 70 Miss. 598. §§ 1232, 1270.
v. S., 32 Tex. 651. § 816.
v. S., 2 Tex. Ap. 460. §§ 307, 314.
v. S., 6 Tex. Ap. 485. § 546.
v. S., 7 Tex. Ap. 150. § 427.
v. S., 8 Tex. Ap. 119. § 872.
v. S., 18 Tex. Ap. 640. § 303.
v. S., 26 Tex. Ap. 99. § 1037.
v. S., 27 Tex. Ap. 472. §§ 216, 590.
v. S., 28 Tex. Ap. 1. § 590.
v. S., 1 Wis. 209. § 1114.
S. v., 1 Houst. Cr. C. 371. §§ 172, 316, 416.
S. v., 14 Lea, 38. § 909.
S. v., 42 Minn. 147. § 6.
S. v., 69 Mo. 401. § 395.
Westbeer, Rex v., 2 Stra. 1133, 1 Leach, 12. § 543.
Westbrook v. P., 126 Ill. 81. § 426.
v. S., 23 Tex. Ap. 401. § 796.
Westcott v. S., 31 Fla. 458. § 358.
Western, etc. R. Co., S. v., 89 N. C. 584. § 180.
S. v., 95 N. C. 602. §§ 183, 185.
Western U. Tel. Co. v. Yopst, 118 Ind. 248. § 1323.
Westfall, S. v., 49 Ia. 328. §§ 194, 425.
Westfield, S. v., 1 Bailey, 132. § 210.
Westlake, P. v., 62 Cal. 303. § 309.
Westley, Reg. v., 11 Cox, 139. § 252.
Westmoreland v. S., 45 Ga. 225. § 179.
v. U. S., 155 U. S. 545. §§ 378, 388.

Weston v. C., 111 Pa. St. 251. §§ 114, 196, 299.
Reg. v., 14 Cox, 346. §§ 305. 307, 351.
S. v., 9 Conn. 527. §§ 571, 617, 713.
Westwood, Rex v., Russ. & Ry. 495. §§ 494, 498.
Wetherbee, C. v., 105 Mass. 149. § 41.
C. v., 153 Mass. 159. § 33.
Wetherhead, C. v., 110 Mass. 175. § 46.
Wetmore v. S., 55 Ala. 198. § 1284.
Wetzler v. S., 18 Ind. 416. § 1324.
Weydeman, S. v., 3 Wash. 399. § 636.
Weyrich v. P., 89 Ill. 90. § 416.
Whalen v. C., 90 Va. 544. §§ 585, 595, 610.
C. v., 131 Mass. 419. § 499.
S. v., 54 Ia. 753. § 1273.
S. v., 85 Me. 469. § 1267.
Whaley, C. v., 6 Bush, 266. § 1079.
P. v., 6 Cow. 661. § 914.
v. S., 87 Ala. 83. § 1247.
S. v., 2 Harr. 538. § 489.
U. S. v., 37 Fed. R. 145. § 132.
Whalley, Rex v., 7 C. & P. 245. § 795.
Wharton v. King, 69 Ala. 365. § 1227.
v. S., 73 Ala. 366. § 416.
Whateley, Rex v., 4 M. & Rob. 431. § 827.
Whatley v. S., 91 Ala. 108. § 313.
Wheat v. Brown, 1 Q. B. D. (1892) 418. § 34.
v. S., 63 Vt. 673. §§ 442, 464.
Wheatland, Reg. v., 8 C. & P. 238. § 891.
Wheatley, Rex v., 1 W. Bl. 272. §§ 660, 670.
S. v., 4 Lea, 230. § 1141.
v. Thorn, 23 Miss. 62. § 11.
Wheatly, Rex v., 2 Burr. 1125. §§ 10, 16.
Wheeldon, Reg. v., 8 C. & P. 747. § 502.
Wheeler, P. v., 73 Cal. 252. § 906.
P. v., 96 Mich. 1. § 1264.
Rex v., 3 C. & P. 585. § 499.
Rex v., 7 C. & P. 170. § 609.
v. S., 42 Md. 563. §§ 1295, 1296, 1309.
v. S., 64 Miss. 462. § 96.
v. S., 16 Tex. Ap. 607. § 572.
S. v., 25 Conn. 290. § 104.
S. v., 19 Minn. 98. § 759.
S. v., 27 Minn. 76. § 1216.
S. v., 108 Mo. 658. §§ 1113, 1119.
S. v., 44 N. J. 88. § 30.
S. v., 104 N. C. 893. § 1129.
S. v., 20 Oreg. 192. § 764.
S. v., 15 Rich. 362. § 591.
S. v., 3 Vt. 344. § 814.
S. v., 35 Vt. 261. § 799.
S. v., 62 Vt. 439. §§ 1243, 1277.
Wheeling, etc. Bridge, Pennsylvania v., 13 How. (U. S.) 518. § 1195.
Wheelock v. S., 15 Tex. 260. § 1302.
Whelan, C. v., 134 Mass. 206. §§ 1223, 1225, 1266.
Whelchell v. S., 23 Ind. 89. § 380.
Whilden v. S., 25 Ga. 396. § 262.
Whiley, Reg. v., 1 C. & K. 150. § 1077.
Rex v., Russ. & Ry. 90. § 764.
Whipple, S. v., 57 Vt. 637. § 1272.
Whisenhurst, S. v., 2 Hawks, 458. § 854.
Whisenhunt v. S., 18 Tex. Ap. 491. § 1232.
Whisner, S. v., 35 Kan. 271. §§ 1207, 1273, 1274.
Whissenhunt, S. v., 98 N. C. 682. § 1254.
Whitaker v. English, 1 Bay, 15. § 210.
v. S., 79 Ga. 87. § 426.
v. S., 12 Tex. Ap. 436. § 391.
S. v., 89 N. C. 472. § 609.
S. v., 107 N. C. 802. § 828.
Whitcher v. S., 2 Wash. 286. § 464.
Whitchurch, Reg. v., 24 Q. B. D. 420. § 967.
Whitcomb, C. v., 107 Mass. 486. § 695.
S. v., 52 Ia. 85. §§ 1090, 1091.
T. v., 1 Mont. 358. § 1094.
Whitcomb Metallic Bedstead Co., U. S. v., 45 Fed. R. 89. § 1343.
White v. C., 4 Binn. 418. § 774.
v. C., 6 Binn. 179. §§ 361, 362.
v. C., 9 Bush, 178. § 377.
v. C., 87 Ky. 454. § 498.
C. v., 18 B. Mon. 492. § 1270.
C. v., 11 Cush. 483. §§ 550, 562, 570.
C. v., 110 Mass. 407. § 233.
C. v., 123 Mass. 430. §§ 715, 720.
C. v., 145 Mass. 392. §§ 754, 808.
C. v., 162 Mass. 403. § 741.
C. v., 10 Met. 14. §§ 1221, 1273.
C. v., 133 Pa. St. 183. § 478.
v. Fort, 3 Hawks, 251. § 11.
v. Murtland, 71 Ill. 250. § 1149.
v. P., 81 Ill. 333. § 194.
v. P., 139 Ill. 143. § 265.
v. P., 32 N. Y. 465. § 1001.
P. v., 34 Cal. 183. §§ 778, 790.
P. v., 24 Wend. 520. §§ 354, 357, 383.
v. Reg., 13 Cox, 318. § 707.
Reg. v., 2 C. & K. 404. § 762.
Reg. v., 3 C. & K. 363. §§ 542, 548.
Reg. v., 8 C. & P. 742. §§ 626, 640, 653.
Reg. v., 9 C. & P. 282. § 753.
Reg. v., 9 C. & P. 344. §§ 556, 558.
Reg. v., 5 Cox, 290. § 764.
Reg. v., 1 F. & F. 665. § 716.
Reg. v., 2 F. & F. 554. § 764.
Reg. v., L. R. 1 C. C. 311. § 58.
Rex v., 4 C. & P. 46. §§ 629, 630.
Rex v., 2 East, P. C. 513, 780. § 508.
Rex v., Moody & M. 271. § 865.
Rex v., Russ. & Ry. 99. § 197.
v. Spettigue, 13 M. & W. 603. § 11.
v. S., 30 Ala. 518. § 363.
v. S., 49 Ala. 344. § 500.
v. S., 72 Ala. 195. §§ 508, 619.
v. S., 84 Ala. 421. § 351.
v. S., 86 Ala. 69. § 703.
v. S., 87 Ala. 24. § 683.
v. S., 103 Ala. 72. §§ 161, 899.
v. S., 51 Ga. 285. § 502.
v. S., 56 Ga. 385. § 914.
v. S., 93 Ga. 47. §§ 1233, 1272.
v. S., 136 Ind. 308. § 463.
v. S., 9 Miss. 149. §§ 859, 861.

White v. S., 11 Tex. 769. §§ 562, 614.
v. S., 13 Tex. 133. § 930.
v. S., 16 Tex. 206. § 362.
v. S., 22 Tex. 608. §§ 223, 265, 269.
v. S., 4 Tex. Ap. 488. § 389.
v. S., 11 Tex. Ap. 476. §§ 1270, 1273.
v. S., 13 Tex. Ap. 259. § 274.
v. S., 14 Tex. Ap. 449. § 825.
v. S., 23 Tex. Ap. 643. § 564.
v. S., 24 Tex. Ap. 231. § 604.
v. S., 28 Tex. Ap. 71. § 618.
v. S., 29 Tex. Ap. 530. § 239.
v. S., 30 Tex. Ap. 652. §§ 391. 414, 429.
v. S., 32 Tex. Ap. 625. § 419.
v. S., 33 Tex. Ap. 94. § 546.
v. S., 20 Wis. 233. § 644.
S. v., 23 Ark. 275. § 1223.
S. v., 7 Baxt. 158. § 1255.
S. v., 129 Ind. 153. § 593.
S. v., 45 Ia. 325. §§ 271, 278, 335.
S. v., 6 Ired. 418. §§ 1060, 1070.
S. v., 7 Ired. 180. § 1051.
S. v., 4 Jones, 349. §§ 497, 504.
S. v., 14 Kan. 538. § 161.
S. v., 31 Kan. 342. § 1271.
S. v., 44 Kan. 514. §§ 443, 444, 449, 452.
S. v., 7 La. An. 531. § 213.
S. v., 30 La. An., Pt. I. 364. § 339.
S. v., 35 Mo. 500. § 460.
S. v., 76 Mo. 96. §§ 128, 1152.
S. v., 126 Mo. 591. §§ 571, 617.
S. v., 64 N. H. 48. §§ 39, 128, 1016.
S. v., 68 N. C. 158. § 614.
S. v., 89 N. C. 462. § 614.
S. v., 18 R. I. 473. § 245.
S. v., 2 Tyler, 352. § 554.
S. v., 64 Vt. 372. § 1018.
S. v., 10 Wash. 611. §§ 195, 214.
S. v., 66 Wis. 343. §§ 636, 648.
v. T., 1 Wash. 279. § 797.
U. S. v., 25 Fed. R. 716. § 775.
U. S. v., 27 Fed. R. 200. §§ 775, 790.
U. S. v., 42 Fed. R. 138. §§ 1237, 1251, 1253.
White Oak River Corp., S. v., 111 N. C. 661. § 1195.
Whiteford v. C., 6 Rand. 721. § 358.
Whitehead, Reg. v., 3 C. & K. 202. § 418.
Reg. v., 9 C. & P. 429. § 509.
v. S., 20 Fla. 841. § 582.
v. S., 4 Humph. 278. § 216.
Whitehouse, Reg. v., 3 Cox, 86. § 880.
Reg. v., 6 Cox, 38. §§ 960, 988.
Whitehurst v. S., 43 Ind. 473. § 96.
Whiteley, Rex v., 1 Lewin, 173. § 342.
Whitely, P. v., 64 Cal. 211. § 588.
Whiteman, Reg. v., Dears. 353. § 834.
Whitener, S. v., 92 N. C. 798. § 821.
Whiteside v. S., 4 Coldw. 175. § 520.
Whitesides v. S., 11 Lea, 474. § 221.
S. v., 1 Swan, 88. § 993.
Whitfield v. S., 4 Ark. 171. § 1295.
Whitford v. S., 24 Tex. Ap. 489. § 511.
Whithorne, Rex v., 3 C. & P. 394. § 195.
Whiting, P. v., 64 Cal. 67. § 100.
Whitley's Case, 1 Lewin, 123. § 258.
Whitley v. S., 38 Ga. 50. § 428.
v. S., 66 Ga. 656. § 996.
v. S., 33 Tex. Ap. 172. § 242.
Whitlock v. C., 89 Va. 337. § 36.
Whitman, C. v., 118 Mass. 458. §§ 1161, 1163, 1164.
C. v., 121 Mass. 361. § 562.
v. S., 80 Md. 410. § 1232.
Whitmer, S. v., 77 Ia. 557. § 617.
Whitmore, S. v., 53 Kan. 343. § 1070.
Whitney, C. v., 11 Cush. 477. § 1018.
C. v., 5 Gray, 85. § 1018.
Reg. v., 1 Moody, 3. § 815.
v. S., 10 Ind. 404. § 1318.
v. S., 35 Ind. 503. § 455.
v. S., 10 Tex. Ap. 377. §§ 1283, 1285. 1296.
Whitson v. Franklin, 34 Ind. 392. § 70.
S. v., 111 N. C. 695. §§ 333, 429.
Whitt, S. v., 113 N. C. 716. § 216.
Whittaker v. C., 95 Ky. 632. § 1121.
C. v., 131 Mass. 224. §§ 1106*a*, 1118.
Reg. v., 1 Den. 310. § 210.
Rex v., 2 C. & K. 636. § 195.
v. S., 50 Wis. 518. § 441.
Whitted, S. v., 3 Ala. 102. § 1273.
Whittemore, P. v., 102 Mich. 519. §§ 737, 738.
S. v., 50 N. H. 245. §§ 852, 858, 859, 865, 877, 885.
Whitten v. S., 29 Tex. Ap. 504. § 299.
Whittier, S. v., 21 Me. 341. § 830.
U. S. v., 5 Dill. 35. §§ 118, 1330, 1335.
Whittingham, Reg. v., 9 C. & P. 234. § 817.
Rex v., 2 Leach, 912. § 643.
Whittington, Ex parte, 34 Ark. 394. § 1228.
Whitton v. S., 37 Miss. 379. § 1238.
Whitworth, Reg. v., 1 F. & F. 382. § 426.
v. S., 11 Tex. Ap. 414. §§ 609, 625.
S. v., 8 Port. 434. §§ 1310, 1311.
Whyte, S. v., 2 Nott & M. 174. § 548.
Wiborg v. U. S., 163 U. S. 632. § 1341.
Wickes v. Clutterbuck, 2 Bing. 483. § 538.
Wickham v. Gatrill, 2 Sm. & G. 353. § 11.
Reg. v., 10 A. & E. 34. § 675.
Wicks, Rex v., Russ. & Ry. 149. § 756.
v. S., 44 Ala. 398. §§ 194, 204, 509.
Widenhouse, S. v., 71 N. C. 279. § 820.
Widner v. S., 25 Ind. 234. § 602.
Wiedemann v. P., 92 Ill. 314. § 1262.
Wieger, P. v., 100 Cal. 352. § 689.
Wieners, S. v., 66 Mo. 13. §§ 357, 358, 365.
Wiggin, S. v., 72 Me. 425. § 1280.
S. v., 20 N. H. 449. §§ 191, 1233.
S. v., 64 N. H. 508. §§ 38, 77.
Wiggins v. Utah, 93 U. S. 465. § 307.
v. S., 23 Fla. 180. § 358.
Wiggs, Rex v., 1 Leach, 379. § 348.
Wight, In re, 134 U. S. 136. § 1330.
U. S. v., 38 Fed. R. 106. §§ 1330. 1338.
Wightman, U. S. v., 29 Fed. R. 636. § 1332.

Wilborn v. S., 8 Sm. & M. 345. § 588.
Wilbur v. Crane, 13 Pick. 284. § 1126.
v. T., 3 Wyo. 268. § 554.
Wilburn v. S., 60 Ark. 141. § 708.
v. S., 41 Tex. 237. §§ 505, 509.
S. v., 7 Baxt. 57. § 1030.
Wilcox, Rex v., 2 Russ. Cr. 479. § 752.
Rex v., Russ. & Ry. 50. § 801.
v. S., 3 Heisk. 110. §§ 589, 617.
v. S., 94 Tenn. 106. §§ 156, 158, 162.
v. S., 26 Tex. 145. §§ 1301, 1303.
v. S., 31 Tex. 586. § 511.
S. v., 42 Conn. 364. § 1210.
S. v., 66 Ind. 557. § 1224.
S. v., 111 Mo. 569. § 455.
S. v., 3 Yerg. 277. § 829.
U. S. v., 4 Blatch. 385. § 752.
U. S. v., 4 Blatch. 391. §§ 873, 875, 879.
U. S. v., 4 Blatch. 393. § 893.
Wilcoxson v. S., 60 Ga. 184. § 758.
Wild's Case, 2 Lewin, 214. § 347.
Wilde, C. v., 5 Gray, 83. § 559.
Wilder v. S., 3 Mo. 291. § 96.
Wiles v. S., 33 Ind. 306. § 1223.
Wiley, P. v., 3 Hill (N. Y.), 194. §§ 543, 567, 595, 714.
Reg. v., 2 Den. 37. § 714.
Wilford, Rex v., Russ. & Ry. 517. § 495.
Wilforth, S. v., 74 Mo. 528. §§ 132, 1030.
Wilgus, C. v., 4 Pick. 177. § 680.
Wilke, Ex parte, 34 Tex. 155. § 536.
Wilkerson v. C., 88 Ky. 29. §§ 160, 162, 331.
v. Rahrer, 140 U. S. 545. § 76.
v. S., 91 Ga. 729. §§ 309, 427.
v. S., 2 Ind. 546. § 53.
v. S., 2 Tex. Ap. 255. § 380.
v. S., 31 Tex. Ap. 86. §§ 411, 416.
S. v., 72 N. C. 376. § 614.
S. v., 103 N. C. 337. § 676.
v. Utah, 99 U. S. 130. § 80.
Wilkes, Rex v., 4 Burr. 2527. § 1049.
Wilkins, C. v., 121 Mass. 356. § 62.
Reg. v., 10 Cox, 363. § 474.
Reg. v., L. & C. 89. § 236.
Rex v., 2 East, P. C. 673. § 546.
S. v., 17 Vt. 151. § 803.
S. v., 66 Vt. 1. § 455.
Wilkinson, C. v., 16 Pick. 275. §§ 1184, 1191.
C. v., 139 Pa. St. 298. § 46.
v. Dutton, 3 B. & S. 821. § 255.
v. Gill, 10 Hun, 156. § 1315.
Rex v., Russ. & Ry. 470. § 547.
v. S., 10 Ind. 372. § 786.
v. S., 59 Ind. 416. § 1321.
S. v., 121 Mo. 485. § 1106*a*.
Wilks, Rex v., 2 East, P. C. 957. § 764.
v. S., 3 Tex. Ap. 34. § 257.
Will, S. v., 1 Dev. & B. 121. § 339.
Willard, C. v., 22 Pick. 476. §§ 199, 1241.
P. v., 92 Cal. 482. § 726.
v. S., 4 Ind. 407. § 1246.
S. v., 109 Mo. 242. §§ 674, 681.
Willers, S. v., 27 La. An. 246. § 1062.
Willet v. C., 13 Bush, 230. § 150.
Willett, P. v., 102 N. Y. 251. §§ 382, 608.
Willey v. S., 46 Ind. 363. § 327.
v. S., 22 Tex. Ap. 408. § 557.
Williams, Case of, Whart. St. Tr. 651. § 14.
v. Augusta, 4 Ga. 509. § 6.
v. C., 80 Ky. 313. § 304.
v. C., 29 Pa. St. 102. §§ 408, 616.
v. C., 34 Pa. St. 178. § 987.
v. C., 91 Pa. St. 493. §§ 892, 947.
C. v., 2 Ashm. 69. § 426.
C. v., 13 Bush, 267. § 801.
C. v., 2 Cush. 582. §§ 504, 508, 592.
C. v., 3 Gray, 461. § 654.
C. v., 6 Gray, 1. § 1215.
C. v., 7 Gray, 337. § 546.
C. v., 110 Mass. 401. §§ 121, 812, 821, 826.
C. v., 161 Mass. 442. § 605.
C. v., 9 Met. 273. §§ 543, 585.
C. v., 1 Va. Cas. 14. § 602.
v. P., 44 Ill. 478. § 588.
v. P., 54 Ill. 422. §§ 206, 418.
v. P., 101 Ill. 382. §§ 718, 724.
v. P., 121 Ill. 84. § 36.
v. P., 24 N. Y. 405. § 109.
v. P., 33 N. Y. 688. § 88.
P. v., 32 Cal. 280. §§ 303, 306.
P. v., 35 Cal. 671. § 536.
P. v., 43 Cal. 344. §§ 162, 360.
P. v., 57 Cal. 108. § 612.
P. v., 59 Cal. 397. § 1154.
P. v., 60 Cal. 1. § 636.
P. v., 73 Cal. 531. § 359.
P. v., 4 Hill (N. Y.), 9. § 687.
P. v., 24 Mich. 156. §§ 543, 553, 620.
v. Reg., 7 Q. B. 251. § 589.
Reg. v., 1 C. & K. 195. §§ 118, 557.
Reg. v., 1 C. & K. 589. §§ 225, 227.
Reg. v., 2 C. & K. 51. § 753.
Reg. v., Car. & M. 259. § 785.
Reg. v., 8 C. & P. 286. §§ 249, 446, 462, 463.
Reg v., 8 C. & P. 434. § 806.
Reg. v., 1 Cox, 16. § 733.
Reg. v., 6 Cox, 49. § 543.
Reg. v., 9 Cox, 338. § 834.
Reg. v., 11 Cox, 684. § 1152.
Reg. v., 2 Den. 61. § 753.
Reg. v., 1 Q. B. D. (1893) 320. §§ 449, 465.
Rex v., 5 B. & Ald. 595. § 1044.
Rex v., 9 B. & C. 549. §§ 839, 841.
Rex v., 6 C. & P. 390. § 560.
Rex v., 7 C. & P. 338. § 640.
Rex v., 7 C. & P. 354. § 689.
Rex v., 2 East, P. C. 937. § 764.
Rex v., 26 How. St. Tr. 656. §§ 1049, 1159.
Rex v., 1 Moody, 107. § 541.
Rex v., 1 Moody, 387. § 255.
v. S., 44 Ala. 24. §§ 1077, 1085.
v. S., 44 Ala. 396. §§ 564, 586.
v. S., 54 Ala. 131. § 1083.
v. S., 68 Ala. 551. § 862.
v. S., 74 Ala. 18. § 307.

Williams v. S., 81 Ala. 1. §§ 162, 196, 291, 420.
v. S., 83 Ala. 16. § 368.
v. S., 90 Ala. 649. § 758.
v. S., 91 Ala. 14. §§ 83, 1235.
v. S., 98 Ala. 52. § 1133.
v. S., 35 Ark. 430. § 1218.
v. S., 50 Ark. 511. §§ 156, 167, 172, 175, 178.
v. S., 20 Fla. 777. § 449.
v. S., 34 Fla. 217. § 294.
v. S., 46 Ga. 212. §§ 504, 577.
v. S., 51 Ga. 535. § 758.
v. S., 52 Ga. 580. § 500.
v. S., 55 Ga. 391. §§ 118, 201.
v. S., 61 Ga. 417. § 1033.
v. S., 69 Ga. 11. § 416.
v. S., 86 Ga. 548. §§ 1088, 1089.
v. S., 89 Ga. 483. §§ 1273, 1274.
v. S., 3 Heisk. 37. § 361.
v. S., 3 Heisk. 376. §§ 303, 306, 382.
v. S., 4 Humph. 584. § 268.
v. S., 7 Humph. 47. § 880.
v. S., 8 Humph. 584. §§ 268, 461, 466.
v. S., 9 Humph. 79. § 766.
v. S., 54 Ill. 422. § 206.
v. S., 2 Ind. 439. § 1123.
v. S., 47 Ind. 568. §§ 196, 213, 268, 270, 275.
v. S., 48 Ind. 306. § 1257.
v. S., 49 Ind. 367. § 563.
v. S., 3 Ind. Ap. 350. § 1113.
v. S., 60 Md. 402. § 362.
v. S., 64 Md. 384. § 330.
v. S., 20 Miss. 58. §§ 210, 1288.
v. S., 42 Miss. 328. § 275.
v. S., 47 Miss. 609. § 442.
v. S., 63 Miss. 58. § 548.
v. S., 9 Mo. 268. § 995.
v. S., 6 Neb. 334. § 333.
v. S., 14 Ohio, 222. §§ 449, 450, 1153.
v. S., 35 Ohio St. 175. § 377.
v. S., 2 Sneed, 159. § 914.
v. S., 3 Sneed, 313. § 1024.
v. S., 92 Tenn. 275. § 1297.
v. S., 41 Tex. 649. § 577.
v. S., 42 Tex. 392. § 377.
v. S., 43 Tex. 382. § 274.
v. S., 1 Tex. Ap. 90. §§ 439, 448, 452.
v. S., 2 Tex. Ap. 271. §§ 292, 303.
v. S., 3 Tex. Ap. 123. § 409.
v. S., 3 Tex. Ap. 316. § 274.
v. S., 5 Tex. Ap. 116. § 597.
v. S., 7 Tex. Ap. 396. § 391.
v. S., 10 Tex. Ap. 8. §§ 472, 481.
v. S., 11 Tex. Ap. 275. §§ 616, 818.
v. S., 12 Tex. Ap. 240. § 470.
v. S., 13 Tex. Ap. 285. § 731.
v. S., 14 Tex. Ap. 102. § 307.
v. S., 15 Tex. Ap. 617. § 338.
v. S., 19 Tex. Ap. 276. § 557.
v. S., 22 Tex. Ap. 497. § 311.
v. S., 23 Tex. Ap. 70. § 1257.
v. S., 24 Tex. Ap. 17. § 930.
v. S., 24 Tex. Ap. 69. § 509.
v. S., 24 Tex. Ap. 342. § 759.
v. S., 24 Tex. Ap. 412. § 615.
Williams v. S., 25 Tex. Ap. 216. §§ 267, 339.
v. S., 25 Tex. Ap. 733. § 644.
v. S., 27 Tex. Ap. 258. §§ 846, 848, 850.
v. S., 28 Tex. Ap. 301. § 864.
v. S., 30 Tex. Ap. 153. § 554.
v. S., 30 Tex. Ap. 330. § 617.
v. S., 30 Tex. Ap. 429. §§ 274, 305, 311.
S. v., 5 Baxt. 655. § 278.
S. v., 3 Hill (S. C.), 91. § 1269.
S. v., 10 Humph. 101. § 551.
S. v., 4 Ind. 234. § 53.
S. v., 139 Ind. 43. § 789.
S. v., 8 Ia. 533. § 774.
S. v., 20 Ia. 98. §§ 1076, 1080, 1082.
S. v., 61 Ia. 517. § 611.
S. v., 66 Ia. 573. §§ 766, 789.
S. v., 70 Ia. 52. § 1032.
S. v., 4 Ired. 400. § 1319.
S. v., 12 Ired. 172. § 909.
S. v., 2 Jones, 194. § 617.
S. v., 7 Jones, 446. §§ 377, 396, 398.
S. v., 30 La. An., Pt. II, 843. § 376.
S. v., 32 La. An. 335. § 452.
S. v., 34 La. An. 87. §§ 1153, 1154.
S. v., 37 La. An. 776. § 382.
S. v., 40 La. An. 168. § 307.
S. v., 45 La. An. 936. § 605.
S. v., 46 La. An. 709. § 303.
S. v., 46 La. An. 922. § 41.
S. v., 25 Me. 561. § 942.
S. v., 30 Me. 484. § 843.
S. v., 32 Minn. 537. § 846.
S. v., 19 Mo. 389. § 571.
S. v., 30 Mo. 364. §§ 866, 891.
S. v., 35 Mo. 229. §§ 552, 562.
S. v., 54 Mo. 170. § 617.
S. v., 77 Mo. 310. § 80.
S. v., 95 Mo. 247. § 565.
S. v., 9 Mont. 179. §§ 449, 452.
S. v., 23 N. H. 321. § 274.
S. v., 30 N. J. 102. §§ 1137, 1141.
S. v., 65 N. C. 398. § 145.
S. v., 86 N. C. 671. § 748.
S. v., 90 N. C. 724. § 494.
S. v., 97 N. C. 455. § 98.
S. v., 106 N. C. 646. § 848.
S. v., 6 R. I. 207. § 1244.
S. v., 32 S. C. 123. § 10.
S. v., 2 Strobh. 229. § 546.
S. v., 2 Strobh. 474. § 536.
S. v., 36 Tex. 352. § 377.
S. v., 41 Tex. 98. §§ 503, 509.
v. Troop, 17 Wis. 463. § 1227.
v. Warsaw, 60 Ind. 457. § 1283.
U. S. v., 4 Biss. 302. § 796.
U. S. v., 1 Clif. 5. § 396.
U. S. v., 1 Cranch, C. C. 174. § 210.
U. S. v., 2 Fed. R. 61. § 257.
U. S. v., 14 Fed. R. 550. § 774.
Williamson, C. v., 2 Va. Cas. 211. § 215.
Reg. v., 11 Cox, 328. § 670.
Rex v., 3 C. & P. 635. § 287.
v. S., 13 Tex. Ap. 514. § 601.
v. S., 30 Tex. Ap. 330. § 616.

Williamson, S. v., 3 Heisk. 483. § 505.
S. v., 1 Houst. Cr. C. 155. § 561.
S. v., 68 Ia. 351. § 829.
S. v., 106 Mo. 162. §§ 173, 416.
S. v., 118 Mo. 146. § 635.
S. v., 43 Tex. 500. § 607.
Willingham v. S., 33 Tex. Ap. 98. §§ 1148, 1151.
Willis v. C., 32 Grat. 929. §§ 162, 360.
Reg. v., 1 C. & K. 722. § 373*a*.
Rex v., 1 Moody, 375. § 558.
v. S., 89 Ga. 188. § 152.
v. S., 24 Tex. Ap. 487. § 605.
v. S., 24 Tex. Ap. 586. § 619.
v. S., 32 Tex. Ap. 534. § 526.
v. S., 33 Tex. Ap. 168. § 503.
S. v., Busbee, 223. § 1188.
S. v., 7 Jones, 190. § 500.
S. v., 43 La. An. 407. §§ 162, 505.
S. v., 78 Me. 70. §§ 1316, 1318.
S. v., 63 N. C. 26. § 332.
S. v., 104 N. C. 764. § 46.
U. S v., 1 Cranch, C. C. 511. § 1283.
v. Warren, 1 Hilton, 590. § 1312.
Willot, Reg. v., 12 Cox, 68. § 683.
Willoughby, Ex parte, 14 Nev. 451. § 200.
Rex v., 1 East, P. C. 288. § 338.
Rex v., 2 East, P. C. 944. § 753.
Wills v. S., 74 Ala. 21. § 323.
v. S., 69 Ind. 286. § 1273.
v. S., 40 Tex. 69. §§ 190, 601.
v. S., 24 Tex. Ap. 400. § 702.
Willshire, Reg. v., 6 Q. B. D. 366. § 1084.
Wilson, Ex parte, 114 U. S. 417. § 19.
In re, 18 Fed. R. 33. § 782.
v. Boerem, 15 Johns. 286. § 425.
v. C., 12 B. Mon. 2. § 1137.
v. C., 3 Bush, 105. §§ 256, 257.
v. C., 14 Bush, 159. § 1274.
v. C., 96 Pa. St. 56. §§ 12, 953, 955.
v. C., 10 Serg. & R. 373. §§ 907, 913, 914, 916.
v. C., 86 Va. 666. § 78.
C. v., 2 Gray, 70. § 797.
C. v., 89 Ky. 157. § 752.
C. v., 9 Leigh, 648. § 1302.
v. Middleton, 2 Cal. 54. § 11.
v. Noonan, 35 Wis. 321. § 111.
v. P., 94 Ill. 299. §§ 412, 988.
v. P., 24 Mich. 410. § 279.
v. P., 39 N. Y. 459. § 569.
P. v., 49 Cal. 13. §§ 177, 178.
P. v., 145 N. Y. 628. § 326.
v. Rastall, 4 Term R. 753. § 7.
Reg. v., 2 C. & K. 527. § 765.
Reg. v., 8 C. & P. 111. §§ 560, 563.
Reg. v., Dears. & B. 127. § 1148.
Reg. v., Dears. & B. 157. § 618.
Reg. v., Dears. & B. 558. § 756.
Reg. v., 3 F. & F. 119. § 1074.
Reg. v., 2 Moody, 52. § 713.
Rex v., 3 A. & E. 817. 838.
Rex v., 1 Leach, 285. § 774.
Rex v., Russ. & Ry. 115. § 508.
Rex v., 8 Term R. 357. § 836.
v. S., 31 Ala. 371. § 1303.
Wilson v. S., 52 Ala. 299. §§ 943, 950, 951.
v. S., 61 Ala. 151. § 934.
v. S., 68 Ala. 41. § 1036.
v. S., 73 Ala. 527. §§ 1113, 1114, 1117, 1119.
v. S., 5 Ark. 513. § 543.
v. S., 33 Ark. 557. § 1039.
v. S., 35 Ark. 414. § 1224.
v. S., 30 Fla. 234. §§ 306, 307.
v. S., 53 Ga. 205. §§ 223, 269.
v. S., 58 Ga. 328. § 1112.
v. S., 66 Ga. 591. § 596.
v. S., 69 Ga. 224. § 333.
v. S., 11 Lea, 310. § 328.
v. S., 43 Neb. 745. §§ 586, 589, 851.
v. S., 18 Ohio, 143. § 271.
v. S., 2 Ohio St. 319. § 1148.
v. S., 34 Ohio St. 199. §§ 495, 508.
v. S., 1 Port. 118. §§ 543, 560, 586.
v. S., 5 Tex. 21. § 1304.
v. S., 25 Tex. 169. § 271.
v. S., 43 Tex. 472. § 398.
v. S., 3 Tex. Ap. 206. § 546.
v. S., 4 Tex. Ap. 637. §§ 267, 274.
v. S., 6 Tex. Ap. 427. § 365.
v. S., 12 Tex. Ap. 481. § 716.
v. S., 15 Tex. Ap. 150. § 257.
v. S., 17 Tex. Ap. 525. § 460.
v. S., 18 Tex. Ap. 270. § 507.
v. S., 18 Tex. Ap. 576. § 304.
v. S., 20 Tex. Ap. 662. § 569.
v. S., 27 Tex. Ap. 47. § 892.
v. S., 1 Wis. 184. § 18.
S. v., 3 Brev. 196. § 543.
S. v., 30 Conn. 500. §§ 226, 228, 228*a*, 573, 979.
S. v., 38 Conn. 126. § 139.
S. v., Coxe, 439. §§ 493, 500.
S. v., 1 Hayw. 242. § 498.
S. v., 22 Ia. 364. §§ 1093, 1096.
S. v., 1 Ired. 32. § 1000.
S. v., 24 Kan. 189. §§ 425, 426, 429.
S. v., 23 La. An. 558. § 425.
S. v., 3 McCord, 187. § 586.
S. v., 42 Me. 9. §§ 1190, 1195.
S. v., 28 Minn. 52. § 762.
S. v., 3 Mo. 91. §§ 12, 1014.
S. v., 3 Mo. 125. §§ 12, 821.
S. v., 80 Mo. 303. § 1219.
S. v., 98 Mo. 440. § 368.
S. v., 121 Mo. 434. § 426.
S. v., 43 N. H. 415. §§ 95, 1169.
S. v., 47 N. H. 101. §§ 84, 578.
S. v., 1 N. J. 439. § 500.
S. v., 93 N. C. 608. § 1143.
S. v., 94 N. C. 1015. §§ 814, 1168.
S. v., 101 N. C. 730. § 626.
S. v., 106 N. C. 718. § 63.
S. v., 116 N. C. 979. § 703.
S. v., 6 Oreg. 428. § 602.
S. v., Phill. 238. § 1010.
S. v., 5 R. I. 291. § 1279.
S. v., 15 R. I. 180. § 1215.
S. v., Treadw. Const. 495. § 543.
S. v., 9 Wash. 16. § 1296.
S. v., 10 Wash. 402. § 313.

Wilson v. U. S., 162 U. S. 613. §§ 406, 411, 421.
U. S. v., Baldw. 78. §§ 84, 205, 478.
U. S. v., 44 Fed. R. 593. § 1330.
U. S. v., 44 Fed. R. 751. § 774.
U. S. v., 58 Fed. R. 768. §§ 86, 1332.
U. S. v., 60 Fed. R. 890. §§ 956, 966.
U. S. v., 69 Fed. R. 144. § 1219.
Wiltberger, U. S. v., 3 Wash. C. C. 515. §§ 139, 303, 400.
U. S. v., 5 Wheat. 76. §§ 14, 84.
Wilton, Reg. v., 1 F. & F. 391. § 752.
Wimberly, S. v., 3 McCord, 190. §§ 381, 382.
Wimbish v. S., 89 Ga. 294. § 509.
Wimple, S. v., 8 Blackf. 214. § 252.
Wims v. S., 90 Ala. 623. § 275.
Winbow, Reg. v., 5 Cox, 346. § 556.
Winburn v. S., 28 Fla. 339. § 271.
Winch, S. v., 45 Ohio St. 663. § 77.
Wincroft, S. v., 76 N. C. 38. § 509.
Windell, S. v., 60 Ind. 300. § 1299.
Windham v. S., 26 Ala. 69. § 1303.
v. S., 19 Tex. Ap. 413. § 618.
Windsor v. S., 13 Ind. 375. § 825.
S. v., 5 Harr. 512. § 156.
Wine v. S., 25 Ohio St. 69. § 502.
Winehart v. S., 6 Ind. 30. § 132.
Wing, C. v., 9 Pick. 1. § 811.
Wingard v. S., 13 Ga. 396. §§ 1289, 1291.
S. v., 40 La. An. 733. § 758.
Wingo, S. v., 89 Ind. 204. §§ 89, 556, 624.
S. v., 66 Mo. 181. § 316.
Winkelmeier, S. v., 35 Mo. 103. § 1216.
Winkler, P. v., 9 Cal. 234. § 586.
Winlock v. S., 121 Ind. 531. § 822.
Winn v. S., 43 Ark. 151. § 1220.
v. S., 11 Tex. Ap. 304. § 572.
v. S., 17 Tex. Ap. 284. § 564.
Winnall, Reg. v., 5 Cox, 326. § 626.
Winningham, S. v., 124 Mo. 423. § 1124.
Winright, S. v., 12 Mo. 410. § 915.
Winslow, P. v., 39 Mich. 505. § 676.
Reg. v., 8 Cox, 397. § 418.
v. S., 92 Ala. 78. § 51.
v. S., 5 Ind. Ap. 306. § 1145.
v. S., 26 Neb. 308. §§ 505, 508.
S. v., 95 N. C. 649. § 828.
U. S. v., 2 Cranch, C. C. 47. § 752.
U. S. v., 3 Sawy. 337. § 1263.
Winsor, In re, 6 B. & S. 522. § 755.
Winston v. S., 9 Tex. Ap. 143. § 481.
Winter, Rex v., Russ. & Ry. 295. § 520.
S. v., 72 Ia. 627. § 405.
Winterbottom, Reg. v., 2 C. & K. 37. § 752.
Winters, P. v., 29 Cal. 658. § 516.
P. v., 93 Cal. 277. § 506.
P. v., 2 Park. Cr. 10. § 243.
v. S., 9 Ind. 172. § 1168.
v. S., 33 Tex. Ap. 395. § 1302.
S. v., 44 Kan. 723. § 1204.
Wintermute, P. v., 1 Dak. T. 60. § 102.
Winterton v. S., 65 Miss. 238. § 1216.
Winthrop, S. v., 43 Ia. 519. § 294.
Wintzingerode, S. v., 9 Oreg. 153. § 416.
Wisdom, S. v., 84 Mo. 177. §§ 359, 365.
Wisdom, S. v., 119 Mo. 539. § 420.
S. v., 8 Port. 511. §§ 548, 615.
Wise, C. v., 110 Mass. 181. § 1139.
v. S., 2 Kan. 419. § 412.
S. v., 3 Lea, 38. § 876.
Wiseman v. S., 14 Tex. Ap. 74. § 1057.
Wish, S. v., 15 Neb. 448. § 96.
Wishon, S. v., 15 Mo. 503. § 1229.
Wiswell v. S., 21 Ohio St. 658. § 536.
Witchell, Rex v., 2 East, P. C. 830. § 670.
Withal, Rex v., 2 East, P. C. 515. § 511.
Witham, S. v., 47 Me. 165. § 794.
S. v., 6 Oreg. 366. § 873.
S. v., 70 Wis. 473. §§ 58, 78.
Witherby v. S., 39 Ala. 702. § 466.
Withers, Ex parte, 3 Brev. 83. § 1191.
Rex v., 4 C. & P. 446. § 256.
Rex v., 1 East, P. C. 295. § 340.
Rex v., 3 Term R. 428. § 1070.
S. v., 7 Baxt. 16. § 904.
Withrow, S. v., 47 Ark. 551. § 1193.
Witt, Rex v., 1 Moody, 248. § 508.
v. S., 6 Coldw. 5. §§ 359, 377, 382.
v. S., 9 Mo. 663. § 564.
S. v., 39 Ark. 216. §§ 1220, 1273.
Witten, S. v., 100 Mo. 525. § 455.
Wittig, U. S. v., 2 Low. 466. §§ 1234, 1240.
Wo Tai Li, In re, 48 Fed. R. 668. § 1345.
Wofford v. S., 29 Tex. Ap. 536. § 597.
Wohlford v. P., 148 Ill. 296. § 125.
Wohlman, S. v., 34 Mo. 482. § 620.
Wolcott, C. v., 10 Cush. 61. § 904.
Wolf, Ex parte, 14 Neb. 24. § 1217.
In re, 27 Fed. R. 606. § 972.
C. v., 3 Serg. & R. 48. § 1319.
P. v., 95 Mich. 625. §§ 332, 416.
v. S., 41 Ala. 412. § 609.
v. S., 59 Ark. 297. §§ 1220, 1265.
v. S., 19 Ohio St. 248. § 377.
v. S., 4 Tex. Ap. 332. § 613.
v. S., 14 Tex. Ap. 210. § 569.
S. v., 112 N. C. 889. § 1169.
Wolfenberger v. S., 20 Ind. 242. § 518.
Wolff v. Cohen, 8 Rich. 144. § 11.
S. v., 34 La. An. 1153. § 622.
S. v., 15 Mo. 168. §§ 619, 620.
S. v., 46 Mo. 584. § 1274.
Wollaston, Reg. v., 12 Cox, 180. §§ 238, 249, 1153.
Wollez, Reg. v., 8 Cox, 337. § 611.
Wolstenholme, Reg. v., 11 Cox, 313. § 640.
Wolverton v. C., 75 Va. 909. § 582.
v. S., 16 Ohio, 173. § 1083.
Wolz v. S., 33 Tex. 331. § 1310.
Womack v. S., 7 Coldw. 508. § 375.
v. S., 6 Lea, 146. § 499.
S. v., 4 Wash. 19. §§ 897, 901.
Wong Ah Hung, U. S. v., 62 Fed. R. 1005. § 1345.
Wong Ark, P. v., 96 Cal. 125. § 414.
Wong Ah Teak, P. v., 63 Cal. 544. § 310.
Wong Sing, U. S. v., 51 Fed. R. 79. § 1344.
Wong Wing v. U. S., 163 U. S. 228. § 1344.

Wong You Ting, Ex parte, 106 Cal. 296. §§ 5, 6.
Wonson v. Sayward, 13 Pick. 402. § 542.
Wood v. C., 12 Serg. & R. 213. § 95.
C. v., 4 Gray, 11. § 1270.
C. v., 11 Gray, 85. §§ 199, 1148, 1149, 1151.
C. v., 97 Mass. 225. §§ 148, 1140.
C. v., 111 Mass. 408. § 1163.
C. v., 142 Mass. 459. § 696.
v. Mathews, 47 Ia. 409. § 1111.
v. P., 53 N. Y. 511. § 28.
v. P., 59 N. Y. 117. §§ 865, 883.
P. v., 99 Mich. 620. § 514.
Reg. v., 14 Cox, 46. § 456.
Reg. v., 1 F. & F. 497. § 716.
Rex v., 4 C. & P. 381. § 256.
Rex v., 2 East. P. C. 732. § 470.
v. Smith, 23 Vt. 706. § 1253.
v. S., 34 Ark. 341. § 161.
v. S., 18 Fla. 967. §§ 499, 505.
v. S., 46 Ga. 322. § 504.
v. S., 48 Ga. 192. §§ 1112, 1113, 1115.
v. S., 5 Ind. 433. § 1181.
v. S., 21 Ind. 276. § 1246.
v. S., 92 Ind. 269. §§ 307, 381.
v. S., 64 Miss. 761. §§ 241, 268, 274.
v. S., 47 N. J. 180. § 966.
v. S., 47 N. J. 461. § 971.
v. S., 1 Oreg. 223. § 1235.
v. S., 11 Tex. Ap. 318. § 1024.
v. S., 27 Tex. Ap. 393. § 275.
v. S., 32 Tex. Ap. 476. § 1057.
S. v., 1 Bay, 351. § 241.
S. v., 17 Ia. 18. §§ 881, 892.
S. v., 46 Ia. 116. §§ 569, 583, 587.
S. v., 1 Mill. Const. 29. § 587.
S. v., 53 N. H. 484. § 1149.
S. v., 53 Vt. 560. § 292.
U. S. v., 2 Cranch, C. C. 164. § 765.
U. S. v., 44 Fed. R. 753. § 881.
U. S. v., 70 Fed. R. 485. § 860.
U. S. v., 14 Pet. 430. §§ 890, 892.
U. S. v., 3 Wash. C. C. 440. § 478.
v. Wood, 2 Paige, 108. § 1094.
Woodard v. S., 9 Tex. Ap. 412. § 575.
Woodbury v. S., 69 Ala. 242. § 686.
S. v., 35 N. H. 230. § 909.
S. v., 67 Vt. 602. § 1170.
Woodcock, Rex v., 1 East. P. C. 356. § 426.
Wooden v. Shotwell, 23 N. J. 465. § 1315.
Wooderd, S. v., 20 Ia. 541. §§ 765, 767.
Woodfall, Rex v., 5 Burr. 2661. §§ 123, 1070.
Rex v., Lofft, 776. § 1048.
Woodfin, S. v., 87 N. C. 526. § 1039.
Woodford v. P., 62 N. Y. 117. §§ 524, 526, 529, 531.
Woodhead, Rex v., 1 M. & Rob. 549. § 817.
Woodhurst, Reg. v., 12 Cox, 443. § 447.
Woodley, S. v., 25 Ga. 235. § 601.
Woodman, Reg. v., 14 Cox, 179. § 667.
Woodrow, Reg. v., 15 M. & W. 404. § 128.
Woodruff, S. v., 47 Kan. 151. § 562.
S. v., 67 N. C. 89. § 1129.
U. S. v., 68 Fed. R. 536. § 1327.
Woods v. C., 1 B. Mon. 74. § 1249.
C. v., 10 Gray, 477. §§ 765, 793.
Woods v. P., 55 N. Y. 515. § 460.
v. S., 36 Ark. 36. § 1253.
v. S., 14 Lea, 460. § 873.
v. S., 67 Miss. 575. 1015.
v. S., 3 Tex. Ap. 204. § 488.
S. v., 49 Kan. 237. §§ 443, 444.
S. v., 31 La. An. 267. § 506.
S. v., 68 Me. 409. § 78.
S. v., 124 Mo. 412. § 271.
S. v., 104 N. C. 898. § 846.
U. S. v., 4 Cranch, C. C. 484. § 426.
Woodsides v. S., 2 How. (Miss.) 655. §§ 376, 425.
Woodson's Case, 9 Leigh, 669. § 256.
Woodson v. S., 24 Tex. Ap. 153. § 887.
S. v., 99 Ala. 201. § 1127.
S. v., 5 Humph. 55. § 704.
Woodward, C. v., 102 Mass. 155. § 347.
P. v., 45 Cal. 293. §§ 194, 224.
Reg. v., 8 C. & P. 561. § 145.
Reg. v., L. & C. 122. § 714.
Rex v., 2 East, P. C. 563. § 830.
Rex v., 1 Moody, 323. §§ 520, 527.
v. S., 4 Baxt. 322. § 403.
v. S., 33 Tex. Ap. 554. §§ 828, 830.
S. v., 1 Houst. Cr. C. 455. §§ 338, 413.
S. v., 89 Ind. 110. § 75.
S. v., 84 Ia. 172. § 275.
S. v., 34 Me. 293. §§ 1252, 1281.
S. v., 50 N. H. 527. § 142.
v. Turnbull, 4 Ill. 1. § 1216.
U. S. v., 44 Fed. R. 592. § 1328.
Woodworth v. S., 4 Ohio St. 487. § 1270.
v. S., 26 Ohio St. 196. §§ 84, 922.
v. S., 20 Tex. Ap. 375. §§ 971, 981.
Woody, P. v., 45 Cal. 289. §§ 194, 409.
v. S., 32 Ga. 595. § 1244.
v. S., 16 Tex. Ap. 252. § 1043.
S. v., 2 Jones, 335. § 1009.
Woodyard v. S., 19 Tex. Ap. 516. § 823.
Wool, S. v., 86 N. C. 708. § 1252.
Woolcock, Rex v., 5 C. & P. 516. §§ 997, 1004.
Wooley, P. v., 44 Cal. 494. §§ 527, 529.
Woolfolk v. S., 81 Ga. 551. § 404.
v. S., 85 Ga. 69. § 404.
Woolford, Rex v., 1 M. & Rob. 384. § 719.
Woolley, Reg. v., 3 C. & K. 98. § 687.
Reg. v., 4 Cox, 251. §§ 626, 631.
Woolmer, Rex v., 1 Moody, 334. § 328.
Woolridge v. S., 13 Tex. Ap. 443. § 392.
Woolsey v. S., 30 Tex. Ap. 346. §§ 523, 529.
S. v., 92 Ind. 131. § 1247.
Woolston, Rex v., 2 Stra. 834. § 1159.
Woolverton, S. v., 8 Blackf. 452. § 868.
Woolweaver v. S., 50 Ohio St. 277. § 195.
Wooster v. S., 6 Baxt. 533. § 1248.
Wooten v. S., 24 Fla. 335. §§ 1308, 1309.
v. Wilkins, 39 Ga. 223. § 425.
Wootten, U. S. v., 29 Fed. R. 702. §§ 956, 966, 1331.
Worcester, C. v., 126 Mass. 256. § 33.
C. v., 3 Pick. 462. § 70.
Word v. C., 3 Leigh, 743. § 1293.
v. S., 12 Tex. Ap. 174. §§ 449, 450, 452.

Word, S. v., 68 Me. 409. § 78.
Worden, S. v., 46 Conn. 349. § 442.
Wordin, S. v., 56 Conn. 216. § 73.
Workingmen's Amalgamated Council, U. S. v., 54 Fed. R. 994. § 963.
Workman, S. v., 35 W. Va. 367. § 1030.
World v. S., 50 Md. 49. §§ 25, 580.
Worley v. Spurgeon, 38 Ia. 465. § 1218.
Worrall, Rex v., 7 C. & P. 516. § 578.
U. S. v., 2 Dall. 384. §§ 14, 896, 900.
Worrell, S. v., 25 Mo. 205. §§ 164, 326, 355, 382.
Worth, S. v., R. M. Charl. 5. § 1309.
Wortham v. C., 5 Rand. 669. § 1304.
v. S., 70 Ga. 336. § 303.
v. S., 59 Miss. 179. § 1313.
Worthen, In re, 58 Fed. R. 467. §§ 34, 76.
Worthington, P. v., 105 Cal. 166. §§ 136, 172.
v. S., 58 Md. 403. § 553.
Wortley, Reg. v., 2 C. & K. 283. § 546.
Reg. v., 1 Den. 162. §§ 499, 509.
Reg. v., 2 Den. 333. § 631.
Worton, Reg. v., 1 Q. B. D. (1895) 227. § 1307.
Wray, Ex parte, 30 Miss. 673. § 322.
S. v., 109 Mo. 594. § 464.
S. v., 72 N. C. 253. §§ 136, 1252.
Wreden, P. v., 59 Cal. 392. § 168.
Wreford v. P., 14 Mich. 41. § 1169.
Wren v. C., 26 Grat. 952. § 209.
v. S., 70 Ala. 1. § 1310.
Wright v. C., 33 Grat. 880. § 358.
v. C., 77 Pa. St. 470. § 1030.
v. C., 75 Va. 914. §§ 357. 358.
C. v., 12 Allen, 187. § 1326.
C. v., 1 Cush. 46. §§ 1043, 1061, 1069.
C. v., 137 Mass. 250. § 1315.
C. v., 139 Mass. 382. § 1158.
v. Lindsay, 20 Ala. 428. § 554.
v. P., 61 Ill. 382. § 639.
v. P., 101 Ill. 126. § 1253.
P. v., 93 Cal. 564. § 435.
P. v., 38 Mich. 744. § 146.
P. v., 9 Wend. 193. §§ 751, 792, 793, 801, 803.
v. Reg., 14 Q. B. 148. § 977.
Reg. v., 9 C. & P. 754. §§ 294, 1152.
Reg. v., Dears. & B. 431. § 556.
Reg. v., 4 F. & F. 967. §§ 451, 463.
Rex v., 1 East, P. C. 396. § 435.
Rex v., Russ. & Ry. 456. § 172.
Rex v., 8 Term R. 293. §§ 1051, 1052.
v. S., 79 Ala. 262. § 759.
v. S., 5 Blackf. 358. § 1087.
v. S., 30 Ga. 325. § 826.
v. S., 4 Humph. 194. §§ 441, 443, 460.
v. S., 8 Lea, 563. § 1026.
v. S., 43 Tex. 170. § 195.
v. S., 44 Tex. 645. § 298.
v. S., 7 Tex. Ap. 574. § 117.
v. S., 18 Tex. Ap. 358. § 573.
v. S., 31 Tex. Ap. 354. §§ 1116, 1119.
v. S., 5 Yerg. 154. § 714.
v. S., 9 Yerg. 342. § 256.
S. v., 52 Ind. 307. § 235.
S. v., 6 Jones, 25. § 1137.
Wright, S. v., 46 La. An. 1403. § 333.
S. v., 25 Neb. 38. §§ 443, 444.
S. v., 14 Oreg. 365. § 1206.
S. v., 19 Oreg. 258. § 508.
U. S. v., 2 Cranch, C. C. 68. § 784.
U. S. v., 2 Cranch, C. C. 296. § 791.
U. S. v., 16 Fed. R. 112. § 949.
Wrightson, Reg. v., 11 Mod. 166. § 1057.
Wroe v. S., 8 Md. 416. § 1193.
v. S., 20 Ohio St. 460. §§ 428, 431.
Wroxton, Rex v., 4 B. & Ad. 640. § 1074.
Wusnig v. S., 33 Tex. 651. § 150.
Wyatt, C. v., 6 Rand. 693. §§ 80, 1310.
Rex v., Russ. & Ry. 230. § 394.
v. S., 2 Swan, 394. § 446.
S. v., 2 Hayw. 56. § 858.
S. v., 76 Ia. 328. § 241.
S. v., 124 Mo. 537. § 476.
Wycherly, Reg. v., 8 C. & P. 262. § 1146.
Wyckoff, S. v., 31 N. J. 65. §§ 207, 213.
Wyers v. S., 21 Tex. Ap. 448. § 613.
Wyl, S. v., 55 Mo. 67. § 1254.
Wylde, S. v., 110 N. C. 500. §§ 1082, 1083.
Wylie, Rex v., 1 N. R. 92. § 808.
Wyman, C. v., 12 Cush. 237. § 91.
C. v., 8 Met. 247. §§ 82, 87, 632, 654, 655.
P. v., 15 Cal. 70. § 389.
P. v., 102 Cal. 552. § 639.
v. S., 13 Wis. 663. § 1189.
S. v., 80 Me. 117. § 1273.
S. v., 42 Minn. 182. § 1246.
Wymberly, S. v., 40 La. An. 460. § 858.
Wymer, Rex v., 4 C. & P. 391. § 546.
Wynehamer v. P., 13 N. Y. 378. §§ 29, 74, 104, 1207.
Wynn, Reg. v., 2 C. & K. 859. §§ 542. 568, 1330.
v. S., 82 Ala. 55. § 10.
v. S., 63 Miss. 260. § 196.
v. S., 81 Ga. 744. § 514.
Wynne, Rex v., 2 East, P. C. 664, 697. § 545.
S. v., 116 N. C. 981. § 1126.
Wyse, S. v., 32 S. C. 45. § 424.
S. v., 33 S. C. 582. § 306.

Yager, S. v., 72 Ia. 421. § 1219.
Yakel v. S., 30 Tex. Ap. 391. § 1258.
Yancey, S. v., 74 N. C. 244. § 245.
Yancy, S. v., 3 Brev. 142. § 392.
S. v., 1 Car. Law Repos. 519. § 247.
S. v., 1 Treadw. 241. § 212.
Yarberry, T. v., 2 N. M. 391. §§ 194, 292, 362.
Yarborough v. S., 41 Ala. 405. § 615.
v. S., 86 Ga. 396. §§ 495. 511.
S. v., 39 Kan. 581. § 343.
S. v., 70 N. C. 250. § 828.
S. v., 77 N. C. 524. §§ 906, 917.
S. v., 19 Tex. 161. § 1028.
Yardley, S. v., 95 Tenn. 546. §§ 663a, 692.
Yarrell, S. v., 12 Ired. 130. § 1188.
Yates v. P., 32 N. Y. 509. §§ 133, 418.
Reg. v., Car. & M. 132. §§ 859, 892.
Reg. v., 6 Cox, 441. §§ 730, 975.
Rex v., 1 Moody, 170. § 693.

Yates v. S., 26 Fla. 484. § 359.
v. S., 37 Tex. 202. § 617.
v. S., 10 Yerg. 548. § 546.
S. v., 10 Cr. L. Mag. 439. § 539.
S. v., 21 W. Va. 761. § 269.
Ybanez, U. S. v., 53 Fed. R. 536. § 1341.
Ybarra, P. v., 17 Cal. 166. §§ 377, 426.
Ye Park, P. v., 62 Cal. 204. § 315.
Ye Wan, T. v., 2 Mont. 478. § 12.
Yeadon, Reg. v., L. & C. 81. § 262.
Yeager, Ex parte, 11 Grat. 655. § 1228.
Yeaton, S. v., 53 Me. 125. § 142.
Yee Lung, In re, 61 Fed. R. 641. § 1345.
Yeiter, S. v., 54 Kan. 288. § 626.
Yellowstone Kit v. S., 88 Ala. 196. § 1315.
Yeoman v. S., 21 Neb. 171. § 1121.
Yepperson v. S., 39 Tex. 48. § 1308.
Yerkes, C. v., 29 Leg. Int. 60; 119 Pa. St. 266. §§ 543, 562.
Yewell, S. v., 63 Md. 120. § 1216.
Yick Wo v. Hopkins, 118 U. S. 356. § 72.
Yoes v. S., 9 Ark. 42. § 246.
Yohe, S. v., 87 Ia. 33. § 505.
Yopp, S. v., 97 N. C. 477. § 39.
York's Case, Foster, 70. § 150.
York, C. v., 9 Met. 93. §§ 121, 321, 329, 333.
v. S., 17 Tex. Ap. 441. § 618.
S. v., 5 Harr. 493. § 566.
S. v., 37 N. H. 175. §§ 212, 217.
S. v., 70 N. C. 66. § 992.
York Street, etc. Co., U. S. v., 17 Blatch. 138. § 1351.
Yorke, Reg. v., 2 C. & K. 841. § 571.
Young v. C., 6 Bush, 312. § 426.
v. C., 8 Bush, 366. § 213.
v. C., 12 Bush, 243. §§ 526, 529.
v. C., 14 Bush, 161. §§ 1232, 1272.
C. v., 9 Gray, 5. § 626.
C. v., 135 Mass. 526. § 62.
v. P., 6 Ill. Ap. 434. § 262.
P. v., 31 Cal. 563. § 859.
P. v., 64 Cal. 212. § 316.
P. v., 65 Cal. 225. §§ 499, 500, 509.
P. v., 102 Cal. 411. §§ 161, 398.
P. v., 72 Ill. 411. §§ 1188, 1193.
Reg. v., 2 C. & K. 466. §§ 557, 1330, 1335.
Reg. v., 8 C. & P. 644. §§ 205, 324.
Reg. v., 10 Cox, 371. § 1013.
Reg. v., 38 L. T. 540. § 445.
v. Rex, 3 Term R. 98. §§ 668, 697.
v. S., 58 Ala. 358. § 1233.
v. S., 100 Ala. 126. § 495.
v. S., 50 Ark. 501. § 468.
v. S., 24 Fla. 147. § 617.
v. S., 95 Ga. 456. § 619.
v. S., 11 Humph. 200. § 302.
v. S., 34 Ind. 46. § 1225.
v. S., 10 Lea, 165. §§ 1159, 1160.
v. S., 42 Tex. 462. § 1038.
v. S., 44 Tex. 98. § 268.
Young v. S., 7 Tex. Ap. 75. § 257.
v. S., 30 Tex. Ap. 308. § 605.
v. S., 31 Tex. Ap. 24. § 255.
S. v., 5 Coldw. 51. § 1270.
S. v., 26 Ia. 122. §§ 731, 732, 738, 741.
S. v., 55 Kan. 349. §§ 13, 326, 1147.
S. v., 99 Mo. 284. § 1100.
S. v., 18 N. H. 543. § 932.
S. v., 46 N. H. 266. §§ 755, 756.
S. v., 47 N. H. 402. § 758.
S. v., 37 N. J. 184. §§ 962, 975, 977.
S. v., 76 N. C. 258. § 669.
S. v., 1 Wins. 126. § 4 0.
T. v., 5 Mont. 242. § 378.
U. S. v., 25 Fed. R. 710. § 156.
Youngblood v. Sexton, 32 Mich. 406. § 1212.
Younger, Rex v., 5 Term R. 449. § 1321.
S. v., 1 Dev. 357. § 960.
Yount v. S., 64 Ind. 443. § 769.
Yowell v. S., 41 Ark. 355. § 1236.
Yslas, P. v., 27 Cal. 630. § 232.
Yundt v. P., 65 Ill. 372. § 1147.
Yung Jon, Ex parte, 28 Fed. R. 308. § 29.
Yung Sing Hee, In re, 36 Fed. R. 437. § 79.

Zabriskie v. S., 43 N. J. 640. §§ 1118, 1119.
Zallner v. S., 15 Tex. Ap. 23. § 1035.
Zaner v. S., 90 Ala. 651. § 309.
Zanone v. Mound City, 103 Ill. 552. 1228.
Zapf v. S., 11 Ind. Ap. 360. § 1253.
Zarresseller v. P., 17 Ill. 101. § 1273.
Zeibart, S. v., 40 Ia. 169. §§ 196, 214, 328, 332.
Zeigert, Reg. v., 10 Cox, 555. § 808.
Zeigler, S. v., 32 N. J. 262. § 62.
S. v., 46 N. J. 307. § 63.
Zeisler, U. S. v., 30 Fed. R. 499. § 1334.
Zeitler, S. v., 63 Ind. 441. §§ 1247, 1256.
Zeizer v. S., 47 Ind. 129. § 1262.
Zell v. C., 94 Pa. St. 258. § 354.
Zeller v. S., 46 Ind. 304. § 1239.
Zellers, S. v., 7 N. J. 220. §§ 142, 337, 338.
Zelt, C. v., 138 Pa. St. 615. §§ 1204, 1256, 1257.
Zes Cloya, U. S. v., 35 Fed. R. 493. § 1104.
Zielke v. S., 42 Neb. 750. § 1223.
Zimmerman v. S., 4 Ind. Ap. 583. § 1191.
v. S., 14 Neb. 568. § 358.
S. v., 47 Kan. 242. § 803.
Zink v. P., 77 N. Y. 114. § 563.
v. S., 34 Neb. 37. § 629.
Zinner v. C., —— Pa. ——, 14 Atl. R. 431. § 1231.
Ziord, S. v., 30 La. An., Pt. II, 867. § 597.
Zoldoske v. S., 82 Wis. 580. §§ 396, 418.
Zook v. S., 47 Ind. 463. §§ 59, 1314.
Zschocke v. P., 62 Ill. 127. § 554.
Zug v. C., 70 Pa. St. 138. § 1195.

INDEX.

References are to sections, which are numbered continuously throughout the two volumes, §§ 1–742 being in Vol. I, and §§ 743–1359 in Vol. II.

Abandonment of wife or child, § 58.
of criminal design or intent, §§ 198, 223, 224.
of stolen property, effect of, § 548.
Abatement of nuisance by order of court, §§ 1181, 1182.
by private party, § 1182.
of obstruction in highway, § 1184.
of liquor nuisance, § 1249.
Abduction of child, § 486, n.
of female, §§ 1100–1108.
Abortion, procuring of, when criminal, §§ 1146–1152.
attempt to procure, §§ 122, 1148.
effect of impossibility, § 226.
the woman subject not deemed an accomplice, § 199.
whether death resulting is homicide, § 289.
whether death resulting is manslaughter or murder, §§ 325, n., 327, 347.
death in procuring by poison, murder in first degree, § 354.
Absence of consort as defense in bigamy, § 1080.
Abuse of official authority, § 905.
Abusive language causing affray, § 1007.
as constituting breach of the peace, §§ 1017, 1020.
Accessories, see Principal and accessory.
Accident causing death, whether homicide, § 285.
as excuse for homicide, § 300.
Accidental killing, when murder, § 323.
Accomplice, who deemed, liability of, § 199.
acts or declarations of, as evidence, § 203.
evidence of, requires corroboration, §§ 203, 397, 990, 1151, 1296.
one who pays a consideration to stifle prosecution, is not, § 940.
in procuring abortion, woman not deemed, § 1151.
consenting party in sodomy deemed, § 1155.
purchaser of liquor, not deemed, § 1241.
see also Principal and accessory.
Account books, whether subject of larceny, § 543.
false entries in, as indicating embezzlement, § 640.
forgery of, § 755.
Accounting, failure in, as constituting embezzlement, §§ 639, 640, 651.
Accusation of crime, threatening, when criminal, §§ 737, 741.
Acknowledgment, forgery of, § 750.

Acquittal of one, in prosecution for joint offense, §§ 981, 996, 1010.
Act, variance of, from intent, § 126.
in connection with intent necessary to constitute crime, §§ 219–225.
what sufficient to constitute embezzlement, §§ 637, 655.
Action to recover penalty in criminal proceedings, § 5.
Actions, *qui tam*, § 7.
Acts of co-conspirators, when evidence of admissible, § 988.
of parties, evidence of, in prosecution for homicide, §§ 413, 414.
of accused, evidence of, in prosecution for homicide, §§ 420, 421.
as evidence in larceny, § 614.
admissible on question of sanity, § 168.
Administration of poison or drug, to procure abortion, § 1148.
Administrators, embezzlement by. § 629.
Admiralty jurisdiction, exercise of, as to crimes, § 1347.
Admissions of accused in prosecution for homicide, § 420.
in bigamy, § 1083.
of third persons, not admissible in prosecution for larceny, § 614.
of co-conspirators, when admissible, § 988.
Adulteration of food or drink, § 33.
knowledge of, must be shown, § 128, n.
Adultery, what constitutes, §§ 1086–1090.
intent involved in, §§ 1091, 1092.
prosecution for, on complaint of husband or wife, § 1093.
indictment for, §§ 1094, 1095.
mistake as defense in, § 134.
solicitation to commit, not criminal, §§ 220, 225.
person committing cannot make self-defense against husband, § 309.
as provocation for homicide, §§ 341, 365.
classified with other like crimes, § 1110.
as included in charge of seduction, § 1115.
Advertisements of lotteries, provisions as to, §§ 1315–1318.
sending through mails, § 1334.
Advice of counsel, whether a defense, § 132.
as a defense in perjury, § 870.
Affidavit, forgery of, § 750.
false swearing in, as perjury, §§ 859, 861, 877, 879.
as to pension claim, falsity of, § 1348.
false, in support of claims against the United States, § 1352.
Affinity, relationship by, in incest, § 1120.
Affray, what constitutes, §§ 1006–1008.
procedure in, §§ 1009–1011.
indictment for, § 1009.
included offense in, § 1011.
as constituting breach of the peace, § 1012.
right to resist, § 139.
Age, proof of to show capacity, §§ 152, 153.
of person guilty of embezzlement, § 633.
of person to whom intoxicating liquors are sold, knowledge of, evidence, §§ 1257, 1260.

Age — continued.
of minor, evidence of, § 1314.
of girl, knowledge of, in case of abduction, § 1105.
Age of consent, in rape, §§ 443, 444.
in case of rape, mistake as to, § 451.
Agency as affecting criminal liability, §§ 186–192.
Agent, criminal liability of, §§ 186, 190.
commission of crime through, § 207.
crime committed through, jurisdiction of, §§ 207, 211.
wife acting in presence of husband not deemed, § 145.
of corporations, criminal liability of, §§ 180, 184.
innocent or criminal, larceny through, § 548.
embezzlement by, §§ 626–628.
of corporation, when guilty of embezzlement, §§ 632, 639.
false pretenses made by or to, when criminal, § 683.
liability of, for receipt of stolen goods, § 714.
liability for acts of, in libel, § 1056.
sale of liquor by, protected by license of principal, § 1227.
liability of employer for sale of intoxicating liquors by, § 1237. And see Master and servant.
liability of, for illegal sale of intoxicating liquors, § 1239.
minor as, in purchase of intoxicating liquor for another, § 1258.
Aggravated assaults, see Assaults.
Aggravation of assault, what constitutes, § 255.
matter of, in prosecution for robbery, § 478.
in burglary, § 512.
elements of, in larceny, § 574.
Agreement to stifle prosecution, § 940.
Aiders and abettors, who are, § 199. See, also, Principal and accessory.
in manslaughter, § 200.
how indicted, § 213.
who deemed, in keeping house of ill-fame, § 1141.
in violations of law by bank officers, § 1339.
Aiding and abetting, indictment for, § 218. And see Principal and accessory.
Aiding or procuring in illegal gaming, § 1288.
Air, corruption of, as constituting nuisance, §§ 1169, 1171.
Alcohol, whether deemed intoxicating liquor, §§ 1218–1222.
within provision as to sale of goods, wares and merchandise on Sunday, § 1321, n.
Alibi of alleged deceased in homicide, § 399.
Allegiance, violation of, as constituting treason, § 1354.
not material in piracy, § 1359.
Alleys, deemed highways, § 1192.
Alteration of instrument as constituting forgery, § 765.
of invalid instrument, not forgery, § 756.
Ambassador, violence to, § 1342.
Amusements, on Sunday, whether permitted, § 1325.
"And," in construction of statutes, § 108.
Animal, what deemed, § 1162.

Animals, cruelty to, §§ 1161–1164.
malicious injuries to, § 815.
regulations as to transportation of, §§ 1161, 1338.
diseased, sale of, § 56.
vicious, death caused by, from negligence of owner, § 351.
feræ naturæ, larceny of, § 538.
tamed, when subject of larceny, § 538.
domestic, subject of larceny, § 540.
carcasses of, subject of larceny, § 541.
trespassing, larceny of, § 546, n.
domestic, killing of, without removed, whether larceny, § 548.
special provisions as to larceny of, § 589.
sufficiency of description of, in indictment for larceny, §§ 593, 594.
Animus furandi in larceny, § 564.
Answer in chancery, false oath to, as constituting perjury, § 859.
Apology, effect of, in libel, § 1054.
Apparent danger justifying killing in self-defense, § 304.
Apparent legal efficacy of forged instrument sufficient, § 757.
Appeal, repeal of statute pending, § 99.
Appeals of felony, § 2.
Apprehension of danger as justifying killing in self-defense, §§ 304–306.
Appropriation, what sufficient, in larceny, §§ 566, 567.
subsequent to rightful taking, § 569.
Appurtenant buildings, in burglary, §§ 496, 498.
Arms, carrying of, see Weapons.
Arrest without warrant, resistance to, § 141.
with unnecessary violence, resistance to, § 302.
with unnecessary violence constitutes assault, § 255.
death caused in resisting, §§ 328, 340.
homicide justifiable in making, § 298.
homicide by undue violence in making, § 348.
unlawful, resistance to, §§ 141, 241.
as constituting provocation in homicide, § 340.
death caused in making, § 347.
escape from, § 931.
as constituting false imprisonment, §§ 487, 488, 906.
Arson, definition of, § 517.
as to what buildings, §§ 518–521.
intent to defraud insurance companies, § 522.
what burning necessary to constitute, § 523.
aggravation of, § 524.
degrees of, § 525.
intent, § 526.
indictment for, §§ 527–531.
included offenses in, § 532.
evidence in prosecution for, § 533.
attempt to commit, §§ 223, 225.
murder in committing, first degree, § 355.
recent possession of stolen goods, as evidence of, § 616.

Asportation, what sufficient in larceny, §§ 548–563.
how alleged, § 607.
Assault, in general, §§ 230–253.
what constitutes, §§ 231–234.
what intent necessary, § 239.
intent alone, not sufficient, § 219.
form of attempt, §§ 224, 225.
justification for, §§ 241–247.
prosecution for, not barred by civil action, § 247.
consent to, § 249.
principal and accessory in, § 250.
jurisdiction of, § 251.
extent of right to resist, § 139.
as constituting provocation for manslaughter, § 339.
allegation of, in indictment for homicide, § 378.
resistance to officer, as constituting, § 921.
not included in riot, § 1001.
included in robbery, § 484.
as constituting breach of the peace, § 1012.
mitigation of, § 248.
aggravated, §§ 230, 248, 254–262.
intent in case of, § 259.
indictment for, §§ 260, 261.
offense included in, § 262.
indecent, § 238.
involved in assault with intent to commit rape, § 465.
with unloaded weapon, § 226.
with deadly weapon, § 257.
intoxication no defense for, § 161, n.
with specific intent, § 122.
with felonious intent, §§ 263–272.
justification or mitigation for, § 267.
indictment for, §§ 268–270.
what offense included in, § 271.
to kill or murder, general discussion of, §§ 273–279.
impossibility, as affecting, § 226.
felonies included in, § 271.
to murder, intoxication as affecting, § 161.
to do great bodily injury, § 280.
with intent to rob, § 281.
with intent to commit rape, general discussion of, §§ 462–467.
forms of indictment for, § 467.
intoxication no defense for, § 161.
with intent to commit sodomy, § 1153.
Assault and battery, general discussion of, §§ 231–253.
indictment for, §§ 252, 253.
Assembly, unlawful, what constitutes, §§ 1003–1005.
constituting riot or rout, §§ 991, 992.
for destruction of property, § 993.

Assignment of liquor license, § 1227.
Association, misappropriation of funds by member, not embezzlement, § 631.
unincorporated, ownership by, how charged, in indictment for larceny, § 604.
furnishing of liquors to members of, § 1240.
Attempt, what criminal, §§ 220–229.
impossibility as affecting, § 226.
indictment for, §§ 228, 229.
as an included offense, § 229.
assault deemed, §§ 231–233.
to obtain property by false pretense, when criminal, § 680.
to procure perjury, §§ 893–895.
to corrupt juror, § 899.
to violate election laws, §§ 943, 948, n.
to commit incest, § 1122.
to procure abortion, when criminal, § 1148.
to commit sodomy, § 1153.
Attorneys, regulation of business of, § 37.
regulation of by municipalities, § 73.
embezzlement by, §§ 627–629.
extortion by, § 914.
excessive charges by, in procuring pensions, § 1348.
Auctioneer, embezzlement by, §§ 636, 639.
Authority as defense for crime, § 115.
misrepresentation of, when criminal, § 673.
forgery of instrument executed without, § 759.
claim of, in wilful trespass, § 828.

Bailee, larceny from, § 546.
deemed owner in case of larceny, §§ 547–549.
misappropriation by, whether larceny, § 554.
larceny by, § 555.
distinguished from servant in larceny, § 556.
of lost property, not guilty of larceny in unlawful appropriation, § 571.
of stolen property, ownership laid in, § 603.
embezzlement by, §§ 623, 644.
Ballots, refusal or alteration of, § 945.
as evidence in prosecutions for violating election laws, § 951.
Bank bills or notes, whether subject of larceny, § 543.
subject of larceny, § 543.
description of, in indictment for larceny, § 596.
embezzlement of, before issue, § 636.
receipt of, when stolen, § 715.
forgery of, §§ 752, 757, 758.
Bankers, regulation of business of, § 42.
Banking act, offenses under, §§ 1339, 1340.
Barbers, validity of special regulations as to, § 55.
legislation as to, unconstitutional for want of uniformity, § 77.

Barn, part of dwelling, with reference to burglary, § 497.
subject of arson, § 519.
Barratry, §§ 27, 1169.
Bastard, concealing birth of, § 1152.
Bastardy, as a crime, § 1126.
liability of father for support of child, § 1126.
Battery, is a completed assault, § 235.
not included in assault with intent to commit felony, § 271.
danger of, does not justify killing in defense, § 302.
see Assault and battery.
Bawd, definition of, § 1106*a*.
Bawdy house, see House of ill-fame.
Beer, whether deemed intoxicating liquor, §§ 1218-1222.
Bees, larceny of, § 538.
Belief of danger as justifying killing in self-defense, §§ 305, 306.
as to age of girl in prosecution for rape, § 451.
Belligerent rights, acts of insurgents on the high seas, without, deemed piracy, § 1359.
Benefit of clergy as distinguishing between murder and manslaughter, § 319.
Best evidence in prosecution for homicide, § 410.
Betting, what criminal, §§ 1282-1299.
on elections, § 947.
on games in public place, §§ 1301-1304.
Beverage, regulation of sale of liquor as, see Intoxicating liquors.
Bicycles, licenses for, §§ 39, 70.
deemed vehicles, § 1197.
Bigamy, definition of, what constitutes, §§ 1071-1076.
jurisdiction and venue in, § 1077.
limitation of prosecution for, § 1078.
indictment for, §§ 1079-1081.
evidence in prosecution for, §§ 1082-1085.
mistake of fact, as a defense in, § 133.
may constitute also adultery, § 1095.
classified among sexual crimes, §§ 1109, 1110.
Bill in chancery, false oath to, as constituting perjury, § 859.
Bill of particulars in prosecution for conspiracy, § 976.
Billiard saloons, allowing minors to remain in, §§ 59, 1314.
Bills of attainder, § 79.
Bills and notes, whether subject of larceny, § 543.
description of, in indictment for larceny, § 595.
whether deemed property in false pretenses, § 693.
forgery of, § 752.
Birth of bastard, concealment of, § 1152.
Black Act, § 812.
Blackmail as a crime, §§ 728-742.
Blank, filling after execution, constitutes forgery, § 765.
Blasphemous publications, as libel, § 1049.
Blasphemy and profanity, what constitutes, §§ 1159, 1160.
Board of health, regulations of, enforced, § 30.

Books of account, forgery of, § 755.
Borrowing of property with the intent to appropriate, § 562.
Boundaries, protection of, § 45.
Boundary trees, injury to, § 819.
destruction of, intent, § 826.
Boxing-match, may be lawful, § 249.
Boy, under fourteen years of age, whether competent to commit rape, § 449.
whether may be guilty of assault with intent to commit rape, § 465.
Boycotting, § 963, n.
Brands, protection of, § 47.
as evidence in larceny, §§ 594, 613.
falsification of, as constituting false pretenses, § 661.
of animals, altering, § 816.
Breach of contract, not usually criminal, § 10.
Breach of the peace, what constitutes, §§ 1012–1021.
indictment for, § 1021.
improper language as constituting, § 26.
involved in forcible trespass, §§ 820, 823.
in case of unlawful assembly, § 1003.
slander or libel as leading to, §§ 1040, 1055.
Bread, regulation of weight of loaves, § 48.
Breaking, what sufficient in burglary, § 500.
constructive, § 501.
Breaking and entry, statutory provisions as to, § 499. And see Burglary.
Breaking bulk by carrier or bailee, larceny, § 555.
Breaking jail, §§ 930–936.
Breaking out, as constituting burglary, § 502.
Brewers, sale of liquors by, § 1254.
Bribe, offering or accepting, §§ 896–903.
attempt to extort, § 914.
Bribery, what constitutes, §§ 896–899.
venue in, § 900.
indictment for, §§ 901, 902.
evidence of, § 903.
punished as contempt, § 920, n.
of electors, § 947.
Bridges, obstruction of navigable rivers by, § 1195.
Buggery, see Sodomy.
Buildings, appurtenant to dwelling, breaking and entering of, as constituting burglary, § 496.
adjacent to dwelling, with reference to burglary, § 498.
not appurtenant to dwelling, with reference to burglary, § 499.
what subject of arson, §§ 518–521.
larceny from, § 578.
malicious injury to, § 821.
Burden of proof, as to intoxication, § 162.
as to insanity, §§ 175, 176.
as to self-defense, § 316.
in homicide not shifted by presumption of malice, § 333.

Burden of proof — continued.
of provocation for homicide, § 346.
in prosecution for rape, § 461.
as to possession of stolen goods, in larceny, § 617.
as to guilty knowledge, in receipt of stolen goods, § 716.
as to chastity in prosecution for slander imputing unchastity to female, § 1057.
as to chastity, in seduction, § 1118.
in prosecution under liquor laws, § 1281.
Burglar's tools, possession of, criminal, §§ 221, 516.
Burglary, definition of, § 493.
what buildings subject of, §§ 494–499.
breaking and entering, constituting, §§ 500–503.
in night-time, § 504.
intent, what necessary to constitute, §§ 505–507.
indictment for, §§ 508–513.
venue in prosecution for, § 509*a*.
what offenses included in, § 511.
degrees of, § 512.
evidence in prosecution for, §§ 514–516.
whether connivance of servant of owner is a defense, § 118.
intent essential in, § 122.
furnishing tools for, criminal, § 200, n.
attempt to commit, § 223.
effect of impossibility, § 226.
murder in committing, first degree, § 355.
recent possession of stolen goods, as evidence in, § 616.
receipt of goods procured by, whether criminal, § 713.
Burial of dead bodies, §§ 1165–1168.
Burial grounds, desecration of, §§ 1167, 1168.
Burning, statutory, § 520. And see Arson.
what constitutes, in arson, §§ 522, 523.
Business, regulation of under police power, § 29.
regulation of in particular localities, § 39.
regulation of by municipalities, § 73.
Butter, imitation, sale of, § 34.
manufacturers of to make returns to those furnishing milk, § 42.

Camp meeting, regulation of business near, § 39.
disturbance of, §§ 1022–1028.
Capacity, criminal, in case of infants, §§ 149–153.
to commit crime, in case of insanity or intoxication, §§ 154–179.
of deaf and dumb person to commit crime, § 155.
age of, in case of rape, § 449.
Car, larceny from, § 578.
Cards, swindling by means of, § 662.
Carelessness, criminal, liability for, §§ 129, 130.
of person defrauded, whether material in false pretenses, § 687.

Carnal knowledge, involved in rape, §§ 438, 443, 450.
whether necessary to constitute incest, § 1122.
Carrier, regulation of charges of, § 40.
game laws as affecting, § 46.
regulations as to colored passengers, § 54.
larceny from, § 546.
larceny by, § 555.
embezzlement by, § 644.
regulation of transportation of animals by, §§ 1161, 1338.
regulations of, as to interstate commerce, §§ 1336–1338*a*.
of mails, robbery of, § 1329.
of intoxicating liquors, see Transportation.
Carrying away, how alleged, in larceny, § 607.
Carrying concealed weapons, §§ 1029–1039.
Cashier of banking corporation, embezzlement by, § 632.
Cattle, running at large, larceny of, § 546.
stealing of, value immaterial, § 589.
description of, in indictment for larceny, § 594.
malicious injuries to, § 815.
driving from range, § 816.
meaning of term, § 1162.
Causation, in case of homicide, §§ 283–292.
Cause of death, § 292.
Cemeteries, desecration of, §§ 1167, 1168.
Certificate of acknowledgment, forgery of, § 750.
of character, not subject of forgery, § 756.
Challenging to fight a duel, § 324.
Chance, involved in lottery, § 1315.
Change, mistake in making, as constituting larceny, § 561.
Character, bad, of defendant, evidence of, in larceny, § 615.
good, proof of, in prosecution for receiving stolen goods, § 716.
obtaining property by threats of injury to, § 736.
of deceased, as bearing on the right of self-defense, § 307.
evidence of, in prosecution for homicide, § 423.
as affecting credibility of dying declarations, § 431.
as affecting provocation in homicide, § 344.
of defendant, evidence of, in prosecution for homicide, § 422.
in prosecution for adultery, § 1097.
of prosecutrix, evidence of, in case of rape, § 460.
not involved in libel, § 1054.
of third person, not admissible, in prosecution for larceny, § 614.
Charity, obtaining by false pretenses, whether criminal, § 695.
works of, excepted from Sunday laws, § 1321.
Charivari, whether constitutes provocation for manslaughter, § 339.
Chaste character, when lost may be regained, § 1113.
Chastisement, when lawful, § 242.
of wife by husband, § 243.
Chastity, definition of, what constitutes, §§ 1113, 1118.
evidence of, in case of rape, § 460.

Chastity — continued.
reputation as to, in prosecution for slander in imputing unchastity to female, § 1057.
imputation against, deemed slander, § 1057.
in case of abduction, §§ 1106, 1106*a*.
in seduction, § 1113.
should be alleged in indictment for seduction, § 1114.
evidence of, § 1118.
Chattel mortgage, as constituting fraudulent conveyance, § 842.
removal of property covered by, §§ 846, 847.
Chattels, value of, in larceny, § 543.
what subject of larceny, see Larceny.
Cheats and frauds, when criminal, §§ 657–665. And see False pretenses.
Checks, whether subject of larceny, § 543.
not genuine, use of as constituting false pretense, § 661.
false, when constitute false pretenses, § 674.
whether deemed property, in false pretenses, § 693.
forgery of, § 752.
falsely certifying, § 1340.
Cheese, manufacturers of, to make returns to those furnishing milk, § 42.
imitation, sale of, § 34.
Chemist, negligence of, as constituting homicide, § 287.
Child, stealing of, § 486, n.
ill-treatment of, as showing malice, § 330.
neglect of, § 58.
neglect or exposure of, causing death, §§ 286, 351.
death of, from undue violence in chastisement, § 348.
female, consent of, as affecting assault with intent to commit rape, § 464.
violation of, as constituting rape, see Rape.
illegitimate, how described in indictment for homicide, § 373*a*.
concealing birth of, § 1152.
unborn, not subject of homicide, § 294.
causing death of, by abortion, §§ 1146, 1147.
exhibition to jury, as evidence in prosecution for seduction, § 1117.
in prosecution for bastardy, § 1129.
Children, assaults upon, § 255.
Chimney, entry through, deemed breaking, § 500.
Chinese, exclusion of, §§ 1344, 1345.
Christian religion, offenses against, §§ 1159, 1160.
Church buildings, malicious injury to, § 821.
Churches, sale of liquor near, § 1266.
Circumstantial evidence in homicide cases, §§ 408–410.
to identify defendant in larceny, § 614.
of recent possession of stolen goods, § 616.
by way of corroboration, in prosecution for perjury, § 892.
admissible to show conspiracy, § 989.
in bigamy, to prove husband or wife still alive, § 1084.
in adultery, § 1097.

Circumstantial evidence — continued.
as to intercourse, in prosecution for illicit cohabitation, § 1132.
in prosecution for lewdness, § 1135.
Cities and towns, police power of, see Municipalities.
City ordinances, see Ordinances.
Civil action for assault does not bar criminal prosecution. § 247.
Civil code, provisions of, applicable in construing criminal statute, § 88.
Civil remedy not merged in crime, § 11.
Civil rights, protection of, § 54.
Claim of right as a defense, § 113.
resistance to trespass under, § 142.
as showing want of criminal intent in larceny, §§ 564, 565.
as defense for malicious trespass, § 827.
as defense for resisting officer, § 924.
Class legislation, validity of, § 77.
Clerk, larceny by, § 556.
embezzlement by, §§ 626–628.
liability of employer for acts of, see Master and servant.
Clothing, introduction of, as evidence in homicide cases, § 405.
of wife, taking of, as husband's property, § 558.
Club room, whether deemed public place, in prosecution for gaming, § 1303.
Clubs, sale of liquors in, § 1240.
Coal, regulations as to weighing, §§ 48, 55.
Coasting trade, regulations as to, § 1347.
Cock-fighting, punishable as cruelty to animals, § 1161.
Coercion of wife by husband, presumption of, §§ 145–148.
Cohabitation, as proof of marriage, §§ 1074, 1082.
whether involved in abduction, § 1104.
illicit, when criminal, §§ 1130–1132.
Coin, description of, in indictment for larceny, § 597.
whether charged as goods and chattels in larceny, § 543, n.
evidence of identity of, in prosecution for larceny, § 599.
description of, in indictment for embezzlement, § 652.
counterfeiting of, §§ 774–776.
tools for counterfeiting, possession of, §§ 777–779.
counterfeiting, uttering, passing or having in possession, §§ 780–789.
Collateral facts, false swearing as to, § 862.
Collection agency, libel by, § 1055.
envelopes, use of, § 1333.
Collectors, embezzlement by, § 629.
Colloquium, in libel, § 1060.
Color blindness, examination for, required, § 38, n.
Combat, as constituting provocation for manslaughter, § 339.
Combination, unlawful, when punishable, §§ 952, 953. And see Conspiracy.
criminal liability of those who participate in, §§ 193–203.
joint liability of each participant for acts of others, §§ 195–203.
in false pretenses, § 697.
in restraint of trade, § 963.
in restraint of commerce, § 1337.

Command, as defense for crime, §§ 115, 136.
Commerce, regulations of, federal statutes as to, §§ 1336–1338*a*. And see Interstate commerce.
with Indians, regulation of, § 1338*a*.
Commercial agency, false statement to, whether criminal, § 679.
Commission merchant, embezzlement by, §§ 636, 639.
Common barrator, offense of being, §§ 27, 1169.
Common gambler, who deemed, § 1300.
Common law as to crimes, § 12.
where in force, § 12.
modified by statute, § 12.
how far recognized, §§ 13, 14.
definitions of, as applicable to statutes, § 15.
as affected by statute, § 95.
whether revived by repeal of statute superseding, § 102.
meaning of terms in construction of statutes, § 105.
Common railer and brawler, the offense of being, § 26.
Common scold, the offense of being, §§ 26, 1169.
Common seller of intoxicating liquors, § 1244.
Common thief, offense of being, § 580.
Complaint, meaning of term, § 110.
of husband or wife, in prosecution for adultery, § 1093.
in bastardy proceedings, § 1128.
evidence of, in prosecution for rape, §§ 455, 456.
in prosecution for sodomy, § 1155.
Compound larcenies, §§ 574–580.
Compound liquors, sale of, § 1219.
Compounding offenses, §§ 938–940.
Compulsion as defense for crime, §§ 116, 136–144.
Concealed weapons, carrying of, §§ 1029–1039.
Concealing property to defraud creditors, § 843.
Concealment of crime, when criminal, § 209.
of fact of incumbrance, when criminal, §§ 671, 685.
of receipt of stolen goods, when criminal, § 714.
of birth of bastard, § 1152.
Conception, does not show consent in rape, § 440.
Concubinage, what constitutes, § 1104.
abduction for purpose of, §§ 1104, 1106*a*.
Condonation, in adultery, not affected by marriage of parties, § 1093.
Confederates, acts or declarations of, as evidence, § 203. And see Accomplices.
Confession of infants as to age or capacity, § 152.
in homicide, § 420.
of accused without corroboration, not sufficient to prove *corpus delicti* in homicide, § 397.
of guilt of third person, in prosecution for homicide, § 404.
Conflict of laws, as to taking of stolen property from one state to another, § 553.

Congregation assembled for worship, disturbance of, § 1024.
Congressional elections, regulation of, § 948.
Consanguinity, relationship by, in incest, § 1120.
Consent to crime, effect of, §§ 199, 202.
to assault, § 249.
to unlawful act, obtained by fraud, § 249.
no defense, in case of murder, § 324.
to fight, §§ 1007, 1013.
as affecting breaking and entry in burglary, §§ 501, 503.
of owner, as preventing conversion of property from constituting larceny, §§ 550, 557–563.
of employer, as disproving embezzlement, § 643.
of mortgagee, to disposal of property covered by chattel mortgage, §§ 847, 851.
as disproving rape, §§ 439–448.
to intercourse, procured by fraud, whether disproves rape, § 446.
effect of proof of, in prosecution for attempt to commit rape, §§ 249, 463, 464.
effect of, in case of abduction of girls, § 1102.
to indecent assault. § 338.
to illicit intercourse, in case of seduction, § 1117.
to abortion, § 1149.
in sodomy, § 1155.
Consideration for sale of intoxicating liquor, § 1234.
Conspiracy, general nature and definition, what constitutes, §§ 952–955.
what combination sufficient to constitute, §§ 968, 969.
intent in, § 971.
procedure in, §§ 972–987.
indictment for, §§ 974–986.
punishment of, § 987.
evidence in prosecution for, §§ 988–990.
proof of existence of, § 989.
to charge with crime, § 957.
to commit a crime, § 956.
joint liability of those participating, §§ 194–203.
to extort, evidence of, § 742.
to defraud, § 960.
to obtain property by false pretenses, § 697.
to deprive of civil rights, § 961.
to injure the public, § 962.
to defraud or overthrow government, §§ 964, 965.
to commit treason, § 1357.
to interfere with interstate commerce, § 1337.
in restraint of trade, § 963.
to slander, § 958.
to secure admission in case of burglary, § 501.
to seduce or entice female, § 959.
liability of each party for acts of others, §§ 195–203, 970.

Conspiracy — continued.
death resulting from, § 291.
causing death, joint liability for, § 196.
jurisdiction of conspirators, § 211.
proof of acts and threats by joint conspirators, in homicide, § 419.
proof of, in prosecution for forgery or counterfeiting, § 810.
overt act, § 966.
impossibility of effecting the object intended, § 967.
Constitutional law, validity of regulation of sales of liquor and opium, § 29.
regulation of sale of imitation butter, cheese and lard, § 34.
validity of inspection laws, § 35.
validity of statutes requiring licenses, § 38.
validity of regulations as to railroads, § 40.
validity of license tax, § 44.
validity of regulations as to colored passengers, § 54.
validity of regulations as to employees, § 55.
validity of regulations as to freedom of contract, § 55.
validity of statutes as to miscegenation, § 57.
authority of municipalities, § 62.
uniformity of operation of statute, § 77.
ex post facto laws, § 78.
right to be confronted with witnesses, rule as to dying declarations, § 425.
as to carrying concealed weapons, § 1030.
freedom of the press, § 1050.
regulations as to use of mails, §§ 1332–1334.
religious freedom, recognition of Christianity, § 1159.
truth as a defense, in libel, § 1051.
functions of jury in prosecution for libel, § 1070.
enforcement of payment of fine, in bastardy proceedings, § 1126.
validity of liquor legislation, §§ 1200–1215.
validity of statutes regulating lotteries, § 1317.
validity of Sunday laws, § 1319.
exercise of power to regulate postoffices and post-roads, § 1327.
definition of treason, §§ 1354, 1355.
Constitutional limitations, §§ 74–80.
Constitutionality of statutes, effect of partial invalidity, § 104.
Construction of penal statutes, §§ 81–110.
Construction of statutes according to legislative intent, § 86.
in pari materia, § 87.
general and special provisions, §§ 89, 90.
with reference to common law, § 95.
as to particular terms, §§ 105–110.
as affected by grammar and punctuation, § 106.
as to sale of liquors, § 1216.
Contempt, whether criminal, § 9.
corporation liable for, § 183.

Continuance of nuisance, § 1173.
how charged, § 1180.
of obstruction of highway, § 1188.
Continuous crimes, statute providing for punishment of, not *ex post facto,* § 78.
Contract, breach of, whether punishable as crime, § 10.
freedom of, § 55.
obligation of, how far protected against criminal legislation, § 75.
whether constitutes false pretense, § 678.
to compound offense, invalid, §§ 939, 940.
Contract labor, federal regulations as to importation of, § 1343.
Contribution to nuisance, effect of, § 1175.
Conversion, what sufficient to constitute larceny, §§ 550, 562.
subsequent to rightful taking, in larceny, § 569.
allegation of, not sufficient to show larceny, § 607.
by servant, when constitutes embezzlement, § 621.
as an element in embezzlement, §§ 623, 638.
in embezzlement, how described, § 655.
of property received by virtue of employment, § 634.
of money, what sufficient to constitute embezzlement, § 639.
whether failure to pay or deliver amounts to, § 640.
by public officer, what constitutes, § 649.
Conviction, repeal of statute after, § 98.
meaning of term, § 110.
of accessory before principal, §§ 215–218.
of principal, record of, on trial of accessory, § 216.
of one, in prosecution for conspiracy, § 981.
in prosecution for riot, § 996.
in prosecution for affray, § 1010.
Conveyances, fraudulent, when criminal, §§ 842–851.
Cool blood, killing in, notwithstanding provocation, §§ 342, 343.
Cooling time, after provocation, in case of homicide, § 343.
Coroner's inquest, preventing, § 1165.
Corporate business, regulation of, § 43.
Corporation, regulation of business of § 43.
foreign, required to procure permit, § 43.
regulation of contracts of with employees, § 55.
term does not include municipality, § 110.
whether indictable, § 180.
criminal liability of, §§ 180–185.
whether deemed persons, §§ 110, 181, 705.
existence of, how proved, in prosecution for larceny, § 604.
ownership in, how charged, in indictment for larceny, § 604.
embezzlement of funds by member, § 631.
embezzlement by officers or agents of, §§ 632, 639.
ownership by, in prosecution for embezzlement, § 653.
deemed person, as to false pretenses, § 705.
existence of, how alleged and proved in forgery, § 772.
public, see Municipal corporation.

Corpus delicti, proof of, in homicide, § 396.
not to be proved by uncorroborated confessions, § 397.
in larceny, evidence of, § 612.
not proved, by possession of stolen goods, § 616.
in prosecution for receiving stolen goods, § 724.
Corroboration of evidence of accomplices, §§ 203, 990, 1151, 1296. And see Accomplice.
required as to *corpus delicti* in homicide, § 397.
what sufficient in perjury, §§ 891, 892.
not required in prosecution for adultery, § 1097.
whether necessary in prosecution for abduction, § 1108.
in prosecution for seduction, § 1119.
of woman upon whom abortion procured, not necessary, § 1151.
of testimony of party consenting, in sodomy, § 1155.
of testimony of purchaser as to illegal sale of intoxicating liquor, not required, § 1241.
of accomplice, in prosecution for gaming, § 1296.
of witness, when necessary, see Accomplice.
Cotton, regulation of sale of, § 50.
Counseling, to commit crime, when criminal, § 207.
Counterfeit money, intoxication as bearing upon intent in passing, § 161
passing of, as constituting false pretenses, §§ 661, 675.
uttering, passing or having in possession, §§ 780–789.
procedure in prosecutions for passing, §§ 790–804.
sending through the mails circulars as to sale of, § 1331.
Counterfeiting, general nature of crime, § 743.
what constitutes, §§ 774–776.
jurisdiction and venue in prosecutions for, §§ 790, 791.
procedure in prosecutions for, §§ 790–804.
indictment for, §§ 792–804.
evidence in prosecution for, §§ 805–810.
Counterfeiting tools, possession of, §§ 777–779.
Counts for larceny and receiving stolen goods in same indictment, § 722.
separate, in indictment for embezzlement, § 656.
in indictment for perjury, § 883.
Court, jurisdiction of, in proceeding in which perjury is committed, § 858.
Court and jury, materiality in perjury is for the court, § 866.
functions of, in libel, § 1070.
respective provinces of, in determining character of liquors, § 1218.
Courts, power to punish contempt, § 9.
federal, jurisdiction of, as to forgery and counterfeiting, § 790.
Courtship, evidence of, in seduction, §§ 1112, 1117.
Coverture, as a defense, §§ 145–148.
Credibility and weight of dying declarations, § 431.
of witness, false swearing as to, § 864.
Credit, obtaining by false pretenses, when criminal, §§ 667–682.
obtaining false indorsement of, not criminal, § 692.
Creditors, conveyances in fraud of, §§ 842–851.

Crime, definition of, § 4.
how distinguished from tort, §§ 2, 4.
includes misdemeanor, § 4, n.
under municipal ordinances, § 6.
distinguished from tort or breach of contract, § 10.
civil remedy not merged in, § 11.
power of legislature to prescribe constitutional limitations on, § 74.
intent as an element of, §§ 111–128.
distinguished from tort as to intent, § 111.
conspiracy to commit or charge with, §§ 956, 957.
publication imputing, deemed libelous, § 1043.
against nature, see Sodomy.
Crimes, common-law or statutory, § 12.
what acts punishable as, § 16.
classification of into felonies and misdemeanors, §§ 17–19.
punishable under the police power, §§ 23–73.
created by ordinances, § 63.
Criminal contempts, § 9.
Criminal intent, see Intent.
Criminal law, history and origin of, § 2.
definition of, §§ 4, 5.
is branch of public law, § 3.
substantive and adjective, § 3.
place of, in jurisprudence, § 3.
Criminal offense, see Crime.
Criminal procedure, bastardy proceedings, when deemed, § 1126.
Criminal proceedings, what deemed, § 5.
Crops, larceny of, § 536.
malicious destruction of, § 813.
Cruel punishments, § 80.
Cruelty to animals, §§ 1161–1164.
Curtilage, what constitutes, § 576.
protection of building within, as part of dwelling, § 144, n.
defense of buildings within, § 312.
buildings within, burglary as to, § 497.
subject of arson, § 519.
Custodian, larceny by, § 556.
consent of, to taking, as affecting larceny, § 558.
embezzlement by, § 630.
of building, right of, to protect, § 143.
of premises, authority of, § 244.
Customs duties, enforcement of, § 1351.

Dam, see Mill-dam.
Damages, exemplary, for criminal wrong, § 11.
Dangerous acts causing death, § 325.
Dangerous weapon, assault with, § 257.
forcible breaking into a dwelling, armed with, § 511.
Day-time, breaking and entry in, § 504.

Dead bodies, burial or disposal of, §§ 1165–1168.
whether subject of larceny, § 542.
Dead person, signature of name of, forgery, § 764.
libel upon, § 1046.
Deadly weapon, assault with, §§ 255, 257.
use of, as showing intent to kill or murder, §§ 274–276.
use of, as indicating intent to do great bodily injury, § 280.
use of in making arrests, § 298, n.
necessity for resort to, in self-defense, § 308.
use of, as indicating malice, § 332.
combat with, as provocation for manslaughter, § 339.
use of, as indicating intent to kill without provocation, § 342.
negligent use of, causing death, § 351.
use of, presumptive of intent to kill, § 357.
description of, in indictment for homicide, §§ 377, 378.
Deaf and dumb person, whether criminally accountable, § 155.
preliminary investigation as to condition, § 166.
Death, time of, in homicide, § 293.
causing of, in protection of person or property, when excused, §§ 136–144.
caused by negligence of railroad company, liability for, § 288.
from negligence or undue violence, deemed manslaughter, §§ 348–351.
in one jurisdiction from wound inflicted in another, § 369.
allegation of, in indictment for homicide, § 381.
proof of place of, in homicide, § 395.
evidence of cause of, in homicide, §§ 400, 402.
sense of impending, essential to admissibility of dying declarations, § 426.
not libel to falsely publish, § 1046.
in general, see Homicide.
Death penalty, regulation of, whether *ex post facto*, § 78, n.
Deaths, report of, § 36.
Debts, collection of, by threatening letters, § 1333.
Deceased, in prosecution for homicide, evidence of threats, character and declarations of, §§ 423, 424.
dying declarations of, §§ 425–431.
Decency as to burial of dead bodies, §§ 1165, 1166.
Declarations as part of *res gestæ* in homicide, §§ 412–415.
in presence of accused, admissible in homicide, § 420.
of deceased, evidence of, in prosecution for homicide, §§ 424–431. And see Dying declarations.
of defendant as evidence in larceny, § 614.
as to recent possession of stolen goods, § 618.
of co-conspirators, when admissible, § 988.
Decoy letters, larceny or embezzlement of, by postal servant, § 1330.
for detecting postal crimes, §§ 1334, 1335.
Decoying to crime, §§ 118, 557.
Dedication of highway, § 1190.

Deed, signature to, obtained by threats, § 738.
forgery of, § 751.
invalid, forgery of, § 757.
forged, uttering of, § 781.
De facto officer, embezzlement by, § 647. And see Officer.
Defamatory matter, sending of, through mail, § 1333.
Defense, want of intent as, §§ 110–128.
of insanity, how interposed and proved, §§ 164–179.
of person or property as an excuse for criminal act, 138–144.
of family, § 140.
of others, extent of right of, § 313.
Defilement of female child, § 1100.
what constitutes, § 448, n.
abducting for purpose of, §§ 1106*a*, 1111.
Definition of crime, § 4.
of criminal proceedings, § 5.
of common-law crime as applied to statute, § 15.
of murder, § 320, n.
of robbery, § 468.
of burglary, § 493.
of arson, § 517.
of embezzlement, § 622.
of cheats, § 660.
of false pretenses, § 666.
of forgery, § 744.
of perjury, § 852.
of riot, § 992.
of conspiracy, § 953.
of libel, §§ 1041, 1042.
of bigamy, § 1071.
of nuisance, § 1169.
of treason, §§ 1355, 1356.
Defrauding, by use of mails, § 1331.
by false representations, see False pretenses.
Degrees of murder and manslaughter, §§ 352–368.
of robbery, § 478.
of burglary, § 512.
of arson, § 525.
of larceny, §§ 581–589, 609.
Delegation of legislative authority to municipalities, § 62.
Deliberation not essential to malice aforethought, § 329.
as negativing provocation in homicide, § 342.
constituting murder in first degree, §§ 353, 356–360.
how charged, in indictment for murder, §§ 382, 383.
Delirium tremens as constituting insanity, § 159.
presumption as to continuance of, § 169.
Delivery to carrier or bailee, proof of, in case of embezzlement, § 644.
of instrument, need not be proved in forgery, § 760.

Demand and refusal as indicating conversion, §§ 638, 639.
whether necessary, in prosecution of carrier or bailee for embezzlement, § 644.
Dentists, regulation of business of, § 36.
Deportation of Chinese, §§ 1344, 1345.
Deputy officer, whether authorized to administer oath, § 855.
protection extended to, § 922.
Description of means and method of killing, in case of homicide, §§ 377, 378.
of wound, in indictment for homicide, § 380.
of property, in prosecution for burglary, § 508.
in indictment for larceny, §§ 592-600.
in embezzlement, § 652.
in false pretenses, § 708.
in indictment for receiving stolen goods, § 718.
in prosecution for malicious mischief or trespass, §§ 830-834.
in indictment for forcible entry and detainer, § 840.
involved in conspiracy, § 983.
in prosecution for riot, § 1000.
of person, in indictment for libel, § 1066.
of locality, in indictment for nuisance, § 1181.
of highway, in indictment, § 1193.
of kind and quantity of intoxicating liquor, in prosecution under liquor laws, § 1273.
Desecration of graves or cemeteries, §§ 1167, 1168.
Deserting seamen, regulations as to, § 1347.
Destruction of gaming implements, § 1312.
of fish and game, § 46.
Detection of crime, what permissible in, § 118.
Detectives, criminal liability of, §§ 117, 118, 201.
decoying to crime, § 557.
acts of, in securing evidence of postal crimes, § 1335.
Detention of mail, when criminal, § 1330.
Direct and collateral attack on validity of liquor license, § 1225.
Discrimination in granting licenses, § 38.
Disfiguring, see Maiming.
Disorderly house, the offense of keeping, §§ 1137-1145. And see House of ill-fame.
place for illegal sale of intoxicating liquors, deemed, § 1249.
Disorderly persons, punishment of, § 1018.
Dispensary act, as to sale of liquors, validity of, §§ 76, n., 1205, 1214.
Disposing of property to defraud creditors, § 843.
covered by chattel mortgage, §§ 846, 847.
Disqualification for voting, § 944.
Distillers, sale of liquors by, § 1254.
Distinct crime, evidence of, see Other crimes.
Distrained property, rescue of, § 52.

Disturbance, public, as constituting breach of the peace, § 1016.
of meeting, what constitutes, §§ 1022–1027.
indictment for, § 1028.
as constituting riot, § 993.
Divorce as terminating marriage, in bigamy, §§ 1075, 1076.
in prosecution for adultery, § 1090.
Dog fighting, punishable as cruelty to animals, § 1161.
Dogs, whether subject of larceny, § 539.
obtaining of by false pretenses, not criminal, § 692.
whether malicious injuries to, criminal, § 815.
owner not liable for injury by, § 823.
is within the term "tame animal," § 1162.
Domestic animal, what deemed, § 1162.
Domestic manufacture of liquors, protection of, § 1202.
Double crime, same act may constitute, § 122.
Double damages, deemed penal, § 5, n.
whether statute giving, for previous injury, *ex post facto*. § 78, n.
Double punishment, in prosecution under liquor laws, § 1277.
Draft, forgery of, § 753.
Drinks, adulterated, sale of, § 33.
Driving away stock, punishment for, § 609.
Druggists, regulation of business of, § 36.
sale of intoxicating liquors by, § 1253.
Drugs, regulation of sale of, § 36.
injurious, administering constitutes assault and battery, § 236.
administration of, to procure abortion, § 1148.
Drunkards, punishment of, § 1018.
sale of liquor to, §§ 1255–1262.
Drunkenness, punishment of, § 1018.
Due-bill, forgery of, § 753.
Dueling, criminal, § 324.
Due process of law, improper interference with business or property prohibited, § 75.
liquor legislation not violation of, §§ 1201, 1207.
provisions as to evidence, in prosecution under liquor laws, in violation of, § 1215.
Duplicity, charging larceny and receipt of stolen goods in same indictment, § 722.
in indictment for assault, § 252.
for burglary, §§ 506, 511.
for embezzlement, § 656.
for forgery, § 803.
for resisting officer, § 928.
for escape or rescue, § 934.
for conspiracy, § 978.
for libel, § 1068.
for gaming, §§ 1295, 1309.
Duress as an excuse for crime, §§ 136–144.
in case of rape, what sufficient, § 448.

Duress — continued.
what sufficient, to constitute false imprisonment or kidnapping, §§ 486–489.
taking property by, constitutes larceny, § 559.
larceny in obtaining property by, § 563.
as a defense in perjury, § 869.
as an excuse for treasonable acts, § 1357.
Duty, omission of, when criminal, § 129.
Dwelling, right to defend, § 139.
protection of, § 144.
against invasion, § 312.
use of improper language in, punishable, § 1017.
Dwelling-house, what constitutes in prosecution for burglary, §§ 494, 495.
breaking and entering, as constituting burglary, § 494.
what deemed, in arson, § 518.
larceny from the, § 576.
malicious injury to, § 821.
Dying declarations as evidence in prosecution for homicide, §§ 425–431.
Dynamiting, 524.

Educational institutions, sale of liquor near, § 1266.
Eight-hour laws, validity of, § 55.
Election, what deemed, § 942.
to determine adoption of local-option liquor law, § 1232.
Election day, sale of liquor upon, liability of agent for, § 1239.
sale of liquor upon, § 1265.
Election laws, violation of, §§ 941–951.
Elections, bets upon, § 1298.
bribery of officers of, § 897.
Electors, bribery of, § 947.
Elevator charges, regulation of, § 40.
Embassador, violence to, § 1342.
Embezzlement, what constitutes, definition, §§ 621, 622.
how distinguished from larceny, §§ 623–625.
not included in larceny, § 625.
by servant, clerk or agent, §§ 626–643.
value of property in, § 636.
by carrier or bailee, § 644.
by public officers, §§ 645–649.
indictment for, §§ 650–656*a*.
procedure in, §§ 650–656.
venue in, § 650.
allegation of time as to, § 651.
description of money or property in indictment for, § 652.
misappropriation by bailee, § 554.
by clerk or bailee, distinguished from larceny, § 556.
not included in larceny, § 609.
by public officer, as misconduct, § 906.
receipt of goods procured by, whether criminal, § 713.

Embezzlement — continued.
of funds of United States, by postal officers, § 1327.
by postal servants, § 1330.
from national bank, § 1340.
by national bank officers, § 1340.
Embracery, § 899.
Emission, whether necessary to prove, in prosecution for rape, § 450.
whether necessary, to constitute incest, § 1122.
whether essential, in sodomy, § 1153.
Emotional insanity, § 157.
Employees, protection of health of, §§ 30, 31.
enticing away, § 51.
protection of, § 55.
regulation of payment of, § 55.
liability of employer for acts of, see Master and servant.
Employment, embezzlement by virtue of, § 634.
Employments, special, regulation of, § 55.
regulation of by municipalities, § 73.
discriminations in, § 77.
Encumbrance, see Incumbrance.
Englishry, presentment of, in homicide, § 319.
Enlistment laws, violation of, § 1341.
Entering dwelling with criminal intent, § 576.
Enticing persons out of the state for enlistment, § 489, n.
Entries, false, as indicating embezzlement, § 640.
Entry, what sufficient to constitute burglary, § 503.
Entry and detainer, forcible, §§ 836–841.
Equality under the law, § 77.
Escape from jail, §§ 930–936.
from arrest, resistance of justifiable, § 298.
from unlawful arrest, § 141.
Estate, larceny of property of, § 546.
Estray, larceny of, § 546.
Evidence of intent, in assault, §§ 239, 259, 265, 275.
in homicide, §§ 330–333.
in rape, § 451.
in assault to rape, § 463.
in burglary, § 506.
in false pretenses, §§ 688–691.
in receiving stolen goods, § 716.
in keeping or selling intoxicating liquors, §§ 1243, 1246–1248.
of defendant as to intent, §§ 125, 259.
of age to show capacity of infant, §§ 152, 153.
of boy, in rape, § 449.
of girl under age of consent, in rape, § 444.
of minor, allowed in gaming place or billiard saloon, § 1314.
of insanity, §§ 167–179.
of acts or declarations of accomplice, § 203.

Evidence — continued.
corroboration of accomplice, §§ 203, 990, 1151, 1296.
whether required in rape, § 458.
in seduction, § 1119.
in adultery, § 1097.
in abduction, § 1108.
in sodomy, § 1155.
of purchaser in prosecution for selling intoxicating liquors, § 1241.
of guilt of principal, on trial of accessory, § 216.
of *corpus delicti*, in homicide, § 396.
in larceny, § 612.
of *res gestæ*, in homicide, §§ 411–415.
of malice, in homicide, §§ 330–333.
of provocation, for homicide, § 346.
of deliberation and premeditation, in homicide, § 359.
of threats or bad character of deceased, as bearing on right of self-defense, § 307.
of venue, in homicide, § 395.
circumstantial, see Circumstantial evidence.
presumptive, see Presumptions.
real, in prosecution for homicide, §§ 405–407.
photographs, § 406.
experiments, § 407.
improperly obtained, whether admissible, § 405, n.
of eye-witness, in homicide, § 410.
dying declarations, §§ 425–431.
how introduced, § 429.
credibility and weight of, § 431.
hearsay, to identify defendant, in larceny, § 614.
recent possession of stolen property, §§ 514, 616–620.
tampering with witness, § 937.
of outcry or complaint, in rape, §§ 455, 456.
in sodomy, § 1155.
of chastity, §§ 460, 1118.
exhibition of child to jury, in seduction, § 1117.
in bastardy, § 1129.
competency of wife as witness against husband, in prosecution for bigamy, § 1185.
for adultery, § 1099.
for abduction, § 1108.
for incest, § 1124.
of other crimes, in rape, § 461.
in larceny, § 615.
in embezzlement, § 642.
in false pretenses, § 691.
in receiving stolen goods, § 726.
of overt act, in conspiracy, § 977.
in treason, § 1358.

Evidence — continued.
in prosecution, for homicide, §§ 330–333, 346, 359, 395–431.
for rape, §§ 455–461.
outcry or complaint, §§ 455, 456.
chastity, § 460.
for burglary, §§ 506, 514, 515.
for arson, § 533.
for larceny, §§ 612-620.
for embezzlement, §§ 639, 640.
for false pretenses, §§ 688–691, 699–710.
for receiving stolen goods, §§ 716, 724–726.
for threats, § 743.
for forgery, counterfeiting or uttering, §§ 799, 805–810.
for perjury, §§ 886–892.
for resisting officer, § 929.
for escape or rescue, § 936.
for violating election laws, § 951.
for conspiracy, §§ 977, 988–990.
for carrying weapons, § 1039.
for bigamy, §§ 1082–1085.
for adultery, §§ 1096–1099.
for abduction, § 1108.
for seduction, §§ 1117–1119.
for incest, § 1124.
for bastardy, § 1129.
for illicit cohabitation, § 1132.
for keeping disorderly house, § 1145.
for abortion, § 1151.
for sodomy, § 1155.
for obscenity or indecency, § 1158.
for illegally selling or keeping intoxicating liquors, §§ 1215, 1229, 1241, 1243, 1246–1248, 1260–1262, 1279–1281.
for gaming, § 1296.
for gaming in public place, § 1304.
for keeping gaming house, § 1309.
for using mails to defraud, § 1331.
for mailing lottery advertisements, § 1334.
for smuggling, § 1351.
Evil course of life, § 25.
Exceptions, statutory, as to sale of intoxicating liquors, how pleaded, § 1252.
negativing, in prosecution under liquor laws, § 1278.
Exclusion of Chinese, §§ 1344, 1345.
Excusable homicide, §§ 296–316.
Execution, lawful, is justifiable homicide, § 297.
of instrument, not necessary to prove, in forgery, §§ 758–763.
resisting sale of goods under, § 923.
Exemplary damages for criminal wrong, § 11.
Experiments, as evidence in homicide, § 407.
evidence of, in arson, 533.

Expert, opinion of, in homicide cases, § 407.
testimony of, as to handwriting, in forgery, § 806.
Expert evidence, as to sanity, §§ 172, 173.
Explanation of recent possession of stolen goods, in larceny, §§ 617, 618.
Exposing for sale, what constitutes, § 34.
Ex post facto laws, what are, § 78.
effect of repeal of statute as to offense already committed, § 96.
statutes not construed to be, § 103.
Exposure of the person, indecent, see Indecent exposure.
of another to injury, constitutes assault and battery, § 237.
of child, causing death, constitutes manslaughter, § 351.
Express companies, license tax upon, § 44, n.
as affected by game laws, § 46.
Expulsion of Chinese, §§ 1344, 1345.
Extortion, by officer, § 914.
by threats or blackmail, §§ 728–742.
Eye-witnesses, in case of homicide, calling of, § 410.

Factories, regulation of business of, § 42.
Facts, duty to know, § 134.
misrepresentation of, when criminal, §§ 668–670.
Fairs, sale of liquor at, prohibited, § 1266.
False claims against United States, presentation of, § 1352.
False entries in books of account, constituting forgery, § 755.
in bank books, § 1339.
False imprisonment, general discussion of, §§ 485–488.
indictment for, § 492.
False instrument, see Forgery.
False oath, under naturalization laws, § 1346. And see Perjury.
False packing, when criminal, § 663.
False personation, obtaining property by, § 562.
when criminal, § 664.
as constituting forgery, § 744.
False pretenses, nature of the offense, §§ 657–665.
what pretense criminal, §§ 666–679.
fraud as constituting, §§ 680–687.
intent and knowledge as elements of the crime, §§ 688–691.
the fraud perpetrated, §§ 692–695.
venue in prosecution for, § 696.
indictment for, §§ 697–712.
must show reliance upon, § 684.
must show intent and knowledge, §§ 688–690
evidence in prosecutions for, §§ 699–710.
receipt of goods secured by, whether criminal, § 713.
attempt to obtain money by, § 223.
obtaining property by, as distinct from larceny, §§ 562, 563.
restitution of property obtained by, § 611.
False promise, as an element in seduction, §§ 1109, 1112.
False swearing, see Perjury.

False tokens, cheating by, § 661. And see False pretenses.
False weights and measures, use of, § 48.
False writing, see Forgery.
Falsehood, when constitutes false pretenses, § 666.
Falsity of oath as constituting perjury, § 867.
how averred, in perjury, §§ 880, 881.
Falsity of pretenses, how alleged, § 702.
Family, defense of, § 140.
husband deemed head of, § 148.
disturbance of, by improper conduct, § 1020.
Fear, causing, whether assault, § 233.
causing death, whether constituting homicide, § 284.
what necessary, to constitute robbery, § 470.
obtaining property by threats inducing, §§ 728–742.
Federal courts, common-law crimes not recognized by, § 14.
jurisdiction of larceny in, § 590.
as to forgery and counterfeiting, § 790.
as to offenses against election laws, § 948.
as to offenses against national banking act, § 632.
Federal election laws, violation of, § 948.
Federal government, jurisdiction of, as to forgery and counterfeiting, § 790.
Federal statute, authority under, for state officers to administer oaths, § 857.
Fee bill, forgery of, § 752.
Fees, illegal exaction of, as criminal misconduct, § 906.
extortion of, § 914.
"**Feloniously,**" whether necessary in indictment for burglary, § 510.
not necessary, in indictment for forgery, § 802.
Felony, appeal of, § 2.
what is, §§ 17, 18.
civil remedy for, not postponed, § 11.
whether misdemeanor merged in, § 22.
assault with intent to commit, § 230.
killing in resisting commission of, § 299.
person committing cannot make self-defense, § 309.
resistance of, § 312.
attempt to commit causing death, § 326.
killing in perpetration of, when murder in first degree, §§ 353–355.
murder in first degree in committing, how charged, § 361.
killing in commission of, when murder in second degree, § 365.
breaking and entry with intent to commit, deemed burglary, § 505.
how described, in indictment for burglary, § 509.
misprision of, §§ 938–940.
does not merge conspiracy to commit, § 979.
Female labor, regulations as to, §§ 55, 77.
Female relative, insult to, as provocation for homicide, § 341.
Females, indignities to, constituting assault, § 238.
assaults upon, § 255.

Females — continued.
under age of consent, abuse of, constituting rape, §§ 443, 444.
conspiracy to seduce or entice, § 959.
imputing unchastity to, deemed slander, § 1057.
abduction of, §§ 1100–1106.
using obscene language in presence of, § 1156.
not allowed to be employed in saloons, § 1255.
sales of liquors to, in saloons, § 1255.
Fences, malicious injury to, § 823.
Ferrymen, regulation of charges of, § 40.
Fictitious name, use of, in forgery, § 764.
Fighting by consent, whether lawful, § 249.
as constituting affray, § 1007.
in public place. constituting affray, § 1008.
criminal, § 1013.
as constituting disturbance of meeting, § 1026.
Financial standing, false statement as to, when criminal, § 679.
Finder of lost property, appropriation by, § 571.
Finding as to degree of murder, §§ 359, 362.
as to value of property in larceny, §§ 587, 588.
Fine, recovery of, in civil action, § 5.
enforcement of, in bastardy proceedings, § 1126.
Fire, what constitutes, in arson, § 523.
false alarms of, § 72.
Fire limits, authority of municipalities as to, § 62.
regulation of by municipalities, § 72.
Fish, protection of, § 46.
larceny of, § 538.
Fishing, regulation of, § 46.
without permission, when unlawful, § 822.
Fixtures, whether subject of larceny, § 536.
Flight, as evidence of guilt, in prosecution for homicide, § 421.
Food, unwholesome, sale of, § 32.
adulterated, sale of, § 33.
Force, what sufficient, in rape, §§ 438, 439.
Forcible entry and detainer, §§ 836–841.
Forcible trespass, §§ 811–835.
Foreign coin, counterfeiting of, § 775.
Foreign language, setting out libelous instrument in, § 1062.
Foreign ministers, violence to, § 1342.
Forfeiture of nets for illegal fishing, § 46.
of liquor license, § 1226.
of property for violation of revenue laws, § 1349.
Forgery, general nature and definition, what constitutes, §§ 743–773.
joint uttering of forged instrument, § 788.
jurisdiction and venue in prosecutions for, §§ 790, 791.
possession or uttering, as evidence of, § 791.
indictment for, §§ 792–804.
charging intent to defraud, §§ 768–773.

Forgery — continued.
evidence in prosecution for, §§ 805–810.
of postoffice order, § 1327.
Form of indictment for attempt, § 228*a*.
for assault and battery, § 252*a*.
for aggravated assault, § 261.
for assault with felonious intent, § 270.
for homicide, §§ 387, 388.
for mayhem, § 436*a*.
for rape, § 453.
for assault with intent to commit rape, § 467.
for robbery, § 483.
for false imprisonment or kidnapping, § 492.
for burglary, § 513.
for arson, § 531.
for larceny, § 610.
for embezzlement, § 656*a*.
for false pretenses, §§ 698, 711.
for receiving stolen goods, § 727.
for obtaining property by threats, § 741.
for forging and uttering, § 804.
for perjury, § 885.
for subornation of perjury, § 895.
for bribery, § 902.
for violating election laws, § 950, n.
for conspiracy, § 986.
for riot, § 999.
for breach of the peace, § 1021.
for libel, § 1069.
for lewdness, § 1132, n.
for keeping disorderly house, § 1144.
for procuring abortion, § 1150, n.
for sodomy, § 1154, n.
for desecration of cemetery, § 1168, n.
for nuisance, § 1183.
for sale of liquor on election day, § 1266, n.
Former jeopardy, see Jeopardy.
Fornication, criminal, §§ 1109, 1110, 1125–1129.
involved in illicit cohabitation, §§ 1130, 1132.
solicitation to, not criminal, § 225.
as included in adultery, § 1095.
as included in charge of seduction, § 1115.
Fowls, domestic, subject of larceny, § 540.
Fox Libel Act, § 1070.
Franking privilege, regulation of, § 1327.
Fraud, by adulteration, prevention of, § 33.
in use of false weights and measures, § 48.
statutes for suppression of, liberally construed, § 83.

Fraud — continued.
as affecting criminality in prosecution for rape, § 446.
in securing admission constitutes breaking. in burglary, § 501.
taking property by, as constituting larceny, §§ 559, 560.
upon hotel-keepers, § 663*a*.
as constituting false pretenses, § 680.
what involved in forgery, §§ 766-773.
involving fraudulent conveyance or concealment of property, §§ 842-851.
in removing or disposing of property covered by chattel mortgage, §§ 846, 847.
conspiracy to commit, § 960.
how charged, §§ 975, 982.
perpetration of, by use of mails, § 1331.
when criminal in general, §§ 657-665. And see False pretenses.
Fraudulent conveyances, when criminal, §§ 842-851.
Freedom of contract, § 55.
Freedom of the press, discussion of, with reference to libel, § 1050.
whether violated by statutes as to use of the mail, §§ 1332-1334.
Freedom of religion, § 1159.
as affected by Sunday laws, § 1319.
Fruit, larceny of, § 536.
Funds, public, see Public funds.
Furnishing intoxicating liquors, what criminal, §§ 1233-1235.
to minor or intoxicated person, § 1259.

Gambler, punishment for being, § 25.
Gambling, see Gaming.
Gambling devices, swindling by, § 662.
Gambling house, deemed disorderly house, § 1137.
keeping of, §§ 1306-1309.
Game, protection of, § 46.
Game laws, discrimination in, against non-residents, constitutional, § 77.
Games of chance, when criminal, see Gaming.
allowing to be played on premises, § 1313.
Gaming, what criminal, §§ 1282-1288.
indictment for, §§ 1289-1295.
in public place, §§ 1301-1304.
liability of husband for, on wife's premises, § 148.
criminal to visit house for purpose of, § 223.
by minors, § 1314.
Gaming devices, the keeping of, §§ 1310-1312.
swindling by, § 662.
Gaming house, keeping of, §§ 1137, 1306-1309.
Gaming implements, destruction of, § 1312.
Gaming tables, the keeping of, §§ 1310-1312.
Gas, illuminating, larceny of, §§ 542, 548.
General and special provisions in statute, construction of, §§ 89, 90.
Gestation, evidence to show period of, § 1117.

Girls, carnal abuse of, when rape, §§ 439, 442–444.
under age, consent of, as affecting assault with intent to commit rape, § 464.
connection with, not seduction, § 1115.
abduction of, §§ 1100–1106.
see, also, Females.
Giving away intoxicating liquor, when criminal, § 1235.
Good faith, see Intent.
Goods, what subject of larceny, see Larceny.
stolen, recent possession of, as evidence in larceny, §§ 616–620.
Goods and chattels, whether coin deemed, in larceny, § 543, n.
in indictment for larceny, term includes what, §§ 598–601.
Government, libel against, §§ 1048, 1069.
Grain, larceny of, § 536.
see Crops.
Grammar and punctuation in construction of statutes, § 106.
Grand jury, false swearing before, as constituting perjury, § 859.
Graves, violation of, § 1167.
Great bodily harm or injury, assault to commit, §§ 256, 280.
danger of, justifying self-defense, §§ 302, 303.
Guardian, larceny from, § 546.
embezzlement by, § 629.
abduction of girl from control of, §§ 1100–1106.
consent of, to sale of liquor to minor, § 1261.
Guilty, plea of, under indictment for murder in first degree, how punishment fixed, § 364.
Gunpowder, keeping of, as a nuisance, § 1170.

Habitation, offenses against, in general, including burglary and arson, §§ 493–533.
Habitual criminals, § 28.
Half-blood, relationship by, in incest, § 1120.
Handwriting, counterfeiting of, in forgery, § 761.
comparison of, in prosecution for forgery, § 806.
Harbor, obstruction of, as nuisance, § 1195.
Health, public, see Public health.
Heat of blood as reducing homicide to manslaughter, §§ 337–346.
Hereditary insanity, proof of, § 170.
Hides, inspection of, § 35.
High crimes, what deemed, § 19.
Highway, corporation liable for failure to construct, §§ 182, 183.
shooting in, as breach of the peace, § 1015.
whether deemed public place, § 1136.
obstruction of, as constituting nuisance, § 1169.
obstruction or non-repair of, §§ 1184–1194.
fast driving in, as constituting nuisance, § 1184.
right of public to use land adjoining, § 1189.
what deemed, § 1190.
arising by dedication or prescription, § 1190.

Highway — continued.
turning to the right upon, § 1197.
racing upon, § 1198.
deemed part of premises, in prosecution for selling liquor to be drunk on the premises, § 1247.
whether deemed part of premises, in prosecution for allowing gambling, § 1313.
Hiring as an element, in case of embezzlement by servant or agent, § 628.
History of criminal law, § 2.
Holiday, selling liquor upon, § 1264.
Home, protection of, as against invasion, § 312.
Homicide, the discussion of, in general, §§ 282-431.
in case of conspiracy, § 291.
death from wound, § 292.
time of death, § 293.
justifiable or excusable, §§ 296-316.
accidental killing, § 300.
self-defense as justification for, §§ 301-316.
division of, into murder and manslaughter, § 318.
killing of person unintended, § 323.
justifiable, though intentional, § 330.
provocation, reducing to manslaughter, §§ 337-346.
jurisdiction and venue in prosecutions for, §§ 369, 370.
evidence in prosecution for, §§ 395-431.
presumption of intent in, § 123.
degree of, as affected by insanity, § 158.
effect of intoxication in determining, § 162.
in carrying out criminal conspiracy, joint liability for, § 196.
resulting from prize-fight, liability for, § 196.
in killing officer making arrest, § 924.
resulting from abortion, § 1147.
see, also, Murder and manslaughter.
Horse, description of, in indictment for larceny, § 594.
false representations in sale of, as constituting false pretenses, § 677.
malicious injuries to, § 815.
Horse races, betting upon, criminal, § 1297.
selling pools for, § 1305.
Horse stealing, value of property immaterial in, § 589.
Hotel, not deemed dwelling, in prosecution for burglary, § 495.
Hotel-keepers, frauds upon, § 663*a*.
Hours of labor, regulation of, § 55.
of minors, regulation as to, § 59.
regulation of by municipalities, § 73.
House, breaking and entering, as constituting burglary, § 494.
what deemed, in arson, § 518.
what deemed, as to larceny from, § 577.
meaning of term with reference to keeping disorderly house, § 1139.

House of ill-fame, what constitutes, in case of abduction, § 1106*a*.
keeping of, classified with similar crimes, §§ 1109, 1110.
frequenting, § 1134.
the offense of keeping, §§ 1137–1145.
enticing females to, § 1106*a*.
Human being, who deemed, in homicide, § 294.
description of, in indictment for homicide, § 374.
Hunting and fishing, regulation of, § 46.
Hunting without permission, § 822.
Husband and wife, abandonment of wife, § 58.
acts of wife in presence of husband excused, §§ 145–148.
crimes committed by wife in separate business, § 148.
husband deemed liable for conducting illegal business by wife, § 148.
liability of husband for illegal sales of liquor by wife, §§ 194, 1238.
communication of venereal disease by one to the other, §§ 238, 249.
correction of wife by husband, § 243.
neglect of wife by husband causing death, § 286.
correction of wife by husband causing death, § 348.
husband may be guilty of rape as aider and abettor, § 449.
premises occupied by, described as those of husband in prosecution for burglary, § 495.
burning of dwelling by wife, not arson, § 521.
larceny of property by wife, § 546.
consent of wife to taking, as affecting larceny, § 558.
to taking of husband's property, § 558.
receipt of stolen goods by wife, § 714.
defamation of one by the other, not libel, § 1045.
communication of libel concerning one to the other, § 1055.
speaking slanderous words of husband in wife's presence, § 1055.
testimony of one in prosecution of the other for bigamy, § 1085.
complaint of one against the other in prosecution for adultery, § 1093.
complaint of, in prosecution for adultery, § 1093.
competency of wife as witness in prosecution for adultery, § 1099.
wife competent witness in prosecution for abduction and marriage, § 1108.
competency of wife as witness in prosecution for incest, § 1124.
persons unlawfully holding themselves out to be, punishable, §§ 1130–1132.
Hypnotism not recognized as a defense, § 136, n.

Ice, when subject of larceny, § 536.
unlawful taking of, as constituting criminal trespass, § 823.
Idem sonans, doctrine of, as to name of deceased, in indictment for homicide, § 373*a*.
as to name of owner, in prosecution for larceny, § 605.
as applicable to name in forged instrument, § 799.
Ignorance or mistake, whether a defense, §§ 114, 131–135.
Illegal voting, as a crime, §§ 943, 944.
Illegitimate kinship, relationship by, in incest, § 1120.
Illicit cohabitation, when criminal, §§ 1130–1132.

Illuminating oil, inspection of, § 35.
Imbecility as a defense for crime, § 154.
of female, in case of rape. § 447.
Immigration laws, violation of, § 1343.
Imminent danger, what sufficient to constitute assault, §§ 232, 233.
as justification for assault, § 246.
in case of self-defense. § 303.
Impeachment of dying declarations. § 431.
Importation of oleomargarine, § 34.
of intoxicating liquors, §§ 1202-1205.
regulation of, see Interstate commerce.
Impossibility as affecting the criminality of attempt, § 226.
of doing injury, does not negative assault, §§ 232-234, 257.
in case of assault with felonious intent, § 266.
of carrying out intent, immaterial in prosecution for burglary. § 506.
Imprisonment for non-payment of damages for trespass, § 5, n.
under municipal ordinances, § 64.
regulation of, as to crime already committed, whether *ex post facto*, § 78, n.
escape from, §§ 930-936.
to compel payment of allowance, in bastardy proceedings, § 1126.
unlawful, see False imprisonment.
Incest, what constitutes, §§ 1120-1122.
indictment for, § 1123.
evidence of, § 1124.
solicitation to commit, not criminal, § 220.
what constitutes attempt to commit, § 225.
marriage void on account of, in bigamy, § 1074, n.
whether may constitute also adultery, § 1092.
classified with other like crimes, § 1110.
Inciting to crime, liability for, §§ 200, 201.
Included offense, in case of attempts, § 229.
assault as, § 253.
in case of aggravated assault, § 262.
second degree of murder in first degree, § 367.
in prosecution for homicide, § 389.
in case of mayhem, § 437.
in case of rape, § 454.
in case of robbery, § 484.
in case of burglary, § 511.
in case of arson, § 532.
larceny deemed, when, § 609.
embezzlement not deemed, in larceny, § 625.
in case of riot, § 1001.
in case of affray, § 1011.
in case of adultery, § 1095.
in case of seduction, § 1115.
in prosecution under liquor laws, § 1277.
Incomplete act, when criminal, §§ 219-229.

Incumbrance, false statemen' ... L.
concealment of fact of, § 685.
Indebtedness, false statements as to, when criminal, §§ 670, 679.
Indecent assault, what constitutes, § 238.
Indecent exhibitions and prints, when criminal, § 1157.
Indecent exposure, the crime of, § 1136.
does not include indecent exhibition or prints, § 1157.
Indecent language, setting out in indictment, §§ 1158, 1166.
how alleged in indictment for libel, § 1064.
in indictment for sending such matter through the mails, § 1332.
Indecent publications, §§ 60, 1156–1158.
Indians, sale of liquor to, §§ 77, 1217, 1263.
regulation as to trading with, § 1338*a*.
in intoxicating liquors, § 1217.
Indictment, meaning of term, § 110.
following language of statute, whether sufficient, §§ 386, 436, 466, 698, 800, 950, 975, 984, 1013, 1028, 1136, 1179, 1270, 1318, 1326.
statutory regulations as to, §§ 361, 482, 591, 652, 698, 771, 800, 872, 984.
charging intent, § 124.
obscene or indecent matter need not be set out, §§ 1064, 1158, 1160, 1332.
of corporation, § 180.
of principal and accessory jointly, § 212.
of person aiding and abetting, § 213.
as principal, proof of act committed through agent, § 213.
of accessory as principal under statute, § 217.
for attempt, § 228.
for assault and battery, §§ 252, 253.
for aggravated assault, §§ 260, 261.
for assault with felonious intent, §§ 268–270.
for murder in first degree, §§ 355, 361.
for criminal homicide, §§ 371–388.
for murder, statutory regulations as to, § 386.
for mayhem, §§ 436, 436*a*.
for rape, §§ 443, 452.
for assault with intent to commit rape, § 466.
for robbery, §§ 480–483.
for false imprisonment or kidnapping, § 492.
for burglary, §§ 508–513.
for arson, §§ 527–531.
for larceny, charging the intent in, § 572.
statement of value in, § 586.
common-law form, § 591.
description of property and ownership in, §§ 592–606.
objection to, cured by verdict, § 606.
allegation of act, § 607.
allegation of intent, § 608.
does not include embezzlement, § 625.

Indictment — continued.
for embezzlement, description of money or property and ownership in, §§ 652-654.
description of act in, § 655.
joinder of counts in, § 656.
for false pretenses, §§ 696-711.
must show fraud established, § 684.
must show intent and knowledge, §§ 688-690.
setting out instrument, § 700.
allegation of intent, § 703.
for receiving stolen goods, §§ 718-727.
for obtaining property by threats, §§ 740, 741.
for forgery, charging intent to defraud, §§ 768-773.
for uttering forged instrument, naming person to be defrauded, § 771.
for having in possession counterfeiting tools, § 779.
for forgery, counterfeiting or passing, §§ 792-804.
setting out instrument in foreign language, § 795.
duplicity in, § 803.
for malicious mischief or wilful trespass, §§ 830-835.
in prosecution for forcible entry and detainer, § 840.
for fraudulent conveyance or removal of property covered by chattel mortgage, § 851.
for perjury, §§ 871-885.
joinder, duplicity, §§ 883, 884.
for subornation of perjury, § 895.
for bribery, §§ 901, 902.
for extortion, § 914.
for official misconduct or neglect, §§ 915-918.
for resisting officer, §§ 925-928.
for escape or rescue, § 934.
for violating election laws, § 950.
for conspiracy, §§ 974-986.
for riot, §§ 998-1001.
for affray, § 1009.
for breach of the peace or disorderly conduct, § 1021.
for disturbance of meeting, § 1028.
for carrying weapons, § 1038.
for slander, in imputing unchastity to female, § 1057.
for libel, §§ 1059-1069.
for bigamy, §§ 1079-1081.
for adultery, in general, §§ 1094, 1095.
found only on complaint of husband or wife, § 1093.
for abducting or enticing female, §§ 1106*a*, 1107.
for seduction, § 1114.
for incest, what sufficient, § 1123.
joinder of defendants, § 1121.
for illicit cohabitation, §§ 1131, 1132.
for lewdness, § 1135.
for keeping disorderly house, §§ 1142-1144.

Indictment — continued.
for procuring or attempting to procure abortion, §§ 1149, 1150.
for concealing birth of bastard, § 1152.
for sodomy, § 1154.
for obscenity or indecency, § 1158.
setting out obscene or profane language, §§ 1158, 1160.
for blasphemy and profanity, § 1160.
for cruelty to animals, § 1164.
for violation of right of sepulture, §§ 1167, 1168.
for nuisance, §§ 1178–1183.
for obstruction of highway, § 1193.
for obstructing navigable rivers, § 1195.
for sale of liquor without license, § 1229.
for sale of intoxicating liquors by small measure, § 1246.
for sale of intoxicating liquor to minor or intoxicated person, §§ 1260–1262.
for sale of liquor on election day, § 1266.
for sale of liquor near church or school-house, § 1266.
under liquor laws, §§ 1270–1275.
for illegal gaming, §§ 1289–1295.
for betting, § 1299.
for gaming in public place, § 1304.
for keeping gaming house, § 1309.
for keeping gaming devices or tables, § 1311.
for allowing gaming on premises, § 1313.
for violation of statutes as to lotteries, § 1318.
for violation of Sunday laws, § 1326.
for using mails to defraud, § 1331.
for sending obscene matter through the mails, § 1332.
for mailing lottery advertisements, § 1334.
for embezzlement from national banks, § 1340.
forms of, see Forms of indictment.
Infamous crimes, what are, § 20.
Infancy as a defense, §§ 149–153.
Information, false swearing in, as constituting perjury, § 859.
Informer, proceedings by, § 7.
Injunctions, to prevent combinations in restraint of commerce, § 1337.
Injuries to property, malicious, §§ 811–835.
Injury, what sufficient to constitute assault and battery, §§ 235–238.
Innkeepers, regulation of, § 38.
frauds upon, § 663*a*.
may sell liquor on Sunday, § 1321, n.
Innuendo, in libel, § 1060.
Inquest, prevention of, criminal, §§ 920, 1165.
Insane delusion as constituting mistake of fact, §§ 133, 158.
Insanity as a defense, general doctrine, §§ 154–179.
degrees of, §§ 156–158.
caused by intoxication, § 159.
defense of, how interposed and proved, §§ 164–179.

Insanity — continued.
evidence of, §§ 167–179.
proof of as bearing on malice in homicide, § 331.
as affecting provocation in homicide, § 344.
as bearing on degree of murder, § 360.
of female in case of rape, § 447.
as a defense in forgery, § 767.
Inspection laws, validity of, § 35.
Instructions as to insanity, §§ 164, 165.
as to lower degree or included offense in homicide, §§ 390, 391.
as to self-defense, § 315.
as to malice aforethought, § 334.
as to circumstantial evidence, § 409.
as to weight of dying declarations, § 431.
Instruments, written, see Written instruments.
Insulting language, use of, criminal, §§ 1017, 1020.
Insults to female relative as constituting provocation for homicide, § 341.
Insurance, regulation of business of, § 41.
rates of, discrimination in, prohibited, § 41.
Insurance companies, burning property with intent to defraud, § 522.
destroying vessels with intent to defraud, § 1347.
Intent of statute to be preserved, in construction, §§ 84, 86, 105.
criminal, general discussion of, §§ 111–128.
distinguished from motive, § 120.
specific, when essential, § 122.
to defraud, how alleged, § 122, n.
presumed, § 123.
allegation and proof of, § 124.
to do different act from that done, § 126.
alone, not punishable, § 127.
in statutory offenses, § 128.
lack of, supplied by proof of negligence, §§ 129, 130.
ignorance or mistake as showing want of, §§ 131–135.
necessity or compulsion as showing want of, §§ 136–144.
specific, intoxication as bearing upon, § 161.
on part of corporation, § 184.
how far must be acted upon to be criminal, § 219.
what involved in attempt, § 222.
without act, not criminal, § 223.
not alone sufficient to constitute assault, § 232.
in case of assault, § 239.
in case of aggravated assault, §§ 254, 259.
felonious, assaults with, §§ 263–272.
specific, in case of assault, § 265.
in case of assault to commit felony, how charged, § 269.
specific, in case of assault with felonious intent, § 269.
involved in assault to kill or murder, §§ 274–276.
involved in assault to do great bodily injury, § 280.
involved in assault to rob, § 281.

Intent — continued.
to kill, as constituting malice aforethought, § 323.
not inconsistent with manslaughter, § 336.
whether essential to murder in first degree, §§ 354, 355.
necessary to render the killing wilful and premeditated, §§ 357, 358.
when renders murder of first degree, § 357.
how charged, in indictment for murder, § 383.
allegation of, in indictment for homicide, § 382.
in homicide, evidence of, § 418.
in prosecution for mayhem, § 435.
in case of rape, § 451.
involved in assault with intent to commit rape, §§ 462, 463.
what essential, in case of robbery, § 470.
necessary, to constitute false imprisonment or kidnapping, § 491.
in burglary, what sufficient, §§ 505-507.
how described, in indictment for burglary, § 509.
what necessary, in arson, § 526.
allegation of, in case of arson, § 530.
to appropriate as an element in larceny, §§ 562-573.
in larceny, how charged, §§ 572, 608.
evidence of, § 615.
what necessary in embezzlement, § 641.
in case of embezzlement by public officer, § 649.
in false pretenses, what essential, §§ 688-691.
how charged, § 703.
and knowledge, as elements in receipt of stolen goods, §§ 716, 717.
how alleged, in indictment for receiving stolen goods, § 721.
evidence of, in prosecution for receiving stolen goods, § 726.
to defraud, what necessary, in forgery, §§ 766-768.
what necessary, in counterfeiting, § 776.
in possession of counterfeiting tools, § 778.
involved in uttering counterfeit money, §§ 788, 789.
in forgery, how alleged, § 802.
involved in malicious trespass or mischief, §§ 826-829.
in malicious mischief or trespass, how alleged, § 833.
involved in fraudulent conveyance or removal of property covered by chattel mortgage, § 849.
what sufficient, in perjury, §§ 869, 870.
how averred, in prosecution for perjury, § 881.
in case of official misconduct, § 913.
in extortion, § 914.
in resistance of officer, §§ 924, 927.
in escape or rescue, § 933.
in violation of election laws, §§ 949, 950.
what essential, in crime of unlawful assembly, § 1004.
as an element in crime of disturbing meeting, § 1027.
in crime of carrying weapons, § 1032.
in libel, what essential, § 1053.
allegation of, § 1067.

Intent — continued.
in bigamy, § 1076.
allegation of, § 1081.
what essential in case of adultery, §§ 1091, 1092.
mutuality of, whether essential in adultery, incest and illicit cohabitation, §§ 1092, 1121, 1131.
in incest, what necessary, §§ 1121, 1123.
mutuality of, § 1121.
in case of illicit cohabitation, § 1131.
in keeping house of ill-fame, § 1138.
in attempt to procure abortion, § 1148.
as an element in obscenity and indecency, § 1158.
in offense of cruelty to animals, § 1163.
in violation of grave, § 1167.
as an element in the crime of nuisance, § 1176.
in obstruction of highway, § 1189.
in obstruction of railroad, § 1196.
in sale of intoxicating liquor, § 1222.
as to illegal sale of intoxicating liquors, § 1243.
as to intoxicating liquors being drunk on the premises, § 1247.
in sale of intoxicating liquor, § 1251.
in case of sale of intoxicating liquors to prohibited persons, § 1257.
with which intoxicating liquors are kept, § 1267.
essential, in treason, § 1357.
involved in piracy, § 1359.
Interference with elections, what criminal, § 946.
Internal revenue tax, see Revenue tax.
International law, violation of, when criminal, §§ 1341, 1342.
as affecting treason, § 1354.
Interpretation of statute, see Construction.
Interpreter on trial of deaf and dumb person, § 155.
Interstate commerce, regulations as to, by congress, §§ 1336–1338*a*.
how far sale of oleomargarine protected under, § 34.
Sunday laws as applicable to, § 40.
mercantile agencies not instruments of, § 42.
validity under, of requirements as to license, § 44.
validity of game laws affecting, § 46.
regulations as to colored passengers, § 54.
constitutional protection of, § 76.
regulations under, as to transportation of live-stock, § 1161.
liquor laws as affecting, §§ 1202–1205.
regulation of operation of freight trains on Sunday as affecting, § 1323.
Intoxicated persons, sale of liquor to, §§ 1255, 1261.
punishment of, § 1018. And see Intoxication.
Intoxicating liquors, general relations as to sale of, constitutionality and construction, §§ 29, 76, 1199–1216.
sale of in original package, §§ 76, 1204, 1205.
federal, state and city regulation of sale of, § 1217.
what deemed, §§ 1218–1222.

Intoxicating liquors — continued.
license of sale of, local option, §§ 1223-1232
regulation of sale of, by license or local option, §§ 1223-1232.
illegal selling or keeping for sale, §§ 1233-1251.
liability for sale of, by servant, agent, partuer or wife, §§ 1237-1239.
sale of, in clubs, § 1240.
purchasers of, not punishable, § 1241.
transportation of, § 1242.
common seller of, § 1244.
retailing or wholesaling, § 1245.
sale of, by small measure, § 1246.
sale of, to be drunk on the premises, § 1247.
nuisance committed in the illegal selling or keeping for sale, §§ 1248, 1249.
regulation of the method and place of sale, § 1250.
exceptions to regulations as to sale of, § 1252.
sales of, by physicians and druggists, § 1253.
sales of, by producers or manufacturers, § 1254.
sales of, to prohibited persons or in prohibited localities, §§ 1255-1266.
sale of, to minors, §§ 1256-1261.
to drunkards or intoxicated persons, §§ 1256, 1262.
to Indians, § 1263.
on Sundays or holidays, § 1264.
on election day, § 1265.
near churches or schools, § 1266.
seizure of, § 1267.
second offense of illegal sale or keeping, § 1268.
venue in prosecution for illegal selling or keeping, § 1269.
indictment for violations of statutes as to, §§ 1270-1275.
evidence of illegal sale, variance, election, § 1276.
illegal sale, double punishment, included offense, § 1277.
description of, in indictment under liquor laws, § 1273.
prosecution for illegal sale, negativing exceptions, § 1278.
evidence in prosecution for illegal sale or keeping, §§ 1279-1281.
constitutionality of statute regulating sale of, §§ 29, 76.
drinking, of not criminal, § 29.
regulation of sale of by federal government, § 29.
regulation of sale of under police power, § 29.
adulterated, sale of, § 33.
regulation of sale of within particular localities, § 39.
regulation of sale of to minors, § 59.
regulation of sale of by municipalities, §§ 63, 68.
municipal power to regulate sale of does not include power to prohibit, § 69.
transportation of protected, § 76.
regulation of sale of in certain localities, § 77.
criminal intent not essential in prosecution for sale of, § 128.
sale to minor, mistake as to age, § 128.
adulterated, sale of, mistake as defense, § 128, n.

Intoxicating liquors — continued.
liability of husband for sale of on wife's premises, § 148.
illegal sale of by corporation, § 183.
liability of principal for sale by servant, § 189.
liability of husband for illegal sale by wife, § 194.
person to whom sold not an accomplice, § 199.
illegal sale, purchaser not criminal, § 220.
attempt to introduce into Alaska, § 225.
house for sale of, deemed disorderly house, § 1137.
federal license for sale of, §§ 29, 1217, 1245, 1250, 1280, 1350.
Intoxication as a defense, §§ 159–163.
as bearing upon a specific intent, § 161.
voluntary or involuntary, § 163.
not punishable where not intentional, § 163, n.
proof of, as bearing on malice in homicide, § 331.
as affecting provocation in homicide, § 344.
as bearing on degree of murder, § 360.
as a defense in larceny, § 572.
in forgery, § 767.
in perjury, § 869.
punishment of, § 1018.
Invalidity of statutes, effect of, § 104.
when partial, § 1100.
of forged instrument, effect of, §§ 756–760.
Itinerant merchants, licensing, § 44.
Itinerant vendors, regulation of, § 36.

Jail, burning of, to escape, whether arson, § 526.
Jail breach, as a crime, §§ 930–936.
Jeopardy, conviction of lower degree in homicide as constituting, § 390.
previous, in prosecution under liquor laws, § 1277.
in prosecution for being common thief, § 580.
as between burglary and larceny, § 511.
Joinder of principal and accessory, § 212.
of offenses in indictment for burglary, § 511.
what permitted, in indictment for larceny, § 609.
of counts, in indictment for embezzlement, § 656.
of offenses, in indictment for receiving stolen goods, § 722.
for malicious mischief or trespass, § 835.
of defendants, in prosecution for perjury, § 884.
of offense, in conspiracy, § 980.
of defendants, in prosecution for conspiracy, § 981.
in prosecution for adultery, § 1095.
in prosecution for incest, § 1121.
in prosecution for illicit cohabitation, § 1131.
not necessary, in prosecution for lewdness, § 1135.
of different acts, in indictment for nuisance, § 1180.
of offenses, in prosecution under liquor law, § 1275.
of defendants or offenses, in prosecution for gaming, §§ 1294, 1295.

Joint liability of participants in crime, §§ 194–203.
Joint offense, conviction of one, in prosecution for, §§ 981, 996, 1010.
Judgment, repeal of statute after, § 99.
Judicial functions, misconduct in discharge of, § 907.
Judicial notice, as to whether liquor intoxicating, § 1218.
of adoption of local-option liquor law, § 1232.
Judicial proceedings, perjury in, § 859.
publication in, privileged, § 1052.
Jurisdiction in case of accessories, §§ 207, 211.
in cases of conspiracy, § 211.
of assault, § 251.
in prosecutions for homicide, § 369.
in larceny by the taking of goods from one county or state to another, § 552.
in prosecutions for larceny, § 590.
for receiving stolen goods, § 720.
for forgery, counterfeiting or passing, § 790.
in perjury, § 871.
of court before which proceeding is pending in which perjury is committed, §§ 858, 876.
to issue warrant, as affecting the crime of resisting, § 922.
in prosecutions for conspiracy, § 972.
for bigamy, § 1077.
in bastardy proceedings, § 1127.
of the crime of advising the procuring of abortion, § 1150.
of federal courts, as to combinations in restraint of commerce, § 1337.
in prosecutions for violation of immigration laws, § 1343.
of piracy, § 1359.
Jurisprudence, place of criminal law in, § 3.
Jurors, false swearing by, as constituting perjury, § 859.
bribery of, § 899.
Jury, finding by, as to degree of murder, § 362.
finding of, as to value of property, in larceny, §§ 587, 588.
judges of the law, in libel, § 1070.
Jury trial as to prisoner's sanity, § 166.
in proceedings to abate nuisance, in sale of intoxicating liquors, § 1208.
Justice, obstruction of, in general, § 920.
by resisting officer, §§ 921–929.
by breaking jail, escape, etc., §§ 930, 936.
by tampering with witnesses, § 937.
Justice of the peace administering oath under federal statute, § 857.
Justifiable homicide, what constitutes, §§ 296–316.
self-defense as constituting, §§ 301–316.
Justification for assault, §§ 241–247.
for assault with felonious intent, § 267.
for assault with intent to kill, § 277.
in homicide, burden of proof as to, § 333.
in libel, § 1051.
for procuring abortion, § 1149.

Keeper of house of ill-fame, who deemed, §§ 1139–1142.
of gaming house, who deemed, § 1308.
of gaming place, allowing minor therein, § 1314.
Keeping gaming devices or tables, §§ 1310–1312.
Keeping intoxicating liquors for sale, when criminal, §§ 1233–1251. And see Intoxicating liquors.
Kidnapping, general discussion of, §§ 485, 489–491.
indictment for, § 492.
abduction as constituting, § 1102, n.
Killing, what constitutes, §§ 283–295.
accidental, § 300.
presumption of malice from, § 333.
intentional, when manslaughter, § 336.
dying declarations as to, in prosecution for homicide, § 427.
King's peace, violation of, § 295.
Kinship, degrees of, in incest, § 1120.
Kleptomania as a defense in larceny, § 572.
Knowledge as indicating intent, § 124.
want of, whether a defense under statute, § 128.
of law, presumption of, §§ 132–135.
negatived by proof of intoxication, § 161.
what material in false pretenses, §§ 688–691.
as element in receiving stolen goods, §§ 716, 717.
how alleged, in indictment for receiving stolen goods, § 721.
evidence of, in prosecution for receiving stolen goods, § 726.
essential in passing counterfeit money, § 789.
how proved, in prosecution for passing counterfeit money, § 808.
how averred, in prosecution for perjury, § 881.
essential in subornation of perjury, § 893.
of law, presumed in case of violation of election laws, §§ 944, 949.
involved in bigamy, § 1076.
as to age of girl in case of abduction, § 1105.
of relationship, essential, in incest, §§ 1121, 1123.
of character of disorderly house, must be shown to convict for keeping, §§ 1140, 1142.
as an element in the crime of nuisance, § 1176.
as to character of intoxicating liquor, § 1222.
of character of person to whom intoxicating liquors are sold, § 1257.
of age of minor allowed in gaming places, § 1314.
not essential, in crime of obstructing mails, § 1328.

Label, to prevent adulteration, § 33.
Labor organizations, validity of contracts prohibiting employees from belonging to, § 55.
Laborer, Chinese, exclusion of, § 1345.
Laborers, federal statutes as to importation of, § 1343.
Lager beer, whether deemed intoxicating liquor, §§ 1218–1222.
Land laws, violation of, § 1353.

Landlord, guilty of arson as to premises in possession of tenant, § 521.
liability of, for house of ill-fame kept by tenant, §§ 1141, 1142.
lease of premises by, for purpose constituting nuisance, § 1174.
liability of, for gaming allowed on premises, § 1313.
Landmarks, removal of, § 45.
Language, improper, use of as criminal, § 26.
Larceny, definition of, §§ 534, 535.
degrees of, §§ 581–589, 609.
grand, §§ 581–589.
compound, §§ 574–580.
petit, §§ 581–589.
jurisdiction and venue in case of, § 590.
procedure in, § 590.
indictment for, §§ 591–610.
indictment, charging intent, § 572.
does not include embezzlement, § 625.
from the person as an included offense, § 575.
involved in robbery, §§ 468, 471–475, 484.
included in robbery, §§ 482, 484.
connivance at, § 118.
intent in, as affected by intoxication, § 161.
petit, no accessories in, § 210.
attempt to commit, § 225.
when complete, § 223.
effect of impossibility, § 226.
presumed to be intended on proof of breaking and entering dwelling, § 506.
how charged, in indictment for burglary, §§ 509, 511.
what property subject of, §§ 536–543.
ownership of property stolen, §§ 544–547.
intent to charge another with property, § 547.
what acts sufficient to constitute taking and carrying away, §§ 548–563.
jurisdiction in case of goods taken from one county or state to another, §§ 552, 553.
intent in, §§ 564–573.
petit, accessory not recognized in, § 573.
aggravation, § 574.
from the person, § 575.
included in stealing from a person or dwelling-house, §§ 575, 576.
from the dwelling-house, § 576.
from a house or store, §§ 577, 578.
in night-time, § 579.
included in larceny from a building, etc., § 578.
punishment for, depending on value, §§ 581–589.
indictments, statement of value in, § 586.
restitution in, § 611.
corpus delicti, § 612.
identification of property, § 613.
identification of thief, § 614.

Larceny — continued.
evidence of other crimes, § 615.
recent possession of stolen goods as evidence, §§ 616-620.
embezzlement distinguished from, §§ 621, 625.
distinguished from false pretenses, § 659.
whether receiver of stolen goods accessory to, § 713.
description of, in indictment for receiving stolen goods, § 719.
charge of, joined with receiving stolen goods, § 722.
proof of, in prosecution for receiving stolen goods, § 724.
indictment charging in connection with receiving stolen goods, § 727.
distinguished from malicious trespass, § 813.
in postoffice building, § 1329.
by postal servants, § 1330.
receiving goods obtained by, see Receiving stolen goods.
Lard, imitation, sale of, § 34.
Lascivious cohabitation, when criminal, §§ 1130-1132.
Lascivious lewdness, what constitutes, § 1135.
Laundries, regulation of, § 39.
Law, practice of, regulation of, § 37.
ignorance or mistake of, as a defense, § 132.
knowledge of, presumed, § 132.
Law of nations, counterfeiting as an offense against, § 790.
violation of, §§ 1341, 1342.
Law or fact, whether intoxicating character of liquor deemed question of, § 1218.
"Lawfully," meaning of term, § 110.
Lease of premises for purpose constituting nuisance, § 1174.
Leasing house for improper purposes, §§ 1140-1142.
Legal advice as a defense, § 114.
as excuse for violating election laws, § 914.
Legal efficacy of instrument forged, §§ 756-760.
Legal process, resistance to, § 142.
Legislative power, delegation of to municipalities, § 62.
Legislative proceedings, publication of, privileged, § 1052.
Lessor, not liable for criminal acts of lessee on the premises, § 192.
Letter, false pretenses accomplished by means of, § 696.
larceny or embezzlement of, §§ 542, 1330.
containing threats, the obtaining of property by, criminal, § 729.
obscene, crime of sending, § 1332.
Letter and spirit of statute in construction, § 85.
Levying war, what sufficient, to constitute treason, § 1357.
Lewd pictures or prints, §§ 1157, 1158.
Lewdness, classified with sexual crimes, §§ 1109, 1110.
when cohabitation deemed criminal, §§ 1130-1132.
what constitutes, §§ 1135, 1138.
keeping house for purpose of, criminal, § 1138.
Libel, the crime of, §§ 1040-1049.
intent in, §§ 123, 1053.
good faith as defense, §§ 1050-1054.

Libel — continued.
truth as a defense, § 1051.
mitigation, § 1054.
publication of, § 1055.
by agent or servant, § 1056.
venue in, § 1058.
indictment for, §§ 1059–1069.
functions of court and jury in prosecution for, § 1070.
corporation punishable for, § 183.
liability of principal for sale by agent, § 188.
License for practicing profession, § 36.
required under police power, § 38.
for conducting insurance business, § 41.
by municipalities, § 69.
to sell liquors, not a contract, § 75, n.
for sale of intoxicating liquors, how procured, effect of, §§ 1223–1232.
for sale of intoxicating liquors by physicians and druggists, § 1253.
possession of, as evidence, in prosecution under liquor laws, § 1280.
federal, for sale of intoxicating liquors, §§ 29, 1217, 1245, 1250, 1280, 1350.
for sale of intoxicating liquors, see Intoxicating liquors.
License tax for vehicles, § 39.
on peddlers, § 44.
Lien, selling or removing property subject to, § 848.
Limitation of prosecution, whether regulation of is *ex post facto,* § 78.
for embezzlement, § 649.
for conspiracy, § 973.
for bigamy, § 1078.
Liquor, regulations as to sale, etc., see Intoxicating liquors.
Live-stock, transportation of, regulated, §§ 1161, 1338.
Loaded weapon, offense of carrying, § 1033.
Local laws, as to sale of intoxicating liquors, § 1210.
Local option, as a means of regulating sale of intoxicating liquors, §§ 1199, 1210, 1223.
as to sale of intoxicating liquors, § 1232.
Locus pœnitentiæ, see Abandonment.
Lord Campbell's Act, as to libel, § 1051.
Lost property, larceny of, § 545.
unlawful keeping, in larceny, § 571.
Lotteries, what deemed, §§ 1315-1317.
sending advertisements of, through mails, § 1315.
statutory regulation of, § 1316.
constitutionality of statutes regulating, §§ 75, 1317.
indictment for keeping, § 1318.
Lottery advertisements, sending through mails, § 1334.
Lottery scheme, what deemed, § 1334.
Lottery tickets, regulation of sale of, by municipalities, § 66.
regulation of sale of, § 1316.
Lucri causa in larceny, § 568.
Lying in wait, killing by, murder in first degree, § 354.

Machinery, dangerous, death caused by, § 351.
Mail, sending dunning letters by, as constituting libel, § 1055.
transmission of libel by, § 1055.
Mail matter, larceny of, § 542.
Mails, sending offer of bribery through, § 900.
sending medicine through, to procure abortion, § 1148.
publication of libel by means of, § 1058.
use of, for transmitting lottery advertisements, § 1315.
regulation of crimes relating to, §§ 1327–1335.
Maiming, general discussion of, §§ 432–437.
Maiming of animals punishable, § 1161.
Mala in se, acts which are, § 23.
Mala prohibita, acts which are, § 23.
Malice, what constitutes, § 121.
intoxication as bearing upon, § 161.
as constituting aggravation of assault, § 255.
necessary in assault with felonious intent, § 265.
in homicide, meaning of, § 321.
express or implied, § 322.
how proved, in homicide, § 330.
in homicide, evidence of, § 418.
what sufficient, in malicious mischief, §§ 826–829.
inferred, in libel, § 1053.
involved in obstruction of railroad, § 1196.
Malice aforethought, what constitutes, § 319.
meaning of term, §§ 320, 321, 329.
express or implied, § 322.
attempt to commit felony constitutes, § 326.
evidence of, § 330.
presumption as to, §§ 332, 333.
instructions as to, § 334.
whether attempt to perpetrate a felony deemed, § 355.
how charged, in indictment for murder, § 382.
whether necessary to constitute assault with intent to kill, § 279.
Malicious mischief, when criminal, §§ 811–835.
indictment for, §§ 830–835.
as distinguished from cruelty to animals, § 1161.
"Maliciously," meaning of term, § 110.
Malt liquors, see Intoxicating liquors.
Manslaughter, what constitutes, §§ 335–351.
voluntary or involuntary, §§ 335, 368.
included in murder, § 335.
how distinguished from murder, §§ 318, 335.
statutory degrees of, §§ 352, 368.
evidence in prosecution for, §§ 395–431.
indictment for, in general, §§ 371–388.
forms of indictment for, § 388.
what offenses included in indictment for, § 389.
in careless handling of deadly weapon, § 130.

Manslaughter — continued.
in causing death by attempt to procure abortion, § 1147.
in making arrest, § 298.
accidental killing, § 300.
aider and abettor in, § 200.
no accessory in, § 208.
assault with intent to commit, § 278.
as an included offense, § 271.
negligence as amounting to, § 286.
effect of conviction for lower degree of, § 390.
Manufactories, regulation of, § 30.
Manufacture of intoxicating liquors, regulation of, see Intoxicating liquors.
Manufacturers of intoxicating liquors, sale by, § 1254.
Manufacturing, annoyance caused by, whether nuisance, § 1171.
contamination of water by, § 1175.
Maritime jurisdiction, exercise of, as to crimes, § 1347.
Markets, regulation of, by municipalities, § 71.
Marks, falsification of, as constituting false pretenses, § 661. And see Brands.
Marriage, regulation of, § 57.
forgery of certificate, to secure license, § 750, n.
forgery of certificate of, § 756.
false swearing in license to procure, § 860.
conspiracy to procure, § 959.
when constitutes bigamy, §§ 1073–1076.
validity of, how shown in prosecution for bigamy, §§ 1074–1076, 1082–1085.
allegation of, in bigamy, § 1079.
proof of, in bigamy, § 1082.
validity of, in prosecution for adultery, § 1088.
proof of, in prosecution for adultery, § 1096.
abducting for purpose of, §§ 1106*a*, 1111.
promise of, as element in seduction, § 1112.
as a bar to prosecution for seduction, § 1116.
what constitutes, such as to disprove seduction, § 1117.
incestuous, §§ 1120, 1122.
proof of, in prosecution for incest, § 1124.
illegal, whether cohabitation under, criminal, § 1131.
between whites and blacks, when illegal, § 1131.
should be negatived in prosecution for lewdness, § 1135.
Married women, criminal liability of, §§ 145–148. And see Husband and wife.
Master and servant, liability of master for acts of servant, in libel, § 1056.
liability of master for nuisance maintained by servant, § 1174.
for illegal sale by servant of intoxicating liquor, § 1237.
liability of servant for sale of intoxicating liquors, § 1239.
see, also, Servant.
Materiality of false oath, essential to perjury, §§ 861, 866.
how alleged, §§ 878, 879.
how proved, § 889.

"May," in construction of statutes, § 109.
Mayhem, general discussion of, §§ 432-437.
attempt to commit, criminal, § 221, n.
murder in committing, first degree, § 355.
Mechanical purposes, sale of intoxicating liquors for, § 1253.
Medical preparations containing alcohol, whether deemed intoxicating liquors, § 1219.
Medicine, regulation of practice of, § 36.
administration of, to procure abortion, § 1148.
sale of intoxicating liquors as, § 1253.
deemed retailing, § 1245.
what constitutes, under exceptions as to sales on Sunday, § 1321, n.
Meeting, public, what deemed, § 1023.
violently breaking into, as constituting riot, § 993.
disturbance of, see Disturbance of meeting.
Menaces, obtaining property by, §§ 728-742.
Mens rea as an essential element of crime, § 112.
Mental weakness as a defense for crime, § 156.
Mercantile agencies, regulation of, § 42.
Merger of offense in conspiracy, § 979.
of misdemeanor into felony, § 22.
Mile posts, duty to erect and maintain, § 1185.
Military command, as justifying homicide, § 297*a*.
Military power, arrest under, § 487.
Milk, adulterated, sale of, § 33.
regulation of sale of by municipalities, § 66.
regulation as to reports by those who purchase for manufacturing, etc., § 42.
Mill-dam, as creating a nuisance, § 1170.
Mineral lands, cutting or removing timber from, § 1353.
Minister, foreign, violence to, § 1342.
Minor, employment of, § 59.
enticing from employment, § 51.
municipal regulations for protection of, § 66.
clothing of, charged as property of parent, § 546.
criminal liability of, §§ 149-153.
may be guilty of larceny as bailee, § 554.
validity of marriage of, in bigamy, § 1074.
sale of liquor to, §§ 1255-1261.
permitting drinking or gaming by, or allowing in gaming place, §§ 59, 1314.
evidence of age of, §§ 153, 1314.
mistake as to age of, § 128.
Misappropriation of property in larceny, §§ 549, 554-556.
whether larceny, §§ 554-556.
when constitutes embezzlement, § 639.
Miscarriage, see Abortion.
Miscegenation, punishment for, §§ 54, 57, 1131, n.
statutes as to, not invalid for want of uniformity, § 77.

Misconduct of officer, what criminal, §§ 904–919.
Misdemeanor, included in crime, § 4, n.
civil remedy for, not postponed, § 11.
what is, §§ 17–21.
whether merged in felony, § 22.
as included crime in felony, § 22.
whether statutes for punishment strictly construed, § 83.
no accessories in, § 210.
jurisdiction of participants in, § 211.
attempts to commit felony deemed, § 221.
taking life in resisting, not justified, § 299.
death caused in commission of, deemed manslaughter, § 347.
Misfeasance, liability of corporation for, § 183.
Misfeasance in office, what criminal, §§ 904–919.
Misprision of felony, whether criminal, §§ 938–940.
Misrepresentation of fact, when criminal, §§ 668–670.
Mistake, in general, as a defense, §§ 131–135.
whether a defense under statute, § 128.
as to age of girl abducted or maltreated, §§ 134, 1105.
in rape, § 451.
due to insanity, effect of, § 158.
in case of homicide as to person to be killed, § 196.
in case of assault, § 239.
obtaining property by, with subsequent appropriation, whether larceny, § 561.
as a defense in larceny, § 565.
in indictment for larceny, as to name of owner, § 605.
as to title, in prosecution for malicious trespass, § 826.
as to continuance in life of consort, in case of adultery, § 1091.
as to validity of marriage as affecting criminality of cohabitation thereunder, § 1131.
Mistake of fact as a defense, § 133.
in bigamy, § 1076.
for violating election laws, §§ 944, 949.
Mistake of law as a defense, § 132.
no defense for violating election laws, § 949.
Mitigation in case of assault, § 248.
in case of assault with felonious intent, § 267.
of guilt, in homicide, burden of proof as to, § 333.
in libel, §§ 1051–1054.
Mixed liquors, sale of, § 1219.
Mock auction as constituting a cheat, § 661.
Money, depreciation in value of, § 534.
larceny of, § 543.
description of, in indictment for larceny, §§ 596–598.
evidence of identity of, in prosecution for larceny, § 599.
embezzlement of, § 621.
illegally received, embezzlement of, § 635.
conversion of, as constituting embezzlement, § 639.

Money — continued.
description of, in embezzlement, § 652.
receipt of, when stolen, § 715.
procuring of, by forgery, § 752.
obtaining by false pretenses, see False pretenses.
Money order, forgery of, § 1327.
Monomania as a defense, § 158.
Monopolies, statutes against, § 963.
Moral insanity, whether a defense, § 157.
Mortgage, whether subject of larceny, § 543.
forgery of, § 751.
fraudulent, when criminal, § 844.
chattel, removal of property covered by, §§ 846, 847.
Motive, distinguished from intent, § 120.
evidence of, in prosecution for homicide, § 416.
in sending obscene matter through mails, § 1332.
Municipal corporations, criminal liability of, § 183.
ownership by, how charged, in indictment for larceny, § 604.
embezzlement by officers of, §§ 632, 645–649.
liability of, for failure to keep highway in repair, § 1185.
Municipal regulations, under police power, § 62. And see Ordinances.
Municipalities, power of to pass ordinances, §§ 62, 63.
general police power of, §§ 62–73.
suppression of nuisances by, § 66.
power of to regulate, does not include power to prohibit, § 69.
powers of not to be delegated to mayor, § 77.
authority of to punish keeping houses of ill-fame, § 1138.
power of to declare and abate nuisances, § 1169.
regulation by, of obnoxious manufactories, § 1172.
removal of nuisance by, § 1172.
regulations by, as to sale of liquors, §§ 1216, 1217.
Murder, definition of, § 320, n.
discussion of in full, §§ 317–334.
statutory degrees of, §§ 352, 353.
first degree, §§ 353–364.
second degree, §§ 365–367.
first degree includes second degree, § 367.
distinguished from manslaughter, §§ 318, 319.
distinguished from manslaughter as to indictment, § 371.
manslaughter included in, § 335.
indictment for, in general, §§ 371–388.
forms of indictment for, § 388.
first degree, indictment for, §§ 355, 361.
what offenses included in indictment for, § 389.
in a duel, § 324.
coverture no defense in prosecution for, § 146.
evidence of intoxication, § 162.
solicitation to commit, § 220, n.
attempt to commit, what constitutes, § 223.

Murder — continued.
assault to commit, in general, §§ 273–279.
deemed felony, § 230.
justification or mitigation, § 267.
felonies included in, § 271.
in making arrest, § 298.
by poison or lying in wait, § 354.
finding as to degree by jury, § 362.
fixing punishment for first degree, §§ 363, 364.
effect of conviction of lower degree, or included offense, § 390.
evidence in prosecution for, §§ 395–431.
petit treason as constituting, § 1354.
Mutilation, see Maiming.

Name of person killed, how alleged, in indictment for homicide, § 373*a*.
of owner, mistake as to, in indictment for larceny, § 605.
Naphtha, regulation of sale of, § 29.
illegal sale of, want of knowledge, § 128, n.
keeping of, as a nuisance, § 1170.
Narrative of past transactions as evidence in prosecution for homicide, § 414.
National bank notes, description of, in indictment for larceny, § 596.
National Banking Act, prosecutions for forgery under, § 790.
offenses under, §§ 1339, 1340.
Naturalization, false swearing in proceedings for, § 859.
Naturalization laws, violation of, § 1346.
Navigable rivers, see Rivers.
Navigation laws, violation of, § 1347.
Necessity as a defense, §§ 136–144.
justifying killing in self-defense, §§ 302–316.
as a defense in larceny, § 572.
abortion procured under, § 1149.
works of, exempt from Sunday laws, § 1321.
duress as an excuse for treasonable acts, § 1357.
Neglect of duty, official, § 909.
Negligence, criminal, §§ 129, 130.
as amounting to assault, § 240.
of physician amounting to assault, § 237.
causing death, § 325.
when amounting to homicide, §§ 286–288.
death from, deemed manslaughter, §§ 349–351.
allegation of, in indictment for homicide, § 379.
prima facie evidence of, in case of killing stock, § 77.
Neutrality, violations of, §§ 1341, 1342.
Newspapers, regulation of, as to indecent publications, § 60.
sale of, on Sunday, § 1321, n.
containing obscene or defamatory matter or lottery advertisements, not to be sent through mails, §§ 1332–1334.
Night-walking, as a crime, §§ 25, 1133.

Night-time, in burglary, § 504.
in arson, § 525.
as aggravation in larceny, § 579.
Noise, as constituting breach of the peace, § 1016.
Non-residents, privileges denied to, § 77.
Notes, whether subject of larceny, § 543.
description of, in indictment for larceny, § 595.
whether deemed property, in false pretenses, § 693.
receipt of, when stolen, § 715.
forgery of, § 752.
Nudity as an element in indecent exhibitions, §§ 1136, 1157.
Nuisance, what constitutes, §§ 1169, 1170.
whether public benefit a defense, § 1171.
acts under public authority, § 1172.
illegal continuance of, § 1173.
liability of owner for acts of servant, § 1174.
contribution to, § 1175.
intent and knowledge involved in, § 1176.
venue, § 1177.
indictment for, §§ 1178-1183.
abatement of, § 1182.
common scold and common barrator as, §§ 26, 27, 1169.
indecent and profane language as, § 60.
profane swearing as constituting, § 1159.
regulation as to, by municipalities, § 63.
suppression of by municipalities, § 66.
liability of principal for acts of agent in causing, §§ 188-192.
disorderly house deemed, § 1137.
in keeping disorderly house, how charged, §§ 1142-1144.
evidence of, § 1145.
involved in violation of liquor laws, prosecution for, equitable proceedings, §§ 1199, 1201.
liability of servant for, in illegal sale of intoxicating liquor, § 1239.
keeping intoxicating liquors for sale, deemed, § 1243.
involved in keeping place for illegal sale of intoxicating liquors, §§ 1248, 1249.
gaming house deemed, §§ 1306-1309.

Oath, what sufficient, in perjury, §§ 854-857.
false taking of, see Perjury.
Oaths, profane, as constituting nuisance, § 1159.
Obligation of contracts, how far protected against criminal legislation, § 75.
impairment of, by liquor legislation, § 1209.
Obscene exhibition, what criminal, § 1136.
Obscene exposure, classified with other like crimes, § 1110.
Obscene language as constituting provocation for homicide, § 341.
use of, criminal, §§ 1017, 1020.
Obscene letters or publications, transmission of, by mail, criminal, § 1327.

Obscene matter, sending by mail, § 1332.
Obscene pictures, want of knowledge as defense for sale of, § 128, n.
Obscene publications, as libel, § 1049.
classified with other like crimes, § 1110.
Obscenity, §§ 1156–1158.
Obstructing justice, see Justice, obstruction of.
Obstruction of highway, see Highway.
Obstruction of mails in transmission, §§ 1327, 1328.
Obstruction of railroads, what criminal, § 1196.
carrying United States mails, § 1328.
Obstruction of rivers, what criminal, § 1195.
Obtaining property by false pretenses, distinguished from larceny, §§ 562, 563.
when criminal, §§ 680–687.
by threats, §§ 728–742.
Occupation tax, validity of provisions as to, § 44.
Offenses, compounding, §§ 938–940.
see, also, Crimes.
Offensive language, no justification for assault, § 241.
Officer, public, purchase of warrants by, § 45.
wrongful acts of, in detecting crime, § 118.
resistance to, when acting unlawfully, § 245.
resistance of, constitutes aggravated assault, § 255.
justified in killing to make arrest, § 298.
resistance of, causing death, § 328.
who kills in making unlawful arrest, guilty of manslaughter, § 347.
causing death by undue violence in making arrest, guilty of manslaughter, § 348.
larceny from, §§ 546, 547.
embezzlement by, §§ 621, 645–649.
de facto, embezzlement by, § 647.
liability of, for wilful trespass, § 828.
oath before, what sufficient, in perjury, §§ 854–857.
de facto, oath before, as constituting perjury, §§ 856, 887.
authority of, to administer oath, how stated in indictment for perjury, § 875.
bribery of, §§ 896–903.
misconduct of, what criminal, §§ 904–919.
de facto, misconduct of, § 912.
extortion by, § 914.
de facto, extortion by, § 914.
obstruction of, in discharge of duty, § 920.
resistance of, §§ 921–929.
de facto, evidence in prosecution for resisting, § 929.
escape from, §§ 930–936.
carrying of weapons by, § 1037.
libel against, § 1047.
publication as to acts of, privileged, § 1052.

Officer of corporation, criminal liability of, §§ 180, 184.
embezzlement by, §§ 632, 639.
Officers of elections, violation of law by, §§ 941–951.
mistaken exercise of judgment by, not punishable, § 949.
Officers of vessel, authority of, § 351.
criminal liability of, for ill-treating crew, § 1347.
Official misconduct, what criminal, §§ 904–919.
indictment for, §§ 915–918.
Oil, inspection of, see Illuminating oil.
Oleomargarine, regulation of sale of, § 34.
illegal sale of, want of knowledge, § 128, n.
Omission of legal duty as constituting negligence in homicide, § 350.
Opening and conclusion of indictment for homicide, § 384.
Opinion, evidence of as to sanity, §§ 172, 173.
false statement as to, constituting perjury, § 868.
false statement as to, when criminal, § 669.
Opinions, not admissible as dying declarations, § 428.
Opium, regulation of sale of, § 29.
"**Or**" in construction of statutes, § 108.
Orders for goods, forgery of, § 753.
for payment of money, forgery of, § 753.
Ordinances, of city, for punishment of crime, § 6.
validity of under police power, § 62.
repeal of, § 62.
in conflict with statutes, validity of, § 63.
reasonableness of, § 65.
power to regulate by, does not include power to prohibit, § 69.
as to sale of intoxicating liquors, §§ 1216, 1217.
Original packages, sale of intoxicating liquors in, §§ 76, 1204, 1205.
Other crimes, evidence of, in prosecution for homicide, §§ 416, 418.
in prosecution for rape, § 461.
in prosecution for assault with intent to commit rape, § 463.
in prosecution for burglary, § 515.
in prosecution for arson, § 533.
in prosecution for larceny, § 615.
in prosecution for embezzlement, § 642.
in prosecution for false pretenses, § 691.
in prosecution for receiving stolen goods, § 726.
in prosecution for threats, § 742.
in prosecution for forgery, § 808.
in prosecution for adultery, § 1098.
in prosecution for seduction, § 1117.
in prosecution for incest, § 1124.
to show intent, in case of indecent exposure, § 1136.
in prosecution for attempting to procure abortion, § 1151.
not admissible in proof of obscenity or indecency, § 1158.
Outlawry, § 2.
Overt act, necessary in crime, §§ 223, 224.
necessary to show imminent danger justifying killing in self-defense, §§ 303, 307.

Overt act — continued.
of wrong as debarring from self-defense, § 309.
whether necessary in conspiracy, § 966.
in conspiracy, as determining jurisdiction, § 972.
as determining limitation of prosecution, § 973.
allegation of, in indictment for conspiracy, §§ 975, 977.
necessary to constitute violation of neutrality laws, § 1341.
in treason, § 1358.
Owners, distinct, taking property of, whether one larceny, § 551.
Ownership, how alleged, in prosecution for robbery, § 481.
of premises, allegation and proof of, in prosecution for burglary, § 495.
how alleged and proved, in prosecution for burglary, § 508.
in prosecution for arson, § 521.
in indictment for arson, how described, § 529.
of property, in case of larceny, §§ 544–547.
how charged, in indictment for larceny, §§ 600–605.
in prosecution for embezzlement by public officer, § 648.
in embezzlement, how charged, § 653.
in false pretenses, how alleged, § 707.
in prosecution for receiving stolen goods, § 718.
in prosecution for malicious mischief or trespass, § 830.
Oysters, regulations as to taking, §§ 44, 46.

Pains and penalties, bills of, § 79.
Paramour, eloping with wife, whether guilty of larceny as to property taken, § 558.
Parent, abandonment of child by, § 58.
chastisement by, when lawful, § 242.
causing death by unreasonable chastisement, guilty of manslaughter, § 348.
control of, over minor child, § 487.
deemed owner of clothing furnished to minor, § 546.
abduction of girl, from control of, §§ 1100–1106.
consent of, to sale of liquor to minor, § 1261.
Pari materia, statutes in, construction, § 87.
Particeps criminis, who deemed, § 202.
cannot complain of false pretenses, § 682.
Participation in crime, what sufficient to render punishable, § 194.
what sufficient to render criminally liable, § 199, 200.
what necessary to make one a principal, §§ 205, 206.
as accessory after the fact, § 209.
in homicide, § 291.
what sufficient in robbery, § 476.
what necessary in riot, § 995.
Particularity in description of property in indictment for larceny, §§ 592–594.
Particulars, bill of, in prosecution for conspiracy, § 976.
Partner, criminal liability of one for acts of another, § 191.
ownership by, how charged in larceny, § 602.

Partner — continued.
misappropriation of funds by, not embezzlement, § 631.
allegation of ownership by, in prosecution for embezzlement, § 653.
sale of liquor by, protected by license of copartner, § 1227.
illegal sale of intoxicating liquors by, liability for, § 1238.
Party in the wrong cannot make self-defense, § 309.
cannot claim provocation as reducing homicide to manslaughter, § 339.
Passing counterfeit money, what criminal, §§ 780-789.
jurisdiction and venue in prosecutions for, §§ 790, 791.
indictment for, §§ 792-804.
evidence in prosecution for, §§ 805-810.
Patent rights, discrimination as to sale of, § 44.
regulation as to notes given for, § 50.
how far protected against state regulation, § 75.
Paternity of child, in proceedings for seduction or bastardy, evidence of, §§ 1117, 1129.
Payment of employees, regulation of, § 55.
Peddler, who deemed, § 44.
license tax on, §§ 44.
Penal actions, what are, § 7.
construction and repeal of, §§ 81-110.
strict construction of, § 83.
Penalty, proceedings to recover, § 5.
whether exclusive of criminal punishment, § 8.
Penetration, necessity of, in case of rape, § 450.
what necessary, to constitute incest, § 1122.
essential in sodomy, § 1153.
Pension laws, violations of, § 1348.
Perjury, what constitutes, §§ 852, 853.
the oath, §§ 854-857.
jurisdiction of the court, § 858.
in case where oath authorized, §§ 859, 860.
materiality of false testimony, §§ 861-866.
falsity of testimony, §§ 867, 868.
intent, §§ 869, 870.
as affected by duress, § 137.
as affected by intoxication, § 161.
indictment for, §§ 871-885.
jurisdiction in, § 871.
materiality, how averred, §§ 878, 879.
how proved, § 889.
evidence in prosecution for, §§ 886-892.
subornation of, §§ 893-895.
attempt to suborn, effect of impossibility, § 226.
in connection with voting, § 950.
under naturalization laws, § 1346.
in connection with procuring pension, § 1348.
Person, meaning of term, § 110.
whether corporation deemed, § 181.

Person — continued.
who deemed, in homicide, § 294.
intended to be injured, name in indictment for conspiracy, § 982.
Person, the, taking from, in robbery, § 474.
larceny from, § 575.
Personalty, subject of larceny, § 536.
Personation, false, obtaining property by, § 562.
Petit larceny, deemed felony in prosecution for burglary, § 505.
Pharmacists, regulation of business of, § 36.
sale of intoxicating liquors by, § 1253.
Photographs as evidence, § 406.
Physical condition, declarations as to, § 415.
Physician, regulation of business of, § 36.
regulation of business of by municipalities, § 73.
discriminations as to license to, § 77.
criminal liability of, for negligence, § 130.
injurious treatment by, constitutes assault, § 237.
consent of patient to improper treatment by, no defense, § 249.
negligence of, as constituting homicide, § 287.
negligence of, in treating wound as cause of death, § 292.
negligence of, causing death, constitutes manslaughter, § 351.
sale of intoxicating liquors by, § 1253.
Piggery, keeping of, as a nuisance, § 1170.
Pilotage, regulations as to, § 1347.
Pimping, § 1106*a*.
Piracy, as a crime, § 1359.
Place, allegation of, in indictment for homicide, § 376.
of death, allegation of, in indictment for murder, § 381.
how averred, in perjury, § 882.
description of, in indictment for nuisance, § 1181.
allegation of, in prosecution under liquor laws, § 1272.
of sale of intoxicating liquor, what deemed, §§ 1231, 1236.
public, see Public place.
Plea of insanity, § 164.
of guilty in murder in first degree, § 364.
Pleading, false oath to, as perjury, § 859.
Plural when used for singular, § 107.
Poison, use of, to prevent trespass, § 142.
attempt to administer, §§ 225, 227.
administration of, constitutes assault and battery, § 236.
with intent to murder, § 276, n.
killing by, murder in first degree, §§ 353, 354.
death by, deemed deliberate and premeditated, § 356.
allegation of death by, in indictment for homicide, § 378.
administration of, to procure abortion, § 1148.
Poisoning, evidence of, in prosecution for homicide, § 418.
injury to animals by, § 815.
Police power, vested in the state, § 23.
constitutional limitations upon, §§ 75–80.
as affecting interstate commerce, § 76.

Police regulations of municipalities, validity of, § 63.
liquor laws deemed, § 1200.
as to place for sale of intoxicating liquors, § 1250.
Sunday laws deemed, § 1319.
Polygamy, religious belief as to, § 121, n.
Pool selling, § 1305.
Poor-house, burning of, with intent to escape, whether arson, § 526.
Possession, what sufficient, in case of larceny, §§ 544-546.
in thief, necessary, in larceny, § 548.
of stolen property, continuous. § 552.
of property obtained by fraud or trick, whether larceny, § 560.
sufficient to support charge of ownership in indictment for larceny, § 603.
of stolen goods as evidence in larceny, §§ 616-620.
when deemed exclusive, § 620.
of burglar's tools, criminal, § 516.
of counterfeiting tools, §§ 777-779.
of counterfeit money, §§ 780-789.
of counterfeit money or forged instrument, presumption from, § 809.
of realty, criminal interference with, § 825.
in prosecution for forcible entry and detainer, § 839.
of intoxicating liquors, as evidence of intent to sell illegally, § 1243.
Post-offices, regulation of, §§ 1327-1335.
Post-roads, what are, § 1328.
Postal crimes, general discussion of, §§ 1327-1335.
Postal routes, regulation of, § 1327.
Pound breach, when criminal, § 932.
Practice of law, regulation of, § 37.
Preliminary examination, perjury committed in, § 858.
Preliminary investigation as to insanity, § 166.
as to capacity of deaf and dumb person, § 166.
Premeditation not essential to malice aforethought, § 329.
constituting murder in the first degree, §§ 353, 356-360.
how charged, in indictment for murder, §§ 382, 383.
Preparation to commit wrong will not debar from making self-defense, § 309.
Preparation for crime distinguished from attempt, § 224.
what constitutes, § 225.
Preponderance of evidence as to insanity, § 178.
Prescription, nuisance not supported by, § 1173.
highway by, § 1190.
for intoxicating liquors as medicine, § 1253.
Presence, taking from, in robbery, § 474.
Presence at commission of crime, constructive, §§ 195, 206.
Present ability, whether necessary in assault, §§ 232-234.
in case of assault with deadly weapon, § 257.
in case of assault with felonious intent, § 266.
Presumption, as to intent, § 123.
as to coercion in acts of married women, § 147.

Presumption — continued.
of innocence, in case of infancy, §§ 149–153.
as to sanity, § 174.
as to continuance of sanity or insanity, § 169.
of malice, from use of deadly weapon, §§ 332, 333.
as to degree of murder, § 365.
of intent to kill, from use of deadly weapon, § 357.
of life, in prosecution for homicide, § 399.
as to suicide, in prosecution for homicide, § 401.
as to intent, in prosecution for burglary, § 506.
from recent possession of stolen goods, in burglary and larceny, §§ 514, 617.
of guilty knowledge, in prosecution for receiving stolen goods, § 726.
as to intent, in forgery, § 767.
in violation of election laws, § 951.
as to life of husband or wife, in prosecution for bigamy, § 1084.
of continuance of marriage relation, in prosecution for adultery, § 1089.
of continuance of criminal intercourse, in adultery, § 1098.
as to chastity, in seduction, § 1118.
as to marriage, in illicit cohabitation, § 1132.
as to intent to sell intoxicating liquors, § 1243.
Previous adjudication as to material fact in criminal prosecution, § 890, n.
Previous conviction proved in prosecution for second offense, § 28.
Previous jeopardy, see Jeopardy.
Principal and agent, criminal liability of principal for agent's acts, §§ 186–192.
in case of libel, § 1056.
in case of maintaining nuisance, § 1174.
in case of illegal sales of liquor, § 1237.
Principal and accessory, distinction between, § 204.
general doctrine as to, §§ 204–210.
principals in first and second degree, § 205.
constructive presence, § 206.
accessory before the fact, § 207.
accessory in manslaughter, § 208.
accessory after the fact, § 209.
crimes in which accessory is not recognized, § 210.
procedure as to accessories, §§ 211–218.
indictment of, §§ 212–214.
order of trial, §§ 215–218.
in cases of assault, § 250.
accessory before the fact to murder in second degree, § 365.
in prosecution for rape, § 449.
in robbery, § 476.
in larceny, § 573.
whether receiver of stolen goods deemed accessory to larceny, § 713.
one who procures perjury guilty as accessory before the fact, § 893.
rules applicable to, do not apply between co-conspirators, § 981.

Prisoner, permitting escape of, § 910.
escape or rescue of, §§ 930–936.
Privileged publications, §§ 1050–1054.
Privileges and immunities of citizens, how far protected, § 77.
Prize-fight, criminal liability of those participating or others, §§ 196, 249, 1013.
Prize system among shop-keepers, §§ 1315, 1317.
Procedure, statutes applicable to, not unconstitutional as *ex post facto*, § 78.
statutes as to, not strictly construed, § 83.
as to accessories, §§ 211–218.
in prosecutions for homicide, §§ 389–394.
in prosecutions for larceny, §§ 590–611.
in case of embezzlement, §§ 650–656.
for forgery, counterfeiting or passing, §§ 790–804.
as to riot, §§ 996–1002.
Process, forgery of, § 750.
obstruction of service of, § 923.
Procurement of commission of crime, when criminal, § 200.
of crime through agent, § 207.
death caused by, § 291.
of perjury, §§ 893–895.
Procuring, the offense of, § 1106*a*.
Procuring abortion, see Abortion.
Profanity, punishment of, §§ 1159, 1160.
Professions, regulation of, § 36.
Prohibitory liquor laws, §§ 29, 1199, 1213, 1223.
Producers of intoxicating liquors, sale by, § 1254.
Promise, false, whether constitutes false pretense, §§ 676, 678.
Promise of marriage, as element in seduction, § 1112.
Promissory notes, whether subject of larceny, § 543.
description of, in indictment for larceny, § 595.
whether deemed property in false pretenses, § 693.
receipt of, when stolen, § 715.
forgery of, § 752.
Property, protection of, when authorized, § 245.
what subject of robbery, § 473.
description of, in robbery, § 481.
in burglary, § 508.
in arson, §§ 528, 529.
what subject of larceny, §§ 536–543.
unlawfully acquired or held, larceny of, § 542.
ownership of, in case of larceny, §§ 544–547.
value of, as determining punishment in larceny, §§ 581–589.
description of, in indictment for larceny, §§ 592–600.
ownership of, how described, in prosecution for larceny, §§ 600–605.
identification of, in larceny, §§ 612, 613.
what subject of embezzlement, value, §§ 634, 636.
illegally received, embezzlement of, § 635.
conversion of, as constituting embezzlement, § 638.

Property — continued.
ownership of, in prosecution for embezzlement by public officer, § 648.
description of, in embezzlement, § 652.
ownership of, in embezzlement, how charged, § 653.
what constitutes, in false pretenses, §§ 692–695.
ownership and description of, in false pretenses, §§ 707–709.
obtained by false pretenses, restitution of, § 712.
description of, in indictment for receiving stolen goods, § 718.
obtaining by threats, §§ 728–742.
personal, injuries to, § 814.
description of, in prosecution for malicious mischief or trespass, §§ 830–834.
disposing of, to defraud creditors, § 843.
value of, in prosecution for malicious mischief or trespass, § 834.
involved in conspiracy, description of, § 983.
description of, in prosecution for riot, § 1000.
injury to, as constituting breach of the peace, § 1014.
in intoxicating liquors, § 1267.
the crime of obtaining by false pretenses, see False pretenses.
Prosecution for crime in behalf of the public, § 4, n.
for violation of city ordinances, whether criminal, § 6.
for crime, does not affect civil remedy, § 11.
repeal of statute as affecting, § 97.
threats of, when criminal, § 737.
compounding or stifling, §§ 938–940.
Prostitution, definition of, what constitutes, §§ 1104, 1106*a*, 1133, 1138.
abduction for purpose of, §§ 1104, 1106*a*.
classified with sexual crimes, §§ 1109, 1110.
as a crime, § 1133.
keeping house for purpose of, criminal, § 1138. See, also, Houses of ill-fame.
Protection of property, when authorized, § 245.
Provisions, unwholesome, sale of, §§ 32, 1170.
Provocation for assault with felonious intent, § 267.
of insulting language, will not debar from self-defense, § 309.
to show want of malice in homicide, § 330.
insanity or intoxication as affecting, in homicide, § 331.
as excuse for use of deadly weapon, §§ 332, 333.
reducing intentional homicide to manslaughter, §§ 336–346.
for homicide, burden of proof of, § 346.
sufficiency of, a question of fact, § 345.
to reduce murder to second degree, §§ 365, 366.
Proximate cause in homicide, §§ 282, 292.
Public benefit, as a defense in nuisance, § 1171.
for obstructing navigable river, § 1195.
Public callings, regulation of, § 40.
Public corporation, see Municipal corporation.
Public exposure, indecent, what deemed, § 1136.

Public funds, misuse of, as constituting embezzlement, § 649.
what deemed, in embezzlement, § 648.
Public health, protection of, §§ 30–33.
that which is injurious to, as nuisance, §§ 1169–1183.
Public highways, see Highways.
Public interests, protection of, § 45.
Public lands, inclosure of, § 45.
violation of federal regulations as to, § 1353.
Public law, criminal law as a branch of, § 3.
Public notices, obliteration or tearing down of, §§ 45, 819.
Public officers, embezzlement by, §§ 621, 645-649.
see, also, Officers.
Public places, regulation of, by municipalities, § 70.
intoxication or disorderly conduct in, §§ 1018, 1019.
what deemed, with reference to indecent exposure, § 1136.
with reference to gaming, §§ 1302–1304.
gaming in, §§ 1301–1304.
Public property, malicious injury to, § 819.
Public records, forgery of, § 750.
Public squares, obstruction of, § 1192.
Publication of libel, § 1055.
how alleged, § 1065.
of information as to procuring abortion, § 1150.
of indecent matter, §§ 1157, 1158.
of lottery advertisements, §§ 1315–1318.
Publications, indecent, prohibition of, § 60.
what deemed libelous, § 1043.
obscene, §§ 1156–1158.
obscene, transmission of, by mail, criminal, §§ 1327, 1332.
defamatory, sending through mails, § 1334.
containing lottery advertisements, sending through mails, § 1334.
Punctuation as affecting construction of statutes, § 106.
"**Punishable,**" meaning of term, § 110.
Punishment, basis of provision as to cruel and unusual, § 1, n.
theory and object of, §§ 1, 2.
criminal, what deemed, § 5.
for contempt, § 9.
for violation of ordinances, § 63.
power of municipality to impose, § 64.
change of form of, whether *ex post facto*, § 78.
cruel, § 80.
excessive, constitutes assault, § 242.
for murder in first degree, how fixed, §§ 363, 364.
for different forms of homicide, § 393.
for larceny, how fixed, § 588.
for conspiracy, § 987.
for riot, § 1002.
Purchaser of intoxicating liquors not punishable for illegal sale, § 1241.

Purport of written instrument, in forgery, when sufficient, §§ 794, 796.
Putting in fear as constituting assault, § 233.
in robbery, § 470.

Quarantine, enforcement of by municipalities, § 67.
regulations as to, § 1347.
Qui tam actions, nature of, § 7.

Racing on the highway, § 1198.
betting involved in, § 1297.
sale of pools in connection with, § 1305.
Railroad bridges, burning of, § 520, n.
Railroad companies, prosecution of by indictment for negligence causing death, § 184.
Railroad pass, forgery of, § 752.
Railroad property, malicious injury to, § 819.
Railroad tickets, subject of larceny, § 543.
forgery of, § 752.
Railroad train, firing at, intoxication no defense for, § 161.
Railroads, regulation of, § 40.
in streets, regulation of by municipalities, § 70.
killing of stock by, may be made criminal, § 77.
negligence of, causing death, § 288.
obstruction of highway by, § 1187.
interference with operation of, § 1196.
malicious injury to property of, § 819.
attempts to place obstructions on tracks of, § 223.
operation of on Sunday, § 1323.
carrying United States mails, obstruction of, § 1328.
Railway, see Railroad.
Rape, definition, what constitutes, § 438.
force involved, resistance, §§ 439, 440.
must be without consent, §§ 441, 442.
whether connection with girl under age of consent constitutes, §§ 443, 444.
by means of insensibility of female, or fraud, imbecility or fear, §§ 445, 448.
what acts sufficient to constitute, § 450.
intent involved, § 451.
indictment for, §§ 452, 453.
offenses included in, § 454.
not included in seduction, § 1115.
duress as an excuse for attempt, § 137.
intoxication no defense for, § 161.
connection with female under age of consent, solicitation not criminal, § 220.
attempt, impossibility, § 226.
murder in committing, first degree, § 355.
whether may also constitute adultery, § 1092.
whether same act may constitute incest, § 1121.
classified among sexual crimes, §§ 1109, 1110.

Rape — continued.
assault with intent to commit, general discussion of, §§ 462–467.
by boy under fourteen, § 226.
deemed felony, § 230.
Reading the riot act, when authorized, effect of, § 997.
Real evidence in prosecution for homicide, §§ 405–407.
in prosecution for rape, § 459.
exhibition of child to jury, in prosecution for seduction or bastardy, §§ 1117, 1129.
Real property, injuries to, § 823.
Realty, not subject to larceny, § 536.
forcible entry or detainer of, §§ 836–841.
Reason of the statute taken into account in construction, § 82.
Reasonable belief of danger as justifying killing in self-defense, § 306.
Reasonable doubt as to insanity, §§ 177, 179.
in cases of self-defense, § 316.
as to malice, in homicide, § 333.
as to sufficiency of provocation, in homicide, § 346.
as to *corpus delicti*, in homicide, § 396.
as to chastity of prosecutrix, in prosecution for seduction, § 1118.
Rebellion, treason in case of, § 1357.
Receipts, whether subject of larceny, § 543.
forgery of, §§ 754, 756.
Receiver of stolen goods not guilty of larceny, § 573.
Receiving stolen goods, crime of, §§ 713–727.
whether receiver deemed accessory after the fact, § 209.
covers goods obtained by robbery, § 471, n.
distinct crime from larceny, § 609.
charge of, joined with that of larceny, § 609.
Recent possession of fruits of crime, evidence of, in prosecution for homicide, § 421, n.
of stolen goods, evidence of, in prosecution for robbery, § 476.
evidence of, in prosecution for burglary, § 514.
as evidence in larceny, §§ 616–620.
what deemed, § 619.
as evidence in prosecution for receiving, §§ 725, 726.
Recklessness causing death, § 325.
Recommendation, false making of, not forgery, § 756.
Records, public, whether subject of larceny, § 543.
forgery of, § 750.
destruction of, § 920.
Registration, violation of law as to, § 945.
Regulation of business under police power, § 29.
in particular localities, § 39.
Relation of parties, evidence of, in prosecution for homicide, § 417.
Relationship, what sufficient, in incest, § 1120.
Religion, offense against, §§ 1159, 1160.
Religious assemblies, disturbance of, § 1024. And see Disturbance of meeting.

Religious belief no excuse for crime, § 120, n.
Religious freedom, as affected by Sunday laws, § 1319.
Religious worship, disturbance of, see Disturbance of meeting.
Removal, what necessary to constitute larceny, § 548.
of property covered by chattel mortgage, §§ 846, 847.
from office as penalty for misconduct, § 919.
of dead bodies, §§ 1165–1168.
Rendering establishments, regulation of, § 39.
Repeal of statutes, implied, §§ 91–95.
as to offense already committed, § 96.
as affecting pending prosecutions, § 97.
after conviction, § 98.
pending an appeal, § 99.
partial, § 100.
effect of saving clause, § 101.
effect of repeal of repealing statute, § 102.
Repeated offenses, additional punishment for, § 28.
Reputation not admissible on question of sanity, § 171.
of prosecutrix, evidence of, in prosecution for rape, § 460.
not admissible to prove marriage, in prosecution for adultery, § 1096.
as to chastity, not admissible in seduction, § 1118.
of place, evidence of, in prosecution for keeping place for illegal sale of intoxicating liquors, § 1215.
not sufficient to show illicit cohabitation, § 1132
not sufficient evidence, in prosecution for lewdness, § 1135.
of house, in offense of keeping house of ill-fame, § 1138.
of disorderly house, may be shown, § 1145.
as evidence of intent, with reference to sale of intoxicating liquors, § 1249.
as evidence of age of minor to whom intoxicating liquor is sold, § 1260.
as evidence, in prosecution for being common gambler, § 1300.
Rescue of distrained property, § 52.
from jail, §§ 930–936.
Res gestæ, in prosecution for homicide, §§ 411–415.
threats as part of, § 423.
proof of stealing other property admissible, in prosecution for larceny, § 615.
declarations as to recent possession of stolen goods, admissible as, § 618.
proof of, in perjury, § 890.
Residents, privileges granted to, § 77.
Resistance, in rape, what essential, § 440.
when sufficiently overcome by duress, § 448.
proof of complaint as showing, § 455.
Resisting felony by taking life, § 299.
Resisting officer, offense of, §§ 921–929.
Responsibility, criminal, theory of, § 1.
Restaurants, regulation of, § 38.

Restitution of property in case of larceny, § 611.
obtained by false pretenses, § 712.
in prosecution for forcible entry or detainer, § 841.
Restoration of stolen property, effect of, § 572.
Restraint of trade, conspiracy in, § 963.
Retailer of intoxicating liquors, required to post revenue receipt, § 1250.
Retailing of intoxicating liquors, regulation of, § 1245. And see **Intoxicating** liquors.
Retraction, effect of, in libel, § 1054.
Retreat of party assailed before making self-defense, §§ 310, 311.
burden of proof as to, in self-defense, § 316.
Return of property in larceny, effect of, § 572.
Revenue laws, violation of, §§ 1349–1352.
Revenue license, for retail of intoxicating liquors, §§ 29, 1245, 1250, 1280, 1350.
Revenue tax, federal, on sale of intoxicating liquors, § 1217.
for sale of intoxicating liquors, posting of receipt, § 1250.
as to imports, § 1349.
on sale of intoxicating liquors, § 1350.
Revocation of liquor license, § 1226.
Reward, receiving stolen goods to secure, criminal, § 717.
Right to vote, not a privilege or immunity, § 948.
Ringing the changes, larceny by, § 560.
Riot, nature of offense, definition, what constitutes, §§ 991–995.
procedure in prosecution for, §§ 996–1001.
indictment for, §§ 998, 999.
what crimes included in, § 1001.
punishment for, § 1002.
as constituting breach of the peace, § 1012.
River, obstruction of, as constituting nuisance, §§ 1169, 1195.
Road, law of, § 1197.
see Highway.
Road tax, failure to work, § 45.
Robbery, definition and elements of, §§ 468–479.
degrees of, § 478.
indictment, §§ 480–483.
offenses included in, § 484.
includes larceny from the person, § 575.
connivance at, § 118.
who deemed principal in, § 206.
attempt to commit, effect of impossibility, § 226.
assault with intent to commit, deemed felony, §§ 230, 281.
murder in committing, first degree, § 355.
larceny included in, § 609.
recent possession of stolen goods, as evidence in, § 616.
receipt of goods procured by, whether criminal, § 713.
on the sea, as constituting piracy, § 1359.
of graves, § 1167.
of mails, § 1329.
Rout, nature and definition of, § 991, n.

Sabbath, breach of, see Sunday.
Sacramental purposes, sale of intoxicating liquors for, § 1253.
Sales, of dangerous articles, regulation of, § 29.
of intoxicating liquor, what deemed, regulation of, §§ 1233–1251. And see Intoxicating liquors.
by small measure, § 1246.
to be drunk on the premises, § 1247.
to prohibited classes of persons or in prohibited places, §§ 1255–1266.
to Indians, § 1263.
on Sundays or holidays, § 1264.
of property, regulations for protection of, § 50.
Saloons, allowing minors to remain in, § 59. See, also, Intoxicating liquors.
Salvation Army, disturbance of meeting of, § 1024.
Samples as evidence of adulteration, § 33.
Sanity, presumption as to, § 174. See, also, Insanity.
Saving clause in statute, effect of, § 101.
School, disturbance of, § 1025. And see Disturbance of meeting.
School-houses, sale of liquor near, § 1266.
Screens in saloons, regulation of, § 1250.
Seamen, deserting, harboring of, criminal, § 1347.
arrest of, § 1347, n.
Searches and seizures, unreasonable, as to intoxicating liquors, § 1206.
Second offense, additional punishment for, § 28.
first offense included in, § 28.
statute providing additional punishment for, not *ex post facto,* § 78.
heavier punishment for, § 80, n.
previous jeopardy in, § 580.
under liquor laws, § 1268.
Securities for payment of money, whether subject of larceny, § 543.
Seduction, what constitutes, §§ 1109–1113.
indictment for, § 1114.
what offenses included in, § 1115.
not included in crime of procuring, § 1106*a*.
marriage a bar to prosecution for, § 1116.
evidence in prosecution for, §§ 1117–1119.
conspiracy to commit, § 959.
Seizure of liquor, unlawfully kept for sale, § 1267.
Self-defense as a branch of the law of necessity, §§ 136–144.
as justification for assault, § 246.
as justification for homicide, §§ 301–316.
duty to retreat, § 311.
as against felony or invasion of home, § 312.
right to pursue assailant, § 314.
burden of proof as to, § 316.
excessive violence in making, causing death, § 348.
Self-preservation as an excuse for crime, § 137.
Sentence on conviction for criminal homicide, § 394.
Sepulture, violation of right of, §§ 1165–1168.

Servant, enticing away, § 51.
criminal liability for carelessness in employing, § 130.
not excused for crime by command of master, § 136.
criminal liability of for acts under master's order, § 190.
liability of master for death caused by act of, § 291.
admission by, not deemed breaking, in burglary, § 501.
possession of, deemed that of master, § 529.
larceny by, § 556.
consent of, to taking, as affecting larceny, § 558.
conversion by, as constituting embezzlement, § 621.
when taking by, deemed embezzlement, §§ 623, 626–628.
of corporation, embezzlement by, § 632.
receipt of stolen goods by, § 714.
see, also, Master and servant.
Servants, regulations as to importation of, § 1343.
Severance from realty, in case of larceny, §§ 536, 537.
Sexual crimes, classification of, § 1109.
table of, § 1110.
Sexual intercourse, what sufficient to constitute rape, § 450.
Shade trees, injury to, § 823.
Shooting, punishment for, § 256.
Shooting across the line, jurisdiction as to crime of, §§ 251, 369.
Shooting in public place, as constituting breach of the peace, § 1015.
Sidewalks, use of by adjoining owners for business purposes, § 71.
riding or driving upon, § 1197.
Sign-boards, duty to erect or maintain, § 1185.
Signature to an instrument, falsely obtaining, when criminal, §§ 665, 694.
to deed obtained by threat, § 738.
false making, when forgery, §§ 745, 746, 761.
without authority, whether forgery, § 762.
fictitious, in forgery, § 764.
to forged instrument, allegation of, § 801.
proof of, § 799.
evidence as to handwriting of, in forgery, § 806.
Similitude, what necessary, in counterfeiting, § 774.
Singular for plural in construction of statutes, § 107.
Slander, conspiracy to commit, § 958.
when criminal, §§ 1040, 1057.
Slaughter-houses, regulation of, § 39.
as constituting nuisance, § 1170.
Slave, killing of master by, under provocation, § 339.
Small measure, sale of intoxicating liquors by, § 1246.
Smuggling, the crime of, § 1351.
Societies, misappropriation of funds by member, not embezzlement, § 631.
Sodomy, what constitutes, §§ 1153–1155.
attempt to commit, § 238.
effect of consent to, § 249.
classified with other like crimes, § 1110.

Solicitation to commit crime, when criminal, § 220.
to fornication or adultery not criminal, § 225.
not sufficient to show intent to commit rape, § 463.
involved in abduction, § 1103.
Special owner, larceny from, § 546.
Specific intent, when essential, § 122.
when inferred, § 123.
whether material under statute, § 128.
intoxication as bearing upon, § 161.
Spirituous liquors, see Intoxicating liquors.
Spring-gun, use of, to prevent trespass, § 142.
death caused by, § 325.
near highway, as constituting nuisance, § 1184.
Squares, public, obstruction of, § 1192.
Stabbing, as constituting aggravated assault, § 256.
Stake, involved in game of chance, § 1286.
Stallion, keeping of, as a nuisance, § 1170.
Stamp to prevent adulteration, § 33.
Stamps, registration of, § 47.
postal, regulation of sale of, § 1327.
use of, in violation of revenue laws, § 1350.
Statement, false, when constitutes false pretenses, § 666.
Statutes as affecting common law as to crimes, § 12.
felonies under, § 18.
conflict of ordinances with, § 62.
uniformity of operation of, § 77.
when unconstitutional as *ex post facto*, § 78.
penal, construction and repeal of, §§ 81–110.
penal, strict construction of, § 83.
construction of, according to legislative intent, § 86.
in pari materia, construction of, §§ 87, 105.
construction of, general and special provisions, §§ 89, 90.
implied repeal of, §§ 91, 95.
construed with reference to common law, § 95.
repeal of, as to offenses committed, § 96.
in part repealed or invalid, effect of, § 100.
repealing, effect of repeal of, § 102.
prospectively construed, § 103.
construction of, as affected by grammar and punctuation, § 106.
whether intent material under, § 128.
knowledge of, presumed, § 132.
as to sale of intoxicating liquors, construction of, § 1216. And see Intoxicating liquors.
indictment under, see Indictment.
Statutory forms of indictment, see Indictment.
Statutory law as to crimes, § 12.
Stealing, how charged in larceny, § 607.
Stock, killing of by railroads may be made criminal, § 77.
transportation of, regulated, §§ 1161, 1338.

Stock, corporate, subject to embezzlement, § 636.
Stolen property, restitution of, § 611.
recent possession of, as evidence in larceny, §§ 616–620.
crime of receiving, see Receiving stolen goods.
Store building, breaking and entering of, § 499.
Store-house, breaking and entering, as constituting burglary, § 494.
larceny from, § 578.
Stream, obstruction of, as constituting nuisance, § 1169.
contamination of, by several, § 1175.
damming of, so as to obstruct highway, as constituting nuisance, § 1186.
obstruction of, as nuisance, §§ 1169, 1195.
Street railways, regulation of for protection of employees, § 31.
regulation of by municipalities, § 70.
obstruction of, § 1196.
operation of on Sunday, § 1323.
Streets, regulation of use of by abutting owner, § 39.
regulations as to working, § 64.
regulation of by municipalities, § 70.
shooting in, as breach of the peace, § 1015.
obstruction of, as constituting nuisance, §§ 1184–1194.
deemed highways, § 1192.
fast driving in, as constituting nuisance, § 1184. And see Highways.
Strict construction of penal statutes, § 83.
Strikers, obstructing transmission of mails, § 1328.
Strikes, conspiracy to engage in, § 963.
Subornation of perjury, what constitutes, §§ 893–895.
Suicide, intoxication as bearing on attempt to commit, § 161.
inciting to commit, § 207.
attempt to commit, § 221, n.
whether criminal, § 290.
evidence of, in prosecution for homicide, § 401.
Sunday, regulations as to observance of, §§ 1319–1326.
what constitutes, § 1320.
regulation of running of trains upon, § 40.
corporation punishable for violating, § 183.
violation of, as constituting breach of the peace, § 1012.
sale of liquors upon, §§ 1229, 1264.
sale of liquor upon, liability of agent for, § 1239.
Sunday school, disturbance of, § 1024.
Support, failure to furnish, when criminal, § 130.
as constituting assault, § 237, n.
causing death, § 286.
when constitutes murder, § 325, n.
causing death, constitutes manslaughter, § 351.
Surgeon, negligence of in treating wound as causing death, § 292. See, also, Physician.
Swearing, punishment for, §§ 1159, 1160.
Swindling, when criminal, §§ 662–664.

Table of homicide, § 282*a*.
of sexual crimes, § 1110.
Taking and carrying away, in robbery, §§ 471–475.
what sufficient, in larceny, §§ 548–563.
must be continuous, §§ 536, 537.
how alleged, in larceny, § 607.
Taking private property for public use, liquor legislation not deemed, §§ 1201, 1207.
Tame animal, what deemed, § 1162.
Tavern, license for, covering sale of liquor thereat, § 1230.
Tavern-keepers, regulation of, § 38.
Tax on occupations, § 44.
on peddlers, § 44.
Taxation, untrue listing of property, § 45.
false swearing in connection with, § 860.
by municipalities by means of licenses, § 69.
uniformity of, as affected by liquor laws, § 1211.
Teacher, chastisement by, when lawful, § 242.
causing death by unreasonable chastisement, guilty of manslaughter, § 348.
Teacher's certificate, forgery of, § 752.
Telegraph companies, license tax on, § 44, n.
Telegraphs, operation of, on Sunday, § 1323.
Temporary use, wrongful taking for, whether larceny, § 566.
Tenant, deemed owner, in prosecution for burglary, § 495.
in prosecution for arson, § 521.
Tenant in common cannot eject co-tenant, § 245.
Tenement, meaning of term, §§ 1139, 1181.
Tenements, regulation of for public health, § 30.
Tenor, setting out instruments by, in prosecution for false pretenses, § 700.
in prosecution for obtaining property by threats, § 740.
in prosecution for forgery, § 794.
in prosecution for perjury, § 877.
Terms of art and science, construction of, § 105.
Test oath, invalid as *ex post facto* legislation, § 78.
Theater ticket, forgery of, § 752.
Theft, see Larceny.
Thief, larceny from, § 546.
Thief, common, punishment for being, §§ 25, 580.
Threatening language, use of, criminal, §§ 1017, 1020.
Threatening letters, the crime of sending, §§ 729, 1333.
Threats not sufficient alone to constitute assault, § 232.
causing death, whether constituting homicide, § 284.
not sufficient to show danger justifying killing in self-defense, § 303.
of deceased, as bearing on the right of self-defense, § 307.
as evidence of malice in homicide, § 330.
by accused, evidence of, in prosecution for homicide, §§ 418, 419.
of deceased, evidence of, in prosecution for homicide, § 423.
effect of, in rape, §§ 440, 448.

Threats — continued.
sexual connection procured by, as constituting defilement, § 448, n.
may constitute constructive breaking in burglary, § 501.
obtaining property by, §§ 728–742.
procuring money by, § 914.
Tickets, forgery of, § 752.
Timber, cutting or removing from public lands, § 1353.
Time, how far material, in prosecution for embezzlement, § 651.
Time and place, allegation of, in indictment for homicide, § 376.
of death, in indictment for homicide, § 381.
how averred, in perjury, § 882.
allegation and proof of, in prosecution under liquor law, § 1272.
allegation of, in prosecution for gaming, § 1293.
allegation of, in prosecution for keeping gaming house, § 1307.
Title, immaterial in forcible trespass, § 820.
not involved in prosecution for trespass, § 825.
in question, in determining existence of public highway, § 1194.
Title deeds, whether subject of larceny, § 543.
Token, false, what constitutes, § 661.
Tools for counterfeiting, possession of, §§ 777–779.
Tort, distinguished from crime, §§ 2, 4, 10, 111.
Trades, regulation of, § 38.
Translation of written instrument in foreign language, in indictment, § 795.
Transportation of intoxicating liquors, regulation of, §§ 76, 1203–1205, 1242, 1267.
of live animals, regulation of, §§ 1161, 1338.
Travelers, carrying of weapons by, § 1036.
Traveling upon Sunday, legality of, § 1322.
Treason, definition of, what constitutes, §§ 1354–1358.
petit, § 1354.
piracy as constituting, § 1359.
deemed a felony, § 17.
compulsion as an excuse for, § 137.
no accessories recognized in, § 210.
counterfeiting deemed, § 743.
Treasure trove, concealment of, as constituting treason, § 1356.
Treasury notes, deemed personal property or bank-notes in case of larceny, § 543.
description of, in indictment for larceny, § 596.
Trees, malicious destruction of, § 813.
Trespass, criminal, belief of right to enter, § 113, n.
under mistake as to ownership, § 135.
resistance to, when lawful, § 142.
not sufficient to constitute provocation for manslaughter, § 338.
essential to constitute larceny, §§ 549, 550.
continuous, in larceny, §§ 551–553.
by reason of subsequent wrongful act, § 570.
as distinguishing larceny from embezzlement, § 623.

Trespass — continued.
wilful, §§ 811–835.
after warning, § 824.
Trespasser, ejection of, when lawful, § 245.
death of, from unnecessary violence in resisting, manslaughter, § 347.
Trespassing animals, injuries to, § 815.
Trial of accessories, §§ 215–218.
Trick, obtaining property by, as constituting larceny, § 560.
swindling by means of, when criminal, § 662.
Truck-store statutes, constitutionality of, § 55.
Trustees, larceny from, § 546.
embezzlement by, § 629.
Trusts, statutes against, § 963.
Truth as a defense in libel, § 1051.
Turning to the right on highways, § 1197.
Turnpike, obstruction of, as constituting nuisance, § 1184. And see Highway.
failure to keep in repair, § 1185.
deemed public highway, § 1191.

Unchastity, evidence of, in prosecution for rape, § 460. And see Chastity.
Undertakers, license for, § 73.
Underwriters, burning property with intent to defraud, § 522.
destroying vessels with intent to defraud, § 1347.
Uniformity of operation of statutes, § 77.
in case of liquor laws, §§ 1210, 1211.
Unincorporated association, ownership in, how charged, in indictment for larceny, § 604.
United States, jurisdiction of courts of, see Federal courts.
Unlawful act, death from, deemed manslaughter, § 347.
Unlawful assembly, see Assembly.
Usurpation in office, what criminal, § 904.
Usury, punishable, § 53.
Uttering of forged instrument or counterfeit money, §§ 771, 730–789, 791.

Vagabonds, place of resort for, deemed nuisance, § 1137.
Vagrants, punishment of, §§ 61, 1018.
place of resort for, deemed nuisance, § 1137.
Validity of writing, essential in forgery, §§ 756, 760.
Value of property in prosecution for robbery, §§ 472, 481.
in prosecution for larceny, § 543.
not essential in larceny from a building, § 578.
as determining punishment in larceny, §§ 581–589.
in larceny, how determined, § 585.
in embezzlement, what essential, § 636.
false statements as to, when criminal, § 670.
allegation of, in false pretenses, § 709.
finding of, in prosecution for receiving stolen goods, § 723.
in prosecution for malicious mischief or trespass, § 834.

Variance between indictment and proof as to name of owner in larceny, § 605.
as to ownership in embezzlement, § 653.
in prosecution for false pretenses, §§ 699-710.
as to forged instrument, § 798.
in prosecution for forgery, §§ 798, 799.
as to the proceedings in which perjury is committed, § 873.
in prosecution for conspiracy, § 985.
in prosecution under liquor laws, § 1276.
Vengeance, private, right of, § 2.
Venue in case of accessory or conspirator, § 211.
allegation of, in indictment for homicide, § 376.
evidence of, in prosecution for homicide, § 395.
in prosecutions for homicide, § 370.
for burglary, § 509*a*.
for arson, § 527.
for larceny, § 590.
for embezzlement, § 650.
for false pretenses, § 696.
for receiving stolen goods, § 720.
for obtaining property by threats, § 739.
for forgery, counterfeiting or passing, § 791.
for fraudulent conveyance or removal of property covered by chattel mortgage, § 850.
for bribery, § 900.
for conspiracy, § 972.
for libel, § 1058.
for bigamy, § 1077.
for abduction of female, § 1100.
for bastardy, § 1127.
for publishing information as to procuring abortion, § 1150.
for nuisance, § 1177.
under liquor laws, § 1269.
for sending lottery advertisements through mails, § 1334.
Verdict as to degree of murder, § 362.
in prosecution for homicide, § 392.
Vessel, larceny from, § 578.
injuries to, § 818.
Vested rights, how far protected against criminal legislation, § 75.
Vinegar, colored, sale of, § 33.
Violence, involved in rape, §§ 438, 439.
what necessary, to constitute robbery, § 469.
Void instrument, forgery of, §§ 756-760.
Voting, mistake in belief as to right of, § 135.
illegal, §§ 943, 944.

Wager, fraudulent, as constituting larceny, § 560.
as an element in the crime of gaming, §§ 1283-1286.
War, what constitutes, with reference to treason, § 1357.

Warehouse, larceny from, § 578.
Warehouse receipts, protection of, § 49.
Warehousemen, regulation of charges of, § 40.
regulation of, § 49.
Warrant, sufficiency of, in prosecution for resistance, § 922.
Warrants, whether subject of larceny, § 543.
forgery of, § 752.
Warranty, false, whether constituting false pretenses, §§ 676, 677.
Wash-houses, regulation of, § 39.
Water, when subject of larceny, §§ 536, 548.
contamination of, as a nuisance, §§ 30, 1170, 1175.
Ways, private, § 1191.
Weapon, nature of as indicating intent, § 123.
loaded, assault with, § 258.
description of, in indictment for homicide, §§ 377, 378.
see Deadly weapon, also Dangerous weapon.
Weapons, concealed, carrying of, §§ 1029–1039.
Weights and measures, regulation of, § 48.
Weregild, in Anglo-Saxon law, § 2.
Wharfingers, regulation of charges of, § 40.
Wharves, regulation of use of by municipalities, § 70.
Whisky, as intoxicating liquor, §§ 1218, 1220. And see Intoxicating liquors.
White-cap Act, what acts covered by, § 993.
Wholesale dealer, manufacturer of liquor not deemed, § 1254.
Wife, see Husband and wife.
Wild animals, larceny of, § 538.
Wilful trespass, as a crime, §§ 811–835.
indictment for, §§ 830–835.
Wilfulness necessary to constitute murder in first degree, §§ 353, 356–360.
how charged, in indictment for murder, §§ 382, 383.
Wills, forgery of, §§ 743, 750.
Wilson law, in regard to importation of intoxicating liquors, §§ 76, 1205.
Wine, regulation of sale of, see Intoxicating liquors.
Withdrawal of party in wrong before making self-defense, § 310.
Witness, tampering with, when criminal, § 937.
self-crimination, as to violating election laws, § 951.
corroboration of, see Evidence.
Witnesses, more than one required, in perjury, § 892.
bribery of, § 898.
Women, regulation of employment of, § 55.
restricting hours of labor as to, unconstitutional, § 77.
equal rights of, as affecting criminal liability, § 145, n.
assaults upon, § 255.
indignities to, constituting assault, § 238.
insults to, as provocation for homicide, § 341.
see, also, Females.
Words, not sufficient to constitute assault, § 232.
offensive, not sufficient to justify assault, § 241.
will not justify killing in self-defense, § 303.

Words — continued.
not sufficient wrong to debar from self-defense, § 309.
not sufficient to constitute provocation for manslaughter, § 338.
when sufficient to reduce murder to second degree, § 365.
not constituting affray, § 1007.
threatening or insulting, as constituting breach of the peace, §§ 1017, 1020.
Workmen, combinations of, § 963.
Worship, disturbance of, see Disturbance of meeting.
Wound, death from, when homicide, § 292.
mortal, place of inflicting, determines jurisdiction for homicide, § 369.
description of, in indictment for homicide, § 380.
Wounding as constituting aggravated assault, § 256.
Written instruments, subject of larceny, § 543.
valuation of, in larceny, § 585.
description of, in indictment for larceny, § 595.
subject to embezzlement, § 636.
obtaining false signature to, when criminal, § 665.
whether deemed property in false pretenses, § 693.
falsely obtaining signature to, whether deemed criminal, § 694.
how set out in indictment for false pretenses, § 700.
in indictment for obtaining property by threats, § 740.
forgery of, §§ 743-754.
invalidity of, as affecting forgery, §§ 756-760.
description of, in indictment for forgery, §§ 793-798.
in foreign language, how set out, § 795.
production of, in prosecution for forgery, § 805.
in which perjury is committed, how set out, § 877.
how proved, in prosecution for perjury, § 890.
constituting libel, how set out, § 1061.
Written law as to crimes, § 12.